P9-CKD-929

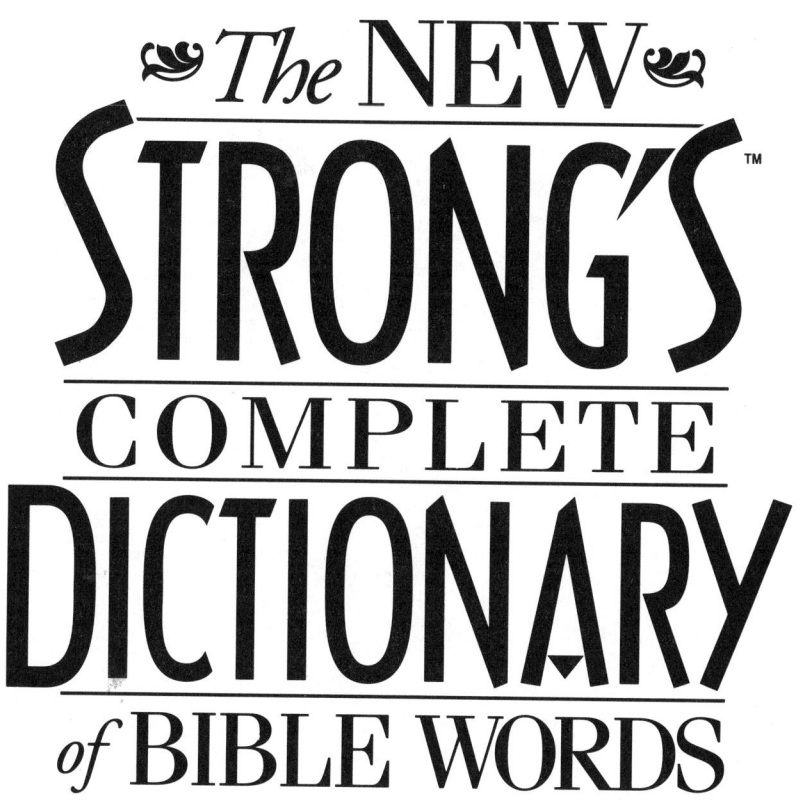

The NEW STRONG'S
COMPLETE
DICTIONARY
of BIBLE WORDS

JAMES STRONG, LL.D., S.T.D.

Introduction by John R. Kohlenberger, III

THOMAS NELSON PUBLISHERS
Nashville • Atlanta • London • Vancouver

Copyright © 1996 by Thomas Nelson Publishers

All rights reserved. Written permission must be secured from the publisher to use or repro-duce any part of this book, except for brief quotations in critical reviews or articles.

Published in Nashville, Tennessee, by Thomas Nelson, Inc. Distributed in Canada by Nelson/Word Inc.

The publisher wishes to acknowledge the editorial and composition services of John R. Kohlenberger III and Multnomah Graphics.

ISBN 0–7852–1147–0 (hardcover)

Printed in the United States of America

Contents

Read this first!

How to Use *The New Strong's™ Complete Dictionary of Bible Words*

Strong's unique system of numbers continues to be *the* bridge between the original languages of the Bible and English translations for many Bible students. *The New Strong's™ Complete Dictionary of Bible Words* combines a completely new and exclusive English Index to the Biblical Languages with newly typeset, corrected, and enlarged print editions of *The New Strong's™ Hebrew and Aramaic Dictionary* and *The New Strong's™ Greek Dictionary* to offer a unique and valuable tool for biblical word studies.

1. What the *Dictionary* Is

The New Strong's™ Complete Dictionary of Bible Words is a fully integrated collection of three key Bible study tools. It is an essential companion to *The New Strong's™ Exhaustive Concordance* or any other edition of this classic concordance. The English Index to the Biblical Languages contains every major word in the *KJV* in alphabetical order, with a list of every Hebrew, Aramaic, and Greek word that each English word translates. This unique Index shows at a glance the range of meaning of each English word and provides a key to the biblical language dictionaries. The Introduction to the English Index follows on page v. *The Hebrew and Aramaic Dictionary* contains a wealth of information about the original languages of the Old Testament. It is keyed to the English Index by *Strong's* numbering system, as well as by the complete list of *KJV* renderings within each *Dictionary* entry. The Introduction to *The Hebrew and Aramaic Dictionary* appears on page 289. *The Greek Dictionary* contains a wealth of information about the original language of the New Testament. It is also keyed to the English Index by *Strong's* numbering system, as well as by the complete list of *KJV* renderings within each *Dictionary* entry. The Introduction to *The Greek Dictionary* appears on page 561.

2. Using the *Dictionary* Independently

To use this *Dictionary*, look up any *KJV* word in the English Index. Within each entry is a listing of every Hebrew, Aramaic, and Greek word that the English word translates. Because each original language word

has a concise English definition, you immediately see the range of meaning of the English words. "Earnest," for example, is used as an adjective describing sincere emotions and is also used as a noun, as in "earnest money" or "pledge." Because each original language word is keyed to *Strong's* numbering system, you can find further information in the *Hebrew and Aramaic* and *Greek Dictionaries*. If *Strong's* number is not italicized (e.g., **1001**), consult the *Hebrew and Aramaic Dictionary*. If *Strong's* number is italicized (e.g., *1001*), consult the *Greek Dictionary*. These dictionaries provide further definitions and explanations of the original languages. They also list every English word in the *KJV* that translates each original language word. These features of *The New Strong's™ Complete Dictionary of Bible Words* allow it to function as a complete dictionary and thesaurus to the original biblical languages and to the *KJV*.

3. Using the *Dictionary* with *The New Strong's™ Exhaustive Concordance*

The New Strong's™ Complete Dictionary of Bible Words provides word meanings for the *KJV* and for the original biblical languages. Although its *Dictionaries* do cite many biblical texts, it by no means replaces *The New Strong's™ Exhaustive Concordance* as an exhaustive index to every appearance of every English word in the *KJV*. The English Index provides a quick and easy summary of the hundreds of thousands of contexts in *Strong's Exhaustive Concordance*, while the *Concordance* lists every context for every word of the *KJV*, allowing you to study the use of the word in the Bible itself. The *Hebrew and Aramaic* and *Greek Dictionaries* duplicate the corrected and improved *Dictionaries* of *The New Strong's™ Exhaustive Concordance*, but do so in a much more generous print size. Further, with both books open, you can do context research in the *Concordance* and, without losing your place, consult the *Dictionaries* of *The New Strong's™ Complete Dictionary of Bible Words*.

The publisher trusts you will soon find *The New Strong's™ Complete Dictionary of Bible Words* an invaluable and constant companion to your study of God's Word.

How to Use the English Index to the Biblical Languages

1. What the Index Is

The English Index to the Biblical Languages contains every major word in the *KJV* with a list of every Hebrew, Aramaic, and Greek word that each English word translates. Words that are omitted from this list include words that appear in the Appendix of Articles in the original *Strong's Exhaustive Concordance* (such as "a," "and," and "the") and words that do not directly translate a Hebrew, Aramaic, or Greek word (such as "aileth", "letting," and "shouldest"). English words are listed in alphabetical order, exactly as they are spelled in the *KJV*.

Under each English entry is a listing of every Hebrew, Aramaic, and Greek word that the English word translates. These lists are organized in alphabetical order (which is also *Strong's* number order): Old Testament words first, then New Testament words. Each line has four elements: (1) *Strong's* number, (2) the original language word in transliteration, (3) the total number of times the word is so translated, and (4) a brief definition. (See the enlarged example on page vi.)

(1) If *Strong's* number is not italicized, it refers to an original word in the *Hebrew and Aramaic Dictionary*. If Strong's number and the transliterated word are ***italicized***, it refers to an original word in the *Greek Dictionary*.

(2) Words are transliterated exactly as in the *Dictionaries,* according to the schemes outlined on pages 292-293 and 564-565. If more than one Strong's number is listed on an entry line (**4672+1767** under "able," for example), in the interest of saving space, only the first word is transliterated. The additional word(s) are transliterated in the *Dictionaries.*

(3) The total number of occurrences is given to show patterns of *KJV* usage and in case you wish to study the original language words in the order of their frequency. For example, Greek word **25** (*agapaō*) is translated "love" 70 times in the *KJV* and may be a more significant or interesting word than **2309** (*thělō*), which is translated as "love" only once.

(4) The brief definition summarizes *Strong's* fuller dictionary entries. These definitions actually function as a dictionary to the vocabulary of the *KJV*, informing you that a "habergeon" is a "coat of mail" or that "unction" is a "special endowment of the Holy Spirit." Sometimes these definitions update the scholarship of the *KJV*, as in the case of "unicorn," which is defined as "wild bull." As is the case of the occurrences statistics, the definition may also point out a key Hebrew, Aramaic, or Greek word that you may want to study in more detail by referring to the *Dictionaries.*

2. Using the Index with the Dictionaries

Because the Index lists every Hebrew, Aramaic, and Greek word that is translated by any English word of the *KJV*, it functions as a concise dictionary and thesaurus of the biblical languages. Quickly scanning the entry for the word "love" shows that the word is used of general positive affection, deep compassion, fraternal affection, love for husbands, love for children, and greedy love of money. Reading the appropriate *Dictionary* entries will enlarge on these definitions. Again, if a *Strong's* number is not italicized (e.g., **157**), consult the *Hebrew and Aramaic Dictionary*. If a *Strong's* number is italicized (e.g., **26**), consult the *Greek Dictionary*. Each entry in the *Dictionaries* also provides a complete list of *KJV* words that translate the original language word, following the :— symbol. Greek word **26** (*agapē*), for example, lists four English words: charitably, charity, dear, and love. This shows the range of meaning the *KJV* translators assigned to *agapē*. By returning to the Index and looking up each of these English words, you find even more original language words to study.

3. Using the Index with *The New Strong's™ Exhaustive Concordance*

The English Index provides a quick and easily used summary of the hundreds of thousands of contexts in *The New Strong's™ Exhaustive Concordance*, while the *Concordance* lists every context for every word of the *KJV*. This allows you to study the use of the word in the Bible itself, which is the most important way to understand how a specific word is used in a specific context. Although *Strong's Hebrew and Aramaic* and *Greek Dictionaries* offer definitions for each word of the original languages, these words do not have the sum total of every definition in every context. Greek word **26** (*agapē*), for example, cannot mean "affection" *and* "love-feast" every time it occurs. It means "affection" in such contexts as Philemon 7 and "love-feast" in Jude 12. Similarly, the historical or etymological materials that *Strong's Dictionaries* often present at the beginning of an entry may show something of the origin of a word, but are not necessarily its *definition* in every biblical context. For example, when Greek word **314** (*anaginōskō*) is used in the New Testament, it means "to read," rather than "to know again," as *Strong's Dictionary* describes its origin.

In short, the wealth of materials contained in *The New Strong's™ Complete Dictionary of Bible Words* is truly maximized in conjunction with *The New Strong's™ Exhaustive Concordance* when carefully applied to the study of God's Word.

An Example
from the English Index

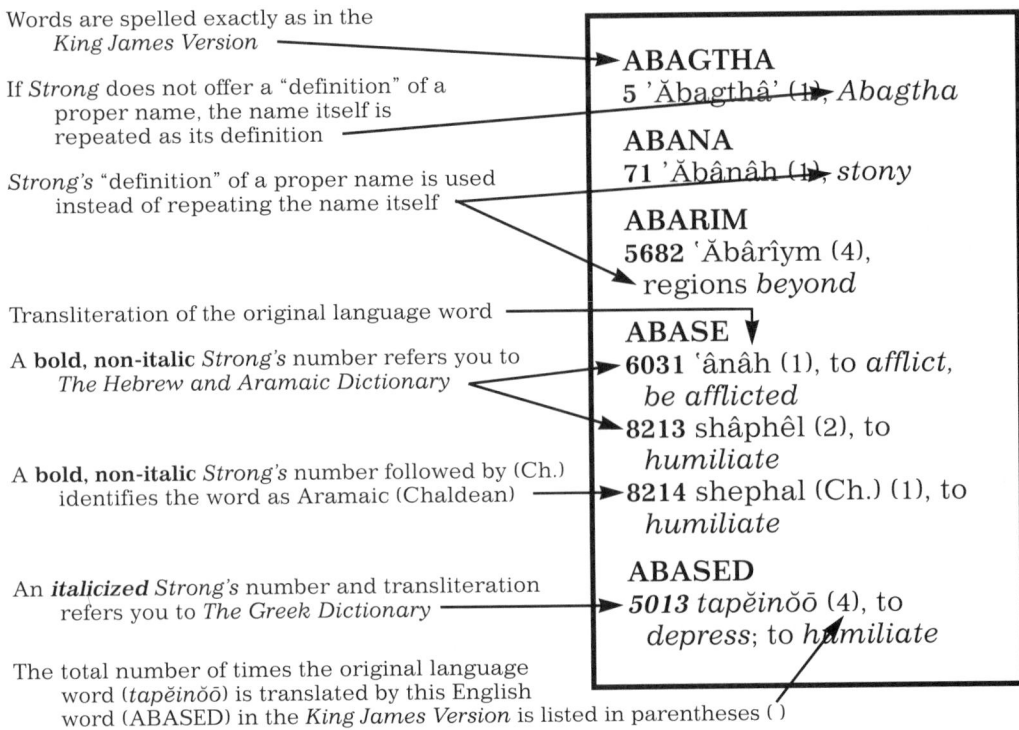

Words are spelled exactly as in the *King James Version*

If *Strong* does not offer a "definition" of a proper name, the name itself is repeated as its definition

Strong's "definition" of a proper name is used instead of repeating the name itself

ABAGTHA
5 'Ăbagthâ' (1), *Abagtha*

ABANA
71 'Ăbânâh (1), *stony*

ABARIM
5682 'Ăbârîym (4), regions *beyond*

Transliteration of the original language word

A **bold, non-italic** *Strong's* number refers you to *The Hebrew and Aramaic Dictionary*

A **bold, non-italic** *Strong's* number followed by (Ch.) identifies the word as Aramaic (Chaldean)

ABASE
6031 'ânâh (1), to *afflict, be afflicted*
8213 shâphêl (2), to *humiliate*
8214 shephal (Ch.) (1), to *humiliate*

An *italicized* *Strong's* number and transliteration refers you to *The Greek Dictionary*

ABASED
5013 tapĕinŏō (4), to *depress*; to *humiliate*

The total number of times the original language word (*tapĕinŏō*) is translated by this English word (ABASED) in the *King James Version* is listed in parentheses ( )

Words Omitted from the English Index

ENGLISH INDEX TO THE BIBLICAL LANGUAGES

AARON
175 'Ahărôwn (315), Aharon
2 Aarōn (4), Aaron

AARON'S
175 'Ahărôwn (30), Aharon
2 Aarōn (1), Aaron

AARONITES
175 'Ahărôwn (2), Aharon

ABADDON
3 Abaddōn (1), destroying angel

ABAGTHA
5 'Ăbagthâ' (1), Abagtha

ABANA
71 'Ăbânâh (1), stony

ABARIM
5682 'Ăbârîym (4), regions beyond

ABASE
6031 'ânâh (1), to afflict, be afflicted
8213 shâphêl (2), to humiliate
8214 shephal (Ch.) (1), to humiliate

ABASED
5013 tapĕinŏŏ (4), to depress; to humiliate

ABASING
5013 tapĕinŏŏ (1), to depress; to humiliate

ABATED
1639 gâra' (1), to remove, lessen, withhold
2637 châçêr (1), to lack; to fail, want, make less
5127 nûwç (1), to vanish away, flee
7043 qâlal (2), to be, make light
7503 râphâh (1), to slacken

ABBA
5 Abba (3), father

ABDA
5653 'Abdâ' (2), work

ABDEEL
5655 Abde'êl (1), serving God

ABDI
5660 'Abdîy (3), serviceable

ABDIEL
5661 'Abdîy'êl (1), servant of God

ABDON
5658 'Abdôwn (8), servitude

ABED-NEGO
5664 'Ăbêd Negôw (1), servant of -Nego
5665 'Ăbêd Negôw' (Ch.) (14), servant of -Nego

ABEL
59 'Âbêl (2), meadow

62 'Âbêl Bêyth-Mă'akâh (2), meadow of Beth-Maakah
1893 Hebel (8), emptiness or vanity
6 Abĕl (4), emptiness or vanity

ABEL-BETH-MAACHAH
62 'Âbêl Bêyth-Mă'akâh (2), meadow of Beth-Maakah

ABEL-MAIM
66 'Âbêl Mayim (1), meadow of water

ABEL-MEHOLAH
65 'Âbêl Mechôwlâh (3), meadow of dancing

ABEL-MIZRAIM
67 'Âbêl Mitsrayim (1), meadow of Egypt

ABEL-SHITTIM
63 'Âbêl hash-Shiṭṭîym (1), meadow of the acacias

ABEZ
77 'Ebets (1), Ebets

ABHOR
887 bâ'ash (1), to be a moral stench
1602 gâ'al (4), to detest; to reject; to fail
2194 zâ'am (1), to be enraged
3988 mâ'aç (1), to spurn; to disappear
5006 nâ'ats (1), to scorn
8374 tâ'ab (1), to loathe
8581 tâ'ab (9), to loathe, i.e. detest
655 apŏstugĕŏ (1), to detest utterly, hate

ABHORRED
887 bâ'ash (2), to be a moral stench
973 bâchal (1), to loathe, detest
1602 gâ'al (1), to detest; to reject; to fail
2194 zâ'am (1), to be enraged
3988 mâ'aç (2), to spurn; to disappear
5006 nâ'ats (2), to scorn
5010 nâ'ar (1), to reject
6973 qûwts (2), to be, make disgusted
8262 shâqats (1), to loathe, pollute
8581 tâ'ab (3), to loathe, i.e. detest

ABHORREST
6973 qûwts (1), to be, make disgusted
948 bdĕlussŏ (1), to detest, abhor

ABHORRETH
2092 zâham (1), to loathe, make loatheful
3988 mâ'aç (1), to spurn; to disappear
5006 nâ'ats (1), to scorn

8581 tâ'ab (2), to loathe, i.e. detest

ABHORRING
1860 derâ'ôwn (1), aversion, loathing

ABI
21 'Ăbîy (1), fatherly

ABI-ALBON
45 'Ăbîy-'albôwn (1), valiant, strong

ABI-EZER
44 'Ăbîy'ezer (2), helpful

ABI-EZRITE
33 'Ăbîy hâ-'Ezrîy (1), father of the Ezrite

ABI-EZRITES
33 'Ăbîy hâ-'Ezrîy (2), father of the Ezrite

ABIA
29 'Ăbîyâh (1), worshipper of Jehovah
7 Abia (3), knowing

ABIAH
29 'Ăbîyâh (4), worshipper of Jehovah

ABIASAPH
23 'Ăbîy'âçâph (1), gatherer

ABIATHAR
54 'Ebyâthâr (29), abundant, liberal
8 Abiathar (1), abundant, liberal

ABIATHAR'S
54 'Ebyâthâr (1), abundant, liberal

ABIB
24 'âbîyb (6), head of grain; month of Abib

ABIDA
28 'Ăbîydâ' (1), knowing

ABIDAH
28 'Ăbîydâ' (1), knowing

ABIDAN
27 'Ăbîydân (5), judge

ABIDE
935 bôw' (1), to go or come
1481 gûwr (2), to sojourn, live as an alien
1692 dâbaq (1), to cling or adhere
2342 chûwl (1), to wait
2583 chânâh (1), to encamp for abode
3427 yâshab (31), to dwell, remain; to settle
3557 kûwl (3), to keep in; to maintain
3867 lâvâh (1), to unite; to remain
3885 lûwn (5), to be obstinate
5975 'âmad (2), to stand
6965 qûwm (1), to rise
7937 shâkar (1), to become tipsy, to satiate
1961 ĕpimĕnō (3), to remain; to persevere

8581 tâ'ab (2), to loathe, i.e. detest

ABHORRING
1860 derâ'ôwn (1), aversion, loathing

3306 mĕnō (27), to stay, remain
3887 paramĕnō (1), to be permanent, persevere
4357 prŏsmĕnō (1), to remain; to adhere to

ABIDETH
935 bôw' (1), to go or come
3427 yâshab (4), to dwell, to remain; to settle
3885 lûwn (3), to be obstinate
5975 'âmad (2), to stand
3306 mĕnō (20), to stay, remain

ABIDING
3427 yâshab (2), to dwell, to remain; to settle
4723 miqveh (1), confidence; collection
5596 çâphach (1), to associate; be united
7931 shâkan (1), to reside
63 agraulĕō (1), to camp out, live outdoors
1304 diatribō (1), to remain, stay
3306 mĕnō (2), to stay, remain

ABIEL
22 'Ăbîy'êl (3), possessor of God

ABIEZER
44 'Ăbîy'ezer (5), helpful

ABIGAIL
26 'Ăbîygayil (17), source of joy

ABIHAIL
32 'Ăbîyhayil (6), possessor of might

ABIHU
30 'Ăbîyhûw' (12), worshipper of Him

ABIHUD
31 'Ăbîyhûwd (1), possessor of renown

ABIJAH
29 'Ăbîyâh (20), worshipper of Jehovah

ABIJAM
38 'Ăbîyâm (5), seaman

ABILENE
9 Abilēnē (1), Abilene

ABILITY
1767 day (1), enough, sufficient
3581 kôach (2), force, might; strength
5381 nâsag (1), to reach
1411 dunamis (1), force, power, miracle
2141 ĕupŏrĕō (1), to have means, have ability
2479 ischus (1), forcefulness, power

ABIMAEL
39 'Ăbîymâ'êl (2), father of Mael

ABIMELECH
40 'Ăbîymelek (65),
father of the king

ABIMELECH'S
40 'Ăbîymelek (2), father
of the king

ABINADAB
41 'Ăbîynâdâb (13),
generous, i.e. liberal

ABINOAM
42 'Ăbîynô'am (4),
gracious

ABIRAM
48 'Ăbîyrâm (11), lofty,
high

ABISHAG
49 'Ăbîyshag (5),
blundering

ABISHAI
52 'Ăbîyshay (25), (poss.)
generous

ABISHALOM
53 'Ăbîyshâlôwm (2),
friendly

ABISHUA
50 'Ăbîyshûwa' (5),
prosperous

ABISHUR
51 'Ăbîyshûwr (2), (poss.)
mason

ABITAL
37 'Ăbîyṭal (2), fresh

ABITUB
36 'Ăbîyṭûwb (1), good

ABIUD
10 Abiŏud (2), possessor
of renown

ABJECTS
5222 nêkeh (1), smiter;
attacker

ABLE
2296 châgar (1), to gird
on a belt; put on armor
2428 chayil (4), army;
wealth; virtue; strength
3201 yâkôl (44), to be able
3202 yᵉkêl (Ch.) (4), to be
able
3318 yâtsâ' (15), to go,
bring out
3320 yâtsab (3), to
station, offer, continue
3546 kᵉhal (Ch.) (2), to be
able
3581 kôach (1), force,
might; strength
4672+1767 mâtsâ' (2), to
find or acquire
4979+3027 mâttânâh (1),
present; offering; bribe
4991+3027 mattâth (2),
present
5060+1767 nâga' (1), to
strike
5375 nâsâ' (2), to lift up
5381 nâsag (6), to reach
5975 'âmad (1), to stand
6113 'âtsar (1), to hold
back; to maintain
6113+3581 'âtsar (2), to
hold back; to maintain
7272 regel (1), foot; step
1410 dunamai (41), to be
able or possible

1415 dunatŏs (10), ,
powerful or capable
1840 ĕxischuŏ (1), to be
entirely competent
2192 ĕchō (1), to have;
hold; keep
2425 hikanŏs (1), ample;
fit
2427 hikanŏō (1), to
make competent
2480 ischuŏ (6), to have
or exercise force

ABNER
74 'Abnêr (62),
enlightening

ABNER'S
74 'Abnêr (1),
enlightening

ABOARD
1910 ĕpibainō (1), to
mount, embark, arrive

ABODE
1961 hâyâh (2), to exist,
i.e. be or become
2583 chânâh (3), to
encamp
3427 yâshab (33), to
dwell, remain; to settle
5975 'âmad (1), to stand
7931 shâkan (6), to reside
390 anastrĕphō (1), to
remain, to live
835 aulizŏmai (1), to
pass the night
1304 diatribō (4), to
remain, stay
1961 ĕpimĕnō (1), to
remain; to persevere
2476 histēmi (1), to
stand, establish
2650 katamĕnō (1), to
reside, stay, live
3306 mĕnō (12), to stay,
remain
3438 mŏnē (1), residence,
dwelling place
4160 pŏiĕō (1), to make
or do
5278 hupŏmĕnō (1), to
undergo (trials)

ABODEST
3427 yâshab (1), to dwell,
to remain; to settle

ABOLISH
2498 châlaph (1), to
hasten away

ABOLISHED
2865 châthath (1), to
break down
4229 mâchâh (1), to erase
2673 katargĕō (3), to be,
render entirely useless

ABOMINABLE
2194 zâ'am (1), to be
enraged
6292 piggûwl (3),
unclean, fetid
8251 shiqqûwts (2),
disgusting idol
8262 shâqats (2), to
loathe, pollute
8263 sheqets (2), filthy
idolatrous object
8441 tôw'êbâh (4),
something disgusting
8581 tâ'ab (6), to loathe

111 athĕmitŏs (1),
illegal; detestable
947 bdĕluktŏs (1),
detestable, abominable
948 bdĕlussō (1), to
detest, abhor

ABOMINABLY
8581 tâ'ab (1), to loathe

ABOMINATION
887 bâ'ash (1), to be a
moral stench
6292 piggûwl (1),
unclean, fetid
8251 shiqqûwts (7),
disgusting idol
8262 shâqats (2), to
loathe, pollute
8263 sheqets (9), filthy
idolatrous object
8441 tôw'êbâh (52),
something disgusting
946 bdĕlugma (4),
detestable, abominable

ABOMINATIONS
8251 shiqqûwts (13),
disgusting idol
8441 tôw'êbâh (61),
something disgusting
946 bdĕlugma (2),
detestable, abominable

ABOUND
7227 rab (1), great
4052 pĕrissĕuō (12), to
superabound
4121 plĕŏnazō (4), to
superabound
4129 plēthunō (1), to
increase in numbers
5248 hupĕrpĕrissĕuō (1),
to superabound

ABOUNDED
4052 pĕrissĕuō (4), to
superabound
4121 plĕŏnazō (1), to
superabound

ABOUNDETH
7227 rab (1), great
4052 pĕrissĕuō (1), to
superabound
4121 plĕŏnazō (1), to
superabound

ABOUNDING
3513 kâbad (1), to be
rich, glorious
4052 pĕrissĕuō (2), to
superabound

ABOVE
4480 min (2), from, out of
4605 ma'al (55), upward,
above, overhead
4791 mârôwm (7),
elevation; elation
5921 'al (67), above, over,
upon, or against
5922 'al (Ch.) (1), above,
over, upon, or against
507 anō (5), upward or
on the top, heavenward
509 anōthĕn (5), from
above; from the first
511 anŏtĕrŏs (1), upper
part; former part
1883 ĕpanō (2), over or on
1909 ĕpi (5), on, upon
3844 para (4), from; with;
besides; on account of

4012 pĕri (1), about;
around
4117 plĕgma (1), plait or
braid of hair
4253 prŏ (4), before in
time or space
5228 hupĕr (13), over;
above; beyond
5231 hupĕranō (2),
above, upward

ABRAHAM
85 'Abrâhâm (160),
father of a multitude
11 Abraam (68), father of
a multitude

ABRAHAM'S
85 'Abrâhâm (14), father
of a multitude
11 Abraam (5), father of
a multitude

ABRAM
87 'Abrâm (54), high
father

ABRAM'S
87 'Abrâm (7), high
father

ABROAD
1980 hâlak (1), to walk;
live a certain way
2351 chûwts (21),
outside, outdoors
3318 yâtsâ' (1), to go,
bring out
5074 nâdad (1), to rove,
flee; to drive away
5203 nâṭash (1), to
disperse; to thrust off
5310 nâphats (1), to dash
to pieces; to scatter
6327 pûwts (4), to dash
in pieces; to disperse
6340 pâzar (1), to scatter
6504 pârad (1), to spread
6524 pârach (1), to break
forth; to bloom
6527 pâraṭ (5), to scatter
words, i.e. prate
6555 pârats (3), to break
out
6566 pâras (5), to break
apart, disperse, scatter
6581 pâsâh (3), to spread
6584 pâshaṭ (1), to strip
7350 râchôwq (1),
remote, far
7554 râqa' (2), to pound
7849 shâṭach (1), to
expand
864 aphiknĕŏmai (1), to
go forth by rumor
1096+5456 ginŏmai (1),
to be, become
1232 diagnōrizō (1), to
tell abroad
1255 dialalĕō (1), to
converse, discuss
1287 diaskŏrpizō (2), to
scatter; to squander
1289 diaspĕirō (3), to
scatter like seed
1290 diaspŏra (1),
dispersion
1310 diaphēmizō (2), to
spread news
1330 diĕrchŏmai (1), to
traverse, travel through

1519+1096 ĕis (1), *to or into*
1519+5318 ĕis (2), *to or into*
1632 ĕkchĕō (1), *to pour forth; to bestow*
1831 ĕxĕrchŏmai (4), *to issue; to leave*
4496 rhiptō (1), *to fling, toss; to lay out*
4650 skŏrpizō (2), *dissipate, be liberal*

ABSALOM
53 'Ăbîyshâlôwm (102), *friendly*

ABSALOM'S
53 'Ăbîyshâlôwm (5), *friendly*

ABSENCE
666 apŏusia (1), *being away, absence*
817 atĕr (1), *apart from, without*

ABSENT
5641 çâthar (1), *to hide by covering*
548 apĕimi (7), *to be away, be absent*
553 apĕkdĕchŏmai (3), *to expect fully, await*

ABSTAIN
567 apĕchŏmai (6), *to hold oneself off*

ABSTINENCE
776 asitia (1), *state of food fasting*

ABUNDANCE
369+4557 'ayin (1), *there is no, none*
1995 hâmôwn (3), *noise, tumult; many, crowd*
2123 zîyz (1), *fulness of the breast*
3502 yithrâh (1), *wealth, abundance*
4342 makbîyr (1), *plenty*
6109 'otsmâh (1), *numerousness*
6283 'ăthereth (1), *copiousness*
7227 rab (1), *great*
7230 rôb (35), *abundance*
7235 râbâh (2), *to increase*
7647 sâbâ' (1), *copiousness*
7962 shalvâh (1), *security, ease*
8228 shepha' (1), *abundance*
8229 shiph'âh (3), *copiousness*
8317 shârats (1), *to swarm, or abound*
100 hadrŏtēs (1), *liberality*
1411 dunamis (1), *force, power, miracle*
4050 pĕrissĕia (2), *superabundance*
4051 pĕrissĕuma (4), *superabundance*
4052 pĕrissĕuō (5), *to superabound*
5236 hupĕrbŏlē (1), *supereminence*

ABUNDANT
1419 gâdôwl (1), *great*
7227 rab (2), *great*
4052 pĕrissĕuō (2), *to superabound*
4055 pĕrissŏtĕrŏs (3), *more superabundant*
4056 pĕrissŏtĕrŏs (2), *more superabundantly*
4121 plĕŏnazō (1), *o superabound*
4183 pŏlus (1), *much*
5250 hupĕrplĕŏnazō (1), *to superabound*

ABUNDANTLY
1288 bârak (1), *to bless*
3381 yârad (1), *to descend*
5042 nâba' (1), *to gush forth; to utter*
6524 pârach (1), *to break forth; to flourish*
7227 rab (2), *great*
7230 rôb (4), *abundance*
7235 râbâh (1), *to increase*
7301 râvâh (2), *to slake thirst or appetites*
7937 shâkar (1), *to become tipsy, to satiate*
8317 shârats (6), *to swarm, or abound*
1519+4050 ĕis (1), *to or into*
1537+4053 ĕk (1), *out of*
4053 pĕrissŏs (1), *superabundant*
4054 pĕrissŏtĕrŏn (2), *superabundant way*
4056 pĕrissŏtĕrŏs (4), *more superabundantly*
4146 plŏusiōs (2), *copiously, abundantly*

ABUSE
5953 'âlal (2), *to glean; to overdo*
2710 katachraŏmai (1), *to overuse*

ABUSED
5953 'âlal (1), *to glean; to overdo*

ABUSERS
733 arsĕnŏkŏitēs (1), *sodomite*

ABUSING
2710 katachraŏmai (1), *to overuse*

ACCAD
390 'Akkad (1), *Accad*

ACCEPT
1878 dâshên (1), *to be fat, thrive; to satisfy*
3947 lâqach (1), *to take*
5375 nâsâ' (8), *to lift up*
7306 rûwach (1), *to smell or perceive*
7521 râtsâh (13), *to be pleased with; to satisfy*
588 apŏdĕchŏmai (1), *welcome persons*

ACCEPTABLE
977 bâchar (1), *select, chose, prefer*
2656 chêphets (1), *pleasure; desire*
7522 râtsôwn (9), *delight*

8232 shᵉphar (Ch.) (1), *to be beautiful*
587 apŏdĕktŏs (2), *agreeable, pleasant*
1184 dĕktŏs (2), *approved, favorable*
2101 ĕuarĕstŏs (4), *fully agreeable, pleasing*
2144 ĕuprŏsdĕktŏs (2), *approved, favorable*
5285 hupŏpnĕō (1), *to breathe gently*

ACCEPTABLY
2102 ĕuarĕstōs (1), *quite agreeably*

ACCEPTANCE
7522 râtsôwn (1), *delight*

ACCEPTATION
594 apŏdŏchē (2), *acceptance, approval*

ACCEPTED
3190 yâṭab (2), *to be, make well*
5307 nâphal (2), *to fall*
5375 nâsâ' (3), *to lift up*
7521 râtsâh (7), *to be pleased with; to satisfy*
7522 râtsôwn (4), *delight*
7613 sᵉ'êth (1), *elevation; swelling leprous scab*
1184 dĕktŏs (3), *approved, favorable*
1209 dĕchŏmai (2), *to receive, welcome*
2101 ĕuarĕstŏs (1), *fully agreeable, pleasing*
2144 ĕuprŏsdĕktŏs (3), *approved, favorable*
5487 charitŏō (1), *one highly favored*

ACCEPTEST
2983 lambanō (1), *to take, receive*

ACCEPTETH
5375 nâsâ' (1), *to lift up*
7521 râtsâh (2), *to be pleased with; to satisfy*
2983 lambanō (1), *to take, receive*

ACCEPTING
4327 prŏsdĕchŏmai (1), *to receive; to await for*

ACCESS
4318 prŏsagōgē (3), *admission, access*

ACCHO
5910 'Akkôw (1), *to hem in*

ACCOMPANIED
2064+4862 ĕrchŏmai (1), *to go or come*
4311 prŏpĕmpō (1), *to escort or aid in travel*
4902 sunĕpŏmai (1), *to travel in company with*
4905 sunĕrchŏmai (1), *to go with*

ACCOMPANY
2192 ĕchō (1), *to have; hold; keep*

ACCOMPANYING
5973 'îm (1), *with*

ACCOMPLISH
3615 kâlâh (5), *to complete, prepare*

4390 mâlê' (1), *to fill*
6213 'âsâh (2), *to do or make*
6381 pâlâ' (1), *to be, make great, difficult*
6965 qûwm (1), *to rise*
7521 râtsâh (1), *to be pleased with; to satisfy*
8552 tâmam (1), *to complete, finish*
4137 plērŏō (1), *to fill, make complete*

ACCOMPLISHED
1961 hâyâh (1), *to exist, i.e. be or become*
3615 kâlâh (7), *to complete, prepare*
4390 mâlê' (6), *to fill*
8552 tâmam (1), *to complete, finish*
1822 ĕxartizō (1), *to finish out; to equip fully*
2005 ĕpitĕlĕō (1), *to terminate; to undergo*
4130 plēthō (4), *to fulfill, complete*
5055 tĕlĕō (4), *to end, i.e. complete, execute*

ACCOMPLISHING
2005 ĕpitĕlĕō (1), *to terminate; to undergo*

ACCOMPLISHMENT
1604 ĕkplērōsis (1), *completion, end*

ACCORD
5599 çâphîyach (1), *self-sown crop; freshet*
6310 peh (1), *mouth; opening*
830 authairĕtŏs (1), *self-chosen*
844 autŏmatŏs (1), *spontaneous, by itself*
3661 hŏmŏthumadŏn (11), *in togetherness*
4861 sumpsuchŏs (1), *united in spirit*

ACCORDING
413 'êl (2), *to, toward*
834 'âsher (1), *because, in order that*
1767 day (1), *enough, sufficient*
3605 kôl (1), *all, any*
3644 kᵉmôw (2), *like, as*
3651 kên (1), *just; right, correct*
4481 min (Ch.) (1), *from or out of*
5921 'al (39), *above, over, upon, or against*
6310 peh (21), *mouth; opening*
6903 qᵉbêl (Ch.) (1), *on account of, so as, since*
7272 regel (1), *foot; step*
2526 kathŏ (2), *precisely as, in proportion as*
2530 kathŏti (1), *as far or inasmuch as*
2531 kathōs (5), *just or inasmuch as, that*
2596 kata (109), *down; according to*
4314 prŏs (3), *for; on, at; to, toward; against*
5613 hōs (2), *which, how*

ADER
5738 'Ēder (1), arrangement

ADIEL
5717 'Ădîy'êl (3), ornament of God

ADIN
5720 'Ădîyn (4), voluptuous

ADINA
5721 'Ădîynâ' (1), effeminacy

ADINO
5722 'ădîynôw (1), his spear

ADITHAIM
5723 'Ădîythayim (1), double prey

ADJURE
7650 shâba' (2), to swear
1844 ĕxŏrkizō (1), to charge under oath
3726 hŏrkizō (2), to solemnly enjoin

ADJURED
422 'âlâh (1), imprecate, utter a curse
7650 shâba' (1), to swear

ADLAI
5724 'Adlay (1), Adlai

ADMAH
126 'Admâh (5), earthy

ADMATHA
133 'Admâthâ' (1), Admatha

ADMINISTERED
1247 diakŏnĕō (2), to act as a deacon

ADMINISTRATION
1248 diakŏnia (1), attendance, aid, service

ADMINISTRATIONS
1248 diakŏnia (1), attendance, aid, service

ADMIRATION
2295 thauma (1), wonder, marvel
2296 thaumazō (1), to wonder; to admire

ADMIRED
2296 thaumazō (1), to wonder; to admire

ADMONISH
3560 nŏuthĕtĕō (3), to caution or reprove

ADMONISHED
2094 zâhar (2), to enlighten
5749 'ûwd (1), to protest, testify; to restore
3867 parainĕō (1), to recommend or advise
5537 chrēmatizō (1), to utter an oracle

ADMONISHING
3560 nŏuthĕtĕō (1), to caution or reprove

ADMONITION
3559 nŏuthĕsia (3), mild rebuke or warning

ADNA
5733 'Adnâ' (2), pleasure

ADNAH
5734 'Adnâh (2), pleasure

ADO
2350 thŏrubĕō (1), to disturb; clamor

ADONI-BEZEK
137 'Ădônîy-Bezeq (3), lord of Bezek

ADONI-ZEDEK
139 'Ădônîy-Tsedeq (2), lord of justice

ADONIJAH
138 'Ădônîyâh (25), worshipper of Jehovah

ADONIKAM
140 'Ădônîyqâm (3), high, lofty

ADONIRAM
141 'Ădônîyrâm (2), lord of height

ADOPTION
5206 huiŏthĕsia (5), adoption

ADORAIM
115 'Ădôwrayim (1), double mound

ADORAM
151 'Ădôrâm (2), Adoram

ADORN
2885 kŏsmĕō (2), to decorate; to snuff

ADORNED
5710 'âdâh (1), to remove; to bedeck
2885 kŏsmĕō (3), to decorate; to snuff

ADORNETH
5710 'âdâh (1), to remove; to bedeck

ADORNING
2889 kŏsmŏs (2), world

ADRAMMELECH
152 'Adrammelek (3), splendor of (the) king

ADRAMYTTIUM
98 Adramuttēnŏs (1), Adramyttene

ADRIA
99 Adrias (1), Adriatic Sea

ADRIEL
5741 'Adrîy'êl (2), flock of God

ADULLAM
5725 'Ădullâm (8), Adullam

ADULLAMITE
5726 'Ădullâmîy (3), Adullamite

ADULTERER
5003 nâ'aph (3), to commit adultery

ADULTERERS
5003 nâ'aph (5), to commit adultery
3432 mŏichŏs (4), male paramour

ADULTERESS
802+376 'ishshâh (1), woman, wife
5003 nâ'aph (2), to commit adultery

3428 mŏichalis (2), adulteress

ADULTERESSES
5003 nâ'aph (2), to commit adultery
3428 mŏichalis (1), adulteress

ADULTERIES
5004 nî'ûph (2), adultery
5005 na'ăphûwph (1), adultery
3430 mŏichĕia (2), adultery

ADULTEROUS
5003 nâ'aph (1), to commit adultery
3428 mŏichalis (3), adulteress

ADULTERY
5003 nâ'aph (17), to commit adultery
3428 mŏichalis (1), adulteress
3429 mŏichaō (6), to commit adultery
3430 mŏichĕia (2), adultery
3431 mŏichĕuō (14), to commit adultery

ADUMMIM
131 'Ădummîym (2), red spots

ADVANCED
1431 gâdal (1), to be great, make great
5375 nâsâ' (2), to lift up
6213 'âsâh (1), to do or make

ADVANTAGE
5532 çâkan (1), to be serviceable to
4053 pĕrissŏs (1), superabundant
4122 plĕŏnĕktĕō (1), to be covetous
5622 ŏphĕlĕia (1), value, advantage

ADVANTAGED
5623 ŏphĕlĕō (1), to benefit, be of use

ADVANTAGETH
3786 ŏphĕlŏs (1), accumulate or benefit

ADVENTURE
5254 nâçâh (1), to test, attempt
1325 didōmi (1), to give

ADVENTURED
7993 shâlak (1), to throw out, down or away

ADVERSARIES
6696 tsûwr (1), to cramp, i.e. confine; to harass
6862 tsar (21), trouble; opponent
6887 tsârar (2), to cramp
7378 rîyb (1), to hold a controversy; to defend
7853 sâṭan (5), to attack by accusation
7854 sâṭân (1), opponent
480 antikĕimai (4), be adverse to
5227 hupĕnantiŏs (1), opposed; opponent

ADVERSARY
376+7379 'îysh (1), man; male; someone
1166+4941 bâ'al (1), to be master; to marry
6862 tsar (6), trouble; opponent
6869 tsârâh (1), trouble; rival-wife
6887 tsârar (1), to cramp
7854 sâṭân (6), opponent
476 antidikŏs (5), opponent
480 antikĕimai (1), be adverse to

ADVERSITIES
6869 tsârâh (1), trouble; rival-wife
7451 ra' (1), bad; evil

ADVERSITY
6761 tsela' (1), limping
6862 tsar (1), trouble; opponent
6869 tsârâh (4), trouble; rival-wife
7451 ra' (3), bad; evil
2558 kakŏuchĕō (1), to maltreat; to torment

ADVERTISE
1540+241 gâlâh (1), to denude; to reveal
3289 yâ'ats (1), to advise

ADVICE
1697 dâbâr (2), word; matter; thing
2940 ṭa'am (1), intelligence; mandate
3289 yâ'ats (2), to advise
5779 'ûwts (1), to consult
6098 'êtsâh (1), advice; plan; prudence
8458 tachbûlâh (1), guidance; plan
1106 gnōmē (1), cognition, opinion

ADVISE
3045 yâda' (1), to know
3289 yâ'ats (1), to advise
7200 râ'âh (1), to see

ADVISED
3289 yâ'ats (1), to advise
1012+5087 bŏulē (1), purpose, plan, decision

ADVISEMENT
6098 'êtsâh (1), advice; plan; prudence

ADVOCATE
3875 paraklētŏs (1), intercessor, consoler

AENEAS
132 Ainĕas (2), (poss.) praise

AENON
137 Ainōn (1), springs

AFAR
4801 merchâq (3), distant place; from afar
7350 râchôwq (29), remote, far
7368 râchaq (1), to recede; remove
3112 makran (2), at a distance, far away
3113 makrŏthĕn (13), from a distance or afar

3467 muŏpazŏ (1), to *see
indistinctly, be myopic*
4207 pŏrrhŏthĕn (2),
distantly, at a distance

AFFAIRS
1697 dâbâr (2), *word;
matter; thing*
5673 'ăbîydâh (Ch.) (2),
labor or business
2596 kata (1), *down;
according to*
4012 pĕri (2), *about;
around*
4230 pragmatĕia (1),
transaction

AFFECT
2206 zēlŏŏ (2), to *have
warmth of feeling for*

AFFECTED
2206 zēlŏŏ (1), to *have
warmth of feeling for*
2559 kakŏŏ (1), to *injure;
to oppress; to embitter*

AFFECTETH
5953 'âlal (1), to *glean; to
overdo*

AFFECTION
7521 râtsâh (1), to *be
pleased with; to satisfy*
794 astŏrgŏs (2),
hard-hearted
3806 pathŏs (1), *passion,
concupiscence*
4698 splagchnŏn (1),
intestine; affection, pity
5426 phrŏnĕŏ (1), to *be
mentally disposed*

AFFECTIONATELY
2442 himĕirŏmai (1), to
long for, desire

AFFECTIONED
5387 philŏstŏrgŏs (1),
lovingly devoted

AFFECTIONS
3804 pathēma (1),
passion; suffering
3806 pathŏs (1), *passion,
concupiscence*

AFFINITY
2859 châthan (3), to
become related

AFFIRM
1226 diabĕbaiŏŏmai (2),
to *confirm thoroughly*
5346 phēmi (1), to *speak
or say*

AFFIRMED
1340 diïschurizŏmai (2),
to *asseverate*
5335 phaskŏ (1), to
assert a claim

AFFLICT
3013 yâgâh (1), to *grieve;
to torment*
3513 kâbad (1), to *be
heavy, severe, dull*
3905 lâchats (1), to *press;
to distress*
6031 'ânâh (28), to *afflict,
be afflicted*
6887 tsârar (2), to *cramp*
7489 râ'a' (2), to *break to
pieces*

AFFLICTED
1790 dak (1), *injured,
oppressed*
3013 yâgâh (3), to *grieve;
to torment*
4523 mâç (1),
disconsolate
6031 'ânâh (21), to *afflict,
be afflicted*
6040 'ŏnîy (1),
depression, i.e. misery
6041 'ânîy (15), *depressed*
6862 tsar (1), *trouble;
opponent*
6887 tsârar (2), to *cramp*
7043 qâlal (1), to *be easy,
trifling, vile*
7489 râ'a' (3), to *break to
pieces*
2346 thlibŏ (3), to *crowd,
press, trouble*
2347 thlipsis (1),
pressure, trouble
2553 kakŏpathĕŏ (1), to
undergo hardship
5003 talaipōrĕŏ (1), to *be
wretched*

AFFLICTEST
6031 'ânâh (1), to *afflict,
be afflicted*

AFFLICTION
205 'âven (3), *trouble,
vanity, wickedness*
3905 lâchats (3), to *press;
to distress*
4157 mûw'âqâh (1),
pressure; distress
6039 'ênûwth (1),
affliction
6040 'ŏnîy (33),
depression, i.e. misery
6862 tsar (3), *trouble;
opponent*
6869 tsârâh (7), *trouble;
rival-wife*
6887 tsârar (1), to *cramp*
7451 ra' (5), *bad; evil*
7667 sheber (2), *fracture;
ruin*
2347 thlipsis (11),
pressure, trouble
2552 kakŏpathĕia (1),
hardship, suffering
2561 kakōsis (1),
maltreatment
4797 sugchĕŏ (1), to
throw into disorder

AFFLICTIONS
6031 'ânâh (1), to *afflict,
be afflicted*
7451 ra' (1), *bad; evil*
2347 thlipsis (6),
pressure, trouble
2553 kakŏpathĕŏ (1), to
undergo hardship
3804 pathēma (3),
passion; suffering
4777 sugkakŏpathĕŏ (1),
to *suffer hardship*

AFFORDING
6329 pûwq (1), to *issue;
to furnish; to secure*

AFFRIGHT
3372 yârê' (1), to *fear; to
revere*

AFFRIGHTED
270+8178 'âchaz (1), to
seize, grasp; possess
926 bâhal (1), to *tremble;
be, make agitated*
1204 bâ'ath (1), to *fear*
2865 châthath (1), to
break down
6206 'ârats (1), to *awe; to
dread; to harass*
1568 ĕkthambĕŏ (2), to
astonish utterly
1719 ĕmphŏbŏs (2),
alarmed, terrified

AFOOT
3978 pĕzĕuŏ (1), to *travel
by land, i.e. on foot*
3979 pĕzĕi (1), *on foot*

AFORE
3808 lô' (1), no, *not*
6440 pânîym (2), *face;
front*
6924 qedem (1), *before,
anciently*
4270 prŏgraphŏ (1), to
write previously
4279 prŏĕpaggĕllŏmai
(1), to *promise from
before*
4282 prŏĕtŏimazŏ (1), to
fit up in advance

AFOREHAND
4301 prŏlambanŏ (1), to
take before

AFORETIME
4481+6928+1836 min
(Ch.) (1), *from or out of*
6440 pânîym (2), *face;
front*
6924 qedem (1), *before,
anciently*
7223 rî'shôwn (1), *first, in
place, time or rank*
4218 pŏtĕ (1), *at some
time, ever*
4270 prŏgraphŏ (1), to
write previously

AFRAID
926 bâhal (3), to *tremble;
be, make agitated;
hasten, hurry anxiously*
1204 bâ'ath (10), to *fear*
1481 gûwr (6), to *sojourn,
live as an alien*
1672 dâ'ag (3), *be
anxious, be afraid*
1763 dᵉchal (Ch.) (1), to
fear; be formidable
2119 zâchal (1), to *crawl;
glide*
2296 châgar (1), to *gird
on a belt; put on armor*
2342 chûwl (1), to *dance,
whirl; to writhe*
2727 chârag (1), to *be
dismayed, tremble*
2729 chârad (20), to
shudder with terror
2730 chârêd (1), *fearful*
2865 châthath (6), to
*break down, either by
violence, or by fear*
3025 yâgôr (5), to *fear*
3372 yârê' (78), to *fear; to
revere*
3373 yârê' (3), *fearing;
reverent*

AFFRIGHTED
6206 'ârats (3), to *awe; to
dread; to harass*
6342 pâchad (9), to *be
startled; to fear*
7264 râgaz (1), to *quiver*
7297 râhâh (1), to *fear*
7493 râ'ash (1), to
undulate, quake
8175 sâ'ar (3), to *storm;
to shiver, i.e. fear*
1168 dĕiliaŏ (1), to *be
timid, cowardly*
1630 ĕkphŏbŏs (1),
frightened out of one's
wits
1719 ĕmphŏbŏs (3),
alarmed, terrified
5141 trĕmŏ (1), to
tremble or fear
5399 phŏbĕŏ (29), to *fear,
be frightened*

AFRESH
388 anastaurŏŏ (1), to
re-crucify

AFTER
167 'âhal (1), to *pitch a
tent*
310 'achar (492), *after*
311 'achar (Ch.) (3), *after*
314 'achărôwn (5), *late
or last; behind; western*
413 'êl (4), *to, toward*
834 'âsher (2), *because,
in order that*
870 'âthar (Ch.) (3), *after*
1767 day (2), *enough,
sufficient*
1863 dardar (1), *thorn*
3602 kâkâh (4), *just so*
4480 min (1), *from, out of*
4481 min (Ch.) (1), *from
or out of*
5921 'al (18), *above, over,
upon, or against*
6256 'êth (1), *time*
6310 peh (1), *mouth;
opening*
7093 qêts (10), *extremity;
after*
7097 qâtseh (1), *extremity*
7272 regel (4), *foot; step*
516 axiŏs (1),
appropriately, suitable
1207 dĕutĕrŏprŏtŏs (1),
second-first
1223 dia (3), *through, by
means of; because of*
1230 diaginŏmai (1), to
have time elapse
1377 diōkŏ (1), to *pursue;
to persecute*
1534 ĕita (3), *then,
moreover*
1567 ĕkzĕtĕŏ (2), to *seek
out*
1722 ĕn (1), *in; during;
because of*
1836 hĕxēs (1),
successive, next
1872 ĕpakŏlŏuthĕŏ (1), to
accompany, follow
1887 ĕpauriŏn (1),
to-morrow
1894 ĕpĕidē (1), *when,
whereas*
1899 ĕpĕita (3),
thereafter, afterward
1905 ĕpĕrōtaŏ (1), to
inquire, seek

English

1909 ĕpi (3), *on, upon*
1934 ĕpizētĕō (4), *to search (inquire) for*
1938 ĕpithumētēs (1), *craver*
1971 ĕpipŏthĕō (3), *intensely crave*
2089 ĕti (1), *yet, still*
2517 kathĕxēs (1), *in a sequence*
2569 kalŏpŏiĕō (3), *to do well*
2596 kata (58), *down; according to*
2614 katadiōkō (1), *to search for, look for*
2628 katakŏlŏuthĕō (1), *to accompany closely*
3195 mĕllō (2), *to intend, i.e. be about to be*
3326 mĕta (96), *with, among; after, later*
3693 ŏpisthĕn (2), *at the back; after*
3694 ŏpisō (22), *behind, after, following*
3753 hŏtĕ (3), *when; as*
3765 ŏukĕti (1), *not yet, no longer*
3779 hŏutō (2), *in this way; likewise*
4023 pĕriĕchō (1), *to clasp; to encircle*
4137 plērŏō (1), *to fill, make complete*
4329 prŏsdŏkia (1), *apprehension*
4459 pōs (1), *in what way?; how?; how* much!
5225 huparchō (1), *to come into existence*
5613 hōs (3), *which, how, i.e. in that manner*
5615 hōsautōs (1), *in the same way*
5618 hōspĕr (1), *exactly like*

AFTERNOON
5186+3117 nâṭâh (1), *to stretch* or spread out

AFTERWARD
310 'achar (21), *after*
314 'achărôwn (2), *late* or *last; behind; western*
1208 dĕutĕrŏs (1), *second; secondly*
1534 ĕita (1), *then, moreover*
1899 ĕpĕita (2), *thereafter, afterward*
2517 kathĕxēs (1), *in a sequence*
2547 kakĕithĕn (1), *from that place (or time)*
3347 mĕtĕpĕita (1), *thereafter*
5305 hustĕrŏn (7), *more lately, i.e. eventually*

AFTERWARDS
268 'âchôwr (1), *behind, backward; west*
310 'achar (5), *after*
310+3651 'achar (2), *after*
314 'achărôwn (1), *late* or *last; behind; western*
1899 ĕpĕita (1), *thereafter, afterward*

5305 hustĕrŏn (1), *more lately, i.e. eventually*

AGABUS
13 Agabŏs (2), *locust*

AGAG
90 'Ăgag (8), *flame*

AGAGITE
91 'Ăgăgîy (5), *Agagite*

AGAIN
310 'achar (1), *after*
322 'ăchôrannîyth (1), *by turning around*
1571 gam (2), *also; even*
1906 hêd (1), *shout of joy*
1946 hûwk (Ch.) (1), *to go, come*
3138 yôwreh (2), *autumn rain showers*
3254 yâçaph (49), *to add or augment*
3284 ya'ănâh (1), *ostrich*
5437 çâbab (1), *to surround*
5750 'ôwd (51), *again; repeatedly; still; more*
7725 shûwb (246), *to turn back; to return*
7999 shâlam (3), *to reciprocate*
8138 shânâh (1), *to fold; to transmute*
8145 shênîy (7), *second; again*
8579 tinyânûwth (Ch.) (1), *second time*
313 anagĕnnaō (2), *to beget or bear again*
321 anagō (2), *to lead up; to bring out*
326 anazaō (3), *to recover life, live again*
330 anathallō (1), *to flourish; to revive*
344 anakamptō (1), *to turn back, come back*
364 anamnēsis (1), *recollection*
375 anapĕmpō (2), *to send up or back*
386 anastasis (2), *resurrection* from death
450 anistēmi (15), *to come back to life*
456 anŏikŏdŏmĕō (2), *to rebuild*
467 antapŏdidōmi (2), *to require good or evil*
470 antapŏkrinŏmai (1), *to contradict or dispute*
479 antikalĕō (1), *to reciprocate*
483 antilĕgō (1), *to dispute, refuse*
486 antilŏidŏrĕō (1), *to rail in reply, retaliate*
488 antimĕtrĕō (1), *to measure in return*
509 anōthĕn (2), *from the first; anew*
518 apaggĕllō (2), *to announce, proclaim*
523 apaitĕō (1), *to demand back*
560 apĕlpizō (1), *to fully expect* in return
591 apŏdidōmi (2), *to give away*

600 apŏkathistēmi (1), *to reconstitute*
618 apŏlambanō (1), *to receive; be repaid*
654 apŏstrĕphō (2), *to turn away or back*
1208 dĕutĕrŏs (3), *second; secondly*
1364 dis (2), *twice*
1453 ĕgĕirō (8), *to waken, i.e. rouse*
1458 ĕgkalĕō (1), *to charge*
1515 ĕirēnē (1), *peace; health; prosperity*
1880 ĕpanĕrchŏmai (1), *return home*
1994 ĕpistrĕphō (5), *to revert, turn back to*
3326 mĕta (1), *with, among; after, later*
3825 palin (141), *anew, i.e. back; once more*
4388 prŏtithĕmai (2), *to place before*
4762 strĕphō (2), *to turn around or reverse*
5290 hupŏstrĕphō (6), *to return*

AGAINST
413 'êl (144), *to, toward*
431 'ălûw (Ch.) (1), *lo!*
834 'âsher (1), *because, in order that*
4136 mûwl (19), *in front of, opposite*
4775 mârad (1), *to rebel*
5048 neged (33), *over against or before*
5227 nôkach (1), *opposite, in front of*
5704 'ad (3), *as far (long) as; during; while; until*
5921 'al (525), *above, over, upon,* or *against*
5922 'al (Ch.) (7), *above, over, upon,* or *against*
5971 'am (1), *people; tribe; troops*
5973 'îm (35), *with*
5978 'immâd (1), *along with*
5980 'ummâh (26), *near, beside, along with*
6440 pânîym (11), *face; front*
6640 tsᵉbûw (Ch.) (1), *affair; matter of determination*
6655 tsad (Ch.) (1), *at or upon the side of; against*
6903 qᵉbêl (Ch.) (1), *in front of, before*
6965 qûwm (1), *to rise*
7125 qîr'âh (41), *to encounter; to happen*
210 akōn (1), *unwilling*
368 anantirrhētŏs (1), *indisputable*
470 antapŏkrinŏmai (1), *to contradict or dispute*
471 antĕpō (1), *to refute*
481 antikru (1), *opposite*
483 antilĕgō (5), *to dispute, refuse*
495 antipĕran (1), *on the opposite side*

497 antistratĕuŏmai (1), *to wage war against*
561 apĕnanti (2), *before or against*
1519 ĕis (24), *to or into*
1690 ĕmbrimaŏmai (1), *to blame, warn sternly*
1693 ĕmmainŏmai (1), *to rage at*
1715 ĕmprŏsthĕn (1), *in front of*
1722 ĕn (1), *in; during*
1727 ĕnantiŏs (1), *opposite*
1909 ĕpi (38), *on, upon*
2018 ĕpiphĕrō (1), *to inflict, bring upon*
2019 ĕpiphōnĕō (1), *to exclaim, shout*
2596 kata (59), *down; according to*
2620 katakauchaŏmai (2), *to exult against*
2649 katamarturĕō (1), *to testify against*
2691 katastrēniaō (1), *to be voluptuous against*
2702 kataphĕrō (1), *to bear down*
2713 katĕnanti (4), *directly opposite*
2729 katischuŏ (1), *to overpower, prevail*
3326 mĕta (4), *with, among; after, later*
3844 para (2), *from; with; besides; on account of*
4012 pĕri (2), *around*
4314 prŏs (23), *for; on, at; to, toward; against*
4366 prŏsrĕgnumi (1), *to burst upon*
5396 phluarĕō (1), *to berate*

AGAR
28 Agar (2), *Hagar*

AGATE
3539 kadkôd (1), *(poss.) sparkling ruby*
7618 shᵉbûw (2), *agate*

AGATES
3539 kadkôd (1), *(poss.) sparkling ruby*

AGE
582 'ĕnôwsh (1), *man; person, human*
1121 bên (3), *son, descendant; people*
1755 dôwr (2), *dwelling*
2207 zôqen (1), *old age*
2209 ziqnâh (1), *old age*
2465 cheled (7), *fleeting time; this world*
3117 yôwm (6), *day; time period*
3485 Yissâˢkâr (1), *he will bring a reward*
3624 kelach (2), *maturity*
7869 sêyb (1), *old age*
7872 sêybâh (6), *old age*
2244 hēlikia (4), *maturity*
2250 hēmĕra (1), *day; period of time*
5046 tĕlĕiŏs (1), *complete; mature*
5230 hupĕrakmŏs (1), *past the prime of youth*

AGED
2204 zâqên (1), *to be old*
2205 zâqên (4), *old*
3453 yâshîysh (1), *old man*
4246 prĕsbutēs (2), *old man*
4247 prĕsbutis (1), *old woman*

AGEE
89 'Âgê' (1), *Agee*

AGES
165 aiōn (2), *perpetuity, ever; world*
1074 gĕnĕa (2), *generation; age*

AGO
3117 yôwm (1), *day; time period*
6928 qadmâh (Ch.) (1), *former time; formerly*
7350 râchôwq (3), *remote, far*
575 apô (4), *from, away*
3819 palai (2), *formerly; sometime since*
4253 prŏ (1), *before in time or space*

AGONY
74 agōnia (1), *anguish, anxiety*

AGREE
1526 ĕisi (1), they *are*
2132 ĕunŏĕō (1), to *reconcile*
2470 isŏs (1), *similar*
4160+3391+1106 pŏiĕō (1), to *make* or *do*
4856 sumphōnĕō (3), to *be harmonious*

AGREED
3259 yâ'ad (1), to *meet; to summon; to direct*
800 asumphōnŏs (1), *disagreeable*
2470 isŏs (1), *similar*
3982 pĕithō (1), to *pacify* or *conciliate*
4856 sumphōnĕō (2), to *be harmonious*
4934 suntithĕmai (2), to *consent, concur, agree*

AGREEMENT
2374 chôzeh (1), *beholder* in vision
2380 châzûwth (1), *revelation; compact*
4339 mêyshâr (1), *straightness; rectitude*
4783 sugkatathĕsis (1), *accord* with

AGREETH
3662 hŏmŏiazō (1), to *resemble, be like*
4856 sumphōnĕō (1), to *be harmonious*

AGRIPPA
67 Agrippas (12), *wild-horse* tamer

AGROUND
2027 ĕpŏkĕllō (1), to *beach* a ship vessel

AGUE
6920 qaddachath (1), *inflammation*

AGUR
94 'Âgûwr (1), *one received*

AH
162 'ăhâhh (8), *Oh!, Alas!, Woe!*
253 'âch (2), *Oh!; Alas!*
1945 hôwy (7), *oh!, woe!*
3758 ŏua (1), *ah!; so!*

AHA
253 'âch (7), *Oh!; Alas!*

AHAB
256 'Ach'âb (90), *friend of* (his) *father*

AHAB'S
256 'Ach'âb (2), *friend of* (his) *father*

AHARAH
315 'Achrach (1), *after* (his) *brother*

AHARHEL
316 'Acharchêl (1), *safe*

AHASAI
273 'Achzay (1), *seizer*

AHASBAI
308 'Ăchaçbay (1), *Achasbai*

AHASUERUS
325 'Ăchashvêrôwsh (30), *Xerxes*

AHASUERUS'
325 'Ăchashvêrôwsh (1), *Xerxes*

AHAVA
163 'Ăhăvâ' (3), *Ahava*

AHAZ
271 'Âchâz (41), *possessor*

AHAZIAH
274 'Ăchazyâh (37), *Jehovah has seized*

AHBAN
257 'Achbân (1), *one who understands*

AHER
313 'Achêr (1), *Acher*

AHI
277 'Ăchîy (2), *brotherly*

AHIAH
281 'Ăchiyâh (4), *worshipper of Jehovah*

AHIAM
279 'Ăchîy'âm (2), *uncle*

AHIAN
291 'Achyân (1), *brotherly*

AHIEZER
295 'Ăchîy'ezer (6), *brother of help*

AHIHUD
282 'Ăchîyhûwd (1), *possessor of renown*
284 'Ăchîychûd (1), *mysterious*

AHIJAH
281 'Ăchiyâh (20), *worshipper of Jehovah*

AHIKAM
296 'Ăchîyqâm (20), *high, exalted*

AHILUD
286 'Ăchîylûwd (5), *brother of one born*

AHIMAAZ
290 'Ăchîyma'ats (15), *brother of anger*

AHIMAN
289 'Ăchîyman (4), *gift*

AHIMELECH
288 'Ăchîymelek (16), *brother of* (the) *king*

AHIMELECH'S
288 'Ăchîymelek (1), *brother of* (the) *king*

AHIMOTH
287 'Ăchîymôwth (1), *brother of death*

AHINADAB
292 'Ăchîynâdâb (1), *brother of liberality*

AHINOAM
293 'Ăchîynô'am (7), *brother of pleasantness*

AHIO
283 'Achyôw (6), *brotherly*

AHIRA
299 'Ăchîyra' (5), *brother of wrong*

AHIRAM
297 'Ăchîyrâm (1), *high, exalted*

AHIRAMITES
298 'Ăchîyrâmîy (1), *Achiramite*

AHISAMACH
294 'Ăchîyçâmâk (3), *brother of support*

AHISHAHAR
300 'Achîyshachar (1), *brother of* (the) *dawn*

AHISHAR
301 'Ăchîyshâr (1), *brother of* (the) *singer*

AHITHOPHEL
302 'Ăchîythôphel (20), *brother of folly*

AHITUB
285 'Ăchîyṭûwb (15), *brother of goodness*

AHLAB
303 'Achlâb (1), *fertile*

AHLAI
304 'Achlay (2), *wishful*

AHOAH
265 'Ăchôwach (1), *brotherly*

AHOHITE
266 'Ăchôwchîy (4), *Achochite*
1121+266 bên (1), *son, descendant; people*

AHOLAH
170 'Ohŏlâh (5), *her tent* (idolatrous *sanctuary*)

AHOLIAB
171 'Ohŏlîy'âb (5), *tent of* (his) *father*

AHOLIBAH
172 'Ohŏlîybâh (6), *my tent* (is) *in her*

AHOLIBAMAH
173 'Ohŏlîybâmâh (8), *tent of* (the) *height*

AHUMAI
267 'Ăchûwmay (1), *neighbor of water*

AHUZAM
275 'Ăchuzzâm (1), *seizure*

AHUZZATH
276 'Ăchuzzath (1), *possession*

AI
5857 'Ay (34), *ruin*
5892 'îyr (1), *city, town,* unwalled-*village*

AIAH
345 'Ayâh (5), *hawk*

AIATH
5857 'Ay (1), *ruin*

AIDED
2388+3027 châzaq (1), to *be strong; courageous*

AIJA
5857 'Ay (1), *ruin*

AIJALON
357 'Ayâlôwn (7), *deer-field*

AIJELETH
365 'ayeleth (1), *doe deer*

AIN
5871 'Ayin (5), *fountain*

AIR
7307 rûwach (1), *breath; wind; life*-spirit
8064 shâmayim (21), *sky; unseen celestial places*
109 aēr (7), *air, sky*
3772 ŏuranŏs (10), *sky; air; heaven*

AJAH
345 'Ayâh (1), *hawk*

AJALON
357 'Ayâlôwn (3), *deer-field*

AKAN
6130 'Âqân (1), *crooked*

AKKUB
6126 'Aqqûwb (8), *insidious*

AKRABBIM
6137 'aqrâb (2), *scorpion*

ALABASTER
211 alabastrŏn (3), *alabaster*

ALAMETH
5964 'Âlemeth (1), *covering*

ALAMMELECH
487 'Allammelek (1), *oak of* (the) *king*

ALAMOTH
5961 'Ălâmôwth (2), *soprano*

ALARM
7321 rûwa' (4), to *shout for alarm or joy*
8643 t°rûw'âh (6), *battle-cry; clangor*

ALAS
160 'ahăbâh (7),
affection, love
188 'ŏwy (1), *Oh!, Woe!*
253 'âch (1), *Oh!; Alas!*
994 bîy (1), *Oh that!*
1930 hôw (1), *oh! ah!*
1945 hôwy (2), *oh!, woe!*
3758 ŏua (5), *ah!; so!*

ALBEIT
2443 hina (1), in order
that

ALEMETH
5964 'Ălemeth (3),
covering

ALEXANDER
223 Alĕxandrŏs (5),
man-defender

ALEXANDRIA
221 Alĕxandrĕus (3), *of
Alexandria*

ALEXANDRIANS
221 Alĕxandrĕus (1), *of
Alexandria*

ALGUM
418 'algûwmmîym (3),
Algum-wood

ALIAH
5933 'Alvâh (1), *moral
perverseness*

ALIAN
5935 'Alvân (1), *lofty*

ALIEN
1616 gêr (1), *foreigner*
5236 nêkâr (1), *foreigner*
5237 nokrîy (3), *foreign;
non-relative*

ALIENATE
5674 'âbar (1), to *cross
over; to transition*

ALIENATED
3363 yâqa' (2), to *be
dislocated*
5361 nâqa' (3), to *feel
aversion*
526 apallŏtriŏō (2), to *be
excluded*

ALIENS
5237 nokrîy (1), *foreign;
non-relative*
245 allŏtriŏs (1), *not
one's own*
526 apallŏtriŏō (1), to *be
excluded*

ALIKE
259 'echâd (1), *first*
834 'ăsher (1), *who,
which, what, that*
1571 gam (1), *also; even*
3162 yachad (5), *unitedly*
7737 shâvâh (1), to
equalize; to resemble

ALIVE
2416 chay (30), *alive;
raw; fresh; life*
2418 chăyă' (Ch.) (1), to
live
2421 châyâh (34), to *live;
to revive*
8300 sârîyd (1), *survivor;
remainder*
326 anazaō (2), to
recover life, live again
2198 zaō (15), to *live*

ALL
622 'âçaph (1), to *gather,
collect*
1571 gam (1), *also; even*
3162 yachad (1), *unitedly*
3605 kôl (4194), *all, any*
3606 kôl (Ch.) (50), *all,
any or every*
3632 kâlîyl (2), *whole,
entire; complete; whole*
3885 lûwn (14), to *be
obstinate with*
4393 mᵉlô' (9), *fulness*
4557 miçpâr (3), *number*
5973 'îm (2), *with*
7230 rôb (1), *abundance*
8552 tâmam (2), to
complete, finish
537 hapas (39), *all, every
one, whole*
1273 dianuktĕrĕuō (1), to
pass, spend the night
2178 ĕphapax (1), *once
for all*
2527 kathŏlŏu (1),
entirely, completely
3122 malista (1), *in the
greatest degree*
3364 ŏu mē (7), *not at all,
absolutely not*
3367 mēdĕis (1), *not even
one*
3650 hŏlŏs (62), *whole* or
all, i.e. complete
3654 hŏlōs (2), *completely*
3745 hŏsŏs (6), *as much
as*
3762 ŏudĕis (4), *none,
nobody, nothing*
3779 hŏutō (1), *in this
way; likewise*
3829 pandŏchĕiŏn (1),
public *lodging-place*
3832 panŏiki (1), *with
the whole family*
3833 panŏplia (1), *full
armor*
3837 pantachŏu (1),
universally, everywhere
3843 pantōs (2), *entirely;
at all events*
3956 pas (947), *all, any,
every, whole*
4219 pŏtĕ (1), *at what
time?*
4561 sarx (1), *flesh*

ALLEGING
3908 paratithēmi (1), to
present something

ALLEGORY
238 allĕgŏrĕō (1), to
allegorize

ALLELUIA
239 allĕlŏuïa (4), *praise
Jehovah!*

ALLIED
7138 qârôwb (1), *near,
close*

ALLON
438 'Allôwn (2), *oak*

ALLON-BACHUTH
439 'Allôwn Bâkûwth (1),
oak of weeping

ALLOW
1097 ginōskō (1), to *know*
4327 prŏsdĕchŏmai (1),
to *receive; to await for*
4909 sunĕudŏkĕō (1), to
assent to, *feel gratified*

ALLOWANCE
737 'ărûchâh (1), *ration,
portion* of food

ALLOWED
1381 dŏkimazō (1), to
test; to approve

ALLOWETH
1381 dŏkimazō (1), to
test; to approve

ALLURE
6601 pâthâh (1), to *be,
make simple; to delude*
1185 dĕlĕazō (1), to
delude, seduce

ALMIGHTY
7706 Shadday (48), the
Almighty God
3841 pantŏkratōr (9),
Absolute *sovereign*

ALMODAD
486 'Almôwdâd (2),
Almodad

ALMON
5960 'Almôwn (1), *hidden*

ALMON-DIBLATHAIM
5963 'Almôn
Diblâthâyᵉmâh (2),
*Almon toward
Diblathajim*

ALMOND
8247 shâqêd (2), *almond*
tree or nut

ALMONDS
8246 shâqad (6), to *be,
almond-shaped*
8247 shâqêd (2), *almond*
tree or nut

ALMOST
4592 mᵉ'aṭ (5), *little* or
few
3195 mĕllō (1), to *intend,
i.e. be about to*
4975 schĕdŏn (3), *nigh,
i.e. nearly*

ALMS
1654 ĕlĕĕmŏsunē (13),
benefaction

ALMSDEEDS
1654 ĕlĕĕmŏsunē (1),
benefaction

ALMUG
484 'almuggiym (3),
Almug-wood

ALOES
174 'ăhâlîym (4),
aloe-wood sticks
250 alŏē (1), *aloes*

ALONE
259 'echâd (4), *first*
905 bad (42), *apart, only,
besides*
909 bâdad (9), to *be
solitary, be alone*
2308 châdal (2), to *desist,
stop; be fat*
4422 mâlaṭ (1), to *escape
as if by slipperiness*

ALAS
7503 râphâh (4), to
slacken
7662 shᵉbaq (Ch.) (1), to
allow to remain
7896 shîyth (1), to *place,
put*
863 aphiēmi (6), to *leave;
to pardon, forgive*
1439 ĕaō (3), to *let be,* i.e.
permit or *leave* alone
2651 katamŏnas (2),
separately, alone
3440 mŏnŏn (3), *merely,
just*
3441 mŏnŏs (21), *single,
only; by oneself*

ALONG
1980 hâlak (3), to *walk;
live a certain way*

ALOOF
5048 neged (1), *over
against* or *before*

ALOTH
1175 Bᵉ'âlôwth (1),
mistresses

ALOUD
1419+3605 gâdôwl (1),
great
1627 gârôwn (1), *throat*
1993 hâmâh (1), to *be in
great commotion*
2429 chayil (Ch.) (3),
strength; loud sound
5414+854+6963 nâthan
(1), to *give*
6670 tsâhal (2), to *be
cheerful; to sound*
6963+1419 qôwl (1), *voice
or sound*
7311+1419 rûwm (1), to
be high; to rise or raise
7321 rûwa' (1), to *shout
for alarm or joy*
7442 rânan (5), to *shout
for joy*
7452 rêa' (1), *crash;
noise; shout*
7768 shâva' (1), to
halloo, call for help
310 anabŏaō (1), to *cry
out*

ALPHA
1 A (4), *first*

ALPHAEUS
256 Alphaiŏs (5),
Alphæus

ALREADY
3528 kᵉbâr (5), *long ago,
formerly, hitherto*
2235 ēdē (18), *even now*
4258 prŏamartanō (1), to
sin previously
5348 phthanō (1), to *be
beforehand*

ALTAR
741 'ărî'êyl (3), *altar*
4056 madbach (Ch.) (1),
sacrificial altar
4196 mizbêach (347),
altar
1041 bōmŏs (1), *altar*
2379 thusiastēriŏn (21),
altar

ALTARS
4196 mizbêach (52), *altar*

2379 thusiastērĭŏn (1), *altar*

ALTASCHITH
516 'Al tashchêth (4), *"Thou must not destroy"*

ALTER
2498 châlaph (1), to *hasten* away; to *pass*
8133 shᵉnâ' (Ch.) (2), to *alter, change*
8138 shânâh (1), to *transmute*

ALTERED
5674 'âbar (1), to *cross over*; to *transition*
1096+2087 ginŏmai (1), to *be, become*

ALTERETH
5709 'ădâ' (Ch.) (2), to *pass* on or *continue*

ALTHOUGH
272 'ăchuzzâh (2), *possession*
3588 kîy (7), *for, that because*
2543 kaitŏi (1), *nevertheless*

ALTOGETHER
259 'echâd (1), *first*
1571 gam (1), *also; even*
3162 yachad (5), *unitedly*
3605 kôl (4), *all, any*
3617 kâlâh (3), *complete destruction*
3650 hŏlŏs (1), *whole* or *all, i.e. complete*
3843 pantōs (2), *entirely; at all events*

ALUSH
442 'Âlûwsh (2), *Alush*

ALVAH
5933 'Alvâh (1), *moral perverseness*

ALVAN
5935 'Alvân (1), *lofty*

ALWAY
3605+3117 kôl (4), *all, any* or *every*
5331 netsach (1), *splendor; lasting*
5769 'ôwlâm (2), *eternity; ancient; always*
8548 tâmîyd (4), *constantly, regularly*
104 aĕi (8), *ever, always*
1275 diapantŏs (2), *constantly, continually*
3842 pantŏtĕ (1), *at all times*
3956+2250 pas (1), *all, any, every, whole*

ALWAYS
3605+3117 kôl (4), *all, any* or *every*
3605+6256 kôl (4), *all, any* or *every*
5331 netsach (2), *splendor; lasting*
5769 'ôwlâm (3), *eternity; ancient; always*
8548 tâmîyd (6), *constantly, regularly*
104 aĕi (3), *ever, always*

1223+3956 dia (3), *through*, by means of
1275 diapantŏs (3), *constantly, continually*
1539 hĕkastŏtĕ (1), at *every time*
1722+3956+2540 ĕn (2), *in; during; because of*
3839 pantē (1), *wholly*
3842 pantŏtĕ (29), *at all times*

AMAD
6008 'Am'âd (1), *people of time*

AMAL
6000 'Âmâl (1), *wearing effort; worry*

AMALEK
6002 'Ămâlêq (24), *Amalek*

AMALEKITE
6003 'Ămâlêqîy (3), *Amalekite*

AMALEKITES
6003 'Ămâlêqîy (24), *Amalekite*

AMAM
538 'Ămâm (1), *gathering-spot*

AMANA
549 'Ămânâh (1), *covenant*

AMARIAH
568 'Ămaryâh (14), *Jehovah has promised*

AMASA
6021 'Ămâsâ' (16), *burden*

AMASAI
6022 'Ămâsay (5), *burdensome*

AMASHAI
6023 'Ămashçay (1), *burdensome*

AMASIAH
6007 'Ămaçyâh (1), *Jehovah has loaded*

AMAZED
926 bâhal (2), to *tremble; be, make agitated*
2865 châthath (1), to *break down*
8074 shâmêm (1), to *devastate; to stupefy*
8539 tâmahh (1), to *be astounded*
1096+2285 ginŏmai (1), to *be, become*
1568 ĕkthambĕō (2), to *astonish utterly*
1605 ĕkplēssō (3), to *astonish*
1611 ĕkstasis (1), *astonishment*
1611+2983 ĕkstasis (1), *astonishment*
1839 ĕxistēmi (6), to *become astounded*
2284 thambĕō (2), to *astound, be amazed*

AMAZEMENT
1611 ĕkstasis (1), *astonishment*

4423 ptŏĕsis (1), *something alarm*

AMAZIAH
558 'Ămatsyâh (40), *strength of Jehovah*

AMBASSADOR
6735 tsîyr (3), *hinge; herald* or *errand-doer*
4243 prĕsbĕuō (1), to *act as a representative*

AMBASSADORS
3887 lûwts (1), to *scoff;* to *interpret*; to *intercede*
4397 mal'âk (4), *messenger*
6735 tsîyr (2), *hinge; herald* or *errand-doer*
4243 prĕsbĕuō (1), to *act as a representative*

AMBASSAGE
4242 prĕsbĕia (1), *ambassadors*

AMBER
2830 chashmal (3), *bronze*

AMBUSH
693 'ârab (7), to *ambush, lie in wait*

AMBUSHES
693 'ârab (1), to *ambush, lie in wait*

AMBUSHMENT
3993 ma'ărâb (2), *ambuscade, ambush*

AMBUSHMENTS
693 'ârab (1), to *ambush, lie in wait*

AMEN
543 'âmên (22), *truly, "may it be so!"*
281 amēn (51), *surely; so be it*

AMEND
2388 châzaq (1), to *fasten* upon; to *seize*
3190 yâṭab (4), to *be, make well*
2192+2866 ĕchō (1), to *have; hold; keep*

AMENDS
7999 shâlam (1), to *be friendly;* to *reciprocate*

AMERCE
6064 'ânash (1), to *inflict* a penalty, to *fine*

AMETHYST
306 'achlâmâh (2), *amethyst*
271 amĕthustŏs (1), *amethyst*

AMI
532 'Âmîy (1), *skilled craftsman*

AMIABLE
3039 yᵉdîyd (1), *loved*

AMINADAB
284 Aminadab (3), *people of liberality*

AMISS
5753 'âvâh (1), to *be crooked*
7955 shâlâh (Ch.) (1), *wrong*

824 atŏpŏs (1), *improper; injurious; wicked*
2560 kakŏs (1), *badly; wrongly; ill*

AMITTAI
573 'Ămittay (2), *veracious*

AMMAH
522 'Ammâh (1), *cubit*

AMMI
5971 'am (1), *people*

AMMI-NADIB
5993 'Ammîy Nâdîyb (1), *my people* (are) *liberal*

AMMIEL
5988 'Ammîy'êl (6), *people of God*

AMMIHUD
5989 'Ammîyhûwd (10), *people of splendor*

AMMINADAB
5992 'Ammîynâdâb (13), *people of liberality*

AMMISHADDAI
5996 'Ammîyshadday (5), *people of* (the) *Almighty*

AMMIZABAD
5990 'Ammîyzâbâd (1), *people of endowment*

AMMON
5983 'Ammôwn (91), *inbred*

AMMONITE
5984 'Ammôwnîy (9), *Ammonite*

AMMONITES
1121+5984 bên (7), *son, descendant; people*
5984 'Ammôwnîy (16), *Ammonite*

AMMONITESS
5984 'Ammôwnîy (4), *Ammonite*

AMNON
550 'Amnôwn (25), *faithful*

AMNON'S
550 'Amnôwn (3), *faithful*

AMOK
5987 'Âmôwq (2), *deep*

AMON
526 'Âmôwn (17), *skilled craftsman*
300 Amōn (2), *skilled craftsman*

AMONG
413 'êl (7), *to, toward*
854 'êth (8), *with; among*
996 bêyn (33), *between*
997 bêyn (Ch.) (1), *between; "either...or"*
1460 gêv (1), *middle, inside, in, on, etc.*
1767 day (1), *enough, sufficient*
4480 min (4), *from, out of*
5921 'al (7), *above, over, upon,* or *against*
5973 'îm (8), *with*
7130 qereb (74), *nearest part, i.e. the center*

English

AMONGST

7310 rᵉvâyâh (1), *satisfaction*
8432 tâvek (142), *center, middle*
575 apŏ (1), *from, away*
1223 dia (1), *through*, by means of; *because of*
1519 ĕis (1), *to or into*
1537 ĕk (5), *out, out of*
1722 ĕn (115), *in; during; because of*
1909 ĕpi (4), *on, upon*
2596 kata (2), *down; according to*
3319 mĕsŏs (7), *middle*
3326 mĕta (5), *with, among; after, later*
3844 para (2), *from; with; besides; on account of*
4045 pĕripiptō (1), *to fall into the hands of*
4314 prŏs (19), *for; on, at; to, toward; against*
4315 prŏsabbatŏn (1), *Sabbath-eve*
5259 hupŏ (1), *under; by means of; at*

AMONGST

8432 tâvek (2), *center, middle*

AMORITE

567 'Ĕmôrîy (14), *mountaineer*

AMORITES

567 'Ĕmôrîy (73), *mountaineer*

AMOS

5986 'Âmôwç (7), *burdensome*
301 Amŏs (1), *strong*

AMOZ

531 'Âmôwts (13), *strong*

AMPHIPOLIS

295 Amphipŏlis (1), *city surrounded* by a river

AMPLIAS

291 Amplias (1), *enlarged*

AMRAM

2566 Chamrân (1), *red*
6019 'Amrâm (13), *high people*

AMRAM'S

6019 'Amrâm (1), *high people*

AMRAMITES

6020 'Amrâmîy (2), *Amramite*

AMRAPHEL

569 'Amrâphel (2), *Amraphel*

AMZI

557 'Amtsîy (2), *strong*

ANAB

6024 'Ănâb (2), *fruit*

ANAH

6034 'Ănâh (12), *answer*

ANAHARATH

588 'Ănâchărâth (1), *gorge* or *narrow pass*

ANAIAH

6043 'Ănâyâh (2), *Jehovah has answered*

ANAK

6061 'Ânâq (9), *necklace chain*

ANAKIMS

6062 'Ănâqîy (9), *Anakite*

ANAMIM

6047 'Ănâmîm (2), *Anamim*

ANAMMELECH

6048 'Ănammelek (1), *Anammelek*

ANAN

6052 'Ânân (1), *cloud*

ANANI

6054 'Ănânîy (1), *cloudy*

ANANIAH

6055 'Ănanyâh (2), *Jehovah has covered*

ANANIAS

367 Ananias (11), *Jehovah has favored*

ANATH

6067 'Ănâth (2), *answer*

ANATHEMA

331 anathĕma (1), *excommunicated*

ANATHOTH

6068 'Ănâthôwth (16), *answers*

ANCESTORS

7223 rî'shôwn (1), *first*, in place, time or rank

ANCHOR

45 agkura (1), *anchor*

ANCHORS

45 agkura (2), *anchor*

ANCIENT

2204 zâqên (6), *to be old, venerated*
3453 yâshîysh (1), *old man*
5769 'ôwlâm (6), *eternity; ancient; always*
6267 'attîyq (1), *weaned; antique*
6268 'attîyq (Ch.) (3), *venerable, old*
6917 qâdûwm (1), *pristine hero*
6924 qedem (8), *East, eastern; antiquity; before, anciently*

ANCIENTS

2204 zâqên (9), *to be old, venerated*
6931 qadmôwnîy (1), *anterior* time; *oriental*

ANCLE

4974 sphurŏn (1), *ankle*

ANCLES

657 'epheç (1), *end; no further*

ANDREW

406 Andrĕas (13), *manly*

ANDRONICUS

408 Andrŏnikŏs (1), *man of victory*

ANEM

6046 'Ănêm (1), *two fountains*

ANER

6063 'Ânêr (3), *Aner*

ANETHOTHITE

6069 'Anthôthîy (1), *Antothite*

ANETOTHITE

6069 'Anthôthîy (1), *Antothite*

ANGEL

4397 mal'âk (100), *messenger*
4398 mal'ak (Ch.) (2), *messenger*
32 aggĕlŏs (95), *messenger; angel*

ANGEL'S

32 aggĕlŏs (2), *messenger; angel*

ANGELS

430 'ĕlôhîym (1), *the true God; gods; great ones*
4397 mal'âk (10), *messenger*
8136 shin'ân (1), *change, i.e. repetition*
32 aggĕlŏs (80), *messenger; angel*
2465 isaggĕlŏs (1), *angelic, like an angel*

ANGELS'

47 'abbîyr (1), *mighty*

ANGER

639 'aph (173), *nose or nostril; face; person*
2195 za'am (1), *fury, anger*
2534 chêmâh (1), *heat; anger; poison*
3707 kâ'aç (42), *to grieve, rage, be indignant*
3708 ka'aç (2), *vexation, grief*
5006 nâ'ats (1), *to scorn*
5674 'âbar (1), *to cross over; to transition*
5678 'ebrâh (1), *outburst of passion*
6440 pânîym (3), *face; front*
7307 rûwach (1), *breath; wind; life-spirit*
3709 ŏrgē (3), *ire; punishment*
3949 parŏrgizō (1), *to enrage, exasperate*

ANGERED

7107 qâtsaph (1), *to burst out in rage*

ANGLE

2443 chakkâh (2), *fish hook*

ANGRY

599 'ânaph (13), *be enraged, be angry*
639 'aph (4), *nose or nostril; face; person*
1149 bᵉnaç (Ch.) (1), *to be enraged, be angry*
2194 zâ'am (2), *to be enraged*
2734 chârâh (10), *to blaze up*
3707 kâ'aç (2), *to grieve, rage, be indignant*
3708 ka'aç (1), *vexation, grief*
4751+5315 mar (1), *bitter; bitterness; bitterly*

ANETHOTHITE

6225 'âshan (1), *to envelope in smoke*
7107 qâtsaph (2), *to burst out in rage*
3710 ŏrgizō (5), *to become exasperated, enraged*
3711 ŏrgilŏs (1), *irascible, hot-tempered*
5520 chŏlaŏ (1), *irritable, enraged*

ANGUISH

2342 chûwl (1), *to dance, whirl; to writhe* in pain
4689 mâtsôwq (1), *confinement; disability*
4691 mᵉtsûwqâh (1), *trouble, anguish*
6695 tsôwq (3), *distress*
6862 tsar (1), *trouble; opponent*
6869 tsârâh (5), *trouble; rival-wife*
7115 qôtser (1), *shortness* (of spirit)
7661 shâbâts (1), *intanglement*
2347 thlipsis (1), *pressure, trouble*
4730 stĕnŏchôria (1), *calamity, distress*
4928 sunŏchē (1), *anxiety, distress*

ANIAM

593 'Ănîy'âm (1), *groaning of* (the) *people*

ANIM

6044 'Ănîym (1), *fountains*

ANISE

432 anēthŏn (1), *dill seed for seasoning*

ANNA

451 Anna (1), *favored*

ANNAS

452 Annas (4), *Jehovah has favored*

ANOINT

4886 mâshach (25), *to rub or smear*
5480 çûwk (5), *to smear*
218 alĕiphō (3), *to oil with perfume, anoint*
1472 ĕgchriō (1), *to besmear, anoint*
3462 murizō (1), *to apply perfumed unguent to*

ANOINTED

1101 bâlal (1), *to mix*
1121+3323 bên (1), *son, descendant; people*
4473 mimshach (1), *with outstretched wings*
4886 mâshach (43), *to rub or smear with oil*
4888 mishchâh (1), *unction; gift*
4899 mâshîyach (37), *consecrated* person; *Messiah*
5480 çûwk (2), *to smear*
218 alĕiphō (5), *to oil with perfume, anoint*
2025 ĕpichriō (1), *to smear over, anoint*

2025+1909 ĕpichriō (1), to *smear over, anoint*
5548 chriō (5), to *smear* or *rub* with oil

ANOINTEDST
4886 mâshach (1), to *rub* or *smear* with oil

ANOINTEST
1878 dâshên (1), to *anoint; to satisfy*

ANOINTING
4888 mishchâh (24), *unction; gift*
8081 shemen (1), *olive*
218 alĕiphō (1), to *oil* with perfume, *anoint*
5545 chrisma (2), special *endowment*

ANON
2112 ĕuthĕōs (1), *at once* or *soon*
2117 ĕuthus (1), *at once, immediately*

ANOTHER
250 'Ezrâchîy (22), *Ezrachite*
251 'âch (1), *brother; relative*
259 'echâd (35), *first*
269 'achôwth (6), *sister*
312 'achêr (58), *other, another, different; next*
317 'ochŏrîy (Ch.) (5), *other, another*
321 'ochŏrân (Ch.) (1), *other, another*
376 'îysh (5), *man; male; someone*
1668 dâ' (Ch.) (2), *this*
1836 dên (Ch.) (1), *this*
2088 zeh (10), *this or that*
2090 zôh (1), *this or that*
2114 zûwr (3), to *be foreign, strange*
3671 kânâph (1), *edge or extremity; wing*
5234 nâkar (2), to *treat as a foreigner*
5997 'âmîyth (2), *comrade or kindred*
7453 rêa' (20), *associate*
7468 rᵉ'ûwth (2), *female associate*
8145 shênîy (7), *second; again*
8264 shâqaq (1), to *seek greedily*
240 allēlōn (70), *one another*
243 allŏs (60), *different, other*
245 allŏtriŏs (4), *not one's own*
246 allŏphulŏs (1), *Gentile, foreigner*
1438 hĕautŏu (7), *himself, herself, itself*
1520 hĕis (2), *one*
2087 hĕtĕrŏs (44), *other or different*
3588 hŏ (1), *"the," i.e. the definite article*
3739 hŏs (6), *who, which*
4299 prŏkrima (1), *prejudgment*
4835 sumpathēs (1), *commiserative*

ANOTHER'S
7453 rêa' (2), *associate; one close*
240 allēlōn (2), *one another*
2087 hĕtĕrŏs (1), *other or different*

ANSWER
559 'âmar (9), to *say, speak*
1696 dâbar (1), to *speak, say; to subdue*
1697 dâbâr (7), *word; matter; thing*
3045 yâda' (1), to *know*
4405 millâh (1), *word; discourse; speech*
4617 ma'ăneh (7), *reply, answer*
6030 'ânâh (60), to *respond, answer;*
6600 pithgâm (Ch.) (2), *decree; report*
7725 shûwb (12), to *turn back; to return*
8421 tûwb (Ch.) (2), to *reply, answer*
470 antapŏkrinŏmai (1), to *contradict* or *dispute*
611 apŏkrinŏmai (12), to *respond*
612 apŏkrisis (3), *response*
626 apŏlŏgĕŏmai (4), to *give an account* of self
627 apŏlŏgia (4), *plea* or verbal *defense*
1906 ĕpĕrōtēma (1), *inquiry*
2036 ĕpō (1), to *speak*
5538 chrēmatismŏs (1), *divine response*

ANSWERABLE
5980 'ummâh (1), *near, beside, along with*

ANSWERED
559 'âmar (90), to *say, speak*
1697 dâbâr (4), *word; matter; thing*
6030 'ânâh (175), to *respond, answer*
6032 'ănâh (Ch.) (16), to *respond, answer*
6039 'ĕnûwth (1), *affliction*
7725 shûwb (2), to *turn back; to return*
8421 tûwb (Ch.) (1), to *reply, answer*
611 apŏkrinŏmai (201), to *respond*
626 apŏlŏgĕŏmai (2), to *give an account* of self

ANSWEREDST
6030 'ânâh (2), to *respond, answer*

ANSWEREST
6030 'ânâh (2), to *respond, answer*
611 apŏkrinŏmai (4), to *respond*

ANSWERETH
6030 'ânâh (6), to *respond, answer*
7725 shûwb (1), to *turn back; to return*

ANSWERING
488 antimĕtrĕō (1), to *measure in return*
611 apŏkrinŏmai (29), to *respond*
5274 hupŏlambanō (1), to *take up,* i.e. *continue*

ANSWERS
8666 tᵉshûwbâh (2), *reply*
612 apŏkrisis (1), *response*

ANT
5244 nᵉmâlâh (1), *ant*

ANTICHRIST
500 antichristŏs (4), *opponent of Messiah*

ANTICHRISTS
500 antichristŏs (1), *opponent of Messiah*

ANTIOCH
490 Antiŏchĕia (18), *Antiochia*
491 Antiŏchĕus (1), *inhabitant of Antiochia*

ANTIPAS
493 Antipas (1), *instead of father*

ANTIPATRIS
494 Antipatris (1), *Antipatris*

ANTIQUITY
6927 qadmâh (1), *priority in time; before; past*

ANTOTHIJAH
6070 'Anthôthîyâh (1), *answers of Jehovah*

ANTOTHITE
6069 'Anthôthîy (2), *Antothite*

ANTS
5244 nᵉmâlâh (1), *ant*

ANUB
6036 'Ânûwb (1), *borne*

ANVIL
6471 pa'am (1), *time; step; occurence*

ANY
259 'echâd (18), *first*
376 'îysh (25), *man*
1697 dâbâr (2), *thing*
1991 hêm (1), *wealth*
3254 yâçaph (2), to *add*
3605 kôl (175), *all, any*
3606 kôl (Ch.) (8), *all, any or every*
3792 kᵉthâb (Ch.) (1), *writing, record or book*
3972 mᵉ'ûwmâh (12), *something; anything*
4310 mîy (1), *who?*
5315 nephesh (3), *life; breath; soul; wind*
5750 'ôwd (9), *again; repeatedly; still; more*
5769 'ôwlâm (1), *eternity; ancient; always*
1520 hĕis (2), *one*
1535 ĕitĕ (1), *if too*
1536 ĕi tis (52), *if any*
1538 hĕkastŏs (1), *each*

ANY
2089 ĕti (10), *yet, still*
3361 mē (1), *not; lest*
3362 ĕan mē (2), *if not*
3364 ŏu mē (2), *not at all*
3367 mĕdĕis (5), *not even one*
3370 Mēdŏs (2), *inhabitant of Media*
3379 mēpŏtĕ (7), *not ever; if, or lest ever*
3381 mēpōs (4), *lest somehow*
3387 mētis (6), *whether any*
3588 hŏ (1), *"the," i.e. the definite article*
3762 ŏudĕis (12), *none, nobody, nothing*
3763 ŏudĕpŏtĕ (2), *never at all*
3765 ŏukĕti (4), *not yet, no longer*
3956 pas (9), *all, any, every, whole*
4218 pŏtĕ (4), *at some time, ever*
4455 pōpŏtĕ (3), *at no time*
4458 -pōs (4), *particle used in composition*
5100 tis (122), *some or any person or object*
5150 trimēnŏn (1), *three months' space*

APART
905 bad (6), *apart, only, besides*
5079 niddâh (3), *time of menstrual impurity*
5674 'âbar (1), to *cross over; to transition*
6395 pâlâh (1), to *distinguish*
659 apŏtithēmi (1), to *put away; get rid of*
2596 kata (7), *down; according to*

APELLES
559 Apĕllēs (1), *Apelles*

APES
6971 qôwph (2), *ape or monkey*

APHARSACHITES
671 Ăpharçᵉkay (Ch.) (2), *Apharsekite*

APHARSATHCHITES
671 Ăpharçᵉkay (Ch.) (1), *Apharsekite*

APHARSITES
670 Ăphârᵉçay (Ch.) (1), *Apharesite*

APHEK
663 Ăphêq (8), *fortress*

APHEKAH
664 'Ăphêqâh (1), *fortress*

APHIAH
647 'Ăphîyach (1), *breeze*

APHIK
663 Ăphêq (1), *fortress*

APHRAH
1036 Bêyth lᵉ-'Aphrâh (1), *house of dust*

APHSES
6483 Pitstsêts (1), *dispersive*

English

APIECE
259 'echâd (1), *first*
5982+259 'ammûwd (1), *column, pillar*
303 *ana* (2), *each; in turn; among*

APOLLONIA
624 *Apŏllōnia* (1), *sun*

APOLLOS
625 *Apŏllōs* (10), *sun*

APOLLYON
623 *Apŏlluōn* (1), *Destroyer*

APOSTLE
652 *apŏstŏlŏs* (19), *commissioner* of Christ

APOSTLES
652 *apŏstŏlŏs* (53), *commissioner* of Christ
5570 *psĕudapŏstŏlŏs* (1), *pretended preacher*

APOSTLES'
652 *apŏstŏlŏs* (5), *commissioner* of Christ

APOSTLESHIP
651 *apŏstŏlē* (4), *office of apostle*

APOTHECARIES
7543 râqach (1), to *perfume, blend spice*

APOTHECARIES'
4842 mirqachath (1), *unguent; unguent-pot*

APOTHECARY
7543 râqach (4), to *perfume, blend spice*

APPAIM
649 'Appayim (2), *two nostrils*

APPAREL
899 beged (4), *clothing; treachery or pillage*
1264 bᵉrôwm (1), *damask*
3830 lᵉbûwsh (8), *garment; wife*
3847 lâbash (1), to *clothe*
4254 machălâtsâh (1), *mantle, garment*
4403 malbûwsh (4), *garment, clothing*
8071 simlâh (2), *dress, mantle*
2066 ĕsthēs (3), to *clothe; dress*
2440 himatiŏn (1), to *put on clothes*
2441 himatismŏs (1), *clothing*
2689 katastŏlē (1), *costume or apparel*

APPARELLED
3847 lâbash (1), to *clothe*
2441 himatismŏs (1), *clothing*

APPARENTLY
4758 mar'eh (1), *appearance; vision*

APPEAL
1941 ĕpikalĕŏmai (2), to *invoke*

APPEALED
1941 ĕpikalĕŏmai (4), to *invoke*

APPEAR
1540 gâlâh (1), to *denude; uncover*
1570 gâlash (2), to *caper*
4286 machsôph (1), *peeling, baring*
6524 pârach (1), to *break forth; to bloom; to fly*
7200 râ'âh (24), to *see*
82 adēlŏs (1), *indistinct, not clear*
398 anaphainō (1), to *appear*
1718 ĕmphanizō (1), to *show forth*
2064 ĕrchŏmai (1), to *go or come*
3700 ŏptanŏmai (2), to *appear*
5316 phainō (9), to *show; to appear, be visible*
5318+5600 phanĕrŏs (1), *apparent, visible, clear*
5319 phanĕrŏō (9), to *render apparent*

APPEARANCE
4758 mar'eh (30), *appearance; vision*
5869 'ayin (1), *eye; sight; fountain*
1491 ĕidŏs (1), *form, appearance, sight*
3799 ŏpsis (1), *face; appearance*
4383 prŏsōpŏn (2), *face, presence*

APPEARANCES
4758 mar'eh (2), *appearance; vision*

APPEARED
1540 gâlâh (1), to *denude; uncover*
3318 yâtsâ' (1), to *go, bring out*
6437 pânâh (1), to *turn, to face*
7200 râ'âh (39), to *see*
1718 ĕmphanizō (1), to *show forth*
2014 ĕpiphainō (3), to *become visible*
3700 ŏptanŏmai (15), to *appear*
5316 phainō (5), to *show; to appear, be visible*
5319 phanĕrŏō (3), to *render apparent*

APPEARETH
1540 gâlâh (1), to *denude; uncover*
4758 mar'eh (1), *appearance; vision*
7200 râ'âh (3), to *see*
8259 shâqaph (1), to *peep or gaze*
5316 phainō (3), to *show; to appear, be visible*

APPEARING
602 apŏkalupsis (1), *disclosure, revelation*
2015 ĕpiphanĕia (5), *manisfestation*

APPEASE
3722+6440 kâphar (1), to *cover; to expiate*

APPEASED
7918 shâkak (1), to *lay a trap; to allay*
2687 katastĕllō (1), to *quell, quiet*

APPEASETH
8252 shâqaṭ (1), to *repose*

APPERTAIN
2969 yâ'âh (1), to *be suitable, proper*

APPETITE
2416 chay (1), *alive; raw; fresh; life*
5315 nephesh (2), *life; breath; soul; wind*
8264 shâqaq (1), to *seek greedily*

APPHIA
682 Apphia (1), *Apphia*

APPII
675 'Appiŏs (1), *Appius*

APPLE
380 'îyshôwn (2), *pupil, eyeball*
380+1323 'îyshôwn (1), *pupil, eyeball*
892 bâbâh (1), *pupil of the eye*
1323 bath (1), *daughter, descendant, woman*
8598 tappûwach (3), *apple*

APPLES
8598 tappûwach (3), *apple*

APPLIED
5414 nâthan (2), to *give*
5437 çâbab (1), to *surround*

APPLY
935 bôw' (2), to *go, come*
5186 nâṭâh (1), to *stretch or spread out*
7896 shîyth (1), to *place, put*

APPOINT
559 'âmar (1), to *say, speak*
977 bâchar (1), *select, chose, prefer*
3259 yâ'ad (2), to *meet; to summon; to direct*
5344 nâqab (1), to *specify, designate, libel*
5414 nâthan (4), to *give*
5975 'âmad (2), to *stand*
6485 pâqad (10), to *visit, care for, count*
6680 tsâvâh (1), to *constitute, enjoin*
7136 qârâh (1), to *bring about; to impose*
7760 sûwm (11), to *put*
7896 shîyth (2), to *place*
7971 shâlach (1), to *send away*
1303 diatithēmai (1), to *put apart, i.e. dispose*
2525 kathistēmi (1), to *designate, constitute*
5087 tithēmi (2), to *place, put*

APPOINTED
559 'âmar (2), to *say*

561 'ēmer (1), *something said*
1121 bên (3), *son, people of a class or kind*
1696 dâbar (1), to *speak, say; to subdue*
2163 zâman (3), to *fix a time*
2296 châgar (3), to *gird on a belt; put on armor*
2706 chôq (1), *appointment; allotment*
2708 chuqqâh (1), to *delineate*
2710 châqaq (1), to *enact laws; to prescribe*
2764 chêrem (1), *doomed object*
3045 yâda' (1), to *know*
3198 yâkach (2), to *decide, justify*
3245 yâçad (1), *settle, consult, establish*
3259 yâ'ad (3), to *meet; to summon; to direct*
3677 keçe' (2), *full moon*
4150 môw'êd (20), *assembly, congregation*
4151 môw'âd (1), *ranking of troop*
4152 mûw'âdâh (1), *appointed place*
4487 mânâh (4), to *allot; to enumerate or enroll*
4662 miphqâd (1), *designated spot; census*
5324 nâtsab (1), to *station*
5414 nâthan (7), to *give*
5567 çâman (1), to *designate*
5975 'âmad (10), to *stand*
6213 'âsâh (2), to *do or make*
6485 pâqad (4), to *visit, care for, count*
6635 tsâbâ' (3), *army, military host*
6680 tsâvâh (4), to *constitute, enjoin*
6942 qâdâsh (1), to *be, make clean*
7760 sûwm (8), to *put*
7896 shîyth (1), to *place*
322 anadĕiknumi (1), to *indicate, appoint*
606 apŏkĕimai (1), to *be reserved; to await*
1299 diatassō (4), to *institute, prescribe*
1303 diatithēmai (1), to *put apart, i.e. dispose*
1476 hĕdraiŏs (1), *immovable; steadfast*
1935 ĕpithanatiŏs (1), *doomed to death*
2476 histēmi (1), to *stand, establish*
2749 kĕimai (1), to *lie outstretched*
4160 pŏiĕō (1), to *do*
4287 prŏthĕsmiŏs (1), *designated day or time*
4384 prŏtassō (1), to *prescribe beforehand*
4929 suntassō (2), to *direct, instruct*
5021 tassō (3), to *assign or dispose*

5081 tĕlaugōs (1), in a far-shining manner
5087 tithēmi (3), to *put*

APPOINTETH
6966 qûwm (Ch.) (1), to rise

APPOINTMENT
3259 yâ'ad (1), to *meet;* to *summon;* to *direct*
3883 lûwl (1), *spiral* step
6310 peh (2), *mouth; opening*

APPREHEND
2638 katalambanō (1), to *seize;* to *understand*
4084 piazō (1), to *seize, arrest,* or *capture*

APPREHENDED
2638 katalambanō (2), to *seize;* to *possess;* to *understand*
4084 piazō (1), to *seize, arrest,* or *capture*

APPROACH
5066 nâgash (5), to *be, come, bring near*
7126 qârab (12), to *approach, bring near*
7138 qârôwb (1), *near, close*
676 aprŏsitŏs (1), *unapproachable*

APPROACHED
5066 nâgash (1), to *be, come, bring near*
7126 qârab (1), to *approach, bring near*

APPROACHETH
1448 ĕggizō (1), to *approach*

APPROACHING
7132 qᵉrâbâh (1), *approach*
1448 ĕggizō (1), to *approach*

APPROVE
7520 râtsad (1), to *look askant;* to *be jealous*
1381 dŏkimazō (2), to *test;* to *approve*

APPROVED
584 apŏdĕiknumi (1), to *accredit*
1384 dŏkimŏs (6), *acceptable, approved*
4921 sunistaō (1), to *introduce* (favorably)

APPROVEST
1381 dŏkimazō (1), to *test;* to *approve*

APPROVETH
7200 râ'âh (1), to *see*

APPROVING
4921 sunistaō (1), to *introduce* (favorably)

APRONS
2290 chăgôwr (1), *belt* for the waist
4612 simikinthiŏn (1), narrow *apron*

APT
6213 'âsâh (1), to *do*
1317 didaktikŏs (2), *instructive*

AQUILA
207 Akulas (6), *eagle*

AR
6144 'Âr (6), *city*

ARA
690 'Ărâ' (1), *lion*

ARAB
694 'Ărâb (1), *ambush*

ARABAH
6160 'ărâbâh (2), *desert, wasteland*

ARABIA
6152 'Ărâb (6), *Arabia*
688 *Arabia* (2), *Arabia*

ARABIAN
6153 'ereb (1), *dusk*
6163 'Ărăbîy (3), *Arabian*

ARABIANS
6163 'Ărăbîy (5), *Arabian*
690 *'Araps* (1), *native of Arabia*

ARAD
6166 'Ărâd (5), *fugitive*

ARAH
733 'Ărach (4), *way-faring*

ARAM
758 'Arâm (7), *highland*
689 *Aram* (3), *high*

ARAM-NAHARAIM
763 'Ăram Nahărayim (1), *Aram of* (the) *two rivers*

ARAM-ZOBAH
760 'Ăram Tsôwbâh (1), *Aram of* Coele-Syria

ARAMITESS
761 'Ărammîy (1), *Aramite*

ARAN
765 'Ărân (2), *stridulous*

ARARAT
780 'Ărâraṭ (2), *Ararat*

ARAUNAH
728 'Ăravnâh (9), *Aravnah* or *Ornah*

ARBA
704 'Arba' (2), *four*

ARBAH
704 'Arba' (1), *four*

ARBATHITE
6164 'Arbâthîy (2), *Arbathite*

ARBITE
701 'Arbîy (1), *Arbite*

ARCHANGEL
743 archaggĕlŏs (2), *chief angel*

ARCHELAUS
745 Archĕlaŏs (1), *people-ruling*

ARCHER
1869 dârak (1), to *walk, lead;* to *string* a bow
7198 qesheth (1), *bow; rainbow*

ARCHERS
1167+2671 ba'al (1), *master; husband*
1869+7198 dârak (1), to *walk;* to *string* a bow

ARCHES
361 'êylâm (15), *portico, porch*

ARCHEVITES
756 'Arkᵉvay (Ch.) (1), *Arkevite*

ARCHI
757 'Arkîy (1), *Arkite*

ARCHIPPUS
751 Archippŏs (2), *horse-ruler*

ARCHITE
757 'Arkîy (5), *Arkite*

ARCTURUS
5906 'Ayish (2), Great *Bear* constellation

ARD
714 'Ard (3), *fugitive*

ARDITES
716 'Ardîy (1), *Ardite*

ARDON
715 'Ardôwn (1), *roaming*

ARELI
692 'Ar'êlîy (2), *heroic*

ARELITES
692 'Ar'êlîy (1), *heroic*

AREOPAGITE
698 Arĕŏpagitēs (1), *Areopagite*

AREOPAGUS
697 Arĕiŏs Pagŏs (1), *rock of Ares*

ARETAS
702 Arĕtas (1), *Aretas*

ARGOB
709 'Argôb (5), *stony*

ARGUING
3198 yâkach (1), to *be correct;* to *argue*

ARGUMENTS
8433 tôwkêchâh (1), *correction, refutation*

ARIDAI
742 'Ărîyday (1), *Aridai*

ARIDATHA
743 'Ărîydâthâ' (1), *Aridatha*

ARIEH
745 'Aryêh (1), *lion*

ARIEL
740 'Ărî'êl (5), *Lion of God*

ARIGHT
3190 yâṭab (1), to *be, make well*
3559 kûwn (1), to *render sure, proper*
3651 kên (1), *just; right; correct*

4339 mêyshâr (1), straightness; rectitude

ARIMATHAEA
707 Arimathaia (4), *height*

ARIOCH
746 'Ăryôwk (7), *Arjok*

ARISAI
747 'Ărîyçay (1), *Arisai*

ARISE
2224 zârach (3), to *rise;* to *be bright*
5782 'ûwr (1), to *awake*
5927 'âlâh (2), to *ascend, be high, mount*
5975 'âmad (1), to *stand*
6965 qûwm (106), to *rise*
6966 qûwm (Ch.) (3), to *rise*
6974 qûwts (1), to *awake*
7721 sôw' (1), *rising*
305 anabainō (1), to *go up, rise*
393 anatĕllō (1), to *cause to arise*
450 anistēmi (14), to *stand up;* to *come back to life*
1453 ĕgĕirō (13), to *waken,* i.e. *rouse*

ARISETH
2224 zârach (4), to *rise;* to *be bright*
5927 'âlâh (1), to *ascend, be high, mount*
6965 qûwm (2), to *rise*
450 anistēmi (1), to *stand up;* to *come back to life*
1096 ginŏmai (2), to *be, become*
1453 ĕgĕirō (1), to *waken,* i.e. *rouse*

ARISING
6965 qûwm (1), to *rise*

ARISTARCHUS
708 Aristarchŏs (5), *best ruling*

ARISTOBULUS'
711 Aristŏbŏulŏs (1), *best counselling*

ARK
727 'ârôwn (194), *box*
8392 têbâh (28), *box, basket*
2787 kibōtŏs (6), *ark; chest* or *box*

ARKITE
6208 'Arqîy (2), *tush*

ARM
248 'ezrôwa (2), *arm*
2220 zᵉrôwa (59), *arm; foreleg; force, power*
2502 châlats (1), to *depart;* to *equip*
3802 kâthêph (1), *side-piece*
1023 brachiōn (3), *arm*
3695 hŏplizō (1), to *equip*

ARMAGEDDON
717 Armagĕddōn (1), *hill of the rendezvous*

ARMED
2502 châlats (16), to *equip;* to *present*

English

ARMENIA
2571 châmûsh (3), able-bodied *soldiers*
3847 lâbash (3), to *clothe*
4043 mâgên (2), small *shield* (*buckler*)
5401 nâshaq (3), to *kiss;* to *equip* with weapons
5402 nesheq (1), military *arms, arsenal*
7324 rûwq (1), to *pour* out, i.e. *empty*
2528 kathŏplizō (1), to *equip fully* with armor

ARMENIA
780 'Ărâraṭ (2), *Ararat*

ARMHOLES
679+3027 'atstsîyl (2), *joint* of the hand

ARMIES
1416 gᵉdûwd (1), *band* of soldiers
2428 chayil (4), *army; wealth; virtue; valor*
4264 machăneh (4), *encampment*
4630 ma'ărâh (1), *open* spot
4634 ma'ărâkâh (6), *row; pile*; military *array*
6635 tsâbâ' (22), *army, military host*
3925 parĕmbŏlē (1), *battle-array*
4753 stratĕuma (3), body of *troops*
4760 stratŏpĕdŏn (1), body of *troops*

ARMONI
764 'Armônîy (1), *palatial*

ARMOUR
2185 zônôwth (1), *harlots*
2290 chăgôwr (1), *belt* for the waist
2488 chăliytsâh (1), *spoil, booty* of the dead
3627 kᵉlîy (11), *implement, thing*
4055 mad (2), *vesture, garment; carpet*
5402 nesheq (3), military *arms, arsenal*
3696 hŏplŏn (2), *implement*, or *utensil* or *tool*
3833 panŏplia (3), *full armor*

ARMOURBEARER
5375+3627 nâsâ' (18), to *lift up*

ARMOURY
214 'ôwtsâr (1), *depository*
5402 nesheq (1), military *arms, arsenal*
8530 talpîyâh (1), *something tall*

ARMS
1672 dâ'ag (1), *be anxious, be afraid*
2220 zᵉrôwa (24), *arm; foreleg; force, power*
2684 chôtsen (1), *bosom*
43 agkalē (1), *arm*
1723 ĕnagkalizŏmai (2), to *take into one's arms*

ARMY
1416 gᵉdûwd (4), *band* of soldiers
2426 chêyl (1), *rampart, battlement*
2426+6635 chêyl (1), *rampart, battlement*
2428 chayil (52), *army; wealth; virtue; valor*
2429 chayil (Ch.) (2), *army; strength*
2502 châlats (1), to *deliver, equip*
4634 ma'ărâkâh (7), *row; pile*; military *array*
4675 matstsâbâh (1), military *guard*
6635 tsâbâ' (7), *army, military host*
4753 stratĕuma (3), body of *troops*

ARNAN
770 'Arnân (1), *noisy*

ARNON
769 'Arnôwn (25), *brawling* stream

AROD
720 'Ărôwd (1), *fugitive*

ARODI
722 'Ărôwdîy (1), *Arodite*

ARODITES
722 'Ărôwdîy (1), *Arodite*

AROER
6177 'Ărôw'êr (16), *nudity* of situation

AROERITE
6200 'Ărô'êrîy (1), *Aroërite*

AROSE
2224 zârach (2), to *rise;* to *be bright*
5927 'âlâh (2), to *ascend, be high, mount*
5975 'âmad (1), to *stand*
6965 qûwm (107), to *rise*
6966 qûwm (Ch.) (1), to *rise*
7925 shâkam (7), to *start early* in the morning
305 anabainō (1), to *go up, rise*
450 anistēmi (24), to *stand up;* to *come back to life*
906 ballō (1), to *throw*
1096 ginŏmai (11), to *be, become*
1326 diĕgĕirō (2), to *arouse, stimulate*
1453 ĕgĕirō (13), to *waken,* i.e. *rouse*
1525 ĕisĕrchŏmai (1), to *enter*

ARPAD
774 'Arpâd (4), *spread out*

ARPHAD
774 'Arpâd (2), *spread out*

ARPHAXAD
775 'Arpakshad (9), *Arpakshad*
742 Arphaxad (1), *Arphaxad*

ARRAY
631 'âçar (1), to *fasten;* to *join* battle
3847 lâbash (2), to *clothe*
5844 'âṭâh (1), to *wrap,* i.e. *cover, veil, clothe*
6186 'ârak (26), to set in a *row,* i.e. *arrange,*
7896 shîyth (1), to *place*
2441 himatismŏs (1), *clothing*

ARRAYED
3847 lâbash (4), to *clothe*
1746 ĕnduō (1), to *invest* with clothing
4016 pĕriballō (6), to *wrap around, clothe*

ARRIVED
2668 kataplĕō (1), to *sail down*
3846 paraballō (1), to *reach* a place; to *liken*

ARROGANCY
1347 gâ'ôwn (3), *ascending; majesty*
6277 'âthâq (1), *impudent*

ARROW
1121+7198 bên (1), *people* of a class or kind
2671 chêts (11), *arrow; shaft* of a spear
2678 chitstsîy (4), *arrow*

ARROWS
1121 bên (1), *people* of a class or kind
2671 chêts (36), *arrow; wound; shaft* of a spear
2678 chitstsîy (1), *arrow*
2687 châtsâts (1), *gravel, grit*
7565 resheph (1), *flame*

ARTAXERXES
783 'Artachshastâ' (Ch.) (14), *Artaxerxes*

ARTAXERXES'
783 'Artachshastâ' (Ch.) (1), *Artaxerxes*

ARTEMAS
734 Artĕmas (1), *gift of Artemis*

ARTIFICER
2794 chôrêsh (1), skilled *fabricator* worker
2796 chârâsh (1), skilled *fabricator* or *worker*

ARTIFICERS
2796 chârâsh (2), skilled *fabricator* or *worker*

ARTILLERY
3627 kᵉlîy (1), *implement, thing*

ARTS
4021 pĕriĕrgŏs (1), *magic, sorcery*

ARUBOTH
700 'Ărubbôwth (1), *Arubboth*

ARUMAH
725 'Ărûwmâh (1), *height*

ARVAD
719 'Arvad (2), refuge for the *roving*

ARVADITE
721 'Arvâdîy (2), *Arvadite*

ARZA
777 'artsâ' (1), *earthiness*

ASA
609 'Âçâ' (57), *Asa*
760 Asa (2), *Asa*

ASA'S
609 'Âçâ' (1), *Asa*

ASAHEL
760 'Ăram Tsôwbâh (1), *Aram* of Coele-Syria
6214 'Ăsâh'êl (17), *God has made*

ASAHIAH
6222 'Ăsâyâh (2), *Jehovah has made*

ASAIAH
6222 'Ăsâyâh (6), *Jehovah has made*

ASAPH
623 'Âçâph (44), *collector*

ASAPH'S
623 'Âçâph (1), *collector*

ASAREEL
840 'Ăsar'êl (1), *right of God*

ASARELAH
841 'Ăsar'êlâh (1), *right toward God*

ASCEND
5927 'âlâh (9), to *ascend, be high, mount*
305 anabainō (4), to *go up, rise*

ASCENDED
5927 'âlâh (10), to *ascend, be high, mount*
305 anabainō (9), to *go up, rise*

ASCENDETH
305 anabainō (2), to *go up, rise*

ASCENDING
5927 'âlâh (2), to *ascend, be high, mount*
305 anabainō (3), to *go up, rise*

ASCENT
4608 ma'ăleh (2), *elevation; platform*
5930 'ôlâh (1), *sacrifice wholly consumed in fire*
5944 'ăliyâh (1), *upper things; second-story*

ASCRIBE
3051 yâhab (1), to *give*
5414 nâthan (2), to *give*

ASCRIBED
5414 nâthan (2), to *give*

ASENATH
621 'Âçᵉnath (3), *Asenath*

ASER
768 Asēr (2), *happy*

ASH
766 'ôren (1), *ash* tree

ASHAMED
954 bûwsh (79), to be *ashamed; disappointed*
1322 bôsheth (1), *shame*
2659 châphêr (4), to *be ashamed, disappointed*
3637 kâlam (12), to *taunt* or *insult*

153 aischunŏmai (5), to
feel shame for oneself
422 anĕpaischuntŏs (1),
unashamed
1788 ĕntrĕpō (2), to
respect; to confound
1870 ĕpaischunŏmai
(11), to feel shame
2617 kataischunō (7), to
disgrace or shame

ASHAN
6228 'Āshân (4), smoke

ASHBEA
791 'Ashbêa' (1), adjurer

ASHBEL
788 'Ashbêl (3), flowing

ASHBELITES
789 'Ashbêlîy (1),
Ashbelite

ASHCHENAZ
813 'Ashkᵉnaz (2),
Ashkenaz

ASHDOD
795 'Ashdôwd (21),
ravager

ASHDODITES
796 'Ashdôwdîy (1),
Ashdodite

ASHDOTH-PISGAH
798+6449 'Ashdôwth
hap-Piçgâh (3), ravines
of the Pisgah

ASHDOTHITES
796 'Ashdôwdîy (1),
Ashdodite

ASHER
836 'Āshêr (42), happy

ASHERITES
843 'Āshêrîy (1), Asherite

ASHES
665 'êpher (24), ashes
1878 dâshên (2), to be
fat, thrive; to fatten
1880 deshen (8), fat;
fatness, ashes
6083 'âphâr (2), dust,
earth, mud; clay,
6368 piyach (2), powder
dust or ashes
4700 spŏdŏs (3), ashes
5077 tĕphrŏō (1), to
incinerate

ASHIMA
807 'Ăshîymâ' (1),
Ashima

ASHKELON
831 'Ashqᵉlôwn (9),
Ashkelon

ASHKENAZ
813 'Ashkᵉnaz (1),
Ashkenaz

ASHNAH
823 'Ashnâh (2), Ashnah

ASHPENAZ
828 'Ashpᵉnaz (1),
Ashpenaz

ASHRIEL
845 'Asrî'êlîy (1), Asrielite

ASHTAROTH
6252 'Ashtârôwth (11),
increases

ASHTERATHITE
6254 'Ashtᵉrâthîy (1),
Ashterathite

ASHTEROTH
6255 'Ashtᵉrôth
Qarnayim (1),
Ashtaroth of (the)
double horns

ASHTORETH
6252 'Ashtârôwth (3),
increases

ASHUR
804 'Ashshûwr (2),
successful

ASHURITES
843 'Āshêrîy (2), Asherite

ASHVATH
6220 'Ashvâth (1), bright

ASIA
773 Asia (20), Asia Minor
775 Asiarchēs (1), ruler
in Asia

ASIDE
2015 hâphak (1), to turn
about or over
3943 lâphath (1), to
clasp; to turn aside
5186 nâṭâh (16), to
stretch or spread out
5265 nâça' (1), start on a
journey
5437 çâbab (2), to
surround
5493 çûwr (4), to turn off
5844 'âṭâh (1), to wrap,
i.e. cover, veil, clothe
6437 pânâh (1), to turn,
to face
7750 sûwṭ (1), become
derelict
7847 sâṭâh (5), to deviate
from duty, go astray
402 anachōrĕō (3), to
retire, withdraw
565 apĕrchŏmai (1), to
go off, i.e. depart
659 apŏtithēmi (2), to put
away; get rid of
863 aphiēmi (1), to leave;
to pardon, forgive
1824 ĕxautēs (2),
instantly, at once
2596 kata (1), down;
according to
5087 tithēmi (1), to
place, put
5298 hupŏchōrĕō (1), to
vacate down, i.e. retire

ASIEL
6221 'Ăsîy'êl (1), made of
God

ASK
1156 bᵉ'â' (Ch.) (2), to
seek or ask
1245 bâqash (1), to
search out
1875 dârash (1), to
pursue or search
7592 shâ'al (41), to ask
154 aitĕō (38), to ask for
523 apaitĕō (1), to
demand back
1833 ĕxĕtazō (1), to
ascertain or interrogate
1905 ĕpĕrōtaō (8), to
inquire, seek

2065 ĕrōtaō (11), to
interrogate; to request
4441 punthanŏmai (2), to
ask for information

ASKED
1156 bᵉ'â' (Ch.) (1), to
seek or ask
1245 bâqash (1), to
search out
7592 shâ'al (49), to ask
7593 shᵉ'êl (Ch.) (3), to
ask
154 aitĕō (4), to ask for
1905 ĕpĕrōtaō (45), to
inquire, seek
2065 ĕrōtaō (11), to
interrogate; to request
3004 lĕgō (1), to say
4441 punthanŏmai (4), to
ask for information

ASKELON
831 'Ashqᵉlôwn (3),
Ashkelon

ASKEST
7592 shâ'al (1), to ask
154 aitĕō (1), to ask for
1905 ĕpĕrōtaō (1), to
inquire, seek

ASKETH
7592 shâ'al (5), to ask
154 aitĕō (5), to ask for
2065 ĕrōtaō (1), to
interrogate; to request

ASKING
7592 shâ'al (3), to ask
350 anakrinō (2), to
interrogate, determine
1905 ĕpĕrōtaō (1), to
inquire, seek
2065 ĕrōtaō (1), to
interrogate; to request

ASLEEP
3463 yâshên (2), sleepy
7290 râdam (2), to
stupefy
879 aphupnŏō (1), to
drop (off) in slumber
2518 kathĕudō (5), to fall
asleep
2837 kŏimaō (6), to
slumber; to decease

ASNAH
619 'Açnâh (1), Asnah

ASNAPPER
620 'Oçnappar (Ch.) (1),
Osnappar

ASP
6620 pethen (1), asp

ASPATHA
630 'Açpâthâ' (1),
Aspatha

ASPS
6620 pethen (3), asp
785 aspis (1), serpent,
(poss.) asp

ASRIEL
844 'Asrîy'êl (2), right of
God

ASRIELITES
845 'Asrî'êlîy (1), Asrielite

ASS
860 'âthôwn (16), female
donkey, ass

2543 chămôwr (55), male
donkey or ass
5601 çappîyr (1),
sapphire
5895 'ayîr (2), young
robust donkey or ass
6171 'ârôwd (1), onager
or wild donkey
6501 pere' (3), onager,
wild donkey
3678 ŏnariŏn (1), little
donkey
3688 ŏnŏs (5), donkey
5268 hupŏzugiŏn (2),
donkey

ASS'S
860 'âthôwn (1), female
donkey, ass
2543 chămôwr (1), male
donkey or ass
6501 pere' (1), onager,
wild donkey
3688 ŏnŏs (1), donkey

ASSAULT
6696 tsûwr (1), to cramp,
i.e. confine; to harass
3730 hŏrmē (1), violent
impulse, i.e. onset

ASSAULTED
2186 ĕphistēmi (1), to be
present; to approach

ASSAY
5254 nâçâh (1), to test,
attempt

ASSAYED
2974 yâ'al (1), to assent;
to undertake, begin
5254 nâçâh (1), to test,
attempt
3985 pĕirazō (1), to
endeavor, scrutinize,
entice, discipline
3987 pĕiraō (1), to
attempt, try

ASSAYING
3984+2983 pĕira (1),
attempt, experience

ASSEMBLE
622 'âçaph (10), to
gather, collect
1481 gûwr (1), to sojourn,
live as an alien
2199 zâ'aq (2), to call
out, convene publicly
3259 yâ'ad (1), to meet;
to summon; to direct
5789 'ûwsh (1), to hasten
6908 qâbats (5), to
collect, assemble

ASSEMBLED
622 'âçaph (4), to gather,
collect
662 'âphaq (1), to abstain
1413 gâdad (1), to gash,
slash oneself
2199 zâ'aq (1), to call
out, convene publicly
3259 yâ'ad (3), to meet;
to summon; to direct
6633 tsâbâ' (1), to mass
an army or servants
6638 tsâbâh (1), to array
an army against
6908 qâbats (1), to
collect, assemble

6950 qâhal (11), to *convoke, gather*
7284 rᵉgash (Ch.) (3), to *gather tumultuously*
1096 ginŏmai (1), to *be, become*
4863 sunagō (6), to *gather together*
4871 sunalizō (1), to *accumulate*
4905 sunĕrchŏmai (1), to *gather together*

ASSEMBLIES
627 'ăçuppâh (1), *collection* of sayings
4150 môw'êd (1), *assembly, congregation*
4744 miqrâ' (2), *public meeting*
5712 'êdâh (1), *assemblage; family*
6116 'ătsârâh (1), *assembly*

ASSEMBLING
6633 tsâbâ' (1), to *mass an army or servants*
1997 ĕpisunagōgē (1), *meeting, gathering*

ASSEMBLY
4150 môw'êd (3), *assembly, congregation*
4186 môwshâb (1), *seat; site; abode*
5475 çôwd (5), *intimacy; consultation; secret*
5712 'êdâh (8), *assemblage; family*
6116 'ătsârâh (9), *assembly*
6951 qâhâl (17), *assemblage*
6952 qᵉhillâh (1), *assemblage*
1577 ĕkklēsia (3), *congregation*
3831 panēguris (1), *mass-meeting*
4864 sunagōgē (1), *assemblage*

ASSENT
6310 peh (1), *mouth; opening*

ASSENTED
4934 suntithĕmai (1), to *place jointly*

ASSES
860 'âthôwn (17), female *donkey, ass*
2543 chămôwr (40), male *donkey or ass*
5895 'ayîr (2), young *robust donkey or ass*
6167 'ărâd (Ch.) (1), *onager or wild donkey*
6501 pere' (4), *onager, wild donkey*

ASSHUR
804 'Ashshûwr (8), *successful*

ASSHURIM
805 'Ăshûwrîy (1), *Ashurite*

ASSIGNED
5414 nâthan (2), to *give*

ASSIR
617 'Aççîyr (5), *prisoner*

ASSIST
3936 paristēmi (1), to *stand beside, present*

ASSOCIATE
7489 râ'a' (1), to *break to pieces; to make*

ASSOS
789 Assŏs (2), *Assus*

ASSUR
804 'Ashshûwr (2), *successful*

ASSURANCE
539 'âman (1), to *be firm, faithful, true; to trust*
983 beṭach (1), *safety, security, trust*
4102 pistis (1), *faithfulness; faith, belief*
4136 plērŏphŏria (4), *full assurance*

ASSURE
3983 pĕinaō (1), to *famish; to crave*

ASSURED
571 'emeth (1), *certainty, truth, trustworthiness*
6966 qûwm (Ch.) (1), to *rise*
4104 pistŏō (1), to *assure*

ASSUREDLY
571 'emeth (1), *certainty, truth, trustworthiness*
3045 yâda' (1), to *know*
3318 yâtsâ' (1), to *go, bring out*
3588 kîy (3), *for, that because*
8354 shâthâh (1), to *drink, imbibe*
806 asphalŏs (1), *securely*
4822 sumbibazō (1), to *unite; to infer, show*

ASSWAGE
2820 châsak (1), to *refuse, spare, preserve*

ASSWAGED
2820 châsak (1), to *refuse, spare, preserve*
7918 shâkak (1), to *lay a trap; to allay*

ASSYRIA
804 'Ashshûwr (118), *successful*

ASSYRIAN
804 'Ashshûwr (13), *successful*

ASSYRIANS
804 'Ashshûwr (10), *successful*

ASTAROTH
6252 'Ashtârôwth (1), *increases*

ASTONIED
1724 dâham (1), to *be astounded*
7672 shᵉbash (Ch.) (1), to *perplex, be baffled*
8074 shâmêm (6), to *devastate; to stupefy*
8075 shᵉmam (Ch.) (1), to *devastate; to stupefy*
8429 tᵉvahh (Ch.) (1), to *amaze, take alarm*

ASTONISHED
8074 shâmêm (14), to *devastate; to stupefy*
8539 tâmahh (1), to *be astounded*
1605 ĕkplēssō (10), to *astonish*
1839 ĕxistēmi (6), to *become astounded*
2284 thambĕō (2), to *astound, be amazed*
4023+2285 pĕriĕchō (1), to *clasp; to encircle*

ASTONISHMENT
8047 shammâh (14), *ruin; consternation*
8074 shâmêm (1), to *devastate; to stupefy*
8078 shimmâmôwn (2), *stupefaction, despair*
8541 timmâhôwn (2), *consternation, panic*
8653 tar'êlâh (1), *reeling, staggering*
1611 ĕkstasis (1), *bewilderment, ecstasy, astonishment*

ASTRAY
5080 nâdach (1), to *push off, scattered*
7683 shâgag (1), to *stray*
7686 shâgâh (2), to *stray*
8582 tâ'âh (13), to *vacillate, stray*
4105 planaō (5), to *roam, wander from safety*

ASTROLOGER
826 'ashshâph (Ch.) (1), *conjurer, enchanter*

ASTROLOGERS
825 'ashshâph (2), *conjurer, enchanter*
826 'ashshâph (Ch.) (5), *conjurer, enchanter*
1895+8064 hâbar (1), to *be a horoscopist*

ASUNDER
996 bêyn (1), *between*
673 apŏchōrizō (1), to *rend apart; to separate*
1288 diaspaō (1), to *sever or dismember*
1371 dichŏtŏmĕō (1), to *flog severely*
2997 laschō (1), to *crack open*
4249 prizō (1), to *saw in two*
5563 chōrizō (2), to *place room between*

ASUPPIM
624 'ăçûph (2), *stores of goods*

ASYNCRITUS
799 Asugkritŏs (1), *incomparable*

ATAD
329 'âṭâd (2), *buckthorn tree*

ATARAH
5851 'Ăṭârâh (1), *crown*

ATAROTH
5852 'Ăṭârôwth (5), *crowns*

ATAROTH-ADAR
5853 'Aṭrôwth 'Addâr (1), *crowns of Addar*

ATAROTH-ADDAR
5853 'Aṭrôwth 'Addâr (1), *crowns of Addar*

ATE
398 'âkal (2), to *eat*
2719 katĕsthiō (1), to *devour*

ATER
333 'Âṭêr (5), *maimed*

ATHACH
6269 'Ăthâk (1), *lodging*

ATHAIAH
6265 'Ăthâyâh (1), *Jehovah has helped*

ATHALIAH
6271 'Ăthalyâh (17), *Jehovah has constrained*

ATHENIANS
117 Athēnaiŏs (1), *inhabitant of Athenæ*

ATHENS
116 Athēnai (6), city *Athenæ*
117 Athēnaiŏs (1), *inhabitant of Athenæ*

ATHIRST
6770 tsâmê' (2), to *thirst*
1372 dipsaō (3), to *thirst for*

ATHLAI
6270 'Athlay (1), *compressed*

ATONEMENT
3722 kâphar (73), to *cover; to expiate*
3725 kippûr (7), *expiation*
2643 katallagē (1), *restoration*

ATONEMENTS
3725 kippûr (1), *expiation*

ATROTH
5855 'Aṭrôwth Shôwphân (1), *crowns of Shophan*

ATTAI
6262 'Attay (4), *timely*

ATTAIN
3201 yâkôl (1), to *be able*
5381 nâsag (1), to *reach*
7069 qânâh (1), to *create; to procure*
2658 katantaō (2), to *attain or reach*

ATTAINED
935 bôw' (4), to *go or come*
5381 nâsag (1), to *reach*
2638 katalambanō (1), to *seize; to possess*
2983 lambanō (1), to *take, receive*
3877 parakŏlŏuthĕō (1), to *attend; trace out*
5348 phthanō (2), to *anticipate or precede*

ATTALIA
825 Attalĕia (1), *Attaleia*

English

ATTEND
6440 pânîym (1), *face; front*
7181 qâshab (9), to *prick up* the ears
2145 ĕuprŏsĕdrŏs (1), *diligent service*

ATTENDANCE
4612 ma'ămâd (2), *position; attendant*
4337 prŏsĕchō (2), to *pay attention to*

ATTENDED
995 bîyn (1), to *understand; discern*
7181 qâshab (1), to *prick up* the ears
4337 prŏsĕchō (1), to *pay attention to*

ATTENDING
4343 prŏskartĕrēsis (1), *persistency*

ATTENT
7183 qashshâb (2), *hearkening*

ATTENTIVE
7183 qashshâb (3), *hearkening*
1582 ĕkkrĕmamai (1), to *listen closely*

ATTENTIVELY
8085 shâma' (1), to *hear* intelligently

ATTIRE
2871 tâbûwl (1), *turban*
7196 qishshûr (1), *girdle* or *sash* for women
7897 shîyth (1), *garment*

ATTIRED
6801 tsânaph (1), to *wrap*, i.e. *roll* or *dress*

AUDIENCE
241 'ôzen (7), *ear*
189 akŏĕ (1), *hearing; thing heard*
191 akŏuō (4), to *hear; obey*

AUGMENT
5595 çâphâh (1), to *scrape*; to *accumulate*

AUGUSTUS
828 Augŏustŏs (3), *revered one*

AUGUSTUS'
828 Augŏustŏs (1), *revered one*

AUL
4836 martsêa' (2), *awl* for piercing

AUNT
1733 dôwdâh (1), *aunt*

AUSTERE
840 austērŏs (2), *severe, harsh; exacting*

AUTHOR
159 aitiŏs (1), *causer*
747 archēgŏs (1), *chief leader; founder*

AUTHORITIES
1849 ĕxŏusia (1), *authority, power, right*

AUTHORITY
7235 râbâh (1), to *increase*
8633 tôqeph (1), *might*
831 authĕntĕō (1), to *have authority*
1413 dunastēs (1), *ruler* or *officer*
1849 ĕxŏusia (28), *authority, power, right*
1850 ĕxŏusiazō (1), to *control, master another*
2003 ĕpitagē (1), *injunction* or *decree*
2715 katĕxŏusiazō (2), to *wield full privilege over*
5247 hupĕrŏchē (1), *superiority*

AVA
5755 'Ivvâh (1), *overthrow, ruin*

AVAILETH
7737 shâvâh (1), to *level*; to *resemble*; to *adjust*
2480 ischuō (3), to *have* or *exercise force*

AVEN
206 'Âven (3), *idolatry*

AVENGE
5358 nâqam (8), to *avenge* or *punish*
5358+5360 nâqam (1), to *avenge* or *punish*
5414+5360 nâthan (1), to *give*
6485 pâqad (1), to *visit, care for, count*
1556 ĕkdikĕō (4), to *vindicate; retaliate*
4160+3588+1557 pŏiĕō (2), to *make* or *do*

AVENGED
3467 yâsha' (1), to *make safe, free*
5358 nâqam (9), to *avenge* or *punish*
5414+5360 nâthan (1), to *give*
8199 shâphaṭ (2), to *judge*
1556 ĕkdikĕō (1), to *vindicate; retaliate*
2919+3588+2917 krinō (1), to *decide*; to *try*

AVENGER
1350 gâ'al (6), to *redeem*; to *be the next of kin*
5358 nâqam (2), to *avenge* or *punish*
1558 ĕkdikŏs (1), *punisher, avenger*

AVENGETH
5414+5360 nâthan (2), to *give*

AVENGING
3467 yâsha' (2), to *make safe, free*
6544+6546 pâra' (1), to *absolve, begin*

AVERSE
7725 shûwb (1), to *turn back*; to *return*

AVIM
5761 'Avvîym (1), *Avvim*

AVIMS
5757 'Avvîy (1), *Avvite*

AVITES
5757 'Avvîy (2), *Avvite*

AVITH
5762 'Ăvîyth (2), *ruin*

AVOID
6544 pâra' (1), to *loosen*; to *expose, dismiss*
1223 dia (1), *through*, by means of; *because* of
1578 ĕkklinō (1), to *shun*; to *decline*
3868 paraitĕŏmai (1), to *deprecate, decline*
4026 pĕriistēmi (1), to *stand around*; to *avoid*

AVOIDED
5437 çâbab (1), to *surround*

AVOIDING
1624 ĕktrĕpō (1), to *turn away*
4724 stĕllō (1), to *repress, abstain* from

AVOUCHED
559 'âmar (2), to *say, speak*

AWAIT
1917 ĕpibŏulē (1), *plot, plan*

AWAKE
5782 'ûwr (20), to *awake*
6974 qûwts (11), to *awake*
1235 diagrēgŏrĕō (1), to *waken thoroughly*
1326 diĕgĕirō (1), to *arouse, stimulate*
1453 ĕgĕirō (2), to *waken*, i.e. *rouse*
1594 ĕknēphō (1), to *rouse* (oneself) *out*
1852 ĕxupnizō (1), to *waken, rouse*

AWAKED
3364 yâqats (4), to *awake*
6974 qûwts (4), to *awake*

AWAKEST
5782 'ûwr (1), to *awake*
6974 qûwts (1), to *awake*

AWAKETH
6974 qûwts (3), to *awake*

AWAKING
1096+1853 ginŏmai (1), to *be, become*

AWARE
3045 yâda' (2), to *know*
1097 ginōskō (2), to *know*
1492 ĕidō (1), to *know*

AWAY
310 'achar (1), *after*
1197 bâ'ar (16), to *be brutish, be senseless*
1272 bârach (1), to *flee suddenly*
1473 gôwlâh (7), *exile; captive*
1497 gâzal (4), to *rob*
1540 gâlâh (17), to *denude; uncover*
1541 gᵉlâh (Ch.) (1), to *reveal mysteries*
1546 gâlûwth (4), *captivity; exiles*
1589 gânab (1), to *thieve*; to *deceive*

1639 gâra' (1), to *shave, remove, lessen*
1870 derek (1), *road; course* of life
1898 hâgâh (2), to *remove, expel*
1920 hâdaph (1), to *push away* or *down; drive out*
2219 zârâh (1), to *toss about*; to *diffuse*
2763 charam (1), to *devote* to destruction
2846 châthâh (1), to *lay hold* of; to *take away*
2862 châthaph (1), to *clutch, snatch*
3212 yâlak (4), to *walk*; to *live*; to *carry*
3318 yâtsâ' (4), to *go, bring out*
3988 mâ'aç (1), to *spurn*; to *disappear*
4422 mâlaṭ (1), to *escape* as if by *slipperiness*
5074 nâdad (1), to *rove, flee*; to *drive away*
5077 nâdâh (1), to *exclude*, i.e. *banish*
5111 nûwd (Ch.) (1), to *flee*
5186 nâṭâh (1), to *stretch* or *spread out*
5265 nâça' (3), *start* on a journey
5493 çûwr (70), to *turn off*
5496 çûwth (1), to *stimulate*; to *seduce*
5674 'âbar (7), to *cross over*; to *transition*
5709 'ădâ' (Ch.) (3), to *remove*; to *bedeck*
5710 'âdâh (1), to *pass on* or *continue*; to *remove*
7311 rûwm (2), to *be high*; to *rise* or *raise*
7368 râchaq (3), to *recede; remove*
7617 shâbâh (7), to *transport* into captivity
7628 shᵉbîy (1), *exile; booty*
7673 shâbath (1), to *repose*; to *desist* from
7726 shôwbâb (1), *apostate*, i.e. *idolatrous*
7953 shâlâh (1), to *draw out* or *off*, i.e. *remove*
115 athĕtēsis (1), *cancellation*
142 airō (12), to *lift, take up*
337 anairĕō (1), to *take away*, i.e. *abolish*
343 anakaluptō (1), to *unveil*
520 apagō (12), to *take away*
522 apairō (1), to *remove, take away*
565 apĕrchŏmai (15), to *go off*, i.e. *depart*
577 apŏballō (2), to *throw off*; fig. to *lose*
580 apŏbŏlē (1), *rejection, loss*
595 apŏthĕsis (1), *laying aside*
617 apŏkuliō (3), to *roll away, roll back*

English

628 apŏlŏuō (1), to *wash fully*
630 apŏluō (27), to *relieve, release*
645 apŏspaō (1), to *withdraw* with force
646 apŏstasia (1), *defection* from truth
649 apŏstĕllō (4), to *send out* on a mission
654 apŏstrĕphō (6), to *turn away* or *back*
657 apŏtassŏmai (1), to *say adieu; to renounce*
659 apŏtithēmi (1), to *put away; get rid of*
665 apŏtrĕpō (1), to *deflect, avoid*
667 apŏhĕrō (3), to *bear off, carry away*
683 apŏthĕŏmai (4), to *push off; to reject*
726 harpazō (2), to *seize*
851 aphairĕō (8), to *remove, cut off*
863 aphiēmi (4), to *leave; to pardon, forgive*
868 aphistēmi (2), *instigate* to revolt
1294 diastrĕphō (1), to *distort*
1544 ĕkballō (1), to *throw out*
1593 ĕknĕuō (1), to *quietly withdraw*
1599 ĕkpĕmpō (1), to *despatch, send out*
1601 ĕkpiptō (1), to *drop away*
1602 ĕkplĕō (1), to *depart* by ship
1808 ĕxairō (1), to *remove, drive away*
1813 ĕxalĕiphō (2), to *obliterate*
1821 ĕxapŏstĕllō (4), to *despatch*, or to *dismiss*
1831 ĕxĕrchŏmai (1), to *issue; to leave*
1854 ĕxō (1), *out, outside*
2210 zēmiŏō (1), to *experience detriment*
2673 katargĕō (6), to *be, render entirely useless*
3179 mĕthistēmi (1), to *move*
3334 mĕtakinĕō (1), to *be removed, shifted from*
3350 mĕtŏikĕsia (3), *expatriation, exile*
3351 mĕtŏikizō (1), to *transfer* as a *settler* or *captive*
3895 parapiptō (1), to *apostatize, fall away*
3911 paraphĕrō (1), to *carry off; to avert*
3928 parĕrchŏmai (5), to *go by; to perish*
4014 pĕriairĕō (3), to *cast off* anchor; to *expiate*
4879 sunapagō (2), to *take off together*
5217 hupagō (3), to *withdraw* or *retire*

AWE
1481 gûwr (1), to *sojourn, live as an alien*

6342 pâchad (1), to *be startled; to fear*
7264 râgaz (1), to *quiver*

AWOKE
3364 yâqats (6), to *awake*
1326 diĕgĕirō (1), to *arouse, stimulate*
1453 ĕgĕirō (1), to *waken*, i.e. *rouse*

AX
1270 barzel (1), *iron; iron implement*
1631 garzen (2), *axe*
4601 Ma'ăkâh (1), *depression*
4621 ma'ătsâd (1), *axe*
7134 qardôm (1), *axe*
513 axinē (1), *axe*

AXE
1631 garzen (2), *axe*
7134 qardôm (1), *axe*
513 axinē (1), *axe*

AXES
2719 chereb (1), *knife, sword*
3781 kashshîyl (1), *axe*
4037 magzêrâh (1), *cutting blade, ax*
4050 mᵉgêrâh (1), *stone cutting saw*
7134 qardôm (3), *axe*

AXLETREES
3027 yâd (2), *hand; power*

AZAL
682 'Âtsêl (1), *noble*

AZALIAH
683 'Ătsalyâhûw (2), *Jehovah has reserved*

AZANIAH
245 'Ăzanyâh (1), *heard by Jehovah*

AZARAEL
5832 'Ăzar'êl (1), *God has helped*

AZAREEL
5832 'Ăzar'êl (5), *God has helped*

AZARIAH
5838 'Ăzaryâh (47), *Jehovah has helped*
5839 'Ăzaryâh (Ch.) (1), *Jehovah has helped*

AZAZ
5811 'Âzâz (1), *strong*

AZAZIAH
5812 'Ăzazyâhûw (3), *Jehovah has strengthened*

AZBUK
5802 'Azbûwq (1), *stern depopulator*

AZEKAH
5825 'Ăzêqâh (7), *tilled*

AZEL
682 'Âtsêl (6), *noble*

AZEM
6107 'Etsem (2), *bone*

AZGAD
5803 'Azgâd (4), *stern troop*

AZIEL
5815 'Ăzîy'êl (1), *strengthened of God*

AZIZA
5819 'Ăzîyzâ' (1), *strengthfulness*

AZMAVETH
5820 'Azmâveth (8), *strong* (one) *of death*

AZMON
6111 'Atsmôwn (3), *bone-like*

AZNOTH-TABOR
243 'Aznôwth Tâbôwr (1), *flats of Tabor*

AZOR
107 Azōr (2), *helpful*

AZOTUS
108 Azōtŏs (1), *Azotus*, i.e. *Ashdod*

AZRIEL
5837 'Azrîy'êl (3), *help of God*

AZRIKAM
5840 'Azrîyqâm (6), *help of an enemy*

AZUBAH
5806 'Ăzûwbâh (4), *forsaking*

AZUR
5809 'Azzûwr (2), *helpful*

AZZAH
5804 'Azzâh (3), *strong*

AZZAN
5821 'Azzân (1), *strong one*

AZZUR
5809 'Azzûwr (1), *helpful*

BAAL
1168 Ba'al (61), *master*
896 Baal (1), *master*

BAAL'S
1168 Ba'al (1), *master*

BAAL-BERITH
1170 Ba'al Bᵉrîyth (2), *Baal of* (the) *covenant*

BAAL-GAD
1171 Ba'al Gâd (3), *Baal of Fortune*

BAAL-HAMON
1174 Ba'al Hâmôwn (1), *possessor of a multitude*

BAAL-HANAN
1177 Ba'al Chânân (5), *possessor of grace*

BAAL-HAZOR
1178 Ba'al Châtsôwr (1), *possessor of a village*

BAAL-HERMON
1179 Ba'al Chermôwn (2), *possessor of Hermon*

BAAL-MEON
1186 Ba'al Mᵉ'ôwn (3), *Baal of* (the) *habitation*

BAAL-PEOR
1187 Ba'al Pᵉ'ôwr (6), *Baal of Peor*

BAAL-PERAZIM
1188 Ba'al Pᵉ'râtsîym (4), *possessor of breaches*

BAAL-SHALISHA
1190 Ba'al Shâlîshâh (1), *Baal of Shalishah*

BAAL-TAMAR
1193 Ba'al Tâmâr (1), *possessor of* (the) *palm-tree*

BAAL-ZEBUB
1176 Ba'al Zᵉbûwb (4), *Baal of* (the) *Fly*

BAAL-ZEPHON
1189 Ba'al Tsᵉphôwn (3), *Baal of winter*

BAALAH
1173 Ba'ălâh (5), *mistress*

BAALATH
1191 Ba'ălâth (3), office of *mistress*

BAALATH-BEER
1192 Ba'ălath Bᵉ'êr (1), *mistress of a well*

BAALE
1184 Ba'ălêy Yᵉhûwdâh (1), *masters of Judah*

BAALI
1180 Ba'ălîy (1), *my master*

BAALIM
1168 Ba'al (18), *master*

BAALIS
1185 Ba'ălîç (1), *in exultation*

BAANA
1195 Ba'ănâ' (2), *in affliction*

BAANAH
1195 Ba'ănâ' (10), *in affliction*

BAARA
1199 Bâ'ărâ' (1), *brutish*

BAASEIAH
1202 Ba'ăsêyâh (1), *in* (the) *work of Jehovah*

BAASHA
1201 Ba'shâ' (28), *offensiveness*

BABBLER
1167+3956 ba'al (1), *master; husband*
4691 spĕrmŏlŏgŏs (1), *gossip* or *trifler* in talk

BABBLING
7879 sîyach (1), uttered *contemplation*

BABBLINGS
2757 kĕnŏphōnia (2), *fruitless discussion*

BABE
5288 na'ar (1), male *child; servant*
1025 brĕphŏs (4), *infant*
3516 nēpiŏs (1), *infant; simple-minded* person

BABEL
894 Bâbel (2), *confusion*

BABES
5768 'ôwlêl (2), *suckling child*
8586 ta'ălûwl (1), *caprice* (as a fit *coming on*)
1025 brĕphŏs (1), *infant*

3516 *nēpiŏs* (5), *infant; simple-minded* person

BABYLON
894 Bâbel (247), *confusion*
895 Bâbel (Ch.) (25), *confusion*
897 Babulōn (12), *Babylon*

BABYLON'S
894 Bâbel (8), *confusion*

BABYLONIANS
896 Bablîy (Ch.) (1), *Babylonian*
1121+894 bên (3), *people of a class or kind*

BABYLONISH
8152 Shin'âr (1), *Shinar*

BACA
1056 Bâkâ' (1), *Baca*

BACHRITES
1076 Bakrîy (1), *Bakrite*

BACK
268 'âchôwr (16), *behind, backward; west*
310 'achar (1), *after*
322 'âchôrannîyth (1), *backwardly, by turning*
1354 gab (1), *mounded or rounded: top or rim*
1355 gab (Ch.) (1), *back*
1458 gav (7), *back*
1639 gâra' (1), *to shave, remove, lessen*
1973 hâl'âh (1), *far away; thus far*
2015 hâphak (2), *to turn about or over*
2820 châsak (4), *to restrain or refrain*
3607 kâlâ' (1), *to hold back or in; to prohibit*
4185 mûwsh (1), *to withdraw*
4513 mâna' (4), *to deny, refuse*
5253 nâçag (1), *to retreat*
5437 çâbab (1), *to surround*
5472 çûwg (3), *to go back, to retreat*
5493 çûwr (2), *to turn off*
5637 çârar (1), *to be refractory, stubborn*
6203 'ôreph (1), *nape or back of the neck*
6437 pânâh (6), *to turn, to face*
6544 pâra' (1), *to loosen; to expose, dismiss*
7725 shûwb (70), *to turn back; to return*
7926 sh'kem (2), *neck; spur of a hill*
617 apŏkuliō (2), *to roll away, roll back*
650 apŏstĕrĕō (1), *to deprive; to despoil*
3557 nŏsphizŏmai (2), *to sequestrate*
3577 nōtŏs (1), *back*
3694 ŏpisō (5), *behind, after, following*
4762 strĕphō (1), *to turn quite around or reverse*
5288 hupŏstĕllō (2), *cower or shrink*

5289 hupŏstŏlē (1), *shrinkage, timidity*
5290 hupŏstrĕphō (3), *to turn under, behind*

BACKBITERS
2637 katalalŏs (1), *slanderer*

BACKBITETH
7270 râgal (1), *to reconnoiter; to slander*

BACKBITING
5643 çêther (1), *cover, shelter*

BACKBITINGS
2636 katalalia (1), *defamation, slander*

BACKBONE
6096 'âtseh (1), *spine*

BACKS
268 'âchôwr (1), *behind, backward; west*
1354 gab (1), *mounded or rounded: top or rim*
1458 gav (1), *back*
6203 'ôreph (4), *nape of the neck*

BACKSIDE
268 'âchôwr (1), *behind, backward; west*
310 'achar (1), *after*
3693 ŏpisthĕn (1), *at the back; after*

BACKSLIDER
5472 çûwg (1), *to go back, to apostatize*

BACKSLIDING
4878 m'shûwbâh (7), *apostasy*
5637 çârar (1), *to be refractory, stubborn*
7726 shôwbâb (2), *apostate, i.e. idolatrous*
7728 shôwbêb (2), *apostate, heathenish*

BACKSLIDINGS
4878 m'shûwbâh (4), *apostasy*

BACKWARD
268 'âchôwr (11), *behind, backward; west*
322 'âchôrannîyth (6), *backwardly, by turning*
1519+3588+3694 ĕis (1), *to or into*

BAD
873 bi'ûwsh (Ch.) (1), *wicked, evil*
7451 ra' (13), *bad; evil*
2556 kakŏs (1), *bad, evil*
4190 pŏnĕrŏs (1), *malice, wicked, bad; crime*
4550 saprŏs (1), *rotten, i.e. worthless*

BADE
559 'âmar (6), *to say, speak*
1696 dâbar (1), *to speak, say; to subdue*
6680 tsâvâh (3), *to constitute, enjoin*
657 apŏtassŏmai (1), *to say adieu; to renounce*
2036 ĕpō (3), *to speak*
2564 kalĕō (4), *to call*

BADEST
1696 dâbar (1), *to speak, say; to subdue*

BADGERS'
8476 tachash (14), (poss.) *antelope*

BADNESS
7455 rôa' (1), *badness*

BAG
3599 kîyç (4), *cup; utility bag*
3627 k'lîy (2), *implement, thing*
6872 ts'rôwr (3), *parcel; kernel or particle*
1101 glōssŏkŏmŏn (2), *money purse*

BAGS
2754 chârîyṭ (1), *pocket*
6696 tsûwr (1), *to cramp, i.e. confine; to harass*
905 balantiŏn (1), *money pouch*

BAHARUMITE
978 Bachărûwmîy (1), *Bacharumite*

BAHURIM
980 Bachûrîym (5), *young men*

BAJITH
1006 Bayith (1), *house; temple; family, tribe*

BAKBAKKAR
1230 Baqbaqqar (1), *searcher*

BAKBUK
1227 Baqbûwq (2), *bottle*

BAKBUKIAH
1229 Baqbuqyâh (3), *wasting of Jehovah*

BAKE
644 'âphâh (6), *to bake*
1310 bâshal (1), *to boil up, cook; to ripen*
5746 'ûwg (1), *to bake*

BAKED
644 'âphâh (2), *to bake*
1310 bâshal (1), *to boil up, cook; to ripen*

BAKEMEATS
3978+4639+644 ma'ăkâl (1), *food*

BAKEN
644 'âphâh (4), *to bake*
7246 râbak (1), *to soak bread in oil*
8601 tûphîyn (1), *baked cake*

BAKER
644 'âphâh (8), *to bake*

BAKERS
644 'âphâh (2), *to bake*

BAKERS'
644 'âphâh (1), *to bake*

BAKETH
644 'âphâh (1), *to bake*

BALAAM
1109 Bil'âm (57), *foreigner*
903 Balaam (3), *foreigner*

BALAAM'S
1109 Bil'âm (3), *foreigner*

BALAC
904 Balak (1), *waster*

BALADAN
1081 Bal'ădân (2), *Bel (is his) lord*

BALAH
1088 Bâlâh (1), *failure*

BALAK
1111 Bâlâq (42), *waster*

BALAK'S
1111 Bâlâq (1), *waster*

BALANCE
3976 mô'zên (7), *pair of balance scales*
7070 qâneh (1), *reed*

BALANCES
3976 mô'zên (8), *pair of balance scales*
3977 mô'zên (Ch.) (1), *pair of balance scales*

BALANCINGS
4657 miphlâs (1), *poising*

BALD
1371 gibbêach (1), *bald forehead*
1372 gabbachath (3), *baldness on forehead*
5556 çol'âm (1), *destructive locust kind*
7139 qârach (4), *to depilate, shave*
7142 qêrêach (3), *bald on the back of the head*
7144 qorchâh (1), *baldness*
7146 qârachath (1), *bald spot; threadbare spot*

BALDNESS
7144 qorchâh (9), *baldness*

BALL
1754 dûwr (1), *circle; ball*

BALM
6875 ts'rîy (6), *balsam*

BAMAH
1117 Bâmâh (1), *elevation, high place*

BAMOTH
1120 Bâmôwth (2), *heights*

BAMOTH-BAAL
1120 Bâmôwth (1), *heights of Baal*

BAND
613 'ĕçûwr (Ch.) (2), *manacles, chains*
1416 g'dûwd (5), *band of soldiers*
2428 chayil (2), *army; wealth; virtue; valor*
5688 'ăbôth (1), *entwined things: a string, wreath*
8193 sâphâh (1), *lip, language, speech*
4686 spĕira (7), *tenth of a Roman Legion*

BANDED
4160+4963 pŏiĕō (1), *to make or do*

BANDS
102 'aggâph (7), *crowds of troops*

English

612 'êçûwr (2), *manacles, chains*
631 'âçar (1), to *fasten*; to *join* battle
1416 gᵉdûwd (8), *band* of soldiers
2256 chebel (3), *company, band*
2683 chêtsen (1), *bosom*
2784 chartsubbâh (2), *fetter; pain*
4133 môwṭâh (2), *pole; ox-bow; yoke*
4147 môwçêr (6), *halter; restraint*
4189 môwshᵉkâh (1), *cord, band*
4264 machăneh (2), *encampment*
5688 'ăbôth (3), *entwined* things: a *string, wreath*
7218 rô'sh (2), *head*
1199 dĕsmŏn (3), *shackle; impediment*
2202 zĕuktĕria (1), *tiller-rope, band*
4886 sundĕsmŏs (1), *ligament; control*

BANI
1137 Bânîy (15), *built*

BANISHED
5080 nâdach (2), to *push* off, *scattered*

BANISHMENT
4065 maddûwach (1), *seduction, misleading*
8331 sharshâh (1), *chain*

BANK
5550 çôlᵉlâh (3), siege mound, i.e. *rampart*
8193 sâphâh (10), *lip; edge, margin*
5132 trapĕza (1), *table* or *stool*

BANKS
1415 gâdâh (3), *border, bank* of a river
1428 gidyâh (1), *border, bank* of a river

BANNER
1714 degel (1), *flag, standard, banner*
5251 nêç (2), *flag; signal; token*

BANNERS
1713 dâgal (3), to *be conspicuous*

BANQUET
3738 kârâh (1), to *dig*; to *plot*; to *bore, hew*
4797 mirzach (1), *cry* of *joy; revel* or *feast*
4960 mishteh (10), *drink; banquet* or *feast*
4961 mishteh (Ch.) (1), *drink; banquet* or *feast*
8354 shâthâh (1), to *drink, imbibe*

BANQUETING
3196 yayin (1), *wine; intoxication*

BANQUETINGS
4224 pŏtŏs (1), *drinking-bout*

BAPTISM
908 baptisma (22), *baptism*

BAPTISMS
909 baptismŏs (1), *baptism*

BAPTIST
907 baptizō (1), *baptize*
910 Baptistēs (13), *baptizer*

BAPTIST'S
910 Baptistēs (1), *baptizer*

BAPTIZE
907 baptizō (9), *baptize*

BAPTIZED
907 baptizō (57), *baptize*

BAPTIZEST
907 baptizō (1), *baptize*

BAPTIZETH
907 baptizō (2), *baptize*

BAPTIZING
907 baptizō (4), *baptize*

BAR
270 'âchaz (1), to *seize, grasp; possess*
1280 bᵉrîyach (4), *bolt; cross-bar* of a door
4132 môwṭ (2), *pole; yoke*

BAR-JESUS
919 Bariēsŏus (1), *son of Joshua*

BAR-JONA
920 Bariōnas (1), *son of Jonah*

BARABBAS
912 Barabbas (11), *son of Abba*

BARACHEL
1292 Bârak'êl (2), *God has blessed*

BARACHIAS
914 Barachias (1), *blessing* of *Jehovah*

BARAK
1301 Bârâq (13), *(flash of) lightning*
913 Barak (1), *(flash of) lightning*

BARBARIAN
915 barbarŏs (3), *foreigner, non-Greek*

BARBARIANS
915 barbarŏs (2), *foreigner, non-Greek*

BARBAROUS
915 barbarŏs (1), *foreigner, non-Greek*

BARBED
7905 sukkâh (1), *dart, harpoon*

BARBER'S
1532 gallâb (1), *barber*

BARE
2029 hârâh (1), to *conceive, be pregnant*
2308 châdal (1), to *desist, stop; be fat*
2342 chûwl (1), to *dance, whirl*; to *writhe* in pain
2554 châmaç (1), to *be violent; to maltreat*

2834 châsaph (4), to *drain* away or *bail* up
3205 yâlad (110), to *bear young*; to *father a child*
4910 mâshal (1), to *rule*
5190 nâṭal (1), to *lift*; to *impose*
5375 nâsâ' (34), to *lift up*
6181 'eryâh (4), *nudity*
6209 'ârar (1), to *bare*; to *demolish*
6544 pâra' (1), to *loosen*; to *expose, dismiss*
7146 qârachath (1), *bald* spot; *threadbare* spot
7287 râdâh (2), to *subjugate*; to *crumble*
7980 shâlaṭ (1), to *dominate*, i.e. *govern*
399 anaphĕrō (1), to *take up*; to *lead up*
941 bastazō (4), to *lift, bear*
1080 gĕnnaō (1), to *procreate, regenerate*
1131 gumnŏs (1), *nude* or *not well clothed*
3140 marturĕō (9), to *testify; to commend*
4160 pŏiĕō (2), to *make* or *do*
5342 phĕrō (1), to *bear* or *carry*
5576 psĕudŏmarturĕō (2), to *offer false evidence*

BAREFOOT
3182 yâchêph (4), *not wearing sandals*

BAREST
4910 mâshal (1), to *rule*
5375 nâsâ' (1), to *lift up*
3140 marturĕō (1), to *testify; to commend*

BARHUMITE
1273 Barchûmîy (1), *Barchumite*

BARIAH
1282 Bârîyach (1), *Bariach*

BARK
5024 nâbach (1), to *bark*

BARKED
7111 qᵉtsâphâh (1), *fragment*

BARKOS
1302 Barqôwç (2), *Barkos*

BARLEY
8184 sᵉ'ôrâh (33), *barley*
2915 krithē (1), *barley*
2916 krithinŏs (2), *consisting of barley*

BARN
1637 gôren (1), *open area*
4035 mᵉgûwrâh (1), *fright; granary*
596 apŏthēkē (2), *granary, grain barn*

BARNABAS
921 Barnabas (29), *son of prophecy*

BARNFLOOR
1637 gôren (1), *open area*

BARNS
618 'âçâm (1), *barn*

4460 mammᵉgûrâh (1), *granary, grain pit*
596 apŏthēkē (2), *granary, grain barn*

BARREL
3537 kad (3), *jar, pitcher*

BARRELS
3537 kad (1), *jar, pitcher*

BARREN
4420 mᵉlêchâh (1), *salted* land, i.e. a *desert*
6115 'ôtser (1), *closure; constraint*
6135 'âqâr (11), *sterile, barren*
6723 tsîyâh (1), *arid desert*
7909 shakkuwl (2), *bereaved*
7921 shâkôl (2), to *miscarry*
692 argŏs (1), *lazy; useless*
4722 stĕgō (4), to *endure patiently*

BARRENNESS
4420 mᵉlêchâh (1), *salted* land, i.e. a *desert*

BARS
905 bad (1), *limb, member; bar; chief*
1280 bᵉrîyach (35), *bolt; cross-bar* of a door
4800 merchâb (1), *open space; liberty*

BARSABAS
923 Barsabas (2), *son of Sabas*

BARTHOLOMEW
918 Barthŏlŏmaiŏs (4), *son of Tolmai*

BARTIMAEUS
924 Bartimaiŏs (1), *son of the unclean*

BARUCH
1263 Bârûwk (26), *blessed*

BARZILLAI
1271 Barzillay (12), *iron-hearted*

BASE
1097+8034 bᵉlîy (1), *without, not yet*
3653 kên (2), *pedestal* or *station* of a basin
4350 mᵉkôwnâh (7), *pedestal; spot* or *place*
4369 mᵉkûnâh (1), *spot*
7034 qâlâh (1), to *be light*
8217 shâphâl (4), *depressed, low*
36 agĕnēs (1), *ignoble, lowly*
5011 tapĕinŏs (1), *humiliated, lowly*

BASER
60 agŏraiŏs (1), *people* of the *market place*

BASES
4350 mᵉkôwnâh (13), *pedestal; spot* or *place*
4369 mᵉkûnâh (1), *spot*

BASEST
8215 sh°phal (Ch.) (1),
low
8217 shâphâl (1),
depressed, low

BASHAN
1316 Bâshân (59), *Bashan*

BASHAN-HAVOTH-JAIR
1316+2334 Bâshân (1),
Bashan

BASHEMATH
1315 Bosmath (6),
fragrance

BASKET
1731 dûwd (2), *pot,
kettle; basket*
2935 ţene' (4), *basket*
3619 k°lûwb (2),
bird-trap; basket
5536 çal (12), *basket*
4553 sarganē (1), *wicker
basket*
4711 spuris (1), *hamper
or lunch-receptacle*

BASKETS
1731 dûwd (1), *pot,
kettle; basket*
1736 dûwday (1), *basket*
5536 çal (2), *basket*
5552 çalçillâh (1), *twig*
2894 kŏphinŏs (6), *small
basket*
4711 spuris (4), *hamper
or lunch-receptacle*

BASMATH
1315 Bosmath (1),
fragrance

BASON
3713 k°phôwr (2), *bowl;
white frost*
5592 çaph (2), *dish*
3537 niptēr (1), *basin for
washing*

BASONS
101 'aggân (1), *bowl*
3713 k°phôwr (3), *bowl;
white frost*
4219 mîzrâq (11), *bowl
for sprinkling*
5592 çaph (2), *dish*

BASTARD
4464 mamzêr (2),
mongrel

BASTARDS
3541 nŏthŏs (1), *spurious
or illegitimate son*

BAT
5847 'ăţallêph (2),
mammal, bat

BATH
1324 bath (6), *liquid
measure*

BATH-RABBIM
1337 Bath Rabbîym (1),
city of Rabbah

BATH-SHEBA
1339 Bath-Sheba' (11),
daughter of an oath

BATH-SHUA
1340 Bath-Shûwa' (1),
daughter of wealth

BATHE
7364 râchats (18), to
lave, bathe

BATHED
7301 râvâh (1), to *slake
thirst or appetites*

BATHS
1324 bath (8), *liquid
measure*
1325 bath (Ch.) (1), *liquid
measure*

BATS
5847 'ăţallêph (1), *bat*

BATTERED
7843 shâchath (1), to
decay; to ruin

BATTLE
3593 kîydôwr (1), (poss.)
tumult, battle
4221 môach (1), *bone
marrow*
4264 machăneh (1),
encampment
4421 milchâmâh (143),
battle; war; fighting
4661 mappêts (1),
war-club
5402 nesheq (1), *military
arms, arsenal*
5430 ç°'ôwn (1), *military
boot*
6635 tsâbâ' (5), *army,
military host*
6635+4421 tsâbâ' (1),
army, military host
7128 q°râb (5), *hostile
encounter*
4171 pŏlĕmŏs (5),
warfare; battle; fight

BATTLEMENT
4624 ma'ăqeh (1),
parapet

BATTLEMENTS
5189 n°ţîyshâh (1),
tendril plant shoot

BATTLES
4421 milchâmâh (6),
battle; war; fighting

BAVAI
942 Bavvay (1), *Bavvai*

BAY
249 'ezrâch (1), *native
born*
554 'âmôts (2), *red*
3956 lâshôwn (3),
tongue; tongue-shaped

BAZLITH
1213 Batslûwth (1),
peeling

BAZLUTH
1213 Batslûwth (1),
peeling

BDELLIUM
916 b°dôlach (2),
bdellium, amber; pearl

BEACON
8650 tôren (1), *mast
pole; flag-staff pole*

BEALIAH
1183 B°'alyâh (1),
Jehovah (is) master

BEALOTH
1175 B°'âlôwth (1),
mistresses

BEAM
708 'ereg (1), *weaving;
braid; also shuttle*

3714 kâphîyç (1), *girder,
beam*
4500 mânôwr (4), *frame
of a loom*
5646 'âb (1), *architrave*
6982 qôwrâh (2), *rafter;
roof*
1385 dŏkŏs (6), *stick or
plank*

BEAMS
1356 gêb (1), *well, cistern*
3773 kârûthâh (3), *hewn
timber beams*
6763 tsêlâ' (1), *side of a
person or thing*
6982 qôwrâh (2), *rafter;
roof*
7136 qârâh (4), to *bring
about; to impose*

BEANS
6321 pôwl (2), *beans*

BEAR
1319 bâsar (4), to
announce (good news)
1677 dôb (10), *bear*
1678 dôb (Ch.) (1), *bear*
2398 châţâ' (2), to *sin*
3205 yâlad (16), to *bear
young; to father a child*
3212 yâlak (1), to *walk;
to live; to carry*
3318 yâtsâ' (1), to *go,
bring out*
3557 kûwl (1), to *keep in;
to measure*
4910 mâshal (1), to *rule*
5187 n°ţîyl (1), *laden*
5201 nâţar (1), to *guard;
to cherish anger*
5375 nâsâ' (100), to *lift up*
5445 çâbal (3), to *carry*
5749 'ûwd (1), to *protest,
testify; to encompass*
6030 'ânâh (2), to
respond, answer
6213 'âsâh (4), to *do*
7287 râdâh (1), to
subjugate; to crumble
7981 sh°lêţ (Ch.) (1), to
dominate, i.e. govern
8323 sârar (1), to *have,
exercise, get dominion*
8382 tâ'am (1), to *be
twinned, i.e. duplicate*
8505 tâkan (1), to
balance, i.e. measure
142 airō (4), to *lift, to
take up*
399 anaphérō (1), to *take
up; to lead up*
430 anĕchŏmai (4), *put
up with, endure*
503 antŏphthalmĕō (1),
to face into the wind
715 arktŏs (1), *bear*
(animal)
941 bastazō (11), to *lift,
bear*
1080 gĕnnaō (1), to
procreate, regenerate
3114 makrŏthumĕō (1),
to be forbearing, patient
3140 marturĕō (21), to
testify; to commend
4160 pŏiĕō (2), to *do*
5041 tĕknŏgŏnĕō (1), to
be a child bearer

5297 hupŏphérō (1), to
bear from underneath
5342 phérō (4), to *bear*
5409 phŏrĕō (1), to *wear*
5576 psĕudŏmarturĕō
(4), to offer *falsehood in
evidence*

BEARD
2206 zâqân (14), *beard*
8222 sâphâm (1), *beard*

BEARDS
2206 zâqân (4), *beard*

BEARERS
5449 çabbâl (3), *porter,
carrier*

BEAREST
3205 yâlad (1), to *bear
young; to father a child*
941 bastazō (1), to *lift,
bear*
3140 marturĕō (1), to
testify; to commend
5088 tiktō (1), to *produce
from seed*

BEARETH
3205 yâlad (2), to *bear
young; to father a child*
4910 mâshal (1), to *rule*
5375 nâsâ' (7), to *lift up*
6030 'ânâh (2), to
respond, answer
6509 pârâh (1), to *bear
fruit*
6779 tsâmach (1), to
sprout
8382 tâ'am (1), to *be
twinned, i.e. duplicate*
1627 ĕkphérō (1), to *bear
out; to produce*
2592 karpŏphŏrĕō (1), to
be fertile
3140 marturĕō (3), to
testify; to commend
4722 stĕgō (1), to *endure
patiently*
4828 summarturĕō (1), to
testify jointly
5342 phérō (1), to *bear or
carry*
5409 phŏrĕō (1), to *wear*

BEARING
2232 zâra' (1), to *sow
seed; to disseminate*
3205 yâlad (3), to *bear
young; to father a child*
5375 nâsâ' (10), to *lift up*
941 bastazō (3), to *lift,
bear*
4064 pĕriphĕrō (1), to
transport
4828 summarturĕō (2), to
testify jointly
4901 sunĕpimarturĕō (1),
to testify further jointly
5342 phérō (1), to *bear or
carry*

BEARS
1677 dôb (2), *bear*

BEAST
929 b°hêmâh (83),
animal, beast
1165 b°'îyr (1), *cattle,
livestock*
2123 zîyz (1), *moving
creature*

English

2416 chay (34), *alive; raw; fresh; life*
2423 chêyvâ' (Ch.) (6), wild *animal; monster*
5038 nᵉbêlâh (1), *carcase* or *carrion*
5315 nephesh (1), *life; breath; soul; wind*
5315+929 nephesh (1), *life; breath; soul; wind*
7409 rekesh (1), *relay* of animals
2226 zôôn (7), *living animal*
2342 thêriŏn (40), *dangerous animal*
2934 ktēnŏs (1), *domestic animal*

BEAST'S
2423 chêyvâ' (Ch.) (1), wild *animal; monster*

BEASTS
338 'îy (3), solitary wild creature that *howls*
929 bᵉhêmâh (51), *animal, beast*
1165 bᵉ'îyr (3), *cattle, livestock*
2123 zîyz (1), *moving creature*
2416 chay (42), *alive; raw; fresh; life*
2423 chêyvâ' (Ch.) (13), wild *animal; monster*
2874 ṭebach (1), *butchery*
2966 ṭᵉrêphâh (5), *torn prey*
3753 karkârâh (1), *cow-camel*
4806 mᵉrîy' (2), *stall-fed* animal
6728 tsîyîy (3), wild *beast*
2226 zôôn (16), *living animal*
2341 thêriŏmachĕō (1), to *be a beast fighter*
2342 thêriŏn (6), *dangerous animal*
2934 ktēnŏs (3), *domestic animal*
4968 sphagiŏn (1), *offering for slaughter*
5074 tĕtrapŏus (2), *quadruped* animal

BEAT
1743 dûwk (1), to *pulverize in a mortar*
1792 dâkâ' (1), to *pulverize; be contrite*
1849 dâphaq (1), to *knock; to press* severely
1854 dâqaq (2), to *crush*
2040 hâraç (1), to *pull down; break, destroy*
2251 châbaṭ (2), to *knock out or off, thresh* a tree
3807 kâthath (4), to *bruise or strike, beat*
5221 nâkâh (4), to *strike, kill*
5422 nâthats (3), to *tear down*
7554 râqa' (1), to *pound*
7833 shâchaq (3), to *grind or wear away*
1194 dĕrō (5), to *flay,* i.e. to *scourge or thrash*

1911 ĕpiballō (1), to *throw upon*
4350 prŏskŏptō (1), to *trip up;* to *strike*
4363 prŏspiptō (1), to *beat or strike*
4366 prŏsrēgnumi (2), to *burst upon*
4463 rhabdizō (1), to *strike with a stick*
5180 tuptō (2), to *strike, beat, wound*

BEATEN
1643 geres (2), *grain*
1851 daq (1), *crushed; small or thin*
1986 hâlam (1), to *strike, beat, stamp, conquer*
2251 châbaṭ (1), to *knock out or off, thresh* a tree
2865 châthath (1), to *break down*
3795 kâthîyth (4), *pure oil from beaten olives*
3807 kâthath (3), to *bruise or strike, beat*
4347 makkâh (1), *blow; wound; pestilence*
4749 miqshâh (8), work molded by *hammering*
5060 nâga' (1), to *strike*
5062 nâgaph (1), to *strike*
5221 nâkâh (4), to *strike, kill*
5310 nâphats (1), to *dash to pieces;* to *scatter*
7820 shâchaṭ (5), to *hammer* out
1194 dĕrō (5), to *flay,* i.e. to *scourge or thrash*
4463 rhabdizō (1), to *strike with a stick*

BEATEST
2251 châbaṭ (1), to *knock out or off, thresh* a tree
5221 nâkâh (1), to *strike, kill*

BEATETH
1194 dĕrō (1), to *flay,* i.e. to *scourge or thrash*

BEATING
1986 hâlam (1), to *strike, beat, stamp, conquer*
1194 dĕrō (1), to *flay,* i.e. to *scourge or thrash*
5180 tuptō (1), to *strike, beat, wound*

BEAUTIES
1926 hâdâr (1), *magnificence*

BEAUTIFUL
2896 ṭôwb (1), *good; well*
2896+4758 ṭôwb (1), *good; well*
3303 yâpheh (7), *beautiful; handsome*
3303+8389 yâpheh (2), *beautiful; handsome*
4998 nâ'âh (1), to be *pleasant,* i.e. *beautiful*
6643 tsᵉbîy (1), *conspicuous splendor*
8597 tiph'ârâh (6), *ornament*
5611 hŏraiŏs (4), *flourishing, beauteous*

BEAUTIFY
6286 pâ'ar (3), to *shake a* tree

BEAUTY
1926 hâdâr (3), *magnificence*
1927 hădârâh (4), *decoration, ornament*
1935 hôwd (1), *grandeur, majesty*
2530 châmad (1), to *delight* in; *lust for*
3308 yŏphîy (20), *beauty*
4758 mar'eh (1), *appearance; vision*
5276 nâ'êm (1), to be *agreeable*
5278 no'am (4), *delight, suitableness*
6287 pᵉ'êr (1), *fancy head-dress*
6643 tsᵉbîy (2), *conspicuous splendor*
6736 tsîyr (1), *carved idolatrous image*
8597 tiph'ârâh (10), *ornament*

BEBAI
893 Bêbay (6), *Bebai*

BECAUSE
413 'êl (3), *to, toward*
834 'ăsher (42), *because, in order that*
1115 biltîy (3), *except, without, unless, besides*
1558 gâlâl (2), *on account of, because of*
1697 dâbâr (1), *word; matter; thing*
1768 dîy (Ch.) (2), *that; of*
1870 derek (1), *road; course* of life
3027 yâd (2), *hand; power*
3282 ya'an (59), *because, for this reason*
3588 kîy (455), *for, that because*
3605 kôl (1), *all, any*
4480 min (2), *from, out of*
4481 min (Ch.) (1), *from or out of*
4616 ma'an (11), *on account of*
5668 'âbûwr (7), *on account of*
5921 'al (45), *above, over, upon,* or *against*
6118 'êqeb (1), *unto the end; for ever*
6119 'âqêb (1), *track, footprint*
6440 pânîym (67), *face; front*
6448 pâçag (1), to *contemplate*
8478 tachath (1), *bottom; underneath; in lieu of*
575 apô (1), *from, away*
1063 gar (5), *for, indeed, but, because*
1223 dia (54), *through, by means of; because of*
1360 diŏti (13), *on the very account that*
1537 ĕk (2), *out, out of*
1722 ĕn (3), *in; during; because of*
1893 ĕpĕi (7), *since*

1894 ĕpĕidē (2), *when, whereas*
1909 ĕpi (1), *on, upon*
2443 hina (1), *in order that*
2530 kathŏti (2), *as far or inasmuch as*
3704 hŏpōs (1), *in the manner that*
3754 hŏti (184), *that; because; since*
4314 prŏs (2), *for; on, at; to, toward; against*
5484 charin (2), *on account of, because of*

BECHER
1071 Beker (5), *young bull camel*

BECHORATH
1064 Bᵉkôwrath (1), *primogeniture*

BECKONED
1269 dianĕuō (1), to *nod or express by signs*
2656 katanĕuō (1), to *make a sign or signal*
2678 katasĕiō (2), to *motion a signal or sign*
3506 nĕuō (2), *nod,* i.e. *signal*

BECKONING
2678 katasĕiō (2), to *motion a signal or sign*

BED
3326 yâtsûwa' (3), *bed; wing or lean-to*
3331 yâtsa' (1), to *strew*
4296 miṭṭâh (23), *bed; sofa, litter or bier*
4702 matstsâ' (1), *couch*
4903 mishkab (Ch.) (6), *bed*
4904 mishkâb (29), *bed; sleep; intercourse*
6170 'ărûwgâh (1), *parterre, kind of garden*
6210 'eres (4), *canopy couch*
6210+3326 'eres (1), *canopy couch*
2825 klinē (8), *couch*
2845 kŏitē (2), *couch; conception*
2895 krabbatŏs (10), *sleeping mat*
4766 strōnnumi (1), to *spread a couch*

BED'S
4296 miṭṭâh (1), *bed; sofa, litter or bier*

BEDAD
911 Bᵉdad (2), *separation*

BEDAN
917 Bᵉdân (2), *servile*

BEDCHAMBER
2315+4296 cheder (3), *apartment, chamber*
2315+4904 cheder (3), *apartment, chamber*

BEDEIAH
912 Bêdᵉyâh (1), *servant of Jehovah*

BEDS
4296 miṭṭâh (2), *bed; sofa, litter or bier*

4904 mishkâb (5), *bed; sleep; intercourse*
6170 'ărûwgâh (1), *parterre, kind of garden*
2825 klínē (1), *couch*
2895 krabbatŏs (1), *sleeping mat*

BEDSTEAD
6210 'eres (1), *canopy couch*

BEE
1682 dᵉbôwrâh (1), *bee*

BEELIADA
1182 Bᵉ'elyâdâ' (1), *Baal has known*

BEELZEBUB
954 Bĕĕlzĕbŏul (7), *dung-god*

BEER
876 Bᵉ'êr (2), *well, cistern*

BEER-ELIM
879 Bᵉ'êr 'Êlîym (1), *well of heroes*

BEER-LAHAI-ROI
883 Bᵉ'êr la-Chay Rô'îy (1), *well of a living (One) my seer*

BEER-SHEBA
884 Bᵉ'êr Sheba' (34), *well of an oath*

BEERA
878 Bᵉ'êrâ' (1), *well*

BEERAH
880 Bᵉ'êrâh (1), *well*

BEERI
882 Bᵉ'êrîy (2), *fountain*

BEEROTH
881 Bᵉ'êrôwth (6), *wells*

BEEROTHITE
886 Bᵉ'êrôthîy (4), *Beërothite*

BEEROTHITES
886 Bᵉ'êrôthîy (1), *Beërothite*

BEES
1682 dᵉbôwrâh (3), *bee*

BEESH-TERAH
1203 Bᵉ'eshtᵉrâh (1), *with Ashtoreth*

BEETLE
2728 chargôl (1), *leaping insect*

BEEVES
1241 bâqâr (7), *plowing ox; herd*

BEFALL
579 'ânâh (1), *to meet, to happen*
4672 mâtsâ' (1), *to find or acquire; to occur, meet or be present*
7122 qârâ' (4), *to encounter, to happen*
7136 qârâh (2), *to bring about; to impose*
4876 sunantaō (1), *to meet with; to occur*

BEFALLEN
4672 mâtsâ' (3), *to find or acquire; to occur*
4745 miqreh (1), *accident or fortune*

BEFALL
7122 qârâ' (1), *to encounter, to happen*
7136 qârâh (1), *to bring about; to impose*
4876 sunantaō (1), *to meet with; to occur*

BEFALLETH
4745 miqreh (2), *accident or fortune*

BEFELL
935 bôw' (1), *to go, come*
4672 mâtsâ' (1), *to find or acquire; to occur*
7136 qârâh (1), *to bring about; to impose*
1096 ginŏmai (1), *to be, become*
4819 sumbainō (1), *to concur, happen*

BEFORE
413 'êl (8), *to, toward*
639 'aph (2), *nose or nostril; face; person*
854 'êth (4), *with; by; at*
865 'ethmôwl (1), *heretofore, formerly*
2958 tᵉrôwm (1), *not yet, before*
2962 terem (41), *not yet or before*
3808 lô' (2), *no, not*
3942 liphnay (1), *anterior, in front of*
4136 mûwl (1), *in front of, opposite*
4551 maççâ' (1), *stone quarry; projectile*
4608 ma'ăleh (1), *elevation; platform*
5048 neged (70), *over against or before*
5084 nâdân (1), *sheath*
5226 nêkach (1), *opposite*
5227 nôkach (ɔ), *opposite, in front of*
5703 'ad (1), *perpetuity; ancient*
5704 'ad (1), *as far (long) as; during; while; until*
5869 'ayin (8), *eye; sight; fountain*
5921 'al (12), *above, over, upon, or against*
5973 'îm (5), *with*
6440 pânîym (1110), *face; front*
6471 pa'am (1), *time; step; occurence*
6903 qᵉbêl (Ch.) (3), *in front of, before*
6905 qâbâl (1), *in front of*
6924 qedem (10), *before, anciently*
6925 qŏdâm (Ch.) (29), *before*
6931 qadmôwnîy (1), *anterior time*
7130 qereb (1), *nearest part, i.e. the center*
7223 rî'shôwn (3), *first, in place, time or rank*
561 apĕnanti (2), *opposite, before*
575 apŏ (2), *from, away*
1519 ĕis (2), *to or into*
1715 ĕmprŏsthĕn (41), *in front of*

1722 ĕn (1), *in; during; because of*
1725 ĕnanti (1), *before, in presence of*
1726 ĕnantiŏn (4), *in the presence of*
1773 ĕnnuchŏn (1), *by night*
1799 ĕnōpiŏn (63), *in the face of, before*
1909 ĕpi (17), *on, upon*
2596 kata (2), *down; according to*
2713 katĕnanti (1), *directly opposite*
2714 katĕnōpiŏn (3), *directly in front of*
3319 mĕsŏs (1), *middle*
3764 ŏudĕpō (1), *not even yet*
3844 para (3), *from; with; besides; on account of*
3908 paratithēmi (9), *to present something*
3936 paristēmi (2), *to stand beside, present*
4250 prin (7), *prior, sooner, before*
4253 prŏ (43), *before in time or space*
4254 prŏagō (15), *to lead forward; to precede*
4256 prŏaitiaŏmai (1), *to previously charge*
4257 prŏakŏuō (1), *to hear beforehand*
4264 prŏbibazō (1), *to bring to the front*
4267 prŏginōskō (1), *know beforehand*
4270 prŏgraphō (1), *to write previously*
4275 prŏĕidō (1), *to foresee*
4277 prŏĕpō (1), *to say already, to predict*
4278 prŏĕnarchŏmai (1), *to commence already*
4280 prŏĕrĕō (8), *to say already, predict*
4281 prŏĕrchŏmai (4), *to go onward, precede*
4282 prŏĕtŏimazō (1), *to fit up in advance*
4283 prŏĕuaggĕlizŏmai (1), *to announce in advance*
4293 prŏkataggĕllō (3), *to predict, promise, foretell*
4295 prŏkĕimai (3), *to be present to the mind*
4296 prŏkĕrussō (1), *to proclaim in advance*
4299 prŏkrima (1), *prejudgment*
4300 prŏkurŏō (1), *to ratify previously*
4301 prŏlambanō (1), *to take before*
4302 prŏlĕgō (2), *to predict, forewarn*
4304 prŏmĕlĕtaō (1), *to premeditate*
4308 prŏŏraō (1), *to notice previously*
4309 prŏŏrizō (1), *to predetermine*

4310 prŏpaschō (1), *to undergo previously*
4313 prŏpŏrĕuŏmai (1), *to precede as guide*
4314 prŏs (2), *for; on, at; to, toward; against*
4315 prŏsabbatŏn (1), *Sabbath-eve*
4363 prŏspiptō (5), *to prostrate oneself*
4384 prŏtassō (1), *to prescribe beforehand*
4386 prŏtĕrŏn (4), *previously*
4391 prŏüparchō (1), *to be or do previously*
4401 prŏchĕirŏtŏnĕō (1), *to elect in advance*
4412 prōtŏn (1), *firstly*
4413 prōtŏs (2), *foremost*

BEFOREHAND
4271 prŏdēlŏs (2), *obvious, evident*
4294 prŏkatartizō (1), *to prepare in advance*
4303 prŏmarturŏmai (1), *to witness beforehand*
4305 prŏmĕrimnaō (1), *to care in advance*

BEFORETIME
865+832 'ethmôwl (1), *heretofore, formerly*
6440 pânîym (5), *face; front*
7223 rî'shôwn (1), *first, in place, time or rank*
8543+8032 tᵉmôwl (2), *yesterday*
4391 prŏüparchō (1), *to be or do previously*

BEG
7592 shâ'al (2), *to ask*
1871 ĕpaitĕō (1), *to ask for, beg*

BEGAN
2490 châlal (34), *to profane, defile*
2974 yâ'al (1), *to assent; to undertake, begin*
3246 yᵉˢûd (1), *foundation; beginning)*
5927 'âlâh (1), *to ascend, be high, mount*
6751 tsâlal (1), *to shade; to grow dark*
8271 shᵉrê' (Ch.) (1), *to unravel, commence*
756 archŏmai (64), *to begin*
2020 ĕpiphōskō (1), *grow light*
2192 ĕchō (1), *to have; hold; keep*

BEGAT
3205 yâlad (176), *to bear young; to father a child*
616 apŏkuĕō (1), *to generate, bring to being*
1080 gĕnnaō (43), *to procreate, regenerate*

BEGET
3205 yâlad (10), *to bear young; to father a child*

BEGETTEST
3205 yâlad (2), *to bear young; to father a child*

BEGETTETH
3205 yâlad (3), to *bear young*; to *father a child*

BEGGAR
34 'ebyôwn (1), *destitute; poor*
4434 ptōchŏs (2), *pauper, beggar*

BEGGARLY
4434 ptōchŏs (1), *pauper, beggar*

BEGGED
154 aitĕō (2), to *ask for*
4319 prŏsaitĕō (1), to *solicit, beg*

BEGGING
1245 bâqash (1), to *search*; to *strive after*
4319 prŏsaitĕō (2), to *solicit, beg*

BEGIN
2490 châlal (12), to *profane, defile*
8462 tᵉchillâh (1), *original; originally*
756 archŏmai (11), to *begin*
3195 mĕllō (1), to *intend*, i.e. *be about* to be

BEGINNEST
2490 châlal (1), to *profane, defile*

BEGINNING
227 'âz (3), *at that time* or *place; therefore*
1931 hûw' (2), *he, she, it; this* or *that*
5769 'ôwlâm (1), *eternity; ancient; always*
7218 rô'sh (12), *head*
7223 rî'shôwn (4), *first*
7225 rê'shîyth (18), *first*
8462 tᵉchillâh (14), *original; originally*
509 anōthĕn (1), *from above; from the first*
746 archē (39), *first in rank; first in time*
756 archŏmai (8), to *begin*
4412 prōtŏn (1), *firstly*
4413 prōtŏs (1), *foremost*

BEGINNINGS
7218 rô'sh (2), *head*
7221 rî'shâh (1), *beginning*
746 archē (1), *first*

BEGOTTEN
3205 yâlad (7), to *bear young*; to *father a child*
3318 yâtsâ' (1), to *go, bring out*
4138 môwledeth (1), *lineage, offspring*
313 anagĕnnaō (2), to *beget* or *bear again*
1080 gĕnnaō (7), to *procreate, regenerate*
3439 mŏnŏgĕnēs (6), *sole, one and only*
4416 prōtŏtŏkŏs (1), *first-born*

BEGUILE
2603 katabrabĕuō (1), to *award a price against*

BEGUILE (cont.)
3884 paralŏgizŏmai (1), to *delude, deceive*

BEGUILED
5230 nâkal (1), to *act treacherously*
5377 nâshâ' (1), to *lead astray, to delude*
7411 râmâh (2), to *hurl; to shoot; to delude*
1818 ĕxapataō (1), to *seduce wholly, deceive*

BEGUILING
1185 dĕlĕazō (1), to *delude, seduce*

BEGUN
2490 châlal (6), to *profane, defile*
756 archŏmai (1), to *begin*
1728 ĕnarchŏmai (2), to *commence on, begin*
2691 katastrēniaō (1), to *be voluptuous against*
4278 prŏĕnarchŏmai (2), to *commence already*

BEHALF
854 'êth (1), *with; by; at*
5973 'îm (1), *with*
8478 tachath (1), *bottom; underneath; in lieu of*
1909 ĕpi (1), *on, upon*
3313 mĕrŏs (2), *division or share*
4012 pĕri (1), *about; around*
5228 hupĕr (4), *over; in behalf of*

BEHAVE
2388 châzaq (1), to *fasten upon; to seize*
5234 nâkar (1), to *care for, respect, revere*
7292 râhab (1), to *urge severely*
7919 sâkal (1), to *be circumspect*
390 anastrĕphō (1), to *remain, to live*
807 aschēmŏnĕō (1), to *be, act unbecoming*

BEHAVED
1980 hâlak (1), to *walk; live a certain way*
7489 râ'a' (1), to *be good for nothing*
7737 shâvâh (1), to *level*, i.e. *equalize*
7919 sâkal (4), to *be circumspect*
812 ataktĕō (1), to *be, act irregular*
1096 ginŏmai (1), to *be, become*

BEHAVETH
807 aschēmŏnĕō (1), to *be, act unbecoming*

BEHAVIOUR
2940 ta'am (2), *taste; perception*
2688 katastēma (1), *demeanor*
2887 kŏsmiŏs (1), *orderly*

BEHEADED
5493+7218 çûwr (1), to *turn off*

BEHEADED (cont.)
6202 'âraph (1), to *break the neck, to destroy*
607 apŏkĕphalizō (4), to *decapitate*
3990 pĕlĕkizō (1), to *remove the head*

BEHELD
2370+934 chăzâ' (Ch.) (6), to *gaze* upon
5027 nâbat (2), to *scan; to regard* with favor
7200 râ'âh (23), to *see*
333 anathĕōrĕō (1), to *look again*
991 blĕpō (2), to *look at*
1492 ĕidō (10), to *know*
1689 ĕmblĕpō (3), to *observe; to discern*
2300 thĕaŏmai (2), to *look closely at*
2334 thĕōrĕō (4), to *see; to discern*

BEHEMOTH
930 bᵉhêmôwth (1), *hippopotamus*

BEHIND
268 'âchôwr (5), *behind, backward; west*
310 'achar (49), *after*
3498 yâthar (1), to *remain or be left*
5975 'âmad (1), to *stand*
2641 katalĕipō (1), to *abandon*
3693 ŏpisthĕn (4), *at the back; after*
3694 ŏpisō (6), *behind, after, following*
5278 hupŏmĕnō (1), to *undergo (trials)*
5302 hustĕrĕō (4), to *be inferior; to fall short*

BEHOLD
431 'ălûw (Ch.) (5), *lo!*
718 'ărûw (Ch.) (4), *lo!, behold!*
1887 hê' (1), *Lo!, Look!*
2005 hên (237), *lo!; if!*
2009 hinnêh (770), *lo!; Look!*
2205 zâqên (2), *old, venerated*
2209 ziqnâh (1), *old age*
2372 châzâh (7), to *gaze at; to perceive*
5027 nâbat (9), to *scan; to regard* with favor
6822 tsâphâh (1), to *peer into the distance*
7200 râ'âh (58), to *see*
7789 shûwr (5), to *spy out, survey*
7891 shîyr (1), to *sing*
816 atĕnizō (1), to *gaze intently*
991 blĕpō (3), to *look at*
1492 ĕidō (5), to *know*
1689 ĕmblĕpō (3), to *observe; to discern*
1896 ĕpĕidŏn (1), to *regard*
2029 ĕpŏptĕuō (2), to *watch, observe*
2334 thĕōrĕō (3), to *see; to discern*
2396 idĕ (24), *surprise!, lo!, look!*

BEHOLD (cont.)
2400 idŏu (180), *lo!, note!, see!*
2657 katanŏĕō (2), to *observe fully*

BEHOLDEST
5027 nâbat (1), to *scan; to regard* with favor
991 blĕpō (3), to *look at*

BEHOLDETH
6437 pânâh (1), to *turn, to face*
7200 râ'âh (2), to *see*
2657 katanŏĕō (1), to *observe fully*

BEHOLDING
6822 tsâphâh (1), to *peer; to observe, await*
7200 râ'âh (2), to *see*
816 atĕnizō (2), to *gaze intently*
991 blĕpō (2), to *look at*
1689 ĕmblĕpō (1), to *observe; to discern*
2334 thĕōrĕō (4), to *see; to discern*
2657 katanŏĕō (1), to *observe fully*
2734 katŏptrizŏmai (1), to *see reflected*
3708 hŏraō (1), to *stare, see clearly*

BEHOVED
1163 dĕi (1), *it is (was) necessary*
3784 ŏphĕilō (1), to *owe; to be under obligation*

BEING
1961 hâyâh (4), to *exist*, i.e. *be or become*
5750 'ôwd (2), *again; repeatedly; still; more*
1096 ginŏmai (5), to *be, become*
1909 ĕpi (1), *on, upon*
2070 ĕsmĕn (1), *we are*
2192 ĕchō (1), to *have; hold; keep*
5225 huparchō (13), to *come into existence*
5605 ōdinō (1), to *experience labor pains*
5607 ōn (35), *being, existence*

BEKAH
1235 beqa' (1), *half shekel*

BEL
1078 Bêl (3), *Bel (Baal)*

BELA
1106 Bela' (13), *gulp; destruction*

BELAH
1106 Bela' (1), *gulp; destruction*

BELAITES
1108 Bal'îy (1), *Belaite*

BELCH
5042 nâba' (1), to *gush forth; emit* a foul odor

BELIAL
1100 bᵉlîya'al (16), *wickedness, trouble*
955 Bĕlial (1), *worthlessness*

BELIED
3584 kâchash (1), to *lie,
disown;* to *disappoint*

BELIEF
4102 pistis (1), *faith,
belief; conviction*

BELIEVE
539 'âman (19), to *be
firm, faithful, true*
544 apĕithĕō (1), to
disbelieve
569 apistĕō (2), to
disbelieve, disobey
571 apistŏs (4), *without
faith; untrustworthy*
4100 pistĕuō (109), to
have faith, i.e. credit; to
entrust
4100+1722 pistĕuō (1), to
have faith, i.e. credit
4100+1909 pistĕuō (1), to
have faith, i.e. credit
4102 pistis (1), *faith,
belief; conviction*
4103 pistŏs (2), *trustful;
reliable*

BELIEVED
539 'âman (21), to *be
firm, faithful, true*
540 'âman (Ch.) (1), to *be
firm, faithful, true*
544 apĕithĕō (6), to
disbelieve
569 apistĕō (3), to
disbelieve, disobey
569+4100 apistĕō (1), to
disbelieve, disobey
3982 pĕithō (3), to *rely* by
inward certainty
4100 pistĕuō (76), to *have
faith, i.e. credit*
4103 pistŏs (2),
trustworthy; reliable
4135 plĕrŏphŏrĕō (1), to
assure or *convince*

BELIEVERS
4100 pistĕuō (1), to *have
faith, i.e. credit*
4103 pistŏs (1),
trustworthy; reliable

BELIEVEST
4100 pistĕuō (8), to *have
faith, i.e. credit*

BELIEVETH
539 'âman (4), to *be firm,
faithful, true;* to *trust*
544 apĕithĕō (1), to
disbelieve
569 apistĕō (1), to
disbelieve, disobey
571 apistŏs (3), *without
faith; untrustworthy*
1537+4102 ĕk (1), *out of*
4100 pistĕuō (33), to *have
faith, i.e. credit*
4103 pistŏs (2),
trustworthy; reliable

BELIEVING
4100 pistĕuō (6), to *have
faith, i.e. credit*
4103 pistŏs (2),
trustworthy; reliable

BELL
6472 pa'ămôn (3), *bell*

BELLIES
1064 gastēr (1), *stomach;
womb; gourmand*

BELLOW
6670 tsâhal (1), to *be
cheerful;* to *sound*

BELLOWS
4647 mappûach (1),
bellows

BELLS
4698 mᵉtsillâh (1), *small
bell*
6472 pa'ămôn (3), *bell*

BELLY
990 beţen (30), *belly;
womb; body*
1512 gâchôwn (2), *belly*
3770 kᵉrês (1), *paunch*
4577 mᵉ'âh (Ch.) (1),
bowels, belly
4578 mê'âh (3), *viscera;
anguish, tenderness*
6897 qôbâh (1), *abdomen*
2836 kŏilia (10),
abdomen, womb, heart

BELONG
1510 ĕimi (1), I *exist,* I *am*

BELONGED
4490 mânâh (1), *ration;
lot* or *portion*
1510 ĕimi (1), I *exist,* I *am*

BELONGETH
1510 ĕimi (1), I *exist,* I *am*

BELOVED
157 'âhab (6), to *have
affection, love*
1730 dôwd (29), *beloved,
friend; relative*
2530 châmad (3), to
delight in; *lust for*
3033 yᵉdîdûwth (1),
darling object
3039 yᵉdîyd (5), *loved*
4261 machmâd (1),
object of *affection* or
desire
25 agapaō (5), to *love*
27 agapētŏs (57), *beloved*

BELOVED'S
1730 dôwd (2), *beloved,
friend; relative*

BELSHAZZAR
1113 Bêlsha'tstsar (Ch.)
(8), *Belshatstsar*

BELTESHAZZAR
1095 Bêlţᵉsha'tstsar (2),
Belteshatstsar
1096 Bêlţᵉsha'tstsar
(Ch.) (8), *Belteshatstsar*

BEMOAN
5110 nûwd (5), to
deplore; to *taunt*

BEMOANED
5110 nûwd (1), to
deplore; to *taunt*

BEMOANING
5110 nûwd (1), to
deplore; to *taunt*

BEN
1122 Bên (1), *son*

BEN-AMMI
1151 Ben-'Ammîy (1),
son of my people

BEN-HADAD
1130 Ben-Hădad (18),
son of Hadad
1131 Binnûwy (7), *built*

BEN-HAIL
1134 Ben-Chayil (1), *son
of might*

BEN-HANAN
1135 Ben-Chânân (1),
son of Chanan

BEN-ONI
1126 Ben-'Ôwnîy (1), *son
of my sorrow*

BEN-ZOHETH
1132 Ben-Zôwchêth (1),
son of Zocheth

BENAIAH
1141 Bᵉnâyâh (42),
Jehovah has built

BENCHES
7175 qeresh (1), *slab* or
plank; deck of a ship

BEND
1869 dârak (7), to *tread,
trample;* to *string* a bow
3719 kâphan (1), to *bend*

BENDETH
1869 dârak (2), to *walk,
lead;* to *string* a bow

BENDING
7817 shâchach (1), to
sink or *depress*

BENE-BERAK
1138 Bunnîy (1), *built*

BENE-JAAKAN
1142 Bᵉnêy Ya'ăqân (2),
sons of Yaakan

BENEATH
4295 maţţâh (7), *below*
or *beneath*
8478 tachath (17),
bottom; underneath
2736 katō (3), *downwards*

BENEFACTORS
2110 ĕuĕrgĕtēs (1),
philanthropist

BENEFIT
1576 gᵉmûwl (1), *act;
service; reward*
3190 yâţab (1), to *be,
make well*
18 agathŏs (1), *good*
2108 ĕuĕrgĕsia (1),
beneficence
5485 charis (1),
gratitude; benefit given

BENEFITS
1576 gᵉmûwl (1), *act;
service; reward*
8408 tagmûwl (1),
bestowment

BENEVOLENCE
2133 ĕunŏia (1), *eagerly,
with a whole heart*

BENINU
1148 Bᵉnîynûw (1), *our
son*

BENJAMIN
1144 Binyâmîyn (158),
son of (the) *right hand*
953 bĕbēlŏō (4), to
desecrate, profane

BENJAMIN'S
1144 Binyâmîyn (4), *son
of* (the) *right hand*

BENJAMITE
1145 Ben-yᵉmîynîy (9),
son of (the) *right hand*

BENJAMITES
1145 Ben-yᵉmîynîy (8),
son of (the) *right hand*

BENO
1121 bên (2), *son,
descendant; people*

BENT
1869 dârak (7), to *walk,
lead;* to *string* a bow
8511 tâlâ' (1), to *suspend;*
to *be uncertain*

BEON
1194 Bᵉ'ôn (1), *Beon*

BEOR
1160 Bᵉ'ôwr (10), *lamp*

BERA
1298 Bera' (1), *Bera*

BERACHAH
1294 Bᵉrâkâh (3),
benediction, blessing

BERACHIAH
1296 Berekyâh (1),
blessing of Jehovah

BERAIAH
1256 Bᵉrâ'yâh (1),
Jehovah has created

BEREA
960 Bĕrŏia (3), region
beyond the coast-line

BEREAVE
2637 châçêr (1), to *lack;*
to *fail, want, make less*
3782+(7921) kâshal (1), to
totter, waver; to *falter*
7921 shâkôl (4), to
miscarry

BEREAVED
7909 shakkuwl (2),
bereaved
7921 shâkôl (3), to
miscarry

BEREAVETH
7921 shâkôl (1), to
miscarry

BERECHIAH
1296 Berekyâh (10),
blessing of Jehovah

BERED
1260 Bered (2), *hail*

BERI
1275 Bêrîy (1), *Beri*

BERIAH
1283 Bᵉrîy'âh (11), *in
trouble*

BERIITES
1284 Bᵉrîy'îy (1), *Beriite*

BERITES
1276 Bêrîy (1), *Berites*

BERITH
1286 Bᵉrîyth (1), *Berith*

BERNICE
959 Bĕrnikē (3),
victorious

BERODACH-BALADAN
1255 Bᵉrôˈdak Balˈădân (1), *Berodak-Baladan*

BEROTHAH
1268 Bêrôwthâh (1), *cypress-like*

BEROTHAI
1268 Bêrôwthâh (1), *cypress-like*

BEROTHITE
1307 Bêrôthîy (1), *Berothite*

BERRIES
1620 gargar (1), *berry*
1636 ĕlaia (1), *olive*

BERYL
8658 tarshîysh (7), (poss.) *topaz*
969 bᵉrullŏs (1), *beryl*

BESAI
1153 Bᵉçay (2), *domineering*

BESEECH
577 ˈânnâ' (8), *I ask you!*
2470+6440 châlâh (1), *to be weak, sick, afflicted*
4994 nâ' (26), *I pray!, please!, I beg you!*
1189 dĕŏmai (6), *to beg, petition, ask*
2065 ĕrōtaō (4), *to interrogate; to request*
3870 parakalĕō (20), *to call, invite*

BESEECHING
2065 ĕrōtaō (1), *to interrogate; to request*
3870 parakalĕō (2), *to call, invite*

BESET
3803 kâthar (1), *to enclose, besiege; to wait*
5437 çâbab (3), *to surround*
6696 tsûwr (1), *to cramp, i.e. confine; to harass*
2139 ĕupĕristatŏs (1), *entangling, obstructing*

BESIDE
310 ˈachar (1), *after*
413 ˈêl (2), *to, toward*
657 ˈepheç (3), *end; no further*
681 ˈêtsel (12), *side; near*
854 ˈêth (2), *with; by; at; among*
905 bad (45), *apart, only, besides*
1107 bilˈădêy (7), *except, without, besides*
1115 biltîy (3), *except, without, unless, besides*
2108 zûwlâh (6), *except; apart from; besides*
3027 yâd (1), *hand; power*
5921 ˈal (17), *above, over, upon, or against*
5973 ˈîm (4), *with*
5980 ˈummâh (2), *near, beside, along with*
6654 tsad (3), *side; adversary*
846 autŏs (1), *he, she, it*
1839 ĕxistēmi (2), *to astound*
1909 ĕpi (3), *on, upon*

BESIDES
905 bad (1), *apart, only, besides*
2108 zûwlâh (1), *except; apart from; besides*
5750 ˈôwd (4), *again; repeatedly; still; more*
5921 ˈal (1), *above, over, upon, or against*
3063 lŏipŏn (1), *something remaining; finally*
4359 prŏsŏphĕilō (1), *to be indebted*

BESIEGE
6696 tsûwr (8), *to cramp, i.e. confine; to harass*
6887 tsârar (3), *to cramp*

BESIEGED
935+4692 bôw' (3), *to go or come*
4692 mâtsôwr (1), *siege-mound; distress*
4693 mâtsôwr (2), *limit, border*
5341 nâtsar (2), *to guard, protect, maintain*
5437 çâbab (1), *to surround*
6696 tsûwr (14), *to cramp, i.e. confine*

BESODEIAH
1152 Bᵉçôwdᵉyâh (1), *in (the) counsel of Jehovah*

BESOM
4292 matˈătê' (1), *broom*

BESOR
1308 Bᵉsôwr (3), *cheerful*

BESOUGHT
1245 bâqash (2), *to search out*
2470 châlâh (5), *to be weak, sick, afflicted*
2603 chânan (4), *to implore*
1189 dĕŏmai (3), *to beg, petition, ask*
2065 ĕrōtaō (9), *to interrogate; to request*
3870 parakalĕō (21), *to call, invite*

BEST
2173 zimrâh (1), *choice*
2459 cheleb (5), *fat; choice part*
2896 tôwb (8), *good; well*
3190 yâṭab (1), *to be, make well*
4315 mêyṭâb (6), *best*
5324 nâtsab (1), *to station*
6338 pâzaz (1), *to refine gold*
2909 krĕittōn (1), *stronger, i.e. nobler*
4413 prōtŏs (1), *foremost*

BESTIR
2782 chârats (1), *to be alert, to decide*

BESTOW
5414 nâthan (2), *to give*

BESTOW
5415 nᵉthan (Ch.) (2), *to give*
6213 ˈâsâh (1), *to do or make*
4060 pĕritithēmi (1), *to present*
4863 sunagō (2), *to gather together*
5595 psōmizō (1), *to nourish, feed*

BESTOWED
1580 gâmal (2), *to benefit or requite; to wean*
3240 yânach (2), *to allow to stay*
5414 nâthan (2), *to give*
6485 pâqad (1), *to visit, care for, count*
1325 didōmi (2), *to give*
2872 kŏpiaō (3), *to feel fatigue; to work hard*

BETAH
984 Beṭach (1), *safety, security, trust*

BETEN
991 Beṭen (1), *belly; womb; body*

BETH-ANATH
1043 Bêyth ˈĂnâth (3), *house of replies*

BETH-ANOTH
1042 Bêyth ˈĂnôwth (1), *house of replies*

BETH-ARABAH
1026 Bêyth hâ-ˈĂrâbâh (3), *house of the desert*

BETH-ARAM
1027 Bêyth hâ-Râm (1), *house of the height*

BETH-ARBEL
1009 Bêyth ˈArbê'l (1), *house of God's ambush*

BETH-AVEN
1007 Bêyth ˈĂven (7), *house of vanity*

BETH-AZMAVETH
1041 Bêyth ˈAzmâveth (1), *house of Azmaveth*

BETH-BAAL-MEON
1010 Bêyth Ba'al Mᵉˈôwn (1), *house of Baal of (the) habitation*

BETH-BARAH
1012 Bêyth Bârâh (2), *house of (the) river ford*

BETH-BIREI
1011 Bêyth Bir'îy (1), *house of a creative one*

BETH-CAR
1033 Bêyth Kar (1), *house of pasture*

BETH-DAGON
1016 Bêyth-Dâgôwn (2), *house of Dagon*

BETH-DIBLATHAIM
1015 Bêyth Diblâthayim (1), *house of (the) two figcakes*

BETH-EL
1008 Bêyth-'Êl (66), *house of God*

BETH-ELITE
1017 Bêyth hâ-ˈĔlîy (1), *Beth-elite*

BETH-EMEK
1025 Bêyth hâ-ˈÊmeq (1), *house of the valley*

BETH-EZEL
1018 Bêyth hâ-ˈÊtsel (1), *house of the side*

BETH-GADER
1013 Bêyth-Gâdêr (1), *house of (the) wall*

BETH-GAMUL
1014 Bêyth Gâmûwl (1), *house of (the) weaned*

BETH-HACCEREM
1021 Bêyth hak-Kerem (2), *house of the vineyard*

BETH-HARAN
1028 Bêyth hâ-Rân (1), *house of the height*

BETH-HOGLA
1031 Bêyth Choglâh (1), *house of a partridge*

BETH-HOGLAH
1031 Bêyth Choglâh (2), *house of a partridge*

BETH-HORON
1032 Bêyth Chôwrôwn (14), *house of hollowness*

BETH-JESHIMOTH
1020 Bêyth ha-Yᵉshîy-môwth (3), *house of the deserts*

BETH-JESIMOTH
1020 Bêyth ha-Yᵉshîy-môwth (1), *house of the deserts*

BETH-LEBAOTH
1034 Bêyth Lᵉbâ'ôwth (1), *house of lionesses*

BETH-LEHEM
1035 Bêyth Lechem (30), *house of bread*

BETH-LEHEM-JUDAH
1035 Bêyth Lechem (10), *house of bread*

BETH-LEHEMITE
1022 Bêyth hal-Lachmîy (4), *Beth-lechemite*

BETH-MAACHAH
1038 Bêyth Ma'ăkâh (2), *house of Maakah*

BETH-MARCABOTH
1024 Bêyth ham-Markâbôwth (2), *place of (the) chariots*

BETH-MEON
1010 Bêyth Ba'al Mᵉˈôwn (1), *house of Baal of (the) habitation*

BETH-NIMRAH
1039 Bêyth Nimrâh (2), *house of (the) leopard*

BETH-PALET
1046 Bêyth Peleṭ (1), *house of escape*

BETH-PAZZEZ
1048 Bêyth Patstsêts (1), *house of dispersion*

BETH-PEOR
1047 Bêyth Pᵉ'ôwr (4), house of Peor

BETH-PHELET
1046 Bêyth Peleṭ (1), house of escape

BETH-RAPHA
1051 Bêyth Râphâ' (1), house of (the) giant

BETH-REHOB
1050 Bêyth Rᵉchôwb (2), house of (the) street

BETH-SHAN
1052 Bêyth Shᵉ'ân (3), house of ease

BETH-SHEAN
1052 Bêyth Shᵉ'ân (6), house of ease

BETH-SHEMESH
1053 Bêyth Shemesh (21), house of (the) sun

BETH-SHEMITE
1030 Bêyth hash-Shimshîy (2), Beth-shimshite

BETH-SHITTAH
1029 Bêyth hash-Shiṭṭâh (1), house of the acacia

BETH-TAPPUAH
1054 Bêyth Tappûwach (1), house of (the) apple

BETH-ZUR
1049 Bêyth Tsûwr (4), house of (the) rock

BETHABARA
962 Bēthabara (1), ferry-house

BETHANY
963 Bēthania (11), date-house

BETHER
1336 Bether (1), section

BETHESDA
964 Bēthesda (1), house of kindness

BETHINK
7725+413+3820 shûwb (2), to turn back

BETHLEHEM
1035 Bêyth Lechem (1), house of bread
965 Bêthlĕĕm (8), house of bread

BETHPHAGE
967 Bēthphagē (3), fig-house

BETHSAIDA
966 Bēthsaïda (7), fishing-house

BETHUEL
1328 Bᵉthûw'êl (10), destroyed of God

BETHUL
1329 Bᵉthûwl (1), Bethuel

BETIMES
7836 shâchar (3), to search for
7925 shâkam (2), to load up, i.e. to start early

BETONIM
993 Bᵉṭônîym (1), hollows

BETRAY
7411 râmâh (1), to hurl; to shoot; to delude
3860 paradidōmi (17), to hand over

BETRAYED
3860 paradidōmi (18), to hand over

BETRAYERS
4273 prŏdŏtēs (1), betraying

BETRAYEST
3860 paradidōmi (1), to hand over

BETRAYETH
3860 paradidōmi (3), to hand over

BETROTH
781 'âras (4), to engage for matrimony, betroth

BETROTHED
781 'âras (6), to engage for matrimony, betroth
2778 châraph (1), to spend the winter
3259 yâ'ad (2), to engage for marriage

BETTER
2896 ṭôwb (75), good; well
3027 yâd (1), hand; power
3148 yôwthêr (1), moreover; rest; gain
3190 yâṭab (4), to be, make well
3504 yithrôwn (1), preeminence, gain
1308 diaphĕrō (3), to differ; to surpass
2570 kalŏs (5), good; beautiful; valuable
2573 kalŏs (1), well
2909 krĕittōn (18), stronger, i.e. nobler
3081 lusitĕlĕi (1), it is advantageous
4052 pĕrissĕuō (1), to superabound
4284 prŏĕchŏmai (1), to excel
4851 sumphĕrō (1), to collect; advantage
5242 hupĕrĕchō (1), excel; superior
5543 chrēstŏs (1), employed, i.e. useful

BETTERED
5623 ōphĕlĕō (1), benefit, be of use

BETWEEN
996 bêyn (190), between
997 bêyn (Ch.) (1), between; "either...or"
5921 'al (1), upon, against
5973 'îm (2), with
8432 tâvek (3), center, middle
1722 ĕn (1), in; during; because of
3307 mĕrizō (1), to apportion, bestow
3342 mĕtaxu (6), betwixt
4314 prŏs (2), for; on, at; to, toward; against

BETWIXT
996 bêyn (13), between
6293 pâga' (1), to impinge

1537 ĕk (1), out, out of

BEULAH
1166 bâ'al (1), to be master; to marry

BEWAIL
1058 bâkâh (4), to weep, moan
2799 klaiō (1), to sob, wail
3996 pĕnthĕō (1), to grieve

BEWAILED
1058 bâkâh (1), to weep, moan
2875 kŏptō (2), to beat the breast

BEWAILETH
3306 yâphach (1), to breathe hard, gasp

BEWARE
6191 'âram (1), to be cunning; be prudent
8104 shâmar (9), to watch
991 blĕpō (6), to look at
4337 prŏsĕchō (7), to pay attention to
5442 phulassō (2), to watch, i.e. be on guard

BEWITCHED
940 baskainō (1), to fascinate, bewitch
1839 ĕxistēmi (2), to astound; to be insane

BEWRAY
1540 gâlâh (1), to denude; uncover

BEWRAYETH
5046 nâgad (1), to announce
7121 qârâ' (1), to call out
1212+4160 dēlŏs (1), clear, plain, evident

BEYOND
1973 hâl'âh (5), far away; thus far
5674 'âbar (4), to cross over; to transition
5675 'ăbar (Ch.) (7), region across
5676 'êber (21), opposite side; east
5921 'al (2), above, over
1900 ĕpĕkĕina (1), on the further side of, beyond
4008 pĕran (7), across, beyond
5228 hupĕr (1), over; above; beyond
5233 hupĕrbainō (1), to transcend
5238 hupĕrĕkĕina (1), beyond, still farther
5239 hupĕrĕktĕinō (1), to overreach
5249 hupĕrpĕrissōs (1), exceedingly

BEZAI
1209 Bêtsay (3), Betsai

BEZALEEL
1212 Bᵉtsal'êl (9), in (the) protection of God

BEZEK
966 Bezeq (3), lightning

BEZER
1221 Betser (5), inaccessible spot

BICHRI
1075 Bikrîy (8), youthful

BID
559 'âmar (6), to say
1696 dâbar (2), to speak, say; to subdue
6942 qâdâsh (1), to be, make clean
479 antikalĕō (1), invite in return
657 apŏtassŏmai (1), to say adieu; to renounce
2036 ĕpō (2), to speak
2564 kalĕō (2), to call
2753 kĕlĕuō (1), to order
3004 lĕgō (1), to say

BIDDEN
559 'âmar (1), to say
7121 qârâ' (2), to call out
2564 kalĕō (10), to call
4367 prŏstassō (1), to arrange towards

BIDDETH
3004 lĕgō (1), to say

BIDDING
4928 mishma'ath (1), royal court; obedience

BIDKAR
920 Bidqar (1), stabbing assassin

BIER
4296 miṭṭâh (1), bed; sofa, litter or bier
4673 sŏrŏs (1), funeral bier

BIGTHA
903 Bigthâ' (1), Bigtha

BIGTHAN
904 Bigthân (1), Bigthan

BIGTHANA
904 Bigthân (1), Bigthana

BIGVAI
902 Bigvay (6), Bigvai

BILDAD
1085 Bildad (5), Bildad

BILEAM
1109 Bil'âm (1), foreigner

BILGAH
1083 Bilgâh (3), desistance

BILGAI
1084 Bilgay (1), desistant

BILHAH
1090 Bilhâh (11), timid

BILHAN
1092 Bilhân (4), timid

BILL
5612 çêpher (4), writing
975 bibliŏn (1), scroll; certificate
1121 gramma (2), writing; education

BILLOWS
1530 gal (1), heap; ruins
4867 mishbâr (1), breaker

BILSHAN
1114 Bilshân (2), Bilshan

English

BIMHAL
1118 Bimhâl (1), *with pruning*

BIND
631 'âçar (13), to *fasten;* to *join* battle
2280 châbash (6), to *wrap* firmly, *bind*
3729 kᵉphath (Ch.) (1), to *fetter, bind*
6029 'ânad (1), to *lace fast, bind*
6887 tsârar (3), to *cramp*
7164 qâraç (1), to *hunch*
7194 qâshar (10), to *tie, bind*
7405 râkaç (2), to *tie, bind*
7573 râtham (1), to *yoke*
1195 děsmĕuō (1), to *enchain, tie on*
1210 děō (9), to *bind*
5265 hupŏdĕō (1), to *put on shoes or sandals*

BINDETH
247 'âzar (1), to *belt*
631 'âçar (1), to *fasten;* to *join* battle
2280 châbash (4), to *wrap* firmly, *bind*
6014 'âmar (1), to *gather grain into sheaves*
6887 tsârar (2), to *cramp*

BINDING
481 'âlam (1), to be *tongue-tied, be silent*
632 'ĕçâr (1), *obligation, vow, pledge*
681 'êtsel (1), *side; near*
8193 sâphâh (1), *lip, edge, margin*
1195 děsmĕuō (1), to *enchain, tie on*

BINEA
1150 Bin'â' (2), *Bina*

BINNUI
1131 Binnûwy (7), *built*

BIRD
1167+3671 ba'al (1), *master; owner; citizen*
5775 'ôwph (3), *bird*
5861 'ayiṭ (2), bird of prey (poss.) *hawk*
6833 tsippôwr (21), little *hopping bird*
3732 ŏrnĕŏn (1), *bird*

BIRD'S
6833 tsippôwr (1), little *hopping bird*

BIRDS
5775 'ôwph (6), winged *bird*
5861 'ayiṭ (1), bird of prey (poss.) *hawk*
6833 tsippôwr (10), little *hopping bird*
4071 pětĕinŏn (5), *bird which flies*
4421 ptĕnŏn (1), *bird*

BIRDS'
6853 tsᵉphar (Ch.) (1), *bird*

BIRSHA
1306 Birsha' (1), *with wickedness*

BIRTH
3205 yâlad (2), to *bear young;* to *father a child*
4351 mᵉkûwrâh (1), *origin*
4866 mishbêr (2), vaginal *opening*
5309 nephel (3), *abortive miscarriage*
7665 shâbar (1), to *burst*
8435 tôwlᵉdâh (1), family *descent,* family *record*
1079 gĕnĕtĕ (1), *birth*
1083 gĕnnĕsis (2), *nativity*
5605 ōdinō (2), to *experience labor pains*

BIRTHDAY
3117+3205 yôwm (1), *day; time period*
1077 gĕnĕsia (2), *birthday* ceremonies

BIRTHRIGHT
1062 bᵉkôwrâh (9), *state of, rights of first born*
4415 prōtŏtŏkia (1), *primogeniture* rights

BIRZAVITH
1269 Birzôwth (1), *holes*

BISHLAM
1312 Bishlâm (1), *Bishlam*

BISHOP
1984 ĕpiskŏpē (1), *episcopate*
1985 ĕpiskŏpŏs (5), *overseer, supervisor*

BISHOPRICK
1984 ĕpiskŏpē (1), *episcopate*

BISHOPS
1985 ĕpiskŏpŏs (1), *overseer, supervisor*

BIT
4964 metheg (1), *bit*
5391 nâshak (2), to *strike;* to *oppress*

BITE
5391 nâshak (6), to *strike;* to *oppress*
1143 daknō (1), to *bite*

BITETH
5391 nâshak (2), to *strike;* to *oppress*

BITHIAH
1332 Bithyâh (1), *worshipper of Jehovah*

BITHRON
1338 Bithrôwn (1), *craggy spot*

BITHYNIA
978 Bithunia (2), *Bithynia*

BITS
5469 chalinŏs (1), *curb* or *head-stall,* i.e. *bit*

BITTEN
5391 nâshak (2), to *strike;* to *oppress*

BITTER
4751 mar (20), *bitter; bitterness; bitterly*
4784 mârâh (1), to *rebel* or *resist;* to *provoke*

BITTER
4805 mᵉrîy (1), *rebellion, rebellious*
4815 mᵉrîyrîy (1), *bitter,* i.e. *poisonous*
4843 mârar (2), to *be, make bitter*
4844 mᵉrôr (2), *bitter herb*
4846 mᵉrôrâh (2), bitter *bile; venom* of a serpent
8563 tamrûwr (2), *bitterness*
4087 pikrainō (4), to *embitter, turn sour*
4089 pikrŏs (2), *sharp, pungent,* i.e. *bitter*

BITTERLY
779 'ârar (1), to *execrate,* place a *curse*
4751 mar (3), *bitter; bitterness; bitterly*
4843 mârar (2), to *be, make bitter*
8563 tamrûwr (1), *bitterness*
4090 pikrŏs (2), *bitterly,* i.e. *violently*

BITTERN
7090 qippôwd (3), *bittern*

BITTERNESS
4470 memer (1), *sorrow*
4472 mamrôr (1), *bitterness, misery*
4751 mar (10), *bitter; bitterness; bitterly*
4814 mᵉrîyrûwth (1), *bitterness*
4843 mârar (4), to *be, make bitter*
4844 mᵉrôr (1), *bitter herb*
4088 pikria (4), *acridity, bitterness*

BIZJOTHJAH
964 bizyôwthᵉyâh (1), *contempts of Jehovah*

BIZTHA
968 Bizthâ' (1), *Biztha*

BLACK
380 'îyshôwn (1), *pupil, eyeball; middle*
3648 kâmar (1), to *shrivel* with heat
5508 çôchereth (1), (poss.) black *tile*
6937 qâdar (4), to be *dark-colored*
7835 shâchar (1), to *be dim* or dark in color
7838 shâchôr (6), *dusky, jet black*
7840 shᵉcharchôreth (1), *swarthy, dark*
3189 mĕlas (3), *black*

BLACKER
2821 châshak (1), to be *dark;* to *darken*

BLACKISH
6937 qâdar (1), to be *dark-colored*

BLACKNESS
3650 kimrîyr (1), *obscuration, eclipse*
6289 pâ'rûwr (2), *flush* of anxiety

BLADE
3851 lahab (2), *flame* of fire; *flash* of a *blade*
7929 shikmâh (1), *shoulder-bone*
5528 chŏrtŏs (2), *pasture, herbage* or *vegetation*

BLAINS
76 'âba'bû'âh (2), *pustule, skin eruption*

BLAME
2398 châṭâ' (2), to *sin*
299 amōmŏs (1), *unblemished, blameless*
3469 mōmaŏmai (1), to *carp at,* i.e. to *censure*

BLAMED
2607 kataginōskō (1), to *find fault with*
3469 mōmaŏmai (1), to *carp at,* i.e. to *censure*

BLAMELESS
5352 nâqâh (1), to be, *make clean;* to be *bare*
5355 nâqîy (2), *innocent*
273 amĕmptŏs (3), *irreproachable*
274 amĕmptŏs (1), *faultlessly*
298 amōmĕtŏs (1), *unblamable*
338 anaitiŏs (1), *innocent*
410 anĕglētŏs (4), *irreproachable*
423 anĕpilēptŏs (2), *not open to blame*

BLASPHEME
1288 bârak (2), to *bless*
5006 nâ'ats (2), to *scorn*
987 blasphēmĕō (6), to *speak impiously*

BLASPHEMED
1442 gâdaph (5), to *revile, blaspheme*
2778 châraph (1), to *spend the winter*
5006 nâ'ats (2), to *scorn*
5344 nâqab (1), to *specify, designate, libel*
987 blasphēmĕō (7), to *speak impiously*

BLASPHEMER
989 blasphēmŏs (1), *slanderous*

BLASPHEMERS
987 blasphēmĕō (1), to *speak impiously*
989 blasphēmŏs (1), *slanderous*

BLASPHEMEST
987 blasphēmĕō (1), to *speak impiously*

BLASPHEMETH
1442 gâdaph (1), to *revile, blaspheme*
5344 nâqab (2), to *specify, designate, libel*
987 blasphēmĕō (2), to *speak impiously*

BLASPHEMIES
5007 nᵉ'âtsâh (1), *scorn; to bloom*
988 *blasphēmia* (5), *impious speech*

BLASPHEMING
987 *blasphēmĕō* (1), to *speak impiously*

BLASPHEMOUS
989 *blasphēmŏs* (2), *slanderous*

BLASPHEMOUSLY
987 *blasphēmĕō* (1), to *speak impiously*

BLASPHEMY
5007 nᵉ'âtsâh (2), *scorn; to bloom*
987 *blasphēmĕō* (1), to *speak impiously*
988 *blasphēmia* (11), *impious speech*

BLAST
5397 nᵉshâmâh (3), *breath, life*
7307 rûwach (4), *breath; wind; life-spirit*

BLASTED
7709 shᵉdêmâh (1), *cultivated field*
7710 shâdaph (3), to *scorch*
7711 shᵉdêphâh (1), *blight; scorching*

BLASTING
7711 shᵉdêphâh (5), *blight; scorching*

BLASTUS
986 *Blastŏs* (1), (poss.) to *yield fruit*

BLAZE
1310 *diaphēmizō* (1), to *spread news*

BLEATING
6963 qôwl (1), *voice or sound*

BLEATINGS
8292 shᵉrûwqâh (1), *whistling; scorn*

BLEMISH
3971 m'ûwm (15), *blemish; fault*
8400 tᵉballûl (1), *cataract in the eye*
8549 tâmîym (44), *entire, complete; integrity*
299 *amōmŏs* (2), *unblemished, blameless*

BLEMISHES
3971 m'ûwm (1), *blemish; fault*
3470 *mōmŏs* (1), *flaw or blot*

BLESS
1288 bârak (115), to *bless*
2127 *ĕulŏgĕō* (10), to *invoke a benediction*

BLESSED
833 'âshar (7), to *be honest, prosper*
835 'esher (27), *how happy!*
1288 bârak (175), to *bless*
1289 bᵉrak (Ch.) (4), to *bless*

1293 bᵉrâkâh (3), *benediction, blessing*
1757 *ĕnĕulŏgĕō* (2), to *confer a benefit, bless*
2127 *ĕulŏgĕō* (30), to *invoke a benediction*
2128 *ĕulŏgētŏs* (8), *adorable, praised*
3106 *makarizō* (1), to *pronounce fortunate*
3107 *makariŏs* (43), *fortunate, well off*

BLESSEDNESS
3108 *makarismŏs* (3), *fortunate*

BLESSEST
1288 bârak (3), to *bless*

BLESSETH
1288 bârak (8), to *bless*

BLESSING
1288 bârak (1), to *bless*
1293 bᵉrâkâh (51), *benediction, blessing*
2127 *ĕulŏgĕō* (1), to *invoke a benediction*
2129 *ĕulŏgia* (12), *benediction*

BLESSINGS
1293 bᵉrâkâh (11), *benediction, blessing*
2129 *ĕulŏgia* (1), *benediction*

BLEW
8628 tâqa' (18), to *clatter, slap, drive, clasp*
1920 *ĕpiginŏmai* (1), to *come up, happen*
4154 pnĕō (3), to *breeze*
5285 *hupŏpnĕō* (1), to *breathe gently*

BLIND
5786 'âvar (1), to *blind*
5787 'ivvêr (26), *blind*
5788 'ivvârôwn (1), *blindness*
5956 'âlam (1), to *veil from sight, i.e. conceal*
5185 *tuphlŏs* (52), *blindness; blind person*

BLINDED
4456 *pōrŏō* (2), to *render stupid or callous*
5186 *tuphlŏō* (3), to *cause blindness*

BLINDETH
5786 'âvar (1), to *blind*

BLINDFOLDED
4028 *pĕrikaluptō* (1), to *cover eyes*

BLINDNESS
5575 çanvêr (3), *blindness*
5788 'ivvârôwn (2), *blindness*
4457 *pōrōsis* (2), *stupidity or callousness*

BLOOD
1818 dâm (337), *blood; juice; life*
5332 nêtsach (1), blood *(as if red juice)*
129 *haima* (97), *blood*
130 *haimatĕkchusia* (1), *pouring of blood*

131 *haimŏrrhĕō* (1), to *have a hemorrhage*

BLOODGUILTINESS
1818 dâm (1), *blood; juice; life*

BLOODTHIRSTY
582+1818 'ĕnôwsh (1), *man; person, human*

BLOODY
1818 dâm (15), *blood; juice; life*
1420 *dusĕntĕria* (1), *dysentery*

BLOOMED
6692 tsûwts (1), to *blossom, flourish*

BLOSSOM
6524 pârach (4), to *bloom; to fly; to flourish*
6525 perach (1), *calyx flower; bloom*
6692 tsûwts (1), to *blossom, flourish*

BLOSSOMED
6692 tsûwts (1), to *blossom, flourish*

BLOSSOMS
5322 nêts (1), *flower*
6731 tsîyts (1), burnished *plate; bright flower*

BLOT
3971 m'ûwm (2), *blemish; fault*
4229 mâchâh (10), to *erase; to grease*
1813 *ĕxalĕiphō* (1), to *obliterate*

BLOTTED
4229 mâchâh (5), to *erase; to grease*
1813 *ĕxalĕiphō* (1), to *obliterate*

BLOTTETH
4229 mâchâh (1), to *erase; to grease*

BLOTTING
1813 *ĕxalĕiphō* (1), to *obliterate*

BLOW
2690 châtsar (1), to *blow the trumpet*
4347 makkâh (1), *blow; wound; pestilence*
5265 nâça' (1), *start on a journey*
5301 nâphach (3), to *inflate, blow hard*
5380 nâshab (1), to *blow; to disperse*
5398 nâshaph (2), to *breeze as the wind*
6315 pûwach (2), to *blow, to fan, kindle; to utter*
7321 rûwa' (1), to *shout*
8409 tigrâh (1), *strife, i.e. infliction*
8628 tâqa' (23), to *clatter, slap, drive, clasp*
8643 tᵉrûw'âh (1), *battle-cry; clangor*
4154 pnĕō (2), to *breeze*

BLOWETH
5301 nâphach (1), to *inflate, blow hard*

5380 nâshab (1), to *blow; to disperse*
8628 tâqa' (1), to *clatter, slap, drive, clasp*
4154 pnĕō (1), to *breeze*

BLOWING
8628 tâqa' (2), to *clatter, slap, drive, clasp*
8643 tᵉrûw'âh (2), *battle-cry; clangor*

BLOWN
5301 nâphach (1), to *inflate, blow hard*
8628 tâqa' (3), to *clatter, slap, drive, clasp*

BLUE
8504 tᵉkêleth (50), *color violet*

BLUENESS
2250 chabbûwrâh (1), *weal, bruise*

BLUNT
6949 qâhâh (1), to *be dull; be blunt*

BLUSH
3637 kâlam (3), to *taunt or insult*

BOANERGES
993 *Bŏanĕrgĕs* (1), *sons of commotion*

BOAR
2386 chăzîyr (1), *hog, boar*

BOARD
7175 qeresh (17), *slab or plank; deck of a ship*

BOARDS
3871 lûwach (4), *tablet*
6763 tsêlâ' (2), *side*
7175 qeresh (33), *slab*
7713 sᵉdêrâh (1), *row, i.e. rank of soldiers*
4548 sanis (1), *planked timber, board*

BOAST
559 'âmar (1), to *say*
1984 hâlal (6), to *boast*
3235 yâmar (1), to *exchange*
3513 kâbad (1), to *be heavy, severe, dull*
6286 pâ'ar (1), to *shake a tree*
2620 *katakauchaŏmai* (1), to *exult against*
2744 *kauchaŏmai* (8), to *glory in; to boast*

BOASTED
1431 gâdal (1), to *be great, make great*
2744 *kauchaŏmai* (1), to *glory in; to boast*

BOASTERS
213 *alazōn* (2), *braggart*

BOASTEST
1984 hâlal (1), to *boast*

BOASTETH
1984 hâlal (3), to *boast*
3166 *mĕgalauchĕō* (1), to *be arrogant, egotistic*

BOASTING
2744 *kauchaŏmai* (1), to *glory in; to boast*

English

2745 kauchēma (1),
boast; brag
2746 kauchēsis (6),
boasting; bragging
3004 lĕgō (1), to say

BOASTINGS
212 alazŏnĕia (1),
boasting

BOAT
5679 'ăbârâh (1),
crossing-place
4142 plŏiariŏn (2), small
boat
4627 skaphē (3), skiff or
yawl, i.e. life boat

BOATS
4142 plŏiariŏn (1), small
boat

BOAZ
1162 Bô'az (24), Boaz

BOCHERU
1074 Bôkᵉrûw (2),
first-born

BOCHIM
1066 Bôkîym (2), weepers

BODIES
1354 gab (1), mounded
or rounded: top or rim
1472 gᵉvîyâh (7), dead
body
1480 gûwphâh (1), corpse
1655 geshem (Ch.) (2),
body
5038 nᵉbêlâh (2), carcase
or carrion
6297 peger (6), carcase;
corpse
4430 ptōma (3), corpse,
carrion
4983 sōma (11), body

BODILY
4983 sōma (1), body
4984 sōmatikŏs (2),
corporeal or physical
4985 sōmatikōs (1),
corporeally

BODY
990 beten (8), belly;
womb; body
1320 bâsâr (2), flesh;
body; person
1460 gêv (1), middle,
inside, in, on, etc.
1465 gêvâh (1), back
1472 gᵉvîyâh (3), dead
body
1480 gûwphâh (1), corpse
1655 geshem (Ch.) (3),
body
3409 yârêk (1), leg or
shank, flank; side
5038 nᵉbêlâh (4), carcase
or carrion
5085 nidneh (Ch.) (1),
sheath; body
5315 nephesh (9), life;
breath; soul; wind
6106 'etsem (2), bone;
body; substance
7607 shᵉ'êr (1), flesh,
meat; kindred by blood
4954 sussōmŏs (1),
fellow-member
4983 sōma (131), body
5559 chrōs (1), skin

BODY'S
4983 sōma (1), body

BOHAN
932 Bôhan (2), thumb

BOIL
1158 bâ'âh (1), to ask; be
bulging, swelling
1310 bâshal (4), to boil
up, cook; to ripen
7570 râthach (2), to boil,
churn
7822 shᵉchîyn (9),
inflammation, ulcer

BOILED
1310 bâshal (2), to boil
7570 râthach (1), to boil,
churn

BOILING
4018 mᵉbashshᵉlâh (1),
cooking hearth

BOILS
7822 shᵉchîyn (2),
inflammation, ulcer

BOISTEROUS
2478 ischurŏs (1),
forcible, powerful

BOLD
982 bâṭach (1), to trust,
be confident or sure
662 apŏtŏlmaō (1), to
bring forth boldly
2292 tharrhĕō (2), to be
bold
3954 parrhēsia (1),
frankness, boldness
3955 parrhēsiazŏmai (2),
to be frank, confident
5111 tŏlmaō (4), to be
bold, courageous

BOLDLY
983 betach (1), safety,
security, trust
2292 tharrhĕō (1), to be
bold
3954 parrhēsia (3),
frankness, boldness
3955 parrhēsiazŏmai (6),
to be frank, confident
5111 tŏlmaō (1), to be
bold, courageous
5112 tŏlmērŏtĕrŏn (1),
with greater confidence

BOLDNESS
5797 'ôz (1), strength
3954 parrhēsia (9),
frankness, boldness

BOLLED
1392 gib'ôl (1), calyx

BOLSTER
4763 mᵉra'ăshâh (6),
headpiece; head-rest

BOLT
5274 nâ'al (1), to fasten
up, lock

BOLTED
5274 nâ'al (1), to fasten
up, lock

BOND
632 'êçâr (7), obligation,
vow, pledge
4148 mûwçâr (1),
reproof, warning
4562 mâçôreth (1), band

1199 dĕsmŏn (1),
shackle; impediment
1401 dŏulŏs (6), slave,
servant
4886 sundĕsmŏs (3),
ligament; control

BONDAGE
3533 kâbash (2), to
conquer, subjugate
5647 'âbad (1), to do,
work, serve
5650 'ebed (10), servant
5656 'ăbôdâh (8), work
5659 'abdûwth (3),
servitude
1397 dŏulĕia (5), slavery,
bondage
1398 dŏulĕuō (4), to
serve as a slave
1402 dŏulŏō (4), to
enslave
2615 katadŏulŏō (2), to
enslave utterly

BONDMAID
8198 shiphchâh (1),
household female slave
3814 paidiskē (1), female
slave or servant

BONDMAIDS
519 'âmâh (2), female
servant or slave

BONDMAN
5650 'ebed (5), servant
1401 dŏulŏs (1), slave,
servant

BONDMEN
5647 'âbad (1), to do,
work, serve
5650 'ebed (16), servant

BONDS
632 'êçâr (3), obligation,
vow, pledge
4147 môwçêr (5), halter;
restraint
254 halusis (1), fetter or
manacle
1198 dĕsmiŏs (2), bound
captive; one arrested
1199 dĕsmŏn (14),
shackle; impediment
or disability
1210 dĕō (1), to bind

BONDSERVANT
5656+5650 'ăbôdâh (1),
work of any kind

BONDSERVICE
5647 'âbad (1), to do,
work, serve

BONDWOMAN
519 'âmâh (4),
maid-servant or
female slave
3814 paidiskē (4), female
slave or servant

BONDWOMEN
8198 shiphchâh (3),
household female slave

BONE
1634 gerem (1), bone; self
6106 'etsem (14), bone;
body; substance
7070 qâneh (1), reed
3747 ŏstĕŏn (1), bone

BONES
1633 gâram (1), to
crunch the bones
1634 gerem (2), bone; self
1635 gerem (Ch.) (1),
bone
6106 'etsem (89), bone;
body; substance
3747 ŏstĕŏn (4), bone
4974 sphurŏn (1), ankle

BONNETS
4021 migbâ'âh (4), cap
wrapped around head
6287 pᵉ'êr (2), fancy
head-dress

BOOK
1697 dâbâr (7), word;
matter; thing
5609 çᵉphar (Ch.) (3),
book
5612 çêpher (136),
writing
974 bibliaridiŏn (4), little
scroll
975 bibliŏn (23), scroll;
certificate
976 biblŏs (15), scroll

BOOKS
5609 çᵉphar (Ch.) (1),
book
5612 çêpher (2), writing
975 bibliŏn (4), scroll;
certificate
976 biblŏs (1), scroll of
writing

BOOTH
5521 çukkâh (2),
tabernacle; shelter

BOOTHS
5521 çukkâh (8),
tabernacle; shelter

BOOTIES
4933 mᵉshiççâh (1),
plunder

BOOTY
957 baz (1), plunder, loot
4455 malqôwach (1),
spoil, plunder
4953 mashrôwqîy (Ch.)
(1), musical pipe

BOOZ
1003 Bŏŏz (3), Boöz

BORDER
1366 gᵉbûwl (136),
boundary, border
1379 gâbal (2), to set a
boundary line, limit
3027 yâd (1), hand; power
3411 yᵉrêkâh (1),
recesses, far away
4526 miçgereth (6),
margin; stronghold
7093 qêts (2), extremity;
after
7097 qâtseh (2), extremity
8193 sâphâh (3), lip;
edge, margin
2899 kraspĕdŏn (2),
margin

BORDERS
1366 gᵉbûwl (20),
boundary, border
1367 gᵉbûwlâh (1),
boundary marker
1552 gᵉlîylâh (3), circuit
or region

3027 yâd (1), *hand; power*
3671 kânâph (2), *edge or extremity; wing*
4526 miçgereth (7), *margin; stronghold*
5299 nâphâh (1), *height*
7093 qêts (1), *extremity*
7097 qâtseh (1), *extremity*
8444 tôwtsâ'âh (1), *exit,* i.e. *boundary*
8447 tôwr (1), *succession, order*
2899 kraspĕdŏn (1), *margin*
3181 mĕthŏriŏs (1), *frontier* region
3725 hŏriŏn (1), *region, area, vicinity*

BORE
5344 nâqab (1), *to puncture, perforate*
7527 râtsa' (1), *to pierce*

BORED
5344 nâqab (1), *to puncture, perforate*

BORN
249 'ezrâch (11), *native born*
990 beṭen (1), *belly; womb; body*
1121 bên (2), *son, descendant*
3205 yâlad (80), *to bear young; to father a child*
3209 yillôwd (4), *born*
3211 yâliyd (6), *born; descendants*
4138 môwledeth (2), *offspring, family*
313 anagĕnnaŏ (1), *to beget or bear again*
1080 gĕnnaŏ (3), *to procreate, regenerate*
1084 gĕnnētŏs (2), *pertaining to birth*
1085 gĕnŏs (2), *kin, offspring in kind*
1626 ĕktrōma (1), *untimely birth*
5088 tiktŏ (3), *to produce from seed*

BORNE
3205 yâlad (3), *to bear young; to father a child*
5190 nâṭal (1), *to lift; to impose*
5375 nâsâ' (14), *to lift up*
5445 çâbal (1), *to carry*
5564 çâmak (1), *to lean upon; take hold* of
6006 'âmaç (1), *to impose* a burden
142 airŏ (1), *to lift, to take up*
941 bastazŏ (4), *to lift, bear*
1418 dus- (2), *hard,* i.e. *with difficulty*
5409 phŏrĕŏ (1), *to wear*

BORROW
3867 lâvâh (1), *to borrow; to lend*
5670 'âbaṭ (1), *to pawn; to lend; to entangle*
7592 shâ'al (4), *to ask*
1155 danĕizŏ (1), *to loan* on interest; *to borrow*

BORROWED
3867 lâvâh (1), *to borrow; to lend*
7592 shâ'al (2), *to ask*

BORROWER
3867 lâvâh (2), *to borrow; to lend*

BORROWETH
3867 lâvâh (1), *to borrow; to lend*

BOSCATH
1218 Botsqath (1), *swell* of ground

BOSOM
2243 chôb (1), *bosom*
2436 chêyq (32), *bosom, heart*
2683 chêtsen (1), *bosom*
6747 tsallachath (2), *bosom*
2859 kŏlpŏs (5), *lap* area

BOSOR
1007 Bŏsŏr (1), *lamp*

BOSSES
1354 gab (1), *mounded* or *rounded: top* or *rim*

BOTCH
7822 shᵉchîyn (2), *inflammation, ulcer*

BOTH
413 'êl (1), *to, toward*
1571 gam (30), *also; even; "both...and"*
3162 yachad (1), *unitedly*
8147 shᵉnayim (78), *two-fold*
8174 Sha'aph (2), *fluctuation*
297 amphŏtĕrŏs (14), *both*
1417 duŏ (2), *two*
1538 hĕkastŏs (1), *each* or *every*
2532 kai (45), *and; or; even; also*
5037 tĕ (39), *both* or *also*

BOTTLE
1228 baqbûk (2), *bottle*
2573 chêmeth (4), skin *bottle*
4997 nô'd (4), skin *bag*
5035 nebel (5), skin *bag*

BOTTLES
178 'ôwb (1), *wineskin; necromancer, medium*
2573 chêmeth (1), skin *bottle*
4997 nô'd (3), skin *bag*
5035 nebel (3), skin *bag*
779 askŏs (12), *leather bottle* or *bag*

BOTTOM
773 'ar'îyth (Ch.) (1), *bottom, dirt floor*
2436 chêyq (2), *bosom, heart*
3247 yᵉçôwd (10), *foundation*
4688 mᵉtsôwlâh (1), *deep* place
4699 mᵉtsullâh (1), *shade, deep*
7172 qarqa' (1), *floor*
7507 rᵉphîydâh (1), *railing*

8328 sheresh (1), *root*
2736 katŏ (2), *downwards*

BOTTOMLESS
12 abussŏs (7), *deep place, abyss*

BOTTOMS
7095 qetseb (1), *shape; base*

BOUGH
534 'âmîyr (1), *top*
1121 bên (2), *son, descendant; people*
2793 chôresh (1), *wooded forest*
6288 pᵉ'ôrâh (1), *foliage, branches*
7754 sôwk (2), *branch*

BOUGHS
5577 çançin (1), *twig*
5589 çᵉ'appâh (2), *twig*
5634 çar'appâh (1), *twig*
5688 'ăbôth (3), *entwined* things: *foliage*
6056 'ănaph (Ch.) (1), *bough, branch*
6057 'ânâph (3), *twig*
6288 pᵉ'ôrâh (2), *foliage, branches*
6529 pᵉrîy (1), *fruit*
7105 qâtsîyr (3), *harvest; limb of a tree*
7730 sôwbek (1), *thicket*

BOUGHT
3739 kârâh (1), *to purchase* by bargaining
4736 miqnâh (7), *acquisition*
7069 qânâh (21), *to create; to procure*
7666 shâbar (1), *to deal* in cereal grain
59 agŏrazŏ (13), *to purchase; to redeem*
5608 ônĕŏmai (1), *to purchase, buy*

BOUND
615 'âçîyr (2), *captive, prisoner*
631 'âçar (33), *to fasten; to join* battle
640 'âphad (1), *to fasten, gird*
1366 gᵉbûwl (4), *boundary, border*
2280 châbash (4), *to wrap firmly, bind*
3256 yâçar (1), *to chastise; to instruct*
3729 kᵉphath (Ch.) (3), *to fetter, bind*
4205 mâzôwr (1), *sore* needing a bandage
6123 'âqad (1), *to tie the feet with thongs*
6616 pâthîyl (1), *twine, cord*
6887 tsârar (7), *to cramp*
7194 qâshar (4), *to tie, bind*
7576 râthaq (1), *to fasten, bind*
8244 sâqad (1), *to fasten, bind*
8379 ta'ăvâh (1), *limit,* i.e. *full extent*
332 anathĕmatizŏ (3), *to declare or vow an oath*

1196 dĕsmĕŏ (1), *shackle; bind*
1210 dĕŏ (28), *to bind*
2611 katadĕŏ (1), *to bandage* a wound
3784 ŏphĕilŏ (2), *to owe; to be under obligation*
4019 pĕridĕŏ (1), *to wrap around*
4029 pĕrikĕimai (1), *to enclose, encircle*
4385 prŏtĕinŏ (1), *to tie prostrate for scourging*
4887 sundĕŏ (1), *to be a fellow-prisoner*

BOUNDS
1366 gᵉbûwl (1), *boundary, border*
1367 gᵉbûwlâh (2), *boundary marker*
1379 gâbal (2), *to set a boundary*
2706 chôq (2), *appointment; allotment*
3734 hŏrŏthĕsia (1), *boundary-line*

BOUNTIFUL
2896 ṭôwb (1), *good; well*
7771 shôwa' (1), *noble,* i.e. *liberal; opulent*

BOUNTIFULLY
1580 gâmal (4), *to benefit* or *requite; to wean*
2129 ĕulŏgia (1), *benediction*

BOUNTIFULNESS
572 haplŏtēs (1), *sincerity; generosity*

BOUNTY
3027 yâd (1), *hand; power*
2129 ĕulŏgia (2), *benediction*

BOW
86 'abrêk (1), *kneel*
3721 kâphaph (2), *to curve, bow*
3766 kâra' (9), *to prostrate*
5186 nâṭâh (6), *to stretch* or *spread out*
5791 'âvath (1), *to wrest, twist*
7198 qesheth (55), *bow, rainbow*
7812 shâchâh (17), *to prostrate* in homage
7817 shâchach (2), *to sink or depress*
2578 kamptŏ (3), *to bend*
4781 sugkamptŏ (1), *to afflict*
5115 tŏxŏn (1), *bow*

BOWED
3721 kâphaph (3), *to curve, bow*
3766 kâra' (11), *to prostrate; to make miserable*
5186 nâṭâh (5), *to stretch* or *spread out*
5791 'âvath (1), *to wrest, twist*
6915 qâdad (13), *to bend*
7743 shûwach (1), *to sink*
7812 shâchâh (35), *to prostrate* in homage

English

7817 shâchach (4), to *sink* or *depress*
1120 *gŏnupĕtĕō* (1), to *fall* on the knee, *kneel*
2578 *kamptō* (1), to *bend*
2827 *klinō* (2), to *slant* or *slope*
4794 *sugkuptō* (1), to be *completely overcome*

BOWELS
4578 mê'âh (26), *viscera; anguish, tenderness*
7130 qereb (1), *nearest part*, i.e. the *center*
7358 rechem (2), *womb*
4698 *splagchnŏn* (9), *intestine; affection, pity*

BOWETH
3766 kâra' (2), to *prostrate*
7817 shâchach (1), to *sink* or *depress*

BOWING
5186 nâṭâh (2), to *stretch* or *spread out*
5087 *tithēmi* (1), to *put*

BOWL
1543 gullâh (3), *fountain; bowl* or *globe*
4219 mîzrâq (13), *bowl* for sprinkling
5602 çêphel (1), *basin, bowl*

BOWLS
1375 gᵉbîya' (8), *goblet; bowl*
1543 gullâh (3), *fountain; bowl* or *globe*
4219 mîzrâq (8), *bowl* for sprinkling
4518 mᵉnaqqîyth (3), *sacrificial basin*
5592 çaph (2), *dish*

BOWMEN
7411+7198 râmâh (1), to *hurl; to shoot*

BOWS
7198 qesheth (13), *bow, rainbow*

BOWSHOT
2909+7198 ṭâchâh (1), to *stretch* a bow

BOX
6378 pak (2), *flask, jug*
8391 tᵉ'ashshûwr (2), *cedar*
211 alabastrŏn (4), *alabaster, vase*

BOY
3206 yeled (1), *young male*

BOYS
3206 yeled (1), *young male*
5288 na'ar (1), *male child; servant*

BOZEZ
949 Bôwtsêts (1), *shining*

BOZKATH
1218 Botsqath (1), *swell* of ground

BOZRAH
1224 Botsrâh (9), *sheep-fold, animal pen*

BRACELET
685 'ets'âdâh (1), *bracelet*

BRACELETS
2397 châch (1), *ring* for the nose or lips
6616 pâthîyl (2), *twine, cord*
6781 tsâmîyd (6), *bracelet; lid*
8285 shêrâh (1), *wrist-band*

BRAKE
1234 bâqa' (3), to *cleave, break, tear open*
1518 gîyach (1), to *issue forth; to burst forth*
1855 dᵉqaq (Ch.) (5), to *crumble; crush*
1961 hâyâh (1), to *exist,* i.e. *be* or *become*
3807 kâthath (1), to *bruise* or *strike, beat*
5310 nâphats (1), to *dash* to pieces; to *scatter*
5422 nâthats (12), to *tear down*
5423 nâthaq (3), to *tear off*
6555 pârats (4), to *break out*
6561 pâraq (1), to *break off* or *crunch;* to *deliver*
6565 pârar (2), to *break up;* to *violate, frustrate*
7323 rûwts (1), to *run*
7533 râtsats (1), to *crack in pieces, smash*
7665 shâbar (20), to *burst*
1284 *diarrhēssō* (2), to *tear asunder*
2608 *katagnumi* (2), to *crack apart*
2622 *kataklaō* (2), to *divide* in pieces
2806 *klaō* (9), to *break bread*
4937 *suntribō* (1), to *crush completely*

BRAKEST
7533 râtsats (1), to *crack in pieces, smash*
7665 shâbar (4), to *burst*

BRAMBLE
329 'âṭâd (3), *buckthorn*
942 *batŏs* (1), *brier*

BRAMBLES
2336 chôwach (1), *thorn; hook; ring* for the nose

BRANCH
534 'âmîyr (1), *top*
1121 bên (1), *son, descendant; people*
2156 zᵉmôwrâh (3), *twig, vine branch*
2158 zâmîyr (1), *song*
3127 yôwneqeth (3), *sprout, new shoot*
3712 kippâh (3), *leaf*
5342 nêtser (4), *shoot* of a plant; *descendant*
5929 'âleh (1), *leaf; foliage*
6057 'ânâph (1), *twig*
6780 tsemach (5), *sprout, branch*
6788 tsammereth (2), *foliage*

BRANCHES
905 bad (3), *limb, member; bar; chief*
1121 bên (1), *son, descendant; people*
1808 dâlîyâh (8), *bough, branch*
2156 zᵉmôwrâh (1), pruned *twig, branch*
3127 yôwneqeth (3), *sprout, new shoot*
3709 kaph (1), *hollow of hand; paw; sole*
5189 nᵉṭîyshâh (1), *tendril* plant shoot
5585 çâ'îyph (2), *fissure* of rocks; *bough*
5688 'ăbôth (1), *entwined things: string* or *foliage*
5929 'âleh (3), *leaf; foliage*
6056 'ănaph (Ch.) (3), *bough, branch*
6057 'ânâph (3), *twig*
6058 'ânêph (1), *branching*
6073 'ophe' (1), *bough*
6288 pᵉ'ôrâh (4), *foliage, branches*
7070 qâneh (19), *reed*
7641 shibbôl (1), *stream; ear* of grain
7976 shilluchâh (1), *shoot* of a vine
8299 sârîyg (3), *entwining tendril*
902 baiŏn (1), *palm twig*
2798 *kladŏs* (9), *twig* or *bough*
2814 *klēma* (1), *limb* or *shoot*
4746 *stŏibas* (1), *bough* of a tree so employed

BRAND
181 'ûwd (1), *poker stick* for a *fire*

BRANDISH
5774 'ûwph (1), to *cover,* to *fly;* to *faint*

BRANDS
3940 lappîyd (1), *flaming torch, lamp* or *flame*

BRASEN
5178 nᵉchôsheth (27), *copper; bronze*
5473 chalkiŏn (1), *copper dish* or *kettle*

BRASS
5153 nâchûwsh (1), *coppery,* i.e. *hard*
5154 nᵉchûwshâh (7), *copper; bronze*
5174 nᵉchâsh (Ch.) (9), *copper*
5178 nᵉchôsheth (102), *copper; bronze*
5470 chalkĕŏs (1), *copper*
5474 chalkŏlibanŏn (2), *burnished copper*
5475 chalkŏs (3), *copper*

BRAVERY
8597 tiph'ârâh (1), *ornament*

BRAWLER
269 amachŏs (1), *not quarrelsome*

BRAWLERS
269 amachŏs (1), *not quarrelsome*

BRAWLING
4090 mᵉdân (2), *contest* or *quarrel*

BRAY
3806 kâthash (1), to *pound* in a mortar
5101 nâhaq (1), to *bray;* to *scream* from hunger

BRAYED
5101 nâhaq (1), to *bray;* to *scream* from hunger

BREACH
919 bedeq (1), *gap*
1234 bâqa' (2), to *cleave, break, tear open*
6555 pârats (1), to *break out*
6556 perets (10), *break, gap*
7667 sheber (5), *fracture; ruin*
8569 tᵉnûw'âh (1), *enmity*

BREACHES
919 bedeq (7), *gap*
1233 bᵉqîya' (1), *fissure, breach*
4664 miphrâts (1), *haven, cove*
6555 pârats (1), to *break out*
6556 perets (3), *break, gap*
7447 râçîyç (1), *ruin; dew-drop*
7667 sheber (1), *fracture; ruin*

BREAD
3899 lechem (236), *food, bread*
740 artos (72), *loaf* of *bread*

BREADTH
2947 ṭêphach (1), *palm-breadth*
2948 ṭôphach (3), *palm-breadth*
4800 merchâb (1), *open space; liberty*
6613 pᵉthay (Ch.) (2), *width*
7338 rachab (1), *width, expanse*
7341 rôchab (75), *width*
4114 *platŏs* (4), *width*

BREAK
215 'ôwr (1), to *be luminous*
1234 bâqa' (3), to *cleave, break, tear open*
1633 gâram (2), to *crunch* the bones
1758 dûwsh (1), to *trample* or *thresh*
1792 dâkâ' (3), to *pulverize; be contrite*
1854 dâqaq (3), to *crush; crumble*

1986 hâlam (1), to *strike, beat, stamp, conquer*
2000 hâmam (1), to *disturb, drive, destroy*
2040 hâraç (7), to *pull down; break, destroy*
2490 châlal (3), to *profane, defile*
3318 yâtsâ' (1), to *go, bring out*
5003 nâ'aph (1), to *commit adultery*
5106 nûw' (1), to *refuse, forbid, dissuade*
5214 nîyr (2), to *till* the soil
5310 nâphats (10), to *dash* to pieces
5422 nâthats (6), to *tear down*
5423 nâthaq (2), to *tear off*
5670 'âbaṭ (1), to *pawn; to lend; to entangle*
6202 'âraph (3), to *break the neck, to destroy*
6206 'ârats (1), to *awe; to dread; to harass*
6315 pûwach (2), to *blow, to fan, kindle; to utter*
6476 pâtsach (6), to *break out in sound*
6524 pârach (2), to *break forth; to bloom; to fly*
6555 pârats (7), to *break out*
6561 pâraq (3), to *break off or crunch; to deliver*
6562 pᵉraq (Ch.) (1), to *discontinue, stop*
6565 pârar (14), to *break up; to violate, frustrate*
6605 pâthach (1), to *open wide; to loosen, begin*
6743 tsâlach (1), to *push forward*
6746 tsᵉlôchîyth (1), *vial* or salt-*cellar*
7489 râ'a' (3), to *break* to pieces
7533 râtsats (1), to *crack in pieces, smash*
7665 shâbar (33), to *burst*
7702 sâdad (2), to *break ground*
827 augē (1), *radiance, dawn*
1358 diŏrussō (2), to *penetrate burglariously*
2608 katagnumi (1), to *crack apart*
2806 klaō (2), to *break bread*
3089 luō (1), to *loosen*
4486 rhēgnumi (2), to *break, burst forth*
4919 sunthruptō (1), to *crush together*

BREAKER
6555 pârats (1), to *break out*
3848 parabatēs (1), *violator, lawbreaker*

BREAKEST
7665 shâbar (1), to *burst*

BREAKETH
1234 bâqa' (1), to *cleave, break, tear open*

1638 gâraç (1), to *crush, break; to dissolve*
1855 dᵉqaq (Ch.) (1), to *crumble; crush*
2040 hâraç (1), to *pull down; break, destroy*
5927 'âlâh (1), to *ascend, be high, mount*
6327 pûwts (1), to *dash in pieces; to disperse*
6555 pârats (3), to *break out*
6566 pâras (1), to *break apart, disperse, scatter*
7665 shâbar (5), to *burst*
7779 shûwph (1), to *gape,* i.e. *snap* at
7940 Sâkar (1), *recompense*

BREAKING
4290 machtereth (1), *burglary*
4866 mishbêr (1), *vaginal opening*
5927 'âlâh (1), to *ascend, be high, mount*
6524 pârach (2), to *break forth; to bloom; to fly*
6556 perets (3), *break, gap*
6565 pârar (2), to *break up; to violate, frustrate*
6979 qûwr (1), to *throw forth; to wall up*
7667 sheber (2), *fracture; ruin*
7670 shibrôwn (1), *ruin*
2800 klasis (2), *fracturing*
2806 klaō (1), to *break bread*
3847 parabasis (1), *violation, breaking*

BREAKINGS
7667 sheber (1), *fracture; ruin*

BREAST
2306 chădîy (Ch.) (1), *breast*
2373 châzeh (11), animal *breast* meat
7699 shad (3), female *breast*
4738 stēthŏs (3), area of the human *chest*

BREASTPLATE
2833 chôshen (25), *gorget*
8302 shiryôwn (1), *corslet, coat of mail*
2382 thōrax (2), *corslet, chest*

BREASTPLATES
2382 thōrax (3), *corslet, chest*

BREASTS
1717 dad (2), female *breast* or *bosom*
2373 châzeh (2), animal *breast* meat
3824 lêbâb (1), *heart*
5845 'ăṭîyn (1), *receptacle* for milk
7699 shad (19), female *breast*
4738 stēthŏs (2), area of the human *chest*

BREATH
5315 nephesh (1), *life; breath; soul; wind*
5396 nishmâ' (Ch.) (1), *breath, life*
5397 nᵉshâmâh (12), *breath, life*
7307 rûwach (27), *breath; wind; life*-spirit
4157 pnŏē (1), *breeze; breath*

BREATHE
3307 yâphêach (1), *puffing; breathing out*
5301 nâphach (1), to *inflate, blow hard*
5397 nᵉshâmâh (2), *breath, life*

BREATHED
5301 nâphach (1), to *inflate, blow hard*
5397 nᵉshâmâh (2), *breath, life*
1720 ĕmphusaō (1), to *blow at or on*

BREATHETH
5397 nᵉshâmâh (1), *breath, life*

BREATHING
7309 rᵉvâchâh (1), *relief*
1709 ĕmpnĕō (1), to *be animated by*

BRED
7311 rûwm (1), to *be high; to rise or raise*

BREECHES
4370 miknâç (5), *drawers concealing* the privates

BREED
1121 bên (1), *people* of a class or kind
8317 shârats (1), to *swarm, or abound*

BREEDING
4476 mimshâq (1), *possession*

BRETHREN
251 'âch (329), *brother; relative; member*
252 'ach (Ch.) (1), *brother; relative*
80 adĕlphŏs (225), *brother*
81 adĕlphŏtēs (1), *fraternity, brotherhood*
5360 philadĕlphia (1), *fraternal affection*
5361 philadĕlphŏs (1), *fraternal*
5569 psĕudadĕlphŏs (2), *pretended associate*

BRETHREN'S
251 'âch (1), *brother; relative; member*

BRIBE
3724 kôpher (2), *redemption*-price

BRIBERY
7810 shachad (1), to *bribe; gift*

BRIBES
7810 shachad (3), to *bribe; gift*

BRICK
3835 lâban (3), to *make bricks*
3843 lᵉbênâh (4), *brick*

BRICKKILN
4404 malbên (3), *brick-kiln*

BRICKS
3843 lᵉbênâh (4), *brick*

BRIDE
3618 kallâh (9), *bride; son's wife*
3565 numphē (5), *young married woman*

BRIDECHAMBER
3567 numphōn (3), *bridal room*

BRIDEGROOM
2860 châthân (8), *bridegroom*
3566 numphiŏs (15), *bridegroom*

BRIDEGROOM'S
3566 numphiŏs (1), *bridegroom*

BRIDLE
4269 machçôwm (1), *muzzle*
4964 metheg (3), *bit*
7448 reçen (4), *jaw restraint* of a horse
5469 chalinŏs (1), *bit or bridle*

BRIDLES
5469 chalinŏs (1), *bit or bridle*

BRIDLETH
5468 chalinagōgĕō (1), to *curb, hold in check*

BRIEFLY
346 anakĕphalaiŏmai (1), to *sum up*
1223+3641 dia (1), *through,* by means of

BRIER
2312 chêdeq (1), *prickly plant*
5544 çillôwn (1), *prickle*
5636 çarpâd (1), *stinging nettle*

BRIERS
1303 barqân (2), *thorn, biers*
5621 çârâb (1), *thistle*
8068 shâmîyr (8), *thorn;* (poss.) *diamond*
5146 tribŏlŏs (1), *thorny caltrop plant*

BRIGANDINE
5630 çiyrôn (1), coat of *mail, scale armor*

BRIGANDINES
5630 çiyrôn (1), coat of *mail, scale armor*

BRIGHT
216 'ôwr (1), *luminary; lightning; happiness*
925 bâhîyr (1), *shining, bright*
934 bôhereth (11), *whitish, bright spot*
1300 bârâq (1), *lightning; flash of lightning*

English

1305 bârar (1), to *brighten; purify*
2385 chăzîyz (1), *flash of lightning*
3851 lahab (1), *flame of fire; flash of a blade*
3974 mâ'ôwr (1), *luminary, light source*
4803 mâraṭ (1), to *polish; to make bald*
4838 mâraq (1), to *polish; to sharpen; to rinse*
5051 nôgahh (1), *brilliancy*
6219 'âshôwth (1), *polished*
6247 'esheth (1), *fabric*
7043 qâlal (1), to *be, make light*
796 astrapē (1), *lightning; light's glare*
2986 lamprŏs (2), *radiant; clear*
5460 phōtĕinŏs (1), *well-illuminated*

BRIGHTNESS
2096 zôhar (2), *brilliancy, shining*
2122 zîyv (Ch.) (2), *cheerfulness*
3314 yiph'âh (2), *splendor, beauty*
3368 yâqâr (1), *valuable*
5051 nôgahh (11), *brilliancy*
5054 nᵉgôhâh (1), *splendor, luster*
541 apaugasma (1), *effulgence, radiance*
2015 ĕpiphanĕia (1), *manisfestation*
2987 lamprŏtēs (1), *brilliancy*

BRIM
7097 qâtseh (1), *extremity*
8193 sâphâh (7), *lip; edge, margin*
507 anō (1), *upward or on the top, heavenward*

BRIMSTONE
1614 gophrîyth (7), *sulphur*
2303 thĕiŏn (7), *sulphur*
2306 thĕiōdēs (1), *sulphurous yellow*

BRING
338 'îy (1), solitary wild *creature that howls*
503 'âlaph (1), *increase by thousands*
622 'âçaph (2), to *gather, collect*
858 'âthâh (Ch.) (2), to *arrive; go*
935 bôw' (248), to *go or come*
1069 bâkar (1), to *give the birthright*
1431 gâdal (1), to *be great, make great*
1518 gîyach (1), to *issue forth; to burst forth*
1876 dâshâ' (1), to *sprout new plants*
1980 hâlak (1), to *walk; live a certain way*
2142 zâkar (2), to *remember; to mention*

2342 chûwl (1), to *dance, whirl; to writhe* in pain
2381 Chăzîy'êl (1), *seen of God*
2986 yâbal (5), to *bring*
3051 yâhab (2), to *give*
3205 yâlad (17), to *bear young; to father a child*
3212 yâlak (3), to *walk; to live; to carry*
3254 yâçaph (1), to *add or augment*
3318 yâtsâ' (73), to *go, bring out*
3381 yârad (24), to *descend*
3513 kâbad (1), to be *heavy, severe, dull*
3533 kâbash (1), to *conquer, subjugate*
3665 kâna' (3), to *humiliate, vanquish*
3947 lâqach (17), to *take*
4608 ma'ăleh (1), *elevation; platform*
4672 mâtsâ' (1), to *find or acquire; to occur*
5060 nâga' (3), to *strike*
5066 nâgash (14), to *be, come, bring near*
5080 nâdach (1), to *push off, scattered*
5107 nûwb (1), to *(make) flourish; to utter*
5375 nâsâ' (10), to *lift up*
5381 nâsag (1), to *reach*
5414 nâthan (11), to *give*
5437 çâbab (2), to *surround*
5647 'âbad (1), to *do, work, serve*
5674 'âbar (1), to *cross over; to transition*
5924 'êllâ' (Ch.) (3), *above*
5927 'âlâh (35), to *ascend, be high, mount*
6049 'ânan (1), to *cover, becloud; to act covertly*
6213 'âsâh (9), to *do or make*
6315 pûwach (1), to *blow, to fan, kindle; to utter*
6398 pâlach (1), to *slice; to break* open; to *pierce*
6509 pârâh (2), to *bear fruit*
6779 tsâmach (1), to *sprout*
6805 tsâ'ad (1), to *pace, step regularly*
7034 qâlâh (1), to *hold in contempt*
7126 qârab (36), to *approach, bring near*
7311 rûwm (1), to be *high; to rise or raise*
7392 râkab (1), to *ride*
7665 shâbar (1), to *burst*
7725 shûwb (72), to *turn back; to return*
7760 sûwm (1), to *put, place*
7817 shâchach (1), to *sink or depress*
7896 shîyth (1), to *place*
7971 shâlach (1), to *send away*
8045 shâmad (1), to *desolate*

8074 shâmêm (2), to *devastate; to stupefy*
8213 shâphêl (4), to *humiliate*
8317 shârats (3), to *wriggle, swarm*
71 agō (14), to *lead; to bring, drive; to weigh*
114 athĕtĕō (1), to *disesteem, neutralize*
321 anagō (2), to *lead up; to bring out; to sail*
363 anamimnēskō (1), to *remind; to recollect*
518 apaggĕllō (2), to *announce, proclaim*
520 apagō (1), to *take away*
667 apŏhĕrō (1), to *bear off, carry away*
1295 diasōzō (1), to *cure, preserve, rescue*
1396 dŏulagōgĕō (1), to *enslave, subdue*
1402 dŏulŏō (1), to *enslave*
1521 ĕisagō (1), to *lead into*
1533 ĕisphĕrō (2), to *carry inward*
1625 ĕktrĕphō (1), to *cherish or train*
1627 ĕkphĕrō (1), to *bear out; to produce*
1863 ĕpagō (2), *inflict; charge*
2018 ĕpiphĕrō (1), to *inflict, bring upon*
2036 ĕpō (1), to *speak or say*
2097 ĕuaggĕlizō (2), to *announce good news*
2592 karpŏphŏrĕō (4), to *be fertile*
2609 katagō (3), to *lead down; to moor a vessel*
2615 katadŏulŏō (2), to *enslave utterly*
2673 katargĕō (1), to *be, render entirely useless*
3919 parĕisagō (1), to *lead in aside*
4160 pŏiĕō (6), to *do*
4311 prŏpĕmpō (3), to *send forward*
4317 prŏsagō (2), to *bring near*
4374 prŏsphĕrō (2), to *present to; to treat as*
5062 tĕssarakŏnta (1), *forty*
5088 tiktō (3), to *produce from seed*
5179 tupŏs (1), *shape*, i.e. *statue or resemblance*
5342 phĕrō (17), to *bear or carry*
5461 phōtizō (1), to *shine or to brighten up*

BRINGERS
539 'âman (1), to *be firm, faithful, true; to trust*

BRINGEST
935 bôw' (1), to *go, come*
1319 bâsar (3), to *announce* (good news)
1533 ĕisphĕrō (1), to *carry inward*

BRINGETH
935 bôw' (6), to *go or come*
1069 bâkar (1), to *give the birthright*
1319 bâsar (5), to *announce* (good news)
2142 zâkar (1), to *remember*
2659 châphêr (1), to *shamë, reproach*
3318 yâtsâ' (18), to *go, bring out*
3381 yârad (2), to *descend*
3615 kâlâh (1), to *complete, prepare*
5060 nâga' (1), to *strike*
5107 nûwb (1), to *(make) flourish; to utter*
5148 nâchâh (2), to *guide*
5414 nâthan (3), to *give*
5927 'âlâh (3), to *ascend, be high, mount*
6213 'âsâh (1), to *do or make*
6331 pûwr (1), to *crush*
6445 pânaq (1), to *enervate, reduce vigor*
6779 tsâmach (1), to *sprout*
7725 shûwb (3), to *turn back; to return*
7737 shâvâh (1), to *level, equalize; to resemble*
7817 shâchach (1), to *sink or depress*
8213 shâphêl (1), to *humiliate*
399 anaphĕrō (1), to *take up; to lead up*
616 apŏkuĕō (1), to *bring into being*
1521 ĕisagō (1), to *lead into*
1544 ĕkballō (3), to *throw out*
2592 karpŏphŏrĕō (2), to *be fertile*
4160 pŏiĕō (7), to *do*
4393 prŏphĕrō (2), to *bear forward*
4992 sōtēriŏn (1), *defender or defence*
5088 tiktō (2), to *produce from seed*
5342 phĕrō (2), to *bear or carry*

BRINGING
935 bôw' (6), to *go, come*
2142 zâkar (1), to *remember; to mention*
3318 yâtsâ' (3), to *go, bring out*
5375 nâsâ' (3), to *lift up*
7725 shûwb (2), to *turn back; to return*
71 agō (1), to *lead; to bring, drive; to weigh*
163 aichmalōtizō (2), to *make captive*
1863 ĕpagō (1), *inflict; charge*
1898 ĕpĕisagōgē (1), *introduction*
4160 pŏiĕō (1), to *do*
5342 phĕrō (3), to *bear or carry*

BRINK
7097 qâtseh (1), *extremity*
8193 sâphâh (5), *lip; edge, margin*

BROAD
7338 rachab (1), *width, expanse*
7338+3027 rachab (1), *width, expanse*
7339 rᵉchôb (3), *myriad*
7341 rôchab (21), *width*
7342 râchâb (5), *roomy, spacious*
7554 râqa' (1), to *pound*
7555 riqqûa' (1), *thin metallic plate*
2149 ĕuruchŏrŏs (1), spacious, wide
4115 platunō (1), to widen

BROADER
7342 râchâb (1), *roomy, spacious*

BROIDED
4117 plĕgma (1), plait or braid of hair

BROIDERED
7553 riqmâh (7), *embroidery*
8665 tashbêts (1), *checkered stuff*

BROILED
3702 ŏptŏs (1), roasted, broiled

BROKEN
6 'âbad (1), *perish; destroy*
1234 bâqa' (6), to *cleave, break, tear open*
1638 gâraç (1), to *crush, break; to dissolve*
1792 dâkâ' (3), to *pulverize; be contrite*
1794 dâkâh (3), to *collapse; contrite*
1854 dâqaq (1), to *crush; crumble*
1986 hâlam (2), to *strike, beat, stamp, conquer*
2040 hâraç (4), to *pull down; break, destroy*
2490 châlal (1), to *profane, defile*
2844 chath (6), *terror*
2865 châthath (6), to *break down*
3807 kâthath (1), to *bruise or strike*
4535 maççâch (1), *cordon; barrier; in turn*
4790 mᵉrôwach (1), *bruised, pounded*
5181 nâchath (2), to *sink, descend; to press*
5218 nâkê' (3), *smitten; afflicted*
5310 nâphats (1), to *dash to pieces; to scatter*
5421 nâtha' (1), to *tear out*
5422 nâthats (5), to *tear down*
5423 nâthaq (7), to *tear off*
5927 'âlâh (1), to *ascend, be high, mount*

6105 'âtsam (1), to *be, make powerful*
6209 'ârar (1), to *bare; to demolish*
6331 pûwr (1), to *crush*
6480 pâtsam (1), to *rend, tear* by earthquake
6524 pârach (2), to *break forth; to bloom*
6531 perek (1), *severity*
6555 pârats (12), to *break out*
6565 pârar (9), to *break up; to violate, frustrate*
7280 râga' (1), to *stir up*
7462 râ'âh (1), to *tend a flock, i.e. pasture it*
7465 rô'âh (1), *breakage*
7489 râ'a' (2), to *break to pieces*
7533 râtsats (4), to *crack in pieces, smash*
7616 shâbâb (1), *fragment, i.e. ruin*
7665 shâbar (65), to *burst*
8406 tᵉbar (Ch.) (1), to *be fragile*
1358 diŏrussō (2), to penetrate burglariously
1575 ĕkklaō (3), to exscind, cut off
1846 ĕxŏrussō (1), to dig out
2608 katagnumi (1), to crack apart
2801 klasma (2), piece, bit
2806 klaō (3), to break bread
3089 luō (6), to loosen
4917 sunthlaō (2), to dash together, shatter
4937 suntribō (3), to crush completely
4977 schizō (1), to split or sever

BROKENFOOTED
7667+7272 sheber (1), *fracture; ruin*

BROKENHANDED
7667+3027 sheber (1), *fracture; ruin*

BROKENHEARTED
7665+3820 shâbar (1), to *burst*
4937+2588 suntribō (1), to crush completely

BROOD
3555 nŏssia (1), hen's brood

BROOK
4323 mîykâl (1), *brook*
5158 nachal (37), *valley, ravine; mine shaft*
5493 chĕimarrhŏs (1), winter-torrent

BROOKS
650 'âphîyq (1), *valley; stream; mighty, strong*
2975 yᵉ'ôr (4), Nile *River*; Tigris *River*
5158 nachal (9), *valley, ravine; mine shaft*

BROTH
4839 mârâq (2), *soup-broth*

6564 pârâq (1), *fragments* in soup

BROTHER
251 'âch (244), *brother; relative; member*
1730 dôwd (1), *beloved, friend; relative*
2992 yâbam (2), to *marry* a brother's widow
2993 yâbâm (2), *husband's brother*
7453 rêa' (1), *associate; one close*
80 adĕlphŏs (109), brother

BROTHER'S
251 'âch (25), *brother; relative; member*
2994 yᵉbêmeth (3), dead brother's widow, i.e. *sister-in-law*
80 adĕlphŏs (7), brother

BROTHERHOOD
264 'achăvâh (1), *fraternity; brotherhood*
81 adĕlphŏtēs (1), fraternity, brotherhood

BROTHERLY
251 'âch (1), *brother; relative; member*
5360 philadĕlphia (5), fraternal affection

BROTHERS'
1730 dôwd (1), *beloved, friend; relative*

BROUGHT
539 'âman (5), to *be firm, faithful, true; to trust*
622 'âçaph (3), to *gather, collect*
656 'âphêç (1), to *cease*
857 'âthâh (1), to *arrive; go*
858 'âthâh (Ch.) (7), to *arrive; go*
935 bôw' (264), to *go or come*
1197 bâ'ar (1), to *be brutish; be senseless*
1310 bâshal (1), to *boil up, cook; to ripen*
1319 bâsar (2), to *announce* (good news)
1431 gâdal (6), to *be great, make great*
1468 gûwz (1), to *pass rapidly*
1540 gâlâh (1), to *denude; uncover*
1541 gᵉlâh (Ch.) (1), to *reveal mysteries*
1589 gânab (1), to *thieve; to deceive*
1809 dâlal (3), to *slacken, dangle*
1820 dâmâh (2), to *be silent; to fail, cease*
1946 hûwk (Ch.) (1), to *go, come*
1961 hâyâh (2), to *exist, i.e. be or become*
2254 châbal (2), to *bind* by a pledge; to *pervert*
2342 chûwl (3), to *dance, whirl; to writhe* in pain
2659 châphêr (3), to *be ashamed, disappointed*

2986 yâbal (7), to *bring*
2987 yᵉbal (Ch.) (2), to *bring*
3205 yâlad (12), to *bear young; to father a child*
3212 yâlak (8), to *walk; to live; to carry*
3218 yekeq (1), young *locust*
3318 yâtsâ' (127), to *go, bring out*
3381 yârad (17), to *descend*
3467 yâsha' (2), to *make safe, free*
3474 yâshar (1), to *be straight; to make right*
3533 kâbash (3), to *conquer, subjugate*
3665 kâna' (4), to *humiliate, vanquish*
3766 kâra' (2), to *make miserable*
3947 lâqach (8), to *take*
4161 môwtsâ' (2), *going forth*
4355 mâkak (2), to *tumble; to perish*
4551 maççâ' (1), *stone quarry; projectile*
5060 nâga' (1), to *strike*
5066 nâgash (13), to *be, come, bring near*
5090 nâhag (4), to *drive forth; to carry away*
5148 nâchâh (2), to *guide*
5265 nâça' (3), *start* on a journey
5375 nâsâ' (13), to *lift up*
5414 nâthan (3), to *give*
5437 çâbab (1), to *surround*
5493 çûwr (1), to *turn off*
5674 'âbar (6), to *cross over; to transition*
5927 'âlâh (65), to *ascend, be high, mount*
5954 'ălal (Ch.) (4), to *go in; to lead in*
6030 'ânâh (1), to *respond, answer*
6213 'âsâh (3), to *do or make*
6565 pârar (1), to *break up; to violate, frustrate*
6819 tsâ'ar (6), to *be small; be trivial*
6908 qâbats (1), to *collect, assemble*
7126 qârab (27), to *approach, bring near*
7127 qᵉrêb (Ch.) (1), to *approach, bring near*
7136 qârâh (1), to *bring about; to impose*
7235 râbâh (1), to *increase*
7311 rûwm (1), to *be high; to rise or raise*
7323 rûwts (1), to *run*
7392 râkab (1), to *ride*
7617 shâbâh (1), to *transport* into captivity
7725 shûwb (39), to *turn back; to return*
7760 sûwm (4), to *put, place*
7817 shâchach (3), to *sink or depress*

English

7971 shâlach (1), to *send away*
8213 shâphêl (3), to *humiliate*
8239 shâphath (1), to *place* or *put*
8317 shârats (2), to *swarm*, or *abound*
71 agō (32), to *lead*; to *bring, drive*; to *weigh*
321 anagō (4), to *lead up*; to *bring out*; to *sail*
397 anatrĕphō (1), to *rear, care for*
654 apŏstrĕphō (1), to *turn away* or *back*
985 blastanō (1), to *yield fruit*
1080 gĕnnaō (1), to *procreate, regenerate*
1096 ginŏmai (2), to *be, become*
1325 didōmi (1), to *give*
1402 dŏulŏō (1), to *enslave*
1521 ĕisagō (7), to *lead into*
1533 ĕisphĕrō (2), to *carry inward*
1627 ĕkphĕrō (1), to *bear out*; to *produce*
1806 ĕxagō (6), to *lead forth, escort*
1850 ĕxŏusiazō (1), to *control, master another*
2018 ĕpiphĕrō (2), to *inflict, bring upon*
2049 ĕrēmŏō (2), to *lay waste*
2064 ĕrchŏmai (1), to *go*
2097 ĕuaggĕlizō (1), to *announce good news*
2164 ĕuphŏrĕō (1), to *be fertile, produce a crop*
2476 histēmi (1), to *stand, establish*
2601 katabibazō (1), to *cause to bring down*
2609 katagō (4), to *lead down*; to *moor a vessel*
2865 kŏmizō (1), to *provide for*
2989 lampō (1), to *radiate brilliancy*
3350 mĕtŏikĕsia (1), *exile, deportation*
3860 paradidōmi (1), to *hand over*
3920 parĕisaktŏs (1), *smuggled in, infiltrated*
3930 parĕchō (2), to *hold near*, i.e. to *present*
3936 paristēmi (2), to *stand beside, present*
4160 pŏiĕō (1), to *make*
4254 prŏagō (3), to *lead forward; to precede*
4311 prŏpĕmpō (4), to *send forward*
4317 prŏsagō (1), to *bring near*
4374 prŏsphĕrō (15), to *present to; to treat as*
4851 sumphĕrō (1), to *collect; to conduce*
4939 suntrŏphŏs (1), one *brought up with*
5013 tapĕinŏō (1), to *depress; to humiliate*

5044 tĕknŏtrŏphĕō (1), to *be a child-rearer*
5088 tiktō (4), to *produce from seed*
5142 trĕphō (1), to *nurse, feed, care for*
5342 phĕrō (17), to *bear or carry*
5461 phōtizō (1), to *shine* or to *brighten* up

BROUGHTEST
935 bōw' (4), to *go or come*
3318 yâtsâ' (7), to *go, bring out*
5927 'âlâh (2), to *ascend, be high, mount*

BROW
4696 mêtsach (1), *forehead*
3790 ŏphrus (1), eye-*brow*

BROWN
2345 chûwm (4), *sunburnt* or *swarthy*

BRUISE
1792 dâkâ' (1), to *pulverize*; be *contrite*
1854 dâqaq (1), to *crush; crumble*
7490 r^e'a' (Ch.) (1), to *shatter, dash to pieces*
7667 sheber (2), *fracture; ruin*
7779 shûwph (2), to *gape*, i.e. *snap* at
4937 suntribō (1), to *crush completely*

BRUISED
1792 dâkâ' (1), to *pulverize*; be *contrite*
1854 dâqaq (1), to *crush; crumble*
4600 mâ'ak (1), to *press, to pierce, emasculate*
6213 'âsâh (2), to *do or make*
7533 râtsats (2), to *crack in pieces, smash*
2352 thrauō (1), to *crush*
4937 suntribō (1), to *crush completely*

BRUISES
2250 chabbûwrâh (1), *weal, bruise*

BRUISING
6213 'âsâh (1), to *do or make*
4937 suntribō (1), to *crush completely*

BRUIT
8052 sh^emûw'âh (1), *announcement*
8088 shêma' (1), *something heard*

BRUTE
249 alŏgŏs (2), *irrational, not reasonable*

BRUTISH
1197 bâ'ar (11), to *be brutish, be senseless*

BUCKET
1805 d^elîy (1), *pail, bucket*

BUCKETS
1805 d^elîy (1), *pail, bucket*

BUCKLER
4043 mâgên (6), small *shield (buckler); skin*
5507 çôchêrâh (1), *surrounding shield*
6793 tsinnâh (3), large *shield; piercing cold*
7420 rômach (1), iron *pointed spear*

BUCKLERS
4043 mâgên (3), small *shield (buckler); skin*
6793 tsinnâh (2), large *shield; piercing cold*

BUD
4161 môwtsâ' (1), *going forth*
5132 nûwts (1), to *fly away, leave*
6524 pârach (2), to *break forth; to bloom*
6525 perach (1), *calyx flower; bloom*
6779 tsâmach (6), to *sprout*

BUDDED
5132 nûwts (1), to *fly away, leave*
6524 pârach (3), to *break forth; to bloom*
985 blastanō (1), to *yield fruit*

BUDS
6525 perach (1), *calyx flower; bloom*

BUFFET
2852 kŏlaphizō (2), to *strike*

BUFFETED
2852 kŏlaphizō (3), to *strike*

BUILD
1124 b^enâ' (Ch.) (6), to *build*
1129 bânâh (140), to *build; to establish*
456 anŏikŏdŏmĕō (2), to *rebuild*
2026 ĕpŏikŏdŏmĕō (2), to *rear up, build up*
3618 ŏikŏdŏmĕō (12), *construct; edification*

BUILDED
1124 b^enâ' (Ch.) (10), to *build*
1129 bânâh (36), to *build; to establish*
2680 kataskĕuazō (2), to *construct; to arrange*
3618 ŏikŏdŏmĕō (1), *construct; edification*
4925 sunŏikŏdŏmĕō (1), to *construct*

BUILDEDST
1129 bânâh (1), to *build; to establish*

BUILDER
5079 tĕchnitēs (1), *artisan, craftsman*

BUILDERS
1129 bânâh (9), to *build; to establish*
3618 ŏikŏdŏmĕō (5), *construct; edification*

BUILDEST
1129 bânâh (3), to *build; to establish*
3618 ŏikŏdŏmĕō (2), *construct; edification*

BUILDETH
1129 bânâh (7), to *build; to establish*
2026 ĕpŏikŏdŏmĕō (2), to *rear up, build up*

BUILDING
1124 b^enâ' (Ch.) (3), to *build*
1129 bânâh (15), to *build; to establish*
1140 binyâh (1), *structure*
1146 binyân (7), *edifice, building*
1147 binyân (Ch.) (1), *edifice, building*
4746 m^eqâreh (1), *frame of timbers*
1739 ĕndōmēsis (1), *structure*
2026 ĕpŏikŏdŏmĕō (1), to *rear up, build up*
2937 ktisis (1), *formation*
3618 ŏikŏdŏmĕō (1), *construct; edification*
3619 ŏikŏdŏmē (3), *structure; edification*

BUILDINGS
3619 ŏikŏdŏmē (3), *structure; edification*

BUILT
1124 b^enâ' (Ch.) (1), to *build*
1129 bânâh (155), to *build; to establish*
2026 ĕpŏikŏdŏmĕō (3), to *rear up, build up*
2680 kataskĕuazō (1), to *construct; to arrange*
3618 ŏikŏdŏmĕō (10), *construct; edification*

BUKKI
1231 Buqqiy (5), *wasteful*

BUKKIAH
1232 Buqqîyâh (2), *wasting of Jehovah*

BUL
945 Bûwl (1), *rain*

BULL
7794 shôwr (1), *bullock*
8377 t^e'ôw (1), *antelope*

BULLOCK
1121+1241 bên (3), *son, descendant*
1241 bâqâr (1), *plowing ox; herd*
5695 'êgel (1), bull-*calf*
6499 par (89), *bullock*
7794 shôwr (10), *bullock*

BULLOCK'S
6499 par (3), *bullock*

BULLOCKS
1241 bâqâr (4), *plowing ox; herd*
5695 'êgel (1), bull-*calf*
6499 par (36), *bullock*
7794 shôwr (1), *bullock*
8450 tôwr (Ch.) (3), *bull*

BULLS
47 'abbîyr (4), *mighty*

1241 bâqâr (1), *plowing ox; herd*
6499 par (2), *bullock*
5022 taurŏs (2), *bullock, ox*

BULRUSH
100 'agmôwn (1), *rush; rope of rushes*

BULRUSHES
1573 gôme' (2), *papyrus plant*

BULWARKS
2426 chêyl (1), *entrenchment, rampart*
2430 chêylâh (1), *entrenchment, rampart*
4685 mâtsôwd (1), *net or snare; besieging tower*
4692 mâtsôwr (1), *siege-mound; distress*
6438 pinnâh (1), *pinnacle; chieftain*

BUNAH
946 Bûwnâh (1), *discretion*

BUNCH
92 'ăguddâh (1), *band; bundle; knot; arch*

BUNCHES
1707 dabbesheth (1), *hump of a camel*
6778 tsammûwq (2), *lump of dried grapes*

BUNDLE
6872 tsᵉrôwr (3), *parcel; kernel or particle*
4128 plēthŏs (1), *large number, throng*

BUNDLES
6872 tsᵉrôwr (1), *parcel; kernel or particle*
1197 dĕsmē (1), *bundle*

BUNNI
1137 Bânîy (3), *built*

BURDEN
3053 yᵉhâb (1), *lot given*
4853 massâ' (52), *burden, utterance*
4858 massâ'âh (1), *conflagration from the rising of smoke*
4864 mas'êth (1), *raising; beacon; present*
5445 çâbal (1), to *carry*
5448 çôbel (3), *load, burden*
5449 çabbâl (1), *porter, carrier*
6006 'âmaç (1), to *impose a burden*
922 barŏs (3), *load, abundance, authority*
1117 gŏmŏs (1), *cargo, wares or freight*
2599 katabarĕŏ (1), to *be a burden*
5413 phŏrtiŏn (2), *burden, task or service*

BURDENED
916 barĕŏ (1), to *weigh down, cause pressure*
2347 thlipsis (1), *pressure, trouble*

BURDENS
92 'ăguddâh (1), *band; bundle; knot; arch*
4853 massâ' (5), *burden, utterance*
4864 mas'êth (2), *raising; beacon; present*
4942 mishpâth (1), *pair of stalls for cattle*
5447 çêbel (1), *load; forced labor*
5449 çabbâl (5), *porter, carrier*
5450 çᵉbâlâh (6), *porterage; forced labor*
922 barŏs (1), *load, abundance, authority*
5413 phŏrtiŏn (3), *burden, task or service*

BURDENSOME
4614 ma'ămâçâh (1), *burdensomeness*
4 abarēs (1), *not burdensome*
1722+922 ĕn (1), *in; during; because of*
2655 katanarkaŏ (2), to *be a burden*

BURIAL
6900 qᵉbûwrâh (4), *sepulchre*
1779 ĕntaphiazō (1), to *enswathe for burial*

BURIED
6912 qâbar (96), to *inter, pile up*
2290 thaptō (7), to *celebrate funeral rites*
4916 sunthaptō (2), to *be buried with*

BURIERS
6912 qâbar (1), to *inter, pile up*

BURN
1197 bâ'ar (19), to *be brutish, be senseless*
1754 dûwr (1), *circle; ball; pile*
2734 chârâh (1), to *blaze*
2787 chârar (1), to *melt, burn, dry up*
3344 yâqad (3), to *burn*
3857 lâhaṭ (1), to *blaze*
4729 miqṭâr (1), *hearth*
5400 nâsaq (1), to *catch fire*
5927 'âlâh (2), to *ascend, be high, mount*
6702 tsûwth (1), to *blaze, set on fire*
6999 qâṭar (59), to *turn into fragrance by fire*
8313 sâraph (40), to *be, set on fire*
2370 thumiaŏ (1), to *offer aromatic fumes*
2545 kaiō (1), to *set on fire*
2618 katakaiō (4), to *consume wholly by burning*
4448 purŏō (2), to *be ignited, glow; inflamed*

BURNED
1197 bâ'ar (8), to *be brutish, be senseless*

BURDENS *(col 2 continues)*

2787 chârar (7), to *melt, burn, dry up*
3341 yâtsath (9), to *burn or set on fire*
3554 kâvâh (2), to *blister, be scorched*
3857 lâhaṭ (2), to *blaze*
5375 nâsâ' (2), to *lift up*
6866 tsârab (1), to *burn*
6999 qâṭar (19), to *turn into fragrance by fire*
8313 sâraph (33), to *be, set on fire*
8314 sârâph (1), *poisonous serpent*
8316 sᵉrêphâh (1), *cremation*
1572 ĕkkaiō (1), to *inflame deeply*
1714 ĕmprēthō (1), to *burn, set on fire*
2545 kaiō (3), to *set on fire*
2618 katakaiō (6), to *consume wholly by burning*
2740 kausis (1), *act of burning*
4448 purŏō (1), to *be ignited, glow; inflamed*

BURNETH
1197 bâ'ar (4), to *be brutish, be senseless*
2142 zâkar (1), to *remember; to mention*
3344 yâqad (1), to *burn*
3857 lâhaṭ (2), to *blaze*
4348 mikvâh (1), *burn*
5635 çâraph (1), to *cremate*
6919 qâdach (1), to *inflame*
6999 qâṭar (2), to *turn into fragrance by fire*
8313 sâraph (4), to *be, set on fire*
2545 kaiō (1), to *set on fire*

BURNING
784 'êsh (3), *fire*
1197 bâ'ar (6), to *be brutish, be senseless*
1513 gechel (1), *ember, hot coal*
1814 dâlaq (1), to *flame; to pursue*
1815 dᵉlaq (Ch.) (1), to *flame, burn*
2746 charchûr (1), *hot fever*
3344 yâqad (3), to *burn*
3345 yᵉqad (Ch.) (10), to *burn*
3346 yᵉqêdâ' (Ch.) (1), *consuming fire*
3350 yᵉqôwd (1), *burning, blazing*
3555 kᵉvîyâh (1), *branding, scar*
3587 kîy (1), *brand or scar*
3940 lappîyd (1), *flaming torch, lamp or flame*
4169 môwqᵉdâh (1), *fuel*
4348 mikvâh (4), *burn*
6867 tsârebeth (2), *conflagration*
6920 qaddachath (1), *inflammation*

BUSH *(col 4)*

6999 qâṭar (1), to *turn into fragrance by fire*
7565 resheph (1), *flame*
8316 sᵉrêphâh (9), *cremation*
2545 kaiō (6), to *set on fire*
2742 kausōn (1), *burning heat, hot day*
4451 purōsis (2), *ignition; conflagration, calamity*

BURNINGS
4168 môwqêd (1), *conflagration, burning*
4955 misrâphâh (2), *cremation*

BURNISHED
7044 qâlâl (1), *brightened, polished*

BURNT
398 'âkal (1), to *eat*
1197 bâ'ar (6), to *be brutish, be senseless*
3632 kâlîyl (1), *whole, entire; complete; whole*
4198 mâzeh (1), *exhausted, empty*
5927 'âlâh (1), to *ascend, be high, mount*
5928 'ălâh (Ch.) (1), *wholly consumed in fire*
5930 'ôlâh (284), *sacrifice wholly consumed in fire*
6999 qâṭar (24), to *turn into fragrance by fire*
8313 sâraph (36), to *be, set on fire*
8316 sᵉrêphâh (2), *cremation*
2618 katakaiō (2), to *consume wholly by burning*
3646 hŏlŏkautōma (3), *wholly-consumed*

BURST
1234 bâqa' (1), to *cleave, break, tear open*
5423 nâthaq (4), to *tear off*
6555 pârats (1), to *break out*
2997 laschō (1), to *crack open*
4486 rhēgnumi (2), to *break, burst forth*

BURSTING
4386 mᵉkittâh (1), *fracture*

BURY
6912 qâbar (33), to *inter, pile up*
1779 ĕntaphiazō (1), to *enswathe for burial*
2290 thaptō (4), to *celebrate funeral rites*
5027 taphē (1), *burial*

BURYING
6912 qâbar (2), to *inter, pile up*
1780 ĕntaphiasmŏs (2), *preparation for burial*

BURYINGPLACE
6913 qeber (7), *sepulchre*

BUSH
5572 çᵉneh (6), *bramble*
942 batŏs (5), *brier*

English

BUSHEL
3426 mŏdiŏs (3), dry measure of volume

BUSHES
5097 nahălôl (1), pasture
7880 sîyach (2), shrubbery

BUSHY
8534 taltal (1), wavy

BUSINESS
1697 dâbâr (8), word; matter; thing
4399 mᵉlâ'kâh (12), work; property
4639 ma'ăseh (1), action; labor
6045 'inyân (2), employment, labor
2398 idiŏs (1), private or separate
4229 pragma (1), matter, deed, affair
4710 spŏudē (1), despatch; eagerness
5532 chrĕia (1), affair; occasion, demand

BUSY
6213 'âsâh (1), to do or make

BUSYBODIES
4020 pĕriĕrgazŏmai (1), to meddle
4021 pĕriĕrgŏs (1), busybody; magic

BUSYBODY
244 allotriĕpiskŏpŏs (1), meddler, busybody

BUTLER
4945 mashqeh (8), butler; drink; well-watered

BUTLERS
4945 mashqeh (1), butler; drink; well-watered

BUTLERSHIP
4945 mashqeh (1), butler; drink; well-watered

BUTTER
2529 chem'âh (10), curds, milk or cheese
4260 machămâ'âh (1), buttery; flattery

BUTTOCKS
4667 miphsâ'âh (1), crotch area
8357 shêthâh (2), seat i.e. buttock

BUY
3739 kârâh (1), to purchase by bargaining
3947 lâqach (2), to take
7066 qᵉnâ' (Ch.) (1), to purchase
7069 qânâh (24), to create; to procure
7666 shâbar (14), to deal in cereal grain
59 agŏrazō (13), to purchase; to redeem
1710 ĕmpŏrĕuŏmai (1), to trade, do business

BUYER
7069 qânâh (3), to create; to procure

BUYEST
7069 qânâh (2), to create; to procure

BUYETH
3947 lâqach (1), to take
59 agŏrazō (2), to purchase; to redeem

BUZ
938 Bûwz (3), disrespect, scorn

BUZI
941 Bûwzîy (1), Buzi

BUZITE
940 Bûwzîy (2), Buzite

BYWAYS
734+6128 'ôrach (1), well-traveled road

BYWORD
4405 millâh (1), word; discourse; speech
4912 mâshâl (1), pithy maxim; taunt
4914 mᵉshôl (1), satire
8148 shᵉnîynâh (3), gibe, verbal taunt

CAB
6894 qab (1), dry measure of volume

CABBON
3522 Kabbôwn (1), hilly

CABINS
2588 chânûwth (1), vault or cell

CABUL
3521 Kâbûwl (2), sterile

CAESAR
2541 Kaisar (21), Cæsar

CAESAR'S
2541 Kaisar (9), Cæsar

CAESAREA
2542 Kaisarĕia (17), of Cæsar

CAGE
3619 kᵉlûwb (1), bird-trap; basket
5438 phulakē (1), guarding or guard

CAIAPHAS
2533 Kaïaphas (9), dell

CAIN
7014 Qayin (17), lance
2535 Kaïn (3), lance

CAINAN
7018 Qêynân (5), fixed
2536 Kaïnan (2), fixed

CAKE
1690 dᵉbêlâh (1), cake of pressed figs
2471 challâh (7), cake shaped as a ring
4580 mâ'ôwg (1), cake of bread, provision
5692 'uggâh (3), round-cake
6742 tsᵉlûwl (1), round or flattened cake

CAKES
1690 dᵉbêlâh (2), cake of pressed figs
2471 challâh (8), cake shaped as a ring
3561 kavvân (2), sacrificial wafer

3823 lâbab (1), to make cakes
3834 lâbîybâh (3), fried or turned cake
4682 matstsâh (4), unfermented cake
5692 'uggâh (4), round-cake
7550 râqîyq (1), thin cake, wafer

CALAH
3625 Kelach (2), maturity

CALAMITIES
343 'êyd (1), misfortune, ruin, disaster
1942 havvâh (1), desire; craving
7451 ra' (1), bad; evil

CALAMITY
343 'êyd (16), misfortune, ruin, disaster
1942 havvâh (3), desire; craving

CALAMUS
7070 qâneh (3), reed

CALCOL
3633 Kalkôl (1), sustenance

CALDRON
100 'agmôwn (1), rush; rope of rushes
5518 çîyr (3), thorn; hook
7037 qallachath (2), kettle

CALDRONS
1731 dûwd (1), pot, kettle; basket
5518 çîyr (2), thorn; hook

CALEB
3612 Kâlêb (32), forcible

CALEB'S
3612 Kâlêb (4), forcible

CALEB-EPHRATAH
3613 Kâlêb 'Ephrâthâh (1), Caleb-Ephrathah

CALF
1121+1241 bên (2), son, descendant
5695 'êgel (21), calf
3447 mŏschŏpŏiĕō (1), to fabricate a bullock-idol
3448 mŏschŏs (4), young bullock

CALF'S
5695 'êgel (1), calf

CALKERS
2388+919 châzaq (2), to fasten upon; to seize

CALL
559 'âmar (2), to say, speak
833 'âshar (5), to go forward; guide
2142 zâkar (3), to remember; to mention
5493 çûwr (1), to turn off
5749 'ûwd (3), to duplicate or repeat
7121 qârâ' (131), to call out
7725 shûwb (1), to turn back; to return
8085 shâma' (2), to hear intelligently

363 anamimnēskō (1), to remind; to recollect
1941 ĕpikalĕŏmai (9), to invoke
2564 kalĕō (17), to call
2840 kŏinŏō (2), to make profane
2983 lambanō (1), to take, receive
3004 lĕgō (4), to say
3106 makarizō (1), to pronounce fortunate
3333 mĕtakalĕō (2), to summon for, call for
3343 mĕtapĕmpō (2), to summon or invite
3687 ŏnŏmazō (1), to give a name
4341 prŏskalĕŏmai (1), to call toward oneself
4779 sugkalĕō (1), to convoke, call together
5455 phōnĕō (4), to emit a sound

CALLED
559 'âmar (4), to say, speak
935 bôw' (1), to go or come
2199 zâ'aq (3), to call out, announce
6817 tsâ'aq (2), to shriek; to proclaim
7121 qârâ' (380), to call out
7123 qᵉrâ' (Ch.) (1), to call out
7760 sûwm (1), to put, place
8085 shâma' (1), to hear intelligently
154 aitĕō (1), to ask for
363 anamimnēskō (1), to remind; to recollect
1458 ĕgkalĕō (1), to charge, criminate
1528 ĕiskalĕō (1), to invite in
1941 ĕpikalĕŏmai (4), to invoke
1951 ĕpilĕgŏmai (1), to surname, select
2028 ĕpŏnŏmazō (1), to be called, denominate
2036 ĕpō (1), to speak
2046 ĕrĕō (1), to utter
2564 kalĕō (103), to call
2822 klētŏs (11), appointed, invited
2919 krinō (2), to decide; to try, condemn, punish
3004 lĕgō (36), to say
3044 Linŏs (1), (poss.) flax linen
3333 mĕtakalĕō (2), to summon for, call for
3686 ŏnŏma (4), name
3687 ŏnŏmazō (1), to give a name
3739+2076 hŏs (1), who, which, what, that
3870 parakalĕō (1), to call, invite
4316 prŏsagŏrĕuō (1), to designate a name
4341 prŏskalĕŏmai (25), to call toward oneself
4377 prŏsphōnĕō (2), to address, exclaim

4779 sugkalĕŏ (5), to convoke, call together
4867 sunathrŏizō (1), to convene
5455 phōnĕŏ (16), to emit a sound
5537 chrēmatizō (2), to utter an oracle
5581 psĕudōnumŏs (1), untruly named

CALLEDST
6485 pâqad (1), to visit, care for, count
7121 qârâ' (3), to call out

CALLEST
3004 lĕgō (3), to say

CALLETH
7121 qârâ' (13), to call out
2564 kalĕō (6), to call
3004 lĕgō (4), to say
4341 prŏskalĕŏmai (1), to call toward oneself
4779 sugkalĕō (2), to convoke, call together
5455 phōnĕŏ (4), to emit a sound

CALLING
2142 zâkar (1), to remember; to mention
4744 miqrâ' (1), public meeting
7121 qârâ' (3), to call out
363 anamimnēskō (1), to remind; to recollect
1941 ĕpikalĕŏmai (2), to invoke
2564 kalĕō (1), to call
2821 klēsis (10), invitation; station in life
4341 prŏskalĕŏmai (2), to call toward oneself
4377 prŏsphōnĕŏ (2), to address, exclaim
5455 phōnĕŏ (1), to emit a sound

CALM
1827 dᵉmâmâh (1), quiet
8367 shâthaq (2), to subside
1055 galēnē (3), tranquillity, calm

CALNEH
3641 Kalneh (2), Calneh or Calno

CALNO
3641 Kalneh (1), Calneh or Calno

CALVARY
2898 kraniŏn (1), skull

CALVE
2342 chûwl (2), to dance, whirl; to writhe in pain

CALVED
3205 yâlad (1), to bear young; to father a child

CALVES
1121 bên (2), son, descendant
1121+1241 bên (1), son, descendant
5695 'êgel (10), bull calf
5697 'eglâh (2), cow calf
6499 par (1), bullock

3448 mŏschŏs (2), young bullock

CALVETH
6403 pâlaṭ (1), to slip out, i.e. escape; to deliver

CAME
857 'âthâh (4), to arrive; go
858 'âthâh (Ch.) (3), to arrive; go
935 bôw' (668), to go or come
1061 bikkûwr (1), first-fruits of the crop
1518 gîyach (1), to issue forth; to burst forth
1691 Diblayim (1), two cakes
1916 hădôm (2), foot-stool
1946 hûwk (Ch.) (1), to go, come
1961 hâyâh (527), to exist, i.e. be or become
1980 hâlak (7), to walk; live a certain way
2015 hâphak (1), to turn about or over
3212 yâlak (6), to walk; to live; to carry
3318 yâtsâ' (106), to go, bring out
3329 yâtsîy' (1), issue forth, i.e. offspring
3381 yârad (42), to descend
3847 lâbash (3), to clothe
3996 mâbôw' (1), entrance; sunset; west
4161 môwtsâ' (1), going forth
4291 mᵉṭâ' (Ch.) (4), to arrive, to extend
4672 mâtsâ' (2), to find or acquire; to occur
5060 nâga' (5), to strike
5066 nâgash (27), to be, come, bring near
5182 nᵉchath (Ch.) (1), to descend; to depose
5312 nᵉphaq (Ch.) (3), to issue forth; to bring out
5437 çâbab (1), to surround
5559 çᵉlìq (Ch.) (5), to ascend, go up
5674 'âbar (4), to cross over; to transition
5927 'âlâh (82), to ascend, be high, mount
5954 'ălal (Ch.) (4), to go in; to lead in
5957 'âlam (Ch.) (1), forever
6293 pâga' (1), to impinge
6473 pâ'ar (1), to open wide
6555 pârats (1), to break out
6743 tsâlach (5), to push forward
7122 qârâ' (1), to encounter, to happen
7126 qârab (20), to approach, bring near
7127 qᵉrêb (Ch.) (5), to approach, bring near
7131 qârêb (1), near

7725 shûwb (16), to turn back; to return
191 akŏuō (1), to hear; obey
305 anabainō (3), to go up, rise
565 apĕrchŏmai (1), to go off, i.e. depart
1096 ginŏmai (88), to be, become
1237 diadĕchŏmai (1), succeed, receive in turn
1448 ĕggizō (3), to approach
1525 ĕisĕrchŏmai (10), to enter
1531 ĕispŏrĕuŏmai (1), to enter
1607 ĕkpŏrĕuŏmai (1), to depart, be discharged
1831 ĕxĕrchŏmai (38), to issue; to leave
1904 ĕpĕrchŏmai (1), to supervene
1910 ĕpibainō (1), to mount, ascend
1994 ĕpistrĕphō (1), to revert, turn back to
1998 ĕpisuntrĕchō (1), to hasten together upon
2064 ĕrchŏmai (199), to go or come
2113 ĕuthudrŏmĕŏ (1), to sail direct
2186 ĕphistēmi (7), to be present; to approach
2240 hēkō (3), to arrive, i.e. be present
2597 katabainō (16), to descend
2658 katantaō (8), to arrive at; to attain
2718 katĕrchŏmai (6), to go, come down
2944 kuklŏō (1), to surround, encircle
2983 lambanō (1), to take, receive
3415 mnaŏmai (1), to bear in mind
3719 ŏrthrizō (1), to get up early in the morning
3854 paraginŏmai (16), to arrive; to appear
3918 parĕimi (1), to be present; to have come
3922 parĕisĕrchŏmai (1), to supervene
3928 parĕrchŏmai (1), to go by; to perish
4130 plēthō (1), to fulfill, complete
4334 prŏsĕrchŏmai (65), to come near, visit
4370 prŏstrĕchō (1), to hasten by running
4836 sumparaginŏmai (1), to convene
4863 sunagō (6), to gather together
4872 sunanabainō (2), to ascend in company
4905 sunĕrchŏmai (8), to gather together
5342 phĕrō (3), to bear or carry

CAMEL
1581 gâmâl (5), camel
2574 kamēlŏs (4), camel

CAMEL'S
1581 gâmâl (1), camel
2574 kamēlŏs (2), camel

CAMELS
327 'ăchastârân (2), mule
1581 gâmâl (44), camel

CAMELS'
1581 gâmâl (3), camel

CAMEST
935 bôw' (8), to go, come
1518 gîyach (1), to issue forth; to burst forth
1980 hâlak (3), to walk; live a certain way
3318 yâtsâ' (7), to go, bring out
3381 yârad (3), to descend
7126 qârab (1), to approach, bring near
7725 shûwb (1), to turn back; to return
1096 ginŏmai (1), to be, become
1525 ĕisĕrchŏmai (1), to enter
1831 ĕxĕrchŏmai (1), to issue; to leave
2064 ĕrchŏmai (1), to go or come

CAMON
7056 Qâmôwn (1), elevation

CAMP
2583 chânâh (3), to encamp
4264 machăneh (127), encampment
8466 tachănâh (1), encampment
3925 parĕmbŏlē (3), encampment

CAMPED
2583 chânâh (1), to encamp

CAMPHIRE
3724 kôpher (2), village; bitumen; henna

CAMPS
4264 machăneh (7), encampment

CAN
3045 yâda' (1), to know
3201 yâkôl (18), to be able
3202 yᵉkêl (Ch.) (2), to be able
1097 ginōskō (1), to know
1410 dunamai (65), to be able or possible
1492 ĕidō (2), to know
2480 ischuō (1), to have or exercise force

CANA
2580 Kana (4), Cana

CANAAN
3667 Kᵉna'an (90), humiliated
5478 Chanaanaiŏs (1), Kenaanite

CANAANITE
3669 Kᵉna'ănîy (12), Kenaanite; merchant
2581 Kananitēs (2), zealous

English

CANAANITES
3669 Kᵉna'ăniy (55), *Kenaanite; merchant*

CANAANITESS
3669 Kᵉna'ănîy (1), *Kenaanite; merchant*

CANAANITISH
3669 Kᵉna'ăniy (2), *Kenaanite; merchant*

CANDACE
2582 *Kandakē* (1), *Candacë*

CANDLE
5216 nîyr (8), *lamp; lamplight*
3088 luchnŏs (8), portable *lamp*

CANDLES
5216 nîyr (1), *lamp; lamplight*

CANDLESTICK
4501 mᵉnôwrâh (34), *chandelier, lamp-stand*
5043 nebrᵉshâ' (Ch.) (1), *lamp-stand*
3087 luchnia (6), *lamp-stand*

CANDLESTICKS
4501 mᵉnôwrâh (6), *chandelier, lamp-stand*
3087 luchnia (6), *lamp-stand*

CANE
7070 qâneh (2), *reed*

CANKER
1044 gaggraina (1), *ulcer*, i.e. gangrene

CANKERED
2728 katiŏō (1), to *corrode, tarnish*

CANKERWORM
3218 yekeq (6), young *locust*

CANNEH
3656 Kanneh (1), *Canneh*

CANNOT
369 'ayin (1), *there is no*, i.e., *not exist, none*
408 'al (2), *not; nothing*
518 'îm (1), *whether?; if, although; Oh that!*
1077 bal (2), *nothing; not at all; lest*
1097 bᵉlîy (1), *without, not yet; lacking*;
1115 biltîy (1), *not, except, without, unless*
3201 yâkôl (3), to *be able*
3308 yŏphîy (2), *beauty*
3808 lô' (57), *no, not*
176 akatagnōstŏs (1), *unblamable*
180 akatapaustŏs (1), *unrefraining, unceasing*
215 alalētŏs (1), *unspeakable*
368 anantirrhētŏs (1), *indisputable*
551 apĕirastŏs (1), *not temptable*
761 asalĕutŏs (1), *immovable, fixed*
893 apsĕudēs (1), *veracious, free of deceit*
1492 ĕidō (2), to *know*

3361 mē (2), *not; lest*
3467 muōpazō (1), to *see indistinctly, be myopic*
3756 ŏu (3), *no* or *not*

CANST
3201 yâkôl (6), to *be able*
3202 yᵉkêl (Ch.) (2), to *be able*
1097 ginōskō (1), to *know*
1410 dunamai (9), to *be able* or *possible*
1492 ĕidō (1), to *know*

CAPERNAUM
2584 Kapĕrnaŏum (16), walled *village* which is *comfortable*

CAPHTHORIM
3732 Kaphtôriy (1), *Caphtorite*

CAPHTOR
3731 Kaphtôr (3), *wreath-shaped island*

CAPHTORIM
3732 Kaphtôriy (1), *Caphtorite*

CAPHTORIMS
3732 Kaphtôriy (1), *Caphtorite*

CAPPADOCIA
2587 Kappadŏkia (2), *Cappadocia*

CAPTAIN
1167 ba'al (1), *master; husband; owner; citizen*
2951 ţiphçar (1), military *governor*
5057 nâgîyd (5), *commander, official*
5387 nâsîy' (12), *leader; rising mist, fog*
5921 'al (1), *above, over, upon*, or *against*
6346 pechâh (2), *prefect, officer*
7101 qâtsîyn (2), *magistrate*
7218 rô'sh (4), *head*
7227 rab (23), *great*
7229 rab (Ch.) (1), *great*
7990 shallîyţ (Ch.) (1), *premier, sovereign*
7991 shâlîysh (2), *officer; of the third rank*
8269 sar (51), *head person, ruler*
747 archēgŏs (1), *chief leader; founder*
4755 stratēgŏs (3), military *governor*
4759 stratŏpĕdarchēs (1), military *commander*
5506 chiliarchŏs (18), *colonel*

CAPTAINS
441 'allûwph (1), *friend, one familiar; chieftain*
2951 ţiphçar (1), military *governor*
3733 kar (1), *ram sheep; battering ram*
3746 kârîy (2), *life-guardsman*
5057 nâgîyd (1), *commander, official*
6346 pechâh (7), *prefect, officer*

6347 pechâh (Ch.) (4), *prefect, officer*
7101 qâtsîyn (1), *magistrate*
7218 rô'sh (6), *head*
7991 shâlîysh (9), *officer; of the third rank*
8269 sar (80), *head person, ruler*
4755 stratēgŏs (2), military *governor*
5506 chiliarchŏs (4), *colonel*

CAPTIVE
1473 gôwlâh (4), *exile; captive*
1540 gâlâh (24), to *denude; uncover*
1546 gâlûwth (2), *captivity; exiles*
6808 tsâ'âh (1), to *depopulate; imprison*
7617 shâbâh (21), to *transport into captivity*
7628 shᵉbîy (3), *exile; booty*
162 aichmalōtĕuō (2), to *capture*
163 aichmalōtizō (1), to *make captive*
2221 zōgrĕō (1), to *capture* or *ensnare*

CAPTIVES
1123+1547 bên (Ch.) (1), *son*
1473 gôwlâh (3), *exile; captive*
1540 gâlâh (3), to *denude; uncover*
1546 gâlûwth (3), *captivity; exiles*
7617 shâbâh (16), to *transport into captivity*
7628 shᵉbîy (8), *exile; booty*
7633 shibyâh (8), *exile; captive*
164 aichmalōtŏs (1), *captive*

CAPTIVITY
1473 gôwlâh (28), *exile; captive*
1540 gâlâh (9), to *denude; uncover*
1546 gâlûwth (11), *captivity; exiles*
1547 gâlûwth (Ch.) (3), *captivity; exiles*
2925 ţaltêlâh (1), *overthrow or rejection*
7622 shᵉbûwth (31), *exile; prisoners*
7628 shᵉbîy (30), *exile; booty*
7633 shibyâh (6), *exile; captive*
161 aichmalōsia (2), *captivity*
163 aichmalōtizō (2), to *make captive*

CARBUNCLE
1304 bârᵉqath (3), *flashing gem* (poss.) *emerald*

CARBUNCLES
68+688 'eben (1), *stone*

CARCAS
3752 Karkaç (1), *Karkas*

CARCASE
1472 gᵉvîyâh (2), *dead body*
4658 mappeleth (1), down-*fall; ruin; carcase*
5038 nᵉbêlâh (29), *carcase or carrion*
6297 peger (1), *carcase; corpse*
4430 ptōma (1), *corpse, carrion*

CARCASES
5038 nᵉbêlâh (7), *carcase or carrion*
6297 peger (13), *carcase; corpse*
2966 kōlŏn (1), *corpse*

CARCHEMISH
3751 Karkᵉmîysh (2), *Karkemish*

CARE
983 beţach (1), *safety, security, trust*
1674 dᵉ'âgâh (1), *anxiety*
1697 dâbâr (1), *word; matter; thing*
2731 chărâdâh (1), *fear, anxiety*
7760+3820 sûwm (2), to *put, place*
1959 ĕpimĕlĕŏmai (3), to *care for*
3199 mĕlō (3), *it is a care or concern*
3308 mĕrimna (3), *solicitude; worry*
3309 mĕrimnaō (2), to *be anxious about*
4710 spŏudē (2), *despatch; eagerness*
5426 phrŏnĕō (1), to *be mentally disposed*

CAREAH
7143 Qârêach (1), *bald*

CARED
1875 dârash (1), to *pursue or search*
3199 mĕlō (2), *it is a care or concern*

CAREFUL
1672 dâ'ag (1), *be anxious, be afraid*
2729 chârad (1), to *hasten with anxiety*
2818 chăshach (Ch.) (1), to *need*
3309 mĕrimnaō (2), to *be anxious about*
5426 phrŏnĕō (1), to *be mentally disposed*
5431 phrŏntizō (1), *be anxious; to be careful*

CAREFULLY
2470 châlâh (1), to *be weak, sick, afflicted*
8085 shâma' (1), to *hear intelligently*
1567 ĕkzētĕō (1), to *seek out*
4708 spŏudaiŏtĕrōs (1), *more speedily*

CAREFULNESS
1674 dᵉ'âgâh (2), *anxiety*

275 amĕrimnŏs (1), *not anxious, free of care*
4710 spŏudē (1), *despatch; eagerness*

CARELESS
982 bâṭach (3), *to trust, be confident or sure*
983 beṭach (2), *safety, security, trust*

CARELESSLY
983 beṭach (3), *safety, security, trust*

CARES
3303 mĕn (3), not translated

CAREST
3199 mēlō (3), *it is a care or concern*

CARETH
1875 dârash (1), *to pursue or search*
3199 mēlō (2), *it is a care or concern*
3309 mĕrimnaō (4), *to be anxious about*

CARMEL
3760 Karmel (26), planted *field; garden*

CARMELITE
3761 Karmᵉlîy (5), *Karmelite*

CARMELITESS
3762 Karmᵉlîyth (2), *Karmelitess*

CARMI
3756 Karmîy (8), *gardener*

CARMITES
3757 Karmîy (1), *Karmite*

CARNAL
4559 sarkikŏs (9), *pertaining to flesh*
4561 sarx (2), *flesh*

CARNALLY
7902+2233 shᵉkâbâh (2), *lying* down
7903+2233 shᵉkôbeth (1), sexual *lying* down with
4561 sarx (1), *flesh*

CARPENTER
2796 chârâsh (1), skilled *fabricator* or worker
2796+6086 chârâsh (1), skilled *fabricator*
5045 tĕktōn (1), *craftsman* in wood

CARPENTER'S
5045 tĕktōn (1), *craftsman* in wood

CARPENTERS
2796 chârâsh (6), skilled *fabricator* or worker
2796+6086 chârâsh (2), skilled *fabricator*
6086 'ēts (1), *wood*, things made of *wood*

CARPUS
2591 Karpŏs (1), (poss.) *fruit*

CARRIAGE
3520 kᵉbûwddâh (1), *magnificence, wealth*

3627 kᵉlîy (2), *implement, thing*

CARRIAGES
3627 kᵉlîy (1), *implement, thing*
5385 nᵉsûw'âh (1), *load, burden*
643 apŏskĕuazō (1), to *pack up baggage*

CARRIED
935 bôw' (10), *to go, come*
1473 gôwlâh (10), *exile; captive*
1540 gâlâh (35), *to denude; uncover*
1541 gᵉlâh (Ch.) (1), to *reveal mysteries*
1546 gâlûwth (3), *captivity; exiles*
1980 hâlak (1), to *walk; live a certain way*
2986 yâbal (3), *to bring*
3212 yâlak (3), *to walk; to live; to carry*
3318 yâtsâ' (3), *to go, bring out*
3947 lâqach (3), *to take*
4116 mâhar (1), *to hurry; promptly*
4131 môwṭ (1), *to slip, shake, fall*
5090 nâhag (3), *to drive; to lead, carry away*
5095 nâhal (1), to *conduct; to protect*
5186 nâṭâh (2), to *stretch* or spread out
5375 nâsâ' (15), *to lift up*
5376 nᵉsâ' (Ch.) (1), to *lift* up
5437 çâbab (3), to *surround*
5445 çâbal (1), to *carry*
5674 'âbar (1), *to cross over; to transition*
5927 'âlâh (3), *to ascend, be high, mount*
7392 râkab (3), *to ride*
7617 shâbâh (18), to *transport* into captivity
7725 shûwb (2), *to turn back; to return*
71 agō (1), *to lead; to bring, drive; to weigh*
339 anakathizō (1), *to sit up*
520 apagō (1), *to take away*
667 apŏhĕrō (4), *to bear off, carry away*
941 bastazō (1), *to lift, bear*
1580 ĕkkŏmizō (1), to *bear forth to burial*
1627 ĕkphĕrō (1), *to bear out; to produce*
1643 ĕlaunō (1), *to push*
3346 mĕtatithēmi (1), to *transport; to exchange*
3350 mĕtŏikĕsia (1), *exile, deportation*
4064 pĕriphĕrō (3), to *transport*
4216 pŏtamŏphŏrētŏs (1), *overwhelmed by a stream*
4792 sugkŏmizō (1), to *convey together*

4879 sunapagō (1), *to take off together*

CARRIEST
2229 zâram (1), *to gush* water, *pour forth*

CARRIETH
1589 gânab (1), *to thieve; to deceive*
5375 nâsâ' (1), *to lift up*
941 bastazō (1), *to lift, bear*

CARRY
935 bôw' (7), *to go or come*
1319 bâsar (1), to *announce* (good news)
1540 gâlâh (5), *to denude; uncover*
1980 hâlak (1), to *walk; live a certain way*
2904 ṭûwl (1), *to cast down or out, hurl*
2986 yâbal (1), *to bring*
2987 yᵉbal (Ch.) (1), *to bring*
3212 yâlak (3), *to walk; to live; to carry*
3318 yâtsâ' (18), *to go, bring out*
3381 yârad (2), *to descend*
3947 lâqach (2), *to take*
4853 massâ' (1), *burden, utterance*
5182 nᵉchath (Ch.) (1), to *descend; to depose*
5375 nâsâ' (18), *to lift up*
5445 çâbal (3), *to carry*
5674 'âbar (2), *to cross over; to transition*
5927 'âlâh (4), *to ascend, be high, mount*
6403 pâlaṭ (1), *to slip* out, i.e. *escape; to deliver*
7400 râkîyl (1), *scandal-monger*
7617 shâbâh (5), to *transport* into captivity
7725 shûwb (4), *to turn back; to return*
142 airō (1), *to lift, to take up*
941 bastazō (1), *to lift, bear*
1308 diaphĕrō (1), to *bear, carry; to differ*
1627 ĕkphĕrō (2), *to bear out; to produce*
3351 mĕtŏikizō (1), to *transfer* as a *captive*
4046 pĕripŏiĕŏmai (1), to *acquire; to gain*
5342 phĕrō (1), *to bear or carry*

CARRYING
1540 gâlâh (1), *to denude; uncover*
5375 nâsâ' (3), *to lift up*
7411 râmâh (1), *to hurl; to shoot; to delude*
1627 ĕkphĕrō (1), *to bear out; to produce*
3350 mĕtŏikĕsia (2), *exile, deportation*

CARSHENA
3771 Karshᵉnâ' (1), *Karshena*

CART
5699 'ăgâlâh (15), wheeled *vehicle*

CARVED
2405 châṭûbâh (1), *tapestry*
2707 châqah (1), *to carve; to delineate*
4734 miqla'ath (1), *bas-relief sculpture*
6456 pᵉçîyl (3), *idol*
6459 peçel (2), *idol*
6603 pittûwach (2), *sculpture; engraving*
7049 qâla' (3), *to sling* a stone; *to carve*

CARVING
2799 chărôsheth (2), skilled *work*

CARVINGS
4734 miqla'ath (1), *bas-relief sculpture*

CASE
1697 dâbâr (1), *word; matter; thing*
3602 kâkâh (1), *just so*
7725 shûwb (2), *to turn back; to return*
156 aitia (1), logical *reason; legal crime*
3364 ŏu mē (1), *not at all, absolutely not*

CASEMENT
822 'eshnâb (1), latticed *window*

CASIPHIA
3703 Kâçiphyâ' (2), *silvery*

CASLUHIM
3695 Kaçlûchîym (2), *Casluchim*

CASSIA
6916 qiddâh (2), *cassia*
7102 qᵉtsîy'âh (1), *cassia*

CAST
1299 bâraq (1), *to flash* lightning
1457 gâhar (1), *to prostrate* oneself
1602 gâ'al (1), *to detest; to reject; to fail*
1644 gârash (9), *to drive* out; *to expatriate*
1740 dûwach (1), *to rinse clean, wash*
1760 dâchâh (1), *to push* down; *to totter*
1920 hâdaph (2), *to push* away or down; *drive out*
1972 hâlâ' (1), *to remove* or be *remote*
2186 zânach (17), *to reject, forsake, fail*
2219 zârâh (1), *to toss* about; *to diffuse*
2490 châlal (1), *to profane, defile*
2904 ṭûwl (12), *to cast down or out, hurl*
3032 yâdad (3), *to throw* lots
3034 yâdâh (2), *to throw; to revere or worship*
3240 yânach (1), *to allow to stay*

English

3332 yâtsaq (10), to *pour out*
3333 yᵉtsûqâh (1), *poured* out into a mold
3381 yârad (3), to *descend*
3384 yârâh (4), to *throw, shoot* an arrow
3423 yârash (10), to *inherit;* to *impoverish*
3766 kâra' (1), to *prostrate*
3782 kâshal (3), to *totter, waver;* to *falter*
3874 lûwṭ (1), to *wrap* up
3988 mâ'aç (10), to *spurn;* to *disappear*
4048 mâgar (1), to *yield up, be thrown*
4054 migrâsh (1), *open country*
4131 môwṭ (1), to *slip, shake, fall*
4166 mûwtsâqâh (1), *casting* of metal; *tube*
4788 mârûwd (1), *outcast; destitution*
5060 nâga' (1), to *strike*
5077 nâdâh (1), to *exclude,* i.e. *banish*
5080 nâdach (4), to *push off, scattered*
5203 nâṭash (1), to *disperse;* to *thrust* off
5221 nâkâh (1), to *strike, kill*
5307 nâphal (24), to *fall*
5375 nâsâ' (1), to *lift up*
5390 nᵉshîyqâh (1), *kiss*
5394 nâshal (1), to *divest, eject,* or *drop*
5414 nâthan (5), to *give*
5422 nâthats (3), to *tear down*
5437 çâbab (1), to *surround*
5499 çᵉchâbâh (2), *rag*
5549 çâlal (4), to *mound up;* to *exalt;* to *oppose*
5619 çâqal (1), to *throw large stones*
5927 'âlâh (2), to *ascend, be high, mount*
6080 'âphar (1), to *be dust*
6327 pûwts (2), to *dash in pieces;* to *disperse*
6437 pânâh (1), to *turn,* to *face*
6696 tsûwr (1), to *cramp,* i.e. *confine;* to *harass*
7290 râdam (1), to *stupefy*
7324 rûwq (1), to *pour out,* i.e. *empty*
7368 râchaq (1), to *recede; remove*
7412 rᵉmâh (Ch.) (11), to *throw;* to *set;* to *assess*
7760 sûwm (1), to *put, place*
7817 shâchach (4), to *sink* or *depress*
7843 shâchath (1), to *decay;* to *ruin*
7921 shâkôl (3), to *miscarry*
7933 sheken (4), *residence*

7971 shâlach (14), to *send away*
7993 shâlak (113), to *throw out, down*
7995 shalleketh (1), *felling* of trees
7998 shâlâl (1), *booty*
8210 shâphak (8), to *spill forth;* to *expend*
8213 shâphêl (1), to *humiliate*
8628 tâqa' (1), to *clatter, slap, drive, clasp*
114 athĕtĕō (1), to *disesteem, neutralize*
577 apŏballō (1), to *throw off;* fig. to *lose*
641 apŏrrhiptō (1), to *throw oneself into*
656 apŏsunagōgŏs (1), *excommunicated*
683 apōthĕŏmai (2), to *push off;* to *reject*
906 ballō (81), to *throw*
1000 bŏlē (1), *throw* as a measure
1260 dialŏgizŏmai (1), to *deliberate*
1544 ĕkballō (51), to *throw out*
1601 ĕkpiptō (1), to *drop away*
1614 ĕktĕinō (1), to *stretch*
1620 ĕktithēmi (1), to *expose;* to *declare*
1685 ĕmballō (1), to *throw in*
1911 ĕpiballō (2), to *throw upon*
1977 ĕpirrhiptō (1), to *throw upon*
2210 zēmiŏō (1), to *experience detriment*
2598 kataballō (2), to *throw down*
2630 katakrēmnizō (1), to *precipitate down*
2975 lagchanō (1), to *determine* by lot
3036 lithŏbŏlĕō (1), to *throw stones*
3679 ŏnĕidizō (1), to *rail at, chide, taunt*
3860 paradidōmi (1), to *hand over*
4016 pĕriballō (3), to *wrap around, clothe*
4406 prŏïmŏs (1), *autumnal* showering
4496 rhiptō (5), to *fling, toss;* to *lay out*
5011 tapĕinŏs (1), *humiliated, lowly*
5020 tartarŏō (1), to *incarcerate* in Tartaros

CASTAWAY
96 adŏkimŏs (1), *failing the test, worthless*

CASTEDST
5307 nâphal (1), to *fall*

CASTEST
2186 zânach (1), to *reject, forsake, fail*
6565 pârar (1), to *break up;* to *violate, frustrate*
7993 shâlak (1), to *throw out, down or away*

CASTETH
1920 hâdaph (1), to *push away or down; drive out*
3381 yârad (1), to *descend*
3384 yârâh (1), to *throw, shoot* an arrow
5307 nâphal (1), to *fall*
6884 tsâraph (1), to *fuse* metal; to *refine*
6979 qûwr (2), to *throw forth;* to *wall up*
7921 shâkôl (1), to *miscarry*
7993 shâlak (1), to *throw out, down or away*
8213 shâphêl (1), to *humiliate*
906 ballō (2), to *throw*
1544 ĕkballō (4), to *throw out*

CASTING
2866 chăthath (1), *dismay*
3445 yeshach (1), *hunger*
4165 mûwtsâq (1), *casting* of metal
5307 nâphal (1), to *fall*
7901 shâkab (1), to *lie down*
8210 shâphak (1), to *spill forth;* to *expend*
577 apŏballō (1), to *throw off;* fig. to *lose*
580 apŏbŏlē (1), *rejection, loss*
906 ballō (6), to *throw*
1544 ĕkballō (3), to *throw out*
1977 ĕpirrhiptō (1), to *throw upon*
2507 kathairĕō (1), to *lower,* or *demolish*

CASTLE
759 'armôwn (1), *citadel, high fortress*
4679 mᵉtsad (1), *stronghold*
4686 mâtsûwd (1), *net* or *capture; fastness*
3925 parĕmbŏlē (6), *encampment*

CASTLES
1003 bîyrânîyth (2), *fortress, citadel*
2918 ṭîyrâh (3), *fortress; hamlet*
4026 migdâl (1), *tower; rostrum*

CASTOR
1359 Diŏskŏurŏi (1), *twins of Zeus*

CATCH
1641 gârar (1), to *drag off roughly*
2414 châṭaph (3), to *seize* as a prisoner
2480 châlaṭ (1), to *snatch at, seizing*
2963 ṭâraph (2), to *pluck off* or *pull* to pieces
3920 lâkad (2), to *catch;* to *capture*
4672 mâtsâ' (1), to *find* or *acquire;* to *occur*
5367 nâqash (1), to *entrap* with a noose

8610 tâphas (1), to *manipulate,* i.e. *seize*
64 agrĕuŏ (1), to *entrap, catch*
2221 zōgrĕō (1), to *capture* or *ensnare*
2340 thērĕuŏ (1), to *carp at*

CATCHETH
6679 tsûwd (1), to *lie* in wait; to *catch*
726 harpazō (2), to *seize*

CATERPILLER
2625 chaçîyl (5), *locust*

CATERPILLERS
2625 chaçîyl (1), *locust*
3218 yekeq (3), *young locust*

CATTLE
926 bâhal (1), to *tremble; be, make agitated*
929 bᵉhêmâh (56), *animal, beast*
1165 bᵉ'îyr (2), *cattle, livestock*
1241 bâqâr (1), *plowing* ox; *herd*
4399 mᵉlâ'kâh (1), *work; property*
4734 miqla'ath (1), *bas-relief sculpture*
4735 miqneh (57), *live-stock*
4806 mᵉrîy' (3), *stall-fed* animal
6629 tsô'n (13), *flock* of sheep or goats
7069 qânâh (1), to *create;* to *procure*
7716 seh (7), *sheep* or *goat*
2353 thrĕmma (1), *stock*
4165 pŏimainō (1), to *tend* as a shepherd

CAUGHT
270 'âchaz (4), to *seize, grasp; possess*
962 bâzaz (1), to *plunder, take booty*
1497 gâzal (1), to *rob*
2388 châzaq (8), to *fasten* upon; to *seize*
3920 lâkad (2), to *catch;* to *capture*
8610 tâphas (3), to *manipulate,* i.e. *seize*
726 harpazō (5), to *seize*
1949 ĕpilambanŏmai (2), to *seize*
2983 lambanō (3), to *take, receive*
4084 piazō (2), to *seize, arrest,* or *capture*
4815 sullambanō (1), to *seize (arrest, capture)*
4884 sunarpazō (4), to *snatch together*

CAUL
3508 yôthereth (11), *lobe* or *flap* of the liver
5458 çᵉgôwr (1), *breast*

CAULS
7636 shâbîyç (1), *netting*

CAUSE
657 'epheç (1), *end; no further*

834 'ăsher (1), *because, in order that*
1697 dâbâr (6), *word; matter; thing*
1700 dibrâh (1), *because, on account of*
1779 dîyn (7), *judge; judgment; law suit*
1961 hâyâh (1), *to exist, i.e. be or become*
2600 chinnâm (15), *gratis, free*
3651 kên (1), *just; right, correct*
4616 ma'an (1), *on account of*
4941 mishpâṭ (12), *verdict; formal decree*
5252 nᵉçibbâh (1), *turn of affairs*
5414 nâthan (5), *to give*
5438 çibbâh (1), *turn of affairs*
5668 'âbûwr (1), *on account of*
7379 rîyb (23), *contest, personal or legal*
7387 rêyqâm (2), *emptily; ineffectually*
7945 shel (1), *on account of; what*soever
8267 sheqer (1), *untruth; sham*
156 aitia (9), *logical reason; legal crime*
158 aitiŏn (2), *reason, basis; crime*
846 autŏs (1), *he, she, it*
873 aphŏrizō (1), *to limit, exclude, appoint*
1223 dia (13), *because of, for the sake of*
1352 diŏ (2), *consequently, therefore*
1432 dōrĕan (1), *gratuitously, freely*
1500 ĕikĕ (1), *idly, i.e. without reason or effect*
1752 hĕnĕka (4), *on account of*
2289 thanatŏō (3), *to kill*
3056 lŏgŏs (1), *word, matter, thing*
4160 pŏiĕō (3), *to do*
5484 charin (3), *on account of, because of*

CAUSED
1961 hâyâh (1), *to exist, i.e. be or become*
5414 nâthan (7), *to give*
3076 lupĕō (1), *to distress; to be sad*
4160 pŏiĕō (2), *to do*

CAUSELESS
2600 chinnâm (2), *gratis, free*

CAUSES
182 'ôwdôwth (1), *on account of; because*
1697 dâbâr (2), *word; matter; thing*
7379 rîyb (1), *contest, personal or legal*
1752 hĕnĕka (1), *on account of*

CAUSETH
5414 nâthan (1), *to give*

2358 thriambĕuō (1), *to lead in triumphal procession*
2716 katĕrgazŏmai (1), *to finish; to accomplish*
4160 pŏiĕō (3), *to do*

CAUSEWAY
4546 mᵉçillâh (2), *main thoroughfare; viaduct*

CAVE
4631 mᵉ'ârâh (32), *dark cavern*
4693 spēlaiŏn (1), *cavern; hiding-place*

CAVE'S
4631 mᵉ'ârâh (1), *dark cavern*

CAVES
2356 chôwr (1), *cavity, socket, den*
4247 mᵉchillâh (1), *cavern, hole*
4631 mᵉ'ârâh (3), *dark cavern*
3692 ŏpē (1), *hole, i.e. cavern; spring of water*

CEASE
988 bâṭêl (1), *to desist from labor, cease*
989 bᵉṭêl (Ch.) (3), *to stop*
1820 dâmâh (1), *to be silent; to fail, cease*
1826 dâmam (1), *to stop, cease; to perish*
2308 châdal (12), *to desist, stop; be fat*
2790 chârash (1), *to be silent; to be deaf*
3254 yâçaph (1), *to add or augment*
3615 kâlâh (1), *to complete, consume*
4185 mûwsh (1), *to withdraw*
6565 pârar (1), *to break up; to violate, frustrate*
7503 râphâh (1), *to slacken*
7647 sâbâ' (1), *copiousness*
7673 shâbath (37), *to repose; to desist*
7725 shûwb (1), *to turn back; to return*
7918 shâkak (1), *to lay a trap; to allay*
8552 tâmam (1), *to complete, finish*
180 akatapaustŏs (1), *unrefraining, unceasing*
3973 pauō (4), *to stop, i.e. restrain, quit*

CEASED
989 bᵉṭêl (Ch.) (1), *to stop*
1826 dâmam (1), *to stop, cease; to perish*
1934+989 hăvâ' (Ch.) (1), *to be, to exist*
2308 châdal (6), *to desist, stop; be fat*
5117 nûwach (1), *to rest; to settle down*
5307 nâphal (1), *to fall*
5975 'âmad (1), *to stand*
6313 pûwg (1), *to be sluggish; be numb*

7673 shâbath (6), *to repose; to desist*
1257 dialĕipō (1), *to intermit, stop*
2270 hēsuchazō (1), *to refrain*
2664 katapauō (1), *to cause to desist*
2673 katargĕō (1), *to be, render entirely useless*
2869 kŏpazō (3), *to tire, i.e. to relax*
3973 pauō (7), *to stop, i.e. restrain, quit*

CEASETH
1584 gâmar (1), *to end; to complete; to fail*
1820 dâmâh (1), *to be silent; to fail, cease*
2308 châdal (1), *to desist, stop; be fat*
3615 kâlâh (1), *to cease, be finished, perish*
7673 shâbath (4), *to repose; to desist*
8367 shâthaq (1), *to subside*
3973 pauō (1), *to stop, i.e. restrain, quit*

CEASING
2308 châdal (1), *to desist, stop; be fat*
83 adēlŏtēs (1), *uncertainty*
89 adialĕiptōs (4), *without omission*
1618 ĕktĕnēs (1), *intent, earnest*

CEDAR
729 'âraz (1), *of cedar*
730 'erez (49), *cedar tree*
731 'arzâh (1), *cedar paneling*

CEDARS
730 'erez (24), *cedar tree*

CEDRON
2748 Kĕdrōn (1), *dusky place*

CELEBRATE
1984 hâlal (1), *to speak words of thankfulness*
2278 chăbereth (1), *consort, companion*
7673 shâbath (1), *to repose*

CELESTIAL
2032 ĕpŏuraniŏs (2), *above the sky, celestial*

CELLARS
214 'ôwtsâr (2), *depository*

CENCHREA
2747 Kĕgchrĕai (2), *millet*

CENSER
4289 machtâh (7), *pan for live coals*
4730 miqṭereth (1), *incense coal-pan*
2369 thumiastĕriŏn (1), *altar of incense*
3031 libanōtŏs (2), *censer for incense*

CENSERS
4289 machtâh (8), *pan for live coals*

CENTURION
1543 hĕkatŏntarchēs (17), *captain of a hundred*
2760 kĕnturiōn (3), *captain of a hundred*

CENTURION'S
1543 hĕkatŏntarchēs (1), *captain of a hundred*

CENTURIONS
1543 hĕkatŏntarchēs (1), *captain of a hundred*

CEPHAS
2786 Kēphas (6), *rock*

CEREMONIES
4941 mishpâṭ (1), *verdict; formal decree; justice*

CERTAIN
259 'echâd (9), *first*
376 'îysh (4), *man; male; someone*
582 'ĕnôwsh (8), *man; person, human*
592 'ănîyâh (2), *groaning*
1400 gᵉbar (Ch.) (2), *person; someone*
1697 dâbâr (2), *word; matter; thing*
3045 yâda' (3), *to know*
3330 yatstsîyb (Ch.) (1), *fixed, sure*
3559 kûwn (2), *to render sure, proper*
6256 'êth (1), *time*
6422 palmôwnîy (1), *a certain one*
444 anthrōpŏs (2), *human being; mankind*
444+5100 anthrōpŏs (1), *human being; mankind*
790 astatĕō (1), *homeless, vagabond*
804 asphalēs (1), *secure; certain*
1212 dēlŏs (1), *clear, plain, evident*
1520 hĕis (5), *one*
4225 pŏu (2), *somewhere, i.e. nearly*
5100 tis (112), *some or any person or object*

CERTAINLY
389 'ak (1), *surely; only, however*
403 'âkên (1), *surely!, truly!; but*
3588 kîy (1), *for, that because*
3689 ŏntōs (1), *really, certainly*

CERTAINTY
3330 yatstsîyb (Ch.) (1), *fixed, sure*
3559 kûwn (1), *to render sure, proper*
7189 qôsheṭ (1), *reality*
803 asphalĕia (1), *security; certainty*
804 asphalēs (2), *secure; certain*

CERTIFIED
559 'âmar (1), *to say*
3064 Yᵉhûwdîy (1), *Jehudite*

English

CERTIFY
3046 y^{e}da' (Ch.) (3), to
know
5046 nâgad (1), to
announce
1107 gnŏrizō (1), to
make known, reveal

CHAFED
4751 mar (1), bitter;
bitterness; bitterly

CHAFF
2842 châshash (2), dry
grass, chaff
4671 môts (8), chaff
5784 'ûwr (Ch.) (1), chaff
8401 teben (1), threshed
stalks of cereal grain
892 achurŏn (2), chaff of
grain

CHAIN
2002 hamnîyk (Ch.) (3),
necklace
5178 n^{e}chôsheth (1),
copper; bronze
6059 'ânaq (1), to collar;
to fit out
6060 'ânâq (1), necklace
chain
7242 râbîyd (2), collar
spread around the neck
7659 shib'âthayim (1),
seven-fold
8333 sharsh^{e}râh (1),
chain
254 halusis (3), fetter or
manacle

CHAINS
246 'ăziqqîym (2),
manacles, chains
685 'ets'âdâh (1), bracelet
2131 zîyqâh (3), burning
arrow; bond, fetter
2397 châch (2), ring for
the nose or lips
2737 chârûwz (1), strung
beads
3574 kôwshârâh (1),
prosperity
5178 n^{e}chôsheth (2),
copper; bronze
5188 n^{e}ṭîyphâh (1),
pendant for the ears
5688 'ăbôth (3), entwined
things: string, wreath
6060 'ânâq (2), necklace
chain
7569 rattôwq (2), chain
8333 sharsh^{e}râh (6),
chain
8337 shêsh (1), six; sixth
254 halusis (7), fetter or
manacle
1199 dĕsmŏn (1),
shackle; impediment
4577 sĕira (1), chain, as
binding or drawing

CHALCEDONY
5472 chalkēdŏn (1),
copper-like, chalcedony

CHALCOL
3633 Kalkôl (1),
sustenance

CHALDAEANS
5466 Chaldaiŏs (1),
native or the region of
the lower Euphrates

CHALDEA
3778 Kasdîy (7),
astrologer

CHALDEAN
3777 Kesed (2), Kesed

CHALDEANS
3778 Kasdîy (48),
astrologer
3779 Kasday (Ch.) (17),
magian or astrologer

CHALDEANS'
3778 Kasdîy (1),
astrologer

CHALDEES
3778 Kasdîy (13),
astrologer

CHALDEES'
3778 Kasdîy (1),
astrologer

CHALKSTONES
68+1615 'eben (1), stone

CHALLENGETH
559 'âmar (1), to say

CHAMBER
2315 cheder (15),
apartment, chamber
2646 chuppâh (1), canopy
3326 yâtsûwa' (1), bed;
wing or lean-to
3957 lishkâh (14), room
5393 nishkâh (2), room,
cell
5944 'ălîyâh (6),
second-story room
5952 'allîyth (Ch.) (1),
second-story room
6763 tsêlâ' (3), side of a
person or thing
8372 tâ' (4), room
5253 hupĕrō̆ŏn (3), third
story apartment

CHAMBERING
2845 kŏitē (1), couch;
conception

CHAMBERLAIN
5631 çârîyç (4), eunuch;
official of state
1909+3588+2846 ĕpi (1),
on, upon
3623 ŏikŏnŏmŏs (1),
overseer, manager

CHAMBERLAINS
5631 çârîyç (9), eunuch;
official of state

CHAMBERS
2315 cheder (8),
apartment, chamber
3326 yâtsûwa' (2), bed;
wing or lean-to of a
building
3957 lishkâh (31), room
in a building
5393 nishkâh (1), room,
cell
5944 'ălîyâh (6), upper
things; second-story
room
6763 tsêlâ' (8), side of a
person or thing
8372 tâ' (9), room
5009 tamĕiŏn (1), room

CHAMELEON
3581 kôach (1), large
lizard

CHAMOIS
2169 zemer (1), gazelle

CHAMPAIGN
6160 'ărâbâh (1), desert,
wasteland

CHAMPION
376+1143 'îysh (2), man;
male; someone
1368 gibbôwr (1),
powerful; great warrior

CHANAAN
5477 Chanaan (2),
humiliated

CHANCE
4745 miqreh (1),
accident or fortune
6294 pega' (1), casual
impact
7122 qârâ' (2), to
encounter, to happen
4795 sugkuria (1),
chance occurrence
5177 tugchanō (1), to
happen; perhaps

CHANCELLOR
1169+2942 b^e'êl (Ch.) (3),
master

CHANCETH
4745 miqreh (1),
accident or fortune

CHANGE
2015 hâphak (1), to
change, overturn
2487 chălîyphâh (4),
alternation, change
2498 châlaph (4), to
pierce; to change
4171 mûwr (5), to alter;
to barter, to dispose of
4254 machălâtsâh (1),
mantle, garment
7760 sûwm (1), to put,
place
8133 sh^{e}nâ' (Ch.) (1), to
alter, change
8138 shânâh (3), to fold,
i.e. duplicate; to
transmute
8545 t^{e}mûwrâh (1),
barter, compensation
236 allassō (2), to make
different, change
3331 mĕtathĕsis (1),
transferral,
disestablishment
3337 mĕtallassō (1), to
exchange
3345 mĕtaschēmatizō
(1), to transfigure or
disguise; to apply

CHANGEABLE
4254 machălâtsâh (1),
mantle, garment

CHANGED
2015 hâphak (2), to
change, overturn
2498 châlaph (6), to pass
on; to change
2664 châphas (1), to
seek; to mask
4171 mûwr (6), to alter;
to barter, to dispose of
5437 çâbab (2), to
surround
8132 shânâ' (3), to alter,
change

8133 sh^{e}nâ' (Ch.) (12), to
alter, change
8138 shânâh (3), to fold,
to transmute
236 allassō (4), to make
different, change
3328 mĕtaballō (1), to
turn about in opinion
3337 mĕtallassō (1), to
exchange
3339 mĕtamŏrphŏō (1),
to transform, i.e.
metamorphose
3346 mĕtatithēmi (1), to
transport; to exchange

CHANGERS
2773 kĕrmatistēs (1),
money-broker

CHANGERS'
2855 kŏllubistēs (1),
coin-dealer

CHANGES
2487 chălîyphâh (7),
alternation, change

CHANGEST
8138 shânâh (1), to fold,
to transmute

CHANGETH
4171 mûwr (1), to alter;
to barter, to dispose of
8133 sh^{e}nâ' (Ch.) (1), to
alter, change

CHANGING
8545 t^{e}mûwrâh (1),
barter, compensation

CHANNEL
7641 shibbôl (1), stream;
ear of grain

CHANNELS
650 'âphîyq (3), valley;
stream; mighty, strong

CHANT
6527 pâraṭ (1), to scatter
words, i.e. prate

CHAPEL
4720 miqdâsh (1),
sanctuary of deity

CHAPITER
3805 kôthereth (12),
capital of a column
6858 tsepheth (1),
capital of a column

CHAPITERS
3805 kôthereth (12),
capital of a column
7218 rô'sh (4), head

CHAPMEN
582+8846 'ĕnôwsh (1),
man; person; human

CHAPT
2865 châthath (1), to
break down

CHARASHIM
2798 Chărâshîym (1),
skilled worker

CHARCHEMISH
3751 Kark^{e}mîysh (1),
Karkemish

CHARGE
3027 yâd (1), hand; power
4931 mishmereth (46),
watch, sentry, post

CHARGEABLE

4941 mishpâṭ (1), *verdict;* formal *decree; justice*
5414 nâthan (1), to *give*
5447 çêbel (1), *load; forced labor*
5749 'ûwd (1), to *protest, testify*
5921 'al (3), *above, over, upon,* or *against*
6213 'âsâh (1), to *do or make*
6485 pâqad (1), to *visit, care for, count*
6486 pᵉquddâh (2), *visitation; punishment*
6496 pâqîyd (1), *superintendent, officer*
6680 tsâvâh (16), to *constitute, enjoin*
7130 qereb (1), *nearest part, i.e.* the *center*
7592 shâ'al (1), to *ask*
7650 shâba' (7), to *swear*
77 adapanŏs (1), *free of charge*
1263 diamarturŏmai (2), to *attest* or *protest*
1458+2596 ĕgkalĕŏ (1), to *charge, criminate*
1462 ĕgklēma (1), *accusation*
1781 ĕntĕllŏmai (2), to *enjoin, give orders*
1909 ĕpi (1), *on, upon*
2004 ĕpitassŏ (1), to *order, command*
2476 histēmi (1), to *stand, establish*
3049 lŏgizŏmai (1), to *take an inventory*
3726 hŏrkizŏ (1), to *solemnly enjoin*
3852 paraggĕlia (2), *mandate, order*
3853 paraggĕllŏ (4), to *enjoin; to instruct*

CHARGEABLE

3513 kâbad (2), to *be rich, glorious*
1912 ĕpibarĕŏ (2), to *be severe toward*
2655 katanarkaŏ (1), to *be a burden*

CHARGED

559 'âmar (1), to *say*
5414 nâthan (1), to *give*
5674+5921 'âbar (1), to *cross over; to transition*
6485 pâqad (3), to *visit, care for, count*
6680 tsâvâh (23), to *constitute, enjoin*
7650 shâba' (2), to *swear*
7760 sûwm (1), to *put, place*
916 barĕŏ (1), to *weigh down, cause pressure*
1291 diastĕllŏmai (6), to *distinguish*
1690 ĕmbrimaŏmai (2), to *blame, warn sternly*
1781 ĕntĕllŏmai (1), to *enjoin, give orders*
2008 ĕpitimaŏ (5), to *rebuke, warn, forbid*
3146 mastigŏŏ (1), to punish by *flogging*
3853 paraggĕllŏ (3), to *enjoin; to instruct*

CHARGEDST

5749 'ûwd (1), to *protest, testify; to encompass*

CHARGER

7086 qᵉ'ârâh (13), *bowl*
4094 pinax (4), *plate, platter, dish*

CHARGERS

105 'ăgarṭâl (2), *basin*
7086 qᵉ'ârâh (1), *bowl*

CHARGES

4931 mishmereth (4), *watch, sentry, post*
1159 dapanaŏ (1), to *incur cost; to waste*
3800 ŏpsŏniŏn (1), *rations, stipend* or *pay*

CHARGEST

6485 pâqad (1), to *visit, care for, count*

CHARGING

1263 diamarturŏmai (1), to *attest* or *protest*
3853 paraggĕllŏ (1), to *enjoin; to instruct*

CHARIOT

668 'appiryôwn (1), *palanquin, carriage*
4818 merkâbâh (23), *chariot*
5699 'ăgâlâh (1), *wheeled vehicle*
7393 rekeb (28), *vehicle for riding*
7395 rakkâb (2), *charioteer*
7398 rᵉkûwb (1), *vehicle ridden on*
716 harma (3), *chariot, carriage*

CHARIOTS

2021 hôtsen (1), *weapon*
4817 merkâb (1), *chariot; seat* in chariot
4818 merkâbâh (20), *chariot*
7393 rekeb (87), *vehicle for riding*
7396 rikbâh (1), *chariot*
716 harma (1), *chariot, carriage*
4480 rhĕda (1), *wagon* for riding

CHARITABLY

2596+26 kata (1), *down; according to*

CHARITY

26 agapē (28), *love; love-feast*

CHARMED

3908 lachash (1), *incantation; amulet*

CHARMER

2266+2267 châbar (1), to *fascinate* by spells

CHARMERS

328 'aṭ (1), *gently, softly*
3907 lâchash (1), to *whisper* a magic spell

CHARMING

2266+2267 châbar (1), to *fascinate* by spells

CHARRAN

5488 Charrhan (2), *parched*

CHASE

1760 dâchâh (1), to *push down; to totter*
7291 râdaph (5), to *run after* with hostility

CHASED

1272 bârach (1), to *flee suddenly*
5074 nâdad (2), to *rove, flee; to drive away*
5080 nâdach (1), to *push off, scattered*
6679 tsûwd (1), to *lie in wait; to catch*
7291 râdaph (8), to *run after* with hostility

CHASETH

1272 bârach (1), to *flee suddenly*

CHASING

1814 dâlaq (1), to *flame; to pursue*

CHASTE

53 hagnŏs (3), *innocent, modest, perfect, pure*

CHASTEN

3198 yâkach (1), to *decide, justify, convict*
3256 yâçar (3), to *chastise; to instruct*
6031 'ânâh (1), to *afflict, be afflicted*
3811 paidĕuŏ (1), to *educate* or *discipline*

CHASTENED

3198 yâkach (1), to *decide, justify, convict*
3256 yâçar (2), to *chastise; to instruct*
8433 tôwkêchâh (1), *chastisement*
3811 paidĕuŏ (3), to *educate* or *discipline*

CHASTENEST

3256 yâçar (1), to *chastise; to instruct*

CHASTENETH

3256 yâçar (2), to *chastise; to instruct*
4148 mûwçâr (1), *reproof, warning*
3811 paidĕuŏ (2), to *educate* or *discipline*

CHASTENING

4148 mûwçâr (3), *reproof, warning*
3809 paidĕia (3), *disciplinary correction*

CHASTISE

3256 yâçar (6), to *chastise; to instruct*
3811 paidĕuŏ (2), to *educate* or *discipline*

CHASTISED

3256 yâçar (5), to *chastise; to instruct*

CHASTISEMENT

4148 mûwçâr (3), *reproof, warning*
3809 paidĕia (1), *disciplinary correction*

CHASTISETH

3256 yâçar (1), to *chastise; to instruct*

CHATTER

6850 tsâphaph (1), to *coo* or *chirp* as a bird

CHEBAR

3529 Kᵉbâr (8), *length*

CHECK

4148 mûwçâr (1), *reproof, warning*

CHECKER

7639 sᵉbâkâh (1), *net-work balustrade*

CHEDORLAOMER

3540 Kᵉdorlâ'ômer (5), *Kedorlaomer*

CHEEK

3895 lᵉchîy (6), *jaw;* area of the *jaw*
4973 mᵉthallᵉ'âh (1), *tooth*
4600 siagŏn (2), *cheek*

CHEEKS

3895 lᵉchîy (5), *jaw;* area of the *jaw*

CHEER

3190 yâṭab (1), to *be, make well*
8055 sâmach (1), to *be, make gleesome*
2114 ĕuthumĕŏ (3), to *be cheerful*
2293 tharsĕŏ (5), to *have courage; take heart!*

CHEERETH

8055 sâmach (1), to *be, make gleesome*

CHEERFUL

2896 ṭôwb (1), *good; well*
3190 yâṭab (1), to *be, make well*
5107 nûwb (1), to *(make) flourish; to utter*
2431 hilarŏs (1), *prompt* or *willing*

CHEERFULLY

2115 ĕuthumŏs (1), *cheerful, encouraged*

CHEERFULNESS

2432 hilarŏtēs (1), *cheerful readiness*

CHEESE

1385 gᵉbînah (1), *curdled milk*
8194 shâphâh (1), *cheese*

CHEESES

2757+2461 chârîyts (1), *slice, portion*

CHELAL

3636 Kᵉlâl (1), *complete*

CHELLUH

3622 Kᵉlûwhay (1), *completed*

CHELUB

3620 Kᵉlûwb (2), *bird-trap; basket*

CHELUBAI

3621 Kᵉlûwbay (1), *forcible*

CHEMARIMS

3649 kâmâr (1), *pagan priest*

English

CHEMOSH
3645 Kᵉmôwsh (8), *powerful*

CHENAANAH
3668 Kᵉna'ănâh (5), *humiliated*

CHENANI
3662 Kᵉnânîy (1), *planted*

CHENANIAH
3663 Kᵉnanyâh (3), *Jehovah has planted*

CHEPHAR-HAAMMONAI
3726 Kᵉphar hâ-'Ammôwnîy (1), *village of the Ammonite*

CHEPHIRAH
3716 Kᵉphîyrâh (4), *village*

CHERAN
3763 Kᵉrân (2), *Keran*

CHERETHIMS
3774 Kᵉrêthîy (1), *executioner*

CHERETHITES
3746 kârîy (1), *life-guardsman*
3774 Kᵉrêthîy (8), *executioner*

CHERISH
5532 çâkan (1), to *be familiar with*

CHERISHED
5532 çâkan (1), to *be familiar with*

CHERISHETH
2282 thalpō (2), to *foster, care for*

CHERITH
3747 Kᵉrîyth (2), *cut*

CHERUB
3742 kᵉrûwb (26), *cherub*
3743 Kᵉrûwb (2), *cherub*

CHERUBIM
3742 kᵉrûwb (2), *cherub*

CHERUBIMS
3742 kᵉrûwb (61), *cherub*
5502 chĕrŏubim (1), *cherubs or kerubim*

CHERUBIMS'
3742 kᵉrûwb (1), *cherub*

CHESALON
3693 Kᵉçâlôwn (1), *fertile*

CHESED
3777 Kesed (1), *Kesed*

CHESIL
3686 Kᵉçîyl (1), *stupid or silly*

CHESNUT
6196 'armôwn (2), *plane tree*

CHEST
727 'ârôwn (6), *box*

CHESTS
1595 genez (1), *treasury coffer*

CHESULLOTH
3694 Kᵉçullôwth (1), *fattened*

CHEW
5927 'âlâh (3), to *ascend, be high, mount*

CHEWED
3772 kârath (1), to *cut (off, down or asunder)*

CHEWETH
1641 gârar (1), to *chew*
5927 'âlâh (6), to *ascend, be high, mount*

CHEZIB
3580 Kᵉzîyb (1), *falsified*

CHICKENS
3556 nŏssiŏn (1), *birdling, chick-bird*

CHIDE
7378 rîyb (4), to *hold a controversy; to defend*

CHIDING
7379 rîyb (1), *contest, personal or legal*

CHIDON
3592 Kîydôwn (1), *dart, javelin*

CHIEF
1 'âb (3), *father*
441 'allûwph (1), *friend, chieftain, leader*
678 'âtsîyl (1), *extremity; noble*
1167 ba'al (1), *master; husband; owner; citizen*
1368 gibbôwr (1), *powerful; great warrior*
3548 kôhên (2), one *officiating as a priest*
5051 nôgahh (1), *brilliancy*
5057 nâgîyd (1), *commander, official*
5059 nâgan (1), to *play; to make music*
5329 nâtsach (55), i.e. to *be eminent*
5387 nâsîy' (8), *leader; rising mist, fog*
6260 'attûwd (1), *he-goats; leaders* of the *people*
6438 pinnâh (2), *pinnacle; chieftain*
7217 rê'sh (Ch.) (1), *head*
7218 rô'sh (97), *head*
7223 rî'shôwn (3), *first*
7225 rê'shîyth (5), *first*
7229 rab (Ch.) (1), *great*
7725 shûwb (3), to *turn back; to return*
8269 sar (33), *head person, ruler*
204 akrŏgōniaiŏs (2), *corner, cornerstone*
749 archiĕrĕus (65), *high-priest, chief priest*
750 archipŏimēn (1), *head shepherd*
752 archisunagōgŏs (2), *director* of the *synagogue services*
754 architĕlōnēs (1), *chief tax-gatherer*
758 archōn (3), *first in rank or power*
775 Asiarchēs (1), *ruler in Asia*
2233 hēgĕŏmai (3), to *lead, i.e. the chief*
4410 prōtŏkathĕdria (2), *place of pre-eminence*
4411 prōtŏklisia (2), *pre-eminence at meals*
4413 prōtŏs (10), *foremost*
5506 chiliarchŏs (19), *colonel*

CHIEFEST
47 'abbîyr (1), *mighty*
1713 dâgal (1), to *be conspicuous*
4608 ma'ăleh (1), *elevation; platform*
7218 rô'sh (1), *head*
7225 rê'shîyth (1), *first*
3390 mētrŏpŏlis (1), *main city*
4413 prōtŏs (1), *foremost*
5228+3029 hupĕr (2), *over; above; beyond*

CHIEFLY
3122 malista (2), *in the greatest degree*
4412 prōtŏn (1), *firstly*

CHILD
1121 bên (10), *son, descendant*
2029 hârâh (2), to *conceive, be pregnant*
2030 hâreh (12), *pregnant*
2056 vâlâd (1), *boy*
2233 zera' (2), *seed; fruit*
3173 yâchîyd (1), *only son; alone; beloved*
3205 yâlad (5), to *bear young; to father a child*
3206 yeled (39), *young male*
4392 mâlê' (1), *full; filling; fulness; fully*
5288 na'ar (44), *male child; servant*
5290 nô'ar (1), *boyhood*
5768 'ôwlêl (1), *suckling child*
1025 brĕphŏs (1), *infant*
1471 ĕgkuŏs (1), *pregnant*
1722+1064+2192 ĕn (7), *in; during; because of*
3439 mŏnŏgĕnēs (2), *sole, one and only*
3516 nēpiŏs (4), *infant; simple-minded person*
3812 paidiŏthĕn (1), *from infancy*
3813 paidiŏn (28), *child: immature*
3816 pais (5), *child; slave or servant*
5043 tĕknŏn (5), *child*
5088 tiktō (1), to *produce from seed*
5207 huiŏs (3), *son*

CHILD'S
3206 yeled (2), *young male*
5290 nô'ar (1), *boyhood*
3813 paidiŏn (1), *child: immature*

CHILDBEARING
5042 tĕknŏgŏnia (1), *maternity, childbearing*

CHILDHOOD
3208 yaldûwth (1), *boyhood or girlhood*
5271 nâ'ûwr (1), *youth; juvenility; young people*

CHILDISH
3516 nēpiŏs (1), *infant; simple-minded* person

CHILDLESS
6185 'ărîyrîy (4), *barren of child*
7921 shâkôl (2), to *miscarry*
815 atĕknŏs (1), *childless*

CHILDREN
1121 bên (1523), *son, descendant*
1123 bên (Ch.) (4), *son*
1129 bânâh (2), to *build; to establish*
2945 ṭaph (12), *family of children and women*
3205 yâlad (1), to *bear young; to father a child*
3206 yeled (31), *young male*
3211 yâlîyd (4), *born; descendants*
5288 na'ar (7), *male child; servant*
5768 'ôwlêl (12), *suckling child*
6768 Tseleq (1), *fissure*
815 atĕknŏs (2), *childless*
1025 brĕphŏs (1), *infant*
3515 nēpiazō (1), to *act as a baby*
3516 nēpiŏs (2), *infant; simple-minded person*
3808 paidariŏn (1), *little boy*
3813 paidiŏn (17), *child: immature*
3816 pais (2), *child; slave or servant*
5027 taphē (2), *act of burial*
5040 tĕkniŏn (9), *infant, i.e. a darling*
5041 tĕknŏgŏnĕō (1), to *be a child bearer*
5043 tĕknŏn (70), *child*
5044 tĕknŏtrŏphĕō (1), to *be a child-rearer*
5206 huiŏthĕsia (1), *adoption*
5207 huiŏs (44), *son*
5388 philŏtĕknŏs (1), *loving one's child(ren)*

CHILDREN'S
1121 bên (16), *son, descendant*
3813 paidiŏn (1), *child: immature* Christian
5043 tĕknŏn (2), *child*

CHILEAB
3609 Kil'âb (1), *restraint of (his) father*

CHILION
3630 Kilyôwn (2), *pining, destruction*

CHILION'S
3630 Kilyôwn (1), *pining, destruction*

CHILMAD
3638 Kilmâd (1), *Kilmad*

CHIMHAM
3643 Kimhâm (4), *pining*

CHIMNEY
699 'ărubbâh (1), *window; chimney*

CHINNERETH
3672 Kinn⁰rôwth (4),
(poss.) *harp*-shaped

CHINNEROTH
3672 Kinn⁰rôwth (2),
(poss.) *harp*-shaped

CHIOS
5508 *Chiŏs* (1), *Chios*

CHISLEU
3691 Kîçlêv (2), *Hebrew
month*

CHISLON
3692 Kiçlôwn (1), *hopeful*

CHISLOTH-TABOR
3696 Kiçlôth Tâbôr (1),
flanks of Tabor

CHITTIM
3794 Kittîy (6), *islander*

CHIUN
3594 Kîyûwn (1), *deity*
(poss.) *Priapus or
Baal-peor*

CHLOE
5514 *Chlŏē* (1), *green*

CHODE
7378 rîyb (2), to *hold a
controversy; to defend*

CHOICE
970 bâchûwr (3), *male
youth; bridegroom*
977 bâchar (4), *select,
chose, prefer*
1249 bar (1), *beloved;
pure; empty*
1305 bârar (2), to
examine; select
4005 mibchâr (9), *select*
8321 sôrêq (1), *choice
vine stock*
1586 ĕklĕgŏmai (1), to
select, choose, pick out

CHOICEST
4055 mad (1), *vesture,
garment; carpet*
8321 sôrêq (1), *choice
vine stock*

CHOKE
4846 sumpnigō (2), to
drown; to crowd

CHOKED
638 apŏpnigō (3), to *stifle
or choke*
4155 pnigō (1), to *throttle
or strangle; to drown*
4846 sumpnigō (2), to
drown; to crowd

CHOLER
4843 mârar (2), to *be,
make bitter*

CHOOSE
972 bâchîyr (1), *selected
one*
977 bâchar (53), *select,
chose, prefer*
1254 bârâ' (2), to *create;
fashion*
1262 bârâh (1), to *feed*
6901 qâbal (1), to *take*
138 hairĕŏmai (1), to
prefer, choose

CHOOSEST
977 bâchar (2), *select,
chose, prefer*

CHOOSETH
977 bâchar (3), *select,
chose, prefer*

CHOOSING
138 hairĕŏmai (1), to
prefer, choose

CHOP
6566 pâras (1), to *break
apart, disperse, scatter*

CHOR-ASHAN
3565 Kôwr 'Âshân (1),
furnace of smoke

CHORAZIN
5523 Chŏrazin (2),
Chorazin

CHOSE
977 bâchar (24), *select,
chose, prefer*
1586 ĕklĕgŏmai (4), to
select, choose, pick out
1951 ĕpilĕgŏmai (1), to
surname, select

CHOSEN
970 bâchûwr (21), *male
youth; bridegroom*
972 bâchîyr (8), *selected
one*
977 bâchar (58), *select,
chose, prefer*
1305 bârar (2), to
examine; select
4005 mibchâr (4), *select*
138 hairĕŏmai (1), to
prefer, choose
140 hairĕtizō (1), to
make a choice
1586 ĕklĕgŏmai (15), to
select, choose, pick out
1588 ĕklĕktŏs (7),
selected; chosen
1589 ĕklŏgē (1),
selection, choice
4400 prŏchĕirizŏmai (1),
to *purpose*
4401 prŏchĕirŏtŏnĕō (1),
to *elect in advance*
4758 stratŏlŏgĕō (1), to
enlist in the army
5500 chĕirŏtŏnĕō (1), to
select or appoint

CHOZEBA
3578 Kôzⁱbâ' (1),
fallacious

CHRIST
5477 Chanaan (1),
humiliated
5547 Christŏs (551),
Anointed One

CHRIST'S
5547 Christŏs (15),
Anointed One

CHRISTIAN
5546 Christianŏs (2),
follower of Christ

CHRISTIANS
5546 Christianŏs (1),
follower of Christ

CHRISTS
5580 psĕudŏchristŏs (2),
spurious Messiah

CHRONICLES
1697+3117 dâbâr (38),
word; matter; thing

CHRYSOLITE
5555 chrusŏlithŏs (1),
yellow chrysolite

CHRYSOPRASUS
5556 chrusŏprasŏs (1),
*greenish-yellow
chrysoprase*

CHUB
3552 Kûwb (1), *Kub*

CHUN
3560 Kûwn (1),
established

CHURCH
1577 ĕkklēsia (80),
congregation

CHURCHES
1577 ĕkklēsia (36),
congregation
2417 hiĕrŏsulŏs (1),
temple-despoiler

CHURL
3596 kîylay (2),
begrudging

CHURLISH
7186 qâsheh (1), *severe*

CHURNING
4330 mîyts (1), *pressure*

CHUSHAN-RISHATHAIM
3573 Kûwshan
Rish'âthâyim (4),
*Cushan of double
wickedness*

CHUZA
5529 Chŏuzas (1),
Chuzas

CIELED
2645 châphâh (1), to
cover; to veil, to encase
5603 çâphan (2), to *hide
by covering; to roof*
7824 shâchîyph (1),
board, panel

CIELING
5604 çippûn (1),
wainscot, paneling

CILICIA
2791 Kilikia (8), *Cilicia*

CINNAMON
7076 qinnâmôwn (3),
cinnamon spice
2792 kinamōmŏn (1),
cinnamon

CINNEROTH
3672 Kinn⁰rôwth (1),
(poss.) *harp*-shaped

CIRCLE
2329 chûwg (1), *circle*

CIRCUIT
2329 chûwg (1), *circle*
5437 çâbab (1), to
surround
8622 tⁱqûwphâh (1),
revolution, course

CIRCUITS
5439 çâbîyb (1), *circle;
neighbor; environs*

CIRCUMCISE
4135 mûwl (5), to
circumcise
5243 nâmal (1), to *be
circumcised*
4059 pĕritĕmnō (4), to
circumcise

CIRCUMCISED
4135 mûwl (23), to
circumcise
203 akrŏbustia (1),
uncircumcised
4059 pĕritĕmnō (13), to
circumcise
4061 pĕritŏmē (1),
circumcision; Jews

CIRCUMCISING
4135 mûwl (1), to
circumcise
4059 pĕritĕmnō (1), to
circumcise

CIRCUMCISION
4139 mûwlâh (1),
circumcision
4061 pĕritŏmē (35),
circumcision; Jews

CIRCUMSPECT
8104 shâmar (1), to
watch

CIRCUMSPECTLY
199 akribŏs (1), *exactly,
carefully*

CIS
2797 Kis (1), *bow*

CISTERN
953 bôwr (4), *pit hole,
cistern, well*

CISTERNS
877 bô'r (1), *well, cistern*

CITIES
5892 'îyr (419), *city, town,
unwalled-village*
7141 Qôrach (1), *ice*
8179 sha'ar (2), *opening,
i.e. door or gate*
4172 pŏlis (19), *town*

CITIZEN
4177 pŏlitēs (2), *citizen*

CITIZENS
4177 pŏlitēs (1), *citizen*

CITY
4062 madhêbâh (1), *gold
making*
5892 'îyr (650), *city, town,
unwalled-village*
5982 'ammûwd (1),
column, pillar
7149 qiryâ' (Ch.) (6), *city*
7151 qiryâh (32), *city*
7176 qereth (5), *city*
7179 qash (1), *dry straw*
8179 sha'ar (1), *opening,
i.e. door or gate*
3390 mētrŏpŏlis (1),
main city
4172 pŏlis (143), *town*
4173 pŏlitarchēs (2),
magistrate, city official

CLAD
3680 kâçâh (1), to *cover*
5844 'âţâh (1), to *wrap,
i.e. cover, veil, clothe*

CLAMOROUS
1993 hâmâh (1), to *be in
great commotion*

CLAMOUR
2906 kraugē (1), *outcry*

CLAP
4222 mâcha' (2), to *strike
the hands together*

English

CLAPPED
5606 çâphaq (2), to *clap*
the hands
8628 tâqa' (2), to *clatter,
slap, drive, clasp*

CLAPPED
4222 mâchâ' (1), to *strike*
the hands together
5221 nâkâh (1), to *strike,
kill*

CLAPPETH
5606 çâphaq (1), to *clap*
the hands

CLAUDA
2802 *Klaudē* (1), *Claude*

CLAUDIA
2803 *Klaudia* (1), *Claudia*

CLAUDIUS
2804 *Klaudiŏs* (3),
Claudius

CLAVE
1234 bâqa' (6), to *cleave,
break, tear open*
1692 dâbaq (6), to *cling*
or *adhere*
2388 châzaq (1), to
fasten upon; to *seize;* to
be strong; courageous
2853 *kŏllaō* (1), to *glue
together*

CLAWS
6541 parçâh (2), split
hoof

CLAY
2563 chômer (11), *clay;*
dry *measure*
2635 chăçaph (Ch.) (9),
clay
2916 tîyṭ (3), *mud* or *clay*
4423 meleṭ (1), smooth
clay *cement floor*
4568 ma'ăbeh (1),
compact part of soil
5671 'abṭîyṭ (1),
something *pledged,* i.e.
(collect.) *pawned* goods
4081 *pēlŏs* (6), lump of
clay

CLEAN
656 'âphêç (1), to *cease*
1249 bar (3), *beloved;
pure; empty*
1305 bârar (1), to
brighten; purify
2134 zak (2), *pure; clear*
2135 zâkâh (4), to *be
translucent*
2141 zâkak (2), to *be
transparent; clean, pure*
2548 châmîyts (1), *salted*
provender or fodder
2889 ṭâhôwr (49), *pure,
clean, flawless*
2891 ṭâhêr (41), to *be
pure, unadulterated*
5355 nâqîy (1), *innocent*
6565 pârar (1), to *break
up;* to *violate, frustrate*
8552 tâmam (3), to
complete, finish
2511 *katharizō* (5), to
cleanse
2513 *katharŏs* (10),
clean, pure
2889 *kŏsmŏs* (3), *world*
3689 *ŏntōs* (1), *really,
certainly*

CLEANNESS
1252 bôr (4), *purity,
cleanness*
5356 niqqâyôwn (1),
clearness; cleanness

CLEANSE
1305 bârar (1), to
brighten; purify
2135 zâkâh (1), to *be
translucent*
2398 châṭâ' (7), to *sin*
2891 ṭâhêr (15), to *be
pure, unadulterated*
5352 nâqâh (3), to *be,
make clean;* to *be bare*
2511 *katharizō* (6), to
cleanse

CLEANSED
2135 zâkâh (1), to *be
translucent*
2891 ṭâhêr (23), to *be
pure, unadulterated*
2893 ṭohŏrâh (1),
purification; purity
3722 kâphar (1), to
cover; to *expiate*
5352 nâqâh (1), to *be,
make clean;* to *be bare*
6663 tsâdaq (1), to *be,
make right*
2511 *katharizō* (9), to
cleanse

CLEANSETH
2891 ṭâhêr (1), to *be
pure, unadulterated*
8562 tamrûwq (1),
scouring, i.e. *soap*
2511 *katharizō* (1), to
cleanse

CLEANSING
2893 ṭohŏrâh (8),
purification; purity
2512 *katharismŏs* (2),
ablution; expiation

CLEAR
216 'ôwr (1), *luminary;
lightning; happiness*
1249 bar (1), *beloved;
pure; empty*
2135 zâkâh (1), to *be
translucent*
3368 yâqâr (1), *valuable*
5352 nâqâh (3), to *be,
make clean;* to *be bare*
5355 nâqîy (1), *innocent*
6663 tsâdaq (1), to *be,
make right*
6703 tsach (1), *dazzling,*
i.e. *sunny, bright*
53 hagnŏs (1), *innocent,
modest, perfect, pure*
2513 *katharŏs* (1), *clean,
pure*
2929 *krustallizō* (1), to
appear as ice
2986 *lamprŏs* (1),
radiant; clear

CLEARER
6965 qûwm (1), to *rise*

CLEARING
5352 nâqâh (1), to *be,
make clean;* to *be bare*
627 *apŏlŏgia* (1), *plea* or
verbal *defense*

CLEARLY
1305 bârar (1), to
brighten; purify
1227 *diablĕpō* (2), *see
clearly*
2529 *kathŏraō* (1), to
distinctly apprehend
5081 *tēlaugōs* (1), *plainly*

CLEARNESS
2892 ṭôhar (1),
brightness; purification

CLEAVE
1234 bâqa' (3), to *cleave,
break, tear open*
1692 dâbaq (18), to *cling*
or *adhere;* to *catch*
1693 dᵉbaq (Ch.) (1), to
stick; to *be united*
1695 dâbêq (1),
adhering, sticking to
3867 lâvâh (1), to *unite*
5596 çâphach (1), to
associate; be united
8156 shâça' (1), to *split*
or *tear;* to *upbraid*
2853 *kŏllaō* (1), to *glue
together*
4347 *prŏskŏllaō* (3), to
glue to, i.e. to *adhere*

CLEAVED
1692 dâbaq (3), to *cling*
or *adhere;* to *catch*

CLEAVETH
1234 bâqa' (2), to *cleave,
break, tear open*
1692 dâbaq (6), to *cling*
or *adhere;* to *catch*
3332 yâtsaq (1), to *pour
out*
6398 pâlach (1), to *slice;*
to *break* open; to *pierce*
6821 tsâphad (1), to
adhere, join
8157 sheça' (1), *fissure,
split*
2853 *kŏllaō* (1), to *glue
together*

CLEFT
1234 bâqa' (1), to *cleave,
break, tear open*
8156 shâça' (1), to *split*
or *tear;* to *upbraid*

CLEFTS
1233 bᵉqîya' (1), *fissure,
breach*
2288 chăgâv (3), *rift, cleft*
in rocks
5366 nᵉqârâh (1), *fissure*

CLEMENCY
1932 *ĕpiĕikĕia* (1),
mildness, gentleness

CLEMENT
2815 *Klēmēs* (1), *merciful*

CLEOPAS
2810 *Klĕŏpas* (1), *renown
father*

CLEOPHAS
2832 *Klōpas* (1), cf. *friend
of* (his) *father*

CLIFF
4608 ma'ăleh (1),
elevation; platform

CLIFFS
6178 'ârûwts (1), *feared;
horrible* place or *chasm*

CLIFT
5366 nᵉqârâh (1), *fissure*

CLIFTS
5585 çâ'îyph (1), *fissure*
of rocks; *bough*

CLIMB
5927 'âlâh (4), to *ascend,
be high, mount*

CLIMBED
5927 'âlâh (1), to *ascend,
be high, mount*
305 anabainō (1), to *go
up, rise*

CLIMBETH
305 anabainō (1), to *go
up, rise*

CLIPPED
1639 gâra' (1), to *shave,
remove, lessen*

CLODS
1487 gûwsh (1), *mass* of
earth, dirt *clod*
4053 migrâphâh (1), *clod*
of cultivated dirt
7263 regeb (2), *lump* of
clay
7702 sâdad (2), to
harrow a field

CLOKE
4598 mᵉ'îyl (1), outer
garment or robe
1942 *ĕpikaluma* (1),
pretext, covering
2440 *himatiŏn* (2), to *put
on clothes*
4392 *prŏphasis* (2),
pretext, excuse
5341 *phĕlŏnēs* (1), outer
garment, *mantle, cloak*

CLOSE
681 'êtsel (1), *side; near*
1443 gâdar (1), to *build a
stone wall*
1692 dâbaq (1), to *cling*
or *adhere;* to *catch*
4526 miçgereth (2),
margin; stronghold
5641 çâthar (1), to *hide*
by covering
5956 'âlam (1), to *veil*
from sight, i.e. *conceal*
6113 'âtsar (1), to *hold
back;* to *maintain*
6862 tsar (1), *trouble;
opponent*
788 assŏn (1), *more
nearly,* i.e. *very near*
4601 sigaō (1), to *keep
silent*

CLOSED
2115 zûwr (1), to *press
together, tighten*
3680 kâçâh (1), to *cover*
5437 çâbab (1), to
surround
5462 çâgar (2), to *shut
up;* to *surrender*
5640 çâtham (1), to *stop
up;* to *keep secret*
6105 'âtsam (1), to *be,
make powerful*
6113 'âtsar (1), to *hold
back;* to *maintain*
2576 kammuō (2), to
close or *shut* the eyes

4428 ptussō (1), to fold,
i.e. furl or roll a scroll

CLOSEST
8474 tachârâh (1), to vie
with a rival

CLOSET
2646 chuppâh (1), canopy
5009 tamĕiŏn (1), room

CLOSETS
5009 tamĕiŏn (1), room

CLOTH
899 beged (9), clothing;
treachery or pillage
4346 makbâr (1),
netted-cloth
8071 simlâh (2), dress,
mantle
4470 rhakŏs (2), piece of
cloth
4616 sindōn (3), byssos,
i.e. bleached linen

CLOTHE
3847 lâbash (12), to
clothe
294 amphiĕnnumi (2), to
enrobe, clothe

CLOTHED
3680 kâçâh (1), to cover
3736 karbêl (1), to gird
or clothe
3830 lᵉbûwsh (1),
garment; wife
3847 lâbash (39), to
clothe
3848 lᵉbash (Ch.) (3), to
clothe
294 amphiĕnnumi (2), to
enrobe, clothe
1463 ĕgkŏmbŏŏmai (1),
to wear, be clothed
1737 ĕndiduskō (1), to
clothe
1746 ĕnduō (6), to invest
with clothing, i.e. to
dress
1902 ĕpĕnduŏmai (2), to
clothe
2439 himatizō (2), to
dress, clothe
4016 pĕriballō (14), to
wrap around, clothe

CLOTHES
899 beged (69), clothing;
treachery or pillage
1545 gᵉlôwm (1),
clothing, fabric
4055 mad (1), vesture,
garment; carpet
5497 çûwth (1), clothing
8008 salmâh (3), clothing
8071 simlâh (6), dress,
mantle
2440 himatiŏn (12), to
put on clothes
3608 ŏthŏniŏn (5), strips
of linen bandage
4683 sparganŏō (2), to
wrap with cloth
5509 chitōn (1), tunic or
shirt

CLOTHEST
3847 lâbash (1), to clothe

CLOTHING
899 beged (1), clothing;
treachery or pillage

3830 lᵉbûwsh (9),
garment; wife
4374 mᵉkaççeh (1),
covering
8071 simlâh (2), dress,
mantle
8516 talbôsheth (1),
garment
1742 ĕnduma (1),
apparel, outer robe
2066 ĕsthēs (2), to clothe
4749 stŏlē (1),
long-fitting gown

CLOTHS
899 beged (4), clothing;
treachery or pillage

CLOUD
5645 'âb (9), thick
clouds; thicket
5743 'ûwb (1), to darkly
becloud
6051 'ânân (75), nimbus
cloud
6053 'ănânâh (1),
cloudiness
6205 'ărâphel (1), gloom,
darkness
3507 nĕphĕlē (18), cloud
3509 nĕphŏs (1), cloud

CLOUDS
2385 chăzîyz (1), flash of
lightning
3709 kaph (1), hollow of
hand; paw; sole of foot
5387 nâsîy' (1), leader;
rising mist, fog
5645 'âb (20), thick
clouds; thicket
6050 'ănan (Ch.) (1),
nimbus cloud
6051 'ânân (5), nimbus
cloud
6053 'ănânâh (1),
cloudiness
7834 shachaq (11),
firmament, clouds
3507 nĕphĕlē (8), cloud

CLOUDY
6051 'ânân (6), nimbus
cloud

CLOUTED
2921 ţâlâ' (1), to be
spotted or variegated

CLOUTS
5499 çᵉchâbâh (2), rag

CLOVEN
8156 shâça' (1), to split
or tear; to upbraid
1266 diamĕrizō (1), to
distribute

CLOVENFOOTED
8156+8157 shâça' (1), to
split or tear; to upbraid
8156+8157+6541 shâça'
(2), to split or tear

CLUSTER
811 'eshkôwl (5), bunch
of grapes

CLUSTERS
811 'eshkôwl (4), bunch
of grapes
6778 tsammûwq (2),
lump of dried grapes
1009 bŏtrus (1), bunch,
cluster of grapes

CNIDUS
2834 Knidŏs (1), Cnidus

COAL
1513 gechel (2), ember,
hot coal
7531 ritspâh (1), hot
stone; pavement
7815 shᵉchôwr (1), soot

COALS
1513 gechel (16), ember,
hot coal
6352 pechâm (3), black
coal, charcoal
7529 retseph (1), red-hot
stone for baking
7565 resheph (2), flame
439 anthrakia (2), fire
bed of burning coals
440 anthrax (1), live coal

COAST
1366 gᵉbûwl (47),
boundary, border
2256 chebel (4),
company, band
2348 chôwph (1), cove,
sheltered bay
3027 yâd (5), hand; power
5299 nâphâh (1), height;
sieve
7097 qâtseh (1), extremity
3864 parathalassiŏs (1),
by the lake
3882 paraliŏs (1),
maritime; seacoast

COASTS
1366 gᵉbûwl (23),
boundary, border
1367 gᵉbûwlâh (5), region
1552 gᵉlîylâh (1), circuit
or region
2348 chôwph (1), cove,
sheltered bay
3027 yâd (1), hand; power
3411 yᵉrêkâh (3), far
away places
7097 qâtseh (1), extremity
7098 qâtsâh (1),
termination; fringe
3313 mĕrŏs (3), division
or share
3725 hŏriŏn (10), region,
area, vicinity
5117 tŏpŏs (1), place
5561 chōra (1), territory

COAT
3801 kᵉthôneth (16),
garment that covers
4598 mᵉ'îyl (1), outer
garment or robe
8302 shiryôwn (3),
corslet, coat of mail
1903 ĕpĕndutēs (1), outer
garment, coat
5509 chitōn (4), tunic or
shirt

COATS
3801 kᵉthôneth (7),
garment that covers
5622 çarbal (Ch.) (2),
cloak
5509 chitōn (5), tunic or
shirt

COCK
220 alĕktōr (12), rooster

COCKATRICE
6848 tsepha' (1), hissing
viper

COCKATRICES
6848 tsepha' (1), hissing
viper

COCKCROWING
219 alektŏrŏphōnia (1),
rooster-crowing

COCKLE
890 bo'shâh (1), weed

COFFER
712 'argâz (3), box, chest

COFFIN
727 'ârôwn (1), box

COGITATIONS
7476 ra'yôwn (Ch.) (1),
mental conception

COLD
2779 chôreph (1),
autumn (and winter)
6793 tsinnâh (1), large
shield; piercing cold
7119 qar (2), cool; quiet;
cool-headed
7120 qôr (1), cold
7135 qârâh (5), coolness,
cold
5592 psuchŏs (3),
coolness, cold
5593 psuchrŏs (4), chilly,
cold
5594 psuchō (1), to chill,
grow cold

COLHOZEH
3626 Kol-Chôzeh (2),
every seer

COLLAR
6310 peh (1), mouth;
opening

COLLARS
5188 nᵉţîyphâh (1),
pendant for the ears

COLLECTION
4864 mas'êth (2), raising;
beacon; present
3048 lŏgia (1),
contribution, collection

COLLEGE
4932 mishneh (2),
duplicate copy; double

COLLOPS
6371 pîymâh (1), obesity

COLONY
2862 kŏlōnia (1), colony

COLORS
6320 pûwk (1), stibium

COLOSSE
2857 Kŏlŏssai (1),
colossal

COLOSSIANS
2858 Kŏlŏssaĕus (1),
inhabitant of Colossæ

COLOUR
5869 'ayin (11), eye;
sight; fountain
4392 prŏphasis (1),
pretext, excuse

COLOURS
2921 ţâlâ' (1), to be
spotted or variegated
6446 paç (5), long
-sleeved tunic

English

6648 tseba' (3), *dye*
7553 riqmâh (2),
  variegation of color

COLT
1121 bên (1), *son,
  descendant*
5895 'ayîr (2), *young
  robust donkey* or *ass*
4454 pôlŏs (12), *young
  donkey*

COLTS
1121 bên (1), *son,
  descendant*
5895 'ayîr (2), *young
  robust donkey* or *ass*

COME
270 'âchaz (1), to *seize,
  grasp; possess*
314 'achărôwn (8), *late
  or last; behind; western*
635 'Ȩçtêr (1), *Esther*
835 'esher (3), *how
  happy!*
857 'âthâh (12), to *arrive*
858 'âthâh (Ch.) (3), to
  arrive; go
935 bôw' (681), to *go,
  come*
1869 dârak (1), to *walk,
  lead;* to *string* a bow
1934 hăvâ' (Ch.) (3), to
  be, to *exist*
1961 hâyâh (131), to
  exist, i.e. *be* or *become*
1980 hâlak (7), to *walk;
  live a certain way*
3045 yâda' (3), to *know*
3051 yâhab (1), to *give*
3205 yâlad (1), to *bear
  young;* to *father a child*
3212 yâlak (72), to *walk;
  *to *live;* to *carry*
3318 yâtsâ' (84), to *go,
  bring out*
3381 yârad (57), to
  descend
4279 mâchar (8),
  tomorrow; hereafter
4291 mᵉṭâ' (Ch.) (1), to
  arrive, to *extend*
4609 ma'ălâh (1),
  thought arising
4672 mâtsâ' (8), to *find
  or acquire;* to *occur*
5060 nâga' (13), to *strike*
5066 nâgash (28), to *be,
  come, bring near*
5181 nâchath (2), to *sink,
  descend*
5185 nâchêth (1),
  descending
5312 nᵉphaq (Ch.) (1), to
  issue forth; to *bring out*
5506 çᵉchôrâh (1), *traffic*
5674 'âbar (14), to *cross
  over;* to *transition*
5927 'âlâh (104), to
  ascend, be high, mount
6213 'âsâh (1), to *do* or
  make
6264 'âthîyd (1),
  prepared; treasure
6631 tse'ĕtsâ' (1),
  produce, children
6743 tsâlach (1), to *push
  forward*
6923 qâdam (5), to
  anticipate, hasten

7122 qârâ' (4), to
  encounter, to *happen*
7125 qir'âh (1), to
  encounter, to *happen*
7126 qârab (33), to
  approach, bring near
7131 qârêb (2), *near*
7136 qârâh (2), to *bring
  about;* to *impose*
7138 qârôwb (1), *near,
  close*
7725 shûwb (30), to *turn
  back;* to *return*
8175 sâ'ar (1), to *storm;*
  to shiver, i.e. *fear*
8622 tᵉqûwphâh (1),
  revolution, course
191 akŏuō (1), to *hear;
  obey*
305 anabainō (7), to *go
  up, rise*
565 apérchŏmai (3), to
  go off, i.e. *depart*
576 apŏbainō (1), to
  eventuate, become
864 aphiknĕŏmai (1), to
  go forth by rumor
1096 ginŏmai (43), to *be,
  become*
1204 dĕurŏ (8), *hither!;
  hitherto*
1205 dĕutĕ (12), *come
  hither!*
1224 diabainō (1), to
  pass by, over, across
1330 diĕrchŏmai (1), to
  traverse, travel through
1448 ĕggizō (9), to
  approach
1511 ĕinai (8), to *exist*
1525 ĕisĕrchŏmai (18), to
  enter
1531 ĕispŏrĕuŏmai (1), to
  enter
1607 ĕkpŏrĕuŏmai (3), to
  depart, be discharged
1684 ĕmbainō (2), to
  embark, to *reach*
1764 ĕnistēmi (1), to *be
  present*
1831 ĕxĕrchŏmai (24), to
  issue; to *leave*
1834 ĕxēgĕŏmai (1), to
  tell, relate again
1880 ĕpanĕrchŏmai (1),
  return home
1904 ĕpĕrchŏmai (8), to
  supervene
1910 ĕpibainō (1), to
  ascend, embark, arrive
1975 ĕpipŏrĕuŏmai (1),
  to *go, come* to
2049 ĕrēmŏō (1), to *lay
  waste*
2064 ĕrchŏmai (290), to
  go or *come*
2186 ĕphistēmi (2), to *be
  present;* to *approach*
2240 hēkō (24), to *arrive,*
  i.e. *be present*
2597 katabainō (20), to
  descend
2638 katalambanō (1), to
  seize; to *possess*
2647 kataluō (1), to *halt
  for the night
2658 katantaō (3), to
  arrive at; to *attain*

2673 katargĕō (1), to *be,
  render entirely useless*
2718 katĕrchŏmai (2), to
  go, come down
3195 mĕllō (16), to
  intend, i.e. *be about to*
3854 paraginŏmai (15),
  to *arrive;* to *appear*
3918 parĕimi (6), to *be
  present;* to *have come*
3928 parĕrchŏmai (1), to
  go by; to *perish*
3936 paristēmi (1), to
  stand beside, present
4137 plērŏō (1), to *fill,
  make complete*
4301 prŏlambanō (1), to
  take before
4331 prŏsĕggizō (1), to
  approach near
4334 prŏsĕrchŏmai (6),
  to *come near, visit*
4365 prŏspŏrĕuŏmai (1),
  to *come towards*
4845 sumplērŏō (2), to *be
  complete, fulfill*
4905 sunĕrchŏmai (14),
  to *go with*
4940 suntugchanō (1), to
  come together
5290 hupŏstrĕphō (1), to
  turn under, behind
5302 hustĕrĕō (3), to be
  inferior; to *fall short*
5348 phthanō (4), to *be
  anticipate* or *precede*
5562 chōrĕō (1), to *pass,
  enter;* to *hold, admit*

COMELINESS
1926 hâdâr (3),
  magnificence
1935 hôwd (1), *grandeur,
  majesty*
2157 ĕuschēmŏsunē (1),
  decorousness

COMELY
2433 chîyn (1), *graceful
  beauty*
3190 yâṭab (1), to *be,
  make well*
3303 yâpheh (1),
  beautiful; handsome
4998 nâ'âh (1), to *be
  pleasant* or *suitable*
5000 nâ'veh (7), *suitable
  *or *beautiful*
8389 tô'ar (1), *outline,
  figure* or *appearance*
8597 tiph'ârâh (1),
  ornament
2158 ĕuschēmōn (2),
  decorous, proper; noble
4241 prĕpō (1), to *be
  suitable* or *proper*

COMERS
4334 prŏsĕrchŏmai (1),
  to *come near, visit*

COMEST
935 bôw' (22), to *go* or
  come
2199 zâ'aq (1), to *call
  out, announce*
7126 qârab (2), to
  approach, bring near
2064 ĕrchŏmai (3), to *go
  *or *come*

COMETH
857 'âthâh (3), to *arrive*
935 bôw' (89), to *go, come*
1961 hâyâh (1), to *exist,*
  i.e. *be* or *become*
1980 hâlak (2), to *walk;
  live a certain way*
3318 yâtsâ' (19), to *go,
  bring out*
3381 yârad (1), to
  descend
4672 mâtsâ' (1), to *occur,
  meet* or *be present*
5034 nâbêl (1), to *wilt;* to
  fall away
5060 nâga' (1), to *strike*
5414 nâthan (1), to *give*
5674 'âbar (1), to *cross
  over;* to *transition*
5927 'âlâh (10), to
  ascend, be high, mount
6293 pâga' (1), to *impinge*
6437 pânâh (1), to *turn,
  *to *face*
6627 tsâ'âh (2), *human
  excrement*
6631 tse'ĕtsâ' (1),
  produce, children
7131 qârêb (5), *near*
7698 sheger (1), *what
  comes forth*
7725 shûwb (3), to *turn
  back;* to *return*
305 anabainō (1), to *go
  up, rise*
1096 ginŏmai (2), to *be,
  become*
1511 ĕinai (1), to *exist*
1607 ĕkpŏrĕuŏmai (2), to
  depart, be discharged
1831 ĕxĕrchŏmai (1), to
  issue; to *leave*
1999 ĕpisustasis (1),
  insurrection
2064 ĕrchŏmai (97), to *go
  *or *come*
2186 ĕphistēmi (1), to *be
  present;* to *approach*
2591 Karpŏs (1), (poss.)
  fruit
2597 katabainō (3), to
  descend
3854 paraginŏmai (3), to
  arrive; to *appear*
4334 prŏsĕrchŏmai (1),
  to *come near, visit*
4905 sunĕrchŏmai (1), to
  gather together

COMFORT
1082 bâlag (2), to *be
  comforted*
4010 mablîygîyth (1),
  desolation
5162 nâcham (33), to *be
  sorry;* to *pity, console*
5165 nechâmâh (1),
  consolation
5582 çâ'ad (3), to *support*
7502 râphad (1), to
  spread a bed; to *refresh*
2174 ĕupsuchĕō (1), to
  feel encouraged
2293 tharsĕō (3), to *have
  courage; take heart!*
3870 parakalĕō (9), to
  call, invite
3874 paraklēsis (6),
  imploring, exhortation

3888 paramuthĕŏmai (2), to *console*
3889 paramuthia (1), *consolation*
3890 paramuthiŏn (1), *consolation*
3931 parēgŏria (1), *consolation, comfort*

COMFORTABLE
4496 mᵉnûwchâh (1), *peacefully; consolation*
5150 nichûwm (1), *consoled; solace*

COMFORTABLY
5921+3820 'al (4), *above, over, upon, or against*
5921+3824 'al (1), *above, over, upon, or against*

COMFORTED
5162 nâcham (20), to *be sorry; to pity, console*
3870 parakalĕŏ (13), to *call, invite*
3888 paramuthĕŏmai (2), to *console*
4837 sumparakalĕŏ (1), to *console jointly*

COMFORTEDST
5162 nâcham (1), to *be sorry; to pity, console*

COMFORTER
5162 nâcham (3), to *be sorry; to pity, console*
3875 paraklētŏs (4), *intercessor, consoler*

COMFORTERS
5162 nâcham (5), to *be sorry; to pity, console*

COMFORTETH
5162 nâcham (3), to *be sorry; to pity, console*
3870 parakalĕŏ (2), to *call, invite*

COMFORTLESS
3737 ŏrphanŏs (1), *parentless, orphaned*

COMFORTS
5150 nichûwm (1), *consoled; solace*
8575 tanchûwm (1), *compassion, solace*

COMING
857 'âthâh (1), to *arrive*
935 bôw' (19), to *go, come*
1980 hâlak (1), to *walk; live a certain way*
3318 yâtsâ' (2), to *go, bring out*
3381 yârad (2), to *descend*
3996 mâbôw' (1), *entrance; sunset; west*
4126 môwbâ' (1), *entrance*
5182 nᵉchath (Ch.) (1), to *descend; to depose*
5674 'âbar (1), to *cross over; to transition*
7122 qârâ' (1), to *encounter, to happen*
7272 regel (1), *foot; step*
305 anabainŏ (2), to *go up, rise*
602 apŏkalupsis (1), *disclosure, revelation*

1525 ĕisĕrchŏmai (3), to *enter*
1529 ĕisŏdŏs (1), *entrance*
1531 ĕispŏrĕuŏmai (1), to *enter*
1660 ĕlĕusis (1), *advent, coming*
1831 ĕxĕrchŏmai (1), to *issue; to leave*
1904 ĕpĕrchŏmai (1), to *supervene*
2064 ĕrchŏmai (27), to *go or come*
2186 ĕphistēmi (1), to *be present; to approach*
2597 katabainŏ (1), to *descend*
3854 paraginŏmai (1), to *arrive; to appear*
3952 parŏusia (22), *advent, coming*
4334 prŏsĕrchŏmai (3), to *come near, visit*

COMINGS
4126 môwbâ' (1), *entrance*

COMMAND
559 'âmar (2), to *say*
6310 peh (1), *mouth; opening*
6680 tsâvâh (84), to *constitute, enjoin*
1781 ĕntĕllŏmai (4), to *enjoin, give orders*
2004 ĕpitassŏ (1), to *order, command*
2036 ĕpŏ (3), to *speak*
2753 kĕlĕuŏ (1), to *order, direct*
3853 paraggĕllŏ (8), to *enjoin; to instruct*

COMMANDED
559 'âmar (25), to *say*
560 'âmar (Ch.) (12), to *say,* speak
1696 dâbar (4), to *speak, say; to subdue*
4480+2941 min (1), *from or out of*
4687 mitsvâh (2), *command*
6680 tsâvâh (333), to *constitute, enjoin*
7761+2942 sûwm (Ch.) (3), to *put, place*
1291 diastĕllŏmai (1), to *enjoin*
1299 diatassŏ (6), to *institute, prescribe*
1781 ĕntĕllŏmai (6), to *enjoin, give orders*
2004 ĕpitassŏ (4), to *order, command*
2036 ĕpŏ (5), to *speak*
2750 kĕiria (1), *swathe of cloth*
2753 kĕlĕuŏ (20), to *order, direct*
3853 paraggĕllŏ (11), to *enjoin; to give instruction*
4367 prŏstassŏ (6), to *enjoin*
4483 rhĕŏ (1), to *utter, i.e. speak or say*

COMMANDEDST
6680 tsâvâh (4), to *constitute, enjoin*

COMMANDER
6680 tsâvâh (1), to *constitute, enjoin*

COMMANDEST
6680 tsâvâh (2), to *constitute, enjoin*
2753 kĕlĕuŏ (1), to *order, direct*

COMMANDETH
559 'âmar (3), to *say,* speak
6680 tsâvâh (6), to *constitute, enjoin*
2004 ĕpitassŏ (3), to *order, command*
3853 paraggĕllŏ (1), to *enjoin; to instruct*

COMMANDING
6680 tsâvâh (1), to *constitute, enjoin*
1299 diatassŏ (1), to *institute, prescribe*
2753 kĕlĕuŏ (1), to *order, direct*

COMMANDMENT
559 'âmar (2), to *say*
565 'imrâh (1), *something said*
1697 dâbâr (15), *word; matter; thing*
1881 dâth (2), royal *edict or statute*
2941 ṭa'am (Ch.) (2), *sentence, command*
2942 ṭᵉ'êm (Ch.) (2), *judgment; account*
3318 yâtsâ' (1), to *go, bring out*
3982 ma'ămar (2), *edict, command*
4406 millâh (Ch.) (1), *word, command*
4662 miphqâd (1), *appointment*
4687 mitsvâh (43), *command*
6310 peh (37), *mouth; opening*
6673 tsav (1), *injunction*
6680 tsâvâh (9), to *constitute, enjoin*
1291 diastĕllŏmai (1), to *enjoin*
1297 diatagma (1), *authoritative edict*
1781 ĕntĕllŏmai (2), to *enjoin, give orders*
1785 ĕntŏlē (42), *prescription, regulation*
2003 ĕpitagē (6), *injunction or decree*
2753 kĕlĕuŏ (2), to *order, direct*
3852 paraggĕlia (1), *mandate, order*
3853 paraggĕllŏ (1), to *enjoin; to instruct*

COMMANDMENTS
1697 dâbâr (5), *word; matter; thing*
2706 chôq (1), *appointment; allotment*
4687 mitsvâh (130), *command*

COMMANDEDST
6680 tsâvâh (4), to *constitute, enjoin*
1778 ĕntalma (3), *precept, command*
1781 ĕntĕllŏmai (1), to *enjoin, give orders*
1785 ĕntŏlē (27), *prescription, regulation*
3852 paraggĕlia (1), *mandate, order*

COMMEND
3908 paratithēmi (2), to *present something*
4921 sunistaŏ (5), to *set together*

COMMENDATION
4956 sustatikŏs (2), *recommendatory*

COMMENDED
1984 hâlal (2), to *speak words of thankfulness*
7623 shâbach (1), to *address in a loud tone*
1867 ĕpainĕŏ (1), to *applaud, commend*
3908 paratithēmi (1), to *present something*
4921 sunistaŏ (1), to *set together*

COMMENDETH
3936 paristēmi (1), to *stand beside, present*
4921 sunistaŏ (3), to *set together*

COMMENDING
4921 sunistaŏ (1), to *set together*

COMMISSION
2011 ĕpitrŏpē (1), *permission*

COMMISSIONS
1881 dâth (1), royal *edict or statute*

COMMIT
1556 gâlal (2), to *roll; to commit*
2181 zânâh (11), to *commit adultery*
4560 mâçar (1), to *set apart; apostatize*
4603 mâ'al (4), to *act treacherously*
5003 nâ'aph (6), to *commit adultery*
5414 nâthan (1), to *give*
5753 'âvâh (2), to *be crooked*
6213 'âsâh (14), to *do or make*
6313 pûwg (1), to *be sluggish; be numb*
6466 pâ'al (1), to *do, make or practice*
6485 pâqad (2), to *visit, care for, count*
7760 sûwm (1), to *put, place*
2038 ĕrgazŏmai (1), to *toil*
2416 hiĕrŏsulĕŏ (1), to *be a temple-robber*
3429 mŏichaŏ (2), to *commit adultery*
3431 mŏichĕuŏ (10), to *commit adultery*

English

COMMITTED

3908 paratithēmi (3), to
present something
4100 pisteúō (2), to *have
faith, to entrust*
4160 pŏiĕō (2), to *make*
4203 pŏrnĕuō (3), to
indulge unlawful *lust*
4238 prassō (2), to
execute, accomplish

COMMITTED
1961 hâyâh (2), to *exist*,
i.e. *be or become*
2181 zânâh (5), to
commit adultery
2398 châṭâ' (6), to *sin*
4600 mâ'ak (6), to *pierce,
emasculate, handle*
5003 nâ'aph (5), to
commit adultery
5414 nâthan (5), to *give*
5753 'âvâh (2), to *be
crooked*
6213 'âsâh (28), to *do or
make*
6485 pâqad (4), to *visit,
care for, count*
7561 râsha' (1), to *be, do,
declare wrong*
8581 tâ'ab (1), to *loathe*,
i.e. *detest*
764 asĕbĕō (1), to *be, act
impious or wicked*
1325 didōmi (1), to *give*
1439 ĕaō (1), to *let be*, i.e.
permit or leave alone
3431 mŏichĕuō (1), to
commit adultery
3860 paradidōmi (2), to
hand over
3866 parathēkē (1), *trust,
deposit entrusted*
3872 parakatathēkē (2),
deposit, trust
3908 paratithēmi (1), to
present something
4100 pisteúō (5), to *have
faith; to entrust*
4160 pŏiĕō (4), to *make*
4203 pŏrnĕuō (4), to
indulge unlawful *lust*
4238 prassō (3), to
execute, accomplish
5087 tithēmi (1), to *place*

COMMITTEST
2181 zânâh (1), to
commit adultery

COMMITTETH
5003 nâ'aph (4), to
commit adultery
5800 'âzab (1), to *loosen;
relinquish; permit*
6213 'âsâh (4), to *do or
make*
3429 mŏichaō (4), to
commit adultery
3431 mŏichĕuō (2), to
commit adultery
4160 pŏiĕō (3), to *make*
or *do*
4203 pŏrnĕuō (1), to
indulge unlawful *lust*

COMMITTING
5003 nâ'aph (1), to
commit adultery
6213 'âsâh (1), to *do or
make*

COMMODIOUS
428 anĕuthĕtŏs (1),
inconvenient

COMMON
776 'erets (1), *earth,
land, soil; country*
1121 bên (1), *people* of a
class or kind
2455 chôl (2), *profane,
common, not holy*
2490 châlal (1), to
profane, defile
7227 rab (1), *great*
7230 rôb (1), *abundance*
442 anthrōpinŏs (1),
human
1219 dēmŏsiŏs (1),
public; in public
2839 kŏinŏs (8),
common, i.e. *profane*
2840 kŏinŏō (1), to *make
profane*
4183 pŏlus (1), *much,
many*
4232 praitōriŏn (1),
governor's court-room

COMMONLY
1310 diaphēmizō (1), to
spread news
3654 hŏlōs (1), *altogether*

COMMONWEALTH
4174 pŏlitĕia (1),
citizenship

COMMOTION
7494 ra'ash (1),
bounding, uproar

COMMOTIONS
181 akatastasia (1),
disorder, riot

COMMUNE
559 'âmar (1), to *say*
1696 dâbar (4), to *speak,
say; to subdue*
1697 dâbâr (1), *word;
matter; thing*
5608 çâphar (1), to
enumerate; to recount
7878 sîyach (1), to
ponder, muse aloud

COMMUNED
1696 dâbar (14), to
speak, say; to subdue
1255 dialalĕō (1), to
converse, discuss
3656 hŏmilĕō (2), to
converse, talk
4814 sullalĕō (1), to *talk
together*, i.e. *converse*

COMMUNICATE
2841 kŏinōnĕō (1), to
share or participate
2842 kŏinōnia (1),
benefaction; sharing
2843 kŏinōnikŏs (1),
liberal
4790 sugkŏinōnĕō (1), to
co-participate in

COMMUNICATED
394 anatithēmai (1), to
propound, set forth
2841 kŏinōnĕō (1), to
share or participate

COMMUNICATION
1697 dâbâr (1), *word;
matter; thing*

COMMODIOUS (cont.)
7879 sîyach (1), *uttered
contemplation*
148 aischrŏlŏgia (1), *vile
conversation*
2842 kŏinōnia (1),
benefaction; sharing
3056 lŏgŏs (2), *word,
matter, thing; Word*

COMMUNICATIONS
3056 lŏgŏs (1), *word,
matter, thing*
3657 hŏmilia (1),
associations

COMMUNING
1696 dâbar (2), to *speak,
say; to subdue*

COMMUNION
2842 kŏinōnia (4),
benefaction; sharing

COMPACT
2266 châbar (1), to
fascinate by spells

COMPACTED
4822 sumbibazō (1), to
drive together

COMPANIED
4905 sunĕrchŏmai (1), to
gather together

COMPANIES
736 'ôrᵉchâh (1), *caravan*
1416 gᵉdûwd (1), *band* of
soldiers
1979 hălîykâh (1),
walking; procession
4256 machălôqeth (1),
section or *division*
4264 machăneh (1),
encampment
6951 qâhâl (1),
assemblage
7218 rô'sh (7), *head*
4849 sumpŏsiŏn (1),
group

COMPANION
2270 châbêr (2),
associate, friend
2278 châbereth (1),
consort, companion
4828 mêrêa' (3), close
friend
7453 rêa' (3), *associate;
one close*
7462 râ'âh (2), to
associate as a friend
4791 sugkŏinōnŏs (1),
co-participant
4904 sunĕrgŏs (1),
fellow-worker

COMPANIONS
2269 chăbar (Ch.) (1),
associate, friend
2270 châbêr (5),
associate, friend
2271 chabbâr (1), *partner*
3675 kᵉnâth (Ch.) (8),
colleague
4828 mêrêa' (1), close
friend
7453 rêa' (1), *associate;
one close*
7464 rê'âh (2), female
associate
2844 kŏinōnŏs (1),
associate, partner
4898 sunĕkdēmŏs (1),
fellow-traveller

COMPANIONS'
7453 rêa' (1), *associate;
one close*

COMPANY
736 'ôrᵉchâh (1), *caravan*
1323 bath (1), *daughter,
descendant, woman*
1416 gᵉdûwd (3), *band* of
soldiers
1995 hâmôwn (1), *noise,
tumult; many, crowd*
2199 zâ'aq (1), to
convene publicly
2256 chebel (2),
company, band
2267 cheber (1), *society,
group; magic spell*
2274 chebrâh (1),
association
2416 chay (1), *alive; raw;
fresh; life*
2428 chayil (1), *army;
wealth; virtue; valor;
strength*
3862 lahăqâh (1),
assembly
4246 mᵉchôwlâh (1),
round-dance
4264 machăneh (5),
encampment
5712 'êdâh (13),
assemblage; crowd
6635 tsâbâ' (1), *army,
military host*
6951 qâhâl (16),
assemblage
7218 rô'sh (5), *head*
7285 regesh (1),
tumultuous crowd
7462 râ'âh (1), to
associate as a friend
8229 shiph'âh (2),
copiousness
2398 idiŏs (1), *private* or
separate
2828 klisia (1), *party* or
group
2853 kŏllaō (1), to *glue
together*
3461 murias (1),
ten-thousand
3588+4012 hŏ (1), "the"
3658 hŏmilŏs (1),
multitude
3792 ŏchlŏpŏiĕō (1), to
raise a disturbance
3793 ŏchlŏs (7), *throng*
4012 pĕri (1), *about;
around*
4128 plēthŏs (1), *large
number, throng*
4874 sunanamignumi
(3), to *associate with*
4923 sunŏdia (1),
traveling company

COMPARABLE
5577 çançin (1), *twig*

COMPARE
4911 mâshal (1), to *use
figurative language*
6186 'ârak (1), to *set in a
row*, i.e. *arrange,*
3846 paraballō (1), to
reach a place; to *liken*
4793 sugkrinō (1), to
combine

COMPARED
1819 dâmâh (1), to
resemble, liken
6186 'ârak (1), to set in a
row, i.e. arrange,
7737 shâvâh (2), to
resemble; to adjust

COMPARING
4793 sugkrinō (2), to
combine

COMPARISON
3644 kᵉmôw (1), like, as;
for; with
3850 parabŏlē (1),
fictitious narrative

COMPASS
247 'âzar (1), to belt
2329 chûwg (1), circle
3749 karkôb (2), rim,
ledge, or top margin
3803 kâthar (2), to
enclose, besiege; to wait
4230 mᵉchûwgâh (1),
compass
4524 mêçab (1), around,
surround
5362 nâqaph (3), to
surround or circulate
5437 çâbab (22), to
surround
5439 çâbîyb (2), circle;
environs; around
5849 'âţar (1), to encircle,
enclose in; to crown
4013 pĕriagō (1), to walk
around
4022 pĕriĕrchŏmai (1), to
stroll, vacillate, veer
4033 pĕrikuklŏō (1), to
blockade completely

COMPASSED
661 'âphaph (5), to
surround
2328 chûwg (1), to
describe a circle
5362 nâqaph (4), to
surround or circulate
5437 çâbab (28), to
surround
5849 'âţar (1), to encircle,
enclose in; to crown
2944 kuklŏō (3), to
surround, encircle
4029 pĕrikĕimai (2), to
enclose, encircle

COMPASSEST
2219 zârâh (1), to toss
about; to diffuse

COMPASSETH
5437 çâbab (4), to
surround
6059 'ânaq (1), to collar;
to fit out

COMPASSING
5362 nâqaph (2), to
surround or circulate
5437 çâbab (2), to
surround

COMPASSION
2550 châmal (5), to
spare, have pity on
7349 rachûwm (5),
compassionate
7355 râcham (8), to be
compassionate

7356 racham (2),
compassion; womb
1653 ĕlĕĕŏ (3), to give out
compassion
3356 mĕtriŏpathĕō (1), to
deal gently
3627 ŏiktĕirō (1), to
exercise pity
4697 splagchnizŏmai
(12), to feel sympathy
4834 sumpathĕō (1), to
commiserate
4835 sumpathēs (1),
commiserative

COMPASSIONS
7355 râcham (1), to be
compassionate
7356 racham (1),
compassion; womb

COMPEL
597 'ânaç (1), to insist,
compel
5647 'âbad (1), to do,
work, serve
29 aggarĕuō (2), to press
into public service
315 anagkazō (1), to
necessitate, compel

COMPELLED
5080 nâdach (1), to push
off, scattered
6555 pârats (1), to break
out
29 aggarĕuō (1), to press
into public service
315 anagkazō (3), to
necessitate, compel

COMPELLEST
315 anagkazō (1), to
necessitate, compel

COMPLAIN
596 'ânan (1), complain
1058 bâkâh (1), to weep,
moan
7378 rîyb (1), to hold a
controversy; to defend
7878 sîyach (1), to
ponder, muse aloud

COMPLAINED
596 'ânan (1), complain
7878 sîyach (1), to
ponder, muse aloud

COMPLAINERS
3202 mĕmpsimŏirŏs (1),
discontented

COMPLAINING
6682 tsᵉvâchâh (1),
screech of anguish

COMPLAINT
7878 sîyach (9), to
ponder, muse aloud

COMPLAINTS
157 aitiama (1), thing
charged

COMPLETE
8549 tâmîym (1), entire,
complete; integrity
4137 plĕrŏō (2), to fill,
make complete

COMPOSITION
4971 mathkôneth (2),
proportion

COMPOUND
4842 mirqachath (1),
unguent; unguent-pot

COMPOUNDETH
7543 râqach (1), to
perfume, blend spice

COMPREHEND
3045 yâda' (1), to know
2638 katalambanō (1), to
possess; to understand

COMPREHENDED
3557 kûwl (1), to
measure; to maintain
346 anakĕphalaiŏmai
(1), to sum up
2638 katalambanō (1), to
possess; to understand

CONANIAH
3562 Kôwnanyâhûw (1),
Jehovah has sustained

CONCEAL
2790 chârash (1), to be
silent; to be deaf
3582 kâchad (2), to
destroy; to hide
3680 kâçâh (2), to cover
5641 çâthar (1), to hide

CONCEALED
3582 kâchad (2), to
destroy; to hide

CONCEALETH
3680 kâçâh (2), to cover

CONCEIT
4906 maskîyth (1),
carved figure
5869 'ayin (4), eye; sight;
fountain

CONCEITS
3844+1438 para (2), from;
with; besides

CONCEIVE
2029 hârâh (3), to
conceive, be pregnant
2030 hâreh (4), pregnant
2232 zâra' (1), to sow
seed; to disseminate
3179 yâcham (4), to
conceive
2602 katabŏlē (1),
conception, beginning
4815 sullambanō (1), to
conceive; to aid

CONCEIVED
2029 hârâh (1), to
conceive, be pregnant
2030 hâreh (33), pregnant
2232 zâra' (1), to sow
seed; to disseminate
2803 châshab (1), to plot;
to think, regard
3179 yâcham (2), to
conceive
3254 yâçaph (1), to add
or augment
1080 gĕnnaō (1), to
procreate, regenerate
2845+2192 kŏitē (1),
couch; conception
4815 sullambanō (4), to
conceive; to aid
5087 tithēmi (1), to place

CONCEIVING
2030 hâreh (1), pregnant

CONCEPTION
2032 hêrôwn (3),
pregnancy

CONCERN
4012 pĕri (2), about;
around

CONCERNETH
1157 bᵉ'ad (1), at, beside,
among, behind, for

CONCERNING
413 'êl (15), to, toward
854 'êth (1), with; by; at;
among
5921 'al (78), above, over,
upon, or against
5922 'al (Ch.) (6), above,
over, upon, or against
6655 tsad (Ch.) (1), at the
side of; against
1519 ĕis (5), to or into
2596 kata (5), down;
according to
3754 hŏti (1), that;
because; since
4012 pĕri (44), about;
around
4314 prŏs (1), for; on, at;
to, toward; against
5228 hupĕr (1), over;
above; beyond

CONCISION
2699 katatŏmē (1),
mutilation, cutting

CONCLUDE
3049 lŏgizŏmai (1), to
credit; to think, regard

CONCLUDED
2919 krinō (1), to decide;
to try, condemn, punish
4788 sugklĕiō (2), to net
fish; to lock up persons

CONCLUSION
5490 çôwph (1),
termination; end

CONCORD
4857 sumphōnēsis (1),
accordance, agreement

CONCOURSE
1993 hâmâh (1), to be in
great commotion
4963 sustrŏphē (1),
riotous crowd

CONCUBINE
6370 pîylegesh (22),
concubine

CONCUBINES
3904 lᵉchênâh (Ch.) (3),
concubine
6370 pîylegesh (14),
concubine

CONCUPISCENCE
1939 ĕpithumia (3),
longing

CONDEMN
7561 râsha' (11), to be,
do, declare wrong
8199 shâphaṭ (1), to judge
2607 kataginŏskō (2), to
condemn
2618 katakaiō (1), to
consume wholly by
burning
2632 katakrinō (7), to
judge against
2633 katakrisis (1), act of
sentencing adversely
2919 krinō (1), to decide;
to try, condemn, punish

English

CONDEMNATION
2631 katakrima (3), *adverse sentence*
2633 katakrisis (1), act of *sentencing adversely*
2917 krima (5), *decision*
2920 krisis (2), *decision; tribunal; justice*
5272 hupŏkrisis (1), *deceit, hypocrisy*

CONDEMNED
3318+7563 yâtsâ' (1), to *go, bring out*
6064 'ânash (2), to *inflict a penalty, to fine*
7561 râsha' (1), to *be, do, declare wrong*
176 akatagnōstŏs (1), *unblamable*
843 autŏkatakritŏs (1), *self-condemned*
1519+2917 ĕis (1), *to or into*
2613 katadikazō (4), to *condemn*
2632 katakrinō (8), to *judge against*
2919 krinō (2), to *decide; to try, condemn, punish*

CONDEMNEST
2632 katakrinō (1), to *judge against*

CONDEMNETH
7561 râsha' (2), to *be, do, declare wrong*
2632 katakrinō (1), to *judge against*
4314 prŏs (1), *for; on, at; to, toward; against*

CONDEMNING
7561 râsha' (1), to *be, do, declare wrong*
2919 krinō (1), to *decide; to try, condemn, punish*

CONDESCEND
4879 sunapagō (1), to *take off together*

CONDITIONS
4314 prŏs (1), *for; on, at; to, toward; against*

CONDUCT
5674 'âbar (1), to *cross over; to transition*
7971 shâlach (1), to *send away*
4311 prŏpĕmpō (1), to *send forward*

CONDUCTED
5674 'âbar (1), to *cross over; to transition*
2525 kathistēmi (1), to *designate, constitute*

CONDUIT
8585 tᵉ'âlâh (4), *irrigation channel; bandage or plaster*

CONEY
8227 shâphân (2), *rock-rabbit*, (poss.) *hyrax*

CONFECTION
7545 rôqach (1), *aromatic, fragrance*

CONFECTIONARIES
7543 râqach (1), to *perfume, blend spice*

CONFEDERACY
1285 bᵉrîyth (1), *compact, agreement*
7195 qesher (2), *unlawful alliance*

CONFEDERATE
1167+1285 ba'al (1), *master; owner; citizen*
1285+3772 bᵉrîyth (1), *compact, agreement*
5117 nûwach (1), to *rest; to settle down*

CONFERENCE
4323 prŏsanatithēmi (1), to *add; to consult*

CONFERRED
1961+1697 hâyâh (1), to *exist, i.e. be or become*
4323 prŏsanatithēmi (1), to *add; to consult*
4814 sullalĕō (1), to *talk together, i.e. converse*
4820 sumballō (1), to *converse, consult*

CONFESS
3034 yâdâh (11), to *revere or worship*
1843 ĕxŏmŏlŏgĕō (5), to *acknowledge or agree*
3670 hŏmŏlŏgĕō (12), to *acknowledge, agree*

CONFESSED
3034 yâdâh (3), to *throw; to revere or worship*
1843 ĕxŏmŏlŏgĕō (1), to *acknowledge or agree*
3670 hŏmŏlŏgĕō (3), to *acknowledge, agree*

CONFESSETH
3034 yâdâh (1), to *throw; to revere or worship*
3670 hŏmŏlŏgĕō (2), to *acknowledge, agree*

CONFESSING
3034 yâdâh (1), to *throw; to revere or worship*
1843 ĕxŏmŏlŏgĕō (2), to *acknowledge or agree*

CONFESSION
3034 yâdâh (2), to *throw; to revere or worship*
8426 tôwdâh (2), *expressions of thanks*
3670 hŏmŏlŏgĕō (1), to *acknowledge, agree*
3671 hŏmŏlŏgia (1), *confession*

CONFIDENCE
982 bâṭach (4), to *trust, be confident or sure*
983 beṭach (1), *safety, security, trust*
985 biṭchâh (1), *trust*
986 biṭṭâchôwn (2), *trust*
3689 keçel (1), *loin; back; viscera; trust*
3690 kiçlâh (1), *trust*
4009 mibṭâch (8), *security; assurance*
2292 tharrhĕō (1), to *exercise courage*
3954 parrhēsia (6), *frankness, boldness*
3982 pĕithō (6), to *rely*
4006 pĕpŏithēsis (5), *reliance, trust*

CONFIDENCES
4009 mibṭâch (1), *security; assurance*

CONFIDENT
982 bâṭach (2), to *trust, be confident or sure*
2292 tharrhĕō (2), to *exercise courage*
3982 pĕithō (3), to *rely*
5287 hupŏstasis (1), *essence; assurance*

CONFIDENTLY
1340 diïschurizŏmai (1), to *asserverate*

CONFIRM
553 'âmats (1), to *be strong; be courageous*
1396 gâbar (1), to *be strong; to prevail*
2388 châzaq (2), to *bind, restrain, conquer*
3559 kûwn (1), to *set up: establish, fix, prepare*
4390 mâlĕ' (1), to *fill; be full*
6965 qûwm (4), to *rise*
950 bĕbaiŏō (2), to *stabilitate, keep strong*
2964 kurŏō (1), to *ratify, validate a treaty*

CONFIRMATION
951 bĕbaiōsis (2), *confirmation*

CONFIRMED
2388 châzaq (1), to *bind, restrain, conquer*
3559 kûwn (2), to *render sure, proper or prosperous*
5975 'âmad (2), to *stand*
6965 qûwm (2), to *rise*
950 bĕbaiŏō (2), to *stabilitate, keep strong*
1991 ĕpistērizō (1), to *re-establish, strengthen*
2964 kurŏō (1), to *ratify, validate a treaty*
3315 mĕsitĕuō (1), to *ratify as surety, confirm*
4300 prŏkurŏō (1), to *ratify previously*

CONFIRMETH
6965 qûwm (3), to *rise*

CONFIRMING
950 bĕbaiŏō (1), to *stabilitate, keep strong*
1991 ĕpistērizō (2), to *re-establish, strengthen*

CONFISCATION
6065 'ănash (Ch.) (1), *fine, penalty, mulct*

CONFLICT
73 agōn (2), *contest, struggle*

CONFORMABLE
4832 summŏrphŏs (1), *similar, conformed to*

CONFORMED
4832 summŏrphŏs (1), *similar, conformed to*
4964 suschēmatizō (1), to *conform*

CONFOUND
1101 bâlal (2), to *mix; confuse*
2865 châthath (1), to *break down*
2617 kataischunō (2), to *disgrace or shame*

CONFOUNDED
954 bûwsh (21), be *ashamed; disappointed*
2659 châphêr (6), to *be ashamed, disappointed*
3001 yâbêsh (9), to *dry up; to wither*
3637 kâlam (11), to *taunt or insult*
2617 kataischunō (1), to *disgrace or shame*
4797 sugchĕō (2), to *throw into disorder*

CONFUSED
7494 ra'ash (1), *bounding, uproar*
4797 sugchĕō (1), to *throw into disorder*

CONFUSION
954 bûwsh (1), be *ashamed, disappointed*
1322 bôsheth (7), *shame*
2659 châphêr (2), to *be ashamed, disappointed*
3637 kâlam (1), to *taunt or insult*
3639 kᵉlimmâh (6), *disgrace, scorn*
7036 qâlôwn (1), *disgrace*
8397 tebel (2), confused *mixture*
8414 tôhûw (3), *waste, desolation, formless*
181 akatastasia (2), *disorder, riot*
4799 sugchusis (1), *riotous disturbance*

CONGEALED
7087 qâphâ' (1), to *thicken, congeal*

CONGRATULATE
1288 bârak (1), to *bless*

CONGREGATION
482 'êlem (1), *silence*
2416 chay (2), *alive; raw; fresh; life*
4150 môw'êd (147), *assembly, congregation*
5712 'êdâh (123), *assemblage; crowd*
6951 qâhâl (85), *assemblage*
6952 qᵉhillâh (1), *assemblage*
4865 sunagōnizŏmai (1), to *be a partner*

CONGREGATIONS
4150 môw'êd (1), *assembly, congregation*
4721 maqhêl (2), *assembly*

CONIAH
3659 Konyâhûw (3), *Jehovah will establish*

CONIES
8226 sâphan (2), to *conceal*

CONONIAH
3562 Kôwnanyâhûw (2), *Jehovah has sustained*

CONQUER
3528 nikaō (1), to *subdue, conquer*

CONQUERING
3528 nikaō (1), to *subdue, conquer*

CONQUERORS
5245 hupĕrnikaō (1), to *gain* a decisive *victory*

CONSCIENCE
4893 sunĕidēsis (31), moral *consciousness*

CONSCIENCES
4893 sunĕidēsis (1), moral *consciousness*

CONSECRATE
2763 charam (1), to *devote* to destruction
4390+3027 mâlê' (10), to *fill; be full*
5144 nâzar (1), to *devote*
6942 qâdâsh (2), to *be, make clean*

CONSECRATED
4390+3027 mâlê' (7), to *fill; be full*
6942 qâdâsh (4), to *be, make clean*
6944 qôdesh (1), *sacred* place or thing
1457 ĕgkainizō (1), to *inaugurate*
5048 tĕlĕiŏō (1), to *perfect, complete*

CONSECRATION
4394 millû' (7), *fulfilling; setting; consecration*
5145 nezer (1), *set apart; dedication*

CONSECRATIONS
4394 millû' (4), *fulfilling; setting; consecration*

CONSENT
14 'âbâh (4), to *be acquiescent*
225 'ûwth (3), to *assent*
376 'îysh (1), *man; male*
3820 lêb (1), *heart*
7926 shᵉkem (2), *neck; spur* of a hill
4334 prŏsĕrchŏmai (1), to *assent to*
4852 sumphēmi (1), to *assent to*
4859 sumphōnŏs (1), *agreeing; agreement*

CONSENTED
225 'ûwth (1), to *assent; agree*
8085 shâma' (1), to *hear*
1962 ĕpinĕuō (1), to *assent, give consent*
4784 sugkatatithĕmai (1), to *accord* with

CONSENTEDST
7521 râtsâh (1), to *be pleased with; to satisfy*

CONSENTING
4909 sunĕudŏkĕō (2), to *assent to, feel gratified*

CONSIDER
559 'âmar (1), to *say*
995 bîyn (20), to *understand; discern*
3045 yâda' (4), to *know*
5027 nâbaṭ (5), to *scan; to regard* with favor
6448 pâçag (1), to *contemplate*
7200 râ'âh (15), to *see*
7725 shûwb (1), to *turn* back; to *return*
7760 sûwm (2), to *put*
7760+3820 sûwm (4), to *put, place*
7760+3820+5921 sûwm (2), to *put, place*
7919 sâkal (2), to *be or act circumspect*
357 analŏgizŏmai (1), to *contemplate*
1260 dialŏgizŏmai (1), to *deliberate*
1492 ĕidō (1), to *know*
2334 thĕōrĕō (1), to *see; to discern*
2648 katamanthanō (1), to *note carefully*
2657 katanŏĕō (4), to *observe fully*
3539 nŏiĕō (1), to *exercise* the *mind*

CONSIDERED
995 bîyn (1), to *understand; discern*
2803 châshab (1), to *think, regard; to value*
5414 nâthan (1), to *give*
7200 râ'âh (4), to *see*
7760+3820 sûwm (2), to *put, place*
7896+3820 shîyth (1), to *place, put*
7920 sᵉkal (Ch.) (1), to *be or act circumspect*
8085 shâma' (1), to *hear*
2657 katanŏĕō (2), to *observe fully*
4894 sunĕidō (1), to *understand*
4920 suniēmi (1), to *comprehend*

CONSIDEREST
7200 râ'âh (1), to *see*
2657 katanŏĕō (1), to *observe fully*

CONSIDERETH
995 bîyn (1), to *understand; discern*
2161 zâmam (1), to *plan*
3045 yâda' (2), to *know*
7200 râ'âh (2), to *see*
7725 shûwb (1), to *turn* back; to *return*
7919 sâkal (2), to *be or act circumspect*

CONSIDERING
995 bîyn (2), to *understand; discern*
333 anathĕōrĕō (1), to *look again*
4648 skŏpĕō (1), to *watch* out for, i.e. to *regard*

CONSIST
4921 sunistaō (1), to *set together*

CONSISTETH
2076 ĕsti (1), he (she or it) *is; they are*

CONSOLATION
8575 tanchûwm (1), *compassion, solace*
3874 paraklēsis (14), *imploring, solace*

CONSOLATIONS
8575 tanchûwm (3), *compassion, solace*

CONSORTED
4845 sumplērŏō (1), to be *complete, fulfill*

CONSPIRACY
7195 qesher (9), unlawful *alliance*
4945 sunōmŏsia (1), *plot, conspiracy*

CONSPIRATORS
7194 qâshar (1), to *tie, bind*

CONSPIRED
5320 Naphtûchîym (1), *Naphtuchim*
7194 qâshar (18), to *tie, bind*

CONSTANT
2388 châzaq (1), to *fasten* upon; to *seize*

CONSTANTLY
5331 netsach (1), *splendor; lasting*
1226 diabĕbaiŏŏmai (1), to *confirm thoroughly*
1340 diïschurizŏmai (1), to *asseverate*

CONSTELLATIONS
3685 Kᵉçîyl (1), *constellation Orion*

CONSTRAIN
315 anagkazō (1), to *necessitate, compel*

CONSTRAINED
2388 châzaq (1), to *fasten* upon; to *seize*
315 anagkazō (3), to *necessitate, compel*
3849 parabiazŏmai (2), to *compel* by entreaty

CONSTRAINETH
6693 tsûwq (1), to *oppress, distress*
4912 sunĕchō (1), to *hold together*

CONSTRAINT
317 anagkastōs (1), *compulsorily*

CONSULT
3289 yâ'ats (1), to *advise*

CONSULTATION
4824 sumbŏuliŏn (1), *advisement*

CONSULTED
3272 yᵉ'aṭ (Ch.) (1), to *counsel*
3289 yâ'ats (8), to *advise*
4427 mâlak (1), to *reign* as *king*
7592 shâ'al (1), to *ask*
1011 bŏulĕuō (1), to *deliberate; to resolve*
4823 sumbŏulĕuō (1), to *recommend, deliberate*

CONSULTER
7592 shâ'al (1), to *ask*

CONSULTETH
1011 bŏulĕuō (1), to *deliberate; to resolve*

CONSUME
398 'âkal (9), to *eat*
402 'oklâh (1), *food*
1086 bâlâh (1), to *wear out, decay; consume*
1497 gâzal (1), to *rob*
2000 hâmam (1), to *disturb, drive, destroy*
2628 châçal (1), to *eat off, consume*
3423 yârash (1), to *inherit; to impoverish*
3615 kâlâh (23), to *complete, consume*
4529 mâçâh (1), to *dissolve, melt*
4743 mâqaq (4), to *melt; to flow, dwindle, vanish*
5486 çûwph (4), to *terminate*
5487 çûwph (Ch.) (1), to *come to an end*
5595 çâphâh (1), to *scrape; to accumulate*
8046 shᵉmad (Ch.) (1), to *desolate*
8552 tâmam (2), to *complete, finish*
355 analiskō (2), *destroy*
1159 dapanaō (1), to *incur cost; to waste*

CONSUMED
398 'âkal (21), to *eat*
622 'âçaph (1), to *gather*
1846 dâ'ak (1), to *be extinguished; to expire*
3615 kâlâh (37), to *complete, consume*
4127 mûwg (1), to *soften, flow down, disappear*
5486 çûwph (1), to *terminate*
5595 çâphâh (5), to *scrape; to accumulate*
6244 'âshêsh (3), to *fail*
6789 tsâmath (1), to *extirpate, root out*
8552 tâmam (24), to *complete, finish*
355 analiskō (1), *destroy*

CONSUMETH
398 'âkal (2), to *eat*
1086 bâlâh (1), to *wear out, decay; consume*
7503 râphâh (1), to *slacken*

CONSUMING
398 'âkal (2), to *eat*
2654 katanaliskō (1), to *consume utterly*

CONSUMMATION
3617 kâlâh (1), *complete destruction*

CONSUMPTION
3617 kâlâh (2), *complete destruction*
3631 killâyôwn (1), *pining, destruction*
7829 shachepheth (2), *wasting disease*

English

CONTAIN
1004 bayith (1), *house; temple; family, tribe*
3557 kûwl (3), *to keep in; to maintain*
5375 nâsâ' (1), *to lift up*
1467 ĕgkratĕuŏmai (1), *to exercise self-restraint*
5562 chōrĕō (1), *to pass, enter; to hold, admit*

CONTAINED
3557 kûwl (2), *to keep in; to maintain*
4023 pĕriĕchō (1), *to encircle; to contain*

CONTAINETH
3557 kûwl (1), *to keep in; to maintain*

CONTAINING
5562 chōrĕō (1), *to pass, enter; to hold, admit*

CONTEMN
3988 mâ'aç (1), *to spurn; to disappear*
5006 nâ'ats (1), *to scorn*

CONTEMNED
936 bûwz (1), *to disrespect, scorn*
959 bâzâh (1), *to disesteem, ridicule*
5006 nâ'ats (1), *to scorn*
7034 qâlâh (1), *to hold in contempt*

CONTEMNETH
3988 mâ'aç (1), *to spurn; to disappear*

CONTEMPT
937 bûwz (7), *disrespect, scorn*
963 bizzâyôwn (1), *disesteem, disrespect*
1860 dᵉrâ'ôwn (1), *object of loathing*
7043 qâlal (1), *to be easy, trifling, vile*

CONTEMPTIBLE
959 bâzâh (3), *to disesteem, ridicule*
1848 ĕxŏuthĕnĕō (1), *to treat with contempt*

CONTEMPTUOUSLY
937 bûwz (1), *disrespect*

CONTEND
1624 gârâh (3), *to provoke to anger*
1777 dîyn (1), *to judge; to strive or contend for*
3401 yârîyb (1), *contentious; adversary*
7378 rîyb (7), *to hold a controversy; to defend*
8474 tachârâh (1), *to vie with a rival*
1864 ĕpagōnizŏmai (1), *to struggle for, fight for*

CONTENDED
4695 matstsûwth (1), *quarrel, contention*
7378 rîyb (4), *to hold a controversy; to defend*
1252 diakrinō (1), *to decide; to hesitate*

CONTENDEST
7378 rîyb (1), *to hold a controversy; to defend*

CONTENDETH
3401 yârîyb (1), *contentious; adversary*
7378 rîyb (1), *to hold a controversy; to defend*
8199 shâphaṭ (1), *to judge*

CONTENDING
1252 diakrinō (1), *to decide; to hesitate*

CONTENT
14 'âbâh (1), *to be acquiescent*
2974 yâ'al (7), *to assent; to undertake, begin*
3190+5869 yâṭab (1), *to be, make well*
8085 shâma' (1), *to hear intelligently*
714 arkĕō (4), *to avail; be satisfactory*
842 autarkēs (1), *contented*
2425+3588+4160 hikanŏs (1), *ample; fit*

CONTENTION
4066 mâdôwn (3), *contest or quarrel*
4683 matstsâh (1), *quarrel*
7379 rîyb (2), *contest, personal or legal*
73 agōn (1), *contest, struggle*
2052 ĕrithĕia (1), *faction, strife, selfish ambition*
3948 parŏxusmŏs (1), *incitement; dispute*

CONTENTIONS
4079 midyân (4), *contest or quarrel*
2054 ĕris (2), *quarrel, i.e. wrangling*

CONTENTIOUS
4066 mâdôwn (3), *contest or quarrel*
1537+2052 ĕk (1), *out of*
5380 philŏnĕikŏs (1), *disputatious*

CONTENTMENT
841 autarkeia (1), *contentedness*

CONTINUAL
1115+5627 biltîy (1), *not, except, without, unless*
2956 ṭârad (1), *to drive on*
8548 tâmîyd (27), *constantly, regularly*
88 adialĕiptŏs (1), *permanent, constant*
1519+5056 ĕis (1), *to or into*

CONTINUALLY
1980 hâlak (1), *to walk; live a certain way*
1980+7725 hâlak (1), *to walk; live a certain way*
3605+3117 kôl (10), *all, any or every*
6256 'êth (1), *time*
8411 tᵉdîyrâ' (Ch.) (2), *constantly, faithfully*
8544 tᵉmûwnâh (1), *something fashioned*
8548 tâmîyd (52), *constantly, regularly*

CONTENDETH
1275 diapantŏs (1), *constantly, continually*
1519+1336 ĕis (2), *to or into*
1725 ĕnanti (1), *before, in presence of*
4342 prŏskartĕrĕō (3), *to be constantly diligent*

CONTINUANCE
539 'âman (2), *to be firm; to be permanent*
3117 yôwm (1), *day; time period*
5769 'ôwlâm (1), *eternity; ancient; always*
5281 hupŏmŏnē (1), *endurance, constancy*

CONTINUE
309 'âchar (1), *to remain; to delay*
1961 hâyâh (2), *to exist, i.e. be or become*
3427 yâshab (2), *to dwell, to remain; to settle*
3885 lûwn (1), *to be obstinate*
4900 mâshak (1), *to draw out; to be tall*
5975 'âmad (4), *to stand*
6965 qûwm (3), *to rise*
7931 shâkan (1), *to reside*
1265 diamĕnō (2), *to stay constantly*
1696 ĕmmĕnō (1), *to remain; to persevere*
1961 ĕpimĕnō (5), *to remain; to persevere*
2476 histēmi (1), *to stand, establish*
3306 mĕnō (7), *to stay, remain*
3887 paramĕnō (1), *to be permanent, persevere*
4160 pŏiĕō (2), *to do*
4342 prŏskartĕrĕō (1), *to persevere*
4357 prŏsmĕnō (1), *to remain; to adhere to*
4839 sumparamĕnō (1), *to remain in company*

CONTINUED
1961 hâyâh (3), *to exist, i.e. be or become*
2388 châzaq (1), *to fasten upon; to seize*
3254 yâçaph (2), *to add or augment*
3427 yâshab (3), *to dwell, to remain; to settle*
5125 nûwn (1), *to be perpetual*
5975 'âmad (1), *to stand*
7235 râbâh (1), *to increase*
1096 ginŏmai (1), *to be, become*
1265 diamĕnō (1), *to stay constantly*
1273 dianuktĕrĕuō (1), *to pass, spend the night*
1300 diatĕlĕō (1), *to persist, continue*
1304 diatribō (2), *to remain, stay*
1696 ĕmmĕnō (1), *to remain; to persevere*
1961 ĕpimĕnō (2), *to remain; to persevere*

CONTINUETH
5975 'âmad (1), *to stand*
1696 ĕmmĕnō (1), *to remain; to persevere*
3306 mĕnō (1), *to stay, remain*
3887 paramĕnō (1), *to be permanent, persevere*
4357 prŏsmĕnō (1), *to remain; to adhere to*

CONTINUING
1641 gârar (1), *to ruminate; to saw*
3306 mĕnō (1), *to stay, remain*
4342 prŏskartĕrĕō (2), *to persevere; to adhere*

CONTRADICTING
483 antilĕgō (1), *to dispute, refuse*

CONTRADICTION
485 antilŏgia (2), *dispute, disobedience*

CONTRARIWISE
5121 tŏunantiŏn (3), *on the contrary*

CONTRARY
2016 hephek (2), *reverse, perversion*
7147 qᵉrîy (7), *hostile encounter*
480 antikĕimai (2), *be adverse to*
561 apĕnanti (1), *opposite, against*
1727 ĕnantiŏs (6), *opposite*
3844 para (3), *from; with; besides; on account of*
3891 paranŏmĕō (1), *transgress, violate law*
5227 hupĕnantiŏs (1), *opposed; opponent*

CONTRIBUTION
2842 kŏinōnia (1), *benefaction; sharing*

CONTRITE
1792 dâkâ' (1), *to be contrite, be humbled*
1793 dakkâ' (2), *contrite, humbled*
1794 dâkâh (1), *to collapse; contrite*
5223 nâkeh (1), *maimed; dejected*

CONTROVERSIES
7379 rîyb (1), *contest, personal or legal*

CONTROVERSY
7379 rîyb (12), *contest, personal or legal*
3672 hŏmŏlŏgŏumĕnōs (1), *confessedly*

CONVENIENT
2706 chôq (1), *appointment; allotment*
3477 yâshâr (2), *straight*

433 anēkō (2), *be proper, fitting*
2119 ĕukairĕō (1), *to have opportunity*
2121 ĕukairŏs (1), *opportune, suitable*
2520 kathēkō (1), *becoming, proper*
2540 kairŏs (1), *occasion, set or proper*

CONVENIENTLY
2122 ĕukairōs (1), *opportunely*

CONVERSANT
1980 hâlak (2), *to walk; live a certain way*

CONVERSATION
1870 derek (2), *road; course of life*
390 anastrĕphō (2), *to remain, to live*
391 anastrŏphē (13), *behavior*
4175 pŏlitĕuma (1), *citizenship*
4176 pŏlitĕuŏmai (1), *to behave as a citizen*
5158 trŏpŏs (1), *deportment, character*

CONVERSION
1995 ĕpistrŏphē (1), *moral revolution*

CONVERT
7725 shûwb (1), *to turn back; to return*
1994 ĕpistrĕphō (1), *to revert, turn back to*

CONVERTED
2015 hâphak (1), *to turn about or over*
7725 shûwb (1), *to turn back; to return*
1994 ĕpistrĕphō (6), *to revert, turn back to*
4762 strĕphō (1), *to turn around or reverse*

CONVERTETH
1994 ĕpistrĕphō (1), *to revert, turn back to*

CONVERTING
7725 shûwb (1), *to turn back; to return*

CONVERTS
7725 shûwb (1), *to turn back; to return*

CONVEY
5674 'âbar (1), *to cross over; to transition*
7760 sûwm (1), *to put*

CONVEYED
1593 ĕknĕuō (1), *to quietly withdraw*

CONVICTED
1651 ĕlĕgchō (1), *to confute, admonish*

CONVINCE
1651 ĕlĕgchō (1), *to confute, admonish*
1827 ĕxĕlĕgchō (1), *to punish*

CONVINCED
3198 yâkach (1), *to be correct; to argue*

1246 diakatĕlĕgchŏmai (1), *to prove downright*
1651 ĕlĕgchō (2), *to confute, admonish, rebuke*

CONVINCETH
1651 ĕlĕgchō (1), *to confute, admonish*

CONVOCATION
4744 miqrâ' (15), *public meeting*

CONVOCATIONS
4744 miqrâ' (3), *public meeting*

COOK
2876 ṭabbâch (2), *butcher, cook*

COOKS
2876 ṭabbâch (1), *butcher, cook*

COOL
7307 rûwach (1), *breath; wind; life-spirit*
2711 katapsuchō (1), *to refresh, cool off*

COOS
2972 Kōs (1), *Cos*

COPIED
6275 'âthaq (1), *to grow old; to transcribe*

COPING
2947 ṭĕphach (1), *palm-breadth*

COPPER
5178 nᵉchôsheth (1), *copper; bronze*

COPPERSMITH
5471 chalkĕus (1), *copper-worker*

COPULATION
7902 shᵉkâbâh (3), *lying down*

COPY
4932 mishneh (2), *duplicate copy; double*
6572 parshegen (3), *transcript*
6573 parshegen (Ch.) (4), *transcript*

COR
3734 kôr (1), *dry measure*

CORAL
7215 râ'mâh (2), *high in value, (poss.) coral*

CORBAN
2878 kŏrban (1), *votive offering or gift*

CORD
2256 chebel (4), *company, band*
2339 chûwṭ (1), *string; measuring tape; line*
3499 yether (1), *remainder; small rope*

CORDS
2256 chebel (12), *company, band*
4340 mêythâr (8), *tent-cord; bow-string*
5688 'ăbôth (5), *entwined things*
4979 schŏiniŏn (1), *rushlet, i.e. grass-withe*

CORE
2879 Kŏrĕ (1), *ice*

CORIANDER
1407 gad (2), *coriander*

CORINTH
2882 Kŏrinthŏs (6), *Corinthus*

CORINTHIANS
2881 Kŏrinthiŏs (4), *inhabitant of Corinth*

CORINTHUS
2882 Kŏrinthŏs (1), *Corinthus*

CORMORANT
6893 qâ'ath (2), *pelican*
7994 shâlâk (2), *bird of prey (poss.) pelican*

CORN
1098 bᵉlîyl (1), *feed, fodder*
1121 bên (1), *son, descendant*
1250 bâr (9), *cereal grain*
1637 gôren (1), *open area*
1643 geres (2), *grain*
1715 dâgân (37), *grain*
3759 karmel (1), *planted field; garden produce*
5669 'âbûwr (2), *kept over; stored grain*
6194 'ârêm (1), *heap, mound; sheaf*
7054 qâmâh (7), *stalk of cereal grain*
7383 rîyphâh (1), *grits cereal*
7668 sheber (7), *grain*
7688 shâgach (1), *to glance sharply at*
2848 kŏkkŏs (1), *kernel*
4621 sitŏs (2), *grain, especially wheat*
4702 spŏrimŏs (3), *field planted with seed*
4719 stachus (3), *head of grain*

CORNELIUS
2883 Kŏrnēliŏs (10), *Cornelius*

CORNER
2106 zâvîyth (1), *angle, corner (as projecting)*
3671 kânâph (1), *edge or extremity; wing*
3802 kâthêph (2), *shoulder-piece; wall*
4742 mᵉquts'âh (1), *angle*
6285 pê'âh (5), *direction; region; extremity*
6434 pên (1), *angle*
6437 pânâh (1), *to turn, to face*
6438 pinnâh (17), *pinnacle; chieftain*
204 akrŏgōniaiŏs (2), *corner, cornerstone*
1137 gōnia (6), *angle; cornerstone*

CORNERS
2106 zâvîyth (1), *angle, corner (as projecting)*
3671 kânâph (2), *edge or extremity; wing*
4740 maqtsôwa' (1), *angle*
4742 mᵉquts'âh (6), *angle*

CORE
2879 Kŏrĕ (1), *ice*

6284 pâ'âh (1), *to blow away*
6285 pê'âh (11), *region; extremity*
6438 pinnâh (6), *pinnacle; chieftain*
6471 pa'am (3), *time; step; occurence*
6763 tsêlâ' (2), *side*
7098 qâtsâh (1), *termination; fringe*
7106 qâtsa' (1), *to strip off, i.e. (partially) scrape*
746 archē (2), *first in rank; first in time*
1137 gōnia (2), *angle; cornerstone*

CORNET
7162 qeren (Ch.) (4), *horn*
7782 shôwphâr (3), *curved ram's horn*

CORNETS
4517 mᵉna'na' (1), *rattling instrument*
7782 shôwphâr (1), *curved ram's horn*

CORNFLOOR
1637+1715 gôren (1), *open area*

CORPSE
4430 ptōma (1), *corpse, carrion*

CORPSES
1472 gᵉvîyâh (2), *dead body*
6297 peger (2), *carcase; corpse*

CORRECT
3198 yâkach (1), *to be correct; to argue*
3256 yâçar (6), *to chastise; to instruct*

CORRECTED
3256 yâçar (1), *to chastise; to instruct*
3810 paidĕutēs (1), *teacher or discipliner*

CORRECTETH
3198 yâkach (2), *to be correct; to argue*

CORRECTION
3198 yâkach (1), *to be correct; to argue*
4148 mûwçâr (8), *reproof, warning*
7626 shêbeṭ (1), *stick; clan, family*
8433 tôwkêchâh (1), *correction*
1882 ĕpanŏrthōsis (1), *rectification, correction*

CORRUPT
1605 gâ'ar (1), *to chide, reprimand*
2254 châbal (1), *to bind by a pledge; to pervert*
2610 chânêph (1), *to soil, be defiled*
4167 mûwq (1), *to blaspheme, scoff*
4743 mâqaq (1), *to melt; to flow, dwindle, vanish*
7843 shâchath (11), *to decay; to ruin*
7844 shᵉchath (Ch.) (1), *to decay; to ruin*

English

CORRUPTED

853 aphanizō (2), to
consume (becloud)
1311 diaphthĕirō (1), to
ruin, to pervert
2585 kapēlĕuō (1), to
retail, i.e. to adulterate
2704 kataphthĕirō (1), to
spoil entirely
4550 saprŏs (6), rotten,
i.e. worthless
5351 phthĕirō (4), to
spoil; to deprave

CORRUPTED

7843 shâchath (11), to
decay; to ruin
4595 sēpō (1), to putrefy,
rot
5351 phthĕirō (2), to
spoil; to deprave

CORRUPTERS

7843 shâchath (2), to
decay; to ruin

CORRUPTETH

1311 diaphthĕirō (1), to
ruin, to pervert

CORRUPTIBLE

862 aphthartŏs (1),
undecaying, immortal
5349 phthartŏs (6),
perishable, not lasting

CORRUPTING

7843 shâchath (1), to
decay; to ruin

CORRUPTION

1097 bᵉliy (1), without,
not yet; lacking;
4889 mashchîyth (2),
destruction; corruption
4893 mishchâth (1),
disfigurement
7845 shachath (4), pit;
destruction
1312 diaphthŏra (6),
decay, corruption
5356 phthŏra (7), ruin;
depravity, corruption

CORRUPTLY

2254 châbal (1), to bind
by a pledge; to pervert
7843 shâchath (1), to
decay; to ruin

COSAM

2973 Kōsam (1), Cosam

COST

2600 chinnâm (2), free
1160 dapanē (1),
expense, cost

COSTLINESS

5094 timiŏtēs (1),
expensiveness

COSTLY

3368 yâqâr (4), valuable
4185 pŏlutĕlēs (1),
extremely expensive
4186 pŏlutimŏs (1),
extremely valuable

COTES

220 ʾăvêrâh (1), stall, pen

COTTAGE

4412 mᵉlûwnâh (1), hut
5521 çukkâh (1),
tabernacle; shelter

COTTAGES

3741 kârâh (1), meadow

COUCH

3326 yâtsûwaʾ (1), bed;
wing or lean-to
4904 mishkâb (1), bed;
sleep
6210 ʾeres (2), canopy
couch
7742 sûwach (1), to muse
pensively
2826 klinidiŏn (2), pallet
or little couch

COUCHED

3766 kâraʾ (1), to
prostrate
7257 râbats (1), to
recline, repose, brood

COUCHES

6210 ʾeres (1), canopy
couch
2895 krabbatŏs (1),
sleeping mat

COUCHETH

7257 râbats (1), to
recline, repose, brood

COUCHING

7257 râbats (1), to
recline, repose, brood

COUCHINGPLACE

4769 marbêts (1), resting
place

COULD

3045 yâdaʾ (2), to know
3201 yâkôl (46), to be able
3202 yᵉkêl (Ch.) (1), to be
able
3546 kᵉhal (Ch.) (1), to be
able
5074 nâdad (1), to rove,
flee; to drive away
5234 nâkar (1), to
acknowledge
5346 Neqeb (1), dell
102 adunatŏs (1), weak;
impossible
1410 dunamai (29), to be
able or possible
1415 dunatŏs (1),
powerful or capable
2192 ĕchō (3), to have;
hold; keep
2480 ischuō (7), to have
or exercise force
2489 Iōanna (1),
Jehovah-favored
5342 phĕrō (1), to bear or
carry

COULDEST

3201 yâkôl (1), to be able
2480 ischuō (1), to have
or exercise force

COULDST

3202 yᵉkêl (Ch.) (1), to be
able

COULTER

855 ʾêth (1), digging
implement

COULTERS

855 ʾêth (1), digging
implement

COUNCIL

7277 rigmâh (1), throng
4824 sumbŏuliŏn (2),
deliberative body
4892 sunĕdriŏn (20),
tribunal

COUNCILS

4891 sunĕgĕirō (2), to
raise up with

COUNSEL

1697 dâbâr (1), word;
matter; thing
3245 yâçad (2), settle,
consult
3289 yâʿats (21), to advise
4431 mᵉlak (Ch.) (1),
counsel, advice
5475 çôwd (6), intimacy;
consultation; secret
5843 ʾêṭâʾ (Ch.) (1),
prudence
6098 ʾêtsâh (80), advice;
plan; prudence
8458 tachbûlâh (2),
guidance; plan
1011 bŏulĕuō (1), to
deliberate; to resolve
1012 bŏulē (9), purpose,
plan, decision
4823 sumbŏulĕuō (4), to
recommend; deliberate
4824 sumbŏuliŏn (5),
deliberative body

COUNSELED

3289 yâʿats (1), to advise

COUNSELLED

3289 yâʿats (3), to advise

COUNSELLOR

3289 yâʿats (10), to advise
6098 ʾêtsâh (1), advice;
plan; prudence
1010 bŏulĕutēs (2),
adviser, councillor
4825 sumbŏulŏs (1),
adviser

COUNSELLORS

1884 dᵉthâbâr (Ch.) (2),
skilled in law; judge
1907 haddâbâr (Ch.) (4),
vizier, high official
3272 yᵉʿaṭ (Ch.) (2), to
counsel
3289 yâʿats (12), to advise
6098 ʾêtsâh (1), advice;
plan; prudence

COUNSELS

4156 môwʿêtsâh (6),
purpose, plan
6098 ʾêtsâh (2), advice;
plan; prudence
8458 tachbûlâh (3),
guidance; plan
1012 bŏulē (1), purpose,
plan, decision

COUNT

1961 hâyah (1), to exist,
i.e. be or become
2803 châshab (3), to
think; to compute
3699 kâçaç (1), to
estimate, determine
4487 mânâh (1), to allot;
to enumerate or enroll
5414 nâthan (1), to give
5608 çâphar (4), to
inscribe; to enumerate
515 axiŏō (1), to deem
entitled or fit, worthy
2192 ĕchō (2), to have;
hold; keep
2233 hēgĕŏmai (7), to
deem, i.e. consider

COUNCILS

3049 lŏgizŏmai (1), to
credit; to think, regard
3106 makarizō (1), to
esteem fortunate
5585 psēphizō (1), to
compute, estimate

COUNTED

2803 châshab (18), to
think; to compute
5608 çâphar (2), to
inscribe; to enumerate
6485 pâqad (3), to visit,
care for, count
515 axiŏō (2), to deem
entitled or fit, worthy
1075 gĕnĕalŏgĕō (1),
trace in genealogy
2192 ĕchō (2), to have;
hold; keep
2233 hēgĕŏmai (3), to
deem, i.e. consider
2661 kataxiŏō (2), to
deem entirely deserving
3049 lŏgizŏmai (4), to
credit; to think, regard
4860 sumpsēphizō (1), to
compute jointly

COUNTENANCE

639 ʾaph (1), nose or
nostril; face; person
1921 hâdar (1), to favor
or honor; to be proud
2122 zîyv (Ch.) (4),
cheerfulness
4758 marʾeh (8),
appearance; vision
5869 ʾayin (1), eye; sight;
fountain
6440 pânîym (30), face
8389 tôʾar (1), outline,
figure or appearance
2397 idĕa (1), sight
3799 ŏpsis (1), face;
appearance
4383 prŏsōpŏn (3), face,
presence
4659 skuthrōpŏs (1),
gloomy or mournful

COUNTENANCES

4758 marʾeh (2),
appearance; vision

COUNTERVAIL

7737 shâvâh (1), to
resemble; to adjust

COUNTETH

2803 châshab (2), to
think; to compute
5585 psēphizō (1), to
compute, estimate

COUNTRIES

776 ʾerets (48), earth,
land, soil; country
5316 nepheth (1), height
5561 chōra (1), space of
territory

COUNTRY

127 ʾădâmâh (1), soil;
land
249 ʾezrâch (5), native
born
339 ʾîy (1), dry land;
coast; island
776 ʾerets (91), earth,
land, soil; country
1552 gᵉlîylâh (1), circuit
or region

2256 chebel (1),
company, band
4725 mâqôwm (1),
general *locality, place*
6521 pᵉrâzîy (1), *rustic*
7704 sâdeh (17), *field*
68 agrŏs (8), *farm*land,
countryside
589 apŏdēmĕŏ (4), *visit a
foreign land*
1085 gĕnŏs (1), *kin,
offspring in kind*
1093 gē (2), *soil, region,
whole earth*
3968 patris (8),
hometown
4066 pĕrichōrŏs (4),
surrounding country
5561 chōra (15), *space of
territory*

COUNTRYMEN
1085 gĕnŏs (1), *kin,
offspring in kind*
4853 sumphulĕtēs (1), *of
the same country*

COUPLE
2266 châbar (5), to
fascinate by spells
6776 tsemed (4), *paired
yoke*
8147 shᵉnayim (1),
two-fold

COUPLED
2266 châbar (7), to
fascinate by spells
8382 tâ'am (2), to *be
twinned*, i.e. *duplicate*
8535 tâm (2), morally
pious; gentle, dear

COUPLETH
2279 chôbereth (2), *joint*

COUPLING
2279 chôbereth (2), *joint*
4225 machbereth (8),
junction

COUPLINGS
4226 mᵉchabbᵉrâh (1),
joiner

COURAGE
553 'âmats (9), to *be
strong; be courageous*
2388 châzaq (8), to *be
strong; courageous*
3824 lêbâb (1), *heart*
7307 rûwach (1), *breath;
wind; life-spirit*
2294 tharsŏs (1),
boldness, courage

COURAGEOUS
533+3820 'ammîyts (1),
strong; mighty; brave
553 'âmats (2), to *be
strong; be courageous*
2388 châzaq (2), to *be
strong; courageous*

COURAGEOUSLY
2388 châzaq (1), to *be
strong; courageous*

COURSE
4131 môwṭ (1), to *slip,
shake, fall*
4256 machălôqeth (19),
section or division
4794 mᵉrûwtsâh (2), *race*
165 aiōn (1), *perpetuity,
ever; world*

1408 drŏmŏs (3), *career,
course of life*
2113 ĕuthudrŏmĕŏ (1), to
sail direct
2183 ĕphēmĕria (2),
rotation or class
3313 mĕrŏs (1), *division
or share*
4144 plŏŏs (2),
navigation, voyage
5143 trĕchō (1), to *run or
walk hastily; to strive*
5164 trŏchŏs (1), *wheel;
circuitous course of life*

COURSES
2487 chălîyphâh (1),
alternation, change
2988 yâbâl (1), *stream*
4255 machlᵉqâh (Ch.) (1),
section or division
4256 machălôqeth (14),
section or division
4546 mᵉçillâh (1), *main
thoroughfare; viaduct*

COURT
1004 bayith (1), *house;
temple; family, tribe*
2681 châtsîyr (1), *court
or abode*
2691 châtsêr (114),
enclosed yard
5835 'ăzârâh (2),
enclosure; border
5892 'îyr (1), *city, town,
unwalled-village*
833 aulē (1), *palace;
house; courtyard*

COURTEOUS
5391 philŏphrŏn (1),
kind, well-disposed

COURTEOUSLY
5364 philanthrōpōs (1),
fondly to mankind
5390 philŏphrŏnōs (1),
friendliness of mind

COURTS
2691 châtsêr (24),
enclosed yard

COUSIN
4773 suggĕnēs (1),
relative; countryman

COUSINS
4773 suggĕnēs (1),
relative; countryman

COVENANT
1285 bᵉrîyth (264),
compact, agreement
1242 diathēkē (17),
contract; devisory will

COVENANTBREAKERS
802 asunthĕtŏs (1),
untrustworthy

COVENANTED
3772 kârath (2), to *make
an agreement*
2476 histēmi (1), to
stand, establish
4934 suntithĕmai (1), to
consent, concur, agree

COVENANTS
1242 diathēkē (3),
contract; devisory will

COVER
2645 châphâh (1), to
cover; to veil, to encase

3680 kâçâh (50), to *cover*
4374 mᵉkaççeh (1),
covering
5258 nâçak (4), to *pour a
libation; to anoint*
5526 çâkak (5), to *fence
in; cover over; protect*
7159 qâram (1), to *cover*
7779 shûwph (1), to
gape, to overwhelm
2572 kaluptō (2), to *cover*
2619 katakaluptō (1),
cover with a veil
4028 pĕrikaluptō (1), to
cover eyes

COVERED
1104 bâla' (1), to
swallow; to destroy
2645 châphâh (7), to
cover; to veil, to encase
2926 ṭâlal (1), to *cover,
roof*
3271 yâ'aṭ (1), to *clothe,
cover*
3680 kâçâh (61), to *cover*
3728 kâphash (1), to
tread down
3780 kâsâh (1), to *grow
fat*
3813 lâ'aṭ (1), to *muffle,
cover*
4374 mᵉkaççeh (1),
covering
5526 çâkak (8), to *fence
in; cover over; protect*
5603 çâphan (3), to *hide
by covering; to roof*
5743 'ûwb (1), to *darkly
becloud*
5844 'âṭâh (3), to *wrap,
i.e. cover, veil, clothe*
5848 'âṭaph (1), to
shroud, clothe
6632 tsâb (1), *covered
cart*
6823 tsâphâh (5), to
sheet over with metal
7159 qâram (1), to *cover*
1943 ĕpikaluptō (1), to
forgive
2572 kaluptō (2), to *cover*
2596 kata (1), *down*
2619 katakaluptō (2),
cover with a veil
4780 sugkaluptō (1), to
conceal altogether

COVEREDST
3680 kâçâh (1), to *cover*

COVEREST
3680 kâçâh (1), to *cover*
5844 'âṭâh (1), to *wrap,
i.e. cover, veil, clothe*

COVERETH
3680 kâçâh (20), to *cover*
4374 mᵉkaççeh (2),
covering
5526 çâkak (2), to *fence
in; cover over; protect*
5844 'âṭâh (1), to *wrap,
i.e. cover, veil, clothe*
5848 'âṭaph (1), to
shroud, i.e. clothe
2572 kaluptō (1), to *cover*

COVERING
168 'ôhel (1), *tent*

3680 kâçâh (2), to *cover*
3681 kâçûwy (2), *covering*
3682 kᵉçûwth (6), *cover;
veiling*
3875 lôwṭ (1), *veil*
4372 mikçeh (16),
covering
4539 mâçâk (7), *veil;
shield*
4540 mᵉçukkâh (1),
covering
4541 maççêkâh (2), *cast
image); woven coverlet*
4817 merkâb (1), *chariot;
seat in chariot*
5526 çâkak (2), to *fence
in; cover over; protect*
5643 çêther (1), *cover,
shelter*
5844 'âṭâh (1), to *wrap,
i.e. cover, veil, clothe*
6781 tsâmîyd (1),
bracelet; lid
6826 tsippûwy (3),
encasement with metal
4018 pĕribŏlaiŏn (1),
mantle, veil

COVERINGS
4765 marbad (2),
coverlet, covering

COVERS
7184 qâsâh (3), *jug*

COVERT
4329 mêyçâk (1),
covered portico
4563 miçtôwr (1), *refuge,
hiding place*
5520 çôk (1), *hut of
entwined boughs; lair*
5521 çukkâh (1),
tabernacle; shelter
5643 çêther (5), *cover,
shelter*

COVET
183 'âvâh (1), to *wish for,
desire*
2530 châmad (3), to
delight in; lust for
1937 ĕpithumĕŏ (2), to
long for
2206 zēlŏŏ (2), to *have
warmth of feeling for*

COVETED
2530 châmad (1), to
delight in; lust for
1937 ĕpithumĕŏ (1), to
long for
3713 ŏrĕgŏmai (1), to
reach out after, long for

COVETETH
183 'âvâh (1), to *wish for,
desire*
1214 bâtsa' (1), to
plunder; to finish

COVETOUS
1214 bâtsa' (1), to
plunder; to finish
866 aphilargurŏs (1), *not
greedy*
4123 plĕŏnĕktēs (4),
eager for gain, greedy
4124 plĕŏnĕxia (1),
fraudulence, extortion
5366 philargurŏs (2),
avaricious

English

COVETOUSNESS
1215 betsa' (10), *plunder; unjust gain*
866 aphilargurŏs (1), *not greedy*
4124 plĕŏnĕxia (8), *fraudulence, avarice*

COVOCATION
4744 miqrâ' (1), *public meeting*

COW
5697 'eglâh (1), *cow calf*
6510 pârâh (2), *heifer*
7794 shôwr (2), *bullock*

COW'S
1241 bâqâr (1), *plowing ox; herd*

COZ
6976 Qôwts (1), *thorns*

COZBI
3579 Kozbîy (2), *false*

CRACKLING
6963 qôwl (1), *voice or sound*

CRACKNELS
5350 niqqud (1), *crumb, morsel; biscuit*

CRAFT
4820 mirmâh (1), *fraud*
1388 dŏlŏs (1), *wile, deceit, trickery*
2039 ĕrgasia (1), *occupation; profit*
3313 mĕrŏs (1), *division or share*
3673 hŏmŏtĕchnŏs (1), *fellow-artificer*
5078 tĕchnē (1), *trade, craft; skill*

CRAFTINESS
6193 'ôrem (1), *stratagem, craftiness*
3834 panŏurgia (4), *trickery or sophistry*

CRAFTSMAN
2976 yâ'ash (1), *to despond, despair*
5079 tĕchnitēs (1), *skilled craftsman*

CRAFTSMEN
2796 chârâsh (5), *skilled fabricator or worker*
5079 tĕchnitēs (2), *skilled craftsman*

CRAFTY
6175 'ârûwm (2), *cunning; clever*
6191 'âram (1), *to be cunning; be prudent*
3835 panŏurgŏs (1), *shrewd, clever*

CRAG
8127 shên (1), *tooth; ivory; cliff*

CRANE
5483 çûwç (2), *horse; bird swallow*

CRASHING
7667 sheber (1), *fracture; ruin*

CRAVED
154 aitĕŏ (1), *to ask for*

CRAVETH
404 'âkaph (1), *to urge*

CREATE
1254 bârâ' (8), *to create; fashion*

CREATED
1254 bârâ' (33), *to create; fashion*
2936 ktizō (12), *to fabricate, create*

CREATETH
1254 bârâ' (1), *to create; fashion*

CREATION
2937 ktisis (6), *formation*

CREATOR
1254 bârâ' (3), *to create; fashion*
2936 ktizō (1), *to fabricate, create*
2939 ktistēs (1), *founder*

CREATURE
2416 chay (6), *alive; raw; fresh; life*
5315 nephesh (9), *life; breath; soul; wind*
8318 sherets (1), *swarm, teeming mass*
2937 ktisis (11), *formation*
2938 ktisma (2), *created product*

CREATURES
255 'ôach (1), *creature that howls;*
2416 chay (9), *alive; raw; fresh; life*
2938 ktisma (2), *created product*

CREDITOR
1167+4874+3027 ba'al (1), *master; owner; citizen*
5383 nâshâh (1), *to lend or borrow*
1157 danĕistēs (1), *money lender*

CREDITORS
5383 nâshâh (1), *to lend or borrow*

CREEK
2859 kŏlpŏs (1), *lap area; bay*

CREEP
7430 râmas (2), *to glide swiftly, i.e. crawl*
8317 shârats (2), *to wriggle, swarm*
8318 sherets (2), *swarm, teeming mass*
1744+1519 ĕndunō (1), *to sneak in, creep in*

CREEPETH
7430 râmas (9), *to glide swiftly, i.e. crawl*
7431 remes (1), *any rapidly moving animal*
8317 shârats (4), *to wriggle, swarm*

CREEPING
7431 remes (15), *any rapidly moving animal*
8318 sherets (11), *swarm, teeming mass*
2062 hĕrpĕtŏn (3), *reptile*

CREPT
3921 parĕisdunō (1), *to slip in secretly*

CRESCENS
2913 Krēskēs (1), *growing*

CRETE
2914 Krētē (5), *Cretë*

CRETES
2912 Krēs (1), *inhabitant of Crete*

CRETIANS
2912 Krēs (2), *inhabitant of Crete*

CREW
5455 phōnĕō (5), *to emit a sound*

CRIB
18 'êbûwç (3), *manger or stall*

CRIED
2199 zâ'aq (31), *to call out, announce*
2200 zᵉ'îq (Ch.) (1), *to make an outcry, shout*
2980 yâbab (1), *to bawl, cry out*
5414 nâthan (1), *to give*
6817 tsâ'aq (29), *to shriek; to proclaim*
7121 qârâ' (54), *to call out*
7123 qᵉrâ' (Ch.) (3), *to call out*
7321 rûwa' (2), *to shout for alarm or joy*
7768 shâva' (10), *to halloo, call for help*
310 anabŏaō (2), *to cry out*
349 anakrazō (5), *to scream aloud*
863 aphiēmi (1), *to leave; to pardon, forgive*
994 bŏaō (3), *to shout for help*
2019 ĕpiphōnĕō (2), *to exclaim, shout*
2896 krazō (43), *to call aloud*
2905 kraugazō (6), *to clamor, shout*
5455 phōnĕō (5), *to emit a sound*

CRIES
995 bŏē (1), *to call for aid*

CRIEST
2199 zâ'aq (2), *to call out, announce*
6817 tsâ'aq (1), *to shriek; to proclaim*
7121 qârâ' (2), *to call out*

CRIETH
2199 zâ'aq (1), *to call out, announce*
5414+6963 nâthan (1), *to give*
6817 tsâ'aq (2), *to shriek; to proclaim*
7121 qârâ' (4), *to call out*
7442 rânan (3), *to shout for joy*
7768 shâva' (2), *to halloo, call for help*
2896 krazō (4), *to call aloud*

CRIME
2154 zimmâh (1), *bad plan*
1462 ĕgklēma (1), *accusation*

CRIMES
4941 mishpât (1), *verdict; formal decree; justice*
156 aitia (1), *logical reason; legal crime*

CRIMSON
3758 karmîyl (3), *carmine, deep red*
8144 shânîy (1), *crimson dyed stuffs*
8438 tôwlâ' (1), *maggot worm; crimson-grub*

CRIPPLE
5560 chōlŏs (1), *limping, crippled*

CRISPING
2754 chârîyt (1), *pocket*

CRISPUS
2921 Krispŏs (2), *crisp*

CROOKBACKT
1384 gibbên (1), *hunch-backed*

CROOKED
1281 bârîyach (1), *fleeing, gliding serpent*
1921 hâdar (1), *to favor or honor; to be high*
4625 ma'ăqâsh (1), *crook in a road*
5753 'âvâh (1), *to be crooked*
5791 'âvath (2), *to wrest, twist*
6121 'âqôb (1), *fraudulent; tracked*
6128 'ăqalqal (1), *crooked*
6129 'ăqallâthôwn (1), *crooked*
6140 'âqash (1), *to knot or distort; to pervert*
6141 'iqqêsh (1), *distorted, warped, false*
6618 pᵉthaltôl (1), *tortuous, perverse*
4646 skŏliŏs (2), *crooked; perverse*

CROP
4760 mur'âh (1), *craw or crop of a bird*
6998 qâtaph (1), *to strip off, pick off*

CROPPED
6998 qâtaph (1), *to strip off, pick off*

CROSS
4716 staurŏs (28), *pole or cross*

CROSSWAY
6563 pereq (1), *rapine; fork in roads*

CROUCH
7812 shâchâh (1), *to prostrate in homage*

CROUCHETH
1794 dâkâh (1), *to collapse; contrite*

CROW
5455 phōnĕō (7), *to emit a sound*

CROWN
2213 zêr (10), border molding on a building
3804 kether (3), royal headdress
5145 nezer (11), royal chaplet
5850 'ăṭârâh (20), crown
6936 qodqôd (7), crown of the head
4735 stĕphanŏs (15), chaplet, wreath

CROWNED
3803 kâthar (1), to enclose, besiege; to wait
4502 minnᵉzâr (1), prince
5849 'âṭar (2), to encircle, enclose in; to crown
4737 stephanŏō (2), to adorn with a wreath

CROWNEDST
4737 stephanŏō (1), to adorn with a wreath

CROWNEST
5849 'âṭar (1), to encircle, enclose in; to crown

CROWNETH
5849 'âṭar (1), to encircle, enclose in; to crown

CROWNING
5849 'âṭar (1), to encircle, enclose in; to crown

CROWNS
5850 'ăṭârâh (3), crown
1238 diadĕma (3), crown or diadem
4735 stĕphanŏs (3), chaplet, wreath

CRUCIFIED
4362 prŏspēgnumi (1), to fasten to a cross
4717 staurŏō (31), to crucify
4957 sustaurŏō (5), to crucify with

CRUCIFY
388 anastaurŏō (1), to re-crucify
4717 staurŏō (13), to crucify

CRUEL
393 'akzâr (3), violent, deadly; brave
394 'akzârîy (8), terrible, cruel
395 'akzᵉrîyûwth (1), fierceness, cruelty
2555 châmâç (1), violence; malice
2556 châmêts (1), to be fermented; be soured
7185 qâshâh (2), to be tough or severe
7186 qâsheh (1), severe

CRUELLY
6233 'ôsheq (1), injury; fraud; distress

CRUELTY
2555 châmâç (4), violence; malice
6531 perek (1), severity

CRUMBS
5589 psichiŏn (3), little bit or morsel

CRUSE
1228 baqbûk (1), bottle
6746 tsᵉlôchîyth (1), vial or salt-cellar
6835 tsappachath (7), flat saucer

CRUSH
1792 dâkâ' (1), to pulverize; be contrite
2115 zûwr (1), to press together, tighten
7533 râtsats (1), to crack in pieces, smash
7665 shâbar (1), to burst

CRUSHED
1792 dâkâ' (2), to pulverize; be contrite
2000 hâmam (1), to disturb, drive, destroy
2116 zûwreh (1), trodden on
3807 kâthath (1), to bruise, strike, beat
3905 lâchats (1), to press; to distress
7533 râtsats (1), to crack in pieces, smash

CRY
602 'ânaq (3), to shriek, cry out in groaning
1993 hâmâh (1), to be in great commotion
2199 zâ'aq (25), to call out, announce
2201 za'aq (18), shriek, outcry, lament
5414+6963 nâthan (1), to give
6030 'ânâh (2), to respond, answer
6165 'ârag (1), to long for, pant for
6463 pâ'âh (1), to scream in childbirth
6670 tsâhal (3), to be cheerful; to sound
6682 tsᵉvâchâh (1), screech of anguish
6817 tsâ'aq (15), to shriek; to proclaim
6818 tsa'ăqâh (19), shriek, wail
6873 tsârach (1), to whoop
6963 qôwl (1), voice or sound
7121 qârâ' (37), to call out
7321 rûwa' (5), to shout for alarm or joy
7440 rinnâh (12), shout
7442 rânan (1), to shout for joy
7768 shâva' (8), to call for help
7769 shûwa' (1), call
7773 sheva' (1), call
7775 shav'âh (11), call
8173 shâ'a' (1), to fondle, please or amuse (self)
994 bŏaō (2), to shout for help
2896 krazō (3), to call
2905 kraugazō (1), to clamor, shout
2906 kraugē (3), outcry

CRYING
603 'ănâqâh (1), shrieking, groaning
2201 za'aq (2), shriek, outcry, lament
4191 mûwth (1), to die; to kill
6682 tsᵉvâchâh (1), screech of anguish
6818 tsa'ăqâh (2), shriek, wail
7121 qârâ' (1), to call out
7771 shôwa' (1), call
8663 tᵉshû'âh (1), crashing or clamor
310 anabŏaō (1), to cry out
994 bŏaō (6), to shout for help
1916 ĕpibŏaō (1), to cry out loudly
2896 krazō (9), to call
2906 kraugē (2), outcry

CRYSTAL
2137 zᵉkûwkîyth (1), transparent glass
7140 qerach (1), ice; hail; rock crystal
2929 krustallizō (1), to appear as ice
2930 krustallŏs (2), rock crystal

CUBIT
520 'ammâh (35), cubit
1574 gômed (1), measurement of length
4083 pēchus (2), measure of time or length

CUBITS
520 'ammâh (197), cubit
521 'ammâh (Ch.) (4), cubit
4088 pikria (1), acridity, bitterness

CUCKOW
7828 shachaph (2), gull

CUCUMBERS
4750 miqshâh (1), cucumber field
7180 qishshû' (1), cucumber

CUD
1625 gêrâh (11), cud

CUMBERED
4049 pĕrispaō (1), to be distracted

CUMBERETH
2673 katargĕō (1), to be, render entirely useless

CUMBRANCE
2960 ṭôrach (1), burden

CUMI
2891 kŏumi (1), rise!

CUMMIN
3646 kammôn (3), cummin
2951 kuminŏn (1), dill or fennel

CUNNING
542 'âmân (1), expert artisan, craftsman
995 bîyn (1), to understand; discern
1847 da'ath (1), understanding

CUP
1375 gᵉbîya' (4), goblet; bowl
3563 kôwç (29), cup; (poss.) owl
3599 kîyç (1), cup; utility bag
5592 çaph (1), dish
4221 pŏtēriŏn (31), drinking-vessel

CUPBEARER
4945 mashqeh (1), butler; drink; well-watered

CUPBEARERS
4945 mashqeh (2), butler; drink; well-watered

CUPS
101 'aggân (1), bowl
3563 kôwç (1), cup
4518 mᵉnaqqîyth (1), sacrificial basin
7184 qâsâh (1), jug
4221 pŏtēriŏn (2), drinking-vessel

CURDLED
7087 qâphâ' (1), to thicken, congeal

CURE
1455 gâhâh (1), to heal
7495 râphâ' (1), to cure, heal
2323 thĕrapĕuō (2), to relieve disease

CURED
8585 tᵉ'âlâh (1), bandage or plaster
2323 thĕrapĕuō (3), to relieve disease

CURES
2392 iasis (1), curing

CURIOUS
4284 machăshâbâh (1), contrivance; plan
4021 pĕriĕrgŏs (1), meddlesome, busybody

CURIOUSLY
7551 râqam (1), variegation; embroider

CURRENT
5674 'âbar (1), to cross over; to transition

CURSE
423 'âlâh (9), imprecation: curse
779 'ârar (15), to execrate, place a curse
1288 bârak (3), to bless
2764 chêrem (4), doomed object
3994 mᵉ'êrâh (4), execration, curse
5344 nâqab (4), to specify, designate, libel
6895 qâbab (7), to stab with words
7043 qâlal (17), to be easy, trifling, vile

CRITICAL
2450 châkâm (10), wise, intelligent, skillful
2803 châshab (11), to plot; to think, regard
3045 yâda' (4), to know
4284 machăshâbâh (3), contrivance; plan

English

CURSED
7045 qᵉlâlâh (24), *vilification*
7621 shᵉbûw'âh (1), *sworn oath*
8381 ta'ălâh (1), *imprecation*
332 anathĕmatizō (3), to *declare* or *vow an oath*
2652 katanathĕma (1), *imprecation*
2653 katanathĕmatizō (1), to *imprecate*
2671 katara (3), *imprecation, execration*
2672 kataraŏmai (4), to *execrate, curse*

CURSED
779 'ârar (44), to *execrate, place a curse*
1288 bârak (1), to *bless*
2764 chêrem (3), *doomed object*
5344 nâqab (1), to *specify, designate, libel*
6895 qâbab (1), to *stab with words*
7043 qâlal (17), to *be easy, trifling, vile*
1944 ĕpikataratŏs (3), *execrable, cursed*
2671 katara (1), *imprecation, execration*
2672 kataraŏmai (1), to *execrate, curse*

CURSEDST
422 'âlâh (1), *imprecate, utter a curse*
2672 kataraŏmai (1), to *execrate, curse*

CURSES
423 'âlâh (5), *imprecation: curse*
7045 qᵉlâlâh (3), *vilification*

CURSEST
779 'ârar (1), to *execrate, place a curse*

CURSETH
779 'ârar (2), to *execrate, place a curse*
7043 qâlal (6), to *be easy, trifling, vile*
2551 kakŏlŏgĕō (2), to *revile, curse*

CURSING
423 'âlâh (4), *imprecation: curse*
3994 mᵉ'êrâh (1), *execration, curse*
7045 qᵉlâlâh (4), *vilification*
685 ara (1), *imprecation, curse*
2671 katara (2), *imprecation, execration*

CURSINGS
7045 qᵉlâlâh (1), *vilification*

CURTAIN
1852 dôq (1), *fine, thin cloth*
3407 yᵉrîy'âh (23), *drapery*
4539 mâçâk (1), *veil; shield*

CURTAINS
3407 yᵉrîy'âh (31), *drapery*

CUSH
3568 Kûwsh (8), *Cush*

CUSHAN
3572 Kûwshân (1), *Cushan*

CUSHI
3569 Kûwshîy (10), *Cushite*

CUSTODY
3027 yâd (4), *hand; power*
6486 pᵉquddâh (1), *visitation; punishment*

CUSTOM
1870 derek (1), *road; mode of action*
1983 hălâk (Ch.) (3), *toll, duty on goods at a road*
2706 chôq (2), *appointment; allotment*
4941 mishpâṭ (2), *verdict; formal decree; justice*
1480 ĕthizō (1), *customary, required*
1485 ĕthŏs (2), *usage*
3588+1486 hŏ (1), "the" i.e. the definite article
4914 sunĕthĕia (2), *usage, custom*
5056 tĕlŏs (2), *conclusion* of an act or state
5058 tĕlōniŏn (3), *tax-gatherer's booth*

CUSTOMS
2708 chuqqâh (2), to *delineate*
1485 ĕthŏs (5), *usage*

CUT
1214 bâtsa' (3), to *plunder; to finish*
1219 bâtsar (1), to *be inaccessible*
1254 bârâ' (2), to *create; fashion*
1413 gâdad (5), to *gash, slash oneself*
1438 gâda' (21), to *fell a tree; to destroy*
1494 gâzaz (2), to *shear; shave; destroy*
1504 gâzar (8), to *cut down; to destroy*
1505 gᵉzar (Ch.) (2), to *quarry rock*
1629 gâraz (1), to *cut off*
1820 dâmâh (5), to *be silent; to fail, cease*
1826 dâmam (5), to *stop, cease; to perish*
2404 châṭab (1), to *chop or carve wood*
2498 châlaph (1), to *pierce; to change*
2672 châtsab (1), to *cut stone or carve wood*
2686 châtsats (1), to *curtail*
3582 kâchad (10), to *destroy; to hide*
3683 kâçach (2), to *cut off*
3772 kârath (175), to *cut (off, down or asunder)*
4135 mûwl (2), to *circumcise*

CUT
5243 nâmal (4), to *be circumcised*
5352 nâqâh (2), to *be, make clean; to be bare*
5362 nâqaph (1), to *strike; to surround*
5408 nâthach (7), to *dismember, cut up*
5648 'ăbad (Ch.) (2), to *do, work, serve*
5927 'âlâh (1), to *ascend, be high, mount*
6780 tsemach (1), *sprout, branch*
6789 tsâmath (7), to *extirpate, destroy*
6990 qâṭaṭ (1), to *destroy*
6998 qâṭaph (2), to *strip off, pick off*
7059 qâmaṭ (1), to *pluck, i.e. destroy*
7082 qâçaç (1), to *lop off*
7088 qâphad (1), to *roll together*
7094 qâtsab (1), to *clip, or chop*
7096 qâtsâh (1), to *cut off; to destroy*
7112 qâtsats (10), to *chop off; to separate*
7113 qᵉtsats (Ch.) (1), to *chop off, lop off*
7167 qâra' (1), to *rend*
7787 sûwr (1), to *saw*
8295 sâraṭ (1), to *gash oneself*
8456 tâzaz (1), to *lop off*
581 apŏgĕnŏmĕnŏs (1), *deceased*
609 apŏkŏptō (6), *mutilate* the genitals
851 aphairĕō (1), to *remove, cut off*
1282 diapriō (2), to *be furious*
1371 dichŏtŏmĕō (2), to *flog severely*
1581 ĕkkŏptō (7), to *cut off; to frustrate*
2875 kŏptō (2), to *beat* the breast
4932 suntĕmnō (1), to *cut short, i.e. do speedily*

CUTH
3575 Kûwth (1), *Cuth or Cuthah*

CUTHAH
3575 Kûwth (1), *Cuth or Cuthah*

CUTTEST
7114 qâtsar (1), to *curtail, cut short*

CUTTETH
1234 bâqa' (1), to *cleave, break, tear open*
3772 kârath (1), to *cut (off, down or asunder)*
6398 pâlach (1), to *slice; to break open; to pierce*
7096 qâtsâh (1), to *cut off; to destroy*
7112 qâtsats (1), to *chop off; to separate*
7167 qâra' (1), to *rend*

CUTTING
1824 dᵉmîy (1), *quiet, peacefulness*

CUTTING
2799 chărôsheth (2), *skilled work*
7096 qâtsâh (1), to *cut off; to destroy*
2629 katakŏptō (1), to *mangle, cut up*

CUTTINGS
1417 gᵉdûwd (1), *furrow ridge*
8296 sereṭ (2), *incision*

CYMBAL
2950 kumbalŏn (1), *cymbal*

CYMBALS
4700 mᵉtsêleth (13), *pair of cymbals*
6767 tsᵉlâtsal (3), *whirring*

CYPRESS
8645 tirzâh (1), (poss.) *cypress*

CYPRUS
2954 Kuprŏs (8), *Cyprus*

CYRENE
2957 Kurēnē (4), *Cyrenë*

CYRENIAN
2956 Kurēnaiŏs (2), *inhabitant of Cyrene*

CYRENIANS
2956 Kurēnaiŏs (1), *inhabitant of Cyrene*

CYRENIUS
2958 Kurēniŏs (1), *Quirinus*

CYRUS
3566 Kôwresh (15), *Koresh*
3567 Kôwresh (Ch.) (8), *Koresh*

DABAREH
1705 Dâbᵉrath (1), *Daberath*

DABBASHETH
1708 Dabbesheth (1), *hump of a camel*

DABERATH
1705 Dâbᵉrath (2), *Daberath*

DAGGER
2719 chereb (3), *knife, sword*

DAGON
1712 Dâgôwn (11), *fish-god*

DAGON'S
1712 Dâgôwn (1), *fish-god*

DAILY
3117 yôwm (20), *day; time period*
3117+259 yôwm (1), *day; time period*
3119 yôwmâm (2), *daily*
3605+3117 kôl (11), *all, any or every*
8548 tâmîyd (7), *constantly, regularly*
1967 ĕpiŏusiŏs (2), *for subsistence, i.e. needful*
2184 ĕphēmĕrŏs (1), *diurnal, i.e. daily*
2522 kathēmĕrinŏs (1), *quotidian, i.e. daily*

2596+1538+2250 kata (1), down; according to
2596+2250 kata (15), down; according to
2596+3956+2250 kata (1), down; according to
3956+2250 pas (1), all, any, every, whole

DAINTIES
4303 maț'am (1), *delicacy*
4516 man'am (1), *delicacy eaten*
4574 ma'ădân (1), *delicacy; pleasure*

DAINTY
4303 maț'am (1), *delicacy*
8378 ta'ăvâh (1), *longing; delight*
3045 liparŏs (1), *costly, rich*

DALAIAH
1806 Dᵉlâyâh (1), *Jehovah has delivered*

DALE
6010 'ēmeq (2), broad *depression or valley*

DALMANUTHA
1148 Dalmanŏutha (1), *Dalmanutha*

DALMATIA
1149 Dalmatia (1), *Dalmatia*

DALPHON
1813 Dalphôwn (1), *dripping*

DAM
517 'ēm (5), *mother*

DAMAGE
2257 chăbal (Ch.) (1), *harm, wound*
2555 châmâç (1), *violence; malice*
5142 nᵉzaq (Ch.) (1), to *suffer, inflict loss*
5143 nêzeq (1), *injure, loss*
2209 zēmia (1), *detriment; loss*
2210 zēmiŏō (1), to *experience detriment*

DAMARIS
1152 Damaris (1), *gentle*

DAMASCENES
1159 dapanaō (1), to *incur cost; to waste*

DAMASCUS
1833 dᵉmesheq (1), *damask fabric*
1834 Dammeseq (44), *Damascus*
1154 Damaskŏs (15), *Damascus*

DAMNABLE
684 apŏlĕia (1), *ruin or loss*

DAMNATION
684 apŏlĕia (1), *ruin or loss*
2917 krima (7), *decision*
2920 krisis (3), *decision; tribunal; justice*

DAMNED
2632 katakrinō (2), to *judge against*

2919 krinō (1), to *decide; to try, condemn, punish*

DAMSEL
3207 yaldâh (1), *young female*
5291 na'ărâh (24), *female child; servant*
7356 racham (1), *womb; maiden*
2877 kŏrasiŏn (6), *little girl*
3813 paidiŏn (4), *child: boy or girl; immature*
3814 paidiskĕ (4), *female slave or servant*

DAMSEL'S
5291 na'ărâh (8), *female child; servant*

DAMSELS
5291 na'ărâh (2), *female child; servant*
5959 'almâh (1), *lass, young woman*

DAN
1835 Dân (71), *judge*

DAN-JAAN
1842 Dân Ya'an (1), *judge of purpose*

DANCE
2342 chûwl (1), to *dance, whirl; to writhe*
4234 mâchôwl (4), *(round) dance*
7540 râqad (3), to *spring about wildly or for joy*

DANCED
2342 chûwl (1), to *dance, whirl; to writhe in pain; to wait; to pervert*
3769 kârar (1), to *dance in whirling motion*
3738 ŏrchĕŏmai (4), to *dance*

DANCES
4246 mᵉchôwlâh (5), *round-dance*

DANCING
2287 châgag (1), to *observe a festival*
3769 kârar (1), to *dance in whirling motion*
4234 mâchôwl (1), *(round) dance*
4246 mᵉchôwlâh (2), *round-dance*
7540 râqad (1), to *spring about wildly or for joy*
5525 chŏrŏs (1), *round dance; dancing*

DANDLED
8173 shâ'a' (1), to *fondle, please or amuse* (self)

DANGER
1777 ĕnŏchŏs (5), *liable*
2793 kindunĕuō (2), to *undergo peril*

DANGEROUS
2000 ĕpisphalēs (1), *insecure, unsafe*

DANIEL
1840 Dânîyê'l (29), *judge of God*
1841 Dânîyê'l (Ch.) (50), *judge of God*

1158 Daniēl (2), *judge of God*

DANITES
1839 Dânîy (4), *Danite*

DANNAH
1837 Dannâh (1), *Dannah*

DARA
1873 Dâra' (1), *Dara*

DARDA
1862 Darda' (1), *pearl of knowledge*

DARE
5111 tŏlmaō (4), to be *bold; to dare*

DARIUS
1867 Dârᵉyâvêsh (10), *Darejavesh*
1868 Dârᵉyâvêsh (Ch.) (15), *Darejavesh*

DARK
651 'âphêl (1), *dusky, dark*
653 'ăphêlâh (1), *duskiness, darkness*
2420 chîydâh (5), *puzzle; conundrum; maxim*
2821 châshak (5), to be *dark; to darken*
2822 chôshek (7), *darkness; misery*
2824 cheshkâh (1), *darkness, dark*
2841 chashrâh (1), *gathering of clouds*
3544 kêheh (5), *feeble; obscure*
4285 machshâk (3), *darkness; dark place*
5399 nesheph (1), *dusk, dawn*
5939 'ălâțâh (1), *dusk*
6205 'ărâphel (2), *gloom, darkness*
6751 tsâlal (1), to *shade; to grow dark*
6937 qâdar (4), to be *dark-colored*
7087 qâphâ' (1), to *thicken, congeal*
850 auchmērŏs (1), *obscure, dark*
4652 skŏtĕinŏs (1), *dark, very dark*
4653 skŏtia (2), *dimness*

DARKEN
2821 châshak (1), to be *dark; to darken*

DARKENED
2821 châshak (7), to be *dark; to darken*
3543 kâhâh (1), to *grow dull, fade; to be faint*
6150 'ârab (1), to *grow dusky at sundown*
6272 'âtham (1), *be desolated by scorching*
6937 qâdar (1), to be *dark-colored*
4654 skŏtizō (8), to be, *become dark*

DARKENETH
2821 châshak (1), to be *dark; to darken*

DARKISH
3544 kêheh (1), *feeble; obscure*

DARKLY
1722+135 ĕn (1), *in; during; because of*

DARKNESS
652 'ôphel (6), *dusk, darkness*
653 'ăphêlâh (6), *duskiness, darkness*
2816 chăshôwk (Ch.) (1), *dark, darkness*
2821 châshak (1), to be *dark; to darken*
2822 chôshek (69), *darkness; misery*
2825 chăshêkâh (5), *darkness; misery*
3990 ma'ăphêl (1), *opaque, dark*
3991 ma'ĕhᵉyâh (1), *opaqueness, darkness*
4285 machshâk (4), *darkness; dark place*
5890 'êyphâh (2), *covering of darkness*
6205 'ărâphel (13), *gloom, darkness*
2217 zŏphŏs (2), *gloom*
4652 skŏtĕinŏs (2), *dark, very dark*
4653 skŏtia (13), *dimness*
4655 skŏtŏs (31), *darkness*
4656 skŏtŏō (1), to *make dark, i.e. blind*

DARKON
1874 Darqôwn (2), *Darkon*

DARLING
3173 yâchîyd (2), *only son; alone; beloved*

DART
2671 chêts (1), *arrow; wound; shaft* of a spear
4551 maççâ' (1), *stone quarry; projectile*
1002 bŏlis (1), *javelin, projectile*

DARTS
7626 shêbeț (1), *stick; clan, family*
7973 shelach (1), *spear; shoot of growth*
8455 tôwthâch (1), *stout club*
956 bĕlŏs (1), *spear or arrow*

DASH
5062 nâgaph (1), to *strike*
5310 nâphats (2), to *dash to pieces; to scatter*
7376 râțash (2), to *dash down*
4350 prŏskŏptō (2), to *trip up; to strike*

DASHED
7376 râțash (4), to *dash down*
7492 râ'ats (1), to *break in pieces; to harass*

DASHETH
5310 nâphats (1), to *dash to pieces; to scatter*

6327 pûwts (1), to *dash in pieces*; to *disperse*

DATHAN
1885 Dâthân (10), *Dathan*

DAUB
2902 ṭûwach (1), to *whitewash*

DAUBED
2560 châmar (1), to *glow*; to *smear*
2902 ṭûwach (6), to *whitewash*

DAUBING
2915 ṭîyach (1), *plaster, whitewash coating*

DAUGHTER
1004 bayith (1), *house; temple; family, tribe*
1121 bên (1), *son, descendant*
1323 bath (270), *daughter, descendant*
3618 kallâh (13), *bride; son's wife*
2364 thugatēr (24), *female child*
2365 thugatriŏn (2), *little daughter*
3565 numphē (3), young *married* woman

DAUGHTER'S
1323 bath (3), *daughter, descendant, woman*

DAUGHTERS
1121 bên (244), *son, descendant*
3618 kallâh (3), *bride*
2364 thugatēr (5), *female child, or descendant*
5043 tĕknŏn (1), *child*

DAVID
1732 Dâvîd (1019), *loving*
1138 Dabid (58), *loving*

DAVID'S
1732 Dâvîd (53), *loving*
1138 Dabid (1), *loving*

DAWN
1306 diaugazō (1), to *dawn, shine through*
2020 ĕpiphōskō (1), to *grow light*

DAWNING
5399 nesheph (2), *dusk, dawn*
5927 'âlâh (1), to *ascend, be high, mount*
6079 'aph'aph (1), *morning ray*
6437 pânâh (1), to *turn, to face*

DAY
215 'ôwr (1), to *be luminous*
216 'ôwr (1), *luminary; lightning; happiness*
1242 bôqer (4), *morning*
3117 yôwm (1250), *day; time period*
3118 yôwm (Ch.) (4), *day; time period*
3119 yôwmâm (53), *daily*
4283 mochŏrâth (2), *tomorrow, next day*
5399 nesheph (1), *dusk, dawn*

7837 shachar (6), *dawn*
737 arti (1), just *now; at once*
827 augē (1), *radiance, dawn*
839 auriŏn (1), *to-morrow*
1773 ĕnnuchŏn (1), *by night*
1887 ĕpauriŏn (8), *to-morrow*
2250 hēmĕra (200), *day; period of time*
3574 nuchthēmĕrŏn (1), full *day*
3588+2596+2250 hŏ (2), *"the,"* definite article
4594 sēmĕrŏn (38), *this day, today, now*
4594+2250 sēmĕrŏn (1), *this day, today, now*
4595 sēpō (1), to *putrefy, rot*
5459 phōsphŏrŏs (1), *morning-star*
5610 hōra (1), *hour,* i.e. a *unit of time*

DAY'S
3117 yôwm (6), *day; time period*
2250 hēmĕra (1), *day; period of time*
4594 sēmĕrŏn (1), *this day, today, now*

DAYS
3117 yôwm (665), *day; time period*
3118 yôwm (Ch.) (9), *day; time period*
8543 tᵉmôwl (1), (day before) *yesterday*
1909 ĕpi (2), *on, upon*
2250 hēmĕra (154), *day; period of time*
5066 tĕtartaiŏs (1), of the *fourth day*

DAYS'
3117 yôwm (13), *day; time period*

DAYSMAN
3198 yâkach (1), to *decide, justify, convict*

DAYSPRING
7837 shachar (1), *dawn*
395 anatŏlē (1), *dawn of sun; east*

DAYTIME
3119 yôwmâm (8), *daily*

DEACON
1247 diakŏnĕō (2), to *act as a deacon*

DEACONS
1249 diakŏnŏs (3), *attendant, deacon(-ess)*

DEAD
1472 gᵉvîyâh (1), *dead body*
1478 gâva' (1), to *expire, die*
4191 mûwth (136), to *die; to kill*
4194 mâveth (7), *death; dead*
5038 nᵉbêlâh (7), *carcase or carrion*
5315 nephesh (8), *life; breath; soul; wind*

6297 peger (6), *carcase; corpse*
7496 râphâ' (7), *dead*
7703 shâdad (1), to *ravage*
581 apŏgĕnŏmĕnŏs (1), *deceased*
599 apŏthnēskō (29), to *die off*
2258 ēn (1), I *was*
2289 thanatŏō (1), to *kill*
2348 thnēskō (12), to *die, be dead*
2837 kŏimaō (1), to *slumber; to decease*
3498 nĕkrŏs (130), *corpse; dead*
3499 nĕkrŏō (2), to *deaden,* i.e. to *subdue*
4430 ptōma (3), *corpse, carrion*
4880 sunapŏthnēskō (1), to *decease with*
5053 tĕlĕutaō (3), to *finish life,* i.e. *expire*

DEADLY
4194 mâveth (1), *death; dead*
5315 nephesh (1), *life; breath; soul; wind*
2286 thanasimŏs (1), *poisonous, deadly*
2287 thanatēphŏrŏs (1), *fatal,* i.e. *bringing death*
2288 thanatŏs (2), *death*

DEADNESS
3500 nĕkrōsis (1), *death, deadness*

DEAF
2790 chârash (1), to *be silent; to be deaf*
2795 chêrêsh (9), *deaf*
2974 kōphŏs (5), *deaf or silent*

DEAL
1580 gâmal (2), to *benefit or requite; to wean*
6213 'âsâh (26), to *do*
6536 pâraç (1), to *split, distribute*
4054 pĕrissŏtĕrŏn (1), *more superabundantly*

DEALEST
6213 'âsâh (1), to *do*

DEALETH
6213 'âsâh (7), to *do*
4374 prŏsphĕrō (1), to *present to; to treat as*

DEALINGS
1697 dâbâr (1), *word; matter; thing*
4798 sugchraŏmai (1), to *have dealings with*

DEALT
1580 gâmal (2), to *benefit or requite; to wean*
2505 châlaq (2), to *be smooth; be slippery*
6213 'âsâh (18), to *do or make*
1793 ĕntugchanō (1), to *entreat, petition*
2686 katasŏphizŏmai** (1), to *be crafty against*
3307 mĕrizō (1), to *apportion, bestow*

4160 pŏiĕō (2), to *do*

DEAR
3357 yaqqîyr (1), *precious*
26 agapē (1), *love*
27 agapētŏs (3), *beloved*
1784 ĕntimŏs (1), *valued, considered precious*
5093 timiŏs (1), *honored, esteemed,* or *beloved*

DEARTH
1226 batstsôreth (1), *drought*
7458 râ'âb (5), *hunger*
3042 limŏs (2), *scarcity, famine*

DEATH
4191 mûwth (82), to *die; to kill*
4192 Mûwth (1), *"To die for the son"*
4193 môwth (Ch.) (1), *death*
4194 mâveth (126), *death; dead*
6757 tsalmâveth (18), *shade of death*
7523 râtsach (1), to *murder*
8546 tᵉmûwthâh (1), *execution, death*
336 anairĕsis (5), act of *killing*
337 anairĕō (2), to *take away,* i.e. *abolish, murder*
520 apagō (1), to *take away*
599 apŏthnēskō (1), to *die off*
615 apŏktĕinō (6), to *kill outright; to destroy*
1935 ĕpithanatiŏs (1), *doomed to death*
2079 ĕschatōs (1), *finally,* i.e. *at the extremity*
2288 thanatŏs (113), *death*
2289 thanatŏō (7), to *kill*
5054 tĕlĕutē (1), *deceasedness, death*

DEATHS
4194 mâveth (1), *death; dead*
4463 mâmôwth (2), *mortal disease, death*
2288 thanatŏs (1), *death*

DEBASE
8213 shâphêl (1), to *humiliate*

DEBATE
4683 matstsâh (1), *quarrel*
7378 rîyb (2), to *hold a controversy; to defend*
2054 ĕris (1), *quarrel,* i.e. *wrangling*

DEBATES
2054 ĕris (1), *quarrel,* i.e. *wrangling*

DEBIR
1688 Dᵉbîyr (14), *inmost part of the sanctuary*

DEBORAH
1683 Dᵉbôwrâh (10), *bee*

DEBT
3027 yâd (1), *hand; power*

English

5378 nâshâ' (1), to *lend* on interest
5386 nᵉshîy (1), *debt*
1156 danĕiŏn (1), *loan; debt*
3782 ŏphĕilē (1), *sum owed; obligation*
3783 ŏphĕilēma (1), *due; moral fault*
3784 ŏphĕilō (1), to *owe;* to *be under obligation*

DEBTOR
2326 chôwb (1), *debt*
3781 ŏphĕilĕtēs (2), person *indebted*
3784 ŏphĕilō (1), to *owe;* to *be under obligation*

DEBTORS
3781 ŏphĕilĕtēs (3), person *indebted*
5533 chrĕŏphĕilĕtēs (2), *indebted* person

DEBTS
4859 mashshâ'âh (1), secured *loan*
3783 ŏphĕilēma (1), *due; moral fault*

DECAPOLIS
1179 Dĕkapŏlis (3), *ten-city* region

DECAY
4131 môwṭ (1), to *slip, shake, fall*

DECAYED
2723 chorbâh (1), *desolation, dry* desert
3782 kâshal (1), to *totter, waver;* to *falter*

DECAYETH
2717 chârab (1), to *parch; desolate, destroy*
4355 mâkak (1), to *tumble* in ruins
3822 palaiŏō (1), to *become worn out*

DECEASE
1841 ĕxŏdŏs (2), *exit,* i.e. *death*

DECEASED
7496 râphâ' (1), *dead*
5053 tĕlĕutaō (1), to *finish life,* i.e. *expire*

DECEIT
4820 mirmâh (19), *fraud*
4860 mashshâ'ôwn (1), *dissimulation*
7423 rᵉmîyâh (2), *remissness; treachery*
8267 sheqer (1), *untruth*
8496 tôk (2), *oppression*
8649 tormâh (4), *fraud*
539 apatē (1), *delusion*
1387 dŏliŏō (1), to *practice deceit*
1388 dŏlŏs (2), *wile, deceit, trickery*
4106 planē (1), *fraudulence; straying*

DECEITFUL
3577 kâzâb (1), *falsehood; idol*
4820 mirmâh (8), *fraud*
6121 'âqôb (1), *fraudulent; tracked*

6280 'âthar (1), to *be, make abundant*
7423 rᵉmîyâh (4), *remissness; treachery*
8267 sheqer (2), *untruth; sham*
8501 tâkâk (1), to *dissever,* i.e. *crush*
8649 tormâh (1), *fraud*
539 apatē (1), *delusion*
1386 dŏliŏs (1), *guileful, tricky*

DECEITFULLY
898 bâgad (2), to *act covertly*
2048 hâthal (1), to *deride, mock*
4820 mirmâh (3), *fraud*
6231 'âshaq (1), to *oppress;* to *defraud*
7423 rᵉmîyâh (3), *remissness; treachery*
1389 dŏlŏō (1), to *adulterate, falsify*

DECEITFULNESS
539 apatē (3), *delusion*

DECEITS
4123 mahăthallâh (1), *delusion*
4820 mirmâh (1), *fraud*

DECEIVABLENESS
539 apatē (1), *delusion*

DECEIVE
2048 hâthal (1), to *deride, mock*
3884 lûwlê' (1), *if not*
5377 nâshâ' (7), to *lead astray,* to *delude*
6601 pâthâh (2), to *be, make simple;* to *delude*
7952 shâlâh (1), to *mislead*
538 apataō (1), to *cheat, delude*
1818 ĕxapataō (3), to *seduce wholly, deceive*
4105 planaō (10), to *wander;* to *deceive*
4106 planē (1), *fraudulence; straying*

DECEIVED
2048 hâthal (2), to *deride, mock*
5377 nâshâ' (5), to *lead astray,* to *delude*
6231 'âshaq (1), to *oppress;* to *defraud*
6601 pâthâh (6), to *be, make simple;* to *delude*
7411 râmâh (4), to *hurl;* to *shoot;* to *delude*
7683 shâgag (1), to *stray;* to *sin*
7686 shâgâh (1), to *stray, wander;* to *transgress*
8582 tâ'âh (1), to *vacillate, reel* or *stray*
538 apataō (2), to *cheat, delude*
1818 ĕxapataō (1), to *seduce wholly, deceive*
4105 planaō (10), to *wander;* to *deceive*

DECEIVER
5230 nâkal (1), to *act treacherously*

7686 shâgâh (1), to *stray, wander;* to *transgress*
8591 tâ'a' (1), to *cheat;* to *maltreat*
4108 planŏs (2), *roving; impostor* or *misleader*

DECEIVERS
4108 planŏs (2), *roving; impostor* or *misleader*
5423 phrĕnapatēs (1), *seducer, misleader*

DECEIVETH
7411 râmâh (1), to *hurl;* to *shoot;* to *delude*
538 apataō (1), to *cheat, delude*
4105 planaō (3), to *roam, wander;* to *deceive*
5422 phrĕnapataō (1), to *delude, deceive*

DECEIVING
3884 paralŏgizŏmai (1), to *delude, deceive*
4105 planaō (1), to *roam, wander;* to *deceive*

DECEIVINGS
539 apatē (1), *delusion*

DECENTLY
2156 ĕuschēmŏnŏs (1), *fittingly, properly*

DECIDED
2782 chârats (1), to *be alert,* to *decide*

DECISION
2742 chârûwts (2), *diligent, earnest*

DECK
3302 yâphâh (1), to *be beautiful*
5710 'âdâh (1), to *remove;* to *bedeck*

DECKED
5710 'âdâh (3), to *remove;* to *bedeck*
7234 râbad (1), to *spread*
5558 chrusŏō (2), to *guild, bespangle*

DECKEDST
5710 'âdâh (1), to *remove;* to *bedeck*
6213 'âsâh (1), to *do*

DECKEST
5710 'âdâh (1), to *remove;* to *bedeck*

DECKETH
3547 kâhan (1), to *officiate* as a *priest*

DECLARATION
262 'achvâh (1), *utterance*
6575 pârâshâh (1), *exposition*
1335 diēgĕsis (1), *recital, written account*

DECLARE
560 'âmar (Ch.) (1), to *say,* speak
874 bâ'ar (1), to *explain*
952 bûwr (1), to *examine*
1696 dâbar (1), to *speak, say;* to *subdue*
3045 yâda' (3), to *know*
5046 nâgad (46), to *announce*

5608 çâphar (20), to *enumerate;* to *recount*
7878 sîyach (1), to *ponder, muse aloud*
8085 shâma' (1), to *hear intelligently*
312 anaggĕllō (2), to *announce, report*
518 apaggĕllō (2), to *announce, proclaim*
1107 gnŏrizō (3), to *make known, reveal*
1213 dēlŏō (1), to *make plain* by words
1334 diēgĕŏmai (1), to *relate fully, describe*
1555 ĕkdiēgĕŏmai (1), to *narrate through wholly*
1718 ĕmphanizō (1), to *show forth*
1732 ĕndĕixis (2), *demonstration*
2097 ĕuaggĕlizō (1), to *announce good news*
2605 kataggĕllō (1), to *proclaim, promulgate*
3853 paraggĕllō (1), to *enjoin;* to *instruct*
5419 phrazō (2), to *indicate,* to *expound*

DECLARED
559 'âmar (1), to *say,* speak
1696 dâbar (1), to *speak, say;* to *subdue*
3045 yâda' (3), to *know*
5046 nâgad (13), to *announce*
5608 çâphar (4), to *enumerate;* to *recount*
6567 pârash (1), to *separate;* to *specify*
8085 shâma' (1), to *hear*
312 anaggĕllō (1), to *announce, report*
394 anatithĕmai (1), to *set forth a declaration*
518 apaggĕllō (1), to *announce, proclaim*
1107 gnŏrizō (1), to *make known, reveal*
1213 dēlŏō (2), to *make plain* by words
1229 diaggĕllō (1), to *herald thoroughly*
1334 diēgĕŏmai (2), to *relate fully, describe*
1834 ĕxēgĕŏmai (4), to *tell, relate again*
2097 ĕuaggĕlizō (1), to *announce good news*
3724 hŏrizō (1), to *appoint, decree, specify*
5319 phanĕrŏō (1), to *render apparent*

DECLARETH
5046 nâgad (4), to *announce*

DECLARING
5046 nâgad (1), to *announce*
1555 ĕkdiēgĕŏmai (1), to *narrate through wholly*
1834 ĕxēgĕŏmai (1), to *tell, relate again*
2605 kataggĕllō (1), to *proclaim, promulgate*

DECLINE
5186 nâṭâh (3), to *stretch or spread out*
5493 çûwr (1), to *turn off*
7847 sâṭâh (1), to *deviate from duty, go astray*

DECLINED
5186 nâṭâh (3), to *stretch or spread out*
5493 çûwr (1), to *turn off*

DECLINETH
5186 nâṭâh (2), to *stretch or spread out*

DECREASE
4591 mâ'aṭ (1), to *be, make small or few*
1642 ĕlattŏō (1), to *lessen*

DECREASED
2637 châçêr (1), to *lack; to fail, want, make less*

DECREE
633 'ĕçâr (Ch.) (7), *edict, decree*
1504 gâzar (1), to *exclude; decide*
1510 gᵉzêrâh (Ch.) (2), *decree, decision*
1697 dâbâr (1), *word; matter; thing*
1881 dâth (9), *royal edict or statute*
1882 dâth (Ch.) (3), *Law; royal edict or statute*
2706 chôq (7), *appointment; allotment*
2710 châqaq (2), to *engrave; to enact laws*
2940 ṭa'am (1), *taste; intelligence; mandate*
2942 ṭᵉ'êm (Ch.) (13), *judgment; account*
3982 ma'ămar (1), *edict, command*
6599 pithgâm (1), *judicial sentence; edict*
1378 dŏgma (1), *law*

DECREED
1504 gâzar (1), to *destroy, exclude; decide*
2706 chôq (1), *appointment; allotment*
2782 chârats (1), to *be alert, to decide*
6965 qûwm (1), to *rise*
2919 krinō (1), to *decide; to try, condemn, punish*

DECREES
2711 chêqeq (1), *enactment, resolution*
1378 dŏgma (2), *law*

DEDAN
1719 Dᵉdân (11), *Dedan*

DEDANIM
1720 Dᵉdânîym (1), *Dedanites*

DEDICATE
2596 chânak (1), to *initiate or discipline*
6942 qâdâsh (3), to *be, make clean*

DEDICATED
2596 chânak (3), to *initiate or discipline*
2764 chêrem (1), *doomed object*

DECLINE (second column)
6942 qâdâsh (7), to *be, make clean*
6944 qôdesh (12), *sacred place or thing*
1457 ĕgkainizō (1), to *inaugurate*

DEDICATING
2598 chănukkâh (2), *dedication*

DEDICATION
2597 chănukkâ' (Ch.) (4), *dedication*
2598 chănukkâh (6), *dedication*
1456 ĕgkainia (1), Feast of *Dedication*

DEED
199 'ûwlâm (2), *however or on the contrary*
1697 dâbâr (3), *word; matter; thing*
3559 kûwn (1), to *set up: establish, fix, prepare*
4639 ma'ăseh (1), *action; labor*
2041 ĕrgŏn (6), *work*
2108 ĕuĕrgĕsia (1), *beneficence*
4162 pŏiēsis (1), *action, i.e. performance*
4334 prŏsĕrchŏmai (1), to *come near, visit*

DEEDS
1578 gᵉmûwlâh (1), *act; service; reward*
1697 dâbâr (2), *word; matter; thing*
4639 ma'ăseh (2), *action; labor*
5949 'ălîylâh (2), *opportunity, action*
6467 pô'al (2), *act or work, deed*
1411 dunamis (1), *force, power, miracle*
2041 ĕrgŏn (16), *work*
2735 katŏrthōma (1), *made fully upright*
3739+4238 hŏs (1), *who, which, what, that*
4234 praxis (3), *act; function*

DEEMED
5282 hupŏnŏĕō (1), to *think; to expect*

DEEP
4113 mahămôrâh (1), (poss.) *abyss, pits*
4278 mechqâr (1), *recess, unexplored place*
4615 ma'ămâq (2), *deep place*
4688 mᵉtsôwlâh (5), *deep place*
4950 mishqâ' (1), *clear pond with settled water*
5994 'ămîyq (Ch.) (1), *profound, unsearchable*
6009 'âmaq (5), to *be, make deep*
6013 'âmôq (8), *deep, profound*
6683 tsûwlâh (1), *watery abyss*
7290 râdam (2), to *stupefy*

DEEP (third column)
8257 shâqa' (1), to *be overflowed; to cease*
8328 sheresh (1), *root*
8415 tᵉhôwm (20), *abyss of the sea, i.e. the deep*
8639 tardêmâh (7), *trance, deep sleep*
12 abussŏs (2), *deep place, abyss*
899 bathŏs (3), *extent; mystery, i.e. deep*
901 bathus (2), *deep, profound*
1037 buthŏs (1), *deep sea*
2532+900 kai (1), *and; or; even; also*

DEEPER
6012 'âmêq (1), *deep, obscure*
6013 'âmôq (8), *deep, profound*

DEEPLY
6009 'âmaq (2), to *be, make deep*
389 anastĕnazō (1), to *sigh deeply*

DEEPNESS
899 bathŏs (1), *extent; mystery, i.e. deep*

DEEPS
4688 mᵉtsôwlâh (3), *deep place*
8415 tᵉhôwm (1), *abyss of the sea, i.e. the deep*

DEER
3180 yachmûwr (1), *deer*

DEFAMED
987 blasphĕmĕō (1), to *speak impiously*

DEFAMING
1681 dibbâh (1), *slander, bad report*

DEFEAT
6565 pârar (2), to *break up; to violate, frustrate*

DEFENCE
1220 betser (1), *gold*
2646 chuppâh (1), *canopy*
4043 mâgên (2), *small shield (buckler); animal skin*
4686 mâtsûwd (1), *net or capture; fastness*
4692 mâtsôwr (2), *siege-mound; distress*
4869 misgâb (7), *refuge*
5526 çâkak (1), to *fence in; cover over; protect*
6738 tsêl (3), *shade; protection*
626 apŏlŏgĕŏmai (1), to *give an account*
627 apŏlŏgia (3), *plea or verbal defense*

DEFENCED
1219 bâtsar (5), to *be inaccessible*
4013 mibtsâr (4), *fortification; defender*

DEFEND
1598 gânan (7), to *protect*
3467 yâsha' (1), to *make safe, free*
7682 sâgab (2), to *be, make lofty; be safe*

DEFEND (fourth column)
8199 shâphaṭ (1), to *judge*

DEFENDED
5337 nâtsal (1), to *deliver*
292 amunŏmai (1), to *protect, help*

DEFENDEST
5526 çâkak (1), to *fence in; cover over; protect*

DEFENDING
1598 gânan (1), to *protect*

DEFER
309 'âchar (2), to *remain; to delay*
748 'ârak (1), to *be, make long*

DEFERRED
309 'âchar (1), to *remain; to delay*
4900 mâshak (1), to *draw out; to be tall*
306 anaballŏmai (1), to *put off, adjourn*

DEFERRETH
748 'ârak (1), to *be, make long*

DEFIED
2194 zâ'am (1), to *be enraged*
2778 châraph (5), to *spend the winter*

DEFILE
1351 gâ'al (2), to *soil, stain; desecrate*
2490 châlal (2), to *profane, defile*
2930 ṭâmê' (25), to *be morally contaminated*
2936 ṭânaph (1), to *soil, make dirty*
733 arsĕnŏkŏitēs (1), *sodomite*
2840 kŏinŏō (6), to *make profane*
3392 miainō (1), to *contaminate*
5351 phthĕirō (1), to *spoil, ruin; to deprave*

DEFILED
1351 gâ'al (2), to *soil, stain; desecrate*
2490 châlal (5), to *profane, defile*
2610 chânêph (3), to *soil, be defiled*
2930 ṭâmê' (44), to *be morally contaminated*
2931 ṭâmê' (5), *foul; ceremonially impure*
2933 ṭâmâh (1), to *be ceremonially impure*
5953 'âlal (1), to *glean; to overdo*
6031 'ânâh (1), to *afflict, be afflicted*
6942 qâdâsh (1), to *be, make clean*
2839 kŏinŏs (1), *common, i.e. profane*
3392 miainō (4), to *contaminate*
3435 mŏlunō (3), to *soil, make impure*

DEFILEDST
2490 châlal (1), to *profane, defile*

English

DEFILETH
2490 châlal (1), to profane, defile
2610 chânêph (1), to soil, be defiled
2930 ţâmê' (1), to be foul; be morally contaminated
2840 kŏinŏō (5), to make profane
4695 spilŏō (1), to stain or soil

DEFRAUD
6231 'âshaq (1), to oppress; to defraud
650 apŏstěrěō (3), to despoil or defraud
4122 plěŏněktěō (1), to be covetous

DEFRAUDED
6231 'âshaq (2), to oppress; to defraud
650 apŏstěrěō (1), to despoil or defraud
4122 plěŏněktěō (1), to be covetous

DEFY
2194 zâ'am (2), to be enraged
2778 châraph (3), to spend the winter

DEGENERATE
5494 çûwr (1), turned off; deteriorated

DEGREE
898 bathmŏs (1), grade of dignity
5011 tapěinŏs (2), humiliated, lowly

DEGREES
4609 ma'ălâh (24), thought arising

DEHAVITES
1723 Dahăvâ' (Ch.) (1), Dahava

DEKAR
1857 Deqer (1), stab

DELAIAH
1806 Dᵉlâyâh (6), Jehovah has delivered

DELAY
309 'âchar (1), to remain; to delay; to procrastinate
311 anabŏlē (1), putting off, delay
3635 ŏkněō (1), to be slow, delay

DELAYED
954 bûwsh (1), to be disappointed; delayed
4102 mâhahh (1), to be reluctant

DELAYETH
5549 chrŏnizŏ (2), to take time, i.e. linger

DELECTABLE
2530 châmad (1), delight in; lust for

DELICACIES
4764 strēnŏs (1), luxury, sensuality

DELICATE
6026 'ânag (1), to be soft or pliable
6028 'ânôg (3), luxurious
8588 ta'ănûwg (1), luxury; delight

DELICATELY
4574 ma'ădân (2), delicacy; pleasure
6445 pânaq (1), to enervate, reduce vigor
5172 truphē (1), luxury or debauchery

DELICATENESS
6026 'ânag (1), to be soft or pliable

DELICATES
5730 'êden (1), pleasure

DELICIOUSLY
4763 strēniaō (2), to be luxurious, live sensually

DELIGHT
1523 gîyl (1), rejoice
2530 châmad (1), to delight in; lust for
2531 chemed (1), delight
2654 châphêts (17), to be pleased with, desire
2655 châphêts (1), pleased with
2656 chêphets (3), pleasure; desire
2836 châshaq (1), to join; to love, delight
4574 ma'ădân (1), delicacy; pleasure
5276 nâ'êm (1), to be agreeable
6026 'ânag (6), to be soft or pliable
6027 'ôneg (1), luxury
7521 râtsâh (2), to be pleased with
7522 râtsôwn (5), delight
8173 shâ'a' (4), to fondle, please or amuse (self)
dismay, i.e. stare
8191 sha'shûa' (4), enjoyment
8588 ta'ănûwg (1), luxury; delight
4913 sunēdŏmai (1), to rejoice in with oneself

DELIGHTED
2654 châphêts (10), to be pleased with, desire
5727 'âdan (1), to be soft or pleasant
6026 'ânag (1), to be soft or pliable

DELIGHTEST
7521 râtsâh (1), to be pleased with

DELIGHTETH
2654 châphêts (12), to be pleased with, desire
7521 râtsâh (2), to be pleased with

DELIGHTS
5730 'êden (1), pleasure
8191 sha'shûa' (3), enjoyment
8588 ta'ănûwg (2), luxury; delight

DELIGHTSOME
2656 chêphets (1), pleasure; desire

DELILAH
1807 Dᵉlîylâh (6), languishing

DELIVER
579 'ânâh (1), to meet, to happen
1350 gâ'al (1), to redeem; to be the next of kin
2502 châlats (5), to depart; to deliver
3467 yâsha' (3), to make safe, free
4042 mâgan (2), to rescue, to surrender
4422 mâlaţ (17), to be delivered; be smooth
4672 mâtsâ' (1), to find or acquire; to occur
5186 nâţâh (1), to stretch or spread out
5337 nâtsal (115), to deliver
5338 nᵉtsal (Ch.) (2), to extricate, deliver
5414 nâthan (78), to give
5462 çâgar (10), to shut up; to surrender
6299 pâdâh (3), to ransom; to release
6308 pâda' (1), to retrieve
6403 pâlaţ (11), to escape; to deliver
6561 pâraq (1), to break off or crunch; to deliver
7725 shûwb (5), to turn back; to return
7804 shᵉzab (Ch.) (6), to leave; to free
8000 shᵉlam (Ch.) (1), to restore; be safe
8199 shâphaţ (1), to judge
525 apallassō (1), to release; be reconciled
1325 didŏmi (1), to give
1807 ěxairěō (2), to tear out; to select; to release
3860 paradidōmi (15), to hand over
4506 rhuŏmai (8), to rescue
5483 charizŏmai (2), to grant as a favor, rescue

DELIVERANCE
2020 hatstsâlâh (1), rescue, deliverance
3444 yᵉshûw'âh (2), deliverance; aid
6405 pallêţ (1), escape
6413 pᵉlêyţâh (5), escaped portion
8668 tᵉshûw'âh (5), rescue, deliverance
629 apŏlutrōsis (1), ransom in full
859 aphěsis (1), pardon, freedom

DELIVERANCES
3444 yᵉshûw'âh (1), deliverance; aid

DELIVERED
2502 châlats (9), to depart; to deliver
3052 yᵉhab (Ch.) (1), to give

DELIGHTEST [col4?]
3205 yâlad (6), to bear young; to father a child
3467 yâsha' (8), to make safe, free
4042 mâgan (1), to rescue, to surrender
4422 mâlaţ (16), to be delivered; be smooth
4560 mâçar (1), to set apart; apostatize
4672 mâtsâ' (1), to find or acquire; to occur
5234 nâkar (1), to acknowledge, care for
5337 nâtsal (58), to deliver
5414 nâthan (98), to give
5462 çâgar (6), to shut up; to surrender
5674 'âbar (1), to cross over; to transition
6299 pâdâh (2), to ransom; to release
6403 pâlaţ (3), to slip out, i.e. escape; to deliver
6487 piqqâdôwn (2), deposit
7804 shᵉzab (Ch.) (2), to leave; to free
325 anadidōmi (1), to hand over, deliver
525 apallassō (1), to release; be reconciled
591 apŏdidōmi (2), to give away
1080 gěnnaō (1), to procreate, regenerate
1325 didōmi (2), to give
1560 ěkdŏtŏs (1), surrendered
1659 ělěuthěrŏō (1), to exempt, liberate
1807 ěxairěō (2), to tear out; to select; to release
1825 ěxěgěirō (1), to resuscitate; release
1929 ěpididōmi (2), to give over
2673 katargěō (1), to be, render entirely useless
3860 paradidōmi (44), to hand over
4506 rhuŏmai (9), to rescue
5088 tiktō (5), to produce from seed

DELIVEREDST
5414 nâthan (1), to give
3860 paradidōmi (2), to hand over

DELIVERER
3467 yâsha' (2), to make safe, free
5337 nâtsal (1), to deliver
6403 pâlaţ (5), to slip out, i.e. escape; to deliver
3086 lutrōtēs (1), redeemer, deliverer
4506 rhuŏmai (1), to rescue

DELIVEREST
5337 nâtsal (1), to deliver
6403 pâlaţ (1), to slip out, i.e. escape; to deliver

DELIVERETH
2502 châlats (2), to depart; to deliver
5337 nâtsal (7), to deliver

English

5414 nâthan (1), to *give*
6403 pâlaṭ (1), to *slip* out,
i.e. *escape*; to *deliver*
6475 pâtsâh (1), to *rend*,
i.e. *open*
7804 sh\ᵉzab (Ch.) (1), to
leave; to *free*

DELIVERING
1807 ĕxairĕō (1), to *tear
out*; to *select*; to *release*
3860 paradidōmi (2), to
hand over

DELIVERY
3205 yâlad (1), to *bear
young*; to *father a child*

DELUSION
4106 planē (1),
fraudulence; *straying*

DELUSIONS
8586 ta'ălûwl (1), *caprice*
(as a fit *coming on*)

DEMAND
7592 shâ'al (3), to *ask*
7595 sh\ᵉêl (Ch.) (1),
judicial *decision*

DEMANDED
559 'âmar (1), to *say*
7592 shâ'al (1), to *ask*
7593 sh\ᵉêl (Ch.) (1), to
ask
1905 ĕpĕrōtaō (2), to
inquire, seek
4441 punthanŏmai (2), to
ask for information

DEMAS
1214 Dēmas (3), *Demas*

DEMETRIUS
1216 Dēmētriŏs (3),
Demetrius

DEMONSTRATION
585 apŏdĕixis (1),
manifestation, proof

DEN
1358 gôb (Ch.) (10), lion
pit
3975 m\ᵉ'ûwrâh (1),
serpent's *hole* or *den*
4583 mâ'ôwn (2), *retreat*
or asylum *dwelling*
4585 m\ᵉôwnâh (1), *abode*
4631 m\ᵉ'ârâh (1), dark
cavern
5520 çôk (1), *hut* of
entwined boughs
4693 spēlaiŏn (3),
cavern; hiding-place

DENIED
3584 kâchash (2), to *lie,
disown*; to *disappoint*
4513 mâna' (1), to *deny,
refuse*
533 aparnĕŏmai (2),
disown, deny
720 arnĕŏmai (14), to
disavow, reject

DENIETH
720 arnĕŏmai (4), to
disavow, reject

DENOUNCE
5046 nâgad (1), to
announce

DENS
695 'ereb (1), *hiding
place; lair*

4492 minhârâh (1),
cavern, fissure
4585 m\ᵉ'ôwnâh (4), *abode*
4631 m\ᵉ'ârâh (1), dark
cavern
4693 spēlaiŏn (2),
cavern; hiding-place

DENY
3584 kâchash (3), to *lie,
disown*; to *disappoint,
cringe*
4513 mâna' (1), to *deny,
refuse*
7725 shûwb (1), to *turn*
back; to *return*
483 antilĕgō (1), to
dispute, refuse
533 aparnĕŏmai (11),
disown, deny
720 arnĕŏmai (7), to
disavow, reject

DENYING
720 arnĕŏmai (4), to
disavow, reject

DEPART
1540 gâlâh (1), to
denude; uncover
1980 hâlak (3), to *walk;
live a certain way*
3212 yâlak (15), to *walk;
to live; to carry*
3249 yâçûwr (1),
departing
3318 yâtsâ' (3), to *go,
bring out*
3363 yâqa' (1), to *be
dislocated*
3868 lûwz (2), to *depart;
to be perverse*
4185 mûwsh (8), to
withdraw
5493 çûwr (42), to *turn off*
5927 'âlâh (2), to *ascend,
be high, mount*
6852 tsâphar (1), to
return
7971 shâlach (4), to *send
away*
8159 shâ'âh (1), to *be
nonplussed, bewildered*
321 anagō (1), to *lead
up; to bring out; to sail*
360 analuō (1), to *depart*
565 apĕrchŏmai (4), to
go off, i.e. *depart*
630 apŏluō (2), to *relieve,
release*
672 apŏchōrĕō (1), to *go
away, leave*
868 aphistēmi (4), to
desist, desert
1607 ĕkpŏrĕuŏmai (2), to
depart, be discharged
1633 ĕkchōrĕō (1), to
depart, go away
1826 ĕxĕimi (1), *leave;
escape*
1831 ĕxĕrchŏmai (7), to
issue; to leave
3327 mĕtabainō (3), to
depart, move from
4198 pŏrĕuŏmai (5), to
go, come; to travel
5217 hupagō (1), to
withdraw or retire
5562 chōrĕō (6), to *pass,
enter; to hold, admit*

DEPARTED
935 bôw' (1), to *go, come*
1540 gâlâh (3), to
denude; uncover
1980 hâlak (3), to *walk;
live a certain way*
3212 yâlak (47), to *walk;
to live; to carry*
3318 yâtsâ' (10), to *go,
bring out*
4185 mûwsh (2), to
withdraw
5074 nâdad (1), to *rove,
flee; to drive away*
5265 nâça' (30), *start on
a journey*
5493 çûwr (31), to *turn off*
5709 'ădâ' (Ch.) (1), to
pass on or continue
5927 'âlâh (1), to *ascend,
be high, mount*
321 anagō (2), to *lead
up; to bring out; to sail*
402 anachōrĕō (8), to
retire, withdraw
525 apallassō (1), to
release; be reconciled
565 apĕrchŏmai (24), to
go off, i.e. *depart*
630 apŏluō (1), to *relieve,
release; to let die,
pardon or divorce*
673 apŏchōrizō (2), to
rend apart; to separate
868 aphistēmi (6), to
desist, desert
1316 diachōrizŏmai (1),
to *remove* (oneself)
1330 diĕrchŏmai (1), to
traverse, travel through
1607 ĕkpŏrĕuŏmai (1), to
depart, be discharged
1826 ĕxĕimi (1), *leave;
escape*
1831 ĕxĕrchŏmai (22), to
issue; to leave
2718 katĕrchŏmai (1), to
go, come down
3327 mĕtabainō (3), to
depart, move from
3332 mĕtairō (2), to
move on, leave
3855 paragō (1), to *go
along or away*
4198 pŏrĕuŏmai (6), to
go, come; to travel
5562 chōrĕō (1), to *pass,
enter; to hold, admit*
5563 chōrizō (1), to *part;
to go away*

DEPARTETH
3212 yâlak (2), to *walk;
to live; to carry*
4185 mûwsh (1), to
withdraw
5493 çûwr (3), to *turn off*
672 apŏchōrĕō (1), to *go
away, leave*

DEPARTING
3318 yâtsâ' (2), to *go,
bring out*
5253 nâçag (1), to *retreat*
5493 çûwr (2), to *turn off*
672 apŏchōrĕō (1), to *go
away, leave*
867 aphixis (1),
departure, leaving
868 aphistēmi (1), to
desist, desert

1831 ĕxĕrchŏmai (1), to
issue; to leave
1841 ĕxŏdŏs (1), *exit*, i.e.
death
5217 hupagō (1), to
withdraw or retire

DEPARTURE
3318 yâtsâ' (1), to *go,
bring out*
359 analusis (1),
departure

DEPOSED
5182 n\ᵉchath (Ch.) (1), to
descend; to depose

DEPRIVED
5382 nâshâh (1), to *forget*
6485 pâqad (1), to *visit,
care for, count*
7921 shâkôl (1), to
miscarry

DEPTH
6009 'âmaq (1), to *be,
make deep*
6012 'âmêq (1), *deep,
obscure*
8415 t\ᵉhôwm (5), *abyss*
of the sea, i.e. the *deep*
899 bathŏs (4), *extent;
mystery*, i.e. *deep*
3989 pĕlagŏs (1), deep or
open sea

DEPTHS
4615 ma'ămâq (3), *deep
place*
4688 m\ᵉtsôwlâh (2), *deep
place*
6010 'êmeq (1), broad
depression or valley
8415 t\ᵉhôwm (10), *abyss*
of the sea, i.e. the *deep*
899 bathŏs (1), *extent;
mystery*, i.e. *deep*

DEPUTIES
6346 pechâh (2), *prefect,
officer*
446 anthupatŏs (1),
Roman *proconsul*

DEPUTY
5324 nâtsab (1), to *station*
446 anthupatŏs (4),
Roman *proconsul*

DERBE
1191 Dĕrbē (4), *Derbe*

DERIDE
7832 sâchaq (1), to
laugh; to scorn; to play

DERIDED
1592 ĕkmuktĕrizō (2), to
sneer at, ridicule

DERISION
3887 lûwts (1), to *scoff; to
interpret; to intercede*
3932 lâ'ag (5), to *deride;
to speak unintelligibly*
7047 qeleç (3),
laughing-stock
7814 s\ᵉchôwq (5),
laughter; scorn
7832 sâchaq (1), to
laugh; to scorn; to play

DESCEND
3381 yârad (6), to
descend
2597 katabainō (4), to
descend

DESCENDED
3381 yârad (12), to *descend*
2597 katabainō (7), to *descend*

DESCENDETH
2718 katĕrchŏmai (1), to *go, come down*

DESCENDING
3381 yârad (1), to *descend*
2597 katabainō (7), to *descend*

DESCENT
35 agĕnĕalŏgētŏs (1), *unregistered* as to birth
1075 gĕnĕalŏgĕō (1), *trace in genealogy*
2600 katabasis (1), *declivity, slope*

DESCRIBE
3789 kâthab (4), to *write*

DESCRIBED
3789 kâthab (2), to *write*

DESCRIBETH
1125 graphō (1), to *write*
3004 lĕgō (1), to *say*

DESCRY
8446 tûwr (1), to *wander, meander* for trade

DESERT
1576 gᵉmûwl (1), *act; service; reward*
2723 chorbâh (1), *desolation, dry* desert
3452 yᵉshîymôwn (4), *desolation*
4057 midbâr (13), *desert*; also *speech; mouth*
6160 'ărâbâh (8), *desert, wasteland*
6728 tsîyȳ (3), *desert-dweller; beast*
2048 ĕrēmŏs (12), *remote place, deserted place*

DESERTS
2723 chorbâh (2), *desolation, dry* desert
4941 mishpâṭ (1), *verdict; formal decree; justice*
6160 'ărâbâh (1), *desert, wasteland*
2047 ĕrēmia (1), place of *solitude, remoteness*
2048 ĕrēmŏs (1), *remote place, deserted place*

DESERVING
1576 gᵉmûwl (1), *act; service; reward*

DESIRABLE
2531 chemed (3), *delight*

DESIRE
15 'âbeh (1), *longing*
35 'ăbîyôwnáh (1), *caper-berry*
183 'âvâh (7), to *wish* for, *desire*
1156 bᵉ'â' (Ch.) (1), to *seek or ask*
1245 bâqash (1), to *search* out; to *strive*
2530 châmad (4), to *delight* in; *lust for*
2532 chemdâh (3), *delight*

2654 châphêts (6), to *be pleased* with, *desire*
2655 châphêts (2), *pleased* with
2656 chêphêts (9), *pleasure; desire*
2836 châshaq (1), to *join*; to *love, delight*
2837 chêsheq (1), *delight, desired* thing
3700 kâçaph (1), to *pine* after; to *fear*
4261 machmâd (3), *object of desire*
5315 nephesh (3), *life; breath; soul; wind*
5375+5315 nâsâ' (2), to *lift up*
7522 râtsôwn (3), *delight*
7592 shâ'al (3), to *ask*
7602 shâ'aph (1), to *be angry*; to *hasten*
8378 ta'ăvâh (14), *longing; delight*
8420 tâv (1), *mark, signature*
8669 tᵉshûwqâh (3), *longing*
154 aitĕō (5), to *ask* for
515 axiŏō (1), to *deem entitled* or *fit, worthy*
1934 ĕpizētĕō (2), to *demand*, to *crave*
1937 ĕpithumĕō (4), to *long for*
1939 ĕpithumia (3), *longing*
1971 ĕpipŏthĕō (1), *intensely crave*
1972 ĕpipŏthēsis (2), *longing for*
1974 ĕpipŏthia (1), *intense longing*
2065 ĕrōtaō (1), to *interrogate; to request*
2107 ĕudŏkia (1), *delight, kindness, wish*
2206 zēlŏō (2), to *have warmth of feeling for*
2309 thĕlō (9), to *will; to desire; to choose*
3713 ŏrĕgŏmai (2), to *reach* out after, *long* for

DESIRED
183 'âvâh (5), to *wish* for, *desire*
559 'âmar (1), to *say, speak*
1156 bᵉ'â' (Ch.) (2), to *seek or ask*
2530 châmad (5), to *delight* in; *lust for*
2532 chemdâh (1), *delight*
2654 châphêts (1), to *be pleased* with, *desire*
2656 chêphets (2), *pleasure; desire*
2836 châshaq (2), to *join*; to *love, delight*
3700 kâçaph (1), to *pine* after; to *fear*
7592 shâ'al (4), to *ask*
154 aitĕō (10), to *ask* for
1809 ĕxaitĕŏmai (1), to *demand*
1905 ĕpĕrōtaō (1), to *inquire, seek*

1934 ĕpizētĕō (1), to *demand*, to *crave*
1937 ĕpithumĕō (1), to *long for*
1939 ĕpithumia (1), *longing*
2065 ĕrōtaō (4), to *interrogate; to request*
2212 zētĕō (1), to *seek*
2309 thĕlō (1), to *will*; to *desire*; to *choose*
3870 parakalĕō (5), to *call, invite*

DESIREDST
7592 shâ'al (1), to *ask*
3870 parakalĕō (1), to *call, invite*

DESIRES
3970 ma'ăvay (1), *desire*
4862 mish'âlâh (1), *request*
2307 thĕlēma (1), *purpose; inclination*

DESIREST
2654 châphêts (2), to *be pleased* with, *desire*

DESIRETH
183 'âvâh (4), to *wish* for, *desire*
559 'âmar (1), to *say, speak*
2530 châmad (2), to *delight* in; *lust for*
2655 châphêts (1), *pleased* with
2656 chêphets (1), *pleasure; desire*
7592 shâ'al (1), to *ask*
7602 shâ'aph (1), to *be angry*; to *hasten*
8378 ta'ăvâh (3), *longing; delight*
1937 ĕpithumĕō (1), to *long for*
2065 ĕrōtaō (1), to *interrogate; to request*
2309 thĕlō (1), to *will*; to *desire*; to *choose*

DESIRING
154 aitĕō (2), to *ask* for
1937 ĕpithumĕō (1), to *long for*
1971 ĕpipŏthĕō (3), *intensely crave*
2212 zētĕō (2), to *seek*
2309 thĕlō (2), to *will*; to *desire*; to *choose*
3870 parakalĕō (2), to *call, invite*

DESIROUS
183 'âvâh (1), to *wish* for, *desire*
2309 thĕlō (3), to *will*; to *desire*; to *choose*
2442 himĕirŏmai (1), to *long for, desire*
2755 kĕnŏdŏxŏs (1), *self-conceited*

DESOLATE
490 'almânáh (2), *widow*
816 'âsham (6), to *be guilty*; to *be punished*
820 'ashmân (1), *uninhabited places*
910 bâdâd (1), *separate, alone*

1934 ĕpizētĕō (1), to *demand*, to *crave*
1937 ĕpithumĕō (1), to *long for*
1939 ĕpithumia (1), *longing*
2065 ĕrōtaō (4), to *interrogate; to request*
2212 zētĕō (1), to *seek*
2309 thĕlō (1), to *will*; to *desire*; to *choose*
3870 parakalĕō (5), to *call, invite*

1327 battâh (1), area of *desolation*
1565 galmûwd (2), *sterile, barren, desolate*
2717 chârab (5), to *parch* through drought; *desolate, destroy*
2723 chorbâh (7), *desolation, dry* desert
3173 yâchîyd (1), *only son; alone; beloved*
3341 yâtsath (1), to *burn* or *set on fire*
3456 yâsham (4), to *lie waste*
3582 kâchad (1), to *destroy*; to *hide*
4923 mᵉshammâh (2), *waste; object of horror*
5352 nâqâh (1), to *be, make clean*; to *be bare*
7722 shôw' (2), *tempest; devastation*
8047 shammâh (11), *ruin; consternation*
8074 shâmêm (43), to *devastate; to stupefy*
8076 shâmêm (8), *ruined, deserted*
8077 shᵉmâmâh (42), *devastation*
2048 ĕrēmŏs (4), *remote place, deserted place*
2049 ĕrēmŏō (2), to *lay waste*
3443 mŏnŏō (1), to *isolate*, i.e. *bereave*

DESOLATION
2721 chôreb (1), *ruined; desolate*
2723 chorbâh (5), *desolation, dry* desert
4875 mᵉshôw'âh (1), *ruin*
7584 sha'ăvâh (1), *rushing tempest*
7612 shê'th (1), *devastation*
7701 shôd (2), *violence, ravage, destruction*
7722 shôw' (4), *tempest; devastation*
8047 shammâh (12), *ruin; consternation*
8074 shâmêm (3), to *devastate; to stupefy*
8077 shᵉmâmâh (11), *devastation*
2049 ĕrēmŏō (2), to *lay waste*
2050 ĕrēmōsis (3), *despoliation, desolation*

DESOLATIONS
2723 chorbâh (3), *desolation, dry* desert
4876 mashshûw'âh (1), *ruin*
8047 shammâh (1), *ruin; consternation*
8074 shâmêm (4), to *devastate; to stupefy*
8077 shᵉmâmâh (2), *devastation*

DESPAIR
2976 yâ'ash (2), to *despond, despair*
1820 ĕxapŏrĕŏmai (1), to *be utterly at a loss*

DESPAIRED
1820 ĕxapŏrĕŏmai (1), to *be utterly at a loss*

DESPERATE
605 'ânash (1), to *be frail, feeble*
2976 yâ'ash (1), to *despond, despair*

DESPERATELY
605 'ânash (1), to *be frail, feeble*

DESPISE
936 bûwz (4), to *disrespect, scorn*
959 bâzâh (6), to *ridicule, scorn*
2107 zûwl (1), to *treat lightly*
3988 mâ'aç (9), to *spurn; to disappear*
5006 nâ'ats (1), to *scorn*
7043 qâlal (1), to *be easy, trifling, vile*
7590 shâ'ṭ (2), *reject by maligning*
114 athĕtĕō (1), to *disesteem, neutralize*
1848 ĕxŏuthĕnĕō (3), to *treat with contempt*
2706 kataphrŏnĕō (7), to *disesteem, despise*
3643 ŏligŏrĕō (1), to *disesteem, despise*
4065 pĕriphrŏnĕō (1), to *depreciate, contemn*

DESPISED
937 bûwz (4), *disrespect, scorn*
939 bûwzâh (1), something *scorned*
959 bâzâh (26), to *ridicule, scorn*
3988 mâ'aç (12), to *spurn; to disappear*
5006 nâ'ats (6), to *scorn*
7034 qâlâh (1), to *be, hold in contempt*
7043 qâlal (2), to *be easy, trifling, vile*
7590 shâ'ṭ (1), *reject by maligning*
114 athĕtĕō (1), to *disesteem, set aside*
818 atimazō (1), to *maltreat, dishonor*
820 atimŏs (1), *without honor*
1519+3762+3049 ĕis (1), to or into
1848 ĕxŏuthĕnĕō (3), to *treat with contempt*

DESPISERS
865 aphilagathŏs (1), *hostile to virtue*
2707 kataphrŏntēs (1), *contemner, scoffer*

DESPISEST
2706 kataphrŏnĕō (1), to *disesteem, despise*

DESPISETH
936 bûwz (4), to *disrespect, scorn*
959 bâzâh (4), to *ridicule, scorn*
960 bâzôh (1), *scorned*
3988 mâ'aç (3), to *spurn; to disappear*

DESPISING
2706 kataphrŏnĕō (1), to *disesteem, despise*

DESPITE
7589 shᵉ'âṭ (1), *contempt*
1796 ĕnubrizō (1), to *insult*

DESPITEFUL
7589 shᵉ'âṭ (2), *contempt*
5197 hubristēs (1), *maltreater*

DESPITEFULLY
1908 ĕpĕrĕazō (2), to *insult, slander*
5195 hubrizō (1), to *exercise violence*

DESTITUTE
2638 châçêr (1), *lacking*
5800 'âzab (1), to *loosen; relinquish; permit*
6168 'ârâh (1), to *empty, pour out; demolish*
6199 'ar'âr (1), *naked; poor*
8047 shammâh (1), *ruin; consternation*
650 apŏstĕrĕō (1), to *deprive; to despoil*
3007 lĕipō (1), to *fail or be absent*
5302 hustĕrĕō (1), to *be inferior; to fall short*

DESTROY
6 'âbad (38), *perish; destroy*
7 'âbad (Ch.) (4), *perish; destroy*
9 'âbêdâh (1), *destruction*
622 'âçaph (1), to *gather, collect*
816 'âsham (1), to *be guilty; to be punished*
1104 bâla' (7), to *swallow; to destroy*
1641 gârar (1), to *ruminate; to saw*
1792 dâkâ' (1), to *be contrite, be humbled*
1820 dâmâh (1), to *be silent; to fail, cease*
1949 hûwm (1), to *make an uproar; agitate*
2000 hâmam (3), to *disturb, drive, destroy*
2040 hâraç (1), to *pull down; break, destroy*
2254 châbal (5), to *pervert, destroy*
2255 chăbal (Ch.) (2), to *ruin, destroy*
2763 charam (14), to *devote to destruction*
3238 yânâh (1), to *rage or be violent*
3423 yârash (1), to *inherit; to impoverish*
3615 kâlâh (1), to *complete, consume*
3772 kârath (1), to *cut (off, down or asunder)*
4049 mᵉgar (Ch.) (1), to *overthrow, depose*
4135 mûwl (3), to *circumcise*

DESTROY (continued)
4191 mûwth (1), to *die; to kill*
4229 mâchâh (2), to *erase; to grease*
4889 mashchîyth (4), *destruction; corruption*
5255 nâçach (1), to *tear away*
5362 nâqaph (1), to *strike; to surround*
5395 nâsham (1), to *destroy*
5422 nâthats (4), to *tear down*
5595 çâphâh (3), to *scrape; to remove*
6789 tsâmath (4), to *extirpate, destroy*
6979 qûwr (1), to *throw forth; to wall up*
7665 shâbar (2), to *burst*
7703 shâdad (1), to *ravage*
7722 shôw' (1), *tempest; devastation*
7843 shâchath (68), to *decay; to ruin*
7921 shâkôl (1), to *miscarry*
8045 shâmad (40), to *desolate*
8074 shâmêm (2), to *devastate; to stupefy*
622 apŏllumi (19), to *destroy fully; to perish*
1311 diaphthĕirō (1), to *ruin, to decay*
2647 kataluō (6), to *demolish; to halt*
2673 katargĕō (3), to *be, render entirely useless*
3089 luō (2), to *loosen*
5351 phthĕirō (1), to *spoil, ruin; to deprave*

DESTROYED
6 'âbad (17), *perish; destroy*
7 'âbad (Ch.) (1), *perish; destroy*
1104 bâla' (1), to *swallow; to destroy*
1696 dâbar (1), to *speak, say; to subdue*
1792 dâkâ' (1), to *pulverize; be contrite*
1820 dâmâh (1), to *be silent; to fail, cease*
1822 dummâh (1), *desolation*
2026 hârag (1), to *kill, slaughter*
2040 hâraç (3), to *pull down; break, destroy*
2254 châbal (2), to *pervert, destroy*
2255 chăbal (Ch.) (3), to *ruin, destroy*
2717 chârab (1), to *desolate, destroy*
2718 chărab (Ch.) (1), to *demolish*
2763 charam (23), to *devote to destruction*
2764 chêrem (1), *extermination*
3615 kâlâh (1), to *cease, be finished, perish*
3772 kârath (2), to *cut (off, down or asunder)*

DESTROYED (continued)
3807 kâthath (3), to *bruise, strike, beat*
4229 mâchâh (3), to *erase; to grease*
5422 nâthats (1), to *tear down*
5428 nâthash (1), to *tear away, be uprooted*
5595 çâphâh (2), to *scrape; to remove*
5642 çᵉthar (Ch.) (1), to *demolish*
6658 tsâdâh (1), to *desolate*
6789 tsâmath (1), to *extirpate, destroy*
7321 rûwa' (1), to *shout*
7665 shâbar (7), to *burst*
7703 shâdad (1), to *ravage*
7843 shâchath (21), to *decay; to ruin*
8045 shâmad (43), to *desolate*
8074 shâmêm (1), to *devastate; to stupefy*
622 apŏllumi (7), to *destroy fully; to perish*
1311 diaphthĕirō (1), to *ruin, to pervert*
1842 ĕxŏlŏthrĕuō (1), to *extirpate*
2507 kathairĕō (2), to *lower, or demolish*
2647 kataluō (1), to *demolish; to halt*
2673 katargĕō (2), to *be, render entirely useless*
3645 ŏlŏthrĕuō (1), to *slay, destroy*
4199 pŏrthĕō (2), to *ravage, pillage*
5356 phthŏra (1), *ruin; depravity, corruption*

DESTROYER
2717 chârab (1), to *desolate, destroy*
6530 pᵉrîyts (1), *violent, i.e. a tyrant*
7703 shâdad (1), to *ravage*
7843 shâchath (3), to *decay; to ruin*
3644 ŏlŏthrĕutēs (1), serpent which *destroys*

DESTROYERS
2040 hâraç (1), to *pull down; break, destroy*
4191 mûwth (1), to *die; to kill*
7843 shâchath (1), to *decay; to ruin*
8154 shâçâh (1), to *plunder*

DESTROYEST
6 'âbad (1), *perish; destroy*
7843 shâchath (1), to *decay; to ruin*
2647 kataluō (2), to *demolish; to halt*

DESTROYETH
6 'âbad (4), *perish; destroy*
3615 kâlâh (1), to *complete, consume*
4229 mâchâh (1), to *erase; to grease*

7843 shâchath (2), to *decay;* to *ruin*

DESTROYING
1104 bâla' (1), to *swallow;* to *destroy*
2763 charam (5), to *devote* to destruction
4889 mashchîyth (1), *destruction; corruption*
4892 mashchêth (1), *destruction*
6986 qeṭeb (1), *ruin*
7843 shâchath (5), to *decay;* to *ruin*

DESTRUCTION
6 'âbad (1), *perish; destroy*
10 'ăbaddôh (1), *perishing*
11 'ăbaddôwn (5), *perishing*
12 'abdân (1), *perishing*
13 'obdân (1), *perishing*
343 'êyd (7), *misfortune, ruin, disaster*
1793 dakkâ' (1), *crushed, destroyed; contrite*
2035 hărîyçûwth (1), *demolition, destruction*
2041 hereç (1), *demolition, destruction*
2256 chebel (1), *company, band*
2475 chălôwph (1), *destitute orphans*
2764 chêrem (2), *extermination*
3589 kîyd (1), *calamity, destruction*
4103 mᵉhûwmâh (3), *confusion or uproar*
4288 mᵉchittâh (7), *ruin; consternation*
4876 mashshûw'âh (1), *ruin*
4889 mashchîyth (2), *destruction; corruption*
6365 pîyd (2), *misfortune*
6986 qeṭeb (2), *ruin*
6987 qôṭeb (1), *extermination*
7089 qᵉphâdâh (1), *terror*
7171 qerets (1), *extirpation*
7591 shᵉ'îyâh (1), *desolation*
7667 sheber (20), *fracture; ruin*
7670 shibrôwn (1), *ruin*
7701 shôd (7), *violence, ravage, destruction*
7722 shôw' (2), *tempest; devastation*
7843 shâchath (1), to *decay;* to *ruin*
7845 shachath (2), *pit; destruction*
8045 shâmad (1), to *desolate*
8395 tᵉbûwçâh (1), *ruin*
8399 tablîyth (1), *consumption*
684 apôlĕia (5), *ruin or loss*
2506 kathairĕsis (2), *demolition*
3639 ŏlĕthrŏs (4), *death, punishment*

4938 *suntrimma* (1), complete *ruin*

DESTRUCTIONS
2723 chorbâh (1), *desolation, dry* desert
7722 shôw' (1), *tempest; devastation*
7825 shᵉchîyth (1), *pit*-fall

DETAIN
6113 'âtsar (2), to *hold back;* to *maintain*

DETAINED
6113 'âtsar (1), to *hold back;* to *maintain*

DETERMINATE
3724 hŏrizō (1), to *appoint, decree, specify*

DETERMINATION
4941 mishpâṭ (1), *verdict; formal decree; justice*

DETERMINED
559 'âmar (1), to *say*
2782 chârats (6), to *be alert, to decide*
2852 châthak (1), to *decree*
3289 yâ'ats (2), to *advise*
3615 kâlâh (5), to *cease, be finished, perish*
7760 sûwm (1), to *put, place*
1011 bŏulĕuō (1), to *deliberate;* to *resolve*
1956 ĕpiluō (1), to *explain;* to *decide*
2919 krinō (7), to *decide;* to *try, condemn, punish*
3724 hŏrizō (3), to *appoint, decree, specify*
4309 prŏŏrizō (1), to *predetermine*
5021 tassō (1), to *assign or dispose*

DETEST
8262 shâqats (1), to *loathe, pollute*

DETESTABLE
8251 shiqqûwts (6), *disgusting idol*

DEUEL
1845 Dᵉ'ûw'êl (4), *known of God*

DEVICE
1902 higgâyôwn (1), *musical notation*
2808 cheshbôwn (1), *contrivance; plan*
4209 mᵉzimmâh (1), *plan; sagacity*
4284 machăshâbâh (4), *contrivance; plan*
1761 ĕnthumēsis (1), *deliberation; idea*

DEVICES
2154 zimmâh (1), bad *plan*
4156 môw'êtsâh (1), *purpose, plan*
4209 mᵉzimmâh (5), *plan; sagacity*
4284 machăshâbâh (8), *contrivance; plan*
3540 nŏēma (1), *perception, purpose*

DEVIL
1139 daimŏnizŏmai (7), to *be demonized*
1140 daimŏniŏn (18), *demonic being*
1142 daimōn (1), evil supernatural *spirit*
1228 diabŏlŏs (35), *traducer,* i.e. *Satan*

DEVILISH
1141 daimŏniōdēs (1), *demon-like, of the devil*

DEVILS
7700 shêd (2), *demon*
8163 sâ'îyr (2), *shaggy; he-goat; goat idol*
1139 daimŏnizŏmai (6), to *be demonized*
1140 daimŏniŏn (40), *demonic being*
1142 daimōn (4), evil supernatural *spirit*

DEVISE
2790 chârash (3), to *engrave;* to *plow*
2803 châshab (13), to *weave, fabricate*

DEVISED
908 bâdâ' (1), to *invent;* to *choose*
1819 dâmâh (1), to *resemble, liken*
2161 zâmam (3), to *plan*
2803 châshab (5), to *plot;* to *think, regard*
4284 machăshâbâh (1), *contrivance; plan*
4679 sŏphizō (1), to *make wise*

DEVISETH
2790 chârash (2), to *engrave;* to *plow*
2803 châshab (4), to *plot;* to *think, regard*
3289 yâ'ats (2), to *advise*

DEVOTE
2763 charam (1), to *devote* to destruction

DEVOTED
2763 charam (1), to *devote* to destruction
2764 chêrem (5), *doomed* object

DEVOTIONS
4574 sĕbasma (1), *object of worship*

DEVOUR
398 'âkal (57), to *eat*
399 'ăkal (Ch.) (2), to *eat*
402 'oklâh (2), *food*
7462 râ'âh (1), to *tend* a flock, i.e. *pasture* it
7602 shâ'aph (1), to *be angry;* to *hasten*
2068 ĕsthiō (1), to *eat*
2666 katapinō (1), to *devour by swallowing*
2719 katĕsthiō (6), to *devour*

DEVOURED
398 'âkal (42), to *eat*
399 'ăkal (Ch.) (2), to *eat*
402 'oklâh (1), *food*
1104 bâla' (2), to *swallow;* to *destroy*

3898 lâcham (1), to *fight* a *battle,* i.e. *consume*
2719 katĕsthiō (5), to *devour*

DEVOURER
398 'âkal (1), to *eat*

DEVOUREST
398 'âkal (1), to *eat*

DEVOURETH
398 'âkal (6), to *eat*
1104 bâla' (2), to *swallow;* to *destroy*
3216 yâla' (1), to *blurt* or utter inconsiderately
2719 katĕsthiō (1), to *devour*

DEVOURING
398 'âkal (5), to *eat*
1105 bela' (1), *gulp; destruction*

DEVOUT
2126 ĕulabēs (3), *circumspect, pious*
2152 ĕusĕbēs (3), *pious*
4576 sĕbŏmai (3), to *revere,* i.e. *adore*

DEW
2919 ṭal (30), *dew, morning mist*
2920 ṭal (Ch.) (5), *dew, morning mist*

DIADEM
4701 mitsnepheth (1), *turban*
6797 tsânîyph (2), *head-dress, turban*
6843 tsᵉphîyrâh (1), *encircling crown*

DIAL
4609 ma'ălâh (2), *thought* arising

DIAMOND
3095 yahălôm (3), (poss.) *onyx*
8068 shâmîyr (1), *thorn;* (poss.) *diamond*

DIANA
735 Artĕmis (5), *prompt*

DIBLAIM
1691 Diblayim (1), *two cakes*

DIBLATH
1689 Diblâh (1), *Diblah*

DIBON
1769 Dîybôwn (9), *pining*

DIBON-GAD
1769 Dîybôwn (2), *pining*

DIBRI
1704 Dibrîy (1), *wordy*

DID
1580 gâmal (2), to *benefit* or *requite;* to *wean*
1961 hâyâh (1), to *exist,* i.e. *be or become*
2052 Vâhêb (1), *Vaheb*
5648 'ăbad (Ch.) (1), to do, *work, serve*
6213 'âsâh (327), to *do or make*
6313 pûwg (1), to *be sluggish; be numb*
7965 shâlôwm (2), *safe; well; health, prosperity*

15 agathŏpŏiĕō (1), to be
a well-doer
91 adikĕō (1), to do
wrong
1731 ĕndĕiknumi (1), to
show, display
3000 latrĕuō (1), to
minister to God
4160 pŏiĕō (54), to make
or do
4238 prassō (1), to
execute, accomplish

DIDDEST
387 anastatŏō (1), to
disturb, cause trouble

DIDST
6213 'âsâh (14), to do or
make
6466 pâ'al (1), to do,
make or practice

DIDYMUS
1324 Didumŏs (3), twin

DIE
1478 gâva' (8), to expire,
die
4191 mûwth (255), to die;
to kill
4194 mâveth (7), death;
dead
8546 tᵉmûwthâh (1),
execution, death
599 apŏthnēskō (40), to
die off
622 apŏllumi (1), to
destroy fully; to perish
684 apŏlĕia (1), ruin or
loss
4880 sunapŏthnēskō (2),
to decease with
5053 tĕlĕutaō (3), to
finish life, i.e. expire

DIED
1478 gâva' (3), to expire,
die
4191 mûwth (154), to die;
to kill
4194 mâveth (7), death;
dead
5038 nᵉbêlâh (1), carcase
or carrion
5307 nâphal (1), to fall
599 apŏthnēskō (32), to
die off
5053 tĕlĕutaō (2), to
finish life, i.e. expire

DIEST
4191 mûwth (1), to die; to
kill

DIET
737 'ărûchâh (2), ration,
portion of food

DIETH
4191 mûwth (16), to die;
to kill
4194 mâveth (4), death;
dead
5038 nᵉbêlâh (4), carcase
or carrion
599 apŏthnēskō (2), to
die off
5053 tĕlĕutaō (3), to
finish life, i.e. expire

DIFFER
1252 diakrinō (1), to
decide; to hesitate

DIFFERENCE
914 bâdal (3), to divide,
separate, distinguish
6395 pâlâh (1), to
distinguish
1252 diakrinō (2), to
decide; to hesitate
1293 diastŏlē (2),
variation, distinction
3307 mĕrizō (1), to
disunite, differ

DIFFERENCES
1243 diairĕsis (1),
distinction or variety

DIFFERETH
1308 diaphĕrō (2), to
bear, carry; to differ

DIFFERING
1313 diaphŏrŏs (1),
varying; surpassing

DIG
2658 châphar (3), to
delve, to explore
2672 châtsab (1), to cut
stone or carve wood
2864 châthar (5), to
break or dig into
3738 kârâh (2), to dig; to
plot; to bore, hew
4626 skaptō (2), to dig

DIGGED
2658 châphar (13), to
delve, to explore
2672 châtsab (3), to cut
stone or carve wood
2864 châthar (2), to
break or dig into
3738 kârâh (8), to dig; to
plot; to bore, hew
5365 nâqar (3), to bore;
to gouge
5737 'âdar (2), to hoe a
vineyard
6131 'âqar (1), to pluck
up; to hamstring
2679 kataskaptō (1), to
destroy, be ruined
3736 ŏrussō (3), to
burrow, i.e. dig out
4626 skaptō (1), to dig

DIGGEDST
2672 châtsab (1), to cut
stone or carve wood

DIGGETH
2658 châphar (1), to
delve, to explore
3738 kârâh (1), to dig; to
plot; to bore, hew

DIGNITIES
1391 Ĕpaphrŏditŏs (2),
devoted to Venus

DIGNITY
1420 gᵉdûwlâh (1),
greatness, grandeur
4791 mârôwm (1),
elevation; haughtiness
7613 sᵉ'êth (2), elevation;
swelling scab

DIKLAH
1853 Diqlâh (2), Diklah

DILEAN
1810 Dil'ân (1), Dilan

DILIGENCE
4929 mishmâr (1), guard;
deposit; usage; example

2039 ĕrgasia (1),
occupation; profit
4704 spŏudazō (2), to
make effort
4710 spŏudē (6),
despatch; eagerness

DILIGENT
2742 chârûwts (5),
diligent, earnest
3190 yâṭab (1), to be,
make well
3966 mᵉ'ôd (1), very,
utterly
4106 mâhîyr (1), skillful
4704 spŏudazō (2), to
make effort
4705 spŏudaiŏs (1),
prompt, energetic
4707 spŏudaiŏtĕrŏs (1),
more earnest

DILIGENTLY
149 'adrazdâ' (Ch.) (1),
carefully, diligently
995 bîyn (1), to
understand; discern
3190 yâṭab (2), to be,
make well
3966 mᵉ'ôd (4), very,
utterly
5172 nâchash (1), to
prognosticate
7182 qesheb (1),
hearkening
7836 shâchar (2), to
search for
8150 shânan (1), to
pierce; to inculcate
199 akribōs (2), exactly,
carefully
1567 ĕkzētĕō (1), to seek
out
1960 ĕpimĕlōs (1),
carefully, diligently
4706 spŏudaiŏtĕrŏn (1),
more earnestly
4709 spŏudaiōs (1),
earnestly, promptly

DIM
2821 châshak (1), to be
dark; to darken
3513 kâbad (1), to be
heavy, severe, dull
3543 kâhâh (3), to grow
dull, fade; to be faint
3544 kêheh (1), feeble;
obscure
6004 'âmam (1), to
overshadow
6965 qûwm (1), to rise
8159 shâ'âh (1), to
inspect, consider

DIMINISH
1639 gâra' (6), to shave,
remove, lessen
4591 mâ'aṭ (2), to be,
make small or few

DIMINISHED
1639 gâra' (2), to shave,
remove, lessen
4591 mâ'aṭ (3), to be,
make small or few

DIMINISHING
2275 hĕttēma (1), failure
or loss

DIMNAH
1829 Dimnâh (1),
dung-heap

DIMNESS
4155 mûw'âph (1),
obscurity; distress
4588 mâ'ûwph (1),
darkness, gloom

DIMON
1775 Dîymôwn (2),
Dimon

DIMONAH
1776 Dîymôwnâh (1),
Dimonah

DINAH
1783 Dîynâh (7), justice

DINAH'S
1783 Dîynâh (1), justice

DINAITES
1784 Dîynay (Ch.) (1),
Dinaite

DINE
398 'âkal (1), to eat
709 aristaō (2), to eat a
meal

DINED
709 aristaō (1), to eat a
meal

DINHABAH
1838 Dinhâbâh (2),
Dinhabah

DINNER
737 'ărûchâh (1), ration,
portion of food
712 aristŏn (3), breakfast
or lunch; feast

DIONYSIUS
1354 Diŏnusiŏs (1),
reveller

DIOTREPHES
1361 Diŏtrĕphēs (1),
Zeus-nourished

DIP
2881 ṭâbal (9), to dip
911 baptō (1), to
overwhelm, cover

DIPPED
2881 ṭâbal (6), to dip
4272 mâchats (1), to
crush; to subdue
911 baptō (2), to
overwhelm, cover
1686 ĕmbaptō (1), to wet

DIPPETH
1686 ĕmbaptō (2), to wet

DIRECT
3384 yârâh (1), to point;
to teach
3474 yâshar (3), to be
straight; to make right
3559 kûwn (1), to set up;
establish, fix, prepare
3787 kâshêr (1), to be
straight or right
5414 nâthan (1), to give
6186 'ârak (1), to set in a
row, i.e. arrange,
2720 katĕuthunō (2), to
direct, lead, direct

DIRECTED
3559 kûwn (1), to set up;
establish, fix, prepare
6186 'ârak (1), to set in a
row, i.e. arrange,
8505 tâkan (1), to
balance, i.e. measure

DIRECTETH
3474 yâshar (1), to be straight; to make right
3559 kûwn (2), to set up: establish, fix, prepare

DIRECTLY
413+5227 'êl (1), to, toward
1903 hâgîyn (1), (poss.) suitable or turning

DIRT
2916 țîyț (2), mud or clay
6574 parsheḏôn (1), crotch or anus

DISALLOW
5106 nûw' (1), to refuse, forbid, dissuade

DISALLOWED
5106 nûw' (3), to refuse, forbid, dissuade
593 apŏḏŏkimazō (2), to repudiate, reject

DISANNUL
6565 pârar (2), to break up; to violate, frustrate
208 akurŏō (1), to invalidate, nullify

DISANNULLED
3722 kâphar (1), to placate or cancel

DISANNULLETH
114 athĕtĕō (1), to neutralize or set aside

DISANNULLING
115 athĕtēsis (1), cancellation

DISAPPOINT
6923 qâdam (1), to anticipate, hasten

DISAPPOINTED
6565 pârar (1), to break up; to violate, frustrate

DISAPPOINTETH
6565 pârar (1), to break up; to violate, frustrate

DISCERN
995 bîyn (2), to understand; discern
3045 yâda' (3), to know
5234 nâkar (4), to acknowledge
7200 râ'âh (1), to see
8085 shâma' (2), to hear intelligently
1252 diakrinō (1), to decide; to hesitate
1253 diakrisis (1), estimation
1381 dŏkimazō (1), to test; to approve

DISCERNED
995 bîyn (1), to understand; discern
5234 nâkar (2), to acknowledge
350 anakrinō (1), to interrogate, determine

DISCERNER
2924 kritikŏs (1), discriminative

DISCERNETH
3045 yâda' (1), to know

DISCERNING
1252 diakrinō (1), to decide; to hesitate
1253 diakrisis (1), estimation

DISCHARGE
4917 mishlachath (1), mission; release; army

DISCHARGED
5310 nâphats (1), to dash to pieces; to scatter

DISCIPLE
3100 mathĕteuō (1), to become a student
3101 mathētēs (27), pupil, student
3102 mathētria (1), female pupil, student

DISCIPLES
3928 limmûwd (1), instructed one
3101 mathētēs (240), pupil, student

DISCIPLES'
3101 mathētēs (1), pupil, student

DISCIPLINE
4148 mûwçâr (1), reproof, warning

DISCLOSE
1540 gâlâh (1), to denude; uncover

DISCOMFITED
1949 hûwm (3), to make an uproar; agitate
2000 hâmam (2), to put in commotion
2522 châlash (1), to prostrate, lay low
2729 chârad (1), to shudder with terror
3807 kâthath (1), to bruise, strike, beat
4522 maç (1), forced labor

DISCOMFITURE
4103 mehûwmâh (1), confusion or uproar

DISCONTENTED
4751+5315 mar (1), bitter; bitterness; bitterly

DISCONTINUE
8058 shâmaț (1), to let alone, desist, remit

DISCORD
4066 mâḏôwn (1), contest or quarrel
4090 meḏân (1), contest or quarrel

DISCOURAGE
5106 nûw' (1), to refuse, forbid, dissuade

DISCOURAGED
2865 châthath (1), to break down
4549 mâçaç (1), to waste; to faint
5106 nûw' (1), to refuse, forbid, dissuade
7114 qâtsar (1), to curtail, cut short
7533 râtsats (1), to crack in pieces; smash

120 athumĕō (1), to be disheartened

DISCOVER
1540 gâlâh (10), to denude; uncover
2834 châsaph (1), to drain away or bail up
6168 'ârâh (1), to be, make bare; to empty

DISCOVERED
1540 gâlâh (18), to denude; uncover
3045 yâda' (1), to know
6168 'ârâh (1), to be, make bare; to empty
398 anaphainō (1), to appear
2657 katanŏĕō (1), to observe fully

DISCOVERETH
1540 gâlâh (1), to denude; uncover
2834 châsaph (1), to drain away or bail up

DISCOVERING
6168 'ârâh (1), to be, make bare; to empty

DISCREET
995 bîyn (2), to understand; discern
4998 sōphrōn (1), self-controlled

DISCREETLY
3562 nŏunĕchōs (1), prudently

DISCRETION
2940 ța'am (1), taste; intelligence; mandate
4209 mezimmâh (4), plan; sagacity
4941 mishpâț (2), verdict; formal decree; justice
7922 sekel (1), intelligence; success
8394 tâbûwn (1), intelligence; argument

DISDAINED
959 bâzâh (1), to ridicule, scorn
3988 mâ'aç (1), to spurn; to disappear

DISEASE
1697 dâbâr (1), word; matter; thing
2483 chŏlîy (7), malady; anxiety; calamity
4245 machăleh (1), sickness
3119 malakia (3), enervation, debility
3553 nŏsēma (1), ailment, disease

DISEASED
2456 châlá' (2), to be sick
2470 châlâh (2), to be weak, sick, afflicted
770 asthĕnĕō (1), to be feeble
2560+2192 kakōs (2), badly; wrongly; ill

DISEASES
4064 madveh (2), sickness
4245 machăleh (1), sickness

4251 machlûy (1), disease
8463 tachălûw' (2), malady, disease
769 asthĕnĕia (1), feebleness of body
3554 nŏsŏs (6), malady, disease

DISFIGURE
853 aphanizō (1), to consume (becloud)

DISGRACE
5034 nâbêl (1), to be foolish or wicked

DISGUISE
2664 châphas (2), to let be sought; to mask
8138 shânâh (1), to transmute

DISGUISED
2664 châphas (5), to let be sought; to mask

DISGUISETH
5643 çêther (1), cover, shelter

DISH
5602 çêphel (1), basin, bowl
6747 tsallachath (1), bowl
5165 trubliŏn (2), bowl

DISHAN
1789 Dîyshân (5), antelope

DISHES
7086 qe'ârâh (3), bowl

DISHON
1788 dîyshôn (7), antelope

DISHONEST
1215 betsa' (2), plunder; unjust gain

DISHONESTY
152 aischunē (1), shame or disgrace

DISHONOUR
3639 kelimmâh (3), disgrace, scorn
6173 'arvâh (Ch.) (1), nakedness
7036 qâlôwn (1), disgrace
818 atimazō (2), to maltreat, dishonor
819 atimia (4), disgrace

DISHONOUREST
818 atimazō (1), to maltreat, dishonor

DISHONOURETH
5034 nâbêl (1), to wilt; to be foolish or wicked
2617 kataischunō (2), to disgrace or shame

DISINHERIT
3423 yârash (1), to inherit; to impoverish

DISMAYED
926 bâhal (1), to tremble; hurry anxiously
2844 chath (1), terror
2865 châthath (26), to break down
8159 shâ'âh (2), to be bewildered

English

DISMAYING
4288 mᵉchittâh (1), *ruin; consternation*

DISMISSED
6362 pâṭar (1), *to burst through; to emit*
630 apŏluō (2), *to relieve, release; to divorce*

DISOBEDIENCE
543 apeítheia (3), *disbelief*
3876 parakŏē (3), *disobedience*

DISOBEDIENT
4784 mârâh (2), *to rebel or resist; to provoke*
506 anupŏtaktŏs (1), *insubordinate*
544 apeithĕō (4), *to disbelieve*
545 apeíthēs (6), *willful disobedience*

DISOBEYED
4784 mârâh (1), *to rebel or resist; to provoke*

DISORDERLY
812 ataktĕō (1), *to be, act irregular*
814 ataktōs (2), *morally irregularly*

DISPATCH
1254 bârâ' (1), *to create; fashion*

DISPENSATION
3622 ŏikŏnŏmia (4), *administration*

DISPERSE
2219 zârâh (7), *to toss about; to diffuse*
6327 pûwts (1), *to dash in pieces; to disperse*

DISPERSED
2219 zârâh (1), *to toss about; to diffuse*
5310 nâphats (1), *to dash to pieces; to scatter*
6327 pûwts (2), *to dash in pieces; to disperse*
6340 pâzar (1), *to scatter*
6504 pârad (1), *to spread or separate*
6555 pârats (1), *to break out*
1287 diaskŏrpizō (1), *to scatter; to squander*
1290 diaspŏra (1), *dispersion*
4650 skŏrpizō (1), *to dissipate*

DISPERSIONS
8600 tᵉphôwtsâh (1), *dispersal*

DISPLAYED
5127 nûwç (1), *to vanish away, flee*

DISPLEASE
2734 chârâh (1), *to blaze up*
6213+7451+5869 'âsâh (1), *to do or make*
7489+5869 râ'a' (3), *to be good for nothing*

DISPLEASED
599 'ânaph (1), *be enraged, be angry*
888 bᵉ'êsh (Ch.) (1), *to be displeased*
2198 zâ'êph (2), *angry, raging*
2734 chârâh (3), *to blaze up*
3415+5869 yâra' (1), *to fear*
6087 'âtsab (1), *to worry, have pain or anger*
7107 qâtsaph (3), *to burst out in rage*
7451+241 ra' (1), *bad; evil*
7489+5869 râ'a' (7), *to be good for nothing*
23 aganaktĕō (3), *to be indignant*
2371 thumŏmachĕō (1), *to be exasperated*

DISPLEASURE
2534 chêmâh (3), *heat; anger; poison*
2740 chârôwn (1), *burning of anger*
7451 ra' (1), *bad; evil*

DISPOSED
7760 sûwm (2), *to put, place*
1014 bŏulŏmai (1), *to be willing, desire*
2309 thĕlō (1), *to will; to desire; to choose*

DISPOSING
4941 mishpâṭ (1), *verdict; formal decree; justice*

DISPOSITION
1296 diatagē (1), *putting into effect*

DISPOSSESS
3423 yârash (2), *to inherit; to impoverish*

DISPOSSESSED
3423 yârash (2), *to inherit; to impoverish*

DISPUTATION
4803 suzētēsis (1), *discussion, dispute*

DISPUTATIONS
1253 diakrisis (1), *estimation*

DISPUTE
3198 yâkach (1), *to be correct; to argue*

DISPUTED
1256 dialĕgŏmai (3), *to discuss*
1260 dialŏgizŏmai (1), *to deliberate*
4802 suzētĕō (1), *to discuss, controvert*

DISPUTER
4804 suzētētēs (1), *sophist*

DISPUTING
1256 dialĕgŏmai (3), *to discuss*
4802 suzētĕō (1), *to discuss, controvert*
4803 suzētēsis (1), *discussion, dispute*

DISPUTINGS
1261 dialŏgismŏs (1), *consideration; debate*
3859 paradiatribē (1), *meddlesomeness*

DISQUIET
7264 râgaz (1), *to quiver*

DISQUIETED
1993 hâmâh (4), *to be in great commotion*
7264 râgaz (2), *to quiver*

DISQUIETNESS
5100 nᵉhâmâh (1), *snarling, growling*

DISSEMBLED
3584 kâchash (1), *to lie, disown; to disappoint*
8582 tâ'âh (1), *to vacillate, reel or stray*
4942 sunupŏkrinŏmai (1), *to act hypocritically*

DISSEMBLERS
5956 'âlam (1), *to veil from sight, i.e. conceal*

DISSEMBLETH
5234 nâkar (1), *to treat as a foreigner*

DISSENSION
4714 stasis (3), *one leading an uprising*

DISSIMULATION
505 anupŏkritŏs (1), *sincere, genuine*
5272 hupŏkrisis (1), *deceit, hypocrisy*

DISSOLVE
8271 shᵉrê' (Ch.) (1), *to unravel, commence*

DISSOLVED
4127 mûwg (3), *to soften, flow down, disappear*
4743 mâqaq (1), *to melt; to flow, dwindle, vanish*
6565 pârar (1), *to break up; to violate, frustrate*
2647 kataluō (1), *to demolish; to halt*
3089 luō (2), *to loosen*

DISSOLVEST
4127 mûwg (1), *to soften, flow down, disappear*

DISSOLVING
8271 shᵉrê' (Ch.) (1), *to free, separate*

DISTAFF
6418 pelek (1), *spindle-whorl; crutch*

DISTANT
7947 shâlab (1), *to make equidistant*

DISTIL
5140 nâzal (1), *to drip, or shed by trickling*
7491 râ'aph (1), *to drip*

DISTINCTION
1293 diastŏlē (1), *variation, distinction*

DISTINCTLY
6567 pârash (1), *to separate; to specify*

DISTRACTED
6323 pûwn (1), *to be perplexed*

DISTRACTION
563 apĕrispastōs (1), *undistractedly*

DISTRESS
4689 mâtsôwq (1), *confinement; disability*
4691 mᵉtsûwqâh (1), *trouble, anguish*
4712 mêtsar (1), *trouble*
6693 tsûwq (5), *to oppress, distress*
6696 tsûwr (2), *to cramp, i.e. confine; to harass*
6862 tsar (4), *trouble; opponent*
6869 tsârâh (8), *trouble; rival-wife*
6887 tsârar (5), *to cramp*
7451 ra' (1), *bad; evil*
318 anagkē (3), *constraint; distress*
4730 stĕnŏchōria (1), *calamity, distress*
4928 sunŏchē (1), *anxiety, distress*

DISTRESSED
3334 yâtsar (4), *to be in distress*
5065 nâgas (2), *to exploit; to tax, harass*
6696 tsûwr (1), *to cramp, i.e. confine; to harass*
6887 tsârar (1), *to cramp*
6973 qûwts (1), *to be, make disgusted*
4729 stĕnŏchōrĕō (1), *to hem in closely*

DISTRESSES
4691 mᵉtsûwqâh (5), *trouble, anguish*
6862 tsar (1), *trouble; opponent*
4730 stĕnŏchōria (2), *calamity, distress*

DISTRIBUTE
2505 châlaq (1), *to be smooth; be slippery*
5157 nâchal (1), *to inherit*
5414 nâthan (1), *to give*
1239 diadidōmi (1), *to divide up, distribute*
2130 ĕumĕtadŏtŏs (1), *liberal, generous*

DISTRIBUTED
2505 châlaq (2), *to be smooth; be slippery*
5157 nâchal (1), *to inherit*
1239 diadidōmi (1), *to divide up, distribute*
3307 mĕrizō (2), *to apportion, bestow*

DISTRIBUTETH
2505 châlaq (1), *to be smooth; be slippery*

DISTRIBUTING
2841 kŏinōnĕō (1), *to share or participate*

DISTRIBUTION
1239 diadidōmi (1), *to divide up, distribute*
2842 kŏinōnia (1), *benefaction; sharing*

DITCH
4724 miqvâh (1), *water reservoir*
7745 shûwchâh (1), *chasm*
7845 shachath (2), *pit; destruction*

999 bŏthunŏs (2), *cistern, pit-hole*

DITCHES
1356 gêb (1), *well, cistern; pit*

DIVERS
582 'ĕnôwsh (1), *man; person, human*
2921 ṭâlâ' (1), to *be spotted or variegated*
3610 kil'ayim (1), *two different kinds of thing*
6446 paç (2), *long -sleeved tunic*
6648 tseba' (3), *dye*
7553 riqmâh (2), *variegation of color*
8162 sha'aṭnêz (1), *linen and woolen*
1313 diaphŏrŏs (1), *varying; surpassing*
4164 pŏikilŏs (8), *various in character or kind*
4187 pŏlutrŏpŏs (1), *in many ways*
5100 tis (2), *some or any*

DIVERSE
3610 kil'ayim (1), *two different kinds of thing*
8133 shᵉnâ' (Ch.) (5), to *alter, change*
8138 shânâh (2), to *duplicate; to transmute*

DIVERSITIES
1085 gĕnŏs (1), *kin, offspring in kind*
1243 diairĕsis (2), *distinction or variety*

DIVIDE
914 bâdal (5), to *divide, separate, distinguish*
1234 bâqa' (2), to *cleave, break, tear open*
1504 gâzar (2), to *destroy, divide*
2505 châlaq (17), to *be smooth; be slippery*
2673 châtsâh (3), to *cut or split in two; to halve*
5157 nâchal (3), to *inherit*
5307 nâphal (4), to *fall*
5312 nᵉphaq (Ch.) (2), to *issue forth; to bring out*
6385 pâlag (1), to *split*
6536 pâraç (4), to *break in pieces; to split*
6565 pârar (1), to *break up; to violate, frustrate*
1266 diamĕrizō (1), to *distribute*
3307 mĕrizō (1), to *apportion, bestow*

DIVIDED
914 bâdal (2), to *divide, separate, distinguish*
1234 bâqa' (2), to *cleave, break, tear open*
1334 bâthar (2), to *chop up, cut up*
1504 gâzar (1), to *destroy, divide*
2505 châlaq (21), to *be smooth; be slippery*
2673 châtsâh (8), to *cut or split in two; to halve*
5307 nâphal (2), to *fall*

5408 nâthach (1), to *dismember, cut up*
5504 çachar (1), *profit from trade*
6385 pâlag (3), to *split*
6386 pᵉlag (Ch.) (1), *dis-united*
6504 pârad (2), to *spread or separate*
6537 pᵉraç (Ch.) (1), to *split up*
7280 râga' (1), to *settle, to stir up*
7323 rûwts (1), to *run*
1096 ginŏmai (1), to *be, become*
1244 diairĕō (1), *distribute, apportion*
1266 diamĕrizō (4), to *distribute*
2624 kataklērŏdŏtĕō (1), to *apportion an estate*
3307 mĕrizō (8), to *apportion, bestow*
4977 schizō (2), to *split or sever*

DIVIDER
3312 mĕristēs (1), *apportioner*

DIVIDETH
2672 châtsab (1), to *cut stone or carve wood*
6536 pâraç (5), to *break; to split, distribute*
7280 râga' (2), to *settle, to stir up*
873 aphŏrizō (1), to *limit, exclude, appoint*
1239 diadidōmi (1), to *divide up, distribute*

DIVIDING
1234 bâqa' (1), to *cleave, break, tear open*
2505 châlaq (1), to *be smooth; be slippery*
6387 pᵉlag (Ch.) (1), *half-time unit*
1244 diairĕō (1), *distribute, apportion*
3311 mĕrismŏs (1), *separation, distribution*
3718 ŏrthŏtŏmĕō (1), to *expound correctly*

DIVINATION
4738 miqçâm (2), *augury, divination*
7080 qâçam (1), to *divine magic*
7081 qeçem (8), *divination*
4436 Puthōn (1), *inspiration in soothsaying*

DIVINATIONS
7081 qeçem (1), *divination*

DIVINE
5172 nâchash (1), to *prognosticate*
7080 qâçam (5), to *divine magic*
7081 qeçem (1), *divination*
7181 qâshab (1), to *prick up the ears*
2304 thĕiŏs (2), *divinity*
2999 latrĕia (1), *worship, ministry service*

DIVINERS
7080 qâçam (7), to *divine magic*

DIVINETH
5172 nâchash (1), to *prognosticate*

DIVINING
7080 qâçam (1), to *divine magic*

DIVISION
2515 châluqqâh (1), *distribution, portion*
6304 pᵉdûwth (1), *distinction; deliverance*
1267 diamĕrismŏs (1), *disunion*
4978 schisma (3), *dissension, i.e. schism*

DIVISIONS
4256 machălôqeth (8), *section or division*
4653 miphlaggâh (1), *classification, division*
6391 pᵉluggâh (3), *section*
6392 pᵉluggâh (Ch.) (1), *section*
1370 dichŏstasia (2), *dissension*
4978 schisma (2), *dissension, i.e. schism*

DIVORCE
3748 kᵉrîythûwth (1), *divorce*

DIVORCED
1644 gârash (3), to *drive out; to divorce*
630 apŏluō (1), to *relieve, release; to divorce*

DIVORCEMENT
3748 kᵉrîythûwth (3), *divorce*
647 apŏstasiŏn (3), *marriage divorce*

DIZAHAB
1774 Dîy zâhâb (1), *of gold*

DO
1167 ba'al (1), *master; husband; owner; citizen*
1580 gâmal (1), to *benefit or requite; to wean*
3190 yâṭab (2), to *be, make well*
3318 yâtsâ' (1), to *go, bring out*
4640 Ma'say (1), *operative*
5647 'âbad (17), to *do, work, serve*
5648 'ăbad (Ch.) (5), to *do, work, serve*
5674 'âbar (1), to *cross over; to transition*
5953 'âlal (2), to *glean; to overdo*
6213 'âsâh (617), to *do*
6466 pâ'al (6), to *do*
6467 pô'al (1), *act or work, deed*
14 agathŏĕrgĕō (1), to do *good work*
15 agathŏpŏiĕō (6), to *be a well-doer*
17 agathŏpŏiŏs (1), *virtuous one*

91 adikĕō (2), to *do wrong*
1107 gnōrizō (1), to *make known, reveal*
1286 diasĕiō (1), to *intimidate*
1398 dŏulĕuō (1), to *serve as a slave*
1754 ĕnĕrgĕō (1), to *be active, efficient, work*
2005 ĕpitĕlĕō (1), to *terminate; to undergo*
2038 ĕrgazŏmai (2), to *toil*
2140 ĕupŏiïa (1), *beneficence, doing good*
2192 ĕchō (1), to *have; hold; keep*
2480 ischuō (1), to *have or exercise force*
2554 kakŏpŏiĕō (2), to *injure; to sin, do wrong*
2698 katatithēmi (1), to *place down*
2716 katĕrgazŏmai (3), to *finish; to accomplish*
3930 parĕchō (1), to *hold near, i.e. to present*
4160 pŏiĕō (199), to *do*
4238 prassō (15), to *execute, accomplish*
4704 spŏudazō (2), to *make effort*
4982 sōzō (1), to *deliver; to protect*

DOCTOR
3547 nŏmŏdidaskalŏs (1), *Rabbi*

DOCTORS
1320 didaskalŏs (1), *instructor*
3547 nŏmŏdidaskalŏs (1), *Rabbi*

DOCTRINE
3948 leqach (4), *instruction*
4148 mûwçâr (1), *reproof, warning*
8052 shᵉmûw'âh (1), *announcement*
1319 didaskalia (15), *instruction*
1322 didachē (28), *instruction*
3056 lŏgŏs (1), *word, matter, thing*

DOCTRINES
1319 didaskalia (4), *instruction*
1322 didachē (1), *instruction*

DODAI
1739 dâveh (1), *menstrual; fainting*

DODANIM
1721 Dôdânîym (2), *Dodanites*

DODAVAH
1735 Dôwdâvâhûw (1), *love of Jehovah*

DODO
1734 Dôwdôw (5), *loving*

DOEG
1673 Dô'êg (6), *anxious*

English

DOER
6218 'âsôwr (3), group of ten
2557 kakŏurgŏs (1), criminal, evildoer
4163 pŏiētēs (3), performer; poet

DOERS
6213 'âsâh (2), to do or make
6466 pâ'al (1), to do, make or practice
4163 pŏiētēs (2), performer; poet

DOEST
5648 'ăbad (Ch.) (1), to do, work, serve
6213 'âsâh (18), to do or make
6466 pâ'al (1), to do, make or practice
7965 shâlôwm (1), safe; well; health, prosperity
4160 pŏiĕō (14), to do
4238 prassō (1), to execute, accomplish

DOETH
1580 gâmal (1), to benefit or requite; to wean
5648 'ăbad (Ch.) (1), to do, work, serve
6213 'âsâh (44), to do
7760 sûwm (1), to put, place
15 agathŏpŏiĕō (1), to be a well-doer
91 adikĕō (1), to do wrong
2554 kakŏpŏiĕō (1), to injure; to sin, do wrong
4160 pŏiĕō (34), to do
4238 prassō (3), to execute, accomplish
4374 prŏsphĕrō (1), to present to; to treat as

DOG
3611 keleb (14), dog; male prostitute
2965 kuōn (1), dog

DOG'S
3611 keleb (2), dog; male prostitute

DOGS
3611 keleb (16), dog; male prostitute
2952 kunariŏn (4), small dog
2965 kuōn (4), dog

DOING
854 'êth (1), with; by; at; among
4640 Ma'say (1), operative
5949 'ălîylâh (1), opportunity, action
6213 'âsâh (14), to do or make
15 agathŏpŏiĕō (2), to be a well-doer
16 agathŏpŏiïa (1), virtue, doing good
92 adikĕma (1), wrong done
1096 ginŏmai (2), to be, become
1398 dŏuleuō (1), to serve as a slave

DOINGS
4611 ma'ălâl (35), act, deed
4640 Ma'say (3), operative
5949 'ălîylâh (13), opportunity, action

DOLEFUL
255 'ôach (1), creature that howls;
5093 nihyâh (1), lamentation

DOMINION
1166 bâ'al (1), to be master; to marry
1196 Ba'ănâh (1), in affliction
3027 yâd (2), hand; power
4474 mimshâl (2), ruler; dominion, rule
4475 memshâlâh (10), rule; realm or a ruler
4896 mishțâr (1), jurisdiction, rule
4910 mâshal (7), to rule
4915 môshel (2), empire; parallel
7287 râdâh (9), to subjugate
7300 rûwd (1), to ramble free or disconsolate
7980 shâlaṭ (1), to dominate, i.e. govern
7985 sholṭân (Ch.) (11), official
2634 katakuriĕuō (1), to control, subjugate
2904 kratŏs (4), vigor, strength
2961 kuriĕuō (4), to rule, be master of
2963 kuriŏtēs (2), rulers, masters

DOMINIONS
7985 sholṭân (Ch.) (1), official
2963 kuriŏtēs (1), rulers, masters

DONE
466 'Ĕlîyphᵉlêhûw (1), God of his distinction
1254 bârâ' (1), to create; fashion
1580 gâmal (1), to benefit or requite; to wean
1639 gâra' (1), to shave, remove, lessen
1697 dâbâr (1), word; matter; thing
1961 hâyâh (2), to exist, i.e. be or become
3254 yâçaph (1), to add or augment
3615 kâlâh (9), to complete, prepare
5414 nâthan (1), to give
5647 'âbad (1), to do, work, serve

2041 ĕrgŏn (1), work
2109 ĕuĕrgĕtĕō (1), to be philanthropic
2554 kakŏpŏiĕō (1), to injure; to sin, do wrong
2569 kalŏpŏiĕō (1), to do well
4160 pŏiĕō (8), to do

5648 'ăbad (Ch.) (4), to do, work, serve
5953 'âlal (3), to glean; to overdo
6213 'âsâh (318), to do or make
6466 pâ'al (21), to do, make or practice
7760 sûwm (1), to put, place
8552 tâmam (2), to complete, finish
91 adikĕō (3), to do wrong
1096 ginŏmai (61), to be, become
1796 ĕnubrizō (1), to insult
2673 katargĕō (4), to be, render entirely useless
2716 katĕrgazŏmai (2), to finish; to accomplish
4160 pŏiĕō (52), to do
4238 prassō (6), to execute, accomplish

DOOR
1004 bayith (1), house; temple; family, tribe
1817 deleth (21), door; gate
4201 mᵉzûwzâh (2), door-post
4947 mashqôwph (1), lintel
5592 çaph (11), dish
6607 pethach (114), opening; door
6907 qubba'ath (2), goblet, cup
8179 sha'ar (1), opening, i.e. door or gate
2374 thura (28), entrance, i.e. door, gate
2377 thurŏrŏs (2), doorkeeper

DOORKEEPER
5605 çâphaph (1), to wait at (the) threshold

DOORKEEPERS
7778 shôw'êr (2), janitor, door-keeper

DOORS
1817 deleth (48), door; gate
5592 çaph (2), dish
6607 pethach (11), opening; door
8179 sha'ar (1), opening, i.e. door or gate
2374 thura (9), entrance, i.e. door, gate

DOPHKAH
1850 Dophqâh (2), knock

DOR
1756 Dôwr (6), dwelling

DORCAS
1393 Dŏrkas (2), gazelle

DOTE
2973 yâ'al (1), to be or act foolish

DOTED
5689 'âgab (6), to lust sensually

DOTHAN
1886 Dôthân (3), Dothan

DOTING
3552 nŏsĕō (1), to be sick, be ill

DOUBLE
3717 kâphal (2), to fold together; to repeat
3718 kephel (3), duplicate, double
4932 mishneh (8), duplicate copy; double
8147 shᵉnayim (5), two-fold
1362 diplŏus (2), two-fold
1374 dipsuchŏs (2), vacillating
3588+1362 hŏ (1), "the," i.e. the definite article

DOUBLED
3717 kâphal (3), to fold together; to repeat
8138 shânâh (1), to fold, i.e. duplicate

DOUBLETONGUED
1351 dilŏgŏs (1), insincere

DOUBT
551 'omnâm (1), verily, indeed, truly
142+5590 airō (1), to lift, to take up
639 apŏrĕō (1), be at a mental loss, be puzzled
686 ara (1), then, so, therefore
1063 gar (1), for, indeed, but, because
1252 diakrinō (2), to decide; to hesitate
1280 diapŏrĕō (1), to be thoroughly puzzled
1365 distazō (1), to waver in opinion
3843 pantŏs (1), at all events; in no event

DOUBTED
639 apŏrĕō (1), be at a mental loss, be puzzled
1280 diapŏrĕō (2), to be thoroughly puzzled
1365 distazō (1), to waver in opinion

DOUBTETH
1252 diakrinō (1), to decide; to hesitate

DOUBTFUL
1261 dialŏgismŏs (1), consideration; debate
3349 mĕtĕōrizō (1), to be anxious

DOUBTING
639 apŏrĕō (1), be at a mental loss, be puzzled
1252 diakrinō (2), to decide; to hesitate
1261 dialŏgismŏs (1), consideration; debate

DOUBTLESS
518 'îm (1), whether?; if, although; Oh that!
3588 kîy (1), for, that because
1065 gĕ (1), particle of emphasis
1211 dē (1), now, then; indeed, therefore

3304 měnŏungě (1), *so then at least*

DOUBTS
7001 qᵉṭar (Ch.) (2), *riddle*

DOUGH
1217 bâtsêq (4), *fermenting dough*
6182 'ărîyçâh (4), *ground-up meal*

DOVE
3123 yôwnâh (14), *dove*
4058 pěristěra (4), *pigeon, dove*

DOVE'S
1686 dibyôwn (1), (poss.) *vegetable or root*

DOVES
3123 yôwnâh (5), *dove*
4058 pěristěra (5), *pigeon, dove*

DOVES'
3123 yôwnâh (2), *dove*

DOWN
935 bôw' (11), *to go or come*
1288 bârak (1), *to bless*
1438 gâda' (9), *to fell a tree; to destroy*
1457 gâhar (1), *to prostrate, bow down*
1760 dâchâh (1), *to push down; to totter*
2040 hâraç (22), *to pull down; break, destroy*
2904 ṭûwl (2), *to cast down or out, hurl*
3212 yâlak (1), *to walk; to live; to carry*
3281 Ya'lâm (1), *occult*
3332 yâtsaq (1), *to pour out*
3381 yârad (339), *to descend*
3665 kâna' (3), *to humiliate, vanquish*
3766 kâra' (9), *to prostrate*
3782 kâshal (4), *to totter, waver, stumble*
3996 mâbôw' (2), *entrance; sunset; west; towards*
4174 môwrâd (3), *descent, slope*
4295 maṭṭâh (1), *below or beneath*
4535 maççâch (1), *cordon; military barrier*
4606 mê'al (Ch.) (1), *setting of the sun*
4769 marbêts (2), *resting place*
5117 nûwach (1), *to rest; to settle down*
5128 nûwa' (1), *to waver*
5181 nâchath (4), *to sink, descend; to lead down*
5182 nᵉchath (Ch.) (2), *to descend; to depose*
5183 nachath (1), *descent; quiet*
5186 nâṭâh (8), *to stretch or spread out*
5242 Nᵉmûw'êlîy (2), *Nemuelite*

5243 nâmal (1), *to be circumcised*
5307 nâphal (9), *to fall*
5422 nâthats (29), *to tear down*
5456 çâgad (4), *to prostrate oneself*
5493 çûwr (1), *to turn off*
6131 'âqar (1), *to pluck up; to hamstring*
6201 'âraph (1), *to drip*
6915 qâdad (5), *to bend*
7250 râba' (2), *to lay down*
7252 reba' (1), *prostration for sleep*
7257 râbats (13), *to recline, repose, brood*
7323 rûwts (1), *to run*
7491 râ'aph (1), *to drip*
7503 râphâh (2), *to slacken*
7665 shâbar (1), *to burst*
7673 shâbath (1), *to repose; to desist*
7743 shûwach (1), *to sink*
7812 shâchâh (20), *to prostrate in homage*
7817 shâchach (12), *to sink or depress*
7821 shᵉchîyṭâh (1), *slaughter*
7901 shâkab (40), *to lie down*
7971 shâlach (2), *to send away*
8045 shâmad (2), *to desolate*
8058 shâmaṭ (2), *to jostle; to let alone*
8213 shâphêl (7), *to humiliate*
8214 shᵉphal (Ch.) (1), *to humiliate*
8231 shâphar (1), *to be, make fair*
8257 shâqa' (1), *to be overflowed; to cease*
8497 tâkâh (1), *to strew, i.e. encamp*
345 anakĕimai (2), *to recline at a meal*
347 anaklinō (7), *to lean back, recline*
377 anapiptō (10), *lie down, lean back*
387 anastatŏō (1), *to disturb, cause trouble*
1308 diaphěrō (1), *to bear, carry; to differ*
1581 ěkkŏptō (5), *to cut off; to frustrate*
1931 ěpiduō (1), *to set*
2504 kagō (1), *and also*
2506 kathairěsis (1), *demolition*
2507 kathairěō (6), *to lower, or demolish*
2521 kathēmai (4), *to sit down; to remain, reside*
2523 kathizō (14), *to seat down, dwell*
2524 kathiěmi (4), *to lower, let down*
2596 kata (3), *down; according to*
2597 katabainō (64), *to descend*

2598 kataballō (2), *to throw down*
2601 katabibazō (2), *to cause to bring down*
2609 katagō (5), *to lead down; to moor a vessel*
2621 katakěimai (1), *to lie down; to recline*
2625 kataklinō (2), *to take a place at table*
2630 katakrēmnizō (1), *to precipitate down*
2647 kataluō (3), *to halt for the night*
2662 katapatěō (1), *to trample down; to reject*
2667 katapiptō (1), *to fall down*
2673 katargěō (1), *to be, render entirely useless*
2679 kataskaptō (1), *to destroy, be ruined*
2701 katatrěchō (1), *to hasten, run*
2718 katěrchŏmai (6), *to go, come down*
2736 katō (5), *downwards*
2778 kēnsŏs (1), *enrollment*
2875 kŏptō (2), *to beat the breast*
3879 parakuptō (3), *to lean over*
3935 pariěmi (1), *to neglect; to be weakened*
4098 piptō (2), *to fall*
4496 rhiptō (2), *to fling, toss; to lay out*
4776 sugkathizō (1), *to give, take a seat with*
4781 sugkamptō (1), *to afflict*
4782 sugkatabainō (1), *to descend with*
5011 tapěinŏs (1), *humiliated, lowly*
5294 hupŏtithēmi (1), *to hazard; to suggest*
5465 chalaō (5), *to lower as into a void*

DOWNSITTING
3427 yâshab (1), *to dwell, to remain; to settle*

DOWNWARD
4295 maṭṭâh (5), *below or beneath*

DOWRY
2065 zebed (1), *gift*
4119 môhar (3), *wife-price*

DRAG
4365 mikmereth (2), *fishing-net*

DRAGGING
4951 surō (1), *to trail, drag, sweep*

DRAGON
8577 tannîyn (6), *sea-serpent; jackal*
1404 drakōn (13), *fabulous kind of serpent*

DRAGONS
8568 tannâh (1), female *jackal*
8577 tannîyn (15), *sea-serpent; jackal*

DRAMS
150 'ădarkôn (2), *daric*
1871 darkᵉmôwn (4), *coin*

DRANK
4960 mishteh (2), *drink; banquet or feast*
8354 shâthâh (8), *to drink, imbibe*
8355 shᵉthâh (Ch.) (3), *to drink, imbibe*
4095 pinō (5), *to imbibe, drink*

DRAUGHT
4280 machărâ'âh (1), *privy sink, latrine*
61 agra (2), *haul of fish in a net*
856 aphědrōn (2), *privy or latrine*

DRAVE
1644 gârash (3), *to drive out; to expatriate*
3423 yârash (2), *to impoverish; to ruin*
5071 nᵉdâbâh (1), *abundant gift*
5090 nâhag (4), *to drive forth; to lead*
5394 nâshal (1), *to divest, eject, or drop*
556 apělaunō (1), *to dismiss, eject*
1856 ěxōthěō (1), *to expel; to propel*

DRAW
748 'ârak (1), *to be, make long*
1518 gîyach (1), *to issue forth; to burst forth*
1802 dâlâh (1), *to draw out water); to deliver*
2502 châlats (1), *to pull off; to strip; to depart*
2834 châsaph (1), *to drain away or bail up*
3318 yâtsâ' (1), *to go, bring out*
4900 mâshak (11), *to draw out; to be tall*
5423 nâthaq (1), *to tear off*
5498 çâchab (3), *to trail along*
6329 pûwq (1), *to issue; to furnish; to secure*
7324 rûwq (8), *to pour out, i.e. empty*
7579 shâ'ab (9), *to bale up water*
8025 shâlaph (4), *to pull out, up or off*
501 antlěō (3), *dip water*
502 antlēma (1), *bucket for drawing water*
645 apŏspaō (1), *unsheathe a sword*
1670 hělkuō (4), *to drag, draw, pull in*
4334 prŏsěrchŏmai (1), *to come near, visit*
5288 hupŏstěllō (1), *to cower or shrink*
5289 hupŏstŏlē (1), *shrinkage, timidity*

DRAWER
7579 shâ'ab (1), *to bale up water*

DRAWERS
7579 shâ'ab (3), to *bale up* water

DRAWETH
4900 mâshak (2), to *draw out; to be tall*
7503 râphâh (1), to *slacken*

DRAWING
4857 mash'âb (1), water *trough* for cattle
1096 ginŏmai (1), to *be, become*

DRAWN
3318 yâtsâ' (1), to *go, bring out*
3947 lâqach (1), to *take*
4900 mâshak (2), to *draw out; to be tall*
5080 nâdach (1), to *push off, scattered*
5203 nâtash (1), to *disperse; to thrust off*
5423 nâthaq (3), to *tear off*
5498 çâchab (1), to *trail along*
6267 'attîyq (1), *weaned; antique*
6605 pâthach (2), to *open wide; to loosen, begin*
6609 pᵉthîchâh (1), *drawn sword*
7579 shâ'ab (1), to *bale up* water
7725 shûwb (1), to *turn back; to return*
8025 shâlaph (5), to *pull out, up or off*
8388 tâ'ar (5), to *delineate; to extend*
385 anaspaŏ (1), to *take up or extricate*
1828 ĕxĕlkō (1), to *drag away*, i.e. *entice*

DREAD
367 'êymâh (1), *fright*
2844 chath (1), *terror*
3372 yârê' (1), to *fear; to revere*
4172 môwrâ' (1), *fearful*
6206 'ârats (2), to *awe; to dread; to harass*
6343 pachad (3), *sudden alarm, fear*

DREADFUL
1763 dᵉchal (Ch.) (2), to *fear; be formidable, awesome*
3372 yârê' (5), to *fear; to revere*
3374 yir'âh (1), *fear; reverence*
6343 pachad (1), *sudden alarm, fear*

DREAM
2472 chălôwm (44), *dream; dreamer*
2492 châlam (1), to *dream*
2493 chêlem (Ch.) (21), *dream*
1798 ĕnupniŏn (1), *dream, vision*
3677 ŏnar (6), *dream*

DREAMED
2492 châlam (19), to *dream*

DREAMER
1167+2472 ba'al (1), *master; owner; citizen*
2492 châlam (3), to *dream*

DREAMERS
2492 châlam (1), to *dream*
1797 ĕnupniazŏmai (1), to *dream*

DREAMETH
2492 châlam (2), to *dream*

DREAMS
2472 chălôwm (19), *dream; dreamer*
2493 chêlem (Ch.) (1), *dream*
1797 ĕnupniazŏmai (1), to *dream*

DREGS
6907 qubba'ath (2), *goblet, cup*
8105 shemer (1), *settlings* of wine, *dregs*

DRESS
5647 'âbad (2), to *do, work, serve*
6213 'âsâh (7), to *do or make*

DRESSED
6213 'âsâh (6), to *do or make*
1090 gĕŏrgĕō (1), to *till the soil*

DRESSER
289 ampĕlŏurgŏs (1), *vineyard caretaker*

DRESSERS
3755 kôrêm (1), *vinedresser*

DRESSETH
3190 yâtab (1), to *be, make well*

DREW
748 'ârak (2), to *be, make long*
1802 dâlâh (2), to *draw out* water); to *deliver*
1869 dârak (1), to *walk, lead; to string* a bow
3318 yâtsâ' (1), to *go, bring out*
4871 mâshâh (3), to *pull out*
4900 mâshak (6), to *draw out; to be tall*
7579 shâ'ab (4), to *bale up* water
7725 shûwb (2), to *turn back; to return*
8025 shâlaph (15), to *pull out, up or off*
307 anabibazō (1), *haul up* a net
501 antlĕō (1), *dip* water
645 apŏspaō (1), *unsheathe* a sword
868 aphistēmi (1), to *desist, desert*
1670 hĕlkuō (4), to *drag, draw, pull in*

DRIED
1809 dâlal (1), to *slacken, dangle*
2717 chârab (9), to *parch; desolate, destroy*
2787 chârar (1), to *melt, burn, dry up*
3001 yâbêsh (22), to *dry up; to wither*
3002 yâbêsh (1), *dry*
6704 tsîcheh (1), *parched*
7033 qâlâh (1), to *toast, scorch*
3583 xêrainō (3), to *shrivel, to mature*

DRIEDST
3001 yâbêsh (1), to *dry up; to wither*

DRIETH
3001 yâbêsh (3), to *dry up; to wither*

DRINK
1572 gâmâ' (1), to *swallow*
4469 mamçâk (1), *mixed-wine*
4945 mashqeh (2), *butler; drink; well-watered*
4960 mishteh (3), *drink; banquet* or *feast*
5257 nᵉçîyk (1), *libation; molten image; prince*
5261 nᵉçak (Ch.) (1), *libation*
5262 neçek (59), *libation; cast idol*
5435 çôbe' (1), *wine*
7937 shâkar (2), to *become tipsy, to satiate*
7941 shêkâr (21), *liquor*
8248 shâqâh (42), to *quaff*, i.e. to *irrigate*
8249 shiqqûv (1), *draught, drink*
8250 shiqqûwy (1), *beverage; refreshment*
8353 shêth (Ch.) (1), *six; sixth*
8354 shâthâh (161), to *drink, imbibe*
8355 shᵉthâh (Ch.) (1), to *drink, imbibe*
4095 pinō (50), to *imbibe, drink*
4188 pŏma (1), *beverage, drink*
4213 pŏsis (3), *draught, drink*
4222 pŏtizō (9), to *furnish drink, irrigate*
4608 sikĕra (1), *intoxicant*
4844 sumpinō (1), to *partake a beverage*

DRIED (col 3 top)
2020 ĕpiphōskō (1), to *grow light*
4264 prŏbibazō (1), to *bring to the front*
4317 prŏsagō (1), to *bring near*
4334 prŏsĕrchŏmai (1), to *come near, visit*
4358 prŏsŏrmizō (1), to *moor to*, i.e. *land at*
4685 spaō (2), to *draw* a *sword*
4951 surō (3), to *trail, drag, sweep*

DRINKERS
8354 shâthâh (1), to *drink, imbibe*

DRINKETH
6231 'âshaq (1), to *overflow*
8354 shâthâh (8), to *drink, imbibe*
4095 pinō (7), to *imbibe, drink*

DRINKING
4945 mashqeh (2), *butler; drink; well-watered*
8354 shâthâh (12), to *drink, imbibe*
8360 shᵉthîyâh (1), *manner of drinking*
4095 pinō (6), to *imbibe, drink*

DRINKS
4188 pŏma (1), *beverage, drink*

DRIVE
1644 gârash (12), to *drive out; to divorce*
1920 hâdaph (2), to *push away or down; drive out*
2957 tᵉrad (Ch.) (2), to *expel, drive on*
3423 yârash (30), to *impoverish; to ruin*
5080 nâdach (5), to *push off, scattered*
5086 nâdaph (1), to *disperse, be windblown*
5090 nâhag (2), to *drive forth; to carry away*
6327 pûwts (1), to *dash in pieces; to disperse*
1929 ĕpididŏmi (1), to *give over*

DRIVEN
1644 gârash (5), to *drive out; to divorce*
1760 dâchâh (2), to *push down; to totter*
1920 hâdaph (1), to *push away or down; drive out*
2957 tᵉrad (Ch.) (2), to *expel, drive on*
3423 yârash (2), to *impoverish; to ruin*
5080 nâdach (23), to *push off, scattered*
5086 nâdaph (4), to *disperse, be windblown*
5437 çâbab (2), to *surround*
5472 çûwg (1), to *go back, to retreat*
5590 çâ'ar (1), to *rush upon; to toss about*
7617 shâbâh (1), to *transport into captivity*
416 anemizō (1), to *toss with the wind*
1308 diaphĕrō (1), to *bear, carry; to differ*
1643 ĕlaunō (2), to *push*
5342 phĕrō (1), to *bear or carry*

DRIVER
5065 nâgas (1), to *exploit; to tax, harass*

7395 rakkâb (1),
charioteer

DRIVETH
2342 chûwl (1), to *dance,
whirl;* to *writhe*
5086 nâdaph (1), to
disperse, be windblown
5090 nâhag (1), to *drive*
forth; to *carry away*
1544 ĕkballō (1), to
throw out

DRIVING
1644 gârash (1), to *drive*
out; to *divorce*
3423 yârash (1), to
impoverish; to *ruin*
4491 minhâg (2),
chariot-*driving*

DROMEDARIES
1070 beker (1), young
bull *camel*
7409 rekesh (1), *relay* of
animals on a post-route
7424 rammâk (1), brood
mare

DROMEDARY
1072 bikrâh (1), young
she-*camel*

DROP
4752 mar (1), *drop* in a
bucket
5140 nâzal (1), to *drip,* or
shed by trickling
5197 nâṭaph (7), to *fall in
drops*
6201 'âraph (2), to *drip*
7491 râ'aph (4), to *drip*

DROPPED
1982 hêlek (1), *wayfarer,
visitor; flowing*
5197 nâṭaph (5), to *fall in
drops*
5413 nâthak (1), to *flow*
forth, *pour* out

DROPPETH
1811 dâlaph (1), to *drip*

DROPPING
1812 deleph (2), *dripping*
5197 nâṭaph (1), to *fall in
drops*

DROPS
96 'egel (1), *reservoir*
5197 nâṭaph (1), to *fall in
drops*
7447 râçîyç (1), *ruin;*
dew-*drop*
2361 thrŏmbŏs (1), *clot* of
blood

DROPSY
5203 hudrōpikŏs (1), to
suffer edema

DROSS
5509 çîyg (8), *refuse,
scoria*

DROUGHT
1226 batstsôreth (1),
drought
2721 chôreb (3),
parched; ruined
2725 chârâbôwn (1),
parching *heat*
6710 tsachtsâchâh (1),
dry desert place
6723 tsîyâh (2), arid
desert

6774 tsimmâ'ôwn (1),
desert
8514 tal'ûwbâh (1),
dehydration

DROVE
1272 bârach (1), to *flee*
suddenly
1644 gârash (3), to *drive*
out; to *divorce*
3423 yârash (2), to
impoverish; to *ruin*
4264 machăneh (1),
encampment
5380 nâshab (1), to *blow;*
to *disperse*
5425 nâthar (1), to *jump;*
to *terrify; shake* off
5739 'êder (3), *muster,
flock*
1544 ĕkballō (1), to
throw out

DROVES
5739 'êder (1), *muster,
flock*

DROWN
7857 shâṭaph (1), to
gush; to *inundate*
1036 buthizō (1), to *sink;*
to *plunge*

DROWNED
2823 châshôk (1), *obscure*
8248 shâqâh (2), to *quaff,*
i.e. to *irrigate*
2666 katapinō (1), to
devour by swallowing
2670 katapŏntizō (1), to
submerge, be drowned

DROWSINESS
5124 nûwmâh (1),
sleepiness

DRUNK
7301 râvâh (1), to *slake*
thirst or appetites
7910 shikkôwr (2),
intoxicated
7937 shâkar (4), to
become tipsy, to *satiate*
8354 shâthâh (15), to
drink, imbibe
8355 shᵉthâh (Ch.) (1), to
drink, imbibe
3182 mĕthuskō (2), to
become drunk
3184 mĕthuō (1), to *get
drunk*
4095 pinō (2), to *imbibe,
drink*

DRUNKARD
5435 çôbe' (2), *wine*
7910 shikkôwr (2),
intoxicated
3183 mĕthusŏs (1),
drunkard

DRUNKARDS
5435 çôbe' (1), *wine*
7910 shikkôwr (3),
intoxicated
8354+7941 shâthâh (1), to
drink, imbibe
3183 mĕthusŏs (1),
drunkard

DRUNKEN
5435 çôbe' (1), *wine*
7301 râvâh (1), to *slake*
thirst or appetites

7910 shikkôwr (6),
intoxicated
7937 shâkar (13), to
become tipsy, to *satiate*
7943 shikkârôwn (2),
intoxication
8354 shâthâh (3), to
drink, imbibe
3182 mĕthuskō (1), to
become drunk
3184 mĕthuō (5), to *get
drunk*
4095 pinō (1), to *imbibe,
drink*

DRUNKENNESS
7302 râveh (1), *sated, full*
with drink
7943 shikkârôwn (2),
intoxication
8358 shᵉthîy (1),
intoxication
3178 mĕthē (3),
intoxication

DRUSILLA
1409 Drŏusilla (1),
Drusilla

DRY
954 bûwsh (1), be
ashamed; disappointed
2717 chârab (3), to
parch, desolate, destroy
2720 chârêb (3),
parched; ruined
2721 chôreb (3),
parched; ruined
2724 chârâbâh (8),
desert, dry land
3001 yâbêsh (9), to *dry*
up; to *wither*
3002 yâbêsh (7), *dry*
3004 yabbâshâh (14), *dry*
ground
3006 yabbesheth (2), *dry*
ground
5424 netheq (1), *scurf,*
i.e. diseased skin
6703 tsach (1), *dazzling,*
i.e. *sunny, bright*
6707 tsᵉchîychâh (1),
parched desert region
6723 tsîyâh (10), arid
desert
6724 tsîyôwn (2), *desert*
6774 tsimmâ'ôwn (1),
desert
6784 tsâmaq (1), to *dry*
up, *shrivel* up
504 anudrŏs (2), *dry,* arid
3584 xērŏs (2), *scorched;
arid; withered*

DRYSHOD
5275 na'al (1), *sandal*

DUE
1167 ba'al (1), *master;
husband; owner; citizen*
1697 dâbâr (1), *word;
matter; thing*
2706 chôq (2),
appointment; allotment
4941 mishpâṭ (1), *verdict;
formal decree; justice*
514 axiŏs (1), *deserving,
comparable* or *suitable*
2398 idiŏs (3), *private* or
separate
3784 ŏphĕilō (2), to *owe;*
to *be under obligation*

DUES
3782 ŏphĕilē (1), *sum*
owed; *obligation*

DUKE
441 'allûwph (20), *friend,*
one *familiar; chieftain*

DUKES
441 'allûwph (13), *friend,*
one *familiar; chieftain*
5257 nᵉçîyk (1), *libation;*
molten *image; prince*

DULCIMER
5481 çûwmpôwnᵉyâh
(Ch.) (3), *bagpipe*

DULL
917 barĕŏs (2), *heavily,
with difficulty*
3576 nōthrŏs (1), *lazy;
stupid*

DUMAH
1746 Dûwmâh (4),
silence; death

DUMB
481 'âlam (7), to be
tongue-tied, be silent
483 'illêm (6), *speechless*
1748 dûwmâm (1),
silently
216 alalŏs (3), *mute, not
able to speak*
880 aphōnŏs (3), *mute,
silent; unmeaning*
2974 kōphŏs (8), *deaf* or
silent
4623 siōpaō (1), to *be
quiet*

DUNG
830 'ashpôth (4), heap of
rubbish; Dung gate
1557 gâlâl (1), *dung*
pellets
1561 gêlel (4), *dung;
dung* pellets
1828 dômen (6), *manure,
dung*
2716+(6675) chere' (2),
excrement
2755 chărêy-yôwnîym
(1), *excrements of
doves* or a vegetable
6569 peresh (7),
excrement
6832 tsᵉphûwa' (1),
excrement
906+2874 ballō (1), to
throw
4657 skubalŏn (1), what
is *thrown* to the *dogs*

DUNGEON
953 bôwr (13), pit *hole,
cistern, well; prison*

DUNGHILL
830 'ashpôth (2), heap of
rubbish; Dung gate
4087 madmênâh (1),
dunghill
5122 nᵉvâlûw (Ch.) (3), to
be foul; *sink*
2874 kŏpria (1), *manure*
or *rubbish pile*

DUNGHILLS
830 'ashpôth (1), heap of
rubbish; Dung gate

DURA
1757 Dûwrâ' (Ch.) (1), *circle* or *dwelling*

DURABLE
6266 'âthîyq (1), *venerable* or *splendid*
6276 'âthêq (1), *enduring value*

DURETH
2076 êsti (1), he (she or it) *is; they are*

DURST
3372 yârê' (1), to *fear;* to *revere*
5111 tôlmaō (7), to be *bold;* to *dare*

DUST
80 'âbâq (5), *fine dust; cosmetic powder*
1854 dâqaq (1), to *crush; crumble*
6083 'âphâr (91), *dust, earth, mud; clay,*
7834 shachaq (1), *firmament, clouds*
2868 kŏniŏrtŏs (5), *blown* dust
5522 chŏŏs (2), loose *dirt*

DUTY
1697 dâbâr (2), *word; matter; thing*
3784 ŏphĕilō (2), to *owe; to fail* in duty

DWARF
1851 daq (1), *crushed; small* or *thin*

DWELL
1481 gûwr (11), to *sojourn, live as an alien*
1752 dûwr (1), *remain*
1753 dûwr (Ch.) (3), to *reside, live in*
2073 zᵉbûwl (1), *residence, dwelling*
2082 zâbal (1), to *reside*
3427 yâshab (210), to *dwell,* to *remain*
3488 yᵉthîb (Ch.) (1), to *sit* or *dwell*
3885 lûwn (1), to *be obstinate*
4186 môwshâb (1), *seat; site; abode*
5975 'âmad (1), to *stand*
7931 shâkan (69), to *reside*
7932 shᵉkan (Ch.) (1), to *reside*
1774 ĕnŏikĕō (2), to *inhabit, live with*
2521 kathēmai (1), to *sit down; to remain, reside*
2730 katŏikĕō (19), to *reside, live in*
3306 mĕnō (2), to *stay, remain*
3611 ŏikĕō (4), to *reside, inhabit, remain*
4637 skēnŏō (4), to *occupy; to reside*
4924 sunŏikĕō (1), to *reside together* as a family

DWELLED
3427 yâshab (6), to *dwell,* to *remain;* to *settle*

DWELLERS
7931 shâkan (1), to *reside*
2730 katŏikĕō (2), to *reside, live in*

DWELLEST
3427 yâshab (14), to *dwell,* to *remain*
7931 shâkan (3), to *reside*
2730 katŏikĕō (1), to *reside, live in*
3306 mĕnō (1), to *stay, remain*

DWELLETH
1481 gûwr (1), to *sojourn, live as an alien*
3427 yâshab (20), to *dwell,* to *remain*
4908 mishkân (1), *residence*
7931 shâkan (9), to *reside*
8271 shᵉrê' (Ch.) (1), to *free, separate;* to *reside*
1774 ĕnŏikĕō (2), to *inhabit, live with*
2730 katŏikĕō (7), to *reside, live in*
3306 mĕnō (9), to *stay, remain*
3611 ŏikĕō (4), to *reside, inhabit, remain*

DWELLING
168 'ôhel (3), *tent*
2073 zᵉbûwl (1), *residence, dwelling*
3427 yâshab (17), to *dwell,* to *remain*
4070 mᵉdôwr (Ch.) (4), *dwelling*
4186 môwshâb (5), *seat; site; abode*
4349 mâkôwn (2), *basis; place*
4583 mâ'ôwn (6), *retreat* or asylum *dwelling*
4585 mᵉ'ôwnâh (1), *abode*
4908 mishkân (4), *residence*
5116 nâveh (3), *at home; lovely; home*
7931 shâkan (1), to *reside*
1460 ĕgkatŏikĕō (1), *reside, live among*
2730 katŏikĕō (3), to *reside, live in*
2731 katŏikēsis (1), *residence*
3611 ŏikĕō (1), to *reside, inhabit, remain*

DWELLINGPLACE
4186 môwshâb (1), *seat; site; abode*
790 astatĕō (1), *homeless, vagabond*

DWELLINGPLACES
4186 môwshâb (2), *seat; site; abode*
4908 mishkân (3), *residence*

DWELLINGS
4033 mâgûwr (2), *abode*
4186 môwshâb (8), *seat; site; abode*
4908 mishkân (6), *residence*
5116 nâveh (1), *at home; lovely; home*

DWELT
1753 dûwr (Ch.) (2), to *reside, live in*
2583 chânâh (2), to *encamp*
3427 yâshab (189), to *dwell,* to *remain*
4186 môwshâb (2), *seat; site; abode*
7931 shâkan (11), to *reside*
1774 ĕnŏikĕō (1), to *inhabit, live with*
2730 katŏikĕō (12), to *reside, live in*
3306 mĕnō (2), to *stay, remain*
3940 parŏikia (1), *foreign residence*
4039 pĕriŏikĕō (1), to be a *neighbor*
4637 skēnŏō (1), to *occupy; to reside*

DYED
2556 châmêts (1), to be *fermented; be soured*
2871 ṭâbûwl (1), *turban*

DYING
1478 gâva' (1), to *expire, die*
599 apŏthnēskō (4), to *die off*
3500 nĕkrōsis (1), *death, deadness*

EACH
259 'echâd (10), *first*
376 'îysh (5), *man; male; someone*
802 'ishshâh (2), *woman, wife; women, wives*
905 bad (1), *limb, member; bar; chief*
240 allēlōn (2), *one another*
303 ana (1), *each; in turn; among*
1538 hĕkastŏs (2), *each* or *every*

EAGLE
5404 nesher (19), large *bird of prey*
7360 râchâm (2), kind of *vulture*
105 aĕtŏs (2), *eagle, vulture*

EAGLE'S
5403 nᵉshar (Ch.) (1), large *bird of prey*
5404 nesher (1), large *bird of prey*

EAGLES
5404 nesher (5), large *bird of prey*
105 aĕtŏs (2), *eagle, vulture*

EAGLES'
5403 nᵉshar (Ch.) (1), large *bird of prey*
5404 nesher (1), large *bird of prey*

EAR
24 'âbîyb (1), *head of grain;* month of *Abib*
238 'âzan (33), to *listen*
241 'ôzen (63), *ear*

EARRING
2790 chârash (1), to be *silent;* to *be deaf*
5647 'âbad (1), to do, *work, serve*
8085 shâma' (1), to *hear intelligently*
3775 ŏus (13), *ear; listening*
4719 stachus (2), *head of* grain
5621 ōtiŏn (5), *earlet, ear (-lobe)*

EARED
5647 'âbad (1), to do, *work, serve*

EARING
2758 chârîysh (2), *plowing; plowing season*

EARLY
1242 bôqer (3), *morning*
6852 tsâphar (1), to *return*
7836 shâchar (6), to *search* for
7837 shachar (2), *dawn*
7925 shâkam (62), to *start early*
8238 shᵉpharphar (Ch.) (1), *dawn*
260+4404 hama (1), *at the same time, together*
3719 ŏrthrizō (1), to *get up early in the morning*
3721 ŏrthriŏs (1), up *at day-break*
3722 ŏrthrŏs (3), *dawn, daybreak*
4404 prōï (3), *at dawn; day-break* watch
4405 prōïa (1), *day-dawn, early morn*
4406 prōïmŏs (1), *autumnal showering*

EARNEST
603 apŏkaradŏkia (2), *intense anticipation*
728 arrhabōn (3), *pledge, security*
1972 ĕpipŏthēsis (1), *longing for*
4056 pĕrissŏtĕrōs (1), *more superabundantly*
4710 spŏudē (1), *eagerness, earnestness*

EARNESTLY
2734 chârâh (1), to *blaze* up
3190 yâṭab (1), to be, *make well*
816 atĕnizō (3), to *gaze intently*
1617 ĕktĕnĕstĕrŏn (1), *more earnest*
1864 ĕpagōnizŏmai (1), to *struggle for, fight for*
1971 ĕpipŏthĕō (1), *intensely crave*
2206 zēlŏō (1), to *have warmth* of feeling for
4335 prŏsĕuchē (1), *prayer; prayer chapel*

EARNETH
7936 sâkar (1), to *hire*

EARRING
5141 nezem (5), *nose-ring*

EARRINGS
3908 lachash (1),
incantation; amulet
5141 nezem (9),
nose-*ring*
5694 'âgîyl (2), ear-*ring*

EARS
24 'âbîyb (1), *head of
grain;* month of *Abib*
241 'ôzen (100), *ear*
3759 karmel (3), *planted
field;* garden *produce*
4425 mᵉlîylâh (1), *cut*-off
head of cereal grain
7641 shibbôl (13),
stream; ear of grain
189 akŏē (4), *hearing;
thing heard*
191 akŏuō (1), to *hear;
obey*
3775 ŏus (24), *ear;
listening*
4719 stachus (3), *head of
grain*

EARTH
127 'ădâmâh (52), *soil;
land*
772 'ăra' (Ch.) (20),
earth, ground, land
776 'erets (710), *earth,
land, soil; country*
778 'ăraq (Ch.) (1), *earth*
2789 cheres (1), *piece of
earthenware pottery*
3007 yabbesheth (Ch.)
(1), *dry* land
6083 'âphâr (7), *dust,
earth, mud; clay,*
1093 gē (186), *soil,
region, whole earth*
1919 ĕpigĕiŏs (1),
worldly, earthly
2709 katachthŏniŏs (1),
infernal
3625 ŏikŏumĕnē (1),
Roman empire
3749 ŏstrakinŏs (1),
made of clay

EARTHEN
2789 cheres (8), *piece of
earthenware pottery*
3335 yâtsar (1), to *form;
potter; to determine*
3749 ŏstrakinŏs (1),
made of clay

EARTHLY
1537+3588+1093 ĕk (1),
out, out of
1919 ĕpigĕiŏs (4),
worldly, earthly

EARTHQUAKE
7494 ra'ash (6),
vibration, uproar
4578 sĕismŏs (10), *gale
storm; earthquake*

EARTHQUAKES
4578 sĕismŏs (3), *gale
storm; earthquake*

EARTHY
5517 chŏïkŏs (4), *dusty,
dirty,* i.e. *terrene*

EASE
2896 ţôwb (1), *good; well*
3427 yâshab (1), to *dwell,
to remain; to settle*

4496 mᵉnûwchâh (1),
peacefully; consolation
5162 nâcham (1), to *be
sorry;* to *pity, console*
5375 nâsâ' (1), to *lift up*
7043 qâlal (2), to *be easy,
trifling, vile*
7280 râga' (1), to *settle,*
i.e. *quiet;* to *wink*
7599 shâ'an (2), to *loll,*
i.e. *be peaceful*
7600 sha'ănân (6),
secure; haughty
7946 shal'ănân (1),
tranquil
7961 shâlêv (2), *carefree;
security, at ease*
373 anapauō (1), to
repose; to *refresh*

EASED
1980 hâlak (1), to *walk;
live a certain way*
425 anĕsis (1),
relaxation; relief

EASIER
7043 qâlal (1), to *be easy,
trifling, vile*
2123 ĕukŏpŏtĕrŏs (7),
better for toil

EAST
2777 charçûwth (1),
pottery
4161 môwtsâ' (1), *going
forth*
4217 mizrâch (33), *place
of sunrise; east*
4217+8121 mizrâch (2),
place of sunrise; east
6921 qâdîym (61), *east;
eastward; east wind*
6924 qedem (42), *east,
eastern; antiquity*
6926 qidmâh (3), *east;* on
the *east, in front*
6930 qadmôwn (1),
eastern
6931 qadmôwnîy (4),
oriental, eastern
395 anatŏlē (9), *dawn of
sun; east*

EASTER
3957 pascha (1),
Passover events

EASTWARD
1870+6921 derek (1),
road; course of life
4217 mizrâch (19), *place
of sunrise; east*
4217+8121 mizrâch (1),
place of sunrise; east
6921 qâdîym (7), *East;
eastward; east wind*
6924 qedem (11), *east,
eastern; antiquity*
6926 qidmâh (1), *east;* on
the *east, in front*

EASY
7043 qâlal (1), to *be easy,
trifling, vile*
2138 ĕupĕithēs (1),
compliant, submissive
2154 ĕusēmŏs (1),
significant
5543 chrēstŏs (1),
employed, i.e. *useful*

EAT
398 'âkal (497), to *eat*

399 'ăkal (Ch.) (1), to *eat*
402 'oklâh (2), *food*
1262 bârâh (4), to *feed*
2490 châlal (1), to
profane, defile
2939 ţᵉ'am (Ch.) (2), to
feed
3898 lâcham (5), to *fight
a battle,* i.e. *consume*
3899 lechem (1), *food,
bread*
6310 peh (1), *mouth;
opening*
7462 râ'âh (2), to *tend a
flock,* i.e. *pasture it*
1089 gĕuŏmai (1), to
taste; to *eat*
2068 ĕsthiō (39), to *eat*
2719 katĕsthiō (1), to
devour
3335 mĕtalambanō (1),
to *participate*
3542+2192 nŏmē (1),
pasture, feeding
4906 sunĕsthiō (4), to
take food with
5315 phagō (88), to *eat*

EATEN
398 'âkal (86), to *eat*
935+413+7130 bôw' (2), to
go or come
1197 bâ'ar (2), to *be
brutish, be senseless*
2490 châlal (1), to
profane, defile
7462 râ'âh (1), to *tend a
flock,* i.e. *pasture it*
977 bibrōskō (1), to *eat*
1089 gĕuŏmai (2), to
taste; to *eat*
2068 ĕsthiō (1), to *eat*
2719 katĕsthiō (1), to
devour
2880 kŏrĕnnumi (1), to
cram, i.e. *glut or sate*
4662 skōlĕkŏbrōtŏs (1),
diseased with maggots
5315 phagō (5), to *eat*

EATER
398 'âkal (3), to *eat*

EATERS
2151 zâlal (1), to *be loose
morally, worthless*

EATEST
398 'âkal (3), to *eat*

EATETH
398 'âkal (31), to *eat*
1104 bâla' (1), to
swallow; to *destroy*
2068 ĕsthiō (13), to *eat*
4906 sunĕsthiō (1), to
take food with
5176 trōgō (5), to *gnaw
or chew,* i.e. to *eat*

EATING
398 'âkal (13), to *eat*
400 'ôkel (4), *food*
3894 lâchûwm (1), *flesh
as food*
1035 brōsis (1), *food;
rusting corrosion*
2068 ĕsthiō (6), to *eat*
5176 trōgō (1), to *gnaw
or chew,* i.e. to *eat*
5315 phagō (1), to *eat*

EBAL
5858 'Êybâl (8), *bare, bald*

EBED
5651 'Ebed (6), *servant*

EBED-MELECH
5663 'Ebed Melek (6),
servant of a king

EBEN-EZER
72 'Eben hâ-'êzer (3),
stone of the help

EBER
5677 'Êber (13), *regions
beyond*

EBIASAPH
43 'Ebyâçâph (3),
Ebjasaph

EBONY
1894 hôben (1), *ebony*

EBRONAH
5684 'Ebrônâh (2),
Ebronah

EDAR
5740 'Êder (1), *flock*

EDEN
5731 'Êden (20), *pleasure*

EDER
5740 'Êder (3), *flock*

EDGE
5310 nâphats (1), to *dash
to pieces;* to *scatter*
6310 peh (34), *mouth;
opening*
6440 pânîym (1), *face;
front*
6697 tsûwr (1), *rock*
6949 qâhâh (3), to *be
dull; be blunt*
7097 qâtseh (8), *extremity*
8193 sâphâh (5), *lip;
edge, margin*
4750 stŏma (2), *mouth;
edge*

EDGES
6366 pêyâh (1), *edge*
7098 qâtsâh (1),
termination; fringe
7099 qetsev (1), *limit,
borders*
1366 distŏmŏs (1),
double-edged

EDIFICATION
3619 ŏikŏdŏmē (4),
edification

EDIFIED
3618 ŏikŏdŏmĕō (2), to
construct, edify

EDIFIETH
3618 ŏikŏdŏmĕō (3), to
construct, edify

EDIFY
3618 ŏikŏdŏmĕō (2), to
construct, edify
3619 ŏikŏdŏmē (1),
edification

EDIFYING
3618 ŏikŏdŏmĕō (1), to
construct, edify
3619 ŏikŏdŏmē (7),
edification

EDOM
123 'Êdôm (87), *red*

EDOMITE
130 'Êdômîy (6), *Edomite*

English

EDOMITES
130 'Ĕdômîy (12), *Edomite*

EDREI
154 'edre'îy (8), *mighty*

EFFECT
1697 dâbâr (1), *word; matter; thing*
5106 nûw' (1), *to refuse, forbid, dissuade*
5656 'ăbôdâh (1), *work of any kind*
6213 'âsâh (1), *to do or make*
6565 pârar (1), *to break up; to violate, frustrate*
208 akurŏŏ (2), *to invalidate, nullify*
1601 ĕkpiptō (1), *to drop away*
2673 katargĕō (4), *to be, render entirely useless*
2758 kĕnŏō (1), *to make empty*

EFFECTED
6743 tsâlach (1), *to push forward*

EFFECTUAL
1753 ĕnĕrgĕia (2), *efficiency, energy*
1754 ĕnĕrgĕō (2), *to be active, efficient, work*
1756 ĕnĕrgēs (2), *active, operative*

EFFECTUALLY
1754 ĕnĕrgĕō (2), *to be active, efficient, work*

EFFEMINATE
3120 malakŏs (1), *soft; catamite homosexual*

EGG
2495 challâmûwth (1), *(poss.) purslain plant*
5609 ŏōn (1), *egg*

EGGS
1000 bêytsâh (6), *egg*

EGLAH
5698 'Eglâh (2), *heifer*

EGLAIM
97 'Eglayim (1), *double pond*

EGLON
5700 'Eglôwn (13), *vituline*

EGYPT
4713 Mitsrîy (1), *Mitsrite*
4714 Mitsrayim (585), *double border*
125 Aiguptŏs (24), *Ægyptus*

EGYPTIAN
4713 Mitsrîy (18), *Mitsrite*
4714 Mitsrayim (2), *double border*
124 Aiguptiŏs (3), *inhabitant of Ægyptus*

EGYPTIAN'S
4713 Mitsrîy (4), *Mitsrite*

EGYPTIANS
4713 Mitsrîy (7), *Mitsrite*
4714 Mitsrayim (88), *double border*
124 Aiguptiŏs (2), *inhabitant of Ægyptus*

EHI
278 'Êchîy (1), *Echi*

EHUD
261 'Êchûwd (10), *united*

EIGHT
8083 shᵉmôneh (74), *eight; eighth*
3638 ŏktō (6), *eight*

EIGHTEEN
7239+8083 ribbôw (1), *myriad*
8083+6240 shᵉmôneh (18), *eight; eighth*
1176+2532+3638 dĕka (3), *ten*

EIGHTEENTH
8083+6240 shᵉmôneh (11), *eight; eighth*

EIGHTH
8066 shᵉmîynîy (28), *eight, eighth*
8083 shᵉmôneh (4), *eight; eighth*
3590 ŏgdŏŏs (5), *eighth*
3637 ŏktaēmĕrŏs (1), *eighth-day*

EIGHTIETH
8084 shᵉmônîym (1), *eighty; eightieth*

EIGHTY
8084 shᵉmônîym (3), *eighty; eightieth*

EITHER
176 'ôw (7), *or, whether; desire*
376 'îysh (3), *man; male; someone*
518 'îm (1), *whether?; if, although; Oh that!*
1571 gam (1), *also; even; "both...and"*
3588 kîy (1), *for, that because*
8145 shênîy (1), *second; again*
2228 ē (9), *or; than*

EKER
6134 'Êqer (1), *naturalized citizen*

EKRON
6138 'Eqrôwn (22), *eradication*

EKRONITES
6139 'Eqrôwnîy (2), *Ekronite*

EL-BETH-EL
416 'Êl Bêyth-'Êl (1), *God of Bethel*

EL-ELOHE-ISRAEL
415 'Êl 'ĕlôhêy Yisrâ'êl (1), *mighty God of Israel*

EL-PARAN
364 'Êyl Pâ'rân (1), *oak of Paran*

ELADAH
497 'El'âdâh (1), *God has decked*

ELAH
425 'Êlâh (17), *oak*

ELAM
5867 'Êylâm (28), *distant*

ELAMITES
5962 'Almîy (Ch.) (1), *Elamite*
1639 Ĕlamîtēs (1), *distant ones*

ELASAH
501 'El'âsâh (2), *God has made*

ELATH
359 'Êylôwth (5), *grove (of palms)*

ELDAAH
420 'Eldâ'âh (2), *God of knowledge*

ELDAD
419 'Eldâd (2), *God has loved*

ELDER
1419 gâdôwl (8), *great*
2205+3117 zâqên (1), *old, venerated*
7227 rab (1), *great*
3187 mĕizōn (1), *larger, greater*
4245 prĕsbutĕrŏs (7), *elderly; older; presbyter*
4850 sumprĕsbutĕrŏs (1), *co-presbyter*

ELDERS
2205 zâqên (113), *old, venerated*
7868 sîyb (Ch.) (5), *to become aged*
4244 prĕsbutĕriŏn (2), *order of elders*
4245 prĕsbutĕrŏs (58), *elderly; older; presbyter*

ELDEST
1060 bᵉkôwr (5), *firstborn, i.e. oldest son*
1419 gâdôwl (6), *great*
2205 zâqên (1), *old, venerated*
7223 rî'shôwn (1), *first, in place, time or rank*
4245 prĕsbutĕrŏs (1), *elderly; older; presbyter*

ELEAD
496 'El'âd (1), *God has testified*

ELEALEH
500 'El'âlê' (5), *God (is) going up*

ELEASAH
501 'El'âsâh (4), *God has made*

ELEAZAR
499 'El'âzâr (71), *God (is) helper*
1648 Ĕlĕazar (2), *God (is) helper*

ELECT
972 bâchîyr (4), *selected one*
1588 ĕklĕktŏs (13), *selected; chosen*

ELECT'S
1588 ĕklĕktŏs (3), *selected; chosen*

ELECTED
4899 sunĕklĕktŏs (1), *co-elected*

ELECTION
1589 ĕklŏgē (6), *selection, choice*

ELEMENTS
4747 stŏichĕiŏn (4), *elements, elementary*

ELEPH
507 'Eleph (1), *thousand*

ELEVEN
259+6240 'echâd (9), *first*
505+3967 'eleph (3), *thousand*
6249+6240 'ashtêy (6), *eleven; eleventh*
1733 hĕndĕka (6), *eleven*

ELEVENTH
259+6240 'echâd (4), *first*
6249+6240 'ashtêy (12), *eleven; eleventh*
1734 hĕndĕkatŏs (3), *eleventh*

ELHANAN
445 'Elchânân (4), *God (is) gracious*

ELI
5941 'Êlîy (32), *lofty*
2241 ĕli (1), *my God*

ELI'S
5941 'Êlîy (1), *lofty*

ELIAB
446 'Ĕlîy'âb (20), *God of (his) father*

ELIAB'S
446 'Ĕlîy'âb (1), *God of (his) father*

ELIADA
450 'Elyâdâ' (3), *God (is) knowing*

ELIADAH
450 'Elyâdâ' (1), *God (is) knowing*

ELIAH
452 'Êlîyâh (2), *God of Jehovah*

ELIAHBA
455 'Elyachbâ' (2), *God will hide*

ELIAKIM
471 'Elyâqîym (12), *God of raising*
1662 Ĕliakĕim (3), *God of raising*

ELIAM
463 'Êlîy'âm (2), *God of (the) people*

ELIAS
2243 Hēlias (30), *God of Jehovah*

ELIASAPH
460 'Elyâçâph (6), *God (is) gatherer*

ELIASHIB
475 'Elyâshîyb (17), *God will restore*

ELIATHAH
448 'Ĕlîy'âthâh (2), *God of (his) consent*

ELIDAD
449 'Ĕlîydâd (1), *God of (his) love*

ELIEL
447 'Ĕlîy'êl (10), *God of*
(his) *God*

ELIENAI
462 'Ĕlîy'êynay (1),
Elienai

ELIEZER
461 'Ĕlîy'ezer (14), *God
of help*
1663 Ĕlîĕzĕr (1), *God of
help*

ELIHOENAI
454 'Ely⁰hôw'êynay (1),
toward Jehovah (are)
my eyes

ELIHOREPH
456 'Ĕlîychôreph (1),
God of autumn

ELIHU
453 'Ĕlîyhûw (11), *God of
him*

ELIJAH
452 'Ĕlîyâh (69), *God of
Jehovah*

ELIKA
470 'Ĕlîyqâ' (1), *God of
rejection*

ELIM
362 'Êylîm (6), palm-*trees*

ELIMELECH
458 'Ĕlîymelek (4), *God
of* (the) *king*

ELIMELECH'S
458 'Ĕlîymelek (2), *God
of* (the) *king*

ELIOENAI
454 'Ely⁰hôw'êynay (8),
toward Jehovah (are)
my eyes

ELIPHAL
465 'Ĕlîyphâl (1), *God of
judgment*

ELIPHALET
467 'Ĕlîyphelĕṭ (2), *God
of deliverance*

ELIPHAZ
464 'Ĕlîyphaz (15), *God
of gold*

ELIPHELEH
466 'Ĕlîyph⁰lêhûw (2),
God of his distinction

ELIPHELET
467 'Ĕlîyphelĕṭ (6), *God
of deliverance*

ELISABETH
1665 Ĕlisabĕt (8), *God of*
(the) *oath*

ELISABETH'S
1665 Ĕlisabĕt (1), *God of*
(the) *oath*

ELISEUS
1666 Ĕlissaiŏs (1), *Elisha*

ELISHA
477 'Ĕlîyshâ' (58), *Elisha*

ELISHAH
473 'Ĕlîyshâh (3), *Elishah*

ELISHAMA
476 'Ĕlîyshâmâ' (17), *God
of hearing*

ELISHAPHAT
478 'Ĕlîyshâphâṭ (1), *God
of judgment*

ELISHEBA
472 'Ĕlîysheba' (1), *God
of* (the) *oath*

ELISHUA
474 'Ĕlîyshûwa' (2), *God
of supplication* (or *of
riches*)

ELIUD
1664 Ĕliŏud (2), *God of
majesty*

ELIZAPHAN
469 'Ĕlîytsâphân (4), *God
of treasure*

ELIZUR
468 'Ĕlîytsûwr (5), *God of*
(the) *rock*

ELKANAH
511 'Elqânâh (20), *God
has obtained*

ELKOSHITE
512 'Elqôshîy (1),
Elkoshite

ELLASAR
495 'Ellâçâr (2), *Ellasar*

ELMODAM
1678 Ĕlmôdam (1),
Elmodam

ELMS
424 'êlâh (1), *oak*

ELNAAM
493 'Elna'am (1), *God* (is
his) *delight*

ELNATHAN
494 'Elnâthân (7), *God* (is
the) *giver*

ELOI
1682 ĕlōï (1), *my God*

ELON
356 'Êylôwn (7),
oak-grove

ELON-BETH-HANAN
358 'Êylôwn Bêyth
Chânân (1), *oak-grove
of* (the) *house of favor*

ELONITES
440 'Êlôwnîy (1), *Elonite*

ELOQUENT
376+1697 'îysh (1), *man;
male; someone*
995 bîyn (1), *to
understand; discern*
3052 lŏgiŏs (1), *fluent,
i.e. an orator*

ELOTH
359 'Êylôwth (3), *grove*
(of palms)

ELPAAL
508 'Elpa'al (3), *God* (is)
act

ELPALET
467 'Ĕlîyphelĕṭ (1), *God
of deliverance*

ELSE
369 'ayin (1), *there is no,
i.e., not exist, none*
518 'îm (1), *whether?; if,
although; Oh that!*
3588 kîy (3), *for, that
because*

ELTEKEH
514 'Elt⁰qê' (2), *Eltekeh*

ELTEKON
515 'Elt⁰qôn (1), *God* (is)
straight

ELTOLAD
513 'Eltôwlad (2), *God*
(is) *generator*

ELUL
435 'Ĕlûwl (1), *Elul*

ELUZAI
498 'El'ûwzay (1), *God*
(is) *defensive*

ELYMAS
1681 Ĕlumas (1), *Elymas*

ELZABAD
443 'Elzâbâd (2), *God
has bestowed*

ELZAPHAN
469 'Ĕlîytsâphân (2), *God
of treasure*

EMBALM
2590 chânaṭ (1), *to
embalm; to ripen*

EMBALMED
2590 chânaṭ (3), *to
embalm; to ripen*

EMBOLDENED
3618 ŏikŏdŏmĕō (1), *to
construct, edify*

EMBOLDENETH
4834 mârats (1), *to be
pungent or vehement*

EMBRACE
2263 châbaq (8), *to clasp
the hands, embrace*

EMBRACED
2263 châbaq (3), *to clasp
the hands, embrace*
782 aspazŏmai (2), *to
salute, welcome*

EMBRACING
2263 châbaq (1), *to clasp
the hands, embrace*
4843 sumpĕrilambanō
(1), *to embrace*

EMBROIDER
7660 shâbats (1), *to
interweave*

EMBROIDERER
7551 râqam (2),
variegation; embroider

EMERALD
5306 nôphek (3), (poss.)
garnet
4664 smaragdinŏs (1), *of
emerald*
4665 smaragdŏs (1),
green emerald

EMERALDS
5306 nôphek (1), (poss.)
garnet

EMERODS
2914 ṭ⁰chôr (2), *piles,
tumor*
6076 'ôphel (6), *tumor;
fortress*

EMIMS
368 'Êymîym (3), *terrors*

EMINENT
1354 gab (3), *mounded
or rounded: top or rim*
8524 tâlal (1), *to elevate*

EMMANUEL
1694 Ĕmmanŏuēl (1),
God with us

EMMAUS
1695 Ĕmmaŏus (1),
Emmaüs

EMMOR
1697 Ĕmmŏr (1), male
donkey or *ass*

EMPIRE
4438 malkûwth (1), *rule;
dominion*

EMPLOY
935+6440 bôw' (1), *to go
or come*

EMPLOYED
5921 'al (1), *above, over,
upon, or against*
5975 'âmad (1), *to stand*

EMPTIED
1238 bâqaq (2), *to
depopulate, ruin*
1809 dâlal (1), *to
slacken, dangle*
6168 'ârâh (2), *to be,
make bare; to empty*
7324 rûwq (2), *to pour
out, i.e. empty*
7386 rêyq (1), *empty;
worthless*

EMPTIERS
1238 bâqaq (1), *to
depopulate, ruin*

EMPTINESS
922 bôhûw (1), *ruin,
desolation*

EMPTY
950 bûwqâh (1), *empty,
pillaged*
1238 bâqaq (3), *to
depopulate, ruin*
6437 pânâh (1), *to turn,
to face*
6485 pâqad (3), *to visit,
care for, count*
7324 rûwq (5), *to pour
out, i.e. empty*
7385 rîyq (5), *emptiness;
worthless thing; in vain*
7386 rêyq (2), *empty;
worthless*
7387 rêyqâm (12),
emptily; ineffectually
8414 tôhûw (1), *waste,
desolation, formless*
2756 kĕnŏs (4), *empty;
vain; useless*
4980 schŏlazō (1), *to
take a holiday*

EMULATION
3863 parazēlŏō (1), *to
excite to rivalry*

EMULATIONS
2205 zêlŏs (1), zeal,
ardor; jealousy, malice

EN-DOR
5874 'Êyn-Dô'r (3),
fountain of dwelling

EN-EGLAIM
5882 'Êyn 'Eglayim (1),
fountain of two calves

EN-GANNIM
5873 'Êyn Gannîym (3),
fountain of gardens

EN-GEDI
5872 'Êyn Gedîy (6),
fountain of a kid

EN-HADDAH
5876 'Êyn Chaddâh (1),
fountain of sharpness

EN-HAKKORE
5875 'Êyn haq-Qôwrê'
(1), fountain of One
calling

EN-HAZOR
5877 'Êyn Châtsôwr (1),
fountain of a village

EN-MISHPAT
5880 'Êyn Mishpâṭ (1),
fountain of judgment

EN-RIMMON
5884 'Êyn Rimmôwn (1),
fountain of a
pomegranate

EN-ROGEL
5883 'Êyn Rôgêl (4),
fountain of a traveller

EN-SHEMESH
5885 'Êyn Shemesh (2),
fountain of (the) sun

EN-TAPPUAH
5887 'Êyn Tappûwach
(1), fountain of an
apple tree

ENABLED
1743 ĕndunamŏō (1), to
empower, strengthen

ENAM
5879 'Êynayim (1),
double fountain

ENAN
5881 'Êynân (5), having
eyes

ENCAMP
2583 chânâh (11), to
encamp for abode or
siege

ENCAMPED
2583 chânâh (33), to
encamp

ENCAMPETH
2583 chânâh (2), to
encamp

ENCAMPING
2583 chânâh (1), to
encamp

ENCHANTER
5172 nâchash (1), to
prognosticate

ENCHANTERS
6049 'ânan (1), to cover,
becloud; to act covertly

ENCHANTMENT
3908 lachash (1),
incantation; amulet
5172 nâchash (2), to
prognosticate

ENCHANTMENTS
2267 cheber (2), society,
group; magic spell
3858 lahaṭ (1), blaze;
magic
3909 lâṭ (3), incantation;
secrecy; covertly
5172 nâchash (4), to
prognosticate

ENCOUNTERED
4820 sumballō (1), to
consider; to aid; to join

ENCOURAGE
2388 châzaq (4), to be
strong; courageousd,
restrain, conquer

ENCOURAGED
2388 châzaq (5), to be
strong; courageous

END
319 'achărîyth (21),
future; posterity
657 'epheç (1), end; no
further
1104 bâla' (1), to
swallow; to destroy
1584 gâmar (1), to end;
to complete; to fail
1700 dibrâh (1), reason,
suit or style; because
2583 chânâh (1), to
encamp
2856 châtham (1), to
close up; to affix a seal
3318 yâtsâ' (1), to go,
bring out
3615 kâlâh (56), to
complete, prepare
4390 mâlê' (1), to fill; be
full
4616 ma'an (8), in order
that
5239 nâlâh (1), to
complete, attain
5331 netsach (2),
splendor; lasting
5486 çûwph (1), to
terminate
5490 çôwph (3),
termination; end
5491 çôwph (Ch.) (5), end
5704+5769+5703 'ad (1),
during; while; until
6118 'êqeb (2), on
account of
6285 pê'âh (1), direction;
region; extremity
6310 peh (3), mouth;
opening
7078 qenets (1),
perversion
7093 qêts (51), extremity;
after
7097 qâtseh (48),
extremity
7098 qâtsâh (4),
termination; fringe
7117 qᵉtsâth (3),
termination; portion
7118 qᵉtsâth (Ch.) (2),
termination; portion

7999 shâlam (2), to be
safe; complete
8503 taklîyth (2),
extremity
8537 tôm (1),
completeness
8552 tâmam (2), to
complete, finish
8622 tᵉqûwphâh (2),
revolution, course
165+3588+165 aiōn (1),
perpetuity, ever; world
206 akrŏn (1), extremity:
end, top
1519 eis (4), to or into
1545 ĕkbasis (1), exit,
way out
2078 ĕschatŏs (1),
farthest, final
3796 ŏpsĕ (1), late in the
day
4009 pĕras (1), extremity,
end, limit
4930 suntĕlĕia (6), entire
completion
5049 tĕlĕiŏs (1),
completely
5055 tĕlĕō (1), to end, i.e.
complete, conclude
5056 tĕlŏs (34),
conclusion

ENDAMAGE
5142 nᵉzaq (Ch.) (1), to
suffer, inflict loss

ENDANGER
2325 chûwb (1), to tie, to
owe; to forfeit

ENDANGERED
5533 çâkan (1), to
damage; to grow

ENDEAVOUR
4704 spŏudazō (1), to
make effort

ENDEAVOURED
2212 zētĕō (1), to seek
4704 spŏudazō (1), to
make effort

ENDEAVOURING
4704 spŏudazō (1), to
make effort

ENDEAVOURS
4611 ma'ălâl (1), act,
deed

ENDED
3615 kâlâh (7), to cease,
be finished, perish
7999 shâlam (2), to be
safe; be complete
8552 tâmam (5), to
complete, finish
1096 ginŏmai (1), to be,
become
4137 plērŏō (2), to fill,
make complete
4931 suntĕlĕō (4), to
complete entirely

ENDETH
2308 châdal (1), to desist,
stop; be fat

ENDING
5056 tĕlŏs (1), conclusion
of an act or state

ENDLESS
179 akatalutŏs (1),
permanent

562 apĕrantŏs (1),
without a finish

ENDOW
4117 mâhar (1), to wed a
wife by bargaining

ENDS
657 'epheç (13), end; no
further
1383 gablûth (2), twisted
chain or lace
3671 kânâph (2), edge or
extremity; wing
4020 migbâlâh (1),
border on garb
7097 qâtseh (7), extremity
7098 qâtsâh (17),
termination; fringe
7099 qetsev (4), limit,
borders
7218 rô'sh (2), head
2078 ĕschatŏs (1),
farthest, final
4009 pĕras (1), extremity,
end, limit
5056 tĕlŏs (1), conclusion
of an act or state

ENDUED
2064 zâbad (1), to confer,
bestow a gift
3045 yâda' (2), to know
1746 ĕnduō (1), to dress
1990 ĕpistēmōn (1),
intelligent, learned

ENDURE
1961 hâyâh (3), to exist,
i.e. be or become
3201 yâkôl (2), to be able
3427 yâshab (2), to dwell,
to remain; to settle
3885 lûwn (1), to be
obstinate
5975 'âmad (3), to stand
6440 pânîym (1), face;
front
6965 qûwm (1), to rise
7272 regel (1), foot; step
430 anĕchŏmai (2), put
up with, endure
2076 ĕsti (1), he (she or
it) is; they are
2553 kakŏpathĕō (2), to
undergo hardship
5278 hupŏmĕnō (5), to
undergo (trials)
5297 hupŏphĕrō (1), to
undergo hardship
5342 phĕrō (1), to bear or
carry

ENDURED
1961 hâyâh (1), to exist,
i.e. be or become
2594 kartĕrĕō (1), to be
steadfast or patient
3114 makrŏthumĕō (1),
to be forbearing, patient
5278 hupŏmĕnō (3), to
undergo (trials)
5297 hupŏphĕrō (1), to
undergo hardship
5342 phĕrō (1), to bear or
carry

ENDURETH
1097 bᵉlîy (1), without,
not yet; lacking;
5975 'âmad (4), to stand
3306 mĕnō (2), to stay,
remain

5278 hupŏmĕnō (3), to
undergo (trials)

ENDURING
5975 'âmad (1), to *stand*
3306 mĕnō (1), to *stay,*
remain
5281 hupŏmŏnē (1),
endurance, constancy

ENEMIES
341 'ôyêb (199),
adversary, enemy
6145 'âr (1), *foe*
6146 'âr (Ch.) (1), *foe*
6862 tsar (26), *trouble;*
opponent
6887 tsârar (9), to *cramp*
6965 qûwm (1), to *rise*
7790 shûwr (1), *foe as*
lying in wait
8130 sânê' (3), to *hate*
8324 shârar (5), *opponent*
2190 ĕchthrŏs (19),
adversary

ENEMIES'
341 'ôyêb (3), *adversary,*
enemy

ENEMY
340 'âyab (1), to *be*
hostile, be an enemy
341 'ôyêb (78),
adversary, enemy
6145 'âr (1), *foe*
6862 tsar (9), *trouble;*
opponent
6887 tsârar (5), to *cramp*
8130 sânê' (2), to *hate*
2190 ĕchthrŏs (11),
adversary

ENEMY'S
341 'ôyêb (1), *adversary,*
enemy
6862 tsar (2), *trouble;*
opponent

ENFLAMING
2552 châmam (1), to *be*
hot; to be in a rage

ENGAGED
6148 'ârab (1), to *intermix*

ENGINES
2810 chishshâbôwn (1),
machination, scheme
4239 mᵉchîy (1), *stroke of*
a battering-ram

ENGRAFTED
1721 ĕmphutŏs (1),
implanted

ENGRAVE
6605 pâthach (2), to *open*
wide; to plow, carve

ENGRAVEN
1795 ĕntupŏō (1), to
engrave, carve

ENGRAVER
2796 chârâsh (3), skilled
fabricator or worker

ENGRAVINGS
6603 pittûwach (5),
sculpture; engraving

ENJOIN
2004 ĕpitassō (1), to
order, command

ENJOINED
6485 pâqad (1), to *visit,*
care for, count

6965 qûwm (1), to *rise*
1781 ĕntĕllŏmai (1), to
enjoin, give orders

ENJOY
1086 bâlâh (1), to *wear*
out; consume, spend
1961 hâyâh (1), to *exist,*
i.e. be or become
3423 yârash (2), to
inherit; to impoverish
7200 râ'âh (4), to *see*
7521 râtsâh (3), to *be*
pleased with; to satisfy
619 apŏlausis (1), full
enjoyment, pleasure
2192+619 ĕchō (1), to
have; hold; keep
5177 tugchanō (1), to
take part in; to obtain

ENJOYED
7521 râtsâh (1), to *be*
pleased with; to satisfy

ENLARGE
6601 pâthâh (1), to *be,*
make simple; to delude
7235 râbâh (1), to
increase
7337 râchab (7), to
broaden
3170 mĕgalunō (1), to
increase or extol

ENLARGED
7337 râchab (8), to
broaden
3170 mĕgalunō (1), to
increase or extol
4115 platunō (2), to
widen

ENLARGEMENT
7305 revach (1), *room;*
deliverance

ENLARGETH
7337 râchab (2), to
broaden
7849 shâtach (1), to
expand

ENLARGING
7337 râchab (1), to
broaden

ENLIGHTEN
5050 nâgahh (1), to
illuminate

ENLIGHTENED
215 'ôwr (4), to *be*
luminous
5461 phōtizō (2), to *shine*
or to brighten up

ENLIGHTENING
215 'ôwr (1), to *be*
luminous

ENMITY
342 'êybâh (2), *hostility*
2189 ĕchthra (5),
hostility; opposition

ENOCH
2585 Chănôwk (9),
initiated
1802 Ēnōch (3), *initiated*

ENOS
583 'Ēnôwsh (6), *man;*
person, human
1800 Ēnōs (1), *man*

ENOSH
583 'Ēnôwsh (1), *man;*
person, human

ENOUGH
1767 day (6), *enough,*
sufficient
1952 hôwn (2), *wealth*
3027 yâd (1), *hand; power*
3605 kôl (1), *all, any or*
every
4672 mâtsâ' (1), to *find*
or acquire; to occur
7227 rab (7), *great*
7654 sob'âh (2), *satiety*
566 apĕchĕi (1), *it is*
sufficient
713 arkĕtŏs (1),
satisfactory, enough
714 arkĕō (1), to *avail; be*
satisfactory
2425 hikanŏs (1), *ample;*
fit
2880 kŏrĕnnumi (1), to
cram, i.e. glut or sate
4052 pĕrissĕuō (1), to
superabound

ENQUIRE
1158 bâ'âh (2), to *ask; be*
bulging, swelling
1239 bâqar (2), to
inspect, admire, care
for, consider
1240 bᵉqar (Ch.) (1), to
inspect, admire, care
for, consider
1875 dârash (32), to
pursue or search; to
seek or ask; to worship
7592 shâ'al (7), to *ask*
1231 diaginōskō (1),
ascertain exactly
1833 ĕxĕtazō (1), to
ascertain or interrogate
1934 ĕpizĕtĕō (1), to
search (inquire) for
2212 zĕtĕō (2), to *seek*
4441 punthanŏmai (1), to
ask for information
4802 suzĕtĕō (1), to
discuss, controvert

ENQUIRED
1245 bâqash (2), to
search; to strive after
1875 dârash (10), to
pursue or search
7592 shâ'al (15), to *ask*
7836 shâchar (1), to
search for
198 akribŏō (2), to
ascertain, find out
1567 ĕkzĕtĕō (1), to *seek*
4441 punthanŏmai (1), to
ask for information

ENQUIREST
1245 bâqash (1), to
search; to strive after

ENQUIRY
1239 bâqar (1), to
inspect, admire, care
1331 diĕrōtaō (1), to
question throughout

ENRICH
6238 'âshar (2), to *grow,*
make rich

ENRICHED
4148 plŏutizō (2), to
make wealthy

ENRICHEST
6238 'âshar (1), to *grow,*
make rich

ENSAMPLE
5179 tupŏs (1), *shape or*
resemblance; "type"
5262 hupŏdĕigma (1),
exhibit, specimen

ENSAMPLES
5179 tupŏs (3), *shape or*
resemblance; "type"

ENSIGN
226 'ôwth (1), *signal, sign*
5251 nêç (6), *flag; signal*
5264 nâçaç (1), to *gleam;*
to flutter a flag

ENSIGNS
226 'ôwth (1), *signal, sign*

ENSNARED
4170 môwqêsh (1), *noose*
for catching animals

ENSUE
1377 diōkō (1), to *pursue;*
to persecute

ENTANGLE
3802 pagidĕuō (1), to
ensnare, entrap

ENTANGLED
943 bûwk (1), to *be*
confused
1707 ĕmplĕkō (1), to
involve with
1758 ĕnĕchō (1), to *keep*
a grudge

ENTANGLETH
1707 ĕmplĕkō (1), to
involve with

ENTER
935 bôw' (81), to *go or*
come
1980 hâlak (1), to *walk;*
live a certain way
5674 'âbar (1), to *cross*
over; to transition
1525 ĕisĕrchŏmai (63), to
enter
1529 ĕisŏdŏs (1),
entrance
1531 ĕispŏrĕuŏmai (1), to
enter

ENTERED
935 bôw' (38), to *go or*
come
305 anabainō (2), to *go*
up, rise
1524 ĕisĕimi (1), to *enter*
1525 ĕisĕrchŏmai (53), to
enter
1531 ĕispŏrĕuŏmai (3), to
enter
1684 ĕmbainō (7), to
embark; to reach
2064 ĕrchŏmai (2), to *go*
or come
3922 parĕisĕrchŏmai (1),
to supervene

ENTERETH
935 bôw' (9), to *go or*
come
5181 nâchath (1), to *sink,*
descend; to press down
1531 ĕispŏrĕuŏmai (5), to
enter
1535 ĕitĕ (4), *if too*

English

ENTERING
935 bôw' (15), to go, come
3996 mâbôw' (3), entrance; sunset; west
6607 pethach (17), opening; entrance way
1525 ĕisĕrchŏmai (4), to enter
1529 ĕisŏdŏs (1), entrance
1531 ĕispŏrĕuŏmai (4), to enter
1684 ĕmbainō (1), to embark; to reach
1910 ĕpibainō (1), to mount, arrive

ENTERPRISE
8454 tûwshîyâh (1), ability, undertaking

ENTERTAIN
5381 philŏnĕxia (1), hospitableness

ENTERTAINED
3579 xĕnizō (1), to be a host; to be a guest

ENTICE
5496 çûwth (1), tɔ stimulate; to seduce
6601 pâthâh (7), to be, make simple; to delude

ENTICED
6601 pâthâh (2), to be, make simple; to delude
1185 dĕlĕazō (1), to delude, seduce

ENTICETH
6601 pâthâh (1), to be, make simple; to delude

ENTICING
3981 pĕithŏs (1), persuasive
4086 pithanŏlŏgia (1), persuasive language

ENTIRE
3648 hŏlŏklĕrŏs (1), entirely sound in body

ENTRANCE
935 bôw' (2), to go or come
2978 yeʾîthôwn (1), entry
3996 mâbôw' (3), entrance; sunset; west
6607 pethach (2), opening; entrance way
6608 pêthach (1), opening
1529 ĕisŏdŏs (2), entrance

ENTRANCES
6607 pethach (1), opening; entrance way

ENTREAT
6293 pâga' (1), to impinge
2559 kakŏō (1), to injure; to oppress; to embitter

ENTREATED
818 atimazō (1), to maltreat, dishonor
2559 kakŏō (1), to injure; to oppress; to embitter
5195 hubrizō (1), to exercise violence
5530 chraŏmai (1), to employ or to act toward

ENTRIES
6607 pethach (1), opening; entrance way

ENTRY
872 beʾâh (1), entrance
3996 mâbôw' (6), entrance; sunset; west
6310 peh (1), mouth; opening
6607 pethach (7), opening; entrance way

ENVIED
7065 qânâ' (5), to be, make jealous, envious
7068 qin'âh (1), jealousy or envy

ENVIES
5355 phthŏnŏs (1), spiteful jealousy, envy

ENVIEST
7065 qânâ' (1), to be, make jealous, envious

ENVIETH
2206 zēlŏō (1), to have warmth of feeling for

ENVIOUS
7065 qânâ' (4), to be, make jealous, envious

ENVIRON
5437 çâbab (1), to surround

ENVY
7065 qânâ' (3), to be, make zealous, jealous or envious
7068 qin'âh (7), jealousy or envy
2205 zēlŏs (1), zeal, ardor; jealousy; malice
2206 zēlŏō (2), to have warmth of feeling for
5355 phthŏnŏs (7), spiteful jealousy, envy

ENVYING
2205 zēlŏs (4), zeal, ardor; jealousy; malice
5354 phthŏnĕō (1), to be jealous of

ENVYINGS
2205 zēlŏs (1), zeal, ardor; jealousy; malice
5355 phthŏnŏs (1), spiteful jealousy, envy

EPAENETUS
1866 Ĕpainĕtŏs (1), praised

EPAPHRAS
1889 Ĕpaphras (3), devoted to Venus

EPAPHRODITUS
1891 Ĕpaphrŏditŏs (3), devoted to Venus

EPHAH
374 'êyphâh (34), dry grain measure
5891 'Êyphâh (5), obscurity

EPHAI
5778 'Ôwphay (1), birdlike

EPHER
6081 'Êpher (4), gazelle

EPHES-DAMMIM
658 'Epheç Dammîym (1), boundary of blood

EPHESIAN
2180 Ĕphĕsiŏs (1), Ephesian

EPHESIANS
2180 Ĕphĕsiŏs (5), Ephesian

EPHESUS
2181 Ĕphĕsŏs (17), Ephesus

EPHLAL
654 'Ephlâl (2), judge

EPHOD
641 'Êphôd (1), Ephod
642 'êphuddâh (2), plating
646 'êphôwd (49), ephod

EPHPHATHA
2188 ĕphphatha (1), be opened!

EPHRAIM
669 'Ephrayim (171), double fruit
2187 Ĕphraïm (1), double fruit

EPHRAIM'S
669 'Ephrayim (4), double fruit

EPHRAIMITE
673 'Ephrâthîy (1), Ephrathite or Ephraimite

EPHRAIMITES
669 'Ephrayim (5), double fruit

EPHRAIN
6085 'Ephrôwn (1), fawn-like

EPHRATAH
672 'Ephrâth (5), fruitfulness

EPHRATH
672 'Ephrâth (5), fruitfulness

EPHRATHITE
673 'Ephrâthîy (3), Ephrathite or Ephraimite

EPHRATHITES
673 'Ephrâthîy (1), Ephrathite or Ephraimite

EPHRON
6085 'Ephrôwn (13), fawn-like

EPICUREANS
1946 Ĕpikŏurĕiŏs (1), servant

EPISTLE
1992 ĕpistŏlē (13), written message

EPISTLES
1992 ĕpistŏlē (2), written message

EQUAL
1809 dâlal (1), to slacken, dangle
4339 mêyshâr (1), straightness; rectitude

6186 'ârak (2), to set in a row, i.e. arrange
6187 'êrek (1), pile, equipment, estimate
7737 shâvâh (3), to level, i.e. equalize
8505 tâkan (7), to balance, i.e. measure
2465 isaggĕlŏs (1), angelic, like an angel
2470 isŏs (4), similar
2471 isŏtēs (1), likeness; fairness

EQUALITY
2471 isŏtēs (2), likeness; fairness

EQUALLY
7947 shâlab (1), to make equidistant

EQUALS
4915 sunēlikiōtēs (1), alike, contemporary

EQUITY
3476 yôsher (1), right
3477 yâshâr (1), straight
3788 kishrôwn (1), success; advantage
4334 mîyshôwr (2), plain; justice
4339 mêyshâr (4), straightness; rectitude
5229 nekôchâh (1), integrity; truth

ER
6147 'Êr (10), watchful
2262 Ēr (1), watchful

ERAN
6197 'Êrân (1), watchful

ERANITES
6198 'Êrânîy (1), Eranite

ERASTUS
2037 Ĕrastŏs (3), beloved

ERE
2962 țerem (4), not yet or before
3808 lô' (4), no, not
4250 prin (1), prior, sooner, before

ERECH
751 'Erek (1), length

ERECTED
5324 nâtsab (1), to station

ERI
6179 'Êrîy (2), watchful

ERITES
6180 'Êrîy (1), Erite

ERR
7686 shâgâh (4), to stray, wander; to transgress
8582 tâ'âh (14), to vacillate, i.e. stray
4105 planaō (6), to roam, wander; to deceive

ERRAND
1697 dâbâr (3), word; matter; thing

ERRED
7683 shâgag (5), to stray; to sin
7686 shâgâh (2), to stray, wander; to transgress
8582 tâ'âh (2), to vacillate, i.e. stray

635 apŏplanaō (1), to
lead astray; to *wander*
795 astŏchĕō (2), *deviate*
or *wander* from truth

ERRETH
7686 shâgâh (1), to *stray,
wander;* to *transgress*
8582 tâ'âh (1), to
vacillate, i.e. *stray*

ERROR
4879 mᵉshûwgâh (1),
mistake
7684 shᵉgâgâh (2),
mistake
7944 shal (1), *fault*
7960 shâlûw (Ch.) (1),
fault, error
8432 tâvek (1), *center,
middle*
4106 planē (7),
fraudulence; straying

ERRORS
7691 shᵉgîy'âh (1), moral
mistake
8595 ta'tûa' (2), *fraud*
51 agnŏēma (1), *sin
committed in ignorance*

ESAIAS
2268 Hēsaïas (21),
Jehovah has saved

ESAR-HADDON
634 'Êçar-Chaddôwn (3),
Esar-chaddon

ESAU
6215 'Êsâv (84), *rough*
2269 Ēsau (3), *rough*

ESAU'S
6215 'Êsâv (12), *rough*

ESCAPE
3318 yâtsâ' (1), to *go,
bring out*
4422 mâlaṭ (22), to
escape; be delivered
4498+6 mânôwç (1),
fleeing; place of refuge
4655 miphlâṭ (1), *escape,
shelter*
5337 nâtsal (1), to
deliver; to be snatched
5674 'âbar (1), to *cross
over;* to *transition*
6403 pâlaṭ (2), to *slip out,*
i.e. *escape;* to *deliver*
6405 pallêṭ (1), *escape*
6412 pâlîyṭ (12), *refugee*
6413 pᵉlêyṭâh (9),
escaped portion
1309 diaphĕugō (1), to
escape, flee
1545 ĕkbasis (1), *exit,
way out*
1628 ĕkphĕugō (4), to
flee out, escape
5343 phĕugō (1), to *run
away;* to *vanish*
5343+575 phĕugō (1), to
run away; to *vanish*

ESCAPED
3318 yâtsâ' (1), to *go,
bring out*
4422 mâlaṭ (25), to
escape; be delivered
5337 nâtsal (1), to
deliver; to *be snatched*
6412 pâlîyṭ (8), *refugee*

6413 pᵉlêyṭâh (11),
escaped portion
7611 shᵉ'êrîyth (1),
remainder or *residual*
668 apŏphĕugō (3), to
escape from
1295 diasōzō (3), to *cure,
preserve, rescue*
1628 ĕkphĕugō (1), to
flee out, escape
1831 ĕxĕrchŏmai (1), to
issue; to *leave*
5343 phĕugō (2), to *run
away;* to *vanish*

ESCAPETH
4422 mâlaṭ (3), to *escape;*
be delivered; be smooth
6412 pâlîyṭ (2), *refugee*
6413 pᵉlêyṭâh (1),
escaped portion

ESCAPING
6413 pᵉlêyṭâh (1),
escaped portion

ESCHEW
1578 ĕkklinō (1), to *shun;*
to *decline*

ESCHEWED
5493 çûwr (1), to *turn off*

ESCHEWETH
5493 çûwr (2), to *turn off*

ESEK
6230 'Êseq (1), *strife*

ESH-BAAL
792 'Eshba'al (2), *man of
Baal*

ESHBAN
790 'Eshbân (2), *vigorous*

ESHCOL
812 'Eshkôl (6), *bunch of
grapes*

ESHEAN
824 'Esh'ân (1), *support*

ESHEK
6232 'Êsheq (1),
oppression

ESHKALONITES
832 'Eshqᵉlôwnîy (1),
Ashkelonite

ESHTAOL
847 'Eshtâ'ôl (7), *entreaty*

ESHTAULITES
848 'Eshtâ'ûlîy (1),
Eshtaolite

ESHTEMOA
851 'Eshtᵉmôa' (5),
Eshtemoa or *Eshtemoh*

ESHTEMOH
851 'Eshtᵉmôa' (1),
Eshtemoa or *Eshtemoh*

ESHTON
850 'Eshtôwn (2), *restful*

ESLI
2069 Ēsli (1), *Esli*

ESPECIALLY
3966 mᵉ'ôd (1), *very,
utterly*
3122 malista (4), *in the
greatest degree*

ESPIED
7200 râ'âh (1), to *see*
8446 tûwr (1), to *wander,
meander*

ESPOUSALS
2861 chăthunnâh (1),
wedding
3623 kᵉlûwlâh (1),
bridehood

ESPOUSED
781 'âras (1), to *engage*
for matrimony, betroth
718 harmŏzō (1), to
betroth for marriage
3423 mnēstĕuō (3), to
betroth, be engaged

ESPY
6822 tsâphâh (1), to *peer;*
to *observe, await*
7270 râgal (1), to
reconnoiter; to *slander*

ESROM
2074 Ēsrōm (3),
court-yard

ESTABLISH
3322 yâtsag (1), to *place*
permanently
3427 yâshab (1), to *dwell,*
to *remain;* to *settle*
3559 kûwn (14), to *set up:
establish, fix, prepare*
5324 nâtsab (1), to *station*
5582 çâ'ad (1), to *support*
5975 'âmad (3), to *stand*
6965 qûwm (17), to *rise*
6966 qûwm (Ch.) (2), to
rise
2476 histēmi (3), to
stand, establish
4741 stērizō (1), to *turn
resolutely;* to *confirm*

ESTABLISHED
539 'âman (7), to *be firm,
faithful, true;* to *trust*
553 'âmats (1), to *be
strong; be courageous*
2388 châzaq (1), to
fasten upon; to *seize*
3245 yâçad (2), *settle,
establish a foundation*
3559 kûwn (44), to *set up:
establish, fix, prepare*
5564 çâmak (1), to *lean*
upon; *take hold* of
5975 'âmad (1), to *stand*
6965 qûwm (9), to *rise*
8627 tᵉqan (Ch.) (1), to
straighten up, *confirm*
950 bĕbaiŏō (1), to
stabilitate, keep strong
2476 histēmi (2), to
stand, establish
3549 nŏmŏthĕtĕō (1), to
be founded, enacted
4732 stĕrĕŏō (1), to *be,
become strong*
4741 stērizō (2), to *turn
resolutely;* to *confirm*

ESTABLISHETH
5975 'âmad (1), to *stand*
6965 qûwm (1), to *rise*
6966 qûwm (Ch.) (1), to
rise

ESTABLISHMENT
571 'emeth (1), *certainty,
truth, trustworthiness*

ESTATE
1700 dibrâh (1), *reason,
suit* or *style; because*

3653 kên (5), *pedestal* or
station of a basin
8448 tôwr (1), *manner*
3588+4012 hŏ (1), *"the,"*
i.e. the definite article

ESTEEM
2803 châshab (1), to *plot;*
to *think, regard*
6186 'ârak (1), to set in a
row, i.e. *arrange,*
2233 hēgĕŏmai (2), to
deem, i.e. *consider*

ESTEEMED
2803 châshab (3), to *plot;*
to *think, regard*
5034 nâbêl (1), to *wilt;* to
fall away; to *be foolish*
6845 tsâphan (1), to
deny; to *protect;* to *lurk*
7043 qâlal (2), to *be,
make light*
1848 ĕxŏuthĕnĕō (1), to
treat with contempt

ESTEEMETH
2803 châshab (1), to *plot;*
to *think, regard*
2919 krinō (2), to *decide;*
to *try, condemn, punish*
3049 lŏgizŏmai (1), to
credit; to *think, regard*

ESTEEMING
2233 hēgĕŏmai (1), to
lead; to *deem, consider*

ESTHER
635 'Eçtêr (52), *Esther*

ESTHER'S
635 'Eçtêr (3), *Esther*

ESTIMATE
6186 'ârak (2), to set in a
row, i.e. *arrange,*

ESTIMATION
6187 'êrek (23), *pile,
equipment, estimate*

ESTIMATIONS
6187 'êrek (1), *pile,
equipment, estimate*

ESTRANGED
2114 zûwr (4), to *be
foreign, strange*
5234 nâkar (1), to *treat
as a foreigner*

ETAM
5862 'Êyṭâm (5),
hawk-ground

ETERNAL
5769 'ôwlâm (1), *eternity;
ancient; always*
6924 qedem (1), *eastern;
antiquity; before*
126 aïdiŏs (1),
everduring, eternal
165 aiōn (2), *perpetuity,
ever; world*
166 aiōniŏs (42),
perpetual, long ago

ETERNITY
5703 'ad (1), *perpetuity;
ancient*

ETHAM
864 'Êthâm (4), *Etham*

ETHAN
387 'Êythân (8),
permanent

English

ETHANIM
388 Êythânîym (1), *permanent* brooks

ETHBAAL
856 'Ethba'al (1), *with Baal*

ETHER
6281 'Ether (2), *abundance*

ETHIOPIA
3568 Kûwsh (19), *Cush*
128 Aithiŏps (1), *inhabitant of Æthiop*

ETHIOPIAN
3569 Kûwshîy (8), *Cushite*

ETHIOPIANS
3569 Kûwshîy (12), *Cushite*
128 Aithiŏps (1), *inhabitant of Æthiop*

ETHNAN
869 'Ethnan (1), *gift price of harlotry*

ETHNI
867 'Ethnîy (1), *munificence, lavishness*

EUBULUS
2103 Êubŏulŏs (1), *good-willer*

EUNICE
2131 Êunikē (1), *victorious*

EUNUCH
5631 çârîyç (2), *eunuch; official of state*
2135 ĕunŏuchŏs (5), *castrated; impotent*

EUNUCHS
5631 çârîyç (15), *eunuch; official of state*
2134 ĕunŏuchizō (3), *to castrate*
2135 ĕunŏuchŏs (2), *castrated; impotent*

EUODIAS
2136 Êuŏdia (1), *fine travelling*

EUPHRATES
6578 Pᵉrâth (19), *rushing*
2166 Êuphratēs (2), *Euphrates*

EUROCLYDON
2148 Êurŏkludōn (1), *wind from the east*

EUTYCHUS
2161 Êutuchŏs (1), *fortunate*

EVANGELIST
2099 ĕuaggĕlistēs (2), *preacher of the gospel*

EVANGELISTS
2099 ĕuaggĕlistēs (1), *preacher of the gospel*

EVE
2332 Chavvâh (2), *life-giver*
2096 Êua (2), *life-giver*

EVEN
227 'âz (1), *at that time or place; therefore*
389 'ak (2), *surely; only, however*

518 'îm (1), *whether?; if, although; Oh that!*
637 'aph (7), *also or yea; though*
853 'êth (25), *not translated*
1571 gam (50), *also; even; yea; though*
1887 hê' (1), *Lo!, Look!*
3588 kîy (7), *for, that because*
3602 kâkâh (5), *just so*
3651 kên (3), *just; right, correct*
4334 mîyshôwr (1), *plain; justice*
5704 'ad (3), *as far (long) as; during; while; until*
5705 'ad (Ch.) (2), *as far (long) as; during*
6153 'ereb (71), *dusk*
6664 tsedeq (1), *right*
7535 raq (1), *merely; although*
737 arti (1), just *now; at once*
891 achri (1), *until or up to*
1063 gar (1), *for, indeed, but, because*
1161 dĕ (3), *but, yet; and then*
2089 ĕti (1), *yet, still*
2193 hĕōs (2), *until*
2504 kagō (7), *and also, even*
2509 kathapĕr (2), *exactly as*
2531 kathōs (24), *just or inasmuch as, that*
2532 kai (108), *and; or; even; also*
2548 kakĕinŏs (2), *likewise that or those*
3303 mĕn (1), *not translated*
3483 nai (4), *yes*
3676 hŏmōs (1), *at the same* time, *yet still*
3761 ŏudĕ (3), *neither, nor, not even*
3779 hŏutō (3), *in this way; likewise*
3796 ŏpsĕ (2), *late* in the day
3798 ŏpsiŏs (8), *late; early eve; later eve*
5037 tĕ (1), *both or also*
5613 hōs (5), *which, how,* i.e. *in that manner*
5615 hōsautōs (1), *in the same way*
5618 hōspĕr (2), *exactly like*

EVENING
6150 'ârab (2), *to grow dusky at sundown*
6153 'ereb (49), *dusk*
2073 hĕspĕra (2), *evening*
3798 ŏpsiŏs (5), *late; early eve; later eve*

EVENINGS
6160 'ărâbâh (1), *desert, wasteland*

EVENINGTIDE
6256+6153 'êth (2), *time*

EVENT
4745 miqreh (3), *accident or fortune*

EVENTIDE
6153 'ereb (1), *dusk*
6256+6153 'êth (2), *time*
2073 hĕspĕra (1), *evening*

EVER
753+3117 'ôrek (2), *length*
3605+3117 kôl (18), *all, any or every*
3808 lô' (1), *no, not*
3809 lâ' (Ch.) (1), *as nothing*
5331 netsach (23), *splendor; lasting*
5703 'ad (40), *perpetuity; ancient*
5704+5769 'ad (1), *as far (long) as; during; while*
5750 'ôwd (1), *again; repeatedly; still; more*
5757 'Avvîy (1), *Avvite*
5769 'ôwlâm (266), *ancient; always*
5769+5703 'ôwlâm (1), *ancient; always*
5865 'êylôwm (1), *forever*
5957 'âlam (Ch.) (11), *forever*
6783 tsᵉmîythûth (2), *perpetually*
6924 qedem (1), *eastern; antiquity; before*
8548 tâmîyd (3), *constantly, regularly*
104 aĕi (1), *ever, always*
165 aiōn (49), *perpetuity, ever; world*
166 aiōniŏs (1), *perpetual, long ago*
1336 diēnĕkĕs (2), *perpetually, endless*
2250+165 hēmĕra (1), *day; period of time*
3364 ŏu mē (1), *not at all, absolutely* not
3745 hŏsŏs (3), *as much as*
3842 pantŏtĕ (6), *at all times*
3956+165 pas (1), *all, any, every, whole*
4218 pŏtĕ (1), *at some time, ever*
4253 prŏ (1), *before in time or space*

EVERLASTING
5703 'ad (2), *perpetuity; ancient*
5769 'ôwlâm (60), *ancient; always*
5957 'âlam (Ch.) (4), *forever*
6924 qedem (1), *eastern; antiquity; before*
126 aïdiŏs (1), *everduring, eternal*
166 aiōniŏs (25), *perpetual, long ago*

EVERMORE
1755 dôwr (1), *dwelling*
3605+3117 kôl (2), *all, any or every*
5331 netsach (1), *splendor; lasting*
5703 'ad (1), *perpetuity; ancient*

5769 'ôwlâm (15), *ancient; always*
8548 tâmîyd (1), *constantly, regularly*
3588+165 hŏ (3), *"the,"* i.e. the definite article
3842 pantŏtĕ (2), *at all times*

EVERY
259 'echâd (5), *first*
376 'îysh (125), *man; male; someone*
802 'ishshâh (4), *woman, wife; women, wives*
1397 geber (1), *person, man*
3605 kôl (451), *all, any or every*
3606 kôl (Ch.) (4), *all, any or every*
3632 kâlîyl (1), *whole, entire; complete; whole*
5437 çâbab (26), *to surround*
7218 rô'sh (1), *head*
303 ana (2), *each; in turn; among*
376 anapērŏs (1), *maimed; crippled*
537 hapas (2), *all, every one, whole*
1330 diĕrchŏmai (1), *to traverse, travel through*
1538 hĕkastŏs (73), *each or every*
2596 kata (15), *down; according to*
3596 hŏdŏipŏrĕō (2), *to travel*
3650 hŏlŏs (2), *whole or all,* i.e. *complete*
3836 pantachŏthĕn (1), *from all directions*
3837 pantachŏu (6), *universally, everywhere*
3840 pantŏthĕn (1), *from, on all sides*
3956 pas (162), *all, any, every, whole*
5100 tis (2), *some or any person or object*
5101 tis (1), *who?, which? or what?*

EVI
189 'Ēvîy (2), *desirous*

EVIDENCE
5612 çêpher (6), *writing*
1650 ĕlĕgchŏs (1), *proof, conviction*

EVIDENCES
5612 çêpher (2), *writing*

EVIDENT
5921+6440 'al (1), *above, over, upon, or against*
1212 dēlŏs (1), *clear, plain, evident*
1732 ĕndĕixis (1), *demonstration*
2612 katadēlŏs (1), *manifest, clear*
4271 prŏdēlŏs (1), *obvious, evident*

EVIDENTLY
4270 prŏgraphō (1), *to announce, prescribe*
5320 phanĕrŏs (1), *plainly,* i.e. *clearly*

EVIL
205 'âven (1), *trouble, vanity, wickedness*
1100 beliya'al (1), *wickedness, trouble*
1681 dibbâh (1), *slander, bad report*
7451 ra' (434), *bad; evil*
7455 rôa' (11), *badness, evil*
7462 râ'âh (1), to *associate* with
7489 râ'a' (24), to *be good for nothing*
92 adikēma (1), *wrong done*
987 blasphēmĕŏ (9), to *speak impiously*
988 blasphēmia (1), *impious speech*
1426 dusphēmia (1), *defamation, slander*
2549 kakia (1), *depravity; malignity*
2551 kakŏlŏgĕŏ (1), to *revile, curse*
2554 kakŏpŏiĕŏ (4), to *injure; to sin, do wrong*
2556 kakŏs (44), *bad, evil, wrong*
2557 kakŏurgŏs (1), *criminal, evildoer*
2559 kakŏŏ (3), to *injure; to oppress; to embitter*
2560 kakŏs (2), *badly; wrongly; ill*
2635 katalalĕŏ (4), to speak *slander*
2636 katalalia (1), *defamation, slander*
4190 pŏnērŏs (49), *malice, wicked, bad*
4190+4487 pŏnērŏs (1), *malice, wicked, bad*
5337 phaulŏs (4), *foul or flawed*, i.e. *wicked*

EVIL-MERODACH
192 'Ĕvîyl Merôdak (2), *Evil-Merodak*

EVILDOER
7489 râ'a' (1), to *be good for nothing*
2555 kakŏpŏiŏs (1), *bad-doer; criminal*

EVILDOERS
7489 râ'a' (9), to *be good for nothing*
2555 kakŏpŏiŏs (3), *bad-doer; criminal*

EVILFAVOUREDNESS
1697+7451 dâbâr (1), *word; matter; thing*

EVILS
7451 ra' (8), *bad; evil*
4190 pŏnērŏs (1), *malice, wicked, bad; crime*

EWE
3535 kibsâh (6), *ewe sheep*
7716 seh (1), *sheep or goat*

EWES
5763 'ûwl (1), to *suckle*, i.e. *give milk*
7353 râchêl (2), *ewe*

EXACT
5065 nâgas (3), to *exploit; to tax, harass*
5378 nâshâ' (2), to *lend* on *interest*
5383 nâshâh (2), to *lend or borrow*
4238 prassō (1), to *execute, accomplish*

EXACTED
3318 yâtsâ' (1), to *go, bring out*
5065 nâgas (1), to *exploit; to tax, harass*

EXACTETH
5382 nâshâh (1), to *forget*

EXACTION
4855 mashshâ' (1), *loan; interest* on a *debt*

EXACTIONS
1646 gerûshâh (1), *dispossession*

EXACTORS
5065 nâgas (1), to *exploit; to tax, harass*

EXALT
1361 gâbahh (3), to *be lofty; to be haughty*
5375 nâsâ' (2), to *lift up*
5549 çâlal (1), to *mound up; to exalt; to oppose*
7311 rûwm (17), to *be high; to rise or raise*
1869 ĕpairō (1), to *raise up, look up*
5312 hupsŏŏ (2), to *elevate; to exalt*

EXALTED
1361 gâbahh (5), to *be lofty; to be haughty*
5375 nâsâ' (8), to *lift up*
5927 'âlâh (2), to *ascend, be high, mount*
7311 rûwm (28), to *be high; to rise or raise*
7426 râmam (2), to *rise*
7682 sâgab (5), to *be, make lofty; be safe*
5229 hupĕrairŏmai (2), to *raise* oneself *over*
5251 hupĕrupsŏŏ (1), to *raise* to the *highest*
5311 hupsŏs (1), *altitude; sky; dignity*
5312 hupsŏŏ (10), to *elevate; to exalt*

EXALTEST
5549 çâlal (1), to *mound up; to exalt; to oppose*

EXALTETH
1361 gâbahh (1), to *be lofty; to be haughty*
7311 rûwm (3), to *be high; to rise or raise*
7682 sâgab (1), to *be, make lofty; be safe*
1869 ĕpairō (1), to *raise up, look up*
5229 hupĕrairŏmai (1), to *raise* oneself *over*
5312 hupsŏŏ (2), to *elevate; to exalt*

EXAMINATION
351 anakrisis (1), *judicial investigation*

EXAMINE
974 bâchan (1), to *test; to investigate*
1875 dârash (1), to *seek or ask; to worship*
350 anakrinō (1), to *interrogate, determine*
1381 dŏkimazō (1), to *test; to approve*
3985 pĕirazō (1), to *endeavor, scrutinize*

EXAMINED
350 anakrinō (4), to *interrogate, determine*
426 anĕtazō (2), to *investigate; to question*

EXAMINING
350 anakrinō (1), to *interrogate, determine*

EXAMPLE
1164 dĕigma (1), *specimen, example*
3856 paradĕigmatizō (1), to *expose to infamy*
5179 tupŏs (1), *shape, resemblance; "type"*
5261 hupŏgrammŏs (1), *copy, example, model*
5262 hupŏdĕigma (4), *exhibit; specimen*

EXAMPLES
5179 tupŏs (1), *shape, resemblance; "type"*

EXCEED
3254 yâçaph (2), to *add or augment*
4052 pĕrissĕuō (2), to *superabound*

EXCEEDED
1396 gâbar (1), to *be strong; to prevail*
1431 gâdal (2), to *be great, make great*

EXCEEDEST
3254 yâçaph (1), to *add or augment*

EXCEEDETH
3254 yâçaph (1), to *add or augment*

EXCEEDING
430 'ĕlôhîym (1), the true *God; gods; great ones*
1419 gâdôwl (1), *great*
2302 châdâh (1), to *rejoice, be glad*
2493 chêlem (Ch.) (1), *dream*
3493 yattîyr (Ch.) (1), *preeminent; very*
3499 yether (1), *remainder; small rope*
3966 me'ôd (18), *very, utterly*
4605 ma'al (2), *upward, above, overhead*
5628 çârach (1), to *extend even to excess*
7235 râbâh (1), to *increase*
7235+3966 râbâh (1), to *increase*
7689 saggîy' (1), *mighty*
8057 simchâh (1), *blithesomeness or glee*
1519+5236 ĕis (1), *to or into*

EXAMINE — 2596+5236 kata (1), *down; according to*
3029 lian (5), *very much*
3588+2316 hŏ (1), *"the,"* i.e. the *definite article*
4036 pĕrilupŏs (3), *intensely sad*
4970 sphŏdra (4), *vehemently, much*
5228 hupĕr (1), *over; above; beyond*
5235 hupĕrballō (3), to *surpass*
5248 hupĕrpĕrissĕuō (1), to *superabound*
5250 hupĕrplĕŏnazō (1), to *superabound*

EXCEEDINGLY
413+1524 'êl (1), *to, toward*
1419 gâdôwl (5), *great*
1419+3966 gâdôwl (1), *great*
3493 yattîyr (Ch.) (1), *preeminent; very*
3966 me'ôd (9), *very, utterly*
4605 ma'al (4), *upward, above, overhead*
7227 rab (2), *great*
7235 râbâh (1), to *increase*
7235+3966 râbâh (1), to *increase*
8057 simchâh (1), *blithesomeness or glee*
1613 ĕktarassō (1), to *disturb wholly*
1630 ĕkphŏbŏs (1), *frightened out* of one's *wits*
4056 pĕrissŏtĕrŏs (3), *more superabundantly*
4057 pĕrissŏs (1), *superabundantly*
4970 sphŏdra (1), *vehemently, much*
4971 sphŏdrŏs (1), *very much*
5228+1537+4053 hupĕr (1), *over; above; beyond*
5401+3173 phŏbŏs (1), *alarm, or fright*

EXCEL
1368 gibbôwr (1), *powerful; great warrior*
3498 yâthar (1), to *remain or be left*
5329 nâtsach (1), i.e. to *be eminent*
4052 pĕrissĕuō (1), to *superabound*

EXCELLED
7227 rab (1), *great*

EXCELLENCY
1346 ga'ăvâh (3), *arrogance; majesty*
1347 gâ'ôwn (10), *ascending; majesty*
1363 gôbahh (1), *height; grandeur; arrogance*
1926 hâdâr (1), *magnificence*
3499 yether (2), *remainder; small rope*
3504 yithrôwn (1), *preeminence, gain*

EXCELLENT

7613 se'êth (2), *elevation; swelling* scab
7863 sîy' (1), *elevation*
5236 hupĕrbŏlē (1), *super-eminence*
5242 hupĕrĕchō (1), to *excel; be superior*
5247 hupĕrŏchē (1), *superiority*

EXCELLENT

117 'addîyr (4), *powerful; majestic*
977 bâchar (1), *select, chose, prefer*
1347 gâ'ôwn (1), *ascending; majesty*
1348 gê'ûwth (1), *ascending; majesty*
1420 gᵉdûwlâh (1), *greatness, grandeur*
1431 gâdal (1), to *be great, make great*
3368 yâqâr (1), *valuable*
3493 yattîyr (Ch.) (5), *preeminent; very*
3499 yether (1), *remainder;* small *rope*
5057 nâgîyd (1), *commander, official*
5716 'ădîy (1), *finery; outfit; headstall*
7119 qar (1), *cool; quiet; cool*-headed
7218 rô'sh (1), *head*
7230 rôb (1), *abundance*
7682 sâgab (1), to *be, make lofty; be safe*
7689 saggîy' (1), *mighty*
7991 shâlîysh (1), *officer; of the third rank*
8446 tûwr (1), to *wander, meander*
1308 diaphĕrō (2), to *differ; to surpass*
1313 diaphŏrŏs (2), *varying; surpassing*
2596+5236 kata (1), *down; according to*
2903 kratistŏs (2), *very honorable*
3169 mĕgalŏprĕpēs (1), *befitting greatness*
4119 plĕiŏn (1), *more*

EXCELLEST

5927 'âlâh (1), to *ascend, be high, mount*

EXCELLETH

3504 yithrôwn (2), *preeminence, gain*
5235 hupĕrballō (1), to *surpass*

EXCEPT

369 'ayin (1), *there is no, i.e., not exist, none*
905 bad (1), *chief; apart, only, besides*
1115 biltîy (3), *not, except, without, unless*
3588 kîy (2), *for, that because*
3861 lâhên (Ch.) (3), *therefore; except*
3884 lûwlê' (3), *if not*
7535 raq (1), *merely; although*
1508 ĕi mē (7), *if not*
1509 ĕi mē ti (3), *if not somewhat*

EXCEPTED

2228 ē (1), *or; than*
3362 ĕan mē (33), *if not, i.e. unless*
3923 parĕisphĕrō (1), to *bear in alongside*
4133 plēn (1), *albeit, save that, rather, yet*

EXCEPTED

1622 ĕktŏs (1), *aside from, besides; except*

EXCESS

192 akrasia (1), *lack of control of self*
401 anachusis (1), *excessively pour out*
810 asōtia (1), *profligacy, debauchery*
3632 ŏinŏphlugia (1), *drunkenness*

EXCHANGE

4171 mûwr (1), to *alter; to barter, to dispose of*
8545 tᵉmûwrâh (2), *barter, compensation*
465 antallagma (2), *equivalent* exchange

EXCHANGERS

5133 trapĕzitēs (1), *money-broker*

EXCLUDE

1576 ĕkklĕiō (1), to *shut out, exclude*

EXCLUDED

1576 ĕkklĕiō (1), to *shut out, exclude*

EXCUSE

379 anapŏlŏgētŏs (1), *without excuse*
626 apŏlŏgĕŏmai (1), to *give an account*
3868 paraitĕŏmai (1), to *deprecate, decline*

EXCUSED

3868 paraitĕŏmai (2), to *deprecate, decline*

EXCUSING

626 apŏlŏgĕŏmai (1), to *give an account*

EXECRATION

423 'âlâh (2), *curse, oath, public agreement*

EXECUTE

1777 dîyn (1), to *judge;* to *strive or contend for*
5647 'âbad (1), to *do, work, serve*
6213 'âsâh (25), to *do or make*
8199 shâphaṭ (2), to *judge*
4160 pŏiĕō (2), to *do*

EXECUTED

5648 'âbad (Ch.) (1), to *do, work, serve*
6213 'âsâh (15), to *do or make*
2407 hiĕratĕuō (1), to *be a priest*

EXECUTEDST

6213 'âsâh (1), to *do*

EXECUTEST

6213 'âsâh (1), to *do*

EXECUTETH

6213 'âsâh (5), to *do*

EXECUTING

6213 'âsâh (1), to *do*

EXECUTION

6213 'âsâh (1), to *do*

EXECUTIONER

4688 spĕkŏulatōr (1), *life-guardsman*

EXEMPTED

5355 nâqîy (1), *innocent*

EXERCISE

1980 hâlak (1), to *walk; live a certain way*
6213 'âsâh (1), to *do or make*
778 askĕō (1), to *strive for one's best*
1128 gumnazō (1), to *train by exercise*
1129 gumnasia (1), *training of the body*
1850 ĕxŏusiazō (1), to *control, master another*
2634 katakuriĕuō (2), to *control, subjugate*
2715 katĕxŏusiazō (2), to *wield full privilege over*
2961 kuriĕuō (1), to *rule, be master of*

EXERCISED

6031 'ânâh (2), to *afflict, be afflicted*
1128 gumnazō (3), to *train by exercise*

EXERCISETH

4160 pŏiĕō (1), to *do*

EXHORT

3867 parainĕō (1), to *recommend or advise*
3870 parakalĕō (14), to *call, invite*

EXHORTATION

3870 parakalĕō (2), to *call, invite*
3874 paraklēsis (8), *imploring, exhortation*

EXHORTED

3870 parakalĕō (3), to *call, invite*

EXHORTETH

3870 parakalĕō (1), to *call, invite*

EXHORTING

3870 parakalĕō (3), to *call, invite*
4389 prŏtrĕpŏmai (1), to *encourage*

EXILE

1540 gâlâh (1), to *denude; uncover*
6808 tsâ'âh (1), to *tip over; to depopulate*

EXORCISTS

1845 ĕxŏrkistēs (1), *exorcist, i.e. conjurer*

EXPECTATION

4007 mabbâṭ (3), *expectation, hope*
8615 tiqvâh (7), *cord; expectancy*
603 apŏkaradŏkia (2), *intense anticipation*
4328 prŏsdŏkaō (1), to *anticipate; to await*

EXPECTED

8615 tiqvâh (1), *cord; expectancy*

EXPECTING

1551 ĕkdĕchŏmai (1), to *await, expect*
4328 prŏsdŏkaō (1), to *anticipate; to await*

EXPEDIENT

4851 sumphĕrō (7), to *collect; to conduce*

EXPEL

1644 gârash (1), to *drive out; to expatriate*
1920 hâdaph (1), to *push away or down; drive out*

EXPELLED

3423 yârash (2), to *inherit; to impoverish*
5080 nâdach (1), to *push off, scattered*
1544 ĕkballō (1), to *throw out*

EXPENCES

5313 niphqâ' (Ch.) (2), *outgo, i.e. expense*

EXPERIENCE

5172 nâchash (1), to *prognosticate*
7200 râ'âh (1), to *see*
1382 dŏkimē (2), *test, i.e. trustiness*

EXPERIMENT

1382 dŏkimē (1), *test, i.e. trustiness*

EXPERT

3925 lâmad (1), to *teach, train*
6186 'ârak (3), to *set in a row, i.e. arrange,*
7919 sâkal (1), to *be or act circumspect*
1109 gnōstēs (1), *knower, expert*

EXPIRED

3615 kâlâh (1), to *cease, be finished, perish*
4390 mâlê' (3), to *fill; be full*
8666 tᵉshûwbâh (3), *recurrence; reply*
4137 plērŏō (1), to *fill, make complete*
5055 tĕlĕō (1), to *end, i.e. complete, execute*

EXPOUND

5046 nâgad (1), to *announce*

EXPOUNDED

5046 nâgad (1), to *announce*
1329 diĕrmēnĕuō (1), to *explain thoroughly*
1620 ĕktithēmi (3), to *expose; to declare*
1956 ĕpiluō (1), to *explain; to decide*

EXPRESS

5481 charaktēr (1), *exact copy or representation*

EXECUTING

4329 prŏsdŏkia (1), *apprehension* of evil

English

EXPRESSED
5344 nâqab (5), to
specify, designate, libel

EXPRESSLY
559 'âmar (1), to say
4490 rhētōs (1),
out-spoken, distinctly

EXTEND
4900 mâshak (1), to draw
out; to be tall
5186 nâṭâh (1), to stretch
or spread out

EXTENDED
5186 nâṭâh (2), to stretch
or spread out

EXTINCT
1846 dâ'ak (1), to be
extinguished; to expire
2193 zâ'ak (1), to
extinguish

EXTOL
5549 çâlal (1), to mound
up; to exalt; to oppose
7311 rûwm (2), to be
high; to rise or raise
7313 rûwm (Ch.) (1),
elation, arrogance

EXTOLLED
5375 nâsâ' (1), to lift up
7318 rôwmâm (1),
exaltation, praise

EXTORTION
6233 'ôsheq (1), fraud;
distress; unjust gain
724 harpagē (1), pillage;
greediness; robbery

EXTORTIONER
4160 mûwts (1), to
oppress
5383 nâshâh (1), to lend
or borrow
727 harpax (1),
rapacious; robbing

EXTORTIONERS
727 harpax (3),
rapacious; robbing

EXTREME
2746 charchûr (1), hot
fever

EXTREMITY
6580 pash (1), stupidity
as a result of grossness

EYE
5869 'ayin (73), eye;
sight; fountain
5870 'ayin (Ch.) (1), eye;
sight
3442 mŏnŏphthalmŏs
(2), one-eyed
3788 ŏphthalmŏs (29),
eye
5168 trumalia (2),
needle's eye
5169 trupēma (1),
needle's eye

EYE'S
5869 'ayin (1), eye; sight;
fountain

EYEBROWS
1354+5869 gab (1),
rounded: top or rim;
arch

EYED
5770 'âvan (1), to watch
with jealousy
5869 'ayin (1), eye; sight;
fountain

EYELIDS
6079 'aph'aph (9),
fluttering eyelash

EYES
5869 'ayin (417), eye;
sight; fountain
5870 'ayin (Ch.) (5), eye;
sight
3659 ŏmma (1), eye
3788 ŏphthalmŏs (70),
eye

EYESALVE
2854 kŏllŏuriŏn (1),
poultice

EYESERVICE
3787 ŏphthalmŏdŏulĕia
(2), service that needs
watching

EYESIGHT
5869 'ayin (1), eye; sight;
fountain

EYEWITNESSES
845 autŏptēs (1),
eyewitness
2030 ĕpŏptēs (1),
looker-on

EZAR
687 'Etser (1), treasure

EZBAI
229 'Ezbay (1),
hyssop-like

EZBON
675 'Etsbôwn (2), Etsbon

EZEKIAS
1478 Ĕzĕkias (2),
strengthened of
Jehovah

EZEKIEL
3168 Yᵉchezqê'l (2), God
will strengthen

EZEL
237 'ezel (1), departure

EZEM
6107 'Etsem (1), bone

EZER
687 'Etser (4), treasure
5827 'Ezer (1), help
5829 'Êzer (4), aid

EZION-GABER
6100 'Etsyôwn (short (4),
backbone-like of a man

EZION-GEBER
6100 'Etsyôwn (short (3),
backbone-like of a man

EZNITE
6112 'Êtsen (1), spear

EZRA
5830 'Ezrâ' (26), aid

EZRAHITE
250 'Ezrâchîy (3),
Ezrachite

EZRI
5836 'Ezrîy (1), helpful

FABLES
3454 muthŏs (5), tale,
fiction, myth

FACE
600 'ănaph (Ch.) (1), face
639 'aph (19), nose or
nostril; face; person
5869 'ayin (9), eye; sight;
fountain
6440 pânîym (313), face;
front
1799 ĕnōpiŏn (1), in the
face of, before
3799 ŏpsis (1), face;
appearance
4383 prŏsōpŏn (48), face,
presence
4750 stŏma (4), mouth;
edge

FACES
639 'aph (3), nose or
nostril; face; person
6440 pânîym (62), face;
front
4383 prŏsōpŏn (5), face,
presence

FADE
5034 nâbêl (5), to wilt; to
fall away; to be foolish
3133 marainō (1), to pass
away, fade away

FADETH
5034 nâbêl (5), to wilt; to
fall away; to be foolish
262 amarantinŏs (1),
fadeless
263 amarantŏs (1),
perpetual, never fading

FADING
5034 nâbêl (2), to wilt; to
fall away; to be foolish

FAIL
235 'âzal (1), to disappear
656 'âphêç (1), to cease
1238 bâqaq (1), to
depopulate, ruin
1584 gâmar (1), to end;
to complete; to fail
1809 dâlal (1), to
slacken, dangle
2637 châçêr (3), to lack;
to fail, want, make less
2638 châçêr (1), lacking
3543 kâhâh (1), to grow
dull, fade; to be faint
3576 kâzab (1), to lie,
deceive
3584 kâchash (2), to lie,
disown; to disappoint
3615 kâlâh (14), to cease,
be finished, perish
3772 kârath (6), to cut
(off, down or asunder)
3808+539 lô' (1), no, not
5307 nâphal (2), to fall
5405 nâshath (1), to dry
up
5674 'âbar (2), to cross
over; to transition
5737 'âdar (1), to
arrange as a battle
5848 'âṭaph (1), to
shroud, to languish
6461 paçaç (1), to
disappear
6565 pârar (1), to break
up; to violate, frustrate
7503 râphâh (4), to
slacken

7673 shâbath (2), to
repose; to desist
7960 shâlûw (Ch.) (2),
fault, error
8266 shâqar (1), to cheat,
i.e. be untrue in words
1587 ĕklĕipō (3), to die;
to spot
1952 ĕpilĕipō (1), to be
insufficient for
2673 katargĕō (1), to be,
render entirely useless
4098 piptō (1), to fall
5302 hustĕrĕō (1), to be
inferior; to fall short

FAILED
6 'âbad (1), perish;
destroy
2308 châdal (1), to desist,
stop; be fat
3318 yâtsâ' (2), to go,
bring out
3615 kâlâh (1), to cease,
be finished, perish
5307 nâphal (4), to fall
5405 nâshath (1), to dry
up
8552 tâmam (2), to
complete, finish

FAILETH
6 'âbad (1), perish;
destroy
369 'ayin (1), there is no,
i.e., not exist, none
656 'âphêç (1), to cease
1602 gâ'al (1), to detest;
to reject; to fail
2638 châçêr (1), lacking
3584 kâchash (1), to lie,
disown; to disappoint
3615 kâlâh (4), to cease,
be finished, perish
3782 kâshal (1), to totter,
waver; to falter
5405 nâshath (1), to dry
up
5737 'âdar (3), to
arrange as a battle
5800 'âzab (2), to loosen;
relinquish; permit
413 anĕklĕiptŏs (1), not
failing
1601 ĕkpiptō (1), to drop
away

FAILING
3631 killâyôwn (1),
pining, destruction
674 apŏpsuchō (1), to
faint

FAIN
1272 bârach (1), to flee
suddenly
1937 ĕpithumĕō (1), to
long for

FAINT
1738 dâvâh (1), to be in
menstruation cycle
1739 dâveh (1),
menstrual; fainting
1742 davvây (3), sick;
troubled, afflicted
3286 yâ'aph (1), to tire
3287 yâ'êph (2),
exhausted
3543 kâhâh (1), to grow
dull, fade; to be faint

FAINTED
4127 mûwg (3), to *soften, flow down, disappear*
4549 mâçaç (1), to *waste*; to *faint*
5774 'ûwph (3), to *cover*, to *fly*; to *faint*
5848 'âṭaph (1), to *shroud*, to *languish*
5889 'âyêph (6), *languid*
5968 'âlaph (1), to *be languid, faint*
6296 pâgar (2), to *become exhausted*
7401 râkak (2), to *soften*
7503 râphâh (2), to *slacken*
1573 ĕkkakĕō (4), to *be weak, fail*
1590 ĕkluō (5), to *lose heart*

FAINTED
1961 hâyâh (1), to *exist*, i.e. *be* or *become*
3021 yâga' (1), to *be exhausted*, to *tire*,
3856 lâhahh (1), to *languish*
5848 'âṭaph (2), to *shroud*, to *languish*
5968 'âlaph (2), to *be languid, faint*
5969 'ulpeh (1), *mourning*
6313 pûwg (1), to *be sluggish; be numb*
1590 ĕkluō (1), to *lose heart*
2577 kamnō (1), to *tire*; to *faint, sicken*

FAINTEST
3811 lâ'âh (1), to *tire*; to *be, make disgusted*

FAINTETH
3286 yâ'aph (1), to *tire*
3615 kâlâh (2), to *cease, be finished, perish*
4549 mâçaç (1), to *waste*; to *faint*

FAINTHEARTED
3824+7401 lêbâb (1), *heart*
4127 mûwg (1), to *soften*; to *fear, faint*
7390+3824 rak (1), *tender; weak*

FAINTNESS
4816 môrek (1), *despondent fear*

FAIR
2091 zâhâb (1), *gold, golden colored*
2603 chânan (1), to *implore*
2889 ṭâhôwr (2), *pure, clean, flawless*
2896 ṭôwb (6), *good; well*
2896+4758 ṭôwb (1), *good; well*
2897+4758 Ṭôwb (1), *good*
2898 ṭûwb (1), *good; goodness, beauty*
3302 yâphâh (12), to *be beautiful*
3303 yâpheh (14), *beautiful; handsome*
3303+8389 yâpheh (1), *beautiful; handsome*

FAIRER
2896 ṭôwb (2), *good; well*
3302 yâphâh (1), to *be beautiful*

FAIREST
3303 yâpheh (3), *beautiful; handsome*

FAIRS
5801 'izzâbôwn (6), *trade, merchandise*

FAITH
529 'êmûwn (1), *trustworthiness; faithful*
530 'ĕmûwnâh (1), *fidelity; steadiness*
1680 ĕlpis (1), *expectation; hope*
3640 ŏligŏpistŏs (5), *lacking full confidence*
4102 pistis (238), *faithfulness; faith, belief*

FAITHFUL
529 'êmûwn (3), *trustworthiness; faithful*
530 'ĕmûwnâh (3), *fidelity; steadiness*
539 'âman (20), to *be firm, faithful, true*
540 'âman (Ch.) (1), to *be firm, faithful, true*
571 'emeth (1), *certainty, truth, trustworthiness*
4103 pistŏs (53), *trustworthy; reliable*

FAITHFULLY
530 'ĕmûwnâh (5), *fidelity; steadiness*
571 'emeth (2), *certainty, truth, trustworthiness*
4103 pistŏs (1), *trustworthy; reliable*

FAITHFULNESS
530 'ĕmûwnâh (18), *fidelity; steadiness*
3559 kûwn (1), to *render sure, proper*

FAITHLESS
571 apistŏs (4), *without faith; untrustworthy*

FALL
2342 chûwl (2), to *dance, whirl*; to *writhe* in pain
3318 yâtsâ' (1), to *go, bring out*
3381 yârad (1), to *descend*

3304 yᵉphêh-phîyâh (1), *very beautiful*
3948 leqach (1), *instruction*
6320 pûwk (1), *stibium*
8209 sappîyr (Ch.) (2), *beautiful*
8597 tiph'ârâh (3), *ornament*
791 astĕiŏs (1), *handsome*
2105 ĕudia (1), *clear sky*, i.e. *fine weather*
2129 ĕulŏgia (1), *benediction*
2146 ĕuprŏsōpĕō (1), to *make a good display*
2568 Kalŏi Limĕnĕs (1), *Good Harbors*

3782 kâshal (22), to *totter, waver*; to *falter*
3783 kishshâlôwn (1), *ruin*
3832 lâbaṭ (3), to *overthrow*; to *fall*
3872 Lûwchîyth (1), *floored*
4131 môwṭ (1), to *slip, shake, fall*
4383 mikshôwl (1), *stumbling-block*
4658 mappeleth (7), *down-fall; ruin; carcase*
5034 nâbêl (1), to *wilt*; to *fall away*; to *be foolish*
5064 nâgar (1), to *pour* out; to *deliver* over
5203 nâṭash (1), to *disperse*; to *thrust* off
5307 nâphal (149), to *fall*
5308 nᵉphal (Ch.) (3), to *fall*
5456 çâgad (2), to *prostrate* oneself
6293 pâga' (8), to *impinge*
7264 râgaz (1), to *quiver*
7812 shâchâh (2), to *prostrate* in homage
7997 shâlal (1), to *drop* or *strip*; to *plunder*
868 aphistēmi (1), to *desist, desert*
1601 ĕkpiptō (4), to *drop away*
1706 ĕmpiptō (3), to *be entrapped by*
3895 parapiptō (1), to *apostatize, fall away*
3900 paraptōma (2), *error; transgression*
4045 pĕripiptō (1), to *fall into the hands of*
4098 piptō (22), to *fall*
4417 ptaiō (1), to *trip up, stumble* morally
4431 ptōsis (2), *downfall, crash*
4625 skandalŏn (1), *snare*

FALLEN
935 bôw' (1), to *go* or *come*
3782 kâshal (2), to *totter, waver*; to *falter*
4131+3027 môwṭ (1), to *slip, shake, fall*
4803 mâraṭ (2), to *polish*; to *make bald*
5307 nâphal (55), to *fall*
1601 ĕkpiptō (3), to *drop away*
1706 ĕmpiptō (1), to *be entrapped by*
1968 ĕpipiptō (1), to *embrace*; to *seize*
2064 ĕrchŏmai (1), to *go* or *come*
2667 katapiptō (2), to *fall down*
2702 kataphĕrō (1), to *bear down*
2837 kŏimaō (2), to *slumber*; to *decease*
4098 piptō (4), to *fall*

FALLEST
5307 nâphal (1), to *fall*

FALLETH
3918 layish (1), *lion*
5034 nâbêl (1), to *wilt*; to *fall away*; to *be foolish*
5307 nâphal (15), to *fall*
5308 nᵉphal (Ch.) (2), to *fall*
5456 çâgad (2), to *prostrate* oneself
7122 qârâ' (1), to *encounter*, to *happen*
1601 ĕkpiptō (2), to *drop away*
1911 ĕpiballō (1), to *throw upon*
4098 piptō (3), to *fall*

FALLING
1762 dᵉchîy (2), *stumbling fall*
3782 kâshal (1), to *totter, waver*; to *falter*
4131 môwṭ (1), to *slip, shake, fall*
5034 nâbêl (1), to *wilt*; to *fall away*; to *be foolish*
5307 nâphal (3), to *fall*
646 apŏstasia (1), *defection, rebellion*
679 aptaistŏs (1), *not stumbling, without sin*
2597 katabainō (1), to *descend*
4045 pĕripiptō (1), to *fall into the hands of*
4098 piptō (1), to *fall*
4248+1096 prēnēs (1), *headlong*
4363 prŏspiptō (1), to *prostrate* oneself

FALLOW
3180 yachmûwr (1), kind of *deer*
5215 nîyr (2), freshly *plowed* land

FALLOWDEER
3180 yachmûwr (1), kind of *deer*

FALSE
205 'âven (1), *trouble, vanity, wickedness*
2555 châmâç (2), *violence; malice*
3577 kâzâb (1), *falsehood; idol*
4820 mirmâh (2), *fraud*
7423 rᵉmîyâh (1), *remissness; treachery*
7723 shâv' (5), *ruin; guile; idolatry*
8267 sheqer (20), *untruth; sham*
1228 diabŏlŏs (2), *traducer*, i.e. *Satan*
4811 sukŏphantĕō (1), to *defraud, extort*
5569 psĕudadĕlphŏs (2), *pretended associate*
5570 psĕudapŏstŏlŏs (1), *pretended preacher*
5571 psĕudēs (1), *erroneous, deceitful*
5572 psĕudŏdidaskalŏs (1), *propagator of erroneous doctrine*
5573 psĕudŏlŏgŏs (4), *promulgating erroneous doctrine*

5575 *pseŭdŏmartur* (3), bearer of *untrue testimony*
5576 *pseŭdŏmartureō* (6), to offer *falsehood*
5577 *pseŭdŏmarturia* (1), *untrue testimony*
5578 *pseŭdŏprŏphētēs* (6), *pretended foreteller*
5580 *pseŭdŏchristŏs* (2), *spurious Messiah*

FALSEHOOD
4604 ma'al (1), *sinful treachery*
8267 sheqer (13), *untruth; sham*

FALSELY
3584 kâchash (1), to *lie, disown;* to *disappoint*
5921+8267 'al (1), *above, over, upon,* or *against*
7723 shâv' (1), *ruin; guile; idolatry*
8266 shâqar (2), to *cheat,* i.e. *be untrue* in words
8267 sheqer (12), *untruth; sham*
5574 *pseŭdŏmai* (1), to *utter an untruth*
5581 *pseŭdŏnumŏs* (1), *untruly named*

FALSIFYING
5791 'âvath (1), to *wrest, twist*

FAME
6963 qôwl (1), *voice* or *sound*
8034 shêm (4), *appellation,* i.e. name
8052 shemûw'âh (2), *announcement*
8088 shêma' (1), *something heard*
8089 shôma' (4), *report; reputation*
189 akŏē (3), *hearing; thing heard*
1310 *diaphēmizō* (1), to *spread news*
2279 *ēchŏs* (1), *roar; rumor*
3056 *lŏgŏs* (1), *word, matter, thing; Word*
5345 *phēmē* (2), *news, report*

FAMILIAR
3045 yâda' (1), to *know*
7965 shâlôwm (1), *safe; well; health, prosperity*

FAMILIARS
7965 shâlôwm (1), *safe; well; health, prosperity*

FAMILIES
1004 bayith (2), *house; temple; family, tribe*
1004+1 bayith (2), *house; temple; family, tribe*
2945 ṭaph (1), *family of children and women*
4940 mishpâchâh (169), *family, clan, people*

FAMILY
504 'eleph (1), *ox; cow* or *cattle*
1004 bayith (1), *house; temple; family, tribe*

4940 mishpâchâh (120), *family, clan, people*
3965 patria (1), *family, race, nation*

FAMINE
3720 kâphân (2), *hunger*
7458 râ'âb (86), *hunger*
7459 re'âbôwn (3), *famine*
3042 limŏs (4), *scarcity of food, famine*

FAMINES
3042 limŏs (3), *scarcity of food, famine*

FAMISH
7329 râzâh (1), to *make, become thin*
7456 râ'êb (1), to *hunger*

FAMISHED
7456 râ'êb (1), to *hunger*
7458 râ'âb (1), *hunger*

FAMOUS
117 'addîyr (2), *powerful; majestic*
3045 yâda' (1), to *know*
7121 qârâ' (2), to *call* out
7148 qârîy' (1), *called,* i.e. *select*
8034 shêm (4), *appellation,* i.e. name

FAN
2219 zârâh (4), to *toss about;* to *winnow*
4214 mizreh (1), *winnowing shovel*
4425 ptuŏn (2), *winnowing-fork*

FANNERS
2114 zûwr (1), to *be foreign, strange*

FAR
1419 gâdôwl (1), *great*
2008 hênnâh (2), *from here; from there*
2186 zânach (1), to *reject, forsake, fail*
2486 châlîylâh (9), *far be it!, forbid!*
3966 me'ôd (3), *very, utterly*
4801 merchâq (15), *distant place; from afar*
5048 neged (3), *over against* or *before*
5079 niddâh (1), *time of menstrual impurity*
7350 râchôwq (59), *remote, far*
7352 rachîyq (Ch.) (1), *far away; aloof*
7368 râchaq (39), to *recede; remove*
7369 râchêq (2), *remote, far*
891 achri (2), *until* or *up to*
1519 eis (1), to or *into*
2193 heŏs (4), *until*
2436 hileŏs (1), God be *gracious!, far* be it!
3112 makran (6), *at a distance, far away*
3113 makrŏthĕn (1), *from a distance* or *afar*
3117 makrŏs (2), *long,* in place or time

4054 perissŏtĕrŏn (1), in a superabundant way
4183 pŏlus (3), *much, many*
4206 pŏrrhō (2), *forwards, at a distance*
5231 hupĕranō (2), *above, upward*

FARE
7939 sâkâr (1), *payment, salary; compensation*
7965 shâlôwm (1), *safe; well; health, prosperity*
4517 rhônnumi (1), to *strengthen*

FARED
2165 eŭphrainō (1), to *rejoice, be glad*

FAREWELL
657 apŏtassŏmai (2), to *say adieu;* to *renounce*
4517 rhônnumi (1), to *strengthen*
5463 chairō (1), to be *cheerful*

FARM
68 agrŏs (1), *farmland, countryside*

FARTHER
4008 pĕran (1), *across, beyond*
4260 prŏbainō (1), to *advance*
4281 prŏĕrchŏmai (1), to *go onward, precede*

FARTHING
787 assariŏn (1), *assarius*
2835 kŏdrantēs (2), *quadrans*

FARTHINGS
787 assariŏn (1), *assarius*

FASHION
1823 demûwth (1), *resemblance, likeness*
3559 kûwn (1), to *set up: establish, fix, prepare*
4941 mishpâṭ (2), *verdict; formal decree; justice*
8498 tekûwnâh (1), *structure; equipage*
1491 eidŏs (1), *form, appearance, sight*
3778 hŏutŏs (1), *this* or *that*
4383 prŏsŏpŏn (1), *face, presence*
4976 schēma (2), *form* or *appearance*
5179 tupŏs (1), *shape, resemblance; "type"*

FASHIONED
3335 yâtsar (3), to *form; potter;* to *determine*
3559 kûwn (2), to *set up: establish, fix, prepare*
6213 'âsâh (1), to *do* or *make*
4832 summŏrphŏs (1), *similar, conformed to*

FASHIONETH
3335 yâtsar (3), to *form; potter;* to *determine*

FASHIONING
4964 suschēmatizō (1), to *conform* to the same

FASHIONS
4941 mishpâṭ (1), *verdict; formal decree; justice*

FAST
629 'oçparnâ' (Ch.) (1), *diligently*
3966 me'ôd (1), *very, utterly*
6684 tsûwm (8), to *fast from food*
6685 tsôwm (16), *fast from food*
472 antĕchŏmai (1), to *adhere to;* to *care for*
805 asphalizō (1), to *render secure*
2722 katĕchō (3), to *hold down fast*
3521 nēstĕia (1), *abstinence*
3522 nēstĕuō (16), to *abstain* from food

FASTED
6684 tsûwm (12), to *fast from food*
3522 nēstĕuō (3), to *abstain* from food

FASTEN
2388 châzaq (1), to *fasten upon;* to *seize*
5414 nâthan (3), to *give*
8628 tâqa' (1), to *clatter, slap, drive, clasp*

FASTENED
270 'âchaz (3), to *seize, grasp; possess*
2388 châzaq (1), to *fasten upon;* to *seize*
2883 ṭâba' (1), to *sink;* to *be drowned*
3559 kûwn (1), to *set up: establish, fix, prepare*
5193 nâṭa' (1), to *plant*
5414 nâthan (2), to *give*
6775 tsâmad (1), to *link,* i.e. *gird*
6795 tsânach (1), to *descend,* i.e. *drive* down
8628 tâqa' (4), to *clatter, slap, drive, clasp*
816 atĕnizō (2), to *gaze intently*
2510 kathaptō (1), to *seize upon*

FASTENING
816 atĕnizō (1), to *gaze intently*

FASTEST
2522 kathēmĕrinŏs (1), *quotidian,* i.e. *daily*

FASTING
2908 ṭevâth (Ch.) (1), *hunger*
6685 tsôwm (8), *fast*
777 asitŏs (1), *without taking food*
3521 nēstĕia (4), *abstinence*
3522 nēstĕuō (1), to *abstain* from food
3523 nēstis (2), *abstinent from food*

FASTINGS
6685 tsôwm (1), *fast*
3521 nēstĕia (3), *abstinence*

English

FAT
1254 bârâ' (1), to create; fashion
1277 bârîy' (6), fatted or plump; healthy
1878 dâshên (7), to be fat, thrive; to fatten
1879 dâshên (3), fat; rich, fertile
2459 cheleb (79), fat; choice part
2502 châlats (1), to pull off; to strip; to depart
2954 ţâphash (1), to be stupid
3368 yâqâr (1), valuable
4220 mêach (1), fat; rich
4770 marbêq (1), stall
4806 mᵉrîy' (4), stall-fed animal
4924 mashmân (2), fatness; rich dish; fertile field; robust man
4945 mashqeh (1), butler; drink; well-watered
6309 peder (3), suet
6335 pûwsh (1), to spread; to act proudly
6371 pîymáh (1), obesity
8080 shâman (3), to be, make oily or gross
8081 shemen (4), olive oil, wood, lotions
8082 shâmên (10), rich; fertile

FATFLESHED
1277 bârîy' (2), fatted or plump; healthy

FATHER
1 'âb (504), father
2 'ab (Ch.) (13), father
25 'Ăbîy Gib'ôwn (67), founder of Gibon
1121 bên (1), son, descendant; people
2524 châm (4), father-in-law
2589 channôwth (1), supplication
2859 châthan (20), to become related
540 apatōr (1), of unrecorded paternity
3962 patēr (344), father
3995 pĕnthĕrŏs (1), wife's father

FATHER'S
1 'âb (126), father
1730 dôwd (3), beloved, friend; relative
1733 dôwdâh (1), aunt
3962 patēr (17), father

FATHERLESS
369+1 'ayin (1), there is no, i.e., not exist, none
3490 yâthôwm (41), child alone, fatherless child
3737 ŏrphanŏs (1), parentless, orphaned

FATHERS
1 'âb (475), father
2 'ab (Ch.) (3), father
3962 patēr (52), father
3964 patralǫ̆as (1), killing of father
3967 patrikŏs (1), ancestral, paternal

3970 patrŏparadŏtŏs (1), traditionary
3971 patrǭŏs (3), from forefathers

FATHERS'
1 'âb (10), father
3962 patēr (1), father

FATHOMS
3712 ŏrguia (2), measure of about six feet

FATLING
4806 mᵉrîy' (1), stall-fed animal

FATLINGS
4220 mêach (1), fat; rich
4806 mᵉrîy' (2), stall-fed animal
4932 mishneh (1), duplicate copy; double
4619 sitistŏs (1), grained, i.e. fatted

FATNESS
1880 deshen (7), fat; fatness, abundance
2459 cheleb (4), fat; choice part
4924 mashmân (3), fatness; fertile; robust
8081 shemen (1), olive oil, wood, lotions
8082 shâmên (10), rich; fertile
4096 piŏtēs (1), oiliness, i.e. nourishing sap

FATS
3342 yeqeb (2), wine-vat, wine-press

FATTED
75 'âbaç (1), to feed; be fattened with feed
4770 marbêq (1), stall
4618 sitĕutŏs (3), fattened, i.e. stall-fed

FATTER
1277 bârîy' (1), fatted or plump; healthy

FATTEST
4924 mashmân (2), fatness; fertile; robust

FAULT
2398 châţâ' (1), to sin
3972 mᵉ'ûwmâh (1), something; anything
5771 'âvôn (2), moral evil
7564 rish'âh (1), moral wrong
7844 shᵉchath (Ch.) (2), to decay; to ruin
156 aitia (3), logical reason; legal crime
158 aitiŏn (2), reason, basis; crime
299 amŏmŏs (1), unblemished, blameless
1651 ĕlĕgchŏ (1), to confute, admonish
2275 hēttēma (1), failure or loss
3201 mĕmphŏmai (3), to blame
3900 paraptōma (1), error; transgression

FAULTLESS
278 amĕtamĕlētŏs (1), irrevocable
299 amŏmŏs (1), unblemished, blameless

FAULTS
2399 chēţ' (1), crime or its penalty
264 hamartanō (1), to miss the mark, to err
3900 paraptōma (1), error; transgression

FAULTY
816 'âsham (1), to be guilty; to be punished
818 'âshêm (1), bearing guilt, guilty

FAVOUR
2580 chên (26), graciousness; beauty
2594 chănîynâh (1), graciousness, kindness
2603 chânan (8), to implore
2617 cheçed (3), kindness, favor
2655 châphêts (1), pleased with
2896 tôwb (2), good; well
3190 yâţab (1), to be, make well
6440 pânîym (4), face; front
7520 râtsad (1), to look askant; to be jealous
7522 râtsôwn (15), delight
7965 shâlôwm (1), safe; well; health, prosperity
8467 tᵉchinnâh (1), gracious entreaty
5485 charis (6), gratitude; benefit given

FAVOURABLE
2603 chânan (1), to implore
7520 râtsad (3), to look askant; to be jealous

FAVOURED
2603 chânan (1), to implore
4758 mar'eh (7), appearance; vision
8389 tô'ar (2), outline, i.e. figure or appearance
5487 charitŏŏ (1), to give special honor; one highly favored

FAVOUREST
2654 châphêts (1), to be pleased with, desire

FAVOURETH
2654 châphêts (1), to be pleased with, desire

FEAR
367 'êymâh (5), fright
1481 gûwr (2), to sojourn, live as an alien
1674 dᵉ'âgâh (1), anxiety
1763 dᵉchal (Ch.) (1), to fear; be formidable, awesome
2342 chûwl (2), to dance, whirl; to writhe in pain; to wait; to pervert
2731 chărâdâh (2), fear, anxiety
2844 chath (1), terror
3025 yâgôr (1), to fear
3372 yârê' (148), to fear; to revere

3373 yârê' (35), fearing; reverent
3374 yir'âh (41), fear; reverence
4032 mâgôwr (6), fright, horror
4034 mᵉgôwrâh (1), affright, dread
4172 môwrâ' (6), fearful
6206 'ârats (2), to awe; to dread; to harass
6342 pâchad (9), to be startled; to fear
6343 pachad (41), sudden alarm, fear
6345 pachdâh (1), awe
6440 pânîym (8), face; front
7267 rôgez (1), disquiet; anger
7374 reţeţ (1), terror, panic
7461 ra'ad (1), shudder
820 atimŏs (1), dishonoured; without honor
870 aphŏbŏs (3), fearlessly
1167 dĕilia (1), timidity, cowardice
1630+1510 ĕkphŏbŏs (1), frightened out of one's wits
2124 ĕulabĕia (1), reverence; submission
2125 ĕulabĕŏmai (1), to have reverence
5399 phŏbĕŏ (35), to fear, be frightened; to revere
5401 phŏbŏs (40), alarm, or fright; reverence
5401+2192 phŏbŏs (1), fright; reverence

FEARED
1481 gûwr (1), to sojourn, live as an alien
1763 dᵉchal (Ch.) (1), to fear; be formidable
3372 yârê' (38), to fear; to revere
3373 yârê' (8), fearing; reverent
4172 môwrâ' (1), fearful
6206 'ârats (1), to awe; to dread; to harass
6342 pâchad (3), to be startled; to fear
8175 sâ'ar (1), to storm; to shiver, i.e. fear
2124 ĕulabĕia (1), reverence; submission
5399 phŏbĕŏ (17), to fear, to be in awe of, revere
5399+5401 phŏbĕŏ (1), to fear, be in awe of

FEAREST
1481 gûwr (1), to sojourn, live as an alien
3372 yârê' (1), to fear; to revere
3373 yârê' (1), fearing; reverent

FEARETH
3372 yârê' (2), to fear; to revere
3373 yârê' (13), fearing; reverent

6342 pâchad (1), to *be startled; to fear*
5399 phŏbĕŏ (4), to *fear, be in awe of, revere*

FEARFUL
3372 yârê' (2), to *fear; to revere*
3373 yârê' (2), *fearing; reverent*
4116 mâhar (1), to *hurry; promptly*
1169 dĕilŏs (3), *timid,* i.e. *faithless*
5398 phŏbĕrŏs (2), *frightful,* i.e. *formidable*
5400 phŏbĕtrŏn (1), *frightening* thing

FEARFULLY
3372 yârê' (1), to *fear; to revere*

FEARFULNESS
3374 yir'âh (1), *fear; reverence*
6427 pallâtsûwth (1), *affright, trembling fear*
7461 ra'ad (1), *shudder*

FEARING
3372 yârê' (1), to *fear; to revere*
2125 ĕulabĕŏmai (1), to *have reverence*
5399 phŏbĕŏ (6), to *fear, be in awe of, revere*

FEARS
2849 chathchath (1), *terror, horror*
4035 mᵉgûwrâh (2), *fright; granary*
5401 phŏbŏs (1), *alarm, or fright; reverence*

FEAST
2282 chag (53), solemn *festival*
2287 châgag (4), to *observe* a festival
3899 lechem (1), *food, bread*
3900 lᵉchem (Ch.) (1), *food, bread*
4150 môw'êd (3), *assembly, congregation*
4960 mishteh (21), *drink; banquet or feast*
755 architriklinŏs (3), *director of the entertainment*
1408 drŏmŏs (2), *career, course of life*
1456 ĕgkainia (1), Feast of *Dedication*
1858 hĕŏrtazŏ (1), to *observe a festival*
1859 hĕŏrtē (26), *festival*
4910 sunĕuōchĕŏ (2), to *feast together*

FEASTED
6213+4960 'âsâh (1), to *do or make*

FEASTING
4960 mishteh (7), *drink; banquet or feast*

FEASTS
2282 chag (5), solemn *festival*
4150 môw'êd (19), *assembly, congregation*

4580 mâ'ôwg (1), *cake of* bread, *provision*
4960 mishteh (2), *drink; banquet or feast*
1173 dĕipnŏn (3), *principal meal*

FEATHERED
3671 kânâph (2), *edge or extremity; wing*

FEATHERS
84 'ebrâh (2), *pinion*
2624 chăçîydâh (1), *stork*
5133 nôwtsâh (3), *plumage*

FED
398 'âkal (5), to *eat*
1277 bârîy' (1), *fatted or plump; healthy*
2109 zûwn (1), to *nourish; feed*
2110 zûwn (Ch.) (1), to *nourish; feed*
2939 ṭᵉ'am (Ch.) (1), to *feed*
3557 kûwl (3), to *keep in; to measure*
4806 mᵉrîy' (1), *stall-fed* animal
5095 nâhal (1), to *flow; to protect, sustain*
7462 râ'âh (10), to *tend a* flock, i.e. *pasture it*
1006 bŏskŏ (2), to *pasture a flock*
4222 pŏtizŏ (1), to *furnish drink, irrigate*
5142 trĕphō (1), to *nurse, feed, care for*
5526 chŏrtazō (1), to *supply food*

FEEBLE
535 'âmal (1), to *be weak; to be sick*
537 'ămêlâl (1), *languid, feeble*
2826 châshal (1), to *make unsteady*
3766 kâra' (1), to *make miserable*
3782 kâshal (4), to *totter, waver; to falter*
3808+3524 lô' (1), no, *not*
3808+6099 lô' (1), no, *not*
5848 'âṭaph (1), to *shroud; to languish*
6313 pûwg (1), to *be sluggish; be numb*
7503 râphâh (6), to *slacken*
772 asthĕnēs (1), *strengthless, weak*
3886 paraluŏ (1), to *be paralyzed or enfeebled*

FEEBLEMINDED
3642 ŏligŏpsuchŏs (1), *timid, faint-hearted*

FEEBLENESS
7510 riphyôwn (1), *slackness*

FEEBLER
5848 'âṭaph (1), to *shroud, to languish*

FEED
398 'âkal (8), to *eat*
1197 bâ'ar (1), to *be brutish, be senseless*

2963 ṭâraph (1), to *supply, provide food*
3557 kûwl (3), to *keep in; to measure*
3938 lâ'aṭ (1), to *swallow greedily, gulp*
7462 râ'âh (55), to *tend a* flock, i.e. *pasture it*
1006 bŏskŏ (3), to *pasture a flock*
4165 pŏimainō (4), to *tend as a shepherd*
5142 trĕphō (1), to *nurse, feed, care for*
5595 psōmizō (2), to *nourish, feed*

FEEDEST
398 'âkal (1), to *eat*
7462 râ'âh (1), to *tend a* flock, i.e. *pasture it*

FEEDETH
7462 râ'âh (5), to *tend a* flock, i.e. *pasture it*
4165 pŏimainō (1), to *tend as a shepherd*
5142 trĕphō (2), to *nurse, feed, care for*

FEEDING
7462 râ'âh (4), to *tend a* flock, i.e. *pasture it*
1006 bŏskŏ (3), to *pasture a flock*
4165 pŏimainō (2), to *tend as a shepherd*

FEEL
995 bîyn (1), to *understand; discern*
3045 yâda' (2), to *know*
4184 mûwsh (2), to *touch, feel*
4959 mâshash (1), to *feel of; to grope*
5584 psēlaphaō (1), to *verify* by contac

FEELING
524 apalgĕŏ (1), *become apathetic, callous*
4834 sumpathĕŏ (1), to *commiserate*

FEET
4772 margᵉlâh (5), *at the foot*
6471 pa'am (6), *time; step; occurence*
7166 qarçôl (2), *ankles*
7271 rᵉgal (Ch.) (7), *pair of feet*
7272 regel (151), *foot; step*
939 basis (1), *foot*
4228 pŏus (76), *foot*

FEIGN
5234 nâkar (1), to *treat as a foreigner*
5271 hupŏkrinŏmai (1), to *pretend*

FEIGNED
4820 mirmâh (1), *fraud*
4112 plastŏs (1), *artificial, fabricated*

FEIGNEDLY
8267 sheqer (1), *untruth; sham*

FEIGNEST
908 bâdâ' (1), to *invent; to choose*

FELIX
5344 Phēlix (8), *happy*

FELIX'
5344 Phēlix (1), *happy*

FELL
1961 hâyâh (7), to *exist,* i.e. *be or become*
3318 yâtsâ' (2), to *go, bring out*
3381 yârad (2), to *descend*
3766 kâra' (2), to *prostrate*
3782 kâshal (2), to *totter, waver; to falter*
5307 nâphal (122), to *fall*
5308 nᵉphal (Ch.) (5), to *fall*
5927 'âlâh (2), to *ascend, be high, mount*
6293 pâga' (4), to *impinge*
6298 pâgash (1), to *come in contact with*
6584 pâshat (2), to *strip,* i.e. *unclothe, plunder*
7257 râbats (1), to *recline, repose, brood*
7812 shâchâh (2), to *prostrate*
634 apŏpiptō (1), to *fall off, drop off*
1096 ginŏmai (1), to *be, become*
1356 diŏpĕtēs (1), *sky-fallen*
1601 ĕkpiptō (1), to *drop away*
1706 ĕmpiptō (1), to *be entrapped by*
1968 ĕpipiptō (10), to *embrace; to seize*
2597 katabainō (1), to *descend*
4045 pĕripiptō (1), to *fall into the hands of*
4098 piptō (56), to *fall*
4363 prŏspiptō (6), to *prostrate oneself*

FELLED
5307 nâphal (1), to *fall*

FELLER
3772 kârath (1), to *cut* (off, down or asunder)

FELLEST
5307 nâphal (1), to *fall*

FELLING
5307 nâphal (1), to *fall*

FELLOES
2839 chishshûq (1), *wheel-spoke*

FELLOW
376 'îysh (1), *man; male; someone*
2270 châbêr (2), *associate, friend*
5997 'âmîyth (1), *comrade or kindred*
7453 rêa' (9), *associate; one close*

FELLOW'S
7453 rêa' (1), *associate; one close*

FELLOWCITIZENS
4847 sumpŏlitēs (1), *fellow citizen*

English

FELLOWDISCIPLES
4827 summathētēs (1), co-learner

FELLOWHEIRS
4789 sugklērŏnŏmŏs (1), participant in common

FELLOWHELPER
4904 sunĕrgŏs (1), fellow-worker

FELLOWHELPERS
4904 sunĕrgŏs (1), fellow-worker

FELLOWLABOURER
4904 sunĕrgŏs (2), fellow-worker

FELLOWLABOURERS
4904 sunĕrgŏs (2), fellow-worker

FELLOWPRISONER
4869 sunaichmalōtŏs (2), co-captive

FELLOWPRISONERS
4869 sunaichmalōtŏs (1), co-captive

FELLOWS
582 'ĕnôwsh (1), man; person, human
2269 chăbar (Ch.) (2), associate, friend
2270 châbêr (3), associate, friend
2273 chabrâh (Ch.) (1), similar, associated
7453 rêa' (1), associate; one close
7464 rê'âh (1), female associate
435 anēr (1), man; male
2083 hĕtairŏs (1), comrade, friend
3353 mĕtŏchŏs (1), sharer, associate

FELLOWSERVANT
4889 sundŏulŏs (6), servitor of the same master

FELLOWSERVANTS
4889 sundŏulŏs (4), servitor of the same master

FELLOWSHIP
2266 châbar (1), to fascinate by spells
8667+3027 t°sûwmeth (1), deposit, i.e. pledging
2842 kŏinōnia (12), benefaction; sharing
2844 kŏinōnŏs (1), associate, partner
3352 mĕtŏchē (1), something in common
4790 sugkŏinōnĕō (1), to co-participate

FELLOWSOLDIER
4961 sustratiōtēs (1), soldier together with

FELT
3045 yâda' (1), to know
4959 mâshash (2), to feel of; to grope
1097 ginōskō (1), to know
3958 paschō (1), to experience pain

FEMALE
802 'ishshâh (2), woman, wife; women, wives
5347 n°qêbâh (19), female, woman
2338 thēlus (3), female

FENCE
1447 gâdêr (1), enclosure, wall or fence

FENCED
1211 betsel (1), onion
1219 bâtsar (15), to be inaccessible
1443 gâdar (1), to build a stone wall
4013 mibtsâr (12), fortification; defender
4390 mâlê' (1), to fill; be full
4692 mâtsôwr (1), siege-mound; distress
4694 m°tsûwrâh (5), rampart, fortification
5823 'âzaq (1), to grub over, dig
7753 sûwk (1), to shut in with hedges

FENS
1207 bitstsâh (1), swamp, marsh

FERRET
604 'ănâqâh (1), gecko

FERRY
5679 'ăbârâh (1), crossing-place

FERVENT
1618 ĕktĕnēs (1), intent, earnest
2204 zĕō (2), to be fervid or earnest
2205 zēlŏs (1), zeal, ardor; jealousy, malice

FERVENTLY
1619 ĕktĕnōs (1), intently, earnestly

FESTUS
5347 Phēstŏs (12), festal

FESTUS'
5347 Phēstŏs (1), festal

FETCH
935 bôw' (1), to go or come
3318 yâtsâ' (1), to go, bring out
3947 lâqach (20), to take
5375 nâsâ' (1), to lift up
5437 çâbab (1), to surround
5670 'âbaṭ (1), to pawn; to lend; to entangle
5927 'âlâh (1), to ascend, be high, mount
7725 shûwb (1), to turn back; to return
1806 ĕxagō (1), to lead forth, escort

FETCHED
622 'âçaph (1), to gather, collect
3318 yâtsâ' (1), to go, bring out
3947 lâqach (10), to take
5375 nâsâ' (1), to lift up
5927 'âlâh (1), to ascend, be high, mount

FETCHETH
5080 nâdach (1), to push off, scattered

FETCHT
3947 lâqach (1), to take

FETTERS
2131 zîyqâh (1), arrow; bond, fetter
3525 kebel (2), fetter, shackles
5178 n°chôsheth (5), copper; bronze
3976 pĕdē (3), shackle for the feet

FEVER
6920 qaddachath (1), inflammation
4445 purĕssō (2), to burn with a fever
4446 purĕtŏs (6), fever

FEW
259 'echâd (3), first
4213 miz'âr (1), fewness, smallness
4557 miçpâr (5), number
4591 mâ'aṭ (4), to be, make small or few
4592 m°'aṭ (24), little or few
4962 math (4), men
7116 qâtsêr (1), short
1024 brachus (1), little, short
3641 ŏligŏs (20), puny, small
4935 suntŏmōs (1), briefly

FEWER
4592 m°'aṭ (1), little or few

FEWEST
4592 m°'aṭ (1), little or few

FEWNESS
4591 mâ'aṭ (1), to be, make small or few

FIDELITY
4102 pistis (1), faithfulness; faith, belief

FIELD
776 'erets (1), earth, land, soil; country
1251 bar (Ch.) (8), field
2513 chelqâh (3), flattery; allotment
7704 sâdeh (246), field
68 agrŏs (22), farmland, countryside
5564 chōriŏn (3), spot or plot of ground

FIELDS
2351 chûwts (2), outside, outdoors; countryside
3010 yâgêb (1), plowed field
7704 sâdeh (46), field
7709 sh°dêmâh (4), cultivated field
8309 sh°rêmâh (1), common
68 agrŏs (1), farmland, countryside
5561 chōra (2), space of territory

FIERCE
393 'akzâr (1), violent, deadly; brave
2300 châdad (1), to be, make sharp; fierce
2740 chârôwn (23), burning of anger
2750 chŏrîy (3), burning anger
3267 yâ'az (1), to be obstinate, be arrogant
5794 'az (4), strong, vehement, harsh
7826 shachal (3), lion
434 anēmĕrŏs (1), brutal, savage
2001 ĕpischuō (1), to insist stoutly
4642 sklērŏs (1), hard or tough; harsh, severe
5467 chalĕpŏs (1), difficult, furious

FIERCENESS
2740 chârôwn (9), burning of anger
7494 ra'ash (1), bounding, uproar
2372 thumŏs (2), passion, anger

FIERCER
7185 qâshâh (1), to be tough or severe

FIERY
784 'êsh (1), fire
799 'eshdâth (1), fire-law
5135 nûwr (Ch.) (10), fire
8314 sârâph (5), poisonous serpent
4442 pur (1), fire
4448 purŏŏ (1), to be ignited, glow
4451 purōsis (1), ignition, conflagration, calamity

FIFTEEN
2568+6240 châmêsh (16), five
6235+2568 'eser (1), ten
7657+2568 shib'îym (3), seventy
1178 dĕkapĕntĕ (3), fifteen
1440+4002 hĕbdŏ-mēkŏnta (1), seventy

FIFTEENTH
2568+6240 châmêsh (17), five
4003 pĕntĕkaidĕkatŏs (1), five and tenth

FIFTH
2549 chămîyshîy (44), fifth; fifth part
2567 châmash (1), to tax a fifth
2568 châmêsh (6), five
2569 chômesh (1), fifth tax
2570 chômesh (4), abdomen, belly
3991 pĕmptŏs (4), fifth

FIFTIES
2572 chămishshîym (5), fifty
4004 pĕntēkŏnta (2), fifty

FIFTIETH
2572 chămishshîym (4), fifty

FIFTY
2572 chămishshîym
(148), *fifty*
4002+3461 pĕntĕ (1), *five*
4004 pĕntēkŏnta (5), *fifty*

FIG
8384 tᵉ'ên (24), *fig tree
or fruit*
4808 sukē (16), *fig-tree*

FIGHT
3898 lâcham (85), to *fight
a battle*, i.e. *consume*
4421 milchâmâh (5),
battle; war; fighting
4634 ma'ărâkâh (1), *row;
pile;* military *array*
6633 tsâbâ' (4), to *mass*
an army or servants
73 agōn (1), *contest,
struggle*
75 agōnizŏmai (2), to
struggle; to *contend*
119 athlēsis (1), *struggle,
contest*
2313 thĕŏmachĕō (1), to
resist deity
2314 thĕŏmachŏs (1),
opponent of deity
3164 machŏmai (1), to
war, i.e. to *quarrel*
4170 pŏlĕmĕō (1), to
battle, make war
4171 pŏlĕmŏs (1),
warfare; battle; fight
4438 puktĕō (1), to *box*
as a sporting event

FIGHTETH
3898 lâcham (3), to *fight
a battle*, i.e. *consume*

FIGHTING
3898 lâcham (2), to *fight
a battle*, i.e. *consume*
6213+4421 'âsâh (1), to
do or make

FIGHTINGS
3163 machē (2),
controversy, conflict

FIGS
6291 pag (1), *unripe fig*
8384 tᵉ'ên (15), *fig tree
or fruit*
3653 ŏlunthŏs (1), *unripe
fig*
4810 sukŏn (4), *fig*

FIGURE
5566 çemel (1), *likeness*
8403 tabnîyth (1), *model,
resemblance*
499 antitupŏn (1),
representative
3345 mĕtaschēmatizō
(1), to *transfigure*
3850 parabŏlē (2),
fictitious narrative
5179 tupŏs (1), *shape,
resemblance;* "*type*"

FIGURES
4734 miqla'ath (1),
bas-relief *sculpture*
499 antitupŏn (1),
representative
5179 tupŏs (1), *shape,
resemblance;* "*type*"

FILE
6477+6310 pᵉtsîyrâh (1),
bluntness

FILL
4390 mâlê' (33), to *fill; be
full*
4393 mᵉlô' (2), *fulness*
5433 çâbâ' (1), to *quaff* to
satiety
7301 râvâh (1), to *slake*
thirst or appetites
7646 sâba' (1), *fill* to
satiety
7648 sôba' (2),
satisfaction
466 antanaplērŏō (1), to
fill up
878 aphrōn (1), *ignorant;
egotistic; unbelieving*
1072 gĕmizō (1), to *fill*
entirely
2767 kĕrannumi (1), to
mingle, i.e. to *pour*
4137 plērŏō (3), to *fill,
make complete*
4138 plērōma (1), *what
fills; what is filled*
5526 chŏrtazō (1), to
supply food

FILLED
4390 mâlê' (74), to *fill; be
full*
4391 mᵉlâ' (Ch.) (1), to
fill; be full
7059 qâmaṭ (1), to *pluck,*
i.e. *destroy*
7301 râvâh (1), to *slake*
thirst or appetites
7646 sâba' (22), *fill* to
satiety
1072 gĕmizō (7), to *fill*
entirely
1705 ĕmpiplēmi (3), to
satisfy
2767 kĕrannumi (1), to
mingle, i.e. to *pour*
4130 plēthō (17), to *fulfill,
complete*
4137 plērŏō (17), to *fill,
make complete*
4138 plērōma (1), *what
fills; what is filled*
4845 sumplērŏō (1), to be
complete, fulfill
5055 tĕlĕō (1), to *end*, i.e.
complete, execute
5526 chŏrtazō (11), to
supply food

FILLEDST
4390 mâlê' (1), to *fill; be
full*
7646 sâba' (1), *fill* to
satiety

FILLEST
4390 mâlê' (1), to *fill; be
full*

FILLET
2339 chûwṭ (1), *string;*
measuring *tape; line*

FILLETED
2836 châshaq (3), to *join;*
to *love, delight*

FILLETH
4390 mâlê' (2), to *fill; be
full*
5844 'âṭâh (1), to *wrap,*
i.e. *cover, veil, clothe*
7646 sâba' (2), *fill* to
satiety

FILLETS
2838 châshûq (8),
fence-*rail* or *rod*

FILLING
1705 ĕmpiplēmi (1), to
satisfy

FILTH
6675 tsôw'âh (1),
pollution
4027 pĕrikatharma (1),
refuse, scum
4509 rhupŏs (1), *dirt*, i.e.
moral *depravity*

FILTHINESS
2932 ṭum'âh (7),
ceremonial *impurity*
5079 niddâh (2), time of
menstrual *impurity*
5178 nᵉchôsheth (1),
copper; bronze
6675 tsôw'âh (2),
pollution
151 aischrŏtēs (1),
obscenity
168 akathartēs (1), state
of *impurity*
3436 mŏlusmŏs (1),
contamination
4507 rhuparia (1), moral
dirtiness

FILTHY
444 'âlach (3), to *be* or
turn morally *corrupt*
4754 mârâ' (1), to *rebel;*
to *lash* with whip; *flap*
5708 'êd (1), periodical
menstrual flux
6674 tsôw' (2),
excrementitious, soiled
147 aischrŏkĕrdōs (1),
sordidly, greedily
148 aischrŏlŏgia (1),
filthy speech
150 aischrŏs (2),
shameful thing, *base*
766 asĕlgĕia (1),
debauchery, lewdness
4510 rhupŏō (2), to
become morally *dirty*

FINALLY
3063 lŏipŏn (5), *finally*
5056 tĕlŏs (1), *conclusion*

FIND
2803 châshab (1), to
think, regard; to *value*
4672 mâtsâ' (100), to *find
or acquire;* to *occur*
7912 shᵉkach (Ch.) (6), to
discover, find out
2147 hĕuriskō (46), to
find

FINDEST
4672 mâtsâ' (2), to *find
or acquire;* to *occur*

FINDETH
4672 mâtsâ' (11), to *find
or acquire;* to *occur*
2147 hĕuriskō (12), to
find

FINDING
2714 chêqer (1),
examination
4672 mâtsâ' (2), to *find
or acquire;* to *occur*

FILLETS
4131 plĕktēs (1),
pugnacious

FILLETS
2838 châshûq (8),
fence-*rail* or *rod*

421 anĕxichniastŏs (1),
unsearchable
429 anĕuriskō (1), to *find
out*
2147 hĕuriskō (4), to *find*

FINE
2212 zâqaq (1), to *strain,
refine; extract, clarify*
2869 ṭâb (Ch.) (1), *good*
2896 ṭôwb (2), *good; well*
6668 tsâhab (1), to be
golden in color
8305 sᵉrîyqâh (1), *linen
cloth*
4585 sĕmidalis (1), fine
wheat *flour*

FINER
6884 tsâraph (1), to *fuse*
metal; to *refine*

FINEST
2459 cheleb (2), *fat;
choice* part

FINGER
676 'etsba (19), *finger;
toe*
1147 daktulŏs (5), *finger*

FINGERS
676 'etsba (11), *finger;
toe*
677 'etsba' (Ch.) (1),
finger; toe
1147 daktulŏs (3), *finger*

FINING
4715 mitsrêph (2),
crucible

FINISH
1214 bâtsa' (1), to
plunder; to *finish*
3607 kâlâ' (1), to *hold
back or in;* to *prohibit*
3615 kâlâh (1), to *cease,
be finished, perish*
535 apartismŏs (1),
completion
1615 ĕktĕlĕō (2), to
complete fully, finish
2005 ĕpitĕlĕō (1), to
terminate; to *undergo*
4931 suntĕlĕō (1), to
complete entirely
5048 tĕlĕiŏō (3), to
perfect, complete

FINISHED
3319 yᵉtsâ' (Ch.) (1), to
complete
3615 kâlâh (19), to *cease,
be finished, perish*
3635 kᵉlal (Ch.) (1), to
complete
7999 shâlam (3), to be
safe; be complete
8000 shᵉlam (Ch.) (2), to
complete, to *restore*
8552 tâmam (4), to
complete, finish
658 apŏtĕlĕō (1), to *bring
to completion*
1096 ginŏmai (1), to *be,
become*
1274 dianuō (1), to
accomplish thoroughly
5048 tĕlĕiŏō (1), to
perfect, complete
5055 tĕlĕō (8), to *end,
complete, conclude*

FINISHER
5047 tĕlĕiŏtēs (1), *completeness; maturity*

FINS
5579 ç^{e}nappîyr (5), *fin*

FIR
1265 b^{e}rôwsh (20), (poss.) *cypress*
1266 b^{e}rôwth (1), (poss.) *cypress*

FIRE
215 'ôwr (1), to *be luminous*
217 'ûwr (4), *flame; East*
784 'êsh (375), *fire*
1200 b^{e}'êrâh (1), *burning*
3857 lâhaṭ (4), to *blaze*
5135 nûwr (Ch.) (8), *fire*
4442 pur (73), *fire*
4443 pura (2), *fire*
4447 purinŏs (1), *fiery*, i.e. *flaming*
4448 purŏō (1), to *be ignited, glow*
5394 phlŏgizō (2), to *cause a blaze*
5457 phōs (2), *luminousness, light*

FIREBRAND
181 'ûwd (1), *poker stick for a fire*
3940 lappîyd (1), *flaming torch, lamp* or *flame*

FIREBRANDS
181 'ûwd (1), *poker stick for a fire*
2131 zîyqâh (1), *flash* of fire
3940 lappîyd (1), *flaming torch, lamp* or *flame*

FIREPANS
4289 machtâh (4), *pan* for live coals

FIRES
217 'ûwr (1), *flame; East*

FIRKINS
3355 mĕtrētēs (1), liquid *measure:* 8-10 gallons

FIRM
1277 bârîy' (1), *fatted* or *plump; healthy*
3332 yâtsaq (2), to *pour* out
3559 kûwn (2), to *set up: establish, fix, prepare*
8631 t^{e}qêph (Ch.) (1), to *become, make mighty*
949 bĕbaiŏs (1), *stable, certain, binding*

FIRMAMENT
7549 râqîya' (17), *expanse*

FIRST
259 'echâd (34), *first*
1061 bikkûwr (1), *first-fruits* of the crop
1069 bâkar (1), *bear the first born*
1073 bakkûrâh (1), *first-ripe fruit* of a fig
1121 bên (51), *son, descendant*
1323 bath (3), *daughter, descendant, woman*
2298 chad (Ch.) (4), *one; single; first; at once*
2490 châlal (1), to *profane, defile*
3138 yôwreh (1), autumn *rain* showers
4395 m^{e}lê'âh (1), *fulfilled; abundance*
6440 pânîym (1), *face; front*
6933 qadmay (Ch.) (3), *first*
7218 rô'sh (6), *head*
7223 rî'shôwn (130), *first*, in place, time or rank
7224 rî'shônîy (1), *first*
7225 rê'shîyth (11), *first*
8462 t^{e}chillâh (7), *original; originally*
509 anōthĕn (1), *from above; from the first*
746 archē (4), *first in rank; first in time*
1207 dĕutĕrŏprōtŏs (1), *second-first*
1722+4413 ĕn (1), *in; during; because of*
3391 mia (7), *one* or *first*
3891 paranŏmĕō (1), to *transgress, violate law*
4272 prŏdidōmi (1), to *give before*
4276 prŏĕlpizō (1), to *hope in advance* of
4295 prŏkĕimai (1), to *be present* to the mind
4386 prŏtĕrŏn (3), *previously*
4412 prōtŏn (58), *firstly*
4413 prōtŏs (84), *foremost*
4416 prōtŏtŏkŏs (1), *first-born*

FIRSTBEGOTTEN
4416 prōtŏtŏkŏs (1), *first-born*

FIRSTBORN
1060 b^{e}kôwr (101), *firstborn*
1062 b^{e}kôwrâh (1), *state of, rights of first born*
1067 b^{e}kîyrâh (6), *first born, eldest* daughter
1069 bâkar (1), *bear the first born*
4416 prōtŏtŏkŏs (7), *first-born*

FIRSTFRUIT
7225 rê'shîyth (1), *first*
536 aparchē (1), *first-fruit*

FIRSTFRUITS
1061 bikkûwr (13), *first-fruits* of the crop
7225 rê'shîyth (11), *first*
536 aparchē (7), *first-fruit*

FIRSTLING
1060 b^{e}kôwr (8), *firstborn*, i.e. oldest son
1069 bâkar (1), *bear the first born*
6363 peṭer (4), *firstling, first born*

FIRSTLINGS
1060 b^{e}kôwr (1), *firstborn*, i.e. oldest son
1062 b^{e}kôwrâh (5), *state of, rights of first born*

FIRSTRIPE
1061 bikkûwr (1), *first-fruits* of the crop
1063 bikkûwrâh (3), *early* fig

FISH
1709 dâg (11), *fish; fishes*
1710 dâgâh (14), *fish; fishes*
1770 dîyg (1), to catch *fish*
5315 nephesh (1), *life; breath; soul; wind*
2486 ichthus (5), *fish*
3795 ŏpsariŏn (3), *small fish*

FISH'S
1710 dâgâh (1), *fish; fishes*

FISHER'S
1903 ĕpĕndutēs (1), *outer garment, coat*

FISHERMEN
231 haliĕus (1), one who *fishes for a living*

FISHERS
1728 davvâg (2), *fisherman*
1771 dayâg (1), *fisherman*
231 haliĕus (4), one who *fishes for a living*

FISHES
1709 dâg (8), *fish; fishes*
2485 ichthudiŏn (2), *little fish*
2486 ichthus (15), *fish*
3795 ŏpsariŏn (2), *small fish*

FISHHOOKS
5518+1729 çîyr (1), *thorn; hook*

FISHING
232 haliĕuō (1), to catch *fish*

FISHPOOLS
1295 b^{e}rêkâh (1), *reservoir, pool*

FIST
106 'egrôph (2), *clenched* hand

FISTS
2651 chôphen (1), pair of *fists*

FIT
6257 'âthad (1), to *prepare*
6261 'ittîy (1), *timely*
433 anēkō (1), *be proper, fitting*
2111 ĕuthĕtŏs (2), *appropriate, suitable*
2520 kathēkō (1), *becoming, proper*

FITCHES
3698 kuççemeth (1), *spelt*
7100 qetsach (3), *fennel-flower*

FITLY
5921+655 'al (1), *above, over, upon*, or *against*
5921+4402 'al (1), *above, over, upon*, or *against*
4883 sunarmŏlŏgĕō (2), to *render close-jointed*

FITTED
3474 yâshar (1), to *be straight; to make right*
3559 kûwn (1), to *render sure, proper*
2675 katartizō (1), to *repair;* to *prepare*

FITTETH
6213 'âsâh (1), to *do* or *make*

FIVE
2568 châmêsh (271), *five*
3999 pĕntakis (1), *five times*
4000 pĕntakischiliŏi (16), *five times a thousand*
4001 pĕntakŏsiŏi (2), *five hundred*
4002 pĕntĕ (25), *five*

FIXED
3559 kûwn (4), to *render sure, proper*
4741 stērizō (1), to *turn resolutely;* to *confirm*

FLAG
260 'âchûw (1), *bulrush* or any marshy grass

FLAGON
809 'ăshîyshâh (2), *cake* of raisins

FLAGONS
809 'ăshîyshâh (2), *cake* of raisins
5035 nebel (1), skin-*bag* for liquids; *vase; lyre*

FLAGS
5488 çûwph (3), *papyrus* reed; *reed*

FLAKES
4651 mappâl (1), *chaff; flap* or *fold* of skin

FLAME
785 'êsh (Ch.) (1), *fire*
3632 kâlîyl (1), *whole, entire; complete; whole*
3827 labbâh (1), *flame*
3851 lahab (6), *flame* of fire; *flash* of a *blade*
3852 lehâbâh (12), *flame; flash*
4864 mas'êth (2), *raising; beacon; present*
7631 s^{e}bîyb (Ch.) (2), *flame* tongue
7957 shalhebeth (3), *flare, flame* of fire
5395 phlŏx (6), *flame; blaze*

FLAMES
3851 lahab (2), *flame* of fire; *flash* of a *blade*
3852 lehâbâh (1), *flame; flash*

FLAMING
784 'êsh (1), *fire*
3852 lehâbâh (5), *flame; flash*
3857 lâhaṭ (1), to *blaze*
3858 lahaṭ (1), *blaze; magic*
5395 phlŏx (1), *flame; blaze*

FLANKS
3689 keçel (6), *loin; back; viscera*

FLASH
965 bâzâq (1), *flash* of lightning

FLAT
2763 charam (1), to devote to destruction
8478 tachath (2), bottom; underneath; in lieu of

FLATTER
2505 châlaq (1), to be smooth; be slippery
6601 pâthâh (1), to be, make simple; to delude

FLATTERETH
2505 châlaq (5), to be smooth; be slippery
6601 pâthâh (1), to be, make simple; to delude

FLATTERIES
2514 chălaqqâh (1), smoothness; flattery
2519 chălaqlaqqâh (2), smooth; treacherous

FLATTERING
2506 chêleq (1), smoothness of tongue
2509 châlâq (2), smooth, slippery of tongue
2513 chelqâh (2), smoothness; flattery
3665 kâna' (2), to humiliate, vanquish
2850 kŏlakĕia (1), flattery

FLATTERY
2506 chêleq (1), smoothness of tongue
2513 chelqâh (1), smoothness; flattery

FLAX
6593 pishteh (7), linen, made of carded thread
6594 pishtâh (3), flax; flax wick
3043 linŏn (1), flax linen

FLAY
6584 pâshaṭ (3), to strip, i.e. unclothe, flay

FLAYED
6584 pâshaṭ (1), to strip, i.e. unclothe, flay

FLEA
6550 par'ôsh (2), flea

FLED
1272 bârach (40), to flee suddenly
5074 nâdad (8), to rove, flee; to drive away
5127 nûwç (83), to vanish away, flee
5132 nûwts (1), to fly away, leave
1628 ĕkphĕugō (2), to flee out, escape
2703 kataphĕugō (2), to flee down
5343 phĕugō (11), to run away; to shun

FLEDDEST
1272 bârach (1), to flee suddenly
5127 nûwç (1), to vanish away, flee

FLEE
1227 Baqbûwq (1), gurgling bottle
1272 bârach (14), to flee suddenly
3680 kâçâh (1), to cover

4498 mânôwç (1), fleeing; place of refuge
5074 nâdad (4), to rove, flee; to drive away
5110 nûwd (1), to waver; to wander, flee
5127 nûwç (62), to vanish away, flee
5323 nâtsâ' (1), to go away
5756 'ûwz (1), to save by fleeing
7368 râchaq (1), to recede; remove
5343 phĕugō (15), to run away; to shun

FLEECE
1488 gêz (2), shorn fleece; mown grass
1492 gazzâh (7), wool fleece

FLEEING
4499 mᵉnuwçâh (1), retreat, fleeing
5127 nûwç (1), to vanish away, flee
6207 'âraq (1), to gnaw; a pain

FLEETH
1272 bârach (1), to flee suddenly
5127 nûwç (4), to vanish away, flee
5211 nîyç (1), fugitive
5775 'ôwph (1), bird
5343 phĕugō (2), to run away; to shun

FLESH
829 'eshpâr (2), measured portion
1320 bâsâr (253), flesh; body; person
1321 bᵉsar (Ch.) (3), flesh; body; person
2878 ṭibehâh (1), butchery
3894 lâchûwm (1), flesh
7607 shᵉêr (7), flesh, meat; kindred by blood
2907 krĕas (2), butcher's meat
4561 sarx (143), flesh

FLESHHOOK
4207 mazlêg (2), three-tined meat fork

FLESHHOOKS
4207 mazlêg (5), three-tined meat fork

FLESHLY
4559 sarkikŏs (2), pertaining to flesh

FLESHY
4560 sarkinŏs (1), similar to flesh

FLEW
5774 'ûwph (1), to cover, to fly; to faint
6213 'âsâh (1), to do or make

FLIES
2070 zᵉbûwb (1), stinging fly
6157 'ârôb (2), swarming mosquitoes

FLIETH
1675 dâ'âh (1), to fly rapidly, soar
5774 'ûwph (2), to cover, to fly; to faint
5775 'ôwph (1), bird

FLIGHT
1272 bârach (1), to flee suddenly
4498 mânôwç (1), fleeing; place of refuge
4499 mᵉnuwçâh (1), retreat, fleeing
5127 nûwç (1), to vanish away, flee
7291 râdaph (1), to run after with hostility
5437 phugē (2), escape, flight, fleeing

FLINT
2496 challâmîysh (3), flint, flinty rock
6864 tsôr (2), flint-stone knife

FLINTY
2496 challâmîysh (1), flint, flinty rock

FLOATS
1702 dôbᵉrâh (1), raft, collection of logs

FLOCK
5739 'êder (16), muster, flock
6629 tsô'n (83), flock
4167 pŏimnē (4), flock
4168 pŏimniŏn (5), flock

FLOCKS
2835 châsîph (1), small company, flock
4735 miqneh (1), stock
4830 mir'îyth (1), pasturage; flock
5739 'êder (16), muster, flock
6251 'ashtᵉrâh (4), flock of ewes
6629 tsô'n (54), flock

FLOOD
2229 zâram (1), to gush water, pour forth
2230 zerem (1), gush of water, flood
2975 yᵉ'ôr (6), Nile River; Tigris River
3999 mabbûwl (13), deluge
5104 nâhâr (8), stream; Nile; Euphrates; Tigris
5158 nachal (3), valley, ravine; mine shaft
7858 sheṭeph (3), deluge, torrent
2627 kataklusmŏs (4), inundation, flood
4182 pŏlupŏikilŏs (1), many-sided
4215 pŏtamŏs (2), current, brook
4216 pŏtamŏphŏrētŏs (1), overwhelmed by a stream

FLOODS
5104 nâhâr (10), stream; Nile; Euphrates; Tigris
5140 nâzal (3), to drip, or shed by trickling

5158 nachal (2), valley, ravine; mine shaft
7641 shibbôl (1), stream; ear of grain
7858 sheṭeph (1), deluge, torrent
4215 pŏtamŏs (2), current, brook

FLOOR
1637 gôren (10), open area
7136 qârâh (1), to bring about; to impose
7172 qarqa' (6), floor of a building or a sea
257 halôn (2), threshing-floor

FLOORS
1637 gôren (1), open area

FLOTES
7513 raphçôdâh (1), log raft

FLOUR
1217 bâtsêq (1), fermenting dough
5560 çôleth (52), fine flour
7058 qemach (4), flour
4585 sĕmidalis (1), fine wheat flour

FLOURISH
5006 nâ'ats (1), to scorn
6524 pârach (9), to break forth; to bloom, flourish
6692 tsûwts (3), to blossom, flourish

FLOURISHED
6524 pârach (1), to break forth; to bloom, flourish
330 anathallô (1), to flourish; to revive

FLOURISHETH
6692 tsûwts (2), to blossom, flourish

FLOURISHING
7487 ra'ânan (Ch.) (1), prosperous
7488 ra'ănân (1), verdant; prosperous

FLOW
2151 zâlal (1), to be loose morally, worthless
3212 yâlak (2), to walk; to live; to carry
5064 nâgar (1), to pour out; to deliver over
5102 nâhar (5), to sparkle; to flow
5140 nâzal (3), to drip, or shed by trickling
4482 rhĕō (1), to flow water

FLOWED
2151 zâlal (1), to be loose morally, worthless
3212 yâlak (1), to walk; to live; to carry
6687 tsûwph (1), to overflow

FLOWER
582 'ĕnôwsh (1), man; person, human
5328 nitstsâh (2), blossom
6525 perach (5), calyx flower; bloom

6731 tsîyts (6), burnished plate; bright *flower*
6733 tsîytsâh (1), *flower*
438 anthŏs (4), flower blossom
5230 hupĕrakmŏs (1), past the *bloom* of youth

FLOWERS
4026 migdâl (1), *tower; rostrum*
5079 niddâh (2), time of menstrual *impurity;* idolatry
5339 nitstsân (1), *blossom*
6525 perach (9), *calyx flower; bloom*
6731 tsîyts (4), burnished plate; bright *flower*

FLOWETH
2100 zûwb (12), to *flow* freely, *gush*

FLOWING
2100 zûwb (9), to *flow* freely, *gush*
5042 nâba' (1), to *gush* forth; to *utter*
5140 nâzal (1), to *drip,* or *shed* by trickling
7857 shâṭaph (1), to *gush;* to *inundate*

FLUTE
4953 mashrôwqîy (Ch.) (4), musical *pipe*

FLUTTERETH
7363 râchaph (1), to *brood;* to *be relaxed*

FLUX
1420 dusĕntĕria (1), *dysentery*

FLY
82 'âbar (1), to *soar*
1675 dâ'âh (3), to *fly* rapidly, *soar*
2070 zᵉbûwb (1), *fly*
3286 yâ'aph (1), to *tire*
5774 'ûwph (13), to *cover,* to *fly;* to *faint*
5860 'îyṭ (1), to *swoop* down upon; to *insult*
6524 pârach (2), to *break* forth; to *bloom;* to *fly*
4072 pĕtŏmai (3), to *fly*

FLYING
3671 kânâph (1), *edge* or *extremity; wing*
5774 'ûwph (6), to *cover,* to *fly;* to *faint*
5775 'ôwph (2), *bird*
4072 pĕtŏmai (2), to *fly*

FOAL
1121 bên (1), *son, descendant*
5895 'ayîr (1), young donkey or *ass*
5207 huiŏs (1), *son*

FOALS
5895 'ayîr (1), young donkey or *ass*

FOAM
7110 qetseph (1), *rage* or *strife*

FOAMETH
875 aphrizō (1), to *froth* at the mouth

876 aphrŏs (1), *froth, foam*

FOAMING
875 aphrizō (1), to *froth* at the mouth
1890 ĕpaphrizō (1), to *foam upon*

FODDER
1098 bᵉlîyl (1), *feed, fodder*

FOES
341 'ôyêb (2), *adversary, enemy*
6862 tsar (2), *trouble; opponent*
8130 sânê' (1), to *hate*
2190 ĕchthrŏs (2), *adversary*

FOLD
1699 dôber (1), grazing *pasture*
4356 miklâ'âh (1), sheep or goat *pen*
5116 nâveh (3), *at home; lovely; home*
7257 râbats (1), to *recline, repose, brood*
833 aulē (1), *palace; house; sheepfold*
1667 hĕlissō (1), to *coil, roll up,* or *wrap*
4167 pŏimnē (1), *flock*

FOLDEN
5440 çâbak (1), to *entwine*

FOLDETH
2263 châbaq (1), to *clasp* the hands, *embrace*

FOLDING
1550 gâlîyl (2), *valve* of a folding door
2264 chibbûq (2), *folding*

FOLDS
1448 gᵉdêrâh (3), *enclosure* for flocks
4356 miklâ'âh (1), sheep or goat *pen*
5116 nâveh (1), *at home; lovely; home*

FOLK
3816 lᵉ'ôm (1), *community, nation*
5971 'am (2), *people; tribe; flock*

FOLLOW
310 'achar (5), *after*
935+310 bôw' (1), to *go or come*
1692 dâbaq (1), to *cling* or *adhere;* to *catch*
1961 hâyâh (3), to *exist,* i.e. *be* or *become*
1961+310 hâyâh (1), to *exist,* i.e. *be* or *become*
1980+310 hâlak (1), to *walk; live a certain way*
1980+7272 hâlak (1), to *walk; live a certain way*
3212+310 yâlak (8), to *walk;* to *live;* to *carry*
7272 regel (3), *foot; step*
7291 râdaph (11), to *run after* with hostility
190 akŏlŏuthĕō (30), to *accompany, follow*

1205+3694 dĕutĕ (1), *come hither!*
1377 diōkō (8), to *pursue;* to *persecute*
1811 ĕxakŏlŏuthĕō (1), to *imitate, obey*
1872 ĕpakŏlŏuthĕō (2), to *accompany, follow*
2071 ĕsŏmai (1), *will be*
2517 kathĕxēs (1), *in a sequence*
3326+5023 mĕta (1), *with, among; after, later*
3401 mimĕŏmai (4), to *imitate,* i.e. *model*
3877 parakŏlŏuthĕō (1), to *attend; trace out*
4870 sunakŏlŏuthĕō (1), to *follow, accompany*

FOLLOWED
310 'achar (16), *after*
1692 dâbaq (4), to *cling* or *adhere;* to *catch*
1961+310 hâyâh (2), to *exist,* i.e. *be* or *become*
1980+310 hâlak (7), to *walk; live a certain way*
3112+310 Yôwyâkîyn (1), *Jehovah will establish*
3212+310 yâlak (9), to *walk;* to *live;* to *carry*
3318+310 yâtsâ' (1), to *go, bring out*
6213 'âsâh (1), to *do or make*
7272 regel (1), *foot; step*
7291 râdaph (2), to *run after* with hostility
190 akŏlŏuthĕō (53), to *accompany, follow*
1096 ginŏmai (1), to *be, become*
1377 diōkō (2), to *pursue;* to *persecute*
1811 ĕxakŏlŏuthĕō (1), to *imitate, obey*
1872 ĕpakŏlŏuthĕō (1), to *accompany, follow*
2076+3326 ĕsti (1), he (she or it) *is*
2614 katadiōkō (1), to *search for, look for*
2628 katakŏlŏuthĕō (2), to *accompany closely*
4870 sunakŏlŏuthĕō (1), to *follow, accompany*

FOLLOWEDST
3212+310 yâlak (1), to *walk;* to *live;* to *carry*

FOLLOWERS
3402 mimētēs (7), *imitator, example*
4831 summimētēs (1), *co-imitator*

FOLLOWETH
310 'achar (1), *after*
935+310 bôw' (2), to *go or come*
1692 dâbaq (1), to *cling* or *adhere;* to *catch*
7291 râdaph (6), to *run after* with hostility
190 akŏlŏuthĕō (5), to *accompany, follow*

FOLLOWING
310 'achar (26), *after*
310+3651 'achar (1), *after*

312 'achêr (1), *other, another, different; next*
314 'achărôwn (1), *late* or *last; behind; western*
3212+310 yâlak (2), to *walk;* to *live;* to *carry*
190 akŏlŏuthĕō (3), to *accompany, follow*
1811 ĕxakŏlŏuthĕō (1), to *imitate, obey*
1836 hĕxēs (1), *successive, next*
1872 ĕpakŏlŏuthĕō (1), to *accompany, follow*
1887 ĕpauriŏn (2), *to-morrow*
1966 ĕpiŏusa (1), *ensuing*
2192 ĕchō (1), to *have; hold; keep*

FOLLY
200 'ivveleth (13), *silliness, foolishness*
3689 keçel (2), *loin; back; viscera; silliness*
3690 kiçlâh (1), *trust; silliness*
5039 nᵉbâlâh (10), moral *wickedness; crime*
5529 çekel (1), *silliness; dolts*
5531 çiklûwth (5), *silliness*
8417 tohŏlâh (1), *bluster, braggadocio,* i.e. *fatuity*
8604 tiphlâh (2), *frivolity, foolishness*
454 anŏia (1), *stupidity; rage*
877 aphrŏsunē (1), *senselessness*

FOOD
398 'âkal (1), to *eat*
400 'ôkel (16), *food*
402 'oklâh (1), *food*
944 bûwl (1), *produce*
3899 lechem (21), *food, bread*
3978 ma'ăkâl (5), *food, something to eat*
4361 makkôleth (1), *nourishment*
6718 tsayid (1), hunting *game; lunch, food*
7607 shᵉ'êr (1), *flesh, meat; kindred* by blood
1035 brōsis (1), *food; rusting corrosion*
1304 diatribō (1), to *remain, stay*
5160 trŏphē (2), *nourishment; rations*

FOOL
191 'ĕvîyl (11), *silly; fool*
3684 kᵉçîyl (34), *stupid* or *silly*
5030 nâbîy' (1), *prophet; inspired* man
5036 nâbâl (6), *stupid; impious*
5528 çâkal (1), to *be silly*
5530 çâkâl (3), *silly*
5536 çal (1), *basket*
876 aphrŏs (6), *froth, foam*
3474 mōrŏs (2), *heedless, moral blockhead*
3912 paraphrŏnĕō (1), to *be insane*

FOOL'S
191 'ĕvîyl (2), *silly; fool*
3684 kᵉçîyl (5), *stupid or silly*

FOOLISH
191 'ĕvîyl (6), *silly; fool*
196 'ĕvîlîy (1), *silly, foolish*
200 'ivveleth (1), *silliness, foolishness*
1198 ba'ar (1), *brutishness; stupidity*
1984 hâlal (2), *to boast*
2973 yâ'al (1), *to be or act foolish*
3684 kᵉçîyl (9), *stupid or silly*
3687 kᵉçîylûwth (1), *silliness, stupidity*
3688 kâçal (1), *silly, stupid*
5036 nâbâl (6), *stupid; impious*
5039 nᵉbâlâh (1), *moral wickedness; crime*
5528 çâkal (1), *to be silly*
5530 çâkâl (2), *silly*
6612 pᵉthîy (1), *silly, i.e. seducible*
8602 tâphêl (1), *to plaster; frivolity*
453 anŏētŏs (4), *unintelligent, senseless*
801 asunĕtŏs (2), *senseless, dull; wicked*
878 aphrōn (2), *ignorant; egotistic; unbelieving*
3471 mōrainō (1), *to become insipid*
3473 mōrŏlŏgia (1), *buffoonery, foolish talk*
3474 mōrŏs (7), *heedless, moral blockhead*

FOOLISHLY
200 'ivveleth (1), *silliness, foolishness*
1984 hâlal (1), *to boast*
2973 yâ'al (1), *to be or act foolish*
5034 nâbêl (1), *to wilt; to fall away; to be foolish or wicked*
5528 çâkal (5), *to be silly*
8604 tiphlâh (1), *frivolity, foolishness*
1722+877 ĕn (2), *in; during; because of*

FOOLISHNESS
200 'ivveleth (10), *silliness, foolishness*
5528 çâkal (1), *to be silly*
5531 çiklûwth (2), *silliness*
877 aphrŏsunē (1), *senselessness*
3472 mŏria (5), *absurdity, foolishness*
3474 mōrŏs (1), *heedless, moral blockhead*

FOOLS
191 'ĕvîyl (7), *silly; fool*
1984 hâlal (2), *to boast*
2973 yâ'al (1), *to be or act foolish*
3684 kᵉçîyl (22), *stupid or silly*
5036 nâbâl (2), *stupid; impious*

453 anŏētŏs (1), *unintelligent, senseless*
781 asŏphŏs (1), *unwise, foolish*
878 aphrōn (2), *ignorant; egotistic; unbelieving*
3471 mōrainō (1), *to become insipid*
3474 mōrŏs (3), *heedless, moral blockhead*

FOOT
947 bûwç (2), *to trample down; oppress*
3653 kên (8), *pedestal or station of a basin*
4001 mᵉbûwçâh (1), *trampling, oppression*
4823 mirmâç (1), *abasement*
5541 çâlâh (1), *to contemn, reject*
7272 regel (61), *foot; step*
7273 raglîy (1), *footman soldier*
2662 katapatĕō (2), *to trample down; to reject*
3979 pĕzē₁ (1), *on foot*
4158 pŏdērēs (1), *robe reaching the ankles*
4228 pŏus (9), *foot*

FOOTBREADTH
3709+4096+7272 kaph (1), *sole of foot*

FOOTMEN
376+7273 'îysh (4), *man; male; someone*
7273 raglîy (7), *footman soldier*
7328 râz (Ch.) (1), *mystery*

FOOTSTEPS
6119 'âqêb (3), *track, footprint; rear position*
6471 pa'am (1), *time; step; occurence*

FOOTSTOOL
1916+7272 hădôm (6), *foot-stool*
3534 kebesh (1), *footstool*
5286 hupŏpŏdiŏn (1), *under the feet*
5286+3588+4228 hupŏpŏdiŏn (8), *under the feet, i.e. a foot-rest*

FORASMUCH
310 'achar (1), *after*
310+834 'achar (2), *after*
854+834 'êth (1), *with; by; at; among*
3282 ya'an (1), *because, for this reason*
3282+365 ya'an (2), *because, for this reason*
3282+834 ya'an (5), *because, for this reason*
3588 kîy (1), *for, that because*
3588+5921+3651 kîy (1), *for, that because*
3606+6903+1768 kôl (Ch.) (8), *all, any or every*
5704 'ad (1), *as far (long) as; during; while; until*
1487 ĕi (1), *if, whether, that*
1893 ĕpĕi (2), *since*

1894 ĕpĕidē (1), *when, whereas*
1895 ĕpĕidēpĕr (1), *since indeed*
5607 ōn (1), *being, existence*

FORBAD
6680 tsâvâh (1), *to constitute, enjoin*
1254 diakōluō (1), *utterly prohibit or prevent*
2967 kōluō (3), *to stop*

FORBARE
2308 châdal (3), *to desist, stop; be fat*

FORBEAR
1826 dâmam (1), *to stop, cease; to perish*
2308 châdal (15), *to desist, stop; be fat*
2820 châsak (1), *to restrain or refrain*
4900 mâshak (1), *to draw out; to be tall*
3361 mē (1), *not; lest*
4722 stĕgō (2), *to endure patiently*
5339 phĕidŏmai (1), *to abstain; treat leniently*

FORBEARANCE
463 anŏchē (2), *tolerance, clemency*

FORBEARETH
2308 châdal (1), *to desist, stop; be fat*
2310 châdêl (1), *ceasing or destitute*

FORBEARING
639 'aph (1), *nose or nostril; face; person*
3557 kûwl (1), *to maintain*
430 anĕchŏmai (2), *put up with, endure*
447 aniēmi (1), *to slacken, loosen*

FORBID
2486 châlîylâh (12), *far be it!, forbid!*
3607 kâlâ' (1), *to hold back or in; to prohibit*
2967 kōluō (9), *to stop*
3361+1096 mē (14), *not; lest*

FORBIDDEN
3808 lô' (1), *no, not*
6680 tsâvâh (1), *to constitute, enjoin*
2967 kōluō (1), *to stop*

FORBIDDETH
2967 kōluō (1), *to stop*

FORBIDDING
209 akōlutŏs (1), *in an unhindered manner*
2967 kōluō (3), *to stop*

FORBORN
2308 châdal (1), *to desist, stop; be fat*

FORCE
153 'edra' (Ch.) (1), *power*
202 'ôwn (1), *ability, power; wealth*
1369 gᵉbûwrâh (1), *force; valor; victory*
1497 gâzal (1), *to rob*

2388 châzaq (1), *to fasten upon; to seize*
2394 chozqâh (2), *vehemence, harshness*
3027 yâd (2), *hand; power*
3533 kâbash (1), *to conquer, subjugate*
3581 kôach (3), *force, might; strength*
3893 lêach (1), *fresh strength, vigor*
6031 'ânâh (1), *to afflict, be afflicted*
726 harpazō (3), *to seize*
949 bĕbaiŏs (1), *stable, certain, binding*

FORCED
662 'âphaq (1), *to abstain*
3905 lâchats (1), *to press; to distress*
5080 nâdach (1), *to push off, scattered*
6031 'ânâh (4), *to afflict, be afflicted*

FORCES
2428 chayil (14), *army; wealth; virtue; valor*
3981 ma'ămâts (1), *strength; resources*
4581 mâ'ôwz (1), *fortified place; defense*

FORCIBLE
4834 mârats (1), *to be pungent or vehement*

FORCING
4330 mîyts (1), *pressure*
5080 nâdach (1), *to push off, scattered*

FORD
4569 ma'ăbâr (1), *crossing-place*

FORDS
4569 ma'ăbâr (3), *crossing-place*

FORECAST
2803 châshab (2), *to plot; to think, regard*

FOREFATHERS
4269 prŏgŏnŏs (1), *ancestor*

FOREFRONT
4136+6440 mûwl (1), *in front of, opposite*
4136+6440 mûwl (3), *in front of, opposite*
6440 pânîym (4), *face; front*
7218 rô'sh (1), *head*
8127 shên (1), *tooth; ivory; cliff*

FOREHEAD
639 'aph (1), *nose or nostril; face; person*
1371 gibbêach (1), *bald forehead*
1372 gabbachath (3), *baldness on forehead*
4696 mêtsach (9), *forehead*
3359 mĕtŏpŏn (2), *forehead*

FOREHEADS
4696 mêtsach (2), *forehead*

English

3359 mĕtōpŏn (6),
forehead

FOREIGNER
5237 nokrîy (1), *foreign;*
non-relative; different
8453 tôwshâb (1),
temporary *dweller*

FOREIGNERS
5237 nokrîy (1), *foreign;*
non-relative; different
3941 *parŏikŏs* (1),
strange; stranger

FOREKNEW
4267 prŏginōskō (1), to
know beforehand

FOREKNOW
4267 prŏginōskō (1), to
know beforehand

FOREKNOWLEDGE
4268 prŏgnōsis (2),
forethought

FOREMOST
7223 ri'shôwn (3), *first*

FOREORDAINED
4267 prŏginōskō (1), to
know beforehand

FOREPART
6440 pânîym (4), *face;*
front
4408 prōra (1), *prow*, i.e.
forward part of a vessel

FORERUNNER
4274 prŏdrŏmŏs (1),
runner ahead

FORESAW
4308 prŏŏraō (1), to
notice previously

FORESEEING
4375 prŏsphilēs (1),
acceptable, pleasing

FORESEETH
7200 râ'âh (2), to *see*

FORESHIP
4408 prōra (1), *prow*, i.e.
forward part of a vessel

FORESKIN
6188 'ârêl (1), to *refrain*
from using
6190 'orlâh (8), *prepuce*
or penile foreskin

FORESKINS
6190 'orlâh (5), *prepuce*
or penile foreskin

FOREST
3293 ya'ar (37), *honey* in
the *comb*
6508 pardêç (1), *park*,
cultivated garden area

FORESTS
2793 chôresh (1),
wooded *forest*
3293 ya'ar (1), *honey* in
the *comb*
3295 ya'ărâh (1), *honey*
in the *comb*

FORETELL
4302 prŏlĕgō (1), to
predict, forewarn

FORETOLD
4280 prŏĕrĕō (1), to *say*
already, predict
4293 prŏkataggĕllō (1),
to *predict, foretell*

FOREWARN
5263 hupŏdĕiknumi (1),
to *exemplify, instruct*

FOREWARNED
4277 prŏĕpō (1), to *say*
already, to *predict*

FORFEITED
2763 charam (1), to
devote to destruction

FORGAT
5382 nâshâh (1), to *forget*
7911 shâkach (7), to be
oblivious of, forget

FORGAVE
3722 kâphar (1), to
cover; to *expiate*
863 aphiēmi (2), to *leave;*
to *pardon, forgive*
5483 charizŏmai (4), to
grant as a *favor, pardon*

FORGAVEST
5375 nâsâ' (2), to *lift up*

FORGED
2950 tâphal (1), to
impute falsely

FORGERS
2950 tâphal (1), to
impute falsely

FORGET
5382 nâshâh (2), to *forget*
7911 shâkach (48), to be
oblivious of, forget
7913 shâkêach (2),
oblivious, forgetting
1950 ĕpilanthanŏmai (2),
to *lose out* of mind

FORGETFUL
1950 ĕpilanthanŏmai (1),
to *lose out* of mind
1953 ĕpilēsmŏnē (1),
negligence

FORGETFULNESS
5388 nᵉshîyâh (1),
oblivion

FORGETTEST
7911 shâkach (2), to be
oblivious of, forget

FORGETTETH
7911 shâkach (2), to be
oblivious of, forget
7913 shâkêach (1),
oblivious, forgetting
1950 ĕpilanthanŏmai (1),
to *lose out* of mind

FORGETTING
1950 ĕpilanthanŏmai (1),
to *lose out* of mind

FORGIVE
3722 kâphar (1), to
cover; to *expiate*
5375 nâsâ' (8), to *lift up*
5545 çâlach (18), to
forgive
5546 çallâch (1),
placable, tolerant
630 apŏluō (1), to *relieve,*
release; to *pardon*
863 aphiēmi (22), to
leave; to *pardon, forgive*
5483 charizŏmai (3), to
grant as a *favor, pardon*

FORGIVEN
3722 kâphar (1), to
cover; to *expiate*

5375 nâsâ' (4), to *lift up*
5545 çâlach (13), to
forgive
630 apŏluō (1), to *relieve,*
release; to *pardon*
863 aphiēmi (21), to
leave; to *pardon, forgive*
5483 charizŏmai (2), to
grant as a *favor, pardon*

FORGIVENESS
5547 çᵉlîychâh (1),
pardon
859 aphĕsis (6), *pardon,*
freedom

FORGIVENESSES
5547 çᵉlîychâh (1),
pardon

FORGIVETH
5545 çâlach (1), to *forgive*
863 aphiēmi (1), to *leave;*
to *pardon, forgive*

FORGIVING
5375 nâsâ' (2), to *lift up*
5483 charizŏmai (2), to
grant as a *favor, pardon*

FORGOT
7911 shâkach (1), to be
oblivious of, forget

FORGOTTEN
5382 nâshâh (1), to *forget*
7911 shâkach (39), to be
oblivious of, forget
7913 shâkêach (1),
oblivious, forgetting
1585 ĕklanthanŏmai (1),
to *forget*
1950 ĕpilanthanŏmai (3),
to *lose out* of mind
3024+2983 lēthē (1),
forgetfulness

FORKS
7969+7053 shâlôwsh (1),
three; third; thrice

FORM
3335 yâtsar (1), to *form;*
potter; to *determine*
4758 mar'eh (1),
appearance; vision
4941 mishpât (1), *verdict;*
formal *decree; justice*
6440 pânîym (1), *face;*
front
6699 tsûwrâh (2), *rock;*
form as if *pressed* out
6755 tselem (Ch.) (1),
idolatrous *figure*
7299 rêv (Ch.) (2), *aspect,*
appearance
8389 tô'ar (3), *outline,*
i.e. *figure, appearance*
8403 tabnîyth (3), *model,*
resemblance
8414 tôhûw (2), *waste,*
desolation, formless
3444 mŏrphē (3), *shape,*
form; nature, character
3446 mŏrphōsis (2),
appearance; semblance
5179 tupŏs (1), *shape*
resemblance; "type"
5296 hupŏtupōsis (1),
example, pattern

FORMED
2342 chûwl (5), to *dance,*
whirl; to *writhe* in pain

3335 yâtsar (23), to *form;*
potter; to *determine*
7169 qârats (1), to *bite*
the lips, *blink* the eyes
3445 mŏrphŏŏ (1), to
fashion, take on a form
4110 plasma (2), *molded,*
what is *formed*
4111 plassō (1), to *mold,*
i.e. *shape* or *fabricate*

FORMER
570 'emesh (1), *last night*
3138 yôwreh (2), autumn
rain showers
3335 yâtsar (2), to *form;*
potter; to *determine*
4175 môwreh (2), *archer;*
teaching; early rain
6440 pânîym (1), *face;*
front
6927 qadmâh (3), *priority*
in time; *before; past*
6931 qadmôwnîy (2),
anterior time; eastern
7223 ri'shôwn (32), *first*
4386 prŏtĕrŏn (2),
previously
4387 prŏtĕrŏs (1), *prior*
or *previous*
4413 prōtŏs (2), *foremost*

FORMETH
3335 yâtsar (2), to *form;*
potter; to *determine*

FORMS
6699 tsûwrâh (2), *rock;*
form as if *pressed* out

FORNICATION
2181 zânâh (3), to
commit adultery
8457 taznûwth (1),
harlotry
1608 ĕkpŏrnĕuō (1), to
fornicate
4202 pŏrnĕia (24), *sexual*
immorality
4203 pŏrnĕuō (7), to
indulge unlawful *lust*

FORNICATIONS
8457 taznûwth (1),
harlotry
4202 pŏrnĕia (2), *sexual*
immorality

FORNICATOR
4205 pŏrnŏs (2), *sexually*
immoral person

FORNICATORS
4205 pŏrnŏs (3), *sexually*
immoral person

FORSAKE
2308 châdal (1), to *desist,*
stop; be fat
5203 nâtash (7), to
disperse; to *abandon*
5800 'âzab (45), to
loosen; relinquish
7503 râphâh (2), to
slacken
646+575 apŏstasia (1),
defection, rebellion
1459 ĕgkatalĕipō (1), to
desert, abandon

FORSAKEN
488 'almân (1),
discarded, forsaken
5203 nâtash (6), to
disperse; to *abandon*

FORSAKETH

5428 nâthash (1), to *tear away, be uprooted*
5800 'âzab (60), to *loosen; relinquish*
7971 shâlach (1), to *send away*
863 aphíēmi (2), to *leave; to pardon, forgive*
1459 ĕgkataleípō (4), to *desert, abandon*
2641 kataleípō (1), to *abandon*

FORSAKETH

5800 'âzab (5), to *loosen; relinquish; permit*
657 apŏtassŏmai (1), to *say adieu; to renounce*

FORSAKING

5805 'ăzûwbâh (1), *desertion, forsaking*
1459 ĕgkataleípō (1), to *desert, abandon*

FORSOMUCH

2530 kathŏti (1), *as far or inasmuch as*

FORSOOK

5203 nâṭash (2), to *disperse; to abandon*
5800 'âzab (16), to *loosen; relinquish*
863 aphíēmi (4), to *leave; to pardon, forgive*
1459 ĕgkataleípō (1), to *desert, abandon*
2641 kataleípō (1), to *abandon*

FORSOOKEST

5800 'âzab (2), to *loosen; relinquish; permit*

FORSWEAR

1964 ĕpiŏrkĕō (1), to *commit perjury*

FORT

1785 dâyêq (3), *battering*-tower
4581 mâ'ôwz (1), *fortified place; defense*
4686 mâtsûwd (1), *net or capture; fastness*
4869 misgâb (1), *high refuge*

FORTH

935 bôw' (1), to *go or come*
1310 bâshal (1), to *boil up, cook; to ripen*
1319 bâsar (1), to *announce* (good news)
1518 gîyach (4), to *issue forth; to burst forth*
1645 geresh (1), *produce, yield*
1876 dâshâ' (1), to *sprout new plants*
1921 hâdar (1), to *favor or honor; to be high*
2254 châbal (2), to *writhe in labor pain*
2315 cheder (1), *apartment, chamber*
2330 chûwd (4), to *propound a riddle*
2342 chûwl (4), to *dance, whirl; to writhe in pain*
2590 chânaṭ (1), to *embalm; to ripen*

2904 ṭûwl (3), to *cast down or out, hurl*
2986 yâbal (1), to *bring*
3205 yâlad (26), to *bear young; to father a child*
3209 yillôwd (1), *born*
3318 yâtsâ' (403), to *go, bring out*
3329 yâtsîy' (1), *issue forth*, i.e. offspring
4161 môwtsâ' (11), *going forth*
4163 môwtsâ'âh (3), *family descent*
4866 mishbêr (1), *vaginal opening*
5066 nâgash (2), to *be, come, bring near*
5107 nûwb (2), to (*make*) *flourish; to utter*
5132 nûwts (1), to *fly away, leave*
5221 nâkâh (1), to *strike, kill*
5265 nâça' (5), *start on a journey*
5312 nᵉphaq (Ch.) (7), to *issue forth; to bring out*
5375 nâsâ' (2), to *lift up*
5414 nâthan (1), to *give*
5608 çâphar (1), to *inscribe; to enumerate*
5674 'âbar (2), to *cross over; to transition*
5975 'âmad (1), to *stand*
6213 'âsâh (10), to *do or make*
6398 pâlach (1), to *slice; to break open; to pierce*
6440 pânîym (1), *face; front*
6509 pârâh (1), to *bear fruit*
6556 perets (1), *break, gap*
6566 pâras (1), to *break apart, disperse, scatter*
6605 pâthach (1), to *open wide; to loosen, begin*
6631 tse'ĕtsâ' (1), *produce, children*
6779 tsâmach (4), to *sprout*
7126 qârab (1), to *approach, bring near*
7737 shâvâh (1), to *level, i.e. equalize*
7971 shâlach (27), to *send away*
8317 shârats (5), to *swarm, or abound*
8444 tôwtsâ'âh (2), *exit, boundary; deliverance*
321 anagō (3), to *lead up; to bring out; to sail*
392 anatassŏmai (1), to *arrange*
584 apŏdĕiknumi (1), to *demonstrate*
616 apŏkuĕō (1), to *bring into being*
649 apŏstĕllō (11), to *send out on a mission*
669 apŏphthĕggŏmai (1), *declare, address*
985 blastanō (1), to *yield fruit*
1032 bruō (1), to *gush, pour forth*

1080 gĕnnaō (1), to *procreate, regenerate*
1544 ĕkballō (7), to *throw out*
1554 ĕkdidōmi (2), to *lease, rent*
1584 ĕklampō (1), to *be resplendent, shine*
1599 ĕkpĕmpō (1), to *despatch, send out*
1600 ĕkpĕtannumi (1), to *extend, spread out*
1607 ĕkpŏrĕuŏmai (4), to *depart, be discharged*
1614 ĕktĕinō (17), to *stretch*
1627 ĕkphĕrō (3), to *bear out; to produce*
1631 ĕkphuō (2), to *sprout up, put forth*
1632 ĕkchĕō (1), to *pour forth; to bestow*
1731 ĕndĕiknumi (1), to *show, display*
1754 ĕnĕrgĕō (2), to *be active, efficient, work*
1804 ĕxaggĕllō (1), to *declare, proclaim*
1806 ĕxagō (1), to *lead forth, escort*
1821 ĕxapŏstĕllō (4), to *despatch, or to dismiss*
1831 ĕxĕrchŏmai (32), to *issue; to leave*
1854 ĕxō (8), *out, outside*
1901 ĕpĕktĕinŏmai (1), to *stretch oneself forward*
1907 ĕpĕchō (1), to *retain; to detain*
1911 ĕpiballō (1), to *throw upon*
2164 ĕuphŏrĕō (1), to *be fertile, produce a crop*
2564 kalĕō (1), to *call*
2592 karpŏphŏrĕō (2), to *be fertile*
2604 kataggĕlĕus (1), *proclaimer*
2609 katagō (1), to *lead down; to moor a vessel*
3004 lĕgō (1), to *say*
3318 Mĕsŏpŏtamia (2), *between the Rivers*
3855 paragō (1), to *go along or away*
3860 paradidōmi (1), to *hand over*
3908 paratithēmi (2), to *present something*
3928 parĕrchŏmai (1), to *go by; to perish*
4160 pŏiĕō (14), to *do*
4198 pŏrĕuŏmai (1), to *go, come; to travel*
4254 prŏagō (2), to *lead forward; to precede*
4261 prŏballō (1), to *push to the front, germinate*
4270 prŏgraphō (1), to *announce, prescribe*
4295 prŏkĕimai (1), to *stand forth*
4311 prŏpĕmpō (1), to *send forward*
4388 prŏtithĕmai (1), to *place before, exhibit*
4393 prŏphĕrō (2), to *bear forward*

4486 rhĕgnumi (1), to *break, burst forth*
5087 tithēmi (1), to *place*
5088 tiktō (9), to *produce from seed*
5319 phanĕrŏō (1), to *render apparent*
5348 phthanō (1), to *be beforehand, precede*

FORTHWITH

629 'oçparnâ' (Ch.) (1), *with diligence*
2112 ĕuthĕōs (7), *at once or soon*
2117 ĕuthus (1), *at once, immediately*
3916 parachrēma (1), *instantly, immediately*

FORTIETH

705 'arbâ'îym (4), *forty*

FORTIFIED

2388 châzaq (2), to *fasten upon; be strong*
4692 mâtsôwr (1), *siege-mound; distress*
5800 'âzab (1), to *loosen; relinquish; permit*

FORTIFY

553 'âmats (1), to *be strong; be courageous*
1219 bâtsar (2), to *be inaccessible*
2388 châzaq (1), to *fasten upon; be strong*
5800 'âzab (1), to *loosen; relinquish; permit*
6696 tsûwr (1), to *cramp, i.e. confine; to harass*

FORTRESS

4013 mibtsâr (4), *fortification; defender*
4581 mâ'ôwz (3), *fortified place; defense*
4686 mâtsûwd (6), *net or capture; fastness*
4693 mâtsôwr (2), *limit, border*

FORTRESSES

4013 mibtsâr (2), *fortification; defender*

FORTS

1785 dâyêq (3), *battering*-tower
4679 mᵉtsad (1), *stronghold*
4694 mᵉtsûwrâh (1), *rampart, fortification*
6076 'ôphel (1), *tumor; fortress*

FORTUNATUS

5415 Phŏrtŏunatŏs (2), *fortunate*

FORTY

702+7239 'arba' (2), *four*
705 'arbâ'îym (126), *forty*
5062 tĕssarakŏnta (22), *forty*
5063 tĕssarakŏntaĕtēs (2), *of forty years of age*

FORTY'S

705 'arbâ'îym (1), *forty*

FORUM

675 'Appiŏs (1), *Appius*

English

FORWARD
1973 hâl°âh (5), *far*
away; thus far
1980 hâlak (1), to *walk;*
live a certain way
3276 yâ'al (1), to *be*
valuable
4605 ma'al (2), *upward,*
above, overhead
5265 nâça' (18), *start on*
a *journey*
5921 'al (3), *above, over,*
upon, or against
6440 pânîym (4), *face;*
front
6584 pâshaṭ (1), to *strip,*
i.e. *unclothe, plunder*
6924 qedem (1), *eastern;*
antiquity; before
2309 thĕlō (1), to *will;* to
desire; to choose
4261 prŏballō (1), to *push*
to the front, germinate
4281 prŏĕrchŏmai (1), to
go onward, precede
4311 prŏpĕmpō (1), to
send forward
4704 spŏudazō (1), to
make effort
4707 spŏudaiŏtĕrŏs (1),
more earnest

FORWARDNESS
4288 prŏthumia (1),
alacrity, eagerness
4710 spŏudē (1),
despatch; eagerness

FOUGHT
3898 lâcham (58), to fight
a *battle*, i.e. *consume*
6633 tsâbâ' (1), to *mass*
an army or servants
75 agōnizŏmai (1), to
struggle; to contend
2341 thēriŏmachĕō (1),
to *be a beast fighter*
4170 pŏlĕmĕō (2), to
battle, make war

FOUL
2560 châmar (1), to
ferment, foam; to *glow*
7515 râphas (1), to
trample, i.e. *roil* water
169 akathartŏs (2),
impure; evil
5494 chĕimōn (1), *winter*
season; *stormy weather*

FOULED
4833 mirpâs (1),
muddied water

FOULEDST
7515 râphas (1), to
trample, i.e. *roil* water

FOUND
2713 châqar (2), to
examine, search
4672 mâtsâ' (267), to *find*
or *acquire;* to *occur*
7912 sh°kach (Ch.) (11),
to *discover, find out*
429 anĕuriskō (1), to *find*
out
1096 ginŏmai (1), to *be,*
become
2147 hĕuriskō (111), to
find
2638 katalambanō (1), to
seize; to possess

FOUNDATION
787 'ôsh (Ch.) (1),
foundation
3245 yâçad (15), *settle,*
establish a foundation
3247 y°çôwd (7),
foundation
3248 y°çûwdâh (5),
foundation
4143 mûwçâd (2),
foundation
4527 maççad (1),
foundation
2310 thĕmĕliŏs (12),
substruction
2311 thĕmĕliŏō (1), to
erect; to *consolidate*
2602 katabŏlē (10),
conception, beginning

FOUNDATIONS
134 'eden (1), *base,*
footing
787 'ôsh (Ch.) (2),
foundation
803 'ăshûwyâh (1),
foundation
808 'âshîysh (1), (ruined)
foundation
3245 yâçad (4), *settle,*
establish a foundation
3247 y°çôwd (3),
foundation
4146 môwçâdâh (13),
foundation
4328 m°yuççâdâh (1),
foundation
4349 mâkôwn (1), *basis;*
place
8356 shâthâh (1), *basis*
2310 thĕmĕliŏs (4),
substruction

FOUNDED
3245 yâçad (8), *settle,*
establish a foundation
2311 thĕmĕliŏō (2), to
erect; to *consolidate*

FOUNDER
6884 tsâraph (5), to *fuse*
metal; to *refine*

FOUNDEST
4672 mâtsâ' (1), to *find*
or *acquire;* to *occur*

FOUNTAIN
953 bôwr (1), pit *hole,*
cistern, well
4002 mabbûwa' (1),
fountain, water spring
4599 ma'yân (9),
fountain; source
4726 mâqôwr (11), *flow*
5869 'ayin (7), *eye; sight;*
fountain
4077 pēgē (4), *source* or
supply

FOUNTAINS
4599 ma'yân (7),
fountain; source
5869 'ayin (4), *eye; sight;*
fountain
4077 pēgē (4), *source* or
supply

FOUR
702 'arba' (258), *four*
703 'arba' (Ch.) (8), *four*
5064 tĕssarĕs (43), *four*
5066 tĕtartaiŏs (1), of the
fourth day

5067 tĕtartŏs (1), *fourth*
5070 tĕtrakischiliŏi (5),
four times a thousand
5071 tĕtrakŏsiŏi (2), *four*
hundred
5072 tĕtramēnŏn (1),
four months' time

FOURFOLD
706 'arba'tayim (1),
fourfold
5073 tĕtraplŏŏs (1),
quadruple, i.e. *four-fold*

FOURFOOTED
5074 tĕtrapŏus (3),
quadruped

FOURSCORE
8084 sh°mônîym (34),
eighty; eightieth
3589 ŏgdŏĕkŏnta (2), *ten*
times eight

FOURSQUARE
7243 r°bîy'îy (1), *fourth;*
fourth
7251 râba' (8), to *be four*
sided, to *be quadrate*
5068 tĕtragōnŏs (1),
four-cornered

FOURTEEN
702+6240 'arba' (2), *four*
702+6246 'arba' (4), *four*
702+7657 'arba' (3), *four*
1180 dĕkatĕssarĕs (5),
fourteen

FOURTEENTH
702+6240 'arba' (23), *four*
5065 tĕssarĕskaidĕkatŏs
(2), *fourteenth*

FOURTH
702 'arba' (5), *four*
7243 r°bîy'îy (55), *fourth;*
fourth
7244 r°bîy'ay (Ch.) (5),
fourth; fourth
7253 reba' (2), *fourth*
part or side
7255 rôba' (2), *quarter*
7256 ribbêa' (2), *fourth;*
fourth generation
5067 tĕtartŏs (9), *fourth*

FOWL
1257 barbûr (1), *fowl*
5775 'ôwph (23), *bird*
5776 'ôwph (Ch.) (1), *bird*
5861 'ayiṭ (1), bird of
prey (poss.) *hawk*
6833 tsippôwr (5), little
hopping bird

FOWLER
3353 yâqûwsh (3),
snarer, trapper of fowl

FOWLERS
3369 yâqôsh (1), to
ensnare, trap

FOWLS
5775 'ôwph (36), *winged*
bird
5776 'ôwph (Ch.) (1),
winged bird
5861 'ayiṭ (3), bird of
prey (poss.) *hawk*
6833 tsippôwr (1), little
hopping bird
6853 ts°phar (Ch.) (3),
bird
3732 ŏrnĕŏn (2), *bird*

4071 pĕtĕinŏn (9), *bird*
which *flies*

FOX
7776 shûw'âl (1), *jackal*
258 alōpĕx (1), *fox*

FOXES
7776 shûw'âl (6), *jackal*
258 alōpĕx (2), *fox*

FRAGMENTS
2801 klasma (7), *piece,*
bit

FRAIL
2310 châdêl (1), *ceasing*
or *destitute*

FRAME
3335 yâtsar (1), to *form;*
potter; to *determine*
3336 yêtser (1), *form*
3559 kûwn (1), to *set up:*
establish, fix, prepare
4011 mibneh (1), *building*
5414 nâthan (1), to *give*

FRAMED
3335 yâtsar (1), to *form;*
potter; to *determine*
3336 yêtser (1), *form*
2675 katartizō (1), to
repair; to *prepare*
4883 sunarmŏlŏgĕō (1),
to *render close-jointed*

FRAMETH
3335 yâtsar (1), to *form;*
potter; to *determine*
6775 tsâmad (1), to *link,*
i.e. *gird*

FRANKINCENSE
3828 l°bôwnâh (15),
frankincense
3030 libanŏs (2), fragrant
incense resin or gum

FRANKLY
5435 Phrugia (1), *Phrygia*

FRAUD
8496 tôk (1), *oppression*
650 apŏstĕrĕō (1), to
deprive; to *despoil*

FRAY
2729 chârad (3), to
shudder; to *hasten*

FRECKLED
933 bôhaq (1), white
scurf, rash

FREE
2600 chinnâm (1), *gratis,*
free
2666 châphash (1), to
loose; free from slavery
2670 chophshîy (16),
exempt, free
5071 n°dâbâh (2),
abundant gift
5081 nâdîyb (1),
magnanimous
5082 n°dîybâh (1),
nobility, i.e. reputation
5352 nâqâh (2), to *be,*
make clean; to *be bare*
5355 nâqîy (1), *innocent*
6362 pâṭar (1), to *burst*
through; to *emit*
6605 pâthach (1), to *open*
wide; to *loosen, begin*
1658 ĕlĕuthĕrŏs (20), *not*
a *slave*

1659 ĕleuthĕrŏŏ (6), to *exempt, liberate*
5486 charisma (2), spiritual *endowment*

FREED
3772 kârath (1), to *cut* (off, down or asunder)
1344 dikaiŏŏ (1), *show* or *regard* as *innocent*

FREEDOM
2668 chuphshâh (1), *liberty* from slavery
4174 pŏlitĕia (1), *citizenship*

FREELY
2600 chinnâm (1), *gratis, free*
5071 nᵉdâbâh (2), *abundant* gift
1432 dōrĕan (6), *gratuitously, freely*
3326+3954 mĕta (1), *with, among; after, later*
3955 parrhēsiazŏmai (1), to *be confident*

FREEMAN
558 apĕlĕuthĕrŏs (1), *freedman*

FREEWILL
5069 nᵉdab (Ch.) (2), *be, give without coercion*
5071 nᵉdâbâh (15), *abundant* gift

FREEWOMAN
1658 ĕleuthĕrŏs (2), *not a slave*

FREQUENT
4056 pĕrissŏtĕrŏs (1), *more superabundantly*

FRESH
2319 châdâsh (1), *new, recent*
3955 lᵉshad (1), *juice; vigor; sweet or fat cake*
7488 ra'ănân (1), *new; prosperous*
1099 glukus (1), *sweet, fresh*

FRESHER
7375 rûwṭăphash (1), to *be rejuvenated*

FRET
2734 chârâh (4), to *blaze* up
6356 pᵉchetheth (1), *mildewed garment hole*
7107 qâtsaph (1), to *burst* out in rage
7481 râ'am (1), to *crash thunder; to irritate*

FRETTED
7264 râgaz (1), to *quiver*

FRETTETH
2196 zâ'aph (1), to *be angry*

FRETTING
3992 mâ'ar (3), to *be painful; destructive*

FRIED
7246 râbak (2), to *soak* bread in oil

FRIEND
157 'âhab (4), to *have affection, love*

7451 ra' (1), *bad; evil*
7453 rêa' (27), *associate; one close*
7462 râ'âh (1), to *associate* as a friend
7463 rê'eh (3), male *advisor*
2083 hĕtairŏs (3), *comrade, friend*
3982 pĕithō (1), to *pacify* or *conciliate*
5384 philŏs (12), *friend; friendly*

FRIENDLY
3820 lêb (2), *heart*
7489 râ'a' (1), to *make, be good for nothing*

FRIENDS
157 'âhab (8), to *have affection, love*
441 'allûwph (2), *friend, one familiar; chieftain*
605+7965 'ânash (1), to *be frail, feeble*
4828 mêrêa' (3), close *friend*
4962 math (1), *men*
7453 rêa' (14), *associate; one close*
3588+3844 hŏ (1), "*the*," i.e. the definite article
4674 sŏs (1), things that are *yours*
5384 philŏs (17), *friend; friendly*

FRIENDSHIP
7462 râ'âh (1), to *associate* as a friend
5373 philia (1), *fondness*

FRINGE
6734 tsîytsîth (2), *fore-lock* of hair; *tassel*

FRINGES
1434 gᵉdîl (1), *tassel; festoon*
6734 tsîytsîth (1), *fore-lock* of hair; *tassel*

FRO
235 'âzal (1), to *disappear*
7725 shûwb (1), to *turn* back; to *return*
7751 shûwṭ (8), to *travel, roam*
8264 shâqaq (1), to *seek greedily*
2831 kludōnizŏmai (1), to *fluctuate back and forth on the waves*

FROGS
6854 tsᵉphardêa' (13), *frog, leaper*
944 batrachŏs (1), *frog*

FRONT
6440 pânîym (2), *face; front*

FRONTIERS
7097 qâtseh (1), *extremity*

FRONTLETS
2903 ṭôwphâphâh (3), *sign* or *symbolic box*

FROST
2602 chănâmâl (1), *aphis* or plant-louse
3713 kᵉphôwr (3), *bowl; white frost*

7140 qerach (3), *ice; hail; rock crystal*

FROWARD
2019 hăphakpak (1), *very perverse, crooked*
3868 lûwz (2), to *depart; to be perverse*
6141 'iqqêsh (6), *distorted, warped, false*
6143 'iqqᵉshûwth (2), *perversity*
6617 pâthal (3), to *struggle; to be tortuous*
8419 tahpûkâh (6), *perversity* or *fraud*
4646 skŏliŏs (1), *crooked; perverse*

FROWARDLY
7726 shôwbâb (1), *apostate,* i.e. *idolatrous*

FROWARDNESS
8419 tahpûkâh (3), *perversity* or *fraud*

FROZEN
3920 lâkad (1), to *catch; to capture*

FRUIT
4 'êb (Ch.) (3), *green plant*
1061 bikkûwr (2), *first-fruits* of the crop
2981 yᵉbûwl (3), *produce, crop; harvest*
3206 yeled (1), *young male*
3899 lechem (1), *food, bread*
3978 ma'ăkâl (1), *food, something to eat*
4395 mᵉlê'âh (1), *fulfilled; abundance*
5107 nûwb (1), to (*make*) *flourish; to utter*
5108 nôwb (2), *agricultural produce*
6509 pârâh (1), to *bear fruit*
6529 pᵉrîy (106), *fruit*
7920 sᵉkal (Ch.) (1), to *be* or *act circumspect*
8270 shôr (1), *umbilical cord; strength*
8393 tᵉbûw'âh (7), *income,* i.e. *produce*
8570 tᵉnûwbâh (1), *crop, produce*
175 akarpŏs (1), *barren, unfruitful*
1081 gĕnnēma (3), *offspring; produce*
2590 karpŏs (54), *fruit; crop*
2592 karpŏphŏrĕŏ (7), to *be fertile*
5052 tĕlĕsphŏrĕŏ (1), to *ripen fruit*
5352 phthinŏpōrinŏs (1), *autumnal*

FRUITFUL
1121+8081 bên (1), *people* of a class or kind
2233 zera' (1), *seed; fruit, plant, sowing-time*
3759 karmel (7), *planted field; garden produce*
6500 pârâ' (1), to *bear fruit*

6509 pârâh (21), to *bear fruit*
6529 pᵉrîy (2), *fruit*
2592 karpŏphŏrĕŏ (1), to *be fertile*
2593 karpŏphŏrŏs (1), *fruitbearing*

FRUITS
3 'êb (1), *green* plant
1061 bikkûwr (1), *first-fruits* of the crop
2173 zimrâh (1), *choice* fruit
3581 kôach (1), *force, might; strength*
4395 mᵉlê'âh (1), *fulfilled; abundance*
6529 pᵉrîy (7), *fruit*
8393 tᵉbûw'âh (6), *income,* i.e. *produce*
8570 tᵉnûwbâh (1), *crop, produce*
1081 gĕnnēma (2), *offspring; produce*
2590 karpŏs (12), *fruit; crop*
3703 ŏpōra (1), *ripe* fruit

FRUSTRATE
656 'âphêç (1), to *cease*
114 athĕtĕŏ (1), to *disesteem, neutralize*

FRUSTRATETH
6565 pârar (1), to *break* up; to *violate, frustrate*

FRYING
4802 marchesheth (1), *stew*-pan

FRYINGPAN
4802 marchesheth (1), *stew*-pan

FUEL
402 'oklâh (3), *food*
3980 ma'ăkôleth (2), *fuel* for fire

FUGITIVE
5128 nûwa' (2), to *waver*

FUGITIVES
1280 bᵉrîyach (1), *bolt; cross-bar* of a door
4015 mibrâch (1), *refugee*
5307 nâphal (1), to *fall*
6412 pâlîyṭ (1), *refugee*

FULFIL
3615 kâlâh (1), to *complete, consume*
4390 mâlê' (7), to *fill; be full*
6213 'âsâh (2), to *do* or *make*
378 anaplĕrŏŏ (1), to *complete; to occupy*
4137 plĕrŏŏ (6), to *fill, make complete*
4160 pŏiĕŏ (2), to *make* or *do*
5055 tĕlĕŏ (3), to *end,* i.e. *complete, execute*

FULFILLED
1214 bâtsa' (1), to *finish; to stop*
3615 kâlâh (2), to *complete, consume*
4390 mâlê' (20), to *fill; be full*
5487 çûwph (Ch.) (1), to *come to an end*

FULFILLING

6213 'âsâh (1), to do
378 anaplēróō (1), to complete; accomplish
1096 ginŏmai (3), to be, become
1603 ĕkplēróō (1), to accomplish, fulfill
4137 plērŏō (45), to fill, make complete
4931 suntĕlĕō (1), to complete entirely
5048 tĕlĕiŏō (2), to perfect, complete
5055 tĕlĕō (4), to end, i.e. complete, execute

FULFILLING

6213 'âsâh (1), to do or make
4138 plērōma (1), what fills; what is filled
4160 pŏiĕō (1), to do

FULL

3117 yôwm (10), day; time period
3624 kelach (1), maturity
3759 karmel (1), planted field; garden produce
4390 mâlê' (50), to fill; be full
4391 mᵉlâ' (Ch.) (1), to fill; be full
4392 mâlê' (58), full; filling; fulness; fully
4393 mᵉlô' (11), fulness
7227 rab (1), great
7235 râbâh (1), to increase
7646 sâba' (20), fill to satiety
7648 sôba' (3), satisfaction
7649 sâbêa' (2), satiated
7654 sob'âh (3), satiety
7999 shâlam (1), to be safe; be, make complete
8003 shâlêm (2), complete; friendly; safe
8537 tôm (1), completeness
8549 tâmîym (1), entire, complete; integrity
8552 tâmam (1), complete, finish
1072 gĕmizō (1), to fill entirely
1073 gĕmō (11), to swell out, i.e. be full
1705 ĕmpiplēmi (1), to satisfy
2880 kŏrennumi (1), to cram, i.e. glut or sate
3324 mĕstos (8), replete, full
3325 mĕstŏō (1), to intoxicate
4130 plēthō (1), to fulfill, complete
4134 plērēs (17), replete, full, complete
4135 plērŏphŏrĕō (1), fill completely
4136 plērŏphŏria (3), full assurance
4137 plērŏō (9), to fill, make complete
4138 plērōma (1), what fills; what is filled
5046 tĕlĕiŏs (1), complete; mature

FULLER

1102 gnaphĕus (1), cloth-dresser

FULLER'S

3526 kâbaç (3), to wash

FULLERS'

3526 kâbaç (3), to wash

FULLY

3615 kâlâh (1), to complete, consume
4390 mâlê' (3), to fill; be full
4392 mâlê' (1), full; filling; fulness; fully
5046 nâgad (1), to announce
3877 parakŏlŏuthĕō (1), to attend; trace out
4135 plērŏphŏrĕō (3), to fill completely
4137 plērŏō (1), to fill, make complete
4845 sumplērŏō (1), to be complete, fulfill

FULNESS

4390 mâlê' (1), to fill; be full
4393 mᵉlô' (8), fulness
4395 mᵉlê'âh (1), fulfilled; abundance
7648 sôba' (1), satisfaction
7653 sib'âh (1), satiety
4138 plērōma (13), what fills; what is filled

FURBISH

4838 mâraq (1), to polish; to sharpen; to rinse

FURBISHED

4803 mâraṭ (5), to polish; to sharpen

FURIOUS

1167+2534 ba'al (1), master; owner; citizen
2534 chêmâh (4), heat; anger; poison
7108 qᵉtsaph (Ch.) (1), to become enraged

FURIOUSLY

2534 chêmâh (1), heat; anger; poison
7697 shiggâ'ôwn (1), craziness

FURLONGS

4712 stadiŏn (5), length of about 200 yards

FURNACE

861 'attûwn (Ch.) (10), fire furnace
3536 kibshân (4), smelting furnace
3564 kûwr (9), smelting furnace
5948 'ălîyl (1), (poss.) crucible
8574 tannûwr (2), fire-pot
2575 kaminŏs (4), furnace

FURNACES

8574 tannûwr (2), fire-pot

FURNISH

4390 mâlê' (1), to fill; be full
6059 'ânaq (1), to collar; to fit out
6186 'ârak (1), to set in a row, i.e. arrange,
6213+3627 'âsâh (1), to do or make

FURNISHED

5375 nâsâ' (1), to lift up
6186 'ârak (1), to set in a row, i.e. arrange,
1822 ĕxartizō (1), to finish out; to equip fully
4130 plēthō (1), to fulfill, complete
4766 strōnnumi (2), strew, spread a carpet

FURNITURE

3627 kᵉlîy (7), implement, thing
3733 kar (1), saddle bag

FURROW

8525 telem (1), bank or terrace

FURROWS

1417 gᵉdûwd (1), furrow ridge
4618 ma'ănâh (1), furrow, plow path
5869 'ayin (1), eye; sight; fountain
6170 'ărûwgâh (2), parterre, kind of garden
8525 telem (3), bank or terrace

FURTHER

3148 yôwthêr (1), moreover; rest; gain
3254 yâçaph (4), to add or augment
5750 'ôwd (2), again; repeatedly; still; more
6329 pûwq (1), to issue; to furnish; to secure
1339 diïstēmi (1), to remove, intervene
2089 ĕti (6), yet, still
4206 pŏrrhō (1), forwards, at a distance

FURTHERANCE

4297 prŏkŏpē (2), progress, advancement

FURTHERED

5375 nâsâ' (1), to lift up

FURTHERMORE

637 'aph (1), also or yea; though
5750 'ôwd (1), again; repeatedly; still; more
1161 dĕ (1), but, yet; and then
1534 ĕita (1), succession, then, moreover
3063 lŏipŏn (1), remaining; finally

FURY

2528 chĕmâ' (Ch.) (2), anger
2534 chêmâh (67), heat; anger; poison
2740 chârôwn (1), burning of anger

GAAL

1603 Ga'al (9), loathing

GAASH

1608 Ga'ash (4), quaking

GABA

1387 Geba' (3), Geba

GABBAI

1373 Gabbay (1), collective

GABBATHA

1042 gabbatha (1), knoll

GABRIEL

1403 Gabrîy'êl (2), man of God
1043 Gabriël (2), man of God

GAD

1410 Gâd (71), Gad
1045 Gad (1), Gad

GADARENES

1046 Gadarēnŏs (3), inhabitant of Gadara

GADDEST

235 'âzal (1), to disappear

GADDI

1426 Gaddîy (1), Gaddi

GADDIEL

1427 Gaddîy'êl (1), fortune of God

GADI

1424 Gâdîy (2), fortunate

GADITE

1425 Gâdîy (1), Gadite

GADITES

1425 Gâdîy (14), Gadite

GAHAM

1514 Gacham (1), flame

GAHAR

1515 Gachar (2), lurker

GAIN

1214 bâtsa' (9), to plunder; to finish; to stop
2084 zᵉban (Ch.) (1), to acquire by purchase
4242 mᵉchîyr (1), price, payment, wages
8393 tᵉbûw'âh (1), income, i.e. produce
8636 tarbîyth (1), percentage or bonus
2039 ĕrgasia (2), occupation; profit
2770 kĕrdainō (9), to gain; to spare
2771 kĕrdŏs (2), gain, profit
4122 plĕŏnĕktĕō (2), to be covetous
4200 pŏrismŏs (2), money-getting

GAINED

1214 bâtsa' (2), to plunder; to finish
1281 diapragmatĕuŏmai (1), to earn, make gain
2770 kĕrdainō (5), to gain; to spare
4160 pŏiĕō (1), to make or do
4333 prŏsĕrgazŏmai (1), to acquire besides

GAINS

2039 ĕrgasia (1), occupation; profit

GAINSAY
471 antĕpō (1), to *refute* or *deny*

GAINSAYERS
483 antilĕgō (1), to *dispute, refuse*

GAINSAYING
369 anantirrhĕtōs (1), *without raising objection*
483 antilĕgō (1), to *dispute, refuse*
485 antilŏgia (1), *dispute, disobedience*

GAIUS
1050 Gaïos (5), *Gaïus*

GALAL
1559 Gâlâl (3), *great*

GALATIA
1053 Galatia (4), *Galatia*
1054 Galatikŏs (2), relating to *Galatia*

GALATIANS
1052 Galatēs (2), *inhabitant of Galatia*

GALBANUM
2464 chelbᵉnâh (1), *fragrant resin gum*

GALEED
1567 Gal'êd (2), *heap of testimony*

GALILAEAN
1057 Galilaiŏs (3), belonging to *Galilæa*

GALILAEANS
1057 Galilaiŏs (5), belonging to *Galilæa*

GALILEE
1551 Gâliyl (6), *circle as a special circuit*
1056 Galilaia (66), heathen *circle*

GALL
4845 mᵉrêrâh (1), bitter *bile of the gall bladder*
4846 mᵉrôrâh (2), bitter *bile; venom* of a serpent
7219 rô'sh (9), *poisonous plant; poison*
5521 chŏlē (2), *gall* or *bile; bitterness*

GALLANT
117 'addîyr (1), *powerful; majestic*

GALLERIES
862 'attûwq (3), *ledge or offset*
7298 rahaṭ (1), *ringlet of hair*

GALLERY
862 'attûwq (1), *ledge or offset*

GALLEY
590 'ŏnîy (1), *ship; fleet of ships*

GALLIM
1554 Gallîym (2), *springs*

GALLIO
1058 Galliōn (3), *Gallion,* i.e. *Gallio*

GALLOWS
6086 'êts (8), *wood, things made of wood*

GAMALIEL
1583 Gamliy'êl (5), *reward of God*
1059 Gamaliēl (2), *reward of God*

GAMMADIMS
1575 Gammâd (1), *warrior*

GAMUL
1577 Gâmûwl (1), *rewarded*

GAP
6556 perets (1), *break, gap*

GAPED
6473 pâ'ar (1), to *open wide*
6475 pâtsâh (1), to *rend,* i.e. *open*

GAPS
6556 perets (1), *break, gap*

GARDEN
1588 gan (39), *garden*
1593 gannâh (3), *garden, grove*
1594 ginnâh (4), *garden, grove*
2779 kēpŏs (5), *garden, grove*

GARDENER
2780 kēpŏurŏs (1), *gardener*

GARDENS
1588 gan (3), *garden*
1593 gannâh (9), *garden, grove*

GAREB
1619 Gârêb (3), *scabby*

GARLANDS
4725 stĕmma (1), *wreath*

GARLICK
7762 shûwm (1), *garlic*

GARMENT
155 'addereth (4), *large; splendid*
899 beged (36), *clothing; treachery* or *pillage*
3801 kᵉthôneth (2), *garment that covers*
3830 lᵉbûwsh (7), *garment; wife*
3831 lᵉbûwsh (Ch.) (1), *garment*
4055 mad (3), *vesture, garment; carpet*
4594 ma'ăṭeh (1), *vestment, garment*
7897 shîyth (1), *garment*
8008 salmâh (4), *clothing*
8071 simlâh (4), *dress, mantle*
8162 sha'aṭnêz (1), *linen and woolen*
8509 takrîyk (1), *wrapper or robe*
1742 ĕnduma (2), *apparel, outer robe*
2440 himatiŏn (15), to *put on clothes*
4158 pŏdērēs (1), robe *reaching the ankles*
4749 stŏlē (1), long-fitting *gown* as a mark of dignity

GARMENTS
899 beged (69), *clothing; treachery* or *pillage*
3801 kᵉthôneth (3), *garment that covers*
3830 lᵉbûwsh (2), *garment; wife*
3831 lᵉbûwsh (Ch.) (1), *garment*
4055 mad (1), *vesture, garment; carpet*
4060 middâh (1), *portion; vestment; tribute*
4063 medev (2), *dress, garment*
8008 salmâh (4), *clothing*
8071 simlâh (2), *dress, mantle*
2067 ĕsthēsis (1), *clothing*
2440 himatiŏn (15), to *put on clothes*

GARMITE
1636 Garmîy (1), *strong*

GARNER
596 apŏthēkē (2), *granary, grain barn*

GARNERS
214 'ôwtsâr (1), *depository*
4200 mezev (1), *granary*

GARNISH
2885 kŏsmĕō (1), to *decorate; to snuff*

GARNISHED
6823 tsâphâh (1), to *sheet* over with metal
8235 shiphrâh (1), *brightness* of skies
2885 kŏsmĕō (3), to *decorate; to snuff*

GARRISON
4673 matstsâb (7), *spot; office; military post*
4675 matstsâbâh (1), *military guard*
5333 nᵉtsîyb (4), *military post; statue*
5432 phrŏurĕō (1), to *post spies at gates*

GARRISONS
4676 matstsêbâh (1), *column or stone*
5333 nᵉtsîyb (5), *military post; statue*

GASHMU
1654 Geshem (1), *rain downpour*

GAT
622 'âçaph (1), to *gather, collect*
935 bôw' (2), to *go or come*
3212 yâlak (4), to *walk; to live; to carry*
5927 'âlâh (7), to *ascend, be high, mount*
6213 'âsâh (1), to *do or make*
7392 râkab (1), to *ride*

GATAM
1609 Ga'tâm (3), *Gatam*

5509 *chitōn* (1), *tunic* or *shirt*

GATE
6607 pethach (4), *opening; door; entrance*
8179 sha'ar (240), *opening, door or gate*
8651 tᵉra' (Ch.) (1), *door*
2374 thura (1), *entrance,* i.e. *door, gate*
4439 pulē (8), *gate*
4440 pulōn (5), *gate-way, door-way*

GATES
1817 deleth (14), *door; gate*
5592 çaph (2), *dish*
6607 pethach (3), *opening; door, entrance*
8179 sha'ar (112), *opening, door or gate*
4439 pulē (2), *gate*
4440 pulōn (11), *gate-way, door-way*

GATH
1661 Gath (33), *wine-press* or *vat*

GATH-HEPHER
1662 Gath-ha-Chêpher (1), *wine-press of* (the) *well*

GATH-RIMMON
1667 Gath-Rimmôwn (4), *wine-press of* (the) *pomegranate*

GATHER
103 'âgar (1), to *harvest*
622 'âçaph (36), to *gather, collect*
1219 bâtsar (2), to *gather grapes*
1413 gâdad (2), to *gash, slash oneself*
1481 gûwr (3), to *sojourn, live as an alien*
1716 dâgar (1), to *brood over; to care for young*
2490 châlal (1), to *profane, defile*
3259 yâ'ad (1), to *meet; to summon; to direct*
3664 kânaç (5), to *collect; to enfold*
3673 kânash (Ch.) (1), to *assemble*
3950 lâqaṭ (13), to *pick up, gather; to glean*
3953 lâqash (1), to *gather the after crop*
4390 mâlê' (2), to *fill; be full*
5619 çâqal (1), to *throw large stones*
5756 'ûwz (3), to *strengthen*
6908 qâbats (56), to *collect, assemble*
6910 qᵉbûtsâh (1), *hoard, gathering*
6950 qâhal (8), to *convoke, gather*
7197 qâshash (4), to *assemble*
346 anakĕphalaiŏmai (1), to *sum up*
1996 ĕpisunagō (2), to *collect upon*
4816 sullĕgō (6), to *collect, gather*

GATHERED
4863 sunagō (11), *to gather together*
5166 trugaō (2), *to collect* the vintage

GATHERED
622 'âçaph (97), *to gather, collect*
626 'ăçêphâh (1), (collect) *together*
717 'ârâh (1), *to pluck, pick fruit*
1219 bâtsar (1), *to gather grapes*
1481 gûwr (2), *to sojourn, live as an alien*
2199 zâ'aq (4), *to call out, announce*
3254 yâçaph (1), *to add or augment*
3259 yâ'ad (3), *to meet; to summon; to direct*
3664 kânaç (2), *to collect; to enfold*
3673 kânash (Ch.) (2), *to assemble*
3950 lâqat (11), *to pick up, gather; to glean*
4390 mâlê' (1), *to fill; be full*
5413 nâthak (2), *to flow forth, pour out*
5596 çâphach (1), *to associate; be united*
6192 'âram (1), *to pile up*
6213 'âsâh (1), *to do or make*
6651 tsâbar (2), *to aggregate, gather*
6817 tsâ'aq (5), *to shriek; to proclaim*
6908 qâbats (57), *to collect, assemble*
6950 qâhal (19), *to convoke, gather*
6960 qâvâh (2), *to collect; to expect*
7035 qâlahh (1), *to assemble*
7197 qâshash (1), *to assemble*
7408 râkash (1), *to lay up, i.e. collect*
8085 shâma' (1), *to hear intelligently*
1865 ĕpathrŏizō (1), *to accumulate, increase*
1996 ĕpisunagō (4), *to collect upon*
3792 ŏchlŏpŏiĕō (1), *to raise a disturbance*
4816 sullĕgō (2), *to collect, gather*
4863 sunagō (29), *to gather together*
4867 sunathrŏizō (1), *to convene*
4896 sunĕimi (1), *to assemble, gather*
4962 sustrĕphō (1), *to collect a bundle, crowd*
5166 trugaō (1), *to collect* the vintage

GATHERER
1103 bâlaç (1), *to pinch* sycamore figs

GATHEREST
1219 bâtsar (1), *to gather* grapes

GATHERETH
103 'âgar (2), *to harvest*
622 'âçaph (4), *to gather, collect*
3664 kânaç (2), *to collect; to enfold*
3950 lâqat (1), *to pick up, gather; to glean*
6908 qâbats (4), *to collect, assemble*
1996 ĕpisunagō (1), *to collect upon*
4863 sunagō (3), *to gather together*

GATHERING
625 'ôçeph (2), fruit *harvest collection*
962 bâzaz (1), *to plunder, take booty*
3349 yiqqâhâh (1), *obedience*
4723 miqveh (1), *confidence; collection*
7197 qâshash (3), *to assemble*
1997 ĕpisunagōgē (1), *meeting, gathering*
4822 sumbibazō (1), *drive together*
4863 sunagō (1), *to gather together*

GATHERINGS
3048 lŏgia (1), *contribution, collection*

GAVE
935 bôw' (1), *to go, come*
1696 dâbar (3), *to speak, say; to subdue*
3052 yᵉhab (Ch.) (4), *to give*
3254 yâçaph (1), *to add or augment*
3289 yâ'ats (2), *to advise*
5414 nâthan (252), *to give*
5462 çâgar (3), *to shut up; to surrender*
7121 qârâ' (3), *to call out*
7311 rûwm (4), *to be high; to rise or raise*
7725 shûwb (1), *to turn back; to return*
7760 sûwm (4), *to put, place*
7971 shâlach (1), *to send away*
437 anthŏmŏlŏgĕōmai (1), *to give thanks*
591 apŏdidōmi (2), *to give away*
1291 diastĕllŏmai (1), *to distinguish*
1325 didōmi (77), *to give*
1433 dōrĕōmai (1), *to bestow* gratuitously
1502 ĕikō (1), *to be weak, i.e. yield*
1781 ĕntĕllŏmai (1), *to enjoin, give orders*
1788 ĕntrĕpō (1), *to respect; to confound*
1907 ĕpĕchō (1), *to retain; to detain*
1929 ĕpididōmi (2), *to give over*
2010 ĕpitrĕpō (3), *allow, permit*
2702 kataphĕrō (1), *to bear down*

2753 kĕlĕuō (1), *to order, direct*
3140 marturĕō (3), *to testify; to commend*
3860 paradidōmi (7), *to hand over*
4160 pŏiĕō (2), *to make or do*
4222 pŏtizō (5), *to furnish drink, irrigate*
4337 prŏsĕchō (3), *to pay attention to*
4823 sumbŏulĕuō (1), *to recommend, deliberate*
5483 charizōmai (2), *to grant as a favor, pardon*

GAVEST
5414 nâthan (21), *to give*
7760 sûwm (1), *to put, place*
1325 didōmi (11), *to give*

GAY
2986 lamprŏs (1), *clear; magnificent*

GAZA
5804 'Azzâh (18), *strong*
1048 Gaza (1), *strong*

GAZATHITES
5841 'Azzâthîy (1), *Azzathite*

GAZE
7200 râ'âh (1), *to see*

GAZER
1507 Gezer (2), *portion, piece*

GAZEZ
1495 Gâzêz (2), *shearer*

GAZING
1689 ĕmblĕpō (1), *to observe; to discern*

GAZINGSTOCK
7210 rô'îy (1), *sight; spectacle*
2301 thĕatrizō (1), *to expose as a spectacle*

GAZITES
5841 'Azzâthîy (1), *Azzathite*

GAZZAM
1502 Gazzâm (2), *devourer*

GEBA
1387 Geba' (12), *Geba*

GEBAL
1381 Gᵉbâl (2), *mountain*

GEBER
1398 Geber (2), *(valiant) man*

GEBIM
1374 Gêbîym (1), *cisterns*

GEDALIAH
1436 Gᵉdalyâh (32), *Jehovah has become great*

GEDEON
1066 Gĕdĕōn (1), *warrior*

GEDER
1445 Geder (1), *wall or fence*

GEDERAH
1449 Gᵉdêrâh (1), *enclosure* for flocks

GEDERATHITE
1452 Gᵉdêrâthîy (1), *Gederathite*

GEDERITE
1451 Gᵉdêriy (1), *Gederite*

GEDEROTH
1450 Gᵉdêrôwth (2), *walls*

GEDEROTHAIM
1453 Gᵉdêrôthayim (1), *double wall*

GEDOR
1446 Gᵉdôr (7), *enclosure*

GEHAZI
1522 Gêychăzîy (12), *valley of a visionary*

GELILOTH
1553 Gᵉlîylôwth (1), *circles*

GEMALLI
1582 Gᵉmalliy (1), *camel-driver*

GEMARIAH
1587 Gᵉmaryâh (5), *Jehovah has perfected*

GENDER
7250 râba' (1), *to lay down; have sex*
1080 gĕnnaō (1), *to procreate, regenerate*

GENDERED
3205 yâlad (1), *to bear young; to father a child*

GENDERETH
5674 'âbar (1), *to cross over; to transition*
1080 gĕnnaō (1), *to procreate, regenerate*

GENEALOGIES
3187 yâchas (6), *to enroll* by *family list*
1076 gĕnĕalŏgia (2), *genealogy, lineage*

GENEALOGY
3188 yachas (15), *family list*

GENERAL
8269 sar (1), *head person, ruler*
3831 panēguris (1), *mass-meeting*

GENERALLY
3605 kôl (1), *all, any or every*

GENERATION
1755 dôwr (50), *dwelling*
1859 dâr (Ch.) (2), *age; generation*
1074 gĕnĕa (30), *generation; age*
1078 genesis (1), *nativity, nature*
1081 gĕnnēma (4), *offspring; produce*
1085 gĕnŏs (1), *kin, offspring in kind*

GENERATIONS
1755 dôwr (73), *dwelling*
8435 tôwlᵉdâh (39), *family descent*, family *record*

English

1074 gĕnĕa (6), generation; age

GENNESARET
1082 Gĕnnēsarĕt (3), (poss.) harp-shaped

GENTILE
1672 Hĕllēn (2), Greek (-speaking)

GENTILES
1471 gôwy (30), foreign nation; Gentiles
1483 ĕthnikōs (1), as a Gentile
1484 ĕthnŏs (93), race; tribe; pagan
1672 Hĕllēn (5), Greek (-speaking)

GENTLE
1933 ĕpiĕikēs (3), mild, gentle
2261 ēpiŏs (2), affable, i.e. mild or kind

GENTLENESS
6031 'ânâh (1), to afflict, be afflicted
6038 'ănâvâh (1), modesty, clemency
1932 ĕpiĕikĕia (1), mildness, gentleness
5544 chrēstŏtēs (1), moral excellence

GENTLY
3814 lâ'ṭ (1), silently

GENUBATH
1592 Gᵉnûbath (2), theft

GERA
1617 Gêrâ' (9), cereal grain

GERAHS
1626 gêrâh (5), measure

GERAR
1642 Gᵉrâr (10), rolling country

GERGESENES
1086 Gĕrgĕsēnŏs (1), Gergesene

GERIZIM
1630 Gᵉrîzîym (4), rocky

GERSHOM
1648 Gêrᵉshôwn (14), refugee

GERSHON
1647 Gêrᵉshôm (17), refugee

GERSHONITE
1649 Gerᵉshunnîy (3), Gereshonite

GERSHONITES
1649 Gerᵉshunnîy (9), Gereshonite

GESHAM
1529 Gêyshân (1), lumpish

GESHEM
1654 Geshem (3), rain downpour

GESHUR
1650 Gᵉshûwr (8), bridge

GESHURI
1651 Gᵉshûwrîy (2), Geshurite

GESHURITES
1651 Gᵉshûwrîy (5), Geshurite

GET
776 'erets (1), earth, land, soil; country
935 bôw' (8), to go or come
1214 bâtsa' (1), to plunder; to finish
1245 bâqash (1), to search; to strive after
1980 hâlak (1), to walk; live a certain way
3212 yâlak (17), to walk; to live; to carry
3318 yâtsâ' (7), to go, bring out
3381 yârad (9), to descend
3513 kâbad (1), to be heavy, severe, dull
3947 lâqach (5), to take
4422 mâlaṭ (1), to escape as if by slipperiness
4672 mâtsâ' (2), to find or acquire; to occur
5110 nûwd (1), to waver; to wander, flee
5111 nûwd (Ch.) (1), to flee
5265 nâça' (1), start on a journey
5381 nâsag (6), to reach
5674 'âbar (1), to cross over; to transition
5927 'âlâh (18), to ascend, be high, mount
6213 'âsâh (2), to do or make
6965 qûwm (1), to rise
7069 qânâh (8), to create; to procure
7426 râmam (1), to rise
7725 shûwb (1), to turn back; to return
1684 ĕmbainō (2), to embark; to reach
1826 ĕxĕimi (1), leave; escape
1831 ĕxĕrchŏmai (3), to issue; to leave
2147 hĕuriskō (1), to find
2597 katabainō (1), to descend
4122 plĕŏnĕktĕō (1), to be covetous
5217 hupagō (4), to withdraw or retire

GETHER
1666 Gether (2), Gether

GETHSEMANE
1068 Gĕthsēmanē (2), oil-press

GETTETH
3947 lâqach (1), to take
5060 nâga' (1), to strike
5927 'âlâh (1), to ascend, be high, mount
6213 'âsâh (1), to do or make
6329 pûwq (1), to issue; to furnish; to secure
7069 qânâh (3), to create; to procure

GETTING
6467 pô'al (1), act or work, deed
7069 qânâh (1), to create; to procure
7075 qinyân (1), acquisition, purchase

GEUEL
1345 Gᵉ'ûw'êl (1), majesty of God

GEZER
1507 Gezer (13), portion, piece

GEZRITES
1511 Gizrîy (1), Gezerite; Girzite

GHOST
1478 gâva' (9), to expire, die
5315 nephesh (2), life; breath; soul; wind
1606 ĕkpnĕō (3), to expire
1634 ĕkpsuchō (3), to expire, die
4151 pnĕuma (92), spirit

GIAH
1520 Gîyach (1), fountain

GIANT
1368 gibbôwr (1), powerful; great warrior
7497 râphâ' (7), giant

GIANTS
1368 gibbôwr (1), powerful; great warrior
5303 nᵉphîyl (2), bully or tyrant
7497 râphâ' (10), giant

GIBBAR
1402 Gibbâr (1), Gibbar

GIBBETHON
1405 Gibbᵉthôwn (6), hilly spot

GIBEA
1388 Gib'â' (1), hill

GIBEAH
1390 Gib'âh (48), hillock

GIBEATH
1394 Gib'ath (1), hilliness

GIBEATHITE
1395 Gib'âthîy (1), Gibathite

GIBEON
1391 Gib'ôwn (35), hilly

GIBEONITE
1393 Gib'ônîy (2), Gibonite

GIBEONITES
1393 Gib'ônîy (6), Gibonite

GIBLITES
1382 Giblîy (1), Gebalite

GIDDALTI
1437 Giddaltîy (2), I have made great

GIDDEL
1435 Giddêl (4), stout

GIDEON
1439 Gid'ôwn (39), warrior

GIDEONI
1441 Gid'ônîy (5), warlike

GIDOM
1440 Gid'ôm (1), desolation

GIER
7360 râchâm (2), kind of vulture

GIFT
4503 minchâh (1), tribute; offering
4976 mattân (4), present, gift
4979 mâttânâh (5), present; offering; bribe
4991 mattâth (3), present
5379 nissê'th (1), present
7810 shachad (6), to bribe; gift
1390 dŏma (1), present, gift
1394 dŏsis (1), gift
1431 dôrĕa (11), gratuity, gift
1434 dôrēma (1), bestowment, gift
1435 dôrŏn (10), sacrificial present
5485 charis (1), gratitude; benefit given
5486 charisma (10), spiritual endowment

GIFTS
814 'eshkâr (1), gratuity, gift; payment
4503 minchâh (6), tribute; offering
4864 mas'êth (1), tribute; reproach
4976 mattân (1), present, gift
4978 mattᵉnâ' (Ch.) (3), present, gift
4979 mâttânâh (11), present; offering; bribe
5078 nêdeh (1), bounty, reward for prostitution
5083 nâdân (1), present for prostitution
7810 shachad (4), to bribe; gift
8641 tᵉrûwmâh (1), tribute, present
334 anathēma (1), votive offering to God
1390 dŏma (2), present, gift
1435 dôrŏn (9), sacrificial present
3311 mĕrismŏs (1), distribution
5486 charisma (7), spiritual endowment

GIHON
1521 Gîychôwn (6), stream

GILALAI
1562 Gîlălay (1), dungy

GILBOA
1533 Gilbôa' (8), bubbling fountain

GILEAD
1568 Gil'âd (100), Gilad

GILEAD'S
1568 Gil'âd (1), Gilad

GILEADITE
1569 Gil'âdîy (9), Giladite

English

GILEADITES
1569 Gil'âdîy (4), *Giladite*

GILGAL
1537 Gilgâl (39), *wheel*

GILOH
1542 Gîlôh (2), *open*

GILONITE
1526 Gîylônîy (2), *Gilonite*

GIMZO
1579 Gimzôw (1), Gimzo

GIN
4170 môwqêsh (1), *noose*
6341 pach (2), thin metallic *sheet; net*

GINATH
1527 Gîynath (2), *Ginath*

GINNETHO
1599 Ginnᵉthôwn (1), *gardener*

GINNETHON
1599 Ginnᵉthôwn (2), *gardener*

GINS
4170 môwqêsh (2), *noose*

GIRD
247 'âzar (4), to *belt*
640 'âphad (1), to *fasten, gird*
2290 chăgôwr (1), *belt* for the waist
2296 châgar (16), to *gird* on a belt; *put on* armor
328 anazônnumi (1), *gird, bind afresh*
2224 zônnumi (2), to *bind about*
4024 pĕrizônnumi (2), to *fasten on one's belt*

GIRDED
247 'âzar (7), to *belt*
631 'âçar (1), to *fasten;* to *join* battle
2280 châbash (1), to *wrap* firmly, *bind*
2289 chăgôwr (1), *belted* around waist
2296 châgar (18), to *gird* on a belt; *put on* armor
8151 shânaç (1), to *compress*
1241 diazônnumi (2), to *gird tightly, wrap*
4024 pĕrizônnumi (2), to *fasten on one's belt*

GIRDEDST
2224 zônnumi (1), to *bind about*

GIRDETH
247 'âzar (1), to *belt*
631 'âçar (1), to *fasten;* to *join* battle
2296 châgar (2), to *gird* on a belt; *put on* armor

GIRDING
2296 châgar (1), to *gird* on a belt; *put on* armor
4228 machăgôreth (1), *girdle* of sackcloth

GIRDLE
73 'abnêṭ (6), *belt*
232 'êzôwr (13), *belt; band around waist*

GILEADITES
2290 chăgôwr (5), *belt* for the waist
2805 chêsheb (8), *belt, waistband*
4206 mâzîyach (1), leather *belt*
2223 zônē (5), *belt, sash*

GIRDLES
73 'abnêṭ (3), *belt*
232 'êzôwr (1), *belt; band around waist*
2289 chăgôwr (1), *belted* around waist
2223 zônē (1), *belt, sash*

GIRGASHITE
1622 Girgâshîy (1), *Girgashite*

GIRGASHITES
1622 Girgâshîy (5), *Girgashite*

GIRGASITE
1622 Girgâshîy (1), *Girgashite*

GIRL
3207 yaldâh (1), *young female*

GIRLS
3207 yaldâh (1), *young female*

GIRT
247 'âzar (1), to *belt*
1241 diazônnumi (1), to *gird tightly, wrap*
4024 pĕrizônnumi (2), to *fasten on one's belt*

GISPA
1658 Gishpâ' (1), *Gishpa*

GITTAH-HEPHER
1662 Gath-ha-Chêpher (1), *wine-press of* (the) *well*

GITTAIM
1664 Gittayim (2), *double wine-press*

GITTITE
1663 Gittîy (8), *Gittite*

GITTITES
1663 Gittîy (2), *Gittite*

GITTITH
1665 Gittîyth (3), *harp*

GIVE
1262 bârâh (1), to *feed*
1478 gâva' (3), to *expire, die*
1696 dâbar (1), to *speak, say;* to *subdue*
1961+413 hâyâh (1), to *exist,* i.e. be or *become*
3051 yâhab (24), to *give*
3052 yᵉhab (Ch.) (2), to *give*
3190 yâṭab (1), to *be, make well*
4900 mâshak (1), to *draw out;* to *be tall*
4991 mattâth (2), *present*
5066 nâgash (1), to *be, come, bring near*
5414 nâthan (482), to *give*
5415 nᵉthan (Ch.) (2), to *give*
5441 çôbek (1), *copse* or *thicket*

GILEADITES
5534 çâkar (1), to *shut up;* to *surrender*
6213 'âsâh (1), to *do* or *make*
7311 rûwm (1), to be *high;* to *rise* or *raise*
7725 shûwb (3), to *turn* back; to *return* or restore
7760 sûwm (5), to *put, place*
7761 sûwm (Ch.) (1), to *put, place*
7999 shâlam (1), to be *safe;* be, make complete
402 anachôrēŏ (1), to *retire, withdraw*
591 apŏdidōmi (8), to *give away*
1096 ginŏmai (1), to *be, become*
1239 diadidōmi (1), to *divide up, distribute*
1325 didōmi (139), to *give*
1929 ĕpididōmi (5), to *give over*
2014 ĕpiphainō (1), to *become known*
2468 isthi (1), *be thou*
3330 mĕtadidōmi (1), to *share, distribute*
3844 para (1), *from; with; besides; on account of*
3860 paradidōmi (1), to *hand over*
3930 parĕchō (1), to *hold near,* i.e. to *present*
3936 paristēmi (1), to *stand beside, present*
4222 pŏtizō (3), to *furnish drink, irrigate*
4342 prŏskartĕrĕŏ (1), to *attend;* to *adhere*
4980 schŏlazō (1), to *devote oneself* wholly to
5461 phōtizō (1), to *shine* or to *brighten* up
5483 charizŏmai (1), to *grant as a favor*

GIVEN
1167 ba'al (2), *master; husband; owner; citizen*
1478 gâva' (1), to *expire, die*
1576 gᵉmûwl (1), *act; reward, recompense*
2505 châlaq (1), to be *smooth;* be *slippery*
2603 chânan (1), to *implore*
3052 yᵉhab (Ch.) (16), to *give*
3254 yâçaph (1), to *add* or *augment*
3289 yâ'ats (2), to *advise*
5221 nâkâh (3), to *strike, kill*
5301 nâphach (1), to *inflate, blow, scatter*
5375 nâsâ' (1), to *lift up*
5414 nâthan (253), to *give*
5462 çâgar (1), to *shut up;* to *surrender*
6213 'âsâh (1), to *do* or *make*
7760 sûwm (1), to *put, place*
7761 sûwm (Ch.) (1), to *put, place*

GILEADITES
1325 didōmi (123), to *give*
1377 diōkō (1), to *pursue;* to *persecute*
1402 dŏulŏō (1), to *enslave*
1433 dōrĕŏmai (2), to *bestow* gratuitously
1547 ĕkgamizō (1), to *marry off* a daughter
2227 zōŏpŏiĕō (1), to (re-)*vitalize, give life*
3860 paradidōmi (2), to *hand over*
3930 parĕchō (1), to *present, afford, exhibit*
3943 parŏinŏs (2), *tippling*
4272 prŏdidōmi (1), to *give before*
4337 prŏsĕchō (1), to *pay attention to*
4369 prŏstithēmi (1), to *lay beside, repeat*
5483 charizŏmai (5), to *grant as a favor*

GIVER
1395 dŏtēs (1), *giver*

GIVEST
5414 nâthan (7), to *give*
7971 shâlach (1), to *send away*

GIVETH
1478 gâva' (1), to *expire, die*
3052 yᵉhab (Ch.) (1), to *give*
5414 nâthan (77), to *give*
5415 nᵉthan (Ch.) (3), to *give*
1325 didōmi (13), to *give*
3330 mĕtadidōmi (1), to *share, distribute*
3930 parĕchō (1), to *present, afford, exhibit*
5087 tithēmi (1), to *place*
5524 chŏrēgĕō (1), to *furnish, supply, provide*

GIVING
4646 mappâch (1), *expiring, dying*
5414 nâthan (5), to *give*
632 apŏnĕmō (1), *bestow, treat with respect*
1325 didōmi (3), to *give*
1394 dŏsis (1), *gift*
3004 lĕgō (1), to *say*
3548 nŏmŏthĕsia (1), *legislation, law*
3923 parĕisphĕrō (1), to *bear in alongside*

GIZONITE
1493 Gizôwnîy (1), *Gizonite*

GLAD
1523 gîyl (6), *rejoice*
1528 gîyr (Ch.) (4), *lime* for plaster
2302 châdâh (1), to *rejoice, be glad*
2868 ṭᵉ'êb (Ch.) (1), to *rejoice, be pleased*
2896 ṭôwb (2), *good; well*
7796 Sôwrêq (2), *vine*
7797 sûws (1), to be *bright;* to be *cheerful*
7996 Shalleketh (1), *felling* of trees

8056 sâmêach (49), *blithe* or *gleeful*
8190 Sha'ashgaz (1), *Shaashgaz*
21 agalliaō (2), to *exult*
2097 ĕuaggĕlizō (4), to *announce good news*
2165 ĕuphrainō (1), to *rejoice, be glad*
5463 chairō (14), to be *cheerful*

GLADLY
780 asmĕnōs (2), *with pleasure, gladly*
2234 hēdĕōs (3), *with pleasure, with delight*
2236 hēdista (2), *with great pleasure*

GLADNESS
1524 gĭyl (1), *age, stage in life*
2304 chedvâh (1), *rejoicing, joy*
2898 ṭûwb (1), *good; goodness; gladness*
7440 rinnâh (1), *shout*
8057 simchâh (34), *blithesomeness* or *glee*
8342 sâsôwn (2), *cheerfulness; welcome*
20 agalliasis (3), *exultation, delight*
2167 ĕuphrŏsunē (1), *joyfulness, cheerfulness*
5479 chara (3), *calm delight, joy*

GLASS
7209 re'îy (1), *mirror*
2072 ĕsŏptrŏn (2), *mirror for looking into*
2734 katŏptrizŏmai (1), to *see reflected*
5193 hualinŏs (3), *pertaining to glass*
5194 hualŏs (2), *glass, crystal*

GLASSES
1549 gĭllâyôwn (1), *tablet for writing; mirror*

GLEAN
3950 lâqaṭ (7), to *pick up, gather; to glean*
5953 'âlal (3), to *glean; to overdo*

GLEANED
3950 lâqaṭ (5), to *pick up, gather; to glean*
5953 'âlal (1), to *glean; to overdo*

GLEANING
3951 leqeṭ (1), *gleaning after a harvest*
5955 'ôlêlâh (4), *gleaning; gleaning-time*

GLEANINGS
3951 leqeṭ (1), *gleaning*

GLEDE
7201 râ'âh (1), bird of prey (poss. *vulture*)

GLISTERING
6320 pûwk (1), *stibium*
1823 ĕxastraptō (1), to be *radiant*

GLITTER
1300 bârâq (1), *lightning; flash of lightning*

GLITTERING
1300 bârâq (5), *lightning; flash of lightning*
3851 lahab (1), *flame of fire; flash* of a *blade*

GLOOMINESS
653 'ăphêlâh (2), *duskiness, darkness*

GLORIEST
1984 hâlal (1), to *shine, flash, radiate*

GLORIETH
1984 hâlal (1), to *shine, flash, radiate*
2744 kauchaŏmai (2), to *glory in, rejoice in*

GLORIFIED
1922 hădar (Ch.) (1), to *magnify, glorify*
3513 kâbad (6), to be *heavy, severe, dull; to be rich, glorious*
6286 pâ'ar (6), to *shake a tree*
1392 dŏxazō (34), to *render, esteem glorious*
1740 ĕndŏxazō (2), to *glorify*
4888 sundŏxazō (1), to *share glory with*

GLORIFIETH
3513 kâbad (1), to be *rich, glorious*

GLORIFY
3513 kâbad (7), to be *rich, glorious*
6286 pâ'ar (1), to *shake a tree*
1392 dŏxazō (17), to *render, esteem glorious*

GLORIFYING
1392 dŏxazō (3), to *render, esteem glorious*

GLORIOUS
117 'addîyr (1), *powerful; majestic*
142 'âdar (2), *magnificent; glorious*
215 'ôwr (1), to be *luminous*
1921 hâdar (1), to *favor* or *honor; to be high* or *proud*
1926 hâdâr (1), *magnificence*
1935 hôwd (1), *grandeur, majesty*
3513 kâbad (5), to be *rich, glorious*
3519 kâbôwd (11), *splendor, wealth*
3520 kebûwddâh (1), *magnificence, wealth*
6643 tsebîy (5), *conspicuous* splendor
8597 tiph'ârâh (3), *ornament*
1223+1391 dia (1), *through*, by means of
1391 dŏxa (6), *glory; brilliance*
1392 dŏxazō (1), to *render, esteem glorious*

1722+1391 ĕn (3), *in; during; because of*
1741 ĕndŏxŏs (2), *splendid; noble*

GLORIOUSLY
3519 kâbôwd (1), *splendor, copiousness*

GLORY
155 'addereth (1), *large; splendid*
1925 heder (1), *honor*
1926 hâdâr (7), *magnificence*
1935 hôwd (9), *grandeur, majesty*
1984 hâlal (12), to *shine, flash, radiate*
2892 ṭôhar (1), *brightness; purification*
3367 yeqâr (Ch.) (5), *glory, honor*
3513 kâbad (1), to be *rich, glorious*
3519 kâbôwd (155), *splendor, wealth*
6286 pâ'ar (1), to *shake a tree*
6643 tsebîy (7), *conspicuous* splendor
7623 shâbach (1), to *address; to pacify*
8597 tiph'ârâh (22), *ornament*
1391 dŏxa (146), *glory; brilliance*
1392 dŏxazō (3), to *render, esteem glorious*
2620 katakauchaŏmai (1), to *exult against*
2744 kauchaŏmai (18), to *glory in, rejoice in*
2745 kauchēma (3), *boast; brag*
2746 kauchēsis (1), *boasting; bragging*
2755 kĕnŏdŏxŏs (1), *self-conceited*
2811 klĕŏs (1), *renown, credited honor*

GLORYING
2744 kauchaŏmai (1), to *glory in, rejoice in*
2745 kauchēma (2), *boast; brag*
2746 kauchēsis (1), *boasting; bragging*

GLUTTON
2151 zâlal (2), to be *loose morally, worthless*

GLUTTONOUS
5314 phagŏs (2), *glutton*

GNASH
2786 chârâq (2), to *grate, grind* the teeth

GNASHED
2786 chârâq (1), to *grate, grind* the teeth
1031 bruchō (1), to *grate, grind* teeth

GNASHETH
2786 chârâq (2), to *grate, grind* the teeth
5149 trizō (1), to *grate* the teeth in frenzy

GNASHING
1030 brugmŏs (7), *grinding* of teeth

GNAT
2971 kōnōps (1), stinging *mosquito*

GNAW
1633 gâram (1), to *crunch* the bones

GNAWED
3145 massaŏmai (1), to *chew, gnaw*

GO
236 'ăzal (Ch.) (1), to *depart*
258 'âchad (1), to *unify,* i.e. *collect*
833 'âshar (2), to *go forward; guide*
935 bôw' (154), to *go, come*
1718 dâdâh (1), to *walk gently; lead*
1869 dârak (2), to *tread, trample; to walk, lead*
1946 hûwk (Ch.) (1), to *go, come*
1961 hâyâh (2), to *exist,* i.e. *be* or *become*
1980 hâlak (83), to *walk; live a certain way*
1982 hêlek (1), *wayfarer, visitor; flowing*
2498 châlaph (1), to *hasten away; to pass on*
2559 châmaq (1), to *depart,* i.e. turn about
3051 yâhab (4), to *give*
3212 yâlak (351), to *walk; to live; to carry*
3312 Yephunneh (1), *he will be prepared*
3318 yâtsâ' (185), to *go, bring out*
3381 yârad (73), to *descend*
3518 kâbâh (1), to *extinguish*
4161 môwtsâ' (1), *going forth*
4609 ma'ălâh (1), *thought* arising
4994 nâ' (2), *I pray!, please!, I beg you!*
5066 nâgash (2), to be, *come, bring near*
5181 nâchath (1), to *sink, descend; to press down*
5186 nâṭâh (1), to *stretch* or *spread out*
5265 nâċa' (7), *start* on a journey
5362 nâqaph (2), to *strike; to surround*
5437 çâbab (7), to *surround*
5472 çûwg (1), to *go back, to retreat*
5493 çûwr (4), to *turn off*
5503 çâchar (1), to *travel* round; to *palpitate*
5674 'âbar (51), to *cross over; to transition*
5927 'âlâh (129), to *ascend, be high, mount*
5930 'ôlâh (1), *sacrifice wholly consumed in fire*
6213 'âsâh (1), to *do*

6310 peh (1), *mouth;
opening*
6485 pâqad (1), *to visit,
care for, count*
6544 pâra'* (1), *to
absolve, begin*
6585 pâsa'* (1), *to stride*
6805 tsâ'ad (1), *to pace,
step regularly*
6806 tsa'ad (1), *pace or
regular step*
6923 qâdam (1), *to
hasten, meet*
7126 qârab (3), *to
approach, bring near*
7368 râchaq (3), *to
recede; remove*
7503 râphâh (4), *to
slacken*
7686 shâgâh (2), *to stray,
wander; to transgress*
7725 shûwb (15), *to turn
back; to return*
7751 shûwṭ (1), *to travel,
roam*
7847 sâṭâh (1), *to deviate
from duty, go astray*
7971 shâlach (76), *to
send away*
8582 tâ'âh (4), *to
vacillate, reel or stray*
8637 tirgal (1), *to cause
to walk*
33 agē (2), *to come on*
71 agō (6), *to lead; to
bring, drive; to weigh*
305 anabainō (9), *to go
up, rise*
565 apĕrchŏmai (25), *to
go off, i.e. depart,
withdraw*
630 apŏluō (13), *to
relieve, release*
863 aphiĕmi (1), *to leave;
to pardon, forgive*
1330 diĕrchŏmai (4), *to
traverse, travel through*
1524 ĕisĕimi (1), *to enter*
1525 ĕisĕrchŏmai (11), *to
enter*
1607 ĕkpŏrĕuŏmai (1), *to
depart, proceed, project*
1830 ĕxĕrĕunaō (1), *to
explore*
1831 ĕxĕrchŏmai (14), *to
issue; to leave*
1881 ĕpanistamai (2), *to
stand up on, to attack*
1931 ĕpiduō (1), *to set*
1994 ĕpistrĕphō (1), *to
revert, turn back to*
2064 ĕrchŏmai (2), *to go
or come*
2212 zētĕō (1), *to seek*
2597 katabainō (2), *to
descend*
3327 mĕtabainō (1), *to
depart, move from*
3928 parĕrchŏmai (1), *to
go by; to perish*
4043 pĕripatĕō (1), *to
walk; to live a life*
4198 pŏrĕuŏmai (74), *to
go, come; to travel*
4254 prŏagō (5), *to lead
forward; to precede*
4281 prŏĕrchŏmai (2), *to
go onward; precede*

4313 prŏpŏrĕuŏmai (2),
to precede
4320 prŏsanabainō (1),
to be promoted
4334 prŏsĕrchŏmai (1),
to come near, visit
4782 sugkatabainō (1),
to descend with
4905 sunĕrchŏmai (1), *to
go with*
5217 hupagō (54), *to
withdraw or retire*
5233 hupĕrbainō (1), *to
transcend, to overreach*
5342 phĕrō (1), *to bear or
carry*

GOAD

4451 malmâd (1),
ox-goad

GOADS

1861 dorbôwn (2), *iron
goad stick*

GOAT

689 'aqqôw (1), *ibex*
5795 'êz (9), *she-goat;
goat's hair*
6842 tsâphîyr (3), *male
goat*
8163 sâ'îyr (21), *shaggy;
he-goat; goat idol*
8495 tayish (1), *buck or
he-goat*

GOATH

1601 Gô'âh (1), *lowing,
bellowing*

GOATS

3277 yâ'êl (3), *ibex
animal*
5795 'êz (45), *she-goat;
goat's hair*
6260 'attûwd (26),
he-goats; leaders
6842 tsâphîyr (1), *he-goat*
8163 sâ'îyr (3), *shaggy;
he-goat; goat idol*
8495 tayish (3), *he-goat*
2055 ĕriphiŏn (1), *goat*
2056 ĕriphŏs (1), *kid or
goat*
5131 tragŏs (4), *he-goat*

GOATS'

5795 'êz (10), *she-goat;
goat's hair*

GOATSKINS

122+1192 aigĕiŏs (1),
belonging to a goat

GOB

1359 Gôb (2), *pit*

GOBLET

101 'aggân (1), *bowl*

GOD

136 'Ădônây (1), *the Lord*
401 'Ûkâl (1), *devoured*
410 'êl (217), *mighty; the
Almighty*
426 'ĕlâhh (Ch.) (79), *God*
430 'ĕlôhîym (2340), *God;
gods; great ones*
433 'ĕlôwahh (55), *the
true God; god*
1008 Bêyth-'Êl (5), *house
of God*
3068 Yᵉhôvâh (4),
*Jehovah, the
self-Existent or Eternal*

3069 Yᵉhôvîh (301),
*Jehovah, (the)
self-Existent or Eternal*
3609 Kil'âb (1), *restraint
of* (his) *father*
4010 mablîygîyth (1),
desolation
6697 tsûwr (2), *rock*
112 athĕŏs (1), *godless*
2312 thĕŏdidaktŏs (1),
divinely instructed
2313 thĕŏmachĕō (1), *to
resist deity*
2314 thĕŏmachŏs (1),
opponent of deity
2315 thĕŏpnĕustŏs (1),
divinely breathed in
2316 thĕŏs (1292), *deity;
the Supreme Deity*
2318 thĕŏsĕbēs (1), *pious,
devout, God-fearing*
2319 thĕŏstugēs (1),
impious, God-hating
2962 kuriŏs (1), *supreme,
controller, Mr.*
3361+1096 mē (15), *not;
lest*
5377 philŏthĕŏs (1),
pious, i.e. loving God
5537 chrēmatizō (1), *to
utter an oracle*

GOD'S

410 'êl (2), *mighty; the
Almighty*
430 'ĕlôhîym (7), *the true
God; gods; great ones*
433 'ĕlôwahh (1), *the
true God; god*
2316 thĕŏs (15), *deity;
the Supreme Deity*

GOD-WARD

4136+430 mûwl (1), *in
front of, opposite*
4314+2316 prŏs (2), *for;
on, at; to, toward*

GODDESS

430 'ĕlôhîym (2), *god;
gods; great ones*
2299 thĕa (3), *female
deity, goddess*

GODHEAD

2304 thĕiŏs (1), *divinity*
2305 thĕiŏtēs (1), *divinity*
2320 thĕŏtēs (1), *divinity*

GODLINESS

2150 ĕusĕbĕia (14), *piety,
religious*
2317 thĕŏsĕbĕia (1),
piety, worship of deity

GODLY

430 'ĕlôhîym (1), *the true
God; gods; great ones*
2623 châçîyd (3),
religiously pious, godly
516+2316 axiōs (1),
appropriately, suitable
2152 ĕusĕbēs (1), *pious*
2153 ĕusĕbōs (2), *piously*
2316 thĕŏs (3), *deity; the
Supreme Deity*
2596+2316 kata (3),
down; according to

GODS

410 'êl (2), *mighty; the
Almighty*
426 'ĕlâhh (Ch.) (14), *God*

430 'ĕlôhîym (214), *God;
gods; judges, great ones*
1140 daimŏniŏn (1),
demonic being; god
2316 thĕŏs (8), *deity; the
Supreme Deity*

GOEST

935 bôw' (13), *to go or
come*
1980 hâlak (5), *to walk;
live a certain way*
3212 yâlak (13), *to walk;
to live; to carry*
3318 yâtsâ' (7), *to go,
bring out*
5927 'âlâh (1), *to ascend,
be high, mount*
565 apĕrchŏmai (1), *to
go off, i.e. depart*
5217 hupagō (5), *to
withdraw or retire*

GOETH

732 'ârach (1), *to travel,
wander*
925 bâhîyr (1), *shining,
bright*
935 bôw' (14), *to go or
come*
1869 dârak (1), *to tread,
trample; to walk, lead*
1980 hâlak (19), *to walk;
live a certain way*
3212 yâlak (2), *to walk;
to live; to carry*
3318 yâtsâ' (31), *to go,
bring out*
3381 yârad (5), *to
descend*
3518 kâbâh (2), *to
extinguish*
3996 mâbôw' (1),
entrance; sunset; west
4609 ma'ălâh (1),
thought arising
5186 nâṭâh (1), *to stretch
or spread out*
5493 çûwr (1), *to turn off*
5648 'ăbad (Ch.) (1), *to
do, work, serve*
5674 'âbar (3), *to cross
over; to transition*
5927 'âlâh (10), *to
ascend, be high, mount*
6437 pânâh (1), *to turn,
to face*
7126 qârab (1), *to
approach, bring near*
7847 sâṭâh (1), *to deviate
from duty, go astray*
305 anabainō (1), *to go
up, rise*
565 apĕrchŏmai (1), *to
go off, i.e. depart*
1525 ĕisĕrchŏmai (1), *to
enter*
1607 ĕkpŏrĕuŏmai (3), *to
depart, be discharged*
2212 zētĕō (1), *to seek*
3597 hŏdŏipŏria (1),
traveling
4198 pŏrĕuŏmai (7), *to
go/come; to travel*
4254 prŏagō (2), *to lead
forward; to precede*
4334 prŏsĕrchŏmai (1),
to come near, visit
5217 hupagō (9), *to
withdraw or retire*

5562 chŏrĕŏ (1), to *pass, enter*; to *hold, admit*

GOG
1463 Gôwg (10), *Gog*
1136 Gôg (1), *Gog*

GOING
235 'âzal (1), to *disappear*
838 'âshshûwr (1), *step; track*
935 bôw' (7), to *go or come*
1980 hâlak (8), to *walk; live a certain way*
3212 yâlak (5), to *walk; to live; to carry*
3318 yâtsâ' (13), to *go, bring out*
3381 yârad (3), to *descend*
3996 mâbôw' (5), *entrance; sunset; west*
4161 môwtsâ' (5), *going forth*
4174 môwrâd (3), *descent, slope*
4606 mê'al (Ch.) (1), *setting of the sun*
4608 ma'ăleh (9), *elevation; platform*
5362 nâqaph (1), to *strike; to surround*
5674 'âbar (2), to *cross over; to transition*
5927 'âlâh (4), to *ascend, be high, mount*
5944 'ălîyâh (2), *upper things; second-story*
6807 tse'âdâh (2), *stepping march*
7751 shûwṭ (2), to *travel, roam*
8444 tôwtsâ'âh (1), *exit, boundary; deliverance*
8582 tâ'âh (1), to *vacillate, reel or stray*
71 agō (1), to *lead*; to *bring, drive*; to *weigh*
305 anabainō (2), to *go up, rise*
565 apérchŏmai (1), to *go off, i.e. depart*
1330 diérchŏmai (1), to *traverse, travel through*
1607 ĕkpŏrĕuŏmai (1), to *depart, be discharged*
2212 zētĕŏ (1), to *seek*
2597 katabainō (1), to *descend*
4105 planaō (1), to *roam, wander; to deceive*
4108 planŏs (1), *roving; impostor or misleader*
4198 pŏrĕuŏmai (1), to *go/come; to travel*
4254 prŏagō (2), to *lead forward; to precede*
4260 prŏbainō (1), to *advance*
4281 prŏérchŏmai (1), to *go onward, precede*
5217 hupagō (1), to *withdraw or retire*

GOINGS
838 'âshshûwr (2), *step; track*
1979 hălîykâh (2), *walking; procession*

4161 môwtsâ' (4), *going forth*
4163 môwtsâ'âh (1), *family descent*
4570 ma'gâl (2), *circular track or camp rampart*
4703 mits'âd (1), *step; companionship*
6471 pa'am (1), *time; step; occurence*
6806 tsa'ad (1), *pace or regular step*
8444 tôwtsâ'âh (12), *exit, boundary; deliverance*

GOLAN
1474 Gôwlân (4), *captive*

GOLD
1220 betser (2), *gold*
1222 bᵉtsar (1), *gold*
1722 dᵉhab (Ch.) (14), *gold*
2091 zâhâb (340), *gold, golden colored*
2742 chârûwts (6), *mined gold; trench*
3800 kethem (7), *pure gold*
5458 çᵉgôwr (1), *breast; gold*
6337 pâz (9), *pure gold*
5552 chrusĕŏs (3), *made of gold*
5553 chrusiŏn (9), *golden thing*
5554 chrusŏdaktuliŏs (1), *gold-ringed*
5557 chrusŏs (13), *gold; golden article*

GOLDEN
1722 dᵉhab (Ch.) (9), *gold*
2091 zâhâb (38), *gold, golden colored*
3800 kethem (1), *pure gold*
4062 madhêbâh (1), *gold making*
5552 chrusĕŏs (15), *made of gold*

GOLDSMITH
6884 tsâraph (3), to *fuse metal; to refine*

GOLDSMITH'S
6885 Tsôrᵉphîy (1), *refiner*

GOLDSMITHS
6884 tsâraph (2), to *fuse metal; to refine*

GOLGOTHA
1115 Golgŏtha (3), *skull knoll*

GOLIATH
1555 Golyath (6), *exile*

GOMER
1586 Gômer (6), *completion*

GOMORRAH
6017 'Ămôrâh (19), *(ruined) heap*
1116 Gŏmŏrrha (1), *ruined heap*

GOMORRHA
1116 Gŏmŏrrha (4), *ruined heap*

GONE
230 'ăzad (Ch.) (2), *firm, assured*

235 'âzal (2), to *disappear*
369 'ayin (4), *there is no, i.e., not exist, none*
656 'âphêç (1), to *cease*
935 bôw' (10), to *go or come*
1540 gâlâh (1), to *denude; uncover*
1961 hâyâh (1), to *exist, i.e. be or become*
1980 hâlak (22), to *walk; live a certain way*
2114 zûwr (1), to *be foreign, strange*
3212 yâlak (17), to *walk; to live; to carry*
3318 yâtsâ' (31), to *go, bring out*
3381 yârad (14), to *descend*
4059 middad (1), *flight*
4161 môwtsâ' (2), *going forth*
4185 mûwsh (1), to *withdraw*
5128 nûwa' (1), to *waver*
5186 nâṭâh (1), to *stretch or spread out*
5312 nᵉphaq (Ch.) (1), to *issue forth; to bring out*
5362 nâqaph (2), to *surround or circulate*
5437 çâbab (1), to *surround*
5472 çûwg (1), to *go back, to retreat*
5493 çûwr (2), to *turn off*
5674 'âbar (16), to *cross over; to transition*
5927 'âlâh (22), to *ascend, be high, mount*
6805 tsâ'ad (1), to *pace, step regularly*
7725 shûwb (2), to *turn back; to return*
7751 shûwṭ (1), to *travel, roam*
7847 sâṭâh (2), to *deviate from duty, go astray*
8582 tâ'âh (2), to *vacillate, reel or stray*
305 anabainō (2), to *go up, rise*
402 anachōrĕŏ (1), to *retire, withdraw*
565 apérchŏmai (4), to *go off, i.e. depart*
576 apŏbainō (1), to *disembark*
1276 diapĕraō (1), to *cross over*
1330 diérchŏmai (4), to *traverse, travel through*
1339 diïstēmi (1), to *remove, intervene*
1525 éisérchŏmai (1), to *enter*
1578 ĕkklinō (1), to *shun; to decline*
1607 ĕkpŏrĕuŏmai (1), to *depart, proceed, project*
1826 ĕxĕimi (1), *leave; escape*
1831 ĕxérchŏmai (11), to *issue; to leave*
3985 pĕirazō (1), to *endeavor, scrutinize*
4105 planaō (2), to *roam, wander*

4198 pŏrĕuŏmai (3), to *go, come; to travel*
4260 prŏbainō (1), to *advance*
4570 sbĕnnumi (1), to *extinguish, snuff out*
5055 tĕlĕŏ (1), to *end, i.e. complete, execute*

GOOD
1319 bâsar (7), to *announce* (good news)
1390 Gib'âh (1), *hillock*
1580 gâmal (1), to *benefit or requite; to wean*
2492 châlam (1), to *be, make plump; to dream*
2617 cheçed (1), *kindness, favor*
2623 châçîyd (1), *religiously pious, godly*
2869 ṭâb (Ch.) (1), *good*
2895 ṭowb (6), to *be good*
2896 ṭôwb (363), *good; well*
2898 ṭûwb (11), *good; goodness; beauty; gladness, welfare*
3190 yâṭab (20), to *be, make well*
3191 yᵉṭab (Ch.) (1), to *be, make well*
3276 yâ'al (1), to *be valuable*
3474 yâshar (1), to *be straight; to make right*
3788 kishrôwn (1), *success; advantage*
3966 mᵉ'ôd (3), *very, utterly*
5750 'ôwd (1), *again; repeatedly; still; more*
6743 tsâlach (1), to *push forward*
7368 râchaq (2), to *recede; remove*
7522 râtsôwn (2), *delight*
7965 shâlôwm (1), *safe; well; health, prosperity*
7999 shâlam (6), to *be safe; be, make complete*
8232 shᵉphar (Ch.) (1), to *be beautiful*
14 agathŏĕrgĕŏ (1), to *do good work*
15 agathŏpŏiĕŏ (6), to *be a well-doer*
18 agathŏs (98), *good*
515 axiŏō (1), to *deem entitled or fit, worthy*
865 aphilagathŏs (1), *hostile to virtue*
979 biŏs (1), *livelihood; property*
2095 ĕu (1), *well*
2097 ĕuaggĕlizō (2), to *announce good news*
2106 ĕudŏkĕŏ (1), to *think well, i.e. approve*
2107 ĕudŏkia (3), *delight, kindness, wish*
2108 ĕuĕrgĕsia (1), *beneficence*
2109 ĕuĕrgĕtĕŏ (1), to *be philanthropic*
2133 ĕunŏia (1), *eagerly, with a whole heart*
2140 ĕupŏiïa (1), *beneficence, doing good*

English

2162 ĕuphēmia (1), *good repute*
2163 ĕuphēmŏs (1), *reputable*
2425 hikanŏs (1), *ample; fit*
2480 ischuō (1), to *have* or *exercise force*
2565 kalliĕlaiŏs (1), *cultivated olive*
2567 kalŏdidaskalŏs (1), *teacher of* the *right*
2570 kalŏs (78), *good; beautiful; valuable*
2573 kalŏs (3), *well*, i.e. *rightly*
2750 kĕiria (2), *swathe of cloth*
3112 makran (1), *at a distance, far away*
4851 sumphĕrō (1), to *collect; to conduce*
5358 philagathŏs (1), *promoter of virtue*
5542 chrēstŏlŏgia (1), *fair speech, plausibility*
5543 chrēstŏs (1), *employed*, i.e. *useful*
5544 chrēstŏtēs (1), moral *excellence*

GOODLIER
2896 ţôwb (1), *good; well*

GOODLIEST
2896 ţôwb (2), *good; well*

GOODLINESS
2617 cheçed (1), *kindness, favor*

GOODLY
117 'addîyr (1), *powerful; majestic*
145 'eder (1), *mantle; splendor*
155 'addereth (1), *large; splendid*
410 'êl (1), *mighty;* the *Almighty*
1926 hâdâr (1), *magnificence*
1935 hôwd (1), *grandeur, majesty*
2530 châmad (1), to *delight* in; *lust for*
2532 chemdâh (1), *delight*
2896 ţôwb (11), *good; well*
4261 machmâd (1), *delightful*
4758 mar'eh (1), *appearance; vision*
6287 pᵉ'êr (1), *fancy head-dress*
6643 tsᵉbîy (1), *conspicuous splendor*
7443 renen (1), *female ostrich*
8231 shâphar (1), to *be, make fair*
8233 shepher (1), *beauty*
2573 kalŏs (2), *well*, i.e. *rightly*
2986 lamprŏs (2), *radiant; magnificent*

GOODMAN
376 'îysh (1), *man; male; someone*
3611 ŏikĕŏ (5), to *reside, inhabit, remain*

GOODNESS
2617 cheçed (12), *kindness, favor*
2896 ţôwb (16), *good; well*
2898 ţûwb (13), *good; goodness; beauty*
19 agathōsunē (4), *virtue* or *beneficence*
5543 chrēstŏs (1), *employed*, i.e. *useful*
5544 chrēstŏtēs (4), moral *excellence*

GOODNESS'
2898 ţûwb (1), *good; goodness; beauty*

GOODS
202 'ôwn (1), *ability, power; wealth*
2428 chayil (2), *army; wealth; virtue; valor*
2896 ţôwb (2), *good; well*
2898 ţûwb (3), *good; goodness; beauty*
4399 mᵉlâ'kâh (2), *work; property*
5232 nᵉkaç (Ch.) (2), *treasure, riches*
7075 qinyân (2), *purchase, wealth*
7399 rᵉkûwsh (12), *property*
18 agathŏs (2), *good*
3776 ŏusia (1), *wealth, property, possessions*
4147 plŏutĕō (1), to *be, become wealthy*
4632 skĕuŏs (2), *vessel, implement, equipment*
4674 sŏs (1), *things that* are *yours*
5223 huparxis (1), *property, wealth*
5224 huparchŏnta (7), *property* or *possessions*

GOPHER
1613 gôpher (1), (poss.) *cypress*

GORE
5055 nâgach (1), to *butt* with bull's *horns*

GORED
5055 nâgach (2), to *butt* with bull's *horns*

GORGEOUS
2986 lamprŏs (1), *radiant; magnificent*

GORGEOUSLY
4358 miklôwl (1), *perfection; splendidly*
1741 ĕndŏxŏs (1), *splendid; noble*

GOSHEN
1657 Gôshen (15), *Goshen*

GOSPEL
2097 ĕuaggĕlizō (24), to *announce good news*
2098 ĕuaggĕliŏn (73), *good message*
4283 prŏĕuaggĕlizŏmai (1), to *announce* glad news *in advance*

GOSPEL'S
2098 ĕuaggĕliŏn (3), *good message*

GOT
3318 yâtsâ' (2), to *go, bring out*
3423 yârash (1), to *inherit; to impoverish*
7069 qânâh (3), to *create; to procure*
7408 râkash (1), to *lay up*, i.e. *collect*

GOTTEN
622 'âçaph (1), to *gather, collect*
3254 yâçaph (1), to *add* or *augment*
4069 maddûwa' (1), *why?, what?*
4672 mâtsâ' (2), to *find* or *acquire; to occur*
5414 nâthan (1), to *give*
6213 'âsâh (8), to *do* or *make*
7069 qânâh (1), to *create; to procure*
7408 râkash (3), to *lay up*, i.e. *collect*
645 apŏspaō (1), *unsheathe; withdraw*

GOURD
7021 qîyqâyôwn (5), *gourd plant*

GOURDS
6498 paqqû'âh (1), *wild cucumber*

GOVERN
2280 châbash (1), to *wrap firmly, bind*
5148 nâchâh (1), to *guide*
6213 'âsâh (1), to *do*

GOVERNMENT
4475 memshâlâh (1), *rule; realm* or a *ruler*
4951 misrâh (2), *empire*
2963 kuriŏtēs (1), *rulers, masters*

GOVERNMENTS
2941 kubĕrnēsis (1), *directorship*

GOVERNOR
441 'allûwph (1), *friend, one familiar; chieftain*
4910 mâshal (3), to *rule*
5057 nâgîyd (3), *commander, official*
5387 nâsîy' (1), *leader; rising mist, fog*
5921 'al (1), *above, over, upon*, or *against*
6346 pechâh (10), *prefect, officer*
6347 pechâh (Ch.) (6), *prefect, officer*
6485 pâqad (5), to *visit, care for, count*
7989 shalliyţ (1), *prince* or *warrior*
8269 sar (4), *head person, ruler*
755 architriklinŏs (2), *director of* the *entertainment*
1481 ĕthnarchēs (1), *governor of a district*
2116 ĕuthunō (1), to *straighten* or *level*
2230 hēgĕmŏnĕuō (3), to *act as ruler*

GOVERNOR'S
2232 hēgĕmŏn (15), *chief person*
2233 hēgĕŏmai (2), to *lead*, i.e. *command*

GOVERNOR'S
2232 hēgĕmŏn (1), *chief person*

GOVERNORS
441 'allûwph (2), *friend, one familiar; chieftain*
2710 châqaq (2), to *engrave; to enact laws*
4910 mâshal (1), to *rule*
5461 çâgân (5), *prfect of a province*
6346 pechâh (7), *prefect, officer*
8269 sar (2), *head person, ruler*
2232 hēgĕmŏn (2), *chief person*
3623 ŏikŏnŏmŏs (1), *overseer, manager*

GOZAN
1470 Gôwzân (5), *quarry*

GRACE
2580 chên (37), *graciousness; beauty*
8467 tᵉchinnâh (1), *gracious entreaty, supplication*
2143 ĕuprĕpĕia (1), *gracefulness*
5485 charis (127), *gratitude; benefit given*

GRACIOUS
2580 chên (2), *graciousness; beauty*
2587 channûwn (14), *gracious*
2589 channôwth (1), *supplication*
2603 chânan (11), to *implore*
5485 charis (1), *gratitude; benefit given*
5543 chrēstŏs (1), *employed*, i.e. *useful*

GRACIOUSLY
2603 chânan (3), to *implore*
2896 ţôwb (1), *good; well*

GRAFF
1461 ĕgkĕntrizō (1), to *engraft*

GRAFFED
1461 ĕgkĕntrizō (5), to *engraft*

GRAIN
6872 tsᵉrôwr (1), *parcel; kernel* or *particle*
2848 kŏkkŏs (6), *kernel*

GRANDMOTHER
3125 mammē (1), *grandmother*

GRANT
5414 nâthan (12), to *give*
7558 rîshyôwn (1), *permit*
1325 didōmi (7), to *give*
2036 ĕpō (1), to *speak* or *say*

GRANTED
935 bôw' (1), to *go* or *come*
5414 nâthan (9), to *give*

6213 'âsâh (1), to *do* or *make*
1325 didōmi (3), to *give*
5483 charizŏmai (1), to grant as a *favor*

GRAPE
1154 beçer (1), *immature, sour* grapes
1155 bôçer (3), *immature, sour* grapes
5563 çᵉmâdar (2), vine *blossom*
6025 'ênâb (1), *grape* cluster
6528 pereṭ (1), *stray* or *single* berry

GRAPEGATHERER
1219 bâtsar (1), to *gather* grapes

GRAPEGATHERERS
1219 bâtsar (2), to *gather* grapes

GRAPEGLEANINGS
5955 'ôlêlâh (1), *gleaning; gleaning-time*

GRAPES
891 bᵉ'ûshîym (2), *rotten fruit*
1154 beçer (1), *immature, sour* grapes
5563 çᵉmâdar (1), vine *blossom*
6025 'ênâb (15), *grape* cluster
4718 staphulē (3), *cluster* of grapes

GRASS
1758 dûwsh (1), to *trample* or *thresh*
1877 deshe' (7), *sprout; green grass*
1883 dethe' (Ch.) (2), *sprout; green grass*
2682 châtsîyr (17), *grass; leek* plant
3418 yereq (1), *green* grass or *vegetation*
6211 'âsh (5), *moth*
6212 'eseb (16), *grass,* or any green, tender shoot
5528 chŏrtŏs (12), *pasture, herbage*

GRASSHOPPER
697 'arbeh (1), *locust*
2284 châgâb (2), *locust*

GRASSHOPPERS
697 'arbeh (3), *locust*
1462 gôwb (2), *locust*
2284 châgâb (2), *locust*

GRATE
4345 makbêr (6), *grate, lattice*

GRAVE
1164 bᵉ'îy (1), *prayer*
6603 pittûwach (1), *sculpture; engraving*
6605 pâthach (3), to *open* wide; to *loosen, begin*
6900 qᵉbûwrâh (4), *sepulchre*
6913 qeber (19), *sepulchre*
7585 shᵉ'ôwl (30), abode of the *dead*
7845 shachath (1), *pit; destruction*

86 haⱼdēs (1), *Hades,* i.e. place of the dead
3419 mnēmĕiŏn (4), *place of interment*
4586 sĕmnŏs (3), *honorable, noble*

GRAVE'S
7585 shᵉ'ôwl (1), abode of the *dead*

GRAVECLOTHES
2750 kĕiria (1), *swathe of cloth*

GRAVED
6605 pâthach (2), to *loosen, plow, carve*

GRAVEL
2687 châtsâts (2), *gravel, grit*
4579 mê'âh (1), *belly*

GRAVEN
2672 châtsab (1), to *cut* stone or *carve* wood
2710 châqaq (1), to *engrave;* to *enact* laws
2790 chârash (1), to *engrave;* to *plow*
2801 chârath (1), to *engrave*
6456 pᵉçîyl (18), *idol*
6458 pâçal (1), to *carve,* to *chisel*
6459 peçel (29), *idol*
6605 pâthach (2), to *loosen, plow, carve*
5480 charagma (1), *mark, sculptured figure*

GRAVES
6913 qeber (16), *sepulchre*
3418 mnēma (1), *sepulchral monument*
3419 mnēmĕiŏn (4), *place of interment*

GRAVETH
2710 châqaq (1), to *engrave;* to *enact* laws

GRAVING
2747 chereṭ (1), *chisel; style* for writing
6603 pittûwach (2), *sculpture; engraving*

GRAVINGS
4734 miqla'ath (1), *bas-relief sculpture*

GRAVITY
4587 sĕmnŏtēs (2), *venerableness*

GRAY
7872 sêybâh (5), old *age*

GRAYHEADED
7867 sîyb (2), to *become aged,* i.e. to *grow gray*

GREASE
2459 cheleb (1), *fat; choice* part

GREAT
410 'êl (1), *mighty;* the Almighty
417 'elgâbîysh (3), *hail*
430 'ĕlôhîym (2), the true God; gods; great ones
679 'atstsîyl (1), *joint* of the hand

1004 bayith (1), *house; temple; family, tribe*
1167 ba'al (1), *master; husband; owner; citizen*
1241 bâqâr (1), *plowing* ox; *herd*
1396 gâbar (2), to *be strong;* to *prevail;* to *act insolently*
1419 gâdôwl (413), *great*
1420 gᵉdûwlâh (3), *greatness, grandeur*
1431 gâdal (33), to *be great, make great*
1432 gâdêl (2), *large, powerful*
1462 gôwb (1), *locust*
1560 gᵉlâl (Ch.) (2), *large* stones
2030 hâreh (1), *pregnant*
2342 chûwl (1), to *dance, whirl;* to *writhe* in pain
2750 chŏrîy (2), *burning anger*
3244 yanshûwph (2), *bird*
3514 kôbed (1), *weight, multitude, vehemence*
3515 kâbêd (8), *numerous; severe*
3699 kâçaç (1), to *estimate, determine*
3833 lâbîy' (3), *lion, lioness*
3966 mᵉ'ôd (11), *very, utterly*
4306 mâṭâr (1), *rain, shower of rain*
4459 maltâ'âh (1), *grinder, molar tooth*
4766 marbeh (1), *increasing; greatness*
5006 nâ'ats (1), to *scorn*
6099 'âtsûwm (1), *powerful; numerous*
6105 'âtsam (1), to *be, make powerful*
6343 pachad (1), *sudden alarm, fear*
7091 qippôwz (1), *arrow-snake*
7227 rab (125), *great*
7229 rab (Ch.) (7), *great*
7230 rôb (7), *abundance*
7235 râbâh (9), to *increase*
7236 rᵉbâh (Ch.) (1), to *increase*
7239 ribbôw (1), *myriad, indefinite large number*
7260 rabrab (Ch.) (8), *huge; domineering*
7350 râchôwq (2), *remote, far*
7451 ra' (1), *bad; evil*
7689 saggîy' (1), *mighty*
7690 saggîy' (Ch.) (3), *large*
7991 shâlîysh (2), *officer;* of the *third* rank
8514 tal'ûwbâh (1), *desiccation*
1974 ĕpipŏthia (1), *intense longing*
2245 hēlikŏs (2), *how much, how great*
2425 hikanŏs (2), *ample; fit*
3029 lian (1), very *much*

3112 makran (1), *at a distance, far away*
3123 mallŏn (1), *in a greater degree*
3166 mĕgalauchĕŏ (1), to *be arrogant, egotistic*
3167 mĕgalĕiŏs (1), *great things, wonderful works*
3170 mĕgalunō (1), to *increase or extol*
3171 mĕgalōs (1), *much, greatly*
3173 mĕgas (149), *great, many*
3175 mĕgistanĕs (2), *great person*
3176 mĕgistŏs (1), *greatest or very great*
3745 hŏsŏs (6), *as much as*
3819 palai (1), *formerly; sometime since*
3827 pampŏlus (1), *full many,* i.e. *immense*
4080 pēlikŏs (1), *how much, how great*
4118 plĕistŏs (1), *largest number or very large*
4183 pŏlus (60), *much, many*
4185 pŏlutĕlēs (2), *extremely expensive*
4186 pŏlutimŏs (1), *extremely valuable*
4214 pŏsŏs (1), *how much?; how much!*
5082 tēlikŏutŏs (3), *so vast*
5118 tŏsŏutŏs (5), *such great*
5246 hupĕrŏgkŏs (2), *insolent, boastful*

GREATER
1419 gâdôwl (20), *great*
1431 gâdal (3), to *be great, make great*
1980 hâlak (1), to *walk; live a certain way*
7227 rab (4), *great*
7235 râbâh (2), to *increase*
3186 mĕizŏtĕrŏs (1), *still larger, greater*
3187 mĕizŏn (34), *larger, greater*
4055 pĕrissŏtĕrŏs (3), *more superabundant*
4119 plĕiŏn (6), *more*

GREATEST
1419 gâdôwl (9), *great*
4768 marbîyth (1), *multitude; offspring*
3173 mĕgas (2), *great, many*
3187 mĕizŏn (9), *larger, greater*

GREATLY
3966 mᵉ'ôd (49), *very, utterly*
7227 rab (3), *great*
7230 rôb (1), *abundance*
7690 saggîy' (Ch.) (1), *large*
1568 ĕkthambĕō (1), to *astonish* utterly
1569 ĕkthambŏs (1), *utterly astounded*

1971 ĕpipŏthĕō (3), *intensely crave*

3029 lian (4), *very much*

3171 mĕgalōs (1), *much, greatly*

4183 pŏlus (4), *much, many*

4970 sphŏdra (2), *high degree, much*

5479 chara (1), *calm delight, joy*

GREATNESS

1419 gâdôwl (1), *great*

1420 geᵈûwlâh (7), *greatness, grandeur*

1433 gôdel (11), *magnitude, majesty*

4768 marbîyth (1), *multitude; offspring*

7230 rôb (9), *abundance*

7238 rᵉbûw (Ch.) (2), *increase*

3174 mĕgĕthŏs (1), *greatness*

GREAVES

4697 mitschâh (1), *shin-piece* of armor

GRECIA

3120 Yâvân (3), *effervescent*

GRECIANS

3125 Yᵉvânîy (1), *Jevanite*

1675 Hĕllēnistēs (3), *Hellenist or Greek-speaking Jew*

GREECE

3120 Yâvân (1), *effervescent*

1671 Hĕllas (1), *Hellas*

GREEDILY

8378 ta'ăvâh (1), *longing; delight*

1632 ĕkchĕō (1), *to pour forth; to bestow*

GREEDINESS

4124 plĕŏnĕxia (1), *extortion, avarice*

GREEDY

1214 bâtsa' (2), *to plunder; to finish*

3700 kâçaph (1), *to pine after; to fear*

5794+5315 'az (1), *strong, vehement, harsh*

146 aischrŏkĕrdēs (1), *sordid, greedy*

866 aphilargurŏs (1), *unavaricious*

GREEK

1672 Hĕllēn (7), *Greek (-speaking)*

1673 Hĕllēnikŏs (2), *Grecian* language

1674 Hĕllēnis (1), *Grecian* woman

1676 Hĕllēnisti (1), *Hellenistically*, i.e. *in the Grecian language*

GREEKS

1672 Hĕllēn (13), *Greek (-speaking)*

1674 Hĕllēnis (1), *Grecian* woman

GREEN

1877 deshe' (1), *sprout; green grass*

3387 yârôwq (1), *green plant*

3410 yarkâ' (Ch.) (1), *thigh*

3418 yereq (5), *green grass or vegetation*

3419 yârâq (1), *vegetable greens*

3768 karpaç (1), *byssus linen*

3892 lach (5), *fresh cut*

6291 pag (1), *unripe fig*

7373 râṭôb (1), *moist with sap*

7488 ra'ănân (18), *verdant; new*

5200 hugrŏs (1), *fresh and moist*

5515 chlōrŏs (3), *greenish*, i.e. *verdant*

GREENISH

3422 yᵉraqraq (2), *yellowishness*

GREENNESS

3 'êb (1), *green plant*

GREET

7592+7965 shâ'al (1), *to ask*

782 aspazŏmai (14), *to salute, welcome*

GREETETH

782 aspazŏmai (1), *to salute, welcome*

GREETING

5463 chairō (3), *salutation, "be well"*

GREETINGS

783 aspasmŏs (3), *greeting*

GREW

1431 gâdal (9), *to be great, make great*

1432 gâdêl (2), *large, powerful*

6509 pârâh (1), *to bear fruit*

6555 pârats (1), *to break out*

6779 tsâmach (2), *to sprout*

6780 tsemach (2), *sprout, branch*

7236 rᵉbâh (Ch.) (2), *to increase*

305 anabainō (1), *to go up, rise*

837 auxanō (6), *to grow*, i.e. *enlarge*

2064 ĕrchŏmai (1), *to go or come*

GREY

7872 sêybâh (1), *old age*

GREYHEADED

7872 sêybâh (1), *old age*

GREYHOUND

2223+4975 zarzîyr (1), *fleet animal (slender)*

GRIEF

2470 châlâh (2), *to be weak, sick, afflicted*

2483 chŏlîy (3), *malady; anxiety; calamity*

3013 yâgâh (1), *to grieve; to torment*

3015 yâgôwn (2), *affliction, sorrow*

3511 kᵉ'êb (2), *suffering; adversity*

3708 ka'aç (7), *vexation, grief*

4341 mak'ôb (2), *anguish; affliction*

4786 môrâh (1), *bitterness; trouble*

6330 pûwqâh (1), *stumbling-block*

7451 ra' (1), *bad; evil*

3076 lupĕō (1), *to distress; to be sad*

3077 lupē (1), *sadness, grief*

4727 stĕnazō (1), *to sigh, murmur, pray* inaudibly

GRIEFS

2483 chŏlîy (1), *malady; anxiety; calamity*

GRIEVANCE

5999 'âmâl (1), *wearing effort; worry*

GRIEVE

109 'âdab (1), *to languish, grieve*

3013 yâgâh (1), *to grieve; to torment*

6087 'âtsab (2), *to worry, have pain or anger*

3076 lupĕō (1), *to distress; to be sad*

GRIEVED

2342 chûwl (2), *to dance, whirl; to writhe* in pain

2470 châlâh (2), *to be weak, sick, afflicted*

2556 châmêts (1), *to be fermented; be soured*

2734 chârâh (1), *to blaze up*

3512 kâ'âh (1), *to despond; to deject*

3707 kâ'aç (1), *to grieve, rage, be indignant*

3735 kârâ' (Ch.) (1), *to grieve, be anxious*

3811 lâ'âh (1), *to tire; to be, make disgusted*

4784 mârâh (1), *to rebel or resist; to provoke*

4843 mârar (1), *to be, make bitter*

5701 'âgam (1), *to be sad*

6087 'âtsab (8), *to worry, have pain or anger*

6962 qûwṭ (3), *to detest*

6973 qûwts (1), *to be, make disgusted*

7114 qâtsar (1), *to curtail, cut short*

7489 râ'a' (2), *to break; to be good for nothing*

1278 diapŏnĕō (2), *to be worried*

3076 lupĕō (5), *to distress; to be sad*

4360 prŏsŏchthizō (2), *to be vexed* with

4818 sullupĕō (1), *to afflict jointly, sorrow at*

3013 yâgâh (1), *to grieve; to torment*

3015 yâgôwn (2), *affliction, sorrow*

3511 kᵉ'êb (2), *suffering; adversity*

GRIEVETH

3811 lâ'âh (1), *to tire; to be, make disgusted*

4843 mârar (1), *to be, make bitter*

GRIEVING

3510 kâ'ab (1), *to feel pain; to grieve; to spoil*

GRIEVOUS

2342 chûwl (2), *to dance, whirl; to writhe* in pain

2470 châlâh (4), *to be weak, sick, afflicted*

3415 yâra' (1), *to fear*

3513 kâbad (1), *to be heavy, severe, dull*

3515 kâbêd (8), *severe, difficult, stupid*

4834 mârats (1), *to be vehement; to irritate*

5493 çûwr (1), *to turn off*

6089 'etseb (1), *earthen vessel; painful toil*

6277 'âthâq (1), *impudent*

7185 qâshâh (2), *to be tough or severe*

7186 qâsheh (3), *severe*

7451 ra' (2), *bad; evil*

7489 râ'a' (2), *to break; to be good for nothing*

8463 tachălûw' (1), *malady, disease*

926 barus (3), *weighty*

1418 dus- (2), *hard*, i.e. *with difficulty*

3077 lupē (1), *sadness, grief*

3636 ŏknērŏs (1), *irksome; lazy*

4190 pŏnērŏs (1), *malice, wicked, bad; crime*

GRIEVOUSLY

2342 chûwl (1), *to dance, whirl; to writhe* in pain

2399 chêṭ' (1), *crime or its penalty*

3513 kâbad (1), *to be heavy, severe, dull*

4604 ma'al (1), *sinful treachery*

4784 mârâh (1), *to rebel or resist; to provoke*

1171 dĕinōs (1), *terribly*, i.e. *excessively, fiercely*

2560 kakōs (1), *badly; wrongly; ill*

GRIEVOUSNESS

3514 kôbed (1), *weight, multitude, vehemence*

5999 'âmâl (1), *wearing effort; worry*

GRIND

2911 ṭᵉchôwn (1), *hand mill; millstone*

2912 ṭâchan (4), *to grind flour meal*

3039 likmaō (2), *to grind to powder*

GRINDERS

2912 ṭâchan (1), *to grind flour meal*

GRINDING

2913 ṭachănâh (1), *chewing, grinding*

229 alēthō (2), *to grind grain*

GRISLED
1261 bârôd (4), *spotted, dappled*

GROAN
584 'ânach (1), to *sigh, moan*
602 'ânaq (1), to *shriek, cry out in groaning*
5008 nâ'aq (2), to *groan*
4727 stĕnazō (3), to *sigh, murmur, pray* inaudibly

GROANED
1690 ĕmbrimaŏmai (1), to *blame, to sigh*

GROANETH
4959 sustĕnazō (1), to *moan jointly*

GROANING
585 'ănâchâh (4), *sighing, moaning*
603 'ănâqâh (1), *shrieking, groaning*
5009 nᵉ'âqâh (2), *groaning*
1690 ĕmbrimaŏmai (1), to *blame, to sigh*
4726 stĕnagmŏs (1), *sigh, groan*

GROANINGS
5009 nᵉ'âqâh (2), *groaning*
4726 stĕnagmŏs (1), *sigh, groan*

GROPE
1659 gâshash (2), to *feel about, grope around*
4959 mâshash (3), to *feel of; to grope*

GROPETH
4959 mâshash (1), to *feel of; to grope*

GROSS
6205 'ărâphel (2), *gloom, darkness*
3975 pachunō (2), to *fatten; to render callous*

GROUND
127 'ădâmâh (44), *soil; land*
776 'erets (97), *earth, land, soil; country*
2513 chelqâh (1), *smoothness; allotment*
2758 chârîysh (1), *plowing (season)*
2912 ṭâchan (3), to *grind flour meal*
6083 'âphâr (1), *dust, earth, mud; clay,*
7383 rîyphâh (1), *grits cereal*
7704 sâdeh (4), *field*
68 agrŏs (1), *farm*land, *countryside*
1093 gē (18), *soil, region, whole earth*
1474 ĕdaphizō (1), to *raze, dash to the ground*
1475 ĕdaphŏs (1), *soil, ground*
1477 hĕdraiōma (1), *basis, foundation*
5476 chamai (2), *toward the ground*
5561 chōra (1), space of *territory*

5564 chōriŏn (1), *spot or plot of ground*

GROUNDED
4145 mûwçâdâh (1), *foundation*
2311 thĕmĕliŏō (2), to *erect; to consolidate*

GROVE
815 'êshel (1), *tamarisk tree*
842 'ăshêrâh (16), *happy; Astarte (goddess)*

GROVES
842 'ăshêrâh (24), *happy; Astarte (goddess)*

GROW
1342 gâ'âh (1), to *rise; to grow tall; be majestic*
1431 gâdal (2), to *be great, make great*
1711 dâgâh (1), to *become numerous*
3212 yâlak (1), to *walk; to live; to carry*
3318 yâtsâ' (1), to *go, bring out*
5599 çâphîyach (2), *self-sown* crop; *freshet*
5927 'âlâh (2), to *ascend, be high, mount*
6335 pûwsh (1), to *spread; to act proudly*
6509 pârâh (1), to *bear fruit*
6524 pârach (2), to *break forth; to bloom; flourish*
6779 tsâmach (9), to *sprout*
7235 râbâh (1), to *increase*
7680 sᵉgâ' (Ch.) (1), to *increase*
7685 sâgâh (1), to *enlarge, be prosperous*
7735 sûwg (1), to *hedge in, make grow*
7971 shâlach (1), to *send away*
837 auxanō (5), to *grow, i.e. enlarge*
1096 ginŏmai (2), to *be, become*
3373 mēkunō (1), to *enlarge, grow long*
4886 sundĕsmŏs (1), *ligament; control*

GROWETH
2498 châlaph (2), to *spring up; to change*
2583 chânâh (1), to *encamp*
3332 yâtsaq (1), to *pour out*
5599 çâphîyach (3), *self-sown* crop; *freshet*
5927 'âlâh (1), to *ascend, be high, mount*
6524 pârach (1), to *break forth; to bloom; flourish*
6779 tsâmach (1), to *sprout*
8025 shâlaph (1), to *pull out, up or off*
305 anabainō (1), to *go up, rise*
837 auxanō (1), to *grow, i.e. enlarge*

5232 hupĕrauxanō (1), to *increase above*

GROWN
648 'âphîyl (1), *unripe*
1431 gâdal (9), to *be great, make great*
5927 'âlâh (1), to *ascend, be high, mount*
6335 pûwsh (1), to *spread; to act proudly*
6779 tsâmach (4), to *sprout*
6965 qûwm (2), to *rise*
7236 rᵉbâh (Ch.) (3), to *increase*
837 auxanō (1), to *grow, i.e. enlarge*

GROWTH
3954 leqesh (2), *after crop, second crop*

GRUDGE
3885 lûwn (1), to *be obstinate*
5201 nâṭar (1), to *guard; to cherish anger*
4727 stĕnazō (1), to *sigh, murmur, pray* inaudibly

GRUDGING
1112 gŏggusmŏs (1), *grumbling*

GRUDGINGLY
1537+3077 ĕk (1), *out, out of*

GUARD
2876 ṭabbâch (29), *king's guard, executioner*
2877 ṭabbâch (Ch.) (1), *king's guard, executioner*
4928 mishma'ath (2), *royal court; subject*
4929 mishmâr (3), *guard; deposit; usage; example*
7323 rûwts (14), to *run*
4759 stratŏpĕdarchēs (1), *military commander*

GUARD'S
2876 ṭabbâch (1), *king's guard, executioner*

GUDGODAH
1412 Gudgôdâh (2), *cleft*

GUEST
2647 kataluō (1), to *halt for the night*

GUESTCHAMBER
2646 kataluma (2), *lodging-place*

GUESTS
7121 qârâ' (4), to *call out*
345 anakĕimai (2), to *recline at a meal*

GUIDE
441 'allûwph (4), *friend, one familiar; leader*
833 'âshar (1), to *go forward; guide*
1869 dârak (1), to *tread, trample; to walk, lead*
3289 yâ'ats (1), to *advise*
3557 kûwl (1), to *keep in; to measure*
5090 nâhag (1), to *drive forth; to lead*
5095 nâhal (3), to *flow; to conduct; to protect*

5148 nâchâh (4), to *guide*
7101 qâtsîyn (1), *magistrate, leader*
2720 katĕuthunō (1), to *direct, lead, direct*
3594 hŏdēgĕō (2), to *show the way, guide*
3595 hŏdēgŏs (2), *conductor, guide*
3616 ŏikŏdĕspŏtĕō (1), to *be the head of a family*

GUIDED
5090 nâhag (1), to *drive forth; to lead*
5095 nâhal (2), to *flow; to conduct; to protect*
5148 nâchâh (2), to *guide*

GUIDES
3595 hŏdēgŏs (2), *conductor, guide*

GUILE
4820 mirmâh (2), *fraud*
6195 'ormâh (1), *trickery; discretion*
7423 rᵉmîyâh (1), *remissness; treachery*
1388 dŏlŏs (7), *wile, deceit, trickery*

GUILTINESS
817 'âshâm (1), *guilt; fault; sin-offering*

GUILTLESS
5352 nâqâh (5), to *be, make clean; to be bare*
5355 nâqîy (4), *innocent*
338 anaitiŏs (1), *innocent*

GUILTY
816 'âsham (16), to *be guilty; to be punished*
7563 râshâ' (1), *morally wrong; bad person*
1777 ĕnŏchŏs (4), *liable*
3784 ŏphĕilō (1), to *owe; to be under obligation*
5267 hupŏdikŏs (1), *under sentence*

GULF
5490 chasma (1), *chasm or vacancy*

GUNI
1476 Gûwnîy (4), *protected*

GUNITES
1477 Gûwnîy (1), *Gunite*

GUR
1483 Gûwr (1), *cub*

GUR-BAAL
1485 Gûwr-Ba'al (1), *dwelling of Baal*

GUSH
5140 nâzal (1), to *drip, or shed by trickling*

GUSHED
2100 zûwb (3), to *flow freely, gush*
8210 shâphak (1), to *spill forth; to expend*
1632 ĕkchĕō (1), to *pour forth; to bestow*

GUTTER
6794 tsinnûwr (1), *culvert, water-shaft*

GUTTERS
7298 rahaṭ (2), *ringlet* of *hair*

HA
1889 he'âch (1), *aha!*

HAAHASHTARI
326 'ăchashtârîy (1), *courier*

HABAIAH
2252 Chăbayâh (2), *Jehovah has hidden*

HABAKKUK
2265 Chăbaqqûwq (2), *embrace*

HABAZINIAH
2262 Chăbatstsanyâh (1), *Chabatstsanjah*

HABERGEON
8302 shiryôwn (1), *corslet, coat of mail*
8473 tachărâ' (2), *linen corslet*

HABERGEONS
8302 shiryôwn (2), *corslet, coat of mail*

HABITABLE
8398 têbêl (1), *earth; world; inhabitants*

HABITATION
1628 gêrûwth (1), *(temporary) residence*
2073 zᵉbûwl (3), *residence, dwelling*
2918 ṭîyrâh (1), *fortress; hamlet*
3427 yâshab (3), to *dwell*, to *remain;* to *settle*
4186 môwshâb (4), *seat; site; abode*
4349 mâkôwn (2), *basis; place*
4351 mᵉkûwrâh (1), *origin*
4583 mâ'ôwn (9), *retreat* or asylum *dwelling*
4907 mishkan (Ch.) (1), *residence*
4908 mishkân (3), *residence*
5115 nâvâh (1), to *rest* as at *home*
5116 nâveh (21), *at home; lovely; home*
7931 shákan (1), to *reside*
7932 shᵉkan (Ch.) (1), to *reside*
7933 sheken (1), *residence*
1886 ĕpaulis (1), *dwelling,residence*
2732 katŏikētēriŏn (2), *dwelling-place, home*
2733 katŏikia (1), *residence, dwelling*
3613 ŏikētēriŏn (1), *residence, home*

HABITATIONS
4186 môwshâb (8), *seat; site; abode*
4380 mᵉkêrâh (1), *stabbing-sword*
4583 mâ'ôwn (1), *retreat* or asylum *dwelling*
4585 mᵉ'ôwnâh (1), *abode*
4908 mishkân (2), *residence*

GUTTERS
4999 nâ'âh (5), *home, dwelling; pasture*
5116 nâveh (1), *at home; lovely; home*
4638 skēnōma (1), *dwelling:* the *Temple*

HABOR
2249 Châbôwr (3), *united*

HACHALIAH
2446 Chăkalyâh (2), *darkness* (of) *Jehovah*

HACHILAH
2444 Chakîylâh (3), *dark*

HACHMONI
2453 Chakmôwnîy (1), *skillful*

HACHMONITE
2453 Chakmôwnîy (1), *skillful*

HAD
935 bôw' (1), to *go, come*
1961 hâyâh (104), to *exist,* i.e. *be* or *become*
2370 chăzâ' (Ch.) (1), to *gaze* upon; to *dream*
3426 yêsh (5), there *is*
3884 lûwlê' (1), *if not*
7760 sûwm (1), to *put*
1096 ginŏmai (1), to *be, become*
1510 ĕimi (8), I *exist,* I *am*
1746 ĕnduō (1), to *dress*
2192 ĕchō (106), to *have*
2722 katĕchō (1), to *hold down fast*
2983 lambanō (2), to *take, receive*
3844 para (1), *from; with; besides; on account of*
5607 ōn (1), *being, existence*

HADAD
1908 Hădad (13), *Hadad*
2301 Chădad (1), *fierce*

HADADEZER
1909 Hădad'ezer (9), *Hadad* (is his) *help*

HADADRIMMON
1910 Hădadrimmôwn (1), *Hadad-Rimmon*

HADAR
1924 Hădar (2), *magnificence*

HADAREZER
1928 Hădar'ezer (12), *Hadad is his help*

HADASHAH
2322 Chădâshâh (1), *new*

HADASSAH
1919 Hădaççâh (1), *Esther*

HADATTAH
2675 Châtsôwr Chădattâh (1), *new village*

HADID
2307 Châdîyd (3), *peak*

HADLAI
2311 Chadlay (1), *idle*

HADORAM
1913 Hădôwrâm (4), *Hadoram*

HADRACH
2317 Chadrâk (1), *Syrian deity*

HAFT
5325 nitstsâb (1), *handle* of a *sword* or *dagger*

HAGAB
2285 Châgâb (1), *locust*

HAGABA
2286 Chăgâbâ' (1), *locust*

HAGABAH
2286 Chăgâbâ' (1), *locust*

HAGAR
1904 Hâgâr (12), *Hagar*

HAGARENES
1905 Hagrîy (1), *Hagrite*

HAGARITES
1905 Hagrîy (3), *Hagrite*

HAGERITE
1905 Hagrîy (1), *Hagrite*

HAGGAI
2292 Chaggay (11), *festive*

HAGGERI
1905 Hagrîy (1), *Hagrite*

HAGGI
2291 Chaggîy (2), *festive*

HAGGIAH
2293 Chaggîyâh (1), *festival of Jehovah*

HAGGITES
2291 Chaggîy (1), *festive*

HAGGITH
2294 Chaggiyîth (5), *festive*

HAI
5857 'Ay (2), *ruin*

HAIL
1258 bârad (1), to *rain hail*
1259 bârâd (26), *hail, hailstones*
5463 chairō (6), *salutation, "be well"*
5464 chalaza (4), *frozen ice crystals,* i.e. *hail*

HAILSTONES
68+417 'eben (3), *stone*
68+1259 'eben (2), *stone*

HAIR
1803 dallâh (1), *loose thread; loose hair*
4748 miqsheh (1), *curl* of beautiful *tresses*
4803 mâraṭ (2), to *polish;* to *make bald*
5145 nezer (1), *set apart; royal chaplet*
8177 sᵉ'ar (Ch.) (2), *hair*
8181 sê'âr (23), *tossed hair*
8185 sa'ărâh (5), *hairiness*
2359 thrix (9), *hair; single hair*
2863 kŏmaō (2), to *wear long hair*
2864 kŏmē (1), *long hair*
4117 plĕgma (1), *plait* or *braid* of *hair*
5155 trichinŏs (1), *made* of *hair*

HAIRS
8177 sᵉ'ar (Ch.) (1), *hair*
8181 sê'âr (1), *tossed hair*
8185 sa'ărâh (2), *hairiness*
2359 thrix (5), *hair*

HAIRY
1167+8181 ba'al (1), *master; owner; citizen*
8163 sâ'îyr (2), *shaggy; he-goat; goat idol*
8181 sê'âr (2), *tossed hair*

HAKKATAN
6997 Qâṭân (1), *small*

HAKKOZ
6976 Qôwts (1), *thorns*

HAKUPHA
2709 Chăqûwphâ' (2), to *bend, crooked*

HALAH
2477 Chălach (3), *Chalach*

HALAK
2510 Châlâq (2), *bare*

HALE
2694 katasurō (1), to *arrest judicially*

HALF
1235 beqa' (1), *half shekel*
2673 châtsâh (1), to *cut* or *split* in two; to *halve*
2677 chêtsîy (106), *half* or *middle, midst*
4275 mechĕtsâh (2), *halving, half*
4276 machătsîyth (14), *halving* or the *middle*
8432 tâvek (1), *center, middle*
2253 hēmithanēs (1), *entirely exhausted*
2255 hēmisu (5), *half*
2256 hēmiŏriŏn (1), *half-hour*

HALHUL
2478 Chalchûwl (1), *contorted*

HALI
2482 Chălîy (1), *polished trinket, ornament*

HALING
4951 surō (1), to *trail, drag, sweep*

HALL
833 aulē (1), *palace; house; courtyard*
4232 praitōriŏn (6), *governor's court-room*

HALLOHESH
3873 Lôwchêsh (1), *enchanter*

HALLOW
6942 qâdâsh (15), to *be, make clean*

HALLOWED
4720 miqdâsh (1), *sanctuary of deity*
6942 qâdâsh (10), to *be, make clean*
6944 qôdesh (9), *sacred place or thing*
37 hagiazō (2), to *purify* or *consecrate*

HALOHESH
3873 Lôwchêsh (1),
enchanter

HALT
6452 pâçach (1), to hop,
skip over; to hesitate
6761 tsela' (1), limping
5560 chôlôs (4), limping,
crippled

HALTED
6761 tsela' (2), limping

HALTETH
6761 tsela' (2), limping

HALTING
6761 tsela' (1), limping

HAM
1990 Hâm (1), Ham
2526 Châm (16), hot

HAMAN
2001 Hâmân (50), Haman

HAMAN'S
2001 Hâmân (3), Haman

HAMATH
2574 Chămâth (33),
walled
2579 Chămath Rabbâh
(1), walled of Rabbah

HAMATH-ZOBAH
2578 Chămath Tsôwbâh
(1), walled of Tsobah

HAMATHITE
2577 Chămâthîy (2),
Chamathite

HAMMATH
2575 Chammath (1), hot
springs

HAMMEDATHA
4099 Mᵉdâthâ (5),
Medatha

HAMMELECH
4429 Melek (2), king

HAMMER
1989 halmûwth (1),
hammer or mallet
4717 maqqâbâh (1),
hammer
4718 maqqebeth (1),
hammer
6360 paṭṭîysh (3),
hammer which pounds

HAMMERS
3597 kêylaph (1), club or
sledge-hammer
4717 maqqâbâh (2),
hammer

HAMMOLEKETH
4447 Môleketh (1), queen

HAMMON
2540 Chammôwn (2),
warm spring

HAMMOTH-DOR
2576 Chammôth Dô'r
(1), hot springs of Dor

HAMON-GOG
1996 Hămôwn Gôwg (2),
multitude of Gog

HAMONAH
1997 Hămôwnâh (1),
multitude

HAMOR
2544 Chămôwr (12),
male donkey or ass

HAMOR'S
2544 Chămôwr (1), male
donkey or ass

HAMUEL
2536 Chammûw'êl (1),
anger of God

HAMUL
2538 Châmûwl (3), pitied

HAMULITES
2539 Châmûwlîy (1),
Chamulite

HAMUTAL
2537 Chămûwṭal (3),
father-in-law of dew

HANAMEEL
2601 Chănam'êl (4), God
has favored

HANAN
2605 Chânân (12), favor

HANANEEL
2606 Chănan'êl (4), God
has favored

HANANI
2607 Chănânîy (11),
gracious

HANANIAH
2608 Chănanyâh (29),
Jehovah has favored

HAND
405 'ekeph (1), stroke,
blow
854 'êth (1), with; by; at;
among
2026 hârag (1), to kill,
slaughter
2651 chôphen (1), pair of
fists
2947 ṭephach (1),
palm-breadth
2948 ṭôphach (4),
palm-breadth
3027 yâd (1086), hand;
power
3028 yad (Ch.) (12),
hand; power
3079 Yᵉhôwyâqîym (2),
Jehovah will raise
3221 yâm (Ch.) (1), sea;
basin; west
3225 yâmîyn (87), right;
south
3227 yᵉmîynîy (1), right
3235 yâmar (1), to
exchange
3325 Yitshârîy (1),
Jitsharite
3709 kaph (52), hollow of
hand; paw; sole of foot
4672 mâtsâ' (1), to find
or acquire; to occur
7126 qârab (4), to
approach, bring near
7138 qârôwb (5), near,
close
8040 sᵉmô'wl (14), north;
left hand
8041 sâma'l (1), to use
the left hand or go left
8042 sᵉmâ'liy (2), on the
left side; northern
1448 ĕggizō (9), to
approach
1451 ĕggus (6), near,
close
1764 ĕnistēmi (1), to be
present

HAMOR
2021 ĕpichĕirĕō (1), to
undertake, try
2186 ĕphistēmi (1), to be
present; to approach
5495 chĕir (87), hand
5496 chĕiragōgĕō (2), to
guide a blind person by
the hand
5497 chĕiragōgŏs (1),
conductor of a blind
person by the hand

HANDBREADTH
2947 ṭephach (2),
palm-breadth
2948 ṭôphach (1),
palm-breadth

HANDED
3027 yâd (1), hand; power

HANDFUL
4390+3709 mâlê' (3), to
fill; be full
4393+7062 mᵉlô' (2),
fulness
5995 'âmîyr (1), bunch of
cereal new-cut grain
6451 piççâh (1),
abundance
7061 qâmats (1), to grasp
a handful
7062 qômets (1),
handful; abundance

HANDFULS
4393+2651 mᵉlô' (1),
fulness
6653 tsebeth (1), lock of
stalks, bundle of grain
7062 qômets (1),
handful; abundance
8168 shô'al (2), palm of
hand; handful

HANDKERCHIEFS
4676 sŏudariŏn (1), towel

HANDLE
270 'âchaz (1), to seize,
grasp; possess
4184 mûwsh (1), to
touch, feel
4900 mâshak (1), to draw
out; to be tall
6186 'ârak (1), to set in a
row, i.e. arrange,
8610 tâphas (5), to
manipulate, i.e. seize
2345 thigganō (1), to
touch
5584 psēlaphaō (1), to
manipulate

HANDLED
8610+3709 tâphas (1), to
manipulate, i.e. seize
821 atimŏō (1), to
maltreat, disgrace
5584 psēlaphaō (1), to
manipulate

HANDLES
3709 kaph (1), hollow of
hand; paw; sole of foot

HANDLETH
5921 'al (1), above, over,
upon, or against
8610 tâphas (2), to
manipulate, i.e. seize

HANDLING
8610 tâphas (1), to
manipulate, i.e. seize

HAMOR
1389 dŏlŏŏ (1), to
adulterate, falsify

HANDMAID
519 'âmâh (22), female
servant or slave
8198 shiphchâh (22),
household female slave
1399 dŏulē (1), female
slave

HANDMAIDEN
1399 dŏulē (1), female
slave

HANDMAIDENS
8198 shiphchâh (2),
household female slave
1399 dŏulē (1), female
slave

HANDMAIDS
519 'âmâh (1), female
servant or slave
8198 shiphchâh (7),
household female slave

HANDS
2651 chôphen (3), pair of
fists
3027 yâd (274), hand;
power
3028 yad (Ch.) (4), hand;
power
3709 kaph (67), hollow of
hand; paw; sole of foot
849 autôchĕir (1),
self-handed, personally
886 achĕirŏpŏiētŏs (3),
unmanufactured
2902 kratĕō (2), to seize
4084 piazō (1), to seize,
arrest, or capture
4475 rhapisma (1), slap,
strike
5495 chĕir (90), hand
5499 chĕirŏpŏiētŏs (6), of
human construction

HANDSTAVES
4731+3027 maqqêl (1),
shoot; stick; staff

HANDWRITING
5498 chĕirŏgraphŏn (1),
document or bond

HANDYWORK
4639+3027 ma'ăseh (1),
action; labor

HANES
2609 Chânêç (1), Chanes

HANG
3363 yâqa' (2), to be
dislocated; to impale
3381 yârad (1), to
descend
5414 nâthan (3), to give
5628 çârach (2), to
extend even to excess
8511 tâlâ' (1), to suspend;
to be uncertain
8518 tâlâh (7), to
suspend, hang
2910 krĕmannumi (2), to
hang
3935 pariēmi (1), to
neglect; to be weakened

HANGED
2614 chânaq (1), to
choke oneself
3363 yâqa' (2), to be
dislocated; to impale

English

HANGETH

4223 mᵉchâ' (Ch.) (1), to strike; to impale
8511 tâlâ' (1), to suspend; to be uncertain
8518 tâlâh (18), to suspend, hang
519 apagchŏmai (1), to strangle oneself
2910 krĕmannumi (4), to hang
4029 pĕrikĕimai (2), to enclose, encircle

HANGETH

8518 tâlâh (1), to suspend, hang
2910 krĕmannumi (1), to hang

HANGING

4539 mâçâk (17), veil; shield
8518 tâlâh (1), to suspend, hang

HANGINGS

1004 bayith (1), house; temple; family, tribe
7050 qela' (15), slinging weapon; door screen

HANIEL

2592 Chănnîy'êl (1), favor of God

HANNAH

2584 Channâh (13), favored

HANNATHON

2615 Channâthôn (1), favored

HANNIEL

2592 Chănnîy'êl (1), favor of God

HANOCH

2585 Chănôwk (5), initiated

HANOCHITES

2599 Chănôkîy (1), Chanokite

HANUN

2586 Chânûwn (11), favored

HAP

4745 miqreh (1), accident or fortune

HAPHRAIM

2663 Chăphârayîm (1), double pit

HAPLY

3863 lûw' (1), if; would that!
686 ara (2), then, so, therefore
3379 mĕpŏtĕ (2), not ever; if, or lest ever
3381 mĕpōs (1), lest somehow

HAPPEN

579 'ânâh (1), to meet, to happen
7136 qârâh (2), to bring about; to impose
4819 sumbainō (1), to concur, happen

HAPPENED

1961 hâyâh (1), to exist, i.e. be or become

7122 qârâ' (2), to encounter, to happen
7136 qârâh (2), to bring about; to impose
1096 ginŏmai (1), to be, become
4819 sumbainō (5), to concur, happen

HAPPENETH

4745 miqreh (1), accident or fortune
5060 nâga' (2), to strike
7136 qârâh (3), to bring about; to impose

HAPPIER

3107 makariŏs (1), fortunate, well off

HAPPY

833 'âshar (2), to be honest, prosper
835 'esher (16), how happy!
837 'ôsher (1), happiness, blessedness
7951 shâlâh (1), to be tranquil, i.e. secure
3106 makarizō (1), to esteem fortunate
3107 makariŏs (5), fortunate, well off

HARA

2024 Hârâ' (1), mountainousness

HARADAH

2732 Chărâdâh (2), fear, anxiety

HARAN

2039 Hârân (1), mountaineer
2309 chedel (6), state of the dead, deceased
2771 Chârân (12), parched

HARARITE

2043 Hărârîy (5), mountaineer

HARBONA

2726 Charbôwnâ' (1), Charbona, Charbonah

HARBONAH

2726 Charbôwnâ' (1), Charbona, Charbonah

HARD

280 'ăchîydâh (Ch.) (1), enigma
386 'êythân (1), never-failing; eternal
681 'êtsel (1), side; near
1692 dâbaq (4), to cling or adhere; to catch
2420 chîydâh (2), puzzle; conundrum; maxim
3332 yâtsaq (1), to pour out
3515 kâbêd (2), severe, difficult, stupid
5066 nâgash (1), to be, come, bring near
5221 nâkâh (1), to strike, kill
5564 çâmak (1), to lean upon; take hold of
5980 'ummâh (1), near, beside, along with
6277 'âthâq (1), impudent

6381 pâlâ' (5), to be, make great, difficult
7185 qâshâh (5), to be tough or severe
7186 qâsheh (6), severe
1421 dusĕrmĕnĕutŏs (1), difficult to explain
1422 duskŏlŏs (1), impracticable, difficult
1425 dusnŏĕtŏs (1), difficult of perception
4642 sklērŏs (5), hard or tough; harsh, severe
4927 sunŏmŏrĕō (1), to border together

HARDEN

533 'ammîyts (1), strong; mighty; brave
2388 châzaq (4), to be obstinate; to bind
5513 Çîynîy (1), Sinite
5539 çâlad (1), to leap with joy
7185 qâshâh (2), to be tough or severe
4645 sklērunō (3), to indurate, be stubborn

HARDENED

553 'âmats (1), to be strong; be courageous
2388 châzaq (9), to be obstinate; to bind
3513 kâbad (4), to be heavy, severe, dull
3515 kâbêd (3), severe, difficult, stupid
7185 qâshâh (8), to be tough or severe
7188 qâshach (2), to be, make unfeeling
8631 tᵉqêph (Ch.) (1), to be obstinate
4456 pōrŏō (3), to render stupid or callous
4645 sklērunō (1), to indurate, be stubborn

HARDENETH

5810 'âzaz (1), to be stout; be bold
7185 qâshâh (2), to be tough or severe
4645 sklērunō (1), to indurate, be stubborn

HARDER

2388 châzaq (1), to be obstinate; to bind
2389 châzâq (1), strong; severe, hard, violent

HARDHEARTED

7186+3820 qâsheh (1), severe

HARDLY

6031 'ânâh (1), to afflict, be afflicted
7185 qâshâh (2), to be tough or severe
1423 duskŏlōs (3), impracticably, with difficulty
3425 mŏgis (1), with difficulty
3433 mŏlis (1), with difficulty

HARDNESS

4165 mûwtsâq (1), casting of metal

2553 kakŏpathĕō (1), to undergo hardship
4457 pōrōsis (1), stupidity or callousness
4641 sklērŏkardia (3), hard-heartedness
4643 sklērŏtēs (1), stubbornness

HARE

768 'arnebeth (2), hare, rabbit

HAREPH

2780 Chârêph (1), reproachful

HARETH

2802 Chereth (1), forest

HARHAIAH

2736 Charhăyâh (1), fearing Jehovah

HARHAS

2745 Charchaç (1), sun

HARHUR

2744 Charchûwr (2), inflammation

HARIM

2766 Chârîm (11), snub-nosed

HARIPH

2756 Chârîyph (2), autumnal

HARLOT

2181 zânâh (33), to commit adultery
6948 qᵉdêshâh (3), sacred female prostitute
4204 pŏrnē (4), strumpet, i.e. prostitute; idolater

HARLOT'S

2181 zânâh (2), to commit adultery

HARLOTS

2181 zânâh (2), to commit adultery
6948 qᵉdêshâh (1), sacred female prostitute
4204 pŏrnē (4), strumpet, i.e. prostitute; idolater

HARLOTS'

2181 zânâh (1), to commit adultery

HARM

1697+7451 dâbâr (1), word; matter; thing
2398 châțâ' (1), to sin
3415 yâra' (1), to fear
7451 ra' (4), bad; evil
7489 râ'a' (3), to make, be good for nothing
824 atŏpŏs (1), improper; injurious; wicked
2556 kakŏs (2), bad, evil, wrong
2559 kakŏō (1), to injure; to oppress; to embitter
4190 pŏnērŏs (1), malice, wicked, bad; crime
5196 hubris (1), insult; injury

HARMLESS

172 akakŏs (1), innocent, blameless

185 akĕraiŏs (2), *innocent*

HARNEPHER
2774 Charnepher (1), *Charnepher*

HARNESS
631 'âçar (1), to *fasten*; to *join* battle
5402 nesheq (1), *military arms, arsenal*
8302 shiryôwn (2), *corslet, coat of mail*

HARNESSED
2571 châmûsh (1), *able-bodied soldiers*

HAROD
5878 'Êyn Chărôd (1), *fountain of trembling*

HARODITE
2733 Chărôdîy (1), *Charodite*

HAROEH
7204 Rô'êh (1), *seer*

HARORITE
2033 Hărôwrîy (1), *mountaineer*

HAROSHETH
2800 Chărôsheth (3), *skilled worker*

HARP
3658 kinnôwr (25), *harp*
7030 qîythârôç (Ch.) (4), *lyre*
2788 kithara (1), *lyre*

HARPED
2789 kitharizō (1), to *play a lyre*

HARPERS
2790 kitharōِdŏs (2), one who *plays a lyre*

HARPING
2789 kitharizō (1), to *play a lyre*

HARPS
3658 kinnôwr (17), *harp*
2788 kithara (3), *lyre*

HARROW
7702 sâdad (1), to *harrow* a field

HARROWS
2757 chârîyts (2), *threshing-sledge; slice*

HARSHA
2797 Charshâ' (2), *magician*

HART
354 'ayâl (9), *stag* deer

HARTS
354 'ayâl (2), *stag* deer

HARUM
2037 Hârûm (1), *high, exalted*

HARUMAPH
2739 Chărûwmaph (1), *snub-nosed*

HARUPHITE
2741 Chărûwphîy (1), *Charuphite*

HARUZ
2743 Chârûwts (1), *earnest*

HARVEST
7105 qâtsîyr (47), *harvest; limb* of a tree
2326 thĕrismŏs (13), *harvest, crop*

HARVESTMAN
7105 qâtsîyr (1), *harvest; limb* of a tree
7114 qâtsar (1), to *curtail, cut short*

HASADIAH
2619 Chăçadyâh (1), *Jehovah has favored*

HASENUAH
5574 Çᵉnûw'âh (1), *pointed*

HASHABIAH
2811 Chăshabyâh (15), *Jehovah has regarded*

HASHABNAH
2812 Chăshabnâh (1), *inventiveness*

HASHABNIAH
2813 Chăshabnᵉyâh (2), *thought of Jehovah*

HASHBADANA
2806 Chashbaddânâh (1), *considerate judge*

HASHEM
2044 Hâshêm (1), *wealthy*

HASHMONAH
2832 Chashmônâh (2), *fertile*

HASHUB
2815 Chashshûwb (4), *intelligent*

HASHUBAH
2807 Chăshûbâh (1), *estimation*

HASHUM
2828 Châshûm (5), *enriched*

HASHUPHA
2817 Chăsûwphâ' (1), *nakedness*

HASRAH
2641 Chaçrâh (1), *want*

HASSENAAH
5570 Çᵉnâ'âh (1), *thorny*

HASSHUB
2815 Chashshûwb (1), *intelligent*

HAST
1961 hâyâh (2), to *exist*, i.e. *be* or *become*
3426 yêsh (3), there *is* or *are*
2076 ĕsti (1), he (she or it) *is*; they *are*
2192 ĕchō (28), to *have; hold; keep*
5224 huparchŏnta (1), *property* or *possessions*

HASTE
213 'ûwts (1), to *be close, hurry, withdraw*
924 bᵉhîylûw (Ch.) (1), *hastily, at once*
926 bâhal (1), to *hasten, hurry anxiously*
927 bᵉhal (Ch.) (3), to *terrify; hasten*

1272 bârach (1), to *flee suddenly*
2363 chûwsh (11), to *hurry; to be eager*
2439 chîysh (1), to *hurry, hasten*
2648 châphaz (5), to *hasten away, to fear*
2649 chîppâzôwn (3), *hasty flight*
4116 mâhar (20), to *hurry; promptly*
5169 nâchats (1), to *be urgent*
4692 spĕudō (4), to *urge on diligently*
4710 spŏudē (2), *despatch; eagerness*

HASTED
213 'ûwts (2), to *be close, hurry, withdraw*
926 bâhal (1), to *hasten, hurry anxiously*
1765 dâchaph (2), to *urge; to hasten*
2363 chûwsh (2), to *hurry; to be eager*
2648 châphaz (2), to *hasten away, to fear*
4116 mâhar (14), to *hurry; promptly*
4692 spĕudō (1), to *urge on diligently*

HASTEN
2363 chûwsh (4), to *hurry; to be eager*
4116 mâhar (3), to *hurry; promptly*
8245 shâqad (1), to *be alert*, i.e. *sleepless*

HASTENED
213 'ûwts (2), to *be close, hurry, withdraw*
926 bâhal (1), to *hasten, hurry anxiously*
1765 dâchaph (1), to *urge; to hasten*
4116 mâhar (2), to *hurry; promptly*

HASTENETH
4116 mâhar (1), to *hurry; promptly*

HASTETH
213 'ûwts (1), to *be close, hurry, withdraw*
926 bâhal (1), to *hasten, hurry anxiously*
2363 chûwsh (1), to *hurry; to be eager*
2648 châphaz (1), to *hasten away, to fear*
2907 ṭûws (1), to *pounce* or *swoop upon*
4116 mâhar (3), to *hurry; promptly*
7602 shâ'aph (1), to *be angry; to hasten*

HASTILY
926 bâhal (1), to *hasten, hurry anxiously*
4116 mâhar (2), to *hurry; promptly*
4118 mahêr (2), *in a hurry*
4120 mᵉhêrâh (1), *hurry; promptly*
7323 rûwts (1), to *run*

5030 tachĕōs (1), *speedily, rapidly*

HASTING
4106 mâhîyr (1), *skillful*
4692 spĕudō (1), to *urge on diligently*

HASTY
213 'ûwts (2), to *be close, hurry, withdraw*
926 bâhal (2), to *hasten, hurry anxiously*
1061 bikkûwr (1), *first-fruits* of the crop
2685 chătsaph (Ch.) (1), to *be severe*
4116 mâhar (2), to *hurry; promptly*
7116 qâtsêr (1), *short*

HASUPHA
2817 Chăsûwphâ' (1), *nakedness*

HATACH
2047 Hăthâk (4), *Hathak*

HATCH
1234 bâqa' (2), to *cleave, break, tear open*

HATCHETH
3205 yâlad (1), to *bear young; to father a child*

HATE
7852 sâṭam (2), to *persecute*
8130 sânê' (67), to *hate*
8131 sᵉnê' (Ch.) (1), *enemy*
3404 misĕō (16), to *detest, to love less*

HATED
7852 sâṭam (2), to *persecute*
8130 sânê' (42), to *hate*
8135 sin'âh (2), *hate, malice*
8146 sânîy' (1), *hated*
3404 misĕō (12), to *detest; to love less*

HATEFUL
8130 sânê' (1), to *hate*
3404 misĕō (1), to *detest, persecute; to love less*
4767 stugnētŏs (1), *hated*, i.e. *odious*

HATEFULLY
8135 sin'âh (1), *hate, malice*

HATERS
8130 sânê' (1), to *hate*
2319 thĕŏstugĕs (1), *impious, God-hating*

HATEST
8130 sânê' (5), to *hate*
3404 misĕō (1), to *detest, persecute; to love less*

HATETH
7852 sâṭam (1), to *persecute*
8130 sânê' (20), to *hate*
3404 misĕō (9), to *detest, persecute; to love less*

HATH
413 'êl (1), *to, toward*
1167 ba'al (3), *master; husband; owner; citizen*

English

1172 ba'ălāh (2), *mistress; female owner*
1933 hăvā' (1), to *be, to exist*
1961 hâyâh (6), to *exist,* i.e. *be* or *become*
3426 yêsh (3), there *is* or *are*
4672 mâtsâ' (1), to *find* or *acquire; to occur, meet* or *be present*
2192 ĕchō (128), to *have; hold; keep*
5220 hupandrŏs (1), *married* woman
5224 huparchŏnta (2), *property* or *possessions*

HATHATH
2867 Chăthath (1), *dismay*

HATING
8130 sânê' (1), to *hate*
3404 misĕō (2), to *detest, persecute; to love less*

HATIPHA
2412 Chătĭyphâ' (2), *robber*

HATITA
2410 Chătĭyṭa' (2), *explorer*

HATRED
342 'êybâh (2), *hostility*
4895 mastêmâh (2), *enmity*
8135 sin'âh (13), *hate, malice*
2189 ĕchthra (1), *hostility; opposition*

HATS
3737 karb'lâ' (Ch.) (1), *mantle*

HATTIL
2411 Chaṭṭîyl (2), *fluctuating*

HATTUSH
2407 Chaṭṭûwsh (5), *Chattush*

HAUGHTILY
7317 rôwmâh (1), *proudly*

HAUGHTINESS
1346 ga'ăvâh (2), *arrogance; majesty*
7312 rùwm (3), *elevation; elation*

HAUGHTY
1361 gâbahh (5), to *be lofty; to be haughty*
1363 gôbahh (1), *height; grandeur; arrogance*
1364 gâbôahh (1), *high; powerful; arrogant*
3093 yâhîyr (1), *arrogant*
4791 mârôwm (1), *elevation; haughtiness*
7311 rûwm (1), to *be high; to rise or raise*

HAUNT
1980 hâlak (1), to *walk; live a certain way*
3427 yâshab (1), to *dwell, to remain; to settle*
7272 regel (1), *foot; step*

HAURAN
2362 Chavrân (2), *cavernous*

HAVE
270 'âchaz (1), to *seize, grasp; possess*
383 'îythay (Ch.) (3), there *is*
935 bôw' (1), to *go, come*
1167 ba'al (1), *master; husband; owner; citizen*
1934 hăvâ' (Ch.) (2), to *be, to exist*
1961 hâyâh (87), to *exist,* i.e. *be* or *become*
3045 yâda' (2), to *know*
3318 yâtsâ' (3), to *go, bring out*
3426 yêsh (12), there *is*
3947 lâqach (1), to *take*
4672 mâtsâ' (1), to *find* or *acquire; to occur*
5307 nâphal (1), to *fall*
5375 nâsâ' (1), to *lift up*
5674 'âbar (1), to *cross over; to transition*
5921 'al (1), *above, over, upon,* or *against*
474 antiballō (1), to *exchange words*
568 apĕchō (4), to *be distant*
1096 ginŏmai (1), to *be, become*
1099 glukus (1), *sweet, fresh*
1526 ĕisi (1), they *are*
1699 ĕmŏs (1), *my*
1751 ĕnĕimi (1), to *be within*
2070 ĕsmĕn (1), we *are*
2071 ĕsŏmai (6), *will be*
2076 ĕsti (11), he (she or it) *is;* they *are*
2192 ĕchō (266), to *have; hold; keep*
2701 katatrĕchō (1), to *hasten, run*
2983 lambanō (1), to *take, receive*
3335 mĕtalambanō (1), to *accept* and use
3918 parĕimi (1), to *be present; to have come*
5224 huparchŏnta (1), *property* or *possessions*
5225 huparchō (1), to *come into existence*

HAVEN
2348 chôph (2), *cove, sheltered bay*
4231 mâchôwz (1), *harbor*
3040 limēn (2), *harbor*

HAVENS
2568 Kalŏi Limĕnĕs (1), *Good Harbors*

HAVILAH
2341 Chăvîylâh (7), *circular*

HAVING
1167 ba'al (2), *master; husband; owner; citizen*
5414 nâthan (1), to *give*
1746 ĕnduō (1), to *dress*
2192 ĕchō (85), to *have; hold; keep*

HAVOCK
3075 lumainŏmai (1), to *insult, maltreat*

HAVOTH-JAIR
2334 Chavvôwth Yâ'îyr (2), *hamlets of Jair*

HAWK
5322 nêts (3), *flower; hawk*
8464 tachmâç (2), *unclean bird* (poss.) *owl*

HAY
2682 châtsîyr (2), *grass; leek plant*
5528 chŏrtŏs (1), *pasture, herbage* or *vegetation*

HAZAEL
2371 Chăzâ'êl (23), *God has seen*

HAZAIAH
2382 Chăzâyâh (1), *Jehovah has seen*

HAZAR-ADDAR
2692 Chătsar 'Addâr (1), *village of Addar*

HAZAR-ENAN
2703 Chătsar 'Êynôwn (1), *village of springs*
2704 Chătsar 'Êynân (3), *village of springs*

HAZAR-GADDAH
2693 Chătsar Gaddâh (1), *village of Fortune*

HAZAR-HATTICON
2694 Chătsar hat-Tîykôwn (1), *village of the middle*

HAZAR-SHUAL
2705 Chătsar Shûw'âl (4), *village of* (the) *fox*

HAZAR-SUSAH
2701 Chătsar Çûwçâh (1), *village of cavalry*

HAZAR-SUSIM
2702 Chătsar Çûwçîym (1), *village of horses*

HAZARDED
3860 paradidōmi (1), to *hand over*

HAZARMAVETH
2700 Chătsarmâveth (2), *village of death*

HAZAZON-TAMAR
2688 Chats'ᵉtsôwn Tâmâr (1), *row of* (the) *palm-tree*

HAZEL
3869 lûwz (1), *nut-tree,* (poss.) *almond*

HAZELELPONI
6753 Tsᵉlelpôwnîy (1), *shade-facing*

HAZERIM
2699 Chătsêrîym (1), *yards*

HAZEROTH
2698 Chătsêrowth (6), *yards*

HAZEZON-TAMAR
2688 Chats'ᵉtsôwn Tâmâr (1), *row of* (the) *palm-tree*

HAZIEL
2381 Chăzîy'êl (1), *seen of God*

HAZO
2375 Chăzow (1), *seer*

HAZOR
2674 Châtsôwr (18), *village*
2675 Châtsôwr Chădattâh (1), *new village*

HEAD
1270 barzel (2), *iron; iron implement*
1538 gulgôleth (1), *skull*
3852 lehâbâh (1), *flame; flash*
4763 mᵉra'ăshâh (1), *headpiece; head-rest*
6936 qodqôd (8), *crown of the head*
7217 rê'sh (Ch.) (11), *head*
7218 rô'sh (262), *head*
2775 kĕphalaiŏō (1), to *strike on the head*
2776 kĕphalē (55), *head*

HEADBANDS
7196 qishshûr (1), *girdle* or *sash* for women

HEADLONG
2630 katakrēmnizō (1), to *precipitate down*
4248 prēnēs (1), *head foremost, headlong*

HEADS
7217 rê'sh (Ch.) (1), *head*
7218 rô'sh (83), *head*
2776 kĕphalē (19), *head*

HEADSTONE
68+7222 'eben (1), *stone*

HEADY
4312 prŏpĕtēs (1), *falling forward headlong*

HEAL
7495 râphâ' (21), to *cure, heal*
1295 diasōzō (1), to *cure, preserve, rescue*
2323 thĕrapĕuō (10), to *relieve disease*
2390 iaŏmai (6), to *cure, heal*
2392 iasis (2), *curing*

HEALED
5414+7499 nâthan (1), to *give*
7495 râphâ' (31), to *cure, heal*
2323 thĕrapĕuō (25), to *relieve disease*
2390 iaŏmai (18), to *cure, heal*
4982 sōzō (3), to *deliver; to protect*

HEALER
2280 châbash (1), to *wrap firmly, bind*

HEALETH
7495 râphâ' (4), to *cure, heal*

HEALING
3545 kêhâh (1), *alleviation,* i.e. a *cure*
4832 marpê' (3), *cure; deliverance; placidity*
8585 tᵉ'âlâh (1), *bandage* or *plaster*

3771 ŏuranŏthĕn (2), *from the sky or heaven*
3772 ŏuranŏs (248), *sky; air; heaven*

HEAVEN'S
3772 ŏuranŏs (1), *sky; air; heaven*

HEAVENLY
1537+3772 ĕk (1), *out, out of*
2032 ĕpŏuraniŏs (16), *above the sky, celestial*
3770 ŏuraniŏs (6), *belonging to or coming from the sky or heaven*

HEAVENS
6160 'ărâbâh (1), *desert, wasteland*
6183 'ărîyph (1), *sky*
8064 shâmayim (107), *sky; unseen celestial places*
8065 shâmayin (Ch.) (3), *sky; unseen celestial places*
3772 ŏuranŏs (19), *sky; air; heaven*

HEAVIER
3513 kâbad (3), *to be heavy, severe, dull*

HEAVILY
3513 kâbad (1), *to be heavy, severe, dull*
3517 kᵉbêdûth (1), *difficulty*
6957 qav (1), *rule for measuring; rim*

HEAVINESS
1674 dᵉ'âgâh (1), *anxiety*
3544 kêheh (1), *feeble; obscure*
5136 nûwsh (1), *to be sick*
6440 pânîym (1), *face; front*
8386 ta'ănîyâh (1), *lamentation*
8424 tûwgâh (3), *depression; grief*
8589 ta'ănîyth (1), *affliction of self, fasting*
85 adēmŏnĕō (1), *to be in mental distress*
2726 katēphĕia (1), *sadness, dejection*
3076 lupĕō (1), *to distress; to be sad*
3077 lupē (2), *sadness, grief*

HEAVY
3513 kâbad (16), *to be heavy, severe, dull*
3514 kôbed (2), *weight, multitude, vehemence*
3515 kâbêd (8), *severe, difficult, stupid*
4133 môwţâh (1), *pole; ox-bow; yoke*
4751 mar (1), *bitter; bitterness; bitterly*
5620 çar (2), *peevish, sullen*
7186 qâsheh (1), *severe*
7451 ra' (1), *bad; evil*
85 adēmŏnĕō (2), *to be in mental distress*
916 barĕō (3), *to weigh down, cause pressure*

926 barus (1), *weighty*

HEBER
2268 Cheber (10), *community*
5677 'Êber (2), *regions beyond*
1443 Ĕbĕr (1), *regions beyond*

HEBER'S
2268 Cheber (1), *community*

HEBERITES
2277 Chebrîy (1), *Chebrite*

HEBREW
5680 'Ibrîy (14), *Eberite (i.e. Hebrew)*
1444 Hĕbraïkŏs (1), *Hebraïc or the Jewish language*
1446 Hĕbraïs (4), *Hebrew or Jewish language*
1447 Hĕbraïsti (6), *Hebraistically or in the Jewish language*

HEBREWESS
5680 'Ibrîy (1), *Eberite (i.e. Hebrew)*

HEBREWS
5680 'Ibrîy (17), *Eberite (i.e. Hebrew)*
1445 Hĕbraiŏs (3), *Hebrew or Jew*

HEBREWS'
5680 'Ibrîy (1), *Eberite (i.e. Hebrew)*

HEBRON
2275 Chebrôwn (72), *seat of association*

HEBRONITES
2276 Chebrôwnîy (6), *Chebronite*

HEDGE
1447 gâdêr (3), *enclosure, wall or fence*
4534 mᵉçûwkâh (1), *thorn-hedge*
4881 mᵉsûwkâh (2), *thorn hedge*
7753 sûwk (2), *to shut in with hedges*
5418 phragmŏs (1), *fence or enclosing barrier*

HEDGED
1443 gâdar (1), *to build a stone wall*
5526 çâkak (1), *to entwine; to fence in*
5418+4060 phragmŏs (1), *fence or barrier*

HEDGES
1447 gâdêr (1), *enclosure, wall or fence*
1448 gᵉdêrâh (4), *enclosure for flocks*
5418 phragmŏs (1), *fence or enclosing barrier*

HEED
238 'âzan (1), *to listen*
2095 zᵉhar (Ch.) (1), *be admonished, be careful*
5414+3820 nâthan (1), *to give*
5535 çâkath (1), *to be silent*

7181 qâshab (3), *to prick up the ears*
7182 qesheb (1), *hearkening*
7200 râ'âh (2), *to see*
8104 shâmar (35), *to watch*
433 anēkō (1), *be proper, fitting*
991 blĕpō (14), *to look at*
1907 ĕpĕchō (2), *to detain; to pay attention*
3708 hŏraō (5), *to stare, see clearly; to discern*
4337 prŏsĕchō (11), *to pay attention to*
4648 skŏpĕō (1), *to watch out for, i.e. to regard*

HEEL
6117 'âqab (1), *to seize by the heel; to circumvent*
6119 'âqêb (4), *track, footprint; rear position*
4418 ptĕrna (1), *heel*

HEELS
6119 'âqêb (2), *track, footprint; rear position*
6120 'âqêb (1), *one who lies in wait*
8328 sheresh (1), *root*

HEGAI
1896 Hêgê' (3), *Hege or Hegai*

HEGE
1896 Hêgê' (1), *Hege or Hegai*

HEIFER
5697 'eglâh (11), *cow calf*
6510 pârâh (6), *heifer*
1151 damalis (1), *heifer*

HEIFER'S
5697 'eglâh (1), *cow calf*

HEIGHT
1361 gâbahh (2), *to be lofty; to be haughty*
1363 gôbahh (8), *height; grandeur; arrogance*
1364 gâbôahh (8), *high; powerful; arrogant*
4791 mârôwm (9), *elevation; elation*
6967 qôwmâh (30), *height*
7218 rô'sh (1), *head*
7312 rûwm (2), *elevation; elation*
7314 rûwm (Ch.) (4), *altitude, tallness*
7419 râmûwth (1), *heap of carcases*
5311 hupsŏs (2), *altitude; sky; dignity*
5313 hupsōma (1), *altitude; barrier*

HEIGHTS
1116 bâmâh (1), *elevation, high place*
4791 mârôwm (1), *elevation; elation*

HEINOUS
2154 zimmâh (1), *bad plan*

HEIR
3423 yârash (9), *to inherit; to impoverish*
2816 klērŏnŏmĕō (1), *to be an heir to, inherit*

2818 klērŏnŏmŏs (8), *possessor by inheritance*

HEIRS
3423 yârash (1), *to inherit; to impoverish*
2816 klērŏnŏmĕō (1), *to be an heir to, inherit*
2818 klērŏnŏmŏs (7), *possessor by inheritance*
4789 sugklērŏnŏmŏs (2), *participant in common*

HELAH
2458 Chel'âh (2), *rust*

HELAM
2431 Chêylâm (2), *fortress*

HELBAH
2462 Chelbâh (1), *fertility*

HELBON
2463 Chelbôwn (1), *fruitful*

HELD
270 'âchaz (3), *to seize, grasp; possess*
631 'âçar (1), *to fasten; to join battle*
1102 bâlam (1), *to muzzle, control*
1826 dâmam (1), *to be silent; to be astonished*
2244 châba' (1), *to secrete*
2388 châzaq (6), *to fasten upon; to seize*
2790 chârash (10), *to engrave; to plow*
2814 châshâh (2), *to hush or keep quiet*
2820 châsak (1), *to restrain or refrain*
3447 yâshaţ (2), *to extend*
3557 kûwl (1), *to keep in; to measure*
5582 çâ'ad (1), *to support*
6213 'âsâh (1), *to do*
6901 qâbal (1), *to admit; to take*
7311 rûwm (2), *to be high; to rise or raise*
8557 temeç (1), *melting disappearance*
2192 ĕchō (1), *to have; hold; keep*
2258 ēn (1), *I was*
2270 hēsuchazō (2), *to refrain*
2722 katĕchō (1), *to hold down fast*
2902 kratĕō (2), *to seize*
2983 lambanō (1), *to take, receive*
4160 pŏiĕō (1), *to make*
4601 sigaō (1), *to keep silent*
4623 siōpaō (4), *to be quiet*
4912 sunĕchō (1), *to hold together*

HELDAI
2469 Chelday (2), *worldliness*

HELEB
2460 Chêleb (1), *fatness*

HELED
2466 Chêled (1), *fleeting time; this world*

HELEK
2507 Chêleq (2), *portion*

HELEKITES
2516 Chelqîy (1), *Chelkite*

HELEM
2494 Chêlem (2), *dream*

HELEPH
2501 Cheleph (1), *change*

HELEZ
2503 Chelets (5), *strength*

HELI
2242 Hêli (1), *lofty*

HELKAI
2517 Chelqay (1), *apportioned*

HELKATH
2520 Chelqath (2), *smoothness*

HELKATH-HAZZURIM
2521 Chelqath hats-Tsûrîym (1), *smoothness of the rocks*

HELL
7585 sheʾôwl (31), *abode of the dead*
86 haidēs (10), *Hades, i.e. place of the dead*
1067 gĕĕnna (12), *valley of (the son of) Hinnom, fig. hell*
5020 tartaroŏ (1), *to incarcerate in Tartaros*

HELM
4079 pēdaliŏn (1), *blade of an oar which steers*

HELMET
3553 kôwbaʾ (4), *helmet*
6959 qôwbaʾ (2), *helmet*
4030 pĕrikĕphalaia (2), *helmet*

HELMETS
3553 kôwbaʾ (2), *helmet*

HELON
2497 Chêlôn (5), *strong*

HELP
2388 châzaq (2), *to fasten upon; to seize*
3444 yeshûwʾâh (2), *deliverance, aid*
3447 yâshaṭ (1), *to extend*
3467 yâshaʾ (9), *to make safe, free*
5375 nâsâʾ (1), *to lift up*
5800 ʿâzab (2), *to loosen; relinquish; permit*
5826 ʿâzar (44), *to protect or aid*
5828 ʿêzer (21), *aid*
5833 ʿezrâh (24), *aid*
6965 qûwm (2), *to rise*
7125 qîrʾâh (1), *to encounter, to happen*
8668 teshûwʾâh (5), *rescue, deliverance*
996 bŏĕthĕia (1), *aid*
997 bŏĕthĕŏ (5), *to aid or relieve*
1947 ĕpikŏuria (1), *assistance, aid*
4815 sullambanŏ (2), *to conceive; to aid*

HELPED
4878 sunantilambanŏmai (1), *assist*

HELPED
3467 yâshaʾ (2), *to make safe, free*
5375 nâsâʾ (1), *to lift up*
5826 ʿâzar (18), *to protect or aid*
5833 ʿezrâh (1), *aid*
997 bŏĕthĕŏ (1), *to aid or relieve*
4820 sumballŏ (1), *to aid; to join, attack*

HELPER
5826 ʿâzar (7), *to protect or aid*
998 bŏĕthŏs (1), *succorer, helper*
4904 sunĕrgŏs (1), *fellow-worker*

HELPERS
5826 ʿâzar (4), *to protect or aid*
5833 ʿezrâh (1), *aid*
4904 sunĕrgŏs (2), *fellow-worker*

HELPETH
5826 ʿâzar (2), *to protect or aid*
4878 sunantilambanŏmai (1), *co-operate, assist*
4903 sunĕrgĕŏ (1), *to be a fellow-worker*

HELPING
3467 yâshaʾ (1), *to make safe, free*
5582 çâʾad (1), *to support*
4943 sunupŏurgĕŏ (1), *assist, join to help*

HELPS
484 antilĕpsis (1), *relief, aid*
996 bŏĕthĕia (1), *aid*

HELVE
6086 ʿêts (1), *wood, things made of wood*

HEM
7757 shûwl (5), *skirt; bottom edge*
2899 kraspĕdŏn (2), *margin*

HEMAM
1967 Hêymâm (1), *raging*

HEMAN
1968 Hêymân (16), *faithful*

HEMATH
2574 Chămâth (3), *walled*

HEMDAN
2533 Chemdân (1), *pleasant*

HEMLOCK
3939 laʿănâh (1), *poisonous wormwood*
7219 rôʾsh (1), *poisonous plant; poison*

HEMS
7757 shûwl (1), *skirt; bottom edge*

HEN
2581 Chên (1), *grace*
3733 ŏrnis (2), *hen*

HENA
2012 Hênaʾ (3), *Hena*

HENADAD
2582 Chênâdâd (4), *favor of Hadad*

HENCE
2088 zeh (14), *this or that*
3212 yâlak (1), *to walk; to live; to carry*
3318 yâtsâʾ (1), *to go, bring out*
1782 ĕntĕuthĕn (9), *hence, from here*
1821 ĕxapŏstĕllŏ (1), *to despatch, or to dismiss*
3326+5025 mĕta (1), *with, among; after, later*
5217 hupagŏ (1), *to withdraw or retire*

HENCEFORTH
3254 yâçaph (5), *to add or augment*
5750 ʿôwd (2), *again; repeatedly; still; more*
6258 ʿattâh (5), *at this time, now*
534 aparti (1), *henceforth, from now*
575+737 apŏ (2), *from, away*
575+3588+3568 apŏ (1), *from, away*
737 arti (1), *just now; at once*
2089 ĕti (1), *yet, still*
3063 lŏipŏn (4), *remaining; finally*
3371 mĕkĕti (4), *no further*
3568 nun (4), *now; the present or immediate*
3765 ŏukĕti (1), *not yet, no longer*

HENCEFORWARD
1973 hâlʾeâh (1), *far away; thus far*
3371 mĕkĕti (1), *no further*

HENOCH
2585 Chănôwk (2), *initiated*

HEPHER
2660 Chêpher (9), *pit or shame*

HEPHERITES
2662 Chephrîy (1), *Chephrite*

HEPHZI-BAH
2657 Chephtsîy bâhh (2), *my delight (is) in her*

HERALD
3744 kârôwz (Ch.) (1), *herald*

HERB
1877 desheʾ (6), *sprout; green grass*
2682 châtsîyr (1), *grass; leek plant*
6212 ʿeseb (12), *grass, or any green, tender shoot*

HERBS
216 ʾôwr (1), *luminary; lightning; happiness*
219 ʾôwrâh (2), *luminousness, light*
3419 yârâq (3), *vegetable greens*

HEREIN
6212 ʿeseb (5), *grass, or any green, tender shoot*
1008 bŏtanĕ (1), *grazing herbage, vegetation*
3001 lachanŏn (4), *vegetable*

HERD
1241 bâqâr (14), *plowing ox; herd*
34 agĕlĕ (8), *drove, herd*

HERDMAN
951 bôwkêr (1), *herder, cattle-tender*

HERDMEN
5349 nôqêd (1), *owner or tender of sheep*
7462 râʿâh (6), *to tend a flock, i.e. pasture it*

HERDS
1241 bâqâr (30), *plowing ox; herd*
4735 miqneh (1), *live-stock*
5739 ʿêder (2), *muster, flock*

HERE
645 ʾêphôw (1), *then*
1988 hălôm (2), *hither, to here*
2005 hên (5), *lo!; if!*
2008 hênnâh (2), *from here; from there*
2009 hinnêh (12), *lo!; Look!*
2088 zeh (12), *this or that*
2236 zâraq (1), *to sprinkle, scatter*
3541 kôh (4), *thus*
4672 mâtsâʾ (1), *to find or acquire; to occur,*
6311 pôh (43), *here or hence*
8033 shâm (2), *where, there*
8552 tâmam (1), *to complete, finish*
848 hautŏu (1), *self*
1759 ĕnthadĕ (3), *here, hither*
3918 parĕimi (2), *to be present; to have come*
3936 paristĕmi (1), *to stand beside, present*
4840 sumparĕimi (1), *to be at hand together*
5602 hŏdĕ (44), *here or hither*

HEREAFTER
268 ʾâchôwr (1), *behind, backward; west*
310 ʾachar (1), *after*
737 arti (1), *just now; at once*
2089 ĕti (1), *yet, still*
3195 mĕllŏ (1), *to intend, i.e. be about to*
3370 Mêdŏs (1), *inhabitant of Media*

HEREBY
2063 zôʾth (4), *this*
1537+5124 ĕk (1), *out, out of*
1722+5129 ĕn (8), *in; during; because of*

HEREIN
2063 zôʾth (1), *this*

HEREOF
5921+2063 'al (1), *above, over, upon,* or *against*
1722+5129 ĕn (7), *in; during; because of*

HEREOF
3778 hŏutŏs (1), *this* or *that*
5026 tautē₁ (1), (*toward* or *of*) *this*

HERES
2776 Chereç (1), *shining*

HERESH
2792 Cheresh (1), magical *craft; silence*

HERESIES
139 hairĕsis (3), *party, sect; disunion* or *heresy*

HERESY
139 hairĕsis (1), *party, sect; disunion* or *heresy*

HERETICK
141 hairĕtikŏs (1), *schismatic, division*

HERETOFORE
865 'ethmôwl (1), *heretofore, formerly*
8543 tᵉmôwl (6), *yesterday*
4258 prŏamartanō (1), to *sin previously*

HEREUNTO
1519+5124 ĕis (1), *to* or *into*

HEREWITH
2063 zô'th (2), *this*

HERITAGE
3425 yᵉrushâh (1), *conquest*
4181 môwrâshâh (1), *possession*
5157 nâchal (1), to *inherit*
5159 nachălâh (26), *occupancy*
2819 klērŏs (1), *lot, portion*

HERITAGES
5159 nachălâh (1), *occupancy*

HERMAS
2057 Hĕrmas (1), *born of god Hermes*

HERMES
2060 Hĕrmēs (1), *born of god Hermes*

HERMOGENES
2061 Hĕrmŏgĕnēs (1), *born of god Hermes*

HERMON
2768 Chermôwn (13), *abrupt*

HERMONITES
2769 Chermôwnîym (1), *peaks of Hermon*

HEROD
2264 Hĕrōdēs (40), *heroic*

HEROD'S
2264 Hĕrōdēs (4), *heroic*

HERODIANS
2265 Hĕrōdianŏi (3), *Herodians*

HERODIAS
2266 Hĕrōdias (4), *heroic*

HERODIAS'
2266 Hĕrōdias (2), *heroic*

HERODION
2267 Hĕrōdiōn (1), *heroic*

HERON
601 'ănâphâh (2), (poss.) *parrot*

HESED
2618 Cheçed (1), *favor*

HESHBON
2809 Cheshbôwn (38), *contrivance; plan*

HESHMON
2829 Cheshmôwn (1), *opulent*

HETH
2845 Chêth (14), *terror*

HETHLON
2855 Chethlôn (2), *enswathed*

HEW
1414 gᵉdad (Ch.) (2), to *cut* down
1438 gâda' (1), to *fell* a tree; to *destroy*
2404 châṭab (1), to *chop* or *carve* wood
2672 châtsab (2), to *cut* stone or *carve* wood
3772 kârath (3), to *cut* (off, down or asunder)
6458 pâçal (3), to *carve,* to *chisel*

HEWED
1496 gâzîyth (5), *dressed* stone
2672 châtsab (3), to *cut* stone or *carve* wood
4274 machtsêb (1), *quarry* stone
5408 nâthach (1), to *dismember, cut up*
6458 pâçal (2), to *carve,* to *chisel*
8158 shâçaph (1), to *hack* in pieces, i.e. *kill*

HEWER
2404 châṭab (1), to *chop* or *carve* wood

HEWERS
2404 châṭab (5), to *chop* or *carve* wood
2672 châtsab (4), to *cut* stone or *carve* wood

HEWETH
2672 châtsab (2), to *cut* stone or *carve* wood
3772 kârath (1), to *cut* (off, down or asunder)

HEWN
1438 gâda' (1), to *fell* a tree; to *destroy*
1496 gâzîyth (5), *dressed* stone
2672 châtsab (2), to *cut* stone or *carve* wood
4274 machtsêb (2), *quarry* stone
7060 qâmal (1), to *wither*
1581 ĕkkŏptō (3), to *cut* off; to *frustrate*
2991 laxĕutŏs (1), *rock-quarried*
2998 latŏmĕō (2), to *quarry*

HEZEKI
2395 Chizqîy (1), *strong*

HEZEKIAH
2396 Chizqîyâh (128), *strengthened of Jehovah*

HEZION
2383 Chezyôwn (1), *vision*

HEZIR
2387 Chêzîyr (2), *protected*

HEZRAI
2695 Chetsrôw (1), *enclosure*

HEZRO
2695 Chetsrôw (1), *enclosure*

HEZRON
2696 Chetsrôwn (17), *court-yard*

HEZRON'S
2696 Chetsrôwn (1), *court-yard*

HEZRONITES
2697 Chetsrôwnîy (2), *Chetsronite*

HID
2244 châbâ' (25), to *secrete*
2934 ṭâman (16), to *hide*
3582 kâchad (6), to *destroy;* to *hide*
3680 kâçâh (2), to *cover*
4301 maṭmôwn (2), *secret storehouse*
5641 çâthar (30), to *hide* by covering
5956 'âlam (11), to *veil* from sight, i.e. *conceal*
6845 tsâphan (8), to *hide;* to *hoard* or *reserve*
8587 ta'ălummâh (1), *secret*
613 apŏkruptō (5), to *keep secret, conceal*
614 apŏkruphŏs (2), *secret, hidden* things
1470 ĕgkruptō (2), *incorporate with, mix in*
2572 kaluptō (1), to *cover* up
2927 kruptŏs (3), *private, unseen*
2928 kruptō (10), to *conceal*
2990 lanthanō (2), to *lie hid; unwittingly*
3871 parakaluptō (1), to *veil, be hidden*
4032 pĕrikruptō (1), to *conceal all around*

HIDDAI
1914 Hidday (1), *Hiddai*

HIDDEKEL
2313 Chiddeqel (2), *Tigris river*

HIDDEN
2664 châphas (1), to *seek;* to *mask*
2934 ṭâman (1), to *hide*
4301 maṭmôwn (1), *secret storehouse*
4710 mitspûn (1), *secret*

HEZEKI
2395 Chizqîy (1), *strong*

HIDE
2244 châbâ' (6), to *secrete*
2247 châbah (5), to *hide*
2934 ṭâman (5), to *hide*
3582 kâchad (10), to *destroy;* to *hide*
3680 kâçâh (3), to *cover*
5127 nûwç (1), to *vanish away, flee*
5641 çâthar (33), to *hide* by covering
5785 'ôwr (2), *skin, leather*
5956 'âlam (8), to *veil* from sight, i.e. *conceal*
6004 'âmam (2), to *overshadow* by *huddling* together
6845 tsâphan (5), to *hide;* to *hoard* or *reserve*
2572 kaluptō (1), to *cover*
2928 kruptō (2), to *conceal*

HIDEST
5641 çâthar (5), to *hide* by covering
5956 'âlam (1), to *veil* from sight, i.e. *conceal*

HIDETH
2244 châbâ' (1), to *secrete*
2821 châshak (1), to *be dark;* to *darken*
2934 ṭâman (2), to *hide*
3680 kâçâh (1), to *cover*
5641 çâthar (5), to *hide* by covering
5848 'âṭaph (1), to *shroud,* i.e. *clothe*
5956 'âlam (2), to *veil* from sight, i.e. *conceal*
6845 tsâphan (1), to *hide;* to *hoard* or *reserve*
2928 kruptō (1), to *conceal*

HIDING
2253 chebyôwn (1), *concealment, hiding*
2934 ṭâman (1), to *hide*
4224 machăbê' (1), *refuge, shelter*
5643 çêther (3), *cover, shelter*

HIEL
2419 Chîy'êl (1), *living of God*

HIERAPOLIS
2404 Hiĕrapŏlis (1), *holy city*

HIGGAION
1902 higgâyôwn (1), *musical notation*

HIGH
376 'îysh (2), *man; male; someone*
753 'ôrek (1), *length*
1111 Bâlâq (1), *waster*
1116 bâmâh (99), *elevation, high place*
1361 gâbahh (4), to *be lofty; to be haughty*
1362 gâbâhh (3), *high; lofty*
1363 gôbahh (2), *height; grandeur; arrogance*
1364 gâbôahh (25), *high; powerful; arrogant*
1386 gabnôn (2), *peak of hills*
1419 gâdôwl (22), *great*
1870 derek (1), *road; course of life*
4546 mᵉçillâh (1), *main thoroughfare; viaduct*
4605 maʿal (7), *upward, above, overhead*
4608 maʿăleh (1), *elevation; platform*
4791 mârôwm (33), *elevation; elation*
4796 Mârôwth (1), *bitter springs*
4869 misgâb (4), high *refuge*
5375 nâsâʾ (1), to *lift up*
5920 ʿal (3), the *Highest God*
5943 ʿillay (Ch.) (9), the *supreme God*
5945 ʿelyôwn (37), *loftier, higher; Supreme God*
5946 ʿelyôwn (Ch.) (4), the *Supreme God*
6381 pâlâʾ (1), to *be, make great, difficult*
6877 tsᵉrîyach (1), *citadel*
6967 qôwmâh (5), *height*
7218 rôʾsh (3), *head*
7311 rûwm (25), to *be high; to rise or raise*
7312 rûwm (3), *elevation; elation*
7315 rôwm (1), *aloft, on high*
7319 rôwmᵉmâh (1), *exaltation, i.e. praise*
7413 râmâh (4), *height; high seat of idolatry*
7682 sâgab (6), to *be, make high; be safe*
8192 shâphâh (1), to *bare*
8203 Shᵉphaṭyâh (2), *Jehovah has judged*
8205 shᵉphîy (7), *bare hill or plain*
8564 tamrûwr (1), *erection, i.e. pillar*
8643 tᵉrûwʿâh (1), *battle-cry; clangor*
507 anō (1), *upward or on the top, heavenward*
749 archiĕrĕus (59), *high-priest, chief priest*
2032 ĕpŏuraniŏs (1), *above the sky, celestial*
2409 hiĕrĕus (1), *priest*
3173 mĕgas (2), *great, many*

5308 hupsēlŏs (9), *lofty* in place or character
5310 hupsistŏs (5), the *Supreme God*
5311 hupsŏs (3), *altitude; sky; dignity*
5313 hupsōma (1), *altitude; barrier*

HIGHER
1354 gab (1), *mounded or rounded: top or rim*
1361 gâbahh (4), to *be lofty; to be haughty*
1364 gâbôahh (5), *high; powerful; arrogant*
3201 yâkôl (1), to *be able*
5945 ʿelyôwn (4), *loftier, higher; Supreme God*
6706 tsᵉchîyach (1), *glaring*
7311 rûwm (2), to *be high; to rise or raise*
511 anōtĕrŏs (1), *upper part; former part*
5242 hupĕrĕchō (1), to *excel; superior*
5308 hupsēlŏs (1), *lofty*

HIGHEST
1364 gâbôahh (1), *high; powerful; arrogant*
4791 mârôwm (1), *elevation; elation*
5945 ʿelyôwn (3), *loftier, higher; Supreme God*
6788 tsammereth (2), *foliage*
7218 rôʾsh (1), *head*
4410 prōtŏkathĕdria (1), *pre-eminence in council*
4411 prōtŏklisia (1), *pre-eminence at meals*
5310 hupsistŏs (8), the *Supreme God*

HIGHLY
1537+4053 ĕk (1), *out of*
2371 thumŏmachĕō (1), to *be exasperated*
5251 hupĕrupsŏō (1), to *raise to the highest*
5252 hupĕrphrŏnĕō (1), to *esteem oneself overmuch*
5308 hupsēlŏs (1), *lofty* in place or character

HIGHMINDED
5187 tuphŏō (1), to *inflate with self-conceit*
5309 hupsēlŏphrŏnĕō (2), to *be lofty in mind*

HIGHNESS
1346 gaʾăvâh (1), *arrogance; majesty*
7613 sᵉʾêth (1), *elevation; swelling leprous scab*

HIGHWAY
4546 mᵉçillâh (13), main *thoroughfare; viaduct*
4547 maçlûwl (1), main *thoroughfare*
3598 hŏdŏs (1), *road*

HIGHWAYS
734 'ôrach (1), *well-traveled road; manner of life*
2351 chûwts (1), *outside, outdoors; open market*

4546 mᵉçillâh (6), main *thoroughfare; viaduct*
1327+3598 diĕxŏdŏs (1), *open square*
3598 hŏdŏs (2), *road*

HILEN
2432 Chîylên (1), *fortress*

HILKIAH
2518 Chilqîyâh (33), *portion (of) Jehovah*

HILKIAH'S
2518 Chilqîyâh (1), *portion (of) Jehovah*

HILL
1389 gibʿâh (30), *hillock*
2022 har (34), *mountain or range of hills*
4608 maʿăleh (1), *elevation; platform*
7161 qeren (1), *horn*
697 Arĕiŏs Pagŏs (1), *rock of Ares*
1015 bŏunŏs (1), small *hill*
3714 ŏrĕinŏs (2), *Highlands of Judæa*
3735 ŏrŏs (3), *hill, mountain*

HILL'S
2022 har (1), *mountain or range of hills*

HILLEL
1985 Hillêl (2), *praising (God)*

HILLS
1389 gibʿâh (39), *hillock*
2022 har (23), *mountain or range of hills*
2042 hârâr (2), *mountain*
1015 bŏunŏs (1), small *hill*

HIN
1969 hîyn (22), liquid *measure*

HIND
355 'ayâlâh (1), *doe deer*
365 'ayeleth (1), *doe deer*

HINDER
268 'âchôwr (3), *behind, backward; west*
309 'âchar (1), to *remain; to delay*
310 'achar (1), *after*
314 'achărôwn (1), *late or last; behind; western*
4513 mânaʿ (1), to *deny, refuse*
5490 çôwph (1), *termination; end*
6213+8442 ʿâsâh (1), to *do or make*
7725 shûwb (2), to *turn back; to return*
348 anakŏptō (1), to *beat back, i.e. check*
2967 kōluō (1), to *stop*
4403 prumna (2), *stern of a ship*
5100+1464+1325 tis (1), *some or any person*

HINDERED
989 bᵉṭêl (Ch.) (1), to *stop*
1465 ĕgkŏptō (2), to *impede, detain*

1581 ĕkkŏptō (1), to *cut off; to frustrate*
2967 kōluō (1), to *stop*

HINDERETH
2820 châsak (1), to *restrain or refrain*

HINDERMOST
314 'achărôwn (1), *late or last; behind; western*
319 'achărîyth (1), *future; posterity*

HINDMOST
314 'achărôwn (1), *late or last; behind; western*
2179 zânab (2), militarily *attack the rear position*

HINDS
355 'ayâlâh (4), *doe deer*

HINDS'
355 'ayâlâh (3), *doe deer*

HINGES
6596 pôth (1), *hole; hinge; female genitals*
6735 tsîyr (1), *hinge*

HINNOM
2011 Hinnôm (13), *Hinnom*

HIP
7785 shôwq (1), lower *leg*

HIRAH
2437 Chîyrâh (2), *splendor*

HIRAM
2438 Chîyrâm (22), *noble*

HIRAM'S
2438 Chîyrâm (1), *noble*

HIRE
868 'ethnan (7), *gift price of harlotry*
4242 mᵉchîyr (1), *price, payment, wages*
7936 sâkar (2), to *hire*
7939 sâkâr (8), *payment, salary; compensation*
3408 misthŏs (3), *pay for services*
3409 misthŏō (1), to *hire*

HIRED
7916 sâkîyr (11), man at *wages, hired hand*
7917 sᵉkîyrâh (1), *hiring*
7936 sâkar (14), to *hire*
8566 tânâh (2), to *bargain with a harlot*
3407 misthiŏs (2), *hired-worker*
3409 misthŏō (1), to *hire*
3410 misthōma (1), *rented building*
3411 misthōtŏs (1), *wage-worker*

HIRELING
7916 sâkîyr (6), man at *wages, hired hand*
3411 misthōtŏs (2), *wage-worker*

HIRES
868 'ethnan (1), *gift price of harlotry*

HIREST
7806 shâzar (1), to *twist a thread of straw*

HISS
8319 shâraq (12), *to whistle or hiss*

HISSING
8292 sh^erûwqâh (1), *whistling; scorn*
8322 sh^erêqâh (7), *derision*

HIT
4672 mâtsâ' (2), *to find or acquire; to occur*

HITHER
1988 hălôm (6), *hither, to here*
2008 hênnâh (2), *from here; from there*
5066 nâgash (7), *to be, come, bring near*
6311 pôh (1), *here or hence*
1204 děurŏ (2), *hither!; hitherto*
1759 ěnthadě (4), *here, hither*
3333 mětakalěō (1), *to summon for, call for*
5602 hŏdě (14), *here or hither*

HITHERTO
227 'âz (1), *at that time or place; therefore*
1973 hâl^eâh (2), *far away; thus far*
1988 hălôm (2), *hither, to here*
5704+2008 'ad (6), *as far (long) as; during*
5704+3541 'ad (2), *as far (long) as; during*
5704+6311 'ad (1), *as far (long) as; during*
5705+3542 'ad (Ch.) (1), *as far (long) as; during*
891+1204 achri (1), *until or up to*
2193+737 hěōs (2), *until*
3768 ŏupŏ (1), *not yet*

HITTITE
2850 Chittîy (26), *Chittite*

HITTITES
2850 Chittîy (22), *Chittite*

HIVITE
2340 Chivvîy (9), *villager*

HIVITES
2340 Chivvîy (16), *villager*

HIZKIAH
2396 Chizqîyâh (1), *strengthened of Jehovah*

HIZKIJAH
2396 Chizqîyâh (1), *strengthened of Jehovah*

HO
1945 hôwy (3), *oh!, woe!*

HOAR
3713 k^ephôwr (2), *bowl; white frost*
7872 sêybâh (3), *old age*

HOARY
3713 k^ephôwr (1), *bowl; white frost*
7872 sêybâh (3), *old age*

HOBAB
2246 Chôbâb (2), *cherished*

HOBAH
2327 chôwbâh (1), *hiding place*

HOD
1963 hêyk (1), *how?*

HODAIAH
1939 Howday^evâhûw (1), *majesty of Jehovah*

HODAVIAH
1938 Hôwdavyâh (3), *majesty of Jehovah*

HODESH
2321 Chôdesh (1), *new moon*

HODEVAH
1937 Hôwd^evâh (1), *majesty of Jehovah*

HODIAH
1940 Hôwdîyâh (1), *Jewess*

HODIJAH
1940 Hôwdîyâh (5), *Jewess*

HOGLAH
2295 Choglâh (4), *partridge*

HOHAM
1944 Hôwhâm (1), *Hoham*

HOISED
1869 ěpairō (1), *to raise up, look up*

HOLD
270 'âchaz (26), *to seize, grasp; possess*
816 'âsham (1), *to be guilty; to be punished*
1225 bitstsârôwn (1), *fortress*
2013 hâçâh (2), *to hush, be quiet*
2388 châzaq (35), *to fasten upon; to seize*
2790 chârash (16), *to engrave; to plow*
2814 châshâh (6), *to hush or keep quiet*
3447 yâshaṭ (1), *to extend*
3557 kûwl (1), *to keep in; to maintain*
3905 lâchats (1), *to press; to distress*
3943 lâphath (1), *to clasp; to turn around*
4013 mibtsâr (2), *fortification; defender*
4581 mâ'ôwz (1), *fortified place; defense*
4672 mâtsâ' (1), *to find or acquire; to occur*
4679 m^etsad (2), *stronghold*
4686 mâtsûwd (7), *net or capture; fastness*
4692 mâtsôwr (1), *distress; fastness*
5253 nâçag (1), *to retreat*
5375 nâsâ' (1), *to lift up*
5381 nâsag (5), *to reach*
5553 çela' (1), *craggy rock; fortress*
5582 çâ'ad (1), *to support*

HOLD (cont.)
6076 'ôphel (1), *tumor; fortress*
6877 ts^erîyach (3), *citadel*
6901 qâbal (1), *to admit; to take*
6965 qûwm (1), *to rise*
8551 tâmak (4), *to obtain, keep fast*
8610 tâphas (7), *to manipulate, i.e. seize*
472 antěchŏmai (2), *to adhere to; to care for*
1949 ěpilambanŏmai (5), *to seize*
2192 ěchō (3), *to have; hold; keep*
2722 katěchō (5), *to hold down fast*
2902 kratěō (19), *to seize*
4601 sigaō (2), *to keep silent*
4623 siōpaō (5), *to be quiet*
5083 tērěō (1), *to keep, guard, obey*
5084 tērēsis (1), *observance; prison*
5392 phimŏō (2), *to restrain to silence*
5438 phulakē (1), *guarding or guard*

HOLDEN
270 'âchaz (1), *to seize, grasp; possess*
2388 châzaq (1), *to fasten upon; to seize*
2814 châshâh (1), *to hush or keep quiet*
3920 lâkad (1), *to catch; to capture*
5564 çâmak (1), *to lean upon; take hold of*
5582 çâ'ad (1), *to support*
6213 'âsâh (2), *to do or make*
8551 tâmak (1), *to obtain, keep fast*
2902 kratěō (2), *to seize*

HOLDEST
270 'âchaz (1), *to seize, grasp; possess*
2790 chârash (2), *to engrave; to plow*
2803 châshab (1), *to weave, fabricate*
8610 tâphas (1), *to manipulate, i.e. seize*
2902 kratěō (1), *to seize*

HOLDETH
270 'âchaz (1), *to seize, grasp; possess*
2388 châzaq (2), *to fasten upon; to seize*
2790 chârash (2), *to engrave; to plow*
7760 sûwm (1), *to put, place*
8551 tâmak (2), *to obtain, keep fast*
2902 kratěō (1), *to seize*

HOLDING
3557 kûwl (1), *to keep in; to measure*
8551 tâmak (1), *to obtain, keep fast*
472 antěchŏmai (1), *to adhere to; to care for*

HOLDS
4013 mibtsâr (11), *fortification; defender*
4581 mâ'ôwz (1), *fortified place; defense*
4679 m^etsad (6), *stronghold*
4686 mâtsûwd (1), *net or capture; fastness*
4694 m^etsûwrâh (1), *rampart, fortification*

HOLE
2356 chôwr (4), *cavity, socket, den*
4718 maqqebeth (1), *hammer*
5357 nâqîyq (1), *cleft, crevice*
6310 peh (6), *mouth; opening*

HOLE'S
6354 pachath (1), *pit*

HOLES
2356 chôwr (4), *cavity, socket, den*
4526 miçgereth (1), *margin; stronghold*
4631 m^e'ârâh (1), *dark cavern*
5344 nâqab (1), *to puncture, perforate*
5357 nâqîyq (2), *cleft, crevice*
5454 phôlěŏs (2), *burrow, den hole*

HOLIER
6942 qâdâsh (1), *to be, make clean*

HOLIEST
39 hagiŏn (3), *sacred thing, place or person*

HOLILY
3743 hŏsiōs (1), *piously*

HOLINESS
6944 qôdesh (30), *sacred place or thing*
38 hagiasmŏs (5), *state of purity*
41 hagiŏtēs (1), *state of holiness*
42 hagiōsunē (3), *quality of holiness*
2150 ěusěběia (1), *piety, religious*
2412 hiěrŏprěpēs (1), *reverent*
3742 hŏsiŏtēs (2), *piety*

HOLLOW
3709 kaph (4), *hollow of hand; paw; sole of foot*
4388 maktêsh (1), *mortar; socket*
5014 nâbab (3), *to be hollow; be foolish*
8168 shô'al (1), *palm of hand; handful*
8258 sh^eqa'rûwrah (1), *depression*

HOLON
2473 Chôlôwn (3), *sandy*

HOLPEN
2220 zᵉrôwa' (1), *arm; foreleg; force, power*
5826 'âzar (3), to *protect or aid*
482 antilambanŏmai (1), to *come to the aid*

HOLY
2623 châçîyd (5), *religiously pious, godly*
4720 miqdâsh (3), *sanctuary of deity*
6918 qâdôwsh (100), *sacred*
6922 qaddîysh (Ch.) (7), *sacred*
6942 qâdâsh (7), to *be, make clean*
6944 qôdesh (297), *sacred place or thing*
37 hagiazō (1), to *purify or consecrate*
39 hagiŏn (3), *sacred thing, place or person*
40 hagiŏs (162), *sacred, holy*
2413 hiĕrŏs (2), *sacred, set apart for God*
3741 hŏsiŏs (6), *hallowed, pious, sacred*

HOLYDAY
2287 châgag (1), to *observe a festival*
1859 hĕŏrtĕ (1), *festival*

HOMAM
1950 Hôwmâm (1), *raging*

HOME
168 'ôhel (1), *tent*
1004 bayith (26), *house; temple; family, tribe*
4725 mâqôwm (3), *general locality, place*
5115 nâvâh (1), to *rest as at home*
7725 shûwb (5), to *turn back; to return*
8432 tâvek (1), *center, middle*
1438 hĕautŏu (1), *himself, herself, itself*
1736 ĕndĕmĕō (1), to *be at home*
2398 idiŏs (2), *private or separate*
3614 ŏikia (1), *abode; family*
3624 ŏikŏs (4), *dwelling; family*
3626 ŏikŏurŏs (1), *domestically inclined*

HOMEBORN
249 'ezrâch (1), *native born*
1004 bayith (1), *house; temple; family, tribe*

HOMER
2563 chômer (10), *clay; dry measure*

HOMERS
2563 chômer (1), *clay; dry measure*

HONEST
2570 kalŏs (5), *good; valuable; virtuous*
4586 sĕmnŏs (1), *honorable, noble*

HONESTLY
2156 ĕuschēmŏnŏs (2), *fittingly, properly*
2573 kalōs (1), *well, i.e. rightly*

HONESTY
4587 sĕmnŏtēs (1), *venerableness*

HONEY
1706 dᵉbash (52), *honey*
3192 mĕli (4), *honey*

HONEYCOMB
3293 ya'ar (1), *honey in the comb*
3295+1706 ya'ărâh (1), *honey in the comb*
5317 nôpheth (4), *honey from the comb*
5317+6688 nôpheth (1), *honey from the comb*
6688+1706 tsûwph (1), *comb of dripping honey*
3193+2781 mĕlissiŏs (1), *honeybee comb*

HONOUR
1921 hâdar (2), to *favor or honor; to be high*
1922 hădar (Ch.) (1), to *magnify, glorify*
1923 hădar (Ch.) (2), *magnificence, glory*
1926 hâdâr (5), *magnificence*
1927 hădârâh (1), *ornament; splendor*
1935 hôwd (6), *grandeur, majesty*
3366 yᵉqâr (12), *wealth; costliness; dignity*
3367 yᵉqâr (Ch.) (2), *glory, honor*
3513 kâbad (22), to *be rich, glorious*
3515 kâbêd (1), *severe, difficult, stupid*
3519 kâbôwd (32), *splendor, wealth*
8597 tiph'ârâh (4), *ornament*
820 atimŏs (2), *dishonoured*
1391 dŏxa (6), *glory; brilliance*
5091 timaō (14), to *revere, honor*
5092 timē (31), *esteem; nobility; money*

HONOURABLE
142 'âdar (1), *magnificent; glorious*
1935 hôwd (2), *grandeur, majesty*
3368 yâqâr (1), *valuable*
3513 kâbad (13), to *be rich, glorious*
3519 kâbôwd (2), *splendor, wealth*
5375+6440 nâsâ' (4), to *lift up*
820 atimŏs (1), *dishonoured*
1741 ĕndŏxŏs (1), *noble; honored*
1784 ĕntimŏs (1), *valued, considered precious*
2158 ĕuschēmōn (3), *decorous, proper; noble*

HONESTLY
5093 timiŏs (1), *costly; honored, esteemed*

HONOURED
1921 hâdar (1), to *favor or honor; to be high*
1922 hădar (Ch.) (1), to *magnify, glorify*
3513 kâbad (5), to *be rich, glorious*
1392 dŏxazō (1), to *render, esteem glorious*
5092 timē (1), *esteem; nobility; money*

HONOUREST
3513 kâbad (1), to *be rich, glorious*

HONOURETH
3513 kâbad (4), to *be rich, glorious*
1392 dŏxazō (1), to *render, esteem glorious*
5091 timaō (3), to *revere, honor, show respect*

HONOURS
5091 timaō (1), to *revere, honor, show respect*

HOODS
6797 tsânîyph (1), *head-dress, turban*

HOOF
6541 parçâh (12), *split hoof*

HOOFS
6536 pâraç (1), to *break in pieces; to split*
6541 parçâh (5), *split hoof*

HOOK
100 'agmôwn (1), *rush; rope of rushes*
2397 châch (2), *ring for the nose or lips*
2443 chakkâh (1), *fish hook*
44 agkistrŏn (1), *fish hook*

HOOKS
2053 vâv (13), *hook*
2397 châch (2), *ring for the nose or lips*
6793 tsinnâh (1), *large shield; piercing cold*
8240 shâphâth (1), *two-pronged hook*

HOPE
982 bâṭach (1), to *trust, be confident or sure*
983 beṭach (1), *safety, security, trust*
986 biṭṭâchôwn (1), *trust*
2342 chûwl (1), to *dance, whirl; to wait; to pervert*
2620 châçâh (1), to *flee to; to confide in*
2976 yâ'ash (3), to *despond, despair*
3176 yâchal (19), to *wait; to be patient, hope*
3689 keçel (3), *loin; back; viscera; trust*
4009 mibṭâch (1), *security; assurance*
4268 machăçeh (2), *shelter; refuge*
4723 miqveh (4), *confidence; collection*

HOPE
5093 timiŏs (1), *costly; honored, esteemed*
7663 sâbar (1), to *expect with hope*
7664 sêber (2), *expectation*
8431 tôwcheleth (6), *hope, expectation*
8615 tiqvâh (23), *cord; expectancy*
1679 ĕlpizō (7), to *expect or confide, hope for*
1680 ĕlpis (51), *hope; confidence*

HOPE'S
1679 ĕlpizō (1), to *expect or confide, hope for*

HOPED
982 bâṭach (1), to *trust, be confident or sure*
3176 yâchal (3), to *wait; to be patient, hope*
7663 sâbar (2), to *expect with hope*
1679 ĕlpizō (4), to *expect or confide, hope for*

HOPETH
1679 ĕlpizō (1), to *expect or confide, hope for*

HOPHNI
2652 Chophnîy (5), *pair of fists*

HOPING
560 apĕlpizō (1), to *fully expect in return*
1679 ĕlpizō (1), to *expect or confide, hope for*

HOR
2023 Hôr (12), *mountain*

HOR-HAGIDGAD
2735 Chôr hag-Gidgâd (2), *hole of the cleft*

HORAM
2036 Hôrâm (1), *high, exalted*

HOREB
2722 Chôrêb (17), *desolate*

HOREM
2765 Chŏrêm (1), *devoted*

HORI
2753 Chôrîy (4), *cave-dweller*

HORIMS
2752 Chôrîy (2), *cave-dweller*

HORITE
2752 Chôrîy (1), *cave-dweller*

HORITES
2752 Chôrîy (3), *cave-dweller*

HORMAH
2767 Chormâh (9), *devoted*

HORN
7161 qeren (28), *horn*
7162 qeren (Ch.) (5), *horn*
2768 kĕras (1), *horn*

HORNET
6880 tsir'âh (2), *wasp*

HORNETS
6880 tsir'âh (1), *wasp*

English

HORNS
3104 yôwbêl (3), *blast of a ram's horn*
7160 qâran (1), to *protrude out horns*
7161 qeren (46), *horn*
7162 qeren (Ch.) (5), *horn*
2768 kĕras (10), *horn*

HORONAIM
2773 Chôrônayim (4), *double cave-town*

HORONITE
2772 Chôrônîy (3), *Choronite*

HORRIBLE
2152 zal'âphâh (1), *glow; famine*
7588 shâ'ôwn (1), *uproar; destruction*
8186 sha'ărûwrâh (4), something *fearful*

HORRIBLY
8175 sâ'ar (1), to *storm; to shiver*, i.e. *fear*
8178 sa'ar (1), *tempest; terror*

HORROR
367 'êymâh (1), *fright*
2152 zal'âphâh (1), *glow; famine*
6427 pallâtsûwth (2), *affright, trembling fear*

HORSE
5483 çûwç (35), *horse*
2462 hippŏs (8), *horse*

HORSEBACK
5483 çûwç (1), *horse*
7392 râkab (2), to *ride*
7392+5483 râkab (2), to *ride*

HORSEHOOFS
6119+5483 'âqêb (1), *track, footprint*

HORSELEACH
5936 'ălûwqâh (1), *leech*

HORSEMAN
6571 pârâsh (1), *horse; chariot driver*
7395 rakkâb (1), *charioteer*

HORSEMEN
6571 pârâsh (56), *horse; chariot driver*
2460 hippĕus (2), member of a *cavalry*
2461 hippikŏn (1), *cavalry force*

HORSES
5483 çûwç (96), *horse*
5484 çûwçâh (1), *mare*
2462 hippŏs (7), *horse*

HORSES'
5483 çûwç (1), *horse*
2462 hippŏs (1), *horse*

HOSAH
2621 Chôçâh (5), *hopeful*

HOSANNA
5614 hōsanna (6), "oh save!"

HOSEA
1954 Hôwshêä' (3), *deliverer*

HOSEN
6361 paṭṭîysh (Ch.) (1), *garment*

HOSHAIAH
1955 Hôwshi'yâh (3), *Jehovah has saved*

HOSHAMA
1953 Hôwshâmâ' (1), *Jehovah has heard*

HOSHEA
1954 Hôwshêä' (11), *deliverer*

HOSPITALITY
5381 philŏnĕxia (1), *hospitableness*
5382 philŏxĕnŏs (3), *hospitable*

HOST
2426 chêyl (2), *rampart, battlement*
2428 chayil (28), *army; wealth; virtue; valor*
4264 machăneh (54), *encampment*
6635 tsâbâ' (100), *army, military host*
3581 xĕnŏs (1), *alien; guest or host*
3830 pandŏchĕus (1), *innkeeper*
4756 stratia (2), *army; celestial luminaries*

HOSTAGES
1121+8594 bên (2), *son, descendant; people*

HOSTS
2428 chayil (1), *army; wealth; virtue; valor*
4264 machăneh (4), *encampment*
6635 tsâbâ' (293), *army, military host*

HOT
228 'ăzâ' (Ch.) (1), to *heat*
784 'êsh (1), *fire*
2525 châm (1), *hot, sweltering*
2527 chôm (4), *heat*
2534 chêmâh (3), *heat; anger; poison*
2552 châmam (3), to *be hot; to be in a rage*
2734 chârâh (10), to *blaze up*
3179 yâcham (2), to *conceive*
7565 resheph (1), *flame*
2200 zĕstŏs (3), *hot*, i.e. *fervent*
2743 kautēriazō (1), to *brand or cauterize*

HOTHAM
2369 Chôwthâm (1), *seal*

HOTHAN
2369 Chôwthâm (1), *seal*

HOTHIR
1956 Hôwthîyr (2), *he has caused to remain*

HOTLY
1814 dâlaq (1), to *flame; to pursue*

HOTTEST
2389 châzâq (1), *strong; severe, hard, violent*

HOUGH
6131 'âqar (1), to *pluck up roots; to hamstring*

HOUGHED
6131 'âqar (3), to *pluck up roots; to hamstring*

HOUR
8160 shâ'âh (Ch.) (5), *immediately*
734 Artĕmas (1), *gift of Artemis*
2256 hēmiōriŏn (1), *half-hour*
5610 hōra (85), *hour*, i.e. *a unit of time*

HOURS
5610 hōra (3), *hour*, i.e. *a unit of time*

HOUSE
1004 bayith (1745), *house; temple; family*
1005 bayith (Ch.) (41), *house; temple; family*
1008 Bêyth-'Êl (5), *house of God*
1035 Bêyth Lechem (1), *house of bread*
5854 'Aṭrôwth Bêyth Yôw'âb (1), *crowns of* (the) *house of Joäb*
3609 ŏikĕiŏs (1), *of the household*
3613 ŏikētēriŏn (1), *residence, home*
3614 ŏikia (84), *abode; family*
3616 ŏikŏdĕspŏtĕō (1), to *be the head of a family*
3617 ŏikŏdĕspŏtēs (7), *head of a family*
3624 ŏikŏs (96), *dwelling; family*
3832 panŏiki (1), *with the whole family*

HOUSEHOLD
1004 bayith (47), *house; temple; family, tribe*
5657 'ăbuddâh (1), *service*
2322 thĕrapĕia (2), *cure, healing; domestics*
3609 ŏikĕiŏs (2), *of the household*
3610 ŏikĕtēs (1), menial *domestic servant*
3614 ŏikia (1), *abode; family*
3615 ŏikiakŏs (2), *relatives*
3624 ŏikŏs (3), *dwelling; family*

HOUSEHOLDER
3617 ŏikŏdĕspŏtēs (4), *head of a family*

HOUSEHOLDS
1004 bayith (7), *house; temple; family, tribe*

HOUSES
490 'almânâh (1), *widow*
1004 bayith (116), *house; temple; family, tribe*
1005 bayith (Ch.) (2), *house; temple; family*
4999 nâ'âh (1), *home, dwelling; pasture*

3614 ŏikia (8), *abode; family*
3624 ŏikŏs (5), *dwelling; family*

HOUSETOP
1406 gâg (2), *roof; top*
1430 dōma (5), *roof, housetop*

HOUSETOPS
1406 gâg (5), *roof; top*
1430 dōma (2), *roof, housetop*

HOW
335 'ay (1), *where?*
346 'ayêh (2), *where?*
349 'êyk (75), *how?* or *how!; where?*
434 'ĕlûwl (1), good for *nothing*
637 'aph (18), *also or yea; though*
834 'ăsher (26), *how, because, in order that*
1963 hêyk (2), *how?*
3588 kîy (11), *for, that because*
4069 maddûwa' (1), *why?, what?*
4100 mâh (59), *how?, how!; what, whatever*
4101 mâh (Ch.) (3), *how?, how!; what, whatever*
5704 'ad (47), *as far (long) as; during*
2193 hĕōs (6), *until*
2245 hēlikŏs (1), *how much, how great*
2531 kathōs (1), *just or inasmuch as, that*
3386 mētigĕ (1), *not to say* (*the rather still*)
3704 hŏpōs (4), *in the manner that*
3745 hŏsŏs (7), *as much as*
3754 hŏti (14), *that; because; since*
4012 pĕri (1), *about; around*
4080 pēlikŏs (2), *how much, how great*
4212 pŏsakis (2), *how many times*
4214 pŏsŏs (26), *how much?; how much!*
4219 pŏtĕ (1), *at what time?*
4459 pōs (96), *in what way?; how?; how much!*
4559 sarkikŏs (2), *pertaining to flesh*
5101 tis (11), *who?, which? or what?*
5613 hōs (19), *which, how*, i.e. *in that manner*

HOWBEIT
199 'ûwlâm (1), *however or on the contrary*
389 'ak (1), *surely; only, however*
657 'epheç (1), *end; no further*
3651 kên (1), *just; right, correct*
7535 raq (1), *merely; although*
235 alla (8), *but, yet, except, instead*

1161 dĕ (1), *but, yet*
3305 mĕntŏi (1), *however*

HOWL
3213 yâlal (27), to *howl, wail, yell*
3649 ŏlŏluzŏ (1), to *howl,* i.e. *shriek or wail*

HOWLED
3213 yâlal (1), to *howl, wail, yell*

HOWLING
3213 yâlal (5), to *howl, wail, yell*
3214 yᵉlêl (1), *howl, wail*

HOWLINGS
3213 yâlal (1), to *howl, wail, yell*

HOWSOEVER
1961+4101 hâyâh (1), to *exist,* i.e. *be or become*
3605+834 kôl (1), *all, any or every*
7535 raq (1), *merely; although*

HUGE
7230 rôb (1), *abundance*

HUKKOK
2712 Chuqqôq (1), *appointed*

HUKOK
2712 Chuqqôq (1), *appointed*

HUL
2343 Chûwl (2), *circle*

HULDAH
2468 Chuldâh (2), *weasel*

HUMBLE
3665 kâna' (2), to *humiliate, vanquish, subdue*
6031 'ânâh (4), to *afflict, be afflicted*
6041 'ânîy (5), *depressed*
7511 râphaç (1), to *trample; to prostrate*
7807+5869 shach (1), *sunk,* i.e. *downcast*
8213 shâphêl (2), to *humiliate*
8217 shâphâl (3), *depressed, low*
5011 tapĕinŏs (2), *humiliated, lowly*
5013 tapĕinŏŏ (5), to *depress; to humiliate*

HUMBLED
1792 dâkâ' (1), to be *contrite, be humbled*
3665 kâna' (13), to *humiliate, vanquish*
6031 'ânâh (7), to *afflict, be afflicted*
7743 shûwach (1), to *sink*
8213 shâphêl (4), to *humiliate*
8214 shᵉphal (Ch.) (1), to *humiliate*
5013 tapĕinŏŏ (1), to *depress; to humiliate*

HUMBLEDST
3665 kâna' (1), to *humiliate, vanquish*

HUMBLENESS
5012 tapĕinŏphrŏsunē (1), *modesty, humility*

HUMBLETH
3665 kâna' (2), to *humiliate, vanquish*
7817 shâchach (1), to *sink or depress*
8213 shâphêl (2), to *humiliate*
5013 tapĕinŏŏ (2), to *depress; to humiliate*

HUMBLY
6800 tsâna' (1), to *humiliate*
7812 shâchâh (1), to *prostrate* in homage

HUMILIATION
5014 tapĕinōsis (1), *humbleness, lowliness*

HUMILITY
6038 'ănâvâh (3), *condescension*
5012 tapĕinŏphrŏsunē (4), *modesty, humility*

HUMTAH
2457 chel'âh (1), *rust*

HUNDRED
520 'ammâh (1), *cubit*
3967 mê'âh (545), *hundred*
3969 mᵉ'âh (Ch.) (7), *hundred*
1250 diakŏsiŏi (8), *two hundred*
1540 hĕkatŏn (14), *hundred*
1541 hĕkatŏntaĕtēs (1), *centenarian*
3461 murias (1), *ten-thousand*
4001 pĕntakŏsiŏi (2), *five hundred*
5071 tĕtrakŏsiŏi (4), *four hundred*
5145 triakŏsiŏi (2), *three hundred*
5516 chi xi stigma (2), 666

HUNDREDFOLD
3967+8180 mê'âh (1), *hundred*
1540 hĕkatŏn (2), *hundred*
1542 hĕkatŏntaplasiōn (3), *hundred times*

HUNDREDS
3967 mê'âh (27), *hundred*
1540 hĕkatŏn (1), *hundred*

HUNDREDTH
3967 mê'âh (3), *hundred*

HUNGER
7456 râ'êb (5), to *hunger*
7457 râ'êb (8), *hungry*
3042 limŏs (3), *scarcity, famine*
3983 pĕinaō (8), to *famish; to crave*

HUNGERBITTEN
7457 râ'êb (1), *hungry*

HUNGERED
3983 pĕinaō (2), to *famish; to crave*

HUNGRED
3983 pĕinaō (9), to *famish; to crave*

HUNGRY
7456 râ'êb (25), to *hunger*
3983 pĕinaō (4), to *famish; to crave*
4361 prŏspĕinŏs (1), *intensely hungry*

HUNT
6679 tsûwd (11), to *lie in* wait; to *catch*
7291 râdaph (1), to *run after* with hostility

HUNTED
4686 mâtsûwd (1), *net or capture; fastness*

HUNTER
6718 tsayid (4), *hunting game; lunch, food*

HUNTERS
6719 tsayâd (1), *huntsman*

HUNTEST
6658 tsâdâh (1), to *desolate*
6679 tsûwd (1), to *lie in* wait; to *catch*

HUNTETH
6679 tsûwd (1), to *lie in* wait; to *catch*

HUNTING
6718 tsayid (2), *hunting game; lunch, food*

HUPHAM
2349 Chûwphâm (1), *protection*

HUPHAMITES
2350 Chûwphâmîy (1), *Chuphamite*

HUPPAH
2647 Chuppâh (1), *canopy*

HUPPIM
2650 Chuppîym (3), *canopies*

HUR
2354 Chûwr (16), *cell* of a prison *or white linen*

HURAI
2360 Chûwray (1), *linen*-worker

HURAM
2361 Chûwrâm (6), *noble*
2438 Chîyrâm (6), *noble*

HURI
2359 Chûwrîy (1), *linen*-worker

HURL
7993 shâlak (1), to *throw out, down or away*

HURLETH
8175 sâ'ar (1), to *storm;* to *shiver,* i.e. *fear*

HURT
1697 dâbâr (1), *word; matter; thing*
2248 chăbûwlâh (Ch.) (1), *crime, wrong*
2250 chabbûwrâh (1), *weal, bruise*
2255 chăbal (Ch.) (1), to *ruin, destroy*
2257 chăbal (Ch.) (2), *harm, wound*
3637 kâlam (2), to *taunt or insult*
5062 nâgaph (2), to *inflict a disease*
5142 nᵉzaq (Ch.) (1), to *suffer, inflict loss*
6031 'ânâh (1), to *afflict, be afflicted*
6087 'âtsab (1), to *worry, have pain or anger*
6485 pâqad (1), to *visit, care for, count*
7451 ra' (20), *bad; evil*
7489 râ'a' (7), to *break to pieces*
7665 shâbar (3), to *burst*
7667 sheber (4), *fracture; ruin*
91 adikĕŏ (10), to *do wrong*
984 blaptō (2), to *hinder,* i.e. to *injure*
2559 kakŏŏ (1), to *injure; to oppress; to embitter*
5196 hubris (1), *insult; injury*

HURTFUL
5142 nᵉzaq (Ch.) (1), to *suffer, inflict loss*
7451 ra' (1), *bad; evil*
983 blabĕrŏs (1), *injurious, harmful*

HURTING
7489 râ'a' (1), to *break to pieces*

HUSBAND
376 'îysh (66), *man; male; someone*
1167 ba'al (13), *master; husband; owner; citizen*
2860 châthân (2), *bridegroom*
435 anēr (38), *man; male*
5220 hupandrŏs (1), *married* woman

HUSBAND'S
376 'îysh (2), *man; male; someone*
2992 yâbam (2), to *marry* a dead brother's widow
2993 yâbâm (2), *husband's brother*

HUSBANDMAN
376+127 'îysh (1), *man; male; someone*
406 'ikkâr (2), *farmer*
5647 'âbad (1), to *do, work, serve*
1092 gĕōrgŏs (3), *farmer; tenant farmer*

HUSBANDMEN
406 'ikkâr (3), *farmer*
1461 gûwb (1), to *dig*
3009 yâgab (1), to *dig or plow*
1092 gĕōrgŏs (16), *farmer; tenant farmer*

HUSBANDRY
127 'ădâmâh (1), *soil; land*
1091 gĕōrgiŏn (1), *cultivate,* i.e. *farm*

HUSBANDS
376 'îysh (1), *man; male*

English

582 'ĕnôwsh (3), *man;
person, human*
1167 ba'al (2), *master;
husband; owner; citizen*
435 anêr (12), *man; male*
5362 philandrŏs (1),
affectionate as a wife
to her *husband*

HUSHAH
2364 Chûwshâh (1), *haste*

HUSHAI
2365 Chûwshay (14),
hasty

HUSHAM
2367 Chûwshâm (4),
hastily

HUSHATHITE
2843 Chûshâthîy (5),
Chushathite

HUSHIM
2366 Chûwshîym (4),
those who *hasten*

HUSK
2085 zâg (1), grape *skin*
6861 tsiqlôn (1), tied up
sack

HUSKS
2769 kĕratiŏn (1), *pod*

HUZ
5780 'Ûwts (1),
consultation

HUZZAB
5324 nâtsab (1), to *station*

HYMENAEUS
5211 Humĕnaiŏs (2), one
dedicated to the god of
weddings

HYMN
5214 humnĕŏ (1), to
celebrate God in song

HYMNS
5215 humnŏs (2), *hymn*
or religious *ode*

HYPOCRISIES
5272 hupŏkrisis (1),
deceit, hypocrisy

HYPOCRISY
2612 chôneph (1), moral
filth, i.e. *wickedness*
505 anupŏkritŏs (1),
sincere, genuine
5272 hupŏkrisis (4),
deceit, hypocrisy

HYPOCRITE
120+2611 'âdâm (1),
human being; mankind
2611 chânêph (6), *soiled*
(i.e. with sin), *impious*
5273 hupŏkritēs (3),
dissembler, hypocrite

HYPOCRITE'S
2611 chânêph (1), *soiled*
(i.e. with sin), *impious*

HYPOCRITES
120+2611 'âdâm (1),
human being; mankind
2611 chânêph (2), *soiled*
(i.e. with sin), *impious*
5273 hupŏkritēs (17),
dissembler, hypocrite

HYPOCRITICAL
2611 chânêph (2), *soiled*
(i.e. with sin), *impious*

HYSSOP
231 'êzôwb (10), *hyssop*
5301 hussōpŏs (2),
hyssop plant

I-CHABOD
350 Îy-kâbôwd (1),
inglorious

I-CHABOD'S
350 Îy-kâbôwd (1),
inglorious

IBHAR
2984 Yibchar (3), *choice*

IBLEAM
2991 Yibleʻâm (3),
devouring people

IBNEIAH
2997 Yibneyâh (1), *built
of Jehovah*

IBNIJAH
2998 Yibnîyâh (1),
building of Jehovah

IBRI
5681 'Ibrîy (1), *Eberite*
(i.e. *Hebrew*)

IBZAN
78 'Ibtsân (2), *splendid*

ICE
7140 qerach (3), *ice; hail;*
rock *crystal*

ICONIUM
2430 Ikŏniŏn (6),
image-like

IDALAH
3030 Yidʻălâh (1), *Jidalah*

IDBASH
3031 Yidbâsh (1),
honeyed

IDDO
112 'Iddôw (2), *Iddo*
3035 Yiddôw (1), *praised*
3260 Yeʻdîy (1), *appointed*
5714 'Iddôw (10), *timely*

IDLE
7423 remîyâh (1),
remissness; treachery
7504 râpheh (2), *slack*
692 argŏs (6), *lazy;
useless*
3026 lērŏs (1), *twaddle*,
i.e. an *incredible* story

IDLENESS
6104 'atslûwth (1),
indolence
8220 shiphlûwth (1),
remissness, idleness
8252 shâqaṭ (1), to *repose*

IDOL
205 'âven (1), *trouble,
vanity, wickedness*
457 'ĕlîyl (1), *vain idol*
4656 miphletseth (4),
terror idol
5566 çemel (2), *likeness*
6089 'etseb (1), earthen
vessel; painful *toil*
6090 'ôtseb (1),
fashioned *idol; pain*
1494 ĕidōlŏthuton (1),
idolatrous offering
1497 ĕidōlŏn (4), *idol*, or
the *worship* of such

IDOL'S
1493 ĕidōlĕiŏn (1), *idol
temple*

IDOLATER
1496 ĕidōlŏlatrēs (2),
image-worshipper

IDOLATERS
1496 ĕidōlŏlatrēs (5),
image-worshipper

IDOLATRIES
1495 ĕidōlŏlatrĕia (1),
image-worship

IDOLATROUS
3649 kâmâr (1), pagan
priest

IDOLATRY
8655 terâphîym (1),
healer
1495 ĕidōlŏlatrĕia (3),
image-worship
2712 katĕidōlŏs (1),
utterly idolatrous

IDOLS
367 'êymâh (1), *fright*
410 'êl (1), *mighty;* the
Almighty
457 'ĕlîyl (16), *vain idol*
1544 gillûwl (47), *idol*
2553 chammân (1),
sun-pillar
6091 'âtsâb (16), *image,
idol*
6736 tsîyr (1), *carved*
idolatrous *image*
8251 shiqqûwts (1),
disgusting; idol
8655 teráphîym (1),
healer
1494 ĕidōlŏthutŏn (9),
idolatrous offering
1497 ĕidōlŏn (7), *idol,* or
the *worship* of such

IDUMAEA
2401 Idŏumaia (1),
Idumæa, i.e. *Edom*

IDUMEA
123 'Ĕdôm (4), *red*

IF
176 'ôw (3), *or, whether*
194 'ûwlay (9), *if not*
432 'illûw (1), *if*
518 'îm (557), *whether?; if*
834 'ăsher (19), *who,
which, what, that*
2005 hên (3), *lo!; if!*
2006 hên (Ch.) (11), *lo;
whether, but, if*
3588 kîy (159), *for, that
because*
3808 lô' (1), *no, not*
3863 lûw' (7), *if; would
that!*
3883 lûwl (1), *spiral* step
3884 lûwlê' (2), *if not*
6112 'Êtsen (1), *spear*
148 aischrŏlŏgia (3), *vile
conversation*
1437 ĕan (216), *in case
that, provided*
1477 hĕdraiōma (5),
basis, foundation
1487 ĕi (305), *if, whether*
1489 ĕigĕ (5), *if indeed*
1490 ĕi dĕ mē(gĕ) (4), *but
if not*
1499 ĕi kai (6), *if also*

1512 ĕi pĕr (4), *if perhaps*
1513 ĕi pōs (4), *if
somehow*
1535 ĕitĕ (1), *if too*
2579 kan (5), *and if*
3379 mēpŏtĕ (1), *not
ever; if,* or *lest ever*

IGAL
3008 Yig'âl (2), *avenger*

IGDALIAH
3012 Yigdalyâhûw (1),
magnified of Jehovah

IGEAL
3008 Yig'âl (1), *avenger*

IGNOMINY
7036 qâlôwn (1), *disgrace*

IGNORANCE
7684 sheĝâgâh (12),
mistake, transgression
7686 shâgâh (1), to
transgress by mistake
52 agnŏia (4), *ignorance*
56 agnōsia (1), state of
ignorance

IGNORANT
3808+3045 lô' (3), no, *not
know; not understand*
50 agnŏĕō (10), to *not
know; not understand*
2399 idiōtēs (1), *not
initiated; untrained*
2990 lanthanō (2), to *lie
hid; unwittingly*

IGNORANTLY
1097+1847 belîy (1), *not
yet; lacking;*
7683 shâgag (1), to *sin
through oversight*
50 agnŏĕō (2), to *not
know; not understand*

IIM
5864 'Iyîym (2), *ruins*

IJE-ABARIM
5863 'Iyêy hâ-ʻĂbârîym
(2), *ruins of the passers*

IJON
5859 'Iyôwn (3), *ruin*

IKKESH
6142 'Iqqêsh (3), *perverse*

ILAI
5866 'Îylay (1), *elevated*

ILL
3415 yâra' (2), to *fear*
6709 tsachănâh (1),
stench
7451 ra' (8), *bad; evil*
7489 râ'a' (3), to *be good
for nothing*
2556 kakŏs (1), *bad, evil,
wrong*

ILLUMINATED
5461 phōtizō (1), to *shine*
or to *brighten* up

ILLYRICUM
2437 Illurikŏn (1),
Illyricum

IMAGE
4676 matstsêbâh (3),
column or *stone*
4906 maskîyth (1),
carved figure
5566 çemel (2), *likeness*
6459 peçel (2), *idol*
6676 tsavva'r (Ch.) (1),
back of the *neck*

6754 tselem (6), *phantom; idol*
6755 tselem (Ch.) (16), idolatrous *figure*
6816 tsa'tsûa' (1), *sculpture* work
8544 tᵉmûwnâh (1), something *fashioned*
8655 tᵉrâphîym (2), *healer*
1504 ĕikōn (22), likeness
5481 charaktēr (1), exact copy or representation

IMAGE'S
6755 tselem (Ch.) (1), idolatrous *figure*

IMAGERY
4906 maskîyth (1), carved *figure*

IMAGES
457 'ĕlîyl (1), *vain idol*
1544 gillûwl (1), *idol*
2553 chammân (6), *sun*-pillar
4676 matstsêbâh (14), *column* or *stone*
6091 'âtsâb (1), *image, idol*
6456 pᵉçîyl (2), *idol*
6754 tselem (9), *phantom; idol*
8655 tᵉrâphîym (5), *healer*

IMAGINATION
3336 yêtser (4), *form*
8307 shᵉrîyrûwth (9), *obstinacy*
1271 dianŏia (1), mind or thought

IMAGINATIONS
3336 yêtser (1), *form*
4284 machăshâbâh (3), *contrivance; plan*
1261 dialŏgismŏs (1), consideration; debate
3053 lŏgismŏs (1), reasoning; conscience

IMAGINE
1897 hâgâh (2), to *murmur, ponder*
2050 hâthath (1), to *assail, verbally attack*
2554 châmaç (1), to *be violent; to maltreat*
2790 chârash (1), to *be silent; to be deaf*
2803 châshab (5), to *plot; to think, regard*
3191 mĕlĕtaō (1), to *plot, think about*

IMAGINED
2161 zâmam (1), to *plan*
2803 châshab (2), to *plot; to think, regard*

IMAGINETH
2803 châshab (1), to *plot; to think, regard*

IMLA
3229 Yimlâ' (2), *full*

IMLAH
3229 Yimlâ' (2), *full*

IMMANUEL
6005 'Immânûw'êl (2), *with us* (is) *God*

IMMEDIATELY
1824 ĕxautēs (3), instantly, at once
2112 ĕuthĕōs (35), at once or soon
2117 ĕuthus (3), at once, immediately
3916 parachrēma (13), instantly, immediately

IMMER
564 'Immêr (10), *talkative*

IMMORTAL
862 aphthartŏs (1), undecaying, immortal

IMMORTALITY
110 athanasia (3), deathlessness
861 aphtharsia (2), unending existence

IMMUTABILITY
276 amĕtathĕtŏs (1), unchangeable

IMMUTABLE
276 amĕtathĕtŏs (1), unchangeable

IMNA
3234 Yimnâ' (1), *he will restrain*

IMNAH
3232 Yimnâh (2), *prosperity*

IMPART
3330 mĕtadidōmi (2), to share, distribute

IMPARTED
2505 châlaq (1), to *be smooth; be slippery*
3330 mĕtadidōmi (1), to share, distribute

IMPEDIMENT
3424 mŏgilalŏs (1), hardly talking

IMPENITENT
279 amĕtanŏētŏs (1), unrepentant

IMPERIOUS
7986 shalleṭeth (1), *dominant woman*

IMPLACABLE
786 aspŏndŏs (1), not reconcilable

IMPLEAD
1458 ĕgkalĕō (1), to charge, criminate

IMPORTUNITY
335 anaidĕia (1), importunity, boldness

IMPOSE
7412 rᵉmâh (Ch.) (1), to *throw; to set; to assess*

IMPOSED
1942 ĕpikaluma (1), pretext, covering

IMPOSSIBLE
101 adunatĕō (2), to be impossible
102 adunatŏs (6), weak; impossible
418 anĕndĕktŏs (1), impossible

IMPOTENT
102 adunatŏs (1), weak; impossible
770 asthĕnĕō (2), to be feeble
772 asthĕnēs (1), strengthless, weak

IMPOVERISH
7567 râshash (1), to *demolish*

IMPOVERISHED
1809 dâlal (1), to *be feeble; to be oppressed*
5533 çâkan (1), to *grow, make poor*
7567 râshash (1), to *demolish*

IMPRISONED
5439 phulakizō (1), to incarcerate, imprison

IMPRISONMENT
613 'ĕçûwr (Ch.) (1), *manacles, chains*
5438 phulakē (1), watch; prison; haunt

IMPRISONMENTS
5438 phulakē (1), watch; prison; haunt

IMPUDENT
2389+4696 châzâq (1), *severe, hard, violent*
5810 'âzaz (1), to *be stout; be bold*
7186+6440 qâsheh (1), *severe*

IMPUTE
2803 châshab (1), to *regard; to compute*
7760 sûwm (1), to *put, place*
3049 lŏgizŏmai (1), to credit; to think, regard

IMPUTED
2803 châshab (2), to *think, regard; compute*
1677 ĕllŏgĕō (1), to *charge to one's account*
3049 lŏgizŏmai (5), to credit; to think, regard

IMPUTETH
2803 châshab (1), to *think, regard; compute*
3049 lŏgizŏmai (1), to credit; to think, regard

IMPUTING
3049 lŏgizŏmai (1), to credit; to think, regard

IMRAH
3236 Yimrâh (1), *interchange*

IMRI
556 'amtsâh (2), *strength, force*

INASMUCH
1115 biltîy (1), except, without, unless, besides
3588 kîy (1), for, that because
2526 kathŏ (1), precisely as, in proportion as

INCENSE
3828 lᵉbôwnâh (6), *frankincense*

IMPOVERISH — (column right)

6999 qâṭar (58), to *turn into fragrance* by fire
7002 qiṭṭêr (1), *perfume*
7004 qᵉṭôreth (57), *fumigation*
2368 thumiama (4), incense offering
2370 thumiaō (1), to offer aromatic fumes

INCENSED
2734 chârâh (2), to *blaze*

INCLINE
5186 nâṭâh (15), to *stretch* or *spread out*
7181 qâshab (1), to *prick up* the ears

INCLINED
5186 nâṭâh (13), to *stretch* or *spread out*

INCLINETH
7743 shûwach (1), to *sink*

INCLOSE
6696 tsûwr (1), to *cramp,* i.e. *confine; to harass*

INCLOSED
1443 gâdar (1), to *build a stone wall*
3803 kâthar (1), to *enclose, besiege; to wait*
4142 mûwçabbâh (2), *backside; fold*
5274 nâ'al (1), to *fasten up, lock*
5362 nâqaph (1), to *surround* or *circulate*
5462 çâgar (1), to *shut up; to surrender*
4788 suglĕiŏ (1), to net fish; to lock up persons

INCLOSINGS
4396 millû'âh (2), *setting*

INCONTINENCY
192 akrasia (1), lack of control of self

INCONTINENT
193 akratēs (1), without self-control

INCORRUPTIBLE
862 aphthartŏs (4), undecaying, immortal

INCORRUPTION
861 aphtharsia (4), unending existence

INCREASE
2981 yᵉbûwl (10), *produce, crop; harvest*
3254 yâçaph (6), to *add* or *augment*
4768 marbîyth (3), *interest on money*
5107 nûwb (1), to (*make*) *flourish; to utter*
6555 pârats (1), to *break out*
7235 râbâh (18), to *increase*
7239 ribbôw (1), *myriad, indefinite large number*
7685 sâgâh (2), to *enlarge, be prosperous*
7698 sheger (4), *what comes forth*
8393 tᵉbûw'âh (23), *income,* i.e. *produce*

8570 t^enûwbâh (2), *crop, produce*
8635 tarbûwth (6), *progeny, brood*
837 auxanō (4), *to grow, i.e. enlarge*
838 auxēsis (2), *growth, increase*
4052 pĕrissĕuō (1), *to superabound*
4121 plĕŏnazō (1), *to increase; superabound*
4298 prŏkŏptō (1), *to go ahead, advance*
4369 prŏstithēmi (1), *to lay beside, annex*

INCREASED
1431 gâdal (1), *to be great, make great*
3254 yâçaph (5), *to add or augment*
5927 'âlâh (3), *to ascend, be high, mount*
6105 'âtsam (4), *to be, make numerous*
6509 pârâh (3), *to bear fruit*
6555 pârats (4), *to break out*
7227 rab (2), *great*
7230 rôb (2), *abundance*
7231 râbab (3), *to increase; to multiply*
7235 râbâh (15), *to increase*
8317 shârats (1), *to swarm, or abound*
837 auxanō (3), *to grow, i.e. enlarge*
1743 ĕndunamŏō (1), *to empower, strengthen*
4052 pĕrissĕuō (1), *to superabound*
4147 plŏutĕō (1), *to be, become wealthy*
4298 prŏkŏptō (1), *to go ahead, advance*

INCREASEST
7235 râbâh (1), *to increase*

INCREASETH
553 'âmats (1), *to be strong; be courageous*
1342 gâ'âh (1), *to rise; to grow tall; be majestic*
3254 yâçaph (4), *to add or augment*
5927 'âlâh (1), *to ascend, be high, mount*
7235 râbâh (5), *to increase*
7679 sâgâ' (1), *to laud, extol*
837 auxanō (1), *to grow, i.e. enlarge*

INCREASING
837 auxanō (1), *to grow, i.e. enlarge*

INCREDIBLE
571 apistŏs (1), *without faith; incredible*

INCURABLE
369+4832 'ayin (1), *there is no, i.e., not exist*
605 'ânash (5), *to be frail, feeble*

INDEBTED
3784 ŏphĕilō (1), *to owe; to be under obligation*

INDEED
61 'ăbâl (2), *truly, surely; yet, but*
389 'ak (1), *surely; only, however*
546 'omnâh (2), *surely*
551 'omnâm (2), *verily, indeed, truly*
552 'umnâm (3), *verily, indeed, truly*
1571 gam (1), *also; even; yea; though*
230 alēthōs (6), *truly, surely*
235 alla (1), *but, yet, except, instead*
1063 gar (2), *for, indeed, but, because*
2532 kai (2), *and; or; even; also*
3303 mĕn (22), *indeed*
3689 ŏntōs (6), *really, certainly*

INDIA
1912 Hôdûw (2), *India*

INDIGNATION
2194 zâ'am (4), *to be enraged*
2195 za'am (20), *fury, anger*
2197 za'aph (2), *anger, rage*
2534 chêmâh (1), *heat; anger; poison*
3707 kâ'aç (1), *to grieve, rage, be indignant*
3708 ka'aç (1), *vexation, grief*
7110 qetseph (3), *rage or strife*
23 aganaktĕō (4), *to be indignant*
24 aganaktēsis (1), *indignation*
2205 zēlŏs (2), *zeal, ardor; jealousy, malice*
2372 thumŏs (1), *passion, anger*
3709 ŏrgē (1), *ire; punishment*

INDITING
7370 râchash (1), *to gush*

INDUSTRIOUS
6213+4399 'âsâh (1), *to do or make*

INEXCUSABLE
379 anapŏlŏgētŏs (1), *without excuse*

INFAMOUS
2931+8034 țâmê' (1), *foul; ceremonially impure*

INFAMY
1681 dibbâh (2), *slander, bad report*

INFANT
5764 'ûwl (1), *nursing babe*
5768 'ôwlêl (1), *suckling child*

INFANTS
5768 'ôwlêl (2), *suckling child*
1025 brĕphŏs (1), *infant*

INFERIOR
772 'ăra' (Ch.) (1), *earth, ground, land; inferior*
5307 nâphal (2), *to fall*
2274 hēttaō (1), *to rate lower, be inferior*

INFIDEL
571 apistŏs (2), *without faith; untrustworthy*

INFINITE
369+4557 'ayin (1), *there is no, i.e., not exist*
369+7093 'ayin (2), *there is no, i.e., not exist*

INFIRMITIES
769 asthĕnĕia (10), *feebleness; malady*
771 asthĕnēma (1), *failing, weakness*
3554 nŏsŏs (1), *malady, disease*

INFIRMITY
1738 dâvâh (1), *to be in menstruation cycle*
2470 châlâh (1), *to be weak, sick, afflicted*
4245 machăleh (1), *sickness*
769 asthĕnĕia (7), *feebleness; malady*

INFLAME
1814 dâlaq (1), *to flame; to pursue*

INFLAMMATION
1816 dalleqeth (1), *burning fever*
6867 tsârebeth (1), *conflagration*

INFLUENCES
4575 ma'ădannâh (1), *bond, i.e. group*

INFOLDING
3947 lâqach (1), *to take*

INFORM
3384 yârâh (1), *to point; to teach*

INFORMED
995 bîyn (1), *to understand; discern*
1718 ĕmphanizō (3), *to show forth*
2727 katēchĕō (2), *to indoctrinate*

INGATHERING
614 'âçîyph (2), *harvest, gathering in of crops*

INHABIT
3427 yâshab (8), *to dwell, to remain; to settle*
7931 shâkan (2), *to reside*

INHABITANT
1481 gûwr (1), *to sojourn, live as an alien*
3427 yâshab (31), *to dwell, to remain*
7934 shâkên (1), *resident; fellow-citizen*

INHABITANTS
1753 dûwr (Ch.) (2), *to reside, live in*
3427 yâshab (190), *to dwell, to remain*
7934 shâkên (2), *resident; fellow-citizen*

8453 tôwshâb (1), *temporary dweller*
2730 katŏikĕō (1), *to reside, live in*

INHABITED
1509 g^ezêrâh (1), *desert, unfertile place*
3427 yâshab (29), *to dwell, to remain*
4186 môwshâb (1), *seat; site; abode*
7931 shâkan (1), *to reside*

INHABITERS
2730 katŏikĕō (2), *to reside, live in*

INHABITEST
3427 yâshab (1), *to dwell, to remain; to settle*

INHABITETH
3427 yâshab (1), *to dwell, to remain; to settle*
7931 shâkan (1), *to reside*

INHABITING
6728 tsîyîy (1), *desert-dweller; wild beast*

INHERIT
3423 yârash (21), *to inherit; to impoverish*
5157 nâchal (25), *to inherit*
5159 nachălâh (2), *occupancy*
2816 klērŏnŏmĕō (14), *to be an heir to, inherit*

INHERITANCE
2490 châlal (1), *to profane, defile*
2506 chêleq (1), *allotment*
3423 yârash (1), *to inherit; to impoverish*
3425 y^erushâh (2), *conquest*
4181 môwrâshâh (2), *possession*
5157 nâchal (18), *to inherit*
5159 nachălâh (189), *occupancy*
2817 klērŏnŏmia (14), *inherited possession*
2819 klērŏs (2), *lot, portion*
2820 klērŏō (2), *to allot*

INHERITANCES
5159 nachălâh (1), *occupancy*

INHERITED
3423 yârash (2), *to inherit; to impoverish*
5157 nâchal (3), *to inherit*
2816 klērŏnŏmĕō (1), *to be an heir to, inherit*

INHERITETH
5157 nâchal (1), *to inherit*

INHERITOR
3423 yârash (1), *to inherit; to impoverish*

INIQUITIES
1647+5771 Gêr^eshôm (1), *refugee*
5758 'ivyâ' (Ch.) (1), *perverseness*
5766 'evel (1), moral *evil*
5771 'âvôn (47), *evil*

92 adikēma (1), *wrong done*
458 anŏmia (3), *violation of law, wickedness*
4189 pŏnēria (1), *malice, evil, wickedness*

INIQUITY
205 'âven (47), *trouble, vanity, wickedness*
1942 havvâh (1), *desire; craving*
5753 'âvâh (4), to *be crooked*
5766 'evel (35), moral *evil*
5771 'âvôn (170), moral *evil*
5932 'alvâh (1), *moral perverseness*
5999 'âmâl (1), *wearing effort; worry*
7562 resha' (1), moral *wrong*
93 adikia (6), *wrongfulness*
458 anŏmia (8), *violation of law, wickedness*
3892 paranŏmia (1), *transgression*

INJURED
91 adikĕŏ (1), to *do wrong*

INJURIOUS
5197 hubristēs (1), *maltreater, violent*

INJUSTICE
2555 châmâç (1), *violence; malice*

INK
1773 dᵉyôw (1), *ink*
3188 mĕlan (3), *black ink*

INKHORN
7083 qeçeth (3), *ink-stand*

INN
4411 mâlôwn (3), *lodgment for night*
2646 kataluma (1), *lodging-place*
3829 pandŏchĕiŏn (1), public *lodging*-place

INNER
2315 cheder (4), *apartment, chamber*
6441 pᵉnîymâh (1), *indoors, inside*
6442 pᵉnîymîy (30), *interior, inner*
2080 ĕsŏ (1), *inside, inner, in*
2082 ĕsŏtĕrŏs (1), *interior, inner*

INNERMOST
2315 cheder (2), *apartment, chamber*

INNOCENCY
2136 zâkûw (Ch.) (1), *purity; justice*
5356 niqqâyôwn (4), *clearness; cleanness*

INNOCENT
2600 chinnâm (1), *gratis, free*
2643 chaph (1), *pure, clean*

5352 nâqâh (5), to *be, make clean; to be bare*
5355 nâqîy (29), *innocent*
121 athŏŏs (2), *not guilty*

INNOCENTS
5355 nâqîy (2), *innocent*

INNUMERABLE
369+4557 'ayin (4), *there is no, i.e., not exist*
382 anarithmētŏs (1), *without number*
3461 murias (2), *ten-thousand*

INORDINATE
5691 'ăgâbâh (1), *love, amorousness*
3806 pathŏs (1), *passion, concupiscence*

INQUISITION
1245 bâqash (1), to *search; to strive after*
1875 dârash (2), to *pursue or search*

INSCRIPTION
1924 ĕpigraphō (1), to *inscribe, write upon*

INSIDE
1004 bayith (1), *house; temple; family, tribe*

INSOMUCH
1519 ĕis (1), *to or into*
5620 hōstĕ (17), *thus, therefore*

INSPIRATION
5397 nᵉshâmâh (1), *breath, life*
2315 thĕŏpnĕustŏs (1), *divinely breathed in*

INSTANT
6621 petha' (2), *wink, i.e. moment; quickly*
7281 rega' (2), very *short space* of time
1945 ĕpikĕimai (1), to *rest upon; press upon*
2186 ĕphistēmi (1), to *be present; to approach*
4342 prŏskartĕrĕŏ (1), to *attend; to adhere*
5610 hōra (1), *hour, i.e. a unit of time*

INSTANTLY
1722+1616 ĕn (1), *in; during; because of*
4705 spŏudaiŏs (1), *prompt, energetic*

INSTEAD
8478 tachath (35), *underneath; in lieu of*

INSTRUCT
995 bîyn (1), to *understand; discern*
3250 yiççôwr (1), *reprover, corrector*
3256 yâçar (3), to *chastise; to instruct*
3925 lâmad (1), to *teach, train*
7919 sâkal (2), to *be or act circumspect*
4822 sumbibazō (1), to *unite; to show, teach*

INSTRUCTED
995 bîyn (2), to *understand; discern*

3045 yâda' (1), to *know*
3245 yâçad (1), *settle, consult, establish*
3256 yâçar (5), to *chastise; to instruct*
3384 yârâh (1), to *point; to teach*
3925 lâmad (2), to *teach, train*
7919 sâkal (1), to *be or act circumspect*
2727 katēchĕŏ (3), to *indoctrinate*
3100 mathētĕuŏ (1), to *become a student*
3453 muĕŏ (1), to *initiate*
4264 prŏbibazō (1), to *bring to the front*

INSTRUCTER
3913 lâţash (1), to *sharpen; to pierce*

INSTRUCTERS
3807 paidagōgŏs (1), *tutor, cf. pedagogue*

INSTRUCTING
3811 paidĕuŏ (1), to *educate or discipline*

INSTRUCTION
4148 mûwçâr (30), *reproof, warning*
4561 môçâr (1), *admonition*
3809 paidĕia (1), *disciplinary correction*

INSTRUCTOR
3810 paidĕutēs (1), *teacher or discipliner*

INSTRUMENT
3627 kᵉlîy (2), *implement, thing*

INSTRUMENTS
1761 dachăvâh (Ch.) (1), *musical instrument*
3627 kᵉlîy (37), *implement, thing*
4482 mên (1), *part; musical chord*
7991 shâlîysh (1), *triangle instrument*
3696 hŏplŏn (2), *implement, or utensil*

INSURRECTION
5376 nᵉsâ' (Ch.) (1), to *lift up*
7285 regesh (1), *tumultuous crowd*
2721 katĕphistēmi (1), to *rush upon* in an *assault*
4714 stasis (1), one leading an *uprising*
4955 sustasiastēs (1), *fellow-insurgent*

INTEGRITY
8537 tôm (11), *prosperity; innocence*
8538 tummâh (5), *innocence*

INTELLIGENCE
995 bîyn (1), to *understand; discern*

INTEND
559 'âmar (2), to *say*
1014 bŏulŏmai (1), to *be willing, desire; choose*

3195 mĕllŏ (1), to *intend, i.e. be about* to

INTENDED
5186 nâţâh (1), to *stretch or spread out*

INTENDEST
559 'âmar (1), to *say*

INTENDING
1011 bŏulĕuŏ (1), to *deliberate; to resolve*
2309 thĕlŏ (1), to *will; to desire; to choose*
3195 mĕllŏ (1), to *intend, i.e. be about* to

INTENT
1701 dibrâh (Ch.) (1), *because, on account of*
4616 ma'an (2), *on account of; in order*
5668 'âbûwr (1), on *account of; in order*
2443 hina (2), in *order that*
3056 lŏgŏs (1), *word, matter, thing*

INTENTS
4209 mᵉzimmâh (1), *plan; sagacity*
1771 ĕnnŏia (1), moral *understanding*

INTERCESSION
6293 pâga' (4), to *impinge*
1793 ĕntugchanŏ (4), to *entreat, petition*
5241 hupĕrĕntugchanŏ (1), to *intercede*

INTERCESSIONS
1783 ĕntĕuxis (1), *intercession*

INTERCESSOR
6293 pâga' (1), to *impinge*

INTERMEDDLE
6148 'ârab (1), to *intermix*

INTERMEDDLETH
1566 gâla' (1), to *be obstinate; to burst forth*

INTERMISSION
2014 hăphûgâh (1), *relaxation*

INTERPRET
6622 pâthar (4), to *interpret a dream*
1329 diĕrmĕnĕuŏ (4), to *explain thoroughly*

INTERPRETATION
4426 mᵉlîytsâh (1), *aphorism, saying*
6591 pᵉshar (Ch.) (30), *interpretation*
6592 pêsher (1), *interpretation*
6623 pithrôwn (5), *interpretation*
7667 sheber (1), *solution of a dream*
1329 diĕrmĕnĕuŏ (1), to *explain thoroughly*
1955 ĕpilusis (1), *interpretation*
2058 hĕrmēnĕia (2), *translation*
2059 hĕrmēnĕuŏ (3), to *translate*
3177 mĕthĕrmēnĕuō (1), to *translate*

INTERPRETATIONS
6591 pᵉshar (Ch.) (1), *interpretation*
6623 pithrôwn (1), *interpretation*

INTERPRETED
6622 pâthar (3), to *interpret* a dream
8638 tirgam (1), to *translate, interpret*
2059 hĕrmēnĕuō (1), to *translate*
3177 mĕthĕrmēnĕuō (6), to *translate*

INTERPRETER
3887 lûwts (2), to *scoff*; to *interpret*; to *intercede*
6622 pâthar (1), to *interpret* a dream
1328 diĕrmēnĕutēs (1), *explainer, translator*

INTERPRETING
6591 pᵉshar (Ch.) (1), *interpretation*

INTREAT
2470 châlâh (3), to *be weak, sick, afflicted*
6279 'âthar (6), *intercede*
6293 pâga' (2), to *impinge*
6419 pâlal (1), to *intercede, pray*
2065 ĕrōtaō (1), to *interrogate;* to *request*
3870 parakalĕō (2), to *call, invite*

INTREATED
2470 châlâh (1), to *be weak, sick, afflicted*
2589 channôwth (1), *supplication*
2603 chânan (1), to *implore*
6279 'âthar (12), *intercede* in prayer
2138 ĕupĕithēs (1), *compliant, submissive*
3862 paradŏsis (1), *precept; tradition*
3870 parakalĕō (1), to *call, invite*

INTREATIES
8469 tachănûwn (1), earnest *prayer, plea*

INTREATY
3874 paraklēsis (1), *imploring, exhortation*

INTRUDING
1687 ĕmbatĕuō (1), to *intrude on*

INVADE
935 bôw' (1), to *go or come*
1464 gûwd (1), to *attack*

INVADED
935 bôw' (1), to *go or come*
6584 pâshaṭ (4), to *strip,* i.e. *unclothe, plunder*

INVASION
6584 pâshaṭ (1), to *strip,* i.e. *unclothe, plunder, flay*

INVENT
2803 châshab (1), to *weave, fabricate*

INVENTED
2803 châshab (1), to *weave, fabricate*

INVENTIONS
2810 chishshâbôwn (1), *machination, scheme*
4209 mᵉzimmâh (1), *plan; sagacity*
4611 ma'ălâl (2), *act, deed*
5949 'ălîylâh (1), *opportunity, action*

INVENTORS
2182 ĕphĕurĕtēs (1), *contriver, inventor*

INVISIBLE
517 aŏratŏs (5), *invisible, not seen*

INVITED
7121 qârâ' (3), to *call out*

INWARD
1004 bayith (7), *house; temple; family, tribe*
2315 cheder (2), *apartment, chamber*
2910 tûwchâh (2), inmost *thought*
5475 çôwd (1), *intimacy; consultation; secret*
6441 pᵉnîymâh (2), *indoors, inside*
6442 pᵉnîymîy (1), *interior, inner*
7130 qereb (5), *nearest part,* i.e. the *center*
2080 ĕsō (1), *inside, inner, in*
2081 ĕsōthĕn (2), *from inside; inside*
4698 splagchnŏn (1), *intestine; affection, pity* or *sympathy*

INWARDLY
7130 qereb (1), *nearest part,* i.e. the *center*
1722+2927 ĕn (1), *in; during; because of*
2081 ĕsōthĕn (1), *from inside; inside*

INWARDS
7130 qereb (19), *nearest part,* i.e. the *center*

IPHEDEIAH
3301 Yiphdᵉyâh (1), *Jehovah will liberate*

IR
5893 'Îyr (1), *city, town,* unwalled-*village*

IR-NAHASH
5904 'Îyr Nâchâsh (1), *city of a serpent*

IR-SHEMESH
5905 'Îyr Shemesh (1), *city of* (the) *sun*

IRA
5896 'Îyrâ' (6), *wakefulness*

IRAD
5897 'Îyrâd (2), *fugitive*

IRAM
5902 'Îyrâm (2), *city-wise*

IRI
5901 'Îyrîy (1), *urbane*

IRIJAH
3376 Yir'îyâyh (2), *fearful of Jehovah*

IRON
1270 barzel (72), *iron; iron implement*
3375 Yir'ôwn (1), *fearfulness*
6523 parzel (Ch.) (19), *iron*
4603 sidērŏĕs (5), made *of iron*
4604 sidērŏs (1), *iron*

IRONS
7905 sukkâh (1), *dart, harpoon*

IRPEEL
3416 Yirpᵉ'êl (1), *God will heal*

IRU
5902 'Îyrâm (1), *city-wise*

ISAAC
3327 Yitschâq (104), *laughter*
3446 Yischâq (4), *he will laugh*
2464 Isaak (20), *he will laugh*

ISAAC'S
3327 Yitschâq (4), *laughter*

ISAIAH
3470 Yᵉsha'yâh (32), *Jehovah has saved*

ISCAH
3252 Yiçkâh (1), *observant*

ISCARIOT
2469 Iskariōtēs (11), *inhabitant of Kerioth*

ISH-BOSHETH
378 'Îysh-Bôsheth (11), *man of shame*

ISH-TOB
382 'Îysh-Ṭôwb (2), *man of Tob*

ISHBAH
3431 Yishbach (1), *he will praise*

ISHBAK
3435 Yishbâq (2), *he will leave*

ISHBI-BENOB
3430 Yishbôw bᵉ-Nôb (1), *his dwelling* (is) *in Nob*

ISHI
376 'îysh (1), *man; male; someone*
3469 Yish'îy (5), *saving*

ISHIAH
3449 Yishshîyâh (1), *Jehovah will lend*

ISHIJAH
3449 Yishshîyâh (1), *Jehovah will lend*

ISHMA
3457 Yishmâ' (1), *desolate*

ISHMAEL
3458 Yishmâ'ê'l (47), *God will hear*

ISHMAEL'S
3458 Yishmâ'ê'l (1), *God will hear*

ISHMAELITE
3458 Yishmâ'ê'l (1), *God will hear*

ISHMAELITES
3459 Yishmâ'ê'lîy (2), *Jishmaëlite*

ISHMAIAH
3460 Yishma'yâh (1), *Jehovah will hear*

ISHMEELITE
3459 Yishmâ'ê'lîy (1), *Jishmaëlite*

ISHMEELITES
3459 Yishmâ'ê'lîy (4), *Jishmaëlite*

ISHMERAI
3461 Yishmᵉray (1), *preservative*

ISHOD
379 'Îyshhôwd (1), *man of renown*

ISHPAN
3473 Yishpân (1), *he will hide*

ISHUAH
3438 Yishvâh (1), *he will level*

ISHUAI
3440 Yishvîy (1), *level*

ISHUI
3440 Yishvîy (1), *level*

ISLAND
336 'îy (1), *not*
338 'îy (1), solitary wild creature that *howls*
3519 nēsiŏn (1), small *island*
3520 nēsŏs (6), *island*

ISLANDS
338 'îy (1), solitary wild creature that *howls*
339 'îy (6), dry *land; coast; island*

ISLE
339 'îy (3), *coast; island*
3520 nēsŏs (3), *island*

ISLES
339 'îy (27), dry *land; coast; island*

ISMACHIAH
3253 Yiçmakyâhûw (1), *Jehovah will sustain*

ISMAIAH
3460 Yishma'yâh (1), *Jehovah will hear*

ISPAH
3472 Yishpâh (1), *he will scratch*

ISRAEL
3478 Yisrâ'êl (2477), *he will rule* (as) *God*
3479 Yisrâ'êl (Ch.) (8), *he will rule* (as) *God*
3481 Yisrᵉ'êlîy (1), *Jisreëlite*
2474 Israēl (70), *he will rule* (as) *God*
2475 Israēlitēs (5), *descendants of Israel*

English

ISRAEL'S
3478 Yisrâ'êl (10), *he will rule* (as) *God*

ISRAELITE
1121+3478 bên (1), *son, descendant; people*
3481 Yisre'êlîy (1), *Jisreëlite*
2475 Israēlitēs (2), descendants *of Israel*

ISRAELITES
3478 Yisrâ'êl (16), *he will rule* (as) *God*
2475 Israēlitēs (2), descendants *of Israel*

ISRAELITISH
3482 Yisre'êlîyth (3), *Jisreëlitess*

ISSACHAR
3485 Yissâ'kâr (43), *he will bring a reward*
2466 Isachar (1), *he will bring a reward*

ISSHIAH
3449 Yishshîyâh (2), *Jehovah will lend*

ISSUE
2100 zûwb (16), *to flow freely, gush*
2101 zôwb (11), *flux or discharge*
2231 zirmâh (1), *emission* of semen
3318 yâtsâ' (3), *to go, bring out*
4138 môwledeth (1), *offspring, family*
4726 mâqôwr (1), *flow*
6849 tse'phî'âh (1), *outcast* thing, *offshoots*
131 haimŏrrhĕŏ (1), *to have a hemorrhage*
4511 rhusis (3), *flux*
4690 spĕrma (1), *seed, offspring*

ISSUED
3318 yâtsâ' (4), *to go, bring out*
5047 ne̓gad (Ch.) (1), *to flow*
1607 ĕkpŏrĕuŏmai (2), *to depart, be discharged*

ISSUES
8444 tôwtsâ'âh (2), *exit, boundary; source*

ISUAH
3440 Yishvîy (1), *level*

ISUI
3440 Yishvîy (1), *level*

ITALIAN
2483 Italikŏs (1), belonging to *Italia*

ITALY
2482 Italia (4), *Italia*

ITCH
2775 chereç (1), *itch; sun*

ITCHING
2833 knēthŏ (1), *to tickle, feel an itch*

ITHAI
863 'Ittay (1), *near*

ITHAMAR
385 'Îythâmâr (21), *coast* of the *palm*-tree

ITHIEL
384 'Îythîy'êl (3), *God has arrived*

ITHMAH
3495 Yithmâh (1), *orphanage*

ITHNAN
3497 Yithnân (1), *extensive*

ITHRA
3501 Yithrâ' (1), *wealth*

ITHRAN
3506 Yithrân (3), *excellent*

ITHREAM
3507 Yithre'âm (2), *excellence of people*

ITHRITE
3505 Yithrîy (4), *Jithrite*

ITHRITES
3505 Yithrîy (1), *Jithrite*

ITTAH-KAZIN
6278 'Êth Qâtsîyn (1), *time of a judge*

ITTAI
863 'Ittay (8), *near*

ITURAEA
2434 hilasmŏs (1), *atonement, expiator*

IVAH
5755 'Ivvâh (3), *overthrow, ruin*

IVORY
8127 shên (10), *tooth; ivory; cliff*
8143 shenhabbîym (2), *elephant's ivory tusk*
1661 ĕlĕphantinŏs (1), *of ivory*

IZEHAR
3324 Yitshâr (1), olive *oil; anointing*

IZEHARITES
3325 Yitshârîy (1), *Jitsharite*

IZHAR
3324 Yitshâr (8), olive *oil; anointing*

IZHARITES
3325 Yitshârîy (3), *Jitsharite*

IZRAHIAH
3156 Yizrachyâh (2), *Jehovah will shine*

IZRAHITE
3155 Yizrâch (1), *Ezrachite or Zarchite*

IZRI
3342 yeqeb (1), wine-*vat*, wine-*press*

JAAKAN
3292 Ya'ăqân (1), *Jaakan*

JAAKOBAH
3291 Ya'ăqôbâh (1), *heel-catcher*

JAALA
3279 Ya'ălâ' (1), *to be valuable*

JAALAH
3279 Ya'ălâ' (1), *to be valuable*

JAALAM
3281 Ya'lâm (4), *occult*

JAANAI
3285 Ya'ănay (1), *responsive*

JAARE-OREGIM
3296 Ya'ărêy 'Ore̓gîym (1), *woods of weavers*

JAASAU
3299 Ya'ăsûw (1), *they will do*

JAASIEL
3300 Ya'ăsîy'êl (1), *made of God*

JAAZANIAH
2970 Ya'ăzanyâh (4), *heard of Jehovah*

JAAZER
3270 Ya'ăzêyr (2), *helpful*

JAAZIAH
3269 Ya'ăzîyâhûw (2), *emboldened of Jehovah*

JAAZIEL
3268 Ya'ăzîy'êl (1), *emboldened of God*

JABAL
2989 Yâbâl (1), *stream*

JABBOK
2999 Yabbôq (7), *pouring forth*

JABESH
3003 Yâbêsh (12), *dry*

JABESH-GILEAD
3003+1568 Yâbêsh (12), *dry*

JABEZ
3258 Ya'bêts (4), *sorrowful*

JABIN
2985 Yâbîyn (7), *intelligent*

JABIN'S
2985 Yâbîyn (1), *intelligent*

JABNEEL
2995 Yabne'êl (2), *built of God*

JABNEH
2996 Yabneh (1), *building*

JACHAN
3275 Ya'kân (1), *troublesome*

JACHIN
3199 Yâkîyn (8), *he* (or *it*) *will establish*

JACHINITES
3200 Yâkîynîy (1), *Jakinite*

JACINTH
5191 huakinthinŏs (1), deep *blue* color
5192 huakinthŏs (1), *blue* gem, (poss.) *zircon*

JACOB
3290 Ya'ăqôb (331), *heel-catcher*
2384 Iakōb (26), *heel-catcher*

JACOB'S
3290 Ya'ăqôb (17), *heel-catcher*

2384 Iakōb (1), *heel-catcher*

JADA
3047 Yâdâ' (2), *knowing*

JADAU
3035 Yiddôw (1), *praised*

JADDUA
3037 Yaddûwa' (3), *knowing*

JADON
3036 Yâdôwn (1), *thankful*

JAEL
3278 Yâ'êl (6), *ibex* animal

JAGUR
3017 Yâgûwr (1), *lodging*

JAH
3050 Yâhh (1), *Jehovah*, (the) self-*Existent* or Eternal One

JAHATH
3189 Yachath (8), *unity*

JAHAZ
3096 Yahats (5), *threshing*-floor

JAHAZA
3096 Yahats (1), *threshing*-floor

JAHAZAH
3096 Yahats (2), *threshing*-floor

JAHAZIAH
3167 Yachze̓yâh (1), *Jehovah will behold*

JAHAZIEL
3166 Yachăzîy'êl (6), *beheld of God*

JAHDAI
3056 Yehday (1), *Judaistic*

JAHDIEL
3164 Yachdîy'êl (1), *unity of God*

JAHDO
3163 Yachdôw (1), *his unity*

JAHLEEL
3177 Yachle'êl (2), *expectant of God*

JAHLEELITES
3178 Yachle'êlîy (1), *Jachleëlite*

JAHMAI
3181 Yachmay (1), *hot*

JAHZAH
3096 Yahats (1), *threshing*-floor

JAHZEEL
3183 Yachtse'êl (2), *God will allot*

JAHZEELITES
3184 Yachtse'êlîy (1), *Jachtseëlite*

JAHZERAH
3170 Yachzêrâh (1), *protection*

JAHZIEL
3185 Yachtsîy'êl (1), *allotted of God*

English

JAILER
1200 dĕsmŏphulax (1),
jailer

JAIR
2971 Yâ'îyr (10),
enlightener

JAIRITE
2972 Yâ'îrîy (1), *Jaïrite*

JAIRUS
2383 Iaĕirŏs (2),
enlightener

JAKAN
3292 Ya'ăqân (1), *Jaakan*

JAKEH
3348 Yâqeh (1), *obedient*

JAKIM
3356 Yâqîym (2), *he will
raise*

JALON
3210 Yâlôwn (1), *lodging*

JAMBRES
2387 Iambrĕs (1),
Jambres

JAMES
2385 Iakōbŏs (41),
heel-catcher

JAMIN
3226 Yâmîyn (6), *right;
south*

JAMINITES
3228 Yᵉmîynîy (1),
Jeminite

JAMLECH
3230 Yamlêk (1), *he will
make king*

JANGLING
3150 mataiŏlŏgia (1),
*babble, meaningless
talk*

JANNA
2388 Ianna (1), *Janna*

JANNES
2389 Iannēs (1), *Jannes*

JANOAH
3239 Yânôwach (1), *quiet*

JANOHAH
3239 Yânôwach (2), *quiet*

JANUM
3241 Yânîym (1), *asleep*

JAPHETH
3315 Yepheth (11),
expansion

JAPHIA
3309 Yâphîya' (5), *bright*

JAPHLET
3310 Yaphlêṭ (3), *he will
deliver*

JAPHLETI
3311 Yaphlêṭîy (1),
Japhletite

JAPHO
3305 Yâphôw (1),
beautiful

JARAH
3294 Ya'râh (2), *honey* in
the *comb*

JAREB
3377 Yârêb (2), *he will
contend*

JARED
3382 Yered (5), *descent*
2391 Iarĕd (1), *descent*

JARESIAH
3298 Ya'ăreshyâh (1),
Jaareshjah

JARHA
3398 Yarchâ' (2), *Jarcha*

JARIB
3402 Yârîyb (3),
contentious; adversary

JARMUTH
3412 Yarmûwth (7),
elevation

JAROAH
3386 Yârôwach (1), (born
at the) new *moon*

JASHEN
3464 Yâshên (1), *sleepy*

JASHER
3477 yâshâr (2), *straight*

JASHOBEAM
3434 Yâshob'âm (3),
people will return

JASHUB
3437 Yâshûwb (3), *he
will return*

JASHUBI-LEHEM
3433 Yâshûbîy Lechem
(1), *returner of bread*

JASHUBITES
3432 Yâshûbîy (1),
Jashubite

JASIEL
3300 Ya'ăsîy'êl (1), *made
of God*

JASON
2394 Iasōn (5), *about to
cure*

JASPER
3471 yâshᵉphêh (3),
jasper stone
2393 iaspis (4), *jasper*

JATHNIEL
3496 Yathnîy'êl (1),
continued of God

JATTIR
3492 Yattîyr (4),
redundant

JAVAN
3120 Yâvân (7),
effervescent

JAVELIN
2595 chănîyth (6), *lance,
spear*
7420 rômach (1), iron
pointed spear

JAW
3895 lᵉchîy (3), *jaw;
jaw*-bone
4973 mᵉthallᵉ'âh (1),
tooth

JAWBONE
3895 lᵉchîy (3), *jaw;
jaw*-bone

JAWS
3895 lᵉchîy (4), *jaw;
jaw*-bone
4455 malqôwach (1),
spoil, plunder
4973 mᵉthallᵉ'âh (1),
tooth

JAZER
3270 Ya'ăzêyr (11),
helpful

JAZIZ
3151 Yâzîyz (1), *he will
make prominent*

JEALOUS
7065 qânâ' (11), to *be,
make zealous, jealous*
7067 qannâ' (4), *jealous*
7072 qannôw' (2), *jealous*
2206 zēlŏō (1), to *have
warmth* of feeling for

JEALOUSIES
7068 qin'âh (1), *jealousy*
or *envy*

JEALOUSY
7065 qânâ' (5), to *be,
make zealous, jealous*
7068 qin'âh (23), *jealousy*
7069 qânâh (1), to *create;*
to *procure*
2205 zēlŏs (1), *zeal,
ardor; jealousy, malice*

JEARIM
3297 Yᵉ'ârîym (1), *forests*

JEATERAI
2979 Yᵉ'âthᵉray (1),
stepping

JEBERECHIAH
3000 Yᵉberekyâhûw (1),
blessed of Jehovah

JEBUS
2982 Yᵉbûwç (4), *trodden*

JEBUSI
2983 Yᵉbûwçîy (2),
Jebusite

JEBUSITE
2983 Yᵉbûwçîy (14),
Jebusite

JEBUSITES
2983 Yᵉbûwçîy (25),
Jebusite

JECAMIAH
3359 Yᵉqamyâh (1),
Jehovah will rise

JECHOLIAH
3203 Yᵉkolyâh (1),
Jehovah will enable

JECHONIAS
2423 Iĕchŏnias (2),
Jehovah will establish

JECOLIAH
3203 Yᵉkolyâh (1),
Jehovah will enable

JECONIAH
3204 Yᵉkonyâh (7),
Jehovah will establish

JEDAIAH
3042 Yᵉdâyâh (2),
praised of Jehovah
3048 Yᵉda'yâh (11),
Jehovah has known

JEDIAEL
3043 Yᵉdîy'ă'êl (6),
knowing God

JEDIDAH
3040 Yᵉdîydâh (1),
beloved

JEDIDIAH
3041 Yᵉdîydᵉyâh (1),
beloved of Jehovah

JEDUTHUN
3038 Yᵉdûwthûwn (16),
laudatory

JEEZER
372 'Îy'ezer (1), *helpless*

JEEZERITES
373 'Îy'ezrîy (1), *Iezrite*

JEGAR-SAHADUTHA
3026 Yᵉgar Sahădûwthâ'
(Ch.) (1), *heap of the
testimony*

JEHALELEEL
3094 Yᵉhallel'êl (1),
praising God

JEHALELEL
3094 Yᵉhallel'êl (1),
praising God

JEHDEIAH
3165 Yechdîyâhûw (2),
unity of Jehovah

JEHEZEKEL
3168 Yᵉchezqê'l (1), *God
will strengthen*

JEHIAH
3174 Yᵉchîyâh (1),
Jehovah will live

JEHIEL
3171 Yᵉchîy'êl (14), *God
will live*
3273 Yᵉ'îy'êl (2), *carried
away of God*

JEHIELI
3172 Yᵉchîy'êlîy (2),
Jechiëlite

JEHIZKIAH
3169 Yᵉchizqîyâh (1),
*strengthened of
Jehovah*

JEHOADAH
3085 Yᵉhôw'addâh (2),
Jehovah-adorned

JEHOADDAN
3086 Yᵉhôw'addîyn (2),
Jehovah-pleased

JEHOAHAZ
3059 Yᵉhôw'âchâz (21),
Jehovah-seized
3099 Yôw'âchâz (1),
Jehovah-seized

JEHOASH
3060 Yᵉhôw'âsh (17),
Jehovah-fired

JEHOHANAN
3076 Yᵉhôwchânân (6),
Jehovah-favored

JEHOIACHIN
3078 Yᵉhôwyâkîyn (10),
Jehovah will establish

JEHOIACHIN'S
3112 Yôwyâkîyn (1),
Jehovah will establish

JEHOIADA
3111 Yôwyâdâ' (52),
Jehovah-known

JEHOIAKIM
3079 Yᵉhôwyâqîym (37),
Jehovah will raise

JEHOIARIB
3080 Yᵉhôwyârîyb (2),
Jehovah will contend

JEHONADAB
3082 Yᵉhôwnâdâb (3), *Jehovah-largessed*

JEHONATHAN
3083 Yᵉhôwnâthân (3), *Jehovah-given*

JEHORAM
3088 Yᵉhôwrâm (23), *Jehovah-raised*

JEHOSHABEATH
3090 Yᵉhôwshab'ath (2), *Jehovah-sworn*

JEHOSHAPHAT
3046 yᵉda' (Ch.) (1), to *know*
3092 Yᵉhôwshâphâṭ (84), *Jehovah-judged*

JEHOSHEBA
3089 Yᵉhôwsheba' (1), *Jehovah-sworn*

JEHOSHUA
3091 Yᵉhôwshûw'a (1), *Jehovah-saved*

JEHOSHUAH
3091 Yᵉhôwshûw'a (1), *Jehovah-saved*

JEHOVAH
3068 Yᵉhôvâh (4), (the) self-*Existent* or Eternal

JEHOVAH-JIREH
3070 Yᵉhôvâh Yir'eh (1), *Jehovah will see* (to it)

JEHOVAH-NISSI
3071 Yᵉhôvâh Niççîy (1), *Jehovah* (is) *my banner*

JEHOVAH-SHALOM
3073 Yᵉhôvâh Shâlôwm (1), *Jehovah* (is) *peace*

JEHOZABAD
3075 Yᵉhôwzâbâd (4), *Jehovah-endowed*

JEHOZADAK
3087 Yᵉhôwtsâdâq (2), *Jehovah-righted*

JEHU
3058 Yêhûw' (57), *Jehovah* (is) *He*

JEHUBBAH
3160 Yᵉchubbâh (1), *hidden*

JEHUCAL
3081 Yᵉhûwkal (1), *potent*

JEHUD
3055 Yᵉhûd (1), *celebrated*

JEHUDI
3065 Yᵉhûwdîy (4), *Jehudite*

JEHUDIJAH
3057 Yᵉhûdîyâh (1), *celebrated*

JEHUSH
3266 Yᵉ'ûwsh (1), *hasty*

JEIEL
3273 Yᵉ'îy'êl (11), *carried away of God*

JEKABZEEL
3343 Yᵉqabtsᵉ'êl (1), *God will gather*

JEKAMEAM
3360 Yᵉqam'âm (2), *people will rise*

JEKAMIAH
3359 Yᵉqamyâh (2), *Jehovah will rise*

JEKUTHIEL
3354 Yᵉqûwthîy'êl (1), *obedience of God*

JEMIMA
3224 Yᵉmîymâh (1), *dove*

JEMUEL
3223 Yᵉmûw'êl (2), *day of God*

JEOPARDED
2778 châraph (1), to spend the *winter*

JEOPARDY
2793 kinduněuō (2), to undergo peril

JEPHTHAE
2422 Iěphthaě (1), *he will open*

JEPHTHAH
3316 Yiphtâch (29), *he will open*

JEPHUNNEH
3312 Yᵉphunneh (16), *he will be prepared*

JERAH
3392 Yerach (2), *lunar month*

JERAHMEEL
3396 Yᵉrachmᵉ'êl (8), *God will be compassionate*

JERAHMEELITES
3397 Yᵉrachmᵉ'êlîy (2), *Jerachmeëlite*

JERED
3382 Yered (2), *descent*

JEREMAI
3413 Yᵉrêmay (1), *elevated*

JEREMIAH
3414 Yirmᵉyâh (146), *Jehovah will rise*

JEREMIAH'S
3414 Yirmᵉyâh (1), *Jehovah will rise*

JEREMIAS
2408 Hiěrěmias (1), *Jehovah will rise*

JEREMOTH
3406 Yᵉrîymôwth (5), *elevations*

JEREMY
2408 Hiěrěmias (2), *Jehovah will rise*

JERIAH
3404 Yᵉrîyâh (2), *Jehovah will throw*

JERIBAI
3403 Yᵉrîybay (1), *contentious*

JERICHO
3405 Yᵉrîychôw (57), *its month,* or *fragrant*
2410 Hiěrichô (7), *its month* or *fragrant*

JERIEL
3400 Yᵉrîy'êl (1), *thrown of God*

JERIJAH
3404 Yᵉrîyâh (1), *Jehovah will throw*

JERIMOTH
3406 Yᵉrîymôwth (8), *elevations*

JERIOTH
3408 Yᵉrîy'ôwth (1), *curtains*

JEROBOAM
3379 Yârob'âm (102), *people will contend*

JEROBOAM'S
3379 Yârob'âm (2), *people will contend*

JEROHAM
3395 Yᵉrôchâm (10), *compassionate*

JERUBBAAL
3378 Yᵉrubba'al (14), *Baal will contend*

JERUBBESHETH
3380 Yᵉrubbesheth (1), the idol *will contend*

JERUEL
3385 Yᵉrûw'êl (1), *founded of God*

JERUSALEM
3389 Yᵉrûwshâlaim (640), *founded peaceful*
3390 Yᵉrûwshâlêm (Ch.) (26), *founded peaceful*
2414 Hiěrŏsŏluma (61), *founded peaceful*
2419 Hiěrŏusalēm (81), *founded peaceful*

JERUSALEM'S
3389 Yᵉrûwshâlaim (3), *founded peaceful*

JERUSHA
3388 Yᵉrûwshâ' (1), *possessed*

JERUSHAH
3388 Yᵉrûwshâ' (1), *possessed*

JESAIAH
3470 Yᵉsha'yâh (2), *Jehovah has saved*

JESHAIAH
3740 kêrâh (5), *purchase*

JESHANAH
3466 Yᵉshânâh (1), *old*

JESHARELAH
3480 Yᵉsar'êlâh (1), *right towards God*

JESHEBEAB
3434 Yâshob'âm (1), *people will return*

JESHER
3475 Yêsher (1), *right*

JESHIMON
3452 yᵉshîymôwn (5), *desolation*

JESHISHAI
3454 Yᵉshîyshay (1), *aged*

JESHOHAIAH
3439 Yᵉshôwchâyâh (1), *Jehovah will empty*

JESHUA
3442 Yêshûwa' (28), *he will save*
3443 Yêshûwa' (Ch.) (2), *he will save*

JESHURUN
3484 Yᵉshûrûwn (3), *upright*

JESIAH
3449 Yishshîyâh (2), *Jehovah will lend*

JESIMIEL
3450 Yᵉsîymâ'êl (1), *God will place*

JESSE
3448 Yîshay (41), *extant*
2421 Iěssai (5), *extant*

JESTING
2160 ěutrapělia (1), *ribaldry*

JESUI
3440 Yishvîy (1), *level*

JESUITES
3441 Yishvîy (1), *Jishvite*

JESURUN
3484 Yᵉshûrûwn (1), *upright*

JESUS
846 autŏs (1), *he, she, it*
2424 Iēsŏus (967), *Jehovah-saved*

JESUS'
2424 Iēsŏus (10), *Jehovah-saved*

JETHER
3500 Yether (8), *remainder*

JETHETH
3509 Yᵉthêyth (2), *Jetheth*

JETHLAH
3494 Yithlâh (1), *be high*

JETHRO
3503 Yithrôw (10), *his excellence*

JETUR
3195 Yᵉṭûwr (3), *enclosed*

JEUEL
3262 Yᵉ'ûw'êl (1), *carried away of God*

JEUSH
3266 Yᵉ'ûwsh (8), *hasty*

JEUZ
3263 Yᵉ'ûwts (1), *counselor*

JEW
3064 Yᵉhûwdîy (10), *Jehudite*
2453 Iŏudaiŏs (22), *belonging to Jehudah*

JEWEL
3627 kᵉlîy (1), *implement, thing*
5141 nezem (2), *nose-ring*

JEWELS
2484 chelyâh (2), *trinket, ornament*
3627 kᵉlîy (18), *implement, thing*
5141 nezem (1), *nose-ring*
5459 çᵉgullâh (1), *wealth*

English

JEWESS
2453 Iŏudaiŏs (2),
belonging to *Jehudah*

JEWISH
2451 Iŏudaïkŏs (1),
resembling a *Judæan*

JEWRY
3061 Yᵉhûwd (Ch.) (1),
celebrated
2449 Iŏudaia (2),
Judæan land

JEWS
3054 yâhad (1), to
become Jewish
3062 Yᵉhûwdâ'îy (Ch.)
(8), *Jew*
3064 Yᵉhûwdîy (65),
Jehudite
2450 Iŏudaïzō (1), to
Judaize, live as a Jew
2452 Iŏudaïkŏs (1), in a
Judæan manner
2453 Iŏudaiŏs (167),
belonging to *Jehudah*

JEWS'
3064 Yᵉhûwdîy (4),
Jehudite
3066 Yᵉhûwdîyth (4), in
the *Jewish language*
2453 Iŏudaiŏs (4),
belonging to *Jehudah*
2454 Iŏudaismŏs (2),
Jewish faith

JEZANIAH
3153 Yᵉzanyâh (2), *heard
of Jehovah*

JEZEBEL
348 'Îyzebel (21), *chaste*
2403 Iĕzabēl (1), *chaste*

JEZEBEL'S
348 'Îyzebel (1), *chaste*

JEZER
3337 Yêtser (3), *form*

JEZERITES
3339 Yitsrîy (1),
formative

JEZIAH
3150 Yizzîyâh (1),
sprinkled of Jehovah

JEZIEL
3149 Yᵉzav'êl (1),
sprinkled of God

JEZLIAH
3152 Yizlîy'ah (1), *he will
draw out*

JEZOAR
3328 Yitschar (1), *he will
shine*

JEZRAHIAH
3156 Yizrachyâh (1),
Jehovah will shine

JEZREEL
3157 Yizrᵉ'ê'l (36), *God
will sow*

JEZREELITE
3158 Yizrᵉ'ê'lîy (8),
Jizreëlite

JEZREELITESS
3159 Yizrᵉ'ê'lîyth (5),
Jezreëlitess

JIBSAM
3005 Yibsâm (1), *fragrant*

JIDLAPH
3044 Yidlâph (1), *tearful*

JIMNA
3232 Yimnâh (1),
prosperity

JIMNAH
3232 Yimnâh (1),
prosperity

JIMNITES
3232 Yimnâh (1),
prosperity

JIPHTAH
3316 Yiphtâch (1), *he
will open*

JIPHTHAH-EL
3317 Yiphtach-'êl (2),
God will open

JOAB
3097 Yôw'âb (137),
Jehovah-fathered
5854 'Aṭrôwth Bêyth
Yôw'âb (1), *crowns of
(the) house of Joäb*

JOAB'S
3097 Yôw'âb (8),
Jehovah-fathered

JOAH
3098 Yôw'âch (11),
Jehovah-brothered

JOAHAZ
3098 Yôw'âch (1),
Jehovah-brothered

JOANNA
2489 Iŏanna (3),
Jehovah-favored

JOASH
3101 Yôw'âsh (47),
Jehovah-fired
3135 Yôw'âsh (2),
Jehovah-hastened

JOATHAM
2488 Iŏatham (2),
Jehovah (is) perfect

JOB
347 'Îyôwb (57),
persecuted
3102 Yôwb (1), *Job*
2492 Iōb (1), *persecuted*

JOB'S
347 'Îyôwb (1), *persecuted*

JOBAB
3103 Yôwbâb (9), *howler*

JOCHEBED
3115 Yôwkebed (2),
Jehovah-gloried

JOED
3133 Yôw'êd (1),
appointer

JOEL
3100 Yôw'êl (19),
Jehovah (is his) God
2493 Iōēl (1), *Jehovah (is
his) God*

JOELAH
3132 Yôw'ê'lâh (1),
furthermore

JOEZER
3134 Yôw'ezer (1),
Jehovah (is his) help

JOGBEHAH
3011 Yogbᵉhâh (2),
hillock

JOGLI
3020 Yoglîy (1), *exiled*

JOHA
3109 Yôwchâ' (2),
Jehovah-revived

JOHANAN
3076 Yᵉhôwchânân (3),
Jehovah-favored
3110 Yôwchânân (24),
Jehovah-favored

JOHN
2491 Iōannēs (131),
Jehovah-favored

JOHN'S
2491 Iōannēs (2),
Jehovah-favored

JOIADA
3111 Yôwyâdâ' (4),
Jehovah-known

JOIAKIM
3113 Yôwyâqîym (4),
Jehovah will raise

JOIARIB
3114 Yôwyârîyb (5),
Jehovah will contend

JOIN
2266 châbar (2), to
fascinate by spells
2859 châthan (1), to
become related
3254 yâçaph (1), to *add
or augment*
3867 lâvâh (2), to *unite;
to remain; to borrow*
5060 nâga' (1), to *strike*
5526 çâkak (1), to
entwine; to fence in
7126 qârab (1), to
approach, bring near
2853 kŏllaō (3), to *glue
together*

JOINED
977 bâchar (1), *select,
chose, prefer*
1692 dâbaq (2), to *cling
or adhere; to catch*
2266 châbar (8), to
fascinate by spells
2302 châdâh (1), to
rejoice, be glad
2338 chûwṭ (Ch.) (1), to
repair; lay a foundation
2859 châthan (1), to
become related
3161 yâchad (1), to be,
become one
3867 lâvâh (8), to *unite;
to remain; to borrow*
5208 nîychôwach (Ch.)
(1), *pleasure*
5595 çâphâh (1), to
scrape; to accumulate
6186 'ârak (1), to set in a
row, i.e. arrange,
6775 tsâmad (3), to *link,
i.e. gird*
7000 qâṭar (1), to *enclose*
7126 qârab (1), to
approach, bring near
7194 qâshar (1), to *tie,
bind*
2675 katartizō (1), to
repair; to prepare
2853 kŏllaō (3), to *glue
together*

JOINING
1692 dâbaq (1), to *cling
or adhere; to catch*

JOININGS
4226 mᵉchabbᵉrâh (1),
joiner, brace or cramp

JOINT
3363 yâqa' (1), to *be
dislocated*
4154 mûw'edeth (1),
dislocated
6504 pârad (1), to *spread
or separate*
860 haphē (1), *fastening
ligament, joint*

JOINT-HEIRS
4789 sugklērŏnŏmŏs (1),
participant in common

JOINTS
1694 debeq (2), *joint*
2542 chammûwq (1),
wrapping, i.e. drawers
7001 qᵉṭar (Ch.) (1),
riddle; vertebra
719 harmŏs (1),
articulation, body-joint
860 haphē (1), *fastening
ligament, joint*

JOKDEAM
3347 Yoqdᵉ'âm (1),
burning of (the) people

JOKIM
3137 Yôwqîym (1),
Jehovah will raise

JOKMEAM
3361 Yoqmᵉ'âm (1),
people will be raised

JOKNEAM
3362 Yoqnᵉ'âm (4),
people will be lamented

JOKSHAN
3370 Yoqshân (4),
insidious

JOKTAN
3355 Yoqtân (6), *he will
be made little*

JOKTHEEL
3371 Yoqthᵉ'êl (2),
veneration of God

JONA
2495 Iōnas (1), *dove*

JONADAB
3082 Yᵉhôwnâdâb (4),
Jehovah-largessed
3122 Yôwnâdâb (8),
Jehovah-largessed

JONAH
3124 Yôwnâh (19), *dove*

JONAN
2494 Iōnan (1), *Jehovah-
favored or a dove*

JONAS
2495 Iōnas (12), *dove*

JONATH-ELEM-RECHOKIM
3128 Yôwnath 'êlem rᵉchôqîym (1), *dove of (the) silence*

JONATHAN
3083 Yᵉhôwnâthân (81), *Jehovah-given*
3129 Yôwnâthân (37), *Jehovah-given*

JONATHAN'S
3129 Yôwnâthân (3), *Jehovah-given*

JOPPA
3305 Yâphôw (3), *beautiful*
2445 Iŏppē (10), *beautiful*

JORAH
3139 Yôwrâh (1), *rainy*

JORAI
3140 Yôwray (1), *rainy*

JORAM
3141 Yôwrâm (19), *Jehovah-raised*
3088 Yᵉhôwrâm (7), *Jehovah-raised*
2496 Iōram (2), *Jehovah-raised*

JORDAN
3383 Yardên (182), *descender*
2446 Iŏrdanēs (15), *descender*

JORIM
2497 Iōrĕim (1), (poss.) *Jehovah-raised*

JORKOAM
3421 Yorqᵉ'âm (1), *people will be poured forth*

JOSABAD
3107 Yôwzâbâd (1), *Jehovah-endowed*

JOSAPHAT
2498 Iōsaphat (2), *Jehovah-judged*

JOSE
2499 Iōsē (1), (poss.) *let him add*

JOSEDECH
3087 Yᵉhôwtsâdâq (6), *Jehovah-righted*

JOSEPH
3084 Yᵉhôwçêph (1), *let him add or adding*
3130 Yôwçêph (193), *let him add or adding*
2501 Iōsēph (33), *let him add or adding*

JOSEPH'S
3130 Yôwçêph (20), *let him add or adding*
2501 Iōsēph (2), *let him add or adding*

JOSES
2500 Iōsēs (6), (poss.) *let him add*

JOSHAH
3144 Yôwshâh (1), *Joshah*

JOSHAPHAT
3146 Yôwshâphâṭ (1), *Jehovah-judged*

JOSHAVIAH
3145 Yôwshavyâh (1), *Jehovah-set*

JOSHBEKASHAH
3436 Yoshbᵉqâshâh (2), *hard seat*

JOSHUA
3091 Yᵉhôwshûw'a (215), *Jehovah-saved*

JOSIAH
2977 Yô'shîyâh (53), *founded of Jehovah*

JOSIAS
2502 Iōsias (2), *founded of Jehovah*

JOSIBIAH
3143 Yôwshîbyâh (1), *Jehovah will cause to dwell*

JOSIPHIAH
3131 Yôwçiphyâh (1), *Jehovah (is) adding*

JOT
2503 iōta (1), *iota*

JOTBAH
3192 Yoṭbâh (1), *pleasantness*

JOTBATH
3193 Yoṭbâthâh (1), *pleasantness*

JOTBATHAH
3193 Yoṭbâthâh (2), *pleasantness*

JOTHAM
3147 Yôwthâm (24), *Jehovah (is) perfect*

JOURNEY
1870 derek (23), *road; course of life; mode of action*
4109 mahălâk (3), *passage or a distance*
4550 maçça' (1), *departure*
5265 nâça' (12), *start on a journey*
5575+7272 çanvêr (1), *blindness*
589 apŏdēmĕŏ (2), *visit a foreign land*
590 apŏdēmŏs (1), *foreign traveller*
1279 diapŏrĕuŏmai (1), *to travel through*
2137 ĕuŏdŏŏ (1), *to succeeʹ in business*
3596 hŏdŏipŏrĕŏ (1), *to travel*
3597 hŏdŏipŏria (1), *traveling*
3598 hŏdŏs (6), *road*
4198 pŏrĕuŏmai (2), *to go, come; to travel*

JOURNEYED
5265 nâça' (28), *start on a journey*
6213+1870 'âsâh (1), *to do or make*
3593 hŏdĕuŏ (1), *to travel*
4198 pŏrĕuŏmai (2), *to go/come; to travel*
4922 sunŏdĕuŏ (1), *to travel in company with*

JOURNEYING
4550 maçça' (1), *departure*
5265 nâça' (1), *start on a journey*
4197+4160 pŏrĕia (1), *journey; life's conduct*

JOURNEYINGS
4550 maçça' (1), *departure*
3597 hŏdŏipŏria (1), *traveling*

JOURNEYS
4550 maçça' (9), *departure*

JOY
1523 gîyl (2), *rejoice*
1524 gîyl (3), *age, stage in life*
1525 gîylâh (1), *joy, delight*
2304 chedvâh (1), *rejoicing, joy*
2305 chedvâh (Ch.) (1), *rejoicing, joy*
2898 ṭûwb (1), *good; beauty, gladness*
4885 mâsôws (12), *delight*
7440 rinnâh (3), *shout*
7442 rânan (3), *to shout for joy*
7796 Sôwrêq (1), *vine*
8055 sâmach (4), *to be, make gleesome*
8056 sâmêach (2), *blithe or gleeful*
8057 simchâh (43), *blithesomeness or glee*
8342 sâsôwn (14), *cheerfulness; welcome*
8643 tᵉrûw'âh (1), *battle-cry; clangor*
20 agalliasis (2), *exultation, delight*
21 agalliaō (1), *to exult*
2167 ĕuphrŏsunē (1), *joyfulness, cheerfulness*
2744 kauchaŏmai (1), *to glory in, rejoice in; to boast*
3685 ŏninēmi (1), *to gratify, derive pleasure*
5468 chalinagōgĕŏ (3), *to curb, hold in check*
5479 chara (51), *calm delight, joy*
5485 charis (1), *gratitude; benefit given*

JOYED
5463 chairō (1), *to be cheerful*

JOYFUL
1523 gîyl (4), *rejoice*
2896 ṭôwb (1), *good; well*
5937 'âlaz (2), *to jump for joy*
5970 'âlats (1), *to jump for joy*
7442 rânan (1), *to shout for joy*
7445 rᵉnânâh (2), *shout for joy*
8055 sâmach (2), *to be, make gleesome*
8056 sâmêach (3), *blithe or gleeful*

8643 tᵉrûw'âh (1), *battle-cry; clangor of trumpets*
5479 chara (1), *calm delight, joy*

JOYFULLY
2416 chay (1), *alive; raw; fresh; life*
3326+5479 mĕta (1), *with, among; after, later*
5463 chairō (1), *to be cheerful*

JOYFULNESS
8057 simchâh (1), *blithesomeness or glee*
5479 chara (1), *calm delight, joy*

JOYING
5463 chairō (1), *to be cheerful*

JOYOUS
5947 'allîyz (3), *exultant; reveling*
5479 chara (1), *calm delight, joy*

JOZABAD
3107 Yôwzâbâd (9), *Jehovah-endowed*

JOZACHAR
3108 Yôwzâkâr (1), *Jehovah-remembered*

JOZADAK
3136 Yôwtsâdâq (5), *Jehovah-righted*

JUBAL
3106 Yûwbâl (1), *stream*

JUBILE
3104 yôwbêl (21), *blast of a ram's horn*
8643 tᵉrûw'âh (1), *battle-cry; clangor*

JUCAL
3116 Yûwkal (1), *potent*

JUDA
2448 Iŏuda (1), *celebrated*
2455 Iŏudas (7), *celebrated*

JUDAEA
2449 Iŏudaia (41), *Judæan land*
2453 Iŏudaiŏs (1), *belonging to Jehudah*
2499 Iōsē (1), (poss.) *let him add*

JUDAH
3061 Yᵉhûwd (Ch.) (5), *celebrated*
3063 Yᵉhûwdâh (806), *celebrated*
3064 Yᵉhûwdîy (1), *Jehudite*
2455 Iŏudas (1), *celebrated*

JUDAH'S
3063 Yᵉhûwdâh (4), *celebrated*

JUDAS
2455 Iŏudas (33), *celebrated*

JUDE
2455 Iŏudas (1), *celebrated*

JUDEA
3061 Yᵉhûwd (Ch.) (1),
celebrated

JUDGE
430 'ĕlôhîym (1), *God;*
magistrates, judges
1777 dîyn (14), to *judge;*
to *strive* or *contend for*
1781 dayân (1), *judge;*
advocate
1784 Dîynay (Ch.) (1),
Dinaite
3198 yâkach (1), to
decide, justify, convict
6416 pᵉlîylîy (1), *judicial*
8199 shâphaṭ (102), to
judge
350 *anakrinō* (1), to
interrogate, determine
1252 *diakrinō* (3), to
decide; to hesitate
1348 *dikastēs* (3), one
who judges
2919 *krinō* (45), to
decide; to try
2922 *kritērion* (1), *rule;*
tribunal; lawsuit
2923 *kritēs* (13), *judge*

JUDGED
1777 dîyn (2), to *judge;* to
strive or *contend for*
4941 mishpâṭ (1), *verdict;*
formal *decree; justice*
5307 nâphal (1), to *fall*
6419 pâlal (1), to
intercede, pray
8199 shâphaṭ (28), to
judge
350 *anakrinō* (3), to
interrogate, determine
2233 *hēgĕomai* (1), to
deem, i.e. consider
2919 *krinō* (26), to
decide; to try,
condemn, punish

JUDGES
148 'ădargâzêr (Ch.) (2),
chief diviner
430 'ĕlôhîym (4), *God;*
magistrates, judges
1782 dayân (Ch.) (1),
judge
6414 pâlîyl (3),
magistrate
8199 shâphaṭ (38), to
judge
2923 *kritēs* (4), *judge*

JUDGEST
8199 shâphaṭ (2), to *judge*
2919 *krinō* (6), to *decide;*
to *try, condemn, punish*

JUDGETH
1777 dîyn (1), to *judge;* to
strive or *contend for*
8199 shâphaṭ (5), to *judge*
350 *anakrinō* (1), to
interrogate, determine
2919 *krinō* (10), to *try,*
condemn, punish

JUDGING
8199 shâphaṭ (4), to *judge*
2919 *krinō* (2), to *decide;*
to *try, condemn, punish*

JUDGMENT
1777 dîyn (1), to *judge;* to
strive or *contend for*

1779 dîyn (9), *judge;*
judgment; law suit
1780 dîyn (Ch.) (5),
judge; judgment
2940 ṭa'am (1),
perception; mandate
4055 mad (1), *vesture,*
garment; carpet
4941 mishpâṭ (187),
verdict; decree; justice
6415 pᵉlîylâh (1), *justice*
6417 pᵉlîylîyâh (1),
judgment
6419 pâlal (1), to
intercede, pray
6485 pâqad (2), to *visit,*
care for, count
8196 shᵉphôwṭ (2),
sentence, punishment
8199 shâphaṭ (2), to *judge*
8201 shepheṭ (2),
criminal sentence
144 *aisthēsis* (1),
discernment
968 *bēma* (10), *tribunal*
platform; judging place
1106 *gnōmē* (3),
cognition, opinion
1341 *dikaiŏkrisia* (1),
just sentence
1345 *dikaiōma* (1),
statute or decision
1349 *dikē* (1), *justice*
2250 *hēmĕra* (1), *day;*
period of time
2917 *krima* (12), *decision*
2920 *krisis* (39), *decision;*
tribunal; justice
2922 *kritērion* (1), *rule;*
tribunal; lawsuit
4232 *praitōriŏn* (5),
governor's court-room

JUDGMENTS
4941 mishpâṭ (108),
verdict; decree; justice
8201 shepheṭ (14),
criminal sentence
1345 *dikaiōma* (1), *deed;*
statute or decision
2917 *krima* (1), *decision*
2920 *krisis* (2), *decision;*
tribunal; justice
2922 *kritērion* (1), *rule;*
tribunal; lawsuit

JUDITH
3067 Yᵉhûwdîyth (1),
Jewess

JUICE
6071 'âçîyç (1), *expressed*
fresh grape-juice

JULIA
2456 *Iŏulia* (1), *Julia*

JULIUS
2457 *Iŏuliŏs* (2), *Julius*

JUMPING
7540 râqad (1), to *spring*
about wildly or for joy

JUNIA
2458 *Iŏunias* (1), *Junias*

JUNIPER
7574 rethem (4), *broom*
tree

JUPITER
1356 *diŏpĕtēs* (1),
sky-fallen

2203 *Zĕus* (2), *Jupiter* or
Jove

JURISDICTION
1849 *ĕxŏusia* (1),
authority, dominion

JUSHAB-HESED
3142 Yûwshab Cheçed
(1), *kindness will be*
returned

JUST
3477 yâshâr (1), *straight*
4941 mishpâṭ (1), *verdict;*
formal *decree; justice*
6662 tsaddîyq (42), *just*
6663 tsâdaq (3), to *be,*
make right
6664 tsedeq (8), *right*
8003 shâlêm (1),
complete; friendly; safe
1342 *dikaiŏs* (33),
equitable, holy
1738 *ĕndikŏs* (2),
equitable, deserved, just

JUSTICE
4941 mishpâṭ (1), *verdict;*
formal *decree; justice*
6663 tsâdaq (2), to *be,*
make right
6664 tsedeq (10), *right*
6666 tsᵉdâqâh (15),
rightness

JUSTIFICATION
1345 *dikaiōma* (1), *deed;*
statute or decision
1347 *dikaiōsis* (2),
acquittal, vindication

JUSTIFIED
6663 tsâdaq (12), to *be,*
make right
1344 *dikaiŏō* (31), *show*
or *regard as just*

JUSTIFIER
1344 *dikaiŏō* (1), *show or*
regard as just

JUSTIFIETH
6663 tsâdaq (2), to *be,*
make right
1344 *dikaiŏō* (2), *show or*
regard as just

JUSTIFY
6663 tsâdaq (7), to *be,*
make right
1344 *dikaiŏō* (4), *show or*
regard as just

JUSTIFYING
6663 tsâdaq (2), to *be,*
make right

JUSTLE
8264 shâqaq (1), to *seek*
greedily

JUSTLY
4941 mishpâṭ (1), *verdict;*
formal *decree; justice*
1346 *dikaiŏs* (2),
equitably

JUSTUS
2459 *Iŏustŏs* (3), *just*

JUTTAH
3194 Yuṭṭâh (2), *extended*

KABZEEL
6909 Qabtsᵉ'êl (3), *God*
has gathered

KADESH
6946 Qâdêsh (17),
sanctuary

KADESH-BARNEA
6947 Qâdêsh Barnêa'
(10), Kadesh of (the)
Wilderness of
Wandering

KADMIEL
6934 Qadmîy'êl (8),
presence of God

KADMONITES
6935 Qadmônîy (1),
ancient

KALLAI
7040 Qallay (1), *frivolous*

KANAH
7071 Qânâh (3), *reediness*

KAREAH
7143 Qârêach (13), *bald*

KARKAA
7173 Qarqa' (1),
ground-floor

KARKOR
7174 Qarqôr (1),
foundation

KARTAH
7177 Qartâh (1), *city*

KARTAN
7178 Qartân (1), *city-plot*

KATTATH
7005 Qaṭṭâth (1),
littleness

KEDAR
6938 Qêdâr (12), *dusky*

KEDEMAH
6929 Qêdᵉmâh (2),
precedence

KEDEMOTH
6932 Qᵉdêmôwth (4),
beginnings

KEDESH
6943 Qedesh (11),
sanctum

KEDESH-NAPHTALI
6943+5321 Qedesh (1),
sanctum

KEEP
1692 dâbaq (3), to *cling*
or *adhere;* to *catch*
1961 hâyâh (1), to *exist,*
i.e. *be* or *become*
2287 châgag (12), to
observe a festival
2820 châsak (1), to
refuse, spare, preserve
3533 kâbash (1), to
conquer, subjugate
3607 kâlâ' (1), to *hold*
back or in; to *prohibit*
4513 mâna' (2), to *deny,*
refuse
4931 mishmereth (1),
watch, sentry, post
5201 nâṭar (3), to *guard;*
to *cherish* anger
5341 nâtsar (26), to
guard, protect
5647 'âbad (1), to *do,*
work, serve
5737 'âdar (2), to
arrange as a battle

6113 'âtsar (1), *to hold back; to maintain, rule*
6213 'âsâh (30), *to do or make*
6485 pâqad (1), *to visit, care for, count*
6942 qâdâsh (1), *to be, make clean*
7069 qânâh (1), *to create; to procure*
7368 râchaq (1), *to recede; remove*
8104 shâmar (186), *to watch*
1301 *diatērĕō* (1), *to observe strictly*
1314 *diaphulassō* (1), *to protect, guard carefully*
1858 *hĕŏrtazō* (1), *to observe a festival*
2722 *katĕchō* (3), *to hold down fast*
2853 *kŏllaō* (1), *to glue together*
3557 *nŏsphizŏmai* (1), *to sequestrate, embezzle*
4160 *pŏiĕō* (2), *to do*
4238 *prassō* (1), *to execute, accomplish*
4601 *sigaō* (2), *to keep silent*
4874 *sunanamignumi* (1), *to associate with*
4912 *sunĕchō* (1), *to hold together*
5083 *tērĕō* (32), *to keep, guard, obey*
5299 *hupōpiazō* (1), *to beat up; to wear out*
5432 *phrŏurĕō* (1), *to hem in, protect*
5442 *phulassō* (13), *to watch, i.e. be on guard*

KEEPER
5201 nâṭar (1), *to guard; to cherish* anger
5341 nâtsar (1), *to guard, protect, maintain*
7462 râ'âh (1), *to tend a flock, i.e. pasture it*
8104 shâmar (13), *to watch*
8269 sar (3), *head person, ruler*
1200 *dĕsmŏphulax* (2), *jailer*

KEEPERS
5201 nâṭar (1), *to guard; to cherish* anger
8104 shâmar (15), *to watch*
3626 *ŏikŏurŏs* (1), *domestically inclined*
5083 *tērĕō* (1), *to keep, guard, obey*
5441 *phulax* (3), *watcher or sentry*

KEEPEST
8104 shâmar (3), *to watch*
5442 *phulassō* (1), *watch, i.e. be on guard*

KEEPETH
2820 châsak (1), *to refuse, spare, preserve*
4513 mâna' (1), *to deny, refuse*
5307 nâphal (1), *to fall*

5341 nâtsar (7), *to guard, protect, maintain*
7462 râ'âh (1), *to tend a flock, i.e. pasture it*
7623 shâbach (1), *to address; to pacify*
8104 shâmar (18), *to watch*
4160 *pŏiĕō* (1), *to do*
5083 *tērĕō* (10), *to keep, guard, obey*
5442 *phulassō* (1), *watch, i.e. be on guard*

KEEPING
5341 nâtsar (1), *to guard, protect, maintain*
7462 râ'âh (1), *to tend a flock, i.e. pasture it*
8104 shâmar (7), *to watch*
5084 *tērēsis* (1), *observance; prison*
5442 *phulassō* (1), *watch, i.e. be on guard*

KEHELATHAH
6954 Qᵉhêlâthâh (2), *convocation*

KEILAH
7084 Qᵉ'îylâh (18), *citadel*

KELAIAH
7041 Qêlâyâh (1), *insignificance*

KELITA
7042 Qᵉlîyṭâ' (3), *maiming*

KEMUEL
7055 Qᵉmûw'êl (3), *raised of God*

KENAN
7018 Qêynân (1), *fixed*

KENATH
7079 Qᵉnâth (2), *possession*

KENAZ
7073 Qᵉnaz (11), *hunter*

KENEZITE
7074 Qᵉnizzîy (3), *Kenizzite*

KENITE
7014 Qayin (2), *lance*
7017 Qêynîy (4), *Kenite*

KENITES
7017 Qêynîy (8), *Kenite*

KENIZZITES
7074 Qᵉnizzîy (1), *Kenizzite*

KEPT
631 'âçar (1), *to fasten; to join battle*
680 'âtsal (1), *to select; refuse; narrow*
1639 gâra' (1), *to shave, remove, or withhold*
1692 dâbaq (1), *to cling or adhere; to catch*
2287 châgag (1), *to observe a festival*
2790 chârash (2), *to engrave; to plow*
2820 châsak (2), *to refuse, spare, preserve*
3607 kâlâ' (1), *to hold back or in; to prohibit*

4513 mâna' (2), *to deny, refuse*
4931 mishmereth (6), *watch, sentry, post*
5201 nâṭar (1), *to guard; to cherish* anger
5202 nᵉṭar (Ch.) (1), *to retain*
5341 nâtsar (4), *to guard, protect, maintain*
5641 çâthar (2), *to hide by covering*
5648 'âbad (Ch.) (1), *to do, work, serve*
6113 'âtsar (2), *to hold back; to maintain, rule*
6213 'âsâh (18), *to do or make*
6942 qâdâsh (1), *to be, make clean*
7462 râ'âh (3), *to tend a flock, i.e. pasture it*
7673 shâbath (1), *to repose; to desist*
8104 shâmar (70), *to watch*
71 agō (1), *to lead; to bring, drive; to weigh*
650 *apŏstĕrĕō* (1), *to deprive; to despoil*
1006 *bŏskō* (1), *to pasture a flock*
1096 *ginŏmai* (1), *to be, become*
1301 *diatĕrĕō* (1), *to observe strictly*
2192 *ĕchō* (1), *to have; hold; keep*
2343 *thēsaurizō* (1), *to amass or reserve, store*
2377 *thurōrŏs* (2), *doorkeeper*
2621 *katakĕimai* (1), *to lie down in bed*
2902 *kratĕō* (1), *to seize*
2967 *kōluō* (1), *to stop*
3557 *nŏsphizŏmai* (1), *to sequestrate, embezzle*
3930 *parĕchō* (1), *to hold near, i.e. to present*
4160 *pŏiĕō* (1), *to do*
4601 *sigaō* (2), *to keep silent*
4933 *suntērĕō* (1), *to protect*
5083 *tērĕō* (15), *to keep, guard, obey*
5288 *hupŏstĕllō* (1), *to conceal (reserve)*
5432 *phrŏurĕō* (3), *to hem in, protect*
5442 *phulassō* (8), *to watch, i.e. be on guard*

KERCHIEFS
4556 miçpachath (2), *scurf, rash*

KEREN-HAPPUCH
7163 Qeren Hap-pûwk (1), *horn of cosmetic*

KERIOTH
7152 Qᵉrîyôwth (3), *buildings*

KERNELS
2785 chartsan (1), *sour, tart grape*

KEROS
7026 Qêyrôç (2), *ankled*

KETTLE
1731 dûwd (1), *pot, kettle; basket*

KETURAH
6989 Qᵉṭûwrâh (4), *perfumed*

KEY
4668 maphtêach (2), *opening; key*
2807 klĕis (4), *key*

KEYS
2807 klĕis (2), *key*

KEZIA
7103 Qᵉtsîy'âh (1), *cassia*

KEZIZ
7104 Qᵉtsîyts (1), *abrupt*

KIBROTH-HATTAAVAH
6914 Qibrôwth hat-Ta'ăvâh (5), *graves of the longing*

KIBZAIM
6911 Qibtsayim (1), *double heap*

KICK
1163 bâ'aṭ (1), *kick*
2979 laktizō (2), *to recalcitrate, kick back*

KICKED
1163 bâ'aṭ (1), *kick*

KID
1423 gᵉdîy (8), *young male goat*
1423+5795 gᵉdîy (5), *young male goat*
5795 'êz (1), *she-goat; goat's hair*
8163 sâ'îyr (26), *shaggy; he-goat; goat idol*
8166 sᵉ'îyrâh (2), *she-goat*
2056 *ĕriphŏs* (1), *kid or goat*

KIDNEYS
3629 kilyâh (18), *kidney; mind, heart, spirit*

KIDRON
6939 Qidrôwn (11), *dusky place*

KIDS
1423 gᵉdîy (4), *young male goat*
5795 'êz (1), *she-goat; goat's hair*
8163 sâ'îyr (2), *shaggy; he-goat; goat idol*

KILL
2026 hârag (17), *to kill, slaughter*
2076 zâbach (3), *to (sacrificially) slaughter*
2491 châlâl (2), *pierced to death, one slain*
2873 ṭâbach (1), *to kill, butcher*
4191 mûwth (24), *to die; to kill*
5221 nâkâh (4), *to strike, kill*
5362 nâqaph (1), *to strike; to surround*
7523 râtsach (4), *to murder*
7819 shâchaṭ (22), *to slaughter; butcher*

English

KILLED
337 anairĕō (6), to *abolish, murder*
615 apŏktĕinō (28), to *kill* outright; to *destroy*
1315 diachĕirizŏmai (1), to *lay hands upon*
2380 thuō (3), to *kill*; to *butcher*; to *sacrifice*
4969 sphazō (1), to *slaughter* or to *maim*
5407 phŏnĕuō (8), to *commit murder*

KILLED
2026 hârag (3), to *kill, slaughter*
2076 zâbach (1), to (sacrificially) *slaughter*
2873 ţâbach (3), to *kill, butcher*
3076 Yᵉhôwchânân (1), *Jehovah-favored*
4191 mûwth (6), to *die*; to *kill*
5221 nâkâh (3), to *strike, kill*
7523 râtsach (1), to *murder*
7819 shâchaţ (15), to *slaughter*; *butcher*
337 anairĕō (3), to *take away, murder*
615 apŏktĕinō (22), to *kill* outright; to *destroy*
2289 thanatŏō (2), to *kill*
2380 thuō (5), to *kill*; to *butcher*; to *sacrifice*
5407 phŏnĕuō (2), to *commit murder*

KILLEDST
2026 hârag (2), to *kill, slaughter*

KILLEST
615 apŏktĕinō (2), to *kill* outright; to *destroy*

KILLETH
2026 hârag (1), to *kill, slaughter*
4191 mûwth (2), to *die*; to *kill*
5221 nâkâh (13), to *strike, kill*
6991 qâţal (1), to *put to death*
7819 shâchaţ (3), to *slaughter*; *butcher*
615 apŏktĕinō (3), to *kill* outright; to *destroy*

KILLING
2026 hârag (1), to *kill, slaughter*
7523 râtsach (1), to *murder*
7819 shâchaţ (1), to *slaughter*; *butcher*
7821 shᵉchîyţâh (1), *slaughter*
615 apŏktĕinō (1), to *kill* outright; to *destroy*

KIN
1320 bâsâr (2), *flesh; body; person*
7138 qârôwb (1), *near, close*
7607 shᵉʾêr (2), *flesh, meat; kindred* by *blood*
4773 suggĕnēs (1), *blood relative; countryman*

KINAH
7016 Qîynâh (1), *dirge*

KIND
2896 ţôwb (1), *good; well*
4327 mîyn (29), *sort, i.e. species*
1085 gĕnŏs (3), *kin, offspring in kind*
5100 tis (1), *some or any person or object*
5449 phusis (1), *genus or sort*
5541 chrēstĕuŏmai (1), to *show oneself useful*
5543 chrēstŏs (2), *employed, i.e. useful*

KINDLE
215 ʾôwr (1), to *be luminous*
1197 bâʿar (4), to *be brutish, be senseless*
1814 dâlaq (2), to *flame; to pursue*
2787 chârar (1), to *melt, burn, dry up*
3341 yâtsath (8), to *burn or set on fire*
3344 yâqad (1), to *burn*
6919 qâdach (1), to *inflame*
6999 qâţar (1), to *turn into fragrance* by fire

KINDLED
1197 bâʿar (9), to *be brutish, be senseless*
2734 chârâh (43), to *blaze* up
3341 yâtsath (4), to *burn or set on fire*
3648 kâmar (1), to *shrivel* with heat
5400 nâsaq (1), to *catch fire*
6919 qâdach (3), to *inflame*
8313 sâraph (1), to *be, set on fire*
381 anaptō (2), to *kindle, set on fire*
681 haptō (1), to *set on fire*

KINDLETH
3857 lâhaţ (1), to *blaze*
5400 nâsaq (1), to *catch fire*
381 anaptō (1), to *kindle, set on fire*

KINDLY
2617 cheçed (5), *kindness, favor*
2896 ţôwb (2), *good; well*
5921+3820 ʿal (2), *above, over, upon, or against*
5387 philŏstŏrgŏs (1), *fraternal, devoted*

KINDNESS
2617 cheçed (40), *kindness, favor*
2896 ţôwb (1), *good; well*
5360 philadĕlphia (2), *fraternal affection*
5363 philanthrōpia (1), *benevolence*
5544 chrēstŏtēs (4), *moral excellence*

KINDRED
250 ʾEzrâchîy (1), *Ezrachite*
1353 gᵉullâh (1), *blood relationship*
4130 môwdaʿath (1), *distant relative*
4138 môwledeth (11), *lineage, family*
4940 mishpâchâh (6), *family, clan, people*
1085 gĕnŏs (3), *kin*
4772 suggĕneia (3), *relatives; one's people*
5443 phulē (2), *race or clan*

KINDREDS
4940 mishpâchâh (3), *family, clan, people*
3965 patria (1), *family, group, race, i.e. nation*
5443 phulē (4), *race or clan*

KINDS
2177 zan (5), *form or sort*
4327 mîyn (1), *sort, i.e. species*
4940 mishpâchâh (2), *family, clan, people*
1085 gĕnŏs (2), *kin, offspring in kind*

KINE
504 ʾeleph (4), *ox; cow or cattle*
1241 bâqâr (2), *plowing ox; herd*
6510 pârâh (18), *heifer*

KING
4427 mâlak (43), to *reign as king*
4428 melek (1957), *king*
4430 melek (Ch.) (140), *king*
935 basilĕus (86), *sovereign*

KING'S
4410 mᵉlûwkâh (2), *realm, rulership*
4428 melek (259), *king*
4430 melek (Ch.) (18), *king*
4467 mamlâkâh (1), *royal dominion*
935 basilĕus (2), *sovereign*
937 basilikŏs (1), *befitting the sovereign*

KINGDOM
4410 mᵉlûwkâh (18), *realm, rulership*
4437 malkûw (Ch.) (45), *dominion*
4438 malkûwth (47), *rule; dominion*
4467 mamlâkâh (61), *royal dominion*
4468 mamlâkûwth (8), *royal dominion*
932 basilĕia (155), *rule; realm*

KINGDOMS
4437 malkûw (Ch.) (2), *dominion*
4438 malkûwth (1), *rule; dominion*
4467 mamlâkâh (49), *royal dominion*

932 *basilĕia* (5), *rule; realm*

KINGLY
4437 malkûw (Ch.) (1), *dominion*

KINGS
4428 melek (283), *king*
4430 melek (Ch.) (13), *king*
935 basilĕus (29), *sovereign*
936 basilĕuō (1), to *rule*

KINGS'
4428 melek (3), *king*
933 basilĕiŏn (1), *royal palace*
935 basilĕus (1), *sovereign*

KINSFOLK
7138 qârôwb (1), *near, close*
4773 suggĕnēs (1), *blood relative; countryman*

KINSFOLKS
1350 gâʾal (1), to *redeem; to be the next of kin*
3045 yâdaʿ (1), to *know*
4773 suggĕnēs (1), *blood relative; countryman*

KINSMAN
1350 gâʾal (12), to *be the next of kin*
3045 yâdaʿ (1), to *know*
7607 shᵉʾêr (1), *flesh, meat; kindred* by *blood*
4773 suggĕnēs (2), *blood relative; countryman*

KINSMAN'S
1350 gâʾal (1), to *redeem; to be the next of kin*

KINSMEN
1350 gâʾal (1), to *redeem; to be the next of kin*
7138 qârôwb (1), *near, close*
4773 suggĕnēs (5), *blood relative; countryman*

KINSWOMAN
4129 môwdaʿ (1), *distant relative*
7607 shᵉʾêr (2), *flesh, meat; kindred* by *blood*

KINSWOMEN
7608 shaʾărâh (1), *female kindred* by *blood*

KIR
7024 Qîyr (5), *fortress*

KIR-HARASETH
7025 Qîyr Cheres (1), *fortress of earthenware*

KIR-HARESETH
7025 Qîyr Cheres (1), *fortress of earthenware*

KIR-HARESH
7025 Qîyr Cheres (1), *fortress of earthenware*

KIR-HERES
7025 Qîyr Cheres (2), *fortress of earthenware*

KIRIATHAIM
7156 Qiryâthayim (3), *double city*

7741 Shâvêh Qiryâthayim (1), *plain of a double city*

KIRIOTH
7152 Qᵉrîyôwth (1), *buildings*

KIRJATH
7157 Qiryath Yᵉ'ârîym (1), *city of forests*

KIRJATH-ARBA
7153 Qiryath 'Arba' (6), *city of Arba* or *of the four* (giants)

KIRJATH-ARIM
7157 Qiryath Yᵉ'ârîym (1), *city of forests* or *of towns*

KIRJATH-BAAL
7154 Qiryath Ba'al (2), *city of Baal*

KIRJATH-HUZOTH
7155 Qiryath Chûtsôwth (1), *city of streets*

KIRJATH-JEARIM
7157 Qiryath Yᵉ'ârîym (18), *city of forests*

KIRJATH-SANNAH
7158 Qiryath Çannâh (1), *city of branches* or *of a book*

KIRJATH-SEPHER
7158 Qiryath Çannâh (4), *city of branches* or *of a book*

KIRJATHAIM
7156 Qiryâthayim (3), *double city*

KISH
7027 Qîysh (20), *bow*

KISHI
7029 Qîyshîy (1), *bowed*

KISHION
7191 Qishyôwn (1), *hard ground*

KISHON
7028 Qîyshôwn (5), *winding*
7191 Qishyôwn (1), *hard ground*

KISON
7028 Qîyshôwn (1), *winding*

KISS
5401 nâshaq (9), to *kiss*
2705 kataphilĕō (1), to *kiss earnestly*
5368 philĕō (3), to *be a friend, to kiss*
5370 philēma (7), *kiss*

KISSED
5401 nâshaq (21), to *kiss*
2705 kataphilĕō (5), to *kiss earnestly*

KISSES
5390 nᵉshîyqâh (2), *kiss*

KITE
344 'ayâh (2), *hawk*

KITHLISH
3798 Kithlîysh (1), *wall of a man*

KITRON
7003 Qiṭrôwn (1), *fumigative*

KITTIM
3794 Kittîy (2), *islander*

KNEAD
3888 lûwsh (2), to *knead*

KNEADED
3888 lûwsh (3), to *knead*

KNEADINGTROUGHS
4863 mish'ereth (2), *kneading-trough*

KNEE
1290 berek (1), *knee*
1119 gŏnu (3), *knee*

KNEEL
1288 bârak (2), to *bless*

KNEELED
1288 bârak (1), to *bless*
1289 bᵉrak (Ch.) (1), to *bless*
1120 gŏnupĕtĕō (1), to *fall on the knee, kneel*
5087+1119 tithēmi (5), to *place, put*

KNEELING
3766 kâra' (1), to *prostrate*
1120 gŏnupĕtĕō (2), to *fall on the knee, kneel*

KNEES
755 'arkûbâh (Ch.) (1), *knees*
1290 berek (24), *knee*
1291 berek (Ch.) (1), *knee*
1119 gŏnu (4), *knee joint*

KNEW
1847 da'ath (1), *knowledge*
3045 yâda' (83), to *know*
3046 yᵉda' (Ch.) (2), to *know*
5234 nâkar (9), to *acknowledge*
50 agnŏĕō (1), to *not know; understand*
1097 ginōskō (30), to *know*
1492 ĕidō (27), to *know*
1912 ĕpibarĕō (1), to *be severe toward*
1921 ĕpiginōskō (13), to *acknowledge*
4267 prŏginōskō (1), to *know beforehand*

KNEWEST
3045 yâda' (5), to *know*
3046 yᵉda' (Ch.) (1), to *know*
1097 ginōskō (1), to *know*
1492 ĕidō (3), to *know*

KNIFE
2719 chereb (2), *knife, sword*
3979 ma'ăkeleth (3), *knife*
7915 sakkîyn (1), *knife*

KNIT
2270 châbêr (1), *associate, friend*
3162 yachad (1), *unitedly*
7194 qâshar (1), to *tie, bind*
1210 dĕō (1), to *bind*

4822 sumbibazō (2), to *drive together*

KNIVES
2719 chereb (3), *knife, sword*
3979 ma'ăkeleth (1), *knife*
4252 machălâph (1), butcher *knife*

KNOCK
2925 krŏuō (4), to *rap, knock*

KNOCKED
2925 krŏuō (1), to *rap, knock*

KNOCKETH
1849 dâphaq (1), to *knock; to press* severely
2925 krŏuō (3), to *rap, knock*

KNOCKING
2925 krŏuō (1), to *rap, knock*

KNOP
3730 kaphtôr (10), *capital; button* or *disk*

KNOPS
3730 kaphtôr (6), *capital; button* or *disk*
6497 peqa' (3), *ornamental semi-globe*

KNOW
995 bîyn (1), to *understand; discern*
1847 da'ath (4), *knowledge*
3045 yâda' (429), to *know*
3046 yᵉda' (Ch.) (15), to *know*
5234 nâkar (9), to *acknowledge*
50 agnŏĕō (2), to *not know; not understand*
1097 ginōskō (92), to *know*
1110 gnōstŏs (1), *well-known*
1231 diaginōskō (1), *ascertain exactly*
1492 ĕidō (176), to *know*
1921 ĕpiginōskō (8), to *acknowledge*
1987 ĕpistamai (9), to *be acquainted with*
2467 isēmi (2), to *know*
4267 prŏginōskō (1), to *know beforehand*
4892 sunĕdriŏn (1), head Jewish *tribunal*

KNOWEST
1847 da'ath (1), *knowledge*
3045 yâda' (66), to *know*
1097 ginōskō (5), to *know*
1492 ĕidō (15), to *know*
1921 ĕpiginōskō (1), to *acknowledge*
2589 kardiŏgnōstēs (1), *heart-knower*

KNOWETH
854 'êth (1), *with; by; at; among*
3045 yâda' (59), to *know*
3046 yᵉda' (Ch.) (1), to *know*

KNOWING
3045 yâda' (2), to *know*
50 agnŏĕō (1), to *not know; not understand*
1097 ginōskō (5), to *know*
1492 ĕidō (38), to *know*
1921 ĕpiginōskō (2), to *acknowledge*
1987 ĕpistamai (3), to *comprehend*

KNOWLEDGE
998 bîynâh (3), *understanding*
1843 dêa' (2), *knowledge*
1844 dê'âh (6), *knowledge*
1847 da'ath (82), *knowledge*
3045 yâda' (19), to *know*
4093 maddâ' (4), *intelligence*
5234 nâkar (2), to *treat as a foreigner*
5869 'ayin (1), *eye; sight; fountain*
7922 sekel (1), *intelligence; success*
56 agnōsia (1), state of *ignorance*
1097 ginōskō (1), to *know*
1108 gnōsis (28), *knowledge*
1492 ĕidō (1), to *know*
1921 ĕpiginōskō (3), to *acknowledge*
1922 ĕpignōsis (16), full *discernment*
1990 ĕpistēmōn (1), *intelligent, learned*
4907 sunĕsis (1), *intelligence, intellect*

KNOWN
3045 yâda' (105), to *know*
3046 yᵉda' (Ch.) (24), to *know*
5234 nâkar (2), to *acknowledge*
319 anagnōrizŏmai (1), to *make* oneself *known*
1097 ginōskō (46), to *know*
1107 gnōrizō (16), to *make known, reveal*
1110 gnōstŏs (11), *well-known*
1232 diagnōrizō (1), to *tell abroad*
1492 ĕidō (6), to *know*
1921 ĕpiginōskō (4), to *acknowledge*
3877 parakŏlŏuthĕō (1), to *attend; trace out*
4135 plērŏphŏrĕō (1), to *assure* or *convince*
5318 phanĕrŏs (3), *apparent, visible, clear*

English

KOA
6970 Qôwa' (1), *curtailment*

KOHATH
6955 Qᵉhâth (32), *allied*

KOHATHITES
6956 Qŏhâthîy (15), *Kohathite*

KOLAIAH
6964 Qôwlâyâh (2), *voice of Jehovah*

KORAH
7141 Qôrach (37), *ice*

KORAHITE
7145 Qorchîy (1), *Korchite*

KORAHITES
7145 Qorchîy (1), *Korchite*

KORATHITES
7145 Qorchîy (1), *Korchite*

KORE
6981 Qôwrê' (3), *crier*
7145 Qorchîy (1), *Korchite*

KORHITES
7145 Qorchîy (4), *Korchite*

KOZ
6976 Qôwts (4), *thorns*

KUSHAIAH
6984 Qûwshâyâhûw (1), *entrapped of Jehovah*

LAADAH
3935 La'dâh (1), *Ladah*

LAADAN
3936 La'dân (7), *Ladan*

LABAN
3837 Lâbân (51), *white*

LABAN'S
3837 Lâbân (4), *white*

LABOUR
213 'ûwts (1), to *be close, hurry, withdraw*
1518 gîyach (1), to *issue forth; to burst forth*
3018 yᵉgîya (12), *toil, work; produce, property*
3021 yâga' (8), to *be exhausted, to tire,*
3023 yâgêa' (1), *tiresome*
3027 yâd (1), *hand; power*
3205 yâlad (2), to *bear young; to father a child*
4399 mᵉlâ'kâh (1), *work; property*
4639 ma'ăseh (1), *action; labor*
5445 çâbal (1), to *carry*
5647 'âbad (2), to *do, work, serve*
5656 'ăbôdâh (1), *work of any kind*
5998 'âmal (2), to *work severely, put forth effort*
5999 'âmâl (25), *wearing effort; worry*
6001 'âmêl (1), *toiling; laborer; sorrowful*
6089 'etseb (1), *earthen vessel; painful toil*
6213 'âsâh (2), to *do*

LABOURED
3021 yâga' (4), to *be exhausted, to tire,*
3022 yâgâ' (1), *earnings, i.e. the product of toil*
5998 'âmal (5), to *work severely, put forth effort*
6001 'âmêl (1), *toiling; laborer; sorrowful*
6213 'âsâh (1), to *do or make*
7712 shᵉdar (Ch.) (1), to *endeavor, strive*
2872 kŏpiaō (5), to *feel fatigue; to work hard*
4866 sunathlĕō (1), to *wrestle with*

LABOURER
2040 ĕrgatēs (2), *toiler, worker*

LABOURERS
2040 ĕrgatēs (8), *toiler, worker*
4904 sunĕrgŏs (1), *fellow-worker*

LABOURETH
5998 'âmal (1), to *work severely, put forth effort*
6001 'âmêl (2), *toiling; laborer; sorrowful*
2872 kŏpiaō (2), to *feel fatigue; to work hard*

LABOURING
5647 'âbad (1), to *do, work, serve*
75 agōnizŏmai (1), to *struggle; to contend*
2872 kŏpiaō (1), to *feel fatigue; to work hard*
2873 kŏpŏs (1), *toil; pains*

LABOURS
3018 yᵉgîya (3), *toil, work; produce, property*
4639 ma'ăseh (3), *action; labor*
6089 'etseb (1), *earthen vessel; painful toil; mental pang*
6092 'âtsêb (1), *hired workman*
2873 kŏpŏs (5), *toil; pains*

LACE
6616 pâthîyl (4), *twine, cord*

LACHISH
3923 Lâchîysh (24), *Lakish*

LACK
1097 bᵉlîy (3), *without, not yet; lacking;*
2637 châçêr (4), to *lack; to fail, want, make less*

LABOUR
6468 pᵉ'ullâh (2), *work, deed*
2038 ĕrgazŏmai (1), to *toil*
2041 ĕrgŏn (1), *work*
2872 kŏpiaō (11), to *feel fatigue; to work hard*
2873 kŏpŏs (8), *toil; pains*
4704 spŏudazō (1), to *make effort*
4904 sunĕrgŏs (1), *fellow-worker*
5389 philŏtimĕŏmai (1), to *be eager or earnest*

LACKED
3021 yâga' (4), to *be exhausted, to tire,*

LACK
4270 machçôwr (1), *impoverishment*
7326 rûwsh (1), to *be destitute*
1641 ĕlattŏnĕō (1), to *fall short, have too little*
3007 lĕipō (1), to *fail or be absent*
5302 hustĕrĕō (1), to *be inferior; to fall short*
5303 hustĕrēma (1), *deficit; poverty; lacking*
5332 pharmakĕus (1), *magician, sorcerer*

LACKED
2637 châçêr (2), to *lack; to fail, want, make less*
2638 châçêr (1), *lacking*
5737 'âdar (2), to *arrange as a battle*
6485 pâqad (1), to *visit, care for, count*
170 akairĕŏmai (1), to *fail of a proper occasion*
1729 ĕndĕēs (1), *lacking; deficient in; needy*
3361+2192 mē (1), *not; lest*
5302 hustĕrĕō (2), to *be inferior; to fall short*

LACKEST
3007 lĕipō (1), to *fail or be absent*
5302 hustĕrĕō (1), to *be inferior; to fall short*

LACKETH
2638 châçêr (3), *lacking*
6485 pâqad (1), to *visit, care for, count*
3361+3918 mē (1), *not; lest*

LACKING
5737 'âdar (1), to *arrange as a battle*
6485 pâqad (2), to *visit, care for, count*
7038 qâlaṭ (1), to *be maim*
7673 shâbath (1), to *repose; to desist*
5303 hustĕrēma (3), *deficit; poverty; lacking*

LAD
5288 na'ar (32), *male child; servant*
3808 paidariŏn (1), *little boy*

LAD'S
5288 na'ar (1), *male child; servant*

LADDER
5551 çullâm (1), *stair-case*

LADE
2943 ṭâ'an (1), to *load a beast*
6006 'âmaç (1), to *impose a burden*
5412 phŏrtizō (1), to *overburden*

LADED
5375 nâsâ' (1), to *lift up*
6006 'âmaç (2), to *impose a burden*
2007 ĕpitithēmi (1), to *impose*

LADEN
3515 kâbêd (1), *severe, difficult, stupid*
5375 nâsâ' (2), to *lift up*
4987 sōrĕuō (1), to *pile up, load up*
5412 phŏrtizō (1), to *overburden*

LADETH
3515 kâbêd (1), *severe, difficult, stupid*

LADIES
8282 sârâh (2), *female noble*

LADING
6006 'âmaç (1), to *impose a burden*
5414 phŏrtŏs (1), *cargo of a ship*

LADS
5288 na'ar (1), *male child; servant*

LADY
1404 gᵉbereth (2), *mistress, noblewoman*
2959 Kuria (2), *Lady*

LAEL
3815 Lâ'êl (1), *belonging to God*

LAHAD
3854 lahag (1), *mental application*

LAHAI-ROI
883 Bᵉ'êr la-Chay Rô'îy (2), *well of a living (One) my seer*

LAHMAM
3903 Lachmâç (1), *food-like*

LAHMI
3902 Lachmîy (1), *foodful*

LAID
935 bôw' (1), to *go or come*
2470 châlâh (1), to *be weak, sick, afflicted*
2630 châçan (1), to *hoard, store up*
2934 ṭâman (2), to *hide*
3052 yᵉhab (Ch.) (1), to *give*
3240 yânach (1), to *allow to stay*
3241 Yânîym (8), *asleep*
3318 yâtsâ' (2), to *go, bring out*
3332 yâtsaq (1), to *pour out*
3369 yâqôsh (1), to *ensnare, trap*
3384 yârâh (1), to *point; to teach*
3515 kâbêd (1), *numerous; severe*
3647 kâmaç (1), to *store away*
5060 nâga' (1), to *strike*
5182 nᵉchath (Ch.) (1), to *descend; to depose*
5186 nâṭâh (1), to *stretch or spread out*
5324 nâtsab (1), to *station*
5375 nâsâ' (4), to *lift up*
5414 nâthan (13), to *give*

5446 çᵉbal (Ch.) (1), to *raise*

5493 çûwr (1), to *turn off*

5564 çâmak (6), to *lean upon*; *take hold* of

5674 'âbar (1), to *cross over*; to *transition*

5927 'âlâh (1), to *ascend, be high, mount*

6293 pâga' (1), to *impinge*

6485 pâqad (2), to *visit, care for, count*

6486 pᵉquddâh (1), *visitation; punishment*

6845 tsâphan (3), to *hide*; to *hoard or reserve*; to *deny*; to *protect*; to *lurk*

7737 shâvâh (3), to *level*, i.e. *equalize*

7760 sûwm (38), to *put, place*

7896 shîyth (8), to *place, put*

7901 shâkab (17), to *lie down*

7971 shâlach (6), to *send away*

8371 shâthath (1), to *place*, i.e. *array*; to *lie*

8610 tâphas (1), to *manipulate*, i.e. *seize*

347 anaklinō (1), to *lean back, recline*

606 apŏkĕimai (3), to be *reserved*; to *await*

659 apŏtithēmi (1), to *put away; get rid of*

906 ballō (3), to *throw*

1096 ginŏmai (1), to be, become

1462 ĕgklēma (2), accusation

1911 ĕpiballō (7), to *throw upon*

1945 ĕpikĕimai (2), to *rest upon; press upon*

2007 ĕpitithēmi (13), to *impose*

2071 ĕsŏmai (1), *will be*

2698 katatithēmi (1), to *place down*

2749 kĕimai (6), to *lie outstretched*

3049 lŏgizŏmai (1), to *credit; to think, regard*

4369 prŏstithēmi (1), to *lay beside, annex*

5087 tithēmi (29), to *place, put*

5294 hupŏtithēmi (1), to *hazard; to suggest*

5342 phĕrō (1), to *bear*

LAIDST
7760 sûwm (1), to *put*

LAIN
3045+4904 yâda' (1), to *know*

5414+7903 nâthan (1), to *give*

7901 shâkab (2), to *lie down*

2749 kĕimai (1), to *lie outstretched*

LAISH
3919 Layish (7), *lion*

LAKE
3041 limnē (10), *pond; lake*

LAKUM
3946 Laqqûwm (1), (poss.) *fortification*

LAMA
2982 lama (2), *why?*

LAMB
2924 ṭâleh (2), *lamb*

3532 kebes (44), *young ram*

3535 kibsâh (5), *ewe sheep*

3733 kar (1), *ram sheep; battering ram*

3775 keseb (3), *young ram sheep*

3776 kisbâh (1), *young ewe sheep*

6629 tsô'n (1), *flock of sheep or goats*

7716 seh (17), *sheep or goat*

286 amnŏs (4), *lamb*

721 arniŏn (27), *lamb, sheep*

LAMB'S
721 arniŏn (2), *lamb, sheep*

LAMBS
563 'immar (Ch.) (3), *lamb*

1121+6629 bên (2), *son, descendant; people*

2922 ṭᵉlâ' (1), *lamb*

3532 kebes (60), *young ram*

3535 kibsâh (3), *ewe sheep*

3733 kar (9), *ram sheep; battering ram*

3775 keseb (1), *young ram sheep*

704 arēn (1), *male lamb*

721 arniŏn (1), *lamb, sheep*

LAME
5223 nâkeh (2), *maimed; dejected*

6452 pâçach (1), to *hop, skip over*; to *hesitate*

6455 piççêach (14), *lame*

5560 chōlŏs (10), *limping, crippled*

LAMECH
3929 Lemek (11), *Lemek*

2984 Lamĕch (1), *Lemek*

LAMENT
56 'âbal (2), to *bewail*

421 'âlâh (1), to *bewail, mourn*

578 'ânâh (1), to *groan, lament*

5091 nâhâh (1), to *bewail; to assemble*

5594 çâphad (9), to *tear the hair, wail*

6969 qûwn (4), to *chant or wail at a funeral*

8567 tânâh (1), to *ascribe praise*, i.e. *celebrate*

2354 thrēnĕō (1), to *bewail, lament*

2875 kŏptō (1), to *beat the breast*

LAMENTABLE
6088 'ătsab (Ch.) (1), to *afflict; be afflicted*

LAMENTATION
592 'ănîyâh (1), *groaning*

1058 bâkâh (1), to *weep, moan*

4553 miçpêd (3), *lamentation, howling*

5092 nᵉhîy (3), *elegy*

7015 qîynâh (14), *dirge*

2355 thrēnŏs (1), *wailing, funeral song*

2870 kŏpĕtŏs (1), *mourning*

LAMENTATIONS
7015 qîynâh (3), *dirge*

LAMENTED
56 'âbal (1), to *bewail*

5091 nâhâh (1), to *bewail; to assemble*

5594 çâphad (4), to *tear the hair, wail*

6969 qûwn (3), to *chant or wail at a funeral*

2354 thrēnĕō (1), to *bewail, lament*

2875 kŏptō (1), to *beat the breast*

LAMP
3940 lappîyd (3), *flaming torch, lamp or flame*

5216 nîyr (9), *lamp; lamplight*

2985 lampas (1), *lamp, lantern, torch*

LAMPS
3940 lappîyd (5), *flaming torch, lamp or flame*

5216 nîyr (26), *lamp; lamplight*

2985 lampas (6), *lamp, lantern, torch*

LANCE
3591 kîydôwn (1), *dart, javelin*

LANCETS
7420 rômach (1), *iron pointed spear*

LAND
127 'ădâmâh (123), *soil; land*

249 'ezrâch (2), *native born*

776 'erets (1505), *earth, land, soil; country*

3004 yabbâshâh (1), *dry ground*

7704 sâdeh (7), *field*

68 agrŏs (1), *farmland, countryside*

1093 gē (42), *soil, region, whole earth*

3584 xērŏs (1), *scorched; arid; withered*

5561 chōra (3), *space of territory*

5564 chōriŏn (2), *spot or plot of ground*

LANDED
2609 katagō (1), to *lead down; to moor a vessel*

2718 katĕrchŏmai (1), to *go/come down*

LANDING
2609 katagō (1), to *lead down; to moor a vessel*

LANDMARK
1366 gᵉbûwl (4), *boundary, border*

LANDMARKS
1367 gᵉbûwlâh (1), *boundary marker*

LANDS
127 'ădâmâh (3), *soil; land*

776 'erets (34), *earth, land, soil; country, nation*

7704 sâdeh (4), *field*

68 agrŏs (3), *farmland, countryside*

5564 chōriŏn (1), *spot or plot of ground*

LANES
4505 rhumē (1), *alley or crowded avenue*

LANGUAGE
1697 dâbâr (1), *word; matter; thing*

3937 lâ'az (1), to *speak in a foreign tongue*

3956 lâshôwn (9), *tongue; tongue-shaped*

3961 lishshân (Ch.) (1), *nation*

8193 sâphâh (7), *lip, language, speech*

1258 dialĕktŏs (1), *known language*

LANGUAGES
3956 lâshôwn (1), *tongue; tongue-shaped*

3961 lishshân (Ch.) (6), *nation*

LANGUISH
535 'âmal (5), to be *weak; to be sick*

LANGUISHED
535 'âmal (1), to be *weak; to be sick*

LANGUISHETH
535 'âmal (8), to be *weak; to be sick*

LANGUISHING
1741 dᵉvay (1), *sickness*

LANTERNS
5322 phanŏs (1), *light; lantern*, i.e. *torch*

LAODICEA
2993 Laŏdikĕia (5), *Laodicea*

LAODICEANS
2994 Laŏdikĕus (2), *inhabitant of Laodicea*

LAP
899 beged (1), *clothing; treachery or pillage*

2436 chêyq (1), *bosom, heart*

2684 chôtsen (1), *bosom*

LAPIDOTH
3941 Lappîydôwth (1), *flaming torch, lamp*

LAPPED
3952 lâqaq (2), to *lick or lap*

LAPPETH
3952 lâqaq (2), to *lick or lap*

LAPWING
1744 dûwkîyphath (2), *hoopoe;* (poss.) *grouse*

LARGE
4800 merchâb (5), *open space; liberty*
7304 râvach (1), to *revive;* to *have ample room*
7337 râchab (2), to *broaden*
7342 râchâb (5), *roomy, spacious*
2425 hikanŏs (1), *ample; fit*
3173 mĕgas (2), *great, many*
4080 pēlikŏs (1), *how much, how great*
5118 tŏsŏutŏs (1), *such great*

LARGENESS
7341 rôchab (1), *width*

LASCIVIOUSNESS
766 asĕlgĕia (6), *licentiousness*

LASEA
2996 Lasaia (1), *Lasæa*

LASHA
3962 Lesha' (1), *boiling spring*

LASHARON
8289 Shârôwn (1), *plain*

LAST
314 'achărôwn (20), *late* or *last; behind; western*
318 'ochŏreyn (Ch.) (1), *at last, finally*
319 'achărîyth (10), *future; posterity*
6119 'âqêb (1), *track, footprint; rear* position
2078 ĕschatŏs (48), *farthest, final*
4218 pŏtĕ (1), at *some time, ever*
5305 hustĕrŏn (4), *more lately,* i.e. *eventually*

LASTED
1961 hâyâh (1), to *exist,* i.e. *be* or *become*

LASTING
5769 'ôwlâm (1), *eternity; ancient; always*

LATCHET
8288 sᵉrôwk (1), *sandal thong*
2438 himas (3), *strap; lash*

LATE
309 'âchar (1), to *delay;* to *procrastinate*
865 'ethmôwl (1), *formerly; yesterday*
3568 nun (1), *now;* the *present* or *immediate*

LATELY
4373 prŏsphatŏs (1), *recently*

LATIN
4513 Rhōmaïkŏs (2), *Latin*

LATTER
314 'achărôwn (8), *late* or *last; behind; western*
319 'achărîyth (20), *future; posterity*
320 'achărîyth (Ch.) (1), *later, end*
3954 leqesh (2), *after crop, second crop*
4456 malqôwsh (8), *spring rain*
2078 ĕschatŏs (1), *farthest, final*
3797 ŏpsimŏs (1), *later,* i.e. *vernal* showering
5305 hustĕrŏn (1), *more lately,* i.e. *eventually*

LATTICE
822 'eshnâb (1), *latticed window*
2762 cherek (1), *window lattice*
7639 sᵉbâkâh (1), *net-work balustrade*

LAUD
1867 ĕpainĕō (1), to *applaud, commend*

LAUGH
3932 lâ'ag (4), to *deride;* to *speak unintelligibly*
6711 tsâchaq (3), to *laugh;* to *scorn*
6712 tsᵉchôq (1), *laughter; scorn*
7832 sâchaq (8), to *laugh;* to *scorn;* to *play*
1070 gĕlaō (2), to *laugh*

LAUGHED
3932 lâ'ag (3), to *deride;* to *speak unintelligibly*
6711 tsâchaq (3), to *laugh;* to *scorn*
6712 tsᵉchôq (1), *laughter; scorn*
7832 sâchaq (3), to *laugh;* to *scorn;* to *play*
2606 katagelaō (3), to *laugh down,* i.e. *deride*

LAUGHETH
7832 sâchaq (1), to *laugh;* to *scorn;* to *play*

LAUGHING
7814 sᵉchôwq (1), *laughter; scorn*

LAUGHTER
7814 sᵉchôwq (6), *laughter; scorn*
1071 gĕlōs (1), *laughter*

LAUNCH
1877 ĕpanagō (1), to *put out* to sea; to *return*

LAUNCHED
321 anagō (4), to *bring out;* to *sail away*

LAVER
3595 kîyôwr (15), *caldron; washbowl*

LAVERS
3595 kîyôwr (5), *caldron; washbowl*

LAVISH
2107 zûwl (1), to *treat lightly*

LAW
1881 dâth (6), *royal edict* or *statute*
1882 dâth (Ch.) (9), *Law; royal edict* or *statute*
2524 châm (4), *father-in-law*
2545 chămôwth (11), *mother-in-law*
2706 chôq (4), *appointment; allotment*
2710 châqaq (1), to *engrave;* to *enact laws;* to *prescribe*
2859 châthan (32), to *become related*
2860 châthân (5), *relative* by *marriage*
2994 yᵉbêmeth (2), *sister-in-law*
3618 kallâh (17), *bride; son's wife*
4687 mitsvâh (1), *command*
4941 mishpâṭ (2), *verdict; formal decree; justice*
8451 tôwrâh (206), *precept* or *statute*
60 agŏraiŏs (1), *people* of the *market place*
458 anŏmia (1), *violation* of *law, wickedness*
459 anŏmŏs (3), *without* Jewish *law*
460 anŏmŏs (1), *lawlessly*
1772 ĕnnŏmŏs (1), *legal,* or *subject* to law
2917 krima (1), *decision*
2919 krinō (2), to *decide;* to *try, condemn, punish*
3544 nŏmikŏs (1), *expert* in the (Mosaic) *law*
3547 nŏmŏdidaskalŏs (3), a *Rabbi*
3548 nŏmŏthĕsia (1), *legislation, law*
3549 nŏmŏthĕtĕō (1), to *be given law*
3551 nŏmŏs (192), *law*
3565 numphē (3), *young married woman*
3891 paranŏmĕō (1), to *transgress, violate law*
3994 pĕnthĕra (3), *wife's mother, mother-in-law*
3995 pĕnthĕrŏs (1), *wife's father*
4160+458 pŏiĕō (1), to *make* or *do*

LAWFUL
4941 mishpâṭ (7), *verdict; formal decree; justice*
6662 tsaddîyq (1), *just*
7990 shallîyṭ (Ch.) (1), *premier, sovereign*
1772 ĕnnŏmŏs (1), *legal,* or *subject* to law
1832 ĕxĕsti (12), *it is right, it is proper*
1833 ĕxĕtazō (17), to *ascertain* or *interrogate*

LAWFULLY
3545 nŏmimŏs (2), *agreeably to the rules*

LAWGIVER
2710 châqaq (6), to *engrave;* to *enact* laws

LAW
3550 nŏmŏthĕtēs (1), *legislator, lawgiver*

LAWLESS
459 anŏmŏs (1), *without* Jewish *law*

LAWS
1881 dâth (3), *royal edict* or *statute*
1882 dâth (Ch.) (2), *Law; royal edict* or *statute*
8451 tôwrâh (12), *precept* or *codified statute*
8541 timmâhôwn (1), *consternation, panic*
3551 nŏmŏs (2), *law*

LAWYER
3544 nŏmikŏs (3), *expert* in the (Mosaic) *law*

LAWYERS
3544 nŏmikŏs (5), *expert* in the (Mosaic) *law*

LAY
3241 Yânîym (10), *asleep*
3331 yâtsa' (1), to *strew* as a surface
3885 lûwn (1), to *be obstinate*
4422 mâlaṭ (1), to *be delivered; be smooth*
5117 nûwach (1), to *rest;* to *settle* down
5186 nâṭâh (1), to *stretch* or *spread out*
5307 nâphal (4), to *fall*
5414 nâthan (20), to *give*
5493 çûwr (1), to *turn* off
5564 çâmak (12), to *lean* upon; *take hold* of
6651 tsâbar (1), to *aggregate, gather*
6845 tsâphan (2), to *hide;* to *hoard* or *reserve*
7126 qârab (1), to *approach, bring near*
7257 râbats (3), to *recline, repose, brood*
7258 rebets (1), *place* of *repose*
7760 sûwm (26), to *put, place*
7871 shîybâh (1), *residence*
7896 shîyth (5), to *place, put*
7901 shâkab (45), to *lie down*
7902 shᵉkâbâh (2), *lying down*
7931 shâkan (1), to *reside*
7971 shâlach (8), to *send away*
659 apŏtithēmi (2), to *put away; get rid of*
1458 ĕgkalĕō (1), to *charge, criminate*
1474 ĕdaphizō (1), to *dash to the ground*
1911 ĕpiballō (2), to *throw upon*
1945 ĕpikĕimai (2), to *rest upon; press upon*
1949 ĕpilambanŏmai (2), to *seize*
2007 ĕpitithēmi (7), to *impose*
2343 thēsaurizō (1), to *amass* or *reserve, store*

2476 hístēmi (1), to
stand, establish
2621 katakĕimai (5), to
lie down; to recline
2749 kĕimai (1), to *lie*
outstretched
2827 klinō (2), to *slant* or
slope
5087 tithēmi (13), to *place*

LAYEDST
5087 tithēmi (1), to *place*

LAYEST
7760 sûwm (1), to *put*

LAYETH
5381 nâsag (1), to *reach*
5414 nâthan (1), to *give*
6845 tsâphan (2), to *hide;*
to *hoard* or *reserve*
7760 sûwm (5), to *place*
7896 shîyth (1), to *place*
7971 shâlach (1), to *send*
away
2007 ĕpitithēmi (1), to
impose

LAYING
2934 ţâman (1), to *hide*
597 apŏthēsaurizō (1), to
store treasure away
659 apŏtithēmi (1), to *put*
away; get rid of
863 aphiēmi (1), to *leave;*
to *pardon, forgive*
1748 ĕnĕdrĕuō (1), to *lurk*
1917 ĕpibŏulē (1), *plot,*
plan
1936 ĕpithĕsis (3),
imposition
2598 kataballō (1), to
throw down
4160 pŏiĕō (1), to *make*
or *do*

LAZARUS
2976 Lazarŏs (15), *God*
(is) *helper*

LEAD
833 'âshar (1), to *go*
forward; guide
1869 dârak (2), to *tread,*
trample; to walk, lead
1980 hâlak (1), to *walk;*
live a certain way
2986 yâbal (1), to *bring*
3212 yâlak (2), to *walk;*
to *live; to carry*
3318 yâtsâ' (1), to *go,*
bring out
5090 nâhag (9), to *drive*
forth; to *lead, carry*
5095 nâhal (2), to *flow;* to
conduct; to protect
5148 nâchâh (16), to
guide
5777 'ôwphereth (9),
mineral *lead*
7218 rô'sh (1), *head*
71 agō (1), to *lead;* to
bring, drive; to weigh
162 aichmalōtĕuō (1), to
capture
520 apagō (2), to *take*
away
1236 diagō (1), to *pass*
time, *conduct one's life*
1533 ĕisphĕrō (2), to
carry inward
1806 ĕxagō (1), to *lead*
forth, escort

3594 hŏdĕgĕō (3), to
show the *way,* i.e. *lead*
4013 pĕriagō (1), to *take*
around as a companion
5497 chĕiragōgŏs (1),
conductor of the *blind*

LEADER
5057 nâgîyd (3),
commander, official

LEADERS
833 'âshar (1), to *go*
forward; guide
5057 nâgîyd (1),
commander, official
3595 hŏdĕgŏs (1),
conductor, guide

LEADEST
5090 nâhag (1), to *drive*
forth; to *lead away*

LEADETH
1869 dârak (1), to *tread,*
trample; to *walk, lead*
3212 yâlak (3), to *walk;*
to *live; to carry*
5090 nâhag (1), to *drive*
forth; to *lead away*
5095 nâhal (1), to *flow;* to
conduct; to *protect*
71 agō (1), to *lead;* to
bring, drive; to *weigh*
399 anaphĕrō (1), to *take*
up; to *lead up*
520 apagō (2), to *take*
away
1806 ĕxagō (1), to *lead*
forth, escort
4863 sunagō (1), to
gather together
5342 phĕrō (1), to *bear* or
carry

LEAF
5929 'âleh (11), *leaf;*
foliage

LEAGUE
1285 bᵉrîyth (17),
compact, agreement
2266 châbar (1), to
fascinate by spells
3772 kârath (1), to *cut*
(off, down or asunder)

LEAH
3812 Lê'âh (29), *weary*

LEAH'S
3812 Lê'âh (5), *weary*

LEAN
1800 dal (1), *weak, thin;*
humble, needy
5564 çâmak (2), to *lean*
upon; *take hold* of
7329 râzâh (1), to *make,*
become thin
7330 râzeh (2), *thin, lean*
7534 raq (1), *emaciated,*
lank
8172 shâ'an (4), to
support, rely on

LEANED
5564 çâmak (1), to *lean*
upon; *take hold* of
8172 shâ'an (4), to
support, rely on
377 anapiptō (1), *lie*
down, lean back

LEANETH
2388 châzaq (1), to
fasten upon; to *seize*
8127 shên (1), *tooth;*
ivory; cliff

LEANFLESHED
1851+1320 daq (2),
crushed; small or *thin*
7534 raq (1), *emaciated,*
lank

LEANING
7514 râphaq (1), to
recline
345 anakĕimai (1), to
recline at a meal

LEANNESS
3585 kachash (1),
emaciation; hypocrisy
7332 râzôwn (2), *thinness*
7334 râzîy (1), *thinness*

LEANNOTH
6030 'ânâh (1), to *sing,*
shout

LEAP
1801 dâlag (2), to *spring*
up, ascend
2178 zan (Ch.) (1), *sort,*
kind
4422 mâlaţ (1), to *escape*
as if by *slipperiness*
5425 nâthar (1), to *jump;*
to *be agitated*
5927 'âlâh (1), to *ascend,*
be high, mount
7520 râtsad (1), to *look*
askant; to be jealous
7540 râqad (1), to *spring*
about wildly or for joy
4640 skirtaō (1), to *jump*

LEAPED
1801 dâlag (2), to *spring*
up, ascend
5927 'âlâh (1), to *ascend,*
be high, mount
6452 pâçach (1), to *hop,*
skip over; to *limp*
242 hallŏmai (1), to *jump*
up; to *gush up*
2177 ĕphallŏmai (1), to
spring upon, leap upon
4640 skirtaō (2), to *jump*

LEAPING
1801 dâlag (1), to *spring*
up, ascend
6339 pâzaz (1), to *solidify*
by *refining;* to *spring*
242 hallŏmai (1), to *jump*
up; to *gush up*
1814 ĕxallŏmai (1), to
spring forth

LEARN
502 'âlaph (1), to *learn;*
to *teach*
3925 lâmad (17), to
teach, train
3129 manthanō (13), to
learn
3811 paidĕuō (1), to
educate or *discipline*

LEARNED
3045+5612 yâda' (3), to
know
3925 lâmad (5), to *teach,*
train
3928 limmûwd (2),
instructed one

5172 nâchash (1), to
prognosticate
3129 manthanō (10), to
learn
3811 paidĕuō (1), to
educate or *discipline*

LEARNING
3948 leqach (4),
instruction
5612 çĕpher (2), *writing*
1121 gramma (1),
writing; education
1319 didaskalia (1),
instruction
3129 manthanō (1), to
learn

LEASING
3577 kâzâb (2),
falsehood; idol

LEAST
176 'ôw (1), *or, whether;*
desire
389 'ak (1), *surely; only,*
however
4591 mâ'aţ (1), to *be,*
make small or *few*
6810 tsâ'îyr (4), *little* in
number; few in age
6994 qâţôn (1), to *be,*
make diminutive
6996 qâţân (10), *small,*
least, youngest
7535 raq (1), *merely;*
although
1646 ĕlachistŏs (9), *least*
1647 ĕlachistŏtĕrŏs (1),
far less
1848 ĕxŏuthĕnĕō (1), to
treat with contempt
2534 kaigĕ (1), *and at*
least (or *even, indeed*)
2579 kan (1), *and if*
3398 mikrŏs (6), *small,*
little

LEATHER
5785 'ôwr (1), *skin,*
leather

LEATHERN
1193 dĕrmatinŏs (1),
made of leather *hide*

LEAVE
2308 châdal (3), to *desist,*
stop; be fat
3241 Yânîym (14), *asleep*
3322 yâtsag (1), to *place*
3498 yâthar (7), to
remain or *be left*
3499 yether (1),
remainder; small *rope*
5157 nâchal (1), to *inherit*
5203 nâţash (6), to
disperse; to *thrust* off
5414 nâthan (2), to *give*
5800 'âzab (30), to
loosen; relinquish
6168 'ârâh (1), to *be,*
make bare; to *empty*
7503 râphâh (1), to
slacken
7592 shâ'al (1), to *ask*
7604 shâ'ar (13), to *leave,*
remain
7662 shᵉbaq (Ch.) (3), to
allow to remain
8338 shâwshâw (1),
(poss.) to *annihilate*

447 aniēmi (1), to *desert, desist* from
657 apŏtassŏmai (2), to *say adieu*; to *renounce*
782 aspazŏmai (1), to *give salutation*
863 aphiēmi (11), to *leave*; to *pardon, forgive*
1459 ĕgkataleipō (1), to *desert, abandon*
1544 ĕkballō (1), to *throw out*
2010 ĕpitrĕpō (2), *allow, permit*
2641 kataleipō (6), to *abandon*

LEAVED
1817 deleth (1), *door; gate*

LEAVEN
2557 châmêts (5), *ferment, yeasted*
4682 matstsâh (1), *unfermented cake*
7603 se'ôr (4), yeast-cake for *fermentation*
2219 zumē (13), *ferment*

LEAVENED
2557 châmêts (11), *ferment, yeasted*
7603 se'ôr (1), yeast-cake for *fermentation*
2220 zumŏō (2), to *cause to ferment*

LEAVENETH
2220 zumŏō (2), to *cause to ferment*

LEAVES
1817 deleth (3), *door; gate*
2529 chem'âh (1), *curds, milk* or *cheese*
2964 ţereph (1), *fresh torn prey*
6074 'ŏphîy (Ch.) (3), *foliage*
6763 tsêlâ' (1), *side*
7050 qela' (1), *slinging weapon*; *door screen*
5444 phullŏn (6), *leaf*

LEAVETH
5800 'âzab (2), to *loosen; relinquish; permit*
863 aphiēmi (2), to *leave*; to *pardon, forgive*

LEAVING
863 aphiēmi (3), to *leave*; to *pardon, forgive*
2641 kataleipō (1), to *abandon*
5277 hupŏlimpanō (1), to *leave behind*

LEBANA
3848 le bash (Ch.) (1), to *clothe*

LEBANAH
3848 le bash (Ch.) (1), to *clothe*

LEBANON
3844 Le bânôwn (71), *white snow mountain*

LEBAOTH
3822 Le bâ'ôwth (1), *lionesses*

LEBBAEUS
3002 Lĕbbaiŏs (1), *Lebbæus*

LEBONAH
3829 Le bôwnâh (1), *frankincense*

LECAH
3922 Lêkâh (1), *journey*

LED
833 'âshar (1), to *go forward; guide*
935 bôw' (2), to *go*
1869 dârak (2), to *tread, trample*; to *walk, lead*
2986 yâbal (1), to *bring*
3212 yâlak (13), to *walk*; to *live*; to *carry*
5090 nâhag (4), to *drive forth*; to *lead away*
5148 nâchâh (6), to *guide*
5437 çâbab (3), to *surround*
71 agō (11), to *lead*; to *bring, drive*; to *weigh*
162 aichmalōtĕuō (1), to *capture*
163 aichmalōtizō (1), to *make captive*
321 anagō (2), to *lead up*; to *bring out*
520 apagō (8), to *take away*
1521 eisagō (1), to *lead into*
1806 ĕxagō (3), to *lead forth, escort*
4879 sunapagō (1), to *take off together*
5496 chĕiragōgĕō (2), to *guide* a blind person

LEDDEST
3318 yâtsâ' (2), to *go, bring out*
5148 nâchâh (2), to *guide*
1806 ĕxagō (1), to *lead forth, escort*

LEDGES
3027 yâd (2), *hand; power*
7948 shâlâb (3), *interval*

LEEKS
2682 châtsîyr (1), *grass; leek plant*

LEES
8105 shemer (4), *settlings* of wine, *dregs*

LEFT
2308 châdal (7), to *desist, stop; be fat*
2790 chârash (1), to *be silent*; to *be deaf*
3240 yânach (8), to *allow to stay*
3241 Yânîym (3), *asleep*
3498 yâthar (7), to *remain* or *be left*
3499 yether (3), *remainder; small rope*
3615 kâlâh (3), to *cease, be finished, perish*
3885 lûwn (1), to *be obstinate with*
4672 mâtsâ' (2), to *find* or *acquire*; to *occur*
5203 nâţash (7), to *disperse*; to *thrust* off
5414 nâthan (1), to *give*

5493 çûwr (1), to *turn off*
5800 'âzab (43), to *loosen; relinquish*
5975 'âmad (2), to *stand*
6275 'âthaq (1), to *remove*; to *grow old*
7604 shâ'ar (65), to *leave, remain*
7611 she'êrîyth (1), *remainder* or *residual*
7662 she baq (Ch.) (1), to *allow to remain*
7673 shâbath (1), to *repose*; to *desist*
7971 shâlach (1), to *send away*
8040 se mô'wl (55), *north; left* hand
8041 sâma'l (4), to *use* the *left* hand or go *left*
8042 se mâ'lîy (9), on the *left* side; *northern*
8300 sârîyd (3), *survivor; remainder*
620 apŏleipō (3), to *leave* behind; to *forsake*
710 aristĕrŏs (3), *left* hand
863 aphiēmi (36), to *leave*; to *pardon, forgive*
1439 eaō (1), to *let be*, i.e. *permit* or *leave* alone
1459 ĕgkataleipō (1), to *desert, abandon*
2176 ĕuōnumŏs (10), *left; at the left* hand; *south*
2641 kataleipō (15), to *abandon*
3973 pauō (2), to *stop*, i.e. *restrain, quit*
4051 pĕrissĕuma (1), *superabundance*
4052 pĕrissĕuō (1), to *superabound*
5275 hupŏleipō (1), to *remain, survive*

LEFTEST
5800 'âzab (1), to *loosen; relinquish; permit*

LEFTHANDED
334+3027+3225 'iţţêr (2), *impeded* (as to the right hand), *left-handed*

LEG
7640 shôbel (1), lady's garment *train*

LEGION
3003 lĕgĕōn (3), *legion*

LEGIONS
3003 lĕgĕōn (1), *legion*

LEGS
3767 kârâ' (9), *leg*
6807 tse'âdâh (1), *march; ankle-chain*
7272 regel (1), *foot; step*
7785 shôwq (4), lower *leg*
8243 shâq (Ch.) (1), *shank*, or *whole leg*
4628 skĕlŏs (3), *leg*

LEHABIM
3853 Le hâbîym (2), *flames*

LEHI
3896 Lechîy (3), *jaw-*bone

LEISURE
2119 ĕukairĕō (1), to *have leisure*

LEMUEL
3927 Le mûw'êl (2), (belonging) *to God*

LEND
3867 lâvâh (4), to *unite*; to *remain*; to *lend*
5383 nâshâh (2), to *lend* or *borrow*
5391 nâshak (3), to *strike*; to *oppress*
5414 nâthan (1), to *give*
5670 'âbaţ (2), to *pawn*; to *lend*; to *entangle*
1155 daneizō (3), to *loan* on interest; to *borrow*
5531 chraō (1), to *loan, lend*

LENDER
3867 lâvâh (2), to *unite*; to *borrow*; to *lend*

LENDETH
3867 lâvâh (3), to *unite*; to *borrow*; to *lend*
5383 nâshâh (1), to *lend* or *borrow*

LENGTH
319 'achărîyth (1), *future; posterity*
753 'ôrek (70), *length*
3372 mêkŏs (3), *length*
4218 pŏtĕ (1), at *some time, ever*

LENGTHEN
748 'ârak (2), to *be, make long*

LENGTHENED
748 'ârak (1), to *be, make long*

LENGTHENING
754 'arkâ' (Ch.) (1), *length*

LENT
5383 nâshâh (2), to *lend* or *borrow*
5391 nâshak (1), to *strike*; to *oppress*
7592 shâ'al (4), to *ask*

LENTILES
5742 'âdâsh (4), *lentil* bean

LEOPARD
5245 ne mar (Ch.) (1), *leopard*
5246 nâmêr (4), *leopard*
3917 pardalis (1), *leopard, panther*

LEOPARDS
5246 nâmêr (2), *leopard*

LEPER
6879 tsâra' (13), to *be stricken with leprosy*
3015 lĕprŏs (4), *leper*

LEPERS
6879 tsâra' (1), to *be stricken with leprosy*
3015 lĕprŏs (5), *leper*

LEPROSY
6883 tsâra'ath (35), *leprosy*
3014 lĕpra (4), *leprosy*

LEPROUS
6879 tsâra' (6), to *be stricken with leprosy*

LESHEM
3959 Leshem (2), *jacinth stone*

LESS
657 'epheç (1), *end; no further*
4295 maṭṭâh (1), *below or beneath*
4591 mâ'aṭ (4), *to be, make small or few*
6996 qâṭân (3), *small, least, youngest*
253 alupŏtĕrŏs (1), *more without grief*
820 atimŏs (1), *without honor*
1640 ĕlassŏn (1), *smaller*
1647 ĕlachistŏtĕrŏs (1), *far less*
2276 hēttŏn (1), *worse; less*
3398 mikrŏs (2), *small, little*

LESSER
6996 qâṭân (2), *small, least, youngest*
7716 seh (1), *sheep or goat*

LEST
1077 bal (1), *nothing; not at all; lest*
1115 biltîy (3), *not, except, without, unless*
3808 lô' (12), *no, not*
6435 pên (120), *lest, not*
3361 mē (13), *not; lest*
3379 mĕpŏtĕ (20), *not ever; if, or lest ever*
3381 mĕpŏs (12), *lest somehow*

LET
3212 yâlak (1), *to walk; to live; to carry*
3240 yânach (3), *to allow to stay*
3381 yârad (7), *to descend*
5117 nûwach (1), *to rest; to settle down*
5186 nâṭâh (1), *to stretch or spread out*
5414 nâthan (3), *to give*
6544 pâra' (1), *to loosen*
7503 râphâh (2), *to slacken*
7725 shûwb (1), *to turn back; to return*
7971 shâlach (2), *to send away*
630 apŏluō (10), *to relieve, release*
863 aphiēmi (16), *to leave; to pardon, forgive*
1439 ĕaō (4), *to let be, i.e. permit or leave alone*
1554 ĕkdidōmi (4), *to lease, rent*
1832 ĕxĕsti (1), *it is right, it is proper*
1929 ĕpididōmi (1), *give over*
2010 ĕpitrĕpō (1), *allow, permit*
2524 kathiēmi (1), *to lower, let down*
2722 katĕchō (2), *to hold down fast*
2967 kōluō (1), *to stop*

5465 chalaō (5), *to lower as into a void*

LETTER
104 'iggᵉrâ' (Ch.) (3), *epistle, letter*
107 'iggereth (4), *epistle, letter*
5406 nishtᵉvân (2), *written epistle*
5407 nishtᵉvân (Ch.) (3), *written epistle*
5612 çêpher (13), *writing*
6600 pithgâm (Ch.) (1), *decree; report*
1121 gramma (6), *writing; education*
1989 ĕpistĕllō (1), *to communicate by letter*
1992 ĕpistŏlē (3), *written message*

LETTERS
107 'iggereth (6), *epistle, letter*
5612 çêpher (16), *writing*
1121 gramma (3), *writing; education*
1992 ĕpistŏlē (6), *written message*

LETTEST
8257 shâqa' (1), *to be overflowed; to cease*
630 apŏluō (1), *to relieve, release*

LETTETH
6362 pâṭar (1), *to burst through; to emit*
2722 katĕchō (1), *to hold down fast*

LETUSHIM
3912 Lᵉṭûwshîm (1), *oppressed ones*

LEUMMIM
3817 Lᵉummîym (1), *communities*

LEVI
3878 Lêvîy (64), *attached*
3017 Lĕui (5), *attached*
3018 Lĕuïs (3), *attached*

LEVIATHAN
3882 livyâthân (5), *serpent (crocodile)*

LEVITE
3881 Lêvîyîy (26), *Levite*
3019 Lĕuitēs (2), *descendants of Levi*

LEVITES
3878 Lêvîy (1), *attached*
3879 Lêvîy (Ch.) (4), *attached*
3881 Lêvîyîy (259), *Levite*
3019 Lĕuitēs (1), *descendants of Levi*

LEVITICAL
3020 Lĕuitikŏs (1), *relating to the Levites*

LEVY
4522 maç (4), *forced labor*
5927 'âlâh (1), *to ascend, be high, mount*
7311 rûwm (1), *to be high; to rise or raise*

LEWD
2154 zimmâh (2), *bad plan*

4190 pŏnērŏs (1), *malice, wicked, bad; crime*

LEWDLY
2154 zimmâh (1), *bad plan*

LEWDNESS
2154 zimmâh (14), *bad plan*
4209 mᵉzimmâh (1), *plan; sagacity*
5040 nablûwth (1), *female genitals*
4467 rhaᵢdiŏurgēma (1), *crime, legal fraction*

LIAR
376+3576 'îysh (1), *man; male; someone*
391 'akzâb (1), *deceit; treachery*
3576 kâzab (2), *to lie, deceive*
8267 sheqer (1), *untruth; sham*
5583 psĕustēs (8), *falsifier*

LIARS
907 bad (2), *brag or lie; liar, boaster*
3576 kâzab (1), *to lie, deceive*
3584 kâchash (1), *to lie, disown; to disappoint*
5571 psĕudēs (2), *erroneous, deceitful*
5583 psĕustēs (2), *falsifier*

LIBERAL
1293 bᵉrâkâh (1), *benediction, blessing*
5081 nâdîyb (3), *generous*
572 haplŏtēs (1), *sincerity; generosity*

LIBERALITY
572 haplŏtēs (1), *sincerity; generosity*
5485 charis (1), *graciousness*

LIBERALLY
6059 'ânaq (1), *to collar; to fit out*
574 haplŏs (1), *bountifully, generously*

LIBERTINES
3032 Libĕrtinŏs (1), *Freedman*

LIBERTY
1865 dᵉrôwr (7), *freedom; clear, pure*
2670 chophshîy (1), *exempt from bondage*
7342 râchâb (1), *roomy, spacious*
425 anĕsis (1), *relaxation; relief*
630 apŏluō (2), *to relieve, release; to pardon*
859 aphĕsis (1), *pardon, freedom*
1657 ĕlĕuthĕria (11), *freedom*
1658 ĕlĕuthĕrŏs (1), *unrestrained*
1849 ĕxŏusia (1), *authority, power, right*
2010 ĕpitrĕpō (1), *to allow*

LIBNAH
3841 Libnâh (18), *storax-tree*

LIBNI
3845 Libnîy (5), *white*

LIBNITES
3864 Lûwbîy (2), *dry region*

LIBYA
6316 Pûwṭ (2), *Put, person*
3033 Libuē (1), *south region*

LIBYANS
3864 Lûwbîy (2), *dry region*
6316 Pûwṭ (2), *Put, person*

LICE
3654 kên (6), *stinging bug*

LICENCE
2010 ĕpitrĕpō (1), *allow, permit*
5117 tŏpŏs (1), *place*

LICK
3897 lâchak (4), *to lick*
3952 lâqaq (1), *to lick*

LICKED
3897 lâchak (1), *to lick*
3952 lâqaq (2), *to lick*
621 apŏlĕichō (1), *to lick off clean*

LICKETH
3897 lâchak (1), *to lick*

LID
1817 deleth (1), *door; gate*

LIE
391 'akzâb (1), *deceit; treachery*
693 'ârab (2), *to ambush, lie in wait*
2583 chânâh (2), *to encamp*
3576 kâzab (12), *to lie, deceive*
3584 kâchash (1), *to lie, disown; to disappoint*
3885 lûwn (2), *to be obstinate*
4769 marbêts (1), *reclining or resting place*
5203 nâṭash (1), *to disperse; to abandon*
5307 nâphal (1), *to fall*
5414+7903 nâthan (3), *to give*
6658 tsâdâh (1), *to desolate*
7250 râba' (2), *to lay down; have sex*
7257 râbats (15), *to recline, repose, brood*
7258 rebets (1), *place of repose*
7693 shâgal (1), *to copulate*
7901 shâkab (59), *to lie down*
7931 shâkab (59) *(see above)*
8266 shâqar (5), *to cheat, i.e. be untrue in words*
8267 sheqer (8), *untruth; sham*
893 apsĕudēs (1), *veracious, free of deceit*
2621 katakĕimai (1), *to lie down; to recline*

2749 kĕimai (1), *to lie*
outstretched
3180 mĕthŏdĕia (1),
trickery, scheming
3582 xĕstēs (1), *vessel*
5574 psĕudŏmai (11), *to
utter an untruth*
5579 psĕudŏs (7),
falsehood

LIED
3576 kâzab (2), *to lie,
deceive*
3584 kâchash (1), *to lie,
disown; to disappoint*
5574 psĕudŏmai (1), *to
utter an untruth*

LIEN
7693 shâgal (1), *to
copulate with*
7901 shâkab (2), *to lie
down*

LIES
907 bad (3), *brag or lie;
liar, boaster*
1697+3576 dâbâr (1),
word; matter; thing
1697+8267 dâbâr (1),
word; matter; thing
3576 kâzab (22), *to lie,
deceive*
3585 kachash (4),
emaciation; hypocrisy
7723 shâv' (1), *ruin;
guile; idolatry*
8267 sheqer (17),
untruth; sham
8383 tᵉ'ûn (1), *toil*
5573 psĕudŏlŏgŏs (1),
*promulgating
erroneous doctrine*

LIEST
5307 nâphal (1), *to fall*
7901 shâkab (4), *to lie
down*

LIETH
3318 yâtsâ' (3), *to go,
bring out*
3584 kâchash (1), *to lie,
disown; to disappoint*
4904 mishkâb (1), *bed;
sleep; intercourse*
5564 çâmak (1), *to lean
upon; take hold of*
6437 pânâh (1), *to turn,
to face*
7257 râbats (2), *to
recline, repose, brood*
7901 shâkab (20), *to lie
down*
8172 shâ'an (1), *to
support, rely on*
906 ballō (1), *to throw*
991 blĕpō (1), *to look at*
2192 ĕchō (1), *to have;
hold; keep*
2749 kĕimai (2), *to lie
outstretched*

LIEUTENANTS
323 'ăchashdarpan (4),
satrap

LIFE
2416 chay (143), *alive;
raw; fresh; life*
2417 chay (Ch.) (1), *alive;
life*
2421 châyâh (10), *to live;
to revive*

2425 châyay (1), *to live;
to revive*
3117 yôwm (3), *day; time
period*
3117+5921 yôwm (1),
day; time period
5315 nephesh (90), *life;
breath; soul; wind*
6106 'etsem (1), *bone;
body; substance*
72 agōgē (1), *mode of
living, way of life*
895 apsuchŏs (1), *lifeless,
i.e. inanimate*
979 biŏs (5), *present
state of existence*
981 biŏsis (1), *mode of
living*
982 biōtikŏs (3), *relating
to the present existence*
2198 zaō (1), *to live*
2222 zōē (132), *life*
2227 zōŏpŏiĕō (2), *to (re-)
vitalize, give life*
4151 pnĕuma (1), *spirit*
5590 psuchē (36), *soul,
vitality; heart, mind*

LIFETIME
2416 chay (1), *alive; raw;
fresh; life*
2198 zaō (1), *to live*
2222 zōē (1), *life*

LIFT
5127 nûҫ (1), *to vanish
away, flee*
5130 nûwph (3), *to
quiver, vibrate, rock*
5375 nâsâ' (66), *to lift up*
5414 nâthan (1), *to give*
6030 'ânâh (1), *to
respond, answer*
6670 tsâhal (1), *to be
cheerful; to sound*
6965 qûwm (3), *to rise*
7311 rûwm (18), *to be
high; to rise or raise*
352 anakuptō (1), *to
straighten up*
461 anŏrthŏō (1), *to
straighten up*
1458 ĕgkalĕō (1), *to
charge, criminate*
1869 ĕpairō (4), *to raise
up, look up*
5312 hupsŏō (1), *to
elevate; to exalt*

LIFTED
935 bôw' (1), *to go or
come*
1361 gâbahh (7), *to be
lofty; to be haughty*
1431 gâdal (1), *to be
great, make great*
1802 dâlâh (1), *to draw
out water); to deliver*
5130 nûwph (1), *to
quiver, vibrate, rock*
5191 nᵉṭal (Ch.) (2), *to
raise; to repent*
5264 nâçaç (1), *to gleam;
to flutter a flag*
5375 nâsâ' (92), *to lift up*
5423 nâthaq (1), *to tear
off*
5782 'ûwr (3), *to awake*
5927 'âlâh (1), *to ascend,
be high, mount*

6075 'âphal (1), *to swell;
be elated*
7213 râ'am (1), *to rise*
7311 rûwm (15), *to be
high; to rise or raise*
7313 rûwm (Ch.) (2),
elation, arrogance
7426 râmam (2), *to rise*
142 airō (4), *to lift, to
take up*
352 anakuptō (2), *to
straighten up*
450 anistēmi (1), *to
stand up; to come back
to life*
1453 ĕgĕirō (3), *to
waken, i.e. rouse*
1869 ĕpairō (10), *to raise
up, look up*
5188 tuphō (1), *to make
a smoke*
5312 hupsŏō (5), *to
elevate; to exalt*

LIFTER
7311 rûwm (1), *to be
high; to rise or raise*

LIFTEST
5375 nâsâ' (1), *to lift up*
5414 nâthan (1), *to give*
7311 rûwm (2), *to be
high; to rise or raise*

LIFTETH
4754 mârâ' (1), *to rebel;
to lash with whip; flap*
5375 nâsâ' (2), *to lift up*
5749 'ûwd (1), *to
duplicate or repeat*
5927 'âlâh (2), *to ascend,
be high, mount*
7311 rûwm (4), *to be
high; to rise or raise*

LIFTING
1348 gê'ûwth (1),
ascending; majesty
1466 gêvâh (1),
exaltation; arrogance
4607 mô'al (1), *raising of
the hands*
4864 mas'êth (1), *raising;
beacon; present*
5375 nâsâ' (1), *to lift up*
5782 'ûwr (1), *to awake*
7311 rûwm (1), *to be
high; to rise or raise*
7427 rômêmûth (1),
exaltation
1869 ĕpairō (1), *to raise
up, look up*

LIGHT
215 'ôwr (1), *to be
luminous*
216 'ôwr (126), *luminary;
lightning; happiness*
217 'ûwr (1), *flame; East*
219 'ôwrâh (2),
luminousness, light
3313 yâpha' (1), *to shine*
3974 mâ'ôwr (15),
luminary, light source
4237 mechĕzâh (2),
window
5051 nôgahh (1),
brilliancy
5094 nᵉhîyr (Ch.) (3),
illumination
5105 nᵉhârâh (1),
daylight

5117 nûwach (1), *to rest;
to settle down*
5216 nîyr (4), *lamp;
lamplight*
5927 'âlâh (2), *to ascend,
be high, mount*
6348 pâchaz (2), *to be
unimportant*
7031 qal (1), *rapid, swift*
7034 qâlâh (1), *to be light*
7043 qâlal (7), *to be,
make light*
7052 qᵉlôqêl (1),
insubstantial food
7136 qârâh (1), *to bring
about; to impose*
7837 shachar (1), *dawn*
272 amĕlĕō (1), *to be
careless of, neglect*
681 haptō (1), *to set on
fire*
1645 ĕlaphrŏs (2), *light,
i.e. easy*
2014 ĕpiphainō (1), *to
become visible*
2017 ĕpiphauō (1), *to
illuminate, shine on*
2545 kaiō (1), *to set on
fire*
2989 lampō (1), *to
radiate brilliancy*
3088 luchnŏs (5), *lamp
or other illuminator*
4098 piptō (1), *to fall*
5338 phĕggŏs (3),
brilliancy, radiance
5457 phōs (65),
luminousness, light
5458 phōstēr (1),
celestial luminary
5460 phōtĕinŏs (4),
well-illuminated
5461 phōtizō (4), *to shine
or to brighten up*
5462 phōtismŏs (2), *light;
illumination*

LIGHTED
3381 yârad (2), *to
descend*
4672 mâtsâ' (1), *to find
or acquire; to occur*
5307 nâphal (3), *to fall*
5927 'âlâh (2), *to ascend,
be high, mount*
6293 pâga' (1), *to impinge*
6795 tsânach (2), *to
descend, i.e. drive down*
681 haptō (2), *to set on
fire*

LIGHTEN
215 'ôwr (2), *to be
luminous*
5050 nâgahh (1), *to
illuminate*
7043 qâlal (2), *to be,
make light*
602 apŏkalupsis (1),
disclosure, revelation
5461 phōtizō (1), *to shine
or to brighten up*

LIGHTENED
215 'ôwr (1), *to be
luminous*
5102 nâhar (1), *to
sparkle; to be cheerful*
1546+4160 ĕkbŏlē (1),
jettison of cargo

2893 kŏuphizō (1), to
unload, make lighter
5461 phōtizō (1), to shine
or to brighten up

LIGHTENETH
215 'ôwr (1), to be
luminous
797 astraptō (1), to flash
as lightning

LIGHTER
7043 qâlal (4), to be,
make light

LIGHTEST
5927 'âlâh (1), to ascend,
be high, mount

LIGHTETH
4672 mâtsâ' (1), to find
or acquire; to occur
5927 'âlâh (1), to ascend,
be high, mount
5461 phōtizō (1), to shine
or to brighten up

LIGHTING
5183 nachath (1),
descent; quiet
2064 ĕrchŏmai (1), to go
or come

LIGHTLY
4592 mᵉ'aṭ (1), little or
few
5034 nâbêl (1), to wilt; to
fall away; to be foolish
7034 qâlâh (1), to be light
7043 qâlal (3), to be,
make light
5035 tachu (1), without
delay, soon, suddenly

LIGHTNESS
6350 pachăzûwth (1),
frivolity
6963 qôwl (1), voice or
sound
1644 ĕlaphria (1),
fickleness

LIGHTNING
216 'ôwr (1), luminary;
lightning; happiness
965 bâzâq (1), flash of
lightning
1300 bârâq (5), lightning;
flash of lightning
2385 chăzîyz (2), flash of
lightning
796 astrapē (4),
lightning; light's glare

LIGHTNINGS
1300 bârâq (9), lightning;
flash of lightning
3940 lappîyd (1), flaming
torch, lamp or flame
796 astrapē (4),
lightning; light's glare

LIGHTS
216 'ôwr (1), luminary;
lightning; happiness
3974 mâ'ôwr (4),
luminary, light source
8261 shâqûph (1),
opening
2985 lampas (1), lamp,
lantern, torch
3088 luchnŏs (1), lamp
or other illuminator
5457 phōs (1),
luminousness, light

5458 phōstēr (1),
celestial luminary

LIGURE
3958 leshem (2), (poss.)
jacinth

LIKE
251 'âch (1), brother;
relative; member
1571 gam (2), also; even
1819 dâmâh (16), to
resemble, liken
1821 dᵉmâh (Ch.) (2), to
resemble; be like
1823 dᵉmûwth (2),
resemblance, likeness
1825 dimyôwn (1),
resemblance, likeness
1922 hădar (Ch.) (1), to
magnify, glorify
2088 zeh (1), this or that
2421 châyâh (1), to live;
to revive
2654 châphêts (2), to be
pleased with, desire
2803 châshab (1), to
think, regard; to value
3541 kôh (1), thus
3644 kᵉmôw (61), like,
as; for; with
3651 kên (7), just; right,
correct
4711 mâtsats (1), to suck
4911 mâshal (5), to use
figurative language
4915 môshel (1), empire;
parallel
5973 'îm (2), with
5974 'îm (Ch.) (1), with
7737 shâvâh (2), to
resemble; to adjust
407 andrizŏmai (1), to
act manly
499 antitupŏn (1),
representative
871 aphŏmŏiŏō (1), to be
like
1381 dŏkimazō (1), to
test; to approve
1503 ĕikō (2), to
resemble, be like
2470 isŏs (1), similar
2472 isŏtimŏs (1), of
equal value or honor
2504 kagō (1), and also
2532 kai (1), and; or
3663 hŏmŏiŏpathēs (2),
similarly affected
3664 hŏmŏiŏs (47),
similar
3665 hŏmŏiŏtēs (1),
resemblance, similarity
3666 hŏmŏiŏō (4), to
become like
3667 hŏmŏiōma (1),
form; resemblance
3779 hŏutō (2), in this
way; likewise
3945 parŏmŏiazō (2), to
resemble, be like
3946 parŏmŏiŏs (2),
similar, like
4832 summŏrphŏs (1),
similar, conformed to
5024 tauta (1), in the
same way
5108 tŏiŏutŏs (1), truly
this, i.e. of this sort
5613 hōs (10), which,
how, i.e. in that manner

5615 hōsautōs (2), in the
same way
5616 hōsĕi (6), as if
5618 hōspĕr (1), exactly
like

LIKED
7521 râtsâh (1), to be
pleased with; to satisfy

LIKEMINDED
2473 isŏpsuchŏs (1), of
similar spirit
3588+846+5426 hŏ (2),
"the," definite article

LIKEN
1819 dâmâh (4), to
resemble, liken
3666 hŏmŏiŏō (5), to
become like

LIKENED
1819 dâmâh (2), to
resemble, liken
3666 hŏmŏiŏō (4), to
become like

LIKENESS
1823 dᵉmûwth (19),
resemblance, likeness
8403 tabnîyth (5),
resemblance
8544 tᵉmûwnâh (5),
something fashioned
3666 hŏmŏiŏō (1), to
become like
3667 hŏmŏiōma (3),
form; resemblance

LIKETH
157 'âhab (1), to have
affection, love
2896 ṭôwb (2), good; well

LIKEWISE
1571 gam (15), also;
even; yea; though
2063 zō'th (2), this
3162 yachad (1), unitedly
3651 kên (14), just; right
36 agĕnēs (1), ignoble,
lowly
437 anthŏmŏlŏgĕŏmai
(1), respond in praise
2532 kai (11), and; or
3668 hŏmŏiōs (29), in the
same way
3779 hŏutō (5), in this
way; likewise
3898 paraplēsiōs (1), in a
manner near by
5615 hōsautōs (13), in
the same way

LIKHI
3949 Liqchîy (1), learned

LIKING
2492 châlam (1), to be,
make plump; to dream

LILIES
7799 shûwshan (8), white
lily; straight trumpet
2918 krinŏn (2), lily

LILY
7799 shûwshan (5), white
lily; straight trumpet

LIME
7875 sîyd (2), lime

LIMIT
1366 gᵉbûwl (1),
boundary, border

LIMITED
8428 tâvâh (1), to grieve,
bring pain

LIMITETH
3724 hŏrizō (1), to
appoint, decree, specify

LINE
2256 chebel (5),
company, band
2339 chûwṭ (1), string;
line
6616 pâthîyl (1), twine,
cord
6957 qav (14), rule;
musical string
8279 sered (1),
scribing-awl
8515 Tᵉla'ssar (1),
Telassar
8615 tiqvâh (1), cord;
expectancy
2583 kanōn (1), rule,
standard

LINEAGE
3965 patria (1), family,
group, race, i.e. nation

LINEN
906 bad (23), linen
garment
948 bûwts (9), Byssus,
(poss.) cotton
4723 miqveh (4),
confidence; collection
5466 çâdîyn (2), shirt
6593 pishteh (9), linen,
from carded thread
8162 sha'aṭnêz (1), linen
and woolen
8336 shêsh (37), white
linen; white marble
1039 bussinŏs (4), linen
1040 bussŏs (2), white
linen
3043 linŏn (1), flax linen
3608 ŏthŏniŏn (5), strips
of linen bandage
4616 sindōn (6), byssos,
i.e. bleached linen

LINES
2256 chebel (2),
company, band

LINGERED
4102 mâhahh (2), to be
reluctant

LINGERETH
691 argĕō (1), to delay,
grow weary

LINTEL
352 'ayîl (1), chief; ram;
oak tree
3730 kaphtôr (1), capital;
wreath-like button
4947 mashqôwph (2),
lintel

LINTELS
3730 kaphtôr (1), capital;
wreath-like button

LINUS
3044 Linŏs (1), (poss.)
flax linen

LION
738 'ărîy (56), lion
739 'ărîy'êl (2), Lion of
God

3715 kᵉphîyr (16), walled village; young lion
3833 lâbîy' (9), lion, lioness
3918 layish (3), lion
7826 shachal (6), lion
3023 lĕōn (6), lion

LION'S
738 'ărîy (4), lion
3833 lâbîy' (1), lion, lioness
7830 shachats (1), haughtiness; dignity

LIONESS
3833 lâbîy' (1), lion, lioness

LIONESSES
3833 lâbîy' (1), lion, lioness

LIONLIKE
739 'ărîy'êl (2), Lion of God

LIONS
738 'ărîy (17), lion
744 'aryêh (Ch.) (8), lion
3715 kᵉphîyr (14), walled village; young lion
3833 lâbîy' (1), lion, lioness
3023 lĕōn (3), lion

LIONS'
738 'ărîy (2), lion
744 'aryêh (Ch.) (1), lion

LIP
822 'eshnâb (1), latticed window
8193 sâphâh (2), lip, language, speech

LIPS
2193 zâ'ak (1), to extinguish
8193 sâphâh (109), lip, language, speech
8222 sâphâm (3), beard
5491 chĕîlŏs (6), lip

LIQUOR
4197 mezeg (1), tempered wine
4952 mishrâh (1), steeped juice

LIQUORS
1831 dema' (1), juice

LISTED
2309 thĕlō (2), to will; to desire; to choose

LISTEN
8085 shâma' (1), to hear intelligently

LISTETH
2309 thĕlō (1), to will; to desire; to choose
3730+1014 hŏrmē (1), impulse, i.e. onset

LITTERS
6632 tsâb (1), lizard; covered cart

LITTLE
1851 daq (1), crushed; small or thin
2191 zᵉ'êyr (3), small, little
2192 zᵉ'êyr (Ch.) (1), small, little

2835 châsîph (1), small company, flock
2945 ṭaph (32), family of children and women
3530 kibrâh (3), measure of length
3563 kôwç (2), cup; (poss.) owl
4591 mâ'aṭ (3), to be, make small or few
4592 mᵉ'aṭ (52), little or few
4704 mitstsᵉʿîyrâh (1), diminutive
4705 mits'âr (3), little; short time
5759 'ăvîyl (1), infant, young child
5768 'ôwlêl (1), suckling child
6810 tsâ'îyr (4), little in number; few in age
6819 tsâ'ar (1), to be small; be trivial
6966 qûwm (Ch.) (1), to rise
6995 qôṭen (2), little finger
6996 qâṭân (20), small, least, youngest
8102 shemets (2), inkling
8241 shetseph (1), outburst of anger
8585 tᵉ'âlâh (1), channel; bandage or plaster
974 bibliaridiŏn (4), little scroll
1024 brachus (6), little, short
1646 ĕlachistŏs (1), least
2365 thugatriŏn (1), little daughter
2485 ichthudiŏn (1), little fish
3357 mĕtriŏs (1), moderately, i.e. slightly
3397 mikrŏn (14), small space of time or degree
3398 mikrŏs (16), small, little
3640 ŏligŏpistŏs (5), little confidence
3641 ŏligŏs (9), puny, small
3813 paidiŏn (12), child: immature
4142 plŏiariŏn (2), small boat
5040 tĕkniŏn (9), infant, i.e. a darling Christian
5177 tugchanō (1), to take part in; to obtain

LIVE
2414 châṭaph (3), to seize as a prisoner
2416 chay (44), alive; raw; fresh; life
2418 chăyâ' (Ch.) (2), to live
2421 châyâh (110), to live; to revive
2425 châyay (15), to live; to revive
3117 yôwm (2), day; time period
7531 ritspâh (1), hot stone; pavement
390 anastrĕphō (2), to remain, to live

980 biŏō (1), to live life
1514 ĕirēnĕuō (2), to be, act peaceful
2068 ĕsthiō (1), to eat
2071+3118 ĕsŏmai (1), will be
2198 zaō (53), to live
2225 zōŏgŏnĕō (1), to rescue; be saved
4800 suzaō (3), to live in common with
5225 huparchō (1), to come into existence

LIVED
2416 chay (5), alive; raw; fresh; life
2421 châyâh (39), to live; to revive
2425 châyay (5), to live; to revive
326 anazaō (1), to recover life, live again
2198 zaō (4), to live
4176 pŏlitĕuŏmai (1), to behave as a citizen
5171 truphaō (1), to live indulgently

LIVELY
2416 chay (1), alive; raw; fresh; life
2422 châyeh (1), vigorous
2198 zaō (3), to live

LIVER
3516 kâbêd (14), liver

LIVES
2416 chay (2), alive; raw; fresh; life
2417 chay (Ch.) (1), alive; life
2421 châyâh (2), to live; to revive
5315 nephesh (18), life; breath; soul; wind
5590 psuchē (5), soul, vitality; heart, mind

LIVEST
2416 chay (1), alive; raw; fresh; life
3117 yôwm (1), day; time period
2198 zaō (2), to live

LIVETH
2416 chay (61), alive; raw; fresh; life
2421 châyâh (1), to live; to revive
2425 châyay (2), to live; to revive
3117 yôwm (1), day; time period
2198 zaō (24), to live

LIVING
2416 chay (98), alive; raw; fresh; life
2417 chay (Ch.) (4), alive; life
2424 chayûwth (1), life, lifetime
979 biŏs (5), present state of existence
1236 diagō (1), to pass time or life
2198 zaō (34), to live

LIZARD
3911 lᵉṭâ'âh (1), kind of lizard

LO
718 'ărûw (Ch.) (1), lo!, behold!
1883 dethe' (Ch.) (1), sprout; green grass
1888 hê' (Ch.) (1), Lo!, Look!
2005 hên (13), lo!; if!
2009 hinnêh (103), lo!; Look!
2114 zûwr (1), to be foreign, strange
7200 râ'âh (3), to see
2395 iatrŏs (1), physician
2396 idĕ (2), surprise!, lo!, look!
2400 idŏu (29), lo!, note!, see!

LO-AMMI
3818 Lô' 'Ammîy (1), not my people

LO-DEBAR
3810 Lô' Dᵉbar (3), pastureless

LO-RUHAMAH
3819 Lô' Rûchâmâh (2), not pitied

LOADEN
6006 'âmaç (1), to impose a burden

LOADETH
6006 'âmaç (1), to impose a burden

LOAF
3603 kikkâr (2), round loaf; talent
740 artos (1), loaf of bread

LOAN
7596 shᵉ'êlâh (1), petition

LOATHE
3988 mâ'aç (1), to spurn; to disappear

LOATHETH
947 bûwç (1), to trample down; oppress
6973 qûwts (1), to be, make disgusted

LOATHSOME
887 bâ'ash (1), to be a moral stench
2214 zârâ' (1), disgusting, loathing
3988 mâ'aç (1), to spurn; to disappear
7033 qâlâh (1), to toast, scorch

LOAVES
3603 kikkâr (2), round loaf; talent
3899 lechem (5), food, bread
740 artos (22), loaf of bread

LOCK
4514 man'ûwl (1), bolt on door
6734 tsîytsîth (1), fore-lock of hair; tassel

LOCKED
5274 nâ'al (2), to fasten up, lock

LOCKS
4253 machlâphâh (2), *ringlet* or *braid*, of hair
4514 man'ûwl (5), *bolt* on door
6545 pera' (2), *hair* as *dishevelled*
6777 tsammâh (4), *veil*
6977 qᵉvutstsâh (2), *forelock* of hair

LOCUST
697 'arbeh (9), *locust*
5556 çol'âm (1), destructive *locust* kind
6767 tsᵉlâtsal (1), *cricket*

LOCUSTS
697 'arbeh (11), *locust*
1357 gêb (1), *locust swarm*
2284 châgâb (1), *locust*
200 akris (4), *locust*

LOD
3850 Lôd (4), *Lod*

LODGE
3885 lûwn (22), to *be obstinate*
4412 mᵉlûwnâh (1), *hut*
2647 kataluō (1), to *halt for the night*
2681 kataskĕnŏō (2), to *remain, live*
3579 xĕnizō (1), to *be a host*; to *be a guest*

LODGED
3885 lûwn (12), to *be obstinate*
4411 mâlôwn (1), *lodging for night*
7901 shâkab (1), to *lie down*
835 aulizŏmai (1), to *pass the night*
2681 kataskĕnŏō (1), to *remain, live*
3579 xĕnizō (4), to *be a host*; to *be a guest*
3580 xĕnŏdŏchĕō (1), to *be hospitable*

LODGEST
3885 lûwn (1), to *be obstinate*

LODGETH
3579 xĕnizō (1), to *be a host*; to *be a guest*

LODGING
3885 lûwn (1), to *be obstinate*
4411 mâlôwn (3), *lodgment* for night
3578 xĕnia (2), *place of entertainment*

LODGINGS
4411 mâlôwn (1), *lodgment* for night

LOFT
5944 'ălîyâh (1), *upper things; second-story*

LOFTILY
4791 mârôwm (1), *elevation; elation*

LOFTINESS
1363 gôbahh (1), *height; grandeur; arrogance*
1365 gabhûwth (1), *pride, arrogance*

LOFTY
1364 gâbôahh (2), *high; powerful; arrogant*
1365 gabhûwth (1), *pride, arrogance*
5375 nâsâ' (1), to *lift up*
7311 rûwm (3), to *be high*; to *rise* or *raise*
7682 sâgab (1), to *be, make lofty*; be *safe*

LOG
3849 lôg (5), *liquid measure*

LOINS
2504 châlâts (9), *loins, areas of the waist*
2788 chârêr (1), *arid, parched*
3409 yârêk (2), *leg* or *shank, flank; side*
3689 keçel (2), *loin; back; viscera*
4975 môthen (42), *loins*
3751 ŏsphus (8), *loin; belt*

LOIS
3090 Lŏïs (1), *Loïs*

LONG
748 'ârak (4), to *be, make long*
752 'ârôk (2), *long*
753 'ôrek (23), *length*
954 bûwsh (1), to *be delayed*
1419 gâdôwl (1), *great*
2442 châkâh (1), to *await; hope for*
3117 yôwm (16), *day; time period*
4101 mâh (Ch.) (1), *what?, how?, why?*
4900 mâshak (2), to *draw out*; to *be tall*
4970 mâthay (1), *when; when?, how long?*
5704 'ad (51), *as far (long) as; during*
5750 'ôwd (4), *again; repeatedly; still; more*
5769 'ôwlâm (3), *eternity; ancient; always*
5973 'îm (1), *with*
6256 'êth (1), *time*
6440 pânîym (1), *face; front*
7221 rî'shâh (1), *beginning*
7227 rab (11), *great*
7230 rôb (2), *abundance*
7235 râbâh (3), to *increase*
7350 râchôwq (3), *remote, far*
8615 tiqvâh (1), *cord; expectancy*
1909 ĕpi (1), *on, upon*
1909+4119 ĕpi (1), *on, upon*
1971 ĕpipŏthĕō (3), *intensely crave*
2118 ĕuthutēs (1), *rectitude, uprightness*
2193 hĕōs (7), *until*
2425 hikanŏs (6), *ample; fit*
2863 kŏmaō (2), to *wear long hair*
3114 makrŏthumĕō (3), to *be forbearing, patient*

LOFTY
1364 gâbôahh (2), *high; powerful; arrogant*
3117 makrŏs (3), *long, in place or time*
3752 hŏtan (1), *inasmuch as, at once*
3756+3641 ŏu (1), *no or not*
3819 palai (1), *formerly; sometime since*
4183 pŏlus (4), *much, many*
4214 pŏsŏs (1), *how much?; how much!*
5118 tŏsŏutŏs (2), *such great*
5550 chrŏnŏs (4), *space of time, period*

LONGED
183 'âvâh (2), to *wish for, desire*
2968 yâ'ab (1), to *desire, long for*
3615 kâlâh (1), to *cease, be finished, perish*
8373 tâ'ab (2), to *desire*
1971 ĕpipŏthĕō (1), *intensely crave*
1973 ĕpipŏthētŏs (1), *yearned upon*

LONGEDST
3700 kâçaph (1), to *pine after*; to *fear*

LONGER
752 'ârôk (1), *long*
3254 yâçaph (1), to *add* or *augment*
5750 'ôwd (4), *again; repeatedly; still; more*
2089 ĕti (4), *yet, still*
3370 Mēdŏs (5), *inhabitant of Media*
4119 plĕïōn (1), *more*

LONGETH
183 'âvâh (1), to *wish for, desire*
2836 châshaq (1), to *join; to love, delight*
3642 kâmahh (1), to *pine after, long for*
3700 kâçaph (1), to *pine after*; to *fear*

LONGING
8264 shâqaq (1), to *seek greedily*
8375 ta'ăbâh (1), *desire*

LONGSUFFERING
750+639 'ârêk (4), *patient*
3114 makrŏthumĕō (1), to *be forbearing, patient*
3115 makrŏthumia (12), *forbearance; fortitude*

LONGWINGED
750+83 'ârêk (1), *patient*

LOOK
2342 chûwl (1), to *wait; to pervert*
2372 châzâh (3), to *gaze at; to perceive*
2376 chêzev (Ch.) (1), *sight, revelation*
4758 mar'eh (6), *appearance; vision*
5027 nâbaṭ (24), to *scan; to regard with favor*
5869 'ayin (3), *eye; sight*
6437 pânâh (13), to *turn, to face*

LOOKED
5027 nâbaṭ (12), to *scan; to regard with favor*
6437 pânâh (18), to *turn, to face*
6440 pânîym (1), *face; front*
6960 qâvâh (8), to *collect; to expect*
6970 Qôwa' (1), *curtailment*
7200 râ'âh (55), to *see*
7805 shâzaph (1), to *scan*
8159 shâ'âh (1), to *inspect, consider*
8259 shâqaph (12), to *peep or gaze*
8559 Tâmâr (1), *palm tree*
308 anablĕpō (6), to *look up; to recover sight*
816 atĕnizō (4), to *gaze intently*
991 blĕpō (1), to *look at*
1492 ĕidō (7), to *know*
1551 ĕkdĕchŏmai (1), to *await, expect*
1689 ĕmblĕpō (2), to *observe; to discern*

LONGTH
183 'âvâh (1), to *wish for, desire*
6440 pânîym (1), *face; front*
6485 pâqad (1), to *visit, care for, count*
6822 tsâphâh (2), to *peer into the distance*
6960 qâvâh (4), to *collect; to expect*
7200 râ'âh (53), to *see*
7210 rô'îy (1), *sight; spectacle*
7688 shâgach (1), to *glance sharply at*
7760 sûwm (2), to *put, place*
7789 shûwr (1), to *spy out, survey*
7896 shîyth (1), to *place, put*
8159 shâ'âh (4), to *inspect, consider*
8259 shâqaph (3), to *peep or gaze*
308 anablĕpō (1), to *look up; to recover sight*
352 anakuptō (1), to *straighten up*
553 apĕkdĕchŏmai (2), to *expect fully*
816 atĕnizō (2), to *gaze intently*
991 blĕpō (5), to *look at*
1492 ĕidō (1), to *know*
1551 ĕkdĕchŏmai (1), *await, expect*
1914 ĕpiblĕpō (2), to *gaze at*
1980 ĕpiskĕptŏmai (1), to *inspect; to go to see*
2300 thĕaŏmai (1), to *look closely at*
3700 ŏptanŏmai (2), to *appear*
3706 hŏrasis (1), *vision*
3879 parakuptō (1), to *lean over to peer within*
4328 prŏsdŏkaō (5), to *anticipate; to await*
4648 skŏpĕō (2), to *watch out for*, i.e. to *regard*

English

1869 ĕpairō (1), to *raise up, look up*
2300 thĕaŏmai (1), to *look closely at*
4017 pĕriblĕpō (6), to *look all around*
4327 prŏsdĕchŏmai (1), to *receive; to await for*
4328 prŏsdŏkaō (2), to *anticipate; to await*

LOOKEST
5027 nâbaṭ (1), to *scan; to regard with favor*
8104 shâmar (1), to *watch*

LOOKETH
995 bîyn (1), to *understand; discern*
4758+5869 mar'eh (1), *appearance; vision*
5027 nâbaṭ (3), to *scan; to regard with favor*
6437 pânâh (8), to *turn, to face*
6440 pânîym (2), *face; front*
6822 tsâphâh (2), to *peer into the distance*
6960 qâvâh (1), to *collect; to expect*
7200 râ'âh (4), to *see*
7688 shâgach (2), to *glance sharply at*
7789 shùwr (1), to *spy out, survey*
8259 shâqaph (4), to *peep or gaze*
991 blĕpō (1), to *look at*
3879 parakuptō (1), to *lean over to peer within*
4328 prŏsdŏkaō (2), to *anticipate; to await*

LOOKING
6437 pânâh (9), to *turn, to face*
7209 rᵉ'îy (1), *mirror*
8259 shâqaph (1), to *peep or gaze*
308 anablĕpō (3), to *look up; to recover sight*
816 atĕnizō (1), to *gaze intently*
872 aphŏraō (1), to *consider attentively*
991 blĕpō (1), to *look at*
1561 ĕkdŏchē (1), *expectation*
1689 ĕmblĕpō (2), to *observe; to discern*
1983 ĕpiskŏpĕō (1), to *oversee; to beware*
2334 thĕōrĕō (1), to *see; to discern*
4017 pĕriblĕpō (1), to *look all around*
4327 prŏsdĕchŏmai (3), to *receive; to await for*
4328 prŏsdŏkaō (1), to *anticipate; to await*
4329 prŏsdŏkia (1), *apprehension* of evil

LOOKINGGLASSES
4759 mar'âh (1), *vision; mirror*

LOOKS
5869 'ayin (3), *eye; sight; fountain*

6400 pelach (2), *slice*

LOOPS
3924 lûlâ'âh (13), curtain *loop*

LOOSE
2502 châlats (1), to *pull off; to strip; to depart*
5394 nâshal (1), to *divest, eject, or drop*
5425 nâthar (1), to *terrify; shake off; untie*
6605 pâthach (7), to *open wide; to loosen, begin*
7971 shâlach (3), to *send away*
8271 shᵉrê' (Ch.) (1), to *free, separate; unravel*
3089 luō (15), to *loosen*

LOOSED
2118 zâchach (2), to *shove or displace*
2502 châlats (1), to *pull off; to strip; to depart*
4549 mâçaç (1), to *waste with disease; to faint*
5203 nâṭash (1), to *disperse; to thrust* off
5425 nâthar (1), to *terrify; shake off; untie*
6605 pâthach (5), to *open wide; to loosen, begin*
7368 râchaq (1), to *recede; remove*
8271 shᵉrê' (Ch.) (1), to *free, separate; unravel*
321 anagō (2), to *lead up; to bring out; to sail*
447 aniēmi (2), to *slacken, loosen*
630 apŏluō (2), to *relieve, release; to pardon*
2673 katargĕō (1), to *be, render entirely useless*
3080 lusis (1), *divorce*
3089 luō (10), to *loosen*

LOOSETH
5425 nâthar (1), to *terrify; shake off; untie*
6605 pâthach (1), to *open wide; to loosen, begin*

LOOSING
142 airō (1), to *lift, to take up*
321 anagō (1), to *lead up; to bring out; to sail*
3089 luō (2), to *loosen*

LOP
5586 çâ'aph (1), to *dis-branch* a tree

LORD
113 'âdôwn (201), *sovereign, i.e. controller*
136 'Ădônây (430), the *Lord*
1376 gᵉbîyr (2), *master*
3050 Yâhh (50), *Jehovah, self-Existent* or Eternal
3068 Yᵉhôvâh (6394), *Jehovah, self-Existent*
4756 mârê' (Ch.) (4), *master*
7229 rab (Ch.) (1), *great*
7991 shâlîysh (3), *officer; of the third* rank
1203 dĕspŏtēs (4), *absolute ruler*

2961 kuriĕuō (1), to *rule, be master of*
2962 kuriŏs (694), *supreme, controller, Mr.*
4462 rhabbŏni (1), *my master*

LORD'S
113 'âdôwn (8), *sovereign, i.e. controller*
136 'Ădônây (1), the *Lord*
3068 Yᵉhôvâh (108), *Jehovah, self-Existent*
2960 kuriakŏs (2), *belonging to the Lord*
2962 kuriŏs (15), *supreme, controller, Mr.*

LORDLY
117 'addîyr (1), *powerful; majestic*

LORDS
113 'âdôwn (4), *sovereign, i.e. controller*
1167 ba'al (2), *master; husband; owner; citizen*
5633 çeren (21), *axle; peer*
7261 rabrᵉbân (Ch.) (6), *magnate, noble*
7300 rûwd (1), to *ramble* free or disconsolate
7991 shâlîysh (1), *officer; of the third rank*
8269 sar (1), *head person, ruler*
2634 katakuriĕuō (1), to *control, subjugate, lord*
2961 kuriĕuō (1), to *rule, be master of*
2962 kuriŏs (3), *supreme, controller, Mr.*
3175 mĕgistanĕs (1), *great person*

LORDSHIP
2634 katakuriĕuō (1), to *subjugate, lord over*
2961 kuriĕuō (1), to *rule, be master of*

LOSE
6 'âbad (1), *perish; destroy*
622 'âçaph (1), to *gather, collect*
3772 kârath (1), to *cut (off, down or asunder)*
5307 nâphal (1), to *fall*
7843 shâchath (1), to *decay; to ruin*
622 apŏllumi (17), to *perish or lose*
2210 zēmiŏō (2), to *suffer loss*

LOSETH
622 apŏllumi (1), to *perish or lose*

LOSS
2398 châṭâ' (1), to *sin*
7674 shebeth (1), *rest, interruption, cessation*
7921 shâkôl (2), to *miscarry*
580 apŏbŏlē (1), *rejection, loss*
2209 zēmia (3), *detriment; loss*
2210 zēmiŏō (2), to *suffer loss*

LOST
6 'âbad (9), to *perish*
9 'âbêdâh (4), *destruction*
5307 nâphal (2), to *fall*
7908 shᵉkôwl (1), *bereavement*
7923 shikkûlîym (1), *childlessness*
358+1096 analŏs (1), *saltless, i.e. insipid*
622 apŏllumi (13), to *perish or lose*
3471 mōrainō (2), to *become insipid*

LOT
1486 gôwrâl (60), *lot, allotment*
2256 chebel (3), *company, band*
3876 Lôwṭ (32), *veil*
2624 katakĕrŏdŏtĕō (1), to *apportion an estate*
2819 klērŏs (2), *lot, portion*
2975 lagchanō (1), to *determine* by lot
3091 Lōt (3), *veil*

LOT'S
3876 Lôwṭ (1), *veil*

LOTAN
3877 Lôwṭân (5), *covering*

LOTAN'S
3877 Lôwṭân (2), *covering*

LOTHE
3811 lâ'âh (1), to *tire; to be, make disgusted*
6962 qûwṭ (3), to *detest*

LOTHED
1602 gâ'al (2), to *detest; to reject; to fail*
7114 qâtsar (1), to *curtail, cut short*

LOTHETH
1602 gâ'al (1), to *detest; to reject; to fail*

LOTHING
1604 gô'al (1), *abhorrence*

LOTS
1486 gôwrâl (16), *lot, allotment*
2819 klērŏs (6), *lot, portion*
2975 lagchanō (1), to *determine* by lot

LOUD
1419 gâdôwl (19), *great*
1993 hâmâh (1), to *be in great commotion*
2389 châzâq (1), *strong; severe, hard, violent*
5797 'ôz (1), *strength*
7311 rûwm (1), to *be high; to rise or raise*
8085 shâma' (2), to *hear*
3173 mĕgas (33), *great, many*

LOUDER
3966 mᵉ'ôd (1), *very, utterly*

LOVE
157 'âhab (73), to *have affection, love*
160 'ahăbâh (34), *affection, love*

1730 dôwd (7), *beloved,
friend; uncle, relative*
2836 châshaq (3), *to join;
to love, delight*
5690 'egeb (1), *amative
words, words of love*
5691 'ăgâbâh (1), *love,
amorousness*
7355 râcham (1), *to be
compassionate*
7474 ra'yâh (9), *female
associate*
25 agapaō (70), *to love*
26 agapē (85), *love;
love-feast*
2309 thĕlō (1), *to will; to
desire; to choose*
5360 philadĕlphia (4),
fraternal affection
5361 philadĕlphŏs (1),
fraternal
5362 philandrŏs (1),
*affectionate as a wife
to her husband*
5363 philanthrōpia (1),
benevolence
5365 philarguria (1),
*avarice, greedy love of
possessions*
5368 philĕō (10), *to be a
friend, have affection*
5388 philŏtĕknŏs (1),
loving one's child(ren)

LOVE'S
26 agapē (1), *love*

LOVED
157 'âhab (48), *to have
affection, love*
160 'ahăbâh (7),
affection, love
2245 châbab (1), *to
cherish*
25 agapaō (37), *to love*
26 agapē (1), *love*
5368 philĕō (3), *to be a
friend, have affection*

LOVEDST
157 'âhab (1), *to have
affection, love*
25 agapaō (1), *to love*

LOVELY
157 'âhab (1), *to have
affection, love*
4261 machmâd (1),
object of affection
5690 'egeb (1), *amative
words, words of love*
4375 prŏsphilēs (1),
acceptable, pleasing

LOVER
157 'âhab (2), *to have
affection, love*
5358 philagathŏs (1),
promoter of virtue
5382 philŏxĕnŏs (1),
hospitable

LOVERS
157 'âhab (17), *to have
affection, love*
158 'ahab (1), *affection,
love*
5689 'âgab (1), *to lust
sensually*
7453 rêa' (1), *associate;
one close*
5367 philautŏs (1), *selfish*

5369 philēdŏnŏs (1),
loving pleasure
5377 philŏthĕŏs (1),
pious, i.e. loving God

LOVES
159 'ôhab (1), *affection,
love*
1730 dôwd (1), *beloved,
friend; uncle, relative*
3039 yᵉdîyd (1), *loved*

LOVEST
157 'âhab (7), *to have
affection, love*
25 agapaō (2), *to love*
5368 philĕō (3), *to be a
friend, have affection*

LOVETH
157 'âhab (37), *to have
affection, love*
25 agapaō (19), *to love*
5368 philĕō (6), *to be a
friend, have affection*
5383 philŏprōtĕuō (1),
loving to be first

LOVING
157 'âhab (1), *to have
affection, love*
158 'ahab (1), *affection,
love*
2896 tôwb (1), *good; well*

LOVINGKINDNESS
2617 cheçed (26),
kindness, favor

LOVINGKINDNESSES
2617 cheçed (4),
kindness, favor

LOW
120 'âdâm (1), *human
being; mankind*
1809 dâlal (3), *to
slacken, dangle*
3665 kâna' (2), *to
humiliate, subdue*
3766 kâra' (1), *to
prostrate*
4295 mattâh (1), *below
or beneath*
4355 mâkak (2), *to
tumble in ruins*
6030 'ânâh (1), *to
respond, answer*
6819 tsâ'ar (1), *to be
small; be trivial*
7817 shâchach (3), *to
sink or depress*
8213 shâphêl (11), *to
humiliate*
8216 shĕphel (1), *humble
state or rank*
8217 shâphâl (5),
depressed, low
8219 shᵉphêlâh (5),
lowland,
8482 tachtîy (2),
lowermost; depths
5011 tapĕinŏs (3),
humiliated, lowly
5013 tapĕinŏō (1), *to
depress; to humiliate*
5014 tapĕinōsis (2),
humbleness, lowliness

LOWER
2637 châçêr (1), *to lack;
to fail, want, make less*
8213 shâphêl (1), *to
humiliate*

8217 shâphâl (4),
depressed, low
8481 tachtôwn (5),
bottommost
8482 tachtîy (4),
lowermost; depths
1642 ĕlattŏō (2), *to lessen*
2737 katōtĕrŏs (1),
inferior, lower

LOWEST
7098 qâtsâh (3),
termination; fringe
8481 tachtôwn (2),
bottommost
8482 tachtîy (4),
lowermost; depths
2078 ĕschatŏs (2),
farthest, final

LOWETH
1600 gâ'âh (1), *to bellow,
i.e. low of a cow*

LOWING
1600 gâ'âh (1), *to bellow,
i.e. low of a cow*
6963 qôwl (1), *voice or
sound*

LOWLINESS
5012 tapĕinŏphrŏsunē
(2), *modesty, humility*

LOWLY
6041 'ânîy (3), *depressed*
6800 tsâna' (1), *to
humiliate*
8217 shâphâl (1),
depressed, low
5011 tapĕinŏs (1),
humiliated, lowly

LOWRING
4768 stugnazō (1), *to be
overcast, somber*

LUBIM
3864 Lûwbîy (2), *dry
region*

LUBIMS
3864 Lûwbîy (1), *dry
region*

LUCAS
3065 Lŏukas (2), *Lucanus*

LUCIFER
1966 hêylêl (1), *Venus
(i.e. morning star)*

LUCIUS
3066 Lŏukiŏs (2),
illuminative

LUCRE
1215 betsa' (1), *plunder;
unjust gain*
146 aischrŏkĕrdēs (2),
shamefully greedy
147 aischrŏkĕrdōs (1),
sordidly, greedily
866 aphilargurŏs (1),
unavaricious

LUCRE'S
2771 kĕrdŏs (1), *gain,
profit*

LUD
3865 Lûwd (4), *Lud*

LUDIM
3866 Lûwdîy (2), *Ludite*

LUHITH
3872 Lûwchîyth (2),
floored

LUKE
3065 Lŏukas (2), *Lucanus*

LUKEWARM
5513 chliarŏs (1), *tepid*

LUMP
1690 dᵉbêlâh (2), *cake of
pressed figs*
5445 phurama (5), *lump
of clay; mass of dough*

LUNATICK
4583 sĕlēniazŏmai (2), *to
be moon-struck*

LURK
6845 tsâphan (2), *to hide;
to hoard; to lurk*

LURKING
3427 yâshab (1), *to dwell,
to remain; to settle*
3993 ma'ărâb (1),
ambuscade, ambush
4224 machăbê' (1),
refuge, shelter

LUST
2530 châmad (1), *to
delight in; lust for*
5315 nephesh (2), *life;
breath; soul; wind*
8307 shᵉrîyrûwth (1),
obstinacy
8378 ta'ăvâh (1), *longing;
delight*
1511+1938 ĕinai (1), *to
exist*
1937 ĕpithumĕō (2), *to
long for*
1939 ĕpithumia (9),
longing
3715 ŏrĕxis (1), *longing
after, lust, desire*
3806 pathŏs (1), *passion,
especially
concupiscence*

LUSTED
183 'âvâh (2), *to wish for,
desire*
1937 ĕpithumĕō (2), *to
long for*

LUSTETH
183 'âvâh (4), *to wish for,
desire*
1937 ĕpithumĕō (1), *to
long for*
1971 ĕpipŏthĕō (1),
intensely crave

LUSTING
8378 ta'ăvâh (1), *longing;
delight*

LUSTS
1939 ĕpithumia (22),
longing
2237 hēdŏnē (2), *delight;
desire*

LUSTY
8082 shâmên (1), *rich;
fertile*

LUZ
3870 Lûwz (7), *Luz*

LYCAONIA
3071 Lukaŏnia (2),
Lycaonia

LYCIA
3073 Lukia (1), *Lycia*

LYDDA
3069 Ludda (3), *Lod*

English

LYDIA
3865 Lûwd (1), *Lud*
3070 Ludia (2), *Lydian* in
Asia Minor

LYDIANS
3866 Lûwdîy (1), *Ludite*

LYING
3538 kᵉdab (Ch.) (1),
false, misleading
3576 kâzab (1), to *lie,
deceive*
3577 kâzâb (2),
falsehood; idol
3584 kâchash (2), to *lie,
disown; to disappoint*
3585 kachash (1),
emaciation; hypocrisy
3586 kechâsh (1),
faithless
4904 mishkâb (4), *bed;
sleep; intercourse*
5307 nâphal (1), to *fall*
7252 reba' (1),
prostration for sleep
7257 râbats (2), to
recline, repose, brood
7723 shâv' (2), *ruin;
guile; idolatry*
7901 shâkab (3), to *lie
down*
8267 sheqer (21),
untruth; sham
345 anakĕimai (1), to
recline at a meal
906 ballō (1), to *throw*
1968 ĕpipiptō (1), to
embrace; to seize
2749 kĕimai (4), to *lie
outstretched*
5579 psĕudōs (2),
falsehood

LYSANIAS
3078 Lusanias (1),
grief-dispelling

LYSIAS
3079 Lusias (3), *Lysias*

LYSTRA
3082 Lustra (6), *Lystra*

MAACAH
4601 Ma'ăkâh (3),
depression

MAACHAH
4601 Ma'ăkâh (18),
depression

MAACHATHI
4602 Ma'ăkâthîy (1),
Maakathite

MAACHATHITE
4602 Ma'ăkâthîy (4),
Maakathite

MAACHATHITES
4602 Ma'ăkâthîy (4),
Maakathite

MAADAI
4572 Ma'ăday (1),
ornamental

MAADIAH
4573 Ma'adyâh (1),
ornament of Jehovah

MAAI
4597 Mâ'ay (1),
sympathetic

MAALEH-ACRABBIM
4610 Ma'ălêh
'Aqrabbîym (1), *Steep
of Scorpions*

MAARATH
4638 Ma'ărâth (1), *waste*

MAASEIAH
4271 Machçêyâh (2),
refuge in Jehovah
4641 Ma'ăsêyâh (23),
work of Jehovah

MAASIAI
4640 Ma'say (1),
operative

MAATH
3092 Maath (1), *Maath*

MAAZ
4619 Ma'ats (1), *closure*

MAAZIAH
4590 Ma'azyâh (2),
rescue of Jehovah

MACEDONIA
3109 Makĕdŏnia (24),
Macedonia
3110 Makĕdōn (4), *of
Macedonia*

MACEDONIAN
3110 Makĕdōn (1), *of
Macedonia*

MACHBANAI
4344 Makbannay (1),
Macbannite

MACHBENAH
4343 Makbênâ' (1), *knoll*

MACHI
4352 Mâkîy (1), *pining*

MACHIR
4353 Mâkîyr (22),
salesman

MACHIRITES
4354 Mâkîyrîy (1),
Makirite

MACHNADEBAI
4367 Maknadbay (1),
what (is) *like* (a) *liberal*
(man)?

MACHPELAH
4375 Makpêlâh (6), *fold*

MAD
1984 hâlal (8), to *shine,
flash, radiate; boast*
3856 lâhahh (1), to
languish
7696 shâga' (7), to *rave*
through insanity
1519+3130 ĕis (1), *to* or
into
1693 ĕmmainŏmai (1), to
rage at
3105 mainŏmai (4), to
rave; to act insane

MADAI
4074 Mâday (2), *Madai*

MADE
1129 bânâh (3), to *build;
to establish*
1443 gâdar (1), to *build a
stone wall*
1961 hâyâh (5), to *exist,*
i.e. *be* or *become*
2342 chûwl (1), to *dance,
whirl; to writhe* in pain

2672 châtsab (1), to *cut
stone* or *carve* wood
3322 yâtsag (2), to *place
permanently*
3335 yâtsar (2), to *form;
potter; to determine*
3627 kᵉlîy (1),
implement, thing
3738 kârâh (2), to *dig; to
plot; to bore, hew*
3772 kârath (50), to *cut
(off, down or asunder)*
3835 lâban (1), to *make
bricks*
4399 mᵉlâ'kâh (1), *work;
property*
4639 ma'ăseh (2), *action;
labor*
5221 nâkâh (1), to *strike,
kill*
5414 nâthan (42), to *give*
5648 'ăbad (Ch.) (7), to
do, work, serve
5975 'âmad (1), to *stand*
6087 'âtsab (1), to
fabricate or *fashion*
6213 'âsâh (394), to *make*
6235 'eser (1), *ten*
6466 pâ'al (3), to *do,
make* or *practice*
6555 pârats (1), to *break
out*
6743 tsâlach (1), to *push
forward*
7194 qâshar (1), to *tie,
bind*
7236 rᵉbâh (Ch.) (1), to
increase
7495 râphâ' (1), to *cure,
heal*
7502 râphad (1), to
spread a bed; to *refresh*
7543 râqach (1), to
perfume, blend spice
7737 shâvâh (1), to *level;
to resemble; to adjust*
7739 shᵉvâh (Ch.) (1), to
resemble
7760 sûwm (50), to *put,
place*
7761 sûwm (Ch.) (10), to
put, place
7896 shîyth (5), to *place*
208 akurŏō (1), to
invalidate, nullify
272 amĕlĕō (1), to *be
careless* of, *neglect*
319 anagnōrizŏmai (1),
to *make* oneself *known*
347 anaklinō (1), to *lean
back, recline*
461 anŏrthŏō (1), to
strengthen, build
591 apŏdidōmi (1), to
give away
626 apŏlŏgĕŏmai (1), to
give an account
770 asthĕnĕō (1), to *be
feeble*
805 asphalizō (3), to
render secure
871 aphŏmŏiŏō (1), to
assimilate closely
886 achĕirŏpŏiētŏs (2),
unmanufactured
1080 gĕnnaō (1), to
procreate, regenerate
1096 ginŏmai (72), to *be,
become*

1107 gnōrizō (9), to
make known, reveal
1165 dĕigmatizō (1), to
expose to spectacle
1215 dēmēgŏrĕō (1), to
address an assembly
1232 diagnōrizō (1), to
tell abroad
1239 diadidōmi (2), to
divide up, distribute
1295 diasōzō (1), to *cure,
preserve, rescue*
1303 diatithĕmai (1), to
put apart, i.e. *dispose*
1392 dŏxazō (1), to
render, esteem glorious
1402 dŏulŏō (1), to
enslave
1511 ĕinai (1), to *exist*
1517 ĕirēnŏpŏiĕō (1), to
harmonize, make peace
1519 ĕis (2), *to* or *into*
1586 ĕklĕgŏmai (1), to
select, choose, pick out
1642 ĕlattŏō (1), to *lessen*
1659 ĕlĕuthĕrŏō (4), to
exempt, liberate
1743 ĕndunamŏō (1), to
empower, strengthen
1770 ĕnnĕuŏ (1), to
gesture, i.e. *signal*
1839 ĕxistēmi (1), to
astound; to be insane
1861 ĕpaggĕllŏ (2), to
engage to do
2005 ĕpitĕlĕō (1), to
terminate; to undergo
2049 ĕrēmŏō (1), to *lay
waste*
2090 hĕtŏimazō (4), to
prepare
2092 hĕtŏimŏs (1), *ready,
prepared*
2134 ĕunŏuchizō (2), to
*castrate; to live
unmarried*
2227 zōŏpŏiĕō (1), to *(re-)
vitalize, give life*
2301 thĕatrizō (1), to
expose as a spectacle
2390 iaŏmai (1), to *cure,
heal*
2427 hikanŏō (2), to
make competent
2525 kathistēmi (7), to
designate, constitute
2559 kakŏō (1), to *injure;
to oppress; to embitter*
2673 katargĕō (1), to *be,
render entirely useless*
2680 kataskĕuazŏ (1), to
prepare thoroughly
2721 katĕphistēmi (1), to
rush upon in an assault
2722 katĕchŏō (1), to *hold
down fast*
2749 kĕimai (1), to *lie
outstretched*
2758 kĕnŏō (2), to *make
empty*
2841 kŏinōnĕō (1), to
share or *participate*
3021 lĕukainō (1), to
whiten
3076 lupĕō (5), to
distress; to be sad
3182 mĕthuskō (1), to
become drunk

3421 mnēmŏnĕuō (1), to
exercise memory
3447 mŏschŏpŏiĕō (1), to
fabricate a bull image
3471 mōrainō (1), to
become insipid
3489 nauagĕō (1), to be
shipwrecked
3666 hŏmŏiŏō (2), to
become like
3670 hŏmŏlŏgĕō (1), to
acknowledge, agree
3822 palaiŏō (1), to
make, become worn out
3903 paraskĕuazō (1), to
get ready, prepare
3982 pĕithō (1), to pacify
or conciliate
4087 pikrainō (1), to
embitter, turn sour
4147 plŏutĕō (2), to be,
become wealthy
4160 pŏiĕō (51), to make
4161 pŏiĕma (1), what is
made, product
4198 pŏrĕuŏmai (1), to
go, come; to travel
4222 pŏtizō (2), to
furnish drink, irrigate
4364 prŏspŏiĕŏmai (1), to
pretend as if about to
4483 rhĕō (1), to utter,
i.e. speak or say
4692 spĕudō (1), to urge;
to await eagerly
4732 stĕrĕŏō (1), to be,
become strong
4776 sugkathizō (1), to
give, take a seat in
company with
4832 summŏrphŏs (1),
similar, conformed to
4955 sustasiastēs (1),
fellow-insurgent
4982 sōzō (9), to deliver;
to protect
5014 tapĕinōsis (1),
humbleness, lowliness
5048 tĕlĕiŏō (9), to
perfect, complete
5055 tĕlĕō (1), to end, i.e.
complete, execute
5087 tithēmi (3), to place
5293 hupŏtassō (2), to
subordinate; to obey
5319 phanĕrŏō (13), to
render apparent
5487 charitŏō (1), to give
special honor
5499 chĕirŏpŏiētŏs (6), of
human construction

MADEST
3045 yâda' (1), to know
3772 kârath (1), to cut
(off, down or asunder)
6213 'âsâh (1), to make
387 anastatŏō (1), to
disturb, cause trouble
1642 ĕlattŏō (1), to lessen

MADIAN
3099 Madian (1), contest
or quarrel

MADMANNAH
4089 Madmannâh (2),
dunghill

MADMEN
4086 Madmên (1),
dunghill

MADMENAH
4088 Madmênâh (1),
dunghill

MADNESS
1947 hôwlêlâh (4), folly,
delusion
1948 hôwlêlûwth (1),
folly, delusion
7697 shiggâ'ôwn (2),
craziness
454 anŏia (1), stupidity;
rage
3913 paraphrŏnia (1),
foolhardiness, insanity

MADON
4068 Mâdôwn (2), height

MAGBISH
4019 Magbîysh (1),
stiffening

MAGDALA
3093 Magdala (1), tower

MAGDALENE
3094 Magdalēnē (12), of
Magdala

MAGDIEL
4025 Magdîy'êl (2),
preciousness of God

MAGICIAN
2749 chartŏm (Ch.) (1),
horoscopist, magician

MAGICIANS
2748 chartŏm (11),
horoscopist, magician
2749 chartŏm (Ch.) (4),
horoscopist, magician

MAGISTRATE
3423+6114 yârash (1), to
inherit; to impoverish
758 archōn (1), first

MAGISTRATES
8200 shᵉphaṭ (Ch.) (1), to
judge
746 archē (1), first in
rank; first in time
3980 pĕitharchĕō (1), to
submit to authority
4755 stratēgŏs (5),
military governor

MAGNIFICAL
1431 gâdal (1), to be
great, make great

MAGNIFICENCE
3168 mĕgalĕiŏtēs (1),
grandeur or splendor

MAGNIFIED
1431 gâdal (17), to be
great, make great
5375 nâsâ' (1), to lift up
3170 mĕgalunō (3), to
increase or extol

MAGNIFY
1431 gâdal (15), to be
great, make great
7679 sâgâ' (1), to laud,
extol
1392 dŏxazō (1), to
render, esteem glorious
3170 mĕgalunō (2), to
increase or extol

MAGOG
4031 Mâgôwg (4), Magog
3098 Magōg (1), Magog

MAGOR-MISSABIB
4036 Mâgôwr
miç-Çâbîyb (1), affright
from around

MAGPIASH
4047 Magpîy'âsh (1),
exterminator of (the)
moth

MAHALAH
4244 Machlâh (1),
sickness

MAHALALEEL
4111 Mahălal'êl (7),
praise of God

MAHALATH
4257 Machălath (2),
sickness
4258 Machălath (2),
sickness

MAHALI
4249 Machlîy (1), sick

MAHANAIM
4266 Machănayim (13),
double camp

MAHANEH-DAN
4265 Machănêh-Dân (1),
camp of Dan

MAHARAI
4121 Mahăray (3), hasty

MAHATH
4287 Machath (3),
erasure

MAHAVITE
4233 Machăvîym (1),
Machavite

MAHAZIOTH
4238 Machăzîy'ôwth (2),
visions

MAHER-SHALAL-HASH-BAZ
4122 Mahêr Shâlâl
Châsh Baz (2), hasting
is he to the booty, swift
to the prey

MAHLAH
4244 Machlâh (4),
sickness

MAHLI
4249 Machlîy (10), sick

MAHLITES
4250 Machlîy (2),
Machlite

MAHLON
4248 Machlôwn (3), sick

MAHLON'S
4248 Machlôwn (1), sick

MAHOL
4235 Mâchôwl (1),
(round) dance

MAID
519 'âmâh (5), female
servant or slave
1330 bᵉthûwlâh (4),
virgin maiden
1331 bᵉthûwlîym (2),
virginity
5291 na'ărâh (4), female
child; servant
5347 nᵉqêbâh (1), female,
woman
5959 'almâh (2), lass,
young woman

8198 shiphchâh (12),
household female slave
2877 kŏrasiŏn (2), little
girl
3814 paidiskē (2), female
slave or servant
3816 pais (1), child; slave
or servant

MAID'S
5291 na'ărâh (1), female
child; servant

MAIDEN
1330 bᵉthûwlâh (2),
virgin maiden
5291 na'ărâh (3), female
child; servant
8198 shiphchâh (2),
household female slave
3816 pais (1), child; slave
or servant

MAIDENS
1330 bᵉthûwlâh (3),
virgin maiden
5291 na'ărâh (13),
female child; servant
8198 shiphchâh (1),
household female slave
3814 paidiskē (1), female
slave or servant

MAIDS
519 'âmâh (3), female
servant or slave
1330 bᵉthûwlâh (3),
virgin maiden
5291 na'ărâh (2), female
child; servant
3814 paidiskē (1), female
slave or servant

MAIDSERVANT
519 'âmâh (13), female
servant or slave
8198 shiphchâh (3),
household female slave

MAIDSERVANT'S
519 'âmâh (1), female
servant or slave

MAIDSERVANTS
519 'âmâh (4), female
servant or slave
8198 shiphchâh (5),
household female slave

MAIDSERVANTS'
519 'âmâh (1), female
servant or slave

MAIL
7193 qasqeseth (2), fish
scales; coat of mail

MAIMED
2782 chârats (1), to be
alert, to decide
376 anapērŏs (2),
maimed; crippled
2948 kullŏs (4), crippled,
i.e. maimed

MAINSAIL
736 artĕmōn (1), foresail
or jib

MAINTAIN
2388 châzaq (1), to bind,
restrain, conquer
3198 yâkach (1), to be
correct; to argue
6213 'âsâh (6), to do or
make

MAINTAINED (continued)

4291 prŏïstēmi (2), to preside; to practice

MAINTAINED

6213 'âsâh (1), to do or make

MAINTAINEST

8551 tâmak (1), to obtain, keep fast

MAINTENANCE

2416 chay (1), alive; raw; fresh; life
4415 mᵉlach (Ch.) (1), to eat salt

MAJESTY

1347 gâ'ôwn (7), ascending; majesty
1348 gê'ûwth (2), ascending; majesty
1420 gᵉdûwlâh (1), greatness, grandeur
1923 hădar (Ch.) (1), magnificence, glory
1926 hâdâr (7), magnificence
1935 hôwd (4), grandeur, majesty
7238 rᵉbûw (Ch.) (3), increase
3168 mĕgălĕiŏtēs (1), grandeur or splendor
3172 mĕgalōsunē (3), divinity, majesty

MAKAZ

4739 Mâqats (1), end

MAKE

1124 bᵉnâ' (Ch.) (1), to build
1254 bârâ' (1), to create; fashion
1443 gâdar (2), to build a stone wall
2015 hâphak (1), to change, overturn
3331 yâtsa' (1), to strew as a surface
3335 yâtsar (1), to form; potter; to determine
3635 kᵉlal (Ch.) (2), to complete
3772 kârath (31), to cut (off, down or asunder)
3823 lâbab (1), transport with love; to stultify
5414 nâthan (64), to give
5674 'âbar (2), to cross over; to transition
6014 'âmar (1), to gather grain into sheaves
6213 'âsâh (238), to make
6381 pâlâ' (1), to be, make great, wonderful
7760 sûwm (65), to put, place
7761 sûwm (Ch.) (5), to put, place
7896 shîyth (9), to place
8074 shâmêm (1), to devastate; to stupefy
142 airō (1), to lift, to take up
347 anaklinō (2), to lean back, recline
805 asphalizō (1), to render secure
1107 gnōrizō (6), to make known, reveal

1303 diatithĕmai (2), to put apart, i.e. dispose
1325 didōmi (2), to give
1510 ĕimi (1), I exist, I am
1519 ĕis (1), to or into
1659 ĕlĕuthĕrŏō (2), to exempt, liberate
1710 ĕmpŏrĕuŏmai (1), to trade, do business
1793 ĕntugchanō (1), to entreat, petition
2005 ĕpitĕlĕō (1), to terminate; to undergo
2090 hĕtŏimazō (6), to prepare
2116 ĕuthunō (1), to straighten or level
2146 ĕuprŏsōpĕō (1), to make a good display
2165 ĕuphrainō (3), to rejoice, be glad
2350 thŏrubĕō (1), to disturb; clamor
2433 hilaskŏmai (1), to conciliate, to atone for
2476 histēmi (1), to stand, establish
2511 katharizō (5), to cleanse
2525 kathistēmi (6), to designate, constitute
2625 kataklinō (1), to recline, take a place
2673 katargĕō (3), to be, render entirely useless
2675 katartizō (2), to repair; to prepare
2758 kĕnŏō (1), to make empty
2936 ktizō (1), to fabricate, create
3076 lupĕō (1), to distress; to be sad
3753 hŏtĕ (1), when; as
3856 paradĕigmatizō (1), to expose to infamy
3868 paraitĕŏmai (1), to deprecate, decline
4052 pĕrissĕuō (1), to superabound
4062 pĕritrĕpō (1), to drive crazy
4087 pikrainō (1), to embitter, turn sour
4115 platunō (1), to widen
4121 plĕŏnazō (1), to increase; superabound
4122 plĕŏnĕktĕō (2), to be covetous
4135 plērŏphŏrĕō (1), fill completely; assure
4137 plērŏō (1), to fill, make complete
4160 pŏiĕō (48), to make
4170 pŏlĕmĕō (3), to battle, make war
4294 prŏkatartizō (1), to prepare in advance
4336 prŏsĕuchŏmai (3), to supplicate, pray
4400 prŏchĕirizŏmai (1), to purpose
4624 skandalizō (2), to entrap, i.e. trip up
4679 sŏphizō (1), to be cleverly invented
4692 spĕudō (2), to urge on

4766 strōnnumi (1), strew, i.e. spread
4820 sumballō (1), to aid; to join, attack
4921 sunistaō (1), to set together, to introduce
4931 suntĕlĕō (1), to complete entirely
5055 tĕlĕō (3), to end, i.e. complete, execute
5087 tithĕmi (6), to place
5319 phanĕrŏō (2), to render apparent
5461 phōtizō (1), to shine or to brighten up

MAKER

3335 yâtsar (4), to form; potter; to determine
6213 'âsâh (13), to make
6466 pâ'al (1), to make
6467 pô'al (1), act or work, deed
1217 dēmiŏurgŏs (1), worker, mechanic

MAKERS

2796 chârâsh (1), skilled fabricator or worker

MAKEST

6213 'âsâh (6), to make
7760 sûwm (1), to place
7896 shîyth (1), to place
2744 kauchaŏmai (2), to glory in, rejoice in
4160 pŏiĕō (4), to make

MAKETH

3772 kârath (1), to cut (off, down or asunder)
5414 nâthan (2), to give
6213 'âsâh (23), to make
6466 pâ'al (1), to make
7706 Shadday (1), the Almighty God
7737 shâvâh (2), to level, i.e. equalize
7760 sûwm (6), to place
393 anatĕllō (1), to cause to arise
1252 diakrinō (1), to decide; to hesitate
1308 diaphĕrō (1), to bear, carry; to differ
1793 ĕntugchanō (3), to entreat, petition
2165 ĕuphrainō (1), to rejoice, be glad
2390 iaŏmai (1), to cure, heal
2525 kathistēmi (1), to designate, constitute
2617 kataischunō (1), to disgrace or shame
4160 pŏiĕō (6), to make
4977 schizō (1), to split or sever
5241 hupĕrĕntugchanō (1), to intercede in behalf of
5319 phanĕrŏō (1), to render apparent

MAKHELOTH

4721 maqhêl (2), assembly

MAKING

3772 kârath (1), to cut (off, down or asunder)
4639 ma'ăseh (2), action; labor

6213 'âsâh (1), to make
208 akurŏō (1), to invalidate, nullify
1189 dĕŏmai (3), to beg, petition, ask
1252 diakrinō (1), to decide; to hesitate
2350 thŏrubĕō (1), to disturb; clamor
4148 plŏutizō (1), to make wealthy
4160 pŏiĕō (7), to make
5567 psallō (1), to play a stringed instrument

MAKKEDAH

4719 Maqqêdâh (9), herding-fold

MAKTESH

4389 Maktêsh (1), dell

MALACHI

4401 Mal'âkîy (1), ministrative

MALCHAM

4445 Malkâm (2), Malcam or Milcom

MALCHI-SHUA

4444 Malkîyshûwa' (3), king of wealth

MALCHIAH

4441 Malkîyâh (9), appointed by Jehovah

MALCHIEL

4439 Malkîy'êl (3), appointed by God

MALCHIELITES

4440 Malkîy'êlîy (1), Malkiëlite

MALCHIJAH

4441 Malkîyâh (6), appointed by Jehovah

MALCHIRAM

4443 Malkîyrâm (1), king of a high one

MALCHUS

3124 Malchŏs (1), king

MALE

376 'îysh (2), man; male
2138 zâkûwr (1), male
2142 zâkar (1), to be male
2145 zâkâr (37), male
730 arrhēn (4), male

MALEFACTOR

2555 kakŏpŏiŏs (1), bad-doer; criminal

MALEFACTORS

2557 kakŏurgŏs (3), criminal, evildoer

MALELEEL

3121 Malĕlĕêl (1), praise of God

MALES

2138 zâkûwr (2), male
2145 zâkâr (30), male

MALICE

2549 kakia (6), depravity; malignity

MALICIOUS

4190 pŏnērŏs (1), malice, wicked, bad; crime

MALICIOUSNESS

2549 kakia (2), depravity; malignity

MALIGNITY
2550 kakŏĕthĕia (1), *mischievousness*

MALLOTHI
4413 Mallôwthîy (2), *loquacious*

MALLOWS
4408 mallûwach (1), *salt-purslain*

MALLUCH
4409 Mallûwk (6), *regnant*

MAMMON
3126 mammōnas (4), *wealth, riches*

MAMRE
4471 Mamrê' (10), *lusty*

MAN
120 'âdâm (388), *human being; mankind*
375 'êyphôh (1), *where?; when?; how?*
376 'îysh (967), *man; male; someone*
376+2145 'îysh (1), *man; male; someone*
582 'ĕnôwsh (32), *man; person, human*
606 'ĕnâsh (Ch.) (8), *man*
935 bôw' (1), *to go, come*
1121 bên (3), *son, descendant; people*
1121+120 bên (1), *son, descendant; people*
1167 ba'al (5), *master; husband; owner; citizen*
1201 Ba'shâ' (1), *offensiveness*
1396 gâbar (1), *to be strong; to prevail*
1397 geber (54), *person, man*
1400 gᵉbar (Ch.) (2), *person; someone*
1538 gulgôleth (2), *skull*
2145 zâkâr (11), *male*
5315 nephesh (3), *life; breath; soul; wind*
5958 'elem (1), *lad, young man*
435 anēr (75), *man; male*
442 anthrōpinŏs (2), *human*
444 anthrōpŏs (347), *human being; mankind*
730 arrhēn (2), *male*
1520 hĕis (3), *one*
1538 hĕkastŏs (3), *each or every*
2478 ischurŏs (1), *forcible, powerful*
3367 mēdĕis (33), *not even one*
3494 nĕanias (4), *youth*
3495 nĕaniskŏs (5), *youth*
3762 ŏudĕis (96), *none, nobody, nothing*
3956 pas (3), *all, any, every, whole*
5100 tis (40), *some or any*

MAN'S
120 'âdâm (17), *human being; mankind*
312 'achêr (1), *other, another, different*
376 'îysh (42), *man; male; someone*

582 'ĕnôwsh (3), *man; person, human*
606 'ĕnâsh (Ch.) (3), *man*
1167 ba'al (1), *master; husband; owner; citizen*
1397 geber (2), *person, man*
245 allŏtriŏs (4), *not one's own*
435 anēr (1), *man; male*
442 anthrōpinŏs (3), *human*
444 anthrōpŏs (10), *human being; mankind*
3494 nĕanias (1), *youth*
3762 ŏudĕis (1), *none, nobody, nothing*
5100 tis (3), *some or any*

MANAEN
3127 Manaēn (1), *Manaën*

MANAHATH
4506 Mânachath (3), *rest*

MANAHETHITES
2679 Chătsîy ham-Mᵉnûchôwth (1), *midst of the resting-places*
2680 Chătsîy ham-Mᵉnachtîy (1), *Chatsi-ham-Menachtite*

MANASSEH
4519 Mᵉnashsheh (141), *causing to forget*
4520 Mᵉnashshîy (2), *Menashshite*

MANASSEH'S
4519 Mᵉnashsheh (4), *causing to forget*

MANASSES
3128 Manassēs (3), *causing to forget*

MANASSITES
4519 Mᵉnashsheh (1), *causing to forget*
4520 Mᵉnashshîy (2), *Menashshite*

MANDRAKES
1736 dûwday (6), *mandrake*

MANEH
4488 mâneh (1), *weight*

MANGER
5336 phatnē (3), *crib; stall*

MANIFEST
1305 bârar (1), *to examine; select*
852 aphanēs (1), *non-apparent, invisible*
1212 dēlŏs (1), *clear, plain, evident*
1552 ĕkdēlŏs (1), *wholly evident, clear*
1717 ĕmphanēs (1), *apparent, seen, visible*
1718 ĕmphanizō (2), *to show forth*
4271 prŏdēlŏs (1), *obvious, evident*
5318 phanĕrŏs (7), *apparent, visible, clear*
5319 phanĕrŏō (23), *to render apparent*

MANIFESTATION
602 apŏkalupsis (1), *disclosure, revelation*
5321 phanĕrōsis (2), *manifestation*

MANIFESTED
5319 phanĕrŏō (10), *to render apparent*

MANIFESTLY
5319 phanĕrŏō (1), *to render apparent*

MANIFOLD
7227 rab (3), *great*
7231 râbab (1), *to increase*
4164 pŏikilŏs (2), *various*
4179 pŏllaplasiōn (1), *very much more*
4182 pŏlupŏikilŏs (1), *multifarious*

MANKIND
1320+376 bâsâr (1), *flesh; body; person*
2145 zâkâr (2), *male*
733 arsĕnŏkŏitēs (2), *sodomite*
5449+442 phusis (1), *genus or sort*

MANNA
4478 mân (14), *manna, i.e. a "whatness?"*
3131 manna (5), *edible gum-like food*

MANNER
734 'ôrach (1), *road; manner of life*
1571 gam (1), *also; even; yea; though*
1697 dâbâr (15), *word; matter; thing*
1699 dôber (1), *grazing pasture*
1823 dᵉmûwth (1), *resemblance, likeness*
1870 derek (8), *road; course of life*
1881 dâth (1), *royal edict or statute*
2177 zan (1), *form or sort*
3541 kôh (6), *thus*
3605 kôl (1), *all, any or every*
3651 kên (3), *just; right, correct*
3654 kên (1), *stinging bug*
4941 mishpâṭ (36), *verdict; decree; justice*
8452 tôwrâh (1), *custom*
72 agōgē (1), *mode of living, way of life*
195 akribĕia (1), *thoroughness*
442 anthrōpinŏs (1), *human*
686 ara (3), *then, so, therefore*
981 biōsis (1), *mode of living*
1483 ĕthnikōs (1), *as a Gentile*
1485 ĕthŏs (5), *usage prescribed*
1486 ĕthō (1), *to be used by habit or convention*
3592 hŏdĕ (1), *this or that; these or those*

MANIFESTATION — column 4:

3634 hŏiŏs (2), *such or what sort of*
3697 hŏpŏiŏs (2), *what kind of, what sort of*
3779 hŏutō (5), *in this way; likewise*
4012 pĕri (1), *about; around*
4169 pŏiŏs (1), *what sort of?; which one?*
4217 pŏtapŏs (6), *of what possible sort?*
4458 -pōs (1), *particle used in composition*
5158 trŏpŏs (2), *deportment, character*
5179 tupŏs (1), *shape, resemblance; "type"*
5615 hōsautōs (1), *in the same way*

MANNERS
2708 chuqqâh (1), *to delineate*
4941 mishpâṭ (2), *verdict; formal decree; justice*
2239 ēthŏs (1), *usage, i.e. moral habits*
4187 pŏlutrŏpōs (1), *in many ways*
5159 trŏpŏphŏrĕō (1), *to endure one's habits*

MANOAH
4495 Mânôwach (18), *rest*

MANSERVANT
5650 'ebed (12), *servant*

MANSERVANT'S
5650 'ebed (1), *servant*

MANSERVANTS
5650 'ebed (1), *servant*

MANSIONS
3438 mŏnē (1), *residence, dwelling place*

MANSLAYER
7523 râtsach (2), *to murder*

MANSLAYERS
409 andrŏphŏnŏs (1), *murderer*

MANTLE
155 'addereth (5), *large; splendid*
4598 mᵉ'îyl (7), *outer garment or robe*
8063 sᵉmîykâh (1), *rug*

MANTLES
4595 ma'ăṭâphâh (1), *cloak*

MANY
1995 hâmôwn (3), *noise, tumult; many, crowd*
3513 kâbad (2), *to be heavy, severe, dull*
3605 kôl (1), *all, any or every*
7227 rab (196), *great*
7230 rôb (4), *abundance*
7231 râbab (6), *to increase; to multiply*
7233 rᵉbâbâh (1), *myriad*
7235 râbâh (27), *to increase*
7690 saggîy' (Ch.) (2), *large*
2425 hikanŏs (11), *ample; fit*

3745 hŏsŏs (31), *as much as*
4119 plĕiōn (14), *more*
4183 pŏlus (207), *much, many*
4214 pŏsŏs (11), *how much?; how much!*
5118 tŏsŏutŏs (6), *such great*

MAOCH
4582 Mâ'ôwk (1), *oppressed*

MAON
4584 Mâ'ôwn (7), *residence*

MAONITES
4584 Mâ'ôwn (1), *residence*

MAR
3510 kâ'ab (1), to feel *pain; to grieve; to spoil*
5420 nâthaç (1), to *tear up*
7843 shâchath (4), to *decay; to ruin*

MARA
4755 Mârâ' (1), *bitter*

MARAH
4785 Mârâh (5), *bitter*

MARALAH
4831 Mar'ălâh (1), (poss.) *earthquake*

MARANATHA
3134 maran atha (1), *Come, Lord!*

MARBLE
7898 shayith (1), wild *growth* of weeds
8336 shêsh (2), *white* linen; *white* marble
8338 shâwshâw (1), (poss.) to *annihilate*
3139 marmarŏs (1), sparkling *white marble*

MARCH
1980 hâlak (1), to *walk; live a certain way*
3212 yâlak (2), to *walk; to live; to carry*
6805 tsâ'ad (2), to *pace, step* regularly

MARCHED
5265 nâça' (1), *start* on a journey

MARCHEDST
6805 tsâ'ad (1), to *pace, step* regularly

MARCUS
3138 Markŏs (3), *Marcus*

MARESHAH
4762 Mar'êshâh (8), *summit*

MARINERS
4419 mallâch (4), *salt*-water *sailor*
7751 shûwṭ (1), to *travel, roam*

MARISHES
1360 gebe' (1), *reservoir; marsh*

MARK
226 'ôwth (1), *signal, sign*

995 bîyn (1), to *understand; discern*
3045 yâda' (3), to *know*
4307 maṭṭârâ' (3), *jail* (*guard*-house); *aim*
4645 miphgâ' (1), *object of attack, target*
6437 pânâh (1), to *turn, to face*
7181 qâshab (1), to *prick up* the ears
7200 râ'âh (1), to *see*
7760 sûwm (2), to *place*
7896 shîyth (1), to *place*
8104 shâmar (4), to *watch*
8420 tâv (2), *mark; signature*
3138 Markŏs (5), *Marcus*
4648 skŏpĕō (2), to *watch out for*, i.e. to *regard*
4649 skŏpŏs (1), *goal*
5480 charagma (8), *mark, stamp*

MARKED
2856 châtham (1), to *close* up; to *affix a seal*
3799 kâtham (1), to *inscribe* indelibly
7181 qâshab (1), to *prick up* the ears
8104 shâmar (2), to *watch*
1907 ĕpĕchō (1), to *pay attention to*

MARKEST
8104 shâmar (1), to *watch*

MARKET
4627 ma'ărâb (4), mercantile *goods*
58 agŏra (2), *town*-square, *market*

MARKETH
8104 shâmar (1), to *watch*
8388 tâ'ar (2), to *delineate; to extend*

MARKETPLACE
58 agŏra (3), *town*-square, *market*

MARKETPLACES
58 agŏra (1), *town*-square, *market*

MARKETS
58 agŏra (4), *town*-square, *market*

MARKS
7085 qa'ăqa' (1), *incision* or *gash*
4742 stigma (1), *mark, scar* of service

MAROTH
4796 Mârôwth (1), *bitter* springs

MARRED
4893 mishchâth (1), *disfigurement*
7843 shâchath (3), to *decay; to ruin*
622 apŏllumi (1), to *destroy* fully

MARRIAGE
1984 hâlal (1), to *shine, flash, radiate*

5772 'ôwnâh (1), *marital cohabitation*
1061 gamiskō (1), to *espouse*
1062 gamŏs (9), *nuptials*
1547 ĕkgamizō (3), to *marry off* a daughter
1548 ĕkgamiskō (4), to *marry off* a daughter

MARRIAGES
2859 châthan (3), to *be related* by marriage

MARRIED
802 'ishshâh (3), *woman, wife; women, wives*
1166 bâ'al (7), to *be master; to marry*
1166+802 bâ'al (1), to *be master; to marry*
3427 yâshab (1), to *dwell, to remain; to settle*
3947 lâqach (4), to *take*
5375 nâsâ' (1), to *lift up*
1060 gamĕō (9), to *wed*
1096 ginŏmai (3), to *be, become*

MARRIETH
1166 bâ'al (1), to *be master; to marry*
1060 gamĕō (3), to *wed*

MARROW
2459 cheleb (1), *fat; choice* part
4221 môach (1), bone *marrow*
4229 mâchâh (1), to *erase; to grease*
8250 shiqqûwy (1), *beverage; refreshment*
3452 muĕlŏs (1), *marrow*

MARRY
802 'ishshâh (2), *woman, wife; women, wives*
1166 bâ'al (1), to *be master; to marry*
1961+376 hâyâh (1), to *exist*, i.e. *be* or *become*
2992 yâbam (1), to *marry* a dead brother's widow
1060 gamĕō (16), to *wed*
1918 ĕpigambrĕuō (1), to *form an affinity with*

MARRYING
3427 yâshab (1), to *dwell, to remain; to settle*
1060 gamĕō (1), to *wed*

MARS'
697 Arĕiŏs Pagŏs (1), *rock of Ares*

MARSENA
4826 Marçᵉnâ' (1), *Marsena*

MART
5505 çâchar (1), *profit* from trade

MARTHA
3136 Martha (12), *mistress*, i.e. *lady lord*

MARTYR
3144 martus (2), *witness*

MARTYRS
3144 martus (1), *witness*

MARVEL
8539 tâmahh (1), to *be astounded*

2296 thaumazō (9), to *wonder; to admire*
2298 thaumastŏs (1), *wonderful, marvelous*

MARVELLED
8539 tâmahh (2), to *be astounded*
2296 thaumazō (21), to *wonder; to admire*

MARVELLOUS
6381 pâlâ' (16), to *be, make great, wonderful*
6382 pele' (1), *miracle*
6395 pâlâh (1), to *distinguish*
2298 thaumastŏs (6), *wonderful, marvelous*

MARVELLOUSLY
6381 pâlâ' (2), to *be, make great, wonderful*
8539 tâmahh (1), to *be astounded*

MARVELS
6381 pâlâ' (1), to *be, make great, wonderful*

MARY
3137 Maria (54), *rebelliously*

MASCHIL
4905 maskîyl (13), *instructional* poem

MASH
4851 Mash (1), *Mash*

MASHAL
4913 Mâshâl (1), *request*

MASONS
1443 gâdar (2), to *build a* stone *wall*
2672 châtsab (3), to *cut* stone or *carve* wood

MASREKAH
4957 Masrêqâh (2), *vineyard*

MASSA
4854 Massâ' (1), *burden*

MASSAH
4532 Maççâh (4), *testing*

MAST
2260 chibbêl (1), ship's *mast*
8650 tôren (1), mast ship *pole; flag*-staff *pole*

MASTER
113 'âdôwn (75), *sovereign*, i.e. *controller*
729 'âraz (2), of *cedar*
1167 ba'al (3), *master; husband; owner; citizen*
5782 'ûwr (1), to *awake*
7227 rab (1), *great*
8269 sar (1), *head* person, *ruler*
1320 didaskalŏs (47), *instructor*
1988 ĕpistatēs (6), *commander*
2519 kathēgētēs (2), *teacher*
2942 kubĕrnētēs (1), *helmsman, captain*
2962 kuriŏs (4), *supreme, controller, Mr.*
3617 ŏikŏdĕspŏtēs (2), *head of a family*

4461 rhabbi (8), *my master*

MASTER'S
113 'âdôwn (22), *sovereign,* i.e. *controller*
1167 ba'al (1), *master; husband; owner; citizen*
1203 dĕspŏtēs (1), absolute *ruler*

MASTERBUILDER
753 architĕktōn (1), *architect, expert builder*

MASTERS
113 'âdôwn (5), *sovereign,* i.e. *controller*
1167 ba'al (1), *master; husband; owner; citizen*
1203 dĕspŏtēs (4), absolute *ruler*
1320 didaskalŏs (1), *instructor*
2519 kathēgētēs (1), *teacher*
2962 kuriŏs (8), *supreme, controller, Mr.*

MASTERS'
113 'âdôwn (1), *sovereign,* i.e. *controller*
2962 kuriŏs (1), *supreme, controller, Mr.*

MASTERY
1369 gᵉbûwrâh (1), *force; valor; victory*
6981 Qôwrê' (1), *crier*

MASTS
8650 tôren (1), mast ship *pole; flag-staff pole*

MATE
7468 rᵉ'ûwth (2), female *associate*

MATHUSALA
3103 Mathŏusala (1), *man of a dart*

MATRED
4308 Maṭrêd (2), *propulsive*

MATRI
4309 Maṭrîy (1), *rainy*

MATRIX
7358 rechem (5), *womb*

MATTAN
4977 Mattân (3), *present, gift*

MATTANAH
4980 Mattânâh (2), *present; sacrificial offering; bribe*

MATTANIAH
4983 Mattanyâh (16), *gift of Jehovah*

MATTATHA
3160 Mattatha (1), *gift of Jehovah*

MATTATHAH
4992 Mattattâh (1), *gift of Jehovah*

MATTATHIAS
3161 Mattathias (2), *gift of Jehovah*

MATTENAI
4982 Mattᵉnay (3), *liberal*

MATTER
1697 dâbâr (48), *word; matter; thing*
1836 dên (Ch.) (1), *this*
2659 châphêr (1), to *shame, reproach*
2941 ṭa'am (Ch.) (1), *sentence, command*
3602 kâkâh (1), *just so*
4405 millâh (1), *word; discourse; speech*
4406 millâh (Ch.) (4), *command, discourse*
6600 pithgâm (Ch.) (2), *decree; report*
1308 diaphĕrō (1), to *bear, carry;* to *differ*
2596 kata (1), *down; according to*
3056 lŏgŏs (4), *word, matter, thing*
4229 pragma (3), *matter, deed, affair*
5208 hulē (1), *forest,* i.e. wood *fuel*

MATTERS
1419 gâdôwl (1), *great*
1697 dâbâr (15), *word; matter; thing*
4406 millâh (Ch.) (1), *word, command*

MATTHAN
3157 Matthan (2), *present, gift*

MATTHAT
3158 Matthat (2), *gift of Jehovah*

MATTHEW
3156 Matthaiŏs (5), *gift of Jehovah*

MATTHIAS
3159 Matthias (2), *gift of Jehovah*

MATTITHIAH
4993 Mattithyâh (8), *gift of Jehovah*

MATTOCK
4281 machărêshâh (1), (poss.) *pick-*axe
4576 ma'dêr (1), *hoe*

MATTOCKS
2719 chereb (1), *knife, sword*
4281 machărêshâh (1), (poss.) *pick-*axe

MAUL
4650 mêphîyts (1), *mallet-*club

MAW
6896 qêbâh (1), *paunch cavity; stomach*

MAY
194 'ûwlay (4), *if not; perhaps*
3201 yâkôl (11), to *be able*
1410 dunamai (9), to *be able or possible*
1832 ĕxĕsti (1), *it is right, it is proper*
2481 isŏs (1), *perhaps*

MAYEST
3201 yâkôl (5), to *be able*
1410 dunamai (2), to *be able or possible*

1832 ĕxĕsti (1), *it is right, it is proper*

MAZZAROTH
4216 Mazzârâh (1), *constellation*

ME-JARKON
4313 Mêy hay-Yarqôwn (1), *water of the yellowness*

MEADOW
260 'âchûw (2), *bulrush or any marshy grass*

MEADOWS
4629 ma'ăreh (1), *nude place,* i.e. a *common*

MEAH
3968 Mê'âh (2), *hundred*

MEAL
7058 qemach (9), *flour*
7058+5560 qemach (1), *flour*
224 alĕurŏn (2), *flour*

MEALTIME
6256+400 'êth (1), *time*

MEAN
120 'âdâm (3), *human being; mankind*
2823 châshôk (1), *obscure*
5704+3541 'ad (1), *as far (long) as; during*
767 asēmŏs (1), *ignoble,* i.e. *ordinary*
1498 ĕiēn (1), *might could, would*
2076 ĕsti (1), *he (she or it) is; they are*
2309+1511 thĕlō (1), to *will;* to *desire;* to *choose*
3342 mĕtaxu (2), *betwixt; meanwhile*
4160 pŏiĕō (1), to *make*

MEANETH
1819 dâmâh (1), to *resemble, liken*
2076 ĕsti (2), *he (she or it) is; they are*
2309+1511 thĕlō (1), to *will;* to *desire;* to *choose*

MEANING
998 bîynâh (1), *understanding*
1411 dunamis (1), *force, power, miracle*
3195 mĕllō (1), to *intend,* i.e. *be about to*

MEANS
1157 bᵉ'ad (1), *at, beside, among, behind, for*
3027 yâd (4), *hand; power*
4284 machăshâbâh (1), *contrivance; plan*
6903 qᵉbêl (Ch.) (1), *on account of, so as, since*
1096 ginŏmai (1), to *be, become*
3361 mē (1), *not; lest*
3364 ŏu mē (1), *not at all, absolutely not*
3843 pantŏs (2), *entirely; at all events*
4458 -pōs (9), particle used in composition
4459 pōs (2), *in what way?; how?; how* much!

5158 trŏpŏs (2), *deportment, character*

MEANT
2803 châshab (1), to *think, regard;* to *value*
1498 ĕiēn (2), *might could, would be*

MEARAH
4632 Mᵉ'ârâh (1), *cave*

MEASURE
374 'êyphâh (2), dry *grain measure*
520 'ammâh (1), *cubit*
2706 chôq (1), *appointment; allotment*
4055 mad (1), *vesture, garment; carpet*
4058 mâdad (7), to *measure*
4060 middâh (15), *measure; portion*
4884 mᵉsûwrâh (4), *liquid measure*
4941 mishpât (2), *verdict; formal decree; justice*
4971 mathkôneth (1), *proportion*
5429 çᵉ'âh (3), *volume measure for grain*
5432 ça'çᵉ'âh (1), *moderation*
7991 shâlîysh (2), *three-fold measure*
8506 tôken (1), *fixed quantity*
280 amĕtrŏs (2), *immoderate*
3354 mĕtrĕō (3), to *admeasure*
3358 mĕtrŏn (13), *what is apportioned*
4053 pĕrissŏs (1), *superabundant*
4057 pĕrissŏs (1), *superabundantly*
5234 hupĕrballŏntōs (1), *to a greater degree*
5236 hupĕrbŏlē (2), *super-eminence*
5249 hupĕrpĕrissŏs (1), *beyond all measure*
5518 chŏinix (1), *about a dry quart measure*

MEASURED
4058 mâdad (40), to *measure*
4128 mûwd (1), to *shake*
488 antimĕtrĕō (2), to *measure in return*
3354 mĕtrĕō (3), to *admeasure*

MEASURES
374 'êyphâh (2), dry *grain measure*
3734 kôr (8), dry *measure*
4055 mad (1), *vesture, garment; carpet*
4060 middâh (12), *measure; portion*
4461 mêmad (1), *measurement*
5429 çᵉ'âh (6), *volume measure for grain*
943 batŏs (1), *measure for liquids*
2884 kŏrŏs (1), *dry bushel measure*

English

4568 satŏn (2), *measure of about 12 dry quarts*
5518 chŏinix (1), *about a dry quart measure*

MEASURING
4060 middâh (10), *measure; portion*
3354 mĕtrĕŏ (1), to *admeasure*

MEAT
396 'ăkîylâh (1), *food*
398 'âkal (5), to *eat*
400 'ôkel (18), *food*
402 'oklâh (8), *food*
1262 bârâh (1), to *feed*
1267 bârûwth (1), *food*
1279 biryâh (3), *food*
2964 ţereph (3), *fresh torn prey*
3899 lechem (18), *food, bread*
3978 ma'ăkâl (22), *food, something to eat*
4202 mâzôwn (1), *food, provisions*
4203 mâzôwn (Ch.) (2), *food, provisions*
6595 path (1), *bit, morsel*
6598 pathbag (6), *dainty food*
6720 tsêydâh (1), *food, supplies*
1033 brōma (10), *food*
1034 brōsimŏs (1), *eatable*
1035 brōsis (7), *food; rusting corrosion*
4371 prŏsphagiŏn (1), *little fish*
4620 sitŏmĕtrŏn (1), *allowance or ration*
5132 trapĕza (1), *four-legged table*
5160 trŏphē (13), *nourishment; rations*
5315 phagō (3), outer *garment, i.e. a mantle*

MEATS
1033 brōma (6), *food*

MEBUNNAI
4012 M͏ᵉbunnay (1), *built up*

MECHERATHITE
4382 M͏ᵉkêrâthîy (1), *Mekerathite*

MEDAD
4312 Mêydâd (2), *affectionate*

MEDAN
4091 M͏ᵉdân (2), *contest or quarrel*

MEDDLE
1624 gârâh (4), to *provoke to anger*
6148 'ârab (2), to *intermix*

MEDDLED
1566 gâla' (1), to *be obstinate; to burst forth*

MEDDLETH
5674 'âbar (1), to *cross over; to transition*

MEDDLING
1566 gâla' (1), to *be obstinate; to burst forth*

MEDE
4075 Mâday (1), *Madian*

MEDEBA
4311 Mêyd͏ᵉbâ' (5), *water of quiet*

MEDES
4074 Mâday (9), *Madai*
4076 Mâday (Ch.) (4), *Madai*
3370 Mēdŏs (1), *inhabitant of Media*

MEDIA
4074 Mâday (6), *Madai*

MEDIAN
4077 Mâday (Ch.) (1), *Madian*

MEDIATOR
3316 mĕsitēs (6), *reconciler, intercessor*

MEDICINE
1456 gêhâh (1), *medicinal cure*
8644 t͏ᵉrûwphâh (1), *remedy, healing*

MEDICINES
7499 r͏ᵉphû'âh (2), *medicament, healing*

MEDITATE
1897 hâgâh (6), to *murmur, ponder*
7742 sûwach (1), to *muse pensively*
7878 sîyach (5), to *ponder, muse aloud*
3191 mĕlĕtaō (1), to *plot, think about*
4304 prŏmĕlĕtaō (1), to *premeditate*

MEDITATION
1900 hâgûwth (1), *musing, meditation*
1901 hâgîyg (1), *complaint, sighing*
1902 higgâyôwn (1), *musical notation*
7879 sîyach (1), *uttered contemplation*
7881 sîychâh (2), *reflection; devotion*

MEEK
6035 'ânâv (13), *needy; oppressed*
4235 praⱼŏs (1), *gentle, i.e. humble*
4239 praüs (3), *mild, humble, gentle*

MEEKNESS
6037 'anvâh (1), *mildness; oppressed*
6038 'ănâvâh (1), *modesty, clemency*
4236 praⱼŏtēs (9), *gentleness, humility*
4240 praütēs (3), *humility, meekness*

MEET
749 'ăraq (Ch.) (1), to *suit*
1121 bên (1), *son, descendant; people*
3259 yâ'ad (8), to *meet; to summon; to direct*
3474 yâshar (1), to *be straight; to make right*
3476 yôsher (1), *right*
3477 yâshâr (1), *straight*

3559 kûwn (1), to *set up: establish, fix, prepare*
4672 mâtsâ' (2), to *find or acquire; to occur*
5828 'êzer (2), *aid*
6213 'âsâh (2), to *make*
6293 pâga' (5), to *impinge*
6298 pâgash (6), to *come in contact with*
6440 pânîym (3), *face; front*
6743 tsâlach (1), to *push forward*
7125 qîr'âh (70), to *encounter, to happen*
7136 qârâh (1), to *bring about; to impose*
7200 râ'âh (1), to *see*
514 axiŏs (4), *deserving, comparable or suitable*
528 apantaō (2), *encounter, meet*
529 apantēsis (4), *friendly encounter*
1163 dĕi (2), *it is (was) necessary*
1342 dikaiŏs (2), *equitable, holy*
2111 ĕuthĕtŏs (1), *appropriate, suitable*
2173 ĕuchrēstŏs (1), *useful, serviceable*
2425 hikanŏs (1), *ample; fit*
2427 hikanoō (1), to *make competent*
2570 kalŏs (2), *good; beautiful; valuable*
4876 sunantaō (1), to *meet with; to occur*
4877 sunantēsis (1), *meeting with*
5222 hupantēsis (1), *encounter; concurrence*

MEETEST
3477 yâshâr (1), *straight*
6293 pâga' (1), to *impinge*

MEETETH
6293 pâga' (2), to *impinge*
6298 pâgash (1), to *come in contact with*

MEETING
6116 'ătsârâh (1), *assembly*
7125 qîr'âh (1), to *encounter, to happen*

MEGIDDO
4023 M͏ᵉgiddôwn (11), *rendezvous*

MEGIDDON
4023 M͏ᵉgiddôwn (1), *rendezvous*

MEHETABEEL
4105 M͏ᵉhêyţab'êl (1), *bettered of God*

MEHETABEL
4105 M͏ᵉhêyţab'êl (2), *bettered of God*

MEHIDA
4240 M͏ᵉchîydâ' (2), *junction*

MEHIR
4243 M͏ᵉchîyr (1), *price*

MEHOLATHITE
4259 M͏ᵉchôlâthîy (2), *Mecholathite*

MEHUJAEL
4232 M͏ᵉchûwyâ'êl (2), *smitten of God*

MEHUMAN
4104 M͏ᵉhûwmân (1), *Mehuman*

MEHUNIM
4586 M͏ᵉ'ûwnîy (1), *Menite*

MEHUNIMS
4586 M͏ᵉ'ûwnîy (1), *Menite*

MEKONAH
4368 M͏ᵉkônâh (1), *base*

MELATIAH
4424 M͏ᵉlaţyâh (1), *Jehovah has delivered*

MELCHI
3197 Mĕlchi (2), *king*

MELCHI-SHUA
4444 Malkîyshûwa' (2), *king of wealth*

MELCHIAH
4441 Malkîyâh (1), *appointed by Jehovah*

MELCHISEDEC
3198 Mĕlchisĕdĕk (9), *king of right*

MELCHIZEDEK
4442 Malkîy-Tsedeq (2), *king of right*

MELEA
3190 Mĕlĕas (1), *Meleas*

MELECH
4429 Melek (2), *king*

MELICU
4409 Mallûwk (1), *regnant*

MELITA
3194 Mĕlitē (1), *Melita*

MELODY
2172 zimrâh (2), *song*
5059 nâgan (1), to *play; to make music*
5567 psallō (1), to *play a stringed instrument*

MELONS
20 'ăbaţţîyach (1), *melon*

MELT
3988 mâ'aç (1), to *spurn; to disappear*
4127 mùwg (4), to *soften, flow down, disappear*
4529 mâçâh (1), to *dissolve, melt*
4549 mâçaç (6), to *waste; to faint*
5413 nâthak (2), to *pour out; to liquefy, melt*
6884 tsâraph (1), to *fuse metal; to refine*
3089 luŏ (1), to *loosen*
5080 tēkō (1), to *liquefy, melt*

MELTED
2046 hittûwk (1), *melting*
4127 mùwg (3), to *soften, flow down, disappear*
4549 mâçaç (6), to *waste; to faint fear or grief*
5140 nâzal (1), to *drip, or shed by trickling*
5413 nâthak (2), to *pour out; to liquefy, melt*

MELTETH
1811 dâlaph (1), to *drip*
4549 mâçaç (3), to *waste*;
to *faint*
5258 nâçak (1), to *pour* a
libation
6884 tsâraph (1), to *fuse*
metal; to *refine*
8557 temeç (1), *melting
disappearance*

MELTING
2003 hâmâç (1), dry *twig*
or *brushwood*

MELZAR
4453 Meltsâr (2), court
officer (poss.) *butler*

MEMBER
3196 mĕlŏs (5), *limb* or
part of the body

MEMBERS
3338 yâtsûr (1),
structure, human frame
3196 mĕlŏs (29), *limb* or
part of the body

MEMORIAL
234 'azkârâh (7),
remembrance-offering
2143 zêker (5),
*recollection;
commemoration*
2146 zikrôwn (17),
commemoration
3422 mnĕmŏsunŏn (3),
memorandum

MEMORY
2143 zêker (5),
commemoration

MEMPHIS
4644 Môph (1), *Moph*

MEMUCAN
4462 Mᵉmûwkân (3),
Memucan or Momucan

MEN
120 'âdâm (107), *human
being; mankind*
376 'îysh (211), *man;
male; someone*
582 'ĕnôwsh (491), *man;
person, human*
606 'ĕnâsh (Ch.) (12),
man
1121 bên (16), *son,
descendant; people*
1167 ba'al (20), *master;
husband; owner; citizen*
1368 gibbôwr (1),
powerful; great warrior
1397 geber (6), *person,
man*
1400 gᵉbar (Ch.) (18),
person; someone
2145 zâkâr (1), *male*
2388 châzaq (1), to *be
strong; courageous*
4962 math (14), *men*
4974 mᵉthôm (1),
completely
407 andrizŏmai (1), to
act manly
435 anêr (79), *man; male*
442 anthrŏpinŏs (1),
human
444 anthrŏpŏs (192),
human being; mankind
730 arrhēn (3), *male*
3495 nĕaniskŏs (5), *youth*

MERAIAH
4811 Mᵉrâyâh (1),
rebellion

MERAIOTH
4812 Mᵉrâyôwth (7),
rebellious

MERARI
4847 Mᵉrârîy (39), *bitter*

MERARITES
4848 Mᵉrârîy (1),
Merarite

MERATHAIM
4850 Mᵉrâthayim (1),
double bitterness

MERCHANDISE
4267 machănaq (1),
choking, strangling
4627 ma'ărâb (4),
mercantile goods
4819 markôleth (1),
mart, market
5504 çachar (4), *profit
from trade*
5505 çâchar (2), *profit
from trade*
5506 çᵉchôrâh (1), *traffic*
6014 'âmar (2), to *gather*
grain into sheaves
7404 rᵉkullâh (2),
peddled trade
1117 gŏmŏs (2), *cargo,
wares* or *freight*
1711 ĕmpŏria (1), *traffic,
business trade*
1712 ĕmpŏriŏn (1),
emporium marketplace

MERCHANT
3667 Kᵉna'an (3),
humiliated
5503 çâchar (4), to *travel*
round; to *palpitate*
7402 râkal (3), to *travel*
for trading
1713 ĕmpŏrŏs (1),
tradesman, merchant

MERCHANTMEN
5503 çâchar (1), to *travel*
round; to *palpitate*
8446 tûwr (1), to wander,
meander for trade

MERCHANTS
3669 Kᵉna'ănîy (1),
Kenaanite; merchant
5503 çâchar (9), to *travel*
round; to *palpitate*
7402 râkal (14), to *travel*
for trading
1713 ĕmpŏrŏs (4),
tradesman, merchant

MERCHANTS'
5503 çâchar (1), to *travel*
round; to *palpitate*

MERCIES
2617 cheçed (9),
kindness, favor
7356 racham (25),
compassion; womb
7359 rᵉchêm (Ch.) (1),
pity
3628 ŏiktirmŏs (4), *pity,
compassion*
3741 hŏsiŏs (1),
hallowed, pious, sacred

MEN'S
120 'âdâm (10), *human
being; mankind*
582 'ĕnôwsh (2), *man;
person, human*
444 anthrŏpŏs (4),
human being; mankind
4283 prŏĕuaggĕlizŏmai
(1), to *announce* glad
news *in advance*

MENAHEM
4505 Mᵉnachêm (8),
comforter

MENAN
3104 Maïnan (1), *Maïnan*

MEND
2388 châzaq (1), to
fasten upon; to *bind*

MENDING
2675 katartizō (2), to
repair; to *prepare*

MENE
4484 menê' (Ch.) (2),
numbered

MENPLEASERS
441 anthrŏparĕskŏs (2),
man-courting, fawning

MENSERVANTS
5650 'ebed (9), *servant*
3816 pais (1), *child; slave*
or *servant*

MENSTEALERS
405 andrapŏdistēs (1),
enslaver, kidnapper

MENSTRUOUS
1739 dâveh (1),
menstrual; fainting
5079 niddâh (2), *time of*
menstrual *impurity*

MENTION
2142 zâkar (18), to
remember; to *mention*
3417 mnĕia (4),
recollection; recital
3421 mnēmŏnĕuō (1), to
exercise memory

MENTIONED
935 bôw' (1), to *go, come*
2142 zâkar (3), to
remember; to *mention*
5927 'âlâh (1), to *ascend,
be high, mount*
7121 qârâ' (1), to *call out*
8052 shᵉmûw'âh (1),
announcement

MEONENIM
6049 'ânan (1), to *cover,
becloud*; to *act covertly*

MEONOTHAI
4587 Mᵉ'ôwnôthay (1),
habitative

MEPHAATH
4158 Môwpha'ath (4),
illuminative

MEPHIBOSHETH
4648 Mᵉphîybôsheth
(15), *dispeller of Shame*

MERAB
4764 Mêrâb (3), *increase*

MERCIES'
2617 cheçed (3),
kindness, favor
7356 racham (1),
compassion; womb

MERCIFUL
2551 chemlâh (1),
commiseration, pity
2603 chânan (11), to
implore
2616 châçad (2), to
reprove, shame
2617 cheçed (5),
kindness, favor
2623 châçîyd (3),
religiously pious, godly
3722 kâphar (2), to
cover; to expiate
7349 rachûwm (8),
compassionate
7355 râcham (1), to *be
compassionate*
1655 ĕlĕĕmōn (2),
compassion
2433 hilaskŏmai (1), to
conciliate, to atone for
2436 hilĕōs (1), God be
gracious!, far be it!
3629 ŏiktirmōn (2),
compassionate

MERCURIUS
2060 Hĕrmēs (1), *born of*
god *Hermes*

MERCY
2603 chânan (16), to
implore
2604 chânan (Ch.) (1), to
favor
2617 cheçed (137),
kindness, favor
3727 kappôreth (27), *lid,
cover*
7355 râcham (31), to *be
compassionate*
7356 racham (4),
compassion; womb
448 anilĕŏs (1),
inexorable, merciless
1653 ĕlĕĕō (27), to *give*
out *compassion*
1656 ĕlĕŏs (28),
compassion
3628 ŏiktirmŏs (1), *pity,
compassion*
3629 ŏiktirmōn (1),
compassionate

MERCYSEAT
2435 hilastēriŏn (1),
expiatory place

MERED
4778 Mered (2), *rebellion*

MEREMOTH
4822 Mᵉrêmôwth (6),
heights

MERES
4825 Mereç (1), *Meres*

MERIB-BAAL
4807 Mᵉrîyb Ba'al (3),
quarreller of Baal
4810 Mᵉrîy Ba'al (1),
rebellion against Baal

MERIBAH
4809 Mᵉrîybâh (6),
quarrel

English

MERIBAH-KADESH
4809+6946 Mᵉrîybâh (1),
quarrel

MERODACH
4781 Mᵉrôdâk (1),
Merodak

MERODACH-BALADAN
4757 Mᵉrô'dak Bal'âdân
(1), *Merodak-Baladan*

MEROM
4792 Mêrôwm (2), *height*

MERONOTHITE
4824 Mêrônôthîy (2),
Meronothite

MEROZ
4789 Mêrôwz (1), *Meroz*

MERRILY
8056 sâmêach (1), *blithe*
or *gleeful*

MERRY
1974 hillûwl (1), *harvest
celebration*
2896 ţôwb (7), *good; well*
3190 yâţab (5), *to be,
make well*
7832 sâchaq (2), *to
laugh; to scorn; to play*
7937 shâkar (1), *to
become tipsy, to satiate*
8055 sâmach (2), *to be,
make gleesome*
8056 sâmêach (3), *blithe*
or *gleeful*
2114 ĕuthumĕō (1), *to be
cheerful; keep courage*
2165 ĕuphrainō (6), *to
rejoice, be glad*

MERRYHEARTED
8056+3820 sâmêach (1),
blithe or *gleeful*

MESECH
4902 Meshek (1), *Meshek*

MESHA
4331 Mêyshâ' (1),
departure
4337 Mêyshâ' (1), *safety*
4338 Mêysha' (1), *safety*
4852 Mêshâ' (1), *Mesha*

MESHACH
4335 Mêyshak (1),
Meshak
4336 Mêyshak (Ch.) (14),
Meshak

MESHECH
4902 Meshek (8), *Meshek*

MESHELEMIAH
4920 Mᵉshelemyâh (4),
ally of Jehovah

MESHEZABEEL
4898 Mᵉshêyzab'êl (3),
delivered of God

MESHILLEMITH
4921 Mᵉshillêmîyth (1),
reconciliation

MESHILLEMOTH
4919 Mᵉshillêmôwth (2),
reconciliations

MESHOBAB
4877 Mᵉshôwbâb (1),
returned

MESHULLAM
4918 Mᵉshullâm (25),
allied

MESHULLEMETH
4922 Mᵉshullemeth (1),
Meshullemeth

MESOBAITE
4677 Mᵉtsôbâyâh (1),
found of Jehovah

MESOPOTAMIA
763 'Ăram Nahărayim
(5), *Aram of* (the) *two
rivers*
3318 Mĕsŏpŏtamia (2),
between the Rivers

MESS
4864 mas'êth (2), *raising;
beacon; present*

MESSAGE
1697 dâbâr (3), *word;
matter; thing*
4400 mal'ăkûwth (1),
message
31 aggĕlia (1), *message*
1860 ĕpaggĕlia (1),
divine assurance
4242 prĕsbĕia (1),
delegates

MESSENGER
1319 bâsar (1), *to
announce* (good news)
4397 mal'âk (24),
messenger
5046 nâgad (2), *to
announce*
6680 tsâvâh (1), *to
constitute, enjoin*
6735 tsîyr (1), *hinge;
herald or errand-doer*
32 aggĕlŏs (4),
messenger; angel
652 apŏstŏlŏs (1),
commissioner of Christ

MESSENGERS
4397 mal'âk (74),
messenger
6735 tsîyr (1), *hinge;
herald or errand-doer*
32 aggĕlŏs (3),
messenger; angel
652 apŏstŏlŏs (1),
commissioner of Christ

MESSES
4864 mas'êth (1), *raising;
beacon; present*

MESSIAH
4899 mâshîyach (2),
consecrated; Messiah

MESSIAS
3323 Mĕssias (2),
consecrated

MET
3259 yâ'ad (1), *to meet;
to summon; to direct*
4672 mâtsâ' (3), *to occur,
meet* or *be present*
6293 pâga' (4), *to impinge*
6298 pâgash (7), *to come
in contact with*
6923 qâdam (2), *to
anticipate, meet*
7122 qârâ' (2), *to
encounter, to happen*
7125 qir'âh (3), *to
encounter, to happen*
7135 qârâh (1), *coolness,
cold*
7136 qârâh (4), *to bring
about; to impose*

296 amphŏdŏn (1), *fork*
in the road
528 apantaō (5),
encounter, meet
3909 paratugchanō (1),
to chance near
4820 sumballō (1), *to aid;
to join, attack*
4876 sunantaō (4), *to
meet with; to occur*
5221 hupantaō (5), *to
meet, encounter*

METE
4058 mâdad (3), *to
measure*
3354 mĕtrĕō (3), *to
admeasure*

METED
6978 qav-qav (2), *stalwart*
8505 tâkan (1), *to
balance, i.e. measure*

METEYARD
4060 middâh (1),
measure; portion

METHEG-AMMAH
4965 Metheg
hâ-'Ammâh (1), *bit of
the metropolis*

METHUSAEL
4967 Mᵉthûwshâ'êl (2),
man who (is) *of God*

METHUSELAH
4968 Mᵉthûwshelach (6),
man of a dart

MEUNIM
4586 Mᵉ'ûwnîy (1), *Menite*

MEZAHAB
4314 Mêy Zâhâb (2),
water of gold

MIAMIN
4326 Mîyâmin (2), *from*
(the) *right hand*

MIBHAR
4006 Mibchâr (1), *select,
i.e. best*

MIBSAM
4017 Mibsâm (3),
fragrant

MIBZAR
4014 Mibtsâr (2),
fortification; defender

MICAH
4316 Mîykâ' (1), *who* (is)
like Jehovah?
4318 Mîykâh (22), *who*
(is) *like Jehovah?*
4319 Mîykâhûw (4), *who*
(is) *like Jehovah?*
4320 Mîykâyâh (1), *who*
(is) *like Jehovah?*

MICAH'S
4318 Mîykâh (3), *who* (is)
like Jehovah?

MICAIAH
4318 Mîykâh (1), *who* (is)
like Jehovah?
4319 Mîykâhûw (1), *who*
(is) *like Jehovah?*
4321 Mîykâyᵉhûw (16),
who (is) *like Jehovah?*

MICE
5909 'akbâr (4), *mouse*

MICHA
4316 Mîykâ' (4), *who* (is)
like Jehovah?

MICHAEL
4317 Mîykâ'êl (13), *who*
(is) *like God?*
3413 Michaĕl (2), *who* (is)
like God?

MICHAH
4318 Mîykâh (3), *who* (is)
like Jehovah?

MICHAIAH
4320 Mîykâyâh (3), *who*
(is) *like Jehovah?*
4321 Mîykâyᵉhûw (2),
who (is) *like Jehovah?*
4322 Mîykâyâhûw (2),
who (is) *like Jehovah?*

MICHAL
4324 Mîykâl (18), *rivulet*

MICHMAS
4363 Mikmâç (2), *hidden*

MICHMASH
4363 Mikmâç (9), *hidden*

MICHMETHAH
4366 Mikmᵉthâth (2),
concealment

MICHRI
4381 Mikrîy (1),
salesman

MICHTAM
4387 Miktâm (6), *poem*

MIDDAY
4276+3117 machătsîyth
(1), *halving* or *middle*
6672 tsôhar (1), *window:
noon time*
2250+3319 hēmĕra (1),
day; period of time

MIDDIN
4081 Middîyn (1), *contest*
or *quarrel*

MIDDLE
2677 chêtsîy (1), *half* or
middle, midst
2872 ţabbûwr (1), *summit*
8432 tâvek (6), *center,
middle*
8484 tîykôwn (9), *central,
middle*
3320 mᵉsŏtŏichŏn (1),
partition wall

MIDDLEMOST
8484 tîykôwn (2), *central,
middle*

MIDIAN
4080 Midyân (39),
contest or *quarrel*

MIDIANITE
4084 Midyânîy (1),
Midjanite

MIDIANITES
4080 Midyân (20),
contest or *quarrel*
4084 Midyânîy (3),
Midjanite
4092 Mᵉdânîy (1),
Midjanite

MIDIANITISH
4084 Midyânîy (3),
Midjanite

MIDNIGHT
2676+3915 châtsôwth (3), *middle* of the night
2677+3916 chêtsîy (3), *half* or *middle, midst*
8432+3915 tâvek (1), *center, middle*
3317 mĕsŏnuktiŏn (4), midnight watch
3319+3571 mĕsŏs (2), middle

MIDST
1459 gav (Ch.) (10), *middle*
2436 chêyq (1), *bosom, heart*
2673 châtsâh (1), to *cut* or *split* in two; to *halve*
2677 chêtsîy (8), *half* or *middle, midst*
2686 châtsats (1), to *curtail;* to *distribute*
2872 ṭabbûwr (1), *summit*
3820 lêb (12), *heart*
3824 lêbâb (1), *heart*
7130 qereb (73), *nearest* part, i.e. the *center*
8432 tâvek (209), *center, middle*
8484 tîykôwn (1), *central, middle*
3319 mĕsŏs (41), *middle*
3321 mĕsŏuranēma (3), *mid-sky, mid-heaven*
3322 mĕsŏō (1), to *be at midpoint*

MIDWIFE
3205 yâlad (3), to *bear* young; to *father a child*

MIDWIVES
3205 yâlad (7), to *bear* young; to *father a child*

MIGDAL-EL
4027 Migdal-'Êl (1), *tower of God*

MIGDAL-GAD
4028 Migdal-Gâd (1), *tower of Fortune*

MIGDOL
4024 Migdôwl (4), *tower*

MIGHT
202 'ôwn (2), *ability, power; wealth*
410 'êl (1), *mighty;* the *Almighty*
1369 gᵉbûwrâh (27), *force; valor; victory*
1370 gᵉbûwrâh (Ch.) (2), *power, strength*
2428 chayil (6), *army; wealth; virtue; strength*
3201 yâkôl (2), to *be able*
3581 kôach (7), *force, might; strength*
3966 mᵉ'ôd (2), *very, utterly*
5797 'ôz (2), *strength*
5807 'ĕzûwz (1), *forcibleness*
6108 'ôtsem (1), *power;* framework of the *body*
8632 tᵉqôph (Ch.) (1), *power*
1410 dunamai (6), to *be able* or *possible*
1411 dunamis (4), *force, power, miracle*

2479 ischus (2), *forcefulness, power*
2480 ischuō (1), to *have* or *exercise force*

MIGHTIER
117 'addîyr (1), *powerful; majestic*
6099 'âtsûwm (7), *powerful; numerous*
6105 'âtsam (1), to *be, make powerful*
8623 taqqîyph (1), *powerful*
2478 ischurŏs (3), *forcible, powerful*

MIGHTIES
1368 gibbôwr (2), *powerful;* great *warrior*

MIGHTIEST
1368 gibbôwr (1), *powerful;* great *warrior*

MIGHTILY
2393 chezqâh (2), *prevailing power*
3966 mᵉ'ôd (2), *very, utterly*
1722+1411 ĕn (1), *in; during; because of*
1722+2479 ĕn (1), *in; during; because of*
2159 eutŏnŏs (1), *intensely, cogently*
2596+2904 kata (1), *down; according to*

MIGHTY
46 'âbîyr (6), *mighty*
47 'abbîyr (4), *mighty*
117 'addîyr (5), *powerful; majestic*
193 'ûwl (1), *powerful; mighty*
352 'ayil (2), *chief; ram; oak tree*
376 'îysh (2), *man; male; someone*
386 'êythân (4), *never-failing; eternal*
410 'êl (5), *mighty;* the *Almighty*
430 'ĕlôhîym (2), the true *God;* great *ones*
533 'ammîyts (1), *strong; mighty; brave*
650 'âphîyq (1), *valley; stream; mighty, strong*
1121+410 bên (1), *son, descendant; people*
1219 bâtsar (1), to *be inaccessible*
1368 gibbôwr (135), *powerful;* great *warrior*
1369 gᵉbûwrâh (7), *force; valor; victory*
1396 gâbar (1), to *be strong;* to *prevail*
1397 geber (2), *person, man*
1401 gibbâr (Ch.) (1), *valiant man,* or *warrior*
1419 gâdôwl (7), *great*
2220 zᵉrôwa' (1), *arm; foreleg; force, power*
2388 châzaq (2), to *be strong; courageous*
2389 châzâq (20), *strong; severe, hard, violent*

2428 chayil (1), *army; wealth; virtue; strength*
3524 kabbîyr (5), *mighty; aged; mighty*
3966 mᵉ'ôd (1), *very, utterly*
5794 'az (3), *strong, vehement, harsh*
5797 'ôz (1), *strength*
5868 'ăyâm (1), (poss.) *strength*
6099 'âtsûwm (8), *powerful; numerous*
6105 'âtsam (4), to *be, make powerful*
6184 'ârîyts (1), *powerful* or *tyrannical*
6697 tsûwr (2), *rock*
7227 rab (5), *great*
7989 shallîyṭ (1), *prince* or *warrior*
8624 taqqîyph (Ch.) (2), *powerful*
972 biaiŏs (1), *violent*
1411 dunamis (14), *force, power, miracle*
1413 dunastēs (1), *ruler* or *officer*
1414 dunatĕō (1), to *be efficient, able, strong*
1415 dunatŏs (7), *powerful* or *capable*
1754 ĕnĕrgĕō (1), to *be active, efficient, work*
2478 ischurŏs (7), *forcible, powerful*
2479 ischus (1), *forcefulness, power*
2900 krataiŏs (1), *powerful, mighty*
3168 mĕgalĕiŏtēs (1), *grandeur* or *splendor*
3173 mĕgas (1), *great, many*
5082 tēlikŏutŏs (1), *so vast*

MIGRON
4051 Migrôwn (2), *precipice*

MIJAMIN
4326 Mîyâmîn (2), *from* (the) *right hand*

MIKLOTH
4732 Miqlôwth (4), *rods*

MIKNEIAH
4737 Miqnêyâhûw (2), *possession of Jehovah*

MILALAI
4450 Mîlălay (1), *talkative*

MILCAH
4435 Milkâh (11), *queen*

MILCH
3243 yânaq (1), to *suck;* to *give milk*
5763 'ûwl (2), to *suckle,* i.e. *give milk*

MILCOM
4445 Malkâm (3), *Malcam* or *Milcom*

MILDEW
3420 yêrâqôwn (5), *paleness; mildew*

MILE
3400 miliŏn (1), about 4,850 feet, Roman *mile*

MILETUM
3399 Milētŏs (1), *Miletus*

MILETUS
3399 Milētŏs (2), *Miletus*

MILK
2461 châlâb (42), *milk*
4711 mâtsats (1), to *suck*
1051 gala (5), *milk*

MILL
7347 rêcheh (1), *mill*-stone
3459 mulŏn (1), *mill-house*

MILLET
1764 dôchan (1), *millet* cereal *grain*

MILLIONS
7233 rᵉbâbâh (1), *myriad* number

MILLO
4407 millôw' (10), *citadel*

MILLS
7347 rêcheh (1), *mill*-stone

MILLSTONE
7347 rêcheh (1), *mill*-stone
7393 rekeb (2), *upper millstone*
3037+3457 lithŏs (1), *stone*
3458 mulŏs (2), *grinder millstone*
3458+3684 mulŏs (2), *grinder millstone*

MILLSTONES
7347 rêcheh (2), *mill*-stone

MINCING
2952 ṭâphaph (1), to *trip* or *step*

MIND
3336 yêtser (1), *form*
3820 lêb (12), *heart*
3824 lêbâb (4), *heart*
5315 nephesh (11), *life; breath; soul; wind*
5973 'îm (1), *with*
6310 peh (1), *mouth; opening*
7307 rûwach (6), *breath; wind;* life-spirit
363 anamimnēskō (1), to *remind;* to *recollect*
1106 gnōmē (2), *cognition, opinion*
1271 dianŏia (7), *mind* or *thought*
1771 ĕnnŏia (1), *moral understanding*
1878 ĕpanamimnēskō (1), to *remind again of*
3563 nŏus (15), *intellect, mind; understanding*
3661 hŏmŏthumadŏn (1), *unanimously*
3675 hŏmŏphrōn (1), *like-minded*
4288 prŏthumia (4), *alacrity, eagerness*
4290 prŏthumōs (1), *with alacrity, with eagerness*
4993 sōphrŏnĕō (2), to *be in a right state of mind*

English

4995 sōphrŏnismŏs (1), self-discipline
5012 tapĕinŏphrŏsunē (1), modesty, humility
5279 hupŏmimnēskō (1), to suggest to memory
5426 phrŏnĕō (9), to be mentally disposed
5427 phrŏnēma (2), inclination or purpose
5590 psuchē (1), soul, vitality; heart, mind

MINDED
5973+3820 'îm (1), with
1011 bŏulĕuō (1), to deliberate; to resolve
1014 bŏulŏmai (3), to be willing, desire
1374 dipsuchŏs (2), vacillating
4993 sōphrŏnĕō (1), to be in a right state of mind
5426 phrŏnĕō (3), to be mentally disposed
5427 phrŏnēma (2), mental inclination

MINDFUL
2142 zākar (6), to remember; to mention
3403 mimnēskō (3), to remind or to recall
3421 mnēmŏnĕuō (1), to exercise memory

MINDING
3195 mĕllō (1), to intend, i.e. be about to

MINDS
5315 nephesh (4), life; breath; soul; wind
1271 dianŏia (2), mind or thought
3540 nŏēma (4), perception, i.e. purpose
3563 nŏus (2), intellect, mind; understanding
5590 psuchē (2), soul, vitality; heart, mind

MINGLE
4537 mâçak (1), to mix
6151 'ărab (Ch.) (1), to co-mingle, mix

MINGLED
1101 bâlal (37), to mix; confuse; to feed
3610 kil'ayim (2), two different kinds of thing
3947 lâqach (1), to take
4537 mâçak (4), to mix
6148 'ârab (2), to intermix
6154 'êreb (4), mixed or woven things
3396 mignumi (4), to mix, mingle

MINIAMIN
4509 Minyâmîyn (3), from (the) right hand

MINISH
1639 gâra' (1), to shave, remove, lessen

MINISHED
4591 mâ'aṭ (1), to be, make small or few

MINISTER
1777 dîyn (1), to judge; to strive or contend for

8334 shârath (50), to attend as a menial
8335 shârêth (1), service
1247 diakŏnĕō (8), to act as a deacon
1248 diakŏnia (1), attendance, aid, service
1249 diakŏnŏs (14), waiter; deacon (-ess)
1325 didōmi (1), to give
2038 ĕrgazŏmai (1), to toil
3008 lĕitŏurgĕō (1), to perform religious or charitable functions
3011 lĕitŏurgŏs (2), functionary in the Temple or Gospel
3930 parĕchō (1), to hold near, i.e. to present
5256 hupĕrĕtĕō (1), to be a subordinate
5257 hupĕrĕtēs (3), servant, attendant
5524 chŏrēgĕō (1), to furnish, supply, provide

MINISTERED
8120 shĕmash (Ch.) (1), to serve
8334 shârath (15), to attend as a menial
1247 diakŏnĕō (14), to wait upon, serve
2023 ĕpichŏrēgĕō (2), to fully supply; to aid
3008 lĕitŏurgĕō (1), to perform religious or charitable functions
3011 lĕitŏurgŏs (1), functionary in the Temple or Gospel
5256 hupĕrĕtĕō (1), to be a subordinate

MINISTERETH
2023 ĕpichŏrēgĕō (2), to fully supply; to aid

MINISTERING
5656 'ăbôdâh (1), work of any kind
8334 shârath (1), to attend as a menial
1247 diakŏnĕō (1), to wait upon, serve
1248 diakŏnia (3), attendance, aid, service
2418 hiĕrŏurgĕō (1), officiate as a priest
3008 lĕitŏurgĕō (1), to perform religious or charitable functions
3010 lĕitŏurgikŏs (1), engaged in holy service

MINISTERS
6399 pĕlach (Ch.) (1), to serve or worship
8334 shârath (15), to attend as a menial
1249 diakŏnŏs (6), attendant, deacon
3011 lĕitŏurgŏs (2), functionary in the Temple or Gospel
5257 hupĕrĕtēs (2), servant, attendant

MINISTRATION
1248 diakŏnia (6), attendance, aid, service

3009 lĕitŏurgia (1), service, ministry

MINISTRY
3027 yâd (2), hand; power
5656 'ăbôdâh (1), work
8335 shârêth (1), service in the Temple
1248 diakŏnia (16), attendance, aid, service
3009 lĕitŏurgia (2), service, ministry

MINNI
4508 Minnîy (1), Minni

MINNITH
4511 Minnîyth (2), enumeration

MINSTREL
5059 nâgan (2), to play; to make music

MINSTRELS
834 aulētēs (1), flute-player

MINT
2238 hēduŏsmŏn (2), sweet-scented, mint

MIPHKAD
4663 Miphqâd (1), assignment

MIRACLE
4159 môwphêth (1), miracle; token or omen
1411 dunamis (1), force, power, miracle
4592 sēmĕiŏn (7), indication, sign, signal

MIRACLES
226 'ôwth (2), signal, sign
4159 môwphêth (1), miracle; token or omen
6381 pâlâ' (1), to be, make great, wonderful
1411 dunamis (8), force, power, miracle
4592 sēmĕiŏn (15), indication, sign, signal

MIRE
1206 bôts (1), mud
1207 bitstsâh (1), swamp, marsh
2563 chômer (2), clay; dry measure
2916 ṭîyṭ (8), mud or clay
3121 yâvên (1), mud, sediment
7516 rephesh (1), mud of the sea
1004 bŏrbŏrŏs (1), mud

MIRIAM
4813 Miryâm (15), rebelliously

MIRMA
4821 Mirmâh (1), fraud

MIRTH
4885 mâsôws (3), delight
7797 sûws (1), to be bright, i.e. cheerful
8057 simchâh (8), blithesomeness or glee
8342 sâsôwn (3), cheerfulness; welcome

MIRY
1207 bitstsâh (1), swamp, marsh

2917 ṭîyn (Ch.) (2), wet clay
3121 yâvên (1), mud, sediment

MISCARRYING
7921 shâkôl (1), to miscarry

MISCHIEF
205 'âven (4), trouble, vanity, wickedness
611 'âçôwn (5), hurt, injury
1943 hôvâh (2), ruin, disaster
2154 zimmâh (3), bad plan
4827 mêra' (1), wickedness
5771 'âvôn (1), moral evil
5999 'âmâl (9), wearing effort; worry
7451 ra' (19), bad; evil
7489 râ'a' (1), to be good for nothing
4468 rhaⁱdiŏurgia (1), malignity, trickery

MISCHIEFS
1942 havvâh (1), desire; craving
7451 ra' (2), bad; evil

MISCHIEVOUS
1942 havvâh (2), desire; craving
4209 mᵉzimmâh (2), plan; sagacity
7451 ra' (1), bad; evil

MISERABLE
5999 'âmâl (1), wearing effort; worry
1652 ĕlĕĕinŏs (2), worthy of mercy

MISERABLY
2560 kakōs (1), badly; wrongly; ill

MISERIES
4788 mârûwd (1), outcast; destitution
5004 talaipōria (1), calamity, distress

MISERY
4788 mârûwd (1), outcast; destitution
5999 'âmâl (3), wearing effort; worry
6001 'âmêl (1), toiling; laborer; sorrowful
7451 ra' (1), bad; evil
5004 talaipōria (1), calamity, distress

MISGAB
4869 misgâb (1), high refuge

MISHAEL
4332 Mîyshâ'êl (8), who (is) what God (is)?

MISHAL
4861 Mish'âl (1), request

MISHAM
4936 Mish'âm (1), inspection

MISHEAL
4861 Mish'âl (1), request

MISHMA
4927 Mishmâ' (4), report

MISHMANNAH
4925 Mishmannâh (1), *fatness*

MISHRAITES
4954 Mishrâ'îy (1), *extension*

MISPERETH
4559 Miçpereth (1), *enumeration*

MISREPHOTH-MAIM
4956 Misr^ephôwth Mayim (2), *burnings of water*

MISS
2398 châṭâ' (1), to *sin*
6485 pâqad (1), to *visit, care for, count*

MISSED
6485 pâqad (3), to *visit, care for, count*

MISSING
6485 pâqad (2), to *visit, care for, count*

MIST
108 'êd (1), *fog*
887 achlus (1), *dimness of sight*, i.e. *cataract*
2217 zŏphŏs (1), *gloom*

MISTRESS
1172 ba'ălâh (2), *mistress; female owner*
1404 g^ebereth (7), *mistress, noblewoman*

MISUSED
8591 tâ'a' (1), to *cheat*; to *maltreat*

MITE
3016 lĕptŏn (1), small *coin*

MITES
3016 lĕptŏn (2), small *coin*

MITHCAH
4989 Mithqâh (2), *sweetness*

MITHNITE
4981 Mithnîy (1), *slenderness*

MITHREDATH
4990 Mithr^edâth (2), *Mithredath*

MITRE
4701 mitsnepheth (11), royal/priestly *turban*
6797 tsânîyph (2), *head-dress, turban*

MITYLENE
3412 Mitulēnē (1), *abounding in shell-fish*

MIXED
1101 bâlal (1), to *mix; confuse; to feed*
4107 mâhal (1), to *dilute a mixture*
4469 mamçâk (1), *mixed-wine*
6151 'ărab (Ch.) (3), to *co-mingle, mix*
6154 'êreb (2), *mixed or woven threads*
4786 sugkĕrannumi (1), to *combine; assimilate*

MIXTURE
4538 meçek (1), wine *mixture with spices*
194 akratŏs (1), *undiluted*
3395 migma (1), *compound, mixture*

MIZAR
4706 Mits'âr (1), *little*

MIZPAH
4708 Mitspeh (5), *observatory*
4709 Mitspah (18), *observatory*

MIZPAR
4558 Miçpâr (1), *number*

MIZPEH
4708 Mitspeh (9), *observatory*
4709 Mitspah (14), *observatory*

MIZRAIM
4714 Mitsrayim (4), double *border*

MIZZAH
4199 Mizzâh (3), *terror*

MNASON
3416 Mnasōn (1), *Mnason*

MOAB
4124 Môw'âb (165), *from mother's father*
4125 Môw'âbîy (2), *Moäbite or Moäbitess*

MOABITE
4125 Môw'âbîy (3), *Moäbite or Moäbitess*

MOABITES
4124 Môw'âb (16), *from mother's father*
4125 Môw'âbîy (3), *Moäbite or Moäbitess*

MOABITESS
4125 Môw'âbîy (6), *Moäbite or Moäbitess*

MOABITISH
4125 Môw'âbîy (1), *Moäbite or Moäbitess*

MOADIAH
4153 Môw'adyâh (1), *assembly of Jehovah*

MOCK
2048 hâthal (1), to *deride, mock*
3887 lûwts (1), to *scoff*; to *interpret; to intercede*
3932 lâ'ag (2), to *deride; to speak unintelligibly*
5953 'âlal (1), to *glean*; to *overdo*
6711 tsâchaq (2), to *scorn; to make sport of*
7046 qâlaç (1), to *disparage*, i.e. *ridicule*
7832 sâchaq (1), to *laugh; to scorn; to play*
1702 ĕmpaizō (3), *deride, ridicule*

MOCKED
2048 hâthal (4), to *deride, mock*
3931 lâ'ab (1), to *deride, mock*
3932 lâ'ag (2), to *deride; to speak unintelligibly*

5953 'âlal (1), to *glean*; to *overdo*
6711 tsâchaq (1), to *scorn; to make sport of*
7046 qâlaç (1), to *disparage*, i.e. *ridicule*
7832 sâchaq (1), to *laugh; to scorn; to play*
1702 ĕmpaizō (8), *deride, ridicule*
3456 muktērizō (1), to *ridicule*
5512 chlĕuazō (1), *jeer at, sneer at*

MOCKER
3887 lûwts (1), to *scoff*; to *interpret; to intercede*

MOCKERS
2049 hâthôl (1), *derision, mockery*
3887 lûwts (1), to *scoff*; to *interpret; to intercede*
3934 lâ'êg (1), *buffoon; foreigner*
7832 sâchaq (1), to *laugh; to scorn; to play*
1703 ĕmpaiktēs (1), *derider; false teacher*

MOCKEST
3932 lâ'ag (1), to *deride; to speak unintelligibly*

MOCKETH
2048 hâthal (1), to *deride, mock*
3932 lâ'ag (3), to *deride; to speak unintelligibly*
7832 sâchaq (1), to *laugh; to scorn; to play*

MOCKING
6711 tsâchaq (1), to *scorn; to make sport of*
7048 qallâçâh (1), *ridicule*
1702 ĕmpaizō (2), to *deride, ridicule*
5512 chlĕuazō (1), *jeer at, sneer at*

MOCKINGS
1701 ĕmpaigmŏs (1), *derision, jeering*

MODERATELY
6666 ts^edâqâh (1), *rightness*

MODERATION
1933 ĕpiĕikēs (1), *mild, gentle*

MODEST
2887 kŏsmiŏs (1), *orderly*

MOIST
3892 lach (1), *fresh cut*, i.e. unused or undried

MOISTENED
8248 shâqâh (1), to *quaff*, i.e. to *irrigate*

MOISTURE
3955 l^eshad (1), *juice; vigor; sweet or fat cake*
2429 hikmas (1), *dampness, dampness*

MOLADAH
4137 Môwlâdâh (4), *birth*

MOLE
8580 tanshemeth (1), (poss.) *tree-toad*

MOLECH
4432 Môlek (8), *king*

MOLES
2661 chăphôr (1), *hole*, i.e. a *burrowing rat*

MOLID
4140 Môwlîyd (1), *genitor*

MOLLIFIED
7401 râkak (1), to *soften*

MOLOCH
4432 Môlek (1), *king*
3434 Mŏlŏch (1), *king*

MOLTEN
3332 yâtsaq (6), to *pour out*
4541 maççêkâh (25), *cast image); libation*
4549 mâçaç (1), to *waste; to faint*
5258 nâçak (1), to *pour a libation*
5262 neçek (4), *libation; cast idol*
5413 nâthak (1), to *flow forth, pour out*
6694 tsûwq (1), to *pour out; melt*

MOMENT
7281 rega' (19), very *short space of time*
823 atŏmŏs (1), *indivisible unit of time*
3901 pararrhuĕō (1), to *flow by*
4743 stigmē (1), *point of time*, i.e. an *instant*

MONEY
3701 keçeph (112), *silver money*
3702 k^eçaph (Ch.) (1), *silver money*
7192 q^esîytah (2), *coin* of unknown weight
694 arguriŏn (11), *silver; silver money*
2772 kĕrma (1), *coin*
2773 kĕrmatistēs (1), *money-broker*
3546 nŏmisma (1), *coin*
4715 statēr (1), *coin worth four day's wage*
5365 philarguria (1), *avarice*
5475 chalkŏs (2), *copper*
5536 chrēma (4), *wealth, price*

MONEYCHANGERS
2855 kŏllubistēs (2), *coin-dealer*

MONSTERS
8577 tannîyn (1), *sea-serpent; jackal*

MONTH
2320 chôdesh (215), *new moon; month*
3391 yerach (6), *lunar month*
3393 y^erach (Ch.) (1), *lunar month*
3376 mēn (4), *month; month's time*

MONTHLY
2320 chôdesh (1), *new moon; month*

MONTHS
2320 chôdesh (37), *new moon; month*
3391 yerach (5), *lunar month*
3393 yᵉrach (Ch.) (1), *lunar* month
3376 mên (14), month; month's time
5072 tĕtramēnŏn (1), four months' time
5150 trimēnŏn (1), three months' space

MONUMENTS
5341 nâtsar (1), to *guard, protect, maintain*

MOON
2320 chôdesh (9), *new moon; month*
3391 yerach (2), *lunar month*
3394 yârêach (26), *moon*
3842 lᵉbânâh (3), *white moon*
3561 nŏumēnia (1), festival of new moon
4582 sĕlēnē (9), moon

MOONS
2320 chôdesh (11), *new moon; month*

MORASTHITE
4183 Mowrashtîy (2), *Morashtite*

MORDECAI
4782 Mordᵉkay (58), *Mordecai*

MORDECAI'S
4782 Mordᵉkay (2), *Mordecai*

MORE
637 'aph (1), *also or yea; though*
1058 bâkâh (1), to *weep, moan*
1490 gizbâr (Ch.) (3), *treasurer*
1980 hâlak (1), to *walk; live a certain way*
2351 chûwts (1), *outside, outdoors; open market; countryside*
3148 yôwthêr (3), *moreover; rest; gain*
3254 yâçaph (59), to *add or augment*
3499 yether (1), *remainder;* small *rope*
3513 kâbad (1), to *be heavy, severe, dull*
3651 kên (2), *just; right, correct*
4480 min (4), *from, out of*
4481 min (Ch.) (1), *from or out of*
5674 'âbar (1), to *cross over; to transition*
5720 'Âdîyn (1), *voluptuous*
5736 'âdaph (1), to *be redundant, have surplus*
5750 'ôwd (196), *again; repeatedly; still; more*
5922 'al (Ch.) (1), *above, over, upon,* or *against*
5973 'îm (1), *with*

6105 'âtsam (2), to *be, make numerous*
6440 pânîym (1), *face; front*
7138 qârôwb (1), *near, close*
7227 rab (14), *great*
7230 rôb (1), *abundance*
7231 râbab (2), to *increase*
7235 râbâh (11), to *increase*
7608 sha'ărâh (1), female *kindred by blood*
7725 shûwb (1), to *turn back; to return*
8145 shênîy (3), *second; again*
197 akribĕstĕrŏn (4), more exactly
243 allŏs (1), different, other
316 anagkaiŏs (1), necessary
414 anĕktŏtĕrŏs (6), more bearable
1065 gĕ (1), particle of emphasis
1308 diaphĕrō (2), to differ; to surpass
1508 ĕi mē (1), if not
1617 ĕktĕnĕstĕrŏn (1), more intently
1833 ĕxĕtazō (1), to ascertain or interrogate
2001 ĕpischuō (7), to insist stoutly
2089 ĕti (39), yet, still
2115 ĕuthumŏs (1), cheerful, encouraged
3122 malista (1), in the greatest degree
3123 mallŏn (47), in a greater degree
3185 mĕizōn (1), in greater degree
3187 mĕizŏn (1), larger, greater
3370 Mēdŏs (3), inhabitant of Media
3745 hŏsŏs (1), as much as
3761 ŏudĕ (1), neither, nor, not even
3765 ŏukĕti (17), not yet, no longer
3844 para (2), from; with; besides; on account of
4053 pĕrissŏs (1), superabundant
4054 pĕrissŏtĕrŏn (1), more superabundant
4055 pĕrissŏtĕrŏs (10), more superabundant
4056 pĕrissŏtĕrōs (10), more superabundantly
4057 pĕrissōs (1), superabundantly
4065 pĕriphrŏnĕō (1), to depreciate, contemn
4119 plĕiōn (25), more
4179 pŏllaplasiōn (1), very much more
4325 prŏsdapanaō (1), to expend additionally
4369 prŏstithēmi (2), to lay beside, repeat
4707 spŏudaiŏtĕrŏs (2), more prompt

5112 tŏlmērŏtĕrŏn (1), more daringly
5228 hupĕr (4), over; above; beyond
5245 hupĕrnikaō (1), to gain a decisive victory

MOREH
4176 Môwreh (3), *archer; teaching; early rain*

MOREOVER
518 'îm (1), *whether?; if, although; Oh that!*
637 'aph (2), *also or yea; though*
1571 gam (25), *also; even; yea; though*
3148 yôwthêr (1), *moreover; rest; gain*
3254 yâçaph (1), to *add or augment*
5750 'ôwd (6), *again; repeatedly; still; more*
1161 dĕ (12), but, yet; and then
2089 ĕti (1), yet, still
2532 kai (1), and; or; even; also

MORESHETH-GATH
4182 Môwresheth Gath (1), *possession of Gath*

MORIAH
4179 Môwrîyâh (2), *seen of Jehovah*

MORNING
216 'ôwr (1), *luminary; lightning; happiness*
1242 bôqer (187), *morning*
4891 mishchâr (1), *dawn*
5053 nôgahh (Ch.) (1), *dawn*
6843 tsᵉphîyrâh (2), *mishap*
7836 shâchar (1), to *search for*
7837 shachar (12), *dawn*
7904 shâkâh (1), to *roam because of lust*
7925 shâkam (1), to *start early in the morning*
3720 ŏrthrinŏs (1), matutinal, i.e. early
4404 prōï (6), at dawn; day-break watch
4405 prōïa (3), day-dawn, early morn
4407 prōïnŏs (1), matutinal, i.e. early

MORROW
1242 bôqer (7), *morning*
4279 mâchar (45), *tomorrow; hereafter*
4283 mochŏrâth (28), *tomorrow, next day*
839 auriŏn (14), to-morrow
1836 hĕxēs (1), successive, next
1887 ĕpauriŏn (8), to-morrow

MORSEL
3603 kikkâr (1), *round loaf; talent*
6595 path (8), *bit, morsel*
1035 brōsis (1), food; rusting corrosion

MORSELS
6595 path (1), *bit, morsel*

MORTAL
582 'ĕnôwsh (1), *man; person, human*
2349 thnētŏs (5), liable to die, i.e. *mortal*

MORTALITY
2349 thnētŏs (1), liable to die, i.e. *mortal*

MORTALLY
5315 nephesh (1), *life; breath; soul; wind*

MORTAR
4085 mᵉdôkâh (1), *mortar for bricks*
4388 maktêsh (1), *mortar; socket*

MORTER
2563 chômer (4), *clay; dry measure*
6083 'âphâr (2), *dust, earth, mud; clay,*

MORTGAGED
6148 'ârab (1), to *intermix; to give or be security*

MORTIFY
2289 thanatŏō (1), to kill
3499 nĕkrŏō (1), to *deaden,* i.e. to *subdue*

MOSERA
4149 Môwçêrâh (1), *corrections*

MOSEROTH
4149 Môwçêrâh (2), *corrections*

MOSES
4872 Môsheh (749), *drawing out of the water*
4873 Môsheh (Ch.) (1), *drawing out of the water*
3475 Mōsĕus (77), drawing out of the water

MOSES'
4872 Môsheh (16), *drawing out of the water*
3475 Mōsĕus (3), drawing out of the water

MOST
2429 chayil (Ch.) (1), *army; strength*
2896 tôwb (1), *good; well*
3524 kabbîyr (1), *mighty; aged; mighty*
3800 kethem (1), *pure gold*
4581 mâ'ôwz (1), *fortified place; defense*
4971 mathkôneth (1), *proportion*
5920 'al (2), the *Highest God*
5943 'illay (Ch.) (9), the *supreme God*
5945 'elyôwn (25), *loftier, higher; Supreme God*
5946 'elyôwn (Ch.) (3), the *Supreme God*

6579 partam (1),
grandee, noble
6944 qôdesh (48), *sacred
place or thing*
7230 rôb (1), *abundance*
8077 sh^emâmâh (1),
devastation
8563 tamrûwr (1),
bitterness
40 hagiŏs (1), *sacred,
holy*
2236 hēdista (1), *with
great pleasure*
2903 kratistŏs (4), *very
honorable*
3122 malista (1), *in the
greatest degree*
4118 plĕistŏs (1), *very
large,* i.e. *the most*
4119 plĕiŏn (3), *more*
5310 hupsistŏs (5),
highest; the Supreme
God

MOTE
2595 karphŏs (6), *dry
twig* or *straw*

MOTH
6211 'âsh (7), *moth*
4597 sēs (3), *moth* insect

MOTHEATEN
4598 sētŏbrōtŏs (1),
moth-eaten

MOTHER
517 'êm (143), *mother*
2545 chămôwth (11),
mother-in-law
2859 châthan (1), to
become related by
marriage,
282 amētōr (1), *of
unknown maternity*
3384 mētēr (76), *mother*
3994 pĕnthĕra (6), *wife's
mother*

MOTHER'S
517 'êm (67), *mother*
3384 mētēr (7), *mother*

MOTHERS
517 'êm (3), *mother*
3384 mētēr (2), *mother*
3389 mētralōịas (1),
matricide

MOTHERS'
517 'êm (1), *mother*

MOTIONS
3804 pathēma (1),
passion; suffering

MOULDY
5350 niqqud (2), *crumb,
morsel; biscuit*

MOUNT
55 'âbak (1), to *coil
upward*
1361 gâbahh (1), to *be
lofty;* to *be haughty*
2022 har (222), *mountain*
or *range* of hills
2042 hârâr (1), *mountain*
4674 mutstsâb (1),
station, military *post*
5550 çôl^elâh (5), military
siege mound, rampart
5927 'âlâh (4), to *ascend,
be high, mount*
7311 rûwm (1), to *be
high;* to *rise* or *raise*

3735 ŏrŏs (21), *hill,
mountain*

MOUNTAIN
2022 har (104), *mountain*
or *range* of hills
2042 hârâr (2), *mountain*
2906 ţûwr (Ch.) (2), *rock*
or *hill*
3735 ŏrŏs (28), *hill,
mountain*

MOUNTAINS
2022 har (155), *mountain*
or *range* of hills
2042 hârâr (8), *mountain*
3735 ŏrŏs (13), *hill,
mountain*

MOUNTED
7426 râmam (1), to *rise*

MOUNTING
4608 ma'ăleh (1),
elevation; platform

MOUNTS
5550 çôl^elâh (3), military
siege mound, rampart

MOURN
56 'âbal (15), to *bewail*
57 'âbêl (3), *lamenting*
578 'ânâh (1), to *groan,
lament*
584 'ânach (1), to *sigh,
moan*
1897 hâgâh (4), to
murmur, utter a sound
5098 nâham (2), to *growl,
groan*
5110 nûwd (1), to
deplore; to *taunt*
5594 çâphad (9), to *tear
the hair, wail*
6937 qâdar (2), to *mourn*
in *dark* garments
7300 rûwd (1), to *ramble*
2875 kŏptŏ (1), to *beat
the breast*
3996 pĕnthĕŏ (5), to
grieve

MOURNED
56 'âbal (10), to *bewail*
1058 bâkâh (2), to *weep,
moan*
5594 çâphad (6), to *tear
the hair, wail*
2354 thrēnĕŏ (2), to
bewail, lament
3996 pĕnthĕŏ (2), to
grieve

MOURNER
56 'âbal (1), to *bewail*

MOURNERS
57 'âbêl (2), *lamenting*
205 'âven (1), *trouble,
vanity, wickedness*
5594 çâphad (1), to *tear
the hair, wail*

MOURNETH
56 'âbal (8), to *bewail*
57 'âbêl (1), *lamenting*
1669 dâ'ab (1), to *pine,
feel sorrow*
5594 çâphad (1), to *tear
the hair, wail*

MOURNFULLY
6941 q^edôrannîyth (1), *in
sackcloth*

MOURNING
56 'âbal (2), to *bewail*
57 'âbêl (2), *lamenting*
60 'êbel (24), *lamentation*
205 'âven (1), *trouble,
vanity, wickedness*
585 'ănâchâh (1),
sighing, moaning
1086 bâlâh (1), to *wear
out, decay; consume*
1899 hegeh (1),
muttering; mourning
1993 hâmâh (1), to *be in
great commotion*
3382 Yered (1), *descent*
4553 miçpêd (6),
lamentation, howling
4798 marzêach (1), *cry* of
lamentation
6937 qâdar (4), to *mourn*
in *dark* garments
6969 qûwn (1), to *chant*
or *wail* at a funeral
8386 ta'ănîyâh (1),
lamentation
3602 ŏdurmŏs (2),
lamentation
3997 pĕnthŏs (2), *grief,
mourning, sadness*

MOUSE
5909 'akbâr (2), *mouse*

MOUTH
1627 gârôwn (1), *throat*
2441 chêk (14), area of
mouth
5716 'ădîy (2), *finery;
outfit; headstall*
6310 peh (326), *mouth;
opening*
6433 pûm (Ch.) (5),
mouth
8651 t^era' (Ch.) (1), *door;
palace*
3056 lŏgŏs (1), *word,
matter, thing*
4750 stŏma (69), *mouth;
edge*

MOUTHS
6310 peh (12), *mouth;
opening*
6433 pûm (Ch.) (1),
mouth
1993 ĕpistŏmizō (1), to
silence
4750 stŏma (4), *mouth;
edge*

MOVE
2782 chârats (1), to *be
alert,* to *decide*
5110 nûwd (1), to *waver;*
to *wander, flee*
5128 nûwa' (1), to *waver*
5130 nûwph (1), to
quiver, vibrate, rock
6328 pûwq (1), to *waver*
6470 pâ'am (1), to *tap;* to
impel or *agitate*
7264 râgaz (2), to *quiver*
8318 sherets (1), *swarm,
teeming mass*
2795 kinĕŏ (2), to *stir,
move, remove*
3056+4160 lŏgŏs (1),
word, matter, thing

MOVEABLE
5128 nûwa' (1), to *waver*

MOVED
1607 gâ'ash (3), to
agitate violently, *shake*
1949 hûwm (1), to *make
an uproar; agitate*
1993 hâmâh (1), to *be in
great commotion*
2111 zûwa' (1), to *shake*
with fear, *tremble*
2782 chârats (1), to *be
alert,* to *decide*
4131 môwţ (19), to *slip,
shake, fall*
4132 môwţ (3), *pole; yoke*
5074 nâdad (1), to *rove,
flee;* to *drive away*
5120 nûwţ (1), to *quake*
5128 nûwa' (5), to *waver*
5425 nâthar (1), to *jump;*
to *be agitated*
5496 çûwth (4), to
stimulate; to *seduce*
5648 'ăbad (Ch.) (1), to
do, work, serve
7043 qâlal (1), to *be,
make light, swift*
7264 râgaz (5), to *quiver*
7363 râchaph (1), to
brood; to *be relaxed*
7430 râmas (1), to *glide
swiftly, move, swarm*
7493 râ'ash (2), to
undulate, quake
23 aganaktĕŏ (1), to *be
indignant*
383 anasĕiŏ (1), to
excite, stir up
761 asalĕutŏs (1),
immovable, fixed
2125 ĕulabĕŏmai (1), to
have reverence
2206 zēlŏŏ (2), to *have
warmth* of feeling for
2795 kinĕŏ (2), to *stir,
move, remove*
3334 mĕtakinĕŏ (1), to *be
removed, shifted from*
4525 sainō (1), to *shake;*
to *disturb*
4531 salĕuŏ (1), to *waver,*
i.e. *agitate, rock, topple*
4579 sĕiŏ (1), to *vibrate;*
to *agitate*
4697 splagchnizŏmai (5),
to *feel sympathy,* to *pity*
5342 phĕrō (1), to *bear* or
carry

MOVEDST
5496 çûwth (1), to
stimulate; to *seduce*

MOVER
2795 kinĕŏ (1), to *stir,
move, remove*

MOVETH
1980 hâlak (1), to *walk;
live a certain way*
2654 châphêts (1), to *be
pleased with, desire*
7430 râmas (5), to *glide
swiftly,* i.e. *crawl,
move, swarm*
8317 shârats (1), to
wriggle, swarm

MOVING
5205 nîyd (1), *motion* of
the lips in speech
7169 qârats (1), to *bite
the lips, blink the eyes*

MOWER
7430 râmas (1), to *glide swiftly, crawl, move*
8318 sherets (1), *swarm, teeming mass*
2796 kinēsis (1), *stirring, motion*

MOWER
7114 qâtsar (1), to *curtail, cut short*

MOWINGS
1488 gêz (1), *shorn fleece; mown grass*

MOWN
1488 gêz (1), *shorn fleece; mown grass*

MOZA
4162 Môwtsâ' (5), *going forth*

MOZAH
4681 Môtsâh (1), *drained*

MUCH
634 'Êçar-Chaddôwn (1), *Esar-chaddon*
637 'aph (15), *also or yea; though*
834 'ăsher (2), *how, because, in order that*
1431 gâdal (2), to *be great, make great*
1571 gam (2), *also; even; yea; though*
1767 day (2), *enough, sufficient*
1931 hûw' (1), *he, she, it; this or that*
2479 chalchâlâh (1), *writhing in childbirth*
3254 yâçaph (1), to *add or augment*
3498 yâthar (1), to *remain or be left*
3515 kâbêd (2), *numerous; severe*
3524 kabbîyr (2), *mighty; aged; mighty*
3605 kôl (1), *all, any*
3966 mᵉ'ôd (9), *very, utterly*
4276 machătsîyth (1), *halving or the middle*
4767 mirbâh (1), *great quantity*
5704 'ad (2), *as far (long) as; during; while; until*
6079 'aph'aph (1), *fluttering eyelash*
6581 pâsâh (4), to *spread*
7114 qâtsar (1), to *curtail, cut short*
7225 rê'shîyth (1), *first*
7227 rab (38), *great*
7230 rôb (7), *abundance*
7235 râbâh (31), to *increase*
7335 râzam (1), to *twinkle the eye*
7690 saggîy' (Ch.) (4), *large*
23 aganaktĕō (2), to be *indignant*
1280 diapŏrĕō (1), to *be thoroughly puzzled*
2425 hikanŏs (6), *ample*
2470 isŏs (1), *similar*
2579 kan (1), *and (or even) if*

3123 mallŏn (3), *in a greater degree*
3366 mĕdĕ (1), *but not, not even; nor*
3383 mĕtĕ (1), *neither or nor; not even*
3386 mĕtigĕ (1), *not to say (the rather still)*
3433 mŏlis (1), *with difficulty*
3588 hŏ (2), *"the," i.e. the definite article*
3745 hŏsŏs (4), *as much as*
3761 ŏudĕ (4), *neither, nor, not even*
4055 pĕrissŏtĕrŏs (1), *more superabundant*
4056 pĕrissŏtĕrŏs (1), *more superabundantly*
4124 plĕŏnĕxia (2), *extortion, avarice*
4180 pŏlulŏgia (1), *prolixity, wordiness*
4183 pŏlus (73), *much, many*
4214 pŏsŏs (11), *how much?; how much!*
5118 tŏsŏutŏs (7), *such great*
5248 hupĕrpĕrissĕuō (2), to *super-abound*

MUFFLERS
7479 ra'ălâh (1), *long veil*

MULBERRY
1057 bâkâ' (4), *(poss.) balsam tree*

MULE
6505 pered (6), *mule*
6506 pirdâh (3), *she-mule*

MULES
3222 yêm (1), *warm spring*
6505 pered (8), *mule*
7409 rekesh (2), *relay of animals on a post-route*

MULES'
6505 pered (1), *mule*

MULTIPLIED
1995 hâmôwn (1), *noise, tumult; many, crowd*
6280 'âthar (1), to *be, make abundant*
7231 râbab (3), to *increase*
7235 râbâh (29), to *increase*
7680 sᵉgâ' (Ch.) (2), to *increase*
4129 plēthunō (8), to *increase*

MULTIPLIEDST
7235 râbâh (1), to *increase*

MULTIPLIETH
3527 kâbar (1), to *augment; accumulate*
7235 râbâh (2), to *increase*

MULTIPLY
7227 rab (1), *great*
7231 râbab (1), to *increase*
7233 rᵉbâbâh (1), *myriad number*

7235 râbâh (41), to *increase*
4129 plēthunō (2), to *increase*

MULTIPLYING
7235 râbâh (1), to *increase*
4129 plēthunō (1), to *increase*

MULTITUDE
527 'âmôwn (4), *throng of people, crowd*
582 'ĕnôwsh (1), *man; person, human*
628 'açpᵉçûph (1), *assemblage*
1995 hâmôwn (55), *noise, tumult; many, crowd*
2416 chay (1), *alive; raw; fresh; life*
4392 mâlê' (1), *full; filling; fulness; fully*
4393 mᵉlô' (2), *fulness*
4768 marbîyth (1), *multitude; offspring*
5519 çâk (1), *crowd*
5712 'êdâh (1), *assemblage; crowd*
6154 'êreb (1), *mixed or woven things*
6951 qâhâl (3), *assemblage*
7227 rab (7), *great*
7230 rôb (68), *abundance*
7379 rîyb (1), *contest*
7393 rekeb (1), *upper millstone*
8229 shiph'âh (1), *copiousness*
3461 murias (1), *ten-thousand*
3793 ŏchlŏs (59), *throng*
4128 plēthos (29), *large number, throng*

MULTITUDES
1995 hâmôwn (2), *noise, tumult; many, crowd*
3793 ŏchlŏs (20), *throng*
4128 plēthos (1), *large number, throng*

MUNITION
4685 mâtsôwd (1), *net or snare; besieging tower*
4694 mᵉtsûwrâh (1), *rampart; fortification*

MUNITIONS
4679 mᵉtsad (1), *stronghold*

MUPPIM
4649 Muppîym (1), *wavings*

MURDER
2026 hârag (1), to *kill, slaughter*
7523 râtsach (3), to *murder*
5407 phŏnĕuō (1), to *commit murder*
5408 phŏnŏs (4), *slaying; murder*

MURDERER
2026 hârag (1), to *kill, slaughter*
7523 râtsach (13), to *murder*

443 anthrōpŏktŏnŏs (3), *killer of humans*
5406 phŏnĕus (3), *murderer*

MURDERERS
2026 hârag (1), to *kill, slaughter*
5221 nâkâh (1), to *strike, kill*
7523 râtsach (1), to *murder*
3389 mētralō₁as (1), *matricide*
3964 patralō₁as (1), *parricide*
4607 sikariŏs (1), *dagger-man*
5406 phŏnĕus (4), *murderer*

MURDERS
5408 phŏnŏs (4), *slaying; murder*

MURMUR
3885 lûwn (7), to *be obstinate with words*
1111 gŏgguzō (2), to *grumble, mutter*

MURMURED
3885 lûwn (7), to *be obstinate with words*
7279 râgan (3), to *grumbling rebel*
1111 gŏgguzō (6), to *grumble, mutter*
1234 diagŏgguzō (2), to *complain throughout*
1690 ĕmbrimaŏmai (1), to *blame, warn sternly*

MURMURERS
1113 gŏggustēs (1), *grumbler*

MURMURING
1112 gŏggusmŏs (2), *grumbling*

MURMURINGS
8519 tᵉlûwnâh (8), *grumbling*
1112 gŏggusmŏs (1), *grumbling*

MURRAIN
1698 deber (1), *pestilence, plague*

MUSE
7878 sîyach (1), to *ponder, muse aloud*

MUSED
1260 dialŏgizŏmai (1), to *deliberate*

MUSHI
4187 Mûwshîy (8), *sensitive*

MUSHITES
4188 Mûwshîy (2), *Mushite*

MUSICAL
7705 shiddâh (1), *wife (as mistress of the house)*
7892 shîyr (2), *song; singing*

MUSICIAN
5329 nâtsach (55), i.e. to *be eminent*

MUSICIANS
3451 mŏusikŏs (1), *minstrel, musician*

MUSICK
*2170 z*ᵉ*mâr* (Ch.) (4), instrumental *music*
4485 mangîynâh (1), *satire, mocking*
*5058 n*ᵉ*gîynâh* (1), stringed *instrument*
7892 shîyr (7), *song; singing*
4858 sumphōnia (1), *concert* of instruments

MUSING
1901 hâgîyg (1), *complaint, sighing*

MUST
318 anagkē (1), *constraint; distress*
1163 dĕi (63), *it is (was) necessary*
2192 ĕchō (1), to *have; hold; keep*
2443 hina (1), *in order that*
3784 ŏphĕilō (1), to *owe; to be under obligation*

MUSTARD
4615 sinapi (5), *mustard*

MUSTERED
6633 tsâbâ' (2), to *mass* an army or servants

MUSTERETH
6485 pâqad (1), to *visit, care for, count*

MUTH-LABBEN
4192 Mûwth (1), "*To die for the son*"

MUTTER
1897 hâgâh (1), to *murmur, utter a sound*

MUTTERED
1897 hâgâh (1), to *murmur, utter a sound*

MUTUAL
1722+240 ĕn (1), *in; during; because of*

MUZZLE
2629 châçam (1), to *muzzle; block*
5392 phimŏō (2), to *muzzle; silence*

MYRA
3460 Mura (1), *Myra*

MYRRH
3910 lôṭ (2), *sticky gum resin* (poss.) *ladanum*
4753 môr (12), *myrrh*
4666 smurna (2), *myrrh*
4669 smurnizō (1), to *mix with myrrh*

MYRTLE
1918 hădaç (6), *myrtle*

MYSIA
3463 muriŏi (2), *ten thousand*

MYSTERIES
3466 mustēriŏn (5), *secret*

MYSTERY
3466 mustēriŏn (22), *secret*

NAAM
5277 Na'am (1), *pleasure*

NAAMAH
5279 Na'ămâh (5), *pleasantness*

NAAMAN
5283 Na'ămân (15), *pleasantness*
3497 Nĕĕman (1), *pleasantness*

NAAMAN'S
5283 Na'ămân (1), *pleasantness*

NAAMATHITE
5284 Na'ămâthîy (4), *Naamathite*

NAAMITES
5280 Na'ămîy (1), *Naamanite*

NAARAH
5292 Na'ărâh (3), female *child; servant*

NAARAI
5293 Na'ăray (1), *youthful*

NAARAN
5295 Na'ărân (1), *juvenile*

NAARATH
5292 Na'ărâh (1), female *child; servant*

NAASHON
5177 Nachshôwn (1), *enchanter*

NAASSON
3476 Naassōn (3), *enchanter*

NABAL
5037 Nâbâl (18), *dolt*

NABAL'S
5037 Nâbâl (4), *dolt*

NABOTH
5022 Nâbôwth (22), *fruits*

NACHON'S
5225 Nâkôwn (1), *prepared*

NACHOR
5152 Nâchôwr (1), *snorer*
3493 Nachōr (1), *snorer*

NADAB
5070 Nâdâb (20), *liberal*

NAGGE
3477 Naggai (1), (poss.) *brilliancy*

NAHALAL
5096 Nahălâl (1), *pasture*

NAHALIEL
5160 Nachălîy'êl (2), *valley of God*

NAHALLAL
5096 Nahălâl (1), *pasture*

NAHALOL
5096 Nahălâl (1), *pasture*

NAHAM
5163 Nacham (1), *consolation*

NAHAMANI
5167 Nachămânîy (1), *consolatory*

NAHARAI
5171 Nacharay (1), *snorer*

NAHARI
5171 Nacharay (1), *snorer*

NAHASH
5176 Nâchâsh (9), *snake*

NAHATH
5184 Nachath (5), *quiet*

NAHBI
5147 Nachbîy (1), *occult*

NAHOR
5152 Nâchôwr (15), *snorer*

NAHOR'S
5152 Nâchôwr (2), *snorer*

NAHSHON
5177 Nachshôwn (9), *enchanter*

NAHUM
5151 Nachûwm (1), *comfortable*

NAIL
3489 yâthêd (8), tent *peg*

NAILING
4338 prŏsēlŏō (1), to *nail* to something

NAILS
2953 ṭᵉphar (Ch.) (2), finger-*nail; claw*
4548 maçmêr (4), *peg*
4930 masmᵉrâh (1), *pin* on the end of a goad
6856 tsippôren (1), *nail; point* of a pen
2247 hēlŏs (2), *stud*, i.e. *spike* or *nail*

NAIN
3484 Naïn (1), cf. a *home, dwelling; pasture*

NAIOTH
5121 Nâvîyth (6), *residence*

NAKED
4636 ma'ărôm (1), *bare, stripped*
5783 'ûwr (1), to *(be) bare*
5903 'êyrôm (9), *naked; nudity*
6168 'ârâh (1), to *be, make bare; to empty*
6174 'ârôwm (16), *nude; partially stripped*
6181 'eryâh (1), *nudity*
6544 pâra' (3), to *loosen; to expose, dismiss*
1130 gumnētĕuō (1), go *poorly clad, be in rags*
1131 gumnŏs (14), *nude or poorly clothed*

NAKEDNESS
4589 mâ'ôwr (1), *nakedness; exposed*
4626 ma'ar (1), *bare place; nakedness*
5903 'êyrôm (1), *naked; nudity*
6172 'ervâh (50), *nudity; disgrace; blemish*
1132 gumnŏtēs (3), *nudity or poorly clothed*

NAME
559 'âmar (2), to *say*
8034 shêm (735), *appellation*
8036 shum (Ch.) (8), *name*

2564 kalĕō (1), to *call*
3686 ŏnŏma (170), *name*

NAME'S
8034 shêm (19), *appellation*, i.e. name
3686 ŏnŏma (11), *name*

NAMED
559 'âmar (1), to *say*
1696 dâbar (1), to *speak, say; to subdue*
5344 nâqab (1), to *specify, designate, libel*
7121 qârâ' (5), to *call* out
7121+8034 qârâ' (1), to *call* out
8034 shêm (4), *appellation*, i.e. name
8034+7121 shêm (1), *appellation*, i.e. name
8036 shum (Ch.) (1), *name*
2564 kalĕō (2), to *call*
3004 lĕgō (2), to *say*
3686 ŏnŏma (28), *name*
3687 ŏnŏmazō (7), to *give a name*

NAMELY
1722 ĕn (1), *in; during; because of*

NAMES
8034 shêm (82), *appellation*, i.e. name
8036 shum (Ch.) (3), *name*
3686 ŏnŏma (11), *name*

NAMETH
3687 ŏnŏmazō (1), to *give a name*

NAOMI
5281 No'ŏmîy (20), *pleasant*

NAOMI'S
5281 No'ŏmîy (1), *pleasant*

NAPHISH
5305 Nâphîysh (2), *refreshed*

NAPHTALI
5321 Naphtâlîy (49), *my wrestling*

NAPHTUHIM
5320 Naphtûchîym (1), *Naphtuchim*

NAPKIN
4676 sŏudariŏn (3), *towel*

NAPHTHTUHIM
5320 Naphtûchîym (1), *Naphtuchim*

NARCISSUS
3488 Narkissŏs (1), *stupefaction*

NARROW
213 'ûwts (1), to *be close, hurry, withdraw*
331 'âṭam (4), to *close*
3334 yâtsar (1), to *be in distress*
6862 tsar (2), *trouble; opponent*
2346 thlibō (1), to *crowd, press, trouble*

NARROWED
4052 migrâ'âh (1), *ledge or offset*

NARROWER
6887 tsârar (1), to *cramp*

NARROWLY
8104 shâmar (1), to *watch*

NATHAN
5416 Nâthân (42), *given*
3481 Nathan (1), *given*

NATHAN-MELECH
5419 Nᵉthan-Melek (1), *given of* (the) *king*

NATHANAEL
3482 Nathanaël (6), *given of God*

NATION
249 'ezrâch (1), *native born*
524 'ummâh (Ch.) (1), *community, clan, tribe*
1471 gôwy (105), *foreign nation; Gentiles*
3816 lᵉ'ôm (1), *community, nation*
5971 'am (2), *people; tribe; troops*
246 allŏphulŏs (1), *Gentile, foreigner*
1074 gĕnĕa (1), *generation; age*
1085 gĕnŏs (2), *kin,* offspring in kind
1484 ĕthnŏs (24), *race; tribe; pagan*

NATIONS
523 'ummâh (1), *community, clan, tribe*
524 'ummâh (Ch.) (7), *community, clan, tribe*
776 'erets (1), *earth, land, soil; nation*
1471 gôwy (266), *foreign nation; Gentiles*
3816 lᵉ'ôm (9), *community, nation*
5971 'am (14), *people; tribe; troops*
1484 ĕthnŏs (37), *race; tribe; pagan*

NATIVE
4138 môwledeth (1), *lineage, native country*

NATIVITY
4138 môwledeth (6), *lineage, native country*
4351 mᵉkûwrâh (1), *origin*

NATURAL
3893 lêach (1), *fresh strength, vigor*
1083 gĕnnēsis (1), *nativity*
2596+6449 kata (2), *down; according to*
5446 phusikŏs (3), *instinctive, natural*
5591 psuchikŏs (1), *physical* and *brutish*

NATURALLY
1103 gnēsiŏs (1), *genuine, true*
5447 phusikōs (1), *instinctively, naturally*

NATURE
1078 genesis (1), *nativity, nature*

NAUGHT
7451 ra' (2), *bad; evil*

NAUGHTINESS
1942 havvâh (1), *desire; craving*
7455 rôa' (1), *badness, evil*
2549 kakia (1), *depravity; malignity; trouble*

NAUGHTY
1100 bᵉlîya'al (1), *wickedness, trouble*
1942 havvâh (1), *desire; craving*
7451 ra' (1), *bad; evil*

NAUM
3486 Naŏum (1), *comfortable*

NAVEL
8270 shôr (2), umbilical *cord; strength*
8306 shârîyr (1), *sinew*
8326 shôrer (1), umbilical *cord*

NAVES
1354 gab (1), *mounded: top, rim; arch, bulwarks*

NAVY
590 'ŏnîy (6), *ship; fleet of ships*

NAY
408 'al (8), *not; nothing*
1571 gam (2), *also; even*
3808 lô' (17), *no, not*
6440 pânîym (1), *face; front*
235 alla (4), *but, yet*
3304 mĕnŏungĕ (1), *so then at least*
3756 ŏu (8), *no or not*
3780 ŏuchi (5), *not indeed*

NAZARENE
3480 Nazōraiŏs (1), *inhabitant of Nazareth*

NAZARENES
3480 Nazōraiŏs (1), *inhabitant of Nazareth*

NAZARETH
3478 Nazarĕth (29), *Nazareth or Nazaret*

NAZARITE
5139 nâzîyr (9), *prince; separated Nazirite*

NAZARITES
5139 nâzîyr (3), *prince; separated Nazirite*

NEAH
5269 Nê'âh (1), *motion*

NEAPOLIS
3496 Nĕapŏlis (1), *new town*

NEAR
413 'êl (1), *to, toward*
681 'êtsel (3), *side; near*
3027 yâd (2), *hand; power*
5060 nâga' (4), to *strike*
5066 nâgash (58), to *be, come, bring near*
5921 'al (1), *above, over, upon,* or *against*
5973 'îm (1), *with*

7126 qârab (54), to *approach, bring near*
7127 qᵉrêb (Ch.) (5), to *approach, bring near*
7131 qârêb (2), *near*
7132 qᵉrâbâh (1), *approach*
7138 qârôwb (42), *near, close*
7200 râ'âh (1), to *see*
7607 shᵉ'êr (4), *flesh, meat; kindred* by blood
7608 sha'ărâh (1), female *kindred* by blood
316 anagkaiŏs (1), *necessary*
1448 ĕggizō (10), to *approach*
1451 ĕggus (4), *near, close*
4139 plēsiŏn (1), *neighbor, fellow*
4317 prŏsagō (1), to *bring near*
4334 prŏsĕrchŏmai (3), to *come near, visit*

NEARER
7138 qârôwb (1), *near, close*
1452 ĕggutĕrŏn (1), *nearer, closer*

NEARIAH
5294 Nᵉ'aryâh (3), *servant of Jehovah*

NEBAI
5109 Nôwbay (1), *fruitful*

NEBAIOTH
5032 Nᵉbâyôwth (2), *fruitfulnesses*

NEBAJOTH
5032 Nᵉbâyôwth (3), *fruitfulnesses*

NEBALLAT
5041 Nᵉballâṭ (1), *foolish secrecy*

NEBAT
5028 Nᵉbâṭ (25), *regard*

NEBO
5015 Nᵉbôw (13), *Nebo*

NEBUCHADNEZZAR
5019 Nᵉbûwkadne'tstsar (29), *Nebukadnetstsar*
5020 Nᵉbûwkadnetstsar (Ch.) (31), *Nebukadnetstsar*

NEBUCHADREZZAR
5019 Nᵉbûwkadne'tstsar (31), *Nebukadnetstsar*

NEBUSHASBAN
5021 Nᵉbûwshazbân (1), *Nebushazban*

NEBUZAR-ADAN
5018 Nᵉbûwzar'ădân (15), *Nebuzaradan*

NECESSARY
2706 chôq (1), *appointment; allotment*
316 anagkaiŏs (5), *necessary*
318 anagkē (1), *constraint; distress*
1876 ĕpanagkĕs (1), *necessarily*
4314+3588+5532 prŏs (1), *for; on, at; to, toward*

NECESSITIES
318 anagkē (2), *constraint; distress*
5532 chrĕia (1), *demand, requirement*

NECESSITY
316 anagkaiŏs (1), *necessary*
318 anagkē (6), *constraint; distress*
2192+318 ĕchō (1), to *have; hold; keep*
5532 chrĕia (2), *demand, requirement*

NECHO
5224 Nᵉkôw (3), *Neko*

NECK
1621 gargᵉrôwth (4), *throat*
1627 gârôwn (1), *throat*
4665 miphreketh (1), *vertebra* of the neck
6202 'âraph (3), to *break the neck,* to *destroy*
6203 'ôreph (12), *nape* or back of the neck
6676 tsavva'r (Ch.) (5), back of the *neck*
6677 tsavvâ'r (30), back of the *neck*
5137 trachēlŏs (6), *throat* or *neck; life*

NECKS
1627 gârôwn (1), *throat*
6203 'ôreph (6), *nape* or back of the neck
6677 tsavvâ'r (10), back of the *neck*
5137 trachēlŏs (1), *throat* or *neck; life*

NECROMANCER
1875+4191 dârash (1), to *seek* or *ask;* to *worship*

NEDABIAH
5072 Nᵉdabyâh (1), *largess of Jehovah*

NEED
2637 châcêr (1), to *lack;* to *fail, want, make less*
2638 châcêr (1), *lacking*
2818 châshach (Ch.) (1), to *need*
4270 machçôwr (1), *impoverishment*
6878 tsôrek (1), *need*
1163 dĕi (1), *it is* (was) *necessary*
2121 ĕukairŏs (1), *opportune, suitable*
2192+5532 ĕchō (8), to *have; hold; keep*
3784 ŏphĕilō (1), to *owe;* to *be under obligation*
5532 chrĕia (26), *demand, requirement*
5535 chrēizō (4), to *have necessity, be in want of*

NEEDED
2192+5532 ĕchō (1), to *have; hold; keep*
4326 prŏsdĕŏmai (1), to *require additionally*

NEEDEST
2192+5532 ĕchō (1), to *have; hold; keep*

NEEDETH
422 anĕpaischuntŏs (1),
unashamed
2192+318 ĕchō (1), to
have; hold; keep
2192+5532 ĕchō (1), to
have; hold; keep
5532 chrĕia (1), *demand,*
requirement
5535 chrē₁zō (1), to *have*
necessity, be in want of

NEEDFUL
2819 chashchûwth (1),
necessity
316 anagkaiŏs (1),
necessary
318 anagkē (1),
constraint; distress
1163 dĕi (1), *it is (was)*
necessary
2006 ĕpitēdĕiŏs (1),
requisite, needful
5532 chrĕia (1), *demand,*
requirement

NEEDLE
4476 rhaphis (2), *sewing*
needle

NEEDLE'S
4476 rhaphis (1), *sewing*
needle

NEEDLEWORK
4639+7551 ma'ăseh (1),
action; labor
7551 râqam (5),
variegation; embroider
7553 riqmâh (3),
variegation of color;
embroidery

NEEDS
318 anagkē (3),
constraint; distress
3843 pantŏs (1), *entirely;*
at all events

NEEDY
34 'ebyôwn (35),
destitute; poor
1800 dal (2), *weak, thin;*
humble, needy
7326 rûwsh (1), to *be*
destitute

NEESINGS
5846 'ăṭîyshâh (1),
sneezing

NEGINAH
5058 nᵉgîynâh (1),
stringed *instrument*

NEGINOTH
5058 nᵉgîynâh (6),
stringed *instrument*

NEGLECT
272 amĕlĕō (2), to *be*
careless of, *neglect*
3878 parakŏuō (2), to
disobey

NEGLECTED
3865 parathĕōrĕō (1), to
overlook or *disregard*

NEGLECTING
857 aphĕidia (1),
austerity, asceticism

NEGLIGENT
7952 shâlâh (1), to
mislead
272 amĕlĕō (1), to *be*
careless of, *neglect*

NEHELAMITE
5161 Nechĕlâmîy (3),
dreamed

NEHEMIAH
5166 Nᵉchemyâh (8),
consolation of Jehovah

NEHILOTH
5155 Nᵉchîylâh (1), *flute*

NEHUM
5149 Nᵉchûwm (1),
comforted

NEHUSHTA
5179 Nᵉchushtâ' (1),
copper

NEHUSHTAN
5180 Nᵉchushtân (1),
copper serpent

NEIEL
5272 Nᵉ'îy'êl (1), *moved*
of God

NEIGHBOUR
5997 'âmîyth (7),
comrade or *kindred*
7138 qârôwb (2), *near,*
close
7453 rêa' (74), *associate;*
one close
7468 rᵉ'ûwth (2), female
associate
7934 shâkên (6),
resident; fellow-*citizen*
4139 plēsiŏn (16),
neighbor, fellow

NEIGHBOUR'S
5997 'âmîyth (2),
comrade or *kindred*
7453 rêa' (26), *associate;*
one close

NEIGHBOURS
7138 qârôwb (3), *near,*
close
7453 rêa' (2), *associate;*
one close
7934 shâkên (11),
resident; fellow-*citizen*
1069 gĕitōn (4),
neighbour
4040 pĕriŏikŏs (1),
neighbor

NEIGHBOURS'
7453 rêa' (1), *associate;*
one close

NEIGHED
6670 tsâhal (1), to *be*
cheerful; to *sound*

NEIGHING
4684 matshâlâh (1),
whinnying

NEIGHINGS
4684 matshâlâh (1),
whinnying

NEITHER
369 'ayin (40), *there is*
no, i.e., not exist, none
408 'al (66), *not; nothing*
518 'îm (5), *whether?; if,*
although; Oh that!
1077 bal (3), *nothing; not*
at all; lest
1115 biltîy (4), *not,*
except, without, unless
1571 gam (5), *also; even*
3608 kele' (2), *prison*

NEHELAMITE

3804 kether (1), *royal*
headdress
3808 lô' (475), no, *not*
3809 lâ' (Ch.) (3), *as*
nothing
4480 min (2), *from, out of*
2228 ē (4), *or; than*
3361 mē (5), *not; lest*
3366 mēdĕ (34), *but not,*
not even; nor
3383 mētĕ (19), *neither*
or nor; not even
3756 ŏu (12), *no or not*
3761 ŏudĕ (67), *neither,*
nor, not even
3763 ŏudĕpŏtĕ (1), *never*
at all
3777 ŏutĕ (39), *not even*

NEKEB
5346 Neqeb (1), *dell*

NEKODA
5353 Nᵉqôwdâ' (4),
distinction

NEMUEL
5241 Nᵉmûw'êl (3), *day*
of God

NEMUELITES
5242 Nᵉmûw'êlîy (1),
Nemuelite

NEPHEG
5298 Nepheg (4), *sprout*

NEPHEW
5220 neked (2), *offspring*

NEPHEWS
1121 bên (1), *son,*
descendant; people
1549 ĕkgŏnŏn (1),
grandchild

NEPHISH
5305 Nâphîysh (1),
refreshed

NEPHISHESIM
5300 Nᵉphûwshᵉçîym (1),
expansions

NEPHTHALIM
3508 Nĕphthalĕim (2),
my wrestling

NEPHTOAH
5318 Nephtôwach (2),
spring

NEPHUSIM
5304 Nᵉphîyçîym (1),
expansions

NEPTHALIM
3508 Nĕphthalĕim (1),
my wrestling

NER
5369 Nêr (16), *lamp*

NEREUS
3517 Nērĕus (1), *wet*

NERGAL
5370 Nêrgal (1), *Nergal*

NERGAL-SHAREZER
5371 Nêrgal Shar'etser
(3), *Nergal-Sharetser*

NERI
3518 Nēri (1), *light of*
Jehovah

NERIAH
5374 Nêrîyâh (10), *light*
of Jehovah

NERO
3505 Nĕrōn (1), *Nero*

NEST
7064 qên (12), *nest;*
nestlings; chamber
7077 qânan (3), to *nestle*

NESTS
7077 qânan (2), to *nestle*
2682 kataskēnōsis (2),
perch or *nest*

NET
2764 chêrem (5),
doomed object
4364 makmâr (1),
hunter's snare-net
4685 mâtsôwd (2), *net* or
snare; besieging *tower*
4686 mâtsûwd (2), *net* or
capture; fastness
7568 resheth (20),
hunting *net; network*
293 amphiblēstrŏn (2),
fishing *net* which is cast
1350 diktuŏn (6), *drag*
net
4522 sagēnē (1), *seine*

NETHANEEL
5417 Nᵉthan'êl (14),
given of God

NETHANIAH
5418 Nᵉthanyâh (20),
given of Jehovah

NETHER
7347 rêcheh (1),
mill-stone
8481 tachtôwn (5),
bottommost
8482 tachtîy (9),
lowermost; depths

NETHERMOST
8481 tachtôwn (1),
bottommost

NETHINIMS
5411 Nâthîyn (17), ones
given to duty
5412 Nᵉthîyn (Ch.) (1),
ones *given* to duty

NETOPHAH
5199 Nᵉṭôphâh (2),
distillation

NETOPHATHI
5200 Nᵉṭôphâthîy (1),
Netophathite

NETOPHATHITE
5200 Nᵉṭôphâthîy (8),
Netophathite

NETOPHATHITES
5200 Nᵉṭôphâthîy (2),
Netophathite

NETS
2764 chêrem (4),
doomed object
4364 makmâr (1),
hunter's snare-net
4365 mikmereth (1),
fishing-net
7638 sâbâk (1), *netting*
1350 diktuŏn (6), *drag*
net

NETTLES
2738 chârûwl (3),
bramble, thorny *weed*
7057 qimmôwsh (2),
prickly plant

English

NETWORK
4640+7568 Ma'say (2),
operative
7639 sᵉbâkâh (5),
net-work balustrade

NETWORKS
2355 chôwr (1), *white
linen*
7639 sᵉbâkâh (2),
net-work balustrade

NEVER
369 'ayin (2), *there is no,
i.e., not exist, none*
408 'al (1), *not; nothing*
1253 bôr (1), *vegetable
lye as soap; flux*
1755 dôwr (1), *dwelling*
3808 lô' (17), *no, not*
165 aiōn (1), *perpetuity,
ever; world*
3361 mē (1), *not; lest*
3364 ŏu mē (1), *not at all,
absolutely not*
3368 mēdĕpŏtĕ (1), *not
even ever*
3756 ŏu (5), *no or not*
3762 ŏudĕis (1), *none,
nobody, nothing*
3763 ŏudĕpŏtĕ (14),
never at all
3764 ŏudĕpō (2), *not
even yet*

NEVERTHELESS
61 'ăbâl (2), *truly, surely;
yet, but*
389 'ak (11), *surely; only,
however*
403 'âkên (1), *surely!,
truly!; but*
657 'epheç (1), *end; no
further*
1297 bᵉram (Ch.) (1),
however, but
1571 gam (3), *also; even*
3588 kîy (4), *for, that
because*
7535 raq (5), *merely;
although*
235 alla (10), *but, yet,
except, instead*
1161 dĕ (11), *but, yet;
and then*
2544 kaitŏigĕ (1),
although really
3305 mĕntŏi (1), *however*
4133 plēn (8), *albeit, save
that, rather, yet*

NEW
1069 bâkar (1), *bear the
first born*
1278 bᵉrîy'âh (1), *creation*
2319 châdâsh (50), *new,
recent*
2320 chôdesh (20), *new
moon; month*
2323 chădath (Ch.) (1),
new
2961 ṭârîy (1), *fresh*
8492 tîyrôwsh (11), *fresh
squeezed grape-juice*
46 agnaphŏs (2), *new,
unshrunk cloth*
1098 glĕukŏs (1), *sweet
wine*
2537 kainŏs (44),
freshness, i.e. new
3501 nĕŏs (11), *new*

3561 nŏumēnia (1),
festival of new moon
4372 prŏsphatŏs (1),
lately made, i.e. new

NEWBORN
738 artigĕnnētŏs (1), *new
born; young convert*

NEWLY
6965 qûwm (1), *to rise*
7138 qârôwb (1), *near,
close*

NEWNESS
2538 kainŏtēs (2),
renewal, newness

NEWS
8052 shᵉmûw'âh (1),
announcement

NEXT
312 'achêr (2), *other,
another, different; next*
4283 mochŏrâth (3),
tomorrow, next day
4932 mishneh (7),
duplicate copy; double
7138 qârôwb (5), *near,
close*
839 auriŏn (1), *to-morrow*
1206 dĕutĕraiŏs (1), *on
the second day*
1836 hĕxēs (2),
successive, next
1887 ĕpauriŏn (7),
to-morrow
1966 ĕpiŏusa (3), *ensuing*
2064 ĕrchŏmai (1), *to go
or come*
2087 hĕtĕrŏs (2), *other or
different*
2192 ĕchō (3), *to have;
hold; keep*
3342 mĕtaxu (1), *betwixt;
meanwhile*

NEZIAH
5335 Nᵉtsîyach (2),
conspicuous

NEZIB
5334 Nᵉtsîyb (1), *station*

NIBHAZ
5026 Nibchaz (1),
Nibchaz

NIBSHAN
5044 Nibshân (1),
Nibshan

NICANOR
3527 Nikanōr (1),
victorious

NICODEMUS
3530 Nikŏdēmŏs (5),
*victorious among his
people*

NICOLAITANES
3531 Nikŏlaïtēs (2),
adherent of Nicolaüs

NICOLAS
3532 Nikŏlaŏs (1),
*victorious over the
people*

NICOPOLIS
3533 Nikŏpŏlis (2),
victorious city

NIGER
3526 Nigĕr (1), *black*

NIGH
4952 mishrâh (1),
steeped juice
5060 nâga' (3), *to strike*
5066 nâgash (12), *to be,
come, bring near*
7126 qârab (32), *to
approach, bring near*
7138 qârôwb (4), *near,
close*
7607 shᵉ'êr (1), *flesh,
meat; kindred by blood*
7934 shâkên (1),
resident; fellow-citizen
1448 ĕggizō (21), *to
approach*
1451 ĕggus (18), *near,
close*
3844 para (2), *from; with;
besides; on account of*
3897 paraplēsiŏn (1),
almost
4314 prŏs (1), *for; on, at;
to, toward; against*

NIGHT
956 bûwth (Ch.) (1), *to
lodge over night*
2822 chôshek (1),
darkness; misery
3915 layil (208), *night;
adversity*
3916 leylᵉyâ' (Ch.) (4),
night
5399 nesheph (3), *dusk,
dawn*
6153 'ereb (4), *dusk*
6916 qiddâh (1), *cassia
bark*
8464 tachmâç (2),
unclean bird (poss.) owl
1273 dianuktĕrĕuō (1), *to
pass, spend the night*
3571 nux (60), *night*
3574 nuchthēmĕrŏn (1),
full day

NIGHTS
3915 layil (15), *night;
adversity*
3571 nux (3), *night*

NIMRAH
5247 Nimrâh (1), *clear
water*

NIMRIM
5249 Nimrîym (2), *clear
waters*

NIMROD
5248 Nimrôwd (4),
Nimrod

NIMSHI
5250 Nimshîy (5),
extricated

NINE
8672 têsha' (44), *nine;
ninth*
1767 ĕnnĕa (1), *nine*
1768 ĕnnĕnēkŏntaĕnnĕa
(4), *ninety-nine*

NINETEEN
8672+6240 têsha' (3),
nine; ninth

NINETEENTH
8672+6240 têsha' (4),
nine; ninth

NINETY
8673 tish'îym (20), *ninety*

1768 ĕnnĕnēkŏntaĕnnĕa
(4), *ninety-nine*

NINEVE
3535 Ninĕuï (1), *Nineveh*

NINEVEH
5210 Nîynᵉvêh (17),
Nineveh
3536 Ninĕuïtēs (1),
inhabitant of Nineveh

NINEVITES
3536 Ninĕuïtēs (1),
inhabitant of Nineveh

NINTH
8671 tᵉshîy'îy (18), *ninth*
8672 têsha' (6), *nine;
ninth*
1766 ĕnnatŏs (10), *ninth*

NISAN
5212 Nîyçân (2), *Nisan*

NISROCH
5268 Niçrôk (2), *Nisrok*

NITRE
5427 nether (2), *mineral
potash for washing*

NOADIAH
5129 Nôw'adyâh (2),
convened of Jehovah

NOAH
5146 Nôach (44), *rest*
5270 Nô'âh (4),
movement
3575 Nŏē (3), *rest*

NOAH'S
5146 Nôach (2), *rest*

NOB
5011 Nôb (6), *fruit*

NOBAH
5025 Nôbach (3), *bark*

NOBLE
3358 yaqqîyr (Ch.) (1),
precious
6579 partam (1),
grandee, noble
2104 ĕugĕnēs (2), *high in
rank; generous*
2908 krĕissŏn (2), *better,
i.e. greater advantage*

NOBLEMAN
937 basilikŏs (2),
befitting the sovereign
2104+444 ĕugĕnēs (1),
high in rank; generous

NOBLES
117 'addîyr (7), *powerful;
majestic*
678 'âtsîyl (1), *extremity;
noble*
1281 bârîyach (1),
fleeing, gliding serpent
1419 gâdôwl (1), *great*
2715 chôr (13), *noble, i.e.
in high rank*
3513 kâbad (1), *to be
rich, glorious*
5057 nâgîyd (1),
commander, official
5081 nâdîyb (4),
magnanimous
6579 partam (1),
grandee, noble

NOD
5113 Nôwd (1), *vagrancy*

NODAB
5114 Nôwdâb (1), *noble*

NOE
3575 Nōĕ (5), *rest*

NOGAH
5052 Nôgahh (2), *brilliancy*

NOHAH
5119 Nôwchâh (1), *quietude*

NOISE
1949 hûwm (2), *to make an uproar; agitate*
1993 hâmâh (4), *to be in great commotion*
1995 hâmôwn (4), *noise, tumult; many, crowd*
1998 hemyâh (1), *sound, tone*
6476 pâtsach (1), *to break out in sound*
6963 qôwl (48), *voice or sound*
7267 rôgez (1), *disquiet; anger*
7452 rêa' (1), *crash; noise; shout*
7588 shâ'ôwn (8), *uproar; destruction*
8085 shâma' (2), *to hear intelligently*
8643 tᵉrûw'âh (1), *battle-cry; clangor*
8663 tᵉshû'âh (1), *crashing or clamor*
2350 thŏrubĕō (1), *to disturb; clamor*
4500 rhŏizĕdŏn (1), *with a crash, with a roar*
5456 phōnē (1), *voice, sound*

NOISED
191 akŏuō (1), *to hear; obey*
1096+5408 ginŏmai (1), *to be, become*
1255 dialalĕō (1), *to converse, discuss*

NOISOME
1942 havvâh (1), *desire; craving*
7451 ra' (2), *bad; evil*
2556 kakŏs (1), *bad, evil, wrong*

NON
5126 Nûwn (1), *perpetuity*

NOON
6672 tsôhar (11), *window: noon time*
3314 mĕsĕmbria (1), *midday; south*

NOONDAY
6672 tsôhar (10), *window: noon time*

NOONTIDE
6256+6672 'êth (1), *time*

NOPH
5297 Nôph (7), *Noph*

NOPHAH
5302 Nôphach (1), *gust*

NORTH
4215 mᵉzâreh (1), *north wind*
6828 tsâphôwn (128), *north, northern*

NORTH
1005 borrhas (2), *north*
5566 chōrŏs (1), *north-west* wind

NORTHERN
6828 tsâphôwn (1), *north, northern*
6830 tsᵉphôwnîy (1), *northern*

NORTHWARD
6828 tsâphôwn (24), *north, northern*

NOSE
639 'aph (11), *nose or nostril; face; person*
2763 charam (1), *to devote to destruction*

NOSES
639 'aph (1), *nose or nostril; face; person*

NOSTRILS
639 'aph (13), *nose or nostril; face; person*
5156 nᵉchîyr (1), *pair of nostrils*
5170 nachar (1), *snorting*

NOTABLE
2380 châzûwth (2), *striking appearance*
1110 gnōstŏs (1), *well-known*
1978 ĕpisēmŏs (1), *eminent, prominent*
2016 ĕpiphanēs (1), *conspicuous*

NOTE
2710 châqaq (1), *to engrave; to enact laws*
1978 ĕpisēmŏs (1), *eminent, prominent*
4593 sēmĕiŏō (1), *to mark for avoidance*

NOTED
7559 râsham (1), *to record*

NOTHING
369 'ayin (23), *there is no, i.e., not exist, none*
408 'al (3), *not; nothing*
657 'epheç (2), *end; no further*
1099 bᵉlîymâh (1), *nothing whatever*
1115 biltîy (3), *not, except, without, unless*
1697 dâbâr (2), *word; matter; thing*
2600 chinnâm (2), *gratis, free*
3605 kôl (1), *all, any or every*
3808 lô' (25), *no, not*
3809 lâ' (Ch.) (1), *as nothing*
4591 mâ'aṭ (1), *to be, make small or few*
7535 raq (1), *merely; although*
8414 tôhûw (1), *waste, desolation, formless*
114 athĕtĕō (1), *to disesteem, neutralize*
3361 mē (1), *not; lest*
3367 mēdĕis (27), *not even one*
3385 mēti (2), *whether at all*

NORTH
3756 ŏu (4), *no or not*
3762 ŏudĕis (66), *none, nobody, nothing*
3777 ŏutĕ (1), *not even*

NOTICE
5234 nâkar (1), *to acknowledge*
4293 prŏkataggĕllō (1), *to predict, promise*

NOTWITHSTANDING
389 'ak (6), *surely; only, however*
657 'epheç (1), *end; no further*
7535 raq (2), *merely; although*
235 alla (1), *but, yet, except, instead*
4133 plēn (4), *albeit, save that, rather, yet*

NOUGHT
205 'âven (1), *trouble, vanity, wickedness*
369 'ayin (1), *there is no, i.e., not exist, none*
408+3972 'al (1), *not; nothing*
434 'ĕlûwl (1), *good for nothing*
656 'âphêç (1), *to cease*
657 'epheç (1), *end; no further*
659 'êpha' (1), *nothing*
2600 chinnâm (6), *gratis, free*
3808 lô' (1), *no, not*
3808+1697 lô' (1), *no, not*
3808+1952 lô' (1), *no, not*
5034 nâbêl (1), *to wilt; to fall away; to be foolish*
6331 pûwr (1), *to crush*
6544 pâra' (1), *to loosen; to expose, dismiss*
6565 pârar (2), *to break up; to violate, frustrate*
8045 shâmad (1), *to desolate*
8414 tôhûw (2), *waste, desolation, formless*
557 apĕlĕgmŏs (1), *refutation, discrediting*
1432 dōrĕan (1), *gratuitously, freely*
1847 ĕxŏudĕnŏō (1), *to be treated with contempt*
1848 ĕxŏuthĕnĕō (3), *to treat with contempt*
2049 ĕrēmŏō (1), *to lay waste*
2647 kataluō (1), *to demolish*
2673 katargĕō (2), *to be, render entirely useless*
3762 ŏudĕis (1), *none, nobody, nothing*

NOURISH
1431 gâdal (1), *to be great, make great*
2421 châyâh (1), *to live; to revive*
3557 kûwl (2), *to keep in; to maintain*

NOURISHED
1431 gâdal (1), *to be great, make great*

NORTH
2421 châyâh (1), *to live; to revive*
3557 kûwl (1), *to keep in; to measure*
7235 râbâh (1), *to increase*
397 anatrĕphō (2), *to rear, care for*
1789 ĕntrĕphō (1), *to educate; to be trained*
5142 trĕphō (3), *to nurse, feed, care for*

NOURISHER
3557 kûwl (1), *to keep in; to measure*

NOURISHETH
1625 ĕktrĕphō (1), *to cherish or train*

NOURISHING
1431 gâdal (1), *to be great, make great*

NOURISHMENT
2023 ĕpichŏrĕgĕō (1), *to fully supply; to aid*

NOVICE
3504 nĕŏphutŏs (1), *young convert*

NOW
116 'ĕdayin (Ch.) (2), *then*
227 'âz (1), *at that time or place; therefore*
645 'êphôw (10), *then*
1768 dîy (Ch.) (1), *that; of*
2008 hênnâh (1), *from here; from there*
2088 zeh (3), *this or that*
3117 yôwm (4), *day; time period*
3528 kᵉbâr (4), *long ago, formerly, hitherto*
3588 kîy (2), *for, that because*
3705 kᵉ'an (Ch.) (14), *now*
4994 nâ' (172), *I pray!, please!, I beg you!*
6254 'Ashtᵉrâthîy (1), *Ashterathite*
6258 'attâh (401), *at this time, now*
6288 pᵉ'ôrâh (3), *foliage, branches*
6471 pa'am (5), *time; step; occurence*
737 arti (25), *just now; at once*
1160 dapanē (2), *expense, cost*
1161 dĕ (160), *but, yet; and then*
1211 dē (1), *now, then; indeed, therefore*
2235 ēdē (3), *even now*
2236 hēdista (38), *with great pleasure*
2532 kai (5), *and; or; even; also*
3063 lŏipŏn (2), *remaining; finally*
3568 nun (127), *now; the present or immediate*
3570 nuni (20), *just now, indeed, in fact*
3765 ŏukĕti (5), *not yet, no longer*
3767 ŏun (12), *certainly; accordingly*

English

NUMBER
2714 chêqer (1), *examination*
3187 yâchas (1), to *enroll by family list*
4373 mikçâh (1), *valuation* of a thing
4487 mânâh (7), to *allot; to enumerate* or enroll
4507 Mᵉnîy (1), *Apportioner*, i.e. Fate
4510 minyân (Ch.) (1), *enumeration, number*
4557 miçpâr (108), *number*
4557+3187 miçpâr (1), *number*
4662 miphqâd (2), designated *spot; census*
5608 çâphar (10), to *inscribe; to enumerate*
5736 'âdaph (1), to *be redundant*
6485 pâqad (14), to *visit, care for, count*
705 arithmĕō (1), to *enumerate or count*
706 arithmŏs (18), reckoned *number*
1469 ĕgkrinō (1), to *count among*
2639 katalĕgō (1), to *enroll, put on a list*
3793 ŏchlŏs (2), *throng*

NUMBERED
4483 mᵉnâ' (Ch.) (1), to *count, appoint*
4487 mânâh (7), to *allot; to enumerate* or enroll
4557 miçpâr (1), *number*
5608 çâphar (11), to *inscribe; to enumerate*
6485 pâqad (102), to *visit, care for, count*
705 arithmĕō (2), to *enumerate or count*
2674 katarithmĕō (1), to *be numbered among*
3049 lŏgizŏmai (1), to *credit; to think, regard*
4785 sugkatapsēphizō (1), to *number with*

NUMBEREST
5608 çâphar (1), to *inscribe; to enumerate*
6485 pâqad (2), to *visit, care for, count*

NUMBERING
5608 çâphar (1), to *inscribe; to enumerate*
5610 çᵉphâr (1), *census*

NUMBERS
4557 miçpâr (1), *number*
5615 çᵉphôrâh (1), *numeration*
6486 pᵉquddâh (1), *visitation; punishment*

NUN
5126 Nûwn (29), *perpetuity*

NURSE
539 'âman (2), to be *firm, faithful, true; to trust*
3243 yânaq (7), to *suck; to give milk*
5162 trŏphŏs (1), *nurse-mother*

NURSED
539 'âman (1), to be *firm, faithful, true; to trust*
5134 nûwq (1), to *suckle*

NURSING
539 'âman (2), to be *firm, faithful, true; to trust*
3243 yânaq (1), to *suck; to give milk*

NURTURE
3809 paidĕia (1), *disciplinary correction*

NUTS
93 'ĕgôwz (1), *nut*
992 bôṭen (1), *pistachio*

NYMPHAS
3564 Numphas (1), *nymph-born*

OAK
424 'êlâh (11), *oak*
427 'allâh (1), *oak*
437 'allôwn (3), *oak*

OAKS
352 'ayîl (1), *chief; ram; oak tree*
437 'allôwn (5), *oak*

OAR
4880 mâshôwṭ (1), *oar*

OARS
4880 mâshôwṭ (1), *oar*
7885 shayiṭ (1), *oar*

OATH
423 'âlâh (14), *curse, oath*
7621 shᵉbûw'âh (26), *sworn oath*
7650 shâba' (7), to *swear*
332 anathĕmatizō (1), to *declare* or *vow an oath*
3727 hŏrkŏs (7), sacred *restraint*, i.e. an *oath*
3728 hŏrkōmŏsia (4), *asseveration on oath*

OATH'S
3727 hŏrkŏs (2), sacred *restraint*, i.e. an *oath*

OATHS
7621 shᵉbûw'âh (2), *sworn oath*
3727 hŏrkŏs (1), sacred *restraint*, i.e. an *oath*

OBADIAH
5662 'Ôbadyâh (20), *serving Jehovah*

OBAL
5745 'Ôwbâl (1), *Obal*

OBED
5744 'Ôwbêd (9), *serving*
5601 Obēd (3), *serving*

OBED-EDOM
5654 'Ôbêd 'Ĕdôwm (20), *worker of Edom*

OBEDIENCE
5218 hupakŏē (11), *compliance, submission*
5293 hupŏtassō (1), to *subordinate; to obey*

OBEDIENT
8085 shâma' (8), to *hear intelligently*
5218 hupakŏē (2), *compliance, submission*
5219 hupakŏuō (2), to *heed or conform*

NURSED (col 2)
5255 hupēkŏŏs (2), to *listen attentively*
5293 hupŏtassō (2), to *subordinate; to obey*

OBEISANCE
7812 shâchâh (9), to *prostrate* in homage

OBEY
3349 yiqqâhâh (1), *obedience*
4928 mishma'ath (1), *obedience;* royal *subject*
8085 shâma' (40), to *hear intelligently*
8086 shᵉma' (Ch.) (1), to *hear* intelligently
544 apĕithĕō (3), to *disbelieve*
3980 pĕitharchĕō (3), to *submit to authority*
3982 pĕithō (5), to *pacify* or *conciliate; to assent*
5218 hupakŏē (1), *compliance, submission*
5219 hupakŏuō (13), to *heed or conform*
5255+1036 hupēkŏŏs (1), to *listen attentively*

OBEYED
8085 shâma' (34), to *hear*
3982 pĕithō (2), to *pacify* or *conciliate; to assent*
5219 hupakŏuō (5), to *heed or conform*

OBEYEDST
8085 shâma' (2), to *hear*

OBEYETH
8085 shâma' (3), to *hear*

OBEYING
8085 shâma' (2), to *hear*
5218 hupakŏē (1), *compliance, submission*

OBIL
179 'Ôwbîyl (1), *mournful*

OBJECT
2723 katēgŏrĕō (1), to *bring a charge*

OBLATION
4503 minchâh (5), *tribute; offering*
4541 maççêkâh (1), *libation; woven coverlet*
7133 qorbân (11), sacrificial *present*
8641 tᵉrûwmâh (17), *sacrifice, tribute*
8642 tᵉrûwmîyâh (1), sacrificial *offering*

OBLATIONS
4503 minchâh (1), sacrificial *offering*
4864 mas'êth (1), *raising; beacon; present*
7133 qorbân (1), sacrificial *present*
8641 tᵉrûwmâh (2), *sacrifice, tribute*

OBOTH
88 'Ôbôth (4), *water-skins*

OBSCURE
380 'îyshôwn (1), *pupil, eyeball; middle*

OBSCURITY
652 'ôphel (1), *dusk, darkness*
2822 chôshek (2), *darkness; misery*

OBSERVATION
3907 paratērēsis (1), *careful observation*

OBSERVE
5172 nâchash (1), to *prognosticate*
5341 nâtsar (1), to *guard, protect, maintain*
6049 'ânan (1), to *cover, becloud; to act covertly*
6213 'âsâh (3), to *do or make*
7789 shûwr (1), to *spy out, survey*
8104 shâmar (41), to *watch*
3906 paratērĕō (1), to *note insidiously*
4160 pŏiĕō (1), to *make*
5083 tērĕō (3), to *keep, guard, obey*
5442 phulassō (1), to *watch*, i.e. be on *guard*

OBSERVED
6049 'ânan (2), to *cover, becloud; to act covertly*
6213 'âsâh (3), to *do or make*
7789 shûwr (1), to *spy out, survey*
8104 shâmar (3), to *watch*
8107 shimmûr (2), *observance*
4933 suntērĕō (1), to *preserve in memory*
5442 phulassō (1), to *watch*, i.e. be on *guard*

OBSERVER
6049 'ânan (1), to *cover, becloud; to act covertly*

OBSERVERS
6049 'ânan (1), to *cover, becloud; to act covertly*

OBSERVEST
8104 shâmar (1), to *watch*

OBSERVETH
8104 shâmar (1), to *watch*

OBSTINATE
553 'âmats (1), to *be strong; be courageous*
7186 qâsheh (1), *severe*

OBTAIN
1129 bânâh (1), to *build; to establish*
2388 châzaq (1), to *fasten upon; to seize*
5381 nâsag (2), to *reach*
6329 pûwq (1), to *issue; to furnish; to secure*
1653 ĕlĕĕō (2), to give out *compassion*
2013 ĕpitugchanō (1), to *attain, obtain*
2638 katalambanō (1), to *seize; to possess*
2983 lambanō (2), to *take, receive*

4047 pĕripŏiēsis (1), acquisition
5177 tugchanō (3), to take part in; to obtain

OBTAINED
5375 nâsâ' (5), to *lift up*
7592 shâ'al (1), to *ask*
1653 ĕlĕĕō (6), to *give out compassion*
2013 ĕpitugchanō (4), to attain, *obtain*
2147 hĕuriskō (1), to *find*
2816 klērŏnŏmĕō (1), to be an heir to, *inherit*
2820 klērŏō (1), to *allot*
2902 kratĕō (1), to *seize*
2932 ktaŏmai (1), to *get*, i.e. *acquire*
2975 lagchanō (2), to determine by lot
3140 marturĕō (3), to *testify; to commend*
5177 tugchanō (2), to *take part in; to obtain*

OBTAINETH
6329 pûwq (2), to *issue; to furnish; to secure*

OBTAINING
4047 pĕripŏiēsis (1), acquisition

OCCASION
1556 gâlal (1), to *roll; to commit*
4672 mâtsâ' (2), to *find or acquire; to occur*
5308 nᵉphal (Ch.) (1), to *fall*
5931 'illâh (Ch.) (3), *pretext, legal grounds*
8385 ta'ănâh (2), *opportunity; purpose*
874 aphŏrmē (6), *opportunity, pretext*
1223 dia (1), *through*, by *means* of; *because* of
4625 skandalŏn (2), *snare*

OCCASIONED
5437 çâbab (1), to *surround*

OCCASIONS
5949 'ălîylâh (2), *opportunity, action*
8569 tᵉnûw'âh (1), *enmity*

OCCUPATION
4399 mᵉlâ'kâh (1), *work; property*
4639 ma'âseh (2), *action; labor*
5078 tĕchnē (1), *trade, craft; skill*

OCCUPIED
5414 nâthan (3), to *give*
5503 çâchar (1), to *travel round; to palpitate*
6213 'âsâh (1), to *do or make*
6213+4399 'âsâh (1), to *do or make*
4043 pĕripatĕō (1), to *walk; to live a life*

OCCUPIERS
6148 'ârab (1), to *intermix*

OCCUPIETH
378 anaplērŏō (1), to *complete; to occupy*

OCCUPY
6148 'ârab (1), to *intermix*
4231 pragmatĕuŏmai (1), to *trade, do business*

OCCURRENT
6294 pega' (1), *casual impact*

OCRAN
5918 'Okrân (5), *muddler*

ODD
5736 'âdaph (1), to be *redundant*

ODED
5752 'Ôwdêd (3), *reiteration*

ODIOUS
887 bâ'ash (1), to *smell bad; be a moral stench*
8130 sânê' (1), to *hate*

ODOUR
3744 ŏsmē (2), *fragrance; odor*

ODOURS
1314 besem (2), *spice; fragrance; balsam*
5207 nîchôwach (1), *pleasant; delight*
5208 nîychôwach (Ch.) (1), *pleasure*
2368 thumiama (2), *incense offering*

OFF
5921 'al (65), *above, over, upon*, or *against*
114 athĕtĕō (1), to *neutralize* or *set aside*
554 apĕkduŏmai (2), to *divest wholly* oneself
568 apĕchō (1), to be *distant*
575 apŏ (13), *from, away*
595 apŏthĕsis (1), *laying aside*
609 apŏkŏptō (8), *mutilate* the *genitals*
631 apŏmassŏmai (1), to *scrape away, wipe off*
659 apŏtithēmi (3), to *put away; get rid of*
660 apŏtinassō (1), to *brush off, shake off*
851 aphairĕō (2), to *remove, cut off*
1537 ĕk (1), *out, out of*
1562 ĕkduō (1), to *divest*
1575 ĕkklaō (4), to *exscind, cut off*
1581 ĕkkŏptō (4), to *cut off; to frustrate*
1601 ĕkpiptō (2), to *drop away*
1621 ĕktinassō (3), to *shake* violently
3089 luō (1), to *loosen*
3112 makran (1), at a *distance, far away*
4048 pĕrirrhĕgnumi (1), to *tear completely away*
4496 rhiptō (1), to *fling, toss; to lay out*

OFFENCE
816 'âsham (1), to be *guilty; to be punished*
4383 mikshôwl (2), *stumbling-block*
266 hamartia (1), *sin*

OCCUPY 677 aprŏskŏpŏs (3), faultless
3900 paraptōma (5), *error; transgression*
4348 prŏskŏmma (1), *occasion of apostasy*
4349 prŏskŏpē (1), *occasion of sin*
4625 skandalŏn (5), *snare*

OFFENCES
2399 chêṭ' (1), *crime* or its *penalty*
3900 paraptōma (2), *error; transgression*
4625 skandalŏn (4), *snare*

OFFEND
816 'âsham (4), to be *guilty; to be punished*
898 bâgad (1), to *act treacherously*
2254 châbal (1), to *pervert, destroy*
4383 mikshôwl (1), *stumbling-block*
4417 ptaiō (3), to *trip up, stumble* morally
4624 skandalizō (14), to *entrap*, i.e. *trip* up
4625 skandalŏn (1), *snare*

OFFENDED
816 'âsham (2), to be *guilty; to be punished*
819 'ashmâh (1), *guiltiness*
2398 châṭâ' (4), to *sin*
6586 pâsha' (1), to *break away from authority*
264 hamartanō (1), to *miss the mark, to sin*
4624 skandalizō (16), to *entrap*, i.e. *trip* up

OFFENDER
2398 châṭâ' (1), to *sin*
91 adikĕō (1), to *do wrong*

OFFENDERS
2400 chaṭṭâ' (1), *criminal, guilty*

OFFER
2076 zâbach (20), to *(sacrificially) slaughter*
2077 zebach (1), *animal flesh; sacrifice*
5066 nâgash (4), to be, *come, bring near*
5130 nûwph (3), to *quiver, vibrate, rock*
5186 nâṭâh (1), to *stretch* or *spread out*
5190 nâṭal (1), to *lift; to impose*
5258 nâçak (2), to *pour a libation*
5260 nᵉçak (Ch.) (1), to *pour out a libation*
5375 nâsâ' (1), to *lift up*
5414 nâthan (2), to *give*
5927 'âlâh (34), to *ascend, be high, mount*
6213 'âsâh (41), to *do or make*
6999 qâṭar (1), to *turn into fragrance* by *fire*

7126 qârab (79), to *approach, bring near*
7127 qᵉrêb (Ch.) (2), to *approach, bring near*
7311 rûwm (14), to be *high; to rise or raise*
7819 shâchaṭ (1), to *slaughter; butcher*
399 anaphĕrō (3), to *lead up; to offer sacrifice*
1325 didōmi (2), to *give*
1929 ĕpididōmi (1), to *give over*
3930 parĕchō (1), to *hold near*, i.e. to *present*
4374 prŏsphĕrō (10), to *present to; to treat as*

OFFERED
1684 dᵉbach (Ch.) (1), to *sacrifice an animal*
2076 zâbach (17), to *(sacrificially) slaughter*
2398 châṭâ' (1), to *sin*
4639 ma'âseh (1), *action; labor*
5066 nâgash (2), to be, *come, bring near*
5068 nâdab (1), to *volunteer; to present*
5069 nᵉdab (Ch.) (1), be, *give without coercion*
5130 nûwph (2), to *quiver, vibrate, rock*
5927 'âlâh (38), to *ascend, be high, mount*
6213 'âsâh (6), to *do or make*
6999 qâṭar (2), to *turn into fragrance* by *fire*
7126 qârab (16), to *approach, bring near*
7127 qᵉrêb (Ch.) (1), to *approach, bring near*
7133 qorbân (1), *sacrificial present*
7311 rûwm (2), to be *high; to rise or raise*
8641 tᵉrûwmâh (1), *sacrifice, tribute*
321 anagō (1), to *lead up; to bring out; to sail*
399 anaphĕrō (3), to *lead up; to offer sacrifice*
1494 ĕidōlŏthutŏn (8), *idolatrous offering*
4374 prŏsphĕrō (14), to *present to; to treat as*
4689 spĕndō (2), to *pour out as a libation*

OFFERETH
2076 zâbach (1), to *(sacrificially) slaughter*
2398 châṭâ' (1), to *sin*
5066 nâgash (1), to be, *come, bring near*
5926 'illĕg (1), *stuttering, stammering*
5927 'âlâh (2), to *ascend, be high, mount*
7126 qârab (9), to *approach, bring near*

OFFERING
817 'âshâm (1), *guilt; fault; sin-offering*
2076 zâbach (1), to *(sacrificially) slaughter*
4503 minchâh (147), *tribute; offering*

English

OFFERINGS
5927 'âlâh (9), to *ascend, be high, mount*
5930 'ôlâh (1), *sacrifice wholly consumed in fire*
6213 'âsâh (2), to *make*
7126 qârab (1), to *approach, bring near*
7133 qorbân (66), sacrificial *present*
8573 t\u1d49nûwphâh (6), *undulation* of offerings
8641 t\u1d49rûwmâh (40), *sacrifice, tribute*
4374 prŏsphĕrō (2), to *present to; to treat as*
4376 prŏsphŏra (8), *presentation; oblation*

OFFERINGS
1890 habhâb (1), *gift given as a sacrifice*
2077 zebach (5), animal *flesh; sacrifice*
4503 minchâh (16), *tribute; offering*
5262 neçek (1), *libation; cast idol*
7133 qorbân (1), sacrificial *present*
8641 t\u1d49rûwmâh (10), *sacrifice, tribute*
1435 dōrŏn (1), sacrificial *present*
3646 hŏlŏkautōma (3), *wholly-consumed sacrifice*
4376 prŏsphŏra (1), *presentation; oblation*

OFFICE
3653 kên (1), *pedestal* or *station* of a basin
4612 ma'ămâd (1), *position; attendant*
5656 'ăbôdâh (1), *work*
6486 p\u1d49quddâh (3), *visitation; punishment*
1247 diakŏnĕŏ (2), to *wait upon, serve*
1248 diakŏnia (1), *attendance, aid, service*
1984 ĕpiskŏpē (1), *episcopate*
2405 hiĕratĕia (2), *priestly office*
2407 hiĕratĕuō (1), to *be a priest*
4234 praxis (1), *act; function*

OFFICER
5324 nâtsab (1), to *station*
5333 n\u1d49tsîyb (1), military *post; statue*
5631 çârîyç (5), *eunuch; official* of state
6496 pâqîyd (2), *superintendent, officer*
4233 praktŏr (2), official *collector*
5257 hupērĕtēs (1), *servant, attendant*

OFFICERS
5324 nâtsab (6), to *station*
5631 çârîyç (7), *eunuch; official* of state
6213 'âsâh (1), to *do*
6485 pâqad (3), to *visit, care for, count*
6486 p\u1d49quddâh (3), *visitation; punishment*

OFFICES
4929 mishmâr (1), *guard; deposit; usage; example*
4931 mishmereth (1), *watch, sentry, post*
6486 p\u1d49quddâh (2), *visitation; punishment*

OFFSCOURING
5501 ç\u1d49chîy (1), *refuse*
4067 pĕripsōma (1), *scum, garbage*

OFFSPRING
6631 tse'ĕtsâ' (9), *produce, children*
1085 gĕnŏs (3), *kin*

OFT
1767 day (1), *enough, sufficient*
3740 hŏsakis (1), *as often as, when*
4178 pŏllakis (5), *many times, i.e. frequently*
4183 pŏlus (1), *much, many*
4212 pŏsakis (1), *how many times*
4435 pugmē (1), *with the fist*

OFTEN
3740 hŏsakis (6), *as often as, when*
4178 pŏllakis (3), *many times, i.e. frequently*
4212 pŏsakis (2), *how many times*
4437 puknŏs (2), *frequent; frequently*

OFTENER
4437 puknŏs (1), *frequent; frequently*

OFTENTIMES
6471+7227 pa'am (1), *time; step; occurence*
6471+7969 pa'am (1), *time; step; occurence*
4178 pŏllakis (3), *many times, i.e. frequently*
4183+5550 pŏlus (1), *much, many*

OFTTIMES
4178 pŏllakis (3), *many times, i.e. frequently*

OG
5747 'Ôwg (22), *round*

OH
518 'îm (1), *whether?; if, although; Oh that!*
577 'ânnâ' (1), *oh now!, I ask you!*
994 bîy (7), *Oh that!*
3863 lûw' (2), *if; would that!*
4994 nâ' (6), *I pray!, please!, I beg you!*

OHAD
161 'Ôhad (2), *unity*

OHEL
169 'Ôhel (1), *Ohel*

OIL
3323 yitshâr (21), *olive oil; anointing*
4887 m\u1d49shach (Ch.) (2), *olive oil*
6671 tsâhar (1), to *press out olive oil*
8081 shemen (163), *olive oil, wood, lotions*
1637 ĕlaiŏn (11), olive *oil*

OILED
8081 shemen (2), *olive oil, wood, lotions*

OINTMENT
4841 merqâchâh (1), *unguent-kettle*
4842 mirqachath (1), *aromatic unguent*
4888 mishchâh (1), *unction; gift*
7545 rôqach (1), *aromatic, fragrance*
8081 shemen (11), *olive oil, wood, lotions*
3464 murŏn (12), *perfumed oil*

OINTMENTS
8081 shemen (3), *olive oil, wood, lotions*
3464 murŏn (2), *perfumed oil*

OLD
227 'âz (2), *at that time* or *place; therefore*
865 'ethmôwl (1), *heretofore, formerly*
1086 bâlâh (11), to *wear out, decay; consume*
1087 bâleh (5), *worn out*
1094 b\u1d49lôw' (3), *rags, worn out fabric*
1121 bên (132), *son, descendant; people*
1247 bar (Ch.) (1), *son, child; descendant*
1323 bath (1), *daughter, descendant, woman*
2204 zâqên (26), to *be old, venerated*
2205 zâqên (41), *old, venerated*
2208 zâqûn (4), *old age*
2209 ziqnâh (6), *old age*
2416 chay (1), *alive; raw; fresh; life*
3117 yôwm (1), *day; time period*
3117+8140+3117 yôwm (1), *day; time period*
3453 yâshîysh (1), *old man*
3462 yâshên (2), to *sleep; to grow old, stale*
3465 yâshân (7), *old*
3833 lâbîy' (1), *lion, lioness*
3918 layish (1), *lion*
5288 na'ar (1), *male child; servant*
5669 'âbûwr (2), *kept over; stored grain*
5703 'ad (1), *perpetuity; ancient*
5769 'ôwlâm (26), *eternity; ancient*
5957 'âlam (Ch.) (2), *forever*

OIL
6275 'âthaq (2), to *remove; to grow old*
6440 pânîym (3), *face; front*
6924 qedem (17), *East, eastern; antiquity*
6927 qadmâh (1), *priority in time; before; past*
6931 qadmôwnîy (2), *anterior* time; *oriental*
7223 rî'shôwn (2), *first*
7350 râchôwq (2), *remote, far*
7872 sêybâh (6), *old age*
7992 sh\u1d49lîyshîy (2), *third*
8027 shâlash (3), to *be, triplicate*
744 archaiŏs (11), *original or primeval*
1088 gĕrōn (1), *aged, old person*
1094 gĕras (1), *senility, old age*
1095 gĕraskō (2), to *be senescent, grow old*
1126 graŏdēs (1), *old lady-like, i.e. silly*
1332 diĕtēs (1), *of two years in age*
1541 hĕkatŏntaĕtēs (1), *centenarian*
1597 ĕkpalai (1), *long ago, for a long while*
3819 palai (2), *formerly; sometime since*
3820 palaiŏs (19), *not recent, worn out, old*
3822 palaiŏō (3), to *become worn out*
4218 pŏtĕ (2), *at some time, ever*
4245 prĕsbutĕrŏs (1), *elderly; older; presbyter*
4246 prĕsbutēs (1), *old man*
5550 chrŏnŏs (1), *space of time, period*

OLDNESS
3821 palaiŏtēs (1), *antiquatedness*

OLIVE
2132 zayith (27), *olive*
8081 shemen (4), *olive oil, wood, lotions*
65 agriĕlaiŏs (2), *wild olive tree*
1636 ĕlaia (4), *olive*
2565 kalliĕlaiŏs (1), *cultivated olive*

OLIVES
2132 zayith (4), *olive*
1636 ĕlaia (11), *olive*

OLIVET
2132 zayith (1), *olive*
1638 ĕlaiōn (1), *Mt. of Olives*

OLIVEYARD
2132 zayith (1), *olive*

OLIVEYARDS
2132 zayith (5), *olive*

OLYMPAS
3632 ŏinŏphlugia (1), *drunkenness*

OMAR
201 'Ôwmâr (3), *talkative*

OMEGA
5598 Ō (4), last letter of the Greek alphabet

OMER
6016 'ômer (5), *sheaf* of grain; dry *measure*

OMERS
6016 'ômer (1), *sheaf* of grain; dry *measure*

OMITTED
863 aphíēmi (1), to *leave*; to *pardon, forgive*

OMNIPOTENT
3841 pantŏkratŏr (1), Absolute *sovereign*

OMRI
6018 'Omrîy (18), *heaping*

ONAM
208 'Ôwnâm (4), *strong*

ONAN
209 'Ôwnân (8), *strong*

ONCE
227 'âz (1), *at that time* or *place; therefore*
259 'echâd (15), *first*
996 bêyn (1), *between; "either...or"*
3162 yachad (1), *unitedly*
4118 mahêr (1), *in a hurry*
5750 'ôwd (1), *again; repeatedly; still; more*
6471 pa'am (10), *time; step; occurence*
6471+259 pa'am (1), *time; step; occurence*
530 hapax (15), *once for all*
2178 ĕphapax (5), *upon one occasion*
3366 mēdĕ (1), *but not, not even; nor*
3826 pamplēthĕi (1), in *full multitude*
4218 pŏtĕ (2), *at some time, ever*

ONE
259 'echâd (658), *first*
376 'îysh (173), *man; male; someone*
428 'êl-leh (2), *these or those*
492 'almônîy (1), *certain so and so, whoever*
802 ishshâh (8), *woman, wife; women, wives*
1397 geber (1), *person, man*
1571 gam (1), *also; even*
1668 dâ' (Ch.) (2), *this*
1836 dên (Ch.) (1), *this*
2063 zō'th (1), *this*
2088 zeh (10), *this or that*
2297 chad (1), *one*
2298 chad (Ch.) (5), *one; single; first; at once*
3605 kôl (1), *all, any*
3627 k°lîy (1), *implement, thing*
3671 kânâph (1), *edge* or *extremity; wing*
5315 nephesh (1), *life; breath; soul; wind*
6918 qâdôwsh (2), *sacred*
240 allēlōn (77), *one another*

243 allŏs (4), *different, other*
1438 hĕautŏu (6), *himself, herself, itself*
1515 ĕirēnē (1), *peace; health; prosperity*
1520 hĕis (231), *one*
2087 hĕtĕrŏs (1), *other or different*
3303 mĕn (2), *not translated*
3391 mia (56), *one or first*
3442 mŏnŏphthalmŏs (2), *one-eyed*
3661 hŏmŏthumadŏn (12), *unanimously*
3675 hŏmŏphrōn (1), *like-minded*
3739 hŏs (1), *who, which, what, that*
3956 pas (2), *all, any, every, whole*
4861 sumpsuchŏs (1), *similar in sentiment*
5100 tis (35), *some or any* person or object
5129 tŏutōi (1), in *this* person or thing

ONES
1121 bên (1), *son, descendant; people*

ONESIMUS
3682 Ŏnēsimŏs (4), *profitable*

ONESIPHORUS
3683 Ŏnēsiphŏrŏs (2), *profit-bearer*

ONIONS
1211 betsel (1), *onion*

ONLY
259 'echâd (2), *first*
389 'ak (33), *surely; only, however*
905 bad (35), *apart, only, besides*
910 bâdâd (1), *separate, alone*
2108 zûwlâh (1), *except; apart from; besides*
3162 yachad (2), *unitedly*
3173 yâchîyd (7), *only son; alone; beloved*
3535 kibsâh (1), *ewe sheep*
3697 kâçam (1), to *shear, clip*
7535 raq (52), *merely; although*
1520 hĕis (1), *one*
3439 mŏnŏgĕnēs (9), *sole, one and only*
3440 mŏnŏn (62), *merely, just*
3441 mŏnŏs (24), *single, only; by oneself*

ONO
207 'Ôwnôw (5), *strong*

ONYCHA
7827 sh°chêleth (1), *scale or shell, mussel*

ONYX
7718 shôham (11), (poss.) *pale green beryl* stone

OPEN
1540 gâlâh (6), to *denude; uncover*

3605 kôl (1), *all, any or every*
4725 mâqôwm (1), general *locality, place*
5869 'ayin (1), *eye; sight; fountain*
6358 pâtûwr (4), *opened; bud*
6363 peţer (1), *firstling, first born*
6440 pânîym (13), *face; front*
6475 pâtsâh (3), to *rend,* i.e. *open*
6491 pâqach (10), to *open* the eyes
6555 pârats (1), to *break out*
6566 pâras (1), to *break apart, disperse, scatter*
6605 pâthach (49), to *open wide; to loosen*
6606 p°thach (Ch.) (1), to *open*
6610 pithchôwn (1), act of *opening* the mouth
8365 shâtham (2), to *unveil,* i.e. *open*
71 agō (1), to *lead; to bring, drive; to weigh*
343 anakaluptō (1), to *unveil*
455 anŏigō (21), to *open up*
1722+457 ĕn (1), *in; during; because of*
3856 paradĕigmatizō (1), to *expose to infamy*
4271 prŏdēlŏs (1), *obvious, evident*

OPENED
1540 gâlâh (3), to *denude; uncover*
3738 kârâh (1), to *dig; to plot; to bore, hew*
6473 pâ'ar (3), to *open wide*
6475 pâtsâh (7), to *rend,* i.e. *open*
6491 pâqach (7), to *open* the eyes
6589 pâsaq (1), to *dispart,* i.e., *spread*
6605 pâthach (51), to *open* wide; to *loosen*
6606 p°thach (Ch.) (1), to *open*
380 anaptussō (1), to *unroll* a scroll
455 anŏigō (53), to *open up*
1272 dianŏigō (6), to *open thoroughly*
4977 schizō (1), to *split* or *sever*
5136 trachēlizō (1), to *lay bare*

OPENEST
6605 pâthach (2), to *open* wide; to *loosen, begin*

OPENETH
1540 gâlâh (3), to *denude; uncover*
6363 peţer (7), *firstling, first born*
6491 pâqach (2), to *open* the eyes

6589 pâsaq (1), to *dispart,* i.e., *spread*
6605 pâthach (4), to *open* wide; to *loosen, begin*
455 anŏigō (3), to *open up*
1272 dianŏigō (1), to *open thoroughly*

OPENING
4668 maphtêach (1), *opening; key*
4669 miphtâch (1), *utterance of lips*
6491 pâqach (1), to *open* the eyes
6495 p°qach-qôwach (1), *jail-delivery; salvation*
6605 pâthach (1), to *open* wide; to *loosen, begin*
6610 pithchôwn (1), act of *opening* the mouth
1272 dianŏigō (1), to *open thoroughly*

OPENINGS
6607 pethach (1), *opening; door, entrance*

OPENLY
5879 'Êynayim (1), *double fountain*
1219 dēmŏsiŏs (1), *public; in public*
1717 ĕmphanēs (1), *apparent in self, seen*
1722+3588+5318 ĕn (3), *in; during; because of*
1722+3954 ĕn (2), *in; during; because of*
3954 parrhēsia (4), *frankness, boldness*
5320 phanĕrōs (2), *plainly,* i.e. *clearly*

OPERATION
4639 ma'ăseh (2), *action; labor*
1753 ĕnĕrgĕia (1), *efficiency, energy*

OPERATIONS
1755 ĕnĕrgēma (1), *effect, activity*

OPHEL
6077 'Ôphel (5), *fortress*

OPHIR
211 'Ôwphîyr (13), *Ophir*

OPHNI
6078 'Ophnîy (1), *Ophnite*

OPHRAH
6084 'Ophrâh (8), *female fawn*

OPINION
1843 dêa' (3), *knowledge*

OPINIONS
5587 çâ'îph (1), *divided* in mind; *sentiment*

OPPORTUNITY
170 akairĕŏmai (1), to *fail of a proper occasion*
2120 ĕukairia (2), *favorable occasion*
2540 kairŏs (2), *occasion, set time*

OPPOSE
475 antidiatithĕmai (1), *be disputatious*

OPPOSED
498 antitassŏmai (1),
oppose, resist

OPPOSEST
7852 sâṭam (1), to
persecute

OPPOSETH
480 antikĕimai (1), to be
an *opponent*

OPPOSITIONS
477 antithĕsis (1),
opposition

OPPRESS
1792 dâkâ' (1), to
pulverize; be contrite
3238 yânâh (5), to
suppress; to maltreat
3905 lâchats (5), to *press;*
to *distress*
6206 'ârats (1), to *awe;* to
dread; to harass
6231 'âshaq (9), to
oppress; to defraud
7703 shâdad (1), to
ravage
2616 katadunastĕuō (1),
to *oppress, exploit*

OPPRESSED
1790 dak (3), *injured,*
oppressed
2541 châmôwts (1),
violent
3238 yânâh (3), to
suppress; to maltreat
3905 lâchats (7), to *press;*
to *distress*
5065 nâgas (2), to
exploit; to tax, harass
6217 'âshûwq (1), *used*
tyranny
6231 'âshaq (11), to
oppress; to defraud
6234 'oshqâh (1),
anguish, trouble
7533 râtsats (6), to *crack*
in pieces, *smash*
2616 katadunastĕuō (1),
to *oppress, exploit*
2669 katapŏnĕō (1), to
harass, oppress

OPPRESSETH
3905 lâchats (1), to *press;*
to *distress*
6231 'âshaq (3), to
oppress; to defraud
6887 tsârar (1), to *cramp*

OPPRESSING
3238 yânâh (3), to
suppress; to maltreat

OPPRESSION
3238 yânâh (1), to
suppress; to maltreat
3906 lachats (7), *distress*
4939 mispâch (1),
slaughter
6115 'ôtser (1), *closure;*
constraint
6125 'âqâh (1), *constraint*
6233 'ôsheq (12), *injury;*
fraud; distress
7701 shôd (1), *violence,*
ravage, destruction

OPPRESSIONS
4642 ma'ăshaqqâh (1),
oppression

6217 'âshûwq (2), *used*
tyranny

OPPRESSOR
376+2555 'îysh (1), *man;*
male; someone
3238 yânâh (1), to
suppress; to maltreat
4642 ma'ăshaqqâh (1),
oppression
5065 nâgas (5), to
exploit; to tax, harass
6184 'ârîyts (1), *powerful*
or *tyrannical*
6216 'âshôwq (1), *tyrant*
6231 'âshaq (2), to
oppress; to defraud
6693 tsûwq (2), to
oppress, distress

OPPRESSORS
3905 lâchats (1), to *press;*
to *distress*
5065 nâgas (2), to
exploit; to tax, harass
6184 'ârîyts (2), *powerful*
or *tyrannical*
6231 'âshaq (2), to
oppress; to defraud
7429 râmaç (1), to *tread*
upon

ORACLE
1687 dᵉbîyr (16), *inmost*
part of the sanctuary
1697 dâbâr (1), *word;*
matter; thing

ORACLES
3051 lŏgiŏn (4),
utterance of God

ORATION
1215 dēmēgŏrĕō (1), to
address an assembly

ORATOR
3908 lachash (1),
incantation; amulet
4489 rhētōr (1), *legal*
advocate

ORCHARD
6508 pardêç (1), *park,*
cultivated garden area

ORCHARDS
6508 pardêç (1), *park,*
cultivated garden area

ORDAIN
3245 yâçad (1), *settle,*
establish a foundation
7760 sûwm (1), to *put,*
place
8239 shâphath (1), to
place or put
1299 diatassō (1), to
institute, prescribe
2525 kathistēmi (1), to
designate, constitute

ORDAINED
3245 yâçad (1), *settle,*
establish a foundation
3559 kûwn (1), to *set up:*
establish, fix, prepare
4483 mᵉnâ' (Ch.) (1), to
count, appoint
5414 nâthan (2), to *give*
5975 'âmad (1), to *stand*
6186 'ârak (2), to set in a
row, i.e. arrange,
6213 'âsâh (3), to *do or*
make
6965 qûwm (1), to *rise*

7760 sûwm (2), to *put,*
place
1096 ginŏmai (1), to *be,*
become
1299 diatassō (2), to
institute, prescribe
2525 kathistēmi (2), to
designate, constitute
2680 kataskĕuazō (1), to
prepare thoroughly
2919 krinō (1), to *decide;*
to *try, condemn, punish*
3724 hŏrizō (2), to
appoint, decree, specify
4160 pŏiĕō (1), to *make*
or *do*
4270 prŏgraphō (1), to
announce, prescribe
4282 prŏĕtŏimazō (1), to
fit up in advance
4304 prŏmĕlĕtaō (1), to
premeditate
5021 tassō (2), to
arrange, assign
5087 tithēmi (2), to *place*
5500 chĕirŏtŏnĕō (3), to
select or appoint

ORDAINETH
6466 pâ'al (1), to *do,*
make or practice

ORDER
631 'âçar (1), to *fasten;* to
join battle
1700 dibrâh (1), *reason,*
suit or style; because
3027 yâd (2), *hand; power*
3559 kûwn (3), to *set up:*
establish, fix, prepare
4634 ma'ărâkâh (1),
arrangement, row; pile
4941 mishpâṭ (5), *verdict;*
formal *decree; justice*
5468 çeder (1), to
arrange, order
6186 'ârak (19), to set in
a *row, i.e. arrange,*
6187 'êrek (1), *pile,*
equipment, estimate
6471 pa'am (1), *time;*
step; occurence
6680 tsâvâh (3), to
constitute, enjoin
7947 shâlab (1), to *make*
equidistant
8626 tâqan (1), to
straighten; to compose
1299 diatassō (3), to
institute, prescribe
1930 ĕpidiŏrthŏō (1), to
arrange additionally
2517 kathĕxēs (3), *in a*
sequence, subsequent
5001 tagma (1), *series or*
succession
5010 taxis (10),
succession; kind

ORDERED
3559 kûwn (1), to *set up:*
establish, fix, prepare
4634 ma'ărâkâh (1),
arrangement, row; pile
6186 'ârak (2), to set in a
row, i.e. arrange,

ORDERETH
7760 sûwm (1), to *put,*
place

ORDERINGS
6486 pᵉquddâh (1),
visitation; punishment

ORDERLY
4748 stŏichĕō (1), to
follow, walk; to conform

ORDINANCE
2706 chôq (6),
appointment; allotment
2708 chuqqâh (12), to
delineate
3027 yâd (1), *hand; power*
4931 mishmereth (3),
watch, sentry, post
4941 mishpâṭ (5), *verdict;*
formal *decree; justice*
1296 diatagĕ (1),
institution
2937 ktisis (1), *formation*

ORDINANCES
2706 chôq (3),
appointment; allotment
2708 chuqqâh (10), to
delineate
4687 mitsvâh (1),
command
4941 mishpâṭ (6), *verdict;*
formal *decree; justice*
1345 dikaiōma (3),
statute or decision
1378 dŏgma (2), *law*
1379 dŏgmatizō (1), to
submit to a certain rule
3862 paradŏsis (1),
precept; tradition

ORDINARY
2706 chôq (1),
appointment; allotment

OREB
6157 'ârôb (6), *swarming*
mosquitoes

OREN
767 'Ôren (1), *ash* tree

ORGAN
5748 'ûwgâb (3),
reed-instrument

ORGANS
5748 'ûwgâb (1),
reed-instrument

ORION
3685 Kᵉçîyl (3),
constellation Orion

ORNAMENT
642 'êphuddâh (1),
plating
2481 chălîy (1), *polished*
trinket, ornament
3880 livyâh (2), *wreath*
5716 'ădîy (2), *finery;*
outfit; headstall

ORNAMENTS
5716 'ădîy (9), *finery;*
outfit; headstall
5914 'ekeç (1), *anklet,*
bangle
6287 pᵉ'êr (1), *fancy*
head-dress
6807 tsᵉ'âdâh (1), *march;*
ankle-chain
7720 sahărôn (2), round
pendant or crescent

ORNAN
771 'Ornân (11), *strong*

ORPAH
6204 'Orpâh (2), *mane*

ORPHANS
3490 yâthôwm (1), child alone, fatherless child

OSEE
5617 Hōsēĕ (1), deliverer

OSHEA
1954 Hôwshêä' (2), deliverer

OSPRAY
5822 'oznîyâh (2), (poss.) sea-eagle

OSSIFRAGE
6538 pereç (2), kind of eagle

OSTRICH
5133 nôwtsâh (1), plumage

OSTRICHES
3283 yâ'ên (1), ostrich

OTHER
251 'âch (1), brother; relative; member
259 'echâd (32), first
269 'achôwth (1), sister
312 'achêr (99), other, another, different; next, more
317 'ochŏrîy (Ch.) (1), other, another
321 'ochŏrân (Ch.) (3), other, another
428 'êl-leh (3), these or those
2063 zô'th (2), this
2088 zeh (16), this or that
3541 kôh (1), thus
3671 kânâph (1), edge or extremity; wing
5048 neged (2), over against or before
5676 'êber (25), opposite side; east
6311 pôh (5), here or hence
7453 rêa' (2), associate; one close
7605 shᵉ'âr (1), remainder
8145 shênîy (36), second; again
237 allachŏthĕn (1), from elsewhere
240 allēlōn (5), one another
243 allŏs (51), different, other
244 allotriĕpiskŏpŏs (1), meddler, busybody
245 allŏtriŏs (2), not one's own
492 antiparĕrchŏmai (2), to go along opposite
846 autŏs (1), he, she, it
1520 hĕis (7), one
1565 ĕkĕinŏs (2), that one
1622 ĕktŏs (1), aside from, besides; except
2084 hĕtĕrŏglōssŏs (1), foreigner
2085 hĕtĕrŏdidaskalĕō (1), to instruct differently
2087 hĕtĕrŏs (34), other or different
2548 kakĕinŏs (2), likewise that or those

3062 lŏipŏi (16), remaining ones
3739 hŏs (2), who, which, what, that
4008 pĕran (12), across, beyond

OTHERS
312 'achêr (9), other, another, different; next
428 'êl-leh (1), these
243 allŏs (29), different, other
245 allŏtriŏs (1), not one's own
2087 hĕtĕrŏs (11), other or different
3062 lŏipŏi (9), remaining ones
3588 hŏ (2), "the," i.e. the definite article
3739 hŏs (1), who, which

OTHERWISE
176 'ôw (1), or, whether
3808 lô' (1), no, not
243 allŏs (1), different, other
247 allŏs (1), differently
1490 ĕi dĕ mē(gĕ) (3), but if not
1893 ĕpĕi (4), since
2085 hĕtĕrŏdidaskalĕō (1), to instruct differently
2088 hĕtĕrŏs (1), differently, otherly

OTHNI
6273 'Otnîy (1), forcible

OTHNIEL
6274 'Othnîy'êl (7), force of God

OUCHES
4865 mishbᵉtsâh (8), reticulated setting

OUGHT
1697 dâbâr (2), word; matter; thing
3972 mᵉ'ûwmâh (6), something; anything
4465 mimkâr (1), merchandise
1163 dĕi (29), it is (was) necessary
3762 ŏudĕis (1), none, nobody, nothing
3784 ŏphĕilō (15), to owe; to be under obligation
5100 tis (8), some or any
5534 chrē (1), it needs (must or should) be

OUGHTEST
1163 dĕi (3), it is (was) necessary

OUTCAST
5080 nâdach (1), to push off, scattered

OUTCASTS
1760 dâchâh (3), to push down; to totter
5080 nâdach (4), to push off, scattered

OUTER
2435 chîytsôwn (1), outer wall side; exterior; secular
1857 ĕxŏtĕrŏs (3), exterior, outer

OUTGOINGS
4161 môwtsâ' (1), going forth
8444 tôwtsâ'âh (7), exit, boundary; deliverance

OUTLANDISH
5237 nokrîy (1), foreign; non-relative

OUTLIVED
748+3117+310 'ârak (1), to be, make long

OUTMOST
7020 qîytsôwn (1), terminal, end
7097 qâtseh (2), extremity

OUTRAGEOUS
7858 sheṭeph (1), deluge, torrent

OUTRUN
4370+5032 prŏstrĕchō (1), to hasten by running

OUTSIDE
2351 chûwts (2), outside, outdoors; open market
7097 qâtseh (3), extremity
1623 hĕktŏs (1), sixth
1855 ĕxŏthĕn (2), outside, external (-ly)

OUTSTRETCHED
5186 nâṭâh (3), to stretch or spread out

OUTWARD
2435 chîytsôwn (8), outer wall side; exterior
5869 'ayin (1), eye; sight; fountain
1722+3588+5318 ĕn (1), in; during; because of
1854 ĕxō (1), out, outside
1855 ĕxŏthĕn (2), outside, external (-ly)
4383 prŏsōpŏn (1), face, presence

OUTWARDLY
1722+5318 ĕn (1), in; during; because of
1855 ĕxŏthĕn (1), outside, external (-ly)

OUTWENT
4281 prŏĕrchŏmai (1), to go onward, precede

OVEN
8574 tannûwr (10), fire-pot
2823 klibanŏs (2), earthen pot

OVENS
8574 tannûwr (1), fire-pot

OVER
413 'êl (19), to, toward
1157 bᵉ'ad (1), up to or over against
1541 gᵉlâh (Ch.) (1), to reveal mysteries
1591 gᵉnêbâh (1), something stolen
1869 dârak (1), to tread, trample; to walk, lead
2498 châlaph (1), to hasten away; to pass on
3148 yôwthêr (1), moreover; rest; gain
4136 mûwl (14), in front of, opposite
4480 min (1), from, out of

4605 ma'al (3), upward, above, overhead
5048 neged (27), over against or before
5226 nêkach (1), opposite
5227 nôkach (9), opposite, in front of
5414 nâthan (1), to give
5462 çâgar (2), to shut up; to surrender
5534 çâkar (1), to shut up; to surrender
5674 'âbar (171), to cross over; to transition
5736 'âdaph (3), to have surplus
5764 'ûwl (2), nursing babe
5848 'âṭaph (1), to shroud, i.e. clothe
5921 'al (406), above, over, upon, or against
5922 'al (Ch.) (12), above, over, upon, or against
5924 'êllâ' (Ch.) (1), above
5927 'âlâh (1), to ascend, be high, mount
5975 'âmad (1), to stand
5980 'ummâh (23), near, beside, along with
6440 pânîym (2), face; front
6743 tsâlach (1), to push forward
6903 qᵉbêl (Ch.) (1), in front of, before
7235 râbâh (2), to increase
481 antikru (1), opposite of
495 antipĕran (1), on the opposite side
561 apĕnanti (2), opposite, before
1224 diabainō (1), to pass by, over, across
1276 diapĕraō (2), to cross over
1277 diaplĕō (1), to sail through, across
1330 diĕrchŏmai (4), to traverse, travel through
1537 ĕk (3), out, out of
1608 ĕkpŏrnĕuō (1), to be utterly unchaste
1722 ĕn (1), in; during; because of
1883 ĕpanō (6), over or on
1909 ĕpi (49), on, upon
1924 ĕpigraphō (1), to inscribe, write upon
2596 kata (2), down; according to
2634 katakuriĕuō (1), to control, lord over
2713 katĕnanti (4), directly opposite
3346 mĕtatithēmi (1), to transport; to exchange
3860 paradidōmi (2), to hand over
3928 parĕrchŏmai (1), to go by; to perish
4008 pĕran (3), across, beyond
4012 pĕri (2), about; around
4052 pĕrissĕuō (1), to superabound

English

4121 plĕŏnazō (1), to
superabound
4291 prŏïstēmi (1), to
preside; to practice
5055 tĕlĕō (1), to end, i.e.
complete, execute
5228 hupĕr (1), over;
above; beyond
5231 hupĕranō (1),
above, upward
5240 hupĕrĕkchunō (1),
to overflow

OVERCAME
2634 katakuriĕuō (1), to
control, lord over
3528 nikaō (2), to
subdue, conquer

OVERCHARGE
1912 ĕpibarĕō (1), to be
severe toward

OVERCHARGED
925 barunō (1), to
burden; to grieve

OVERCOME
1464 gûwd (2), to attack
1986 hâlam (1), to strike,
beat, stamp, conquer
2476 chălûwshâh (1),
defeat
3201 yâkôl (1), to be able
3898 lâcham (2), to fight
a battle
5674 'âbar (1), to cross
over; to transition
7292 râhab (1), to urge
severely, i.e. importune
2274 hēttaō (2), to rate
lower, be inferior
3528 nikaō (10), to
subdue, conquer

OVERCOMETH
3528 nikaō (11), to
subdue, conquer

OVERDRIVE
1849 dâphaq (1), to
knock; to press severely

OVERFLOW
6687 tsûwph (1), to
overflow
7783 shûwq (2), to
overflow
7857 shâṭaph (10), to
gush; to inundate

OVERFLOWED
7857 shâṭaph (1), to
gush; to inundate
2626 katakluzō (1), to
deluge, flood

OVERFLOWETH
4390 mâlê' (1), to fill; be
full

OVERFLOWING
1065 bᵉkîy (1), weeping
2230 zerem (1), gush of
water, flood
7857 shâṭaph (8), to
gush; to inundate
7858 sheṭeph (1), deluge,
torrent

OVERFLOWN
3332 yâtsaq (1), to pour
out
4390 mâlê' (1), to fill; be
full

7857 shâṭaph (1), to
gush; to inundate

OVERLAID
2645 châphâh (4), to
cover; to veil, to encase
5968 'âlaph (1), to be
languid, faint
6823 tsâphâh (28), to
sheet over with metal
7901 shâkab (1), to lie
down
4028 pĕrikaluptō (1), to
cover eyes; to plait

OVERLAY
2902 ṭûwach (1), to
whitewash
6823 tsâphâh (12), to
sheet over with metal

OVERLAYING
6826 tsippûwy (2),
encasement with metal

OVERLIVED
748+3117+310 'ârak (1),
to be, make long

OVERMUCH
4055 pĕrissŏtĕrŏs (1),
more superabundant

OVERPASS
5674 'âbar (1), to cross
over; to transition

OVERPAST
5674 'âbar (2), to cross
over; to transition

OVERPLUS
5736 'âdaph (1), to have
surplus

OVERRAN
5674 'âbar (1), to cross
over; to transition

OVERRUNNING
5674 'âbar (1), to cross
over; to transition

OVERSEE
5329 nâtsach (1), i.e. to
be eminent

OVERSEER
6485 pâqad (2), to visit,
care for, count
6496 pâqîyd (4),
superintendent, officer
7860 shôṭêr (1), to write;
official who is a scribe

OVERSEERS
5329 nâtsach (2), i.e. to
be eminent
6485 pâqad (2), to visit,
care for, count
6496 pâqîyd (1),
superintendent, officer
1985 ĕpiskŏpŏs (1),
overseer, supervisor

OVERSHADOW
1982 ĕpiskiazō (2), to
cast a shade upon

OVERSHADOWED
1982 ĕpiskiazō (3), to
cast a shade upon

OVERSIGHT
4870 mishgeh (1), error
5414 nâthan (1), to give
5921 'al (2), above, over,
upon, or against
6485 pâqad (4), to visit,
care for, count

6486 pᵉquddâh (2),
visitation; punishment
1983 ĕpiskŏpĕō (1), to
oversee; to beware

OVERSPREAD
5310 nâphats (1), to dash
to pieces; to scatter

OVERSPREADING
3671 kânâph (1), edge or
extremity; wing

OVERTAKE
5066 nâgash (2), to be,
come, bring near
5381 nâsag (14), to reach
2638 katalambanō (1), to
seize; to possess

OVERTAKEN
5381 nâsag (1), to reach
4301 prŏlambanō (1), to
take before

OVERTAKETH
5381 nâsag (1), to reach

OVERTHREW
2015 hâphak (4), to
change, overturn
4114 mahpêkâh (3),
destruction
5286 nâ'ar (1), to growl
5287 nâ'ar (1), to tumble
about
390 anastrĕphō (1), to
remain, to live
2690 katastrĕphō (2), to
upset, overturn

OVERTHROW
1760 dâchâh (1), to push
down; to totter
2015 hâphak (5), to
change, overturn
2018 hăphêkâh (1),
destruction, demolition
2040 hâraç (2), to pull
down; break, destroy
4073 mᵉdachphâh (1),
ruin
4114 mahpêkâh (2),
destruction
5186 nâṭâh (1), to stretch
or spread out
5307 nâphal (2), to fall
5422 nâthats (1), to tear
down
396 anatrĕpō (1), to
overturn, destroy
2647 kataluō (1), to
demolish
2692 katastrŏphē (1),
catastrophical ruin

OVERTHROWETH
2040 hâraç (1), to pull
down; break, destroy
5557 çâlaph (4), to
wrench; to subvert

OVERTHROWN
2015 hâphak (4), to
change, overturn
2040 hâraç (2), to pull
down; break, destroy
3782 kâshal (2), to totter,
waver; to falter
4114 mahpêkâh (1),
destruction
5307 nâphal (3), to fall
5791 'âvath (1), to wrest,
twist

8045 shâmad (1), to
desolate
8058 shâmaṭ (1), to
jostle; to let alone
2693 katastrŏnnumi (1),
to prostrate, i.e. slay

OVERTOOK
1692 dâbaq (3), to cling
or adhere; to catch
5381 nâsag (7), to reach

OVERTURN
2015 hâphak (1), to
change, overturn
5754 'avvâh (1),
overthrow, ruin

OVERTURNED
2015 hâphak (1), to
change, overturn

OVERTURNETH
2015 hâphak (3), to
change, overturn

OVERWHELM
5307 nâphal (1), to fall

OVERWHELMED
3680 kâçâh (2), to cover
5848 'âṭaph (5), to
shroud, i.e. clothe
7857 shâṭaph (1), to
gush; to inundate

OWE
3784 ŏphĕilō (1), to owe;
to be under obligation

OWED
3781 ŏphĕilĕtēs (1),
person indebted
3784 ŏphĕilō (2), to owe;
to be under obligation

OWEST
3784 ŏphĕilō (3), to owe;
to be under obligation
4359 prŏsŏphĕilō (1), to
be indebted

OWETH
3784 ŏphĕilō (1), to owe;
to be under obligation

OWL
1323+3284 bath (2),
daughter, descendant
3244 yanshûwph (3), bird
3563 kôwç (3), cup;
(poss.) owl
3917 lîylîyth (1), night
spectre (spirit)
7091 qippôwz (1),
arrow-snake

OWLS
1323+3284 bath (6),
daughter, descendant

OWN
249 'ezrâch (15), native
born
3548 kôhên (2), one
officiating as a priest
5315 nephesh (1), life;
breath; soul; wind
7522 râtsôwn (1), delight
830 authairĕtŏs (1),
self-chosen
846 autŏs (1), he, she, it
848 hautŏu (15), self
849 autŏchĕir (1),
self-handed, personally
1103 gnēsiŏs (2),
genuine, true

1438 hĕautŏu (24),
himself, herself, itself
1683 ĕmautŏu (2), *myself*
1699 ĕmŏs (2), *my*
2398 idiŏs (76), *private or separate*
2596 kata (1), *down; according to*
4572 sĕautŏu (2), *of yourself*

OWNER
113 'ádôwn (1),
sovereign, i.e. controller
1167 ba'al (10), *master; husband; owner; citizen*
7069 qânâh (1), *to create; to procure*
3490 nauklērŏs (1), *ship captain*

OWNERS
1167 ba'al (4), *master; husband; owner; citizen*
2962 kuriŏs (1), *supreme, controller, Mr.*

OWNETH
2076 ĕsti (1), *he (she or it) is; they are*

OX
441 'allûwph (1), *friend, one familiar; chieftain, leader*
1241 bâqâr (3), *plowing ox; herd*
7794 shôwr (53), *bullock*
8377 tᵉ'ôw (1), *antelope*
1016 bŏus (4), *ox, cattle*

OXEN
441 'allûwph (1), *friend, one familiar; chieftain*
504 'eleph (2), *ox; cow or cattle*
1241 bâqâr (74), *plowing ox; herd*
5091 nâhâh (1), *to bewail; to assemble*
6499 par (2), *bullock*
7794 shôwr (8), *bullock*
8450 tôwr (Ch.) (4), *bull*
1016 bŏus (4), *ox, cattle*
5022 taurŏs (2), *bullock, ox*

OZEM
684 'Ôtsem (2), *strong*

OZIAS
3604 Ŏzias (2), *strength of Jehovah*

OZNI
244 'Oznîy (1), *having (quick) ears*

OZNITES
244 'Oznîy (1), *having (quick) ears*

PAARAI
6474 Pa'ăray (1), *yawning*

PACATIANA
3818 Pakatianē (1), *Pacatianian*

PACES
6806 tsa'ad (1), *pace or regular step*

PACIFIED
3722 kâphar (1), *to placate or cancel*
7918 shâkak (1), *to lay a trap; to allay*

PACIFIETH
3240 yânach (1), *to allow to stay*
3711 kâphâh (1), *to tame or subdue*

PACIFY
3722 kâphar (1), *to cover; to placate*

PADAN
6307 Paddân (1), *table-land of Aram*

PADAN-ARAM
6307 Paddân (10), *table-land of Aram*

PADDLE
3489 yâthêd (1), *tent peg*

PADON
6303 Pâdôwn (2), *ransom*

PAGIEL
6295 Pag'îy'êl (5), *accident of God*

PAHATH-MOAB
6355 Pachath Môw'âb (6), *pit of Moäb*

PAI
6464 Pâ'ûw (1), *screaming*

PAID
3052 yᵉhab (Ch.) (1), *to give*
5414 nâthan (1), *to give*
591 apŏdidōmi (2), *to give away*

PAIN
2256 chebel (1), *company, band*
2342 chûwl (6), *to dance, whirl; to writhe in pain*
2427 chîyl (3), *throe of painful childbirth*
2470 châlâh (1), *to be weak, sick, afflicted*
2479 chalchâlâh (4), *writhing in childbirth*
3510 kâ'ab (1), *to feel pain; to grieve; to spoil*
3511 kᵉ'êb (1), *suffering; adversity*
4341 mak'ôb (2), *anguish; affliction*
5999 'âmâl (1), *wearing effort; worry*
4192 pŏnŏs (2), *toil, i.e. anguish*

PAINED
2342 chûwl (3), *to dance, whirl; to writhe in pain*
3176 yâchal (1), *to wait; to be patient, hope*
928 basanizō (1), *to torture, torment*

PAINFUL
5999 'âmâl (1), *wearing effort; worry*

PAINFULNESS
3449 mŏchthŏs (1), *sadness*

PAINS
4712 mêtsar (1), *trouble*
6735 tsîyr (1), *hinge; trouble*
4192 pŏnŏs (1), *toil, i.e. anguish*

PAINTED
4886 mâshach (1), *to rub or smear with oil*
7760+6320 sûwm (1), *to put, place*

PAINTEDST
3583 kâchal (1), *to paint the eyes with stibnite*

PAINTING
6320 pûwk (1), *stibium*

PAIR
2201 zĕugŏs (1), *team, pair*
2218 zugŏs (1), *coupling, yoke*

PALACE
643 'appeden (1), *pavilion or palace-tent*
759 'armôwn (4), *citadel, high fortress*
1002 bîyrâh (17), *palace, citadel*
1004 bayith (1), *house; temple; family, tribe*
1055 bîythân (3), *large house*
1964 hêykâl (8), *palace; temple; hall*
1965 hêykal (Ch.) (4), *palace; temple*
2038 harmôwn (1), *high castle or fortress*
2918 tîyrâh (1), *fortress; hamlet*
833 aulē (7), *palace; house; courtyard*
4232 praitōriŏn (1), *court-room or palace*

PALACES
759 'armôwn (27), *citadel, high fortress*
1964 hêykâl (3), *palace; temple; hall*
2918 tîyrâh (2), *fortress; hamlet*

PALAL
6420 Pâlâl (1), *judge*

PALE
2357 châvar (1), *to blanch with shame*
5515 chlōrŏs (1), *greenish, verdant*

PALENESS
3420 yêrâqôwn (1), *paleness; mildew*

PALESTINA
6429 Pᵉlesheth (3), *migratory*

PALESTINE
6429 Pᵉlesheth (1), *migratory*

PALLU
6396 Pallûw' (4), *distinguished*

PALLUITES
6384 Pallû'îy (1), *Palluïte*

PALM
3709 kaph (2), *hollow of hand; paw; sole of foot*
8558 tâmâr (12), *palm tree*

PALMERWORM
1501 gâzâm (3), *kind of locust*

PALMS
3709 kaph (4), *hollow of hand; paw; sole of foot*
4474 rhapizō (1), *to slap, rap, strike*
4475 rhapisma (1), *slap, strike*
5404 phŏinix (1), *palm-tree*

PALSIES
3886 paraluŏ (1), *to be paralyzed or enfeebled*

PALSY
3885 paralutikŏs (10), *lame person*
3886 paraluŏ (3), *to be paralyzed or enfeebled*

PALTI
6406 Palţîy (1), *delivered*

PALTIEL
6409 Palţîy'êl (1), *deliverance of God*

PALTITE
6407 Palţîy (1), *Paltite*

PAMPHYLIA
3828 Pamphulia (5), *every-tribal, i.e. heterogeneous*

PAN
3595 kîyôwr (1), *caldron; washbowl*
4227 machăbath (6), *metal pan for baking in*
4958 masrêth (1), *pan*

PANGS
2256 chebel (2), *company, band*
2427 chîyl (2), *throe of painful childbirth*
6735 tsîyr (3), *hinge; herald, trouble*
6887 tsârar (2), *to cramp*

PANNAG
6436 Pannag (1), *food, (poss.) pastry*

PANS
2281 châbêth (1), *griddle-cake*
5518 çîyr (1), *thorn; hook*
6517 pârûwr (1), *skillet*
6745 tsêlâchâh (1), *flattened out platter*

PANT
7602 shâ'aph (1), *to be angry; to hasten*

PANTED
7602 shâ'aph (1), *to be angry; to hasten*
8582 tâ'âh (1), *to vacillate, i.e. reel*

PANTETH
5503 çâchar (1), *to travel round; to palpitate*

5604 ōdin (1), *pang of childbirth; agony*

PAINTED

English

PAPER
6165 'ârag (2), to long
for, pant for

PAPER
6169 'ârâh (1), bulrushes,
reeds
5489 chartēs (1), sheet of
papyrus paper

PAPHOS
3974 Paphŏs (2), Paphus

PAPS
7699 shad (1), female
breast
3149 mastŏs (3), female
breast; chest area

PARABLE
4912 mâshâl (17), pithy
maxim; taunt
3850 parabŏlē (31),
fictitious narrative
3942 parŏimia (1),
illustration; adage

PARABLES
4912 mâshâl (1), pithy
maxim; taunt
3850 parabŏlē (15),
fictitious narrative

PARADISE
3857 paradĕisŏs (3), park

PARAH
6511 Pârâh (1), heifer

PARAMOURS
6370 pîylegesh (1),
concubine; paramour

PARAN
6290 Pâ'rân (11),
ornamental

PARBAR
6503 Parbâr (2), Parbar
or Parvar

PARCEL
2513 chelqâh (5),
allotment
5564 chŏriŏn (1), spot or
plot of ground

PARCHED
2788 chârêr (1), arid,
parched
7039 qâlîy (6), roasted
ears of cereal grain
8273 shârâb (1), glow of
the hot air; mirage

PARCHMENTS
3200 mĕmbrana (1),
sheep-skin for writing

PARDON
3722 kâphar (1), to
cover; to expiate
5375 nâsâ' (3), to lift up
5545 çâlach (11), to
forgive
5547 çᵉlîychâh (1),
pardon

PARDONED
5545 çâlach (2), to forgive
7521 râtsâh (1), to be
pleased with; to satisfy

PARDONETH
5375 nâsâ' (1), to lift up

PARE
6213 'âsâh (1), to do or
make

PARENTS
1118 gŏnĕus (19), parents

PARLOUR
3957 lishkâh (1), room
5944 'ălîyâh (4), upper
things; second-story

PARLOURS
2315 cheder (1),
apartment, chamber

PARMASHTA
6534 Parmashtâ' (1),
Parmashta

PARMENAS
3937 Parmĕnas (1),
constant

PARNACH
6535 Parnak (1), Parnak

PAROSH
6551 Par'ôsh (5), flea

PARSHANDATHA
6577 Parshandâthâ' (1),
Parshandatha

PART
2505 châlaq (3), to be
smooth; be slippery
2506 chêleq (19),
allotment
2513 chelqâh (1),
flattery; allotment
2673 châtsâh (1), to cut
or split in two; to halve
2677 chêtsîy (3), half or
middle, midst
4481 min (Ch.) (5), from
or out of
4490 mânâh (1), ration;
lot or portion
4940 mishpâchâh (2),
family, clan, people
5337 nâtsal (1), to
deliver; snatched away
6418 pelek (7),
spindle-whorl; crutch
6447 paç (Ch.) (2), palm
of the hand
6504 pârad (1), to spread
or separate
6626 pâthath (1), to
break, crumble
7117 qᵉtsâth (1),
termination; portion
2819 klērŏs (2), lot,
portion
3307 mĕrizō (1), to
apportion, share
3310 mĕris (5), portion,
share, participation
3313 mĕrŏs (17), division
or share
3348 mĕtĕchō (1), to
share or participate
4119 plēiŏn (1), more
4403 prumna (1), stern of
a ship

PARTAKER
2506 chêleq (1),
smoothness; allotment
2841 kŏinōnĕō (2), to
share or participate
2844 kŏinōnŏs (1),
associate, partner
3335 mĕtalambanō (1),
to participate
3348 mĕtĕchō (2),
share or participate

PARTAKERS
482 antilambanŏmai (1),
to succor; aid
2841 kŏinōnĕō (3), to
share or participate
2844 kŏinōnŏs (4),
associate, partner
3310 mĕris (1), portion,
share, participation
3335 mĕtalambanō (1),
to participate
3348 mĕtĕchō (3), to
share or participate
3353 mĕtŏchŏs (4),
sharer, associate
4790 sugkŏinōnĕō (1), to
co-participate in
4791 sugkŏinōnŏs (1),
co-participant
4829 summĕrizŏmai (1),
to share jointly
4830 summĕtŏchŏs (2),
co-participant

PARTAKEST
1096+4791
Bêlᵗᵉsha'tstsar (Ch.)
(1), Belteshatstsar

PARTED
2505 châlaq (2), to be
smooth; be slippery
2673 châtsâh (1), to cut
or split in two; to halve
6504 pârad (1), to spread
or separate
1266 diamĕrizō (6), to
have dissension
1339 diïstēmi (1), to
remove, intervene

PARTETH
6504 pârad (1), to spread
or separate
6536 pâraç (2), to break
in pieces; to split

PARTHIANS
3934 Parthŏs (1),
inhabitant of Parthia

PARTIAL
5375+6440 nâsâ' (1), to
lift up
1252 diakrinō (1), to
decide; to hesitate

PARTIALITY
87 adiakritŏs (1),
impartial
4346 prŏsklisis (1),
favoritism

PARTICULAR
3313 mĕrŏs (1), division
or share
3588+1520 hŏ (1), "the,"
i.e. the definite article

PARTICULARLY
1520+1538+2596 hĕis (1),
one
2596+3313 kata (1),
down; according to

PARTING
517 'êm (1), mother

PARTITION
5674 'âbar (1), to cross
over; to transition

PARTLY
7118 qᵉtsâth (Ch.) (1),
termination; portion
1161 dĕ (1), but, yet
3313+5100 mĕrŏs (1),
division or share
5124+3303 tŏutŏ (1), that
thing

PARTNER
2505 châlaq (1), to be
smooth; be slippery
2844 kŏinōnŏs (2),
associate, partner

PARTNERS
2844 kŏinōnŏs (1),
associate, partner
3353 mĕtŏchŏs (1),
sharer, associate

PARTRIDGE
7124 qôrê' (2), calling
partridge

PARTS
905 bad (1), limb,
member; bar
1335 bether (2), section,
piece
1506 gezer (1), portion,
piece
1697 dâbâr (1), word;
matter; thing
2506 chêleq (6),
smoothness; allotment
2677 chêtsîy (1), half or
middle, midst
3027 yâd (3), hand; power
3411 yᵉrêkâh (2),
recesses, far places
5409 nêthach (1),
fragment
6310 peh (1), mouth;
opening
7098 qâtsâh (1),
termination; fringe
2825 klinē (1), couch
3313 mĕrŏs (6), division
or share

PARUAH
6515 Pârûwach (1),
blossomed

PARVAIM
6516 Parvayim (1),
Parvajim

PAS-DAMMIM
6450 Paç Dammîym (1),
dell of bloodshed

PASACH
6457 Pâçak (1), divider

PASEAH
6454 Pâçêach (3), limping

PASHUR
6583 Pashchûwr (14),
liberation

PASS
935 bôw' (3), to go or
come
1980 hâlak (1), to walk;
live a certain way
2498 châlaph (2), to
hasten away; to pass on
2499 chălaph (Ch.) (4), to
have time pass by
3615 kâlâh (1), to cease,
be finished, perish

4569 ma'ăbâr (1),
crossing-place
5674 'âbar (153), to *cross*
over; to *transition*
5709 'ădâ' (Ch.) (1), to
pass on or *continue*
6213 'âsâh (5), to *do* or
make
6452 pâçach (2), to *hop*,
skip over; to *hesitate*
390 anastrĕphō (1), to
remain, to *live*
1224 diabainō (1), to
pass by, *over*, *across*
1276 diapĕraō (1), to
cross over
1279 diapŏrĕuŏmai (1),
to *travel through*
1330 diĕrchŏmai (7), to
traverse, *travel through*
3928 parĕrchŏmai (19),
to *go by*; to *perish*
5230 hupĕrakmŏs (1),
past the *bloom* of youth

PASSAGE
1552 gᵉlîylâh (1), *circuit*
or *region*
4569 ma'ăbâr (2),
crossing-place
5674 'âbar (1), to *cross*
over; to *transition*

PASSAGES
4569 ma'ăbâr (4),
crossing-place
5676 'êber (1), *opposite*
side; *east*

PASSED
1431 gâdal (1), to *be*
great, make great
2498 châlaph (2), to
hasten away; to *pass* on
5674 'âbar (117), to *cross*
over; to *transition*
5709 'ădâ' (Ch.) (1), to
pass on or *continue*
5710 'âdâh (1), to *pass* on
or *continue*; to *remove*
6437 pânâh (1), to *turn*,
to *face*
6452 pâçach (1), to *hop*,
skip over; to *hesitate*
492 antiparĕrchŏmai (2),
to *go along opposite*
565 apĕrchŏmai (1), to
go off, i.e. *depart*
1224 diabainō (1), to
pass by, *over*, *across*
1276 diapĕraō (3), to
cross over
1330 diĕrchŏmai (11), to
traverse, *travel through*
1353 diŏdĕuō (1), to
travel through
3327 mĕtabainō (2), to
depart, *move from*
3855 paragō (6), to *go*
along or *away*
3899 parapŏĕruŏmai (4),
to *travel near*
3928 parĕrchŏmai (3), to
go by; to *perish*, *neglect*
4281 prŏĕrchŏmai (1), to
go onward, *precede*

PASSEDST
5674 'âbar (1), to *cross*
over; to *transition*

PASSENGERS
5674 'âbar (4), to *cross*
over; to *transition*
5674+1870 'âbar (1), to
cross over; to *transition*

PASSEST
5674 'âbar (5), to *cross*
over; to *transition*

PASSETH
1980 hâlak (4), to *walk*;
live a certain way
2498 châlaph (1), to
hasten away; to *pass* on
5674 'âbar (28), to *cross*
over; to *transition*
3855 paragō (2), to *go*
along or *away*
3928 parĕrchŏmai (1), to
go by; to *perish*
5235 hupĕrballō (1), to
surpass
5242 hupĕrĕchō (1), to
excel; *superior*

PASSING
5674 'âbar (7), to *cross*
over; to *transition*
1330 diĕrchŏmai (2), to
traverse, *travel through*
2064 ĕrchŏmai (1), to *go*,
come
3881 paralĕgŏmai (1), to
sail past
3928 parĕrchŏmai (1), to
go by; to *perish*

PASSION
3958 paschō (1), to
experience pain

PASSIONS
3663 hŏmŏiŏpathēs (2),
similarly affected

PASSOVER
6453 Peçach (48),
Passover
3957 pascha (28),
Passover events

PASSOVERS
6453 Peçach (1), *Passover*

PAST
369 'ayin (1), *there is no*,
i.e., *not exist*, *none*
5493 çûwr (2), to *turn* off
5674 'âbar (8), to *cross*
over; to *transition*
6924 qedem (1), *eastern*;
antiquity; *before*
7223 rî'shôwn (1), *first*
7291 râdaph (1), to *run*
after with hostility
7725 shûwb (1), to *turn*
back; to *return*
8032 shilshôwm (9), *day*
before yesterday
421 anĕxichniastŏs (1),
untraceable
524 apalgĕō (1), *become*
apathetic
565 apĕrchŏmai (2), to
go off, i.e. *depart*
1096 ginŏmai (2), to *be*,
become
1230 diaginŏmai (1), to
have time elapse
1330 diĕrchŏmai (1), to
traverse, travel through
3819 palai (1), *formerly*;
sometime since

3844 para (1), *from*; *with*;
besides; *on account of*
3855 paragō (1), to *go*
along or *away*
3928 parĕrchŏmai (3), to
go by; to *perish*
3944 parŏichŏmai (1), to
escape along
4266 prŏginŏmai (1), to
have previously
transpired
4302 prŏlĕgō (1), to
predict, forewarn

PASTOR
7462 râ'âh (1), to *tend* a
flock, i.e. *pasture* it

PASTORS
7462 râ'âh (7), to *tend* a
flock, i.e. *pasture* it
4166 pŏimēn (1),
shepherd

PASTURE
4829 mir'eh (11),
pasture; *haunt*
4830 mir'îyth (8),
pasturage; *flock*
3542 nŏmē (1), *pasture*,
i.e. the act of *feeding*

PASTURES
3733 kar (2), *ram sheep*
4829 mir'eh (1), *pasture*;
haunt
4830 mir'îyth (1),
pasturage; *flock*
4945 mashqeh (1), *butler*;
drink; *well-watered*
4999 nâ'âh (5), *home*,
dwelling; *pasture*
7471 rᵉ'îy (1), *pasture*

PATARA
3959 Patara (1), *Patara*

PATE
6936 qodqôd (1), *crown*
of the head

PATH
734 'ôrach (9), *road*;
manner of life
4546 mᵉçillâh (1), main
thoroughfare; *viaduct*
4570 ma'gâl (1), *circular*
track or camp *rampart*
4934 mish'ôwl (1),
narrow passage
5410 nâthîyb (8),
(beaten) *track, path*
7635 shâbîyl (1), *track* or
passage-way

PATHROS
6624 Pathrôwç (5),
Pathros

PATHRUSIM
6625 Pathrûçîy (2),
Pathrusite

PATHS
734 'ôrach (16), *road*;
manner of life
4546 mᵉçillâh (1), main
thoroughfare; *viaduct*
4570 ma'gâl (6), *circular*
track or camp *rampart*
5410 nâthîyb (14),
(beaten) *track, path*
7635 shâbîyl (1), *track* or
passage-way
5147 tribŏs (3), *rut*, or
worn track

5163 trŏchia (1), *course*
of conduct, *path* of life

PATHWAY
1870+5410 derek (1),
road; *course* of life

PATIENCE
3114 makrŏthumĕō (3),
to *be forbearing, patient*
3115 makrŏthumia (2),
forbearance; *fortitude*
5281 hupŏmŏnē (29),
endurance, *constancy*

PATIENT
750 'ârêk (1), *patient*
420 anĕxikakŏs (1),
forbearing
1933 ĕpiĕikēs (1), *mild*,
gentle
3114 makrŏthumĕō (3),
to *be forbearing, patient*
5278 hupŏmĕnō (1), to
undergo, bear (trials)
5281 hupŏmŏnē (2),
perseverence

PATIENTLY
2342 chûwl (1), to *dance*,
whirl; to *wait*; to *pervert*
6960 qâvâh (1), to *collect*;
to *expect*
3114 makrŏthumĕō (1),
to *be forbearing, patient*
3116 makrŏthumōs (1),
with long, enduring
temper, i.e. *leniently*
5278 hupŏmĕnō (2), to
undergo, bear (trials)

PATMOS
3963 Patmŏs (1), *Patmus*

PATRIARCH
3966 patriarchēs (2),
progenitor or patriarch

PATRIARCHS
3966 patriarchēs (2),
progenitor or patriarch

PATRIMONY
1+5921 'âb (1), *father*

PATROBAS
3969 Patrŏbas (1),
father's life

PATTERN
4758 mar'eh (1),
appearance; *vision*
8403 tabnîyth (9),
structure; *model*
8508 toknîyth (1),
admeasurement
5179 tupŏs (2), *shape*,
resemblance; "*type*"
5296 hupŏtupōsis (1),
example, pattern

PATTERNS
5262 hupŏdĕigma (1),
exhibit; *specimen*

PAU
6464 Pâ'ûw (1),
screaming

PAUL
3972 Paulŏs (157), *little*

PAUL'S
3972 Paulŏs (6), *little*

PAULUS
3972 Paulŏs (1), *little*

English

PAVED
3840 libnâh (1),
transparency
7528 râtsaph (1), to
tessellate, embroider

PAVEMENT
4837 martsepheth (1),
pavement, stone base
7531 ritspâh (7), *hot*
stone; pavement
3037 lithŏs (1), *stone*

PAVILION
5520 çôk (1), *hut of*
entwined boughs
5521 çukkâh (2),
tabernacle; shelter
8237 shaphrûwr (1),
tapestry or *canopy*

PAVILIONS
5521 çukkâh (3),
tabernacle; shelter

PAW
3027 yâd (2), *hand; power*

PAWETH
2658 châphar (1), to
delve, to *explore*

PAWS
3709 kaph (1), hollow of
hand; paw; sole of foot

PAY
5414 nâthan (2), to *give*
5414+4377 nâthan (1), to
give
5415 nᵉthan (Ch.) (1), to
give
5927 'âlâh (1), to *ascend,*
be high, mount
7725 shûwb (1), to *turn*
back; to *return*
7999 shâlam (19), to *be*
safe; be, make complete
8254 shâqal (4), to
suspend in trade
586 apŏdĕkatŏō (1), to
tithe, give a tenth
591 apŏdidōmi (7), to
give away
5055 tĕlĕō (2), to *end,*
discharge (a debt)

PAYED
7999 shâlam (1), to *be*
safe; be, make complete
1183 dĕkatŏō (1), to *give*
or *take a tenth*

PAYETH
7999 shâlam (1), to *be*
safe; be, make complete

PAYMENT
591 apŏdidōmi (1), to
give away

PEACE
1826 dâmam (1), to *be*
silent; to *be astonished*
2013 hâçâh (2), to *hush,*
be quiet
2790 chârash (26), to *be*
silent; to *be deaf*
2814 châshâh (9), to
hush or *keep quiet*
6963 qôwl (1), *voice* or
sound
7962 shalvâh (1),
security, ease
7965 shâlôwm (169),
safe; well; health, peace

PEACEABLE
7961 shâlêv (1), *careless,*
carefree; security
7965 shâlôwm (2), *safe;*
well; health, peace
7999 shâlam (1), to *be*
safe; be, make complete
8003 shâlêm (1),
complete; friendly; safe
1516 ĕirēnikŏs (2),
pacific, peaceful
2272 hēsuchiŏs (1), *still,*
undisturbed

PEACEABLY
7962 shalvâh (2),
security, ease
7965 shâlôwm (9), *safe;*
well; health, peace
1518 ĕirēnŏpŏiŏs (1),
peaceable

PEACEMAKERS
1518 ĕirēnŏpŏiŏs (1),
peaceable

PEACOCKS
7443 renen (1), female
ostrich
8500 tukkîy (2), (poss.)
peacock

PEARL
3135 margaritēs (2), *pearl*

PEARLS
1378 gâbîysh (1), *crystal*
3135 margaritēs (7), *pearl*

PECULIAR
5459 çᵉgullâh (5), *wealth*
1519+4047 ĕis (1), *to* or
into
4041 pĕriŏusiŏs (1),
special, one's very own

PEDAHEL
6300 Pᵉdah'êl (1), *God*
has ransomed

PEDAHZUR
6301 Pᵉdâhtsûwr (5),
Rock has ransomed

PEDAIAH
6305 Pᵉdâyâh (8),
Jehovah has ransomed

PEDIGREES
3205 yâlad (1), to *bear*
young; to *father a child*

PEELED
4178 môwrâṭ (2),
obstinate, independent
4803 mâraṭ (1), to *polish;*
to *make bald*

PEEP
6850 tsâphaph (1), to *coo*
or *chirp* as a bird

PEEPED
6850 tsâphaph (1), to *coo*
or *chirp* as a bird

PEKAH
6492 Peqach (11), *watch*

PEKAHIAH
6494 Pᵉqachyâh (3),
Jehovah has observed

PEKOD
6489 Pᵉqôwd (2),
punishment

PELAIAH
6411 Pᵉlâyâh (3),
Jehovah has
distinguished

PELALIAH
6421 Pᵉlalyâh (1),
Jehovah has judged

PELATIAH
6410 Pᵉlaṭyâh (5),
Jehovah has delivered

PELEG
6389 Peleg (7),
earthquake

PELET
6404 Peleṭ (2), *escape*

PELETH
6431 Peleth (2), *swiftness*

PELETHITES
6432 Pᵉlêthîy (7), *courier*
or official *messenger*

PELICAN
6893 qâ'ath (3), *pelican*

PELONITE
6397 Pᵉlôwnîy (3),
separate

PEN
2747 chereṭ (1), *chisel;*
style for writing
5842 'êṭ (4), *stylus; reed*
pen
7626 shêbeṭ (1), *stick;*
clan, family
2563 kalamŏs (1), *reed;*
pen

PENCE
1220 dēnariŏn (5),
denarius

PENIEL
6439 Pᵉnûw'êl (1), *face of*
God

PENINNAH
6444 Pᵉninnâh (3), *round*
pearl

PENKNIFE
8593 ta'ar (1), *knife;*
razor; scabbard

PENNY
1220 dēnariŏn (9),
denarius

PENNYWORTH
1220 dēnariŏn (2),
denarius

PENTECOST
4005 pĕntĕkŏstē (3), the
festival of *Pentecost*

PENUEL
6439 Pᵉnûw'êl (7), *face of*
God

PENURY
4270 machçôwr (1),
impoverishment
5303 hustĕrēma (1),
deficit; poverty; lacking

PEOPLE
376 'îysh (1), *man; male;*
someone
523 'ummâh (1),
community, clan, tribe
528 'Âmôwn (1), *Amon*
582 'ĕnôwsh (1), *man;*
person, human
1121 bên (1), *son,*
descendant; people
1471 gôwy (11), foreign
nation; Gentiles
3816 lᵉ'ôm (24),
community, nation
5712 'êdâh (1),
assemblage; family
5971 'am (1827), *people;*
tribe; troops
5972 'am (Ch.) (15),
people, nation
1218 dēmŏs (4), *public,*
crowd
1484 ĕthnŏs (2), *race;*
tribe; pagan
2992 laŏs (138), *people;*
public
3793 ŏchlŏs (83), *throng*

PEOPLE'S
5971 'am (2), *people;*
tribe; troops
2992 laŏs (2), *people;*
public

PEOPLES
2992 laŏs (2), *people;*
public

PEOR
6465 Pe'ôwr (4), *gap*

PEOR'S
6465 Pe'ôwr (1), *gap*

PERADVENTURE
194 'ûwlay (23), *if not;*
perhaps
3863 lûw' (1), *if; would*
that!
6435 pên (1), *lest, not*
3379 mēpŏtĕ (1), *not*
ever; if, or *lest ever*
5029 tacha (1), *shortly,*
i.e. *possibly*

PERAZIM
6559 Pᵉrâtsîym (1),
breaks

PERCEIVE
995 bîyn (1), to
understand; discern
3045 yâda' (7), to *know*
7200 râ'âh (1), to *see*
8085 shâma' (1), to *hear*
intelligently
991 blĕpō (1), to *look at*
1097 ginōskō (2), to *know*
1492 ĕidō (3), to *know*
2334 thĕōrĕō (4), to *see;*
to *discern*

2638 katalambanō (1), to seize; to possess
3539 nŏiĕō (2), to exercise the mind
3708 hŏraō (1), to stare, see clearly; to discern

PERCEIVED
238 'âzan (1), to listen
995 bîyn (3), to understand; discern
3045 yâda' (11), to know
5234 nâkar (1), to acknowledge
7200 râ'âh (4), to see
8085 shâma' (1), to hear intelligently
143 aisthanŏmai (1), to apprehend
1097 ginōskō (7), to know
1921 ĕpiginōskō (3), to become fully acquainted with
2147 hĕuriskō (1), to find
2638 katalambanō (1), to possess; to understand
2657 katanŏĕō (1), to observe fully

PERCEIVEST
3045 yâda' (1), to know
2657 katanŏĕō (1), to observe fully

PERCEIVETH
995 bîyn (1), to understand; discern
2938 ţâ'am (1), to taste; to perceive, experience
7789 shûwr (1), to spy out, survey

PERCEIVING
1492 ĕidō (3), to know

PERDITION
684 apŏlĕia (8), ruin or loss

PERES
6537 pᵉraç (Ch.) (1), to split up

PERESH
6570 Peresh (1), excrement

PEREZ
6557 Perets (3), breech

PEREZ-UZZA
6560 Perets 'Uzzâ' (1), break of Uzza

PEREZ-UZZAH
6560 Perets 'Uzzâ' (1), break of Uzza

PERFECT
1584 gâmar (1), to end; to complete; to fail
1585 gᵉmar (Ch.) (1), to complete
3559 kûwn (1), to render sure, proper
3632 kâlîyl (3), whole, entire; complete; whole
3634 kâlal (1), to complete
4357 miklâh (1), wholly, solidly
7999 shâlam (1), to be safe; be, make complete
8003 shâlêm (15), complete; friendly; safe

8503 taklîyth (1), extremity
8535 tâm (9), morally pious; gentle, dear
8537 tôm (1), prosperity
8549 tâmîym (18), entire, complete; integrity
8552 tâmam (2), to complete, finish
195 akribĕia (1), exactness
197 akribĕstĕrŏn (1), more exactly
199 akribōs (1), exactly, carefully
739 artiŏs (1), complete, thorough, capable
2005 ĕpitĕlĕō (1), to terminate; to undergo
2675 katartizō (5), to repair; to prepare
3647 hŏlŏklēria (1), wholeness
4137 plērŏō (1), to fill, make complete
5046 tĕlĕiŏs (17), complete; mature
5048 tĕlĕiŏō (13), to perfect, complete

PERFECTED
3634 kâlal (1), to complete
5927+724 'âlâh (1), to ascend, be high, mount
8003 shâlêm (1), complete; friendly; safe
2675 katartizō (1), to repair; to prepare
5048 tĕlĕiŏō (4), to perfect, complete

PERFECTING
2005 ĕpitĕlĕō (1), to terminate; to undergo
2677 katartismŏs (1), complete furnishing

PERFECTION
3632 kâlîyl (1), whole, entire; complete; whole
4359 miklâl (1), perfection of beauty
4512 minleh (1), wealth
8502 tiklâh (1), completeness
8503 taklîyth (2), extremity
8537 tôm (1), completeness
2676 katartisis (1), thorough equipment
5050 tĕlĕiōsis (1), completion; verification
5051 tĕlĕiŏtēs (1), consummator, perfecter
5052 tĕlĕsphŏrĕō (1), to ripen fruit

PERFECTLY
998 bîynâh (1), discernment
197 akribĕstĕrŏn (3), more exactly
199 akribōs (1), exactly, carefully
1295 diasōzō (1), to cure, preserve, rescue
2675 katartizō (1), to repair; to prepare

PERFECTNESS
5047 tĕlĕiŏtēs (1), completeness; maturity

PERFORM
5414 nâthan (1), to give
6213 'âsâh (12), to do or make
6633 tsâbâ' (1), to mass an army or servants
6965 qûwm (13), to rise
7999 shâlam (4), to be safe; be, make complete
591 apŏdidōmi (1), to give away
2005 ĕpitĕlĕō (2), to terminate; to undergo
2716 katĕrgazŏmai (1), to finish; to accomplish
4160 pŏiĕō (2), to do

PERFORMANCE
2005 ĕpitĕlĕō (1), to terminate; to undergo
5050 tĕlĕiōsis (1), completion; verification

PERFORMED
1214 bâtsa' (1), to plunder; to finish
6213 'âsâh (5), to do or make
6965 qûwm (11), to rise
7999 shâlam (1), to be safe; be, make complete
1096 ginŏmai (1), to be, become
2005 ĕpitĕlĕō (1), to terminate; to undergo
5055 tĕlĕō (1), to end, i.e. complete, execute

PERFORMETH
1584 gâmar (1), to end; to complete; to fail
6965 qûwm (1), to rise
7999 shâlam (2), to be safe; be, make complete

PERFORMING
6381 pâlâ' (2), to be, make great, wonderful

PERFUME
7004 qᵉţôreth (3), fumigation

PERFUMED
5130 nûwph (1), to quiver, vibrate, rock
6999 qâţar (1), to turn into fragrance by fire

PERFUMES
7547 raqqûach (1), scented ointment

PERGA
4011 Pĕrgē (3), tower

PERGAMOS
4010 Pĕrgamŏs (2), fortified

PERHAPS
686 ara (1), then, so, therefore
3381 mēpōs (1), lest somehow
5029 tacha (1), shortly, i.e. possibly

PERIDA
6514 Pᵉrûwdâ' (1), dispersion

PERIL
2794 kindunŏs (1), danger, risk

PERILOUS
5467 chalĕpŏs (1), difficult, i.e. dangerous

PERILS
2794 kindunŏs (8), danger, risk

PERISH
6 'âbad (73), perish; destroy
7 'âbad (Ch.) (2), perish; destroy
8 'ôbêd (2), wretched; destruction
1478 gâva' (1), to expire, die
1820 dâmâh (2), to be silent; to fail, cease
3772 kârath (1), to cut (off, down or asunder)
5307 nâphal (1), to fall
5486 çûwph (1), to terminate
5595 çâphâh (2), to scrape; to remove
5674 'âbar (1), to cross over; to transition
6544 pâra' (1), to loosen; to expose, dismiss
7843 shâchath (1), to decay; to ruin
622 apŏllumi (25), to destroy fully; to perish
853 aphanizō (1), to disappear, be destroyed
1311 diaphthĕirō (1), to ruin, to decay
1510+1519+604 ĕimi (1), I exist, I am
2704 kataphthĕirō (1), to spoil entirely
5356 phthŏra (1), ruin; depravity, corruption

PERISHED
6 'âbad (17), perish; destroy
1478 gâva' (1), to expire, die
8045 shâmad (1), to desolate
599 apŏthnēskō (1), to die off
622 apŏllumi (5), to destroy fully; to perish
4881 sunapŏllumi (1), to destroy, be slain with

PERISHETH
6 'âbad (6), perish; destroy
622 apŏllumi (3), to destroy fully; to perish

PERISHING
5674 'âbar (1), to cross over; to transition

PERIZZITE
6522 Pᵉrîzzîy (5), of the open country

PERIZZITES
6522 Pᵉrîzziy (18), of the open country

PERJURED
1965 ĕpiŏrkŏs (1), forswearer, perjurer

PERMISSION
4774 suggnṓmē (1), concession

PERMIT
2010 ĕpitrĕpō (2), allow, permit

PERMITTED
2010 ĕpitrĕpō (2), allow, permit

PERNICIOUS
684 apṓlĕia (1), ruin or loss

PERPETUAL
5331 netsach (4), splendor; lasting
5769 'ôwlâm (22), eternity; always
8548 tâmîyd (2), constantly, regularly

PERPETUALLY
3605+3711 kôl (2), all, any or every
5703 'ad (1), perpetuity

PERPLEXED
943 bûwk (2), to be confused
639 apŏrĕō (1), be at a mental loss, be puzzled
1280 diapŏrĕō (2), to be thoroughly puzzled

PERPLEXITY
3998 mᵉbûwkâh (2), perplexity, confusion
640 apŏria (1), state of quandary, perplexity

PERSECUTE
1814 dâlaq (1), to flame; to pursue
7291 râdaph (14), to run after with hostility
7921+310 shâkôl (1), to miscarry
1377 diŏkō (8), to pursue; to persecute
1559 ĕkdiŏkō (1), to expel or persecute

PERSECUTED
4783 murdâph (1), persecuted
7291 râdaph (5), to run after with hostility
1377 diŏkō (13), to pursue; to persecute
1559 ĕkdiŏkō (1), to expel or persecute

PERSECUTEST
1377 diŏkō (6), to pursue; to persecute

PERSECUTING
1377 diŏkō (1), to pursue; to persecute

PERSECUTION
7291 râdaph (1), to run after with hostility
1375 diŏgmŏs (5), persecution
1377 diŏkō (3), to pursue; to persecute
2347 thlipsis (1), pressure, trouble

PERSECUTIONS
1375 diŏgmŏs (5), persecution

PERSECUTOR
1376 diŏktēs (1), persecutor

PERSECUTORS
1814 dâlaq (1), to flame; to pursue
7291 râdaph (7), to run after with hostility

PERSEVERANCE
4343 prŏskartĕrēsis (1), perseverance

PERSIA
6539 Pâraç (27), Paras
6540 Pâraç (Ch.) (2), Paras

PERSIAN
6523 parzel (Ch.) (1), iron
6542 Parçîy (1), Parsite

PERSIANS
6539 Pâraç (1), Paras
6540 Pâraç (Ch.) (4), Paras

PERSIS
4069 Pĕrsis (1), Persis

PERSON
120 'âdâm (2), human being; mankind
376 'îysh (3), man; male; someone
376+120 'îysh (1), man; male; someone
1167 ba'al (1), master; husband; owner; citizen
5315 nephesh (14), life; breath; soul; wind
6440 pânîym (10), face; front
4383 prŏsōpŏn (5), face, presence
5287 hupŏstasis (1), essence; assurance

PERSONS
120 'âdâm (3), human being; mankind
376 'îysh (8), man; male; someone
582 'ĕnôwsh (2), man; person, human
4962 math (1), men
5315 nephesh (12), life; breath; soul; wind
5315+120 nephesh (4), life; breath; soul; wind
6440 pânîym (11), face; front
678 aprŏsōpŏlēptŏs (2), without prejudice
4380 prŏsōpŏlēptĕō (1), to show partiality
4381 prŏsōpŏlēptēs (1), exhibiting partiality
4382 prŏsōpŏlēpsia (4), favoritism
4383 prŏsōpŏn (2), face, presence

PERSUADE
5496 çûwth (3), to stimulate; to seduce
6601 pâthâh (3), to be, make simple; to delude
3982 pĕithō (3), to assent to evidence

PERSUADED
5496 çûwth (1), to stimulate; to seduce

PERSUADEST
3982 pĕithō (1), to assent to evidence

PERSUADETH
5496 çûwth (1), to stimulate; to seduce
374 anapĕithō (1), to incite, persuade

PERSUADING
3982 pĕithō (2), to assent to evidence

PERSUASION
3988 pĕismŏnē (1), persuadableness

PERTAINED
1961 hâyâh (1), to exist

PERTAINETH
1961 hâyâh (1), to exist
3627 kᵉlîy (1), implement, thing
3348 mĕtĕchō (1), to share or participate

PERTAINING
4012 pĕri (1), about

PERUDA
6514 Pᵉrûwdâ' (1), dispersion

PERVERSE
1942 havvâh (1), desire; craving
2015 hâphak (1), to change, pervert
3399 yârat (1), to be rash
3868 lûwz (1), to depart; to be perverse
3891 lᵉzûwth (1), perverseness
5753 'âvâh (2), to be crooked
5773 'av'eh (1), perversity
6140 'âqash (2), to knot or distort; to pervert
6141 'iqqêsh (4), distorted, warped, false
8419 tahpûkâh (1), perversity or fraud
1294 diastrĕphō (4), to be morally corrupt
3859 paradiatribē (1), meddlesomeness

PERVERSELY
5753 'âvâh (2), to be crooked
5791 'âvath (1), to wrest, twist

PERVERSENESS
3868 lûwz (1), to depart; to be perverse
4297 mutteh (1), distortion; iniquity
5558 çeleph (2), distortion; viciousness
5766 'evel (1), moral evil
5999 'âmâl (1), wearing effort; worry

PERVERT
5186 nâtâh (2), to stretch or spread out

PEULTHAI 6469 Pᵉ'ull'thay (1), laborious

6601 pâthâh (1), to be, make simple; to delude
3982 pĕithō (16), to assent to evidence
4135 plērŏphŏrĕō (2), to assure or convince

PERSUADEST
3982 pĕithō (1), to assent to evidence

PERSUADETH
5496 çûwth (1), to stimulate; to seduce
374 anapĕithō (1), to incite, persuade

PERSUADING
3982 pĕithō (2), to assent to evidence

PERSUASION
3988 pĕismŏnē (1), persuadableness

PERTAINED
1961 hâyâh (1), to exist

PERTAINETH
1961 hâyâh (1), to exist
3627 kᵉlîy (1), implement, thing
3348 mĕtĕchō (1), to share or participate

PERTAINING
4012 pĕri (1), about

PERUDA
6514 Pᵉrûwdâ' (1), dispersion

PERVERTED
2015 hâphak (1), to change, pervert
5186 nâtâh (1), to stretch or spread out
5753 'âvâh (2), to be crooked
7725 shûwb (1), to turn back; to return

PERVERTETH
5186 nâtâh (1), to stretch or spread out
5557 çâlaph (2), to wrench; to subvert
6140 'âqash (1), to knot or distort; to pervert
654 apŏstrĕphō (1), turn away or back

PERVERTING
1294 diastrĕphō (1), to be morally corrupt

PESTILENCE
1698 deber (47), pestilence, plague

PESTILENCES
3061 lŏimŏs (2), plague; disease; pest

PESTILENT
3061 lŏimŏs (1), plague; disease; pest

PESTLE
5940 'ĕlîy (1), mortar pestle

PETER
4074 Pĕtrŏs (157), piece of rock

PETER'S
4074 Pĕtrŏs (4), piece of rock

PETHAHIAH
6611 Pᵉthachyâh (4), Jehovah has opened

PETHOR
6604 Pᵉthôwr (2), Pethor

PETHUEL
6602 Pᵉthûw'êl (1), enlarged of God

PETITION
1159 bâ'ûw (Ch.) (2), request; prayer
7596 shᵉ'êlâh (10), petition

PETITIONS
4862 mish'âlâh (1), request
155 aitēma (1), thing asked, request

PEULTHAI
6469 Pᵉ'ull'thay (1), laborious

PHALEC
5317 Phalĕk (1),
earthquake

PHALLU
6396 Pallûw' (1),
distinguished

PHALTI
6406 Palṭiy (1), delivered

PHALTIEL
6409 Palṭiy'êl (1),
deliverance of God

PHANUEL
5323 Phanŏuēl (1), face
of God

PHARAOH
6547 Par'ôh (221), Paroh
5328 Pharaō (3), Pharaoh

PHARAOH'S
6547 Par'ôh (46), Paroh
5328 Pharaō (2), Pharaoh

PHARAOH-HOPHRA
6548 Par'ôh Chophra'
(1), Paroh-Chophra

PHARAOH-NECHO
6549 Par'ôh Nᵉkôh (1),
Paroh-Nekoh (or -Neko)

PHARAOH-NECHOH
6549 Par'ôh Nᵉkôh (4),
Paroh-Nekoh (or -Neko)

PHARES
5329 Pharĕs (3), breech

PHAREZ
6557 Perets (12), breech

PHARISEE
5330 Pharisaiŏs (10),
separatist

PHARISEE'S
5330 Pharisaiŏs (2),
separatist

PHARISEES
5330 Pharisaiŏs (86),
separatist

PHARISEES'
5330 Pharisaiŏs (1),
separatist

PHAROSH
6551 Par'ôsh (1), flea

PHARPAR
6554 Parpar (1), rapid

PHARZITES
6558 Partsiy (1), Partsite

PHASEAH
6454 Pâçêach (1), limping

PHEBE
5402 Phŏibē (2), bright

PHENICE
5403 Phŏinikē (2),
palm-country
5405 Phŏinix (1),
palm-tree

PHENICIA
5403 Phŏinikē (1),
palm-country

PHICHOL
6369 Pîykôl (3), mouth of
all

PHILADELPHIA
5359 Philadĕlphĕia (2),
fraternal

PHILEMON
5371 Philēmōn (2),
friendly

PHILETUS
5372 Philētŏs (1), amiable

PHILIP
5376 Philippŏs (33), fond
of horses

PHILIP'S
5376 Philippŏs (3), fond
of horses

PHILIPPI
5375 Philippŏi (8),
Philippi

PHILIPPIANS
5374 Philippēsiŏs (1),
native of Philippi

PHILISTIA
6429 Pᵉlesheth (3),
migratory

PHILISTIM
6430 Pᵉlishtiy (1),
Pelishtite

PHILISTINE
6430 Pᵉlishtiy (33),
Pelishtite

PHILISTINES
6430 Pᵉlishtiy (250),
Pelishtite

PHILISTINES'
6430 Pᵉlishtiy (4),
Pelishtite

PHILOLOGUS
5378 Philŏlŏgŏs (1),
argumentative, learned

PHILOSOPHERS
5386 philŏsŏphŏs (1), one
fond of wise things, i.e.
philosopher

PHILOSOPHY
5385 philŏsŏphia (1),
wise things

PHINEHAS
6372 Pîynᵉchâç (24),
mouth of a serpent

PHINEHAS'
6372 Pîynᵉchâç (1),
mouth of a serpent

PHLEGON
5393 Phlĕgōn (1), blazing

PHRYGIA
5435 Phrugia (4), Phrygia

PHURAH
6513 Pûrâh (2), foliage

PHUT
6316 Pûwṭ (2), Put

PHUVAH
6312 Pûw'âh (1), blast

PHYGELLUS
5436 Phugĕllŏs (1),
fugitive

PHYLACTERIES
5440 phulaktēriŏn (1),
guard-case

PHYSICIAN
7495 râphâ' (1), to cure,
heal
2395 iatrŏs (5), physician

PHYSICIANS
7495 râphâ' (4), to cure,
heal

2395 iatrŏs (2), physician

PI-BESETH
6364 Pîy-Beçeth (1),
Pi-Beseth

PI-HAHIROTH
6367 Piy ha-Chîrôth (4),
mouth of the gorges

PICK
5365 nâqar (1), to bore;
to gouge

PICTURES
4906 maskîyth (2),
carved figure
7914 sᵉkîyâh (1),
conspicuous object

PIECE
95 'ăgôwrâh (1), coin
829 'eshpâr (2), portion
915 bâdâl (1), part
1335 bether (1), piece
2513 chelqâh (3),
flattery; allotment
3603 kikkâr (2), round
loaf; talent
4060 middâh (7),
measure; portion
4749 miqshâh (1), work
molded by hammering
5409 nêthach (2),
fragment
6400 pelach (6), slice
6595 path (2), bit, morsel
1406 drachmē (2), coin
1915 ĕpiblēma (4), patch
3313 mĕrŏs (1), division
or share
4138 plērōma (1), what
fills; what is filled

PIECES
1506 gezer (1), portion,
piece
1917 haddâm (Ch.) (2),
bit, piece
5409 nêthach (9),
fragment
6595 path (3), bit, morsel
7168 qera' (3), rag, torn
pieces
7518 rats (1), fragment
1288 diaspaō (1), to sever
or dismember
1406 drachmē (1), coin

PIERCE
4272 mâchats (1), to
crush; to subdue
5344 nâqab (2), to
puncture, perforate
1330 diĕrchŏmai (1), to
traverse, travel through

PIERCED
738 'ărîy (1), lion
1856 dâqar (1), to stab,
pierce
4272 mâchats (1), to
crush; to subdue
5365 nâqar (1), to bore;
to gouge
1574 ĕkkĕntĕō (2), to
pierce or impale
3572 nussŏ (1), to pierce,
stab
4044 pĕripĕirō (1), to
penetrate entirely

PIERCETH
5344 nâqab (1), to
puncture, perforate

2395 iatrŏs (2), physician

PIERCING
1281 bârîyach (1),
fleeing, gliding serpent
1338 diïknĕŏmai (1),
penetrate, pierce

PIERCINGS
4094 madqârâh (1),
wound

PIETY
2151 ĕusĕbĕō (1), to put
show piety toward

PIGEON
1469 gôwzâl (1), young of
a bird
3123 yôwnâh (1), dove

PIGEONS
3123 yôwnâh (9), dove
4058 pĕristĕra (1),
pigeon, dove

PILATE
4091 Pilatŏs (55), firm

PILDASH
6394 Pildâsh (1), Pildash

PILE
4071 mᵉdûwrâh (2), pile

PILEHA
6401 Pilchâ' (1), slicing

PILGRIMAGE
4033 mâgûwr (4), abode

PILGRIMS
3927 parepidēmŏs (2),
resident foreigner

PILLAR
4676 matstsêbâh (10),
column or stone
4678 matstsebeth (4),
stock of a tree
5324 nâtsab (1), to station
5333 nᵉtsîyb (1), military
post; statue
5982 'ammûwd (29),
column, pillar
4769 stulŏs (2),
supporting pillar; leader

PILLARS
547 'ômᵉnâh (1), column
4552 miç'âd (1),
balustrade for stairs
4676 matstsêbâh (2),
column or stone
4690 mâtsûwq (1),
column; hilltop
5982 'ammûwd (79),
column, pillar
8490 tîymârâh (2),
column, i.e. cloud
4769 stulŏs (2),
supporting pillar; leader

PILLED
6478 pâtsal (2), to peel

PILLOW
3523 kᵉbîyr (2), matrass,
quilt of animal hair
4344 prŏskĕphalaiŏn (1),
cushion pillow

PILLOWS
3704 keçeth (2), cushion
or pillow
4763 mᵉra'ăshâh (2),
headpiece; head-rest

PILOTS
2259 chôbêl (4), sailor

PILTAI
6408 Pilṭay (1), *Piltai*

PIN
3489 yâthêd (3), tent *peg*

PINE
2100 zûwb (1), to *waste away*
4743 mâqaq (4), to *melt; to flow, dwindle, vanish*
6086+8081 'êts (1), *wood*
8410 tidhâr (2), *lasting tree* (poss.) *oak*

PINETH
3583 xērainō (1), to *shrivel, to mature*

PINING
1803 dallâh (1), loose *hair; indigent, needy*

PINNACLE
4419 ptĕrugiŏn (2), *winglet*, i.e. *extremity*

PINON
6373 Pîynôn (2), *Pinon*

PINS
3489 yâthêd (10), tent *peg*

PIPE
2485 châlîyl (3), *flute*
836 aulŏs (1), *flute*

PIPED
2490 châlal (1), to *play the flute*
832 aulĕō (3), to play the *flute*

PIPERS
834 aulētēs (1), *flute-player*

PIPES
2485 châlîyl (3), *flute instrument*
4166 mûwtsâqâh (1), *tube*
5345 neqeb (1), *bezel, gem mounting*
6804 tsantârâh (1), *tube, pipe*

PIRAM
6502 Pir'âm (1), *wildly*

PIRATHON
6552 Pir'âthôwn (1), *chieftaincy*

PIRATHONITE
6553 Pir'âthôwnîy (5), *Pirathonite*

PISGAH
6449 Piçgâh (5), *cleft*

PISIDIA
4099 Pisidia (2), *Pisidia*

PISON
6376 Pîyshôwn (1), *dispersive*

PISPAH
6462 Piçpâh (1), *dispersion*

PISS
7890 shayin (2), *urine*

PISSETH
8366 shâthan (6), to *urinate* as a male

PIT
875 bᵉ'êr (3), *well, cistern*
953 bôwr (41), pit *hole, cistern, well; prison*
1360 gebe' (1), *reservoir*

1475 gûwmmâts (1), *pit*
6354 pachath (8), *pit* for catching animals
7585 shᵉ'ôwl (3), abode of the *dead*
7743+7882 shûwach (1), to *sink*
7745 shûwchâh (2), *chasm*
7816 shᵉchûwth (1), *pit*
7845 shachath (14), *pit; destruction*
7882 shîychâh (1), *pit*-fall
999 bŏthunŏs (1), *cistern, pit-hole*
5421 phrĕar (5), *cistern* or water *well; abyss*

PITCH
167 'âhal (1), to pitch a *tent*
2203 zepheth (3), *asphalt*
2583 chânâh (11), to *encamp*
3724 kôpher (1), *village; bitumen; henna*
6965 qûwm (1), to *rise*
8628 tâqa' (1), to *clatter, slap, drive, clasp*

PITCHED
167 'âhal (1), to pitch a *tent*
2583 chânâh (70), to *encamp*
5186 nâṭâh (8), to *stretch* or spread out
8628 tâqa' (2), to *clatter, slap, drive, clasp*
4078 pĕgnumi (1), to *set up* a tent

PITCHER
3537 kad (10), *jar, pitcher*
2765 kĕramiŏn (2), *earthenware vessel*

PITCHERS
3537 kad (4), *jar, pitcher*
5035 nebel (1), skin-*bag* for liquids; *vase; lyre*

PITHOM
6619 Pîthôm (1), *Pithom*

PITHON
6377 Pîythôwn (2), *expansive*

PITIED
2347 chûwç (1), to be *compassionate*
2550 châmal (4), to *spare, have pity on*
7356 racham (1), *compassion; womb*

PITIETH
4263 machmâl (1), *delight*
7355 râcham (2), to be *compassionate*

PITIFUL
7362 rachmânîy (1), *compassionate*
2155 ĕusplagchnŏs (1), *compassionate*
4184 pŏlusplagchnŏs (1), *extremely compassionate*

PITS
953 bôwr (1), pit *hole, cistern, well; prison*

1356 gêb (1), *well, cistern; pit*
7745 shûwchâh (1), *chasm*
7825 shᵉchîyth (1), *pit-fall*
7882 shîychâh (1), *pit-fall*

PITY
2347 chûwç (6), to be *compassionate*
2550 châmal (14), to *spare, have pity on*
2551 chemlâh (1), *commiseration, pity*
2603 chânan (3), to *implore*
2617 cheçed (1), *kindness, favor*
5110 nûwd (1), to *console, deplore; to taunt*
7355 râcham (1), to be *compassionate*
7356 racham (1), *compassion; womb*
1653 ĕlĕĕō (1), to give out *compassion*

PLACE
870 'âthar (Ch.) (5), *after*
1004 bayith (7), *house; temple; family, tribe*
1367 gᵉbûwlâh (1), *region*
3027 yâd (7), *hand; power*
3241 Yânîym (1), *asleep*
3427 yâshab (2), to *dwell, to remain; to settle*
3653 kên (1), *pedestal* or *station* of a basin
4349 mâkôwn (11), *basis; place*
4612 ma'ămâd (1), *position; attendant*
4634 ma'ărâkâh (1), *arrangement, row; pile*
4724 miqvâh (1), water *reservoir*
4725 mâqôwm (373), general *locality, place*
4800 merchâb (1), *open space; liberty*
5182 nᵉchath (Ch.) (1), to *descend; to depose*
5414 nâthan (3), to *give*
5977 'ômed (6), fixed *spot*
6607 pethach (1), *opening; door*
7675 shebeth (1), *abode* or *locality*
7760 sûwm (1), to *place*
7931 shâkan (5), to *reside*
8414 tôhûw (1), *waste, desolation, formless*
8478 tachath (17), *bottom; underneath*
201 akrŏatēriŏn (1), *audience-room*
402 anachōrĕō (1), to *retire, withdraw*
1502 ĕikō (1), to be weak, i.e. *yield*
1564 ĕkĕithĕn (1), *from there*
1786 ĕntŏpiŏs (1), local *resident*
3692 ŏpē (1), *hole*, i.e. *cavern; spring* of water
3699 hŏpŏu (1), *at whichever* spot
4042 pĕriŏchē (1), *passage* of Scripture

5117 tŏpŏs (74), *place*
5562 chōrĕō (1), to *pass, enter; to hold, admit*
5564 chōriŏn (2), *spot* or *plot* of ground
5602 hōdĕ (2), *here*

PLACED
776 'erets (1), *earth, land, soil; country*
3240 yânach (2), to *allow to stay*
3427 yâshab (5), to *dwell, to remain; to settle*
3947 lâqach (1), to *take*
5414 nâthan (5), to *give*
5975 'âmad (1), to *stand*
7760 sûwm (1), to *place*
7931 shâkan (2), to *reside*

PLACES
168 'ôhel (1), *tent*
1004 bayith (9), *house; temple; family, tribe*
2723 chorbâh (1), *desolation, dry* desert
3027 yâd (1), *hand; power*
4585 mᵉ'ôwnâh (1), *abode*
4725 mâqôwm (20), general *locality, place*
5439 çâbîyb (1), *circle; environs; around*
8478 tachath (1), *bottom; underneath; in lieu of*
3837 pantachŏu (1), *universally, everywhere*
5117 tŏpŏs (7), *place*

PLAGUE
4046 maggêphâh (20), *pestilence; defeat*
4347 makkâh (1), *blow; wound; pestilence*
5061 nega' (64), *infliction, affliction; leprous spot*
5063 negeph (7), *infliction* of disease
3148 mastix (2), *flogging device*
4127 plĕgē (2), *stroke; wound; calamity*

PLAGUED
4046 maggêphâh (1), *pestilence; defeat*
5060 nâga' (3), to *strike*
5062 nâgaph (2), to *inflict* a disease

PLAGUES
1698 deber (1), *pestilence, plague*
4046 maggêphâh (1), *pestilence; defeat*
4347 makkâh (8), *blow; wound; pestilence*
5061 nega' (1), *infliction, affliction; leprous spot*
3148 mastix (2), *flogging device*
4127 plĕgē (10), *stroke; wound; calamity*

PLAIN
58 'âbêl (1), *meadow*
436 'êlôwn (7), *oak*
874 bâ'ar (1), to *explain*
1236 biq'â' (Ch.) (1), wide level *valley*
1237 biq'âh (7), wide level *valley*

3603 kikkâr (13), *tract* or
region; round *loaf*
4334 mîyshôwr (14),
plain; justice
5228 nâkôach (1),
equitable, correct
5549 çâlal (1), to *mound
up;* to *exalt;* to *oppose*
6160 'ărâbâh (22), *desert,
wasteland*
7737 shâvâh (1), to *level,*
i.e. *equalize*
8219 sh°phêlâh (3),
lowland,
8535 tâm (1), morally
pious; gentle, dear
3723 ŏrthōs (1), *correctly,
rightly*
5117+3977 tŏpŏs (1),
place

PLAINLY
559 'âmar (1), to *say*
874 bâ'ar (1), to *explain*
1540 gâlâh (1), to
denude; uncover
5046 nâgad (1), to
announce
6568 p°rash (Ch.) (1), to
specify, translate
6703 tsach (1), *dazzling,*
i.e. *sunny, bright*
1718 ĕmphanizō (1), to
show forth
3954 parrhēsia (4),
frankness, boldness

PLAINNESS
3954 parrhēsia (1),
frankness, boldness

PLAINS
436 'êlôwn (2), *oak*
4334 mîyshôwr (1), *plain;
justice*
6160 'ărâbâh (20), *desert,
wasteland*
8219 sh°phêlâh (2),
lowland,

PLAISTER
1528 gîyr (Ch.) (1), *lime
for plaster*
2902 ţûwach (1), to
whitewash
4799 mârach (1), to
apply by rubbing
7874 sîyd (2), to *plaster,
whitewash* with lime

PLAISTERED
2902 ţûwach (2), to
whitewash

PLAITING
1708 ĕmplŏkē (1),
braiding of the hair

PLANES
4741 maqtsû'âh (1),
wood-carving *chisel*

PLANETS
4208 mazzâlâh (1),
constellations

PLANKS
5646 'âb (1), *architrave*
6086 'êts (1), *wood,*
things made of *wood*
6763 tsêlâ' (1), *side*

PLANT
4302 maţţâ' (1),
something *planted*
5193 nâţa' (31), to *plant*

5194 neţa' (3), *plant;
plantation; planting*
5414 nâthan (1), to *give*
7880 sîyach (1),
shrubbery
8362 shâthal (2), to
transplant
5451 phuţěia (1), *shrub*
or *vegetable*

PLANTATION
4302 maţţâ' (1),
something *planted*

PLANTED
5193 nâţa' (21), to *plant*
8362 shâthal (8), to
transplant
4854 sumphutŏs (1),
closely *united* to
5452 phuţěuō (8), to
implant, i.e. to *instill*
doctrine

PLANTEDST
5193 nâţa' (2), to *plant*

PLANTERS
5193 nâţa' (1), to *plant*

PLANTETH
5192 nêţel (2), *burden*
5452 phuţěuō (3), to
implant, i.e. to *instill*

PLANTING
4302 maţţâ' (2),
something *planted*

PLANTINGS
4302 maţţâ' (1),
something *planted*

PLANTS
4302 maţţâ' (1),
something *planted*
5189 n°ţîyshâh (1),
tendril plant shoot
5194 neţa' (2), *plant;
plantation; planting*
5195 nâţîya' (1), *plant*
7973 shelach (1), *spear;
shoot* of growth
8291 sarûwq (1), choice
grapevine
8363 sh°thîyl (1), *sucker*
plant

PLAT
2513 chelqâh (2),
smoothness; flattery

PLATE
6731 tsîyts (3), burnished
plate; bright *flower*

PLATES
3871 lûwach (1), *tablet*
5633 çeren (1), *axle; peer*
6341 pach (2), thin
metallic *sheet; net*

PLATTED
4120 plěkō (3), to *twine*
or *braid*

PLATTER
3953 parŏpsis (2),
side-dish receptacle
4094 pinax (1), *plate,
platter, dish*

PLAY
5059 nâgan (4), to *play;*
to *make music*
6711 tsâchaq (1), to
laugh; to *make sport* of

7832 sâchaq (5), to
laugh; to *scorn;* to *play*
8173 shâ'a' (1), to *fondle,
please* or *amuse* (self)
3815 paizō (1), to *indulge
in* (sexual) *revelry*

PLAYED
5059 nâgan (4), to *play;*
to *make music*
7832 sâchaq (3), to
laugh; to *scorn;* to *play*

PLAYER
5059 nâgan (1), to *play;*
to *make music*

PLAYERS
2490 châlal (1), to *play*
the flute
5059 nâgan (1), to *play;*
to *make music*

PLAYING
5059 nâgan (1), to *play;*
to *make music*
7832 sâchaq (2), to
laugh; to *scorn;* to *play*

PLEA
1779 dîyn (1), *judge;
judgment; law suit*

PLEAD
1777 dîyn (2), to *judge;* to
strive or *contend for*
3198 yâkach (3), to *be
correct;* to *argue*
7378 rîyb (23), to *hold a
controversy;* to *defend*
8199 shâphaţ (9), to *judge*

PLEADED
7378 rîyb (2), to *hold a
controversy;* to *defend*
8199 shâphaţ (1), to *judge*

PLEADETH
7378 rîyb (1), to *hold a
controversy;* to *defend*
8199 shâphaţ (1), to *judge*

PLEADINGS
7379 rîyb (1), *contest,*
personal or legal

PLEASANT
2530 châmad (3), to
delight in; *lust for*
2531 chemed (2), *delight*
2532 chemdâh (11),
delight
2580 chên (1),
graciousness; beauty
2656 chêphets (1),
pleasure; desire
2896 ţôwb (2), *good; well*
3303 yâpheh (1),
beautiful; handsome
4022 meged (3), *valuable*
4261 machmâd (5),
delightful
4262 machmûd (3),
desired; valuable
4999 nâ'âh (1), *home,
dwelling; pasture*
5116 nâveh (1), *at home;
lovely; home*
5273 nâ'îym (8),
delightful; sweet
5276 nâ'êm (5), to *be
agreeable*
5278 no'am (2),
agreeableness, delight
6027 ôneg (1), *luxury*
6148 'ârab (1), to *intermix*

6643 ts°bîy (1),
conspicuous splendor
8191 sha'shûa' (2),
enjoyment
8378 ta'ăvâh (1), *longing;
delight*
8588 ta'ănûwg (1),
luxury; delight

PLEASANTNESS
5278 no'am (1),
agreeableness

PLEASE
2654 châphêts (5), to *be
pleased* with, *desire*
2655 châphêts (1),
pleased with
2894 ţûw' (3), to *sweep
away*
2895 ţowb (6), to *be good*
2896 ţôwb (2), *good; well*
3190 yâţab (2), to *be,
make well*
3477+5869 yâshâr (1),
straight
5606 çâphaq (1), to *be
enough;* to *vomit*
7451+5869 ra' (1), *bad;
evil*
7521 râtsâh (3), to *be
pleased with;* to *satisfy*
700 arĕskō (11), to *seek
to please*
701 arĕstŏs (1),
agreeable; desirable; fit
2001+1511 ĕpischuō (1),
to *insist stoutly*
2100 ĕuarĕstĕō (1), to
gratify entirely, please

PLEASED
2654 châphêts (8), to *be
pleased* with, *desire*
2895 ţowb (1), to *be good*
2896+5869 ţôwb (1),
good; well
2974 yâ'al (1), to *assent;*
to *undertake, begin*
3190 yâţab (2), to *be,
make well*
3190+5869 yâţab (10), to
be, make well
3477+5869 yâshâr (7),
straight
7451+5869 ra' (1), *bad;
evil*
7521 râtsâh (4), to *be
pleased with;* to *satisfy*
8232 sh°phar (Ch.) (1), to
be beautiful
700 arĕskō (5), to *seek to
please*
701 arĕstŏs (1),
agreeable; desirable; fit
1380 dŏkĕō (2), to *think,
regard, seem good*
2100 ĕuarĕstĕō (2), to
gratify entirely, please
2106 ĕudŏkĕō (12), to
think well, i.e. *approve*
2309 thĕlō (2), to *will;* to
desire; to *choose*
4909 sunĕudŏkĕō (2), to
assent to, feel gratified

PLEASETH
2654 châphêts (1), to *be
pleased* with, *desire*
2896+5869 ţôwb (2),
good; well

English

2896+6440 ṭôwb (1), *good; well*
3190+5869 yâṭab (1), to *be, make well*
3477+5869 yâshâr (1), *straight*

PLEASING
2896 ṭôwb (1), *good; well*
6148 'ârab (1), to *give or be security*
699 arĕskĕia (1), *complaisance, amiable*
700 arĕskŏ (2), to *seek to please*
701 arĕstŏs (1), *agreeable; desirable; fit*

PLEASURE
185+5315 'avvâh (1), *longing*
2654 châphêts (3), to be *pleased* with, *desire*
2655 châphêts (2), *pleased* with
2656 chêphets (16), *pleasure; desire*
2837 chêsheq (1), *delight, desired* thing
2896 ṭôwb (2), *good; well*
5315 nephesh (2), *life; breath; soul; wind*
5730 'êden (1), *pleasure*
6148 'ârab (1), to *give or be security*
7470 rᵉ'ûwth (Ch.) (1), *desire*
7521 râtsâh (6), to be *pleased with; to satisfy* a debt
7522 râtsôwn (5), *delight*
8057 simchâh (1), *blithesomeness* or *glee*
2106 ĕudŏkĕō (6), to *think well*, i.e. *approve*
2107 ĕudŏkia (4), *delight, kindness, wish*
2237 hēdŏnē (1), *delight; desire*
2307 thĕlēma (1), *decree; inclination*
3588+1380 hŏ (1), *"the,"* i.e. the definite article
4684 spatalaŏ (1), to *live in luxury*
4909 sunĕudŏkĕō (1), to *assent to, feel gratified*
5171 truphaŏ (1), to *indulge in luxury*
5485 charis (2), *gratitude; benefit given*

PLEASURES
5273 nâ'iym (2), *delightful; sweet*
5719 'âdiyn (1), *voluptuous*
5730 'êden (1), *pleasure*
2237 hēdŏnē (2), *delight; desire*
5569 psĕudadĕlphŏs (1), *pretended associate*

PLEDGE
2254 châbal (10), to *bind* by a *pledge;* to *pervert*
2258 châbôl (4), *pawn, pledge* as security
5667 'ăbôwṭ (4), *pledged* item
6161 'ărubbâh (1), as *security; bondsman*

6162 'ărâbôwn (3), *pawn, security pledge*

PLEDGES
6148 'ârab (2), to *give or be security*

PLEIADES
3598 Kîymâh (2), *cluster* of stars, *Pleiades*

PLENTEOUS
1277 bârîy' (1), *fatted* or *plump; healthy*
3498 yâthar (2), to *remain* or be *left*
7227 rab (3), *great*
7235 râbâh (1), to *increase*
7647 sâbâ' (2), *copiousness*
8082 shâmên (1), *rich; fertile*
4180 pŏlulŏgia (1), *prolixity, wordiness*

PLENTEOUSNESS
4195 môwthar (1), *gain; superiority*
7647 sâbâ' (1), *copiousness*

PLENTIFUL
3759 karmel (3), planted field; garden *produce*
5071 nᵉdâbâh (1), *abundant* gift

PLENTIFULLY
3499 yether (1), *remainder; small rope*
7230 rôb (1), *abundance*
2164 ĕuphŏrĕō (1), to be *fertile, produce a crop*

PLENTY
398 'âkal (1), to *eat*
4723 miqveh (1), *confidence; collection*
7230 rôb (3), *abundance*
7235 râbâh (1), to *increase*
7646 sâba' (2), *fill to satiety*
7647 sâbâ' (4), *copiousness*
8443 tôw'âphâh (1), *treasure; speed*

PLOTTETH
2161 zâmam (1), to *plan*

PLOUGH
723 arŏtrŏn (1), *plow*

PLOW
2790 chârash (6), to *engrave; to plow*
722 arŏtriŏŏ (1), to *plough, make furrows*

PLOWED
2790 chârash (5), to *engrave; to plow*

PLOWERS
2790 chârash (1), to *engrave; to plow*

PLOWETH
722 arŏtriŏŏ (1), to *plough, make furrows*

PLOWING
2790 chârash (2), to *engrave; to plow*
5215 nîyr (1), freshly *plowed* land

722 arŏtriŏŏ (1), to *plough, make furrows*

PLOWMAN
2790 chârash (2), to *engrave; to plow*

PLOWMEN
406 'ikkâr (2), *farmer*

PLOWSHARES
855 'êth (3), *digging implement*

PLUCK
717 'ârâh (1), to *pluck, pick fruit*
1497 gâzal (2), to *rob*
3318 yâtsâ' (1), to *go, bring out*
3615 kâlâh (1), to *cease, be finished, perish*
5255 nâçach (1), to *tear away*
5375 nâsâ' (1), to *lift up*
5423 nâthaq (2), to *tear off*
5428 nâthash (10), to *tear away, be uprooted*
5493 çûwr (1), to *turn off*
6131 'âqar (1), to *pluck up roots; to hamstring*
6998 qâṭaph (1), to *strip off, pick off*
8045 shâmad (1), to *desolate*
726 harpazō (2), to *seize*
1544 ĕkballō (1), to *throw out*
1807 ĕxairĕō (1), to *tear out; to select; to release*
1808 ĕxairō (1), to *remove, drive away*
5089 tillō (2), to *pull off* grain heads

PLUCKED
1497 gâzal (2), to *rob*
3318 yâtsâ' (1), to *go, bring out*
4803 mâraṭ (3), to *polish; to make bald*
4804 mᵉraṭ (Ch.) (1), to *pull off, tear off*
5255 nâçach (1), to *tear away*
5337 nâtsal (2), to be *snatched away*
5423 nâthaq (1), to *tear off*
5428 nâthash (4), to *tear away, be uprooted*
6132 'âqar (Ch.) (1), to *pluck up roots*
7993 shâlak (1), to *throw out, down or away*
8025 shâlaph (1), to *pull out, up or off*
1288 diaspaŏ (1), to *sever or dismember*
1610 ĕkrizŏŏ (2), to *uproot*
1846 ĕxŏrussŏ (1), to *dig out*
5089 tillō (1), to *pull off* grain heads

PLUCKETH
2040 hâraç (1), to *pull down; break, destroy*

PLUCKT
2965 ṭârâph (1), freshly *picked vegetation*

PLUMBLINE
594 'ănâk (4), *plumb-line, plummet*

PLUMMET
68+913 'eben (1), *stone*
4949 mishqeleth (2), *plummet* weight

PLUNGE
2881 ṭâbal (1), to *dip*

POCHERETH
6380 Pôkereth Tsᵉbâyîym (2), *trap of gazelles*

POETS
4163 pŏiētēs (1), *performer; poet*

POINT
19 'ibchâh (1), *brandishing* of a sword
184 'âvâh (1), to *extend* or *mark* out
1980 hâlak (1), to *walk; live a certain way*
6856 tsippôren (1), *nail; point* of a style or pen
8376 tâ'âh (2), to *mark off*, i.e. *designate*
2079 ĕschatŏs (1), *finally*, i.e. *at the extremity*
3195 mĕllō (1), to *intend*, i.e. *be about to*

POINTED
2742 chârûwts (1), *threshing-sledge*

POINTS
5980 'ummâh (1), *near, beside, along with*

POISON
2534 chêmâh (5), *heat; anger; poison*
7219 rô'sh (1), *poisonous plant; poison*
2447 iŏs (2), *corrosion; venom*

POLE
5251 nêç (2), *flag; signal; token*

POLICY
7922 sekel (1), *intelligence; success*

POLISHED
1305 bârar (1), to *brighten; purify*
2404 châṭab (1), to *chop or carve* wood
7044 qâlâl (1), *brightened, polished*

POLISHING
1508 gizrâh (1), *figure, appearance; enclosure*

POLL
1494 gâzaz (1), to *shear; shave; destroy*
1538 gulgôleth (1), *skull*
3697 kâçam (1), to *shear, clip*

POLLED
1548 gâlach (3), to *shave; to lay waste*

POLLS
1538 gulgôleth (6), *skull*

POLLUTE
2490 châlal (8), to *profane, defile*

2610 chânêph (1), to *soil, be defiled*
2930 ţâmê' (2), to *be morally contaminated*

POLLUTED
947 bûwç (2), to *trample down; oppress*
1351 gâ'al (7), to *soil, stain; desecrate*
2490 châlal (13), to *profane, defile*
2610 chânêph (3), to *soil, be defiled*
2930 ţâmê' (12), to *be morally contaminated*
2931 ţâmê' (1), *foul; ceremonially impure*
6121 'âqôb (1), *fraudulent; tracked*
2840 kŏinŏŏ (1), to *make profane*

POLLUTING
2490 châlal (2), to *profane, defile*

POLLUTION
2931 ţâmê' (1), *foul; ceremonially impure*

POLLUTIONS
234 alisgĕma (1), *ceremonially polluted*
3393 miasma (1), *foulness, corruption*

POLLUX
1359 Diŏskŏurŏi (1), *twins of Zeus*

POMEGRANATE
7416 rimmôwn (10), *pomegranate*

POMEGRANATES
7416 rimmôwn (22), *pomegranate*

POMMELS
1543 gullâh (3), *fountain; bowl or globe*

POMP
1347 gâ'ôwn (5), *ascending; majesty*
7588 shâ'ôwn (1), *uproar; destruction*
5325 phantasia (1), vain *show, i.e. pomp*

PONDER
6424 pâlaç (2), to *weigh mentally*

PONDERED
4820 sumballō (1), to *consider; to aid; to join, attack*

PONDERETH
6424 pâlaç (1). to *weigh mentally*
8505 tâkan (2), to *balance, i.e. measure*

PONDS
98 'ăgam (2), *marsh; pond; pool*
99 'âgêm (1), *sad*

PONTIUS
4194 Pŏntiŏs (4), *bridged*

PONTUS
4195 Pŏntŏs (3), *sea*

POOL
98 'ăgam (2), *marsh; pond; pool*

1295 bᵉrêkâh (15), *reservoir, pool*
2861 kŏlumbēthra (5), *pond*

POOLS
98 'ăgam (2), *marsh; pond; pool*
1293 bᵉrâkâh (1), *benediction, blessing*
1295 bᵉrêkâh (1), *reservoir, pool*
4723 miqveh (1), *confidence; collection*

POOR
34 'ebyôwn (25), *destitute; poor*
1800 dal (44), *weak, thin; humble, needy*
1803 dallâh (4), *indigent, needy*
2489 chêlᵉkâ' (3), *unhappy wretch*
3423 yârash (2), to *impoverish; to ruin*
4134 mûwk (4), to *be impoverished*
4270 machçôwr (1), *impoverishment*
4542 miçkên (4), *indigent, needy*
6033 'ănâh (Ch.) (1), to *afflict, be afflicted*
6035 'ânâv (1), *needy; oppressed*
6035+6041 'ânâv (3), *needy; oppressed*
6041 'ânîy (56), *depressed*
7326 rûwsh (21), to *be destitute*
3993 pĕnēs (1), *poor*
3998 pĕnichrŏs (1), *needy, impoverished*
4433 ptōchĕuŏ (1), to *become indigent, poor*
4434 ptōchŏs (31), *pauper, beggar*

POORER
4134 mûwk (1), to *be impoverished*

POOREST
1803 dallâh (1), *indigent, needy*

POPLAR
3839 libneh (1), *whitish tree, (poss.) storax*

POPLARS
3839 libneh (1), *whitish tree, (poss.) storax*

POPULOUS
527 'âmôwn (1), *crowd*
7227 rab (1), *great*

PORATHA
6334 Pôwrâthâ' (1), *Poratha*

PORCH
197 'ûwlâm (33), *vestibule, portico*
4528 miçdᵉrôwn (1), *colonnade or portico*
4259 prŏauliŏn (1), *vestibule, i.e. alley-way*
4440 pulōn (1), *gate-way, door-way*
4745 stŏa (3), *colonnade or interior piazza*

PORCHES
197 'ûwlâm (1), *vestibule, portico*
4745 stŏa (1), *colonnade or interior piazza*

PORCIUS
4201 Pŏrkiŏs (1), *swinish*

PORT
8179 sha'ar (1), *opening, i.e. door or gate*

PORTER
7778 shôw'êr (4), *janitor, door-keeper*
2377 thurōrŏs (2), *gate-warden, doorkeeper*

PORTERS
7778 shôw'êr (31), *janitor, door-keeper*
8179 sha'ar (1), *opening, i.e. door or gate*
8652 târâ' (Ch.) (1), *doorkeeper*

PORTION
270 'âchaz (2), to *seize, grasp; possess*
1697 dâbâr (4), *word; matter; thing*
2256 chebel (2), *company, band*
2505 châlaq (1), to *be smooth; be slippery*
2506 chêleq (36), *allotment*
2508 chălâq (Ch.) (3), *part, portion*
2513 chelqâh (6), *allotment*
2706 chôq (3), *appointment; allotment*
4490 mânâh (4), *ration; lot or portion*
4521 mᵉnâth (4), *allotment*
6310 peh (2), *mouth; opening*
6598 pathbag (5), *dainty food*
7926 shᵉkem (1), *neck; spur of a hill*
3313 mĕrŏs (3), *division or share*
4620 sitŏmĕtrŏn (1), *allowance or ration*

PORTIONS
2256 chebel (2), *company, band*
2506 chêleq (4), *allotment*
4256 machălôqeth (1), *section or division*
4490 mânâh (6), *ration; lot or portion*
4521 mᵉnâth (3), *allotment*

POSSESS
423 'âlâh (2), *public agreement*
2631 chăçan (Ch.) (1), to *take possession*
3423 yârash (93), to *inherit; to impoverish*
5157 nâchal (5), to *inherit*
2932 ktaŏmai (3), to *get*

POSSESSED
270 'âchaz (1), to *seize, grasp; possess*

2631 chăçan (Ch.) (1), to *take possession*
3423 yârash (19), to *inherit; to impoverish*
7069 qânâh (3), to *create; to procure*
1139 daimŏnizŏmai (11), *to be demon-possessed*
2192 ĕchō (2), to *have; hold; keep*
2722 katĕchō (1), to *hold down fast*
5224 huparchŏnta (1), *property or possessions*

POSSESSEST
3423 yârash (1), to *inherit; to impoverish*

POSSESSETH
3423 yârash (1), to *inherit; to impoverish*
5224 huparchŏnta (1), *property or possessions*

POSSESSING
2722 katĕchō (1), to *hold down fast*

POSSESSION
270 'âchaz (1), to *seize, grasp; possess*
272 'ăchuzzâh (64), *possession*
3423 yârash (6), to *inherit; to impoverish*
3424 yᵉrêshâh (2), *occupancy*
3425 yᵉrushâh (11), *conquest*
4180 môwrâsh (1), *possession*
4181 môwrâshâh (6), *possession*
4735 miqneh (3), *live-stock*
4736 miqnâh (1), *acquisition*
5157 nâchal (1), to *inherit*
5159 nachălâh (1), *occupancy*
7272 regel (1), *foot; step*
2697 kataschĕsis (2), *occupancy, possession*
2933 ktēma (3), *estate; wealth, possessions*
4047 pĕripŏiēsis (1), *acquisition*

POSSESSIONS
270 'âchaz (3), to *seize, grasp; possess*
272 'ăchuzzâh (2), *possession*
4180 môwrâsh (1), *possession*
4639 ma'ăseh (1), *action; labor*
4735 miqneh (2), *live-stock*
2933 ktēma (3), *estate; wealth, possessions*
5564 chōriŏn (1), *spot or plot of ground*

POSSESSOR
7069 qânâh (3), to *create; to procure*

POSSESSORS
7069 qânâh (1), to *create; to procure*
2935 ktētŏr (1), land *owner*

English

POSSIBLE
102 adunatŏs (1), *weak; impossible*
1410 dunamai (1), to *be able* or *possible*
1415 dunatŏs (13), *capable; possible*

POST
352 'ayîl (4), *chief; ram; oak* tree
4201 m°zûwzâh (4), *door-post*
4947 mashqôwph (1), *lintel*
7323 rûwts (2), to *run*

POSTERITY
310 'achar (4), *after*
319 'achărîyth (3), *future; posterity*
1755 dôwr (1), *dwelling*
7611 sh°'êrîyth (1), *remainder* or *residual*

POSTS
352 'ayîl (17), *chief; ram; oak* tree
520 'ammâh (1), *cubit*
4201 m°zûwzâh (15), *door-post*
5592 çaph (3), *dish*
7323 rûwts (6), to *run*

POT
610 'âçûwk (1), oil-*flask*
1731 dûwd (1), *pot, kettle; basket*
3627 k°lîy (1), *implement, thing*
4715 mitsrêph (2), *crucible*
5518 çîyr (12), *thorn; hook*
6517 pârûwr (2), *skillet*
6803 tsintseneth (1), *vase, receptacle*
4713 stamnŏs (1), *jar* or earthen *tank*

POTENTATE
1413 dunastēs (1), *ruler* or *officer*

POTI-PHERAH
6319 Pôwṭîy Phera' (3), *Poti-Phera*

POTIPHAR
6318 Pôwṭîyphar (2), *Potiphar*

POTS
1375 g°bîya' (1), *goblet; bowl*
1731 dûwd (1), *pot, kettle; basket*
5518 çîyr (9), *thorn; hook*
8240 shâphâth (1), *hook; hearth*
3582 xěstēs (2), *vessel; measure*

POTSHERD
2789 cheres (4), *piece of earthenware pottery*

POTSHERDS
2789 cheres (1), *piece of earthenware pottery*

POTTAGE
5138 nâzîyd (6), *boiled soup* or *stew*

POTTER
3335 yâtsar (8), to *form; potter; to determine*
2763 kěramēus (1), *potter*
2764 kěramikŏs (1), *made of clay*

POTTER'S
3335 yâtsar (7), to *form; potter; to determine*
2763 kěramēus (2), *potter*

POTTERS
3335 yâtsar (1), to *form; potter; to determine*

POTTERS'
3335 yâtsar (1), to *form; potter; to determine*
6353 pechâr (Ch.) (1), *potter*

POUND
4488 mâneh (2), *fixed weight*
3046 litra (2), *12 oz. measure, i.e. a pound*
3414 mna (4), *certain weight*

POUNDS
4488 mâneh (2), *fixed weight*
3414 mna (5), *certain weight*

POUR
2212 zâqaq (1), to *strain, refine; extract, clarify*
3332 yâtsaq (13), to *pour* out
5042 nâba' (1), to *gush forth; to utter*
5064 nâgar (2), to *pour out; to deliver* over
5140 nâzal (2), to *drip, or shed* by trickling
5258 nâçak (6), to *pour* a *libation; to anoint*
5414 nâthan (1), to *give*
7324 rûwq (1), to *pour out, i.e. empty*
8210 shâphak (33), to *spill* forth; to *expend*
1632 ěkchěō (3), to *pour forth; to bestow*

POURED
2229 zâram (1), to *gush water, pour forth*
3251 yâçak (1), to *pour*
3332 yâtsaq (13), to *pour*
5064 nâgar (1), to *pour out; to deliver* over
5258 nâçak (10), to *pour* a *libation; to anoint*
5413 nâthak (13), to *flow forth, pour out*
6168 'ârâh (2), to *empty, pour out; demolish*
6694 tsûwq (2), to *pour out; melt*
7324 rûwq (1), to *pour out, i.e. empty*
8210 shâphak (25), to *spill* forth
8211 shephek (2), ash-*heap, dump*
906 ballō (1), to *throw*
1632 ěkchěō (9), to *pour forth; to bestow*
2708 katachěō (2), to *pour down* or *out*

POUREDST
8210 shâphak (1), to *spill* forth; to *expend*

POURETH
1811 dâlaph (1), to *drip*
5042 nâba' (2), to *gush forth; to utter*
5064 nâgar (1), to *pour out; to deliver* over
8210 shâphak (6), to *spill* forth; to *expend*
906 ballō (1), to *throw*

POURING
8210 shâphak (1), to *spill* forth; to *expend*

POURTRAY
2710 châqaq (1), to *engrave; to enact* laws

POURTRAYED
2707 châqah (2), to *carve; to delineate*
2710 châqaq (1), to *engrave; to enact* laws

POVERTY
2639 cheçer (1), *lack; destitution*
3423 yârash (3), to *impoverish; to ruin*
4270 machçôwr (1), *impoverishment*
7389 rêysh (7), *poverty*
4432 ptōchěia (3), *indigence, poverty*

POWDER
80 'âbâq (1), *fine dust; cosmetic powder*
1854 dâqaq (2), to *crush; crumble*
6083 'âphâr (3), *dust, earth, mud; clay*,
3039 likmaō (2), to *grind to powder*

POWDERS
81 'ăbâqâh (1), *cosmetic powder*

POWER
410 'êl (3), *mighty; the Almighty*
1369 g°bûwrâh (9), *force; valor; victory*
2220 z°rôwa' (3), *arm; foreleg; force, power*
2428 chayil (9), *army; wealth; virtue; strength*
2429 chayil (Ch.) (1), *army; strength; loud sound*
2632 chêçen (Ch.) (2), *strength, powerful rule*
3027 yâd (13), *hand; power*
3028 yad (Ch.) (1), *hand; power*
3201 yâkôl (1), to *be able*
3581 kôach (47), *force, might; strength*
3709 kaph (1), *hollow of hand; paw; sole of foot*
4475 memshâlâh (1), *rule; realm* or a *ruler*
4910 mâshal (2), to *rule*
5794 'az (1), *strong, vehement, harsh*
5797 'ôz (11), *strength*
5808 'izzûwz (1), *forcible; army*
6184 'ârîyts (1), *powerful* or *tyrannical*
7786 sûwr (1), to *rule, crown*
7980 shâlaṭ (3), to *dominate, i.e. govern*
7981 sh°lêṭ (Ch.) (1), to *dominate, i.e. govern*
7983 shiltôwn (2), *potentate*
7989 shallîyṭ (1), *prince* or *warrior*
8280 sârâh (2), to *prevail, contend*
8592 ta'ătsûmâh (1), *might*
8617 t°qûwmâh (1), *resistfulness*
8633 tôqeph (1), *might*
746 archē (1), *first in rank; first in time*
1325 didōmi (2), to *give*
1410 dunamai (1), to *be able* or *possible*
1411 dunamis (71), *force, power, miracle*
1415 dunatŏs (1), *powerful* or *capable; possible*
1849 ěxŏusia (61), *authority, power, right*
1850 ěxŏusiazō (3), to *control, master another*
2479 ischus (2), *forcefulness, power*
2904 kratŏs (6), *vigor, strength*
3168 měgalěiŏtēs (1), *grandeur* or *splendor*

POWERFUL
3581 kôach (1), *force, might; strength*
1756 ěněrgēs (1), *active, operative*
2478 ischurŏs (1), *forcible, powerful*

POWERS
1411 dunamis (6), *force, power, miracle*
1849 ěxŏusia (8), *authority, power, right*

PRACTISE
5953 'âlal (1), to *glean; to overdo*
6213 'âsâh (3), to *do* or *make*

PRACTISED
2790 chârash (1), to *engrave; to plow*
6213 'âsâh (1), to *do*

PRAETORIUM
4232 praitōriŏn (1), *governor's court-room*

PRAISE
1288 bârak (1), to *bless*
1974 hillûwl (1), *harvest celebration*
1984 hâlal (92), to *praise; thank; boast*
2167 zâmar (4), to *play music*
3034 yâdâh (52), to *revere* or *worship*
4110 mahălâl (1), *fame, good reputation*

7623 shâbach (4), to
address; to pacify
7624 sh^ebach (Ch.) (2), to
adulate, i.e. adore
8416 t^ehillâh (52),
laudation; hymn
8426 tôwdâh (5),
expressions of thanks
133 ainĕsis (1),
thank-offering. praise
134 ainĕō (3), to praise
136 ainŏs (2), praise
1391 dŏxa (4), glory;
brilliance
1867 ĕpainĕō (3), to
applaud, commend
1868 ĕpainŏs (12),
laudation
5214 humnĕō (1), to
celebrate in song

PRAISED
1288 bârak (1), to bless
1984 hâlal (19), to praise;
thank; boast
3034 yâdâh (1), to throw;
to revere or worship
7623 shâbach (1), to
address
7624 sh^ebach (Ch.) (3), to
adulate, i.e. adore
2127 ĕulŏgĕō (1), to
invoke a benediction

PRAISES
1984 hâlal (1), to praise;
thank; boast
8416 t^ehillâh (5),
laudation; hymn
8426 tôwdâh (1),
expressions of thanks
703 arĕtē (1), excellence,
virtue

PRAISETH
1984 hâlal (1), to praise;
thank; boast

PRAISING
1984 hâlal (4), to praise;
thank; boast
134 ainĕō (6), to praise

PRANSING
1725 dâhar (1), to prance

PRANSINGS
1726 dahăhar (2), gallop

PRATING
8193 sâphâh (2), lip,
language, speech
5396 phluarĕō (1), to
berate

PRAY
577 'ânnâ' (2), oh now!, I
ask you!
2470 châlâh (3), to be
weak, sick, afflicted
2603 chânan (1), to
implore
3863 lûw' (1), if; would
that!
4994 nâ' (195), I pray!,
please!, I beg you!
6279 'âthar (1), intercede
6293 pâga' (1), to impinge
6419 pâlal (34), to
intercede, pray
6739 ts^elâ' (Ch.) (1), pray
7592 shâ'al (2), to ask
7878 sîyach (1), to
ponder, muse aloud

1189 dĕŏmai (7), to beg,
petition, ask
2065 ĕrōtaō (10), to
interrogate; to request
2172 ĕuchŏmai (2), to
wish for; to pray
3870 parakalĕō (4), to
call, invite
4336 prŏsĕuchŏmai (42),
to supplicate, pray

PRAYED
6419 pâlal (30), to
intercede, pray
6739 ts^elâ' (Ch.) (1), pray
1189 dĕŏmai (3), to beg,
petition, ask
2065 ĕrōtaō (4), to
interrogate; to request
3870 parakalĕō (2), to
call, invite
4336 prŏsĕuchŏmai (25),
to supplicate, pray

PRAYER
2470 châlâh (1), to be
weak, sick, afflicted
3908 lachash (1),
incantation; amulet
6279 'âthar (1), intercede
in prayer
6419 pâlal (2), to
intercede, pray
7878 sîyach (1), to
ponder, muse aloud
7879 sîyach (1), uttered
contemplation
8605 t^ephillâh (75),
intercession
1162 dĕēsis (7), petition,
request
1783 ĕntĕuxis (1),
intercession
2171 ĕuchē (1), wish,
petition
4335 prŏsĕuchē (21),
prayer; prayer chapel
4336 prŏsĕuchŏmai (1),
to supplicate, pray

PRAYERS
8605 t^ephillâh (2),
intercession
1162 dĕēsis (5), petition,
request
4335 prŏsĕuchē (15),
prayer; prayer chapel
4336 prŏsĕuchŏmai (2),
to supplicate, pray

PRAYEST
4336 prŏsĕuchŏmai (2),
to supplicate, pray

PRAYETH
6419 pâlal (4), to
intercede, pray
4336 prŏsĕuchŏmai (3),
to supplicate, pray

PRAYING
1156 b^e'â' (Ch.) (1), to
seek or ask
6419 pâlal (5), to
intercede, pray
1189 dĕŏmai (2), to beg,
petition, ask
4336 prŏsĕuchŏmai (12),
to supplicate, pray

PREACH
1319 bâsar (1), to
announce (good news)
7121 qârâ' (2), to call out

1229 diaggĕllō (1), to
herald thoroughly
2097 ĕuaggĕlizō (18), to
announce good news
2605 kataggĕllō (4), to
proclaim, promulgate
2784 kērussō (22), to
herald
2980 lalĕō (1), to talk

PREACHED
1319 bâsar (1), to
announce (good news)
189 akŏē (1), hearing;
thing heard
1256 dialĕgŏmai (1), to
discuss
2097 ĕuaggĕlizō (22), to
announce good news
2605 kataggĕllō (6), to
proclaim, promulgate
2784 kērussō (20), to
herald
2907 krĕas (1), meat
2980 lalĕō (4), to talk
3954 parrhēsia (1),
frankness, boldness
4137 plērŏō (1), to fill,
make complete
4283 prŏĕuaggĕlizŏmai
(1), to announce glad
news in advance
4296 prŏkērussō (2), to
proclaim in advance

PREACHER
6953 qôheleth (7),
assembler i.e. lecturer
2783 kērux (3), herald
2784 kērussō (1), to
herald

PREACHEST
2784 kērussō (1), to
herald

PREACHETH
2097 ĕuaggĕlizō (1), to
announce good news
2784 kērussō (2), to
herald

PREACHING
7150 q^erîy'âh (1),
proclamation
1256 dialĕgŏmai (1), to
discuss
2097 ĕuaggĕlizō (6), to
announce good news
2782 kērugma (8),
proclamation
2784 kērussō (8), to
herald
2980 lalĕō (1), to talk
3056 lŏgŏs (1), word,
matter, thing; Word

PRECEPT
4687 mitsvâh (1),
command
6673 tsav (4), injunction
1785 ĕntŏlē (2),
prescription, regulation

PRECEPTS
4687 mitsvâh (3),
command
6490 piqqûwd (21),
mandate of God, Law

PRECIOUS
2530 châmad (3), to
delight in; lust for

2532 chemdâh (1),
delight
2580 chên (1),
graciousness; beauty
2667 chôphesh (1), carpet
2896 tôwb (4), good; well
3365 yâqar (8), to be
valuable; to make rare
3366 y^eqâr (4), wealth;
costliness; dignity
3368 yâqâr (25), valuable
4022 meged (5), valuable
4030 migdânâh (3),
preciousness, i.e. a gem
4901 meshek (1), sowing;
possession
5238 n^ekôth (2),
valuables
927 barutimŏs (1), highly
valuable
1784 ĕntimŏs (2), valued,
considered precious
2472 isŏtimŏs (1), of
equal value or honor
4185 pŏlutĕlēs (1),
extremely expensive
5092 timē (1), esteem;
nobility; money
5093 timiŏs (11), costly;
honored, esteemed

PREDESTINATE
4309 prŏŏrizō (2), to
predetermine

PREDESTINATED
4309 prŏŏrizō (2), to
predetermine

PREEMINENCE
4195 môwthar (1), gain;
superiority
4409 prōtĕuō (1), to be
first
5383 philŏprōtĕuō (1),
loving to be first

PREFER
5927 'âlâh (1), to ascend,
be high, mount

PREFERRED
5330 n^etsach (Ch.) (1), to
become chief
8138 shânâh (1), to fold,
to transmute
1096 ginŏmai (3), to be,
become

PREFERRING
4285 prŏēgĕŏmai (1), to
show deference
4299 prŏkrima (1),
prejudgment, partiality

PREMEDITATE
3191 mĕlĕtaō (1), to plot,
think about

PREPARATION
3559 kûwn (2), to set up:
establish, fix, prepare
2091 hĕtŏimasia (1),
preparation
3904 paraskĕuē (6),
readiness

PREPARATIONS
4633 ma'ărâk (1), mental
disposition, plan

PREPARE
631 'âçar (1), to fasten; to
join battle
3559 kûwn (41), to set up:
establish, fix, prepare

English

4487 mânâh (1), to *allot;* to *enumerate* or enroll
6186 'ârak (2), to set in a row, i.e. *arrange,*
6213 'âsâh (9), to *do* or *make*
6437 pânâh (4), to *turn,* to *face*
6942 qâdâsh (7), to *be, make clean*
2090 hĕtŏimazō (11), to *prepare*
2680 kataskĕuazō (3), to *prepare thoroughly*
3903 paraskĕuazō (1), to *get ready, prepare*

PREPARED
2164 zᵉman (Ch.) (1), to *agree, conspire*
2502 châlats (2), to *deliver, equip*
3559 kûwn (53), to *set up: establish, fix, prepare*
3739 kârâh (1), to *purchase* by bargaining
4487 mânâh (4), to *allot;* to *enumerate* or enroll
6186 'ârak (2), to set in a row, i.e. *arrange,*
6213 'âsâh (13), to *do* or *make*
6437 pânâh (1), to *turn,* to *face*
7543 râqach (1), to *perfume, blend spice*
2090 hĕtŏimazō (18), to *prepare*
2092 hĕtŏimŏs (1), *ready, prepared*
2675 katartizō (1), to *repair;* to *prepare*
2680 kataskĕuazō (2), to *prepare thoroughly*
4282 prŏĕtŏimazō (1), to *fit up in advance*

PREPAREDST
6437 pânâh (1), to *turn,* to *face*

PREPAREST
3559 kûwn (1), to *set up: establish, fix, prepare*
6186 'ârak (1), to set in a row, i.e. *arrange,*
6213 'âsâh (1), to *do* or *make*

PREPARETH
3559 kûwn (3), to *set up: establish, fix, prepare*

PREPARING
6213 'âsâh (1), to *do* or *make*
2680 kataskĕuazō (1), to *prepare thoroughly*

PRESBYTERY
4244 prĕsbutĕriŏn (1), *order of elders*

PRESCRIBED
3789 kâthab (1), to *write*

PRESCRIBING
3792 kᵉthâb (Ch.) (1), *writing, record* or *book*

PRESENCE
5048 neged (8), *over against* or *before*
5869 'ayin (9), *eye; sight; fountain*

5921 'al (1), *above, over, upon,* or *against*
6440 pânîym (76), *face; front*
6925 qŏdâm (Ch.) (1), *before*
561 apĕnanti (1), *before* or *against*
1715 ĕmprŏsthĕn (1), *in front of*
1799 ĕnōpiŏn (9), *in the face* of, before
2714 katĕnōpiŏn (1), *directly in front of*
3952 parŏusia (2), *coming; presence*
4383 prŏsōpŏn (7), *face, presence*

PRESENT
814 'eshkâr (1), *gratuity, gift; payment*
1293 bᵉrâkâh (3), *benediction, blessing*
3320 yâtsab (5), to *station, offer, continue*
3557 kûwl (1), to *keep in;* to *measure*
4503 minchâh (22), *tribute; offering*
4672 mâtsâ' (17), to *find* or *acquire;* to *occur*
5307 nâphal (3), to *fall*
5324 nâtsab (1), to *station*
5975 'âmad (6), to *stand*
7810 shachad (2), to *bribe; gift*
7862 shay (1), *gift*
7964 shillûwach (1), daughter's *dower*
8670 tᵉshûwrâh (1), *gift*
737 arti (2), just *now; at once*
1736 ĕndēmĕō (2), to be *at home*
1764 ĕnistēmi (5), to be *present*
2186 ĕphistēmi (1), to be *present;* to *approach*
2476 histēmi (1), to *stand, establish*
3306 mĕnō (1), to *stay, remain*
3568 nun (4), *now;* the *present* or *immediate*
3854 paraginŏmai (1), to *arrive;* to *appear*
3873 parakĕimai (2), to be *at hand*
3918 parĕimi (14), to be *present;* to *have come*
3936 paristēmi (7), to *stand beside, present*
4840 sumparĕimi (1), to be *now present*

PRESENTED
3320 yâtsab (4), to *station, offer, continue*
3322 yâtsag (1), to *place*
4672 mâtsâ' (3), to *find meet* or *be present*
5066 nâgash (1), to *be, come, bring near*
5307 nâphal (1), to *fall*
5414 nâthan (1), to *give*
5975 'âmad (1), to *stand*
7126 qârab (2), to *approach, bring near*
7200 râ'âh (1), to *see*

3936 paristēmi (2), to *stand beside, present*
4374 prŏsphĕrō (1), to *present to;* to *treat as*

PRESENTING
5307 nâphal (1), to *fall*

PRESENTLY
3117 yôwm (2), *day; time period*
1824 ĕxautēs (1), *instantly, at once*
3916 parachrēma (1), *instantly, immediately*
3936 paristēmi (1), to *stand beside, present*

PRESENTS
4030 migdânâh (1), *preciousness,* i.e. a *gem*
4503 minchâh (6), *tribute; offering*
7862 shay (2), *gift*
7964 shillûwach (1), daughter's *dower*

PRESERVE
2421 châyâh (4), to *live;* to *revive*
3498 yâthar (1), to *remain* or *be left*
4241 michyâh (1), *preservation of life*
4422 mâlaṭ (1), to *escape* as if by *slipperiness*
5341 nâtsar (11), to *guard, protect*
7760 sûwm (1), to *put*
8104 shâmar (9), to *watch*
2225 zōŏgŏnĕō (1), to *rescue; be saved*
4982 sōzō (1), to *deliver;* to *protect*

PRESERVED
3467 yâsha' (4), to make *safe, free*
5336 nâtsîyr (1), *delivered*
5337 nâtsal (1), to *deliver;* to *be snatched*
8104 shâmar (6), to *watch*
4933 suntērĕō (2), to *preserve in memory*
5083 tērĕō (2), to *keep, guard, obey*

PRESERVER
5314 nâphash (1), to be *refreshed*

PRESERVEST
2421 châyâh (1), to *live;* to *revive*
3467 yâsha' (1), to make *safe, free*

PRESERVETH
2421 châyâh (1), to *live;* to *revive*
5341 nâtsar (1), to *guard, protect, maintain*
8104 shâmar (6), to *watch*

PRESIDENTS
5632 çârêk (Ch.) (5), *emir, high official*

PRESS
1660 gath (1), wine-*press* or *vat*
6333 pûwrâh (1), *wine-press trough*

598 apŏthlibō (1), to *crowd, press up* against
1377 diōkō (1), to *pursue;* to *persecute*
3793 ŏchlŏs (5), *throng,* i.e. *crowd* or *mob*

PRESSED
1765 dâchaph (1), to *urge;* to *hasten*
4600 mâ'ak (1), to *press*
5781 'ûwq (2), to *pack, be pressed*
6484 pâtsar (2), to *stun* or *dull*
6555 pârats (2), to *break out*
6693 tsûwq (1), to *oppress, distress*
7818 sâchaṭ (1), to *tread out,* i.e. *squeeze* grapes
916 barĕō (1), to *weigh down, cause pressure*
1945 ĕpikĕimai (1), to *rest upon; press upon*
1968 ĕpipiptō (1), to *embrace;* to *seize*
4085 piĕzō (1), to *pack down firm*
4912 sunĕchō (1), to *hold together, compress*

PRESSES
3342 yeqeb (2), wine-*vat,* wine-*press*

PRESSETH
5181 nâchath (1), to *sink, descend;* to *press* down
971 biazō (1), to *crowd oneself* into

PRESSFAT
3342 yeqeb (1), wine-*vat,* wine-*press*

PRESUME
2102 zûwd (1), to be *insolent*
4390 mâlê' (1), to *fill; be full*

PRESUMED
6075 'âphal (1), to *swell; be elated*

PRESUMPTUOUS
2086 zêd (1), *arrogant, proud*
5113 tŏlmētēs (1), *daring* (audacious) man

PRESUMPTUOUSLY
2087 zâdôwn (2), *arrogance, pride*
2102 zûwd (3), to be *insolent*
3027 yâd (1), *hand; power*

PRETENCE
4392 prŏphasis (3), *pretext, excuse*

PREVAIL
1396 gâbar (5), to *act insolently*
2388 châzaq (2), to *bind, restrain, conquer*
3201 yâkôl (13), to *be able*
3898 lâcham (1), to *fight* a *battle*
5810 'âzaz (1), to be *stout; be bold*
6113 'âtsar (1), to *hold back;* to *maintain, rule*

6206 'ărats (1), to *awe*; to *dread*; to *harass*
8630 tâqaph (2), to *overpower*
2729 katischuō (1), to *overpower, prevail*
5623 ŏphĕlĕō (2), to *benefit, be of use*

PREVAILED
553 'âmats (1), to be *strong; be courageous*
1396 gâbar (9), to be *strong; to prevail*
2388 châzaq (8), to *bind, restrain, conquer*
3201 yâkôl (9), to be able
3202 yᵉkêl (Ch.) (1), to be able
3513 kâbad (1), to be *heavy, severe, dull*
5810 'âzaz (2), to be *stout; be bold*
7186 qâsheh (1), *severe*
2480 ischuō (3), to have or *exercise force*
2729 katischuō (1), to *overpower, prevail*
3528 nikaō (1), to *subdue, conquer*

PREVAILEST
8630 tâqaph (1), to *overpower*

PREVAILETH
7287 rᵉdâh (1), to *subjugate; to crumble*

PREVENT
6923 qâdam (6), to *anticipate, hasten*
5348 phthanō (1), to *anticipate or precede*

PREVENTED
6923 qâdam (8), to *anticipate, hasten*
4399 prŏphthanō (1), to *anticipate*

PREVENTEST
6923 qâdam (1), to *anticipate, hasten*

PREY
400 'ôkel (2), *food*
957 baz (17), *plunder, loot*
961 bizzâh (4), *booty, plunder*
962 bâzaz (9), to *plunder, take booty*
2863 chetheph (1), *robber or robbery*
2963 țâraph (1), to *pluck off or pull to pieces*
2964 țereph (18), *fresh torn prey*
4455 malqôwach (6), *spoil, plunder*
5706 'ad (3), *booty*
7997 shâlal (1), to *drop or strip; to plunder*
7998 shâlâl (11), *booty*

PRICE
3365 yâqar (1), to be *valuable; to make rare*
3701 keçeph (3), *silver money*
4242 mᵉchîyr (11), *price, payment, wages*
4377 meker (1), *merchandise; value*

4736 miqnâh (2), *acquisition*
4901 meshek (1), *sowing; possession*
6187 'êrek (1), *pile, equipment, estimate*
7939 sâkâr (2), *payment, salary; compensation*
4185 pŏlutĕlēs (1), *extremely expensive*
4186 pŏlutimŏs (1), *extremely valuable*
5092 timē (7), *esteem; nobility; money*

PRICES
5092 timē (1), *esteem; nobility; money*

PRICKED
8150 shânan (1), to *pierce; to inculcate*
2669 katapŏnĕō (1), to *harass, oppress*

PRICKING
3992 mâ'ar (1), to be *painful; destructive*

PRICKS
7899 sêk (1), *brier* of a hedge
2759 kĕntrŏn (2), *sting; goad*

PRIDE
1344 gê'âh (1), *arrogance, pride*
1346 ga'ăvâh (9), *arrogance; majesty*
1347 gâ'ôwn (20), *ascending; majesty*
1348 gê'ûwth (2), *ascending; majesty*
1363 gôbahh (2), *height; grandeur; arrogance*
1466 gêvâh (3), *arrogance, pride*
2087 zâdôwn (6), *arrogance, pride*
2103 zûwd (Ch.) (1), to be *proud*
7407 rôkeç (1), *snare* as of *tied meshes*
7830 shachats (1), *haughtiness; dignity*
212 alazŏnĕia (1), *boasting*
5187 tuphŏō (1), to *inflate with self-conceit*
5243 hupĕrēphania (1), *haughtiness, arrogance*

PRIEST
3547 kâhan (2), to *officiate* as a *priest*
3548 kôhên (423), one *officiating as a priest*
3549 kâhên (Ch.) (1), one *officiating as a priest*
748 archiĕratikŏs (1), *high-priestly*
749 archiĕrĕus (53), *high-priest, chief priest*
2409 hiĕrĕus (16), *priest*

PRIEST'S
3547 kâhan (20), to *officiate* as a *priest*
3548 kôhên (17), one *officiating as a priest*
3550 kᵉhunnâh (4), *priesthood*

749 archiĕrĕus (4), *high-priest, chief priest*
2405 hiĕratĕia (1), *priestly office*
2407 hiĕratĕuō (1), to be a *priest*

PRIESTHOOD
3550 kᵉhunnâh (9), *priesthood*
2405 hiĕratĕia (1), *priestly office*
2406 hiĕratĕuma (2), *priestly order*
2420 hiĕrōsunē (4), *priestly office*

PRIESTS
3548 kôhên (300), one *officiating as a priest*
3549 kâhên (Ch.) (6), one *officiating as a priest*
3649 kâmâr (1), *pagan priest*
749 archiĕrĕus (67), *high-priest, chief priest*
2409 hiĕrĕus (15), *priest*

PRIESTS'
3548 kôhên (8), one *officiating as a priest*

PRINCE
5057 nâgîyd (8), *commander, official*
5081 nâdîyb (4), *grandee or tyrant*
5387 nâsîy' (56), *leader; rising mist, fog*
7101 qâtsîyn (2), *magistrate; leader*
7333 râzôwn (1), *dignitary*
8269 sar (19), *head person, ruler*
8323 sârar (1), to *have, exercise, get dominion*
747 archēgŏs (2), *chief leader; founder*
758 archōn (8), *first*

PRINCE'S
5081 nâdîyb (1), *grandee or tyrant*
5387 nâsîy' (2), *leader; rising mist, fog*

PRINCES
324 ăchashdarpan (Ch.) (9), *satrap*
2831 chashmân (1), (poss.) *wealthy*
3548 kôhên (1), one *officiating as a priest*
5057 nâgîyd (1), *commander, official*
5081 nâdîyb (10), *grandee or tyrant*
5257 nᵉçîyk (3), *libation; molten image; prince*
5387 nâsîy' (40), *leader; rising mist, fog*
5461 çâgan (1), *prfect of a province*
6579 partam (1), *grandee, noble*
7101 qâtsîyn (2), *magistrate; leader*
7227 rab (2), *great*
7261 rabrᵉbân (Ch.) (2), *magnate, noble*
7336 râzan (5), *honorable*

749 archiĕrĕus (4), *high-priest, chief priest*
7991 shâlîysh (1), *officer; of the third rank*
8269 sar (190), *head person, ruler*
758 archōn (3), *first*
2232 hēgĕmōn (1), *chief*

PRINCESS
8282 sârâh (1), *female noble*

PRINCESSES
8282 sârâh (1), *female noble*

PRINCIPAL
1 'âb (1), *father*
117 'addîyr (3), *powerful; majestic*
3548 kôhên (1), one *officiating as a priest*
5257 nᵉçîyk (1), *libation; molten image; prince*
7218 rô'sh (5), *head*
7225 rê'shîyth (1), *first*
7795 sôwrâh (1), *row*
8269 sar (2), *head person, ruler*
8291 sarûwq (1), *choice grapevine*

PRINCIPALITIES
4761 mar'âshâh (1), *headship, dominion*
746 archē (6), *first in rank; first in time*

PRINCIPALITY
746 archē (2), *first in rank; first in time*

PRINCIPLES
746 archē (1), *first in rank; first in time*
4747 stŏichĕiŏn (1), *basic principles*

PRINT
2707 châqah (1), to *carve; to delineate*
5414 nâthan (1), to *give*
5179 tupŏs (2), *shape, resemblance; "type"*

PRINTED
2710 châqaq (1), to *engrave; to enact laws*

PRISCA
4251 Priska (1), *ancient*

PRISCILLA
4252 Priskilla (5), *little Prisca*

PRISED
3365 yâqar (1), to be *valuable; to make rare*

PRISON
631 'âçar (2), to *fasten; to join battle*
1004+612 bayith (3), *house; temple; family*
1004+3608 bayith (7), *house; temple; family*
1004+5470 bayith (8), *house; temple; family*
1004+6486 bayith (1), *house; temple; family*
3608 kele' (4), *prison*
4115 mahpeketh (1), *stocks for punishment*
4307 maṭṭârâ' (13), *jail (guard-house); aim*
4525 maçgêr (3), *prison; craftsman*

4929 mishmâr (1), *guard; deposit; usage; example*
6115 'ôtser (1), *closure; constraint*
6495 pᵉqach-qôwach (1), *jail-delivery; salvation*
1200 dĕsmŏphulax (2), *jailer*
1201 dĕsmōtēriŏn (4), *dungeon, jail*
3612 ŏikēma (1), *jail cell*
3860 paradidōmi (2), *to hand over*
5084 tērēsis (1), *observance; prison*
5438 phulakē (33), *night watch; prison; haunt*

PRISONER
615 'âçîyr (1), *captive, prisoner*
616 'aççîyr (1), *captive, prisoner*
1198 dĕsmiŏs (11), *bound captive; one arrested*

PRISONERS
615 'âçîyr (8), *captive, prisoner*
616 'aççîyr (3), *captive, prisoner*
631 'âçar (2), *to fasten; to join battle*
7628 shᵉbîy (2), *exile; booty*
1198 dĕsmiŏs (3), *bound captive; one arrested*
1202 dĕsmōtēs (2), *captive*

PRISONS
5438 phulakē (3), *night watch; prison; haunt*

PRIVATE
2398 idiŏs (1), *private or separate*

PRIVATELY
2596+2398 kata (8), *down; according to*

PRIVILY
652 'ôphel (1), *dusk, darkness*
2934 ţâman (3), *to hide*
3909 lâţ (1), *incantation; secrecy; covertly*
5643 çêther (1), *cover, shelter*
6845 tsâphan (1), *to hide; to protect; to lurk*
8649 tormâh (1), *fraud*
2977 lathra (3), *privately, secretly*
3918 parĕimi (1), *to be present; to have come*
3922 parĕisĕrchŏmai (1), *to supervene stealthily*

PRIVY
2314 châdar (1), *to enclose; to beset*
3045 yâda' (1), *to know*
8212 shophkâh (1), *penis*
4894 sunĕidō (1), *to understand*

PRIZE
1017 brabĕiŏn (2), *prize in the public games*

PROCEED
3254 yâçaph (2), *to add or augment*

3318 yâtsâ' (8), *to go, bring out*
1607 ĕkpŏrĕuŏmai (3), *to proceed, project*
1831 ĕxĕrchōmai (1), *to issue; to leave*
4298 prŏkŏptō (1), *to go ahead, advance*

PROCEEDED
3254 yâçaph (1), *to add or augment*
3318 yâtsâ' (2), *to go, bring out*
4161 môwtsâ' (1), *going forth*
1607 ĕkpŏrĕuŏmai (3), *to proceed, project*
1831 ĕxĕrchōmai (1), *to issue; to leave*
4369 prŏstithēmi (1), *to annex, repeat*

PROCEEDETH
3318 yâtsâ' (6), *to go, bring out*
4161 môwtsâ' (1), *going forth*
1607 ĕkpŏrĕuŏmai (3), *to proceed, project*
1831 ĕxĕrchōmai (1), *to issue; to leave*

PROCEEDING
1607 ĕkpŏrĕuŏmai (1), *to proceed, project*

PROCESS
7093 qêts (1), *extremity; after*
7227 rab (1), *great*
7235 râbâh (1), *to increase*

PROCHORUS
4402 Prŏchŏrŏs (1), *before the dance*

PROCLAIM
5674 'âbar (1), *to cross over; to transition*
6942 qâdâsh (1), *to be, make clean*
7121 qârâ' (21), *to call out*

PROCLAIMED
2199 zâ'aq (1), *to call out, announce*
5674 'âbar (1), *to cross over; to transition*
7121 qârâ' (11), *to call out*
8085 shâma' (1), *to hear*
2784 kērussō (1), *to herald*

PROCLAIMETH
7121 qârâ' (1), *to call out*

PROCLAIMING
7121 qârâ' (2), *to call out*
2784 kērussō (1), *to herald*

PROCLAMATION
3745 kᵉraz (Ch.) (1), *to proclaim*
5674+6963 'âbar (4), *to cross over; to transition*
6963 qôwl (1), *voice or sound*
7121 qârâ' (1), *to call out*
7440 rinnâh (1), *shout*
8085 shâma' (1), *to hear*

PROCURE
6213 'âsâh (2), *to make*

PROCURED
6213 'âsâh (2), *to make*

PROCURETH
1245 bâqash (1), *to search out*

PRODUCE
7126 qârab (1), *to approach, bring near*

PROFANE
2455 chôl (4), *profane, common, not holy*
2490 châlal (18), *to profane, defile*
2491 châlâl (3), *pierced to death, one slain*
2610 chânêph (1), *to soil, be defiled*
952 bĕbēlŏs (5), *irreligious, profane*
953 bĕbēlŏō (2), *to desecrate, profane*

PROFANED
2490 châlal (15), *to profane, defile*

PROFANENESS
2613 chănûphâh (1), *impiety, ungodliness*

PROFANETH
2490 châlal (1), *to profane, defile*

PROFANING
2490 châlal (2), *to profane, defile*

PROFESS
5046 nâgad (1), *to announce*
3670 hŏmŏlŏgĕō (2), *to acknowledge, declare*

PROFESSED
3670 hŏmŏlŏgĕō (1), *to acknowledge, declare*
3671 hŏmŏlŏgia (1), *acknowledgment*

PROFESSING
1861 ĕpaggĕllō (2), *to assert*
5335 phaskō (1), *to assert a claim*

PROFESSION
3671 hŏmŏlŏgia (4), *acknowledgment*

PROFIT
1215 betsa' (3), *plunder; unjust gain*
3148 yôwthêr (1), *moreover; rest; gain*
3276 yâ'al (18), *to be valuable*
3504 yithrôwn (5), *preeminence, gain*
4195 môwthar (1), *gain; superiority*
7737 shâvâh (1), *to resemble; to adjust*
3786 ŏphĕlŏs (2), *accumulate or benefit*
4851 sumphĕrō (4), *to collect; advantage*
5539 chrēsimŏs (1), *useful, valued*
5622 ŏphĕlĕia (1), *value, advantage*

5623 ŏphĕlĕō (4), *to benefit, be of use*

PROFITABLE
3276 yâ'al (1), *to be valuable*
3504 yithrôwn (1), *preeminence, gain*
5532 çâkan (2), *to be serviceable to*
6743 tsâlach (1), *to push forward*
2173 ĕuchrēstŏs (2), *useful, serviceable*
4851 sumphĕrō (3), *to conduce; advantage*
5624 ŏphĕlimŏs (3), *advantageous, useful*

PROFITED
7737 shâvâh (1), *to resemble; to adjust*
4298 prŏkŏptō (1), *to go ahead, advance*
5623 ŏphĕlĕō (4), *to benefit, be of use*

PROFITETH
3276 yâ'al (1), *to be valuable*
5532 çâkan (1), *to be serviceable to*
5623 ŏphĕlĕō (3), *to benefit, be of use*
5624+2076 ŏphĕlimŏs (1), *useful, valuable*

PROFITING
4297 prŏkŏpē (1), *progress, advancement*

PROFOUND
6009 'âmaq (1), *to be, make deep*

PROGENITORS
2029 hârâh (1), *to conceive, be pregnant*

PROGNOSTICATORS
3045 yâda' (1), *to know*

PROLONG
748 'ârak (12), *to be, make long*
3254 yâçaph (1), *to add or augment*
5186 nâţâh (1), *to stretch or spread out*

PROLONGED
748 'ârak (5), *to be, make long*
754+3052 'arkâ (Ch.) (1), *length*
4900 mâshak (3), *to draw out; to be tall*

PROLONGETH
748 'ârak (1), *to be, make long*
3254 yâçaph (1), *to add or augment*

PROMISE
562 'ômer (1), *something said*
1697 dâbâr (6), *word; matter; thing*
1860 ĕpaggĕlia (40), *divine assurance*
1861 ĕpaggĕllō (3), *to assert*
1862 ĕpaggĕlma (1), *self-committal*

PROMISED
559 'âmar (5), to *say*
1696 dâbar (29), to
speak, say; to *subdue*
1843 ĕxŏmŏlŏgĕō (1), to
acknowledge or *agree*
1861 ĕpaggĕllō (10), to
assert
3670 hŏmŏlŏgĕō (1), to
acknowledge, agree
4279 prŏĕpaggĕllŏmai
(1), to *promise before*

PROMISEDST
559 'âmar (1), to *say*
1696 dâbar (2), to *speak*

PROMISES
1860 ĕpaggĕlia (12),
divine *assurance*
1862 ĕpaggĕlma (1),
self-committal

PROMISING
2421 châyâh (1), to *live;*
to *revive*

PROMOTE
1431 gâdal (1), to *make*
great, enlarge
3513 kâbad (3), to *be*
rich, glorious
7311 rûwm (1), to *be*
high; to *rise* or *raise*

PROMOTED
1431 gâdal (1), to *make*
great, enlarge
5128 nûwa' (3), to *waver*
6744 tsᵉlach (Ch.) (1), to
advance; promote

PROMOTION
7311 rûwm (2), to *be*
high; to *rise* or *raise*

PRONOUNCE
981 bâṭâ' (1), to *babble,*
speak rashly
1696 dâbar (1), to *speak*

PRONOUNCED
1691 Diblayim (2), *two*
cakes
1696 dâbar (11), to *speak*
7126 qârab (1), to
approach, bring near

PRONOUNCING
981 bâṭâ' (1), to *babble,*
speak rashly

PROOF
1382 dŏkimē (3), *test,* i.e.
trustiness
1732 ĕndĕixis (1),
demonstration
4135 plērŏphŏrĕō (1), to
assure or *convince*

PROOFS
5039 tĕkmēriŏn (1),
criterion of certainty

PROPER
5459 çᵉgullâh (1), *wealth*
791 astĕiŏs (1),
handsome
2398 idiŏs (2), *private* or
separate

PROPHECIES
4394 prŏphētĕia (2),
prediction

PROPHECY
4853 massâ' (2), *burden,*
utterance

5016 nᵉbûw'âh (3),
prediction
5030 nâbîy' (1), *prophet;*
inspired man
4394 prŏphētĕia (14),
prediction
4397 prŏphētikŏs (1),
prophetic

PROPHESIED
5012 nâbâ' (40), to speak
as a *prophet*
5013 nᵉbâ' (Ch.) (1), to
speak as a *prophet*
4395 prŏphētĕuō (9), to
foretell events, *divine*

PROPHESIETH
5012 nâbâ' (3), to speak
as a *prophet*
4395 prŏphētĕuō (4), to
foretell events, *divine*

PROPHESY
2372 châzâh (2), to *gaze*
at; *have a vision*
5012 nâbâ' (66), to speak
as a *prophet*
5197 nâṭaph (5), to *speak*
by inspiration
4395 prŏphētĕuō (14), to
foretell events, *divine*

PROPHESYING
5012 nâbâ' (2), to speak
as a *prophet*
5017 nᵉbûw'âh (Ch.) (1),
inspired *teaching*
4394 prŏphētĕia (2),
prediction
4395 prŏphētĕuō (1), to
foretell events, *divine*

PROPHESYINGS
4394 prŏphētĕia (1),
prediction

PROPHET
5012 nâbâ' (2), to speak
as a *prophet*
5029 nᵉbîy' (Ch.) (2),
prophet
5030 nâbîy' (164),
prophet; inspired man
5197 nâṭaph (1), to *speak*
by inspiration
4396 prŏphētēs (67),
foreteller
5578 psĕudŏprŏphētēs
(4), *pretended foreteller*

PROPHET'S
5030 nâbîy' (1), *prophet;*
inspired man
4396 prŏphētēs (1),
foreteller

PROPHETESS
5031 nᵉbîy'âh (6),
prophetess
4398 prŏphētis (2),
female foreteller

PROPHETS
2374 chôzeh (1),
beholder in vision
5029 nᵉbîy' (Ch.) (2),
prophet
5030 nâbîy' (147),
prophet; inspired man
4396 prŏphētēs (80),
foreteller
4397 prŏphētikŏs (1),
prophetic

5578 psĕudŏprŏphētēs
(7), *pretended foreteller*

PROPITIATION
2434 hilasmŏs (2),
atonement
2435 hilastēriŏn (1),
expiatory place

PROPORTION
4626 ma'ar (1), *vacant*
space
6187 'êrek (1), *pile,*
equipment, estimate
356 analŏgia (1),
proportion

PROSELYTE
4339 prŏsēlutŏs (2),
convert, i.e. *proselyte*

PROSELYTES
4339 prŏsēlutŏs (2),
convert, i.e. *proselyte*

PROSPECT
6440 pânîym (6), *face;*
front

PROSPER
3787 kâshêr (1), to *be*
straight or *right*
6743 tsâlach (37), to *push*
forward
7919 sâkal (7), to *be* or
act circumspect
7951 shâlâh (3), to *be*
secure or *successful*
2137 ĕuŏdŏō (1), to
succeed in business

PROSPERED
1980 hâlak (1), to *walk;*
live a certain way
6743 tsâlach (6), to *push*
forward
6744 tsᵉlach (Ch.) (2), to
advance; promote
7919 sâkal (1), to *be* or
act circumspect
7965 shâlôwm (1), *safe;*
well; health, prosperity
7999 shâlam (1), to *be*
safe; be, make complete
2137 ĕuŏdŏō (1), to
succeed in business

PROSPERETH
6743 tsâlach (1), to *push*
forward
6744 tsᵉlach (Ch.) (1), to
advance; promote
7919 sâkal (1), to *be* or
act circumspect
2137 ĕuŏdŏō (1), to
succeed in business

PROSPERITY
2896 ṭôwb (6), *good; well*
6743 tsâlach (1), to *push*
forward
7961 shâlêv (2), *careless,*
carefree; security
7962 shalvâh (3),
security, ease
7965 shâlôwm (4), *safe;*
well; health, prosperity

PROSPEROUS
6743 tsâlach (5), to *push*
forward
7965 shâlôwm (1), *safe;*
well; health, prosperity
7999 shâlam (1), to *be*
safe; be, make complete

2137 ĕuŏdŏō (1), to
succeed in business

PROSPEROUSLY
6743 tsâlach (2), to *push*
forward

PROSTITUTE
2490 châlal (1), to
profane, defile

PROTECTION
5643 çêther (1), *cover,*
shelter

PROTEST
5749 'ûwd (2), to *protest*
3513 nē (1), *as sure as*

PROTESTED
5749 'ûwd (3), to *protest*

PROTESTING
5749 'ûwd (1), to *protest*

PROUD
1341 gê' (2), *haughty,*
proud
1343 gê'eh (8), *arrogant,*
haughty
1346 ga'ăvâh (1),
arrogance; majesty
1347 gâ'ôwn (1),
ascending; majesty
1349 ga'ăyôwn (1),
haughty, arrogant
1362 gâbâhh (2), *high;*
lofty
1364 gâbôahh (1), *high;*
powerful; arrogant
1419 gâdôwl (1), *great*
2086 zêd (12), *arrogant,*
proud
2087 zâdôwn (3),
arrogance, pride
2102 zûwd (1), to *seethe,*
to *be insolent*
2121 zêydôwn (1),
boiling, raging wave
3093 yâhîyr (1), *arrogant*
7293 rahab (2), *bluster*
7295 râhâb (2), *insolent*
7311 rûwm (1), to *be*
high; to *rise* or *raise*
7342 râchâb (3), *roomy,*
spacious
5187 tuphŏō (1), to
inflate with self-conceit
5244 hupĕrēphanŏs (5),
haughty, arrogant

PROUDLY
1346 ga'ăvâh (1),
arrogance; majesty
1348 gê'ûwth (1),
ascending; majesty
1364 gâbôahh (1), *high;*
powerful; arrogant
1431 gâdal (1), to *be*
great, make great
2102 zûwd (4), to *seethe;*
to *be insolent*
7292 râhab (1), to *urge,*
embolden

PROVE
974 bâchan (1), to *test;* to
investigate
5254 nâçâh (14), to *test,*
attempt
584 apŏdĕiknumi (1), to
demonstrate
1381 dŏkimazō (6), to
test; to *approve*

3936 *paristēmi* (1), to *stand beside, present*
3985 *pĕirazō* (1), to *endeavor, scrutinize*

PROVED
974 *bâchan* (6), to *test; to investigate*
5254 *nâçâh* (5), to *test, attempt*
1381 *dŏkimazō* (3), to *test; to approve*
4256 *prŏaitiaŏmai* (1), to *previously charge*

PROVENDER
1098 *bᵉlîyl* (1), *feed, fodder*
1101 *bâlal* (1), to *mix; confuse; to feed*
4554 *miçpôw'* (5), *fodder, animal feed*

PROVERB
2420 *chîydâh* (1), *puzzle; conundrum; maxim*
4911 *mâshal* (4), to *use figurative language*
4912 *mâshâl* (12), *pithy maxim; taunt*
3850 *parabŏlē* (1), *fictitious narrative*
3942 *parŏimia* (2), *illustration; adage*

PROVERBS
4911 *mâshal* (2), to *use figurative language*
4912 *mâshâl* (5), *pithy maxim; taunt*
3942 *parŏimia* (2), *illustration; adage*

PROVETH
5254 *nâçâh* (1), to *test, attempt*

PROVIDE
2372 *châzâh* (1), to *gaze at; to perceive*
3559 *kûwn* (2), to *set up: establish, fix, prepare*
6213 *'âsâh* (1), to *do*
7200 *râ'âh* (2), to *see*
2532 *kai* (1), *and; or*
3936 *paristēmi* (1), to *stand beside, present*
4160 *pŏiĕō* (1), to *do*
4306 *prŏnŏĕō* (2), to *look out for beforehand*

PROVIDED
3559 *kûwn* (1), to *set up: establish, fix, prepare*
6213 *'âsâh* (1), to *do*
7200 *râ'âh* (2), to *see*
2090 *hĕtŏimazō* (1), to *prepare*
4265 *prŏblĕpō* (1), to *furnish in advance*

PROVIDENCE
4307 *prŏnŏia* (1), *provident care, supply*

PROVIDETH
3559 *kûwn* (2), to *set up: establish, fix, prepare*

PROVIDING
4306 *prŏnŏĕō* (1), to *look out for beforehand*

PROVINCE
4082 *mᵉdîynâh* (20), *governmental region*

4083 *mᵉdîynâh* (Ch.) (5), *governmental region*
1885 *ĕparchia* (2), Roman *præfecture*

PROVINCES
4082 *mᵉdîynâh* (29), *governmental region*
4083 *mᵉdîynâh* (Ch.) (1), *governmental region*

PROVING
1381 *dŏkimazō* (1), to *test; to approve*
4822 *sumbibazō* (1), to *infer, show, teach*

PROVISION
1697 *dâbâr* (1), *word; matter; thing*
3557 *kûwl* (1), to *measure; to maintain*
3559 *kûwn* (1), to *set up: establish, fix, prepare*
3740 *kêrâh* (1), *purchase*
3899 *lechem* (1), *food, bread*
6679 *tsûwd* (1), to *lie in wait; to catch*
6718 *tsayid* (2), *hunting game; lunch, food*
6720 *tsêydâh* (2), *food, supplies*
4307 *prŏnŏia* (1), *provident care, supply*

PROVOCATION
3708 *ka'aç* (4), *vexation, grief*
4784 *mârâh* (1), to *rebel or resist; to provoke*
4808 *mᵉrîybâh* (1), *quarrel*
3894 *parapikrasmŏs* (2), *irritation*

PROVOCATIONS
3708 *ka'aç* (1), *vexation, grief*
5007 *nᵉ'âtsâh* (2), *scorn; to bloom*

PROVOKE
4784 *mârâh* (2), to *rebel or resist; to provoke*
4843 *mârar* (1), to *be, make bitter*
5006 *nâ'ats* (2), to *scorn*
7264 *râgaz* (1), to *quiver*
653 *apŏstŏmatizō* (1), to *question carefully*
2042 *ĕrĕthizō* (1), to *stimulate, provoke*
3863 *parazēlŏō* (4), to *excite to rivalry*
3893 *parapikrainō* (1), to *embitter alongside*
3948 *parŏxusmŏs* (1), *incitement to good*
3949 *parŏrgizō* (1), to *enrage, exasperate*

PROVOKED
3707 *kâ'aç* (4), to *grieve, rage, be indignant*
4784 *mârâh* (4), to *rebel or resist; to provoke*
5006 *nâ'ats* (2), to *scorn*
5496 *çûwth* (1), to *stimulate; to seduce*
7265 *rᵉgaz* (Ch.) (1), to *quiver*
2042 *ĕrĕthizō* (1), to *stimulate, provoke*

3947 *parŏxunō* (1), to *exasperate*

PROVOKETH
5674 *'âbar* (1), to *cross over; to transition*

PROVOKING
3707 *kâ'aç* (1), to *grieve, rage, be indignant*
4784 *mârâh* (1), to *rebel or resist; to provoke*
4292 *prŏkalĕŏmai* (1), to *irritate*

PRUDENCE
6195 *'ormâh* (1), *trickery; discretion*
7922 *sekel* (1), *intelligence; success*
5428 *phrŏnēsis* (1), *moral insight, understanding*

PRUDENT
995 *bîyn* (8), to *understand; discern*
6175 *'ârûwm* (8), *cunning; clever*
6191 *'âram* (1), to *be cunning; be prudent*
7080 *qâçam* (1), to *divine magic*
7919 *sâkal* (2), to *be or act circumspect*
4908 *sunĕtŏs* (4), *sagacious, learned*

PRUDENTLY
7919 *sâkal* (1), to *be or act circumspect*

PRUNE
2168 *zâmar* (2), to *trim or a vine*

PRUNED
2167 *zâmar* (1), to *play music*

PRUNINGHOOKS
4211 *mazmêrâh* (4), *pruning-knife*

PSALM
2172 *zimrâh* (2), *song*
4210 *mizmôwr* (58), *poem set to music*
5568 *psalmŏs* (2), *psalm; book of the Psalms*

PSALMIST
2158 *zâmîyr* (1), *song*

PSALMS
2158 *zâmîyr* (1), *song*
2167 *zâmar* (2), to *play music*
5567 *psallō* (1), to *play a stringed instrument*
5568 *psalmŏs* (5), *psalm; book of the Psalms*

PSALTERIES
3627 *kᵉlîy* (1), *implement, thing*
5035 *nebel* (13), *skin-bag for liquids; vase; lyre*

PSALTERY
3627 *kᵉlîy* (1), *implement, thing*
5035 *nebel* (8), *skin-bag for liquids; vase; lyre*
6460 *pᵉçantêrîyn* (Ch.) (4), *lyre instrument*

PTOLEMAIS
4424 *Ptŏlĕmaïs* (1), of *Ptolemy*

PUA
6312 *Pûw'âh* (1), *blast*

PUAH
6312 *Pûw'âh* (2), *blast*
6326 *Pûw'âh* (1), *brilliancy*

PUBLICAN
5057 *tĕlōnēs* (6), *collector of revenue*

PUBLICANS
754 *architĕlōnēs* (1), *chief tax-gatherer*
5057 *tĕlōnēs* (16), *collector of revenue*

PUBLICK
3856 *paradĕigmatizō* (1), to *expose to infamy*

PUBLICKLY
1219 *dēmŏsiŏs* (2), *public; in public*

PUBLISH
1319 *bâsar* (2), to *announce* (good news)
7121 *qârâ'* (1), to *call* out
8085 *shâma'* (11), to *hear*
2784 *kērussō* (2), to *herald*

PUBLISHED
559 *'âmar* (1), to *say*
1319 *bâsar* (1), to *announce* (good news)
1540 *gâlâh* (2), to *reveal*
1696 *dâbar* (1), to *speak*
8085 *shâma'* (1), to *hear*
1096 *ginŏmai* (1), to *be, become*
1308 *diaphĕrō* (1), to *bear, carry; to differ*
2784 *kērussō* (3), to *herald*

PUBLISHETH
8085 *shâma'* (4), to *hear*

PUBLIUS
4196 *Pŏpliŏs* (2), *popular*

PUDENS
4227 *Pŏudēs* (1), *modest*

PUFFED
5448 *phusiŏō* (6), to *inflate*, i.e. *make proud*

PUFFETH
6315 *pûwach* (2), to *blow, to fan, kindle; to utter*
5448 *phusiŏō* (1), to *inflate*, i.e. *make proud*

PUHITES
6336 *Pûwthîy* (1), *hinge*

PUL
6322 *Pûwl* (4), *Pul*, i.e. a *person or tribe*

PULL
2040 *hâraç* (3), to *pull down; break, destroy*
3318 *yâtsâ'* (1), to *go, bring out*
5422 *nâthats* (2), to *tear down*
5423 *nâthaq* (2), to *tear off*
6584 *pâshaṭ* (1), to *strip*, i.e. *unclothe, plunder*

7725 shûwb (1), to *turn* back; to *return*
385 anaspaō (1), to *take up* or *extricate*
1544 ĕkballō (3), to *throw out*
2507 kathairĕō (1), to *lower*, or *demolish*

PULLED
935 bôw' (1), to *go, come*
4026 migdâl (1), *tower; rostrum*
5256 nᵉçach (Ch.) (1), to *tear* away
5414 nâthan (1), to *give*
5428 nâthash (1), to *tear* away, *be uprooted*
6582 pâshach (1), to *tear* in pieces
1288 diaspaō (1), to *sever* or *dismember*

PULLING
726 harpazō (1), to *seize*
2506 kathairĕsis (1), *demolition*

PULPIT
4026 migdâl (1), *tower; rostrum*

PULSE
2235 zêrôa' (2), *vegetable*

PUNISH
3256 yâçar (1), to *chastise;* to *instruct*
5221 nâkâh (1), to *strike, kill*
6064 'ânash (1), to *inflict* a penalty, to *fine*
6485 pâqad (27), to *visit, care for, count*
7489 râ'a' (1), to *break to* pieces
2849 kŏlazō (1), to *chastise, punish*

PUNISHED
2820 châsak (1), to *restrain* or *refrain*
5358 nâqam (2), to *avenge* or *punish*
6064 'ânash (4), to *inflict* a penalty, to *fine*
6485 pâqad (4), to *visit, care for, count*
1349+5099 dikē (1), *justice*
2849 kŏlazō (1), to *chastise, punish*
5097 timōrĕō (2), to *avenge*

PUNISHMENT
2399 chêṭ' (1), *crime* or its *penalty*
2403 chaṭṭâ'âh (3), *offence; sin* offering
5771 'âvôn (9), moral *evil*
6066 'ônesh (1), *fine*
1557 ĕkdikēsis (1), *retaliation, punishment*
2009 ĕpitimia (1), *penalty*
2851 kŏlasis (1), *infliction, punishment*
5098 timōria (1), *penalty, punishment*

PUNISHMENTS
5771 'âvôn (2), moral *evil*

PUNITES
6324 Pûwnîy (1), *turn*

PUNON
6325 Pûwnôn (2), *perplexity*

PUR
6332 Pûwr (3), *lot* cast

PURCHASE
1350 gâ'al (1), to *redeem;* to *be the next of kin*
4736 miqnâh (6), *acquisition*
4046 pĕripŏiĕŏmai (1), to *acquire;* to *gain*

PURCHASED
7069 qânâh (5), to *create;* to *procure*
2932 ktaŏmai (2), to *get,* i.e. *acquire*
4046 pĕripŏiĕŏmai (1), to *acquire;* to *gain*
4047 pĕripŏiēsis (1), *acquisition*

PURE
1249 bar (2), *beloved; pure; empty*
1305 bârar (3), to *brighten; purify*
1865 dᵉrôwr (1), *freedom; clear, pure*
2134 zak (9), *pure; clear*
2135 zâkâh (1), to *be innocent*
2141 zâkak (1), to *be transparent; clean, pure*
2561 chemer (1), *fermenting wine*
2888 Ṭabbath (2), *Tabbath*
2889 ṭâhôwr (40), *pure, clean, flawless*
2891 ṭâhêr (2), to *be pure, unadulterated*
3795 kâthîyth (1), pure oil from *beaten* olives
5343 nᵉqê' (Ch.) (1), *clean, pure*
5462 çâgar (8), to *shut* up; to *surrender*
6337 pâz (1), *pure gold*
6884 tsâraph (2), to *fuse* metal; to *refine*
53 hagnŏs (4), *innocent, modest, perfect, pure*
1506 ĕilikrinēs (1), tested as *genuine,* i.e. *pure*
2513 katharŏs (16), *clean, pure*

PURELY
1252 bôr (1), *purity, cleanness*

PURENESS
1252 bôr (1), *purity, cleanness*
2890 ṭᵉhôwr (1), *purity*
54 hagnŏtēs (1), *blamelessness, purity*

PURER
2141 zâkak (1), to *be transparent; clean, pure*
2889 ṭâhôwr (1), *pure, clean, flawless*

PURGE
1305 bârar (2), to *brighten; purify*
2212 zâqaq (1), to *strain, refine; extract, clarify*
2398 châṭâ' (1), to *sin*

2891 ṭâhêr (1), to *be pure, unadulterated*
3722 kâphar (4), to *cover;* to *expiate*
6884 tsâraph (1), to *fuse* metal; to *refine*
1245 diakatharizō (2), to *cleanse perfectly*
1571 ĕkkathairō (2), to *cleanse thoroughly*
2511 katharizō (1), to *cleanse*

PURGED
1740 dûwach (1), to *rinse clean, wash*
2891 ṭâhêr (4), to *be pure, unadulterated*
3722 kâphar (5), to *cover;* to *expiate*
2508 kathairō (1), to *prune dead* wood
2511 katharizō (1), to *cleanse*
2512 katharismŏs (1), *ablution; expiation*
4160+2512 pŏiĕō (1), to *make* or *do*

PURGETH
2508 kathairō (1), to *prune dead* wood

PURGING
2511 katharizō (1), to *cleanse*

PURIFICATION
2403 chaṭṭâ'âh (2), *offence; sin* offering
2893 ṭohŏrâh (2), ceremonial *purification*
8562 tamrûwq (2), *scouring, perfumery*
49 hagnismŏs (1), *purification*
2512 katharismŏs (1), *ablution; expiation*

PURIFICATIONS
4795 mârûwq (1), *rubbing*

PURIFIED
1305 bârar (1), to *brighten; purify*
2212 zâqaq (1), to *strain, refine; extract, clarify*
2398 châṭâ' (3), to *sin*
2891 ṭâhêr (3), to *be pure, unadulterated*
6942 qâdâsh (1), to *be, make clean*
48 hagnizō (2), *sanctify;* to *cleanse* in ritual
2511 katharizō (1), to *cleanse*

PURIFIER
2891 ṭâhêr (1), to *be pure, unadulterated*

PURIFIETH
2398 châṭâ' (1), to *sin*
48 hagnizō (1), *sanctify;* to *cleanse* in ritual

PURIFY
2398 châṭâ' (7), to *sin*
2891 ṭâhêr (3), to *be pure, unadulterated*
48 hagnizō (3), *sanctify;* to *cleanse* in ritual
2511 katharizō (1), to *cleanse*

PURIFYING
2403 chaṭṭâ'âh (1), *offence; sin* offering
2892 ṭôhar (2), ceremonial *purification*
2893 ṭohŏrâh (3), ceremonial *purification*
8562 tamrûwq (1), *scouring, perfumery*
48 hagnizō (1), *sanctify;* to *cleanse* in ritual
2511 katharizō (1), to *cleanse*
2512 katharismŏs (2), *ablution; expiation*
2514 katharŏtēs (1), *cleanness*

PURIM
6332 Pûwr (5), *lot* cast

PURITY
47 hagnĕia (2), moral *chastity, purity*

PURLOINING
3557 nŏsphizŏmai (1), to *embezzle*

PURPLE
710 'argᵉvân (1), *purple*
713 'argâmân (38), *purple*
4209 pŏrphura (5), *red-blue color*
4210 pŏrphurŏus (3), *bluish-red*
4211 pŏrphurŏpōlis (1), *trader in bluish-red cloth*

PURPOSE
559 'âmar (2), to *say*
1697 dâbâr (1), *word; matter; thing*
2656 chêphets (3), *pleasure; desire*
2803 châshab (2), to *plot;* to *think, regard*
4284 machăshâbâh (3), *contrivance; plan*
4639 ma'ăseh (1), *action; labor*
6098 'êtsâh (2), *advice; plan; prudence*
6640 tsᵉbûw (Ch.) (1), *determination*
7385 rîyq (1), *emptiness; worthless* thing; *in vain*
7997 shâlal (1), to *drop* or *strip;* to *plunder*
1011 bŏulĕuō (2), to *deliberate;* to *resolve*
1013 bŏulēma (1), *resolve, willful choice*
4286 prŏthĕsis (8), *setting forth*

PURPOSED
2161 zâmam (2), to *plan*
2803 châshab (4), to *plot;* to *think, regard*
3289 yâ'ats (5), to *advise*
3335 yâtsar (1), to *form; potter;* to *determine*
6440 pânîym (1), *face; front*
7760 sûwm (1), to *put, place*
1096+1106 ginŏmai (1), to *be, become*
4160 pŏiĕō (1), to *do*
4388 prŏtithĕmai (2), to *propose, determine*

English

5087 tithēmi (1), to *place*

PURPOSES
2154 zimmâh (1), *plan*
4284 machăshâbâh (3), *contrivance; plan*
8356 shâthâh (1), *basis*

PURPOSETH
4255 prŏairĕŏmai (1), to *propose, intend, decide*

PURSE
3599 kîyç (1), *cup;* utility *bag*
905 balantiŏn (3), money *pouch*
2223 zōnē (1), *belt, sash*

PURSES
2223 zōnē (1), *belt, sash*

PURSUE
3212 yâlak (1), to *walk;* to *live;* to *carry*
7291 râdaph (28), to *run after* with hostility

PURSUED
1692 dâbaq (1), to *cling* or *adhere;* to *catch*
1814 dâlaq (2), to *flame;* to *pursue*
7291 râdaph (35), to *run after* with hostility

PURSUER
7291 râdaph (1), to *run after* with hostility

PURSUERS
7291 râdaph (5), to *run after* with hostility

PURSUETH
7291 râdaph (7), to *run after* with hostility

PURSUING
310 'achar (2), *after*
7291 râdaph (4), to *run after* with hostility
7873 sîyg (1), *withdrawal* into a private place

PURTENANCE
7130 qereb (1), *nearest* part, i.e. the *center*

PUSH
5055 nâgach (6), to *butt*
5056 naggâch (2), act of *butting*
7971 shâlach (1), to *send away*

PUSHED
5055 nâgach (1), to *butt*

PUSHING
5055 nâgach (1), to *butt*

PUT
622 'âçaph (2), to *gather, collect*
935 bôw' (10), to *go, come*
1197 bâ'ar (13), to *be brutish, be senseless*
1396 gâbar (1), to *be strong;* to *prevail*
1644 gârash (2), to *drive* out; to *divorce*
1645 geresh (1), *produce, yield*
1846 dâ'ak (6), to *be extinguished;* to *expire*
1911 hâdah (1), to *stretch forth* the hand

1921 hâdar (1), to *favor* or *honor;* to *be high*
2026 hârag (1), to *kill, slaughter*
2280 châbash (2), to *wrap* firmly, *bind*
2296 châgar (1), to *gird* on a belt; *put on* armor
2330 chûwd (4), to *propound* a riddle
2502 châlats (1), to *pull* off; to *strip;* to *depart*
3240 yânach (5), to *allow to stay*
3254 yâçaph (5), to *add* or *augment*
3318 yâtsâ' (2), to *go, bring out*
3322 yâtsag (2), to *place*
3381 yârad (2), to *descend*
3455 yâsam (1), to *put*
3518 kâbâh (3), to *extinguish*
3637 kâlam (1), to *taunt* or *insult*
3722 kâphar (1), to *cover;* to *expiate*
3847 lâbash (41), to *clothe*
3947 lâqach (1), to *take* kill
4191 mûwth (3), to *die;* to kill
4229 mâchâh (3), to *touch,* i.e. reach to
4916 mishlôwach (1), *sending* out
5056 naggâch (1), act of *butting*
5079 niddâh (2), time of menstrual *impurity*
5114 Nôwdâh (3), *noble*
5148 nâchâh (1), to *guide*
5186 nâṭâh (1), to *stretch* or spread out
5365 nâqar (2), to *bore;* to *gouge*
5381 nâsag (1), to *reach*
5394 nâshal (2), to *divest, eject,* or *drop*
5411 Nâthîyn (1), ones *given* to duty
5414 nâthan (187), to *give*
5493 çûwr (19), to *turn* off
5564 çâmak (5), to *lean* upon; *take hold* of
5595 çâphâh (1), to *scrape;* to *remove*
5596 çâphach (1), to *associate; be united*
5674 'âbar (4), to *cross* over; to *transition*
5786 'âvar (3), to *blind*
5927 'âlâh (3), to *ascend, be high, mount*
6006 'âmaç (1), to *impose* a burden
6186 'ârak (1), to *set in a* row, i.e. *arrange,*
6213 'âsâh (1), to *do*
6316 Pûwṭ (2), *Put*
6319 Pôwṭîy Phera' (2), *Poti-Phera*
6584 pâshaṭ (6), to *strip,* i.e. *unclothe, plunder*
6605 pâthach (1), to *open* wide; to *loosen, begin*
6695 tsôwq (1), *distress*

7368 râchaq (4), to *recede; remove*
7392 râkab (2), to *ride*
7673 shâbath (2), to *repose;* to *desist*
7725 shûwb (7), to *turn* back; to *return*
7760 sûwm (150), to *put*
7896 shîyth (11), to *put*
7971 shâlach (45), to *send away*
7972 shᵉlach (Ch.) (1), to *send away*
7973 shelach (1), *spear; shoot* of growth
8214 shᵉphal (Ch.) (1), to *humiliate*
115 athĕtēsis (1), *cancellation*
142 airō (1), to *lift,* to *take up*
337 anairĕō (2), to *take away,* i.e. *abolish*
363 anamimnēskō (1), to *remind;* to *recollect*
506 anupŏtaktŏs (1), *independent*
520 apagō (1), to *take away*
554 apĕkduŏmai (1), to *divest wholly* oneself
595 apŏthĕsis (1), *laying aside*
615 apŏktĕinō (6), to *kill* outright; to *destroy*
630 apŏluō (13), to *relieve, release*
654 apŏstrĕphō (1), to *turn away* or *back*
659 apŏtithēmi (2), to *put away; get rid of*
683 apōthĕŏmai (2), to *push off;* to *reject*
863 aphiēmi (2), to *leave;* to *pardon, forgive*
906 ballō (14), to *throw*
1096 ginŏmai (1), to *be, become*
1252 diakrinō (1), to *decide;* to *hesitate*
1325 didōmi (5), to *give*
1544 ĕkballō (4), to *throw out*
1614 ĕktĕinō (3), to *stretch*
1677 ĕllŏgĕō (1), *attribute*
1688 ĕmbibazō (1), to *transfer*
1746 ĕnduō (16), to *dress*
1749 ĕnĕdrŏn (1), *ambush*
1808 ĕxairō (1), to *remove, drive away*
1911 ĕpiballō (1), to *throw upon*
2007 ĕpitithēmi (9), to *impose*
2289 thanatŏō (7), to *kill*
2507 kathairĕō (1), to *lower,* or *demolish*
2673 katargĕō (2), to *be, render entirely useless*
3004 lĕgō (1), to *say*
3089 luō (1), to *loosen*
3179 mĕthistēmi (1), to *move*
3856 paradĕigmatizō (1), to *expose to infamy*

3860 paradidōmi (1), to *hand over*
3908 paratithēmi (2), to *present*
3982 pĕithō (1), to *pacify* or *conciliate*
4016 pĕriballō (1), to *wrap around, clothe*
4060 pĕritithēmi (5), to *present*
4160 pŏiĕō (3), to *do*
4374 prŏsphĕrō (1), to *present to;* to *treat as*
5087 tithēmi (15), to place, put
5279 hupŏmimnēskō (4), to *suggest to memory*
5293 hupŏtassō (9), to *subordinate;* to *obey*
5294 hupŏtithēmi (1), to *hazard;* to *suggest*
5392 phimŏō (1), to *restrain to silence*
5562 chōrĕō (2), to *pass, enter;* to *hold, admit*

PUTEOLI
4223 Pŏtiŏlŏi (1), *little wells*

PUTIEL
6317 Pûwṭîy'êl (1), *contempt of God*

PUTRIFYING
2961 ṭârîy (1), *fresh*

PUTTEST
4916 mishlôwach (2), *presentation; seizure*
5414 nâthan (1), to *give*
5596 çâphach (1), to *associate; be united*
7673 shâbath (1), to *repose;* to *desist*
7760 sûwm (2), to *put, place*

PUTTETH
2590 chânaṭ (1), to *embalm;* to *ripen*
5414 nâthan (4), to *give*
5844 'âṭâh (1), to *wrap,* i.e. *cover, veil, clothe*
6605 pâthach (1), to *open* wide; to *loosen, begin*
7760 sûwm (5), to *put*
7971 shâlach (2), to *send away*
8213 shâphêl (1), to *humiliate*
630 apŏluō (1), to *relieve, release; divorce*
649 apŏstĕllō (1), to *send out* on a mission
906 ballō (2), to *throw*
1544 ĕkballō (1), to *throw out*
1631 ĕkphuō (2), to *sprout up, put forth*
1911 ĕpiballō (2), to *throw upon*
5087 tithēmi (2), to place, put

PUTTING
5414 nâthan (1), to *give*
7760 sûwm (1), to *put, place*
7971 shâlach (2), to *send away*
555 apĕkdusis (1), *divestment, removal*

595 apŏthĕsis (1), *laying
aside*
659 apŏtithēmi (1), *to put
away; get rid of*
1745 ĕndusis (1),
investment
1746 ĕnduō (1), *to dress*
1878 ĕpanamimnēskō
(1), *to remind again of*
1936 ĕpithĕsis (1),
imposition
2007 ĕpitithēmi (2), *to
impose*
4261 prŏballō (1), *to push
to the front, germinate*
5087 tithēmi (1), *to
place, put*
5279 hupŏmimnēskō (1),
to suggest to memory

PYGARG
1787 Dîyshôwn, (1),
antelope

QUAILS
7958 sᵉlâv (4), *quail bird*

QUAKE
7264 râgaz (1), *to quiver*
7493 râ'ash (1), *to
undulate, quake*
1790 ĕntrŏmŏs (1),
terrified
4579 sĕiō (1), *to vibrate;
to agitate*

QUAKED
2729 chârad (1), *to
shudder*
7264 râgaz (1), *to quiver*

QUAKING
2731 chărâdâh (1), *fear,
anxiety*
7494 ra'ash (1),
vibration, uproar

QUARREL
579 'ânâh (1), *to meet, to
happen*
5359 nâqâm (1), *revenge*
1758 ĕnĕchō (1), *to keep
a grudge*
3437 mŏmphē (1), *blame*

QUARRIES
6456 pᵉçîyl (2), *idol*

QUARTER
5676 ' êber (1), *opposite
side; east*
6285 pê'âh (4), *region;
extremity*
7098 qâtsâh (2),
termination; fringe
3836 pantachŏthĕn (1),
from all directions

QUARTERS
1366 gᵉbûwl (1),
boundary, border
3411 yᵉrêkâh (1), *far
away places*
3671 kânâph (1), *edge or
extremity; wing*
7098 qâtsâh (1),
termination; fringe
7307 rûwach (1), *breath;
wind; life*-spirit
1137 gōnia (1), *angle;
cornerstone*
5117 tŏpŏs (2), *place*

QUARTUS
2890 Kŏuartŏs (1), *fourth*

QUATERNIONS
5069 tĕtradiŏn (1), *squad
of four Roman soldiers*

QUEEN
1377 gᵉbîyrâh (6),
mistress
4427 mâlak (2), *to reign
as king*
4433 malkâ' (Ch.) (2),
queen
4436 malkâh (33), *queen*
4446 mᵉleketh (5), *queen*
7694 shêgâl (2), *queen*
938 basilissa (4), *queen*

QUEENS
4436 malkâh (2), *queen*
8282 sârâh (1), *female
noble*

QUENCH
3518 kâbâh (8), *to
extinguish*
7665 shâbar (1), *to burst*
4570 sbĕnnumi (3), *to
extinguish, snuff out*

QUENCHED
1846 dâ'ak (1), *to be
extinguished; to expire*
3518 kâbâh (9), *to
extinguish*
8257 shâqa' (1), *to be
overflowed; to cease*
762 asbĕstŏs (2), *not
extinguished*
4570 sbĕnnumi (4), *to
extinguish, snuff out*

QUESTION
1458 ĕgkalĕō (1), *to bring
crimination*
2213 zētēma (2), *debate,
dispute*
2214 zētēsis (1), *dispute
or its theme*
2919 krinō (2), *to decide;
to try, condemn, punish*
3056 lŏgŏs (1), *word,
matter, thing; Word*
4802 suzētĕō (2), *to
discuss, controvert*

QUESTIONED
1875 dârash (1), *to seek
or ask; to worship*
1905 ĕpĕrōtaō (1), *to
inquire, seek*
4802 suzētĕō (1), *to
discuss, controvert*

QUESTIONING
4802 suzētĕō (2), *to
discuss, controvert*

QUESTIONS
1697 dâbâr (2), *word;
matter; thing*
2420 chîydâh (2), *puzzle;
conundrum; maxim*
1905 ĕpĕrōtaō (1), *to
inquire, seek*
2213 zētēma (3), *debate,
dispute*
2214 zētēsis (5), *dispute*

QUICK
2416 chay (3), *alive; raw;
fresh; life*
4241 michyâh (2),
preservation of life
2198 zaō (4), *to live*

QUICKEN
2421 châyâh (12), *to live*

2227 zōŏpŏiĕō (1), *to* (re-)
vitalize, give life

QUICKENED
2421 châyâh (2), *to live*
2227 zōŏpŏiĕō (2), *to* (re-)
vitalize, give life
4806 suzōŏpŏiĕō (2), *to
reanimate conjointly*

QUICKENETH
2227 zōŏpŏiĕō (5), *to* (re-)
vitalize, give life

QUICKENING
2227 zōŏpŏiĕō (1), *to* (re-)
vitalize, give life

QUICKLY
3966 mᵉ'ôd (1), *very*
4116 mâhar (3), *to hurry*
4118 mahêr (8), *in a
hurry*
4120 mᵉhêrâh (10),
hurry; promptly
1722+5034 ĕn (2), *in;
during; because of*
5030 tachĕōs (2),
speedily, rapidly
5032 tachiŏn (1), *more
rapidly, more speedily*
5035 tachu (12), *without
delay, soon, suddenly*

QUICKSANDS
4950 surtis (1), *sand
drawn by the waves*

QUIET
2790 chârash (1), *to be
silent; to be deaf*
4496 mᵉnûwchâh (1),
peacefully; consolation
5117 nûwach (1), *to rest;
to settle down*
5183 nachath (1),
descent; quiet
7282 râgêa' (1), *restful,
i.e. peaceable*
7599 shâ'an (2), *to loll,
i.e. be peaceful*
7600 sha'ănân (2),
secure; haughty
7961 shâlêv (1), *carefree;
security, at ease*
8003 shâlêm (1),
complete; friendly; safe
8252 shâqat (15), *to
repose*
8367 shâthaq (1), *to
subside*
2263 ĕrĕmŏs (1),
tranquil, peaceful
2270 hēsuchazō (1), *to
refrain*
2272 hēsuchiŏs (1), *still,
undisturbed*
2687 katastĕllō (1), *to
quell, quiet*

QUIETED
1826 dâmam (1), *to be
silent; to stop, cease*
5117 nûwach (1), *to rest;
to settle down*

QUIETETH
8252 shâqat (1), *to repose*

QUIETLY
7987 shᵉlîy (1), *privacy*

QUIETNESS
5183 nachath (1), *quiet*
7961 shâlêv (1), *carefree;
security, at ease*

7962 shalvâh (1),
security, ease
8252 shâqat (4), *to repose*
8253 sheqet (1),
tranquillity
1515 ĕirēnē (1), *peace;
health; prosperity*
2271 hēsuchia (1),
stillness

QUIT
1961 hâyâh (1), *to exist,
i.e. be or become*
5352 nâqâh (1), *to be
bare, i.e. extirpated*
5355 nâqîy (2), *innocent*
407 andrizŏmai (1), *to
act manly*

QUITE
3615 kâlâh (1), *to cease,
be finished, perish*
5080 nâdach (1), *to push
off, scattered*
6181 'eryâh (1), *nudity*

QUIVER
827 'ashpâh (6), *quiver*
8522 tᵉlîy (1), *quiver*

QUIVERED
6750 tsâlal (1), *to tinkle,
to rattle together*

RAAMAH
7484 Ra'mâh (5), *horse's
mane*

RAAMIAH
7485 Ra'amyâh (1),
Jehovah has shaken

RAAMSES
7486 Ra'mᵉçêç (1),
Rameses or Raamses

RAB-MAG
7248 Rab-Mâg (2), *chief
Magian*

RAB-SARIS
7249 Rab-Çârîyç (3),
chief chamberlain

RAB-SHAKEH
7262 Rabshâqêh (8),
chief butler

RABBAH
7237 Rabbâh (13), *great*

RABBATH
7237 Rabbâh (2), *great*

RABBI
4461 rhabbi (7), *my
master*

RABBITH
7245 Rabbîyth (1),
multitude

RABBONI
4462 rhabbŏni (1), *my
master*

RABSHAKEH
7262 Rabshâqêh (8),
chief butler

RACA
4469 rhaka (1), *O empty
one, i.e. worthless*

RACE
734 'ôrach (1), *road;
manner of life*
4793 mêrôwts (1),
running foot-race
73 agŏn (1), *contest,
struggle*

English

4712 stadiŏn (1), *length of about 200 yards*

RACHAB
4477 Rhachab (1), *proud*

RACHAL
7403 Râkâl (1), *merchant*

RACHEL
7354 Râchêl (41), *ewe*
4478 Rhachêl (1), *ewe*

RACHEL'S
7354 Râchêl (5), *ewe*

RADDAI
7288 Radday (1), *domineering*

RAFTERS
7351 rᵉchîyṭ (1), *panel*

RAGAU
4466 Rhagau (1), *friend*

RAGE
1984 hâlal (2), to *boast*
2195 za'am (1), *fury*
2197 za'aph (2), *anger*
2534 chêmâh (2), *heat; anger; poison*
5678 'ebrâh (2), *outburst*
7264 râgaz (5), to *quiver*
7266 rᵉgaz (Ch.) (1), *violent anger*
7267 rôgez (1), *disquiet; anger*
7283 râgash (1), to *be tumultuous*
5433 phruassō (1), to *make a tumult*

RAGED
1993 hâmâh (1), to *be in great commotion*

RAGETH
5674 'âbar (1), to *cross over; to transition*

RAGING
1348 gê'ûwth (1), *ascending; majesty*
1993 hâmâh (1), to *be in great commotion*
2197 za'aph (1), *anger, rage*
66 agriŏs (1), *wild (country)*
2830 kludōn (1), *surge, raging*

RAGS
899 beged (1), *clothing; treachery or pillage*
4418 mâlâch (2), *rag or old garment*
7168 qera' (1), *rag, torn pieces*

RAGUEL
7467 Rᵉ'ûw'êl (1), *friend of God*

RAHAB
7294 Rahab (3), *boaster*
7343 Râchâb (5), *proud*
4460 Rhaab (2), *proud*

RAHAM
7357 Racham (1), *pity*

RAHEL
7354 Râchêl (1), *ewe*

RAIL
2778 châraph (1), to *spend the winter*

RAILED
5860 'îyṭ (1), to *swoop down upon; to insult*
987 blasphēmĕō (2), to *speak impiously*

RAILER
3060 lŏidŏrŏs (1), *verbal abuser*

RAILING
988 blasphēmia (1), *impious speech*
989 blasphēmŏs (1), *slanderous*
3059 lŏidŏria (1), *slander*

RAILINGS
988 blasphēmia (1), *impious speech*

RAIMENT
899 beged (12), *clothing; treachery or pillage*
3682 kᵉçûwth (1), *cover; veiling*
3830 lᵉbûwsh (1), *garment; wife*
4055 mad (1), *vesture, garment; carpet*
4254 machălâtsâh (1), *mantle, garment*
4403 malbûwsh (3), *garment, clothing*
7553 riqmâh (1), *variegation of color*
8008 salmâh (5), *clothing*
8071 simlâh (11), *dress*
1742 ĕnduma (1), *apparel, outer robe*
2066 ĕsthēs (1), to *clothe*
2440 himatiŏn (12), to *put on clothes*
2441 himatismŏs (2), *clothing*
4629 skĕpasma (1), *clothing; covering*

RAIN
1653 geshem (30), *rain*
3138 yôwreh (1), *autumn rain showers*
3384 yârâh (2), to *throw, shoot an arrow*
4175 môwreh (3), *archer; teaching; early rain*
4305 mâṭar (11), to *rain*
4306 mâṭar (37), *rain, shower of rain*
4456 malqôwsh (6), *spring rain*
8164 sâ'îyr (1), *shower*
1026 brĕchō (2), to *make wet; to rain*
1026+5205 brĕchō (1), to *make wet; to rain*
1028 brŏchē (2), *rain*
5205 huĕtŏs (5), *rain; rain shower*

RAINBOW
2463 iris (2), *rainbow*

RAINED
1656 gôshem (1), *rain downpour*
4305 mâṭar (6), to *rain*
1026 brĕchō (2), to *make wet; to rain*

RAINY
5464 çagrîyd (1), *pouring rain*

RAISE
5375 nâsâ' (2), to *lift up*
5549 çâlal (2), to *mound up; to exalt*
5782 'ûwr (6), to *awake*
6965 qûwm (30), to *rise*
450 anistēmi (8), to *rise; to come to life*
1453 ĕgĕirō (8), to *waken, i.e. rouse*
1817 ĕxanistēmi (2), to *beget, raise up*
1825 ĕxĕgĕirō (1), to *resuscitate; release*

RAISED
1361 gâbahh (1), to *be lofty; to be haughty*
5782 'ûwr (12), to *awake*
5927 'âlâh (3), to *ascend, be high, mount*
5975 'âmad (1), to *stand*
6209 'ârar (1), to *bare; to demolish*
6965 qûwm (10), to *rise*
6966 qûwm (Ch.) (1), to *rise*
386 anastasis (1), *resurrection from death*
450 anistēmi (6), to *rise; to come to life*
1326 diĕgĕirō (1), to *arouse, stimulate*
1453 ĕgĕirō (45), to *waken, i.e. rouse*
1825 ĕxĕgĕirō (1), to *resuscitate; release*
1892 ĕpĕgĕirō (1), to *excite against, stir up*
4891 sunĕgĕirō (1), to *raise up with*

RAISER
5674 'âbar (1), to *cross over; to transition*

RAISETH
2210 zâqaph (2), to *lift up, comfort*
5975 'âmad (1), to *stand*
6965 qûwm (2), to *rise*
7613 sᵉ'êth (1), *elevation; swelling leprous scab*
1453 ĕgĕirō (2), to *waken, i.e. rouse*

RAISING
5872 'Êyn Gedîy (1), *fountain of a kid*
4160+1999 pŏiĕō (1), to *do*

RAISINS
6778 tsammûwq (4), *lump of dried grapes*

RAKEM
7552 Reqem (1), *versi-color*

RAKKATH
7557 Raqqath (1), *beach (as expanded shingle)*

RAKKON
7542 Raqqôwn (1), *thinness*

RAM
352 'ayîl (89), *chief; ram*
7410 Râm (7), *high*

RAM'S
3104 yôwbêl (1), *blast of a ram's horn*

RAMA
4471 Rhama (1), *height*

RAMAH
7414 Râmâh (36), *height*

RAMATH
7418 Râmôwth-Negeb (1), *heights of* (the) *South*

RAMATH-LEHI
7437 Râmath Lechîy (1), *height of* (a) *jaw-bone*

RAMATH-MIZPEH
7434 Râmath ham-Mitspeh (1), *height of the watch-tower*

RAMATHAIM-ZOPHIM
7436 Râmâthayim Tsôwphîym (1), *double height of watchers*

RAMATHITE
7435 Râmâthîy (1), *Ramathite*

RAMESES
7486 Ra'mᵉçêç (4), *Rameses or Raamses*

RAMIAH
7422 Ramyâh (1), *Jehovah has raised*

RAMOTH
3406 Yᵉrîymôwth (1), *elevations*
7216 Râ'môwth (6), *heights*
7418 Râmôwth-Negeb (1), *heights of* (the) *South*

RAMOTH-GILEAD
7433 Râmôth Gil'âd (19), *heights of Gilad*

RAMPART
2426 chêyl (2), *rampart, battlement*

RAMS
352 'ayîl (61), *chief; ram*
1798 dᵉkar (Ch.) (3), *male sheep*
3733 kar (2), *ram sheep; battering ram*
6260 'attûwd (2), *he-goats; leaders*

RAMS'
352 'ayîl (5), *chief; ram*
3104 yôwbêl (4), *blast of a ram's horn*

RAN
1272 bârach (1), to *flee suddenly*
1980 hâlak (2), to *walk; live a certain way*
3331 yâtsa' (1), to *strew as a surface*
3332 yâtsaq (1), to *pour out*
5064 nâgar (1), to *pour out; to deliver over*
6379 pâkâh (1), to *pour, trickle*
6584 pâshaṭ (1), to *strip, i.e. unclothe, plunder*
7323 rûwts (30), to *run*
7519 râtsâ' (1), to *run; to delight in*
7857 shâṭaph (1), to *gush; to inundate*

1530 ĕispēdaō (1), to
rush in
1532 ĕistrĕchō (1), to
hasten inward
1632 ĕkchĕō (1), to *pour
forth; to bestow*
2027 ĕpŏkĕllō (1), to
beach a ship vessel
2701 katatrĕchō (1), to
hasten, run
3729 hŏrmaō (4), to *dash
or plunge, stampede*
4063 pĕritrĕchō (1), to
traverse, run about
4370 prŏstrĕchō (1), to
hasten by running
4390 prŏtrĕchō (1), to *run
ahead*, i.e. to *precede*
4890 sundrŏmē (1),
(riotous) *concourse*
4936 suntrĕchō (2), to
rush together
5143 trĕchō (6), to *run or
walk hastily; to strive*

RANG
1949 hûwm (2), to *make
an uproar; agitate*

RANGE
3491 yâthûwr (1),
gleaning

RANGES
3600 kîyr (1), portable
cooking *range*
7713 sᵉdêrâh (3), *row*, i.e.
rank of soldiers; *story*

RANGING
8264 shâqaq (1), to *seek*

RANK
1277 bârîy' (2), *fatted or
plump; healthy*
4634 ma'ărâkâh (1), *row;
pile*; military *array*
5737 'âdar (1), to
arrange; hoe a vineyard

RANKS
734 'ôrach (1), *road;
manner of life*
6471 pa'am (2), *time;
step; occurence*
4237 prasia (1),
arranged group

RANSOM
3724 kôpher (8), *village;
redemption*-price
6299 pâdâh (1), to
ransom; to release
6306 pidyôwm (1),
ransom; payment
487 antilutrŏn (1),
redemption-price
3083 lutrŏn (2),
redemption-price

RANSOMED
1350 gâ'al (2), to *redeem;
to be the next of kin*
6299 pâdâh (1), to
ransom; to release

RAPHA
7498 Râphâ' (2), *giant*

RAPHU
7505 Râphûw' (1), *cured*

RARE
3358 yaqqîyr (Ch.) (1),
precious

RASE
6168 'ârâh (1), to *be,
make bare; demolish*

RASH
926 bâhal (1), to *tremble;
hasten, hurry anxiously*
4116 mâhar (1), to *hurry;
promptly*

RASHLY
4312 prŏpĕtēs (1), falling
forward *headlong*

RASOR
8593 ta'ar (1), *knife;
razor; scabbard*

RATE
1697 dâbâr (5), *word;
matter; thing*

RATHER
408 'al (2), *not; nothing*
977 bâchar (1), *select,
chose, prefer*
2228 ē (3), *or; than*
2309 thĕlō (1), to *will*; to
desire; to choose
3123 mallŏn (34), *in a
greater degree*
3304 mĕnŏungĕ (1), *so
then at least*
4056 pĕrissŏtĕrōs (1),
more superabundantly
4133 plēn (2), *rather, yet*

RATTLETH
7439 rânâh (1), to *whiz,
rattle*

RATTLING
7494 ra'ash (1),
vibration, bounding

RAVEN
6158 'ôrêb (6),
dusky-hue *raven*

RAVENING
2963 țâraph (3), to *pluck
off or pull* to pieces
724 harpagē (1), *pillage;
greediness; robbery*
727 harpax (1),
rapacious; robbing

RAVENOUS
5861 'ayiț (2), bird of
prey (poss.) *hawk*
6530 pᵉrîyts (1), *violent*

RAVENS
6158 'ôrêb (4),
dusky-hue *raven*
2876 kŏrax (1), *crow* or
raven

RAVIN
2963 țâraph (1), to *pluck
off or pull* to pieces
2966 țᵉrêphâh (1), *torn
prey*

RAVISHED
3823 lâbab (2), *transport
with love; to stultify*
6031 'ânâh (1), to *afflict,
be afflicted*
7686 shâgâh (2), to *stray,
wander; to transgress*
7693 shâgal (2), to
copulate with

RAW
2416 chay (6), *alive; raw;
fresh; life*
4995 nâ' (1), *uncooked*

RAZOR
4177 môwrâh (3), *razor*
8593 ta'ar (2), *knife;
razor; scabbard*

REACH
1272 bârach (1), to *flee
suddenly*
1961 hâyâh (1), to *exist*,
i.e. *be or become*
4229 mâchâh (1), to
touch, i.e. reach to
5060 nâga' (5), to *strike*
5381 nâsag (2), to *reach*
2185 ĕphiknĕŏmai (1), to
extend to, reach to
5342 phĕrō (2), to *bear or
carry*

REACHED
4291 mᵉțâ' (Ch.) (2), to
arrive, to extend
5060 nâga' (1), to *strike*
6293 pâga' (1), to *impinge*
6642 tsâbaț (1), to *hand
out food*
190 akŏlŏuthĕō (1), to
accompany, follow
2185 ĕphiknĕŏmai (1), to
extend to, reach to

REACHETH
4291 mᵉțâ' (Ch.) (1), to
arrive, to extend
5060 nâga' (4), to *strike*
6293 pâga' (5), to *impinge*
7971 shâlach (1), to *send
away*

REACHING
5060 nâga' (3), to *strike*
1901 ĕpĕktĕinŏmai (1), to
stretch oneself forward

READ
7121 qârâ' (35), to *call
out*
7123 qᵉrâ' (Ch.) (7), to
call out
314 anaginōskō (28), to
read aloud in public

READEST
314 anaginōskō (2), to
read aloud in public

READETH
7121 qârâ' (1), to *call out*
314 anaginōskō (3), to
read aloud in public

READINESS
2092 hĕtŏimŏs (1), *ready,
prepared*
4288 prŏthumia (2),
alacrity, eagerness

READING
4744 miqrâ' (1), public
meeting
7121 qârâ' (2), to *call out*
320 anagnōsis (3), act of
public *reading*

READY
631 'âçar (4), to *fasten*; to
join battle
1951 hûwn (1), to *be, act
light*
2363 chûwsh (1), to
hurry; to be eager
2896 țôwb (1), *good; well*
3559 kûwn (17), to *set up;
establish, fix, prepare*
4106 mâhîyr (2), *skillful*

4116 mâhar (2), to *hurry;
promptly*
4131 môwț (1), to *slip,
shake, fall*
4672 mâtsâ' (1), to *find
or acquire; to occur*
5750 'ôwd (1), *again;
repeatedly; still; more*
6257 'âthad (1), to
prepare
6263 'ăthîyd (Ch.) (1),
prepared
6264 'âthîyd (4),
prepared; treasure
7126 qârab (1), to
approach, bring near
7138 qârôwb (1), *near,
close*
8003 shâlêm (1),
complete; friendly; safe
1451 ĕggus (1), *near,
close*
2090 hĕtŏimazō (10), to
prepare
2092 hĕtŏimŏs (15),
ready, prepared
2093 hĕtŏimōs (3), *in
readiness*
2130 ĕumĕtadŏtŏs (1),
liberal, generous
3195 mĕllō (4), to *intend*,
i.e. *be about* to
3903 paraskĕuazō (3), to
get ready, prepare
4288 prŏthumia (1),
alacrity, eagerness
4289 prŏthumŏs (3),
alacrity, eagerness
4689 spĕndō (1), to *pour
out as a libation*

REAIA
7211 Rᵉâyâh (1),
Jehovah has seen

REAIAH
7211 Rᵉâyâh (3),
Jehovah has seen

REALM
4437 malkûw (Ch.) (3),
dominion
4438 malkûwth (4), *rule;
dominion*

REAP
7114 qâtsar (18), to
curtail, cut short
2325 thĕrizō (13), to
harvest, reap a crop

REAPED
7114 qâtsar (1), to
curtail, cut short
270 amaō (1), *reap, mow
down grain*
2325 thĕrizō (2), to
harvest, reap a crop

REAPER
7114 qâtsar (1), to
curtail, cut short

REAPERS
7114 qâtsar (7), to
curtail, cut short
2327 thĕristēs (2),
harvester, reaper

REAPEST
7114 qâtsar (1), to
curtail, cut short
2325 thĕrizō (1), to
harvest, reap a crop

English

REAPETH
7114 qâtsar (1), to
curtail, cut short
2325 thĕrizō (3), to
harvest, reap a crop

REAPING
7114 qâtsar (1), to
curtail, cut short
2325 thĕrizō (2), to
harvest, reap a crop

REAR
6965 qûwm (3), to rise
1453 ĕgĕirō (1), to
waken, i.e. rouse

REARED
5324 nâtsab (1), to station
6965 qûwm (9), to rise

REASON
413 'êl (1), to, toward
1697 dâbâr (1), word;
matter; thing
2808 cheshbôwn (1),
intelligent plan
2940 ṭa'am (1), taste;
intelligence; mandate
3198 yâkach (3), to be
correct; to argue
4480 min (5), from, out of
4486 manda' (Ch.) (1),
wisdom or intelligence
5921 'al (2), above, over,
upon, or against
5973 'îm (1), with
6440 pânîym (9), face;
front
6903 qᵉbêl (Ch.) (1), on
account of, so as, since
8199 shâphaṭ (1), to judge
701 arĕstŏs (1),
agreeable; desirable; fit
1223 dia (1), through, by
means of; because of
1260 dialŏgizŏmai (5), to
deliberate
1537 ĕk (1), out, out of
1752 hĕnĕka (1), on
account of
3056 lŏgŏs (2), word,
matter, thing; Word

REASONABLE
3050 lŏgikŏs (1),
rational, logical

REASONED
1256 dialĕgŏmai (4), to
discuss
1260 dialŏgizŏmai (5), to
deliberate
3049 lŏgizŏmai (1), to
credit; to think, regard
4802 suzētĕō (1), to
discuss, controvert
4817 sullŏgizŏmai (1), to
reckon together

REASONING
8433 tôwkêchâh (1),
correction, refutation
1260 dialŏgizŏmai (1), to
deliberate
1261 dialŏgismŏs (1),
consideration; debate
4802 suzētĕō (1), to
discuss, controvert
4803 suzētēsis (1),
discussion, dispute

REASONS
8394 tâbûwn (1),
intelligence; argument

REBA
7254 Reba' (2), fourth

REBECCA
4479 Rhĕbĕkka (1),
fettering (by beauty)

REBEKAH
7259 Ribqâh (28),
fettering (by beauty)

REBEKAH'S
7259 Ribqâh (2), fettering
(by beauty)

REBEL
4775 mârad (9), to rebel
4784 mârâh (4), to rebel
or resist; to provoke
5493 çûwr (1), to turn off

REBELLED
4775 mârad (12), to rebel
4784 mârâh (16), to rebel
or resist; to provoke
6586 pâsha' (5), to break
away from authority
6856 tsippôren (1), nail;
point of a style or pen

REBELLEST
4775 mârad (2), to rebel

REBELLION
4776 mᵉrad (Ch.) (1),
rebellion
4779 mârâd (Ch.) (1),
rebellious
4805 mᵉrîy (4), rebellion,
rebellious
5627 çârâh (2), apostasy;
crime; remission
6588 pesha' (1), revolt

REBELLIOUS
4775 mârad (1), to rebel
4779 mârâd (Ch.) (2),
rebellious
4780 mardûwth (1),
rebelliousness
4784 mârâh (9), to rebel
or resist; to provoke
4805 mᵉrîy (17),
rebellion, rebellious
5637 çârar (6), to be
refractory, stubborn

REBELS
4775 mârad (1), to rebel
4784 mârâh (1), to rebel
or resist; to provoke
4805 mᵉrîy (1), rebellion,
rebellious

REBUKE
1605 gâ'ar (7), to chide,
reprimand
1606 gᵉ'ârâh (12),
chiding, rebuke
2781 cherpâh (2),
contumely, disgrace
3198 yâkach (8), to be
correct; to argue
4045 mig'ereth (1),
reproof (i.e. a curse)
8433 tôwkêchâh (4),
refutation, proof
298 amōmētŏs (1),
unblemished
1651 ĕlĕgchō (4), to
admonish, rebuke

1969 ĕpiplēssō (1), to
upbraid, rebuke
2008 ĕpitimaō (6), to
rebuke, warn, forbid

REBUKED
1605 gâ'ar (4), to chide,
reprimand
3198 yâkach (1), to be
correct; to argue
7378 rîyb (1), to hold a
controversy; to defend
1651 ĕlĕgchō (1), to
admonish, rebuke
2008 ĕpitimaō (17), to
rebuke, warn, forbid
2192+1649 ĕchō (1), to
have; hold; keep

REBUKER
4148 mûwçâr (1),
reproof, warning

REBUKES
8433 tôwkêchâh (3),
correction, refutation

REBUKETH
1605 gâ'ar (1), to chide,
reprimand
3198 yâkach (3), to be
correct; to argue

REBUKING
1606 gᵉ'ârâh (1), chiding,
rebuke
2008 ĕpitimaō (1), to
rebuke, warn, forbid

RECALL
7725 shûwb (1), to turn
back; to return

RECEIPT
5058 tĕlōniŏn (3),
tax-gatherer's booth

RECEIVE
1878 dâshên (1), to
fatten; to satisfy
3557 kûwl (2), to keep in;
to measure
3947 lâqach (35), to take
5162 nâcham (1), to be
sorry; to pity, console
5375 nâsâ' (3), to lift up
6901 qâbal (3), to admit;
to take
6902 qᵉbal (Ch.) (1), to
acquire
8254 shâqal (1), to
suspend in trade
308 anablĕpō (7), to look
up; to recover sight
568 apĕchō (1), to be
distant
588 apŏdĕchŏmai (1), to
welcome; approve
618 apŏlambanō (8), to
receive; be repaid
1209 dĕchŏmai (24), to
receive, welcome
1325 didōmi (1), to give
1523 ĕisdĕchŏmai (1), to
take into one's favor
1926 ĕpidĕchŏmai (1), to
admit, welcome
2210 zēmiŏō (1), to
experience detriment
2865 kŏmizō (6), to
provide for
2983 lambanō (61), to
take, receive

3858 paradĕchŏmai (4),
to accept, receive
3880 paralambanō (1), to
assume an office
4327 prŏsdĕchŏmai (2),
to receive; to await for
4355 prŏslambanō (4), to
welcome, receive
5562 chōrĕō (5), to pass,
enter; to hold, admit

RECEIVED
622 'âçaph (1), to gather,
collect
1961 hâyâh (2), to exist,
i.e. be or become
2388 châzaq (1), to
fasten upon; to seize
2505 châlaq (1), to be
smooth; be slippery
3947 lâqach (22), to take
4672 mâtsâ' (1), to find
or acquire; to occur
6901 qâbal (3), to admit;
to take
308 anablĕpō (8), to look
up; to recover sight
324 anadĕchŏmai (2), to
entertain as a guest
353 analambanō (3), to
take up, bring up
354 analēpsis (1),
ascension
568 apĕchō (1), to be
distant
588 apŏdĕchŏmai (4),
welcome; approve
618 apŏlambanō (1), to
receive; be repaid
1183 dĕkatŏō (1), to give
or take a tenth
1209 dĕchŏmai (16), to
receive, welcome
1653 ĕlĕĕō (1), to give out
compassion
2865 kŏmizō (3), to
provide for, to carry off
2983 lambanō (56), to
take, receive
3336 mĕtalēmpsis (1),
participation, sharing
3549 nŏmŏthĕtĕō (1), to
be given law
3880 paralambanō (13),
to assume an office
4355 prŏslambanō (3), to
welcome, receive
4687 spĕirō (4), to
scatter, i.e. sow seed
4732 stĕrĕŏō (1), to be,
become strong
5264 hupŏdĕchŏmai (4),
to entertain hospitably
5274 hupŏlambanō (1),
to take up, i.e. continue

RECEIVEDST
618 apŏlambanō (1), to
receive; be repaid

RECEIVER
8254 shâqal (1), to
suspend in trade

RECEIVETH
622 'âçaph (1), to gather,
collect
3947 lâqach (4), to take
1209 dĕchŏmai (8), to
receive, welcome
1926 ĕpidĕchŏmai (1), to
admit, welcome

2983 lambanō (14), *to take, receive*
3335 mĕtalambanō (1), *to participate*
3858 paradĕchŏmai (1), *to accept, receive*
4327 prŏsdĕchŏmai (1), *to receive; to await for*

RECEIVING
3947 lâqach (1), *to take*
618 apŏlambanō (1), *to receive; be repaid*
2865 kōmizō (1), *to provide* for, *to carry* off
2983 lambanō (1), *to take, receive*
3028 lēmpsis (1), act of receipt
3880 paralambanō (1), *to assume* an office
4356 prŏslēpsis (1), *admission, acceptance*

RECHAB
7394 Rêkâb (13), *rider*

RECHABITES
7397 Rêkâh (4), *softness*

RECHAH
7397 Rêkâh (1), *softness*

RECKON
2803 châshab (3), to *think, regard;* to *value*
5608 çâphar (1), to *inscribe;* to *enumerate*
6485 pâqad (1), to *visit, care for, count*
3049 lŏgizŏmai (2), to *credit;* to *think, regard*
4868 sunairō (1), to *compute* an account

RECKONED
2803 châshab (4), to *think, regard;* to *value*
3187 yâchas (12), to *enroll* by *family list*
7737 shâvâh (1), to *resemble;* to *adjust*
3049 lŏgizŏmai (4), to *credit;* to *think, regard*

RECKONETH
4868+3056 sunairō (1), to *compute* an account

RECKONING
2803 châshab (1), to *think, regard;* to *value*
6486 pᵉquddâh (1), *visitation; punishment*

RECOMMENDED
3860 paradidōmi (2), to *hand over*

RECOMPENCE
1576 gᵉmûwl (9), *act; reward, recompense*
7966 shillûwm (1), *requital; retribution; fee*
8005 shillêm (1), *requital*
8545 tᵉmûwrâh (1), *barter, compensation*
468 antapŏdŏma (2), *requital, recompense*
489 antimisthia (2), *correspondence*
3405 misthapŏdŏsia (3), *requital, good or bad*

RECOMPENCES
1578 gᵉmûwlâh (1), *act; reward, recompense*
7966 shillûwm (1), *requital; retribution; fee*

RECOMPENSE
1580 gâmal (2), to *benefit* or *requite;* to *wean*
5414 nâthan (9), to *give*
7725 shûwb (3), to *return* or restore
7999 shâlam (7), to *be safe;* to *reciprocate*
467 antapŏdidōmi (3), to *requite* good or evil
591 apŏdidōmi (1), to *give away*

RECOMPENSED
5414 nâthan (1), to *give*
7725 shûwb (5), to *return* or restore
7999 shâlam (2), to *be safe;* to *reciprocate*
467 antapŏdidōmi (2), to *requite* good or evil

RECOMPENSEST
7999 shâlam (1), to *be safe;* to *reciprocate*

RECOMPENSING
5414 nâthan (1), to *give*

RECONCILE
3722 kâphar (2), to *placate* or *cancel*
7521 râtsâh (1), to *be pleased with;* to *satisfy*
604 apŏkatallassō (2), to *reconcile fully, reunite*

RECONCILED
604 apŏkatallassō (1), to *reconcile fully, reunite*
1259 diallassō (1), to *be reconciled*
2644 katallassō (5), to *change mutually*

RECONCILIATION
2398 châṭâ' (1), to *sin*
3722 kâphar (4), to *placate* or *cancel*
2433 hilaskŏmai (1), to *conciliate,* to *atone* for
2643 katallagē (2), *restoration*

RECONCILING
3722 kâphar (1), to *cover;* to *expiate*
2643 katallagē (1), *restoration*
2644 katallassō (1), to *change mutually*

RECORD
1799 dikrôwn (Ch.) (1), *official register*
2142 zâkar (2), to *remember;* to *mention*
5749 'ûwd (3), to *duplicate* or *repeat*
7717 sâhêd (1), *witness*
3140 marturĕō (13), to *testify;* to *commend*
3141 marturia (7), *evidence given*
3143 marturŏmai (1), to *witness*
3144 martus (2), *witness*

RECORDED
3789 kâthab (1), to *write*

RECORDER
2142 zâkar (9), to *remember;* to *mention*

RECORDS
1799 dikrôwn (Ch.) (2), *official register*
2146 zikrôwn (1), *commemoration*

RECOUNT
2142 zâkar (1), to *remember;* to *mention*

RECOVER
622 'âçaph (4), to *gather, collect*
1082 bâlag (1), to *be comforted*
2421 châyâh (6), to *live;* to *revive*
2492 châlam (1), to *be, make plump;* to *dream*
4241 michyâh (1), *preservation of life; sustenance*
5337 nâtsal (3), to *deliver;* to *be snatched*
6113 'âtsar (1), to *hold back;* to *maintain, rule*
7069 qânâh (1), to *create;* to *procure*
7725 shûwb (1), to *turn* back; to *return*
366 ananēphō (1), to *regain* one's *senses*
2192+2573 ĕchō (1), to *have; hold; keep*

RECOVERED
2388 châzaq (1), to *fasten* upon; to *seize*
2421 châyâh (2), to *live;* to *revive*
5337 nâtsal (2), to *deliver;* to *be snatched*
5927 'âlâh (1), to *ascend, be high, mount*
7725 shûwb (5), to *turn* back; to *return*

RECOVERING
309 anablĕpsis (1), *restoration of sight*

RED
119 'âdam (9), to *be red in the face*
122 'âdôm (7), *rosy, red*
132 'admônîy (1), *reddish, ruddy*
923 bahaṭ (1), *white marble*
2447 chaklîyl (1), *darkly flashing eyes; brilliant*
2560 châmar (1), to *ferment, foam;* to *glow*
2561 chemer (1), *fermenting wine*
5488 çûwph (24), *papyrus reed; reed*
5489 Çûwph (1), *reed*
5492 çûwphâh (1), *hurricane wind*
2281 thalassa (2), *sea or lake*
4449 purrhazō (2), to *redden*
4450 purrhŏs (2), *fire-like, flame-colored*

REDDISH
125 'âdamdâm (6), *reddish*

REDEEM
1350 gâ'al (23), to *redeem; be next of kin*
1353 gᵉullâh (5), *redemption*
6299 pâdâh (24), to *ransom;* to *release*
6304 pᵉdûwth (1), *distinction; deliverance*
1805 ĕxagŏrazō (1), to *buy up, ransom*
3084 lutrŏō (1), to *free* by *paying a ransom*

REDEEMED
1350 gâ'al (24), to *redeem; be next of kin*
1353 gᵉullâh (2), *redemption*
6299 pâdâh (23), to *ransom;* to *release*
6302 pâdûwy (2), *ransom*
6306 pidyôwm (2), *ransom payment*
6561 pâraq (1), to *break* off or *crunch;* to *deliver*
7069 qânâh (1), to *create;* to *procure*
59 agŏrazō (3), to *purchase;* to *redeem*
1805 ĕxagŏrazō (1), to *buy up, ransom*
3084 lutrŏō (2), to *free* by *paying a ransom*
4160+3085 pŏiĕō (1), to *make or do*

REDEEMEDST
6299 pâdâh (1), to *ransom;* to *release*

REDEEMER
1350 gâ'al (18), to *redeem; be next of kin*

REDEEMETH
1350 gâ'al (1), to *redeem;* to *be the next of kin*
6299 pâdâh (1), to *ransom;* to *release*

REDEEMING
1353 gᵉullâh (1), *redemption*
1805 ĕxagŏrazō (2), to *buy up, ransom*

REDEMPTION
1353 gᵉullâh (5), *redemption*
6304 pᵉdûwth (2), *distinction; deliverance*
6306 pidyôwm (2), *ransom payment*
629 apŏlutrōsis (9), *ransom in full*
3085 lutrōsis (2), *ransoming*

REDNESS
2498 châlaph (1), to *hasten* away; to *pass on*

REDOUND
4052 pĕrissĕuō (1), to *superabound*

REED
7070 qâneh (21), *reed*
2563 kalamŏs (11), *reed*

REEDS
98 'ăgam (1), *marsh; pond; pool*
7070 qâneh (6), *reed*

English

REEL
2287 châgag (1), to
observe a festival
5128 nûwa' (1), to waver

REELAIAH
7480 Rᵉ'êlâyâh (1),
fearful of Jehovah

REFINE
6884 tsâraph (1), to fuse
metal; to refine

REFINED
2212 zâqaq (3), to strain,
refine; extract, clarify
6884 tsâraph (2), to fuse
metal; to refine

REFINER
6884 tsâraph (1), to fuse
metal; to refine

REFINER'S
6884 tsâraph (1), to fuse
metal; to refine

REFORMATION
1357 diŏrthōsis (1),
Messianic restoration

REFORMED
3256 yâçar (1), to
chastise; to instruct

REFRAIN
662 'âphaq (2), to abstain
2413 châṭam (1), to stop,
restrain
2820 châsak (1), to
restrain or refrain
4513 mâna' (2), to deny
7368 râchaq (1), to
recede; remove
868 aphistēmi (1), to
desist, desert
3973 pauō (1), to stop

REFRAINED
662 'âphaq (3), to abstain
2820 châsak (1), to
restrain or refrain
3601 kîyshôwr (1),
spindle
3607 kâlâ' (1), to hold
back; to prohibit, stop
6113 'âtsar (1), to hold
back; to maintain, rule

REFRAINETH
2820 châsak (1), to
restrain or refrain

REFRESH
5582 çâ'ad (1), to support
373 anapauō (1), to
repose; to refresh
1958+5177 ĕpimĕlĕia (1),
carefulness

REFRESHED
5314 nâphash (3), to be
refreshed
7304 râvach (2), to
revive; to have room
373 anapauō (3), to
repose; to refresh
404 anapsuchō (1), to
relieve
4875 sunanapauŏmai
(1), to recruit oneself

REFRESHETH
7725 shûwb (1), to return
or restore

REFRESHING
4774 margê'âh (1), place
of rest
403 anapsuxis (1),
revival, relief

REFUGE
2620 châçâh (1), to flee
to; to confide in
4268 machâçeh (15),
shelter; refuge
4498 mânôwç (4), fleeing;
place of refuge
4585 mᵉ'ôwnâh (1), abode
4733 miqlâṭ (20), asylum,
place of protection
4869 misgâb (5), high
refuge
2703 kataphĕugō (1), to
flee down

REFUSE
3973 mâ'ôwç (1), refuse
3985 mâ'ên (10), to
refuse, reject
3986 mâ'ên (4),
unwilling, refusing
3987 mê'ên (1),
refractory, stubborn
3988 mâ'aç (3), to spurn;
to disappear
4549 mâçaç (1), to waste;
to faint
4651 mappâl (1), chaff;
flap or fold of skin
6544 pâra' (1), to loosen;
to expose, dismiss
3868 paraitĕŏmai (4), to
deprecate, decline

REFUSED
3985 mâ'ên (24), to
refuse, reject
3988 mâ'aç (5), to spurn;
to disappear
579 apŏblētŏs (1),
rejected
720 arnĕŏmai (2), to
disavow, reject
3868 paraitĕŏmai (1), to
deprecate, decline

REFUSEDST
3985 mâ'ên (1), to refuse,
reject

REFUSETH
3985 mâ'ên (5), to refuse,
reject
3988 mâ'aç (1), to spurn;
to disappear
5800 'âzab (1), to loosen;
relinquish; permit
6544 pâra' (2), to loosen;
to expose, dismiss

REGARD
995 bîyn (4), to
understand; discern
1875 dârash (1), to
pursue or search
2803 châshab (1), to
think, regard; to value
3820 lêb (3), heart
5027 nâbaṭ (4), to scan;
to regard with favor
5375 nâsâ' (3), to lift up
5375+6440 nâsâ' (1), to
lift up
5869+2437+5921 'ayin (1),
eye; sight; fountain
5921+1700 'al (1), above,
over, upon, or against

REFRESHING
6437 pânâh (3), to turn,
to face
7200 râ'âh (1), to see
7789 shûwr (1), to spy
out, survey
8104 shâmar (2), to
watch
8159 shâ'âh (1), to
inspect, consider
1788 ĕntrĕpō (1), to
respect; to confound
4337 prŏsĕchō (1), to pay
attention to
5426 phrŏnĕō (1), to be
mentally disposed

REGARDED
3820 lêb (1), heart
7181 qâshab (1), to prick
up the ears
7182 qesheb (1),
hearkening
7200 râ'âh (2), to see
7761+2942 sûwm (Ch.)
(1), to put, place
272 amĕlĕō (1), to be
careless of, neglect
1788 ĕntrĕpō (1), to
respect; to confound
1914 ĕpiblĕpō (1), to gaze
at

REGARDEST
995 bîyn (1), to
understand; discern
991 blĕpō (2), to look at

REGARDETH
995 bîyn (1), to
understand; discern
2803 châshab (1), to
think, regard; to value
3045 yâda' (1), to know
5234 nâkar (1), to
respect, revere
5375 nâsâ' (1), to lift up
6437 pânâh (1), to turn,
to face
7200 râ'âh (1), to see
7761+2942 sûwm (Ch.)
(1), to put, place
8085 shâma' (1), to hear
8104 shâmar (3), to
watch
5426 phrŏnĕō (2), to be
mentally disposed

REGARDING
7760 sûwm (1), to put,
place
3851 parabŏulĕuŏmai
(1), to misconsult, i.e.
disregard

REGEM
7276 Regem (1),
stone-heap

REGEM-MELECH
7278 Regem Melek (1),
king's heap

REGENERATION
3824 paliggĕnĕsia (2),
renovation; restoration

REGION
2256 chebel (3),
company, band
5299 nâphâh (1), height;
sieve
4066 pĕrichōrŏs (6),
surrounding country
5561 chōra (4), territory

REGIONS
2825 klinĕ (2), couch
5561 chōra (1), territory

REGISTER
3791 kâthâb (2), writing,
record or book
5612 çêpher (1), writing

REHABIAH
7345 Rᵉchabyâh (5),
Jehovah has enlarged

REHEARSE
7760 sûwm (1), to put,
place
8567 tânâh (1), to
commemorate

REHEARSED
1696 dâbar (1), to speak,
say; to subdue
5046 nâgad (1), to
announce
312 anaggĕllō (1), to
announce in detail
756 archŏmai (1), to
begin

REHOB
7340 Rᵉchôb (10), myriad

REHOBOAM
7346 Rᵉchab'âm (50),
people has enlarged

REHOBOTH
7344 Rᵉchôbôwth (4),
streets

REHUM
7348 Rᵉchûwm (8),
compassionate

REI
7472 Rê'îy (1), social

REIGN
4427 mâlak (117), to
reign as king
4437 malkûw (Ch.) (4),
dominion
4438 malkûwth (21),
rule; dominion
4467 mamlâkâh (2),
royal dominion
4468 mamlâkûwth (1),
royal dominion
4910 mâshal (3), to rule
6113 'âtsar (1), to hold
back; to rule, assemble
7287 râdâh (1), to
subjugate
757 archō (1), to rule, be
first in rank
936 basilĕuō (13), to rule
2231 hēgĕmŏnia (1),
rulership, leadership
4821 sumbasilĕuō (2), to
be co-regent

REIGNED
4427 mâlak (159), to
reign as king
4910 mâshal (3), to rule
7786 sûwr (1), to rule,
crown
936 basilĕuō (6), to rule

REIGNEST
4910 mâshal (1), to rule

REIGNETH
4427 mâlak (11), to reign
as king
936 basilĕuō (1), to rule
2192+932 ĕchō (1), to
have; hold; keep

REIGNING
4427 mâlak (1), to *reign as king*

REINS
2504 châlâts (1), *loins, areas of the waist*
3629 kilyâh (13), *kidney; mind, heart, spirit*
3510 nĕphrŏs (1), inmost mind

REJECT
3988 mâ'aç (1), to *spurn; to disappear*
114 athĕtĕō (2), to *disesteem, neutralize*
3868 paraitĕŏmai (1), to *deprecate, decline*

REJECTED
2310 châdêl (1), *ceasing or destitute*
3988 mâ'aç (17), to *spurn; to disappear*
96 adŏkimŏs (1), *failing the test, worthless*
114 athĕtĕō (1), to *disesteem, neutralize*
593 apŏdŏkimazō (7), to *repudiate, reject*
1609 ĕkptuō (1), to *spurn, scorn*

REJECTETH
14 agathŏĕrgĕō (1), to do *good work*

REJOICE
1523 gîyl (23), *rejoice*
1524 gîyl (2), *age, stage in life*
4885 mâsôws (1), *delight*
5937 'âlaz (8), to *jump for joy*
5947 'allîyz (3), *exultant; reveling*
5965 'âlaç (1), to *leap for joy, i.e. exult, wave*
5970 'âlats (4), to *jump for joy*
7442 rânan (11), to *shout for joy*
7797 sûws (14), to be *bright, i.e. cheerful*
7832 sâchaq (1), to *laugh; to scorn; to play*
8055 sâmach (70), to be, *make gleesome*
8056 sâmêach (5), *blithe or gleeful*
8057 simchâh (4), *blithesomeness or glee*
21 agalliaō (4), to *exult*
2165 ĕuphrainō (5), to *rejoice, be glad*
2744 kauchaŏmai (4), to *glory in, rejoice in*
2745 kauchēma (1), *boast; brag*
4796 sugchairō (5), to *sympathize in gladness*
5463 chairō (24), to be *cheerful*

REJOICED
1523 gîyl (2), *rejoice*
2302 châdâh (1), to *rejoice, be glad*
5937 'âlaz (2), to *jump for joy*
6670 tsâhal (1), to be *cheerful*

REJOICEST
7797 sûws (3), to be *bright, i.e. cheerful*
8055 sâmach (20), to be, *make gleesome*
8056 sâmêach (3), *blithe or gleeful*
8057 simchâh (1), *blithesomeness or glee*
21 agalliaō (4), to *exult*
2165 ĕuphrainō (1), to *rejoice, be glad*
4796 sugchairō (1), to *sympathize in gladness*
5463 chairō (8), to be *cheerful*

REJOICEST
5937 'âlaz (1), to *jump for joy*

REJOICETH
1523 gîyl (1), *rejoice*
4885 mâsôws (1), *delight*
5937 'âlaz (1), to *jump for joy*
5938 'âlêz (1), *exultant*
5970 'âlats (2), to *jump for joy*
7797 sûws (3), to be *bright, i.e. cheerful*
8055 sâmach (4), to be, *make gleesome*
2620 katakauchaŏmai (1), to *exult over*
4796 sugchairō (1), to *sympathize in gladness*
5463 chairō (3), to be *cheerful*

REJOICING
1524 gîyl (1), *age, stage in life*
1525 gîylâh (1), *joy, delight*
5947 'allîyz (1), *exultant; reveling*
5951 'ălîytsûwth (1), *exultation*
7440 rinnâh (3), *shout*
7832 sâchaq (2), to *laugh; to scorn; to play*
8055 sâmach (1), to be, *make gleesome*
8056 sâmêach (1), *blithe or gleeful*
8057 simchâh (2), *blithesomeness or glee*
8342 sâsôwn (1), *cheerfulness; welcome*
8643 t*e*rûw'âh (1), *battle-cry; clangor*
2745 kauchēma (4), *boast; brag*
2746 kauchēsis (4), *boasting; bragging*
5463 chairō (5), to be *cheerful*

REKEM
7552 Reqem (5), *versi-color*

RELEASE
2010 hănâchâh (1), *quiet*
8058 shâmaṭ (2), to *let alone, desist, remit*
8059 sh*e*miṭṭâh (5), *remission of debt*
630 apŏluō (13), to *relieve, release*

RELEASED
630 apŏluō (4), to *relieve, release; to divorce*

RELIED
8172 shâ'an (3), to *support, rely on*

RELIEF
1248 diakŏnia (1), *attendance, aid, service*

RELIEVE
833 'âshar (1), to *go forward; guide; prosper*
2388 châzaq (1), to *bind, restrain, conquer*
7725 shûwb (3), to *turn back; to return*
1884 ĕparkĕō (2), to *help*

RELIEVED
1884 ĕparkĕō (1), to *help*

RELIEVETH
5749 'ûwd (1), to *protest, testify; to restore*

RELIGION
2356 thrēskĕia (3), *observance, religion*
2454 Iŏudaismŏs (2), *Jewish faith*

RELIGIOUS
2357 thrēskŏs (1), *ceremonious, pious*
4576 sĕbŏmai (1), to *revere, i.e. adore*

RELY
8172 shâ'an (1), to *support, rely on*

REMAIN
1481 gûwr (1), to *sojourn, live as an alien*
1961 hâyâh (1), to *exist, i.e. be or become*
3241 Yânîym (1), *asleep*
3427 yâshab (11), to *dwell, to remain*
3498 yâthar (13), to *remain or be left*
3885 lûwn (5), to be *obstinate with*
5117 nûwach (1), to *rest; to settle down*
5975 'âmad (3), to *stand*
6965 qûwm (1), to *rise*
7604 shâ'ar (15), to *leave, remain*
7611 sh*e*'êrîyth (1), *remainder or residual*
7931 shâkan (3), to *reside*
8245 shâqad (1), to be *alert, i.e. sleepless*
8300 sârîyd (8), *survivor; remainder*
3062 lŏipŏi (1), *remaining ones*
3306 mĕnō (8), to *remain*
4035 pĕrilĕipō (2), to *survive, be left, remain*
4052 pĕrissĕuō (1), to *superabound*

REMAINDER
3498 yâthar (4), to *remain or be left*
7611 sh*e*'êrîyth (2), *remainder or residual*

REMAINED
1961 hâyâh (1), to *exist, i.e. be or become*

REMAINEST
3427 yâshab (10), to *dwell, to remain*
3462 yâshên (1), to *sleep; to grow old, stale*
3498 yâthar (5), to *remain or be left*
5975 'âmad (4), to *stand*
7604 shâ'ar (23), to *leave, remain*
8277 sârad (1), to *escape or survive*
8300 sârîyd (1), *survivor; remainder*
1265 diamĕnō (1), to *stay constantly*
3306 mĕnō (3), to *remain*
4052 pĕrissĕuō (3), to *superabound*

REMAINEST
3427 yâshab (1), to *dwell, to remain; to settle*
1265 diamĕnō (1), to *stay constantly*

REMAINETH
3117 yôwm (1), *day; time period*
3427 yâshab (1), to *dwell, to remain; to settle*
3498 yâthar (4), to *remain or be left*
3885 lûwn (2), to be *obstinate with*
5736 'âdaph (4), to be *redundant*
5975 'âmad (1), to *stand*
7604 shâ'ar (8), to *leave, remain*
7931 shâkan (1), to *reside*
8300 sârîyd (3), *survivor; remainder*
620 apŏlĕipō (3), to *leave behind; to forsake*
3306 mĕnō (5), to *stay, remain*
3588+3063 hŏ (1), "the," i.e. the definite article

REMAINING
3320 yâtsab (1), to *station, offer, continue*
3498 yâthar (1), to *remain or be left*
7931 shâkan (1), to *reside*
8300 sârîyd (9), *survivor; remainder*
3306 mĕnō (1), to *remain*

REMALIAH
7425 R*e*malyâhûw (11), *Jehovah has bedecked*

REMALIAH'S
7425 R*e*malyâhûw (2), *Jehovah has bedecked*

REMEDY
4832 marpê' (3), *cure; deliverance; placidity*

REMEMBER
2142 zâkar (120), to *remember; to mention*
6485 pâqad (1), to *visit, care for, count*
3403 mimnēskō (1), to *remind or to recall*
3415 mnaŏmai (9), to *bear in mind*
3421 mnēmŏnĕuō (16), to *exercise memory*
5279 hupŏmimnēskō (1), to *suggest to memory*

English

REMEMBERED
2142 zâkar (48), to
remember; to mention
2143 zêker (1),
commemoration
3415 mnaŏmai (6), to
recollect
3421 mnēmŏnĕuō (1), to
recall
5279 hupŏmimnēskō (1),
to *remind oneself*

REMEMBEREST
2142 zâkar (1), to
remember; to mention
3415 mnaŏmai (1), to
recollect

REMEMBERETH
2142 zâkar (3), to
remember; to mention
363 anamimnēskō (1), to
remind; to recollect
3421 mnēmŏnĕuō (1), to
recall

REMEMBERING
2142 zâkar (1), to
remember; to mention
3421 mnēmŏnĕuō (1), to
recall

REMEMBRANCE
2142 zâkar (13), to
remember; to mention
2143 zêker (11),
recollection
2146 zikrôwn (5),
commemoration
6485 pâqad (1), to *visit,
care for, count*
363 anamimnēskō (3), to
remind; to recollect
364 anamnēsis (5),
recollection
3415 mnaŏmai (3), to
recollect
3417 mnĕia (3),
recollection; recital
3418 mnēma (1),
sepulchral monument
5179 tupŏs (2), *shape,
resemblance; "type"*
5279 hupŏmimnēskō (2),
to *remind oneself*
5280 hupŏmnēsis (3),
reminding
5294 hupŏtithēmi (1), to
hazard; to suggest

REMEMBRANCES
2146 zikrôwn (1),
commemoration

REMETH
7432 Remeth (1), *height*

REMISSION
859 aphĕsis (9), *pardon,
freedom*
3929 parĕsis (1),
toleration, passing over

REMIT
863 aphiĕmi (1), to *leave;
to pardon, forgive*

REMITTED
863 aphiĕmi (1), to *leave;
to pardon, forgive*

REMMON
7417 Rimmôwn (1),
pomegranate

REMMON-METHOAR
7417 Rimmôwn (1),
pomegranate

REMNANT
310 'achar (1), *after*
319 'achărîyth (1), *future;
posterity*
3498 yâthar (4), to
remain or be left
3499 yether (14),
remainder; small rope
5629 çerach (1),
redundancy
6413 pᵉlêytâh (1),
escaped portion
7604 shâ'ar (4), to *leave,
remain*
7605 shᵉ'âr (11),
remainder
7611 shᵉ'êrîyth (44),
remainder or residual
8293 shêrûwth (1),
freedom
8300 sârîyd (2), *survivor;
remainder*
2640 katalĕimma (1),
few, remnant
3005 lĕimma (1),
remainder, remnant
3062 lŏipŏi (4),
remaining ones

REMOVE
1540 gâlâh (2), to
denude; uncover
1556 gâlal (1), to *roll; to
commit*
4185 mûwsh (4), to
withdraw
5110 nûwd (4), to *waver;
to wander, flee*
5253 nâçag (4), to *retreat*
5265 nâça' (1), *start*
5437 çâbab (2), to
surround
5472 çûwg (1), to *go
back, to retreat*
5493 çûwr (15), to *turn* off
7368 râchaq (5), to
recede; remove
7493 râ'ash (1), to
undulate, quake
2795 kinĕō (1), to *stir,
move, remove*
3179 mĕthistēmi (1), to
move
3327 mĕtabainō (2), to
depart, move from
3911 paraphĕrō (1), to
carry off; to avert

REMOVED
167 'âhal (1), to *pitch a
tent*
1540 gâlâh (3), to
denude; uncover
1556 gâlal (1), to *roll; to
commit*
2186 zânach (1), to
reject, forsake, fail
2189 za'ăvâh (6),
*agitation,
maltreatment*
3014 yâgâh (1), to *push
away, be removed*
3670 kânaph (1), to
withdraw
4131 môwṭ (5), to *slip,
shake, fall*

REMOVETH
5253 nâçag (1), to *retreat*
5265 nâça' (1), *start*
5493 çûwr (1), to *turn* off
5709 'ădâ' (Ch.) (1), to
pass on or continue
6275 'âthaq (1), to *remove*

REMOVING
1473 gôwlâh (2), *exile;
captive*
5493 çûwr (2), to *turn* off
3331 mĕtathĕsis (1),
transferral to heaven

REMPHAN
4481 Rhĕmphan (1),
Kijun (a pagan god)

REND
1234 bâqa' (3), to *cleave,
break, tear open*
6533 pâram (2), to *tear,
be torn*
7167 qâra' (11), to *rend*
4486 rhēgnumi (1), to
tear to pieces
4977 schizō (1), to *split
or sever*

RENDER
5415 nᵉthan (Ch.) (1), to
give
7725 shûwb (16), to *turn
back; to return*
7999 shâlam (7), to *be
safe; be, make complete*
467 antapŏdidōmi (1), to
requite good or evil
591 apŏdidōmi (8), to
give away

RENDERED
7725 shûwb (4), to *turn
back; to return*

RENDEREST
7999 shâlam (1), to *be
safe; be, make complete*

RENDERETH
7999 shâlam (1), to *be
safe; be, make complete*

RENDERING
591 apŏdidōmi (1), to
give away

RENDING
6561 pâraq (1), to *break
off or crunch; to deliver*

RENEW
2318 châdash (3), to *be
new, renew; to rebuild*
2498 châlaph (2), to
spring up; to change
340 anakainizō (1), to
restore, bring back

RENEWED
2318 châdash (2), to *be
new, renew; to rebuild*
2498 châlaph (1), to
spring up; to change
341 anakainŏō (2), to
renovate, renew
365 ananĕŏō (1), to
renovate, i.e. reform

RENEWEST
2318 châdash (2), to *be
new, renew; to rebuild*

RENEWING
342 anakainōsis (2),
renovation, renewal

RENOUNCED
550 apĕipŏmēn (1), to
disown

RENOWN
8034 shêm (7), *name,
appellation*

RENOWNED
1984 hâlal (1), to *boast*
7121 qârâ' (3), to *call out*

RENT
1234 bâqa' (5), to *cleave,
break, tear open*
2963 ṭâraph (1), to *pluck
off or pull to pieces*
5364 niqpâh (1), *rope*
6533 pâram (1), to *tear,
be torn*
6561 pâraq (1), to *break
off or crunch; to deliver*
7167 qâra' (43), to *rend*
8156 shâça' (2), to *split
or tear; to upbraid*
1284 diarrhēssō (3), to
tear asunder
4048 pĕrirrhēgnumi (1),
to *tear all around*
4682 sparassō (1), to
convulse with epilepsy
4977 schizō (5), to *split
or sever*
4978 schisma (2),
divisive dissension

RENTEST
7167 qâra' (1), to *rend*

REPAID
7999 shâlam (1), to *be
safe; to reciprocate*

REPAIR
918 bâdaq (1), to *mend a
breach*
2318 châdash (3), to *be
new, renew; to rebuild*
2388 châzaq (8), to
fasten upon; to seize
2393 chezqâh (1),
prevailing power
5975 'âmad (1), to *stand*

REPAIRED
1129 bânâh (2), to *build*;
to *establish*
2388 châzaq (39), to
fasten upon; to *seize*
2421 râyâh (1), to *live*;
to *revive*
5462 çâgar (1), to *shut*
up; to *surrender*
7495 râphâ' (1), to *cure,*
heal

REPAIRER
1443 gâdar (1), to *build a*
stone wall

REPAIRING
3247 yᵉçôwd (1),
foundation

REPAY
7999 shâlam (5), to *be*
complete; to *reciprocate*
457 anŏixis (1), *act of*
opening
591 apŏdidōmi (1), to
give away
661 apŏtinō (1), to *pay in*
full, *make restitution*

REPAYETH
7999 shâlam (1), to *be*
complete; to *reciprocate*

REPEATETH
8138 shânâh (1), to *fold,*
i.e. *duplicate*

REPENT
5162 nâcham (19), to *be*
sorry; to *pity, rue*
7725 shûwb (3), to *turn*
back; to *return*
3338 mĕtamĕllŏmai (2),
to *regret*
3340 mĕtanŏĕō (21), to
reconsider

REPENTANCE
5164 nôcham (1),
ruefulness
278 amĕtamĕlētŏs (1),
irrevocable
3341 mĕtanŏia (24),
reversal

REPENTED
5162 nâcham (17), to *be*
sorry; to *pity, rue*
278 amĕtamĕlētŏs (1),
irrevocable
3338 mĕtamĕllŏmai (3),
to *regret*
3340 mĕtanŏĕō (11), to
reconsider

REPENTEST
5162 nâcham (1), to *be*
sorry; to *pity, rue*

REPENTETH
5162 nâcham (3), to *be*
sorry; to *pity, rue*
3340 mĕtanŏĕō (2), to
reconsider

REPENTING
5162 nâcham (1), to *be*
sorry; to *pity, rue*

REPENTINGS
5150 nichûwm (1),
consoled; solace

REPETITIONS
945 battŏlŏgĕō (1), to
prate tediously, *babble*

REPHAEL
7501 Rᵉphâ'êl (1), *God*
has cured

REPHAH
7506 Rephach (1),
support

REPHAIAH
7509 Rᵉphâyâh (5),
Jehovah has cured

REPHAIM
7497 râphâ' (6), *giant*

REPHAIMS
7497 râphâ' (2), *giant*

REPHIDIM
7508 Rᵉphîydîym (5),
balusters

REPLENISH
4390 mâlê' (2), to *fill; be*
full

REPLENISHED
4390 mâlê' (5), to *fill; be*
full

REPLIEST
470 antapŏkrinŏmai (1),
to *contradict* or *dispute*

REPORT
1681 dibbâh (3), *slander,*
bad report
1697 dâbâr (2), *word;*
matter; thing
5046 nâgad (1), to
announce
8034 shêm (1), *name,*
appellation
8052 shᵉmûw'âh (4),
announcement
8088 shêma' (5),
something heard
189 akŏē (2), *hearing;*
thing heard
518 apaggĕllō (1), to
announce, proclaim
1426 dusphēmia (1),
defamation, slander
2162 ĕuphēmia (1), *good*
repute
2163 ĕuphēmŏs (1),
reputable
3140 marturĕō (6), to
testify; to *commend*
3141 marturia (1),
evidence given

REPORTED
559 'âmar (2), to *say*
7725 shûwb (1), to *turn*
back; to *return*
8085 shâma' (2), to *hear*
191 akŏuō (1), to *hear*
312 anaggĕllō (1), to
announce, report
518 apaggĕllō (1), to
announce, proclaim
987 blasphēmĕō (1), to
speak impiously
1310 diaphēmizō (1), to
spread news
3140 marturĕō (2), to
testify; to *commend*

REPROACH
2617 cheçed (1),
kindness, favor
2659 châphêr (1), to
shame, reproach
2778 châraph (10), to
spend the winter

2781 cherpâh (65),
contumely, disgrace
3637 kâlam (1), to *taunt*
or *insult*
3639 kᵉlimmâh (1),
disgrace, scorn
7036 qâlôwn (1), *disgrace*
819 atimia (1), *disgrace*
3679 ŏnĕidizō (2), to *rail*
at, *chide, taunt*
3680 ŏnĕidismŏs (3),
with insult
3681 ŏnĕidŏs (1),
notoriety, i.e. a *taunt*

REPROACHED
2778 châraph (12), to
spend the winter
3637 kâlam (1), to *taunt*
or *insult*
3679 ŏnĕidizō (2), to *rail*
at, *chide, taunt*

REPROACHES
1421 giddûwph (1),
vilification, scorn
2781 cherpâh (1),
contumely, disgrace
3679 ŏnĕidizō (1), to *rail*
at, *chide, taunt*
3680 ŏnĕidismŏs (1),
with insult
5196 hubris (1), *insult*

REPROACHEST
5195 hubrizō (1), to
exercise violence, abuse

REPROACHETH
1442 gâdaph (1), to
revile, blaspheme
2778 châraph (5), to
spend the winter
2781 cherpâh (1),
contumely, disgrace

REPROACHFULLY
2781 cherpâh (1),
contumely, disgrace
5484+3059 charin (1), *on*
account of, because of

REPROBATE
3988 mâ'aç (1), to *spurn*;
to *disappear*
96 adŏkimŏs (3), *failing*
the test, worthless

REPROBATES
96 adŏkimŏs (3), *failing*
the test, worthless

REPROOF
1606 gᵉ'ârâh (2), *chiding,*
rebuke
8433 tôwkêchâh (12),
correction, refutation
1650 ĕlĕgchŏs (1), *proof,*
conviction

REPROOFS
8433 tôwkêchâh (2),
correction, refutation

REPROVE
3198 yâkach (16), to *be*
correct; to *argue*
1651 ĕlĕgchō (3), to
confute, admonish

REPROVED
1605 gâ'ar (1), to *chide,*
reprimand
3198 yâkach (4), to *be*
correct; to *argue*

8433 tôwkêchâh (2),
correction, refutation
1651 ĕlĕgchō (3), to
confute, admonish

REPROVER
3198 yâkach (2), to *be*
correct; to *argue*

REPROVETH
3198 yâkach (3), to *be*
correct; to *argue*
3256 yâçar (1), to
chastise; to instruct

REPUTATION
3368 yâqâr (1), *valuable*
1380 dŏkĕō (1), to *think,*
regard, seem good
1784 ĕntimŏs (1), *valued,*
considered precious
2758 kĕnŏō (1), to *make*
empty
5093 timiŏs (1), *costly;*
honored, esteemed

REPUTED
2804 chăshab (Ch.) (2), to
regard

REQUEST
782 'ăresheth (1),
longing for
1245 bâqash (3), to
search; to *strive after*
1246 baqqâshâh (8),
petition, request
1697 dâbâr (2), *word;*
matter; thing
7596 shᵉ'êlâh (3), *petition*
1162 dĕēsis (1), *petition,*
request
1189 dĕŏmai (1), to *beg,*
petition, ask

REQUESTED
1156 bᵉ'â' (Ch.) (1), to
seek or ask
1245 bâqash (1), to
search; to *strive after*
7592 shâ'al (3), to *ask*

REQUESTS
155 aitēma (1), *thing*
asked, request

REQUIRE
977 bâchar (1), *select,*
chose, prefer
1245 bâqash (10), to
search; to *strive after*
1875 dârash (11), to
pursue or search
3117 yôwm (1), *day; time*
period
7592 shâ'al (3), to *ask*
7593 shᵉ'êl (Ch.) (1), to
ask
154 aitĕō (1), to *ask* for
1096 ginŏmai (1), to *be,*
become

REQUIRED
1245 bâqash (3), to
search; to *strive after*
1875 dârash (3), to
pursue or search
1961 hâyâh (1), to *exist,*
i.e. *be or become*
3117 yôwm (3), *day; time*
period
7592 shâ'al (4), to *ask*
155 aitēma (1), *thing*
asked, request

English

523 apaitĕō (1), to *demand back*
1567 ĕkzētĕō (2), to *seek out*
2212 zētĕō (2), to *seek*
4238 prassō (1), to *execute, accomplish*

REQUIREST
559 'âmar (1), to *say*

REQUIRETH
1245 bâqash (1), to *search*; to *strive after*
7593 she'êl (Ch.) (1), to *ask*

REQUIRING
154 aitĕō (1), to *ask* for

REQUITE
1580 gâmal (1), to *benefit* or *requite*; to *wean*
5414 nâthan (1), to *give*
6213 'âsâh (1), to *do* or *make*
7725 shûwb (2), to *turn back*; to *return*
7999 shâlam (3), to *be safe*; to *reciprocate*
287+591 amŏibē (1), *requital, recompense*

REQUITED
7725 shûwb (1), to *turn back*; to *return*
7999 shâlam (1), to *be safe*; to *reciprocate*

REQUITING
7725 shûwb (1), to *turn back*; to *return*

REREWARD
314 'achărôwn (1), *late* or *last*; *behind*; *western*
622 'âçaph (5), to *gather, collect*

RESCUE
3467 yâsha' (1), to *make safe, free*
5337 nâtsal (1), to *deliver*; to *be snatched*
7725 shûwb (1), to *turn back*; to *return*

RESCUED
5337 nâtsal (1), to *deliver*; to *be snatched*
6299 pâdâh (1), to *ransom*; to *release*
1807 ĕxairĕō (1), to *tear out*; to *select*; to *release*

RESCUETH
5338 neˀtsal (Ch.) (1), to *extricate, deliver*

RESEMBLANCE
5869 'ayin (1), *eye*; *sight*; *fountain*

RESEMBLE
3666 hŏmŏiŏō (1), to *become similar*

RESEMBLED
8389 tô'ar (1), *outline, figure* or *appearance*

RESEN
7449 Reçen (1), *bridle*

RESERVE
5201 nâṭar (1), to *guard*; to *cherish* anger
7604 shâ'ar (1), to *be, make redundant*

5083 tērĕō (1), to *keep, guard, obey*

RESERVED
680 'âtsal (1), to *select*; *refuse*; *narrow*
2820 châsak (2), to *restrain* or *refrain*
3498 yâthar (3), to *remain* or *be left*
3947 lâqach (1), to *take*
2641 katalĕipŏ (1), to *have remaining*
5083 tērĕō (7), to *keep, guard, obey*

RESERVETH
5201 nâṭar (1), to *guard*; to *cherish* anger
8104 shâmar (1), to *watch*

RESHEPH
7566 Resheph (1), *flame*

RESIDUE
319 'achărîyth (1), *future*; *posterity*
3498 yâthar (3), to *remain* or *be left*
3499 yether (8), *remainder*; small *rope*
7605 she'âr (4), *remainder*
7606 she'âr (Ch.) (2), *remainder*
7611 she'êrîyth (13), *remainder* or *residual*
2645 katalŏipŏs (1), *remaining*; *rest*
3062 lŏipŏi (1), *remaining ones*

RESIST
7853 sâṭan (1), to *attack* by *accusation*
436 anthistēmi (7), *oppose, rebel*
496 antipiptō (1), to *oppose, resist*
498 antitassŏmai (1), *oppose, resist*

RESISTED
436 anthistēmi (1), *oppose, rebel*
478 antikathistēmi (1), *withstand, contest*

RESISTETH
436 anthistēmi (1), *oppose, rebel*
498 antitassŏmai (3), *oppose, resist*

RESOLVED
1097 ginōskō (1), to *know*

RESORT
935 bôw' (1), to *go, come*
6908 qâbats (1), to *collect, assemble*
4848 sumpŏrĕuŏmai (1), to *journey together*
4905 sunĕrchŏmai (1), to *gather together*

RESORTED
3320 yâtsab (1), to *station, offer, continue*
2064 ĕrchŏmai (2), to *go*
4863 sunagō (1), to *gather together*
4905 sunĕrchŏmai (1), to *gather together*

RESPECT
3045 yâda' (1), to *know*
4856 massô' (1), *partiality*
5027 nâbaṭ (3), to *scan*; to *regard* with favor
5234 nâkar (3), to *respect, revere*
5375 nâsâ' (2), to *lift up*
6437 pânâh (6), to *turn, to face*
7200 râ'âh (4), to *see*
8159 shâ'âh (3), to *inspect, consider*
578 apŏblĕpō (1), to intently *regard, pay attention*
678 aprŏsŏpŏlēptōs (1), *without prejudice*
1914 ĕpiblĕpō (1), to *gaze at*
2596 kata (1), *down*; *according to*
3313 mĕrŏs (2), *division* or *share*
3382 mērŏs (1), *thigh*
4380 prŏsŏpŏlēptĕō (1), to *show partiality*
4382 prŏsŏpŏlēpsia (3), *favoritism*

RESPECTED
5375 nâsâ' (1), to *lift up*

RESPECTER
4381 prŏsŏpŏlēptēs (1), *exhibiting partiality*

RESPECTETH
6437 pânâh (1), to *turn, to face*
7200 râ'âh (1), to *see*

RESPITE
7309 reˀvâchâh (1), *relief*
7503 râphâh (1), to *slacken*

REST
1824 deˀmîy (1), *quiet, peacefulness*
1826 dâmam (1), to *be silent*; to *be astonished*; to *stop, cease*; to *perish*
2308 châdal (1), to *desist, stop*; *be fat*
2342 chûwl (1), to *wait*; to *pervert*
2790 chârash (1), to *be silent*; to *be deaf*
3498 yâthar (12), to *remain* or *be left*
3499 yether (65), *remainder*; small *rope*
4494 mânôwach (6), *quiet spot*, home
4496 meˀnûwchâh (16), *peacefully*; *consolation*
4771 margôwa' (1), *resting place*
5117 nûwach (44), to *rest*; to *settle* down
5118 nûwach (1), *quiet*
5183 nachath (4), *descent*; *quiet*
6314 pûwgâh (1), *intermission, relief*
7257 râbats (5), to *recline, repose, brood*
7280 râga' (5), to *settle*, i.e. *quiet*; to *wink*
7599 shâ'an (1), to *loll*, i.e. *be peaceful*

7604 shâ'ar (2), to *be, make redundant*
7605 she'âr (10), *remainder*
7606 she'âr (Ch.) (9), *remainder*
7611 she'êrîyth (3), *remainder* or *residual*
7673 shâbath (7), to *repose*; to *desist*
7677 shabbâthôwn (8), *special holiday*
7901 shâkab (2), to *lie down*
7931 shâkan (2), to *reside*
7954 sheˀlâh (Ch.) (1), to *be secure, at rest*
7965 shâlôwm (1), *safe*; *well*; *health, prosperity*
8058 shâmaṭ (1), to *let alone, desist, remit*
8172 shâ'an (2), to *support, rely on*
8252 shâqaṭ (15), to *repose*
8300 sârîyd (1), *survivor*; *remainder*
372 anapausis (4), *recreation, rest*
373 anapauō (6), to *repose*; to *refresh*
425 anĕsis (3), *relaxation*; *relief*
1515 ĕirēnē (1), *peace*; *health*; *prosperity*
1879 ĕpanapauŏmai (1), to *settle on, rely* on
1954 ĕpilŏipŏs (1), *remaining, rest*
1981 ĕpiskēnŏō (1), to *abide with*
2192+372 ĕchō (1), to *have*; *hold*; *keep*
2663 katapausis (9), *abode* for *resting*
2664 katapauō (2), to *settle down*
2681 kataskēnŏō (1), to *remain, live*
3062 lŏipŏi (13), *remaining* ones
4520 sabbatismŏs (1), *sabbatism*

RESTED
270 'âchaz (1), to *seize, grasp*; *possess*
1826 dâmam (1), to *stop, cease*; to *perish*
2583 chânâh (2), to *encamp*
5117 nûwach (7), to *rest*; to *settle* down
5118 nûwach (2), *quiet*
5564 çâmak (1), to *lean upon*; *take hold* of
7673 shâbath (4), to *repose*; to *desist*
7931 shâkan (1), to *reside*
8252 shâqaṭ (1), to *repose*
2270 hēsuchazō (1), to *refrain*

RESTEST
1879 ĕpanapauŏmai (1), to *settle on, rely* on

RESTETH
5117 nûwach (2), to *rest*
8172 shâ'an (1), to *support, rely on*

373 anapauō (1), to
repose; to *refresh*

RESTING
4496 mᵉnûwchâh (2),
peacefully; consolation
5118 nûwach (1), *quiet*
7258 rebets (1), place of
repose

RESTINGPLACE
7258 rebets (1), place of
repose

RESTITUTION
7999 shâlam (4), to *make
complete;* to *reciprocate*
8545 tᵉmûwrâh (1),
barter, compensation
605 apŏkatastasis (1),
reconstitution

RESTORE
5927 'âlâh (1), to *ascend,
be high, mount*
7725 shûwb (27), to
return or restore
7999 shâlam (8), to *make
complete;* to *reciprocate*
591 apŏdidōmi (1), to
give away
600 apŏkathistēmi (2), to
reconstitute
2675 katartizō (1), to
repair; to *prepare*

RESTORED
2421 châyâh (4), to *live;*
to *revive*
5414 nâthan (1), to *give*
7725 shûwb (16), to
return or restore
8421 tûwb (Ch.) (1), to
come back with answer
600 apŏkathistēmi (5), to
reconstitute

RESTORER
7725 shûwb (2), to *return*
or restore

RESTORETH
7725 shûwb (1), to *return*
or restore
600 apŏkathistēmi (1), to
reconstitute

RESTRAIN
1639 gâra' (1), to *shave,
remove, lessen*
2296 châgar (1), to *gird*
on a belt; *put on armor*

RESTRAINED
662 'âphaq (1), to *abstain*
1219 bâtsar (1), to *be
inaccessible*
3543 kâhâh (1), to *grow
dull, fade;* to *be faint*
3607 kâlâ' (2), to *hold
back or in;* to *prohibit*
4513 mâna' (1), to *deny,
refuse*
6113 'âtsar (1), to *hold
back;* to *maintain, rule*
2664 katapauō (1), to
cause to desist

RESTRAINEST
1639 gâra' (1), to *remove,
lessen,* or *withhold*

RESTRAINT
4622 ma'tsôwr (1),
hindrance

RESURRECTION
386 anastasis (39),
resurrection from death
1454 ĕgĕrsis (1),
resurgence from death
1815 ĕxanastasis (1),
rising from death

RETAIN
2388 châzaq (1), to
fasten upon; to *seize;*
3607 kâlâ' (1), to *hold
back or in;* to *prohibit*
6113 'âtsar (1), to *hold
back;* to *maintain, rule*
8551 tâmak (2), to
obtain, keep fast
2192 ĕchō (1), to *have;
hold; keep*
2902 kratĕō (1), to *seize*

RETAINED
2388 châzaq (2), to
fasten upon; to *seize*
6113 'âtsar (2), to *hold
back;* to *maintain, rule*
2722 katĕchō (1), to *hold
down fast*
2902 kratĕō (1), to *seize*

RETAINETH
2388 châzaq (1), to
fasten upon; to *seize*
8551 tâmak (2), to
obtain, keep fast

RETIRE
5756 'ûwz (1), to
strengthen; to *save*
7725 shûwb (1), to *return*
or restore

RETIRED
2015 hâphak (1), to
return, pervert
6327 pûwts (1), to *dash*
in pieces; to *disperse*

RETURN
3427 yâshab (1), to *dwell,
to remain;* to *settle*
6437 pânâh (1), to *turn,*
to *face*
7725 shûwb (242), to *turn*
back; to *return*
8666 tᵉshûwbâh (3),
recurrence; reply
344 anakamptō (1), to
turn back, come back
360 analuō (1), to *depart*
390 anastrĕphō (1), to
remain; to *return*
844 autŏmatŏs (1),
spontaneous, by itself
1994 ĕpistrĕphō (4), to
revert, turn back to
5290 hupŏstrĕphō (5), to
turn under, to *return*

RETURNED
5437 çâbab (2), to
surround
7725 shûwb (151), to *turn*
back; to *return*
8421 tûwb (Ch.) (2), to
reply
344 anakamptō (1), to
turn back, come back
390 anastrĕphō (1), to
remain, to *return*
1877 ĕpanagō (1), to *put
out* to sea; to *return*
1880 ĕpanĕrchŏmai (1),
return home

1994 ĕpistrĕphō (2), to
revert, turn back to
5290 hupŏstrĕphō (24), to
turn under, to *return*

RETURNETH
7725 shûwb (6), to *turn*
back; to *return*
8138 shânâh (1), to *fold,*
to *transmute*

RETURNING
7729 shûwbâh (1),
return, i.e. repentance
5290 hupŏstrĕphō (3), to
turn under, to *return*

REU
7466 Rᵉ'ûw (5), *friend*

REUBEN
7205 Rᵉ'ûwbên (72), *see
ye a son*
7206 Rᵉ'ûwbênîy (1),
Rebenite
4502 Rhŏubēn (1), *see ye
a son*

REUBENITE
7206 Rᵉ'ûwbênîy (1),
Rebenite

REUBENITES
7206 Rᵉ'ûwbênîy (16),
Rebenite

REUEL
7467 Rᵉ'ûw'êl (10), *friend
of God*

REUMAH
7208 Rᵉ'ûwmâh (1),
raised

REVEAL
1540 gâlâh (2), to
denude; to *reveal*
1541 gᵉlâh (Ch.) (1), to
reveal mysteries
601 apŏkaluptō (4),
disclose, reveal

REVEALED
1540 gâlâh (11), to
denude; to *reveal*
1541 gᵉlâh (Ch.) (2), to
reveal mysteries
601 apŏkaluptō (22),
disclose, reveal
602 apŏkalupsis (2),
disclosure, revelation
5537 chrēmatizō (1), to
utter an oracle

REVEALER
1541 gᵉlâh (Ch.) (1), to
reveal mysteries

REVEALETH
1540 gâlâh (3), to
denude; to *reveal*
1541 gᵉlâh (Ch.) (3), to
reveal mysteries

REVELATION
602 apŏkalupsis (10),
disclosure, revelation

REVELATIONS
602 apŏkalupsis (2),
disclosure, revelation

REVELLINGS
2970 kōmŏs (2),
carousal, reveling, orgy

REVENGE
5358 nâqam (1), to
avenge or *punish*

5360 nᵉqâmâh (2),
avengement
1556 ĕkdikĕō (1), to
vindicate; retaliate
1557 ĕkdikēsis (1),
vindication; retaliation

REVENGED
5358 nâqam (1), to
avenge or *punish*

REVENGER
1350 gâ'al (6), to *redeem;
to be the next of kin*
1558 ĕkdikŏs (1),
punisher, avenger

REVENGERS
1350 gâ'al (1), to *redeem;
to be the next of kin*

REVENGES
6546 par'âh (1),
leadership

REVENGETH
5358 nâqam (2), to
avenge or *punish*

REVENGING
5360 nᵉqâmâh (1),
avengement

REVENUE
674 'appᵉthôm (Ch.) (1),
revenue
8393 tᵉbûw'âh (2),
income, i.e. produce

REVENUES
8393 tᵉbûw'âh (3),
income, i.e. produce

REVERENCE
3372 yârê' (2), to *fear;* to
revere
7812 shâchâh (5), to
prostrate in homage
127 aidōs (1), *modesty;
awe*
1788 ĕntrĕpō (4), to
respect; to *confound*
5399 phŏbĕō (1), to *be in
awe of, i.e. revere*

REVERENCED
7812 shâchâh (1), to
prostrate in homage

REVEREND
3372 yârê' (1), to *fear;* to
revere

REVERSE
7725 shûwb (3), to *turn*
back; to *return*

REVILE
7043 qâlal (1), to *be easy,
trifling, vile*
3679 ŏnĕidizō (1), to *rail
at, chide, taunt*

REVILED
486 antilŏidŏrĕō (1), to
rail in reply, retaliate
937 basilikŏs (1),
befitting the sovereign
3058 lŏidŏrĕō (2), *vilify,
insult*
3679 ŏnĕidizō (1), to *rail
at, chide, taunt*

REVILERS
3060 lŏidŏrŏs (1), verbal
abuser

REVILEST
3058 lŏidŏrĕō (1), *vilify,
insult*

English

REVILINGS
1421 giddûwph (2),
vilification, scorn

REVIVE
2421 châyâh (8), to *live;*
to *revive*

REVIVED
2421 châyâh (4), to *live;*
to *revive*
326 anazaō (2), to
recover life, live again

REVIVING
4241 michyâh (2),
preservation of life

REVOLT
5627 çârâh (2), *apostasy;*
crime; remission
6586 pâsha' (1), to *break*
away from authority

REVOLTED
5498 çâchab (1), to *trail*
along
5627 çârâh (1), *apostasy;*
crime; remission
6586 pâsha' (5), to *break*
away from authority

REVOLTERS
5637 çârar (2), to *be*
refractory, stubborn
7846 sêṭ (1), *departure*

REVOLTING
5637 çârar (1), to *be*
refractory, stubborn

REWARD
319 'achărîyth (2), *future;*
posterity
868 'ethnan (3), *gift* price
of harlotry
1309 bᵉsôwrâh (1), glad
tidings, good news
1576 gᵉmûwl (3), *reward,*
recompense
1578 gᵉmûwlâh (1),
reward, recompense
1580 gâmal (1), to *benefit*
or *requite; to wean*
4864 mas'êth (1), *tribute;*
reproach
4909 maskôreth (1),
wages; reward
4991 mattâth (1), *present*
6118 'êqeb (3), *unto the*
end; for ever
6468 pᵉ'ullâh (1), *work,*
deed
6529 pᵉrîy (1), *fruit*
7725 shûwb (2), to *turn*
back; to *return*
7809 shâchad (1), to
bribe; gift
7810 shachad (7), to
bribe; gift
7938 seker (1), *wages,*
reward
7939 sâkâr (5), *payment,*
salary; compensation
7966 shillûwm (1),
requital; retribution; fee
7999 shâlam (6), to *make*
complete; to reciprocate
8011 shillumâh (1),
retribution
469 antapŏdŏsis (1),
requital, reward
514 axiŏs (1), *deserving,*
comparable or suitable

591 apŏdidōmi (6), to
give away
2603 katabrabĕuō (1), to
award the price
3405 misthapŏdŏsia (3),
requital, good or bad
3408 misthŏs (24), *pay*

REWARDED
1580 gâmal (7), to *benefit*
or *requite; to wean*
7760 sûwm (1), to *place*
7939 sâkâr (2), *payment,*
salary; compensation
7999 shâlam (3), to *make*
complete; to reciprocate
591 apŏdidōmi (1), to
give away

REWARDER
3406 misthapŏdŏtēs (1),
rewarder

REWARDETH
7725 shùwb (1), to *turn*
back; to *return*
7936 sâkar (2), to *hire*
7999 shâlam (3), to *make*
complete; to reciprocate

REWARDS
866 'êthnâh (1), *gift* price
of harlotry
5023 nᵉbizbâh (Ch.) (2),
largess, gift
8021 shalmôn (1), *bribe,*
gift

REZEPH
7530 Retseph (2), hot
stone for baking

REZIA
7525 Ritsyâ' (1), *delight*

REZIN
7526 Rᵉtsîyn (10), *delight*

REZON
7331 Rᵉzôwn (1), *prince*

RHEGIUM
4484 Rhēgiŏn (1),
Rhegium

RHESA
4488 Rhēsa (1), (poss.)
Jehovah has cured

RHODA
4498 Rhŏdē (1), *rose*

RHODES
4499 Rhŏdŏs (1), *rose*

RIB
6763 tsêlâ' (1), *side*

RIBAI
7380 Rîybay (2),
contentious

RIBBAND
6616 pâthîyl (1), *twine,*
cord

RIBLAH
7247 Riblâh (11), *fertile*

RIBS
6763 tsêlâ' (2), *side*

RICH
1952 hôwn (1), *wealth*
3513 kâbad (1), to *be*
rich, glorious
5381 nâsag (1), to *reach*
6223 'âshîyr (23), *rich;*
rich person
6238 'âshar (13), to *grow,*
make rich

7771 shôwa' (1), *noble,*
i.e. *liberal; opulent*
4145 plŏusiŏs (28),
wealthy; abounding
4147 plŏutĕō (11), to *be,*
become wealthy
4148 plŏutizō (1), to
make wealthy

RICHER
6238 'âshar (1), to *grow,*
make rich

RICHES
1952 hôwn (9), *wealth*
1995 hâmôwn (1), *noise,*
tumult; many, crowd
2428 chayil (11), *army;*
wealth; virtue; valor
2633 chôçen (1), *wealth,*
stored riches
3502 yithrâh (1), *wealth,*
abundance
4301 maṭmôwn (1),
secret storehouse
5233 nekeç (1), *treasure*
6239 'ôsher (37), *wealth*
7075 qinyân (1),
purchase, wealth
7399 rᵉkûwsh (5),
property
7769 shûwa' (1), *call*
4149 plŏutŏs (22),
abundant riches
5536 chrēma (3), *wealth*

RICHLY
4146 plŏusiŏs (2),
copiously, abundantly

RID
5337 nâtsal (3), to
deliver; to be snatched
6475 pâtsâh (2), to *rend*
7673 shâbath (1), to
repose; to desist

RIDDANCE
3615 kâlâh (1), to *cease,*
be finished, perish
3617 kâlâh (1), *complete*
destruction

RIDDEN
7392 râkab (1), to *ride*

RIDDLE
2420 chîydâh (9), *puzzle;*
conundrum; maxim

RIDE
7392 râkab (20), to *ride*

RIDER
7392 râkab (7), to *ride*

RIDERS
7392 râkab (5), to *ride*

RIDETH
7392 râkab (7), to *ride*

RIDGES
8525 telem (1), *bank* or
terrace

RIDING
7392 râkab (10), to *ride*

RIE
3698 kuççemeth (2), *spelt*

RIFLED
8155 shâçaç (1), to
plunder, ransack

RIGHT
541 'âman (1), to take
the *right hand* road

571 'emeth (3), *certainty,*
truth, trustworthiness
1353 gᵉullâh (1), *blood*
relationship
3225 yâmîyn (136), *right;*
south
3227 yᵉmîynîy (1), *right*
3231 yâman (4), to *be*
right-handed
3233 yᵉmânîy (31), *right*
3474 yâshar (2), to *be*
straight; to make right
3476 yôsher (2), *right*
3477 yâshâr (52), *straight*
3559 kûwn (4), to *render*
sure, proper
3651 kên (3), *just; right*
3787 kâshêr (1), to *be*
straight or right
3788 kishrôwn (1),
success; advantage
4334 mîyshôwr (1), *plain;*
justice
4339 mêyshâr (3),
straightness; rectitude
4941 mishpâṭ (19),
verdict; decree; justice
5227 nôkach (2),
forward, in behalf of
5228 nâkôach (2),
equitable, correct
5229 nᵉkôchâh (2),
integrity; truth
6227 'âshân (1), *smoke*
6437 pânâh (1), to *turn,*
to *face*
6440 pânîym (1), *face;*
front
6664 tsedeq (3), *right*
6666 tsᵉdâqâh (9),
rightness
1188 dĕxiŏs (53), *right*
1342 dikaiŏs (5),
equitable, holy
1849 ĕxŏusia (2),
authority, power, right
2117 ĕuthus (3), *at once,*
immediately
3723 ŏrthōs (1), *rightly*
4993 sōphrŏnĕō (2), to *be*
in a right state of mind

RIGHTEOUS
3477 yâshâr (8), *straight*
6662 tsaddîyq (166), *just*
6663 tsâdaq (8), to *be,*
make right
6664 tsedeq (9), *right*
6666 tsᵉdâqâh (3),
rightness
1341 dikaiŏkrisia (1),
proper judgment
1342 dikaiŏs (39),
equitable, holy
1343 dikaiŏsunē (1),
equity, justification

RIGHTEOUSLY
4334 mîyshôwr (1), *plain;*
justice
4339 mêyshâr (1),
straightness; rectitude
6664 tsedeq (3), *right*
6666 tsᵉdâqâh (1),
rightness
1346 dikaiŏs (2),
equitably

RIGHTEOUSNESS
6663 tsâdaq (1), to *be,*
make right

6664 tsedeq (78), *right*
6665 tsidqâh (Ch.) (1),
beneficence
6666 ts^edâqâh (124),
rightness
*1343 dikaiŏsunē (91),
equity, justification*
*1345 dikaiōma (4),
equitable deed; statute*
*1346 dikaiōs (1),
equitably*
*2118 ĕuthutēs (1),
rectitude, uprightness*

RIGHTEOUSNESS'
6664 tsedeq (1), *right*
6666 ts^edâqâh (1),
rightness
*1343 dikaiŏsunē (2),
equity, justification*

RIGHTEOUSNESSES
6666 ts^edâqâh (3),
rightness

RIGHTLY
3588 kîy (1), *for, that
because*
3723 ŏrthōs (3), rightly

RIGOUR
6531 perek (5), *severity*

RIMMON
7417 Rimmôwn (14),
pomegranate

RIMMON-PAREZ
7428 Rimmôn Perets (2),
pomegranate of (the)
breach

RING
2885 ṭabba'ath (9), *ring;
signet ring* for sealing
*1146 daktuliŏs (1),
finger-ring*
*5554 chrusŏdaktuliŏs
(1), gold-ringed*

RINGLEADER
*4414 prōtŏstatēs (1),
leader, ring leader*

RINGS
1354 gab (2), *mounded
or rounded: top* or *rim*
1550 gâliyl (2), *curtain
ring*
2885 ṭabba'ath (39), *ring;
signet ring* for sealing

RINGSTRAKED
6124 'âqôd (7), *striped,
streaked* animals

RINNAH
7441 Rinnâh (1), *shout*

RINSED
7857 shâṭaph (3), to
inundate, cleanse

RIOT
*810 asōtia (2), profligacy,
debauchery*
5172 truphē (1), luxury
or *debauchery*

RIOTING
*2970 kōmŏs (1),
carousal, reveling, orgy*

RIOTOUS
2151 zâlal (2), to *be loose*
morally, *worthless*
*811 asōtōs (1), with
debauchery*

RIP
1234 bâqa' (1), to *cleave,
break, tear open*

RIPE
1310 bâshal (2), to *boil
up, cook;* to *ripen*
*187 akmazō (1), to be
mature, be ripe*
*3583 xērainō (1), to
shrivel, to mature*

RIPENING
1580 gâmal (1), to *benefit*
or *requite;* to *wean*

RIPHATH
7384 Rîyphath (2),
Riphath

RIPPED
1234 bâqa' (3), to *cleave,
break, tear open*

RISE
2224 zârach (1), to *rise;*
to *be bright*
5927 'âlâh (6), to *ascend,
be high, mount*
6965 qûwm (76), to *rise*
6966 qûwm (Ch.) (1), to
rise
7925 shâkam (5), to *load
up,* i.e. to *start early*
8618 t^eqôwmêm (1),
opponent
*305 anabainō (1), to go
up, rise*
*386 anastasis (1),
resurrection* from death
*393 anatĕllō (2), to cause
to arise*
*450 anistēmi (23), to rise;
to come back to life*
*1453 ĕgĕirō (23), to
waken,* i.e. *rouse*
*1881 ĕpanistamai (2), to
stand up on*

RISEN
1342 gâ'âh (1), to *rise;* to
grow tall; be majestic
2224 zârach (2), to *rise;*
to *be bright*
3318 yâtsâ' (1), to *go,
bring out*
6965 qûwm (16), to *rise*
*393 anatĕllō (1), to cause
to arise*
*450 anistēmi (6), to rise;
to come back to life*
*1453 ĕgĕirō (22), to
waken,* i.e. *rouse*
*4891 sunĕgĕirō (2), to
raise up with*

RISEST
6965 qûwm (2), to *rise*

RISETH
2224 zârach (2), to *rise;*
to *be bright*
5927 'âlâh (1), to *ascend,
be high, mount*
6965 qûwm (9), to *rise*
7837 shachar (1), *dawn*
*1453 ĕgĕirō (1), to
waken,* i.e. *rouse*

RISING
510 'alqûwm (1),
resistlessness
2225 zerach (1), *rising* of
light, *dawning*

4217 mizrâch (8), *place
of sunrise; east*
5927 'âlâh (1), to *ascend,
be high, mount*
6965 qûwm (1), to *rise*
7012 qîymâh (1), *arising*
7613 s^e'êth (7), *elevation;
swelling*
7836 shâchar (1), to
search for
7925 shâkam (14), to
load up, to *start early*
305 anabainō (1), to rise
*386 anastasis (1),
resurrection* from death
*393 anatĕllō (1), to cause
to arise*
*450 anistēmi (1), to rise;
to come back to life*

RISSAH
7446 Riçṣâh (2), *ruin*

RITES
2708 chuqqâh (1), to
delineate

RITHMAH
7575 Rithmâh (2), *broom
tree*

RIVER
180 'ûwbâl (3), *stream*
2975 y^e'ôr (35), Nile
River; Tigris *River*
3105 yûwbal (1), *stream*
5103 n^ehar (Ch.) (14),
river; Euphrates *River*
5104 nâhâr (66), *stream;*
Nile; Euphrates; Tigris
5158 nachal (46), *valley*
4215 pŏtamŏs (6),
current, brook

RIVER'S
2975 y^e'ôr (3), Nile *River;*
Tigris *River*
5104 nâhâr (1), *stream;*
Nile; Euphrates; Tigris

RIVERS
650 'âphîyq (10), *valley;
stream; mighty, strong*
2975 y^e'ôr (15), Nile
River; Tigris *River*
5103 n^ehar (Ch.) (9),
river; Euphrates *River*
5104 nâhâr (22), *stream;*
Nile; Euphrates; Tigris
5158 nachal (8), *valley*
6388 peleg (8), small
irrigation *channel*
6390 p^elaggâh (1), *gully*
8585 t^e'âlâh (1),
irrigation *channel*
4215 pŏtamŏs (3),
current, brook

RIZPAH
7532 Ritspâh (4), hot
stone; pavement

ROAD
6584 pâshaṭ (1), to *strip,*
i.e. *unclothe, plunder*

ROAR
1993 hâmâh (6), to *be in
great commotion*
5098 nâham (2), to *growl,
groan*
6873 tsârach (1), to
whoop
7481 râ'am (2), to *crash*
thunder; to *irritate*

7580 shâ'ag (12), to
rumble or *moan*

ROARED
1993 hâmâh (1), to *be in
great commotion*
7580 shâ'ag (4), to
rumble or *moan*

ROARETH
1993 hâmâh (1), to *be in
great commotion*
7580 shâ'ag (1), to
rumble or *moan*
*3455 mukaŏmai (1), to
roar*

ROARING
1897 hâgâh (1), to
murmur, utter a sound
5098 nâham (1), to *growl,
groan*
5099 naham (2), *snarl,
growl*
5100 n^ehâmâh (1),
snarling, growling
7580 shâ'ag (2), to
rumble or *moan*
7581 sh^e'âgâh (6),
rumbling or *moan*
*2278 ĕchĕŏ (1), to
reverberate, ring out*
5612 ŏruŏmai (1), to roar

ROARINGS
7581 sh^e'âgâh (1),
rumbling or *moan*

ROAST
1310 bâshal (1), to *boil
up, cook;* to *ripen*
6740 tsâlâh (1), to *roast*
6748 tsâlîy (3), *roasted*

ROASTED
1310 bâshal (1), to *boil
up, cook;* to *ripen*
6740 tsâlâh (1), to *roast*
7033 qâlâh (1), to *toast*

ROASTETH
740 'Ărî'êl (1), *Lion of
God*
2760 chârak (1), to *catch*

ROB
962 bâzaz (3), to *plunder,
take booty*
1497 gâzal (2), to *rob*
6906 qâba' (1), to
defraud, rob
7921 shâkôl (1), to
miscarry
8154 shâçâh (1), to
plunder

ROBBED
962 bâzaz (4), to *plunder,
take booty*
1497 gâzal (1), to *rob*
5100 n^ehâmâh (1),
snarling, growling
5749 'ûwd (1), to
encompass, restore
6906 qâba' (2), to
defraud, rob
7909 shakkuwl (2),
bereaved
8154 shâçâh (1), to
plunder
*4813 sulaŏ (1), to despoil,
rob*

ROBBER
6530 p^erîyts (1), *violent*

English

6782 tsammîym (2), *noose, snare*
3027 lē₁stēs (2), *brigand*

ROBBERS
962 bâzaz (1), to *plunder, take booty*
6530 pᵉrîyts (3), *violent*
7703 shâdad (2), to *ravage*
2417 hiĕrŏsulŏs (1), *temple-despoiler*
3027 lē₁stēs (2), *brigand*

ROBBERY
1498 gâzēl (3), *robbery, stealing*
6503 Parbâr (1), *Parbar* or *Parvar*
7701 shôd (2), *violence, ravage, destruction*
725 harpagmŏs (1), *plunder*

ROBBETH
1497 gâzal (1), to *rob*

ROBE
145 'eder (1), *mantle; splendor*
155 'addereth (1), *large; splendid*
3301 Yiphdᵉyâh (1), *Jehovah will liberate*
4598 mᵉʿîyl (17), outer *garment* or *robe*
2066 ĕsthēs (1), to *clothe*
2440 himatiŏn (2), to *put on clothes*
4749 stŏlē (1), long-fitting *gown*
5511 chlamus (2), military *cloak*

ROBES
899 beged (4), *clothing; treachery* or *pillage*
4598 mᵉʿîyl (2), outer *garment* or *robe*
4749 stŏlē (5), long-fitting *gown*

ROBOAM
4497 Rhŏbŏam (2), *people has enlarged*

ROCK
2496 challâmîysh (1), *flint, flinty rock*
4581 mâ'ôwz (1), *fortified place; defense*
5553 çela' (44), craggy *rock; fortress*
5558 çeleph (2), *distortion; viciousness*
6697 tsûwr (56), *rock*
4073 pĕtra (13), mass of *rock*

ROCKS
3710 kêph (2), hollow *rock*
5553 çela' (10), craggy *rock; fortress*
6697 tsûwr (7), *rock*
4073 pĕtra (3), mass of *rock*
5138+5117 trachus (1), *uneven, jagged, rocky*

ROD
2415 chôṭer (2), *twig; shoot of a plant*
4294 maṭṭeh (42), *tribe; rod, scepter; club*

4731 maqqêl (2), *shoot; stick; staff*
7626 shêbeṭ (34), *stick; clan, family*
4464 rhabdŏs (6), *stick, rod*

RODE
7392 râkab (15), to *ride*

RODS
4294 maṭṭeh (8), *tribe; rod, scepter; club*
4731 maqqêl (6), *shoot; stick; staff*
4463 rhabdizŏ (1), to *strike with a stick*

ROE
3280 ya'ălâh (1), *ibex*
6643 tsᵉbîy (6), *gazelle*

ROEBUCK
6643 tsᵉbîy (4), *gazelle*

ROEBUCKS
6643 tsᵉbîy (1), *gazelle*

ROES
6643 tsᵉbîy (3), *gazelle*
6646 tsᵉbîyâh (2), *gazelle*

ROGELIM
7274 Rôgᵉlîym (2), *fullers* as *tramping* the cloth

ROHGAH
7303 Rôwhăgâh (1), *outcry*

ROLL
1549 gillâyôwn (1), *tablet for writing; mirror*
1556 gâlal (4), to *roll; to commit*
4039 mᵉgillâh (14), *roll, scroll*
4040 mᵉgillâh (Ch.) (7), *roll, scroll*
6428 pâlash (1), to *roll in dust*
617 apŏkuliŏ (1), to *roll away, roll back*

ROLLED
1556 gâlal (6), to *roll; to commit*
617 apŏkuliŏ (3), to *roll away, roll back*
1507 hĕilissŏ (1), to *roll, coil* or *wrap*
4351 prŏskuliŏ (2), to *roll towards*

ROLLER
2848 chittûwl (1), *bandage* for a wound

ROLLETH
1556 gâlal (1), to *roll*

ROLLING
1534 galgal (1), *wheel; something round*

ROLLS
5609 çᵉphar (Ch.) (1), *book*

ROMAMTI-EZER
7320 Rôwmamtîy 'Ezer (2), *I have raised* up a *help*

ROMAN
4514 Rhŏmaiŏs (5), *Roman; of Rome*

ROMANS
4514 Rhŏmaiŏs (7), *Roman; of Rome*

ROME
4516 Rhŏmē (15), *strength*

ROOF
1406 gâg (11), *roof; top*
2441 chêk (5), area of *mouth*
6982 qôwrâh (1), *rafter; roof*
4721 stĕgē (3), *roof*

ROOFS
1406 gâg (2), *roof; top*

ROOM
4725 mâqôwm (3), general *locality, place*
4800 merchâb (1), *open space; liberty*
7337 râchab (2), to *broaden*
8478 tachath (11), *bottom; underneath*
473 anti (1), *instead* of , *because* of
508 anŏgĕŏn (1), *dome* or a *balcony*
1240 diadŏchŏs (1), *successor* in office
4411 prŏtŏklisia (1), *pre-eminence at meals*
5117 tŏpŏs (5), *place*
5253 hupĕrŏ₁ŏn (1), *upper room*
5362 philandrŏs (1), *affectionate* as a wife to her *husband*

ROOMS
7064 qên (1), *nest; nestlings; chamber*
8478 tachath (2), *bottom; underneath; in lieu of*
4411 prŏtŏklisia (4), *pre-eminence at meals*

ROOT
5428 nâthash (2), to *tear away, be uprooted*
8327 shârash (7), to *root, insert; to uproot*
8328 sheresh (17), *root*
1610 ĕkrizŏŏ (2), to *uproot*
4491 rhiza (15), *root*

ROOTED
5255 nâçach (1), to *tear away*
5423 nâthaq (1), to *tear off*
5428 nâthash (1), to *tear away, be uprooted*
6131 'âqar (1), to *pluck up roots; to hamstring*
8327 shârash (1), to *root, insert; to uproot*
1610 ĕkrizŏŏ (1), to *uproot*
4492 rhizŏŏ (2), to *root; to become stable*

ROOTS
5428 nâthash (1), to *tear away, be uprooted*
6132 'âqar (Ch.) (1), to *pluck* up roots
8328 sheresh (13), *root*

8330 shôresh (Ch.) (3), *root*
1610 ĕkrizŏŏ (1), to *uproot*
4491 rhiza (1), *root*

ROPE
5688 'ăbôth (1), *entwined things: a string, wreath*

ROPES
2256 chebel (3), *band*
5688 'ăbôth (2), *entwined things: a string, wreath*
4979 schŏiniŏn (1), *withe* or *tie* or *rope*

ROSE
2224 zârach (3), to *rise; to be bright*
2261 chăbatstseleth (2), *meadow-saffron*
5927 'âlâh (2), to *ascend, be high, mount*
6965 qûwm (71), to *rise*
7925 shâkam (29), to *load up,* to *start early*
305 anabainŏ (1), to *go up, rise*
450 anistēmi (18), to *rise; to come back to life*
1453 ĕgĕirŏ (3), to *waken,* i.e. *rouse*
1817 ĕxanistēmi (1), to *beget, raise up*
4911 sunĕphistēmi (1), to *resist* or *assault jointly*

ROSH
7220 Rô'sh (1), *head*

ROT
5307 nâphal (3), to *fall*
7537 râqab (2), to *decay* by worm-eating

ROTTEN
4418 mâlâch (2), *rag* or *old garment*
5685 'âbash (1), to *dry* up
7538 râqâb (1), *decay* by *caries*
7539 riqqâbôwn (1), *decay* by *caries*

ROTTENNESS
4716 maq (1), *putridity, stench*
7538 râqâb (4), *decay* by *caries*

ROUGH
386 'êythân (1), *never-failing; eternal*
5569 çâmâr (1), *shaggy*
7186 qâsheh (1), *severe*
7406 rekeç (1), *ridge*
8163 sâ'îyr (1), *shaggy; he-goat; goat idol*
8181 sê'âr (1), tossed *hair*
5138 trachus (1), *uneven, jagged, rocky, reefy*

ROUGHLY
5794 'az (1), *strong, vehement, harsh*
7186 qâsheh (5), *severe*

ROUND
1754 dûwr (1), *circle; ball; pile*
2636 chaçpaç (1), to *peel; to be scale-like*
3803 kâthar (2), to *enclose, besiege; to wait*

4524 mêçab (3), *divan couch; around*
5362 nâqaph (4), to *strike; to surround*
5437 çâbab (7), to *surround*
5439 çâbîyb (254), *circle; environs; around*
5469 çahar (1), *roundness*
5696 'âgôl (6), *circular*
5921 'al (2), *above, over*
7720 sahârôn (1), round *pendant or crescent*
2943 kuklŏthĕn (10), *from the circle*
2944 kuklŏō (2), to *surround, encircle*
3840 pantŏthĕn (1), *from, on all sides*
4015 pĕriastraptō (2), *to shine around*
4017 pĕriblĕpō (5), to *look all around*
4026 pĕriistēmi (1), to *stand around; to avoid*
4033 pĕrikuklŏō (1), to *blockade completely*
4034 pĕrilampō (2), to *shine all around*
4038 pĕrix (1), all *around*
4039 pĕriŏikĕŏ (1), to *be a neighbor*
4066 pĕrichōrŏs (9), *surrounding country*

ROUSE
6965 qûwm (1), to *rise*

ROW
2905 ṭûwr (14), *row, course built into a wall*
4635 ma'ăreketh (2), *pile of loaves, arrangement*
5073 nidbâk (Ch.) (1), *layer, row*

ROWED
2864 châthar (1), to *row*
1643 ĕlaunō (1), to *push*

ROWERS
7751 shûwṭ (1), to *travel, roam*

ROWING
1643 ĕlaunō (1), to *push*

ROWS
2905 ṭûwr (12), *row, course built into a wall*
2918 ṭîyrâh (1), *fortress; hamlet*
4634 ma'ărâkâh (1), *arrangement, row; pile*
5073 nidbâk (Ch.) (1), *layer, row*
8447 tôwr (1), *succession*

ROYAL
4410 mᵉlûwkâh (4), *realm, rulership*
4428 melek (2), *king*
4430 melek (Ch.) (1), *king*
4438 malkûwth (13), *rule; dominion*
4467 mamlâkâh (4), *royal dominion*
8237 shaphrûwr (1), *tapestry or canopy*
934 basilĕiŏs (1), *royal, kingly* in nature
937 basilikŏs (2), *befitting the sovereign*

RUBBING
5597 psōchō (1), to *rub out grain kernels*

RUBBISH
6083 'âphâr (2), *dust, earth, mud; clay,*

RUBIES
6443 pânîyn (6), (poss.) *round pearl*

RUDDER
4079 pēdaliŏn (1), *blade*

RUDDY
119 'âdam (1), to *red in the face*
132 'admônîy (3), *reddish, ruddy*

RUDE
2399 idiōtēs (1), not *initiated; untrained*

RUDIMENTS
4747 stŏichĕiŏn (2), *elementary* truths

RUE
4076 pēganŏn (1), *rue*

RUFUS
4504 Rhŏuphŏs (2), *red*

RUHAMAH
7355 râcham (1), to *be compassionate*

RUIN
4072 midcheh (1), *overthrow, downfall*
4288 mᵉchittâh (1), *ruin; consternation*
4383 mikshôwl (1), *obstacle; enticement*
4384 makshêlâh (1), *enticement*
4654 mappâlâh (2), *ruin*
4658 mappeleth (2), *down-fall; ruin; carcase*
6365 pîyd (1), *misfortune*
4485 rhēgma (1), *ruin*

RUINED
2040 hâraç (2), to *pull down; break, destroy*
3782 kâshal (1), to *totter, waver; to falter*

RUINOUS
4654 mappâlâh (1), *ruin*
5327 nâtsâh (2), to *be desolate, to lay waste*

RUINS
2034 hărîyçâh (1), *demolished, ruins*
4383 mikshôwl (1), *obstacle; enticement*
2679 kataskaptō (1), to *destroy, be ruined*

RULE
4427 mâlak (1), to *reign as king*
4475 memshâlâh (4), *rule; realm or a ruler*
4623 ma'tsâr (1), *self-control*
4910 mâshal (25), to *rule*
7287 râdâh (10), to *subjugate; to crumble*
7980 shâlaṭ (3), to *dominate, i.e. govern*
7981 shᵉlêṭ (Ch.) (1), to *dominate, i.e. govern*

7990 shallîyṭ (Ch.) (1), *premier, sovereign*
8323 sârar (3), to *have, exercise, get dominion*
746 archē (1), *first*
757 archŏ (1), to *rule, be first in rank*
1018 brabĕuŏ (1), to *govern; to prevail*
2233 hēgĕŏmai (3), to *lead, i.e. command*
2583 kanōn (4), *rule, standard*
4165 pŏimainō (4), to *tend* as a shepherd
4291 prŏïstēmi (2), to *preside; to practice*

RULED
4474 mimshâl (1), *ruler; dominion, rule*
4910 mâshal (5), to *rule*
5401 nâshaq (1), to *kiss; to equip* with weapons
7287 râdâh (3), to *subjugate; to crumble*
7990 shallîyṭ (Ch.) (2), *premier, sovereign*
8199 shâphaṭ (1), to *judge*

RULER
834+5921 'ăsher (1), *who, which, what, that*
4910 mâshal (13), to *rule*
5057 nâgîyd (19), *commander, official*
5387 nâsîy' (3), *leader; rising mist, fog*
6485 pâqad (2), to *visit, care for, count*
7101 qâtsîyn (2), *magistrate; leader*
7287 râdâh (1), to *subjugate; to crumble*
7860 shôṭêr (1), to *write; official who is a scribe*
7981 shᵉlêṭ (Ch.) (4), to *dominate, i.e. govern*
7989 shallîyṭ (1), *prince or warrior*
7990 shallîyṭ (Ch.) (2), *premier, sovereign*
8269 sar (10), *head person, ruler*
752 archisunagōgŏs (6), *director of the synagogue* services
755 architriklinŏs (1), *director of the entertainment*
758 archōn (9), *first*
2525 kathistēmi (6), to *designate, constitute*

RULER'S
4910 mâshal (1), to *rule*
758 archōn (1), *first*

RULERS
4043 mâgên (1), small *shield (buckler)*
4910 mâshal (4), to *rule*
5057 nâgîyd (1), *commander, official*
5387 nâsîy' (3), *leader; rising mist, fog*
5461 çâgân (16), *prefect*
6485 pâqad (2), to *visit, care for, count*
7101 qâtsîyn (2), *magistrate; leader*
7218 rô'sh (2), *head*

7336 râzan (1), *honorable*
7984 shilṭôwn (Ch.) (2), *official*
8269 sar (21), *ruler*
752 archisunagōgŏs (2), *director of the synagogue* services
758 archôn (14), *first*
2232 hēgĕmōn (2), *chief*
2888 kŏsmŏkratŏr (1), *world-ruler*
4178 pŏllakis (2), *many times,* i.e. *frequently*

RULEST
4910 mâshal (2), to *rule*

RULETH
4910 mâshal (7), to *rule*
7300 rûwd (1), to *ramble*
7980 shâlaṭ (4), to *dominate,* i.e. *govern*
4291 prŏïstēmi (2), to *preside; to practice*

RULING
4910 mâshal (2), to *rule*
4291 prŏïstēmi (1), to *preside; to practice*

RUMAH
7316 Rûwmâh (1), *height*

RUMBLING
1995 hâmôwn (1), *noise, tumult; many, crowd*

RUMOUR
8052 shᵉmûw'âh (8), *announcement*
3056 lŏgŏs (1), *word, matter, thing*

RUMOURS
189 akŏē (2), *hearing; thing heard*

RUMP
451 'alyâh (5), fat *tail*

RUN
935 bôw' (1), to *go, come*
1556 gâlal (1), to *roll; to commit*
1980 hâlak (3), to *walk; live a certain way*
2100 zûwb (1), to *flow freely, gush*
3212 yâlak (1), to *walk; to live; to carry*
3381 yârad (6), to *descend*
6293 pâga' (1), to *impinge*
6805 tsâ'ad (1), to *pace*
7323 rûwts (36), to *run*
7325 rûwr (1), to *emit a fluid*
7751 shûwṭ (6), to *travel, roam*
8264 shâqaq (2), to *seek*
4936 suntrĕchō (1), to *rush together*
5143 trĕchō (8), to *run or walk hastily; to strive*

RUNNEST
7323 rûwts (1), to *run*

RUNNETH
935 bôw' (1), to *go, come*
3381 yârad (2), to *descend*
7310 rᵉvâyâh (1), *satisfaction*
7323 rûwts (4), to *run*

English

1632 ĕkchĕō (1), to *pour forth; to bestow*
5143 trĕchō (2), to *run*

RUNNING
1980 hâlak (1), to *walk*
2100 zûwb (2), to *discharge; waste away*
2416 chay (7), *alive; raw*
4794 mᵉrûwtsâh (2), *race*
4944 mashshâq (1), *rapid traversing motion*
5140 nâzal (1), to *drip*
7323 rûwts (6), to *run*
1998 ĕpisuntrĕchō (1), to *hasten together upon*
4370 prŏstrĕchō (2), to *hasten by running*
5143 trĕchō (1), to *run*
5240 hupĕrĕkchunō (1), to *overflow*
5295 hupŏtrĕchō (1), to *run under*

RUSH
100 'agmôwn (2), *rush*
1573 gôme' (1), *papyrus*
7582 shâ'âh (1), to *moan*

RUSHED
6584 pâshaṭ (2), to *strip*
3729 hŏrmaō (1), to *dash*

RUSHES
1573 gôme' (1), *papyrus*

RUSHETH
7857 shâṭaph (1), to *gush*

RUSHING
7494 ra'ash (3), *uproar*
7582 shâ'âh (1), to *moan*
7588 shâ'ôwn (2), *uproar*
5342 phĕrō (1), to *bear*

RUST
1035 brōsis (2), *food; rust*
2447 iŏs (1), *corrosion*

RUTH
7327 Rûwth (12), *friend*
4503 Rhŏuth (1), *friend*

SABACHTHANI
4518 sabachthani (2), *thou hast left me*

SABAOTH
4519 sabaōth (2), *armies*

SABBATH
7673 shâbath (1), to *repose; to desist*
7676 shabbâth (73), *day of rest*
7677 shabbâthôwn (3), *special holiday*
4315 prŏsabbatŏn (1), *Sabbath-eve*
4521 sabbatŏn (59), *day of repose*

SABBATHS
4868 mishbâth (1), *cessation; destruction*
7676 shabbâth (34), *day of rest*

SABEANS
5433 çâbâ' (1), to *quaff*
5436 Çᵉbâ'iy (1), *Sebaite*
7614 Shᵉbâ' (1), *Sheba*
7615 Shᵉbâ'iy (1), *Shebaïte*

SABTA
5454 Çabtâ' (1), *Sabta or Sabtah*

SABTAH
5454 Çabtâ' (1), *Sabta or Sabtah*

SABTECHA
5455 Çabtᵉkâ' (1), *Sabteca*

SABTECHAH
5455 Çabtᵉkâ' (1), *Sabteca*

SACAR
7940 Sâkar (2), *recompense*

SACK
572 'amtêchath (5), *sack*
8242 saq (4), *bag*

SACK'S
572 'amtêchath (3), *sack*

SACKBUT
5443 çabbᵉkâ' (Ch.) (4), *lyre musical instrument*

SACKCLOTH
8242 saq (41), *coarse cloth or sacking; bag*
4526 sakkŏs (4), *sack-cloth*

SACKCLOTHES
8242 saq (1), *coarse cloth or sacking; bag*

SACKS
572 'amtêchath (6), *sack*
3672 Kinnᵉrôwth (1), (poss.) *harp-shaped*
8242 saq (2), *bag*

SACKS'
572 'amtêchath (1), *sack*

SACRIFICE
2076 zâbach (48), to (sacrificially) *slaughter*
2077 zebach (102), *animal flesh; sacrifice*
2282 chag (2), *solemn festival*
4503 minchâh (5), *tribute; offering*
6213 'âsâh (1), to *make*
7133 qorbân (1), *sacrificial present*
1494 ĕidōlŏthutŏn (3), *idolatrous offering*
2378 thusia (17), *sacrifice*
2380 thuō (4), to *sacrifice*

SACRIFICED
2076 zâbach (29), to (sacrificially) *slaughter*
6213 'âsâh (1), to *make*
1494 ĕidōlŏthutŏn (2), *idolatrous offering*
2380 thuō (1), to *kill; to butcher; to sacrifice*

SACRIFICEDST
2076 zâbach (1), to (sacrificially) *slaughter*

SACRIFICES
1685 dᵉbach (Ch.) (1), *animal sacrifice*
2077 zebach (53), *animal flesh; sacrifice*
2282 chag (1), *solemn festival*
2378 thusia (12), *sacrifice, offering*

SACRIFICETH
2076 zâbach (6), to (sacrificially) *slaughter*

SACRIFICING
2076 zâbach (2), to (sacrificially) *slaughter*

SACRILEGE
2416 hiĕrŏsulĕō (1), to be *a temple-robber*

SAD
2196 zâ'aph (1), to be *angry*
3510 kâ'ab (1), to *feel pain; to grieve; to spoil*
3512 kâ'âh (1), to *despond; to deject*
5620 çar (1), *sullen*
7451 ra' (2), *bad; evil*
7489 râ'a' (1), to be *good for nothing*
4659 skuthrōpŏs (2), *gloomy, mournful*
4768 stugnazō (1), to be *overcast; somber*

SADDLE
2280 châbash (3), to *wrap firmly, bind*
4817 merkâb (1), *chariot; seat in chariot*

SADDLED
2280 châbash (10), to *wrap firmly, bind*

SADDUCEES
4523 Saddŏukaiŏs (14), *of Tsadok*

SADLY
7451 ra' (1), *bad; evil*

SADNESS
7455 rôa' (1), *badness*

SADOC
4524 Sadōk (1), *just*

SAFE
983 beṭach (2), *safety*
3467 yâsha' (1), to *make safe, free*
6403 pâlaṭ (1), to *slip out, i.e. escape; to deliver*
7682 sâgab (1), to be *safe*
7965 shâlôwm (3), *safe*
809 aschēmōn (1), *inelegant, indecent*
1295 diasōzō (1), to *cure, preserve, rescue*
5198 hugiainō (1), to *have sound health*

SAFEGUARD
4931 mishmereth (1), *watch, sentry, post*

SAFELY
983 beṭach (17), *safety*
7965 shâlôwm (1), *safe*
806 asphalōs (2), *securely*

SAFETY
983 beṭach (9), *safety*
3468 yesha' (3), *liberty, deliverance, prosperity*
7951 shâlâh (1), to be *secure or successful*
8668 tᵉshûw'âh (4), *rescue, deliverance*
803 asphalĕia (2), *security; certainty*

SAFFRON
3750 karkôm (1), *crocus*

SAID
559 'âmar (2772), to *say*

560 'âmar (Ch.) (41), to *say*
1696 dâbar (85), to *say*
1697 dâbâr (8), *word; matter; thing*
4448 mâlal (1), to *speak*
4449 mᵉlal (Ch.) (1), to *speak, say*
5002 nᵉ'ûm (9), *oracle*
6030 'ânâh (1), to *respond*
7121 qârâ' (1), to *call out*
669 apŏphthĕggŏmai (1), *declare, address*
2036 ĕpō (756), to *speak*
2046 ĕrĕō (21), to *utter*
2063 ĕruthrŏs (3), *red*
2980 lalĕō (7), to *talk*
3004 lĕgō (200), to *say*
4280 prŏĕrĕō (4), to *say already, predict*
4483 rhĕō (15), to *utter*
5346 phēmi (48), to *make known one's thoughts*

SAIDST
559 'âmar (20), to *say*
1696 dâbar (1), to *speak*
2046 ĕrĕō (1), to *utter*

SAIL
5251 nêç (2), *flag; signal*
321 anagō (1), to *sail*
636 apŏplĕō (1), to *set sail, sail away*
3896 paraplĕō (1), to *sail near*
4126 plĕō (2), to *travel in a ship*
4632 skĕuŏs (1), *vessel, implement, equipment*

SAILED
321 anagō (2), to *lead up; to sail away*
636 apŏplĕō (3), to *set sail, sail away*
1020 braduplŏĕō (1), to *sail slowly*
1277 diaplĕō (1), to *sail through, across*
1602 ĕkplĕō (3), to *depart by ship*
3881 paralĕgŏmai (1), to *sail past*
4126 plĕō (2), to *travel in a ship*
5284 hupŏplĕō (2), to *sail under the lee of*

SAILING
1276 diapĕraō (1), to *cross over*
4126 plĕō (1), to *travel in a ship*
4144 plŏŏs (1), *navigation, voyage*

SAILORS
3492 nautēs (1), *sailor*

SAINT
6918 qâdôwsh (3), *sacred*
40 hagiŏs (1), *holy*

SAINTS
2623 châçîyd (19), *religiously pious, godly*
6918 qâdôwsh (9), *sacred*
6922 qaddîysh (Ch.) (6), *sacred*
6944 qôdesh (1), *sacred*
40 hagiŏs (60), *holy*

SAINTS'
40 hagiŏs (1), *holy*

SAITH
559 'âmar (581), *to say*
1696 dâbar (7), *to speak*
5001 nâ'am (10), *to utter as an oracle*
5002 n^e'ûm (353), *oracle*
6310 peh (1), *mouth*
2036 ĕpō (1), *to speak*
2980 laleō (2), *to talk*
3004 legō (297), *to say*
5346 phēmi (5), *to make known one's thoughts*

SAKE
182 'ôwdôwth (1), *on account of; because*
1558 gâlâl (3), *on account of, because of*
1697 dâbâr (2), *word; matter; thing*
4616 ma'an (45), *on account of*
5668 'âbûwr (15), *on account of*
7068 qin'âh (1), *jealousy*
7945 shel (1), *on account of; whatsoever*
8478 tachath (2), *bottom; underneath; in lieu of*
1722 ĕn (1), *because of*
1752 hĕnĕka (14), *on account of*

SAKES
1558 gâlâl (1), *on account of, because of*
1697 dâbâr (1), *matter*
1701 dibrâh (Ch.) (1), *because, on account of*
5668 'âbûwr (1), *on account of*
5921 'al (3), *above, over*
6616 pâthîyl (6), *twine*

SALA
4527 Sala (1), *spear*

SALAH
7974 Shelach (6), *spear*

SALAMIS
4529 Salamis (1), *surge*

SALATHIEL
7597 Sh^e'altîy'êl (1), *I have asked God*
4528 Salathiēl (3), *I have asked God*

SALCAH
5548 Çalkâh (2), *walking*

SALCHAH
5548 Çalkâh (2), *walking*

SALE
4465 mimkâr (3), *merchandise*

SALEM
8004 Shâlêm (2), *peaceful*
4532 Salēm (2), *peaceful*

SALIM
4530 Salĕim (1), (poss.) *waver*

SALLAI
5543 Çallûw (2), *weighed*

SALLU
5543 Çallûw (3), *weighed*

SALMA
8007 Salmâ' (4), *clothing*

SALMON
6756 Tsalmôwn (1), *shady*
8009 Salmâh (1), *clothing*
8012 Salmôwn (1), *investiture*
4533 Salmōn (3), *investiture*

SALMONE
4534 Salmōnē (1), (poss.) *surge on the shore*

SALOME
4539 Salōmē (2), *peace*

SALT
4416 m^elach (Ch.) (2), *salt*
4417 melach (27), *salt*
4420 m^elêchâh (1), *salted land, i.e. a desert*
5898 'Îyr ham-Melach (1), *city of (the) salt*
217 halas (8), *salt*
251 hals (1), *salt*
252 halukŏs (2), *salty*

SALTED
4414 mâlach (1), *to salt*
233 halizō (3), *to salt*

SALTNESS
1096+358 ginŏmai (1), *to be, become*

SALTPITS
4417 melach (1), *salt*

SALU
5543 Çallûw (1), *weighed*

SALUTATION
783 aspasmŏs (6), *greeting*

SALUTATIONS
783 aspasmŏs (1), *greeting*

SALUTE
1288 bârak (4), *to bless*
7592+7965 shâ'al (1), *to ask*
7965 shâlôwm (2), *safe; well; health, prosperity*
782 aspazŏmai (32), *to give salutation*

SALUTED
1288 bârak (1), *to bless*
7592+7965 shâ'al (3), *to ask*
782 aspazŏmai (5), *to give salutation*

SALUTETH
782 aspazŏmai (5), *to give salutation*

SALVATION
3444 y^eshûw'âh (65), *deliverance; aid*
3467 yâsha' (3), *to make safe, free*
3468 yesha' (32), *liberty, deliverance, prosperity*
4190 môwshâ'âh (1), *deliverance*
8668 t^eshûw'âh (17), *rescue, deliverance*
4991 sōtēria (40), *rescue*
4992 sōtēriŏn (5), *defender or defence*

SAMARIA
8111 Shôm^erown (109), *watch-station*

8115 Shomrayin (Ch.) (2), *watch-station*
4540 Samarĕia (13), *watch-station*

SAMARITAN
4541 Samarĕitēs (3), *inhabitant of Samaria*

SAMARITANS
8118 Shôm^erônîy (1), *Shomeronite*
4541 Samarĕitēs (6), *inhabitant of Samaria*

SAME
428 'êl-leh (1), *these*
1459 gav (Ch.) (1), *middle*
1791 dêk (Ch.) (1), *this*
1797 dikkên (Ch.) (1), *this*
1931 hûw' (73), *this*
1933 hâvâ' (1), *to be*
1992 hêm (4), *they*
2063 zô'th (1), *this*
2088 zeh (9), *this or that*
6106 'etsem (6), *selfsame*
8478 tachath (1), *bottom*
846 autŏs (87), *he, she, it*
1565 ĕkĕinŏs (24), *that*
2532 kai (1), *even; also*
3673 hŏmŏtĕchnŏs (1), *of the same trade*
3748 hŏstis (1), *whoever*
3761 ŏudĕ (1), *neither*
3778 hŏutŏs (37), *this*
4954 sussōmŏs (1), *fellow-member*
5023 tauta (2), *these*
5026 tautē₁ (5), (*toward or of*) *this*
5126 tŏutŏn (2), *to this*
5129 tŏutŏ₁ (1), *in this*
5615 hōsautōs (1), *in the same way*

SAMGAR-NEBO
5562 Çamgar N^ebôw (1), *Samgar-Nebo*

SAMLAH
8072 Samlâh (4), *mantle*

SAMOS
4544 Samŏs (1), *Samus*

SAMOTHRACIA
4543 Samŏthra₁kē (1), *Samos of Thrace*

SAMSON
8123 Shimshôwn (35), *sunlight*
4546 Sampsōn (1), *sunlight*

SAMSON'S
8123 Shimshôwn (3), *sunlight*

SAMUEL
8050 Sh^emûw'êl (135), *heard of God*
4545 Samŏuēl (3), *heard of God*

SANBALLAT
5571 Çanballaṭ (10), *Sanballat*

SANCTIFICATION
38 hagiasmŏs (5), *state of purity*

SANCTIFIED
6942 qâdâsh (46), *to be, make clean*
37 hagiazō (16), *to purify*

SANCTIFIETH
37 hagiazō (4), *to purify*

SANCTIFY
6942 qâdâsh (63), *to be, make clean*
37 hagiazō (6), *to purify*

SANCTUARIES
4720 miqdâsh (5), *sanctuary of deity*

SANCTUARY
4720 miqdâsh (64), *sanctuary of deity*
6944 qôdesh (68), *sacred*
39 hagiŏn (4), *sacred*

SAND
2344 chôwl (23), *sand*
285 ammŏs (5), *sand*

SANDALS
4547 sandaliŏn (2), *sandal*

SANG
6030 'ânâh (2), *to sing*
7442 rânan (1), *to shout for joy*
7891 shîyr (7), *to sing*
5214 humnĕō (1), *to celebrate God in song*

SANK
3381 yârad (1), *to descend*
6749 tsâlal (1), *to settle*

SANSANNAH
5578 Çançannâh (1), *bough*

SAPH
5593 Çaph (1), *dish*

SAPHIR
8208 Shâphîyr (1), *beautiful*

SAPPHIRA
4551 Sapphĕirē (1), *sapphire or lapis-lazuli*

SAPPHIRE
5601 çappîyr (8), *sapphire*
4552 sapphĕirŏs (1), *sapphire or lapis-lazuli*

SAPPHIRES
5601 çappîyr (3), *sapphire*

SARA
4564 Sarrha (1), *princess*

SARAH
8283 Sârâh (36), *princess*
8294 Serach (1), *superfluity*
4564 Sarrha (2), *princess*

SARAH'S
8283 Sârâh (2), *princess*
4564 Sarrha (1), *princess*

SARAI
8297 Sâray (16), *dominative*

SARAI'S
8297 Sâray (1), *dominative*

SARAPH
8315 Sâraph (1), *burning one, serpent*

SARDINE
4555 sardinŏs (1), *sard*

English

SARDIS
4554 Sardĕis (3), *Sardis*

SARDITES
5625 Çargîy (1), *Seredite*

SARDIUS
124 ʾôdem (3), *ruby*
4556 sardiŏs (1), *sardian*

SARDONYX
4557 sardŏnux (1),
  sard-onyx

SAREPTA
4558 Sarĕpta (1),
refinement

SARGON
5623 Çargôwn (1),
Sargon

SARID
8301 Sârîyd (2), *survivor*

SARON
4565 Sarōn (1), *plain*

SARSECHIM
8310 Sarçᵉkîym (1),
Sarsekim

SARUCH
4562 Sarŏuch (1), *tendril*

SAT
3427 yâshab (94), to *dwell*
8497 tâkâh (1), to *camp*
339 anakathizō (2), to *sit
up*
345 anakĕimai (6), to
recline at a meal
347 anaklinō (1), to *lean
back, recline*
377 anapiptō (4), *lie
down, lean back*
2516 kathĕzŏmai (4), to
sit down, be seated
2521 kathēmai (43), to
sit down; to remain
2523 kathizō (21), to *seat
down, dwell*
2621 katakĕimai (3), to
lie down; recline
2625 kataklinō (1), to
recline, take a place
3869 parakathizō (1), to
sit down near, beside
4775 sugkathēmai (2), to
seat oneself with
4873 sunanakĕimai (8),
to *recline with*

SATAN
7854 sâṭân (18), *opponent*
4567 Satanas (34),
accuser, i.e. the *Devil*

SATAN'S
4567 Satanas (1),
accuser, i.e. the *Devil*

SATEST
3427 yâshab (2), to *settle*

SATIATE
7301 râvâh (1), to *slake*
7646 sâba' (1), to *fill*

SATIATED
7301 râvâh (1), to *slake*

SATISFACTION
3724 kôpher (2),
redemption-price

SATISFIED
4390 mâlê' (1), to *fill*
7301 râvâh (1), to *slake*
7646 sâba' (36), *fill*

SATISFIEST
7646 sâba' (1), to *fill*

SATISFIETH
7646 sâba' (2), to *fill*
7654 sob'âh (1), *satiety*

SATISFY
4390 mâlê' (1), to *fill*
7301 râvâh (1), to *slake*
7646 sâba' (7), to *fill*
5526 chŏrtazō (1), to
supply food

SATISFYING
7648 sôba' (1),
satisfaction
4140 plēsmŏnē (1),
gratification

SATISIFED
7649 sâbêa' (1), *satiated*

SATYR
8163 sâʿîyr (1), *shaggy;
he-goat; goat* idol

SATYRS
8163 sâʿîyr (1), *shaggy;
he-goat; goat* idol

SAUL
7586 Shâ'ûwl (367), *asked*
4569 Saulŏs (23), *asked*

SAUL'S
7586 Shâ'ûwl (31), *asked*

SAVE
389 'ak (1), *surely; only*
518 'îm (1), *Oh that!*
657 'epheç (1), *end; no
further*
1107 bil'âdêy (4), *except*
1115 biltîy (2), *except*
1115+518 biltîy (1), *not,
except, without, unless*
2108 zûwlâh (6), *except*
2421 châyâh (21), to *live;
to revive*
2425 châyay (1), to *live;
to revive*
3444 yᵉshûw'âh (1),
deliverance; aid
3467 yâsha' (106), to
make safe, free
3588+518 kîy (12), *for,
that because*
3861 lâhên (Ch.) (2),
therefore; except
4422 mâlaṭ (4), to *escape*
7535 raq (3), *although*
8104 shâmar (1), to
watch
235 alla (2), *except*
1295 diasōzō (1), to *cure,
preserve, rescue*
1508 ĕi mē (18), *if not*
2228 ē (1), *or; than*
3844 para (1), *besides*
4133 plēn (1), *save that*
4982 sōzō (41), to *deliver*

SAVED
2421 châyâh (8), to *live;
to revive*
3467 yâsha' (35), to *make
safe, free*
4422 mâlaṭ (1), to *escape*
5337 nâtsal (1), to *deliver*
8104 shâmar (1), to
watch
1295 diasōzō (1), to *cure,
preserve, rescue*

SAVEST
3467 yâsha' (3), to *make
safe, free*

SAVETH
3467 yâsha' (7), to *make
safe, free*

SAVING
518 'îm (1), *Oh that!*
657 'epheç (1), *end; no
further*
2421 châyâh (1), to *live;
to revive*
3444 yᵉshûw'âh (2),
deliverance; aid
3468 yesha' (1), *liberty,
deliverance, prosperity*
1508 ĕi mē (2), *if not*
3924 parĕktŏs (1), *besides*
4047 pĕripŏiēsis (1),
preservation
4991 sōtēria (1), *rescue*

SAVIOUR
3467 yâsha' (13), to *make
safe, free*
4990 sōtēr (24), *Deliverer*

SAVIOURS
3467 yâsha' (2), to *make
safe, free*

SAVOUR
6709 tsachănâh (1),
stench
7381 rêyach (46), *odor*
2175 ĕuōdia (1), *aroma*
3471 mōrainō (2), to
become insipid
3744 ŏsmē (4), *fragrance*

SAVOUREST
5426 phrŏnĕō (2), to be
mentally *disposed*

SAVOURS
5208 nîychôwach (Ch.)
(1), *pleasure*

SAVOURY
4303 maṭ'am (6), *delicacy*

SAW
2370 chăzâ' (Ch.) (9), to
gaze upon; to *dream*
2372 chăzâh (8), to *gaze*
at; to *perceive*
4883 massôwr (1), *saw*
7200 râ'âh (306), to *see*
7805 shâzaph (1), to *scan*
991 blĕpō (9), to *look at*
1492 ĕidō (188), to *know*
1689 ĕmblĕpō (1), to
observe; to discern
2147 hĕuriskō (1), to *find*
2300 thĕaŏmai (8), to
look closely at
2334 thĕōrĕō (9), to *see*
3708 hŏraō (4), to *stare,
see clearly; to discern*

SAWED
1641 gârar (1), to *saw*

SAWEST
2370 chăzâ' (Ch.) (7), to
gaze upon; to *dream*
2372 chăzâh (8), to *gaze*
at; to *perceive*
7200 râ'âh (6), to *see*
1492 ĕidō (7), to *know*

SAWN
4249 prizō (1), to *saw* in
two

SAWS
4050 mᵉgêrâh (3), *saw*

SAY
559 'âmar (573), to *say*
560 'ămar (Ch.) (2), to *say*
1696 dâbar (28), to *speak*
1697 dâbâr (1), *word*
4405 millâh (2), *word*
471 antĕpō (1), to *refute*
2036 ĕpō (66), to *speak*
2046 ĕrĕō (39), to *utter*
2980 lalĕō (6), to *talk*
3004 lĕgō (293), to *say*
3056 lŏgŏs (1), *word*
5335 phaskō (1), to
assert a claim
5346 phēmi (6), to *make
known* one's thoughts

SAYEST
559 'âmar (18), to *say*
2036 ĕpō (1), to *speak*
3004 lĕgō (20), to *say*

SAYING
559 'âmar (916), to *say*
560 'ămar (Ch.) (2), to *say*
1697 dâbâr (1), *word*
2420 chîydâh (1), *puzzle;
conundrum; maxim*
2036 ĕpō (18), to *speak*
2981 lalia (1), *talk*
3004 lĕgō (380), to *say*
3007 lĕipō (5), to *fail*
3056 lŏgŏs (33), *word*
3058 lŏidŏrĕō (1), to
vilify, insult
4487 rhēma (6),
utterance; matter
5335 phaskō (1), to *assert*

SAYINGS
561 'êmer (2), *saying*
1697 dâbâr (5), *word*
2420 chîydâh (1), *puzzle;
conundrum; maxim*
6310 peh (1), *mouth*
3004 lĕgō (1), to *say*
3056 lŏgŏs (16), *word*
4487 rhēma (3),
utterance; matter

SCAB
1618 gârâb (1), *itching*
4556 miçpachath (3),
scurf, rash
5597 çappachath (3),
skin mange

SCABBARD
8593 ta'ar (1), *scabbard*

SCABBED
3217 yallepheth (2), *scurf*

SCAFFOLD
3595 kîyôwr (1), *caldron*

SCALES
650+4043 'âphîyq (1),
valley; stream; mighty
6425 peleç (1), *balance*
7193 qasqeseth (7), *fish
scales; coat of mail*
3013 lĕpis (1), *flake, scale*

SCALETH
5927 'âlâh (1), to *ascend,
be high, mount*

SCALL
5424 netheq (14), *scurf*

SEARCHED

4290 machtereth (1),
  burglary
8446 tûwr (9), to *meander*
1833 *ĕxĕtazō* (1), to
  ascertain or *interrogate*
2045 *ĕrĕunaō* (2), to
  seek, i.e. to *investigate*

SEARCHED

2664 châphas (3), to *seek*
2713 châqar (7), to
  examine intimately
2714 chêqer (1),
  examination
4959 mâshash (2), to *feel*
7270 râgal (1), to
  reconnoiter; to *slander*
8446 tûwr (4), to *meander*
350 anakrinō (1), to
  interrogate, determine
1830 *ĕxĕrĕunaō* (1), to
  explore

SEARCHEST

1875 dârash (1), to *search*
2664 châphas (1), to *seek*

SEARCHETH

1875 dârash (2), to *search*
2713 châqar (3), to *search*
2045 *ĕrĕunaō* (3), to *seek*

SEARCHING

2664 châphas (1), to *seek*
2714 chêqer (2),
  examination
8446 tûwr (1), to *meander*
2045 *ĕrĕunaō* (1), to *seek*

SEARCHINGS

2714 chêqer (1),
  examination

SEARED

2743 *kautēriazō* (1), to
  brand or *cauterize*

SEAS

3220 yâm (24), *sea*
1337 *dithalassŏs* (1),
  having two seas

SEASON

2165 z°mân (1), *time*
2166 z°mân (Ch.) (1),
  time, appointed
3117 yôwm (3), *day; time*
4150 môw'êd (10), *place
  of meeting*
4414 mâlach (1), to
  disappear as dust
6256 'êth (14), *time*
171 akairōs (1),
  inopportunely
741 artuō (1), to *spice*
2121 *ĕukairŏs* (1),
  opportune, suitable
2540 kairŏs (11), *set* or
  proper time
3641 *ŏligŏs* (1), *puny*
4340 *prŏskairŏs* (1),
  temporary
5550 chrŏnŏs (3), *time*
5610 hŏra (3), *hour*

SEASONED

741 artuō (2), to *spice*

SEASONS

2166 z°mân (Ch.) (1),
  time, appointed
4150 môw'êd (3), *place of
  meeting; assembly*
6256 'êth (2), *time*
2540 kairŏs (4), *set* or
  proper time

SEAT

3678 kiççê' (7), *throne*
4186 môwshâb (7), *seat*
7674 shebeth (1), *rest*
7675 shebeth (2), *abode*
8499 t°kûwnâh (1),
  something *arranged*
968 bēma (10), *tribunal
  platform; judging place*
2362 thrŏnŏs (3), *throne*
2515 kathĕdra (1), *bench*

SEATED

5603 çâphan (1), to *roof*

SEATS

2362 thrŏnŏs (4), *throne*
2515 kathĕdra (2), *bench*
4410 prōtŏkathĕdria (4),
  pre-eminence in council

SEBA

5434 Ç°bâ' (4), *Seba*

SEBAT

7627 Sh°bâṭ (1), *Shebat*

SECACAH

5527 Ç°kâkâh (1),
  enclosure

SECHU

7906 Sêkûw (1), *Seku*

SECOND

4932 mishneh (12),
  double; second
8138 shânâh (3), to *fold,*
  i.e. *duplicate*
8145 shênîy (99), *second*
8147 sh°nayim (10),
  two-fold
8578 tinyân (Ch.) (1),
  second
8648 t°rêyn (Ch.) (1), *two*
1207 *dĕutĕrŏprōtŏs* (1),
  second-first
1208 *dĕutĕrŏs* (42),
  second; secondly

SECONDARILY

1208 *dĕutĕrŏs* (1),
  second; secondly

SECRET

328 'aṭ (1), *gently, softly*
2934 ṭâman (1), to *hide*
4565 miçtâr (8), *covert
  hiding place*
5475 çôwd (8), *secret*
5640 çâtham (1), to
  repair; to keep secret
5641 çâthar (4), to *hide*
5642 ç°thar (Ch.) (1), to
  demolish
5643 çêther (15), *cover*
5956 'âlam (2), to *conceal*
6383 pil'îy (1),
  remarkable
6596 pôth (1), *hole; hinge*
6845 tsâphan (2), to *hide*
7328 râz (Ch.) (6),
  mystery
8368 sâthar (1), to *break*
  out as an eruption
614 apŏkruphŏs (1),
  secret, hidden things
2926 kruptē (1), *hidden*
2927 kruptŏs (10), *private*
2928 kruptō (1), to
  conceal
2931 kruphē (1), *in secret*
4601 sigaō (1), to *keep
  silent*

SEAT

5550 chrŏnŏs (1), *time*

SECRETLY

1589 gânab (1), to *deceive*
2244 châbâ' (1), to *secrete*
2644 châphâ' (1), to *act
  covertly*
2790 chârash (1), to
  engrave; to plow
2791 cheresh (1),
  magical *craft; silence*
3909 lâṭ (1), *secrecy*
4565 miçtâr (2), *covert
  hiding place*
5643 çêther (9), *cover*
6845 tsâphan (1), to *hide*
2928 kruptō (1), to
  conceal
2977 lathra (1), *secretly*

SECRETS

4016 mâbûsh (1), *male
  genitals*
5475 çôwd (2), *secret*
7328 râz (Ch.) (3),
  mystery
8587 ta'ălummâh (2),
  secret
2927 kruptŏs (2), *private*

SECT

139 hairĕsis (5), *sect*

SECUNDUS

4580 Sĕkŏundŏs (1),
  second

SECURE

982 bâṭach (4), to *trust*
983 beṭach (1), *security*
987 baṭṭûchôwth (1),
  security
4160+275 mûwts (1), to
  oppress

SECURELY

983 beṭach (2), *safety,
  security, trust*

SECURITY

2425 hikanŏs (1), *ample*

SEDITION

849 'eshtaddûwr (Ch.)
  (2), *rebellion*
4714 stasis (3), one
  leading an *uprising*

SEDITIONS

1370 dichŏstasia (1),
  dissension

SEDUCE

635 apŏplanaō (1), to
  lead astray; to wander
4105 planaō (2), to
  deceive

SEDUCED

2937 ṭâ'âh (1), to *lead
  astray*
8582 tâ'âh (2), to *stray*

SEDUCERS

1114 gŏēs (1), *imposter*

SEDUCETH

8582 tâ'âh (1), to *stray*

SEDUCING

4108 planŏs (1), *roving*

SEE

2009 hinnêh (2), *Look!*
2370 chăzâ' (Ch.) (4), to
  gaze upon; to dream
2372 châzâh (15), to *gaze
  at; to perceive*

SEE

5009 tamĕiŏn (1), *room*

2374 chôzeh (2),
  beholder in vision
4758 mar'eh (1),
  appearance; vision
5027 nâbaṭ (4), to *scan;
  to regard* with favor
7200 râ'âh (346), to *see*
7789 shûwr (1), to *spy
  out, survey*
308 anablĕpō (1), to *look
  up; to recover sight*
542 apĕidō (1), to *see
  fully*
991 blĕpō (46), to *look at*
1227 diablĕpō (2), to *see
  clearly, recover vision*
1492 ĕidō (79), to *know*
1689 ĕmblĕpō (1), to
  observe; to discern
2300 thĕaŏmai (4), to
  look closely at
2334 thĕōrĕō (17), to *see*
2396 idĕ (1), *lo!, look!*
2400 idŏu (3), *lo!, see!*
2477 histŏrĕō (1), to *visit*
3467 muōpazō (1), to *see
  indistinctly, be myopic*
3700 ŏptanŏmai (29), to
  appear
3708 hŏraō (11), to *stare,
  see clearly; to discern*
5461 phōtizō (1), to *shine
  or to brighten* up

SEED

2233 zera' (218), *seed*
2234 z°ra' (Ch.) (1),
  posterity, progeny
6507 p°rûdâh (1), *kernel*
4687 spĕirō (4), to
  scatter, i.e. *sow* seed
4690 spĕrma (41), *seed*
4701 spŏra (1), *sowing*
4703 spŏrŏs (5), *seed*

SEED'S

2233 zera' (1), *seed; fruit*

SEEDS

4690 spĕrma (3), *seed*

SEEDTIME

2233 zera' (1), *seed; fruit*

SEEING

310 'achar (1), *after*
518 'îm (1), *whether?; if*
1768 dîy (Ch.) (1), *that; of*
3282 ya'an (1), *because*
3588 kîy (9), *for, that*
6493 piqqêach (1),
  clear-sighted
7200 râ'âh (16), to *see*
990 blemma (1), *vision*
991 blĕpō (8), to *look at*
1063 gar (1), *for, indeed,
  but, because*
1492 ĕidō (8), to *know*
1512 ĕi pĕr (1), *if perhaps*
1893 ĕpĕi (4), *since*
1894 ĕpĕidē (2), *whereas*
1897 ĕpĕipĕr (1), *since*
2334 thĕōrĕō (2), to *see*
3708 hŏraō (1), to *stare,
  see clearly; to discern*
3754 hŏti (1), *that; since*
4275 prŏĕidō (1), to
  foresee

SEEK

1239 bâqar (3), to
  inspect, admire

1245 bâqash (112), to
  search out; to *strive*
1556 gâlal (1), to *roll*
1875 dârash (56), to *seek*
2713 châqar (1), to *search*
7125 qir'âh (1), to
  encounter, to *happen*
7836 shâchar (8), to
  search for
8446 tûwr (1), to *wander*
327 anazêtêō (1), to
  search out
1567 ĕkzêtêō (2), to *seek
  out*
1934 ĕpizêtêō (6), to
  search (inquire) for
2212 zêtêō (48), to *seek*

SEEKEST
1245 bâqash (7), to
  search out; to *strive*
2212 zêtêō (2), to *seek*

SEEKETH
579 'ânâh (1), to *meet*
1243 baqqârâh (1),
  looking after
1245 bâqash (19), to
  search out; to *strive*
1875 dârash (6), to *seek*
2658 châphar (1), to *delve*
7836 shâchar (1), to
  search for
1567 ĕkzêtêō (1), to *seek
  out*
1934 ĕpizêtêō (3), to
  search (inquire) for
2212 zêtêō (9), to *seek*

SEEKING
1875 dârash (2), to *seek*
2212 zêtêō (12), to *seek*

SEEM
3191 yᵉṭab (Ch.) (1), to
  be, make well
4591 mâ'aṭ (1), to *be,
  make small or few*
4758 mar'eh (1),
  appearance; vision
5869 'ayin (2), *eye; sight*
7034 qâlah (1), to *be light*
7185 qâshâh (1), to *be
  tough* or *severe*
1380 dŏkĕō (5), to *seem*

SEEMED
5869 'ayin (4), *eye; sight*
1380 dŏkĕō (6), to *think,
  regard, seem* good
5316 phainō (1), to
  lighten; to appear

SEEMETH
5869 'ayin (18), *eye; sight*
6440 pânîym (2), *face*
7200 râ'âh (1), to *see*
1380 dŏkĕō (5), to *seem*

SEEMLY
5000 nâ'veh (2), *suitable*

SEEN
2370 chăzâ' (Ch.) (3), to
  gaze upon; to *dream*
2372 châzâh (9), to *gaze*
  at; to *perceive*
7200 râ'âh (162), to *see*
7210 rô'îy (2), *sight*
7805 shâzaph (1), to *scan*
991 blĕpō (9), to *look* at
1492 ĕidō (33), to *know*
2300 thĕaŏmai (8), to
  look closely at

2334 thĕōrĕō (2), to *see*
2529 kathŏraō (1), to *see
  clearly*
3700 ŏptanŏmai (8), to
  appear
3708 hŏraō (32), to *stare,
  see clearly; to discern*
3780 ŏuchi (1), *not indeed*
4308 prŏŏraō (1), to
  notice previously
5316 phainō (2), to
  lighten; be visible

SEER
2374 chôzeh (11),
  beholder in vision
7200 râ'âh (10), to *see*

SEER'S
7200 râ'âh (1), to *see*

SEERS
2374 chôzeh (5),
  beholder in vision
7200 râ'âh (1), to *see*

SEEST
2372 châzâh (2), to *gaze*
  at; to *perceive*
7200 râ'âh (27), to *see*
7210 rô'îy (1), *sight;
  spectacle*
991 blĕpō (5), to *look* at
2334 thĕōrĕō (1), to *see*

SEETH
2372 châzâh (3), to *gaze*
  at; to *perceive*
7200 râ'âh (27), to *see*
7210 rô'îy (1), *sight;
  spectacle*
991 blĕpō (11), to *look* at
2334 thĕōrĕō (9), to *see*
3708 hŏraō (1), to *stare*

SEETHE
1310 bâshal (8), to *boil*

SEETHING
1310 bâshal (1), to *boil*
5301 nâphach (2), to
  inflate, blow, kindle

SEGUB
7687 Sᵉgûwb (3), *aloft*

SEIR
8165 Sê'îyr (39), *rough*

SEIRATH
8167 Sᵉ'îyrâh (1),
  roughness

SEIZE
3423 yârash (1), to
  inherit; to impoverish
3451 yᵉshîymâh (1),
  desolation
3947 lâqach (1), to *take*
2722 katĕchō (1), to *hold
  down fast*

SEIZED
2388 châzaq (1), to *seize*

SELA
5554 Çela' (1), *craggy
  rock; fortress*

SELA-HAMMAHLEKOTH
5555 Çela' ham-
  machlᵉqôwth (1), *rock
  of the divisions*

SELAH
5542 Çelâh (74),
  suspension of music
5554 Çela' (1), *craggy
  rock; fortress*

SELED
5540 Çeled (1),
  exultation

SELEUCIA
4581 Sĕlĕukĕia (1), of
  Seleucus

SELFWILL
7522 râtsôwn (1), *delight*

SELFWILLED
829 authadēs (2),
  self-pleasing, arrogant

SELL
4376 mâkar (24), to *sell*
7666 shâbar (3), to *deal*
1710 ĕmpŏrĕuŏmai (1),
  to *trade, do business*
4453 pōlĕō (7), to *barter*

SELLER
4376 mâkar (3), to *sell*
4211 pŏrphurŏpōlis (1),
  *female trader in
  bluish-red cloth*

SELLERS
4376 mâkar (1), to *sell*

SELLEST
4376 mâkar (1), to *sell*

SELLETH
4376 mâkar (5), to *sell*
7666 shâbar (1), to *deal*
4453 pōlĕō (1), to *barter*

SELVEDGE
7098 qâtsâh (2),
  termination; fringe

SEM
4590 Sēm (1), *name*

SEMACHIAH
5565 Çᵉmakyâhûw (1),
  supported of Jehovah

SEMEI
4584 Sĕmĕï (1), *famous*

SENAAH
5570 Çᵉnâ'âh (2), *thorny*

SENATE
1087 gĕrŏusia (1), Jewish
  Sanhedrin

SENATORS
2205 zâqên (1), *old,
  venerated*

SEND
935 bôw' (1), to *go, come*
5042 nâba' (1), to *gush*
5130 nûwph (1), to *rock*
5414 nâthan (6), to *give*
7136 qârâh (1), to *bring
  about; to impose*
7971 shâlach (157), to
  send away
7972 shᵉlach (Ch.) (1), to
  send away
630 apŏluō (6), to *relieve,
  release; divorce*
649 apŏstĕllō (23), to
  send out on a mission
906 ballō (3), to *throw*
1032 bruō (1), to *gush*
1544 ĕkballō (3), to
  throw out
1821 ĕxapŏstĕllō (1), to
  despatch, or to dismiss
3343 mĕtapĕmpō (2), to
  summon or invite
3992 pĕmpō (25), to *send*

SENDEST
7971 shâlach (6), to *send
  away*

SENDETH
5414 nâthan (2), to *give*
7971 shâlach (8), to *send
  away*
649 apŏstĕllō (4), to *send
  out* on a mission
1026 brĕchō (1), to *make
  wet; to rain*

SENDING
4916 mishlôwach (3),
  sending out
4917 mishlachath (1),
  mission; release; army
7971 shâlach (9), to *send
  away*
3992 pĕmpō (1), to *send*

SENEH
5573 Çeneh (1), *thorn*

SENIR
8149 Shᵉnîyr (2), *peak*

SENNACHERIB
5576 Çanchêrîyb (13),
  Sancherib

SENSE
7922 sekel (1),
  intelligence; success

SENSES
145 aisthētēriŏn (1),
  judgment, sense

SENSUAL
5591 psuchikŏs (2),
  physical and *brutish*

SENT
1980 hâlak (1), to *walk*
2904 ṭûwl (1), to *cast
  down or out, hurl*
3947 lâqach (1), to *take*
5414 nâthan (5), to *give*
5674 'âbar (2), to *cross
  over; to transition*
6680 tsâvâh (1), to
  constitute, enjoin
7725 shûwb (1), to *return*
7964 shillûwach (1),
  divorce; dower
7971 shâlach (459), to
  send away
7972 shᵉlach (Ch.) (12),
  to *send away*
375 anapĕmpō (4), to
  send up or back
628 apŏlŏuō (2), to *wash
  fully*
630 apŏluō (6), to
  release; divorce
640 apŏria (1), state of
  quandary, perplexity
649 apŏstĕllō (104), to
  send out on a mission
652 apŏstŏlŏs (2),
  commissioner of Christ
657 apŏtassŏmai (1), to
  say adieu; to renounce
863 aphiēmi (2), to *leave*
1524 ĕisĕimi (1), to *enter*
1544 ĕkballō (1), to
  throw out
1599 ĕkpĕmpō (2), to
  despatch, send out
1821 ĕxapŏstĕllō (10), to
  despatch, or to dismiss
3343 mĕtapĕmpō (4), to
  summon or invite

3992 pĕmpō (49), *to send*
4842 sumpĕmpō (2), *to dispatch with*
4882 sunapŏstĕllō (1), *to despatch with*

SENTENCE
1697 dâbâr (3), *word*
4941 mishpâṭ (2), *verdict; formal decree; justice*
6310 peh (1), *mouth*
6599 pithgâm (1), *judicial sentence; edict*
7081 qeçem (1), *divination*
610 apŏkrima (1), *decision or sentence*
1948 ĕpikrinō (1), *to adjudge, decide*
2919 krinō (1), *to decide*

SENTENCES
280 'ăchîydâh (Ch.) (1), *enigma*
2420 chîydâh (1), *puzzle*

SENTEST
7971 shâlach (4), *to send away*

SENUAH
5574 Çᵉnûw'âh (1), *pointed*

SEORIM
8188 Sᵉ'ôrîym (1), *barley*

SEPARATE
914 bâdal (7), *to divide*
1508 gizrâh (7), *figure, appearance; enclosure*
2505 châlaq (1), *to be smooth; be slippery*
3995 mibdâlâh (1), *separation; separate*
5139 nâzîyr (1), *prince; separated Nazirite*
5144 nâzar (4), *to set apart, devote*
6381 pâlâ' (1), *to be, make great, difficult*
6504 pârad (2), *to spread*
873 aphŏrizō (5), *to limit, exclude, appoint*
5562 chōrĕō (3), *to pass, enter; to hold, admit*

SEPARATED
914 bâdal (17), *to divide*
5139 nâzîyr (1), *prince; separated Nazirite*
5144 nâzar (1), *to set apart, devote*
6395 pâlâh (2), *to distinguish*
6504 pârad (8), *to spread*
873 aphŏrizō (4), *to limit, exclude, appoint*

SEPARATETH
5144 nâzar (3), *to set apart, devote*
6504 pârad (2), *to spread*

SEPARATING
5144 nâzar (1), *to set apart, devote*

SEPARATION
914 bâdal (1), *to divide*
5079 niddâh (14), *time of menstrual impurity*
5145 nezer (11), *set apart; dedication*

SEPHAR
5611 Çᵉphâr (1), *census*

SEPHARAD
5614 Çᵉphârâd (1), *Sepharad*

SEPHARVAIM
5617 Çᵉpharvayim (6), *Sepharvajim*

SEPHARVITES
5616 Çᵉpharvîy (1), *Sepharvite*

SEPULCHRE
6900 qᵉbûwrâh (5), *sepulchre*
6913 qeber (14), *sepulchre*
3418 mnēma (4), *sepulchral monument*
3419 mnēmĕiŏn (26), *place of interment*
5028 taphŏs (5), *grave*

SEPULCHRES
6913 qeber (12), *sepulchre*
3419 mnēmĕiŏn (3), *place of interment*
5028 taphŏs (1), *grave*

SERAH
8294 Serach (2), *superfluity*

SERAIAH
8304 Sᵉrâyâh (20), *Jehovah has prevailed*

SERAPHIMS
8314 sârâph (2), *saraph*

SERED
5624 Çered (2), *trembling*

SERGIUS
4588 Sĕrgiŏs (1), *Sergius*

SERJEANTS
4465 rhabdŏuchŏs (2), *constable*

SERPENT
5175 nâchâsh (25), *snake*
8314 sârâph (3), *poisonous serpent*
8577 tannîyn (2), *sea-serpent; jackal*
3789 ŏphis (8), *snake*

SERPENT'S
5175 nâchâsh (2), *snake*

SERPENTS
2119 zâchal (1), *to crawl*
5175 nâchâsh (4), *snake*
8577 tannîyn (1), *sea-serpent; jackal*
2062 hĕrpĕtŏn (1), *reptile*
3789 ŏphis (6), *snake*

SERUG
8286 Sᵉrûwg (5), *tendril*

SERVANT
5288 na'ar (30), *servant*
5647 'âbad (1), *to serve*
5649 'ăbad (Ch.) (1), *servant*
5650 'ebed (363), *servant*
7916 sâkîyr (8), *man at wages, hired hand*
8334 shârath (4), *to attend*
1248 diakŏnia (2), *attendance, aid, service*
1249 diakŏnŏs (3), *attendant, deacon*

1401 *dŏulŏs* (66), *servant*
1402 *dŏulŏō* (1), *to enslave*
2324 *thĕrapōn* (1), *menial attendant*
3610 *ŏikĕtēs* (3), *menial domestic servant*
3816 *pais* (8), *servant*

SERVANT'S
5650 'ebed (8), *servant*
1401 *dŏulŏs* (1), *servant*

SERVANTS
582 'ĕnôwsh (1), *man*
5288 na'ar (21), *servant*
5647 'âbad (4), *to serve*
5649 'ăbad (Ch.) (6), *servant*
5650 'ebed (367), *servant*
5657 'ăbuddâh (1), *service*
8334 shârath (1), *to attend as a menial*
341 anakainŏō (1), *to renovate, renew*
1249 diakŏnŏs (2), *attendant, deacon*
1401 *dŏulŏs* (55), *servant*
1402 *dŏulŏō* (2), *to enslave*
3407 *misthiŏs* (2), *hired-worker*
3610 *ŏikĕtēs* (1), *menial domestic servant*
3816 *pais* (1), *servant*
5257 *hupĕrĕtēs* (4), *servant, attendant*

SERVANTS'
5650 'ebed (4), *servant*

SERVE
5647 'âbad (162), *to serve*
5656 'ăbôdâh (1), *work*
5975+6440 'âmad (1), *to stand*
6399 pᵉlach (Ch.) (7), *to serve or worship*
8334 shârath (4), *to attend as a menial*
1247 diakŏnĕō (7), *to wait upon, serve*
1398 dŏulĕuō (13), *to serve as a slave*
3000 latrĕuō (13), *to minister to God*

SERVED
1580 gâmal (1), *to benefit or requite; to wean*
5647 'âbad (61), *to serve*
5975+6440 'âmad (1), *to stand*
6213 'âsâh (1), *to do*
8334 shârath (4), *to attend as a menial*
1247 diakŏnĕō (1), *to wait upon, serve*
1398 dŏulĕuō (1), *serve as a slave*
3000 latrĕuō (2), *to minister to God*
5256 hupĕrĕtĕō (1), *to be a subordinate*

SERVEDST
5647 'âbad (1), *to serve*

SERVEST
6399 pᵉlach (Ch.) (2), *to serve or worship*

SERVETH
5647 'âbad (2), *to serve*
5656 'ăbôdâh (1), *work*
1247 diakŏnĕō (2), *to wait upon, serve*
1398 dŏulĕuō (1), *to serve as a slave*

SERVICE
3027 yâd (2), *hand; power*
5647 'âbad (4), *to serve*
5656 'ăbôdâh (98), *work*
5673 'ăbîydâh (Ch.) (1), *labor or business*
6402 polchân (Ch.) (1), *worship*
6635 tsâbâ' (4), *army, military host*
8278 sᵉrâd (4), *stitching*
8334 shârath (3), *to attend as a menial*
1248 diakŏnia (3), *attendance, aid, service*
1398 dŏulĕuō (3), *to serve as a slave*
2999 latrĕia (5), *worship, ministry service*
3000 latrĕuō (1), *to minister to God*
3009 lĕitŏurgia (3), *service, ministry*

SERVILE
5656 'ăbôdâh (12), *work*

SERVING
5647 'âbad (2), *to serve*
1248 diakŏnia (1), *attendance, aid, service*
1398 dŏulĕuō (1), *serve as a slave*
3000 latrĕuō (1), *to minister to God*

SERVITOR
8334 shârath (1), *to attend as a menial*

SERVITUDE
5656 'ăbôdâh (2), *work*

SET
530 'ĕmûwnâh (5), *fidelity; steadiness*
631 'âçar (1), *to fasten*
935 bôw' (1), *to go, come*
1129 bânâh (2), *to build*
1197 bâ'ar (1), *to be brutish; be senseless*
1379 gâbal (1), *to set a boundary line, limit*
1431 gâdal (2), *to be great, make great*
2211 zᵉqaph (Ch.) (1), *to impale by hanging*
2232 zâra' (1), *to sow seed; to disseminate*
2706 chôq (1), *appointment; allotment*
2710 châqaq (1), *to engrave; to enact laws*
3051 yâhab (1), *to give*
3240 yânach (8), *to allow to stay*
3245 yâçad (1), *settle, consult, establish*
3259 yâ'ad (3), *to meet; to summon; to direct*
3320 yâtsab (5), *to station, offer, continue*
3322 yâtsag (8), *to place*
3332 yâtsaq (1), *to pour out*

English

SHAALABBIN
8169 Sha'albîym (1),
fox-holes

SHAALBIM
8169 Sha'albîym (2),
fox-holes

SHAALBONITE
8170 Sha'albônîy (2),
Shaalbonite

SHAAPH
8174 Sha'aph (2),
fluctuation

SHAARAIM
8189 Sha'ărayim (2),
double gates

SHAASHGAZ
8190 Sha'ashgaz (1),
Shaashgaz

SHABBETHAI
7678 Shabbᵉthay (3),
restful

SHACHIA
7634 Shobyâh (1),
captivation

SHADE
6783 tsᵉmîythûth (1),
perpetually

SHADOW
2927 ṭᵉlal (Ch.) (1), to
cover with shade
6738 tsêl (47), *shade*
6752 tsêlel (1), *shade*
6757 tsalmâveth (16),
shade of death
644 apŏskiasma (1),
shading off
4639 skia (7), *shade*

SHADOWING
6751 tsâlal (1), to *shade*;
to *grow dark*
6767 tsᵉlâtsal (1),
whirring of wings
2683 kataskiazō (1), to
cover, overshadow

SHADOWS
6752 tsêlel (3), *shade*

SHADRACH
7714 Shadrak (1),
Shadrak
7715 Shadrak (Ch.) (14),
Shadrak

SHADY
6628 tse'el (2), *lotus* tree

SHAFT
2671 chêts (1), *shaft*
3409 yârêk (3), *shank*

SHAGE
7681 Shâgê' (1), *erring*

SHAHAR
7837 shachar (1), *dawn*

SHAHARAIM
7842 Shachărayim (1),
double dawn

SHAHAZIMAH
7831 Shachatsôwm (1),
proudly

SHAKE
2554 châmaç (1), to *be
violent*; to *maltreat*
4571 mâ'ad (1), to *waver*
5128 nûwa' (2), to *waver*
5130 nûwph (5), to
quiver, vibrate, rock

5287 nâ'ar (4), to *tumble*
5426 nᵉthar (Ch.) (1), to
tear off; to *shake off*
6206 'ârats (2), to *dread*
6342 pâchad (1), to *fear*
7264 râgaz (1), to *quiver*
7363 râchaph (1), to
brood; to *be relaxed*
7493 râ'ash (14), to *quake*
660 apŏtinassō (1), to
brush off, shake off
1621 ĕktinassō (2), to
shake violently
4531 salĕuō (1), to *waver*
4579 sĕiō (2), to *agitate*

SHAKED
5128 nûwa' (1), to *waver*

SHAKEN
1607 gâ'ash (1), to *agitate*
5086 nâdaph (1), to
disperse, be windblown
5110 nûwd (1), to *waver*
5128 nûwa' (3), to *waver*
5287 nâ'ar (2), to *tumble*
6327 pûwts (1), to *dash*
7477 râ'al (1), to *reel*
4531 salĕuō (11), to *waver*
4579 sĕiō (1), to *agitate*

SHAKETH
2342 chûwl (2), to *writhe*
4131 môwṭ (1), to *shake*
5130 nûwph (2), to *rock*
5287 nâ'ar (1), to *tumble*
7264 râgaz (1), to *quiver*

SHAKING
4493 mânôwd (1), *nod*
5363 nôqeph (2),
threshing of olives
7494 ra'ash (3),
vibration, bounding
8573 tᵉnûwphâh (2),
undulation of offerings

SHALEM
8003 shâlêm (1),
complete; friendly; safe

SHALIM
8171 Sha'ălîym (1), *foxes*

SHALISHA
8031 Shâlîshâh (1),
trebled land

SHALLECHETH
7996 Shalleketh (1),
felling of trees

SHALLUM
7967 Shallûwm (27),
retribution

SHALLUN
7968 Shallûwn (1),
retribution

SHALMAI
8014 Salmay (1), *clothed*
8073 Shamlay (1), *clothed*

SHALMAN
8020 Shalman (1),
Shalman

SHALMANESER
8022 Shalman'eçer (2),
Shalmaneser

SHAMA
8091 Shâmâ' (1), *obedient*

SHAMBLES
3111 makĕllŏn (1),
butcher's stall

SHAME
954 bûwsh (9), be
ashamed
955 bûwshâh (4), *shame*
1317 boshnâh (1),
shamefulness
1322 bôsheth (20), *shame*
2616 châçad (1), to
reprove, shame
2659 châphêr (4), to *be
ashamed*
2781 cherpâh (3),
contumely, disgrace
3637 kâlam (6), to *taunt*
3639 kᵉlimmâh (20),
disgrace, scorn
3640 kᵉlimmûwth (1),
disgrace, scorn
6172 'ervâh (1), *disgrace*
7036 qâlôwn (13),
disgrace
8103 shimtsâh (1),
scornful whispering
149 aischrŏn (3),
shameful thing
152 aischunē (5), *shame*
808 aschēmŏsunē (1),
indecency; shame
818 atimazō (1), to
maltreat, dishonor
819 atimia (1), *disgrace*
1788 ĕntrĕpō (1), to
respect; to confound
1791 ĕntrŏpē (2), *shame*
2617 kataischunō (1), to
disgrace or shame
3856 paradĕigmatizō (1),
to *expose to infamy*

SHAMED
937 bûwz (1), *disrespect*
954 bûwsh (1), to be
ashamed
3001 yâbêsh (1), to *dry
up*; to *wither*
8106 Shemer (1),
settlings of wine, dregs

SHAMEFACEDNESS
127 aidōs (1), *modesty*

SHAMEFUL
1322 bôsheth (1), *shame*
7022 qîyqâlôwn (1),
disgrace

SHAMEFULLY
3001 yâbêsh (1), to *dry
up*; to *wither*
818 atimazō (1), to
maltreat, dishonor
821 atimŏō (1), to
maltreat, disgrace
5195 hubrizō (1), to
exercise violence, abuse

SHAMELESSLY
1540 gâlâh (1), to *denude*

SHAMER
8106 Shemer (2),
settlings of wine, dregs

SHAMETH
3637 kâlam (1), to *taunt*

SHAMGAR
8044 Shamgar (2),
Shamgar

SHAMHUTH
8049 Shamhûwth (1),
desolation

SHAMIR
8053 Shâmûwr (1),
observed
8069 Shâmîyr (3), *thorn*
or (poss.) *diamond*

SHAMMA
8037 Shammâ' (1),
desolation

SHAMMAH
8048 Shammâh (8),
desolation

SHAMMAI
8060 Shammay (6),
destructive

SHAMMOTH
8054 Shammôwth (1),
ruins

SHAMMUA
8051 Shammûwa' (4),
renowned

SHAMMUAH
8051 Shammûwa' (1),
renowned

SHAMSHERAI
8125 Shamshᵉray (1),
sun-like

SHAPE
1491 ĕidŏs (2), *form,
appearance, sight*

SHAPEN
2342 chûwl (1), to *dance,
whirl*; to *writhe* in pain

SHAPES
3667 hŏmŏiōma (1), *form*

SHAPHAM
8223 Shâphâm (1), *baldly*

SHAPHAN
8227 shâphân (30), *hyrax*

SHAPHAT
8202 Shâphâṭ (8), *judge*

SHAPHER
8234 Shepher (2), *beauty*

SHARAI
8298 Shâray (1), *hostile*

SHARAIM
8189 Sha'ărayim (1),
double gates

SHARAR
8325 Shârâr (1), *hostile*

SHARE
4282 machăresheth (1),
(poss.) *hoe*

SHAREZER
8272 Shar'etser (2),
Sharetser

SHARON
8289 Shârôwn (6), *plain*

SHARONITE
8290 Shârôwnîy (1),
Sharonite

SHARP
2299 chad (4), *sharp*
sword
2303 chaddûwd (1),
pointed, jagged
2742 chârûwts (2),
threshing-sledge
3913 lâṭash (1), to
sharpen; to pierce
6697 tsûwr (2), *rock*
6864 tsôr (1), flint-*stone
knife*

8127 shên (2), *tooth*
8150 shânan (4), to *pierce*
3691 ŏxus (7), *sharp*

SHARPEN
3913 lâṭash (1), to *sharpen; to pierce*
5324 nâtsab (1), to *station*

SHARPENED
2300 châdad (3), to *be, make sharp; severe*
8150 shânan (1), to *pierce; to inculcate*

SHARPENETH
2300 châdad (2), to *be, make sharp; severe*
3913 lâṭash (1), to *sharpen; to pierce*

SHARPER
5114 tŏmŏtĕrŏs (1), *more keen*

SHARPLY
2394 chozqâh (1), *vehemence, harshness*
664 apŏtŏmŏs (1), *abruptly, peremptorily*

SHARPNESS
664 apŏtŏmŏs (1), *abruptly, peremptorily*

SHARUHEN
8287 Shârûwchen (1), *abode of pleasure*

SHASHAI
8343 Shâshay (1), *whitish*

SHASHAK
8349 Shâshaq (2), *pedestrian*

SHAUL
7586 Shâ'ûwl (7), *asked*

SHAULITES
7587 Shâ'ûwlîy (1), *Shalite*

SHAVE
1548 gâlach (12), to *shave*
5674+8593 'âbar (1), to *cross* over; to *transition*
3587 xuraō (1), to *shave*

SHAVED
1494 gâzaz (1), to *shave*
1548 gâlach (3), to *shave*

SHAVEH
7740 Shâvêh (1), *plain*
7741 Shâvêh Qiryâthayim (1), *plain of a double city*

SHAVEN
1548 gâlach (5), to *shave*
3587 xuraō (2), to *shave*

SHAVSHA
7798 Shavshâ' (1), *joyful*

SHEAF
485 'ălummâh (2), *sheaf*
5995 'âmîyr (1), *bunch*
6016 'ômer (6), *measure*

SHEAL
7594 She'âl (1), *request*

SHEALTIEL
7597 She'altîy'êl (9), *I have asked God*

SHEAR
1494 gâzaz (4), to *shear*

SHEAR-JASHUB
7610 She'âr Yâshûwb (1), *remnant will return*

SHEARER
2751 kĕirō (1), to *shear*

SHEARERS
1494 gâzaz (3), to *shear*

SHEARIAH
8187 She'aryâh (2), *Jehovah has stormed*

SHEARING
1044 Bêyth 'Êqed (1), *house of* (the) *binding*
1044+7462 Bêyth 'Êqed (1), *house of* (the) *binding*
1494 gâzaz (1), to *shear*

SHEATH
5084 nâdân (1), *sheath*
8593 ta'ar (6), *scabbard*
2336 thēkē (1), *scabbard*

SHEAVES
485 'ălummâh (3), *sheaf*
5995 'âmîyr (2), *bunch*
6016 'ômer (2), *measure*
6194 'ârêm (1), *sheaf*

SHEBA
7614 She'bâ' (22), *Sheba*
7652 Sheba' (10), *seven*

SHEBAH
7656 Shib'âh (1), *seventh*

SHEBAM
7643 Se'bâm (1), *spice*

SHEBANIAH
7645 She'banyâh (7), *Jehovah has prospered*

SHEBARIM
7671 She'bârîym (1), *ruins*

SHEBER
7669 Sheber (1), *crushing*

SHEBNA
7644 Shebnâ' (9), *growth*

SHEBUEL
7619 She'bûw'êl (3), *captive* (or *returned*) of *God*

SHECANIAH
7935 She'kanyâh (2), *Jehovah has dwelt*

SHECHANIAH
7935 She'kanyâh (8), *Jehovah has dwelt*

SHECHEM
7927 She'kem (45), *ridge*
7928 Shekem (17), *shoulder*

SHECHEM'S
7927 She'kem (2), *ridge*

SHECHEMITES
7930 Shikmîy (1), *Shikmite*

SHED
5064 nâgar (1), to *pour*
7760 sûwm (1), to *put*
8210 shâphak (35), to *spill* forth; to *expend;*
1632 ĕkchĕō (11), to *pour*

SHEDDER
8210 shâphak (1), to *spill* forth; to *expend*

SHEDDETH
8210 shâphak (2), to *spill*

SHEDDING
130 haimatĕkchusia (1), *pouring of blood*

SHEDEUR
7707 She'dêy'ûwr (5), *spreader of light*

SHEEP
3532 kebes (2), *young ram*
3775 keseb (9), *young ram sheep*
6629 tsô'n (111), *flock of sheep or goats*
6792 tsône' (2), *flock*
7353 râchêl (2), *ewe*
7716 seh (16), *sheep*
4262 prŏbatikŏs (1), *Sheep Gate*
4263 prŏbatŏn (39), *sheep*

SHEEP'S
4263 prŏbatŏn (1), *sheep*

SHEEPCOTE
5116 nâveh (2), *at home; lovely; home*

SHEEPCOTES
1448+6629 ge'dêrâh (1), *enclosure* for flocks

SHEEPFOLD
833+4263 aulē (1), *house; courtyard; sheepfold*

SHEEPFOLDS
1488+6629 gêz (1), *shorn fleece;* mown *grass*
4356+6629 miklâ'âh (1), *sheep or goat pen*
4942 mishpâth (1), *pair of stalls* for cattle

SHEEPMASTER
5349 nôqêd (1), *owner or tender of sheep*

SHEEPSHEARERS
1494 gâzaz (2), to *shear; shave; destroy*
1494+6629 gâzaz (1), to *shear; shave; destroy*

SHEEPSKINS
3374 mēlōtē (1), *sheep-skin*

SHEET
3607 ŏthŏnē (2), *linen sail cloth*

SHEETS
5466 çâdîyn (2), *shirt*

SHEHARIAH
7841 She'charyâh (1), *Jehovah has sought*

SHEKEL
1235 beqa' (1), *half shekel*
8255 sheqel (41), *standard weight*

SHEKELS
8255 sheqel (45), *standard weight*

SHELAH
7956 Shêlâh (10), *request*
7974 Shelach (1), *spear*

SHELANITES
8024 Shêlânîy (1), *Shelanite*

SHELEMIAH
8018 Shelemyâh (10), *thank-offering of Jehovah*

SHELEPH
8026 Sheleph (2), *extract*

SHELESH
8028 Shelesh (1), *triplet*

SHELOMI
8015 She'lômîy (1), *peaceable*

SHELOMITH
8013 She'lômôwth (4), *pacifications*
8019 She'lômîyth (5), *peaceableness*

SHELOMOTH
8013 She'lômôwth (1), *pacifications*

SHELTER
4268 machăçeh (2), *shelter; refuge*

SHELUMIEL
8017 She'lûmîy'êl (5), *peace of God*

SHEM
8035 Shêm (17), *name*

SHEMA
8087 Shema' (6), *heard*

SHEMAAH
8094 She'mâ'âh (1), *annunciation*

SHEMAIAH
8098 She'ma'yâh (40), *Jehovah has heard*

SHEMARIAH
8114 She'maryâh (4), *Jehovah has guarded*

SHEMEBER
8038 Shem'êber (1), *illustrious*

SHEMER
8106 Shemer (2), *settlings of wine, dregs*

SHEMIDA
8061 She'mîydâ' (2), *name of knowing*

SHEMIDAH
8061 She'mîydâ' (1), *name of knowing*

SHEMIDAITES
8062 She'mîydâ'îy (1), *Shemidaite*

SHEMINITH
8067 she'mîynîyth (3), (poss.) *eight-stringed lyre*

SHEMIRAMOTH
8070 She'mîyrâmôwth (4), *name of heights*

SHEMUEL
8050 She'mûw'êl (3), *heard of God*

SHEN
8129 Shên (1), *crag*

SHENAZAR
8137 Shen'atstsar (1), *Shenatstsar*

SHENIR
8149 She'nîyr (2), *peak*

English

SHEPHAM
8221 Sh⁰phâm (2), *bare*

SHEPHATIAH
8203 Sh⁰phaṭyáh (13), *Jehovah has judged*

SHEPHERD
7462 râʻâh (27), to *tend* a flock, i.e. *pasture* it
7462+6629 râʻâh (1), to *tend* a flock
7473 rôʻîy (1), *shepherd*
750 *archipŏimēn* (1), head *shepherd*
4166 *pŏimēn* (13), *shepherd*

SHEPHERD'S
7462 râʻâh (1), to *tend* a flock, i.e. *pasture* it
7473 rôʻîy (1), *shepherd*

SHEPHERDS
7462 râʻâh (31), to *tend* a flock, i.e. *pasture* it
7462+6629 râʻâh (2), to *tend* a flock
4166 *pŏimēn* (4), *shepherd*

SHEPHERDS'
7462 râʻâh (1), to *tend* a flock, i.e. *pasture* it

SHEPHI
8195 Sh⁰phôw (1), *baldness*

SHEPHO
8195 Sh⁰phôw (1), *baldness*

SHEPHUPHAN
8197 Sh⁰phûwphâm (1), *serpent-like*

SHERAH
7609 Sheʻērâh (1), *kindred* by blood

SHERD
2789 cheres (1), *pottery*

SHERDS
2789 cheres (1), *pottery*

SHEREBIAH
8274 Shêrêbyâh (8), *Jehovah has brought heat*

SHERESH
8329 Sheresh (1), *root*

SHEREZER
8272 Sharʻetser (1), *Sharetser*

SHERIFFS
8614 tiphtay (Ch.) (2), *lawyer, officer*

SHESHACH
8347 Shêshak (2), *Sheshak*

SHESHAI
8344 Shêshay (3), *whitish*

SHESHAN
8348 Shêshân (4), *lily*

SHESHBAZZAR
8339 Shêshbatstsar (4), *Sheshbatstsar*

SHETH
8352 Shêth (2), *put*, i.e. *substituted*

SHETHAR
8369 Shêthâr (1), *Shethar*

SHETHAR-BOZNAI
8370 Sh⁰thar Bôwz⁰nay (4), *Shethar-Bozenai*

SHEVA
7724 Sh⁰vâ' (2), *false*

SHEW
1319 bâsar (3), to *announce* (good news)
1540 gâlâh (5), to *reveal*
1971 hakkârâh (1), *respect*, i.e. partiality
2324 chăvâ' (Ch.) (13), to *show*
2331 châvâh (5), to *show*
3045 yâda' (12), to *know*
3313 yâpha' (1), to *shine*
5046 nâgad (37), to *announce*
5414 nâthan (5), to *give*
5608 çâphar (5), to *inscribe*; to *enumerate*
6213 'âsâh (21), to *do*
6754 tselem (1), *phantom; idol*
7200 râ'âh (27), to *see*
7760 sûwm (1), to *put*
7896 shîyth (1), to *place*
8085 shâma' (3), to *hear*
312 *anaggěllō* (4), to *announce* in detail
322 *anadĕiknumi* (1), to *indicate, appoint*
518 *apaggěllō* (5), to *announce, proclaim*
1165 *dĕigmatizō* (1), to *exhibit, expose*
1166 *dĕiknuō* (20), to *show, make known*
1325 *didōmi* (3), to *give*
1334 *diĕgĕŏmai* (1), to *relate fully, describe*
1731 *ĕndĕiknumi* (7), to *show, display*
1754 *ĕnĕrgĕō* (2), to be *active, efficient, work*
1804 *ĕxaggěllō* (1), to *declare, proclaim*
1925 *ĕpidĕiknumi* (6), to *exhibit, call attention to*
2097 *ĕuaggĕlizō* (1), to *announce good news*
2146 *ĕuprŏsōpĕō* (1), to *make a good display*
2151 *ĕusĕbĕō* (1), to *put religion into practice*
2605 *kataggěllō* (3), to *proclaim, promulgate*
2698 *katatithēmi* (1), to *place down, to deposit*
3004 *lĕgō* (1), to *say*
3056 *lŏgŏs* (1), *word, matter, thing; Word*
3377 *mēnuō* (1), to *report, declare*
3936 *paristēmi* (1), to *stand beside, present*
4392 *prŏphasis* (1), *pretext, excuse*
5263 *hupŏdĕiknumi* (2), to *exemplify*
5319 *phanĕrŏō* (1), to *render apparent*

SHEWBREAD
3899+4635 lechem (4), *food, bread*
3899+6440 lechem (6), *food, bread*
4635 maʻăreketh (3), *pile of loaves, arrangement*
6440 pânîym (1), *face*
740+4286 artos (3), *loaf of bread*
4286+740 prŏthĕsis (1), *setting forth*

SHEWED
1540 gâlâh (2), to *reveal*
3045 yâda' (5), to *know*
3190 yâṭab (1), to be, *make well*
3384 yârâh (1), to *throw*
5046 nâgad (18), to *announce*
5186 nâṭâh (1), to *stretch*
5414 nâthan (1), to *give*
6213 'âsâh (17), to *do*
6567 pârash (1), to *separate; to disperse*
7200 râ'âh (37), to *see*
7760 sûwm (1), to *put*
8085 shâma' (4), to *hear*
312 *anaggěllō* (2), to *announce* in detail
518 *apaggěllō* (6), to *announce, proclaim*
1096 *ginŏmai* (1), to be
1166 *dĕiknuō* (8), to *show, make known*
1213 *dēlŏō* (1), to *make plain* by words
1325+1717+1096 *didōmi* (1), to *give*
1718 *ĕmphanizō* (1), to *show forth*
1731 *ĕndĕiknumi* (1), to *show, display*
1925 *ĕpidĕiknumi* (1), to *exhibit, call attention to*
3170 *mĕgalunō* (1), to *increase or extol*
3377 *mēnuō* (2), to *report, declare*
3700 *ŏptanŏmai* (1), to *appear*
3930 *parĕchō* (1), to *hold near*, i.e. to *present*
3936 *paristēmi* (1), to *stand beside, present*
4160 *pŏiĕō* (4), to *make*
4293 *prŏkataggěllō* (2), to *predict, promise*
5268 *hupŏzugiŏn* (1), *donkey*
5319 *phanĕrŏō* (4), to *render apparent*

SHEWEDST
5414 nâthan (1), to *give*
7200 râ'âh (1), to *see*

SHEWEST
6213 'âsâh (1), to *do*
1166 *dĕiknuō* (1), to *show*
4160 *pŏiĕō* (1), to *make*

SHEWETH
1540+241 gâlâh (2), to *denude; uncover*
2331 châvâh (1), to *show*
5046 nâgad (6), to *announce*
6213 'âsâh (2), to *do*
7200 râ'âh (3), to *see*
1166 *dĕiknuō* (2), to *show*
1658 *ĕlĕuthĕrŏs* (2), *unrestrained*

SHEWING
263 'achăvâh (Ch.) (1), *solution*
5608 çâphar (1), to *inscribe; to enumerate*
6213 'âsâh (2), to *do*
6692 tsûwts (1), to *twinkle*, i.e. *glance*
323 *anadĕixis* (1), act of public *exhibition*
584 *apŏdĕiknumi* (1), to *demonstrate*
1731 *ĕndĕiknumi* (2), to *show, display*
1925 *ĕpidĕiknumi* (2), to *exhibit, call attention to*
3930 *parĕchō* (1), to *hold near*, i.e. to *present*

SHIBBOLETH
7641 shibbôl (1), *stream; ear* of grain

SHIBMAH
7643 S⁰bâm (1), *spice*

SHICRON
7942 Shikk⁰rôwn (1), *drunkenness*

SHIELD
3591 kîydôwn (2), *dart*
4043 mâgên (33), small *shield (buckler)*
6793 tsinnâh (9), large *shield; piercing cold*
2375 *thurĕŏs* (1), large *door*-shaped *shield*

SHIELDS
4043 mâgên (15), small *shield (buckler)*
6793 tsinnâh (1), large *shield; piercing cold*
7982 sheleṭ (7), *shield*

SHIGGAION
7692 Shiggâyôwn (1), *dithyramb* or poem

SHIGIONOTH
7692 Shiggâyôwn (1), *dithyramb* or poem

SHIHON
7866 Shî'yôwn (1), *ruin*

SHIHOR
7883 Shîychôwr (1), *dark*, i.e. *turbid*

SHIHOR-LIBNATH
7884 Shîychôwr Libnâth (1), *darkish whiteness*

SHILHI
7977 Shilchîy (2), *armed*

SHILHIM
7978 Shilchîym (1), *javelins or sprouts*

SHILLEM
8006 Shillêm (2), *requital*

SHILLEMITES
8016 Shillêmîy (1), *Shilemite*

SHILOAH
7975 Shilôach (1), *small stream*

SHILOH
7886 Shîylôh (1), *tranquil*
7887 Shîylôh (32), *tranquil*

SHILONI
8023 Shîlônîy (1), *Shiloni*

SHILONITE
7888 Shiylôwnîy (5), *Shilonite*

SHILONITES
7888 Shiylôwnîy (1), *Shilonite*

SHILSHAH
8030 Shilshâh (1), *triplication*

SHIMEA
8092 Shim'â' (4), *annunciation*

SHIMEAH
8039 Shim'âh (1), *obedient*
8092 Shim'â' (1), *annunciation*
8093 Shim'âh (2), *annunciation*

SHIMEAM
8043 Shim'âm (1), *obedient*

SHIMEATH
8100 Shim'âth (2), *annunciation*

SHIMEATHITES
8101 Shim'âthiy (1), *Shimathite*

SHIMEI
8096 Shim'iy (41), *famous*
8097 Shim'iy (1), *Shimite*

SHIMEON
8095 Shim'ôwn (1), *hearing*

SHIMHI
8096 Shim'iy (1), *famous*

SHIMI
8096 Shim'iy (1), *famous*

SHIMITES
8097 Shim'iy (1), *Shimite*

SHIMMA
8092 Shim'â' (1), *annunciation*

SHIMON
7889 Shîymôwn (1), *desert*

SHIMRATH
8119 Shimrâth (1), *guardship*

SHIMRI
8113 Shimriy (3), *watchful*

SHIMRITH
8116 Shimrîyth (1), *female guard*

SHIMROM
8110 Shimrôwn (1), *guardianship*

SHIMRON
8110 Shimrôwn (4), *guardianship*

SHIMRON-MERON
8112 Shimrôwn M'r'ôwn (1), *guard of lashing*

SHIMRONITES
8117 Shimrônîy (1), *Shimronite*

SHIMSHAI
8124 Shimshay (Ch.) (4), *sunny*

SHINAB
8134 Shin'âb (1), *father has turned*

SHINAR
8152 Shin'âr (7), *Shinar*

SHINE
215 'ôwr (11), to be *luminous*
1984 hâlal (1), to *shine*
2094 zâhar (1), to *enlighten*
3313 yâpha' (4), to *shine*
5050 nâgahh (3), to *illuminate*
5774 'ûwph (1), to *cover*
6245 'âshath (1), to be *sleek; to excogitate*
6670 tsâhal (1), to be *cheerful; to sound*
826 augazō (1), to *beam forth*
1584 ĕklampō (1), to be *resplendent, shine*
2989 lampō (3), to *radiate brilliancy*
5316 phainō (3), to *shine*

SHINED
215 'ôwr (1), to be *luminous*
1984 hâlal (2), to *shine*
3313 yâpha' (2), to *shine*
5050 nâgahh (1), to *illuminate*
2989 lampō (2), to *radiate brilliancy*
4015 pĕriastraptō (1), to *envelop in light, shine*

SHINETH
166 'âhal (1), to be *bright*
215 'ôwr (2), to be *luminous*
2989 lampō (1), to *radiate*
5316 phainō (5), to *shine*

SHINING
5051 nôgahh (6), *brilliancy*
796 astrapē (1), *lightning; light's glare*
797 astraptō (1), to *flash*
4034 pĕrilampō (1), to *shine all around*
4744 stilbō (1), to *gleam*
5316 phainō (1), to *shine*

SHIP
591 'ŏnîyâh (4), *ship*
5600 ç'phîynâh (1), *sea-going vessel*
6716 tsîy (1), *ship*
3490 nauklērŏs (1), ship *captain*
3491 naus (1), *boat*
4142 plŏiariŏn (2), *small boat*
4143 plŏiŏn (58), *ship*

SHIPHI
8230 Shiph'îy (1), *copious*

SHIPHMITE
8225 Shiphmîy (1), *Shiphmite*

SHIPHRAH
8236 Shiphrâh (1), *brightness of skies*

SHIPHTAN
8204 Shiphtân (1), *judge-like*

SHIPMASTER
7227+2259 rab (1), *great*
2942 kubĕrnētēs (1), *helmsman, captain*

SHIPMEN
582+591 'ĕnôwsh (1), *man; person, human*
3492 nautēs (2), *sailor*

SHIPPING
4143 plŏiŏn (1), *ship*

SHIPS
591 'ŏnîyâh (26), *ship*
6716 tsîy (3), *ship*
4142 plŏiariŏn (1), *small boat*
4143 plŏiŏn (8), *boat*

SHIPWRECK
3489 nauagĕō (2), to be *shipwrecked*

SHISHA
7894 Shîyshâ' (1), *whiteness*

SHISHAK
7895 Shîyshaq (7), *Shishak*

SHITRAI
7861 Shiţray (1), *magisterial*

SHITTAH
7848 shiţţâh (1), *acacia*

SHITTIM
7848 shiţţâh (27), *acacia*
7851 Shiţţîym (5), *acacia*

SHIVERS
4937 suntribō (1), to *crush completely*

SHIZA
7877 Shîyzâ' (1), *Shiza*

SHOA
7772 Shôwa' (1), *rich*

SHOBAB
7727 Shôwbâb (4), *rebellious*

SHOBACH
7731 Shôwbâk (2), (poss.) *thicket*

SHOBAI
7630 Shôbay (2), *captor*

SHOBAL
7732 Shôwbâl (9), *overflowing*

SHOBEK
7733 Shôwbêq (1), *forsaking*

SHOBI
7629 Shôbîy (1), *captor*

SHOCHO
7755 Sôwkôh (1), *hedged*

SHOCHOH
7755 Sôwkôh (2), *hedged*

SHOCK
1430 gâdîysh (1), *stack of sheaves, shock of grain*

SHOCKS
1430 gâdîysh (1), *stack of sheaves, shock of grain*

SHOCO
7755 Sôwkôh (1), *hedged*

SHOD
5274 nâ'al (2), to *fasten up, to put on sandals*

SHOE
5265 hupŏdĕō (2), to *put on shoes or sandals*

SHOE
5275 na'al (9), *sandal*

SHOE'S
5266 hupŏdēma (1), *sandal*

SHOELATCHET
8288+5275 s'rôwk (1), sandal *thong*

SHOES
4515 man'âl (1), *bolt on gate*
5275 na'al (11), *sandal*
5266 hupŏdēma (9), *sandal*

SHOHAM
7719 Shôham (1), *beryl*

SHOMER
7763 Shôwmêr (2), *keeper*

SHONE
2224 zârach (1), to *rise; to be bright*
7160 qâran (3), to *shine*
4015 pĕriastraptō (1), to *envelop in light, shine*
4034 pĕrilampō (1), to *shine all around*
5316 phainō (1), to *shine*

SHOOK
1607 gâ'ash (3), to *agitate violently, shake*
5287 nâ'ar (1), to *tumble*
7264 râgaz (1), to *quiver*
7493 râ'ash (2), to *quake*
8058 shâmaţ (1), to *jostle*
660 apŏtinassō (1), to *brush off, shake off*
1621 ĕktinassō (2), to *shake violently*
4531 salĕuō (1), to *waver*

SHOOT
1272 bârach (1), to *flee*
1869 dârak (1), to *tread; to string a bow*
3034 yâdâh (1), to *throw*
3384 yârâh (10), to *throw, shoot an arrow*
5414 nâthan (2), to *give*
6362 pâţar (1), to *burst through; to emit*
7971 shâlach (1), to *send away*
4261 prŏballō (1), to *push to the front, germinate*

SHOOTERS
3384 yârâh (1), to *throw, shoot an arrow*

SHOOTETH
3318 yâtsâ' (1), to *go, bring out*
7971 shâlach (1), to *send away*
4160 pŏiĕō (1), to *do*

SHOOTING
5927 'âlâh (1), to *ascend, be high, mount*

SHOPHACH
7780 Shôwphâk (2), *poured*

English

SHOPHAN
5855 'Aṭrôwth Shôwphân (1), *crowns of Shophan*

SHORE
2348 chôwph (2), *cove*
7097 qâtseh (1), *extremity*
8193 sâphâh (6), *edge*
123 aigialŏs (6), *beach*
4358 prŏsŏrmizō (1), to *moor to*, i.e. *land at*
5491 cheilŏs (1), *lip*

SHORN
7094 qâtsab (1), to *clip*
2751 keirō (3), to *shear*

SHORT
2465 cheled (1), *fleeting*
7114 qâtsar (1), to *curtail*
7138 qârôwb (2), *near*
3641 ŏligŏs (2), *small*
4932 suntemnō (2), to *cut short*, i.e. *do speedily*
4958 sustellō (1), to *draw together*, i.e. *enwrap*
5302 husterĕō (2), to *be inferior; to fall short*
5610 hōra (1), *hour*

SHORTENED
7114 qâtsar (5), to *curtail*
2856 kŏlŏbŏō (4), *shorten*

SHORTER
7114 qâtsar (2), to *curtail*

SHORTLY
4116 mâhar (1), to *hurry*
4120 mehêrâh (1), *hurry*
7138 qârôwb (1), *near*
1722+5034 ĕn (4), *in; during; because of*
2112 ĕuthĕŏs (1), *at once*
5030 tachĕŏs (4), *speedily*
5031 tachinŏs (1), *soon*
5032 tachiŏn (2), *more rapidly, more speedily*

SHOSHANNIM
7799 shûwshan (2), *white lily*; straight *trumpet*

SHOSHANNIM-EDUTH
7802 Shûwshan 'Êdûwth (1), *lily* (or *trumpet) of assemblage*

SHOT
3384 yârâh (7), to *shoot*
5927 'âlâh (1), to *ascend, be high, mount*
7232 râbab (2), to *shoot*
7819 shâchaṭ (1), to *slaughter; butcher*
7971 shâlach (5), to *send away*

SHOULD
1163 dĕi (3), *it is (was) necessary*
3195 mĕllō (25), to *intend*, i.e. *be about to*
3784 ŏpheilō (1), to *owe*

SHOULDER
2220 zerôwa' (2), *arm*
3802 kâthêph (9), *shoulder*-piece; *wall*
7785 shôwq (13), *lower leg*
7926 shekem (12), *neck*
7929 shikmâh (1), *shoulder*-bone

SHOULDERPIECES
3802 kâthêph (4), *shoulder*-piece; *wall*

SHOULDERS
3802 kâthêph (13), *shoulder*-piece; *wall*
7926 shekem (5), *neck*
5606 ŏmŏs (2), *shoulder*

SHOUT
1959 hêydâd (1), *acclamation, shout*
6030 'ânâh (1), to *shout*
6670 tsâhal (1), to *be cheerful; to sound*
6681 tsâvach (1), to *screech* exultingly
7321 rûwa' (12), to *shout*
7442 rânan (6), to *shout*
7768 shâva' (1), to *halloo, call for help*
8643 terûw'âh (9), *battle-cry; clangor*
2019 ĕpiphōnĕō (1), to *exclaim, shout*
2752 kĕlĕuma (1), *cry* of incitement

SHOUTED
7321 rûwa' (11), to *shout*
7442 rânan (1), to *shout*
7452 rêa' (1), *shout*
8643 terûw'âh (1), *battle-cry; clangor*

SHOUTETH
7442 rânan (1), to *shout*

SHOUTING
1959 hêydâd (4), *shout of joy*
7321 rûwa' (1), to *shout*
7440 rinnâh (1), *shout*
8643 terûw'âh (8), *battle-cry; clangor*

SHOUTINGS
8663 teshû'âh (1), *crashing or clamor*

SHOVEL
7371 rachath (1), *winnowing*-fork

SHOVELS
3257 yâ' (9), *shove*

SHOWER
1653 geshem (3), *rain*
3655 ŏmbrŏs (1), *storm*

SHOWERS
1653 geshem (2), *rain*
2230 zerem (1), *flood*
7241 râbîyb (6), *rain*

SHRANK
5384 nâsheh (2), *rheumatic or crippled*

SHRED
6398 pâlach (1), to *slice*

SHRINES
3485 naŏs (1), *shrine*

SHROUD
2793 chôresh (1), *forest*

SHRUBS
7880 sîyach (1), *shrubbery*

SHUA
7770 Shûwa' (1), *halloo*
7774 Shûw'â' (1), *wealth*

SHUAH
7744 Shûwach (2), *dell*

7746 Shûwchâh (1), *chasm*
7770 Shûwa' (2), *halloo*

SHUAL
7777 Shûw'âl (2), *jackal*

SHUBAEL
2619 Chăçadyâh (3), *Jehovah has favored*

SHUHAM
7748 Shûwchâm (1), *humbly*

SHUHAMITES
7749 Shûwchâmîy (2), *Shuchamite*

SHUHITE
7747 Shuchîy (5), *Shuchite*

SHULAMITE
7759 Shûwlammîyth (2), *peaceful*

SHUMATHITES
8126 Shûmâthîy (1), *Shumathite*

SHUN
4026 periistēmi (1), to *avoid, shun*

SHUNAMMITE
7767 Shûwnammîyth (8), *Shunammitess*

SHUNEM
7766 Shûwnêm (3), *quietly*

SHUNI
7764 Shûwnîy (2), *quiet*

SHUNITES
7765 Shûwnîy (1), *Shunite*

SHUNNED
5288 hupŏstĕllō (1), to *cower or shrink*

SHUPHAM
8197 Shephûwphâm (1), *serpent-like*

SHUPHAMITES
7781 Shûwphâmîy (1), *Shuphamite*

SHUPPIM
8206 Shuppîym (3), *serpents*

SHUR
7793 Shûwr (6), *wall*

SHUSHAN
7800 Shûwshan (21), *lily*

SHUSHAN-EDUTH
7802 Shûwshan 'Êdûwth (1), *lily* (or *trumpet) of assemblage*

SHUT
332 'âṭar (1), to *close up*
1479 gûwph (1), to *shut*
2902 ṭûwach (1), to *whitewash*
3607 kâlâ (4), to *stop*
5274 nâ'al (1), to *lock*
5462 çâgar (55), to *shut*
5463 çegar (Ch.) (1), to *close up*
5526 çâkak (1), to *entwine; to fence in*
5640 çâtham (2), to *stop*
6113 'âtsar (16), to *hold*
6887 tsârar (1), to *cramp*

7092 qâphats (3), to *draw together, to leap; to die*
8173 shâ'a' (1), to *fondle, please or amuse* (self)
608 apŏklĕiō (1), to *close*
2623 kataklĕiō (2), to *incarcerate, lock up*
2808 klĕiō (13), to *close*
4788 sugklĕiō (1), to *net fish; to lock up* persons

SHUTHALHITES
8364 Shûthalchîy (1), *Shuthalchite*

SHUTHELAH
7803 Shûwthelach (4), *crash of breakage*

SHUTTETH
331 'âṭam (1), to *close*
5462 çâgar (1), to *shut*
5640 çâtham (1), to *stop*
6095 'âtsâh (1), to *close*
6105 'âtsam (1), to *be, make powerful*
2808 klĕiō (3), to *shut*

SHUTTING
5462 çâgar (1), to *shut*

SHUTTLE
708 'ereg (1), *shuttle*

SIA
5517 Çîy'â' (1), *congregation*

SIAHA
5517 Çîy'â' (1), *congregation*

SIBBECAI
5444 Çibbekay (2), *thicket-like*

SIBBECHAI
5444 Çibbekay (2), *thicket-like*

SIBBOLETH
5451 Çibbôleth (1), *ear of grain*

SIBMAH
7643 Sebâm (4), *spice*

SIBRAIM
5453 Çibrayim (1), *double hope*

SICHEM
7927 Shekem (1), *ridge*

SICK
605 'ânash (1), to *be frail*
1739 dâveh (1), *menstrual; fainting*
2470 châlâh (34), to *be weak, sick, afflicted*
2483 chŏlîy (1), *malady*
8463 tachălûw' (1), *malady, disease*
732 arrhŏstŏs (4), *infirmed, ill*
770 asthĕnĕō (17), to *be feeble*
772 asthĕnēs (6), *weak*
2192+2560 ĕchō (8), to *have; hold; keep*
2577 kamnō (1), to *sicken*
3885 paralutikŏs (11), *lame person*
4445 purĕssō (2), to *burn with a fever*

SICKLE
2770 chermêsh (2), *sickle*
4038 maggâl (2), *sickle*

1407 drĕpanŏn (8), gathering *hook*

SICKLY
732 arrhōstŏs (1), *infirmed, ill*

SICKNESS
1739 dâveh (1), *menstrual; fainting*
2483 chŏlîy (11), *malady*
4245 machăleh (3), *sickness*
769 asthĕnĕia (1), *feebleness* of body
3554 nŏsŏs (3), *malady*

SICKNESSES
2483 chŏlîy (1), *malady*
8463 tachălûw' (1), *malady, disease*
3554 nŏsŏs (2), *malady*

SIDDIM
7708 Siddîym (3), *flats*

SIDE
2296 châgar (1), to *gird*
2348 chôwph (1), *cove*
3027 yâd (5), *hand; power*
3225 yâmîyn (4), *right*
3409 yârêk (7), *side*
3411 yᵉrêkâh (2), *far away places*
3541 kôh (2), *thus*
3802 kâthêph (29), *side-piece*
4217 mizrâch (2), *east*
4975 môthen (4), *loins*
5048 neged (2), *beside*
5437 çâbab (1), to *surround*
5439 çâbîyb (26), *circle*
5675 'ăbar (Ch.) (7), region *across*
5676 'êber (56), *opposite*
6285 pê'âh (50), *direction*
6311 pôh (2), *here*
6654 tsad (20), *side*
6753 Tsᵉlelpôwnîy (2), *shade-facing*
6763 tsêlâ' (22), *side*
6921 qâdîym (1), *East; eastward; east wind*
6924 qedem (3), *East, eastern; antiquity*
6954 Qᵉhêlâthâh (1), *convocation*
7023 qîyr (2), *side-wall*
7097 qâtseh (1), *extremity*
7307 rûwach (5), *breath; wind; life-*spirit
7859 sᵉṭar (Ch.) (1), *side*
8040 sᵉmô'wl (1), *left*
8193 sâphâh (3), *edge*
492 antiparĕrchŏmai (2), to *go along opposite*
1188 dĕxiŏs (2), *right*
1782 ĕntĕuthĕn (2), on both *sides*
3313 *mĕrŏs* (1), *division*
3840 *pantŏthĕn* (1), *from, on all* sides
3844 *para* (15), *besides*
4008 *pĕran* (13), *across*
4125 *plĕura* (5), *side*

SIDES
3411 yᵉrêkâh (19), *far away places*
3802 kâthêph (4), *shoulder-*piece; *wall*
5676 'êber (4), *opposite*

6285 pê'âh (1), *direction*
6654 tsad (9), *side*
6763 tsêlâ' (4), *side*
7023 qîyr (2), *side-wall*
7253 reba' (3), *fourth*
7307 rûwach (1), *breath; wind; life-*spirit

SIDON
6721 Tsîydôwn (2), *fishery*
4605 Sidōn (12), *fishery*

SIDONIANS
6722 Tsîydônîy (5), *Tsidonian*

SIEGE
4692 mâtsôwr (13), *siege-mound; distress*
6696 tsûwr (3), to *cramp*

SIEVE
3531 kᵉbârâh (1), *sieve*
5299 nâphâh (1), *sieve*

SIFT
5128 nûwa' (1), to *waver*
5130 nûwph (1), to *quiver, vibrate, rock*
4617 siniazō (1), to *shake in a sieve*

SIFTED
5128 nûwa' (1), to *waver*

SIGH
584 'ânach (7), to *sigh*

SIGHED
584 'ânach (1), to *sigh*
389 anastĕnazō (1), to *sigh deeply*
4727 stĕnazō (1), to *sigh*

SIGHEST
584 'ânach (1), to *sigh*

SIGHETH
584 'ânach (1), to *sigh*

SIGHING
585 'ănâchâh (5), *sighing*
603 'ănâqâh (2), *shrieking, groaning*

SIGHS
585 'ănâchâh (1), *sighing*

SIGHT
2379 chăzôwth (Ch.) (2), *view, visible sight*
4758 mar'eh (18), *appearance; vision*
5048 neged (2), *before*
5869 'ayin (218), *sight*
6440 pânîym (39), *face*
7200 râ'âh (1), to *see*
308 anablĕpō (15), to *look up; to recover sight*
309 anablĕpsis (1), *restoration of sight*
991 blĕpō (2), to *look at*
1491 ĕidŏs (1), *sight*
1715 ĕmprŏsthĕn (3), *in front of*
1726 ĕnantiŏn (1), *in the presence of*
1799 ĕnōpiŏn (21), *before*
2335 thĕōria (1), *sight*
2714 katĕnōpiŏn (2), *directly in front of*
3705 hŏrama (1), *supernatural spectacle*
3706 hŏrasis (1), *appearance, vision*
3788 ŏphthalmŏs (1), *eye*
3844 *para* (1), *from; with; besides; on account of*

5324 phantazō (1), to *appear; spectacle, sight*

SIGHTS
5400 phŏbētrŏn (1), *frightening* thing

SIGN
226 'ôwth (33), *sign*
4159 môwphêth (8), *miracle; token or omen*
4864 mas'êth (1), *beacon*
5251 nêç (1), *flag; signal*
6725 tsîyûwn (1), *guiding pillar, monument*
7560 rᵉsham (Ch.) (1), to *record*
3902 parasēmŏs (1), *labeled, marked*
4592 sēmĕiŏn (29), *sign*

SIGNED
7560 rᵉsham (Ch.) (4), to *record*

SIGNET
2368 chôwthâm (8), *signature-*ring, *seal*
2858 chôthemeth (1), signet ring *seal*
5824 'izqâ' (Ch.) (2), *signet or signet-*ring

SIGNETS
2368 chôwthâm (1), *signature-*ring, *seal*

SIGNIFICATION
880 aphōnŏs (1), *mute, silent; unmeaning*

SIGNIFIED
4591 sēmainō (2), to *indicate, make known*

SIGNIFIETH
1213 dēlŏō (1), to *make plain* by words

SIGNIFY
1213 dēlŏō (1), to *make plain* by words
1229 diaggĕllō (1), to *herald thoroughly*
1718 ĕmphanizō (1), to *show forth*
4591 sēmainō (1), to *indicate, make known*

SIGNIFYING
1213 dēlŏō (1), to *make plain* by words
4591 sēmainō (3), to *indicate, make known*

SIGNS
226 'ôwth (27), *sign*
852 'âth (Ch.) (3), *sign*
1770 ĕnnĕuō (1), to *signal*
4591 sēmainō (17), to *indicate, make known*
4592 sēmĕiŏn (5), *sign*

SIHON
5511 Çîychôwn (37), *tempestuous*

SIHOR
7883 Shîychôwr (3), *dark,* i.e. *turbid*

SILAS
4609 Silas (13), *sylvan*

SILENCE
481 'âlam (1), to *be silent*
1745 dûwmâh (2), *silence*
1747 dûwmîyâh (1), *silently; quiet, trust*

1820 dâmâh (1), to *be silent; to fail, cease*
1824 dᵉmîy (2), *quiet*
1826 dâmam (6), to *be silent; to be astonished*
1827 dᵉmâmâh (1), *quiet*
2013 hâçâh (3), to *hush*
2790 chârash (5), to *be silent; to be deaf*
2814 châshâh (2), to *hush*
2271 hēsuchia (3), *stillness*
4601 sigaō (3), to *keep silent*
4602 sigē (2), *silence*
5392 phimŏō (2), to *restrain to silence*

SILENT
1748 dûwmâm (1), *silently*
1826 dâmam (4), to *be silent; to be astonished*
1947 hôwlêlâh (1), *folly*
2013 hâçâh (1), to *hush*
2790 chârash (2), to *be silent; to be deaf*

SILK
4897 meshîy (2), *silk*
8336 shêsh (1), *white* linen; *white* marble
2596 kata (1), *down; according to*

SILLA
5538 Çillâ' (1), *embankment*

SILLY
6601 pâthâh (2), to *be, make simple; to delude*
1133 gunaikariŏn (1), *little,* i.e. *foolish woman*

SILOAH
7975 Shilôach (1), *rill*

SILOAM
4611 Silōam (3), *rill*

SILVANUS
4610 Silŏuanŏs (4), *sylvan*

SILVER
3701 keçeph (280), *silver*
3702 kᵉçaph (Ch.) (12), *silver money*
7192 qᵉsîyṭah (1), *coin*
693 argurĕŏs (3), *made of silver*
694 arguriŏn (9), *silver*
696 argurŏs (5), *silver*
1406 drachmē (1), *silver coin*

SILVERLINGS
3701 keçeph (1), *silver*

SILVERSMITH
695 argurŏkŏpŏs (1), *worker of silver*

SIMEON
8095 Shim'ôwn (43), *hearing*
8099 Shim'ônîy (1), *Shimonite*
4826 Sumĕōn (6), *hearing*

SIMEONITES
8099 Shim'ônîy (3), *Shimonite*

SIMILITUDE
1823 dᵉmûwth (2), *resemblance, likeness*

English

SIMILITUDES
8403 tabnîyth (2), *model,
resemblance*
8544 t^emûwnâh (4),
something *fashioned*
3665 hŏmŏiŏtēs (1),
resemblance, similarity
3667 hŏmŏiōma (1),
form; resemblance
3669 hŏmŏiōsis (1),
resemblance, likeness

SIMILITUDES
1819 dâmâh (1), to *liken*

SIMON
4613 Simōn (67), *hearing*

SIMON'S
4613 Simōn (7), *hearing*

SIMPLE
6612 p^ethîy (17), *silly*
6615 p^ethayûwth (1),
silliness, i.e. *seducible*
172 akakŏs (1), *innocent*
185 akĕraiŏs (1),
innocent

SIMPLICITY
6612 p^ethîy (1), *silly*
8537 tôm (1), *innocence*
572 haplŏtēs (3), *sincerity*

SIMRI
8113 Shimriy (1),
watchful

SIN
817 'âshâm (3), *guilt*
819 'ashmâh (2),
guiltiness
2398 châṭâ' (68), to *sin*
2399 chêṭ (22), *crime*
2401 châṭâ'âh (8), *offence*
2402 chaṭṭâ'âh (Ch.) (2),
offence, and *penalty*
2403 chaṭṭâ'âh (215),
offence; sin offering
2409 chaṭṭâyâ' (Ch.) (1),
expiation, sin offering
5512 Çîyn (6), *Sin*
5771 'âvôn (1), moral *evil*
6588 pesha' (1), *revolt*
7686 shâgâh (1), to *stray*
264 hamartanō (15), to
miss the mark, to *err*
265 hamartēma (1), *sin*
266 hamartia (91), *sin*
361 anamartētŏs (1),
sinless

SINA
4614 Sina (2), *Sinai*

SINAI
5514 Çîynay (35), *Sinai*
4614 Sina (2), *Sinai*

SINCE
227 'âz (3), *therefore*
310 'achar (2), *after*
518 'îm (1), *whether?; if,
although; Oh that!*
1767 day (3), *enough,
sufficient*
2008 hênnâh (1), *from
here; from there*
3588 kîy (1), *for, that*
4480 min (12), *from*
4480+227 min (1), *from*
4481 min (Ch.) (1), *from*
5750 'ôwd (2), *more*
575 apŏ (9), *from, away*
575+3769 apŏ (3), *from*
1537 ĕk (1), *out, out of*
1893 ĕpĕi (1), *since*

SINCERE
97 adŏlŏs (1), *pure*
1506 ĕilikrinēs (1), *pure*

SINCERELY
8549 tâmîym (2), *entire*
55 hagnōs (1), *purely*

SINCERITY
8549 tâmîym (1), *integrity*
861 aphtharsia (2),
genuineness
1103 gnēsiŏs (1), *genuine*
1505 ĕilikrinĕia (3),
purity, sincerity

SINEW
1517 gîyd (3), *tendon*

SINEWS
1517 gîyd (4), *tendon*
6207 'âraq (1), to *gnaw*

SINFUL
2398 châṭâ' (1), to *sin*
2400 chaṭṭâ' (1), *guilty*
2401 châṭâ'âh (1),
offence or *sacrifice*
266 hamartia (1), *sin*
268 hamartōlŏs (4),
sinner; sinful

SING
1984 hâlal (2), to *speak
praise; thank*
2167 zâmar (33), to *play
music*
5414+6963 nâthan (1), to
give
6030 'ânâh (4), to *sing*
6031 'ânâh (2), to *afflict*
7440 rinnâh (1), *shout*
7442 rânan (25), to *shout*
7788 shûwr (1), to *travel*
7891 shîyr (32), to *sing*
7892 shîyr (1), *singing*
103 a₁dō (1), to *sing*
5214 humnĕō (1), to
celebrate God in song
5567 psallō (4), to *play* a
stringed instrument

SINGED
2761 chărak (Ch.) (1), to
scorch, singe

SINGER
5329 nâtsach (1), i.e. to
be eminent
7891 shîyr (1), to *sing*

SINGERS
2171 zammâr (Ch.) (1),
musician
7891 shîyr (35), to *sing*
7892 shîyr (1), *singing*

SINGETH
7891 shîyr (1), to *sing*

SINGING
2158 zâmîyr (1), *song*
7440 rinnâh (9), *shout*
7442 rânan (2), to *shout*
for joy
7445 r^enânâh (1), *shout*
for joy
7891 shîyr (5), to *sing*
7892 shîyr (4), *singing*
103 a₁dō (2), to *sing*

SINGLE
573 haplŏus (2), *single*

SINGLENESS
572 haplŏtēs (2), *sincerity*
858 aphĕlŏtēs (1),
simplicity; sincerity

SINGULAR
6381 pâlâ' (1), to *be,
make great, difficult*

SINIM
5515 Çîynîym (1), *Sinim*

SINITE
5513 Çîynîy (2), *Sinite*

SINK
2883 ṭâba' (2), to *sink*
8257 shâqa' (1), to *be
overflowed;* to *abate*
1036 buthizō (1), to *sink*
2670 katapŏntizō (1), to
submerge, be drowned
5087 tithēmi (1), to *place*

SINNED
2398 châṭâ' (102), to *sin*
264 hamartanō (15), to
miss the mark, to *sin*
4258 prŏamartanō (2), to
sin previously

SINNER
2398 châṭâ' (8), to *sin*
2403 chaṭṭâ'âh (1),
offence; sin offering
268 hamartōlŏs (12),
sinner; sinful

SINNERS
2400 chaṭṭâ' (16), *guilty*
268 hamartōlŏs (30),
sinner; sinful
3781 ŏphĕilĕtēs (1),
person *indebted*

SINNEST
2398 châṭâ' (1), to *sin*

SINNETH
2398 châṭâ' (13), to *sin*
6213 'âsâh (1), to *do*
7683 shâgag (1), to *sin*
264 hamartanō (7), to *sin*

SINNING
2398 châṭâ' (2), to *sin*

SINS
819 'ashmâh (2),
guiltiness
2399 chêṭ (8), *crime*
2403 chaṭṭâ'âh (71),
offence; sin offering
2408 chăṭîy (Ch.) (1), *sin*
6588 pesha' (2), *revolt*
265 hamartēma (3), *sin*
266 hamartia (78), *sin*
3900 paraptōma (3),
error; transgression

SION
6726 Tsîyôwn (1), *capital*
7865 Sîy'ôn (1), *peak*
4622 Siōn (7), *capital*

SIPHMOTH
8224 Siphmôwth (1),
Siphmoth

SIPPAI
5598 Çippay (1),
bason-like

SIR
113 'âdôwn (1),
sovereign, i.e. *controller*
2962 kuriŏs (11),
supreme, controller, Mr.

SIRAH
5626 Çîrâh (1), *departure*

SIRION
8304 S^erâyâh (2),
Jehovah has prevailed

SIRS
435 anēr (6), *man; male*
2962 kuriŏs (1), *supreme,
controller,* Mr.

SISAMAI
5581 Çiçmay (2), *Sismai*

SISERA
5516 Çîyç^erâ' (21), *Sisera*

SISTER
269 'achôwth (91), *sister*
1733 dôwdâh (1), *aunt*
2994 y^ebêmeth (2),
sister-in-law
79 adĕlphē (15), *sister*

SISTER'S
269 'achôwth (5), *sister*
79 adĕlphē (1), *sister*
431 anĕpsiŏs (1), *cousin*

SISTERS
269 'achôwth (11), *sister*
79 adĕlphē (8), *sister*

SIT
3427 yâshab (65), to
dwell, to *settle*
3488 y^ethîb (Ch.) (2), to *sit*
5414 nâthan (1), to *give*
5437 çâbab (1), to
surround
7674 shebeth (1), *rest*
347 anaklinō (6), to
recline
377 anapiptō (5), *lie
down, lean back*
2521 kathēmai (12), to
sit down; to *remain*
2523 kathizō (15), to *seat
down, dwell*
2621 katakĕimai (1), to
lie down
2625 kataklinō (2), to
recline, take a place
4776 sugkathizō (1), to
give, take a seat with
4873 sunanakĕimai (1),
to *recline* with at meal

SITH
518 'îm (1), *whether?; if,
although; Oh that!*

SITNAH
7856 Siṭnâh (1),
opposition

SITTEST
3427 yâshab (6), to *settle*
2521 kathēmai (1), to *sit*

SITTETH
1716 dâgar (1), to *brood
over;* to *care for* young
3427 yâshab (25), to *settle*
345 anakĕimai (1), to
recline at a meal
2521 kathēmai (10), to
sit down; or *reside*
2523 kathizō (3), to *seat
down, dwell*

SITTING
3427 yâshab (15), to *settle*
4186 môwshâb (2), *seat*
7257 râbats (1), to *recline*
1910 ĕpibainō (1), to
mount, ascend

2516 kathĕzŏmai (2), to
sit down, be seated
2521 kathēmai (21), to
sit down; to reside
2523 kathizō (1), to seat
down, dwell

SITUATE
3427 yâshab (2), to settle
4690 mâtsûwq (1),
column; hilltop

SITUATION
4186 môwshâb (1), site
5131 nôwph (1), elevation

SIVAN
5510 Çîyvân (1), Sivan

SIX
8337 shêsh (185), six;
sixth
8353 shêth (Ch.) (1), six;
sixth
1803 hĕx (11), six
1812 hĕxakŏsiŏi (1), six
hundred
5516 chi xi stigma (1), 666

SIXSCORE
3967+6242 mê'âh (1),
hundred
8147+6240+7239
sh°nayim (1), two-fold

SIXTEEN
8337+6240 shêsh (22),
six; sixth
1440+1803
hĕbdŏmēkŏnta (1),
seventy

SIXTEENTH
8337+6240 shêsh (3), six;
sixth

SIXTH
8337 shêsh (2), six; sixth
8338 shâwshâw (1),
(poss.) to annihilate
8341 shâshâh (1), to
divide into sixths
8345 shishshîy (26), sixth
8353 shêth (Ch.) (1), six;
sixth
1623 hĕktŏs (14), sixth

SIXTY
8346 shishshîym (11),
sixty
1835 hĕxēkŏnta (3), sixty

SIXTYFOLD
1835 hĕxēkŏnta (1), sixty

SIZE
4060 middâh (3),
measure; portion
7095 qetseb (2), shape

SKIES
7834 shachaq (5), clouds

SKILFUL
995 bîyn (1), to discern
2451 chokmâh (1),
wisdom
2796 chârâsh (1), skilled
fabricator or worker
3045 yâda' (2), to know
3925 lâmad (1), to teach
7919 sâkal (1), to be or
act circumspect

SKILFULLY
3190 yâṭab (1), to be,
make well

SKILFULNESS
8394 tâbûwn (1),
intelligence; argument

SKILL
995 bîyn (1), to discern
3045 yâda' (4), to know
7919 sâkal (2), to be or
act circumspect

SKIN
1320 bâsâr (1), flesh
1539 geled (1), skin
5785 'ôwr (71), skin
1193 dĕrmatinŏs (1),
made of leather hide

SKINS
5785 'ôwr (20), skin

SKIP
7540 râqad (1), to spring

SKIPPED
7540 râqad (2), to spring

SKIPPEDST
5110 nûwd (1), to waver

SKIPPING
7092 qâphats (1), to leap

SKIRT
3671 kânâph (12), wing

SKIRTS
3671 kânâph (2), wing
6310 peh (1), mouth
7757 shûwl (4), skirt

SKULL
1538 gulgôleth (2), skull
2898 kraniŏn (3), skull

SKY
7834 shachaq (2), clouds
3772 ŏuranŏs (5), sky

SLACK
309 'âchar (2), to delay
6113 'âtsar (1), to hold
back; to maintain, rule
7423 r°mîyâh (1),
remissness; treachery
7503 râphâh (3), to
slacken
1019 bradunō (1), to
delay, hesitate

SLACKED
6313 pûwg (1), to be
sluggish; be numb

SLACKNESS
1022 bradutēs (1),
tardiness, slowness

SLAIN
2026 hârag (31), to kill
2027 hereg (1), kill
2076 zâbach (2), to
(sacrificially) slaughter
2490 châlal (1), to
profane, defile
2491 châlâl (75), slain
2717 chârab (1), to
desolate, destroy
2873 ṭâbach (1), to kill
4191 mûwth (18), to kill
5062 nâgaph (2), to strike
5221 nâkâh (20), to kill
6992 q°ṭal (Ch.) (4), to kill
7523 râtsach (3), to
murder
7819 shâchaṭ (5), to
slaughter; butcher
337 anairĕō (3), to take
away, murder
615 apŏktĕinō (7), to kill

1722+5408+599 ĕn (1), in;
during; because of
4968 sphagiŏn (1),
offering for slaughter
4969 sphazō (6), to
slaughter or to maim

SLANDER
1681 dibbâh (3), slander

SLANDERED
7270 râgal (1), to slander

SLANDERERS
1228 diabŏlŏs (1),
traducer, i.e. Satan

SLANDEREST
5414+1848 nâthan (1), to
give

SLANDERETH
3960 lâshan (1), to
calumniate, malign

SLANDEROUSLY
987 blasphēmĕō (1), to
speak impiously

SLANDERS
7400 râkîyl (2),
scandal-monger

SLANG
7049 qâla' (1), to sling

SLAUGHTER
2027 hereg (4), kill
2028 hărēgâh (5), kill
2873 ṭâbach (5), to kill
2875 Ṭebach (9),
massacre
2878 ṭibehâh (1),
butchery
4046 maggêphâh (3),
pestilence; defeat
4293 maṭbêach (1),
slaughter place
4347 makkâh (14), blow;
wound; pestilence
4660 mappâts (1),
striking to pieces
5221 nâkâh (5), to kill
6993 qeṭel (1), death
7524 retsach (1),
crushing; murder-cry
7819 shâchaṭ (1), to
slaughter; butcher
2871 kŏpē (1), carnage
4967 sphagē (3), butchery
5408 phŏnŏs (1), slaying

SLAVES
4983 sōma (1), body

SLAY
1194 B°'ôn (1), Beon
2026 hârag (38), to kill
2717 chârab (1), to
desolate, destroy
2763 charam (1), to
devote to destruction
2873 ṭâbach (1), to kill,
butcher
2875 Ṭebach (1),
massacre
4191 mûwth (43), to kill
5221 nâkâh (11), to kill
5221+5315 nâkâh (1), to
strike, kill
6991 qâṭal (2), to put to
death
6992 q°ṭal (Ch.) (1), to kill
7819 shâchaṭ (9), to
slaughter; butcher

337 anairĕō (2), to take
away, murder
615 apŏktĕinō (3), to kill
2380 thuō (1), to kill
2695 katasphattō (1), to
slaughter, strike down

SLAYER
2026 hârag (1), to kill
5221 nâkâh (1), to kill
7523 râtsach (17), to
murder

SLAYETH
2026 hârag (2), to kill
2490 châlal (1), to
profane, defile
4191 mûwth (1), to kill
7523+5315 râtsach (1), to
murder

SLAYING
2026 hârag (3), to kill
4191 mûwth (1), to kill
5221 nâkâh (2), to kill
7819 shâchaṭ (1), to
slaughter; butcher

SLEEP
3462 yâshên (11), to
sleep; to grow old
3463 yâshên (4), sleepy
7290 râdam (3), to
stupefy
7901 shâkab (11), to lie
8139 sh°nâh (Ch.) (1),
sleep
8142 shênâh (24), sleep
8639 tardêmâh (4),
trance, deep sleep
1852 ĕxupnizō (1), to
waken, rouse
1853 ĕxupnŏs (1), awake
2518 kathĕudō (7), to fall
asleep
2837 kŏimaō (5), to
slumber; to decease
5258 hupnŏs (6), sleep

SLEEPER
7290 râdam (1), to
stupefy

SLEEPEST
3462 yâshên (1), to sleep
7901 shâkab (1), to lie
2518 kathĕudō (2), to fall
asleep

SLEEPETH
3463 yâshên (2), sleepy
7290 râdam (1), to
stupefy
2518 kathĕudō (3), to fall
asleep
2837 kŏimaō (1), to
slumber; to decease

SLEEPING
1957 hâzâh (1), to dream
3463 yâshên (1), sleepy
2518 kathĕudō (2), to fall
asleep
2837 kŏimaō (2), to
slumber; to decease

SLEIGHT
2940 kubĕia (1), artifice
or fraud, deceit

SLEPT
3462 yâshên (5), to sleep
3463 yâshên (1), sleepy
5123 nûwm (1), to
slumber
7901 shâkab (37), to lie

English

SLEW
2518 kathěudō (2), to *fall asleep*
2837 kŏimaō (3), to *slumber; to decease*

SLEW
2026 hârag (55), to *kill*
2076 zâbach (3), to (sacrificially) *slaughter*
2126 Zîynâ' (1), well-*fed*
2490 châlal (1), to *profane, defile*
2491 châlâl (3), *slain*
4191 mûwth (40), to *kill*
5221 nâkâh (57), to *kill*
5307 nâphal (1), to *fall*
6992 qᵉṭal (Ch.) (2), to *kill*
7819 shâchaṭ (21), to *slaughter; butcher*
337 anairěō (3), to *take away, murder*
615 apŏktěinō (4), to *kill*
1315 diachěirizŏmai (1), to *lay hands* upon
4969 sphazō (2), to *slaughter or to maim*
5407 phŏněuō (1), to *commit murder*

SLEWEST
5221 nâkâh (1), to *kill*

SLIDDEN
7725 shûwb (1), to *return*

SLIDE
4131 môwṭ (1), to *slip*
4571 mâ'ad (2), to *waver*

SLIDETH
5637 çârar (1), to be *refractory, stubborn*

SLIGHTLY
7043 qâlal (2), to be, *make light*

SLIME
2564 chêmâr (2), *bitumen*

SLIMEPITS
2564 chêmâr (1), *bitumen*

SLING
4773 margêmâh (1), sling for *stones*
7049 qâla' (3), to *sling*
7050 qela' (4), *sling*

SLINGERS
7051 qallâ' (1), *slinger*

SLINGS
7050 qela' (1), *sling*

SLINGSTONES
68+7050 'eben (1), *stone*

SLIP
4131 môwṭ (1), to *slip*
4571 mâ'ad (3), to *waver*
3901 pararrhuěō (1), to *flow by*, to pass (*miss*)

SLIPPED
6362 pâṭar (1), to *burst through; to emit*
8210 shâphak (1), to *spill forth; to expend*

SLIPPERY
2513 chelqâq (1), *smoothness; flattery*
2519 châlaqlaqqâh (2), *smooth; treacherous*

SLIPPETH
4131 môwṭ (2), to *slip*
5394 nâshal (1), to *drop*

SLIPS
2156 zᵉmôwrâh (1), *twig, vine branch*

SLOTHFUL
6101 'âtsal (1), to be *slack*
6102 'âtsêl (8), *indolent*
7423 rᵉmîyâh (2), *remissness; treachery*
7503 râphâh (1), to *slacken*
3576 nōthrŏs (1), *lazy*
3636 ŏknērŏs (2), *lazy*

SLOTHFULNESS
6103 'atslâh (1), *indolence*

SLOW
750 'ârêk (10), *patient*
3515 kâbêd (1), *stupid*
692 argŏs (1), *lazy*
1021 bradus (2), *slow*

SLOWLY
1020 braduplŏěō (1), to *sail slowly*

SLUGGARD
6102 'âtsêl (6), *indolent*

SLUICES
7938 seker (1), *wages*

SLUMBER
5123 nûwm (5), to *slumber*
8572 tᵉnûwmâh (4), *drowsiness, i.e. sleep*
2659 katanuxis (1), *stupor, bewilderment*

SLUMBERED
3573 nustazō (1), to *fall asleep; to delay*

SLUMBERETH
3573 nustazō (1), to *fall asleep; to delay*

SLUMBERINGS
8572 tᵉnûwmâh (1), *drowsiness, i.e. sleep*

SMALL
1571 gam (1), *also; even*
1639 gâra' (1), to *lessen*
1851 daq (5), *small*
1854 dâqaq (5), to *crush*
3190 yâṭab (1), to be, *make well*
4213 miz'âr (1), *fewness*
4592 mᵉ'aṭ (9), *little*
4705 mits'âr (2), *little; short time*
4962 math (1), *men*
6694 tsûwq (1), to *pour out; melt*
6810 tsâ'îyr (2), *small*
6819 tsâ'ar (1), to be *small; be trivial*
6862 tsar (1), *trouble; opponent*
6994 qâṭôn (2), to be, *make diminutive*
6996 qâṭân (34), *small*
7116 qâtsêr (2), *short*
1646 ělachistŏs (2), *least*
2485 ichthudiŏn (1), *little fish*
3398 mikrŏs (6), *small*
3641 ŏligŏs (5), *small*
3795 ŏpsariŏn (1), *small fish*
4142 plŏiariŏn (1), *small boat*

SLAMMEST *(see below)*

SMALLEST
6996 qâṭân (1), *small*
1646 ělachistŏs (1), *least*

SMART
7321+7451 rûwa' (1), to *shout* for alarm or joy

SMELL
1314 besem (1), *spice*
7306 rûwach (5), to *smell*
7381 rêyach (10), *odor*
7382 rêyach (Ch.) (1), *odor*
2175 ěuōdia (1), *fragrance, aroma*

SMELLED
7306 rûwach (2), to *smell*

SMELLETH
7306 rûwach (1), to *smell*

SMELLING
5674 'âbar (2), to *cross over; to transition*
3750 ŏsphrēsis (1), *smell*

SMITE
1986 hâlam (1), to *strike*
3807 kâthath (1), to *strike*
4272 mâchats (2), to *crush; to subdue*
5062 nâgaph (9), to *strike*
5221 nâkâh (94), to *strike*
5307 nâphal (1), to *fall*
5596 çâphach (1), to *associate; be united*
5606 çâphaq (1), to *clap*
6221 'Ăsîy'êl (2), *made of God*
6375 pîyq (1), *tottering*
1194 děrō (1), to *flay*
3960 patassō (5), to *strike*
4474 rhapizō (1), to *slap*
5180 tuptō (3), to *strike*

SMITERS
5221 nâkâh (1), to *strike*

SMITEST
5221 nâkâh (1), to *strike*
1194 děrō (1), to *flay*

SMITETH
4272 mâchats (1), to *crush; to subdue*
5221 nâkâh (11), to *strike*
5180 tuptō (1), to *strike*

SMITH
2796 chârâsh (2), skilled *fabricator* or worker
2796+1270 chârâsh (1), skilled *fabricator*

SMITHS
4525 maçgêr (4), *prison; craftsman*

SMITING
5221 nâkâh (5), to *strike*

SMITTEN
1792 dâkâ' (1), to *pulverize; be contrite*
3807 kâthath (1), to *strike*
5060 nâga' (1), to *strike*
5062 nâgaph (15), to *inflict; to strike*
5221 nâkâh (43), to *strike*
4141 plēssō (1), to *pound*
5180 tuptō (1), to *strike*

SMOKE
6225 'âshan (5), to *envelope in smoke*

SMALLEST *(see column 2)*

SMOKE
6227 'âshân (24), *smoke*
7008 qîyṭôwr (3), *fume*
2586 kapnŏs (13), *smoke*

SMOKING
3544 kêheh (1), *feeble; obscure*
6226 'âshên (2), *smoky*
6227 'âshân (1), *smoke*
5187 tuphŏō (1), to *inflate* with self-conceit

SMOOTH
2509 châlâq (1), *smooth*
2511 challâq (1), *smooth*
2512 challûq (1), *smooth*
2513 chelqâh (2), *smoothness; flattery*
3006 lêiŏs (1), *smooth*

SMOOTHER
2505 châlaq (1), to be *smooth; be slippery*
2513 chelqâh (1), *smoothness; flattery*

SMOOTHETH
2505 châlaq (1), to be *smooth; be slippery*

SMOTE
1986 hâlam (2), to *strike*
3766 kâra' (1), to *prostrate*
4223 mᵉchâ' (Ch.) (2), to *strike; to impale*
4277 mâchaq (1), to *crush*
4347 makkâh (1), *blow*
5060 nâga' (2), to *strike*
5062 nâgaph (6), to *strike*
5221 nâkâh (194), to *strike*
5368 nᵉqash (Ch.) (1), to *knock; to be frightened*
5606 çâphaq (2), to *clap*
8628 tâqa' (1), to *slap*
851 aphairěō (1), to *remove, cut off*
1194 děrō (1), to *flay, i.e. to scourge or thrash*
1325+4475 didōmi (1), to *give*
3817 paiō (4), to *hit*
3960 patassō (4), to *strike*
4474 rhapizō (1), to *strike*
5180 tuptō (4), to *strike*

SMOTEST
5221 nâkâh (1), to *strike*

SMYRNA
4667 Smurna (1), *myrrh*
4668 Smurnaiŏs (1), *inhabitant of Smyrna*

SNAIL
2546 chômeṭ (1), *lizard*
7642 shablûwl (1), *snail*

SNARE
2256 chebel (1), *band*
3369 yâqôsh (1), to *trap*
4170 môwqêsh (14), *noose*
4686 mâtsûwd (2), *net*
5367 nâqash (1), to *entrap* with a noose
6315 pûwach (1), to *blow, to fan, kindle; to utter*
6341 pach (17), *net*
6354 pachath (1), *pit* for catching animals
6983 qôwsh (1), to *set a trap*
7639 sᵉbâkâh (1), *snare*

1029 brŏchŏs (1), *noose*
3803 pagis (5), *trap; trick*

SNARED
3369 yâqôsh (5), to *trap*
4170 môwqêsh (1), *noose*
5367 nâqash (2), to
   entrap with a noose
6351 pâchach (1), to
   spread a net

SNARES
3353 yâqûwsh (1), *snarer*
4170 môwqêsh (6), *noose*
4685 mâtsôwd (1), *snare*
5367 nâqash (1), to
   entrap with a noose
6341 pach (6), *net*

SNATCH
1504 gâzar (1), to *destroy*

SNEEZED
2237 zârar (1), to *sneeze*

SNORTING
5170 nachar (1), *snorting*

SNOUT
639 'aph (1), *nose, nostril*

SNOW
7949 shâlag (1), to *be
   snow-white*
7950 sheleg (19), *white
   snow*
8517 t^elag (Ch.) (1), *snow*
5510 chiôn (3), *snow*

SNOWY
7950 sheleg (1), *white
   snow*

SNUFFDISHES
4289 machtâh (3), *pan
   for live coals*

SNUFFED
5301 nâphach (1), to
   inflate, blow, expire
7602 shâ'aph (1), to *be
   angry; to hasten*

SNUFFERS
4212 m^ezamm^erâh (5),
   tweezer, trimmer
4457 melqâch (1), *pair of
   tweezers or tongs*

SNUFFETH
7602 shâ'aph (1), to *be
   angry; to hasten*

SOAKED
7301 râvâh (1), to *slake*

SOBER
3524 nêphalĕŏs (2),
   circumspect, temperate
3525 nêphō (4), to
   abstain from wine
4993 sōphrŏnĕŏ (3), to *be
   in a right state of mind*
4994 sōphrŏnizō (1), to
   discipline or *correct*
4998 sōphrōn (2),
   self-controlled

SOBERLY
1519+4993 ĕis (1), *to*
4996 sōphrŏnōs (1), *with
   sound mind*

SOBERNESS
4997 sōphrŏsunē (1),
   self-control, propriety

SOBRIETY
4997 sōphrŏsunē (2),
   self-control, propriety

SOCHO
7755 Sôwkôh (1), *hedged*

SOCHOH
7755 Sôwkôh (1), *hedged*

SOCKET
134 'eden (1), *footing*

SOCKETS
134 'eden (52), *footing*

SOCOH
7755 Sôwkôh (2), *hedged*

SOD
1310 bâshal (1), to *boil*
2102 zûwd (1), to *seethe*

SODDEN
1310 bâshal (5), to *boil*
1311 bâshêl (1), *boiled*

SODERING
1694 debeq (1), *solder*

SODI
5476 Çôwdîy (1),
   confidant

SODOM
5467 Ç^edôm (39),
   volcanic or *bituminous*
4670 Sŏdŏma (9),
   volcanic or *bituminous*

SODOMA
4670 Sŏdŏma (1),
   volcanic or *bituminous*

SODOMITE
6945 qâdêsh (1), *sacred
   male prostitute*

SODOMITES
6945 qâdêsh (3), *sacred
   male prostitute*

SOFT
4127 mûwg (1), to *soften*
7390 rak (3), *tender*
7401 râkak (1), to *soften*
3120 malakŏs (3), *soft*

SOFTER
7401 râkak (1), to *soften*

SOFTLY
328 'aṭ (3), *gently, softly*
3814 lâṭ (1), *silently*
3909 lâṭ (1), *covertly*
5285 hupŏpnĕŏ (1), to
   breathe gently

SOIL
7704 sâdeh (1), *field*

SOJOURN
1481 gûwr (30), to *sojourn*
4033 mâgûwr (1), *abode*
1510+3941 ĕimi (1), *I
   exist, I am*

SOJOURNED
1481 gûwr (11), to *sojourn*
3939 parŏikĕŏ (1), to
   reside as a *foreigner*

SOJOURNER
1616 gêr (1), *foreigner*
8453 tôwshâb (7),
   temporary dweller

SOJOURNERS
1481 gûwr (1), to *sojourn*
8453 tôwshâb (2),
   temporary dweller

SOJOURNETH
1481 gûwr (15), to *sojourn*

SOJOURNING
1481 gûwr (1), to *sojourn*
4186 môwshâb (1), *seat*

3940 parŏikia (1), *foreign
   residence*

SOLACE
5965 'âlaç (1), to *leap* for
   joy, i.e. *exult, wave*

SOLD
935+4242 bôw' (1), to *go*
4376 mâkar (45), to *sell*
4465 mimkâr (5),
   merchandise
7666 shâbar (2), to *deal*
591 apŏdidōmi (3), to
   give away
4097 pipraskō (9), to *sell*
4453 pōlĕŏ (14), to *barter*

SOLDIER
4757 stratiōtēs (4),
   common *warrior*
4758 stratŏlŏgĕŏ (1), to
   enlist in the army

SOLDIERS
1121 bên (1), *son,
   descendant; people*
2428 chayil (1), *army*
2502 châlats (1), to *equip*
6635 tsâbâ' (1), *army*
4753 stratĕuma (1), body
   of *troops*
4754 stratĕuŏmai (1), to
   serve in military
4757 stratiōtēs (21),
   common *warrior*

SOLDIERS'
4757 stratiōtēs (1),
   common *warrior*

SOLE
3709 kaph (12), *sole*

SOLEMN
2282 chag (3), solemn
   festival
2287 châgag (1), to
   observe a festival
4150 môw'êd (14),
   assembly
6116 'ătsârâh (10),
   assembly

SOLEMNITIES
4150 môw'êd (3),
   assembly

SOLEMNITY
2282 chag (1), solemn
   festival
4150 môw'êd (1),
   assembly

SOLEMNLY
5749 'ûwd (2), to *protest,
   testify;* to *encompass*

SOLES
3709 kaph (7), *sole* of foot

SOLITARILY
910 bâdâd (1), *separate*

SOLITARY
910 bâdâd (1), *separate*
1565 galmûwd (2),
   sterile, barren, desolate
3173 yâchîyd (1), *only son*
3452 y^eshîymôwn (1),
   desolation
6723 tsîyâh (1), *desert*
2048 ĕrēmŏs (1), *remote
   place, deserted place*

SOLOMON
8010 Sh^elômôh (271),
   peaceful

4672 Sŏlŏmōn (9),
   peaceful

SOLOMON'S
8010 Sh^elômôh (22),
   peaceful
4672 Sŏlŏmōn (3),
   peaceful

SOME
259 'echâd (7), *first*
428 'êl-leh (3), *these*
582 'ĕnôwsh (3), *person*
1697 dâbâr (1), *thing*
4592 m^e'aṭ (2), *little*
7097 qâtseh (2), *extremity*
243 allŏs (9), *other*
1520 hĕis (2), *one*
2087 hĕtĕrŏs (2), *other*
3381 mēpōs (1), *lest
   somehow*
3588 hŏ (7), *"the,"* i.e. the
   definite article
4218 pŏtĕ (1), *some* time
5100 tis (79), *some*

SOMEBODY
5100 tis (2), *some* or *any*

SOMETHING
4745 miqreh (1),
   accident or *fortune*
5100 tis (5), *some* or *any*

SOMETIME
4218 pŏtĕ (2), *some* time

SOMETIMES
4218 pŏtĕ (3), *some* time

SOMEWHAT
3544 kêheh (5), *feeble*
3972 m^e'ûwmâh (1),
   something; anything
3313 mĕrŏs (1), *division*
5100 tis (6), *some* or *any*

SON
1121 bên (1798), *son,
   descendant; people*
1125 Ben-'Ăbîynâdâb (1),
   (the) *son of Abinadab*
1127 Ben-Geber (1), *son
   of* (the) *hero*
1128 Ben-Deqer (1), *son
   of piercing*
1133 Ben-Chûwr (1), *son
   of Chur*
1136 Ben-Cheçed (1),
   son of kindness
1247 bar (Ch.) (7), *son*
1248 bar (4), *son, heir*
2859 châthan (5), to
   become related
2860 châthân (7),
   relative; bridegroom
3025 yâgôr (1), to *fear*
3173 yâchîyd (1), *only son*
4497 mânôwn (1), *heir*
5209 nîyn (2), *progeny*
5220 neked (1), *offspring*
431 anĕpsiŏs (1), *cousin*
3816 pais (3), *child; slave*
5043 tĕknŏn (14), *child*
5048 tĕlĕiŏō (1), to
   perfect, complete
5207 huiŏs (304), *son*

SON'S
1121 bên (21), *son*
5220 neked (1), *offspring*

SONG
2176 zimrâth (3), *song*
4853 massâ' (3), *burden,
   utterance*

English

SONGS
5058 nᵉgîynâh (4), *instrument, poem*
7892 shîyr (62), *song*
5603 ō¦dē (5), *religious chant or ode*

SONGS
2158 zâmîyr (3), *song*
5058 nᵉgîynâh (1), *instrument; poem*
7438 rôn (1), *shout of deliverance*
7440 rinnâh (1), *shout*
7892 shîyr (12), *song*
5603 ō¦dē (2), *religious chant or ode*

SONS
1121 bên (1024), *son*
1123 bên (Ch.) (3), *son*
2860 châthân (2), *relative; bridegroom*
3206 yeled (3), *young male*
3211 yâlîyd (2), *born; descendants*
5043 tĕknŏn (6), *child*
5206 huiŏthĕsia (1), *placing as a son*
5207 huiŏs (24), *son*

SONS'
1121 bên (26), *son*

SOON
834 'âsher (6), *because, in order that*
1571 gam (1), *also; even*
2440 chîysh (1), *hurry*
4116 mâhar (3), to *hurry*
4120 mᵉhêrâh (1), *hurry*
4592 mᵉ'aṭ (2), *little*
4758 mar'eh (1), *appearance; vision*
7116 qâtsêr (1), *short*
7323 rûwts (1), to *run*
1096 ginŏmai (1), to *be*
2112 ĕuthĕōs (2), *soon*
3711 ŏrgilŏs (1), *irascible, hot-tempered*
3752 hŏtan (2), *inasmuch as, at once*
3753 hŏtĕ (2), *when; as*
3916 parachrēma (1), *instantly, immediately*
5030 tachĕōs (3), *speedily, rapidly*

SOONER
5032 tachiŏn (1), *more rapidly, more speedily*

SOOTHSAYER
7080 qâçam (1), to *divine magic*

SOOTHSAYERS
1505 gᵉzar (Ch.) (4), to *determine by divination*
6049 'ânan (2), to *cover, becloud; to act covertly*

SOOTHSAYING
3132 mantĕuŏmai (1), to *utter spells, fortune-tell*

SOP
5596 psōmiŏn (4), *morsel*

SOPATER
4986 Sōpatrŏs (1), *of a safe father*

SOPE
1287 bôrîyth (2), *alkali soap*

SOPHERETH
5618 Çôphereth (2), *female scribe*

SORCERER
3097 magŏs (2), Oriental *scientist, i.e. magician*

SORCERERS
3784 kâshaph (3), to *enchant*
3786 kashshâph (1), *magician, sorcerer*
5332 pharmakĕus (1), *magician, sorcerer*
5333 pharmakŏs (1), *magician, sorcerer*

SORCERESS
6049 'ânan (1), to *cover, becloud; to act covertly*

SORCERIES
3785 kesheph (2), *sorcery*
3095 magĕia (1), *sorcery*
5331 pharmakĕia (2), *magic, witchcraft*

SORCERY
3096 magĕuō (1), to *practice magic, sorcery*

SORE
1419 gâdôwl (3), *great*
2388 châzaq (4), to *fasten upon; to seize*
2389 châzâq (3), *severe*
2470 châlâh (2), to *be weak, sick, afflicted*
3027 yâd (1), *hand; power*
3510 kâ'ab (2), to feel *pain; to grieve; to spoil*
3513 kâbad (3), to *be heavy, severe, dull*
3515 kâbêd (4), *severe*
3708 ka'aç (1), *vexation*
3966 mᵉ'ôd (22), *very*
4834 mârats (1), to *be pungent or vehement*
5061 nega' (5), *infliction; affliction; leprous spot*
5704+3966 'ad (1), *as far (long) as; during*
7185 qâshâh (1), to *tough or severe*
7186 qâsheh (1), *severe*
7188 qâshach (1), to *be, make unfeeling*
7235 râbâh (1), to *increase*
7451 ra' (9), *bad; evil*
7690 saggîy' (Ch.) (1), *large*
8178 sa'ar (1), *tempest; terror*
23 aganaktĕō (1), to *be indignant*
1568 ĕkthambĕō (1), to *astonish utterly*
1630 ĕkphŏbŏs (1), *frightened out*
1668 hĕlkŏs (1), *sore*
2425 hikanŏs (1), *ample*
2560 kakŏs (1), *badly; wrongly; ill*
3029 lian (1), *very much*
3173 mĕgas (1), *great*
4183 pŏlus (1), *much*
4970 sphŏdra (1), *much*

SOREK
7796 Sôwrêq (1), *vine*

SORELY
4843 mârar (1), to *embitter*

SORER
5501 chĕirōn (1), *more evil or aggravated*

SORES
4347 makkâh (1), *wound*
1668 hĕlkŏs (2), *sore*
1669 hĕlkŏō (1), to *be ulcerous*

SORROW
17 'âbôwy (1), *want*
205 'âven (1), *trouble, vanity, wickedness*
592 'ănîyâh (1), *groaning*
1669 dâ'ab (1), to *pine*
1670 dᵉ'âbâh (1), *pining*
1671 dᵉ'âbôwn (1), *pining*
1674 dᵉ'âgâh (1), *anxiety*
1727 dûwb (1), to *pine*
2342 chûwl (1), to *dance, whirl; to writhe* in pain
2427 chîyl (2), *throe*
2490 châlal (1), to *profane, defile*
3015 yâgôwn (12), *sorrow*
3511 kᵉ'êb (3), *suffering*
3708 ka'aç (4), *vexation*
4044 mᵉginnâh (1), *covering, veil*
4341 mak'ôb (6), *anguish*
4620 ma'ătsêbâh (1), *anguish place*
5999 'âmâl (2), *worry*
6089 'etseb (1), *painful toil; mental pang*
6090 'ôtseb (2), *pain*
6093 'itstsâbôwn (2), *labor or pain*
6094 'atstsebeth (2), *pain or wound, sorrow*
6862 tsar (1), *trouble; opponent*
7451 ra' (1), *bad; evil*
7455 rôa' (1), *badness*
8424 tûwgâh (1), *grief*
3076 lupĕō (1), to *be sad*
3077 lupē (10), *sadness*
3601 ŏdunē (1), *grief*
3997 pĕnthŏs (3), *grief*

SORROWED
3076 lupĕō (2), to *be sad*

SORROWETH
1672 dâ'ag (1), *be anxious, be afraid*

SORROWFUL
1669 dâ'ab (1), to *pine*
1741 dᵉvay (1), *sickness*
2342 chûwl (1), to *dance, whirl; to writhe* in pain
3013 yâgâh (1), to *grieve*
3510 kâ'ab (1), to feel *pain; to grieve; to spoil*
7186 qâsheh (1), *severe*
253 alupŏtĕrŏs (1), *more without grief*
3076 lupĕō (6), to *be sad*
4036 pĕrilupŏs (4), *intensely sad*

SORROWING
3600 ŏdunaō (2), to *grieve*

SORROWS
2256 chebel (10), *company, band*
4341 mak'ôb (5), *anguish*

SOUND
1899 hegeh (1), *muttering; rumbling*
1902 higgâyôwn (1), *musical notation*

SORRY
1672 dâ'ag (1), *be anxious, be afraid*
2470 châlâh (1), to *be weak, sick, afflicted*
5110 nûwd (1), to *console*
6087 'âtsab (1), to *worry*
3076 lupĕō (9), to *be sad*
4036 pĕrilupŏs (1), *intensely sad*

SORT
1524 gîyl (1), *age, stage*
1697 dâbâr (1), *thing*
3660 kᵉnêmâ' (Ch.) (1), *so or thus*
3671 kânâph (2), *edge*
516 axiōs (1), *suitable*
3313 mĕrŏs (1), *division*
3697 hŏpŏiŏs (1), *what kind of, what sort of*

SORTS
4358 miklôwl (1), *perfection; splendidly*
4360 miklûl (1), *perfectly splendid garment*

SOSIPATER
4989 Sōsipatrŏs (1), *of a safe father*

SOSTHENES
4988 Sōsthĕnēs (2), *of safe strength*

SOTAI
5479 Çôwṭay (2), *roving*

SOTTISH
5530 çâkâl (1), *silly*

SOUGHT
1156 bᵉ'â' (Ch.) (1), to *seek or ask*
1158 bâ'âh (3), to *ask*
1245 bâqash (55), to *search; to strive after*
1875 dârash (25), to *seek or ask; to worship*
2713 châqar (1), to *examine, search*
8446 tûwr (1), to *wander*
327 anazētĕō (1), to *search out*
1567 ĕkzētĕō (1), to *seek*
1934 ĕpizētĕō (1), to *search (inquire) for*
2212 zētĕō (36), to *seek*

SOUL
5082 nᵉdîybâh (1), *nobility, i.e. reputation*
5315 nephesh (416), *soul*
5590 psuchē (39), *soul*

SOUL'S
5315 nephesh (1), *soul*

SOULS
5315 nephesh (58), *soul*
5397 nᵉshâmâh (1), *breath, life*
5590 psuchē (19), *soul*

1993 hâmâh (3), to *be in great commotion*
4832 marpê' (1), *cure; deliverance; placidity*
5674 'âbar (2), to *cross over; to transition*
6310 peh (1), *mouth*
6963 qôwl (39), *sound*
7032 qâl (Ch.) (4), *sound*
7321 rûwa' (2), to *shout*
8085 shâma' (3), to *hear*
8454 tûwshîyâh (3), *ability, help*
8549 tâmîym (1), *entire, complete; integrity*
8629 têqa' (1), *blast* of a *trumpet*
8643 t^e^rûw'âh (1), *battle-cry; clangor*
2279 *ēchŏs* (2), *roar*
4537 *salpizō* (5), to *sound a trumpet blast*
4995 *sōphrŏnismŏs* (1), *self-control*
5198 *hugiainō* (8), to *have sound health*
5199 *hugiēs* (1), *well*
5353 *phthŏggŏs* (1), *utterance; musical*
5456 *phōnē* (8), *sound*

SOUNDED
2690 châtsar (3), to *blow* the *trumpet*
2713 châqar (1), to *search*
8628 tâqa' (2), to *clatter, slap, drive, clasp*
1001 *bŏlizō* (2), to *heave a weight*
1096 *ginŏmai* (1), to *be*
1837 *ĕxēchĕŏmai* (1), to *echo forth*, i.e. *resound*
4537 *salpizō* (7), to *sound a trumpet blast*

SOUNDING
1906 hêd (1), *shout of joy*
1995 hâmôwn (1), *noise*
2690 châtsar (1), to *blow* the *trumpet*
8085 shâma' (1), to *hear*
8643 t^e^rûw'âh (2), *battle-cry; clangor*
2278 *ēchĕō* (1), to *reverberate, ring out*

SOUNDNESS
4974 m^e^thôm (3), *wholesomeness*
3647 *hŏlŏklēria* (1), *wholeness*

SOUNDS
5353 *phthŏggŏs* (1), *utterance; musical*

SOUR
1155 bôçer (4), *immature, sour* grapes
5493 çûwr (1), to *turn off*

SOUTH
1864 dârôwm (17), *south; south wind*
2315 cheder (1), *apartment, chamber*
3220 yâm (1), *sea; west*
3225 yâmîyn (3), *south*
4057 midbâr (1), *desert*
5045 negeb (97), *South*
8486 têymân (14), *south; southward; south* wind
3047 *lips* (1), *southwest*

3314 *mĕsēmbria* (1), *midday; south*
3558 *nŏtŏs* (7), *south*

SOUTHWARD
5045 negeb (17), *south*
8486 têymân (7), *south*

SOW
2232 zâra' (28), to *sow seed*; to *disseminate*
4687 *spĕirō* (8), to *scatter*, i.e. *sow* seed
5300 *hus* (1), *swine*

SOWED
2232 zâra' (2), to *sow seed*; to *disseminate*
4687 *spĕirō* (8), to *scatter*, i.e. *sow* seed

SOWEDST
2232 zâra' (1), to *sow seed*; to *disseminate*

SOWER
2232 zâra' (2), to *sow seed*; to *disseminate*
4687 *spĕirō* (6), to *scatter*, i.e. *sow* seed

SOWEST
4687 *spĕirō* (3), to *scatter*, i.e. *sow* seed

SOWETH
2232 zâra' (2), to *sow seed*; to *disseminate*
4900 mâshak (1), to *draw out*; to *be tall*
7971 shâlach (3), to *send away*
4687 *spĕirō* (9), to *scatter*, i.e. *sow* seed

SOWING
2221 zêrûwa' (1), *plant*
2233 zera' (1), *seed; fruit, plant, sowing-time*

SOWN
2221 zêrûwa' (1), *plant*
2232 zâra' (14), to *sow seed*; to *disseminate*
4218 mizrâ' (1), *planted field*
4687 *spĕirō* (15), to *scatter*, i.e. *sow* seed

SPACE
1366 g^e^bûwl (2), *border*
3117 yôwm (3), *day; time*
4390 mâlê' (1), to *fill*
4725 mâqôwm (1), *place*
5750 'ôwd (1), *again*
7281 rega' (1), *very short space* of time
7305 revach (1), *room*
7350 râchôwq (1), *remote*
575 apŏ (1), *from, away*
1024 *brachus* (1), *short*
1292 *diastēma* (1), *interval* of time
1339 *diïstēmi* (1), to *remove, intervene*
1909 *ĕpi* (3), *on, upon*
4158 *pŏdērēs* (1), *robe reaching* the *ankles*
5550 *chrŏnŏs* (2), *space of time, period*

SPAIN
4681 *Spania* (2), *Spania*

SPAKE
559 'âmar (109), to *say*
560 'âmar (Ch.) (1), to *say*

981 bâṭâ' (1), to *babble*
1696 dâbar (318), to *say*
4449 m^e^lal (Ch.) (2), to *speak, say*
5002 n^e^'ûm (1), *oracle*
6030 'ânâh (3), to *respond*
6032 'ănâh (Ch.) (14), to *respond, answer*
400 *anaphōnĕō* (1), to *exclaim*
483 *antilĕgō* (2), to *dispute, refuse*
626 *apŏlŏgĕŏmai* (1), to *give an account*
2036 *ĕpō* (30), to *speak*
2046 *ĕrĕō* (3), to *utter*
2551 *kakŏlŏgĕō* (1), to *revile, curse*
2980 *lalĕō* (72), to *talk*
3004 *lĕgō* (17), to *say*
4227 *Pŏudēs* (1), *modest*
4377 *prŏsphōnĕō* (3), to *address, exclaim*
4814 *sullalĕō* (1), to *talk together*, i.e. *converse*
5537 *chrēmatizō* (1), to *utter an oracle*

SPAKEST
559 'âmar (1), to *say*
1696 dâbar (8), to *speak*
1697 dâbâr (1), *word*

SPAN
2239 zereth (7), *span*
2949 ṭippûch (1), *nursing, caring for*

SPANNED
2946 ṭâphach (1), to *extend, spread out*

SPARE
2347 chûwç (14), to *be compassionate*
2550 châmal (13), to *spare, have pity on*
2820 châsak (3), to *refuse, spare, preserve*
5375 nâsâ' (3), to *lift up*
5545 çâlach (1), to *forgive*
8159 shâ'âh (1), to *inspect, consider*
4052 *pĕrissĕuō* (1), to *superabound*
5339 *phĕidŏmai* (4), to *treat leniently*

SPARED
2347 chûwç (2), to *be compassionate*
2550 châmal (4), to *spare, have pity on*
2820 châsak (2), to *refuse, spare, preserve*
5339 *phĕidŏmai* (4), to *treat leniently*

SPARETH
2550 châmal (1), to *spare, have pity on*
2820 châsak (3), to *refuse, spare, preserve*

SPARING
5339 *phĕidŏmai* (1), to *treat leniently*

SPARINGLY
5340 *phĕidŏmĕnōs* (2), *stingily, sparingly*

SPARK
5213 nîytsôwts (1), *spark*
7632 shâbîyb (1), *flame*

SPARKLED
5340 nâtsats (1), to *be bright*-colored

SPARKS
1121+7565 bên (1), *son, descendant; people*
2131 zîyqâh (2), *flash*
3590 kîydôwd (1), *spark*

SPARROW
6833 tsippôwr (2), *little hopping bird*

SPARROWS
4765 *strŏuthiŏn* (4), *little sparrow*

SPAT
4429 *ptuō* (1), to *spit*

SPEAK
559 'âmar (47), to *say*
560 'âmar (Ch.) (2), to *say*
1680 dâbab (1), to *move slowly*, i.e. *glide*
1696 dâbar (276), to *speak*
1897 hâgâh (3), to *murmur, utter a sound*
2790 chârash (1), to *engrave; to plow*
4405 millâh (1), *word; discourse; speech*
4448 mâlal (1), to *speak*
4449 m^e^lal (Ch.) (1), to *speak, say*
4911 mâshal (2), to *use figurative language*
5608 çâphar (2), to *recount an event*
5790 'ûwth (1), to *succor*
6030 'ânâh (5), to *answer*
6315 pûwach (1), to *utter*
7878 sîyach (4), to *ponder, muse aloud*
653 *apŏstŏmatizō* (1), to *question carefully*
669 *apŏphthĕggŏmai* (1), to *declare, address*
987 *blasphēmĕō* (5), to *speak impiously*
1097 *ginōskō* (1), to *know*
2036 *ĕpō* (6), to *speak*
2046 *ĕrĕō* (2), to *utter*
2551 *kakŏlŏgĕō* (1), to *revile, curse*
2635 *katalalĕō* (3), to *speak slander*
2980 *lalĕō* (101), to *talk*
3004 *lĕgō* (30), to *say*
4354 *prŏslalĕō* (1), *converse with*
5350 *phthĕggŏmai* (2), to *utter* a *clear sound*

SPEAKER
376+3956 'îysh (1), *man*
3056 *lŏgŏs* (1), *word*

SPEAKEST
1696 dâbar (11), to *speak*
2980 *lalĕō* (4), to *talk*
3004 *lĕgō* (2), to *say*

SPEAKETH
559 'âmar (7), to *say*
981 bâṭâ' (1), to *babble*
1696 dâbar (22), to *say*
1897 hâgâh (1), to *murmur, utter a sound*
4448 mâlal (1), to *speak*
5046 nâgad (1), to *announce*

6315 pûwach (5), to *utter*
6963 qôwl (1), *voice*
483 antilĕgō (1), to
  dispute, refuse
1256 dialĕgŏmai (1), to
  discuss
2036 ĕpō (2), to *speak*
2635 katalalĕō (2), to
  speak *slander*
2980 lalĕō (22), to *talk*
3004 lĕgō (4), to *say*

SPEAKING
1696 dâbar (37), to *speak*
2790 chârash (1), to
  engrave; to *plow*
4405 millâh (2), *word;*
  discourse; speech
4449 m^elal (Ch.) (1), to
  speak, say
226 alēthĕuō (1), to *be*
  true
987 blasphēmĕō (1), to
  speak impiously
988 blasphēmia (1),
  impious speech
2980 lalĕō (11), to *talk*
3004 lĕgō (1), to *say*
4180 pŏlulŏgia (1),
  prolixity, wordiness
4354 prŏslalĕō (1), to
  converse with
5350 phthĕggŏmai (1), to
  utter a clear sound
5573 psĕudŏlŏgŏs (1),
  promulgating
  erroneous doctrine

SPEAKINGS
2636 katalalia (1),
  defamation, slander

SPEAR
2595 chănîyth (34),
  lance, spear
3591 kîydôwn (5), *dart,*
  javelin
7013 qayin (1), *lance*
7420 rômach (3), iron
  pointed spear
3057 lŏgchē (1), *lance,*
  spear

SPEAR'S
2595 chănîyth (1), *lance,*
  spear

SPEARMEN
7070 qâneh (1), *reed*
1187 dĕxiŏlabŏs (1),
  guardsman

SPEARS
2595 chănîyth (6), *lance,*
  spear
6767 ts^elâtsal (1),
  whirring of wings
7420 rômach (9), iron
  pointed spear

SPECIAL
5459 ç^egullâh (1), *wealth*
3756+3858+5177 ŏu (1),
  no or not

SPECIALLY
3122 malista (5),
  particularly

SPECKLED
5348 nâqôd (9), *spotted*
6641 tsâbûwa' (1), *hyena*
8320 sâruq (1), *bright*
  red, bay colored

SPECTACLE
2302 thĕatrŏn (1),
  audience-room

SPED
4672 mâtsâ' (1), to *find*
  or *acquire;* to *occur*

SPEECH
562 'ômer (2), something
  said
565 'imrâh (7),
  something *said*
1697 dâbâr (7), *word*
1999 hămullâh (1),
  sound, roar, noise
3066 Y^ehûwdîyth (2), *in*
  the *Jewish language*
3948 leqach (1),
  instruction
4057 midbâr (1), *desert;*
  also *speech; mouth*
4405 millâh (4), *word;*
  discourse; speech
6310 peh (1), *mouth;*
  opening
8088 shêma' (1),
  something *heard*
8193 sâphâh (6), *lip,*
  language, speech
2981 lalia (3), *talk,*
  speech
3056 lŏgŏs (8), *word*
3072 Lukaŏnisti (1), *in*
  Lycaonian language
3424 mŏgilalŏs (1),
  hardly talking

SPEECHES
561 'êmer (2), something
  said
2420 chîydâh (1), *puzzle;*
  conundrum; maxim
4405 millâh (2), *word;*
  discourse; speech
2129 ĕulŏgia (1),
  benediction

SPEECHLESS
1769 ĕnnĕŏs (1),
  speechless, silent
2974 kōphŏs (1), *silent*
5392 phimŏō (1),
  to *restrain to silence*

SPEED
553 'âmats (2), to *be*
  strong; be *courageous*
629 'oçparnâ' (Ch.) (1),
  with diligence
4116 mâhar (2), to *hurry*
4120 m^ehêrâh (2), *hurry*
7136 qârâh (1), to *bring*
  about; to *impose*
5463 chairō (2),
  salutation, *"be well"*
5613+5033 hōs (1), *which,*
  how, i.e. *in that manner*

SPEEDILY
629 'oçparnâ' (Ch.) (4),
  with diligence
926 bâhal (1), to *hasten,*
  hurry anxiously
1980 hâlak (1), to *walk;*
  live a certain way
4116 mâhar (1), to *hurry;*
  promptly
4118 mahêr (4), *in a*
  hurry
4120 m^ehêrâh (4), *hurry;*
  promptly

4422 mâlaṭ (1), to *escape*
  as if by *slipperiness*
5674 'âbar (1), to *cross*
  over; to *transition*
1722+5034 ĕn (1), *in;*
  during; because of

SPEEDY
926 bâhal (1), to *hasten,*
  hurry anxiously

SPEND
3615 kâlâh (4), to *cease,*
  be finished, perish
8254 shâqal (1), to
  suspend in trade
1159 dapanaō (1), to
  incur cost; to *waste*
5551 chrŏnŏtribĕō (1), to
  procrastinate, linger

SPENDEST
4325 prŏsdapanaō (1), to
  expend additionally

SPENDETH
6 'âbad (1), *perish;*
  destroy
1104 bâla' (1), to
  swallow; to *destroy*
6213 'âsâh (1), to *do*

SPENT
235 'âzal (1), to *disappear*
3615 kâlâh (4), to
  complete, consume
7286 râdad (1), to
  conquer; to *overlay*
8552 tâmam (3), to
  complete, finish
1159 dapanaō (2), to
  incur cost; to *waste*
1230 diaginŏmai (1), to
  have time *elapse*
1550 ĕkdapanaō (1), to
  exhaust, be exhausted
2119 ĕukairĕō (1), to
  have opportunity
2827 klinō (1), to *slant*
4160 pŏiĕō (1), to *do*
4298 prŏkŏptō (1), to *go*
  ahead, advance
4321 prŏsanaliskō (1), to
  expend further

SPEWING
7022 qîyqâlôwn (1),
  disgrace

SPICE
1313 bâsâm (1), *balsam*
1314 besem (2), *spice;*
  fragrance; balsam
7402 râkal (1), to *travel*
7543 râqach (1), to
  perfume, blend spice

SPICED
7544 reqach (1), *spice*

SPICERY
5219 n^ekô'th (1), *gum,*
  (poss.) *styrax*

SPICES
1314 besem (22), *spice;*
  fragrance; balsam
5219 n^ekô'th (1), *gum,*
  (poss.) *styrax*
5561 çam (3), *aroma*
759 arōma (4), *scented*
  oils, perfumes, spices

SPIDER
8079 s^emâmîyth (1),
  lizard

SPIDER'S
5908 'akkâbîysh (2),
  web-making *spider*

SPIED
7200 râ'âh (5), to *see*
7270 râgal (1), to
  reconnoiter; to *slander*

SPIES
871 'Ăthârîym (1), *places*
  to step
7270 râgal (10), to
  reconnoiter; to *slander*
8104 shâmar (1), to
  watch
1455 ĕgkathĕtŏs (1), *spy*
2685 kataskŏpŏs (1),
  reconnoiterer, i.e. a *spy*

SPIKENARD
5373 nêrd (3), *nard*
3487+4101 nardŏs (2), oil
  from spike-*nard* root

SPILLED
7843 shâchath (1), to
  decay; to *ruin*
1632 ĕkchĕō (2), to *pour*
  forth; to *bestow*

SPILT
5064 nâgar (1), to *pour*
  out; to *deliver* over

SPIN
2901 ṭâvâh (1), to *spin*
  yarn
3514 nēthō (2), to *spin*
  yarn

SPINDLE
3601 kîyshôwr (1),
  spindle or shank

SPIRIT
178 'ôwb (7), *wineskin;*
  necromancer, medium
5397 n^eshâmâh (2),
  breath, life
7307 rûwach (226),
  breath; wind; life-spirit
7308 rûwach (Ch.) (8),
  breath; wind; life-spirit
4151 pnĕuma (255), *spirit*
5326 phantasma (2),
  spectre, apparition

SPIRITS
178 'ôwb (9), *wineskin;*
  necromancer, medium
7307 rûwach (5), *breath;*
  wind; life-spirit
4151 pnĕuma (32), *spirit*

SPIRITUAL
7307 rûwach (1), *breath;*
  wind; life-spirit
4151 pnĕuma (1), *spirit*
4152 pnĕumatikŏs (25),
  spiritual

SPIRITUALLY
3588+4151 hŏ (1), *"the,"*
  i.e. the definite article
4153 pnĕumatikŏs (2),
  non-physical

SPIT
3417 yâraq (2), to *spit*
7536 rôq (1), *spittle,*
  saliva
7556 râqaq (1), to *spit*
1716 ĕmptuō (5), to *spit*
  at
4429 ptuō (2), to *spit*

SPITE
3708 ka'aç (1), *vexation*

SPITEFULLY
5195 hubrizō (2), to
exercise violence, abuse

SPITTED
1716 ĕmptuō (1), to *spit
at*

SPITTING
7536 rôq (1), *spittle*

SPITTLE
7388 rîyr (1), *saliva; broth*
7536 rôq (1), *spittle*
4427 ptusma (1), *saliva*

SPOIL
957 baz (4), *plunder, loot*
961 bizzâh (6), *plunder*
962 bâzaz (8), to *plunder*
1500 gᵉzêlâh (1), *robbery,
stealing; things stolen*
2254 châbal (1), to
pervert, destroy
2488 châlîytsâh (1), *spoil,
booty of the dead*
2964 ṭereph (1), *fresh
torn prey*
4882 mᵉshûwçâh (1),
spoilation, loot
4933 mᵉshiççâh (3),
plunder
5337 nâtsal (1), to
deliver; to be snatched
6584 pâshaṭ (1), to *strip*
6906 qâba' (1), to
defraud, rob
7701 shôd (5), *violence,
ravage, destruction*
7703 shâdad (8), to
ravage
7921 shâkôl (1), to
miscarry
7997 shâlal (4), to *drop
or strip; to plunder*
7998 shâlâl (62), *booty*
8154 shâçâh (3), to
plunder
8155 shâçaç (1), to
plunder, ransack
1283 diarpazō (4),
plunder, rob
4812 sulagōgĕō (1), to
take captive as booty

SPOILED
957 baz (2), *plunder, loot*
958 bâzâ' (2), to *divide*
962 bâzaz (6), to *plunder*
1497 gâzal (7), to *rob*
5337 nâtsal (1), to
deliver; to be snatched
6906 qâba' (1), to *defraud*
7701 shôd (3), *violence,
ravage, destruction*
7703 shâdad (20), to
ravage
7758 shôwlâl (2),
stripped; captive
7997 shâlal (4), to *drop
or strip; to plunder*
8154 shâçâh (3), to
plunder
8155 shâçaç (3), to
plunder, ransack
554 apĕkduōmai (1), to
despoil

SPOILER
7701 shôd (1), *violence,
ravage, destruction*

7703 shâdad (8), to
ravage

SPOILERS
7703 shâdad (3), to
ravage
7843 shâchath (2), to
decay; to ruin
8154 shâçâh (2), to
plunder

SPOILEST
7703 shâdad (1), to
ravage

SPOILETH
1497 gâzal (1), to *rob*
6584 pâshaṭ (2), to *strip*
7703 shâdad (1), to
ravage

SPOILING
7701 shôd (3), *violence,
ravage, destruction*
7908 shᵉkôwl (1),
bereavement
724 harpagē (1), *pillage*

SPOILS
698 'orôbâh (1),
ambuscades
7998 shâlâl (2), *booty*
205 akrŏthiniŏn (1), *best
of the booty*
4661 skulŏn (1), *plunder*

SPOKEN
559 'âmar (15), to *say*
560 'âmar (Ch.) (1), to *say*
1696 dâbar (174), to
speak, say
1697 dâbâr (2), *word*
6310 peh (1), *mouth*
312 anaggĕllō (1), to
announce, report
369 anantirrhētŏs (1),
without objection
483 antilĕgō (2), to
dispute, refuse
987 blasphēmĕō (5), to
speak impiously
2036 ĕpō (19), to *speak*
2046 ĕrĕō (4), to *utter*
2605 kataggĕllō (1), to
proclaim, promulgate
2980 lalĕō (33), to *talk*
3004 lĕgō (7), to *say*
4280 prŏĕrĕō (2), to *say
already, predict*
4369 prŏstithēmi (1), to
repeat
4483 rhĕō (15), to *utter*

SPOKES
2840 chishshûr (1), *hub*

SPOKESMAN
1696 dâbar (1), to *speak*

SPOON
3709 kaph (12), *bowl;
handle*

SPOONS
3709 kaph (12), *bowl;
handle*

SPORT
6026 'ânag (1), to *be soft
or pliable*
6711 tsâchaq (1), to
laugh; to make sport of
7814 sᵉchôwq (1),
laughter; scorn
7832 sâchaq (3), to
laugh; to scorn; to play

SPORTING
6711 tsâchaq (1), to
laugh; to make sport of
1792 ĕntruphaŏ (1), to
revel in, carouse

SPOT
933 bôhaq (1), *white
scurf, rash*
934 bôhereth (9),
whitish, bright spot
3971 m'ûwm (3),
blemish; fault
8549 tâmîym (6), *entire,
complete; integrity*
299 amōmŏs (1),
unblemished, blameless
784 aspilŏs (3),
unblemished
4696 spilŏs (1), *stain or
blemish*, i.e. *defect*

SPOTS
934 bôhereth (2),
whitish, bright spot
2272 châbarbûrâh (1),
streak, stripe
4694 spilas (1), *ledge or
reef* of rock in the sea
4696 spilŏs (1), *stain or
blemish*, i.e. *defect*

SPOTTED
2921 ṭâlâ' (6), to *be
spotted or variegated*
4695 spilŏō (1), to *soil*

SPOUSE
3618 kallâh (6), *bride;
son's wife*

SPOUSES
3618 kallâh (2), *bride;
son's wife*

SPRANG
305 anabainō (1), to *go
up, rise*
393 anatĕllō (1), to *cause
to arise*
1080 gĕnnaō (1), to
procreate, regenerate
1530 ĕispēdaō (1), to
rush in
1816 ĕxanatĕllō (1), to
germinate, spring forth
4855 sumphuō (1), to
grow jointly
5453 phuō (1), to
germinate or grow

SPREAD
2219 zârâh (2), to *toss
about; to diffuse*
3212 yâlak (2), to *walk;
to live; to carry*
3318 yâtsâ' (1), to *go,
bring out*
3331 yâtsaʻ (2), to *strew*
4894 mishtôwach (2),
spreading-place
5186 nâṭâh (6), to *stretch
or spread out*
5203 nâṭash (4), to
disperse; to thrust off
5259 nâçak (1), to
interweave
6327 pûwts (2), to *dash
in pieces; to disperse*
6335 pûwsh (1), to
spread; to act proudly
6555 pârats (1), to *break
out*

SPRING
6566 pâras (49), to *break
apart, disperse, scatter*
6581 pâsâh (17), to
spread
6584 pâshaṭ (2), to *strip*
6605 pâthach (1), to *open
wide; to loosen, begin*
7286 râdad (1), to
conquer; to overlay
7554 râqa' (4), to *pound*
7849 shâṭach (3), to
expand
1268 dianĕmō (1), to
spread information
1310 diaphēmizō (1), to
spread news
1831 ĕxĕrchŏmai (2), to
issue; to leave
4766 strōnnumi (3),
strew, i.e. *spread*
5291 hupŏstrōnnumi (1),
to *strew underneath*

SPREADEST
4666 miphrâs (1),
expansion

SPREADETH
4969 mâthach (1), to
stretch out
5186 nâṭâh (1), to *stretch
or spread out*
6566 pâras (6), to *break
apart, disperse, scatter*
6576 parshêz (1), to
expand
6581 pâsâh (1), to *spread*
7502 râphad (1), to
spread a bed; to refresh
7554 râqa' (2), to *pound*
7971 shâlach (1), to *send
away*

SPREADING
4894 mishṭôwach (1),
spreading-place
5628 çârach (1), to
extend even to excess
6168 'ârâh (1), to *pour
out; demolish*
6524 pârach (1), to *break
forth; to bloom; to fly*

SPREADINGS
4666 miphrâs (1),
expansion

SPRIGS
2150 zalzal (1), *twig,
shoot*
6288 pᵉ'ôrâh (1), *foliage,
branches*

SPRING
1530 gal (1), *heap; ruins*
1876 dâshâ' (1), to *sprout
new plants*
3318 yâtsâ' (1), to *go,
bring out*
4161 môwtsâ' (2), *going
forth*
4726 mâqôwr (2), *flow of
liquids, or ideas*
5927 'âlâh (3), to *ascend,
be high, mount*
6524 pârach (1), to *break
forth; to bloom; to fly*
6779 tsâmach (10), to
sprout
6780 tsemach (1), *sprout,
branch*
985 blastanō (1), to *yield
fruit*

English

SPRINGETH
3318 yâtsâ' (1), to *go, bring out*
6524 pârach (1), to *break forth; to bloom; to fly*
7823 shâchîyç (2), *after-growth*

SPRINGING
2416 chay (1), *alive; raw; fresh; life*
6780 tsemach (1), *sprout, branch*
242 hallŏmai (1), to *jump up; to gush up*
5453 phuŏ (1), to *germinate or grow*

SPRINGS
794 'âshêdâh (3), *ravine*
1543 gullâh (4), *fountain; bowl or globe*
4002 mabbûwa' (2), *fountain, water spring*
4161 môwtsâ' (1), *going forth*
4599 ma'yân (2), *fountain; source*
4726 mâqôwr (1), *flow*
5033 nêbek (1), *fountain*

SPRINKLE
2236 zâraq (14), to *sprinkle, scatter*
5137 nâzâh (17), to *splash or sprinkle*

SPRINKLED
2236 zâraq (16), to *sprinkle, scatter*
5137 nâzâh (6), to *splash or sprinkle*
4472 rhantizō (3), to *asperse, sprinkle*

SPRINKLETH
2236 zâraq (1), to *sprinkle, scatter*
5137 nâzâh (1), to *splash or sprinkle*

SPRINKLING
4378 prŏschusis (1), *affusion, sprinkling*
4472 rhantizō (1), to *asperse, sprinkle*
4473 rhantismŏs (2), *aspersion, sprinkling*

SPROUT
2498 châlaph (1), to *spring up; to pierce*

SPRUNG
6524 pârach (1), to *break forth; to bloom; to fly*
6779 tsâmach (2), to *sprout*
305 anabainō (1), to *go up, rise*
393 anatĕllō (1), to *cause to arise*
985 blastanō (1), to *yield fruit*
1816 ĕxanatĕllō (1), *germinate, spring forth*
5453 phuŏ (1), to *germinate or grow*

SPUE
6958 qôw' (2), to *vomit*
7006 qâyâh (1), to *vomit*
1692 ĕmĕō (1), to *vomit*

SPUED
6958 qôw' (1), to *vomit*

SPUN
2901 tâvâh (1), to *spin yarn*
4299 matveh (1), *something spun*

SPUNGE
4699 spŏggŏs (3), *sponge*

SPY
7200 râ'âh (2), to *see*
7270 râgal (7), to *reconnoiter; to slander*
8446 tûwr (2), to *wander, meander*
2684 kataskŏpĕō (1), to *inspect, spy on*

SQUARE
7251 râba (3), to *be four sided, to be quadrate*

SQUARED
7251 râba' (1), to *be four sided, to be quadrate*

SQUARES
7253 reba' (2), *fourth*

STABILITY
530 'ĕmûwnâh (1), *fidelity; steadiness*

STABLE
3559 kûwn (1), to *set up: establish, fix, prepare*
5116 nâveh (1), *at home; lovely; home*

STABLISH
3559 kûwn (2), to *set up: establish, fix, prepare*
5324 nâtsab (1), to *station*
6965 qûwm (3), to *rise*
4741 stērizō (6), to *confirm*

STABLISHED
3559 kûwn (2), to *set up: establish, fix, prepare*
5975 'âmad (1), to *stand*
950 bĕbaiŏō (1), to *stabilitate, keep strong*

STABLISHETH
3559 kûwn (1), to *set up: establish, fix, prepare*
950 bĕbaiŏō (1), to *stabilitate, keep strong*

STACHYS
4720 Stachus (1), *head of grain*

STACKS
1430 gâdîysh (1), *stack of sheaves, shock of grain*

STACTE
5198 nâṭâph (1), *drop; aromatic gum resin*

STAFF
2671 chêts (1), *arrow; shaft of a spear*
4132 môwṭ (1), *pole; yoke*
4294 maṭṭeh (15), *tribe; rod, scepter; club*
4731 maqqêl (7), *shoot; stick; staff*
4938 mish'ênâh (11), *walking-stick*
6086 'êts (3), *wood*
6418 pelek (1), *spindle-whorl; crutch*
7626 shêbeṭ (2), *stick*
4464 rhabdŏs (2), *stick, rod*

STAGGER
5128 nûwa' (2), to *waver*
8582 tâ'âh (1), to *vacillate, i.e. reel*

STAGGERED
1252 diakrinō (1), to *decide; to hesitate*

STAGGERETH
8582 tâ'âh (1), to *vacillate, i.e. reel*

STAIN
1350 gâ'al (1), to *redeem; to be the next of kin*
1351 gâ'al (1), to *soil, stain; desecrate*
2490 châlal (1), to *profane, defile*

STAIRS
3883 lûwl (1), *spiral step*
4095 madrêgâh (1), *steep or inaccessible place*
4608 ma'âleh (1), *platform; stairs*
4609 ma'ălâh (5), *thought arising*
304 anabathmŏs (2), *stairway step*

STAKES
3489 yâthêd (2), *tent peg*

STALK
7054 qâmâh (1), *stalk of grain*
7070 qâneh (2), *reed*

STALKS
6086 'êts (1), *wood*

STALL
4770 marbêq (2), *stall*
5336 phatnē (1), *stall*

STALLED
75 'âbaç (1), to *feed*

STALLS
723 'urvâh (3), *herding-place*
7517 repheth (1), *stall for cattle*

STAMMERERS
5926 'illêg (1), *stuttering, stammering*

STAMMERING
3932 lâ'ag (1), to *deride; to speak unintelligibly*
3934 lâ'êg (1), *buffoon; foreigner*

STAMP
1854 dâqaq (1), to *crush*
7554 râqa' (1), to *pound*

STAMPED
1854 dâqaq (3), to *crush*
3807 kâthath (1), to *bruise, strike, beat*
7429 râmaç (2), to *tread*
7512 rephaç (Ch.) (2), to *trample; to ruin*
7554 râqa' (1), to *pound*

STAMPING
8161 sha'âṭâh (1), *clatter of hoofs*

STANCHED
2476 histēmi (1), to *stand, establish*

STAND
539 'âman (1), to *be firm, faithful, true; to trust*

STANDING
1481 gûwr (1), to *sojourn*
1826 dâmam (1), to *stop, cease; to perish*
3318 yâtsâ' (1), to *go, bring out*
3320 yâtsab (22), to *station, offer, continue*
5066 nâgash (1), to *be, come, bring near*
5324 nâtsab (9), to *station*
5564 çâmak (1), to *lean upon; take hold of*
5749 'ûwd (1), to *protest, testify; to restore*
5975 'âmad (144), to *stand*
5976 'âmad (1), to *shake*
6965 qûwm (31), to *rise*
6966 qûwm (Ch.) (2), to *rise*
7126 qârab (1), to *approach, bring near*
8617 t'qûwmâh (1), *resistfulness*
450 anistēmi (2), to *rise; to come back to life*
639 apŏrĕō (1), *be at a mental loss, be puzzled*
1453 ĕgĕirō (1), to *waken, i.e. rouse*
1510 ĕimi (1), I *exist*, I *am*
2476 histēmi (36), to *stand, establish*
3306 mĕnō (1), to *stay*
3936 paristēmi (3), to *stand beside, present*
4026 pĕriistēmi (1), to *stand around; to avoid*
4739 stēkō (7), to *persevere, be steadfast*

STANDARD
1714 degel (10), *flag, standard, banner*
5127 nûwç (1), to *vanish*
5251 nêç (7), *flag; signal*

STANDARD-BEARER
5264 nâçaç (1), to *gleam; to flutter a flag*

STANDARDS
1714 degel (3), *flag, standard, banner*

STANDEST
5975 'âmad (4), to *stand*
2476 histēmi (2), to *stand*

STANDETH
3559 kûwn (1), to *set up*
5324 nâtsab (4), to *station*
5975 'âmad (14), to *stand*
2476 histēmi (8), to *stand*
4739 stēkō (1), to *persevere, be steadfast*

STANDING
98 'ăgam (2), *marsh; pond; pool*
3320 yâtsab (1), to *station, offer, continue*
4613 mo'ŏmâd (1), *foothold*
4676 matstsêbâh (2), *column or stone*
5324 nâtsab (4), to *station*
5975 'âmad (12), to *stand*
5979 'emdâh (1), *station*
7054 qâmâh (5), *stalk*
2186 ĕphistēmi (1), to *be present; to approach*

2192+4174 ĕchō (1), *to have; hold; keep*
2476 histēmi (23), *to stand, establish*
3936 paristēmi (1), *to stand beside, present*
4921 sunistaō (1), *to set together; to stand near*

STANK
887 bâ'ash (4), *to smell bad*

STAR
3556 kôwkâb (2), *star*
792 astēr (11), *star*
798 astrŏn (1), *constellation; star*
5459 phôsphŏrŏs (1), *morning-star*

STARE
7200 râ'âh (1), *to see*

STARGAZERS
2374+3556 chôzeh (1), *beholder in vision*

STARS
3556 kôwkâb (34), *star*
3598 Kîymâh (1), *cluster of stars, the Pleiades*
792 astēr (13), *star*
798 astrŏn (3), *constellation; star*

STATE
3027 yâd (2), *hand; power*
3651 kên (1), *just; right, correct*
4612 ma'ămâd (1), *position; attendant*
4971 mathkôneth (1), *proportion*
5324 nâtsab (1), *to station*
6440 pânîym (1), *face; front*
3588+2596 hŏ (1), *"the,"* i.e. the definite article
3588+4012 hŏ (2), *"the,"* i.e. the definite article

STATELY
3520 kᵉbûwddâh (1), *magnificence, wealth*

STATION
4673 matstsâb (1), fixed *spot; office; post*

STATURE
4055 mad (1), *vesture, garment; carpet*
4060 middâh (4), *measure; portion*
6967 qôwmâh (7), *height*
2244 hēlikia (5), *maturity*

STATUTE
2706 chôq (13), *appointment; allotment*
2708 chuqqâh (20), to *delineate*
7010 qᵉyâm (Ch.) (2), *edict arising* in law

STATUTES
2706 chôq (73), *appointment; allotment*
2708 chuqqâh (58), to *delineate*
6490 piqqûwd (1), *mandate* of God, *Law*

STAVES
905 bad (37), *limb, member; bar; chief*

4133 môwṭâh (1), *pole; ox-bow; yoke*
4294 maṭṭeh (1), *tribe; rod, scepter; club*
4731 maqqêl (2), *shoot; stick; staff*
4938 mish'ênâh (1), *walking-stick*
3586 xulŏn (5), *timber*, i.e. a *stick, club*
4464 rhabdŏs (2), *stick, rod*

STAY
4102 mâhahh (1), *to be reluctant*
4223 mᵉchâ' (Ch.) (1), to *strike; to arrest*
4937 mish'ên (5), *support; protector*
5564 çâmak (2), to *lean* upon; *take hold* of
5702 'âgan (1), to *debar, withdraw*
5975 'âmad (10), to *stand*
6117 'âqab (1), *to seize by the heel; to circumvent*
6438 pinnâh (1), *pinnacle; chieftain*
7503 râphâh (3), to *slacken*
7901 shâkab (1), to *lie down*
8172 shâ'an (5), to *support, rely on*
8551 tâmak (1), to *obtain, keep fast*

STAYED
309 'âchar (1), to *remain*
2342 chûwl (2), to *wait; to pervert*
3176 yâchal (1), to *wait; to be patient, hope*
3322 yâtsag (1), to *place*
3607 kâlâ' (3), to *hold back or in; to prohibit*
5564 çâmak (1), to *lean* upon; *take hold of*
5975 'âmad (9), to *stand*
6113 'âtsar (7), to *hold back; to maintain*
7896 shîyth (1), to *place*
8156 shâça' (1), to *split or tear; to upbraid*
8551 tâmak (1), to *obtain, keep fast*
1907 ĕpĕchō (1), to *retain; to detain*
2722 katĕchō (2), to *hold down fast*

STAYETH
1898 hâgâh (1), to *remove*

STAYS
3027 yâd (4), *hand; power*

STEAD
8478 tachath (91), *in lieu of*
5228 hupĕr (2), *in behalf of*

STEADS
8478 tachath (1), *in lieu of*

STEADY
530 'ĕmûwnâh (1), *fidelity; steadiness*

STEAL
1589 gânab (11), to *thieve; to deceive*
2813 klĕptō (10), to *steal*

STEALETH
1589 gânab (3), to *thieve*

STEALING
1589 gânab (2), to *thieve*

STEALTH
1589 gânab (1), to *thieve*

STEDFAST
539 'âman (2), to *be firm, faithful, true; to trust*
3332 yâtsaq (1), to *pour out*
7011 qayâm (Ch.) (1), *permanent*
949 bĕbaiŏs (4), *stable, certain, binding*
1476 hĕdraiŏs (2), *immovable; steadfast*
4731 stĕrĕŏs (1), *solid, stable*

STEDFASTLY
553 'âmats (1), to *be strong; be courageous*
7760 sûwm (1), to *put*
816 atĕnizō (6), to *gaze intently*
4342 prŏskartĕrĕō (1), to *be constantly* diligent
4741 stĕrizō (1), to *turn resolutely; to confirm*

STEDFASTNESS
4733 stĕrĕōma (1), *stability, firmness*
4740 stĕrigmŏs (1), *stability; firmness*

STEEL
5154 nᵉchûwshâh (3), *copper; bronze*
5178 nᵉchôsheth (1), *copper; bronze*

STEEP
4095 madrêgâh (1), *steep* or *inaccessible place*
4174 môwrâd (1), *descent, slope*
2911 krĕmnŏs (3), *precipice, steep cliff*

STEM
1503 geza' (1), *stump*

STEP
838 'âshshûwr (1), *step*
6587 pesa' (1), *stride, step*

STEPHANAS
4734 Stĕphanas (3), *crowned*

STEPHANUS
4734 Stĕphanas (1), *crowned*

STEPHEN
4736 Stĕphanŏs (7), *wreath*

STEPPED
1684 ĕmbainō (1), to *embark; to reach*

STEPPETH
2597 katabainō (1), to *descend*

STEPS
838 'âshshûwr (5), *step*
1978 hâlîyk (1), *step*

4609 ma'ălâh (11), *thought arising*
4703 mits'âd (2), *step*
6119 'âqêb (1), *track, footprint; rear* position
6471 pa'am (4), *step*
6806 tsa'ad (11), *step*
2487 ichnŏs (3), *track*

STERN
4403 prumna (1), *stern*

STEWARD
376+834+5921 'îysh (1), *man; male; someone*
834+5921 'ăsher (3), *who*
1121+4943 bên (1), *son, descendant; people*
2012 ĕpitrŏpŏs (2), *manager, guardian*
3621 ŏikŏnŏmĕō (1), to *manage a household*
3622 ŏikŏnŏmia (3), *administration*
3623 ŏikŏnŏmŏs (2), *overseer, manager*

STEWARDS
8269 sar (1), *head, ruler*
3623 ŏikŏnŏmŏs (3), *overseer, manager*

STEWARDSHIP
3622 ŏikŏnŏmia (3), *administration*

STICK
1692 dâbaq (2), to *cling* or *adhere; to catch*
3920 lâkad (1), to *catch; to capture*
5181 nâchath (1), to *sink, descend; to press* down
6086 'êts (9), *wood*
8205 shᵉphîy (1), *bare hill or plain*

STICKETH
1695 dâbêq (1), *adhering, sticking to*

STICKS
6086 'êts (5), *wood*
5484 charin (1), *on account* of, *because* of

STIFF
6277 'âthâq (1), *impudent*
7185 qâshâh (1), to *be tough or severe*
7186 qâsheh (1), *severe*

STIFFENED
7185 qâshâh (1), to *be tough or severe*

STIFFHEARTED
2389+3820 châzâq (1), *strong; severe, hard*

STIFFNECKED
7185+6203 qâshâh (2), to *be tough or severe*
7186+6203 qâsheh (6), *severe*
4644 sklĕrŏtrachēlŏs (1), *obstinate*

STILL
1826 dâmam (6), to *be silent; to be astonished*
1827 dᵉmâmâh (1), *quiet*
2790 chârash (1), to *be silent; to be deaf*
2814 châshâh (2), to *hush or keep quiet*

STILLED
4496 mᵉnûwchâh (1), *peacefully; consolation*
5265 nâça' (1), to *start*
5750 'ôwd (19), *still; more*
5975 'âmad (3), to *stand*
7503 râphâh (1), to *slacken*
7673 shâbath (2), to *repose; to desist*
8252 shâqaṭ (2), to *repose*
2089 ĕti (4), *yet, still*
2476 histēmi (4), to *stand, establish*
4357 prŏsmĕnō (1), to *remain in a place*
5392 phimŏō (1), to *restrain to silence*

STILLED
2013 hâçâh (1), to *hush*
2814 châshâh (1), to *hush or keep quiet*

STILLEST
7623 shâbach (1), to *pacify*

STILLETH
7623 shâbach (1), to *pacify*

STING
2759 kĕntrŏn (2), *sting*

STINGETH
6567 pârash (1), to *wound*

STINGS
2759 kĕntrŏn (1), *sting*

STINK
887 bâ'ash (4), to *smell bad*
889 bᵉ'ôsh (3), *stench*
4716 maq (1), *putridity, stench*

STINKETH
887 bâ'ash (1), to *smell bad*
3605 ŏzō (1), to *stink*

STINKING
887 bâ'ash (1), to *smell bad*

STIR
5782 'ûwr (13), to *awake*
5927 'âlâh (1), to *ascend, be high, mount*
6965 qûwm (1), to *rise*
329 anazōpurĕō (1), to *re-enkindle, fan a flame*
1326 diĕgĕirō (3), to *arouse, stimulate*
5017 tarachŏs (2), *disturbance, tumult*

STIRRED
1624 gârâh (3), to *provoke to anger*
5375 nâsâ' (3), to *lift up*
5496 çûwth (2), to *stimulate; to seduce*
5782 'ûwr (5), to *awake*
5916 'âkar (1), to *disturb or afflict*
6965 qûwm (3), to *rise*
1892 ĕpĕgĕirō (1), to *excite against, stir up*
3947 parŏxunō (1), to *exasperate*
3951 parŏtrunō (1), to *stimulate to hostility*

STIRRED
4531 salĕuō (1), to *waver, i.e. agitate, rock, topple*
4787 sugkinĕō (1), to *excite to sedition*
4797 sugchĕō (1), to *throw into disorder*

STIRRETH
1624 gârâh (3), to *provoke to anger*
5782 'ûwr (4), to *awake*
383 anasĕiō (1), to *excite, stir up*

STIRS
8663 tᵉshú'âh (1), *crashing or clamor*

STOCK
944 bûwl (1), *produce*
1503 geza' (2), *stump*
6086 'êts (2), *wood*
6133 'êqer (1), *naturalized citizen*
1085 gĕnŏs (2), *kin*

STOCKS
4115 mahpeketh (2), *stocks for punishment*
5465 çad (2), *stocks*
5914 'ekeç (1), *anklet*
6086 'êts (2), (of) *wood*
6729 tsîynôq (1), *pillory*
3586 xulŏn (1), (of) *timber*

STOICKS
4770 Stŏïkŏs (1), *porch*

STOLE
1589 gânab (4), to *thieve*
2813 klĕptō (2), to *steal*

STOLEN
1589 gânab (14), to *thieve*

STOMACH'S
4751 stŏmachŏs (1), *stomach*

STOMACHER
6614 pᵉthîygîyl (1), fine *mantle for holidays*

STONE
68 'eben (104), *stone*
69 'eben (Ch.) (6), *stone*
1496 gâzîyth (3), *dressed stone*
5619 çâqal (7), to *throw large stones*
6697 tsûwr (1), *rock*
6872 tsᵉrôwr (1), *parcel; kernel or particle*
7275 râgam (10), to *cast stones*
8068 shâmîyr (1), *thorn; (poss.) diamond*
2642 katalithazō (1), to *stone to death*
2991 laxĕutŏs (1), *rock-quarried*
3034 lithazō (4), to *lapidate, to stone*
3035 lithinŏs (3), made of *stone*
3036 lithŏbŏlĕō (1), to *throw stones*
3037 lithŏs (36), *stone*
4074 Pĕtrŏs (1), piece of *rock*
5586 psēphŏs (2), pebble *stone*

STONE'S
3037 lithŏs (1), *stone*

STONED
5619 çâqal (8), to *throw large stones*
7275 râgam (5), to *cast stones*
3034 lithazō (4), to *lapidate, to stone*
3036 lithŏbŏlĕō (5), to *throw stones*

STONES
68 'eben (136), *stone*
69 'eben (Ch.) (2), *stone*
810 'eshek (1), *testicle*
1496 gâzîyth (4), *dressed stone*
2106 zâvîyth (1), *angle, corner* (as *projecting*)
2687 châtsâts (1), *gravel*
2789 cheres (1), piece of *earthenware pottery*
5553 çela' (1), craggy *rock; fortress*
5619 çâqal (1), to *throw large stones*
6344 pachad (1), male *testicle*
6697 tsûwr (1), *rock*
3036 lithŏbŏlĕō (1), to *throw stones*
3037 lithŏs (16), *stone*

STONESQUARERS
1382 Giblîy (1), *Gebalite*

STONEST
3036 lithŏbŏlĕō (2), to *throw stones*

STONING
5619 çâqal (1), to *throw large stones*

STONY
68 'eben (2), *stone*
5553 çela' (1), craggy *rock; fortress*
4075 pĕtrōdēs (4), *rocky*

STOOD
1826 dâmam (1), to *stop, cease; to perish*
3320 yâtsab (7), to *station, offer, continue*
3559 kûwn (1), to *set up*
4673 matstsâb (2), fixed *spot; office; post*
5324 nâtsab (19), to *station*
5568 çâmar (1), to *bristle*
5975 'âmad (189), to *stand*
5977 'ômed (1), fixed *spot*
6965 qûwm (15), to *rise*
6966 qûwm (Ch.) (4), to *rise*
450 anistēmi (7), to *rise; to come back to life*
2186 ĕphistēmi (5), to *be present; to approach*
2476 histēmi (60), to *stand, establish*
2944 kuklŏō (1), to *surround, encircle*
3936 paristēmi (14), to *stand beside, present*
4026 pĕriistēmi (1), to *stand around; to avoid*
4836 sumparaginŏmai (1), to *convene; to appear in aid*
4921 sunistaō (1), to *set together*

STOODEST
5324 nâtsab (1), to *station*
5975 'âmad (2), to *stand*

STOOL
3678 kiççê' (1), *throne*

STOOLS
70 'ôben (1), potter's *wheel; midwife's stool*

STOOP
7164 qâraç (1), to *hunch*
7812 shâchâh (1), to *prostrate in homage*
7817 shâchach (1), to *sink or depress*
2955 kuptō (1), to *bend forward, stoop down*

STOOPED
3486 yâshêsh (1), *gray-haired, aged*
3766 kâra' (1), to *prostrate*
6915 qâdad (2), to *bend*
2955 kuptō (2), to *bend forward, stoop down*
3879 parakuptō (1), to *lean over to peer within*

STOOPETH
7164 qâraç (1), to *hunch*

STOOPING
3879 parakuptō (2), to *lean overto peer within*

STOP
2629 châçam (1), to *muzzle; block*
5462 çâgar (1), to *shut up*
5640 çâtham (2), to *stop up; to repair*
6113 'âtsar (1), to *hold back; to maintain, rule*
7092 qâphats (1), to *draw together, to leap; to die*
5420 phrassō (1), to *fence or enclose, to block up*

STOPPED
2856 châtham (1), to *close up; to affix a seal*
3513 kâbad (1), to *be heavy, severe, dull*
5534 çâkar (2), to *shut up*
5640 çâtham (6), to *stop up; to repair*
8610 tâphas (1), to *manipulate, i.e. seize*
1998 ĕpisuntrĕchō (1), to *hasten together upon*
4912 sunĕchō (1), to *hold together*
5420 phrassō (2), to *fence or enclose, to block up*

STOPPETH
331 'âṭam (3), to *close*
7092 qâphats (1), to *draw together, to leap; to die*

STORE
214 'ôwtsâr (1), *depository*
686 'âtsar (3), to *store up*
1995 hâmôwn (2), *noise, tumult; many, crowd*
3462 yâshên (1), to *sleep; to grow old, stale*
4543 miçkᵉnâh (5), *storage-magazine*
4863 mish'ereth (2), *kneading-trough*

English

6487 piqqâdôwn (1), *deposit*
7235 râbâh (1), to *increase*
8498 tᵉkûwnâh (1), *structure; equipage*
597 apŏthēsaurizō (1), to store *treasure away*
2343 thēsaurizō (2), to *amass, reserve, store up*

STOREHOUSE
214 'ôwtsâr (1), *depository*
5009 tamēiŏn (1), *room*

STOREHOUSES
214 'ôwtsâr (2), *depository*
618 'âçâm (1), *storehouse, barn*
834 'âsher (1), *who, which, what, that*
3965 ma'ăbûwç (1), *granary, barn*
4543 miçkᵉnâh (1), storage-*magazine*

STORIES
4609 ma'ălâh (1), *thought* arising

STORK
2624 chăçîydâh (5), *stork*

STORM
2230 zerem (3), *flood*
5492 çûwphâh (3), *hurricane* wind
5584 çâ'âh (1), to *rush*
5591 ça'ar (1), *hurricane*
7722 shôw' (1), *tempest; devastation*
8178 sa'ar (1), *tempest*
8183 sᵉ'ârâh (1), *hurricane* wind
2978 lailaps (2), *whirlwind; hurricane*

STORMY
5591 ça'ar (4), *hurricane*

STORY
4097 midrâsh (2), *treatise*

STOUT
1433 gôdel (1), *magnitude, majesty*
2388 châzaq (1), to *be strong; courageous*
7229 rab (Ch.) (1), *great*

STOUTHEARTED
47+3820 'abbîyr (2), *mighty*

STOUTNESS
1433 gôdel (1), *magnitude, majesty*

STRAIGHT
3474 yâshar (9), to *be straight; to make right*
4334 mîyshôwr (2), *plain; justice*
5676 'êber (3), *opposite*
8626 tâqan (2), to *straighten; to compose*
461 anŏrthŏō (1), to *straighten up*
2113 ĕuthudrŏmĕō (2), to *sail direct*
2116 ĕuthunō (1), to *straighten or level*
2117 ĕuthus (5), *at once, immediately*

3717 ŏrthŏs (1), *straight*

STRAIGHTWAY
3651 kên (1), *just; right*
4116 mâhar (1), to *hurry*
6258 'attâh (1), *now*
6597 pith'ôwm (1), *instantly, suddenly*
1824 ĕxautēs (1), *instantly, at once*
2112 ĕuthĕŏs (32), *at once or soon*
2117 ĕuthus (2), *at once*
3916 parachrēma (3), *instantly, immediately*

STRAIN
1368 diulizō (1), to *strain out*

STRAIT
6862 tsar (3), *trouble*
6887 tsârar (3), to *cramp*
4728 stĕnŏs (3), *narrow*
4912 sunĕchō (1), to *hold together*

STRAITEN
6693 tsûwq (1), to *oppress*

STRAITENED
680 'âtsal (1), to *select; refuse; narrow*
3334 yâtsar (2), to *be in distress*
4164 mûwtsaq (1), *distress*
7114 qâtsar (1), to *curtail, cut short*
4729 stĕnŏchŏrĕŏ (2), to *hem in closely*
4912 sunĕchō (1), to *hold together*

STRAITENETH
5148 nâchâh (1), to *guide*

STRAITEST
196 akribĕstatŏs (1), *most exact, very strict*

STRAITLY
547 apĕilē (1), *menace, threat*
4183 pŏlus (2), *much*

STRAITNESS
4164 mûwtsaq (1), *distress*
4689 mâtsôwq (4), *confinement; disability*

STRAITS
3334 yâtsar (1), to *be in distress*
4712 mêtsar (1), *trouble*

STRAKE
5465 chalaŏ (1), to *lower* as into a *void*

STRAKES
6479 pᵉtsâlâh (1), *peeling*
8258 shᵉqa'rûwrâh (1), *depression*

STRANGE
312 'achêr (1), *different*
1970 hâkar (1), (poss.) to *injure*
2114 zûwr (22), to *be foreign, strange*
3937 lâ'az (1), to *speak in a foreign tongue*
5234 nâkar (1), to *treat as a foreigner*
5235 neker (1), *calamity*

5236 nêkâr (16), *foreigner; heathendom*
5237 nokrîy (20), *foreign; non-relative; different*
6012 'âmêq (2), *obscure*
245 allŏtriŏs (2), *not one's own*
1854 ĕxō (1), *out, outside*
2087 hĕtĕrŏs (1), *different*
3579 xĕnizō (3), to *be a guest; to be strange*
3581 xĕnŏs (3), *alien*
3861 paradŏxŏs (1), *extraordinary*

STRANGELY
5234 nâkar (1), to *treat as a foreigner*

STRANGER
376+1616 'îysh (1), *man; male; someone*
376+2114 'îysh (3), *man; male; someone*
376+5237 'îysh (2), *man; male; someone*
1121+5235 bên (3), *son, descendant; people*
1121+5236 bên (2), *son, descendant; people*
1616 gêr (69), *foreigner*
2114 zûwr (18), to *be foreign, strange*
4033 mâgûwr (3), *abode*
5235 neker (1), *calamity*
5236 nêkâr (3), *foreigner*
5237 nokrîy (14), *foreign*
8453 tôwshâb (2), *temporary dweller*
241 allŏgĕnēs (1), *foreign, i.e. not a Jew*
245 allŏtriŏs (1), *not one's own*
3581 xĕnŏs (4), *alien*
3939 parŏikĕō (1), to *reside as a foreigner*
3941 parŏikŏs (1), *strange; stranger*

STRANGER'S
1121+5236 bên (1), *son, descendant; people*
1616 gêr (1), *foreigner*

STRANGERS
582+1616 'ĕnôwsh (1), *man; person, human*
1121+5236 bên (6), *son, descendant; people*
1481 gûwr (6), to *sojourn*
1616 gêr (18), *stranger*
2114 zûwr (26), to *be foreign, strange*
4033 mâgûwr (1), *abode*
5236 nêkâr (3), *foreigner*
5237 nokrîy (2), *foreign*
8453 tôwshâb (1), *temporary dweller*
245 allŏtriŏs (3), *not one's own*
1722+3940 ĕn (1), *in; during; because of*
1927 ĕpidēmĕō (1), to *make oneself at home*
3580 xĕnŏdŏchĕō (1), to *be hospitable*
3581 xĕnŏs (4), *alien*
3927 parepidēmŏs (1), *resident foreigner*
3941 parŏikŏs (1), *strange; stranger*

5381 philŏnĕxia (1), *hospitableness to strangers*

STRANGERS'
2114 zûwr (1), to *be foreign, strange*

STRANGLED
2614 chânaq (1), to *choke*
4156 pniktŏs (3), animal *choked* to death

STRANGLING
4267 machănaq (1), *choking, strangling*

STRAW
4963 mathbên (1), *straw*
8401 teben (15), *threshed stalks* of grain

STRAWED
2219 zârâh (1), to *toss about; to winnow*
1287 diaskŏrpizō (2), to *scatter; to squander*
4766 strŏnnumi (2), *strew*, i.e. *spread*

STREAM
650 'âphîyq (1), *valley; stream; mighty, strong*
793 'eshed (1), *stream*
5103 nᵉhar (Ch.) (1), *river*; Euphrates *River*
5158 nachal (7), *valley*
4215 pŏtamŏs (2), *current, brook*

STREAMS
650 'âphîyq (1), *valley; stream; mighty, strong*
2975 yᵉ'ôr (1), Nile *River*; Tigris *River*
2988 yâbâl (1), *stream*
5104 nâhâr (2), *stream*
5140 nâzal (2), to *drip*
5158 nachal (4), *valley*
6388 peleg (1), small irrigation *channel*

STREET
2351 chûwts (8), *outside, outdoors; open market*
2351+6440 chûwts (1), *outside, outdoors*
7339 rᵉchôb (22), *myriad*
7784 shûwq (1), *street*
4113 platĕia (3), *wide, open square*
4505 rhumē (2), *alley* or crowded *avenue*

STREETS
2351 chûwts (34), *outside, outdoors*
7339 rᵉchôb (19), *myriad*
7784 shûwq (3), *street*
58 agŏra (1), *town-square, market*
4113 platĕia (6), *wide, open square*
4505 rhumē (1), *alley* or crowded *avenue*

STRENGTH
193 'ûwl (1), *powerful; mighty*
202 'ôwn (7), *ability, power; wealth*
353 'ĕyâl (1), *strength*
360 'ĕyâlûwth (1), *power*
386 'êythân (2), *never-failing; eternal*

English

556 'amtsâh (1),
strength, force
905 bad (2), *limb,
member; bar; chief*
1082 bâlag (1), to *be
strengthened; invade*
1369 gᵉbûwrâh (17),
force; valor; victory
1679 dôbe' (1), *leisurely*
2220 zᵉrôwa' (1), *arm;
foreleg; force, power*
2388 châzaq (1), to *be
strong; courageous*
2391 chêzeq (1), *help*
2392 chôzeq (5), *power*
2394 chozqâh (1),
vehemence, harshness
2428 chayil (11), *army;
wealth; virtue; strength*
2633 chôçen (2), *wealth,
stored riches*
3027 yâd (1), *hand; power*
3581 kôach (57), *force,
might; strength*
4206 mâzîyach (2), *belt*
4581 mâ'ôwz (24),
fortified place; defense
5326 nitsbâh (Ch.) (1),
firmness, hardness
5331 netsach (2),
splendor; lasting
5332 nêtsach (1), blood
(as if *red juice*)
5797 'ôz (60), *strength*
5807 'ĕzûwz (2),
forcibleness
6106 'etsem (1), *bone;
body; substance*
6109 'otsmâh (2),
powerfulness
6697 tsûwr (5), *rock*
7293 rahab (1), *bluster*
7296 rôhab (1), *pride*
8443 tôw'âphâh (3),
treasure; speed
8510 têl (1), *mound*
8632 tᵉqôph (Ch.) (1),
power
8633 tôqeph (1), *might*
772 asthĕnĕs (1),
strengthless, weak
1411 dunamis (7), *force,
power, miracle*
1743 ĕndunamŏō (1), to
empower, strengthen
1849 ĕxŏusia (1),
authority, power, right
2479 ischus (4),
forcefulness, power
2480 ischuō (1), to *have
or exercise force*
2904 kratŏs (1), *vigor,
strength*
4732 stĕrĕŏō (1), to *be,
become strong*

STRENGTHEN
553 'âmats (7), to *be
strong; be courageous*
1396 gâbar (2), to *be
strong; to prevail*
2388 châzaq (14), to *be
strong; courageous*
4581 mâ'ôwz (1), *fortified
place; defense*
5582 çâ'ad (2), to *support*
5810 'âzaz (2), to *be
stout; be bold*
6965 qûwm (1), to *rise*

4599 sthĕnŏō (1), to
strengthen
4741 stĕrizō (2), to *turn
resolutely; to confirm*

STRENGTHENED
553 'âmats (3), to *be
strong; be courageous*
2388 châzaq (28), to *be
strong; courageous*
2394 chozqâh (1),
vehemence, harshness
5810 'âzaz (3), to *be
stout; be bold*
1412 dunamŏō (1), to
enable, strengthen
1743 ĕndunamŏō (1), to
empower, strengthen
1765 ĕnischuō (1), to
invigorate oneself
2901 krataiŏō (1),
increase in vigor

STRENGTHENEDST
7292 râhab (1), to *urge,
importune, embolden*

STRENGTHENETH
553 'âmats (2), to *be
strong; be courageous*
1082 bâlag (1), to *be
strengthened*
1396 gâbar (1), to *be
strong; to prevail*
5582 çâ'ad (1), to *support*
5810 'âzaz (1), to *be
stout; be bold*
1743 ĕndunamŏō (1), to
empower, strengthen

STRENGTHENING
1765 ĕnischuō (1), to
invigorate oneself
1991 ĕpistĕrizō (1), to
re-establish, strengthen

STRETCH
5186 nâṭâh (28), to
stretch or spread out
5628 çârach (1), to
extend even to excess
6566 pâras (4), to *break
apart, disperse, scatter*
7323 rûwts (1), to *run*
7971 shâlach (10), to
send away
8311 sâra' (1), to *be
deformed*
1614 ĕktĕinō (4), to
stretch
5239 hupĕrĕktĕinō (1), to
extend inordinately

STRETCHED
1457 gâhar (2), to
prostrate, bow down
4058 mâdad (1), to *be
extended*
4900 mâshak (1), to *draw
out; to be tall*
5186 nâṭâh (47), to
stretch or spread out
5203 nâṭash (1), to
disperse; to thrust off
5628 çârach (1), to
extend even to excess
6504 pârad (1), to *spread
or separate*
6566 pâras (2), to *break
apart, disperse, scatter*
7554 râqa' (1), to *pound*
7849 shâṭach (1), to
expand

7971 shâlach (4), to *send
away*
1600 ĕkpĕtannumi (1), to
extend, spread out
1614 ĕktĕinō (7), to
stretch
1911 ĕpiballō (1), to
throw upon

STRETCHEDST
5186 nâṭâh (1), to *stretch*

STRETCHEST
5186 nâṭâh (1), to *stretch*

STRETCHETH
5186 nâṭâh (6), to *stretch*
6566 pâras (1), to *break
apart, disperse, scatter*

STRETCHING
4298 muṭṭâh (1),
expansion, extending
1614 ĕktĕinō (1), to
stretch

STRICKEN
935 bôw' (7), to *go, come*
1856 dâqar (1), to *stab,
pierce; to starve*
2498 châlaph (1), to
pierce; to change
5060 nâga' (1), to *strike*
5061 nega' (1), *infliction,
affliction; leprous spot*
5218 nâkê' (1), *smitten*
5221 nâkâh (3), to *strike,
kill*
8628 tâqa' (1), to *slap*
4260 prŏbainō (2), to
advance

STRIFE
1777 dîyn (1), to *judge; to
strive or contend for*
1779 dîyn (1), *judge;
judgment; law suit*
4066 mâdôwn (7),
contest or quarrel
4683 matstsâh (1),
quarrel
4808 mᵉrîybâh (5),
quarrel
7379 rîyb (14), *contest*
485 antilŏgia (1),
dispute, disobedience
2052 ĕrithĕia (4), *faction,
strife, selfish ambition*
2054 ĕris (4), *quarrel*, i.e.
wrangling
5379 philŏnĕikia (1),
dispute, strife

STRIFES
4090 mᵉdân (1), *contest
or quarrel*
2052 ĕrithĕia (1), *faction,
strife, selfish ambition*
3055 lŏgŏmachia (1),
disputation
3163 machē (1),
controversy, conflict

STRIKE
2498 châlaph (1), *too
pierce; to change*
4272 mâchats (1), to
crush; to subdue
5060 nâga' (1), to *strike*
5130 nûwph (1), to
quiver, vibrate, rock
5221 nâkâh (1), to *strike,
kill*

5344 nâqab (1), to
puncture, perforate
5414 nâthan (1), to *give*
6398 pâlach (1), to *pierce*
8628 tâqa' (2), to *slap*
906 ballō (1), to *throw*

STRIKER
4131 plēktēs (2),
pugnacious

STRIKETH
5606 çâphaq (1), to *clap
the hands*
8628 tâqa' (1), to *clatter,
slap, drive, clasp*
3817 paiō (1), to *hit*

STRING
3499 yether (1),
remainder; small rope
1199 dĕsmŏn (1),
shackle; impediment

STRINGED
4482 mên (1), *part;
musical chord*
5058 nᵉgîynâh (2),
stringed instrument

STRINGS
4340 mêythâr (1),
tent-cord; bow-string

STRIP
6584 pâshaṭ (7), to *strip*

STRIPE
2250 chabbûwrâh (1),
weal, bruise

STRIPES
2250 chabbûwrâh (1),
weal, bruise
4112 mahălummâh (1),
blow
4347 makkâh (2), *blow;
wound; pestilence*
5061 nega' (2), *infliction,
affliction; leprous spot*
5221 nâkâh (2), to *strike,
kill*
3468 mōlōps (1), *black
eye or blow-mark, welt*
4127 plēgē (7), *stroke;
wound; calamity*

STRIPLING
5958 'elem (1), *lad,
young man*

STRIPPED
5337 nâtsal (2), to
deliver; to be snatched
6584 pâshaṭ (6), to *strip*
7758 shôwlâl (1),
bare-foot; stripped
1562 ĕkduō (2), to *divest*

STRIPT
6584 pâshaṭ (1), to *strip*

STRIVE
1777 dîyn (1), to *judge; to
strive or contend for*
3401 yârîyb (1),
contentious; adversary
5327 nâtsâh (2), to
quarrel, fight
7378 rîyb (9), to *hold a
controversy; to defend*
7379 rîyb (1), *contest*
75 agōnizŏmai (1), to
struggle; to contend
118 athlĕō (2), to
contend in games

2051 ĕrizō (1), to wrangle, quarrel
3054 lŏgŏmachĕō (1), to be disputatious
3164 machŏmai (1), to quarrel, dispute
4865 sunagōnizŏmai (1), to struggle with

STRIVED
5389 philŏtimĕŏmai (1), eager or earnest to do

STRIVEN
1624 gârâh (1), to provoke to anger

STRIVETH
7378 rîyb (1), to hold a controversy; to defend
75 agōnizŏmai (1), to struggle; to contend

STRIVING
75 agōnizŏmai (1), to struggle; to contend
464 antagōnizŏmai (1), to struggle against
4866 sunathlĕō (1), to wrestle with

STRIVINGS
7379 rîyb (2), contest
3163 machē (1), controversy, conflict

STROKE
3027 yâd (1), hand; power
4046 maggêphâh (1), pestilence; defeat
4273 machats (1), contusion
4347 makkâh (2), blow; wound; pestilence
5061 nega' (3), infliction, affliction; leprous spot
5607 çêpheq (1), satiety

STROKES
4112 mahălummâh (1), blow

STRONG
47 'abbîyr (3), mighty
386 'êythân (5), never-failing; eternal
410 'êl (1), mighty
533 'ammîyts (4), strong; mighty; brave
553 'âmats (4), to be strong; be courageous
559 'âmar (1), to say
650 'âphîyq (1), valley; stream; mighty, strong
1219 bâtsar (1), to be inaccessible
1225 bitstsârôwn (1), fortress
1368 gibbôwr (5), powerful; great warrior
1634 gerem (1), bone; self
2364 Chûwshâh (1), haste
2388 châzaq (47), to be strong; courageous
2389 châzâq (26), strong; severe, hard, violent
2393 chezqâh (1), power
2394 chozqâh (1), vehemence, harshness
2428 chayil (5), army; wealth; virtue; strength
2626 châçîyn (1), mighty
2634 châçôn (1), strong

3524 kabbîyr (1), mighty; aged; mighty
4013 mibtsâr (14), fortification; defender
4581 mâ'ôwz (5), fortified place; defense
4679 mᵉtsad (5), stronghold
4686 mâtsûwd (2), net or capture; fastness
4692 mâtsôwr (3), siege-mound; distress
4694 mᵉtsûwrâh (1), rampart, fortification
5553 çela' (1), craggy rock; fortress
5794 'az (12), strong, vehement, harsh
5797 'ôz (17), strength
5808 'izzûwz (1), forcible; army
5810 'âzaz (1), to be stout; be bold
6076 'ôphel (1), tumor; fortress
6099 'âtsûwm (13), powerful; numerous
6105 'âtsam (4), to be, make powerful
6108 'ôtsem (1), power; framework of the body
6110 'atstsûmâh (1), defensive argument
6184 'ârîyts (1), powerful or tyrannical
6339 pâzaz (1), to solidify by refining; to spring
6697 tsûwr (1), rock
7682 sâgab (1), to be safe, strong
7941 shêkâr (1), liquor
8624 taqqîyph (Ch.) (3), powerful
8631 tᵉqêph (Ch.) (3), to become, make mighty
1415 dunatŏs (3), powerful or capable
1743 ĕndunamŏō (4), to empower, strengthen
1753 ĕnĕrgĕia (1), energy, power
2478 ischurŏs (11), forcible, powerful
2901 krataiŏō (3), increase in vigor
3173 mĕgas (1), great
3794 ŏchurōma (1), fortress, stronghold
4608 sikĕra (1), intoxicant
4731 stĕrĕŏs (2), solid
4732 stĕrĕŏō (1), to be, become strong

STRONGER
553 'âmats (2), to be strong; be courageous
555 'ômets (1), strength
1396 gâbar (1), to be strong; to prevail
2388 châzaq (6), to be strong; courageous
2389 châzâq (1), strong
2390 châzêq (1), powerful; loud
5794 'az (1), strong
6105 'âtsam (1), to be, make powerful
7194 qâshar (2), to tie, bind

2478 ischurŏs (3), forcible, powerful

STRONGEST
1368 gibbôwr (1), powerful; great warrior

STROVE
1519 gîyach (Ch.) (1), to rush forth
5327 nâtsâh (6), to quarrel, fight
6229 'âsaq (1), to quarrel
7378 rîyb (3), to hold a controversy; to defend
1264 diamachŏmai (1), to fight fiercely
3164 machŏmai (2), to war, quarrel, dispute

STROWED
2236 zâraq (1), to scatter

STRUCK
5062 nâgaph (2), to inflict a disease; strike
5221 nâkâh (1), to strike
8138 shânâh (1), to fold
1325+4475 didōmi (1), to give
3960 patassō (1), to strike
5180 tuptō (1), to strike

STRUGGLED
7533 râtsats (1), to crack in pieces, smash

STUBBLE
7179 qash (16), dry straw
8401 teben (1), threshed stalks of grain
2562 kalamē (1), stubble

STUBBORN
5637 çârar (4), to be refractory, stubborn
7186 qâsheh (1), severe

STUBBORNNESS
6484 pâtsar (1), to stun or dull
7190 qᵉshîy (1), obstinacy

STUCK
1692 dâbaq (1), to cling or adhere; to catch
4600 mâ'ak (1), to press
2043 ĕrĕidō (1), to make immovable

STUDIETH
1897 hâgâh (2), to murmur, ponder

STUDS
5351 nᵉquddâh (1), ornamental boss

STUDY
3854 lahag (1), mental application
4704 spŏudazō (1), to make effort
5389 philŏtimĕŏmai (1), eager or earnest to do

STUFF
3627 kᵉlîy (14), thing
4399 mᵉlâ'kâh (1), work
4632 skĕuŏs (1), vessel

STUMBLE
3782 kâshal (15), to stumble
5062 nâgaph (2), to inflict a disease; strike
6328 pûwq (1), to waver

4350 prŏskŏptō (1), to trip up; to strike

STUMBLED
3782 kâshal (3), to totter
8058 shâmaṭ (1), to jostle; to let alone
4350 prŏskŏptō (1), to trip up; to strike
4417 ptaiō (1), to trip up

STUMBLETH
3782 kâshal (1), to totter
4350 prŏskŏptō (3), to trip up; to strike

STUMBLING
5063 negeph (1), trip
4625 skandalŏn (1), snare

STUMBLINGBLOCK
4383 mikshôwl (7), stumbling-block
4348 prŏskŏmma (2), occasion of apostasy
4625 skandalŏn (3), snare

STUMBLINGBLOCKS
4383 mikshôwl (1), stumbling-block
4384 makshêlâh (1), stumbling-block

STUMBLINGSTONE
3037+4348 lithŏs (2), stone

STUMP
6136 'iqqar (Ch.) (3), stock

SUAH
5477 Çûwach (1), sweeping

SUBDUE
1696 dâbar (1), to subdue
3533 kâbash (3), to conquer, subjugate
3665 kâna' (1), to humiliate, subdue
7286 râdad (1), to conquer; to overlay
8214 shᵉphal (Ch.) (1), to humiliate
5293 hupŏtassō (1), to subordinate; to obey

SUBDUED
3381 yârad (1), to descend
3533 kâbash (5), to conquer, subjugate
3665 kâna' (9), to humiliate, subdue
3766 kâra' (1), to prostrate
2610 katagōnizŏmai (1), to overcome, defeat
5293 hupŏtassō (1), to subordinate; to obey

SUBDUEDST
3665 kâna' (1), to humiliate, subdue

SUBDUETH
1696 dâbar (1), to subdue
2827 châshal (Ch.) (1), to crush, pulverize
7286 râdad (1), to conquer; to overlay

SUBJECT
1379 dŏgmatizō (1), to submit to a certain rule

English

SUBJECTED
1777 ĕnŏchŏs (1), *liable*
3663 hŏmŏiŏpathēs (1), *similarly affected*
5293 hupŏtassō (14), *to subordinate; to obey*

SUBJECTED
5293 hupŏtassō (1), *to subordinate; to obey*

SUBJECTION
3533 kâbash (2), *to conquer, subjugate*
3665 kâna' (1), *to humiliate, subdue*
1396 dŏulagŏgĕō (1), *to enslave, subdue*
5292 hupŏtagē (4), *subordination*
5293 hupŏtassō (6), *to subordinate; to obey*

SUBMIT
3584 kâchash (3), *to lie, disown; to cringe*
6031 'ânâh (1), *to afflict, be afflicted*
7511 râphaç (1), *to trample; to prostrate*
5226 hupĕikō (1), *to surrender, yield*
5293 hupŏtassō (6), *to subordinate; to obey*

SUBMITTED
3584 kâchash (1), *to lie, disown; to cringe*
5414+3027 nâthan (1), *to give*
5293 hupŏtassō (1), *to subordinate; to obey*

SUBMITTING
5293 hupŏtassō (1), *to subordinate; to obey*

SUBORNED
5260 hupŏballō (1), *to throw in stealthily*

SUBSCRIBE
3789 kâthab (2), *to write*

SUBSCRIBED
3789 kâthab (2), *to write*

SUBSTANCE
202 'ôwn (1), *ability, power; wealth*
1564 gôlem (1), *embryo*
1942 havvâh (1), *desire; craving*
1952 hôwn (7), *wealth*
2428 chayil (7), *wealth; virtue; valor; strength*
3351 yᵉqûwm (3), *living thing*
3426 yêsh (1), *there is*
3428 Yesheb'âb (1), *seat of (his) father*
3581 kôach (1), *force, might; strength*
4678 matstsebeth (2), *stock of a tree*
4735 miqneh (2), *stock*
6108 'ôtsem (1), *power; framework of the body*
7009 qîym (1), *opponent*
7075 qinyân (4), *acquisition, purchase*
7399 rᵉkûwsh (11), *property*
7738 shâvâh (1), *to destroy*

SUBSTANCE
3776 ŏusia (1), *wealth, property, possessions*
5223 huparxis (1), *property, possessions*
5224 huparchŏnta (1), *property or possessions*
5287 hupŏstasis (1), *essence; assurance*

SUBTIL
2450 châkâm (1), *wise, intelligent, skillful*
5341 nâtsar (1), *to conceal, hide*
6175 'ârûwm (1), *cunning; clever*

SUBTILLY
5230 nâkal (1), *to act treacherously*
6191 'âram (1), *to be cunning; be prudent*
2686 katasŏphizŏmai (1), *to be crafty against*

SUBTILTY
4820 mirmâh (1), *fraud*
6122 'oqbâh (1), *trickery*
6195 'ormâh (1), *trickery; discretion*
1388 dŏlŏs (2), *wile, deceit, trickery*
3834 panŏurgia (1), *trickery or sophistry*

SUBURBS
4054 migrâsh (110), *open country*
6503 Parbâr (1), *Parbar*

SUBVERT
5791 'âvath (1), *to wrest, twist*
396 anatrĕpō (1), *to overturn, destroy*

SUBVERTED
1612 ĕkstrĕphō (1), *to pervert, be warped*

SUBVERTING
384 anaskĕuazō (1), *to upset, trouble*
2692 katastrŏphē (1), *catastrophical ruin*

SUCCEED
6965 qûwm (1), *to rise*

SUCCEEDED
3423 yârash (3), *to impoverish; to ruin*

SUCCEEDEST
3423 yârash (2), *to impoverish; to ruin*

SUCCESS
7919 sâkal (1), *to be or act circumspect*

SUCCOTH
5523 Çukkôwth (18), *booths*

SUCCOTH-BENOTH
5524 Çukkôwth Bᵉnôwth (1), *brothels*

SUCCOUR
5826 'âzar (2), *to aid*
997 bŏēthĕō (1), *to aid*

SUCCOURED
5826 'âzar (1), *to aid*
997 bŏēthĕō (1), *to aid*

SUCCOURER
4368 prŏstatis (1), *assistant, helper*

SUCHATHITES
7756 Sûwkâthîy (1), *Sukathite*

SUCK
3243 yânaq (13), *to suck*
4680 mâtsâh (1), *to drain; to squeeze out*
5966 'âla' (1), *to sip up*
2337 thēlazō (4), *to suck*

SUCKED
3243 yânaq (1), *to suck*
2337 thēlazō (1), *to suck*

SUCKING
2461 châlâb (1), *milk*
3243 yânaq (3), *to suck*
5764 'ûwl (1), *babe*

SUCKLING
3243 yânaq (3), *to suck*

SUCKLINGS
3243 yânaq (3), *to suck*
2337 thēlazō (1), *to suck*

SUDDEN
6597 pith'ôwm (2), *instantly, suddenly*
160 aiphnidiŏs (1), *suddenly*

SUDDENLY
4116 mâhar (1), *to hurry*
4118 mahêr (1), *in a hurry*
6597 pith'ôwm (22), *instantly, suddenly*
6621 petha' (4), *wink, i.e. moment; quickly*
7280 râga' (2), *to settle, i.e. quiet; to wink*
7281 rega' (1), *very short space of time*
869 aphnō (3), *suddenly*
1810 ĕxaiphnēs (5), *suddenly, unexpectedly*
1819 ĕxapina (1), *unexpectedly*
5030 tachĕōs (1), *rapidly*

SUE
2919 krinō (1), *to decide; to try, condemn, punish*

SUFFER
3201 yâkôl (1), *to be able*
3240 yânach (3), *to allow to stay*
3803 kâthar (1), *to enclose, besiege; to wait*
5375 nâsâ' (5), *to lift up*
5414 nâthan (11), *to give*
430 anĕchŏmai (7), *put up with, endure*
818 atimazō (1), *to maltreat, dishonor*
863 aphiĕmi (8), *to leave; to pardon, forgive*
1325 didōmi (2), *to give*
1377 diōkō (3), *to pursue; to persecute*
1439 ĕaō (2), *to let be, i.e. permit or leave alone*
2010 ĕpitrĕpō (6), *allow*
2210 zēmiŏō (1), *to experience detriment*
2553 kakŏpathĕō (1), *to undergo suffering*
2558 kakŏuchĕō (1), *to maltreat; to torment*
3805 pathētŏs (1), *doomed to pain*

SUFFERED
3240 yânach (2), *to allow to stay*
5203 nâtash (1), *to disperse; to thrust off*
5375 nâsâ' (1), *to lift up*
5414 nâthan (7), *to give*
863 aphiĕmi (6), *to leave; to pardon, forgive*
1439 ĕaō (5), *to let be, i.e. permit or leave alone*
2010 ĕpitrĕpō (4), *allow*
2210 zēmiŏō (1), *to suffer loss*
2967 kōluō (1), *to stop*
3958 paschō (17), *to experience pain*
4310 prŏpaschō (1), *to undergo hardship*
5159 trŏpŏphŏrĕō (1), *to endure one's habits*

SUFFEREST
1439 ĕaō (1), *to let be*

SUFFERETH
5414 nâthan (1), *to give*
971 biazō (1), *to crowd oneself into*
1439 ĕaō (1), *to let be*
3114 makrŏthumĕō (1), *to be forbearing, patient*

SUFFERING
2552 kakŏpathĕia (1), *hardship, suffering*
3804 pathēma (1), *passion; suffering*
3958 paschō (1), *to experience pain*
4330 prŏsĕaō (1), *to permit further progress*
5254 hupĕchō (1), *to endure with patience*

SUFFERINGS
3804 pathēma (10), *passion; suffering*

SUFFICE
4672 mâtsâ' (2), *to find or acquire; to occur*
5606 çâphaq (1), *to be enough; to vomit*
7227 rab (3), *great*
713 arkĕtŏs (1), *enough*

SUFFICED
4672 mâtsâ' (1), *to find or acquire; to occur*
7646 sâba' (1), *fill to satiety*
7648 sôba' (1), *satisfaction*

SUFFICETH
714 arkĕō (1), *to avail; be satisfactory*

SUFFICIENCY
5607 çêpheq (1), *satiety*

841 autarkeia (1), *contentedness*
2426 hikanŏtēs (1), *ability, competence*

SUFFICIENT
1767 day (5), *enough*
7227 rab (1), *great*
713 arkĕtŏs (1), enough
714 arkĕŏ (2), to *avail; be satisfactory*
2425 hikanŏs (3), *ample*

SUFFICIENTLY
4078 madday (1), *sufficiently*
7654 sob'âh (1), *satiety*

SUIT
2470 châlâh (1), to *be weak, sick, afflicted*
6187 'êrek (1), *pile, equipment, estimate*
7379 rîyb (1), *contest*

SUKKIIMS
5525 Çukkîy (1), *hut-dwellers*

SUM
3724 kôpher (1), *redemption*-price
4557 miçpâr (2), *number*
6485 pâqad (1), to *visit, care for, count*
6575 pârâshâh (1), *exposition*
7217 rê'sh (Ch.) (1), *head*
7218 rô'sh (9), *head*
8508 toknîyth (1), *consummation*
8552 tâmam (1), to *complete, finish*
2774 kĕphalaiŏn (2), *principal; amount*
5092 timē (1), *esteem; nobility; money*

SUMMER
4747 mᵉqêrâh (2), *cooling off, coolness*
6972 qûwts (1), to *spend the harvest season*
7007 qáyiṭ (Ch.) (1), *harvest season*
7019 qayits (20), *harvest*
2330 thĕrŏs (3), *summer*

SUMPTUOUSLY
2983 lambanŏ (1), to *take, receive*

SUN
216 'ôwr (1), *luminary*
2535 chammâh (4), *heat of sun*
2775 chereç (3), *itch; sun*
8121 shemesh (120), *sun*
8122 shemesh (Ch.) (1), *sun*
2246 hēliŏs (30), *sun*

SUNDERED
6504 pârad (1), to *spread or separate*

SUNDRY
4181 pŏlumĕrŏs (1), *in many portions*

SUNG
7891 shîyr (1), to *sing*
103 aᵢdō (2), to *sing*
5214 humnĕŏ (2), to *celebrate* God in song

SUNK
2883 ṭâba' (5), to *sink*
3766 kâra' (1), to *prostrate*
2702 kataphĕrō (1), to *bear down*

SUNRISING
4217 mizrâch (1), place of *sunrise; east*
4217+8121 mizrâch (9), place of *sunrise; east*

SUP
4041 mᵉgammâh (1), *accumulation*
1172 dĕipnĕō (2), to *eat the principal meal*

SUPERFLUITY
4050 pĕrissĕia (1), *superabundance*

SUPERFLUOUS
8311 sâra' (2), to *be deformed*
4053 pĕrissŏs (1), *superabundant*

SUPERSCRIPTION
1923 ĕpigraphē (5), *superscription*

SUPERSTITION
1175 dĕisidaimŏnia (1), *religion*

SUPERSTITIOUS
1174 dĕisidaimŏnĕstĕrŏs (1), *more religious*

SUPPED
1172 dĕipnĕō (1), to *eat the principal meal*

SUPPER
1172 dĕipnĕō (1), to *eat the principal meal*
1173 dĕipnŏn (13), *principal meal*

SUPPLANT
6117 'âqab (1), to *seize by the heel; to circumvent*

SUPPLANTED
6117 'âqab (1), to *seize by the heel; to circumvent*

SUPPLE
4935 mish'îy (1), *inspection*

SUPPLIANTS
6282 'âthâr (1), *incense; worshipper*

SUPPLICATION
2420 chîydâh (1), *puzzle; conundrum; maxim*
2603 chânan (10), to *implore*
2604 chănan (Ch.) (1), to *favor*
6419 pâlal (1), to *intercede, pray*
8467 tᵉchinnâh (22), *supplication*
1162 dĕēsis (4), *petition*

SUPPLICATIONS
8467 tᵉchinnâh (1), *supplication*
8469 tachănûwn (17), earnest *prayer, plea*
1162 dĕēsis (2), *petition*
2428 hikĕtēria (1), *entreaty, supplication*

SUPPLIED
378 anaplērŏō (1), to *complete; to supply*
4322 prŏsanaplērŏō (1), to *furnish fully*

SUPPLIETH
2024 ĕpichŏrēgia (1), *contribution, aid*
4322 prŏsanaplērŏō (1), to *furnish fully*

SUPPLY
378 anaplērŏō (1), to *complete; to supply*
2024 ĕpichŏrēgia (1), *contribution, aid*
4137 plērŏō (1), to *fill, make complete*

SUPPORT
472 antĕchŏmai (1), to *adhere to; to care for*
482 antilambanŏmai (1), to *succor; aid*

SUPPOSE
559 'âmar (1), to *say*
1380 dŏkĕō (3), to *think, regard, seem* good
3049 lŏgizŏmai (2), to *credit; to think, regard*
3543 nŏmizō (1), to *deem*
3633 ŏiŏmai (1), to *imagine, opine*
5274 hupŏlambanŏ (2), to *assume, presume*

SUPPOSED
1380 dŏkĕō (2), to *think*
2233 hēgĕŏmai (1), to *deem,* i.e. *consider*
3543 nŏmizō (4), to *deem*
5282 hupŏnŏĕō (1), to *think; to expect*

SUPPOSING
1380 dŏkĕō (2), to *think*
3543 nŏmizō (4), to *deem*
3633 ŏiŏmai (1), to *imagine, opine*

SUPREME
5242 hupĕrĕchō (1), to *excel; be superior*

SUR
5495 Çûwr (1), *deteriorated*

SURE
539 'âman (11), to *be firm, faithful, true*
546 'omnâh (1), *surely*
548 'ămânâh (1), *covenant*
571 'emeth (1), *certainty, truth, trustworthiness*
982 bâṭach (1), to *trust, be confident or sure*
2388 châzaq (1), to *bind*
3045 yâda' (4), to *know*
3245 yâçad (1), *settle, consult, establish*
4009 mibṭâch (1), *security; assurance*
6965 qûwm (2), to *rise*
7011 qayâm (Ch.) (1), *permanent*
7292 râhab (1), to *urge, embolden, capture*
8104 shâmar (1), to *watch*
804 asphalēs (1), *secure*

SWADDLED
2853 châthal (1), to *swathe, wrap in cloth*
2946 ṭâphach (1), to *nurse*

805 asphalizō (3), to *render secure*
949 bĕbaiŏs (3), *stable, certain, binding*
1097 ginŏskō (2), to *know*
1492 ĕidŏ (3), to *know*
4103 pistŏs (1), *trustworthy; reliable*
4731 stĕrĕŏs (1), *solid*

SURETIES
6148 'ârab (1), to *give or be security*

SURETISHIP
8628 tâqa' (1), to *clatter, slap, drive, clasp*

SURETY
389 'ak (1), *surely*
552 'umnâm (1), *verily*
3045 yâda' (1), to *know*
6148 'ârab (8), to *give or be security*
6161 'ărubbâh (1), as *security; bondsman*
230 alēthŏs (1), *surely*
1450 ĕgguŏs (1), *bondsman, guarantor*

SURFEITING
2897 kraipalē (1), *debauch*

SURMISINGS
5283 hupŏnŏia (1), *suspicion*

SURNAME
3655 kânâh (1), to *address, give title*
1941 ĕpikalĕŏmai (6), to *invoke*
2564 kalĕŏ (1), to *call*

SURNAMED
3655 kânâh (1), to *address, give title*
1941 ĕpikalĕŏmai (5), to *invoke*
2007+3686 ĕpitithēmi (2), to *impose*

SURPRISED
270 'âchaz (1), to *seize*
8610 tâphas (2), to *seize*

SUSANCHITES
7801 Shûwshankîy (Ch.) (1), *Shushankite*

SUSANNA
4677 Sŏusanna (1), *lily*

SUSI
5485 Çûwçîy (1), *horse-like*

SUSTAIN
3557 kûwl (4), to *maintain*

SUSTAINED
5564 çâmak (3), to *lean upon; take hold of*

SUSTENANCE
3557 kûwl (1), to *maintain*
4241 michyâh (1), *sustenance*
5527 chŏrtasma (1), *food*

English

SWADDLING
4683 sparganŏŏ (2), to *wrap* with cloth

SWADDLINGBAND
2854 chăthullâh (1), *swathing* cloth to wrap

SWALLOW
1104 bâla' (13), to *swallow; to destroy*
1866 dᵉrôwr (2), *swallow*
3886 lûwa' (1), to *be rash*
5693 'âgûwr (2), *swallow*
7602 shâ'aph (4), to *be angry; to hasten*
2666 katapinō (1), to *devour by swallowing*

SWALLOWED
1104 bâla' (19), to *swallow; to destroy*
1105 bela' (1), *gulp*
3886 lûwa' (1), to *be rash*
7602 shâ'aph (1), to *be angry; to hasten*
2666 katapinō (4), to *devour by swallowing*

SWALLOWETH
1572 gâmâ' (1), to *swallow*
7602 shâ'aph (1), to *be angry; to hasten*

SWAN
8580 tanshemeth (2), (poss.) *water-hen*

SWARE
5375 nâsâ' (1), to *lift up*
7650 shâba' (70), to *swear*
3660 ŏmnuō (7), to *swear, declare on oath*

SWAREST
7650 shâba' (5), to *swear*

SWARM
5712 'êdâh (1), *assemblage; family*
6157 'ârôb (2), swarming *mosquitoes*

SWARMS
6157 'ârôb (5), swarming *mosquitoes*

SWEAR
422 'âlâh (2), *imprecate, utter a curse*
5375 nâsâ' (2), to *lift up*
7650 shâba' (43), to *swear*
3660 ŏmnuō (13), to *swear, declare on oath*

SWEARERS
7650 shâba' (1), to *swear*

SWEARETH
7650 shâba' (7), to *swear*
3660 ŏmnuō (4), to *swear, declare on oath*

SWEARING
422 'âlâh (2), *imprecate, utter a curse*
423 'âlâh (2), *imprecation: curse*

SWEAT
2188 zê'âh (1), *sweat*
3154 yeza' (1), *sweat*
2402 hidrōs (1), *sweat*

SWEEP
2894 ṭûw' (1), to *sweep away*

3261 yâ'âh (1), to *brush aside*
4563 sarŏŏ (1), to *sweep clean*

SWEEPING
5502 çâchaph (1), to *scrape off, sweep* off

SWEET
1314 besem (5), *spice; fragrance; balsam*
2896 ṭôwb (1), *good; well*
3190 yâṭab (1), to *be, make well*
4452 mâlats (1), to *be smooth; to be pleasant*
4477 mamtaq (2), *sweet*
4575 ma'ădannâh (1), *bond, i.e. group*
4840 merqâch (1), *spicy*
4966 mâthôwq (7), *sweet*
4985 mâthaq (5), to *relish; to be sweet*
5207 nîchôwach (43), *pleasant; delight*
5208 nîychôwach (Ch.) (2), *pleasure*
5273 nâ'îym (2), *delightful; sweet*
5276 nâ'êm (1), to *be agreeable*
5561 çam (16), *aroma*
5674 'âbar (2), to *cross over; to transition*
6071 'âçîyç (2), *expressed fresh* grape-juice
6148 'ârab (5), to *intermix*
6149 'ârêb (2), *agreeable*
8492 tîyrôwsh (1), *wine; squeezed grape-juice*
1099 glukus (3), *sweet*
2175 ĕuōdia (2), *fragrance, aroma*

SWEETER
4966 mâthôwq (2), *sweet*

SWEETLY
4339 mêyshâr (1), *straightness; rectitude*
4988 mâthâq (1), sweet *food*

SWEETNESS
4966 mâthôwq (2), *sweet*
4986 metheq (2), *pleasantness*
4987 môtheq (1), *sweetness*

SWEETSMELLING
2175 ĕuōdia (1), *fragrance, aroma*

SWELL
1216 bâtsêq (1), to *blister*
6638 tsâbâh (2), to *array* ⸰ an army against
6639 tsâbeh (1), *swollen*

SWELLED
1216 bâtsêq (1), to *blister*

SWELLING
1158 bâ'âh (1), to *ask; be bulging, swelling*
1346 ga'ăvâh (1), *arrogance; majesty*
1347 gâ'ôwn (3), *ascending; majesty*
5246 hupĕrŏgkŏs (2), *insolent, boastful*

SWELLINGS
5450 phusiōsis (1), *haughtiness, arrogance*

SWEPT
1640 gâraph (1), to *sweep away*
5502 çâchaph (1), to *scrape off, sweep* off
4563 sarŏŏ (2), to *sweep clean*

SWERVED
795 astŏchĕŏ (1), *deviate*

SWIFT
16 'êbeh (1), *papyrus*
3753 karkârâh (1), cow-camel
4116 mâhar (3), to *hurry*
7031 qal (9), *rapid, swift*
7043 qâlal (1), to *be, make light (swift)*
7409 rekesh (1), *relay*
3691 ŏxus (1), *rapid, fast*
5031 tachinŏs (1), *soon, imminent*
5036 tachus (1), *prompt*

SWIFTER
7031 qal (1), *rapid, swift*
7043 qâlal (5), to *be, make light (swift)*

SWIFTLY
3288 yᵉ'âph (1), utterly *exhausted*
4120 mᵉhêrâh (1), *hurry*
7031 qal (2), *rapid, swift*

SWIM
6687 tsûwph (1), to *overflow*
7811 sâchâh (2), to *swim*
7813 sâchûw (1), *pond for swimming*
1579 ĕkkŏlumbaō (1), to *escape* by *swimming*
2860 kŏlumbaō (1), to *plunge* into water

SWIMMEST
6824 tsâphâh (1), *inundation*

SWIMMETH
7811 sâchâh (1), to *swim*

SWINE
2386 chăzîyr (2), *hog*
5519 chŏirŏs (14), *pig*

SWINE'S
2386 chăzîyr (4), *hog*

SWOLLEN
4092 pimprēmi (1), to *become inflamed*

SWOON
5848 'âṭaph (1), to *languish*

SWOONED
5848 'âṭaph (1), to *languish*

SWORD
1300 bârâq (1), *lightning; flash of lightning*
2719 chereb (380), *sword*
7524 retsach (1), *crushing; murder-cry*
7973 shelach (3), *spear*
3162 machaira (22), short *sword*
4501 rhŏmphaia (7), *sabre, cutlass*

SWORDS
2719 chereb (17), *sword*
6609 pᵉthîchâh (1), *drawn* sword
3162 machaira (6), short *sword*

SWORN
1167+7621 ba'al (1), *master; husband*
3027+5920+3676 yâd (1), *hand; power*
5375 nâsâ' (1), to *lift up*
7650 shâba' (42), to *swear*
3660 ŏmnuō (3), to *swear*

SYCAMINE
4807 sukaminŏs (1), *sycamore-fig tree*

SYCHAR
4965 Suchar (1), *liquor*

SYCHEM
4966 Suchĕm (2), *ridge*

SYCOMORE
8256 shâqâm (6), *sycamore tree*
4809 sukŏmōraia (1), *sycamore-fig tree*

SYCOMORES
8256 shâqâm (1), *sycamore tree*

SYENE
5482 Çᵉvênêh (2), the local *Seven*

SYNAGOGUE
656 apŏsunagōgŏs (2), *excommunicated*
752 archisunagōgŏs (7), *director of the synagogue services*
4864 sunagōgē (34), *assemblage*

SYNAGOGUE'S
752 archisunagōgŏs (2), *director of the synagogue services*

SYNAGOGUES
4150 mŏw'êd (1), *place of meeting; congregation*
656 apŏsunagōgŏs (1), *excommunicated*
4864 sunagōgē (22), *assemblage*

SYNTYCHE
4941 Suntuchē (1), *accident*

SYRACUSE
4946 Surakŏusai (1), *Syracuse*

SYRIA
758 'Arâm (66), *highland*
4947 Suria (8), (poss.) *rock*

SYRIA-DAMASCUS
758+1834 'Arâm (1), *highland*

SYRIA-MAACHAH
758 'Arâm (1), *highland*

SYRIACK
762 'Ărâmîyth (1), *in Araman*

SYRIAN
761 'Ărammîy (7), *Aramite*

762 'Ărâmîyth (4), *in Araman*

4948 Surŏs (1), *native of Syria*

SYRIANS
758 'Arâm (57), *highland*
761 'Ărammîy (4), *Aramite*

SYROPHENICIAN
4949 Surŏphŏinissa (1), *native of Phœnicia*

TAANACH
8590 Ta'ănâk (6), *Taanak or Tanak*

TAANATH-SHILOH
8387 Ta'ănath Shîlôh (1), *approach of Shiloh*

TABBAOTH
2884 Ţabbâ'ôwth (2), *rings*

TABBATH
2888 Ţabbath (1), *Tabbath*

TABEAL
2870 Ţâbeʾêl (1), *pleasing* (to) *God*

TABEEL
2870 Ţâbeʾêl (1), *pleasing* (to) *God*

TABERAH
8404 Tabʿêrâh (2), *burning*

TABERING
8608 tâphaph (1), to *drum* on a tambourine

TABERNACLE
168 'ôhel (187), *tent*
4908 mishkân (114), *residence*
5520 çôk (1), *hut of entwined boughs*
5521 çukkâh (3), *tabernacle; shelter*
5522 çikkûwth (1), *idolatrous booth*
7900 sôk (1), *booth*
4633 skēnē (15), *tent*
4636 skēnŏs (2), *tent*
4638 skēnōma (3), *dwelling:* the *Temple*

TABERNACLES
168 'ôhel (11), *tent*
4908 mishkân (5), *residence*
5521 çukkâh (9), *tabernacle; shelter*
4633 skēnē (4), *tent*
4634 skēnŏpēgia (1), *tabernacles, i.e.* booths

TABITHA
5000 Tabitha (2), *gazelle*

TABLE
3871 lûwach (4), *tablet*
4524 mêçab (1), *divan couch; around*
7979 shulchân (56), *table*
345 anakĕimai (1), to *recline at a meal*
4093 pinakidiŏn (1), wooden writing *tablet*
5132 trapĕza (9), four-legged *table or stool*

TABLES
3871 lûwach (34), *tablet*

7979 shulchân (14), *table*
2825 klinē (1), *couch*
4109 plax (3), *tablet*
5132 trapĕza (4), four-legged *table or stool*

TABLETS
1004+5315 bayith (1), *house; temple; family*
3558 kûwmâz (2), *jewel*

TABOR
8396 Tâbôwr (10), *broken*

TABRET
8596 tôph (3), *tambourine*
8611 tôpheth (1), *smiting*

TABRETS
8596 tôph (5), *tambourine*

TABRIMON
2886 Ţabrimmôwn (1), *pleasing* (to) *Rimmon*

TACHES
7165 qereç (10), *knob*

TACHMONITE
8461 Tachkĕmônîy (1), *sagacious*

TACKLING
4631 skĕuē (1), *tackle*

TACKLINGS
2256 chebel (1), *company*

TADMOR
8412 Tadmôr (2), *palm*

TAHAN
8465 Tachan (2), *station*

TAHANITES
8470 Tachănîy (1), *Tachanite*

TAHAPANES
8471 Tachpanchêç (1), *Tachpanches*

TAHATH
8480 Tachath (6), *bottom*

TAHPANHES
8471 Tachpanchêç (5), *Tachpanches*

TAHPENES
8472 Tachpʿnêyç (3), *Tachpenes*

TAHREA
8475 Tachrêa' (1), (poss.) *earth, ground; low*

TAHTIM-HODSHI
8483 Tachtîym Chodshîy (1), *lower* (ones) *monthly*

TAIL
2180 zânâb (8), *tail*
3769 ŏura (1), *tail*

TAILS
2180 zânâb (2), *tail*
3769 ŏura (4), *tail*

TAKE
6 'âbad (1), to *perish*
270 'âchaz (12), to *seize*
622 'âçaph (3), to *gather*
680 'âtsal (1), to *select*
935 bôw' (1), to *go, come*
962 bâzaz (9), to *plunder*
1197 bâ'ar (4), to *be brutish, be senseless*
1497 gâzal (3), to *rob*

1692 dâbaq (1), to *cling or adhere;* to *catch*
1898 hâgâh (2), to *remove, expel*
1961 hâyâh (1), to *exist*
2095 zᵉhar (Ch.) (1), *be admonished, be careful*
2254 châbal (7), to *bind by a pledge;* to *pervert*
2388 châzaq (9), to *fasten* upon; to *seize*
2502 châlats (1), to *present, strengthen*
2834 châsaph (1), to *drain* away or *bail* up
2846 châthâh (3), to *lay hold* of; to *take away*
3051 yâhab (1), to *give*
3212 yâlak (1), to *carry*
3318 yâtsâ' (2), to *go, bring out*
3381 yârad (3), to *descend*
3423 yârash (3), to *inherit*
3615 kâlâh (1), to *complete, prepare*
3920 lâkad (19), to *catch*
3947 lâqach (367), to *take*
5253 nâçag (2), to *retreat*
5267 nᵉçaq (Ch.) (1), to *go up*
5312 nᵉphaq (Ch.) (1), to *issue forth;* to *bring out*
5337 nâtsal (1), to *deliver;* to *be snatched*
5375 nâsâ' (60), to *lift up*
5376 nᵉsâ' (Ch.) (1), to *lift up*
5381 nâsag (5), to *reach*
5414 nâthan (1), to *give*
5493 çûwr (45), to *turn off*
5496 çûwth (1), to *stimulate;* to *seduce*
5535 çâkath (1), to *be silent;* to *observe*
5674 'âbar (2), to *cross over;* to *transition*
5709 'ădâ' (Ch.) (1), to *pass* on or *continue*
5749 'ûwd (2), to *encompass, restore*
5927 'âlâh (4), to *ascend*
5978 'immâd (1), *with*
6213 'âsâh (1), to *do*
6331 pûwr (1), to *crush*
6679 tsûwd (1), to *catch*
6901 qâbal (1), to *admit*
6902 qᵉbal (Ch.) (1), to *acquire*
7061 qâmats (3), to *grasp*
7126 qârab (1), to *approach, bring near*
7200 râ'âh (2), to *see*
7311 rûwm (11), to *be high;* to *rise or raise*
7760 sûwm (2), to *put*
7896 shîyth (1), to *place*
7901 shâkab (2), to *lie*
7997 shâlal (4), to *drop or strip;* to *plunder*
8175 sâ'ar (1), to *storm; to shiver, i.e. fear*
8551 tâmak (2), to *obtain*
8610 tâphas (10), to *manipulate, i.e. seize*
142 airō (35), to *lift up*
353 analambanō (3), to *take up, bring up*
726 harpazō (3), to *seize*

851 aphairĕō (5), to *remove, cut off*
1209 dĕchŏmai (3), to *receive, accept*
1949 ĕpilambanŏmai (2), to *seize*
2507 kathairĕō (1), to *lower, or demolish*
2722 katĕchō (1), to *hold down fast*
2902 kratĕō (4), to *seize*
2983 lambanō (31), to *take, receive*
3335 mĕtalambanō (1), to *accept and use*
3880 paralambanō (5), to *associate with* oneself
3911 paraphĕrō (1), to *carry off;* to *avert*
4014 pĕriairĕō (1), to *unveil;* to *cast off*
4084 piazō (4), to *seize*
4355 prŏslambanō (1), to *take along, receive*
4648 skŏpĕō (1), to *watch out for,* i.e. to *regard*
4815 sullambanō (3), to *seize* (*arrest, capture*)
4838 sumparalambanō (2), to *take along*
4868 sunairō (1), to *compute an account*

TAKEN
247 'âzar (1), to *belt*
270 'âchaz (7), to *seize*
622 'âçaph (7), to *gather*
935 bôw' (1), to *go, come*
1197 bâ'ar (2), to *be brutish, be senseless*
1497 gâzal (5), to *rob*
1639 gâra' (4), to *remove, lessen, or withhold*
2254 châbal (1), to *bind by a pledge;* to *pervert*
2388 châzaq (5), to *fasten* upon; to *seize*
2502 châlats (1), to *pull off;* to *strip;* to *depart*
2974 yâ'al (2), to *assent;* to *undertake, begin*
3289 yâ'ats (2), to *advise*
3381 yârad (1), to *descend*
3427 yâshab (5), to *dwell*
3885 lûwn (1), to *be obstinate with*
3920 lâkad (42), to *catch*
3921 leked (1), *noose*
3947 lâqach (84), to *take*
4672 mâtsâ' (1), to *find*
5267 nᵉçaq (Ch.) (1), to *go up*
5312 nᵉphaq (Ch.) (2), to *issue forth;* to *bring out*
5337 nâtsal (3), to *deliver;* to *be snatched*
5375 nâsâ' (10), to *lift up*
5381 nâsag (1), to *reach*
5414 nâthan (1), to *give*
5493 çûwr (19), to *turn off*
5674 'âbar (1), to *cross over;* to *transition*
5709 'ădâ' (Ch.) (1), to *remove;* to *bedeck*
5927 'âlâh (9), to *ascend*
6001 'âmêl (1), *laborer*
6213 'âsâh (1), to *make*
6679 tsûwd (1), to *catch*
6813 tsâ'an (1), to *load*

7092 qâphats (1), to *draw together, to leap; to die*
7287 râdâh (1), to *subjugate; to crumble*
7311 rûwm (4), to *be high; to rise or raise*
7628 she̱bîy (2), *booty*
7725 shûwb (1), to *turn back; to return*
8610 tâphas (12), to *manipulate, i.e. seize*
142 airō (16), to *lift up*
259 halōsis (1), *capture*
353 analambanō (3), to *take up, bring up*
522 apairō (3), to *remove, take away*
642 apŏrphanizō (1), to *separate*
782 aspazŏmai (1), to *give salutation*
851 aphairĕō (1), to *remove*
1096 ginŏmai (1), to be
1723 ĕnagkalizŏmai (1), *take into one's arms*
1808 ĕxairō (1), to *remove, drive away*
1869 ĕpairō (1), to *raise*
2021 ĕpichĕirĕō (1), to *undertake, try*
2221 zōgrĕō (1), to *capture or ensnare*
2638 katalambanō (2), to *seize; to possess*
2639 katalĕgō (1), to *enroll, put on a list*
2983 lambanō (12), to *take, receive*
3880 paralambanō (5), to *associate with* oneself
4014 pĕriairĕō (3), to *unveil; to cast off*
4084 piazō (2), to *seize*
4355 prŏslambanō (1), to *take along; receive*
4815 sullambanō (2), to *seize (arrest, capture)*
4912 sunĕchō (3), to *hold together*

TAKEST
622 'âçaph (1), to *gather*
1980 hâlak (1), to *walk*
3947 lâqach (1), to *take*
5375 nâsâ' (1), to *lift up*
6001 'âmêl (1), *laborer*
8104 shâmar (1), to *watch*
142 airō (1), to *lift up*

TAKETH
270 'âchaz (2), to *seize*
1197 bâ'ar (1), to be *brutish, be senseless*
2254 châbal (1), to *bind by a pledge; to pervert*
2388 châzaq (4), to *fasten upon; to seize*
2862 châthaph (1), to *clutch, snatch*
3920 lâkad (5), to *catch*
3947 lâqach (11), to *take*
5190 nâṭal (1), to *lift; to impose*
5337 nâtsal (1), to *deliver; to be snatched*
5375 nâsâ' (3), to *lift up*
5493 çûwr (2), to *turn off*
5710 'âdâh (1), to *pass on or continue; to remove*

5998 'âmal (2), to *work severely, put forth effort*
6908 qâbats (1), to *collect, assemble*
7953 shâlâh (1), to *draw out or off, i.e. remove*
8610 tâphas (1), to *manipulate, i.e. seize*
142 airō (11), to *lift up*
337 anairĕō (1), to *take away, i.e. abolish*
851 aphairĕō (1), to *remove, cut off*
1405 drassŏmai (1), to *grasp, i.e. entrap*
2018 ĕpiphĕrō (1), to *inflict, bring upon*
2638 katalambanō (1), to *seize; to possess*
2983 lambanō (4), to *take, receive*
3880 paralambanō (8), to *associate with* oneself
4301 prŏlambanō (1), to *take before; be caught*

TAKING
3947 lâqach (1), to *take*
4727 miqqâch (1), *reception*
8610 tâphas (1), to *manipulate, i.e. seize*
142 airō (1), to *lift up*
321 anagō (1), to *lead up; to bring out*
353 analambanō (1), to *take up, bring up*
1325 didōmi (1), to *give*
2983 lambanō (4), to *take*

TALE
1899 hegeh (1), *muttering*
4557 miçpâr (1), *number*
4971 mathkôneth (1), *proportion*
8506 tôken (1), *quantity*

TALEBEARER
1980+7400 hâlak (1), to *walk; live a certain way*
5372 nirgân (2), *slanderer*
7400 râkîyl (2), *scandal-monger*

TALENT
3603 kikkâr (10), *talent*
5006 talantiaiŏs (1), *weight* of 57-80 lbs.
5007 talantŏn (3), *weight*

TALENTS
3603 kikkâr (38), *talent*
3604 kikkêr (Ch.) (1), *talent* weight
5007 talantŏn (12), *weight* of 57-80 lbs.

TALES
7400 râkîyl (1), *scandal-monger*
3026 lērŏs (1), *twaddle*

TALITHA
5008 talitha (1), *young girl*

TALK
1696 dâbar (11), to *speak*
1697 dâbâr (2), *word*
1897 hâgâh (1), to *murmur, utter a sound*
5608 çâphar (1), to *recount* an event
6310 peh (1), *mouth*

7878 sîyach (5), to *ponder, muse aloud*
8193 sâphâh (1), *lip, language, speech*
2980 lalĕō (1), to *talk*
3056 lŏgŏs (1), *word, matter, thing*

TALKED
559 'âmar (1), to *say*
1696 dâbar (29), to *speak*
2980 lalĕō (8), to *talk*
3656 hŏmilĕō (2), to *talk*
4814 sullalĕō (1), to *talk*
4926 sunŏmilĕō (1), to *converse* mutually

TALKERS
3956 lâshôwn (1), *tongue*
3151 mataiŏlŏgŏs (1), *senseless talker*

TALKEST
1696 dâbar (2), to *speak*
2980 lalĕō (1), to *talk*

TALKETH
1696 dâbar (1), to *speak*
2980 lalĕō (1), to *talk*

TALKING
1696 dâbar (3), to *speak*
4405 millâh (1), *word; discourse; speech*
7879 sîyach (1), *uttered contemplation*
2980 lalĕō (1), to *talk*
3473 mōrŏlŏgia (1), *buffoonery, foolish talk*
4814 sullalĕō (2), to *talk together, i.e. converse*

TALL
6967 qôwmâh (2), *height*
7311 rûwm (3), to *be high*

TALLER
7311 rûwm (1), to *be high*

TALMAI
8526 Talmay (6), *ridged*

TALMON
2929 Ṭalmôwn (5), *oppressive*

TAMAH
8547 Temach (1), *Temach*

TAMAR
8559 Tâmâr (24), *palm*

TAME
1150 damazō (2), to *tame*

TAMED
1150 damazō (2), to *tame*

TAMMUZ
8542 Tammûwz (1), *Tammuz*

TANACH
8590 Ta'ănâk (1), *Taanak or Tanak*

TANHUMETH
8576 Tanchûmeth (2), *compassion, solace*

TANNER
1033 brŏma (3), *food*

TAPHATH
2955 Ṭâphath (1), *dropping* (of ointment)

TAPPUAH
8599 Tappûwach (6), *apple*

TARAH
8646 Terach (2), *Terach*

TARALAH
8634 Tar'ălâh (1), *reeling*

TARE
1234 bâqa' (1), to *cleave, break, tear open*
7167 qâra' (1), to *rend*
4682 sparassō (1), to *convulse* with epilepsy
4952 susparassō (1), to *convulse* violently

TAREA
8390 Ta'ărêa' (1), (poss.) *earth, ground; low*

TARES
2215 zizaniŏn (8), *darnel*

TARGET
3591 kîydôwn (1), *dart*
6793 tsinnâh (2), large *shield; piercing cold*

TARGETS
6793 tsinnâh (3), large *shield; piercing cold*

TARPELITES
2967 Ṭarpeͣlay (Ch.) (1), *Tarpelite*

TARRIED
748 'ârak (2), to be *long*
2342 chûwl (1), to *wait*
3176 yâchal (1), to *wait*
3186 yâchar (1), to *delay*
3427 yâshab (6), to *dwell, to remain; to settle*
3885 lûwn (3), to be *obstinate with*
4102 mâhahh (2), to be *reluctant*
5116 nâveh (1), *at home*
5975 'âmad (1), to *stand*
1304 diatribō (2), to *stay*
1961 ĕpimĕnō (3), to *remain; to persevere*
3306 mĕnō (3), to *stay*
4160 pŏiĕō (1), to *do*
4328 prŏsdŏkaō (1), to *anticipate; to await*
4357 prŏsmĕnō (1), to *remain* in a place
5278 hupŏmĕnō (1), to *undergo, (trials)*
5549 chrŏnizō (2), to *take time, i.e. linger*

TARRIEST
3195 mĕllō (1), to *intend, i.e. be about to*

TARRIETH
3427 yâshab (1), to *dwell, to remain; to settle*
6960 qâvâh (1), to *expect*

TARRY
309 'âchar (4), to *remain; to delay*
1826 dâmam (1), to *stop, cease; to perish*
2442 châkâh (2), to *await; hope for*
3176 yâchal (1), to *wait*
3427 yâshab (13), to *dwell, to remain*
3559 kûwn (1), to *set up: establish, fix, prepare*
3885 lûwn (7), to be *obstinate with*

4102 mâhahh (3), *to be reluctant*
5975 'âmad (1), *to stand*
7663 sâbar (1), *to scrutinize; to expect*
1019 bradunō (1), *to delay, hesitate*
1551 ĕkdĕchŏmai (1), *to await, expect*
1961 ĕpimĕnō (4), *to remain; to persevere*
2523 kathizō (1), *to seat down, dwell*
3306 mĕnō (7), *to stay*
5549 chrŏnizō (1), *to take time, i.e. linger*

TARRYING
309 'âchar (2), *to remain*

TARSHISH
8659 Tarshîysh (24), *merchant* vessel

TARSUS
5018 Tarsĕus (2), *native of Tarsus*
5019 Tarsŏs (3), *flat*

TARTAK
8662 Tartâq (1), *Tartak*

TARTAN
8661 Tartân (2), *Tartan*

TASK
1697 dâbâr (1), *word; matter; thing*
2706 chôq (1), *appointment; allotment*

TASKMASTERS
5065 nâgas (5), *to exploit; to tax, harass*

TASKS
1697 dâbâr (1), *word; matter; thing*

TASTE
2441 chêk (4), *area of mouth*
2938 ţâ'am (6), *to taste*
2940 ţa'am (5), *taste*
1089 gĕuŏmai (7), *to taste*

TASTED
2938 ţâ'am (2), *to taste*
2942 ţe'êm (Ch.) (1), *judgment; account*
1089 gĕuŏmai (5), *to taste; to eat*

TASTETH
2938 ţâ'am (1), *to taste*

TATNAI
8674 Tatt^enay (4), *Tattenai*

TATTLERS
5397 phluarŏs (1), *pratery*

TAUGHT
995 bîyn (1), *to understand; discern*
1696 dâbar (2), *to speak*
3045 yâda' (3), *to know*
3256 yâçar (2), *to instruct*
3384 yârâh (5), *to teach*
3925 lâmad (17), *to teach*
3928 limmûwd (1), *instructed one*
4000 mâbôwn (1), *instructing*
7919 sâkal (1), *to be or act circumspect*

8637 tirgal (1), *to cause to walk*
1318 didaktŏs (1), *instructed, taught*
1321 didaskō (36), *to teach*
1322 didachē (1), *instruction*
2258+1321 ēn (4), *I was*
2312 thĕŏdidaktŏs (1), *divinely instructed*
2727 katēchēō (1), *to indoctrinate*
3100 mathētĕuō (1), *to become a student*
3811 paidĕuō (1), *to educate or discipline*

TAUNT
1422 g^edûwphâh (1), *revilement, taunt*
8148 sh^enîynâh (1), *gibe, verbal taunt*

TAUNTING
4426 m^elîytsâh (1), *aphorism, saying*

TAVERNS
4999 Tabĕrnai (1), *huts*

TAXATION
6187 'êrek (1), *estimate*

TAXED
6186 'ârak (1), *to arrange*
582 apŏgraphē (3), *census registration*

TAXES
5065 nâgas (1), *to exploit; to tax, harass*

TAXING
583 apŏgraphō (2), *enroll, take a census*

TEACH
502 'âlaph (1), *to teach*
2094 zâhar (1), *to enlighten*
3045 yâda' (5), *to know*
3046 y^eda' (Ch.) (1), *to know*
3384 yârâh (33), *to teach*
3925 lâmad (32), *to teach*
8150 shânan (1), *to pierce; to inculcate*
1317 didaktikŏs (2), *instructive*
1321 didaskō (26), *to teach*
2085 hĕtĕrŏdidaskalĕō (2), *to instruct differently*
2605 kataggĕllō (1), *to proclaim, promulgate*
2727 katēchēō (1), *to indoctrinate*
3100 mathētĕuō (1), *to become a student*
4994 sōphrŏnizō (1), *to train up*

TEACHER
995 bîyn (1), *to understand; discern*
3384 yârâh (1), *to teach*
1320 didaskalŏs (4), *instructor*

TEACHERS
3384 yârâh (3), *to teach*
3887 lûwts (1), *to scoff; to interpret; to intercede*
3925 lâmad (1), *to teach*

1320 didaskalŏs (6), *instructor*
2567 kalŏdidaskalŏs (1), *teacher of the right*
3547 nŏmŏdidaskalŏs (1), *Rabbi*
5572 psĕudŏdidaskalŏs (1), *propagator of erroneous doctrine*

TEACHEST
3925 lâmad (1), *to teach*
1321 didaskō (7), *to teach*

TEACHETH
502 'âlaph (1), *to teach*
3384 yârâh (3), *to teach*
3925 lâmad (5), *to teach*
7919 sâkal (1), *to be or act circumspect*
1318 didaktŏs (2), *taught*
1321 didaskō (3), *to teach*
2727 katēchēō (1), *to indoctrinate*

TEACHING
3384 yârâh (1), *to teach*
3925 lâmad (1), *to teach*
1319 didaskalia (1), *instruction*
1321 didaskō (21), *to teach*
3811 paidĕuō (1), *to educate or discipline*

TEAR
1234 bâqa' (1), *to cleave, break, tear open*
1758 dûwsh (1), *to trample or thresh*
2963 ţâraph (5), *to pluck off or pull to pieces*
5498 çâchab (1), *to trail along*
6536 pâraç (1), *to break in pieces; to split*
6561 pâraq (1), *to break off or crunch; to deliver*
7167 qâra' (3), *to rend*

TEARETH
2963 ţâraph (4), *to pluck off or pull to pieces*
4486 rhēgnumi (1), *to tear to pieces*
4682 sparassō (1), *to convulse with epilepsy*

TEARS
1058 bâkâh (1), *to weep*
1832 dim'âh (23), *tears*
1144 dakru (11), *teardrop*

TEATS
1717 dad (2), *female breast or bosom*
7699 shad (1), *breast*

TEBAH
2875 Ţebach (1), *massacre*

TEBALIAH
2882 Ţ^ebalyâhûw (1), *Jehovah has dipped*

TEBETH
2887 Ţêbeth (1), *a month*

TEDIOUS
1465 ĕgkŏptō (1), *to impede, detain*

TEETH
4973 m^ethall^e'âh (3), *tooth*
6374 pîyphîyâh (1), *tooth*

8127 shên (31), *tooth*
8128 shên (Ch.) (3), *tooth*
3599 ŏdŏus (10), *tooth*
3679 ŏnĕidizō (1), *to rail at, chide, taunt*

TEHAPHNEHES
8471 Tachpanchêç (1), *Tachpanches*

TEHINNAH
8468 T^echinnâh (1), *supplication*

TEIL
424 'êlâh (1), *oak*

TEKEL
8625 t^eqal (Ch.) (2), *to weigh in a scale*

TEKOA
8620 T^eqôwa' (6), *trumpet*

TEKOAH
8620 T^eqôwa' (1), *trumpet*
8621 T^eqôw'îy (2), *Tekoite*

TEKOITE
8621 T^eqôw'îy (3), *Tekoite*

TEKOITES
8621 T^eqôw'îy (2), *Tekoite*

TEL-ABIB
8512 Têl 'Âbîyb (1), *mound of green growth*

TEL-HARESHA
8521 Têl Charshâ' (1), *mound of workmanship*

TEL-HARSA
8521 Têl Charshâ' (1), *mound of workmanship*

TEL-MELAH
8528 Têl Melach (2), *mound of salt*

TELAH
8520 Telach (1), *breach*

TELAIM
2923 T^elâ'îym (1), *lambs*

TELASSAR
8515 T^ela'ssar (1), *Telassar*

TELEM
2928 Ţelem (2), *oppression*

TELL
559 'âmar (29), *to say*
560 'ămar (Ch.) (5), *to say*
1696 dâbar (7), *to speak*
3045 yâda' (7), *to know*
5046 nâgad (69), *to announce*
5608 çâphar (12), *to recount an event*
8085 shâma' (2), *to hear*
226 alēthĕuō (1), *to be true*
312 anaggĕllō (2), *to announce, report*
518 apaggĕllō (6), *to announce, proclaim*
1334 diēgĕŏmai (2), *to relate fully, describe*
1492 ĕidō (9), *to know*
1583 ĕklalĕō (1), *to tell*
1650 ĕlĕgchŏs (1), *proof*
2036 ĕpō (28), *to speak*
2046 ĕrĕō (3), *to utter*
2980 lalĕō (2), *to talk*
3004 lĕgō (28), *to say*

4302 prŏlĕgō (1), to
predict, forewarn

TELLEST
5608 çâphar (1), to
recount an event

TELLETH
1696 dâbar (2), to *speak*
4487 mânâh (2), to *allot;*
to *enumerate* or enroll
5046 nâgad (2), to
announce
3004 lĕgō (1), to *say*

TELLING
1696 dâbar (1), to *speak*
4557 miçpâr (1), *number*
5608 çâphar (1), to
recount an event

TEMA
8485 Têymâ' (5), *Tema*

TEMAN
8487 Têymân (11), *south*

TEMANI
8489 Têymânîy (1),
Temanite

TEMANITE
8489 Têymânîy (6),
Temanite

TEMANITES
8489 Têymânîy (1),
Temanite

TEMENI
8488 Têym^enîy (1),
Temeni

TEMPER
7450 râçaç (1), to
moisten with drops

TEMPERANCE
1466 ĕgkratĕia (4),
self-control

TEMPERATE
1467 ĕgkratĕuŏmai (1),
to *exercise self-restraint*
1468 ĕgkratēs (1),
self-controlled
4998 sōphrōn (1),
self-controlled

TEMPERED
1101 bâlal (1), to *mix*
4414 mâlach (1), to *salt*
4786 sugkĕrannumi (1),
to *combine, assimilate*

TEMPEST
2230 zerem (3), *flood*
5492 çûwphâh (1),
hurricane wind
5590 çâ'ar (1), to *rush*
upon; to *toss* about
5591 ça'ar (6), *hurricane*
7307 rûwach (1), *breath;*
wind; life-spirit
8183 s^e'ârâh (1),
hurricane wind
2366 thuĕlla (1), *blowing*
2978 lailaps (1),
whirlwind; hurricane
4578 sĕismŏs (1), *gale*
storm; earthquake
5492 chĕimazō (1), to *be*
battered in a storm
5494 chĕimōn (1), *winter*
season; stormy weather

TEMPESTUOUS
5490 çôwph (2),
termination; end

8175 sâ'ar (1), to *storm*
5189 tuphōnikŏs (1),
stormy

TEMPLE
1004 bayith (11), *house;*
temple; family, tribe
1964 hêykâl (68), *temple*
1965 hêykal (Ch.) (8),
palace; temple
2411 hiĕrŏn (71), *sacred*
place; *sanctuary*
3485 naŏs (43), *temple*
3624 ŏikŏs (1), *dwelling*

TEMPLES
1964 hêykâl (2), *temple*
7451 ra' (5), *bad; evil*
3485 naŏs (2), *temple*

TEMPORAL
4340 prŏskairŏs (1),
temporary

TEMPT
974 bâchan (1), to *test*
5254 nâçâh (4), to *test*
1598 ĕkpĕirazō (3), to
test thoroughly
3985 pĕirazō (6), to
endeavor, scrutinize

TEMPTATION
4531 maççâh (1), *testing*
3986 pĕirasmŏs (15), *test*

TEMPTATIONS
4531 maççâh (3), *testing*
3986 pĕirasmŏs (5), *test*

TEMPTED
5254 nâçâh (8), to *test*
551 apĕirastŏs (1), *not*
temptable
1598 ĕkpĕirazō (1), to
test thoroughly
3985 pĕirazō (14), to
endeavor, scrutinize

TEMPTER
3985 pĕirazō (2), to
endeavor, scrutinize

TEMPTETH
3985 pĕirazō (1), to
endeavor, scrutinize

TEMPTING
3985 pĕirazō (7), to
endeavor, scrutinize

TEN
6218 âsôwr (4), *ten*
6235 'eser (164), *ten*
6236 'ăsar (Ch.) (4), *ten*
7231 râbab (1), to
multiply by the myriad
7233 r^ebâbâh (13),
myriad
7239 ribbôw (2), *myriad*
7240 ribbôw (Ch.) (2),
myriad
1176 dĕka (24), *ten*
3461 murias (3), *ten*
thousand
3463 muriŏi (3), *ten*
thousand; innumerably

TEN'S
6235 'eser (1), *ten*

TENDER
3126 yôwnêq (1), *sucker*
plant; *nursing* infant
3127 yôwneqeth (1),
sprout, new shoot
7390 rak (10), *tender*
7401 râkak (2), to *soften*

527 hapalŏs (2), *tender*
3629 ŏiktirmōn (1),
compassionate
4698 splagchnŏn (1),
intestine; affection, pity

TENDERHEARTED
7390+3824 rak (1),
tender; weak
2155 ĕusplagchnŏs (1),
compassionate

TENDERNESS
7391 rôk (1), *softness*

TENONS
3027 yâd (6), *hand; power*

TENOR
6310 peh (2), *mouth*

TENS
6235 'eser (3), *ten*

TENT
167 'âhal (3), to pitch a
tent
168 'ôhel (89), *tent*
6898 qubbâh (1), *pavilion*

TENTH
4643 ma'ăsêr (4), *tithe,*
one-tenth
6218 âsôwr (13), *ten*
6224 'ăsîyrîy (26), *tenth*
6237 'âsar (3), to *tithe*
6241 'issârôwn (28), *tenth*
1181 dĕkatē (2), *tenth*
1182 dĕkatŏs (3), *tenth*

TENTMAKERS
4635 skēnŏpŏiŏs (1),
manufacturer of tents

TENTS
168 'ôhel (50), *tent*
2583 chânâh (1), to
encamp
4264 machăneh (5),
encampment
4908 mishkân (1),
residence
5521 çukkâh (1),
tabernacle; shelter

TERAH
8646 Terach (11), *Terach*

TERAPHIM
8655 t^erâphîym (6),
healer

TERESH
8657 Teresh (2), *Teresh*

TERMED
559 'âmar (2), to *say*

TERRACES
4546 m^eçillâh (1),
viaduct; staircase

TERRESTRIAL
1919 ĕpigĕiŏs (2),
worldly, earthly

TERRIBLE
366 'âyôm (3), *frightful*
367 'êymâh (2), *fright*
574 'emtânîy (Ch.) (1),
burly or *mighty*
1763 d^echal (Ch.) (1), to
fear; be formidable
2152 zal'âphâh (1), *glow*
3372 yârê' (30), to *fear*
6184 'ârîyts (13),
powerful or *tyrannical*
5398 phŏbĕrŏs (1),
frightful, i.e. *formidable*

TERRIBLENESS
3372 yârê' (1), to *fear*
4172 môwrâ' (1), *fearful*
8606 tiphletseth (1),
fearfulness

TERRIBLY
6206 'ârats (2), to *dread*

TERRIFIED
6206 'ârats (1), to *dread*
4422 ptŏĕō (2), to *be*
scared
4426 pturō (1), to *be*
frightened

TERRIFIEST
1204 bâ'ath (1), to *fear*

TERRIFY
1204 bâ'ath (2), to *fear*
2865 châthath (1), to
break down
1629 ĕkphŏbĕō (1), to
frighten utterly

TERROR
367 'êymâh (4), *fright*
928 behâlâh (1), *sudden*
panic, destruction
1091 ballâhâh (3),
sudden *destruction*
2283 châgâ' (1), *terror*
2847 chittâh (1), *terror*
2851 chittîyth (8), *terror*
4032 mâgôwr (1), *fright*
4172 môwrâ' (2), *fearful*
4288 m^echittâh (2), *ruin;*
consternation
4637 ma'ărâtsâh (1),
terrifying violent power
6343 pachad (2), *fear*
5401 phŏbŏs (3), *alarm,*
or *fright; reverence*

TERRORS
367 'êymâh (3), *fright*
928 behâlâh (1), *sudden*
panic, destruction
1091 ballâhâh (6),
sudden *destruction*
1161 bi'ûwthîym (2),
alarms, startling things
4032 mâgôwr (1), *fright*
4048 mâgar (1), to *yield*
up, be thrown
4172 môwrâ' (1), *fearful*

TERTIUS
5060 Tĕrtiŏs (1), *third*

TERTULLUS
5061 Tĕrtullŏs (2),
Tertullus

TESTAMENT
1242 diathēkē (11),
contract; devisory *will*
1248 diakŏnia (2),
attendance, aid, service

TESTATOR
1303 diatithĕmai (2), to
put apart, i.e. *dispose*

TESTIFIED
5749 'ûwd (7), to *protest,*
testify; to *encompass*
6030 'ânâh (3), to
respond, answer
1263 diamarturŏmai (6),
to *attest earnestly*
3140 marturĕō (6), to
testify; to *commend*
3142 marturiŏn (1),
something *evidential*

4303 prŏmarturŏmai (1),
to *predict beforehand*

TESTIFIEDST
5749 'ûwd (2), to *protest,
testify;* to *encompass*

TESTIFIETH
6030 'ânâh (1), to
respond, answer
3140 *marturĕō* (4), to
testify; to *commend*

TESTIFY
5749 'ûwd (6), to *protest,
testify;* to *encompass*
6030 'ânâh (8), to
respond, answer
1263 diamarturŏmai (4),
to *attest earnestly*
3140 *marturĕō* (8), to
testify; to *commend*
3143 *marturŏmai* (2), to
be witness, i.e. to *obtest*
4828 *summarturĕō* (1), to
testify jointly

TESTIFYING
1263 diamarturŏmai (1),
to *attest earnestly*
1957 *ĕpimarturĕō* (1), to
corroborate
3140 *marturĕō* (1), to
testify; to *commend*

TESTIMONIES
5713 'êdâh (21),
testimony
5715 'êdûwth (15),
testimony

TESTIMONY
5713 'êdâh (1), *testimony*
5715 'êdûwth (40),
testimony
8584 tᵉ'ûwdâh (3),
attestation, precept
3140 *marturĕō* (3), to
testify; to *commend*
3141 *marturia* (14),
evidence given
3142 *marturiŏn* (15),
something *evidential*

TETRARCH
5075 *tĕtrarchĕō* (3), to *be
a tetrarch*
5076 *tĕtrarchēs* (4), *ruler
of a fourth* part

THADDAEUS
2280 *Thaddaiŏs* (2),
Thaddæus

THAHASH
8477 Tachash (1), (poss.)
antelope

THAMAH
8547 Temach (1), *Temach*

THAMAR
2283 Thamar (1), *palm*

THANK
2192+5485 zᵉ'êyr (Ch.)
(3), *small, little*
3029 yᵉdâ' (Ch.) (1), to
praise
3034 yâdâh (4), to *throw;*
to *revere or worship*
8426 tôwdâh (3), *thanks*
1843 ĕxŏmŏlŏgĕō (2), to
acknowledge
2168 ĕucharistĕō (11), to
express gratitude

5485 charis (3),
gratitude; benefit given

THANKED
1288 bârak (1), to *bless*
2168 ĕucharistĕō (1), to
express gratitude
5485 charis (1),
gratitude; benefit given

THANKFUL
3034 yâdâh (1), to *throw;*
to *revere or worship*
2168 ĕucharistĕō (1), to
express gratitude
2170 ĕucharistŏs (1),
grateful, thankful

THANKFULNESS
2169 ĕucharistia (1),
gratitude

THANKING
3034 yâdâh (1), to *throw;*
to *revere or worship*

THANKS
3029 yᵉdâ' (Ch.) (1), to
praise
3034 yâdâh (32), to
throw; to *revere,
worship*
8426 tôwdâh (3), *thanks*
437 anthŏmŏlŏgĕōmai
(1), to *give thanks*
2168 ĕucharistĕō (26), to
express gratitude
2169 ĕucharistia (5),
gratitude
3670 hŏmŏlŏgĕō (1), to
acknowledge, agree
5485 charis (4),
gratitude; benefit given

THANKSGIVING
1960 huyᵉdâh (1), *choir*
3034 yâdâh (2), to *throw;*
to *revere or worship*
8426 tôwdâh (16), *thanks*
2169 ĕucharistia (8),
gratitude; grateful

THANKSGIVINGS
8426 tôwdâh (1), *thanks*
2169 ĕucharistia (1),
gratitude; grateful

THANKWORTHY
5485 charis (1),
gratitude; benefit given

THARA
2291 Thara (1), *Thara*

THARSHISH
8659 Tarshîysh (4),
merchant vessel

THEATRE
2302 thĕatrŏn (2),
audience-room; show

THEBEZ
8405 Têbêts (3),
whiteness

THEFT
1591 gᵉnêbâh (2),
something *stolen*

THEFTS
2804 Klaudiŏs (1),
Claudius
2829 klŏpē (2), *theft*

THELASAR
8515 Tᵉla'ssar (1),
Telassar

THEOPHILUS
2321 Thĕŏphilŏs (2),
friend of God

THERE
2008 hênnâh (1), *from
here; from there*
8033 shâm (440), *there*
8536 tâm (Ch.) (2), *there*
847 autŏu (3), *in this*
1563 ĕkĕi (98), *there*
1564 ĕkĕithĕn (1), *from
there*
1566 ĕkĕisĕ (2), *there*
1759 ĕnthadĕ (1), *here*
1927 ĕpidēmĕō (1), to
make oneself at home
5602 hōdĕ (1), *here*

THEREABOUT
4012+5127 pĕri (1), *about*

THEREAT
1223+846 dia (1),
through, by means of

THEREBY
2004 hên (2), *they*
5921 'al (2), *above, over*

THEREFORE
1571 gam (5), *also; even*
2006 hên (Ch.) (2), *lo;
therefore, unless*
2063 zô'th (1), *this*
3588 kîy (2), *for, that*
3651 kên (170), *just;
right, correct*
235 alla (3), *but, yet*
686 ara (6), *therefore*
1063 gar (1), *for, indeed*
1160 dapanē (1),
expense, cost
1211 dē (1), *therefore*
1352 diŏ (9), *therefore*
1360 diŏti (1), *inasmuch
as*
2532 kai (1), *and; or*
3747 ŏstĕŏn (1), *bone*
3757 hŏu (1), at *which*
3767 ŏun (255), *certainly*
5105 tŏigarŏun (1), *then*
5106 tŏinun (3), *then*
5124 tŏutŏ (1), *that thing*
5620 hōstĕ (9), *thus*

THEREIN
413 'êl (2), *to, toward*
1459 gav (Ch.) (1), *middle*
2004 hên (4), *they*
2007 hênnâh (1),
themselves
4393 mᵉlô' (7), *fulness*
5921 'al (9), *above, over*
7130 qereb (2), *nearest*
8033 shâm (10), *there*
8432 tâvek (3), *center*
5125 tŏutŏis (1), *in these*

THEREINTO
1519+846 ĕis (1), *to*

THEREOF
8033 shâm (1), *there*
846 autŏs (26), *he, she, it*

THEREON
5921 'al (48), *above, over*
846 autŏs (2), *he, she, it*
1911 ĕpiballŏ (1), to
throw upon
1913 ĕpibibazō (1), to
cause to mount
1924 ĕpigraphō (1), to
inscribe, write upon

THEOPHILUS
1945 ĕpikĕimai (1), to
rest upon; press upon
2026 ĕpŏikŏdŏmĕō (1), to
rear up, build up

THEREOUT
8033 shâm (1), *where,
there*

THERETO
5921 'al (8), *above, over*
1928 ĕpidiatassŏmai (1),
to *appoint besides*

THEREUNTO
1519+846+5124 ĕis (1), *to*
1519+5124 ĕis (2), *to*
4334 prŏsĕrchŏmai (1),
to *come near, visit*

THEREUPON
2026 ĕpŏikŏdŏmĕō (2), to
rear up, build up

THEREWITH
854 'êth (1), *with; by; at*
5921 'al (2), *above, over*
1722+846 ĕn (2), *in*
1909+5125 ĕpi (1), *on*
5125 tŏutŏis (1), *in these*

THESSALONIANS
2331 Thĕssalŏnikĕus (5),
of Thessalonice

THESSALONICA
2331 Thĕssalŏnikĕus (1),
of Thessalonice
2332 Thĕssalŏnikē (5),
Thessalonice

THEUDAS
2333 Thĕudas (1),
Theudas

THICK
653 'ăphêlâh (1),
duskiness, darkness
3515 kâbêd (1),
numerous; severe
5441 çôbek (1), *thicket*
5645 'âb (2), *thick clouds*
5666 'âbâh (1), to *be
dense*
5672 'ăbîy (2), *density*
5687 'ăbôth (4), *dense*
5688 'ăbôth (4), *entwined*
6282 'âthâr (1), *incense;
worshipper*
7341 rôchab (1), *width*

THICKER
5666 'âbâh (2), to *be
dense*

THICKET
5441 çôbek (1), *thicket*
5442 çᵉbâk (1), *thicket*

THICKETS
2337 châvâch (1), *dell* or
crevice of rock
5442 çᵉbâk (2), *thicket*
5645 'âb (1), *thick
clouds; thicket*

THICKNESS
5672 'ăbîy (2), *density*
7341 rôchab (2), *width*

THIEF
1590 gannâb (13), *stealer*
2812 klĕptēs (12), *stealer*
3027 lēᵢstēs (3), *brigand*

THIEVES
1590 gannâb (4), *stealer*
2812 klĕptēs (4), *stealer*
3027 lēᵢstēs (8), *brigand*

THIGH
3409 yârêk (19), leg or
shank, flank; side
7785 shôwq (1), lower leg
3382 mĕrŏs (1), thigh

THIGHS
3409 yârêk (2), leg or
shank, flank; side
3410 yarkâ' (Ch.) (1),
thigh

THIMNATHAH
8553 Timnâh (1), portion

THIN
1809 dâlal (1), to
slacken, dangle
1851 daq (5), thin
4174 môwrâd (1),
descent, slope
7534 raq (1), emaciated

THING
562 'ômer (1), something
said
1697 dâbâr (182), thing
3627 kᵉlîy (11), thing
3651 kên (2), just; right
3972 mᵉ'ûwmâh (3),
something; anything
4399 mᵉlâ'kâh (2), work;
property
4406 millâh (Ch.) (9),
word, command
4859 mashshâ'âh (1),
secured loan
5315 nephesh (2), life;
breath; soul; wind
1520 hĕis (1), one
3056 lŏgŏs (2), word,
matter, thing
4110 plasma (1), molded
4229 pragma (2), matter
4487 rhēma (1), matter
5313 hupsōma (1), barrier

THINGS
1697 dâbâr (47), thing
4406 millâh (Ch.) (1),
word or subject
18 agathŏs (1), good
846 autŏs (1), he, she, it
3056 lŏgŏs (3), thing
4229 pragma (4), matter
4487 rhēma (2), thing
5023 tauta (1), these

THINK
559 'âmar (3), to say
995 bîyn (1), to
understand; discern
1819 dâmâh (1), to
consider, think
2142 zâkar (3), to
remember; to mention
2803 châshab (6), to
think, regard; to value
5452 çᵉbar (Ch.) (1), to
bear in mind, i.e. hope
5869 'ayin (2), eye; sight
6245 'âshath (1), to be
sleek; to excogitate
1380 dŏkĕō (22), to think
1760 ĕnthumĕŏmai (1),
ponder, reflect on
2233 hēgĕŏmai (2), to
deem, i.e. consider
3049 lŏgizŏmai (7), to
credit; to think, regard
3539 nŏiĕō (1), to
exercise the mind

3543 nŏmizō (4), to deem
or regard
3633 ŏiŏmai (1), to
imagine, opine
5252 hupĕrphrŏnĕō (1),
to esteem oneself
5282 hupŏnŏĕō (1), to
think; to expect
5316 phainō (1), to
lighten (shine)
5426 phrŏnĕō (4), to be
mentally disposed

THINKEST
2803 châshab (1), to
think, regard; to value
5869 'ayin (2), eye; sight
1380 dŏkĕō (4), to think
3049 lŏgizŏmai (1), to
think, regard
5426 phrŏnĕō (1), to be
mentally disposed

THINKETH
2803 châshab (1), to
think, regard; to value
7200 râ'âh (1), to see
8176 shâ'ar (1), to
estimate
1380 dŏkĕō (2), to think
3049 lŏgizŏmai (1), to
think, regard

THINKING
559 'âmar (1), to say
1931+1961 hûw' (1), this

THIRD
7969 shâlôwsh (9), three;
third; thrice
7992 shᵉlîyshîy (104),
third
8027 shâlash (2), to be
triplicate
8029 shillêsh (5), great
grandchild
8523 tᵉlîythay (Ch.) (2),
third
8531 tᵉlath (Ch.) (3),
tertiary, i.e. third rank
5152 tristĕgŏn (1), third
story place
5154 tritŏs (56), third
part; third time, thirdly

THIRDLY
5154 tritŏs (1), third part

THIRST
6770 tsâmê' (2), to thirst
6771 tsâmê' (1), thirsty
6772 tsâmâ' (16), thirst
6773 tsim'âh (1), thirst
1372 dipsaō (10), to thirst
1373 dipsŏs (1), thirst

THIRSTED
6770 tsâmê' (2), to thirst

THIRSTETH
6770 tsâmê' (2), to thirst
6771 tsâmê' (1), thirsty

THIRSTY
6770 tsâmê' (2), to thirst
6771 tsâmê' (7), thirsty
6772 tsâmâ' (1), thirst
6774 tsimmâ'ôwn (1),
desert
1372 dipsaō (3), to thirst

THIRTEEN
7969 shâlôwsh (2), three
7969+6240 shâlôwsh (13),
three; third; thrice

THIRTEENTH
7969+6240 shâlôwsh (11),
three; third; thrice

THIRTIETH
7970 shᵉlôwshîym (9),
thirty; thirtieth

THIRTY
7970 shᵉlôwshîym (161),
thirty; thirtieth
8533 tᵉlâthîyn (Ch.) (2),
thirty
5144 triakŏnta (9), thirty

THIRTYFOLD
5144 triakŏnta (2), thirty

THISTLE
1863 dardar (1), thorn
2336 chôwach (4), thorn

THISTLES
1863 dardar (1), thorn
2336 chôwach (1), thorn
5146 tribŏlŏs (1), thorny
caltrop plant

THITHER
1988 hălôm (1), hither
2008 hênnâh (3), from
here; from there
5704 'ad (1), until
8033 shâm (63), there
1563 ĕkĕi (8), thither
1904 ĕpĕrchŏmai (1), to
supervene
3854 paraginŏmai (1), to
arrive; to appear
4370 prŏstrĕchō (1), to
hasten by running

THITHERWARD
2008 hênnâh (1), from
here; from there
8033 shâm (1), there
1563 ĕkĕi (1), thither

THOMAS
2381 Thōmas (12), twin

THONGS
2438 himas (1), strap

THORN
2336 chôwach (2), thorn
4534 mᵉçûwkâh (1),
thorn-hedge
5285 na'ătsûwts (1),
brier; thicket
6975 qôwts (2), thorns
4647 skŏlŏps (1), thorn

THORNS
329 'âţâd (1), buckthorn
2312 chêdeq (1), prickly
2336 chôwach (3), thorn
5285 na'ătsûwts (1),
brier; thicket
5518 çîyr (4), thorn; hook
5544 çillôwn (1), prickle
6791 tsên (2), thorn
6975 qôwts (12), thorns
7063 qimmâshôwn (1),
prickly plant
7898 shayith (7), wild
growth of briers
173 akantha (14), thorn
174 akanthinŏs (2),
thorny

THOROUGHLY
3190 yâţab (1), to be,
make well
7495 râphâ' (1), to cure

THOUGHT
559 'âmar (9), to say

1672 dâ'ag (1), be
anxious, be afraid
1696 dâbar (1), to speak
1697 dâbâr (1), word;
matter; thing
1819 dâmâh (4), to think
2154 zimmâh (1), plan
2161 zâmam (5), to plan
2803 châshab (10), to
think, regard; to value
4093 maddâ' (1),
intelligence
4209 mᵉzimmâh (1), plan
4284 machăshâbâh (1),
contrivance; plan
5869 'ayin (3), eye; sight
6246 'ăshîth (Ch.) (1), to
purpose, plan
6248 'ashtûwth (1),
cogitation, thinking
6419 pâlal (1), to
intercede, pray
7454 rêa' (1), thought
7807 shach (1), sunk
8232+6925 shᵉphar (Ch.)
(1), to be beautiful
1260 dialŏgizŏmai (1), to
deliberate
1261 dialŏgismŏs (1),
consideration, debate
1380 dŏkĕō (5), to think
1760 ĕnthumĕŏmai (2),
ponder, reflect on
1911 ĕpiballō (1), to
throw upon
1963 ĕpinŏia (1),
thought, intention
2106 ĕudŏkĕō (1), to
think well, i.e. approve
2233 hēgĕŏmai (2), to
deem, i.e. consider
2919 krinō (1), to decide;
to try, condemn, punish
3049 lŏgizŏmai (1), to
credit; to think, regard
3309 mĕrimnaō (11), to
be anxious about
3540 nŏēma (1),
perception, i.e. purpose
3543 nŏmizō (1), to deem
4305 prŏmĕrimnaō (1), to
care in advance

THOUGHTEST
1819 dâmâh (1), to
consider, think

THOUGHTS
2031 harhôr (Ch.) (1),
mental conception
2711 chêqeq (1),
enactment, resolution
4180 môwrâsh (1),
possession
4209 mᵉzimmâh (2),
plan; sagacity
4284 machăshâbâh (24),
contrivance; plan
5587 çâ'iph (2), divided
in mind; sentiment
5588 çê'êph (1), divided
in mind; skeptic
6250 'eshtônâh (1),
thinking
7454 rêa' (1), thought
7476 ra'yôwn (Ch.) (5),
mental conception
8312 sar'aph (2),
cogitation
1261 dialŏgismŏs (8),
consideration; debate

1270 dianŏēma (1), *sentiment, thought*
1761 ĕnthumēsis (3), *deliberation; idea*
3053 lŏgismŏs (1), *reasoning; conscience*

THOUSAND
505 'eleph (436), *thousand*
506 'ălaph (Ch.) (3), *thousand*
7233 r⁰bâbâh (4), *myriad*
7239 ribbôw (5), *myriad*
7239+505 ribbôw (1), *myriad, large number*
7240 ribbôw (Ch.) (1), *myriad, large number*
1367 dischilioi (1), *two thousand*
2035 hĕptakischiliŏi (1), *seven times a thousand*
3461 murias (3), *ten thousand*
3463 muriŏi (3), *ten thousand*
4000 pĕntakischiliŏi (6), *five times a thousand*
5070 tĕtrakischiliŏi (5), *four times a thousand*
5153 trischiliŏi (1), *three times a thousand*
5505 chilias (21), *one thousand*
5507 chiliŏi (11), *thousand*

THOUSANDS
503 'ălaph (1), *increase by thousands*
505 'eleph (46), *thousand*
506 'ălaph (Ch.) (1), *thousand*
7232 râbab (1), *to shoot*
7233 r⁰bâbâh (7), *myriad*
7239 ribbôw (1), *myriad*
3461 murias (2), *ten thousand*
5505 chilias (1), *one thousand*

THREAD
2339 chûwt (4), *string*
6616 pâthîyl (1), *twine*

THREATEN
546 apĕilĕō (1), *to menace; to forbid*

THREATENED
546 apĕilĕō (1), *to menace; to forbid*
4324 prŏsapĕilĕō (1), *to menace additionally*

THREATENING
547 apĕilē (1), *menace*

THREATENINGS
547 apĕilē (2), *menace*

THREE
7969 shâlôwsh (377), *three; third; thrice*
7991 shâlîysh (1), *triangle, three*
7992 sh⁰lîyshîy (4), *third*
8027 shâlash (6), *to be triplicate*
8032 shilshôwm (1), *day before yesterday*
8532 t⁰lâth (Ch.) (10), *three or third*
5140 trĕis (69), *three*

5145 triakŏsiŏi (2), *three hundred*
5148 triĕtia (1), *three years' period*
5150 trimēnŏn (1), *three months' space*
5151 tris (1), *three times*
5153 trischiliŏi (1), *three times a thousand*

THREEFOLD
8027 shâlash (1), *to be triplicate*

THREESCORE
7239 ribbôw (1), *myriad*
7657 shib'îym (38), *seventy*
8346 shishshîym (42), *sixty*
8361 shittîyn (Ch.) (4), *sixty*
1440 hĕbdŏmēkŏnta (3), *seventy*
1835 hĕxēkŏnta (4), *sixty*
5516 chi xi stigma (1), 666

THRESH
1758 dûwsh (3), *to thresh*
1869 dârak (1), *to tread*

THRESHED
1758 dûwsh (2), *to thresh*
2251 châbaṭ (1), *to thresh*

THRESHETH
248 alŏaō (1), *to tread*

THRESHING
1758 dûwsh (3), *to thresh*
1786 dayîsh (1), *threshing*-time
2742 chârûwts (2), *threshing-sledge*
4098 m⁰dushshâh (1), *down-trodden people*
4173 môwrag (3), *threshing sledge*

THRESHINGFLOOR
1637 gôren (17), *open area*

THRESHINGFLOORS
147 'iddar (Ch.) (1), *threshing-floor*
1637 gôren (1), *open area*

THRESHINGPLACE
1637 gôren (1), *open area*

THRESHOLD
4670 miphtân (8), *sill*
5592 çaph (6), *dish*

THRESHOLDS
624 'âçûph (1), *collection, stores*
5592 çaph (2), *dish*

THREW
5422 nâthats (1), *to tear down*
5619 çâqal (1), *to throw large stones*
8058 shâmaṭ (1), *to jostle*
906 ballō (2), *to throw*
4952 susparassō (1), *to convulse violently*

THREWEST
7993 shâlak (1), *to throw*

THRICE
7969+6471 shâlôwsh (4), *three; third; thrice*
5151 tris (11), *three times*

THROAT
1627 gârôwn (4), *throat*
3930 lôa' (1), *throat*
2995 larugx (1), *throat*
4155 pnigō (1), *to throttle*

THRONE
3678 kiççê' (120), *throne*
3764 korçê' (Ch.) (2), *throne*
968 bēma (1), *tribunal platform; judging place*
2362 thrŏnŏs (50), *throne*

THRONES
3678 kiççê' (4), *throne*
3764 korçê' (Ch.) (1), *throne*
2362 thrŏnŏs (4), *throne*

THRONG
2346 thlibō (1), *to crowd*
4912 sunĕchō (1), *to hold together*

THRONGED
4846 sumpnigō (1), *to drown; to crowd*
4918 sunthlibō (1), *to compress, i.e. to crowd*

THRONGING
4918 sunthlibō (1), *to compress, i.e. to crowd*

THROUGH
413 'êl (2), *to, toward*
1119 b⁰môw (1), *in, with*
1157 b⁰'ad (5), *through*
1234 bâqa' (3), *to cleave*
1811 dâlaph (1), *to drip*
1856 dâqar (2), *to pierce*
1870 derek (1), *road*
2864 châthar (1), *to break or dig into*
2944 ṭâ'an (1), *to stab*
3027 yâd (1), *hand; power*
4480 min (2), *from, out of*
5674 'âbar (10), *to cross*
5921 'al (5), *over, upon*
6440 pânîym (1), *face*
7130 qereb (5), *nearest part, i.e. the center*
7751 shûwṭ (1), *to travel*
8432 tâvek (7), *center*
303 ana (1), *through*
1223 dia (93), *through*
1224 diabainō (1), *to pass by, over, across*
1279 diapŏrĕuŏmai (1), *to travel through*
1330 diĕrchŏmai (8), *to traverse, travel through*
1350 diktuŏn (1), *drag net*
1358 diŏrussō (3), *to penetrate burglariously*
1537 ĕk (3), *out, out of*
1653 ĕlĕĕŏ (1), *to give out compassion*
1722 ĕn (37), *in; during*
1909 ĕpi (2), *on, upon*
2569 kalŏpŏiĕō (1), *to do well*
2596 kata (4), *down; according to*
2700 katatŏxĕuō (1), *to shoot down*
4044 pĕripĕirō (1), *to penetrate entirely*
4063 pĕritrĕchō (1), *to traverse, run about*

THROUGHLY
7235 râbâh (1), *to increase*
1245 diakatharizō (2), *to cleanse perfectly*
1722+3956 ĕn (1), *in*
1822 ĕxartizō (1), *to finish out; to equip fully*

THROUGHOUT
5921 'al (2), *above, over*
1223 dia (3), *through*
1330 diĕrchŏmai (2), *to traverse, travel through*
1519 ĕis (3), *to or into*
1722 ĕn (5), *in; during*
1909 ĕpi (2), *on, upon*
2596 kata (8), *down; according to*

THROW
2040 hâraç (6), *to pull down; break, destroy*
5307 nâphal (1), *to fall*
5422 nâthats (1), *to tear down*
8058 shâmaṭ (1), *to jostle*

THROWING
3027 yâd (1), *hand; power*

THROWN
2040 hâraç (7), *to pull down; break, destroy*
5422 nâthats (3), *to tear down*
7411 râmâh (1), *to hurl*
7993 shâlak (1), *to throw*
906 ballō (1), *to throw*
2647 kataluō (3), *to demolish; to halt*
4496 rhiptō (1), *to toss*

THRUST
926 bâhal (1), *to be, make agitated; hasten*
1333 bâthaq (1), *to cut in pieces, hack up*
1644 gârash (6), *to drive out; to expatriate*
1760 dâchâh (1), *to push down; to totter*
1766 dâchaq (1), *to oppress*
1856 dâqar (8), *to stab*
1920 hâdaph (4), *to push away or down; drive out*
2115 zûwr (1), *to press*
2944 ṭâ'an (1), *to stab*
3238 yânâh (1), *to suppress; to maltreat*
3905 lâchats (1), *to press*
5074 nâdad (1), *to rove, flee; to drive away*
5080 nâdach (2), *to push off, scattered*
5365 nâqar (1), *to bore*
5414 nâthan (1), *to give*
8628 tâqa' (1), *to clatter, slap, drive, clasp*
683 apōthĕŏmai (2), *to push off; to reject*
906 ballō (5), *to throw*
1544 ĕkballō (3), *to throw out*
1856 ĕxōthĕō (1), *to expel; to propel*
1877 ĕpanagō (1), *to put out to sea; to return*
2601 katabibazō (1), *to cause to bring down*

English

2700 *katatŏxĕuō* (1), to *shoot down*
3992 *pĕmpō* (2), to *send*

THRUSTETH
5086 *nâdaph* (1), to *disperse, be windblown*

THUMB
931 *bôhen* (6), *thumb*

THUMBS
931 *bôhen* (1), *thumb*
931+3027 *bôhen* (2), *thumb; big toe*

THUMMIM
8550 *Tummîym* (5), *perfections*

THUNDER
6963 *qôwl* (7), *sound*
7481 *râ'am* (2), to *crash thunder; to irritate*
7482 *ra'am* (6), *peal of thunder*
7483 *ra'mâh* (1), *horse's mane*
1027 *brŏntē* (3), *thunder*

THUNDERBOLTS
7565 *resheph* (1), *flame*

THUNDERED
7481 *râ'am* (3), to *crash thunder; to irritate*
1027+1096 *brŏntē* (1), *thunder*

THUNDERETH
7481 *râ'am* (3), to *crash thunder; to irritate*

THUNDERINGS
6963 *qôwl* (2), *sound*
1027 *brŏntē* (4), *thunder*

THUNDERS
6963 *qôwl* (3), *sound*
1027 *brŏntē* (4), *thunder*

THYATIRA
2363 *Thuatĕira* (4), *Thyatira*

THYINE
2367 *thuïnŏs* (1), of *citron*

TIBERIAS
5085 *Tibĕrias* (3), *Tiberius*

TIBERIUS
5086 *Tibĕriŏs* (1), (poss.) *pertaining to the* river *Tiberis* or *Tiber*

TIBHATH
2880 *Ṭibchath* (1), *slaughter*

TIBNI
8402 *Tibnîy* (3), *strawy*

TIDAL
8413 *Tid'âl* (2), *fearfulness*

TIDINGS
1309 *bᵉsôwrâh* (6), *glad tidings, good news*
1319 *bâsar* (16), to *announce* (good news)
1697 *dâbâr* (4), *word*
8052 *shᵉmûw'âh* (8), *announcement*
8088 *shêma'* (2), *something heard*
2097 *ĕuaggĕlizō* (6), to *announce good news*
3056 *lŏgŏs* (1), *word*
5334 *phasis* (1), *news*

TIE
631 *'âçar* (1), to *fasten*
6029 *'ânad* (1), to *bind*

TIED
631 *'âçar* (3), to *fasten*
5414 *nâthan* (1), to *give*
1210 *dĕō* (4), to *bind*

TIGLATH-PILESER
8407 Tiglath Pil'eçer (3), *Tiglath-Pileser*

TIKVAH
8616 *Tiqvâh* (2), *hope*

TIKVATH
8616 *Tiqvâh* (1), *hope*

TILE
3843 *lᵉbênâh* (1), *brick*

TILGATH-PILNESER
8407 Tiglath Pil'eçer (3), *Tiglath-Pileser*

TILING
2766 *kĕramŏs* (1), *clay roof tile*

TILL
5647 *'âbad* (4), to *work*
5704 *'ad* (90), *until*
5705 *'ad* (Ch.) (1), *until*
6440 *pânîym* (1), *face; front*
891 *achri* (5), *until, up to*
1519 *ĕis* (1), to or *into*
2193 *hĕōs* (41), *until*
3360 *mĕchri* (2), *until*

TILLAGE
5215 *nîyr* (1), *plowed* land
5656 *'ăbôdâh* (2), *work*

TILLED
5647 *'âbad* (2), to *work*

TILLER
5647 *'âbad* (1), to *work*

TILLEST
5647 *'âbad* (1), to *work*

TILLETH
5647 *'âbad* (2), to *work*

TILON
8436 *Tûwlôn* (1), *suspension*

TIMAEUS
5090 *Timaiŏs* (1), (poss.) *foul; impure*

TIMBER
636 *'â'* (Ch.) (3), *wood*
6086 *'êts* (23), *wood*

TIMBREL
8596 *tôph* (5), *tambourine*

TIMBRELS
8596 *tôph* (4), *tambourine*
8608 *tâphaph* (1), to *drum* on a tambourine

TIME
116 *'ĕdayin* (Ch.) (1), *then*
227 *'âz* (5), *at that time*
268 *'âchôwr* (1), *behind, backward; west*
570 *'emesh* (1), *yesterday evening*
1767 *day* (1), *enough*
2165 *zᵉmân* (2), *time*
2166 *zᵉmân* (Ch.) (6), *time, appointed*
3117 *yôwm* (55), *day*
3118 *yôwm* (Ch.) (2), *day*

4150 *môw'êd* (3), *assembly*
4279 *mâchar* (7), *tomorrow; hereafter*
5732 *'iddân* (Ch.) (7), set *time; year*
5769 *'ôwlâm* (1), *eternity*
6256 *'êth* (220), *time*
6258 *'attâh* (3), *now*
6440 *pânîym* (2), *front*
6471 *pa'am* (14), *time*
6635 *tsâbâ'* (2), *army*
7225 *rê'shîyth* (1), *first*
7227 *rab* (2), *great*
7674 *shebeth* (1), *rest*
8032 *shilshôwm* (1), *day before yesterday*
8462 *tᵉchillâh* (2), *original; originally*
8543 *tᵉmôwl* (1), *yesterday*
744 *archaiŏs* (3), *original*
1074 *gĕnĕa* (1), *age*
1208 *dĕutĕrŏs* (1), *second*
1597 *ĕkpalai* (1), *long ago*
1909 *ĕpi* (2), *on, upon*
2119 *ĕukairĕō* (2), to *have opportunity*
2121 *ĕukairŏs* (1), *opportune, suitable*
2235 *ēdē* (1), *even now*
2250 *hēmĕra* (4), *day*
2540 *kairŏs* (54), *set time*
3195 *mĕllō* (1), to *intend*
3379 *mēpŏtĕ* (6), *never*
3568 *nun* (2), *now*
3598 *hŏdŏs* (1), *road*
3819 *palai* (1), *formerly*
4218 *pŏtĕ* (12), *ever*
4287 *prŏthĕsmiŏs* (1), *designated* day or time
4340 *prŏskairŏs* (1), *temporary*
4455 *pōpŏtĕ* (3), *at no time*
5119 *tŏtĕ* (4), *at the time*
5550 *chrŏnŏs* (28), *time*
5551 *chrŏnŏtribĕō* (1), to *procrastinate, linger*
5610 *hōra* (12), *hour*

TIMES
2165 *zᵉmân* (1), *time*
2166 *zᵉmân* (Ch.) (3), *time, appointed*
3027 *yâd* (1), *hand; power*
3117 *yôwm* (5), *day; time*
4150 *môw'êd* (1), *assembly*
4151 *môw'âd* (1), *troop*
4489 *môneh* (2), *instance*
5732 *'iddân* (Ch.) (6), set *time; year*
6256 *'êth* (22), *time*
6471 *pa'am* (42), *time*
8543 *tᵉmôwl* (2), *yesterday*
1074 *gĕnĕa* (1), *age*
1441 *hĕbdŏmēkŏntakis* (1), *seventy times*
2034 *hĕptakis* (4), *seven times*
2540 *kairŏs* (8), *set time*
3999 *pĕntakis* (1), *five times*
4218 *pŏtĕ* (3), *ever*
5151 *tris* (1), *three times*
5550 *chrŏnŏs* (8), *time*

TIMNA
8555 *Timnâ'* (4), *restraint*

TIMNAH
8553 *Timnâh* (3), *portion*
8555 *Timnâ'* (2), *restraint*

TIMNATH
8553 *Timnâh* (8), *portion*

TIMNATH-HERES
8556 Timnath Chereç (1), *portion of* (the) *sun*

TIMNATH-SERAH
8556 Timnath Chereç (2), *portion of* (the) *sun*

TIMNITE
8554 *Timnîy* (1), *Timnite*

TIMON
5096 *Timōn* (1), *valuable*

TIMOTHEOUS
5095 *Timŏthĕŏs* (1), *dear to God*

TIMOTHEUS
5095 *Timŏthĕŏs* (18), *dear to God*

TIMOTHY
5095 *Timŏthĕŏs* (9), *dear to God*

TIN
913 *bᵉdîyl* (5), *tin*

TINGLE
6750 *tsâlal* (3), to *tinkle*

TINKLING
5913 *'âkaç* (1), to *put on anklets*
214 *alalazō* (1), to *clang*

TIP
8571 *tᵉnûwk* (8), *pinnacle, i.e. extremity*
206 *akrŏn* (1), *extremity*

TIPHSAH
8607 *Tiphçach* (2), *ford*

TIRAS
8493 *Tîyrᵉyâ'* (2), *fearful*

TIRATHITES
8654 *Tir'âthîy* (1), *gate*

TIRE
6287 *pᵉ'êr* (1), *head-dress*

TIRED
3190 *yâṭab* (1), to *be, make well; successful*

TIRES
6287 *pᵉ'êr* (1), *fancy head-dress*
7720 *sahărôn* (1), *round pendant* or *crescent*

TIRHAKAH
8640 *Tirhâqâh* (2), *Tirhakah*

TIRHANAH
8647 *Tirchănâh* (1), *Tirchanah*

TIRIA
8493 *Tîyrᵉyâ'* (1), *fearful*

TIRSHATHA
8660 *Tirshâthâ'* (5), deputy or *governor*

TIRZAH
8656 *Tirtsâh* (18), *delightsomeness*

TISHBITE
8664 *Tishbîy* (6), *Tishbite*

TITHE
4643 *ma'ăsêr* (11), *tithe*
6237 *'âsar* (1), to *tithe*

586 *apŏdĕkatŏō* (2), to
tithe

TITHES
4643 ma'ăsêr (16), *tithe*
6237 'âsar (2), to *tithe*
586 *apŏdĕkatŏō* (2), to
tithe, give a tenth
1181 *dĕkatē* (1), *tithe*
1183 *dĕkatŏō* (3), to *give
or take a tenth*

TITHING
4643 ma'ăsêr (1), *tithe*
6237 'âsar (1), to *tithe*

TITLE
6725 tsîyûwn (1), *guiding
pillar, monument*
5102 titlŏs (2), *title*

TITTLE
2762 kĕraia (2), *horn-like*

TITUS
5103 Titŏs (15), *Titus*

TIZITE
8491 Tîytsîy (1), *Titsite*

TOAH
8430 Tôwach (1), *humble*

TOB
2897 Ṭôwb (2), *good*

TOB-ADONIJAH
2899 Ṭôwb Ădônîyâhûw
(1), *pleasing* (to)
Adonijah

TOBIAH
2900 Ṭôwbîyâh (15),
goodness of Jehovah

TOBIJAH
2900 Ṭôwbîyâh (3),
goodness of Jehovah

TOCHEN
8507 Tôken (1), *quantity*

TOE
931 bôhen (6), *big toe*

TOES
676 'etsba' (2), *finger; toe*
677 'etsba' (Ch.) (2), *toe*
931 bôhen (1), *big toe*
931+7272 bôhen (2),
thumb; big toe

TOGARMAH
8425 Tôwgarmâh (4),
Togarmah

TOGETHER
259 'echâd (5), *first*
2298 chad (Ch.) (1), *one*
3162 yachad (125),
unitedly
6776 tsemed (1), *yoke*
240 allēlŏn (1), *one
another*
260 hama (3), *together*
346 anakĕphalaiŏmai
(1), to *sum up*
1794 ĕntulissō (1), *wind
up in, enwrap*
1865 ĕpathrŏizō (1), to
accumulate, increase
1996 ĕpisunagō (6), to
collect upon
1997 ĕpisunagōgē (2),
meeting, gathering
1998 ĕpisuntrĕchō (1), to
hasten together upon
2086 hĕtĕrŏzugĕō (1), to
associate discordantly

2675 katartizō (1), to
prepare, equip
3674 hŏmŏu (3), *at the
same* place or time
4776 sugkathizō (2), to
give, take a seat with
4779 sugkalĕō (8), to
convoke, call together
4786 sugkĕrannumi (1),
to *combine, assimilate*
4789 sugklērŏnŏmŏs (1),
participant in common
4794 sugkuptō (1), to *be
completely overcome*
4801 suzĕugnumi (2), to
conjoin in marriage
4802 suzētĕō (1), to
discuss, controvert
4806 suzōŏpŏiĕō (2), to
reanimate conjointly
4811 sukŏphantĕō (1), to
defraud, i.e. exact
4816 sullĕgō (1), to *gather*
4822 sumbibazō (2), to
drive together, unite
4831 summimētēs (1),
co-imitator
4836 sumparaginŏmai
(1), to *convene*
4837 sumparakalĕō (1),
to *console jointly*
4851 sumphĕrō (1), to
collect; to conduce
4853 sumphulĕtēs (1),
*native of the same
country*
4854 sumphutŏs (1),
closely united to
4856 sumphōnĕō (1), to
be harmonious
4863 sunagō (31), to
gather together
4865 sunagōnizŏmai (1),
to *struggle with*
4866 sunathlĕō (1), to
wrestle with
4867 sunathrŏizō (3), to
convene
4873 sunanakĕimai (1),
to *recline with*
4883 sunarmŏlŏgĕō (2),
to *render close-jointed*
4886 sundĕsmŏs (1),
ligament; uniting
4888 sundŏxazō (1), to
share glory with
4890 sundrŏmē (1),
(riotous) *concourse*
4891 sunĕgĕirō (1), to
raise up with
4896 sunĕimi (1), to
assemble, gather
4897 sunĕisĕrchŏmai (1),
to *enter with*
4899 sunĕklĕktŏs (1),
chosen together with
4903 sunĕrgĕō (2), to *be
a fellow-worker*
4904 sunĕrgŏs (1),
fellow-worker
4905 sunĕrchŏmai (16),
to *gather together*
4911 sunĕphistēmi (1), to
resist or *assault jointly*
4925 sunŏikŏdŏmĕō (1),
to *construct*
4943 sunupŏurgĕō (1),
assist, join to help

4944 sunōdinō (1), to
sympathize

TOHU
8459 Tôchûw (1),
abasement

TOI
8583 Tô'ûw (3), *error*

TOIL
5999 'âmâl (1), *effort*
6093 'itstsâbôwn (1),
labor or pain
2872 kŏpiaō (2), to *feel
fatigue; to work hard*

TOILED
2872 kŏpiaō (1), to *feel
fatigue; to work hard*

TOILING
928 basanizō (1), to
torture, torment

TOKEN
226 'ôwth (10), *sign*
1730 ĕndĕigma (1), *plain
indication*
1732 ĕndĕixis (1),
indication
4592 sēmĕiŏn (1), *sign*
4953 sussēmŏn (1), *sign
in common*

TOKENS
226 'ôwth (4), *signal, sign*

TOLA
8439 Tôwlâ' (6), *worm*

TOLAD
8434 Tôwlâd (1), *posterity*

TOLAITES
8440 Tôwlâ'îy (1), *Tolaite*

TOLD
559 'âmar (13), to *say*
560 'ămar (Ch.) (5), to *say*
1540 gâlâh (2), to *reveal*
1696 dâbar (15), to *speak*
4487 mânâh (1), to *allot;
to enumerate* or enroll
5046 nâgad (152), to
announce
5608 çâphar (27), to
recount an event
8085 shâma' (2), to *hear*
8505 tâkan (1), to
balance, i.e. measure
312 anaggĕllō (4), to
announce, report
513 axinē (3), *axe*
518 apaggĕllō (17), to
announce, proclaim
1285 diasaphĕō (1), to
declare, tell
1334 diēgĕŏmai (2), to
relate fully, describe
1834 ĕxēgĕŏmai (1), to
tell, relate again
2036 ĕpō (13), to *speak*
2046 ĕrĕō (1), to *utter*
2980 lalĕō (10), to *talk*
3004 lĕgō (4), to *say*
3377 mēnuō (1), to *report*
4277 prŏĕpō (1), to *say
already, to predict*
4280 prŏĕrĕō (2), to *say
already, predict*
4302 prŏlĕgō (1), to
predict, forewarn

TOLERABLE
414 anĕktŏtĕrŏs (6),
more endurable

TOLL
4061 middâh (Ch.) (3),
tribute, tax money

TOMB
1430 gâdîysh (1), *stack*
3419 mnēmĕiŏn (2),
place of interment

TOMBS
3418 mnēma (2),
monument
3419 mnēmĕiŏn (3),
place of interment
5028 taphŏs (1), *grave*

TONGS
4457 melqâch (5), *tongs*
4621 ma'ătsâd (1), *axe*

TONGUE
762 'Ărâmîyth (2), *in
Aramean*
2013 hâçâh (1), to *hush*
2790 chârash (4), to *be
silent; to be deaf*
3956 lâshôwn (89),
tongue; tongue-shaped
1100 glōssa (24), *tongue*
1258 dialĕktŏs (5),
language
1447 Hĕbraïsti (3), *in the
Jewish* language

TONGUES
3956 lâshôwn (9), *tongue*
1100 glōssa (26), *tongue*
2084 hĕtĕrŏglōssŏs (1),
foreigner

TOOK
270 'âchaz (6), to *seize*
622 'âçaph (2), to *gather*
680 'âtsal (1), to *select*
935 bôw' (1), to *go, come*
1197 bâ'ar (1), to *be
brutish, be senseless*
1491 gâzâh (1), to *cut off*
1497 gâzal (1), to *rob*
1518 gîyach (1), to *issue
forth; to burst forth*
2388 châzaq (4), to
fasten upon; to seize
3318 yâtsâ' (1), to *bring
out*
3381 yârad (4), to
descend
3920 lâkad (43), to *catch*
3947 lâqach (359), to *take*
4185 mûwsh (1), to
withdraw
5265 nâça' (2), to *start*
5267 nᵉçaq (Ch.) (1), to
go up
5312 nᵉphaq (Ch.) (2), to
issue forth; to bring out
5375 nâsâ' (45), to *lift up*
5384 nâsheh (1),
rheumatic or crippled
5414 nâthan (1), to *give*
5493 çûwr (11), to *turn off*
5674 'âbar (2), to *cross
over; to transition*
5709 'ădâ' (Ch.) (1), to
remove
5927 'âlâh (3), to *ascend*
6901 qâbal (3), to *take*
6902 qᵉbal (Ch.) (1), to
acquire
7287 râdâh (1), to
subjugate; to crumble
7311 rûwm (2), to *be
high; to rise or raise*

7673 shâbath (1), to *repose*; to *desist*
7760 sûwm (1), to *put*
8610 tâphas (18), to *manipulate*, i.e. *seize*
142 airō (18), to *take up*
337 anairĕō (1), to *take away*, i.e. *abolish*
353 analambanō (3), to *take up, bring up*
520 apagō (1), to *take away*
589 apŏdēmĕō (2), *visit a foreign land*
618 apŏlambanō (1), to *receive; be repaid*
643 apŏskĕuazō (1), to *pack up baggage*
657 apŏtassŏmai (1), to *say adieu*; to *renounce*
941 bastazō (1), to *lift*
1011 bŏulĕuō (1), to *deliberate; to resolve*
1209 dĕchŏmai (2), to *receive, welcome*
1453 ĕgĕirō (1), to *waken*
1544 ĕkballō (1), to *throw out*
1562 ĕkduō (2), to *divest*
1723 ĕnagkalizŏmai (1), *take into one's arms*
1921 ĕpiginōskō (1), to *acknowledge*
1949 ĕpilambanŏmai (12), to *seize*
1959 ĕpimĕlĕŏmai (1), to *care for*
2021 ĕpichĕirĕō (1), to *undertake, try*
2192 ĕchō (1), to *have*
2507 kathairĕō (3), to *lower, or demolish*
2902 kratĕō (11), to *seize*
2983 lambanō (57), to *take, receive*
3348 mĕtĕchō (1), to *share or participate*
3830 pandŏchĕus (1), *innkeeper*
3880 paralambanō (16), to *associate with*
4084 piazō (1), to *seize*
4160 pŏiĕō (1), to *make*
4327 prŏsdĕchŏmai (1), to *receive; to await for*
4355 prŏslambanō (5), to *take along*
4815 sullambanō (3), to *seize (arrest, capture)*
4823 sumbŏulĕuō (2), to *recommend, deliberate*
4838 sumparalambanō (2), to *take along with*
4863 sunagō (3), to *gather together*

TOOKEST
3947 lâqach (1), to *take*

TOOL
2719 chereb (1), *knife*
3627 kᵉlîy (1), *thing*

TOOTH
8127 shên (6), *tooth*
3599 ŏdŏus (1), *tooth*

TOOTH'S
8127 shên (1), *tooth*

TOP
1406 gâg (8), *roof; top*

1634 gerem (1), *bone; self*
5585 çâ'îyph (2), *bough*
6706 tsᵉchîyach (4), *exposed* to the sun
6788 tsammereth (3), *foliage*
6936 qodqôd (2), *crown*
7218 rô'sh (67), *head*
206 akrŏn (1), *extremity*
509 anōthĕn (3), *from above; from the first*

TOPAZ
6357 piṭdâh (4), *topaz*
5116 tŏpaziŏn (1), *topaz*

TOPHEL
8603 Tôphel (1), *quagmire*

TOPHET
8612 Tôpheth (8), *smiting*
8613 Tophteh (1), place of *cremation*

TOPHETH
8612 Tôpheth (1), *smiting*

TOPS
1406 gâg (2), *roof; top*
5585 çâ'îyph (1), *bough*
7218 rô'sh (8), *head*

TORCH
3940 lappîyd (1), *torch*

TORCHES
3940 lappîyd (1), *torch*
6393 pᵉlâdâh (1), iron *armature*
2985 lampas (1), *torch*

TORMENT
928 basanizō (3), to *torture, torment*
929 basanismŏs (6), *torture, agony*
931 basanŏs (1), *torture*
2851 kŏlasis (1), *infliction, punishment*

TORMENTED
928 basanizō (5), to *torture, torment*
2558 kakŏuchĕō (1), to *maltreat; to torment*
3600 ŏdunaō (2), to *grieve*

TORMENTORS
930 basanistēs (1), *torturer*

TORMENTS
931 basanŏs (2), *torture*

TORN
1497 gâzal (1), to *rob*
2963 ṭâraph (4), to *pluck*
2966 ṭᵉrêphâh (8), *torn prey*
5478 çûwchâh (1), *filth*
7665 shâbar (2), to *burst*
4682 sparassō (1), to *convulse* with epilepsy

TORTOISE
6632 tsâb (1), *lizard*

TORTURED
5178 tumpanizō (1), to *beat* to death

TOSS
1607 gâ'ash (1), to *agitate* violently, *shake*
6802 tsᵉnêphâh (1), *ball*

TOSSED
5086 nâdaph (1), to *disperse, be windblown*

5287 nâ'ar (1), to *tumble*
928 basanizō (1), to *torture, torment*
2831 kludŏnizŏmai (1), to *fluctuate on waves*
4494 rhipizō (1), to *be tossed about*
5492 chĕimazō (1), to *be battered in a storm*

TOSSINGS
5076 nâdûd (1), *tossing* and *rolling* on the bed

TOTTERING
1760 dâchâh (1), to *totter*

TOU
8583 Tô'ûw (2), *error*

TOUCH
5060 nâga' (31), to *strike*
680 haptŏmai (13), to *touch*
2345 thigganō (2), to *touch*
4379 prŏspsauō (1), to *lay a finger on*

TOUCHED
5060 nâga' (24), to *strike*
5401 nâshaq (1), to *touch*
680 haptŏmai (21), to *touch*
2609 katagō (1), to *lead down*; to *moor* a vessel
4834 sumpathĕō (1), to *commiserate*
5584 psēlaphaō (1), to *manipulate*

TOUCHETH
5060 nâga' (37), to *strike*
7306 rûwach (1), to *smell*
680 haptŏmai (2), to *touch*

TOUCHING
413 'êl (3), *to, toward*
5921 'al (1), against
1909 ĕpi (2), *on, upon*
2596 kata (3), *down; according to*
4012 pĕri (11), *about*

TOW
5296 nᵉ'ôreth (2), *tow*
6594 pishtâh (1), *flax*

TOWEL
3012 lĕntiŏn (2), *linen*

TOWER
969 bâchôwn (1), *assayer*
1431 gâdal (1), to *be great, make great*
4024 Migdôwl (2), *tower*
4026 migdâl (34), *tower*
4692 mâtsôwr (1), *siege-mound; distress*
4869 misgâb (3), *refuge*
6076 'ôphel (1), *fortress*
4444 purgŏs (4), *tower*

TOWERS
971 bachîyn (1), *siege-tower*
975 bachan (1), *watch-tower*
4026 migdâl (13), *tower*
6438 pinnâh (2), *pinnacle*

TOWN
5892 'îyr (3), *city, town*
7023 qîyr (2), *wall*
2968 kōmē (8), *town*

TOWNCLERK
1122 grammatĕus (1), *secretary, scholar*

TOWNS
1323 bath (27), *outlying village*
2333 chavvâh (4), *village*
2691 châtsêr (2), *village*
5892 'îyr (3), *city, town*
6519 pᵉrâzâh (1), *rural*
2968 kōmē (3), town
2969 kōmŏpŏlis (1), *unwalled city*

TRACHONITIS
5139 Trachōnitis (1), *rough* district

TRADE
582 'ĕnôwsh (2), *man; person, human*
5503 çâchar (2), to *travel*
2038 ĕrgazŏmai (1), to *toil*

TRADED
5414 nâthan (4), to *give*
2038 ĕrgazŏmai (1), to *toil*

TRADING
1281 diapragmatĕuŏmai (1), to *earn, make gain*

TRADITION
3862 paradŏsis (11), Jewish *traditional law*

TRADITIONS
3862 paradŏsis (2), Jewish *traditional law*

TRAFFICK
3667 Kᵉna'an (1), *humiliated*
4536 miççhâr (1), *trade*
5503 çâchar (1), to *travel* round; to *palpitate*
7404 rᵉkullâh (1), peddled *trade*

TRAFFICKERS
3669 Kᵉna'ănîy (1), *Kenaanite; pedlar*

TRAIN
2428 chayil (1), *army; wealth; virtue; valor*
2596 kata (3), *down; according to*
7757 shûwl (1), *skirt*

TRAINED
2593 chânîyk (1), *trained*

TRAITOR
4273 prŏdŏtēs (1), *betraying*

TRAITORS
4273 prŏdŏtēs (1), *betraying*

TRAMPLE
7429 râmaç (2), to *tread*
2662 katapatĕō (1), to *trample down; to reject*

TRANCE
1611 ĕkstasis (3), *bewilderment, ecstasy*

TRANQUILITY
7963 shᵉlêvâh (Ch.) (1), *safety*

TRANSFERRED
3345 mĕtaschēmatizō (1), to *transfigure*

TRANSFIGURED
3339 mĕtamŏrphŏō (2),
to *transform*

TRANSFORMED
3339 mĕtamŏrphŏō (1),
to *transform*
3345 mĕtaschēmatizō
(2), to *transfigure*

TRANSFORMING
3345 mĕtaschēmatizō
(1), to *transfigure*

TRANSGRESS
898 bâgad (1), to *act
treacherously*
4603 mâ'al (2), to *act
treacherously*
5647 'âbad (1), to *do*
5674 'âbar (4), to *cross*
6586 pâsha' (3), to *break
away from authority*
3845 parabainō (2), to
violate a command
3848 parabatēs (1),
violator, lawbreaker

TRANSGRESSED
898 bâgad (1), to *act
treacherously*
4603 mâ'al (7), to *act
treacherously*
5674 'âbar (12), to *cross*
6586 pâsha' (13), to
break from authority
3928 parĕrchŏmai (1), to
go by; to perish

TRANSGRESSEST
5674 'âbar (1), to *cross*

TRANSGRESSETH
898 bâgad (1), to *act
treacherously*
4603 mâ'al (1), to *act
treacherously*
458+4160 anŏmia (1),
violation of law
3845 parabainō (1), to
violate a command

TRANSGRESSING
5674 'âbar (1), to *cross*
6586 pâsha' (1), to *break
away from authority*

TRANSGRESSION
4604 ma'al (6), *treachery*
6586 pâsha' (1), to *break
away from authority*
6588 pesha' (38), *revolt*
458 anŏmia (1), *violation
of law, wickedness*
3845 parabainō (1), to
violate a command
3847 parabasis (4),
violation, breaking

TRANSGRESSIONS
6588 pesha' (46), *revolt*
3847 parabasis (2),
violation, breaking

TRANSGRESSOR
898 bâgad (2), to *act
treacherously*
6586 pâsha' (1), to *break
away from authority*
3848 parabatēs (2),
violator, lawbreaker

TRANSGRESSORS
898 bâgad (8), to *act
treacherously*
5674 'âbar (1), to *cross*

6586 pâsha' (8), to *break
away from authority*
459 anŏmŏs (2), *without
Jewish law*
3848 parabatēs (1),
violator, lawbreaker

TRANSLATE
5674 'âbar (1), to *cross*

TRANSLATED
3179 mĕthistēmi (1), to
move
3346 mĕtatithēmi (2), to
transport; to exchange

TRANSLATION
3331 mĕtathĕsis (1),
transferral to heaven

TRANSPARENT
1307 diaphanēs (1),
appearing through

TRAP
4170 môwqêsh (1), *noose*
4434 malkôdeth (1),
snare
4889 mashchîyth (1),
bird snare; corruption
2339 thēra (1), *hunting*

TRAPS
4170 môwqêsh (1), *noose*

TRAVAIL
2342 chûwl (2), to *dance,
whirl; to writhe* in pain
2470 châlâh (1), to *be
weak, sick, afflicted*
3205 yâlad (1), to *bear
young; to father a child*
5999 'âmâl (3), *worry*
6045 'inyân (6), *labor;
affair, care*
8513 tᵉlâ'âh (1), *distress*
3449 mŏchthŏs (2),
sadness
5088 tiktō (1), to *produce
from seed*
5604 ōdin (1), *pang*
5605 ōdinō (1), to
experience labor pains

TRAVAILED
2342 chûwl (2), to *dance,
whirl; to writhe* in pain
3205 yâlad (3), to *bear
young; to father a child*

TRAVAILEST
5605 ōdinō (1), to
experience labor pains

TRAVAILETH
2254 châbal (1), to *writhe*
in labor pain
2342 chûwl (1), to *writhe*
in pain; to *wait*
3205 yâlad (4), to *bear
young; to father a child*
4944 sunōdinō (1), to
sympathize

TRAVAILING
3205 yâlad (2), to *bear
young; to father a child*
5605 ōdinō (1), to
experience labor pains

TRAVEL
8513 tᵉlâ'âh (2), *distress*
4898 sunĕkdēmŏs (2),
fellow-traveller

TRAVELERS
1980+5410 hâlak (1), to
walk

TRAVELLED
1330 diĕrchŏmai (1), to
traverse, travel through

TRAVELLER
734 'ôrach (1), *road*
1982 hêlek (1), *wayfarer*

TRAVELLETH
1980 hâlak (2), to *walk*

TRAVELLING
736 'ôrᵉchâh (1), *caravan*
6808 tsâ'âh (1), to *tip
over; to depopulate*
589 apŏdēmĕō (1), *visit a
foreign land*

TRAVERSING
8308 sârak (1), to
interlace

TREACHEROUS
898 bâgad (6), to *act
treacherously*
900 bôgᵉdôwth (1),
treachery
901 bâgôwd (2),
treacherous

TREACHEROUSLY
898 bâgad (23), to *act
treacherously*

TREACHERY
4820 mirmâh (1), *fraud*

TREAD
947 bûwç (6), to *trample*
1758 dûwsh (1), to
trample or thresh
1759 dûwsh (Ch.) (1), to
trample; destroy
1869 dârak (14), to *tread*
1915 hâdak (1), to *crush*
6072 'âçaç (1), to *trample*
7429 râmaç (6), to *tread*
7760+4823 sûwm (1), to
put, place
3961 patĕō (2), to *trample*

TREADER
1869 dârak (1), to *tread*

TREADERS
1869 dârak (1), to *tread*

TREADETH
1758 dûwsh (1), to
trample or thresh
1869 dârak (4), to *tread*
7429 râmaç (2), to *tread*
248 alŏaō (2), to *tread
out grain*
3961 patĕō (1), to *trample*

TREADING
1318 bâshaç (1), to
trample down
1869 dârak (1), to *tread*
4001 mᵉbûwçâh (1),
trampling, oppression
4823 mirmâç (1),
abasement

TREASON
7195 qesher (5), *unlawful
alliance*

TREASURE
214 'ôwtsâr (11),
depository
1596 gᵉnaz (Ch.) (2),
treasury storeroom
2633 chôçen (2), *wealth*
4301 maṭmôwn (1),
secret storehouse

4543 miçkᵉnâh (1),
storage-magazine
1047 gaza (1), *treasure*
2343 thēsaurizō (2), to
amass or reserve
2344 thēsaurŏs (13),
wealth, what is stored

TREASURED
686 'âtsar (1), to *store up*

TREASURER
1489 gizbâr (1), *treasurer*
5532 çâkan (1), to
minister to

TREASURERS
686 'âtsar (1), to *store up*
1411 gᵉdâbâr (Ch.) (2),
treasurer
1490 gizbâr (Ch.) (1),
treasurer

TREASURES
214 'ôwtsâr (50),
depository
1596 gᵉnaz (Ch.) (1),
treasury storeroom
4301 maṭmôwn (3),
secret storehouse
4362 mikman (1),
hidden-treasure
6259 'âthûwd (1),
prepared
8226 sâphan (1), to
conceal
2344 thēsaurŏs (5),
wealth, what is stored

TREASUREST
2343 thēsaurizō (1), to
amass or reserve

TREASURIES
214 'ôwtsâr (7),
depository
1595 genez (2), treasury
coffer
1597 ginzak (1), *treasury
storeroom*

TREASURY
214 'ôwtsâr (3),
depository
1049 gazŏphulakiŏn (5),
treasure-house
2878 kŏrban (1), votive
offering or gift

TREATISE
3056 lŏgŏs (1), *word*

TREE
363 'îylân (Ch.) (6), *tree*
815 'êshel (2), *tamarisk*
6086 'êts (88), *wood*
65 agriĕlaiŏs (2), *wild
olive tree*
1186 dĕndrŏn (17), *tree*
2565 kalliĕlaiŏs (1),
cultivated olive
3586 xulŏn (10), *timber*
4808 sukē (16), *fig-tree*
4809 sukŏmŏraia (1),
sycamore-fig tree

TREES
352 'ayîl (2), *oak tree*
6086 'êts (77), *wood*
6097 'êtsâh (1), *timber*
1186 dĕndrŏn (9), *tree*

TREMBLE
2111 zûwa' (1), to *tremble*
2112 zûwa' (Ch.) (1), to
shake with fear

2342 chûwl (2), to *writhe*
2648 châphaz (1), to
hasten away, to *fear*
2729 chârad (6), to
shudder with terror
2730 chârêd (2), *fearful*
6426 pâlats (1), to *quiver*
7264 râgaz (9), to *quiver*
7322 rûwph (1), to *quake*
7493 râ'ash (4), to *quake*
5425 phrissō (1), to
shudder in *fear*

TREMBLED
2112 zûwa' (Ch.) (1), to
shake with fear
2342 chûwl (2), to *writhe*
2729 chârad (5), to
shudder with terror
2730 chârêd (2), *fearful*
7264 râgaz (2), to *quiver*
7364 râchats (1), to *bathe*
7493 râ'ash (5), to *quake*
1719+1096 ĕmphŏbŏs (1),
alarmed, terrified
1790+1096 ĕntrŏmŏs (1),
terrified
2192+5156 ĕchō (1), to
have; hold; keep

TREMBLETH
2729 chârad (1), to
shudder with terror
2730 chârêd (2), *fearful*
5568 çâmar (1), to *bristle*
7460 râ'ad (1), to *shudder*

TREMBLING
2729 chârad (1), to
shudder with terror
2731 chărâdâh (4), *fear*
6427 pallâtsûwth (1),
trembling fear
7268 raggâz (1), *timid*
7269 rogzâh (1),
trepidation
7460 râ'ad (6), to
shudder violently
7478 ra'al (1), *reeling*
7578 rᵉthêth (1), *terror*
8653 tar'êlâh (2), *reeling*
1096+1790 ginŏmai (1),
to *be, become*
5141 trĕmō (3), to *tremble*
5156 trŏmŏs (4), *quaking*
with *fear*

TRENCH
2426 chêyl (1),
entrenchment
4570 ma'gâl (3), circular
track or camp *rampart*
8565 tan (2), *jackal*
8585 tᵉ'âlâh (1),
irrigation *channel*
5482 charax (1), *rampart*

TRESPASS
816 'âsham (2), to *be
guilty; to be punished*
817 'âshâm (41), *guilt*
819 'ashmâh (11),
guiltiness
2398 châṭâ' (1), to *sin*
4603 mâ'al (1), to *act
treacherously*
4604 ma'al (18), *sinful
treachery*
6588 pesha' (5), *revolt*
264 hamartanō (3), to *sin*

TRESPASSED
816 'âsham (2), to *be
guilty; to be punished*
819 'ashmâh (1),
guiltiness
4603 mâ'al (8), to *act
treacherously*
4604 ma'al (3), *sinful
treachery*

TRESPASSES
817 'âshâm (1), *guilt*
819 'ashmâh (1),
guiltiness
4604 ma'al (1), *sinful
treachery*
3900 paraptōma (9),
error; transgression

TRESPASSING
819 'ashmâh (1),
guiltiness
4603 mâ'al (1), to *act
treacherously*

TRIAL
974 bâchan (1), to *test*
4531 maççâh (1), *testing*
1382 dŏkimē (1), *test*
1383 dŏkimiŏn (1),
testing; trustworthiness
3984 pĕira (1), *attempt*

TRIBE
4294 maṭṭeh (160), *tribe*
7626 shêbeṭ (57), *clan*
5443 phulē (19), *clan*

TRIBES
4294 maṭṭeh (20), *tribe*
7625 shᵉbaṭ (Ch.) (1), *clan*
7626 shêbeṭ (84), *clan*
1429 dōdĕkaphulŏn (1),
twelve tribes
5443 phulē (6), *clan*

TRIBULATION
6862 tsar (1), *trouble*
6869 tsârâh (2), *trouble*
2346 thlibō (1), to *trouble*
2347 thlipsis (18), *trouble*

TRIBULATIONS
6869 tsârâh (1), *trouble*
2347 thlipsis (3), *trouble*

TRIBUTARIES
4522 maç (4), *labor*

TRIBUTARY
4522 maç (1), *labor*

TRIBUTE
1093 bᵉlôw (Ch.) (3), *tax*
4060 middâh (1), *tribute*
4061 middâh (Ch.) (1),
tribute
4371 mekeç (6),
assessment, census-tax
4522 maç (12), *labor*
4530 miççâh (1), *liberally*
4853 massâ' (1), *burden*
6066 'ônesh (1), *fine*
1323 didrachmŏn (2),
double drachma
2778 kĕnsŏs (4),
enrollment
5411 phŏrŏs (4), *tax, toll*

TRICKLETH
5064 nâgar (1), to *pour*
out; to *deliver* over

TRIED
974 bâchan (4), to *test;* to
investigate
976 bôchan (1), *trial*

6884 tsâraph (7), to *refine*
1381 dŏkimazō (1), to
test; to *approve*
1384 dŏkimŏs (1),
acceptable, approved
3985 pĕirazō (3), to
endeavor, scrutinize
4448 purŏō (1), to *be
ignited, glow*

TRIEST
974 bâchan (3), to *test*

TRIETH
974 bâchan (4), to *test;* to
investigate
1381 dŏkimazō (1), to
test; to *approve*

TRIMMED
6213 'âsâh (1), to *do*
2885 kŏsmĕō (1), to *snuff*

TRIMMEST
3190 yâṭab (1), to *be,
make well*

TRIUMPH
5937 'âlaz (2), to *jump* for
joy
5970 'âlats (1), to *jump*
for joy
7321 rûwa' (3), to *shout*
7440 rinnâh (1), *shout*
7442 rânan (1), to *shout*
for joy
7623 shâbach (1), to
address in a loud tone;
to *pacify*
2358 thriambĕuō (1), to
*give victory, lead in
triumphal procession*

TRIUMPHED
1342 gâ'âh (2), to *be
exalted*

TRIUMPHING
7445 rᵉnânâh (1), *shout*
for joy
2358 thriambĕuō (1), to
*give victory, lead in
triumphal procession*

TROAS
5174 Trōas (6), *plain of
Troy*

TRODDEN
947 bûwç (3), to *trample*
1758 dûwsh (2), to
trample or *thresh*
1869 dârak (7), to *tread*
4001 mᵉbûwçâh (2),
trampling, oppression
4823 mirmâç (4),
abasement
5541 çâlâh (2), to
contemn, reject
7429 râmaç (2), to *tread*
2662 katapatĕō (3), to
trample down; to *reject*
3961 patĕō (2), to *trample*

TRODE
1869 dârak (2), to *tread*
7429 râmaç (5), to *tread*
2662 katapatĕō (1), to
trample down; to *reject*

TROGYLLIUM
5175 Trŏgulliŏn (1),
Trogyllium

TROOP
92 'ăguddâh (2), *band*
1409 gâd (2), *fortune*

1416 gᵉdûwd (7), *band*
2416 chay (2), *alive; raw*

TROOPS
734 'ôrach (1), *road*
1416 gᵉdûwd (3), *band*

TROPHIMUS
5161 Trŏphimŏs (3),
nutritive

TROUBLE
926 bâhal (2), to *tremble*
927 bᵉhal (Ch.) (2), to
terrify; hasten
928 behâlâh (2), *sudden
panic, destruction*
1091 ballâhâh (1),
sudden destruction
1205 bᵉ'âthâh (2), *fear*
1804 dâlach (1), to *roil
water, churn up*
2189 za'ăvâh (1),
agitation
2960 ṭôrach (1), *burden*
4103 mᵉhûwmâh (4),
confusion or uproar
5916 'âkar (4), to *disturb*
5999 'âmâl (3), *worry*
6040 'ŏnîy (3), *misery*
6862 tsar (17), *trouble*
6869 tsârâh (34), *trouble*
6887 tsârar (2), to *cramp*
7186+3117 qâsheh (1),
severe
7267 rôgez (2), *disquiet*
7451 ra' (9), *bad; evil*
7561 râsha' (1), to *be, do,
declare wrong*
8513 tᵉlâ'âh (1), *distress*
387 anastatŏō (1), to
disturb, cause trouble
1613 ĕktarassō (1), to
disturb wholly
1776 ĕnŏchlĕō (1), to
annoy, cause trouble
2346 thlibō (1), to *trouble*
2347 thlipsis (3), *trouble*
2350 thŏrubĕō (1), to
disturb; clamor
2553 kakŏpathĕō (1), to
undergo hardship
2873 kŏpŏs (1), *toil; pains*
2873+3930 kŏpŏs (2), *toil*
3926 parĕnŏchlĕō (1), to
annoy, make trouble
3930 parĕchō (1), to *hold
near,* i.e. to *present*
4660 skullō (2), to *harass*
5015 tarassō (1), to
trouble, disturb

TROUBLED
926 bâhal (12), to *tremble*
927 bᵉhal (Ch.) (6), to
terrify; hasten
1089 bâlahh (1), to *terrify*
1204 bâ'ath (1), to *fear,
be afraid*
1607 gâ'ash (1), to
agitate violently, *shake*
1644 gârash (1), to *drive
out;* to *divorce*
1993 hâmâh (2), to *be in
great commotion*
2000 hâmam (1), to *put
in commotion*
2560 châmar (3), to
ferment, foam
5590 çâ'ar (1), to *rush
upon;* to *toss about*

5753 'âvâh (1), to *be crooked*
5916 'âkar (4), to *disturb*
6031 'ânâh (1), to *afflict*
6470 pâ'am (4), to *impel or agitate*
7114 qâtsar (1), to *curtail, cut short*
7264 râgaz (3), to *quiver*
7481 râ'am (1), to *crash thunder*; to *irritate*
7515 râphas (1), to *trample*, i.e. *roil water*
1298 diatarassō (1), to *disturb wholly*
2346 thlibō (3), to *crowd, press, trouble*
2360 thrŏĕō (3), to *frighten, be alarmed*
5015 tarassō (14), to *trouble, disturb*
5015+1438 tarassō (1), to *trouble, disturb*
5182 turbazō (1), to *make turbid*

TROUBLEDST
1804 dâlach (1), to *roil water, churn up*

TROUBLER
5916 'âkar (1), to *disturb or afflict*

TROUBLES
6869 tsârâh (10), *trouble*
7451 ra' (1), *bad; evil*
5016 tarachē (1), *mob disturbance; roiling*

TROUBLEST
4660 skullō (1), to *harass*

TROUBLETH
598 'ănaç (Ch.) (1), to *distress*
926 bâhal (2), to *tremble*
1204 bâ'ath (1), to *fear, be afraid*
5916 'âkar (4), to *disturb*
3930+2873 parĕchō (1), to *hold near*
5015 tarassō (1), to *trouble, disturb*

TROUBLING
7267 rôgez (1), *disquiet; anger*
5015 tarassō (1), to *trouble, disturb*

TROUBLOUS
5916 'âkar (1), to *disturb or afflict*

TROUGH
8268 shôqeth (1), *watering-trough*

TROUGHS
7298 rahat (1), *ringlet of hair*
8268 shôqeth (1), *watering-trough*

TROW
1380 dŏkĕō (1), to *think, regard, seem good*

TRUCEBREAKERS
786 aspŏndŏs (1), *not reconcilable*

TRUE
551 'omnâm (1), *verily, indeed, truly*

571 'emeth (18), *truth, trustworthiness*
3330 yatstsîyb (Ch.) (2), *fixed, sure*
3651 kên (5), *just; right*
6656 ts\u00b0dâ' (Ch.) (1), (sinister) *design*
227 alēthēs (22), *true; genuine*
228 alēthinŏs (27), *truthful*
1103 gnēsiŏs (1), *genuine, true*
2227 zōŏpŏiĕō (1), to (re-) *vitalize, give life*
3588+225 hŏ (1), "*the*," i.e. the definite article
4103 pistŏs (2), *trustworthy; reliable*

TRULY
199 'ûwlâm (4), *however*
389 'ak (3), *surely; only*
403 'âkên (2), *truly!*
530 'ĕmûwnâh (1), *fidelity; steadiness*
551 'omnâm (1), *truly*
571 'emeth (8), *certainty, truth, trustworthiness*
577 'ânnâ' (1), *oh now!*
3588 kîy (1), *for, that*
227 alēthēs (1), *true*
230 alēthōs (2), *truly*
686 ara (1), *then, so*
1161 dĕ (1), *but, yet*
1909+225 ĕpi (1), *on, upon*
3303 mĕn (12), *truly*

TRUMP
2689 chătsôts\u00b0râh (1), *trumpet*
7782 shôwphâr (1), *curved ram's horn*
4536 salpigx (2), *trumpet*

TRUMPET
3104 yôwbêl (1), *blast of a ram's horn*
7782 shôwphâr (47), *curved ram's horn*
8628 tâqa' (1), to *clatter, slap, drive, clasp*
4536 salpigx (7), *trumpet*
4537 salpizō (1), to *sound a trumpet blast*

TRUMPETERS
2689 chătsôts\u00b0râh (2), *trumpet*
2690 châtsar (1), to *blow the trumpet*
4538 salpistēs (1), *trumpeter*

TRUMPETS
2689 chătsôts\u00b0râh (24), *trumpet*
7782 shôwphâr (20), *curved ram's horn*
4536 salpigx (2), *trumpet*

TRUST
539 'âman (4), to *be firm, faithful, true*; to *trust*
982 bâtach (61), to *trust, be confident or sure*
2342 chûwl (1), to *wait; to pervert*
2620 châçâh (32), to *confide in*
2622 châçûwth (1), *confidence*

3176 yâchal (2), to *wait; to be patient, hope*
4004 mibchôwr (1), *select*, i.e. well fortified
4009 mibtâch (3), *security; assurance*
4268 machăçeh (1), *shelter; refuge*
1679 ĕlpizō (15), to *confide, hope for*
3892 paranŏmia (1), *wrongdoing*
3982 pĕithō (6), to *rely by inward certainty*
4006 pĕpŏithēsis (1), *reliance, trust*
4100 pisteuō (3), to *have faith, credit; to entrust*

TRUSTED
539 'âman (1), to *trust*, to *be permanent*
982 bâtach (18), to *trust, be confident or sure*
1556 gâlal (1), to *roll; to commit*
2620 châçâh (1), to *confide in*
7365 r\u00b0chats (Ch.) (1), to *attend upon, trust*
1679 ĕlpizō (2), to *expect or confide, hope for*
3982 pĕithō (3), to *rely by inward certainty*
4276 prŏĕlpizō (1), to *hope in advance*

TRUSTEDST
982 bâtach (3), to *trust, be confident or sure*

TRUSTEST
982 bâtach (6), to *trust, be confident or sure*

TRUSTETH
982 bâtach (14), to *trust, be confident or sure*
2620 châçâh (2), to *confide in*
1679 ĕlpizō (1), to *expect or confide, hope for*

TRUSTING
982 bâtach (1), to *trust, be confident or sure*

TRUSTY
539 'âman (1), to *be firm, faithful, true*; to *trust*

TRUTH
518+3808 'îm (1), *if, although; Oh that!*
529 'ēmûwn (1), *trustworthiness; faithful*
530 'ĕmûwnâh (13), *fidelity; steadiness*
544 'ômen (1), *verity, faithfulness*
548 'ămânâh (2), *covenant*
551 'omnâm (3), *verily, indeed, truly*
571 'emeth (90), *certainty, truth*
3321 y\u00b0tsêb (Ch.) (1), to *speak surely*
3330 yatstsîyb (Ch.) (1), *fixed, sure*
3588+518 kîy (1), *for, that because*
7187 q\u00b0shôwt (Ch.) (2), *fidelity, truth*

7189 qôshet (1), *reality*
225 alēthĕia (99), *truth, truthfulness*
226 alēthĕuō (8), to *be true*
227 alēthēs (1), *true; genuine*
230 alēthōs (7), *truly, surely*
3483 nai (1), *yes*
3689 ŏntōs (1), *really, certainly*

TRUTH'S
571 'emeth (1), *certainty, truth, trustworthiness*
225 alēthĕia (1), *truth, truthfulness*

TRY
974 bâchan (8), to *test; to investigate*
2713 châqar (1), to *examine, search*
5254 nâçâh (1), to *test, attempt*
6884 tsâraph (3), to *fuse metal; to refine*
1381 dŏkimazō (2), to *test; to approve*
3985 pĕirazō (1), to *endeavor, scrutinize*
4314+3986 prŏs (1), *to, toward; against*

TRYING
1383 dŏkimiŏn (1), *testing; trustworthiness*

TRYPHENA
5170 Truphaina (1), *luxurious*

TRYPHOSA
5173 Truphōsa (1), *luxuriating*

TUBAL
8422 Tûwbal (8), *Tubal*

TUBAL-CAIN
8423 Tûwbal Qayin (2), *offspring of Cain*

TUMBLED
2015 hâphak (1), to *change, overturn*

TUMULT
1993 hâmâh (1), to *be in great commotion*
1995 hâmôwn (4), *noise, tumult; many, crowd*
1999 hămullâh (1), *sound, roar, noise*
4103 m\u00b0hûwmâh (1), *confusion or uproar*
7588 shâ'ôwn (3), *uproar; destruction*
7600 sha'ănân (2), *secure; haughty*
2351 thŏrubŏs (4), *disturbance*

TUMULTS
4103 m\u00b0hûwmâh (1), *confusion or uproar*
181 akatastasia (2), *disorder, riot*

TUMULTUOUS
1121+7588 bên (1), *son, descendant; people*
1993 hâmâh (1), to *be in great commotion*

7588 shâ'ôwn (1), *uproar; destruction*

TURN
2015 hâphak (7), *to turn; to change, overturn*
2186 zânach (1), *to reject, forsake, fail*
5186 nâṭâh (17), *to stretch or spread out*
5414 nâthan (1), *to give*
5437 çâbab (14), *to surround*
5493 çûwr (27), *to turn off*
5627 çârâh (1), *apostasy; crime; remission*
5674 'âbar (2), *to cross over; to transition*
6437 pânâh (18), *to turn, to face*
6801 tsânaph (1), *to wrap, i.e. roll or dress*
7725 shûwb (152), *to turn back; return*
7750 sûwṭ (2), *become derelict*
7760 sûwm (1), *to put, place*
7847 sâṭâh (1), *to deviate from duty, go astray*
8159 shâ'âh (1), *to inspect, consider*
8447 tôwr (2), *string or order*
344 anakamptō (1), *to turn back, come back*
576 apŏbainō (2), *to disembark*
654 apŏstrĕphō (5), *turn away or back*
665 apŏtrĕpō (1), *to deflect, avoid*
1294 diastrĕphō (1), *to be morally corrupt*
1994 ĕpistrĕphō (10), *to revert, turn back to*
3329 mĕtagō (1), *to turn*
4762 strĕphō (4), *to turn or reverse a course*

TURNED
1750 dûwts (1), *to leap*
2015 hâphak (53), *to turn; to change*
3399 yâraṭ (1), *to be rash*
3943 lâphath (2), *to turn around or aside*
5186 nâṭâh (16), *to stretch or spread out*
5253 nâçag (1), *to retreat*
5414 nâthan (1), *to give*
5437 çâbab (31), *to surround*
5472 çûwg (10), *to go back, to retreat*
5493 çûwr (24), *to turn off*
6437 pânâh (36), *to turn, to face*
7725 shûwb (67), *to turn back; return*
7734 sûwg (1), *to retreat*
7760 sûwm (1), *to put, place*
387 anastatŏō (1), *to disturb, cause trouble*
402 anachōrĕō (1), *to retire, withdraw*
654 apŏstrĕphō (2), *turn away or back*
1096 ginŏmai (1), *to be, become*

1624 ĕktrĕpō (1), *to turn away*
1824 ĕxautēs (2), *instantly, at once*
1994 ĕpistrĕphō (11), *to revert, turn back to*
2827 klinō (1), *to slant or slope*
3179 mĕthistēmi (1), *to move*
3329 mĕtagō (1), *to turn*
3344 mĕtastrĕphō (1), *to transmute; corrupt*
4672 Sŏlŏmōn (1), *peaceful*
4762 strĕphō (12), *to turn or reverse a course*
5290 hupŏstrĕphō (2), *to turn under, behind*

TURNEST
6437 pânâh (1), *to turn, to face*
7725 shûwb (2), *to turn back; to return*

TURNETH
2015 hâphak (2), *to turn; to change, overturn*
5186 nâṭâh (2), *to stretch or spread out*
5437 çâbab (2), *to surround*
5493 çûwr (1), *to turn off*
5753 'âvâh (1), *to be crooked*
5791 'âvath (1), *to wrest, twist*
5844 'âṭâh (1), *to wrap, i.e. cover, veil, clothe*
6437 pânâh (4), *to turn, to face*
7725 shûwb (17), *to turn back; to return*
7760 sûwm (1), *to put, place*

TURNING
2015 hâphak (1), *to change, overturn*
2017 hôphek (1), *opposite-ness*
4142 mûwçabbâh (1), *transmutation*
4740 maqtsôwa' (5), *angle; or recess*
4878 mᵉshûwbâh (1), *apostasy*
7257 râbats (1), *to recline, repose, brood*
7725 shûwb (5), *to turn back; to return*
654 apŏstrĕphō (1), *to turn away or back*
1994 ĕpistrĕphō (2), *to revert, turn back to*
3346 mĕtatithēmi (1), *to transport; to exchange*
4762 strĕphō (1), *to turn or reverse a course*
5077 tĕphrŏō (1), *to incinerate*
5157 trŏpē (1), *turn, i.e. revolution (variation)*

TURTLE
8449 tôwr (2), *ring-dove*

TURTLEDOVE
8449 tôwr (3), *ring-dove*

TURTLEDOVES
8449 tôwr (6), *ring-dove*

5167 trugōn (1), *turtle-dove bird*

TURTLES
8449 tôwr (3), *ring-dove*

TUTORS
2012 ĕpitrŏpŏs (1), *manager, guardian*

TWAIN
8147 shᵉnayim (7), *two-fold*
1417 duŏ (10), *two*

TWELFTH
8147+6240 shᵉnayim (20), *two-fold*
1428 dōdĕkatŏs (1), *twelfth*

TWELVE
505 'eleph (1), *thousand*
8147 shᵉnayim (2), *two-fold*
8147+6240 shᵉnayim (107), *two-fold*
8648+6236 tᵉrêyn (Ch.) (2), *two*
1177 dĕkaduŏ (2), *twelve*
1427 dōdĕka (71), *twelve*
1429 dōdĕkaphulŏn (1), *twelve tribes*

TWENTIETH
6242 'esrîym (36), *twenty; twentieth*

TWENTY
6242 'esrîym (275), *twenty; twentieth*
6243 'esrîyn (Ch.) (1), *twenty; twentieth*
7239 ribbôw (3), *myriad, indefinite large number*
1501 ĕikŏsi (12), *twenty*

TWENTY'S
6242 'esrîym (1), *twenty; twentieth*

TWICE
4932 mishneh (3), *duplicate copy; double*
6471 pa'am (5), *time; step; occurence*
8147 shᵉnayim (5), *two-fold*
1364 dis (4), *twice*

TWIGS
3127 yôwneqeth (1), *sprout, new shoot*
3242 yᵉnîqâh (1), *sucker or sapling*

TWILIGHT
5399 nesheph (6), *dusk, dawn*
5939 'ălâṭâh (3), *dusk*

TWINED
7806 shâzar (21), *to twist a thread of straw*

TWINKLING
4493 rhipē (1), *instant*

TWINS
8380 tâ'ôwm (4), *twin, things doubled*
8382 tâ'am (2), *to be twinned, i.e. duplicate*

TWO
2677 chêtsîy (1), *half or middle, midst*
6471 pa'am (1), *time; step; occurence*

6771 tsâmê' (1), *thirsty*
8147 shᵉnayim (527), *two-fold*
8648 tᵉrêyn (Ch.) (1), *two*
296 amphŏdŏn (1), *fork in the road*
1250 diakŏsiŏi (7), *two hundred*
1332 diĕtēs (1), *of two years in age*
1333 diĕtia (2), *interval of two years*
1337 dithalassŏs (1), *having two seas*
1366 distŏmŏs (1), *double-edged*
1367 dischilïoi (1), *two thousand*
1417 duŏ (122), *two*

TWOEDGED
6310 peh (1), *mouth; opening*
6374 pîyphîyâh (1), *edge or tooth*
1366 distŏmŏs (2), *double-edged*

TWOFOLD
1366 distŏmŏs (1), *double-edged*

TYCHICUS
5190 Tuchikŏs (7), *fortunate*

TYRANNUS
5181 Turannŏs (1), *tyrant*

TYRE
6865 Tsôr (20), *rock*
6876 Tsôrîy (5), *Tsorite*
5184 Turŏs (11), *rock*
5185 tuphlŏs (1), *blindness; blind person*

TYRUS
6865 Tsôr (22), *rock*

UCAL
401 'Ûkâl (1), *devoured*

UEL
177 'Ûw'êl (1), *wish of God*

ULAI
195 'Ûwlay (2), *Ulai or Eulus*

ULAM
198 'Ûwlâm (4), *solitary*

ULLA
5925 'Ullâ' (1), *burden*

UMMAH
5981 'Ummâh (1), *association*

UNACCUSTOMED
3808+3925 lô' (1), *no, not*

UNADVISEDLY
981 bâṭâ' (1), *to babble, speak rashly*

UNAWARES
1097+1847 bᵉlîy (1), *without, not yet*
3045 yâda' (1), *to know*
3820+3824 lêb (2), *heart*
7684 shᵉgâgâh (4), *mistake*
160 aiphnidiōs (1), *suddenly*
2990 lanthanō (1), *to lie hid; unwittingly*

3920 *parĕisaktŏs* (1), *smuggled in, infiltrated*
3921 *parĕisdunō* (1), to *slip in secretly*

UNBELIEF
543 *apĕithĕia* (4), *disbelief*
570 *apistia* (12), *disbelief; disobedience*

UNBELIEVERS
571 *apistŏs* (4), *without faith; untrustworthy*

UNBELIEVING
544 *apĕithĕō* (1), to *disbelieve*
571 *apistŏs* (5), *without faith; untrustworthy*

UNBLAMEABLE
299 *amōmŏs* (2), *unblemished, blameless*

UNBLAMEABLY
274 *amĕmptōs* (1), *faultlessly*

UNCERTAIN
82 *adēlŏs* (1), *indistinct, not clear*
83 *adēlŏtēs* (1), *uncertainty*

UNCERTAINLY
82 *adēlŏs* (1), *indistinct, not clear*

UNCHANGEABLE
531 *aparabatŏs* (1), *untransferable*

UNCIRCUMCISED
6189 'ârêl (34), to *be uncircumcised*
6190 'orlâh (2), *prepuce or penile foreskin*
203+2192 *akrŏbustia* (1), *uncircumcised*
564 *apĕritmētŏs* (1), *uncircumcised*
1722+3588+203 *ĕn* (2), *in; during; because of*
1986 *ĕpispaŏmai* (1), to *efface the mark of circumcision*

UNCIRCUMCISION
203 *akrŏbustia* (16), *uncircumcised*

UNCLE
1730 dôwd (10), *beloved, friend; uncle, cousin*

UNCLE'S
1730 dôwd (1), *beloved, friend; uncle, cousin*
1733 dôwdâh (6), *aunt*

UNCLEAN
2930 tâmê' (74), to *be morally contaminated*
2931 tâmê' (78), *foul; ceremonially impure*
2932 ṭum'âh (4), *ceremonial impurity*
5079 niddâh (2), *time of menstrual impurity*
6172 'ervâh (1), *nudity; disgrace; blemish*
6945 qâdêsh (1), *sacred male prostitute*
169 *akathartŏs* (28), *impure; evil*
2839 *kŏinŏs* (3), *common, i.e. profane*

2840 *kŏinŏō* (1), to *make profane*

UNCLEANNESS
2930 tâmê' (1), to *be morally contaminated*
2932 ṭum'âh (25), *ceremonial impurity*
5079 niddâh (1), *time of menstrual impurity*
6172 'ervâh (1), *nudity; disgrace; blemish*
7137 qâreh (1), *accidental occurrence*
167 *akatharsia* (10), *quality of impurity*
3394 *miasmŏs* (1), *act of moral contamination*

UNCLEANNESSES
2932 ṭum'âh (1), *ceremonial impurity*

UNCLOTHED
1562 *ĕkduō* (1), to *divest*

UNCOMELY
807 *aschēmŏnĕō* (1), to *be, act unbecoming*
809 *aschēmōn* (1), *inelegant, indecent*

UNCONDEMNED
178 *akatakritŏs* (2), *without legal trial*

UNCORRUPTIBLE
862 *aphthartŏs* (1), *undecaying, immortal*

UNCORRUPTNESS
90 *adiaphthŏria* (1), *purity of doctrine*

UNCOVER
1540 gâlâh (22), to *denude; uncover*
6168 'ârâh (1), to *be, make bare; to empty*
6544 pâra' (3), to *loosen; to expose, dismiss*

UNCOVERED
1540 gâlâh (10), to *denude; uncover*
2834 châsaph (2), to *drain away or bail up*
6168 'ârâh (1), to *be, make bare; to empty*
177 *akatakaluptŏs* (2), *unveiled*
648 *apŏstĕgazō* (1), to *unroof, make a hole in a roof*

UNCOVERETH
1540 gâlâh (2), to *denude; uncover*
6168 'ârâh (1), to *be, make bare; to empty*

UNCTION
5545 chrisma (1), *special endowment of the Holy Spirit*

UNDEFILED
8535 tâm (2), *morally pious; gentle, dear*
8549 tâmîym (1), *entire, complete; integrity*
283 *amiantŏs* (4), *pure*

UNDER
413 'êl (2), *to, toward*
4295 *maṭṭâh* (1), *below or beneath*

5921 'al (9), *above, over, upon*, or *against*
8460 t\ᵉchôwth (Ch.) (4), *beneath, under*
8478 tachath (231), *bottom; underneath*
332 *anathĕmatizō* (2), to *declare or vow an oath*
506 *anupŏtaktŏs* (1), *independent*
1640 *ĕlassōn* (1), *smaller*
1722 *ĕn* (2), *in; during; because of*
1772 *ĕnnŏmŏs* (1), *legal, or subject to law*
1909 *ĕpi* (3), *on, upon*
2662 *katapatĕō* (2), to *trample down; to reject*
2709 *katachthŏniŏs* (1), *infernal*
2736 katō (1), *downwards*
5259 hupŏ (47), *under; by means of; at*
5270 hupŏkatō (8), *down under*, i.e. *beneath*
5273 hupŏkritēs (1), *dissembler, hypocrite*
5284 hupŏplĕō (2), to *sail under the lee of*
5293 hupŏtassō (4), to *subordinate; to obey*
5295 hupŏtrĕchō (1), to *run under*
5299 hupŏpiazō (1), to *beat up; to wear out*

UNDERGIRDING
5269 hupŏzōnnumi (1), to *gird under*

UNDERNEATH
4295 maṭṭâh (2), *below or beneath*
8478 tachath (1), *bottom; underneath; in lieu of*

UNDERSETTERS
3802 kâthêph (4), *shoulder-piece; wall*

UNDERSTAND
995 bîyn (44), to *understand; discern*
998 bîynâh (1), *understanding*
3045 yâda' (3), to *know*
7919 sâkal (9), to *be or act circumspect*
8085 shâma' (6), to *hear intelligently*
50 *agnŏĕō* (1), to *not know; not understand*
1097 *ginōskō* (3), to *know*
1107 *gnŏrizō* (1), to *make known, reveal*
1492 *ĕidō* (1), to *know*
1987 *ĕpistamai* (1), to *comprehend*
3539 *nŏiĕō* (8), to *exercise the mind*
4920 *suniĕmi* (13), to *comprehend*

UNDERSTANDEST
995 bîyn (2), to *understand; discern*
8085 shâma' (1), to *hear intelligently*
1097 *ginōskō* (1), to *know*

UNDERSTANDETH
995 bîyn (5), to *understand; discern*

7919 sâkal (1), to *be or act circumspect*
191 *akŏuō* (1), to *hear; obey*
1492 *ĕidō* (1), to *know*
4920 *suniĕmi* (3), to *comprehend*

UNDERSTANDING
995 bîyn (33), to *understand; discern*
998 bîynâh (32), *understanding*
999 bîynâh (Ch.) (1), *understanding*
2940 ṭa'am (1), *taste; intelligence; mandate*
3820 lêb (10), *heart*
3824 lêbâb (3), *heart*
4486 manda' (Ch.) (1), *wisdom or intelligence*
7306 rûwach (1), to *smell or perceive*
7919 sâkal (5), to *be or act circumspect*
7922 sekel (7), *intelligence; success*
7924 sokl\ᵉthânûw (Ch.) (3), *intelligence*
8085 shâma' (1), to *hear intelligently*
8394 tâbûwn (38), *intelligence; argument*
801 *asunĕtŏs* (3), *senseless, dull; wicked*
1271 *dianŏia* (3), *mind or thought*
3563 *nŏus* (7), *intellect, mind; understanding*
3877 *parakŏlŏuthĕō* (1), to *attend; trace out*
4907 *sunĕsis* (6), *understanding*
4920 *suniĕmi* (2), to *understand*
5424 *phrēn* (2), *mind or cognitive faculties*

UNDERSTOOD
995 bîyn (11), to *understand; discern*
3045 yâda' (4), to *know*
7919 sâkal (2), to *be or act circumspect*
8085 shâma' (1), to *hear intelligently*
50 *agnŏĕō* (2), to *not know; not understand*
1097 *ginōskō* (4), to *know*
1425 *dusnŏētŏs* (1), *difficult of perception*
2154 *ĕusēmŏs* (1), *significant*
3129 *manthanō* (1), to *learn*
3539 *nŏiĕō* (1), to *exercise the mind*
4441 *punthanŏmai* (1), to *ask for information*
4920 *suniĕmi* (7), to *understand*
5426 *phrŏnĕō* (1), to *be mentally disposed*

UNDERTAKE
6148 'ârab (1), to *intermix; to give or be security*

UNDERTOOK
6901 qâbal (1), to *admit; to take*

English

UNDO
5425 nâthar (1), to
terrify; shake off; untie
6213 'âsâh (1), to do or
make

UNDONE
6 'âbad (1), to perish;
destroy
1820 dâmâh (1), to be
silent; to fail, cease
5493 çûwr (1), to turn off

UNDRESSED
5139 nâzîyr (2), prince;
separated Nazirite

UNEQUAL
3808+8505 lô' (2), no, not

UNEQUALLY
2086 hĕtĕrŏzugĕō (1), to
associate discordantly

UNFAITHFUL
898 bâgad (1), to act
treacherously

UNFAITHFULLY
898 bâgad (1), to act
treacherously

UNFEIGNED
505 anupŏkritŏs (4),
sincere, genuine

UNFRUITFUL
175 akarpŏs (6), barren,
unfruitful

UNGIRDED
6605 pâthach (1), to open
wide; to loosen, begin

UNGODLINESS
763 asĕbĕia (4),
wickedness, impiety

UNGODLY
1100 bᵉlîya'al (4),
wickedness, trouble
3808+2623 lô' (1), no, not
5760 'ăvîyl (1), morally
perverse
7563 râshâ' (8), morally
wrong; bad person
763 asĕbĕia (3),
wickedness, impiety
764 asĕbĕō (2), to be, act
impious or wicked
765 asĕbēs (8), impious
or wicked

UNHOLY
2455 chôl (1), profane,
common, not holy
462 anŏsiŏs (2), wicked,
unholy
2839 kŏinŏs (1),
common, i.e. profane

UNICORN
7214 rᵉ'êm (6), wild bull

UNICORNS
7214 rᵉ'êm (3), wild bull

UNITE
3161 yâchad (1), to be,
become one

UNITED
3161 yâchad (1), to be,
become one

UNITY
3162 yachad (1), unitedly
1775 hĕnŏtēs (2),
unanimity, unity

UNJUST
205 'âven (1), trouble,
vanity, wickedness
5766 'evel (2), moral evil
5767 'avvâl (1), morally
evil
8636 tarbîyth (1),
percentage or bonus
91 adikĕō (1), to do
wrong
93 adikia (2),
wrongfulness
94 adikŏs (8), unjust,
wicked

UNJUSTLY
5765 'âval (1), to morally
distort
5766 'evel (1), moral evil

UNKNOWN
50 agnŏĕō (2), to not
know; not understand
57 agnŏstŏs (1), unknown

UNLADE
670 apŏphŏrtizŏmai (1),
to unload

UNLAWFUL
111 athĕmitŏs (1),
illegal; detestable
459 anŏmŏs (1), without
Jewish law

UNLEARNED
62 agrammatŏs (1),
illiterate, unschooled
261 amathēs (1),
ignorant
521 apaidĕutŏs (1),
stupid, uneducated
2399 idiōtēs (3), not
initiated; untrained

UNLEAVENED
4682 matstsâh (51),
unfermented cake
106 azumŏs (9), made
without yeast; Passover

UNLESS
194 'ûwlay (1), if not;
perhaps
3884 lûwlê' (3), if not

UNLOOSE
3089 luō (3), to loosen

UNMARRIED
22 agamŏs (4),
unmarried

UNMERCIFUL
415 anĕlĕĕmōn (1),
merciless, ruthless

UNMINDFUL
7876 shâyâh (1), to keep
in memory

UNMOVABLE
277 amĕtakinĕtŏs (1),
immovable

UNMOVEABLE
761 asalĕutŏs (1),
immovable, fixed

UNNI
6042 'Unnîy (3), afflicted

UNOCCUPIED
2308 châdal (1), to desist,
stop; be fat

UNPREPARED
532 aparaskĕuastŏs (1),
unready

UNPROFITABLE
5532 çâkan (1), to be
serviceable to
255 alusitĕlēs (1),
gainless, pernicious
512 anōphĕlēs (1), useless
888 achrĕiŏs (2), useless,
i.e. unmeritorious
889 achrĕiŏō (1), render
useless, i.e. spoil
890 achrēstŏs (1),
inefficient, detrimental

UNPROFITABLENESS
512 anōphĕlēs (1), useless

UNPUNISHED
5352 nâqâh (11), to be,
make clean; to be bare

UNQUENCHABLE
762 asbĕstŏs (2), not
extinguished

UNREASONABLE
249 alŏgŏs (1), irrational,
not reasonable
824 atŏpŏs (1), improper;
injurious; wicked

UNREBUKEABLE
423 anĕpilēptŏs (1), not
open to blame

UNREPROVEABLE
410 anĕgklētŏs (1),
irreproachable

UNRIGHTEOUS
205 'âven (2), trouble,
vanity, wickedness
2555 châmâç (1),
violence; malice
5765 'âval (1), to morally
distort
5767 'avvâl (1), morally
evil
94 adikŏs (4), unjust,
wicked

UNRIGHTEOUSLY
5766 'evel (1), moral evil

UNRIGHTEOUSNESS
3808+6664 lô' (1), no, not
5766 'evel (3), moral evil
93 adikia (16),
wrongfulness
458 anŏmia (1), violation
of law, wickedness

UNRIPE
1154 beçer (1),
immature, sour grapes

UNRULY
183 akataschĕtŏs (1),
unrestrainable
506 anupŏtaktŏs (2),
insubordinate
813 ataktŏs (1),
insubordinate

UNSATIABLE
1115+7654 biltîy (1), not,
except, without, unless

UNSAVOURY
6617 pâthal (1), to
struggle; to be tortuous
8602 tâphêl (1), to
plaster; be tasteless

UNSEARCHABLE
369+2714 'ayin (1), there
is no, i.e., not exist
419 anĕxĕrĕunētŏs (1),
inscrutable

421 anĕxichniastŏs (1),
unsearchable

UNSEEMLY
808 aschēmŏsunē (1),
indecency; shame

UNSHOD
3182 mĕthuskō (1), to
intoxicate, become
drunk

UNSKILFUL
552 apĕirŏs (1), ignorant,
not acquainted with

UNSPEAKABLE
411 anĕkdiēgētŏs (1),
indescribable
412 anĕklalētŏs (1),
unutterable
731 arrhētŏs (1),
inexpressible

UNSPOTTED
784 aspilŏs (1),
unblemished

UNSTABLE
6349 pachaz (1),
ebullition, turbulence
182 akatastatŏs (1),
inconstant, restless
793 astēriktŏs (2),
vacillating, unstable

UNSTOPPED
6605 pâthach (1), to open
wide; to loosen, begin

UNTAKEN
3361+348 mē (1), not; lest

UNTEMPERED
8602 tâphêl (5), to be
tasteless; frivolity

UNTHANKFUL
884 acharistŏs (2),
ungrateful

UNTIL
5704 'ad (288), as far
(long) as; during; until
891 achri (16), until or
up to
1519 ĕis (1), to or into
2193 hĕōs (35), until
3360 mĕchri (7), until, to
the point of

UNTIMELY
5309 nephel (3), abortive
miscarriage
3653 ŏlunthŏs (1), unripe
fig

UNTOWARD
4646 skŏliŏs (1), crooked;
perverse

UNWALLED
6519 pᵉrâzâh (1), rural,
open country
6521 pᵉrâzîy (1), rustic

UNWASHEN
449 aniptŏs (3), without
ablution, unwashed

UNWISE
3808+2450 lô' (2), no, not
453 anŏētŏs (1),
unintelligent, senseless
878 aphrōn (1), ignorant;
egotistic; unbelieving

UNWITTINGLY
1097+1847 bᵉlîy (2),
without, not yet

7684 sh°gâgâh (1), *mistake*, inadvertent *transgression*

UNWORTHILY
371 anaxiōs (2), in a manner *unworthy*

UNWORTHY
370 anaxiōs (1), *unfit, unworthy*
3756+514 ŏu (1), *no or not*

UPBRAID
2778 châraph (1), to spend the *winter*
3679 ŏnĕidizō (1), to *rail at, chide, taunt*

UPBRAIDED
3679 ŏnĕidizō (1), to *rail at, chide, taunt*

UPBRAIDETH
3679 ŏnĕidizō (1), to *rail at, chide, taunt*

UPHARSIN
6537 p°raç (Ch.) (1), to *split* up

UPHAZ
210 'Ûwphâz (2), *Uphaz*

UPHELD
5564 çâmak (1), to *lean* upon; *take hold* of

UPHOLD
5564 çâmak (5), to *lean* upon; *take hold* of
8551 tâmak (3), to *obtain, keep fast*

UPHOLDEN
5582 çâ'ad (1), to *support*
6965 qûwm (1), to *rise*

UPHOLDEST
8551 tâmak (1), to *obtain, keep fast*

UPHOLDETH
5564 çâmak (3), to *lean* upon; *take hold* of
8551 tâmak (1), to *obtain, keep fast*

UPHOLDING
5342 phĕrō (1), to *bear or carry*

UPPER
3730 kaphtôr (1), *capital*; wreath-like *button*
4947 mashqôwph (1), *lintel*
5942 'illîy (2), *higher*
5944 'ălîyâh (4), *upper* things; *second-story*
5945 'elyôwn (8), *loftier, higher; Supreme* God
7393 rekeb (1), *upper millstone*
8222 sâphâm (1), *beard*
508 anōgĕŏn (2), *dome* or a *balcony*
510 anōtĕrikŏs (1), *more remote* regions
5250 hupĕrplĕŏnazō (1), to *superabound*
5253 hupĕrō¡ŏn (3), *room* in the *third story*

UPPERMOST
5945 'elyôwn (1), *loftier, higher; Supreme* God
4410 prōtŏkathĕdria (1), *pre-eminence* in council

4411 prōtŏklisia (2), *pre-eminence* at meals

UPRIGHT
3474 yâshar (1), to be *straight*; to *make right*
3476 yôsher (1), *right*
3477 yâshâr (43), *straight*
4339 mêyshâr (1), *straightness; rectitude*
4749 miqshâh (1), work molded by *hammering*
5977 'ōmed (2), fixed *spot*
6968 qôwm°mîyûwth (1), *erectly*, with head high
8535 tâm (1), morally *pious; gentle, dear*
8537 tôm (2), *prosperity; innocence*
8549 tâmîym (8), *entire, complete; integrity*
8549+8552 tâmîym (1), *complete; integrity*
8552 tâmam (2), to *complete, finish*
3717 ŏrthŏs (1), *straight, level*

UPRIGHTLY
3474 yâshar (1), to be *straight*; to *make right*
3477 yâshâr (1), *straight*
4339 mêyshâr (3), *straightness; rectitude*
8537 tôm (2), *prosperity; innocence*
8549 tâmîym (4), *entire, complete; integrity*
3716 ŏrthŏpŏdĕō (1), to act *rightly*

UPRIGHTNESS
3476 yôsher (9), *right*
3477 yâshâr (1), *straight*
3483 yishrâh (1), *moral integrity*
4334 mîyshôwr (1), *plain; justice*
4339 mêyshâr (3), *straightness; rectitude*
5228 nâkôach (1), *equitable, correct*
5229 n°kôchâh (1), *integrity; truth*
8537 tôm (2), *prosperity; innocence*

UPRISING
6965 qûwm (1), to *rise*

UPROAR
1993 hâmâh (1), to be in great *commotion*
387 anastatŏō (1), to *disturb*, cause trouble
2350 thŏrubĕō (1), to *clamor*; start a riot
2351 thŏrubŏs (3), *commotion*
4714 stasis (1), one leading an *uprising*
4797 sugchĕō (1), to *throw into disorder*

UPSIDE
5921+6440 'al (2), *above, over, upon*, or *against*
389 anastĕnazō (1), to *sigh deeply*

UPWARD
1361 gâbahh (1), to be *lofty*; to be *haughty*

4605 ma'al (59), *upward, above, overhead*
4791 mârôwm (1), *elevation; elation*

UR
218 'Ûwr (5), *Ur*

URBANE
3779 hŏutō (1), *in this way; likewise*

URGE
1758 ĕnĕchō (1), to *keep a grudge*

URGED
509 'âlats (1), to *press, urge*
6484 pâtsar (4), to *stun* or *dull*
6555 pârats (1), to *break out*

URGENT
2388 châzaq (1), to *fasten upon*; to *seize*
2685 chătsaph (Ch.) (1), to *be severe*

URI
221 'Ûwrîy (8), *fiery*

URIAH
223 'Ûwrîyâh (27), *flame of Jehovah*

URIAH'S
223 'Ûwrîyâh (1), *flame of Jehovah*

URIAS
3774 Ŏurias (1), *flame of Jehovah*

URIEL
222 'Ûwrîy'êl (4), *flame of God*

URIJAH
223 'Ûwrîyâh (11), *flame of Jehovah*

URIM
224 'Ûwrîym (7), *lights*

US-WARD
413 'êl (1), *to, toward*
1519+2248 ĕis (2), *to or into*

USE
559 'âmar (1), to *say*
3231 yâman (1), to be *right-handed*
3947 lâqach (1), to *take*
4399 m°lâ'kâh (1), *work; property*
4911 mâshal (3), to *use figurative language*
4912 mâshâl (1), pithy *maxim; taunt*
5172 nâchash (1), to *prognosticate*
5656 'ăbôdâh (1), *work*
7080 qâçam (1), to *divine magic*
1838 hĕxis (1), *practice, constant use*
1908 ĕpĕrĕazō (1), to *insult with threats*
5195 hubrizō (1), to *exercise violence, abuse*
5382 philŏxĕnŏs (1), *hospitable*
5530 chraŏmai (7), to *furnish* what is needed

5532 chrĕia (1), *affair; occasion, demand*
5540 chrēsis (2), *employment*

USED
3928 limmûwd (1), *instructed* one
6213 'âsâh (2), to *do or make*
390 anastrĕphō (1), to *remain*, to *live*
1247 diakŏnĕō (1), to *wait upon, serve*
1387 dŏliŏō (1), to *practice deceit*
1510 ĕimi (1), I *exist*, I *am*
3096 magĕuō (1), to *practice magic, sorcery*
4238 prassō (1), to *execute, accomplish*
5530 chraŏmai (3), to *furnish* what is needed

USES
5532 chrĕia (1), *affair; occasion, demand*

USEST
4941 mishpât (1), *verdict*; formal *decree; justice*

USETH
1696 dâbar (1), to *speak, say*; to *subdue*
3348 mĕtĕchō (1), to *share or participate*

USING
671 apŏchrēsis (1), *consumption, using up*
2192 ĕchō (1), to *have*; *hold; keep*

USURER
5383 nâshâh (1), to *lend or borrow*

USURP
831 authĕntĕō (1), to *dominate*

USURY
5378 nâshâ' (1), to *lend* on interest
5383 nâshâh (5), to *lend or borrow*
5391 nâshak (4), to *oppress* through finance
5392 neshek (11), *interest*
5110 tŏkŏs (2), *interest* on money loaned

UTHAI
5793 'Ûwthay (2), *succoring*

UTMOST
314 achărôwn (2). *late or last; behind; western*
7093 qêts (1), *extremity; after*
7097 qâtseh (3), *extremity*
7112 qâtsats (3), to *chop off*; to *separate*
4009 pĕras (1), *extremity, end, limit*

UTTER
1696 dâbar (5), to *speak, say*; to *subdue*
1897 hâgâh (1), to *murmur, utter a sound; ponder*

VANISHETH
3212 yâlak (1), to walk; to live; to carry
853 aphanizō (1), to disappear, be destroyed

VANITIES
1892 hebel (12), emptiness or vanity
3152 mataiŏs (1), profitless, futile; idol

VANITY
205 'âven (6), trouble, vanity, wickedness
1892 hebel (49), emptiness or vanity
7385 rîyq (2), emptiness; worthless thing; in vain
7723 shâv' (22), ruin; guile; idolatry
8414 tôhûw (4), waste, formless; in vain
3153 mataiŏtēs (3), transientness; depravity

VAPORS
5387 nâsîy' (2), leader; rising mist, fog

VAPOUR
108 'êd (1), fog
5927 'âlâh (1), to ascend, be high, mount
822 atmis (2), mist, vapor; billows of smoke

VAPOURS
5387 nâsîy' (1), leader; rising mist, fog
7008 qîyţôwr (1), fume, i.e. smoke cloud

VARIABLENESS
3883 parallagē (1), change or variation

VARIANCE
1369 dichazō (1), to sunder, i.e. alienate
2054 ĕris (1), quarrel, i.e. wrangling

VASHNI
2059 Vashnîy (1), weak

VASHTI
2060 Vashtîy (10), Vashti

VAUNT
6286 pâ'ar (1), to shake a tree

VAUNTETH
4068 pĕrpĕrĕuŏmai (1), to boast, brag

VEHEMENT
2759 chârîyshîy (1), sultry, searing
3050 Yâhh (1), Jehovah, (the) self-Existent or Eternal One
1972 ĕpipŏthēsis (1), longing for

VEHEMENTLY
1171 dĕinōs (1), terribly, i.e. excessively, fiercely
1722+4 ĕn (1), in; during; because of
2159 ĕutŏnōs (1), intensely, cogently
4366 prŏsrēgnumi (2), to burst upon

VEIL
7289 râdîyd (1), veil

2665 katapĕtasma (6), door screen

VEIN
4161 môwtsâ' (1), going forth

VENGEANCE
5358 nâqam (4), to avenge or punish
5359 nâqâm (15), revenge
5360 neqâmâh (19), avengement
1349 dikē (2), justice
1557 ĕkdikēsis (4), retaliation, punishment
3709 ŏrgē (1), ire; punishment

VENISON
6718 tsayid (7), hunting game; lunch, food
6720 tsêydâh (1), food, supplies

VENOM
7219 rô'sh (1), poisonous plant; poison

VENT
6605 pâthach (1), to open wide; to loosen, begin

VENTURE
8537 tôm (2), prosperity; innocence

VERIFIED
539 'âman (3), to be firm, faithful, true; to trust

VERILY
61 'ăbâl (3), truly, surely; yet, but
389 'ak (6), surely; only, however
403 'âkên (2), surely!, truly!; but
518 'îm (1), whether?; if, although; Oh that!
518+3808 'îm (1), Oh that!
530 'ĕmûwnâh (1), fidelity; steadiness
559 'âmar (1), to say
7069 qânâh (1), to create; to procure
230 alēthōs (1), truly, surely
281 amēn (76), surely; so be it
1063 gar (2), for, indeed, but, because
1222 dēpŏu (1), indeed doubtless
2532 kai (1), and; or; even; also
3303 mĕn (13), verily
3303+3767 mĕn (1), verily
3304 mĕnŏungĕ (1), so then at least
3483 nai (1), yes
3689 ŏntōs (1), really, certainly

VERITY
571 'emeth (1), certainty, truth, trustworthiness
225 alētheia (1), truth, truthfulness

VERMILION
8350 shâshar (2), red

VERY
199 'ûwlâm (2), however or on the contrary

430 'ĕlôhîym (1), the true God; great ones
552 'umnâm (1), verily, indeed, truly
651 'âphêl (1), dusky, dark
898 bâgad (1), to act covertly
899 beged (2), clothing; treachery or pillage
1419 gâdôwl (1), great
1767 day (2), enough, sufficient
1851 daq (1), crushed; small or thin
1854 dâqaq (1), to crush; crumble
1942 havvâh (1), desire; craving
2088 zeh (2), this or that
3190 yâţab (2), to be, make well; be successful
3304 yephêh-phîyâh (1), very beautiful
3453 yâshîysh (2), old man
3559 kûwn (1), to render sure, proper
3966 meôd (136), very, utterly
4213 miz'âr (3), fewness, smallness
4295 maţţâh (1), below or beneath
4592 meaţ (1), little or few
4605 ma'al (2), upward, above, overhead
4801 merchâq (1), distant place; from afar
5464 çagrîyd (1), pouring rain
5690 'egeb (1), amative words, words of love
5704 'ad (2), as far (long) as; during; while; until
6106 'etsem (2), bone; substance; selfsame
6621 petha' (1), wink, i.e. moment; quickly
6985 qaţ (1), little, i.e. merely
7023 qîyr (1), wall, side-wall
7230 rôb (1), abundance
7260 rabrab (Ch.) (1), huge, domineering
7690 saggîy' (Ch.) (1), large
85 adĕmŏnĕō (2), to be in mental distress
230 alēthōs (1), truly, surely
662 apŏtŏlmaō (1), to venture plainly
846 autŏs (5), he, she, it
927 barutimōs (1), highly valuable
957 bĕltiŏn (1), better
1565 ĕkĕinŏs (2), that one
1582 ĕkkrĕmamai (1), to listen closely
1646 ĕlachistŏs (3), least
1888 ĕpautŏphōrō̧ (1), in actual crime
2236 hēdista (1), with great pleasure

2532 kai (4), and; or; even; also
2566 kalliŏn (1), better
2735 katŏrthōma (1), made fully upright
3029 lian (2), very much
3827 pampŏlus (1), full many, i.e. immense
4036 pĕrilupŏs (1), intensely sad
4118 plĕistŏs (1), very large, i.e. the most
4119 plĕiŏn (1), more
4184 pŏlusplagchnŏs (1), extremely compassionate
4185 pŏlutĕlēs (1), extremely expensive
4186 pŏlutimŏs (1), extremely valuable
4361 prŏspĕinŏs (1), intensely hungry
4708 spŏudaiŏtĕrōs (1), more speedily
4970 sphŏdra (4), high degree, much
5228 hupĕr (2), over; above; beyond

VESSEL
3627 kelîy (33), implement, thing
5035 nebel (1), skin-bag for liquids; vase; lyre
4632 skĕuŏs (11), vessel, implement, equipment

VESSELS
3627 kelîy (129), implement, thing
3984 mâ'n (Ch.) (7), utensil, vessel
30 aggĕiŏn (2), receptacle, vessel
4632 skĕuŏs (8), vessel, implement, equipment

VESTMENTS
3830 lebûwsh (1), garment; wife
4403 malbûwsh (1), garment, clothing

VESTRY
4458 meltâchâh (1), wardrobe

VESTURE
3682 keçûwth (1), cover; veiling
3830 lebûwsh (2), garment; wife
2440 himatiŏn (2), to put on clothes
2441 himatismŏs (2), clothing
4018 pĕribŏlaiŏn (1), thrown around

VESTURES
899 beged (1), clothing; treachery or pillage

VEX
926 bâhal (1), to tremble; be, make agitated
2000 hâmam (1), to put in commotion
2111 zûwa' (1), to shake with fear, tremble
3013 yâgâh (1), to grieve; to torment
3238 yânâh (2), to rage or be violent

English

VEXATION

3707 kâ'aç (1), to *grieve, rage, be indignant*
6213+7451 'âsâh (1), to *do or make*
6887 tsârar (5), to *cramp*
6973 qûwts (1), to *be, make anxious*
2559 kakôö (1), to *injure; to oppress; to embitter*

VEXATION

2113 z°vâ'âh (1), *agitation, fear*
4103 m°hûwmâh (1), *confusion or uproar*
4164 mûwtsaq (1), *distress*
7469 r°'ûwth (7), *grasping after*
7475 ra'yôwn (3), *desire, chasing after*
7667 sheber (1), *fracture; ruin*

VEXATIONS

4103 m°hûwmâh (1), *confusion or uproar*

VEXED

926 bâhal (3), to *tremble; be, make agitated*
1766 dâchaq (1), to *oppress*
3238 yânâh (2), to *rage or be violent*
3334 yâtsar (1), to *be in distress*
4103 m°hûwmâh (1), *confusion or uproar*
4843 mârar (2), to *be, make bitter*
6087 'âtsab (1), to *worry, have pain or anger*
6887 tsârar (1), to *cramp*
7114 qâtsar (1), to *curtail, cut short*
7489 râ'a' (1), to *be good for nothing*
7492 râ'ats (1), to *break in pieces; to harass*
7561 râsha' (1), to *be, do, declare wrong*
928 basanizō (1), to *torture, torment*
1139 daimōnizōmai (1), to *be exercised by a demon*
2669 katapŏnĕō (1), to *harass, oppress*
3791 ŏchlĕō (2), to *harass, be tormented*
3958 paschō (1), to *experience pain*

VIAL

6378 pak (1), *flask, small jug*
5357 phialē (7), broad shallow *cup*, i.e. a *phial*

VIALS

5357 phialē (5), broad shallow *cup*, i.e. a *phial*

VICTORY

3467 yâsha' (1), to make *safe, free*
5331 netsach (2), *splendor; lasting*
8668 t°shûw'âh (3), *rescue, deliverance*
3528 nikaō (1), to *subdue, conquer*

3529 nikē (1), *conquest, victory, success*
3534 nikŏs (4), *triumph, victory*

VICTUAL

3557 kûwl (1), to *measure; to maintain*
3978 ma'ăkâl (1), *food, something to eat*
4202 mâzôwn (1), *food, provisions*
6720 tsêydâh (2), *food, supplies*

VICTUALS

400 'ôkel (3), *food*
737 'ărûchâh (1), *ration, portion of food*
3557 kûwl (1), to *measure; to maintain*
3899 lechem (2), *food, bread*
4241 michyâh (1), *sustenance; quick*
6718 tsayid (2), *hunting game; lunch, food*
6720 tsêydâh (4), *food, supplies*
7668 sheber (1), *grain*
1033 brōma (1), *food*
1979 ĕpisitismŏs (1), *food*

VIEW

5048 neged (2), *in front of*
7200 râ'âh (1), to *see*
7270 râgal (1), to *reconnoiter; to slander*

VIEWED

995 bîyn (1), to *understand; discern*
7370 râchash (1), to *gush*
7663 sâbar (2), to *scrutinize; to expect*

VIGILANT

1127 grēgŏrĕuō (1), to *watch, guard*
3524 nēphalĕŏs (1), *circumspect, temperate*

VILE

959 bâzâh (2), to *disesteem, ridicule*
2151 zâlal (2), to *be loose morally, worthless*
2933 ţâmâh (1), to *be ceremonially impure*
5034 nâbêl (1), to *wilt; to fall away; to be foolish*
5036 nâbâl (2), *stupid; impious*
5039 n°bâlâh (1), *moral wickedness; crime*
5240 n°mibzeh (1), *despised*
7034 qâlâh (1), to *be, hold in contempt*
7043 qâlal (4), to *be easy, trifling, vile*
8182 shô'âr (1), *harsh or horrid*, i.e. *offensive*
819 atimia (1), *disgrace*
4508 rhuparŏs (1), *shabby, dirty; wicked*
5014 tapĕinōsis (1), *humbleness, lowliness*

VILELY

1602 gâ'al (1), to *detest; to reject; to fail*

VILER

5217 nâkâ' (1), to *smite*, i.e. *drive away*

VILEST

2149 zullûwth (1), (poss.) *tempest*

VILLAGE

2968 kōmē (10), *hamlet, town*

VILLAGES

1323 bath (12), *daughter, outlying village*
2691 châtsêr (47), *yard; walled village*
3715 k°phîyr (1), *walled village; young lion*
3723 kâphâr (2), *walled village*
3724 kôpher (1), *village; bitumen; henna*
6518 pârâz (1), *chieftain*
6519 p°râzâh (1), *rural, open country*
6520 p°râzôwn (2), *magistracy, leadership*
6521 p°râzîy (1), *rustic*
2968 kōmē (7), *hamlet, town*

VILLANY

5039 n°bâlâh (2), *moral wickedness; crime*

VINE

1612 gephen (44), grape *vine*
2156 z°môwrâh (1), *pruned twig, branch*
3196 yayin (1), *wine; intoxication*
3755 kôrêm (1), *vinedresser*
5139 nâzîyr (2), *prince; unpruned vine*
8321 sôrêq (3), *choice vine stock*
288 ampĕlŏs (9), *grape vine*

VINEDRESSERS

3755 kôrêm (4), *vinedresser*

VINEGAR

2558 chômets (6), *vinegar*
3690 ŏxŏs (7), *sour* wine

VINES

1612 gephen (9), grape *vine*
3754 kerem (3), *garden or vineyard*

VINEYARD

3657 kannâh (1), *plant*
3754 kerem (44), *garden or vineyard*
289 ampĕlŏurgŏs (1), *vineyard caretaker*
290 ampĕlōn (23), *vineyard*

VINEYARDS

3754 kerem (45), *garden or vineyard*

VINTAGE

1208 bâtsôwr (1), *inaccessible*
1210 bâtsîyr (7), *grape crop, harvest*
3754 kerem (1), *garden or vineyard*

VIOL

5035 nebel (2), skin-*bag* for liquids; *vase; lyre*

VIOLATED

2554 châmaç (1), to *be violent; to maltreat*

VIOLENCE

1497 gâzal (1), to *rob*
1498 gâzêl (1), *robbery, stealing*
1499 gêzel (1), *violence*
1500 g°zêlâh (3), *robbery, stealing; things stolen*
2554 châmaç (2), to *be violent; to maltreat*
2555 châmâç (39), *violence; malice*
4835 m°rûtsâh (1), *oppression*
6231 'âshaq (1), to *violate; to overflow*
970 bia (4), *force, pounding violence*
971 biazō (1), to *crowd oneself into*
1286 diasĕiō (1), to *intimidate, extort*
1411 dunamis (1), *force, power, miracle*
3731 hŏrmēma (1), *sudden attack*

VIOLENT

1499 gêzel (1), *violence*
2555 châmâç (7), *violence; malice*
6184 'âriyts (1), *powerful or tyrannical*
973 biastēs (1), *energetic, forceful one*

VIOLENTLY

1497 gâzal (4), to *rob*
1500 g°zêlâh (1), *robbery, stealing; things stolen*
2554 châmaç (1), to *be violent; to maltreat*

VIOLS

5035 nebel (2), skin-*bag* for liquids; *vase; lyre*

VIPER

660 'eph'eh (2), *asp*
2191 ĕchidna (1), *adder*

VIPER'S

660 'eph'eh (1), *asp*

VIPERS

2191 ĕchidna (4), *adder*

VIRGIN

1330 b°thûwlâh (24), *virgin*
5959 'almâh (2), *lass, young woman*
3933 parthĕnŏs (7), *virgin*

VIRGIN'S

3933 parthĕnŏs (1), *virgin*

VIRGINITY

1331 b°thûwlîym (8), *virginity; proof of female virginity*
3932 parthĕnia (1), *maidenhood, virginity*

VIRGINS

1330 b°thûwlâh (14), *virgin*
5959 'almâh (2), *lass, young woman*
3933 parthĕnŏs (6), *virgin*

VIRTUE
703 arĕtē (4), *excellence, virtue*
1411 dunamis (3), *force, power, miracle*

VIRTUOUS
2428 chayil (3), *army; wealth; virtue; valor*

VIRTUOUSLY
2428 chayil (1), *army; wealth; virtue; valor*

VISAGE
600 'ănaph (Ch.) (1), *face*
4758 mar'eh (1), *appearance; vision*
8389 tô'ar (1), *outline, appearance*

VISIBLE
3707 hŏratŏs (1), *capable of being seen*

VISION
2376 chêzev (Ch.) (2), *sight, revelation*
2377 cházôwn (32), *sight; revelation*
2380 cházûwth (2), *striking appearance*
2384 chizzâyôwn (6), *dream; vision*
4236 machăzeh (4), *vision*
4758 mar'eh (14), *appearance; vision*
4759 mar'âh (3), *vision; mirror*
7203 rô'eh (1), *seer; vision*
3701 ŏptasia (2), *supernatural vision*
3705 hŏrama (12), *supernatural spectacle*
3706 hŏrasis (1), *appearance, vision*

VISIONS
2376 chêzev (Ch.) (9), *sight, revelation*
2377 cházôwn (3), *sight; revelation*
2378 cházôwth (1), *revelation*
2384 chizzâyôwn (3), *dream; vision*
4759 mar'âh (5), *vision; mirror*
7200 râ'âh (1), *to see*
3701 ŏptasia (1), *supernatural vision*
3706 hŏrasis (1), *appearance, vision*

VISIT
6485 pâqad (33), *to visit, care for, count*
1980 ĕpiskĕptŏmai (4), *inspect, to go to see*

VISITATION
6486 pᵉquddâh (13), *visitation; punishment*
1984 ĕpiskŏpē (2), *episcopate*

VISITED
6485 pâqad (18), *to visit, care for, count*
1980 ĕpiskĕptŏmai (5), *inspect; to go to see*

VISITEST
6485 pâqad (2), *to visit, care for, count*
1980 ĕpiskĕptŏmai (1), *to inspect; to go to see*

VISITETH
6485 pâqad (1), *to visit, care for, count*

VISITING
6485 pâqad (4), *to visit, care for, count*

VOCATION
2821 klēsis (1), *invitation; station in life*

VOICE
6963 qôwl (379), *voice or sound*
7032 qâl (Ch.) (3), *sound, music*
5456 phōnē (116), *voice, sound*
5586 psēphŏs (1), *pebble stone*

VOICES
6963 qôwl (2), *voice or sound*
5456 phōnē (15), *voice, sound*

VOID
6 'âbad (1), *perish; destroy*
922 bôhûw (2), *ruin, desolation*
1238 bâqaq (1), *to depopulate, ruin*
1637 gôren (2), *open area*
2638 châçêr (6), *lacking*
4003 mᵉbûwqâh (1), *emptiness, devastation*
5010 nâ'ar (1), *to reject*
6565 pârar (5), *to break up; to violate, frustrate*
7387 rêyqâm (1), *emptily; ineffectually*
677 aprŏskŏpŏs (1), *not led into sin*
2673 katargĕō (1), *to be, render entirely useless*
2758 kĕnŏō (2), *to make empty*

VOLUME
4039 mᵉgillâh (1), *roll, scroll*
2777 kĕphalis (1), *roll, scroll*

VOLUNTARILY
5071 nᵉdâbâh (1), *abundant gift*

VOLUNTARY
5071 nᵉdâbâh (2), *abundant gift*
7522 râtsôwn (1), *delight*
2309 thĕlō (1), *to will; to desire; to choose*

VOMIT
6892 qê' (4), *vomit*
6958 qôw' (3), *to vomit*
1829 ĕxĕrama (1), *vomit*

VOMITED
6958 qôw' (1), *to vomit*

VOMITETH
6958 qôw' (1), *to vomit*

VOPHSI
2058 Vophçîy (1), *additional*

VOW
5087 nâdar (9), *to promise, vow*
5088 neder (30), *promise to God; thing promised*
2171 ĕuchē (2), *wish, petition*

VOWED
5087 nâdar (16), *to promise, vow*
5088 neder (2), *promise to God; thing promised*

VOWEDST
5087 nâdar (1), *to promise, vow*

VOWEST
5087 nâdar (2), *to promise, vow*

VOWETH
5087 nâdar (1), *to promise, vow*

VOWS
5088 neder (30), *promise to God; thing promised*

VOYAGE
4144 plŏŏs (1), *navigation, voyage*

VULTURE
1676 dâ'âh (1), *kite*
1772 dayâh (1), *falcon*

VULTURE'S
344 'ayâh (1), *hawk*

VULTURES
1772 dayâh (1), *falcon*

WAFER
7550 râqîyq (3), *thin cake, wafer*

WAFERS
6838 tsappîychîth (1), *flat thin cake*
7550 râqîyq (4), *thin cake, wafer*

WAG
5110 nûwd (1), *to waver; to wander, flee*
5128 nûwa' (2), *to waver*

WAGES
2600 chinnâm (1), *gratis, free*
4909 maskôreth (3), *wages; reward*
6468 pᵉ'ullâh (1), *work, deed*
7936 sâkar (1), *to hire*
7939 sâkâr (6), *payment, salary; compensation*
3408 misthŏs (2), *pay for services, good or bad*
3800 ŏpsōniŏn (3), *rations, stipend or pay*

WAGGING
2795 kinĕŏ (2), *to stir, move, remove*

WAGON
5699 'ăgâlâh (1), *wheeled vehicle*

WAGONS
5699 'ăgâlâh (8), *wheeled vehicle*
7393 rekeb (1), *vehicle for riding*

WAIL
5091 nâhâh (1), *to bewail; to assemble*
5594 çâphad (1), *to tear the hair, wail*
2875 kŏptō (1), *to beat the breast*

WAILED
214 alalazō (1), *to wail; to clang*

WAILING
4553 miçpêd (6), *lamentation, howling*
5089 nôahh (1), *lamentation*
5092 nᵉhîy (4), *elegy*
5204 nîy (1), *lamentation*
2805 klauthmŏs (2), *lamentation, weeping*
3996 pĕnthĕō (2), *to grieve*

WAIT
693 'ârab (34), *to ambush, lie in wait*
695 'ereb (1), *hiding place; lair*
696 'ôreb (1), *hiding place; lair*
1748 dûwmâm (1), *silently*
1826 dâmam (1), *to stop, cease; to perish*
2342 chûwl (1), *to wait; to pervert*
2442 châkâh (6), *to await; hope for*
3027 yâd (1), *hand; power*
3176 yâchal (5), *to wait; to be patient, hope*
3993 ma'ărâb (1), *ambuscade, ambush*
6119 'âqêb (1), *track, footprint; rear position*
6633 tsâbâ' (1), *to mass an army or servants*
6658 tsâdâh (1), *to desolate*
6660 tsᵉdîyâh (2), *design, lying in wait*
6960 qâvâh (22), *to collect; to expect*
7663 sâbar (2), *to scrutinize; to expect*
7789 shûwr (1), *to spy out, survey*
8104 shâmar (4), *to watch*
362 anamĕnō (1), *await in expectation*
553 apĕkdĕchŏmai (2), *to expect fully, await*
1096+1917 ginŏmai (1), *to be, become*
1747 ĕnĕdra (1), *ambush*
1748 ĕnĕdrĕuō (2), *to lurk*
1917 ĕpibŏulē (2), *plot, plan*
3180 mĕthŏdĕia (1), *trickery, scheming*
4037 pĕrimĕnō (1), *to await*
4160+1747 pŏiĕō (1), *to make or do*
4327 prŏsdĕchŏmai (1), *to receive; to await for*
4332 prŏsĕdrĕuō (1), *attend as a servant*

English

4342 prŏskartĕrĕō (1), to *persevere*

WAITED
1961+6440 hâyâh (1), to *exist*, i.e. *be* or *become*
2342 chûwl (1), to *wait*; to *pervert*
2442 châkâh (2), to *await*; *hope for*
3176 yâchal (6), to *wait*; to *be patient, hope*
5975 'âmad (5), to *stand*
6822 tsâphâh (1), to *observe, await*
6960 qâvâh (8), to *collect*; to *expect*
8104 shâmar (1), to *watch*
8334 shârath (1), to *attend* as a menial
1551 ĕkdĕchŏmai (2), to *await, expect*
4327 prŏsdĕchŏmai (2), to *receive*; to *await for*
4328 prŏsdŏkaō (2), to *anticipate*; to *await*
4342 prŏskartĕrĕō (1), to *persevere, be constant*

WAITETH
1747 dûwmîyâh (2), *silently; quiet, trust*
2442 châkâh (3), to *await; hope for*
3176 yâchal (1), to *wait*; to *be patient, hope*
8104 shâmar (2), to *watch*
553 apĕkdĕchŏmai (1), to *expect fully, await*
1551 ĕkdĕchŏmai (1), to *await, expect*

WAITING
6635 tsâbâ' (1), *army, military host*
8104 shâmar (1), to *watch*
553 apĕkdĕchŏmai (2), to *expect fully, await*
1551 ĕkdĕchŏmai (1), to *await, expect*
4327 prŏsdĕchŏmai (1), to *receive*; to *await for*
4328 prŏsdŏkaō (1), to *anticipate*; to *await*

WAKE
5782 'ûwr (1), to *awake*
6974 qûwts (2), to *awake*
1127 grĕgŏrĕuō (1), to *watch, guard*

WAKED
5782 'ûwr (1), to *awake*

WAKENED
5782 'ûwr (2), to *awake*

WAKENETH
5782 'ûwr (2), to *awake*

WAKETH
5782 'ûwr (1), to *awake*
8245 shâqad (1), to *be alert*, i.e. *sleepless*

WAKING
8109 shᵉmûrâh (1), *eye-lid*

WALK
1869 dârak (2), to *tread, trample; to walk*

1979 hălîykâh (1), *walking; procession*
1980 hâlak (61), to *walk; live a certain way*
1981 hălak (Ch.) (1), to *walk; live a certain way*
3212 yâlak (79), to *walk*; to *live; to carry*
4108 mahlêk (1), *access; journey*
4109 mahălâk (1), *passage* or a *distance*
5437 çâbab (1), to *surround*
1704 ĕmpĕripatĕō (1), to *be occupied among*
4043 pĕripatĕō (55), to *walk; to live a life*
4198 pŏrĕuŏmai (4), to *go, come; to travel*
4748 stŏichĕō (4), to *follow, walk; to conform*

WALKED
1980 hâlak (67), to *walk; live a certain way*
1981 hălak (Ch.) (1), to *walk; live a certain way*
3212 yâlak (32), to *walk*; to *live; to carry*
3716 ŏrthŏpŏdĕō (1), to *act rightly*
4043 pĕripatĕō (19), to *walk; to live a life*
4198 pŏrĕuŏmai (1), to *go, come; to travel*

WALKEDST
4043 pĕripatĕō (1), to *walk; to live a life*

WALKEST
1980 hâlak (1), to *walk; live a certain way*
3212 yâlak (3), to *walk*; to *live; to carry*
4043 pĕripatĕō (2), to *walk; to live a life*
4748 stŏichĕō (1), to *follow, walk; to conform*

WALKETH
1980 hâlak (31), to *walk; live a certain way*
3212 yâlak (2), to *walk*; to *live; to carry*
1330 diĕrchŏmai (2), to *traverse, travel through*
4043 pĕripatĕō (5), to *walk; to live a life*

WALKING
1980 hâlak (10), to *walk; live a certain way*
1981 hălak (Ch.) (1), to *walk; live a certain way*
3212 yâlak (3), to *walk*; to *live; to carry*
4043 pĕripatĕō (12), to *walk; to live a life*
4198 pŏrĕuŏmai (4), to *go, come; to travel*

WALL
846 'ushsharnâ' (Ch.) (1), *wall*
1444 geder (2), *wall* or *fence*
1447 gâdêr (5), *enclosure*, i.e. *wall*
1448 gᵉdêrâh (1), *enclosure* for flocks
2346 chôwmâh (92), *wall*

2426 chêyl (1), *entrenchment*
2434 chayits (1), *wall*
2742 chârûwts (1), *mined gold; trench*
3796 kôthel (1), *house wall*
3797 kᵉthal (Ch.) (1), *house wall*
7023 qîyr (50), *wall, side-wall*
7791 shûwr (3), *wall*
7794 shôwr (1), *bullock*
5038 tĕichŏs (8), *house wall*
5109 tŏichŏs (1), *wall*

WALLED
1219 bâtsar (2), to *be inaccessible*
2346 chôwmâh (2), *wall*

WALLOW
5606 çâphaq (1), to *be enough; to vomit*
6428 pâlash (3), to *roll in dust*

WALLOWED
1556 gâlal (1), to *roll*; to *commit*
2947 kuliŏō (1), to *roll about*

WALLOWING
2946 kulisma (1), *wallowing* in *filth*

WALLS
846 'ushsharnâ' (Ch.) (1), *wall*
1447 gâdêr (1), *enclosure*, i.e. *wall*
2346 chôwmâh (39), *wall*
2426 chêyl (1), *rampart, battlement*
3797 kᵉthal (Ch.) (1), *house wall*
7023 qîyr (16), *wall, side-wall*
7791 shûwr (4), *wall*
8284 shârâh (1), *fortification*
5038 tĕichŏs (1), *house wall*

WANDER
5074 nâdad (1), to *rove, flee; to drive away*
5128 nûwa' (4), to *waver*
6808 tsâ'âh (1), to *tip over; to depopulate*
7462 râ'âh (1), to *tend a flock*, i.e. *pasture* it
7686 shâgâh (2), to *stray, wander; to transgress*
8582 tâ'âh (5), to *vacillate*, i.e. *reel, stray*

WANDERED
1980 hâlak (1), to *walk; live a certain way*
5128 nûwa' (3), to *waver*
7686 shâgâh (1), to *stray, wander; to transgress*
8582 tâ'âh (3), to *vacillate*, i.e. *reel, stray*
4022 pĕriĕrchŏmai (1), to *stroll, vacillate, veer*
4105 planaō (1), to *roam, wander* from safety

WANDERERS
5074 nâdad (1), to *rove, flee; to drive away*
6808 tsâ'âh (1), to *tip over; to depopulate*

WANDEREST
6808 tsâ'âh (1), to *tip over; to depopulate; to imprison; to lay down*

WANDERETH
5074 nâdad (5), to *rove, flee; to drive away*
8582 tâ'âh (1), to *vacillate*, i.e. *reel, stray*

WANDERING
1981 hălak (Ch.) (1), to *walk; live a certain way*
5074 nâdad (1), to *rove, flee; to drive away*
5110 nûwd (1), to *waver; to wander, flee*
8582 tâ'âh (1), to *vacillate*, i.e. *reel, stray*
4022 pĕriĕrchŏmai (1), to *stroll, vacillate, veer*
4107 planētēs (1), *roving, erratic teacher*

WANDERINGS
5112 nôwd (1), *exile*

WANT
657 'ephĕç (1), *end; no further*
1097 bᵉlîy (2), *without, not yet; lacking*
2637 châçêr (4), to *lack; to fail, want, make less*
2638 châçêr (1), *lacking*
2639 checer (1), *lack; destitution*
2640 chôçer (3), *poverty*
3772 kârath (3), to *cut* (off, down or asunder)
3808 lô' (1), no, *not*
4270 machçôwr (7), *impoverishment*
6485 pâqad (1), to *visit, care for, count*
5302 hustĕrĕō (1), to *be inferior*; to *fall short* (be *deficient*)
5303 hustĕrēma (3), *deficit; poverty; lacking*
5304 hustĕrēsis (2), *penury, lack, need*

WANTED
2637 châçêr (1), to *lack; to fail, want, make less*
5302 hustĕrĕō (2), to *be inferior*; to *fall short*

WANTETH
2308 châdal (1), to *desist, stop; be fat*
2637 châçêr (2), to *lack; to fail, want, make less*
2638 châçêr (4), *lacking*

WANTING
2627 chaççîyr (Ch.) (1), *deficient, wanting*
2642 cheçrôwn (1), *deficiency*
3808 lô' (1), no, *not*
6485 pâqad (2), to *visit, care for, count*
3007 lĕipō (3), to *fail or be absent*

WANTON
8265 sâqar (1), to *ogle*, i.e. *blink* coquettishly
2691 katastrēniaō (1), to *be voluptuous against*
4684 spatalaō (1), to *live in luxury*

WANTONNESS
766 asĕlgĕia (2), *debauchery, lewdness*

WANTS
4270 machçôwr (1), *impoverishment*
5532 chrĕia (1), *affair; requirement*

WAR
2428 chayil (1), *army; wealth; virtue; valor*
2438 Chîyrâm (1), *noble*
3898 lâcham (9), to *fight a battle*
3901 lâchem (1), *battle, war*
4421 milchâmâh (151), *battle; war; fighting*
4421+7128 milchâmâh (1), *battle; war; fighting*
6635 tsâbâ' (41), *army, military host*
6904 qôbel (1), *battering*-ram
7128 qᵉrâb (3), *hostile encounter*
7129 qᵉrâb (Ch.) (1), *hostile encounter*
4170 pŏlĕmĕō (4), to *battle, make war*
4171 pŏlĕmŏs (6), *warfare; battle; fight*
4753 stratĕuma (1), body of *troops*
4754 stratĕuŏmai (4), to *serve* in military

WARD
4929 mishmâr (11), *guard; deposit; usage*
4931 mishmereth (6), *watch, sentry, post*
5474 çûwgar (1), *animal cage*
6488 pᵉqîdûth (1), *supervision*
5438 phulakē (1), *guarding or guard*

WARDROBE
899 beged (2), *clothing; treachery or pillage*

WARDS
4931 mishmereth (3), *watch, sentry, post*

WARE
4377 meker (1), *merchandise; value*
4465 mimkâr (1), *merchandise*
4728 maqqâchâh (1), *merchandise, wares*
1737 ĕndiduskō (1), to *clothe*
4894 sunĕidō (1), to *understand or be aware*
5442 phulassō (1), to *watch*, i.e. *be on guard*

WARES
3627 kᵉlîy (1), *implement, thing*

WARFARE
6635 tsâbâ' (2), *army, military host*
4752 stratĕia (2), *warfare; fight*
4754 stratĕuŏmai (1), to *serve* in military

WARM
2215 zârab (1), to *flow away, be dry*
2525 châm (1), *hot, sweltering*
2527 chôm (1), *heat*
2552 châmam (4), to *be hot; to be in a rage*
3179 yâcham (1), to *conceive*

WARMED
2552 châmam (1), to *be hot; to be in a rage*
2328 thĕrmainō (5), to *heat* oneself

WARMETH
2552 châmam (2), to *be hot; to be in a rage*

WARMING
2328 thĕrmainō (1), to *heat* oneself

WARN
2094 zâhar (8), to *enlighten*
3560 nŏuthĕtĕō (3), to *caution or reprove*

WARNED
2094 zâhar (4), to *enlighten*
5263 hupŏdĕiknumi (2), to *exemplify*
5537 chrēmatizō (4), to *utter an oracle*

WARNING
2094 zâhar (6), to *enlighten*
5749 'ûwd (1), to *duplicate or repeat*
3560 nŏuthĕtĕō (1), to *caution or reprove*

WARP
8359 shᵉthîy (9), *warp* in *weaving*

WARRED
3898 lâcham (7), to *fight a battle*
6633 tsâbâ' (2), to *mass an army or servants*

WARRETH
4754 stratĕuŏmai (1), to *serve* in military

WARRING
3898 lâcham (2), to *fight a battle*
497 antistratĕuŏmai (1), *destroy, wage war*

WARRIOR
5431 çâ'an (1), *soldier wearing boots*

WARRIORS
6213+4421 'âsâh (2), to *do or make*

WARS
4421 milchâmâh (9), *battle; war; fighting*
4171 pŏlĕmŏs (4), *warfare; battle; fight*

WASH
3526 kâbaç (39), to *wash*
7364 râchats (36), to *lave, bathe*
628 apŏlŏuō (1), to *wash fully*
907 baptizō (1), *baptize*
1026 brĕchō (1), to *make wet; to rain*
3538 niptō (11), to *wash, bathe*

WASHED
1740 dûwach (2), to *rinse clean, wash*
3526 kâbaç (7), to *wash*
7364 râchats (17), to *lave, bathe*
7857 shâṭaph (2), to *inundate, cleanse*
628 apŏlŏuō (1), to *wash fully*
633 apŏniptō (1), to *wash off* hands
907 baptizō (1), *baptize*
1026 brĕchō (1), to *make wet; to rain*
3068 lŏuō (6), to *bathe; to wash*
3538 niptō (6), to *wash, bathe*
4150 plunō (1), to *wash or launder* clothing

WASHEST
7857 shâṭaph (1), to *inundate, cleanse*

WASHING
3526 kâbaç (1), to *wash*
4325 mayim (1), *water*
7364 râchats (1), to *lave, bathe*
7367 rachtsâh (2), *bathing* place
637 apŏplunō (1), to *rinse off, wash out*
909 baptismŏs (2), *baptism*
3067 lŏutrŏn (2), *washing, baptism*

WASHINGS
909 baptismŏs (1), *baptism*

WASHPOT
5518+7366 çîyr (2), *thorn; hook*

WAST
1961 hâyâh (13), to *exist*, i.e. *be or become*
2258 ēn (5), I *was*
5607 ŏn (1), *being, existence*

WASTE
1086 bâlâh (1), to *wear out, decay; consume*
1110 bâlaq (2), to *annihilate, devastate*
1326 bâthâh (1), *area of desolation*

WATCH
2717 chârab (13), to *desolate, destroy*
2720 chârêb (6), *ruined; desolate*
2721 chôreb (2), *parched; ruined*
2723 chorbâh (14), *desolation, dry* desert
3615 kâlâh (1), to *complete, prepare*
3765 kirçêm (1), to *lay waste, ravage*
4875 mᵉshôw'âh (2), *ruin*
5327 nâtsâh (1), to *be desolate, to lay waste*
7489 râ'a' (1), to *be good for nothing*
7582 shâ'âh (2), to *moan; to desolate*
7703 shâdad (5), to *ravage*
8047 shammâh (3), *ruin; consternation*
8074 shâmêm (5), to *devastate; to stupefy*
8077 shᵉmâmâh (1), *devastation*
8414 tôhûw (1), *waste, desolation, formless*
684 apŏlĕia (2), *ruin or loss*

WASTED
1197 bâ'ar (1), to *be brutish, be senseless*
2717 chârab (3), to *parch; desolate, destroy*
2723 chorbâh (1), *desolation, dry* desert
3615 kâlâh (1), to *complete, consume*
7582 shâ'âh (1), to *moan; to desolate*
7703 shâdad (2), to *ravage*
7843 shâchath (1), to *decay; to ruin*
8437 tôwlâl (1), *oppressor*
8552 tâmam (2), to *complete, finish*
1287 diaskŏrpizō (2), to *scatter; to squander*
4199 pŏrthĕō (1), to *ravage, pillage*

WASTENESS
7722 shôw' (1), *tempest; devastation*

WASTER
7843 shâchath (2), to *decay; to ruin*

WASTES
2723 chorbâh (7), *desolation, dry* desert

WASTETH
2522 châlash (1), to *prostrate, lay low*
7703 shâdad (1), to *ravage*
7736 shûwd (1), to *devastate*

WASTING
7701 shôd (2), *violence, ravage, destruction*

WATCH
821 'ashmûrâh (4), *night watch*
4707 mitspeh (1), *military observatory*

4929 mishmâr (4), *guard; deposit; usage; example*
4931 mishmereth (5), *watch, sentry, post*
6822 tsâphâh (5), to *observe, await*
8104 shâmar (5), to *watch*
8108 shomrâh (1), *watchfulness*
8245 shâqad (6), to *be on the lookout*
69 agrupnĕō (3), to *be sleepless, keep awake*
1127 grĕgŏrĕuō (16), to *watch, guard*
2892 kŏustōdia (3), *sentry*
3525 nēphō (2), to *abstain* from wine
5438 phulakē (6), *night watch; prison; haunt*

WATCHED
6822 tsâphâh (1), to *observe, await*
8104 shâmar (2), to *watch*
8245 shâqad (2), to *be on the lookout*
1127 grĕgŏrĕuō (2), to *watch, guard*
3906 paratērĕō (5), to *note insidiously*
5083 tērĕō (1), to *keep, guard, obey*

WATCHER
5894 'îyr (Ch.) (2), *watcher-angel*

WATCHERS
5341 nâtsar (1), to *guard, protect, maintain*
5894 'îyr (Ch.) (1), *watcher-angel*

WATCHES
821 'ashmûrâh (3), *night watch*
4931 mishmereth (2), *watch, sentry, post*

WATCHETH
6822 tsâphâh (1), to *observe, await*
6974 qûwts (1), to *awake*
1127 grĕgŏrĕuō (1), to *watch, guard*

WATCHFUL
1127 grĕgŏrĕuō (1), to *watch, guard*

WATCHING
6822 tsâphâh (2), to *observe, await*
8245 shâqad (1), to *be on the lookout*
69 agrupnĕō (1), to *be sleepless, keep awake*
1127 grĕgŏrĕuō (1), to *watch, guard*
5083 tērĕō (1), to *keep, guard, obey*

WATCHINGS
70 agrupnia (2), *keeping awake*

WATCHMAN
6822 tsâphâh (14), to *peer into the distance*
8104 shâmar (4), to *watch*

WATCHMAN'S
6822 tsâphâh (1), to *peer into the distance*

WATCHMEN
5341 nâtsar (3), to *guard, protect, maintain*
6822 tsâphâh (5), to *peer into the distance*
8104 shâmar (4), to *watch*

WATCHTOWER
4707 mitspeh (1), *military observatory*
6844 tsâphîyth (1), *sentry*

WATER
1119 bᵉmôw (1), *in, with, by*
2222 zarzîyph (1), *pouring rain*
4325 mayim (308), *water*
4529 mâçâh (1), to *dissolve, melt*
7301 râvâh (1), to *slake thirst or appetites*
8248 shâqâh (9), to *quaff, i.e. to irrigate*
504 anudrŏs (2), *dry, arid*
5202 hudrŏpŏtĕō (1), to *drink water exclusively*
5204 hudōr (62), *water*

WATERCOURSE
4161+4325 môwtsâ' (1), *going forth*
8585 tᵉ'âlâh (1), *irrigation channel*

WATERED
3384 yârâh (1), to *point; to teach*
4945 mashqeh (1), *butler; drink; well-watered*
7302 râveh (2), *sated, full with drink*
8248 shâqâh (6), to *quaff, i.e. to irrigate*
4222 pŏtizō (1), to *furnish drink, irrigate*

WATEREDST
8248 shâqâh (1), to *quaff, i.e. to irrigate*

WATEREST
7301 râvâh (1), to *slake thirst or appetites*
7783 shûwq (1), to *overflow*

WATERETH
7301 râvâh (2), to *slake thirst or appetites*
8248 shâqâh (1), to *quaff, i.e. to irrigate*
4222 pŏtizō (2), to *furnish drink, irrigate*

WATERFLOOD
7641+4325 shibbôl (1), *stream; ear of grain*

WATERING
4325 mayim (1), *water*
7377 rîy (1), *irrigation*
4222 pŏtizō (1), to *furnish drink, irrigate*

WATERPOT
5201 hudria (1), *water jar, i.e. receptacle*

WATERPOTS
5201 hudria (2), *water jar, i.e. receptacle*

WATERS
4325 mayim (265), *water*
4215 pŏtamŏs (1), *current, brook, running water*
5204 hudōr (15), *water*

WATERSPOUTS
6794 tsinnûwr (1), *culvert, water-shaft*

WATERSPRINGS
4161+4325 môwtsâ' (2), *going forth*

WAVE
5130 nûwph (11), to *quiver, vibrate, rock*
8573 tᵉnûwphâh (19), *official undulation of sacrificial offerings*
2830 kludōn (1), *surge, raging*

WAVED
5130 nûwph (5), to *quiver, vibrate, rock*
8573 tᵉnûwphâh (1), *official undulation of sacrificial offerings*

WAVERETH
1252 diakrinō (1), to *decide; to hesitate*

WAVERING
186 aklinēs (1), *firm, unswerving*
1252 diakrinō (1), to *decide; to hesitate*

WAVES
1116 bâmâh (1), *elevation, high place*
1530 gal (14), *heap; ruins*
1796 dŏkîy (1), *dashing, pounding of surf*
4867 mishbâr (4), *breaker sea-waves*
2949 kuma (5), *bursting or toppling*
4535 salŏs (1), *billow, i.e. rolling motion of waves*

WAX
1749 dôwnag (4), *bees-wax*
2691 katastrēniaō (1), to *be voluptuous against*
3822 palaiŏō (2), to *make, become worn out*
4298 prŏkŏptō (1), to *go ahead, advance*
5594 psuchō (1), to *chill, grow cold*

WAXED
1980 hâlak (5), to *walk; live a certain way*
1096 ginŏmai (2), to *be, become*
2901 krataiŏō (2), *increase in vigor*
3955 parrhēsiazŏmai (1), to *be frank in utterance*
3975 pachunō (2), to *fatten; to render callous*
4147 plŏutĕō (1), to *be, become wealthy*

WAXETH
1095 gēraskō (1), to *be senescent, grow old*

WAXING
3982 pĕithō (1), to *pacify or conciliate; to assent*

WAY
734 'ôrach (18), *road; manner of life*
776 'erets (3), *earth, land, soil; country*
935 bôw' (1), to *go, come*
1870 derek (466), *road; course of life; mode*
2008 hênnâh (1), *from here; from there*
2088 zeh (1), *this or that*
3212 yâlak (6), to *walk; to live; to carry*
3541 kôh (1), *thus*
4498 mânôwç (1), *fleeing; place of refuge*
5265 nâça' (1), *start on a journey*
5410 nâthîyb (2), *(beaten) track, path*
7125 qîr'âh (1), to *encounter, to happen*
7971 shâlach (1), to *send away*
8582 tâ'âh (2), to *vacillate, i.e. reel*
1545 ĕkbasis (1), *exit, way out*
1624 ĕktrĕpō (1), to *turn away*
1722 ĕn (1), *in; during; because of*
3112 makran (2), *at a distance, far away*
3319 mĕsŏs (2), *middle*
3598 hŏdŏs (81), *road*
3938 parŏdŏs (1), *by-road, i.e. a route*
4105 planaō (1), to *roam, wander from safety*
4206 pŏrrhō (1), *forwards*
4311 prŏpĕmpō (5), to *send forward*
5158 trŏpŏs (2), *deportment, character*

WAYFARING
732 'ârach (4), to *travel, wander*
1980+1870 hâlak (1), to *walk; live a certain way*
5674+734 'âbar (1), to *cross over; to transition*

WAYMARKS
6725 tsîyûwn (1), *guiding pillar, monument*

WAYS
734 'ôrach (8), *road; manner of life*
735 'ôrach (Ch.) (2), *road*
1870 derek (161), *road; course of life; mode of action*
1979 hălîykâh (2), *walking; procession or march; caravan*
4546 mᵉçillâh (1), *main thoroughfare; viaduct*
4570 ma'gâl (1), *circular track or camp rampart*
7339 rᵉchôb (1), *myriad*
296 amphŏdŏn (1), *fork in the road*
684 apŏlĕia (1), *ruin or loss*
3598 hŏdŏs (11), *road*

4197 pŏrĕia (1), *journey; life's daily conduct*

WAYSIDE
3027+4570 yâd (1), *hand; power*
3197+1870 yak (1), *hand or side*

WEAK
535 'âmal (1), *to be weak; to be sick*
536 'umlal (1), *sick, faint*
2470 châlâh (4), *to be weak, sick, afflicted*
2523 challâsh (1), *frail, weak*
3212 yâlak (2), *to walk; to live; to carry*
3782 kâshal (1), *to totter, waver; to falter*
7390 rak (1), *tender; weak*
7503 râphâh (1), *to slacken*
7504 râpheh (4), *slack*
102 adunatŏs (1), *weak; impossible*
770 asthĕnĕō (19), *to be feeble*
772 asthĕnēs (8), *strengthless, weak*

WEAKEN
2522 châlash (1), *to prostrate, lay low*

WEAKENED
6031 'ânâh (1), *to afflict, be afflicted*
7503 râphâh (2), *to slacken*

WEAKENETH
7503 râphâh (2), *to slacken*

WEAKER
1800 dal (1), *weak, thin; humble, needy*
772 asthĕnēs (1), *strengthless, weak*

WEAKNESS
769 asthĕnĕia (5), *feebleness; frailty*
772 asthĕnēs (2), *strengthless, weak*

WEALTH
1952 hôwn (5), *wealth*
2428 chayil (10), *army; wealth; virtue; valor*
2896 tôwb (3), *good; well*
3581 kôach (1), *force, might; strength*
5233 nekeç (4), *treasure, riches*
2142 ĕupŏria (1), *resources, prosperity*

WEALTHY
7310 rᵉvâyâh (1), *satisfaction*
7961 shâlêv (1), *careless, carefree; security*

WEANED
1580 gâmal (12), *to benefit or requite*

WEAPON
240 'âzên (1), *spade; paddle*
3627 kᵉlîy (4), *implement, thing*

5402 nesheq (1), *military arms, arsenal*
7973 shelach (2), *spear; shoot of growth*

WEAPONS
3627 kᵉlîy (17), *implement, thing*
5402 nesheq (2), *military arms, arsenal*
3696 hŏplŏn (2), *implement, or utensil*

WEAR
1080 bᵉlâ' (Ch.) (1), *to afflict, torment*
1961 hâyâh (1), *to exist, i.e. be or become*
3847 lâbash (4), *to clothe*
5034 nâbêl (1), *to wilt; to fall away; to be foolish*
5375 nâsâ' (2), *to lift up*
7833 shâchaq (1), *to grind or wear away*
2827 klinō (1), *to slant or slope*
5409 phŏrĕō (1), *to wear*

WEARETH
5409 phŏrĕō (1), *to wear*

WEARIED
3021 yâga' (5), *to be exhausted, to tire,*
3811 lâ'âh (5), *to tire; to be, make disgusted*
5888 'âyêph (1), *to languish*
2577 kamnō (1), *to tire; to faint, sicken*
2872 kŏpiaō (1), *to feel fatigue; to work hard*

WEARIETH
2959 ṭârach (1), *to overburden*
3021 yâga' (1), *to be exhausted, to tire,*

WEARINESS
3024 yᵉgîʿâh (1), *fatigue*
4972 mattᵉlâ'âh (1), *what a trouble!*
2873 kŏpŏs (1), *toil; pains*

WEARING
5375 nâsâ' (1), *to lift up*
4025 pĕrithĕsis (1), *putting all around, i.e. decorating oneself with*
5409 phŏrĕō (1), *to wear*

WEARISOME
5999 'âmâl (1), *wearing effort; worry*

WEARY
3019 yâgîya' (1), *tired, exhausted*
3021 yâga' (7), *to be exhausted, to tire,*
3023 yâgêa' (2), *tiresome*
3286 yâ'aph (5), *to tire*
3287 yâ'êph (1), *exhausted*
3811 lâ'âh (10), *to tire; to be, make disgusted*
5354 nâqaṭ (1), *to loathe*
5774 'ûwph (1), *to cover, to fly; to faint*
5889 'âyêph (8), *languid*
6973 qûwts (2), *to be, make disgusted*
7646 sâba' (1), *fill to satiety*

1573 ĕkkakĕō (2), *to be weak, fail*
5299 hupōpiazō (1), *to beat up; to wear out*

WEASEL
2467 chôled (1), *weasel*

WEATHER
2091 zâhâb (1), *gold, piece of gold*
3117 yôwm (1), *day; time period*
2105 ĕudia (1), *clear sky, i.e. fine weather*
5494 chĕimōn (1), *winter season; stormy weather*

WEAVE
707 'ârag (2), *to plait or weave*

WEAVER
707 'ârag (2), *to plait or weave*

WEAVER'S
707 'ârag (4), *to plait or weave*

WEAVEST
707 'ârag (1), *to plait or weave*

WEB
1004 bayith (1), *house; temple; family, tribe*
4545 maççeketh (2), *length-wise threads*
6980 qûwr (1), spider *web*

WEBS
6980 qûwr (1), spider *web*

WEDDING
1062 gamŏs (7), *nuptials*

WEDGE
3956 lâshôwn (2), *tongue; tongue*-shaped

WEDLOCK
5003 nâ'aph (1), *to commit adultery*

WEEDS
5488 çûwph (1), *papyrus reed; reed*

WEEK
7620 shâbûwa' (4), *seven-day week*
4521 sabbatōn (9), *day of weekly repose*

WEEKS
7620 shâbûwa' (15), *seven-day week*

WEEP
1058 bâkâh (29), *to weep, moan*
1065 bᵉkîy (2), *weeping*
1830 dâma' (1), *to weep*
2799 klaiō (15), *to sob, wail*

WEEPEST
1058 bâkâh (1), *to weep, moan*
2799 klaiō (2), *to sob, wail*

WEEPETH
1058 bâkâh (4), *to weep, moan*

WEEPING
1058 bâkâh (8), *to weep, moan*
1065 bᵉkîy (21), *weeping*

2799 klaiō (9), *to sob, wail*
2805 klauthmŏs (6), *lamentation, weeping*

WEIGH
4948 mishqâl (2), *weight, weighing*
6424 pâlaç (2), *to weigh mentally*
8254 shâqal (2), *to suspend in trade*

WEIGHED
8254 shâqal (12), *to suspend in trade*
8505 tâkan (1), *to balance, i.e. measure*
8625 tᵉqal (Ch.) (1), *to weigh in a balance*

WEIGHETH
8505 tâkan (2), *to balance, i.e. measure*

WEIGHT
68 'eben (4), *stone*
4946 mishqôwl (1), *weight*
4948 mishqâl (44), *weight, weighing*
6425 peleç (1), *balance, scale*
922 barŏs (1), *load, abundance, authority*
3591 ŏgkŏs (1), *burden, hindrance*
5006 talantiaiŏs (1), *weight of 57-80 lbs.*

WEIGHTIER
926 barus (1), *weighty*

WEIGHTS
68 'eben (6), *stone*

WEIGHTY
5192 nêṭel (1), *burden*
926 barus (1), *weighty*

WELFARE
2896 tôwb (1), *good; well*
3444 yᵉshûw'âh (1), *victory; prosperity*
7965 shâlôwm (5), *safe; well; health, prosperity*

WELL
71 'Ăbânâh (1), *stony*
369 'ayin (1), *there is no, i.e., not exist, none*
375 'êyphôh (2), *where?; when?; how?*
875 bᵉ'êr (21), *well, cistern*
883 Bᵉ'êr la-Chay Rô'îy (1), *well of a living (One) my seer*
953 bôwr (6), *pit hole, cistern, well; prison*
995 bîyn (1), *to understand; discern*
2090 zôh (1), *this or that*
2654 châphêts (1), *to be pleased with, desire*
2895 ṭowb (9), *to be good*
2896 ṭôwb (20), *good; well*
2898 ṭûwb (1), *good; goodness; beauty, gladness, welfare*
3190 yâṭab (35), *to be, make well*
3303 yâpheh (5), *beautiful; handsome*

English

3651 kên (4), *just; right, correct*
3966 mᵉʿôd (1), *very, utterly*
4599 maʿyân (2), *fountain; source*
4639 maʾăseh (1), *action; labor*
4726 mâqôwr (1), *flow of liquids, or ideas*
5869 'ayin (9), *eye; sight; fountain*
5878 'Êyn Chărôd (1), *fountain of trembling*
6822 tsâphâh (1), to *peer into the distance*
7181 qâshab (1), to *prick up the ears*
7571 rethach (1), *boiling*
7965 shâlôwm (14), *safe; well; health, prosperity*
15 agathŏpŏiĕŏ (4), *to be a well-doer*
16 agathŏpŏiïa (1), *virtue, doing good*
17 agathŏpŏiŏs (1), *virtuous one*
18 agathŏs (1), *good*
957 bĕltiŏn (1), *better*
1510+2101 ĕimi (1), I *exist, I am*
1921 ĕpiginōskō (1), to *acknowledge*
2095 ĕu (6), *well*
2100 ĕuarĕstĕŏ (1), to *gratify entirely, please*
2101 ĕuarĕstŏs (1), *fully agreeable, pleasing*
2106 ĕudŏkĕŏ (7), to *think well*, i.e. *approve*
2509 kathapĕr (1), *exactly as*
2532 kai (2), *and; or*
2569 kalŏpŏiĕŏ (1), *to do well*
2570 kalŏs (1), *good; beautiful; valuable*
2573 kalŏs (33), *well*, i.e. *rightly*
3140 marturĕŏ (2), to *testify; to commend*
3184 mĕthuŏ (1), to *get drunk*
4077 pēgē (3), *source or supply*
4260 prŏbainō (2), to *advance*
4982 sōzō (1), to *deliver; to protect*
5421 phrĕar (2), *cistern or water well; abyss*

WELL'S
875 bᵉʾêr (6), *well, cistern*

WELLBELOVED
1730 dôwd (1), *beloved, friend; uncle, relative*
3039 yᵉdîyd (2), *loved*
27 agapētŏs (3), *beloved*

WELLFAVOURED
2896+2580 ţôwb (1), *good; well*

WELLPLEASING
2101 ĕuarĕstŏs (2), *fully agreeable, pleasing*

WELLS
875 bᵉʾêr (3), *well, cistern*

---

953 bôwr (3), pit *hole, cistern, well; prison*
4599 maʿyân (3), *fountain; source*
5869 'ayin (1), *eye; sight; fountain*
4077 pēgē (1), *source or supply*

WELLSPRING
4726 mâqôwr (2), *flow*

WEN
2990 yabbêl (1), *having running sores*

WENCH
8198 shiphchâh (1), *household female slave*

WENT
236 'âzal (Ch.) (6), to *depart*
935 bôw' (115), to *go*
980 Bachûrîym (1), *young men*
1718 dâdâh (1), to *walk gently; lead*
1961 hâyâh (4), to *exist*, i.e. *be or become*
1980 hâlak (93), to *walk; live a certain way*
3212 yâlak (281), to *walk; to live; to carry*
3318 yâtsâ' (216), to *go*
3381 yârad (64), to *descend*
3518 kâbâh (1), to *extinguish*
5066 nâgash (4), to *be, come, bring near*
5075 nᵉdad (Ch.) (1), to *depart*
5221 nâkâh (1), to *strike, kill*
5265 nâça' (13), *start on a journey*
5312 nᵉphaq (Ch.) (1), to *issue forth; to bring out*
5437 çâbab (6), to *surround*
5493 çûwr (1), to *turn off*
5674 'âbar (38), to *cross over; to transition*
5927 'âlâh (160), to *ascend, be high, mount*
5954 'ălal (Ch.) (3), to *go in; to lead in*
5974 'îm (Ch.) (1), *with*
6743 tsâlach (1), to *push*
6805 tsâ'ad (1), to *pace, step regularly*
6923 qâdam (2), to *anticipate, hasten*
7121 qârâ' (1), to *call out*
7126 qârab (2), to *approach, bring near*
7311 rûwm (1), to *be high; to rise or raise*
7683 shâgag (1), to *stray; to sin*
7725 shûwb (6), to *turn back; to return*
7751 shûwţ (1), to *travel, roam*
8582 tâ'âh (6), to *vacillate*, i.e. *reel, stray*
305 anabainō (24), to *go up, rise*
402 anachōrĕŏ (1), to *retire, withdraw*

---

424 anĕrchŏmai (3), to *ascend*
549 apĕïmi (1), to *go away*
565 apĕrchŏmai (54), to *go off*, i.e. *depart*
589 apŏdēmĕŏ (3), *visit a foreign land*
1279 diapŏrĕuŏmai (3), to *travel through*
1330 diĕrchŏmai (6), to *traverse, travel through*
1353 diŏdĕuŏ (1), to *travel through*
1524 ĕisĕimi (2), to *enter*
1525 ĕisĕrchŏmai (25), to *enter*
1531 ĕispŏrĕuŏmai (1), to *enter*
1607 ĕkpŏrĕuŏmai (7), to *depart, be discharged, proceed, project*
1681 Ĕlumas (1), *Elymas*
1684 ĕmbainō (2), to *embark; to reach*
1821 ĕxapŏstĕllō (2), to *despatch, or to dismiss*
1831 ĕxĕrchŏmai (86), to *issue; to leave*
1910 ĕpibainō (1), to *embark, arrive*
2021 ĕpichĕirĕŏ (1), to *undertake, try*
2064 ĕrchŏmai (11), to *go, come*
2212 zētĕŏ (1), to *seek*
2597 katabainō (13), to *descend*
2718 katĕrchŏmai (2), to *go, come down*
3596 hŏdŏipŏrĕŏ (1), to *travel*
3854 paraginŏmai (1), to *arrive; to appear*
3899 parapŏrĕuŏmai (1), to *travel near*
3987 pĕiraŏ (1), to *attempt, try*
4013 pĕriagŏ (4), to *walk around*
4105 planaŏ (1), to *roam, wander from safety*
4198 pŏrĕuŏmai (44), to *go, come; to travel*
4254 prŏagŏ (6), to *lead forward; to precede*
4281 prŏĕrchŏmai (4), to *go onward, precede*
4334 prŏsĕrchŏmai (3), to *come near, visit*
4344 prŏskĕphalaiŏn (2), *cushion pillow*
4848 sumpŏrĕuŏmai (3), to *journey together*
4897 sunĕisĕrchŏmai (2), to *enter with*
4905 sunĕrchŏmai (3), to *gather together*
5217 hupagŏ (5), to *withdraw or retire*
5221 hupantaŏ (1), to *meet, encounter*
5298 hupŏchōrĕŏ (1), to *vacate down*, i.e. *retire*

WENTEST
1980 hâlak (6), to *walk; live a certain way*
3212 yâlak (1), to *walk; to live; to carry*

3318 yâtsâ' (3), to *go, bring out*
5927 'âlâh (2), to *ascend, be high, mount*
7788 shûwr (1), i.e. *travel about*
1525 ĕisĕrchŏmai (1), to *enter*

WEPT
1058 bâkâh (57), to *weep, moan*
1145 dakruŏ (1), to *shed tears*
2799 klaiō (11), to *sob, wail*

WERT
1498 ĕiēn (1), *might could, would, or should*

WEST
3220 yâm (51), *sea; basin; west*
3996+8121 mâbôw' (1), *entrance; sunset; west*
4628 ma'ărâb (10), *west*
1424 dusmĕ (5), *western*
3047 lips (1), *southwest*
5566 chŏrŏs (1), *north-west wind*

WESTERN
3220 yâm (1), *sea; basin; west*

WESTWARD
3220 yâm (21), *sea; basin; west*
3996+8121 mâbôw' (1), *entrance; sunset; west*
4628 ma'ărâb (4), *west*

WET
6647 tsᵉba' (Ch.) (5), to *dip, be wet*
7372 râţab (1), to *be moist*

WHALE
8565 tan (1), *jackal*
8577 tannîyn (1), *sea-serpent; jackal*

WHALE'S
2785 kētŏs (1), *huge fish*

WHALES
8577 tannîyn (1), *sea-serpent; jackal*

WHEAT
1250 bâr (5), *grain*
1715 dâgân (2), *grain*
2406 chiţţâh (29), *wheat*
2591 chinţâ' (Ch.) (2), *wheat*
7383 rîyphâh (1), *grits cereal*
4621 sitŏs (12), *grain, especially wheat*

WHEATEN
2406 chiţţâh (1), *wheat*

WHEEL
212 'ôwphân (10), *wheel*
1534 galgal (3), *wheel; something round*
1536 gilgâl (1), *wheel*

WHEELS
70 'ôben (1), *potter's wheel; midwife's stool*
212 'ôwphân (24), *wheel*
1534 galgal (6), *wheel; something round*

1535 galgal (Ch.) (1),
wheel
6471 pa'am (1), time;
step; occurence

WHELP
1482 gûwr (3), cub

WHELPS
1121 bên (2), son,
descendant; people
1482 gûwr (3), cub
1484 gôwr (2), lion cub

WHEN
310 'achar (1), after
518 'îm (19), whether?
834 'ăsher (83), who,
what, that; when
1767 day (3), enough,
sufficient
1768 dîy (Ch.) (4), that; of
1961 hâyâh (4), to exist
3117 yôwm (7), day; time
3588 kîy (280), for, that
3644 kᵉmôw (1), like, as
4970 mâthay (14), when;
when?, how long?
5704 'ad (3), as far (long)
as; during; while; until
5750 'ôwd (2), again;
repeatedly; still; more
5921 'al (1), above, over,
upon, or against
6256 'êth (7), time
6310 peh (2), mouth;
opening
1437 ĕan (2),
indefiniteness
1875 ĕpan (3), whenever
1893 ĕpĕi (1), since
2259 hēnika (2), at which
time, whenever
2531 kathōs (1), just or
inasmuch as, that
3326 mĕta (2), with,
among; after, later
3698 hŏpŏtĕ (1), as soon
as, when
3704 hŏpōs (1), in the
manner that
3752 hŏtan (123),
inasmuch as, at once
3753 hŏtĕ (99), when; as
3756 ŏu (1), no or not
4218 pŏtĕ (13), at some
time, ever
5613 hōs (40), which,
how, i.e. in that manner
5618 hōspĕr (2), exactly
like

WHENCE
335 'ay (1), where?
370 'ayin (19), where
from?, whence?
1992 hêm (1), they
3606 hŏthĕn (4), from
which place or source
3739 hōs (2), who, which,
what, that
4159 pŏthĕn (28), from
which; what

WHENSOEVER
3605 kôl (1), all, any or
every
3752 hŏtan (1),
inasmuch as, at once
5613+1437 hōs (1), which,
how, i.e. in that manner

WHERE
335 'ay (16), where?
346 'ayêh (45), where?
349 'êyk (1), where?
351 'êykôh (1), where
370 'ayin (1), where
from?, whence?
375 'êyphôh (9), where?
413 'êl (2), to, toward
575 'ân (2), where from?
645 'êphôw (5), then
657 'epheç (1), end; no
further
834 'ăsher (58), where
1768 dîy (Ch.) (1), that; of
3027 yâd (1), hand; power
5921 'al (2), above, over,
upon, or against
8033 shâm (20), where
8478 tachath (1), bottom;
underneath; in lieu of
8536 tâm (Ch.) (1), there
296 amphŏdŏn (1), fork
in the road
1330 diĕrchŏmai (1), to
traverse, travel through
1337 dithalassŏs (1),
having two seas
2596 kata (1), down;
according to
3606 hŏthĕn (2), from
which place or source
3699 hŏpŏu (58), at
whichever spot
3757 hŏu (21), at which
place, i.e. where
3837 pantachŏu (5),
universally, everywhere
3838 pantĕlēs (1), entire;
completion
4226 pŏu (37), at what
locality?
5101 tis (1), who?,
which? or what?

WHEREABOUT
834 'ăsher (1), where,
how, because

WHEREAS
518 'îm (1), whether?; if,
although; Oh that!
834 'ăsher (2), because,
in order that
1768 dîy (Ch.) (4), that; of
3588 kîy (5), for, that
because
6258 'attâh (2), at this
time, now
8478 tachath (2), bottom;
underneath; in lieu of
3699 hŏpŏu (2), at
whichever spot
3748 hŏstis (1), whoever

WHEREBY
834 'ăsher (17), because,
in order that
4100 mâh (1), whatever;
that which
4482 mên (1), part;
musical chord
3588 hŏ (1), "the," i.e. the
definite article
3739 hōs (1), who, which,
what, that

WHEREFORE
199 'ûwlâm (1), however
or on the contrary
3651 kên (18), just; right,
correct

3861 lâhên (Ch.) (1),
therefore; except
4069 maddûwa' (28),
why?, what?
4100 mâh (86), what?,
how?, why?, when?
686 ara (1), therefore
1161 dĕ (2), but, yet
1302 diati (4), why?
1352 diŏ (41),
consequently, therefore
1355 diŏpĕr (3), on which
very account
3606 hŏthĕn (4), from
which place or source
3767 ŏun (7), certainly;
accordingly
5101 tis (3), who?,
which? or what?
5105 tŏigarŏun (1),
consequently, then
5620 hōstĕ (17), thus,
therefore

WHEREIN
834 'ăsher (70), when,
where, how, because
1459 gav (Ch.) (1), middle
2098 zûw (2), this or that
4100 mâh (15), what?,
how?, why?, when?
8033 shâm (1), where
3739 hōs (1), what, that
3757 hŏu (3), where

WHEREINSOEVER
1722+3739+302 ĕn (1), in;
during; because of

WHEREINTO
824+8432 'Esh'ân (1),
support
834+413+8432 'ăsher (1),
when, where, how
1519+3739 ĕis (1), to or
into

WHEREOF
834 'ăsher (24), where
3739 hōs (11), who,
which, what, that

WHEREON
834 'ăsher (2), where,
how, because
834+5921 'ăsher (13),
where, how, because
5921 'al (2), above, over,
upon, or against
5921+4100 'al (1), above,
over, upon, or against
1909+3739 ĕpi (4), on,
upon
3739 hōs (1), who, which,
what, that

WHERESOEVER
834 'ăsher (1), where,
how, because
3605 kôl (1), all, any
3699 hŏpŏu (1), at
whichever spot

WHERETO
834 'ăsher (1), where,
how, because
4100 mâh (1), what?,
how?, why?, when?
1519+3739 ĕis (1), to or
into

WHEREUNTO
834 'ăsher (6), where,
how, because

3739 hōs (6), who, which,
what, that
5101 tis (7), who?,
which? or what?

WHEREUPON
413 'êl (1), to, toward
5921 'al (1), above, over,
upon, or against
3606 hŏthĕn (3), from
which place or source

WHEREWITH
834 'ăsher (68), when,
where, how, because
1697 dâbâr (1), word;
matter; thing
4100 mâh (9), what?,
how?, why?, when?
1722+3739 ĕn (2), in;
during; because of
1722+5101 ĕn (3), in;
during; because of
3739 hōs (9), who, which
3745 hŏsŏs (1), as much
as
5101 tis (1), who?,
which? or what?

WHEREWITHAL
5101 tis (1), who?,
which? or what?

WHET
3913 lâṭash (1), to
sharpen; to pierce
7043 qâlal (1), to be,
make light (sharp)
8150 shânan (2), to
pierce; to inculcate

WHETHER
176 'ôw (8), or, whether
335 'ay (1), where?
518 'îm (27), whether?
996 bêyn (4), "either...or"
2006 hên (Ch.) (2),
whether, but, if
3588 kîy (1), for, that
because
4100 mâh (1), what?,
how?, why?, when?
4480 min (3), from, out of
5704 'ad (1), as far (long)
as; during; while; until
5750 'ôwd (2), again;
repeatedly; still; more
1487 ĕi (22), if, whether
1535 ĕitĕ (31), if too
2273 ētŏi (1), either...or
3379 mēpŏtĕ (1), not
ever; if, or lest ever
4220 pŏtĕrŏn (1), which
5037 tĕ (1), both or also
5101 tis (8), who?,
which? or what?

WHILE
518 'îm (1), whether?; if,
although; Oh that!
834 'ăsher (1), when,
where, how, because
3117 yôwm (7), day; time
3541 kôh (1), thus
3588 kîy (3), for, that
because
4705 mits'âr (1), little;
short time
5704 'ad (9), during; while
5750 'ôwd (7), again;
repeatedly; still; more
5751 'ôwd (Ch.) (1),
again; repeatedly; still

7350 râchôwq (1),
remote, far
2193 hĕŏs (8), *until*
2250 hēmĕra (2), *day;
period of time*
2540 kairŏs (1),
occasion, i.e. set time
3153 mataiŏtēs (1),
transientness; depravity
3397 mikrŏn (2), *small
space of time or degree*
3641 ŏligŏs (2), *puny,
small*
3752 hŏtan (1),
inasmuch as, at once
3753 hŏtĕ (1), *when; as*
3819 palai (1), *formerly;
sometime since*
4340 prŏskairŏs (1),
temporary
5550 chrŏnŏs (3), *time*
5613 hōs (4), *which, how,
i.e. in that manner*

WHILES
5750 'ôwd (1), *again;
repeatedly; still; more*
2193+3755 hĕŏs (1), *until*

WHILST
834 'ăsher (1), *when,
where, how, because*
5704 'ad (4), *as far (long)
as; during; while; until*

WHIP
7752 shôwṭ (2), *lash*

WHIPS
7752 shôwṭ (4), *lash*

WHIRLETH
1980 hâlak (1), *to walk;
live a certain way*

WHIRLWIND
5492 çûwphâh (10),
hurricane wind
5590 çâ'ar (3), *to rush
upon; to toss about*
5591 ça'ar (11),
hurricane wind
7307+5591 rûwach (1),
breath; wind; life-spirit
8175 sâ'ar (2), *to storm;
to shiver, i.e. fear*

WHIRLWINDS
5492 çûwphâh (1),
hurricane wind
5591 ça'ar (1), *hurricane*

WHISPER
3907 lâchash (1), *to
whisper a magic spell*
6850 tsâphaph (1), *to coo
or chirp as a bird*

WHISPERED
3907 lâchash (1), *to
whisper a magic spell*

WHISPERER
5372 nirgân (1),
slanderer, gossip

WHISPERERS
5588 psithuristēs (1),
maligning gossip

WHISPERINGS
5587 psithurismŏs (1),
whispering, detraction

WHIT
1697 dâbâr (1), *word;
matter; thing*

3632 kâlîyl (1), *whole,
entire; complete; whole*
3367 mĕdĕis (1), *not even*
3650 hŏlŏs (2), *whole or
all, i.e. complete*

WHITE
1858 dar (1),
*mother-of-pearl or
alabaster*
2353 chûwr (2), *white
linen*
2751 chôrîy (1), *white
bread*
3835 lâban (4), *to be,
become white*
3836 lâbân (29), *white*
6703 tsach (1), *dazzling*
6713 tsachar (1),
whiteness
6715 tsâchôr (1), *white*
7388 rîyr (1), *saliva; broth*
2986 lamprŏs (2),
radiant; clear
3021 lĕukainō (2), *to
whiten*
3022 lĕukŏs (24), *bright
white*

WHITED
2867 kŏniaō (2), *to
whitewash*

WHITER
3835 lâban (1), *to be,
become white*
6705 tsâchach (1), *to be
dazzling white*

WHITHER
413 'êl (2), *to, toward*
575 'ân (20), *where
from?, when?*
834 'ăsher (6), *when,
where, how, because*
8033 shâm (3), *where*
3699 hŏpŏu (9), *at
whichever spot*
3757 hŏu (2), *where*
4226 pŏu (10), *at what?*

WHITHERSOEVER
413+3605+834 'êl (1), *to,
toward*
413+3605+834+8033 'êl
(1), *to, toward*
575 'ân (1), *where from?*
834 'ăsher (2), *where,
how, because*
1870+834 derek (1),
road; course of life
3605+834 kôl (13), *all,
any or every*
3605+834+8033 kôl (1),
all, any or every
4725+834 mâqôwm (1),
general locality, place
5921+834+8033 'al (1),
above, over, upon
5921+3605+834 'al (1),
above, over, upon
3699+302 hŏpŏu (4), *at
whichever spot*
3699+1437 hŏpŏu (1), *at
whichever spot*
3757+1437 hŏu (1), *at
which place, i.e. where*

WHOLE
854+3605 'êth (13), *with;
by; at; among*
2421 châyâh (1), *to live;
to revive*

3117 yôwm (4), *day; time*
3605 kôl (115), *all, any*
3606 kôl (Ch.) (6), *all, any*
3632 kâlîyl (2), *whole*
4749 miqshâh (1), *work
molded by hammering*
7495 râphâ' (2), *to heal*
8003 shâlêm (4),
complete; friendly; safe
8549 tâmîym (4), *entire*
8552 tâmam (1), *to
complete, finish*
537 hapas (3), *whole*
1295 diasōzō (1), *to cure*
2390 iaŏmai (1), *to heal*
2480 ischuō (1), *to have
or exercise force*
3390 mētrŏpŏlis (1),
main city, metropolis
3646 hŏlŏkautōma (1),
wholly-consumed
3648 hŏlŏklērŏs (1),
*sound in the entire
body*
3650 hŏlŏs (43), *whole*
3956 pas (10), *all, any*
3958 paschō (2), *to
experience pain*
4982 sōzō (11), *to deliver;
to protect*
5198 hugiainō (2), *to
have sound health*
5199 hugiēs (13), *well,
healthy; true*

WHOLESOME
4832 marpê' (1), *cure;
deliverance; placidity*
5198 hugiainō (1), *to
have sound health*

WHOLLY
3605 kôl (9), *all, any*
3615 kâlâh (1), *to
complete, prepare*
3632 kâlîyl (4), *whole*
4390 mâlê' (6), *to fill*
5352 nâqâh (1), *to be,
make clean; to be bare*
6942 qâdash (1), *to be,
make clean*
7760 sûwm (1), *to put*
7965 shâlôwm (1), *safe;
well; health, prosperity*
1510+1722 ĕimi (1), *I
exist, I am*
3651 hŏlŏtĕlēs (1),
absolutely perfect

WHORE
2181 zânâh (9), *to
commit adultery*
6948 qĕdêshâh (1),
*sacred female
prostitute*
4204 pŏrnē (4), *prostitute*

WHORE'S
2181 zânâh (1), *to
commit adultery*

WHOREDOM
2181 zânâh (11), *to
commit adultery*
2183 zânûwn (1),
adultery; idolatry
2184 zᵉnûwth (3),
adultery, infidelity
8457 taznûwth (3),
harlotry

WHOREDOMS
2181 zânâh (2), *to
commit adultery*
2183 zânûwn (1),
adultery; idolatry
2184 zᵉnûwth (2),
adultery, infidelity
8457 taznûwth (15),
*harlotry, physical or
spiritual*

WHOREMONGER
4205 pŏrnŏs (1),
debauchee, immoral

WHOREMONGERS
4205 pŏrnŏs (4),
debauchee, immoral

WHORES
2181 zânâh (2), *to
commit adultery*

WHORING
2181 zânâh (19), *to
commit adultery*

WHORISH
2181 zânâh (3), *to
commit adultery*

WHY
4060 middâh (1),
measure
4069 maddûwa' (41),
why?, what?
4100 mâh (119), *what?,
how?, why?, when?*
4101 mâh (Ch.) (2),
what?, how?, why?
1063 gar (4), *for, indeed,
but, because*
1302 diati (23), *why?*
2444 hinati (4), *why?*
3754 hŏti (2), *that;
because; since*
5101 tis (66), *who?,
which? or what?*

WICKED
205 'âven (6), *trouble,
vanity, wickedness*
605 'ânash (1), *to be frail,
feeble*
1100 bᵉlîya'al (5),
wickedness, trouble
2154 zimmâh (2), *bad
plan*
2162 zâmâm (1), *plot*
2617 cheçed (1),
kindness, favor
4209 mᵉzimmâh (3),
plan; sagacity
4849 mirsha'ath (1),
female wicked-doer
5766 'evel (1), *evil*
5767 'avvâl (3), *evil*
6001 'âmêl (1), *toiling;
laborer; sorrowful*
6090 'ôtseb (1), *idol; pain*
7451 ra' (26), *bad; evil*
7489 râ'a' (5), *to be good
for nothing*
7561 râsha' (4), *to be, do,
declare wrong*
7562 resha' (4), *wrong*
7563 râshâ' (252), *wrong;
bad person*
113 athĕsmŏs (2),
criminal
459 anŏmŏs (2), *without
Jewish law*
2556 kakŏs (1), *wrong*

4190 pŏnērŏs (17),
malice, wicked, bad
4191 pŏnērŏtĕrŏs (2),
more evil

WICKEDLY
4209 m[e]zimmâh (1),
plan; sagacity
5753 'âvâh (1), *to be
crooked*
5766 'evel (1), *moral evil*
7451 ra' (1), *bad; evil*
7489 râ'a' (5), *to be good
for nothing*
7561 râsha' (13), *to be,
do, declare wrong*
7564 rish'âh (1), *moral
wrong*

WICKEDNESS
205 'âven (2), *trouble,
vanity, wickedness*
1942 havvâh (3), *desire;
craving*
2154 zimmâh (4), *bad
plan*
5766 'evel (7), *moral evil*
5999 'âmâl (1), *wearing
effort; worry*
7451 ra' (59), *bad; evil*
7455 rôa' (3), *badness*
7561 râsha' (1), *to be, do,
declare wrong*
7562 resha' (25), *wrong*
7564 rish'âh (13), *wrong*
2549 kakia (1),
*depravity; malignity;
trouble*
4189 pŏnēria (6), *malice,
evil, wickedness*
4190 pŏnērŏs (1), *malice,
wicked, bad; crime*
5129+824 tŏutŏ[i] (1), in
this person or thing

WIDE
2267 cheber (2), *society,
group; magic spell;*
4060 middâh (1),
measure; portion
6605 pâthach (3), *to open
wide; to loosen, begin*
7337 râchab (3), *to
broaden*
7342 râchâb (1), *roomy*
7342+3027 râchâb (2),
roomy, spacious
4116 platus (1), *wide*

WIDENESS
7341 rôchab (1), *width*

WIDOW
490 'almânâh (37), *widow*
5503 chēra (13), *widow*

WIDOW'S
490 'almânâh (4), *widow*
491 'almânûwth (1),
widow; widowhood

WIDOWHOOD
489 'almôn (1),
widowhood
491 'almânûwth (3),
widow; widowhood

WIDOWS
490 'almânâh (12), *widow*
5503 chēra (10), *widow*

WIDOWS'
5503 chēra (3), *widow*

WIFE
802 'ishshâh (301),
woman, wife
1166 bâ'al (1), *to be
master; to marry*
1753 dûwr (Ch.) (1), *to
reside, live in*
2994 y[e]bêmeth (3),
sister-in-law
1134 gunaikĕiŏs (1),
feminine
1135 gunē (80), *wife*

WIFE'S
802 'ishshâh (8), *woman,
wife; women, wives*
3994 pĕnthĕra (3), *wife's
mother*

WILD
338 'îy (3), *solitary wild
creature that howls*
689 'aqqôw (1), *ibex*
891 b[e]'ûshîym (2), *rotten
fruit*
2123 zîyz (2), *fulness*
2416 chay (1), *alive; raw*
3277 yâ'êl (3), *ibex*
6167 'ărâd (Ch.) (1),
onager or wild donkey
6171 'ârôwd (1), *onager
or wild donkey*
6501 pere' (10), *onager,
wild donkey*
6728 tsîyîy (3), wild *beast*
7704 sâdeh (8), *field*
8377 t[e]'ôw (2), *antelope*
65 agriĕlaiŏs (2), *wild
olive tree*
66 agriŏs (2), *wild*
2342 thēriŏn (3),
dangerous animal

WILDERNESS
3452 y[e]shîymôwn (2),
desolation
4057 midbâr (255),
desert; also speech
6160 'ărâbâh (4), *desert,
wasteland*
6166 'Ărâd (1), *fugitive*
6723 tsîyâh (2), *desert*
6728 tsîyîy (3), wild *beast*
8414 tôhûw (2), *waste,
desolation, formless*
2047 ĕrēmia (1), *place of
solitude, remoteness*
2048 ĕrēmŏs (32), *remote
place, deserted place*

WILES
5231 nêkel (1), *deceit*
3180 mĕthŏdĕia (1),
trickery, scheming

WILFULLY
1596 hĕkŏusiŏs (1),
voluntarily, willingly

WILILY
6195 'ormâh (1), *trickery;
discretion*

WILL
14 'âbâh (5), *to be
acquiescent*
165 'ĕhîy (3), *Where?*
2654 châphêts (2), *to be
pleased with, desire*
3045 yâda' (1), *to know*
5314 nâphash (1), *to be
refreshed*
5315 nephesh (3), *life;
breath; soul; wind*

WIFE [col 3]
6634 ts[e]bâ' (Ch.) (5), *to
please*
7470 r[e]'ûwth (Ch.) (1),
desire
7522 râtsôwn (15), *delight*
210 akŏn (1), *unwilling*
1012 bŏulē (1), *purpose,
plan, decision*
1013 bŏulēma (1),
resolve, willful choice
1014 bŏulŏmai (12), *to be
willing, desire*
1106 gnōmē (1), *opinion,
resolve*
1479 ĕthĕlŏthrēskĕia (1),
voluntary piety
2107 ĕudŏkia (2),
delight, kindness, wish
2133 ĕunŏia (1), *eagerly,
with a whole heart*
2307 thĕlēma (62),
purpose; decree
2308 thĕlēsis (1),
determination
2309 thĕlō (70), *to will; to
desire; to choose*
3195 mĕllō (6), *to intend,
i.e. be about to*

WILLETH
2309 thĕlō (1), *to will; to
desire; to choose*

WILLING
14 'âbâh (4), *to be
acquiescent*
2655 châphêts (1),
pleased with
5068 nâdab (3), *to
volunteer*
5071 n[e]dâbâh (2),
spontaneous gift
5081 nâdîyb (3),
magnanimous
830 authairĕtŏs (1),
self-chosen, voluntary
1014 bŏulŏmai (5), *to be
willing, desire*
2106 ĕudŏkĕō (2), *to
think well, i.e. approve*
2309 thĕlō (8), *to will; to
desire; to choose*
2843 kŏinōnikŏs (1),
liberal
4288 prŏthumia (1),
alacrity, eagerness
4289 prŏthumŏs (1),
alacrity, eagerness

WILLINGLY
2656 chĕphets (1),
pleasure; desire
2974 yâ'al (1), *to assent;
to undertake, begin*
3820 lêb (1), *heart*
5068 nâdab (13), *to
volunteer*
5071 n[e]dâbâh (1),
spontaneous gift
5414 nâthan (1), *to give*
1596 hĕkŏusiŏs (1),
voluntarily, willingly
1635 hĕkōn (2), *voluntary*
2309 thĕlō (2), *to will*

WILLOW
6851 tsaphtsâphâh (1),
willow tree

WILLOWS
6155 'ârâb (5), *willow*

WILT [col 4]
2309 thĕlō (21), *to will*

WIMPLES
4304 miṭpachath (1),
cloak, shawl

WIN
1234 bâqa' (1), *to cleave*
2770 kĕrdainō (1), *to
gain; to spare*

WIND
7307 rûwach (82),
breath; wind; life-spirit
7308 rûwach (Ch.) (1),
breath; wind; life-spirit
416 anemizō (1), *to toss
with the wind*
417 anĕmŏs (20), *wind*
4151 pnĕuma (1), *spirit*
4154 pnĕō (1), *to breeze*
4157 pnŏē (1), *breeze;
breath*

WINDING
3583 kâchal (1), *to paint*
4141 mûwçâb (1), *circuit*
5437 çâbab (1), *to
surround*

WINDOW
2474 challôwn (13),
window; opening
6672 tsôhar (1), *window*
2376 thuris (2), *window*

WINDOWS
699 'ărubbâh (8),
window; chimney
2474 challôwn (18),
window; opening
3551 kav (Ch.) (1),
window
8121 shemesh (1), *sun*
8260 sheqeph (1),
loophole
8261 shâqûph (1),
opening

WINDS
7307 rûwach (11),
breath; wind; life-spirit
7308 rûwach (Ch.) (1),
breath; wind; life-spirit
417 anĕmŏs (11), *wind*

WINDY
7307 rûwach (1), *breath;
wind; life-spirit*

WINE
2561 chemer (1),
fermenting wine
2562 chămar (Ch.) (6),
wine
3196 yayin (135), *wine*
3342 yeqeb (1), *wine-vat*
4469 mamçâk (1),
mixed-wine
5435 çôbe' (1), *wine*
6025 'ênâb (1), *grape*
6071 'âçîyç (4), *expressed
fresh grape-juice*
7491 râ'aph (1), *to drip*
8492 tîyrôwsh (40), *wine,
squeezed grape-juice*
1098 glĕukŏs (1), *sweet
wine*
3631 ŏinŏs (32), *wine*
3632 ŏinŏphlugia (1),
drunkenness
3943 parŏinŏs (2),
tippling

WINEBIBBER
3630 ŏinŏpŏtēs (1), *tippler*

WINEBIBBERS
5433+3196 çâbâ' (1), to *become tipsy*

WINEFAT
1660 gath (1), wine-*press* or *vat*
5276 hupŏlēniŏn (1), lower *wine vat*

WINEPRESS
1660 gath (2), wine-*press* or *vat*
3342 yeqeb (7), wine-*vat*, wine-*press*
6333 pûwrâh (1), *wine-press* trough
3025 lēnŏs (4), *trough*, i.e. wine-*vat*
3025+3631 lēnŏs (1), *trough*, i.e. wine-*vat*

WINEPRESSES
1660 gath (1), wine-*press*
3342 yeqeb (3), wine-*press*

WINES
8105 shemer (2), *settlings* of wine, *dregs*

WING
3671 kânâph (13), *edge* or *extremity; wing*

WINGED
3671 kânâph (2), *edge* or *extremity; wing*

WINGS
34 'ebyôwn (1), *destitute; poor*
83 'êber (2), *pinion*
84 'ebrâh (1), *pinion*
1611 gaph (Ch.) (3), *wing*
3671 kânâph (60), *edge* or *extremity; wing*
6731 tsîyts (1), *wing*
4420 ptĕrux (5), *wing*

WINK
7169 qârats (1), to *blink*
7335 râzam (1), to *twinkle* the eye

WINKED
5237 hupĕrĕidō (1), to *not punish*

WINKETH
7169 qârats (2), to *blink*

WINNETH
3947 lâqach (1), to *take*

WINNOWED
2219 zârâh (1), to *winnow*

WINNOWETH
2219 zârâh (1), to *winnow*

WINTER
2778 châraph (2), to *spend the winter*
2779 chôreph (3), *autumn, ripeness* of age
5638 çᵉthâv (1), *winter*
3914 parachĕimazō (3), to *spend the winter*
3915 parachĕimasia (1), *wintering* over
5494 chĕimōn (4), *winter*

WINTERED
3916 parachrēma (1), *instantly, immediately*

WINTERHOUSE
2779 chôreph (1), *autumn* (and winter)

WIPE
4229 mâchâh (3), to *erase; to grease*
631 apŏmassŏmai (1), to *scrape away, wipe off*
1591 ĕkmassō (2), to *wipe dry*
1813 ĕxalĕiphō (2), to *obliterate*

WIPED
4229 mâchâh (1), to *erase; to grease*
1591 ĕkmassō (3), to *wipe dry*

WIPETH
4229 mâchâh (2), to *erase; to grease*

WIPING
4229 mâchâh (1), to *erase; to grease*

WIRES
6616 pâthîyl (1), *twine, cord*

WISDOM
998 bîynâh (2), *understanding*
2449 châkam (1), to *be wise*
2451 chokmâh (144), *wisdom*
2452 chokmâh (Ch.) (8), *wisdom*
2454 chokmôwth (4), *wisdom*
2942 ţᵉêm (Ch.) (1), *judgment; account*
3820 lêb (6), *heart*
6195 'ormâh (1), *trickery; discretion*
7919 sâkal (2), to *be* or *act circumspect*
7922 sekel (3), *intelligence; success*
8394 tâbûwn (1), *intelligence; argument*
8454 tûwshîyâh (7), *undertaking*
4678 sŏphia (51), *wisdom*
5428 phrŏnēsis (1), *moral insight, understanding*

WISE
995 bîyn (3), to *understand; discern*
2445 chakkîym (Ch.) (14), *wise one*
2449 châkam (19), to *be wise*
2450 châkâm (122), *wise, intelligent, skillful*
2454 chokmôwth (1), *wisdom*
3198 yâkach (1), to *be correct; to argue*
3823 lâbab (1), *transport* with love; to *stultify*
6031 'ânâh (1), to *afflict, be afflicted*
6493 piqqêach (1), *clear-sighted*
7919 sâkal (12), to *be* or *act circumspect*
7922 sekel (1), *intelligence; success*

WISELY
995 bîyn (1), to *understand; discern*
2449 châkam (2), to *be wise*
2451 chokmâh (2), *wisdom*
7919 sâkal (8), to *be* or *act circumspect*
5430 phrŏnimōs (1), *prudently, shrewdly*

WISER
2449 châkam (4), to *be wise*
2450 châkâm (2), *wise, intelligent, skillful*
4680 sŏphŏs (1), *wise*
5429 phrŏnimōs (1), *sagacious* or *discreet*

WISH
2655 châphêts (1), *pleased* with
4906 maskîyth (1), *carved figure*
6310 peh (1), *mouth*
2172 ĕuchŏmai (3), to *wish for; to pray*

WISHED
7592 shâ'al (1), to *ask*
2172 ĕuchŏmai (1), to *wish for; to pray*

WISHING
7592 shâ'al (1), to *ask*

WIST
3045 yâda' (7), to *know*
1492 ĕidō (6), to *know*

WIT
3045 yâda' (2), to *know*
1107 gnōrizō (1), to *make known, reveal*
5613 hōs (1), *which, how*

WIT'S
2451 chokmâh (1), *wisdom*

WITCH
3784 kâshaph (2), to *enchant*

WITCHCRAFT
3784 kâshaph (1), to *enchant*
7081 qeçem (1), *divination*
5331 pharmakĕia (1), *magic, witchcraft*

WITCHCRAFTS
3785 kesheph (4), *magic, sorcery*

WITHAL
834+3605 'âsher (1), *who, which, what, that*
1992 hêm (1), *they*
2004 hên (3), *they*
3162 yachad (2), *unitedly*
5973 'îm (1), *with*
260 hama (3), *at the same time, together*

WITHDRAW
622 'âçaph (4), to *gather, collect*
3240 yânach (1), to *allow to stay*
3365 yâqar (1), to *be valuable; to make rare*
5493 çûwr (1), to *turn off*
7368 râchaq (1), to *recede*
7725 shûwb (1), to *turn back; to return*
868 aphistēmi (1), to *desist, desert*
4724 stĕllō (1), to *repress*

WITHDRAWEST
7725 shûwb (1), to *turn back; to return*

WITHDRAWETH
1639 gâra' (1), to *shave, remove, lessen*

WITHDRAWN
2502 châlats (1), to *pull off; to strip; to depart*
2559 châmaq (1), to *depart*, i.e. turn about
5080 nâdach (1), to *push off, scattered*
7725 shûwb (2), to *turn back; to return*
645 apŏspaŏ (1), *withdraw* with force

WITHDREW
5414+5437 nâthan (1), to *give*
7725 shûwb (1), to *turn back; to return*
402 anachōrĕō (2), to *retire, withdraw*
5288 hupŏstĕllō (1), to *cower or shrink*
5298 hupŏchōrĕō (1), to *vacate down*, i.e. *retire*

WITHER
3001 yâbêsh (8), to *wither*
5034 nâbêl (2), to *wilt*
7060 qâmal (1), to *wither*

WITHERED
3001 yâbêsh (11), to *wither*
6798 tsânam (1), to *blast*
3583 xērainō (9), to *shrivel, to mature*
3584 xērŏs (4), *withered*

WITHERETH
3001 yâbêsh (5), to *wither*
3583 xērainō (2), to *shrivel, to mature*
5352 phthinŏpōrinŏs (1), *autumnal*

WITHHELD
2820 châsak (3), to *restrain or refrain*
4513 mâna' (3), to *deny, refuse*

WITHHELDEST
4513 mâna' (1), to *deny, refuse*

WITHHOLD
3240 yânach (1), to *allow to stay*
3607 kâlâ' (2), to *hold*
4513 mâna' (5), to *deny*
6113 'âtsar (1), to *hold*

WITHHOLDEN
1219 bâtsar (1), to *be inaccessible*
2254 châbal (1), to *bind by a pledge; to pervert*
4513 mâna' (8), to *deny, refuse*

WITHHOLDETH
2820 châsak (1), to *restrain or refrain*
4513 mâna' (1), to *deny, refuse*
6113 'âtsar (1), to *hold back; to maintain*
2722 katĕchō (1), to *hold down fast*

WITHIN
413 'êl (2), *to, toward*
990 beţen (2), *belly; womb; body*
996 bêyn (1), *between*
1004 bayith (23), *house; temple; family, tribe*
1157 bᵉ'ad (3), *up to or over against*
2315 cheder (1), *apartment, chamber*
2436 chêyq (1), *bosom, heart*
4481 min (Ch.) (1), *from or out of*
5704 'ad (2), *as far (long) as; during; while; until*
5705 'ad (Ch.) (1), *as far (long) as; during*
5750 'ôwd (4), *again; repeatedly; still; more*
5921 'al (8), *above, over, upon, or against*
5978 'immâd (1), *along with*
6440 pânîym (1), *face; front*
6441 pᵉnîymâh (10), *indoors, inside*
6442 pᵉnîymîy (1), *interior, inner*
7130 qereb (26), *nearest part, i.e. the center*
7146 qârachath (1), *bald spot; threadbare spot*
8432 tâvek (20), *center, middle*
8537 tôm (1), *completeness*
1223 dia (1), *through, by means of; because of*
1722 ĕn (13), *in; during; because of*
1737 ĕndiduskō (1), to *clothe*
1787 ĕntŏs (1), *inside, within*
2080 ĕsō (3), *inside, inner, in*
2081 ĕsōthen (10), *from inside; inside*
2082 ĕsōtĕrŏs (1), *interior, inner*
4314 prŏs (1), *for; on, at; to, toward; against*

WITHOUT
268 'âchôwr (1), *behind, backward; west*
369 'ayin (42), *there is no, i.e., not exist, none*
657 'epheç (3), *end; no further*
1097 bᵉlîy (16), *without, not yet; lacking;*
1107 bil'ădêy (4), *except, without, besides*
1115 biltîy (4), *not, except, without, unless*
1372 gabbachath (1), *baldness on forehead*
2351 chûwts (71), *outside, outdoors*
2435 chîytsôwn (5), *outer wall side; exterior*
2600 chinnâm (17), *gratis, free*
2963 ţâraph (1), to *pluck off or pull to pieces*
3808 lô' (29), *no, not*
3809 lâ' (Ch.) (1), *as nothing*
4682 matstsâh (1), *unfermented cake*
5493 çûwr (1), to *turn off*
7387 rêyqâm (2), *emptily; ineffectually*
8267 sheqer (1), *untruth; sham*
8414 tôhûw (2), *waste, desolation, formless*
8549 tâmîym (50), *entire, complete; integrity*
35 agĕnĕalŏgētŏs (1), *unregistered as to birth*
77 adapanŏs (1), *free of charge*
87 adiakritŏs (1), *impartial*
88 adialĕiptŏs (1), *permanent, constant*
89 adialĕiptŏs (4), *without omission*
112 athĕŏs (1), *godless*
175 akarpŏs (1), *barren, unfruitful*
186 aklinēs (1), *firm, unswerving*
194 akratŏs (1), *undiluted*
267 amarturŏs (1), *without witness*
275 amĕrimnŏs (1), *not anxious, free of care*
278 amĕtamĕlētŏs (1), *irrevocable*
280 amĕtrŏs (2), *immoderate*
282 amētōr (1), *of unknown maternity*
298 amōmētŏs (1), *unblemished*
299 amōmŏs (5), *unblemished, blameless*
361 anamartētŏs (1), *sinless*
369 anantirrhētŏs (1), *without raising objection*
379 anapŏlŏgētŏs (1), *without excuse*
427 anĕu (3), *without, apart from*
448 anilĕōs (1), *inexorable, merciless*
459 anŏmŏs (4), *without Jewish law*
460 anŏmŏs (2), *lawlessly, i.e. apart from Jewish Law*
504 anudrŏs (2), *dry, arid*
505 anupŏkritŏs (2), *sincere, genuine*
540 apatōr (1), *of unrecorded paternity*
563 apĕrispastŏs (1), *undistractedly*
677 aprŏskŏpŏs (1), *faultless*
678 aprŏsōpŏlēptŏs (1), *without prejudice*
729 arrhaphŏs (1), *of a single piece, without seam*
772 asthĕnēs (1), *strengthless, weak*
784 aspilŏs (3), *unblemished*
794 astŏrgŏs (2), *hard-hearted*
801 asunĕtŏs (3), *senseless, dull; wicked*
815 atĕknŏs (2), *childless*
817 atĕr (1), *apart from, without*
820 atimŏs (2), *without honor*
866 aphilargurŏs (1), *not greedy*
870 aphŏbŏs (4), *fearlessly*
880 aphōnŏs (1), *mute, silent; unmeaning*
886 achĕirŏpŏiētŏs (2), *unmanufactured*
895 apsuchŏs (1), *lifeless, i.e. inanimate*
1432 dōrĕan (1), *gratuitously, freely*
1500 ĕikē (1), *idly, i.e. without reason or effect*
1618 ĕktĕnēs (1), *intent, earnest*
1622 ĕktŏs (1), *aside from, besides; except*
1854 ĕxō (23), *out, outside*
1855 ĕxōthen (6), *outside, external (-ly)*
2673 katargĕō (1), to *be, render entirely useless*
3361 mē (1), *not; lest*
3672 hŏmŏlŏgŏumĕnōs (1), *confessedly*
3924 parĕktŏs (1), *besides; apart from*
5565 chōris (36), *at a space, i.e. separately*

WITHS
3499 yether (3), *remainder; small rope*

WITHSTAND
2388 châzaq (2), to *bind, restrain, conquer*
3320 yâtsab (1), to *station, offer, continue*
5975 'âmad (4), to *stand*
7854 sâţân (1), *opponent*
436 anthistēmi (1), *oppose, rebel*
2967 kōluō (1), to *stop*

WITHSTOOD
5975 'âmad (2), to *stand*

436 anthistēmi (4), *oppose, rebel*

WITNESS
5707 'êd (45), *witness; testimony*
5711 'Ădâh (1), *ornament*
5713 'êdâh (3), *testimony*
5715 'êdûwth (4), *testimony*
5749 'ûwd (5), to *protest, testify; to encompass*
6030 'ânâh (2), to *respond, answer*
8085 shâma' (1), to *hear intelligently*
267 amarturŏs (1), *without witness*
2649 katamarturĕō (4), to *testify against*
3140 marturĕō (28), to *testify; to commend*
3141 marturia (15), *evidence given*
3142 marturiŏn (4), *something evidential; the Decalogue*
3144 martus (8), *witness*
4828 summarturĕō (3), to *testify jointly*
4901 sunĕpimarturĕō (1), to *testify further jointly*
5576 psĕudŏmarturĕō (6), to *be an untrue testifier*
5577 psĕudŏmarturia (2), *untrue testimony*

WITNESSED
5749 'ûwd (1), to *protest, testify; to encompass*
3140 marturĕō (3), to *testify; to commend*

WITNESSES
5707 'êd (23), *witness; testimony*
3140 marturĕō (1), to *testify; to commend*
3144 martus (21), *witness*
5575 psĕudŏmartur (3), *bearer of untrue testimony*

WITNESSETH
1263 diamarturŏmai (1), to *attest or protest*
3140 marturĕō (1), to *testify; to commend*

WITNESSING
3140 marturĕō (1), to *testify; to commend*

WITTINGLY
7919 sâkal (1), to *be or act circumspect*

WIVES
802 'ishshâh (115), *woman, wife*
5389 nâshîyn (Ch.) (1), *women, wives*
7695 shêgâl (Ch.) (3), *queen*
1135 gunē (12), *woman; wife*

WIVES'
1126 graōdēs (1), *old lady-like, i.e. silly*

WIZARD
3049 yiddeᵉ'ŏnîy (2), *conjurer; ghost*

English

WIZARDS
3049 yidd^e'ônîy (9), conjurer; ghost

WOE
188 'ôwy (22), Oh!, Woe!
190 'ôwyâh (1), Oh!, Woe!
337 'îy (2), alas!
480 'al^{e}lay (2), alas!; woe!
1929 hâhh (1), ah!; woe!
1945 hôwy (36), oh!, woe!
1958 hîy (1), lamentation, woe
3759 ŏuai (39), woe!; woe

WOEFUL
605 'ânash (1), to be frail, feeble

WOES
3759 ŏuai (1), woe!; woe

WOLF
2061 z^e'êb (4), wolf
3074 lukŏs (2), wolf

WOLVES
2061 z^e'êb (3), wolf
3074 lukŏs (4), wolf

WOMAN
802 'ishshâh (211), woman, wife
5291 na'ărâh (1), female child; servant
5347 n^{e}qêbâh (2), female, woman
1135 gunē (96), woman; wife
1658 ĕlĕuthĕrŏs (1), not a slave
2338 thēlus (1), female

WOMAN'S
802 'ishshâh (7), woman

WOMANKIND
802 'ishshâh (1), woman, wife; women, wives

WOMB
990 beţen (31), belly; womb; body
4578 mê'âh (1), viscera; anguish, tenderness
7356 racham (4), compassion; womb
7358 rechem (20), womb
1064 gastēr (1), stomach; womb; gourmand
2836 kŏilia (11), abdomen, womb, heart
3388 mētra (2), womb

WOMBS
7358 rechem (1), womb
2836 kŏilia (1), abdomen, womb, heart

WOMEN
802 'ishshâh (104), woman, wife
5347 n^{e}qêbâh (1), female
1133 gunaikariŏn (1), little woman
1135 gunē (33), woman
2338 thēlus (1), female
4247 prĕsbutis (1), old woman

WOMEN'S
802 'ishshâh (1), woman

WOMENSERVANTS
3198 shiphchâh (3), household female slave

WON
2770 kĕrdainō (1), to gain; to spare

WONDER
4159 môwphêth (6), miracle; token or omen
6382 pele' (1), miracle
8539 tâmahh (3), to be astounded
2285 thambŏs (1), astonishment
2296 thaumazō (2), to wonder; to admire
4592 sēmĕiŏn (2), indication, sign, signal

WONDERED
4159 môwphêth (1), miracle; token or omen
8074 shâmêm (2), to devastate; to stupefy
1839 ĕxistēmi (1), to astound
2296 thaumazō (11), to wonder; to admire

WONDERFUL
6381 pâlâ' (13), to be, make great
6382 pele' (3), miracle
6383 pil'îy (1), remarkable
8047 shammâh (1), ruin, consternation
1411 dunamis (1), force, power, miracle
2297 thaumasiŏs (1), miracle, wondrous act
3167 mĕgalĕiŏs (1), great things, wonderful works

WONDERFULLY
5953 'âlal (1), to glean; to overdo
6381 pâlâ' (1), to be, make wonderful
6382 pele' (1), miracle
6395 pâlâh (1), to distinguish

WONDERING
7583 shâ'âh (1), to be astonished
1569 ĕkthambŏs (1), utterly astounded
2296 thaumazō (1), to wonder; to admire

WONDEROUSLY
6381 pâlâ' (1), to be, make wonderful

WONDERS
4159 môwphêth (19), miracle; token or omen
6381 pâlâ' (9), to be, make wonderful
6382 pele' (7), miracle
8540 t^{e}mahh (Ch.) (3), miracle
4592 sēmĕiŏn (1), indication, sign, signal
5059 tĕras (16), omen or miracle sign

WONDROUS
4652 miphlâ'âh (1), miracle
6381 pâlâ' (14), to be, make wonderful

WONDROUSLY
6381 pâlâ' (1), to be, make wonderful

WONT
1696 dâbar (1), to speak, say; to subdue
1980 hâlak (1), to walk; live a certain way
2370 chăzâ' (Ch.) (1), to gaze upon; to dream
5056 naggâch (1), act of butting
5532 çâkan (1), to be serviceable to
1486 ĕthō (2), to be used by habit
2596+1485 kata (1), down; according to
3543 nŏmizō (1), to deem

WOOD
636 'â' (Ch.) (2), tree; wood; plank
2793 chôresh (4), wooded forest
3293 ya'ar (18), honey in the comb
6086 'êts (106), wood
3585 xulinŏs (2), made of wood
3586 xulŏn (3), timber and its products

WOODS
3264 yâ'ôwr (1), forest

WOOF
6154 'êreb (9), mixed or woven things

WOOL
6015 'ămar (Ch.) (1), wool
6785 tsemer (11), wool
2053 ĕriŏn (2), wool

WOOLLEN
6785 tsemer (5), wool
8162 sha'aţnêz (1), linen and woolen

WORD
562 'ômer (2), something said
565 'imrâh (26), something said
1697 dâbâr (433), word; matter; thing
1699 dôber (2), grazing pasture
3983 mê'mar (Ch.) (1), edict, command
4405 millâh (2), word; discourse; speech
4406 millâh (Ch.) (2), word, command
6310 peh (15), mouth; opening
6600 pithgâm (Ch.) (1), decree; report
518 apaggĕllō (2), to announce, proclaim
2036 ĕpō (1), to speak
3050 lŏgikŏs (1), rational, logical
3056 lŏgŏs (173), word, matter, thing; Word
4487 rhēma (28), utterance; matter

WORD'S
1697 dâbâr (1), word; matter; thing
3056 lŏgŏs (1), word, matter, thing; Word

WORDS
561 'êmer (42), something said
565 'imrâh (3), something said
1697 dâbâr (373), word; matter; thing
1703 dabbârâh (1), word, instruction
4405 millâh (21), word; discourse; speech
4406 millâh (Ch.) (5), word, command
3054 lŏgŏmachĕō (1), to be disputatious
3055 lŏgŏmachia (1), disputation
3056 lŏgŏs (48), word, matter, thing; Word
4086 pithanŏlŏgia (1), persuasive language
4487 rhēma (31), utterance; matter
5542 chrēstŏlŏgia (1), fair speech

WORK
731 'arzâh (1), cedar paneling
1697 dâbâr (1), word; matter; thing
3018 y^{e}gîya' (1), toil, work; produce, property
3027 yâd (1), hand; power
3336 yêtser (1), form
4399 m^{e}lâ'kâh (125), work; property
4639 ma'ăseh (113), action; labor
4640 Ma'say (1), operative
4649 Muppîym (1), wavings
4749 miqshâh (5), work molded by hammering
5627 çârâh (1), apostasy; crime; remission
5647 'âbad (4), to do, work, serve
5656 'ăbôdâh (10), work
5673 'ăbîydâh (Ch.) (3), labor or business
5950 'ălîylîyâh (1), execution, deed
6213 'âsâh (23), to do
6381 pâlâ' (2), to be, make wonderful
6466 pâ'al (5), to do, make or practice
6467 pô'al (28), act or work, deed
6468 p^e'ullâh (8), work
6603 pittûwach (1), sculpture; engraving
7553 riqmâh (5), variegation of color
7639 s^{e}bâkâh (2), reticulated ornament
1411 dunamis (1), force, power, miracle
1754 ĕnĕrgĕō (2), to be active, efficient, work
2038 ĕrgazŏmai (12), to toil
2039 ĕrgasia (1), occupation; profit
2040 ĕrgatēs (1), toiler, worker
2041 ĕrgŏn (45), work

2716 katĕrgazŏmai (1),
to finish; to accomplish
3056 lŏgŏs (2), word,
matter, thing; Word
3433+2480 mŏlis (1), with
difficulty
4229 pragma (1), matter,
deed, affair
4903 sunĕrgĕŏ (1), to be
a fellow-worker

WORK'S
2041 ĕrgŏn (1), work

WORKER
2790 chârash (1), to
engrave; to plow

WORKERS
2796 chârâsh (1), skilled
fabricator or worker
6213 'âsâh (1), to do
6466 pâ'al (19), to do,
make or practice
1411 dunamis (1), force,
power, miracle
2040 ĕrgatēs (3), toiler,
worker
4903 sunĕrgĕŏ (1), to be
a fellow-worker

WORKETH
5648 'ăbad (Ch.) (1), to
work, serve
6213 'âsâh (6), to do or
make
6466 pâ'al (4), to do,
make or practice
1754 ĕnĕrgĕŏ (11), to be
active, efficient, work
2038 ĕrgazŏmai (7), to
toil
2716 katĕrgazŏmai (7),
to finish; to accomplish
4160 pŏiĕŏ (1), to make
or do

WORKFELLOW
4904 sunĕrgŏs (1),
fellow-worker

WORKING
4639 ma'ăseh (1), action;
labor
6213 'âsâh (1), to do or
make
6466 pâ'al (1), to do,
make or practice
8454 tûwshîyâh (1),
ability, i.e. direct help
1753 ĕnĕrgĕia (6),
efficiency, energy
1755 ĕnĕrgēma (1),
effect, activity
2038 ĕrgazŏmai (4), to
toil
2716 katĕrgazŏmai (2),
to finish; to accomplish
4160 pŏiĕŏ (2), to make
or do
4903 sunĕrgĕŏ (1), to be
a fellow-worker

WORKMAN
542 'âmân (1), expert
artisan, craftsman
2796 chârâsh (5), skilled
fabricator or worker
2803 châshab (2), to
weave, fabricate
2040 ĕrgatēs (2), toiler,
worker

WORKMANSHIP
4399 mᵉlâ'kâh (5), work;
property
4639 ma'ăseh (1), action;
labor
4161 pŏiēma (1), what is
made, product

WORKMEN
582+4399 'ĕnôwsh (1),
man; person, human
2796 chârâsh (1), skilled
fabricator or worker
6213+4399 'âsâh (7), to
do or make
2040 ĕrgatēs (2), toiler,
worker

WORKMEN'S
6001 'âmêl (1), toiling;
laborer; sorrowful

WORKS
1697 dâbâr (1), word;
matter; thing
4399 mᵉlâ'kâh (3), work;
property
4566 ma'bâd (1), act,
deed
4567 ma'bâd (Ch.) (1),
act, deed
4611 ma'ălâl (3), act,
deed
4639 ma'ăseh (70),
action; labor
4640 Ma'say (2),
operative
4659 miph'âl (3),
performance, deed
5652 'ăbâd (1), deed
5949 'ălîylâh (3),
opportunity, action
6467 pô'al (2), act or
work, deed
6468 pᵉ'ullâh (1), work,
deed
2041 ĕrgŏn (104), work
4234 praxis (1), act;
function

WORKS'
2041 ĕrgŏn (1), work

WORLD
776 'erets (4), earth,
land, soil; country
2309 chedel (1), state of
the dead, deceased
2465 cheled (2), fleeting
time; this world
5769 'ôwlâm (4), eternity;
ancient; always
8398 têbêl (35), earth;
world; inhabitants
165 aiōn (37), perpetuity,
ever; world
166 aiōniŏs (3),
perpetual, long ago
1093 gē (1), soil, region,
whole earth
2889 kŏsmŏs (183), world
3625 ŏikŏumĕnē (14),
Roman empire

WORLD'S
2889 kŏsmŏs (1), world

WORLDLY
2886 kŏsmikŏs (2),
earthly, worldly

WORLDS
165 aiōn (2), perpetuity,
ever; world

WORM
5580 çâç (1), garment
moth
7415 rimmâh (5), maggot
8438 tôwlâ' (5), maggot
worm; crimson-grub
4663 skōlēx (3), grub,
maggot or earth-worm

WORMS
2119 zâchal (1), to crawl;
glide
7415 rimmâh (2), maggot
8438 tôwlâ' (3), maggot
worm; crimson-grub
4662 skōlēkŏbrōtŏs (1),
diseased with maggots

WORMWOOD
3939 la'ănâh (7),
poisonous wormwood
894 apsinthŏs (2),
wormwood, bitterness

WORSE
2196 zâ'aph (1), to be
angry
5062 nâgaph (5), to
inflict a disease
7451 ra' (1), bad; evil
7489 râ'a' (5), to be good
for nothing
1640 ĕlassōn (1), smaller
2276 hēttōn (1), worse
5302 hustĕrĕŏ (1), to be
inferior; to fall short
5501 chĕirōn (10), more
evil or aggravated

WORSHIP
5457 çᵉgîd (Ch.) (8), to
prostrate oneself
6087 'âtsab (1), to
fabricate or fashion
7812 shâchâh (54), to
prostrate in homage
1391 dŏxa (1), glory;
brilliance
1479 ĕthĕlŏthrēskĕia (1),
voluntary piety
2151 ĕusĕbĕŏ (1), to put
religion into practice
3000 latrĕuō (3), to
minister to God
4352 prŏskunĕŏ (34), to
prostrate oneself
4352+1799 prŏskunĕŏ (1),
to prostrate oneself
4576 sĕbŏmai (3), to
revere, i.e. adore

WORSHIPPED
5457 çᵉgîd (Ch.) (2), to
prostrate oneself
7812 shâchâh (39), to
prostrate in homage
2323 thĕrapĕuō (1), to
adore God
4352 prŏskunĕŏ (24), to
prostrate oneself
4573 sĕbazŏmai (1), to
venerate, worship
4574 sĕbasma (1), object
of worship
4576 sĕbŏmai (2), to
revere, i.e. adore

WORSHIPPER
2318 thĕŏsĕbēs (1), pious,
devout, God-fearing
3511 nĕōkŏrŏs (1),
temple servant

WORSHIPPERS
5647 'âbad (5), to serve
3000 latrĕuō (1), to
minister to God
4353 prŏskunētēs (1),
adorer

WORSHIPPETH
5457 çᵉgîd (Ch.) (2), to
prostrate oneself
7812 shâchâh (3), to
prostrate in homage
4576 sĕbŏmai (1), to
revere, i.e. adore

WORSHIPPING
7812 shâchâh (3), to
prostrate in homage
2356 thrēskĕia (1),
observance, religion
4352 prŏskunĕŏ (1), to
prostrate oneself

WORST
7451 ra' (1), bad; evil

WORTH
3644 kᵉmôw (1), like, as;
for; with
4242 mᵉchîyr (1), price,
payment, wages
4373 mikçâh (1),
valuation of a thing
4392 mâlê' (1), full;
filling; fulness; fully
7939 sâkâr (1), payment,
salary; compensation

WORTHIES
117 'addîyr (1), powerful;
majestic

WORTHILY
2428 chayil (1), army;
wealth; virtue; valor

WORTHY
376 'îysh (1), man; male;
someone
639 'aph (1), nose or
nostril; face; person
1121 bên (2), son,
descendant; people
2428 chayil (1), army;
wealth; virtue; valor
6994 qâṭôn (1), to be,
make diminutive
514 axiŏs (35), deserving,
comparable or suitable
515 axiŏŏ (5), to deem
entitled or fit, worthy
516 axiŏs (3),
appropriately, suitable
2425 hikanŏs (5), ample;
fit
2570 kalŏs (1), good;
beautiful; valuable
2661 kataxiŏŏ (4), to
deem entirely deserving
2735 katŏrthōma (1),
made fully upright

WOT
3045 yâda' (6), to know
1107 gnōrizō (1), to
make known, reveal
1492 ĕidō (3), to know

WOTTETH
3045 yâda' (1), to know

WOULD
14 'âbâh (41), to be
acquiescent
305 'achălay (1), would
that!, Oh that!, If Only!

English

2654 châphêts (1), to be
pleased with, desire
2655 châphêts (1),
pleased with
2974 yâ'al (3), to assent;
to undertake, begin
3863 lûw' (6), would that!
5315 nephesh (1), life;
breath; soul; wind
6634 tsᵉbâ' (Ch.) (5), to
please
1096 ginŏmai (1), to be,
become
2172 ĕuchŏmai (1), to
wish for; to pray
2309 thēlō (73), to will; to
desire; to choose
3195 mĕllō (9), to intend,
i.e. be about to
3785 ŏphĕlŏn (4), I wish

WOULDEST
3426 yêsh (1), there is
2309 thēlō (4), to will; to
desire; to choose

WOUND
2671 chêts (1), arrow;
wound; thunder-bolt
4204 mâzôwr (1), ambush
4205 mâzôwr (2), sore
4272 mâchats (3), to
crush; to subdue
4347 makkâh (8), blow;
wound; pestilence
5061 nega' (1), infliction,
affliction; leprous spot
6482 petsa' (2), wound
1210 dĕō (1), to bind
4127 plēgē (3), stroke;
wound; calamity
4958 sustĕllō (1), to draw
together, i.e. enwrap or
enshroud a corpse
5180 tuptō (1), to strike,
beat, wound

WOUNDED
1214 bâtsa' (1), to
plunder; to finish
1795 dakkâh (1),
mutilated by crushing
1856 dâqar (1), to stab,
pierce; to starve
2342 chûwl (2), to dance,
whirl; to writhe in pain
2470 châlâh (3), to be
weak, sick, afflicted
2490 châlal (3), to
profane, defile
2491 châlâl (10), pierced
to death, one slain
4272 mâchats (2), to
crush; to subdue
4347 makkâh (1), blow;
wound; pestilence
5218 nâkê' (1), smitten;
afflicted
5221 nâkâh (3), to strike,
kill
6481 pâtsa' (2), to wound
4127+2007 plēgē (1),
stroke; wound
4969 sphazō (1), to
slaughter or to maim
5135 traumatizō (2), to
inflict a wound

WOUNDEDST
4272 mâchats (1), to
crush; to subdue

WOUNDETH
4272 mâchats (1), to
crush; to subdue

WOUNDING
6482 petsa' (1), wound

WOUNDS
2250 chabbûwrâh (1),
weal, bruise
3859 lâham (2), to rankle
4347 makkâh (6), blow;
wound; pestilence
6094 'atstsebeth (1), pain
or wound, sorrow
6482 petsa' (4), wound
5134 trauma (1), wound

WOVE
707 'ârag (1), to plait or
weave

WOVEN
707 'ârag (3), to plait or
weave
5307 huphantŏs (1),
knitted, woven

WRAP
3664 kânaç (1), to
collect; to enfold
5686 'âbath (1), to pervert

WRAPPED
1563 gâlam (1), to fold
2280 châbash (1), to
wrap firmly, bind
3874 lûwṭ (2), to wrap up
4593 mâ'ôṭ (1), sharp,
thin-edged
5440 çâbak (1), to
entwine
5968 'âlaph (1), to be
languid, faint
8276 sârag (1), to entwine
1750 ĕnĕilĕō (1), to
enwrap
1794 ĕntulissō (3), wind
up in, enwrap
4683 sparganŏō (2), to
strap or wrap

WRATH
639 'aph (42), nose or
nostril; face; person
2197 za'aph (1), anger,
rage
2534 chêmâh (34), heat;
anger; poison
2740 chârôwn (6),
burning of anger
3707 kâ'aç (1), to grieve,
rage, be indignant
3708 ka'aç (4), vexation,
grief
5678 'ebrâh (31),
outburst of passion
7107 qâtsaph (5), to burst
out in rage
7109 qᵉtsaph (Ch.) (1),
rage
7110 qetseph (23), rage
or strife
7265 rᵉgaz (Ch.) (1), to
quiver
7267 rôgez (1), disquiet;
anger
2372 thumŏs (14),
passion, anger
3709 ŏrgē (31), ire;
punishment
3949 parŏrgizō (1), to
enrage, exasperate

3950 parŏrgismŏs (1),
rage

WRATHFUL
2534 chêmâh (1), heat;
anger; poison
2740 chârôwn (1),
burning of anger

WRATHS
2372 thumŏs (1),
passion, anger

WREATH
7639 sᵉbâkâh (1),
reticulated ornament

WREATHED
8276 sârag (1), to entwine

WREATHEN
5688 'ăbôth (8), entwined
things: a string, wreath
7639 sᵉbâkâh (2),
reticulated ornament

WREATHS
1434 gᵉdîl (1), tassel;
festoon
7639 sᵉbâkâh (2),
reticulated ornament

WREST
5186 nâṭâh (3), to stretch
or spread out
6087 'âtsab (1), to
fabricate or fashion
4761 strĕblŏō (1), to
pervert, twist

WRESTLE
2076+3823 ĕsti (1), he
(she or it) is; they are

WRESTLED
79 'âbaq (2), grapple,
wrestle
6617 pâthal (1), to
struggle; to be tortuous

WRESTLINGS
5319 naphtûwl (1),
struggle

WRETCHED
5005 talaipōrŏs (2),
miserable, wretched

WRETCHEDNESS
7451 ra' (1), bad; evil

WRING
4454 mâlaq (2), to wring
a bird's neck
4680 mâtsâh (1), to
drain; to squeeze out

WRINGED
4680 mâtsâh (1), to
drain; to squeeze out

WRINGING
4330 mîyts (1), pressure

WRINKLE
4512 rhutis (1), face
wrinkle

WRINKLES
7059 qâmaṭ (1), to pluck,
i.e. destroy

WRITE
3789 kâthab (35), to write
3790 kᵉthab (Ch.) (1), to
write
1125 graphō (50), to write
1924 ĕpigraphō (2), to
inscribe, write upon
1989 ĕpistĕllō (1), to
communicate by letter

WRITER
5608 çâphar (2), to
inscribe; to enumerate

WRITER'S
5608 çâphar (2), to
inscribe; to enumerate

WRITEST
3789 kâthab (2), to write

WRITETH
3789 kâthab (1), to write

WRITING
3789 kâthab (1), to write
3791 kâthâb (14),
writing, record or book
3792 kᵉthâb (Ch.) (10),
writing, record or book
4385 miktâb (8), written
thing
975 bibliŏn (1), scroll;
certificate
1125 graphō (1), to write
4093 pinakidiŏn (1),
wooden writing tablet

WRITINGS
1121 gramma (1),
writing; education

WRITTEN
3789 kâthab (138), to
write
3790 kᵉthab (Ch.) (2), to
write
3792 kᵉthâb (Ch.) (1),
writing, record or book
7560 rᵉsham (Ch.) (2), to
record
583 apŏgraphō (1),
enroll, take a census
1123 graptŏs (1),
inscribed, written
1125 graphō (134), to
write
1449 ĕggraphō (2),
inscribe, write
1722+1121 ĕn (1), in;
during; because of
1924 ĕpigraphō (2), to
inscribe, write upon
1989 ĕpistĕllō (2), to
communicate by letter
4270 prŏgraphō (2), to
write previously; to
announce, prescribe

WRONG
2555 châmâç (3),
violence; malice
3238 yânâh (1), to
suppress; to maltreat
3808+4941 lô' (1), no, not
5627 çârâh (1), apostasy;
crime; remission
5753 'âvâh (1), to be
crooked
5792 'avvâthâh (1),
oppression
6127 'âqal (1), to wrest,
be crooked
6231 'âshaq (2), to
violate; to overflow
7451 ra' (1), bad; evil
7563 râshâ' (1), morally
wrong; bad person
91 adikĕō (11), to do
wrong
92 adikēma (1), wrong
93 adikia (1),
wrongfulness

WRONGED
91 adikĕō (2), *to do wrong*

WRONGETH
2554 châmaç (1), *to be violent; to maltreat*

WRONGFULLY
2554 châmaç (1), *to be violent; to maltreat*
3808+4941 lô' (1), *no, not*
8267 sheqer (4), *untruth; sham*
95 adikōs (1), *unjustly*

WROTE
3789 kâthab (34), *to write*
3790 kᵉthab (Ch.) (5), *to write*
1125 graphō (21), *to write*
4270 prŏgraphō (1), *to write previously; to announce, prescribe*

WROTH
2196 zâ'aph (2), *to be angry*
2534 chêmâh (1), *heat; anger; poison*
2734 chârâh (13), *to blaze up*
3707 kâ'aç (1), *to grieve, rage, be indignant*
5674 'âbar (5), *to cross over; to transition*
7107 qâtsaph (22), *to burst out in rage*
7264 râgaz (1), *to quiver*
2373 thumŏō (1), *to enrage*
3710 ŏrgizō (3), *to become exasperated*

WROUGHT
1496 gâzîyth (1), *dressed stone*
1980 hâlak (2), *to walk; live a certain way*
2790 chârash (1), *to engrave; to plow*
4639 ma'âseh (3), *action; labor*
4865 mishbᵉtsâh (1), *reticulated setting*
5647 'âbad (1), *to do, work, serve*
5648 'âbad (Ch.) (1), *to work, serve*
5656 'âbôdâh (1), *work*
5927 'âlâh (1), *to ascend, be high, mount*
5953 'âlal (2), *to glean; to overdo*
6213 'âsâh (52), *to do*
6466 pâ'al (7), *to do, make or practice*
7194 qâshar (1), *to tie, bind*
7551 râqam (1), *variegation; embroider*
7760 sûwm (1), *to put, place*
1096 ginŏmai (2), *to be, become*
1754 ĕnĕrgĕō (2), *to be active, efficient, work*
2038 ĕrgazŏmai (7), *to toil*
2716 katĕrgazŏmai (6), *to finish; to accomplish*

4160 pŏiĕō (5), *to make or do*
4903 sunĕrgĕō (1), *to be a fellow-worker*

WROUGHTEST
6213 'âsâh (1), *to make*

WRUNG
4680 mâtsâh (4), *to drain; to squeeze out*

YARN
4723 miqveh (4), *confidence; collection*

YEA
432 'illûw (1), *if*
637 'aph (39), *also or yea; though*
834 'âsher (1), *who, which, what, that*
1571 gam (66), *also; even; yea; though*
3588 kîy (7), *for, that because*
235 alla (15), *but, yet, except, instead*
1161 dĕ (13), *but, yet; and then*
2089 ĕti (1), *yet, still*
2228 ē (1), *or; than*
2532 kai (5), *and; or; even; also*
3304 mĕnŏungĕ (1), *so then at least*
3483 nai (22), *yes*

YEAR
3117 yôwm (6), *day; time period*
8140 shᵉnâh (Ch.) (5), *year*
8141 shâneh (323), *year*
1763 ĕniautŏs (13), *year*
2094 ĕtŏs (3), *year*
4070 pĕrusi (2), *last year; from last year*

YEAR'S
3117 yôwm (1), *day; time period*
8141 shâneh (3), *year*

YEARLY
3117 yôwm (6), *day; time period*
8141 shâneh (3), *year*

YEARN
3648 kâmar (1), *to shrivel with heat*

YEARNED
3648 kâmar (1), *to shrivel with heat*

YEARS
3027 yâd (1), *hand; power*
3117 yôwm (3), *day; time period*
8027 shâlash (2), *to be, triplicate*
8140 shᵉnâh (Ch.) (2), *year*
8141 shâneh (466), *year*
1096+3173 ginŏmai (1), *to be, become*
1332 diĕtĕs (1), *of two years in age*
1333 diĕtia (2), *interval of two years*
1541 hĕkatŏntaĕtēs (1), *centenarian*
1763 ĕniautŏs (2), *year*
2094 ĕtŏs (46), *year*

2250 hēmĕra (2), *day; period of time*
5063 tĕssarakŏntaĕtēs (2), *of forty years of age*
5148 triĕtia (1), *triennium, three years*

YEARS'
8141 shâneh (2), *year*

YELL
5286 nâ'ar (1), *to growl*

YELLED
5414+6963 nâthan (1), *to give*

YELLOW
3422 yᵉraqraq (1), *yellowishness*
6669 tsâhôb (3), *golden in color*

YES
3304 mĕnŏungĕ (1), *so then at least*
3483 nai (3), *yes*

YESTERDAY
570 'emesh (1), *yesterday evening*
865 'ethmôwl (1), *heretofore, formerly*
8543 tᵉmôwl (4), *yesterday*
5504 chthĕs (3), *yesterday; in time past*

YESTERNIGHT
570 'emesh (3), *yesterday evening*

YET
227 'âz (1), *at that time or place; therefore*
389 'ak (13), *surely; only, however*
559 'âmar (1), *to say*
637 'aph (1), *also or yea*
1297 bᵉram (Ch.) (2), *however, but*
1571 gam (14), *also; even; yea; though*
2962 ţerem (4), *not yet or before*
3588 kîy (14), *for, that because*
5704 'ad (4), *as far (long) as; during; while; until*
5728 'âden (2), *till now, yet*
5750 'ôwd (142), *again; repeatedly; still; more*
7535 raq (2), *merely; although*
188 akmēn (1), *just now, still*
235 alla (11), *but, yet, except, instead*
1063 gar (3), *for, indeed, but, because*
1065 gĕ (2), *particle of emphasis*
1161 dĕ (19), *but, yet; and then*
2089 ĕti (54), *yet, still*
2236 hēdista (2), *with great pleasure*
2532 kai (7), *and; or; even; also*
2539 kaipĕr (1), *nevertheless*
2579 kan (1), *and (or even) if*

2596 kata (2), *down; according to*
3195 mĕllō (1), *to intend, i.e. be about to*
3305 mĕntŏi (2), *however*
3364 ŏu mē (1), *not at all, absolutely not*
3369 mēdĕpō (1), *not even yet*
3380 mēpō (1), *not yet*
3764 ŏudĕpō (4), *not even yet*
3765 ŏukĕti (3), *not yet, no longer*
3768 ŏupō (21), *not yet*

YIELD
3254 yâçaph (1), *to add or augment*
5186 nâţâh (1), *to stretch or spread out*
5375 nâsâ' (1), *to lift up*
5414 nâthan (13), *to give*
5414+3027 nâthan (1), *to give*
6213 'âsâh (6), *to do or make*
1325 didōmi (1), *to give*
3936 paristēmi (4), *to stand beside, present*
3982 pĕithō (1), *to assent to authority*
4160 pŏiĕō (1), *to make or do*

YIELDED
1478 gâva' (1), *to expire, die*
1580 gâmal (1), *to benefit or requite; to wean*
3052 yᵉhab (Ch.) (1), *to give*
591 apŏdidōmi (1), *to give away*
863 aphiēmi (1), *to leave; to pardon, forgive*
1325 didōmi (1), *to give*
1634 ĕkpsuchō (1), *to expire, die*
3936 paristēmi (1), *to stand beside, present*

YIELDETH
5414 nâthan (1), *to give*
7235 râbâh (1), *to increase*
591 apŏdidōmi (1), *to give away*

YIELDING
2232 zâra' (3), *to sow seed; to disseminate*
4832 marpê' (1), *cure; deliverance; placidity*
6213 'âsâh (3), *to do or make*

YOKE
4132 môwţ (1), *pole; yoke*
4133 môwţâh (4), *pole; ox-bow; yoke*
5923 'ôl (39), *neck yoke*
6776 tsemed (7), *paired yoke*
2201 zĕugŏs (1), *team*
2218 zugŏs (5), *coupling, yoke*

YOKED
2086 hĕtĕrŏzugĕō (1), *to associate discordantly*

English

YOKEFELLOW
4805 suzugŏs (1), *colleague*

YOKES
4133 môwṭâh (4), *pole; ox-bow; yoke*

YONDER
1973 hâlĕâh (1), *far away; thus far*
3541 kôh (2), *thus*
5676 ʿêber (1), *opposite side; east*
5704+3541 ʿad (1), *as far (long) as; during; while; until*
1563 ĕkĕi (2), *there, thither*

YOUNG
667 ʿephrôach (4), *brood of a bird*
970 bâchûwr (42), *male youth; bridegroom*
979 bᵉchûrôwth (1), *youth*
1121 bên (20), *son, descendant; people*
1121+1241 bên (34), *son, descendant; people*
1123 bên (Ch.) (1), *son*
1241 bâqâr (1), *plowing ox; herd*
1469 gôwzâl (2), *young of a bird*
1482 gûwr (1), *cub*
3127 yôwneqeth (1), *sprout, new shoot*
3206 yeled (10), *young male*
3242 yᵉnîqâh (1), *sucker or sapling*
3715 kᵉphîyr (25), *walled village; young lion*
3833 lâbîyʿ (1), *lion, lioness*
5288 naʿar (92), *male child; servant*
5288+970 naʿar (1), *male child; servant*
5291 naʿărâh (6), *female child; servant*
5763 ʿûwl (3), *to suckle, i.e. give milk*
5958 ʿelem (1), *lad, young man*
6082 ʿôpher (5), *dusty-colored fawn*
6499 par (1), *bullock*
6810+3117 tsâʿîyr (1), *young in value*
6996 qâṭân (1), *small, least, youngest*
7988 shilyâh (1), *fetus or infant baby*
1025 brĕphŏs (1), *infant*
2365 thugatriŏn (1), *little daughter*
3494 nĕanias (5), *youth, up to about forty years*
3495 nĕaniskŏs (10), *youth under forty*
3501 nĕŏs (4), *new*
3502 nĕŏssŏs (1), *young*
3678 ŏnariŏn (1), *little donkey*
3813 paidiŏn (10), *child; immature*
3816 pais (1), *child; slave or servant*

YOUNGER
6810 tsâʿîyr (7), *little, young*
6810+3117 tsâʿîyr (1), *little, young*
6996 qâṭân (14), *small, least, youngest*
1640 ĕlassŏn (1), *smaller*
3501 nĕŏs (8), *new*

YOUNGEST
6810 tsâʿîyr (3), *little, young*
6996 qâṭân (15), *small, least, youngest*

YOUTH
979 bᵉchûrôwth (2), *youth*
2779 chôreph (1), *autumn (and winter)*
3208 yaldûwth (2), *boyhood or girlhood*
5271 nâʿûwr (46), *youth; juvenility; young people*
5288 naʿar (5), *male child; servant*
5290 nôʿar (2), *boyhood*
5934 ʿâlûwm (4), *adolescence; vigor*
6526 pirchach (1), *progeny, i.e. a brood*
6812 tsᵉʿîyrâh (1), *juvenility*
7839 shachărûwth (1), *juvenescence, youth*
3503 nĕŏtēs (5), *youthfulness*

YOUTHFUL
3512 nĕŏtĕrikŏs (1), *juvenile, youthful*

YOUTHS
1121 bên (1), *son, descendant; people*
5288 naʿar (1), *male child; servant*

ZAANAIM
6815 Tsaʿănannîym (1), *removals*

ZAANAN
6630 Tsaʿănân (1), *sheep pasture*

ZAANANNIM
6815 Tsaʿănannîym (1), *removals*

ZAAVAN
2190 Zaʿăvân (1), *disquiet*

ZABAD
2066 Zâbâd (8), *giver*

ZABBAI
2079 Zabbay (2), *Zabbai*

ZABBUD
2072 Zabbûwd (1), *given*

ZABDI
2067 Zabdîy (6), *giving*

ZABDIEL
2068 Zabdîyʿêl (2), *gift of God*

ZABUD
2071 Zâbûwd (1), *given*

ZABULON
2194 Zaboulŏn (3), *habitation*

ZACCAI
2140 Zakkay (2), *pure*

ZACCHAEUS
2195 Zakchaiŏs (3), *Zacchæus*

ZACCHUR
2139 Zakkûwr (1), *mindful*

ZACCUR
2139 Zakkûwr (8), *mindful*

ZACHARIAH
2148 Zᵉkaryâh (4), *Jehovah has remembered*

ZACHARIAS
2197 Zacharias (11), *Jehovah has remembered*

ZACHER
2144 Zeker (1), *recollection; commemoration*

ZADOK
6659 Tsâdôwq (52), *just*

ZADOK'S
6659 Tsâdôwq (1), *just*

ZAHAM
2093 Zaham (1), *loathing*

ZAIR
6811 Tsâʿîyr (1), *little*

ZALAPH
6764 Tsâlâph (1), *Tsalaph*

ZALMON
6756 Tsalmôwn (2), *shady*

ZALMONAH
6758 Tsalmônâh (2), *shadiness*

ZALMUNNA
6759 Tsalmunnâʿ (12), *shade has been denied*

ZAMZUMMIMS
2157 Zamzôm (1), *intriguing*

ZANOAH
2182 Zânôwach (5), *rejected*

ZAPHNATH-PAANEAH
6847 Tsophnath Paʿnêach (1), *Tsophnath-Paneäch*

ZAPHON
6829 Tsâphôwn (1), *boreal, northern*

ZARA
2196 Zara (1), *rising of light, dawning*

ZARAH
2226 Zerach (2), *rising of light, dawning*

ZAREAH
6881 Tsorʿâh (1), *stinging wasp*

ZAREATHITES
6882 Tsorʿîy (1), *Tsorite or Tsorathite*

ZARED
2218 Zered (1), *lined with shrubbery*

ZAREPHATH
6886 Tsârᵉphath (3), *refinement*

ZARETAN
6891 Tsârᵉthân (1), *Tsarethan*

ZARETH-SHAHAR
6890 Tsereth hash-Shachar (1), *splendor of the dawn*

ZARHITES
2227 Zarchîy (6), *Zarchite*

ZARTANAH
6891 Tsârᵉthân (1), *Tsarethan*

ZARTHAN
6891 Tsârᵉthân (1), *Tsarethan*

ZATTHU
2240 Zattûwʿ (1), *Zattu*

ZATTU
2240 Zattûwʿ (3), *Zattu*

ZAVAN
2190 Zaʿăvân (1), *disquiet*

ZAZA
2117 Zâzâʿ (1), *prominent*

ZEAL
7065 qânâʿ (1), *to be, make zealous, jealous or envious*
7068 qinʿâh (9), *jealousy or envy*
2205 zēlŏs (6), *zeal, ardor; jealousy, malice*

ZEALOUS
7065 qânâʿ (2), *to be, make zealous*
2206 zēlŏō (1), *to have warmth of feeling for*
2207 zēlōtēs (5), *zealot*

ZEALOUSLY
2206 zēlŏō (2), *to have warmth of feeling for*

ZEBADIAH
2069 Zᵉbadyâh (9), *Jehovah has given*

ZEBAH
2078 Zebach (12), *sacrifice*

ZEBAIM
6380 Pôkereth Tsᵉbâyîym (2), *trap of gazelles*

ZEBEDEE
2199 Zĕbĕdaiŏs (10), *Zebedæus*

ZEBEDEE'S
2199 Zĕbĕdaiŏs (2), *Zebedæus*

ZEBINA
2081 Zᵉbîynâʿ (1), *gainfulness*

ZEBOIIM
6636 Tsᵉbôʿiym (2), *gazelles*

ZEBOIM
6636 Tsᵉbôʿiym (3), *gazelles*
6650 Tsᵉbôʿîym (2), *hyenas*

ZEBUDAH
2081 Zᵉbîynâʿ (1), *gainfulness*

ZEBUL
2083 Zᵉbûl (6), *dwelling*

ZEBULONITE
2075 Zᵉbûwlônîy (2), Zebulonite

ZEBULUN
2074 Zᵉbûwlûwn (44), habitation

ZEBULUNITES
2075 Zᵉbûwlônîy (1), Zebulonite

ZECHARIAH
2148 Zᵉkaryâh (39), Jehovah has remembered

ZEDAD
6657 Tsᵉdâd (2), siding

ZEDEKIAH
6667 Tsidqîyâh (61), right of Jehovah

ZEDEKIAH'S
6667 Tsidqîyâh (1), right of Jehovah

ZEEB
2062 Zᵉ'êb (6), wolf

ZELAH
6762 Tsela' (2), limping

ZELEK
6768 Tseleq (2), fissure

ZELOPHEHAD
6765 Tsᵉlophchâd (11), Tselophchad

ZELOTES
2208 Zēlōtēs (2), Zealot, partisan

ZELZAH
6766 Tseltsach (1), clear shade

ZEMARAIM
6787 Tsᵉmârayim (2), double fleece

ZEMARITE
6786 Tsᵉmârîy (2), Tsemarite

ZEMIRA
2160 Zᵉmîyrâh (1), song

ZENAN
6799 Tsᵉnân (1), Tsenan

ZENAS
2211 Zēnas (1), Jove-given

ZEPHANIAH
6846 Tsᵉphanyâh (10), Jehovah has secreted

ZEPHATH
6857 Tsᵉphath (1), watch-tower

ZEPHATHAH
6859 Tsᵉphâthâh (1), watch-tower

ZEPHI
6825 Tsᵉphôw (1), observant

ZEPHO
6825 Tsᵉphôw (2), observant

ZEPHON
6827 Tsᵉphôwn (1), watch-tower

ZEPHONITES
6831 Tsᵉphôwnîy (1), Tsephonite

ZER
6863 Tsêr (1), rock

ZERAH
2226 Zerach (19), rising of light, dawning

ZERAHIAH
2228 Zᵉrachyâh (5), Jehovah has risen

ZERED
2218 Zered (3), lined with shrubbery

ZEREDA
6868 Tsᵉrêdâh (1), puncture

ZEREDATHAH
6868 Tsᵉrêdâh (1), puncture

ZERERATH
6888 Tsᵉrêrâh (1), puncture

ZERESH
2238 Zeresh (4), Zeresh

ZERETH
6889 Tsereth (1), splendor

ZERI
6874 Tsᵉrîy (1), balsam

ZEROR
6872 tsᵉrôwr (1), parcel; kernel or particle

ZERUAH
6871 Tsᵉrûw'âh (1), leprous

ZERUBBABEL
2216 Zᵉrubbâbel (21), from Babylon
2217 Zᵉrubbâbel (Ch.) (1), from Babylon

ZERUIAH
6870 Tsᵉrûwyâh (26), wounded

ZETHAM
2241 Zêthâm (2), seed

ZETHAN
2133 Zêythân (1), olive grove

ZETHAR
2242 Zêthar (1), Zethar

ZIA
2127 Zîya' (1), agitation

ZIBA
6717 Tsîybâ' (16), station

ZIBEON
6649 Tsib'ôwn (8), variegated

ZIBIA
6644 Tsibyâ' (1), female gazelle

ZIBIAH
6645 Tsibyâh (2), female gazelle

ZICHRI
2147 Zikrîy (12), memorable

ZIDDIM
6661 Tsiddîym (1), sides

ZIDKIJAH
6667 Tsidqîyâh (1), right of Jehovah

ZIDON
6721 Tsîydôwn (20), fishery
6722 Tsîydônîy (1), Tsidonian

ZIDONIANS
6722 Tsîydônîy (10), Tsidonian

ZIF
2099 Zîv (2), flowers

ZIHA
6727 Tsîychâ' (3), drought

ZIKLAG
6860 Tsiqlâg (14), Tsiklag or Tsikelag

ZILLAH
6741 Tsillâh (3), Tsillah

ZILPAH
2153 Zilpâh (7), fragrant dropping as myrrh

ZILTHAI
6769 Tsillᵉthay (2), shady

ZIMMAH
2155 Zimmâh (3), bad plan

ZIMRAN
2175 Zimrân (2), musical

ZIMRI
2174 Zimrîy (15), musical

ZIN
6790 Tsîn (10), crag

ZINA
2126 Zîynâ' (1), well-fed

ZION
6726 Tsîyôwn (152), permanent capital or monument

ZION'S
6726 Tsîyôwn (1), permanent capital or monument

ZIOR
6730 Tsîy'ôr (1), small

ZIPH
2128 Zîyph (10), flowing

ZIPHAH
2129 Zîyphâh (1), flowing

ZIPHIMS
2130 Zîyphîy (1), Ziphite

ZIPHION
6837 Tsiphyôwn (1), watch-tower

ZIPHITES
2130 Zîyphîy (2), Ziphite

ZIPHRON
2202 Ziphrôn (1), fragrant

ZIPPOR
6834 Tsippôwr (7), little hopping bird

ZIPPORAH
6855 Tsippôrâh (3), bird

ZITHRI
5644 Çithrîy (1), protective

ZIZ
6732 Tsîyts (1), bloom

ZIZA
2124 Zîyzâ' (2), prominence

ZIZAH
2125 Zîyzâh (1), prominence

ZOAN
6814 Tsô'an (7), Tsoän

ZOAR
6820 Tsô'ar (10), little

ZOBA
6678 Tsôwbâ' (2), station

ZOBAH
6678 Tsôwbâ' (11), station

ZOBEBAH
6637 Tsôbêbâh (1), canopier

ZOHAR
6714 Tsôchar (4), whiteness

ZOHELETH
2120 Zôcheleth (1), serpent

ZOHETH
2105 Zôwchêth (1), Zocheth

ZOPHAH
6690 Tsôwphach (2), breath

ZOPHAI
6689 Tsûwph (1), honey-comb

ZOPHAR
6691 Tsôwphar (4), departing

ZOPHIM
6839 Tsôphîym (1), watchers

ZORAH
6681 tsâvach (8), to screech exultingly

ZORATHITES
6882 Tsor'îy (1), Tsorite or Tsorathite

ZOREAH
6881 Tsor'âh (1), stinging wasp

ZORITES
6882 Tsor'îy (1), Tsorite or Tsorathite

ZOROBABEL
2216 Zŏrŏbabĕl (3), from Babylon

ZUAR
6686 Tsûw'âr (5), small

ZUPH
6689 Tsûwph (3), honey-comb

ZUR
6698 Tsûwr (5), rock

ZURIEL
6700 Tsûwrîy'êl (1), rock of God

ZURISHADDAI
6701 Tsûwrîyshadday (5), rock of (the) Almighty

ZUZIMS
2104 Zûwzîym (1), prominent

∾The NEW *∾*

STRONG'S™

HEBREW &
ARAMAIC

DICTIONARY

of BIBLE WORDS

© 1995, 1996 Thomas Nelson Publishers, Inc.

Read this first!

How to Use the Hebrew and Aramaic Dictionary

For many people Strong's unique system of numbers continues to be *the* bridge between the original languages of the Bible and the English of the *King James Version* (AV). In order to enhance the strategic importance of *Strong's Hebrew and Aramaic Dictionary* for Bible students, it has been significantly improved in this brand-new, up-to-date edition. It is now completely re-typeset with modern, larger type-faces that are kind to the eye, and all known errors in the original typesetting have been corrected, bringing this pivotal work to a new level of usefulness and accuracy.

1. What the Dictionary Is

Strong's Hebrew and Aramaic Dictionary is a fully integrated companion to the English Index. Its compact entries contain a wealth of information about the words of the Bible in their original language. You can enrich your study of the Bible enormously if you will invest the time to understand the various elements included in each entry and their significance. The example that follows identifies many of these entry elements; and the following sections on the transliteration, abbreviations, and special symbols used offer fuller explanations. While no dictionary designed for readers who do not know biblical Hebrew can explain all that a faithful student of the language would know, this *Dictionary* gives the serious student of the English Bible the basic information needed to pursue infinitely deeper and broader studies of God's Word. Vast amounts of biblical insight can be gained by using this *Concordance* alone or in conjunction with other time-proven biblical reference works, such as Thomas Nelson's *Vine's Complete Expository Dictionary of Old and New Testament Words* and *Nelson's New Illustrated Bible Dictionary*, and, of course, *The New Strong's™ Exhaustive Concordance*.

2. Using the Dictionary with the English Index

To use this *Dictionary*, locate the number listed under any word in the English Index. If the number and its transliterated word are in regular [not italic] type, you know that it refers to the *Hebrew and Aramaic Dictionary*. For example, under "SHADY," you find *Strong's* number **6628** representing the Hebrew word tse'el. The English Index offers a concise definition—*lotus* tree—based on the fuller explanations of the *Dictionary*. You may view that enlarged entry on the facing page or on page 496 in this *Dictionary*. The enlarged example that follows, together with the following sections of explanation, identify the kinds of information such entries provide.

3. Using the Dictionary to Do Word Studies

Careful Bible students do word studies, and *The New Strong's™ Complete Dictionary of Bible Words* with this revised, newly-typeset *Hebrew and Aramaic Dictionary* offers unique assistance. Consider the word "love" as found the King James Bible. The English Index lists eight unique Strong's numbers for Hebrew words that the King James Bible translates with the English word "love": 157, 160, 1730, 2836, 5690, 5691, 7355, 7474. By looking up each of these words in the *Dictionary*, you will discover a wide range of meaning for the word "love" used as a noun and a verb.

You can also study the range of meaning for each of these Hebrew words. At the end of each *Dictionary* entry you notice the symbol :—. Following this symbol is a listing of all the ways this word is translated in the King James Bible. Word **157**, for example, is translated as "beloved," "love," "lovely," "lover," "like," and "friend." By looking up each of these words in the English Index, you can find a listing of all the Hebrew (and Aramaic) words they translate. This interaction of the English Index and the *Hebrew and Aramaic Dictionary* allows you to do thorough biblical word studies in English as well as in Hebrew and Aramaic.

Of supreme importance in word studies is examining words in their biblical contexts. To study each occurrence of any word, you would need *The New Strong's™ Exhaustive Concordance*. You may wish to take notes as you look up each occurrence of the word that goes with **157**, and then each occurrence of the word that goes with **160**, and so forth. This method gives you an excellent basis for understanding all that the New Testament signifies with the King James Version's word "earnest."

These three ways of using the *Dictionary* in conjunction with the main concordance show you only a sampling of the many ways *The New Strong's™ Complete Dictionary of Bible Words* can enrich your study of the Bible. And they show you why it is important that you take the time to become familiar with each feature in the *Dictionary* as illustrated in the example on the following page.

An Example
from the
Hebrew and Aramaic Dictionary

Strong's number, corresponding to the numbers at the beginning of each entry in the English Index.

An unnumbered cross-reference entry.

The word as it appears in the original Hebrew (or Aramaic) spelling.

The degree symbol denotes the presence of a textual variation. (See "Special Symbols")

The Hebrew (or Aramaic) word represented in English letters in **bold** type (the transliteration).

Strong's syllable-by-syllable pronunciation in *italics*, with the emphasized syllable marked by the accent.

Information regarding relationship to other Hebrew (or Aramaic) words, usually cited by Strong's numbers. Sometimes a word may refer to a Greek entry (shown by *italic* numbers) or it may come from another language.

צֹאון° **tse'ôn**. See 6629.

6628. צֶאֱל **tse'el**, *tseh´-el;* from an unused root mean. to *be slender;* the *lotus* tree:— shady tree.

6629. צֹאן **tsô'n**, *tsone;* or

צְאוֹן **tse'ôwn** (Psa. 144:13) *tseh-one´;* from an unused root mean. to *migrate;* a collect. name for a flock (of sheep or goats); also fig. (of men):— (small) cattle, flock (+ -s), lamb (+ s), sheep ([-cote, -fold, -shearer, -herds]).

See "Special Symbols."

Occasional, helpful Scripture references.

Improved, consistent abbreviations. All abbreviations occur with their full spelling in the list of abbreviations.

Brief English definitions (shown by italics).

After the long dash (—), there is a complete, alphabetical listing of all renderings of this Hebrew (or Aramaic) word in the KJV. (See also "Special Symbols").

Note that Hebrew (or Aramaic) spelling variations are conveniently indented for easy comparison.

Plan of the Hebrew and Aramaic Dictionary

1. All the original words are presented in their alphabetical order (according to Hebrew and Aramaic). They are numbered for easy matching between this Dictionary and the main part of the Concordance. Many reference books also use these same numbers created by Dr. Strong.

2. Immediately after each word, the exact equivalent of each sound (phoneme) is given in English characters, according to the transliteration system given below.

3. Next follows the precise pronunciation, with the proper stress mark.

4. Then comes the etymology, root meaning, and common uses of the word, along with any other important related details.

5. In the case of proper names, the normal English spelling is given, accompanied by a few words of explanation.

6. Finally, after the colon and the dash (:—), all the different ways that the word appears in the Authorized Version (KJV) are listed in alphabetical order. When the Hebrew or Aramaic word appears in English as a phrase, the main word of the phrase is used to alphabetize it.

By looking up these words in the main concordance and by noting the passages which display the same number in the right-hand column, the reader also possesses a complete *Hebrew Concordance*, expressed in the words of the Authorized Version.

Transliteration and Pronunciation of the Hebrew and Aramaic

The following shows how the Hebrew words are transliterated into English in this Dictionary.

1. The Hebrew and Aramaic read *from right to left*. Both alphabets consist of 22 letters (and their variations), which are all regarded as *consonants*, although four consonants (א ה ו י) sometimes indicate vowel sounds. To help enunciation, vowels are primarily indicated by certain "points" or marks, mostly beneath the letters. Hebrew and Aramaic do not use *capitals, italics*, etc.

2. The Hebrew and Aramaic characters are as follows:

No.	Form	Name	Transliteration and Pronunciation
1.	א	'Aleph (*aw´-lef*)	', silent
2.	ב	Bêyth (*bayth*)	**b**
3.	ג	Gîymel (*ghee´-mel*)	**g** hard = γ
4.	ד	Dâleth (*daw´-leth*)	**d**
5.	ה	Hê' (*hay*)	**h**, often quiescent
6.	ו	Vâv (*vawv*) or Wâw (*waw*)	**v** or **w**, quiescent
7.	ז	Zayin (*zah´-yin*)	**z**, as in *zeal*
8.	ח	Chêyth (*khayth*)	German **ch** = χ (nearly *kh*)
9.	ט	Têyth (*tayth*)	**ṭ** = **T**
10.	י	Yôwd (*yode*)	**y**, often quiescent
11.	כ final ך	Kaph (*caf*)	**k** = ק
12.	ל	Lâmed (*law´-med*)	**l**
13.	מ final ם	Mêm (*mame*)	**m**
14.	נ final ן	Nûwn (*noon*)	**n**
15.	ס	Çâmek (*saw´-mek*)	**ç** = *s* sharp = שׂ
16.	ע	'Ayin (*ah´-yin*)	' peculiar [1]
17.	פ final ף	Phê' (*fay*)	**ph** = *f* = φ
	פ	Pê' (*pay*)	**p**
18.	צ, final ץ	Tsâdêy (*tsaw-day'*)	**ts**
19.	ק	Qôwph (*cofe*)	**q** = *k* = כ
20.	ר	Rêysh (*raysh*)	**r**
21.	שׂ	Sîyn (*seen*)	**s** sharp = ס = σ
	שׁ	Shîyn (*sheen*)	**sh**
22.	ת	Thâv (*thawv*)	**th**, as in *THin* = θ
	ת	Tâv (*tawv*)	**t** = ט = τ

---

[1] The letter *'Ayin*, because Westerners find it difficult to pronounce accurately (it is a deep guttural sound, like that made in *gargling*), is generally passed over silently in reading. We have represented it to the eye (but not exactly to the ear) by the Greek *rough breathing* mark (ʽ) in order to distinguish it from *'Âleph*, which is likewise treated as silent, being similarly represented by the Greek *smooth breathing* (ʼ).

3. The vowel points are as follows:

Form [2]	Name	Transliteration and Pronunciation
בַ	Qâmêts (*caw-mates*)	â, as in *All*
בַ	Pattach (*pat'-takh*)	a, as in *mAn*
בַ	Shevâ'-Pattach (*she-vaw' pat'-takh*)	ă, as in *hAt*
בַ	Tsêrêy (*tsay-ray*)	ê, as in *thEy* = η
בֶ	Çegôwl (*seg-ole*)	e, as in *thEir*
		e, as in *mEn* = ε
בֶ	Shevâ'-Çegôwl (*she-vaw' seg-ole*)	ĕ, as in *mEt*
בַ	Shevâ' (*she-vaw*) [3]	obscure, as in *avErage*
		silent, as *e* in *madE*
בִ	Chîyriq (*khee'-rik*)	î, as in *machIne* [4]
		i, as in *supplIant* (*misery, hit*)
בֹ	Chôwlem (*kho'-lem*) [5]	ô, as in *no* = ω
בָ	Short Qâmêts (*caw-mates*) [6]	o, as in *nor* = o
בָ	Shevâ -Qâmêts (*she-vaw' caw-mates*)	ŏ, as in *not*
וּ	Shûwrêq * (*shoo-rake*) [7]	û, as in *crUel*
בֻ	Qĭbbûts * (*kib'-boots*) [7]	u, as in *fUll, rude*

4. A point in the heart of a letter is called *Dâgêsh'*, and is of two kinds, which must be carefully distinguished.

    a. Dâgêsh *lenè* occurs only in the letters ב, ג, ד, כ, פ, ת (technically vocalized B^egad'-K^ephath), when they *begin* a clause or sentence, or are preceded by a consonant *sound*; and simply has the effect of removing their aspiration. [8]

    b. Dâgêsh *fortè* may occur in any letter except א, ה, ח, ע or ר ; it is equivalent to *doubling* the letter, and at the same time it removes the aspiration of a B^egad-K^ephath letter. [9]

    5. The *Maqqêph'* (־), like a *hyphen*, unites words only for purposes of pronunciation (by removing the primary accent from all except the last word), but it does not affect their meaning or grammatical construction.

Special Symbols

    + (*addition*) denotes a rendering in the A.V. of one or more Hebrew or Aramaic words in connection with the one under consideration. For example, in 2 Kgs. 4:41, No. 1697, דָּבָר (**dâbâr**) is translated as "harm," in connection with No. 7451. Literally, it is "bad thing."

    × (*multiplication*) denotes a rendering in the A.V. that results from an idiom peculiar to the Hebrew or Aramaic. For example, in Psa. 132:15, the whole Hebrew phrase in which בָּרַךְ, **bârak** (1288) appears is a means of expressing a verb root emphatically, i. e. "blessing, I will bless" = "I will abundantly bless."

    ° (*degree*), attached to a Hebrew word, denotes a corrected vowel pointing which is different from the Biblical text. (This mark is set in Hebrew Bibles over syllables in which the vowels of the margin have been inserted instead of those which properly belong to the text.)

    For example, see the difference between the Hebrew text and the scribes' marginal note in Ezek. 40:15 for No. 2978, translated "entrance."

    ( ) (*parentheses*), in the renderings from the A.V., denote a word or syllable which is sometimes given in connection with the principal word to which it is attached. In Num. 34:6, the only occurrence of "western" in the A. V., the underlying Hebrew word is יָם (**yâm**, No. 3220), which is usually translated "sea."

    [ ] (*brackets*), in the rendering from the A.V., denote the inclusion of an additional word in the Hebrew or Aramaic. For example, No. 3117, יוֹם (**yôwm**), is translated as "birthday" in Gen. 40:20, along with No. 3205. So, two Hebrew words are translated by one English word.

    Italics, at the end of a rendering from the A.V., denote an explanation of the variations from the usual form.

---

[2] The same Hebrew/Aramaic consonant (ב) is shown here in order to show the position of the vowel points, whether below, above, or in the middle of Hebrew or Aramaic consonants.

[3] *Silent Sh^evâ'* is not represented by any mark in our method of transliteration, since it is understood whenever there is no other vowel point.

[4] *Chîyriq* is long only when it is followed by a quiescent *yôwd* (either expressed or implied).

[5] *Chôwlem* is written *fully* only over Vâv or Wâw (ׂ), which is then quiescent (w); but when used "defectively" (without the Vâv or Wâw) it may be written either over the left-hand corner of the letter to which it belongs, or over the right-hand corner of the following one.

[6] *Short Qâmêts* is found only in *unaccented syllables ending with a consonant sound.*

[7] *Shûwrêq* is written only in the heart of Vâv or Wâw. Sometimes it is said to be "defectively" written (without the Vâv or Wâw), and then takes the form of *Qĭbbûts*, which in such cases is called *vicarious.*

[8] In our system of transliteration Dâgêsh *lenè* is represented only in the letters פ and ת, because elsewhere it does not affect the pronunciation.

[9] A point in the heart of ה is called *Mappîyq* (*mappeek*). It occurs only in the final vowel-less letter of a few words, and we have represented it by *hh*. A Dâgêsh *fortè* in the heart of ו may easily be distinguished from the vowel *Shûwrêq* by noticing that in the former case the letter has a proper vowel point accompanying it.

    It should be noted that both kinds of Dâgêsh are often omitted in writing (being *implied*), but (in the case at least of Dâgêsh *fortè*) the word is usually pronounced the same as if it were present.

abb. = abbreviated
   abbreviation
abstr. = abstract
   abstractly
act. = active (voice)
   actively
acc. = accusative (case) [1]
adj. = adjective
   adjectivally
adv. = adverb
   adverbial
   adverbially
aff. = affix [2]
   affixed
affin. = affinity
alt. = alternate
   alternately
anal. = analogy
appar. = apparent
   apparently
arch. = architecture
   architectural
   architecturally
art. = article [3]
artif. = artificial
   artificially
Ass. = Assyrian
A.V. = Authorized Version
   (King James Version)
Bab. = Babylon
   Babylonia
   Babylonian
caus. = causative [4]
   causatively
cerem. = ceremony
   ceremonial
   ceremonially
Chald. = Chaldee
   (Aramaic)
   Chaldaism
   (Aramaism)
Chr. = Christian
collat. = collateral
   collaterally
collect. = collective
   collectively
comp. = compare [5]
   comparison
   comparative
   comparatively
concr. = concrete
   concretely
conjec. = conjecture
   conjectural
   conjecturally
conjug. = conjugation [6]
   conjugational
   conjugationally
conjunc. = conjunction
   conjunctional
   conjunctionally
constr. = construct [7]
   construction
   constructive
   constructively

contr. = contracted [8]
   contraction
correl. = correlated
   correlation
   correlative
   correlatively
corresp. = corresponding
   correspondingly
dat. = dative (case) [9]
def. = definite [10]
   definitely
demonstr. = demonstra-
   tive[11]
denom. = denominative [12]
   denominatively
der. = derived
   derivation
   derivative
   derivatively
desc. = descended
   descendant
   descendants
dimin. = diminutive [13]
dir. = direct
   directly
E. = East
   Eastern
eccl. = ecclesiastical
   ecclesiastically
e.g. = for example
Eg. = Egypt
   Egyptian
   Egyptians
ellip. = ellipsis [14]
   elliptical
   elliptically
emphat. = emphatic
   emphatically
equiv. = equivalent
   equivalently
err. = error
   erroneous
   erroneously
espec. = especially
etym. = etymology [15]
   etymological
   etymologically
euphem. = euphemism [16]
   euphemistic
   euphemistically
euphon. = euphonious [17]
   euphonically
extens. = extension [18]
   extensive
extern. = external
   externally
fem. = feminine (gender)
fig. = figurative
   figuratively
for. = foreign
   foreigner
freq. = frequentative
   frequentatively
fut. = future

gen. = general
   generally
   generic
   generical
   generically
Gr. = Greek
   Graecism
gut. = guttural [19]
Heb. = Hebrew
   Hebraism
i.e. = that is
ident. = identical
   identically
immed. = immediate
   immediately
imper. = imperative [20]
   imperatively
imperf. = imperfect [21]
impers. = impersonal
   impersonally
impl. = implied
   impliedly
   implication
incept. = inceptive [22]
   inceptively
incl. = including
   inclusive
   inclusively
indef. = indefinite
   indefinitely
ind. = indicative [23]
   indicatively
indiv. = individual
   individually
infer. = inference
   inferential
   inferentially
infin. = infinitive
inhab. = inhabitant
   inhabitants
ins. = inserted
intens. = intensive
   intensively
interch. = interchangeable
intern. = internal
   internally
interj. = interjection [24]
   interjectional
   interjectionally
interrog. = interrogative [25]
   interrogatively
intr. = intransitive [26]
   intransitively
invol. = involuntary
   involuntarily
irreg. = irregular
   irregularly
Isr. = Israelite
   Israelites
   Israelitish
Lat. = Latin
Levit. = Levitical
   Levitically

lit. = literal
   literally
marg. = margin
   marginal reading
masc. = masculine (gender)
mean. = meaning
ment. = mental
   mentally
metaph. = metaphorical
   metaphorically
mid. = middle (voice) [27]
modif. = modified
   modification
mor. = moral
   morally
mult. = multiplicative [28]
nat. = natural
   naturally
neg. = negative
   negatively
neut. = neuter (gender)
obj. = object
   objective
   objectively
obs. = obsolete
ord. = ordinal [29]
or. = origin
orig. = original
   originally
orth. = orthography [30]
   orthographical
   orthographically
Pal. = Palestine
part. = participle
pass. = passive (voice)
   passively
patron. = patronymic [31]
   patronymical
   patronymically
perh. = perhaps
perm. = permutation [32] (of
   adjacent letters)
pers. = person
   personal
   personally
Pers. = Persia
   Persian
   Persians
phys. = physical
   physically
plur. = plural
poet. = poetry
   poetical
   poetically
pos. = positive
   positively
pref. = prefix
   prefixed
prep. = preposition
   prepositional
   prepositionally
prim. = primitive
prob. = probable
   probably

prol. = prolonged [33]
   prolongation
pron. = pronoun
   pronominal
   pronominally
prop. = properly
prox. = proximate
   proximately
recip. = reciprocal
   reciprocally
redupl. = reduplicated [34]
   reduplication
refl. = reflexive [35]
   reflexively
reg. = regular
rel. = relative
   relatively
relig. = religion
   religious
   religiously
Rom. = Roman
second. = secondary
   secondarily
signif. = signification
   signifying
short. = shorter
   shortened
sing. = singular
spec. = specific
   specifically
streng. = strengthening
subdiv. = subdivision
   subdivisional
   subdivisionally
subj. = subjectively
   subjective
   subject
substit. = substituted
suff. = suffix
superl. = superlative [36]
   superlatively
symb. = symbolic
   symbolical
   symbolically
tech. = technical
   technically
term. = termination
tran. = transitive [37]
   transitively
transc. = transcription
transm. = transmutation [38]
transp. = transposed [39]
   transposition
typ. = typical
   typically
uncert. = uncertain
   uncertainly
var. = various
   variation
voc. = vocative (case) [40]
vol. = voluntary
   voluntarily

---

[1] often indicating the direct object of an action verb

[2] part of a word which, when attached to the beginning of the word is called a prefix; if attaching within a word, an infix; and if at the end, a suffix

[3] "the" is the definite article; "a" and "an" are indefinite articles

[4] expressing or denoting causation

[5] the comparative of an adjective or adverb expresses a greater degree of an attribute, e.g. "higher"; "more slowly"

[6] a systematic array of various verbal forms

[7] the condition in Hebrew and Aramaic when two adjacent nouns are combined semantically as follows, e.g. "sword" + "king" = "(the) sword of (the) king" or "(the) king's sword". These languages tend to throw the stress of the entire noun phrase toward the end of the whole expression.

[8] a shortened form of a word. It is made by omitting or combining some elements or by reducing vowels or syllables, e.g. "is not" becomes "isn't".

[9] often the indirect object of an action verb

[10] the definite article ("the")

[11] demonstrative pronouns which point (show), e.g. "this," "that"

[12] derived from a noun

[13] a grammatical form which expresses smallness and/or endearment

[14] a construction which leaves out understood words

[15] the historical origin of a word

[16] the use of a pleasant, polite, or harmless-sounding word or phrase to hide harsh, rude, or infamous truths, e.g. "to pass away" = "to die"

[17] a linguistic mechanism to make pronunciation easier, e.g. "an" before "hour" instead of "a"

[18] when a general term can denote an entire class of things

[19] speech sounds which are produced deep in the throat

[20] the mood which expresses a command

[21] used of a tense which expresses a continuous but unfinished action or state

[22] used of a verbal aspect which denotes the beginning of an action

[23] used of the mood which expresses a verbal action as actually occurring (not hypothetical)

[24] an exclamation which expresses emotion

[25] indicating a question

[26] referring to verbs which do not govern direct objects

[27] reflexive

[28] capable of multiplying or tending to multiply

[29] This shows the position or the order within a series, e.g. "second"; the corresponding cardinal number is "two".

[30] the written system of spelling in a given language

[31] a name derived from that of a paternal ancestor, often created by an affix in various languages

[32] a rearrangement

[33] lengthening a pronunciation

[34] the repetition of a letter or syllable to form a new, inflected word

[35] denoting an action by the subject upon itself

[36] expressing the highest degree of comparison of the quality indicated by an adjective or an adverb, e.g. "highest"; "most timely"

[37] expressing an action directed toward a person or a thing (the direct object)

[38] the change of one grammatical element to another

[39] switching word order

[40] an inflection which is used when one is addressing a person or a thing directly, e.g. "John, come here!"

א

1. אָב **'âb**, *awb;* a prim. word; *father* in a lit. and immed., or fig. and remote application):— chief, (fore-) father (l-less), × patrimony, principal. Comp. names in "Abi-".

2. אַב **'ab** (Chald.), *ab;* corresp. to 1:— father.

3. אֵב **'êb**, *abe;* from the same as 24; a *green* plant:— greenness, fruit.

4. אֵב **'êb** (Chald.), *abe;* corresp. to 3:— fruit.

אֹב **'ôb.** See 178.

5. אֲבַגְתָא **'Ăbagthâ'**, *ab-ag-thaw';* of for. or.; *Abagtha,* a eunuch of Xerxes:— Abagtha.

6. אָבַד **'âbad**, *aw-bad';* a prim. root; prop. to *wander* away, i.e. *lose* oneself; by impl. to *perish* (caus. *destroy*):— break, destroy (-uction), + not escape, fail, lose, (cause to, make) perish, spend, × and surely, take, be undone, × utterly, be void of, have no way to flee.

7. אֲבַד **'ăbad** (Chald.), *ab-ad';* corresp. to 6:— destroy, perish.

8. אֹבֵד **'ôbêd**, *o-bade';* act. of part. of 6; (concr.) *wretched* or (abstr.) *destruction:*— perish.

9. אֲבֵדָה **'ăbêdâh**, *ab-ay-daw';* from 6; concr. something *lost;* abstr. *destruction,* i.e. Hades:— lost. Comp. 10.

10. אֲבַדֹּה **'ăbaddôh**, *ab-ad-do';* the same as 9, miswritten for 11; a *perishing:*— destruction.

11. אֲבַדּוֹן **'ăbaddôwn**, *ab-ad-done';* intens. from 6; abstr. a *perishing;* concr. Hades:— destruction.

12. אַבְדָן **'abdân**, *ab-dawn';* from 6; a *perishing:*— destruction.

13. אָבְדָן **'obdân**, *ob-dawn';* from 6; a *perishing:*— destruction.

14. אָבָה **'âbâh**, *aw-baw';* a prim. root; to *breathe* after, i.e. (fig.) to *be acquiescent:*— consent, rest content, will, be willing.

15. אָבֶה **'âbeh**, *aw-beh';* from 14; *longing:*— desire.

16. אֵבֶה **'êbeh**, *ay-beh';* from 14 (in the sense of *bending* toward); the *papyrus:*— swift.

17. אֲבוֹי **'ăbôwy**, *ab-o'ee;* from 14 (in the sense of *desiring*); *want:*— sorrow.

18. אֵבוּס **'êbûwç**, *ay-booce';* from 75; a *manger* or *stall:*— crib.

19. אִבְחָה **'ibchâh**, *ib-khaw';* from an unused root (appar. mean. to *turn*); *brandishing* of a sword:— point.

20. אֲבַטִּיחַ **'ăbaṭṭîyach**, *ab-at-tee'-akh;* of uncert. der.; a *melon* (only plur.):— melon.

21. אֲבִי **'Ăbîy**, *ab-ee';* from 1; *fatherly;* Abi, Hezekiah's mother:— Abi.

22. אֲבִיאֵל **'Ăbîy'êl**, *ab-ee-ale';* from 1 and 410; *father* (i.e. *possessor*) *of God;* Abiel, the name of two Isr.:— Abiel.

23. אֲבִיאָסָף **'Ăbîy'âçâph**, *ab-ee-aw-sawf';* from 1 and 622; *father of gathering* (i.e. *gatherer*); Abiasaph, an Isr.:— Abiasaph.

24. אָבִיב **'âbîyb**, *aw-beeb';* from an unused root (mean. to *be tender*); *green,* i.e. a young *ear* of grain; hence, the name of the month Abib or Nisan:— Abib, ear, green ears of corn.

25. אֲבִי גִבְעוֹן **'Ăbîy Gib'ôwn**, *ab-ee' ghib-one';* from 1 and 1391; *father* (i.e. *founder*) *of Gibon;* Abi-Gibon, perh. an Isr.:— father of Gibeon.

26. אֲבִיגֵיל **'Ăbîygayil**, *ab-ee-gah'-yil,* or short.

אֲבִיגַל **'Ăbîygal**, *ab-ee-gal';* from 1 and 1524; *father* (i.e. *source*) *of joy;* Abigail or Abigal, the name of two Israelitesses:— Abigal.

27. אֲבִידָן **'Ăbîydân**, *ab-ee-dawn';* from 1 and 1777; *father of judgment* (i.e. *judge*); Abidan, an Isr.:— Abidan.

28. אֲבִידָע **'Ăbîydâ'**, *ab-ee-daw';* from 1 and 3045; *father of knowledge* (i.e. *knowing*); Abida, a son of Abraham by Keturah:— Abida, Abidah.

29. אֲבִיָה **'Ăbîyâh**, *ab-ee-yaw';* or prol.

אֲבִיָהוּ **'Ăbîyâhûw**, *ab-ee-yaw'-hoo;* from 1 and 3050; *father* (i.e. *worshipper*) *of Jah;* Abijah, the name of several Isr. men and two Israelitesses:— Abiah, Abijah.

30. אֲבִיהוּא **'Ăbîyhûw'**, *ab-ee-hoo';* from 1 and 1931; *father* (i.e. *worshipper*) *of Him* (i.e. *God*); Abihu, a son of Aaron:— Abihu.

31. אֲבִיהוּד **'Ăbîyhûwd**, *ab-ee-hood';* from 1 and 1935; *father* (i.e. *possessor*) *of renown;* Abihud, the name of two Isr.:— Abihud.

32. אֲבִיחַיִל **'Ăbîyhayil**, *ab-ee-hah'-yil;* or (more correctly)

אֲבִיחַיִל **'Ăbîychayil**, *ab-ee-khah'-yil;* from 1 and 2428; *father* (i.e. *possessor*) *of might;* Abihail or Abichail, the name of three Isr. and two Israelitesses:— Abihail.

33. אֲבִי הָעֶזְרִי **'Ăbîy hâ-'Ezrîy**, *ab-ee'-haw-ez-ree';* from 44 with the art. ins.; *father of the Ezrite;* an Abiezrite or desc. of Abiezer:— Abiezrite.

34. אֶבְיוֹן **'ebyôwn**, *eb-yone';* from 14, in the sense of *want* (espec. in feeling); *destitute:*— beggar, needy, poor (man).

35. אֶבְיוֹנָה **'abîyôwnâh**, *ab-ee-yo-naw´;* from 14; provocative of *desire;* the *caper* berry (from its *stimulative* taste):— desire.

אֲבִיחַיִל **'Ăbîychayil.** See 32.

36. אֲבִיטוּב **'Ăbîytûwb**, *ab-ee-toob´;* from 1 and 2898; *father of goodness* (i.e. *good*); *Abitub,* an Isr.:— Abitub.

37. אֲבִיטַל **'Ăbîyṭal**, *ab-ee-tal´;* from 1 and 2919; *father of dew* (i.e. *fresh*); *Abital,* a wife of King David:— Abital.

38. אֲבִיָם **'Ăbîyâm**, *ab-ee-yawm´;* from 1 and 3220; *father of* (the) *sea* (i.e. *seaman*); *Abijam* (or *Abijah*), a king of Judah:— Abijam.

39. אֲבִימָאֵל **'Ăbîymâ'êl**, *ab-ee-maw-ale´;* from 1 and an elsewhere unused (prob. for.) word; *father of Mael* (appar. some Arab tribe); *Abimael,* a son of Joktan:— Abimael.

40. אֲבִימֶלֶךְ **'Ăbîymelek**, *ab-ee-mel´-ek;* from 1 and 4428; *father of* (the) *king; Abimelek,* the name of two Philistine kings and of two Isr.:— Abimelech.

41. אֲבִינָדָב **'Ăbîynâdâb**, *ab-ee-naw-dawb´;* from 1 and 5068; *father of generosity* (i.e. *liberal*); *Abinadab,* the name of four Isr.:— Abinadab.

42. אֲבִינֹעַם **'Ăbîynô'am**, *ab-ee-no´-am;* from 1 and 5278; *father of pleasantness* (i.e. *gracious*); *Abinoam,* an Isr.:— Abinoam.

אֲבִינֵר **'Ăbîynêr.** See 74.

43. אֶבְיָסָף **'Ebyâçâph**, *eb-yaw-sawf´;* contr. from 23; *Ebjasaph,* an Isr.:— Ebiasaph.

44. אֲבִיעֶזֶר **'Ăbîy'ezer**, *ab-ee-ay´-zer;* from 1 and 5829; *father of help* (i.e. *helpful*); *Abiezer,* the name of two Isr.:— Abiezer.

45. אֲבִי־עַלְבוֹן **'Ăbîy-'albôwn**, *ab-ee-al-bone´;* from 1 and an unused root of uncert. der.; prob. *father of strength* (i.e. *valiant*); *Abialbon,* an Isr.:— Abialbon.

46. אָבִיר **'âbîyr**, *aw-beer´;* from 82; *mighty* (spoken of God):— mighty (one).

47. אַבִּיר **'abbîyr**, *ab-beer´;* from 46:— angel, bull, chiefest, mighty (one), stout [-hearted], strong (one), valiant.

48. אֲבִירָם **'Ăbîyrâm**, *ab-ee-rawm´;* from 1 and 7311; *father of height* (i.e. *lofty*); *Abiram,* the name of two Isr.:— Abiram.

49. אֲבִישַׁג **'Ăbîyshag**, *ab-ee-shag´;* from 1 and 7686; *father of error* (i.e. *blundering*); *Abishag,* a concubine of David:— Abishag.

50. אֲבִישׁוּעַ **'Ăbîyshûwa'**, *ab-ee-shoo´-ah;* from 1 and 7771; *father of plenty* (i.e. *prosperous*); *Abishua,* the name of two Isr.:— Abishua.

51. אֲבִישׁוּר **'Ăbîyshûwr**, *ab-ee-shoor´;* from 1 and 7791; *father of* (the) *wall* (i.e. perh. *mason*); *Abishur,* an Isr.:— Abishur.

52. אֲבִישַׁי **'Ăbîyshay**, *ab-ee-shah´ee;* or (short.)

53. אֲבִשַׁי **'Abshay**, *ab-shah´ee;* from 1 and 7862; *father of a gift* (i.e. prob. *generous*); *Abishai,* an Isr.:— Abishai.

53. אֲבִישָׁלוֹם **'Ăbîyshâlôwm**, *ab-ee-shaw-lome´;* or (short.)

אַבְשָׁלוֹם **'Abshâlôwm**, *ab-shaw-lome´;* from 1 and 7965; *father of peace* (i.e. *friendly*); *Abshalom,* a son of David; also (the fuller form) a later Isr.:— Abishalom, Absalom.

54. אֶבְיָתָר **'Ebyâthâr**, *ab-yaw-thawr´;* contr. from 1 and 3498; *father of abundance* (i.e. *liberal*); *Ebjathar,* an Isr.:— Abiathar.

55. אָבַךְ **'âbak**, *aw-bak´;* a prim. root; prob. to *coil* upward:— mount up.

56. אָבַל **'âbal**, *aw-bal´;* a prim. root; to *bewail:*— lament, mourn.

57. אָבֵל **'âbêl**, *aw-bale´;* from 56; *lamenting:*— mourn (-er, -ing).

58. אָבֵל **'âbêl**, *aw-bale´;* from an unused root (mean. to *be grassy*); a *meadow:*— plain. Comp. also the prop. names beginning with Abel-.

59. אָבֵל **'Âbêl**, *aw-bale´;* from 58; a *meadow; Abel,* the name of two places in Pal.:— Abel.

60. אֵבֶל **'êbel**, *ay´-bel;* from 56; *lamentation:*— mourning.

61. אֲבָל **'ăbâl**, *ab-awl´;* appar. from 56 through the idea of *negation; nay* (i.e. *truly* or *yet*):— but, indeed, nevertheless, verily.

62. אָבֵל בֵּית־מַעֲכָה **'Âbêl Bêyth-Mä'akâh**, *aw-bale´ bayth ma-a-kaw´;* from 58 and 1004 and 4601; *meadow of Beth-Maakah; Abel of Beth-maakah,* a place in Pal.:— Abel-beth-maachah, Abel of Beth-maachah.

63. אָבֵל הַשִּׁטִּים **'Âbêl hash-Shiṭṭîym**, *aw-bale´ hash-shit-teem´;* from 58 and the plur. of 7848, with the art. ins.; *meadow of the acacias; Abel hash-Shittim,* a place in Pal.:— Abel-shittim.

64. אָבֵל כְּרָמִים **'Âbêl Kᵉrâmîym**, *aw-bale´ ker-aw-meem´;* from 58 and the plur. of 3754; *meadow of vineyards; Abel-Keramim,* a place in Pal.:— plain of the vineyards.

65. אָבֵל מְחוֹלָה **'Âbêl Mᵉchôwlâh**, *aw-bale´ mekh-o-law´;* from 58 and 4246; *meadow of dancing; Abel-Mecholah,* a place in Pal.:— Abel-meholah.

66. אָבֵל מַיִם **'Âbêl Mayim**, *aw-bale´ mah´-yim;* from 58 and 4325; *meadow of water; Abel-Majim,* a place in Pal.:— Abel-maim.

67. אָבֵל מִצְרַיִם **'Âbêl Mitsrayim**, *aw-bale´ mits-rah´-yim;* from 58 and 4714; *meadow of Egypt; Abel-Mitsrajim,* a place in Pal.:— Abel-mizraim.

68. אֶבֶן **'eben**, *eh´-ben;* from the root of 1129

through the mean. to *build*; a *stone:*— + carbuncle, + mason, + plummet, [chalk-, hail-, head-, sling-] stone (-ny), (divers) weight (-s).

69. אֶבֶן **'eben** (Chald.), *eh´-ben;* corresp. to 68:— stone.

70. אֹבֶן **'ôben**, *o´-ben;* from the same as 68; a *pair of stones* (only dual); a potter's *wheel* or a midwife's *stool* (consisting alike of two horizontal disks with a support between):— wheel, stool.

71. אֲבָנָה **'Ăbânâh**, *ab-aw-naw´;* perh. fem. of 68; *stony; Abanah*, a river near Damascus:— Abana. Comp. 549.

72. אֶבֶן הָעֵזֶר **'Eben hâ-'êzer**, *eh´-ben haw-e´-zer;* from 68 and 5828 with the art. ins.; *stone of the help; Eben-ha-Ezer*, a place in Pal.:— Ebenezer.

73. אַבְנֵט **'abnêṭ**, *ab-nate´;* of uncert. der.; a *belt:*— girdle.

74. אַבְנֵר **'Abnêr**, *ab-nare´;* or (fully)

אֲבִינֵר **'Ăbîynêr**, *ab-ee-nare´;* from 1 and 5216; *father of light* (i.e. *enlightening*); *Abner*, an Isr.:— Abner.

75. אָבַס **'âbaç**, *aw-bas´;* a prim. root; to *fodder:*— fatted, stalled.

76. אֲבַעְבֻּעָה **'ăba'bû'âh**, *ab-ah-boo-aw´;* (by redupl.) from an unused root (mean. to *belch* forth); an inflammatory *pustule* (as *eruption*):— blains.

77. אֶבֶץ **'Ebets**, *eh´-bets;* from an unused root prob. mean. to *gleam; conspicuous; Ebets*, a place in Pal.:— Abez.

78. אִבְצָן **'Ibtsân**, *ib-tsawn´;* from the same as 76; *splendid; Ibtsan*, an Isr.:— Ibzan.

79. אָבַק **'âbaq**, *aw-bak´;* a prim. root, prob. to *float* away (as vapor), but used only as denom. from 80; to *bedust*, i.e. *grapple:*— wrestle.

80. אָבָק **'âbâq**, *aw-bawk´;* from root of 79; light *particles* (as *volatile*):— (small) dust, powder.

81. אֲבָקָה **'ăbâqâh**, *ab-aw-kaw´;* fem. of 80:— powder.

82. אָבַר **'âbar**, *aw-bar´;* a prim. root; to *soar:*— fly.

83. אֵבֶר **'êber**, *ay-ber´;* from 82; a *pinion:*— [long-] wing (-ed).

84. אֶבְרָה **'ebrâh**, *eb-raw´;* fem. of 83:— feather, wing.

85. אַבְרָהָם **'Abrâhâm**, *ab-raw-hawm´;* contr. from 1 and an unused root (prob. mean. to be *populous*); *father of a multitude; Abraham*, the later name of Abram:— Abraham.

86. אַבְרֵךְ **'abrêk**, *ab-rake´;* prob. an Eg. word mean. *kneel:*— bow the knee.

87. אַבְרָם **'Abrâm**, *ab-rawm´;* contr. from 48;

high father; Abram, the original name of Abraham:— Abram.

אַבְשַׁי **'Abshay**. See 52.

אַבְשָׁלוֹם **'Abshâlôwm**. See 53.

88. אֹבֹת **'Ôbôth**, *o-both´;* plur. of 178; *waterskins; Oboth*, a place in the Desert:— Oboth.

89. אָגֵא **'Âgê'**, *aw-gay´;* of uncert. der. [comp. 90]; *Agë*, an Isr.:— Agee.

90. אֲגַג **'Ăgag**, *ag-ag´;* or

אֲגָג **'Ăgâg**, *Ag-awg´;* of uncert. der. [comp. 89]; *flame; Agag*, a title of Amalekitish kings:— Agag.

91. אֲגָגִי **'Ăgâgîy**, *ag-aw-ghee´;* patrial or patron. from 90; an *Agagite* or descendent (subject) of Agag:— Agagite.

92. אֲגֻדָּה **'ăguddâh**, *ag-ood-daw´;* fem. pass. part. of an unused root (mean. to *bind*); a *band, bundle, knot*, or *arch:*— bunch, burden, troop.

93. אֱגוֹז **'ĕgôwz**, *eg-oze´;* prob of Pers. or.; a *nut:*— nut.

94. אָגוּר **'Âgûwr**, *aw-goor´;* pass. part. of 103; *gathered* (i.e. *received* among the sages); *Agur*, a fanciful name for Solomon:— Agur.

95. אֲגוֹרָה **'ăgôwrâh**, *ag-o-raw´;* from the same as 94; prop. something *gathered*, i.e. perh. a *grain* or *berry;* used only of a small (silver) *coin:*— piece [of] silver.

96. אֶגֶל **'egel**, *eh´-ghel;* from an unused root (mean. to *flow* down or together as drops); a *reservoir:*— drop.

97. אֶגְלַיִם **'Eglayim**, *eg-lah´-yim;* dual of 96; a *double pond; Eglajim*, a place in Moab:— Eglaim.

98. אֲגַם **'ăgam**, *ag-am´;* from an unused root (mean. to *collect* as water); a *marsh;* hence, a *rush* (as growing in swamps); hence, a *stockade* of reeds:— pond, pool, standing [water].

99. אֲגֵם **'âgêm**, *aw-game´;* prob. from the same as 98 (in the sense of *stagnant* water); fig. *sad:*— pond.

100. אַגְמוֹן **'agmôwn**, *ag-mone´;* from the same as 98; a marshy *pool* [others from a different root, a *kettle*]; by impl. a *rush* (as growing there); collect. a rope of rushes:— bulrush, caldron, hook, rush.

101. אַגָּן **'aggân**, *ag-gawn´;* prob. from 5059; a *bowl* (as *pounded* out hollow):— basin, cup, goblet.

102. אַגָּף **'aggâph**, *ag-gawf´;* prob. from 5062 (through the idea of *impending*); a *cover* or *heap;* i.e. (only plur.) *wings* of an army, or *crowds* of troops:— bands.

103. אֲגַר 'âgar, aw-gar´; a prim. root; to harvest:— gather.

104. אִגְּרָא 'iggᵉrâ' (Chald.), ig-er-aw´; of Pers. or.; an epistle (as carried by a state courier or postman):— letter.

105. אֲגַרְטָל 'ăgartâl, ag-ar-tawl´; of uncert. der.; a basin:— charger.

106. אֶגְרֹף 'egrôph, eg-rofe´; from 1640 (in the sense of grasping); the clenched hand:— fist.

107. אִגֶּרֶת 'iggereth, ig-eh´-reth; fem. of 104; an epistle:— letter.

108. אֵד 'êd, ade from the same as 181 (in the sense of enveloping); a fog:— mist, vapor.

109. אָדַב 'âdab, aw-dab´; a prim. root; to languish:— grieve.

110. אַדְבְּאֵל 'Adbᵉ'êl, ad-beh-ale´; prob. from 109 (in the sense of chastisement) and 410; disciplined of God; Adbeël, a son of Ishmael:— Adbeel.

111. אֲדַד 'Ădad, ad-ad´; prob. an orth. var. for 2301; Adad (or Hadad), an Edomite:— Hadad.

112. אִדּוֹ 'Iddôw, id-do´; of uncert. der.; Iddo, an Isr.:— Iddo.

אֱדוֹם 'Ĕdôwm. See 123.

אֱדוֹמִי 'Ĕdôwmîy. See 30.

113. אָדוֹן 'âdôwn, aw-done´; or (short.)

אָדֹן 'âdôn, aw-done´; from an unused root (mean. to rule); sovereign, i.e. controller (human or divine):— lord, master, owner. Comp. also names beginning with "Adoni-".

114. אַדּוֹן 'Addôwn, ad-done´; prob. intens. for 113; powerful; Addon, appar. an Isr.:— Addon.

115. אֲדוֹרַיִם 'Ădôwrayim, ad-o-rah´-yim; dual from 142 (in the sense of eminence); double mound; Adorajim, a place in Pal.:— Adoraim.

116. אֱדַיִן 'ĕdayin (Chald.), ed-ah´-yin; of uncert. der.; then (of time):— now, that time, then.

117. אַדִּיר 'addîyr, ad-deer´; from 142; wide or (gen.) large; fig. powerful:— excellent, famous, gallant, glorious, goodly, lordly, mighty (-ier, one), noble, principal, worthy.

118. אֲדַלְיָא 'Ădalyâ', ad-al-yaw´; of Pers. der.; Adalja, a son of Haman:— Adalia.

119. אָדַם 'âdam, aw-dam´; to show blood (in the face), i.e. flush or turn rosy:— be (dyed, made) red (ruddy).

120. אָדָם 'âdâm, aw-dawm´; from 119; ruddy, i.e. a human being (an individual or the species, mankind, etc.):— × another, + hypocrite, + common sort, × low, man (mean, of low degree), person.

121. אָדָם 'Âdâm, aw-dawm´; the same as 120; Adam the name of the first man, also of a place in Pal.:— Adam.

122. אָדֹם 'âdôm, aw-dome´; from 119; rosy:— red, ruddy.

123. אֱדֹם 'Ĕdôm, ed-ome´; or (fully)

אֱדוֹם 'Ĕdôwm, ed-ome´; from 122; red [see Gen. 25:25]; Edom, the elder twin-brother of Jacob; hence, the region (Idumæa) occupied by him:— Edom, Edomites, Idumea.

124. אֹדֶם 'ôdem, o´-dem; from 119; redness, i.e. the ruby, garnet, or some other red gem:— sardius.

125. אֲדַמְדָּם 'ădamdâm, ad-am-dawm´; redupl. from 119; reddish:— (somewhat) reddish.

126. אַדְמָה 'Admâh, ad-maw´; contr. for 127; earthy; Admah, a place near the Dead Sea:— Admah.

127. אֲדָמָה 'ădâmâh, ad-aw-maw´; from 119; soil (from its gen. redness):— country, earth, ground, husband [-man] (-ry), land.

128. אֲדָמָה 'Ădâmâh, ad-aw-maw´; the same as 127; Adamah, a place in Pal.:— Adamah.

אַדְמוֹנִי 'admôwnîy. See 132.

129. אֲדָמִי 'Ădâmîy, ad-aw-mee´; from 127; earthy; Adami, a place in Pal.:— Adami.

130. אֱדֹמִי 'Ĕdômîy, ed-o-mee´; or (fully)

אֱדוֹמִי 'Ĕdôwmîy, ed-o-mee´; patron. from 123; an Edomite, or desc. from (or inhab. of) Edom:— Edomite. See 726.

131. אֲדֻמִּים 'Ădummîym, ad-oom-meem´; plur. of 121; red spots; Adummim, a pass in Pal.:— Adummim.

132. אַדְמֹנִי 'admônîy, ad-mo-nee´; or (fully)

אַדְמוֹנִי 'admôwnîy, ad-mo-nee´; from 119; reddish (of the hair or the complexion):— red, ruddy.

133. אַדְמָתָא 'Admâthâ', ad-maw-thaw´; prob. of Pers. der.; Admatha, a Pers. nobleman:— Admatha.

134. אֶדֶן 'eden, eh´-den; from the same as 113 (in the sense of strength); a basis (of a building, a column, etc.):— foundation, socket.

אָדֹן 'âdôn. See 113.

135. אַדָּן 'Addân, ad-dawn´; intens. from the same as 134; firm; Addan, an Isr.:— Addan.

136. אֲדֹנָי 'Ădônây, ad-o-noy´; am emphat. form of 113; the Lord (used as a proper name of God only):— (my) Lord.

137. אֲדֹנִי־בֶזֶק 'Ădônîy-Bezeq, ad-o´-nee-beh´-zek; from 113 and 966; lord of Bezek; Adoni-Bezek; a Canaanitish king:— Adonibezek.

138. אֲדֹנִיָּה 'Ădônîyâh, ad-o-nee-yaw´; or (prol.)

Hebrew

אֲדֹנִיָּהוּ **'Ădônîyâhûw**, *ad-o-nee-yaw´-hoo;* from 113 and 3050; *lord* (i.e. *worshipper) of Jah; Adonijah,* the name of three Isr.:— Adonijah.

139. אֲדֹנִי־צֶדֶק **'Ădônîy-Tsedeq**, *ad-o´´-nee-tseh´-dek;* from 113 and 6664; *lord of justice; Adoni-Tsedek,* a Canaanitish king:— Adonizedec.

140. אֲדֹנִיקָם **'Ădônîyqâm**, *ad-o-nee-kawm´;* from 113 and 6965; *lord of rising* (i.e. *high); Adonikam,* the name of one or two Isr.:— Adonikam.

141. אֲדֹנִירָם **'Ădônîyrâm**, *ad-o-nee-rawm´;* from 113 and 7311; *lord of height; Adoniram,* an Isr.:— Adoniram.

142. אָדַר **'âdar**, *aw-dar´;* a prim. root; to *expand,* i.e. *be great* or (fig.) *magnificent:*— (become) glorious, honourable.

143. אֲדָר **'Ădâr**, *ad-awr´;* prob. of for. der.; perh. mean. *fire; Adar,* the 12th Heb. month:— Adar.

144. אֲדָר **'Ădâr** (Chald.), *ad-awr´;* corresp. to 143:— Adar.

145. אֶדֶר **'eder**, *eh´-der;* from 142; *amplitude,* i.e. (concr.) a *mantle;* also (fig.) *splendor:*— goodly, robe.

146. אַדָּר **'Addâr**, *ad-dawr´;* intens. from 142; *ample; Addar,* a place in Pal.; also an Isr.:— Addar.

147. אִדַּר **'iddar** (Chald.), *id-dar´;* intens. from a root corresp. to 142; *ample,* i.e. a *threshing-floor:*— threshingfloor.

148. אֲדַרְגָּזֵר **'ădargâzêr** (Chald.), *ad-ar´´-gaw-zare´;* from the same as 147 and 1505; a *chief diviner,* or *astrologer:*— judge.

149. אֲדְרַזְדָּא **'adrazdâ'** (Chald.), *ad-raz-daw´;* prob. of Pers. or.; *quickly* or *carefully:*— diligently.

150. אֲדַרְכֹּן **'ădarkôn**, *ad-ar-kone´;* of Pers. or.; a *daric* or Pers. coin:— dram.

151. אֲדֹרָם **'Ădôrâm**, *ad-o-rawm´;* contr. for 141; *Adoram* (or Adoniram), an Isr.:— Adoram.

152. אַדְרַמֶּלֶךְ **'Adrammelek**, *ad-ram-meh´-lek;* from 142 and 4428; *splendor of* (the) *king; Adrammelek,* the name of an Ass. idol, also of a son of Sennacherib:— Adrammelech.

153. אֶדְרָע **'edra'** (Chald.), *ed-raw´;* an orth. var. for 1872; an *arm,* i.e. (fig.) *power:*— force.

154. אֶדְרֶעִי **'edre'îy**, *ed-reh´-ee;* from the equiv. of 153; *mighty; Edrei,* the name of two places in Pal.:— Edrei.

155. אַדֶּרֶת **'addereth**, *ad-deh´-reth;* fem. of 117; something *ample* (as a *large* vine, a *wide* dress); also the same as 145:— garment, glory, goodly, mantle, robe.

156. אָדַשׁ **'âdash**, *aw-dash´;* a prim. root; to *tread* out (grain):— thresh.

157. אָהַב **'âhab**, *aw-hab´;* or

אָהֵב **'âhêb**, *aw-habe´;* a prim. root; to *have affection* for (sexually or otherwise):— (be-) love (-d, -ly, -r), like, friend.

158. אַהַב **'ahab**, *ah´-hab;* from 157; *affection* (in a good or a bad sense):— love (-r).

159. אֹהַב **'ôhab**, *o´-hab;* from 156; mean. the same as 158:— love.

160. אַהֲבָה **'ahăbâh**, *ă-hab-aw´;* fem. of 158 and mean. the same:— love.

161. אֹהַד **'Ôhad**, *o´-had;* from an unused root mean. to *be united; unity; Ohad,* an Isr.:— Ohad.

162. אֲהָהּ **'ăhâhh**, *ă-haw´;* appar. a prim. word expressing *pain* exclamatorily; *Oh!:*— ah, alas.

163. אַהֲוָא **'Ahăvâ'**, *ă-hav-aw´;* prob. of for. or.; *Ahava,* a river of Bab.:— Ahava.

164. אֵהוּד **'Êhûwd**, *ay-hood´;* from the same as 161; *united; Ehud,* the name of two or three Isr.:— Ehud.

165. אֱהִי **'ĕhîy**, *e-hee´;* appar. an orth. var. for 346; *where:*— I will be (Hos. 13:10, 14) [*which is often the rendering of the same Heb. form from* 1961].

166. אָהַל **'âhal**, *aw-hal´;* a prim. root; to *be clear:*— shine.

167. אָהַל **'âhal**, *aw-hal´;* a denom. from 168; to *tent:*— pitch (remove) a tent.

168. אֹהֶל **'ôhel**, *o´-hel;* from 166; a *tent* (as *clearly* conspicuous from a distance):— covering, (dwelling) (place), home, tabernacle, tent.

169. אֹהֶל **'Ôhel**, *o´-hel;* the same as 168; *Ohel,* an Isr.:— Ohel.

170. אָהֳלָה **'Ohŏlâh**, *ŏ-hol-aw´;* in form a fem. of 168, but in fact for

אָהֳלָהּ **'Ohŏlâhh**, *ŏ-hol-aw´;* from 168; *her tent* (i.e. idolatrous *sanctuary); Oholah,* a symbol. name for Samaria:— Aholah.

171. אָהֳלִיאָב **'Ohŏlîy'âb**, *ŏ´´-hol-e-awb´;* from 168 and 1; *tent of* (his) *father; Oholiab,* an Isr.:— Aholiab.

172. אָהֳלִיבָה **'Ohŏlîybâh**, *ŏ´´-hol-ee-baw´;* (similarly with 170) for

אָהֳלִיבָהּ **'Ohŏlîybâhh**, *ŏ´´-hol-e-baw´;* from 168; *my tent* (is) *in her; Oholibah,* a symb. name for Judah:— Aholibah.

173. אָהֳלִיבָמָה **'Ohŏlîybâmâh**, *ŏ´´-hol-ee-baw-maw´;* from 168 and 1116; *tent of* (the) *height; Oholibamah,* a wife of Esau:— Aholibamah.

174. אֲהָלִים **'ăhâlîym**, *ă-haw-leem´;* or (fem.)

אֲהָלוֹת 'ăhâlôwth, ă-haw-loth´ (only used thus in the plur.); of for. or.; aloe wood (i.e. sticks):— (tree of lign-) aloes.

175. אַהֲרוֹן 'Ahărôwn, ă-har-one´; of uncert. der.; Aharon, the brother of Moses:— Aaron.

176. או 'ôw, o; presumed to be the "constr." or genitival form of

או 'av, av; short. for 185; desire (and so prob. in Prov. 31:4); hence, (by way of alternative) or, also if:— also, and, either, if, at the least, × nor, or, otherwise, then, whether.

177. אוּאֵל 'Ûw'êl, oo-ale´; from 176 and 410; wish of God; Uel, an Isr.:— Uel.

178. אוֹב 'ôwb, obe; from the same as 1 (appar. through the idea of prattling a father's name); prop. a mumble, i.e. a water- skin (from its hollow sound); hence, a necromancer (ventriloquist, as from a jar):— bottle, familiar spirit.

179. אוֹבִיל 'Ôwbîyl, o-beel´; prob. from 56; mournful; Obil, an Ishmaelite:— Obil.

180. אוּבָל 'ûwbâl, oo-bawl´; or (short.)

אֻבָל 'ûbâl, oo-bawl´; from 2986 (in the sense of 2988); a stream:— river.

181. אוּד 'ûwd, ood; from an unused root mean. to rake together; a poker (for turning or gathering embers):— (fire-) brand.

182. אוֹדוֹת 'ôwdôwth, o-dôth´; or (short.)

אֹדוֹת 'ôdôwth, o-dôth´ (only thus in the plur.); from the same as 181; turnings (i.e. occasions); (adv.) on account of:— (be-) cause, concerning, sake.

183. אָוָה 'âvâh, aw-vaw´; a prim. root; to wish for:— covet, (greatly) desire, be desirous, long, lust (after).

184. אָוָה 'âvâh, aw-vaw´; a prim. root; to extend or mark out:— point out.

185. אַוָּה 'avvâh, av-vaw´; from 183; longing:— desire, lust after, pleasure.

186. אוּזַי 'Ûwzay, oo-zah´-ee; perh. by perm. for 5813, strong; Uzai, an Isr.:— Uzai.

187. אוּזָל 'Ûwzâl, oo-zâwl´; of uncert. der.; Uzal, a son of Joktan:— Uzal.

188. אוֹי 'ôwy, ō´-ee; prob. from 183 (in the sense of crying out after); lamentation; also interj. Oh!:— alas, woe.

189. אֱוִי 'Ĕvîy, ev-ee´; prob. from 183; desirous; Evi, a Midianitish chief:— Evi.

אוֹיֵב 'ôwyêb. See 341.

190. אוֹיָה 'ôwyâh, o-yaw´; fem. of 188:— woe.

191. אֱוִיל 'ĕvîyl, ev-eel´; from an unused root (mean. to be perverse); (fig.) silly:— fool (-ish) (man).

192. אֱוִיל מְרֹדַךְ 'Ĕvîyl Mᵉrôdak, ev-eel´ mer-o-dak´; of Chald. der. and prob. mean. soldier

of Merodak; Evil-Merodak, a Bab. king:— Evil-merodach.

193. אוּל 'ûwl, ool; from an unused root mean. to twist, i.e. (by impl.) be strong; the body (as being rolled together); also powerful:— mighty, strength.

194. אוּלַי 'ûwlay, oo-lah´ee; or (short.)

אֻלַי 'ûlay, oo-lah´ee; from 176; if not; hence, perhaps:— if so be, may be, peradventure, unless.

195. אוּלַי 'Ûwlay, oo-lah´ee; of Pers. der.; the Ulai (or Eulæus), a river of Pers.:— Ulai.

196. אֱוִלִי 'ĕvîlîy, ev-ee-lee´; from 191; silly, foolish; hence, (mor.) impious:— foolish.

197. אוּלָם 'ûwlâm, oo-lawm´; or (short.)

אֻלָם 'ûlâm, oo-lawm´; from 481 (in the sense of tying); a vestibule (as bound to the building):— porch.

198. אוּלָם 'Ûwlâm, oo-lawm´; appar. from 481 (in the sense of dumbness); solitary; Ulam, the name of two Isr.:— Ulam.

199. אוּלָם 'ûwlâm, oo-lawm´; appar. a var. of 194; however or on the contrary:— as for, but, howbeit, in very deed, surely, truly, wherefore.

200. אִוֶּלֶת 'ivveleth, iv-veh´-leth; from the same as 191; silliness:— folly, foolishly (-ness).

201. אוֹמָר 'Ôwmâr, o-mawr´; from 559; talkative; Omar, a grandson of Esau:— Omar.

202. אוֹן 'ôwn, ōne; prob. from the same as 205 (in the sense of effort, but successful); ability, power, (fig.) wealth:— force, goods, might, strength, substance.

203. אוֹן 'Ôwn, ōne; the same as 202; On, an Isr.:— On.

204. און 'Ôwn, ōne; or (short.);

אֹן 'Ôn, ōne; of Eg. der.; On, a city of Egypt:— On.

205. אָוֶן 'âven, aw-ven´; from an unused root perh. mean. prop. to pant (hence, to exert oneself, usually in vain; to come to naught); strictly nothingness; also trouble, vanity, wickedness; spec. an idol:— affliction, evil, false, idol, iniquity, mischief, mourners (-ing), naught, sorrow, unjust, unrighteous, vain ,vanity, wicked (-ness). Comp. 369.

206. אָוֶן 'Âven, aw´-ven; the same as 205; idolatry; Aven, the contemptuous synonym of three places, one in Cæle-Syria, one in Egypt (On), and one in Pal. (Bethel):— Aven. See also 204, 1007.

207. אוֹנוֹ 'Ôwnôw, o-no´; or (short.)

אֹנוֹ **'Ônôw**, *o-no´;* prol. from 202; *strong; Ono*, a place in Pal.:— Ono.

208. אוֹנָם **'Ôwnâm**, *o-nawm´;* a var. of 209; *strong; Onam*, the name of an Edomite and of an Isr.:— Onam.

209. אוֹנָן **'Ôwnân**, *o-nawn´;* a var. of 207; *strong; Onan*, a son of Judah:— Onan.

210. אוּפָז **'Ûwphâz**, *oo-fawz´;* perh. a corruption of 211; *Uphaz*, a famous gold region:— Uphaz.

211. אוֹפִיר **'Ôwphîyr**, *o-feer´;* or (short.)

אֹפִיר **'Ôphîyr**, *o-feer´;* and

אוֹפִר **'Ôwphir**, *o-feer´;* of uncert. der.; *Ophir*, the name of a son of Joktan, and of a gold region in the East:— Ophir.

212. אוֹפָן **'Ôwphân**, *o-fawn´;* or (short.)

אֹפָן **'ôphân**, *o-fawn´;* from an unused root mean. to *revolve;* a *wheel:*— wheel.

אוֹפִר **'Ôwphîr**. See 211.

213. אוּץ **'ûwts**, *oots;* a prim. root; to *press;* (by impl.) to *be close, hurry, withdraw:*— (make) haste (-n, -y), labor, be narrow.

214. אוֹצָר **'ôwtsâr**, *o-tsawr´;* from 686; a *depository:*— armory, cellar, garner, store (-house), treasure (-house) (-y).

215. אוֹר **'ôwr**, *ore;* a prim. root; to *be* (caus. *make) luminous* (lit. and metaph.):— × break of day, glorious, kindle, (be, en-, give, show) light (-en, -ened), set on fire, shine.

216. אוֹר **'ôwr**, *ore;* from 215; *illumination* or (concr.) *luminary* (in every sense, incl. *lightning, happiness,* etc.):— bright, clear, + day, light (-ning), morning, sun.

217. אוּר **'ûwr**, *oor;* from 215; *flame,* hence, (in the plur.) the *East* (as being the region of light):— fire, light. See also 224.

218. אוּר **'Ûwr**, *oor;* the same as 217; *Ur,* a place in Chaldæa; also an Isr.:— Ur.

219. אוֹרָה **'ôwrâh**, *o-raw´;* fem. of 216; *luminousness,* i.e. (fig.) *prosperity;* also a plant (as being *bright*):— herb, light.

220. אֻרָה **'ăvêrâh**, *av-ay-raw´;* by transp. for 723; a *stall:*— cote.

221. אוּרִי **'Ûwrîy**, *oo-ree´;* from 217; *fiery; Uri,* the name of three Isr.:— Uri.

222. אוּרִיאֵל **'Ûwrîy'êl**, *oo-ree-ale´;* from 217 and 410; *flame of God; Uriel,* the name of two Isr.:— Uriel.

223. אוּרִיָּה **'Ûwrîyâh**, *oo-ree-yaw´;* or (prol.)

אוּרִיָּהוּ **'Ûwrîyâhûw**, *oo-ree-yaw´-hoo;* from 217 and 3050; *flame of Jah; Urijah,* the name of one Hittite and five Isr.:— Uriah, Urijah.

224. אוּרִים **'Ûwrîym**, *oo-reem´;* plur. of 217; *lights; Urim,* the oracular brilliancy of the figures in the high-priest's breastplate:— Urim.

אוֹרְנָה **'Owrenâh**. See 728.

225. אוּת **'ûwth**, *ooth;* a prim. root; prop. to *come,* i.e. (impl.) to *assent:*— consent.

226. אוֹת **'ôwth**, *ōth;* prob. from 225 (in the sense of *appearing*); a *signal* (lit. or fig.), as a *flag, beacon, monument, omen, prodigy, evidence,* etc.:— mark, miracle, (en-) sign, token.

227. אָז **'âz**, *awz;* a demonstr. adv.; *at that time* or *place;* also as a conjunc., *therefore:*— beginning, for, from, hitherto, now, of old, once, since, then, at which time, yet.

228. אֲזָא **'ăzâ'** (Chald.), *az-zaw´;* or

אֲזָה **'ăzâh** (Chald.), *az-aw´;* to *kindle;* (by impl.) to *heat:*— heat, hot.

229. אֶזְבַּי **'Ezbay**, *ez-bah'ee;* prob. from 231; *hyssop-like; Ezbai,* an Isr.:— Ezbai.

230. אֲזַד **'ăzad** (Chald.), *az-zawd´;* of uncert. der.; *firm:*— be gone.

231. אֵזוֹב **'êzôwb**, *ay-zobe´;* prob. of for. der.; *hyssop:*— hyssop.

232. אֵזוֹר **'êzôwr**, *ay-zore´;* from 246; something *girt;* a *belt,* also a *band:*— girdle.

233. אֲזַי **'ăzay**, *az-ah'ee;* prob. from 227; *at that time:*— then.

234. אַזְכָּרָה **'azkârâh**, *az-kaw-raw´;* from 2142; a *reminder;* spec. *remembrance-offering:*— memorial.

235. אָזַל **'âzal**, *aw-zal´;* a prim. root; to *go away,* hence, to *disappear:*— fail, gad about, go to and fro [*but in Ezek. 27:19 the word is rendered by many "from Uzal," by others "yarn"*], be gone (spent).

236. אֲזַל **'ăzal** (Chald.), *az-al´;* the same as 235; to *depart:*— go (up).

237. אֶזֶל **'ezel**, *eh´-zel;* from 235; *departure; Ezel,* a memorial stone in Pal.:— Ezel.

238. אָזַן **'âzan**, *aw-zan´;* a prim. root; prob. to *expand;* but used only as a denom. from 241; to *broaden out the ear* (with the hand), i.e. (by impl.) to *listen:*— give (perceive by the) ear, hear (-ken). See 239.

239. אָזַן **'âzan**, *aw-zan´;* a prim. root [rather ident. with 238 through the idea of *scales* as if two ears]; to *weigh,* i.e. (fig.) *ponder:*— give good head.

240. אָזֵן **'âzên**, *aw-zane´;* from 238; a *spade* or *paddle* (as having a *broad* end):— weapon.

241. אֹזֶן **'ôzen**, *o´-zen;* from 238; *broadness,* i.e. (concr.) the *ear* (from its form in man):— + advertise, audience, + displease, ear, hearing, + show.

242. אֹזֶן שְׁאֵרָה **'Uzzên She'êrâh**, *ooz-zane´*

sheh-er-aw´; from 238 and 7609; *plat of Sheerah* (i.e. settled by him); *Uzzen-Sheërah,* a place in Pal.:— Uzzen-sherah.

243. אַזְנוֹת תָּבוֹר **'Aznôwth Tâbôwr,** *az-nōth´ taw-bore´;* from 238 and 8396; *flats* (i.e. *tops*) *of Tabor* (i.e. situated on it); *Aznoth-Tabor,* a place in Pal.:— Aznoth-tabor.

244. אׇזְנִי **'Oznîy,** *oz-nee´;* from 241; *having* (quick) *ears; Ozni,* an Isr.; also an *Oznite* (collect.), his desc.:— Ozni, Oznites.

245. אֲזַנְיָה **'Ăzanyâh,** *az-an-yaw´;* from 238 and 3050; *heard by Jah; Azanjah,* an Isr.:— Azaniah.

246. אִזִּקִּים **'ăziqqîym,** *az-ik-keem´;* a var. for 2131; *manacles:—* chains.

247. אָזַר **'âzar,** *aw-zar´;* a prim. root; to *belt:—* bind (compass) about, gird (up, with).

248. אֶזְרוֹעַ **'ezrôwa',** *ez-ro´-ă;* a var. for 2220; the *arm:—* arm.

249. אֶזְרָח **'ezrâch,** *ez-rawkh´;* from 2224 (in the sense of *springing up*); a spontaneous *growth,* i.e. *native* (tree or persons):— bay tree, (home-) born (in the land), of the (one's own) country (nation).

250. אֶזְרָחִי **'Ezrâchîy,** *ez-raw-khee´;* patron. from 2246; an *Ezrachite* or desc. of Zerach:— Ezrahite.

251. אָח **'âch,** *awkh;* a prim. word; a *brother* (used in the widest sense of lit. relationship and metaph. affinity or resemblance [like 1]):— another, brother (-ly), kindred, like, other. Compare also the proper names beginning with "Ah-" or "Ahi-".

252. אָח **'ach** (Chald.), *akh;* corresp. to 251:— brother.

253. אָח **'âch,** *awkh;* a var. for 162; *Oh!* (expressive of grief or surprise):— ah, alas.

254. אָח **'âch,** *awkh;* of uncert. der.; a fire-*pot* or chafing-dish:— hearth.

255. אֹחַ **'ôach,** *o´-akh;* prob. from 253; a *howler* or lonesome wild animal:— doleful creature.

256. אַחְאָב **'Ach'âb,** *akh-awb´;* once (by contr.)

אֶחָב **'Echâb** (Jer. 29:22), *ekh-awb´;* from 251 and 1; *brother* [i.e. *friend*] *of* (his) *father; Achab,* the name of a king of Israel and of a prophet at Bab.:— Ahab.

257. אַחְבָּן **'Achbân,** *akh-bawn´;* from 251 and 995; *brother* (i.e. *possessor*) *of understanding; Achban,* an Isr.:— Ahban.

258. אָחַד **'âchad,** *aw-khad´;* perh. a prim. root; to *unify,* i.e. (fig.) *collect* (one's thoughts):— go one way or other.

259. אֶחָד **'echâd,** *ekh-awd´;* a numeral from 258; prop. *united,* i.e. *one;* or (as an ord.) *first:—* a, alike, alone, altogether, and, any (-thing), apiece, a certain, [dai-lly], each (one),

+ eleven, every, few, first, + highway, a man, once, one, only, other, some, together.

260. אָחוּ **'âchûw,** *aw´-khoo;* of uncert. (perh. Eg.) der.; a *bulrush* or any marshy grass (particularly that along the Nile):— flag, meadow.

261. אֵחוּד **'Êchûwd,** *ay-khood´;* from 258; *united; Echud,* the name of three Isr.:— Ehud.

262. אַחְוָה **'achvâh,** *akh-vaw´;* from 2331 (in the sense of 2324); an *utterance:—* declaration.

263. אַחֲוָה **'achăvâh** (Chald.), *akh-av-aw´;* corresp. to 262; *solution* (of riddles):— showing.

264. אַחֲוָה **'achăvâh,** *akh-av-aw´;* from 251; *fraternity:—* brotherhood.

265. אֲחוֹחַ **'Ăchôwach,** *akh-o´-akh;* by redupl. from 251; *brotherly; Achoach,* an Isr.:— Ahoah.

266. אֲחוֹחִי **'Ăchôwchîy,** *akh-o-khee´;* patron. from 264; an *Achochite* or desc. of Achoach:— Ahohite.

267. אֲחוּמַי **'Ăchûwmay,** *akh-oo-mah´-ee;* perh. from 251 and 4325; *brother* (i.e. *neighbour*) *of water; Achumai,* an Isr.:— Ahumai.

268. אָחוֹר **'âchôwr,** *aw-khore´;* or (short.)

אָחֹר **'âchôr,** *aw-khore´;* from 299; the *hinder* part; hence, (adv.) *behind, backward;* also (as facing north) the *West:—* after (-ward), back (part, -side, -ward), hereafter, (be-) hind (-er part), time to come, without.

269. אָחוֹת **'achôwth,** *aw-khôth´;* irreg. fem. of 251; a *sister* (used very widely [like 250], lit. and fig.):— (an-) other, sister, together.

270. אָחַז **'âchaz,** *aw-khaz´;* a prim. root; to *seize* (often with the accessory idea of holding in possession):— + be affrighted, bar, (catch, lay, take) hold (back), come upon, fasten, handle, portion, (get, have or take) possess (-ion).

271. אָחָז **'Âchâz,** *aw-khawz´;* from 270; *possessor; Achaz,* the name of a Jewish king and of an Isr.:— Ahaz.

272. אֲחֻזָּה **'ăchuzzâh,** *akh-ooz-zaw´;* fem. pass. part. from 270; something *seized,* i.e. a *possession* (espec. of land):— possession.

273. אַחְזַי **'Achzay,** *akh-zah´ee;* from 270; *seizer; Achzai,* an Isr.:— Ahasai.

274. אֲחֻזָּה **'Ăchazyâh,** *akh-az-yaw´;* or (prol.)

אֲחַזְיָהוּ **'Ăchazyâhûw,** *akh-az-yaw´-hoo;* from 270 and 3050; *Jah has seized; Achazjah,* the name of a Jewish and an Isr. king:— Ahaziah.

275. אֲחֻזָּם **'Ăchuzzâm**, *akh-ooz-zawm´*; from 270; *seizure; Achuzzam*, an Isr.:— Ahuzam.

276. אֲחֻזַּת **'Ăchuzzath**, *akh-ooz-zath´*; a var. of 272; *possession; Achuzzath*, a Philistine:— Ahuzzath.

277. אֲחִי **'Ăchîy**, *akh-ee´*; from 251; *brotherly; Achi*, the name of two Isr.:— Ahi.

278. אֵחִי **'Êchîy**, *ay-khee´*; prob. the same as 277; *Echi*, an Isr.:— Ehi.

279. אֲחִיאָם **'Ăchîy'âm**, *akh-ee-awm´*; from 251 and 517; *brother of* (the) *mother* (i.e. *uncle*); *Achiam*, an Isr.:— Ahiam.

280. אֲחִידָה **'ăchîydâh** (Chald.), *akh-ee-daw´*; corresp. to 2420, an *enigma*:— hard sentence.

281. אֲחִיָּה **'Ăchîyâh**, *akh-ee-yaw*; or (prol.)

אֲחִיָּהוּ **'Ăchîyâhûw**, *akh-ee-yaw´-hoo*; from 251 and 3050; *brother* (i.e. *worshipper*) *of Jah; Achijah*, the name of nine Isr.:— Ahiah, Ahijah.

282. אֲחִיהוּד **'Ăchîyhûwd**, *akh-ee-hood´*; from 251 and 1935; *brother* (i.e. *possessor) of renown; Achihud*, an Isr.:— Ahihud.

283. אַחְיוֹ **'Achyôw**, *akh-yo´*; prol. from 251; *brotherly; Achio*, the name of three Isr.:— Ahio.

284. אֲחִיחֻד **'Ăchîychûd**, *akh-ee-khood´*; from 251 and 2330; *brother of a riddle* (i.e. *mysterious); Achichud*, an Isr.:— Ahihud.

285. אֲחִיטוּב **'Ăchîytûwb**, *akh-ee-toob´*; from 251 and 2898; *brother of goodness; Achitub*, the name of several priests:— Ahitub.

286. אֲחִילוּד **'Ăchîylûwd**, *akh-ee-lood´*; from 251 and 3205; *brother of one born; Achilud*, an Isr.:— Ahilud.

287. אֲחִימוֹת **'Ăchîymôwth**, *akh-ee-môth´*; from 251 and 4191; *brother of death; Achimoth*, an Isr.:— Ahimoth.

288. אֲחִימֶלֶךְ **'Ăchîymelek**, *akh-ee-meh´-lek*; from 251 and 4428; *brother of* (the) *king; Achimelek*, the name of an Isr. and of a Hittite:— Ahimelech.

289. אֲחִימָן **'Ăchîyman**, *akh-ee-man´*; or

אֲחִימָן **'Ăchîymân**, *akh-ee-mawn´*; from 251 and 4480; *brother of a portion* (i.e. *gift); Achiman*, the name of an Anakite and of an Isr.:— Ahiman.

290. אֲחִימַעַץ **'Ăchîyma'ats**, *akh-ee-mah´-ats*; from 251 and the equiv. of 4619; *brother of anger; Achimaats*, the name of three Isr.:— Ahimaaz.

291. אַחְיָן **'Achyân**, *akh-yawn´*; from 251; *brotherly; Achjan*, an Isr.:— Ahian.

292. אֲחִינָדָב **'Ăchîynâdâb**, *akh-ee-naw-dawb´*; from 251 and 5068; *brother of liberality; Achinadab*, an Isr.:— Ahinadab.

293. אֲחִינֹעַם **'Ăchîynô'am**, *akh-ee-no´-am*; from 251 and 5278; *brother of pleasantness; Achinoam*, the name of two Israelitesses:— Ahinoam.

294. אֲחִיסָמָךְ **'Ăchîyçâmâk**, *akh-ee-saw-mawk´*; from 251 and 5564; *brother of support; Achisamak*, an Isr.:— Ahisamach.

295. אֲחִיעֶזֶר **'Ăchîy'ezer**, *akh-ee-eh´-zer*; from 251 and 5828; *brother of help; Achiezer*, the name of two Isr.:— Ahiezer.

296. אֲחִיקָם **'Ăchîyqâm**, *akh-ee-kawm´*; from 251 and 6965; *brother of rising* (i.e. *high); Achikam*, an Isr.:— Ahikam.

297. אֲחִירָם **'Ăchîyrâm**, *akh-ee-rawm´*; from 251 and 7311; *brother of height* (i.e. *high); Achiram*, an Isr.:— Ahiram.

298. אֲחִירָמִי **'Ăchîyrâmîy**, *akh-ee-raw-mee´*; patron. from 297; an *Achiramite* or desc. (collect.) of Achiram:— Ahiramites.

299. אֲחִירַע **'Ăchîyra'**, *akh-ee-rah´*; from 251 and 7451; *brother of wrong; Achira*, an Isr.:— Ahira.

300. אֲחִישַׁחַר **'Achîyshachar**, *akh-ee-shakh´-ar*; from 251 and 7837; *brother of* (the) *dawn; Achishachar*, an Isr.:— Ahishar.

301. אֲחִישָׁר **'Ăchîyshâr**, *akh-ee-shawr´*; from 251 and 7891; *brother of* (the) *singer; Achishar*, an Isr.:— Ahishar.

302. אֲחִיתֹפֶל **'Ăchîythôphel**, *akh-ee-tho´-fel*; from 251 and 8602; *brother of folly; Achithophel*, an Isr.:— Ahithophel.

303. אַחְלָב **'Achlâb**, *akh-lawb´*; from the same root as 2459; *fatness* (i.e. *fertile); Achlab*, a place in Pal.:— Ahlab.

304. אַחְלַי **'Achlay**, *akh-lah´ee*; the same as 305; *wishful; Achlai*, the name of an Israelitess and of an Isr.:— Ahlai.

305. אַחֲלַי **'achălay**, *akh-al-ah´ee*; or

אַחֲלֵי **'achălêy**, *akh-al-ay´*; prob. from 253 and a var. of 3863; *would that!*:— O that, would God.

306. אַחְלָמָה **'achlâmâh**, *akh-law´-maw*; perh. from 2492 (and thus *dream-stone*); a gem, prob. the *amethyst*:— amethyst.

307. אַחְמְתָא **'Achmᵉthâ'**, *akh-me-thaw´*; of Pers. der.; *Achmetha* (i.e. *Ecbatana*), the summer capital of Persia:— Achmetha.

308. אַחַסְבַּי **'Ăchaçbay**, *akh-as-bah´ee*; of uncert. der.; *Achasbai*, an Isr.:— Ahasbai.

309. אָחַר **'âchar**, *aw-khar´*; a prim. root; to *loiter* (i.e. *be behind); by impl. to *procrastinate*:— continue, defer, delay, hinder, be late (slack), stay (there), tarry (longer).

310. אַחַר **'achar**, *akh-ar´*; from 309; prop. the *hind* part; gen. used as an adv. or conjunc., *after* (in various senses):— after (that, -ward), again, at, away from, back (from, -side), behind, beside, by, follow (after, -

ing), forasmuch, from, hereafter, hinder end, + out (over) live, + persecute, posterity, pursuing, remnant, seeing, since, thence [-forth], when, with.

311. אַחַר 'achar (Chald.), *akh-ar´*; corresp. to 310; *after:—* [here-] after.

312. אַחֵר 'achêr, *akh-air´*; from 309; prop. *hinder*; gen. *next, other,* etc.:— (an-) other man, following, next, strange.

313. אַחֵר 'Achêr, *akh-air´*; the same as 312; *Acher,* an Isr.:— Aher.

314. אַחֲרוֹן 'achărôwn, *akh-ar-one´*; or (short.)

אַחֲרֹן 'achărôn, *akh-ar-one´*; from 309; *hinder*; gen. *late* or *last*; spec. (as facing the east) *western:—* after (-ward), to come, following, hind (-er, -ermost, -most), last, latter, rereward, ut(ter)most.

315. אַחְרַח 'Achrach, *akh-rakh´*; from 310 and 251; *after* (his) *brother; Achrach,* an Isr.:— Aharah.

316. אַחְרְחֵל 'Acharchêl, *akh-ar-kale´*; from 310 and 2426; *behind* (the) *intrenchment* (i.e. *safe*); *Acharchel,* an Isr.:— Aharhel.

317. אָחֳרִי 'ochŏrîy (Chald.), *okh-or-ee´*; from 311; *other:—* (an-) other.

318. אָחֳרֵין 'ochŏrêyn (Chald.), *okh-or-ane´*; or (short.)

אָחֳרֵן 'ochŏrên (Chald.), *okh-or-ane´*; from 317; *last:—* at last.

319. אַחֲרִית 'achărîyth, *akh-ar-eeth´*; from 310; the *last* or *end,* hence, the *future*; also *posterity:—* (last, latter) end (time), hinder (utter) -most, length, posterity, remnant, residue, reward.

320. אַחֲרִית 'achărîyth (Chald.), *akh-ar-eeth´*; from 311; the same as 319; *later:—* latter.

321. אָחֳרָן 'ochŏrân (Chald.), *okh-or-awn´*; from 311; the same as 317; *other:—* (an-) other.

אָחֳרֵן 'ochŏrên. See 318.

322. אֲחֹרַנִּית 'achôrannîyth, *akh-o-ran-neeth´*; prol. from 268; *backwards:—* back (-ward, again).

323. אֲחַשְׁדַּרְפָּן 'achashdarpan, *akh-ash-dar-pan´*; of Pers. der.; a *satrap* or governor of a main province (of Persia):— lieutenant.

324. אֲחַשְׁדַּרְפָּן ăchashdarpan (Chald.), *akh-ash-dar-pan´*; corresp. to 323:— prince.

325. אֲחַשְׁוֵרוֹשׁ 'Achashvêrôwsh, *akh-ash-vay-rôsh´*; or (short.)

אֲחַשְׁרֹשׁ 'Achashrôsh, *akh-ash-rôsh´* (Esth. 10:1); of Pers. or.; *Achashverosh* (i.e. Ahasuerus or Artaxerxes, but in this case Xerxes), the title (rather than name) of a Pers. king:— Ahasuerus.

326. אֲחַשְׁתָּרִי 'achashtârîy, *akh-ash-taw-ree´*;

prob. of Pers. der.; an *achastarite* (i.e. courier); the designation (rather than name) of an Isr.:— Haakashtari [includ. the art.].

327. אֲחַשְׁתָּרָן 'ăchastârân, *akh-ash-taw-rawn´*; of Pers. or.; a *mule:—* camel.

328. אַט 'at, *at*; from an unused root perh. mean. to *move softly*; (as a noun) a *necromancer* (from their soft incantations), (as an adv.) *gently:—* charmer, gently, secret, softly.

329. אָטָד 'âtâd, *aw-tawd´*; from an unused root prob. mean. to *pierce* or *make fast*; a *thorn*-tree (espec. the *buckthorn*):— Atad, bramble, thorn.

330. אֵטוּן 'êtûwn, *ay-toon´*; from an unused root (prob. mean. to *bind*); prop. *twisted* (yarn), i.e. *tapestry:—* fine linen.

331. אָטַם 'âtam, *aw-tam´*; a prim. root; to *close* (the lips or ears); by anal. to *contract* (a window by bevelled jambs):— narrow, shut, stop.

332. אָטַר 'âtar, *aw-tar´*; a prim. root; to *close up:—* shut.

333. אָטֵר 'Âtêr, *aw-tare´*; from 332; *maimed; Ater,* the name of three Isr.:— Ater.

334. אִטֵּר 'ittêr, *it-tare´*; from 332; *shut* up, i.e. *impeded* (as to the use of the right hand):— + left-handed.

335. אַי 'ay, *ah´ee*; perh. from 370; *where*? hence, *how*?:— how, what, whence, where, whether, which (way).

336. אִי 'îy, *ee*; prob. ident. with 335 (through the idea of a *query*); *not:—* island (Job 22:30).

337. אִי 'îy, *ee*; short. from 188; *alas!:—* woe.

338. אִי 'îy, *ee*; prob. ident. with 337 (through the idea of a *doleful* sound); a *howler* (used only in the plur.), i.e. any solitary wild creature:— wild beast of the islands.

339. אִי 'îy, *ee*; from 183; prop. a *habitable* spot (as *desirable*); dry *land,* a *coast,* an *island:—* country, isle, island.

340. אָיַב 'âyab, *aw-yab´*; a prim. root; to *hate* (as one of an opposite tribe or party); hence, to *be hostile:—* be an enemy.

341. אֹיֵב 'ôyêb, *o-yabe´*; or (fully)

אוֹיֵב 'ôwyêb, *o-yabe´*; act. part. of 340; *hating*; an *adversary:—* enemy, foe.

342. אֵיבָה 'êybâh, *ay-baw´*; from 340; *hostility:—* enmity, hatred.

343. אֵיד 'êyd, *ade*; from the same as 181 (in the sense of *bending* down); *oppression*; by impl. *misfortune, ruin:—* calamity, destruction.

344. אַיָּה 'ayâh, *ah-yaw´*; perh. from 337; the *screamer,* i.e. a *hawk:—* kite, vulture.

345. אַיָּה **'Ayâh**, *ah-yaw´;* the same as 344; *Ajah*, the name of two Isr.:— Aiah, Ajah.

346. אַיֵּה **'ayêh**, *ah-yay´;* prol. from 335; *where?:*— where.

347. אִיּוֹב **'Îyôwb**, *ee-yobe´;* from 340; *hated* (i.e. *persecuted*); *Ijob*, the patriarch famous for his patience:— Job.

348. אִיזֶבֶל **'Îyzebel**, *ee-zeh´-bel;* from 336 and 2083; *chaste; Izebel*, the wife of king Ahab:— Jezebel.

349. אֵיךְ **'êyk**, *ake;* also

אֵיכָה **'êykâh**, *ay-kaw´;* and

אֵיכָכָה **'êykâkâh**, *ay-kaw´-kah;* prol. from 335; *how?* or *how!;* also *where:*— how, what.

350. אִי־כָבוֹד **Îy-kâbôwd**, *ee-kaw-bode´;* from 336 and 3519; (there is) *no glory*, i.e. *inglorious; Ikabod*, a son of Phineas:— I-chabod.

351. אֵיכֹה **'êykôh**, *ay-kō;* prob. a var. for 349, but not as an interrogative; *where:*— where.

אֵיכָה **'êykâh;**

אֵיכָכָה **'êykâkâh**. See 349.

352. אַיִל **'ayil**, *ah´-yil;* from the same as 193; prop. *strength;* hence, anything *strong;* spec. a *chief* (politically); also a *ram* (from his strength); a *pilaster* (as a strong support); an *oak* or other strong tree:— mighty (man), lintel, oak, post, ram, tree.

353. אֱיָל **'êyâl**, *eh-yawl´;* a var. of 352; *strength:*— strength.

354. אַיָּל **'ayâl**, *ah-yawl´;* an intens. form of 352 (in the sense of *ram*); a *stag* or male deer:— hart.

355. אַיָּלָה **'ayâlâh**, *ah-yaw-law´;* fem. of 354; a *doe* or female deer:— hind.

356. אֵילוֹן **'Êylôwn**, *ay-lone´;* or (short.)

אֵלוֹן **'Êlôwn**, *ay-lone´;* or

אֵילֹן **'Êylôn**, *ay-lone´;* from 352; *oak-grove; Elon*, the name of a place in Pal., and also of one Hittite, two Isr.:— Elon.

357. אַיָּלוֹן **'Ayâlôwn**, *ah-yaw-lone´;* from 354; *deer-field; Ajalon*, the name of five places in Pal.:— Aijalon, Ajalon.

358. אֵילוֹן בֵּית חָנָן **'Êylôwn Bêyth Chânân**, *ay-lone´ bayth chaw-nawn´;* from 356, 1004, and 2603; *oak-grove of* (the) *house of favor; Elon of Beth-chanan*, a place in Pal.:— Elon-beth-ha-nan.

359. אֵילוֹת **'Êylôwth**, *ay-lōth´;* or

אֵילַת **'Êylath**, *ay-lath´;* from 352; *trees* or a *grove* (i.e. *palms*); *Eloth* or *Elath*, a place on the Red Sea:— Elath, Eloth.

360. אֱיָלוּת **'ĕyâlûwth**, *eh-yaw-looth´;* fem. of 353; *power;* by impl. *protection:*— strength.

361. אֵילָם **'êylâm**, *ay-lawm´;* or (short.)

אֵלָם **'êlâm**, *ay-lawm´;* or (fem.)

אֱלַמָּה **'êlammâh**, *ay-lam-maw´;* prob. from 352; a *pillar-space* (or colonnade), i.e. a *pale* (or portico):— arch.

362. אֵילִם **'Êylîm**, *ay-leem´;* plur. of 352; *palm-trees; Elim*, a place in the Desert:— Elim.

363. אִילָן **'îylân** (Chald.), *ee-lawn´;* corresp. to 356; a *tree:*— tree.

364. אֵיל פָּארָן **'Êyl Pâ'rân**, *ale paw-rawn´;* from 352 and 6290; *oak of Paran; El-Paran*, a portion of the district of Paran:— El-paran.

אֵילֹן **'Êylôn**. See 356.

365. אַיֶּלֶת **'ayeleth**, *ah-yeh´-leth;* the same as 355; a *doe:*— hind, Aijeleth.

אַיִם **'ayim**. See 368.

366. אָיֹם **'âyôm**, *aw-yome´;* from an unused root (mean. to *frighten*); *frightful:*— terrible.

367. אֵימָה **'êymâh**, *ay-maw´;* or (short.)

אֵמָה **'êmah**, *ay-maw´;* from the same as 366; *fright;* concr. an *idol* (as a bugbear):— dread, fear, horror, idol, terrible, terror.

368. אֵימִים **'Êymîym**, *ay-meem´;* plur. of 367; *terrors; Emim*, an early Canaanitish (or Moabitish) tribe:— Emims.

369. אַיִן **'ayin**, *ah´-yin;* as if from a prim. root mean. to *be nothing* or *not exist;* a *non-entity;* gen. used as a neg. particle:— else, except, fail, [father-]less, be gone, in[-curable], neither, never, no (where), none, nor, (any, thing), not, nothing, to nought, past, un[-searchable], well-nigh, without. Comp. 370.

370. אַיִן **'ayin**, *ah´-yin;* prob. ident. with 369 in the sense of *query* (comp. 336); *where?* (only in connection with prep. pref., *whence*):— whence, where.

371. אִין **'îyn**, *een;* appar. a short. form of 369; but (like 370) interrog.; *is it not?:*— not.

372. אִיעֶזֶר **'Îy'ezer**, *ee-eh´-zer;* from 336 and 5828; *helpless; Iezer*, an Isr.:— Jeezer.

373. אִיעֶזְרִי **'Îy'ezriy**, *ee-ez-ree´;* patron. from 372; an *Iezrite* or desc. of Iezer:— Jezerite.

374. אֵיפָה **'êyphâh**, *ay-faw´;* or (short.)

אֵפָה **'êphâh**, *ay-faw´;* of Eg. der.; an *ephah* or measure for grain; hence, a *measure* in gen.:— ephah, (divers) measure (-s).

375. אֵיפֹה **'êyphôh**, *ay-fō´;* from 335 and 6311; *what place?;* also (of time) *when?;* or (of means) *how?:*— what manner, where.

376. אִישׁ **'îysh**, *eesh;* contr. for 582 [or perh. rather from an unused root mean. to *be extant*]; a *man* as an individual or a male person; often used as an adjunct to a more

def. term (and in such cases frequently not expressed in translation):— also, another, any (man), a certain, + champion, consent, each, every (one), fellow, [foot-, husband-] man, (good-, great, mighty) man, he, high (degree), him (that is), husband, man [-kind], + none, one, people, person, + steward, what (man) soever, whoso (-ever), worthy. Comp. 802.

377. אִישׁ 'îysh, eesh; denom. from 376; to be a man, i.e. act in a manly way:— show (one) self a man.

378. אִישׁ־בֹּשֶׁת 'Îysh-Bôsheth, eesh-bō'-sheth; from 376 and 1322; man of shame; Ish-Bosheth, a son of King Saul:— Ish-bosheth.

379. אִישְׁהוֹד 'Îyshhôwd, eesh-hode'; from 376 and 1935; man of renown; Ishod, an Isr.:— Ishod.

380. אִישׁוֹן 'îyshôwn, ee-shone'; dimin. from 376; the little man of the eye; the pupil or ball; hence, the middle (of night):— apple [of the eye], black, obscure.

אִישׁ־חַי 'Îysh-Chay. See 381.

381. אִישׁ־חַיִל 'Îysh-Chayil, eesh-khah'-yil; from 376 and 2428; man of might; by defect. transc. (2 Sam. 23:20)

אִישׁ־חַי 'Îysh-Chay, eesh-khah'ee; as if from 376 and 2416; living man; Ish-chail (or Ish-chai), an Isr.:— a valiant man.

382. אִישׁ־טוֹב 'Îysh-Tôwb, eesh-tobe'; from 376 and 2897; man of Tob; Ish-Tob, a place in Pal.:— Ish-tob.

אִישַׁי 'Îshay. See 3448.

אִיתוֹן 'îthôwn. See 2978.

383. אִיתַי 'îythay (Chald.), ee-thah'ee; corresp. to 3426; prop. entity; used only as a particle of affirmation, there is:— art thou, can, do ye, have, it be, there is (are), × we will not.

384. אִיתִיאֵל 'Îythîy'êl, eeth-ee-ale'; perh. from 837 and 410; God has arrived; Ithiel, the name of an Isr., also of a symb. person:— Ithiel.

385. אִיתָמָר 'Îythâmâr, eeth-aw-mawr'; from 339 and 8558; coast of the palm-tree; Ithamar, a son of Aaron:— Ithamar.

386. אֵיתָן 'êythân, ay-thawn'; or (short.)

אֵתָן 'êthân, ay-thawn'; from an unused root (mean. to continue); permanence; hence, (concr.) permanent; spec. a chieftain:— hard, mighty, rough, strength, strong.

387. אֵיתָן 'Êythân, ay-thawn'; the same as 386; permanent; Ethan, the name of four Isr.:— Ethan.

388. אֵיתָנִים Êythânîym, ay-thaw-neem'; plur. of 386; always with the art.; the permanent brooks; Ethanim, the name of a month:— Ethanim.

389. אַךְ 'ak, ak; akin to 403; a particle of af-

firmation, surely; hence, (by limitation) only:— also, in any wise, at least, but, certainly, even, howbeit, nevertheless, notwithstanding, only, save, surely, of a surety, truly, verily, + wherefore, yet (but).

390. אַכַּד 'Akkad, ak-kad'; from an unused root prob. mean. to strengthen; a fortress; Accad, a place in Bab.:— Accad.

391. אַכְזָב 'akzâb, ak-zawb'; from 3576; falsehood; by impl. treachery:— liar, lie.

392. אַכְזִיב 'Akzîyb, ak-zeeb'; from 391; deceitful (in the sense of a winter-torrent which fails in summer); Akzib, the name of two places in Pal.:— Achzib.

393. אַכְזָר 'akzâr, ak-zawr'; from an unused root (appar. mean. to act harshly); violent; by impl. deadly; also (in a good sense) brave:— cruel, fierce.

394. אַכְזָרִי 'akzârîy, ak-zaw-ree'; from 393; terrible:— cruel (one).

395. אַכְזְרִיּוּת 'akzᵉrîyûwth, ak-ze-ree-ooth'; from 394; fierceness:— cruel.

396. אֲכִילָה 'ăkîylâh, ak-ee-law'; fem. from 398; something eatable, i.e. food:— meat.

397. אָכִישׁ 'Âkîysh, aw-keesh'; of uncert. der.; Akish, a Philistine king:— Achish.

398. אָכַל 'âkal, aw-kal'; a prim. root; to eat (lit. or fig.):— × at all, burn up, consume, devour (-er, up), dine, eat (-er, up), feed (with), food, × freely, × in … wise (-deed, plenty), (lay) meat, × quite.

399. אֲכַל 'ăkal (Chald.), ak-al'; corresp. to 398:— + accuse, devour, eat.

400. אֹכֶל 'ôkel, o'-kel; from 398; food:— eating, food, meal [-time], meat, prey, victuals.

401. אֻכָל 'Ûkâl, oo-kawl'; or

אֻכָּל 'Ukkâl, ook-kawl'; appar. from 398; devoured; Ucal, a fancy name:— Ucal.

402. אָכְלָה 'oklâh, ok-law'; fem. of 401; food:— consume, devour, eat, food, meat.

403. אָכֵן 'âkên, aw-kane'; from 3559 [comp. 3651]; firmly; fig. surely; also (advers.) but:— but, certainly, nevertheless, surely, truly, verily.

404. אָכַף 'âkaph, aw-kaf'; a prim. root; appar. mean. to curve (as with a burden); to urge:— crave.

405. אֶכֶף 'ekeph, eh'-kef; from 404; a load; by impl. a stroke (others dignity):— hand.

406. אִכָּר 'ikkâr, ik-kawr'; from an unused root mean. to dig; a farmer:— husbandman, ploughman.

407. אַכְשָׁף 'Akshâph, ak-shawf'; from 3784; fascination; Acshaph, a place in Pal.:— Achshaph.

408. אַל 'al, al; a neg. particle [akin to 3808];

not (the qualified negation, used as a deprecative); once (Job 24:25) as a noun, *nothing:*— nay, neither, + never, no, nor, not, nothing [worth], rather than.

409. אַל **'al** (Chald.), *al;* corresp. to 408:— not.

410. אֵל **'êl**, *ale;* short. from 352; *strength;* as adj. *mighty;* espec. the *Almighty* (but used also of any *deity*):— God (god), × goodly, × great, idol, might (-y one), power, strong. Comp. names in "-el."

411. אֵל **'êl**, *ale;* a demonstr. particle (but only in a plur. sense) *these* or *those:*— these, those. Comp. 428.

412. אֵל **'êl** (Chald.), *ale;* corresp. to 411:— these.

413. אֵל **'êl**, *ale;* (but only used in the short. constr. form

אֶל **'el**, *el*); a prim. particle; prop. denoting motion *towards*, but occasionally used for a quiescent position, i.e. *near, with* or *among;* often in general, *to:*— about, according to, after, against, among, as for, at, because (-fore, -side), both ... and, by, concerning, for, from, × hath, in (-to), near, (out) of, over, through, to (-ward), under, unto, upon, whether, with (-in).

414. אֵלָא **'Êlâ**, *ay-law';* a var. of 424; *oak; Ela*, an Isr.:— Elah.

415. אֵל אֱלֹהֵי יִשְׂרָאֵל **'Êl 'ĕlôhêy Yisrâ'êl**, *ale el-o-hay' yis-raw-ale';* from 410 and 430 and 3478; the *mighty God of Jisrael; El-Elohi-Jisrael*, the title given to a consecrated spot by Jacob:— El-elohe-israel.

416. אֵל בֵּית־אֵל **'Êl Bêyth-'Êl**, *ale bayth-ale';* from 410 and 1008; the *God of Bethel; El-Bethel*, the title given to a consecrated spot by Jacob:— El-beth-el.

417. אֶלְגָּבִישׁ **'elgâbîysh**, *el-gaw-beesh';* from 410 and 1378; *hail* (as if a *great pearl*):— great hail [-stones].

418. אַלְגּוּמִּים **'algûwmmîym**, *al-goom-meem';* by transp. for 484; *sticks of algum wood:*— algum [trees].

419. אֶלְדָּד **'Eldâd**, *el-dâd';* from 410 and 1730; *God has loved; Eldad*, an Isr.:— Eldad.

420. אֶלְדָּעָה **'Eldâ'âh**, *el-daw-aw';* from 410 and 3045; *God of knowledge; Eldaah*, a son of Midian:— Eldaah.

421. אָלָה **'âlâh**, *aw-law';* a prim. root [rather ident. with 422 through the idea of *invocation*]; to *bewail:*— lament.

422. אָלָה **'âlâh**, *aw-law';* a prim. root; prop. to *adjure*, i.e. (usually in a bad sense) *imprecate:*— adjure, curse, swear.

423. אָלָה **'âlâh**, *aw-law';* from 422; an *imprecation:*— curse, cursing, execration, oath, swearing.

424. אֵלָה **'êlâh**, *ay-law';* fem. of 352; an *oak* or other strong tree:— elm, oak, teil tree.

425. אֵלָה **'Êlâh**, *ay-law';* the same as 424; *Elah*, the name of an Edomite, of four Isr., and also of a place in Pal.:— Elah.

426. אֱלָהּ **'ĕlâhh** (Chald.), *el-aw';* corresp. to 433; *God:*— God, god.

427. אַלָּה **'allâh**, *al-law';* a var. of 424:— oak.

428. אֵלֶּה **'êl-leh**, *ale'-leh;* prol. from 411; *these* or *those:*— an(the) other; one sort, so, some, such, them, these (same), they, this, those, thus, which, who (-m).

429. אֵלֶּה **'êlleh** (Chald.), *ale'-leh;* corresp. to 428:— these.

אֱלָהּ **'ĕlôahh**. See 433.

430. אֱלֹהִים **'ĕlôhîym**, *el-o-heem';* plur. of 433; *gods* in the ordinary sense; but spec. used (in the plur. thus, espec. with the art.) of the supreme *God;* occasionally applied by way of deference to *magistrates;* and sometimes as a superlative:— angels, × exceeding, God (gods) (-dess, -ly), × (very) great, judges, × mighty.

431. אֲלוּ **'ălûw** (Chald.), *al-oo';* prob. prol. from 412; *lo!:*— behold.

432. אִלּוּ **'illûw**, *il-loo';* prob. from 408; *nay*, i.e. (softened) *if:*— but if, yea though.

433. אֱלוֹהַּ **'ĕlôwahh**, *el-o'-ah;* rarely (short.)

אֱלֹהַּ **'ĕlôahh**, *el-o'-ah;* prob. prol. (emphat.) from 410; a *deity* or the *Deity:*— God, god. See 430.

434. אֱלוּל **'ĕlûwl**, *el-ool';* for 457; *good for nothing:*— thing of nought.

435. אֱלוּל **'Êlûwl**, *el-ool';* prob. of for. der.; *Elul*, the sixth Jewish month:— Elul.

436. אֵלוֹן **'êlôwn**, *ay-lone';* prol. from 352; an *oak* or other strong tree:— plain. See also 356.

437. אַלּוֹן **'allôwn**, *al-lone';* a var. of 436:— oak.

438. אַלּוֹן **'Allôwn**, *al-lone';* the same as 437; *Allon*, an Isr., also a place in Pal.:— Allon.

439. אַלּוֹן בָּכוּת **'Allôwn Bâkûwth**, *al-lone' baw-kooth';* from 437 and a var. of 1068; *oak of weeping; Allon-Bakuth*, a monumental tree:— Allon-bachuth.

440. אֵלוֹנִי **'Êlôwnîy**, *ay-lo-nee';* or rather (short.)

אֵלֹנִי **'Êlônîy**, *ay-lo-nee';* patron. from 438; an *Elonite* or desc. (collect.) of Elon:— Elonites.

441. אַלּוּף **'allûwph**, *al-loof';* or (short.)

אַלֻּף **'allûph**, *al-loof';* from 502; *familiar;* a *friend*, also *gentle;* hence, a *bullock* (as being tame; applied, although masc., to a *cow*); and so, a *chieftain* (as notable, like neat cattle):— captain, duke, (chief) friend, governor, guide, ox.

442. אֵלוּשׁ **'Âlûwsh**, *aw-loosh'*; of uncert. der.; *Alush*, a place in the Desert:— Alush.

443. אֶלְזָבָד **'Elzâbâd**, *el-zaw-bawd'*; from 410 and 2064; *God has bestowed; Elzabad*, the name of two Isr.:— Elzabad.

444. אָלַח **'âlach**, *aw-lakh'*; a prim. root; to *muddle*, i.e. (fig. and intr.) to *turn* (morally) *corrupt:*— become filthy.

445. אֶלְחָנָן **'Elchânân**, *el-khaw-nawn'*; from 410 and 2603; *God (is) gracious; Elchanan*, an Isr.:— Elkanan.

אֵלִי **'Êlîy**. See 1017.

446. אֱלִיאָב **'Elîy'âb**, *el-ee-awb'*; from 410 and 1; *God of (his) father; Eliab*, the name of six Isr.:— Eliab.

447. אֱלִיאֵל **'Elîy'êl**, *el-ee-ale'*; from 410 repeated; *God of (his) God; Eliel*, the name of nine Isr.:— Eliel.

448. אֱלִיאָתָה **'Elîy'âthâh**, *el-ee-aw-thaw'*; or (contr.)

אֱלִיתָה **'Elîyâthâh**, *el-ee-yaw-thaw'*; from 410 and 225; *God of (his) consent; Eliathah*, an Isr.:— Eliathah.

449. אֱלִידָד **'Elîydâd**, *el-ee-dawd'*; from the same as 419; *God of (his) love; Elidad*, an Isr.:— Elidad.

450. אֶלְיָדָע **'Elyâdâ'**, *el-yaw-daw'*; from 410 and 3045; *God (is) knowing; Eljada*, the name of two Isr. and of an Aramaean leader:— Eliada.

451. אַלְיָה **'alyâh**, *al-yaw'*; from 422 (in the orig. sense of *strength*); the *stout* part, i.e. the fat *tail* of the Oriental sheep:— rump.

452. אֵלִיָּה **'Êlîyâh**, *ay-lee-yaw'*; or prol.

אֵלִיָּהוּ **'Êlîyâhûw**, *ay-lee-yaw'-hoo*; from 410 and 3050; *God of Jehovah; Elijah*, the name of the famous prophet and of two other Isr.:— Elijah, Eliah.

453. אֱלִיהוּ **'Elîyhûw**, *el-ee-hoo'*; or (fully)

אֱלִיהוּא **'Elîyhûw'**, *el-ee-hoo'*; from 410 and 1931; *God of him; Elihu*, the name of one of Job's friends, and of three Isr.:— Elihu.

454. אֶלְיְהוֹעֵינַי **'Elyᵉhôw'êynay**, *el-ye-ho-ay-nah'ee*; or (short.)

אֶלְיוֹעֵינַי **'Elyôw'êynay**, *el-yo-ay-nah'ee*; from 413 and 3068 and 5869; *toward Jehovah (are) my eyes; Eljehoenai* or *Eljoenai*, the name of seven Isr.:— Elihoenai, Elionai.

455. אֶלְיַחְבָּא **'Elyachbâ'**, *el-yakh-baw'*; from 410 and 2244; *God will hide; Eljachba*, an Isr.:— Eliahbah.

456. אֱלִיחֹרֶף **'Elîychôreph**, *el-ee-kho'-ref*; from 410 and 2779; *God of autumn; Elichoreph*, an Isr.:— Elihoreph.

457. אֱלִיל **'ĕlîyl**, *el-eel'*; appar. from 408; good for *nothing*, by anal. *vain* or *vanity*; spec. an *idol:*— idol, no value, thing of nought.

458. אֱלִימֶלֶךְ **'Elîymelek**, *el-ee-meh'-lek*; from 410 and 4428; *God of (the) king; Elimelek*, an Isr.:— Elimelech.

459. אִלֵּין **'illêyn** (Chald.), *il-lane'*; or short.

אִלֵּן **'illên**, *il-lane'*; prol. from 412; *these:*— the, these.

460. אֶלְיָסָף **'Elyâçâph**, *el-yaw-sawf'*; from 410 and 3254; *God (is) gatherer; Eljasaph*, the name of two Isr.:— Eliasaph.

461. אֱלִיעֶזֶר **'Elîy'ezer**, *el-ee-eh'-zer*; from 410 and 5828; *God of help; Eliezer*, the name of a Damascene and of ten Isr.:— Eliezer.

462. אֱלִיעֵינַי **'Elîy'êynay**, *el-ee-ay-nah'ee*; prob. contr. for 454; *Elienai*, an Isr.:— Elienai.

463. אֱלִיעָם **'Elîy'âm**, *el-ee-awm'*; from 410 and 5971; *God of (the) people; Eliam*, an Isr.:— Eliam.

464. אֱלִיפַז **'Elîyphaz**, *el-ee-faz'*; from 410 and 6337; *God of gold; Eliphaz*, the name of one of Job's friends, and of a son of Esau:— Eliphaz.

465. אֱלִיפָל **'Elîyphâl**, *el-ee-fawl'*; from 410 and 6419; *God of judgment; Eliphal*, an Isr.:— Eliphal.

466. אֱלִיפְלֵהוּ **'Elîyphᵉlêhûw**, *el-ee-fe-lay'-hoo*; from 410 and 6395; *God of his distinction; Eliphelehu*, an Isr.:— Elipheleh.

467. אֱלִיפֶלֶט **'Elîyphele**ṭ, *el-ee-feh'-let*; or (short.)

אֶלְפֶּלֶט **'Elpele**ṭ, *el-peh'-let*; from 410 and 6405; *God of deliverance; Eliphelet* or *Elpelet*, the name of six Isr.:— Eliphalet, Eliphelet, Elpalet.

468. אֱלִיצוּר **'Elîytsûwr**, *el-ee-tsoor'*; from 410 and 6697; *God of (the) rock; Elitsur*, an Isr.:— Elizur.

469. אֱלִיצָפָן **'Elîytsâphân**, *el-ee-tsaw-fawn'*; or (short.)

אֶלְצָפָן **'Eltsâphân**, *el-tsaw-fawn'*; from 410 and 6845; *God of treasure; Elitsaphan* or *Eltsaphan*, an Isr.:— Elizaphan, Elzaphan.

470. אֱלִיקָא **'Elîyqâ'**, *el-ee-kaw'*; from 410 and 6958; *God of rejection; Elika*, an Isr.:— Elika.

471. אֶלְיָקִים **'Elyâqîym**, *el-yaw-keem'*; from 410 and 6965; *God of raising; Eljakim*, the name of four Isr.:— Eliakim.

472. אֱלִישֶׁבַע **'Elîysheba'**, *el-ee-sheh'-bah*; from 410 and 7651 (in the sense of 7650); *God of (the) oath; Elisheba*, the wife of Aaron:— Elisheba.

473. אֱלִישָׁה **'Elîyshâh**, *el-ee-shaw´*; prob. of for. der.; *Elishah*, a son of Javan:— Elishah.

474. אֱלִישׁוּעַ **'Elîyshûwa'**, *el-ee-shoo´-ah*; from 410 and 7769; *God of supplication* (or *of riches*); *Elishua*, a son of King David:— Elishua.

475. אֶלְיָשִׁיב **'Elyâshîyb**, *el-yaw-sheeb´*; from 410 and 7725; *God will restore*; *Eljashib*, the name of six Isr.:— Eliashib.

476. אֱלִישָׁמָע **'Elîyshâmâ'**, *el-ee-shaw-maw´*; from 410 and 8085; *God of hearing*; *Elishama*, the name of seven Isr.:— Elishama.

477. אֱלִישָׁע **'Elîyshâ'**, *el-ee-shaw´*; contr. for 474; *Elisha*, the famous prophet:— Elisha.

478. אֱלִישָׁפָט **'Elîyshâphât**, *el-ee-shaw-fawt´*; from 410 and 8199; *God of judgment*; *Elishaphat*, an Isr.:— Elishaphat.

אֱלִיָּתָה **'Elîyâthâh**. See 448.

479. אִלֵּךְ **'illêk** (Chald.), *il-lake´*; prol. from 412; *these*:— these, those.

480. אַלְלַי **'al°lay**, *al-le-lah´ee*; by redupl. from 421; *alas!*:— woe.

481. אָלַם **'âlam**, *aw-lam´*; a prim. root; to *tie fast*; hence, (of the mouth) to be *tongue-tied*:— bind, be dumb, put to silence.

482. אֵלֶם **'êlem**, *ay´-lem*; from 481; *silence* (i.e. mute justice):— congregation. Comp. 3128.

אֵלָם **'êlâm**. See 361.

אָלֻם **'âlûm**. See 485.

483. אִלֵּם **'illêm**, *il-lame´*; from 481; *speechless*:— dumb (man).

484. אַלְמֻגִּים **'almuggiym**, *al-moog-gheem´*; prob. of for. der. (used thus only in the plur.); *almug* (i.e. prob. sandal-wood) sticks:— almug trees. Comp. 418.

485. אֲלֻמָּה **'ălummâh**, *al-oom-maw´*; or (masc.)

אָלֻם **'âlûm**, *aw-loom´*; pass. part. of 481; something *bound*; a *sheaf*:— sheaf.

486. אַלְמוֹדָד **'Almôwdâd**, *al-mo-dawd´*; prob. of for. der.; *Almodad*, a son of Joktan:— Almodad.

487. אַלַּמֶּלֶךְ **'Allammelek**, *al-lam-meh´-lek*; from 427 and 4428; *oak of* (the) *king*; *Allammelek*, a place in Pal.:— Alammelech.

488. אַלְמָן **'almân**, *al-mawn´*; prol. from 481 in the sense of *bereavement*; *discarded* (as a divorced person):— forsaken.

489. אַלְמֹן **'almôn**, *al-mone´*; from 481 as in 488; *bereavement*:— widowhood.

490. אַלְמָנָה **'almânâh**, *al-maw-naw´*; fem. of 488; a *widow*; also a *desolate* place:— desolate house (palace), widow.

491. אַלְמָנוּת **'almânûwth**, *al-maw-nooth´*; fem. of 488; concr. a *widow*; abstr. *widowhood*:— widow, widowhood.

492. אַלְמֹנִי **'almônîy**, *al-mo-nee´*; from 489 in the sense of *concealment*; *some* one (i.e. *so and so*, without giving the name of the person or place):— one, and such.

אִלֵּן **'illên**. See 459.

אֵלֹנִי **'Êlônîy**. See 440.

493. אֶלְנַעַם **'Elna'am**, *el-nah´-am*; from 410 and 5276; *God* (is his) *delight*; *Elnaam*, an Isr.:— Elnaam.

494. אֶלְנָתָן **'Elnâthân**, *el-naw-thawn´*; from 410 and 5414; *God* (is the) *giver*; *Elnathan*, the name of four Isr.:— Elnathan.

495. אֶלָּסָר **'Ellâçâr**, *el-law-sawr´*; prob. of for. der.; *Ellasar*, an early country of Asia:— Ellasar.

496. אֶלְעָד **'El'âd**, *el-awd´*; from 410 and 5749; *God has testified*; *Elad*, an Isr.:— Elead.

497. אֶלְעָדָה **'El'âdâh**, *el-aw-daw´*; from 410 and 5710; *God has decked*; *Eladah*, an Isr.:— Eladah.

498. אֶלְעוּזַי **'El'ûwzay**, *el-oo-zah´ee*; from 410 and 5756 (in the sense of 5797); *God* (is) *defensive*; *Eluzai*, an Isr.:— Eluzai.

499. אֶלְעָזָר **'El'âzâr**, *el-aw-zawr´*; from 410 and 5826; *God* (is) *helper*; *Elazar*, the name of seven Isr.:— Eleazar.

500. אֶלְעָלֵא **'El'âlê'**, *el-aw-lay´*; or (more prop.)

אֶלְעָלֵה **'El'âlêh**, *el-aw-lay´*; from 410 and 5927; *God* (is) *going up*; *Elale* or *Elaleh*, a place east of the Jordan:— Elealeh.

501. אֶלְעָשָׂה **'El'âsâh**, *el-aw-saw´*; from 410 and 6213; *God has made*; *Elasah*, the name of four Isr.:— Elasah, Eleasah.

502. אָלַף **'âlaph**, *aw-laf´*; a prim. root, to *associate* with; hence, to *learn* (and caus. to *teach*):— learn, teach, utter.

503. אָלַף **'âlaph**, *aw-laf´*; denom. from 505; caus. to *make a thousandfold*:— bring forth thousands.

504. אֶלֶף **'eleph**, *eh´-lef*; from 502; a *family*; also (from the sense of *yoking* or *taming*) an *ox* or *cow*:— family, kine, oxen.

505. אֶלֶף **'eleph**, *eh´-lef*; prop. the same as 504; hence, (the ox's head being the first letter of the alphabet, and this eventually used as a numeral) a *thousand*:— thousand.

506. אֲלַף **'ălaph** (Chald.), *al-af´*; or

אֶלֶף **'eleph** (Chald.), *eh´-lef*; corresp. to 505:— thousand.

507. אֶלֶף **'Eleph**, *eh´-lef*; the same as 505; *Eleph*, a place in Pal.:— Eleph.

אַלֻּף **'allûph**. See 441.

אֶלְפֶּלֶט **'Elpelet**. See 467.

508. אֶלְפַּעַל **'Elpa'al**, *el-pah´-al;* from 410 and 6466; *God* (is) *act; Elpaal*, an Isr.:— Elpaal.

509. אָלַץ **'âlats**, *aw-lats´;* a prim. root; to *press:*— urge.

אֶלְצָפָן **'Eltsâphân**. See 469.

510. אַלְקוּם **'alqûwm**, *al-koom´;* prob. from 408 and 6965; a *non-rising* (i.e. *resistlessness*):— no rising up.

511. אֶלְקָנָה **'Elqânâh**, *el-kaw-naw´;* from 410 and 7069; *God has obtained; Elkanah,* the name of several Isr.:— Elkanah.

512. אֶלְקֹשִׁי **'Elqôshîy**, *el-ko-shee´;* patrial from a name of uncert. der.; an *Elkoshite* or native of Elkosh:— Elkoshite.

513. אֶלְתּוֹלַד **'Eltôwlad**, *el-to-lad´;* prob. from 410 and a masc. form of 8435 [comp. 8434]; *God* (is) *generator; Eltolad,* a place in Pal.:— Eltolad.

514. אֶלְתְּקֵא **'Elt^eqê'**, *el-te-kay´;* or (more prop.)

אֶלְתְּקֵה **'Elt^eqêh**, *el-te-kay´;* of uncert. der.; *Eltekeh* or *Elteke,* a place in Pal.:— Eltekeh.

515. אֶלְתְּקֹן **'Elt^eqôn**, *el-te-kone´;* from 410 and 8626; *God* (is) *straight; Eltekon,* a place in Pal.:— Eltekon.

516. אַל תַּשְׁחֵת **'Al tashchêth**, *al tash-kayth´;* from 408 and 7843; *Thou must not destroy;* prob. the opening words of a popular song:— Al-taschith.

517. אֵם **'êm**, *ame;* a prim. word; a *mother* (as the *bond* of the family); in a wide sense (both lit. and fig. [like 1]:— dam, mother, × parting.

518. אִם **'îm**, *eem;* a prim. particle; used very widely as demonstr., *lo!;* interrog., *whether?;* or conditional, *if, although;* also *Oh that!, when;* hence, as a neg., *not:*— (and, can-, doubtless, if, that) (not), + but, either, + except, + more (-over if, than), neither, nevertheless, nor, oh that, or, + save (only, -ing), seeing, since, sith, + surely (no more, none, not), though, + of a truth, + unless, + verily, when, whereas, whether, while, + yet.

519. אָמָה **'âmâh**, *aw-maw´;* appar. a prim. word; a *maid-servant* or female *slave:*— (hand-) bondmaid (-woman), maid (-servant).

אֵמָה **'êmâh**. See 367.

520. אַמָּה **'ammâh**, *am-maw´;* prol. from 517; prop. a *mother* (i.e. *unit* of measure, or the *fore-arm* (below the elbow), i.e. a *cubit;* also a door-*base* (as a *bond* of the entrance):— cubit, + hundred [by exchange for 3967], measure, post.

521. אַמָּה **'ammâh** (Chald.), *am-maw´;* corresp. to 520:— cubit.

522. אַמָּה **'Ammâh**, *am-maw´;* the same as 520; *Ammah,* a hill in Pal.:— Ammah.

523. אֻמָּה **'ummâh**, *oom-maw´;* from the same as 517; a *collection,* i.e. community of persons:— nation, people.

524. אֻמָּה **'ummâh** (Chald.), *oom-maw´;* corresp. to 523:— nation.

525. אָמוֹן **'âmôwn**, *aw-mone´;* from 539, prob. in the sense of *training; skilled,* i.e. an architect [like 542]:— one brought up.

526. אָמוֹן **'Âmôwn**, *aw-mone´;* the same as 525; *Amon,* the name of three Isr.:— Amon.

527. אָמוֹן **'âmôwn**, *aw-mone´;* a var. for 1995; a *throng* of people:— multitude.

528. אָמוֹן **'Âmôwn**, *aw-mone´;* of Eg. der.; *Amon* (i.e. Ammon or Amn), a deity of Egypt (used only as an adjunct of 4996):— multitude, populous.

529. אֵמוּן **'êmûwn**, *ay-moon´;* from 539; *established,* i.e. (fig.) *trusty;* also (abstr.) *trustworthiness:*— faith (-ful), truth.

530. אֱמוּנָה **'ĕmûwnâh**, *em-oo-naw´;* or (short.)

אֱמֻנָה **'ĕmûnâh**, *em-oo-naw´;* fem. of 529; lit. *firmness;* fig. *security;* mor. *fidelity:*— faith (-ful, -ly, -ness, [man]), set office, stability, steady, truly, truth, verily.

531. אָמוֹץ **'Âmôwts**, *aw-mohts´;* from 553; *strong; Amots,* an Isr.:— Amoz.

532. אָמִי **'Âmîy**, *aw-mee´;* an abbrev. for 526; *Ami,* an Isr.:— Ami.

אֲמִינוֹן **'Ămîynôwn**. See 550.

533. אַמִּיץ **'ammîyts**, *am-meets´;* or (short.)

אַמִּץ **'ammîts**, *am-meets´;* from 553; *strong* or (abstr.) *strength:*— courageous, mighty, strong (one).

534. אָמִיר **'âmîyr**, *aw-meer´;* appar. from 559 (in the sense of *self-exaltation*); a *summit* (of a tree or mountain:— bough, branch.

535. אָמַל **'âmal**, *aw-mal´;* a prim. root; to *droop;* by impl. to *be sick,* to *mourn:*— languish, be weak, wax feeble.

536. אֻמְלַל **'umlal**, *oom-lal´;* from 535; *sick:*— weak.

537. אֲמֵלָל **'ămêlâl**, *am-ay-lawl´;* from 535; *languid:*— feeble.

538. אָמָם **'Âmâm**, *am-awm´;* from 517; *gathering*-spot; *Amam,* a place in Pal.:— Amam.

539. אָמַן **'âman**, *aw-man´;* a prim. root; prop. to *build up* or *support;* to *foster* as a parent or nurse; fig. to *render* (or *be*) *firm* or faithful, to *trust* or believe, to *be permanent* or quiet; mor. to *be true* or certain; once (Isa. 30:21; interch. for 541) to *go to the right hand:*— hence, assurance, believe,

bring up, establish, + fail, be faithful (of long continuance, stedfast, sure, surely, trusty, verified), nurse, (-ing father), (put), trust, turn to the right.

540. אֲמַן **'ăman** (Chald.), *am-an´;* corresp. to 539:— believe, faithful, sure.

541. אָמַן **'âman**, *aw-man´;* denom. from 3225; to take the *right hand* road:— turn to the right. See 539.

542. אָמָן **'âmân**, *aw-mawn´;* from 539 (in the sense of *training*); an *expert:*— cunning workman.

543. אָמֵן **'âmên**, *aw-mane´;* from 539; *sure;* abstr. *faithfulness;* adv. *truly:*— Amen, so be it, truth.

544. אֹמֶן **'ômen**, *oh-men´;* from 539; *verity:*— truth.

545. אָמְנָה **'omnâh**, *om-naw´;* fem. of 544 (in the spec. sense of *training*); *tutelage:*— brought up.

546. אָמְנָה **'omnâh**, *om-naw´;* fem. of 544 (in its usual sense); adv. *surely:*— indeed.

547. אֹמְנָה **'ômᵉnâh**, *om-me-naw´;* fem. act. part. of 544 (in the orig. sense of *supporting*); a *column:*— pillar.

548. אֲמָנָה **'ămânâh**, *am-aw-naw´;* fem. of 543; something *fixed*, i.e. a *covenant*, an *allowance:*— certain portion, sure.

549. אֲמָנָה **'Ămânâh**, *am-aw-naw´;* the same as 548; *Amanah*, a mountain near Damascus:— Amana.

אֱמוּנָה **'ĕmûnâh**. See 530.

550. אַמְנוֹן **'Amnôwn**, *am-nohn´;* or

אֲמִינוֹן **'Ămîynôwn**, *am-ee-nohn´;* from 539; *faithful; Amnon* (or Aminon), a son of David:— Amnon.

551. אָמְנָם **'omnâm**, *om-nawm´;* adv. from 544; *verily:*— indeed, no doubt, surely, (it is, of a) true (-ly, -th).

552. אֻמְנָם **'umnâm**, *oom-nawm´;* an orth. var. of 551:— in (very) deed; of a surety.

553. אָמַץ **'âmats**, *aw-mats´;* a prim. root; to *be alert*, phys. (on foot) or ment. (in courage):— confirm, be courageous (of good courage, stedfastly minded, strong, stronger), establish, fortify, harden, increase, prevail, strengthen (self), make strong (obstinate, speed).

554. אָמֹץ **'âmôts**, *aw-mohts´;* prob. from 553; of a *strong* color, i.e. *red* (others *fleet*):— bay.

555. אֹמֶץ **'ômets**, *o´-mets;* from 553; *strength:*— stronger.

אַמִּיץ **'ammîts**. See 533.

556. אַמְצָה **'amtsâh**, *am-tsaw´;* from 553; *force:*— strength.

557. אַמְצִי **'Amtsîy**, *am-tsee´;* from 553; *strong; Amtsi*, an Isr.:— Amzi.

558. אֲמַצְיָה **'Ămatsyâh**, *am-ats-yaw´;* or

אֲמַצְיָהוּ **'Ămatsyâhûw**, *am-ats-yaw´-hoo;* from 553 and 3050; *strength of Jah; Amatsjah*, the name of four Isr.:— Amaziah.

559. אָמַר **'âmar**, *aw-mar´;* a prim. root; to *say* (used with great latitude):— answer, appoint, avouch, bid, boast self, call, certify, challenge, charge, + (at the, give) command (-ment), commune, consider, declare, demand, × desire, determine, × expressly, × indeed, × intend, name, × plainly, promise, publish, report, require, say, speak (against, of), × still, × suppose, talk, tell, term, × that is, × think, use [speech], utter, × verily, × yet.

560. אֲמַר **'ămar** (Chald.), *am-ar´;* corresp. to 559:— command, declare, say, speak, tell.

561. אֵמֶר **'êmer**, *ay´-mer;* from 559; something *said:*— answer, × appointed unto him, saying, speech, word.

562. אֹמֶר **'ômer**, *o´-mer;* the same as 561:— promise, speech, thing, word.

563. אִמַּר **'immar** (Chald.), *im-mar´;* perh. from 560 (in the sense of *bringing forth*); a *lamb:*— lamb.

564. אִמֵּר **'Immêr**, *im-mare´;* from 559; *talkative; Immer*, the name of five Isr.:— Immer.

565. אִמְרָה **'imrâh**, *im-raw´;* or

אֶמְרָה **'emrâh**, *em-raw´;* fem. of 561, and mean. the same:— commandment, speech, word.

566. אִמְרִי **'Imrîy**, *im-ree´;* from 564; *wordy; Imri*, the name of two Isr.:— Imri.

567. אֱמֹרִי **'Ĕmôrîy**, *em-o-ree´;* prob. a patron. from an unused name derived from 559 in the sense of *publicity*, i.e. prominence; thus, a *mountaineer*; an *Emorite*, one of the Canaanitish tribes:— Amorite.

568. אֲמַרְיָה **'Ămaryâh**, *am-ar-yaw´;* or prol.

אֲמַרְיָהוּ **'Ămaryâhûw**, *am-ar-yaw´-hoo;* from 559 and 3050; *Jah has said* (i.e. promised); *Amarjah*, the name of nine Isr.:— Amariah.

569. אַמְרָפֶל **'Amrâphel**, *am-raw-fel´;* of uncert. (perh. for.) der.; *Amraphel*, a king of Shinar:— Amraphel.

570. אֶמֶשׁ **'emesh**, *eh´-mesh;* time *past*, i.e. *yesterday* or *last night:*— former time, yesterday (-night).

571. אֱמֶת **'emeth**, *eh´-meth;* contr. from 539; *stability;* fig. *certainty, truth, trustworthiness:*— assured (-ly), establishment, faithful, right, sure, true (-ly, -th), verity.

572. אַמְתַּחַת 'amtêchath, *am-taykh´-ath;* from 4969; prop. something *expansive,* i.e. a *bag:*—sack.

573. אֲמִתַּי 'Ămittay, *am-it-tah´ee;* from 571; *veracious; Amittai,* an Isr.:— Amittai.

574. אֵמְתָנִי 'emtânîy (Chald.), *em-taw-nee´;* from a root corresp. to that of 4975; *well-loined* (i.e. burly) or *mighty:*— terrible.

575. אָן 'ân, *awn;* or

אָנָה 'ânâh, *aw-naw´;* contr. from 370; *where?;* hence, *whither?, when?;* also *hither* and *thither:*— + any (no) whither, now, where, whither (-soever).

אָן 'Ôn. See 204.

576. אֲנָא 'ănâ' (Chald.), *an-aw´;* or

אֲנָה 'ănâh (Chald.), *an-aw´;* corresp. to 589; *I:*— I, as for me.

577. אָנָּא 'ânnâ', *awn-naw´;* or

אָנָּה 'ânnâh, *awn-naw´;* appar. contr. from 160 and 4994; *oh now!:*— I (me) beseech (pray) thee, O.

אֲנָה 'ănâh. See 576.

אָנָה 'ânâh. See 575.

578. אָנָה 'ânâh, *aw-naw´;* a prim. root; to *groan:*— lament, mourn.

579. אָנָה 'ânâh, *aw-naw´;* a prim. root [perh. rather ident. with 578 through the idea of *contraction* in anguish]; to *approach;* hence, to *meet* in various senses:— befall, deliver, happen, seek a quarrel.

אָנָּה 'ânnâh. See 577.

580. אֲנוּ 'ănûw, *an-oo´;* contr. for 587; *we:*— we.

אֹנוֹ 'Ônôw. See 207.

581. אִנּוּן 'innûwn (Chald.), *in-noon´;* or (fem.)

אִנִּין 'innîyn (Chald.), *in-neen´;* corresp. to 1992; *they:*— × are, them, these.

582. אֱנוֹשׁ 'ĕnôwsh, *en-oshe´;* from 605; prop. a *mortal* (and thus differing from the more dignified 120); hence, a *man* in gen. (singly or collect.):— another, × [blood-] thirsty, certain, chap [-man]; divers, fellow, × in the flower of their age, husband, (certain, mortal) man, people, person, servant, some (× of them), + stranger, those, + their trade. It is often unexpressed in the English Version, espec. when used in apposition with another word. Comp. 376.

583. אֱנוֹשׁ 'Ĕnôwsh, *en-ohsh´;* the same as 582; *Enosh,* a son of Seth:— Enos.

584. אָנַח 'ânach, *aw-nakh´;* a prim. root; to *sigh:*— groan, mourn, sigh.

585. אֲנָחָה 'ănâchâh, *an-aw-khaw´;* from 584; *sighing:*— groaning, mourn, sigh.

586. אֲנַחְנָא 'ănachnâ' (Chald.), *an-akh´-naw;* or

587. אֲנַחְנָה 'ănachnâh (Chald.), *an-akh-naw´;* corresp. to 587; *we:*— we.

587. אֲנַחְנוּ 'ănachnûw, *an-akh´-noo;* appar. from 595; *we:*— ourselves, us, we.

588. אֲנָחֲרָת 'Ănâchărâth, *an-aw-khaw-rawth´;* prob. from the same root as 5170; a *gorge* or narrow pass; *Anacharath,* a place in Pal.:— Anaharath.

589. אֲנִי 'ănîy, *an-ee´;* contr. from 595; *I:*— I, (as for) me, mine, myself, we, × which, × who.

590. אֳנִי 'ŏnîy, *on-ee´;* prob. from 579 (in the sense of *conveyance);* a *ship* or (collect.) a *fleet:*— galley, navy (of ships).

591. אֳנִיָּה 'ŏnîyâh, *on-ee-yaw´;* fem. of 590; a *ship:*— ship (l-men]).

592. אֲנִיָּה 'ănîyâh, *an-ee-yaw´;* from 578; *groaning:*— lamentation, sorrow.

אַנִּין 'innîyn. See 581.

593. אֲנִיעָם 'Ănîy'âm, *an-ee-awm´;* from 578 and 5971; *groaning of* (the) *people; Aniam,* an Isr.:— Aniam.

594. אֲנָךְ 'ănâk, *an-awk´;* prob. from an unused root mean. to *be narrow;* according to most a *plumb-line,* and to others a *hook:*— plumb-line.

595. אָנֹכִי 'ânôkîy, *aw-no-kee´* (sometimes *aw-no´-kee);* a prim. pron.; *I:*— I, me, × which.

596. אָנַן 'ânan, *aw-nan´;* a prim. root; to *mourn,* i.e. *complain:*— complain.

597. אָנַס 'ânaç, *aw-nas´;* to *insist:*— compel.

598. אֲנַס 'ănaç (Chald.), *an-as´;* corresp. to 597; fig. to *distress:*— trouble.

599. אָנַף 'ânaph, *aw-naf´;* a prim. root; to *breathe* hard, i.e. *be enraged:*— be angry (displeased).

600. אֲנַף 'ănaph (Chald.), *an-af´;* corresp. to 639 (only in the plur. as a sing.); the *face:*— face, visage.

601. אֲנָפָה 'ănâphâh, *an-aw-faw´;* from 599; an unclean bird, perh. the *parrot* (from its *irascibility):*— heron.

602. אָנַק 'ânaq, *aw-nak´;* a prim. root; to *shriek:*— cry, groan.

603. אֲנָקָה 'ănâqâh, *an-aw-kaw´;* from 602; *shrieking:*— crying out, groaning, sighing.

604. אֲנָקָה 'ănâqâh, *an-aw-kaw´;* the same as 603; some kind of lizard, prob. the *gecko* (from its *wail):*— ferret.

605. אֲנַשׁ 'ânash, *aw-nash´;* a prim. root; to *be frail, feeble,* or (fig.) *melancholy:*— desperate (-ly wicked), incurable, sick, woeful.

606. אֱנָשׁ 'ĕnâsh (Chald.), *en-awsh´;* or

אֱנָשׁ **'ĕnash** (Chald.), *en-ash´;* corresp. to 582; a *man:*— man, + whosoever.

אֲנָה **'ant**. See 859.

607. אַנְתָּה **'antâh** (Chald.), *an-taw´;* corresp. to 859; *thou:*— as for thee, thou.

608. אַנְתּוּן **'antûwn** (Chald.), *an-toon´;* plur. of 607; *ye:*— ye.

609. אָסָא **'Âçâ**, *aw-saw´;* of uncert. der.; *Asa,* the name of a king and of a Levite:— Asa.

610. אָסוּךְ **'âçûwk**, *aw-sook´;* from 5480; *anointed,* i.e. an oil-*flask:*— pot.

611. אָסוֹן **'âçôwn**, *aw-sone´;* of uncert. der.; *hurt:*— mischief.

612. אֵסוּר **'êçûwr**, *ay-soor´;* from 631; a *bond* (espec. *manacles* of a prisoner):— band, + prison.

613. אֱסוּר **'ĕçûwr** (Chald.), *es-oor´;* corresp. to 612:— band, imprisonment.

614. אָסִיף **'âçîyph**, *aw-seef´;* or

אָסִף **'âçiph**, *aw-seef´;* from 622; *gathered,* i.e. (abstr.) a *gathering* in of crops:— ingathering.

615. אָסִיר **'âçîyr**, *aw-sere´;* from 631; *bound,* i.e. a *captive:*— (those which are) bound, prisoner.

616. אַסִּיר **'açç̂îyr**, *as-sere´;* for 615:— prisoner.

617. אַסִּיר **'Açç̂îyr**, *as-sere´;* the same as 616; *prisoner; Assir,* the name of two Isr.:— Assir.

618. אָסָם **'âçâm**, *aw-sawm´;* from an unused root mean. to *heap* together; a *storehouse* (only in the plur.):— barn, storehouse.

619. אַסְנָה **'Açnâh**, *as-naw´;* of uncert. der.; *Asnah,* one of the Nethinim:— Asnah.

620. אָסְנַפַּר **'Oçnappar** (Chald.), *os-nap-par´;* of for. der.; *Osnappar,* an Ass. king:— Asnapper.

621. אָסְנַת **'Âçᵉnath**, *aw-se-nath´;* of Eg. der.; *Asenath,* the wife of Joseph:— Asenath.

622. אָסַף **'âçaph**, *aw-saf´;* a prim. root; to *gather* for any purpose; hence, to *receive, take away,* i.e. remove (destroy, leave behind, put up, restore, etc.):— assemble, bring, consume, destroy, fetch, gather (in, together, up again), × generally, get (him), lose, put all together, receive, recover [another from leprosy], (be) reward, × surely, take (away, into, up), × utterly, withdraw.

623. אָסָף **'Âçâph**, *aw-sawf´;* from 622; *collector; Asaph,* the name of three Isr., and of the family of the first:— Asaph.

אָסִף **'âçiph**. See 614.

624. אָסֻף **'âçûph**, *aw-soof´;* pass. part. of 622; *collected* (only in the plur.), i.e. a *collection* (of offerings):— threshold, Asuppim.

625. אֹסֶף **'ôçeph**, *o´-sef;* from 622; a *collection* (of fruits):— gathering.

626. אֲסֵפָה **'ăçêphâh**, *as-ay-faw´;* from 622; a *collection* of people (only adv.):— × together.

627. אֲסֻפָּה **'ăçuppâh**, *as-up-paw´;* fem. of 624.; a *collection* of (learned) men (only in the plur.):— assembly.

628. אֲסַפְסֻף **'ăçpᵉçuph**, *as-pes-oof´;* by redupl. from 624; *gathered* up *together,* i.e. a promiscuous *assemblage* (of people):— mixt multitude.

629. אָסְפַּרְנָא **'oçparnâ** (Chald.), *os-par-naw´;* of Pers. der.; *diligently:*— fast, forthwith, speed (-ily).

630. אַסְפָּתָא **'Açpâthâ'**, *as-paw-thaw´;* of Pers. der.; *Aspatha,* a son of Haman:— Aspatha.

631. אָסַר **'âçar**, *aw-sar´;* a prim. root; to *yoke* or *hitch;* by anal. to *fasten* in any sense, to *join* battle:— bind, fast, gird, harness, hold, keep, make ready, order, prepare, prison (-er), put in bonds, set in array, tie.

632. אֱסָר **'ĕçâr**, *es-sawr´;* or

אִסָּר **'içç̂âr**, *is-sawr´;* from 631; an *obligation* or *vow* (of abstinence):— binding, bond.

633. אֱסָר **'ĕçâr** (Chald.), *es-sawr´;* corresp. to 632 in a legal sense; an *interdict:*— decree.

634. אֵסַר־חַדּוֹן **'Êçar-Chaddôwn**, *ay-sar´ chad-dohn´;* of for. der.; *Esar-chaddon,* an Ass. king:— Esar-haddon.

635. אֶסְתֵּר **'Eçtêr**, *es-tare´;* of Pers. der.; *Ester,* the Jewish heroine:— Esther.

636. עָע **'â'** (Chald.), *aw;* corresp. to 6086; a *tree* or *wood:*— timber, wood.

637. אַף **'aph**, *af;* a prim. particle; mean. *accession* (used as an adv. or conjunc.); *also* or *yea;* adversatively *though:*— also, + although, and (furthermore, yet), but, even, + how much less (more, rather than), moreover, with, yea.

638. אַף **'aph** (Chald.), *af;* corresp. to 637:— also.

639. אַף **'aph**, *af;* from 599; prop. the *nose* or *nostril;* hence, the *face,* and occasionally a *person;* also (from the rapid breathing in passion) *ire:*— anger (-gry), + before, countenance, face, + forebearing, forehead, + [long-] suffering, nose, nostril, snout, × worthy, wrath.

640. אָפַד **'âphad**, *aw-fad´;* a prim. root [rather a denom. from 646]; to *gird* on (the ephod):— bind, gird.

אֵפֹד **'êphôd**. See 646.

Hebrew

641. אֵפֹד **'Êphôd,** *ay-fode´;* the same as 646 short.; *Ephod,* an Isr.:— Ephod.

642. אֲפֻדָּה **'êphuddâh,** *ay-food-daw´;* fem. of 646; a *girding* on (of the ephod); hence, gen. a *plating* (of metal):— ephod, ornament.

643. אַפֶּדֶן **'appeden,** *ap-peh´-den;* appar. of for. der.; a *pavilion* or palace-tent:— palace.

644. אָפָה **'âphâh,** *aw-faw´;* a prim. root; to *cook,* espec. to *bake:*— bake (-r, [-meats]).

אֵפֹה **'êphâh.** See 374.

645. אֵפֹו **'êphôw,** *ay-fo´;* or

אֵפֹוא **'êphôw',** *ay-fo´;* from 6311; strictly a demonstr. particle, *here;* but used of time, *now* or *then:*— here, now, where?

646. אֵפֹוד **'êphôwd,** *ay-fode´;* rarely

אֵפֹד **'êphôd,** *ay-fode´;* prob. of for. der.; a *girdle;* spec. the *ephod* or high-priest's shoulder-piece; also gen. an *image:*— ephod.

647. אֲפִיחַ **'Ăphîyach,** *af-ee´-akh;* perh. from 6315; *breeze; Aphiach,* an Isr.:— Aphiah.

648. אָפִיל **'âphîyl,** *aw-feel´;* from the same as 651 (in the sense of *weakness*); *unripe:*— not grown up.

649. אַפַּיִם **'Appayim,** *ap-pah´-yim;* dual of 639; *two nostrils; Appajim,* an Isr.:— Appaim.

650. אָפִיק **'âphîyq,** *aw-feek´;* from 622; prop. *containing,* i.e. a *tube;* also a *bed* or *valley* of a stream; also a *strong* thing or a *hero:*— brook, channel, mighty, river, + scale, stream, strong piece.

אֹפִיר **'Ôphîyr.** See 211.

651. אָפֵל **'âphêl,** *aw-fale´;* from an unused root mean. to *set* as the sun; *dusky:*— very dark.

652. אֹפֶל **'ôphel,** *o´fel;* from the same as 651; *dusk:*— darkness, obscurity, privily.

653. אֲפֵלָה **'ăphêlâh,** *af-ay-law´;* fem. of 651; *duskiness,* fig. *misfortune;* concr. *concealment:*— dark, darkness, gloominess, × thick.

654. אֶפְלָל **'Ephlâl,** *ef-lawl´;* from 6419; *judge; Ephlal,* an Isr.:— Ephlal.

655. אֹפֶן **'ôphen,** *o´-fen;* from an unused root mean. to *revolve;* a *turn,* i.e. a *season:*— + fitly.

אֹפָן **'ôphân.** See 212.

656. אָפֵס **'âphêç,** *aw-face´;* a prim. root; to *disappear,* i.e. *cease:*— be clean gone (at an end, brought to nought), fail.

657. אֶפֶס **'epheç,** *eh´-fes;* from 656; *cessation,* i.e. an *end* (espec. of the earth); often used adv. *no further;* also (like 6466) the *ankle* (in the dual), as being the extremity of the leg or foot:— ankle, but (only), end, howbeit, less than nothing, nevertheless (where), no, none (beside), not (any, -withstanding), thing of nought, save (-ing), there, uttermost part, want, without (cause).

658. אֶפֶס דַּמִּים **'Epheç Dammîym,** *eh´-fes dam-meem´;* from 657 and the plur. of 1818; *boundary of blood*-drops; *Ephes-Dammim,* a place in Pal.:— Ephes-dammim.

659. אֶפַע **'êpha',** *eh´-fah;* from an unused root prob. mean. to *breathe;* prop. a *breath,* i.e. *nothing:*— of nought.

660. אֶפְעֶה **'eph'eh,** *ef-eh´;* from 659 (in the sense of *hissing*); an *asp* or other venomous serpent:— viper.

661. אָפַף **'âphaph,** *aw-faf´;* a prim. root; to *surround:*— compass.

662. אָפַק **'âphaq,** *aw-fak´;* a prim. root; to *contain,* i.e. (reflex.) *abstain:*— force (oneself), restrain.

663. אֲפֵק **'Ăphêq,** *af-ake´;* or

אֲפִיק **'Ăphîyq,** *af-eek´;* from 662 (in the sense of *strength*); *fortress; Aphek* (or *Aphik*), the name of three places in Pal.:— Aphek, Aphik.

664. אֲפֵקָה **'Ăphêqâh,** *af-ay-kaw´;* fem. of 663; *fortress; Aphekah,* a place in Pal.:— Aphekah.

665. אֵפֶר **'êpher,** *ay´-fer;* from an unused root mean. to *bestrew; ashes:*— ashes.

666. אֲפֵר **'ăphêr,** *af-ayr´;* from the same as 665 (in the sense of *covering*); a *turban:*— ashes.

667. אֶפְרֹחַ **'ephrôach,** *ef-ro´-akh;* from 6524 (in the sense of *bursting* the shell); the *brood* of a bird:— young (one).

668. אַפִּרְיֹון **'appiryôwn,** *ap-pir-yone´;* prob. of Eg. der.; a *palanquin:*— chariot.

669. אֶפְרַיִם **'Ephrayim,** *ef-rah´-yim;* dual of a masc. form of 672; *double fruit; Ephrajim,* a son of Joseph; also the tribe descended from him, and its territory:— Ephraim, Ephraimites.

670. אֲפָרְסַי **'Ăphâr^eçay** (Chald.), *af-aw-re-sah´ee;* of for. or. (only in the plur.); an *Apharesite* or inhab. of an unknown region of Assyria:— Apharsite.

671. אֲפַרְסְכַי **'Ăpharç^ekay** (Chald.), *af-ar-sek-ah´ee;* or

אֲפַרְסַתְכַי **'Ăpharçathkay** (Chald.), *af-ar-sath-kah´ee;* of for. or. (only in the plur.); an *Apharsekite* or *Apharsathkite,* an unknown Ass. tribe:— Apharsachites, Apharsathchites.

672. אֶפְרָת **'Ephrâth,** *ef-rawth´;* or

אֶפְרָתָה **'Ephrâthâh,** *ef-raw´-thaw;* from 6509; *fruitfulness; Ephrath,* another name for Bethlehem; once (Psa. 132:6) perh. for *Ephraim;* also of an Isr. woman:— Ephrath, Ephratah.

673. אֶפְרָתִי **'Ephrâthîy,** *ef-rawth-ee´;* patrial

from 672; an *Ephrathite* or an *Ephraimite*:— Ephraimite, Ephrathite.

674. אַפְּתֹם **'app^ethôm** (Chald.), *ap-pe-thome´*; of Pers. or.; *revenue; others at the last*:— revenue.

675. אֶצְבּוֹן **'Etsbôwn**, *ets-bone´*; or

אֶצְבֹּן **'Etsbôn**, *ets-bone´*; of uncert. der.; *Etsbon*, the name of two Isr.:— Ezbon.

676. אֶצְבַּע **'etsba'**, *ets-bah´*; from the same as 6648 (in the sense of *grasping*); something to *seize* with, i.e. a *finger*; by anal. a *toe*:— finger, toe.

677. אֶצְבַּע **'etsba'** (Chald.), *ets-bah´*; corresp. to 676:— finger, toe.

678. אָצִיל **'âtsîyl**, *aw-tseel´*; from 680 (in its second. sense of *separation*); an *extremity* (Isa. 41:9), also a *noble*:— chief man, noble.

679. אַצִּיל **'atstsîyl**, *ats-tseel´*; from 680 (in its primary sense of *uniting*); a *joint* of the hand (i.e. *knuckle*); also (according to some) a *party-wall* (Ezek. 41:8):— [arm] hole, great.

680. אָצַל **'âtsal**, *aw-tsal´*; a prim. root; prop. to *join*; used only as a denom. from 681; to *separate*; hence, to *select, refuse, contract*:— keep, reserve, straiten, take.

681. אֵצֶל **'êtsel**, *ay´-tsel*; from 680 (in the sense of *joining*); a *side*; (as a prep.) *near*:— at, (hard) by, (from) (beside), near (unto), toward, with. See also 1018.

682. אָצֵל **'Âtsêl**, *aw-tsale´*; from 680; *noble*; *Atsel*, the name of an Isr., and of a place in Pal.:— Azal, Azel.

683. אֲצַלְיָהוּ **'Ătsalyâhûw**, *ats-al-yaw´-hoo*; from 680 and 3050 prol.; *Jah has reserved*; *Atsaljah*, an Isr.:— Azaliah.

684. אֹצֶם **'Ôtsem**, *o´-tsem*; from an unused root prob. mean. to *be strong*; *strength* (i.e. *strong*); *Otsem*, the name of two Isr.:— Ozem.

685. אֶצְעָדָה **'ets'âdâh**, *ets-aw-daw´*; a var. from 6807; prop. a *step-chain*; by anal. a *bracelet*:— bracelet, chain.

686. אָצַר **'âtsar**, *aw-tsar´*; a prim. root; to *store up*:— (lay up in) store, (make) treasure (-r).

687. אֶצֶר **'Etser**, *ay´-tser*; from 686; *treasure*; *Etser*, an Idumæan:— Ezer.

688. אֶקְדָּח **'eqdâch**, *ek-dawkh´*; from 6916; *burning*, i.e. a *carbuncle* or other fiery gem:— carbuncle.

689. אַקּוֹ **'aqqôw**, *ak-ko´*; prob. from 602; *slender*, i.e. the *ibex*:— wild goat.

690. אֲרָא **'Ărâ'**, *ar-aw´*; prob. for 738; *lion*; *Ara*, an Isr.:— Ara.

691. אֶרְאֵל **'er'êl**, *er-ale´*; prob. for 739; a *hero* (collect.):— valiant one.

692. אַרְאֵלִי **'Ar'êlîy**, *ar-ay-lee´*; from 691; *he-*

roic; *Areli* (or an *Arelite*, collect.), an Isr. and his desc.:— Areli, Arelites.

693. אָרַב **'ârab**, *aw-rab´*; a prim. root; to *lurk*:— (lie in) ambush (-ment), lay (lie in) wait.

694. אֲרָב **'Ărâb**, *ar-awb´*; from 693; *ambush*; *Arab*, a place in Pal.:— Arab.

695. אֶרֶב **'ereb**, *eh´-reb*; from 693; *ambuscade*:— den, lie in wait.

696. אֹרֶב **'ôreb**, *o´-reb*; the same as 695:— wait.

אַרְבֵּאל **'Arbê'l**. See 1009.

697. אַרְבֶּה **'arbeh**, *ar-beh´*; from 7235; a *locust* (from its rapid *increase*):— grasshopper, locust.

698. אָרֳבָה **'orŏbâh**, *or-ob-aw´*; fem. of 696 (only in the plur.); *ambuscades*:— spoils.

699. אֲרֻבָּה **'ărubbâh**, *ar-oob-baw´*; fem. part. pass. of 693 (as if for *lurking*); a *lattice*; (by impl.) a *window, dove-cot* (because of the pigeon-holes), *chimney* (with its apertures for smoke), *sluice* (with openings for water):— chimney, window.

700. אֲרֻבּוֹת **'Ărubbôwth**, *ar-oob-both´*; plur. of 699; *Arubboth*, a place in Pal.:— Aruboth.

701. אַרְבִּי **'Arbîy**, *ar-bee´*; patrial from 694; an *Arbite* or native of Arab:— Arbite.

702. אַרְבַּע **'arba'**, *ar-bah´*; masc.

אַרְבָּעָה **'arbâ'âh**, *ar-baw-aw´*; from 7251; *four*:— four.

703. אַרְבַּע **'arba'** (Chald.), *ar-bah´*; corresp. to 702:— four.

704. אַרְבַּע **'Arba'**, *ar-bah´*; the same as 702; *Arba*, one of the Anakim:— Arba.

אַרְבָּעָה **'arbâ'âh**. See 702.

705. אַרְבָּעִים **'arbâ'îym**, *ar-baw-eem´*; multiple of 702; *forty*:— forty.

706. אַרְבַּעְתַּיִם **'arba'tayim**, *ar-bah-tah´-yim*; dual of 702; *fourfold*:— fourfold.

707. אָרַג **'ârag**, *aw-rag´*; a prim. root; to *plait* or *weave*:— weaver (-r).

708. אֶרֶג **'ereg**, *eh´-reg*; from 707; a *weaving*; a *braid*; also a *shuttle*:— beam, weaver's shuttle.

709. אַרְגֹּב **'Argôb**, *ar-gobe´*; from the same as 7263; *stony*; *Argob*, a district of Pal.:— Argob.

710. אַרְגְּוָן **'arg^evân**, *arg-ev-awn´*; a var. for 713; *purple*:— purple.

711. אַרְגְּוָן **'arg^evân** (Chald.), *arg-ev-awn´*; corresp. to 710:— purple.

712. אַרְגָּז **'argâz**, *ar-gawz´*; perh. from 7264 (in the sense of being *suspended*); a *box* (as a pannier):— coffer.

713. אַרְגָּמָן **'argâmân**, *ar-gaw-mawn´*; of for-

or.; *purple* (the color or the dyed stuff):— purple.

714. אַרְדְּ **'Ard**, *ard;* from an unused root prob. mean. to *wander; fugitive; Ard*, the name of two Isr.:— Ard.

715. אַרְדּוֹן **'Ardôwn**, *ar-dohn´;* from the same as 714; *roaming; Ardon*, an Isr.:— Ardon.

716. אַרְדִּי **'Ardîy**, *ar-dee;* patron. from 714; an *Ardite* (collect.) or desc. of Ard:— Ardites.

717. אָרָה **'ârâh**, *aw-raw´;* a prim. root; to *pluck:*— gather, pluck.

718. אֲרוּ **'ărûw** (Chald.), *ar-oo´;* prob. akin to 431; *lo!:*— behold, lo.

719. אַרְוַד **'Arvad**, *ar-vad´;* prob. from 7300; a *refuge* for the *roving; Arvad*, an island-city of Pal.:— Arvad.

720. אֲרוֹד **'Ărôwd**, *ar-ode´;* an orth. var. of 719; *fugitive; Arod*, an Isr.:— Arod.

721. אַרְוָדִי **'Arvâdîy**, *ar-vaw-dee´;* patrial from 719; an *Arvadite* or citizen of Arvad:— Arvadite.

722. אֲרוֹדִי **'Ărôwdîy**, *ar-o-dee´;* patron. from 721; an *Arodite* or desc. of Arod:— Arodi, Arodites.

723. אֻרְוָה **'urvâh**, *oor-vaw´;* or

אֲרָיָה **'ărâyâh**, *ar-aw-yah´;* from 717 (in the sense of *feeding*); a *herding-place* for an animal:— stall.

724. אֲרוּכָה **'ărûwkâh**, *ar-oo-kaw´;* or

אֲרֻכָה **'ărûkâh**, *ar-oo-kaw´;* fem. pass. part. of 748 (in the sense of *restoring* to soundness); *wholeness* (lit. or fig.):— health, made up, perfected.

725. אֲרוּמָה **'Ărûwmâh**, *ar-oo-maw´;* a var. of 7316; *height; Arumah*, a place in Pal.:— Arumah.

726. אֲרוֹמִי° **'Ărôwmîy**, *ar-o-mee´;* a clerical err. for 130; an *Edomite* (as in the marg.):— Syrian.

727. אָרוֹן **'ârôwn**, *aw-rone´;* or

אָרֹן **'ârôn**, *aw-rone´;* from 717 (in the sense of *gathering*); a *box:*— ark, chest, coffin.

728. אֲרַוְנָה **'Ăravnâh**, *ar-av-naw´;* or (by transp.)

אוֹרְנָה° **'Ôwrnâh**, *ore-naw´;* or

אַרְנִיָה **'Arnîyah**, *ar-nee-yaw´;* all by orth. var. for 771; *Aravnah* (or *Arnijah* or *Ornah*), a Jebusite:— Araunah.

729. אָרַז **'âraz**, *aw-raz´;* a prim. root; to *be firm;* used only in the pass. part. as a denom. from 730; of *cedar:*— made of cedar.

730. אֶרֶז **'erez**, *eh-rez´;* from 729; a *cedar* tree (from the tenacity of its roots):— cedar (tree).

731. אַרְזָה **'arzâh**, *ar-zaw´;* fem. of 730; *cedar paneling:*— cedar work.

732. אָרַח **'ârach**, *aw-rakh´;* a prim. root; to *travel:*— go, wayfaring (man).

733. אָרַח **'Ârach**, *aw-rakh´;* from 732; *wayfaring; Arach*, the name of three Isr.:— Arah.

734. אֹרַח **'ôrach**, *o´-rakh;* from 732; a *well-trodden road* (lit. or fig.); also a *caravan:*— manner, path, race, rank, traveller, troop, [by-, high-] way.

735. אֹרַח **'ôrach** (Chald.), *o´-rakh;* corresp. to 734; a *road:*— way.

736. אֹרְחָה **'ôreᶜhâh**, *o-rekh-aw´;* fem. act. part. of 732; a *caravan:*— (travelling) company.

737. אֲרֻחָה **'ărûchâh**, *ar-oo-khaw´;* fem. pass. part. of 732 (in the sense of *appointing*); a *ration* of food:— allowance, diet, dinner, victuals.

738. אֲרִי **'ărîy**, *ar-ee´;* or (prol.)

אַרְיֵה **'aryêh**, *ar-yay´;* from 717 (in the sense of *violence*); a *lion:*— (young) lion, + pierce [from the marg.].

739. אֲרִיאֵל **'ărîy'êl**, *ar-ee-ale´;* or

אֲרִאֵל **'ărî'êl**, *ar-ee-ale´;* from 738 and 410; *lion of God*, i.e. *heroic:*— lionlike men.

740. אֲרִיאֵל **'Ărî'êl**, *ar-ee-ale´;* the same as 739; *Ariel*, a symb. name for Jerusalem, also the name of an Isr.:— Ariel.

741. אֲרִיאֵיל **'ărî'êyl**, *ar-ee-ale´;* either by transp. for 739 or, more prob. an orth. var. for 2025; the *altar* of the Temple:— altar.

742. אֲרִידַי **'Ărîyday**, *ar-ee-dah´-ee;* of Pers. or.; *Aridai*, a son of Haman:— Aridai.

743. אֲרִידָתָא **'Ărîydâthâ'**, *ar-ee-daw-thaw´;* of Pers. or.; *Aridatha*, a son of Haman:— Aridatha.

אַרְיֵה **'aryêh.** See 738.

744. אַרְיֵה **'aryêh** (Chald.), *ar-yay´;* corresp. to 738:— lion.

745. אַרְיֵה **'Aryêh**, *ar-yay´;* the same as 738; *lion; Arjeh*, an Isr.:— Arieh.

אֲרָיָה **'ărâyâh.** See 723.

746. אַרְיוֹךְ **'Aryôwk**, *ar-yoke´;* of for. or.; *Ariok*, the name of two Babylonians:— Arioch.

747. אֲרִיסַי **'Ărîyçay**, *ar-ee-sah´-ee;* of Pers. or.; *Arisai*, a son of Haman:— Arisai.

748. אָרַךְ **'ârak**, *aw-rak´;* a prim. root; to *be* (caus. *make*) *long* (lit. or fig.):— defer, draw out, lengthen, (be, become, make, pro-) long, + (out-, over-) live, tarry (long).

749. אֲרַךְ **'ărak** (Chald.), *ar-ak´;* prop. corresp. to 748, but used only in the sense of *reaching* to a given point; to *suit:*— be meet.

750. אָרֵךְ **'ârêk**, *aw-rake´*; from 748; *long:*— long [-suffering, -winged], patient, slow [to anger].

751. אֶרֶךְ **'Erek**, *eh´-rek*; from 748; *length; Erek*, a place in Bab.:— Erech.

752. אֲרֹךְ **'ârôk**, *aw-roke´*; from 748; *long:*— long.

753. אֹרֶךְ **'ôrek**, *o´rek´*; from 748; *length:*— + for ever, length, long.

754. אַרְכָּא **'arkâ'** (Chald.), *ar-kaw´*; or

אַרְכָה **'arkâh** (Chald.), *ar-kaw´*; from 749; *length:*— lengthening, prolonged.

755. אַרְכֻּבָה **'arkûbâh** (Chald.), *ar-koo-baw´*; from an unused root corresp. to 7392 (in the sense of *bending* the knee); the *knee:*— knee.

אֲרֻכָה **'ărûkâh**. See 724.

756. אַרְכְּוַי **'Arkᵉvay** (Chald.), *ar-kev-ah´ee*; patrial from 751; an *Arkevite* (collect.) or native of Erek:— Archevite.

757. אַרְכִּי **'Arkîy**, *ar-kee´*; patrial from another place (in Pal.) of similar name with 751; an *Arkite* or native of Erek:— Archi, Archite.

758. אֲרָם **'Arâm**, *arawm´*; from the same as 759; the *highland; Aram* or Syria, and its inhab.; also the name of a son of Shem, a grandson of Nahor, and of an Isr.:— Aram, Mesopotamia, Syria, Syrians.

759. אַרְמוֹן **'armôwn**, *ar-mone´*; from an unused root (mean. to *be elevated*); a *citadel* (from its *height*):— castle, palace. Comp. 2038.

760. אֲרַם צוֹבָה **'Ăram Tsôwbâh**, *ar-am´ tso-baw´*; from 758 and 6678; *Aram of Tsoba* (or Cœle-Syria):— Aram-zobah.

761. אֲרַמִּי **'Ărammîy**, *ar-am-mee´*; patrial from 758; an *Aramite* or Aramæan:— Syrian, Aramitess.

762. אֲרָמִית **'Ărâmîyth**, *ar-aw-meeth´*; fem. of 761; (only adv.) in *Aramæan:*— in the Syrian language (tongue), in Syriack.

763. אֲרַם נַהֲרַיִם **'Ăram NahĂrayim**, *ar-am´ nah-har-ah´-yim*; from 758 and the dual of 5104; *Aram of* (the) *two rivers* (Euphrates and Tigris) or *Mesopotamia:*— Aham-naharaim, Mesopotamia.

764. אַרְמֹנִי **'Armônîy**, *ar-mo-nee´*; from 759; *palatial; Armoni*, an Isr.:— Armoni.

765. אֲרָן **'Ărân**, *ar-awn´*; from 7442; *stridulous; Aran*, an Edomite:— Aran.

766. אֹרֶן **'ôren**, *o´-ren*; from the same as 765 (in the sense of *strength*); the *ash* tree (from its toughness):— ash.

767. אֹרֶן **'Ôren**, *o´-ren*; the same as 766; *Oren*, an Isr.:— Oren.

אָרֹן **'ârôn**. See 727.

768. אַרְנֶבֶת **'arnebeth**, *ar-neh´-beth*; of uncert. der.; the *hare:*— hare.

769. אַרְנוֹן **'Arnôwn**, *ar-nohn´*; or

אַרְנֹן **'Arnôn**, *ar-nohn´*; from 7442; a *brawling* stream; the *Arnon*, a river east of the Jordan; also its territory:— Arnon.

אַרְנִיָה° **'Arnîyah**. See 728.

770. אַרְנָן **'Arnân**, *ar-nawn´*; prob. from the same as 769; *noisy; Arnan*, an Isr.:— Arnan.

771. אׇרְנָן **'Ornân**, *or-nawn´*; prob. from 766; *strong; Ornan*, a Jebusite:— Ornan. See 728.

772. אֲרַע **'ăra'** (Chald.), *ar-ah´*; corresp. to 776; the *earth;* by impl. (fig.) *low:*— earth, interior.

773. אַרְעִית **'ar'îyth** (Chald.), *arh-eeth´*; fem. of 772; the *bottom:*— bottom.

774. אַרְפָּד **'Arpâd**, *ar-pawd´*; from 7502; *spread* out; *Arpad*, a place in Syria:— Arpad, Arphad.

775. אַרְפַּכְשַׁד **'Arpakshad**, *ar-pak-shad´*; prob. of for. or.; *Arpakshad*, a son of Noah; also the region settled by him:— Arphaxad.

776. אֶרֶץ **'erets**, *eh´-rets*; from an unused root prob. mean. to *be firm;* the *earth* (at large, or partitively a *land*):— × common, country, earth, field, ground, land, × nations, way, + wilderness, world.

777. אַרְצָא **'artsâ'**, *ar-tsaw´*; from 776; *earthiness; Artsa*, an Isr.:— Arza.

778. אֲרַק **'ăraq** (Chald.), *ar-ak´*; by transm. for 772; the *earth:*— earth.

779. אָרַר **'ârar**, *aw-rar´*; a prim. root; to *execrate:*— × bitterly curse.

780. אֲרָרַט **'Ărârat**, *ar-aw-rat´*; of for. or.; *Ararat* (or rather Armenia):— Ararat, Armenia.

781. אָרַשׂ **'âras**, *aw-ras´*; a prim. root; to *engage* for matrimony:— betroth, espouse.

782. אֲרֶשֶׁת **'ăresheth**, *ar-eh´-sheth*; from 781 (in the sense of *desiring* to possess); a *longing* for:— request.

783. אַרְתַּחְשַׁשְׁתָּא **'Artachshastâ'** (Chald.), *ar-takh-shas-taw´*; or

אַרְתַּחְשַׁשְׁתְּא **'Artachshast'** (Chald.), *ar-takh-shast´*; or by perm.

אַרְתַּחְשַׂסְתְּא **'Artachshaçt'** (Chald.), *ar-takh-shast´*; of for. or.; *Artachshasta* (or Artaxerxes), a title (rather than name) of several Pers. kings:— Artaxerxes.

784. אֵשׁ **'êsh**, *aysh;* a prim. word; *fire* (lit. or fig.):— burning, fiery, fire, flaming, hot.

785. אֵשׁ **'êsh** (Chald.), *aysh;* corresp. to 784:— flame.

786. אִשׁ 'îsh, *eesh;* ident. (in or. and formation) with 784; *entity;* used only adv., there *is* or *are:*— are there, none can. Comp. 3426.

787. אֹשׁ 'ôsh (Chald.), *ohsh;* corresp. (by transp. and abb.) to 803; a *foundation:*— foundation.

788. אַשְׁבֵּל 'Ashbêl, *ash-bale´;* prob. from the same as 7640; *flowing; Ashbel,* an Isr.:— Ashbel.

789. אַשְׁבֵּלִי 'Ashbêlîy, *ash-bay-lee´;* patron. from 788; an *Ashbelite* (collect.) or desc. of Ashbel:— Ashbelites.

790. אֶשְׁבָּן 'Eshbân, *esh-bawn´;* prob. from the same as 7644; *vigorous; Eshban,* an Idumæan:— Eshban.

791. אַשְׁבֵּעַ 'Ashbêa', *ash-bay´-ah;* from 7650; *adjurer; Asbeä,* an Isr.:— Ashbea.

792. אֶשְׁבַּעַל 'Eshba'al, *esh-bah´-al;* from 376 and 1168; *man of Baal; Eshbaal* (or Ishbosheth), a son of King Saul:— Eshbaal.

793. אֶשֶׁד 'eshed, *eh´-shed;* from an unused root mean. to *pour;* an *outpouring:*— stream.

794. אֲשֵׁדָה 'âshêdâh, *ash-ay-daw´;* fem. of 793; a *ravine:*— springs.

795. אַשְׁדּוֹד 'Ashdôwd, *ash-dode´;* from 7703; *ravager; Ashdod,* a place in Pal.:— Ashdod.

796. אַשְׁדּוֹדִי 'Ashdôwdîy, *ash-do-dee´;* patrial from 795; an *Ashdodite* (often collect.) or inhab. of Ashdod:— Ashdodites, of Ashdod.

797. אַשְׁדּוֹדִית 'Ashdôwdîyth, *ash-do-deeth´;* fem. of 796; (only adv.) *in the language of Ashdod:*— in the speech of Ashdod.

798. אַשְׁדּוֹת הַפִּסְגָּה 'Ashdôwth hap-Piçgâh, *ash-doth´ hap-pis-gaw´;* from the plur. of 794 and 6449 with the art. interposed; *ravines of the Pisgah; Ashdoth-Pisgah,* a place east of the Jordan:— Ashdoth-pisgah.

799. אֶשְׁדָּת 'eshdâth, *esh-dawth´;* from 784 and 1881; a *fire-law:*— fiery law.

800. אֵשָׁה 'eshshâh, *esh-shaw´;* fem. of 784; *fire:*— fire.

801. אִשָּׁה 'ishshâh, *ish-shaw´;* the same as 800, but used in a liturgical sense; prop. a *burntoffering;* but occasionally of any *sacrifice:*— (offering, sacrifice), (made) by fire.

802. אִשָּׁה 'ishshâh, *ish-shaw´;* fem. of 376 or 582; irreg. plur.

נָשִׁים nâshîym, *naw-sheem´;* a *woman* (used in the same wide sense as 582):— [adulterless, each, every, female, × many, + none, one, + together, wife, woman. [Often unexpressed in English.]

803. אֲשׁוּיָה° 'âshûwyâh, *ash-oo-yah´;* fem. pass. part. from an unused root mean. to *found; foundation:*— foundation.

804. אַשּׁוּר 'Ashshûwr, *ash-shoor´;* or

אַשֻּׁר 'Ashshûr, *ash-shoor´;* appar. from 833 (in the sense of *successful*); *Ashshur,* the second son of Shem; also his desc. and the country occupied by them (i.e. Assyria), its region and its empire:— Asshur, Assur, Assyria, Assyrians. See 838.

805. אַשּׁוּרִי 'Ăshûwrîy, *ash-oo-ree´;* or

אַשּׁוּרִי 'Ashshûwrîy, *ash-shoo-ree´;* from a patrial word of the same form as 804; an *Ashurite* (collect.) or inhab. of Ashur, a district in Pal.:— Asshurim, Ashurites.

806. אַשְׁחוּר 'Ashchûwr, *ash-khoor´;* prob. from 7835; *black; Ashchur,* an Isr.:— Ashur.

807. אֲשִׁימָא 'Ăshîymâ', *ash-ee-maw´;* of for. or.; *Ashima,* a deity of Hamath:— Ashima.

אֲשֵׁירָה 'ăshêyrâh. See 842.

808. אָשִׁישׁ 'âshîysh, *aw-sheesh´;* from the same as 784 (in the sense of *pressing* down firmly; comp. 803); a (ruined) *foundation:*— foundation.

809. אֲשִׁישָׁה 'ăshîyshâh, *ash-ee-shaw´;* fem. of 808; something closely *pressed* together, i.e. a *cake* of raisins or other comfits:— flagon.

810. אֶשֶׁךְ 'eshek, *eh´-shek;* from an unused root (prob. mean. to *bunch* together); a *testicle* (as a *lump*):— stone.

811. אֶשְׁכּוֹל 'eshkôwl, *esh-kole´;* or

אֶשְׁכֹּל 'eshkôl, *esh-kole´;* prob. prol. from 810; a *bunch of grapes* or other fruit:— cluster (of grapes).

812. אֶשְׁכֹּל 'Eshkôl, *esh-kole´;* the same as 811; *Eshcol,* the name of an Amorite, also of a valley in Pal.:— Eshcol.

813. אַשְׁכְּנַז 'Ashkᵉnaz, *ash-ken-az´;* of for. or.; *Ashkenaz,* a Japhethite, also his desc.:— Ashkenaz.

814. אֶשְׁכָּר 'eshkâr, *esh-kawr´;* for 7939; a *gratuity:*— gift, present.

815. אֵשֶׁל 'êshel, *ay´-shel;* from a root of uncert. signif.; a *tamarisk* tree; by extens. a *grove* of any kind:— grove, tree.

816. אָשַׁם 'âsham, *aw-sham´;* or

אָשֵׁם 'âshêm, *aw-shame´;* a prim. root; to *be guilty;* by impl. to *be punished* or *perish:*— × certainly, be (-come, made) desolate, destroy, × greatly, be (-come, found, hold) guilty, offend (acknowledge offence), trespass.

817. אָשָׁם 'âshâm, *aw-shawm´;* from 816; *guilt;* by impl. a *fault;* also a *sin-offering:*— guiltiness, (offering for) sin, trespass (offering).

818. אָשֵׁם 'âshêm, *aw-shame´;* from 816; *guilty;* hence, *presenting a sin-offering:*— one which is faulty, guilty.

Hebrew

819. אַשְׁמָה **'ashmâh**, *ash-maw´*; fem. of 817; *guiltiness*, a *fault*, the *presentation of a sin-offering*:— offend, sin, (cause of) trespass (-ing, offering).

אַשְׁמוּרָה **'ashmûwrâh**. See 821.

820. אַשְׁמָן **'ashmân**, *ash-mawn´*; prob. from 8081; a *fat* field:— desolate place.

821. אַשְׁמֻרָה **'ashmûrâh**, *ash-moo-raw´*; or

אַשְׁמוּרָה **'ashmûwrâh**, *ash-moo-raw´*; or

אַשְׁמֹרֶת **'ashmôreth**, *ash-mo´-reth*; fem. from 8104; a night *watch*:— watch.

822. אֶשְׁנָב **'eshnâb**, *esh-nawb´*; appar. from an unused root (prob. mean. to *leave small spaces between two things*); a *latticed window*:— casement, lattice.

823. אַשְׁנָה **'Ashnâh**, *ash-naw´*; prob. a var. for 3466; *Ashnah*, the name of two places in Pal.:— Ashnah.

824. אֶשְׁעָן **'Esh'ân**, *esh-awn´*; from 8172; *support*; *Eshan*, a place in Pal.:— Eshean.

825. אַשָּׁף **'ashshâph**, *ash-shawf´*; from an unused root (prob. mean. to *lisp*, i.e. *practice enchantment*); a *conjurer*:— astrologer.

826. אַשָּׁף **'ashshâph** (Chald.), *ash-shawf´*; corresp. to 825:— astrologer.

827. אַשְׁפָּה **'ashpâh**, *ash-paw´*; perh. (fem.) from the same as 825 (in the sense of *covering*); a *quiver* or arrow-case:— quiver.

828. אַשְׁפְּנַז **'Ashpᵉnaz**, *ash-pen-az´*; of for. or.; *Ashpenaz*, a Bab. eunuch:— Ashpenaz.

829. אֶשְׁפָּר **'eshpâr**, *esh-pawr´*; of uncert. der.; a measured *portion*:— good piece (of flesh).

830. אַשְׁפֹּת **'ashpôth**, *ash-pohth´*; or

אַשְׁפּוֹת **'ashpôwth**, *ash-pohth´*; or (contr.)

שְׁפֹת **shᵉphôth**, *shef-ohth´*; plur. of a noun of the same form as 827, from 8192 (in the sense of *scraping*); a *heap* of *rubbish* or *filth*:— dung (hill).

831. אַשְׁקְלוֹן **'Ashqᵉlôwn**, *ash-kel-one´*; prob. from 8254 in the sense of *weighing*-place (i.e. *mart*); *Ashkelon*, a place in Pal.:— Ashkelon, Askalon.

832. אֶשְׁקְלוֹנִי **'Eshqᵉlôwnîy**, *esh-kel-o-nee´*; patrial from 831; an *Ashkelonite* (collect.) or inhab. of Ashkelon:— Eshkalonites.

833. אָשַׁר **'âshar**, *aw-shar´*; or

אָשֵׁר **'âshêr**, *aw-share´*; a prim. root; to *be straight* (used in the widest sense, espec. to *be level, right, happy*); fig. to *go forward, be honest, prosper*:— (call, be) bless (-ed, happy), go, guide, lead, relieve.

834. אֲשֶׁר **'ăsher**, *ash-er´*; a prim. rel. pron. (of every gender and number); *who, which, what, that*; also (as adv. and conjunc.) *when, where, how, because, in order that*, etc.:— × after, × alike, as (soon as), because, × every,

for, + forasmuch, + from whence, + how (-soever), × if, (so) that ([thing] which, wherein), × though, + until, + whatsoever, when, where (+ -as, -in, -of, -on, -soever, -with), which, whilst, + whither (-soever), who (-m, -soever, -se). [As it is indeclinable, it is often accompanied by the personal pron. expletively, used to show the connection.]

835. אֶשֶׁר **'esher**, *eh´-sher*; from 833; *happiness*; only in masc. plur. constr. as interj., how *happy*!:— blessed, happy.

836. אָשֵׁר **'Âshêr**, *aw-share´*; from 833; *happy*; *Asher*, a son of Jacob, and the tribe descended from him, with its territory; also a place in Pal.:— Asher.

837. אֹשֶׁר **'ôsher**, *o´-sher*; from 833; *happiness*:— happy.

838. אָשׁוּר **'âshûwr**, *aw-shoor´*; or

אַשֻּׁר **'ashshûr**, *ash-shoor´*; from 833 in the sense of *going*; a *step*:— going, step.

839. אָשֻׁר **'ăshûr**, *ash-oor´*; contr. for 8391; the *cedar* tree or some other light elastic wood:— Ashurite.

אַשּׁוּר **'Ashshûr**. See 804, 838.

840. אֲשַׂרְאֵל **'Ăsar'êl**, *as-ar-ale´*; by orth. var. from 833 and 410; *right of God*; *Asarel*, an Isr.:— Asareel.

841. אֲשַׂרְאֵלָה **'Ăsar'êlâh**, *as-ar-ale´-aw*; from the same as 840; *right toward God*; *Asarelah*, an Isr.:— Asarelah. Comp. 3480.

842. אֲשֵׁרָה **'ăshêrâh**, *ash-ay-raw´*; or

אֲשֵׁירָה **'ăshêyrâh**, *ash-ay-raw´*; from 833; *happy*; *Asherah* (or Astarte) a Phœnician goddess; also an *image* of the same:— grove. Comp. 6253.

843. אֲשֵׁרִי **'Âshêrîy**, *aw-shay-ree´*; patron. from 836; an *Asherite* (collect.) or desc. of Asher:— Asherites.

844. אַשְׂרִיאֵל **'Asrî'êl**, *as-ree-ale´*; an orth. var. for 840; *Asriel*, the name of two Isr.:— Ashriel, Asriel.

845. אַשְׂרִאֵלִי **'Asrî'êlîy**, *as-ree-ale-ee´*; patron. from 844; an *Asrielite* (collect.) or desc. of Asriel:— Asrielites.

846. אֻשַּׁרְנָא **'ushsharnâ'** (Chald.), *oosh-ar-naw´*; from a root corresp. to 833; a *wall* (from its uprightness):— wall.

847. אֶשְׁתָּאֹל **'Eshtâ'ôl**, *esh-taw-ole´*; or

אֶשְׁתָּאוֹל **'Eshtâ'ôwl**, *esh-taw-ole´*; prob. from 7592; *intreaty*; *Eshtaol*, a place in Pal.:— Eshtaol.

848. אֶשְׁתָּאֻלִי **'Eshtâ'ûlîy**, *esh-taw-oo-lee´*; patrial from 847; an *Eshtaolite* (collect.) or inhab. of Eshtaol:— Eshtaulites.

849. אֶשְׁתַּדּוּר **'eshtaddûwr** (Chald.), *esh-tad-*

dure´; from 7712 (in a bad sense); *rebellion:—* sedition.

850. אֶשְׁתּוֹן **'Eshtôwn,** *esh-tone´;* prob. from the same as 7764; *restful; Eshton,* an Isr.:— Eshton.

851. אֶשְׁתְּמֹעַ **'Esht**ᵉ**môa',** *esh-tem-o´-ah;* or

אֶשְׁתְּמוֹעַ **'Esht**ᵉ**môwa',** *esh-tem-o´-ah;* or

אֶשְׁתְּמֹה **'Esht**ᵉ**môh,** *esh-tem-o´;* from 8085 (in the sense of *obedience); Eshtemoa* or *Eshtemoh,* a place in Pal.:— Eshtemoa, Eshtemoh.

אֵת° **'ath.** See 859.

852. אָת **'âth** (Chald.), *awth;* corresp. to 226; a *portent:—* sign.

853. אֵת **'êth,** *ayth;* appar. contr. from 226 in the demonstr. sense of *entity;* prop. *self* (but gen. used to point out more def. the obj. of a verb or prep., *even* or *namely):—* [*as such unrepresented in English*].

854. אֵת **'êth,** *ayth;* prob. from 579; prop. *nearness* (used only as a prep. or an adv.), *near;* hence, gen. *with, by, at, among,* etc.:— against, among, before, by, for, from, in (-to), (out) of, with. [*Often with another prep. prefixed.*]

855. אֵת **'êth,** *ayth;* of uncert. der.; a *hoe* or other digging implement:— coulter, plowshare.

אַתְּ **'âttâ.** See 859.

אַתָּא **'âthâ'.** See 857.

856. אֶתְבַּעַל **'Ethba'al,** *eth-bah´-al;* from 854 and 1168; *with Baal; Ethbaal,* a Phœnician king:— Ethbaal.

857. אָתָה **'âthâh,** *aw-thaw´;* or

אָתָא **'âthâ',** *aw-thaw´;* a prim. root [collat. to 225 contr.]; to *arrive:—* (be-, things to) come (upon), bring.

858. אֲתָה **'âthâh** (Chald.), *aw-thaw´;* or

אֲתָא **'âthâ'** (Chald.), *aw-thaw´;* corresp. to 857:— (be-) come, bring.

859. אַתָּה **'attâh,** *at-taw´;* or (short.);

אַתָּ **'attâ,** *at-taw´;* or

אַת° **'ath,** *ath;* fem. (irreg.) sometimes

אַתִּי **'attîy,** *at-tee´;* plur. masc.

אַתֶּם **'attem,** *at-tem´;* fem.

אַתֶּן **'atten,** *at-ten´;* or

אַתֵּנָה **'attênâh,** *at-tay´-naw;* or

אַתֵּנָּה **'attênnâh,** *at-tane´-naw;* a prim. pron. of the second pers.; *thou* and *thee,* or (plur.) *ye* and *you:—* thee, thou, ye, you.

860. אָתוֹן **'âthôwn,** *aw-thone´;* prob. from the same as 386 (in the sense of *patience*); a female *ass* (from its docility):— (she) ass.

861. אַתּוּן **'attûwn** (Chald.), *at-toon´;* prob.

from the corresp. to 784; prob. a *fire-place,* i.e. *furnace:—* furnace.

862. אַתּוּק **'attûwq,** *at-tooke´;* or

אַתִּיק **'attîyq,** *at-teek´;* from 5423 in the sense of *decreasing;* a *ledge* or offset in a building:— gallery.

אַתִּי **'attîy.** See 859.

863. אִתַּי **'Ittay,** *it-tah´ee;* or

אִיתַי **'Iythay,** *ee-thah´ee;* from 854; *near; Ittai* or *Ithai,* the name of a Gittite and of an Isr.:— Ithai, Ittai.

864. אֵתָם **'Êthâm,** *ay-thawm´;* of Eg. der.; *Etham,* a place in the Desert:— Etham.

אַתֶּן **'attem.** See 859.

865. אֶתְמוֹל **'ethmôwl,** *eth-mole´;* or

אִתְמוֹל **'ithmôwl,** *ith-mole´;* or

אֶתְמוּל **'ethmûwl,** *eth-mool´;* prob. from 853 or 854 and 4136; *heretofore; def. yesterday:—* + before (that) time, + heretofore, of late (old), + times past, yester[day].

אַתֶּן **'atten.** See 859.

866. אֶתְנָה **'êthnâh,** *eth-naw´;* from 8566; a *present* (as the price of harlotry):— reward.

אַתֵּנָה **'attênâh** or

אַתֵּנָּה **'attênnâh.** See 859.

867. אֶתְנִי **'Ethnîy,** *eth-nee´;* perh. from 866; *munificence; Ethni,* an Isr.:— Ethni.

868. אֶתְנַן **'ethnan,** *eth-nan´;* the same as 866; a *gift* (as the price of harlotry or idolatry):— hire, reward.

869. אֶתְנַן **'Ethnan,** *eth-nan´;* the same as 868 in the sense of 867; *Ethnan,* an Isr.:— Ethnan.

870. אֲתַר **'ăthar** (Chald.), *ath-ar´;* from a root corresp. to that of 871; a *place;* (adv.) *after:—* after, place.

871. אֲתָרִים **'Ăthârîym,** *ath-aw-reem´;* plur. from an unused root (prob. mean. to *step*); *places; Atharim,* a place near Pal.:— spies.

ב

872. בְּאָה **b**ᵉ**'âh,** *bĕ-aw´;* from 935; an *entrance* to a building:— entry.

873. בְּאוּשׁ **bî'ûwsh** (Chald.), *be-oosh´;* from 888; *wicked:—* bad.

874. בָּאַר **bâ'ar,** *baw-ar´;* a prim. root; to *dig;* by anal. to *engrave;* fig. to *explain:—* declare, (make) plain (-ly).

875. בְּאֵר **b**ᵉ**'êr,** *bĕ-ayr´;* from 874; a *pit;* espec. a *well:—* pit, well.

876. בְּאֵר **B**ᵉ**'êr,** *bĕ-ayr´;* the same as 875; *Beër,* a place in the Desert, also one in Pal.:— Beer.

877. בֹּאר **bô'r**, *bore*; from 874; a *cistern*:— cistern.

878. בְּאֵרָא **Bᵉ'êrâ'**, *bĕ-ay-raw´*; from 875; a *well*; *Beëra*, an Isr.:— Beera.

879. בְּאֵר אֵלִים **Bᵉ'êr 'Êlîym**, *bĕ-ayr´ ay-leem´*; from 875 and the plur. of 410; *well of heroes*; *Beër-Elim*, a place in the Desert:— Beer-elim.

880. בְּאֵרָה **Bᵉ'êrâh**, *bĕ-ay-raw´*; the same as 878; *Beërah*, an Isr.:— Beerah.

881. בְּאֵרוֹת **Bᵉ'êrôwth**, *bĕ-ay-rohth´*; fem. plur. of 875; *wells*; *Beëroth*, a place in Pal.:— Beeroth.

882. בְּאֵרִי **Bᵉ'êrîy**, *bĕ-ay-ree´*; from 875; *fountained*; *Beëri*, the name of a Hittite and of an Isr.:— Beeri.

883. בְּאֵר לַחַי רֹאִי **Bᵉ'êr la-Chay Rô'îy**, *bĕ-ayr´ lakh-ah´ee ro-ee´*; from 875 and 2416 (with pref.) and 7203; *well of a living* (One) *my seer*; *Beër-Lachai-Roï*, a place in the Desert:— Beer-lahai-roi.

884. בְּאֵר שֶׁבַע **Bᵉ'êr Sheba'**, *be-ayr´ sheh´-bah*; from 875 and 7651 (in the sense of 7650); *well of an oath*; *Beër-Sheba*, a place in Pal.:— Beer-shebah.

885. בְּאֵרֹת בְּנֵי־יַעֲקָן **Bᵉêrôth Bᵉnêy-Ya'ăqan**, *bĕ-ay-roth´ be-nay´ yah-a-kan´*; from the fem. plur. of 875, and the plur. contr. of 1121, and 3292; *wells of* (the) *sons of Jaakan*; *Beëroth-Bene-Jaakan*, a place in the Desert:— Beeroth of the children of Jaakan.

886. בְּאֵרֹתִי **Bᵉ'êrôthîy**, *bĕ-ay-ro-thee´*; patrial from 881; a *Beërothite* or inhab. of Beëroth:— Beerothite.

887. בָּאַשׁ **bâ'ash**, *baw-ash´*; a prim. root; to *smell bad*; fig. to *be offensive* mor.:— (make to) be abhorred (had in abomination, loathsome, odious), (cause a, make to) stink (-ing savour), × utterly.

888. בְּאֵשׁ **bᵉ'êsh** (Chald.), *bĕ-aysh´*; corresp. to 887:— displease.

889. בְּאֹשׁ **bᵉ'ôsh**, *bĕ-oshe´*; from 877; a *stench*:— stink.

890. בָּאְשָׁה **bo'shâh**, *bosh-aw´*; fem. of 889; *stink-weed* or any other noxious or useless plant:— cockle.

891. בְּאֻשִׁים **bᵉ'ushîym**, *bĕ-oo-sheem´*; plur. of 889; *poison-berries*:— wild grapes.

892. בָּבָה **bâbâh**, *baw-baw´*; fem. act. part. of an unused root mean. to *hollow* out; something *hollowed* (as a gate), i.e. the *pupil* of the eye:— apple [of the eye].

893. בֵּבַי **Bêbay**, *bay-bah´ee*; prob. of for. or.; *Bebai*, an Isr.:— Bebai.

894. בָּבֶל **Bâbel**, *baw-bel´*; from 1101; *confusion*; *Babel* (i.e. Babylon), incl. Babylonia and the Bab. empire:— Babel, Babylon.

895. בָּבֶל **Bâbel** (Chald.), *baw-bel´*; corresp. to 894:— Babylon.

896. בַּבְלִי **Bablîy** (Chald.), *bab-lee´*; patrial from 895; a *Babylonian*:— Babylonia.

897. בַּג **bag**, *bag*; a Pers. word; *food*:— spoil [from the marg. for 957.]

898. בָּגַד **bâgad**, *baw-gad´*; a prim. root; to *cover* (with a garment); fig. to *act covertly*; by impl. to *pillage*:— deal deceitfully (treacherously, unfaithfully), offend, transgress (-or), (depart), treacherous (dealer, -ly, man), unfaithful (-ly, man), × very.

899. בֶּגֶד **beged**, *behg´-ed*; from 898; a *covering*, i.e. clothing; also *treachery* or *pillage*:— apparel, cloth (-es, ing), garment, lap, rag, raiment, robe, × very [treacherously], vesture, wardrobe.

900. בֹּגְדוֹת **bôgᵉdôwth**, *bohg-ed-ōhth´*; fem. plur. act. part. of 898; *treacheries*:— treacherous.

901. בָּגוֹד **bâgôwd**, *baw-gode´*; from 898; *treacherous*:— treacherous.

902. בִּגְוַי **Bigvay**, *big-vah´ee*; prob. of for. or.; *Bigvai*, an Isr.:— Bigvai.

903. בִּגְתָא **Bigthâ'**, *big-thaw´*; of Pers. der.; *Bigtha*, a eunuch of Xerxes:— Bigtha.

904. בִּגְתָן **Bigthân**, *big-thawn´*; or

בִּגְתָנָא **Bigthânâ'**, *big-thaw´naw*; of similar der. to 903; *Bigthan* or *Bigthana*, a eunuch of Xerxes:— Bigthan, Bigthana.

905. בַּד **bad**, *bad*; from 909; prop. *separation*; by impl. a *part* of the body, *branch* of a tree, *bar* for carrying; fig. *chief* of a city; espec. (with prep. pref.) as adv., *apart, only, besides*:— alone, apart, bar, besides, branch, by self, of each alike, except, only, part, staff, strength.

906. בַּד **bad**, *bad*; perh. from 909 (in the sense of *divided* fibres); flaxen *thread* or yarn; hence, a *linen* garment:— linen.

907. בַּד **bad**, *bad*; from 908; a *brag* or *lie*; also a *liar*:— liar, lie.

908. בָּדָא **bâdâ'**, *baw-daw´*; a prim. root; (fig.) to *invent*:— devise, feign.

909. בָּדַד **bâdad**, *baw-dad´*; a prim. root; to *divide*, i.e. (reflex.) *be solitary*:— alone.

910. בָּדָד **bâdâd**, *baw-dawd´*; from 909; *separate*; adv. *separately*:— alone, desolate, only, solitary.

911. בְּדַד **Bᵉdad**, *bed-ad´*; from 909; *separation*; *Bedad*, an Edomite:— Bedad.

912. בְּדְיָה **Bêdᵉyâh**, *bay-dĕ-yaw´*; prob. short. form 5662; *servant of Jehovah*; *Bedejah*, an Isr.:— Bedeiah.

913. בְּדִיל **bᵉdîyl**, *bed-eel´*; from 914; *alloy*

(because *removed* by smelting); by anal. *tin:*— + plummet, tin.

914. בָּדַל **bâdal**, *baw-dal´;* a prim. root; to *divide* (in var. senses lit. or fig., *separate, distinguish, differ, select,* etc.):— (make, put) difference, divide (asunder), (make) separate (self, -ation), sever (out), × utterly.

915. בְּדָל **bâdâl**, *baw-dawl´;* from 914; a *part:*— piece.

916. בְּדֹלַח **bedôlach**, *bed-o´-lakh;* prob. from 914; something in *pieces,* i.e. *bdellium,* a (fragrant) gum (perh. *amber*); others a *pearl:*— bdellium.

917. בְּדָן **Bedân**, *bed-awn´;* prob. short. for 5658; *servile; Bedan,* the name of two Isr.:— Bedan.

918. בָּדַק **bâdaq**, *baw-dak´;* a prim. root; to *gap* open; used only as a denom. from 919; to *mend* a breach:— repair.

919. בֶּדֶק **bedeq**, *beh´-dek;* from 918; a *gap* or *leak* (in a building or a ship):— breach, + calker.

920. בִּדְקַר **Bidqar**, *bid-car´;* prob. from 1856 with prep. pref.; *by stabbing,* i.e. *assassin; Bidkar,* an Isr.:— Bidkar.

921. בְּדַר **bedar** (Chald.), *bed-ar´;* corresp. (by transp.) to 6504; to *scatter:*— scatter.

922. בֹּהוּ **bôhûw**, *bo´-hoo;* from an unused root (mean. to be empty); a *vacuity,* i.e. (superficially) an undistinguishable *ruin:*— emptiness, void.

923. בַּהַט **bahat**, *bah´-hat;* from an unused root (prob. mean. to *glisten*); white *marble* or perh. *alabaster:*— red [marble].

924. בְּהִילוּ **behîylûw** (Chald.), *bĕ-hee-loo´;* from 927; a *hurry;* only adv. *hastily:*— in haste.

925. בָּהִיר **bâhîyr**, *baw-here´;* from an unused root (mean. to be bright); *shining:*— bright.

926. בָּהַל **bâhal**, *baw-hal´;* a prim. root; to *tremble* inwardly (or *palpitate*), i.e. (fig.) be (caus. *make*) (suddenly) *alarmed* or *agitated;* by impl. to *hasten* anxiously:— be (make) affrighted (afraid, amazed, dismayed, rash), (be, get, make) haste (-n, -y, -ily), (give) speedy (-ily), thrust out, trouble, vex.

927. בְּהַל **behal** (Chald.), *bĕ-hal´;* corresp. to 926; to *terrify, hasten:*— in haste, trouble.

928. בֶּהָלָה **behâlâh**, *beh-haw-law´;* from 926; *panic, destruction:*— terror, trouble.

929. בְּהֵמָה **behêmâh**, *bĕ-hay-maw´;* from an unused root (prob. mean. to be mute); prop. a *dumb* beast; espec. any large quadruped or *animal* (often collect.):— beast, cattle.

930. בְּהֵמוֹת **behêmôwth**, *bĕ-hay-mōhth´;* in form a plur. of 929, but really a sing. of Eg. der.; a *water-ox,* i.e. the *hippopotamus* or *Nile-horse:*— Behemoth.

931. בֹּהֶן **bôhen**, *bo´-hen;* from an unused root appar. mean. to *be thick;* the *thumb* of the hand or *great toe* of the foot:— thumb, great toe.

932. בֹּהַן **Bôhan**, *bo´han;* an orth. var. of 931; *thumb, Bohan,* an Isr.:— Bohan.

933. בֹּהַק **bôhaq**, *bo´-hak;* from an unused root mean. to be pale; white *scurf:*— freckled spot.

934. בֹּהֶרֶת **bôhereth**, *bo-heh´-reth;* fem. act. part. of the same as 925; a *whitish* spot on the skin:— bright spot.

935. בּוֹא **bôw'**, *bo;* a prim. root; to *go* or *come* (in a wide variety of applications):— abide, apply, attain, × be, befall, + besiege, bring (forth, in, into, to pass), call, carry, × certainly, (cause, let, thing for) to come (against, in, out, upon, to pass), depart, × doubtless again, + eat, + employ, (cause to) enter (in, into, -tering, -trance, -try), be fallen, fetch, + follow, get, give, go (down, in, to war), grant, + have, × indeed, [in-]vade, lead, lift [up], mention, pull in, put, resort, run (down), send, set, × (well) stricken [in age], × surely, take (in), way.

בּוּב **bûwb**. See 892, 5014.

936. בּוּז **bûwz**, *booz;* a prim. root; to *disrespect:*— contemn, despise, × utterly.

937. בּוּז **bûwz**, *booz;* from 936; *disrespect:*— contempt (-uously), despised, shamed.

938. בּוּז **Bûwz**, *booz;* the same as 937; *Buz,* the name of a son of Nahor, and of an Isr.:— Buz.

939. בּוּזָה **bûwzâh**, *boo-zaw´;* fem. pass. part. of 936; something *scorned;* an obj. of *contempt:*— despised.

940. בּוּזִי **Bûwzîy**, *boo-zee´;* patron. from 938; a *Buzite* or desc. of Buz:— Buzite.

941. בּוּזִי **Bûwzîy**, *boo-zee´;* the same as 940; *Buzi,* an Isr.:— Buzi.

942. בַּוַּי **Bavvay**, *bav-vah´ee;* prob. of Pers. or.; *Bavvai,* an Isr.:— Bavai.

943. בּוּךְ **bûwk**, *book;* a prim. root; to *involve* (lit. or fig.):— be entangled, (perplexed).

944. בּוּל **bûwl**, *bool;* for 2981; *produce* (of the earth, etc.):— food, stock.

945. בּוּל **Bûwl**, *bool;* the same as 944 (in the sense of *rain*); *Bul,* the eighth Heb. month:— Bul.

בּוּם **bûwm**. See 1116.

946. בּוּנָה **Bûwnâh**, *boo-naw´;* from 995; *discretion; Bunah,* an Isr.:— Bunah.

בּוּנִי **Bûwnîy**. See 1138.

947. בּוּס **bûwç**, *boos;* a prim. root; to *tram-*

Hebrew

ple (lit. or fig.):— loath, tread (down, under [foot]), be polluted.

948. בוּץ **bûwts**, *boots;* from an unused root (of the same form) mean. to *bleach*, i.e. (intr.) *be white;* prob. *cotton* (of some sort):— fine (white) linen.

949. בּוֹצֵץ **Bôwtsêts**, *bo-tsates´;* from the same as 948; *shining; Botsets*, a rock near Michmash:— Bozez.

950. בוּקָה **bûwqâh**, *boo-kaw´;* fem. pass. part. of an unused root (mean. to *be hollow*); *emptiness* (as adj.):— empty.

951. בּוֹקֵר **bôwkêr**, *bo-kare´;* prop. act. part. from 1239 as denom. from 1241; a *cattle-tender:*— herdman.

952. בּוּר **bûwr**, *boor;* a prim. root; to *bore*, i.e. (fig.) *examine:*— declare.

953. בּוֹר **bôwr**, *bore;* from 952 (in the sense of 877); a pit *hole* (espec. one used as a *cistern* or a *prison*):— cistern, dungeon, fountain, pit, well.

954. בּוּשׁ **bûwsh**, *boosh;* a prim. root; prop. to *pale*, i.e. by impl. to *be ashamed;* also (by impl.) to *be disappointed*, or *delayed:*— (be, make, bring to, cause, put to, with, a-) shamed (-d), be (put to) confounded (-fusion), become dry, delay, be long.

955. בּוּשָׁה **bûwshâh**, *boo-shaw´;* fem. part. pass. of 954; *shame:*— shame.

956. בּוּת **bûwth** (Chald.), *booth;* appar. denom. from 1005; to *lodge* over night:— pass the night.

957. בַּז **baz**, *baz;* from 962; *plunder:*— booty, prey, spoil (-ed).

958. בָּזָא **bâzâ'**, *baw-zaw´;* a prim. root; prob. to *cleave:*— spoil.

959. בָּזָה **bâzâh**, *baw-zaw´;* a prim. root; to *disesteem:*— despise, disdain, contemn (-ptible), + think to scorn, vile person.

960. בָּזֹה **bâzôh**, *baw-zo´;* from 959; *scorned:*— despise.

961. בִּזָּה **bizzâh**, *biz-zaw´;* fem. of 957; *booty:*— prey, spoil.

962. בָּזַז **bâzaz**, *baw-zaz´;* a prim. root; to *plunder:*— catch, gather, (take) for a prey, rob (-ber), spoil, take (away, spoil), × utterly.

963. בִּזָּיוֹן **bizzâyôwn**, *biz-zaw-yone´;* from 959; *disesteem:*— contempt.

964. בִּזְיוֹתְיָה **bizyôwtheyâh**, *biz-yo-thĕ-yaw´;* from 959 and 3050; *contempts of Jah; Bizjothjah*, a place in Pal.:— Bizjothjah.

965. בָּזָק **bâzâq**, *baw-zawk´;* from an unused root mean. to *lighten;* a *flash* of lightning:— flash of lightning.

966. בֶּזֶק **Bezeq**, *beh´-zek;* from 965; *lightning; Bezek*, a place in Pal.:— Bezek.

967. בָּזַר **bâzar**, *baw-zar´;* a prim. root; to *disperse:*— scatter.

968. בִּזְתָא **Bizthâ'**, *biz-thaw´;* of Pers. or.; *Biztha*, a eunuch of Xerxes:— Biztha.

969. בָּחוֹן **bâchôwn**, *baw-khone´;* from 974; an *assayer* of metals:— tower.

970. בָּחוּר **bâchûwr**, *baw-khoor´;* or

בָּחֻר **bâchur**, *baw-khoor´;* pass. part. of 977; prop. *selected*, i.e. a *youth* (often collect.):— (choice) young (man), chosen, × hole.

בְּחוּרוֹת **bechûwrôwth**. See 979.

בַּחוּרִים **Bachûwrîym**. See 980.

971. בַּחִין **bachîyn**, *bakh-een´;* another form of 975; a watch-*tower* of besiegers:— tower.

972. בָּחִיר **bâchîyr**, *baw-kheer´;* from 977; *select:*— choose, chosen one, elect.

973. בָּחַל **bâchal**, *baw-khal´;* a prim. root; to *loathe:*— abhor, get hastily [from the marg. for 926].

974. בָּחַן **bâchan**, *baw-khan´;* a prim. root; to *test* (espec. metals); gen. and fig. to *investigate:*— examine, prove, tempt, try (trial).

975. בַּחַן **bachan**, *bakh´-an;* from 974 (in the sense of keeping a *look-out*); a watch-*tower:*— tower.

976. בֹּחַן **bôchan**, *bo´-khan;* from 974; *trial:*— tried.

977. בָּחַר **bâchar**, *baw-khar´;* a prim. root; prop. to *try*, i.e. (by impl.) *select:*— acceptable, appoint, choose (choice), excellent, join, be rather, require.

בָּחֻר **bâchur**. See 970.

978. בַּחֲרוּמִי **Bachărûwmîy**, *bakh-ar-oo-mee´;* patrial from 980 (by transp.); a *Bacharumite* or inhab. of Bachurim:— Baharumite.

979. בְּחֻרוֹת **bechûrôwth**, *bekh-oo-rothe´;* or

בְּחוּרוֹת **bechûwrôwth**, *bekh-oo-roth´;* fem. plur. of 970; also (masc. plur.)

בְּחֻרִים **bechûrîym**, *bekh-oo-reem´;* *youth* (collect. and abstr.):— young men, youth.

980. בַּחֻרִים **Bachûrîym**, *bakh-oo-reem´;* or

בַּחוּרִים **Bachûwrîym**, *bakh-oo-reem´;* masc. plur. of 970; *young men; Bachurim*, a place in Pal.:— Bahurim.

981. בָּטָא **bâṭâ'**, *baw-taw´;* or

בָּטָה **bâṭâh**, *baw-taw´;* a prim. root; to *babble;* hence, to *vociferate* angrily:— pronounce, speak (unadvisedly).

982. בָּטַח **bâṭach**, *baw-takh´;* a prim. root; prop. to *hie* for refuge [but not so *precipitately* as 2620]; fig. to *trust*, be confident or

sure:— be bold (confident, secure, sure), careless (one, woman), put confidence, (make to) hope, (put, make to) trust.

983. בֶּטַח **beṭach**, *beh'takh;* from 982; prop. a place of *refuge;* abstr. *safety,* both the fact (*security*) and the feeling (*trust*); often (adv. with or without prep.) *safely:*— assurance, boldly, (without) care (-less), confidence, hope, safe (-ly, -ty), secure, surely.

984. בֶּטַח **Beṭach**, *beh'-takh; the same as 983; Betach, a place in Syria:*— Betah.

985. בִּטְחָה **biṭchâh**, *bit-khaw';* fem. of 984; *trust:*— confidence.

986. בִּטָּחוֹן **biṭṭâchôwn**, *bit-taw-khone';* from 982; *trust:*— confidence, hope.

987. בַּטֻּחוֹת **baṭṭuchôwth**, *bat-too-khōth'; fem. plur.* from 982; *security:*— secure.

988. בָּטֵל **bâṭêl**, *baw-tale';* a prim. root; to *desist* from labor:— cease.

989. בְּטֵל **beṭêl** (Chald.), *bet-ale';* corresp. to 988; to *stop:*— (cause, make to), cease, hinder.

990. בֶּטֶן **beṭen**, *beh'-ten;* from an unused root prob. mean. to *be hollow;* the *belly,* espec. the *womb;* also the *bosom* or *body* of anything:— belly, body, + as they be born, + within, womb.

991. בֶּטֶן **Beṭen**, *beh'-ten; the same as 990; Beten, a place in Pal.:*— Beten.

992. בֹּטֶן **bôṭen**, *bo'-ten;* from 990; (only in plur.) a *pistachio*-nut (from its form):— nut.

993. בְּטֹנִים **Beṭônîym**, *bet-o-neem'; prob. plur.* from 992; *hollows: Betonim, a place in Pal.:*— Betonim.

994. בִּי **bîy**, *bee;* perh. from 1158 (in the sense of *asking*); prop. a *request;* used only adv. (always with "my Lord"); *Oh that!; with leave,* or *if it please:*— alas, O, oh.

995. בִּין **bîyn**, *bene;* a prim. root; to *separate* mentally (or *distinguish*), i.e.(gen.) *understand:*— attend, consider, be cunning, diligently, direct, discern, eloquent, feel, inform, instruct, have intelligence, know, look well to, mark, perceive, be prudent, regard, (can) skill (-full), teach, think, (cause, make to, get, give, have) understand (-ing), view, (deal) wise (-ly, man).

996. בֵּין **bêyn**, *bane* (sometimes in the plur. masc. or fem.); prop. the constr. contr. form of an otherwise unused noun from 995; a *distinction;* but used only as a prep. *between* (repeated before each noun, often with other particles); also as a conj., *either ... or:*— among, asunder, at, between (-twixt ... and), + from (the widest), × in, out of, whether (it be ... or), within.

997. בֵּין **bêyn** (Chald.), *bane;* corresp. to 996:— among, between.

998. בִּינָה **bîynâh**, *bee-naw';* from 995; *under-*

standing:— knowledge, meaning, × perfectly, understanding, wisdom.

999. בִּינָה **bîynâh** (Chald.), *bee-naw';* corresp. to 998:— knowledge.

1000. בֵּיצָה **bêytsâh**, *bay-tsaw';* from the same as 948; an *egg* (from its whiteness):— egg.

1001. בִּירָא **bîyrâ'** (Chald.), *bee-raw';* corresp. to 1002; a *palace:*— palace.

1002. בִּירָה **bîyrâh**, *bee-raw';* of for. or.; a *castle* or *palace:*— palace.

1003. בִּירָנִית **bîyrânîyth**, *bee-raw-neeth';* from 1002; a *fortress:*— castle.

1004. בַּיִת **bayith**, *bah'-yith;* prob. from 1129 abb.; a *house* (in the greatest var. of applications, espec. *family,* etc.):— court, daughter, door, + dungeon, family, + forth of, × great as would contain, hangings, homeborn, [winterlhouse (-hold), inside (-ward), palace, place, + prison, + steward, + tablet, temple, web, + within (-out).

1005. בַּיִת **bayith** (Chald.), *bah-yith;* corresp. to 1004:— house.

1006. בַּיִת **Bayith**, *bah'-yith; the same as 1004; Bajith, a place in Pal.:*— Bajith.

1007. בֵּית אָוֶן **Bêyth 'Âven**, *bayth aw'-ven;* from 1004 and 205; *house of vanity; Beth-Aven, a place in Pal.:*— Beth-aven.

1008. בֵּית־אֵל **Bêyth-'Êl**, *bayth-ale';* from 1004 and 410; *house of God; Beth-El, a place in Pal.:*— Beth-el.

1009. בֵּית אַרְבֵּאל **Bêyth 'Arbê'l**, *bayth ar-bale';* from 1004 and 695 and 410; *house of God's ambush; Beth-Arbel, a place in Pal.:*— Beth-Arbel.

1010. בֵּית בַּעַל מְעוֹן **Bêyth Ba'al Me'ôwn**, *bayth bah'-al mĕ-own';* from 1004 and 1168 and 4583; *house of Baal* of (the) *habitation of* [appar. by transp.]; or (short.)

בֵּית מְעוֹן **Bêyth Me'ôwn**, *bayth mĕ-own'; house of habitation of* (Baal); *Beth-Baal-Meön, a place in Pal.:*— Beth-baal-meon. Comp. 1186 and 1194.

1011. בֵּית בִּראִי **Bêyth Bir'îy**, *bayth bir-ee';* from 1004 and 1254; *house of a creative* one; *Beth-Biri, a place in Pal.:*— Beth-birei.

1012. בֵּית בָּרָה **Bêyth Bârâh**, *bayth baw-raw';* prob. from 1004 and 5679; *house of* (the) *ford; Beth-Barah, a place in Pal.:*— Beth-barah.

1013. בֵּית־גָּדֵר **Bêyth-Gâdêr**, *bayth-gaw-dare';* from 1004 and 1447; *house of* (the) *wall; Beth-Gader, a place in Pal.:*— Beth-gader.

1014. בֵּית גָּמוּל **Bêyth Gâmûwl**, *bayth gaw-mool';* from 1004 and the pass. part. of 1576;

house of (the) *weaned; Beth-Gamul*, a place E. of the Jordan:— Beth-gamul.

1015. בֵּית דִּבְלָתַיִם **Bêyth Diblâthayim**, *bayth dib-law-thah´-yim;* from 1004 and the dual of 1690; *house of* (the) *two figcakes; Beth-Diblathajim*, a place E. of the Jordan:— Beth-diblathaim.

1016. בֵּית־דָּגוֹן **Bêyth-Dâgôwn**, *bayth-daw-gohn´;* from 1004 and 1712; *house of Dagon; Beth-Dagon*, the name of two places in Pal.:— Beth-dagon.

1017. בֵּית הָאֱלִי **Bêyth hâ-'Ĕlîy**, *bayth haw-el-ee´;* patrial from 1008 with the art. interposed; *a Beth-elite*, or inhab. of Bethel:— Bethelite.

1018. בֵּית הָאָצֵל **Bêyth hâ-'Êtsel**, *bayth haw-ay´-tsel;* from 1004 and 681 with the art. interposed; *house of the side; Beth-ha-Etsel*, a place in Pal.:— Beth-ezel.

1019. בֵּית הַגִּלְגָּל **Bêyth hag-Gilgâl**, *bayth hag-gil gawl´;* from 1004 and 1537 with the article interposed; *house of Gilgal* (or *rolling*); *Beth-hag-Gilgal*, a place in Pal.:— Beth-gilgal.

1020. בֵּית הַיְשִׁימוֹת **Bêyth ha-Yeshîy-môwth**, *bayth hah-yesh-ee-mōth´;* from 1004 and the plur. of 3451 with the art. interposed; *house of the deserts; Beth-ha-Jeshimoth*, a town E. of the Jordan:— Beth-jeshimoth.

1021. בֵּית הַכֶּרֶם **Bêyth hak-Kerem**, *bayth hak-keh´-rem;* from 1004 and 3754 with the art. interposed; *house of the vineyard; Beth-hak-Kerem*, a place in Pal.:— Beth-haccerem.

1022. בֵּית הַלַּחְמִי **Bêyth hal-Lachmîy**, *bayth hal-lakh-mee´;* patrial from 1035 with the art. ins.; *a Beth-lechemite*, or native of Bethlechem:— Bethlehemite.

1023. בֵּית הַמֶּרְחָק **Bêyth ham-Merchâq**, *bayth ham-mer-khawk´;* from 1004 and 4801 with the art. interposed; *house of the breadth; Beth-ham-Merchak*, a place in Pal.:— place that was far off.

1024. בֵּית הַמַּרְכָּבוֹת **Bêyth ham-Markâbôwth**, *bayth ham-mar-kaw-both´;* or (short.)

בֵּית מַרְכָּבוֹת **Bêyth Markâbôwth**, *bayth mar-kaw-both´;* from 1004 and the plur. of 4818 (with or without the art. interposed); *place of* (the) *chariots; Beth-ham-Markaboth* or *Beth-Markaboth*, a place in Pal.:— Beth-marcaboth.

1025. בֵּית הָעֵמֶק **Bêyth hâ-'Êmeq**, *bayth haw-ay´-mek;* from 1004 and 6010 with the art. interposed; *house of the valley; Beth-ha-Emek*, a place in Pal.:— Beth-emek.

1026. בֵּית הָעֲרָבָה **Bêyth hâ-'Ărâbâh**, *bayth haw-ar-aw-baw´;* from 1004 and 6160 with the art. interposed; *house of the Desert; Beth-ha-Arabah*, a place in Pal.:— Beth-arabah.

1027. בֵּית הָרָם **Bêyth hâ-Râm**, *bayth haw-rawm´;* from 1004 and 7311 with the art. inter-

posed; *house of the height; Beth-ha-Ram*, a place E. of the Jordan:— Beth-aram.

1028. בֵּית הָרָן **Bêyth hâ-Rân**, *bayth haw-rawn´;* prob. for 1027; *Beth-ha-Ran*, a place E. of the Jordan:— Beth-haran.

1029. בֵּית הַשִּׁטָּה **Bêyth hash-Shiṭṭâh**, *bayth hash-shit-taw´;* from 1004 and 7848 with the art. interposed; *house of the acacia; Beth-hash-Shittah*, a place in Pal.:— Beth-shittah.

1030. בֵּית הַשֶּׁמֶשׁ **Bêyth hash-Shimshîy**, *bayth hash-shim-shee´;* patrial from 1053 with the art. ins.; *a Beth-shimshite*, or inhab. of Bethshemesh:— Bethshemite.

1031. בֵּית חָגְלָה **Bêyth Choglâh**, *bayth chog-law´;* from 1004 and the same as 2295; *house of a partridge; Beth-Choglah*, a place in Pal.:— Beth-hoglah.

1032. בֵּית חוֹרוֹן **Bêyth Chôwrôwn**, *bayth kho-rone´;* from 1004 and 2356; *house of hollowness; Beth-Choron*, the name of two adjoining places in Pal.:— Beth-horon.

בֵּית חָנָן **Bêyth Chânân**. See 358.

1033. בֵּית כַּר **Bêyth Kar**, *bayth kar;* from 1004 and 3733; *house of pasture; Beth-Car*, a place in Pal.:— Beth-car.

1034. בֵּית לְבָאוֹת **Bêyth Lebâ'ôwth**, *bayth leb-aw-ōth´;* from 1004 and the plural of 3833; *house of lionesses; Beth-Lebaoth*, a place in Pal.:— Beth-lebaoth. Comp. 3822.

1035. בֵּית לֶחֶם **Bêyth Lechem**, *bayth leh´-khem;* from 1004 and 3899; *house of bread; Beth-Lechem*, a place in Pal.:— Beth-lehem.

1036. בֵּית לְעַפְרָה **Bêyth le-'Aphrâh**, *bayth lĕ-af-raw´;* from 1004 and the fem. of 6083 (with prep. interposed); *house to* (i.e. *of*) *dust; Beth-le-Aphrah*, a place in Pal.:— house of Aphrah.

1037. בֵּית מִלּוֹא **Bêyth Millôw'**, *bayth mil-lo´;* or

בֵּית מִלֹּא **Bêyth Millô'**, *bayth mil-lo´;* from 1004 and 4407; *house of* (the) *rampart; Beth-Millo*, the name of two citadels:— house of Millo.

1038. בֵּית מַעֲכָה **Bêyth Ma'âkâh**, *bayth mah-ak-aw´;* from 1004 and 4601; *house of Maakah; Beth-Maakah*, a place in Pal.:— Beth-maachah.

1039. בֵּית נִמְרָה **Bêyth Nimrâh**, *bayth nim-raw´;* from 1004 and the fem. of 5246; *house of* (the) *leopard; Beth-Nimrah*, a place east of the Jordan:— Beth-nimrah. Comp. 5247.

1040. בֵּית עֵדֶן **Bêyth 'Êden**, *bayth ay´-den;* from 1004 and 5730; *house of pleasure; Beth-Eden*, a place in Syria:— Beth-eden.

1041. בֵּית עַזְמָוֶת **Bêyth 'Azmâveth**, *bayth az-*

maw´-veth; from 1004 and 5820; house of Azmaveth, a place in Pal.:— Beth-az-maveth. Comp. 5820.

1042. בֵּית עֲנוֹת **Bêyth 'Ănôwth**, bayth an-ōth´; from 1004 and a plur. from 6030; house of replies; Beth-Anoth, a place in Pal.:— Beth-anoth.

1043. בֵּית עֲנָת **Bêyth 'Ănâth**, bayth an-awth´; an orth. var. for 1042; Beth-Anath, a place in Pal.:— Beth-anath.

1044. בֵּית עֵקֶד **Bêyth 'Êqed**, bayth ay´-ked; from 1004 and a der. of 6123; house of (the) binding (for sheep-shearing); Beth-Eked, a place in Pal.:— shearing house.

1045. בֵּית עַשְׁתָּרוֹת **Bêyth 'Ashtârôwth**, bayth ash-taw-rōth´; from 1004 and 6252; house of Ashtoreths; Beth-Ashtaroth, a place in Pal.:— house of Ashtaroth. Comp. 1203, 6252.

1046. בֵּית פֶּלֶט **Bêyth Peleṭ**, bayth peh´-let; from 1004 and 6412; house of escape; Beth-Palet, a place in Pal.:— Beth-palet.

1047. בֵּית פְּעוֹר **Bêyth Pe'ôwr**, bayth pĕ-ore´; from 1004 and 6465; house of Peor; Beth-Peor, a place E. of the Jordan:— Beth-peor.

1048. בֵּית פַּצֵּץ **Bêyth Patstsêts**, bayth pats-tsates´; from 1004 and a der. from 6327; house of dispersion; Beth-Patstsets, a place in Pal.:— Beth-pazzez.

1049. בֵּית צוּר **Bêyth Tsûwr**, bayth tsoor´; from 1004 and 6697; house of (the) rock; Beth-Tsur, a place in Pal.:— Beth-zur.

1050. בֵּית רְחוֹב **Bêyth Rechôwb**, bayth rĕ-khobe´; from 1004 and 7339; house of (the) street; Beth-Rechob, a place in Pal.:— Beth-rehob.

1051. בֵּית רָפָא **Bêyth Râphâ'**, bayth raw-faw´; from 1004 and 7497; house of (the) giant; Beth-Rapha, an Isr.:— Beth-rapha.

1052. בֵּית שְׁאָן **Bêyth She'ân**, bayth shĕ-awn´; or

בֵּית שָׁן **Bêyth Shân**, bayth shawn´; from 1004 and 7599; house of ease; Beth-Shean or Beth-Shan, a place in Pal.:— Beth-shean, Beth-Shan.

1053. בֵּית שֶׁמֶשׁ **Bêyth Shemesh**, bayth sheh´-mesh; from 1004 and 8121; house of (the) sun; Beth-Shemesh, a place in Pal.:— Beth-she-mesh.

1054. בֵּית תַּפּוּחַ **Bêyth Tappûwach**, bayth tap-poo´-akh; from 1004 and 8598; house of (the) apple; Beth-Tappuach, a place in Pal.:— Beth-tappuah.

1055. בִּיתָן **bîythân**, bee-thawn´; prob. from 1004; a palace (i.e. large house):— palace.

1056. בָּכָא **Bâkâ'**, baw-kaw´; from 1058, weeping; Baca, a valley in Pal.:— Baca.

1057. בָּכָא **bâkâ'**, baw-kaw´; the same as 1056;

the weeping tree (some gum-distilling tree, perh. the balsam):— mulberry tree.

1058. בָּכָה **bâkâh**, baw-kaw´; a prim. root; to weep; gen. to bemoan:— × at all, bewail, complain, make lamentation, × more, mourn, × sore, × with tears, weep.

1059. בֶּכֶה **bekeh**, beh´-keh; from 1058; a weeping:— × sore.

1060. בְּכוֹר **bekôwr**, bek-ore´; from 1069; firstborn; hence, chief:— eldest (son), first-born (-ling).

1061. בִּכּוּר **bikkûwr**, bik-koor´; from 1069; the first-fruits of the crop:— first fruit (-ripe [fig.]), hasty fruit.

1062. בְּכוֹרָה **bekôwrâh**, bek-o-raw´; or (short.)

בְּכֹרָה **bekôrâh**, bek-o-raw´; fem. of 1060; the firstling of man or beast; abstr. primogeniture:— birthright, firstborn (-ling).

1063. בִּכּוּרָה **bikkûwrâh**, bik-koo-raw´; fem. of 1061; the early fig:— firstripe (fruit).

1064. בְּכוֹרַת **Bekôwrath**, bek-o-rath´; fem. of 1062; primogeniture; Bekorath, an Isr.:— Bechorath.

1065. בְּכִי **bekîy**, bek-ee´; from 1058; a weeping; by anal. a dripping:— overflowing, × sore, (continual) weeping, wept.

1066. בֹּכִים **Bôkîym**, bo-keem´; plur. act. part. of 1058; (with the art.) the weepers; Bo-kim, a place in Pal.:— Bochim.

1067. בְּכִירָה **bekîyrâh**, bek-ee-raw´; fem. from 1069; the eldest daughter:— firstborn.

1068. בְּכִית **bekîyth**, bek-eeth´; from 1058; a weeping:— mourning.

1069. בָּכַר **bâkar**, baw-kar´; a prim. root; prop. to burst the womb, i.e. (caus.) bear or make early fruit (of woman or tree); also (as denom. from 1061) to give the birthright:— make firstborn, be firstling, bring forth first child (new fruit).

1070. בֶּכֶר **beker**, beh´-ker; from 1069 (in the sense of youth); a young camel:— dromedary.

1071. בֶּכֶר **Beker**, beh´-ker; the same as 1070; Beker, the name of two Isr.:— Becher.

1072. בִּכְרָה **bikrâh**, bik-raw´; fem. of 1070; a young she-camel:— dromedary.

בְּכֹרָה **bekôrâh**. See 1062.

1073. בַּכֻּרָה **bakkûrâh**, bak-koo-raw´; by orth. var. for 1063; a first-ripe fig:— first-ripe.

1074. בֹּכְרוּ **Bôkerûw**, bo-ker-oo´; from 1069; first-born; Bokeru, an Isr.:— Bocheru.

1075. בִּכְרִי **Bikrîy**, bik-ree´; from 1069; youth-ful; Bikri, an Isr.:— Bichri.

Hebrew

1076. בִּכְרִי **Bakrîy**, *bak-ree´;* patron. from 1071; a *Bakrite* (collect.) or desc. of Beker:— Bachrites.

1077. בַּל **bal**, *bal;* from 1086; prop. a *failure;* by impl. *nothing;* usually (adv.) *not* at all; also *lest:*— lest, neither, no, none (that ...), not (any), nothing.

1078. בֵּל **Bêl**, *bale;* by contr. for 1168; *Bel,* the Baal of the Babylonians:— Bel.

1079. בָּל **bâl** (Chald.), *bawl;* from 1080; prop. *anxiety,* i.e. (by impl.) the *heart* (as its seat):— heart.

1080. בְּלָא **belâ'** (Chald.), *bel-aw´;* corresp. to 1086 (but used only in a ment. sense); to *afflict:*— wear out.

1081. בַּלְאֲדָן **Bal'ădân**, *bal-ad-awn´;* from 1078 and 113 (contr.); *Bel (is his) lord; Baladan,* the name of a Bab. prince:— Baladan.

1082. בָּלַג **bâlag**, *baw-lag´;* a prim. root; to *break off* or *loose* (in a favorable or unfavorable sense), i.e. *desist* (from grief) or *invade* (with destruction):— comfort, (recover) strength (-en).

1083. בִּלְגָּה **Bilgâh**, *bil-gaw´;* from 1082; *desistance; Bilgah,* the name of two Isr.:— Bilgah.

1084. בִּלְגַּי **Bilgay**, *bil-gah´-ee;* from 1082; *desistant; Bilgai,* an Isr.:— Bilgai.

1085. בִּלְדַּד **Bildad**, *bil-dad´;* of uncert. der.; *Bildad,* one of Job's friends:— Bildad.

1086. בָּלָה **bâlâh**, *baw-law´;* a prim. root; to *fail;* by impl. to *wear out, decay* (caus. *consume, spend*):— consume, enjoy long, become (make, wax) old, spend, waste.

1087. בָּלֶה **bâleh**, *baw-leh´;* from 1086; *worn out:*— old.

1088. בָּלָה **Bâlâh**, *baw-law´;* fem. of 1087; *failure; Balah,* a place in Pal.:— Balah.

1089. בָּלַהּ **bâlahh**, *baw-lah´;* a prim. root [rather by transp. for 926]; to *palpitate;* hence, (caus.) to *terrify:*— trouble.

1090. בִּלְהָה **Bilhâh**, *bil-haw´;* from 1089; *timid; Bilhah,* the name of one of Jacob's concubines; also of a place in Pal.:— Bilhah.

1091. בַּלָּהָה **ballâhâh**, *bal-law-haw´;* from 1089; *alarm;* hence, *destruction:*— terror, trouble.

1092. בִּלְהָן **Bilhân**, *bil-hawn´;* from 1089; *timid; Bilhan,* the name of an Edomite and of an Isr.:— Bilhan.

1093. בְּלוֹ **belôw** (Chald.), *bel-o´;* from a root corresp. to 1086; *excise* (on articles consumed):— tribute.

1094. בְּלוֹא **belôw'**, *bel-o´;* or (fully)

בְּלוֹי **belôwy**, *bel-o´-ee;* from 1086; (only in plur. constr.) *rags:*— old.

1095. בֵּלְטְשַׁאצַּר **Bêlteshatsstsar**, *bale-tesh-ats-*

tsar´; of for. der.; *Belteshatstsar,* the Bab. name of Daniel:— Belteshazzar.

1096. בֵּלְטְשַׁאצַּר **Bêlteshatsstsar** (Chald.), *bale-tesh-ats-tsar´;* corresp. to 1095:— Belteshazzar.

1097. בְּלִי **belîy**, *bel-ee´;* from 1086; prop. *failure,* i.e. *nothing* or *destruction;* usually (with prep.) *without, not yet, because not, as long as,* etc.:— corruption, ig[norantly], for lack of, where no ... is, so that no, none, not, un[aware], without.

1098. בְּלִיל **belîyl**, *bel-eel´;* from 1101; *mixed,* i.e. (spec.) *feed* (for cattle):— corn, fodder, provender.

1099. בְּלִימָה **belîymâh**, *bel-ee-mah´;* from 1097 and 4100; (as indef.) *nothing whatever:*— nothing.

1100. בְּלִיַּעַל **belîya'al**, *bel-e-yah´-al;* from 1097 and 3276; *without profit, worthlessness;* by extens. *destruction, wickedness* (often in connection with 376, 802, 1121, etc.):— Belial, evil, naughty, ungodly (men), wicked.

1101. בָּלַל **bâlal**, *baw-lal´;* a prim. root; to *overflow* (spec. with oil); by impl. to *mix;* also (denom. from 1098) to *fodder:*— anoint, confound, × fade, mingle, mix (self), give provender, temper.

1102. בָּלַם **bâlam**, *baw-lam´;* a prim. root; to *muzzle:*— be held in.

1103. בָּלַס **bâlaç**, *baw-las´;* a prim. root; to *pinch* sycamore figs (a process necessary to ripen them):— gatherer.

1104. בָּלַע **bâla'**, *baw-lah´;* a prim. root; to *make away with* (spec. by *swallowing*); gen. to *destroy:*— cover, destroy, devour, eat up, be at end, spend up, swallow down (up).

1105. בֶּלַע **bela'**, *beh´-lah;* from 1104; a *gulp;* fig. *destruction:*— devouring, that which he hath swallowed up.

1106. בֶּלַע **Bela'**, *beh´-lah;* the same as 1105; *Bela,* the name of a place, also of an Edomite and of two Isr.:— Bela.

1107. בִּלְעֲדֵי **bil'ădêy**, *bil-ad-ay´;* or

בַּלְעֲדֵי **bal'ădêy**, *bal-ad-ay´;* constr. plur. from 1077 and 5703, *not till,* i.e. (as prep. or adv.) *except, without, besides:*— beside, not (in), save, without.

1108. בַּלְעִי **Bal'îy**, *bal-ee´;* patron. from 1106; a *Belaite* (collect.) or desc. of Bela:— Belaites.

1109. בִּלְעָם **Bil'âm**, *bil-awm´;* prob. from 1077 and 5971; *not (of the) people,* i.e. *foreigner; Bilam,* a Mesopotamian prophet; also a place in Pal.:— Balaam, Bileam.

1110. בָּלַק **bâlaq**, *baw-lak´*; a prim. root; to *annihilate:*— (make) waste.

1111. בָּלָק **Bâlâq**, *baw-lawk´*; from 1110; *waster; Balak*, a Moabitish king:— Balak.

1112. בֵּלְשַׁאצַּר **Bêlsha'tstsar**, *bale-shats-tsar´*; or

בֵּלְאשַׁצַּר **Bêl'shatstsar**, *bale-shats-tsar´*; of for. or. (comp. 1095); *Belshatstsar*, a Bab. king:— Belshazzar.

1113. בֵּלְשַׁאצַּר **Bêlsha'tstsar** (Chald.), *bale-shats-tsar´*; corresp. to 1112:— Belshazzar.

1114. בִּלְשָׁן **Bilshân**, *bil-shawn´*; of uncert. der.; *Bilshan*, an Isr.:— Bilshan.

1115. בִּלְתִּי **biltîy**, *bil-tee´*; constr. fem. of 1086 (equiv. to 1097); prop. a *failure of*, i.e. (used only as a neg. particle, usually with prep. pref.) *not, except, without, unless, besides, because not, until*, etc.:— because un[sati-able], beside, but, + continual, except, from, lest, neither, no more, none, not, nothing, save, that no, without.

1116. בָּמָה **bâmâh**, *baw-maw´*; from an unused root (mean. to *be high*); an *elevation:*— height, high place, wave.

1117. בָּמָה **Bâmâh**, *baw-maw´*; the same as 1116; *Bamah*, a place in Pal.:— Bamah. See also 1120.

1118. בִּמְהָל **Bimhâl**, *bim-hawl´*; prob. from 4107 with prep. pref.; *with pruning; Bimhal*, an Isr.:— Bimhal.

1119. בְּמוֹ **b°môw**, *bem-o´*; prol. for prep. pref.; *in, with, by*, etc.:— for, in into, through.

1120. בָּמוֹת **Bâmôwth**, *baw-mōth´*; plur. of 1116; *heights;* or (fully)

בָּמוֹת בַּעַל **Bâmôwth Ba'al**, *baw-mōth´ bah´-al*; from the same and 1168; *heights of Baal; Bamoth* or *Bamoth-Baal*, a place E. of the Jordan:— Bamoth, Bamoth-baal.

1121. בֵּן **bên**, *bane*; from 1129; a *son* (as a *builder* of the family name), in the widest sense (of lit. and fig. relationship, incl. *grandson, subject, nation, quality* or *condition*, etc., [like 1, 251, etc.]):— + afflicted, age, [Ahoh-] [Ammon-] [Hachmon-] [Lev-lite, [anoint-] ed one, appointed to, (+) arrow, [Assyr-] [Babylon-] [Egypt-] [Grec-]ian, one born, bough, branch, breed, + (young) bullock, + (young) calf, × came up in, child, colt, × common, × corn, daughter, × of first , + firstborn, foal, + very fruitful, + postage, × in, + kid, + lamb, (+) man, meet, + mighty, + nephew, old, (+) people, + rebel, + robber, × servant born, × soldier, son, + spark, + steward, + stranger, × surely, them of, + tumultuous one, + valiant [-est], whelp, worthy, young (one), youth.

1122. בֵּן **Bên**, *bane*; the same as 1121; *Ben*, an Isr.:— Ben.

1123. בֵּן **bên** (Chald.), *bane*; corresp. to 1121:— child, son, young.

1124. בְּנָא **b°nâ'** (Chald.), *ben-aw´*; or

בְּנָה **b°nâh** (Chald.), *ben-aw´*; corresp. to 1129; to *build:*— build, make.

1125. בֶּן־אֲבִינָדָב **Ben-'Ăbîynâdâb**, *ben-ab-ee´´-naw-dawb´*; from 1121 and 40; (the) *son of Abinadab; Ben-Abinadab*, an Isr.:— the son of Abinadab.

1126. בֶּן־אוֹנִי **Ben-'Ôwniy**, *ben-o-nee´*; from 1121 and 205; *son of my sorrow; Ben-Oni*, the orig. name of Benjamin:— Ben-oni.

1127. בֶּן־גֶּבֶר **Ben-Geber**, *ben-gheh´-ber*; from 1121 and 1397; *son of* (the) *hero; Ben-Geber*, an Isr.:— the son of Geber.

1128. בֶּן־דֶּקֶר **Ben-Deqer**, *ben-deh´-ker*; from 1121 and a der. of 1856; *son of piercing* (or *of a lance*); *Ben-Deker*, an Isr.:— the son of Dekar.

1129. בָּנָה **bânâh**, *baw-naw´*; a prim. root; to *build* (lit. and fig.):— (begin to) build (-er), obtain children, make, repair, set (up), × surely.

1130. בֶּן־הֲדַד **Ben-Hădad**, *ben-had-ad´*; from 1121 and 1908; *son of Hadad; Ben-Hadad*, the name of several Syrian kings:— Benhadad.

1131. בִּנּוּי **Binnûwy**, *bin-noo´-ee*; from 1129; *built* up; *Binnui*, an Isr.:— Binnui.

1132. בֶּן־זוֹחֵת **Ben-Zôwchêth**, *ben-zo-khayth´*; from 1121 and 2105; *son of Zocheth; Ben-Zocheth*, an Isr.:— Ben-zoketh.

1133. בֶּן־חוּר **Ben-Chûwr**, *ben-khoor´*; from 1121 and 2354; *son of Chur; Ben-Chur*, an Isr.:— the son of Hur.

1134. בֶּן־חַיִל **Ben-Chayil**, *ben-khah´-yil*; from 1121 and 2428; *son of might; Ben-Chail*, an Isr.:— Ben-hail.

1135. בֶּן־חָנָן **Ben-Chânân**, *ben-khaw-nawn´*; from 1121 and 2605; *son of Chanan; Ben-Chanan*, an Isr.:— Ben-hanan.

1136. בֶּן־חֶסֶד **Ben-Checed**, *ben-kheh´-sed*; from 1121 and 2617; *son of kindness; Ben-Chesed*, an Isr.:— the son of Hesed.

1137. בָּנִי **Bâniy**, *baw-nee´*; from 1129; *built; Bani*, the name of five Isr.:— Bani.

1138. בֻּנִּי **Bunniy**, *boon-nee´*; or (fuller)

בּוּנִי **Bûwniy**, *boo-nee´*; from 1129; *built; Bunni* or *Buni*, an Isr.:— Bunni.

1139. בְּנֵי־בְרַק **B°nêy-B°raq**, *ben-ay´-ber-ak´*; from the plur. constr. of 1121 and 1300; *sons of lightning, Bene-berak*, a place in Pal.:— Bene-barak.

1140. בִּנְיָה **binyâh**, *bin-yaw´*; fem. from 1129; a *structure:*— building.

1141. בְּנָיָה **B°nâyâh**, *ben-aw-yaw´*; or (prol.)

בְּנָיָהוּ **Bᵉnâyâhûw**, *ben-aw-yaw´-hoo;* from 1129 and 3050; *Jah has built; Benajah,* the name of twelve Isr.:— Benaiah.

1142. בְּנֵי יַעֲקָן **Bᵉnêy Ya'ăqân**, *ben-ay´ yah-ak-awn´;* from the plur. of 1121 and 3292; *sons of Yaakan; Bene-Jaakan,* a place in the Desert:— Bene-jaakan.

1143. בְּנַיִם **bênayim**, *bay-nah´-yim;* dual of 996; a *double interval,* i.e. the space between two armies:— + champion.

1144. בִּנְיָמִין **Binyâmîyn**, *bin-yaw-mene´;* from 1121 and 3225; *son of* (the) *right hand; Binjamin,* youngest son of Jacob; also the tribe descended from him, and its territory:— Benjamin.

1145. בֶּן־יְמִינִי **Ben-yᵉmîyniy**, *ben-yem-ee-nee´;* sometimes (with the art. ins.)

בֶּן־הַיְמִינִי **Ben-ha-yᵉmîyniy**, *ben-hah-yem-ee-nee´;* with 376 ins. (1 Sam. 9:1)

בֶּן־אִישׁ יְמִינִי **Ben-'îysh Yᵉmîyniy**, *ben-eesh´ yem-ee-nee´; son of a man of Jemini;* or short. (1 Sam. 9:4; Esth. 2:5)

אִישׁ יְמִינִי **'îysh Yᵉmîyniy**, *eesh yem-ee-nee´; a man of Jemini,* or (1 Sam. 20:1) simply

יְמִינִי **Yᵉmîyniy**, *yem-ee-nee´; a Jeminite;* (plur.

בְּנֵי יְמִינִי **Bᵉniy Yᵉmîyniy**, *ben-ay´ yem-ee-nee´;* patron. from 1144; a *Benjaminite,* or descendent of Benjamin:— Benjamite, of Benjamin.

1146. בִּנְיָן **binyân**, *bin-yawn´;* from 1129; an *edifice:*— building.

1147. בִּנְיָן **binyân** (Chald.), *bin-yawn´;* corresp. to 1146:— building.

1148. בְּנִינוּ **Bᵉnîynûw**, *ben-ee-noo´;* prob. from 1121 with pron. suff.; *our son; Beninu,* an Isr.:— Beninu.

1149. בְּנַס **bᵉnaç** (Chald.), *ben-as´;* of uncert. affin.; to *be enraged:*— be angry.

1150. בִּנְעָא **Bin'â'**, *bin-aw´;* or

בִּנְעָה **Bin'âh**, *bin-aw´;* of uncert. der.; *Bina* or *Binah,* an Isr.:— Binea, Bineah.

1151. בֶּן־עַמִּי **Ben-'Ammîy**, *ben-am-mee´;* from 1121 and 5971 with pron. suff.; *son of my people; Ben-Ammi,* a son of Lot:— Ben-ammi.

1152. בְּסוֹדְיָה **Bᵉçôwdᵉyâh**, *bes-o-deh-yaw´;* from 5475 and 3050 with prep. pref.; *in* (the) *counsel of Jehovah; Besodejah,* an Isr.:— Besodeiah.

1153. בְּסַי **Bᵉçay**, *bes-ah´-ee;* from 947; *domineering; Besai,* one of the Nethinim:— Besai.

1154. בֶּסֶר **beçer**, *beh´-ser;* from an unused root mean. to *be sour;* an *immature* grape:— unripe grape.

1155. בֹּסֶר **bôçer**, *bo´ser;* from the same as 1154:— sour grape.

1156. בְּעָא **bᵉ'â'** (Chald.), *beh-aw´;* or

בְּעָה **bᵉ'âh** (Chald.), *beh-aw´;* corresp. to 1158; to *seek* or *ask:*— ask, desire, make [petition], pray, request, seek.

1157. בְּעַד **bᵉ'ad**, *beh-ad´;* from 5704 with prep. pref.; *in up to* or *over against;* gen. *at, beside, among, behind, for,* etc.:— about, at, by (means of), for, over, through, up (-on), within.

1158. בָּעָה **bâ'âh**, *baw-aw´;* a prim. root; to *gush* over, i.e. to *swell;* (fig.) to *desire* earnestly; by impl. to *ask:*— cause, inquire, seek up, swell out.

1159. בָּעוּ **bâ'ûw** (Chald.), *baw-oo´;* from 1156; a *request:*— petition.

1160. בְּעוֹר **Bᵉ'ôwr**, *beh-ore´;* from 1197 (in the sense of *burning*); a *lamp; Beôr,* the name of the father of an Edomitish king; also of that of Balaam:— Beor.

1161. בִּעוּתִים **bi'ûwthîym**, *be-oo-theme´;* masc. plur. from 1204; *alarms:*— terrors.

1162. בֹּעַז **Bô'az**, *bo´-az;* from an unused root of uncert. mean.; *Boaz,* the ancestor of David; also the name of a pillar in front of the temple:— Boaz.

1163. בָּעַט **bâ'aṭ**, *baw-at´;* a prim. root; to *trample* down, i.e. (fig.) *despise:*— kick.

1164. בְּעִי **bᵉ'îy**, *beh-ee´;* from 1158; a *prayer:*— grave.

1165. בְּעִיר **bᵉ'îyr**, *beh-ere´;* from 1197 (in the sense of *eating*); *cattle:*— beast, cattle.

1166. בָּעַל **bâ'al**, *baw-al´;* a prim. root; to *be master;* hence, (as denom. from 1167) to *marry:*— have dominion (over), be husband, marry (-ried, × wife).

1167. בַּעַל **ba'al**, *bah´-al;* from 1166; a *master;* hence, a *husband,* or (fig.) *owner* (often used with another noun in modifications of this latter sense):— + archer, + babbler, + bird, captain, chief man, + confederate, + have to do, + dreamer, those to whom it is due, + furious, those that are given to it, great, + hairy, he that hath it, have, + horseman, husband, lord, man, + married, master, person, + sworn, they of.

1168. בַּעַל **Ba'al**, *bah´-al;* the same as 1167; *Baal,* a Phœnician deity:— Baal, [plur.] Baalim.

1169. בְּעֵל **bᵉ'êl** (Chald.), *beh-ale´;* corresp. to 1167:— + chancellor.

1170. בַּעַל בְּרִית **Ba'al Bᵉrîyth**, *bah´-al ber-eeth´;* from 1168 and 1285; *Baal of* (the) *covenant; Baal-Berith,* a special deity of the Shechemites:— Baal-berith.

1171. בַּעַל גָּד **Ba'al Gâd**, *bah´-al gawd;* from 1168 and 1409; *Baal of Fortune; Baal-Gad,* a place in Syria:— Baal-gad.

1172. בַּעֲלָה **ba'ălâh**, *bah-al-aw´*; fem. of 1167; a *mistress*:— that hath, mistress.

1173. בַּעֲלָה **Ba'ălâh**, *bah-al-aw´*; the same as 1172; *Baalah*, the name of three places in Pal.:— Baalah.

1174. בַּעַל הָמוֹן **Ba'al Hâmôwn**, *bah´-al haw-mone´*; from 1167 and 1995; *possessor of a multitude*; *Baal-Hamon*, a place in Pal.:— Baal-hamon.

1175. בְּעָלוֹת **B^eâlôwth**, *beh-aw-lôth´*; plur. of 1172; *mistresses*; *Bealoth*, a place in Pal.:— Bealoth, in Aloth [by mistake for a plur. from 5927 with prep. pref.].

1176. בַּעַל זְבוּב **Ba'al Z^ebûwb**, *bah´-al zeb-oob´*; from 1168 and 2070; *Baal of* (the) *Fly*; *Baal-Zebub*, a special deity of the Ekronites:— Baalzebub.

1177. בַּעַל חָנָן **Ba'al Chânân**, *bah´-al khaw-nawn´*; from 1167 and 2603; *possessor of grace*; *Baal-Chanan*, the name of an Edomite, also of an Isr.:— Baal-hanan.

1178. בַּעַל חָצוֹר **Ba'al Châtsôwr**, *bah´-al khaw-tsore´*; from 1167 and a modif. of 2691; *possessor of a village*; *Baal-Chatsor*, a place in Pal.:— Baal-hazor.

1179. בַּעַל חֶרְמוֹן **Ba'al Chermôwn**, *bah´-al kher-mone´*; from 1167 and 2768; *possessor of Hermon*; *Baal-Chermon*, a place in Pal.:— Baal-hermon.

1180. בַּעֲלִי **Ba'ălîy**, *bah-al-ee´*; from 1167 with pron. suff.; *my master*; *Baali*, a symb. name for Jehovah:— Baali.

1181. בַּעֲלֵי בָּמוֹת **Ba'ălêy Bâmôwth**, *bah-al-ay´ baw-môth´*; from the plur. of 1168 and the plur. of 1116; *Baals of* (the) *heights*; *Baale-Bamoth*, a place E. of the Jordan:— lords of the high places.

1182. בְּעֶלְיָדָע **B^eelyâdâ´**, *beh-el-yaw-daw´*; from 1168 and 3045; *Baal has known*; *Beëljada*, an Isr.:— Beeliada.

1183. בְּעַלְיָה **B^ealyâh**, *beh-al-yaw´*; from 1167 and 3050; *Jah* (is) *master*; *Bealjah*, an Isr.:— Bealiah.

1184. בַּעֲלֵי יְהוּדָה **Ba'ălêy Y^ehûwdâh**, *bah-al-ay´ yeh-hoo-daw´*; from the plural of 1167 and 3063; *masters of Judah*; *Baale-Jehudah*, a place in Pal.:— Baale of Judah.

1185. בַּעֲלִיס **Ba'ălîç**, *bah-al-ece´*; prob. from a der. of 5965 with prep. pref.; *in exultation*; *Baalis*, an Ammonitish king:— Baalis.

1186. בַּעַל מְעוֹן **Ba'al M^eôwn**, *bah-al meh-one´*; from 1168 and 4583; *Baal of* (the) *habitation* (of) [comp. 1010]; *Baal-Meön*, a place E. of the Jordan:— Baal-meon.

1187. בַּעַל פְּעוֹר **Ba'al P^eôwr**, *bah´-al peh-ore´*; from 1168 and 6465; *Baal of Peor*; *Baal-Peör*, a Moabitish deity:— Baal-peor.

1188. בַּעַל פְּרָצִים **Ba'al P^erâtsîym**, *bah´-al per-aw-tseem´*; from 1167 and the plur. of 6556; *possessor of breaches*; *Baal-Peratsim*, a place in Pal.:— Baal-perazim.

1189. בַּעַל צְפוֹן **Ba'al Ts^ephôwn**, *bah´-al tsef-one´*; from 1168 and 6828 (in the sense of *cold*) [according to others an Eg. form of *Typhon*, the destroyer]; *Baal of winter*; *Baal-Tsephon*, a place in Eqypt:— Baalzephon.

1190. בַּעַל שָׁלִשָׁה **Ba'al Shâlîshâh**, *bah´-al shaw-lee-shaw´*; from 1168 and 8031; *Baal of Shalishah*, *Baal-Shalishah*, a place in Pal.:— Baal-shalisha.

1191. בַּעֲלָת **Ba'ălâth**, *bah-al-awth´*; a modif. of 1172; *mistress-ship*; *Baalath*, a place in Pal.:— Baalath.

1192. בַּעֲלַת בְּאֵר **Ba'ălath B^eêr**, *bah-al-ath´ beh-ayr´*; from 1172 and 875; *mistress of a well*; *Baalath-Beër*, a place in Pal.:— Baalath-beer.

1193. בַּעַל תָּמָר **Ba'al Tâmâr**, *bah´-al taw-mawr´*; from 1167 and 8558; *possessor of* (the) *palm-tree*; *Baal-Tamar*, a place in Pal.:— Baal-tamar.

1194. בְּעֹן **B^eôn**, *beh-ohn´*; prob. a contr. of 1010; *Beön*, a place E. of the Jordan:— Beon.

1195. בַּעֲנָא **Ba'ănâ´**, *bah-an-aw´*; the same as 1196; *Baana*, the name of four Isr.:— Baana, Baanah.

1196. בַּעֲנָה **Ba'ănâh**, *bah-an-aw´*; from a der. of 6031 with prep. pref.; *in affliction*; *Baanah*, the name of four Isr.:— Baanah.

1197. בָּעַר **bâ'ar**, *baw-ar´*; a prim. root; to *kindle*, i.e. *consume* (by fire or by eating); also (as denom. from 1198) to *be* (-*come*) *brutish*:— be brutish, bring (put, take) away, burn, (cause to) eat (up), feed, heat, kindle, set ([on fire]), waste.

1198. בַּעַר **ba'ar**, *bah´-ar*; from 1197; prop. *food* (as *consumed*); i.e. (by exten.) of cattle *brutishness*; (concr.) *stupid*:— brutish (person), foolish.

1199. בָּעֲרָא **Bâ'ărâ´**, *bah-ar-aw´*; from 1198; *brutish*; *Baara*, an Isr. woman:— Baara.

1200. בְּעֵרָה **b^eêrâh**, *bě-ay-raw´*; from 1197; a *burning*:— fire.

1201. בַּעְשָׁא **Ba'shâ´**, *bah-shaw´*; from an unused root mean. to *stink*; *offensiveness*; *Basha*, a king of Israel:— Baasha.

1202. בַּעֲשֵׂיָה **Ba'ăsêyâh**, *bah-as-ay-yaw´*; from 6213 and 3050 with a prep. pref.; *in* (the) *work of Jah*; *Baasejah*, an Isr.:— Baaseiah.

1203. בְּעֶשְׁתְּרָה **B^eesht^erâh**, *beh-esh-ter-aw´*; from 6251 (as sing. of 6252) with prep. pref.;

with *Ashtoreth; Beështerah*, a place E. of the Jordan:— Beeshterah.

1204. בָּעַת **bâ'ath**, *baw-ath´*; a prim. root; to *fear*:— affright, be (make) afraid, terrify, trouble.

1205. בְּעָתָה **be'âthâh**, *beh-aw-thaw´*; from 1204; *fear*:— trouble.

1206. בֹּץ **bôts**, *botse*; prob. the same as 948; *mud* (as *whitish* clay):— mire.

1207. בִּצָּה **bitstsâh**, *bits-tsaw´*; intens. from 1206; a *swamp*:— fen, mire (-ry place).

1208. בָּצוֹר° **bâtsôwr**, *baw-tsore´*; from 1219; *inaccessible*, i.e. *lofty*:— vintage [by confusion with 1210].

1209. בֵּצָי **Bêtsay**, *bay-tsah´-ee*; perh. the same as 1153; *Betsai*, the name of two Isr.:— Bezai.

1210. בָּצִיר **bâtsîyr**, *baw-tseer´*; from 1219; *clipped*, i.e. the *grape crop*:— vintage.

1211. בֶּצֶל **betsel**, *beh´-tsel*; from an unused root appar. mean. to *peel*; an *onion*:— onion.

1212. בְּצַלְאֵל **Betsal'êl**, *bets-al-ale´*; prob. from 6738 and 410 with prep. pref.; *in* (the) *shadow* (i.e. *protection*) *of God; Betsalel*, the name of two Isr.:— Bezaleel.

1213. בַּצְלוּת **Batslûwth**, *bats-looth´*; or

בַּצְלִית **Batslîyth**, *bats-leeth´*; from the same as 1211; a *peeling; Batsluth* or *Batslith*, an Isr.:— Bazlith, Bazluth.

1214. בָּצַע **bâtsa'**, *baw-tsah´*; a prim. root to *break* off, i.e. (usually) *plunder;* fig. to *finish*, or (intr.) *stop*:— (be) covet (-ous), cut (off), finish, fulfill, gain (greedily), get, be given to [covetousness], greedy, perform, be wounded.

1215. בֶּצַע **betsa'**, *beh´-tsah;* from 1214; *plunder;* by extens. *gain* (usually unjust):— covetousness, (dishonest) gain, lucre, profit.

1216. בָּצֵק **bâtsêq**, *baw-tsake´*; a prim. root; perh. to *swell* up, i.e. *blister*:— swell.

1217. בָּצֵק **bâtsêq**, *baw-tsake´*; from 1216; *dough* (as *swelling* by fermentation):— dough, flour.

1218. בָּצְקַת **Botsqath**, *bots-cath´;* from 1216; a *swell* of ground; *Botscath*, a place in Pal.:— Bozcath, Boskath.

1219. בָּצַר **bâtsar**, *baw-tsar´*; a prim. root; to *clip* off; spec. (as denom. from 1210) to *gather* grapes; also to *be isolated* (i.e. *inaccessible* by height or fortification):— cut off, (de-) fenced, fortify, (grape) gather (-er), mighty things, restrain, strong, wall (up), withhold.

1220. בֶּצֶר **betser**, *beh´-tser;* from 1219; strictly a *clipping*, i.e. *gold* (as *dug* out):— gold defence.

1221. בֶּצֶר **Betser**, *beh´-tser;* the same as 1220, an *inaccessible* spot; *Betser*, a place in Pal.; also an Isr.:— Bezer.

1222. בְּצַר **betsar**, *bets-ar´;* another form for 1220; *gold:*— gold.

1223. בָּצְרָה **botsrâh**, *bots-raw´;* fem. from 1219; an *enclosure*, i.e. *sheep-fold*:— Bozrah.

1224. בָּצְרָה **Botsrâh**, *bots-raw´;* the same as 1223; *Botsrah*, a place in Edom:— Bozrah.

1225. בִּצָּרוֹן **bitstsârôwn**, *bits-tsaw-rone´*; masc. intens. from 1219; a *fortress*:— stronghold.

1226. בַּצֹּרֶת **batstsôreth**, *bats-tso´-reth;* fem. intens. from 1219; *restraint* (of rain), i.e. *drought*:— dearth, drought.

1227. בַּקְבּוּק **Baqbûwq**, *bak-book´;* the same as 1228; *Bakbuk*, one of the *Nethinim*:— Bakbuk.

1228. בַּקְבֻּק **baqbûk**, *bak-book´;* from 1238; a *bottle* (from the gurgling in *emptying*):— bottle, cruse.

1229. בַּקְבֻּקְיָה **Baqbuqyâh**, *bak-book-yaw´;* from 1228 and 3050; *emptying* (i.e. *wasting*) *of Jah; Bakbukjah*, an Isr.:— Bakbukiah.

1230. בַּקְבַּקַּר **Baqbaqqar**, *bak-bak-kar´;* redupl. from 1239; *searcher; Bakbakkar*, an Isr.:— Bakbakkar.

1231. בֻּקִּי **Buqqîy**, *book-kee´;* from 1238; *wasteful; Bukki*, the name of two Isr.:— Bukki.

1232. בֻּקִּיָּה **Buqqîyâh**, *book-kee-yaw´;* from 1238 and 3050; *wasting of Jah; Bukkijah*, an Isr.:— Bukkiah.

1233. בְּקִיעַ **beqîya'**, *bek-ee´-ah;* from 1234; a *fissure*:— breach, cleft.

1234. בָּקַע **bâqa'**, *baw-kah´*; a prim. root; to *cleave;* gen. to *rend, break, rip* or *open*:— make a breach, break forth (into, out, in pieces, through, up), be ready to burst, cleave (asunder), cut out, divide, hatch, rend (asunder), rip up, tear, win.

1235. בֶּקַע **beqa'**, *beh´-kah;* from 1234; a *section* (half) of a shekel, i.e. a *beka* (a weight and a coin):— bekah, half a shekel.

1236. בִּקְעָא **biq'â'** (Chald.), *bik-aw´;* corresp. to 1237:— plain.

1237. בִּקְעָה **biq'âh**, *bik-aw´;* from 1234; prop. a *split*, i.e. a wide level *valley* between mountains:— plain, valley.

1238. בָּקַק **bâqaq**, *baw-kak´;* a prim. root; to *pour* out, i.e. to *empty*, fig. to *depopulate;* by anal. to *spread* out (as a fruitful vine):— (make) empty (out), fail, × utterly, make void.

1239. בָּקַר **bâqar**, *baw-kar;* a prim. root; prop. to *plow*, or (gen.) *break* forth, i.e. (fig.) to *inspect, admire, care for, consider:*—

(make) inquire (-ry), (make) search, seek out.

1240. בְּקַר **bᵉqar** (Chald.), *bek-ar´*; corresp. to 1239:— inquire, make search.

1241. בָּקָר **bâqâr**, *baw-kawr´*; from 1239; a *beeve* or animal of the ox kind of either gender (as used for *plowing*); collect. a *herd:*— beeve, bull (+ -ock), + calf, + cow, great [cattle], + heifer, herd, kine, ox.

1242. בֹּקֶר **bôqer**, *bo´-ker*; from 1239; prop. *dawn* (as the *break* of day); gen. *morning:*— (+) day, early, morning, morrow.

1243. בַּקָּרָה **baqqârâh**, *bak-kaw-raw´*; intens. from 1239; a *looking after:*— seek out.

1244. בִּקֹּרֶת **biqqôreth**, *bik-ko´-reth*; from 1239; prop. *examination*, i.e. (by impl.) *punishment:*— scourged.

1245. בָּקַשׁ **bâqash**, *baw-kash´*; a prim. root; to *search* out (by any method, spec. in worship or prayer); by impl. to *strive after:*— ask, beg, beseech, desire, enquire, get, make inquisition, procure, (make) request, require, seek (for).

1246. בַּקָּשָׁה **baqqâshâh**, *bak-kaw-shaw´*; from 1245; a *petition:*— request.

1247. בַּר **bar** (Chald.), *bar*; corresp. to 1121; a *son, grandson*, etc.:— × old, son.

1248. בַּר **bar**, *bar*; borrowed (as a title) from 1247; the *heir* (apparent to the throne):— son.

1249. בַּר **bar**, *bar*; from 1305 (in its various senses); *beloved*; also *pure, empty:*— choice, clean, clear, pure.

1250. בָּר **bâr**, *bawr;* or

    בַּר **bar**, *bar*; from 1305 (in the sense of *winnowing*); *grain* of any kind (even while standing in the field); by extens. the open *country:*— corn, wheat.

1251. בַּר **bar** (Chald.), *bar*; corresp. to 1250; a *field:*— field.

1252. בֹּר **bôr**, *bore*; from 1305; *purity:*— cleanness, pureness.

1253. בֹּר **bôr**, *bore*; the same as 1252; vegetable *lye* (from its *cleansing*); used as a *soap* for washing, or a *flux* for metals:— × never so, purely.

1254. בָּרָא **bârâ'**, *baw-raw´*; a prim. root; (absolutely) to *create;* (qualified) to *cut* down (a wood), *select, feed* (as formative processes):— choose, create (creator), cut down, dispatch, do, make (fat).

1255. בְּרֹאדַךְ בַּלְאֲדָן **Bᵉrô'dak Bal'ădân**, *ber-o-dak´ bal-ad-awn´*; a var. of 4757; *Berodak-Baladan*, a Bab. king:— Berodach-baladan.

    בְּרָאִי **Bir'îy**. See 1011.

1256. בְּרָאיָה **Bᵉrâ'yâh**, *ber-aw-yaw´*; from 1254 and 3050; *Jah has created; Berajah*, an Isr.:— Beraiah.

1257. בַּרְבֻּר **barbûr**, *bar-boor´*; by redupl. from 1250; a *fowl* (as fattened on *grain*):— fowl.

1258. בָּרַד **bârad**, *baw-rad´*; a prim. root, to *hail:*— hail.

1259. בָּרָד **bârâd**, *baw-rawd´*; from 1258; *hail:*— hail ([stones]).

1260. בֶּרֶד **Bered**, *beh´red*; from 1258; *hail; Bered*, the name of a place south of Pal., also of an Isr.:— Bered.

1261. בָּרֹד **bârôd**, *baw-rode´*; from 1258; *spotted* (as if with *hail*):— grisled.

1262. בָּרָה **bârâh**, *baw-raw´*; a prim. root; to *select;* also (as denom. from 1250) to *feed;* also (as equiv. to 1305) to *render clear* (Eccl. 3:18):— choose, (cause to) eat, manifest, (give) meat.

1263. בָּרוּךְ **Bârûwk**, *baw-rook´*; pass. part. from 1288; *blessed; Baruk*, the name of three Isr.:— Baruch.

1264. בְּרוֹם **bᵉrôwm**, *ber-ome´*; prob. of for. or.; *damask* (stuff of variegated thread):— rich apparel.

1265. בְּרוֹשׁ **bᵉrôwsh**, *ber-ōsh´*; of uncert. der.; a *cypress* (?) tree; hence, a *lance* or a *musical* instrument (as made of that wood):— fir (tree).

1266. בְּרוֹת **bᵉrôwth**, *ber-ōth´*; a var. of 1265; the *cypress* (or some elastic tree):— fir.

1267. בָּרוּת **bârûwth**, *baw-rooth´*; from 1262; *food:*— meat.

1268. בֵּרוֹתָה **Bêrôwthâh**, *bay-ro-thaw´*; or

    בֵּרֹתַי **Bêrôthay**, *bay-ro-tha´-ee*; prob. from 1266; *cypress* or *cypresslike; Berothah* or *Berothai*, a place north of Pal.:— Berothah, Berothai.

1269. בִּרְזוֹת **Birzôwth**, *beer-zoth´*; prob. fem. plur. from an unused root (appar. mean. to *pierce*); *holes; Birzoth*, an Isr.:— Birzavith [from the marg.].

1270. בַּרְזֶל **barzel**, *bar-zel´*; perh. from the root of 1269; *iron* (as *cutting*); by extens. an iron *implement:*— (ax) head, iron.

1271. בַּרְזִלַּי **Barzillay**, *bar-zil-lah´-ee*; from 1270; *iron*-hearted; *Barzillai*, the name of three Isr.:— Barzillai.

1272. בָּרַח **bârach**, *baw-rakh´*; a prim. root; to *bolt*, i.e. fig. to *flee* suddenly:— chase (away); drive away, fain, flee (away), put to flight, make haste, reach, run away, shoot.

    בְּרַח **bârîach**. See 1281.

1273. בַּרְחֻמִי **Barchûmîy**, *bar-khoo-mee´*; by transp. for 978; a *Barchumite*, or native of *Bachurim:*— Barhumite.

1274. בְּרִי **bᵉrîy**, *ber-ee´*; from 1262; *fat:*— fat.

1275. בְּרִי **Bêrîy**, *bay-ree´*; prob. by contr. from 882; *Beri*, an Isr.:— Beri.

1276. בֵּרִי **Bêrîy**, *bay-ree´*; of uncert. der.; (only in the plur. and with the art.) the *Berites*, a place in Pal.:— Berites.

1277. בָּרִיא **bârîy'**, *baw-ree´*; from 1254 (in the sense of 1262); *fatted* or *plump*:— fat ([fleshed], -ter), fed, firm, plenteous, rank.

1278. בְּרִיאָה **bᵉrîy'âh**, *ber-ee-aw´*; fem. from 1254; a *creation*, i.e. a *novelty*:— new thing.

1279. בִּרְיָה **biryâh**, *beer-yaw´*; fem. from 1262; *food*:— meat.

1280. בְּרִיחַ **bᵉrîyach**, *ber-ee´-akh*; from 1272; a *bolt*:— bar, fugitive.

1281. בָּרִיחַ **bârîyach**, *baw-ree´-akh*; or (short.)

בָּרִחַ **bâriach**, *baw-ree´-akh*; from 1272; a *fugitive*, i.e. the *serpent* (as *fleeing*), and the constellation by that name:— crooked, noble, piercing.

1282. בָּרִיחַ **Bârîyach**, *baw-ree´-akh*; the same as 1281; *Bariach*, an Isr.:— Bariah.

1283. בְּרִיעָה **Bᵉrîy'âh**, *ber-ee-aw´*; appar. from the fem. of 7451 with prep. pref.; *in trouble*; *Beriah*, the name of four Isr.:— Beriah.

1284. בְּרִיעִי **Bᵉrîy'îy**, *ber-ee-ee´*; patron. from 1283; a *Beriite* (collect.) or desc. of Beriah:— Beerites.

1285. בְּרִית **bᵉrîyth**, *ber-eeth´*; from 1262 (in the sense of *cutting* [like 1254]); a *compact* (because made by passing between *pieces* of flesh):— confederacy, [con-]feder[-ate], covenant, league.

1286. בְּרִית **Bᵉrîyth**, *ber-eeth´*; the same as 1285; *Berith*, a Shechemitish deity:— Berith.

1287. בֹּרִית **bôrîyth**, *bo-reeth´*; fem. of 1253; vegetable *alkali*:— sope.

1288. בָּרַךְ **bârak**, *baw-rak´*; a prim. root; to *kneel*; by impl. to *bless* God (as an act of adoration), and (vice-versa) man (as a benefit); also (by euphem.) to *curse* (God or the king, as treason):— × abundantly, × altogether, × at all, blaspheme, bless, congratulate, curse, × greatly, × indeed, kneel (down), praise, salute, × still, thank.

1289. בְּרַךְ **bᵉrak** (Chald.), *ber-ak´*; corresp. to 1288:— bless, kneel.

1290. בֶּרֶךְ **berek**, *beh´-rek*; from 1288; a *knee*:— knee.

1291. בֶּרֶךְ **berek** (Chald.), *beh´-rek*; corresp. to 1290:— knee.

1292. בָּרַכְאֵל **Bârak'êl**, *baw-rak-ale´*; from 1288 and 410, *God has blessed*; *Barakel*, the father of one of Job's friends:— Barachel.

1293. בְּרָכָה **bᵉrâkâh**, *ber-aw-kaw´*; from 1288; *benediction*; by impl. *prosperity*:— blessing, liberal, pool, present.

1294. בְּרָכָה **Bᵉrâkâh**, *ber-aw-kaw´*; the same as 1293; *Berakah*, the name of an Isr., and also of a valley in Pal.:— Berachah.

1295. בְּרֵכָה **bᵉrêkâh**, *ber-ay-kaw´*; from 1288; a *reservoir* (at which camels *kneel* as a resting-place):— (fish-) pool.

1296. בֶּרֶכְיָה **Berekyâh**, *beh-rek-yaw´*; or

בֶּרֶכְיָהוּ **Berekyâhûw**, *beh-rek-yaw´-hoo*; from 1290 and 3050; *knee* (i.e. *blessing*) of *Jah*; *Berekjah*, the name of six Isr.:— Berachiah, Berechiah.

1297. בְּרַם **bᵉram** (Chald.), *ber-am´*; perh. from 7313 with prep. pref.; prop. *highly*, i.e. *surely*; but used adversatively, *however*:— but, nevertheless, yet.

1298. בֶּרַע **Bera'**, *beh´-rah*; of uncert. der.; *Bera*, a Sodomitish king:— Bera.

1299. בָּרַק **bâraq**, *baw-rak´*; a prim. root; to *lighten* (lightning):— cast forth.

1300. בָּרָק **bârâq**, *baw-rawk´*; from 1299; *lightning*; by anal. a *gleam*; concr. a *flashing* sword:— bright, glitter (-ing sword), lightning.

1301. בָּרָק **Bârâq**, *baw-rawk´*; the same as 1300; *Barak*, an Isr.:— Barak.

1302. בַּרְקוֹס **Barqôwç**, *bar-kose´*; of uncert. der.; *Barkos*, one of the Nethinim:— Barkos.

1303. בַּרְקָן **barqân**, *bar-kwan´*; from 1300; a *thorn* (perh. as burning *brightly*):— brier.

1304. בָּרְקַת **bârᵉqath**, *baw-reh´-keth*; or

בָּרְכַת **bârᵉkath**, *baw-rek-ath´*; from 1300; a *gem* (as *flashing*), perh. the *emerald*:— carbuncle.

1305. בָּרַר **bârar**, *baw-rar´*; a prim. root; to *clarify* (i.e. *brighten*), *examine*, *select*:— make bright, choice, chosen, cleanse (be clean), clearly, polished, (shew self) pure (-ify), purge (out).

1306. בִּרְשַׁע **Birsha'**, *beer-shah´*; prob. from 7562 with a prep. pref.; *with wickedness*; *Birsha*, a king of Gomorrah:— Birsha.

1307. בֵּרֹתִי **Bêrôthîy**, *bay-ro-thee´*; patrial from 1268; a *Berothite*, or inhab. of Berothai:— Berothite.

1308. בְּשׂוֹר **Bᵉsôwr**, *bes-ore´*; from 1319; *cheerful*; *Besor*, a stream of Pal.:— Besor.

1309. בְּשׂוֹרָה **bᵉsôwrâh**, *bes-o-raw´*; or (short.)

בְּשׂרָה **bᵉsôrâh**, *bes-o-raw´*; fem. from 1319; glad *tidings*; by impl. *reward for good news*:— reward for tidings.

1310. בָּשַׁל **bâshal**, *baw-shal´*; a prim. root; prop. to *boil* up; hence, to *be done* in cooking; fig. to *ripen*:— bake, boil, bring forth, is ripe, roast, seethe, sod (be sodden).

1311. בָּשֵׁל **bâshêl**, *baw-shale´*; from 1310; *boiled:*— × at all, sodden.

1312. בִּשְׁלָם **Bishlâm**, *bish-lawm´*; of for. der.; *Bishlam*, a Pers.:— Bishlam.

1313. בָּשָׂם **bâsâm**, *baw-sawm´*; from an unused root mean. to be fragrant; [comp. 5561] the *balsam* plant:— spice.

1314. בֶּשֶׂם **besem**, *beh´-sem*; or

     בֹּשֶׂם **bôsem**, *bo´-sem*; from the same as 1313; *fragrance*; by impl. *spicery*; also the *balsam* plant:— smell, spice, sweet (odour).

1315. בָּשְׂמָה **Bosmath**, *bos-math´*; fem. of 1314 (the second form); *fragrance*; *Bosmath*, the name of a wife of Esau, and of a daughter of Solomon:— Bashemath, Basmath.

1316. בָּשָׁן **Bâshân**, *baw-shawn´*; of uncert. der.; *Bashan* (often with the art.), a region E. of the Jordan:— Bashan.

1317. בָּשְׁנָה **boshnâh**, *bosh-naw´*; fem. from 954; *shamefulness:*— shame.

1318. בָּשַׁס **bâshaç**, *baw-shas´*; a prim. root; to *trample* down:— tread.

1319. בָּשַׂר **bâsar**, *baw-sar´*; a prim. root; prop. to *be fresh*, i.e. *full* (rosy, (fig.) *cheerful*); to *announce* (glad news):— messenger, preach, publish, shew forth, (bear, bring, carry, preach, good, tell good) tidings.

1320. בָּשָׂר **bâsâr**, *baw-sawr´*; from 1319; *flesh* (from its *freshness*); by extens. *body, person*; also (by euphem.) the *pudenda* of a man:— body, [fat, lean] flesh [-ed], kin, [man-] kind, + nakedness, self, skin.

1321. בְּשַׁר **besar** (Chald.), *bes-ar´*; corresp. to 1320:— flesh.

     בְּשֹׂרָה **besôrâh**. See 1309.

1322. בֹּשֶׁת **bôsheth**, *bo´-sheth*; from 954; *shame* (the feeling and the condition, as well as its cause); by impl. (spec.) an *idol:*— ashamed, confusion, + greatly, (put to) shame (-ful thing).

1323. בַּת **bath**, *bath*; from 1129 (as fem. of 1121); a *daughter* (used in the same wide sense as other terms of relationship, lit. and fig.):— apple [of the eye], branch, company, daughter, × first, × old, + owl, town, village.

1324. בַּת **bath**, *bath*; prob. from the same as 1327; a *bath* or Heb. measure (as a means of *division*) of liquids:— bath.

1325. בַּת **bath** (Chald.), *bath*; corresp. to 1324:— bath.

1326. בָּתָה **bâthâh**, *baw-thaw´*; prob. an orth. var. for 1327; *desolation:*— waste.

1327. בַּתָּה **battâh**, *bat-taw´*; fem. from an unused root (mean. to *break* in pieces); *desolation:*— desolate.

1328. בְּתוּאֵל **Bethûw'êl**, *beth-oo-ale´*; appar.

from the same as 1326 and 410; *destroyed of God*; *Bethuel*, the name of a nephew of Abraham, and of a place in Pal.:— Bethuel. Comp. 1329.

1329. בְּתוּל **Bethûwl**, *beth-ool´*; for 1328; *Bethul* (i.e. Bethuel), a place in Pal.:— Bethul.

1330. בְּתוּלָה **bethûwlâh**, *beth-oo-law´*; fem. pass. part. of an unused root mean. to *separate*; a *virgin* (from her *privacy*); sometimes (by continuation) a *bride*; also (fig.) a *city* or *state:*— maid, virgin.

1331. בְּתוּלִים **bethûwlîym**, *beth-oo-leem´*; masc. plur. of the same as 1330; (collect. and abstr.) *virginity*; by impl. and concr. the *tokens* of it:— × maid, virginity.

1332. בִּתְיָה **Bithyâh**, *bith-yaw´*; from 1323 and 3050; *daughter* (i.e. worshipper) *of Jah*; *Bithjah*, an Eg. woman:— Bithiah.

1333. בָּתַק **bâthaq**, *baw-thak´*; a prim. root; to *cut* in pieces:— thrust through.

1334. בָּתַר **bâthar**, *baw-thar´*; a prim. root, to *chop* up:— divide.

1335. בֶּתֶר **bether**, *beh´-ther*; from 1334; a *section:*— part, piece.

1336. בֶּתֶר **Bether**, *beh´-ther*; the same as 1335; *Bether*, a (craggy) place in Pal.:— Bether.

1337. בַּת רַבִּים **Bath Rabbîym**, *bath rab-beem´*; from 1323 and a masc. plur. from 7227; the *daughter* (i.e. city) *of Rabbah:*— Bath-rabbim.

1338. בִּתְרוֹן **Bithrôwn**, *bith-rone´*; from 1334; (with the art.) the *craggy* spot; *Bithron*, a place E. of the Jordan:— Bithron.

1339. בַּת־שֶׁבַע **Bath-Sheba'**, *bath-sheh´-bah*; from 1323 and 7651 (in the sense of 7650); *daughter of an oath*; *Bath-Sheba*, the mother of Solomon:— Bath-sheba.

1340. בַּת־שׁוּעַ **Bath-Shûwa'**, *bath-shoo´-ah*; from 1323 and 7771; *daughter of wealth*; *Bath-shuä*, the same as 1339:— Bath-shua.

ג

1341. גֵּא **gê'**, *gay´*; for 1343; *haughty:*— proud.

1342. גָּאָה **gâ'âh**, *gaw-aw´*; a prim. root; to *mount* up; hence, in gen. to *rise*, (fig.) be *majestic:*— gloriously, grow up, increase, be risen, triumph.

1343. גֵּאֶה **gê'eh**, *gay-eh´*; from 1342; *lofty*; fig. *arrogant:*— proud.

1344. גֵּאָה **gê'âh**, *gay-aw´*; fem. from 1342; *arrogance:*— pride.

1345. גְּאוּאֵל **Gᵉ'ûw'êl**, *gheh-oo-ale´*; from 1342 and 410; *majesty of God*; *Geüel*, an Isr.:— Geuel.

1346. גַּאֲוָה **ga'ăvâh**, *gah-av-aw´*; from 1342; *arrogance* or *majesty;* by impl. (concr.) *ornament:*— excellency, haughtiness, highness, pride, proudly, swelling.

1347. גָּאוֹן **gâ'ôwn**, *gaw-ohn´*; from 1342; the same as 1346:— arrogancy, excellency (-lent), majesty, pomp, pride, proud, swelling.

1348. גֵּאוּת **gê'ûwth**, *gay-ooth´*; from 1342; the same as 1346:— excellent things, lifting up, majesty, pride, proudly, raging.

1349. גַּאֲיוֹן **ga'ăyôwn**, *gah-ăh-yone´*; from 1342: *haughty:*— proud.

1350. גָּאַל **gâ'al**, *gaw-al´*; a prim. root, to *redeem* (according to the Oriental law of kinship), i.e. to *be the next of kin* (and as such to *buy back* a relative's property, *marry* his widow, etc.):— × in any wise, × at all, avenger, deliver, (do, perform the part of near, next) kinsfolk (-man), purchase, ransom, redeem (-er), revenger.

1351. גָּאַל **gâ'al**, *gaw-al´*; a prim. root, [rather ident. with 1350, through the idea of *freeing*, i.e. *repudiating*]; to *soil* or (fig.) *desecrate:*— defile, pollute, stain.

1352. גֹּאֶל **gô'el**, *go´-el*; from 1351; *profanation:*— defile.

1353. גְּאֻלָּה **gᵉullâh**, *geh-ool-law´*; fem. pass. part. of 1350; *redemption* (incl. the right and the object); by impl. *relationship:*— kindred, redeem, redemption, right.

1354. גַּב **gab**, *gab;* from an unused root mean. to *hollow* or *curve;* the *back* (as *rounded* [comp. 1460 and 1479]; by anal. the *top* or *rim*, a *boss*, a *vault*, *arch* of eye, *bulwarks*, etc.:— back, body, boss, eminent (higher) place, [eye] brows, nave, ring.

1355. גַּב **gab** (Chald.), *gab;* corresp. to 1354:— back.

1356. גֵּב **gêb**, *gabe;* from 1461; a *log* (as *cut* out); also *well* or *cistern* (as *dug*):— beam, ditch, pit.

1357. גֵּב **gêb**, *gabe;* prob. from 1461 [comp. 1462]; a *locust* (from its *cutting*):— locust.

1358. גֹּב **gôb** (Chald.), *gobe;* from a root corresp. to 1461; a *pit* (for wild animals) (as *cut* out):— den.

1359. גֹּב **Gôb**, *gobe;* or (fully)

גּוֹב **Gôwb**, *gobe;* from 1461; *pit; Gob*, a place in Pal.:— Gob.

1360. גֶּבֶא **gebe'**, *geh´-beh;* from an unused root mean. prob. to *collect;* a *reservoir;* by anal. a *marsh:*— marish, pit.

1361. גָּבַהּ **gâbahh**, *gaw-bah´;* a prim. root; to *soar*, i.e. *be lofty;* fig. to *be haughty:*— exalt, be haughty, be (make) high (-er), lift up, mount up, be proud, raise up great height, upward.

1362. גָּבָהּ **gâbâhh**, *gaw-bawh´;* from 1361; *lofty* (lit. or fig.):— high, proud.

1363. גֹּבַהּ **gôbahh**, *go´-bah;* from 1361; *elation, grandeur, arrogance:*— excellency, haughty, height, high, loftiness, pride.

1364. גָּבֹהַּ **gâbôahh**, *gaw-bo´-ah;* or (fully)

גָּבוֹהַּ **gâbôwahh**, *gaw-bo´-ah;* from 1361; *elevated* (or *elated*), *powerful, arrogant:*— haughty, height, high (-er), lofty, proud, × exceeding proudly.

1365. גַּבְהוּת **gabhûwth**, *gab-hooth´;* from 1361; *pride:*— loftiness, lofty.

1366. גְּבוּל **gᵉbûwl**, *gheb-ool´;* or (short.)

גְּבֻל **gᵉbûl**, *gheb-ool´;* from 1379; prop. a *cord* (as *twisted*), i.e. (by impl.) a *boundary;* by extens. the *territory* inclosed:— border, bound, coast, × great, landmark, limit, quarter, space.

1367. גְּבוּלָה **gᵉbûwlâh**, *gheb-oo-law´;* or (short.)

גְּבֻלָה **gᵉbûlâh**, *gheb-oo-law´;* fem. of 1366; a *boundary, region:*— border, bound, coast, landmark, place.

1368. גִּבּוֹר **gibbôwr**, *ghib-bore´;* or (short.)

גִּבֹּר **gibbôr**, *ghib-bore´;* intens. from the same as 1397; *powerful;* by impl. *warrior, tyrant:*— champion, chief, × excel, giant, man, mighty (man, one), strong (man), valiant man.

1369. גְּבוּרָה **gᵉbûwrâh**, *gheb-oo-raw´;* fem. pass. part. from the same as 1368; *force* (lit. or fig.); by impl. *valor, victory:*— force, mastery, might, power, strength.

1370. גְּבוּרָה **gᵉbûwrâh** (Chald.), *gheb-oo-raw´;* corresp. to 1369; *power:*— might.

1371. גִּבֵּחַ **gibbêach**, *ghib-bay´-akh;* from an unused root mean. to *be high* (in the forehead); *bald* in the forehead:— forehead bald.

1372. גַּבַּחַת **gabbachath**, *gab-bakh´-ath;* from the same as 1371; *baldness* in the forehead; by anal. a *bare spot* on the right side of cloth:— bald forehead, × without.

1373. גַּבַּי **Gabbay**, *gab-bah´-ee;* from the same as 1354; *collective; Gabbai*, an Isr.:— Gabbai.

1374. גֵּבִים **Gêbîym**, *gay-beem´;* plur. of 1356; *cisterns; Gebim*, a place in Pal.:— Gebim.

1375. גְּבִיעַ **gᵉbîya'**, *gheb-ee´-ah;* from an unused root (mean. to *be convex*); a *goblet;* by anal. the *calyx* of a flower:— house, cup, pot.

1376. גְּבִיר **gᵉbîyr**, *gheb-eer´;* from 1396; a *master:*— lord.

1377. גְּבִירָה **gᵉbîyrâh**, *gheb-ee-raw´;* fem. of 1376; a *mistress:*— queen.

1378. גָּבִישׁ **gâbîysh**, *gaw-beesh´;* from an unused root (prob. mean. to *freeze*); *crystal* (from its resemblance to *ice*):— pearl.

1379. גָּבַל **gâbal**, *gaw-bal´;* a prim. root; prop. to *twist* as a rope; only (as a denom. from 1366) to *bound* (as by a line):— be border, set (bounds about).

1380. גְּבַל **Gᵉbal**, *gheb-al´;* from 1379 (in the sense of a *chain* of hills); a *mountain; Gebal,* a place in Phœnicia:— Gebal.

1381. גְּבָל **Gᵉbâl**, *gheb-awl´;* the same as 1380; *Gebal,* a region in Idumæa:— Gebal.

גְּבֻלָה **gᵉbûlâh**. See 1367.

1382. גִּבְלִי **Giblîy**, *ghib-lee´;* patrial from 1380; a *Gebalite,* or inhab. of Gebal:— Giblites, stone-squarer.

1383. גַּבְלֻת **gablûth**, *gab-looth´;* from 1379; a twisted *chain* or *lace:*— end.

1384. גִּבֵּן **gibbên**, *gib-bane´;* from an unused root mean. to *be arched* or *contracted; hunch-backed:*— crookbackt.

1385. גְּבִנָה **gᵉbînah**, *gheb-ee-naw´;* fem. from the same as 1384; *curdled* milk:— cheese.

1386. גַּבְנֹן **gabnôn**, *gab-nohn´;* from the same as 1384; a *hump* or *peak* of hills:— high.

1387. גֶּבַע **Geba'**, *gheh´-bah;* from the same as 1375, a *hillock; Geba,* a place in Pal.:— Gaba, Geba, Gibeah.

1388. גִּבְעָא **Gib'â'**, *ghib-aw´;* by perm. for 1389; a *hill; Giba,* a place in Pal.:— Gibeah.

1389. גִּבְעָה **gib'âh**, *ghib-aw´;* fem. from the same as 1387; a *hillock:*— hill, little hill.

1390. גִּבְעָה **Gib'âh**, *ghib-aw´;* the same as 1389; *Gibah;* the name of three places in Pal.:— Gibeah, the hill.

1391. גִּבְעוֹן **Gib'ôwn**, *ghib-ohn´;* from the same as 1387; *hilly; Gibon,* a place in Pal.:— Gibeon.

1392. גִּבְעֹל **gib'ôl**, *ghib-ole´;* prol. from 1375; the *calyx* of a flower:— bolled.

1393. גִּבְעֹנִי **Gib'ôniy**, *ghib-o-nee´;* patrial from 1391; a *Gibonite,* or inhab. of Gibon:— Gibeonite.

1394. גִּבְעַת **Gib'ath**, *ghib-ath´;* from the same as 1375; *hilliness; Gibath:*— Gibeath.

1395. גִּבְעָתִי **Gib'âthîy**, *ghib-aw-thee´;* patrial from 1390; a *Gibathite,* or inhab. of Gibath:— Gibeathite.

1396. גָּבַר **gâbar**, *gaw-bar´;* a prim. root; to *be strong;* by impl. to *prevail, act insolently:*— exceed, confirm, be great, be mighty, prevail, put to more [strength], strengthen, be stronger, be valiant.

1397. גֶּבֶר **geber**, *gheh´-ber;* from 1396; prop. a

valiant man or *warrior;* gen. a *person* simply:— every one, man, × mighty.

1398. גֶּבֶר **Geber**, *gheh´-ber;* the same as 1397; *Geber,* the name of two Isr.:— Geber.

1399. גֶּבֶר **gᵉbar**, *gheb-ar´;* from 1396; the same as 1397; a person:— man.

1400. גְּבַר **gᵉbar** (Chald.), *gheb-ar´;* corresp. to 1399:— certain, man.

1401. גִּבָּר **gibbâr** (Chald.), *ghib-bawr´;* intens. of 1400; *valiant,* or *warrior:*— mighty.

1402. גִּבָּר **Gibbâr**, *ghib-bawr´;* intens. of 1399; *Gibbar,* an Isr.:— Gibbar.

גְּבוּרָה **gᵉbûrâh**. See 1369.

1403. גַּבְרִיאֵל **Gabrîy'êl**, *gab-ree-ale´;* from 1397 and 410; *man of God; Gabriel,* an archangel:— Gabriel.

1404. גְּבֶרֶת **gᵉbereth**, *gheb-eh´-reth;* fem. of 1376; *mistress:*— lady, mistress.

1405. גִּבְּתוֹן **Gibbᵉthôwn**, *ghib-beth-one´;* intens. from 1389; a *hilly* spot; *Gibbethon,* a place in Pal.:— Gibbethon.

1406. גָּג **gâg**, *gawg;* prob. by redupl. from 1342; a *roof;* by anal. the *top* of an altar:— roof (of the house), (house) top (of the house).

1407. גַּד **gad**, *gad;* from 1413 (in the sense of *cutting*); *coriander* seed (from its furrows):— coriander.

1408. גַּד **Gad**, *gad;* a var. of 1409; *Fortune,* a Bab. deity:— that troop.

1409. גָּד **gâd**, *gawd;* from 1464 (in the sense of *distributing*); *fortune:*— troop.

1410. גָּד **Gâd**, *gawd;* from 1464; *Gad,* a son of Jacob, incl. his tribe and its territory; also a prophet:— Gad.

1411. גְּדָבָר **gᵉdâbâr** (Chald.), *ghed-aw-bawr´;* corresp. to 1489; a *treasurer:*— treasurer.

1412. גֻּדְגֹּדָה **Gudgôdâh**, *gud-go´-daw;* by redupl. from 1413 (in the sense of *cutting*) *cleft; Gudgodah,* a place in the Desert:— Gudgodah.

1413. גָּדַד **gâdad**, *gaw-dad´;* a prim. root [comp. 1464]; to *crowd;* also to *gash* (as if by *pressing* into):— assemble (selves by troops), gather (selves together, self in troops), cut selves.

1414. גְּדַד **gᵉdad** (Chald.), *ghed-ad´;* corresp. to 1413; to *cut* down:— hew down.

גְּדוּדָה **gᵉdûdâh**. See 1417.

1415. גָּדָה **gâdâh**, *gaw-daw´;* from an unused root (mean. to *cut* off); a *border* of a river (as *cut* into by the stream):— bank.

גַּדָּה **Gaddâh**. See 2693.

1416. גְּדוּד **gᵉdûwd**, *ghed-ood´;* from 1413; a

crowd (espec. of soldiers):— army, band (of men), company, troop (of robbers).

1417. גְּדוּד **gᵉdûwd**, *ghed-ood´;* or (fem.)

גְּדֻדָה **gᵉdûdâh**, *ghed-oo-daw´;* from 1413; a *furrow* (as *cut*):— furrow.

1418. גְּדוּדָה **gᵉdûwdâh**, *ghed-oo-daw´;* fem. pass. part. of 1413; an *incision:*— cutting.

1419. גָּדוֹל **gâdôwl**, *gaw-dole´;* or (short.)

גָּדֹל **gâdôl**, *gaw-dole´;* from 1431; *great* (in any sense); hence, *older;* also *insolent:*— + aloud, elder (-est), + exceeding (-ly) + far, (man of) great (man, matter, thing, -er, -ness), high, long, loud, mighty, more, much, noble, proud thing, × sore, (×) very.

1420. גְּדוּלָה **gᵉdûwlâh**, *ghed-oo-law´;* or (short.)

גְּדֻלָּה **gᵉdullâh**, *ghed-ool-law´;* or (less accurately)

גְּדוּלָּה **gᵉdûwllâh**, *ghed-ool-law´;* fem. of 1419; *greatness;* (concr.) *mighty acts:*— dignity, great things (-ness), majesty.

1421. גִּדּוּף **giddûwph**, *ghid-doof´;* or (short.)

גִּדֻּף **giddûph**, *ghid-doof´;* and (fem.)

גִּדּוּפָה **giddûwphâh**, *ghid-doo-faw´;* or

גִּדֻּפָה **giddûphâh**, *ghid-doo-faw´;* from 1422; *vilification:*— reproach, reviling.

1422. גְּדוּפָה **gᵉdûwphâh**, *ghed-oo-faw´;* fem. pass. part. of 1442; a *revilement:*— taunt.

גְּדוֹר **Gᵉdôwr**. See 1446.

1423. גְּדִי **gᵉdiy**, *ghed-ee´;* from the same as 1415; a young *goat* (from *browsing*):— kid.

1424. גָּדִי **Gâdîy**, *gaw-dee´;* from 1409; *fortunate; Gadi*, an Isr.:— Gadi.

1425. גָּדִי **Gâdîy**, *gaw-dee´;* patron. from 1410; a *Gadite* (collect.) or desc. of Gad:— Gadites, children of Gad.

1426. גַּדִּי **Gaddîy**, *gad-dee´;* intens. for 1424; *Gaddi*, an Isr.:— Gaddi.

1427. גַּדִּיאֵל **Gaddîy'êl**, *gad-dee-ale´;* from 1409 and 410; *fortune of God; Gaddiel*, an Isr.:— Gaddiel.

1428. גִּדְיָה° **gidyâh**, *ghid-yaw´;* or

גַּדְיָה° **gadyâh**, *gad-yaw´;* the same as 1415; a river *brink:*— bank.

1429. גְּדִיָּה **gᵉdîyâh**, *ghed-ee-yaw´;* fem. of 1423; a young female *goat:*— kid.

1430. גָּדִישׁ **gâdîysh**, *gaw-deesh´;* from an unused root (mean. to *heap* up); a *stack* of sheaves; by anal. a *tomb:*— shock (stack) (of corn), tomb.

1431. גָּדַל **gâdal**, *gaw-dal´;* a prim. root; prop. to *twist* [comp. 1434], i.e. to *be* (caus. *make*) *large* (in various senses, as in body, mind, estate or honor, also in pride):— advance, boast, bring up, exceed, excellent, be (-come,

do, give, make, wax), great (-er, come to ... estate, + things), grow (up), increase, lift up, magnify (-ifical), be much set by, nourish (up), pass, promote, proudly [spoken], tower.

1432. גָּדֵל **gâdêl**, *gaw-dale´;* from 1431; *large* (lit. or fig.):— great, grew.

1433. גֹּדֶל **gôdel**, *go´-del;* from 1431; *magnitude* (lit. or fig.):— greatness, stout (-ness).

1434. גְּדִל **gᵉdil**, *ghed-eel´;* from 1431 (in the sense of *twisting*); *thread*, i.e. a *tassel* or *festoon:*— fringe, wreath.

1435. גִּדֵּל **Giddêl**, *ghid-dale´;* from 1431; *stout; Giddel*, the name of one of the Nethinim, also of one of "Solomon's servants":— Giddel.

גָּדֹל **gâdôl**. See 1419.

גְּדֻלָּה **gᵉdullâh**. See 1420.

1436. גְּדַלְיָה **Gᵉdalyâh**, *ghed-al-yaw´;* or (prol.)

גְּדַלְיָהוּ **Gᵉdalyâhûw**, *ghed-al-yaw´-hoo;* from 1431 and 3050; *Jah has become great; Gedaljah*, the name of five Isr.:— Gedaliah.

1437. גִּדַּלְתִּי **Giddaltîy**, *ghid-dal´-tee;* from 1431; *I have made great; Giddalti*, an Isr.:— Giddalti.

1438. גָּדַע **gâda'**, *gaw-dah´;* a prim. root; to *fell* a tree; gen. to *destroy* anything:— cut (asunder, in sunder, down, off), hew down.

1439. גִּדְעוֹן **Gid'ôwn**, *ghid-ohn´;* from 1438; *feller* (i.e. *warrior*); *Gidon*, an Isr.:— Gideon.

1440. גִּדְעֹם **Gid'ôm**, *ghid-ohm´;* from 1438; a *cutting* (i.e. *desolation*); *Gidom*, a place in Pal.:— Gidom.

1441. גִּדְעֹנִי **Gid'ônîy**, *ghid-o-nee´;* from 1438; *warlike* [comp. 1439]; *Gidoni*, an Isr.:— Gideoni.

1442. גָּדַף **gâdaph**, *gaw-daf´;* a prim. root; to *hack* (with words), i.e. *revile:*— blaspheme, reproach.

גִּדֻּף **giddûph**, and

גִּדֻּפָה **giddûphâh**. See 1421.

1443. גָּדַר **gâdar**, *gaw-dar´;* a prim. root; to *wall* in or around:— close up, fence up, hedge, inclose, make up [a wall], mason, repairer.

1444. גֶּדֶר **geder**, *gheh´-der;* from 1443; a *circumvallation:*— wall.

1445. גֶּדֶר **Geder**, *gheh´-der;* the same as 1444; *Geder*, a place in Pal.:— Geder.

1446. גְּדֹר **Gᵉdôr**, *ghed-ore´;* or (fully)

גְּדוֹר **Gᵉdôwr**, *ghed-ore´;* from 1443; *inclosure; Gedor*, a place in Pal.; also the name of three Isr.:— Gedor.

1447. גָּדֵר **gâdêr**, *gaw-dare´*; from 1443; a *circumvallation;* by impl. an *inclosure:*— fence, hedge, wall.

1448. גְּדֵרָה **gᵉdêrâh**, *ghed-ay-raw´*; fem. of 1447; *inclosure* (espec. for flocks):— [sheep-] cote (fold) hedge, wall.

1449. גְּדֵרָה **Gᵉdêrâh**, *ghed-ay-raw´*; the same as 1448; (with the art.) *Gederah*, a place in Pal.:— Gederah, hedges.

1450. גְּדֵרוֹת **Gᵉdêrôwth**, *ghed-ay-rohth´*; plur. of 1448; *walls; Gederoth*, a place in Pal.:— Gederoth.

1451. גְּדֵרִי **Gᵉdêrîy**, *ghed-ay-ree´*; patrial from 1445; a *Gederite*, or inhab. of Geder:— Gederite.

1452. גְּדֵרָתִי **Gᵉdêrâthîy**, *ghed-ay-raw-thee´*; patrial from 1449; a *Gederathite*, or inhab. of Gederah:— Gederathite.

1453. גְּדֵרֹתַיִם **Gᵉdêrôthayim**, *ghed-ay-ro-thah´-yim;* dual of 1448; *double wall; Gederothajim*, a place in Pal.:— Gederothaim.

1454. גֶּה **gêh**, *gay;* prob. a clerical err. for 2088; *this:*— this.

1455. גָּהָה **gâhâh**, *gaw-haw´*; a prim. root; to *remove* (a bandage from a wound, i.e. *heal* it):— cure.

1456. גֵּהָה **gêhâh**, *gay-haw´*; from 1455; a *cure:*— medicine.

1457. גָּהַר **gâhar**, *gaw-har´*; a prim. root; to *prostrate* oneself:— cast self down, stretch self.

1458. גַּו **gav**, *gav;* another form for 1460; the *back:*— back.

1459. גַּו **gav** (Chald.), *gav;* corresp. to 1460; the *middle:*— midst, same, there- (where-) in.

1460. גֵּו **gêv**, *gave;* from 1342 [corresp. to 1354]; the *back;* by anal. the *middle:*— + among, back, body.

1461. גּוּב **gûwb**, *goob;* a prim. root; to *dig:*— husbandman.

1462. גּוֹב **gôwb**, *gobe;* from 1461; the *locust* (from its *grubbing* as a larvae):— grasshopper, × great.

1463. גּוֹג **Gôwg**, *gohg;* of uncert. der.; *Gog*, the name of an Isr., also of some northern nation:— Gog.

1464. גּוּד **gûwd**, *goode;* a prim. root [akin to 1413]; to *crowd* upon, i.e. *attack:*— invade, overcome.

1465. גֵּוָה **gêvâh**, *gay-vaw´*; fem. of 1460; the *back*, i.e. (by extens.) the *person:*— body.

1466. גֵּוָה **gêvâh**, *gay-vaw´*; the same as 1465; *exaltation;* (fig.) *arrogance:*— lifting up, pride.

1467. גֵּוָה **gêvâh** (Chald.), *gay-vaw´*; corresp. to 1466:— pride.

1468. גּוּז **gûwz**, *gooz;* a prim. root [comp. 1494]; prop. to *shear* off; but used only in the (fig.) sense of *passing* rapidly:— bring, cut off.

1469. גּוֹזָל **gôwzâl**, *go-zawl´;* or (short.)

גּוֹזָל **gôzâl**, *go-zawl´;* from 1497; a *nestling* (as being comp. *nude* of feathers):— young (pigeon).

1470. גּוֹזָן **Gôwzân**, *go-zawn´;* prob. from 1468; a *quarry* (as a place of *cutting* stones); *Gozan*, a province of Assyria:— Gozan.

1471. גּוֹי **gôwy**, *go´-ee;* rarely (short.)

גּוֹי **gôy**, *go´-ee;* appar. from the same root as 1465 (in the sense of *massing*); a foreign *nation;* hence, a *Gentile;* also (fig.) a *troop* of animals, or a *flight* of locusts:— Gentile, heathen, nation, people.

1472. גְּוִיָּה **gᵉvîyâh**, *ghev-ee-yaw´;* prol. for 1465; a *body*, whether alive or dead:— (dead) body, carcase, corpse.

1473. גּוֹלָה **gôwlâh**, *go-law´;* or (short.)

גֹּלָה **gôlâh**, *go-law´;* act. part. fem. of 1540; *exile;* concr. and collect. *exiles:*— (carried away) captive (-ity), removing.

1474. גּוֹלָן **Gôwlân**, *go-lawn´;* from 1473; *captive; Golan*, a place E. of the Jordan:— Golan.

1475. גּוּמָּץ **gûwmmâts**, *goom-mawts´;* of uncert. der.; a *pit:*— pit.

1476. גּוּנִי **Gûwnîy**, *goo-nee´;* prob. from 1598; *protected; Guni*, the name of two Isr.:— Guni.

1477. גּוּנִי **Gûwnîy**, *goo-nee´;* patron. from 1476; a *Gunite* (collect. with art. pref.) or desc. of Guni:— Gunites.

1478. גָּוַע **gâva´**, *gaw-vah´;* a prim. root; to *breathe* out, i.e. (by impl.) *expire:*— die, be dead, give up the ghost, perish.

1479. גּוּף **gûwph**, *goof;* a prim. root; prop. to *hollow* or *arch*, i.e. (fig.) *close;* to *shut:*— shut.

1480. גּוּפָה **gûwphâh**, *goo-faw´;* from 1479; a *corpse* (as *closed* to sense):— body.

1481. גּוּר **gûwr**, *goor;* a prim. root; prop. to *turn* aside from the road (for a lodging or any other purpose), i.e. *sojourn* (as a guest); also to *shrink, fear* (as in a *strange* place); also to *gather* for hostility (as *afraid*):— abide, assemble, be afraid, dwell, fear, gather (together), inhabitant, remain, sojourn, stand in awe, (be) stranger, × surely.

1482. גּוּר **gûwr**, *goor;* or (short.)

גּוּר **gûr**, *goor;* perh. from 1481; a *cub* (as still *abiding* in the lair), espec. of the lion:— whelp, young one.

1483. גוּר **Gûwr**, *goor;* the same as 1482; *Gur*, a place in Pal.:— Gur.

1484. גּוֹר **gôwr**, *gore;* or (fem.)

גֹּרָה **gôrâh**, *go-raw´;* a var. of 1482:— whelp.

1485. גוּר־בַּעַל **Gûwr-Ba'al**, *goor-bah´-al;* from 1481 and 1168; *dwelling of Baal; Gur-Baal*, a place in Arabia.:— Gur-baal.

1486. גּוֹרָל **gôwrâl**, *go-rawl´;* or (short.)

גֹּרָל **gôral**, *go-ral´;* from an unused root mean. to *be rough* (as stone); prop. a *pebble*, i.e. a *lot* (small stones being used for that purpose); fig. a *portion* or *destiny* (as if determined by lot):— lot.

1487. גּוּשׁ **gûwsh**, *goosh;* or rather (by perm.)

גִּישׁ **gîysh**, *gheesh;* of uncert. der.; a *mass* of earth:— clod.

1488. גֵּז **gêz**, *gaze;* from 1494; a *fleece* (as shorn); also mown *grass:—* fleece, mowing, mown grass.

1489. גִּזְבָּר **gizbâr**, *ghiz-bawr´;* of for. der.; *treasurer:—* treasurer.

1490. גִּזְבָּר **gizbâr** (Chald.), *ghiz-bawr´;* corresp. to 1489:— treasurer.

1491. גָּזָה **gâzâh**, *gaw-zaw´;* a prim. root [akin to 1468]; to *cut* off, i.e. *portion* out:— take.

1492. גִּזָּה **gazzâh**, *gaz-zaw´;* fem. from 1494; a *fleece:—* fleece.

1493. גִּזוֹנִי **Gizôwnîy**, *ghee-zo-nee´;* patrial from the unused name of a place appar. in Pal.; a *Gizonite* or inhab. of Gizoh:— Gizonite.

1494. גָּזַז **gâzaz**, *gaw-zaz´;* a prim. root [akin to 1468]; to *cut* off; spec. to *shear* a flock or *shave* the hair; fig. to *destroy* an enemy:— cut off (down), poll, shave, [sheep-] shear (-er).

1495. גָּזֵז **Gâzêz**, *gaw-zaze´;* from 1494; *shearer; Gazez*, the name of two Isr.:— Gazez.

1496. גָּזִית **gâzîyth**, *gaw-zeeth´;* from 1491; something *cut*, i.e. *dressed* stone:— hewed, hewn stone, wrought.

1497. גָּזַל **gâzal**, *gaw-zal´;* a prim. root; to *pluck* off; spec. to *flay, strip* or *rob:—* catch, consume, exercise [robbery], pluck (off), rob, spoil, take away (by force, violence), tear.

1498. גָּזֵל **gâzêl**, *gaw-zale´;* from 1497; *robbery*, or (concr.) *plunder:—* robbery, thing taken away by violence.

1499. גֵּזֶל **gêzel**, *ghe´-zel;* from 1497; *plunder*, i.e. *violence:—* violence, violent perverting.

גֹּזָל **gôzâl**. See 1469.

1500. גְּזֵלָה **gᵉzêlâh**, *ghez-ay-law´;* fem. of 1498 and mean. the same:— that (he had robbed) [which he took violently away], spoil, violence.

1501. גָּזָם **gâzâm**, *gaw-zawm´;* from an unused root mean. to *devour;* a kind of *locust:—* palmer-worm.

1502. גַּזָּם **Gazzâm**, *gaz-zawm´;* from the same as 1501; *devourer; Gazzam*, one of the Nethinim:— Gazzam.

1503. גֶּזַע **geza'**, *geh´-zah;* from an unused root mean. to *cut* down (trees); the *trunk* or *stump* of a tree (as felled or as planted):— stem, stock.

1504. גָּזַר **gâzar**, *gaw-zar´;* a prim. root; to *cut* down or off; (fig.) to *destroy, divide, exclude,* or *decide:—* cut down (off), decree, divide, snatch.

1505. גְּזַר **gᵉzar** (Chald.), *ghez-ar´;* corresp. to 1504; to *quarry; determine:—* cut out, soothsayer.

1506. גֶּזֶר **gezer**, *gheh´-zer;* from 1504; something *cut* off; a *portion:—* part, piece.

1507. גֶּזֶר **Gezer**, *gheh´-zer;* the same as 1506; *Gezer*, a place in Pal.:— Gazer, Gezer.

1508. גִּזְרָה **gizrâh**, *ghiz-raw´;* fem. of 1506; the *figure* or person (as if *cut* out); also an *inclosure* (as *separated*):— polishing, separate place.

1509. גְּזֵרָה **gᵉzêrâh**, *ghez-ay-raw´;* from 1504; a *desert* (as *separated*):— not inhabited.

1510. גְּזֵרָה **gᵉzêrâh** (Chald.), *ghez-ay-raw´;* from 1505 (as 1504); a *decree:—* decree.

1511. גִּזְרִי **Gizrîy** (in the marg.), *ghiz-ree´;* patrial from 1507; a *Gezerite* (collect.) or inhab. of Gezer; but better (as in the text) by transp.

גִּרְזִי° **Girzîy**, *gher-zee´;* patrial of 1630; a *Girzite* (collect.) or member of a native tribe in Pal.:— Gezrites.

גִּחוֹן **Gichôwn**. See 1521.

1512. גָּחוֹן **gâchôwn**, *gaw-khone´;* prob. from 1518; the external *abdomen, belly* (as the *source* of the fetus [comp. 1521]):— belly.

גְּחֲזִי **Gêchăzîy**. See 1522.

גָּחֹל **gâchol**. See 1513.

1513. גֶּחֶל **gechel**, *geh´-khel;* or (fem.)

גַּחֶלֶת **gacheleth**, *gah-kheh´-leth;* from an unused root mean. to *glow* or *kindle;* an *ember:—* (burning) coal.

1514. גַּחַם **Gacham**, *gah´-kham;* from an unused root mean. to *burn; flame; Gacham*, a son of Nahor:— Gaham.

1515. גַּחַר **Gachar**, *gah´-khar;* from an unused root mean. to *hide; lurker; Gachar*, one of the Nethinim:— Gahar.

גּוֹי **gôy**. See 1471.

1516. גַּיְא **gay'**, *gah-ee´;* or (short.)

גַּי **gay,** *gah´-ee;* prob. (by transm.) from the same root as 1466 (abb.); a *gorge* (from its *lofty* sides; hence, narrow, but not a gully or winter-torrent):— valley.

1517. גִּיד **gîyd,** *gheed;* prob. from 1464; a *thong* (as *compressing*); by anal. a *tendon:*— sinew.

1518. גִּיחַ **gîyach,** *ghee´-akh;* or (short.)

גֹּחַ **gôach,** *go´-akh;* a prim. root; to *gush* forth (as water), gen. to *issue:*— break forth, labor to bring forth, come forth, draw up, take out.

1519. גִּיחַ **gîyach** (Chald.), *ghee´-akh;* or (short.)

גּוּחַ **gûwach** (Chald.), *goo´-akh;* corresp. to 1518; to *rush* forth:— strive.

1520. גִּיחַ **Gîyach,** *ghee´-akh;* from 1518; a *fountain; Giach,* a place in Pal.:— Giah.

1521. גִּיחוֹן **Gîychôwn,** *ghee-khone´;* or (short.)

גִּחוֹן **Gîchôwn,** *ghee-khone´;* from 1518; *stream; Gichon,* a river of Paradise; also a valley (or pool) near Jerusalem:— Gihon.

1522. גֵּיחֲזִי **Gêychăzîy,** *gay-khah-zee´;* or

גֵּחֲזִי **Gêchăzîy,** *gay-khah-zee´;* appar. from 1516 and 2372; *valley of a visionary; Gechazi,* the servant of Elisha:— Gehazi.

1523. גִּיל **gîyl,** *gheel;* or (by perm.)

גּוּל° **gûwl,** *gool;* a prim. root; prop. to *spin* round (under the influence of any violent emotion), i.e. usually *rejoice,* or (as *cringing*) *fear:*— be glad, joy, be joyful, rejoice.

1524. גִּיל **gîyl,** *gheel;* from 1523; a *revolution* (of time, i.e. an *age*); also *joy:*— × exceedingly, gladness, × greatly, joy, rejoice (-ing), sort.

1525. גִּילָה **gîylâh,** *ghee-law´;* or

גִּילַת **gîylath,** *ghee-lath´;* fem. of 1524; *joy:*— joy, rejoicing.

גִּילֹה **Gîylôh.** See 1542.

1526. גִּילֹנִי **Gîylônîy,** *ghee-lo-nee´;* patrial from 1542; a *Gilonite* or inhab. of Giloh:— Gilonite.

1527. גִּינַת **Gîynath,** *ghee-nath´;* of uncert. der.; *Ginath,* an Isr.:— Ginath.

1528. גִּיר **gîyr** (Chald.), *gheer;* corresp. to 1615; *lime:*— plaster.

גֵּיר **gêyr.** See 1616.

1529. גֵּישָׁן **Gêyshân,** *gay-shawn´;* from the same as 1487; *lumpish; Geshan,* an Isr.:— Geshan.

1530. גַּל **gal,** *gal;* from 1556; something *rolled,* i.e. a *heap* of stone or dung (plural *ruins*), by anal. a *spring* of water (plur. *waves*):— billow, heap, spring, wave.

1531. גֹּל **gôl,** *gole;* from 1556; a *cup* for oil (as *round*):— bowl.

גְּלָא **gᵉlâ´.** See 1541.

1532. גַּלָּב **gallâb,** *gal-lawb´;* from an unused root mean. to *shave;* a *barber:*— barber.

1533. גִּלְבֹּעַ **Gilbôa´,** *ghil-bo´-ah;* from 1530 and 1158; *fountain of ebullition; Gilboa,* a mountain of Pal.:— Gilboa.

1534. גַּלְגַּל **galgal,** *gal-gal´;* by redupl. from 1556; a *wheel;* by anal. a *whirlwind;* also *dust* (as *whirled*):— heaven, rolling thing, wheel.

1535. גַּלְגַּל **galgal** (Chald.), *gal-gal´;* corresp. to 1534; a *wheel:*— wheel.

1536. גִּלְגָּל **gilgâl,** *ghil-gawl´;* a var. of 1534:— wheel.

1537. גִּלְגָּל **Gilgâl,** *ghil-gawl´;* the same as 1536 (with the art. as a prop. noun); *Gilgal,* the name of three places in Pal.:— Gilgal. See also 1019.

1538. גֻּלְגֹּלֶת **gulgôleth,** *gul-go´-leth;* by redupl. from 1556; a *skull* (as *round*); by impl. a *head* (in enumeration of persons):— head, every man, poll, skull.

1539. גֶּלֶד **geled,** *ghe´-led;* from an unused root prob. mean. to *polish;* the (human) *skin* (as *smooth*):— skin.

1540. גָּלָה **gâlâh,** *gaw-law´;* a prim. root; to *denude* (espec. in a disgraceful sense); by impl. to *exile* (captives being usually *stripped*); fig. to *reveal:*— + advertise, appear, bewray, bring, (carry, lead, go) captive (into captivity), depart, disclose, discover, exile, be gone, open, × plainly, publish, remove, reveal, × shamelessly, shew, × surely, tell, uncover.

1541. גְּלָה **gᵉlâh** (Chald.), *ghel-aw´;* or

גְּלָא **gᵉlâ´** (Chald.), *ghel-aw´;* corresp. to 1540:— bring over, carry away, reveal.

גֹּלָה **gôlâh.** See 1473.

1542. גִּלֹה **Gîlôh,** *ghee-lo´;* or (fully)

גִּילֹה **Gîylôh,** *ghee-lo´;* from 1540; *open; Giloh,* a place in Pal.:— Giloh.

1543. גֻּלָּה **gullâh,** *gool-law´;* fem. from 1556; a *fountain, bowl* or *globe* (all as *round*):— bowl, pommel, spring.

1544. גִּלּוּל **gillûwl,** *ghil-lool´;* or (short.)

גִּלֻּל **gillûl,** *ghil-lool´;* from 1556; prop. a *log* (as *round*); by impl. an *idol:*— idol.

1545. גְּלוֹם **gᵉlôwm,** *ghel-ome´;* from 1563; *clothing* (as *wrapped*):— clothes.

1546. גָּלוּת **gâlûwth,** *gaw-looth´;* fem. from 1540; *captivity;* concr. *exiles* (collect.):— (they that are carried away) captives (-ity).

1547. גָּלוּת **gâlûwth** (Chald.), *gaw-looth´;* corresp. to 1546:— captivity.

1548. גָּלַח **gâlach,** *gaw-lakh´;* a prim. root; prop. to *be bald,* i.e. (caus.) to *shave;* fig. to *lay waste:*— poll, shave (off).

Hebrew

1549. גִּלָּיוֹן **gîllâyôwn**, *ghil-law-yone´*; or

גִּלְיוֹן **gilyôwn**, *ghil-yone´*; from 1540; a *tablet* for writing (as *bare*); by anal. a *mirror* (as a *plate*):— glass, roll.

1550. גָּלִיל **gâlîyl**, *gaw-leel´*; from 1556; a *valve* of a folding door (as *turning*); also a *ring* (as *round*):— folding, ring.

1551. גָּלִיל **Gâlîyl**, *gaw-leel´*; or (prol.)

גָּלִילָה **Gâlîylâh**, *gaw-lee-law´*; the same as 1550; a *circle* (with the art.); *Galil* (as a special *circuit*) in the North of Pal.:— Galilee.

1552. גְּלִילָה **gelîylâh**, *ghel-ee-law´*; fem. of 1550; a *circuit* or *region*:— border, coast, country.

1553. גְּלִילוֹת **Gelîylôwth**, *ghel-ee-lowth´*; plur. of 1552; *circles*; *Geliloth*, a place in Pal.:— Geliloth.

1554. גַּלִּים **Gallîym**, *gal-leem´*; plur. of 1530; *springs*; *Gallim*, a place in Pal.:— Gallim.

1555. גָּלְיָת **Golyath**, *gol-yath´*; perh. from 1540; *exile*; *Goljath*, a Philistine:— Goliath.

1556. גָּלַל **gâlal**, *gaw-lal´*; a prim. root; to *roll* (lit. or fig.):— commit, remove, roll (away, down, together), run down, seek occasion, trust, wallow.

1557. גָּלָל **gâlâl**, *gaw-lawl´*; from 1556; *dung* (as in *balls*):— dung.

1558. גָּלָל **gâlâl**, *gaw-lawl´*; from 1556; a *circumstance* (as *rolled* around); only used adv., on *account* of:— because of, for (sake).

1559. גָּלָל **Gâlâl**, *gaw-lawl´*; from 1556, in the sense of 1560; *great*; *Galal*, the name of two Isr.:— Galal.

1560. גְּלָל **gelâl** (Chald.), *ghel-awl´*; from a root corresp. to 1556; *weight* or *size* (as if *rolled*):— great.

1561. גֵּלֶל **gêlel**, *gay´-lel*; a var. of 1557; *dung* (plur. *balls* of dung):— dung.

1562. גִּלֲלַי **Gîlălay**, *ghe-lal-ah´-ee*; from 1561; *dungy*; *Gilalai*, an Isr.:— Gilalai.

1563. גָּלַם **gâlam**, *gaw-lam´*; a prim. root; to *fold*:— wrap together.

1564. גֹּלֶם **gôlem**, *go´-lem*; from 1563; a *wrapped* (and unformed *mass*, i.e. as the *embryo*):— substance yet being unperfect.

1565. גַּלְמוּד **galmûwd**, *gal-mood´*; prob. by prol. from 1563; *sterile* (as *wrapped* up too hard); fig. *desolate*:— desolate, solitary.

1566. גָּלַע **gâla'**, *gaw-lah´*; a prim. root; to *be obstinate*:— (inter-) meddle (with).

1567. גַּלְעֵד **Gal'êd**, *gal-ade´*; from 1530 and 5707; *heap of testimony*; *Galed*, a memorial cairn E. of the Jordan:— Galeed.

1568. גִּלְעָד **Gil'âd**, *ghil-awd´*; prob. from 1567; *Gilad*, a region E. of the Jordan; also the name of three Isr.:— Gilead, Gileadite.

1569. גִּלְעָדִי **Gil'âdîy**, *ghil-aw-dee´*; patron. from 1568; a *Giladite* or desc. of Gilad:— Gileadite.

1570. גָּלַשׁ **gâlash**, *gaw-lash´*; a prim. root; prob. to *caper* (as a goat):— appear.

1571. גַּם **gam**, *gam*; by contr. from an unused root mean. to *gather*; prop. *assemblage*; used only adv. *also, even, yea, though*; often repeated as correl. *both ... and*:— again, alike, also, (so much) as (soon), both (so) ... and, but, either ... or, even, for all, (in) likewise (manner), moreover, nay ... neither, one, then (-refore), though, what, with, yea.

1572. גָּמָא **gâmâ'**, *gaw-maw´*; a prim. root (lit. or fig.) to *absorb*:— swallow, drink.

1573. גֹּמֶא **gôme'**, *go´-meh*; from 1572; prop. an *absorbent*, i.e. the *bulrush* (from its *porosity*); spec. the *papyrus*:— (bul-) rush.

1574. גֹּמֶד **gômed**, *go´-med*; from an unused root appar. mean. to *grasp*; prop. a *span*:— cubit.

1575. גַּמָּד **Gammâd**, *gam-mawd´*; from the same as 1574; a *warrior* (as *grasping* weapons):— Gammadims.

1576. גְּמוּל **gemûwl**, *ghem-ool´*; from 1580; *treatment*, i.e. an *act* (of good or ill); by impl. *service* or *requital*:— + as hast served, benefit, desert, deserving, that which he hath given, recompense, reward.

1577. גָּמוּל **Gâmûwl**, *gaw-mool´*; pass. part. of 1580; *rewarded*; *Gamul*, an Isr.:— Gamul. See also 1014.

1578. גְּמוּלָה **gemûwlâh**, *ghem-oo-law´*; fem. of 1576; mean. the same:— deed, recompense, such a reward.

1579. גִּמְזוֹ **Gimzôw**, *ghim-zo´*; of uncert. der.; *Gimzo*, a place in Pal.:— Gimzo.

1580. גָּמַל **gâmal**, *gaw-mal´*; a prim. root; to *treat* a person (well or ill), i.e. *benefit* or *requite*; by impl. (of *toil*), to *ripen*, i.e. (spec.) to *wean*:— bestow on, deal bountifully, do (good), recompense, requite, reward, ripen, + serve, mean, yield.

1581. גָּמָל **gâmâl**, *gaw-mawl´*; appar. from 1580 (in the sense of *labor* or *burden-bearing*); a *camel*:— camel.

1582. גְּמַלִּי **Gemalliy**, *ghem-al-lee´*; prob. from 1581; *camel-driver*; *Gemalli*, an Isr.:— Gemalli.

1583. גַּמְלִיאֵל **Gamliy'êl**, *gam-lee-ale´*; from 1580 and 410; *reward of God*; *Gamliel*, an Isr.:— Gamaliel.

1584. גָּמַר **gâmar**, *gaw-mar´*; a prim. root; to *end* (in the sense of *completion* or *failure*):— cease, come to an end, fail, perfect, perform.

1585. גְּמַר **gᵉmar** (Chald.), *ghem-ar´;* corresp. to 1584:— perfect.

1586. גֹּמֶר **Gômer**, *go´-mer;* from 1584; *completion; Gomer*, the name of a son of Japheth and of his desc.; also of a Hebrewess:— Gomer.

1587. גְּמַרְיָה **Gᵉmaryâh**, *ghem-ar-yaw´;* or

גְּמַרְיָהוּ **Gᵉmaryâhûw**, *ghem-ar-yaw´-hoo;* from 1584 and 3050; *Jah has perfected; Gemarjah*, the name of two Isr.:— Gemariah.

1588. גַּן **gan**, *gan;* from 1598; a *garden* (as *fenced*):— garden.

1589. גָּנַב **gânab**, *gaw-nab´;* a prim. root; to *thieve* (lit. or fig.); by impl. to *deceive:*— carry away, × indeed, secretly bring, steal (away), get by stealth.

1590. גַּנָּב **gannâb**, *gaw-nab´;* from 1589; a *stealer:*— thief.

1591. גְּנֵבָה **gᵉnêbâh**, *ghen-ay-baw´;* from 1589; *stealing*, i.e. (concr.) something *stolen:*— theft.

1592. גְּנֻבַת **Gᵉnûbath**, *ghen-oo-bath´;* from 1589; *theft; Genubath*, an Edomitish prince:— Genubath.

1593. גַּנָּה **gannâh**, *gan-naw´;* fem. of 1588; a *garden:*— garden.

1594. גִּנָּה **ginnâh**, *ghin-naw´;* another form for 1593:— garden.

1595. גֶּנֶז **genez**, *gheh´-nez;* from an unused root mean. to *store; treasure;* by impl. a *coffer:*— chest, treasury.

1596. גְּנַז **gᵉnaz** (Chald.), *ghen-az´;* corresp. to 1595; *treasure:*— treasure.

1597. גִּנְזַךְ **ginzak**, *ghin-zak´;* prol. from 1595; a *treasury:*— treasury.

1598. גָּנַן **gânan**, *gaw-nan´;* a prim. root; to *hedge* about, i.e. (gen.) *protect:*— defend.

1599. גִּנְּתוֹן **Ginnᵉthôwn**, *ghin-neth-ōne´;* or

גִּנְּתוֹ **Ginnᵉthôw**, *ghin-neth-o´;* from 1598; *gardener; Ginnethon* or *Ginnetho*, an Isr.:— Ginnetho, Ginnethon.

1600. גָּעָה **gâ'âh**, *gaw-aw´;* a prim. root; to *bellow* (as cattle):— low.

1601. גֹּעָה **Gô'âh**, *go-aw´;* fem. act. part. of 1600; *lowing; Goah*, a place near Jerusalem:— Goath.

1602. גָּעַל **gâ'al**, *gaw-al´;* a prim. root; to *detest;* by impl. to *reject:*— abhor, fail, lothe, vilely cast away.

1603. גַּעַל **Ga'al**, *gah´-al;* from 1602; *loathing; Gaal*, an Isr.:— Gaal.

1604. גֹּעַל **gô'al**, *go´-al;* from 1602; *abhorrence:*— loathing.

1605. גָּעַר **gâ'ar**, *gaw-ar´;* a prim. root to *chide:*— corrupt, rebuke, reprove.

1606. גְּעָרָה **gᵉ'ârâh**, *gheh-aw-raw´;* from 1605; a *chiding:*— rebuke (-ing), reproof.

1607. גָּעַשׁ **gâ'ash**, *gaw-ash´;* a prim. root to *agitate* violently:— move, shake, toss, trouble.

1608. גַּעַשׁ **Ga'ash**, *ga´-ash;* from 1607; a *quaking; Gaash*, a hill in Pal.:— Gaash.

1609. גַּעְתָּם **Ga'tâm**, *gah-tawm´;* of uncert. der.; *Gatam*, an Edomite:— Gatam.

1610. גַּף **gaph**, *gaf;* from an unused root mean. to *arch;* the *back;* by extens. the *body* or self:— + highest places, himself.

1611. גַּף **gaph** (Chald.), *gaf;* corresp. to 1610; a *wing:*— wing.

1612. גֶּפֶן **gephen**, *gheh´-fen;* from an unused root mean. to *bend;* a *vine* (as *twining*), espec. the grape:— vine, tree.

1613. גֹּפֶר **gôpher**, *go´-fer;* from an unused root, prob. mean. to *house in;* a kind of tree or wood (as used for *building*), appar. the *cypress:*— gopher.

1614. גָּפְרִית **gophrîyth**, *gof-reeth´;* prob. fem. of 1613; prop. cypress-*resin;* by anal. *sulphur* (as equally inflammable):— brimstone.

1615. גִּר **gîr**, *gheer;* perh. from 3564; *lime* (from being *burned* in a kiln):— chalk [-stone].

1616. גֵּר **gêr**, *gare;* or (fully)

גֵּיר **gêyr**, *gare;* from 1481; prop. a *guest;* by impl. a *foreigner:*— alien, sojourner, stranger.

גֻּר **gûr**. See 1482.

1617. גֵּרָא **Gêrâ'**, *gay-raw´;* perh. from 1626; a *grain; Gera*, the name of six Isr.:— Gera.

1618. גָּרָב **gârâb**, *gaw-rawb´;* from an unused root mean. to *scratch; scurf* (from *itching*):— scab, scurvy.

1619. גָּרֵב **Gârêb**, *gaw-rabe´;* from the same as 1618; *scabby; Gareb*, the name of an Isr., also of a hill near Jerusalem:— Gareb.

1620. גַּרְגַּר **gargar**, *gar-gar´;* by redupl. from 1641; a *berry* (as if a pellet of *rumination*):— berry.

1621. גַּרְגְּרוֹת **gargᵉrôwth**, *gar-gher-owth´;* fem. plur. from 1641; the *throat* (as used in *rumination*):— neck.

1622. גִּרְגָּשִׁי **Girgâshîy**, *ghir-gaw-shee´;* patrial from an unused name [of uncert. der.]; a *Girgashite*, one of the native tribes of Canaan:— Girgashite, Girgasite.

1623. גָּרַד **gârad**, *gaw-rad´;* a prim. root; to *abrade:*— scrape.

1624. גָּרָה **gârâh**, *gaw-raw´;* a prim. root; prop. to *grate*, i.e. (fig.) to *anger:*— contend, meddle, stir up, strive.

1625. גֵּרָה **gêrâh**, *gay-raw´;* from 1641; the *cud* (as *scraping* the throat):— cud.

1626. גֵּרָה **gêrâh**, *gay-raw´;* from 1641 (as in 1625); prop. (like 1620) a *kernel* (round as if *scraped*), i.e. a *gerah* or small weight (and coin):— gerah.

גֹּרָה **gôrâh**. See 1484.

1627. גָּרוֹן **gârôwn**, *gaw-rone´;* or (short.)

גָּרֹן **gârôn**, *gaw-rone´;* from 1641; the *throat* [comp. 1621] (as *roughened* by swallowing):— × aloud, mouth, neck, throat.

1628. גֵּרוּת **gêrûwth**, *gay-rooth´;* from 1481; a (temporary) *residence:*— habitation.

1629. גָּרַז **gâraz**, *gaw-raz´;* a prim. root; to *cut off:*— cut off.

1630. גְּרִזִים **Gᵉrîzîym**, *gher-ee-zeem´;* plur. of an unused noun from 1629 [comp. 1511], *cut up* (i.e. *rocky*); *Gerizim*, a mountain of Pal.:— Gerizim.

1631. גַּרְזֶן **garzen**, *gar-zen´;* from 1629; an *axe:*— ax.

1632. גָּרֹל° **gârôl**, *gaw-role´;* from the same as 1486; *harsh:*— man of great [*as in the marg. which reads* 1419].

גֹּרָל **gôrâl**. See 1486.

1633. גָּרַם **gâram**, *gaw-ram´;* a prim. root; to *be spare* or *skeleton-like;* used only as a denom. from 1634; (caus.) to *bone*, i.e. *denude* (by extens. *crunch*) the bones:— gnaw the bones, break.

1634. גֶּרֶם **gerem**, *gheh´-rem;* from 1633; a *bone* (as the *skeleton* of the body); hence, *self*, i.e. (fig.) *very:*— bone, strong, top.

1635. גֶּרֶם **gerem** (Chald.), *gheh´-rem;* corresp. to 1634; a *bone:*— bone.

1636. גַּרְמִי **Garmîy**, *gar-mee´;* from 1634; *bony*, i.e. *strong:*— Garmite.

1637. גֹּרֶן **gôren**, *go´-ren;* from an unused root mean. to *smooth;* a threshing-*floor* (as made *even*); by anal. any open *area:*— (barn, corn, threshing-) floor, (threshing-, void) place.

גָּרֹן **gârôn**. See 1627.

1638. גָּרַס **gâraç**, *gaw-ras´;* a prim. root; to *crush;* also (intr. and fig.) to *dissolve:*— break.

1639. גָּרַע **gâra´**, *gaw-rah´;* a prim. root; to *scrape* off; by impl. to *shave, remove, lessen*, or *withhold:*— abate, clip, (di-) minish, do (take) away, keep back, restrain, make small, withdraw.

1640. גָּרַף **gâraph**, *gaw-raf´;* a prim. root; to *bear* off violently:— sweep away.

1641. גָּרַר **gârar**, *gaw-rar´;* a prim. root; to *drag* off roughly; by impl. to *bring up* the cud (i.e. *ruminate*); by anal. to *saw:*— catch, chew, × continuing, destroy, saw.

1642. גְּרָר **Gᵉrâr**, *gher-awr´;* prob. from 1641; a

rolling country; *Gerar*, a Philistine city:— Gerar.

1643. גֶּרֶשׂ **geres**, *gheh´-res;* from an unused root mean. to *husk;* a *kernel* (collect.), i.e. *grain:*— beaten corn.

1644. גָּרַשׁ **gârash**, *gaw-rash´;* a prim. root; to *drive out* from a possession; espec. to *expatriate* or *divorce:*— cast up (out), divorced (woman), drive away (forth, out), expel, × surely put away, trouble, thrust out.

1645. גֶּרֶשׁ **geresh**, *gheh´-resh;* from 1644; *produce* (as if *expelled*):— put forth.

1646. גְּרֻשָׁה **gᵉrûshâh**, *gher-oo-shaw´;* fem. pass. part. of 1644; (abstr.) *dispossession:*— exaction.

1647. גֵּרְשֹׁם **Gêrᵉshôm**, *gay-resh-ome´;* for 1648; *Gereshom*, the name of four Isr.:— Gershom.

1648. גֵּרְשׁוֹן **Gêrᵉshôwn**, *gay-resh-one´;* or

גֵּרְשׁוֹם **Gêrᵉshôwm**, *gay-resh-ome´;* from 1644; a *refugee; Gereshon* or *Gereshom*, an Isr.:— Gershon, Gershom.

1649. גֵּרְשֻׁנִּי **Gerᵉshunnîy**, *gay-resh-oon-nee´;* patron. from 1648; a *Gereshonite* or desc. of Gereshon:— Gershonite, sons of Gershon.

1650. גְּשׁוּר **Gᵉshûwr**, *ghesh-oor´;* from an unused root (mean. to *join*); *bridge; Geshur*, a district of Syria:— Geshur, Geshurite.

1651. גְּשׁוּרִי **Gᵉshûwrîy**, *ghe-shoo-ree´;* patrial from 1650; a *Geshurite* (also collect.) or inhab. of Geshur:— Geshuri, Geshurites.

1652. גָּשַׁם **gâsham**, *gaw-sham´;* a prim. root; to *shower* violently:— (cause to) rain.

1653. גֶּשֶׁם **geshem**, *gheh´-shem;* from 1652; a *shower:*— rain, shower.

1654. גֶּשֶׁם **Geshem**, *gheh´-shem;* or (prol.)

גַּשְׁמוּ **Gashmûw**, *gash-moo´;* the same as 1653; *Geshem* or *Gashmu*, an Arabian:— Geshem, Gashmu.

1655. גֶּשֶׁם **geshem** (Chald.), *gheh´-shem;* appar. the same as 1653; used in a peculiar sense, the *body* (prob. for the [fig.] idea of a *hard* rain):— body.

1656. גֹּשֶׁם **gôshem**, *go´-shem;* from 1652; equiv. to 1653:— rained upon.

גַּשְׁמוּ **Gashmûw**. See 1654.

1657. גֹּשֶׁן **Gôshen**, *go´-shen;* prob. of Eg. or.; *Goshen*, the residence of the Isr. in Egypt; also a place in Pal.:— Goshen.

1658. גִּשְׁפָּא **Gishpâ'**, *ghish-paw´;* of uncert. der.; *Gishpa*, an Isr.:— Gispa.

1659. גָּשַׁשׁ **gâshash**, *gaw-shash´;* a prim. root; appar. to *feel* about:— grope.

1660. גַּת **gath**, *gath;* prob. from 5059 (in the

sense of *treading* out grapes); a wine-*press* (or vat for holding the grapes in pressing them):— (wine-) press (fat).

1661. גַּת **Gath**, *gath;* the same as 1660; *Gath,* a Philistine city:— Gath.

1662. גַּת־הַחֵפֶר **Gath-ha-Chêpher**, *gath-hah-khay´-fer;* or (abridged)

גִּתָּה־חֵפֶר **Gittâh-Chêpher**, *ghit-taw-khay´-fer;* from 1660 and 2658 with the art. ins.; *wine-press of* (the) *well; Gath-Chepher,* a place in Pal.:— Gath-kephr, Gittah-kephr.

1663. גִּתִּי **Gittîy**, *ghit-tee´;* patrial from 1661; a *Gittite* or inhab. of Gath:— Gittite.

1664. גִּתַּיִם **Gittayim**, *ghit-tah´-yim;* dual of 1660; *double wine-press; Gittajim,* a place in Pal.:— Gittaim.

1665. גִּתִּית **Gittîyth**, *ghit-teeth´;* fem. of 1663; a *Gittite* harp:— Gittith.

1666. גֶּתֶר **Gether**, *gheh´-ther;* of uncert. der.; *Gether,* a son of Aram, and the region settled by him:— Gether.

1667. גַּת־רִמּוֹן **Gath-Rimmôwn**, *gath-rim-mone´;* from 1660 and 7416; *wine-press of* (the) *pomegranate; Gath-Rimmon,* a place in Pal.:— Gath-rimmon.

ד

1668. דָּא **dâ'** (Chald.), *daw;* corresp. to 2088; *this:*— one ... another, this.

1669. דָּאַב **dâ'ab**, *daw-ab´;* a prim. root; to *pine:*— mourn, sorrow (-ful).

1670. דְּאָבָה **de'âbâh**, *děh-aw-baw´;* from 1669; prop. *pining;* by anal. *fear:*— sorrow.

1671. דְּאָבוֹן **de'âbôwn**, *děh-aw-bone´;* from 1669; *pining:*— sorrow.

1672. דָּאַג **dâ'ag**, *daw-ag´;* a prim. root; *be anxious:*— be afraid (careful, sorry), sorrow, take thought.

1673. דֹּאֵג **Dô'êg**, *do-ayg´;* or (fully)

דּוֹאֵג **Dôw'êg**, *do-ayg´;* act. part. of 1672; *anxious; Doëg,* an Edomite:— Doeg.

1674. דְּאָגָה **de'âgâh**, *děh-aw-gaw´;* from 1672; *anxiety:*— care (-fulness), fear, heaviness, sorrow.

1675. דָּאָה **dâ'âh**, *daw-aw´;* a prim. root; to *dart,* i.e. *fly* rapidly:— fly.

1676. דָּאָה **dâ'âh**, *daw-aw´;* from 1675; the *kite* (from its rapid *flight*):— vulture. See 7201.

1677. דֹּב **dôb**, *dobe;* or (fully)

דּוֹב **dôwb**, *dobe;* from 1680; the *bear* (as slow):— bear.

1678. דֹּב **dôb** (Chald.), *dobe;* corresp. to 1677:— bear.

1679. דֹּבֶא **dôbe'**, *do´-beh;* from an unused

root (comp. 1680) (prob. mean. to be *sluggish,* i.e. *restful*); *quiet:*— strength.

1680. דָּבַב **dâbab**, *daw-bab´;* a prim. root (comp. 1679); to *move* slowly, i.e. *glide:*— cause to speak.

1681. דִּבָּה **dibbâh**, *dib-baw´;* from 1680 (in the sense of *furtive* motion); *slander:*— defaming, evil report, infamy, slander.

1682. דְּבוֹרָה **debôwrâh**, *deb-o-raw´;* or (short.)

דְּבֹרָה **debôrâh**, *deb-o-raw´;* from 1696 (in the sense of *orderly* motion); the *bee* (from its *systematic* instincts):— bee.

1683. דְּבוֹרָה **Debôwrâh**, *deb-o-raw´;* or (short.)

דְּבֹרָה **Debôrâh**, *deb-o-raw´;* the same as 1682; *Deborah,* the name of two Hebrewesses:— Deborah.

1684. דְּבַח **debach** (Chald.), *deb-akh´;* corresp. to 2076; to *sacrifice* (an animal):— offer [sacrifice].

1685. דְּבַח **debach** (Chald.), *deb-akh´;* from 1684; a *sacrifice:*— sacrifice.

1686. דִּבְיוֹן **dibyôwn**, *dib-yone´;* in the marg. for the textual reading

חֲרְיוֹן° **cheryôwn**, *kher-yone´;* both (in the plur. only and) of uncert. der.; prob. some cheap vegetable, perh. a bulbous root:— dove's dung.

1687. דְּבִיר **debîyr**, *deb-eer´;* or (short.)

דְּבִר **debîr**, *deb-eer´;* from 1696 (appar. in the sense of *oracle*); the *shrine* or innermost part of the sanctuary:— oracle.

1688. דְּבִיר **Debîyr**, *deb-eer´;* or (short.)

דְּבִר **Debîr** (Josh. 13:26 [but see 3810]), *deb-eer´;* the same as 1687; *Debir,* the name of an Amoritish king and of two places in Pal.:— Debir.

1689. דִּבְלָה **Diblâh**, *dib-law´;* prob. an orth. err. for 7247; *Diblah,* a place in Syria:— Diblath.

1690. דְּבֵלָה **debêlâh**, *deb-ay-law´;* from an unused root (akin to 2082) prob. mean. to *press* together; a *cake* of pressed figs:— cake (lump) of figs.

1691. דִּבְלַיִם **Diblayim**, *dib-lah´-yim;* dual from the masc. of 1690; *two cakes; Diblajim,* a symb. name:— Diblaim.

דִּבְלָתַיִם **Diblâthayim**. See 1015.

1692. דָּבַק **dâbaq**, *daw-bak´;* a prim. root; prop. to *impinge,* i.e. *cling* or *adhere;* fig. to *catch* by pursuit:— abide fast, cleave (fast together), follow close (hard after), be joined (together), keep (fast), overtake, pursue hard, stick, take.

1693. דְּבַק **d^ebaq** (Chald.), *deb-ak´;* corresp. to 1692; to *stick* to:— cleave.

1694. דֶּבֶק **debeq**, *deh´-bek;* from 1692; a *joint;* by impl. *solder:*— joint, solder.

1695. דָּבֵק **dâbêq**, *daw-bake´;* from 1692; *adhering:*— cleave, joining, stick closer.

1696. דָּבַר **dâbar**, *daw-bar´;* a prim. root; perh. prop. to *arrange;* but used fig. (of words), to *speak;* rarely (in a destructive sense) to *subdue:*— answer, appoint, bid, command, commune, declare, destroy, give, name, promise, pronounce, rehearse, say, speak, be spokesman, subdue, talk, teach, tell, think, use [entreaties], utter, × well, × work.

1697. דָּבָר **dâbâr**, *daw-baw´;* from 1696; a *word;* by impl. a *matter* (as *spoken* of) or *thing;* adv. a *cause:*— act, advice, affair, answer, × any such (thing), + because of, book, business, care, case, cause, certain rate, + chronicles, commandment, × commune (-ication), + concern [-ing], + confer, counsel, + dearth, decree, deed, × disease, due, duty, effect, + eloquent, errand, [evil favoured-] ness, + glory, + harm, hurt, + iniquity, + judgment, language, + lying, manner, matter, message, [no] thing, oracle, × ought, × parts, + pertaining, + please, portion, + power, promise, provision, purpose, question, rate, reason, report, request, × (as hast) said, sake, saying, sentence, + sign, + so, some [uncleanness], somewhat to say, + song, speech, × spoken, talk, task, + that, × there done, thing (concerning), thought, + thus, tidings, what [-soever], + wherewith, which, word, work.

1698. דֶּבֶר **deber**, *deh´-ber;* from 1696 (in the sense of *destroying*); a *pestilence:*— murrain, pestilence, plague.

1699. דֹּבֶר **dôber**, *do´-ber;* from 1696 (in its original sense); a *pasture* (from its *arrangement* of the flock):— fold, manner.

דְּבִר **d^ebîr** or

דְּבִר **D^ebîr**. See 1687, 1688.

1699'. דִּבֵּר **dibbêr**, *dib-bare´;* for 1697:— word.

1700. דִּבְרָה **dibrâh**, *dib-raw´;* fem. of 1697; a *reason, suit* or *style:*— cause, end, estate, order, regard.

1701. דִּבְרָה **dibrâh** (Chald.), *dib-raw´;* corresp. to 1700:— intent, sake.

דְּבֹרָה **d^ebôrâh** or

דְּבֹרָה **D^ebôrâh**. See 1682, 1683.

1702. דֹּבְרָה **dôb^erâh**, *do-ber-aw´;* fem. act. part. of 1696 in the sense of *driving* [comp. 1699]; a *raft:*— float.

1703. דַּבָּרָה **dabbârâh**, *dab-baw-raw´;* intens. from 1696; a *word:*— word.

1704. דִּבְרִי **Dibrîy**, *dib-ree´;* from 1697; *wordy;* Dibri, an Isr.:— Dibri.

1705. דָּבְרַת **Dâb^erath**, *daw-ber-ath´;* from 1697 (perh. in the sense of 1699); *Daberath,* a place in Pal.:— Dabareh, Daberath.

1706. דְּבַשׁ **d^ebash**, *deb-ash´;* from an unused root mean. to *be gummy; honey* (from its *stickiness*); by anal. *syrup:*— honey [-comb].

1707. דַּבֶּשֶׁת **dabbesheth**, *dab-beh´-sheth;* intens. from the same as 1706; a sticky *mass,* i.e. the *hump* of a camel:— hunch [of a camel].

1708. דַּבֶּשֶׁת **Dabbesheth**, *dab-beh´-sheth;* the same as 1707; *Dabbesheth,* a place in Pal.:— Dabbesheth.

1709. דָּג **dâg**, *dawg;* or (fully)

דָּאג° **dâ'g** (Neh. 13:16), *dawg;* from 1711; a *fish* (as *prolific*); or perh. rather from 1672 (as *timid*); but still better from 1672 (in the sense of *squirming,* i.e. moving by the vibratory action of the tail); a *fish* (often used collect.):— fish.

1710. דָּגָה **dâgâh**, *daw-gaw´;* fem. of 1709, and mean. the same:— fish.

1711. דָּגָה **dâgâh**, *daw-gaw´;* a prim. root; to *move rapidly;* used only as a denom. from 1709; to *spawn,* i.e. *become numerous:*— grow.

1712. דָּגוֹן **Dâgôwn**, *daw-gohn´;* from 1709; the *fish-god; Dagon,* a Philistine deity:— Dagon.

1713. דָּגַל **dâgal**, *daw-gal´;* a prim. root; to *flaunt,* i.e. *raise a flag;* fig. to *be conspicuous:*— (set up, with) banners, chiefest.

1714. דֶּגֶל **degel**, *deh´-gel;* from 1713; a *flag:*— banner, standard.

1715. דָּגָן **dâgân**, *daw-gawn´;* from 1711; prop. *increase,* i.e. *grain:*— corn ([floor]), wheat.

1716. דָּגַר **dâgar**, *daw-gar´;* a prim. root, to *brood* over eggs or young:— gather, sit.

1717. דַּד **dad**, *dad;* appar. from the same as 1730; the *breast* (as the seat of *love,* or from its shape):— breast, teat.

1718. דָּדָה **dâdâh**, *daw-daw´;* a doubtful root; to *walk gently:*— go (softly, with).

1719. דְּדָן **D^edân**, *ded-awn´;* or (prol.)

דְּדָנֵה **D^edâneh** (Ezek. 25:13), *deh-daw´-neh;* of uncert. der.; *Dedan,* the name of two Cushites and of their territory:— Dedan.

1720. דְּדָנִים **D^edânîym**, *ded-aw-neem´;* plur. of 1719 (as patrial); *Dedanites,* the desc. or inhab. of Dedan:— Dedanim.

1721. דֹּדָנִים **Dôdânîym**, *do-daw-neem´;* or (by orth. err.)

רֹדָנִים **Rôdânîym** (1 Chron. 1:7), *ro-*

daw-neem´; a plur. of uncert. der.; *Dodanites,* or desc. of a son of Javan:— Dodanim.

1722. דְּהַב **d^ehab** (Chald.), *deh-hab´;* corresp. to 2091; *gold:*— gold (-en).

1723. דַּהֲוָא **Dahăvâ'** (Chald.), *dah-hav-aw´;* of uncert. der.; *Dahava,* a people colonized in Samaria:— Dehavites.

1724. דָּהַם **dâham,** *daw-ham´;* a prim. root (comp. 1740); to *be dumb,* i.e. (fig.) *dumbfounded:*— be astonished.

1725. דָּהַר **dâhar,** *daw-har´;* a prim. root; to *curvet* or move irregularly:— pause.

1726. דַּהֲהַר **dahăhar,** *dah-hah-har´;* by redupl. from 1725; a *gallop:*— pransing.

דֹּואֵג **Dôw'êg.** See 1673.

1727. דּוּב **dûwb,** *doob;* a prim. root; to *mope,* i.e. (fig.) *pine:*— sorrow.

דֹּוב **dôwb.** See 1677.

1728. דַּוָּג **davvâg,** *dav-vawg´;* an orth. var. of 1709 as a denom. [1771]; a *fisherman:*— fisher.

1729. דּוּגָה **dûwgâh,** *doo-gaw´;* fem. from the same as 1728; prop. *fishery,* i.e. a *hook* for fishing:— fish [hook].

1730. דֹּוד **dôwd,** *dode;* or (short.)

דֹּד **dôd,** *dode;* from an unused root mean. prop. to *boil,* i.e. (fig.) to *love;* by impl. a *love-token, lover, friend;* spec. an *uncle:*— (well-) beloved, father's brother, love, uncle.

1731. דּוּד **dûwd,** *dood;* from the same as 1730; a *pot* (for *boiling*); also (by resemblance of shape) a *basket:*— basket, caldron, kettle, (seething) pot.

1732. דָּוִד **Dâvîd,** *daw-veed´;* rarely (fully)

דָּוִיד **Dâvîyd,** *daw-veed´;* from the same as 1730; *loving; David,* the youngest son of Jesse:— David.

1733. דֹּודָה **dôwdâh,** *do-daw´;* fem. of 1730; an *aunt:*— aunt, father's sister, uncle's wife.

1734. דֹּודֹו **Dôwdôw,** *do-do´;* from 1730; *loving; Dodo,* the name of three Isr.:— Dodo.

1735. דֹּודָוָהוּ **Dôwdâvâhûw,** *do-daw-vaw´-hoo;* from 1730 and 3050; *love of Jah; Dodavah,* an Isr.:— Dodavah.

1736. דּוּדַי **dûwday,** *doo-dah´-ee;* from 1731; a *boiler* or *basket;* also the *mandrake* (as *aphrodisiac*):— basket, mandrake.

1737. דֹּודַי **Dôwday,** *do-dah´-ee;* formed like 1736; *amatory; Dodai,* an Isr.:— Dodai.

1738. דָּוָה **dâvâh,** *daw-vaw´;* a prim. root; to *be sick* (as if in menstruation):— infirmity.

1739. דָּוֶה **dâveh,** *daw-veh´;* from 1738; *sick* (espec. in menstruation):— faint, menstruous cloth, she that is sick, having sickness.

1740. דּוּחַ **dûwach,** *doo´-akh;* a prim. root; to *thrust away;* fig. to *cleanse:*— cast out, purge, wash.

1741. דְּוַי **d^evay,** *dev-ah´-ee;* from 1739; *sickness;* fig. *loathing:*— languishing, sorrowful.

1742. דַּוָּי **davvây,** *dav-voy´;* from 1739; *sick;* fig. *troubled:*— faint.

דָּוִיד **Dâvîyd.** See 1732.

1743. דּוּךְ **dûwk,** *dook;* a prim. root; to *bruise* in a mortar:— beat.

1744. דּוּכִיפַת **dûwkîyphath,** *doo-kee-fath´;* of uncert. der.; the *hoopoe* or else the *grouse:*— lapwing.

1745. דּוּמָה **dûwmâh,** *doo-maw´;* from an unused root mean. to *be dumb* (comp. 1820); *silence;* fig. *death:*— silence.

1746. דּוּמָה **Dûwmâh,** *doo-maw´;* the same as 1745; *Dumah,* a tribe and region of Arabia:— Dumah.

1747. דּוּמִיָּה **dûwmîyâh,** *doo-me-yaw´;* from 1820; *stillness;* adv. *silently;* abstr. *quiet, trust:*— silence, silent, waiteth.

1748. דּוּמָם **dûwmâm,** *doo-mawm´;* from 1826; *still;* adv. *silently:*— dumb, silent, quietly wait.

דֹּומֶשֶׂק **Dûwmesheq.** See 1833.

1749. דֹּונַג **dôwnag,** *do-nag´;* of uncert. der.; *wax:*— wax.

1750. דּוּץ **dûwts,** *doots;* a prim. root; to *leap:*— be turned.

1751. דּוּק **dûwq** (Chald.), *dook;* corresp. to 1854; to *crumble:*— be broken to pieces.

1752. דּוּר **dûwr,** *dure;* a prim. root; prop. to *gyrate* (or move in a circle), i.e. to *remain:*— dwell.

1753. דּוּר **dûwr** (Chald.), *dure;* corresp. to 1752; to *reside:*— dwell.

1754. דּוּר **dûwr,** *dure;* from 1752; a *circle, ball* or *pile:*— ball, turn, round about.

1755. דֹּור **dôwr,** *dore;* or (short.)

דֹּר **dôr,** *dore;* from 1752; prop. a *revolution* of time, i.e. an *age* or *generation;* also a *dwelling:*— age, × evermore, generation, In-lever, posterity.

1756. דֹּור **Dôwr,** *dore* or (by perm.)

דֹּאר **Dô'r** (Josh. 17:11; 1 Kings 4:11), *dore;* from 1755; *dwelling; Dor,* a place in Pal.:— Dor.

1757. דּוּרָא **Dûwrâ'** (Chald.), *doo-raw´;* prob. from 1753; *circle* or *dwelling; Dura,* a place in Bab.:— Dura.

1758. דּוּשׁ **dûwsh,** *doosh;* or

דֹּושׁ **dôwsh,** *dōsh;* or

דִּישׁ **dîysh,** *deesh;* a prim. root; to *trample* or *thresh:*— break, tear, thresh, tread out (down), at grass [Jer. 50:11, *by mistake for* 1877].

1759. דוּשׁ **dûwsh** (Chald.), *doosh;* corresp. to 1758; to *trample:—* tread down.

1760. דָּחָה **dâchâh,** *daw-khaw´;* or

דָּחַח **dâchach** (Jer. 23:12), *daw-khakh´;* a prim. root; to *push* down:— chase, drive away (on), overthrow, outcast, × sore, thrust, totter.

1761. דַּחֲוָה **dachăvâh** (Chald.), *dakh-av-aw´;* from the equiv. of 1760; prob. a musical *instrument* (as being *struck*):— instrument of music.

1762. דְּחִי **dᵉchîy,** *deh-khee´;* from 1760; a *push,* i.e. (by impl.) a *fall:—* falling.

1763. דְּחַל **dᵉchal** (Chald.), *deh-khal´;* corresp. to 2119; to *slink,* i.e. (by impl.) to *fear,* or (caus.) *be formidable:—* make afraid, dreadful, fear, terrible.

1764. דֹּחַן **dôchan,** *do´-khan;* of uncert. der.; *millet:—* millet.

1765. דָּחַף **dâchaph,** *daw-khaf´;* a prim. root; to *urge,* i.e. *hasten:—* (be) haste (-ned), pressed on.

1766. דָּחַק **dâchaq,** *daw-khak´;* a prim. root; to *press,* i.e. *oppress:—* thrust, vex.

1767. דַּי **day,** *dahee;* of uncert. der.; *enough* (as noun or adv.), used chiefly with prep. in phrases:— able, according to, after (ability), among, as (oft as), (more than) enough, from, in, since, (much as is) sufficient (-ly), too much, very, when.

1768. דִּי **dîy** (Chald.), *dee;* appar. for 1668; *that,* used as rel., conjunc., and espec. (with prep.) in adv. phrases; also as prep. *of:—* × as, but, for (-asmuch +), + now, of, seeing, than, that, therefore, until, + what (-soever), when, which, whom, whose.

1769. דִּיבוֹן **Dîybôwn,** *dee-bome´;* or (short.)

דִּיבֹן **Dîybôn,** *dee-bone´;* from 1727; *pining; Dibon,* the name of three places in Pal.:— Dibon. [Also, *with* 1410 *added,* Dibon-gad.]

1770. דִּיג **dîyg,** *deeg;* denom. from 1709; to *fish:—* fish.

1771. דַּיָּג **dayâg,** *dah-yawg´;* from 1770; a *fisherman:—* fisher.

1772. דַּיָּה **dayâh,** *dah-yaw´;* intens. from 1675; a *falcon* (from its *rapid* flight):— vulture.

1773. דְּיוֹ **dᵉyôw,** *deh-yo´;* of uncert. der.; *ink:—* ink.

1774. דִּי זָהָב **Dîy zâhâb,** *dee zaw-hawb´;* as if from 1768 and 2091; *of gold; Dizahab,* a place in the Desert:— Dizahab.

1775. דִּימוֹן **Dîymôwn,** *dee-mone´;* perh. for 1769; *Dimon,* a place in Pal.:— Dimon.

1776. דִּימוֹנָה **Dîymôwnâh,** *dee-mo-naw´;* fem. of 1775; *Dimonah,* a place in Pal.:— Dimonah.

1777. דִּין **dîyn,** *deen;* or (Gen. 6:3)

דּוּן **dûwn,** *doon;* a prim. root [comp. 113]; to *rule;* by impl. to *judge* (as umpire); also to *strive* (as at law):— contend, execute (judgment), judge, minister judgment, plead (the cause), at strife, strive.

1778. דִּין **dîyn** (Chald.), *deen;* corresp. to 1777; to *judge:—* judge.

1779. דִּין **dîyn,** *deen;* or (Job 19:29)

דּוּן **dûwn,** *doon;* from 1777; *judgement* (the suit, justice, sentence or tribunal); by impl. also *strife:—* cause, judgement, plea, strife.

1780. דִּין **dîyn** (Chald.), *deen;* corresp. to 1779:— judgement.

1781. דַּיָּן **dayân,** *dah-yawn´;* from 1777; a *judge* or *advocate:—* judge.

1782. דַּיָּן **dayân** (Chald.), *dah-yawn´;* corresp. to 1781:— judge.

1783. דִּינָה **Dîynâh,** *dee-naw´;* fem. of 1779; *justice; Dinah,* the daughter of Jacob:— Dinah.

1784. דִּינַי **Dîynay** (Chald.), *dee-nah´-ee;* patrial from an uncert. prim.; a *Dinaite* or inhab. of some unknown Ass. province:— Dinaite.

דִּיפַת **Dîyphath.** See 7384.

1785. דָּיֵק **dâyêq,** *daw-yake´;* from a root corresp. to 1751; a *battering*-tower:— fort.

1786. דַּיִשׁ **dayish,** *dah-yish´;* from 1758; *threshing*-time:— threshing.

1787. דִּישׁוֹן **Dîyshôwn,**

דִּישֹׁן **Dîyshôn,**

דִּשׁוֹן **Dîshôwn,** or

דִּשֹׁן **Dîshôn,** *dee-shone´;* the same as 1788; *Dishon,* the name of two Edomites:— Dishon.

1788. דִּישֹׁן **dîyshôn,** *dee-shone´;* from 1758; the *leaper,* i.e. an *antelope:—* pygarg.

1789. דִּישָׁן **Dîyshân,** *dee-shawn´;* another form of 1787; *Dishan,* an Edomite:— Dishan, Dishon.

1790. דַּךְ **dak,** *dak;* from an unused root (comp. 1794); *crushed,* i.e. (fig.) *injured:—* afflicted, oppressed.

1791. דֵּךְ **dêk** (Chald.), *dake;* or

דָּךְ **dâk** (Chald.), *dawk;* prol. from 1668; *this:—* the same, this.

1792. דָּכָא **dâkâ',** *daw-kaw´;* a prim. root (comp. 1794); to *crumble;* tran. to *bruise* (lit. or fig.):— beat to pieces, break (in pieces), bruise, contrite, crush, destroy, humble, oppress, smite.

1793. דַּכָּא **dakkâ',** *dak-kaw´;* from 1792;

crushed (lit. *powder*, or fig. *contrite*):— contrite, destruction.

1794. דָּכָה **dâkâh**, *daw-kaw´*; a prim. root (comp. 1790, 1792); to *collapse* (phys. or ment.):— break (sore), contrite, crouch.

1795. דַּכָּה **dakkâh**, *dak-kaw´*; from 1794 like 1793; *mutilated:*— + wounded.

1796. דֳּכִי **dŏkîy**, *dok-ee´*; from 1794; a *dashing* of surf:— wave.

1797. דִּכֵּן **dikkên** (Chald.), *dik-kane´*; prol. from 1791; *this:*— same, that, this.

1798. דְּכַר **dᵉkar** (Chald.), *dek-ar´*; corresp. to 2145; prop. a *male*, i.e. of sheep:— ram.

1799. דִּכְרוֹן **dikrôwn** (Chald.), *dik-rone´*; or

דָּכְרָן **dokrân**, *dok-rawn´* (Chald.); corresp. to 2146; a *register:*— record.

1800. דַּל **dal**, *dal*; from 1809; prop. *dangling*, i.e. (by impl.) *weak* or *thin:*— lean, needy, poor (man), weaker.

1801. דָּלַג **dâlag**, *daw-lag´*; a prim. root; to *spring:*— leap.

1802. דָּלָה **dâlâh**, *daw-law´*; a prim. root (comp. 1809); prop. to *dangle*, i.e. to *let down* a bucket (for *drawing* out water); fig. to *deliver:*— draw (out), × enough, lift up.

1803. דַּלָּה **dallâh**, *dal-law´*; from 1802; prop. something *dangling*, i.e. a loose *thread* or *hair*; fig. *indigent:*— hair, pining sickness, poor (-est sort).

1804. דָּלַח **dâlach**, *daw-lakh´*; a prim. root; to *roil* water:— trouble.

1805. דְּלִי **dᵉlîy**, *del-ee´*; or

דֳּלִי **dŏlîy**, *dol-ee´*; from 1802; a *pail* or *jar* (for *drawing* water):— bucket.

1806. דְּלָיָה **Dᵉlâyâh**, *del-aw-yaw´*; or (prol.)

דְּלָיָהוּ **Dᵉlâyâhûw**, *del-aw-yaw´-hoo*; from 1802 and 3050; *Jah has delivered; Delajah*, the name of five Isr.:— Dalaiah, Delaiah.

1807. דְּלִילָה **Dᵉlîylâh**, *del-ee-law´*; from 1809; *languishing; Delilah*, a Philistine woman:— Delilah.

1808. דָּלִיָּה **dâlîyâh**, *daw-lee-yaw´*; from 1802; something *dangling*, i.e. a *bough:*— branch.

1809. דָּלַל **dâlal**, *daw-lal´*; a prim. root (comp. 1802); to *slacken* or *be feeble*; fig. to *be oppressed:*— bring low, dry up, be emptied, be not equal, fail, be impoverished, be made thin.

1810. דִּלְעָן **Dil'ân**, *dil-awn´*; of uncert. der.; *Dilan*, a place in Pal.:— Dilean.

1811. דָּלַף **dâlaph**, *daw-laf´*; a prim. root; to *drip*; by impl. to *weep:*— drop through, melt, pour out.

1812. דֶּלֶף **deleph**, *deh´-lef*; from 1811; a *dripping:*— dropping.

1813. דַּלְפוֹן **Dalphôwn**, *dal-fone´*; from 1811; *dripping; Dalphon*, a son of Haman:— Dalphon.

1814. דָּלַק **dâlaq**, *daw-lak´*; a prim. root; to *flame* (lit. or fig.):— burning, chase, inflame, kindle, persecute (-or), pursue hotly.

1815. דְּלַק **dᵉlaq** (Chald.), *del-ak´*; corresp. to 1814:— burn.

1816. דַּלֶּקֶת **dalleqeth**, *dal-lek´-keth*; from 1814; a *burning* fever:— inflammation.

1817. דֶּלֶת **deleth**, *deh´-leth*; from 1802; something *swinging*, i.e. the *valve* of a door:— door (two-leaved), gate, leaf, lid. [In Psa. 141:3, *dâl*, irreg.].

1818. דָּם **dâm**, *dawm*; from 1826 (comp. 119); *blood* (as that which when shed causes *death*) of man or an animal; by anal. the *juice* of the grape; fig. (espec. in the plur.) *bloodshed* (i.e. *drops* of blood):— blood (-y, -guiltiness, [-thirsty]), + innocent.

1819. דָּמָה **dâmâh**, *daw-maw´*; a prim. root; to *compare*; by impl. to *resemble, liken, consider:*— compare, devise, (be) like (-n), mean, think, use similitudes.

1820. דָּמָה **dâmâh**, *daw-maw´*; a prim. root; to *be dumb* or *silent*; hence, to *fail* or *perish*; trans. to *destroy:*— cease, be cut down (off), destroy, be brought to silence, be undone, × utterly.

1821. דְּמָה **dᵉmâh** (Chald.), *dem-aw´*; corresp. to 1819; to *resemble:*— be like.

1822. דֻּמָּה **dummâh**, *doom-maw´*; from 1820; *desolation*; concr. *desolate:*— destroy.

1823. דְּמוּת **dᵉmûwth**, *dem-ooth´*; from 1819; *resemblance*; concr. *model, shape*; adv. *like:*— fashion, like (-ness, as), manner, similitude.

1824. דְּמִי **dᵉmîy**, *dem-ee´*; or

דֳּמִי **dŏmîy**, *dom-ee´*; from 1820; *quiet:*— cutting off, rest, silence.

1825. דִּמְיוֹן **dimyôwn**, *dim-yone´*; from 1819; *resemblance:*— × like.

1826. דָּמַם **dâmam**, *daw-mam´*; a prim. root [comp. 1724, 1820]; to *be dumb*; by impl. to *be astonished*, to *stop*; also to *perish:*— cease, be cut down (off), forbear, hold peace, quiet self, rest, be silent, keep (put to) silence, be (stand) still, tarry, wait.

1827. דְּמָמָה **dᵉmâmâh**, *dem-aw-maw´*; fem. from 1826; *quiet:*— calm, silence, still.

1828. דֹּמֶן **dômen**, *do´-men*; of uncert. der.; *manure:*— dung.

1829. דִּמְנָה **Dimnâh**, *dim-naw´*; fem. from the same as 1828; a *dung-heap; Dimnah*, a place in Pal.:— Dimnah.

1830. דָּמַע **dâma'**, *daw-mah´*; a prim. root; to *weep*:— × sore, weep.

1831. דֶּמַע **dema'**, *dah´-mah*; from 1830; a *tear*; fig. *juice*:— liquor.

1832. דִּמְעָה **dim'âh**, *dim-aw´*; fem. of 1831; *weeping*:— tears.

1833. דְּמֶשֶׁק **dᵉmesheq**, *dem-eh´-shek*; by orth. var. from 1834; *damask* (as a fabric of Damascus):— in Damascus.

1834. דַּמֶּשֶׂק **Dammeseq**, *dam-meh´-sek*; or

דּוּמֶשֶׂק° **Dûwmeseq**, *doo-meh´-sek*; or

דַּרְמֶשֶׂק **Darmeseq**, *dar-meh´-sek*; of for. or.; *Damascus*, a city of Syria:— Damascus.

1835. דָּן **Dân**, *dawn*; from 1777; *judge*; *Dan*, one of the sons of Jacob; also the tribe descended from him, and its territory; likewise a place in Pal. colonized by them:— Dan.

1836. דֵּן **dên** (Chald.), *dane*; an orth. var. of 1791; *this*:— [afore-] time, + after this manner, here [-after], one ... another, such, there [-fore], these, this (matter), + thus, where [-fore], which.

דָּנִיֵּאל **Dânî'êl**. See 1841.

1837. דַּנָּה **Dannâh**, *dan-naw´*; of uncert. der.; *Dannah*, a place in Pal.:— Dannah.

1838. דִּנְהָבָה **Dinhâbâh**, *din-haw-baw´*; of uncert. der.; *Dinhabah*, an Edomitish town:— Dinhaban.

1839. דָּנִי **Dâniy**, *daw-nee´*; patron. from 1835; a *Danite* (often collect.) or desc. (or inhab.) of Dan:— Danites, of Dan.

1840. דָּנִיֵּאל **Dânîyê'l**, *daw-nee-yale´*; in Ezek.

דָּנִיֵּאל **Dânî'êl**, *daw-nee-ale´*; from 1835 and 410; *judge of God*; *Daniel* or *Danijel*, the name of two Isr.:— Daniel.

1841. דָּנִיֵּאל **Dânîyê'l** (Chald.), *daw-nee-yale´*; corresp. to 1840; *Danijel*, the Heb. prophet:— Daniel.

1842. דָּן יַעַן **Dân Ya'an**, *dawn yah´-an*; from 1835 and (appar.) 3282; *judge of purpose*; *Dan-Jaan*, a place in Pal.:— Dan-jaan.

1843. דֵּעַ **dêa'**, *day´-ah*; from 3045; *knowledge*:— knowledge, opinion.

1844. דֵּעָה **dê'âh**, *day-aw´*; fem. of 1843; *knowledge*:— knowledge.

1845. דְּעוּאֵל **Dᵉ'ûw'êl**, *deh-oo-ale´*; from 3045 and 410; *known of God*; *Deüel*, an Isr.:— Deuel.

1846. דָּעַךְ **dâ'ak**, *daw-ak´*; a prim. root; to *be extinguished*; fig. to *expire* or *be dried up*:— be extinct, consumed, put out, quenched.

1847. דַּעַת **da'ath**, *dah´-ath*; from 3045; *knowledge*:— cunning, [ig-]norantly, know (-ledge), [un-] awares (wittingly).

1848. דֳּפִי **dŏphiy**, *dof-ee´*; from an unused root (mean. to *push* over); a *stumbling-block*:— slanderest.

1849. דָּפַק **dâphaq**, *daw-fak´*; a prim. root; to *knock*; by anal. to *press* severely:— beat, knock, overdrive.

1850. דָּפְקָה **Dophqâh**, *dof-kaw´*; from 1849; a *knock*; *Dophkah*, a place in the Desert:— Dophkah.

1851. דַּק **daq**, *dak*; from 1854; *crushed*, i.e. (by impl.) *small* or *thin*:— dwarf, lean [-fleshed], very little thing, small, thin.

1852. דֹּק **dôq**, *doke*; from 1854; something *crumbling*, i.e. *fine* (as a *thin* cloth):— curtain.

1853. דִּקְלָה **Diqlâh**, *dik-law´*; of for. or.; *Diklah*, a region of Arabia:— Diklah.

1854. דָּקַק **dâqaq**, *daw-kak´*; a prim. root [comp. 1915]; to *crush* (or intr.) *crumble*:— beat in pieces (small), bruise, make dust, (into) × powder, (be, very) small, stamp (small).

1855. דְּקַק **dᵉqaq** (Chald.), *dek-ak´*; corresp. to 1854; to *crumble* or (trans.) *crush*:— break to pieces.

1856. דָּקַר **dâqar**, *daw-kar´*; a prim. root; to *stab*; by anal. to *starve*; fig. to *revile*:— pierce, strike (thrust) through, wound.

1857. דֶּקֶר **Deqer**, *deh´-ker*; from 1856; a *stab*; *Deker*, an Isr.:— Dekar.

1858. דַּר **dar**, *dar*; appar. from the same as 1865; prop. a *pearl* (from its sheen as rapidly *turned*); by anal. *pearl-stone*, i.e. mother-of-pearl or alabaster:— × white.

1859. דָּר **dâr** (Chald.), *dawr*; corresp. to 1755; an *age*:— generation.

דֹּר **dôr**. See 1755.

1860. דְּרָאוֹן **dᵉrâ'ôwn**, *der-aw-one´*; or

דֵּרָאוֹן **dêra'ôwn**, *day-raw-one´*; from an unused root (mean. to *repulse*); an obj. of *aversion*:— abhorring, contempt.

1861. דָּרְבוֹן **dorbôwn**, *dor-bone´* [also *dor-bawn*]; of uncert. der.; a *goad*:— goad.

1862. דַּרְדַּע **Darda'**, *dar-dah´*; appar. from 1858 and 1843; *pearl of knowledge*; *Darda*, an Isr.:— Darda.

1863. דַּרְדַּר **dardar**, *dar-dar´*; of uncert. der.; a *thorn*:— thistle.

1864. דָּרוֹם **dârôwm**, *daw-rome´*; of uncert. der.; the *south*; poet. the *south wind*:— south.

1865. דְּרוֹר **dᵉrôwr**, *der-ore´*; from an unused root (mean. to *move rapidly*); *freedom*; hence, *spontaneity* of outflow, and so *clear*:— liberty, pure.

1866. דְּרוֹר **dᵉrôwr**, *der-ore´*; the same as

1865, applied to a bird; the *swift*, a kind of swallow:— swallow.

1867. דָּרְיָוֵשׁ **Dâr°yâvêsh**, *daw-reh-yaw-vaysh´*; of Pers. or.; *Darejavesh*, a title (rather than name) of several Pers. kings:— Darius.

1868. דָּרְיָוֵשׁ **Dâr°yâvêsh** (Chald.), *daw-reh-yaw-vaysh´*; corresp. to 1867:— Darius.

1869. דָּרַךְ **dârak**, *daw-rak´*; a prim. root; to *tread*; by impl. to *walk*; also to *string* a bow (by treading on it in bending):— archer, bend, come, draw, go (over), guide, lead (forth), thresh, tread (down), walk.

1870. דֶּרֶךְ **derek**, *deh´-rek*; from 1869; a *road* (as *trodden*); fig. a *course* of life or *mode* of action, often adv.:— along, away, because of, + by, conversation, custom, [east-] ward, journey, manner, passenger, through, toward, [high-] [path-] way [-side], whither [-soever].

1871. דַּרְכְּמוֹן **dark°môwn**, *dar-kem-one´*; of Pers. or.; a "*drachma*," or coin:— dram.

1872. דְּרַע **d°râ'** (Chald.), *der-aw´*; corresp. to 2220; an *arm*:— arm.

1873. דָּרַע **Dâra'**, *daw-rah´*; prob. contr. from 1862; *Dara*, an Isr.:— Dara.

1874. דַּרְקוֹן **Darqôwn**, *dar-kone´*; of uncert. der.; *Darkon*, one of "Solomon's servants":— Darkon.

1875. דָּרַשׁ **dârash**, *daw-rash´*; a prim. root; prop. to *tread* or *frequent*; usually to *follow* (for pursuit or search); by impl. to *seek* or *ask*; spec. to *worship*:— ask, × at all, care for, × diligently, inquire, make inquisition, [necro-] mancer, question, require, search, seek [for, out], × surely.

1876. דָּשָׁא **dâshâ'**, *daw-shaw´*; a prim. root; to *sprout*:— bring forth, spring.

1877. דֶּשֶׁא **deshe'**, *deh´-sheh*; from 1876; a *sprout*; by anal. *grass*:— (tender) grass, green, (tender) herb.

1878. דָּשֵׁן **dâshên**, *daw-shane´*; a prim. root; to *be fat*; tran. to *fatten* (or regard as fat); spec. to *anoint*; fig. to *satisfy*; denom. (from 1880) to *remove* (fat) *ashes* (of sacrifices):— accept, anoint, take away the (receive) ashes (from), make (wax) fat.

1879. דָּשֵׁן **dâshên**, *daw-shane´*; from 1878; *fat*; fig. *rich, fertile*:— fat.

1880. דֶּשֶׁן **deshen**, *deh´-shen*; from 1878; the *fat*; abstr. *fatness*, i.e. (fig.) *abundance*; spec. the (fatty) *ashes* of sacrifices:— ashes, fatness.

1881. דָּת **dâth**, *dawth*; of uncert. (perh. for.) der.: a royal *edict* or statute:— commandment, commission, decree, law, manner.

1882. דָּת **dâth** (Chald.), *dawth*; corresp. to 1881:— decree, law.

1883. דֶּתֶא **dethe'** (Chald.), *deh´-thay*; corresp. to 1877:— tender grass.

1884. דְּתָבָר **d°thâbâr** (Chald.), *deth-aw-bawr´*; of Pers. or.; mean. one *skilled in law*; a *judge*:— counsellor.

1885. דָּתָן **Dâthân**, *daw-thawn´*; of uncert. der.; *Dathan*, an Isr.:— Dathan.

1886. דֹּתָן **Dôthân**, *do´-thawn*; or (Chaldaizing dual)

דֹּתַיִן **Dôthayin** (Gen. 37:17), *do-thah´-yin*; of uncert. der.; *Dothan*, a place in Pal.:— Dothan.

ה

1887. הֵא **hê'**, *hay*; a prim. particle; *lo!*:— behold, lo.

1888. הֵא **hê'** (Chald.), *hay*; or

הָא **hâ'** (Chald.), *haw*; corresp. to 1887:— even, lo.

1889. הֶאָח **he'âch**, *heh-awkh´*; from 1887 and 253; *aha!*:— ah, aha, ha.

הָאֲרָרִי **Hâ'râriy**. See 2043.

1890. הַבְהָב **habhâb**, *hab-hawb´*; by redupl. from 3051; *gift* (in sacrifice), i.e. *holocaust*:— offering.

1891. הָבַל **hâbal**, *haw-bal´*; a prim. root; to *be vain* in act, word, or expectation; spec. to *lead astray*:— be (become, make) vain.

1892. הֶבֶל **hebel**, *heh´-bel*; or (rarely in the abs.)

הֲבֵל **hăbêl**, *hab-ale´*; from 1891; *emptiness* or *vanity*; fig. something *transitory* and *unsatisfactory*; often used as an adv.:— × altogether, vain, vanity.

1893. הֶבֶל **Hebel**, *heh´-bel*; the same as 1892; *Hebel*, the son of Adam:— Abel.

1894. הֹבֶן **hôben**, *ho´-ben*; only in plur., from an unused root mean. to *be hard*; *ebony*:— ebony.

1895. הָבַר **hâbar**, *haw-bar´*; a prim. root of uncert. (perh. for.) der.; to *be a horoscopist*:— + (astro-)loger.

1896. הֵגֵא **Hêgê'**, *hay-gay´*; or (by perm.)

הֵגַי **Hêgay**, *hay-gah´-ee*; prob. of Pers. or.; *Hege* or *Hegai*, a eunuch of Xerxes:— Hegai, Hege.

1897. הָגָה **hâgâh**, *haw-gaw´*; a prim. root [comp. 1901]; to *murmur* (in pleasure or anger); by impl. to *ponder*:— imagine, meditate, mourn, mutter, roar, × sore, speak, study, talk, utter.

1898. הָגָה **hâgâh**, *haw-gaw´*; a prim. root; to *remove*:— stay, take away.

1899. הֶגֶה **hegeh**, *heh´-geh*; from 1897; a

muttering (in sighing, thought, or as thunder):— mourning, sound, tale.

1900. הָגוּת **hâgûwth**, *haw-gooth´*; from 1897; *musing:*— meditation.

1901. הָגִיג **hâgîyg**, *haw-gheeg´*; from an unused root akin to 1897; prop. a *murmur*, i.e. *complaint:*— meditation, musing.

1902. הִגָּיוֹן **higgâyôwn**, *hig-gaw-yone´*; intens. from 1897; a *murmuring* sound, i.e. a musical notation (prob. similar to the modern *affettuoso* to indicate solemnity of movement); by impl. a *machination:*— device, Higgaion, meditation, solemn sound.

1903. הָגִין **hâgîyn**, *haw-gheen´*; of uncert. der.; perh. *suitable* or *turning:*— directly.

1904. הָגָר **Hâgâr**, *haw-gawr´*; of uncert. (perhaps for.) der.; *Hagar*, the mother of Ishmael:— Hagar.

1905. הַגְרִי **Hagrîy**, *hag-ree´*; or (prol.)

הַגְרִיא **Hagrîy'**, *hag-ree´*; perh. patron. from 1904; a *Hagrite* or member of a certain Arabian clan:— Hagarene, Hagarite, Haggeri.

1906. הֵד **hêd**, *hade;* for 1959; a *shout:*— sounding again.

1907. הַדְּבָר **haddâbâr** (Chald.), *had-daw-bawr´*; prob. of for. origin; a *vizier:*— counsellor.

1908. הֲדַד **Hădad**, *had-ad´*; prob. of for. or. [comp. 111]; *Hadad*, the name of an idol, and of several kings of Edom:— Hadad.

1909. הֲדַדְעֶזֶר **Hădad'ezer**, *had-ad-eh´-zer;* from 1908 and 5828; *Hadad* (is his) *help; Hadadezer*, a Syrian king:— Hadadezer. Comp. 1928.

1910. הֲדַדְרִמּוֹן **Hădadrimmôwn**, *had-ad-rim-mone´;* from 1908 and 7417; *Hadad-Rimmon*, a place in Pal.:— Hadad-rimmon.

1911. הָדָה **hâdâh**, *haw-daw´*; a prim. root [comp. 3034]; to *stretch forth* the hand:— put.

1912. הֹדוּ **Hôdûw**, *ho´-doo;* of for. or.; *Hodu* (i.e. Hindü-stan):— India.

1913. הֲדוֹרָם **Hădôwrâm**, *had-o-rawm´;* or

הֲדֹרָם **Hădôrâm**, *had-o-rawm´;* prob. of for. der.; *Hadoram*, a son of Joktan, and the tribe descended from him:— Hadoram.

1914. הִדַּי **Hidday**, *hid-dah´ee;* of uncert. der.; *Hiddai*, an Isr.:— Hiddai.

1915. הָדַךְ **hâdak**, *haw-dak´*; a prim. root [comp. 1854]; to *crush* with the foot:— tread down.

1916. הֲדֹם **hădôm**, *had-ome´;* from an unused root mean. to *stamp* upon; a foot-*stool:*— [foot-] stool.

1917. הַדָּם **haddâm** (Chald.), *had-dawm´;* from

a root corresp. to that of 1916; something *stamped* to pieces, i.e. a *bit:*— piece.

1918. הֲדַס **hădaç**, *had-as´;* of uncert. der.; the *myrtle:*— myrtle (tree).

1919. הֲדַסָּה **Hădaççâh**, *had-as-saw´;* fem. of 1918; *Hadassah* (or Esther):— Hadassah.

1920. הָדַף **hâdaph**, *haw-daf´;* a prim root; to *push* away or down:— cast away (out), drive, expel, thrust (away).

1921. הָדַר **hâdar**, *haw-dar´;* a prim. root; to *swell* up (lit. or fig., act. or pass.); by impl. to *favor* or *honour*, *be high* or *proud:*— countenance, crooked place, glorious, honour, put forth.

1922. הֲדַר **hâdar** (Chald.), *had-ar´;* corresp. to 1921; to *magnify* (fig.):— glorify, honour.

1923. הֲדַר **hădar** (Chald.), *had-ar´;* from 1922; *magnificence:*— honour, majesty.

1924. הֲדַר **Hădar**, *had-ar´;* the same as 1926; *Hadar*, an Edomite:— Hadar.

1925. הֶדֶר **heder**, *heh´-der;* from 1921; *honour;* used (fig.) for the *capital* city (Jerusalem):— glory.

1926. הָדָר **hâdâr**, *haw-dawr´;* from 1921; *magnificence*, i.e. ornament or splendor:— beauty, comeliness, excellency, glorious, glory, goodly, honour, majesty.

1927. הֲדָרָה **hădârâh**, *had-aw-raw´;* fem. of 1926; *decoration:*— beauty, honour.

הֲדֹרָם **Hădôrâm**. See 1913.

1928. הֲדַרְעֶזֶר **Hădar'ezer**, *had-ar-eh´-zer;* from 1924 and 5828; *Hadar* (i.e. *Hadad*, 1908) is his *help; Hadarezer* (i.e. Hadadezer, 1909), a Syrian king:— Hadarezer.

1929. הָהּ **hâhh**, *haw;* a short. form of 162; *ah!* expressing grief:— woe worth.

1930. הוֹ **hôw**, *ho;* by perm. from 1929; *oh!:*— alas.

1931. הוּא **hûw'**, *hoo;* of which the fem. (beyond the Pentateuch) is

הִיא **hîy'**, *he;* a prim. word, the third pers. pron. sing., *he* (*she* or *it*); only expressed when emphat. or without a verb; also (intens.) *self*, or (espec. with the art.) the *same;* sometimes (as demonstr.) *this* or *that;* occasionally (instead of copula) *as* or *are:*— he, as for her, him (-self), it, the same, she (herself), such, that (... it), these, they, this, those, which (is), who.

1932. הוּא **hûw'** (Chald.), *hoo;* or (fem.)

הִיא **hîy'** (Chald.), *he;* corresp. to 1931:— × are, it, this.

1933. הֲוָא **hâvâ'**, *haw-vaw´;* or

הֲוָה **hâvâh**, *haw-vaw´;* a prim. root [comp. 183, 1961] supposed to mean prop.

to *breathe;* to *be* (in the sense of existence):— be, × have.

1934.   הֲוָא **hăvâ'** (Chald.), *hav-aw´;* or

הֲוָה **hăvâh** (Chald.), *hav-aw´;* corresp. to 1933; to *exist;* used in a great variety of applications (espec. in connection with other words):— be, become, + behold, + came (to pass), + cease, + cleave, + consider, + do, + give, + have, + judge, + keep, + labour, + mingle (self), + put, + see, + seek, + set, + slay, + take heed, tremble, + walk, + would.

1935.   הוֹד **hôwd**, *hode;* from an unused root; *grandeur* (i.e. an imposing form and appearance):— beauty, comeliness, excellency, glorious, glory, goodly, honour, majesty.

1936.   הוֹד **Hôwd**, *hode;* the same as 1935; *Hod,* an Isr.:— Hod.

1937.   הוֹדְוָה **Hôwdᵉvâh**, *ho-dev-aw´;* a form of 1938; *Hodevah* (or Hodevjah), an Isr.:— Hodevah.

1938.   הוֹדַוְיָה **Hôwdavyâh**, *ho-dav-yaw´;* from 1935 and 3050; *majesty of Jah; Hodavjah,* the name of three Isr.:— Hodaviah.

1939.   הוֹדַוְיָהוּ **Howdayᵉvâhûw**, *ho-dah-yeh-vaw´-hoo;* a form of 1938; *Hodajvah,* an Isr.:— Hodaiah.

1940.   הוֹדִיָּה **Hôwdîyâh**, *ho-dee-yaw´;* a form for the fem. of 3064; a *Jewess:*— Hodiah.

1941.   הוֹדִיָּה **Hôwdîyâh**, *ho-dee-yaw´;* a form of 1938; *Hodijah,* the name of three Isr.:— Hodijah.

הֲוָה **hâvâh.** See 1933.

הֲוָה **hăvâh.** See 1934.

1942.   הַוָּה **havvâh**, *hav-vaw´;* from 1933 (in the sense of eagerly *coveting* and *rushing* upon; by impl. of *falling*); *desire;* also *ruin:*— calamity, iniquity, mischief, mischievous (thing), naughtiness, naughty, noisome, perverse thing, substance, very wickedness.

1943.   הֹוָה **hôvâh**, *ho-vaw´;* another form for 1942; *ruin:*— mischief.

1944.   הוֹהָם **Hôwhâm**, *ho-hawm´;* of uncert. der.; *Hoham,* a Canaanitish king:— Hoham.

1945.   הוֹי **hôwy**, *hoh´-ee;* a prol. form of 1930 [akin to 188]; *oh!:*— ah, alas, ho, O, woe.

1946.   הוּךְ **hûwk** (Chald.), *hook;* corresp. to 1981; to *go;* caus. to *bring:*— bring again, come, go (up).

1947.   הוֹלֵלָה **hôwlêlâh**, *ho-lay-law´;* fem. act. part. of 1984; *folly:*— madness.

1948.   הוֹלֵלוּת **hôwlêlûwth**, *ho-lay-looth´;* from act. part. of 1984; *folly:*— madness.

1949.   הוּם **hûwm**, *hoom;* a prim. root [comp. 2000]; to *make an uproar,* or *agitate* greatly:— destroy, move, make a noise, put, ring again.

1950.   הוֹמָם **Hôwmâm**, *ho-mawm´;* from 2000; *raging; Homam,* an Edomitish chieftain:— Homam. Comp. 1967.

1951.   הוּן **hûwn**, *hoon;* a prim. root; prop. to *be naught,* i.e. (fig.) to *be* (caus. *act*) *light:*— be ready.

1952.   הוֹן **hôwn**, *hone;* from the same as 1951 in the sense of 202; *wealth;* by impl. *enough:*— enough, + for nought, riches, substance, wealth.

1953.   הוֹשָׁמָע **Hôwshâmâ'**, *ho-shaw-maw´;* from 3068 and 8085; *Jehovah has heard; Hoshama,* an Isr.:— Hoshama.

1954.   הוֹשֵׁעַ **Hôwshêä'**, *ho-shay´-ah;* from 3467; *deliverer; Hoshëa,* the name of five Isr.:— Hosea, Hoshea, Oshea.

1955.   הוֹשַׁעְיָה **Hôwshi'yâh**, *ho-shee-yaw´;* from 3467 and 3050; *Jah has saved; Hoshajah,* the name of two Isr.:— Hoshaiah.

1956.   הוֹתִיר **Hôwthîyr**, *ho-theer´;* from 3498; *he has caused to remain; Hothir,* an Isr.:— Hothir.

1957.   הָזָה **hâzâh**, *haw-zaw´;* a prim. root [comp. 2372]; to *dream:*— sleep.

1958.   הִי **hîy**, *he;* for 5092; *lamentation:*— woe.

הִיא **hîy'**. See 1931, 1932.)

1959.   הֵידָד **hêydâd**, *hay-dawd´;* from an unused root (mean. to *shout*); *acclamation:*— shout (-ing).

1960.   הֻיְדָה **huyᵉdâh**, *hoo-yed-aw´;* from the same as 1959; prop. an *acclaim,* i.e. a *choir* of singers:— thanksgiving.

1961.   הָיָה **hâyâh**, *haw-yaw;* a prim. root [comp. 1933]; to *exist,* i.e. *be* or *become, come to pass* (always emphat., and not a mere copula or auxiliary):— beacon, × altogether, be (-come), accomplished, committed, like), break, cause, come (to pass), do, faint, fall, + follow, happen, × have, last, pertain, quit (one-) self, require, × use.

1962.   הַיָּה **hayâh**, *hah-yaw´;* another form for 1943; *ruin:*— calamity.

1963.   הֵיךְ **hêyk**, *hake;* another form for 349; *how?:*— how.

1964.   הֵיכָל **hêykâl**, *hay-kawl´;* prob. from 3201 (in the sense of *capacity*); a large public building, such as a *palace* or *temple:*— palace, temple.

1965.   הֵיכַל **hêykal** (Chald.), *hay-kal´;* corresp. to 1964:— palace, temple.

1966.   הֵילֵל **hêylêl**, *hay-lale´;* from 1984 (in the sense of *brightness*); the *morning-star:*— lucifer.

1967.   הֵימָם **Hêymâm**, *hay-mawm´;* another form for 1950; *Hemam,* an Idumæan:— Hemam.

Hebrew

1968. הֵימָן **Hêymân**, *hay-mawn´*; prob. from 539; *faithful; Heman*, the name of at least two Isr.:— Heman.

1969. הִין **hîyn**, *heen;* prob. of Eg. or.; a *hin* or liquid measure:— hin.

1970. הָכַר **hâkar**, *haw-kar´*; a prim. root; appar. to *injure:*— make self strange.

1971. הַכָּרָה **hakkârâh**, *hak-kaw-raw´*; from 5234; *respect,* i.e. partiality:— shew.

הֵל **hal**. See 1973.

1972. הָלָא **hâlâ'**, *haw-law´*; prob. denom. from 1973; to *remove* or be *remote:*— cast far off.

1973. הָלְאָה **hâleâh**, *haw-leh-aw´*; from the prim. form of the art. [הל **hal**]; *to the distance,* i.e. *far away;* also (of time) *thus far:*— back, beyond, (hence-) forward, hitherto, thenceforth, yonder.

1974. הִלּוּל **hillûwl**, *hil-lool´*; from 1984 (in the sense of *rejoicing*); a *celebration* of thanksgiving for harvest:— merry, praise.

1975. הַלָּז **hallâz**, *hal-lawz´*; from 1976; *this* or *that:*— side, that, this.

1976. הַלָּזֶה **hallâzeh**, *hal-law-zeh´*; from the art. [see 1973] and 2088; *this very:*— this.

1977. הַלֵּזוּ **hallêzûw**, *hal-lay-zoo´*; another form of 1976; *that:*— this.

1978. הָלִיךְ **hâlîyk**, *haw-leek´*; from 1980; a *walk,* i.e. (by impl.) a *step:*— step.

1979. הֲלִיכָה **hălîykâh**, *hal-ee-kaw´*; fem. of 1978; a *walking;* by impl. a *procession* or *march,* a *caravan:*— company, going, walk, way.

1980. הָלַךְ **hâlak**, *haw-lak´*; akin to 3212; a prim. root; to *walk* (in a great variety of applications, lit. and fig.):— (all) along, apace, behave (self), come, (on) continually, be conversant, depart, + be eased, enter, exercise (self), + follow, forth, forward, get, go (about, abroad, along, away, forward, on, out, up and down), + greater, grow, be wont to haunt, lead, march, × more and more, move (self), needs, on, pass (away), be at the point, quite, run (along), + send, speedily, spread, still, surely, + tale-bearer, + travel (-ler), walk (abroad, on, to and fro, up and down, to places), wander, wax, [way-] faring man, × be weak, whirl.

1981. הֲלַךְ **hălak** (Chald.), *hal-ak´*; corresp. to 1980 [comp. 1946]; to *walk:*— walk.

1982. הֵלֶךְ **hêlek**, *hay´-lek;* from 1980; prop. a *journey,* i.e. (by impl.) a *wayfarer;* also a *flowing:*— × dropped, traveller.

1983. הֲלָךְ **hălâk** (Chald.), *hal-awk´*; from 1981; prop. a *journey,* i.e. (by impl.) *toll* on goods at a road:— custom.

1984. הָלַל **hâlal**, *haw-lal´*; a prim. root; to be *clear* (orig. of sound, but usually of color); to

shine; hence, to *make a show,* to *boast;* and thus to *be* (clamorously) *foolish;* to *rave;* caus. to *celebrate;* also to *stultify:*— (make) boast (self), celebrate, commend, (deal, make), fool (-ish, -ly), glory, give [light], be (make, feign self) mad (against), give in marriage, [sing, be worthy of] praise, rage, renowned, shine.

1985. הִלֵּל **Hillêl**, *hil-layl´*; from 1984; *praising* (namely God); *Hillel,* an Isr.:— Hillel.

1986. הָלַם **hâlam**, *haw-lam´*; a prim. root; to *strike* down; by impl. to *hammer, stamp, conquer, disband:*— beat (down), break (down), overcome, smite (with the hammer).

1987. הֵלֶם **Hêlem**, *hay´-lem;* from 1986; *smiter; Helem,* the name of two Isr.:— Helem.

1988. הֲלֹם **hălôm**, *hal-ome´*; from the art. [see 1973]; *hither:*— here, hither (-[to]), thither.

1989. הַלְמוּת **halmûwth**, *hal-mooth´*; from 1986; a *hammer* (or *mallet*):— hammer.

1990. הָם **Hâm**, *hawm;* of uncert. der.; *Ham,* a region of Pal.:— Ham.

1991. הֵם **hêm**, *haym;* from 1993; *abundance,* i.e. *wealth:*— any of theirs.

1992. הֵם **hêm**, *haym;* or (prol.)

הֵמָּה **hêmmâh**, *haym´-maw;* masc. plur. from 1931; *they* (only used when emphat.):— it, like, × (how, so) many (soever, more as) they (be), (the) same, × so, × such, their, them, these, they, those, which, who, whom, withal, ye.

1993. הָמָה **hâmâh**, *haw-maw´*; a prim. root [comp. 1949]; to *make a loud sound* (like the English "hum"); by impl. to *be in great commotion* or *tumult,* to *rage, war, moan, clamor:*— clamorous, concourse, cry aloud, be disquieted, loud, mourn, be moved, make a noise, rage, roar, sound, be troubled, make in tumult, tumultuous, be in an uproar.

1994. הִמּוֹ **himmôw** (Chald.), *him-mo´;* or (prol.)

הִמּוֹן **himmôwn** (Chald.), *him-mone´;* corresp. to 1992; *they:*— × are, them, those.

1995. הָמוֹן **hâmôwn**, *haw-mone´;* or

הָמֹן **hâmôn** (Ezek. 5:7), *haw-mone´;* from 1993; a *noise, tumult, crowd;* also *disquietude, wealth:*— abundance, company, many, multitude, multiply, noise, riches, rumbling, sounding, store, tumult.

הַמְּלֶכֶת **ham-môleketh**. See 4447.

1996. הֲמוֹן גּוֹג **Hămôwn Gôwg**, *ham-one´ gohg;* from 1995 and 1463; the *multitude of*

Gog; the fanciful name of an emblematic place in Pal.:— Hamon-gog.

1997. הֲמוֹנָה **Hămôwnâh,** *ham-o-naw´;* fem. of 1995; *multitude; Hamonah,* the same as 1996:— Hamonah.

הֲמוּנֵךְ° **hămûwnêk.** See 2002.

1998. הֶמְיָה **hemyâh,** *hem-yaw´;* from 1993; *sound:*— noise.

1999. הֲמֻלָּה **hămullâh,** *ham-ool-law´;* or (too fully)

הֲמוּלָה **hămûwllâh** (Jer. 11:16), *ham-ool-law´;* fem. pass. part. of an unused root mean. to *rush* (as rain with a windy roar); a *sound:*— speech, tumult.

הַמֶּלֶךְ **ham-melek.** See 4429.

2000. הָמַם **hâmam,** *haw-mam´;* a prim. root [comp. 1949, 1993]; prop. to *put in commotion;* by impl. to *disturb, drive, destroy:*— break, consume, crush, destroy, discomfit, trouble, vex.

הָמוֹן **hâmôn.** See 1995.

2001. הָמָן **Hâmân,** *haw-mawn´;* of for. der.; *Haman,* a Pers. vizier:— Haman.

2002. הַמְנִיךְ **hamnîyk** (Chald.), *ham-neek´;* but the text is

הֲמוּנֵךְ° **hămûwnêk,** *ham-oo-nayk´;* of for. or.; a *necklace:*— chain.

2003. הָמָס **hâmâç,** *haw-mawce´;* from an unused root appar. mean. to *crackle;* a dry *twig* or *brushwood:*— melting.

2004. הֵן **hên,** *hane;* fem. plur. from 1931; *they* (only used when emphat.):— × in, such like, (with) them, thereby, therein, (more than) they, wherein, in which, whom, withal.

2005. הֵן **hên,** *hane;* a prim. particle; *lo!;* also (as expressing surprise) *if:*— behold, if, lo, though.

2006. הֵן **hên** (Chald.), *hane;* corresp. to 2005: *lo!* also *there* [-fore], [un-] *less, whether, but, if:*— (that) if, or, whether.

2007. הֵנָּה **hênnâh,** *hane´-naw;* prol. for 2004; *themselves* (often used emphat. for the copula, also in indirect relation):— × in, × such (and such things), their, (into) them, thence, therein, these, they (had), on this side, those, wherein.

2008. הֵנָּה **hênnâh,** *hane´-naw;* from 2004; *hither* or *thither* (but used both of place and time):— here, hither [-to], now, on this (that) side, + since, this (that) way, thitherward, + thus far, to … fro, + yet.

2009. הִנֵּה **hinnêh,** *hin-nay´;* prol. for 2005; *lo!:*— behold, lo, see.

2010. הֲנָחָה **hănâchâh,** *han-aw-khaw´;* from 5117; *permission* of rest, i.e. *quiet:*— release.

2011. הִנֹּם **Hinnôm,** *hin-nome´;* prob. of for. or.; *Hinnom,* appar. a Jebusite:— Hinnom.

2012. הֵנַע **Hêna',** *hay-nah´;* prob. of for. der.; *Hena,* a place appar. in Mesopotamia:— Hena.

2013. הָסָה **hâçâh,** *haw-saw´;* a prim. root; to *hush:*— hold peace (tongue), (keep) silence, be silent, still.

2014. הֲפֻגָה **hăphûgâh,** *haf-oo-gaw´;* from 6313; *relaxation:*— intermission.

2015. הָפַךְ **hâphak,** *haw-fak´;* a prim. root; to *turn* about or over; by impl. to *change, overturn, return, pervert:*— × become, change, come, be converted, give, make [a bed], overthrow (-turn), perverse, retire, tumble, turn (again, aside, back, to the contrary, every way).

2016. הֶפֶךְ **hephek,** *heh´-fek;* or

הֵפֶךְ **hêphek,** *hay´-fek;* from 2015; a *turn,* i.e. the *reverse:*— contrary.

2017. הֹפֶךְ **hôphek,** *ho´-fek;* from 2015; an *upset,* i.e. (abstr.) *perversity:*— turning of things upside down.

2018. הֲפֵכָה **hăphêkâh,** *haf-ay-kaw´;* fem. of 2016; *destruction:*— overthrow.

2019. הֲפַכְפַּךְ **hăphakpak,** *haf-ak-pak´;* by redupl. from 2015; *very perverse:*— froward.

2020. הַצָּלָה **hatstsâlâh,** *hats-tsaw-law´;* from 5337; *rescue:*— deliverance.

2021. הֹצֶן **hôtsen,** *ho´-tsen;* from an unused root mean. appar. to *be sharp* or *strong;* a *weapon* of war:— chariot.

2022. הַר **har,** *har;* a short. form of 2042; a *mountain* or *range* of hills (sometimes used fig.):— hill (country), mount (-ain), × promotion.

2023. הֹר **Hôr,** *hore;* another form of 2022; *mountain; Hor,* the name of a peak in Idumæa and of one in Syria:— Hor.

2024. הָרָא **Hârâ',** *haw-raw´;* perh. from 2022; *mountainousness; Hara,* a region of Media:— Hara.

2025. הַרְאֵל **har'êl,** *har-ale´;* from 2022 and 410; *mount of God;* fig. the *altar* of burnt-offering:— altar. Comp. 739.

2026. הָרַג **hârag,** *haw-rag´;* a prim. root; to *smite* with deadly intent:— destroy, out of hand, kill, murder (-er), put to [death], make [slaughter], slay (-er), × surely.

2027. הֶרֶג **hereg,** *heh´-reg;* from 2026; *slaughter:*— be slain, slaughter.

2028. הֲרֵגָה **hărêgâh,** *har-ay-gaw´;* fem. of 2027; *slaughter:*— slaughter.

2029. הָרָה **hârâh,** *haw-raw´;* a prim. root; to *be* (or *become*) *pregnant, conceive* (lit. or fig.):— been, be with child, conceive, progenitor.

2030. הָרֶה **hâreh**, *haw-reh´;* or

הָרִי **hârîy** (Hos. 14:1), *haw-ree´;* from 2029; *pregnant:*— (be, woman) with child, conceive, × great.

2031. הַרְהֹר **harhôr** (Chald.), *har-hor´;* from a root corresp. to 2029; a mental *conception:*— thought.

2032. הֵרוֹן **hêrôwn**, *hay-rone´;* or

הֵרָיוֹן **hêrâyôwn**, *hay-raw-yone´;* from 2029; *pregnancy:*— conception.

2033. הֲרוֹרִי **Hărôwrîy**, *har-o-ree´;* another form for 2043; a *Harorite* or mountaineer:— Harorite.

2034. הֲרִיסָה **hărîçâh**, *har-ee-saw´;* from 2040; something *demolished:*— ruin.

2035. הֲרִיסוּת **hărîçûwth**, *har-ee-sooth´;* from 2040; *demolition:*— destruction.

2036. הֹרָם **Hôrâm**, *ho-rawm´;* from an unused root (mean. to *tower* up); *high;* Horam, a Canaanitish king:— Horam.

2037. הָרֻם **Hârûm**, *haw-room´;* pass. part. of the same as 2036; *high;* Harum, an Isr.:— Harum.

2038. הַרְמוֹן **harmôwn**, *har-mone´;* from the same as 2036; a *castle* (from its height):— palace.

2039. הָרָן **Hârân**, *haw-rawn´;* perh. from 2022; *mountaineer;* Haran, the name of two men:— Haran.

2040. הָרַס **hâraç**, *haw-ras´;* a prim. root; to *pull* down or in pieces, *break, destroy:*— beat down, break (down, through), destroy, overthrow, pluck down, pull down, ruin, throw down, × utterly.

2041. הֶרֶס **hereç**, *heh´-res;* from 2040; *demolition:*— destruction.

2042. הָרָר **hârâr**, *haw-rawr´;* from an unused root mean. to *loom* up; a *mountain:*— hill, mount (-ain).

2043. הֲרָרִי **Hărârîy**, *hah-raw-ree´;* or

הָרָרִי **Hârârîy** (2 Sam. 23:11), *haw-raw-ree´;* or

הָאָרָרִי **Hâ'rârîy** (2 Sam. 23:34, last clause), *haw-raw-ree´;* appar. from 2042; a *mountaineer:*— Hararite.

2044. הָשֵׁם **Hâshêm**, *haw-shame´;* perh. from the same as 2828; *wealthy;* Hashem, an Isr.:— Hashem.

2045. הַשְׁמָעוּת **hâshmâ'ûwth**, *hashmaw-ooth´;* from 8085; *announcement:*— to cause to hear.

2046. הִתּוּךְ **hittûwk**, *hit-took´;* from 5413; a *melting:*— is melted.

2047. הֲתָךְ **Hăthâk**, *hath-awk´;* prob. of for. or.; *Hathak,* a Pers. eunuch:— Hatach.

2048. הָתַל **hâthal**, *haw-thal´;* a prim. root; to *deride;* by impl. to *cheat:*— deal deceitfully, deceive, mock.

2049. הָתֹל **hâthôl**, *haw-thole´;* from 2048 (only in plur. collect.); a *derision:*— mocker.

2050. הָתַת **hâthath**, *haw-thath´;* a prim. root; prop. to *break* in upon, i.e. to *assail:*— imagine mischief.

ו

2051. וְדָן **V⁻dân**, *ved-awn´;* perh. for 5730; *Vedan* (or Aden), a place in Arabia:— Dan also.

2052. וָהֵב **Vâhêb**, *vaw-habe´;* of uncert. der.; *Vaheb,* a place in Moab:— what he did.

2053. וָו **vâv**, *vaw;* prob. a *hook* (the name of the sixth Heb. letter):— hook.

2054. וָזָר **vâzâr**, *vaw-zawr´;* presumed to be from an unused root mean. to *bear* guilt; *crime:*— × strange.

2055. וַיְזָתָא **Vay⁻zâthâ'**, *vah-yez-aw´-thaw;* of for. or.; *Vajezatha,* a son of Haman:— Vajezatha.

2056. וָלָד **vâlâd**, *vaw-lawd´;* for 3206; a *boy:*— child.

2057. וַנְיָה **Vanyâh**, *van-yaw´;* perh. for 6043; *Vanjah,* an Isr.:— Vaniah.

2058. וָפְסִי **Vophçîy**, *vof-see´;* prob. from 3254; *additional;* Vophsi, an Isr.:— Vophsi.

2059. וַשְׁנִי **Vashnîy**, *vash-nee´;* prob. from 3461; *weak;* Vashni, an Isr.:— Vashni.

2060. וַשְׁתִּי **Vashtîy**, *vash-tee´;* of Pers. or.; *Vashti,* the queen of Xerxes:— Vashti.

ז

2061. זְאֵב **z⁻'êb**, *zeh-abe´;* from an unused root mean. to *be yellow;* a *wolf:*— wolf.

2062. זְאֵב **Z⁻'êb**, *zeh-abe´;* the same as 2061; *Zeëb,* a Midianitish prince:— Zeeb.

2063. זֹאת **zô'th**, *zothe´;* irreg. fem. of 2089; *this* (often used adv.):— hereby (-in, -with), it, likewise, the one (other, same), she, so (much), such (deed), that, therefore, these, this (thing), thus.

2064. זָבַד **zâbad**, *zaw-bad´;* a prim. root; to *confer:*— endure.

2065. זֶבֶד **zebed**, *zeh´-bed;* from 2064; a *gift:*— dowry.

2066. זָבָד **Zâbâd**, *zaw-bawd´;* from 2064; *giver;* Zabad, the name of seven Isr.:— Zabad.

Hebrew

2067. זַבְדִּי **Zabdîy**, *zab-dee´;* from 2065; *giving; Zabdi,* the name of four Isr.:— Zabdi.

2068. זַבְדִּיאֵל **Zabdîy'êl**, *zab-dee-ale´;* from 2065 and 410; *gift of God; Zabdiel,* the name of two Isr.:— Zabdiel.

2069. זְבַדְיָה **Zᵉbadyâh**, *zeb-ad-yaw´;* or

זְבַדְיָהוּ **Zᵉbadyâhûw**, *zeb-ad-yaw´-hoo;* from 2064 and 3050; *Jah has given; Zebadjah,* the name of nine Isr.:— Zebadiah.

2070. זְבוּב **zᵉbûwb**, *zeb-oob´;* from an unused root (mean. to *flit*); a *fly* (espec. one of a stinging nature):— fly.

2071. זָבוּד **Zâbûwd**, *zaw-bood´;* from 2064; *given; Zabud,* an Isr.:— Zabud.

2072. זַבּוּד **Zabbûwd**, *zab-bood´;* a form of 2071; *given; Zabbud,* an Isr.:— Zabbud.

2073. זְבוּל **zᵉbûwl**, *ze-bool´;* or

זְבֻל **zᵉbûl**, *zeb-ool´;* from 2082; a *residence:*— dwell in, dwelling, habitation.

2074. זְבוּלוֹן **Zᵉbûwlûwn**, *zeb-oo-loon´;* or

זְבֻלוֹן **Zᵉbûlûwn**, *zeb-oo-loon´;* or

זְבוּלֻן **Zᵉbûwlûn**, *zeb-oo-loon´;* from 2082; *habitation; Zebulon,* a son of Jacob; also his territory and tribe:— Zebulun.

2075. זְבוּלֹנִי **Zᵉbûwlôniy**, *zeb-oo-lo-nee´;* patron. from 2074; a *Zebulonite* or desc. of Zebulun:— Zebulonite.

2076. זָבַח **zâbach**, *zaw-bakh´;* a prim. root; to *slaughter* an animal (usually in sacrifice):— kill, offer, (do) sacrifice, slay.

2077. זֶבַח **zebach**, *zeh´-bakh;* from 2076; prop. a *slaughter,* i.e. the *flesh* of an animal; by impl. a *sacrifice* (the victim or the act):— offer (-ing), sacrifice.

2078. זֶבַח **Zebach**, *zeh´-bakh;* the same as 2077; *sacrifice; Zebach,* a Midianitish prince:— Zebah.

2079. זַבַּי **Zabbay**, *zab-bah´-ee;* prob. by orth. err. for 2140; *Zabbai* (or Zaccai), an Isr.:— Zabbai.

2080. זְבִידָה **Zᵉbîydâh**, *zeb-ee-daw´;* fem. from 2064; *giving; Zebidah,* an Israelitess:— Zebudah.

2081. זְבִינָא **Zᵉbîynâ'**, *zeb-ee-naw´;* from an unused root (mean. to *purchase*); *gainfulness; Zebina,* an Isr.:— Zebina.

2082. זָבַל **zâbal**, *zaw-bal´;* a prim. root; appar. prop. to *inclose,* i.e. to *reside:*— dwell with.

2083. זְבֻל **Zᵉbûl**, *zeb-ool´;* the same as 2073; *dwelling; Zebul,* an Isr.:— Zebul. Comp. 2073.

זְבֻלוֹן **Zᵉbûlûwn**. See 2074.

2084. זְבַן **zᵉban** (Chald.), *zeb-an´;* corresp. to the root of 2081; to *acquire* by purchase:— gain.

2085. זָג **zâg**, *zawg;* from an unused root prob. mean. to *inclose;* the *skin* of a grape:— husk.

2086. זֵד **zêd**, *zade´;* from 2102; *arrogant:*— presumptuous, proud.

2087. זָדוֹן **zâdôwn**, *zaw-done´;* from 2102; *arrogance:*— presumptuously, pride, proud (man).

2088. זֶה **zeh**, *zeh;* a prim. word; the masc. demonstr. pron., *this* or *that:*— he, × hence, × here, it (-self), × now, × of him, the one ... the other, × than the other, (× out of) the (self) same, such (an one) that, these, this (hath, man), on this side ... on that side, × thus, very, which. Comp. 2063, 2090, 2097, 2098.

2089. זֶה **zeh** (1 Sam. 17:34), *zeh;* by perm. for 7716; a *sheep:*— lamb.

2090. זֹה **zôh**, *zo;* for 2088; *this* or *that:*— as well as another, it, this, that, thus and thus.

2091. זָהָב **zâhâb**, *zaw-hawb´;* from an unused root mean. to *shimmer; gold,* fig. something *gold-colored* (i.e. *yellow*), as *oil,* a *clear sky:*— gold (-en), fair weather.

2092. זָהַם **zâham**, *zaw-ham´;* a prim. root; to *be rancid,* i.e. (tran.) to *loathe:*— abhor.

2093. זַהַם **Zaham**, *zah´-ham;* from 2092; *loathing; Zaham,* an Isr.:— Zaham.

2094. זָהַר **zâhar**, *zaw-har´;* a prim. root; to *gleam;* fig. to *enlighten* (by caution):— admonish, shine, teach, (give) warn (-ing).

2095. זְהַר **zᵉhar** (Chald.), *zeh-har´;* corresp. to 2094; (pass.) *be admonished:*— take heed.

2096. זֹהַר **zôhar**, *zo´-har;* from 2094; *brilliancy:*— brightness.

2097. זוֹ **zôw**, *zo;* for 2088; *this* or *that:*— that, this.

2098. זוּ **zûw**, *zoo;* for 2088; *this* or *that:*— that, this, × wherein, which, whom.

2099. זִו **Zîv**, *zeev´;* prob. from an unused root mean. to *be prominent;* prop. *brightness* [comp. 2122], i.e. (fig.) the *month* of *flowers; Ziv* (corresp. to Ijar or May):— Zif.

2100. זוּב **zûwb**, *zoob;* a prim. root; to *flow freely* (as water), i.e. (spec.) to *have a* (sexual) *flux;* fig. to *waste* away; also to *overflow:*— flow, gush out, have a (running) issue, pine away, run.

2101. זוֹב **zôwb**, *zobe;* from 2100; a seminal or menstrual *flux:*— issue.

2102. זוּד **zûwd**, *zood;* or (by perm.)

זִיד **zîyd**, *zeed;* a prim. root; to *seethe;* fig. to *be insolent:*— be proud, deal proudly, presume, (come) presumptuously, sod.

2103. זוּד **zûwd** (Chald.), *zood;* corresp. to 2102; to *be proud:*— in pride.

2104. זוּזִים **Zûwzîym,** *zoo-zeem´;* plur. prob. from the same as 2123; *prominent; Zuzites,* an aboriginal tribe of Pal.:— Zuzims.

2105. זוֹחֵת **Zôwchêth,** *zo-khayth´;* of uncert. or.; *Zocheth,* an Isr.:— Zoheth.

2106. זָוִית **zâvîyth,** *zaw-veeth´;* appar. from the same root as 2099 (in the sense of *prominence*); an *angle* (as *projecting*), i.e. (by impl.) a *corner-column* (or *anta*):— corner (stone).

2107. זוּל **zûwl,** *zool;* a prim. root [comp. 2151]; prob. to *shake* out, i.e. (by impl.) to *scatter* profusely; fig. to *treat lightly:*— lavish, despise.

2108. זוּלָה **zûwlâh,** *zoo-law´;* from 2107; prob. *scattering,* i.e. *removal;* used adv. *except:*— beside, but, only, save.

2109. זוּן **zûwn,** *zoon;* a prim. root; perh. prop. to *be plump,* i.e. (tran.) to *nourish:*— feed.

2110. זוּן **zûwn** (Chald.), *zoon;* corresp. to 2109:— feed.

2111. זוּעַ **zûwâ',** *zoo-ah;* a prim. root; prop. to *shake* off, i.e. (fig.) to *agitate* (as with fear):— move, tremble, vex.

2112. זוּעַ **zûwa'** (Chald.), *zoo´-ah;* corresp. to 2111; to *shake* (with fear):— tremble.

2113. זְוָעָה **z°vâ'âh,** *zev-aw-aw´;* from 2111; *agitation, fear:*— be removed, trouble, vexation. Comp. 2189.

2114. זוּר **zûwr,** *zoor;* a prim. root; to *turn* aside (espec. for lodging); hence, to *be a foreign, strange, profane;* spec. (act. part.) to *commit adultery:*— (come from) another (man, place), fanner, go away, (e-) strange (-r, thing, woman).

2115. זוּר **zûwr,** *zoor;* a prim. root [comp. 6695]; to *press* together, *tighten:*— close, crush, thrust together.

2116. זוּרֶה **zûwreh,** *zoo-reh´;* from 2115; *trodden* on:— that which is crushed.

2117. זָזָא **Zâzâ',** *zaw-zaw´;* prob. from the root of 2123; *prominent; Zaza,* an Isr.:— Zaza.

2118. זָחַח **zâchach,** *zaw-khakh´;* a prim. root; to *shove* or *displace:*— loose.

2119. זָחַל **zâchal,** *zaw-khal´;* a prim. root; to *crawl;* by impl. to *fear:*— be afraid, serpent, worm.

2120. זֹחֶלֶת **Zôcheleth,** *zo-kheh´-leth;* fem. act. part. of 2119; *crawling* (i.e. *serpent*); *Zocheleth,* a boundary stone in Pal.:— Zoheleth.

2121. זֵידוֹן **zêydôwn,** *zay-dohn´;* from 2102; *boiling* of water, i.e. *wave:*— proud.

2122. זִיו **zîyv** (Chald.), *zeev;* corresp. to 2099; (fig.) *cheerfulness:*— brightness, countenance.

2123. זִיז **zîyz,** *zeez;* from an unused root appar. mean. to *be conspicuous; fulness* of the breast; also a moving *creature:*— abundance, wild beast.

2124. זִיזָא **Zîyzâ',** *zee-zaw´;* appar. from the same as 2123; *prominence; Ziza,* the name of two Isr.:— Ziza.

2125. זִיזָה **Zîyzâh,** *zee-zaw´;* another form for 2124; *Zizah,* an Isr.:— Zizah.

2126. זִינָא **Zîynâ',** *zee-naw´;* from 2109; *well-fed;* or perh. an orth. err. for 2124; *Zina,* an Isr.:— Zina.

2127. זִיעַ **Zîya',** *zee´-ah;* from 2111; *agitation; Zia,* an Isr.:— Zia.

2128. זִיף **Zîyph,** *zeef;* from the same as 2203; *flowing; Ziph,* the name of a place in Pal.; also of an Isr.:— Ziph.

2129. זִיפָה **Zîyphâh,** *zee-faw´;* fem. of 2128; a *flowing; Ziphah,* an Isr.:— Ziphah.

2130. זִיפִי **Zîyphîy,** *zee-fee´;* patrial from 2128; a *Ziphite* or inhab. of Ziph:— Ziphims, Ziphite.

2131. זִיקָה **zîyqâh** (Isa. 50:11), *zee-kaw´* (fem.); and

זִק **zîq,** *zeek;* or

זֵק **zêq,** *zake;* from 2187; prop. what *leaps* forth, i.e. *flash* of fire, or a burning *arrow;* also (from the orig. sense of the root) a *bond:*— chain, fetter, firebrand, spark.

2132. זַיִת **zayith,** *zay´-yith;* prob. from an unused root [akin to 2099]; an *olive* (as yielding *illuminating* oil), the tree, the branch or the berry:— olive (tree, -yard), Olivet.

2133. זֵיתָן **Zêythân,** *zay-thawn´;* from 2132; *olive* grove; *Zethan,* an Isr.:— Zethan.

2134. זַך **zak,** *zak;* from 2141; *clear:*— clean, pure.

2135. זָכָה **zâkâh,** *zaw-kaw´;* a prim. root [comp. 2141]; to *be translucent;* fig. to *be innocent:*— be (make) clean, cleanse, be clear, count pure.

2136. זָכוּ **zâkûw** (Chald.), *zaw-koo´;* from a root corresp. to 2135; *purity:*— innocency.

2137. זְכוּכִית **z°kûwkîyth,** *zek-oo-keeth;* from 2135; prop. *transparency,* i.e. *glass:*— crystal.

2138. זָכוּר **zâkûwr,** *zaw-koor´;* prop. pass. part. of 2142, but used for 2145; a *male* (of man or animals):— males, men-children.

2139. זַכּוּר **Zakkûwr,** *zaw-koor´;* from 2142; *mindful; Zakkur,* the name of seven Isr.:— Zaccur, Zacchur.

2140. זַכַּי **Zakkay,** *zak-kah´-ee;* from 2141; *pure; Zakkai,* an Isr.:— Zaccai.

2141. זָכַךְ **zâkak**, *zaw-kak´*; a prim. root [comp. 2135]; to *be transparent* or *clean* (phys. or mor.):— be (make) clean, be pure (-r).

2142. זָכַר **zâkar**, *zaw-kar´*; a prim. root; prop. to *mark* (so as to be recognized), i.e. to *remember*; by impl. to *mention*; also (as denom. from 2145) to *be male*:— × burn [incense], × earnestly, be male, (make) mention (of), be mindful, recount, record (-er), remember, make to be remembered, bring (call, come, keep, put) to (in) remembrance, × still, think on, × well.

2143. זֵכֶר **zêker**, *zay´-ker*; or

זֶכֶר **zeker**, *zeh´-ker*; from 2142; a *memento*, abstr. *recollection* (rarely if ever); by impl. *commemoration:*— memorial, memory, remembrance, scent.

2144. זֶכֶר **Zeker**, *zeh´-ker*; the same as 2143; *Zeker*, an Isr.:— Zeker.

2145. זָכָר **zâkâr**, *zaw-kawr´*; from 2142; prop. *remembered*, i.e. a *male* (of man or animals, as being the most noteworthy sex):— × him, male, man (child, -kind).

2146. זִכְרוֹן **zikrôwn**, *zik-rone´*; from 2142; a *memento* (or memorable thing, day or writing):— memorial, record.

2147. זִכְרִי **Zikrîy**, *zik-ree´*; from 2142; *memorable*; *Zicri*, the name of twelve Isr.:— Zichri.

2148. זְכַרְיָה **Zᵉkaryâh**, *zek-ar-yaw´*; or

זְכַרְיָהוּ **Zᵉkaryâhûw**, *zek-ar-yaw´-hoo*; from 2142 and 3050; *Jah has remembered*; *Zecarjah*, the name of twenty-nine Isr.:— Zachariah, Zechariah.

2149. זְלוּת **zullûwth**, *zool-looth´*; from 2151; prop. a *shaking*, i.e. perh. a *tempest:*— vilest.

2150. זַלְזַל **zalzal**, *zal-zal´*; by redupl. from 2151; *tremulous*, i.e. a *twig:*— sprig.

2151. זָלַל **zâlal**, *zaw-lal´*; a prim. root [comp. 2107]; to *shake* (as in the wind), i.e. to *quake*; fig. to *be loose* morally, *worthless* or *prodigal:*— blow down, glutton, riotous (eater), vile.

2152. זַלְעָפָה **zal'âphâh**, *zal-aw-faw´*; or

זִלְעָפָף **zil'âphâph**, *zil-aw-faw´*; from 2196; a *glow* (of wind or anger); also a *famine* (as *consuming*):— horrible, horror, terrible.

2153. זִלְפָּה **Zilpâh**, *zil-paw´*; from an unused root appar. mean. to *trickle*, as myrrh; *fragrant dropping*; *Zilpah*, Leah's maid:— Zilpah.

2154. זִמָּה **zimmâh**, *zim-maw´*; or

זַמָּה **zammâh**, *zam-maw´*; from 2161; a *plan*, espec. a bad one:— heinous crime, lewd (-ly, -ness), mischief, purpose, thought, wicked (device, mind, -ness).

2155. זִמָּה **Zimmâh**, *zim-maw´*; the same as

2154; *Zimmah*, the name of two Isr.:— Zimmah.

2156. זְמוֹרָה **zᵉmôwrâh**, *zem-o-raw´*; or

זְמֹרָה **zᵉmôrâh**, *zem-o-raw´* (fem.); and

זְמֹר **zᵉmôr**, *zem-ore´* (masc.); from 2168; a *twig* (as *pruned*):— vine, branch, slip.

2157. זַמְזֹם **Zamzôm**, *zam-zome´*; from 2161; *intriguing*; a *Zamzumite*, or native tribe of Pal.:— Zamzummim.

2158. זָמִיר **zâmîyr**, *zaw-meer´*; or

זָמִר **zâmir**, *zaw-meer´*; and (fem.)

זְמִרָה **zᵉmîrâh**, *zem-ee-raw´*; from 2167; a *song* to be accompanied with instrumental music:— psalm (-ist), singing, song.

2159. זָמִיר **zâmîyr**, *zaw-meer´*; from 2168; a *twig* (as *pruned*):— branch.

2160. זְמִירָה **Zᵉmîyrâh**, *zem-ee-raw´*; fem. of 2158; *song*; *Zemirah*, an Isr.:— Zemira.

2161. זָמַם **zâmam**, *zaw-mam´*; a prim. root; to *plan*, usually in a bad sense:— consider, devise, imagine, plot, purpose, think (evil).

2162. זָמָם **zâmâm**, *zaw-mawm´*; from 2161; a *plot:*— wicked device.

2163. זָמַן **zâman**, *zaw-man´*; a prim. root; to *fix* (a time):— appoint.

2164. זְמַן **zᵉman** (Chald.), *zem-an´*; corresp. to 2163; to *agree* (on a time and place):— prepare.

2165. זְמָן **zᵉmân**, *zem-awn´*; from 2163; an *appointed* occasion:— season, time.

2166. זְמָן **zᵉmân** (Chald.), *zem-awn´*; from 2165; the same as 2165:— season, time.

2167. זָמַר **zâmar**, *zaw-mar´*; a prim. root [perh. ident. with 2168 through the idea of *striking* with the fingers]; prop. to *touch* the strings or parts of a musical instrument, i.e. *play* upon it; to make *music*, accompanied by the voice; hence, to *celebrate* in song and music:— give praise, sing forth praises, psalms.

2168. זָמַר **zâmar**, *zaw-mar´*; a prim. root [comp. 2167, 5568, 6785]; to *trim* (a vine):— prune.

2169. זֶמֶר **zemer**, *zeh´-mer*; appar. from 2167 or 2168; a *gazelle* (from its lightly *touching* the ground):— chamois.

2170. זְמָר **zᵉmâr** (Chald.), *zem-awr´*; from a root corresp. to 2167; instrumental *music:*— musick.

זָמִיר **zâmîr**. See 2158.

זְמֹר **zᵉmôr**. See 2156.

2171. זַמָּר **zammâr** (Chald.), *zam-mawr´*;

from the same as 2170; an instrumental *musician:*— singer.

2172. זִמְרָה **zimrâh**, *zim-raw´;* from 2167; a *musical* piece or *song* to be accompanied by an instrument:— melody, psalm.

2173. זִמְרָה **zimrâh**, *zim-raw´;* from 2168; *pruned* (i.e. *choice*) fruit:— best fruit.

זְמִרָה **zᵉmîrâh**. See 2158.

זְמֹרָה **zᵉmôrâh**. See 2156.

2174. זִמְרִי **Zimrîy**, *zim-ree´;* from 2167; *musical; Zimri*, the name of five Isr., and of an Arabian tribe:— Zimri.

2175. זִמְרָן **Zimrân**, *zim-rawn´;* from 2167; *musical; Zimran*, a son of Abraham by Keturah:— Zimran.

2176. זִמְרָת **zimrâth**, *zim-rawth´;* from 2167; instrumental *music;* by impl. *praise:*— song.

2177. זָן **zan**, *zan;* from 2109; prop. *nourished* (or fully *developed*), i.e. a *form* or *sort:*— divers kinds, × all manner of store.

2178. זַן **zan** (Chald.), *zan;* corresp. to 2177; *sort:*— kind.

2179. זָנַב **zânab**, *zaw-nab´;* a prim. root mean. to *wag;* used only as a denom. from 2180; to *curtail*, i.e. *cut* off the rear:— smite the hindmost.

2180. זָנָב **zânâb**, *zaw-nawb´;* from 2179 (in the orig. sense of *flapping*); the *tail* (lit. or fig.):— tail.

2181. זָנָה **zânâh**, *zaw-naw´;* a prim. root [highly-*fed* and therefore *wanton*]; to *commit adultery* (usually of the female, and less often of simple fornication, rarely of involuntary ravishment); fig. to *commit idolatry* (the Jewish people being regarded as the spouse of Jehovah):— (cause to) commit fornication, × continually, × great, (be an, play the) harlot, (cause to be, play the) whore, (commit, fall to) whoredom, (cause to) go a-whoring, whorish.

2182. זָנוֹחַ **Zânôwach**, *zaw-no´-akh;* from 2186; *rejected; Zanoach*, the name of two places in Pal.:— Zanoah.

2183. זָנוּן **zânûwn**, *zaw-noon´;* from 2181; *adultery;* fig. *idolatry:*— whoredom.

2184. זְנוּת **zᵉnûwth**, *zen-ooth´;* from 2181; *adultery*, i.e. (fig.) *infidelity, idolatry:*— whoredom.

2185. זֹנוֹת **zônôwth**, *zo-noth´;* regarded by some as if from 2109 or an unused root, and applied to military *equipments;* but evidently the fem. plur. act. part. of 2181; *harlots:*— armour.

2186. זָנַח **zânach**, *zaw-nakh´;* a prim. root mean. to *push* aside, i.e. *reject, forsake, fail:*— cast away (off), remove far away (off).

2187. זָנַק **zânaq**, *zaw-nak´;* a prim. root; prop. to *draw together* the feet (as an animal about to dart upon its prey), i.e. to *spring* forward:— leap.

2188. זֵעָה **zêʻâh**, *zay-aw´;* from 2111 (in the sense of 3154); *perspiration:*— sweat.

2189. זַעֲוָה **zaʻăvâh**, *zah-av-aw´;* by transp. for 2113; *agitation, maltreatment:*— × removed, trouble.

2190. זַעֲוָן **Zaʻăvân**, *zah-av-awn´;* from 2111; *disquiet; Zaavan*, an Idumæan:— Zaavan.

2191. זְעֵיר **zᵉʻêyr**, *zeh-ayr´;* from an unused root [akin (by perm.) to 6819], mean. to *dwindle; small:*— little.

2192. זְעֵיר **zᵉʻêyr** (Chald.), *zeh-ayr´;* corresp. to 2191:— little.

2193. זָעַךְ **zâʻak**, *zaw-ak´;* a prim. root; to *extinguish:*— be extinct.

2194. זָעַם **zâʻam**, *zaw-am´;* a prim. root; prop. to *foam* at the mouth, i.e. to *be enraged:*— abhor, abominable, (be) angry, defy, (have) indignation.

2195. זַעַם **zaʻam**, *zah´-am;* from 2194; strictly *froth* at the mouth, i.e. (fig.) *fury* (espec. of God's displeasure with sin):— angry, indignation, rage.

2196. זָעַף **zâʻaph**, *zaw-af´;* a prim. root; prop. to *boil* up, i.e. (fig.) to *be peevish* or *angry:*— fret, sad, worse liking, be wroth.

2197. זַעַף **zaʻaph**, *zah´-af;* from 2196; *anger:*— indignation, rage (-ing), wrath.

2198. זָעֵף **zâʻêph**, *zaw-afe´;* from 2196; *angry:*— displeased.

2199. זָעַק **zâʻaq**, *zaw-ak´;* a prim. root; to *shriek* (from anguish or danger); by anal. (as a herald) to *announce* or *convene* publicly:— assemble, call (together), (make a) cry (out), come with such a company, gather (together), cause to be proclaimed.

2200. זְעִק **zᵉʻîq** (Chald.), *zeh-eek´;* corresp. to 2199; to *make an outcry:*— cry.

2201. זַעַק **zaʻaq**, *zah´-ak;* and (fem.)

זְעָקָה **zᵉʻâqâh**, *zeh-aw-kaw´;* from 2199; a *shriek* or *outcry:*— cry (-ing).

2202. זִפְרֹן **Ziphrôn**, *zi-frone´;* from an unused root (mean. to *be fragrant*); *Ziphron*, a place in Pal.:— Ziphron.

2203. זֶפֶת **zepheth**, *zeh´-feth;* from an unused root (mean. to *liquify*); *asphalt* (from its tendency to *soften* in the sun):— pitch.

זִיק **zîq** or

זֵק **zêq**. See 2131.

2204. זָקֵן **zâqên**, *zaw-kane´;* a prim. root; to *be old:*— aged man, be (wax) old (man).

2205. זָקֵן **zâqên**, *zaw-kane´;* from 2204; *old:*— aged, ancient (man), elder (-est), old (man, men and ... women), senator.

2206. זָקָן **zâqân**, *zaw-kawn´*; from 2204; the *beard* (as indicating *age*):— beard.

2207. זֹקֶן **zôqen**, *zo´-ken*; from 2204; old *age:*— age.

2208. זָקֻן **zâqûn**, *zaw-koon´*; prop. pass. part. of 2204 (used only in the plur. as a noun); *old age:*— old age.

2209. זִקְנָה **ziqnâh**, *zik-naw´*; fem. of 2205; old *age:*— old (age).

2210. זָקַף **zâqaph**, *zaw-kaf´*; a prim. root; to *lift*, i.e. (fig.) *comfort:*— raise (up).

2211. זְקַף **zᵉqaph** (Chald.), *zek-af´*; corresp. to 2210; to *hang*, i.e. *impale:*— set up.

2212. זָקַק **zâqaq**, *zaw-kak´*; a prim. root; to *strain*, (fig.) *extract, clarify:*— fine, pour down, purge, purify, refine.

2213. זֵר **zêr**, *zare*; from 2237 (in the sense of *scattering*); a *chaplet* (as *spread* around the top), i.e. (spec.) a border *moulding:*— crown.

2214. זָרָא **zârâ'**, *zaw-raw´*; from 2114 (in the sense of *estrangement*) [comp. 2219]; *disgust:*— loathsome.

2215. זָרַב **zârab**, *zaw-rab´*; a prim. root; to *flow* away:— wax warm.

2216. זְרֻבָּבֶל **Zᵉrubbâbel**, *zer-oob-baw-bel´*; from 2215 and 894; *descended of* (i.e. from) *Babylon*, i.e. born there; *Zerubbabel*, an Isr.:— Zerubbabel.

2217. זְרֻבָּבֶל **Zᵉrubbâbel** (Chald.), *zer-oob-baw-bel´*; corresp. to 2216:— Zerubbabel.

2218. זֶרֶד **Zered**, *zeh´-red*; from an unused root mean. to *be exuberant* in growth; lined with *shrubbery*; *Zered*, a brook E. of the Dead Sea:— Zared, Zered.

2219. זָרָה **zârâh**, *zaw-raw´*; a prim. root [comp. 2114]; to *toss* about; by impl. to *diffuse, winnow:*— cast away, compass, disperse, fan, scatter (away), spread, strew, winnow.

2220. זְרוֹעַ **zᵉrôwa'**, *zer-o´-ah*; or (short.)

זְרֹעַ **zᵉrôa'**, *zer-o´-ah*; and (fem.)

זְרוֹעָה **zᵉrôw'âh**, *zer-o-aw´*; or

זְרֹעָה **zᵉrô'âh**, *zer-o-aw´*; from 2232; the *arm* (as *stretched* out), or (of animals) the *foreleg*; fig. *force:*— arm, + help, mighty, power, shoulder, strength.

2221. זֵרוּעַ **zêrûwa'**, *zay-roo´-ah*; from 2232; something *sown*, i.e. a *plant:*— sowing, thing that is sown.

2222. זַרְזִיף **zarzîyph**, *zar-zeef´*; by redupl. from an unused root mean. to *flow*; a *pouring rain:*— water.

זְרוֹעָה **zᵉrôw'âh**. See 2220.

2223. זַרְזִיר **zarzîyr**, *zar-zeer´*; by redupl. from 2115; prop. tightly *girt*, i.e. prob. a *racer*, or some fleet animal (as being *slender* in the waist):— + greyhound.

2224. זָרַח **zârach**, *zaw-rakh´*; a prim. root; prop. to *irradiate* (or shoot forth beams), i.e. to *rise* (as the sun); spec. to *appear* (as a symptom of leprosy):— arise, rise (up), as soon as it is up.

2225. זֶרַח **zerach**, *zeh´-rakh*; from 2224; a *rising* of light:— rising.

2226. זֶרַח **Zerach**, *zeh´-rakh*; the same as 2225; *Zerach*, the name of three Isr., also of an Idumæan and an Ethiopian prince:— Zarah, Zerah.

2227. זַרְחִי **Zarchîy**, *zar-khee´*; patron. from 2226; a *Zarchite* or desc. of Zerach:— Zarchite.

2228. זְרַחְיָה **Zᵉrachyâh**, *zer-akh-yaw´*; from 2225 and 3050; *Jah has risen; Zerachjah*, the name of two Isr.:— Zerahiah.

2229. זָרַם **zâram**, *zaw-ram´*; a prim. root; to *gush* (as water):— carry away as with a flood, pour out.

2230. זֶרֶם **zerem**, *zeh´-rem*; from 2229; a *gush* of water:— flood, overflowing, shower, storm, tempest.

2231. זִרְמָה **zirmâh**, *zir-maw´*; fem. of 2230; a *gushing* of fluid (semen):— issue.

2232. זָרַע **zâra'**, *zaw-rah´*; a prim. root; to *sow*; fig. to *disseminate, plant, fructify:*— bear, conceive seed, set with, sow (-er), yield.

2233. זֶרַע **zera'**, *zeh´-rah*; from 2232; *seed*; fig. *fruit, plant, sowing-time, posterity:*— × carnally, child, fruitful, seed (-time), sowing-time.

2234. זְרַע **zᵉra'** (Chald.), *zer-ah´*; corresp. to 2233; *posterity:*— seed.

זְרֹעַ **zᵉrôa'**. See 2220.

2235. זֵרֹעַ **zêrôa'**, *zay-ro´-ah*; or

זֵרָעֹן **zêrâ'ôn**, *zay-raw-ohn´*; from 2232; something *sown* (only in the plur.), i.e. a *vegetable* (as food):— pulse.

זְרֹעָה **zᵉrô'âh**. See 2220.

2236. זָרַק **zâraq**, *zaw-rak´*; a prim. root; to *sprinkle* (fluid or solid particles):— be here and there, scatter, sprinkle, strew.

2237. זָרַר **zârar**, *zaw-rar´*; a prim. root [comp. 2114]; perh. to *diffuse*, i.e. (spec.) to *sneeze:*— sneeze.

2238. זֶרֶשׁ **Zeresh**, *zeh´-resh*; of Pers. or.; *Zeresh*, Haman's wife:— Zeresh.

2239. זֶרֶת **zereth**, *zeh´-reth*; from 2219; the *spread* of the fingers, i.e. a *span:*— span.

2240. זַתּוּא **Zattûw'**, *zat-too´*; of uncert. der.; *Zattu*, an Isr.:— Zattu.

2241. זֵתָם **Zêthâm**, *zay-thawm´*; appar. a var. for 2133; *Zetham*, an Isr.:— Zetham.

2242. זֵתַר **Zêthar**, *zay-thar´*; of Pers. or.; *Zethar*, a eunuch of Xerxes:— Zethar.

ח

2243. חֹב **chôb**, *khobe*; by contr. from 2245; prop. a *cherisher*, i.e. the *bosom:*— bosom.

2244. חָבָא **châbâ'**, *khaw-baw´*; a prim. root [comp. 2245]; to *secrete:*— × held, hide (self), do secretly.

2245. חָבַב **châbab**, *khaw-bab´*; a prim. root [comp. 2244, 2247]; prop. to *hide* (as in the bosom), i.e. to *cherish* (with affection):— love.

2246. חֹבָב **Chôbâb**, *kho-bawb´*; from 2245; *cherished*; *Chobab*, father-in-law of Moses:— Hobab.

2247. חָבָה **châbah**, *khaw-baw´*; a prim. root [comp. 2245]; to *secrete:*— hide (self).

2248. חֲבוּלָה **chăbûwlâh** (Chald.), *khab-oo-law´*; from 2255; prop. *overthrown*, i.e. (morally) *crime:*— hurt.

2249. חָבוֹר **Châbôwr**, *khaw-bore´*; from 2266; *united*; *Chabor*, a river of Assyria:— Habor.

2250. חַבּוּרָה **chabbûwrâh**, *khab-boo-raw´*; or

חַבֻּרָה **chabbûrâh**, *khab-boo-raw´*; or

חֲבֻרָה **chăbûrâh**, *khab-oo-raw´*; from 2266; prop. *bound* (with stripes), i.e. a *weal* (or black-and-blue mark itself):— blueness, bruise, hurt, stripe, wound.

2251. חָבַט **châbaṭ**, *khaw-bat´*; a prim. root; to *knock* out or off:— beat (off, out), thresh.

2252. חֲבַיָּה **Chăbayâh**, *khab-ah-yaw´*; or

חֲבָיָה **Chăbâyâh**, *khab-aw-yaw´*; from 2247 and 3050; *Jah has hidden*; *Chabajah*, an Isr.:— Habaiah.

2253. חֶבְיוֹן **chebyôwn**, *kheb-yone´*; from 2247; a *concealment:*— hiding.

2254. חָבַל **châbal**, *khaw-bal´*; a prim. root; to *wind* tightly (as a rope), i.e. to *bind*; spec. by a *pledge*; fig. to *pervert, destroy*; also to *writhe* in pain (espec. of parturition):— × at all, band, bring forth, (deal) corrupt (-ly), destroy, offend, lay to (take a) pledge, spoil, travail, × very, withhold.

2255. חֲבַל **chăbal** (Chald.), *khab-al´*; corresp. to 2254; to *ruin:*— destroy, hurt.

2256. חֶבֶל **chebel**, *kheh´-bel*; or

חֵבֶל **chêbel**, *khay´-bel*; from 2254; a *rope* (as *twisted*), espec. a measuring *line*; by impl. a *district* or *inheritance* (as *measured*); or a *noose* (as of *cords*); fig. a *company* (as if *tied* together); also a *throe* (espec. of parturition); also *ruin:*— band, coast, company, cord, country, destruction, line, lot, pain, pang, portion, region, rope, snare, sorrow, tackling.

2257. חֲבַל **chăbal** (Chald.), *khab-al´*; from

2255; *harm* (personal or pecuniary):— damage, hurt.

2258. חֲבֹל **chăbôl**, *khab-ole´*; or (fem.)

חֲבֹלָה **chăbôlâh**, *khab-o-law´*; from 2254; a *pawn* (as security for debt):— pledge.

2259. חֹבֵל **chôbêl**, *kho-bale´*; act. part. from 2254 (in the sense of handling *ropes*); a *sailor:*— pilot, shipmaster.

2260. חִבֵּל **chibbêl**, *khib-bale´*; from 2254 (in the sense of furnished with *ropes*); a *mast:*— mast.

2261. חֲבַצֶּלֶת **chăbatstseleth**, *khab-ats-tseh´-leth*; of uncert. der.; prob. *meadow-saffron:*— rose.

2262. חֲבַצִּנְיָה **Chăbatstsanyâh**, *khab-ats-tsan-yaw´*; of uncert. der.; *Chabatstsanjah*, a Rechabite:— Habazaniah.

2263. חָבַק **châbaq**, *khaw-bak´*; a prim. root; to *clasp* (the hands or in embrace):— embrace, fold.

2264. חִבֻּק **chibbûq**, *khib-book´*; from 2263; a *clasping* of the hands (in idleness):— fold.

2265. חֲבַקּוּק **Chăbaqqûwq**, *khab-ak-kook´*; by redupl. from 2263; *embrace*; *Chabak-kuk*, the prophet:— Habakkuk.

2266. חָבַר **châbar**, *khaw-bar´*; a prim. root; to *join* (lit. or fig.); spec. (by means of spells) to *fascinate:*— charm (-er), be compact, couple (together), have fellowship with, heap up, join (self, together), league.

2267. חֶבֶר **cheber**, *kheh´-ber*; from 2266; a *society*; also a *spell:*— + charmer (-ing), company, enchantment, × wide.

2268. חֶבֶר **Cheber**, *kheh´-ber*; the same as 2267; *community*; *Cheber*, the name of a Kenite and of three Isr.:— Heber.

2269. חֲבַר **chăbar** (Chald.), *khab-ar´*; from a root corresp. to 2266; an *associate:*— companion, fellow.

2270. חָבֵר **châbêr**, *khaw-bare´*; from 2266; an *associate:*— companion, fellow, knit together.

2271. חַבָּר **chabbâr**, *khab-bawr´*; from 2266; a *partner:*— companion.

2272. חֲבַרְבֻּרָה **chăbarbûrâh**, *khab-ar-boo-raw´*; by redupl. from 2266; a *streak* (like a *line*), as on the tiger:— spot.

2273. חֲבְרָה **chabrâh** (Chald.), *khab-raw´*; fem. of 2269; an *associate:*— other.

2274. חֶבְרָה **chebrâh**, *kheb-raw´*; fem. of 2267; *association:*— company.

2275. חֶבְרוֹן **Chebrôwn**, *kheb-rone´*; from 2267; seat of *association*; *Chebron*, a place in Pal., also the name of two Isr.:— Hebron.

2276. חֶבְרוֹנִי **Chebrôwnîy**, *kheb-ro-nee´*; or

חֶבְרֹנִי **Chebrôniy**, *kheb-ro-nee´*; patron. from 2275; *Chebronite* (collect.), an inhab. of Chebron:— Hebronites.

2277. חֶבְרִי **Chebrîy**, *kheb-ree´*; patron. from 2268; a *Chebrite* (collect.) or desc. of Cheber:— Heberites.

2278. חֲבֶרֶת **chăbereth**, *khab-eh´-reth*; fem. of 2270; a *consort:*— companion.

2279. חֹבֶרֶת **chôbereth**, *kho-beh´-reth;* fem. act. part. of 2266; a *joint:*— which coupleth, coupling.

2280. חָבַשׁ **châbash**, *khaw-bash´;* a prim. root; to *wrap* firmly (espec. a turban, compress, or *saddle*); fig. to *stop,* to *rule:*— bind (up), gird about, govern, healer, put, saddle, wrap about.

2281. חָבֵת **châbêth**, *khaw-bayth´;* from an unused root prob. mean. to *cook* [comp. 4227]; something *fried,* prob. a *griddle-cake:*— pan.

2282. חַג **chag**, *khag;* or

חָג **châg**, *khawg;* from 2287; a *festival,* or a *victim* therefore:— (solemn) feast (day), sacrifice, solemnity.

2283. חָגָא **châgâ'**, *khaw-gaw´;* from an unused root mean. to *revolve* [comp. 2287]; prop. *vertigo,* i.e. (fig.) *fear:*— terror.

2284. חָגָב **châgâb**, *khaw-gawb´;* of uncert. der.; a *locust:*— locust.

2285. חָגָב **Châgâb**, *khaw-gawb´;* the same as 2284; *locust; Chagab,* one of the Nethinim:— Hagab.

2286. חֲגָבָא **Chăgâbâ'**, *khag-aw-baw´;* or

חֲגָבָה **Chăgâbâh**, *khag-aw-baw´;* fem. of 2285; *locust; Chagaba* or *Chagabah,* one of the Nethinim:— Hagaba, Hagabah.

2287. חָגַג **châgag**, *khaw-gag´;* a prim. root [comp. 2283, 2328]; prop. to *move* in a *circle,* i.e. (spec.) to *march* in a sacred procession, to *observe* a festival; by impl. to *be giddy:*— celebrate, dance, (keep, hold) a (solemn) feast (holiday), reel to and fro.

2288. חֲגָו **chăgâv**, *khag-awv´;* from an unused root mean. to *take refuge;* a *rift* in rocks:— cleft.

2289. חָגוֹר **chăgôwr**, *khaw-gore´;* from 2296; *belted:*— girded with.

2290. חֲגוֹר **chăgôwr**, *khag-ore´;* or

חֲגֹר **chăgôr**, *khag-ore´;* and (fem.)

חֲגוֹרָה **chăgôwrâh**, *khag-o-raw´;* or

חֲגֹרָה **chăgôrâh**, *khag-o-raw´;* from 2296; a *belt* (for the waist):— apron, armour, gird (-le).

2291. חַגִּי **Chaggîy**, *khag-ghee´;* from 2287; *festive, Chaggi,* an Isr.; also (patron.) a *Chaggite,* or desc. of the same:— Haggi, Haggites.

2292. חַגַּי **Chaggay**, *khag-gah´-ee;* from 2282; *festive; Chaggai,* a Heb. prophet:— Haggai.

2293. חַגִּיָּה **Chaggîyâh**, *khag-ghee-yaw´;* from 2282 and 3050; *festival of Jah; Chaggijah,* an Isr.:— Haggiah.

2294. חַגִּית **Chaggiyîth**, *khag-gheeth´;* fem. of 2291; *festive; Chaggith,* a wife of David:— Haggith.

2295. חָגְלָה **Choglâh**, *khog-law´;* of uncert. der.; prob. a *partridge; Choglah,* an Israelitess:— Hoglah. See also 1031.

2296. חָגַר **châgar**, *khaw-gar´;* a prim. root; to *gird* on (as a belt, armor, etc.):— be able to put on, be afraid, appointed, gird, restrain, × on every side.

2297. חַד **chad**, *khad;* abridged from 259; *one:*— one.

2298. חַד **chad** (Chald.), *khad;* corresp. to 2297; as card. *one;* as art. *single;* as an ord. *first;* adv. *at once:*— a, first, one, together.

2299. חַד **chad**, *khad;* from 2300; *sharp:*— sharp.

2300. חָדַד **châdad**, *khaw-dad´;* a prim. root; to *be* (caus. *make*) *sharp* or (fig.) *severe:*— be fierce, sharpen.

2301. חֲדַד **Chădad**, *khad-ad´;* from 2300; *fierce; Chadad,* an Ishmaelite:— Hadad.

2302. חָדָה **châdâh**, *khaw-daw´;* a prim. root; to *rejoice:*— make glad, be joined, rejoice.

2303. חַדּוּד **chaddûwd**, *khad-dood´;* from 2300; a *point:*— sharp.

2304. חֶדְוָה **chedvâh**, *khed-vaw´;* from 2302; *rejoicing:*— gladness, joy.

2305. חֶדְוָה **chedvâh** (Chald.), *khed-vaw´;* corresp. to 2304:— joy.

2306. חֲדִי **chădîy** (Chald.), *khad-ee´;* corresp. to 2373; a *breast:*— breast.

2307. חָדִיד **Châdîyd**, *khaw-deed´;* from 2300; a *peak; Chadid,* a place in Pal.:— Hadid.

2308. חָדַל **châdal**, *khaw-dal´;* a prim. root; prop. to *be flabby,* i.e. (by impl.) *desist;* (fig.) *be lacking* or *idle:*— cease, end, fail, forbear, forsake, leave (off), let alone, rest, be unoccupied, want.

2309. חֶדֶל **chedel**, *kheh´-del;* from 2308; *rest,* i.e. the state of the *dead:*— world.

2310. חָדֵל **châdêl**, *khaw-dale´;* from 2308; *vacant,* i.e. *ceasing* or *destitute:*— he that forbeareth, frail, rejected.

2311. חַדְלַי **Chadlay**, *khad-lah´-ee;* from 2309; *idle; Chadlai,* an Isr.:— Hadlai.

2312. חֵדֶק **chêdeq**, *khay´-dek;* from an unused root mean. to *sting;* a *prickly* plant:— brier, thorn.

2313. חִדֶּקֶל **Chiddeqel**, *khid-deh´-kel;* prob.

Hebrew

of for. or.; the *Chiddekel* (or Tigris) river:— Hiddekel.

2314. חָדַר **châdar**, *khaw-dar´*; a prim. root; prop. to *inclose* (as a room), i.e. (by anal.) to *beset* (as in a siege):— enter a privy chamber.

2315. חֶדֶר **cheder**, *kheh´-der*; from 2314; an *apartment* (usually lit.):— [bed] inner) chamber, innermost (-ward) part, parlour, + south, × within.

2316. חֲדַר **Chădar**, *khad-ar´*; another form for 2315; *chamber; Chadar*, an Ishmaelite:— Hadar.

2317. חַדְרָךְ **Chadrâk**, *khad-rawk´*; of uncert. der.; *Chadrak*, a Syrian deity:— Hadrach.

2318. חָדַשׁ **châdash**, *khaw-dash´*; a prim. root; to *be new;* caus. to *rebuild:*— renew, repair.

2319. חָדָשׁ **châdâsh**, *khaw-dawsh´*; from 2318; *new:*— fresh, new thing.

2320. חֹדֶשׁ **chôdesh**, *kho´-desh*; from 2318; the *new* moon; by impl. a *month:*— month (-ly), new moon.

2321. חֹדֶשׁ **Chôdesh**, *kho´-desh;* the same as 2320; *Chodesh*, an Israelitess:— Hodesh.

2322. חֲדָשָׁה **Chădâshâh**, *khad-aw-shaw´*; fem. of 2319; *new; Chadashah*, a place in Pal.:— Hadashah.

2323. חֲדַת **chădath** (Chald.), *khad-ath´*; corresp. to 2319; *new:*— new.

2324. חֲוָא **chăvâ'** (Chald.), *khav-aw´*; corresp. to 2331; to *show:*— shew.

2325. חוּב **chûwb**, *khoob;* also

חָיַב **châyab**, *khaw-yab´*; a prim. root; prop. perh. to *tie*, i.e. (fig. and refl.) to *owe*, or (by impl.) to *forfeit:*— make endanger.

2326. חוֹב **chôwb**, *khobe;* from 2325; *debt:*— debtor.

2327. חוֹבָה **chôwbâh**, *kho-baw´;* fem. act. part. of 2247; *hiding* place; *Chobah*, a place in Syria:— Hobah.

2328. חוּג **chûwg**, *khoog;* a prim. root [comp. 2287]; to *describe* a *circle:*— compass.

2329. חוּג **chûwg**, *khoog;* from 2328; a *circle:*— circle, circuit, compass.

2330. חוּד **chûwd**, *khood;* a prim. root; prop. to *tie* a knot, i.e. (fig.) to *propound* a riddle:— put forth.

2331. חָוָה **châvâh**, *khaw-vah´*; a prim. root; [comp. 2324, 2421]; prop. to *live;* by impl. (intens.) to *declare* or *show:*— show.

2332. חַוָּה **Chavvâh**, *khav-vaw´*; caus. from 2331; *life-giver; Chavvah* (or Eve), the first woman:— Eve.

2333. חַוָּה **chavvâh**, *khav-vaw´;* prop. the same as 2332 (*life-giving*, i.e. *living-place*); by impl. an encampment or *village:*— (small) town.

2334. חַוֺּת יָעִיר **Chavvôwth Yâ'îyr**, *khav-vothe´ yaw-eer´*; from the plural of 2333 and a modif. of 3265; *hamlets of Jair*, a region of Pal.:— [Bashan-] Havoth-jair.

2335. חוֹזַי **Chôwzay**, *kho-zah´-ee;* from 2374; *visionary; Chozai*, an Isr.:— the seers.

2336. חוֹחַ **chôwach**, *kho´-akh;* from an unused root appar. mean. to *pierce; a thorn;* by anal. a *ring* for the nose:— bramble, thistle, thorn.

2337. חָוָח **châvâch**, *khaw-vawkh´;* perh. the same as 2336; a *dell* or *crevice* (as if *pierced* in the earth):— thicket.

2338. חוּט **chûwt** (Chald.), *khoot;* corresp. to the root of 2339, perhaps as a denom.; to *string* together, i.e. (fig.) to *repair:*— join.

2339. חוּט **chûwt**, *khoot;* from an unused root prob. mean. to *sew; a string;* by impl. a *measuring tape:*— cord, fillet, line, thread.

2340. חִוִּי **Chivvîy**, *khiv-vee´;* perh. from 2333; a *villager;* a *Chivvite*, one of the aboriginal tribes of Pal.:— Hivite.

2341. חֲוִילָה **Chăvîylâh**, *khav-ee-law´;* prob. from 2342; *circular; Chavilah*, the name of two or three eastern regions; also perh. of two men:— Havilah.

2342. חוּל **chûwl**, *khool;* or

חִיל **chîyl**, *kheel;* a prim. root; prop. to *twist* or *whirl* (in a circular or spiral manner), i.e. (spec.) to *dance*, to *writhe* in pain (espec. of parturition) or fear; fig. to *wait,* to *pervert:*— bear, (make to) bring forth, (make to) calve, dance, drive away, fall grievously (with pain), fear, form, great, grieve, (be) grievous, hope, look, make, be in pain, be much (sore) pained, rest, shake, shapen, (be) sorrow (-ful), stay, tarry, travail (with pain), tremble, trust, wait carefully (patiently), be wounded.

2343. חוּל **Chûwl**, *khool;* from 2342; a *circle; Chul*, a son of Aram; also the region settled by him:— Hul.

2344. חוֹל **chôwl**, *khole;* from 2342; *sand* (as *round* or whirling particles):— sand.

2345. חוּם **chûwm**, *khoom;* from an unused root mean. to *be warm*, i.e. (by impl.) *sunburnt* or *swarthy* (blackish):— brown.

2346. חוֹמָה **chôwmâh**, *kho-maw´;* fem. act. part. of an unused root appar. mean. to *join;* a *wall* of protection:— wall, walled.

2347. חוּס **chûwç**, *khoos;* a prim. root; prop. to *cover*, i.e. (fig.) to *compassionate:*— pity, regard, spare.

2348. חוֹף **chôwph**, *khofe;* from an unused root mean. to *cover;* a *cove* (as a *sheltered* bay):— coast [of the sea], haven, shore, [sea-] side.

2349. חוּפָם **Chûwphâm**, *khoo-fawm´*; from the same as 2348; *protection: Chupham*, an Isr.:— Hupham.

2350. חוּפָמִי **Chûwphâmîy**, *khoo-faw-mee´*; patron. from 2349; a *Chuphamite* or desc. of Chupham:— Huphamites.

2351. חוּץ **chûwts**, *khoots;* or (short.)

חֻץ **chûts**, *khoots;* (both forms fem. in the plur.) from an unused root mean. to *sever;* prop. *separate* by a wall, i.e. *outside, outdoors:*— abroad, field, forth, highway, more, out (-side, -ward), street, without.

חוֹק **chôwq**. See 2436.

חֻקֹק **Chûwqôq**. See 2712.

2352. חוּר **chûwr**, *khoor;* or (short.)

חֻר **chûr**, *khoor;* from an unused root prob. mean. to *bore;* the *crevice* of a serpent; the *cell* of a prison:— hole.

2353. חוּר **chûwr**, *khoor;* from 2357; *white* linen:— white.

2354. חוּר **Chûwr**, *khoor;* the same as 2353 or 2352; *Chur*, the name of four Isr. and one Midianite:— Hur.

2355. חוֹר **chôwr**, *khore;* the same as 2353; *white* linen:— network. Comp. 2715.

2356. חוֹר **chôwr**, *khore;* or (short.)

חֹר **chôr**, *khore;* the same as 2352; a *cavity, socket, den:*— cave, hole.

2357. חָוַר **châvar**, *khaw-var´;* a prim. root; to *blanch* (as with shame):— wax pale.

2358. חִוָּר **chivvâr** (Chald.), *khiv-vawr´;* from a root corresp. to 2357; *white:*— white.

חוֹרוֹן **Chôwrôwn**. See 1032.

חוֹרִי **chôwrîy**. See 2753.

2359. חוּרִי **Chûwrîy**, *khoo-ree´;* prob. from 2353; *linen*-worker; *Churi*, an Isr.:— Huri.

2360. חוּרַי **Chûwray**, *khoo-rah´ee;* prob. an orth. var. for 2359; *Churai*, an Isr.:— Hurai.

2361. חוּרָם **Chûwrâm**, *khoo-rawm´;* prob. from 2353; *whiteness*, i.e. noble; *Churam*, the name of an Isr. and two Syrians:— Huram. Comp. 2438.

2362. חַוְרָן **Chavrân**, *khav-rawn´;* appar. from 2357 (in the sense of 2352); *cavernous; Chavran*, a region E. of the Jordan:— Hauran.

2363. חוּשׁ **chûwsh**, *koosh;* a prim. root; to *hurry;* fig. to *be eager* with excitement or enjoyment:— (make) haste (-n), ready.

2364. חוּשָׁה **Chûwshâh**, *khoo-shaw´;* from 2363; *haste; Chushah*, an Isr.:— Hushah.

2365. חוּשַׁי **Chûwshay**, *khoo-shah´-ee;* from 2363; *hasty; Chushai*, an Isr.:— Hushai.

2366. חוּשִׁים **Chûwshîym**, *khoo-sheem´;* or

חֻשִׁם **Chûshîym**, *khoo-shem´;* or

2367. חוּשָׁם **Chûwshâm**, *khoo-sheem´;* plur. from 2363; *hasters; Chushim*, the name of three Isr.:— Hushim.

2367. חוּשָׁם **Chûwshâm**, *khoo-shawm´;* or

חֻשָׁם **Chûshâm**, *khoo-shawm´;* from 2363; *hastily; Chusham*, an Idumæan:— Husham.

2368. חוֹתָם **chôwthâm**, *kho-thawm´;* or

חֹתָם **chôthâm**, *kho-thawm´;* from 2856; a *signature*-ring:— seal, signet.

2369. חוֹתָם **Chôwthâm**, *kho-thawm´;* the same as 2368; *seal; Chotham*, the name of two Isr.:— Hotham, Hothan.

2370. חֲזָא **chăzâ'** (Chald.), *khaz-aw´;* or

חֲזָה **chăzâh** (Chald.), *khaz-aw´;* corresp. to 2372; to *gaze* upon; ment. to *dream, be usual* (i.e. *seem*):— behold, have [a dream], see, be wont.

2371. חֲזָאֵל **Chăzâ'êl**, *khaz-aw-ale´;* or

חֲזָהאֵל **Chăzâh'êl**, *khaz-aw-ale´;* from 2372 and 410; *God has seen; Chazaël*, a king of Syria:— Hazael.

2372. חָזָה **châzâh**, *khaw-zaw´;* a prim. root; to *gaze* at; ment. to *perceive, contemplate* (with pleasure); spec. to *have a vision of:*— behold, look, prophesy, provide, see.

2373. חָזֶה **châzeh**, *khaw-zeh´;* from 2372; the *breast* (as most *seen* in front):— breast.

2374. חֹזֶה **chôzeh**, *kho-zeh´;* act. part. of 2372; a *beholder* in vision; also a *compact* (as *looked upon* with approval):— agreement, prophet, see that, seer, [star-] gazer.

חֲזָהאֵל **Chăzâh'êl**. See 2371.

2375. חֲזוֹ **Chăzow**, *khaz-o´;* from 2372; *seer; Chazo*, a nephew of Abraham:— Hazo.

2376. חֵזֵו **chêzev** (Chald.), *khay´-zev;* from 2370; a *sight:*— look, vision.

2377. חָזוֹן **châzôwn**, *khaw-zone´;* from 2372; a *sight* (ment.), i.e. a *dream, revelation*, or *oracle:*— vision.

2378. חָזוֹת **châzôwth**, *khaw-zooth´;* from 2372; a *revelation:*— vision.

2379. חֲזוֹת **chăzôwth** (Chald.), *khaz-oth´;* from 2370; a *view:*— sight.

2380. חָזוּת **châzûwth**, *khaw-zooth´;* from 2372; a *look;* hence, (fig.) striking *appearance, revelation*, or (by impl.) *compact:*— agreement, notable (one), vision.

2381. חֲזִיאֵל **Chăzîy'êl**, *khaz-ee-ale´;* from 2372 and 410; *seen of God; Chaziel*, a Levite:— Haziel.

2382. חֲזָיָה **Chăzâyâh**, *khaz-aw-yaw´;* from 2372 and 3050; *Jah has seen; Chazajah*, an Isr.:— Hazaiah.

Hebrew

2383. חֶזְיוֹן **Chezyôwn**, *khez-yone´;* from 2372; *vision; Chezjon,* a Syrian:— Hezion.

2384. חִזָּיוֹן **chizzâyôwn**, *khiz-zaw-yone´;* from 2372; a *revelation,* espec. by *dream:*— vision.

2385. חָזִיז **châzîyz**, *khaw-zeez´;* from an unused root mean. to *glare; a flash* of lightning:— bright cloud, lightning.

2386. חֲזִיר **châzîyr**, *khaz-eer´;* from an unused root prob. mean. to *inclose; a hog* (perh. as *penned*):— boar, swine.

2387. חֵזִיר **Chêzîyr**, *khay-zeer´;* from the same as 2386; perh. *protected; Chezir,* the name of two Isr.:— Hezir.

2388. חָזַק **châzaq**, *khaw-zak´;* a prim. root; to *fasten* upon; hence, to *seize, be strong* (fig. *courageous,* caus. *strengthen, cure, help, repair, fortify*), *obstinate;* to *bind, restrain, conquer:*— aid, amend, × calker, catch, cleave, confirm, be constant, constrain, continue, be of good (take) courage (-ous, -ly), encourage (self), be established, fasten, force, fortify, make hard, harden, help, (lay) hold (fast), lean, maintain, play the man, mend, become (wax) mighty, prevail, be recovered, repair, retain, seize, be (wax) sore, strengthen (self), be stout, be (make, shew, wax) strong (-er), be sure, take (hold), be urgent, behave self valiantly, withstand.

2389. חָזָק **châzâq**, *khaw-zawk´;* from 2388; *strong* (usually in a bad sense, *hard, bold, violent*):— harder, hottest, + impudent, loud, mighty, sore, stiff [-hearted], strong (-er).

2390. חָזֵק **châzêq**, *khaw-zake´;* from 2388; *powerful:*— × wax louder, stronger.

2391. חֵזֶק **chêzeq**, *khay´-zek;* from 2388; *help:*— strength.

2392. חֹזֶק **chôzeq**, *kho´-zek;* from 2388; *power:*— strength.

2393. חֶזְקָה **chezqâh**, *khez-kaw´;* fem. of 2391; *prevailing power:*— strength (-en self), (was) strong.

2394. חָזְקָה **chozqâh**, *khoz-kaw´;* fem. of 2392; *vehemence* (usually in a bad sense):— force, mightily, repair, sharply.

2395. חִזְקִי **Chizqîy**, *khiz-kee´;* from 2388; *strong; Chizki,* an Isr.:— Hezeki.

2396. חִזְקִיָּה **Chizqîyâh**, *khiz-kee-yaw´;* or

חִזְקִיָּהוּ **Chizqîyâhûw**, *khiz-kee-yaw´-hoo;* also

יְחִזְקִיָּה **Yᵉchizqîyâh**, *yekh-iz-kee-yaw´;* or

יְחִזְקִיָּהוּ **Yᵉchizqîyâhûw**, *yekh-iz-kee-yaw´-hoo;* from 2388 and 3050; *strengthened of Jah; Chizkijah,* a king of Judah, also the name of two other Isr.:— Hezekiah, Hizkiah, Hizkijah. Comp. 3169.

2397. חָח **châch**, *khawkh;* once (Ezek. 29:4)

חָחִי **chăchîy**, *khakh-ee´;* from the same as 2336; a *ring* for the nose (or lips):— bracelet, chain, hook.

חָחִי **chăchîy**. See 2397.

2398. חָטָא **châṭâ´**, *khaw-taw´;* a prim. root; prop. to *miss;* hence, (fig. and gen.) to *sin;* by infer. to *forfeit, lack, expiate, repent,* (caus.) *lead astray, condemn:*— bear the blame, cleanse, commit [sin], by fault, harm he hath done, loss, miss, (make) offend (-er), offer for sin, purge, purify (self), make reconciliation, (cause, make) sin (-ful, -ness), trespass.

2399. חֵטְא **chêṭ´**, *khate;* from 2398; a *crime* or its *penalty:*— fault, × grievously, offence, (punishment of) sin.

2400. חַטָּא **chaṭṭâ´**, *khat-taw´;* intens. from 2398; a *criminal,* or one accounted *guilty:*— offender, sinful, sinner.

2401. חֲטָאָה **chăṭâ´âh**, *khat-aw-aw´;* fem. of 2399; an *offence,* or a *sacrifice* for it:— sin (offering), sinful.

2402. חֲטָאָה **chaṭṭâ´âh** (Chald.), *khat-taw-aw´;* corresp. to 2401; an *offence,* and the *penalty* or *sacrifice* for it:— sin (offering).

2403. חַטָּאָה **chaṭṭâ´âh**, *khat-taw-aw´;* or

חַטָּאת **chaṭṭâ´th**, *khat-tawth´;* from 2398; an *offence* (sometimes habitual *sinfulness*), and its penalty, occasion, sacrifice, or expiation; also (concr.) an *offender:*— punishment (of sin), purifying (-fication for sin), sin (-ner, offering).

2404. חָטַב **châṭab**, *khaw-tab´;* a prim. root; to *chop* or *carve* wood:— cut down, hew (-er), polish.

2405. חֲטֻבָה **chăṭûbâh**, *khat-oo-baw´;* fem. pass. part. of 2404; prop. a *carving;* hence, a *tapestry* (as figured):— carved.

2406. חִטָּה **chiṭṭâh**, *khit-taw´;* of uncert. der.; *wheat,* whether the grain or the plant:— wheat (-en).

2407. חַטּוּשׁ **Chaṭṭûwsh**, *khat-toosh´;* from an unused root of uncert. signif.; *Chattush,* the name of four or five Isr.:— Hattush.

2408. חֲטִי **chăṭîy** (Chald.), *khat-ee´;* from a root corresp. to 2398; an *offence:*— sin.

2409. חֲטָּיָא **chaṭṭâyâ´** (Chald.), *khat-taw-yaw´;* from the same as 2408; an *expiation:*— sin offering.

2410. חֲטִיטָא **Chăṭîyṭâ´**, *khat-ee-taw´;* from an unused root appar. mean. to *dig* out; *explorer; Chatita,* a temple porter:— Hatita.

2411. חַטִּיל **Chaṭṭîyl**, *khat-teel´;* from an unused root appar. mean. to *wave; fluctuating; Chattil,* one of "Solomon's servants":— Hattil.

2412. חֲטִיפָא **Chăṭîyphâ'**, *khat-ee-faw´;* from 2414; *robber; Chatipha,* one of the Nethinim:— Hatipha.

2413. חָטַם **châtam**, *khaw-tam´;* a prim. root; to *stop:*— refrain.

2414. חָטַף **châtaph**, *khaw-taf´;* a prim. root; to *clutch;* hence, to *seize* as a prisoner:— catch.

2415. חֹטֶר **chôṭer**, *kho´-ter;* from an unused root of uncert. signif.; a *twig:*— rod.

2416. חַי **chay**, *khah´-ee;* from 2421; *alive;* hence, *raw* (flesh); *fresh* (plant, water, year), *strong;* also (as noun, espec. in the fem. sing. and masc. plur.) *life* (or living thing), whether lit. or fig.:— + age, alive, appetite, (wild) beast, company, congregation, life (-time), live (-ly), living (creature, thing), maintenance, + merry, multitude, + (be) old, quick, raw, running, springing, troop.

2417. חַי **chay** (Chald.), *khah´-ee;* from 2418; *alive;* also (as noun in plur.) *life:*— life, that liveth, living.

2418. חֲיָא **chăyâ'** (Chald.), *khah-yaw´;* or

חֲיָה **chăyâh** (Chald.), *khah-yaw´;* corresp. to 2421; to *live:*— live, keep alive.

2419. חִיאֵל **Chîy'êl**, *khee-ale´;* from 2416 and 410; *living of God; Chiel,* an Isr.:— Hiel.

חִיב **châyab**. See 2325.

2420. חִידָה **chîydâh**, *khee-daw´;* from 2330; a *puzzle,* hence, a *trick, conundrum,* sententious *maxim:*— dark saying (sentence, speech), hard question, proverb, riddle.

2421. חָיָה **châyâh**, *khaw-yaw´;* a prim. root [comp. 2331, 2421]; to *live,* whether lit. or fig.; caus. to *revive:*— keep (leave, make) alive, × certainly, give (promise) life, (let, suffer to) live, nourish up, preserve (alive), quicken, recover, repair, restore (to life), revive, (× God) save (alive, life, lives), × surely, be whole.

2422. חָיֶה **châyeh**, *khaw-yeh´;* from 2421; *vigorous:*— lively.

2423. חֵיוָא **chêyvâ'** (Chald.), *khay-vaw´;* from 2418; an *animal:*— beast.

2424. חַיּוּת **chayûwth**, *khah-yooth´;* from 2421; *life:*— × living.

2425. חָיַי **châyay**, *khaw-yah´-ee;* a prim. root [comp. 2421]; to *live;* caus. to *revive:*— live, save life.

2426. חֵיל **chêyl**, *khale;* or (short.)

חֵל **chêl**, *khale;* a collat. form of 2428; an *army;* also (by anal.) an *intrenchment:*— army, bulwark, host, + poor, rampart, trench, wall.

חִיל **chîyl**. See 2342.

2427. חִיל **chîyl**, *kheel;* and (fem.)

חִילָה **chîylâh**, *khee-law´;* from 2342; a

throe (espec. of childbirth):— pain, pang, sorrow.

2428. חַיִל **chayil**, *khah´-yil;* from 2342; prob. a *force,* whether of men, means or other resources; an *army, wealth, virtue, valor, strength:*— able, activity, (+) army, band of men (soldiers), company, (great) forces, goods, host, might, power, riches, strength, strong, substance, train, (+) valiant (-ly), valour, virtuous (-ly), war, worthy (-ily).

2429. חַיִל **chayil** (Chald.), *khah´-yil;* corresp. to 2428; an *army,* or *strength:*— aloud, army, × most [mighty], power.

2430. חֵילָה **chêylâh**, *khay-law´;* fem. of 2428; an *intrenchment:*— bulwark.

2431. חֵילָם **Chêylâm**, *khay-lawm´;* or

חֵלָאם **Chêlâ'm**, *khay-lawm´;* from 2428; *fortress; Chelam,* a place E. of Pal.:— Helam.

2432. חִילֵן **Chîylên**, *khee-lane´;* from 2428; *fortress; Chilen,* a place in Pal.:— Hilen.

2433. חִין **chîyn**, *kheen;* another form for 2580; *beauty:*— comely.

2434. חַיִץ **chayits**, *khah´-yits;* another form for 2351; a *wall:*— wall.

2435. חִיצוֹן **chîytsôwn**, *khee-tsone´;* from 2434; prop. the (outer) *wall side;* hence, *exterior;* fig. *secular* (as opposed to sacred):— outer, outward, utter, without.

2436. חֵיק **chêyq**, *khake;* or

חֵק **chêq**, *khake;* and

חוֹק **chôwq**, *khoke;* from an unused root, appar. mean. to *inclose;* the *bosom* (lit. or fig.):— bosom, bottom, lap, midst, within.

2437. חִירָה **Chîyrâh**, *khee-raw´;* from 2357 in the sense of *splendor; Chirah,* an Adullamite:— Hirah.

2438. חִירָם **Chîyrâm**, *khee-rawm´;* or

חִירֹם **Chîyrôm**, *khee-rome´;* another form of 2361; *Chiram* or *Chirom,* the name of two Tyrians:— Hiram, Huram.

2439. חִישׁ **chîysh**, *kheesh;* another form of 2363; to *hurry:*— make haste.

2440. חִישׁ **chîysh**, *kheesh;* from 2439; prop. a *hurry;* hence, (adv.) *quickly:*— soon.

2441. חֵךְ **chêk**, *khake;* prob. from 2596 in the sense of *tasting;* prop. the *palate* or inside of the mouth; hence, the *mouth* itself (as the organ of speech, taste and kissing):— (roof of the) mouth, taste.

2442. חָכָה **châkâh**, *khaw-kaw´;* a prim. root [appar. akin to 2707 through the idea of *piercing*]; prop. to *adhere* to; hence, to *await:*— long, tarry, wait.

Hebrew

2443. חַכָּה **chakkâh**, *khak-kaw';* prob. from 2442; a *hook* (as *adhering*):— angle, hook.

2444. חֲכִילָה **Chakîylâh**, *khak-ee-law';* from the same as 2447; *dark; Chakilah*, a hill in Pal.:— Hachilah.

2445. חַכִּים **chakkîym** (Chald.), *khak-keem';* from a root corresp. to 2449; *wise*, i.e. a *Magian:*— wise.

2446. חֲכַלְיָה **Chăkalyâh**, *khak-al-yaw';* from the base of 2447 and 3050; *darkness* (of) *Jah; Chakaljah*, an Isr.:— Hachaliah.

2447. חַכְלִיל **chaklîyl**, *khak-leel';* by redupl. from an unused root appar. mean. to *be dark; darkly flashing* (only of the eyes); in a good sense, *brilliant* (as stimulated by wine):— red.

2448. חַכְלִלוּת **chaklîlûwth**, *khak-lee-looth';* from 2447; *flash* (of the eyes); in a bad sense, *blearedness:*— redness.

2449. חָכַם **châkam**, *khaw-kam';* a prim. root, to *be wise* (in mind, word or act):— × exceeding, teach wisdom, be (make self, shew self) wise, deal (never so) wisely, make wiser.

2450. חָכָם **châkâm**, *khaw-kawm';* from 2449; *wise*, (i.e. intelligent, skilful or artful):— cunning (man), subtil, (un-)wise ([hearted], man).

2451. חָכְמָה **chokmâh**, *khok-maw';* from 2449; *wisdom* (in a good sense):— skilful, wisdom, wisely, wit.

2452. חָכְמָה **chokmâh** (Chald.), *khok-maw';* corresp. to 2451; *wisdom:*— wisdom.

2453. חַכְמוֹנִי **Chakmôwnîy**, *khak-mo-nee';* from 2449; *skilful; Chakmoni*, an Isr.:— Hachmoni, Hachmonite.

2454. חָכְמוֹת **chokmôwth**, *khok-môth';* or

חַכְמוֹת **chakmôwth**, *khak-môth';* collat. forms of 2451; *wisdom:*— wisdom, every wise [woman].

חֵל **chêl**. See 2426.

2455. חֹל **chôl**, *khole;* from 2490; prop. *exposed;* hence, *profane:*— common, profane (place), unholy.

2456. חָלָא **châlâ'**, *khaw-law';* a prim. root [comp. 2470]; to *be sick:*— be diseased.

2457. חֶלְאָה **chel'âh**, *khel-aw';* from 2456; prop. *disease;* hence, *rust:*— scum.

2458. חֶלְאָה **Chel'âh**, *khel-aw';* the same as 2457; *Chelah*, an Israelitess:— Helah.

2459. חֶלֶב **cheleb**, *kheh'-leb;* or

חֵלֶב **chêleb**, *khay'-leb;* from an unused root mean. to *be fat; fat*, whether lit. or fig.; hence, the *richest* or *choice* part:— × best, fat (-ness), × finest, grease, marrow.

2460. חֵלֶב **Chêleb**, *khay'-leb;* the same as 2459; *fatness; Cheleb*, an Isr.:— Heleb.

2461. חָלָב **châlâb**, *khaw-lawb';* from the same

as 2459; *milk* (as the *richness* of kine):— + cheese, milk, sucking.

2462. חֶלְבָּה **Chelbâh**, *khel-baw';* fem. of 2459; *fertility: Chelbah*, a place in Pal.:— Helbah.

2463. חֶלְבּוֹן **Chelbôwn**, *khel-bone';* from 2459; *fruitful; Chelbon*, a place in Syria:— Helbon.

2464. חֶלְבְּנָה **chelbᵉnâh**, *khel-ben-aw';* from 2459; *galbanam*, an odorous gum (as if *fatty*):— galbanum.

2465. חֶלֶד **cheled**, *kheh'-led;* from an unused root appar. mean. to *glide* swiftly; *life* (as a *fleeting* portion of time); hence, the *world* (as *transient*):— age, short time, world.

2466. חֵלֶד **Chêled**, *khay'-led;* the same as 2465; *Cheled*, an Isr.:— Heled.

2467. חֹלֶד **chôled**, *kho'-led;* from the same as 2465; a *weasel* (from its *gliding* motion):— weasel.

2468. חֻלְדָּה **Chuldâh**, *khool-daw';* fem. of 2467; *Chuldah*, an Israelitess:— Huldah.

2469. חֶלְדַּי **Chelday**, *khel-dah'-ee;* from 2466; *worldliness; Cheldai*, the name of two Isr.:— Heldai.

2470. חָלָה **châlâh**, *khaw-law';* a prim. root [comp. 2342, 2470, 2490]; prop. to *be rubbed* or *worn;* hence, (fig.) to *be weak, sick, afflicted;* or (caus.) to *grieve, make sick;* also to *stroke* (in flattering), *entreat:*— beseech, (be) diseased, (put to) grief, be grieved, (be) grievous, infirmity, intreat, lay to, put to pain, × pray, make prayer, be (fall, make) sick, sore, be sorry, make suit (× supplication), woman in travail, be (become) weak, be wounded.

2471. חַלָּה **challâh**, *khal-law';* from 2490; a *cake* (as usually *punctured*):— cake.

2472. חֲלוֹם **chălôwm**, *khal-ome';* or (short.)

חֲלֹם **chălôm**, *khal-ome';* from 2492; a *dream:*— dream (-er).

2473. חֹלוֹן **Chôlôwn**, *kho-lone';* or (short.)

חֹלֹן **Chôlôn**, *kho-lone';* prob. from 2344; *sandy; Cholon*, the name of two places in Pal.:— Holon.

2474. חַלּוֹן **challôwn**, *khal-lone';* a *window* (as *perforated*):— window.

2475. חֲלוֹף **chălôwph**, *khal-ofe';* from 2498; prop. *surviving;* by impl. (collect.) *orphans:*— × destruction.

2476. חֲלוּשָׁה **chălûwshâh**, *khal-oo-shaw';* fem. pass. part. of 2522; *defeat:*— being overcome.

2477. חֲלַח **Chălach**, *khal-akh';* prob. of for. or.; *Chalach*, a region of Assyria:— Halah.

2478. חַלְחוּל **Chalchûwl,** *khal-khool´;* by re-dupl. from 2342; *contorted; Chalchul,* a place in Pal.:— Halhul.

2479. חַלְחָלָה **chalchâlâh,** *khal-khaw-law´;* fem. from the same as 2478; *writhing* (in childbirth); by impl. *terror:*— (great, much) pain.

2480. חָלַט **châlat,** *khaw-lat´;* a prim. root; to *snatch* at:— catch.

2481. חֲלִי **chălîy,** *khal-ee´;* from 2470; a *trinket* (as *polished*):— jewel, ornament.

2482. חֲלִי **Chălîy,** *khal-ee´;* the same as 2481; *Chali,* a place in Pal.:— Hali.

2483. חֳלִי **chŏlîy,** *khol-ee´;* from 2470; *malady, anxiety, calamity:*— disease, grief, (is) sick (-ness).

2484. חֶלְיָה **chelyâh,** *khel-yaw´;* fem. of 2481; a *trinket:*— jewel.

2485. חָלִיל **châlîyl,** *khaw-leel´;* from 2490; a *flute* (as *perforated*):— pipe.

2486. חָלִילָה **châlîylâh,** *khaw-lee´-law;* or

חָלִלָה **châlîlâh,** *khaw-lee´-law;* a directive from 2490; lit. *for a profaned* thing; used (interj.) *far be it!:*— be far, (× God) forbid.

2487. חֲלִיפָה **chălîyphâh,** *khal-ee-faw´;* from 2498; *alternation:*— change, course.

2488. חֲלִיצָה **chălîytsâh,** *khal-ee-tsaw´;* from 2503; *spoil:*— armour.

2489. חֵלְכָא **chêlᵉkâ',** *khay-lek-aw´;* or

חֵלְכָה **chêlᵉkâh,** *khay-lek-aw´;* appar. from an unused root prob. mean. to *be dark* or (fig.) *unhappy;* a *wretch,* i.e. *unfortunate:*— poor.

2490. חָלַל **châlal,** *khaw-lal´;* a prim. root [comp. 2470]; prop. to *bore,* i.e. (by impl.) to *wound,* to *dissolve;* fig. to *profane* (a person, place or thing), to *break* (one's word), to *begin* (as if by an "opening wedge"); denom. (from 2485) to *play* (the flute):— begin (× men began), defile, × break, defile, × eat (as common things), × first, × gather the grape thereof, × take inheritance, pipe, player on instruments, pollute, (cast as) profane (self), prostitute, slay (slain), sorrow, stain, wound.

2491. חָלָל **châlâl,** *khaw-lawl´;* from 2490; *pierced* (espec. to death); fig. *polluted:*— kill, profane, slain (man), × slew, (deadly) wounded.

חֲלִלָה **châlîlâh.** See 2486.

2492. חָלַם **châlam,** *khaw-lam´;* a prim. root; prop. to *bind* firmly, i.e. (by impl.) to *be* (caus. to *make*) *plump;* also (through the fig. sense of *dumbness*) to *dream:*— (cause to) dream (-er), be in good liking, recover.

2493. חֵלֶם **chêlem** (Chald.), *khay´-lem;* from a root corresp. to 2492; a *dream:*— dream.

2494. חֵלֶם **Chêlem,** *khay´lem;* from 2492; a *dream; Chelem,* an Isr.:— Helem. Comp. 2469.

2495. חַלָּמוּת **challâmûwth,** *khal-law-mooth´;* from 2492 (in the sense of *insipidity*); prob. *purslain:*— egg.

2496. חַלָּמִישׁ **challâmîysh,** *khal-law-meesh´;* prob. from 2492 (in the sense of *hardness*); *flint:*— flint (-y), rock.

2497. חֵלֹן **Chêlôn,** *khay-lone´;* from 2428; *strong; Chelon,* an Isr.:— Helon.

2498. חָלַף **châlaph,** *khaw-laf´;* a prim. root; prop. to *slide* by, i.e. (by impl.) to *hasten away, pass* on, *spring* up, *pierce* or *change:*— abolish, alter, change, cut off, go on forward, grow up, be over, pass (away, on, through), renew, sprout, strike through.

2499. חֲלַף **chălaph** (Chald.), *khal-af´;* corresp. to 2498; to *pass* on (of time):— pass.

2500. חֵלֶף **chêleph,** *khay´-lef;* from 2498; prop. *exchange;* hence, (as prep.) *instead* of:— × for.

2501. חֵלֶף **Cheleph,** *kheh´-lef;* the same as 2500; *change; Cheleph,* a place in Pal.:— Heleph.

2502. חָלַץ **châlats,** *khaw-lats´;* a prim. root; to *pull* off; hence, (intens.) to *strip,* (reflex.) to *depart;* by impl. to *deliver, equip* (for fight); *present, strengthen:*— arm (self), (go, ready) armed (× man, soldier), deliver, draw out, make fat, loose, (ready) prepared, put off, take away, withdraw self.

2503. חֶלֶץ **Chelets,** *kheh´-lets;* or

חֵלֶץ **Chêlets,** *khay´-lets;* from 2502; perh. *strength; Chelets,* the name of two Isr.:— Helez.

2504. חָלָץ **châlâts,** *khaw-lawts´;* from 2502 (in the sense of *strength*); only in the dual; the *loins* (as the seat of vigor):— loins, reins.

2505. חָלַק **châlaq,** *khaw-lak´;* a prim. root; to *be smooth* (fig.); by impl. (as smooth stones were used for *lots*) to *apportion* or *separate:*— deal, distribute, divide, flatter, give, (have, im-) part (-ner), take away a portion, receive, separate self, (be) smooth (-er).

2506. חֵלֶק **chêleq,** *khay´-lek;* from 2505; prop. *smoothness* (of the tongue); also an *allotment:*— flattery, inheritance, part, × partake, portion.

2507. חֵלֶק **Chêleq,** *khay´-lek;* the same as 2506; *portion; Chelek,* an Isr.:— Helek.

2508. חֲלָק **chălâq** (Chald.), *khal-awk´;* from a root corresp. to 2505; a *part:*— portion.

2509. חָלָק **châlâq,** *khaw-lawk´;* from 2505;

smooth (espec. of tongue):— flattering, smooth.

2510. חָלָק **Châlâq,** *khaw-lawk´;* the same as 2509; *bare; Chalak,* a mountain of Idumæa:— Halak.

2511. חַלָּק **challâq,** *khal-lawk´;* from 2505; *smooth:*— smooth.

2512. חַלּוּק **challûq,** *khal-look´;* from 2505; *smooth:*— smooth.

2513. חֶלְקָה **chelqâh,** *khel-kaw´;* fem. of 2506; prop. *smoothness;* fig. *flattery;* also an *allotment:*— field, flattering (-ry), ground, parcel, part, piece of land [ground], plat, portion, slippery place, smooth (thing).

2514. חֲלַקָּה **chălaqqâh,** *khal-ak-kaw´;* fem. from 2505; *flattery:*— flattery.

2515. חֲלֻקָּה **chăluqqâh,** *khal-ook-kaw´;* fem. of 2512; a *distribution:*— division.

2516. חֶלְקִי **Chelqîy,** *khel-kee´;* patron. from 2507; a *Chelkite* or desc. of Chelek:— Helkites.

2517. חֶלְקַי **Chelqay,** *khel-kah´ee;* from 2505; *apportioned; Chelkai,* an Isr.:— Helkai.

2518. חִלְקִיָּה **Chilqîyâh,** *khil-kee-yaw´;* or

חִלְקִיָּהוּ **Chilqîyâhûw,** *khil-kee-yaw´-hoo;* from 2506 and 3050; *portion* (of) *Jah; Chilhijah,* the name of eight Isr.:— Hilkiah.

2519. חֲלַקְלַקָּה **chălaqlaqqâh,** *khal-ak-lak-kaw´;* by redupl. from 2505; prop. something *very smooth;* i.e. a *treacherous* spot; fig. *blandishment:*— flattery, slippery.

2520. חֶלְקַת **Chelqath,** *khel-kath´;* a form of 2513; *smoothness; Chelkath,* a place in Pal.:— Helkath.

2521. חֶלְקַת הַצֻּרִים **Chelqath hats-Tsûrîym,** *khel-kath´ hats-tsoo-reem´;* from 2520 and the plur. of 6697, with the art. ins.; *smoothness of the rocks; Chelkath Hats-tsurim,* a place in Pal.:— Helkath-hazzurim.

2522. חָלַשׁ **châlash,** *khaw-lash´;* a prim. root; to *prostrate;* by impl. to *overthrow, decay:*— discomfit, waste away, weaken.

2523. חַלָּשׁ **challâsh,** *khal-lawsh´;* from 2522; *frail:*— weak.

2524. חָם **châm,** *khawm;* from the same as 2346; a *father-in-law* (as in *affinity*):— father in law.

2525. חָם **châm,** *khawm;* from 2552; *hot:*— hot, warm.

2526. חָם **Châm,** *khawm;* the same as 2525; *hot* (from the tropical habitat); *Cham,* a son of Noah; also (as a patron.) his desc. or their country:— Ham.

2527. חֹם **chôm,** *khome;* from 2552; *heat:*— heat, to be hot (warm).

2528. חֱמָא **chĕmâ'** (Chald.), *khem-aw´;* or

חֱמָה **chĕmâh** (Chald.), *kham-aw´;* corresp. to 2534; *anger:*— fury.

חֵמָא **chêmâ'.** See 2534.

2529. חֶמְאָה **chem'âh,** *khem-aw´;* or (short.)

חֵמָה **chêmâh,** *khay-maw´;* from the same root as 2346; *curdled milk* or *cheese:*— butter.

2530. חָמַד **châmad,** *khaw-mad´;* a prim. root; to *delight* in:— beauty, greatly beloved, covet, delectable thing, (× great) delight, desire, goodly, lust, (be) pleasant (thing), precious (thing).

2531. חֶמֶד **chemed,** *kheh´-med;* from 2530; *delight:*— desirable, pleasant.

2532. חֶמְדָּה **chemdâh,** *khem-daw´;* fem. of 2531; *delight:*— desire, goodly, pleasant, precious.

2533. חֶמְדָּן **Chemdân,** *khem-dawn´;* from 2531; *pleasant; Chemdan,* an Idumæan:— Hemdan.

2534. חֵמָה **chêmâh,** *khay-maw´;* or (Dan. 11:44)

חֵמָא **chêmâ',** *khay-maw´;* from 3179; *heat;* fig. *anger, poison* (from its *fever*):— anger, bottles, hot displeasure, furious (-ly, -ry), heat, indignation, poison, rage, wrath (-ful). See 2529.

2535. חַמָּה **chammâh,** *kham-maw´;* from 2525; *heat;* by impl. the *sun:*— heat, sun.

2536. חַמּוּאֵל **Chammûw'êl,** *kham-moo-ale´;* from 2535 and 410; *anger of God; Chammuel,* an Isr.:— Hamuel.

2537. חֲמוּטַל **Chămûwţal,** *kham-oo-tal´;* or

חֲמִיטַל **Chămîyţal,** *kham-ee-tal´;* from 2524 and 2919; *father-in-law of dew; Chamutal* or *Chamital,* an Israelitess:— Hamutal.

2538. חָמוּל **Châmûwl,** *khaw-mool´;* from 2550; *pitied; Chamul,* an Isr.:— Hamul.

2539. חָמוּלִי **Châmûwlîy,** *khaw-moo-lee´;* patron. from 2538: a *Chamulite* (collect.) or desc. of Chamul:— Hamulites.

2540. חַמּוֹן **Chammôwn,** *kham-mone´;* from 2552; *warm* spring; *Chammon,* the name of two places in Pal.:— Hammon.

2541. חָמוֹץ **châmôwts,** *khaw-motse´;* from 2556; prop. *violent;* by impl. a *robber:*— oppressed.

2542. חַמּוּק **chammûwq,** *kham-mook´;* from 2559; a *wrapping,* i.e. *drawers:*— joints.

2543. חֲמוֹר **chămôwr,** *kham-ore´;* or (short.)

חֲמֹר **chămôr,** *kham-ore´;* from 2560; a *male ass* (from its dun *red*):— (he) ass.

2544. חֲמוֹר **Chămôwr,** *kham-ore´;* the same as 2543; *ass; Chamor,* a Canaanite:— Hamor.

2545. חֲמוֹת **chămôwth**, *kham-ōth´;* or (short.)

חֲמֹת **chămôth**, *kham-ōth´;* fem. of 2524; a *mother-in-law:*— mother in law.

2546. חֹמֶט **chômeṭ**, *kho´-met;* from an unused root prob. mean. to *lie low;* a *lizard* (as *creeping*):— snail.

2547. חֻמְטָה **Chumṭâh**, *khoom-taw´;* fem. of 2546; *low; Chumtah,* a place in Pal.:— Humtah.

2548. חָמִיץ **châmîyts**, *khaw-meets´;* from 2556; *seasoned,* i.e. *salt* provender:— clean.

2549. חֲמִישִׁי **chămîyshîy**, *kham-ee-shee´;* or

חֲמִשִּׁי **chamishshîy**, *kham-ish-shee´;* ord. from 2568; *fifth;* also a *fifth:*— fifth (part).

2550. חָמַל **châmal**, *khaw-mal´;* a prim. root; to *commiserate;* by impl. to *spare:*— have compassion, (have) pity, spare.

2551. חֶמְלָה **chemlâh**, *khem-law´;* from 2550; *commiseration:*— merciful, pity.

2552. חָמַם **châmam**, *khaw-mam´;* a prim. root; to *be hot* (lit. or fig.):— enflame self, get (have) heat, be (wax) hot, (be, wax) warm (self, at).

2553. חַמָּן **chammân**, *kham-mawn´;* from 2535; a *sun*-pillar:— idol, image.

2554. חָמַס **châmaç**, *khaw-mas´;* a prim. root; to *be violent;* by impl. to *maltreat:*— make bare, shake off, violate, do violence, take away violently, wrong, imagine wrongfully.

2555. חָמָס **châmâç**, *khaw-mawce´;* from 2554; *violence;* by impl. *wrong;* by meton. unjust *gain:*— cruel (-ty), damage, false, injustice, × oppressor, unrighteous, violence (against, done), violent (dealing), wrong.

2556. חָמֵץ **châmêts**, *khaw-mates´;* a prim. root; to *be pungent;* i.e. in taste (*sour,* i.e. lit. *fermented,* or fig. *harsh*), in color (*dazzling*):— cruel (man), dyed, be grieved, leavened.

2557. חָמֵץ **châmêts**, *khaw-mates´;* from 2556; *ferment,* (fig.) *extortion:*— leaven, leavened (bread).

2558. חֹמֶץ **chômets**, *kho´-mets;* from 2556; *vinegar:*— vinegar.

2559. חָמַק **châmaq**, *khaw-mak´;* a prim. root; prop. to *enwrap;* hence, to *depart* (i.e. turn about):— go about, withdraw self.

2560. חָמַר **châmar**, *khaw-mar´;* a prim. root; prop. to *boil* up; hence, to *ferment* (with scum); to *glow* (with redness); as denom. (from 2564) to *smear* with pitch:— daub, befoul, be red, trouble.

2561. חֶמֶר **chemer**, *kheh´-mer;* from 2560; *wine* (as *fermenting*):— × pure, red wine.

2562. חֲמַר **chămar** (Chald.), *kham-ar´;* corresp. to 2561; *wine:*— wine.

חֲמֹר **chămôr**. See 2543.

2563. חֹמֶר **chômer**, *kho´mer;* from 2560; prop. a *bubbling* up, i.e. of water, a *wave;* of earth, *mire* or *clay* (cement); also a *heap;* hence, a *chomer* or dry measure:— clay, heap, homer, mire, motion, mortar.

2564. חֵמָר **chêmâr**, *khay-mawr´;* from 2560; *bitumen* (as *rising* to the surface):— slime (-pit).

2565. חֲמֹרָה **chămôrâh**, *kham-o-raw´;* from 2560 [comp. 2563]; a *heap:*— heap.

2566. חַמְרָן **Chamrân**, *kham-rawn´;* from 2560; *red; Chamran,* an Idumæan:— Amran.

2567. חָמַשׁ **châmash**, *khaw-mash´;* a denom. from 2568; to *tax a fifth:*— take up the fifth part.

2568. חָמֵשׁ **châmêsh**, *khaw-maysh´;* masc.

חֲמִשָּׁה **chămishshâh**, *kham-ish-shaw´;* a prim. numeral; *five:*— fif[-teen], fifth, five (× apiece).

2569. חֹמֶשׁ **chômesh**, *kho´-mesh;* from 2567; a *fifth* tax:— fifth part.

2570. חֹמֶשׁ **chômesh**, *kho´-mesh;* from an unused root prob. mean. to *be stout;* the *abdomen* (as *obese*):— fifth [rib].

2571. חָמֻשׁ **châmûsh**, *khaw-moosh´;* pass. part. of the same as 2570; *staunch,* i.e. able-bodied *soldiers:*— armed (men), harnessed.

חֲמִשָּׁה **chămishshâh**. See 2568.

חֲמִישִׁי **chămishshîy**. See 2549.

2572. חֲמִשִּׁים **chămishshîym**, *kham-ish-sheem´;* multiple of 2568; *fifty:*— fifty.

2573. חֵמֶת **chêmeth**, *khay´-meth;* from the same as 2346; a skin *bottle* (as *tied* up):— bottle.

2574. חֲמָת **Chămâth**, *kham-awth´;* from the same as 2346; *walled; Chamath,* a place in Syria:— Hamath, Hemath.

חֲמֹת **chămôth**. See 2545.

2575. חַמַּת **Chammath**, *kham-math´;* a var. for the first part of 2576; *hot* springs; *Chammath,* a place in Pal.:— Hammath.

2576. חַמֹּת דֹּאר **Chammôth Dô'r**, *kham-moth´ dore;* from the plur. of 2535 and 1756; *hot* springs *of Dor; Chammath-Dor,* a place in Pal.:— Hamath-Dor.

2577. חֲמָתִי **Chămâthîy**, *kham-aw-thee´;* patrial from 2574; a *Chamathite* or native of *Chamath:*— Hamathite.

2578. חֲמָת צוֹבָה **Chămath Tsôwbâh**, *kham-ath´ tso-baw´;* from 2574 and 6678; *Chamath of Tsobah; Chamath-Tsobah;* prob. the same as 2574:— Hamath-Zobah.

2579. חֲמָת רַבָּה **Chămath Rabbâh**, *kham-ath´ rab-baw´;* from 2574 and 7237;

Chamath of Rabbah; Chamath-Rabbah, prob. the same as 2574.

2580. חֵן **chên**, *khane;* from 2603; *graciousness,* i.e. subj. (*kindness, favor*) or obj. (*beauty*):— favour, grace (-ious), pleasant, precious, [well-] favoured.

2581. חֵן **Chên**, *khane;* the same as 2580; *grace; Chen,* a fig. name for an Isr.:— Hen.

2582. חֲנָדָד **Chênâdâd**, *khay-naw-dawd';* prob. from 2580 and 1908; *favor of Hadad; Chenadad,* an Isr.:— Henadad.

2583. חָנָה **chânâh**, *khaw-naw';* a prim. root [comp. 2603]; prop. to *incline;* by impl. to *decline* (of the slanting rays of evening); spec. to *pitch* a tent; gen. to *encamp* (for abode or siege):— abide (in tents), camp, dwell, encamp, grow to an end, lie, pitch (tent), rest in tent.

2584. חַנָּה **Channâh**, *khan-naw';* from 2603; *favored; Channah,* an Israelitess:— Hannah.

2585. חֲנוֹךְ **Chǎnôwk**, *khan-oke';* from 2596; *initiated; Chanok,* an antediluvian patriarch:— Enoch.

2586. חָנוּן **Chânûwn**, *khaw-noon';* from 2603; *favored; Chanun,* the name of an Ammonite and of two Isr.:— Hanun.

2587. חַנּוּן **channûwn**, *khan-noon';* from 2603; *gracious:*— gracious.

2588. חָנוּת **chânûwth**, *khaw-nooth';* from 2583; prop. a *vault* or *cell* (with an arch); by impl. a *prison:*— cabin.

2589. חֲנוֹת **channôwth**, *khan-nōth';* from 2603 (in the sense of *prayer*); *supplication:*— be gracious, intreated.

2590. חָנַט **chânaṭ**, *khaw-nat';* a prim. root; to *spice;* by impl. to *embalm;* also to *ripen:*— embalm, put forth.

2591. חִנְטָא **chinṭâ'** (Chald.), *khint-taw';* corresp. to 2406; *wheat:*— wheat.

2592. חַנִּיאֵל **Chǎnnîy'êl**, *khan-nee-ale';* from 2603 and 410; *favor of God; Channiel,* the name of two Isr.:— Hanniel.

2593. חָנִיךְ **chânîyk**, *kaw-neek';* from 2596; *initiated;* i.e. *practiced:*— trained.

2594. חֲנִינָה **chǎnîynâh**, *khan-ee-naw';* from 2603; *graciousness:*— favour.

2595. חֲנִית **chǎnîyth**, *khan-eeth';* from 2583; a *lance* (for *thrusting,* like *pitching* a tent):— javelin, spear.

2596. חָנַךְ **chânak**, *khaw-nak';* a prim. root; prop. to *narrow* (comp. 2614); fig. to *initiate* or *discipline:*— dedicate, train up.

2597. חֲנֻכָּא **chǎnukkâ'** (Chald.), *chan-ook-kaw';* corresp. to 2598; *consecration:*— dedication.

2598. חֲנֻכָּה **chǎnukkâh**, *khan-ook-kaw';* from

2596; *initiation,* i.e. *consecration:*— dedicating (-tion).

2599. חֲנֹכִי **Chǎnôkîy**, *khan-o-kee';* patron. from 2585; a *Chanokite* (collect.) or desc. of Chanok:— Hanochites.

2600. חִנָּם **chinnâm**, *khin-nawm';* from 2580; *gratis,* i.e. devoid of cost, reason or advantage:— without a cause (cost, wages), causeless, to cost nothing, free (-ly), innocent, for nothing (nought), in vain.

2601. חֲנַמְאֵל **Chǎnam'êl**, *khan-am-ale';* prob. by orth. var. for 2606; *Chanamel,* an Isr.:— Hanameel.

2602. חֲנָמָל **chǎnâmâl**, *khan-aw-mawl';* of uncert. der.; perh. the *aphis* or plantlouse:— frost.

2603. חָנַן **chânan**, *khaw-nan';* a prim. root [comp. 2583]; prop. to *bend* or *stoop* in kindness to an inferior; to *favor, bestow;* caus. to *implore* (i.e. move to favor by petition):— beseech, × fair, (be, find, shew) favour (-able), be (deal, give, grant (gracious (-ly), intreat, (be) merciful, have (shew) mercy (on, upon), have pity upon, pray, make supplication, × very.

2604. חֲנַן **chǎnan** (Chald.), *khan-an';* corresp. to 2603; to *favor* or (caus.) to *entreat:*— shew mercy, make supplication.

2605. חָנָן **Chânân**, *khaw-nawn';* from 2603; *favor; Chanan,* the name of seven Isr.:— Canan.

2606. חֲנַנְאֵל **Chǎnan'êl**, *khan-an-ale';* from 2603 and 410; *God has favored; Chananel,* prob. an Isr., from whom a tower of Jerusalem was named:— Hananeel.

2607. חֲנָנִי **Chǎnânîy**, *khan-aw-nee';* from 2603; *gracious; Chanani,* the name of six Isr.:— Hanani.

2608. חֲנַנְיָה **Chǎnanyâh**, *khan-an-yaw';* or

חֲנַנְיָהוּ **Chǎnanyâhûw**, *khan-an-yaw'-hoo;* from 2603 and 3050; *Jah has favored; Chananjah,* the name of thirteen Isr.:— Hananiah.

2609. חָנֵס **Chânêç**, *khaw-nace';* of Eg. der.; *Chanes,* a place in Egypt:— Hanes.

2610. חָנֵף **chânêph**, *khaw-nafe';* a prim. root; to *soil,* espec. in a mor. sense:— corrupt, defile, × greatly, pollute, profane.

2611. חָנֵף **chânêph**, *khaw-nafe';* from 2610; *soiled* (i.e. with sin), *impious:*— hypocrite (-ical).

2612. חֹנֶף **chôneph**, *kho'-nef;* from 2610; moral *filth,* i.e. *wickedness:*— hypocrisy.

2613. חֲנֻפָה **chǎnûphâh**, *khan-oo-faw';* fem. from 2610; *impiety:*— profaneness.

2614. חָנַק **chânaq**, *khaw-nak';* a prim. root [comp. 2596]; to *be narrow;* by impl. to *throttle*, or (reflex.) to *choke* oneself to death (by a rope):— hang self, strangle.

2615. חַנָּתֹן **Channâthôn**, *khan-naw-thone´;* prob. from 2603; *favored; Channathon*, a place in Pal.:— Hannathon.

2616. חָסַד **châcad**, *khaw-sad´;* a prim. root; prop. perh. to *bow* (the neck only [comp. 2603] in courtesy to an equal), i.e. to *be kind;* also (by euphem. [comp. 1288], but rarely) to *reprove:*— shew self merciful, put to shame.

2617. חֶסֶד **checed**, *kheh´-sed;* from 2616; *kindness;* by impl. (toward God) *piety;* rarely (by opposition) *reproof,* or (subj.) *beauty:*— favour, good deed (-liness, -ness), kindly, (loving-) kindness, merciful (kindness), mercy, pity, reproach, wicked thing.

2618. חֶסֶד **Checed**, *kheh´-sed;* the same as 2617: *favor; Chesed,* an Isr.:— Hesed.

2619. חֲסַדְיָה **Chăcadyâh**, *khas-ad-yaw´;* from 2617 and 3050; *Jah has favored; Chasadjâh,* an Isr.:— Hasadiah.

2620. חָסָה **châçâh**, *khaw-saw´;* a prim. root; to *flee* for protection [comp. 982]; fig. to *confide* in:— have hope, make refuge, (put) trust.

2621. חֹסָה **Chôçâh**, *kho-saw´;* from 2620; *hopeful; Chosah,* an Isr.; also a place in Pal.:— Hosah.

2622. חָסוּת **châçûwth**, *khaw-sooth´;* from 2620; *confidence:*— trust.

2623. חָסִיד **châçîyd**, *khaw-seed´;* from 2616; prop. *kind,* i.e. (relig.) *pious* (a saint):— godly (man), good, holy (one), merciful, saint, [un-] godly.

2624. חֲסִידָה **chăçîydâh**, *khas-ee-daw´;* fem. of 2623; the *kind* (maternal) bird, i.e. a *stork:*— × feather, stork.

2625. חָסִיל **châçîyl**, *khaw-seel´;* from 2628; the *ravager,* i.e. a *locust:*— caterpillar.

2626. חָסִין **chăçîyn**, *khas-een´;* from 2630; prop. *firm,* i.e. (by impl.) *mighty:*— strong.

2627. חַסִּיר **chaççîyr** (Chald.), *khas-seer´;* from a root corresp. to 2637; *deficient:*— wanting.

2628. חָסַל **châçal**, *khaw-sal´;* a prim. root; to *eat* off:— consume.

2629. חָסַם **châçam**, *khaw-sam´;* a prim. root; to *muzzle;* by anal. to *stop* the nose:— muzzle, stop.

2630. חָסַן **châçan**, *khaw-san´;* a prim. root; prop. to (*be*) *compact;* by impl. to *hoard:*— lay up.

2631. חֲסַן **chăçan** (Chald.), *khas-an´;* corresp. to 2630; to *hold* in occupancy:— possess.

2632. חֵסֶן **chêçen** (Chald.), *khay´-sen;* from 2631; *strength:*— power.

2633. חֹסֶן **chôçen**, *kho´-sen;* from 2630; *wealth:*— riches, strength, treasure.

2634. חָסֹן **châçôn**, *khaw-sone´;* from 2630; *powerful:*— strong.

2635. חֲסַף **chăçaph** (Chald.), *khas-af´;* from a root corresp. to that of 2636; a *clod:*— clay.

2636. חַסְפַּס **chaçpaç**, *khas-pas´;* redupl. from an unused root mean. appar. to *peel;* a *shred* or *scale:*— round thing.

2637. חָסֵר **châçêr**, *khaw-sare´;* a prim. root; to *lack;* by impl. to *fail, want, lessen:*— be abated, bereave, decrease, (cause to) fail, (have) lack, make lower, want.

2638. חָסֵר **châçêr**, *khaw-sare´;* from 2637; *lacking;* hence, *without:*— destitute, fail, lack, have need, void, want.

2639. חֶסֶר **checer**, *kheh´-ler;* from 2637; *lack;* hence, *destitution:*— poverty, want.

2640. חֹסֶר **chôçer**, *kho´-ser;* from 2637; *poverty:*— in want of.

2641. חַסְרָה **Chaçrâh**, *khas-raw´;* from 2637; *want; Chasrah,* an Isr.:— Hasrah.

2642. חֶסְרוֹן **checrôwn**, *khes-rone´;* from 2637; *deficiency:*— wanting.

2643. חַף **chaph**, *khaf;* from 2653 (in the mor. sense of *covered* from soil); *pure:*— innocent.

2644. חָפָא **châphâ'**, *khaw-faw´;* an orth. var. of 2645; prop. to *cover,* i.e. (in a sinister sense) to *act covertly:*— do secretly.

2645. חָפָה **châphâh**, *khaw-faw´;* a prim. root (comp. 2644, 2653); to *cover;* by impl. to *veil,* to *incase, protect:*— ceil, cover, overlay.

2646. חֻפָּה **chuppâh**, *khoop-paw´;* from 2645; a *canopy:*— chamber, closet, defence.

2647. חֻפָּה **Chuppâh**, *khoop-paw´;* the same as 2646; *Chuppah,* an Isr.:— Huppah.

2648. חָפַז **châphaz**, *khaw-faz´;* a prim. root; prop. to *start* up suddenly, i.e. (by impl.) to *hasten* away, to *fear:*— (make) haste (away), tremble.

2649. חִפָּזוֹן **chippâzôwn**, *khip-paw-zone´;* from 2648; *hasty flight:*— haste.

2650. חֻפִּים **Chuppîym**, *khoop-peem´;* plur. of 2646 [comp. 2349]; *Chuppim,* an Isr.:— Huppim.

2651. חֹפֶן **chôphen**, *kho´-fen;* from an unused root of uncert. signif.; a *fist* (only in the dual):— fists, (both) hands, hand (-ful).

2652. חָפְנִי **Chophnîy**, *khof-nee´;* from 2651; perh. *pugilist; Chophni,* an Isr.:— Hophni.

2653. חָפַף **chôphaph**, *khaw-faf´;* a prim. root (comp. 2645, 3182); to *cover* (in protection):— cover.

2654. חָפֵץ **châphêts**, *khaw-fates´;* a prim. root; prop. to *incline* to; by impl. (lit. but rarely) to *bend;* fig. to *be pleased* with, *desire:*— × any at all, (have, take) delight, desire, favour, like, move, be (well) pleased, have pleasure, will, would.

2655. חָפֵץ **châphêts**, *khaw-fates´*; from 2654; *pleased* with:— delight in, desire, favour, please, have pleasure, whosoever would, willing, wish.

2656. חֵפֶץ **chêphets**, *khay´-fets*; from 2654; *pleasure;* hence, (abstr.) *desire;* concr. a *valuable* thing; hence, (by extens.) a *matter* (as something in mind):— acceptable, delight (-some), desire, things desired, matter, pleasant (-ure), purpose, willingly.

2657. חֶפְצִי בָהּ **Chephtsiy bâhh**, *khef-tsee´-baw;* from 2656 with suffixes; *my delight* (is) *in her; Cheptsi-bah,* a fanciful name for Pal.:— Hephzi-bah.

2658. חָפַר **châphar**, *khaw-far´;* a prim. root; prop. to *pry* into; by impl. to *delve,* to *explore:*— dig, paw, search out, seek.

2659. חָפֵר **châphêr**, *khaw-fare´;* a prim. root [perhaps rath. the same as 2658 through the idea of *detection*]: to *blush;* fig. to be *ashamed, disappointed;* caus. to *shame, reproach:*— be ashamed, be confounded, be brought to confusion (unto shame), come (be put to) shame, bring reproach.

2660. חֵפֶר **Chêpher**, *khay´-fer;* from 2658 or 2659; a *pit* or *shame; Chepher,* a place in Pal.; also the name of three Isr.:— Hepher.

2661. חֲפֹר **chăphôr**, *khaf-ore´;* from 2658; a *hole;* only in connection with 6512, which ought rather to be joined as one word, thus

חֲפַרְפֵּרָה **chăpharpêrâh**, *khaf-ar-pay-raw´;* by redupl. from 2658; a *burrower,* i.e. prob. a *rat:*— + mole.

2662. חֶפְרִי **Chephriy**, *khef-ree´;* patron. from 2660; a *Chephrite* (collect.) or desc. of *Chepher:*— Hepherites.

2663. חֲפָרַיִם **Châphârayim**, *khaf-aw-rah´-yim;* dual of 2660; *double pit; Chapharajim,* a place in Pal.:— Haphraim.

חֲפַרְפֵּרָה **chăpharpêrâh**. See 2661.

2664. חָפַשׂ **châphas**, *khaw-fas´;* a prim. root; to *seek;* caus. to *conceal* oneself (i.e. let be sought), or *mask:*— change, (make) diligent (search), disguise self, hide, search (for, out).

2665. חֵפֶשׂ **chêphes**, *khay´-fes;* from 2664; something *covert,* i.e. a *trick:*— search.

2666. חָפַשׁ **châphash**, *khaw-fash´;* a prim. root; to *spread* loose; fig. to *manumit:*— be free.

2667. חֹפֶשׁ **chôphesh**, *kho´-fesh;* from 2666; something *spread* loosely, i.e. a *carpet:*— precious.

2668. חֻפְשָׁה **chuphshâh**, *khoof-shaw´;* from 2666; *liberty* (from slavery):— freedom.

2669. חָפְשׁוּת **chôphshûwth**, *khof-shooth´;* and

חָפְשִׁית **chophshîyth**, *khof-sheeth´;* from

2666; *prostration* by sickness (with 1004, a *hospital*):— several.

2670. חָפְשִׁי **chophshîy**, *khof-shee´;* from 2666; *exempt* (from bondage, tax or care):— free, liberty.

2671. חֵץ **chêts**, *khayts;* from 2686; prop. a *piercer,* i.e. an *arrow;* by impl. a *wound;* fig. (of God) thunder-*bolt;* (by interchange for 6086) the *shaft* of a spear:— + archer, arrow, dart, shaft, staff, wound.

חֻץ **chûts**. See 2351.

2672. חָצַב **châtsab**, *khaw-tsab´;* or

חָצֵב **châtsêb**, *khaw-tsabe´;* a prim. root; to *cut* or *carve* (wood), stone or other material); by impl. to *hew, split, square, quarry, engrave:*— cut, dig, divide, grave, hew (out, -er), make, mason.

2673. חָצָה **châtsâh**, *khaw-tsaw´;* a prim. root [comp. 2686]; to *cut* or *split* in two; to *halve:*— divide, × live out half, reach to the midst, part.

2674. חָצוֹר **Châtsôwr**, *khaw-tsore´;* a collect. form of 2691; *village; Chatsor,* the name (thus simply) of two places in Pal. and of one in Arabia:— Hazor.

2675. חָצוֹר חֲדַתָּה **Châtsôwr Chădattâh**, *khaw-tsore´ khad-at-taw´;* from 2674 and a Chaldaizing form of the fem. of 2319 [comp. 2323]; *new Chatsor,* a place in Pal.:— Hazor, Hadattah [as if two places].

2676. חָצוֹת **châtsôwth**, *khaw-tsoth´;* from 2673; the *middle* (of the night):— mid [-night].

2677. חֵצִי **chêtsiy**, *khay-tsee´;* from 2673; the *half* or *middle:*— half, middle, mid [-night], midst, part, two parts.

2678. חִצִּי **chitstsîy**, *khits-tsee´;* or

חֵצִי **chêtsiy**, *khay-tsee´;* prol. from 2671; an *arrow:*— arrow.

2679. חֲצִי הַמְּנֻחוֹת **Châtsiy ham-Menûchôwth**, *chat-tsee´ ham-men-oo-khoth´;* from 2677 and the plur. of 4496, with the art. interposed; *midst of the resting-places; Chatsi-ham-Menuchoth,* an Isr.:— half of the Manahethites.

2680. חֲצִי הַמְּנַחְתִּי **Châtsiy ham-Menachtîy**, *khat-see´ ham-men-akh-tee´;* patron. from 2679; a *Chatsi-ham-Menachtite* or desc. of Chatsi-ham-Menuchoth:— half of the Manahethites.

2681. חָצִיר **châtsîyr**, *khaw-tseer´;* a collat. form of 2691; a *court* or *abode:*— court.

2682. חָצִיר **châtsîyr**, *khaw-tseer´;* perh. orig. the same as 2681, from the *greenness* of a courtyard; *grass;* also a *leek* (collect.):— grass, hay, herb, leek.

2683. חֵצֶן **chêtsen**, *khay´-tsen;* from an unused root mean. to hold *firmly;* the *bosom* (as *comprised* between the arms):— bosom.

2684. חֹצֶן **chôtsen,** *kho'tsen;* a collat. form of 2683, and mean. the same:— arm, lap.

2685. חֲצַף **chătsaph** (Chald.), *khats-af';* a prim. root; prop. to *shear* or cut close; fig. to *be severe:*— hasty, be urgent.

2686. חָצַץ **châtsats,** *khaw-tsats';* a prim. root [comp. 2673]; prop. to *chop* into, pierce or sever; hence, to *curtail,* to *distribute* (into ranks); as denom. from 2671, to *shoot* an arrow:— archer, × bands, cut off in the midst.

2687. חָצָץ **châtsâts,** *khaw-tsawts';* from 2687; prop. something *cutting;* hence, *gravel* (as *grit*); also (like 2671) an *arrow:*— arrow, gravel (stone).

2688. חַצְצוֹן תָּמָר **Chatsetsôwn Tâmâr,** *khats-ets-one' taw-mawr';* or

חַצְצֹן תָּמָר **Chatsătsôn Tâmâr,** *khats-ats-one' taw-mawr';* from 2686 and 8558; *division* [i.e. perh. row] of (the) *palm-tree; Chatsetson-tamar,* a place in Pal.:— Hazezon-tamar.

2689. חֲצֹצְרָה **chătsôtserâh,** *khats-o-tser-aw';* by redupl. from 2690; a *trumpet* (from its *sundered* or quavering note):— trumpet (-er).

2690. חָצַר **châtsar,** *khaw-tsar';* a prim. root; prop. to *surround* with a stockade, and thus *separate* from the open country; but used only in the redupl. form

חַצֹּצֵר **chătsôtsêr,** *khast-o-tsare';* or (2 Chron. 5:12)

חַצֹרֵר **chătsôrêr,** *khats-o-rare';* as denom. from 2689; to *trumpet,* i.e. blow on that instrument:— blow, sound, trumpeter.

2691. חָצֵר **châtsêr,** *khaw-tsare'* (masc. and fem.); from 2690 in its orig. sense; a *yard* (as *inclosed* by a fence); also a *hamlet* (as similarly *surrounded* with walls):— court, tower, village.

2692. חֲצַר אַדָּר **Chătsar 'Addâr,** *khats-ar' ad-dawr';* from 2691 and 146; (the) *village of Addar; Chatsar-Addar,* a place in Pal.:— Hazar-addar.

2693. חֲצַר גַּדָּה **Chătsar Gaddâh,** *khats-ar' gad-daw';* from 2691 and a fem. of 1408; (the) *village of* (female) *Fortune; Chatsar-Gaddah,* a place in Pal.:— Hazar-gaddah.

2694. חֲצַר הַתִּיכוֹן **Chătsar hat-Tîykôwn,** *khats-ar' hat-tee-kone';* from 2691 and 8484 with the art. interposed; *village of the middle; Chatsar-hat-Tikon,* a place in Pal.:— Hazar-hatticon.

2695. חֶצְרוֹ **Chetsrôw,** *khets-ro';* by an orth. var. for 2696; *inclosure; Chetsro,* an Isr.:— Hezro, Hezrai.

2696. חֶצְרוֹן **Chetsrôwn,** *khets-rone';* from 2691;

court-yard; *Chetsron,* the name of a place in Pal.; also of two Isr.:— Hezron.

2697. חֶצְרוֹנִי **Chetsrôwnîy,** *khets-ro-nee';* patron. from 2696; a *Chetsronite* or (collect.) desc. of Chetsron:— Hezronites.

2698. חֲצֵרוֹת **Chătsêrowth,** *khats-ay-roth';* fem. plur. of 2691; *yards; Chatseroth,* a place in Pal.:— Hazeroth.

2699. חֲצֵרִים **Chătsêrîym,** *khats-ay-reem';* plur. masc. of 2691; *yards; Chatserim,* a place in Pal.:— Hazerim.

2700. חֲצַרְמָוֶת **Chătsarmâveth,** *khats-ar-maw'-veth;* from 2691 and 4194; *village of death; Chatsarmaveth,* a place in Arabia:— Hazarmaveth.

2701. חֲצַר סוּסָה **Chătsar Çûwçâh,** *khats-ar' soo-saw';* from 2691 and 5484; *village of cavalry; Chatsar-Susah,* a place in Pal.:— Hazar-susah.

2702. חֲצַר סוּסִים **Chătsar Çûwçîym,** *khats-ar' soo-seem';* from 2691 and the plur. of 5483; *village of horses; Chatsar-Susim,* a place in Pal.:— Hazar-susim.

2703. חֲצַר עֵינוֹן **Chătsar 'Êynôwn,** *khats-ar' ay-nōne';* from 2691 and a der. of 5869; *village of springs; Chatsar-Enon,* a place in Pal.:— Hazar-enon.

2704. חֲצַר עֵינָן **Chătsar 'Êynân,** *khats-ar' ay-nawn';* from 2691 and the same as 5881; *village of springs; Chatsar-Enan,* a place in Pal.:— Hazar-enan.

2705. חֲצַר שׁוּעָל **Chătsar Shûw'âl,** *khats-ar' shoo-awl';* from 2691 and 7776; *village of* (the) *fox; Chatsar-Shual,* a place in Pal.:— Hazar-shual.

חֵק **chêq.** See 2436.

2706. חֹק **chôq,** *khoke;* from 2710; an *enactment;* hence, an *appointment* (of time, space, quantity, labor or usage):— appointed, bound, commandment, convenient, custom, decree (-d), due, law, measure, × necessary, ordinance (-nary), portion, set time, statute, task.

2707. חָקָה **châqah,** *khaw-kaw';* a prim. root; to *carve;* by impl. to *delineate;* also to *intrench:*— carved work, portrayed, set a print.

2708. חֻקָּה **chuqqâh,** *khook-kaw';* fem. of 2706, and mean. substantially the same:— appointed, custom, manner, ordinance, site, statute.

2709. חֲקוּפָא **Chăqûwphâ',** *khak-oo-faw';* from an unused root prob. mean. to *bend; crooked; Chakupha,* one of the Nethinim:— Hakupha.

2710. חָקַק **châqaq,** *khaw-kak';* a prim. root; prop. to *hack,* i.e. *engrave* (Judg. 5:14, to *be a scribe* simply); by impl. to *enact* (laws being *cut* in stone or metal tablets in primitive times) or (gen.) *prescribe:*— appoint, decree, governor, grave, lawgiver, note, pourtray, print, set.

2711. חֵקֶק **chêqeq**, *khay´-kek;* from 2710; an *enactment,* a *resolution:*— decree, thought.

2712. חֹקֹק **Chuqqôq**, *Khook-koke´;* or (fully)

חוּקֹק **Chûwqôq**, *khoo-koke´;* from 2710; *appointed; Chukkok* or *Chukok,* a place in Pal.:— Hukkok, Hukok.

2713. חָקַר **châqar**, *khaw-kar´;* a prim. root; prop. to *penetrate;* hence, to *examine* intimately:— find out, (make) search (out), seek (out), sound, try.

2714. חֵקֶר **chêqer**, *khay´-ker;* from 2713; *examination, enumeration, deliberation:*— finding out, number, [un-] search (-able, -ed, out, -ing).

2715. חֹר **chôr**, *khore;* or (fully)

חוֹר **chôwr**, *khore;* from 2787; prop. *white* or *pure* (from the *cleansing* or *shining* power of fire [comp. 2751]; hence, (fig.) *noble* (in rank):— noble.

חֻר **chûr**. See 2352.

2716. חֶרֶא **chere'**, *kheh´-reh;* from an unused (and vulgar) root prob. mean. to *evacuate* the bowels: *excrement:*— dung. Also

חֲרִי° **chărîy**, *khar-ee´.*

2717. חָרַב **charab**, *khaw-rab´;* or

חָרֵב **chârêb**, *khaw-rabe´;* a prim. root; to *parch* (through drought) i.e. (by anal.) to *desolate, destroy, kill:*— decay, (be) desolate, destroy (-er), (be) dry (up), slay, × surely, (lay, lie, make) waste.

2718. חֲרַב **chărab** (Chald.), *khar-ab´;* a root corresp. to 2717; to *demolish:*— destroy.

2719. חֶרֶב **chereb**, *kheh´-reb;* from 2717; *drought;* also a *cutting* instrument (from its *destructive* effect), as a *knife, sword,* or other sharp implement:— axe, dagger, knife, mattock, sword, tool.

2720. חָרֵב **chârêb**, *khaw-rabe´;* from 2717; *parched* or *ruined:*— desolate, dry, waste.

2721. חֹרֶב **chôreb**, *kho´-reb;* a collat. form of 2719; *drought* or *desolation:*— desolation, drought, dry, heat, × utterly, waste.

2722. חֹרֵב **Chôrêb**, *kho-rabe´;* from 2717; *desolate; Choreb,* a (gen.) name for the Sinaitic mountains:— Horeb.

2723. חָרְבָּה **chorbâh**, *khor-baw´;* fem. of 2721; prop. *drought,* i.e. (by impl.) a *desolation:*— decayed place, desolate (place, -tion), destruction, (laid) waste (place).

2724. חֲרָבָה **chârâbâh**, *khaw-raw-baw´;* fem. of 2720; a *desert:*— dry (ground, land).

2725. חֲרָבוֹן **chărâbôwn**, *khar-aw-bone´;* from 2717; parching *heat:*— drought.

2726. חַרְבוֹנָא **Charbôwnâ'**, *khar-bo-naw´;* or

חַרְבוֹנָה **Charbôwnâh**, *khar-bo-naw´;* of Pers. or.; *Charbona* or *Charbonah,* a eunuch of Xerxes:— Harbona, Harbonah.

2727. חָרַג **charag**, *khaw-rag´;* a prim. root; prop. to *leap* suddenly, i.e. (by impl.) to *be dismayed:*— be afraid.

2728. חַרְגֹּל **chargôl**, *khar-gole´;* from 2727; the *leaping* insect, i.e. a *locust:*— beetle.

2729. חָרַד **charad**, *khaw-rad´;* a prim. root; to *shudder* with terror; hence, to *fear;* also to *hasten* (with anxiety):— be (make) afraid, be careful, discomfit, fray (away), quake, tremble.

2730. חָרֵד **chârêd**, *khaw-rade´;* from 2729; *fearful;* also *reverential:*— afraid, trembling.

2731. חֲרָדָה **chărâdâh**, *khar-aw-daw´;* fem. of 2730; *fear, anxiety:*— care, × exceedingly, fear, quaking, trembling.

2732. חֲרָדָה **Chărâdâh**, *khar-aw-daw´;* the same as 2731; *Charadah,* a place in the Desert:— Haradah.

2733. חֲרֹדִי **Chărôdîy**, *khar-o-dee´;* patrial from a der. of 2729 [comp. 5878]; a *Charodite,* or inhab. of *Charod:*— Harodite.

2734. חָרָה **chârâh**, *khaw-raw´;* a prim. root [comp. 2787]; to *glow* or grow *warm;* fig. (usually) to *blaze* up, of anger, zeal, jealousy:— be angry, burn, be displeased, × earnestly, fret self, grieve, be (wax) hot, be incensed, kindle, × very, be wroth. See 8474.

2735. חֹר הַגִּדְגָּד **Chôr hag-Gidgâd**, *khore hag-ghid-gawd´;* from 2356 and a collat. (masc.) form of 1412, with the art. interposed; *hole of the cleft; Chor-hag-Gidgad,* a place in the Desert:— Hor-hagidgad.

2736. חַרְהֲיָה **Charhăyâh**, *khar-hah-yaw´;* from 2734 and 3050; *fearing Jah; Charhajah,* an Isr.:— Harhaiah.

2737. חָרוּז **chârûwz**, *khaw-rooz´;* from an unused root mean. to *perforate;* prop. *pierced,* i.e. a *bead* of pearl, gems or jewels (as strung):— chain.

2738. חָרוּל **chârûwl**, *khaw-rool´;* or (short.)

חָרֻל **chârul**, *khaw-rool´;* appar. a pass. part. of an unused root prob. mean. to *be prickly;* prop. *pointed,* i.e. a *bramble* or other thorny weed:— nettle.

חֹרוֹן **chôrôwn**. See 1032, 2772.

2739. חֲרוּמַף **Chărûwmaph**, *khar-oo-maf´;* from pass. part. of 2763 and 639; *snubnosed; Charumaph,* an Isr.:— Harumaph.

2740. חָרוֹן **chârôwn**, *khaw-rone´;* or (short.)

חָרֹן **chârôn**, *khaw-rone´;* from 2734; a *burning* of anger:— sore displeasure, fierce (-ness), fury, (fierce) wrath (-ful).

2741. חֲרוּפִי **Chăruwphîy**, *khar-oo-fee´;* a patrial from (prob.) a collat. form of 2756; a *Charuphite* or inhab. of Charuph (or Chariph):— Haruphite.

2742. חָרוּץ **chârûwts**, *khaw-roots´;* or

חָרֻץ **chârûts**, *khaw-roots´;* pass. part. of 2782; prop. *incised* or (act.) *incisive;* hence, (as noun masc. or fem.) a *trench* (as dug), *gold* (as mined), a *threshing-sledge* (having sharp teeth); (fig.) *determination;* also *eager:*— decision, diligent, (fine) gold, pointed things, sharp, threshing instrument, wall.

2743. חָרוּץ **Chârûwts**, *khaw-roots´;* the same as 2742; *earnest; Charuts,* an Isr.:— Haruz.

2744. חַרְחוּר **Charchûwr**, *khar-khoor´;* a fuller form of 2746; *inflammation; Charchur,* one of the Nethinim:— Harhur.

2745. חַרְחַס **Charchaç**, *khar-khas´;* from the same as 2775; perh. *shining; Charchas,* an Isr.:— Harhas.

2746. חַרְחֻר **charchûr**, *khar-khoor´;* from 2787; *fever* (as *hot*):— extreme burning.

2747. חֶרֶט **cheret**, *kheh´-ret;* from a prim. root mean. to *engrave;* a *chisel* or *graver;* also a *style* for writing:— graving tool, pen.

חָרִט **chârît**. See 2754.

2748. חַרְטֹם **chartôm**, *khar-tome´;* from the same as 2747; a *horoscopist* (as *drawing* magical lines or circles):— magician.

2749. חַרְטֹם **chartôm** (Chald.), *khar-tome´;* the same as 2748:— magician.

2750. חֳרִי **chŏriy**, *khor-ee´;* from 2734; a *burning* (i.e. intense) anger:— fierce, × great, heat.

חֳרִי° **chăriy**. See 2716.

2751. חֹרִי **chôriy**, *kho-ree´;* from the same as 2353; *white* bread:— white.

2752. חֹרִי **Chôriy**, *kho-ree´;* from 2356; *cave-dweller* or troglodyte; a *Chorite* or aboriginal Idumæan:— Horims, Horites.

2753. חֹרִי **Chôriy**, *kho-ree´;* or

חוֹרִי **Chôwriy**, *kho-ree´;* the same as 2752; *Chori,* the name of two men:— Hori.

2754. חָרִיט **chârîyt**, *khaw-reet´;* or

חָרִט **chârit**, *khaw-reet´;* from the same as 2747; prop. *cut* out (or *hollow*), i.e. (by impl.) a *pocket:*— bag, crisping pin.

2755. חֲרֵי־יוֹנִים **chărêy-yôwnîym**, *khar-ay´-yo-neem´;* from the plur. of 2716 and the plur. of 3123; *excrements of doves* [or perh. rather the plur. of a single word

חֲרָאיוֹן **chârâ'yôwn**, *khar-aw-yone´;* of similar or uncert. deriv.], prob. a kind of vegetable:— doves' dung.

2756. חָרִיף **Chârîyph**, *khaw-reef´;* from 2778; *autumnal; Chariph,* the name of two Isr.:— Hariph.

2757. חָרִיץ **chârîyts**, *khaw-reets´;* or

חָרִץ **chârîts**, *khaw-reets´;* from 2782; prop. *incisure* or (pass.) *incised* [comp. 2742]; hence, a *threshing-sledge* (with sharp teeth): also a *slice* (as cut):— + cheese, harrow.

2758. חָרִישׁ **chârîysh**, *khaw-reesh´;* from 2790; *plowing* or its season:— earing (time), ground.

2759. חֲרִישִׁי **chăriyshîy**, *khar-ee-shee´;* from 2790 in the sense of *silence; quiet,* i.e. *sultry* (as fem. noun, the *sirocco* or hot east wind):— vehement.

2760. חָרַךְ **chârak**, *khaw-rak´;* a prim. root; to *braid* (i.e. to *entangle* or snare) or *catch* (game) in a net:— roast.

2761. חֲרַךְ **chărak** (Chald.), *khar-ak´;* a root prob. allied to the equiv. of 2787; to *scorch:*— singe.

2762. חֶרֶךְ **cherek**, *kheh´-rek;* from 2760; prop. a *net,* i.e. (by anal.) *lattice:*— lattice.

חָרֻל **chârûl**. See 2738.

2763. חָרַם **charam**, *khaw-ram´;* a prim. root; to *seclude;* spec. (by a ban) to *devote* to relig. uses (espec. destruction); phys. and refl. to *be blunt* as to the nose:— make accursed, consecrate, (utterly) destroy, devote, forfeit, have a flat nose, utterly (slay, make away).

2764. חֵרֶם **chêrem**, *khay´-rem;* or (Zech. 14:11)

חֶרֶם **cherem**, *kheh´-rem;* from 2763; phys. (as *shutting in*) a *net* (either lit. or fig.); usually a *doomed* object; abstr. *extermination:*— (ac-) curse (-d, -d thing), dedicated, things which should have been utterly destroyed, (appointed to) utter destruction, devoted (thing), net.

2765. חֳרֵם **Chŏrêm**, *khor-ame´;* from 2763; *devoted; Chorem,* a place in Pal.:— Horem.

2766. חָרִם **Chârîm**, *khaw-reem´;* from 2763; *snub-nosed; Charim,* an Isr.:— Harim.

2767. חָרְמָה **Chormâh**, *khor-maw´;* from 2763; *devoted; Chormah,* a place in Pal.:— Hormah.

2768. חֶרְמוֹן **Chermôwn**, *kher-mone´;* from 2763; *abrupt; Chermon,* a mount of Pal.:— Hermon.

2769. חֶרְמוֹנִים **Chermôwnîym**, *kher-mo-neem´;* plur. of 2768; *Hermons,* i.e. its peaks:— the Hermonites.

2770. חֶרְמֵשׁ **chermêsh**, *kher-mashe´;* from 2763; a *sickle* (as *cutting*):— sickle.

2771. חָרָן **Chârân**, *kaw-rawn´;* from 2787;

parched; Charan, the name of a man and also of a place:— Haran.

חָרֹן **chârôn**. See 2740.

2772. חֹרֹנִי **Chôrônîy**, *kho-ro-nee´*; patrial from 2773; a *Choronite* or inhab. of Choronaim:— Horonite.

2773. חֹרֹנַיִם **Chôrônayim**, *kho-ro-nah´-yim*; dual of a der. from 2356; *double cave-town; Choronajim*, a place in Moab:— Horonaim.

2774. חַרְנֶפֶר **Charnepher**, *khar-neh´fer*; of uncert. der.; *Charnepher*, an Isr.:— Harnepher.

2775. חֶרֶס **chereç**, *kheh´-res*; or (with a directive enclitic)

חַרְסָה **charçâh**, *khar´-saw*; from an unused root mean. to *scrape*; the *itch;* also [perh. from the mediating idea of 2777] the *sun:*— itch, sun.

2776. חֶרֶס **Chereç**, *kheh´-res*; the same as 2775; *shining; Cheres*, a mountain in Pal.:— Heres.

2777. חַרְסוּת **charçûwth**, *khar-sooth´*; from 2775 (appar. in the sense of a red *tile* used for scraping); a *potsherd*, i.e. (by impl.) a *pottery;* the name of a gate at Jerusalem:— east.

2778. חָרַף **châraph**, *khaw-raf´*; a prim. root; to *pull* off, i.e. (by impl.) to *expose* (as by *stripping*); spec. to *betroth* (as if a surrender); fig. to carp at, i.e. *defame;* denom. (from 2779) to spend the *winter:*— betroth, blaspheme, defy, jeopard, rail, reproach, upbraid.

2779. חֹרֶף **chôreph**, *kho´-ref;* from 2778; prop. the *crop* gathered, i.e. (by impl.) the *autumn* (and winter) season; fig. *ripeness* of age:— cold, winter (I-house]), youth.

2780. חָרֵף **Châreph**, *khaw-rafe´;* from 2778; *reproachful; Chareph*, an Isr.:— Hareph.

2781. חֶרְפָּה **cherpâh**, *kher-paw´;* from 2778; *contumely, disgrace,* the *pudenda:*— rebuke, reproach (-fully), shame.

2782. חָרַץ **chârats**, *khaw-rats´;* a prim. root; prop. to *point* sharply, i.e. (lit.) to *wound;* fig. to *be alert,* to *decide:*— bestir self, decide, decree, determine, maim, move.

2783. חֲרַץ **chărats** (Chald.), *khar-ats´;* from a root corresp. to 2782 in the sense of *vigor;* the *loin* (as the seat of strength):— loin.

חָרוּץ **chârûts**. See 2742.

2784. חַרְצֻבָּה **chartsubbâh**, *khar-tsoob-baw´;* of uncert. der.; a *fetter;* fig. a *pain:*— band.

חָרִיץ **chârîts**. See 2757.

2785. חַרְצָן **chartsan**, *khar-tsan´;* from 2782; a *sour* grape (as *sharp* in taste):— kernel.

2786. חָרַק **châraq**, *khaw-rak´;* a prim. root; to *grate* the teeth:— gnash.

2787. חָרַר **chârar**, *khaw-rar´;* a prim. root; to *glow*, i.e. lit. (to *melt, burn, dry* up) or fig. (to

show or *incite* passion):— be angry, burn, dry, kindle.

2788. חָרֵר **chârêr**, *khaw-rare´;* from 2787; *arid:*— parched place.

2789. חֶרֶס **cheres**, *kheh´-res;* a collat. form mediating between 2775 and 2791; a piece of *pottery:*— earth (-en), (pot-) sherd, + stone.

2790. חָרַשׁ **chârash**, *khaw-rash´;* a prim. root; to *scratch*, i.e. (by impl.) to *engrave, plow;* hence, (from the use of tools) to *fabricate* (of any material); fig. to *devise* (in a bad sense); hence, (from the idea of secrecy) to *let alone;* hence, (by impl.) to *be deaf* (as an accompaniment of dumbness):— × altogether, cease, conceal, be deaf, devise, ear, graven, imagine, leave off speaking, hold peace, plow (-er, man), be quiet, rest, practise secretly, keep silence, be silent, speak not a word, be still, hold tongue, worker.

2791. חֶרֶשׁ **cheresh**, *kheh´-resh;* from 2790; magical *craft;* also *silence:*— cunning, secretly.

2792. חֶרֶשׁ **Cheresh**, *kheh´-resh;* the same as 2791; *Cheresh*, a Levite:— Heresh.

2793. חֹרֶשׁ **chôresh**, *kho´-resh;* from 2790; a *forest* (perh. as furnishing the material for fabric):— bough, forest, shroud, wood.

2794. חֹרֵשׁ **chôrêsh**, *kho-rashe´;* act. part. of 2790; a *fabricator* or mechanic:— artificer.

2795. חֵרֵשׁ **chêrêsh**, *khay-rashe´;* from 2790; *deaf* (whether lit. or spir.):— deaf.

2796. חָרָשׁ **chârâsh**, *khaw-rawsh´;* from 2790; a *fabricator* or any material:— artificer, (+) carpenter, craftsman, engraver, maker, + mason, skilful, (+) smith, worker, workman, such as wrought.

2797. חַרְשָׁא **Charshâ´**, *khar-shaw´;* from 2792; *magician; Charsha*, one of the Nethinim:— Harsha.

2798. חֲרָשִׁים **Chărâshîym**, *khar-aw-sheem´;* plur. of 2796; *mechanics*, the name of a valley in Jerusalem:— Charashim, craftsmen.

2799. חֲרֹשֶׁת **chărôsheth**, *khar-o´-sheth;* from 2790; mechanical *work:*— carving, cutting.

2800. חֲרֹשֶׁת **Chărôsheth**, *khar-o´-sheth;* the same as 2799; *Charosheth*, a place in Pal.:— Harosheth.

2801. חָרַת **chârath**, *khaw-rath´;* a prim. root; to *engrave:*— graven.

2802. חֶרֶת **Chereth**, *kheh´-reth;* from 2801 [but equiv. to 2793]; *forest; Chereth*, a thicket in Pal.:— Hereth.

2803. חָשַׁב **châshab**, *khaw-shab´;* a prim. root; prop. to *plait* or interpenetrate, i.e.

(lit.) to *weave* or (gen.) to *fabricate;* fig. to *plot* or contrive (usually in a malicious sense); hence, (from the ment. effort) to *think, regard, value, compute:*— (make) account (of), conceive, consider, count, cunning (man, work, workman), devise, esteem, find out, forecast, hold, imagine, impute, invent, be like, mean, purpose, reckon (-ing be made), regard, think.

2804. חֲשַׁב **chăshab** (Chald.), *khash-ab´;* corresp. to 2803; to *regard:*— repute.

2805. חֵשֶׁב **chêsheb,** *khay´-sheb;* from 2803; a *belt* or strap (as being interlaced):— curious girdle.

2806. חַשְׁבַּדָּנָה **Chashbaddânâh,** *khash-baddaw´-naw;* from 2803 and 1777; *considerate judge; Chasbaddanah,* an Isr.:— Hasbadana.

2807. חֲשֻׁבָה **Chăshûbâh,** *khash-oo-baw´;* from 2803; *estimation; Cashubah,* an Isr.:— Hashubah.

2808. חֶשְׁבּוֹן **cheshbôwn,** *khesh-bone´;* from 2803; prop. *contrivance;* by impl. *intelligence:*— account, device, reason.

2809. חֶשְׁבּוֹן **Cheshbôwn,** *khesh-bone´;* the same as 2808; *Cheshbon,* a place E. of the Jordan:— Heshbon.

2810. חִשָּׁבוֹן **chishshâbôwn,** *khish-shaw-bone´;* from 2803; a *contrivance,* i.e. actual (a warlike *machine)* or ment. (a *machination):*— engine, invention.

2811. חֲשַׁבְיָה **Chăshabyâh,** *khash-ab-yaw´;* or

חֲשַׁבְיָהוּ **Chăshabyâhûw,** *khash-ab-yaw´-hoo;* from 2803 and 3050; *Jah has regarded; Chashabjah,* the name of nine Isr.:— Hashabiah.

2812. חֲשַׁבְנָה **Chăshabnâh,** *khash-ab-naw´;* fem. of 2808; *inventiveness; Chashnah,* an Isr.:— Hashabnah.

2813. חֲשַׁבְנְיָה **Chăshabneyâh,** *khash-ab-neh-yaw´;* from 2808 and 3050; *thought of Jah; Chashabnejah,* the name of two Isr.:— Hashabniah.

2814. חָשָׁה **châshâh,** *khaw-shaw´;* a prim. root; to *hush* or keep quiet:— hold peace, keep silence, be silent, (be) still.

2815. חַשּׁוּב **Chashshûwb,** *khash-shoob´;* from 2803; *intelligent; Chashshub,* the name of two or three Isr.:— Hashub, Hasshub.

2816. חֲשׁוֹךְ **chăshôwk** (Chald.), *khash-oke´;* from a root corresp. to 2821; the *dark:*— darkness.

2817. חֲשׂוּפָא **Chăsûwphâ´,** *khas-oo-faw´;* or

חֲשֻׂפָא **Chăsuphâ´,** *khas-oo-faw´;* from 2834; *nakedness; Chasupha,* one of the Nethinim:— Hashupha, Hasupha.

חָשׂוּק **châshûwq.** See 2838.

2818. חֲשַׁח **chăshach** (Chald.), *khash-akh´;* a

collat. root to one corresp. to 2363 in the sense of *readiness;* to *be necessary* (from the idea of *convenience)* or (tran.) to *need:*— careful, have need of.

2819. חַשְׁחוּת **chashchûwth** (Chald.), *khash-khooth´;* from a root corresp. to 2818; *necessity:*— be needful.

חֲשִׁיכָה **chăshêykăh.** See 2825.

חֻשִׁים **Chûshîym.** See 2366.

2820. חָשַׂךְ **châsak,** *khaw-sak´;* a prim. root; to *restrain* or (reflex.) *refrain;* by impl. to *refuse, spare, preserve;* also (by interch. with 2821) to *observe:*— assuage, × darken, forbear, hinder, hold back, keep (back), punish, refrain, reserve, spare, withhold.

2821. חָשַׁךְ **châshak,** *khaw-shak´;* a prim. root; to *be dark* (as *withholding* light); tran. to *darken:*— be black, (make) dark, darken, cause darkness, be dim, hide.

2822. חֹשֶׁךְ **chôshek,** *kho-shek´;* from 2821; the *dark;* hence, (lit.) *darkness;* fig. *misery, destruction, death, ignorance, sorrow, wickedness:*— dark (-ness), night, obscurity.

2823. חָשֹׁךְ **châshôk,** *khaw-shoke´;* from 2821; *dark* (fig. i.e. *obscure):*— mean.

2824. חֶשְׁכָה **cheshkâh,** *khesh-kaw´;* from 2821; *darkness:*— dark.

2825. חֲשֵׁכָה **chăshêkâh,** *khash-ay-kaw´;* or

חֲשֵׁיכָה **chăshêykâh,** *khash-ay-kaw´;* from 2821; *darkness;* fig. *misery:*— darkness.

2826. חָשַׁל **châshal,** *khaw-shal´;* a prim. root; to *make* (intrans. *be) unsteady,* i.e. *weak:*— feeble.

2827. חֲשַׁל **chăshal** (Chald.), *khash-al´;* a root corresp. to 2826; to *weaken,* i.e. *crush:*— subdue.

2828. חָשֻׁם **Châshum,** *khaw-shoom´;* from the same as 2831; *enriched; Chashum,* the name of two or three Isr.:— Hashum.

חֻשָׁם **Chûshâm.** See 2367.

חֻשִׁים **Chûshîm.** See 2366.

2829. חֶשְׁמוֹן **Cheshmôwn,** *khesh-mone´;* the same as 2831; *opulent; Cheshmon,* a place in Pal.:— Heshmon.

2830. חַשְׁמַל **chashmal,** *khash-mal´;* of uncert. der.; prob. *bronze* or polished spectrum metal:— amber.

2831. חַשְׁמָן **chashmân,** *khash-man´;* from an unused root (prob. mean. *firm* or *capacious* in resources); appar. *wealthy:*— princes.

2832. חַשְׁמֹנָה **Chashmônâh,** *khash-mo-naw´;* fem. of 2831; *fertile; Chasmonah,* a place in the Desert:— Hashmonah.

2833. חֹשֶׁן **chôshen,** *kho´-shen;* from an unused root prob. mean. to *contain* or *sparkle;* perh. a *pocket* (as holding the Urim and Thummim), or *rich* (as containing gems), used only of the *gorget* of the high priest:— breastplate.

2834. חָשַׂף **châsaph,** *khaw-saf´;* a prim. root; to *strip* off, i.e. gen. to *make naked* (for exertion or in disgrace), to *drain* away or *bail* up (a liquid):— make bare, clean, discover, draw out, take, uncover.

2835. חָשִׂף **châsîph,** *khaw-seef´;* from 2834; prop. *drawn off,* i.e. separated; hence, a small *company* (as divided from the rest):— little flock.

2836. חָשַׁק **châshaq,** *khaw-shak´;* a prim. root; to *cling,* i.e. *join,* (fig.) to *love, delight* in; ellip. (or by interch. for 2820) to *deliver:*— have a delight, (have a) desire, fillet, long, set (in) love.

2837. חֵשֶׁק **chêsheq,** *khay´-shek;* from 2836; *delight:*— desire, pleasure.

2838. חָשׁוּק **châshûq,** *khaw-shook´;* or

חָשׁוּק **châshûwq,** *khaw-shook´;* pass. part. of 2836; *attached,* i.e. a fence-*rail* or rod connecting the posts or pillars:— fillet.

2839. חִשֻּׁק **chishshûq,** *khish-shook´;* from 2836; *conjoined,* i.e. a wheel-*spoke* or rod connecting the hub with the rim:— felloe.

2840. חִשֻּׁר **chishshûr,** *khish-shoor´;* from an unused root mean. to *bind* together; *combined,* i.e. the *nave* or hub of a wheel (as holding the spokes together):— spoke.

2841. חַשְׁרָה **chashrâh,** *khash-raw´;* from the same as 2840; prop. a *combination* or gathering, i.e. of watery *clouds:*— dark.

חֲשֻׂפָא **Chăsûphâ´.** See 2817.

2842. חָשַׁשׁ **châshash,** *khaw-shash´;* by var. for 7179; dry *grass:*— chaff.

2843. חֻשָׁתִי **Chûshâthîy,** *khoo-shaw-thee´;* patron. from 2364; a *Chushathite* or desc. of Chushah:— Hushathite.

2844. חַת **chath,** *khath;* from 2865; concr. *crushed;* also *afraid;* abstr. *terror:*— broken, dismayed, dread, fear.

2845. חֵת **Chêth,** *khayth;* from 2865; *terror;* *Cheth,* an aboriginal Canaanite:— Heth.

2846. חָתָה **châthâh,** *khaw-thaw´;* a prim. root; to lay *hold* of; espec. to *pick* up fire:— heap, take (away).

2847. חִתָּה **chittâh,** *khit-taw´;* from 2865; *fear:*— terror.

2848. חִתּוּל **chittûwl,** *khit-tool´;* from 2853; *swathed,* i.e. a *bandage:*— roller.

2849. חַתְחַת **chathchath,** *khath-khath´;* from 2844; *terror:*— fear.

2850. חִתִּי **Chittîy,** *khit-tee´;* patron. from 2845; a *Chittite,* or desc. of Cheth:— Hittite, Hittities.

2851. חִתִּית **chittîyth,** *khit-teeth´;* from 2865; *fear:*— terror.

2852. חָתַךְ **châthak,** *khaw-thak´;* a prim. root; prop. to *cut* off, i.e. (fig.) to *decree:*— determine.

2853. חָתַל **châthal,** *khaw-thal´;* a prim. root; to *swathe:*— × at all, swaddle.

2854. חֲתֻלָּה **chăthullâh,** *khath-ool-law´;* from 2853; a *swathing* cloth (fig.):— swaddling band.

2855. חֶתְלֹן **Chethlôn,** *kheth-lone´;* from 2853; *enswathed;* *Chethlon,* a place in Pal.:— Hethlon.

2856. חָתַם **châtham,** *khaw-tham´;* a prim. root; to *close* up; espec. to *seal:*— make an end, mark, seal (up), stop.

2857. חֲתַם **chătham** (Chald.), *khath-am´;* a root corresp. to 2856; to *seal:*— seal.

חֹתָם **chôthâm.** See 2368.

2858. חֹתֶמֶת **chôthemeth,** *kho-the-meth;* fem. act. part. of 2856; a *seal:*— signet.

2859. חָתַן **châthan,** *khaw-than´;* a prim. root; to *give* (a daughter) *away* in marriage; hence, (gen.) to *contract affinity* by marriage:— join in affinity, father in law, make marriages, mother in law, son in law.

2860. חָתָן **châthân,** *khaw-thawn´;* from 2859; a *relative* by marriage (espec. through the bride); fig. a *circumcised* child (as a species of relig. espousal):— bridegroom, husband, son in law.

2861. חֲתֻנָּה **chăthunnâh,** *khath-oon-naw´;* from 2859; a *wedding:*— espousal.

2862. חָתַף **châthaph,** *khaw-thaf´;* a prim. root; to *clutch:*— take away.

2863. חֶתֶף **chetheph,** *kheh´-thef;* from 2862; prop. *rapine;* fig. *robbery:*— prey.

2864. חָתַר **châthar,** *khaw-thar´;* a prim. root; to *force* a passage, as by burglary; fig. with oars:— dig (through), row.

2865. חָתַת **châthath,** *khaw-thath´;* a prim. root; prop. to *prostrate;* hence, to *break* down, either (lit.) by violence, or (fig.) by confusion and fear:— abolish, affright, be (make) afraid, amaze, beat down, discourage, (cause to) dismay, go down, scare, terrify.

2866. חֲתַת **chăthath,** *khath-ath´;* from 2865; *dismay:*— casting down.

2867. חֲתַת **Chăthath,** *khath-ath´;* the same as 2866; *Chathath,* an Isr.:— Hathath.

ט

2868. טְאֵב ṭe'êb (Chald.), teh-abe´; a prim. root; to rejoice:— be glad.

2869. טָב ṭâb (Chald.), tawb; from 2868; the same as 2896; good:— fine, good.

2870. טָבְאֵל Ṭâbe'êl, taw-beh-ale´; from 2895 and 410; pleasing (to) God; Tabeël, the name of a Syrian and of a Persian:— Tabeal, Tabeel.

2871. טָבוּל ṭâbûwl, taw-bool´; pass. part. of 2881; prop. dyed, i.e. a turban (prob. as of colored stuff):— dyed attire.

2872. טַבּוּר ṭabbûwr, tab-boor´; from an unused root mean. to pile up; prop. accumulated; i.e. (by impl.) a summit:— middle, midst.

2873. טָבַח ṭâbach, taw-bakh´; a prim. root; to slaughter (animals or men):— kill, (make) slaughter, slay.

2874. טֶבַח ṭebach, teh´-bakh; from 2873; prop. something slaughtered; hence, a beast (or meat, as butchered); abstr. butchery (or concr. a place of slaughter):— × beast, slaughter, × slay, × sore.

2875. טֶבַח Ṭebach, teh´-bakh; the same as 2874; massacre; Tebach, the name of a Mesopotamian and of an Isr.:— Tebah.

2876. טַבָּח ṭabbâch, tab-bawkh´; from 2873; prop. a butcher; hence, a lifeguardsman (because acting as an executioner); also a cook (as usually slaughtering the animal for food):— cook, guard.

2877. טַבָּח ṭabbâch (Chald.), tab-bawkh´; the same as 2876; a lifeguardsman:— guard.

2878. טִבְחָה ṭibehâh, tib-khaw´; fem. of 2874 and mean. the same:— flesh, slaughter.

2879. טַבָּחָה ṭabbâchâh, tab-baw-khaw´; fem. of 2876; a female cook:— cook.

2880. טִבְחַת Ṭibchath, tib-khath´; from 2878; slaughter; Tibchath, a place in Syria:— Tibhath.

2881. טָבַל ṭâbal, taw-bal´; a prim. root; to dip:— dip, plunge.

2882. טְבַלְיָהוּ Ṭebalyâhûw, teb-al-yaw´-hoo; from 2881 and 3050; Jah has dipped; Tebaljah, an Isr.:— Tebaliah.

2883. טָבַע ṭâba', taw-bah´; a prim. root; to sink:— drown, fasten, settle, sink.

2884. טַבָּעוֹת Ṭabbâ'ôwth, tab-baw-othe´; plur. of 2885; rings; Tabbaoth, one of the Nethinim:— Tabbaoth.

2885. טַבַּעַת ṭabba'ath, tab-bah´-ath; from 2883; prop. a seal (as sunk into the wax), i.e. signet (for sealing); hence, (gen.) a ring of any kind:— ring.

2886. טַבְרִמּוֹן Ṭabrimmôwn, tab-rim-mone´; from 2895 and 7417; pleasing (to) Rimmon; Tabrimmon, a Syrian:— Tabrimmon.

2887. טֵבֵת Ṭêbeth, tay´-beth; prob. of for. der.; Tebeth, the tenth Heb. month:— Tebeth.

2888. טַבַּת Ṭabbath, tab-bath´; of uncert. der.; Tabbath, a place E. of the Jordan:— Tabbath.

2889. טָהוֹר ṭâhôwr, taw-hore´; or

טָהֹר ṭâhôr, taw-hore´; from 2891; pure (in a physical, chemical, ceremonial or moral sense):— clean, fair, pure (-ness).

2890. טְהוֹר ṭehôwr, teh-hore´; from 2891; purity:— pureness.

2891. טָהֵר ṭâhêr, taw-hare´; a prim. root; prop. to be bright; i.e. (by impl.) to be pure (phys. sound, clear, unadulterated; Levit. uncontaminated; mor. innocent or holy):— be (make, make self, pronounce) clean, cleanse (self), purge, purify (-ier, self).

2892. טֹהַר ṭôhar, to´-har; from 2891; lit. brightness; ceremonial purification:— clearness, glory, purifying.

2893. טָהֳרָה ṭohŏrâh, toh-or-aw´; fem. of 2892; ceremonial purification; moral purity:— × is cleansed, cleansing, purification (-fying).

2894. טוּא ṭûw', too; a prim. root; to sweep away:— sweep.

2895. טוֹב ṭowb, tobe; a prim. root, to be (tran. do or make) good (or well) in the widest sense:— be (do) better, cheer, be (do, seem) good, (make) goodly, × please, (be, do, go, play) well.

2896. טוֹב ṭôwb, tobe; from 2895; good (as an adj.) in the widest sense; used likewise as a noun, both in the masc. and the fem., the sing. and the plur. (good, a good or good thing, a good man or woman; the good, goods or good things, good men or women), also as an adv. (well):— beautiful, best, better, bountiful, cheerful, at ease, × fair (word), (be in) favour, fine, glad, good (deed, -lier, -liest, -ly, -ness, -s), graciously, joyful, kindly, kindness, liketh (best), loving, merry, × most, pleasant, + pleaseth, pleasure, precious, prosperity, ready, sweet, wealth, welfare, (be) well ([-favoured]).

2897. טוֹב Ṭôwb, tobe; the same as 2896; good; Tob, a region appar. E. of the Jordan:— Tob.

2898. טוּב ṭûwb, toob; from 2895; good (as a noun), in the widest sense, espec. goodness (superl. concr. the best), beauty, gladness, welfare:— fair, gladness, good (-ness, thing, -s), joy, go well with.

2899. טוֹב אֲדֹנִיָהוּ Ṭôwb Ădônîyâhûw, tobe

Hebrew

ado-nee-yah´-hoo; from 2896 and 138; *pleasing* (to) *Adonijah; Tob-Adonijah,* an Isr.:— Tob-adonijah.

2900. טוֹבִיָּה **Ṭôwbîyâh,** *to-bee-yaw´;* or

טוֹבִיָּהוּ **Ṭôwbîyâhûw,** *to-bee-yaw´-hoo;* from 2896 and 3050; *goodness of Jehovah; Tobijah,* the name of three Isr. and of one Samaritan:— Tobiah, Tobijah.

2901. טָוָה **ṭâvâh,** *taw-vaw´;* a prim. root; to *spin:*— spin.

2902. טוּחַ **ṭûwach,** *too´-akh;* a prim. root; to *smear,* espec. with lime:— daub, overlay, plaister, smut.

2903. טוֹטָפָה **ṭôwphâphâh,** *to-faw-faw´;* from an unused root mean. to *go around* or *bind;* a *fillet* for the forehead:— frontlet.

2904. טוּל **ṭûwl,** *tool;* a prim. root; to *pitch* over or *reel;* hence, (tran.) to *cast* down or out:— carry away, (utterly) cast (down, forth, out), send out.

2905. טוּר **ṭûwr,** *toor;* from an unused root mean. to *range* in a reg. manner; a *row;* hence, a *wall:*— row.

2906. טוּר **ṭûwr** (Chald.), *toor;* corresp. to 6697; a *rock* or hill:— mountain.

2907. טוּשׂ **ṭûws,** *toos;* a prim. root; to *pounce* as a bird of prey:— haste.

2908. טְוָת **ṭᵉvâth** (Chald.), *tev-awth´;* from a root corresp. to 2901; *hunger* (as *twisting*):— fasting.

2909. טָחָה **ṭâchâh,** *taw-khaw´;* a prim. root; to *stretch* a bow, as an *archer:*— [bow-] shot.

2910. טוּחָה **ṭûwchâh,** *too-khaw´;* from 2909 (or 2902) in the sense of *overlaying;* (in the plur. only) the *kidneys* (as being *covered*); hence, (fig.) the inmost *thought:*— inward parts.

2911. טְחוֹן **ṭᵉchôwn,** *tekh-one´;* from 2912; a hand *mill;* hence, a *millstone:*— to grind.

2912. טָחַן **ṭâchan,** *taw-khan´;* a prim. root; to *grind* meal; hence, to *be a concubine* (that being their employment):— grind (-er).

2913. טַחֲנָה **ṭachănâh,** *takh-an-aw´;* from 2912; a hand *mill;* hence, (fig.) *chewing:*— grinding.

2914. טְחֹר **ṭᵉchôr,** *tekh-ore´;* from an unused root mean. to *burn;* a *boil* or ulcer (from the inflammation), espec. a tumor in the anus or pudenda (the piles):— emerod.

2915. טִיחַ **ṭîyach,** *tee´akh;* from (the equiv. of) 2902; mortar or *plaster:*— daubing.

2916. טִיט **ṭîyṭ,** *teet;* from an unused root mean. appar. to *be sticky* [rather perh. a denom. from 2894, through the idea of dirt to *be swept* away]; *mud* or *clay;* fig. *calamity:*— clay, dirt, mire.

2917. טִין **ṭîyn** (Chald.), *teen;* perh. by inter-

change, for a word corresp. to 2916; *clay:*— miry.

2918. טִירָה **ṭîyrâh,** *tee-raw´;* fem. of (an equiv. to) 2905; a *wall;* hence, a *fortress* or a *hamlet:*— (goodly) castle, habitation, palace, row.

2919. טַל **ṭal,** *tal;* from 2926; *dew* (as *covering* vegetation):— dew.

2920. טַל **ṭal** (Chald.), *tal;* the same as 2919:— dew.

2921. טָלָא **ṭâlâ',** *taw-law´;* a prim. root; prop. to *cover* with pieces; i.e. (by impl.) to *spot* or *variegate* (as tapestry):— clouted, with divers colours, spotted.

2922. טְלָא **ṭᵉlâ',** *tel-aw´;* appar. from 2921 in the (orig.) sense of *covering* (for protection); a *lamb* [comp. 2924]:— lamb.

2923. טְלָאִים **Ṭᵉlâ'îym,** *tel-aw-eem´;* from the plur. of 2922; *lambs; Telaim,* a place in Pal.:— Telaim.

2924. טָלֶה **ṭâleh,** *taw-leh´;* by var. for 2922; a *lamb:*— lamb.

2925. טַלְטֵלָה **ṭalṭêlâh,** *tal-tay-law´;* from 2904; *overthrow* or *rejection:*— captivity.

2926. טָלַל **ṭâlal,** *taw-lal´;* a prim. root; prop. to *strew* over, i.e. (by impl.) to *cover* in or *plate* (with beams):— cover.

2927. טְלַל **ṭᵉlal** (Chald.), *tel-al´;* corresp. to 2926; to *cover* with shade:— have a shadow.

2928. טֶלֶם **Ṭelem,** *teh´-lem;* from an unused root mean. to *break* up or treat violently; *oppression; Telem,* the name of a place in Idumæa, also of a temple doorkeeper:— Telem.

2929. טַלְמוֹן **Ṭalmôwn,** *tal-mone´;* from the same as 2728; *oppressive; Talmon,* a temple doorkeeper:— Talmon.

2930. טָמֵא **ṭâmê',** *taw-may´;* a prim. root; to *be foul,* espec. in a cerem. or mor. sense (*contaminated*):— defile (self), pollute (self), be (make, make self, pronounce) unclean, × utterly.

2931. טָמֵא **ṭâmê',** *taw-may´;* from 2930; *foul* in a relig. sense:— defiled, + infamous, polluted (-tion), unclean.

2932. טֻמְאָה **ṭum'âh,** *toom-aw´;* from 2930; relig. *impurity:*— filthiness, unclean (-ness).

2933. טָמָה **ṭâmâh,** *taw-maw´;* a collat. form of 2930; to *be impure* in a relig. sense:— be defiled, be reputed vile.

2934. טָמַן **ṭâman,** *taw-man´;* a prim. root; to *hide* (by *covering* over):— hide, lay privily, in secret.

2935. טֶנֶא **ṭene',** *teh´-neh;* from an unused root prob. mean. to *weave;* a *basket* (of interlaced osiers):— basket.

2936. טָנַף **ṭânaph**, *taw-naf´;* a prim. root; to *soil:*— defile.

2937. טָעָה **tâ'âh**, *taw-aw´;* a prim. root; to *wander;* caus. to *lead astray:*— seduce.

2938. טָעַם **tâ'am**, *taw-am´;* a prim. root; to *taste;* fig. to *perceive:*— × but, perceive, taste.

2939. טְעַם **tᵉ'am** (Chald.), *teh-am´;* corresp. to 2938; to *taste;* caus. to *feed:*— make to eat, feed.

2940. טַעַם **ṭa'am**, *tah´-am;* from 2938; prop. a *taste,* i.e. (fig.) *perception;* by impl. *intelligence;* tran. a *mandate:*— advice, behaviour, decree, discretion, judgment, reason, taste, understanding.

2941. טַעַם **ṭa'am** (Chald.), *tah´-am;* from 2939; prop. a *taste,* i.e. (as in 2940) a judicial *sentence:*— account, × to be commanded, commandment, matter.

2942. טְעֵם **tᵉ'êm** (Chald.), *teh-ame´;* from 2939, and equiv. to 2941; prop. *flavor;* fig. *judgment* (both subj. and obj.); hence, *account* (both subj. and obj.):— + chancellor, + command, commandment, decree, + regard, taste, wisdom.

2943. טָעַן **tâ'an**, *taw-an´;* a prim. root; to *load* a beast:— lade.

2944. טָעַן **tâ'an**, *taw-an´;* a prim. root; to *stab:*— thrust through.

2945. טַף **ṭaph**, *taf;* from 2952 (perh. referring to the *tripping* gait of children); a *family* (mostly used collect. in the sing.):— (little) children (ones), families.

2946. טָפַח **ṭâphach**, *taw-fakh´;* a prim. root; to *flatten* out or *extend* (as a tent); fig. to *nurse* a child (as *promotive* of growth); or perh. a denom. from 2947, from *dandling* on the palms:— span, swaddle.

2947. טֵפַח **tēphach**, *tay´-fakh;* from 2946; a *spread* of the hand, i.e. a *palm-breadth* (not "span" of the fingers); arch. a *corbel* (as a supporting palm):— coping, hand-breadth.

2948. טֹפַח **tôphach**, *to´-fakh;* from 2946 (the same as 2947):— hand-breadth (broad).

2949. טִפֻּח **tippûch**, *tip-pookh´;* from 2946; *nursing:*— span long.

2950. טָפַל **tâphal**, *taw-fal´;* a prim. root; prop. to *stick* on as a patch; fig. to *impute* falsely:— forge (-r), sew up.

2951. טִפְסַר **tiphçar**, *tif-sar´;* of for. der.; a military *governor:*— captain.

2952. טָפַף **tâphaph**, *taw-faf´;* a prim. root; appar. to *trip* (with short steps) coquettishly:— mince.

2953. טְפַר **tᵉphar** (Chald.), *tef-ar´;* from a root corresp. to 6852, and mean. the same as 6856; a finger-*nail;* also a *hoof* or *claw:*— nail.

2954. טָפַשׁ **tâphash**, *taw-fash´;* a prim. root;

prop. appar. to *be thick;* fig. to *be stupid:*— be fat.

2955. טָפַת **Ṭâphath**, *taw-fath´;* prob. from 5197; a *dropping* (of ointment); *Taphath,* an Israelitess:— Taphath.

2956. טָרַד **târad**, *taw-rad´;* a prim. root; to *drive* on; fig. to *follow* close:— continual.

2957. טְרַד **tᵉrad** (Chald.), *ter-ad´;* corresp. to 2956; to *expel:*— drive.

2958. טְרוֹם **tᵉrôwm**, *ter-ome´;* a var. of 2962; *not yet:*— before.

2959. טָרַח **târach**, *taw-rakh´;* a prim. root; to *overburden:*— weary.

2960. טֹרַח **tôrach**, *to´-rakh;* from 2959; a *burden:*— cumbrance, trouble.

2961. טָרִי **târîy**, *taw-ree´;* from an unused root appar. mean. to *be moist;* prop. *dripping;* hence, *fresh* (i.e. recently made such):— new, putrefying.

2962. טֶרֶם **terem**, *teh´-rem;* from an unused root appar. mean. to *interrupt* or *suspend;* prop. *non-occurrence;* used adv. *not yet* or *before:*— before, ere, not yet.

2963. טָרַף **târaph**, *taw-raf´;* a prim. root; to *pluck off* or *pull* to pieces; caus. to *supply* with food (as in morsels):— catch, × without doubt, feed, ravin, rend in pieces, × surely, tear (in pieces).

2964. טֶרֶף **tereph**, *teh´-ref;* from 2963; something *torn,* i.e. a *fragment,* e.g. a *fresh* leaf, *prey, food:*— leaf, meat, prey, spoil.

2965. טָרָף **târâph**, *taw-rawf´;* from 2963; recently *torn* off, i.e. *fresh:*— pluckt off.

2966. טְרֵפָה **tᵉrêphâh**, *ter-ay-faw´;* fem. (collect.) of 2964; *prey,* i.e. flocks devoured by animals:— ravin, (that which was) torn (of beasts, in pieces).

2967. טַרְפְּלַי **Ṭarpᵉlay** (Chald.), *tar-pel-ah´-ee;* from a name of for. der.; a *Tarpelite* (collect.) or inhab. of Tarpel, a place in Assyria:— Tarpelites.

2968. יָאַב **yâ'ab**, *yaw-ab´;* a prim. root; to *desire:*— long.

2969. יָאָה **yâ'âh**, *yaw-aw´;* a prim. root; to *be suitable:*— appertain.

     יְאוֹר **yᵉ'ôwr**. See 2975.

2970. יַאֲזַנְיָה **Ya'ăzanyâh**, *yah-az-an-yaw´;* or

     יַאֲזַנְיָהוּ **Ya'ăzanyâhûw**, *yah-az-an-yaw´-hoo;* from 238 and 3050; *heard of Jah; Jaazanjah,* the name of four Isr.:— Jaazaniah. Comp. 3153.

2971. יָאִיר **Yâ'îyr**, *yaw-ere´;* from 215; *enlightener; Jair,* the name of four Isr.:— Jair.

2972. יָאִרִי **Yâ'îrîy**, *yaw-ee-ree´*; patron. from 2971; a *Jairite* or desc. of Jair:— Jairite.

2973. יָאַל **yâ'al**, *yaw-al´*; a prim. root; prop. to *be slack*, i.e. (fig.) to *be foolish:*— dote, be (become, do) foolish (-ly).

2974. יָאַל **yâ'al**, *yaw-al´*; a prim. root [prob. rather the same as 2973 through the idea of mental *weakness*]; prop. to *yield*, espec. *assent*; hence, (pos.) to *undertake* as an act of volition:— assay, begin, be content, please, take upon, × willingly, would.

2975. יְאֹר **ye'ôr**, *yeh-ore´*; of Eg. or.; a *channel*, e.g. a fosse, canal, shaft; spec. the *Nile*, as the one river of Egypt, incl. its collat. trenches; also the *Tigris*, as the main river of Assyria:— brook, flood, river, stream.

2976. יָאַשׁ **yâ'ash**, *yaw-ash´*; a prim. root; to *desist*, i.e. (fig.) to *despond:*— (cause to) despair, one that is desperate, be no hope.

2977. יֹאשִׁיָּה **Yô'shîyâh**, *yo-shee-yaw´*; or

יֹאשִׁיָּהוּ **Yô'shîyâhûw**, *yo-she-yaw´-hoo*; from the same root as 803 and 3050; *founded of Jah; Joshijah*, the name of two Isr.:— Josiah.

2978. יְאִתוֹן° **ye'îthôwn**, *yeh-ee-thone´*; from 857; an *entry:*— entrance.

2979. יְאָתְרַי **Ye'âtheray**, *yeh-aw-ther-ah´ee*; from the same as 871; *stepping; Jeätherai*, an Isr.:— Jeaterai.

2980. יָבַב **yâbab**, *yaw-bab´*; a prim. root; to *bawl:*— cry out.

2981. יְבוּל **yebûwl**, *yeb-ool´*; from 2986; *produce*, i.e. a *crop* or (fig.) *wealth:*— fruit, increase.

2982. יְבוּס **Yebûwç**, *yeb-oos´*; from 947; *trodden*, i.e. threshing-place; *Jebus*, the aboriginal name of Jerusalem:— Jebus.

2983. יְבוּסִי **Yebûwçîy**, *yeb-oo-see´*; patrial from 2982; a *Jebusite* or inhab. of Jebus:— Jebusite (-s).

2984. יִבְחַר **Yibchar**, *yib-khar´*; from 977; *choice; Jibchar*, an Isr.:— Ibhar.

2985. יָבִין **Yâbîyn**, *yaw-bene´*; from 995; *intelligent; Jabin*, the name of two Canaanitish kings:— Jabin.

יָבֵשׁ **Yâbêysh**. See 3003.

2986. יָבַל **yâbal**, *yaw-bal´*; a prim. root; prop. to *flow*; caus. to *bring* (espec. with pomp):— bring (forth), carry, lead (forth).

2987. יְבַל **yebal** (Chald.), *yeb-al´*; corresp. to 2986; to *bring:*— bring, carry.

יֹבֵל **yôbêl**. See 3104.

2988. יָבָל **yâbâl**, *yaw-bawl´*; from 2986; a *stream:*— [water-] course, stream.

2989. יָבָל **Yâbâl**, *yaw-bawl´*; the same as 2988; *Jabal*, an antediluvian:— Jabal.

יֹבֵל **yôbêl**. See 3104.

2990. יַבֵּל **yabbêl**, *yab-bale´*; from 2986; having *running* sores:— wen.

2991. יִבְלְעָם **Yible'âm**, *yib-leh-awm´*; from 1104 and 5971; *devouring people; Jibleäm*, a place in Pal.:— Ibleam.

2992. יָבַם **yâbam**, *yaw-bam´*; a prim. root of doubtful mean.; used only as a denom. from 2993; to *marry* a (deceased) brother's widow:— perform the duty of a husband's brother, marry.

2993. יָבָם **yâbâm**, *yaw-bawm´*; from (the orig. of) 2992; a *brother-in-law:*— husband's brother.

2994. יְבֵמֶת **yebêmeth**, *yeb-ay´-meth*; fem. part. of 2992; a *sister-in-law:*— brother's wife, sister in law.

2995. יַבְנְאֵל **Yabne'êl**, *yab-neh-ale´*; from 1129 and 410; *built of God; Jabneël*, the name of two places in Pal.:— Jabneel.

2996. יַבְנֶה **Yabneh**, *yab-neh´*; from 1129; a *building; Jabneh*, a place in Pal.:— Jabneh.

2997. יִבְנְיָה **Yibneyâh**, *yib-neh-yaw´*; from 1129 and 3050; *built of Jah; Jibnejah*, an Isr.:— Ibneiah.

2998. יִבְנִיָּה **Yibnîyâh**, *yib-nee-yaw´*; from 1129 and 3050; *building of Jah; Jibnijah*, an Isr.:— Ibnijah.

2999. יַבֹּק **Yabbôq**, *yab-boke´*; prob. from 1238; *pouring* forth; *Jabbok*, a river E. of the Jordan:— Jabbok.

3000. יְבֶרֶכְיָהוּ **Yeberekyâhûw**, *yeb-eh-rek-yaw´-hoo*; from 1288 and 3050; *blessed of Jah; Jeberekjah*, an Isr.:— Jeberechiah.

3001. יָבֵשׁ **yâbêsh**, *yaw-bashe´*; a prim. root; to *be ashamed, confused* or *disappointed*; also (as failing) to *dry* up (as water) or *wither* (as herbage):— be ashamed, clean, be confounded, (make) dry (up), (do) shame (-fully), × utterly, wither (away).

3002. יָבֵשׁ **yâbêsh**, *yaw-bashe´*; from 3001; *dry:*— dried (away), dry.

3003. יָבֵשׁ **Yâbêsh**, *yaw-bashe´*; the same as 3002 (also

יָבֵישׁ **Yâbêysh**, *yaw-bashe´*; often with the addition of 1568, i.e. *Jabesh of Gilead*); *Jabesh*, the name of an Isr. and of a place in Pal.:— Jabesh (l-Gilead).

3004. יַבָּשָׁה **yabbâshâh**, *yab-baw-shaw´*; from 3001; *dry ground:*— dry (ground, land).

3005. יִבְשָׂם **Yibsâm**, *yib-sawm´*; from the same as 1314; *fragrant; Jibsam*, an Isr.:— Jibsam.

3006. יַבֶּשֶׁת **yabbesheth**, *yab-beh´-sheth*; a var. of 3004; *dry* ground:— dry land.

3007. יַבֶּשֶׁת **yabbesheth** (Chald.), *yab-beh´-sheth;* corresp. to 3006; *dry* land:— earth.

3008. יִגְאָל **Yig'âl**, *yig-awl´;* from 1350; *avenger; Jigal,* the name of three Isr.:— Igal, Igeal.

3009. יָגַב **yâgab**, *yaw-gab´;* a prim. root; to *dig* or *plow:*— husbandman.

3010. יָגֵב **yâgêb**, *yaw-gabe´;* from 3009; a plowed *field:*— field.

3011. יָגְבְּהָה **Yogbᵉhâh**, *yog-beh-haw´;* fem. from 1361; *hillock; Jogbehah,* a place E. of the Jordan:— Jogbehah.

3012. יִגְדַּלְיָהוּ **Yigdalyâhûw**, *yig-dal-yaw´-hoo;* from 1431 and 3050; *magnified of Jah; Jigdaljah,* an Isr.:— Igdaliah.

3013. יָגָה **yâgâh**, *yaw-gaw´;* a prim. root; to *grieve:*— afflict, cause grief, grieve, sorrowful, vex.

3014. יָגָה **yâgâh**, *yaw-gaw´;* a prim. root [prob. rather the same as 3013 through the common idea of *dissatisfaction*]; to *push* away:— be removed.

3015. יָגוֹן **yâgôwn**, *yaw-gohn´;* from 3013; *affliction:*— grief, sorrow.

3016. יָגוֹר **yâgôwr**, *yaw-gore´;* from 3025; *fearful:*— afraid, fearest.

3017. יָגוּר **Yâgûwr**, *yaw-goor´;* prob. from 1481; a *lodging; Jagur,* a place in Pal.:— Jagur.

3018. יְגִיעַ **yᵉgîya'**, *yeg-ee´-ah;* from 3021; *toil;* hence, a *work, produce, property* (as the result of labor):— labour, work.

3019. יָגִיעַ **yâgîya'**, *yaw-ghee´-ah;* from 3021; *tired:*— weary.

3020. יָגְלִי **Yoglîy**, *yog-lee´;* from 1540; *exiled; Jogli,* an Isr.:— Jogli.

3021. יָגַע **yâga'**, *yaw-gah´;* a prim. root; prop. to *gasp;* hence, to *be exhausted,* to *tire,* to *toil:*— faint, (make to) labour, (be) weary.

3022. יָגָע **yâgâ'**, *yaw-gaw´;* from 3021; *earnings* (as the product of toil):— that which he laboured for.

3023. יָגֵעַ **yâgêa'**, *yaw-gay´-ah;* from 3021; *tired;* hence, (tran.) *tiresome:*— full of labour, weary.

3024. יְגִעָה **yᵉgi'âh**, *yeg-ee-aw´;* fem. of 3019; *fatigue:*— weariness.

3025. יָגֹר **yâgôr**, *yaw-gore´;* a prim. root; to *fear:*— be afraid, fear.

3026. יְגַר שָׂהֲדוּתָא **Yᵉgar Sahădûwthâ'** (Chald.), *yegar´ sah-had-oo-thaw´;* from a word derived from an unused root (mean. to *gather*) and a der. of a root corresp. to 7717; *heap of the testimony; Jegar-Sahadutha,* a cairn E. of the Jordan:— Jegar-Sahadutha.

3027. יָד **yâd**, *yawd;* a prim. word; a *hand* (the *open* one [indicating *power, means, direction,*

etc.], in distinction from 3709, the *closed* one); used (as noun, adv., etc.) in a great variety of applications, both lit. and fig., both prox. and remote [as follows]:— (+ be) able, × about, + armholes, at, axletree, because of, beside, border, × bounty, + broad, [broken-] handed, × by, charge, coast, + consecrate, + creditor, custody, debt, dominion, × enough, + fellowship, force, × from, hand [-staves, -y work], × he, himself, × in, labour, + large, ledge, [left-] handed, means, × mine, ministry, near, × of, × order, ordinance, × our, parts, pain, power, × presumptuously, service, side, sore, state, stay, draw with strength, stroke, + swear, terror, × thee, × by them, × themselves, × thine own, × thou, through, × throwing, + thumb, times, × to, × under, × us, × wait on, [way-] side, where, + wide, × with (him, me, you), work, + yield, × yourselves.

3028. יַד **yad** (Chald.), *yad;* corresp. to 3027:— hand, power.

3029. יְדָא **yᵉdâ'** (Chald.), *yed-aw´;* corresp. to 3034; to *praise:*— (give) thank (-s).

3030. יִדְאֲלָה **Yid'ălâh**, *yid-al-aw´;* of uncert. der.; *Jidalah,* a place in Pal.:— Idalah.

3031. יִדְבָּשׁ **Yidbâsh**, *yid-bawsh´;* from the same as 1706; perh. *honeyed; Jidbash,* an Isr.:— Idbash.

3032. יָדַד **yâdad**, *yaw-dad´;* a prim. root; prop. to *handle* [comp. 3034], i.e. to *throw,* e.g. lots:— cast.

3033. יְדִדוּת **yᵉdîdûwth**, *yed-ee-dooth´;* from 3039; prop. *affection;* concr. a *darling* object:— dearly beloved.

3034. יָדָה **yâdâh**, *yaw-daw´;* a prim. root; used only as denom. from 3027; lit. to *use* (i.e. hold out) *the hand;* phys. to *throw* (a stone, an arrow) at or away; espec. to *revere* or *worship* (with extended hands); intens. to *bemoan* (by wringing the hands):— cast (out), (make) confess (-ion), praise, shoot, (give) thank (-ful, -s, -sgiving).

3035. יִדּוֹ **Yiddôw**, *yid-do´;* from 3034; *praised; Jiddo,* an Isr.:— Iddo.

3036. יָדוֹן **Yâdôwn**, *yaw-done´;* from 3034; *thankful; Jadon,* an Isr.:— Jadon.

3037. יַדּוּעַ **Yaddûwa'**, *yad-doo´-ah;* from 3045; *knowing; Jadduä,* the name of two Isr.:— Jaddua.

3038. יְדוּתוּן **Yᵉdûwthûwn**, *yed-oo-thoon´;* or יְדֻתוּן **Yᵉdûthûwn**, *yed-oo-thoon´;* or יְדִיתוּן **Yᵉdîythûwn**, *yed-ee-thoon´;* prob. from 3034; *laudatory; Jeduthun,* an Isr.:— Jeduthun.

3039. יְדִיד **yᵉdîyd**, *yed-eed´;* from the same as 1730; *loved:*— amiable, (well-) beloved, loves.

3040. יְדִידָה **Yᵉdîydâh**, *yed-ee-daw´*; fem. of 3039; *beloved; Jedidah*, an Israelitess:— Jedidah.

3041. יְדִידְיָה **Yᵉdîydᵉyâh**, *yed-ee-deh-yaw´*; from 3039 and 3050; *beloved of Jah; Jedidejah*, a name of Solomon:— Jedidiah.

3042. יְדָיָה **Yᵉdâyâh**, *yed-aw-yaw´*; from 3034 and 3050; *praised of Jah; Jedajah*, the name of two Isr.:— Jedaiah.

3043. יְדִיעֵאל **Yᵉdîy'ă'êl**, *yed-ee-ah-ale´*; from 3045 and 410; *knowing God; Jediaël*, the name of three Isr.:— Jediael.

3044. יִדְלָף **Yidlâph**, *yid-lawf´*; from 1811; *tearful; Jidlaph*, a Mesopotamian:— Jidlaph.

3045. יָדַע **yâda'**, *yaw-dah´*; a prim. root; to *know* (prop. to ascertain by *seeing*); used in a great variety of senses, fig., lit., euphem. and infer. (incl. *observation, care, recognition;* and caus. *instruction, designation, punishment,* etc.) [as follow]:— acknowledge, acquaintance (-ted with), advise, answer, appoint, assuredly, be aware, [un-] awares, can [-not], certainly, for a certainty, comprehend, consider, × could they, cunning, declare, be diligent, (can, cause to) discern, discover, endued with, familiar friend, famous, feel, can have, be [ig-] norant, instruct, kinsfolk, kinsman, (cause to, let, make) know, (come to give, have, take) knowledge, have [knowledge], (be, make, make to be, make self) known, + be learned, + lie by man, mark, perceive, privy to, × prognosticator, regard, have respect, skilful, shew, can (man of) skill, be sure, of a surety, teach, (can) tell, understand, have [understanding], × will be, wist, wit, wot.

3046. יְדַע **yᵉda'** (Chald.), *yed-ah´*; corresp. to 3045:— certify, know, make known, teach.

3047. יָדָע **Yâdâ'**, *yaw-daw´*; from 3045; *knowing; Jada*, an Isr.:— Jada.

3048. יְדַעְיָה **Yᵉda'yâh**, *yed-ah-yaw´*; from 3045 and 3050; *Jah has known; Jedajah*, the name of two Isr.:— Jedaiah.

3049. יִדְּעֹנִי **yiddᵉ'ônîy**, *yid-deh-o-nee´*; from 3045; prop. a *knowing* one; spec. a *conjurer;* (by impl.) a *ghost:*— wizard.

3050. יָהּ **Yâhh**, *yaw*; contr. for 3068, and mean. the same; *Jah*, the sacred name:— Jah, the Lord, most vehement. Comp. names in "-iah," "-jah."

3051. יָהַב **yâhab**, *yaw-hab´*; a prim. root; to *give* (whether lit. or fig.); gen. to *put;* imper. (refl.) *come:*— ascribe, bring, come on, give, go, set, take.

3052. יְהַב **yᵉhab** (Chald.), *yeh-hab´*; corresp. to 3051:— deliver, give, lay, + prolong, pay, yield.

3053. יְהָב **yᵉhâb**, *ye-hawb´*; from 3051; prop.

what is *given* (by Providence), i.e. a *lot:*— burden.

3054. יָהַד **yâhad**, *yaw-had´*; denom. from a form corresp. to 3061; to *Judaize*, i.e. become Jewish:— become Jews.

3055. יְהֻד **Yᵉhûd**, *yeh-hood´*; a briefer form of one corresp. to 3061; *Jehud*, a place in Pal.:— Jehud.

3056. יֶהְדַּי **Yehday**, *yeh-dah´-ee*; perh. from a form corresp. to 3061; *Judaistic; Jehdai*, an Isr.:— Jehdai.

3057. יְהֻדִיָּה **Yᵉhûdîyâh**, *yeh-hoo-dee-yaw´*; fem. of 3064; *Jehudijah*, a Jewess:— Jehudijah.

3058. יֵהוּא **Yêhûw'**, *yay-hoo´*; from 3068 and 1931; *Jehovah (is) He; Jehu*, the name of five Isr.:— Jehu.

3059. יְהוֹאָחָז **Yᵉhôw'âchâz**, *yeh-ho-aw-khawz´*; from 3068 and 270; *Jehovah-seized; Jehoächaz*, the name of three Isr.:— Jehoahaz. Comp. 3099.

3060. יְהוֹאָשׁ **Yᵉhôw'âsh**, *yeh-ho-awsh´*; from 3068 and (perh.) 784; *Jehovah-fired; Jehoäsh*, the name of two Isr. kings:— Jehoash. Comp. 3101.

3061. יְהוּד **Yᵉhûwd** (Chald.), *yeh-hood´*; contr. from a form corresp. to 3063; prop. *Judah*, hence, *Judea:*— Jewry, Judah, Judea.

3062. יְהוּדָאִי **Yᵉhûwdâ'îy** (Chald.), *yeh-hoo-daw-ee´*; patrial from 3061; a *Jehudaïte* (or Judaite), i.e. *Jew:*— Jew.

3063. יְהוּדָה **Yᵉhûwdâh**, *yeh-hoo-daw´*; from 3034; *celebrated; Jehudah* (or Judah), the name of five Isr.; also of the tribe descended from the first, and of its territory:— Judah.

3064. יְהוּדִי **Yᵉhûwdîy**, *yeh-hoo-dee´*; patron. from 3063; a *Jehudite* (i.e. Judaite or Jew), or desc. of Jehudah (i.e. Judah):— Jew.

3065. יְהוּדִי **Yᵉhûwdîy**, *yeh-hoo-dee´*; the same as 3064; *Jehudi*, an Isr.:— Jehudi.

3066. יְהוּדִית **Yᵉhûwdîyth**, *yeh-hoo-deeth´*; fem. of 3064; the *Jewish* (used adv.) language:— in the Jews' language.

3067. יְהוּדִית **Yᵉhûwdîyth**, *yeh-ho-deeth´*; the same as 3066; *Jewess; Jehudith*, a Canaanitess:— Judith.

3068. יְהֹוָה **Yᵉhôvâh**, *yeh-ho-vaw´*; from 1961; (the) self-*Existent* or Eternal; *Jehovah*, Jewish national name of God:— Jehovah, the Lord. Comp. 3050, 3069.

3069. יְהֹוִה **Yᵉhôvîh**, *yeh-ho-vee´*; a var. of 3068 [used after 136, and pronounced by Jews as 430, in order to prevent the repetition of the same sound, since they elsewhere pronounce 3068 as 136]:— God.

3070. יְהֹוָה יִרְאֶה **Yᵉhôvâh Yir'eh**, *yeh-ho-vaw´ yir-eh´*; from 3068 and 7200; *Jehovah will see* (to it); *Jehovah-Jireh*, a symb. name for Mt. Moriah:— Jehovah-jireh.

3071. יְהֹוָה נִסִּי **Yᵉhôvâh Niççîy**, *yeh-ho-vaw´ nis-see´*; from 3068 and 5251 with the pron. suff.; *Jehovah* (is) *my banner; Jehovah-Nissi*, a symb. name of an altar in the Desert:— Jehovah-nissi.

3072. יְהֹוָה צִדְקֵנוּ **Yᵉhôvâh Tsidqênûw**, *ye-ho-vaw´ tsid-kay´-noo;* from 3068 and 6664 with pron. suff.; *Jehovah* (is) *our right; Jehovah-Tsidkenu*, a symb. epithet of the Messiah and of Jerusalem:— the Lord our righteousness.

3073. יְהֹוָה שָׁלוֹם **Yᵉhôvâh Shâlôwm**, *yeh-ho-vaw´ shaw-lome´;* from 3068 and 7965; *Jehovah* (is) *peace; Jehovah-Shalom*, a symb. name of an altar in Pal.:— Jehovah-shalom.

3074. יְהֹוָה שָׁמָּה **Yᵉhôvâh Shâmmâh**, *yeh-ho-vaw´ shawm´-maw;* from 3068 and 8033 with directive enclitic; *Jehovah* (is) *thither; Jehovah-Shammah*, a symbol. title of Jerusalem:— Jehovah-shammah.

3075. יְהוֹזָבָד **Yᵉhôwzâbâd**, *yeh-ho-zaw-bawd´;* from 3068 and 2064; *Jehovah-endowed; Jehozabad*, the name of three Isr.:— Jehozabad. Comp. 3107.

3076. יְהוֹחָנָן **Yᵉhôwchânân**, *yeh-ho-khaw-nawn´;* from 3068 and 2603; *Jehovah-favored; Jehochanan*, the name of eight Isr.:— Jehohanan, Johanan. Comp. 3110.

3077. יְהוֹיָדָע **Yᵉhôwyâdâ'**, *yeh-ho-yaw-daw´;* from 3068 and 3045; *Jehovah-known; Jehojada*, the name of three Isr.:— Jehoiada. Comp. 3111.

3078. יְהוֹיָכִין **Yᵉhôwyâkîyn**, *yeh-ho-yaw-keen´;* from 3068 and 3559; *Jehovah will establish; Jehojakin*, a Jewish king:— Jehoiachin. Comp. 3112.

3079. יְהוֹיָקִים **Yᵉhôwyâqîym**, *yeh-ho-yaw-keem´;* from 3068 abb. and 6965; *Jehovah will raise; Jehojakim*, a Jewish king:— Jehoiakim. Comp. 3113.

3080. יְהוֹיָרִיב **Yᵉhôwyârîyb**, *yeh-ho-yaw-reeb´;* from 3068 and 7378; *Jehovah will contend; Jehojarib*, the name of two Isr.:— Jehoiarib. Comp. 3114.

3081. יוּכַל **Yᵉhûwkal**, *yeh-hoo-kal´;* from 3201; *potent; Jehukal*, an Isr.:— Jehucal. Comp. 3116.

3082. יְהוֹנָדָב **Yᵉhôwnâdâb**, *yeh-ho-naw-dawb´;* from 3068 and 5068; *Jehovah-largessed; Jehonadab*, the name of an Isr. and of an Arab:— Jehonadab, Jonadab. Comp. 3122.

3083. יְהוֹנָתָן **Yᵉhôwnâthân**, *yeh-ho-naw-thawn´;* from 3068 and 5414; *Jehovah-given; Jehonathan*, the name of four Isr.:— Jonathan. Comp. 3129.

3084. יְהוֹסֵף **Yᵉhôwçêph**, *yeh-ho-safe´;* a fuller form of 3130; *Jehoseph* (i.e. Joseph), a son of Jacob:— Joseph.

3085. יְהוֹעַדָּה **Yᵉhôw'addâh**, *yeh-ho-ad-daw´;* from 3068 and 5710; *Jehovah-adorned; Jehoäddah*, an Isr.:— Jehoada.

3086. יְהוֹעַדִּין **Yᵉhôw'addîyn**, *yeh-ho-ad-deen´;* or

יְהוֹעַדָּן **Yᵉhôw'addân**, *yeh-ho-ad-dawn´;* from 3068 and 5727; *Jehovah-pleased; Jehoäddin* or *Jehoäddan*, an Israelitess:— Jehoaddan.

3087. יְהוֹצָדָק **Yᵉhôwtsâdâq**, *yeh-ho-tsaw-dawk´;* from 3068 and 6663; *Jehovah-righted; Jehotsadak*, an Isr.:— Jehozadek, Josedech. Comp. 3136.

3088. יְהוֹרָם **Yᵉhôwrâm**, *yeh-ho-rawm´;* from 3068 and 7311; *Jehovah-raised; Jehoram*, the name of a Syrian and of three Isr.:— Jehoram, Joram. Comp. 3141.

3089. יְהוֹשֶׁבַע **Yᵉhôwsheba'**, *yeh-ho-sheh´-bah;* from 3068 and 7650; *Jehovah-sworn; Jehosheba*, an Israelitess:— Jehosheba. Comp. 3090.

3090. יְהוֹשַׁבְעַת **Yᵉhôwshab'ath**, *yeh-ho-shab-ath´;* a form of 3089; *Jehoshabath*, an Israelitess:— Jehoshabeath.

3091. יְהוֹשׁוּעַ **Yᵉhôwshûw'a**, *yeh-ho-shoo´-ah;* or

יְהוֹשֻׁעַ **Yᵉhôwshû'a**, *yeh-ho-shoo´-ah;* from 3068 and 3467; *Jehovah-saved; Jehoshuä* (i.e. Joshua), the Jewish leader:— Jehoshua, Jehoshuah, Joshua. Comp. 1954, 3442.

3092. יְהוֹשָׁפָט **Yᵉhôwshâphât**, *yeh-ho-shaw-fawt´;* from 3068 and 8199; *Jehovah-judged; Jehoshaphat*, the name of six Isr.; also of a valley near Jerusalem:— Jehoshaphat. Comp. 3146.

3093. יָהִיר **yâhîyr**, *yaw-here´;* prob. from the same as 2022; *elated;* hence, *arrogant:*— haughty, proud.

3094. יְהַלֶּלְאֵל **Yᵉhallel'êl**, *yeh-hal-lel-ale´;* from 1984 and 410; *praising God; Jehallelel*, the name of two Isr.:— Jehaleleel, Jehalelel.

3095. יַהֲלֹם **yahălôm**, *yah-hal-ome´;* from 1986 (in the sense of *hardness*); a precious stone, prob. *onyx:*— diamond.

3096. יַהַץ **Yahats**, *yah´-hats;* or

יַהְצָה **Yahtsâh**, *yah´-tsaw;* or (fem.)

יַהְצָה **Yahtsâh**, *yah-tsaw´;* from an unused root mean. to *stamp;* perh. *threshing-floor; Jahats* or *Jahtsah*, a place E. of the Jordan:— Jahaz, Jahazah, Jahzah.

3097. יוֹאָב **Yôw'âb**, *yo-awb´;* from 3068 and

1; *Jehovah-fathered; Joâb*, the name of three Isr.:— Joab.

3098. יוֹאָח **Yôw'âch**, yo-awkh´; from 3068 and 251; *Jehovah-brothered; Joach*, the name of four Isr.:— Joah.

3099. יוֹאָחָז **Yôw'âchâz**, yo-aw-khawz´; a form of 3059; *Joächaz*, the name of two Isr.:— Jehoahaz, Joahaz.

3100. יוֹאֵל **Yôw'êl**, yo-ale´; from 3068 and 410; *Jehovah* (is his) *God; Joël*, the name of twelve Isr.:— Joel.

3101. יוֹאָשׁ **Yôw'âsh**, yo-awsh´; or

אֹאָשׁ **Yô'âsh** (2 Chron. 24:1), yo-awsh´; a form of 3060; *Joâsh*, the name of six Isr.:— Joash.

3102. יוֹב **Yôwb**, yobe; perh. a form of 3103, but more prob. by err. transc. for 3437; *Job*, an Isr.:— Job.

3103. יוֹבָב **Yôwbâb**, yo-bawb´; from 2980; *howler; Jobab*, the name of two Isr. and of three foreigners:— Jobab.

3104. יוֹבֵל **yôwbêl**, yo-bale´; or

יֹבֵל **yôbêl**, yob-ale´; appar. from 2986; the *blast* of a horn (from its *continuous* sound); spec. the *signal* of the silver trumpets; hence, the instrument itself and the festival thus introduced:— jubile, ram's horn, trumpet.

3105. יוּבַל **yûwbal**, yoo-bal´; from 2986; a *stream:*— river.

3106. יוּבָל **Yûwbâl**, yoo-bawl´; from 2986; *stream; Jubal*, an antediluvian:— Jubal.

3107. יוֹזָבָד **Yôwzâbâd**, yo-zaw-bawd´; a form of 3075; *Jozabad*, the name of ten Isr.:— Josabad, Jozabad.

3108. יוֹזָכָר **Yôwzâkâr**, yo-zaw-kawr´; from 3068 and 2142; *Jehovah-remembered; Jozacar*, an Isr.:— Jozachar.

3109. יוֹחָא **Yôwchâ'**, yo-khaw´; prob. from 3068 and a var. of 2421; *Jehovah-revived; Jocha*, the name of two Isr.:— Joha.

3110. יוֹחָנָן **Yôwchânân**, yo-khaw-nawn´; a form of 3076; *Jochanan*, the name of nine Isr.:— Johanan.

יוּטָה **Yûwṭâh**. See 3194.

3111. יוֹיָדָע **Yôwyâdâ'**, yo-yaw-daw´; a form of 3077; *Jojada*, the name of two Isr.:— Jehoiada, Joiada.

3112. יוֹיָכִין **Yôwyâkîyn**, yo-yaw-keen´; a form of 3078; *Jojakin*, an Isr. king:— Jehoiachin.

3113. יוֹיָקִים **Yôwyâqîym**, yo-yaw-keem´; a form of 3079; *Jojakim*, an Isr.:— Joiakim. Comp. 3137.

3114. יוֹיָרִיב **Yôwyârîyb**, yo-yaw-reeb´; a form of 3080; *Jojarib*, the name of four Isr.:— Joiarib.

3115. יוֹכֶבֶד **Yôwkebed**, yo-keh´-bed; from 3068 contr. and 3513; *Jehovah-gloried; Jokebed*, the mother of Moses:— Jochebed.

3116. יוּכַל **Yûwkal**, yoo-kal´; a form of 3081; *Jukal*, an Isr.:— Jucal.

3117. יוֹם **yôwm**, yome; from an unused root mean. to *be hot*; a *day* (as the *warm* hours), whether lit. (from sunrise to sunset, or from one sunset to the next), or fig. (a space of time defined by an associated term), [often used adv.]:— age, + always, + chronicles, continually (-ance), daily, ([birth-], each, to) day, (now a, two) days (agone), + elder, × end, + evening, + (for) ever (-lasting, -more), × full, life, as (so) long as (... live), (even) now, + old, + outlived, + perpetually, presently, + remaineth, × required, season, × since, space, then, (process of) time, + as at other times, + in trouble, weather, (as) when, (a, the, within a) while (that), × whole (+ age), (full) year (-ly), + younger.

3118. יוֹם **yôwm** (Chald.), yome; corresp. to 3117; a *day:*— day (by day), time.

3119. יוֹמָם **yôwmâm**, yo-mawm´; from 3117; *daily:*— daily, (by, in the) day (-time).

3120. יָוָן **Yâvân**, yaw-vawn´; prob. from the same as 3196; *effervescing* (i.e. hot and active); *Javan*, the name of a son of Joktan, and of the race (*Ionians*, i.e. Greeks) descended from him, with their territory; also of a place in Arabia:— Javan.

3121. יָוֵן **yâvên**, yaw-ven´; from the same as 3196; prop. *dregs* (as *effervescing*); hence, *mud:*— mire, miry.

3122. יוֹנָדָב **Yôwnâdâb**, yo-naw-dawb´; a form of 3082; *Jonadab*, the name of an Isr. and of a Rechabite:— Jonadab.

3123. יוֹנָה **yôwnâh**, yo-naw´; prob. from the same as 3196; a *dove* (appar. from the *warmth* of their mating):— dove, pigeon.

3124. יוֹנָה **Yôwnâh**, yo-naw´; the same as 3123; *Jonah*, an Isr.:— Jonah.

3125. יְוָנִי **Yᵉvânîy**, yev-aw-nee´; patron. from 3121; a *Jevanite*, or desc. of Javan:— Grecian.

3126. יוֹנֵק **yôwnêq**, yo-nake´; act. part. of 3243; a *sucker;* hence, a *twig* (of a tree felled and sprouting):— tender plant.

3127. יוֹנֶקֶת **yôwneqeth**, yo-neh´-keth; fem. of 3126; a *sprout:*— (tender) branch, young twig.

3128. יוֹנַת אֵלֶם רְחֹקִים **Yôwnath 'êlem rᵉchôqîym**, yo-nath´ ay´-lem rekh-o-keem´; from 3123 and 482 and the plur. of 7350; *dove of* (the) *silence* (i.e. *dumb* Israel) *of* (i.e. *among*) *distances* (i.e. *strangers*); the title of a ditty (used for a name of its melody):— Jonath-elem-rechokim.

3129. יוֹנָתָן **Yôwnâthân**, *yo-naw-thawn´;* a form of 3083; *Jonathan,* the name of ten Isr.:— Jonathan.

3130. יוֹסֵף **Yôwçêph**, *yo-safe´;* future of 3254; *let him add* (or perh. simply act. part. *adding*); *Joseph,* the name of seven Isr.:— Joseph. Comp. 3084.

3131. יוֹסִפְיָה **Yôwçiphyâh**, *yo-sif-yaw´;* from act. part. of 3254 and 3050; *Jah (is) adding; Josiphjah,* an Isr.:— Josiphiah.

3132. יוֹעֵאלָה **Yôw'ê'lâh**, *yo-ay-law´;* perh. fem. act. part. of 3276; *furthermore; Joelah,* an Isr.:— Joelah.

3133. יוֹעֵד **Yôw'êd**, *yo-ade´;* appar. the act. part. of 3259; *appointer; Joed,* an Isr.:— Joed.

3134. יוֹעֶזֶר **Yôw'ezer**, *yo-eh´-zer;* from 3068 and 5828; *Jehovah (is his) help; Joezer,* an Isr.:— Joezer.

3135. יוֹעָשׁ **Yôw'âsh**, *yo-awsh´;* from 3068 and 5789; *Jehovah-hastened; Joash,* the name of two Isr.:— Joash.

3136. יוֹצָדָק **Yôwtsâdâq**, *yo-tsaw-dawk´;* a form of 3087; *Jotsadak,* an Isr.:— Jozadak.

3137. יוֹקִים **Yôwqîym**, *yo-keem´;* a form of 3113; *Jokim,* an Isr.:— Jokim.

3138. יוֹרֶה **yôwreh**, *yo-reh´;* act. part. of 3384; *sprinkling;* hence, a *sprinkling* (or autumnal showers):— first rain, former [rain].

3139. יוֹרָה **Yôwrâh**, *yo-raw´;* from 3384; *rainy; Jorah,* an Isr.:— Jorah.

3140. יוֹרַי **Yôwray**, *yo-rah´-ee;* from 3384; *rainy; Jorai,* an Isr.:— Jorai.

3141. יוֹרָם **Yôwrâm**, *yo-rawm´;* a form of 3088; *Joram,* the name of three Isr. and one Syrian:— Joram.

3142. יוּשַׁב חֶסֶד **Yûwshab Cheçed**, *yoo-shab´ kheh´-sed;* from 7725 and 2617; *kindness will be returned; Jushab-Chesed,* an Isr.:— Jushab-hesed.

3143. יוֹשִׁבְיָה **Yôwshîbyâh**, *yo-shib-yaw´;* from 3427 and 3050; *Jehovah will cause to dwell; Josibjah,* an Isr.:— Josibiah.

3144. יוֹשָׁה **Yôwshâh**, *yo-shaw´;* prob. a form of 3145; *Joshah,* an Isr.:— Joshah.

3145. יוֹשַׁוְיָה **Yôwshavyâh**, *yo-shav-yaw´;* from 3068 and 7737; *Jehovah-set; Joshavjah,* an Isr.:— Joshaviah. Comp. 3144.

3146. יוֹשָׁפָט **Yôwshâphât**, *yo-shaw-fawt´;* a form of 3092; *Joshaphat,* an Isr.:— Joshaphat.

3147. יוֹתָם **Yôwthâm**, *yo-thawm´;* from 3068 and 8535; *Jehovah (is) perfect; Jotham,* the name of three Isr.:— Jotham.

3148. יוֹתֵר **yôwthêr**, *yo-thare´;* act. part. of 3498; prop. *redundant;* hence, *over and above,* as adj., noun, adv. or conjunc. [as follows]:— better, more (-over), over, profit.

3149. יְזַוְאֵל° **Yᵉzav'êl**, *yez-av-ale´;* from an unused root (mean. to *sprinkle*) and 410; *sprinkled of God; Jezavel,* an Isr.:— Jeziel [from the marg.].

3150. יִזִּיָּה **Yizzîyâh**, *yiz-zee-yaw´;* from the same as the first part of 3149 and 3050; *sprinkled of Jah; Jizzijah,* an Isr.:— Jeziah.

3151. יָזִיז **Yâzîyz**, *yaw-zeez´;* from the same as 2123; *he will make prominent; Jaziz,* an Isr.:— Jaziz.

3152. יִזְלִיאָה **Yizlîy'ah**, *yiz-lee-aw´;* perh. from an unused root (mean. to *draw up*); *he will draw out; Jizliah,* an Isr.:— Jezliah.

3153. יְזַנְיָה **Yᵉzanyâh**, *yez-an-yaw´;* or

יְזַנְיָהוּ **Yᵉzanyâhûw**, *yez-an-yaw´-hoo;* prob. for 2970; *Jezanjah,* an Isr.:— Jezaniah.

3154. יֵזַע **yeza'**, *yeh´-zah;* from an unused root mean. to *ooze; sweat,* i.e. (by impl.) a *sweating* dress:— any thing that causeth sweat.

3155. יִזְרָח **Yizrâch**, *yiz-rawkh´;* a var. for 250; a *Jizrach* (i.e. Ezrahite or Zarchite) or desc. of Zerach:— Izrahite.

3156. יִזְרַחְיָה **Yizrachyâh**, *yiz-rakh-yaw´;* from 2224 and 3050; *Jah will shine; Jizrachjah,* the name of two Isr.:— Izrahiah, Jezrahiah.

3157. יִזְרְעֵאל **Yizrᵉ'ê'l**, *yiz-reh-ale´;* from 2232 and 410; *God will sow; Jizreël,* the name of two places in Pal. and of two Isr.:— Jezreel.

3158. יִזְרְעֵאלִי **Yizrᵉ'ê'lîy**, *yiz-reh-ay-lee´;* patron. from 3157; a *Jizreëlite* or native of Jizreel:— Jezreelite.

3159. יִזְרְעֵאלִית **Yizrᵉ'ê'lîyth**, *yiz-reh-ay-leeth´;* fem. of 3158; a *Jezreëlitess:*— Jezreelitess.

3160. יְחֻבָּה **Yᵉchubbâh**, *yekh-oob-baw´;* from 2247; *hidden; Jechubbah,* an Isr.:— Jehubbah.

3161. יָחַד **yâchad**, *yaw-khad´;* a prim. root; to *be* (or *become) one:*— join, unite.

3162. יַחַד **yachad**, *yakh´-ad;* from 3161; prop. a *unit,* i.e. (adv.) *unitedly:*— alike, at all (once), both, likewise, only, (al-) together, withal.

3163. יַחְדּוֹ **Yachdôw**, *yakh-doe´;* from 3162 with pron. suff.; *his unity,* i.e. (adv.) *together; Jachdo,* an Isr.:— Jahdo.

3164. יַחְדִּיאֵל **Yachdîy'êl**, *yakh-dee-ale´;* from 3162 and 410; *unity of God; Jachdiël,* an Isr.:— Jahdiel.

3165. יֶחְדִּיָּהוּ **Yechdîyâhûw**, *yekh-dee-yaw´-*

hoo; from 3162 and 3050; *unity of Jah; Jechdijah,* the name of two Isr.:— Jehdeiah.

יָחוּאֵל **Y^echav'êl.** See 3171.

3166. יַחֲזִיאֵל **Yachăzîy'êl,** *yakh-az-ee-ale´;* from 2372 and 410; *beheld of God; Jachaziël,* the name of five Isr.:— Jahaziel, Jahziel.

3167. יַחְזְיָה **Yachz^eyâh,** *yakh-zeh-yaw´;* from 2372 and 3050; *Jah will behold; Jachzejah,* an Isr.:— Jahaziah.

3168. יְחֶזְקֵאל **Y^echezqê'l,** *yekh-ez-kale´;* from 2388 and 410; *God will strengthen; Jechezkel,* the name of two Isr.:— Ezekiel, Jehezekel.

3169. יִחְזְקִיָּה **Y^echizqîyâh,** *yekh-iz-kee-yaw´;* or

יְחִזְקִיָּהוּ **Y^echizqîyâhûw,** *yekh-iz-kee-yaw´-hoo;* from 3388 and 3050; *strengthened of Jah; Jechizkijah,* the name of five Isr.:— Hezekiah, Jehizkiah. Comp. 2396.

3170. יַחְזֵרָה **Yachzêrâh,** *yakh-zay-raw´;* from the same as 2386; perh. *protection; Jachzerah,* an Isr.:— Jahzerah.

3171. יְחִיאֵל **Y^echîy'êl,** *yekh-ee-ale´;* or (2 Chron. 29:14)

יְחֻואֵל° **Y^echav'êl,** *yekh-av-ale´;* from 2421 and 410; *God will live; Jechiël* (or *Jechavel*), the name of eight Isr.:— Jehiel.

3172. יְחִיאֵלִי **Y^echîy'êliy,** *yekh-ee-ay-lee´;* patron. from 3171; a *Jechiëlite* or desc. of Jechiel:— Jehieli.

3173. יָחִיד **yâchîyd,** *yaw-kheed´;* from 3161; prop. *united,* i.e. *sole;* by impl. *beloved;* also *lonely;* (fem.) the *life* (as not to be replaced):— darling, desolate, only (child, son), solitary.

3174. יְחִיָּה **Y^echîyâh,** *yekh-ee-yaw´;* from 2421 and 3050; *Jah will live; Jechijah,* an Isr.:— Jehiah.

3175. יָחִיל **yâchîyl,** *yaw-kheel´;* from 3176; *expectant:*— should hope.

3176. יָחַל **yâchal,** *yaw-chal´;* a prim. root; to *wait;* by impl. to *be patient, hope:*— (cause to, have, make to) hope, be pained, stay, tarry, trust, wait.

3177. יַחְלְאֵל **Yachl^e'êl,** *yakh-leh-ale´;* from 3176 and 410; *expectant of God; Jachleël,* an Isr.:— Jahleel.

3178. יַחְלְאֵלִי **Yachl^e'êliy,** *yakh-leh-ay-lee´;* patron. from 3177; a *Jachleëlite* or desc. of Jachleel:— Jahleelites.

3179. יָחַם **yâcham,** *yaw-kham´;* a prim. root; prob. to *be hot;* fig. to *conceive:*— get heat, be hot, conceive, be warm.

3180. יַחְמוּר **yachmûwr,** *yakh-moor´;* from 2560; a kind of *deer* (from the color; comp. 2543):— fallow deer.

3181. יַחְמַי **Yachmay,** *yakh-mah´-ee;* prob. from 3179; *hot; Jachmai,* an Isr.:— Jahmai.

3182. יָחֵף **yâchêph,** *yaw-khafe´;* from an un-

used root mean. to *take off the shoes; unsandaled:*— barefoot, being unshod.

3183. יַחְצְאֵל **Yachtse^e'êl,** *yakh-tseh-ale´;* from 2673 and 410; *God will allot; Jachtseël,* an Isr.:— Jahzeel. Comp. 3185.

3184. יַחְצְאֵלִי **Yachts^e'êliy,** *yakh-tseh-ay-lee´;* patron. from 3183; a *Jachtseëlite* (collect.) or desc. of Jachtseel:— Jahzeelites.

3185. יַחְצִיאֵל **Yachtsîy'êl,** *yakh-tsee-ale´;* from 2673 and 410; *allotted of God; Jachtsiël,* an Isr.:— Jahziel. Comp. 3183.

3186. יָחַר **yâchar,** *yaw-khar´;* a prim. root; to *delay:*— tarry longer.

3187. יָחַשׂ **yâchas,** *yaw-khas´;* a prim. root; to *sprout;* used only as denom. from 3188; to *enroll* by pedigree:— (number after, number throughout the) genealogy (to be reckoned), be reckoned by genealogies.

3188. יַחַשׂ **yachas,** *yakh´-as;* from 3187; a *pedigree* or family list (as *growing* spontaneously):— genealogy.

3189. יַחַת **Yachath,** *yakh´-ath;* from 3161; *unity; Jachath,* the name of four Isr.:— Jahath.

3190. יָטַב **yâṭab,** *yaw-tab´;* a prim. root; to *be* (caus.) *make well,* lit. (*sound, beautiful*) or fig. (*happy, successful, right*):— be accepted, amend, use aright, benefit, be (make) better, seem best, make cheerful, be comely, + be content, diligent (-ly), dress, earnestly, find favour, give, be glad, do (be, make) good (I-ness]), be (make) merry, please (+ well), shew more [kindness], skilfully, × very small, surely, make sweet, thoroughly, tire, trim, very, be (can, deal, entreat, go, have) well [said, seen].

3191. יְטַב **y^eṭab** (Chald.), *yet-ab´;* corresp. to 3190:— seem good.

3192. יָטְבָה **Yoṭbâh,** *yot-baw´;* from 3190; *pleasantness; Jotbah,* a place in Pal.:— Jotbah.

3193. יָטְבָתָה **Yoṭbâthâh,** *yot-baw´-thaw;* from 3192; *Jotbathah,* a place in the Desert:— Jotbath, Jotbathah.

3194. יֻטָּה **Yuṭṭâh,** *yoo-taw´;* or

יוּטָה **Yûwṭâh,** *yoo-taw´;* from 5186; *extended; Juttah* (or *Jutah*), a place in Pal.:— Juttah.

3195. יְטוּר **Y^eṭûwr,** *yet-oor´;* prob. from the same as 2905; *encircled* (i.e. *inclosed*); *Jetur,* a son of Ishmael:— Jetur.

3196. יַיִן **yayin,** *yah´-yin;* from an unused root mean. to *effervesce; wine* (as fermented); by impl. *intoxication:*— banqueting, wine, wine [-bibber].

3197. יַךְ **yak,** *yak;* by err. transc. for 3027; a *hand* or *side:*— [way-] side.

יְכֹל **yâkôwl**. See 3201.

יְכָנְיָה **Yᵉkôwnᵉyâh**. See 3204.

3198. יְכַח **yâkach**, *yaw-kahh´*; a prim. root; to *be right* (i.e. *correct*); recip. to *argue*; caus. to *decide, justify* or *convict*:— appoint, argue, chasten, convince, correct (-ion), daysman, dispute, judge, maintain, plead, reason (together), rebuke, reprove (-r), surely, in any wise.

יְכִילְיָה **Yᵉkîylᵉyâh**. See 3203.

3199. יָכִין **Yâkîyn**, *yaw-keen´*; from 3559; *he* (or *it*) *will establish; Jakin*, the name of three Isr. and of a temple pillar:— Jachin.

3200. יָכִינִי **Yâkîynîy**, *yaw-kee-nee´*; patron. from 3199; a *Jakinite* (collect.) or desc. of Jakin:— Jachinites.

3201. יָכֹל **yâkôl**, *yaw-kole´*; or (fuller)

יָכֹול **yâkôwl**, *yaw-kole´*; a prim. root; to *be able*, lit. (*can, could*) or mor. (*may, might*):— be able, any at all (ways), attain, can (away with, [-not]), could, endure, might, overcome, have power, prevail, still, suffer.

3202. יְכֵל **yᵉkêl** (Chald.), *yek-ale´*; or

יְכִיל **yᵉkîyl** (Chald.), *yek-eel´*; corresp. to 3201:— be able, can, couldest, prevail.

3203. יְכָלְיָה **Yᵉkolyâh**, *yek-ol-yaw´*; and

יְכָלְיָהוּ **Yᵉkolyâhûw**, *yek-ol-yaw´-hoo*; or (2 Chron. 26:3)

יְכִילְיָה° **Yᵉkîylᵉyâh**, *yek-ee-leh-yaw´*; from 3201 and 3050; *Jah will enable; Jekoljah* or *Jekiljah*, an Israelitess:— Jecholiah, Jecoliah.

3204. יְכָנְיָה **Yᵉkonyâh**, *yek-on-yaw´*; and

יְכָנְיָהוּ **Yᵉkonyâhûw**, *yek-on-yaw´-hoo*; or (Jer. 27:20)

יְכוֹנְיָה° **Yᵉkôwnᵉyâh**, *yek-o-neh-yaw´*; from 3559 and 3050; *Jah will establish; Jekonjah*, a Jewish king:— Jeconiah. Comp. 3659.

3205. יָלַד **yâlad**, *yaw-lad´*; a prim. root; to *bear* young; caus. to *beget*; medically, to *act as midwife*; spec. to *show lineage*:— bear, beget, birth ([-day]), born, (make to) bring forth (children, young), bring up, calve, child, come, be delivered (of a child), time of delivery, gender, hatch, labour, (do the office of a) midwife, declare pedigrees, be the son of, (woman in, woman that) travail (-eth, -ing woman).

3206. יֶלֶד **yeled**, *yeh´-led*; from 3205; something *born*, i.e. a *lad* or *offspring*:— boy, child, fruit, son, young man (one).

3207. יַלְדָּה **yaldâh**, *yal-daw´*; fem. of 3206; a *lass*:— damsel, girl.

3208. יַלְדוּת **yaldûwth**, *yal-dooth´*; abstr. from 3206; *boyhood* (or *girlhood*):— childhood, youth.

3209. יִלּוֹד **yillôwd**, *yil-lode´*; pass. from 3205; *born*:— born.

3210. יָלוֹן **Yâlôwn**, *yaw-lone´*; from 3885; *lodging; Jalon*, an Isr.:— Jalon.

3211. יָלִיד **yâlîyd**, *yaw-leed´*; from 3205; *born*:— ([home-]) born, child, son.

3212. יָלַךְ **yâlak**, *yaw-lak´*; a prim. root [comp. 1980]; to *walk* (lit. or fig.); caus. to *carry* (in various senses):— × again, away, bear, bring, carry (away), come (away), depart, flow, + follow (-ing), get (away, hence, him), (cause to, make) go (away, ing, -ne, one's way, out), grow, lead (forth), let down, march, prosper, + pursue, cause to run, spread, take away ([-journey]), vanish, (cause to) walk (-ing), wax, × be weak.

3213. יָלַל **yâlal**, *yaw-lal´*; a prim. root; to *howl* (with a wailing tone) or *yell* (with a boisterous one):— (make to) howl, be howling.

3214. יְלֵל **yᵉlêl**, *yel-ale´*; from 3213; a *howl*:— howling.

3215. יְלָלָה **yᵉlâlâh**, *yel-aw-law´*; fem. of 3214; a *howling*:— howling.

3216. יָלַע **yâla**', *yaw-lah´*; a prim. root; to *blurt* or utter inconsiderately:— devour.

3217. יַלֶּפֶת **yallepheth**, *yal-leh´-feth*; from an unused root appar. mean. to *stick* or *scrape; scurf* or *tetter*:— scabbed.

3218. יֶקֶק **yekeq**, *yeh´-lek*; from an unused root mean. to *lick* up; a *devourer*; spec. the young *locust*:— cankerworm, caterpillar.

3219. יַלְקוּט **yalqûwṭ**, *yal-koot´*; from 3950; a travelling *pouch* (as if for gleanings):— scrip.

3220. יָם **yâm**, *yawm*; from an unused root mean. to *roar*; a *sea* (as breaking in *noisy* surf) or large body of water; spec. (with the art.), the *Mediterranean*; sometimes a large *river*, or an artificial *basin*; locally, the *west*, or (rarely) the *south*:— sea (× -faring man, [-shore]), south, west (-ern, side, -ward).

3221. יָם **yâm** (Chald.), *yawm*; corresp. to 3220:— sea.

3222. יֵם **yêm**, *yame*; from the same as 3117; a *warm* spring:— mule.

3223. יְמוּאֵל **Yᵉmûw'êl**, *yem-oo-ale´*; from 3117 and 410; *day of God; Jemuel*, an Isr.:— Jemuel.

3224. יְמִימָה **Yᵉmîymâh**, *yem-ee-maw´*; perh. from the same as 3117; prop. *warm*, i.e. *affectionate*; hence, *dove* [comp. 3123]; *Jemimah*, one of Job's daughters:— Jemimah.

3225. יָמִין **yâmîyn**, *yaw-meen´*; from 3231; the *right* hand or side (leg, eye) of a person or other object (as the *stronger* and more dexterous); locally, the *south:*— + left-handed, right (hand, side), south.

3226. יָמִין **Yâmîyn**, *yaw-meen´;* the same as 3225; *Jamin,* the name of three Isr.:— Jamin. See also 1144.

3227. יְמִינִי **yᵉmîynîy**, *yem-ee-nee´;* for 3225; *right:*— (on the) right (hand).

3228. יְמִינִי **Yᵉmîynîy**, *yem-ee-nee´;* patron. from 3226; a *Jeminite* (collect.) or desc. of Jamin:— Jaminites. See also 1145.

3229. יִמְלָא **Yimlâ'**, *yeem-law´;* or

       יִמְלָה **Yimlâh**, *yim-law´;* from 4390; *full; Jimla* or *Jimlah,* an Isr.:— Imla, Imlah.

3230. יַמְלֵךְ **Yamlêk**, *yam-lake´;* from 4427; *he will make king; Jamlek,* an Isr.:— Jamlech.

3231. יָמַן **yâman**, *yaw-man´;* a prim. root; to *be* (phys.) *right* (i.e. firm); but used only as denom. from 3225 and tran. *to be right-handed* or *take the right-hand* side:— go (turn) to (on, use) the right hand.

3232. יִמְנָה **Yimnâh**, *yim-naw´;* from 3231; *prosperity* (as betokened by the *right* hand); *Jimnah,* the name of two Isr.; also (with the art.) of the posterity of one of them:— Imna, Imnah, Jimnah, Jimnites.

3233. יְמָנִי **yᵉmânîy**, *yem-aw-nee´;* from 3231; *right* (i.e. at the right hand):— (on the) right (hand).

3234. יִמְנָע **Yimnâ'**, *yim-naw´;* from 4513; *he will restrain; Jimna,* an Isr.:— Imna.

3235. יָמַר **yâmar**, *yaw-mar´;* a prim. root; to *exchange;* by impl. to *change places:*— boast selves, change.

3236. יִמְרָה **Yimrâh**, *yim-raw´;* prob. from 3235; *interchange; Jimrah,* an Isr.:— Imrah.

3237. יָמַשׁ **yâmash**, *yaw-mash´;* a prim. root; to *touch:*— feel.

3238. יָנָה **yânâh**, *yaw-naw´;* a prim. root; to *rage* or *be violent;* by impl. to *suppress,* to *maltreat:*— destroy, (thrust out by) oppress (-ing, -ion, -or), proud, vex, do violence.

3239. יָנוֹחַ **Yânôwach**, *yaw-no´-akh;* or (with enclitic)

       יָנוֹחָה **Yânôwchâh**, *yaw-no´-khaw;* from 3240; *quiet; Janoäch* or *Janochah,* a place in Pal.:— Janoah, Janohah.

       יָנוּם **Yânûm**. See 3241.

3240. יָנַח **yânach**, *yaw-nakh´;* a prim. root; to *deposit;* by impl. *to allow to stay:*— bestow, cast down, lay (down, up), leave (off), let alone (remain), pacify, place, put, set (down), suffer, withdraw, withhold. (The Hiphil forms with the *dagesh* are here referred to, in accordance with the older grammarians; but if any distinction of the kind is to be made, these

should rather be referred to 5117, and the others here.)

3241. יָנִים° **Yânîym**, *yaw-neem´;* from 5123; *asleep; Janim,* a place in Pal.:— Janum [*from the marg.*].

3242. יְנִיקָה **yᵉnîqâh**, *yen-ee-kaw´;* from 3243; a *sucker* or sapling:— young twig.

3243. יָנַק **yânaq**, *yaw-nak´;* a prim. root; to *suck;* caus. to *give milk:*— milch, nurse (-ing mother), (give, make to) suck (-ing child, -ling).

3244. יַנְשׁוּף **yanshûph**, *yan-shoof´;* or

       יַנְשׁוֹף **yanshôwph**, *yan-shofe´;* appar. from 5398; an unclean (aquatic) bird; prob. the *heron* (perh. from its *blowing* cry, or because the *night*-heron is meant [comp. 5399]):— (great) owl.

3245. יָסַד **yâçad**, *yaw-sad´;* a prim. root; to *set* (lit. or fig.); intens. to *found;* refl. to *sit down together,* i.e. *settle, consult:*— appoint, take counsel, establish, (lay the, lay for a) found (-ation), instruct, lay, ordain, set, × sure.

3246. יְסֻד **yᵉçud**, *yes-ood´;* from 3245; a *foundation* (fig. i.e. *beginning*):— × began.

3247. יְסוֹד **yᵉçôwd**, *yes-ode´;* from 3245; a *foundation* (lit. or fig.):— bottom, foundation, repairing.

3248. יְסוּדָה **yᵉçûwdâh**, *yes-oo-daw´;* fem. of 3246; a *foundation:*— foundation.

3249. יָסוּר **yâçûwr**, *yaw-soor´;* from 5493; *departing:*— they that depart.

3250. יִסּוֹר **yiççôwr**, *yis-sore´;* from 3256; a *reprover:*— instruct.

3251. יָסַךְ **yâçak**, *yaw-sak´;* a prim. root; to *pour* (intr.):— be poured.

3252. יִסְכָּה **Yiçkâh**, *yis-kaw´;* from an unused root mean. to *watch; observant; Jiskah,* sister of Lot:— Iscah.

3253. יִסְמַכְיָהוּ **Yiçmakyâhûw**, *yis-mak-yaw-hoo´;* from 5564 and 3050; *Jah will sustain; Jismakjah,* an Isr.:— Ismachiah.

3254. יָסַף **yâçaph**, *yaw-saf´;* a prim. root; to *add* or *augment* (often adv. to *continue* to do a thing):— add, × again, × any more, × cease, × come more, + conceive again, continue, exceed, × further, × gather together, get more, give more-over, × henceforth, increase (more and more), join, × longer (bring, do, make, much, put), × (the, much, yet) more (and more), proceed (further), prolong, put, be [strong-] er, × yet, yield.

3255. יְסַף **yᵉçaph** (Chald.), *yes-af´;* corresp. to 3254:— add.

3256. יָסַר **yâçar**, *yaw-sar´;* a prim. root; to *chastise,* lit. (with blows) or fig. (with words); hence, to *instruct:*— bind, chasten, chastise, correct, instruct, punish, reform, reprove, sore, teach.

3257. יָע **yâ'**, *yaw*; from 3261; a *shovel*:— shovel.

3258. יַעְבֵּץ **Ya'bêts**, *yah-bates'*; from an unused root prob. mean. to *grieve*; *sorrowful*; *Jabets*, the name of an Isr., and also of a place in Pal.:— Jabez.

3259. יָעַד **yâ'ad**, *yaw-ad'*; a prim. root; to *fix* upon (by agreement or appointment); by impl. to *meet* (at a stated time), to *summon* (to trial), to *direct* (in a certain quarter or position), to *engage* (for marriage):— agree,(make an) appoint (-ment, a time), assemble (selves), betroth, gather (selves, together), meet (together), set (a time).

יְעָדוֹ **Ye'dôw**. See 3260.

3260. יֶעְדִּי **Ye'dîy**, *yed-ee'*; from 3259; *appointed*; *Jedi*, an Isr.:— Iddo [*from the marg.*] See 3035.

3261. יָעָה **yâ'âh**, *yaw-aw'*; a prim. root; appar. to *brush* aside:— sweep away.

3262. יְעוּאֵל **Ye'ûw'êl**, *yeh-oo-ale'*; from 3261 and 410; *carried away of God*; *Jeüel*, the name of four Isr.:— Jehiel, Jeiel, Jeuel. Comp. 3273.

3263. יְעוּץ **Ye'ûwts**, *yeh-oots'*; from 5779; *counsellor*; *Jeüts*, an Isr.:— Jeuz.

3264. יָעוֹר **yâ'ôwr**, *yaw-ore'*; a var. of 3293; a *forest*:— wood.

3265. יָעוּר **Yâ'ûwr**, *yaw-oor'*; appar. pass. part. of the same as 3293; *wooded*; *Jaür*, an Isr.:— Jair [*from the marg.*].

3266. יְעוּשׁ **Ye'ûwsh**, *yeh-oosh'*; from 5789; *hasty*; *Jeüsh*, the name of an Edomite and of four Isr.:— Jehush, Jeush. Comp. 3274.

3267. יָעַז **yâ'az**, *yaw-az'*; a prim. root; to *be bold* or *obstinate*:— fierce.

3268. יַעֲזִיאֵל **Ya'ăzîy'êl**, *yah-az-ee-ale'*; from 3267 and 410; *emboldened of God*; *Jaaziël*, an Isr.:— Jaaziel.

3269. יַעֲזִיָּהוּ **Ya'ăzîyâhûw**, *yah-az-ee-yaw'-hoo*; from 3267 and 3050; *emboldened of Jah*; *Jaazijah*, an Isr.:— Jaaziah.

3270. יַעֲזֵיר **Ya'ăzêyr**, *yah-az-ayr'*; or

יַעְזֵר **Ya'zêr**, *yah-zare'*; from 5826; *helpful*; *Jaazer* or *Jazer*, a place E. of the Jordan:— Jaazer, Jazer.

3271. יָעַט **yâ'aṭ**, *yaw-at'*; a prim. root; to *clothe*:— cover.

3272. יְעַט **ye'aṭ** (Chald.), *yeh-at'*; corresp. to 3289; to *counsel*; refl. to *consult*:— counsellor, consult together.

3273. יְעִיאֵל **Ye'îy'êl**, *yeh-ee-ale'*; from 3261 and 410; *carried away of God*; *Jeïel*, the name of six Isr.:— Jeiel, Jehiel. Comp. 3262.

יָעִיר **Yâ'îyr**. See 3265.

3274. יְעִישׁ **Ye'îysh**, *yeh-eesh'*; from 5789; *hasty*; *Jeïsh*, the name of an Edomite and of an Isr.:— Jeush [*from the marg.*]. Comp. 3266.

3275. יַעְכָּן **Ya'kân**, *yah-kawn'*; from the same as 5912; *troublesome*; *Jakan*, an Isr.:— Jachan.

3276. יָעַל **yâ'al**, *yaw-al'*; a prim. root; prop. to *ascend*; fig. to *be valuable* (obj. *useful*, subj. *benefited*):— × at all, set forward, can do good, (be, have) profit (-able).

3277. יָעֵל **yâ'êl**, *yaw-ale'*; from 3276; an *ibex* (as *climbing*):— wild goat.

3278. יָעֵל **Yâ'êl**, *yaw-ale'*; the same as 3277; *Jaël*, a Canaanite:— Jael.

3279. יַעְלָא **Ya'ălâ'**, *yah-al-aw'*; or

יַעְלָה **Ya'ălâh**, *yah-al-aw'*; the same as 3280 or direct from 3276; *Jaala* or *Jaalah*, one of the Nethinim:— Jaala, Jaalah.

3280. יַעֲלָה **ya'ălâh**, *yah-al-aw'*; fem. of 3277:— roe.

3281. יַעְלָם **Ya'lâm**, *yah-lawm'*; from 5956; *occult*; *Jalam*, an Edomite:— Jalam.

3282. יַעַן **ya'an**, *yah'-an*; from an unused root mean. to *pay attention*; prop. *heed*; by impl. *purpose* (sake or account); used adv. to indicate the *reason* or cause:— because (that), forasmuch (+ as), seeing then, + that, + whereas, + why.

3283. יָעֵן **yâ'ên**, *yaw-ane'*; from the same as 3282; the *ostrich* (prob. from its *answering* cry:— ostrich.

3284. יַעֲנָה **ya'ănâh**, *yah-an-aw'*; fem. of 3283, and mean. the same:— + owl.

3285. יַעֲנַי **Ya'ănay**, *yah-an-ah'ee*; from the same as 3283; *responsive*; *Jaanai*, an Isr.:— Jaanai.

3286. יָעַף **yâ'aph**, *yaw-af'*; a prim. root; to *tire* (as if from wearisome *flight*):— faint, cause to fly, (be) weary (self).

3287. יָעֵף **yâ'êph**, *yaw-afe'*; from 3286; *fatigued*; fig. *exhausted*:— faint, weary.

3288. יְעָף **ye'âph**, *yeh-awf'*; from 3286; *fatigue* (adv. utterly *exhausted*):— swiftly.

3289. יָעַץ **yâ'ats**, *yaw-ats'*; a prim. root; to *advise*; refl. to *deliberate* or *resolve*:— advertise, take advice, advise (well), consult, (give, take) counsel (-lor), determine, devise, guide, purpose.

3290. יַעֲקֹב **Ya'ăqôb**, *yah-ak-obe'*; from 6117; *heel*-catcher (i.e. supplanter); *Jaakob*, the Isr. patriarch:— Jacob.

3291. יַעֲקֹבָה **Ya'ăqôbâh**, *yah-ak-o'-baw*; from 3290; *Jaakobah*, an Isr.:— Jaakobah.

3292. יַעֲקָן **Ya'ăqân**, *yah-ak-awn'*; from the

same as 6130; *Jaakan*, an Idumæan:— Jaakan. Comp. 1142.

3293. יַעַר **ya'ar**, *yah´-ar* from an unused root prob. mean. to *thicken* with verdure; a *copse* of bushes; hence, a *forest;* hence, *honey* in the *comb* (as hived in trees):— [honey-] comb, forest, wood.

3294. יַעְרָה **Ya'râh**, *yah-raw´;* a form of 3295; *Jarah*, an Isr.:— Jarah.

3295. יַעְרָה **ya'ărâh**, *yah-ar-aw´;* fem. of 3293, and mean. the same:— [honey-] comb, forest.

3296. יַעְרֵי אֹרְגִים **Ya'ărêy 'Orᵉgîym**, *yah-ar-ay´ o-reg-eem´;* from the plural of 3293 and the masc. plur. act. part. of 707; *woods of weavers; Jaare-Oregim*, an Isr.:— Jaare-oregim.

3297. יְעָרִים **Yᵉ'ârîym**, *yeh-aw-reem´;* plur. of 3293; *forests; Jeärim*, a place in Pal.:— Jearim. Comp. 7157.

3298. יַעְרֶשְׁיָה **Ya'ăreshyâh**, *yah-ar-esh-yaw´;* from an unused root of uncert. signif. and 3050; *Jaareshjah*, an Isr.:— Jaresiah.

3299. יַעֲשׂוּ **Ya'ăsûw**, *yah-as-oo´;* from 6213; *they will do; Jaasu*, an Isr.:— Jaasau.

3300. יַעֲשִׂיאֵל **Ya'ăsîy'êl**, *yah-as-ee-ale´;* from 6213 and 410; *made of God; Jaasiel*, an Isr.:— Jaasiel, Jasiel.

3301. יִפְדְּיָה **Yiphdᵉyâh**, *yif-deh-yaw´;* from 6299 and 3050; *Jah will liberate; Jiphdejah*, an Isr.:— Iphedeiah.

3302. יָפָה **yâphâh**, *yaw-faw´;* a prim. root; prop. to *be bright*, i.e. (by impl.) *beautiful:*— be beautiful, be (make self) fair (-r), deck.

3303. יָפֶה **yâpheh**, *yaw-feh´;* from 3302; *beautiful* (lit. or fig.):— + beautiful, beauty, comely, fair (-est, one), + goodly, pleasant, well.

3304. יְפֵה־פִיָּה **yᵉphêh-phiyâh**, *yef-eh´ fee-yaw´;* from 3302 by redupl.; *very beautiful:*— very fair.

3305. יָפוֹ **Yâphôw**, *yaw-fo´;* or

יָפוֹא **Yâphôw'** (Ezra 3:7), *yaw-fo´;* from 3302; *beautiful; Japho*, a place in Pal.:— Japha, Joppa.

3306. יָפַח **yâphach**, *yaw-fakh´;* a prim. root; prop. to *breathe* hard, i.e. (by impl.) to *sigh:*— bewail self.

3307. יָפֵחַ **yâphêach**, *yaw-fay´-akh;* from 3306; prop. *puffing*, i.e. (fig.) *meditating:*— such as breathe out.

3308. יֳפִי **yŏphiy**, *yof-ee´;* from 3302; *beauty:*— beauty.

3309. יָפִיעַ **Yâphiya'**, *yaw-fee´-ah;* from 3313; *bright; Japhia*, the name of a Canaanite, an Isr., and a place in Pal.:— Japhia.

3310. יַפְלֵט **Yaphlêṭ**, *yaf-late´;* from 6403; *he will deliver; Japhlet*, an Isr.:— Japhlet.

3311. יַפְלֵטִי **Yaphlêṭiy**, *yaf-lay-tee´;* patron.

from 3310; a *Japhletite* or desc. of Japhlet:— Japhleti.

3312. יְפֻנֶּה **Yᵉphunneh**, *yef-oon-neh´;* from 6437; *he will be prepared; Jephunneh*, the name of two Isr.:— Jephunneh.

3313. יָפַע **yâpha'**, *yaw-fah´;* a prim. root; to *shine:*— be light, shew self, (cause to) shine (forth).

3314. יִפְעָה **yiph'âh**, *yif-aw´;* from 3313; *splendor* or (fig.) *beauty:*— brightness.

3315. יֶפֶת **Yepheth**, *yeh´-feth;* from 6601; *expansion; Jepheth*, a son of Noah; also his posterity:— Japheth.

3316. יִפְתָּח **Yiphtâch**, *yif-tawkh´;* from 6605; *he will open; Jiphtach*, an Isr.; also a place in Pal.:— Jephthah, Jiphtah.

3317. יִפְתַּח־אֵל **Yiphtach-'êl**, *yif-tach-ale´;* from 6605 and 410; *God will open; Jiphtach-el*, a place in Pal.:— Jiphthah-el.

3318. יָצָא **yâtsâ'**, *yaw-tsaw´;* a prim. root; to *go* (caus. *bring*) *out*, in a great variety of applications, lit. and fig., direct and proxim.:— × after, appear, × assuredly, bear out, × begotten, break out, bring forth (out, up), carry out, come (abroad, out, thereat, without), + be condemned, depart (-ing, -ure), draw forth, in the end, escape, exact, fail, fall (out), fetch forth (out), get away (forth, hence, out), (able to, cause to, let) go abroad (forth, on, out), going out, grow, have forth (out), issue out, lay (lie) out, lead out, pluck out, proceed, pull out, put away, be risen, × scarce, send with commandment, shoot forth, spread, spring out, stand out, × still, × surely, take forth (out), at any time, × to [and fro], utter.

3319. יְצָא **yᵉtsâ'** (Chald.), *yets-aw´;* corresp. to 3318:— finish.

3320. יָצַב **yâtsab**, *yaw-tsab´;* a prim. root; to *place* (any thing so as to stay); refl. to *station, offer, continue:*— present selves, remaining, resort, set (selves), (be able to, can, with-) stand (fast, forth, -ing, still, up).

3321. יְצֵב **yᵉtsêb** (Chald.), *yets-abe´;* corresp. to 3320; to *be firm;* hence, to *speak surely:*— truth.

3322. יָצַג **yâtsag**, *yaw-tsag´;* a prim. root; to *place* permanently:— establish, leave, make, present, put, set, stay.

3323. יִצְהָר **yitshâr**, *yits-hawr´;* from 6671; *oil* (as producing *light*); fig. *anointing:*— + anointed oil.

3324. יִצְהָר **Yitshâr**, *yits-hawr´;* the same as 3323; *Jitshar*, an Isr.:— Izhar.

3325. יִצְהָרִי **Yitshâriy**, *yits-haw-ree´;* patron. from 3324; a *Jitsharite* or desc. of Jitshar:— Izeharites, Izharites.

3326. יָצוּעַ **yâtsûwa'**, *yaw-tsoo´-ah;* pass.

part. of 3331; *spread*, i.e. a *bed;* (arch.) an *extension*, i.e. *wing* or *lean-to* (a single story or collect.):— bed, chamber, couch.

3327. יִצְחָק **Yitschâq**, *yits-khawk´;* from 6711; *laughter* (i.e. *mockery*); *Jitschak* (or Isaac), son of Abraham:— Isaac. Comp. 3446.

3328. יִצְהַר **Yitschar**, *yits-khar´;* from the same as 6713; *he will shine; Jitschar,* an Isr.:— and Zehoar [from the marg.].

3329. יָצִיא **yâtsîy´**, *yaw-tsee´;* from 3318; *issue,* i.e. *offspring:*— those that came forth.

3330. יַצִּיב **yatstsîyb** (Chald.), *yats-tseeb´;* from 3321; *fixed, sure;* concr. *certainty:*— certain (-ty), true, truth.

יָצִיעַ **yâtsîyaʻ**. See 3326.

3331. יָצַע **yâtsaʻ**, *yaw-tsah´;* a prim. root; to *strew* as a surface:— make [one's] bed, × lie, spread.

3332. יָצַק **yâtsaq**, *yaw-tsak´;* a prim. root; prop. to *pour* out (tran. or intr.); by impl. to *melt* or *cast* as metal; by extens. to *place* firmly, to *stiffen* or grow hard:— cast, cleave fast, be (as) firm, grow, be hard, lay out, molten, overflow, pour (out), run out, set down, stedfast.

3333. יְצֻקָה **yᵉtsuqâh**, *yets-oo-kaw´;* pass. part. fem. of 3332; *poured* out, i.e. *run* into a mould:— when it was cast.

3334. יָצַר **yâtsar**, *yaw-tsar´;* a prim. root; to *press* (intr.), i.e. *be narrow;* fig. *be in distress:*— be distressed, be narrow, be straitened (in straits), be vexed.

3335. יָצַר **yâtsar**, *yaw-tsar´;* prob. ident. with 3334 (through the *squeezing* into shape); [comp. 3331]; to *mould* into a form; espec. as a *potter;* fig. to *determine* (i.e. form a resolution):— × earthen, fashion, form, frame, make (-r), potter, purpose.

3336. יֵצֶר **yêtser**, *yay´-tser;* from 3335; a *form;* fig. *conception* (i.e. *purpose*):— frame, thing framed, imagination, mind, work.

3337. יֵצֶר **Yêtser**, *yay-tser;* the same as 3336; *Jetser,* an Isr.:— Jezer.

3338. יָצֻר **yâtsûr**, *yaw-tsoor´;* pass. part. of 3335; *structure*, i.e. limb or part:— member.

3339. יִצְרִי **Yitsrîy**, *yits-ree´;* from 3335; *formative; Jitsri,* an Isr.:— Isri.

3340. יִצְרִי **Yitsrîy**, *yits-ree´;* patron. from 3337; a *Jitsrite* (collect.) or desc. of Jetser:— Jezerites.

3341. יָצַת **yâtsath**, *yaw-tsath´;* a prim. root; to *burn* or *set on fire;* fig. to *desolate:*— burn (up), be desolate, set (on) fire [fire], kindle.

3342. יֶקֶב **yeqeb**, *yeh´-keb;* from an unused root mean. to *excavate;* a *trough* (as dug out); spec. a wine-*vat* (whether the lower one, into which the juice drains; or the upper, in which

the grapes are crushed):— fats, presses, press-fat, wine (-press).

3343. יְקַבְצְאֵל **Yᵉqabtseʼêl**, *yek-ab-tseh-ale´;* from 6908 and 410; *God will gather; Jekabtseël,* a place in Pal.:— Jekabzeel. Comp. 6909.

3344. יָקַד **yâqad**, *yaw-kad´;* a prim. root; to *burn:*— (be) burn (-ing), × from the hearth, kindle.

3345. יְקַד **yᵉqad** (Chald.), *yek-ad´;* corresp. to 3344:— burning.

3346. יְקֵדָא **yᵉqêdâʼ** (Chald.), *yek-ay-daw´;* from 3345; a *conflagration:*— burning.

3347. יָקְדְעָם **Yoqdᵉʻâm**, *yok-deh-awm´;* from 3344 and 5971; *burning of* (the) *people; Jokdeäm,* a place in Pal.:— Jokdeam.

3348. יָקֶה **Yâqeh**, *yaw-keh´;* from an unused root prob. mean. to *obey; obedient; Jakeh,* a symb. name (for Solomon):— Jakeh.

3349. יִקְּהָה **yiqqâhâh**, *yik-kaw-haw´;* from the same as 3348; *obedience:*— gathering, to obey.

3350. יְקוֹד **yᵉqôwd**, *yek-ode´;* from 3344; a *burning:*— burning.

3351. יְקוּם **yᵉqûwm**, *yek-oom´;* from 6965; prop. *standing* (extant), i.e. by impl. a *living thing:*— (living) substance.

3352. יָקוֹשׁ **yâqôwsh**, *yaw-koshe´;* from 3369; prop. *entangling;* hence, a *snarer:*— fowler.

3353. יָקוּשׁ **yâqûwsh**, *yaw-koosh´;* pass. part. of 3369; prop. *entangled,* i.e. by impl. (intr.) a *snare,* or (tran.) a *snarer:*— fowler, snare.

3354. יְקוּתִיאֵל **Yᵉqûwthîyʼêl**, *yek-ooth-ee-ale´;* from the same as 3348 and 410; *obedience of God; Jekuthiël,* an Isr.:— Jekuthiel.

3355. יָקְטָן **Yoqṭân**, *yok-tawn´;* from 6994; *he will be made little; Joktan,* an Arabian patriarch:— Joktan.

3356. יָקִים **Yâqîym**, *yaw-keem´;* from 6965; *he will raise; Jakim,* the name of two Isr.:— Jakim. Comp. 3079.

3357. יַקִּיר **yaqqîyr**, *yak-keer´;* from 3365; *precious:*— dear.

3358. יַקִּיר **yaqqîyr** (Chald.), *yak-keer´;* corresp. to 3357:— noble, rare.

3359. יְקַמְיָה **Yᵉqamyâh**, *yek-am-yaw´;* from 6965 and 3050; *Jah will rise; Jekamjah,* the name of two Isr.:— Jekamiah. Comp. 3079.

3360. יְקַמְעָם **Yᵉqamʻâm**, *yek-am´-awm;* from 6965 and 5971; (the) *people will rise; Jekamam,* an Isr.:— Jekameam. Comp. 3079, 3361.

3361. יָקְמְעָם **Yoqmᵉʻâm**, *yok-meh-awm´;* from 6965 and 5971; (the) *people will be raised; Jokmeäm,* a place in Pal.:— Jokmeam. Comp. 3360, 3362.

Hebrew

3362. יָקְנְעָם **Yoqne'âm**, *yok-neh-awm´*; from 6969 and 5971; (the) *people will be lamented; Jokneäm*, a place in Pal.:— Jokneam.

3363. יָקַע **yâqa'**, *yaw-kah´*; a prim. root; prop. to *sever* oneself, i.e. (by impl.) to *be dislocated;* fig. to *abandon;* caus. to *impale* (and thus allow to drop to pieces by *rotting*):— be alienated, depart, hang (up), be out of joint.

3364. יָקַץ **yâqats**, *yaw-kats´*; a prim. root; to *awake* (intr.):— (be) awake (-d).

יָקַף **yâqaph**. See 5362.

3365. יָקַר **yâqar**, *yaw-kar´*; a prim. root; prop. appar. to *be heavy*, i.e. (fig.) *valuable;* caus. to *make rare* (fig. to *inhibit*):— be (make) precious, be prized, be set by, withdraw.

3366. יְקָר **yᵉqâr**, *yek-awr´*; from 3365; *value*, i.e. (concr.) *wealth;* abstr. *costliness, dignity:*— honour, precious (things), price.

3367. יְקָר **yᵉqâr** (Chald.), *yek-awr´*; corresp. to 3366:— glory, honour.

3368. יָקָר **yâqâr**, *yaw-kawr´*; from 3365; *valuable* (obj. or subj.):— brightness, clear, costly, excellent, fat, honourable women, precious, reputation.

3369. יָקֹשׁ **yâqôsh**, *yaw-koshe´*; a prim. root; to *ensnare* (lit. or fig.):— fowler (lay a) snare.

3370. יָקְשָׁן **Yoqshân**, *yok-shawn´*; from 3369; *insidious; Jokshan*, an Arabian patriarch:— Jokshan.

3371. יָקְתְאֵל **Yoqthᵉ'êl**, *yok-theh-ale´*; prob. from the same as 3348 and 410; *veneration of God* [comp. 3354]; *Joktheël*, the name of a place in Pal., and of one in Idumæa:— Joktheel.

יָרָא **yârâ'**. See 3384.

3372. יָרֵא **yârê'**, *yaw-ray´*; a prim. root; to *fear;* mor. to *revere;* caus. to *frighten:*— affright, be (make) afraid, dread (-ful), (put in) fear (-ful, -fully, -ing), (be had in) reverence (-end), × see, terrible (act, -ness, thing).

3373. יָרֵא **yârê'**, *yaw-ray´*; from 3372; *fearing;* mor. *reverent:*— afraid, fear (-ful).

3374. יִרְאָה **yir'âh**, *yir-aw´*; fem. of 3373; *fear* (also used as infin.); mor. *reverence:*— × dreadful, × exceedingly, fear (-fulness).

3375. יִרְאוֹן **Yir'ôwn**, *yir-ohn´*; from 3372; *fearfulness; Jiron*, a place in Pal:— Iron.

3376. יִרְאִיָּיה **Yir'îyâyh**, *yir-ee-yaw´*; from 3373 and 3050; *fearful of Jah; Jirijah*, an Isr.:— Irijah.

3377. יָרֵב **Yârêb**, *yaw-rabe´*; from 7378; *he will contend; Jareb*, a symb. name for Assyria:— Jareb. Comp. 3402.

3378. יְרֻבַּעַל **Yᵉrubba'al**, *yer-oob-bah´-al*; from 7378 and 1168; *Baal will contend; Jerubbaal*, a symbol. name of Gideon:— Jerubbaal.

3379. יָרָבְעָם **Yârob'âm**, *yaw-rob-awm´*; from 7378 and 5971; (the) *people will contend; Jarobam*, the name of two Isr. kings:— Jeroboam.

3380. יְרֻבֶּשֶׁת **Yᵉrubbesheth**, *yer-oob-beh´-sheth;* from 7378 and 1322; *shame* (i.e. the idol) *will contend; Jerubbesheth*, a symbol. name for Gideon:— Jerubbesheth.

3381. יָרַד **yârad**, *yaw-rad´*; a prim. root; to *descend* (lit. to *go downwards;* or conventionally to a lower region, as the shore, a boundary, the enemy, etc.; or fig. to *fall*); caus. to *bring down* (in all the above applications):— × abundantly, bring down, carry down, cast down, (cause to) come (-ing) down, fall (down), get down, go (-ing) down (-ward), hang down, × indeed, let down, light (down), put down (off), (cause to, let) run down, sink, subdue, take down.

3382. יֶרֶד **Yered**, *yeh´-red;* from 3381; a *descent; Jered*, the name of an antediluvian, and of an Isr.:— Jared.

3383. יַרְדֵּן **Yardên**, *yar-dane´;* from 3381; a *descender; Jarden*, the principal river of Pal.:— Jordan.

3384. יָרָה **yârâh**, *yaw-raw´;* or (2 Chron. 26:15)

יָרָא **yârâ'**, *yaw-raw´;* a prim. root; prop. to *flow* as water (i.e. to *rain*); tran. to *lay* or *throw* (espec. an arrow, i.e. to *shoot*); fig. to *point* out (as if by *aiming* the finger), to *teach:*— (+) archer, cast, direct, inform, instruct, lay, shew, shoot, teach (-er,-ing), through.

3385. יְרוּאֵל **Yᵉrûw'êl**, *yer-oo-ale´;* from 3384 and 410; *founded of God; Jeruel*, a place in Pal.:— Jeruel.

3386. יָרוֹחַ **Yârôwach**, *yaw-ro´-akh;* perh. denom. from 3394; (born at the) new *moon; Jaroäch*, an Isr.:— Jaroah.

3387. יָרוֹק **yârôwq**, *yaw-roke´;* from 3417; *green*, i.e. an herb:— green thing.

3388. יְרוּשָׁא **Yᵉrûwshâ'**, *yer-oo-shaw´;* or

יְרוּשָׁה **Yᵉrûwshâh**, *yer-oo-shaw´;* fem. pass. part. of 3423; *possessed; Jerusha* or *Jerushah*, an Israelitess:— Jerusha, Jerushah.

3389. יְרוּשָׁלַם **Yᵉrûwshâlaim**, *yer-oo-shaw-lah´-im;* rarely

יְרוּשָׁלַיִם **Yᵉrûwshâlayim**, *yer-oo-shaw-lah´-yim;* a dual (in allusion to its two main hills [the true pointing, at least of the former reading, seems to be that of 3390]; prob. from (the pass. part. of) 3384 and 7999; *founded peaceful; Jerushalaïm* or *Jerusalem*, the capital city of Pal.:— Jerusalem.

3390. יְרוּשָׁלֵם **Y^erûwshâlêm** (Chald.), *yer-oo-shaw-lame´*; corresp. to 3389:— Jerusalem.

3391. יֶרַח **yerach**, *yeh´-rakh*; from an unused root of uncert. signif.; a *lunation*, i.e. *month*:— month, moon.

3392. יֶרַח **Yerach**, *yeh´-rakh*; the same as 3391; *Jerach*, an Arabian patriarch:— Jerah.

3393. יְרַח **y^erach** (Chald.), *yeh-rakh´*; corresp. to 3391; a *month*:— month.

3394. יָרֵחַ **yârêach**, *yaw-ray´-akh*; from the same as 3391; the *moon*:— moon.

יְרֵחוֹ **Y^erêchôw**. See 3405.

3395. יְרֹחָם **Y^erôchâm**, *yer-o-khawm´*; from 7355; *compassionate*; *Jerocham*, the name of seven or eight Isr.:— Jeroham.

3396. יְרַחְמְאֵל **Y^erachm^eêl**, *yer-akh-meh-ale´*; from 7355 and 410; *God will compassionate*; *Jerachmeël*, the name of three Isr.:— Jerahmeel.

3397. יְרַחְמְאֵלִי **Y^erachm^eêlîy**, *yer-akh-meh-ay-lee´*; patron. from 3396; a *Jerachmeëlite* or desc. of Jerachmeel:— Jerahmeelites.

3398. יַרְחָע **Yarchâ'**, *yar-khaw´*; prob. of Eg. or.; *Jarcha*, an Eg.:— Jarha.

3399. יָרַט **yâraṭ**, *yaw-rat´*; a prim. root; to *precipitate* or *hurl* (*rush*) headlong; (intr.) to *be rash*:— be perverse, turn over.

3400. יְרִיאֵל **Y^erîy'êl**, *yer-ee-ale´*; from 3384 and 410; *thrown of God*; *Jeriël*, an Isr.:— Jeriel. Comp. 3385.

3401. יָרִיב **yârîyb**, *yaw-rebe´*; from 7378; lit. *he will contend*; prop. adj. *contentious*; used as noun, an *adversary*:— that content (-eth), that strive.

3402. יָרִיב **Yârîyb**, *yaw-rebe´*; the same as 3401; *Jarib*, the name of three Isr.:— Jarib.

3403. יְרִיבַי **Y^erîybay**, *yer-eeb-ah´ee*; from 3401; *contentious*; *Jeribai*, an Isr.:— Jeribai.

3404. יְרִיָּה **Y^erîyâh**, *yer-ee-yaw´*; or

יְרִיָּהוּ **Y^erîyâhûw**, *yer-ee-yaw´-hoo*; from 3384 and 3050; *Jah will throw*; *Jerijah*, an Isr.:— Jeriah, Jerijah.

3405. יְרִיחוֹ **Y^erîychôw**, *yer-ee-kho´*; or

יְרֵחוֹ **Y^erêchôw**, *yer-ay-kho´*; or var. (1 Kings 16:34)

יְרִיחֹה **Y^erîychôh**, *yer-ee-kho´*; perh. from 3394; *its month*; or else from 7306; *fragrant*; *Jericho* or *Jerecho*, a place in Pal.:— Jericho.

3406. יְרִימוֹת **Y^erîymôwth**, *yer-ee-mohth´*; or

יְרֵימוֹת **Y^erêymôwth**, *yer-ay-mohth´*; or

יְרֵמוֹת **Y^erêmôwth**, *yer-ay-mohth´*; fem. plur. from 7311; *elevations*; *Jerimoth* or *Jeremoth*, the name of twelve Isr.:— Jeremoth, Jerimoth, and Ramoth [from the marg.].

3407. יְרִיעָה **y^erîy'âh**, *yer-ee-aw´*; from 3415; a *hanging* (as *tremulous*):— curtain.

3408. יְרִיעוֹת **Y^erîy'ôwth**, *yer-ee-ohth´*; plur. of 3407; *curtains*; *Jerioth*, an Israelitess:— Jerioth.

3409. יָרֵךְ **yârêk**, *yaw-rake´*; from an unused root mean. to *be soft*; the *thigh* (from its fleshy *softness*); by euphem. the *generative parts*; fig. a *shank*, *flank*, *side*:— × body, loins, shaft, side, thigh.

3410. יַרְכָא **yarkâ'** (Chald.), *yar-kaw´*; corresp. to 3411; a *thigh*:— thigh.

3411. יְרֵכָה **y^erêkâh**, *yer-ay-kaw´*; fem. of 3409; prop. the *flank*; but used only fig., the *rear* or *recess*:— border, coast, part, quarter, side.

3412. יַרְמוּת **Yarmûwth**, *yar-mooth´*; from 7311; *elevation*; *Jarmuth*, the name of two places in Pal.:— Jarmuth.

יְרֵמוֹת **Y^erêmôwth**. See 3406.

3413. יְרֵמַי **Y^erêmay**, *yer-ay-mah´-ee* from 7311; *elevated*; *Jeremai*, an Isr.:— Jeremai.

3414. יִרְמְיָה **Yirm^eyâh**, *yir-meh-yaw´*; or

יִרְמְיָהוּ **Yirm^eyâhûw**, *yir-meh-yaw´-hoo*; from 7311 and 3050; *Jah will rise*; *Jirmejah*, the name of eight or nine Isr.:— Jeremiah.

3415. יָרַע **yâra'**, *yaw-rah´*; a prim. root; prop. to *be broken* up (with any violent action) i.e. (fig.) to *fear*:— be grievous [only Isa. 15:4; the rest belong to 7489].

3416. יִרְפְּאֵל **Yirp^eêl**, *yir-peh-ale´*; from 7495 and 410; *God will heal*; *Jirpeël*, a place in Pal.:— Irpeel.

3417. יָרַק **yâraq**, *yaw-rak´*; a prim. root; to *spit*:— × but, spit.

3418. יֶרֶק **yereq**, *yeh´-rek*; from 3417 (in the sense of *vacuity* of color); prop. *pallor*, i.e. the yellowish *green* of young and sickly vegetation; concr. *verdure*, i.e. grass or vegetation:— grass, green (thing).

3419. יָרָק **yârâq**, *yaw-rawk´*; from the same as 3418; prop. *green*; concr. a *vegetable*:— green, herbs.

יַרְקוֹן **Yarqôwn**. See 4313.

3420. יֵרָקוֹן **yêrâqôwn**, *yay-raw-kone´*; from 3418; *paleness*, whether of persons (from fright), or of plants (from drought):— greenish, yellow.

3421. יָרְקְעָם **Yorq^e'âm**, *yor-keh-awm´*; from 7324 and 5971; *people will be poured forth*; *Jorkeäm*, a place in Pal.:— Jorkeam.

3422. יְרַקְרַק **y^eraqraq**, *yer-ak-rak´*; from the same as 3418; *yellowishness*:— greenish, yellow.

3423. יָרַשׁ **yârash**, *yaw-rash´*; or

יָרַשׁ **yâresh**, *yaw-raysh´*; a prim. root; to *occupy* (by *driving* out previous tenants, and *possessing* in their place); by impl. to *seize*, to *rob*, to *inherit*; also to *expel*, to *impoverish*, to *ruin*:— cast out, consume, destroy, disinherit, dispossess, drive (-ing) out, enjoy, expel, × without fail, (give to, leave for) inherit (-ance, -or) + magistrate, be (make) poor, come to poverty, (give to, make to) possess, get (have) in (take) possession, seize upon, succeed, × utterly.

3424. יְרֵשָׁה **yᵉrêshâh**, *yer-ay-shaw´*; from 3423; *occupancy:*— possession.

3425. יְרֻשָּׁה **yᵉrushâh**, *yer-oosh-shaw´*; from 3423; something *occupied*; a *conquest*; also a *patrimony:*— heritage, inheritance, possession.

3426. שׁ **yêsh**, *yaysh*; perh. from an unused root mean. to *stand* out, or *exist*; *entity*; used adv. or as a copula for the substantive verb (1961); there *is* or *are* (or any other form of the verb to be, as may suit the connection):— (there) are, (he, it, shall, there, there may, there shall, there should) be, thou do, had, hast, (which) hath, (I, shalt, that) have, (he, it, there) is, substance, it (there) was, (there) were, ye will, thou wilt, wouldest.

3427. יָשַׁב **yâshab**, *yaw-shab´*; a prim. root; prop. to *sit* down (spec. as judgement in ambush, in quiet); by impl. to *dwell*, to *remain*; caus. to *settle*, to *marry:*— (make to) abide (-ing), continue, (cause to, make to) dwell (-ing), ease self, endure, establish, × fail, habitation, haunt, (make to) inhabit (-ant), make to keep [house], lurking, × marry (-ing), (bring again to) place, remain, return, seat, set (-tle), (down-) sit (-down, still, -ting down, -ting [place], -uate), take, tarry.

3428. יְשֶׁבְאָב **Yesheb'âb**, *yeh-sheb-awb´*; from 3427 and 1; *seat of* (his) *father*; Jeshebab, an Isr.:— Jeshebeab.

3429. יֹשֵׁב בַּשֶּׁבֶת **Yôshêb bash-Shebeth**, *yo-shabe´ bash-sheh´-beth*; from the act. part. of 3427 and 7674, with a prep. and the art. interposed; *sitting in the seat*; Josheb-bash-Shebeth, an Isr.:— that sat in the seat.

3430. יִשְׁבּוֹ בְּנֹב° **Yishbôw bᵉ-Nôb**, *yish-bo´ beh-nobe´*; from 3427 and 5011, with a pron. suff. and a prep. interposed; *his dwelling* (is) *in Nob*; Jishbo-be-Nob, a Philistine:— Ishbi-benob [from the marg.].

3431. יִשְׁבַּח **Yishbach**, *yish-bakh´*; from 7623; *he will praise*; Jishbach, an Isr.:— Ishbah.

3432. יָשׁוּבִי **Yâshûbîy**, *yaw-shoo-bee´*; patron. from 3437; a *Jashubite*, or desc. of Jashub:— Jashubites.

3433. יָשֻׁבִי לֶחֶם **Yâshûbîy Lechem**, *yaw-shoo-bee´ leh´-khem*; from 7725 and 3899; *returner*

of bread; Jashubi-Lechem, an Isr.:— Jashubi-lehem. [Prob. the text should be pointed

יֹשְׁבֵי לֶחֶם **Yôshᵉbêy Lechem**, *yo-sheh-bay´ leh´-khem*, and rendered "(they were) inhab. of Lechem," i.e. of Bethlehem (by contr.). Comp. 3902].

3434. יָשָׁבְעָם **Yâshob'âm**, *yaw-shob-awm´*; from 7725 and 5971; *people will return*; Jashobam, the name of two or three Isr.:— Jashobeam.

3435. יִשְׁבָּק **Yishbâq**, *yish-bawk´*; from an unused root corresp. to 7662; *he will leave*; Jishbak, a son of Abraham:— Ishbak.

3436. יָשְׁבְּקָשָׁה **Yoshbᵉqâshâh**, *yosh-bek-aw-shaw´*; from 3427 and 7186; a *hard seat*; Joshbekashah, an Isr.:— Joshbekashah.

3437. יָשׁוּב **Yâshûwb**, *yaw-shoob´*; or

יָשִׁיב **Yâshîyb**, *yaw-sheeb´*; from 7725; *he will return*; Jashub, the name of two Isr.:— Jashub.

3438. יִשְׁוָה **Yishvâh**, *yish-vaw´*; from 7737; *he will level*; Jishvah, an Isr.:— Ishvah, Isvah.

3439. יְשׁוֹחָיָה **Yᵉshôwchâyâh**, *yesh-o-khaw-yaw´*; from the same as 3445 and 3050; *Jah will empty*; Jeshochajah, an Isr.:— Jeshoaiah.

3440. יִשְׁוִי **Yishvîy**, *yish-vee´*; from 7737; *level*; Jishvi, the name of two Isr.:— Ishuai, Ishvi, Isui, Jesui.

3441. יִשְׁוִי **Yishvîy**, *yish-vee´*; patron. from 3440; a *Jishvite* (collect.) or desc. of Jishvi:— Jesuites.

3442. יֵשׁוּעַ **Yêshûwa'**, *yay-shoo´-ah*; for 3091; *he will save*; Jeshua, the name of ten Isr., also of a place in Pal.:— Jeshua.

3443. יֵשׁוּעַ **Yêshûwa'** (Chald.), *yay-shoo´-ah*; corresp. to 3442:— Jeshua.

3444. יְשׁוּעָה **yᵉshûw'âh**, *yesh-oo´-aw*; fem. pass. part. of 3467; something *saved*, i.e. (abstr.) *deliverance*; hence, *aid, victory, prosperity:*— deliverance, health, help (-ing), salvation, save, saving (health), welfare.

3445. יֶשַׁח **yeshach**, *yeh´-shakh*; from an unused root mean. to *gape* (as the empty stomach); *hunger:*— casting down.

3446. יִשְׂחָק **Yischâq**, *yis-khawk´*; from 7831; *he will laugh*; Jischak, the heir of Abraham:— Isaac. Comp. 3327.

3447. יָשַׁט **yâshaṭ**, *yaw-shat´*; a prim. root; to *extend:*— hold out.

3448. יִשַׁי **Yîshay**, *yee-shah´-ee*; by Chald.

אִישַׁי **'Îyshay**, *ee-shah´-ee*; from the same as 3426; *extant*; Jishai, David's father:— Jesse.

יָשִׁיב **Yâshîyb.** See 3437.

3449. יִשִּׁיָּה **Yishshîyâh,** *yish-shee-yaw´;* or

יִשִּׁיָּהוּ **Yishshîyâhûw,** *yish-shee-yaw´-hoo;* from 5383 and 3050; *Jah will lend; Jishshijah,* the name of five Isr.:— Ishiah, Isshiah, Ishijah, Jesiah.

3450. יְשִׂימָאֵל **Yᵉsîymâʼêl,** *yes-eem-aw-ale´;* from 7760 and 410; *God will place; Jesimaël,* an Isr.:— Jesimael.

3451. יְשִׁימָה **yᵉshîymâh,** *yesh-ee-maw´;* from 3456; *desolation:*— let death seize [*from the marg.*].

3452. יְשִׁימוֹן **yᵉshîymôwn,** *yesh-ee-mone´;* from 3456; a *desolation:*— desert, Jeshimon, solitary, wilderness.

יְשִׁימוֹת **yᵉshîymôwth.** See 1020, 3451.

3453. יָשִׁישׁ **yâshîysh,** *yaw-sheesh´;* from 3486; an *old* man:— (very) aged (man), ancient, very old.

3454. יְשִׁישַׁי **Yᵉshîyshay,** *yesh-ee-shah´-ee;* from 3453; *aged; Jeshishai,* an Isr.:— Jeshishai.

3455. יָשַׂם **yâsam,** *yaw-sam´;* a prim. root; to *place;* intr. to *be placed:*— be put (set).

3456. יָשַׁם **yâsham,** *yaw-sham´;* a prim. root; to *lie waste:*— be desolate.

3457. יִשְׁמָא **Yishmâʼ,** *yish-maw´;* from 3456; *desolate; Jishma,* an Isr.:— Ishma.

3458. יִשְׁמָעֵאל **Yishmâʻêʼl,** *yish-maw-ale´;* from 8085 and 410; *God will hear; Jishmaël,* the name of Abraham's oldest son, and of five Isr.:— Ishmael.

3459. יִשְׁמְעֵאלִי **Yishmâʻêʼlîy,** *yish-maw-ay-lee´;* patron. from 3458; a *Jishmaëlite* or desc. of Jishmael:— Ishmaelite.

3460. יִשְׁמַעְיָה **Yishmaʻyâh,** *yish-mah-yaw´;* or

יִשְׁמַעְיָהוּ **Yishmaʻyâhûw,** *yish-mah-yaw´-hoo;* from 8085 and 3050; *Jah will hear; Jishmajah,* the name of two Isr.:— Ishmaiah.

3461. יִשְׁמְרַי **Yishmᵉray,** *yish-mer-ah´-ee;* from 8104; *preservative; Jishmerai,* an Isr.:— Ishmerai.

3462. יָשֵׁן **yâshên,** *yaw-shane´;* a prim. root; prop. to *be slack* or *languid,* i.e. (by impl.) *sleep* (fig. to *die*); also to *grow old, stale* or *inveterate:*— old (store), remain long, (make to) sleep.

3463. יָשֵׁן **yâshên,** *yaw-shane´;* from 3462; *sleepy:*— asleep, (one out of) sleep (-eth, -ing), slept.

3464. יָשֵׁן **Yâshên,** *yaw-shane´;* the same as 3463; *Jashen,* an Isr.:— Jashen.

3465. יָשָׁן **yâshân,** *yaw-shawn´;* from 3462; *old:*— old.

3466. יְשָׁנָה **Yᵉshânâh,** *yesh-aw-naw´;* fem. of 3465; *Jeshanah,* a place in Pal.:— Jeshanah.

3467. יָשַׁע **yâshaʻ,** *yaw-shah´;* a prim. root; prop. to *be open, wide* or *free,* i.e. (by impl.) to *be safe;* caus. to *free* or *succor:*— × at all, avenging, defend, deliver (-er), help, preserve, rescue, be safe, bring (having) salvation, save (-iour), get victory.

3468. יֶשַׁע **yeshaʻ,** *yeh´-shah;* or

יֵשַׁע **yêshaʻ,** *yay´-shah;* from 3467; *liberty, deliverance, prosperity:*— safety, salvation, saving.

3469. יִשְׁעִי **Yishʻîy,** *yish-ee´;* from 3467; *saving; Jishi,* the name of four Isr.:— Ishi.

3470. יְשַׁעְיָה **Yᵉshaʻyâh,** *yesh-ah-yaw´;* or

יְשַׁעְיָהוּ **Yᵉshaʻyâhûw,** *yesh-ah-yaw´-hoo;* from 3467 and 3050; *Jah has saved; Jeshajah,* the name of seven Isr.:— Isaiah, Jesaiah, Jeshaiah.

3471. יָשְׁפֵה **yâshᵉphêh,** *yaw-shef-ay´;* from an unused root mean. to *polish;* a gem supposed to be *jasper* (from the resemblance in name):— jasper.

3472. יִשְׁפָּה **Yishpâh,** *yish-paw´;* perh. from 8192; *he will scratch; Jishpah,* an Isr.:— Ispah.

3473. יִשְׁפָּן **Yishpân,** *yish-pawn´;* prob. from the same as 8227; *he will hide; Jishpan,* an Isr.:— Ishpan.

3474. יָשַׁר **yâshar,** *yaw-shar´;* a prim. root; to *be straight* or *even;* fig. to *be* (caus. to *make*) *right, pleasant, prosperous:*— direct, fit, seem good (meet), + please (will), be (esteem, go) right (on), bring (look, make, take the) straight (way), be upright (-ly).

3475. יֵשֶׁר **Yêsher,** *yay´-sher;* from 3474; *the right; Jesher,* an Isr.:— Jesher.

3476. יֹשֶׁר **yôsher,** *yo´-sher;* from 3474; *the right:*— equity, meet, right, upright (-ness).

3477. יָשָׁר **yâshâr,** *yaw-shawr´;* from 3474; *straight* (lit. or fig.):— convenient, equity, Jasher, just, meet (-est), + pleased well right (-eous), straight, (most) upright (-ly, -ness).

3478. יִשְׂרָאֵל **Yisrâʼêl,** *yis-raw-ale´;* from 8280 and 410; *he will rule* (as) *God; Jisraël,* a symb. name of Jacob; also (typ.) of his posterity:— Israel.

3479. יִשְׂרָאֵל **Yisrâʼêl** (Chald.), *yis-raw-ale´;* corresp. to 3478:— Israel.

3480. יְשַׂרְאֵלָה **Yᵉsarʼêlâh,** *yes-ar-ale´-aw;* by var. from 3477 and 410 with directive enclitic; *right towards God; Jesarelah,* an Isr.:— Jesharelah. Comp. 841.

3481. יִשְׂרְאֵלִי **Yisrᵉʼêlîy,** *yis-reh-ay-lee´;* patron. from 3478; a *Jisreëlite* or desc. of Jisrael:— of Israel, Israelite.

3482. יִשְׂרְאֵלִית **Yisrᵉʼêlîyth,** *yis-reh-ay-leeth´;*

fem. of 3481; a *Jisreëlitess* or female desc. of Jisrael:— Israelitish.

3483. יִשְׁרָה **yishrâh**, *yish-raw´*; fem. or 3477; *rectitude:*— uprightness.

3484. יְשֻׁרוּן **Yeshûrûwn**, *yesh-oo-roon´*; from 3474; *upright; Jeshurun*, a symbol. name for Israel:— Jeshurun.

3485. יִשָּׂשכָר **Yissâskâr**, *yis-saw-kawr´*; (strictly *yis-saws-kawr´*); from 5375 and 7939; *he will bring a reward; Jissaskar*, a son of Jacob:— Issachar.

3486. יָשֵׁשׁ **yâshêsh**, *yaw-shaysh´*; from an unused root mean. to *blanch; gray*-haired, i.e. an *aged* man:— stoop for age.

3487. יָת **yath** (Chald.), *yath;* corresp. to 853; a sign of the object of a verb:— + whom.

3488. יְתִב **yethîb** (Chald.), *yeth-eeb´*; corresp. to 3427; to *sit* or *dwell:*— dwell, (be) set, sit.

3489. יָתֵד **yâthêd**, *yaw-thade´*; from an unused root mean. to *pin* through or fast; a *peg:*— nail, paddle, pin, stake.

3490. יָתוֹם **yâthôwm**, *yaw-thome´*; from an unused root mean. to *be lonely*; a *bereaved* person:— fatherless (child), orphan.

3491. יָתוּר **yâthûwr**, *yaw-thoor´*; pass. part. of 3498; prop. what is *left*, i.e. (by impl.) a *gleaning:*— range.

3492. יַתִּיר **Yattîyr**, *yat-teer´*; from 3498; *redundant; Jattir*, a place in Pal.:— Jattir.

3493. יַתִּיר **yattîyr** (Chald.), *yat-teer´*; corresp. to 3492; *preeminent;* adv. *very:*— exceeding (-ly), excellent.

3494. יִתְלָה **Yithlâh**, *yith-law´*; prob. from 8518; it *will hang*, i.e. *be high; Jithlah*, a place in Pal.:— Jethlah.

3495. יִתְמָה **Yithmâh**, *yith-maw´*; from the same as 3490; *orphanage; Jithmah*, an Isr.:— Ithmah.

3496. יַתְנִיאֵל **Yathnîy'êl**, *yath-nee-ale´*; from an unused root mean. to *endure*, and 410; *continued of God; Jathniël*, an Isr.:— Jathniel.

3497. יִתְנָן **Yithnân**, *yith-nawn´*; from the same as 8577; *extensive; Jithnan*, a place in Pal.:— Ithnan.

3498. יָתַר **yâthar**, *yaw-thar´*; a prim. root; to *jut* over or *exceed;* by impl. to *excel;* (intr.) to *remain* or *be left;* caus. to *leave, cause to abound, preserve:*— excel, leave (a remnant), left behind, too much, make plenteous, preserve, (be, let) remain (-der, -ing, -nant), reserve, residue, rest.

3499. יֶתֶר **yether**, *yeh´-ther;* from 3498; prop. an *overhanging*, i.e. (by impl.) an *excess, superiority, remainder;* also a small *rope* (as hanging free):— + abundant, cord, exceeding, excellency (-ent), what they leave, that

hath left, plentifully , remnant, residue, rest, string, with.

3500. יֶתֶר **Yether**, *yeh´-ther;* the same as 3499; *Jether*, the name of five or six Isr. and of one Midianite:— Jether, Jethro. Comp. 3503.

3501. יִתְרָא **Yithrâ'**, *yith-raw´*; by var. for 3502; *Jithra*, an Isr. (or Ishmaelite):— Ithra.

3502. יִתְרָה **yithrâh**, *yith-raw´*; fem. of 3499; prop. *excellence*, i.e. (by impl.) *wealth:*— abundance, riches.

3503. יִתְרוֹ **Yithrôw**, *yith-ro´*; from 3499 with pron. suff.; *his excellence; Jethro*, Moses' father-in-law:— Jethro. Comp. 3500.

3504. יִתְרוֹן **yithrôwn**, *yith-rone´*; from 3498; *preeminence, gain:*— better, excellency (-leth), profit (-able).

3505. יִתְרִי **Yithrîy**, *yith-ree´*; patron. from 3500; a *Jithrite* or desc. of Jether:— Ithrite.

3506. יִתְרָן **Yithrân**, *yith-rawn´*; from 3498; *excellent; Jithran*, the name of an Edomite and of an Isr.:— Ithran.

3507. יִתְרְעָם **Yithre'âm**, *yith-reh-awm´*; from 3499 and 5971; *excellence of people; Jithreäm*, a son of David:— Ithream.

3508. יֹתֶרֶת **yôthereth**, *yo-theh´-reth;* fem. act. part. of 3498; the *lobe* or *flap* of the liver (as if redundant or outhanging):— caul.

3509. יְתֵת **Yethêyth**, *yeh-thayth´*; of uncert. der.; *Jetheth*, an Edomite:— Jetheth.

כ

3510. כָּאַב **kâ'ab**, *kaw-ab´;* a prim. root; prop. to feel *pain;* by impl. to *grieve;* fig. to *spoil:*— grieving, mar, have pain, make sad (sore), (be) sorrowful.

3511. כְּאֵב **ke'êb**, *keh-abe´;* from 3510; *suffering* (phys. or ment.), *adversity:*— grief, pain, sorrow.

3512. כָּאָה **kâ'âh**, *kaw-aw´;* a prim. root; to *despond;* caus. to *deject:*— broken, be grieved, make sad.

3513. כָּבַד **kâbad**, *kaw-bad´;* or

כָּבֵד **kâbêd**, *kaw-bade´;* a prim. root; to *be heavy*, i.e. in a bad sense (*burdensome, severe, dull*) or in a good sense (*numerous, rich, honorable*); caus. to *make weighty* (in the same two senses):— abounding with, more grievously afflict, boast, be chargeable, × be dim, glorify, be (make) glorious (things), glory, (very) great, be grievous, harden, be (make) heavy, be heavier, lay heavily, (bring to, come to, do, get, be had in) honour (self), (be) honourable (man) , lade, × more be laid, make self many, nobles, prevail, promote (to honour), be rich, be (go) sore, stop.

3514. כֹּבֶד **kôbed**, *ko´-bed;* from 3513; *weight, multitude, vehemence:*— grievousness, heavy, great number.

3515. כָּבֵד **kâbêd**, *kaw-bade´;* from 3513; *heavy;* fig. in a good sense (*numerous*) or in a bad sense (*severe, difficult, stupid*):— (so) great, grievous, hard (-ened), (too) heavy (-ier), laden, much, slow, sore, thick.

3516. כָּבֵד **kâbêd**, *kaw-bade´;* the same as 3515; the *liver* (as the *heaviest* of the viscera):— liver.

כָּבֹד **kâbôd**. See 3519.

3517. כְּבֵדֻת **kebêdûth**, *keb-ay-dooth´;* fem. of 3515; *difficulty:*— × heavily.

3518. כָּבָה **kâbâh**, *kaw-baw´;* a prim. root; to *expire* or (caus.) to *extinguish* (fire, light, anger):— go (put) out, quench.

3519. כָּבוֹד **kâbôwd**, *kaw-bode´;* rarely

כָּבֹד **kâbôd**, *kaw-bode´;* from 3513; prop. *weight,* but only fig. in a good sense, *splendor* or *copiousness:*— glorious (-ly), glory, honour (-able).

3520. כְּבוּדָּה **kebûwddâh**, *keb-ood-daw´;* irreg. fem. pass. part. of 3513; *weightiness,* i.e. *magnificence, wealth:*— carriage, all glorious, stately.

3521. כָּבוּל **Kâbûwl**, *kaw-bool´;* from the same as 3525 in the sense of *limitation; sterile; Cabul,* the name of two places in Pal.:— Cabul.

3522. כַּבּוֹן **Kabbôwn**, *kab-bone´;* from an unused root mean. to *heap* up; *hilly; Cabon,* a place in Pal.:— Cabbon.

3523. כְּבִיר **kebîyr**, *keb-eer;* from 3527 in the orig. sense of *plaiting;* a *matrass* (of intertwined materials):— pillow.

3524. כַּבִּיר **kabbîyr**, *kab-beer´;* from 3527; *vast,* whether in extent (fig. of power, *mighty;* of time, *aged*), or in number, *many:*— + feeble, mighty, most, much, strong, valiant.

3525. כֶּבֶל **kebel**, *keh´-bel;* from an unused root mean. to *twine* or braid together; a *fetter:*— fetter.

3526. כָּבַס **kâbaç**, *kaw-bas´;* a prim. root; to *trample;* hence, to *wash* (prop. by stamping with the feet), whether lit. (incl. the *fulling* process) or fig.:— fuller, wash (-ing).

3527. כָּבַר **kâbar**, *kaw-bar´;* a prim. root; prop. to *plait* together, i.e. (fig.) to *augment* (espec. in number or quantity, to *accumulate*):— in abundance, multiply.

3528. כְּבָר **kebâr**, *keb-awr´;* from 3527; prop. *extent* of time, i.e. a *great while;* hence, *long ago, formerly, hitherto:*— already, (seeing that which) now.

3529. כְּבָר **Kebâr**, *keb-awr´;* the same as 3528;

length; Kebar, a river of Mesopotamia:— Chebar. Comp. 2249.

3530. כִּבְרָה **kibrâh**, *kib-raw´;* fem. of 3528; prop. *length,* i.e. a *measure* (of uncert. dimension):— × little.

3531. כְּבָרָה **kebârâh**, *keb-aw-raw´;* from 3527 in its orig. sense; a *sieve* (as netted):— sieve.

3532. כֶּבֶשׂ **kebes**, *keh-bes´;* from an unused root mean. to *dominate;* a *ram* (just old enough to *butt*):— lamb, sheep.

3533. כָּבַשׁ **kâbash**, *kaw-bash´;* a prim. root; to *tread* down; hence, neg. to *disregard;* pos. to *conquer, subjugate, violate:*— bring into bondage, force, keep under, subdue, bring into subjection.

3534. כֶּבֶשׁ **kebesh**, *keh´-besh;* from 3533; a *footstool* (as trodden upon):— footstool.

3535. כִּבְשָׂה **kibsâh**, *kib-saw´;* or

כַּבְשָׂה **kabsâh**, *kab-saw´;* fem. of 3532; a *ewe:*— (ewe) lamb.

3536. כִּבְשָׁן **kibshân**, *kib-shawn´;* from 3533; a smelting *furnace* (as *reducing* metals):— furnace.

3537. כַּד **kad**, *kad;* from an unused root mean. to *deepen;* prop. a *pail;* but gen. of earthenware; a *jar* for domestic purposes:— barrel, pitcher.

3538. כְּדַב **kedab** (Chald.), *ked-ab´;* from a root corresp. to 3576; *false:*— lying.

3539. כַּדְכֹּד **kadkôd**, *kad-kobe´;* from the same as 3537 in the sense of *striking fire* from a metal forged; a *sparkling* gem, prob. the ruby:— agate.

3540. כְּדָרְלָעֹמֶר **Kedorlâ´ômer**, *ked-or-law-o´-mer;* of for. or.; *Kedorlaomer,* an early Pers. king:— Chedorlaomer.

3541. כֹּה **kôh**, *ko;* from the pref. *k* and 1931; prop. *like this,* i.e. by impl. (of manner) *thus* (or *so*); also (of place) *here* (or *hither*); or (of time) *now:*— also, here, + hitherto, like, on the other side, so (and much), such, on that manner, (on) this (manner, side, way, way and that way), + mean while, yonder.

3542. כָּה **kâh** (Chald.), *kaw;* corresp. to 3541:— hitherto.

3543. כָּהָה **kâhâh**, *kaw-haw´;* a prim. root; to *be weak,* i.e. (fig.) to *despond* (caus. *rebuke*), or (of light, the eye) to *grow dull:*— darken, be dim, fail, faint, restrain, × utterly.

3544. כֵּהֶה **kêheh**, *kay-heh´;* from 3543; *feeble, obscure:*— somewhat dark, darkish, wax dim, heaviness, smoking.

3545. כֵּהָה **kêhâh**, *kay-haw´;* fem. of 3544; prop. a *weakening;* fig. *alleviation,* i.e. *cure:*— healing.

3546. כְּהַל **kᵉhal** (Chald.), *keh-hal´;* a root corresp. to 3201 and 3557; to *be able:*— be able, could.

3547. כָּהַן **kâhan**, *kaw-han´;* a prim. root, appar. mean. to *mediate* in relig. services; but used only as denom. from 3548; to *officiate as a priest;* fig. to *put on regalia:*— deck, be (do the office of a, execute the, minister in the) priest ('s office).

3548. כֹּהֵן **kôhên**, *ko-hane´;* act. part. of 3547; lit. one *officiating,* a *priest;* also (by courtesy) an *acting priest* (although a layman):— chief ruler, × own, priest, prince, principal officer.

3549. כָּהֵן **kâhên** (Chald.), *kaw-hane´;* corresp. to 3548:— priest.

3550. כְּהֻנָּה **kᵉhunnâh**, *keh-hoon-naw´;* from 3547; *priesthood:*— priesthood, priest's office.

3551. כַּו **kav** (Chald.), *kav;* from a root corresp. to 3854 in the sense of *piercing;* a *window* (as a perforation):— window.

3552. כּוּב **Kûwb**, *koob;* of for. der.; *Kub,* a country near Egypt:— Chub.

3553. כּוֹבַע **kôwbaʻ**, *ko´-bah;* from an unused root mean. to be *high* or *rounded;* a *helmet* (as *arched*):— helmet. Comp. 6959.

3554. כָּוָה **kâvâh**, *kaw-vaw´;* a prim. root; prop. to *prick* or *penetrate;* hence, to *blister* (as smarting or eating into):— burn.

כּוּחַ **kôwach.** See 3581.

3555. כְּוִיָה **kᵉvîyâh**, *kev-ee-yaw´;* from 3554; a *branding:*— burning.

3556. כּוֹכָב **kôwkâb**, *ko-kawb´;* prob. from the same as 3522 (in the sense of *rolling*) or 3554 (in the sense of *blazing*); a *star* (as *round* or as *shining*); fig. a *prince:*— star (l-gazer).

3557. כּוּל **kûwl**, *kool;* a prim. root; prop. to *keep in;* hence, to *measure;* fig. to *maintain* (in various senses):— (be able to, can) abide, bear, comprehend, contain, feed, forbearing, guide, hold (-ing in), nourish (-er), be present, make provision, receive, sustain, provide sustenance (victuals).

3558. כּוּמָז **kûwmâz**, *koo-mawz´;* from an unused root mean. to *store* away; a *jewel* (prob. gold beads):— tablet.

3559. כּוּן **kûwn**, *koon;* a prim. root; prop. to be *erect* (i.e. stand perpendicular); hence, (caus.) to *set up,* in a great variety of applications, whether lit. (*establish, fix, prepare, apply*), or fig. (*appoint, render sure, proper* or *prosperous*):— certain (-ty), confirm, direct, faithfulness, fashion, fasten, firm, be fitted, be fixed, frame, be meet, ordain, order, perfect, (make) preparation, prepare (self), provide, make provision, (be, make) ready, right, set (aright, fast, forth), be stable , (e-) stablish, stand, tarry, × very deed.

3560. כּוּן **Kûwn**, *koon;* prob. from 3559; *established; Kun,* a place in Syria:— Chun.

3561. כַּוָּן **kavvân**, *kav-vawn´;* from 3559; something *prepared,* i.e. a sacrificial *wafer:*— cake.

3562. כּוֹנַנְיָהוּ **Kôwnanyâhûw**, *ko-nan-yaw´-hoo;* from 3559 and 3050; *Jah has sustained; Conanjah,* the name of two Isr.:— Conaniah, Cononiah. Comp. 3663.

3563. כּוֹס **kôwç**, *koce;* from an unused root mean. to *hold* together; a *cup* (as a container), often fig. a *lot* (as if a potion); also some unclean bird, prob. an *owl* (perh. from the cup-like cavity of its eye):— cup, (small) owl. Comp. 3599.

3564. כּוּר **kûwr**, *koor;* from an unused root mean. prop. to *dig* through; a *pot* or *furnace* (as if excavated):— furnace. Comp. 3600.

כּוֹר **kôwr.** See 3733.

3565. כּוֹר עָשָׁן **Kôwr ʼÂshân**, *kore aw-shawn´;* from 3564 and 6227; *furnace of smoke; Cor-Ashan,* a place in Pal.:— Chorashan.

3566. כּוֹרֶשׁ **Kôwresh**, *ko´-resh;* or (Ezra 1:1 [last time], 2)

כֹּרֶשׁ **Kôresh**, *ko´-resh;* from the Pers.; *Koresh* (or Cyrus), the Pers. king:— Cyrus.

3567. כּוֹרֶשׁ **Kôwresh** (Chald.), *ko´-resh;* corresp. to 3566:— Cyrus.

3568. כּוּשׁ **Kûwsh**, *koosh;* prob. of for. or.; *Cush* (or Ethiopia), the name of a son of Ham, and of his territory; also of an Isr.:— Chush, Cush, Ethiopia.

3569. כּוּשִׁי **Kûwshîy**, *koo-shee´;* patron. from 3568; a *Cushite,* or desc. of Cush:— Cushi, Cushite, Ethiopian (-s).

3570. כּוּשִׁי **Kûwshîy**, *koo-shee´;* the same as 3569; *Cushi,* the name of two Isr.:— Cushi.

3571. כּוּשִׁית **Kûwshîyth**, *koo-sheeth´;* fem. of 3569; a *Cushite woman:*— Ethiopian.

3572. כּוּשָׁן **Kûwshân**, *koo-shawn´;* perh. from 3568; *Cushan,* a region of Arabia:— Cushan.

3573. כּוּשַׁן רִשְׁעָתַיִם **Kûwshan Rishʻâthayim**, *koo-shan´ rish-aw-thah´-yim;* appar. from 3572 and the dual of 7564; *Cushan of double wickedness; Cushan-Rishathajim,* a Mesopotamian king:— Chushan-rishathayim.

3574. כּוֹשָׁרָה **kôwshârâh**, *ko-shaw-raw´;* from 3787; *prosperity;* in plur. *freedom:*— × chain.

3575. כּוּת **Kûwth**, *kooth;* or (fem.)

כּוּתָה **Kûwthâh**, *koo-thaw´;* of for. or.; *Cuth* or *Cuthah,* a province of Assyria:— Cuth.

3576. כָּזַב **kâzab**, *kaw-zab´;* a prim. root; to *lie* (i.e. *deceive*), lit. or fig.:— fail, (be found a, make a) liar, lie, lying, be in vain.

3577. כָּזָב **kâzâb**, *kaw-zawb´;* from 3576; *falsehood;* lit. (*untruth*) or fig. (*idol*):— deceitful, false, leasing, + liar, lie, lying.

3578. כֹּזְבָא **Kôzᵉbâ'**, *ko-zeb-aw´;* from 3576; *fallacious;* Cozeba, a place in Pal.:— Choseba.

3579. כָּזְבִּי **Kozbîy**, *koz-bee´;* from 3576; *false;* Cozbi, a Midianitess:— Cozbi.

3580. כְּזִיב **Kᵉzîyb**, *kez-eeb´;* from 3576; *falsified;* Kezib, a place in Pal.:— Chezib.

3581. כֹּחַ **kôach**, *ko´-akh;* or (Dan. 11:6)

כּוֹחַ **kôwach**, *ko´-akh;* from an unused root mean. to *be firm; vigor,* lit. (*force,* in a good or a bad sense) or fig. (*capacity, means, produce*); also (from its hardiness) a large *lizard:*— ability, able, chameleon, force, fruits, might, power (-ful), strength, substance, wealth.

3582. כָּחַד **kâchad**, *kaw-khad´;* a prim. root; to *secrete,* by act or word; hence, (intens.) to *destroy:*— conceal, cut down (off), desolate, hide.

3583. כָּחַל **kâchal**, *kaw-khal´;* a prim. root; to *paint* (with stibium):— paint.

3584. כָּחַשׁ **kâchash**, *kaw-khash´;* a prim. root; to *be untrue,* in word (to *lie, feign, disown*) or deed (to *disappoint, fail, cringe*):— deceive, deny, dissemble, fail, deal falsely, be found liars, (be-) lie, lying, submit selves.

3585. כַּחַשׁ **kachash**, *kakh´-ash;* from 3584; lit. a *failure* of flesh, i.e. *emaciation;* fig. *hypocrisy:*— leanness, lies, lying.

3586. כֶּחָשׁ **kechâsh**, *kekh-awsh´;* from 3584; *faithless:*— lying.

3587. כִּי **kîy**, *kee;* from 3554; a *brand* or *scar:*— burning.

3588. כִּי **kîy**, *kee;* a prim. particle [the full form of the prepositional prefix] indicating *causal* relations of all kinds, antecedent or consequent; (by impl.) very widely used as a rel. conjunc. or adv. [as below]; often largely modif. by other particles annexed:— and, + (forasmuch, inasmuch, where-) as, assured [-ly], + but, certainly, doubtless, + else, even, + except, for, how, (because, in, so, than) that, + nevertheless, now, rightly, seeing, since, surely, then, therefore, + (al-) + though, + till, truly, + until, when, whether, while, whom, yea, yet.

3589. כִּיד **kîyd**, *keed;* from a prim. root mean. to *strike;* a *crushing;* fig. *calamity:*— destruction.

3590. כִּידוֹד **kîydôwd**, *kee-dode´;* from the same as 3589 [comp. 3539]; prop. something *struck* off, i.e. a *spark* (as struck):— spark.

3591. כִּידוֹן **kîydôwn**, *kee-dohn´;* from the same as 3589; prop. something to *strike* with, i.e. a *dart* (perh. smaller than 2595):— lance, shield, spear, target.

3592. כִּידוֹן **Kîydôwn**, *kee-dohn´;* the same as 3591; *Kidon,* a place in Pal.:— Chidon.

3593. כִּידוֹר **kîydôwr**, *kee-dore´;* of uncert. der.; perh. *tumult:*— battle.

3594. כִּיּוּן **Kîyûwn**, *kee-yoon´;* from 3559; prop. a *statue,* i.e. idol; but used (by euphem.) for some heathen deity (perh. corresp. to Priapus or Baal-peor):— Chiun.

3595. כִּיּוֹר **kîyôwr**, *kee-yore´;* or

כִּיֹר **kîyôr**, *kee-yore´;* from the same as 3564; prop. something *round* (as *excavated* or *bored*), i.e. a chafing-*dish* for coals or a *caldron* for cooking; hence, (from similarity of form) a *washbowl;* also (for the same reason) a *pulpit* or platform:— hearth, laver, pan, scaffold.

3596. כִּילַי **kîylay**, *kee-lah´-ee;* or

כֵּלַי **kêlay**, *kay-lah´-ee;* from 3557 in the sense of *withholding; niggardly:*— churl.

3597. כֵּילַף **kêylaph**, *kay-laf´;* from an unused root mean. to *clap* or strike with noise; a *club* or sledge-hammer:— hammer.

3598. כִּימָה **Kîymâh**, *kee-maw´;* from the same as 3558; a *cluster* of stars, i.e. the *Pleiades:*— Pleiades, seven stars.

3599. כִּיס **kîyç**, *keece;* a form for 3563; a *cup;* also a *bag* for money or weights:— bag, cup, purse.

3600. כִּיר **kîyr**, *keer;* a form for 3564 (only in the dual); a cooking *range* (consisting of two parallel stones, across which the boiler is set):— ranges for pots.

כִּיֹר **kîyôr.** See 3595.

3601. כִּישׁוֹר **kîyshôwr**, *kee-shore´;* from 3787; lit. a *director,* i.e. the *spindle* or shank of a distaff (6418), by which it is twirled:— spindle.

3602. כָּכָה **kâkâh**, *kaw´-kaw;* from 3541; *just so,* referring to the previous or following context:— after that (this) manner, this matter, (even) so, in such a case, thus.

3603. כִּכָּר **kikkâr**, *kik-kawr´;* from 3769; a *circle,* i.e. (by impl.) a circumjacent *tract* or region, expec. the *Ghôr* or valley of the Jordan; also a (round) *loaf;* also a *talent* (or large [round] coin):— loaf, morsel, piece, plain, talent.

3604. כִּכֵּר **kikkêr** (Chald.), *kik-kare´;* corresp. to 3603; a *talent:*— talent.

3605. כֹּל **kôl**, *kole;* or (Jer. 33:8)

כּוֹל **kôwl**, *kole;* from 3634; prop. the

whole; hence, *all, any* or *every* (in the sing. only, but often in a plur. sense):— (in) all (manner, [ye]), altogether, any (manner), enough, every (one, place, thing), howsoever, as many as, [no-] thing, ought, whatsoever, (the) whole, (whoso (-ever).

3606. כֹּל **kôl** (Chald.), *kole;* corresp. to 3605:— all, any, + (forasmuch) as, + be- (for this) cause, every, + no (manner, -ne), + there (where) -fore, + though, what (where, who) -soever, (the) whole.

3607. כָּלָא **kâlâ'**, *kaw-law';* a prim. root; to *re-strict,* by act (*hold* back or in) or word (*pro-hibit*):— finish, forbid, keep (back), refrain, restrain, retain, shut up, be stayed, withhold.

3608. כֶּלֶא **kele'**, *keh'-leh;* from 3607; a *prison:*— prison. Comp. 3610, 3628.

3609. כִּלְאָב **Kil'âb**, *kil-awb';* appar. from 3607 and 1; *restraint of* (his) *father; Kilab,* an Isr.:— Chileab.

3610. כִּלְאַיִם **kil'ayim**, *kil-ah'-yim;* dual of 3608 in the orig. sense of *separation; two heteroge-neities:*— divers seeds (-e kinds), mingled (seed).

3611. כֶּלֶב **keleb**, *keh'-leb;* from an unused root means. to *yelp,* or else to *attack; a dog;* hence, (by euphem.) a male *prostitute:*— dog.

3612. כָּלֵב **Kâlêb**, *kaw-labe';* perh. a form of 3611, or else from the same root in the sense of *forcible; Caleb,* the name of three Isr.:— Caleb.

3613. כָּלֵב אֶפְרָתָה **Kâlêb 'Ephrâthâh**, *kaw-labe' ef-raw'-thaw;* from 3612 and 672; *Caleb-Ephrathah,* a place in Egypt (if the text is correct):— Caleb-ephrathah.

3614. כָּלֻבּוֹ **Kâlibbôw**, *kaw-lib-bo';* prob. by err. transc. for

כָּלֵבִי° **Kâlêbîy**, *kaw-lay-bee';* patron. from 3612; a *Calebite* or desc. of Caleb:— of the house of Caleb.

3615. כָּלָה **kâlâh**, *kaw-law';* a prim. root; to *end,* whether intr. (to *cease, be finished, per-ish*) or tran. (to *complete, prepare, con-sume*):— accomplish, cease, consume (away), determine, destroy (utterly), be (when ... were) done, (be an) end (of), expire, (cause to) fail, faint, finish, fulfil, × fully, × have, leave (off), long, bring to pass, wholly reap, make clean riddance, spend, quite take away, waste.

3616. כָּלֶה **kâleh**, *kaw-leh';* from 3615; *pin-ing:*— fail.

3617. כָּלָה **kâlâh**, *kaw-law';* from 3615; a *com-pletion;* adv. *completely;* also *destruction:*— altogether, (be, utterly) consume (-d), con-summation (-ption), was determined, (full, utter) end, riddance.

3618. כַּלָּה **kallâh**, *kal-law';* from 3634; a *bride*

(as if *perfect*); hence, a *son's wife:*— bride, daughter-in-law, spouse.

כְּלוּא **kelûw'**. See 3628.

3619. כְּלוּב **kelûwb**, *kel-oob';* from the same as 3611; a bird-*trap* (as furnished with a *clap*-stick or treadle to spring it); hence, a *basket* (as resembling a wicker cage):— basket, cage.

3620. כְּלוּב **Kelûwb**, *kel-oob';* the same as 3619; *Kelub,* the name of two Isr.:— Chelub.

3621. כְּלוּבַי **Kelûwbay**, *kel-oo-bay'-ee;* a form of 3612; *Kelubai,* an Isr.:— Chelubai.

3622. כְּלוּהַי **Kelûwhay**, *kel-oo-hah'-ee;* from 3615; *completed; Keluhai,* an Isr.:— Chel-luh.

3623. כְּלוּלָה **kelûwlâh**, *kel-oo-law';* denom. pass. part. from 3618; *bridehood* (only in the plur.):— espousal.

3624. כֶּלַח **kelach**, *keh'-lakh;* from an un-used root mean. to *be complete; matur-ity:*— full (old) age.

3625. כֶּלַח **Kelach**, *keh'-lakh;* the same as 3624; *Kelach,* a place in Assyria:— Calah.

3626. כָּל־חֹזֶה **Kol-Chôzeh**, *kol-kho-zeh';* from 3605 and 2374; *every seer; Col-Chozeh,* an Isr.:— Col-hozeh.

3627. כְּלִי **kelîy**, *kel-ee';* from 3615; some-thing *prepared,* i.e. any *apparatus* (as an implement, utensil, dress, vessel or weapon):— armour ([-bearer]), artillery, bag, carriage, + furnish, furniture, instru-ment, jewel, that is made of, × one from another, that which pertaineth, pot, + psal-tery, sack, stuff, thing, tool, vessel, ware, weapon, + whatsoever.

3628. כְּלִיא **kelîy'**, *kel-ee';* or

כְּלוּא **kelûw'**, *kel-oo';* from 3607 [comp. 3608]; a *prison:*— prison.

3629. כִּלְיָה **kilyâh**, *kil-yaw';* fem. of 3627 (only in the plur.); a *kidney* (as an essential *organ*); fig. the *mind* (as the interior self):— kidneys, reins.

3630. כִּלְיוֹן **Kilyôwn**, *kil-yone';* a form of 3631; *Kiljon,* an Isr.:— Chilion.

3631. כִּלָּיוֹן **killâyôwn**, *kil-law-yone';* from 3615; *pining, destruction:*— consumption, failing.

3632. כָּלִיל **kâlîyl**, *kaw-leel';* from 3634; *com-plete;* as noun, the *whole* (spec. a sacrifice *entirely consumed*); as adv. *fully:*— all, every whit, flame, perfect (-ion), utterly, whole burnt offering (sacrifice), wholly.

3633. כַּלְכֹּל **Kalkôl**, *kal-kole';* from 3557; *sustenance; Calcol,* an Isr.:— Calcol, Chal-col.

3634. כָּלַל **kâlal**, *kaw-lal';* a prim. root; to *complete:*— (make) perfect.

3635. כְּלַל k^elal (Chald.), *kel-al';* corresp. to 3634; to *complete:*— finish, make (set) up.

3636. כְּלָל K^elâl, *kel-awl';* from 3634; *complete; Kelal,* an Isr.:— Chelal.

3637. כָּלַם kâlam, *kaw-lawm';* a prim. root; prop. to *wound;* but only fig., to *taunt* or *insult:*— be (make) ashamed, blush, be confounded, be put to confusion, hurt, reproach, (do, put to) shame.

3638. כִּלְמָד Kilmâd, *kil-mawd';* of for. der.; *Kilmad,* a place appar. in the Ass. empire:— Chilmad.

3639. כְּלִמָּה k^elimmâh, *kel-im-maw';* from 3637; *disgrace:*— confusion, dishonour, reproach, shame.

3640. כְּלִמּוּת k^elimmûwth, *kel-im-mooth';* from 3639; *disgrace:*— shame.

3641. כַּלְנֶה Kalneh, *kal-neh';* or

כַּלְנֵה Kalnêh, *kal-nay';* also

כַּלְנוֹ Kalnôw, *kal-no';* of for. der.; *Calneh* or *Calno,* a place in the Ass. empire:— Calneh, Calno. Comp. 3656.

3642. כָּמַהּ kâmahh, *kaw-mah';* a prim. root; to *pine* after:— long.

3643. כִּמְהָם Kimhâm, *kim-hawm';* from 3642; *pining; Kimham,* an Isr.:— Chimham.

3644. כְּמוֹ k^emôw, *kem-o';* or

כָּמוֹ kâmôw, *kaw-mo';* a form of the pref. k, but used separately [comp. 3651]; *as, thus, so:*— according to, (such) as (it were, well as), in comp. of, like (as, to, unto), thus, when, worth.

3645. כְּמוֹשׁ K^emôwsh, *kem-oshe';* or (Jer. 48:7)

כְּמִישׁ° K^emîysh, *kem-eesh';* from an unused root mean. to *subdue;* the *powerful; Kemosh,* the god of the Moabites:— Chemosh.

3646. כַּמֹּן kammôn, *kam-mone';* from an unused root mean. to *store* up or *preserve;* "cummin" (from its use as a *condiment*):— cummin.

3647. כָּמַס kâmaç, *kaw-mas';* a prim. root; to *store* away, i.e. (fig.) in the memory:— lay up in store.

3648. כָּמַר kâmar, *kaw-mar';* a prim. root; prop. to *intertwine* or *contract,* i.e. (by impl.) to *shrivel* (as with heat); fig. to be deeply *affected* with passion (love or pity):— be black, be kindled, yearn.

3649. כָּמָר kâmâr, *kaw-mawr';* from 3648; prop. an *ascetic* (as if *shrunk* with self-maceration), i.e. an idolatrous *priest* (only in plur.):— Chemarims (idolatrous) priests.

3650. כִּמְרִיר kimrîyr, *kim-reer';* redupl. from 3648; *obscuration* (as if from *shrinkage* of

light, i.e. an *eclipse* (only in plur.):— blackness.

3651. כֵּן kên, *kane;* from 3559; prop. *set* upright; hence, (fig. as adj.) *just;* but usually (as adv. or conjunc.) *rightly* or *so* (in various applications to manner, time and relation; often with other particles):— + after that (this, -ward, -wards), as ... as, + [for-] as-much as yet, + be (for which) cause, + following, howbeit, in (the) like (manner, -wise), × the more, right, (even) so, state, straightway, such (thing), surely, + there (where)-fore, this, thus, true, well, × you.

3652. כֵּן kên (Chald.), *kane;* corresp. to 3651; *so:*— thus.

3653. כֵּן kên, *kane;* the same as 3651, used as a noun; a *stand,* i.e. pedestal or station:— base, estate, foot, office, place, well.

3654. כֵּן kên, *kane;* from 3661 in the sense of *fastening;* a *gnat* (from infixing its sting; used only in plur. [and irreg. in Exod. 8:17,18; Heb. 13:14]):— lice, × manner.

3655. כָּנָה kânâh, *kaw-naw';* a prim. root; to *address* by an additional name; hence, to *eulogize:*— give flattering titles, surname (himself).

3656. כַּנֶּה Kanneh, *kan-neh';* for 3641; *Canneh,* a place in Assyria:— Canneh.

3657. כַּנָּה kannâh, *kaw-naw';* from 3661; a *plant* (as *set*):— × vineyard.

3658. כִּנּוֹר kinnôwr, *kin-nore';* from an unused root mean. to *twang;* a *harp:*— harp.

3659. כָּנְיָהוּ Konyâhûw, *kon-yaw'-hoo;* for 3204; *Conjah,* an Isr. king:— Coniah.

3660. כְּנֵמָא k^enêmâ' (Chald.), *ken-ay-maw';* corresp. to 3644; *so* or *thus:*— so, (in) this manner (sort), thus.

3661. כָּנַן kânan, *kaw-nan';* a prim. root; to *set* out, i.e. *plant:*— × vineyard.

3662. כְּנָנִי K^enânîy, *ken-aw-nee';* from 3661; *planted; Kenani,* an Isr.:— Chenani.

3663. כְּנַנְיָה K^enanyâh, *ken-an-yaw';* or

כְּנַנְיָהוּ K^enanyâhûw, *ken-an-yaw'-hoo;* from 3661 and 3050; *Jah has planted; Kenanjah,* an Isr.:— Chenaniah.

3664. כָּנַס kânaç, *kaw-nas';* a prim. root; to *collect;* hence, to *enfold:*— gather (together), heap up, wrap self.

3665. כָּנַע kâna', *kaw-nah';* a prim. root; prop. to *bend* the knee; hence, to *humiliate, vanquish:*— bring down (low), into subjection, under, humble (self), subdue.

3666. כִּנְעָה kin'âh, *kin-aw';* from 3665 in the sense of *folding* [comp. 3664]; a *package:*— wares.

3667. כְּנַעַן K^ena'an, *ken-ah'-an;* from 3665; *humiliated; Kenaan,* a son of Ham; also the country inhabited by him:— Canaan, merchant, traffick.

3668. כְּנַעֲנָה **Kᵉna'ănâh**, *ken-ah-an-aw´*; fem. of 3667; *Kenaanah*, the name of two Isr.:— Chenaanah.

3669. כְּנַעֲנִי **Kᵉna'ănîy**, *ken-ah-an-ee´*; patrial from 3667; a *Kenaanite* or inhab. of Kenaan; by impl. a *pedlar* (the Canaanites standing for their neighbors the Ishmaelites, who conducted mercantile caravans):— Canaanite, merchant, trafficker.

3670. כָּנַף **kânaph**, *kaw-naf´*; a prim. root; prop. to *project* laterally, i.e. prob. (refl.) to *withdraw:*— be removed.

3671. כָּנָף **kânâph**, *kaw-nawf´*; from 3670; an *edge* or *extremity*; spec. (of a bird or army) a *wing*, (of a garment or bed-clothing) a *flap*, (of the earth) a *quarter*, (of a building) a *pinnacle:*— + bird, border, corner, end, feather [-ed], × flying, + (one an-) other, overspreading, × quarters, skirt, × sort, uttermost part, wing [-ed].

3672. כִּנְּרוֹת **Kinnᵉrôwth**, *kin-ner-ōth´*; or

כִּנֶּרֶת **Kinnereth**, *kin-neh´-reth*; respectively plur. and sing. fem. from the same as 3658; perh. *harp*-shaped; *Kinneroth* or *Kinnereth*, a place in Pal.:— Chinnereth, Chinneroth, Cinneroth.

3673. כְּנַשׁ **kânash** (Chald.), *kaw-nash´*; corresp. to 3664; to *assemble:*— gather together.

3674. כְּנָת **kᵉnâth**, *ken-awth´*; from 3655; a *colleague* (as having the same title):— companion.

3675. כְּנָת **kᵉnâth** (Chald.), *ken-awth´*; corresp. to 3674:— companion.

3676. כֵּס **kêç**, *kace*; appar. a contr. for 3678, but prob. by err. transc. for 5251:— sworn.

3677. כֶּסֶא **keçe'**, *keh´-seh*; or

כֶּסֶה **keçeh**, *keh´-seh*; appar. from 3680; prop. *fulness* or the *full moon*, i.e. its festival:— (time) appointed.

3678. כִּסֵּא **kiççê'**, *kis-say´*; or

כִּסֵּה **kiççêh**, *kis-say´*; from 3680; prop. *covered*, i.e. a *throne* (as canopied):— seat, stool, throne.

3679. כַּסְדַּי **Kaçday**, *kas-dah´-ee*; for 3778:— Chaldean.

3680. כָּסָה **kâçâh**, *kaw-saw´*; a prim. root; prop. to *plump*, i.e. *fill up* hollows; by impl. to *cover* (for clothing or secrecy):— clad self, close, clothe, conceal, cover (self), (flee to) hide, overwhelm. Comp. 3780.

כְּסֶה **keçeh**. See 3677.

כִּסֶּה **kiççêh**. See 3678.

3681. כָּסוּי **kâçûwy**, *kaw-soo´-ee*; pass. part. of

3680; prop. *covered*, i.e. (as noun) a *covering:*— covering.

3682. כְּסוּת **kᵉçûwth**, *kes-ooth´*; from 3680; a *cover* (garment); fig. a *veiling:*— covering, raiment, vesture.

3683. כָּסַח **kâçach**, *kaw-sakh´*; a prim. root; to *cut off:*— cut down (up).

3684. כְּסִיל **kᵉçîyl**, *kes-eel´*; from 3688; prop. *fat*, i.e. (fig.) stupid or *silly:*— fool (-ish).

3685. כְּסִיל **Kᵉçîyl**, *kes-eel´*; the same as 3684; any notable *constellation*; spec. *Orion* (as if a *burly* one):— constellation, Orion.

3686. כְּסִיל **Kᵉçîyl**, *kes-eel´*; the same as 3684; *Kesil*, a place in Pal.:— Chesil.

3687. כְּסִילוּת **kᵉçîylûwth**, *kes-eel-ooth´*; from 3684; *silliness:*— foolish.

3688. כָּסַל **kâçal**, *kaw-sal´*; a prim. root; prop. to *be fat*, i.e. (fig.) *silly:*— be foolish.

3689. כֶּסֶל **keçel**, *keh´-sel*; from 3688; prop. *fatness*, i.e. by impl. (lit.) the *loin* (as the seat of the leaf fat) or (gen.) the *viscera*; also (fig.) *silliness* or (in a good sense) *trust:*— confidence, flank, folly, hope, loin.

3690. כִּסְלָה **kiçlâh**, *kis-law´*; fem. of 3689; in a good sense, *trust*; in a bad one, *silliness:*— confidence, folly.

3691. כִּסְלֵו **Kiçlêv**, *kis-lave´*; prob. of for. or.; *Kisleu*, the 9th Heb. month:— Chisleu.

3692. כִּסְלוֹן **Kiçlôwn**, *kis-lone´*; from 3688; *hopeful*; *Kislon*, an Isr.:— Chislon.

3693. כְּסָלוֹן **Kᵉçâlôwn**, *kes-aw-lone´*; from 3688; *fertile*; *Kesalon*, a place in Pal.:— Chesalon.

3694. כְּסֻלּוֹת **Kᵉçullôwth**, *kes-ool-lōth´*; fem. plur. of pass. part. of 3688; *fattened*; *Kesulloth*, a place in Pal.:— Chesulloth.

3695. כַּסְלֻחִים **Kaçlûchîym**, *kas-loo´-kheem*; a plur. prob. of for. der.; *Casluchim*, a people cognate to the Eg.:— Casluhim.

3696. כִּסְלֹת תָּבֹר **Kiçlôth Tâbôr**, *kis-lōth´ taw-bore´*; from the fem. plur. of 3689 and 8396; *flanks of Tabor*; *Kisloth-Tabor*, a place in Pal.:— Chisloth-tabor.

3697. כָּסַם **kâçam**, *kaw-sam´*; a prim. root; to *shear:*— × only, poll. Comp. 3765.

3698. כֻּסֶּמֶת **kuççemeth**, *koos-seh´-meth*; from 3697; *spelt* (from its bristliness as if just *shorn*):— fitches, rie.

3699. כָּסַס **kâçaç**, *kaw-sas´*; a prim. root; to *estimate:*— make count.

3700. כָּסַף **kâçaph**, *kaw-saf´*; a prim. root; prop. to *become pale*, i.e. (by impl.) to *pine* after; also to *fear:*— [have] desire, be greedy, long, sore.

3701. כֶּסֶף **keçeph**, *keh´-sef*; from 3700; *sil-*

ver (from its *pale* color); by impl. *money:*— money, price, silver (-ling).

3702. כְּסַף **keçaph** (Chald.), *kes-af´;* corresp. to 3701:— money, silver.

3703. כָּסְפְיָא **Kâçiphyâ',** *kaw-sif-yaw´;* perh. from 3701; *silvery; Casiphja,* a place in Bab.:— Casiphia.

3704. כֶּסֶת **keçeth,** *keh´-seth;* from 3680; a *cushion* or pillow (as *covering* a seat or bed):— pillow.

3705. כְּעַן **ke'an** (Chald.), *keh-an´;* prob. from 3652; *now:*— now.

3706. כְּעֶנֶת **ke'eneth** (Chald.), *keh-eh´-neth;* or

כְּעֶת **ke'eth** (Chald.), *keh-eth´;* fem. of 3705; *thus* (only in the formula "and so forth"):— at such a time.

3707. כָּעַס **kâ'aç,** *kaw-as´;* a prim. root; to *trouble;* by impl. to *grieve, rage, be indignant:*— be angry, be grieved, take indignation, provoke (to anger, unto wrath), have sorrow, vex, be wroth.

3708. כַּעַס **ka'aç,** *kah´-as;* or (in Job)

כַּעַשׂ **ka'as,** *kah´-as;* from 3707; *vexation:*— anger, angry, grief, indignation, provocation, provoking, × sore, sorrow, spite, wrath.

כְּעֶת **ke'eth.** See 3706.

3709. כַּף **kaph,** *kaf;* from 3721; the hollow *hand* or palm (so of the *paw* of an animal, of the *sole,* and even of the *bowl* of a dish or sling, the *handle* of a bolt, the *leaves* of a palm-tree); fig. *power:*— branch, + foot, hand ([-full, -dle, [-led]), hollow, middle, palm, paw, power, sole, spoon.

3710. כֵּף **kêph,** *kafe;* from 3721; a hollow *rock:*— rock.

3711. כָּפָה **kâphâh,** *kaw-faw´;* a prim. root; prop. to *bend,* i.e. (fig.) to *tame* or subdue:— pacify.

3712. כִּפָּה **kippâh,** *kip-paw´;* fem. of 3709; a *leaf* of a palm-tree:— branch.

3713. כְּפוֹר **kephôwr,** *kef-ore´;* from 3722; prop. a *cover,* i.e. (by impl.) a *tankard* (or *covered* goblet); also white *frost* (as *covering* the ground):— bason, hoar (-y) frost.

3714. כָּפִיס **kâphîyç,** *kaw-fece´;* from an unused root mean. to *connect;* a *girder:*— beam.

3715. כְּפִיר **kephîyr,** *kef-eer´;* from 3722; a *village* (as *covered* in by walls); also a young *lion* (perh. as *covered* with a mane):— (young) lion, village. Comp. 3723.

3716. כְּפִירָה **Kephîyrâh,** *kef-ee-raw´;* fem. of 3715; the *village* (always with the art.); *Kephirah,* a place in Pal.:— Chephirah.

3717. כָּפַל **kâphal,** *kaw-fal´;* a prim. root; to *fold* together; fig. to *repeat:*— double.

3718. כֶּפֶל **kephel,** *keh´-fel;* from 3717; a *duplicate:*— double.

3719. כָּפַן **kâphan,** *kaw-fan´;* a prim. root to *bend:*— bend.

3720. כָּפָן **kâphân,** *kaw-fawn´;* from 3719; *hunger* (as making to *stoop* with emptiness and pain):— famine.

3721. כָּפַף **kâphaph,** *kaw-faf´;* a prim. root; to *curve:*— bow down (self).

3722. כָּפַר **kâphar,** *kaw-far´;* a prim. root; to *cover* (spec. with bitumen); fig. to *expiate* or *condone,* to *placate* or *cancel:*— appease, make (an atonement, cleanse, disannul, forgive, be merciful, pacify, pardon, to *pitch,* purge (away), put off, (make) reconcile (-liation).

3723. כָּפָר **kâphâr,** *kaw-fawr´;* from 3722; a *village* (as *protected* by walls):— village. Comp. 3715.

3724. כֹּפֶר **kôpher,** *ko´-fer;* from 3722; prop. a *cover,* i.e. (lit.) a *village* (as *covered* in); (spec.) *bitumen* (as used for *coating*), and the *henna* plant (as used for *dyeing*); fig. a *redemption*-price:— bribe, camphire, pitch, ransom, satisfaction, sum of money, village.

3725. כִּפֻּר **kippûr,** *kip-poor´;* from 3722; *expiation* (only in plur.):— atonement.

3726. כְּפַר הָעַמּוֹנִי **Kephar hâ-'Ammôwnîy,** *kef-ar´ haw-am-mo-nee´;* from 3723 and 5984, with the art. interposed; *village of the Ammonite; Kefar-ha-Ammoni,* a place in Pal.:— Chefar-haammonai.

3727. כַּפֹּרֶת **kappôreth,** *kap-po´-reth;* from 3722; a *lid* (used only of the *cover* of the sacred Ark):— mercy seat.

3728. כָּפַשׁ **kâphash,** *kaw-fash´;* a prim. root; to *tread* down; fig. to *humiliate:*— cover.

3729. כְּפַת **kephath** (Chald.), *kef-ath´;* a root of uncert. correspondence; to *fetter:*— bind.

3730. כַּפְתֹּר **kaphtôr,** *kaf-tore´;* or (Am. 9:1)

כַּפְתּוֹר **kaphtôwr,** *kaf-tore´;* prob. from an unused root mean. to *encircle;* a *chaplet;* but used only in an architectonic sense, i.e. the *capital* of a column, or a wreath-like *button* or *disk* on the candelabrum:— knop, (upper) lintel.

3731. כַּפְתֹּר **Kaphtôr,** *kaf-tore´;* or (Am. 9:7)

כַּפְתּוֹר **Kaphtôwr,** *kaf-tore´;* appar. the same as 3730; *Caphtor* (i.e. a *wreath*-shaped island), the orig. seat of the Philistines:— Caphtor.

3732. כַּפְתֹּרִי **Kaphtôrîy,** *kaf-to-ree´;* patrial from 3731; a *Caphtorite* (collect.) or native of Caphtor:— Caphthorim, Caphtorim (-s).

3733. כַּר **kar,** *kar;* from 3769 in the sense of

plumpness; a *ram* (as *full-grown* and *fat*), incl. a *battering-ram* (as *butting*); hence, a *meadow* (as *for sheep*); also a *pad* or camel's *saddle* (as *puffed out*):— captain, furniture, lamb, (large) pasture, ram. See also 1033, 3746.

3734. כֹּר **kôr**, *kore;* from the same as 3564; prop. a deep round *vessel*, i.e. (spec.) a *cor* or measure for things dry:— cor, measure. Chald. the same.

3735. כְּרָא **kârâ'** (Chald.), *kaw-raw';* prob. corresp. to 3738 in the sense of *piercing* (fig.); to *grieve:*— be grieved.

3736. כַּרְבֵּל **karbêl**, *kar-bale';* from the same as 3525; to *gird* or *clothe:*— clothed.

3737. כַּרְבְּלָא **karbᵉlâ'** (Chald.), *kar-bel-aw';* from a verb corresp. to that of 3736; a *mantle:*— hat.

3738. כָּרָה **kârâh**, *kaw-raw';* a prim. root; prop. to *dig;* fig. to *plot;* gen. to *bore* or *open:*— dig, × make (a banquet), open.

3739. כָּרָה **kârâh**, *kaw-raw';* usually assigned as a prim. root, but prob. only a special application of 3738 (through the common idea of *planning* impl. in a bargain); to *purchase:*— buy, prepare.

3740. כֵּרָה **kêrâh**, *kay-raw';* from 3739; a *purchase:*— provision.

3741. כָּרָה **kârâh**, *kaw-raw';* fem. of 3733; a *meadow:*— cottage.

3742. כְּרוּב **kᵉrûwb**, *ker-oob';* of uncert. der.; a *cherub* or imaginary figure:— cherub, [plur.] cherubims.

3743. כְּרוּב **Kᵉrûwb**, *ker-oob';* the same as 3742; *Kerub*, a place in Bab.:— Cherub.

3744. כָּרוֹז **kârôwz** (Chald.), *kaw-roze';* from 3745; a *herald:*— herald.

3745. כְּרַז **kᵉraz** (Chald.), *ker-az';* prob. of Gr. or. (κηρύσσω); to *proclaim:*— make a proclamation.

3746. כָּרִי **kârîy**, *kaw-ree';* perh. an abridged plur. of 3733 in the sense of *leader* (of the flock); a *life-guardsman:*— captains, Cherethites [from the marg.].

3747. כְּרִית **Kᵉrîyth**, *ker-eeth';* from 3772; a *cut;* *Kerith*, a brook of Pal.:— Cherith.

3748. כְּרִיתוּת **kᵉrîythûwth**, *ker-ee-thooth';* from 3772; a *cutting* (of the matrimonial bond), i.e. *divorce:*— divorce (-ment).

3749. כַּרְכֹּב **karkôb**, *kar-kobe';* expanded from the same as 3522; a *rim* or top margin:— compass.

3750. כַּרְכֹּם **karkôm**, *kar-kome';* prob. of for. or.; the *crocus:*— saffron.

3751. כַּרְכְּמִישׁ **Karkᵉmîysh**, *kar-kem-eesh';* of for. der.; *Karkemish*, a place in Syria:— Carchemish.

3752. כַּרְכַּס **Karkaç**, *kar-kas';* of Pers. or.; *Karkas*, a eunuch of Xerxes:— Carcas.

3753. כַּרְכָּרָה **karkârâh**, *kar-kaw-raw';* from 3769; a *dromedary* (from its *rapid* motion as if dancing):— swift beast.

3754. כֶּרֶם **kerem**, *keh'-rem;* from an unused root of uncert. mean.; a *garden* or *vineyard:*— vines, (increase of the) vineyard (-s), vintage. See also 1021.

3755. כֹּרֵם **kôrêm**, *ko-rame';* act. part. of an imaginary denom. from 3754; a *vinedresser:*— vine dresser [as one or two words].

3756. כַּרְמִי **Karmîy**, *kar-mee';* from 3754; *gardener; Karmi*, the name of three Isr.:— Carmi.

3757. כַּרְמִי **Karmîy**, *kar-mee';* patron. from 3756; a *Karmite* or desc. of *Karmi:*— Carmites.

3758. כַּרְמִיל **karmîyl**, *kar-mele';* prob. of for. or.; *carmine*, a deep red:— crimson.

3759. כַּרְמֶל **karmel**, *kar-mel';* from 3754; a planted *field* (garden, orchard, vineyard or park); by impl. garden *produce:*— full (green) ears (of corn), fruitful field (place), plentiful (field).

3760. כַּרְמֶל **Karmel**, *kar-mel';* the same as 3759; *Karmel*, the name of a hill and of a town in Pal.:— Carmel, fruitful (plentiful) field, (place).

3761. כַּרְמְלִי **Karmᵉlîy**, *kar-mel-ee';* patron. from 3760; a *Karmelite* or inhab. of Karmel (the town):— Carmelite.

3762. כַּרְמְלִית **Karmᵉlîyth**, *kar-mel-eeth';* fem. of 3761; a *Karmelitess* or female inhab. of Karmel:— Carmelitess.

3763. כְּרָן **Kᵉrân**, *ker-awn';* of uncert. der.; *Keran*, an aboriginal Idumæan:— Cheran.

3764. כָּרְסֵא **korçê'** (Chald.), *kor-say';* corresp. to 3678; a *throne:*— throne.

3765. כִּרְסֵם **kirçêm**, *kir-same';* from 3697; to *lay waste:*— waste.

3766. כָּרַע **kâra'**, *kaw-rah';* a prim. root; to *bend* the knee; by impl. to *sink*, to *prostrate:*— bow (down, self), bring down (low), cast down, couch, fall, feeble, kneeling, sink, smite (stoop) down, subdue, × very.

3767. כָּרָע **kârâ'**, *kaw-raw';* from 3766; the *leg* (from the knee to the ankle) of men or locusts (only in the dual):— leg.

3768. כַּרְפַּס **karpaç**, *kar-pas';* of for. or.; *byssus* or fine vegetable wool:— green.

3769. כָּרַר **kârar**, *kaw-rar';* a prim. root; to *dance* (i.e. *whirl*):— dance (-ing).

3770. כְּרֵשׂ **kᵉrês**, *ker-ace';* by var. from 7164; the *paunch* or belly (as *swelling* out):— belly.

כֹּרֶשׁ **Kôresh**. See 3567.

3771. כַּרְשְׁנָא **Karsh^enâ'**, *kar-shen-aw´*; of for. or.; *Karshena*, a courtier of Xerxes:— Carshena.

3772. כָּרַת **kârath**, *kaw-rath´*; a prim. root; to *cut* (off, down or asunder); by impl. to *destroy* or *consume*; spec. to *covenant* (i.e. make an alliance or bargain, orig. by cutting flesh and passing between the pieces):— be chewed, be con- [feder-] ate, covenant, cut (down, off), destroy, fail, feller, be freed, hew (down), make a league ([covenant]), × lose, perish, × utterly, × want.

3773. כְּרֻתָה **kârûthâh**, *kaw-rooth-aw´*; pass. part. fem. of 3772; something *cut*, i.e. a hewn *timber*:— beam.

3774. כְּרֵתִי **K^erêthîy**, *ker-ay-thee´*; prob. from 3772 in the sense of *executioner*; a *Kerethite* or *life-guardsman* [comp. 2876] (only collect. in the sing. as plur.):— Cherethims, Cherethites.

3775. כֶּשֶׂב **keseb**, *keh´-seb*; appar. by transp. for 3532; a young *sheep*:— lamb, sheep.

3776. כִּשְׂבָּה **kisbâh**, *kis-baw´*; fem. of 3775; a young *ewe*:— lamb.

3777. כֶּשֶׂד **Kesed**, *keh´-sed*; from an unused root of uncert. mean.; *Kesed*, a relative of Abraham:— Chesed.

3778. כַּשְׂדִּי **Kasdîy**, *kas-dee´*; (occasionally with enclitic)

כַּשְׂדִּימָה **Kasdîymâh**, *kas-dee´-maw; to-ward* (the) *Kasdites* (into Chaldea), patron. from 3777 (only in the plur.); a *Kasdite*, or desc. of Kesed; by impl. a *Chaldæan* (as if so descended); also an *astrologer* (as if prover-bial of that people):— Chaldeans, Chaldees, inhabitants of Chaldea.

3779. כַּשְׂדָּי **Kasday** (Chald.), *kas-dah´-ee;* cor-resp. to 3778; a *Chaldæan* or inhab. of Chaldæa; by impl. a *Magian* or professional astrologer:— Chaldean.

3780. כָּשָׂה **kâsâh**, *kaw-saw´*; a prim. root; to *grow fat* (i.e. *be covered* with flesh):— be cov-ered. Comp. 3680.

3781. כַּשִּׁיל **kashshîyl**, *kash-sheel´*; from 3782; prop. a *feller*, i.e. an *axe*:— ax.

3782. כָּשַׁל **kâshal**, *kaw-shal´*; a prim. root; to *totter* or *waver* (through weakness of the legs, espec. the ankle); by impl. to *falter, stumble*, faint or fall:— bereave [*from the marg.*], cast down, be decayed, (cause to) fail, (cause, make to) fall (down, -ing), feeble, be (the) ruin (-ed, of), (be) overthrown, (cause to) stumble, × utterly, be weak.

3783. כִּשָּׁלוֹן **kishshâlôwn**, *kish-shaw-lone´*; from 3782; prop. a *tottering*, i.e. *ruin*:— fall.

3784. כָּשַׁף **kâshaph**, *kaw-shaf´*; a prim. root; prop. to *whisper* a spell, i.e. to *inchant* or

practise magic:— sorcerer, (use) witch (-craft).

3785. כֶּשֶׁף **kesheph**, *keh´-shef;* from 3784; *magic:*— sorcery, witchcraft.

3786. כַּשָּׁף **kashshâph**, *kash-shawf´;* from 3784; a *magician:*— sorcerer.

3787. כָּשֵׁר **kâshêr**, *kaw-share´;* a prim. root; prop. to *be straight* or *right;* by impl. to *be acceptable;* also to *succeed* or *prosper:*— direct, be right, prosper.

3788. כִּשְׁרוֹן **kishrôwn**, *kish-rone´;* from 3787; *success, advantage:*— equity, good, right.

3789. כָּתַב **kâthab**, *kaw-thab´;* a prim. root; to *grave*, by impl. to *write* (describe, in-scribe, prescribe, subscribe):— describe, record, prescribe, subscribe, write (-ing, -ten).

3790. כְּתַב **k^ethab** (Chald.), *keth-ab´;* cor-resp. to 3789:— write (-ten).

3791. כָּתָב **kâthâb**, *kaw-thawb´;* from 3789; something *written*, i.e. a *writing, record* or *book:*— register, scripture, writing.

3792. כְּתָב **k^ethâb** (Chald.), *keth-awb´;* cor-resp. to 3791:— prescribing, writing (-ten).

3793. כְּתֹבֶת **k^ethôbeth**, *keth-o´-beth;* from 3789; a *letter* or other *mark* branded on the skin:— × any [mark].

3794. כִּתִּי **Kittîy**, *kit-tee´* or

כִּתִּיִּי **Kittîyîy**, *kit-tee-ee´;* patrial from an unused name denoting Cyprus (only in the plur.); a *Kittite* or Cypriote; hence, an *islander* in gen., i.e. the Greeks or Romans on the shores opposite Pal.:— Chittim, Kit-tim.

3795. כָּתִית **kâthîyth**, *kaw-theeth´;* from 3807; *beaten*, i.e. pure (oil):— beaten.

3796. כֹּתֶל **kôthel**, *ko´-thel;* from an unused root mean. to *compact;* a *wall* (as *gathering* inmates):— wall.

3797. כְּתַל **k^ethal** (Chald.), *keth-al´;* corresp. to 3796:— wall.

3798. כִּתְלִישׁ **Kithlîysh**, *kith-leesh´;* from 3796 and 376; *wall of a man; Kithlish*, a place in Pal.:— Kithlish.

3799. כָּתַם **kâtham**, *kaw-tham´;* a prim. root; prop. to *carve* or *engrave*, i.e. (by impl.) to *inscribe* indelibly:— mark.

3800. כֶּתֶם **kethem**, *keh´-them;* from 3799; prop. something *carved* out, i.e. *ore;* hence, *gold* (pure as orig. mined):— [most] fine, pure) gold (-en wedge).

3801. כְּתֹנֶת **k^ethôneth**, *keth-o´-neth;* or

כֻּתֹּנֶת **kuttôneth**, *koot-to´-neth;* from an unused root mean. to *cover* [comp. 3802]; a *shirt:*— coat, garment, robe.

3802. כָּתֵף **kâthêph**, *kaw-thafe´;* from an un-

Hebrew

used root mean. to *clothe;* the *shoulder* (proper, i.e. upper end of the arm; as being the spot where the garments hang); fig. *side-piece* or lateral projection of anything:— arm, corner, shoulder (-piece), side, undersetter.

3803. כָּתַר **kāthar,** *kaw-thar´;* a prim. root; to *enclose;* hence, (in a friendly sense) to *crown,* (in a hostile one) to *besiege;* also to *wait* (as restraining oneself):— beset round, compass about, be crowned, inclose round, suffer.

3804. כֶּתֶר **kether,** *keh´-ther;* from 3803; prop. a *circlet,* i.e. a *diadem:*— crown.

3805. כֹּתֶרֶת **kôthereth,** *ko-theh´-reth;* fem. act. part. of 3803; the *capital* of a column:— chapiter.

3806. כָּתַשׁ **kāthash,** *kaw-thash´;* a prim. root; to *butt* or *pound:*— bray.

3807. כָּתַת **kāthath,** *kaw-thath´;* a prim. root; to *bruise* or violently *strike:*— beat (down, to pieces), break in pieces, crushed, destroy, discomfit, smite, stamp.

ל

3808. לֹא **lô',** *lo;* or

לוֹא **lôw',** *lo;* or

לֹה **lôh** (Deut. 3:11), *lo;* a prim. particle; *not* (the simple or abs. negation); by impl. *no;* often used with other particles (as follows):— × before, + or else, ere, + except, ig[-norant], much, less, nay, neither, never, no ([-ne], -r, [-thing]), (× as though ... , [can-], for) not (out of), of nought, otherwise, out of, + surely, + as truly as, + of a truth, + verily, for want, + whether, without.

3809. לָא **lā'** (Chald.), *law;* or

לָה **lâh** (Chald.) (Dan. 4:32), *law;* corresp. to 3808:— or even, neither, no (-ne, -r), ([can-]) not, as nothing, without.

לֻא **lû'.** See 3863.

3810. לֹא דְבַר **Lô' Dᵉbar,** *lo deb-ar´;* or

לוֹ דְבַר **Lôw Dᵉbar** (2 Sam. 9:4,5), *lo deb-ar´;* or

לִדְבִר **Lidbîr** (Josh. 13:26), *lid-beer´;* [prob. rather

לֹדְבַר° **Lôdᵉbar,** *lo-deb-ar´*]; from 3808 and 1699; *pastureless;* Lo-Debar, a place in Pal.:— Debir, Lo-debar.

3811. לָאָה **lā'âh,** *law-aw´;* a prim. root; to *tire;* (fig.) to be (or make) *disgusted:*— faint, grieve, lothe, (be, make) weary (selves).

3812. לֵאָה **Lê'âh,** *lay-aw´;* from 3811; *weary;* Leah, a wife of Jacob:— Leah.

לְאֹם **lᵉowm.** See 3816.

3813. לָאַט **lā'aṭ,** *law-at´;* a prim. root; to *muffle:*— cover.

3814. לָאֵט **lâ'ṭ,** *lawt;* from 3813 (or perh. for act. part. of 3874); prop. *muffled,* i.e. *silently:*— softly.

3815. לָאֵל **Lâ'êl,** *law-ale´;* from the prep. pref. and 410; (belonging) *to God;* Laël, an Isr.:— Lael.

3816. לְאֹם **lᵉôm,** *leh-ome´* or

לְאוֹם **lᵉôwm,** *leh-ome´;* from an unused root mean. to *gather;* a *community:*— nation, people.

3817. לְאֻמִּים **Lᵉummîym,** *leh-oom-meem´;* plur. of 3816; *communities;* Leümmim, an Arabian:— Leummim.

3818. לֹא עַמִּי **Lô' 'Ammîy,** *lo am-mee´;* from 3808 and 5971 with pron. suff.; *not my people;* Lo-Ammi, the symbol. name of a son of Hosea:— Lo-ammi.

3819. לֹא רֻחָמָה **Lô' Rûchâmâh,** *lo roo-khaw-maw´;* from 3808 and 7355; *not pitied;* Lo-Ruchamah, the symbol. name of a son of Hosea:— Lo-ruhamah.

3820. לֵב **lêb,** *labe;* a form of 3824; the *heart;* also used (fig.) very widely for the feelings, the will and even the intellect; likewise for the *center* of anything:— + care for, comfortably, consent, × considered, courag[-eous], friend [-ly], ([broken-], [hard-], [merry-], [stiff-], [stout-], double) heart ([-ed]), × heed, × I, kindly, midst, mind (-ed), × regard ([-ed]), × themselves, × unawares, understanding, × well, willingly, wisdom.

3821. לֵב **lêb** (Chald.), *labe;* corresp. to 3820:— heart.

3822. לְבָאוֹת **Lᵉbâ'ôwth,** *leb-aw-ōth´;* plur. of 3833; *lionesses;* Lebaoth, a place in Pal.:— Lebaoth. See also 1034.

3823. לָבַב **lābab,** *law-bab´;* a prim. root; prop. to *be enclosed* (as if with *fat);* by impl. (as denom. from 3824) to *unheart,* i.e. (in a good sense) *transport* (with love), or (in a bad sense) *stultify;* also (as denom. from 3834) to *make cakes:*— make cakes, ravish, be wise.

3824. לֵבָב **lêbâb,** *lay-bawb´;* from 3823; the *heart* (as the most interior organ); used also like 3820:— + bethink themselves, breast, comfortably, courage, ([faint], [ten-der-] heart ([-ed]), midst, mind, × unawares, understanding.

3825. לְבַב **lᵉbab** (Chald.), *leb-ab´;* corresp. to 3824:— heart.

לְבִבָה **lᵉbîbâh.** See 3834.

3826. לִבָּה **libbâh,** *lib-baw´;* fem. of 3820; the *heart:*— heart.

3827. לַבָּה **labbâh,** *lab-baw´;* for 3852; *flame:*— flame.

3828. לְבוֹנָה **lᵉbôwnâh,** *leb-o-naw´;* or

לְבֹנָה **lᵉbonâh,** *leb-o-naw´;* from 3836;

frankincense (from its *whiteness* or perh. that of its *smoke*):— (frank-) incense.

3829. לְבֹנָה **Lᵉbôwnâh**, *leb-o-naw´*; the same as 3828; *Lebonah*, a place in Pal.:— Lebonah.

3830. לְבוּשׁ **lᵉbûwsh**, *leb-oosh´*; or

לְבֻשׁ **lᵉbûsh**, *leb-oosh´*; from 3847; a *garment* (lit. or fig.); by impl. (euphem.) a *wife*:— apparel, clothed with, clothing, garment, raiment, vestment, vesture.

3831. לְבוּשׁ **lᵉbûwsh** (Chald.), *leb-oosh´*; corresp. to 3830:— garment.

3832. לָבַט **lâbaṭ**, *law-bat´*; a prim. root; to *overthrow*; intr. to *fall*:— fall.

לֻבִּי **Lubbîy**. See 3864.

3833. לָבִיא **lâbîy’**, *law-bee´*; or (Ezek. 19:2)

לְבִיָא **lᵉbîyâ’**, *leb-ee-yaw´*; irreg. masc. plur.

לְבָאִים **lᵉbâ’îym**, *leb-aw-eem´*; irreg. fem. plur.

לְבָאוֹת **lᵉbâ’ôwth**, *leb-aw-ōth´*; from an unused root mean. to *roar*; a *lion* (prop. a lio*ness* as the fiercer [although not a *roarer*; comp. 738]):— (great, old, stout) lion, lioness, young [lion].

3834. לְבִיבָה **lâbîybâh**, *law-bee-baw´*; or rather

לְבִבָה **lᵉbîbâh**, *leb-ee-baw´*; from 3823 in its orig. sense of *fatness* (or perh. of *folding*); a *cake* (either as *fried* or *turned*):— cake.

3835. לָבַן **lâban**, *law-ban´*; a prim. root; to *be* (or *become) white*; also (as denom. from 3843) to *make bricks*:— make brick, be (made, make) white (-r).

3836. לָבָן **lâbân**, *law-bawn´*; or (Gen. 49:12)

לָבֵן **lâbên**, *law-bane´*; from 3835; *white*:— white.

3837. לָבָן **Lâbân**, *law-bawn´*; the same as 3836; *Laban*, a Mesopotamian; also a place in the Desert:— Laban.

לַבֵּן **Labbên**. See 4192.

3838. לְבָנָא **Lᵉbânâ’**, *leb-aw-naw´*; or

לְבָנָה **Lᵉbânâh**, *leb-aw-naw´*; the same as 3842; *Lebana* or *Lebanah*, one of the Nethinim:— Lebana, Lebanah.

3839. לִבְנֶה **libneh**, *lib-neh´*; from 3835; some sort of *whitish* tree, perh. the *storax*:— poplar.

3840. לִבְנָה **libnâh**, *lib-naw´*; from 3835; prop. *whiteness*, i.e. (by impl.) *transparency*:— paved.

3841. לִבְנָה **Libnâh**, *lib-naw´*; the same as 3839; *Libnah*, a place in the Desert and one in Pal.:— Libnah.

3842. לְבָנָה **lᵉbânâh**, *leb-aw-naw´*; from 3835; prop. (the) *white*, i.e. the *moon*:— moon. See also 3838.

3843. לְבֵנָה **lᵉbênâh**, *leb-ay-naw´*; from 3835; a *brick* (from the *whiteness* of the clay):— (altar of) brick, tile.

לְבֹנָה **lᵉbônâh**. See 3828.

3844. לְבָנוֹן **Lᵉbânôwn**, *leb-aw-nohn´*; from 3825; (the) *white* mountain (from its *snow*); *Lebanon*, a mountain range in Pal.:— Lebanon.

3845. לִבְנִי **Libnîy**, *lib-nee´*; from 3835; *white*; *Libni*, an Isr.:— Libni.

3846. לִבְנִי **Libnîy**, *lib-nee´*; patron. from 3845; a *Libnite* or desc. of Libni (collect.):— Libnites.

3847. לָבַשׁ **lâbash**, *law-bash´*; or

לָבֵשׁ **lâbêsh**, *law-bashe´*; a prim. root; prop. *wrap* around, i.e. (by impl.) to *put on* a garment or *clothe* (oneself, or another), lit. or fig.:— (in) apparel, arm, array (self), clothe (self), come upon, put (on, upon), wear.

3848. לְבַשׁ **lᵉbash** (Chald.), *leb-ash´*; corresp. to 3847:— clothe.

לְבֻשׁ **lᵉbûsh**. See 3830.

3849. לֹג **lôg**, *lohg*; from an unused root appar. mean. to *deepen* or *hollow* [like 3537]; a *log* or measure for liquids:— log [of oil].

3850. לֹד **Lôd**, *lode*; from an unused root of uncert. signif.; *Lod*, a place in Pal.:— Lod.

לִדְבִר **Lidbîr**. See 3810.

3851. לַהַב **lahab**, *lah´-hab*; from an unused root mean. to *gleam*; a *flash*; fig. a sharply polished *blade* or *point* of a weapon:— blade, bright, flame, glittering.

3852. לֶהָבָה **lehâbâh**, *leh-aw-baw´*; or

לַהֶבֶת **lahebeth**, *lah-eh´-beth*; fem. of 3851, and mean. the same:— flame (-ming), head [of a spear].

3853. לְהָבִים **Lᵉhâbîym**, *leh-haw-beem´*; plur. of 3851; *flames*; *Lehabim*, a son of Mizrain, and his desc.:— Lehabim.

3854. לַהַג **lahag**, *lah´-hag*; from an unused root mean. to *be eager*; intense mental *application*:— study.

3855. לַהַד **Lahad**, *lah´-had*; from an unused root mean. to *glow* [comp. 3851] or else to *be earnest* [comp. 3854]; *Lahad*, an Isr.:— Lahad.

3856. לָהַהּ **lâhahh**, *law-hah´*; a prim. root mean. prop. to *burn*, i.e. (by impl.) to *be rabid* (fig. *insane*); also (from the *exhaustion* of frenzy) to *languish*:— faint, mad.

3857. לָהַט **lâhaṭ**, *law-hat´*; a prim. root; prop. to *lick*, i.e. (by impl.) to *blaze*:— burn (up), set on fire, flaming, kindle.

3858. לַהַט **lahaṭ**, *lah´-hat*; from 3857; a

blaze; also (from the idea of *enwrapping*) *magic* (as *covert*):— flaming, enchantment.

3859. לָהַם **lâham,** *law-ham´;* a prim. root; prop. to *burn* in, i.e. (fig.) to *rankle:*— wound.

3860. לָהֵן **lâhên,** *law-hane´;* from the pref. prep. mean. *to* or *for* and 2005; prop. *for if;* hence, *therefore:*— for them [by mistake for prep. suff.].

3861. לָהֵן **lâhên** (Chald.), *law-hane´;* corresp. to 3860; *therefore;* also *except:*— but, except, save, therefore, wherefore.

3862. לַהֲקָה **lahăqâh,** *lah-hak-aw´;* prob. from an unused root mean. to *gather;* an *assembly:*— company.

לוֹא **lôw'.** See 3808.

3863. לוּא **lûw',** *loo;* or

לֻא **lû',** *loo;* or

לוּ **lûw,** *loo;* a conditional particle; *if;* by impl. (interj. as a wish) *would that!:*— if (haply), peradventure, I pray thee, though, I would, would God (that).

3864. לוּבִי **Lûwbîy,** *loo-bee´;* or

לֻבִּי **Lubbîy** (Dan. 11:43) *loob-bee´;* patrial from a name prob. derived from an unused root mean. to *thirst,* i.e. a *dry* region; appar. a *Libyan* or inhab. of interior Africa (only in plur.):— Lubim (-s), Libyans.

3865. לוּד **Lûwd,** *lood;* prob. of for. der.; *Lud,* the name of two nations:— Lud, Lydia.

3866. לוּדִי **Lûwdîy,** *loo-dee´;* or

לוּדִיִּי **Lûwdîyîy,** *loo-dee-ee´;* patrial from 3865; a *Ludite* or inhab. of Lud (only in plural):— Ludim, Lydians.

3867. לָוָה **lâvâh,** *law-vaw´;* a prim. root; prop. to *twine,* i.e. (by impl.) to *unite,* to *remain;* also to *borrow* (as a form of *obligation*) or (caus.) to *lend:*— abide with, borrow (-er), cleave, join (self), lend (-er).

3868. לוּז **lûwz,** *looz;* a prim. root; to *turn* aside [comp. 3867, 3874 and 3885], i.e. (lit.) to *depart,* (fig.) *be perverse:*— depart, froward, perverse (-ness).

3869. לוּז **lûwz,** *looz;* prob. of for. or.; some kind of *nut*-tree, perh. the *almond:*— hazel.

3870. לוּז **Lûwz,** *looz;* prob. from 3869 (as *growing* there); *Luz,* the name of two places in Pal.:— Luz.

3871. לוּחַ **lûwach,** *loo´-akh;* or

לֻחַ **lûach,** *loo´-akh;* from a prim. root; prob. mean. to *glisten;* a *tablet* (as *polished*), of stone, wood or metal:— board, plate, table.

3872. לוּחִית **Lûwchîyth,** *loo-kheeth´;* or

לֻחוֹת° **Lûchôwth** (Jer. 48:5), *loo-khoth´;* from the same as 3871; *floored; Luchith,* a place E. of the Jordan:— Luhith.

3873. לוֹחֵשׁ **Lôwchêsh,** *lo-khashe´;* act. part. of 3907; (the) *enchanter; Lochesh,* an Isr.:— Hallohesh, Haloshesh [includ. the art.].

3874. לוּט **lûwt,** *loot;* a prim. root; to *wrap* up:— cast, wrap.

3875. לוֹט **lôwt,** *lote;* from 3874; a *veil:*— covering.

3876. לוֹט **Lôwt,** *lote;* the same as 3875; *Lot,* Abraham's nephew:— Lot.

3877. לוֹטָן **Lôwtân,** *lo-tawn´;* from 3875; *covering; Lotan,* an Idumæan:— Lotan.

3878. לֵוִי **Lêvîy,** *lay-vee´;* from 3867; *attached; Levi,* a son of Jacob:— Levi. See also 3879, 3881.

3879. לֵוִי **Lêvîy** (Chald.), *lay-vee´;* corresp. to 3880:— Levite.

3880. לִוְיָה **livyâh,** *liv-yaw´;* from 3867; something *attached,* i.e. a *wreath:*— ornament.

3881. לֵוִיִּי **Lêvîyîy,** *lay-vee-ee´;* or

לֵוִי **Lêvîy,** *lay-vee´;* patron. from 3878; a *Levite* or desc. of Levi:— Levite.

3882. לִוְיָתָן **livyâthân,** *liv-yaw-thawn´;* from 3867; a *wreathed* animal, i.e. a *serpent* (espec. the *crocodile* or some other large sea-monster); fig. the constellation of the *dragon;* also as a symbol of *Babylon:*— leviathan, mourning .

3883. לוּל **lûwl,** *lool;* from an unused root mean. to *fold* back; a *spiral* step:— winding stair. Comp. 3924.

3884. לוּלֵא **lûwlê',** *loo-lay´;* or

לוּלֵי **lûwlêy,** *loo lay´;* from 3863 and 3808; *if not:*— except, had not, if (... not), unless, were it not that.

3885. לוּן **lûwn,** *loon;* or

לִין **lîyn,** *leen;* a prim. root; to *stop* (usually over night); by impl. to *stay* permanently; hence, (in a bad sense) to be *obstinate* (espec. in words, to *complain*):— abide (all night), continue, dwell, endure, grudge, be left, lie all night, (cause to) lodge (all night, in, -ing, this night), (make to) murmur, remain, tarry (all night, that night).

3886. לוּע **lûwa',** *loo´-ah;* a prim. root; to *gulp;* fig. to *be rash:*— swallow down (up).

3887. לוּץ **lûwts,** *loots;* a prim. root; prop. to *make mouths* at, i.e. to *scoff;* hence, (from the effort to pronounce a foreign language) to *interpret,* or (gen.) *intercede:*— ambassador, have in derision, interpreter, make a mock, mocker, scorn (-er, -ful), teacher.

3888. לוּשׁ **lûwsh,** *loosh;* a prim. root; to *knead:*— knead.

3889. לוּשׁ° **Lûwsh,** *loosh;* from 3888; *knead-*

Hebrew

ing; Lush, a place in Pal.:— Laish [*from the marg.*]. Comp. 3919.

3890. לְוָת **leᵛâth** (Chald.), *lev-awth´;* from a root corresp. to 3867; prop. *adhesion*, i.e. (as prep.) *with:*— × thee.

לְחוֹת **Lûchôwth**. See 3872.

לָז **lâz** and

לָזֶה **lâzeh**. See 1975 and 1976.

3891. לְזוּת **leᵛzûwth**, *lez-ooth´;* from 3868; *perverseness:*— perverse.

3892. לַח **lach**, *lakh;* from an unused root mean. to *be new; fresh*, i.e. unused or undried:— green, moist.

3893. לֵחַ **lêach**, *lay´-akh;* from the same as 3892; *freshness*, i.e. vigor:— natural force.

לֻחַ **lûach**. See 3871.

3894. לְחוּם **lâchûwm**, *law-khoom´;* or

לְחֻם **lâchûm**, *law-khoom´;* pass. part. of 3898; prop. *eaten*, i.e. *food;* also *flesh*, i.e. *body:*— while ... is eating, flesh.

3895. לְחִי **lechîy**, *lekh-ee´;* from an unused root mean. to *be soft;* the *cheek* (from its *fleshiness*); hence, the *jaw*-bone:— cheek (bone), jaw (bone).

3896. לֶחִי **Lechîy**, *lekh´-ee;* a form of 3895; *Lechi*, a place in Pal.:— Lehi. Comp. also 7437.

3897. לָחַךְ **lâchak**, *law-khak´;* a prim. root; to *lick:*— lick (up).

3898. לָחַם **lâcham**, *law-kham´;* a prim. root; to *feed* on; fig. to *consume;* by impl. to *battle* (as *destruction*):— devour, eat, × ever, fight (-ing), overcome, prevail, (make) war (-ring).

3899. לֶחֶם **lechem**, *lekh´-em;* from 3898; *food* (for man or beast), espec. *bread*, or *grain* (for making it):— ([shew-] bread, × eat, food, fruit, loaf, meat, victuals. See also 1036.

3900. לְחֶם **leᵛchem** (Chald.), *lekh-em´;* corresp. to 3899:— feast.

3901. לָחֶם **lâchem**, *law-khem´;* from 3898, *battle:*— war.

לְחֻם **lâchûm**. See 3894.

3902. לַחְמִי **Lachmîy**, *lakh-mee´;* from 3899; *foodful; Lachmi*, a Philis.; or rather prob. a brief form (or perh. err. transc.) for 1022:— Lahmi. See also 3433.

3903. לַחְמָס **Lachmâç**, *lakh-maws´;* prob. by err. transc. for

לַחְמָם° **Lachmâm**, *lakh-mawm´;* from 3899; *food-like; Lachmam* or *Lachmas*, a place in Pal.:— Lahmam.

3904. לְחֵנָה **leᵛchênâh** (Chald.), *lekh-ay-naw´;* from an unused root of uncert. mean.; a *concubine:*— concubine.

3905. לָחַץ **lâchats**, *law-khats´;* a prim. root; prop. to *press*, i.e. (fig.) to *distress:*— afflict,

crush, force, hold fast, oppress (-or), thrust self.

3906. לַחַץ **lachats**, *lakh´-ats;* from 3905; *distress:*— affliction, oppression.

3907. לָחַשׁ **lâchash**, *law-khash´;* a prim. root; to *whisper;* by impl. to *mumble* a spell (as a magician):— charmer, whisper (together).

3908. לַחַשׁ **lachash**, *lakh´-ash;* from 3907; prop. a *whisper*, i.e. by impl. (in a good sense) a private *prayer*, (in a bad one) an *incantation;* concr. an *amulet:*— charmed, earring, enchantment, orator, prayer.

3909. לָט **lât**, *lawt;* a form of 3814 or else part. from 3874; prop. *covered*, i.e. *secret;* by impl. *incantation;* also *secrecy* or (adv.) *covertly:*— enchantment, privily, secretly, softly.

3910. לֹט **lôt**, *lote;* prob. from 3874; a *gum* (from its *sticky* nature), prob. *ladanum:*— myrrh.

3911. לְטָאָה **leᵛtâ'âh**, *let-aw-aw´;* from an unused root mean. to *hide;* a kind of *lizard* (from its *covert* habits):— lizard.

3912. לְטוּשִׁם **Leᵛtûwshîm**, *let-oo-sheem´;* masc. plur. of pass. part. of 3913; *hammered* (i.e. *oppressed*) ones; *Letushim*, an Arabian tribe:— Letushim.

3913. לָטַשׁ **lâtash**, *law-tash´;* a prim. root; prop. to *hammer* out (an edge), i.e. to *sharpen:*— instructer, sharp (-en), whet.

3914. לֹיָה **lôyâh**, *lo-yaw´;* a form of 3880; a *wreath:*— addition.

3915. לַיִל **layil**, *lah´-yil;* or (Isa. 21:11)

לֵיל **lêyl**, *lale;* also

לַיְלָה **layᵉlâh**, *lah´-yel-aw;* from the same as 3883; prop. a *twist* (away of the light), i.e. *night;* fig. *adversity:*— [mid-] night (season).

3916. לֵילְיָא **leylᵉyâ'** (Chald.), *lay-leh-yaw´;* corresp. to 3915:— night.

3917. לִילִית **lîylîyth**, *lee-leeth´;* from 3915; a *night* spectre:— screech owl.

3918. לַיִשׁ **layish**, *lah´-yish;* from 3888 in the sense of *crushing;* a *lion* (from his destructive *blows*):— (old) lion.

3919. לַיִשׁ **Layish**, *lah´-yish;* the same as 3918; *Laïsh*, the name of two places in Pal.:— Laish. Comp. 3889.

3920. לָכַד **lâkad**, *law-kad´;* a prim. root; to *catch* (in a net, trap or pit); gen. to *capture* or *occupy;* also to *choose* (by lot); fig. to *cohere:*— × at all, catch (self), be frozen, be holden, stick together, take.

3921. לֶכֶד **leked**, *leh´ked;* from 3920; something to *capture* with, i.e. a *noose:*— being taken.

Hebrew

3922. לְכָה **Lêkâh,** *lay-kaw´;* from 3212; a *journey; Lekah,* a place in Pal.:— Lecah.

3923. לָחִישׁ **Lâchîysh,** *law-keesh´;* from an unused root of uncert. mean.; *Lakish,* a place in Pal.:— Lachish.

3924. לֻלָאָה **lûlâ'âh,** *loo-law-aw´;* from the same as 3883; a *loop:*— loop.

3925. לָמַד **lâmad,** *law-mad´;* a prim. root; prop. to *goad,* i.e. (by impl.) to *teach* (the rod being an Oriental *incentive):*— [un-] accustomed, × diligently, expert, instruct, learn, skilful, teach (-er, ing).

לִמֻד **limmûd.** See 3928.

3926. לְמוֹ **lemôw,** *lem-o´;* a prol. and separable form of the pref. prep.; *to* or *for:*— at, for, to, upon.

3927. לְמוּאֵל **Lemûw'êl,** *lem-oo-ale´;* or

לְמוֹאֵל **Lemôw'êl,** *lem-o-ale´;* from 3926 and 410; (belonging) *to God; Lemuël* or *Lemoël,* a symbol. name of Solomon:— Lemuel.

3928. לִמּוּד **limmûwd,** *lim-mood´;* or

לִמֻד **limmûd,** *lim-mood´;* from 3925; *instructed:*— accustomed, disciple, learned, taught, used.

3929. לֶמֶךְ **Lemek,** *leh´-mek;* from an unused root of uncert. mean.; *Lemek,* the name of two antediluvian patriarchs:— Lamech.

3930. לֹעַ **lôa',** *lo´ah;* from 3886; the *gullet:*— throat.

3931. לָעַב **lâ'ab,** *law-ab´;* a prim. root; to *deride:*— mock.

3932. לָעַג **lâ'ag,** *law-ag´;* a prim. root; to *deride;* by impl. (as if imitating a foreigner) to *speak unintelligibly:*— have in derision, laugh (to scorn), mock (on), stammering.

3933. לַעַג **la'ag,** *lah´-ag;* from 3932; *derision, scoffing:*— derision, scorn (-ing).

3934. לָעֵג **lâ'êg,** *law-ayg´;* from 3932; a *buffoon;* also a *foreigner:*— mocker, stammering.

3935. לַעְדָּה **La'dâh,** *lah-daw´;* from an unused root of uncert. mean.; *Ladah,* an Isr.:— Laadah.

3936. לַעְדָּן **La'dân,** *lah-dawn´;* from the same as 3935; *Ladan,* the name of two Isr.:— Laadan.

3937. לָעַז **lâ'az,** *law-az´;* a prim. root; to *speak in a foreign tongue:*— strange language.

3938. לָעַט **lâ'at,** *law-at´;* a prim. root; to *swallow* greedily; caus. to *feed:*— feed.

3939. לַעֲנָה **la'ănâh,** *lah-an-aw´;* from an unused root supposed to mean to *curse; wormwood* (regarded as *poisonous,* and therefore *accursed):*— hemlock, wormwood.

3940. לַפִּיד **lappîyd,** *lap-peed´;* or

לַפִּד **lappîd,** *lap-peed´;* from an unused root prob. mean. to *shine;* a *flambeau,* lamp or flame:— (fire-) brand, (burning) lamp, lightning, torch.

3941. לַפִּידוֹת **Lappîydôwth,** *lap-pee-dōth´;* fem. plur. of 3940; *Lappidoth,* the husband of Deborah:— Lappidoth.

3942. לִפְנַי **liphnay,** *lif-nah´ee;* from the pref. prep. (*to* or *for*) and 6440; *anterior:*— before.

3943. לָפַת **lâphath,** *law-fath´;* a prim. root; prop. to *bend,* i.e. (by impl.) to *clasp;* also (refl.) to *turn* around or aside:— take hold, turn aside (self).

3944. לָצוֹן **lâtsôwn,** *law-tsone´;* from 3887; *derision:*— scornful (-ning).

3945. לָצַץ **lâtsats,** *law-tsats´;* a prim. root; to *deride:*— scorn.

3946. לַקּוּם **Laqqûwm,** *lak-koom´;* from an unused root thought to mean to *stop* up by a barricade; perh. *fortification; Lakkum,* a place in Pal.:— Lakum.

3947. לָקַח **lâqach,** *law-kakh´;* a prim. root; to *take* (in the widest variety of applications):— accept, bring, buy, carry away, drawn, fetch, get, infold, × many, mingle, place, receive (-ing), reserve, seize, send for, take (away, -ing, up), use, win.

3948. לֶקַח **leqach,** *leh´-kakh;* from 3947; prop. something *received,* i.e. (ment.) *instruction* (whether on the part of the teacher or hearer); also (in an act. and sinister sense) *inveiglement:*— doctrine, learning, fair speech.

3949. לִקְחִי **Liqchîy,** *lik-khee´;* from 3947; *learned; Likchi,* an Isr.:— Likhi.

3950. לָקַט **lâqat,** *law-kat´;* a prim. root; prop. to *pick* up, i.e. (gen.) to *gather;* spec. to *glean:*— gather (up), glean.

3951. לֶקֶט **leqet,** *leh´-ket;* from 3950; the *gleaning:*— gleaning.

3952. לָקַק **lâqaq,** *law-kak´;* a prim. root; to *lick* or *lap:*— lap, lick.

3953. לָקַשׁ **lâqash,** *law-kash´;* a prim. root; to *gather* the *after* crop:— gather.

3954. לֶקֶשׁ **leqesh,** *leh´-kesh;* from 3953; the *after crop:*— latter growth.

3955. לְשַׁד **leshad,** *lesh-ad´;* from an unused root of uncert. mean.; appar. *juice,* i.e. (fig.) *vigor;* also a sweet or fat *cake:*— fresh, moisture.

3956. לָשׁוֹן **lâshôwn,** *law-shone´;* or

לָשׁוֹן **lâshôn,** *law-shone´;* also (in plur.) fem.

לְשֹׁנָה **leshônâh,** *lesh-o-naw´;* from 3960; the *tongue* (of man or animals), used lit. (as the instrument of licking, eating, or speech), and fig. (speech; an ingot, a fork of flame, a cove of water):— + babbler, bay, + evil speaker, language, talker, tongue, wedge.

3957. לִשְׁכָּה **lishkâh**, *lish-kaw'*; from an unused root of uncert. mean.; a *room* in a building (whether for storage, eating, or lodging):— chamber, parlour. Comp. 5393.

3958. לֶשֶׁם **leshem**, *leh'-shem*; from an unused root of uncert. mean.; a *gem*, perh. the *jacinth*:— ligure.

3959. לֶשֶׁם **Leshem**, *leh'-shem*; the same as 3958; *Leshem*, a place in Pal.:— Leshem.

3960. לָשַׁן **lâshan**, *law-shan'*; a prim. root; prop. to *lick*; but used only as a denom. from 3956; to *wag the tongue*, i.e. to *calumniate*:— accuse, slander.

3961. לִשָּׁן **lishshân** (Chald.), *lish-shawn'*; corresp. to 3956; *speech*, i.e. a *nation*:— language.

3962. לֶשַׁע **Lesha'**, *leh'-shah*; from an unused root thought to mean to *break* through; a boiling *spring; Lesha*, a place prob. E. of the Jordan:— Lasha.

3963. לֶתֶךְ **lethek**, *leh'-thek*; from an unused root of uncert. mean.; a *measure* for things dry:— half homer.

מ

מ **ma-**, or

מ **mâ-**. See 4100.

3964. מָא **mâ'** (Chald.), *maw*; corresp. to 4100; (as indef.) *that*:— + what.

3965. מַעֲבוּס **ma'ăbûwç**, *mah-ab-ooce'*; from 75; a *granary*:— storehouse.

3966. מְעֹד **me'ôd**, *meh-ode'*; from the same as 181; prop. *vehemence*, i.e. (with or without prep.) *vehemently*; by impl. *wholly, speedily*, etc. (often with other words as an intens. or superl.; espec. when repeated):— diligently, especially, exceeding (-ly), far, fast, good, great (-ly), × louder and louder, might (-ily, -y), (so) much, quickly, (so) sore, utterly, very (+ much, sore), well.

3967. מֵאָה **mê'âh**, *may-aw'*; or

מֵאיָה **mê'yâh**, *may-yaw'*; prop. a prim. numeral; a *hundred*; also as a multiplicative and a fraction:— hundred ([-fold], -th), + sixscore.

3968. מֵאָה **Mê'âh**, *may-aw'*; the same as 3967; *Meäh*, a tower in Jerusalem:— Meah.

3969. מְאָה **me'âh** (Chald.), *meh-aw'*; corresp. to 3967:— hundred.

3970. מַאֲוַי **ma'ăvay**, *mah-av-ah'ee*; from 183; a *desire*:— desire.

מוֹאל **môw'l**. See 4136.

3971. מאוּם **m'ûwm**, *moom*; usually

מוּם **mûwm**, *moom*; as if pass. part. from an unused root prob. mean. to *stain*; a *blemish* (phys. or mor.):— blemish, blot, spot.

3972. מְאוּמָה **me'ûwmâh**, *meh-oo'-maw*; appar. a form of 3971; prop. a *speck* or *point*, i.e. (by impl.) *something;* with neg. *nothing:*— fault, + no (-ught), ought, somewhat, any ([no-]) thing.

3973. מָאוֹס **mâ'ôwç**, *maw-oce'*; from 3988; *refuse:*— refuse.

3974. מָאוֹר **mâ'ôwr**, *maw-ore'*; or

מָאֹר **mâ'ôr**, *maw-ore'*; also (in plur.) fem.

מְאוֹרָה **me'ôwrâh**, *meh-o-raw'*; or

מְאֹרָה **me'ôrâh**, *meh-o-raw'*; from 215; prop. a *luminous* body or *luminary*, i.e. (abstr.) *light* (as an element); fig. *brightness*, i.e. *cheerfulness;* spec. a *chandelier:*— bright, light.

3975. מְאוּרָה **me'ûwrâh**, *meh-oo-raw'*; fem. pass. part. of 215; something *lighted*, i.e. an *aperture;* by impl. a *crevice* or *hole* (of a serpent):— den.

3976. מֹאזֵן **mô'zên**, *mo-zane'*; from 239; (only in the dual) a pair of *scales:*— balances.

3977. מֹאזֵן **mô'zên** (Chald.), *mo-zane'*; corresp. to 3976:— balances.

מֵאיָה **mê'yâh**. See 3967.

3978. מַאֲכָל **ma'ăkâl**, *mah-ak-awl'*; from 398; an *eatable* (includ. provender, flesh and fruit):— food, fruit, ([bake-] meat (-s), victual.

3979. מַאֲכֶלֶת **ma'ăkeleth**, *mah-ak-eh'-leth*; from. 398; something to *eat* with, i.e. a *knife:*— knife.

3980. מַאֲכֹלֶת **ma'ăkôleth**, *mah-ak-o'-leth*; from 398; something *eaten* (by fire), i.e. *fuel:*— fuel.

3981. מַאֲמָץ **ma'ămâts**, *mah-am-awts'*; from 553; *strength*, i.e. (plur.) *resources:*— force.

3982. מַאֲמָר **ma'ămar**, *mah-am-ar'*; from 559; something (authoritatively) *said*, i.e. an *edict:*— commandment, decree.

3983. מֵאמַר **mê'mar** (Chald.), *may-mar'*; corresp. to 3982:— appointment, word.

3984. מָאן **mâ'n** (Chald.), *mawn*; prob. from a root corresp. to 579 in the sense of an *inclosure* by sides; a *utensil:*— vessel.

3985. מָאֵן **mâ'ên**, *maw-ane'*; a prim. root; to *refuse:*— refuse, × utterly.

3986. מָאֵן **mâ'ên**, *maw-ane'*; from 3985; *unwilling:*— refuse.

3987. מֵאֵן **mê'ên**, *may-ane'*; from 3985; *refractory:*— refuse.

Hebrew

3988. מָאַס **mâ'aç**, *maw-as'*; a prim. root; to *spurn*; also (intr.) to *disappear*:— abhor, cast away (off), contemn, despise, disdain, (become) loathe (some), melt away, refuse, reject, reprobate, × utterly, vile person.

3989. מַאֲפֶה **mâ'ăpheh**, *mah-af-eh'*; from 644; something *baked*, i.e. a *batch*:— baken.

3990. מַאֲפֵל **ma'ăphêl**, *mah-af-ale'*; from the same as 651; something *opaque*:— darkness.

3991. מַאֲפֵלְיָה° **ma'phêleyâh**, *mah-af-ay-leh-yaw'*; prol. fem. of 3990; *opaqueness*:— darkness.

3992. מָאַר **mâ'ar**, *maw-ar'*; a prim. root; to *be bitter* or (caus.) to *embitter*, i.e. *be painful*:— fretting, picking.

מָאֹר **mâ'ôr**. See 3974.

3993. מַאֲרָב **ma'ărâb**, *mah-ar-awb'*; from 693; an *ambuscade*:— lie in ambush, ambushment, lurking place, lying in wait.

3994. מְאֵרָה **me'êrâh**, *meh-ay-raw'*; from 779; an *execration*:— curse.

מְאֹרָה **me'ôrâh**. See 3974.

3995. מִבְדָּלָה **mibdâlâh**, *mib-daw-law'*; from 914; a *separation*, i.e. (concr.) a *separate place*:— separate.

3996. מָבוֹא **mâbôw'**, *maw-bo'*; from 935; an *entrance* (the place or the act); spec. (with or without 8121) *sunset* or the *west*; also (adv. with prep.) *towards*:— by which came, as cometh, in coming, as men enter into, entering, entrance into, entry, where goeth, going down, + westward. Comp. 4126.

3997. מְבוֹאָה **mebôw'âh**, *meb-o-aw'*; fem. of 3996; a *haven*:— entry.

3998. מְבוּכָה **mebûwkâh**, *meb-oo-kaw'*; from 943; *perplexity*:— perplexity.

3999. מַבּוּל **mabbûwl**, *mab-bool'*; from 2986 in the sense of *flowing*; a *deluge*:— flood.

4000. מָבוֹן **mâbôwn**, *maw-bone'*; from 995; *instructing*:— taught.

4001. מְבוּסָה **mebûwçâh**, *meb-oo-saw'*; from 947; a *trampling*:— treading (trodden) down (under foot).

4002. מַבּוּעַ **mabbûwa'**, *mab-boo'-ah*; from 5042; a *fountain*:— fountain, spring.

4003. מְבוּקָה **mebûwqâh**, *meb-oo-kah'*; from the same as 950; *emptiness*:— void.

4004. מִבְחוֹר **mibchôwr**, *mib-khore'*; from 977; *select*, i.e. well *fortified*:— choice.

4005. מִבְחָר **mibchâr**, *mib-khawr'*; from 977; *select*, i.e. *best*:— choice (-st), chosen.

4006. מִבְחָר **Mibchâr**, *mib-khawr'*; the same as 4005; *Mibchar*, an Isr.:— Mibhar.

4007. מַבָּט **mabbâṭ**, *mab-bawt'*; or

מֶבָּט **mebbâṭ**, *meb-bawt'*; from 5027;

something *expected*, i.e. (abstr.) *expectation*:— expectation.

4008. מִבְטָא **mibṭâ'**, *mib-taw'*; from 981; a rash *utterance* (hasty vow):— (that which ...) uttered (out of).

4009. מִבְטָח **mibṭâch**, *mib-tawkh'*; from 982; prop. a *refuge*, i.e. (obj.) *security*, or (subj.) *assurance*:— confidence, hope, sure, trust.

4010. מַבְלִיגִית **mablîygîyth**, *mab-leeg-eeth'*; from 1082; *desistance* (or rather *desolation*):— comfort self.

4011. מִבְנֶה **mibneh**, *mib-neh'*; from 1129; a *building*:— frame.

4012. מְבֻנַּי **Mebunnay**, *meb-oon-hah'-ee*; from 1129; *built up*; *Mebunnai*, an Isr.:— Mebunnai.

4013. מִבְצָר **mibtsâr**, *mib-tsawr'*; also (in plur.) fem. (Dan. 11:15)

מִבְצָרָה **mibtsârâh**, *mib-tsaw-raw'*; from 1219; a *fortification, castle*, or *fortified city*; fig. a *defender*:— (de-, most) fenced, fortress, (most) strong (hold).

4014. מִבְצָר **Mibtsâr**, *mib-tsawr'*; the same as 4013; *Mibtsar*, an Idumæan:— Mibzar.

מִבְצָרָה **mibtsârâh**. See 4013.

4015. מִבְרָח **mibrâch**, *mib-rawkh'*; from 1272; a *refugee*:— fugitive.

4016. מָבֻשׁ **mâbûsh**, *maw-boosh'*; from 954; (plur.) the (male) *pudenda*:— secrets.

4017. מִבְשָׂם **Mibsâm**, *mib-sawm'*; from the same as 1314; *fragrant*; *Mibsam*, the name of an Ishmaelite and of an Isr.:— Mibsam.

4018. מְבַשְּׁלָה **mebashshelâh**, *meb-ash-shel-aw'*; from 1310; a cooking *hearth*:— boiling-place.

מַג **Mâg**. See 7248, 7249.

4019. מַגְבִּישׁ **Magbîysh**, *mag-beesh'*; from the same as 1378; *stiffening*; *Magbish*, an Isr., or a place in Pal.:— Magbish.

4020. מִגְבָּלָה **migbâlâh**, *mig-baw-law'*; from 1379; a *border*:— end.

4021. מִגְבָּעָה **migbâ'âh**, *mig-baw-aw'*; from the same as 1389; a *cap* (as hemispherical):— bonnet.

4022. מֶגֶד **meged**, *meh'-ghed*; from an unused root prob. mean. to *be eminent*; prop. a *distinguished* thing; hence, something *valuable*, as a product or fruit:— pleasant, precious fruit (thing).

4023. מְגִדּוֹן **Megiddôwn** (Zech. 12:11), *meg-id-dōne'*; or

מְגִדּוֹ **Megiddôw**, *meg-id-do'*; from 1413; *rendezvous*; *Megiddon* or *Megiddo*, a place in Pal.:— Megiddo, Megiddon.

4024. מִגְדּוֹל **Migdôwl**, *mig-dole'*; or

מִגְדֹּל **Migdôl**, *mig-dole´;* prob. of Eg. or.; *Migdol,* a place in Egypt:— Migdol, tower.

4025. מַגְדִּיאֵל **Magdîy'êl**, *mag-dee-ale´;* from 4022 and 410; *preciousness of God; Magdiël,* an Idumæan:— Magdiel.

4026. מִגְדָּל **migdâl**, *mig-dawl´;* also (in plur.) fem.

מִגְדָּלָה **migdâlâh**, *mig-daw-law´;* from 1431; a *tower* (from its size or height); by anal. a *rostrum;* fig. a (pyramidal) *bed* of flowers:— castle, flower, tower. Comp. the names following.

מִגְדֹּל **Migdôl**. See 4024.

מִגְדָּלָה **migdâlâh**. See 4026.

4027. מִגְדַּל־אֵל **Migdal-'Êl**, *mig-dal-ale´;* from 4026 and 410; *tower of God; Migdal-El,* a place in Pal.:— Migdal-el.

4028. מִגְדַּל־גָּד **Migdal-Gâd**, *migdal-gawd´;* from 4026 and 1408; *tower of Fortune; Migdal-Gad,* a place in Pal.:— Migdal-gad.

4029. מִגְדַּל־אֵדֶר **Migdal-'Êder**, *mig-dal´-ay´-der;* from 4026 and 5739; *tower of a flock; Migdal-Eder,* a place in Pal.:— Migdal-eder, tower of the flock.

4030. מִגְדָּנָה **migdânâh**, *mig-daw-naw´;* from the same as 4022; *preciousness,* i.e. a *gem:*— precious thing, present.

4031. מָגוֹג **Mâgôwg**, *maw-gogue´;* from 1463; *Magog,* a son of Japheth; also a barbarous northern region:— Magog.

4032. מָגוֹר **mâgôwr**, *maw-gore´;* or (Lam. 2:22)

מָגוּר **mâgûwr**, *maw-goor´;* from 1481 in the sense of *fearing;* a *fright* (obj. or subj.):— fear, terror. Comp. 4036.

4033. מָגוּר **mâgûwr**, *maw-goor´;* or

מָגֻר **mâgur**, *maw-goor´;* from 1481 in the sense of *lodging;* a *temporary abode;* by extens. a *permanent residence:*— dwelling, pilgrimage, where sojourn, be a stranger. Comp. 4032.

4034. מְגוֹרָה **mᵉgôwrâh**, *meg-o-raw´;* fem. of 4032; *affright:*— fear.

4035. מְגוּרָה **mᵉgûwrâh**, *meg-oo-raw´;* fem. of 4032 or of 4033; a *fright;* also a *granary:*— barn, fear.

4036. מָגוֹר מִסָּבִיב **Mâgôwr miç-Çâbîyb**, *maw-gore´ mis-saw-beeb´;* from 4032 and 5439 with the prep. ins.; *affright from around; Magor-mis-Sabib,* a symbol. name of Pashur:— Magor-missabib.

4037. מַגְזֵרָה **magzêrâh**, *mag-zay-raw´;* from 1504; a *cutting* implement, i.e. a *blade:*— axe.

4038. מַגָּל **maggâl**, *mag-gawl´;* from an unused root mean. to *reap;* a *sickle:*— sickle.

4039. מְגִלָּה **mᵉgillâh**, *meg-il-law´;* from 1556; a *roll:*— roll, volume.

4040. מְגִלָּה **mᵉgillâh** (Chald.), *meg-il-law´;* corresp. to 4039:— roll.

4041. מְנַמָּה **mᵉgammâh**, *meg-am-maw´;* from the same as 1571; prop. *accumulation,* i.e. *impulse* or *direction:*— sup up.

4042. מָגַן **mâgan**, *maw-gan´;* a denom. from 4043; prop. to *shield; encompass* with; fig. to *rescue,* to *hand* safely *over* (i.e. *surrender*):— deliver.

4043. מָגֵן **mâgên**, *maw-gane´;* also (in plur.) fem.

מְגִנָּה **mᵉginnâh**, *meg-in-naw´;* from 1598; a *shield* (i.e. the small one or *buckler*); fig. a *protector;* also the scaly *hide* of the crocodile:— × armed, buckler, defence, ruler, + scale, shield.

4044. מְגִנָּה **mᵉginnâh**, *meg-in-naw´;* from 4042; a *covering* (in a bad sense), i.e. *blindness* or obduracy:— sorrow. See also 4043.

4045. מִגְעֶרֶת **mig'ereth**, *mig-eh´-reth;* from 1605; *reproof* (i.e. curse):— rebuke.

4046. מַגֵּפָה **maggêphâh**, *mag-gay-faw´;* from 5062; a *pestilence;* by anal. *defeat:*— (× be) plague (-d), slaughter, stroke.

4047. מַגְפִּיעָשׁ **Magpîy'âsh**, *mag-pee-awsh´;* appar. from 1479 or 5062 and 6211; *exterminator of* (the) *moth; Magpiash,* an Isr.:— Magpiash.

4048. מָגַר **mâgar**, *maw-gar´;* a prim. root; to *yield up;* intens. to *precipitate:*— cast down, terror.

4049. מְגַר **mᵉgar** (Chald.), *meg-ar´;* corresp. to 4048; to *overthrow:*— destroy.

4050. מְגֵרָה **mᵉgêrâh**, *meg-ay-raw´;* from 1641; a *saw:*— axe, saw.

4051. מִגְרוֹן **Migrôwn**, *mig-rone´;* from 4048; *precipice; Migron,* a place in Pal.:— Migron.

4052. מִגְרָעָה **migrâ'âh**, *mig-raw-aw´;* from 1639; a *ledge* or offset:— narrowed rest.

4053. מִגְרָפָה **migrâphâh**, *mig-raw-faw´;* from 1640; something *thrown off* (by the spade), i.e. a *clod:*— clod.

4054. מִגְרָשׁ **migrâsh**, *mig-rawsh´;* also (in plur.) fem. (Ezek. 27:28)

מִגְרָשָׁה **migrâshâh**, *mig-raw-shaw´;* from 1644; a *suburb* (i.e. open country whither flocks are *driven* for pasture); hence, the *area* around a building, or the *margin* of the sea:— cast out, suburb.

4055. מַד **mad**, *mad;* or

מֵד **mêd**, *made;* from 4058; prop. *extent,* i.e. *height;* also a *measure;* by impl. a *vesture* (as measured); also a *carpet:*— armour, clothes, garment, judgment, measure, raiment, stature.

Hebrew

4056. מַדְבַּח **madbach** (Chald.), *mad-bakh´*; from 1684; a sacrificial *altar*:— altar.

4057. מִדְבָּר **midbâr**, *mid-bawr´*; from 1696 in the sense of *driving*; a *pasture* (i.e. open field, whither cattle are driven); by impl. a *desert*; also *speech* (incl. its organs):— desert, south, speech, wilderness.

4058. מָדַד **mâdad**, *maw-dad´*; a prim. root; prop. to *stretch*; by impl. to *measure* (as if by *stretching* a line); fig. to be *extended*:— measure, mete, stretch self.

4059. מָדַד **middad**, *mid-dad´*; from 5074; *flight*:— be gone.

4060. מִדָּה **middâh**, *mid-daw´*; fem. of 4055; prop. *extension*, i.e. height or breadth; also a *measure* (incl. its standard); hence, a *portion* (as measured) or a *vestment*; spec. *tribute* (as measured):— garment, measure (-ing, meteyard, piece, size, (great) stature, tribute, wide.

4061. מִדָּה **middâh** (Chald.), *mid-daw´* or

מִנְדָּה **mindâh** (Chald.), *min-daw´*; corresp. to 4060; *tribute* in money:— toll, tribute.

4062. מַדְהֵבָה **madhêbâh**, *mad-hay-baw´*; perh. from the equiv. of 1722; *goldmaking*, i.e. *exactness*:— golden city.

4063. מְדֵו **medev**, *meh´-dev*; from an unused root mean. to *stretch*; prop. *extent*, i.e. *measure*; by impl. a *dress* (as measured):— garment.

4064. מַדְוֶה **madveh**, *mad-veh´*; from 1738; *sickness*:— disease.

4065. מַדּוּחַ **maddûwach**, *mad-doo´-akh*; from 5080; *seduction*:— cause of banishment.

4066. מָדוֹן **mâdôwn**, *maw-dohn´*; from 1777; a *contest* or quarrel:— brawling, contention (-ous), discord, strife. Comp. 4079, 4090.

4067. מָדוֹן **mâdôwn**, *maw-dohn´*; from the same as 4063; *extensiveness*, i.e. *height*:— stature.

4068. מָדוֹן **Mâdôwn**, *maw-dohn´*; the same as 4067; *Madon*, a place in Pal.:— Madon.

4069. מַדּוּעַ **maddûwa'**, *mad-doo´-ah*; or

מַדֻּעַ **maddua'**, *mad-doo´-ah*; from 4100 and the pass. part. of 3045; *what* (is) *known?*; i.e. (by impl.) (adv.) *why?*:— how, wherefore, why.

4070. מְדוֹר **medôwr** (Chald.), *med-ore´*; or

מְדֹר **medôr** (Chald.), *med-ore´*; or

מְדָר **medâr** (Chald.), *med-awr´*; from 1753; a *dwelling*:— dwelling.

4071. מְדוּרָה **medûwrâh**, *med-oo-raw´*; or

מְדֻרָה **medûrâh**, *med-oo-raw´*; from 1752 in the sense of *accumulation*; a *pile* of fuel:— pile (for fire).

4072. מִדְחֶה **midcheh**, *mid-kheh´*; from 1760; *overthrow*:— ruin.

4073. מְדַחְפָה **medachphâh**, *med-akh-faw´*; from 1765; a *push*, i.e. ruin:— overthrow.

4074. מָדַי **Mâday**, *maw-dah´-ee*; of for. der.; *Madai*, a country of central Asia:— Madai, Medes, Media.

4075. מָדַי **Mâday**, *maw-dah´-ee*; patrial from 4074; a *Madian* or native of Madai:— Mede.

4076. מָדַי **Mâday** (Chald.), *maw-dah´-ee*; corresp. to 4074:— Mede (-s).

4077. מָדַי **Mâday** (Chald.), *maw-dah´-ee*; corresp. to 4075:— Median.

4078. מַדַּי **madday**, *mad-dah´-ee*; from 4100 and 1767; *what* (is) *enough*, i.e. *sufficiently*:— sufficiently.

4079. מִדְיָן **midyân**, *mid-yawn´*; a var. for 4066:— brawling, contention (-ous).

4080. מִדְיָן **Midyân**, *mid-yawn´*; the same as 4079; *Midjan*, a son of Abraham; also his country and (collect.) his desc.:— Midian, Midianite.

4081. מִדִּין **Middîyn**, *mid-deen´*; a var. for 4080:— Middin.

4082. מְדִינָה **medîynâh**, *med-ee-naw´*; from 1777; prop. a *judgeship*, i.e. *jurisdiction*; by impl. a *district* (as ruled by a judge); gen. a *region*:— (× every) province.

4083. מְדִינָה **medîynâh** (Chald.), *med-ee-naw´*; corresp. to 4082:— province.

4084. מִדְיָנִי **Midyânîy**, *mid-yaw-nee´*; patron. or patrial from 4080; a *Midjanite* or descend. (native) of Midjan:— Midianite. Comp. 4092.

4085. מְדֹכָה **medôkâh**, *med-o-kaw´*; from 1743; a *mortar*:— mortar.

4086. מַדְמֵן **Madmên**, *mad-mane´*; from the same as 1828; *dunghill*; *Madmen*, a place in Pal.:— Madmen.

4087. מַדְמֵנָה **madmênâh**, *mad-may-naw´*; fem. from the same as 1828; a *dunghill*:— dunghill.

4088. מַדְמֵנָה **Madmênâh**, *mad-may-naw´*; the same as 4087; *Madmenah*, a place in Pal.:— Madmenah.

4089. מַדְמַנָּה **Madmannâh**, *mad-man-naw´*; a var. for 4087; *Madmannah*, a place in Pal.:— Madmannah.

4090. מְדָן **medân**, *med-awn´*; a form of 4066:— discord, strife.

4091. מְדָן **Medân**, *med-awn´*; the same as 4090; *Medan*, a son of Abraham:— Medan.

4092. מְדָנִי **Medânîy**, *med-aw-nee´*; a var. of 4084:— Midianite.

4093. מַדָּע **maddâ'**, *mad-daw´*; or

מַדָּע **madda'**, *mad-dah´*; from 3045; *intelligence* or *consciousness:*— knowledge, science, thought.

מֹדַע **môdâ'**. See 4129.

מַדֻּע **madua'**. See 4069.

4094. מַדְקָרָה **madqârâh**, *mad-kaw-raw´*; from 1856; a *wound:*— piercing.

מְדֹר **medôr**. See 4070.

4095. מַדְרֵגָה **madrêgâh**, *mad-ray-gaw´*; from an unused root mean. to *step*; prop. a *step*; by impl. a *steep* or inaccessible place:— stair, steep place.

מְדֻרָה **medûrâh**. See 4071.

4096. מִדְרָךְ **midrâk**, *mid-rawk´*; from 1869; a *treading*, i.e. a place for stepping on:— [foot-] breadth.

4097. מִדְרָשׁ **midrâsh**, *mid-rawsh´*; from 1875; prop. an *investigation*, i.e. (by impl.) a *treatise* or elaborate compilation:— story.

4098. מְדֻשָּׁה **medushshâh**, *med-oosh-shaw´*; from 1758; a *threshing*, i.e. (concr. and fig.) *down-trodden* people:— threshing.

4099. מְדָתָא **Medâthâ**, *med-aw-thaw´*; of Pers. or.; *Medatha*, the father of Haman:— Hammedatha [incl. the art.].

4100. מָה **mâh**, *maw*; or

מַה **mah**, *mah*; or

מָ **mâ**, *maw*; or

מַ **ma**, *mah*; also

מֶה **meh**, *meh*; a prim. particle; prop. interrog. *what?* (incl. *how? why? when?*); but also exclamation, *what!* (incl. *how!*), or indef. *what* (incl. *whatever*, and even rel. *that* *which*); often used with prefixes in various adv. or conjunc. senses:— how (long, oft, [-soever]), [no-] thing, what (end, good, purpose, thing), whereby (-fore, -in, -to, -with), (for) why.

4101. מָה **mâh** (Chald.), *maw*; corresp. to 4100:— how great (mighty), that which, what (-soever), why.

4102. מָהַהּ **mâhahh**, *maw-hah´*; appar. a denom. from 4100; prop. to *question* or hesitate, i.e. (by impl.) to *be reluctant:*— delay, linger, stay selves, tarry.

4103. מְהוּמָה **mehûwmâh**, *meh-hoo-maw´*; from 1949; *confusion* or uproar:— destruction, discomfiture, trouble, tumult, vexation, vexed.

4104. מְהוּמָן **Mehûwmân**, *meh-hoo-mawn´*; of Pers. or.; *Mehuman*, a eunuch of Xerxes:— Mehuman.

4105. מְהֵיטַבְאֵל **Mehêyṭab'êl**, *meh-hay-tab-ale´*; from 3190 (augmented) and 410; *bettered of God*; *Mehetabel*, the name of an Edomitish man and woman:— Mehetabeel, Mehetabel.

4106. מָהִיר **mâhîyr**, *maw-here´*; or

מָהִר **mâhir**, *maw-here´*; from 4116; *quick*; hence, *skilful:*— diligent, hasty, ready.

4107. מָהַל **mâhal**, *maw-hal´*; a prim. root; prop. to *cut down* or *reduce*, i.e. by impl. to *adulterate:*— mixed.

4108. מַהְלֵךְ **mahlêk**, *mah-lake´*; from 1980; a *walking* (plur. collect.), i.e. *access:*— place to walk.

4109. מַהֲלָךְ **mahălâk**, *mah-hal-awk´*; from 1980; a *walk*, i.e. a *passage* or a *distance:*— journey, walk.

4110. מַהֲלָל **mahălâl**, *mah-hal-awl´*; from 1984; *fame:*— praise.

4111. מַהֲלַלְאֵל **Mahălal'êl**, *mah-hal-al-ale´*; from 4110 and 410; *praise of God*; *Mahalalel*, the name of an antediluvian patriarch and of an Isr.:— Mahalaleel.

4112. מַהֲלֻמָּה **mahălummâh**, *mah-hal-oom-maw´*; from 1986; a *blow:*— stripe, stroke.

4113. מַהֲמֹרָה **mahămôrâh**, *mah-ham-o-raw´*; from an unused root of uncert. mean.; perh. an *abyss:*— deep pit.

4114. מַהְפֵּכָה **mahpêkâh**, *mah-pay-kaw´*; from 2015; a *destruction:*— when ... overthrew, overthrow (-n).

4115. מַהְפֶּכֶת **mahpeketh**, *mah-peh´-keth*; from 2015; a *wrench*, i.e. the *stocks:*— prison, stocks.

4116. מָהַר **mâhar**, *maw-har´*; a prim. root; prop. to *be liquid* or *flow* easily, i.e. (by impl.); to *hurry* (in a good or a bad sense); often used (with another verb) adv. *promptly:*— be carried headlong, fearful, (cause to make, in, make) haste (-n, -ily), (be) hasty, (fetch, make ready) × quickly, rash, × shortly, (be so) × soon, make speed, × speedily, × straightway, × suddenly, swift.

4117. מָהַר **mâhar**, *maw-har´*; a prim. root (perh. rather the same as 4116 through the idea of *readiness* in assent); to *bargain* (for a wife), i.e. to *wed:*— endow, × surely.

4118. מַהֵר **maher**, *mah-hare´*; from 4116; prop. *hurrying*; hence, (adv.) *in a hurry:*— hasteth, hastily, at once, quickly, soon, speedily, suddenly.

מָהִר **mâhîr**. See 4106.

4119. מֹהַר **môhar**, *mo´-har*; from 4117; a *price* (for a wife):— dowry.

4120. מְהֵרָה **mehêrâh**, *meh-hay-raw´*; fem. of 4118; prop. a *hurry*; hence, (adv.) *promptly:*— hastily, quickly, shortly, soon, make (with) speed (-ily), swiftly.

4121. מַהְרַי **Mahăray**, *mah-har-ah´-ee*; from 4116; *hasty*; *Maharai*, an Isr.:— Maharai.

4122. מַהֵר שָׁלָל חָשׁ בַּז **Maher Shâlâl Châsh**

Hebrew

Baz, *mah-hare´shaw-lawl´khawsh baz;* from 4118 and 7998 and 2363 and 957; *hasting* (is he [the enemy] to the) *booty, swift* (to the) *prey; Maher-Shalal-Chash-Baz;* the symb. name of the son of Isaiah:— Maher-shalal-hash-baz.

4123. מַהֲתַלָּה **mahăthallâh**, *mah-hath-al-law´;* from 2048; a *delusion:*— deceit.

4124. מוֹאָב **Môw'âb**, *mo-awb;* from a prol. form of the prep. pref. *m-* and 1; *from* (her [the mother's]) *father; Moäb,* an incestuous son of Lot; also his territory and desc.:— Moab.

4125. מוֹאָבִי **Môw'âbîy**, *mo-aw-bee´;* fem.

מוֹאָבִיָּה **Môw'âbîyah**, *mo-aw-bee-yaw´;* or

מוֹאָבִית **Môwâbîyth**, *mo-aw-beeth´;* patron. from 4124; a *Moäbite* or *Moäbitess,* i.e. a desc. from Moab:— (woman) of Moab, Moabite (-ish, -ss).

מוֹאָל **môw'l**. See 4136.

4126. מוֹבָא **môwbâ'**, *mo-baw´;* by transp. for 3996; an *entrance:*— coming.

4127. מוּג **mûwg**, *moog;* a prim. root; to *melt,* i.e. lit. (to *soften, flow down, disappear*), or fig. (to *fear, faint*):— consume, dissolve, (be) faint (-hearted), melt (away), make soft.

4128. מוּד **mûwd**, *mood;* a prim. root; to *shake:*— measure.

4129. מוֹדַע **môwda'**, *mo-dah´;* or rather

מֹדַע **môdâ'**, *mo-daw´;* from 3045; an *acquaintance:*— kinswoman.

4130. מוֹדַעַת **môwda'ath**, *mo-dah´-ath;* from 3045; *acquaintance:*— kindred.

4131. מוֹט **môwṭ**, *mote;* a prim. root; to *waver;* by impl. to *slip, shake, fall:*— be carried, cast, be out of course, be fallen in decay, × exceedingly, fall (-ing down), be (re-) moved, be ready, shake, slide, slip.

4132. מוֹט **môwṭ**, *mote;* from 4131; a *wavering,* i.e. *fall;* by impl. a *pole* (as shaking); hence, a *yoke* (as essentially a bent pole):— bar, be moved, staff, yoke.

4133. מוֹטָה **môwṭâh**, *mo-taw´;* fem. of 4132; a *pole;* by impl. an ox-*bow;* hence, a *yoke* (either lit. or fig.):— bands, heavy, staves, yoke.

4134. מוּךְ **mûwk**, *mook;* a prim. root; to *become thin,* i.e. (fig.) *be impoverished:*— be (waxen) poor (-er).

4135. מוּל **mûwl**, *mool;* a prim. root; to *cut short,* i.e. *curtail* (spec. the prepuce, i.e. to *circumcise*); by impl. to *blunt;* fig. to *destroy:*— circumcise (-ing), selves, cut down (in pieces), destroy, × must needs.

4136. מוּל **mûwl**, *mool;* or

מֻל **môwl** (Deut. 1:1), *mole;* or

מוֹאָל **môw'l** (Neh. 12:38), *mole;* or

מֻל **mûl** (Num. 22:5), *mool;* from 4135; prop. *abrupt,* i.e. a *precipice;* by impl. the *front;* used only adv. (with prep. pref.) *opposite:*— (over) against, before, [fore-] front, from, [God-] ward, toward, with.

4137. מוֹלָדָה **Môwlâdâh**, *mo-law-daw´;* from 3205; *birth; Moladah,* a place in Pal.:— Moladah.

4138. מוֹלֶדֶת **môwledeth**, *mo-leh´-deth;* from 3205; *nativity* (plur. *birth-place*); by impl. *lineage, native country;* also *offspring, family:*— begotten, born, issue, kindred, native (-ity).

4139. מוּלָה **mûwlâh**, *moo-law´;* from 4135; *circumcision:*— circumcision.

4140. מוֹלִיד **Môwlîyd**, *mo-leed´;* from 3205; *genitor; Molid,* an Isr.:— Molid.

מוּם **muwm**. See 3971.

מוֹמֻכָן° **Môwmûkân**. See 4462.

4141. מוּסָב **mûwçâb**, *moo-sawb´;* from 5437; a *turn,* i.e. *circuit* (of a building):— winding about.

4142. מוּסַבָּה **mûwçabbâh**, *moo-sab-baw´;* or

מֻסַבָּה **mûçabbâh**, *moo-sab-baw´;* fem. of 4141; a *reversal,* i.e. the *backside* (of a gem), *fold* (of a double-leaved door), *transmutation* (of a name):— being changed, inclosed, be set, turning.

4143. מוּסָד **mûwçâd**, *moo-sawd´;* from 3245; a *foundation:*— foundation.

4144. מוֹסָד **môwçâd**, *mo-sawd´;* from 3245; a *foundation:*— foundation.

4145. מוּסָדָה **mûwçâdâh**, *moo-saw-daw´;* fem. of 4143; a *foundation;* fig. an *appointment:*— foundation, grounded. Comp. 4328.

4146. מוֹסָדָה **môwçâdâh**, *mo-saw-daw´;* or

מֹסָדָה **môçâdâh**, *mo-saw-daw´;* fem. of 4144; a *foundation:*— foundation.

4147. מוֹסֵר **môwçêr**, *mo-sare´;* also (in plur.) fem.

מוֹסֵרָה **môwçêrâh**, *mo-say-raw´;* or

מֹסְרָה **môçᵉrâh**, *mo-ser-aw´;* from 3256; prop. *chastisement,* i.e. (by impl.) a *halter;* fig. *restraint:*— band, bond.

4148. מוּסָר **mûwçâr**, *moo-sawr´;* from 3256; prop. *chastisement;* fig. *reproof, warning* or *instruction;* also *restraint:*— bond, chastening ([-eth]), chastisement, check, correction, discipline, doctrine, instruction, rebuke.

4149. מוֹסֵרָה **Môwçêrâh**, *mo-say-raw´;* or (plur.)

מֹסְרוֹת **Môçᵉrôwth**, *mo-ser-othe´* fem. of 4147; *correction* or *corrections; Moserah* or *Moseroth*, a place in the Desert:— Mosera, Moseroth.

4150. מוֹעֵד **môw'êd**, *mo-ade´*; or

מֹעֵד **mô'êd**, *mo-ade´*; or (fem.)

מוֹעָדָה **môw'âdâh** (2 Chron. 8:13), *mo-aw-daw´*; from 3259; prop. an *appointment*, i.e. a fixed *time* or season; spec. a *festival*; conventionally a *year*; by impl. an *assembly* (as convened for a def. purpose); tech. the *congregation*; by extens. the *place of meeting*; also a *signal* (as appointed beforehand):— appointed (sign, time), (place of, solemn) assembly, congregation, (set, solemn) feast, (appointed, due) season, solemn (-ity), synagogue, (set) time (appointed).

4151. מוֹעָד **môw'âd**, *mo-awd´*; from 3259; prop. an *assembly* [as in 4150]; fig. a *troop*:— appointed time.

4152. מוּעָדָה **mûw'âdâh**, *moo-aw-daw´*; from 3259; an *appointed* place, i.e. *asylum*:— appointed.

4153. מוֹעַדְיָה **Môw'adyâh**, *mo-ad-yaw´*; from 4151 and 3050; *assembly of Jah*; *Moädjah*, an Isr.:— Moadiah. Comp. 4573.

4154. מוּעֶדֶת **mûw'edeth**, *moo-ay´-deth*; fem. pass. part. of 4571; prop. *made to slip*, i.e. *dislocated*:— out of joint.

4155. מוּעָף **mûw'âph**, *moo-awf´*; from 5774; prop. *covered*, i.e. *dark*; abstr. *obscurity*, i.e. *distress*:— dimness.

4156. מוֹעֵצָה **môw'êtsâh**, *mo-ay-tsaw´*; from 3289; a *purpose*:— counsel, device.

4157. מוּעָקָה **mûw'âqâh**, *moo-aw-kaw´*; from 5781; *pressure*, i.e. (fig.) *distress*:— affliction.

4158. מוֹפַעַת° **Môwpha'ath** (Jer. 48:21), *mo-fah´-ath*; or

מֵיפַעַת **Mêyphaath**, *may-fah´-ath*; or

מֵפַעַת **Mêphaath**, *may-fah´-ath*; from 3313; *illuminative*; *Mophaath* or *Mephaath*, a place in Pal.:— Mephaath.

4159. מוֹפֵת **môwphêth**, *mo-faith´*; or

מֹפֵת **môphêth**, *mo-faith´*; from 3302 in the sense of *conspicuousness*; a *miracle*; by impl. a *token* or *omen*:— miracle, sign, wonder (-ed at).

4160. מוּץ **mûwts**, *moots*; a prim. root; to *press*, i.e. (fig.) to *oppress*:— extortioner.

4161. מוֹצָא **môwtsâ'**, *mo-tsaw´*; or

מֹצָא **môtsâ'**, *mo-tsaw´*; from 3318; a *going forth*, i.e. (the act) an *egress*, or (the place) an *exit*; hence, a *source* or *product*; spec. *dawn*, the *rising* of the sun (the *East*), *exportation*, *utterance*, a *gate*, a *fountain*, a *mine*, a *meadow* (as producing grass):— brought out, bud, that which came out, east, going forth, goings out, that which (thing that) is gone out,

outgoing, proceeded out, spring, vein, [water-] course, [springs].

4162. מוֹצָא **Môwtsâ'**, *mo-tsaw´*; the same as 4161; *Motsa*, the name of two Isr.:— Moza.

4163. מוֹצָאָה **môwtsâ'âh**, *mo-tsaw-aw´*; fem. of 4161; a family *descent*; also a *sewer* [marg.; comp. 6675]:— draught house; going forth.

4164. מוּצָק **mûwtsaq**, *moo-tsak´*; or

מוּצָק **mûwtsâq**, *moo-tsawk´*; from 3332; *narrowness*; fig. *distress*:— anguish, is straitened, straitness.

4165. מוּצָק **mûwtsâq**, *moo-tsawk´*; from 5694; prop. *fusion*, i.e. lit. a *casting* (of metal); fig. a *mass* (of clay):— casting, hardness.

4166. מוּצָקָה **mûwtsâqâh**, *moo-tsaw-kaw´*; or

מֻצָקָה **mûtsâqâh**, *moo-tsaw-kaw´*; from 3332; prop. something *poured* out, i.e. a *casting* (of metal); by impl. a *tube* (as cast):— when it was cast, pipe.

4167. מוּק **mûwq**, *mook*; a prim. root; to *jeer*, i.e. (intens.) *blaspheme*:— be corrupt.

4168. מוֹקֵד **môwqêd**, *mo-kade´*; from 3344; a *fire* or *fuel*; abstr. a *conflagration*:— burning, hearth.

4169. מוֹקְדָה° **môwq^edâh**, *mo-ked-aw´*; fem. of 4168; *fuel*:— burning.

4170. מוֹקֵשׁ **môwqêsh**, *mo-kashe´*; or

מֹקֵשׁ **môqêsh**, *mo-kashe´*; from 3369; a *noose* (for catching animals) (lit. or fig.); by impl. a *hook* (for the nose):— be ensnared, gin, (is) snare (-d), trap.

4171. מוּר **mûwr**, *moor*; a prim. root; to *alter*; by impl. to *barter*, to *dispose of*:— × at all, (ex-) change, remove.

4172. מוֹרָא **môwrâ'**, *mo-raw´*; or

מֹרָא **môrâ'**, *mo-raw´*; or

מוֹרָה **môrâh** (Psa. 9:20), *mo-raw´*; from 3372; *fear*; by impl. a *fearful* thing or *deed*:— dread, (that ought to be) fear (-ed), terribleness, terror.

4173. מוֹרַג **môwrag**, *mo-rag´*; or

מֹרַג **môrag**, *mo-rag´*; from an unused root mean. to *triturate*; a *threshing sledge*:— threshing instrument.

4174. מוֹרָד **môwrâd**, *mo-rawd´*; from 3381; a *descent*; arch. an ornamental *appendage*, perh. a *festoon*:— going down, steep place, thin work.

4175. מוֹרֶה **môwreh**, *mo-reh´*; from 3384; an *archer*; also *teacher* or *teaching*; also the *early rain* [see 3138]:— (early) rain.

4176. מוֹרֶה **Môwreh**, *mo-reh´*; or

מֹרֶה **Môreh**, *mo-reh´*; the same as 4175; *Moreh*, a Canaanite; also a hill (perh. named from him):— Moreh.

4177. מוֹרָה **môwrâh**, *mo-raw´*; from 4171 in the sense of *shearing*; a *razor:*— razor.

4178. מוֹרָט **môwrâṭ**, *mo-rawt´*; from 3399; *obstinate*, i.e. independent:— peeled.

4179. מוֹרִיָּה **Môwrîyâh**, *mo-ree-yaw´*; or

מֹרִיָּה **Môrîyâh**, *mo-ree-yaw´*; from 7200 and 3050; *seen of Jah*; *Morijah*, a hill in Pal.:— Moriah.

4180. מוֹרָשׁ **môwrâsh**, *mo-rawsh´*; from 3423; a *possession*; fig. *delight:*— possession, thought.

4181. מוֹרָשָׁה **môwrâshâh**, *mo-raw-shaw´*; fem. of 4180; a *possession:*— heritage, inheritance, possession.

4182. מוֹרֶשֶׁת גַּת **Môwresheth Gath**, *mo-reh´-sheth gath*; from 3423 and 1661; *possession of Gath*; *Moresheth-Gath*, a place in Pal.:— Moresheth-gath.

4183. מוֹרַשְׁתִּי **Mowrashtiy**, *mo-rash-tee´*; patrial from 4182; a *Morashtite* or inhab. of Moresheth-Gath:— Morashthite.

4184. מוּשׁ **mûwsh**, *moosh*; a prim. root; to *touch:*— feel, handle.

4185. מוּשׁ **mûwsh**, *moosh*; a prim. root [perh. rather the same as 4184 through the idea of receding by *contact*]; to *withdraw* (both lit. and fig., whether intr. or tran.):— cease, depart, go back, remove, take away.

4186. מוֹשָׁב **môwshâb**, *mo-shawb´*; or

מֹשָׁב **môshâb**, *mo-shawb´*; from 3427; a *seat*; fig. a *site*; abstr. a *session*; by extens. an *abode* (the place or the time); by impl. *population:*— assembly, dwell in, dwelling (-place), wherein (that) dwelt (in), inhabited place, seat, sitting, situation, sojourning.

4187. מוּשִׁי **Mûwshiy**, *moo-shee´*; or

מֻשִׁי **Mushshiy**, *mush-shee´*; from 4184; *sensitive*; *Mushi*, a Levite:— Mushi.

4188. מוּשִׁי **Mûwshiy**, *moo-shee´*; patron. from 4187; a *Mushite* (collect.) or desc. of Mushi:— Mushites.

4189. מוֹשְׁכָה **môwshᵉkâh**, *mo-shek-aw´*; act. part. fem. of 4900; something *drawing*, i.e. (fig.) a *cord:*— band.

4190. מוֹשָׁעָה **môwshâʿâh**, *mo-shaw-aw´*; from 3467; *deliverance:*— salvation.

4191. מוּת **mûwth**, *mooth*; a prim. root; to *die* (lit. or fig.); caus. to *kill:*— × at all, × crying, (be) dead (body, man, one), (put to, worthy of) death, destroy (-er), (cause to, be like to, must) die, kill, necro [-mancer], × must needs, slay, × surely, × very suddenly, × in [no] wise.

4192. מוּת **Mûwth** (Psa. 48:14), *mooth*; or

מוּת לַבֵּן **Mûwth lab-bên**, *mooth lab-bane´*; from 4191 and 1121 with the prep. and art. interposed; "*To die for the son*", prob. the title of a popular song:— death, Muthlabben.

4193. מוֹת **môwth** (Chald.), *mohth*; corresp. to 4194; *death:*— death.

4194. מָוֶת **mâveth**, *maw´-veth*; from 4191; *death* (nat. or violent); concr. the *dead*, their place or state (*hades*); fig. *pestilence, ruin:*— (be) dead (l-ly], death, die (-d).

מוּת לַבֵּן **Mûwth lab-bên**. See 4192.

4195. מוֹתָר **môwthar**, *mo-thar´*; from 3498; lit. *gain*; fig. *superiority:*— plenteousness, preeminence, profit.

4196. מִזְבֵּחַ **mizbêach**, *miz-bay´-akh*; from 2076; an *altar:*— altar.

4197. מֶזֶג **mezeg**, *meh´-zeg*; from an unused root mean. to *mingle* (water with wine); *tempered* wine:— liquor.

4198. מָזֶה **mâzeh**, *maw-zeh´*; from an unused root mean. to *suck* out; *exhausted:*— burnt.

4199. מִזָּה **Mizzâh**, *miz-zaw´*; prob. from an unused root mean. to *faint* with fear; *terror*; *Mizzah*, an Edomite:— Mizzah.

4200. מֶזֶו **mezev**, *meh´-zev*; prob. from an unused root mean. to *gather* in; a *granary:*— garner.

4201. מְזוּזָה **mᵉzûwzâh**, *mez-oo-zaw´*; or

מְזֻזָה **mᵉzûzâh**, *mez-oo-zaw´*; from the same as 2123; a *door-post* (as *prominent*):— (door, side) post.

4202. מָזוֹן **mâzôwn**, *maw-zone´*; from 2109; *food:*— meat, victual.

4203. מָזוֹן **mâzôwn** (Chald.), *maw-zone´*; corresp. to 4202:— meat.

4204. מָזוֹר **mâzôwr**, *maw-zore´*; from 2114 in the sense of *turning aside* from truth; *treachery*, i.e. a *plot:*— wound.

4205. מָזוֹר **mâzôwr**, *maw-zore´*; or

מָזֹר **mâzôr**, *maw-zore´*; from 2115 in the sense of *binding* up; a *bandage*, i.e. remedy; hence, a *sore* (as needing a compress):— bound up, wound.

מְזֻזָה **mᵉzûzâh**. See 4201.

4206. מָזִיחַ **mâzîyach**, *maw-zee´-akh*; or

מֵזַח **mêzach**, *may-zakh´*; from 2118; a *belt* (as movable):— girdle, strength.

4207. מַזְלֵג **mazlêg**, *maz-layg´*; or (fem.)

מִזְלָגָה **mizlâgâh**, *miz-law-gaw´*; from an unused root mean. to *draw* up; a *fork:*— fleshhook.

4208. מַזָּלָה **mazzâlâh**, *maz-zaw-law´*; appar. from 5140 in the sense of *raining;* a *constellation,* i.e. Zodiacal sign (perh. as affecting the weather):— planet. Comp. 4216.

4209. מְזִמָּה **m^ezimmâh**, *mez-im-maw';* from 2161; a *plan,* usually evil (*machination*), sometimes good (*sagacity*):— (wicked) device, discretion, intent, witty invention, lewdness, mischievous (device), thought, wickedly.

4210. מִזְמוֹר **mizmôwr**, *miz-more';* from 2167; prop. instrumental *music;* by impl. a *poem* set to notes:— psalm.

4211. מַזְמֵרָה **mazmêrâh**, *maz-may-raw';* from 2168; a *pruning-knife:*— pruning-hook.

4212. מְזַמְּרָה **m^ezamm^erâh**, *mez-am-mer-aw';* from 2168; a *tweezer* (only in the plur.):— snuffers.

4213. מִזְעָר **miz'âr**, *miz-awr';* from the same as 2191; *fewness;* by impl. as superl. *diminutiveness:*— few, × very.

מָזוֹר **mâzôr**. See 4205.

4214. מִזְרֶה **mizreh**, *miz-reh';* from 2219; a winnowing *shovel* (as scattering the chaff):— fan.

4215. מְזָרֶה **m^ezâreh**, *mez-aw-reh';* appar. from 2219; prop. a *scatterer,* i.e. the north *wind* (as dispersing clouds; only in plur.):— north.

4216. מַזָּרָה **Mazzârâh**, *maz-zaw-raw';* appar. from 5144 in the sense of *distinction;* some noted *constellation* (only in the plur.), perh. collect. the *zodiac:*— Mazzaroth. Comp. 4208.

4217. מִזְרָח **mizrâch**, *miz-rawkh';* from 2224; *sunrise,* i.e. the *east:*— east (side, -ward), (sun-) rising (of the sun).

4218. מִזְרָע **mizrâ'**, *miz-raw';* from 2232; a planted *field:*— thing sown.

4219. מִזְרָק **mîzrâq**, *miz-rawk';* from 2236; a *bowl* (as if for sprinkling):— bason, bowl.

4220. מֵחַ **mêach**, *may'-akh;* from 4229 in the sense of *greasing; fat;* fig. *rich:*— fatling (one).

4221. מֹחַ **môach**, *mo'-akh;* from the same as 4220; *fat,* i.e. marrow:— marrow.

4222. מָחָא **mâchâ'**, *maw-khaw';* a prim. root; to *rub* or *strike* the hands together (in exultation):— clap.

4223. מְחָא **m^echâ'** (Chald.), *mekh-aw';* corresp. to 4222; to *strike* in pieces; also to *arrest;* spec. to *impale:*— hang, smite, stay.

4224. מַחֲבֵא **machăbê'**, *makh-ab-ay';* or

מַחֲבֹא **machăbô'**, *makh-ab-o';* from 2244; a *refuge:*— hiding (lurking) place.

4225. מַחְבֶּרֶת **machbereth**, *makh-beh'-reth;* from 2266; a *junction,* i.e. seam or sewed piece:— coupling.

4226. מְחַבְּרָה **m^echabb^erâh**, *mekh-ab-ber-aw';*

from 2266; a *joiner,* i.e. brace or cramp:— coupling, joining.

4227. מַחֲבַת **machăbath**, *makh-ab-ath';* from the same as 2281; a *pan* for baking in:— pan.

4228. מַחְגֹּרֶת **machăgôreth**, *makh-ag-o'-reth;* from 2296; a *girdle:*— girding.

4229. מָכָה **mâchâh**, *maw-khaw';* a prim. root; prop. to *stroke* or *rub;* by impl. to *erase;* also to *smooth* (as if with oil), i.e. *grease* or make fat; also to *touch,* i.e. reach to:— abolish, blot out, destroy, full of marrow, put out, reach unto, × utterly, wipe (away, out).

4230. מְחוּגָה **m^echûwgâh**, *mekk-oo-gaw';* from 2328; an instrument for marking a circle, i.e. *compasses:*— compass.

4231. מָחוֹז **mâchôwz**, *maw-khoze';* from an unused root mean. to *enclose;* a *harbor* (as shut in by the shore):— haven.

4232. מְחוּיָאֵל **M^echûwyâ'êl**, *mekh-oo-yaw-ale';* or

מְחִייָּאֵל **M^echîyyâ'êl**, *mekh-ee-yaw-ale';* from 4229 and 410; *smitten of God; Mechujael* or *Mechijael,* an antediluvian patriarch:— Mehujael.

4233. מַחֲוִים **Machăvîym**, *makh-av-eem';* appar. a patrial, but from an unknown place (in the plur. only for a sing.); a *Machavite* or inhab. of some place named Machaveh:— Mahavite.

4234. מָחוֹל **mâchôwl**, *maw-khole';* from 2342; a (round) *dance:*— dance (-cing).

4235. מָחוֹל **Mâchôwl**, *maw-khole';* the same as 4234; *dancing; Machol,* an Isr.:— Mahol.

מְחוֹלָה **m^echôwlâh**. See 65, 4246.

4236. מַחֲזֶה **machăzeh**, *makh-az-eh';* from 2372; a *vision:*— vision.

4237. מֶחֱזָה **mechĕzâh**, *mekh-ez-aw';* from 2372; a *window:*— light.

4238. מַחֲזִיאוֹת **Machăzîy'ôwth**, *makh-az-ee-oth';* fem. plur. from 2372; *visions; Machazioth,* an Isr.:— Mahazioth.

4239. מְחִי **m^echîy**, *mekh-ee';* from 4229; a *stroke,* i.e. battering-*ram:*— engines.

4240. מְחִידָא **M^echîydâ'**, *mek-ee-daw';* from 2330; *junction; Mechida,* one of the Nethinim:— Mehida.

4241. מִחְיָה **michyâh**, *mikh-yaw';* from 2421; *preservation of life;* hence, *sustenance;* also the live flesh, i.e. the *quick:*— preserve life, quick, recover selves, reviving, sustenance, victuals.

מְחִייָאֵל **M^echîyyâ'êl**. See 4232.

4242. מְחִיר **m^echîyr**, *mekk-eer';* from an unused root mean. to *buy; price, payment, wages:*— gain, hire, price, sold, worth.

4243. מְחִיר **Mᵉchîyr**, *mekh-eer´;* the same as 4242; *price; Mechir,* an Isr.:— Mehir.

4244. מַחְלָה **Machlâh**, *makh-law´;* from 2470; *sickness; Machlah,* the name appar. of two Israelitesses:— Mahlah.

4245. מַחֲלֶה **machăleh**, *makh-al-eh´;* or (fem.)

מַחֲלָה **machălâh**, *makk-al-aw´;* from 2470; *sickness:*— disease, infirmity, sickness.

4246. מְחוֹלָה **mᵉchôwlâh**, *mek-o-law´;* fem. of 4284; a *dance:*— company, dances (-cing).

4247. מְחִלָּה **mᵉchillâh**, *mekh-il-law´;* from 2490; a *cavern* (as if excavated):— cave.

4248. מַחְלוֹן **Machlôwn**, *makh-lone´;* from 2470; *sick; Machlon,* an Isr.:— Mahlon.

4249. מַחְלִי **Machliy**, *makh-lee´;* from 2470; *sick; Machli,* the name of two Isr.:— Mahli.

4250. מַחְלִי **Machliy**, *makh-lee´;* patron. from 4249; a *Machlite* or (collect.) desc. of Machli:— Mahlites.

4251. מַחְלֻי **machlûy**, *makh-loo´-ee;* from 2470; a *disease:*— disease.

4252. מַחֲלָף **machălâph**, *makh-al-awf´;* from 2498; a (sacrificial) *knife* (as *gliding* through the flesh):— knife.

4253. מַחְלָפָה **machlâphâh**, *makh-law-faw´;* from 2498; a *ringlet* of hair (as *gliding* over each other):— lock.

4254. מַחֲלָצָה **machălâtsâh**, *makh-al-aw-tsaw´;* from 2502; a *mantle* (as easily *drawn off*):— changeable suit of apparel, change of raiment.

4255. מַחְלְקָה **machlᵉqâh** (Chald.), *makh-lek-aw´;* corresp. to 4256; a *section* (of the Levites):— course.

4256. מַחֲלֹקֶת **machălôqeth**, *makh-al-o´-keth;* from 2505; a *section* (of Levites, people or soldiers):— company, course, division, portion. See also 5555.

4257. מַחֲלַת **Machălath**, *makh-al-ath´;* from 2470; *sickness; Machalath,* prob. the title (initial word) of a popular song:— Mahalath.

4258. מַחֲלַת **Machălath**, *makh-al-ath´;* the same as 4257; *sickness; Machalath,* the name of an Ishmaelitess and of an Israelitess:— Mahalath.

4259. מְחֹלָתִי **Mᵉchôlâthiy**, *mekh-o-law-thee´;* patrial from 65; a *Mecholathite* or inhab. of Abel-Mecholah:— Mecholathite.

4260. מַחֲמָאָה **machămâ´âh**, *makh-am-aw-aw´;* a denom. from 2529; something *buttery* (i.e. unctuous and pleasant), as (fig.) *flattery:*— × than butter.

4261. מַחְמָד **machmâd**, *makh-mawd´;* from 2530; *delightful;* hence, a *delight,* i.e. object of affection or desire:— beloved, desire, goodly, lovely, pleasant (thing).

4262. מַחְמֻד **machmûd**, *makh-mood´;* or

מַחְמוּד **machmûwd**, *makh-mood´;* from 2530; *desired;* hence, a *valuable:*— pleasant thing.

4263. מַחְמָל **machmâl**, *makh-mawl´;* from 2550; prop. *sympathy;* (by paronomasia with 4261) *delight:*— pitieth.

4264. מַחֲנֶה **machăneh**, *makh-an-eh´;* from 2583; an *encampment* (of travellers or troops); hence, an *army,* whether lit. (of soldiers) or fig. (of dancers, angels, cattle, locusts, stars; or even the sacred courts):— army, band, battle, camp, company, drove, host, tents.

4265. מַחֲנֵה־דָן **Machănêh-Dân**, *makh-an-ay´-dawn;* from 4264 and 1835; *camp of Dan; Machaneh-Dan,* a place in Pal.:— Mahaneh-dan.

4266. מַחֲנַיִם **Machănayim**, *makh-an-ah´-yim;* dual of 4264; *double camp; Machanajim,* a place in Pal.:— Mahanaim.

4267. מַחֲנַק **machănaq**, *makh-an-ak´;* from 2614; *choking:*— strangling.

4268. מַחֲסֶה **machăçeh**, *makh-as-eh´;* or

מַחְסֶה **machçeh**, *makh-seh´;* from 2620; a *shelter* (lit. or fig.):— hope, (place of) refuge, shelter, trust.

4269. מַחְסוֹם **machçôwm**, *makh-sohm´;* from 2629; a *muzzle:*— bridle.

4270. מַחְסוֹר **machçôwr**, *makh-sore´;* or

מַחְסֹר **machçôr**, *makh-sore´;* from 2637; *deficiency;* hence, *impoverishment:*— lack, need, penury, poor, poverty, want.

4271. מַחְסֵיָה **Machçêyâh**, *makh-say-yaw´;* from 4268 and 3050; *refuge of* (i.e. in) *Jah; Machsejah,* an Isr.:— Maaseiah.

4272. מָחַץ **mâchats**, *maw-khats´;* a prim. root; to *dash* asunder; by impl. to *crush, smash* or violently *plunge;* fig. to *subdue* or *destroy:*— dip, pierce (through), smite (through), strike through, wound.

4273. מַחַץ **machats**, *makh´-ats;* from 4272; a *contusion:*— stroke.

4274. מַחְצֵב **machtsêb**, *makh-tsabe´;* from 2672; prop. a *hewing;* concr. a *quarry:*— hewed (-n).

4275. מֶחֱצָה **mechĕtsâh**, *mekh-ets-aw´;* from 2673; a *halving:*— half.

4276. מַחֲצִית **machătsîyth**, *makh-ats-eeth´;* from 2673; a *halving* or the *middle:*— half (so much), mid [-day].

4277. מָחַק **mâchaq**, *maw-khak´;* a prim. root; to *crush:*— smite off.

4278. מֶחְקָר **mechqâr**, *mekh-kawr´;* from

2713; prop. *scrutinized*, i.e. (by impl.) a *recess:*— deep place.

4279. מָחָר **machar**, *maw-khar´*; prob. from 309; prop. *deferred*, i.e. the *morrow*; usually (adv.) *tomorrow*; indef. *hereafter:*— time to come, tomorrow.

4280. מַחֲרָאָה **machărâ'âh**, *makh-ar-aw-aw´*; from the same as 2716; a *sink:*— draught house.

4281. מַחֲרֵשָׁה **machărêshâh**, *makh-ar-ay-shaw´*; from 2790; prob. a *pick*-axe:— mattock.

4282. מַחֲרֵשָׁה **machăresheth**, *makh-ar-eh´-sheth*; from 2790; prob. a *hoe:*— share.

4283. מָחֳרָת **mochŏrâth**, *mokh-or-awth´*; or

מָחֳרָתָם **mochŏrâthâm** (1 Sam. 30:17), *mokh-or-aw-thawm´*; fem. from the same as 4279; the *morrow* or (adv.) *tomorrow:*— morrow, next day.

4284. מַחֲשָׁבָה **machăshâbâh**, *makh-ash-aw-baw´*; or

מַחֲשֶׁבֶת **machăshebeth**, *makh-ash-eh´-beth*; from 2803; a *contrivance*, i.e. (concr.) a *texture, machine*, or (abstr.) *intention, plan* (whether bad, a *plot*; or good, *advice*):— cunning (work), curious work, device (-sed), imagination, invented, means, purpose, thought.

4285. מַחְשָׁךְ **machshâk**, *makh-shawk´*; from 2821; *darkness*; concr. a *dark place:*— dark (-ness, place).

4286. מַחְשׂוֹף **machsôph**, *makh-sofe´*; from 2834; a *peeling:*— made appear.

4287. מַחַת **Machath**, *makh´-ath*; prob. from 4229; *erasure*; *Machath*, the name of two Isr.:— Mahath.

4288. מְחִתָּה **mᵉchittâh**, *mekh-it-taw´*; from 2846; prop. a *dissolution*; concr. a *ruin*, or (abstr.) *consternation:*— destruction, dismaying, ruin, terror.

4289. מַחְתָּה **machtâh**, *makh-taw´*; the same as 4288 in the sense of *removal*; a *pan* for live coals:— censer, firepan, snuffdish.

4290. מַחְתֶּרֶת **machtereth**, *makh-teh´-reth*; from 2864; a *burglary*; fig. *unexpected examination:*— breaking up, secret search.

4291. מְטָא **mᵉṭâ'** (Chald.), *met-aw´*; or

מְטָה **mᵉṭâh** (Chald.) *met-aw´*; appar. corresp. to 4672 in the intr. sense of being found *present*; to *arrive, extend* or *happen:*— come, reach.

4292. מַטְאֲטֵא **maṭ'ăṭê'**, *mat-at-ay´*; appar. a denom. from 2916; a *broom* (as removing *dirt* [comp. Engl. "to dust", i.e. remove dust]):— besom.

4293. מַטְבֵּחַ **maṭbêach**, *mat-bay´-akh*; from 2873; *slaughter:*— slaughter.

4294. מַטֶּה **maṭṭeh**, *mat-teh´*; or (fem.)

מַטָּה **maṭṭâh**, *mat-taw´*; from 5186; a *branch* (as *extending*); fig. a *tribe*; also a *rod*, whether for chastising (fig. *correction*), ruling (a *sceptre*), throwing (a *lance*), or walking (a *staff*; fig. a *support* of life, e.g. bread):— rod, staff, tribe.

4295. מַטָּה **maṭṭâh**, *mat´-taw*; from 5786 with directive enclitic appended; *downward, below* or *beneath*; often adv. with or without prefixes:— beneath, down (-ward), less, very low, under (-neath).

4296. מִטָּה **miṭṭâh**, *mit-taw´*; from 5186; a *bed* (as *extended*) for sleeping or eating; by anal. a *sofa, litter* or *bier:*— bed ([-chamber]), bier.

4297. מֻטֶּה **muṭṭeh**, *moot-teh´*; from 5186; a *stretching*, i.e. *distortion* (fig. *iniquity*):— perverseness.

4298. מֻטָּה **muṭṭâh**, *moot-taw´*; from 5186; *expansion:*— stretching out.

4299. מַטְוֶה **matveh**, *mat-veh´*; from 2901; something *spun:*— spun.

4300. מְטִיל **mᵉṭîyl**, *met-eel´*; from 2904 in the sense of *hammering* out; an iron *bar* (as *forged*):— bar.

4301. מַטְמוֹן **matmôwn**, *mat-mone´*; or

מַטְמֹן **matmôn**, *mat-mone´*; or

מַטְמֻן **matmûn**, *mat-moon´*; from 2934; a *secret* storehouse; hence, a *secreted* valuable (buried); gen. *money:*— hidden riches, (hid) treasure (-s).

4302. מַטָּע **maṭṭâ'**, *mat-taw´*; from 5193; something *planted*, i.e. the place (a *garden* or *vineyard*), or the thing (a *plant*, fig. of men); by impl. the act, *planting:*— plant (-ation, -ing).

4303. מַטְעָם **maṭ'am**, *mat-am´*; or (fem.)

מַטְעַמָּה **maṭ'ammâh**, *mat-am-maw´*; from 2938; a *delicacy:*— dainty (meat), savoury meat.

4304. מִטְפַּחַת **miṭpachath**, *mit-pakh´-ath*; from 2946; a wide *cloak* (for a woman):— vail, wimple.

4305. מָטַר **mâṭar**, *maw-tar´*; a prim. root; to *rain:*— (cause to) rain (upon).

4306. מָטָר **mâṭâr**, *maw-tawr´*; from 4305; *rain:*— rain.

4307. מַטָּרָא **maṭṭârâ'**, *mat-taw-raw´*; or

מַטָּרָה **maṭṭârâh**, *mat-taw-raw´*; from 5201; a *jail* (as a *guard*-house); also an *aim* (as being closely *watched*):— mark, prison.

4308. מַטְרֵד **Maṭrêd**, *mat-rade´*; from 2956; *propulsive*; *Matred*, an Edomitess:— Matred.

Hebrew

4309. מַטְרִי **Maṭrîy**, *mat-ree´;* from 4305; *rainy; Matri,* an Isr.:— Matri.

4310. מִי **mîy**, *me;* an interrog. pron. of persons, as 4100 is of things, *who?* (occasionally, by a peculiar idiom, of things); also (indef.) *whoever;* often used in oblique constr. with pref. or suff.:— any (man), × he, × him, + O that! what, which, who (-m, -se, soever), + would to God.

4311. מֵידְבָא **Mêyd͏eb͏â'**, *may-deb-aw´;* from 4325 and 1679; *water of quiet; Medeba,* a place in Pal.:— Medeba.

4312. מֵידָד **Mêydâd**, *may-dawd´;* from 3032 in the sense of *loving; affectionate; Medad,* an Isr.:— Medad.

4313. מֵי הַיַּרְקוֹן **Mêy hay-Yarqôwn**, *may hah´-ee-yar-kone´;* from 4325 and 3420 with the art. interposed; *water of the yellowness; Me-haj-Jarkon,* a place in Pal.:— Me-jarkon.

4314. מֵי זָהָב **Mêy Zâhâb**, *may zaw-hawb´;* from 4325 and 2091, *water of gold; Me-Zahab,* an Edomite:— Mezahab.

4315. מֵיטָב **mêyṭâb**, *may-tawb´;* from 3190; the *best* part:— best.

4316. מִיכָא **Mîykâ'**, *mee-kaw´;* a var. for 4318; *Mica,* the name of two Isr.:— Micha.

4317. מִיכָאֵל **Mîykâ'êl**, *me-kaw-ale´;* from 4310 and (the pref. der. from) 3588 and 410; *who (is) like God?; Mikael,* the name of an archangel and of nine Isr.:— Michael.

4318. מִיכָה **Mîykâh**, *mee-kaw´;* an abbrev. of 4320; *Micah,* the name of seven Isr.:— Micah, Micaiah, Michah.

4319. מִיכָהוּ **Mîykâhûw**, *me-kaw´-hoo;* a contr. for 4321; *Mikehu,* an Isr. prophet:— Micaiah (2 Chron. 18:8).

4320. מִיכָיָה **Mîykâyâh**, *me-kaw-yaw´;* from 4310 and (the pref. der. from) 3588 and 3050; *who (is) like Jah?; Micajah,* the name of two Isr.:— Micah, Michaiah. Comp. 4318.

4321. מִיכָיְהוּ **Mîykây͏ehûw**, *me-kaw-yeh-hoo´;* or

מִכָיְהוּ **Mîkây͏ehûw** (Jer. 36:11), *me-kaw-yeh-hoo´;* abbrev. for 4322; *Mikajah,* the name of three Isr.:— Micah, Micaiah, Michaiah.

4322. מִיכָיָהוּ **Mîykâyâhûw**, *me-kaw-yaw´-hoo;* for 4320; *Mikajah,* the name of an Isr. and an Israelitess:— Michaiah.

4323. מִיכָל **mîykâl**, *me-kawl´;* from 3201; prop. a *container,* i.e. a *streamlet:*— brook.

4324. מִיכָל **Mîykâl**, *me-kawl´;* appar. the same as 4323; *rivulet; Mikal,* Saul's daughter:— Michal.

4325. מַיִם **mayim**, *mah´-yim;* dual of a prim. noun (but used in a sing. sense); *water;* fig. *juice;* by euphem. *urine, semen:*— + piss,

wasting, water (-ing, [-course, -flood, -spring]).

4326. מִיָּמִן **Mîyâmîn**, *me-yaw-meem´;* a form for 4509; *Mijamin,* the name of three Isr.:— Miamin, Mijamin.

4327. מִין **mîyn**, *meen;* from an unused root mean. to *portion* out; a *sort,* i.e. *species:*— kind. Comp. 4480.

4328. מְיֻסָּדָה **m͏eyuççâdâh**, *meh-yoos-saw-daw´;* prop. fem. pass. part. of 3245; something *founded,* i.e. a *foundation:*— foundation.

4329. מִיסָךְ **mêyçâk**, *may-sawk´;* from 5526; a *portico* (as *covered*):— covert.

מֵיפַעַת **Mêypha'ath**. See 4158.

4330. מִיץ **mîyts**, *meets;* from 4160; *pressure:*— churning, forcing, wringing.

4331. מֵישָׁא **Mêyshâ'**, *may-shaw´;* from 4185; *departure; Mesha,* a place in Arabia; also an Isr.:— Mesha.

4332. מִישָׁאֵל **Mîyshâ'êl**, *mee-shaw-ale´;* from 4310 and 410 with the abbrev. insep. rel. [see 834] interposed; *who (is) what God (is)?; Mishaël,* the name of three Isr.:— Mishael.

4333. מִישָׁאֵל **Mîyshâ'êl** (Chald.), *mee-shaw-ale´;* corresp. to 4332; *Mishaël,* an Isr.:— Mishael.

4334. מִישׁוֹר **mîyshôwr**, *mee-shore´;* or

מִישֹׁר **mîyshôr**, *mee-shore´;* from 3474; a *level,* i.e. a *plain* (often used [with the art. pref.] as a prop. name of certain districts); fig. *concord;* also *straightness,* i.e. (fig.) *justice* (sometimes adv. *justly*):— equity, even place, plain, right (-eously), (made) straight, uprightness.

4335. מֵישַׁךְ **Mêyshak**, *may-shak´;* borrowed from 4336; *Meshak,* an Isr.:— Meshak.

4336. מֵישַׁךְ **Mêyshak** (Chald.), *may-shak´;* of for. or. and doubtful signif.; *Meshak,* the Bab. name of 4333:— Meshak.

4337. מֵישָׁא **Mêyshâ'**, *may-shah´;* from 3467; *safety; Mesha,* an Isr.:— Mesha.

4338. מֵישַׁע **Mêysha'**, *may-shaw´;* a var. for 4337; *safety; Mesha,* a Moabite:— Mesha.

4339. מֵישָׁר **mêyshâr**, *may-shawr´;* from 3474; *evenness,* i.e. (fig.) *prosperity* or *concord;* also *straightness,* i.e. (fig.) *rectitude* (only in plur. with sing. sense; often adv.):— agreement, aright, that are equal, equity, (things that are) right (-eously, things), sweetly, upright (-ly, -ness).

4340. מֵיתָר **mêythâr**, *may-thar´;* from 3498; a *cord* (of a tent) [comp. 3499] or the *string* (of a bow):— cord, string.

4341. מַכְאֹב **mak'ôb**, *mak-obe´;* sometimes

מַכְאֹב **mak'ôwb**, *mak-obe'*; also (fem. Isa. 53:3)

מַכְאֵבָה **mak'ôbâh**, *mak-o-baw'*; from 3510; *anguish* or (fig.) *affliction:*— grief, pain, sorrow.

4342. מַכְבִּיר **makbîyr**, *mak-beer'*; tran. part. of 3527; *plenty:*— abundance.

4343. מַכְבֵּנָא **Makbênâ'**, *mak-bay-naw'*; from the same as 3522; *knoll; Macbena*, a place in Pal. settled by him:— Machbenah.

4344. מַכְבַּנַּי **Makbannay**, *mak-ban-nah'-ee*; patrial from 4343; a *Macbannite* or native of Macbena:— Machbanai.

4345. מַכְבֵּר **makbêr**, *mak-bare'*; from 3527 in the sense of *covering* [comp. 3531]; a *grate:*— grate.

4346. מַכְבָּר **makbâr**, *mak-bawr'*; from 3527 in the sense of *covering;* a *cloth* (as *netted* [comp. 4345]):— thick cloth.

4347. מַכָּה **makkâh**, *mak-kaw'*; or (masc.)

מַכֶּה **makkeh**, *mak-keh'*; (plur. only) from 5221; a *blow* (in 2 Chron. 2:10, of the flail); by impl. a *wound;* fig. *carnage*, also *pestilence:*— beaten, blow, plague, slaughter, smote, × sore, stripe, stroke, wound (l-ed]).

4348. מִכְוָה **mikvâh**, *mik-vaw'*; from 3554; a *burn:*— that burneth, burning.

4349. מָכוֹן **mâkôwn**, *maw-kone'*; from 3559; prop. a *fixture*, i.e. a *basis*; gen. a *place*, espec. as an *abode:*— foundation, habitation, (dwelling-, settled) place.

4350. מְכוֹנָה **mᵉkôwnâh**, *mek-o-naw'*; or

מְכֹנָה **mᵉkônâh**, *mek-o-naw'*; fem. of 4349; a *pedestal*, also a *spot:*— base.

4351. מְכוּרָה **mᵉkûwrâh**, *mek-oo-raw'*; or

מְכֹרָה **mᵉkôrâh**, *mek-o-raw'*; from the same as 3564 in the sense of *digging; origin* (as if a mine):— birth, habitation, nativity.

4352. מָכִי **Mâkîy**, *maw-kee'*; prob. from 4134; *pining; Maki*, an Isr.:— Machi.

4353. מָכִיר **Mâkîyr**, *maw-keer'*; from 4376; *salesman; Makir*, an Isr.:— Machir.

4354. מָכִירִי **Mâkîyrîy**, *maw-kee-ree'*; patron. from 4353; a *Makirite* or descend. of Makir:— of Machir.

4355. מָכַךְ **mâkak**, *maw-kak'*; a prim. root; to *tumble* (in ruins); fig. to *perish:*— be brought low, decay.

4356. מִכְלָאָה **miklâ'âh**, *mik-law-aw'*; or

מִכְלָה **miklâh**, *mik-law'*; from 3607; a *pen* (for flocks):— [sheep-] fold. Comp. 4357.

4357. מִכְלָה **miklâh**, *mik-law'*; from 3615; *completion* (in plur. concr. adv. *wholly*):— perfect. Comp. 4356.

4358. מִכְלוֹל **miklôwl**, *mik-lole'*; from 3634; per-fection (i.e. concr. adv. *splendidly*):— most gorgeously, all sorts.

4359. מִכְלָל **miklâl**, *mik-lawl'*; from 3634; *perfection* (of beauty):— perfection.

4360. מִכְלֻל **miklûl**, *mik-lool'*; from 3634; something *perfect*, i.e. a splendid *garment:*— all sorts.

4361. מַכֹּלֶת **makkôleth**, *mak-ko'-leth*; from 398; *nourishment:*— food.

4362. מִכְמָן **mikman**, *mik-man'*; from the same as 3646 in the sense of *hiding; treasure* (as *hidden*):— treasure.

4363. מִכְמָס **Mikmâç** (Ezra 2:27; Neh. 7:31), *mik-maws';* or

מִכְמָשׁ **Mikmâsh**, *mik-mawsh';* or

מִכְמָשׁ **Mikmash** (Neh. 11:31), *mik-mash';* from 3647; *hidden; Mikmas* or *Mikmash*, a place in Pal.:— Mikmas, Mikmash.

4364. מַכְמָר **makmâr**, *mak-mawr';* or

מִכְמֹר **mikmôr**, *mik-more';* from 3648 in the sense of *blackening* by heat; a (hunter's) *net* (as *dark* from concealment):— net.

4365. מִכְמֶרֶת **mikmereth**, *mik-meh'-reth;* or

מִכְמֹרֶת **mikmôreth**, *mik-mo'-reth;* fem. of 4364; a (fisher's) *net:*— drag, net.

מִכְמָשׁ **Mikmâsh**. See 4363.

4366. מִכְמְתָת **Mikmᵉthâth**, *mik-meth-awth';* appar. from an unused root mean. to *hide; concealment; Mikmethath*, a place in Pal.:— Michmethath.

4367. מַכְנַדְבַּי **Maknadbay**, *mak-nad-bah'-ee;* from 4100 and 5068 with a particle interposed; *what* (is) *like* (a) *liberal* (man)?; *Maknadbai*, an Isr.:— Machnadebai.

מְכֹנָה **mᵉkônâh**. See 4350.

4368. מְכֹנָה **Mᵉkônâh**, *mek-o-naw';* the same as 4350; a *base; Mekonah*, a place in Pal.:— Mekonah.

4369. מְכֻנָה **mᵉkûnâh**, *mek-oo-naw';* the same as 4350; a *spot:*— base.

4370. מִכְנָס **miknâç**, *mik-nawce';* from 3647 in the sense of *hiding;* (only in dual) *drawers* (from *concealing* the private parts):— breeches.

4371. מֶכֶס **mekeç**, *meh'-kes;* prob. from an unused root mean. to *enumerate;* an *assessment* (as based upon a *census*):— tribute.

4372. מִכְסֶה **mikçeh**, *mik-seh';* from 3680; a *covering*, i.e. weather-*boarding:*— covering.

4373. מִכְסָה **mikçâh**, *mik-saw';* fem. of 4371; an *enumeration;* by impl. a *valuation:*— number, worth.

Hebrew

4374. מְכַסֶּה **mᵉkaççeh**, *mek-as-seh´;* from 3680; a *covering,* i.e. *garment;* spec. a *coverlet* (for a bed), an *awning* (from the sun); also the *omentum* (as covering the intestines):— clothing, to cover, that which covereth.

4375. מַכְפֵּלָה **Makpêlâh**, *mak-pay-law´;* from 3717; a *fold; Makpelah,* a place in Pal.:— Machpelah.

4376. מָכַר **mâkar**, *maw-kar´;* a prim. root; to *sell,* lit. (as merchandise, a daughter in marriage, into slavery), or fig. (to *surrender*):— × at all, sell (away, -er, self).

4377. מֶכֶר **meker**, *meh´-ker;* from 4376; *merchandise;* also *value:*— pay, price, ware.

4378. מַכָּר **makkâr**, *mak-kawr´;* from 5234; an *acquaintance:*— acquaintance.

4379. מִכְרֶה **mikreh**, *mik-reh´;* from 3738; a *pit* (for salt):— [salt-] pit.

4380. מְכֵרָה **mᵉkêrâh**, *mek-ay-raw´;* prob. from the same as 3564 in the sense of *stabbing;* a *sword:*— habitation.

מְכֹרָה **mᵉkôrâh**. See 4351.

4381. מִכְרִי **Mikrîy**, *mik-ree´;* from 4376; *salesman; Mikri,* an Isr.:— Michri.

4382. מְכֵרָתִי **Mᵉkêrâthîy**, *mek-ay-raw-thee´;* patrial from an unused name (the same as 4380) of a place in Pal.; a *Mekerathite,* or inhab. of Mekerah:— Mecherathite.

4383. מִכְשׁוֹל **mikshôwl**, *mik-shole´;* or

מִכְשֹׁל **mikshôl**, *mik-shole´;* masc. from 3782; a *stumbling-block,* lit. or fig. (*obstacle, enticement* [spec. an idol], *scruple*):— caused to fall, offence, × [no-] thing offered, ruin, stumbling-block.

4384. מַכְשֵׁלָה **makshêlâh**, *mak-shay-law´;* fem. from 3782; a *stumbling-block,* but only fig. (*fall, enticement* [idol]):— ruin, stumbling-block.

4385. מִכְתָּב **miktâb**, *mik-tawb´;* from 3789; a thing *written,* the *characters,* or a *document* (letter, copy, edict, poem):— writing.

4386. מְכִתָּה **mᵉkittâh**, *mek-it-taw´;* from 3807; a *fracture:*— bursting.

4387. מִכְתָּם **Miktâm**, *mik-tawm´;* from 3799; an *engraving,* i.e. (techn.) a *poem:*— Michtam.

4388. מַכְתֵּשׁ **maktêsh**, *mak-taysh´;* from 3806; a *mortar;* by anal. a *socket* (of a tooth):— hollow place, mortar.

4389. מַכְתֵּשׁ **Maktêsh**, *mak-taysh´;* the same as 4388; *dell;* the *Maktesh,* a place in Jerusalem:— Maktesh.

מֻל **mûl**. See 4136.

4390. מָלֵא **mâlê'**, *maw-lay´;* or

מָלָא **mâlâ'** (Esth. 7:5), *maw-law´;* a prim. root, to *fill* or (intr.) *be full* of, in a wide application (lit. and fig.):— accomplish, confirm, + consecrate, be at an end, be expired, be fenced, fill, fulfil, (be, become, × draw, give in, go) full (-ly, -ly set, tale, [over-] flow, fulness, furnish, gather (selves, together), presume, replenish, satisfy, set, space, take a [hand-] full, + have wholly.

4391. מְלָא **mᵉlâ'** (Chald.), *mel-aw´;* corresp. to 4390; to *fill:*— fill, be full.

4392. מָלֵא **mâlê'**, *maw-lay´;* from 4390; *full* (lit. or fig.) or *filling* (lit.); also (concr.) *fulness;* adv. *fully:*— × she that was with child, fill (-ed, -ed with), full (-ly), multitude, as is worth.

4393. מְלֹא **mᵉlô'**, *mel-o´;* rarely

מְלוֹא **mᵉlôw'**, *mel-o´;* or

מְלוֹ **mᵉlôw** (Ezek. 41:8), *mel-o´;* from 4390; *fulness* (lit. or fig.):— × all along, × all that is (there-) in, fill, (× that whereof ... was) full, fulness, [hand-] full, multitude.

מִלֹּא **Millô'**. See 4407.

4394. מִלֻּא **millû'**, *mil-loo´;* from 4390; a *fulfilling* (only in plur.), i.e. (lit.) a *setting* (of gems), or (tech.) *consecration* (also concr. a dedicatory *sacrifice*):— consecration, be set.

4395. מְלֵאָה **mᵉlê'âh**, *mel-ay-aw´;* fem. of 4392; *something fulfilled,* i.e. *abundance* (of produce):— (first of ripe) fruit, fulness.

4396. מִלֻּאָה **millû'âh**, *mil-loo-aw´;* fem. of 4394; a *filling,* i.e. *setting* (of gems):— inclosing, setting.

4397. מַלְאָךְ **mal'âk**, *mal-awk´;* from an unused root mean. to *despatch* as a deputy; a *messenger;* spec. of God, i.e. an *angel* (also a prophet, priest or teacher):— ambassador, angel, king, messenger.

4398. מַלְאַךְ **mal'ak** (Chald.), *mal-ak´;* corresp. to 4397; an *angel:*— angel.

4399. מְלָאכָה **mᵉlâ'kâh**, *mel-aw-kaw´;* from the same as 4397; prop. *deputyship,* i.e. *ministry;* gen. *employment* (never servile) or *work* (abstr. or concr.); also *property* (as the result of *labor*):— business, + cattle, +industrious, occupation, (+ -pied), + officer, thing (made), use, (manner of) work ([-man], -manship).

4400. מַלְאֲכוּת **mal'ăkûwth**, *mal-ak-ooth´;* from the same as 4397; a *message:*— message.

4401. מַלְאָכִי **Mal'âkîy**, *mal-aw-kee´;* from the same as 4397; *ministrative; Malaki,* a prophet:— Malachi.

4402. מִלֵּאת **millê'th**, *mil-layth´;* from 4390; *fulness,* i.e. (concr.) a *plump socket* (of the eye):— × fitly.

4403. מַלְבּוּשׁ **malbûwsh**, *mal-boosh´;* or

מַלְבֻּשׁ **malbûsh**, *mal-boosh´;* from

3847; a *garment*, or (collect.) *clothing*:— apparel, raiment, vestment.

4404. מַלְבֵּן **malbên**, *mal-bane'*; from 3835 (denom.); a *brick-kiln*:— brickkiln.

4405. מִלָּה **millâh**, *mil-law'*; from 4448 (plur. masc. as if from

מִלֶּה **milleh**, *mil-leh'*; a *word*; collect. a *discourse*; fig. a *topic*:— + answer, by-word, matter, any thing (what) to say, to speak (-ing), speak, talking, word.

4406. מִלָּה **millâh** (Chald.), *mil-law'*; corresp. to 4405; a *word, command, discourse*, or *subject*:— commandment, matter, thing, word.

מְלוֹ **melôw**. See 4393.

מְלוֹא **melôw'**. See 4393.

4407. מִלּוֹא **millôw'**, *mil-lo'*; or

מִלּא **millô'** (2 Kings 12:20) *mil-lo'*; from 4390; a *rampart* (as *filled* in), i.e. the *citadel*:— Millo. See also 1037.

4408. מַלּוּחַ **mallûwach**, *mal-loo'-akh*; from 4414; *sea-purslain* (from its *saltness*):— mallows.

4409. מַלּוּךְ **Mallûwk**, *mal-luke'*; or

מַלּוּכִי° **Mallûwkîy** (Neh. 12:14) *mal-loo-kee'*; from 4427; *regnant*; *Malluk*, the name of five Isr.:— Malluch, Melichu [*from the marg.*].

4410. מְלוּכָה **melûwkâh**, *mel-oo-kaw'*; fem. pass. part. of 4427; something *ruled*, i.e. a *realm*:— kingdom, king's, × royal.

4411. מָלוֹן **mâlôwn**, *maw-lone'*; from 3885; a *lodgment*, i.e. *caravanserai* or *encampment*:— inn, place where ... lodge, lodging (place).

4412. מְלוּנָה **melûwnâh**, *mel-oo-naw'*; fem. from 3885; a *hut*, a *hammock*:— cottage, lodge.

4413. מַלּוֹתִי **Mallôwthîy**, *mal-lo'-thee*; appar. from 4448; *I have talked* (i.e. *loquacious*); *Mallothi*, an Isr.:— Mallothi.

4414. מָלַח **mâlach**, *maw-lakh'*; a prim. root; prop. to *rub* to pieces or pulverize; intr. to *disappear* as dust; also (as denom. from 4417) to *salt* whether intern. (to *season* with salt) or extern. (to *rub* with salt):— × at all, salt, season, temper together, vanish away.

4415. מְלַח **melach** (Chald.), *mel-akh'*; corresp. to 4414; to *eat* salt, i.e. (gen.) *subsist*:— + have maintenance.

4416. מְלַח **melach** (Chald.), *mel-akh'*; from 4415; *salt*:— + maintenance, salt.

4417. מֶלַח **melach**, *meh'-lakh*; from 4414; prop. *powder*, i.e. (spec.) *salt* (as easily pulverized and dissolved:— salt (I-pit).

4418. מָלָח **mâlâch**, *maw-lawkh'*; from 4414 in its orig. sense; a *rag* or old garment:— rotten rag.

4419. מַלָּח **mallâch**, *mal-lawkh'*; from 4414 in its second. sense; a *sailor* (as following "the salt"):— mariner.

4420. מְלֵחָה **melêchâh**, *mel-ay-khaw'*; from 4414 in its denom. sense; prop. *salted* (i.e. land [776 being understood]), i.e. a *desert*:— barren land (-ness), salt (land).

4421. מִלְחָמָה **milchâmâh**, *mil-khaw-maw'*; from 3898 (in the sense of *fighting*); a *battle* (i.e. the *engagement*); gen. *war* (i.e. *warfare*):— battle, fight (-ing), war (I-rior).

4422. מָלַט **mâlat**, *maw-lat'*; a prim. root; prop. to *be smooth*, i.e. (by impl.) to *escape* (as if by *slipperiness*); caus. to *release* or *rescue*; spec. to *bring forth* young, *emit* sparks:— deliver (self), escape, lay, leap out, let alone, let go, preserve, save, × speedily, × surely.

4423. מֶלֶט **melet**, *meh'-let*; from 4422, *cement* (from its plastic *smoothness*):— clay.

4424. מְלַטְיָה **Melatyâh**, *mel-at-yaw'*; from 4423 and 3050; (whom) *Jah has delivered*; *Melatjah*, a Gibeonite:— Melatiah.

4425. מְלִילָה **melîylâh**, *mel-ee-law'*; from 4449 (in the sense of *cropping* [comp. 4135]); a *head* of grain (as *cut* off):— ear.

4426. מְלִיצָה **melîytsâh**, *mel-ee-tsaw'*; from 3887; an *aphorism*; also a *satire*:— interpretation, taunting.

4427. מָלַךְ **mâlak**, *maw-lak'*; a prim. root; to *reign*; incept. to *ascend the throne*; caus. to *induct* into royalty; hence, (by impl.) to *take counsel*:— consult, × indeed, be (make, set a, set up) king, be (make) queen, (begin to, make to) reign (-ing), rule, × surely.

4428. מֶלֶךְ **melek**, *meh'-lek*; from 4427; a *king*:— king, royal.

4429. מֶלֶךְ **Melek**, *meh'-lek*; the same as 4428; *king*; *Melek*, the name of two Isr.:— Melech, Hammelech [by incl. the art.].

4430. מֶלֶךְ **melek** (Chald.), *meh'-lek*; corresp. to 4428; a *king*:— king, royal.

4431. מְלַךְ **melak** (Chald.), *mel-ak'*; from a root corresp. to 4427 in the sense of *consultation*; *advice*:— counsel.

4432. מֹלֶךְ **Môlek**, *mo'-lek*; from 4427; *Molek* (i.e. *king*), the chief deity of the Ammonites:— Molech. Comp. 4445.

4433. מַלְכָּא **malkâ'** (Chald.), *mal-kaw'*; corresp. to 4436; a *queen*:— queen.

4434. מַלְכֹּדֶת **malkôdeth**, *mal-ko'-deth*; from 3920; a *snare*:— trap.

4435. מִלְכָּה **Milkâh**, *mil-kaw'*; a form of 4436; *queen*; *Milcah*, the name of a Hebrewess and of an Isr.:— Milcah.

4436. מַלְכָּה **malkâh**, *mal-kaw´*; fem. of 4428; a *queen:*— queen.

4437. מַלְכוּ **malkûw** (Chald.), *mal-koo´*; corresp. to 4438; *dominion* (abstr. or concr.):— kingdom, kingly, realm, reign.

4438. מַלְכוּת **malkûwth**, *mal-kooth´*; or

מַלְכֻת **malkûth**, *mal-kooth´*; or (in plur.)

מַלְכֻיָה **malkûyâh**, *mal-koo-yâh´*; from 4427; a *rule;* concr. a *dominion:*— empire, kingdom, realm, reign, royal.

4439. מַלְכִּיאֵל **Malkîy´êl**, *mal-kee-ale´*; from 4428 and 410; *king of* (i.e. appointed by) *God; Malkiël*, an Isr.:— Malchiel.

4440. מַלְכִּיאֵלִי **Malkîy´êlîy**, *mal-kee-ay-lee´*; patron. from 4439; a *Malkiëlite* or desc. of Malkiel:— Malchielite.

4441. מַלְכִּיָה **Malkîyâh**, *mal-kee-yaw´*; or

מַלְכִּיָהוּ **Malkîyâhûw** (Jer. 38:6), *mal-kee-yaw´-hoo;* from 4428 and 3050; *king of* (i.e. appointed by) *Jah; Malkijah,* the name of ten Isr.:— Malchiah, Malchijah.

4442. מַלְכִּי־צֶדֶק **Malkîy-Tsedeq**, *mal-kee-tseh´-dek;* from 4428 and 6664; *king of right; Malki-Tsedek,* an early king in Pal.:— Melchizedek.

4443. מַלְכִּירָם **Malkîyrâm**, *mal-kee-rawm´;* from 4428 and 7311; *king of a high one* (i.e. of exaltation); *Malkiram,* an Isr.:— Malchiram.

4444. מַלְכִּישׁוּעַ **Malkîyshûwa'**, *mal-kee-shoo´-ah;* from 4428 and 7769; *king of wealth; Malk-ishua,* an Isr.:— Malchishua.

4445. מַלְכָּם **Malkâm**, *mal-kawm´;* or

מִלְכּוֹם **Milkôwm**, *mil-kome´;* from 4428 for 4432; *Malcam* or *Milcom,* the national idol of the Ammonites:— Malcham, Milcom.

4446. מְלֶכֶת **mᵉleketh**, *mel-eh´-keth;* from 4427; a *queen:*— queen.

4447. מֹלֶכֶת **Môleketh**, *mo-leh´-keth;* fem. act. part. of 4427; *queen; Moleketh,* an Israelitess:— Hammoleketh [incl. the art.].

4448. מָלַל **mâlal**, *maw-lal´;* a prim. root; to *speak* (mostly poet.) or *say:*— say, speak, utter.

4449. מְלַל **mᵉlal** (Chald.), *mel-al´;* corresp. to 4448; to *speak:*— say, speak (-ing).

4450. מִלֲלַי **Mîlălay**, *mee-lal-ah´-ee;* from 4448; *talkative; Milalai,* an Isr.:— Milalai.

4451. מַלְמָד **malmâd**, *mal-mawd´;* from 3925; a *goad* for oxen:— goad.

4452. מָלַץ **mâlats**, *maw-lats´;* a prim. root; to *be smooth,* i.e. (fig.) *pleasant:*— be sweet.

4453. מֶלְצָר **Meltsâr**, *mel-tsawr´;* of Pers. der.; the *butler* or other officer in the Bab. court:— Melzar.

4454. מָלַק **mâlaq**, *maw-lak´;* a prim. root; to *crack* a joint; by impl. to *wring* the neck of a fowl (without separating it):— wring off.

4455. מַלְקוֹחַ **malqôwach**, *mal-ko´-akh;* from 3947; tran. (in dual) the *jaws* (as taking food); intr. *spoil* [and captives] (as taken):— booty, jaws, prey.

4456. מַלְקוֹשׁ **malqôwsh**, *mal-koshe´;* from 3953; the *spring rain* (comp. 3954); fig. *eloquence:*— latter rain.

4457. מֶלְקָח **melqâch**, *mel-kawkh´;* or

מַלְקָח **malqâch**, *mal-kawkh´;* from 3947; (only in dual) *tweezers:*— snuffers, tongs.

4458. מֶלְתָּחָה **meltâchâh**, *mel-taw-khaw´;* from an unused root mean. to *spread* out; a *wardrobe* (i.e. room where clothing is spread):— vestry.

4459. מַלְתָּעָה **maltâ´âh**, *mal-taw-aw´;* transp. for 4973; a *grinder,* i.e. back *tooth:*— great tooth.

4460. מַמְּגֻרָה **mammᵉgûrâh**, *mam-meg-oo-raw´;* from 4048 (in the sense of *depositing*); a *granary:*— barn.

4461. מֵמַד **mêmad**, *may-mad´;* from 4058; a *measure:*— measure.

4462. מְמוּכָן **Mᵉmûwkân**, *mem-oo-kawn´;* or (transp.)

מוֹמֻכָן **Môwmûkân** (Esth. 1:16), *mo-moo-kawn´;* of Pers. der.; *Memucan* or *Momucan,* a Pers. satrap:— Memucan.

4463. מָמוֹת **mâmôwth**, *maw-mothe´;* from 4191; a mortal *disease;* concr. a *corpse:*— death.

4464. מַמְזֵר **mamzêr**, *mam-zare´;* from an unused root mean. to *alienate;* a *mongrel,* i.e. born of a Jewish father and a heathen mother:— bastard.

4465. מִמְכָּר **mimkâr**, *mim-kawr´;* from 4376; *merchandise;* abstr. a *selling:*— × ought, (that which cometh of) sale, that which ... sold, ware.

4466. מִמְכֶּרֶת **mimkereth**, *mim-keh´-reth;* fem. of 4465; a *sale:*— + sold as.

4467. מַמְלָכָה **mamlâkâh**, *mam-law-kaw´;* from 4427; *dominion,* i.e. (abstr.) the *estate* (rule) or (concr.) the *country* (realm):— kingdom, king's, reign, royal.

4468. מַמְלָכוּת **mamlâkûwth**, *mam-law-kooth´;* a form of 4467 and equiv. to it:— kingdom, reign.

4469. מַמְסָךְ **mamçâk**, *mam-sawk´;* from 4537; *mixture,* i.e. (spec.) wine *mixed* (with water or spices):— drink-offering, mixed wine.

4470. מֶמֶר **memer**, *meh´-mer;* from an unused root mean. to *grieve; sorrow:*— bitterness.

4471. מַמְרֵא **Mamrê'**, *mam-ray';* from 4754 (in the sense of *vigor*); *lusty; Mamre,* an Amorite:— Mamre.

4472. מַמְרֹר **mamrôr**, *mam-rore';* from 4843; a *bitterness,* i.e. (fig.) *calamity:*— bitterness.

4473. מִמְשַׁח **mimshach**, *mim-shakh';* from 4886, in the sense of *expansion; outspread* (i.e. with outstretched wings):— anointed.

4474. מִמְשָׁל **mimshâl**, *mim-shawl';* from 4910; a *ruler* or (abstr.) *rule:*— dominion, that ruled.

4475. מֶמְשָׁלָה **memshâlâh**, *mem-shaw-law';* fem. of 4474; *rule;* also (concr. in plur.) a *realm* or a *ruler:*— dominion, government, power, to rule.

4476. מִמְשָׁק **mimshâq**, *mim-shawk';* from the same as 4943; a *possession:*— breeding.

4477. מַמְתַּק **mamtaq**, *mam-tak';* from 4985; something *sweet* (lit. or fig.):— (most) sweet.

4478. מָן **mân**, *mawn;* from 4100; lit. a *whatness* (so to speak), i.e. *manna* (so called from the question about it):— manna.

4479. מָן **mân** (Chald.), *mawn;* from 4101; *who* or *what* (prop. interrog., hence, also indef. and rel.):— what, who (-msoever, + -so).

4480. מִן **min**, *min;* or

מִנִּי **minnîy**, *min-nee';* or

מִנֵּי **minnêy** (constr. plur.) *min-nay';* (Isa. 30:11); for 4482; prop. a *part* of; hence, (prep.), *from* or *out of* in many senses (as follows):— above, after, among, at, because of, by (reason of), from (among), in, × neither, × nor, (out) of, over, since, × then, through, × whether, with.

4481. מִן **min** (Chald.), *min;* corresp. to 4480:— according, after, + because, + before, by, for, from, × him, × more than, (out) of, part, since, × these, to, upon, + when.

4482. מֵן **mên**, *mane;* from an unused root mean. to *apportion;* a *part;* hence, a musical *chord* (as parted into strings):— in [the same] (Psa. 68:23), stringed instrument (Psa. 150:4), whereby (Psa. 45:8 [*defective plur.*]).

4483. מְנָא **menâ'** (Chald.), *men-aw';* or

מְנָה **menâh** (Chald.) *men-aw';* corresp. to 4487; to *count, appoint:*— number, ordain, set.

4484. מְנֵא **menê'** (Chald.), *men-ay';* pass. part. of 4483; *numbered:*— Mene.

4485. מַנְגִּינָה **mangîynâh**, *man-ghee-naw';* from 5059; a *satire:*— music.

מִנְדָּה **mindâh**. See 4061.

4486. מַנְדַּע **manda'** (Chald.), *man-dah';* corresp. to 4093; *wisdom* or *intelligence:*— knowledge, reason, understanding.

מְנָה **menâh**. See 4483.

4487. מָנָה **mânâh**, *maw-naw';* a prim. root; prop. to *weigh* out; by impl. to *allot* or constitute officially; also to *enumerate* or enroll:— appoint, count, number, prepare, set, tell.

4488. מָנֶה **mâneh**, *maw-neh';* from 4487; prop. a fixed *weight* or measured amount, i.e. (techn.) a *maneh* or *mina:*— maneh, pound.

4489. מֹנֶה **môneh**, *mo-neh';* from 4487; prop. something *weighed* out, i.e. (fig.) a *portion* of time, i.e. an *instance:*— time.

4490. מָנָה **mânâh**, *maw-naw';* from 4487; prop. something *weighed* out, i.e. (gen.) a *division;* spec. (of food) a *ration;* also a *lot:*— such things as belonged, part, portion.

4491. מִנְהָג **minhâg**, *min-hawg';* from 5090; the *driving* (of a chariot):— driving.

4492. מִנְהָרָה **minhârâh**, *min-haw-raw';* from 5102; prop. a *channel* or fissure, i.e. (by impl.) a *cavern:*— den.

4493. מָנוֹד **mânôwd**, *maw-node';* from 5110 a *nodding* or *toss* (of the head in derision):— shaking.

4494. מָנוֹחַ **mânôwach**, *maw-no'-akh;* from 5117; *quiet,* i.e. (concr.) a *settled spot,* or (fig.) a *home:*— (place of) rest.

4495. מָנוֹחַ **Mânôwach**, *maw-no'-akh;* the same as 4494; *rest; Manoach,* an Isr.:— Manoah.

4496. מְנוּחָה **menûwchâh**, *men-oo-khaw';* or

מְנֻחָה **menûchâh**, *men-oo-khaw';* fem. of 4495; *repose* or (adv.) *peacefully;* fig. *consolation* (spec. *matrimony*); hence, (concr.) an *abode:*— comfortable, ease, quiet, rest (-ing place), still.

4497. מָנוֹן **mânôwn**, *maw-nohn';* from 5125; a *continuator,* i.e. *heir:*— son.

4498. מָנוֹס **mânôwç**, *maw-noce';* from 5127; a *retreat* (lit. or fig.); abstr. a *fleeing:*— × apace, escape, way to flee, flight, refuge.

4499. מְנוּסָה **menuwçâh**, *men-oo-saw';* or

מְנֻסָה **menûçâh**, *men-oo-saw';* fem. of 4498; *retreat:*— fleeing, flight.

4500. מָנוֹר **mânôwr**, *maw-nore';* from 5214; a *yoke* (prop. for *plowing*), i.e. the *frame* of a loom:— beam.

4501. מְנוֹרָה **menôwrâh**, *men-o-raw';* or

מְנֹרָה **menôrâh**, *men-o-raw';* fem. of 4500 (in the orig. sense of 5216); a *chandelier:*— candlestick.

4502. מִנְּזָר **minnezâr**, *min-ez-awr';* from 5144; a *prince:*— crowned.

4503. מִנְחָה **minchâh**, *min-khaw';* from an unused root mean. to *apportion,* i.e. *bestow;* a *donation;* euphem. *tribute;* spec. a sacrificial *offering* (usually bloodless and voluntary):— gift, oblation, (meat) offering, present, sacrifice.

4504. מִנְחָה **minchâh** (Chald.), *min-khaw´*; corresp. to 4503; a sacrificial *offering:*— oblation, meat offering.

מְנֻחָה **menûchâh**. See 4496.

מְנֻחוֹת **Menûchôwth**. See 2679.

4505. מְנַחֵם **Menachêm**, *men-akh-ame´*; from 5162; *comforter; Menachem*, an Isr.:— Menahem.

4506. מָנַחַת **Mânachath**, *maw-nakh´-ath;* from 5117; *rest; Manachath*, the name of an Edomite and of a place in Moab:— Manahath.

מְנַחְתִּי **Menachtîy**. See 2680.

4507. מְנִי **Menîy**, *men-ee´;* from 4487; the *Apportioner*, i.e. Fate (as an idol):— number.

מִנִּי **mînnîy**. See 4480, 4482.

4508. מִנִּי **Minnîy**, *min-nee´;* of for. der.; *Minni*, an Armenian province:— Minni.

מְנָיוֹת **menâyôwth**. See 4521.

4509. מִנְיָמִין **Minyâmîyn**, *min-yaw-meen´;* from 4480 and 3225; *from* (the) *right hand; Minjamin*, the name of two Isr.:— Miniamin. Comp. 4326.

4510. מִנְיָן **minyân** (Chald.), *min-yawn´;* from 4483; *enumeration:*— number.

4511. מִנִּית **Minnîyth**, *min-neeth´;* from the same as 4482; *enumeration; Minnith*, a place E. of the Jordan:— Minnith.

4512. מִנְלֶה **minleh**, *min-leh´;* from 5239; *completion*, i.e. (in produce) *wealth:*— perfection.

מְנֻחָה **menûçâh**. See 4499.

4513. מָנַע **mâna'**, *maw-nah´;* a prim. root; to *debar* (neg. or pos.) from benefit or injury:— deny, keep (back), refrain, restrain, withhold.

4514. מַנְעוּל **man'ûwl**, *man-ool´;* or

מַנְעֻל **man'ûl**, *man-ool´;* from 5274; a *bolt:*— lock.

4515. מַנְעָל **man'âl**, *man-awl´;* from 5274; a *bolt:*— shoe.

4516. מַנְעַם **man'am**, *man-am´;* from 5276; a *delicacy:*— dainty.

4517. מְנַעֲנַע **mena'na'**, *men-ah-ah´;* from 5128; a *sistrum* (so called from its *rattling* sound):— cornet.

4518. מְנַקִּית **menaqqîyth**, *men-ak-keeth´;* from 5352; a *sacrificial basin* (for holding blood):— bowl.

מְנֹרָה **menôrâh**. See 4501.

4519. מְנַשֶּׁה **Menashsheh**, *men-ash-sheh´;* from 5382; *causing to forget; Menashsheh*, a grandson of Jacob, also the tribe descended from him, and its territory:— Manasseh.

4520. מְנַשִּׁי **Menashshîy**, *men-ash-shee´;* from 4519; a *Menashshite* or desc. of Menashsheh:— of Manasseh, Manassites.

4521. מְנָת **menâth**, *men-awth´;* from 4487; an *allotment* (by courtesy, law or providence):— portion.

4522. מַס **maç**, *mas;* or

מִס **miç**, *mees;* from 4549; prop. a *burden* (as causing to *faint*), i.e. a *tax* in the form of forced *labor:*— discomfited, levy, task [-master], tribute (-tary).

4523. מָס **mâç**, *mawce;* from 4549; *fainting*, i.e. (fig.) *disconsolate:*— is afflicted.

4524. מֵסַב **mêçab**, *may-sab´;* plur. masc.

מְסִבִּים **meçîbbîym**, *mes-ib-beem´;* or fem.

מְסִבּוֹת **meçîbbôwth**, *mes-ib-bohht´;* from 5437; a *divan* (as *enclosing* the room); abstr. (adv.) *around:*— that compass about, (place) round about, at table.

מְסֻבָּה **mûçabbâh**. See 4142.

4525. מַסְגֵּר **maçgêr**, *mas-gare´;* from 5462; a *fastener*, i.e. (of a person) a *smith*, (of a thing) a *prison:*— prison, smith.

4526. מִסְגֶּרֶת **miçgereth**, *mis-gheh´-reth;* from 5462; something *enclosing*, i.e. a *margin* (of a region, of a panel); concr. a *stronghold:*— border, close place, hole.

4527. מַסַּד **maççad**, *mas-sad´;* from 3245; a *foundation:*— foundation.

מוֹסָדָה **môçâdâh**. See 4146.

4528. מִסְדְּרוֹן **miçderôwn**, *mis-der-ohn´;* from the same as 5468; a *colonnade* or *internal portico* (from its *rows* of pillars):— porch.

4529. מָסָה **mâçâh**, *maw-saw´;* a prim. root; to *dissolve:*— make to consume away, (make to) melt, water.

4530. מִסָּה **miççâh**, *mis-saw´;* from 4549 (in the sense of *flowing*); *abundance*, i.e. (adv.) *liberally:*— tribute.

4531. מַסָּה **maççâh**, *mas-saw´;* from 5254; a *testing*, of men (judicial) or of God (querulous):— temptation, trial.

4532. מַסָּה **Maççâh**, *mas-saw´;* the same as 4531; *Massah*, a place in the Desert:— Massah.

4533. מַסְוֶה **maçveh**, *mas-veh´;* appar. from an unused root mean. to *cover;* a *veil:*— vail.

4534. מְסוּכָה **meçûwkâh**, *mes-oo-kaw´;* for 4881; a *hedge:*— thorn hedge.

4535. מַסָּח **maççâch**, *mas-sawkh´;* from 5255 in the sense of *staving* off; a *cordon*, (adv.) or (as a) military *barrier:*— broken down.

4536. מִסְחָר **miçchâr**, *mis-khawr´;* from 5503; *trade:*— traffic.

4537. מָסַךְ **mâçak**, *maw-sak´;* a prim. root; to *mix*, espec. wine (with spices):— mingle.

4538. מֶסֶךְ **meçek**, *meh´-sek;* from 4537; a *mixture*, i.e. of wine with spices:— mixture.

4539. מָסָךְ **mâçâk**, *maw-sawk´;* from 5526; a *cover*, i.e. *veil:*— covering, curtain, hanging.

4540. מְסֻכָּה **mᵉçukkâh**, *mes-ook-kaw´;* from 5526; a *covering*, i.e. garniture:— covering.

4541. מַסֵּכָה **maççêkâh**, *mas-say-kaw´;* from 5258; prop. a *pouring* over, i.e. *fusion* of metal (espec. a *cast* image); by impl. a *libation*, i.e. league; concr. a *coverlet* (as if *poured* out):— covering, molten (image), vail.

4542. מִסְכֵּן **miçkên**, *mis-kane´;* from 5531; *indigent:*— poor (man).

4543. מִסְכְּנָה **miçkᵉnâh**, *mis-ken-aw´;* by transp. from 3664; a *magazine:*— store (-house), treasure.

4544. מִסְכְּנֻת **miçkênûth**, *mis-kay-nooth´;* from 4542; *indigence:*— scarceness.

4545. מַסֶּכֶת **maççeketh**, *mas-seh´-keth;* from 5259 in the sense of *spreading* out; something *expanded*, i.e. the *warp* in a loom (as *stretched* out to receive the woof):— web.

4546. מְסִלָּה **mᵉçillâh**, *mes-il-law´;* from 5549; a *thoroughfare* (as *turnpiked*), lit. or fig.; spec. a *viaduct*, a *staircase:*— causeway, course, highway, path, terrace.

4547. מַסְלוּל **maçlûl**, *mas-lool´;* from 5549; a *thoroughfare* (as turnpiked):— highway.

4548. מַסְמֵר **maçmêr**, *mas-mare´;* or

מִסְמֵר **miçmêr**, *mis-mare´;* also (fem.)

מַסְמְרָה **maçmᵉrâh**, *mas-mer-aw´;* or

מִסְמְרָה **miçmᵉrâh**, *mis-mer-aw´;* or even

מַשְׂמְרָה **masmᵉrâh** (Eccles. 12:11), *mas-mer-aw´;* from 5568; a *peg* (as *bristling* from the surface):— nail.

4549. מָסַס **mâçaç**, *maw-sas´;* a prim. root; to *liquefy;* fig. to *waste* (with disease), to *faint* (with fatigue, fear or grief):— discourage, faint, be loosed, melt (away), refuse, × utterly.

4550. מַסַּע **maççaʻ**, *mas-sah´;* from 5265; a *departure* (from *striking* the tents), i.e. march (not necessarily a single day's travel); by impl. a *station* (or point of *departure*):— journey (-ing).

4551. מַסָּע **maççâʻ**, *mas-saw´;* from 5265 in the sense of *projecting;* a *missile* (spear or arrow); also a *quarry* (whence stones are, as it were, *ejected*):— before it was brought, dart.

4552. מִסְעָד **miçʻâd**, *mis-awd´* from 5582; a *balustrade* (for stairs):— pillar.

4553. מִסְפֵּד **miçpêd**, *mis-pade´;* from 5594; a *lamentation:*— lamentation, one mourneth, mourning, wailing.

4554. מִסְפּוֹא **miçpôw'**, *mis-po´;* from an unused root mean. to *collect; fodder:*— provender.

4555. מִסְפָּחָה **miçpâchâh**, *mis-paw-khaw´;* from 5596; a *veil* (as *spread* out):— kerchief.

4556. מִסְפַּחַת **miçpachath**, *mis-pakh´-ath;* from 5596; *scruf* (as *spreading* over the surface):— scab.

4557. מִסְפָּר **miçpâr**, *mis-pawr´;* from 5608; a *number*, def. (arithmetical) or indef. (large, *innumerable;* small, a *few*); also (abstr.) *narration:*— + abundance, account, × all, × few, [in-]finite, (certain) number (-ed), tale, telling, + time.

4558. מִסְפָּר **Miçpâr**, *mis-pawr´;* the same as 4457; *number; Mispar*, an Isr.:— Mizpar. Comp. 4559.

מֹסְרוֹת **Môçᵉrowth**. See 4149.

4559. מִסְפֶּרֶת **Miçpereth**, *mis-peh´-reth;* fem. of 4457; *enumeration; Mispereth*, an Isr.:— Mispereth. Comp. 4458.

4560. מָסַר **mâçar**, *maw-sar´;* a prim. root; to *sunder*, i.e. (tran.) *set apart*, or (reflex.) *apostatize:*— commit, deliver.

4561. מֹסָר **môçâr**, *mo-sawr´;* from 3256; *admonition:*— instruction.

4562. מָסֹרֶת **mâçôreth**, *maw-so´-reth;* from 631; a *band:*— bond.

4563. מִסְתּוֹר **miçtôwr**, *mis-tore´;* from 5641; a *refuge:*— covert.

4564. מַסְתֵּר **maçtêr**, *mas-tare´;* from 5641; prop. a *hider*, i.e. (abstr.) a *hiding*, i.e. *aversion:*— hid.

4565. מִסְתָּר **miçtâr**, *mis-tawr´;* from 5641; prop. a *concealer*, i.e. a *covert:*— secret (-ly), place).

מֵעָא **mᵉʻâ'**. See 4577.

4566. מַעְבָּד **maʻbâd**, *mah-bawd´;* from 5647; an *act:*— work.

4567. מַעְבָּד **maʻbâd** (Chald.), *mah-bawd´;* corresp. to 4566; an *act:*— work.

4568. מַעֲבֶה **maʻăbeh**, *mah-ab-eh´;* from 5666; prop. *compact* (part of soil), i.e. *loam:*— clay.

4569. מַעֲבָר **maʻăbâr**, *mah-ab-awr´;* or fem.

מַעֲבָרָה **maʻăbârâh**, *mah-ab-aw-raw´;* from 5674; a *crossing*-place (of a river, a *ford;* of a mountain, a *pass*); abstr. a *transit*, i.e. (fig.) *overwhelming:*— ford, place where ... pass, passage.

4570. מַעְגָּל **maʻgâl**, *mah-gawl´;* or fem.

מַעְגָּלָה **maʻgâlâh**, *mah-gaw-law´;* from the same as 5696; a *track* (lit. or fig.); also a *rampart* (as *circular*):— going, path, trench, way (I-side).

4571. מָעַד **mâ'ad**, *maw-ad´*; a prim. root; to *waver*:— make to shake, slide, slip.

מוֹעֵד **mô'êd**. See 4150.

4572. מֵעֲדַי **Ma'ăday**, *mah-ad-ah´-ee*; from 5710; *ornamental*; *Maadai*, an Isr.:— Maadai.

4573. מַעֲדְיָה **Ma'adyâh**, *mah-ad-yaw´*; from 5710 and 3050; *ornament of Jah*; *Maadjah*, an Isr.:— Maadiah. Comp. 4153.

4574. מַעֲדָן **ma'ădân**, *mah-ad-awn´*; or (fem.)

מַעֲדַנָּה **ma'ădannâh**, *mah-ad-an-naw´*; from 5727; a *delicacy* or (abstr.) *pleasure* (adv. *cheerfully*):— dainty, delicately, delight.

4575. מַעֲדַנָּה **ma'ădannâh**, *mah-ad-an-naw´*; by tran. from 6029; a *bond*, i.e. *group*:— influence.

4576. מַעְדֵּר **ma'dêr**, *mah-dare´*; from 5737; a (weeding) *hoe*:— mattock.

4577. מְעָה **me'âh** (Chald.), *meh-aw´*; or

מְעָא **me'â'** (Chald.), *meh-aw´*; corresp. to 4578; only in plur. the *bowels*:— belly.

4578. מֵעֶה **mê'âh**, *may-aw´*; from an unused root prob. mean. to *be soft*; used only in plur. the *intestines*, or (collect.) the *abdomen*, fig. *sympathy*; by impl. a *vest*; by extens. the *stomach*, the *uterus* (or of men, the seat of generation), the *heart* (fig.):— belly, bowels, × heart, womb.

4579. מֵעֶה **mê'âh**, *may-aw´*; fem. of 4578; the *belly*, i.e. (fig.) interior:— gravel.

4580. מָעוֹג **mâ'ôwg**, *maw-ogue´*; from 5746; a *cake* of bread (with 3934 a *table-buffoon*, i.e. *parasite*):— cake, feast.

4581. מָעוֹז **mâ'ôwz**, *maw-oze´* (also

מָעוּז **mâ'ûwz**, *maw-ooz´*); or

מָעֹז **mâ'ôz**, *maw-oze´* (also

מָעֻז **mâ'ûz**, *maw-ooz´*); from 5810; a *fortified* place; fig. a *defence*:— force, fort (-ress), rock, strength (-en), (× most) strong (hold).

4582. מָעוֹךְ **Mâ'ôwk**, *maw-oke´*; from 4600; *oppressed*; *Maok*, a Philistine:— Maoch.

4583. מָעוֹן **mâ'ôwn**, *maw-ohn´*; or

מָעִין° **mâ'îyn** (1 Chron. 4:41), *maw-een´*; from the same as 5772; an *abode*, of God (the Tabernacle or the Temple), men (their home) or animals (their lair); hence, a *retreat* (asylum):— den, dwelling ([-] place), habitation.

4584. מָעוֹן **Mâ'ôwn**, *maw-ohn´*; the same as 4583; a *residence*; *Maon*, the name of an Isr. and of a place in Pal.:— Maon, Maonites. Comp. 1010, 4586.

4585. מְעוֹנָה **me'ôwnâh**, *meh-o-naw´*; or

מְעֹנָה **me'ônâh**, *meh-o-naw´*; fem. of 4583, and mean. the same:— den, habitation, (dwelling) place, refuge.

4586. מְעוּנִי **Me'ûwnîy**, *meh-oo-nee´*; or

4587. מְעוֹנֹתַי **Me'ôwnôthay**, *meh-o-no-thah´-ee*; plur. of 4585; *habitative*; *Meonothai*, an Isr.:— Meonothai.

4588. מָעוּף **mâ'ûwph**, *maw-off´*; from 5774 in the sense of *covering* with shade [comp. 4155]; *darkness*:— dimness.

4589. מָעוֹר **mâ'ôwr**, *maw-ore´*; from 5783; *nakedness*, i.e. (in plur.) the *pudenda*:— nakedness.

מָעוֹז **mâ'ôz**. See 4581.

מָעֻז **mâ'ûz**. See 4581.

4590. מַעַזְיָה **Ma'azyâh**, *mah-az-yaw´*; or

מַעַזְיָהוּ **Ma'azyâhûw**, *mah-az-yaw´-hoo*; prob. from 5756 (in the sense of *protection*) and 3050; *rescue of Jah*; *Maazjah*, the name of two Isr.:— Maaziah.

4591. מָעַט **mâ'aṭ**, *maw-at´*; a prim. root; prop. to *pare off*, i.e. *lessen*; intr. to *be* (or caus. to *make*) *small* or *few* (or fig. *ineffective*):— suffer to decrease, diminish, (be, × borrow a, give, make) few (in number, -ness), gather least (little), be (seem) little, (× give the) less, be minished, bring to nothing.

4592. מְעַט **me'aṭ**, *meh-at´*; or

מְעָט **me'âṭ**, *meh-awt´*; from 4591; a *little* or *few* (often adv. or compar.):— almost, (some, very) few (-er, -est), lightly, little (while), (very) small (matter, thing), some, soon, × very.

4593. מָעֹט **mâ'ôṭ**, *maw-ote´*; pass. adj. of 4591; *thinned* (as to the edge), i.e. *sharp*:— wrapped up.

4594. מַעֲטֶה **ma'ăṭeh**, *mah-at-eh´*; from 5844; a *vestment*:— garment.

4595. מַעֲטָפָה **ma'ăṭâphâh**, *mah-at-aw-faw´*; from 5848; a *cloak*:— mantle.

4596. מְעִי **me'îy**, *meh-ee´*; from 5753; a *pile* of rubbish (as *contorted*), i.e. a *ruin* (comp. 5856):— heap.

4597. מָעַי **Mâ'ay**, *maw-ah´-ee*; prob. from 4578; *sympathetic*; *Maai*, an Isr.:— Maai.

4598. מְעִיל **me'îyl**, *meh-eel´*; from 4603 in the sense of *covering*; a *robe* (i.e. upper and outer *garment*):— cloke, coat, mantle, robe.

מֵעִים **mê'îym**. See 4578.

מְעִין **me'îyn** (Chald.). See 4577.

4599. מַעְיָן **ma'yân**, *mah-yawn´*; or

מַעְיְנוֹ **ma'yenôw** (Psa. 114:8) *mah-yeno´*; or (fem.)

מַעְיָנָה **ma'yânâh**, *mah-yaw-naw´*;

from 5869 (as a denom. in the sense of a *spring*); a *fountain* (also collect.), fig. a *source* (of satisfaction):— fountain, spring, well.

מְעִינִי° **Me'îynîy**. See 4586.

4600. מָעַךְ **mâ'ak**, *maw-ak´*; a prim. root; to *press*, i.e. to *pierce, emasculate, handle:*— bruised, stuck, be pressed.

4601. מַעֲכָה **Ma'ăkâh**, *mah-ak-aw´*; or

מַעֲכָת **Ma'ăkâth** (Josh. 13:13), *mah-ak-awth´*; from 4600; *depression; Maakah* (or *Maakath*), the name of a place in Syria, also of a Mesopotamian, of three Isr., and of four Israelitesses and one Syrian woman:— Maachah, Maachathites. See also 1038.

4602. מַעֲכָתִי **Ma'ăkâthîy**, *mah-ak-aw-thee´*; patrial from 4601; a *Maakathite*, or inhab. of Maakah:— Maachathite.

4603. מָעַל **mâ'al**, *maw-al´*; a prim. root; prop. to *cover* up; used only fig. to *act covertly*, i.e. *treacherously:*— transgress, (commit, do a) trespass (-ing).

4604. מַעַל **ma'al**, *mah´-al*; from 4603; *treachery*, i.e. sin:— falsehood, grievously, sore, transgression, trespass, × very.

4605. מַעַל **ma'al**, *mah´al*; from 5927; prop. the *upper* part, used only adv. with pref. *upward, above, overhead, from the top*, etc.:— above, exceeding (-ly), forward, on (× very) high, over, up (-on, -ward), very.

מֵעַל **mê'al**. See 5921.

4606. מֵעַל **mê'al** (Chald.), *may-awl´*; from 5954; (only in plur. as sing.) the *setting* (of the sun):— going down.

4607. מֹעַל **mô'al**, *mo´-al*; from 5927; a *raising* (of the hands):— lifting up.

4608. מַעֲלֶה **ma'ăleh**, *mah-al-eh´*; from 5927; an *elevation*, i.e. (concr.) *acclivity* or *platform*; abstr. (the relation or state) a *rise* or (fig.) *priority:*— ascent, before, chiefest, cliff, that goeth up, going up, hill, mounting up, stairs.

4609. מַעֲלָה **ma'ălâh**, *mah-al-aw´*; fem. of 4608; *elevation*, i.e. the act (lit. a *journey* to a higher place, fig. a *thought* arising), or (concr.) the *condition* (lit. a *step* or *grade*-mark, fig. a *superiority* of station); spec. a climactic *progression* (in certain Psalms):— things that come up, (high) degree, deal, go up, stair, step, story.

4610. מַעֲלֵה עַקְרַבִּים **Ma'ălêh 'Aqrabbîym**, *mah-al-ay´ ak-rab-beem´*; from 4608 and (the plur. of) 6137; *Steep of Scorpions*, a place in the Desert:— Maaleh-accrabim, the ascent (going up) of Akrabbim.

4611. מַעֲלָל **ma'ălâl**, *mah-al-awl´*; from 5953; an *act* (good or bad):— doing, endeavour, invention, work.

4612. מַעֲמָד **ma'ămâd**, *mah-am-awd´*; from 5975; (fig.) a *position:*— attendance, office, place, state.

4613. מׇעֳמָד **mo'ŏmâd**, *moh-om-awd´*; from 5975; lit. a *foothold:*— standing.

4614. מַעֲמָסָה **ma'ămâçâh**, *mah-am-aw-saw´*; from 6006; *burdensomeness:*— burdensome.

4615. מַעֲמָק **ma'ămâq**, *mah-am-awk´*; from 6009; a *deep:*— deep, depth.

4616. מַעַן **ma'an**, *mah´-an*; from 6030; prop. *heed*, i.e. *purpose*; used only adv., *on account of* (as a motive or an aim), teleologically *in order that:*— because of, to the end (intent) that, for (to, … 's sake), + lest, that, to.

4617. מַעֲנֶה **ma'ăneh**, *mah-an-eh´*; from 6030; a *reply* (favorable or contradictory):— answer, × himself.

4618. מַעֲנָה **ma'ănâh**, *mah-an-aw´*; from 6031, in the sense of *depression* or *tilling*; a *furrow:*— + acre, furrow.

מְעֹנָה **me'ônâh**. See 4585.

4619. מַעַץ **Ma'ats**, *mah´-ats*; from 6095; *closure; Maats*, an Isr.:— Maaz.

4620. מַעֲצֵבָה **ma'ătsêbâh**, *mah-ats-ay-baw´*; from 6087; *anguish:*— sorrow.

4621. מַעֲצָד **ma'ătsâd**, *mah-ats-awd´*; from an unused root mean. to *hew*; an *axe:*— ax, tongs.

4622. מַעְצוֹר **ma'tsôwr**, *mah-tsore´*; from 6113; obj. a *hindrance:*— restraint.

4623. מַעְצָר **ma'tsâr**, *mah-tsawr´*; from 6113; subj. *control:*— rule.

4624. מַעֲקֶה **ma'ăqeh**, *mah-ak-eh´*; from an unused root mean. to *repress*; a *parapet:*— battlement.

4625. מַעֲקָשׁ **ma'ăqâsh**, *mah-ak-awsh´*; from 6140; a *crook* (in a road):— crooked thing.

4626. מַעַר **ma'ar**, *mah´-ar*; from 6168; a *nude* place, i.e. (lit.) the *pudenda*, or (fig.) a vacant *space:*— nakedness, proportion.

4627. מַעֲרָב **ma'ărâb**, *mah-ar-awb´*; from 6148, in the sense of *trading; traffic*; by impl. mercantile *goods:*— market, merchandise.

4628. מַעֲרָב **ma'ărâb**, *mah-ar-awb´*; or (fem.)

מַעֲרָבָה **ma'ărâbâh**, *mah-ar-aw-baw´*; from 6150, in the sense of *shading*; the *west* (as a region of the *evening* sun):— west.

4629. מַעֲרֶה **ma'ăreh**, *mah-ar-eh´*; from 6168; a *nude* place, i.e. a *common:*— meadows.

4630. מַעֲרָה° **ma'ărâh**, *mah-ar-aw´*; fem. of 4629; an *open* spot:— army [*from the marg.*].

4631. מְעָרָה **m^e'ârâh**, *meh-aw-raw´*; from 5783; a *cavern* (as dark):— cave, den, hole.

4632. מְעָרָה **M^e'ârâh**, *meh-aw-raw´*; the same as 4631; *cave*; *Meärah*, a place in Pal.:— Mearah.

4633. מַעֲרָךְ **ma'ărâk**, *mah-ar-awk´*; from 6186; an *arrangement*, i.e. (fig.) mental *disposition:*— preparation.

4634. מַעֲרָכָה **ma'ărâkâh**, *mah-ar-aw-kaw´*; fem. of 4633; an *arrangement*; concr. a *pile*; spec. a military *array:*— army, fight, be set in order, ordered place, rank, row.

4635. מַעֲרֶכֶת **ma'ăreketh**, *mah-ar-eh´-keth*; from 6186; an *arrangement*, i.e. (concr.) a *pile* (of loaves):— row, shewbread.

4636. מַעֲרֹם **ma'ărôm**, *mah-ar-ome´*; from 6191, in the sense of *stripping; bare:*— naked.

4637. מַעֲרָצָה **ma'ărâtsâh**, *mah-ar-aw-tsaw´*; from 6206; *violence:*— terror.

4638. מַעֲרָת **Ma'ărâth**, *mah-ar-awth´*; a form of 4630; *waste*; *Maarath*, a place in Pal.:— Maarath.

4639. מַעֲשֶׂה **ma'ăseh**, *mah-as-eh´*; from 6213; an *action* (good or bad); gen. a *transaction*; abstr. *activity*; by impl. a *product* (spec. a *poem*) or (gen.) *property:*— act, art, + bakemeat, business, deed, do (-ing), labour, thing made, ware of making, occupation, thing offered, operation, possession, × well, (handy-, needle-, net-l) work (ing, -manship), wrought.

4640. מַעֲשַׂי **Ma'say**, *mah-as-ah´ee*; from 6213; *operative; Maasai*, an Isr.:— Maasiai.

4641. מַעֲשֵׂיָה **Ma'ăsêyâh**, *mah-as-ay-yaw´*; or

מַעֲשֵׂיָהוּ **Ma'ăsêyâhûw**, *mah-as-ay-yaw´-hoo*; from 4639 and 3050; *work of Jah; Maasejah*, the name of sixteen Isr.:— Maaseiah.

4642. מַעֲשַׁקָּה **ma'ăshaqqâh**, *mah-ash-ak-kaw´*; from 6231; *oppression:*— oppression, × oppressor.

4643. מַעֲשֵׂר **ma'ăsêr**, *mah-as-ayr´*; or

מַעֲשַׂר **ma'ăsar**, *mah-as-ar´*; and (in plur.) fem.

מַעֲשָׂרָה **ma'asrâh**, *mah-as-raw´*; from 6240; a *tenth;* espec. a *tithe:*— tenth (part), tithe (-ing).

4644. מֹף **Môph**, *mofe;* of Eg. or.; *Moph*, the capital of Lower Egypt:— Memphis. Comp. 5297.

מְפִיבֹשֶׁת **M^ephîbôsheth.** See 4648.

4645. מִפְגָּע **miphgâ'**, *mif-gaw´*; from 6293; an *object of attack:*— mark.

4646. מַפָּח **mappâch**, *map-pawkh´*; from 5301; a *breathing out* (of life), i.e. expiring:— giving up.

4647. מַפֻּחַ **mappûach**, *map-poo´-akh;* from

5301; the *bellows* (i.e. *blower*) of a forge:— bellows.

4648. מְפִיבֹשֶׁת **M^ephîybôsheth**, *mef-ee-bo´-sheth;* or

מְפִבֹשֶׁת **M^ephîbôsheth**, *mef-ee-bo´-sheth;* prob. from 6284 and 1322; *dispeller of shame* (i.e. of Baal); *Mephibosheth*, the name of two Isr.:— Mephibosheth.

4649. מֻפִּים **Muppîym**, *moop-peem´;* a plur. appar. from 5130; *wavings; Muppim*, an Isr.:— Muppim. Comp. 8206.

4650. מֵפִיץ **mêphîyts**, *may-feets´;* from 6327; a *breaker*, i.e. mallet:— maul.

4651. מַפָּל **mappâl**, *map-pawl´;* from 5307; a *falling* off, i.e. chaff; also something *pendulous*, i.e. a flap:— flake, refuse.

4652. מִפְלָאָה **miphlâ'âh**, *mif-law-aw´;* from 6381; a *miracle:*— wondrous work.

4653. מִפְלַגָּה **miphlaggâh**, *mif-lag-gaw´;* from 6385; a *classification:*— division.

4654. מַפָּלָה **mappâlâh**, *map-paw-law´;* or

מַפֵּלָה **mappêlâh**, *map-pay-law´;* from 5307; something *fallen*, i.e. a *ruin:*— ruin (-ous).

4655. מִפְלָט **miphlât**, *mif-lawt´;* from 6403; an *escape:*— escape.

4656. מִפְלֶצֶת **miphletseth**, *mif-leh´-tseth;* from 6426; a *terror*, i.e. an idol:— idol.

4657. מִפְלָשׂ **miphlâs**, *mif-lawce´;* from an unused root mean. to *balance*; a *poising:*— balancing.

4658. מַפֶּלֶת **mappeleth**, *map-peh´-leth;* from 5307; *fall*, i.e. *decadence*; concr. a *ruin*; spec. a *carcase:*— carcase, fall, ruin.

4659. מִפְעָל **miph'âl**, *mif-awl´;* or (fem.)

מִפְעָלָה **miph'âlâh**, *mif-aw-law´;* from 6466; a *performance:*— work.

4660. מַפָּץ **mappâts**, *map-pawts´;* from 5310; a *smiting* to pieces:— slaughter.

4661. מַפֵּץ **mappêts**, *map-pates´;* from 5310; a *smiter*, i.e. a war *club:*— battle ax.

4662. מִפְקָד **miphqâd**, *mif-kawd´;* from 6485; an *appointment*, i.e. *mandate*; concr. a designated *spot*; spec. a *census:*— appointed place, commandment, number.

4663. מִפְקָד **Miphqâd**, *mif-kawd´;* the same as 4662; *assignment; Miphkad*, the name of a gate in Jerusalem:— Miphkad.

4664. מִפְרָץ **miphrâts**, *mif-rawts´;* from 6555; a *break* (in the shore), i.e. a *haven:*— breach.

4665. מִפְרֶכֶת **miphreketh**, *mif-reh´-keth;* from 6561; prop. a *fracture*, i.e. *joint* (*vertebra*) of the neck:— neck.

4666. מִפְרָשׂ **miphrâs**, *mif-rawce´;* from 6566;

Hebrew

an *expansion:*— that which ... spreadest forth, spreading.

4667. מִפְשָׂעָה **miphsâ'âh**, *mif-saw-aw´;* from 6585; a *stride,* i.e. (by euphem.) the *crotch:*— buttocks.

מֹפֵת **môphêth.** See 4159.

4668. מַפְתֵּחַ **maphtêach**, *maf-tay´-akh;* from 6605; an *opener,* i.e. a *key:*— key.

4669. מִפְתָּח **miphtâch**, *mif-tawkh´;* from 6605; an *aperture,* i.e. (fig.) *utterance:*— opening.

4670. מִפְתָּן **miphtân**, *mif-tawn´;* from the same as 6620; a *stretcher,* i.e. a *sill:*— threshold.

4671. מֹץ **môts**, *motes;* or

מוֹץ **môwts** (Zeph. 2:2), *motes;* from 4160; *chaff* (as *pressed* out, i.e. *winnowed* or [rather] *threshed loose*):— chaff.

4672. מָצָא **mâtsâ'**, *maw-tsaw´;* a prim. root; prop. *to come forth to,* i.e. *appear* or *exist;* tran. *to attain,* i.e. *find* or *acquire;* fig. *to occur, meet* or *be present:*— + be able, befall, being, catch, × certainly, (cause to) come (on, to, to hand), deliver, be enough (cause to) find (-ing, occasion, out), get (hold upon), × have (here), be here, hit, be left, light (up-) on, meet (with), × occasion serve, (be) present, ready, speed, suffice, take hold on.

מֹצָא **môtsâ'**. See 4161.

4673. מַצָּב **matstsâb**, *mats-tsawb´;* from 5324; a fixed *spot;* fig. an *office,* a military *post:*— garrison, station, place where ... stood.

4674. מֻצָּב **mutstsâb**, *moots-tsawb´;* from 5324; a *station,* i.e. military *post:*— mount.

4675. מַצָּבָה **matstsâbâh**, *mats-tsaw-baw´;* or

מִצָּבָה **mitstsâbâh**, *mits-tsaw-baw´;* fem. of 4673; a military *guard:*— army, garrison.

4676. מַצֵּבָה **matstsêbâh**, *mats-tsay-baw´;* fem. (caus.) part. of 5324; something *stationed,* i.e. a *column* or (memorial *stone*); by anal. an *idol:*— garrison, (standing) image, pillar.

4677. מְצֹבָיָה **Metsôbâyâh**, *mets-o-baw-yaw´;* appar. from 4672 and 3050; *found of Jah;* Metsobajah, a place in Pal.:— Mesobaite.

4678. מַצֶּבֶת **matstsebeth**, *mats-tseh´-beth;* from 5324; something *stationary,* i.e. a monumental *stone;* also the *stock* of a tree:— pillar, substance.

4679. מְצַד **metsad**, *mets-ad´;* or

מְצָד **metsâd**, *mets-awd´;* or (fem.)

מְצָדָה **metsâdâh**, *mets-aw-daw´;* from 6679; a *fastness* (as a *covert* of ambush):— castle, fort, (strong) hold, munition.

מְצֻדָה **metsûdâh.** See 4686.

4680. מָצָה **mâtsâh**, *maw-tsaw´;* a prim. root; to *suck* out; by impl. to *drain,* to *squeeze* out:— suck, wring (out).

4681. מֹצָה **Môtsâh**, *mo-tsaw´;* act. part. fem. of 4680; *drained; Motsah,* a place in Pal.:— Mozah.

4682. מַצָּה **matstsâh**, *mats-tsaw´;* from 4711 in the sense of *greedily* devouring for sweetness; prop. *sweetness;* concr. *sweet* (i.e. not soured or bittered with yeast); spec. an *unfermented cake* or loaf, or (ellip.) the *festival* of *Passover* (because no leaven was then used):— unleavened (bread, cake), without leaven.

4683. מַצָּה **matstsâh**, *mats-tsaw´;* from 5327; a *quarrel:*— contention, debate, strife.

4684. מִצְהָלָה **matshâlâh**, *mats-haw-law´;* from 6670; a *whinnying* (through impatience for battle or lust):— neighing.

4685. מָצוֹד **mâtsôwd**, *maw-tsode´;* or (fem.)

מְצוֹדָה **metsôwdâh**, *mets-o-daw´;* or

מְצֹדָה **metsôdâh**, *mets-o-daw´;* from 6679; a *net* (for *capturing* animals or fishes); also (by interch. for 4679) a *fastness* or (besieging) *tower:*— bulwark, hold, munition, net, snare.

4686. מָצוּד **mâtsûwd**, *maw-tsood´;* or (fem.)

מְצוּדָה **metsûwdâh**, *mets-oo-daw´;* or

מְצֻדָה **metsûdâh**, *mets-oo-daw´;* for 4685; a *net,* or (abstr.) *capture;* also a *fastness:*— castle, defence, fort (-ress), (strong) hold, be hunted, net, snare, strong place.

4687. מִצְוָה **mitsvâh**, *mits-vaw´;* from 6680; a *command,* whether human or divine (collect. the *Law):*— (which was) commanded (-ment), law, ordinance, precept.

4688. מְצוֹלָה **metsôwlâh**, *mets-o-law´;* or

מְצֹלָה **metsôlâh**, *mets-o-law´;* also

מְצוּלָה **metsûwlâh**, *mets-oo-law´;* or

מְצֻלָה **metsûlâh**, *mets-oo-law´;* from the same as 6683; a *deep* place (of water or mud):— bottom, deep, depth.

4689. מָצוֹק **mâtsôwq**, *maw-tsoke´;* from 6693; a *narrow* place, i.e. (abstr. and fig.) *confinement* or *disability:*— anguish, distress, straitness.

4690. מָצוּק **mâtsûwq**, *maw-tsook´;* or

מָצֻק **mâtsûq**, *maw-tsook´;* from 6693; something *narrow,* i.e. a *column* or *hilltop:*— pillar, situate.

4691. מְצוּקָה **metsûwqâh**, *mets-oo-kaw´;* or

מְצֻקָה **metsûqâh**, *mets-oo-kaw´;* fem. of 4690; *narrowness,* i.e. (fig.) *trouble:*— anguish, distress.

4692. מָצוֹר **mâtsôwr**, *maw-tsore´;* or

מָצוּר **mâtsûwr**, *maw-tsoor´;* from 6696; something *hemming* in, i.e. (obj.) a *mound* (of besiegers), (abstr.) a *siege,* (fig.) *distress;* or (subj.) a *fastness:*— besieged, bulwark, defence, fenced, fortress, siege, strong (hold), tower.

4693. מָצוֹר **mâtsôwr**, *maw-tsore´*; the same as 4692 in the sense of a *limit*; *Egypt* (as the *border* of Pal.):— besieged places, defence, fortified.

4694. מְצוּרָה **m^etsûwrâh**, *mets-oo-raw´*; or

מְצֻרָה **m^etsûrâh**, *mets-oo-raw´*; fem. of 4692; a *hemming* in, i.e. (obj.) a *mound* (of siege), or (subj.) a *rampart* (of protection), (abstr.) *fortification*:— fenced (city), fort, munition, strong hold.

4695. מַצּוּת **matstsûwth**, *mats-tsooth´*; from 5327; a *quarrel*:— that contended.

4696. מֵצַח **mêtsach**, *may´-tsakh*; from an unused root mean. to *be clear*, i.e. *conspicuous*; the *forehead* (as *open* and *prominent*):— brow, forehead, + impudent.

4697. מִצְחָה **mitschâh**, *mits-khaw´*; from the same as 4696; a *shin-piece* of armor (as *prominent*), only plur.:— greaves.

מְצֹלָה **m^etsôlâh**. See 4688.

מְצֻלָה **m^etsûlâh**. See 4688.

4698. מְצִלָּה **m^etsillâh**, *mets-il-law´*; from 6750; a *tinkler*, i.e. a *bell*:— bell.

4699. מְצֻלָּה **m^etsullâh**, *mets-ool-law´*; from 6751; *shade*:— bottom.

4700. מְצֵלֶת **m^etsêleth**, *mets-ay´-leth*; from 6750; (only dual) double *tinklers*, i.e. cymbals:— cymbals.

4701. מִצְנֶפֶת **mitsnepheth**, *mits-neh´-feth*; from 6801; a *tiara*, i.e. official *turban* (of a king or high priest):— diadem, mitre.

4702. מַצָּע **matstsâ'**, *mats-tsaw´*; from 3331; a *couch*:— bed.

4703. מִצְעָד **mits'âd**, *mits-awd´*; from 6805; a *step*; fig. *companionship*:— going, step.

4704. מִצְעִירָה **mitsts^e'îyrâh**, *mits-tseh-ee-raw´*; fem. of 4705; prop. *littleness*; concr. *diminutive*:— little.

4705. מִצְעָר **mits'âr**, *mits-awr´*; from 6819; *petty* (in size or number); adv. a *short* (time):— little one (while), small.

4706. מִצְעָר **Mits'âr**, *mits-awr´*; the same as 4705; *Mitsar*, a peak of Lebanon:— Mizar.

4707. מִצְפֶּה **mitspeh**, *mits-peh´*; from 6822; an *observatory*, espec. for military purposes:— watch tower.

4708. מִצְפֶּה **Mitspeh**, *mits-peh´*; the same as 4707; *Mitspeh*, the name of five places in Pal.:— Mizpeh, watch tower. Comp. 4709.

4709. מִצְפָּה **Mitspah**, *mits-paw´*; fem. of 4708; *Mitspah*, the name of two places in Pal.:— Mitspah. [This seems rather to be only an orthographic var. of 4708 when "in pause".]

4710. מִצְפֻּן **mitspûn**, *mits-poon´*; from 6845; a

secret (place or thing, perh. *treasure*):— hidden thing.

4711. מָצַץ **mâtsats**, *maw-tsats´*; a prim. root; to *suck*:— milk.

מוּצָקָה **mûtsâqâh**. See 4166.

4712. מֵצַר **mêtsar**, *may-tsar´*; from 6896; something *tight*, i.e. (fig.) *trouble*:— distress, pain, strait.

מָצוּק **mâtsûq**. See 4690.

מְצוּקָה **m^etsûqâh**. See 4691.

מְצֻרָה **m^etsûrâh**. See 4694.

4713. מִצְרִי **Mitsrîy**, *mits-ree´*; from 4714; a *Mitsrite*, or inhab. of Mitsrajim:— Egyptian, of Egypt.

4714. מִצְרַיִם **Mitsrayim**, *mits-rah´-yim*; dual of 4693; *Mitsrajim*, i.e. Upper and Lower Egypt:— Egypt, Egyptians, Mizraim.

4715. מִצְרֵף **mitsrêph**, *mits-rafe´*; from 6884; a *crucible*:— fining pot.

4716. מַק **maq**, *mak*; from 4743; prop. a *melting*, i.e. *putridity*:— rottenness, stink.

4717. מַקָּבָה **maqqâbâh**, *mak-kaw-baw´*; from 5344; prop. a *perforatrix*, i.e. a *hammer* (as *piercing*):— hammer.

4718. מַקֶּבֶת **maqqebeth**, *mak-keh´-beth*; from 5344; prop. a *perforator*, i.e. a *hammer* (as *piercing*); also (intr.) a *perforation*, i.e. a *quarry*:— hammer, hole.

4719. מַקֵּדָה **Maqqêdâh**, *mak-kay-daw´*; from the same as 5348 in the denom. sense of *herding* (comp. 5349); *fold*; *Makkedah*, a place in Pal.:— Makkedah.

4720. מִקְדָּשׁ **miqdâsh**, *mik-dawsh´*; or

מִקְּדָשׁ **miqq^edâsh** (Exod. 15:17), *mik-ked-awsh´*; from 6942; a *consecrated* thing or place, espec. a *palace*, *sanctuary* (whether of Jehovah or of idols) or *asylum*:— chapel, hallowed part, holy place, sanctuary.

4721. מַקְהֵל **maqhêl**, *mak-hale´*; or (fem.)

מַקְהֵלָה **maqhêlâh**, *mak-hay-law´*; from 6950; an *assembly*:— congregation.

4722. מַקְהֵלֹת **Maqhêlôth**, *mak-hay-loth´*; plur. of 4721 (fem.); *assemblies*; *Makheloth*, a place in the Desert:— Makheloth.

4723. מִקְוֶה **miqveh**, *mik-veh´*; or

מִקְוֵה **miqvêh** (1 Kings 10:28) *mik-vay´*; or

מִקְוֵא° **miqvê'** (2 Chron. 1:16), *mik-vay´*; from 6960; something *waited* for, i.e. *confidence* (obj. or subj.); also a *collection*, i.e. (of water) a *pond*, or (of men and horses) a *caravan* or *drove*:— abiding, gathering together, hope, linen yarn, plenty [of water], pool.

4724. מִקְוֶה **miqvâh**, *mik-vaw´*; fem. of 4723; a *collection*, i.e. (of water) a *reservoir:*— ditch.

4725. מָקוֹם **mâqôwm**, *maw-kome´*; or

מָקֹם **mâqôm**, *maw-kome´*; also (fem.)

מְקוֹמָה **meqôwmâh**, *mek-o-mah´*; or

מְקֹמָה **meqômâh**, *mek-o-mah´*; from 6965; prop. a *standing*, i.e. a *spot*; but used widely of a *locality* (gen. or spec.); also (fig.) of a *condition* (of body or mind):— country, × home, × open, place, room, space, × whither [-soever].

4726. מָקוֹר **mâqôwr**, *maw-kore´*; or

מָקֹר **mâqôr**, *maw-kore´*; from 6979; prop. something *dug*, i.e. a (gen.) *source* (of water, even when naturally flowing; also of tears, blood [by euphem. of the female *pudenda*]; fig. of happiness, wisdom, progeny):— fountain, issue, spring, well (-spring).

4727. מִקָּח **miqqâch**, *mik-kawkh´*; from 3947; *reception:*— taking.

4728. מִקָּחָה **maqqâchâh**, *mak-kaw-khaw´*; from 3947; something *received*, i.e. *merchandise* (purchased):— ware.

4729. מִקְטָר **miqtâr**, *mik-tawr´*; from 6999; something to *fume* (incense) on, i.e. a *hearth place:*— to burn ... upon.

מְקַטְּרָה **meqatterâh**. See 6999.

4730. מִקְטֶרֶת **miqtereth**, *mik-teh´-reth*; fem. of 4729; something to *fume* (incense) in, i.e. a *coal-pan:*— censer.

4731. מַקֵּל **maqqêl**, *mak-kale*; or (fem.)

מַקְּלָה **maqqelâh**, *mak-kel-aw´*; from an unused root mean. appar. to *germinate*; a *shoot*, i.e. *stick* (with leaves on, or for walking, striking, guiding, divining):— rod, [hand-] staff.

4732. מִקְלוֹת **Miqlôwth**, *mik-lohth´*; (or perh. *mik-kel-ohth´*); plur. of (fem.) 4731; *rods*; *Mikloth*, a place in the Desert:— Mikloth.

4733. מִקְלָט **miqlât**, *mik-lawt´*; from 7038 in the sense of *taking* in; an *asylum* (as a *receptacle*):— refuge.

4734. מִקְלַעַת **miqla'ath**, *mik-lah´-ath*; from 7049; a *sculpture* (prob. in bas-relief):— carved (figure), carving, graving.

מָקֹם **mâqôm**. See 4725.

מְקֹמָה **meqômâh**. See 4725.

4735. מִקְנֶה **miqneh**, *mik-neh´*; from 7069; something *bought*, i.e. *property*, but only live stock; abstr. *acquisition:*— cattle, flock, herd, possession, purchase, substance.

4736. מִקְנָה **miqnâh**, *mik-naw´*; fem. of 4735; prop. a *buying*, i.e. *acquisition*; concr. a piece of *property* (land or living); also the *sum* paid:— (he that is) bought, possession, piece, purchase.

4737. מִקְנֵיָהוּ **Miqnêyâhûw**, *mik-nay-yaw´-hoo*; from 4735 and 3050; *possession of Jah*; *Miknejah*, an Isr.:— Mikneiah.

4738. מִקְסָם **miqçâm**, *mik-sawm´*; from 7080; an *augury:*— divination.

4739. מָקַץ **Mâqats**, *maw-kats´*; from 7112; *end*; *Makats*, a place in Pal.:— Makaz.

4740. מַקְצוֹעַ **maqtsôwa'**, *mak-tso´-ah*; or

מַקְצֹעַ **maqtsôa'**, *mak-tso´-ah*; or (fem.)

מַקְצֹעָה **maqtsô'âh**, *mak-tso-aw´*; from 7106 in the denom. sense of *bending*; an *angle* or recess:— corner, turning.

4741. מַקְצֻעָה **maqtsû'âh**, *mak-tsoo-aw´*; from 7106; a *scraper*, i.e. a carving *chisel:*— plane.

4742. מְקֻצְעָה **mequts'âh**, *mek-oots-aw´*; from 7106 in the denom. sense of *bending*; an *angle:*— corner.

4743. מָקַק **mâqaq**, *maw-kak´*; a prim. root; to *melt*; fig. to *flow, dwindle, vanish:*— consume away, be corrupt, dissolve, pine away.

מָקֹר **mâqôr**. See 4726.

4744. מִקְרָא **miqrâ'**, *mik-raw´*; from 7121; something *called* out, i.e. a public *meeting* (the act, the persons, or the place); also a *rehearsal:*— assembly, calling, convocation, reading.

4745. מִקְרֶה **miqreh**, *mik-reh´*; from 7136; something *met* with, i.e. an *accident* or *fortune:*— something befallen, befalleth, chance, event, hap (-peneth).

4746. מְקָרֶה **meqâreh**, *mek-aw-reh´*; from 7136; prop. something *meeting*, i.e. a *frame* (of timbers):— building.

4747. מְקֵרָה **meqêrâh**, *mek-ay-raw´*; from the same as 7119; a *cooling* off:— × summer.

מוֹקֵשׁ **môqêsh**. See 4170.

4748. מִקְשֶׁה **miqsheh**, *mik-sheh´*; from 7185 in the sense of *knotting* up round and hard; something *turned* (rounded), i.e. a *curl* (of tresses):— × well [set] hair.

4749. מִקְשָׁה **miqshâh**, *mik-shaw´*; fem. of 4748; *rounded* work, i.e. moulded by *hammering* (repoussé):— beaten (out of one piece, work), upright, whole piece.

4750. מִקְשָׁה **miqshâh**, *mik-shaw´*; denom. from 7180; lit. a *cucumbered* field, i.e. a *cucumber* patch:— garden of cucumbers.

4751. מַר **mar**, *mar*; or (fem.)

מָרָה **mârâh**, *maw-raw´*; from 4843; *bitter* (lit. or fig.); also (as noun) *bitterness*, or (adv.) *bitterly:*— + angry, bitter (-ly,

-ness), chafed, discontented, × great, heavy.

4752. מַר **mar**, *mar;* from 4843 in its orig. sense of *distillation;* a *drop:*— drop.

4753. מֹר **môr**, *mor;* or

מוֹר **môwr**, *more;* from 4843; *myrrh* (as *distilling* in drops, and also as *bitter*):— myrrh.

4754. מָרָא **mârâ'**, *maw-raw';* a prim. root; to *rebel;* hence, (through the idea of *maltreating*) to *whip,* i.e. *lash* (self with wings, as the ostrich in running):— be filthy, lift up self.

4755. מָרָא **Mârâ'**, *maw-raw';* for 4751 fem.; *bitter; Mara,* a symbol. name of Naomi:— Mara.

4756. מָרֵא **mârê'** (Chald.), *maw-ray';* from a root corresp. to 4754 in the sense of *domineering;* a *master:*— lord, Lord.

מֹרָא **môrâ'**. See 4172.

4757. מְראֹדַךְ בַּלְאָדָן **Merô'dak Bal'âdân**, *mer-o-dak' bal-aw-dawn';* of for. der.; *Merodak-Baladan,* a Bab. king:— Merodach-baladan. Comp. 4781.

4758. מַרְאֶה **mar'eh**, *mar-eh';* from 7200; a *view* (the act of seeing); also an *appearance* (the thing seen), whether (real) a *shape* (espec. if handsome, *comeliness;* often plur. the *looks*), or (ment.) a *vision:*— × apparently, appearance (-reth), × as soon as beautiful (-ly), countenance, fair, favoured, form, goodly, to look (up) on (to), look [-eth], pattern, to see, seem, sight, visage, vision.

4759. מַרְאָה **mar'âh**, *mar-aw';* fem. of 4758; a *vision;* also (caus.) a *mirror:*— looking glass, vision.

4760. מֻרְאָה **mur'âh**, *moor-aw';* appar. fem. pass. caus. part. of 7200; something *conspicuous,* i.e. the *craw* of a bird (from its *prominence*):— crop.

מְראוֹן° **Mer'ôwn**. See 8112.

4761. מַרְאָשָׁה **mar'âshâh**, *mar-aw-shaw';* denom. from 7218; prop. *headship,* i.e. (plur. for collect.) *dominion:*— principality.

4762. מַרְאֵשָׁה **Mar'êshâh**, *mar-ay-shaw';* or

מָרֵשָׁה **Marêshâh**, *mar-ay-shaw';* formed like 4761; *summit; Mareshah,* the name of two Isr. and of a place in Pal.:— Mareshah.

4763. מְרַאֲשָׁה **mera'ăshâh**, *mer-ah-ash-aw';* formed like 4761; prop. a *headpiece,* i.e. (plur. for adv.) *at* (or *as*) the *head-rest* (or pillow):— bolster, head, pillow. Comp. 4772.

4764. מֵרָב **Mêrâb**, *may-rawb';* from 7231; *increase; Merab,* a daughter of Saul:— Merab.

4765. מַרְבַד **marbad**, *mar-bad';* from 7234; a *coverlet:*— covering of tapestry.

4766. מַרְבֶּה **marbeh**, *mar-beh';* from 7235; prop. *increasing;* as noun, *greatness,* or (adv.) *greatly:*— great, increase.

4767. מִרְבָּה **mirbâh**, *meer-baw';* from 7235; *abundance,* i.e. a great quantity:— much.

4768. מַרְבִּית **marbîyth**, *mar-beeth';* from 7235; a *multitude;* also *offspring;* spec. *interest* (on capital):— greatest part, greatness, increase, multitude.

4769. מַרְבֵּץ **marbêts**, *mar-bates';* from 7257; a *reclining* place, i.e. *fold* (for flocks):— couching place, place to lie down.

4770. מַרְבֵּק **marbêq**, *mar-bake';* from an unused root mean. to *tie* up; a *stall* (for cattle):— × fat (-ted), stall.

מֹרַג **môrag**. See 4173.

4771. מַרְגּוֹעַ **margôwa'**, *mar-go'-ah;* from 7280; a *resting* place:— rest.

4772. מַרְגְּלָה **margelâh**, *mar-ghel-aw';* denom. from 7272; (plur. for collect.) a *footpiece,* i.e. (adv.) *at the foot,* or (direct.) the *foot* itself:— feet. Comp. 4763.

4773. מַרְגֵּמָה **margêmâh**, *mar-gay-maw';* from 7275; a *stone*-heap:— sling.

4774. מַרְגֵּעָה **margê'âh**, *mar-gay-aw';* from 7280; *rest:*— refreshing.

4775. מָרַד **mârad**, *maw-rad';* a prim. root; to *rebel:*— rebel (-lious).

4776. מְרַד **merad** (Chald.), *mer-ad';* from a root corresp. to 4775; *rebellion:*— rebellion.

4777. מֶרֶד **mered**, *meh'-red;* from 4775; *rebellion:*— rebellion.

4778. מֶרֶד **Mered**, *meh'-red;* the same as 4777; *Mered,* an Isr.:— Mered.

4779. מָרָד **mârâd** (Chald.), *maw-rawd';* from the same as 4776; *rebellious:*— rebellious.

4780. מַרְדּוּת **mardûwth**, *mar-dooth';* from 4775; *rebelliousness:*— × rebellious.

4781. מְרֹדָךְ **Merôdâk**, *mer-o-dawk';* of for. der.; *Merodak,* a Bab. idol:— Merodach. Comp. 4757.

4782. מָרְדְּכַי **Mordekay**, *mor-dek-ah'-ee;* of for. der.; *Mordecai,* an Isr.:— Mordecai.

4783. מֻרְדָּף **murdâph**, *moor-dawf';* from 7291; *persecuted:*— persecuted.

4784. מָרָה **mârâh**, *maw-raw';* a prim. root; to *be* (caus. *make*) *bitter* (or unpleasant); (fig.) to *rebel* (or resist; caus. to *provoke*):— bitter, change, be disobedient, disobey, grievously, provocation, provoke (-ing), (be) rebel (against, -lious).

4785. מָרָה **Mârâh**, *maw-raw';* the same as 4751 fem.; *bitter; Marah,* a place in the Desert:— Marah.

מֹרֶה **Môreh**. See 4175.

4786. מֹרָה **môrâh**, *mo-raw';* from 4843; *bitterness,* i.e. (fig.) *trouble:*— grief.

4787. מֹרָה **morrâh**, *mor-raw´;* a form of 4786; *trouble:*— bitterness.

4788. מָרוּד **mârûwd**, *maw-rood´;* from 7300 in the sense of *maltreatment;* an *outcast;* (abstr.) *destitution:*— cast out, misery.

4789. מֵרוֹז **Mêrôwz**, *may-roze´;* of uncert. der.; *Meroz,* a place in Pal.:— Meroz.

4790. מֵרוֹחַ **m⁰rôwach**, *mer-o-akh´;* from 4799; *bruised,* i.e. *emasculated:*— broken.

4791. מָרוֹם **mârôwm**, *maw-rome´;* from 7311; *altitude,* i.e. concr. (an *elevated place*), abstr. (*elevation*), fig. (*elation*), or adv. (*aloft*):— (far) above, dignity, haughty, height, (most, on) high (one, place), loftily, upward.

4792. מֵרוֹם **Mêrôwm**, *may-rome´;* formed like 4791; *height; Merom,* a lake in Pal.:— Merom.

4793. מֵרוֹץ **mêrôwts**, *may-rotes´;* from 7323; a *run* (the trial of speed):— race.

4794. מְרוּצָה **m⁰rûwtsâh**, *mer-oo-tsaw´;* or

מְרֻצָה **m⁰rûtsâh**, *mer-oo-tsaw´;* fem. of 4793; a *race* (the act), whether the manner or the progress:— course, running. Comp. 4835.

4795. מָרוּק **mârûwq**, *maw-rook´;* from 4838; prop. *rubbed;* but used abstr. a *rubbing* (with perfumery):— purification.

מְרוֹר **m⁰rôwr**. See 4844.

מְרוֹרָה **m⁰rôwrâh**. See 4846.

4796. מָרוֹת **Mârôwth**, *maw-rohth´;* plur. of 4751 fem.; *bitter* springs; *Maroth,* a place in Pal.:— Maroth.

4797. מִרְזַח **mirzach**, *meer-zakh´;* from an unused root mean. to *scream;* a *cry,* i.e. (of joy), a *revel:*— banquet.

4798. מַרְזֵחַ **marzêach**, *mar-zay´-akh;* formed like 4797; a *cry,* i.e. (of grief) a *lamentation:*— mourning.

4799. מָרַח **mârach**, *maw-rakh´;* a prim. root; prop. to *soften* by rubbing or pressure; hence, (medicinally) to *apply* as an emollient:— lay for a plaister.

4800. מֶרְחָב **merchâb**, *mer-khawb´;* from 7337; *enlargement,* either lit. (an *open space,* usually in a good sense), or fig. (*liberty*):— breadth, large place (room).

4801. מֶרְחָק **merchâq**, *mer-khawk´;* from 7368; *remoteness,* i.e. (concr.) a *distant* place; often (adv.) *from afar:*— (a-, dwell in, very) far (country, off). See also 1023.

4802. מַרְחֶשֶׁת **marchesheth**, *mar-kheh´-sheth;* from 7370; a *stew*-pan:— fryingpan.

4803. מָרַט **mâraṭ**, *maw-rat´;* a prim. root; to *polish;* by impl. to *make bald* (the head), to *gall* (the shoulder); also, to *sharpen:*— bright, furbish, (have his) hair (be) fallen off, peeled, pluck off (hair).

4804. מְרַט **m⁰raṭ** (Chald.), *mer-at´;* corresp. to 4803; to *pull* off:— be plucked.

4805. מְרִי **m⁰rîy**, *mer-ee´;* from 4784; *bitterness,* i.e. (fig.) *rebellion;* concr. *bitter,* or *rebellious:*— bitter, (most) rebel (-lion, -lious).

4806. מְרִיא **m⁰rîy'**, *mer-ee´;* from 4754 in the sense of *grossness,* through the idea of *domineering* (comp. 4756); *stall-fed;* often (as noun) a *beeve:*— fat (fed) beast (cattle, -ling).

4807. מְרִיב בַּעַל **M⁰rîyb Ba'al**, *mer-eeb´ bah´-al;* from 7378 and 1168; *quarreller of Baal; Merib-Baal,* an epithet of Gideon:— Merib-baal. Comp. 4810.

4808. מְרִיבָה **m⁰rîybâh**, *mer-ee-baw´;* from 7378; *quarrel:*— provocation, strife.

4809. מְרִיבָה **M⁰rîybâh**, *mer-ee-baw´;* the same as 4808; *Meribah,* the name of two places in the Desert:— Meribah.

4810. מְרִי בַעַל **M⁰rîy Ba'al**, *mer-ee´ bah´-al;* from 4805 and 1168; *rebellion of* (i.e. *against*) *Baal; Meri-Baal,* an epithet of Gideon:— Meri-baal. Comp. 4807.

4811. מְרָיָה **M⁰râyâh**, *mer-aw-yaw´;* from 4784; *rebellion; Merajah,* an Isr.:— Meraiah. Comp. 3236.

מֹרִיָּה **Môrîyâh**. See 4179.

4812. מְרָיוֹת **M⁰râyôwth**, *mer-aw-yohth´;* plur. of 4811; *rebellious; Merajoth,* the name of two Isr.:— Meraioth.

4813. מִרְיָם **Miryâm**, *meer-yawm´;* from 4805; *rebelliously; Mirjam,* the name of two Israelitesses:— Miriam.

4814. מְרִירוּת **m⁰rîyrûwth**, *mer-ee-rooth´;* from 4843; *bitterness,* i.e. (fig.) *grief:*— bitterness.

4815. מְרִירִי **m⁰rîyrîy**, *mer-ee-ree´;* from 4843; *bitter,* i.e. *poisonous:*— bitter.

4816. מֹרֶךְ **môrek**, *mo´-rek;* perh. from 7401; *softness,* i.e. (fig.) *fear:*— faintness.

4817. מֶרְכָּב **merkâb**, *mer-kawb´;* from 7392; a *chariot;* also a *seat* (in a vehicle):— chariot, covering, saddle.

4818. מֶרְכָּבָה **merkâbâh**, *mer-kaw-baw´;* fem. of 4817; a *chariot:*— chariot. See also 1024.

4819. מַרְכֹּלֶת **markôleth**, *mar-ko´-leth;* from 7402; a *mart:*— merchandise.

4820. מִרְמָה **mirmâh**, *meer-maw´;* from 7411 in the sense of *deceiving; fraud:*— craft, deceit (-ful, -fully), false, feigned, guile, subtilly, treachery.

4821. מִרְמָה **Mirmâh**, *meer-maw´;* the same as 4820; *Mirmah,* an Isr.:— Mirma.

4822. מְרֵמוֹת **M⁰rêmôwth**, *mer-ay-mohth´;*

plur. from 7311; *heights; Meremoth,* the name of two Isr.:— Meremoth.

4823. מִרְמָס **mirmâç**, *meer-mawce´;* from 7429; *abasement* (the act or the thing):— tread (down)-ing, (to be) trodden (down) under foot.

4824. מֵרֹנֹתִי **Mêrônôthîy**, *may-ro-no-thee´;* patrial from an unused noun; a *Meronothite,* or inhab. of some (otherwise unknown) Meronoth.:— Meronothite.

4825. מֶרֶס **Mereç**, *meh´-res;* of for. der.; *Meres,* a Pers.:— Meres.

4826. מַרְסְנָא **Març ͤnâ'**, *mar-sen-aw´;* of for. der.; *Marsena,* a Pers.:— Marsena.

4827. מֶרַע **mêra'**, *may-rah´;* from 7489; used as (abstr.) noun, *wickedness:*— do mischief.

4828. מֵרֵעַ **mêrêa'**, *may-ray´-ah;* from 7462 in the sense of *companionship;* a *friend:*— companion, friend.

4829. מִרְעֶה **mir'eh**, *meer-eh´;* from 7462 in the sense of *feeding; pasture* (the place or the act); also the *haunt* of wild animals:— feeding place, pasture.

4830. מִרְעִית **mir'îyth**, *meer-eeth´;* from 7462 in the sense of *feeding; pasturage;* concr. a *flock:*— flock, pasture.

4831. מַרְעֵלָה **Mar'âlâh**, *mar-al-aw´;* from 7477; perh. *earthquake; Maralah,* a place in Pal.:— Maralah.

4832. מַרְפֵּא **marpê'**, *mar-pay´;* from 7495; prop. *curative,* i.e. lit. (concr.) a *medicine,* or (abstr.) a *cure;* fig. (concr.) *deliverance,* or (abstr.) *placidity:*— (in-l) cure (-able), healing (-lth), remedy, sound, wholesome, yielding.

4833. מִרְפָּשׂ **mirpâs**, *meer-paws´;* from 7515; *muddled* water:— that which ... have fouled.

4834. מָרַץ **mârats**, *maw-rats´;* a prim. root; prop. to *press,* i.e. (fig.) to be *pungent* or vehement; to *irritate:*— embolden, be forcible, grievous, sore.

4835. מְרֻצָה **m ͤrûtsâh**, *mer-oo-tsaw´;* from 7533; *oppression:*— violence. See also 4794.

4836. מַרְצֵעַ **martsêa'**, *mar-tsay´-ah;* from 7527; an *awl:*— aul.

4837. מַרְצֶפֶת **martsepheth**, *mar-tseh´-feth;* from 7528; a *pavement:*— pavement.

4838. מָרַק **mâraq**, *maw-rak´;* a prim. root; to *polish;* by impl. to *sharpen;* also to *rinse:*— bright, furbish, scour.

4839. מָרָק **mârâq**, *maw-rawk´;* from 4838; *soup* (as if a *rinsing*):— broth. See also 6564.

4840. מֶרְקָח **merqâch**, *mer-kawkh´;* from 7543; a *spicy* herb:— × sweet.

4841. מֶרְקָחָה **merqâchâh**, *mer-kaw-khaw´;* fem. of 4840; abstr. a *seasoning* (with spicery);

concr. an *unguent-kettle* (for preparing spiced oil):— pot of ointment, × well.

4842. מִרְקַחַת **mirqachath**, *meer-kakh´-ath;* from 7543; an aromatic *unguent;* also an *unguent-pot:*— prepared by the apothecaries' art, compound, ointment.

4843. מָרַר **mârar**, *maw-rar´;* a prim. root; prop. to *trickle* [see 4752]; but used only as a denom. from 4751; to be (caus. *make*) *bitter* (lit. or fig.):— (be, be in, deal, have, make) bitter (-ly, -ness), be moved with choler, (be, have sorely, it) grieved (-eth), provoke, vex.

4844. מְרֹר **m ͤrôr**, *mer-ore´;* or

מְרוֹר **m ͤrôwr**, *mer-ore´;* from 4843; a *bitter* herb:— bitter (-ness).

4845. מְרֵרָה **m ͤrêrâh**, *mer-ay-raw´;* from 4843; *bile* (from its bitterness):— gall.

4846. מְרֹרָה **m ͤrôrâh**, *mer-o-raw´;* or

מְרוֹרָה **m ͤrôwrâh**, *mer-o-raw´;* from 4843; prop. *bitterness;* concr. a *bitter thing;* spec. *bile;* also *venom* (of a serpent):— bitter (thing), gall.

4847. מְרָרִי **M ͤrârîy**, *mer-aw-ree´;* from 4843; *bitter; Merari,* an Isr.:— Merari. See also 4848.

4848. מְרָרִי **M ͤrârîy**, *mer-aw-ree´;* from 4847; a *Merarite* (collect.), or desc. of Merari:— Merarites.

מָרֵשָׁה **Mârêshâh.** See 4762.

4849. מִרְשַׁעַת **mirsha'ath**, *meer-shah´-ath;* from 7561; a female *wicked doer:*— wicked woman.

4850. מְרָתַיִם **M ͤrâthayim**, *mer-aw-thah´-yim;* dual of 4751 fem.; *double bitterness; Merathajim,* an epithet of Bab.:— Merathaim.

4851. מַשׁ **Mash**, *mash;* of for. der.; *Mash,* a son of Aram, and the people desc. from him:— Mash.

4852. מֵשָׁא **Mêshâ'**, *may-shaw´;* of for. der.; *Mesha,* a place in Arabia:— Mesha.

4853. מַשָּׂא **massâ'**, *mas-saw´;* from 5375; a *burden;* spec. *tribute,* or (abstr.) *porterage;* fig. an *utterance,* chiefly a *doom,* espec. *singing;* ment. *desire:*— burden, carry away, prophecy, × they set, song, tribute.

4854. מַשָּׂא **Massâ'**, *mas-saw´;* the same as 4853; *burden; Massa,* a son of Ishmael:— Massa.

4855. מַשָּׁא **mashshâ'**, *mash-shaw´;* from 5383; a *loan;* by impl. *interest* on a debt:— exaction, usury.

4856. מַשֹּׂא **massô'**, *mas-so´;* from 5375; *partiality* (as a *lifting* up):— respect.

4857. מַשְׁאָב **mash'âb**, *mash-awb´;* from 7579;

a *trough* for cattle to drink from:— place of drawing water.

מְשֹׁאָה **mᵉshô'âh**. See 4875.

4858. מַשָּׂאָה **massâ'âh**, *mas-saw-aw'*; from 5375; a *conflagration* (from the *rising* of smoke):— burden.

4859. מַשָּׁאָה **mashshâ'âh**, *mash-shaw-aw'*; fem. of 4855; a *loan:*— × any [-thing], debt.

מַשֻּׁאָה **mashshû'âh**. See 4876.

4860. מַשָּׁאוֹן **mashshâ'ôwn**, *mash-shaw-ohn'*; from 5377; *dissimulation:*— deceit.

4861. מִשְׁאָל **Mish'âl**, *mish-awl'*; from 7592; *request; Mishal*, a place in Pal.:— Mishal, Misheal. Comp. 4913.

4862. מִשְׁאָלָה **mish'âlâh**, *mish-aw-law'*; from 7592; a *request:*— desire, petition.

4863. מִשְׁאֶרֶת **mish'ereth**, *mish-eh'-reth*; from 7604 in the orig. sense of *swelling*; a *kneading-trough* (in which the dough *rises*):— kneading trough, store.

4864. מַשְׂאֵת **mas'êth**, *mas-ayth'*; from 5375; prop. (abstr.) a *raising* (as of the hands in prayer), or *rising* (of flame); fig. an *utterance*; concr. a *beacon* (as *raised*); a *present* (as *taken*), *mess*, or *tribute*; fig. a *reproach* (as a *burden*):— burden, collection, sign of fire, (great) flame, gift, lifting up, mess, oblation, reward.

מֹשָׁב **môshâb**. See 4186.

מְשֻׁבָה **mᵉshûbâh**. See 4878.

4865. מִשְׁבְּצָה **mishbᵉtsâh**, *mish-bets-aw'*; from 7660; a *brocade*; by anal. a (reticulated) *setting* of a gem:— ouch, wrought.

4866. מִשְׁבֵּר **mishbêr**, *mish-bare'*; from 7665; the *orifice* of the womb (from which the fetus *breaks* forth):— birth, breaking forth.

4867. מִשְׁבָּר **mishbâr**, *mish-bawr'*; from 7665; a *breaker* (of the sea):— billow, wave.

4868. מִשְׁבָּת **mishbâth**, *mish-bawth'*; from 7673; *cessation*, i.e. destruction:— sabbath.

4869. מִשְׂגָּב **misgâb**, *mis-gawb'*; from 7682; prop. a *cliff* (or other *lofty* or *inaccessible* place); abstr. *altitude*; fig. a *refuge:*— defence, high fort (tower), refuge.

4869'. מִשְׂגָּב **misgâb**, *mis-gawb'*; *Misgab*, a place in Moab:— Misgab.

4870. מִשְׁגֶּה **mishgeh**, *mish-gay'*; from 7686; an *error:*— oversight.

4871. מָשָׁה **mâshâh**, *maw-shaw'*; a prim. root; to *pull* out (lit. or fig.):— draw (out).

4872. מֹשֶׁה **Môsheh**, *mo-sheh'*; from 4871; *drawing* out (of the water), i.e. *rescued; Mosheh*, the Isr. lawgiver:— Moses.

4873. מֹשֶׁה **Môsheh** (Chald.), *mo-sheh'*; corresp. to 4872:— Moses.

4874. מַשֶּׁה **mashsheh**, *mash-sheh'*; from 5383; a *debt:*— + creditor.

4875. מְשׁוֹאָה **mᵉshôw'âh**, *meh-o-aw'*; or

מְשֹׁאָה **mᵉshô'âh**, *mesh-o-aw'*; from the same as 7722; (a) *ruin*, abstr. (the act) or concr. (the wreck):— desolation, waste.

4876. מַשּׁוּאָה **mashshûw'âh**, *mash-shoo-aw'*; or

מַשֻּׁאָה **mashshû'âh**, *mash-shoo-aw'*; for 4875; *ruin:*— desolation, destruction.

4877. מְשׁוֹבָב **Mᵉshôwbâb**, *mesh-o-bawb'*; from 7725; *returned; Meshobab*, an Isr.:— Meshobab.

4878. מְשׁוּבָה **mᵉshûwbâh**, *mesh-oo-baw'*; or

מְשֻׁבָה **mᵉshûbâh**, *mesh-oo-baw'*; from 7725; *apostasy:*— backsliding, turning away.

4879. מְשׁוּגָה **mᵉshûwgâh**, *mesh-oo-gaw'*; from an unused root mean. to *stray; mistake:*— error.

4880. מָשׁוֹט **mâshôwṭ**, *maw-shote'*; or

מִשּׁוֹט **mishshôwṭ**, *mish-shote'*; from 7751; an *oar:*— oar.

4881. מְשׂוּכָה **mᵉsûwkâh**, *mes-oo-kaw'*; or

מְשׂכָה **mᵉsûkâh**, *mes-oo-kaw'*; from 7753; a *hedge:*— hedge.

4882. מְשׁוּסָה° **mᵉshûwçâh**, *mesh-oo-saw'*; from an unused root mean. to *plunder; spoilation:*— spoil.

4883. מַשּׂוֹר **massôwr**, *mas-sore'*; from an unused root mean. to *rasp*; a *saw:*— saw.

4884. מְשׂוּרָה **mᵉsûwrâh**, *mes-oo-raw'*; from an unused root mean. appar. to *divide*; a *measure* (for liquids):— measure.

4885. מָשׂוֹשׂ **mâsôws**, *maw-soce'*; from 7797; *delight*, concr. (the cause or object) or abstr. (the feeling):— joy, mirth, rejoice.

4886. מָשַׁח **mâshach**, *maw-shakh'*; a prim. root; to *rub* with oil, i.e. to *anoint*; by impl. to *consecrate*; also to *paint:*— anoint, paint.

4887. מְשַׁח **mᵉshach** (Chald.), *mesh-akh'*; from a root corresp. to 4886; *oil:*— oil.

4888. מִשְׁחָה **mishchâh**, *meesh-khaw'*; or

מָשְׁחָה **moshchâh**, *mosh-khaw'*; from 4886; *unction* (the act); by impl. a consecratory *gift:*— (to be) anointed (-ing), ointment.

4889. מַשְׁחִית **mashchîyth**, *mash-kheeth'*; from 7843; *destructive*, i.e. (as noun) *destruction*, lit. (spec. a *snare*) or fig. (*corruption*):— corruption, (to) destroy (-ing), destruction, trap, × utterly.

4890. מִשְׂחָק **mischâq**, *mis-khawk'*; from 7831; a *laughing-stock:*— scorn.

4891. מִשְׁחָר **mishchâr**, *mish-khawr'*; from

Hebrew

7836 in the sense of day *breaking; dawn:*— morning.

4892. מַשְׁחֵת **mashchêth**, *mash-khayth´;* for 4889; *destruction:*— destroying.

4893. מִשְׁחָת **mishchâth**, *mish-khawth´;* or

מָשְׁחָת **moshchâth**, *mosh-khawth´;* from 7843; *disfigurement:*— corruption, marred.

4894. מִשְׁטוֹחַ **mishṭôwach**, *mish-to´-akh;* or

מִשְׁטַח **mishṭach**, *mish-takh´;* from 7849; a *spreading*-place:— (to) spread (forth, -ing, upon).

4895. מַשְׂטֵמָה **masṭêmâh**, *mas-tay-maw´;* from the same as 7850; *enmity:*— hatred.

4896. מִשְׁטָר **mishṭâr**, *mish-tawr´;* from 7860; *jurisdiction:*— dominion.

4897. מֶשִׁי **meshîy**, *meh´-shee;* from 4871; *silk* (as *drawn* from the cocoon):— silk.

מֻשִׁי **Mushîy**. See 4187.

4898. מְשֵׁיזַבְאֵל **Meshêyzab'êl**, *mesh-ay-zab-ale´;* from an equiv. to 7804 and 410; *delivered of God; Meshezabel*, an Isr.:— Meshezabeel.

4899. מָשִׁיחַ **mâshîyach**, *maw-shee´-akh;* from 4886; *anointed;* usually a *consecrated* person (as a king, priest, or saint); spec. the *Messiah:*— anointed, Messiah.

4900. מָשַׁךְ **mâshak**, *maw-shak´;* a prim. root; to *draw*, used in a great variety of applications (incl. to *sow*, to *sound*, to *prolong*, to *develop*, to *march*, to *remove*, to *delay*, to be *tall*, etc.):— draw (along, out), continue, defer, extend, forbear, × give, handle, make (pro-, sound) long, × sow, scatter, stretch out.

4901. מֶשֶׁךְ **meshek**, *meh´shek;* from 4900; a *sowing;* also a *possession:*— precious, price.

4902. מֶשֶׁךְ **Meshek**, *meh´-shek;* the same in form as 4901, but prob. of for. der.; *Meshek*, a son of Japheth, and the people desc. from him:— Mesech, Meshech.

4903. מִשְׁכַּב **mishkab** (Chald.), *mish-kab´;* corresp. to 4904; a *bed:*— bed.

4904. מִשְׁכָּב **mishkâb**, *mish-kawb´;* from 7901; a *bed* (fig. a *bier*); abstr. *sleep;* by euphem. carnal *intercourse:*— bed ([-chamber]), couch, lieth (lying) with.

מְסֻכָּה **mesûkâh**. See 4881.

4905. מַשְׂכִּיל **maskîyl**, *mas-keel´;* from 7919; *instructive*, i.e. a *didactic* poem:— Maschil.

מַשְׂכִּים **mashkîym**. See 7925.

4906. מַשְׂכִּית **maskîyth**, *mas-keeth´;* from the same as 7906; a *figure* (carved on stone, the wall, or any object); fig. *imagination:*— conceit, image (-ry), picture, × wish.

4907. מִשְׁכַּן **mishkan** (Chald.), *mish-kan´;* corresp. to 4908; *residence:*— habitation.

4908. מִשְׁכָּן **mishkân**, *mish-kawn´;* from 7931; a

residence (incl. a shepherd's *hut*, the *lair* of animals, fig. the *grave;* also the *Temple*); spec. the *Tabernacle* (prop. its wooden walls):— dwelleth, dwelling (place), habitation, tabernacle, tent.

4909. מַשְׂכֹּרֶת **maskôreth**, *mas-koh´-reth;* from 7936; *wages* or a *reward:*— reward, wages.

4910. מָשַׁל **mâshal**, *maw-shal´;* a prim. root; to *rule:*— (have, make to have) dominion, governor, × indeed, reign, (bear, cause to, have) rule (-ing, -r), have power.

4911. מָשַׁל **mâshal**, *maw-shal´;* denom. from 4912; to *liken*, i.e. (tran.) to use fig. language (an allegory, adage, song or the like); intr. to *resemble:*— be (-come) like, compare, use (as a) proverb, speak (in proverbs), utter.

4912. מָשָׁל **mâshâl**, *maw-shawl´;* appar. from 4910 in some orig. sense of *superiority* in mental action; prop. a pithy *maxim*, usually of metaph. nature; hence, a *simile* (as an adage, poem, discourse):— byword, like, parable, proverb.

4913. מָשָׁל **Mâshâl**, *maw-shawl´;* for 4861; *Mashal*, a place in Pal.:— Mashal.

4914. מְשׁוֹל **meshôl**, *mesh-ol´;* from 4911; a *satire:*— byword.

4915. מֹשֶׁל **môshel**, *mo´-shel;* (1) from 4910; *empire;* (2) from 4911; a *parallel:*— dominion, like.

מִשְׁלוֹשׁ **mishlôwsh**. See 7969.

4916. מִשְׁלוֹחַ **mishlôwach**, *mish-lo´-akh;* or

מִשְׁלֹחַ **mishlôach**, *mish-lo´-akh;* also

מִשְׁלָח **mishlâch**, *mish-lawkh´;* from 7971; a *sending* out, i.e. (abstr.) *presentation* (favorable), or *seizure* (unfavorable); also (concr.) a place of *dismissal*, or a *business* to be discharged:— to lay, to put, sending (forth), to set.

4917. מִשְׁלַחַת **mishlachath**, *mish-lakh´-ath;* fem. of 4916; a *mission*, i.e. (abstr.) and favorable) *release*, or (concr. and unfavorable) an *army:*— discharge, sending.

4918. מְשֻׁלָּם **Meshullâm**, *mesh-ool-lawm´;* from 7999; *allied; Meshullam*, the name of seventeen Isr.:— Meshullam.

4919. מְשִׁלֵּמוֹת **Meshillêmôwth**, *mesh-il-lay-mohth´;* plur. from 7999; *reconciliations; Meshillemoth*, an Isr.:— Meshillemoth. Comp. 4921.

4920. מְשֶׁלֶמְיָה **Meshelemyâh**, *mesh-eh-lem-yaw´;* or

מְשֶׁלֶמְיָהוּ **Meshelemyâhûw**, *mesh-eh-lem-yaw´-hoo;* from 7999 and 3050; *ally of Jah; Meshelemjah*, an Isr.:— Meshelemiah.

4921. מְשִׁלֵּמִית **Meshillêmîyth**, *mesh-il-lay-*

meeth'; from 7999; *reconciliation; Meshillemith,* an Isr.:— Meshillemith. Comp. 4919.

4922. מְשֻׁלֶּמֶת **M^eshullemeth,** *mesh-ool-leh'-meth;* fem. of 4918; *Meshullemeth,* an Israelitess:— Meshullemeth.

4923. מְשַׁמָּה **m^eshammâh,** *mesh-am-maw';* from 8074; a *waste* or *amazement:—* astonishment, desolate.

4924. מַשְׁמָן **mashmân,** *mash-mawn';* from 8080; *fat,* i.e. (lit. and abstr.) *fatness;* but usually (fig. and concr.) a *rich* dish, a *fertile* field, a *robust* man:— fat (one, -ness, -test, -test place).

4925. מִשְׁמַנָּה **Mishmannâh,** *mish-man-naw';* from 8080; *fatness; Mashmannah,* an Isr.:— Mishmannah.

4926. מִשְׁמָע **mishmâ',** *mish-maw';* from 8085; a *report:—* hearing.

4927. מִשְׁמָע **Mishmâ',** *mish-maw';* the same as 4926; *Mishma,* the name of a son of Ishmael, and of an Isr.:— Mishma.

4928. מִשְׁמַעַת **mishma'ath,** *mish-mah'-ath;* fem. of 4926; *audience,* i.e. the royal *court;* also *obedience,* i.e. (concr.) a *subject:—* bidding, guard, obey.

4929. מִשְׁמָר **mishmâr,** *mish-mawr';* from 8104; a *guard* (the man, the post, or the *prison*); fig. a *deposit;* also (as observed) a *usage* (abstr.), or an *example* (concr.):— diligence, guard, office, prison, ward, watch.

4930. מַשְׂמְרָה **masm^erâh,** *mas-mer-aw';* for 4548 fem.; a *peg:—* nail.

4931. מִשְׁמֶרֶת **mishmereth,** *mish-meh'-reth;* fem. of 4929; *watch,* i.e. the act (*custody*) or (concr.) the *sentry,* the *post;* obj. *preservation,* or (concr.) *safe;* fig. *observance,* i.e. (abstr.) *duty,* or (obj.) a *usage* or *party:—* charge, keep, to be kept, office, ordinance, safeguard, ward, watch.

4932. מִשְׁנֶה **mishneh,** *mish-neh';* from 8138; prop. a *repetition,* i.e. a *duplicate* (*copy* of a document), or a *double* (in amount); by impl. a *second* (in order, rank, age, quality or location):— college, copy, double, fatlings, next, second (order), twice as much.

4933. מְשִׁסָּה **m^eshiççâh,** *mesh-is-saw';* from 8155; *plunder:—* booty, spoil.

4934. מִשְׁעוֹל **mish'ôwl,** *mish-ole';* from the same as 8168; a *hollow,* i.e. a narrow passage:— path.

4935. מִשְׁעִי **mish'îy,** *mish-ee';* prob. from 8159; *inspection:—* to supple.

4936. מִשְׁעָם **Mish'âm,** *mish-awm';* appar. from 8159; *inspection; Misham,* an Isr.:— Misham.

4937. מִשְׁעֵן **mish'ên,** *mish-ane';* or

מִשְׁעָן **mish'ân,** *mish-awn';* from 8172; a

support (concr.), i.e. (fig.) a *protector* or *sustenance:—* stay.

4938. מִשְׁעֵנָה **mish'ênâh,** *mish-ay-naw';* or

מִשְׁעֶנֶת **mish'eneth,** *mish-eh'-neth;* fem. of 4937; *support* (abstr.), i.e. (fig.) *sustenance* or (concr.) a *walking-stick:—* staff.

4939. מִשְׂפָּח **mispâch,** *mis-pawkh';* from 5596; *slaughter:—* oppression.

4940. מִשְׁפָּחָה **mishpâchâh,** *mish-paw-khaw';* from 8192 [comp. 8198]; a *family,* i.e. circle of relatives; fig. a *class* (of persons), a *species* (of animals) or *sort* (of things); by extens. a *tribe* or *people:—* family, kind (-red).

4941. מִשְׁפָּט **mishpât,** *mish-pawt';* from 8199; prop. a *verdict* (favorable or unfavorable) pronounced judicially, espec. a *sentence* or formal decree (human or [participant's] divine *law,* indiv. or collect.), incl. the act, the place, the suit, the crime, and the penalty; abstr. *justice,* incl. a participant's *right* or *privilege* (statutory or customary), or even a *style:—* + adversary, ceremony, charge, × crime, custom, desert, determination, discretion, disposing, due, fashion, form, to be judged, judgment, just (-ice, -ly), (manner of) law (-ful), manner, measure, (due) order, ordinance, right, sentence, usest, × worthy, + wrong.

4942. מִשְׁפָּת **mishpâth,** *mish-pawth';* from 8192; a *stall* for cattle (only dual):— burden, sheepfold.

4943. מֶשֶׁק **mesheq,** *meh'-shek;* from an unused root mean. to *hold; possession:—* + steward.

4944. מַשָּׁק **mashshâq,** *mash-shawk';* from 8264; a *traversing,* i.e. rapid *motion:—* running to and fro.

4945. מַשְׁקֶה **mashqeh,** *mash-keh';* from 8248; prop. *causing to drink,* i.e. a *butler;* by impl. (intr.), *drink* (itself); fig. a *well-watered* region:— butler (-ship), cupbearer, drink (-ing), fat pasture, watered.

4946. מִשְׁקוֹל **mishqôwl,** *mish-kole';* from 8254; *weight:—* weight.

4947. מַשְׁקוֹף **mashqôwph,** *mash-kofe';* from 8259 in its orig. sense of *overhanging;* a *lintel:—* lintel.

4948. מִשְׁקָל **mishqâl,** *mish-kawl';* from 8254; *weight* (numerically estimated); hence, *weighing* (the act):— (full) weight.

4949. מִשְׁקֶלֶת **mishqeleth,** *mish-keh'-leth;* or

מִשְׁקֹלֶת **mishqôleth,** *mish-ko'-leth;* fem. of 4948 or 4947; a *weight,* i.e. a *plummet* (with line attached):— plummet.

4950. מִשְׁקָע **mishqâ',** *mish-kaw';* from 8257; a *settling* place (of water), i.e. a *pond:—* deep.

Hebrew

4951. מִשְׂרָה **misrâh**, *mis-raw´*; from 8280; *empire*:— government.

4952. מִשְׁרָה **mishrâh**, *mish-raw´*; from 8281 in the sense of *loosening; maceration*, i.e. steeped *juice*:— liquor.

4953. מַשְׁרוֹקִי **mashrôwqîy** (Chald.), *mash-ro-kee´*; from a root corresp. to 8319; a (musical) *pipe* (from its *whistling* sound):— flute.

4954. מִשְׁרָעִי **Mishrâ'îy**, *mish-raw-ee´*; patrial from an unused noun from an unused root; prob. mean. to *stretch* out; *extension*; a *Mishraite*, or inhab. (collect.) of Mishra:— Mishraites.

4955. מִשְׂרָפָה **misrâphâh**, *mis-raw-faw´*; from 8313; *combustion*, i.e. *cremation* (of a corpse), or *calcination* (of lime):— burning.

4956. מִשְׂרְפוֹת מַיִם **Misrephôwth Mayim**, *mis-ref-ohth´ mah´-yim*; from the plur. of 4955 and 4325; *burnings of water*; *Misrephoth-Majim*, a place in Pal.:— Misrephoth-mayim.

4957. מַשְׂרֵקָה **Masrêqâh**, *mas-ray-kaw´*; a form for 7796 used denom.; *vineyard*; *Masrekah*, a place in Idumæa:— Masrekah.

4958. מַשְׂרֵת **masrêth**, *mas-rayth´*; appar. from an unused root mean. to *perforate*, i.e. hollow out; a *pan*:— pan.

4959. מָשַׁשׁ **mâshash**, *maw-shash´*; a prim. root; to *feel* of; by impl. to *grope*:— feel, grope, search.

4960. מִשְׁתֶּה **mishteh**, *mish-teh´*; from 8354; *drink*, by impl. *drinking* (the act); also (by impl.) a *banquet* or (gen.) *feast*:— banquet, drank, drink, feast (I-ed], -ing).

4961. מִשְׁתֶּה **mishteh** (Chald.), *mish-teh´*; corresp. to 4960; a *banquet*:— banquet.

4962. מַת **math**, *math*; from the same as 4970; prop. an *adult* (as of full length); by impl. a *man* (only in the plur.):— + few, × friends, men, persons, × small.

4963. מַתְבֵּן **mathbên**, *math-bane´*; denom. from 8401; *straw* in the heap:— straw.

4964. מֶתֶג **metheg**, *meh-theg*; from an unused root mean. to *curb*; a *bit*:— bit, bridle.

4965. מֶתֶג הָאַמָּה **Metheg hâ-'Ammâh**, *meh´-theg haw-am-maw´*; from 4964 and 520 with the art. interposed; *bit of the metropolis*; *Metheg-ha-Ammah*, an epithet of Gath:— Metheg-ammah.

4966. מָתוֹק **mâthôwq**, *maw-thoke´*; or

מָתוּק **mâthûwq**, *maw-thook´*; from 4985; *sweet*:— sweet (-er, -ness).

4967. מְתוּשָׁאֵל **Methûwshâ'êl**, *meth-oo-shaw-ale´*; from 4962 and 410, with the rel. interposed; *man who* (is) *of God*; *Methushaël*, an antediluvian patriarch:— Methusael.

4968. מְתוּשֶׁלַח **Methûwshelach**, *meth-oo-sheh´-lakh*; from 4962 and 7973; *man of a dart*; *Methushelach*, an antediluvian patriarch:— Methuselah.

4969. מָתַח **mâthach**, *maw-thakh´*; a prim. root; to *stretch* out:— spread out.

4970. מָתַי **mâthay**, *maw-thah´ee*; from an unused root mean. to *extend*; prop. *extent* (of time); but used only adv. (espec. with other particles pref.), *when* (either rel. or interrog.):— long, when.

מְתִים **methîym**. See 4962.

4971. מַתְכֹּנֶת **mathkôneth**, *math-ko´-neth*; or

מַתְכֻּנֶת **mathkûneth**, *math-koo´-neth*; from 8505 in the transferred sense of *measuring*; *proportion* (in size, number or ingredients):— composition, measure, state, tale.

4972. מַתְלָאָה **mattelâ'âh**, *mat-tel-aw-aw´*; from 4100 and 8513; *what a trouble!*:— what a weariness.

4973. מְתַלְּעָה **methalle'âh**, *meth-al-leh-aw´*; contr. from 3216; prop. a *biter*, i.e. a *tooth*:— cheek (jaw) tooth, jaw.

4974. מְתֹם **methôm**, *meth-ohm´*; from 8552; *wholesomeness*; also (adv.) *completely*:— men [by reading 4962], soundness.

מֶתֶן **Methen**. See 4981.

4975. מֹתֶן **môthen**, *mo´-then*; from an unused root mean. to *be slender*; prop. the *waist* or small of the back; only in plur. the *loins*:— + greyhound, loins, side.

4976. מַתָּן **mattân**, *mat-tawn´*; from 5414; a *present*:— gift, to give, reward.

4977. מַתָּן **Mattân**, *mat-tawn´*; the same as 4976; *Mattan*, the name of a priest of Baal, and of an Isr.:— Mattan.

4978. מַתְּנָא **mattenâ'** (Chald.), *mat-ten-aw´*; corresp. to 4979:— gift.

4979. מַתָּנָה **mâttânâh**, *mat-taw-naw´*; fem. of 4976; a *present*; spec. (in a good sense), a sacrificial *offering*, (in a bad sense) a *bribe*:— gift.

4980. מַתָּנָה **Mattânâh**, *mat-taw-naw´*; the same as 4979; *Mattanah*, a place in the Desert:— Mattanah.

4981. מִתְנִי **Mithnîy**, *mith-nee´*; prob. patrial from an unused noun mean. *slenderness*; a *Mithnite*, or inhab. of Methen:— Mithnite.

4982. מַתְּנַי **Mattenay**, *mat-ten-ah´ee*; from 4976; *liberal*; *Mattenai*, the name of three Isr.:— Mattenai.

4983. מַתַּנְיָה **Mattanyâh**, *mat-tan-yaw´*; or

מַתַּנְיָהוּ **Mattanyâhûw**, *mat-tan-yaw´-hoo*; from 4976 and 3050; *gift of Jah*; *Mattanjah*, the name of ten Isr.:— Mattaniah.

מָתְנַיִם **mothnayim**. See 4975.

4984. מִתְנַשֵּׂא **mithnassê'**, *mith-nas-say´*;

from 5375; (used as abstr.) supreme *exaltation:*— exalted.

4985. מָתַק **mâthaq**, *maw-thak´*; a prim. root; to *suck*, by impl. to *relish*, or (intr.) *be sweet:*— be (made, × take) sweet.

4986. מֶתֶק **metheq**, *meh´-thek;* from 4985; fig. *pleasantness* (of discourse):— sweetness.

4987. מֹתֶק **môtheq**, *mo´-thek;* from 4985; *sweetness:*— sweetness.

4988. מָתָק **mâthâq**, *maw-thawk´;* from 4985; a *dainty*, i.e. (gen.) *food:*— feed sweetly.

4989. מִתְקָה **Mithqâh**, *mith-kaw´;* fem. of 4987; *sweetness; Mithkah*, a place in the Desert:— Mithcah.

4990. מִתְרְדָת **Mithrᵉdâth**, *mith-red-awth´;* of Pers. or.; *Mithredath*, the name of two Pers.:— Mithredath.

4991. מַתָּת **mattâth**, *mat-tawth´;* fem. of 4976 abb.; a *present:*— gift.

4992. מַתַּתָּה **Mattattâh**, *mat-tat-taw´;* for 4993; *gift of Jah; Mattattah*, an Isr.:— Mattathah.

4993. מַתִּתְיָה **Mattithyâh**, *mat-tith-yaw´;* or

מַתִּתְיָהוּ **Mattithyâhûw**, *mat-tith-yaw´-hoo;* from 4991 and 3050; *gift of Jah; Mattithjah*, the name of four Isr.:— Mattithiah.

נ

4994. נָא **nâ'**, *naw;* a prim. particle of incitement and entreaty, which may usually be rendered *I pray, now* or *then;* added mostly to verbs (in the imperative or future), or to interj., occasionally to an adv. or conjunc.:— I beseech (pray) thee (you), go to, now, oh.

4995. נָא **nâ'**, *naw;* appar. from 5106 in the sense of *harshness* from refusal; prop. *tough*, i.e. *uncooked* (flesh):— raw.

4996. נֹא **Nô'**, *no;* of Eg. or.; *No* (i.e. *Thebes*), the capital of Upper Egypt:— No. Comp. 528.

4997. נֹאד **nô'd**, *node;* or

נֹאוד **nô'wd**, *node;* also (fem.)

נֹאדָה **nô'dâh**, *no-daw´;* from an unused root of uncert. signif.; a (skin or leather) *bag* (for fluids):— bottle.

נְאֹדְרִי **ne'dârîy**. See 142.

4998. נָאָה **nâ'âh**, *naw-aw´;* a prim. root; prop. to *be at home*, i.e. (by impl.) to be *pleasant* (or *suitable*), i.e. *beautiful:*— be beautiful, become, be comely.

4999. נָאָה **nâ'âh**, *naw-aw´;* from 4998; a *home;* fig. a *pasture:*— habitation, house, pasture, pleasant place.

5000. נָאוֶה **nâ'veh**, *naw-veh´;* from 4998 or 5116; *suitable*, or *beautiful:*— becometh, comely, seemly.

5001. נָאַם **nâ'am**, *naw-am´;* a prim. root; prop.

to *whisper*, i.e. (by impl.) to *utter* as an oracle:— say.

5002. נְאֻם **nᵉ'ûm**, *neh-oom´;* from 5001; an *oracle:*— (hath) said, saith.

5003. נָאַף **nâ'aph**, *naw-af´;* a prim. root; to *commit adultery;* fig. to *apostatize:*— adulterer (-ess), commit (-ing) adultery, woman that breaketh wedlock.

5004. נִאֻף **nî'ûph**, *nee-oof´;* from 5003; *adultery:*— adultery.

5005. נַאֲפוּף **na'ăphûwph**, *nah-af-oof´;* from 5003; *adultery:*— adultery.

5006. נָאַץ **nâ'ats**, *naw-ats´;* a prim. root; to *scorn;* or (Eccles. 12:5) by interchange for 5132, to *bloom:*— abhor, (give occasion to) blaspheme, contemn, despise, flourish, × great, provoke.

5007. נְאָצָה **nᵉ'âtsâh**, *neh-aw-tsaw´;* or

נֶאָצָה **ne'âtsâh**, *neh-aw-tsaw´;* from 5006; *scorn:*— blasphemy.

5008. נָאַק **nâ'aq**, *naw-ak´;* a prim. root; to *groan:*— groan.

5009. נְאָקָה **nᵉ'âqâh**, *neh-aw-kaw´;* from 5008; a *groan:*— groaning.

5010. נָאַר **nâ'ar**, *naw-ar´;* a prim. root; to *reject:*— abhor, make void.

5011. נֹב **Nôb**, *nobe;* the same as 5108; *fruit; Nob*, a place in Pal.:— Nob.

5012. נָבָא **nâbâ'**, *naw-baw´;* a prim. root; to *prophesy*, i.e. speak (or sing) by inspiration (in prediction or simple discourse):— prophesy (-ing), make self a prophet.

5013. נְבָא **nᵉbâ'** (Chald.), *neb-aw´;* corresp. to 5012:— prophesy.

5014. נָבַב **nâbab**, *naw-bab´;* a prim. root; to *pierce;* to *be hollow*, or (fig.) *foolish:*— hollow, vain.

5015. נְבוֹ **Nᵉbôw**, *neb-o´;* prob. of for. der.; *Nebo*, the name of a Bab. deity, also of a mountain in Moab, and of a place in Pal.:— Nebo.

5016. נְבוּאָה **nᵉbûw'âh**, *neb-oo-aw´;* from 5012; a *prediction* (spoken or written):— prophecy.

5017. נְבוּאָה **nᵉbûw'âh** (Chald.), *neb-oo-aw´;* corresp. to 5016; inspired *teaching:*— prophesying.

5018. נְבוּזַרְאֲדָן **Nᵉbûwzar'ădân**, *neb-oo-zar-ad-awn´;* of for. or.; *Nebuzaradan*, a Bab. general:— Nebuzaradan.

5019. נְבוּכַדְנֶאצַּר **Nᵉbûwkadne'tstsar**, *neb-oo-kad-nets-tsar´;* or

נְבֻכַדְנֶאצַּר **Nᵉbûkadne'tstsar** (2 Kings 24:1, 10), *neb-oo-kad-nets-tsar´;* or

נְבוּכַדְנֶצַּר **Nᵉbûwkadnetstsar** (Esth. 2:6; Dan. 1:18), *neb-oo-kad-nets-tsar´;* or

נְבוּכַדְרֶאצַּר **Nebûwkadre'tstsar**, *neb-oo-kad-rets-tsar'*; or

נְבוּכַדְרֶאצּוֹר° **Nebûwkadre'tstsôwr** (Ezra 2:1; Jer. 49:28), *neb-oo-kad-rets-tsore'*; or for. der.; *Nebukadnetstsar* (or *-retstsar*, or *-retstsor*), king of Bab.:— Nebuchadnezzar, Nebuchadrezzar.

5020. נְבוּכַדְנֶצַּר **Nebûwkadnetstsar** (Chald.), *neb-oo-kad-nets-tsar'*; corresp. to 5019:— Nebuchadnezzar.

5021. נְבוּשַׁזְבָּן **Nebûwshazbân**, *neb-oo-shaz-bawn'*; of for. der.; *Nebushazban*, Nebuchadnezzar's chief eunuch:— Nebushazban.

5022. נָבוֹת **Nâbôwth**, *naw-both'*; fem. plur. from the same as 5011; *fruits; Naboth*, an Isr.:— Naboth.

5023. נְבִזְבָּה **nᵉbizbâh** (Chald.), *neb-iz-baw'*; of uncert. der.; a *largess:*— reward.

5024. נָבַח **nâbach**, *naw-bakh'*; a prim. root; to *bark* (as a dog):— bark.

5025. נֹבַח **Nôbach**, *no'-bach*; from 5024; a *bark; Nobach*, the name of an Isr., and of a place E. of the Jordan:— Nobah.

5026. נִבְחַז **Nibchaz**, *nib-khaz'*; of for. or.; *Nibchaz*, a deity of the Avites:— Nibhaz.

5027. נָבַט **nâbat**, *naw-bat'*; a prim. root; to *scan*, i.e. look intently at; by impl. to *regard* with pleasure, favor or care:— (cause to) behold, consider, look (down), regard, have respect, see.

5028. נְבָט **Nebât**, *neb-awt'*; from 5027; *regard; Nebat*, the father of Jeroboam I:— Nebat.

5029. נְבִיא **nᵉbîy'** (Chald.), *neb-ee'*; corresp. to 5030; a *prophet:*— prophet.

5030. נָבִיא **nâbîy'**, *naw-bee'*; from 5012; a *prophet* or (gen.) *inspired* man:— prophecy, that prophesy, prophet.

5031. נְבִיאָה **nᵉbîy'âh**, *neb-ee-yaw'*; fem. of 5030; a *prophetess* or (gen.) *inspired* woman; by impl. a *poetess*; by association a *prophet's wife:*— prophetess.

5032. נְבָיוֹת **Nᵉbâyôwth**, *neb-aw-yoth'*; or

נְבָיֹת **Nᵉbâyôth**, *neb-aw-yoth'*; fem. plur. from 5107; *fruitfulnesses; Nebajoth*, a son of Ismael, and the country settled by him:— Nebaioth, Nebajoth.

5033. נֵבֶךְ **nêbek**, *nay'-bek;* from an unused root mean. to *burst* forth; a *fountain:*— spring.

5034. נָבֵל **nâbêl**, *naw-bale'*; a prim. root; to *wilt*; gen. to *fall* away, *fail, faint*; fig. to *be foolish* or (mor.) *wicked*; caus. to *despise, disgrace:*— disgrace, dishonour, lightly esteem, fade (away, -ing), fall (down, -ling, off), do foolishly, come to nought, × surely, make vile, wither.

5035. נֶבֶל **nebel**, *neh'-bel;* or

נֵבֶל **nêbel**, *nay'-bel;* from 5034; a skinbag for liquids (from *collapsing* when empty); hence, a *vase* (as similar in shape when full); also a *lyre* (as having a body of like form):— bottle, pitcher, psaltery, vessel, viol.

5036. נָבָל **nâbâl**, *naw-bawl'*; from 5034; *stupid; wicked* (espec. *impious*):— fool (-ish, -ish man, -ish woman), vile person.

5037. נָבָל **Nâbâl**, *naw-bawl'*; the same as 5036; *dolt; Nabal*, an Isr.:— Nabal.

5038. נְבֵלָה **nᵉbêlâh**, *neb-ay-law'*; from 5034; a *flabby* thing, i.e. a *carcase* or *carrion* (human or bestial, often collect.); fig. an *idol:*— (dead) body, (dead) carcase, dead of itself, which died, (beast) that (which) dieth of itself.

5039. נְבָלָה **nᵉbâlâh**, *neb-aw-law'*; fem. of 5036; *foolishness*, i.e. (mor.) *wickedness*; concr. a *crime*; by extens. *punishment:*— folly, vile, villany.

5040. נַבְלוּת **nablûwth**, *nab-looth'*; from 5036; prop. *disgrace*, i.e. the (female) *pudenda:*— lewdness.

5041. נְבַלָּט **Nᵉballât**, *neb-al-lawt'*; appar. from 5036 and 3909; *foolish secrecy; Neballat*, a place in Pal.:— Neballat.

5042. נָבַע **nâba'**, *naw-bah'*; a prim. root; to *gush* forth; fig. to *utter* (good or bad words); spec. to *emit* (a foul odor):— belch out, flowing, pour out, send forth, utter (abundantly).

5043. נֶבְרְשָׁא **nebreshâ'** (Chald.), *neb-reh-shaw'*; from an unused root mean. to *shine*; a *light*; plur. (collect.) a *chandelier:*— candlestick.

5044. נִבְשָׁן **Nibshân**, *nib-shawn'*; of uncert. der.; *Nibshan*, a place in Pal.:— Nibshan.

5045. נֶגֶב **negeb**, *neh'-gheb;* from an unused root mean. to *be parched*; the *south* (from its drought); spec. the *Negeb* or southern district of Judah, occasionally, *Egypt* (as south to Pal.):— south (country, side, -ward).

5046. נָגַד **nâgad**, *naw-gad'*; a prim. root; prop. to *front*, i.e. stand boldly out opposite; by impl. (caus.) to *manifest*; fig. to *announce* (always by word of mouth to one present); spec. to *expose, predict, explain, praise:*— bewray, × certainly, certify, declare (-ing), denounce, expound, × fully, messenger, plainly, profess, rehearse, report, shew (forth), speak, × surely, tell, utter.

5047. נְגַד **nᵉgad** (Chald.), *neg-ad'*; corresp. to 5046; to *flow* (through the idea of *clearing* the way):— issue.

5048. נֶגֶד **neged**, *neh'-ghed;* from 5046; a

front, i.e. part opposite; spec. a *counterpart,* or mate; usually (adv., espec. with prep.) *over against* or *before:*— about, (over) against, × aloof, × far (off), × from, over, presence, × other side, sight, × to view.

5049. נֶגֶד **neged** (Chald.), *neh´-ghed;* corresp. to 5048; *opposite:*— toward.

5050. נָגַהּ **nâgahh,** *naw-găh´;* a prim. root; to *glitter;* caus. to *illuminate:*— (en-) lighten, (cause to) shine.

5051. נֹגַהּ **nôgahh,** *no´-găh;* from 5050; *brilliancy* (lit. or fig.):— bright (-ness), light, (clear) shining.

5052. נֹגַהּ **Nôgahh,** *no´-găh;* the same as 5051; *Nogah,* a son of David:— Nogah.

5053. נֹגַהּ **nôgahh** (Chald.), *no´-găh;* corresp. to 5051; *dawn:*— morning.

5054. נְגֹהָה **neฺgôhâh,** *neg-o-haw´;* fem. of 5051; *splendor:*— brightness.

5055. נָגַח **nâgach,** *naw-gakh´;* a prim. root; to *butt* with the horns; fig. to *war* against:— gore, push (down, -ing).

5056. נַגָּח **naggâch,** *nag-gawkh´;* from 5055; *butting,* i.e. *vicious:*— used (wont) to push.

5057. נָגִיד **nâgîyd,** *naw-gheed´;* or

נָגִד **nâgîd,** *naw-gheed´;* from 5046; a *commander* (as occupying the *front*), civil, military or religious; gen. (abstr. plur.), *honorable* themes:— captain, chief, excellent thing, (chief) governor, leader, noble, prince, (chief) ruler.

5058. נְגִינָה **neฺgîynâh,** *neg-ee-naw´;* or

נְגִינַת **neฺgîynath** (Psa. 61:title), *neg-ee-nath´;* from 5059; prop. instrumental *music;* by impl. a stringed *instrument;* by extens. a *poem* set to music; spec. an *epigram:*— stringed instrument, musick, Neginoth [*plur.*], song.

5059. נָגַן **nâgan,** *naw-gan´;* a prim. root; prop. to *thrum,* i.e. *beat* a tune with the fingers; expec. to *play* on a stringed instrument; hence, (gen.), to *make music:*— player on instruments, sing to the stringed instruments, melody, ministrel, play (-er, -ing).

5060. נָגַע **nâga',** *naw-gah´;* a prim. root; prop. to *touch,* i.e. *lay the hand upon* (for any purpose; euphem. to *lie with* a woman); by impl. to *reach* (fig. to *arrive, acquire*); violently, to *strike* (punish, defeat, destroy, etc.):— beat, (× be able to) bring (down), cast, come (nigh), draw near (nigh), get up, happen, join, near, plague, reach (up), smite, strike, touch.

5061. נֶגַע **nega',** *neh´-gah;* from 5060; a *blow* (fig. *infliction*); also (by impl.) a *spot* (concr. a *leprous* person or dress):— plague, sore, stricken, stripe, stroke, wound.

5062. נָגַף **nâgaph,** *naw-gaf´;* a prim. root; to *push, gore, defeat, stub* (the toe), *inflict* (a disease):— beat, dash, hurt, plague, slay, smite (down), strike, stumble, × surely, put to the worse.

5063. נֶגֶף **negeph,** *neh´-ghef;* from 5062; a *trip* (of the foot); fig. an *infliction* (of disease):— plague, stumbling.

5064. נָגַר **nâgar,** *naw-gar´;* a prim. root; to *flow;* fig. to *stretch* out; caus. to *pour* out or down; fig. to *deliver* over:— fall, flow away, pour down (out), run, shed, spilt, trickle down.

5065. נָגַשׂ **nâgas,** *naw-gas´;* a prim. root; to *drive* (an animal, a workman, a debtor, an army); by impl. to *tax, harass, tyrannize:*— distress, driver, exact (-or), oppress (-or), × raiser of taxes, taskmaster.

5066. נָגַשׁ **nâgash,** *naw-gash´;* a prim. root; to *be* or *come* (caus. *bring*) *near* (for any purpose); euphem. to *lie with* a woman; as an enemy, to *attack;* relig. to *worship;* caus. to *present;* fig. to *adduce* an argument; by reversal, to *stand back:*— (make to) approach (nigh), bring (forth, hither, near), (cause to) come (hither, near, nigh), give place, go hard (up), (be, draw, go) near (nigh), offer, overtake, present, put, stand.

5067. נֵד **nêd,** *nade;* from 5110 in the sense of *piling* up; a *mound,* i.e. *wave:*— heap.

5068. נָדַב **nâdab,** *naw-dab´;* a prim. root; to *impel;* hence, to *volunteer* (as a soldier), to *present* spontaneously:— offer freely, be (give, make, offer self) willing (-ly).

5069. נְדַב **neฺdab** (Chald.), *ned-ab´;* corresp. to 5068; *be* (or *give*) *liberal* (-ly):— (be minded of ... own) freewill (offering), offer freely (willingly).

5070. נָדָב **Nâdâb,** *naw-dawb´;* from 5068; *liberal; Nadab,* the name of four Isr.:— Nadab.

5071. נְדָבָה **neฺdâbâh,** *ned-aw-baw´;* from 5068; prop. (abstr.) *spontaneity,* or (adj.) *spontaneous;* also (concr.) a *spontaneous* or (by infer., in plur.) *abundant* gift:— free (-will) offering, freely, plentiful, voluntary (-ily, offering), willing (-ly, offering).

5072. נְדַבְיָה **Neฺdabyâh,** *ned-ab-yaw´;* from 5068 and 3050; *largess of Jah; Nedabjah,* an Isr.:— Nedabiah.

5073. נִדְבָּךְ **nidbâk** (Chald.), *nid-bawk´;* from a root mean. to *stick;* a *layer* (of building materials):— row.

5074. נָדַד **nâdad,** *naw-dad´;* a prim. root; prop. to *wave* to and fro (rarely to *flap* up and down); fig. to *rove, flee,* or (caus.) to *drive* away:— chase (away), × could not, depart, flee (× apace, away), (re-) move, thrust away, wander (abroad, -er, -ing).

Hebrew

5075. נְדַד n°dad (Chald.), *ned-ad´;* corresp. to 5074; to *depart:*— go from.

5076. נָדֻד nâdûd, *naw-dood´;* pass. part. of 5074; prop. *tossed;* abstr. a *rolling* (on the bed):— tossing to and fro.

5077. נָדָה nâdâh, *naw-daw´;* or

נָדָא° nâdâ' (2 Kings 17:21), *naw-daw´;* a prim. root; prop. to *toss;* fig. to *exclude,* i.e. *banish, postpone, prohibit:*— cast out, drive, put far away.

5078. נֵדֶה nêdeh, *nay´-deh;* from 5077 in the sense of freely *flinging* money; a *bounty* (for prostitution):— gifts.

5079. נִדָּה niddâh, *nid-daw´;* from 5074; prop. *rejection;* by impl. *impurity,* espec. pers. (menstruation) or mor. (idolatry, incest):— × far, filthiness, × flowers, menstruous (woman), put apart, × removed (woman), separation, set apart, unclean (-ness, thing, with filthiness).

5080. נָדַח nâdach, *naw-dakh´;* a prim. root; to *push* off; used in a great variety of applications, lit. and fig. (to expel, mislead, strike, inflict, etc.):— banish, bring, cast down (out), chase, compel, draw away, drive (away, out, quite), fetch a stroke, force, go away, outcast, thrust away (out), withdraw.

5081. נָדִיב nâdîyb, *naw-deeb´;* from 5068; prop. *voluntary,* i.e. generous; hence, *magnanimous;* as noun, a *grandee* (sometimes a *tyrant*):— free, liberal (things), noble, prince, willing (lhearted]).

5082. נְדִיבָה n°dîybâh, *ned-ee-baw´;* fem. of 5081; prop. *nobility,* i.e. reputation:— soul.

5083. נָדָן nâdân, *naw-dawn´;* prob. from an unused root mean. to *give;* a *present* (for prostitution):— gift.

5084. נָדָן nâdân, *naw-dawn´;* of uncert. der.; a *sheath* (of a sword):— sheath.

5085. נִדְנֶה nidneh (Chald.), *nid-neh´;* from the same as 5084; a *sheath;* fig. the *body* (as the receptacle of the soul):— body.

5086. נָדַף nâdaph, *naw-daf´;* a prim. root; to *shove* asunder, i.e. *disperse:*— drive (away, to and fro), thrust down, shaken, tossed to and fro.

5087. נָדַר nâdar, *naw-dar´;* a prim. root; to *promise* (pos., to do or give something to God):— (make a) vow.

5088. נֶדֶר neder, *neh´-der;* or

נֵדֶר nêder, *nay´-der;* from 5087; a *promise* (to God); also (concr.) a thing *promised:*— vow (l-ed]).

5089. נֹהַּ nôahh, *no´-ăh;* from an unused root mean. to *lament; lamentation:*— wailing.

5090. נָהַג nâhag, *naw-hag´;* a prim. root; to *drive* forth (a person, an animal or chariot), i.e. *lead, carry away;* refl. to *proceed* (i.e. impel or guide oneself); also (from the *panting* induced by effort), to *sigh:*— acquaint, bring (away), carry away, drive (away), lead (away, forth), (be) guide, lead (away, forth).

5091. נָהָה nâhâh, *naw-haw´;* a prim. root; to *groan,* i.e. *bewail;* hence, (through the idea of *crying* aloud), to *assemble* (as if on proclamation):— lament, wail.

5092. נְהִי n°hîy, *neh-hee´;* from 5091; an *elegy:*— lamentation, wailing.

5093. נִהְיָה nihyâh, *nih-yaw´;* fem. of 5092; *lamentation:*— doleful.

5094. נְהִיר° n°hîyr (Chald.), *neh-heere´;* or

נְהִירוּ nehîyrûw (Chald.), *neh-hee-roo´;* from the same as 5105; *illumination,* i.e. (fig.) *wisdom:*— light.

5095. נָהַל nâhal, *naw-hal´;* a prim. root; prop. to *run* with a *sparkle,* i.e. *flow;* hence, (tran.), to *conduct,* and (by infer.) to *protect, sustain:*— carry, feed, guide, lead (gently, on).

5096. נַהֲלָל Nahălâl, *nah-hal-awl´;* or

נַהֲלֹל Nahălôl, *nah-hal-ole´;* the same as 5097; *Nahalal* or *Nahalol,* a place in Pal.:— Nahalal, Nahallal, Nahalol.

5097. נַהֲלֹל nahălôl, *nah-hal-ole´;* from 5095; *pasture:*— bush.

5098. נָהַם nâham, *naw-ham´;* a prim. root; to *growl:*— mourn, roar (-ing).

5099. נַהַם naham, *nah´-ham;* from 5098; a *snarl:*— roaring.

5100. נְהָמָה n°hâmâh, *neh-haw-maw´;* fem. of 5099; *snarling:*— disquietness, roaring.

5101. נָהַק nâhaq, *naw-hak´;* a prim. root; to *bray* (as an ass), *scream* (from hunger):— bray.

5102. נָהַר nâhar, *naw-har´;* a prim. root; to *sparkle,* i.e. (fig.) *be cheerful;* hence, (from the *sheen* of a running stream) to *flow,* i.e. (fig.) *assemble:*— flow (together), be lightened.

5103. נְהַר n°har (Chald.), *neh-har´;* from a root corresp. to 5102; a *river,* espec. the Euphrates:— river, stream.

5104. נָהָר nâhâr, *naw-hawr´;* from 5102; a *stream* (incl. the *sea;* expec. the Nile, Euphrates, etc.); fig. *prosperity:*— flood, river.

5105. נְהָרָה n°hârâh, *neh-haw-raw´;* from 5102 in its orig. sense; *daylight:*— light.

5106. נוּא nûw', *noo;* a prim. root; to *refuse, forbid, dissuade,* or *neutralize:*— break, disallow, discourage, make of none effect.

5107. נוּב nûwb, *noob;* a prim. root; to *ger-*

minate, i.e. (fig.) to (caus. *make*) *flourish;* also (of words), to *utter:*— bring forth (fruit), make cheerful, increase.

5108. נוֹב° **nôwb**, *nobe;* or

נֵיב **nêyb**, *nabe;* from 5107; *produce*, lit. or fig.:— fruit.

5109. נוֹבַי° **Nôwbay**, *no-bah'ee;* from 5108; *fruitful; Nobai*, an Isr.:— Nebai [*from the marg.*].

5110. נוּד **nûwd**, *nood;* a prim. root; to *nod*, i.e. *waver;* fig. to *wander, flee, disappear;* also (from *shaking* the head in sympathy), to *console, deplore*, or (from *tossing* the head in scorn) *taunt:*— bemoan, flee, get, mourn, make to move, take pity, remove, shake, skip for joy, be sorry, vagabond, way, wandering.

5111. נוּד **nûwd** (Chald.), *nood;* corresp. to 5116; to *flee:*— get away.

5112. נוֹד **nôwd**, *node* [only defect.

נֹד **nôd**, *node*]; from 5110; *exile:*— wandering.

5113. נוֹד **Nôwd**, *node;* the same as 5112; *vagrancy; Nod*, the land of Cain:— Nod.

5114. נוֹדָב **Nôwdâb**, *no-dawb';* from 5068; *noble; Nodab*, an Arab tribe:— Nodab.

5115. נָוָה **nâvâh**, *naw-vaw';* a prim. root; to *rest* (as at home); caus. (through the impl. idea of *beauty* [comp. 5116]), to *celebrate* (with praises):— keep at home, prepare an habitation.

5116. נָוֶה **nâveh**, *naw-veh';* or (fem.)

נָוָה **nâvâh**, *naw-vaw';* from 5115; (adj.) *at home;* hence, (by impl. of satisfaction) *lovely;* also (noun) a *home*, of God (temple), men (residence), flocks (pasture), or wild animals (*den*):— comely, dwelling (place), fold, habitation, pleasant place, sheepcote, stable, tarried.

5117. נוּחַ **nûwach**, *noo'-akh;* a prim. root; to *rest*, i.e. *settle* down; used in a great variety of applications, lit. and fig., intr., tran. and caus. (to *dwell, stay, let fall, place, let alone, withdraw, give comfort*, etc.):— cease, be confederate, lay, let down, (be) quiet, remain, (cause to, be at, give, have, make to) rest, set down. Comp. 3241.

5118. נוּחַ **nûwach**, *noo'-akh;* or

נֹחַ **nôwach**, *no'-akh;* from 5117; *quiet:*— rest (-ed, -ing place).

5119. נוֹחָה **Nôwchâh**, *no-chaw';* fem. of 5118; *quietude; Nochah*, an Isr.:— Nohah.

5120. נוּט **nûwṭ**, *noot;* to *quake:*— be moved.

5121. נָוִית° **Nâvîyth**, *naw-veeth';* from 5115; *residence; Navith*, a place in Pal.:— Naioth [*from the marg.*].

5122. נְוָלוּ **nevâlûw** (Chald.), *nev-aw-loo';* or

נְוָלִי **nevâlîy** (Chald.), *nev-aw-lee';* from an unused root prob. mean. to *be foul;* a *sink:*— dunghill.

5123. נוּם **nûwm**, *noom;* a prim. root; to *slumber* (from drowsiness):— sleep, slumber.

5124. נוּמָה **nûwmâh**, *noo-maw';* from 5123; *sleepiness:*— drowsiness.

5125. נוּן **nûwn**, *noon;* a prim. root; to *resprout*, i.e. propagate by shoots; fig., to *be perpetual:*— be continued.

5126. נוּן **Nûwn**, *noon;* or

נוֹן **Nôwn** (1 Chron. 7:27), *nohn;* from 5125; *perpetuity, Nun* or *Non*, the father of Joshua:— Non, Nun.

5127. נוּס **nûwç**, *noos;* a prim. root; to *flit*, i.e. *vanish* away (subside, escape; caus. chase, impel, deliver):— × abate, away, be displayed, (make to) flee (away, -ing), put to flight, × hide, lift up a standard.

5128. נוּעַ **nûwa'**, *noo'-ah;* a prim. root; to *waver*, in a great variety of applications, lit. and fig. (as subjoined):— continually, fugitive, × make, to [go] up and down, be gone away, (be) move (-able, -d), be promoted, reel, remove, scatter, set, shake, sift, stagger, to and fro, be vagabond, wag, (make) wander (up and down).

5129. נוֹעַדְיָה **Nôw'adyâh**, *no-ad-yaw';* from 3259 and 3050; *convened of Jah; Noadjah*, the name of an Isr., and a false prophetess:— Noadiah.

5130. נוּף **nûwph**, *noof;* a prim. root; to *quiver* (i.e. *vibrate* up and down, or *rock* to and fro); used in a great variety of applications (incl. *sprinkling, beckoning, rubbing, bastinadoing, sawing, waving*, etc.):— lift up, move, offer, perfume, send, shake, sift, strike, wave.

5131. נוֹף **nôwph**, *nofe;* from 5130; *elevation:*— situation. Comp. 5297.

5132. נוּץ **nûwts**, *noots;* a prim. root; prop. to *flash;* hence, to *blossom* (from the brilliancy of color); also, to *fly* away (from the quickness of motion):— flee away, bud (forth).

5133. נוֹצָה **nôwtsâh**, *no-tsaw';* or

נֹצָה **nôtsâh**, *no-tsaw';* fem. act. part. of 5327 in the sense of *flying;* a *pinion* (or wing feather); often (collect.) *plumage:*— feather (-s), ostrich.

5134. נוּק **nûwq**, *nook;* a prim. root; to *suckle:*— nurse.

5135. נוּר **nûwr** (Chald.), *noor;* from an unused root (corresp. to that of 5216) mean. to *shine; fire:*— fiery, fire.

5136. נוּשׁ **nûwsh**, *noosh;* a prim. root; to *be*

sick, i.e. (fig.) *distressed*:— be full of heaviness.

5137. זָה **nâzâh**, *naw-zaw´*; a prim. root; to *spirt*, i.e. *besprinkle* (espec. in expiation):— sprinkle.

5138. זִיד **nâzîyd**, *naw-zeed´*; from 2102; something *boiled*, i.e. *soup*:— pottage.

5139. זִיר **nâzîyr**, *naw-zeer´*; or

זִר **nâzir**, *naw-zeer´*; from 5144; *separate*, i.e. *consecrated* (as *prince*, a *Nazirite*); hence, (fig. from the latter) an *unpruned* vine (like an unshorn Nazirite):— Nazarite [by a false alliteration with Nazareth], separate (-d), vine undressed.

5140. זַל **nâzal**, *naw-zal´*; a prim. root; to *drip*, or *shed* by trickling:— distil, drop, flood, (cause to) flow (-ing), gush out, melt, pour (down), running water, stream.

5141. זֶם **nezem**, *neh´-zem*; from an unused root of uncert. mean.; a nose-*ring*:— earring, jewel.

5142. זֶק **nᵉzaq** (Chald.), *nez-ak´*; corresp. to the root of 5143; to *suffer* (caus. *inflict*) *loss*:— have (en-) damage, hurt (-ful).

5143. זֶק **nêzeq**, *nay´zek*; from an unused root mean. to *injure*; *loss*:— damage.

5144. זַר **nâzar**, *naw-zar´*; a prim. root; to *hold aloof*, i.e. (intr.) *abstain* (from food and drink, from impurity, and even from divine worship [i.e. *apostatize*]); spec. to *set apart* (to sacred purposes), i.e. *devote*:— consecrate, separate (-ing, self).

5145. זֶר **nezer**, *neh´-zer*; or

זֵר **nêzer**, *nay´-zer*; from 5144; prop. something *set apart*, i.e. (abstr.) *dedication* (of a priest or Nazirite); hence, (concr.) unshorn *locks*; also (by impl.) a *chaplet* (espec. of royalty):— consecration, crown, hair, separation.

5146. חַ **Nôach**, *no´-akh*; the same as 5118; *rest*; *Noach*, the patriarch of the flood:— Noah.

5147. חְבִּי **Nachbîy**, *nakh-bee´*; from 2247; *occult*; *Nachbi*, an Isr.:— Nakbi.

5148. חָה **nâchâh**, *naw-khaw´*; a prim. root; to *guide*; by impl. to *transport* (into exile, or as colonists):— bestow, bring, govern, guide, lead (forth), put, straiten.

5149. חוּם **Nᵉchûwm**, *neh-khoom´*; from 5162; *comforted*; *Nechum*, an Isr.:— Nehum.

5150. חוּם **nichûwm**, *nee-khoom´*; or

חֻם **nichûm**, *nee-khoom´*; from 5162; prop. *consoled*; abstr. *solace*:— comfort (-able), repenting.

5151. חוּם **Nachûwm**, *nakh-oom´*; from 5162; *comfortable*; *Nachum*, an Isr. prophet:— Nahum.

5152. חוֹר **Nâchôwr**, *naw-khore´*; from the same as 5170; *snorer*; *Nachor*, the name of the grandfather and a brother of Abraham:— Nahor.

5153. חוּשׁ **nâchûwsh**, *naw-khoosh´*; appar. pass. part. of 5172 (perh. in the sense of *ringing*, i.e. bell-metal; or from the *red* color of the throat of a serpent [5175, as denom.] when hissing); *coppery*, i.e. (fig.) *hard*:— of brass.

5154. חוּשָׁה **nᵉchûwshâh**, *nekh-oo-shaw´*; or

חֻשָׁה **nᵉchûshâh**, *nekh-oo-shaw´*; fem. of 5153; *copper*:— brass, steel. Comp. 5176.

5155. חִילָה **Nᵉchîylâh**, *nekh-ee-law´*; prob. denom. from 2485; a *flute*:— [plur.] Nehiloth.

5156. חִיר **nᵉchîyr**, *nekh-eer´*; from the same as 5170; a *nostril*:— [dual] nostrils.

5157. חַל **nâchal**, *naw-khal´*; a prim. root; to *inherit* (as a [fig.] mode of descent), or (gen.) to *occupy*; caus. to *bequeath*, or (gen.) *distribute*, *instate*:— divide, have ([inheritance]), take as an heritage, (cause to, give to, make to) inherit, (distribute for, divide [for, for an, by], give for, have, leave for, take [for]) inheritance, (have in, cause to, be made to) possess (-ion).

5158. חַל **nachal**, *nakh´-al*; or (fem.)

חְלָה **nachlâh** (Psa. 124:4), *nakh´-law*; or

חְלָה **nachălâh** (Ezek. 47:19; 48:28), *nakh-al-aw´*; from 5157 in its orig. sense; a *stream*, espec. a winter *torrent*; (by impl.) a (narrow) *valley* (in which a brook runs); also a *shaft* (of a mine):— brook, flood, river, stream, valley.

5159. חְלָה **nachălâh**, *nakh-al-aw´*; from 5157 (in its usual sense); prop. something *inherited*, i.e. (abstr.) *occupancy*, or (concr.) an *heirloom*; gen. an *estate, patrimony* or *portion*:— heritage, to inherit, inheritance, possession. Comp. 5158.

5160. חְלִיאֵל **Nachălîy´êl**, *nakh-al-ee-ale´*; from 5158 and 410; *valley of God*; *Nachaliël*, a place in the Desert:— Nahaliel.

5161. חְלָמִי **Nechĕlâmîy**, *nekh-el-aw-mee´*; appar. a patron. from an unused name (appar. pass. part. of 2492); *dreamed*; a *Nechelamite*, or desc. of Nechlam:— Nehelamite.

5162. חַם **nâcham**, *naw-kham´*; a prim. root; prop. to *sigh*, i.e. *breathe* strongly; by impl. to *be sorry*, i.e. (in a favorable sense) to *pity*, *console* or (refl.) *rue*; or (unfavorably) to *avenge* (oneself):— comfort (self), ease [one's self], repent (-er,-ing, self).

5163. חַם **Nacham**, *nakh´-am*; from 5162; *consolation*; *Nacham*, an Isr.:— Naham.

5164. נֹחַם **nôcham**, *no´-kham;* from 5162; *ruefulness,* i.e. *desistance:*— repentance.

5165. נֶחָמָה **nechâmâh**, *nekh-aw-maw´;* from 5162; *consolation:*— comfort.

5166. נְחֶמְיָה **Nechemyâh**, *nekh-em-yaw´;* from 5162 and 3050; *consolation of Jah; Nechemjah,* the name of three Isr.:— Nehemiah.

5167. נַחֲמָנִי **Nachămânîy**, *nakh-am-aw-nee´;* from 5162; *consolatory; Nachamani,* an Isr.:— Nahamani.

5168. נַחְנוּ **nachnûw**, *nakh-noo´;* for 587; *we:*— we.

5169. נָחַץ **nâchats**, *naw-khats´;* a prim. root; to *be urgent:*— require haste.

5170. נַחַר **nachar**, *nakh´-ar;* and (fem.)

נַחֲרָה **nachărâh**, *nakh-ar-aw´;* from an unused root mean. to *snort* or *snore;* a *snorting:*— nostrils, snorting.

5171. נַחֲרַי **Nachăray**, *nakh-ar-ah´-ee;* or

נַחְרַי **Nachray**, *nakh-rah´-ee;* from the same as 5170; *snorer; Nacharai* or *Nachrai,* an Isr.:— Naharai, Nahari.

5172. נָחַשׁ **nâchash**, *naw-khash´;* a prim. root; prop. to *hiss,* i.e. *whisper* a (magic) spell; gen. to *prognosticate:*— × certainly, divine, enchanter, (use) × enchantment, learn by experience, × indeed, diligently observe.

5173. נַחַשׁ **nachash**, *nakh´-ash;* from 5172; an *incantation* or *augury:*— enchantment.

5174. נְחָשׁ **nechâsh** (Chald.), *nekh-awsh´;* corresp. to 5154; *copper:*— brass.

5175. נָחָשׁ **nâchâsh**, *naw-khawsh´;* from 5172; a *snake* (from its *hiss*):— serpent.

5176. נָחָשׁ **Nâchâsh**, *naw-khawsh´;* the same as 5175; *Nachash,* the name of two persons appar. non-Isr.:— Nahash.

נְחֻשָׁה **nechûshâh**. See 5154.

5177. נַחְשׁוֹן **Nachshôwn**, *nakh-shone´;* from 5172; *enchanter; Nachshon,* an Isr.:— Naashon, Nahshon.

5178. נְחֹשֶׁת **nechôsheth**, *nekh-o´-sheth;* for 5154; *copper,* hence, something made of that metal, i.e. *coin,* a *fetter;* fig. *base* (as compared with gold or silver):— brasen, brass, chain, copper, fetter (of brass), filthiness, steel.

5179. נְחֻשְׁתָּא **Nechushtâ'**, *nekh-oosh-taw´;* from 5178; *copper; Nechushta,* an Israelitess:— Nehushta.

5180. נְחֻשְׁתָּן **Nechushtân**, *nekh-oosh-tawn´;* from 5178; something made of *copper,* i.e. the copper *serpent* of the Desert:— Nehushtan.

5181. נָחַת **nâchath**, *naw-khath´;* a prim. root; to *sink,* i.e. *descend;* caus., to *press* or *lead*

down:— be broken, (cause to) come down, enter, go down, press sore, settle, stick fast.

5182. נְחַת **nechath** (Chald.), *nekh-ath´;* corresp. to 5181; to *descend;* caus., to *bring away, deposit, depose:*— carry, come down, depose, lay up, place.

5183. נַחַת **nachath**, *nakh´-ath;* from 5182; a *descent,* i.e. *imposition,* unfavorable (*punishment*) or favorable (*food*); also (intr.) perh. from 5117), *restfulness:*— lighting down, quiet (-ness), to rest, be set on.

5184. נַחַת **Nachath**, *nakh´-ath;* the same as 5183; *quiet; Nachath,* the name of an Edomite and of two Isr.:— Nahath.

5185. נָחֵת **nâchêth**, *naw-khayth´;* from 5181; *descending:*— come down.

5186. נָטָה **nâtâh**, *naw-taw´;* a prim. root; to *stretch* or spread out; by impl. to *bend* away (incl. mor. deflection); used in a great variety of application (as follows):— + afternoon, apply, bow (down, -ing), carry aside, decline, deliver, extend, go down, be gone, incline, intend, lay, let down, offer, outstretched, overthrown, pervert, pitch, prolong, put away, shew, spread (out), stretch (forth, out), take (aside), turn (aside, away), wrest, cause to yield.

5187. נָטִיל **netîyl**, *net-eel´;* from 5190; *laden:*— that bear.

5188. נְטִיפָה **netîyphâh**, *net-ee-faw´;* from 5197; a *pendant* for the ears (espec. of pearls):— chain, collar.

5189. נְטִישָׁה **netîyshâh**, *net-ee-shaw´;* from 5203; a *tendril* (as an offshoot):— battlement, branch, plant.

5190. נָטַל **nâtal**, *naw-tal´;* a prim. root; to *lift;* by impl. to *impose:*— bear, offer, take up.

5191. נְטַל **netal** (Chald.), *net-al´;* corresp. to 5190; to *raise:*— take up.

5192. נֵטֶל **nêtel**, *nay´-tel;* from 5190; a *burden:*— weighty.

5193. נָטַע **nâta'**, *naw-tah´;* a prim. root; prop. to *strike* in, i.e. *fix;* spec. to *plant* (lit. or fig.):— fastened, plant (-er).

5194. נֶטַע **neta'**, *neh´-tah;* from 5193; a *plant;* collect. a *plantation;* abstr. a *planting:*— plant.

5195. נָטִיעַ **nâtîya'**, *naw-tee´-ah;* from 5193; a *plant:*— plant.

5196. נְטָעִים **Netâ'îym**, *net-aw-eem´;* plur. of 5194; *Netaim,* a place in Pal.:— plants.

5197. נָטַף **nâtaph**, *naw-taf´;* a prim. root; to *ooze,* i.e. *distil* gradually; by impl. to *fall in drops;* fig. to *speak* by inspiration:— drop (-ping), prophesy (-et).

5198. נָטָף **nâṭâph**, *naw-tawf´;* from 5197; a *drop;* spec., an aromatic *gum* (prob. *stacte*):— drop, stacte.

5199. נְטֹפָה **Nᵉṭôphâh**, *net-o-faw´;* from 5197; *distillation; Netophah,* a place in Pal.:— Netophah.

5200. נְטֹפָתִי **Nᵉṭôphâthîy**, *net-o-faw-thee´;* patron. from 5199; a *Netophathite,* or inhab. of Netophah:— Netophathite.

5201. נָטַר **nâṭar**, *naw-tar´;* a prim. root; to *guard;* fig., to *cherish* (anger):— bear grudge, keep (-er), reserve.

5202. נְטַר **nᵉṭar** (Chald.), *net-ar´;* corresp. to 5201; to *retain:*— keep.

5203. נָטַשׁ **nâṭash**, *naw-tash´;* a prim. root; prop. to *pound,* i.e. *smite;* by impl. (as if beating out, and thus expanding) to *disperse;* also, to *thrust* off, down, out or upon (incl. *reject, let alone, permit, remit,* etc.):— cast off, drawn, let fall, forsake, join [battle], leave (off), lie still, loose, spread (self) abroad, stretch out, suffer.

5204. נִי **nîy**, *nee;* a doubtful word; appar. from 5091; *lamentation:*— wailing.

5205. נִיד **nîyd**, *need;* from 5110; *motion* (of the lips in speech):— moving.

5206. נִידָה **nîydâh**, *nee-daw´;* fem. of 5205; *removal,* i.e. *exile:*— removed.

5207. נִיחוֹחַ **nîchôwach**, *nee-kho´-akh;* or

נִיחֹחַ **nîychôach**, *nee-kho´-akh;* from 5117; prop. *restful,* i.e. *pleasant;* abstr. *delight:*— sweet (odour).

5208. נִיחוֹחַ **nîychôwach** (Chald.), *nee-kho´-akh;* or (short.)

נִיחֹחַ **nîychôach** (Chald.), *nee-kho´-akh;* corresp. to 5207; *pleasure:*— sweet odour (savour).

5209. נִין **nîyn**, *neen;* from 5125; *progeny:*— son.

5210. נִינְוֵה **Nîynᵉvêh**, *nee-nev-ay´;* of for. or.; *Nineveh,* the capital of Assyria:— Nineveh.

5211. נִיס° **nîyç**, *neece;* from 5127; *fugitive:*— that fleeth.

5212. נִיסָן **Nîyçân**, *nee-sawn´;* prob. of for. or.; *Nisan,* the first month of the Jewish sacred year:— Nisan.

5213. נִיצוֹץ **nîytsôwts**, *nee-tsotes´;* from 5340; a *spark:*— spark.

5214. נִיר **nîyr**, *neer;* a root prob. ident. with that of 5216, through the idea of the *gleam* of a fresh furrow; to *till* the soil:— break up.

5215. נִיר **nîyr**, *neer;* or

נִר **nîr**, *neer;* from 5214; prop. *plowing,* i.e. (concr.) freshly *plowed* land:— fallow ground, ploughing, tillage.

5216. נִיר **nîyr**, *neer* or

נִר **nîr**, *neer;* also

נֵיר **nêyr**, *nare;* or

נֵר **nêr**, *nare;* or (fem.)

נֵרָה **nêrâh**, *nay-raw´;* from a prim. root [see 5214; 5135] prop. mean. to *glisten;* a *lamp* (i.e. the burner) or *light* (lit. or fig.):— candle, lamp, light.

5217. נָכָא **nâkâ'**, *naw-kaw´;* a prim. root; to *smite,* i.e. *drive* away:— be viler.

5218. נָכֵא **nâkê'**, *naw-kay´;* or

נָכָא **nâkâ'**, *naw-kaw´;* from 5217; *smitten,* i.e. (fig.) *afflicted:*— broken, stricken, wounded.

5219. נְכֹאת **nᵉkô'th**, *nek-ohth´;* from 5218; prop. a *smiting,* i.e. (concr.) an aromatic *gum* [perh. *styrax*] (as *powdered*):— spicery (-ces).

5220. נֶכֶד **neked**, *neh´-ked;* from an unused root mean. to *propagate; offspring:*— nephew, son's son.

5221. נָכָה **nâkâh**, *naw-kaw´;* a prim. root; to *strike* (lightly or severely, lit. or fig.):— beat, cast forth, clap, give [wounds], × go forward, × indeed, kill, make [slaughter], murderer, punish, slaughter, slay (-er, -ing), smite (-r, -ing), strike, be stricken, (give) stripes, × surely, wound.

5222. נֵכֶה **nêkeh**, *nay-keh´;* from 5221; a *smiter,* i.e. (fig.) *traducer:*— abject.

5223. נָכֶה **nâkeh**, *naw-keh´; smitten,* i.e. (lit.) *maimed,* or (fig.) *dejected:*— contrite, lame.

5224. נְכוֹ **Nᵉkôw**, *nek-o´;* prob. of Eg. or.; *Neko,* an Eg. king:— Necho. Comp. 6549.

5225. נָכוֹן **Nâkôwn**, *naw-kone´;* from 3559; *prepared; Nakon,* prob. an Isr.:— Nachon.

5226. נֵכַח **nêkach**, *nay´-kakh;* from an unused root mean. to *be straightforward;* prop. the *fore* part; used adv., *opposite:*— before, over against.

5227. נֹכַח **nôkach**, *no´-kakh;* from the same as 5226; prop., the *front* part; used adv. (espec. with prep.), *opposite, in front of, forward, in behalf of:*— (over) against, before, direct [-ly], for, right (on).

5228. נָכֹחַ **nâkôach**, *naw-ko´-akh;* from the same as 5226; *straightforward,* i.e. (fig.), *equitable, correct,* or (abstr.), *integrity:*— plain, right, uprightness.

5229. נְכֹחָה **nᵉkôchâh**, *nek-o-khaw´;* fem. of 5228; prop. *straightforwardness,* i.e. (fig.) *integrity,* or (concr.) a *truth:*— equity, right (thing), uprightness.

5230. נָכַל **nâkal**, *naw-kal´;* a prim. root; to *defraud,* i.e. *act treacherously:*— beguile, conspire, deceiver, deal subtilly.

5231. נְכֵל **nêkel**, *nay´-kel;* from 5230; *deceit:—* wile.

5232. נְכַס **n^ekaç** (Chald.), *nek-as´;* corresp. to 5233:— goods.

5233. נֶכֶס **nekeç**, *neh´-kes;* from an unused root mean. to *accumulate; treasure:—* riches, wealth.

5234. נָכַר **nâkar**, *naw-kar´;* a prim. root; prop. to *scrutinize,* i.e. look intently at; hence (with *recognition* impl.), to *acknowledge, be acquainted with, care for, respect, revere,* or (with *suspicion* impl.), to *disregard, ignore, be strange* toward, *reject, resign, dissimulate* (as if ignorant or disowning):— acknowledge, × could, deliver, discern, dissemble, estrange, feign self to be another, know, take knowledge (notice), perceive, regard, (have) respect, behave (make) self strange (-ly).

5235. נֵכֶר **neker**, *neh´-ker;* or

נֹכֶר **nôker**, *no´-ker;* from 5234; something *strange,* i.e. unexpected *calamity:—* strange.

5236. נֵכָר **nêkâr**, *nay-kawr´;* from 5234; *foreign,* or (concr.) a *foreigner,* or (abstr.) *heathendom:—* alien, strange (+ -er).

5237. נָכְרִי **nokrîy**, *nok-ree´;* from 5235 (second form); *strange,* in a variety of degrees and applications (*foreign, non-relative, adulterous, different, wonderful*):— alien, foreigner, outlandish, strange (-r, woman).

5238. נְכֹת **n^ekôth**, *nek-ōth´;* prob. for 5219; *spicery,* i.e. (gen.) *valuables:—* precious things.

5239. נָלָה **nâlâh**, *naw-law´;* appar. a prim. root; to *complete:—* make an end.

5240. נִמְבְזֶה **n^emibzeh**, *nem-ib-zeh´;* from 959, *despised:—* vile.

5241. נְמוּאֵל **N^emûw'êl**, *nem-oo-ale´;* appar. for 3223; *Nemuel,* the name of two Isr.:— Nemuel.

5242. נְמוּאֵלִי **N^emûw'êlîy**, *nem-oo-ay-lee´;* from 5241; a *Nemuelite,* or desc. of Nemuel:— Nemuelite.

5243. נָמַל **nâmal**, *naw-mal´;* a prim. root; to *become clipped* or (spec.) *circumcised:—* (branch to) be cut down (off), circumcise.

5244. נְמָלָה **n^emâlâh**, *nem-aw-law´;* fem. from 5243; an *ant* (prob. from its almost *bisected* form):— ant.

5245. נְמַר **n^emar** (Chald.), *nem-ar´;* corresp. to 5246:— leopard.

5246. נָמֵר **nâmêr**, *naw-mare´;* from an unused root mean. prop. to *filtrate,* i.e. *be limpid* [comp 5247 and 5249]; and thus to *spot* or *stain* as if by dripping; a *leopard* (from its stripes):— leopard.

נִמְרֹד **Nimrôd**. See 5248.

5247. נִמְרָה **Nimrâh**, *nim-raw´;* from the same

as 5246; *clear* water; *Nimrah,* a place E. of the Jordan:— Nimrah. See also 1039, 5249.

5248. נִמְרוֹד **Nimrôwd**, *nim-rode´;* or

נִמְרֹד **Nimrôd**, *nim-rode´;* prob. of for. or.; *Nimrod,* a son of Cush:— Nimrod.

5249. נִמְרִים **Nimrîym**, *nim-reem´;* plur. of a masc. corresp. to 5247; *clear* waters; *Nimrim,* a place E. of the Jordan:— Nimrim. Comp. 1039.

5250. נִמְשִׁי **Nimshîy**, *nim-shee´;* prob. from 4871; *extricated; Nimshi,* the (grand-) father of Jehu:— Nimshi.

5251. נֵס **nêç**, *nace;* from 5264; a *flag;* also a *sail;* by impl. a *flagstaff;* gen. a *signal;* fig. a *token:—* banner, pole, sail, (en-) sign, standard.

5252. נְסִבָּה **n^eçibbâh**, *nes-ib-baw´;* fem. pass. part. of 5437; prop. an *environment,* i.e. *circumstance* or *turn* of affairs:— cause.

5253. נָסַג **nâçag**, *naw-sag´;* a prim. root; to *retreat:—* departing away, remove, take (hold), turn away.

נְסָה **n^eçâh**. See 5375.

5254. נָסָה **nâçâh**, *naw-saw´;* a prim. root; to *test;* by impl. to *attempt:—* adventure, assay, prove, tempt, try.

5255. נָסַח **nâçach**, *naw-sakh´;* a prim. root; to *tear* away:— destroy, pluck, root.

5256. נְסַח **n^eçach** (Chald.), *nes-akh´;* corresp. to 5255:— pull down.

5257. נְסִיךְ **n^eçîyk**, *nes-eek´;* from 5258; prop. something *poured* out, i.e. a *libation;* also a *molten image;* by impl. a *prince* (as *anointed*):— drink offering, duke, prince (-ipal).

5258. נָסַךְ **nâçak**, *naw-sak´;* a prim. root; to *pour* out, espec. a libation, or to *cast* (metal); by anal. to *anoint* a king:— cover, melt, offer, (cause to) pour (out), set (up).

5259. נָסַךְ **nâçak**, *naw-sak´;* a prim. root [prob. ident. with 5258 through the idea of *fusion*]; to *interweave,* i.e. (fig.) to *overspread:—* that is spread.

5260. נְסַךְ **n^eçak** (Chald.), *nes-ak´;* corresp. to 5258; to *pour* out a libation:— offer.

5261. נְסַךְ **n^eçak** (Chald.), *nes-ak´;* corresp. to 5262; a *libation:—* drink offering.

5262. נֶסֶךְ **neçek**, *neh´-sek;* or

נֵסֶךְ **nêçek**, *nay´-sek;* from 5258; a *libation;* also a *cast idol:—* cover, drink offering, molten image.

נִסְמָן **niçmân**. See 5567.

5263. נָסַס **nâçaç**, *naw-sas´;* a prim. root; to *wane,* i.e. *be sick:—* faint.

5264. נָסַס **nâçaç**, *naw-sas´;* a prim. root; to *gleam* from afar, i.e. to *be conspicuous* as a signal; or rather perh. a denom. from 5251 [and ident. with 5263, through the idea of a flag as *fluttering* in the wind]; to *raise a beacon:*— lift up as an ensign.

5265. נָסַע **nâça'**, *naw-sah´*; a prim. root; prop. to *pull* up, espec. the tent-pins, i.e. *start* on a journey:— cause to blow, bring, get, (make to) go (away, forth, forward, onward, out), (take) journey, march, remove, set aside (forward), × still, be on his (go their) way.

5266. נָסַק **nâçaq**, *naw-sak´*; a prim. root; to *go* up:— ascend.

5267. נְסַק **nᵉçaq** (Chald.), *nes-ak´*; corresp. to 5266:— take up.

5268. נִסְרֹךְ **Niçrôk**, *nis-roke´*; of for. or.; *Nisrok*, a Bab. idol:— Nisroch.

5269. נֵעָה **Nê'âh**, *nay-aw´*; from 5128; *motion; Neäh*, a place in Pal.:— Neah.

5270. נֹעָה **Nô'âh**, *no-aw´*; from 5128; *movement; Noah*, an Israelitess:— Noah.

5271. נָעוּר **nâ'ûwr**, *naw-oor´*; or

נָעֻר **nâ'ûr**, *naw-oor´*; and (fem.)

נְעֻרָה **nᵉ'ûrâh**, *neh-oo-raw´*; prop. pass. part. from 5288 as denom.; (only in plur. collect. or emphat.) *youth*, the state (*juvenility*) or the persons (*young* people):— childhood, youth.

5272. נְעִיאֵל **Nᵉ'îy'êl**, *neh-ee-ale´*; from 5128 and 410; *moved of God; Neiel*, a place in Pal.:— Neiel.

5273. נָעִים **nâ'îym**, *naw-eem´*; from 5276; *delightful* (obj. or subj., lit. or fig.):— pleasant (-ure), sweet.

5274. נָעַל **nâ'al**, *naw-al´*; a prim. root; prop. to *fasten* up, i.e. with a bar or cord; hence, (denom. from 5275), to *sandal*, i.e. furnish with slippers:— bolt, inclose, lock, shoe, shut up.

5275. נַעַל **na'al**, *nah´-al*; or (fem.)

נַעֲלָה **na'âlâh**, *nah-al-aw´*; from 5274; prop. a sandal *tongue;* by extens. a *sandal* or *slipper* (sometimes as a symbol of occupancy, a refusal to marry, or of something valueless):— dryshod, (pair of) shoe (1-latchet1, -s).

5276. נָעֵם **nâ'êm**, *naw-ame´*; a prim. root; to *be agreeable* (lit. or fig.):— pass in beauty, be delight, be pleasant, be sweet.

5277. נַעַם **Na'am**, *nah´-am*; from 5276; *pleasure; Naam*, an Isr.:— Naam.

5278. נֹעַם **no'am**, *no´-am*; from 5276; *agreeableness*, i.e. *delight, suitableness, splendor* or *grace:*— beauty, pleasant (-ness).

5279. נַעֲמָה **Na'âmâh**, *nah-am-aw´*; fem. of 5277; *pleasantness; Naamah*, the name of an antediluvian woman, of an Ammonitess, and of a place in Pal.:— Naamah.

5280. נַעֲמִי **Na'âmîy**, *nah-am-ee´*; patron. from

5283; a *Naamanite*, or desc. of Naaman (collect.):— Naamites.

5281. נָעֳמִי **No'ŏmîy**, *no-ŏm-ee´*; from 5278; *pleasant; Noomi*, an Israelitess:— Naomi.

5282. נַעֲמָן **na'âmân**, *nah-am-awn´*; from 5276; *pleasantness* (plur. as concr.):— pleasant.

5283. נַעֲמָן **Na'âmân**, *nah-am-awn´*; the same as 5282; *Naaman*, the name of an Isr. and of a Damascene:— Naaman.

5284. נַעֲמָתִי **Na'âmâthîy**, *nah-am-aw-thee´*; patrial from a place corresp. in name (but not ident.) with 5279; a *Naamathite*, or inhab. of Naamah:— Naamathite.

5285. נַעֲצוּץ **na'àtsûwts**, *nah-ats-oots´*; from an unused root mean. to *prick;* prob. a *brier;* by impl. a *thicket* of thorny bushes:— thorn.

5286. נָעַר **nâ'ar**, *naw-ar´*; a prim. root; to *growl:*— yell.

5287. נָעַר **nâ'ar**, *naw-ar´*; a prim. root [prob. ident. with 5286, through the idea of the *rustling* of mane, which usually accompanies the lion's roar]; to *tumble* about:— shake (off, out, self), overthrow, toss up and down.

5288. נַעַר **na'ar**, *nah´-ar;* from 5287; (concr.) a *boy* (as act.), from the age of infancy to adolescence; by impl. a *servant;* also (by interch. of sex), a *girl* (of similar latitude in age):— babe, boy, child, damsel [from the marg.], lad, servant, young (man).

5289. נַעַר **na'ar**, *nah´-ar;* from 5287 in its der. sense of *tossing* about; a *wanderer:*— young one.

5290. נֹעַר **nô'ar**, *no´-ar;* from 5287; (abstr.) *boyhood* [comp. 5288]:— child, youth.

נָעֻר **nâ'ûr**. See 5271.

5291. נַעֲרָה **na'àrâh**, *nah-ar-aw´*; fem. of 5288; a *girl* (from infancy to adolescence):— damsel, maid (-en), young (woman).

5292. נַעֲרָה **Na'àrâh**, *nah-ar-aw´*; the same as 5291; *Naarah*, the name of an Israelitess, and of a place in Pal.:— Naarah, Naarath.

נְעֻרָה **nᵉ'ûrâh**. See 5271.

5293. נַעֲרַי **Na'àray**, *nah-ar-ah´-ee;* from 5288; *youthful; Naarai*, an Isr.:— Naarai.

5294. נְעַרְיָה **Nᵉ'aryâh**, *neh-ar-yaw´*; from 5288 and 3050; *servant of Jah; Nearjah*, the name of two Isr.:— Neariah.

5295. נַעֲרָן **Na'àrân**, *nah-ar-awn´*; from 5288; *juvenile; Naaran*, a place in Pal.:— Naaran.

5296. נְעֹרֶת **nᵉ'ôreth**, *neh-o´-reth;* from 5287; something *shaken* out, i.e. *tow* (as the refuse of flax):— tow.

נַעֲרָתָה **Na'àrâthâh**. See 5292.

5297. נֹף **Nôph**, *nofe;* a var. of 4644; *Noph,* the capital of Upper Egypt:— Noph.

5298. נֶפֶג **Nepheg**, *neh´-feg;* from an unused root prob. mean. to *spring* forth; a *sprout; Nepheg,* the name of two Isr.:— Nepheg.

5299. נָפָה **nâphâh**, *naw-faw´;* from 5130 in the sense of *lifting;* a *height;* also a *sieve:*— border, coast, region, sieve.

5300. נְפוּשְׁסִים° **Nephûwshecîym**, *nef-oo-shes-eem´;* for 5304; *Nephushesim,* a Temple-servant:— Nephisesim [*from the marg.*].

5301. נָפַח **nâphach**, *naw-fakh´;* a prim. root; to *puff,* in various applications (lit., to *inflate, blow* hard, *scatter, kindle, expire;* fig., to *disesteem*):— blow, breath, give up, cause to lose [life], seething, snuff.

5302. נֹפַח **Nôphach**, *no´-fakh;* from 5301; a *gust; Nophach,* a place in Moab:— Nophah.

5303. נְפִיל **nephîyl**, *nef-eel´;* or

נְפִל **nephîl**, *nef-eel´;* from 5307; prop., a *feller,* i.e. a *bully* or *tyrant:*— giant.

5304. נְפִיסִים° **Nephîycîym**, *nef-ee-seem´;* plur. from an unused root mean. to *scatter; expansions; Nephisim,* a Temple-servant:— Nephusim [*from the marg.*].

5305. נָפִישׁ **Nâphîysh**, *naw-feesh´;* from 5314; *refreshed; Naphish,* a son of Ishmael, and his posterity:— Naphish.

5306. נֹפֶךְ **nôphek**, *no´-fek;* from an unused root mean. to *glisten; shining;* a gem, prob. the *garnet:*— emerald.

5307. נָפַל **nâphal**, *naw-fal´;* a prim. root; to *fall,* in a great variety of applications (intr. or caus., lit. or fig.):— be accepted, cast (down, self, [lots], out), cease, die, divide (by lot), (let) fail, (cause to, let, make, ready to) fall (away, down, -en, -ing), fell (-ing), fugitive, have [inheritance], inferior, be judged [by mistake for 6419], lay (along), (cause to) lie down, light (down), be (× hast) lost, lying, overthrow, overwhelm, perish, present (-ed, -ing), (make to) rot, slay, smite out, × surely, throw down.

5308. נְפַל **nephal** (Chald.), *nef-al´;* corresp. to 5307:— fall (down), have occasion.

5309. נֶפֶל **nephel**, *neh´-fel;* or

נֵפֶל **nêphel**, *nay´-fel;* from 5307; something *fallen,* i.e. an *abortion:*— untimely birth.

נְפִל **nephîl**. See 5303.

5310. נָפַץ **nâphats**, *naw-fats´;* a prim. root; to *dash* to pieces, or *scatter:*— be beaten in sunder, break (in pieces), broken, dash (in pieces), cause to be discharged, dispersed, be overspread, scatter.

5311. נֶפֶץ **nephets**, *neh´-fets;* from 5310; a *storm* (as dispersing):— scattering.

5312. נְפַק **nephaq** (Chald.), *nef-ak´;* a prim.

root; to *issue;* caus. to *bring out:*— come (go, take) forth (out).

5313. נִפְקָא **niphqâ'** (Chald.), *nif-kaw´;* from 5312; an *outgo,* i.e. expense:— expense.

5314. נָפַשׁ **nâphash**, *naw-fash´;* a prim. root; to *breathe;* pass., to *be breathed* upon, i.e. (fig.) *refreshed* (as if by a current of air):— (be) refresh selves (-ed).

5315. נֶפֶשׁ **nephesh**, *neh´-fesh;* from 5314; prop. a *breathing* creature, i.e. *animal* of (abstr.) *vitality;* used very widely in a lit., accommodated or fig. sense (bodily or ment.):— any, appetite, beast, body, breath, creature, × dead (-ly), desire, × [dis-] contented, × fish, ghost, + greedy, he, heart (-y), (hath, × jeopardy of) life (× in jeopardy), lust, man, me, mind, mortally, one, own, person, pleasure, (her-, him-, my-, thy-) self, them (your)-selves, + slay, soul, + tablet, they, thing, (× she) will, × would have it.

5316. נֶפֶת **nepheth**, *neh´-feth;* for 5299; a *height:*— country.

5317. נֹפֶת **nôpheth**, *no´-feth;* from 5130 in the sense of *shaking* to pieces; a *dripping,* i.e. of *honey* (from the comb):— honeycomb.

5318. נַפְתּוֹחַ **Nephtôwach**, *nef-to´-akh;* from 6605; *opened,* i.e. a *spring; Nephtoach,* a place in Pal.:— Neptoah.

5319. נַפְתּוּל **naphtûwl**, *naf-tool´;* from 6617; prop. *wrestled;* but used (in the plur.) tran., a *struggle:*— wrestling.

5320. נַפְתֻּחִים **Naphtûchîym**, *naf-too-kheem´;* plur. of for. or., *Naphtuchim,* an Eg. tribe:— Naptuhim.

5321. נַפְתָּלִי **Naphtâlîy**, *naf-taw-lee´;* from 6617; *my wrestling; Naphtali,* a son of Jacob, with the tribe desc. from him, and its territory:— Naphtali.

5322. נֵץ **nêts**, *nayts;* from 5340; a *flower* (from its *brilliancy*); also a *hawk* (from it *flashing* speed):— blossom, hawk.

5323. נָצָא **nâtsâ'**, *naw-tsaw´;* a prim. root; to *go away:*— flee.

5324. נָצַב **nâtsab**, *naw-tsab´;* a prim. root; to *station,* in various applications (lit. or fig.):— appointed, deputy, erect, establish, × Huzzah [by mistake for a proper name], lay, officer, pillar, present, rear up, set (over, up), settle, sharpen, stablish, (make to) stand (-ing, still, up, upright), best state.

נְצִיב **netsîb**. See 5333.

5325. נִצָּב **nitstsâb**, *nits-tsawb´;* pass. part. of 5324; *fixed,* i.e. a *handle:*— haft.

5326. נִצְבָּה **nitsbâh** (Chald.), *nits-baw´;* from a root corresp. to 5324; *fixedness,* i.e. *firmness:*— strength.

Hebrew

5327. נָצָה **nâtsâh**, *naw-tsaw´*; a prim. root; prop. to *go forth*, i.e. (by impl.) to *be expelled*, and (consequently) *desolate*; caus. to *lay waste*; also (spec.), to *quarrel*:— be laid waste, ruinous, strive (together).

נֹצָה **nôtsâh**. See 5133.

5328. נִצָּה **nitstsâh**, *nits-tsaw´*; fem. of 5322; a *blossom*:— flower.

נְצוּרָה **n⁰tsûwrâh**. See 5341.

5329. נָצַח **nâtsach**, *naw-tsakh´*; a prim. root; prop. to *glitter* from afar, i.e. to *be eminent* (as a superintendent, espec. of the Temple services and its music); also (as denom. from 5331), to *be permanent*:— excel, chief musician (singer), oversee (-r), set forward.

5330. נְצַח **n⁰tsach** (Chald.), *nets-akh´*; corresp. to 5329; to *become chief*:— be preferred.

5331. נֶצַח **netsach**, *neh´-tsakh*; or

נֵצַח **nêtsach**, *nay´-tsakh*; from 5329; prop. a *goal*, i.e. the bright object at a distance travelled toward; hence, (fig.) *splendor*, or (subj.) *truthfulness*, or (obj.) *confidence*; but usually (adv.), *continually* (i.e. to the most distant point of view):— alway (-s), constantly, end, (+ n-) ever (more), perpetual, strength, victory.

5332. נֵצַח **nêtsach**, *nay´-tsakh*; prob. ident. with 5331, through the idea of *brilliancy* of color; *juice* of the grape (as blood red):— blood, strength.

5333. נְצִיב **n⁰tsîyb**, *nets-eeb´*; or

נְצִב **n⁰tsîb**, *nets-eeb´*; from 5324; something *stationary*, i.e. a *prefect*, a military *post*, a *statue*:— garrison, officer, pillar.

5334. נְצִיב **N⁰tsîyb**, *nets-eeb´*; the same as 5333; *station*; *Netsib*, a place in Pal.:— Nezib.

5335. נְצִיחַ **N⁰tsîyach**, *nets-ee´-akh*; from 5329; *conspicuous*; *Netsiach*, a Temple-servant:— Neziah.

5336. נָצִיר° **nâtsîyr**, *naw-tsere´*; from 5341; prop. *conservative*; but used pass., *delivered*:— preserved.

5337. נָצַל **nâtsal**, *naw-tsal´*; a prim. root; to *snatch* away, whether in a good or a bad sense:— × at all, defend, deliver (self), escape, × without fail, part, pluck, preserve, recover, rescue, rid, save, spoil, strip, × surely, take (out).

5338. נְצַל **n⁰tsal** (Chald.), *nets-al´*; corresp. to 5337; to *extricate*:— deliver, rescue.

5339. נִצָּן **nitstsân**, *nits-tsawn´*; from 5322; a *blossom*:— flower.

5340. נָצַץ **nâtsats**, *naw-tsats´*; a prim. root; to *glare*, i.e. *be bright*-colored:— sparkle.

5341. נָצַר **nâtsar**, *naw-tsar´*; a prim. root; to *guard*, in a good sense (to *protect*, *maintain*, *obey*, etc.) or a bad one (to *conceal*, etc.):— besieged, hidden thing, keep (-er, -ing), monument, observe, preserve (-r), subtil, watcher (-man).

5342. נֵצֶר **nêtser**, *nay´-tser*; from 5341 in the sense of *greenness* as a striking color; a *shoot*; fig. a *descendant*:— branch.

5343. נְקֵא **n⁰qê'** (Chald.), *nek-ay´*; from a root corresp. to 5352; *clean*:— pure.

5344. נָקַב **nâqab**, *naw-kab´*; a prim. root; to *puncture*, lit. (to *perforate*, with more or less violence) or fig. (to *specify*, *designate*, *libel*):— appoint, blaspheme, bore, curse, express, with holes, name, pierce, strike through.

5345. נֶקֶב **neqeb**, *neh´keb*; a *bezel* (for a gem):— pipe.

5346. נֶקֶב **Neqeb**, *neh´-keb*; the same as 5345; *dell*; *Nekeb*, a place in Pal.:— Nekeb.

5347. נְקֵבָה **n⁰qêbâh**, *nek-ay-baw´*; from 5344; *female* (from the sexual form):— female.

5348. נָקֹד **nâqôd**, *naw-kode´*; from an unused root mean. to *mark* (by *puncturing* or *branding*); *spotted*:— speckled.

5349. נֹקֵד **nôqêd**, *no-kade´*; act. part. from the same as 5348; a *spotter* (of sheep or cattle), i.e. the owner or tender (who thus marks them):— herdman, sheepmaster.

5350. נִקֻּד **niqqud**, *nik-kood´*; from the same as 5348; a *crumb* (as *broken* to spots); also a *biscuit* (as *pricked*):— cracknel, mouldy.

5351. נְקֻדָּה **n⁰quddâh**, *nek-ood-daw´*; fem. of 5348; a *boss*:— stud.

5352. נָקָה **nâqâh**, *naw-kaw´*; a prim. root; to *be* (or *make*) *clean* (lit. or fig.); by impl. (in an adverse sense) to *be bare*, i.e. *extirpated*:— acquit × at all, × altogether, be blameless, cleanse, (be) clear (-ing), cut off, be desolate, be free, be (hold) guiltless, be (hold) innocent, × by no means, be quit, be (leave) unpunished, × utterly, × wholly.

5353. נְקוֹדָא **N⁰qôwdâ'**, *nek-o-daw´*; fem. of 5348 (in the fig. sense of *marked*); *distinction*; *Nekoda*, a Temple-servant:— Nekoda.

5354. נָקַט **nâqat**, *naw-kat´*; a prim. root; to *loathe*:— weary.

5355. נָקִי **nâqîy**, *naw-kee´*; or

נָקִיא **nâqîy'** (Joel 4:19; Jonah 1:14), *naw-kee´*; from 5352; *innocent*:— blameless, clean, clear, exempted, free, guiltless, innocent, quit.

5356. נִקָּיוֹן **niqqâyôwn**, *nik-kaw-yone´*; or

נִקָּיֹן **niqqâyôn**, *nik-kaw-yone´*; from 5352; *clearness* (lit. or fig.):— cleanness, innocency.

5357. קיק׃ **nâqîyq**, *naw-keek´*; from an unused root mean. to *bore*; a *cleft*:— hole.

5358. נקם **nâqam**, *naw-kam´*; a prim. root; to *grudge*, i.e. *avenge* or *punish*:— avenge (-r, self), punish, revenge (self), × surely, take vengeance.

5359. נקם **nâqâm**, *naw-kawm´*; from 5358; *revenge*:— + avenged, quarrel, vengeance.

5360. נקמה **neqâmâh**, *nek-aw-maw´*; fem. of 5359; *avengement*, whether the act or the passion:— + avenge, revenge (-ing), vengeance.

5361. נקע **nâqa'**, *naw-kah´*; a prim. root; to *feel aversion*:— be alienated.

5362. נקף **nâqaph**, *naw-kaf´*; a prim. root; to *strike* with more or less violence (*beat, fell, corrode*); by impl. (of attack) to *knock together*, i.e. *surround* or *circulate*:— compass (about, -ing), cut down, destroy, go round (about), inclose, round.

5363. נקף **nôqeph**, *no´-kef*; from 5362; a *threshing* (of olives):— shaking.

5364. נקפה **niqpâh**, *nik-paw´*; from 5362; prob. a *rope* (as *encircling*):— rent.

5365. נקר **nâqar**, *naw-kar´*; a prim. root; to *bore* (*penetrate, quarry*):— dig, pick out, pierce, put (thrust) out.

5366. נקרה **neqârâh**, *nek-aw-raw´*; from 5365, a *fissure*:— cleft, clift.

5367. נקש **nâqash**, *naw-kash´*; a prim. root; to *entrap* (with a noose), lit. or fig.:— catch, (lay a) snare.

5368. נקש **neqash** (Chald.), *nek-ash´*; corresp. to 5367; but used in the sense of 5362; to *knock*:— smote.

נר **nêr**,

נר **nîr**. See 5215, 5216.

5369. נר **Nêr**, *nare*; the same as 5216; *lamp*; *Ner*, an Isr.:— Ner.

5370. נרגל **Nêrgal**, *nare-gal´*; of for. or.; *Nergal*, a Cuthite deity:— Nergal.

5371. נרגל שראצר **Nêrgal Shar'etser**, *nare-gal´ shar-eh´-tser*; from 5370 and 8272; *Nergal-Sharetser*, the name of two Bab.:— Nergalsharezer.

5372. נרגן **nirgân**, *neer-gawn´*; from an unused root mean. to *roll* to pieces; a *slanderer*:— talebearer, whisperer.

5373. נרד **nêrd**, *nayrd*; of for. or.; *nard*, an aromatic:— spikenard.

נרה **nêrâh**. See 5216.

5374. נריה **Nêrîyâh**, *nay-ree-yaw´*; or

נריהו **Nêrîyâhûw**, *nay-ree-yaw´-hoo*; from 5216 and 3050; *light of Jah*; *Nerijah*, an Isr.:— Neriah.

5375. נשא **nâsâ'**, *naw-saw´*; or

נסה **nâçah** (Psa. 4:6 [7]) *naw-saw´*; a prim. root; to *lift*, in a great variety of applications, lit. and fig., absol. and rel. (as follows):— accept, advance, arise, (able to, [armour], suffer to) bear (-er, up), bring (forth), burn, carry (away), cast, contain, desire, ease, exact, exalt (self), extol, fetch, forgive, furnish, further, give, go on, help, high, hold up, honorable (+ man), lade, lay, lift (self) up, lofty, marry, magnify, × needs, obtain, pardon, raise (up), receive, regard, respect, set (up), spare, stir up, + swear, take (away, up), × utterly, wear, yield.

5376. נשא **nesâ'** (Chald.), *nes-aw´*; corresp. to 5375:— carry away, make insurrection, take.

5377. נשא **nâshâ'**, *naw-shaw´*; a prim. root; to *lead astray*, i.e. (ment.) to *delude*, or (mor.) to *seduce*:— beguile, deceive, × greatly, × utterly.

5378. נשא **nâshâ'**, *naw-shaw´*; a prim. root [perh. ident. with 5377, through the idea of *imposition*]; to *lend* on interest; by impl. to *dun* for debt:— × debt, exact, giver of usury.

נשא **nâsî'**. See 5387.

נשאה **nesû'âh**. See 5385.

5379. נשאת **nissê'th**, *nis-sayth´*; pass. part. fem. of 5375; something *taken*, i.e. a *present*:— gift.

5380. נשב **nâshab**, *naw-shab´*; a prim. root; to *blow*; by impl. to *disperse*:— (cause to) blow, drive away.

5381. נשג **nâsag**, *naw-sag´*; a prim. root; to *reach* (lit. or fig.):— ability, be able, attain (unto), (be able to, can) get, lay at, put, reach, remove, wax rich, × surely, (over-) take (hold of, on, upon).

5382. נשה **nâshâh**, *naw-shaw´*; a prim. root; to *forget*; fig. to *neglect*; caus. to *remit, remove*:— forget, deprive, exact.

5383. נשה **nâshâh**, *naw-shaw´*; a prim. root [rather ident. with 5382, in the sense of 5378]; to *lend* or (by reciprocity) *borrow* on security or interest:— creditor, exact, extortioner, lend, usurer, lend on (taker of) usury.

5384. נשה **nâsheh**, *naw-sheh´*; from 5382, in the sense of *failure*; *rheumatic* or *crippled* (from the incident to Jacob):— which shrank.

5385. נשואה **nesûw'âh**, *nes-oo-aw´*; or rather,

נשאה **nesû'âh**, *nes-oo-aw´*; fem.. pass. part. of 5375; something *borne*, i.e. a *load*:— carriage.

5386. נשי **neshîy**, *nesh-ee´*; from 5383; a *debt*:— debt.

5387. נָשִׂיא **nâsîy'**, *naw-see´*; or

נָשִׂא **nâsi'**, *naw-see´*; from 5375; prop. an *exalted* one, i.e. a *king* or *sheik;* also a rising *mist:*— captain, chief, cloud, governor, prince, ruler, vapour.

5388. נְשִׁיָּה **nᵉshîyâh**, *nesh-ee-yaw´*; from 5382; *oblivion:*— forgetfulness.

נָשִׁים **nâshîym**. See 802.

5389. נָשִׁין **nâshîyn** (Chald.), *naw-sheen´*; irreg. plur. fem. of 606:— women.

5390. נְשִׁיקָה **nᵉshîyqâh**, *nesh-ee-kaw´*; from 5401; a *kiss:*— kiss.

5391. נָשַׁךְ **nâshak**, *naw-shak´*; a prim. root; to *strike* with a sting (as a serpent); fig. to *oppress* with interest on a loan:— bite, lend upon usury.

5392. נֶשֶׁךְ **neshek**, *neh´-shek*; from 5391; *interest* on a debt:— usury.

5393. נִשְׁכָּה **nishkâh**, *nish-kaw´*; for 3957; a *cell:*— chamber.

5394. נָשַׁל **nâshal**, *naw-shal´*; a prim. root; to *pluck* off, i.e. *divest, eject,* or *drop:*— cast (out), drive, loose, put off (out), slip.

5395. נָשַׁם **nâsham**, *naw-sham´*; a prim. root; prop. to *blow* away, i.e. *destroy:*— destroy.

5396. נִשְׁמָא **nishmâ'** (Chald.), *nish-maw´*; corresp. to 5397; vital *breath:*— breath.

5397. נְשָׁמָה **nᵉshâmâh**, *nesh-aw-maw´*; from 5395; a *puff,* i.e. *wind,* angry or vital *breath,* divine *inspiration, intellect,* or (concr.) an *animal:*— blast, (that) breath (-eth), inspiration, soul, spirit.

5398. נָשַׁף **nâshaph**, *naw-shaf´*; a prim. root; to *breeze,* i.e. *blow* up fresh (as the wind):— blow.

5399. נֶשֶׁף **nesheph**, *neh´-shef*; from 5398; prop. a *breeze,* i.e. (by impl.) *dusk* (when the evening breeze prevails):— dark, dawning of the day (morning), night, twilight.

5400. נָשַׂק **nâsaq**, *naw-sak´*; a prim. root; to *catch* fire:— burn, kindle.

5401. נָשַׁק **nâshaq**, *naw-shak´*; a prim. root [ident. with 5400, through the idea of *fastening* up; comp. 2388, 2836]; to *kiss,* lit. or fig. (*touch*); also (as a mode of *attachment*), to *equip* with weapons:— armed (men), rule, kiss, that touched.

5402. נֶשֶׁק **nesheq**, *neh´-shek*; or

נֵשֶׁק **nêsheq**, *nay´-shek*; from 5401; military *equipment,* i.e. (collect.) *arms* (offensive or defensive), or (concr.) an *arsenal:*— armed men, armour (-y), battle, harness, weapon.

5403. נְשַׁר **nᵉshar** (Chald.), *nesh-ar´*; corresp. to 5404; an *eagle:*— eagle.

5404. נֶשֶׁר **nesher**, *neh´-sher*; from an unused root mean. to *lacerate;* the *eagle* (or other large bird of prey):— eagle.

5405. נָשַׁת **nâshath**, *naw-shath´*; a prim. root; prop. to *eliminate,* i.e. (intr.) to *dry* up:— fail.

נְתִבָה **nᵉthîbâh**. See 5410.

5406. נִשְׁתְּוָן **nishtᵉvân**, *nish-tev-awn´*; prob. of Pers. or.; an *epistle:*— letter.

5407. נִשְׁתְּוָן **nishtᵉvân** (Chald.), *nish-tev-awn´*; corresp. to 5406:— letter.

נָתוּן **Nâthûwn**. See 5411.

5408. נָתַח **nâthach**, *naw-thakh´*; a prim. root; to *dismember:*— cut (in pieces), divide, hew in pieces.

5409. נֵתַח **nêthach**, *nay´-thakh;* from 5408; a *fragment:*— part, piece.

5410. נָתִיב **nâthîyb**, *naw-theeb´*; or (fem.)

נְתִיבָה **nᵉthîybâh**, *neth-ee-baw´*; or

נְתִבָה **nᵉthîbâh** (Jer. 6:16), *neth-ee-baw´*; from an unused root mean. to *tramp;* a (beaten) *track:*— path ([-way]), × travel [-ler], way.

5411. נָתִין **Nâthîyn**, *naw-theen´*; or

נָתוּן **Nâthûwn** (Ezra 8:17), *naw-thoon´* (the proper form, as pass. part.), from 5414; one *given,* i.e. (in the plur. only) the *Nethinim,* or Temple-servants (as *given* to that duty):— Nethinims.

5412. נְתִין **Nᵉthîyn** (Chald.), *netheen´*; corresp. to 5411:— Nethinims.

5413. נָתַךְ **nâthak**, *naw-thak´*; a prim. root; to *flow* forth (lit. or fig.); by impl. to *liquefy:*— drop, gather (together), melt, pour (forth, out).

5414. נָתַן **nâthan**, *naw-than´*; a prim. root; to *give,* used with greatest latitude of application (*put, make,* etc.):— add, apply, appoint, ascribe, assign, × avenge, × be (healed), bestow, bring (forth, hither), cast, cause, charge, come, commit, consider, count, + cry, deliver (up), direct, distribute, do, × doubtless, × without fail, fasten, frame, × get, give (forth, over, up), grant, hang (up), × have, × indeed, lay (unto charge, up), (give) leave, lend, let (out), + lie, lift up, make, + O that, occupy, offer, ordain, pay, perform, place, pour, print, × pull, put (forth), recompense, render, require, restore, send (out), set (forth), shew, shoot forth (up), + sing, + slander, strike, [sub-] mit, suffer, × surely, × take, thrust, trade, turn, utter, + weep, × willingly, + withdraw, + would (to) God, yield.

5415. נְתַן **nᵉthan** (Chald.), *neth-an´*; corresp. to 5414; *give:*— bestow, give, pay.

5416. נָתָן **Nâthân**, *naw-thawn´*; from 5414;

given; Nathan, the name of five Isr.:— Nathan.

5417. נְתַנְאֵל **N^ethan'êl**, neth-an-ale´; from 5414 and 410; given of God; Nethanel, the name of ten Isr.:— Nethaneel.

5418. נְתַנְיָה **N^ethanyâh**, neth-an-yaw´; or

נְתַנְיָהוּ **N^ethanyâhûw**, neth-an-yaw´-hoo; from 5414 and 3050; given of Jah; Nethanjah, the name of four Isr.:— Nethaniah.

5419. נְתַן־מֶלֶךְ **N^ethan-Melek**, neth-an´ meh´-lek; from 5414 and 4428; given of (the) king; Nethan-Melek, an Isr.:— Nathan-melech.

5420. נָתַס **nâthaç**, naw-thas´; a prim. root; to tear up:— mar.

5421. נָתַע **nâtha'**, naw-thah´; for 5422; to tear out:— break.

5422. נָתַץ **nâthats**, naw-thats´; a prim. root; to tear down:— beat down, break down (out), cast down, destroy, overthrow, pull down, throw down.

5423. נָתַק **nâthaq**, naw-thak´; a prim. root; to tear off:— break (off), burst, draw (away), lift up, pluck (away, off), pull (out), root out.

5424. נֶתֶק **netheq**, neh´-thek; from 5423; scurf:— (dry) scall.

5425. נָתַר **nâthar**, naw-thar´; a prim. root; to jump, i.e. be violently agitated; caus., to terrify, shake off, untie:— drive asunder, leap, (let) loose, × make, move, undo.

5426. נְתַר **n^ethar** (Chald.), neth-ar´; corresp. to 5425:— shake off.

5427. נֶתֶר **nether**, neh´-ther; from 5425; mineral potash (so called from effervescing with acid):— nitre.

5428. נָתַשׁ **nâthash**, naw-thash´; a prim. root; to tear away:— destroy, forsake, pluck (out, up, by the roots), pull up, root out (up), × utterly.

ס

5429. סְאָה **ç^e'âh**, seh-aw´; from an unused root mean. to define; a seah, or certain measure (as determinative) for grain:— measure.

5430. סְאוֹן **ç^e'ôwn**, seh-own´; from 5431; perh. a military boot (as a protection from mud:— battle.

5431. סָאַן **çâ'an**, saw-an´; a prim. root; to be miry; used only as denom. from 5430; to shoe, i.e. (act. part.) a soldier shod:— warrior.

5432. סַאסְאָה° **ça'ç^e'âh**, sah-seh-aw´; for 5429; measurement, i.e. moderation:— measure.

5433. סָבָא **çâbâ'**, saw-baw´; a prim. root; to quaff to satiety, i.e. become tipsy:— drunkard, fill self, Sabean, [wine-]bibber.

5434. סְבָא **Ç^ebâ'**, seb-aw´; of for. or.; Seba, a

son of Cush, and the country settled by him:— Seba.

5435. סֹבֶא **çôbe'**, so´-beh; from 5433; potation, concr. (wine), or abstr. (carousal):— drink, drunken, wine.

5436. סְבָאִי **Ç^ebâ'îy**, seb-aw-ee´; patrial from 5434; a Sebaite, or inhab. of Seba:— Sabean.

5437. סָבַב **çâbab**, saw-bab´; a prim. root; to revolve, surround, or border; used in various applications, lit. and fig. (as follows):— bring, cast, fetch, lead, make, walk, × whirl, × round about, be about on every side, apply, avoid, beset (about), besiege, bring again, carry (about), change, cause to come about, × circuit, (fetch a) compass (about, round), drive, environ, × on every side, beset (close, come, compass, go, stand) round about, inclose, remove, return, set, sit down, turn (self) (about, aside, away, back).

5438. סִבָּה **çibbâh**, sib-baw´; from 5437; a (providential) turn (of affairs):— cause.

5439. סָבִיב **çâbîyb**, saw-beeb´; or (fem.)

סְבִיבָה **ç^ebîybâh**, seb-ee-baw´; from 5437; (as noun) a circle, neighbour, or environs; but chiefly (as adv., with or without prep.) around:— (place, round) about, circuit, compass, on every side.

5440. סָבַךְ **çâbak**, saw-bak´; a prim. root; to entwine:— fold together, wrap.

5441. סֹבֶךְ **çôbek**, so´-bek; from 5440; a copse:— thicket.

5442. סְבָךְ **ç^ebâk**, seb-awk´; from 5440, a copse:— thick (-et).

5443. סַבְּכָא **çabb^ekâ'** (Chald.), sab-bek-aw´; or

שַׂבְּכָא **sabb^ekâ'** (Chald.), sab-bek-aw´; from a root corresp. to 5440; a lyre:— sackbut.

5444. סִבְּכַי **Çibb^ekay**, sib-bek-ah´-ee; from 5440; copse-like; Sibbecai, an Isr.:— Sibbecai, Sibbechai.

5445. סָבַל **çâbal**, saw-bal´; a prim. root; to carry (lit. or fig.), or (refl.) be burdensome; spec. to be gravid:— bear, be a burden, carry, strong to labour.

5446. סְבַל **ç^ebal** (Chald.), seb-al´; corresp. to 5445; to erect:— strongly laid.

5447. סֵבֶל **çêbel**, say´-bel; from 5445; a load (lit. or fig.):— burden, charge.

5448. סֹבֶל **çôbel**, so´-bel; [only in the form

סֻבָּל **çubbâl**, soob-bawl´]; from 5445; a load (fig.):— burden.

5449. סַבָּל **çabbâl**, sab-bawl´; from 5445; a porter:— (to bear, bearer of) burden (-s).

Hebrew

5450. סְבָלָה çᵉbâlâh, *seb-aw-law´*; from 5447; *porterage:*— burden.

5451. סִבֹּלֶת Çibbôleth, *sib-bo´-leth;* for 7641; an *ear* of grain:— Sibboleth.

5452. סְבַר çᵉbar (Chald.), *seb-ar´;* a prim. root; to *bear in mind,* i.e. *hope:*— think.

5453. סְבָרַיִם Çibrayim, *sib-rah´-yim;* dual from a root corresp. to 5452; *double hope; Sibrajim,* a place in Syria:— Sibraim.

5454. סַבְתָּא Çabtâ', *sab-taw´;* or

סַבְתָּה Çabtâh, *sab-taw´;* prob. of for. der.; *Sabta* or *Sabtah,* the name of a son of Cush, and the country occupied by his posterity:— Sabta, Sabtah.

5455. סַבְתְּכָא Çabtᵉkâ', *sab-tek-aw´;* prob. of for. der.; *Sabteca,* the name of a son of Cush, and the region settled by him:— Sabtecha, Sabtechah.

5456. סְגַד çâgad, *saw-gad´;* a prim. root; to *prostrate* oneself (in homage):— fall down.

5457. סְגִד çᵉgîd (Chald.), *seg-eed´;* corresp. to 5456:— worship.

5458. סְגוֹר çᵉgôwr, *seg-ore´;* from 5462; prop. *shut up,* i.e. the *breast* (as inclosing the heart); also *gold* (as gen. *shut* up safely):— caul, gold.

5459. סְגֻלָּה çᵉgullâh, *seg-ool-law´;* fem. pass. part. of an unused root mean. to *shut* up; *wealth* (as closely *shut* up):— jewel, peculiar (treasure), proper good, special.

5460. סְגַן çᵉgan (Chald.), *seg-an´;* corresp. to 5461:— governor.

5461. סָגָן çâgân, *saw-gawn´;* from an unused root mean. to *superintend;* a *præfect* of a province:— prince, ruler.

5462. סָגַר çâgar, *saw-gar´;* a prim. root; to *shut* up; fig. to *surrender:*— close up, deliver (up), give over (up), inclose, × pure, repair, shut (in, self, out, up, up together), stop, × straitly.

5463. סְגַר çᵉgar (Chald.), *seg-ar´;* corresp. to 5462:— shut up.

5464. סַגְרִיד çagrîyd, *sag-reed´;* prob. from 5462 in the sense of *sweeping* away; a *pouring* rain:— very rainy.

5465. סַד çad, *sad;* from an unused root mean. to *estop;* the *stocks:*— stocks.

5466. סָדִין çâdîyn, *saw-deen´;* from an unused root mean. to *envelop;* a *wrapper,* i.e. *shirt:*— fine linen, sheet.

5467. סְדֹם Çᵉdôm, *sed-ome´;* from an unused root mean. to *scorch;* burnt (i.e. *volcanic* or *bituminous*) district; *Sedom,* a place near the Dead Sea:— Sodom.

5468. סֶדֶר çeder, *seh´-der;* from an unused root mean. to *arrange; order:*— order.

5469. סַהַר çahar, *sah´-har;* from an unused root mean. to *be round; roundness:*— round.

5470. סֹהַר çôhar, *so´-har;* from the same as 5469; a *dungeon* (as *surrounded* by walls):— prison.

5471. סוֹא Çôw', *so;* of for. der.; *So,* an Eg. king:— So.

5472. סוּג çûwg, *soog;* a prim. root; prop. to *flinch,* i.e. (by impl.) to *go back,* lit. (to retreat) or fig. (to *apostatize*):— backslider, drive, go back, turn (away, back).

5473. סוּג çûwg, *soog;* a prim. root [prob. rather ident. with 5472 through the idea of *shrinking* from a hedge; comp. 7735]; to *hem* in, i.e. *bind:*— set about.

סוּג° çûwg. See 5509.

5474. סוּגַר çûwgar, *soo-gar´;* from 5462; an *inclosure,* i.e. *cage* (for an animal):— ward.

5475. סוֹד çôwd, *sode;* from 3245; a *session,* i.e. *company* of persons (in close deliberation); by impl. *intimacy, consultation,* a *secret:*— assembly, counsel, inward, secret (counsel).

5476. סוֹדִי Çôwdîy, *so-dee´;* from 5475; a *confidant; Sodi,* an Isr.:— Sodi.

5477. סוּחַ Çûwach, *soo´-akh;* from an unused root mean. to *wipe* away; *sweeping; Suach,* an Isr.:— Suah.

5478. סוּחָה çûwchâh, *soo-khaw´;* from the same as 5477; something *swept* away, i.e. *filth:*— torn.

סוּט° çûwṭ. See 7750.

5479. סוֹטַי Çôwṭay, *so-tah´-ee;* from 7750; *roving; Sotai,* one of the Nethinim:— Sotai.

5480. סוּךְ çûwk, *sook;* a prim. root; prop. to *smear* over (with oil), i.e. *anoint:*— anoint (self), × at all.

סוֹלְלָה° çôwlᵉlâh. See 5550.

5481. סוּמְפּוֹנְיָה çûwmpôwnᵉyâh (Chald.), *soom-po-neh-yaw´;* or

סוּמְפֹּנְיָה çûwmpônᵉyâh (Chald.), *soom-po-neh-yaw´;* or

סִיפֹנְיָא° çîyphônᵉyâ' (Dan. 3:10) (Chald.), *see-fo-neh-yaw´;* of Gr. or. (συμφωνία); a *bagpipe* (with a double pipe):— dulcimer.

5482. סְוֵנֵה Çᵉvênêh, *sev-ay-nay´* [rather to be written

סְוֵנָה Çᵉvênâh, *sev-ay´-naw;* for

סְוֵן Çᵉvên, *sev-ane´;* i.e. *to Seven*]; of Eg. der.; *Seven,* a place in Upper Egypt:— Syene.

5483. סוּס çûwç, *soos;* or

סֻס çûç, *soos;* from an unused root

mean. to *skip* (prop. for joy); a *horse* (as leaping); also a *swallow* (from its rapid *flight*):— crane, horse (I-back, -hoofl). Comp. 6571.

5484. סוּסָה çûwçâh, *soo-saw´*; fem. of 5483; a *mare:*— company of horses.

5485. סוּסִי Çûwçîy, *soo-see´*; from 5483; *horse-like; Susi,* an Isr.:— Susi.

5486. סוּף çûwph, *soof;* a prim. root; to *snatch* away, i.e. *terminate:*— consume, have an end, perish, × be utterly.

5487. סוּף çûwph (Chald.), *soof;* corresp. to 5486; to *come to an end:*— consume, fulfill.

5488. סוּף çûwph, *soof;* prob. of Eg. or.; a *reed,* espec. the *papyrus:*— flag, Red [sea], weed. Comp. 5489.

5489. סוּף Çûwph, *soof;* for 5488 (by ellip. of 3220); the *Reed (Sea):*— Red Sea.

5490. סוֹף çôwph, *sofe;* from 5486; a *termination:*— conclusion, end, hinder part.

5491. סוֹף çôwph (Chald.), *sofe;* corresp. to 5490:— end.

5492. סוּפָה çûwphâh, *soo-faw´;* from 5486; a *hurricane:*— storm, tempest, whirlwind, Red sea.

5493. סוּר çûwr, *soor;* or

שׂוּר sûwr (Hosea 9:12), *soor;* a prim. root; to *turn* off (lit. or fig.):— be [-head], bring, call back, decline, depart, eschew, get [you], go (aside), × grievous, lay away (by), leave undone, be past, pluck away, put (away, down), rebel, remove (to and fro), revolt, × be sour, take (away, off), turn (aside, away, in), withdraw, be without.

5494. סוּר çûwr, *soor;* prob. pass. part. of 5493; *turned* off, i.e. *deteriorated:*— degenerate.

5495. סוּר Çûwr, *soor;* the same as 5494; *Sur,* a gate of the Temple:— Sur.

5496. סוּת çûwth, *sooth;* perh. denom. from 7898; prop. to *prick,* i.e. (fig.) stimulate; by impl. to *seduce:*— entice, move, persuade, provoke, remove, set on, stir up, take away.

5497. סוּת çûwth, *sooth;* prob. from the same root as 4533; *covering,* i.e. *clothing:*— clothes.

5498. סָחַב çâchab, *saw-khab´;* a prim. root; to *trail* along:— draw (out), tear.

5499. סְחָבָה çᵉchâbâh, *seh-khaw-baw´;* from 5498; a *rag:*— cast clout.

5500. סָחָה çâchâh, *saw-khaw´;* a prim. root; to *sweep* away:— scrape.

5501. סְחִי çᵉchîy, *seh-khee´;* from 5500; *refuse* (as *swept* off):— offscouring.

סָחִישׁ çâchîysh. See 7823.

5502. סָחַף çâchaph, *saw-khaf´;* a prim. root; to *scrape* off:— sweep (away).

5503. סָחַר çâchar, *saw-khar´;* a prim. root; to

travel round (spec. as a *pedlar*); intens. to *palpitate:*— go about, merchant (-man), occupy with, pant, trade, traffick.

5504. סַחַר çachar, *sakh´-ar;* from 5503; *profit* (from trade):— merchandise.

5505. סָחַר çâchar, *saw-khar´;* from 5503; an *emporium;* abstr. *profit* (from trade):— mart, merchandise.

5506. סְחֹרָה çᵉchôrâh, *sekh-o-raw´;* from 5503; *traffic:*— merchandise.

5507. סֹחֵרָה çôchêrâh, *so-khay-raw´;* prop. act. part. fem. of 5503; something *surrounding* the person, i.e. a *shield:*— buckler.

5508. סֹחֶרֶת çôchereth, *so-kheh´-reth;* similar to 5507; prob. a (black) *tile* (or *tessara*) for laying borders with:— black marble.

סֵט çêṭ. See 7750.

5509. סִיג çîyg, *seeg;* or

סוּג° çûwg (Ezek. 22:18), *soog;* from 5472 in the sense of *refuse; scoria:*— dross.

5510. סִיוָן Çîyvân, *see-vawn´;* prob. of Pers. or.; *Sivan,* the third Heb. month:— Sivan.

5511. סִיחוֹן Çîychôwn, *see-khone´;* or

סִיחֹן Çîychôn, *see-khone´;* from the same as 5477; *tempestuous; Sichon,* an Amoritish king:— Sihon.

5512. סִין Çîyn, *seen;* of uncert. der.; *Sin,* the name of an Eg. town and (prob.) desert adjoining:— Sin.

5513. סִינִי Çîynîy, *see-nee´;* from an otherwise unknown name of a man; a *Sinite,* or desc. of one of the sons of Canaan:— Sinite.

5514. סִינַי Çîynay, *see-nah´-ee;* of uncert. der.; *Sinai,* a mountain of Arabia:— Sinai.

5515. סִינִים Çîynîym, *see-neem´;* plur. of an otherwise unknown name; *Sinim,* a distant Oriental region:— Sinim.

5516. סִיסְרָא Çîyçᵉrâ´, *see-ser-aw´;* of uncert. der.; *Sisera,* the name of a Canaanitish king and of one of the Nethinim:— Sisera.

5517. סִיעָא Çîy'â´, *see-ah´;* or

סִיעֲהָא Çîy'ăhâ´, *see-ah-haw´;* from an unused root mean. to *converse; congregation; Sia,* or *Siaha,* one of the Nethinim:— Sia, Siaha.

סִיפֹנְיָא° çîyphônᵉyâ´. See 5481.

5518. סִיר çîyr, *seer;* or (fem.)

סִירָה çîyrâh, *see-raw´;* or

סִרָה çîrâh (Jer. 52:18), *see-raw´;* from a prim. root mean. to *boil* up; a *pot;* also a *thorn* (as springing up rapidly); by impl. a *hook:*— caldron, fishhook, pan, ([wash-]) pot, thorn.

5519. סָךְ çâk, *sawk;* from 5526; prop. a *thicket* of men, i.e. a *crowd:*— multitude.

5520. סֹך **çôk**, *soke;* from 5526; a *hut* (as of *entwined* boughs); also a *lair:*— covert, den, pavilion, tabernacle.

5521. סֻכָּה **çukkâh**, *sook-kaw';* fem of 5520; a *hut* or *lair:*— booth, cottage, covert, pavilion, tabernacle, tent.

5522. סִכּוּת **çikkûwth**, *sik-kooth';* fem. of 5519; an (idolatrous) *booth:*— tabernacle.

5523. סֻכּוֹת **Çukkôwth**, *sook-kohth';* or

סֻכֹּת **Çukkôth**, *sook-kohth';* plur. of 5521; *booths; Succoth,* the name of a place in Egypt and of three in Pal.:— Succoth.

5524. סֻכּוֹת בְּנוֹת **Çukkôwth Benôwth**, *sook-kohth' ben-ohth';* from 5523 and the (irreg.) plur. of 1323; *booths of* (the) *daughters; broth-els,* i.e. idolatrous *tents* for impure pur-poses:— Succoth-benoth.

5525. סֻכִּי **Çukkîy**, *sook-kee';* patrial from an unknown name (perh. 5520); a *Sukkite,* or inhab. of some place near Egypt (i.e. *hut-dwellers*):— Sukkiims.

5526. סָכַךְ **çâkak**, *saw-kak';* or

שָׂכַךְ **sâkak** (Exod. 33:22), *saw-kak';* a prim. root; prop. to *entwine* as a screen; by impl. to *fence* in, *cover* over, (fig.) *protect:*— cover, defence, defend, hedge in, join to-gether, set, shut up.

5527. סְכָכָה **Çekâkâh**, *sek-aw-kaw';* from 5526; *inclosure; Secacah,* a place in Pal.:— Seca-cah.

5528. סָכַל **çâkal**, *saw-kal';* for 3688; to *be silly:*— do (make, play the, turn into) fool (-ish, -ishly, -ishness).

5529. סֶכֶל **çekel**, *seh'-kel;* from 5528; *silliness;* concr. and collect. *dolts:*— folly.

5530. סָכָל **çâkâl**, *saw-kawl';* from 5528; *silly:*— fool (-ish), sottish.

5531. סִכְלוּת **çiklûwth**, *sik-looth';* or

שִׂכְלוּת **siklûwth** (Eccl. 1:17) *sik-looth';* from 5528; *silliness:*— folly, foolishness.

5532. סָכַן **çâkan**, *saw-kan';* a prim. root; to *be familiar* with; by impl. to *minister* to, *be serv-iceable* to, *be customary:*— acquaint (self), be advantage, × ever, (be, [un-l) profit (-able), treasurer, be wont.

5533. סָכַן **çâkan**, *saw-kan';* prob. a denom. from 7915; prop. to *cut,* i.e. *damage;* also to *grow* (caus. *make) poor:*— endanger, impov-erish.

5534. סָכַר **çâkar**, *saw-kar';* a prim. root; to *shut* up; by impl. to *surrender:*— stop, give over. See also 5462, 7936.

5535. סָכַת **çâkath**, *saw-kath';* a prim. root; to *be silent;* by impl. to *observe* quietly:— take heed.

סֻכֹּת **Çukkôth**. See 5523.

5536. סַל **çal**, *sal;* from 5549; prop. a *willow twig* (as *pendulous*), i.e. an *osier;* but only as woven into a *basket:*— basket.

5537. סָלָא **çâlâ'**, *saw-law';* a prim. root; to *suspend* in a balance, i.e. *weigh:*— com-pare.

5538. סִלָּא **Çillâ'**, *sil-law';* from 5549; an *em-bankment; Silla,* a place in Jerusalem:— Silla.

5539. סָלַד **çâlad**, *saw-lad';* a prim. root; prob. to *leap* (with joy), i.e. *exult:*— harden self.

5540. סֶלֶד **Çeled**, *seh'-led;* from 5539; *exul-tation; Seled,* an Isr.:— Seled.

5541. סָלָה **çâlâh**, *saw-law';* a prim. root; to *hang* up, i.e. *weigh,* or (fig.) *contemn:*— tread down (under foot), value.

5542. סֶלָה **Çelâh**, *seh'-law;* from 5541; *sus-pension* (of music), i.e. *pause:*— Selah.

5543. סַלּוּ **Çallûw**, *sal-loo';* or

סַלּוּא **Çallûw'**, *sal-loo';* or

סָלוּא **Çâlûw'**, *sal-loo';* or

סַלַּי **Çallay**, *sal-lah'-ee;* from 5541; *weighed; Sallu* or *Sallai,* the name of two Isr.:— Sallai, Sallu, Salu.

5544. סִלּוֹן **çillôwn**, *sil-lone';* or

סַלּוֹן **çallôwn**, *sal-lone';* from 5541; a *prickle* (as if *pendulous*):— brier, thorn.

5545. סָלַח **çâlach**, *saw-lakh';* a prim. root; to *forgive:*— forgive, pardon, spare.

5546. סַלָּח **çallâch**, *saw-lawkh';* from 5545; *placable:*— ready to forgive.

סַלַּי **Çallay**. See 5543.

5547. סְלִיחָה **çelîychâh**, *sel-ee-khaw';* from 5545; *pardon:*— forgiveness, pardon.

5548. סַלְכָה **Çalkâh**, *sal-kaw';* from an un-used root mean. to *walk; walking; Salcah,* a place E. of the Jordan:— Salcah, Salchah.

5549. סָלַל **çâlal**, *saw-lal';* a prim. root; to *mound* up (espec. a turnpike); fig. to *exalt;* refl. to *oppose* (as by a dam):— cast up, exalt (self), extol, make plain, raise up.

5550. סֹלְלָה **çôlelâh**, *so-lel-aw';* or

סוֹלְלָה **çôwlelâh**, *so-lel-aw';* act. part. fem. of 5549, but used pass.; a military *mound,* i.e. *rampart* of besiegers:— bank, mount.

5551. סֻלָּם **çullâm**, *sool-lawm';* from 5549; a *stair-case:*— ladder.

5552. סַלְסִלָּה **çalçillâh**, *sal-sil-law';* from 5541; a *twig* (as *pendulous*):— basket.

5553. סֶלַע **çela'**, *seh'-lah;* from an unused root mean. to be *lofty;* a craggy *rock,* lit. or fig. (a *fortress*):— (ragged) rock, stone (-ny), strong hold.

5554. סֶלַע **Çela'**, *seh´-lah;* the same as 5553; *Sela,* the rock-city of Idumaea:— rock, Sela (-h).

5555. סֶלַע הַמַּחְלְקוֹת **Çela' ham-machlᵉqôwth**, *seh´-lah ham-makh-lek-ōth´;* from 5553 and the plur. of 4256 with the art. interposed; *rock of the divisions; Sela-ham-Machlekoth,* a place in Pal.:— Sela-hammalekoth.

5556. סָלְעָם **çol'âm**, *sol-awm´;* appar. from the same as 5553 in the sense of *crushing* as with a rock, i.e. consuming; a kind of *locust* (from its *destructiveness*):— bald locust.

5557. סָלַף **çâlaph**, *saw-laf´;* a prim. root; prop. to *wrench,* i.e. (fig.) to *subvert:*— overthrow, pervert.

5558. סֶלֶף **çeleph**, *seh´-lef;* from 5557; *distortion,* i.e. (fig.) *viciousness:*— perverseness.

5559. סְלִק **çᵉlîq** (Chald.), *sel-eek´;* a prim. root; to *ascend:*— come (up).

5560. סֹלֶת **çôleth**, *so´-leth;* from an unused root mean. to *strip; flour* (as *chipped* off):— (fine) flour, meal.

5561. סַם **çam**, *sam;* from an unused root mean. to *smell* sweet; an *aroma:*— sweet (spice).

5562. סַמְגַּר נְבוֹ **Çamgar Nᵉbôw**, *sam-gar´ neb-o´;* of for. or.; *Samgar-Nebo,* a Bab. general:— Samgar-nebo.

5563. סְמָדַר **çᵉmâdar**, *sem-aw-dar´;* of uncert. der.; a vine *blossom;* used also adv. *abloom:*— tender grape.

5564. סָמַךְ **çâmak**, *saw-mak´;* a prim. root; to *prop* (lit. or fig.); refl. to *lean* upon or *take hold* of (in a favorable or unfavorable sense):— bear up, establish, (up-) hold, lay, lean, lie hard, put, rest self, set self, stand fast, stay (self), sustain.

5565. סְמַכְיָהוּ **Çᵉmakyâhûw**, *sem-ak-yaw´-hoo;* from 5564 and 3050; *supported of Jah; Semakjah,* an Isr.:— Semachiah.

5566. סֶמֶל **çemel**, *seh´-mel;* or

סֵמֶל **çêmel**, *say´-mel;* from an unused root mean. to *resemble;* a *likeness:*— figure, idol, image.

5567. סָמַן **çâman**, *saw-man´;* a prim. root; to *designate:*— appointed.

5568. סָמַר **çâmar**, *saw-mar´;* a prim. root; to *be erect,* i.e. *bristle* as hair:— stand up, tremble.

5569. סָמָר **çâmâr**, *saw-mar´;* from 5568; *bristling,* i.e. *shaggy:*— rough.

5570. סְנָאָה **Çᵉnâ'âh**, *sen-aw-aw´;* from an unused root mean. to *prick; thorny; Senaah,* a place in Pal.:— Senaah, Hassenaah [with the art.].

סְנֻאָה **çᵉnû'âh**. See 5574.

5571. סַנְבַלָּט **Çanballaṭ**, *san-bal-laṭ´;* of for. or.;

Sanballat, a Pers. satrap of Samaria:— Sanballat.

5572. סְנֶה **çᵉneh**, *sen-eh´;* from an unused root mean. to *prick;* a *bramble:*— bush.

5573. סֶנֶה **Çeneh**, *seh-neh´;* the same as 5572; *thorn; Seneh,* a crag in Pal.:— Seneh.

סַנָּה **Çannâh**. See 7158.

5574. סְנוּאָה **Çᵉnûw'âh**, *sen-oo-aw´;* or

סְנֻאָה **Çᵉnû'âh**, *sen-oo-aw´* from the same as 5570; *pointed;* (used with the art. as a proper name) *Senuah,* the name of two Isr.:— Hasenuah [incl. the art.], Senuah.

5575. סַנְוֵר **çanvêr**, *san-vare´;* of uncert. der.; (in plur.) *blindness:*— blindness.

5576. סַנְחֵרִיב **Çanchêrîyb**, *san-khay-reeb´;* of for. or.; *Sancherib,* an Ass. king:— Sennacherib.

5577. סַנְסִן **çançin**, *san-seen´;* from an unused root mean. to *be pointed;* a *twig* (as *tapering*):— bough.

5578. סַנְסַנָּה **Çançannâh**, *san-san-naw´;* fem. of a form of 5577; a *bough; Sansannah,* a place in Pal.:— Sansannah.

5579. סְנַפִּיר **çᵉnappîyr**, *sen-ap-peer´;* of uncert. der.; a *fin* (collect.):— fins.

5580. סָס **çâç**, *sawce;* from the same as 5483; a *moth* (from the *agility* of the fly):— moth.

סוּס **çûç**. See 5483.

5581. סִסְמַי **Çiçmay**, *sis-mah´-ee;* of uncert. der.; *Sismai,* an Isr.:— Sisamai.

5582. סָעַד **çâ'ad**, *saw-ad´;* a prim. root; to *support* (mostly fig.):— comfort, establish, hold up, refresh self, strengthen, be upholden.

5583. סְעַד **çᵉ'ad** (Chald.), *seh-ad´;* corresp. to 5582; to *aid:*— helping.

5584. סָעָה **çâ'âh**, *saw-aw´;* a prim. root; to *rush:*— storm.

5585. סָעִיף **çâ'îyph**, *saw-eef´;* from 5586; a *fissure* (of rocks); also a *bough* (as *subdivided*):— (outmost) branch, clift, top.

5586. סָעַף **çâ'aph**, *saw-af´;* a prim. root; prop. to *divide* up; but used only as denom. from 5585, to *disbranch* (a tree):— top.

5587. סָעִף **çâ'îph**, *saw-eef´* or

שָׂעִף **sâ'îph**, *saw-eef´;* from 5586; *divided* (in mind), i.e. (abstr.) a *sentiment:*— opinion.

5588. סֵעֵף **çê'êph**, *say-afe´;* from 5586; *divided* (in mind), i.e. (concr.) a *skeptic:*— thought.

5589. סְעַפָּה **çᵉ'appâh**, *seh-ap-paw´;* fem. of 5585; a *twig:*— bough, branch. Comp. 5634.

5590. סָעַר **çâ'ar**, *saw-ar´;* a prim. root; to *rush upon;* by impl. to *toss* (tran. or intr., lit.

or fig.):— be (toss with) tempest (-uous), be sore troubled, come out as a (drive with the, scatter with a) whirlwind.

5591. סַעַר **ça'ar**, *sah´-ar;* or (fem.)

סְעָרָה **çe'ârâh**, *seh-aw-raw´;* from 5590; a *hurricane:*— storm (-y), tempest, whirlwind.

5592. סַף **çaph**, *saf;* from 5605, in its orig. sense of *containing;* a *vestibule* (as a *limit*); also a *dish* (for holding blood or wine):— bason, bowl, cup, door (post), gate, post, threshold.

5593. סַף **Çaph**, *saf;* the same as 5592; *Saph,* a Philistine:— Saph. Comp. 5598.

5594. סָפַד **çâphad**, *saw-fad´;* a prim. root; prop. to *tear* the hair and *beat* the breasts (as Orientals do in grief); gen. to *lament;* by impl. to *wail:*— lament, mourn (-er), wail.

5595. סָפָה **çâphâh**, *saw-faw´;* a prim. root; prop. to *scrape* (lit. to *shave;* but usually fig.) together (i.e. to *accumulate* or *increase*) or away (i.e. to *scatter, remove,* or *ruin;* intr. to *perish*):— add, augment, consume, destroy, heap, join, perish, put.

5596. סָפַח **çâphach**, *saw-fakh´;* or

שָׂפַח **sâphach** (Isa. 3:17) *saw-fakh´;* a prim. root; prop. to *scrape* out, but in certain peculiar senses (of *removal* or *association*):— abiding, gather together, cleave, smite with the scab.

5597. סַפַּחַת **çappachath**, *sap-pakh´-ath;* from 5596; the *mange* (as making the hair fall off):— scab.

5598. סִפַּי **Çippay**, *sip-pah´-ee;* from 5592; *bason-like; Sippai,* a Philistine:— Sippai. Comp. 5593.

5599. סָפִיחַ **çâphîyach**, *saw-fee´-akh;* from 5596; something (spontaneously) *falling* off, i.e. a *self-sown* crop; fig. a *freshet:*— (such) things as (which) grow (of themselves), which groweth of its own accord (itself).

5600. סְפִינָה **çe'phîynâh**, *sef-ee-naw´;* from 5603; a (sea-going) *vessel* (as *ceiled* with a deck):— ship.

5601. סַפִּיר **çappîyr**, *sap-peer´;* from 5608; a *gem* (perh. as used for *scratching* other substances), prob. the *sapphire:*— sapphire.

5602. סֵפֶל **çêphel**, *say´-fel;* from an unused root mean. to *depress;* a *basin* (as *deepened* out):— bowl, dish.

5603. סָפַן **çâphan**, *saw-fan´;* a prim. root; to *hide* by covering; spec. to *roof* (pass. part. as noun, a *roof)* or *paneling;* fig. to *reserve:*— cieled, cover, seated.

5604. סִפֻּן **çippûn**, *sip-poon´;* from 5603; a *wainscot:*— cieling.

5605. סָפַף **çâphaph**, *saw-faf´;* a prim. root; prop. to *snatch* away, i.e. *terminate;* but used only as denom. from 5592 (in the sense of a

vestibule), to *wait at* (the) *threshold:*— be a doorkeeper.

5606. סָפַק **çâphaq**, *saw-fak´;* or

שָׂפַק **sâphaq** (1 Kings 20:10; Job 27:23; Isa. 2:6), *saw-fak´;* a prim. root; to *clap* the hands (in token of compact, derision, grief, indignation, or punishment); by impl. of satisfaction, to *be enough;* by impl. of excess, to *vomit:*— clap, smite, strike, suffice, wallow.

5607. סֶפֶק **çêpheq**, *say´-fek;* or

שֶׂפֶק **sepheq** (Job 20:22; 36:18) *seh´-fek;* from 5606; *chastisement;* also *satiety:*— stroke, sufficiency.

5608. סָפַר **çâphar**, *saw-far´;* a prim. root; prop. to *score* with a mark as a tally or record, i.e. (by impl.) to *inscribe,* and also to *enumerate;* intens. to *recount,* i.e. *celebrate:*— commune, (ac-) count; declare, number, + penknife, reckon, scribe, shew forth, speak, talk, tell (out), writer.

5609. סְפַר **çe'phar** (Chald.), *sef-ar´;* from a root corresp. to 5608; a *book:*— book, roll.

5610. סְפָר **çe'phâr**, *sef-awr´;* from 5608; a *census:*— numbering.

5611. סְפָר **Çe'phâr**, *sef-awr´;* the same as 5610; *Sephar,* a place in Arabia:— Sephar.

5612. סֵפֶר **çêpher**, *say´-fer;* or (fem.)

סִפְרָה **çiphrâh** (Psa. 56:8 [9]), *sif-raw´;* from 5608; prop. *writing* (the art or a document); by impl. a *book:*— bill, book, evidence, × learn [-ed] (-ing), letter, register, scroll.

5613. סָפֵר **çâphêr** (Chald.), *saw-fare´;* from the same as 5609; a *scribe* (secular or sacred):— scribe.

5614. סְפָרָד **Çe'phârâd**, *sef-aw-rawd´;* of for. der.; *Sepharad,* a region of Assyria:— Sepharad.

סִפְרָה **çiphrâh**. See 5612.

5615. סְפֹרָה **çe'phôrâh**, *sef-o-raw´;* from 5608; a *numeration:*— number.

5616. סְפַרְוִי **Çe'pharvîy**, *sef-ar-vee´;* patrial from 5617; a *Sepharvite* or inhab. of Sepharvain:— Sepharvite.

5617. סְפַרְוַיִם **Çe'pharvayim** (dual), *sef-ar-vah´-yim;* or

סְפָרִים° **Çe'phârîym** (plur.), *sef-aw-reem´;* of for. der.; *Sepharvajim* or *Sepharim,* a place in Assyria:— Sepharvaim.

5618. סֹפֶרֶת **Çôphereth**, *so-feh´-reth;* fem. act. part. of 5608; a *scribe* (prop. female); *Sophereth,* a temple servant:— Sophereth.

5619. סָקַל **çâqal**, *saw-kal´;* a prim. root; prop. to *be weighty;* but used only in the sense of *lapidation* or its contrary (as if a delapidation):— (cast, gather out, throw) stone (-s), × surely.

5620. סַר **çar**, *sar*; from 5637 contr.; *peevish:*— heavy, sad.

5621. סָרָב **çârâb**, *saw-rawb'*; from an unused root mean. to *sting*; a thistle:— brier.

5622. סַרְבַּל **çarbal** (Chald.), *sar-bal'*; of uncert. der.; a *cloak:*— coat.

5623. סַרְגוֹן **Çargôwn**, *sar-gone'*; of for. der.; *Sargon*, an Ass. king:— Sargon.

5624. סֶרֶד **Çered**, *seh'-red*; from a prim. root mean. to *tremble*; *trembling*; *Sered*, an Isr.:— Sered.

5625. סַרְדִּי **Çardîy**, *sar-dee'*; patron. from 5624; a *Seredite* (collect.) or desc. of Sered:— Sardites.

5626. סִרָה **Çîrâh**, *see-raw'*; from 5493; *departure*; *Sirah*, a cistern so-called:— Sirah. See also 5518.

5627. סָרָה **çârâh**, *saw-raw'*; from 5493; *apostasy, crime*; fig. *remission:*— × continual, rebellion, revolt (l-ed]), turn away, wrong.

5628. סָרַח **çârach**, *saw-rakh'*; a prim. root; to *extend* (even to *excess*):— exceeding, hand, spread, stretch self, banish.

5629. סֶרַח **çerach**, *seh'-rakh*; from 5628; a *redundancy:*— remnant.

5630. סִרְיֹן **çiyrôn**, *sir-yone'*; for 8302; a coat of *mail:*— brigandine.

5631. סָרִיס **çârîyç**, *saw-reece'*; or

    סָרִס **çârîç**, *saw-reece'*; from an unused root mean. to *castrate*; a *eunuch*; by impl. *valet* (espec. of the female apartments), and thus, a *minister* of state:— chamberlain, eunuch, officer. Comp. 7249.

5632. סָרֵךְ **çârêk** (Chald.), *saw-rake'*; of for. or.; an *emir:*— president.

5633. סֶרֶן **çeren**, *seh'-ren*; from an unused root of uncert. mean.; an *axle*; fig. a *peer:*— lord, plate.

5634. סַרְעַפָּה **çar'appâh**, *sar-ap-paw'*; for 5589; a *twig:*— bough.

5635. סָרַף **çâraph**, *saw-raf'*; a prim. root; to *cremate*, i.e. to *be* (near) *of kin* (such being privileged to kindle the pyre):— burn.

5636. סַרְפָּד **çarpâd**, *sar-pawd'*; from 5635; a *nettle* (as stinging like a *burn*):— brier.

5637. סָרַר **çârar**, *saw-rar'*; a prim. root; to *turn away*, i.e. (mor.) *be refractory:*— × away, backsliding, rebellious, revolter (-ing), slide back, stubborn, withdrew.

5638. סְתָו **çᵉthâv**, *seth-awv'*; from an unused root mean. to *hide*; *winter* (as the dark season):— winter.

5639. סְתוּר **Çᵉthûwr**, *seth-oor'*; from 5641; *hidden*; *Sethur*, an Isr.:— Sethur.

5640. סָתַם **çâtham**, *saw-tham'*; or

    שָׂתַם **sâtham** (Num. 24:15), *saw-tham'*; a prim. root; to *stop* up; by impl. to *repair*; fig. to *keep secret:*— closed up, hidden, secret, shut out (up), stop.

5641. סָתַר **çâthar**, *saw-thar'*; a prim. root; to *hide* (by covering), lit. or fig.:— be absent, keep close, conceal, hide (self), (keep) secret, × surely.

5642. סְתַר **çᵉthar** (Chald.), *seth-ar'*; corresp. to 5641; to *conceal*; fig. to *demolish:*— destroy, secret thing.

5643. סֵתֶר **çêther**, *say'-ther*; or (fem.)

    סִתְרָה **çithrâh** (Deut. 32:38), *sith-raw'*; from 5641; a *cover* (in a good or a bad, a lit. or a fig. sense):— backbiting, covering, covert, × disguise [-th], hiding place, privily, protection, secret (-ly, place).

5644. סִתְרִי **Çithrîy**, *sith-ree'*; from 5643; *protective*; *Sithri*, an Isr.:— Zithri.

ע

5645. עָב **'âb**, *awb* (masc. and fem.); from 5743; prop. an *envelope*, i.e. *darkness* (or *density*, 2 Chron. 4:17); spec. a (scud) *cloud*; also a *copse:*— clay, (thick) cloud, × thick, thicket. Comp. 5672.

5646. עָב **'âb**, *awb*; or

    עֹב **'ôb**, *obe*; from an unused root mean. to *cover*; prop. equiv. to 5645; but used only as an arch. term, an *architrave* (as *shading* the pillars):— thick (beam, plant).

5647. עָבַד **'âbad**, *aw-bad'*; a prim. root; to *work* (in any sense); by impl. to *serve, till*, (caus.) *enslave*, etc.:— × be, keep in bondage, be bondmen, bond-service, compel, do, dress, ear, execute, + husbandman, keep, labour (-ing man, bring to pass, (cause to, make to) serve (-ing, self), (be, become) servant (-s), do (use) service, till (-er), transgress [*from marg.*], (set a) work, be wrought, worshipper.

5648. עֲבַד **'ăbad** (Chald.), *ab-bad'*; corresp. to 5647; to *do, make, prepare, keep*, etc.:— × cut, do, execute, go on, make, move, work.

5649. עֲבַד **'ăbad** (Chald.), *ab-bad'*; from 5648; a *servant:*— servant.

5650. עֶבֶד **'ebed**, *eh'-bed*; from 5647; a *servant:*— × bondage, bondman, [bond-] servant, (man-) servant.

5651. עֶבֶד **'Ebed**, *eh'-bed*; the same as 5650; *Ebed*, the name of two Isr.:— Ebed.

5652. עֲבָד **'ăbâd**, *ab-awd'*; from 5647; a *deed:*— work.

5653. עַבְדָּא **'Abdâ'**, *ab-daw'*; from 5647; *work; Abda*, the name of two Isr.:— Abda.

5654. עֹבֵד אֱדוֹם **'Ôbêd 'Ĕdôwm**, *o-bade' ed-ome'*; from the act. part. of 5647 and 123; *worker of Edom; Obed-Edom*, the name of five Isr.:— Obed-edom.

5655. עַבְדְּאֵל **'Abde'êl**, *ab-deh-ale'*; from 5647 and 410; *serving God; Abdeel*, an Isr.:— Abdeel. Comp. 5661.

5656. עֲבֹדָה **'ăbôdâh**, *ab-o-daw'*; or

עֲבוֹדָה **'ăbôwdâh**, *ab-o-daw'*; from 5647; *work* of any kind:— act, bondage, + bondservant, effect, labour, ministering (-try), office, service (-ile, -itude), tillage, use, work, × wrought.

5657. עֲבֻדָּה **'ăbuddâh**, *ab-ood-daw'*; pass. part. of 5647; *something wrought*, i.e. (concr.) *service*:— household, store of servants.

5658. עַבְדּוֹן **'Abdôwn**, *ab-dohn'*; from 5647; *servitude; Abdon*, the name of a place in Pal. and of four Isr.:— Abdon. Comp. 5683.

5659. עַבְדוּת **'abdûwth**, *ab-dooth'*; from 5647; *servitude*:— bondage.

5660. עַבְדִּי **'Abdîy**, *ab-dee'*; from 5647; *serviceable; Abdi*, the name of two Isr.:— Abdi.

5661. עַבְדִּיאֵל **'Abdîy'êl**, *ab-dee-ale'*; from 5650 and 410; *servant of God; Abdiel*, an Isr.:— Abdiel. Comp. 5655.

5662. עֹבַדְיָה **'Ôbadyâh**, *o-bad-yaw'*; or

עֹבַדְיָהוּ **'Ôbadyâhûw**, *o-bad-yaw'-hoo*; act. part. of 5647 and 3050; *serving Jah; Obadjah*, the name of thirteen Isr.:— Obadiah.

5663. עֶבֶד מֶלֶךְ **'Ebed Melek**, *eh'-bed meh'-lek;* from 5650 and 4428; *servant of a king; Ebed-Melek*, a eunuch of Zedekeah:— Ebed-melech.

5664. עֲבֵד נְגוֹ **'Ăbêd Neֵgôw**, *ab-ade' neg-o';* the same as 5665; *Abed-Nego*, the Bab. name of one of Daniel's companions:— Abed-nego.

5665. עֲבֵד נְגוֹא **'Ăbêd Neֵgôw'** (Chald.), *ab-ade' neg-o';* of for. or.; *Abed-Nego*, the name of Azariah:— Abed-nego.

5666. עָבָה **'âbâh**, *aw-baw'*; a prim. root; to *be dense*:— be (grow) thick (-er).

5667. עֲבוֹט **'ăbôwṭ**, *ab-ote'*; or

עֲבֹט **'ăbôṭ**, *ab-ote'*; from 5670; a *pawn*:— pledge.

5668. עָבוּר **'âbûwr**, *aw-boor'*; or

עָבֻר **'âbûr**, *aw-boor'*; pass. part. of 5674; prop. *crossed*, i.e. (abstr.) *transit*; used only adv. on *account* of, in *order* that:— because of, for (... 's sake), (intent) that, to.

5669. עָבוּר **'âbûwr**, *aw-boor'*; the same as 5668; *passed*, i.e. *kept* over; used only of *stored* grain:— old corn.

5670. עָבַט **'âbaṭ**, *aw-bat'*; a prim. root; to

pawn; caus. to *lend* (on security); fig. to *entangle*:— borrow, break [ranks], fetch [a pledge], lend, × surely.

5671. עַבְטִיט **'abṭîyṭ**, *ab-teet'*; from 5670; something *pledged*, i.e. (collect.) *pawned* goods:— thick clay [by a false etym.].

5672. עֳבִי **'ăbîy**, *ab-ee'*; or

עֳבִי **'ŏbîy**, *ob-ee'*; from 5666; *density*, i.e. *depth* or *width*:— thick (-ness). Comp. 5645.

5673. עֲבִידָה **'ăbîydâh** (Chald.), *ab-ee-daw'*; from 5648; *labor* or *business*:— affairs, service, work.

5674. עָבַר **'âbar**, *aw-bar'*; a prim. root; to *cross* over; used very widely of any *transition* (lit. or fig.; tran., intr., intens., or caus.); spec. to *cover* (in copulation):— alienate, alter, × at all, beyond, bring (over, through), carry over, (over-) come (on, over), conduct (over), convey over, current, deliver, do away, enter, escape, fail, gender, get over, (make) go (away, beyond, by, forth, his way, in, on, over, through), have away (more), lay, meddle, overrun, make partition, (cause to, give, make to, over) pass (-age, along, away, beyond, by, -enger, on, out, over, through), (cause to, make) proclaim (-amation), perish, provoke to anger, put away, rage, + raiser of taxes, remove, send over, set apart, + shave, cause to (make) sound, × speedily, × sweet smelling, take (away), (make to) transgress (-or), translate, turn away, [way-] faring man, be wrath.

5675. עֲבַר **'ăbar** (Chald.), *ab-ar';* corresp. to 5676:— beyond, this side.

5676. עֵבֶר **'êber**, *ay'-ber;* from 5674; prop. a region *across*; but used only adv. (with or without a prep.) on the *opposite* side (espec. of the Jordan; usually mean. the *east*):— × against, beyond, by, × from, over, passage, quarter, (other, this) side, straight.

5677. עֵבֶר **'Êber**, *ay'-ber;* the same as 5676; *Eber*, the name of two patriarchs and four Isr.:— Eber, Heber.

5678. עֶבְרָה **'ebrâh**, *eb-raw'*; fem. of 5676; an *outburst* of passion:— anger, rage, wrath.

5679. עֲבָרָה **'ăbârâh**, *ab-aw-raw'*; from 5674; a *crossing*-place:— ferry, plain [from the marg.].

5680. עִבְרִי **'Ibrîy**, *ib-ree'*; patron. from 5677; an *Eberite* (i.e. Hebrew) or desc. of Eber:— Hebrew (-ess, woman).

5681. עִבְרִי **'Ibrîy**, *ib-ree'*; the same as 5680; *Ibri*, an Isr.:— Ibri.

5682. עֲבָרִים **'Ăbârîym**, *ab-aw-reem'*; plur. of

5676; regions *beyond; Abarim*, a place in Pal.:— Abarim, passages.

5683. עֶבְרֹן **'Ebrôn**, *eb-rone´;* from 5676; *transitional; Ebron*, a place in Pal.:— Hebron. [*Perh. a clerical err. for* 5658.]

5684. עֶבְרֹנָה **'Ebrônâh**, *eb-raw-naw´;* fem. of 5683; *Ebronah*, a place in the Desert:— Ebronah.

5685. עָבַשׁ **'âbash**, *aw-bash´;* a prim. root; to *dry* up:— be rotten.

5686. עָבַת **'âbath**, *aw-bath´;* a prim. root; to *interlace*, i.e. (fig.) to *pervert:*— wrap up.

5687. עָבֹת **'âbôth**, *aw-both´;* or

עָבוֹת **'âbôwth**, *aw-both´;* from 5686; *intwined*, i.e. *dense:*— thick.

5688. עֲבֹת **'ăbôth**, *ab-oth´;* or

עֲבוֹת **'ăbôwth**, *ab-oth´;* or (fem.)

עֲבֹתָה **'ăbôthâh**, *ab-oth-aw´;* the same as 5687; something *intwined*, i.e. a *string, wreath* or *foliage:*— band, cord, rope, thick bough (branch), wreathen (chain).

5689. עָגַב **'âgab**, *aw-gab´;* a prim. root; to *breathe* after, i.e. to *love* (sensually):— dote, lover.

5690. עֶגֶב **'egeb**, *eh´-gheb;* from 5689; *love* (concr.), i.e. *amative* words:— much love, very lovely.

5691. עֲגָבָה **'ăgâbâh**, *ag-aw-baw´;* from 5689; *love* (abstr.), i.e. *amorousness:*— inordinate love.

5692. עֻגָּה **'uggâh**, *oog-gaw´;* from 5746; an *ash-cake* (as *round*):— cake (upon the hearth).

עָגוֹל **'âgôwl**. See 5696.

5693. עָגוּר **'âgûwr**, *aw-goor´;* pass. part. [but with act. sense] of an unused root mean. to *twitter;* prob. the *swallow:*— swallow.

5694. עָגִיל **'âgîyl**, *aw-gheel´;* from the same as 5696; something *round*, i.e. a *ring* (for the ears):— earring.

5695. עֵגֶל **'êgel**, *ay-ghel;* from the same as 5696; a (male) *calf* (as *frisking* round), espec. one nearly grown (i.e. a *steer*):— bullock, calf.

5696. עָגֹל **'âgôl**, *aw-gole´;* or

עָגוֹל **'âgôwl**, *aw-gole´;* from an unused root mean. to *revolve, circular:*— round.

5697. עֶגְלָה **'eglâh**, *eg-law´;* fem. of 5695; a (female) *calf*, espec. one nearly grown (i.e. a *heifer*):— calf, cow, heifer.

5698. עֶגְלָה **'Eglâh**, *eg-law´;* the same as 5697; *Eglah*, a wife of David:— Eglah.

5699. עֲגָלָה **'ăgâlâh**, *ag-aw-law´;* from the same as 5696; something *revolving*, i.e. a wheeled *vehicle:*— cart, chariot, wagon.

5700. עֶגְלוֹן **'Eglôwn**, *eg-lawn´;* from 5695; vi-

tuline; Eglon, the name of a place in Pal. and of a Moabitish king:— Eglon.

5701. עָגַם **'âgam**, *aw-gam´;* a prim. root; to *be sad:*— grieve.

5702. עָגַן **'âgan**, *aw-gan´;* a prim. root; to *debar*, i.e. from marriage:— stay.

5703. עַד **'ad**, *ad;* from 5710; prop. a (peremptory) *terminus*, i.e. (by impl.) *duration*, in the sense of *advance* or *perpetuity* (substantially as a noun, either with or without a prep.):— eternity, ever (-lasting, -more), old, perpetually, + world without end.

5704. עַד **'ad**, *ad;* prop. the same as 5703 (used as a prep., adv. or conjunc.; espec. with a prep.); *as far* (or *long*, or *much*) *as*, whether of space (*even unto*) or time (*during, while, until*) or degree (*equally with*):— against, and, as, at, before, by (that), even (to), for (-asmuch as), [hither-] to, + how long, into, as long (much) as, (so) that, till, toward, until, when, while, (+ as) yet.

5705. עַד **'ad** (Chald.), *ad;* corresp. to 5704:— × and, at, for, [hither-] to, on, till, (un-) to, until, within.

5706. עַד **'ad**, *ad;* the same as 5703 in the sense of the *aim* of an attack; *booty:*— prey.

5707. עֵד **'êd**, *ayd;* contr. from 5749 ; concr. a *witness;* abstr. *testimony;* spec. a *recorder*, i.e. *prince:*— witness.

5708. עֵד **'êd**, *ayd;* from an unused root mean. to *set* a period [comp. 5710, 5749]; the *menstrual* flux (as *periodical*); by impl. (in plur.) *soiling:*— filthy.

עֹד **'ôd**. See 5750.

5709. עֲדָא **'ădâ'** (Chald.), *ad-aw´;* or

עֲדָה **'ădâh** (Chald.), *ad-aw´;* corresp. to 5710:— alter, depart, pass (away), remove, take (away).

עֹדֵד **'Ôdêd**. See 5752.

5710. עָדָה **'âdâh**, *aw-daw´;* a prim. root; to *advance*, i.e. *pass* on or *continue;* caus. to *remove;* spec. to *bedeck* (i.e. bring an ornament upon):— adorn, deck (self), pass by, take away.

5711. עָדָה **'Âdâh**, *aw-daw´;* from 5710; *ornament; Adah*, the name of two women:— Adah.

5712. עֵדָה **'êdâh**, *ay-daw´;* fem. of 5707 in the orig. sense of *fixture*; a stated *assemblage* (spec. a *concourse*, or gen. a *family* or *crowd*):— assembly, company, congregation, multitude, people, swarm. Comp. 5713.

5713. עֵדָה **'êdâh**, *ay-daw´;* fem. of 5707 in its techn. sense; *testimony:*— testimony, witness. Comp. 5712.

5714. עִדּוֹ **'Iddôw**, *id-do´;* or

עִדּוֹא **'Iddôw'**, *id-do´;* or

עִדִּיא° **'Iddîy**, *id-dee´;* from 5710; *timely; Iddo* (or *Iddi*), the name of five Isr.:— Iddo. Comp. 3035, 3260.

5715. עֵדוּת **'êdûwth**, *ay-dooth´;* fem. of 5707; *testimony:*— testimony, witness.

5716. עֲדִי **'ădîy**, *ad-ee´;* from 5710 in the sense of *trappings; finery;* gen. an *outfit;* spec. a *headstall:*— × excellent, mouth, ornament.

5717. עֲדִיאֵל **'Ădîy'êl**, *ad-ee-ale´;* from 5716 and 410; *ornament of God; Adiel*, the name of three Isr.:— Adiel.

5718. עֲדָיָה **'Ădâyâh**, *ad-aw-yaw´;* or

עֲדָיָהוּ **'Ădâyâhûw**, *ad-aw-yaw´-hoo;* from 5710 and 3050; *Jah has adorned; Adajah,* the name of eight Isr.:— Adaiah.

5719. עָדִין **'âdîyn**, *aw-deen´;* from 5727; *voluptuous:*— given to pleasures.

5720. עָדִין **'Âdîyn**, *aw-deen´;* the same as 5719; *Adin*, the name of two Isr.:— Adin.

5721. עֲדִינָא **'Ădîynâ'**, *ad-ee-naw´;* from 5719; *effeminacy; Adina*, an Isr.:— Adina.

5722. עֲדִינוֹ **'ădîynôw**, *ad-ee-no´;* prob. from 5719 in the orig. sense of *slender* (i.e. a *spear*); *his spear:*— Adino.

5723. עֲדִיתַיִם **'Ădîythayim**, *ad-ee-thah´-yim;* dual of a fem. of 5706; *double prey; Adithajim*, a place in Pal.:— Adithaim.

5724. עַדְלָי **'Adlay**, *ad-lah´-ee;* prob. from an unused root of uncert. mean.; *Adlai*, an Isr.:— Adlai.

5725. עֲדֻלָּם **'Ădullâm**, *ad-ool-lawm´;* prob. from the pass. part. of the same as 5724; *Adullam*, a place in Pal.:— Adullam.

5726. עֲדֻלָּמִי **'Ădullâmîy**, *ad-ool-law-mee´;* patrial from 5725; an *Adullamite* or native of Adullam:— Adullamite.

5727. עָדַן **'âdan**, *aw-dan´;* a prim. root; to *be soft* or *pleasant;* fig. and refl. to *live voluptuously:*— delight self.

5728. עֶדֶן **'ăden**, *ad-en´;* or

עֶדֶנָה **'ădennâh**, *ad-en´-naw;* from 5704 and 2004; *till now:*— yet.

5729. עֶדֶן **'Eden**, *eh´-den;* from 5727; *pleasure; Eden*, a place in Mesopotamia:— Eden.

5730. עֵדֶן **'êden**, *ay´-den;* or (fem.)

עֶדְנָה **'ednâh**, *ed-naw´;* from 5727; *pleasure:*— delicate, delight, pleasure. See also 1040.

5731. עֵדֶן **'Êden**, *ay´-den;* the same as 5730 (masc.); *Eden*, the region of Adam's home:— Eden.

5732. עִדָּן **'iddân** (Chald.), *id-dawn´;* from a root corresp. to that of 5708; a *set time;* tech. a *year:*— time.

5733. עַדְנָא **'Adnâ'**, *ad-naw´* from 5727; *pleasure; Adna*, the name of two Isr.:— Adna.

5734. עַדְנָה **'Adnâh**, *ad-naw´;* from 5727; *pleasure; Adnah*, the name of two Isr.:— Adnah.

5735. עֲדָעֲדָה **'Ăd'âdâh**, *ad-aw-daw´;* from 5712; *festival; Adadah*, a place in Pal.:— Adadah.

5736. עָדַף **'ădaph**, *aw-daf´;* a prim. root; to *be* (caus. *have*) *redundant:*— be more, odd number, be (have) over (and above), overplus, remain.

5737. עָדַר **'âdar**, *aw-dar´;* a prim. root; to *arrange*, as a battle, a vineyard (to *hoe*); hence, to *muster* and so to *miss* (or find *wanting*):— dig, fail, keep (rank), lack.

5738. עֶדֶר **'Eder**, *eh´-der;* from 5737; an *arrangement* (i.e. drove); *Eder*, an Isr.:— Ader.

5739. עֵדֶר **'êder**, *ay´-der;* from 5737; an *arrangement*, i.e. *muster* (of animals):— drove, flock, herd.

5740. עֵדֶר **'Êder**, *ay´-der;* the same as 5739; *Eder*, the name of an Isr. and of two places in Pal.:— Edar, Eder.

5741. עַדְרִיאֵל **'Adrîy'êl**, *ad-ree-ale´;* from 5739 and 410; *flock of God; Adriel*, an Isr.:— Adriel.

5742. עָדָשׁ **'âdâsh**, *aw-dawsh´;* from an unused root of uncert. mean.; a *lentil:*— lentile.

עַוָּא **'Avvâ'**. See 5755.

5743. עוּב **'ûwb**, *oob;* a prim. root; to *be dense* or *dark*, i.e. to *becloud:*— cover with a cloud.

5744. עוֹבֵד **'Ôwbêd**, *o-bade´;* act. part. of 5647; *serving; Obed*, the name of five Isr.:— Obed.

5745. עוֹבָל **'Ôwbâl**, *o-bawl´;* of for. der.; *Obal*, a son of Joktan:— Obal.

5746. עוּג **'ûwg**, *oog;* a prim. root; prop. to *gyrate;* but used only as a denom. from 5692, to *bake* (round cakes on the hearth):— bake.

5747. עוֹג **'Ôwg**, *ogue;* prob. from 5746; *round; Og*, a king of Bashan:— Og.

5748. עוּגָב **'ûwgâb**, *oo-gawb´;* or

עֻגָּב **'ûggâb**, *oog-gawb´;* from 5689 in the orig. sense of *breathing;* a *reed*-instrument of music:— organ.

5749. עוּד **'ûwd**, *ood;* a prim. root; to *duplicate* or *repeat;* by impl. to *protest, testify* (as by reiteration); intens. to *encompass, restore* (as a sort of redupl.):— admonish, charge, earnestly, lift up, protest, call (take) to record, relieve, rob, solemnly, stand upright, testify, give warning, (bear, call to, give, take to) witness.

5750. עוֹד **'ôwd**, ode; or

עֹד **'ôd**, ode; from 5749; prop. *iteration* or *continuance;* used only adv. (with or without prep.), *again, repeatedly, still, more:*— again, × all life long, at all, besides, but, else, further (-more), henceforth, (any) longer, (any) more (-over), × once, since, (be) still, when, (good, the) while (having being), (as, because, whether, while) yet (within).

5751. עוֹד **'ôwd** (Chald.), ode; corresp. to 5750:— while.

5752. עוֹדֵד **'Ôwdêd**, o-dade´; or

עֹדֵד **'Ôdêd**, o-dade´; from 5749; *reiteration; Oded*, the name of two Isr.:— Oded.

5753. עָוָה **'âvâh**, aw-vaw´; a prim. root; to *crook*, lit. or fig. (as follows):— do amiss, bow down, make crooked, commit iniquity, pervert, (do) perverse (-ly), trouble, × turn, do wickedly, do wrong.

5754. עַוָּה **'avvâh**, av-vaw´; intens. from 5753 abb.; *overthrow:*— × overturn.

5755. עִוָּה **'Ivvâh**, iv-vaw´; or

עַוָּא **'Avvâ'** (2 Kings 17: 24) av-vaw´; for 5754; *Ivvah* or *Avva*, a region of Assyria:— Ava, Ivah.

עָווֹן **'âvôwn**. See 5771.

5756. עוּז **'ûwz**, ooz; a prim. root; to *be strong;* caus. to *strengthen*, i.e. (fig.) to *save* (by flight):— gather (self, self to flee), retire.

5757. עַוִּי **'Avvîy**, av-vee´; patrial from 5755; an *Avvite* or native of Avvah (only plur.):— Avims, Avites.

5758. עִוְיָא **'ivyâ'** (Chald.), iv-yaw´; from a root corresp. to 5753; *perverseness:*— iniquity.

5759. עֲוִיל **'ăvîyl**, av-eel´; from 5764; a *babe:*— young child, little one.

5760. עֲוִיל **'ăvîyl**, av-eel´; from 5765; *perverse* (morally):— ungodly.

5761. עַוִּים **'Avvîym**, av-veem´; plur. of 5757; *Avvim* (as inhabited by Avvites), a place in Pal. (with the art. pref.):— Avim.

5762. עֲוִית **'Ăvîyth**, av-veeth´; or [perh.

עַיּוֹת° **'Ayôwth**, ah-yōth´, as if plur. of 5857]

עַוִּית° **'Ayûwth**, ah-yōth´; from 5753; *ruin; Avvith* (or *Avvoth*), a place in Pal.:— Avith.

5763. עוּל **'ûwl**, ool; a prim. root; to *suckle*, i.e. *give milk:*— milch, (ewe great) with young.

5764. עוּל **'ûwl**, ool; from 5763; a *babe:*— sucking child, infant.

5765. עָוַל **'âval**, aw-val´; a prim. root; to *distort* (morally):— deal unjustly, unrighteous.

עוּל **'ôwl**. See 5923.

5766. עֶוֶל **'evel**, eh´-vel; or

עָוֶל **'âvel**, aw´-vel; and (fem.)

עַוְלָה **'avlâh**, av-law´; or

עוֹלָה **'ôwlâh**, o-law´; or

עֹלָה **'ôlâh**, o-law´; from 5765; (moral) *evil:*— iniquity, perverseness, unjust (-ly), unrighteousness (-ly), wicked (-ness).

5767. עַוָּל **'avvâl**, av-vawl´; intens. from 5765; *evil* (morally):— unjust, unrighteous, wicked.

עוֹלָה **'ôwlâh**. See 5930.

5768. עוֹלֵל **'ôwlêl**, o-lale´; or

עֹלָל **'ôlâl**, o-lawl´; from 5763; a *suckling:*— babe, (young) child, infant, little one.

5769. עוֹלָם **'ôwlâm**, o-lawm´; or

עֹלָם **'ôlâm**, o-lawm´; from 5956; prop. *concealed,* i.e. the *vanishing* point; gen. time *out of mind* (past or future), i.e. (practically) *eternity;* freq. adv. (espec. with prep. pref.) *always:*— alway (-s), ancient (time), any more, continuance, eternal, (for, [n-]) ever (-lasting, -more, of old), lasting, long (time), (of) old (time), perpetual, at any time, (beginning of the) world (+ without end). Comp. 5331, 5703.

5770. עָוַן **'âvan**, aw-van´; denom. from 5869; to *watch* (with jealousy):— eye.

5771. עָוֺן **'âvôn**, aw-vone´; or

עָווֹן **'âvôwn** (2 Kings 7:9; Psa. 51:5 [7]), aw-vone´; from 5753; *perversity,* i.e. (moral) *evil:*— fault, iniquity, mischief, punishment (of iniquity), sin.

5772. עוֹנָה **'ôwnâh**, o-naw´; from an unused root appar. mean. to *dwell* together; *sexual (cohabitation):*— duty of marriage.

5773. עֲוֶה **'av'eh**, av-eh´; from 5753; *perversity:*— × perverse.

5774. עוּף **'ûwph**, oof; a prim. root; to *cover* (with wings or obscurity); hence, (as denom. from 5775) to *fly;* also (by impl. of dimness) to *faint* (from the darkness of swooning):— brandish, be (wax) faint, flee away, fly (away), × set, shine forth, weary.

5775. עוֹף **'ôwph**, ofe; from 5774; a *bird* (as *covered* with feathers, or rather as *covering* with wings), often collect.:— bird, that flieth, flying, fowl.

5776. עוֹף **'ôwph** (Chald.), ofe; corresp. to 5775:— fowl.

5777. עוֹפֶרֶת **'ôwphereth**, o-feh´-reth; or

עֹפֶרֶת **'ôphereth**, o-feh´-reth; fem. part. act. of 6080; *lead* (from its *dusty* color):— lead.

5778. עוֹפַי° **'Ôwphay**, o-fah´-ee; from 5775;

birdlike; *Ephai*, an Isr.:— Ephai [*from marg.*].

5779. עוּץ **'ûwts**, *oots;* a prim. root; to *consult:*— take advice ([counsel] together).

5780. עוּץ **'Ûwts**, *oots;* appar. from 5779; *consultation; Uts*, a son of Aram, also a Seirite, and the regions settled by them.:— Uz.

5781. עוּק **'ûwq**, *ook;* a prim. root; to *pack:*— be pressed.

5782. עוּר **'ûwr**, *oor;* a prim. root [rather ident. with 5783 through the idea of *opening* the eyes] to *wake* (lit. or fig.):— (a-) wake (-n, up), lift up (self), × master, raise (up), stir up (self).

5783. עוּר **'ûwr**, *oor;* a prim. root; to (*be*) *bare:*— be made naked.

5784. עוּר **'ûwr** (Chald.), *oor; chaff* (as the *naked* husk):— chaff.

5785. עוֹר **'ôwr**, *ore;* from 5783; *skin* (as *naked*); by impl. *hide, leather:*— hide, leather, skin.

5786. עָוַר **'âvar**, *aw-var´;* a prim. root [rather denom. from 5785 through the idea of a *film* over the eyes] to *blind:*— blind, put out. See also 5895.

5787. עִוֵּר **'ivvêr**, *iv-vare´;* intens. from 5786; *blind* (lit. or fig.):— blind (men, people).

עוֹרֵב **'ôwrêb**. See 6159.

5788. עִוָּרוֹן **'ivvârôwn**, *iv-vaw-rone´;* and (fem.)

עַוֶּרֶת **'avvereth**, *av-veh´-reth;* from 5787; *blindness:*— blind (-ness).

5789. עוּשׁ **'ûwsh**, *oosh;* a prim. root; to *hasten:*— assemble self.

5790. עוּת **'ûwth**, *ooth;* for 5789; to *hasten*, i.e. *succor:*— speak in season.

5791. עָוַת **'âvath**, *aw-vath´;* a prim. root; to *wrest:*— bow self, (make) crooked, falsifying, overthrow, deal perversely, pervert, subvert, turn upside down.

5792. עַוָּתָה **'avvâthâh**, *av-vaw-thaw´;* from 5791; *oppression:*— wrong.

5793. עוּתַי **'Ûwthay**, *oo-thah´-ee;* from 5790; *succoring; Uthai*, the name of two Isr.:— Uthai.

5794. עַז **'az**, *az;* from 5810; *strong, vehement, harsh:*— fierce, + greedy, mighty, power, roughly, strong.

5795. עֵז **'êz**, *aze;* from 5810; a she-*goat* (as *strong*), but masc. in plur. (which also is used ellipt. for *goat's hair*):— (she) goat, kid.

5796. עֵז **'êz** (Chald.), *aze;* corresp. to 5795:— goat.

5797. עֹז **'ôz**, *oze;* or (fully)

עוֹז **'ôwz**, *oze;* from 5810; *strength* in various applications (*force, security, majesty, praise*):— boldness, loud, might, power, strength, strong.

5798. עֻזָּא **'Uzzâ'**, *ooz-zaw´;* or

5799. עֲזָאזֵל **'ăzâ'zêl**, *az-aw-zale´;* from 5795 and 235; *goat of departure;* the *scapegoat:*— scapegoat.

5800. עָזַב **'âzab**, *aw-zab´;* a prim. root; to *loosen*, i.e. *relinquish, permit*, etc.:— commit self, fail, forsake, fortify, help, leave (destitute, off), refuse, × surely.

5801. עִזָּבוֹן **'izzâbôwn**, *iz-zaw-bone´;* from 5800 in the sense of *letting go* (for a price, i.e. *selling*); *trade*, i.e. the place (*mart*) or the payment (*revenue*):— fair, ware.

5802. עַזְבּוּק **'Azbûwq**, *az-book´;* from 5794 and the root of 950; *stern depopulator; Azbuk*, an Isr.:— Azbuk.

5803. עַזְגָּד **'Azgâd**, *az-gawd´;* from 5794 and 1409; *stern troop; Azgad*, an Isr.:— Azgad.

5804. עַזָּה **'Azzâh**, *az-zaw´;* fem. of 5794; *strong; Azzah*, a place in Pal.:— Azzah, Gaza.

5805. עֲזוּבָה **'ăzûwbâh**, *az-oo-baw´;* fem. pass. part. of 5800; *desertion* (of inhabitants):— forsaking.

5806. עֲזוּבָה **'Ăzûwbâh**, *az-oo-baw´;* the same as 5805; *Azubah*, the name of two Israelitesses:— Azubah.

5807. עֱזוּז **'ĕzûwz**, *ez-ooz´;* from 5810; *forcibleness:*— might, strength.

5808. עִזּוּז **'izzûwz**, *iz-zooz´;* from 5810; *forcible;* collect. and concr. an *army:*— power, strong.

5809. עַזּוּר **'Azzûwr**, *az-zoor´;* or

עַזֻּר **'Azzûr**, *az-zoor´;* from 5826; *helpful; Azur, Azzur*, the name of three Isr.:— Azur, Azzur.

5810. עָזַז **'âzaz**, *aw-zaz´;* a prim. root; to *be stout* (lit. or fig.):— harden, impudent, prevail, strengthen (self), be strong.

5811. עָזָז **'Âzâz**, *aw-zawz´;* from 5810; *strong; Azaz*, an Isr.:— Azaz.

5812. עֲזַזְיָהוּ **'Ăzazyâhûw**, *az-az-yaw´-hoo;* from 5810 and 3050; *Jah has strengthened; Azazjah*, the name of three Isr.:— Azaziah.

5813. עֻזִּי **'Uzzîy**, *ooz-zee´;* from 5810; *forceful; Uzzi*, the name of six Isr.:— Uzzi.

5814. עֻזִּיָּא **'Uzzîyâ'**, *ooz-zee-yaw´;* perh. for 5818; *Uzzija*, an Isr.:— Uzzia.

5815. עֲזִיאֵל **'Ăzîy'êl**, *az-ee-ale´;* from 5756 and 410; *strengthened of God; Aziël*, an Isr.:— Aziel. Comp. 3268.

5816. עֻזִּיאֵל **'Uzzîy'êl**, *ooz-zee-ale´;* from 5797 and 410; *strength of God; Uzziël*, the name of six Isr.:— Uzziel.

5817. עָזִיאֵלִי **'Ozzîy'êlîy**, *oz-zee-ay-lee´;* patron. from 5816; an *Uzziëlite* (collect.) or desc. of Uzziel:— Uzzielites.

5818. עֻזִּיָּה **'Uzzîyâh,** *ooz-zee-yaw´;* or

עֻזִּיָּהוּ **'Uzzîyâhûw,** *ooz-zee-yaw´-hoo;* from 5797 and 3050; *strength of Jah; Uzzijah,* the name of five Isr.:— Uzziah.

5819. עֲזִיזָא **'Ăzîyzâ,** *az-ee-zaw´;* from 5756; *strengthfulness; Aziza,* an Isr.:— Aziza.

5820. עַזְמָוֶת **'Azmâveth,** *az-maw´-veth;* from 5794 and 4194; *strong* (one) *of death; Azmaveth,* the name of three Isr. and of a place in Pal.:— Azmaveth. See also 1041.

5821. עַזָּן **'Azzân,** *az-zawn´;* from 5794; *strong one; Azzan,* an Isr.:— Azzan.

5822. עָזְנִיָּה **'oznîyâh,** *oz-nee-yaw´;* prob. fem. of 5797; prob. the *sea-eagle* (from its *strength*):— ospray.

5823. עָזַק **'âzaq,** *aw-zak´;* a prim. root; to *grub over:*— fence about.

5824. עִזְקָא **'izqâ'** (Chald.), *iz-kaw´;* from a root corresp. to 5823; a *signet*-ring (as engraved):— signet.

5825. עֲזֵקָה **'Ăzêqâh,** *az-ay-kaw´;* from 5823; *tilled; Azekah,* a place in Pal.:— Azekah.

5826. עָזַר **'âzar,** *aw-zar´;* a prim. root; to *surround,* i.e. *protect* or *aid:*— help, succour.

5827. עֵזֶר **'Ezer,** *eh´-zer;* from 5826; *help; Ezer,* the name of two Isr.:— Ezer. Comp. 5829.

5828. עֵזֶר **'êzer,** *ay´-zer;* from 5826; *aid:*—help.

5829. עֵזֶר **'Êzer,** *ay´-zer;* the same as 5828; *Ezer,* the name of four Isr.:— Ezer. Comp. 5827.

עַזּוּר **'Azzûr.** See 5809.

5830. עֶזְרָא **'Ezrâ',** *ez-raw´;* a var. of 5833; *Ezra,* an Isr.:— Ezra.

5831. עֶזְרָא **'Ezrâ'** (Chald.), *ez-raw´;* corresp. to 5830; *Ezra,* an Isr.:— Ezra.

5832. עֲזַרְאֵל **'Ăzar'êl,** *az-ar-ale´;* from 5826 and 410; *God has helped; Azarel,* the name of five Isr.:— Azarael, Azareel.

5833. עֶזְרָה **'ezrâh,** *ez-raw´;* or

עֶזְרָת **'ezrâth** (Psa. 60:11 [13]; 108:12 [13]), *ez-rawth´;* fem. of 5828; *aid:*— help (-ed, -er).

5834. עֶזְרָה **'Ezrâh,** *ez-raw´;* the same as 5833; *Ezrah,* an Isr.:— Ezrah.

5835. עֲזָרָה **'ăzârâh,** *az-aw-raw´;* from 5826 in its orig. mean. of *surrounding;* an *inclosure;* also a *border:*— court, settle.

5836. עֶזְרִי **'Ezrîy,** *ez-ree´;* from 5828; *helpful; Ezri,* an Isr.:— Ezri.

5837. עַזְרִיאֵל **'Azrîy'êl,** *az-ree-ale´;* from 5828 and 410; *help of God; Azriël,* the name of three Isr.:— Azriel.

5838. עֲזַרְיָה **'Ăzaryâh,** *az-ar-yaw´;* or

עֲזַרְיָהוּ **'Ăzaryâhûw,** *az-ar-yaw´-hoo;* from 5826 and 3050; *Jah has helped; Azarjah,* the name of nineteen Isr.:— Azariah.

5839. עֲזַרְיָה **'Ăzaryâh** (Chald.), *az-ar-yaw´;* corresp. to 5838; *Azarjah,* one of Daniel's companions:— Azariah.

5840. עַזְרִיקָם **'Azrîyqâm,** *az-ree-kawm´;* from 5828 and act. part. of 6965; *help of an enemy; Azrikam,* the name of four Isr.:— Azrikam.

5841. עַזָּתִי **'Azzâthîy,** *az-zaw-thee´;* patrial from 5804; an *Azzathite* or inhab. of Azzah:— Gazathite, Gazite.

5842. עֵט **'êṭ,** *ate;* from 5860 (contr.) in the sense of *swooping,* i.e. *side-long stroke;* a *stylus* or marking stick:— pen.

5843. עֵטָא **'êṭâ'** (Chald.), *ay-taw´;* from 3272; *prudence:*— counsel.

5844. עָטָה **'âṭâh,** *aw-taw´;* a prim. root; to *wrap,* i.e. *cover, veil, clothe,* or *roll:*— array self, be clad, (put a) cover (-ing, self), fill, put on, × surely, turn aside.

5845. עֲטִין **'ăṭîyn,** *at-een´;* from an unused root mean. appar. to *contain;* a *receptacle* (for milk, i.e. *pail;* fig. *breast*):— breast.

5846. עֲטִישָׁה **'ăṭîyshâh,** *at-ee-shaw´;* from an unused root mean. to *sneeze; sneezing:*— sneezing.

5847. עֲטַלֵּף **'ăṭallêph,** *at-al-lafe´;* of uncert. der.; a *bat:*— bat.

5848. עָטַף **'âṭaph,** *aw-taf´;* a prim. root; to *shroud,* i.e. *clothe* (whether tran. or reflex.); hence, (from the idea of *darkness*) to *languish:*— cover (over), fail, faint, feebler, hide self, be overwhelmed, swoon.

5849. עָטַר **'âṭar,** *aw-tar´;* a prim. root; to *encircle* (for attack or protection); espec. to *crown* (lit. or fig.):— compass, crown.

5850. עֲטָרָה **'ăṭârâh,** *at-aw-raw´;* from 5849; a *crown:*— crown.

5851. עֲטָרָה **'Ăṭârâh,** *at-aw-raw´;* the same as 5850; *Atarah,* an Israelitess:— Atarah.

5852. עֲטָרוֹת **'Ăṭârôwth,** *at-aw-rōth´;* or

עֲטָרֹת **'Ăṭârôth,** *at-aw-rōth´;* plur. of 5850; *Ataroth,* the name (thus simply) of two places in Pal.:— Ataroth.

5853. עֲטְרוֹת אַדָּר **'Aṭrôwth 'Addâr,** *at-rōth´ ad-dawr´;* from the same as 5852 and 146; *crowns of Addar; Atroth-Addar,* a place in Pal.:— Ataroth-adar (-addar).

5854. עֲטְרוֹת בֵּית יוֹאָב **'Aṭrôwth Bêyth Yôw'âb,** *at-rōth´ bayth yo-awb´;* from the same as 5852 and 1004 and 3097; *crowns of* (the) *house of Joäb; Atroth-beth-Joäb,* a place in Pal.:— Ataroth, the house of Joab.

5855. עֲטְרוֹת שׁוֹפָן **'Aṭrôwth Shôwphân,** *at-rōth´ sho-fawn´;* from the same as 5852 and a name otherwise unused [being from the same as 8226] mean. *hidden; crowns of Shophan; Atroth-Shophan*, a place in Pal.:— Atroth, Shophan [*as if two places*].

5856. עִי '**îy**, *ee*; from 5753; a *ruin* (as if overturned):— heap.

5857. עַי '**Ay**, *ah'ee*; or (fem.)

עַיָּא '**Ayâ'** (Neh. 11:31), *ah-yaw'*; or

עַיָּת '**Ayâth** (Isa. 10:28), *ah-yawth'*; for 5856; *Ai, Aja* or *Ajath*, a place in Pal.:— Ai, Aija, Aijath, Hai.

5858. עֵיבָל '**Êybâl**, *ay-bawl'*; perh. from an unused root prob. mean. *to be bald; bare; Ebal*, a mountain of Pal.:— Ebal.

עִיָּה '**Ayâh**. See 5857.

5859. עִיּוֹן '**Iyôwn**, *ee-yone'*; from 5856; *ruin; Ijon*, a place in Pal.:— Ijon.

5860. עִיט '**îyt**, *eet*; a prim. root; to *swoop* down upon (lit. or fig.):— fly, rail.

5861. עַיִט '**ayit**, *ah'-yit*; from 5860; a *hawk* or other bird of prey:— bird, fowl, ravenous (bird).

5862. עֵיטָם '**Êytâm**, *ay-tawm'*; from 5861; *hawk-ground; Etam*, a place in Pal.:— Etam.

5863. עִיֵּי הָעֲבָרִים '**Iyêy hâ-'Ăbârîym**, *ee-yay' haw-ab-aw-reem'*; from the plur. of 5856 and the plur. of the act. part. of 5674 with the art. interposed; *ruins of the passers; Ije-ha-Abarim*, a place near Pal.:— Ije-abarim.

5864. עִיִּים '**Iyîym**, *ee-yeem'*; plur. of 5856; *ruins; Ijim*, a place in the Desert:— Iim.

5865. עֵילוֹם '**êylôwm**, *ay-lome'*; for 5769:— ever.

5866. עִילַי '**Îylay**, *ee-lah'-ee*; from 5927; *elevated; Ilai*, an Isr.:— Ilai.

5867. עֵילָם '**Êylâm**, *ay-lawm'*; or

עוֹלָם° '**Ôwlâm** (Ezra 10:2; Jer. 49:36), *o-lawm'*; prob. from 5956; *hidden*, i.e. *distant; Elam*, a son of Shem, and his desc., with their country; also of six Isr.:— Elam.

5868. עֲיָם '**ăyâm**, *ah-yawm'*; of doubtful or. and authenticity; prob. mean. *strength*:— mighty.

5869. עַיִן '**ayin**, *ah'-yin*; prob. a prim. word; an *eye* (lit. or fig.); by anal. a *fountain* (as the *eye* of the landscape):— affliction, outward appearance, + before, + think best, colour, conceit, + be content, countenance, + displease, eye [l-brow], [-d], -sight], face, + favour, fountain, furrow [*from the marg.*], × him, + humble, knowledge, look, (+ well), × me, open (-ly), + (not) please, presence, + regard, resemblance, sight, × thee, × them, + think, × us, well, × you (-rselves).

5870. עַיִן '**ayin** (Chald.), *ah'-yin*; corresp. to 5869; an *eye*:— eye.

5871. עַיִן '**Ayin**, *ah'-yin*; the same as 5869; *fountain; Ajin*, the name (thus simply) of two places in Pal.:— Ain.

5872. עֵין גֶּדִי '**Êyn Gedîy**, *ane geh'-dee*; from 5869 and 1423; *fountain of a kid; En-Gedi*, a place in Pal.:— En-gedi.

5873. עֵין גַּנִּים '**Êyn Gannîym**, *ane gan-neem'*; from 5869 and the plur. of 1588; *fountain of gardens; En-Gannim*, a place in Pal.:— En-gannim.

5874. עֵין־דֹּאר '**Êyn-Dô'r**, *ane-dore'*; or

עֵין דּוֹר '**Êyn Dôwr**, *ane dore*; or

עֵין־דֹּר '**Êyn-Dôr**, *ane-dore'*; from 5869 and 1755; *fountain of dwelling; En-Dor*, a place in Pal.:— En-dor.

5875. עֵין הַקּוֹרֵא '**Êyn haq-Qôwrê'**, *ane-hak-ko-ray'*; from 5869 and the act. part. of 7121; *fountain of One calling; En-hak-Korè*, a place near Pal.:— En-hakhore.

עֵינוֹן '**Êynôwn**. See 2703.

5876. עֵין חַדָּה '**Êyn Chaddâh**, *ane khad-daw'*; from 5869 and the fem. of a der. from 2300; *fountain of sharpness; En-Chaddah*, a place in Pal.:— En-haddah.

5877. עֵין חָצוֹר '**Êyn Châtsôwr**, *ane khaw-tsore'*; from 5869 and the same as 2674; *fountain of a village; En-Chatsor*, a place in Pal.:— En-hazor.

5878. עֵין חֲרֹד '**Êyn Chărôd**, *ane khar-ode'*; from 5869 and a der. of 2729; *fountain of trembling; En-Charod*, a place in Pal.:— well of Harod.

5879. עֵינָיִם '**Êynayim**, *ay-nah'-yim*; or

עֵינָם '**Êynâm**, *ay-nawm'*; dual of 5869; *double fountain; Enajim* or *Enam*, a place in Pal.:— Enaim, openly (Genesis 38:21).

5880. עֵין מִשְׁפָּט '**Êyn Mishpât**, *ane mish-pawt'*; from 5869 and 4941; *fountain of judgment; En-Mishpat*, a place near Pal.:— En-mishpat.

5881. עֵינָן '**Êynân**, *ay-nawn'*; from 5869; *having eyes; Enan*, an Isr.:— Enan. Comp. 2704.

5882. עֵין עֶגְלַיִם '**Êyn 'Eglayim**, *ane eg-lah'-yim*; from 5869 and the dual of 5695; *fountain of two calves; En-Eglajim*, a place in Pal.:— En-eglaim.

5883. עֵין רֹגֵל '**Êyn Rôgêl**, *ane ro-gale'*; from 5869 and the act. part. of 7270; *fountain of a traveller; En-Rogel*, a place near Jerusalem:— En-rogel.

5884. עֵין רִמּוֹן '**Êyn Rimmôwn**, *ane rim-mone'*; from 5869 and 7416; *fountain of a pomegranate; En-Rimmon*, a place in Pal.:— En-rimmon.

5885. עֵין שֶׁמֶשׁ '**Êyn Shemesh**, *ane sheh'-mesh*; from 5869 and 8121; *fountain of (the)* sun; En-Shemesh, a place in Pal.:— En-she-mesh.

5886. עֵין תַּנִּים **'Êyn Tanniym**, ane tan-neem´; from 5869 and the plur. of 8565; *fountain of jackals; En-Tannim*, a pool near Jerusalem:— dragon well.

5887. עֵין תַּפּוּחַ **'Êyn Tappûwach**, ane tap-poo´-akh; from 5869 and 8598; *fountain of an apple tree; En-Tappuách*, a place in Pal.:— En-tappuah.

5888. עָיֵף **'âyêph**, aw-yafe´; a prim. root; to *languish*:— be wearied.

5889. עָיֵף **'âyêph**, aw-yafe´; from 5888; *languid*:— faint, thirsty, weary.

5890. עֵיפָה **'êyphâh**, ay-faw´; fem. from 5774; *obscurity* (as if from *covering*):— darkness.

5891. עֵיפָה **'Êyphâh**, ay-faw´; the same as 5890; *Ephah*, the name of a son of Midian, and of the region settled by him; also of an Isr. and of an Israelitess:— Ephah.

5892. עִיר **'îyr**, eer; or (in the plur.)

עָר **'âr**, awr; or

עָיַר **'âyar** (Judg. 10:4), aw-yar´; from 5782 a *city* (a place guarded by *waking* or a *watch*) in the widest sense (even of a mere *encampment* or *post*):— Ai [from marg.], city, court [from marg.], town.

5893. עִיר **'Îyr**, eer; the same as 5892; *Ir*, an Isr.:— Ir.

5894. עִיר **'îyr** (Chald.), eer; from a root corresp. to 5782; a *watcher*, i.e. an *angel* (as guardian):— watcher.

5895. עַיִר **'ayîr**, ah´-yeer; from 5782 in the sense of *raising* (i.e. *bearing* a burden); prop. a young *ass* (as just broken to a load); hence, an ass-*colt*:— (ass) colt, foal, young ass.

5896. עִירָא **'Îyrâ**, ee-raw´; from 5782; *wakefulness; Ira*, the name of three Isr.:— Ira.

5897. עִירָד **'Îyrâd**, ee-rawd´; from the same as 6166; *fugitive; Irad*, an antediluvian:— Irad.

5898. עִיר הַמֶּלַח **'Îyr ham-Melach**, eer ham-meh´-lakh; from 5892 and 4417 with the art. of substance interp.; *city of* (the) *salt; Ir-ham-Melach*, a place near Pal.:— the city of salt.

5899. עִיר הַתְּמָרִים **'Îyr hat-Temâriym**, eer hat-tem-aw-reem´; from 5892 and the plur. of 8558 with the art. interpolated; *city of the palmtrees; Ir-hat-Temarim*, a place in Pal.:— the city of palmtrees.

5900. עִירוּ **'Îyrûw**, ee-roo´; from 5892; a *citizen; Iru*, an Isr.:— Iru.

5901. עִירִי **'Îyriy**, ee-ree´; from 5892; *urbane; Iri*, an Isr.:— Iri.

5902. עִירָם **'Îyrâm**, ee-rawm´; from 5892; *city-wise; Iram*, an Idumæan:— Iram.

5903. עֵירֹם **'êyrôm**, ay-rome´; or

עֵרֹם **'êrôm**, ay-rome´; from 6191; *nudity*:— naked (-ness).

5904. עִיר נָחָשׁ **'Îyr Nâchâsh**, eer naw-khawsh´; from 5892 and 5175; *city of a serpent; Ir-Nachash*, a place in Pal.:— Ir-nahash.

5905. עִיר שֶׁמֶשׁ **'Îyr Shemesh**, eer sheh´-mesh; from 5892 and 8121; *city of* (the) *sun; Ir-Shemesh*, a place in Pal.:— Ir-shemesh.

5906. עַיִשׁ **'Ayish**, ah´-yish; or

עָשׁ **'Âsh**, awsh; from 5789; the constellation of the Great *Bear* (perh. from its *migration* through the heavens):— Arcturus.

עָיָת **'Ayâth**. See 5857.

5907. עַכְבּוֹר **'Akbôwr**, ak-bore´; prob. for 5909; *Akbor*, the name of an Idumæan and two Isr.:— Achbor.

5908. עַכָּבִישׁ **'akkâbîysh**, ak-kaw-beesh´; prob. from an unused root in the lit. sense of *entangling*; a *spider* (as *weaving* a network):— spider.

5909. עַכְבָּר **'akbâr**, ak-bawr´; prob. from the same as 5908 in the second. sense of *attacking*; a *mouse* (as *nibbling*):— mouse.

5910. עַכּוֹ **'Akkôw**, ak-ko´; appar. from an unused root mean. to *hem* in; *Akko* (from its situation on a *bay*):— Accho.

5911. עָלוֹר **'Âlôwr**, aw-lore´; from 5916; *troubled; Akor*, the name of a place in Pal.:— Achor.

5912. עָכָן **'Âkân**, aw-kawn´; from an unused root mean. to *trouble; troublesome; Akan*, an Isr.:— Achan. Comp. 5917.

5913. עָכַס **'âkaç**, aw-kas´; a prim. root; prop. to *tie*, spec. with fetters; but used only as denom. from 5914; to *put on anklets*:— make a tinkling ornament.

5914. עֶכֶס **'ekeç**, eh´-kes; from 5913; a *fetter*; hence, an *anklet*:— stocks, tinkling ornament.

5915. עַכְסָה **'Akçâh**, ak-saw´; fem. of 5914; *anklet; Aksah*, an Israelitess:— Achsah.

5916. עָכַר **'âkar**, aw-kar´; a prim. root; prop. to *roil* water; fig. to *disturb* or *afflict*:— trouble, stir.

5917. עָכָר **'Âkâr**, aw-kawr´; from 5916; *troublesome; Akar*, an Isr.:— Achar. Comp. 5912.

5918. עָכְרָן **'Okrân**, ok-rawn´; from 5916; *muddler; Okran*, an Isr.:— Ocran.

5919. עַכְשׁוּב **'akshûwb**, ak-shoob´; prob. from an unused root mean. to *coil*; an *asp* (from lurking *coiled* up):— adder.

5920. עַל **'al**, al; from 5927; prop. the *top*;

spec. the *Highest* (i.e. *God*); also (adv.) *aloft, to Jehovah:*— above, high, Most High.

5921. עַל **'al**, *al*; prop. the same as 5920 used as a prep. (in the sing. or plur. often with pref., or as conjunc. with a particle following); *above, over, upon,* or *against* (yet always in this last relation with a downward aspect) in a great variety of applications (as follow):— above, according to (-ly), after, (as) against, among, and, × as, at, because of, beside (the rest of), between, beyond the time, × both and, by (reason of), × had the charge of, concerning for, in (that), (forth, out) of, (from) (off), (up-) on, over, than, through (-out), to, touching, × with.

5922. עַל **'al** (Chald.), *al*; corresp. to 5921:— about, against, concerning, for, [there-]fore, from, in, × more, of, (there-, up-) on, (in-) to, + why with.

5923. עֹל **'ôl**, *ole*; or

עוֹל **'ôwl**, *ole*; from 5953; a *yoke* (as *imposed* on the neck), lit. or fig.:— yoke.

5924. עֵלָּא **'êllâ'** (Chald.), *ale-law'*; from 5922; *above:*— over.

5925. עֻלָּא **'Ullâ'**, *ool-law'*; fem. of 5923; *burden; Ulla,* an Isr.:— Ulla.

5926. עִלֵּג **'illêg**, *il-layg'*; from an unused root mean. to *stutter; stuttering:*— stammerer.

5927. עָלָה **'âlâh**, *aw-law'*; a prim. root; to *ascend,* intr. (*be high*) or act. (*mount*); used in a great variety of senses, primary and second., lit. and fig. (as follow):— arise (up), (cause to) ascend up, at once, break [the day] (up), bring (up), (cause to) burn, carry up, cast up, + shew, climb (up), (cause to, make to) come (up), cut off, dawn, depart, exalt, excel, fall, fetch up, get up, (make to) go (away, up); grow (over), increase, lay, leap, levy, lift (self) up, light, [make] up, × mention, mount up, offer, make to pay, + perfect, prefer, put (on), raise, recover, restore, (make to) rise (up), scale, set (up), shoot forth (up), (begin to) spring (up), stir up, take away (up), work.

5928. עֲלָה **'ălâh** (Chald.), *al-aw'*; corresp. to 5930; a *holocaust:*— burnt offering.

5929. עָלֶה **'âleh**, *aw-leh'*; from 5927; a *leaf* (as *coming up* on a tree); collect. *foliage:*— branch, leaf.

5930. עֹלָה **'ôlâh**, *o-law'*; or

עוֹלָה **'ôwlâh**, *o-law'*; fem. act. part. of 5927; a *step* or (collect. *stairs,* as *ascending*); usually a *holocaust* (as *going up* in smoke):— ascent, burnt offering (sacrifice), go up to. See also 5766.

5931. עִלָּה **'illâh** (Chald.), *il-law'*; fem. from a root corresp. to 5927; a *pretext* (as *arising* artificially):— occasion.

5932. עַלְוָה **'alvâh**, *al-vaw'*; for 5766; *moral perverseness:*— iniquity.

5933. עַלְוָה **'Alvâh**, *al-vaw'*; or

עַלְיָה° **'Alyâh**, *al-yaw'*; the same as 5932; *Alvah* or *Aljah,* an Idumæan:— Aliah, Alvah.

5934. עָלוּם **'âlûwm**, *aw-loom'*; pass. part. of 5956 in the denom. sense of 5958; (only in plur. as abstr.) *adolescence;* fig. *vigor:*— youth.

5935. עַלְוָן **'Alvân**, *al-vawn'*; or

עַלְיָן **'Alyân**, *al-yawn'*; from 5927; *lofty; Alvan* or *Aljan,* an Idumæan:— Alian, Alvan.

5936. עֲלוּקָה **'ălûwqâh**, *al-oo-kaw'*; fem. pass. part. of an unused root mean. to *suck;* the *leech:*— horse-leech.

5937. עָלַז **'âlaz**, *aw-laz'*; a prim. root; to *jump* for joy, i.e. *exult:*— be joyful, rejoice, triumph.

5938. עָלֵז **'âlêz**, *aw-laze'*; from 5937; *exultant:*— that rejoiceth.

5939. עֲלָטָה **'ălâṭâh**, *al-aw-taw'*; fem. from an unused root mean. to *cover; dusk:*— dark, twilight.

5940. עֱלִי **'ĕlîy**, *el-ee'*; from 5927; a *pestle* (as *lifted*):— pestle.

5941. עֵלִי **'Êlîy**, *ay-lee'*; from 5927; *lofty; Eli,* an Isr. high-priest:— Eli.

5942. עִלִּי **'illîy**, *il-lee'*; from 5927; *high;* i.e. comparative:— upper.

5943. עִלַּי **'illay** (Chald.), *il-lah'-ee;* corresp. to 5942; *supreme* (i.e. *God*):— (most) high.

עַלְיָה° **'Alyâh**. See 5933.

5944. עֲלִיָּה **'ălîyâh**, *al-ee-yaw'*; fem. from 5927; something *lofty,* i.e. a *stair-way;* also a *second-story* room (or even one on the roof); fig. the *sky:*— ascent, (upper) chamber, going up, loft, parlour.

5945. עֶלְיוֹן **'elyôwn**, *el-yone'*; from 5927; an *elevation,* i.e. (adj.) *lofty* (comp.); as title, the *Supreme:*— (Most, on) high (-er, -est), upper (-most).

5946. עֶלְיוֹן **'elyôwn** (Chald.), *el-yone'*; corresp. to 5945; the *Supreme:*— Most high.

5947. עַלִּיז **'allîyz**, *al-leez'*; from 5937; *exultant:*— joyous, (that) rejoice (-ing).

5948. עֲלִיל **'ălîyl**, *al-eel'*; from 5953 in the sense of *completing;* prob. a *crucible* (as *working* over the metal):— furnace.

5949. עֲלִילָה **'ălîylâh**, *al-ee-law'*; or

עֲלִלָה **'ălîlâh**, *al-ee-law'*; from 5953 in the sense of *effecting;* an *exploit* (of God), or a *performance* (of man, often in a bad sense); by impl. an *opportunity:*— act (-ion), deed, doing, invention, occasion, work.

5950. עֲלִילָיָה **'ălîylîyâh**, *al-ee-lee-yaw´;* for 5949; (miraculous) *execution:*— work.

עִלָּן **'Alyân.** See 5935.

5951. עֲלִיצֻת **'ălîytsûwth**, *al-ee-tsooth´;* from 5970; *exultation:*— rejoicing.

5952. עֲלִית **'allîyth** (Chald.), *al-leeth´;* from 5927; a *second-story* room:— chamber. Comp. 5944.

5953. עָלַל **'âlal**, *aw-lal´;* a prim. root; to *effect* thoroughly; spec. to *glean* (also fig.); by impl. (in a bad sense) to *overdo*, i.e. maltreat, be saucy to, pain, impose (also lit.):— abuse, affect, × child, defile, do, glean, mock, practise, thoroughly, work (wonderfully).

5954. עֲלַל **'ălal** (Chald.), *al-al´;* corresp. to 5953 (in the sense of *thrusting* oneself in), to *enter;* caus. to *introduce:*— bring in, come in, go in.

עֹלָל **'ôlâl.** See 5768.

עֲלִלָה **'ălîlâh.** See 5949.

5955. עֹלֵלָה **'ôlêlâh**, *o-lay-law´;* fem. act. part. of 5953; only in plur. *gleanings;* by extens. *gleaning-time:*— (gleaning) (of the) grapes, grapegleanings.

5956. עָלַם **'âlam**, *aw-lam´;* a prim. root; to *veil* from sight, i.e. *conceal* (lit. or fig.):— × any ways, blind, dissembler, hide (self), secret (thing).

5957. עָלַם **'âlam** (Chald.), *aw-lam´;* corresp. to 5769; *remote* time, i.e. the *future* or *past* indefinitely; often adv. *forever:*— for ([n-]) ever (lasting), old.

5958. עֶלֶם **'elem**, *eh´-lem;* from 5956; prop. something *kept out of sight* [comp. 5959], i.e. a *lad:*— young man, stripling.

עֹלָם **'ôlâm.** See 5769.

5959. עַלְמָה **'almâh**, *al-maw´;* fem. of 5958; a *lass* (as *veiled* or private):— damsel, maid, virgin.

5960. עַלְמוֹן **'Almôwn**, *al-mone´;* from 5956; *hidden; Almon*, a place in Pal.:— Almon. See also 5963.

5961. עֲלָמוֹת **'Ălâmôwth**, *al-aw-môth´;* plur. of 5959; prop. *girls*, i.e. the *soprano* or female voice, perh. *falsetto:*— Alamoth.

עַלְמוּת **'almûwth.** See 4192.

5962. עַלְמִי **'Almîy** (Chald.), *al-mee´;* patrial from a name corresp. to 5867 contr.; an *Elamite* or inhab. of Elam:— Elamite.

5963. עַלְמֹן דִּבְלָתָיְמָה **'Almôn Diblâthâyᵉmâh**, *al-mone´ dib-law-thaw´-yem-aw;* from the same as 5960 and the dual of 1690 [comp. 1015] with enclitic of direction; *Almon toward Diblatha-jim; Almon-Diblathajemah*, a place in Moab:— Almon-dilathaim.

5964. עָלֶמֶת **'Âlemeth**, *aw-leh´-meth;* from

5956; a *covering; Alemeth*, the name of a place in Pal. and of two Isr.:— Alameth, Alemeth.

5965. עָלַס **'âlaç**, *aw-las´;* a prim. root; to *leap* for joy, i.e. *exult, wave* joyously:— × peacock, rejoice, solace self.

5966. עָלַע **'âla'**, *aw-lah´;* a prim root; to *sip* up:— suck up.

5967. עֲלַע **'ăla'** (Chald.), *al-ah´;* corresp. to 6763; a *rib:*— rib.

5968. עָלַף **'âlaph**, *aw-laf´;* a prim. root; to *veil* or *cover;* fig. to *be languid:*— faint, overlaid, wrap self.

5969. עֻלְפֶּה **'ulpeh**, *ool-peh´;* from 5968; an *envelope*, i.e. (fig.) *mourning:*— fainted.

5970. עָלַץ **'âlats**, *aw-lats´;* a prim. root; to *jump* for joy, i.e. *exult:*— be joyful, rejoice, triumph.

5971. עַם **'am**, *am;* from 6004; a *people* (as a congregated *unit*); spec. a *tribe* (as those of Israel); hence, (collect.) *troops* or *attendants;* fig. a *flock:*— folk, men, nation, people.

5972. עַם **'am** (Chald.), *am;* corresp. to 5971:— people.

5973. עִם **'îm**, *eem;* from 6004; adv. or prep., *with* (i.e. in *conjunction* with), in varied applications; spec. *equally with;* often with prep. pref. (and then usually unrepresented in English):— accompanying, against, and, as (× long as), before, beside, by (reason of), for all, from (among, between), in, like, more than, of, (un-) to, with (-al).

5974. עִם **'îm** (Chald.), *eem;* corresp. to 5973:— by, from, like, to (-ward), with.

5975. עָמַד **'âmad**, *aw-mad´;* a prim. root; to *stand*, in various relations (lit. and fig., intr. and tran.):— abide (behind), appoint, arise, cease, confirm, continue, dwell, be employed, endure, establish, leave, make, ordain, be [over], place, (be) present (self), raise up, remain, repair, + serve, set (forth, over, -tle, up), (make to, make to be at a, with-) stand (by, fast, firm, still, up), (be at a) stay (up), tarry.

5976. עָמַד **'âmad**, *aw-mad´;* for 4571; to *shake:*— be at a stand.

5977. עֹמֶד **'ômed**, *o´-med;* from 5975; a *spot* (as being *fixed*):— place, (+ where) stood, upright.

5978. עִמָּד **'immâd**, *im-mawd´;* prol. for 5973; along *with:*— against, by, from, in, + me, + mine, of, + that I take, unto, upon, with (-in.)

עַמּוּד **'ammûd.** See 5982.

Hebrew

5979. עֶמְדָּה **'emdâh**, *em-daw'*; from 5975; a *station*, i.e. domicile:— standing.

5980. עֻמָּה **'ummâh**, *oom-maw'*; from 6004; *conjunction*, i.e. *society*; mostly adv. or prep. (with prep. pref.), *near, beside, along with:—* (over) against, at, beside, hard by, in points.

5981. עֻמָּה **'Ummâh**, *oom-maw'*; the same as 5980; *association*; *Ummah*, a place in Pal.:— Ummah.

5982. עַמּוּד **'ammûwd**, *am-mood'*; or

עַמֻּד **'ammûd**, *am-mood'*; from 5975; a *column* (as *standing*); also a *stand*, i.e. platform:— × apiece, pillar.

5983. עַמּוֹן **'Ammôwn**, *am-mone'*; from 5971; *tribal*, i.e. *inbred*; *Ammon*, a son of Lot; also his posterity and their country:— Ammon, Ammonites.

5984. עַמּוֹנִי **'Ammôwnîy**, *am-mo-nee'*; patron. from 5983; an *Ammonite* or (adj.) *Ammonitish*:— Ammonite (-s).

5985. עַמּוֹנִית **'Ammôwnîyth**, *am-mo-neeth'*; fem. of 5984; an *Ammonitess*:— Ammonite (-ss).

5986. עָמוֹס **'Âmôwç**, *aw-moce'*; from 6006; *burdensome*; *Amos*, an Isr. prophet:— Amos.

5987. עָמוֹק **'Âmôwq**, *aw-moke'*; from 6009; *deep*; *Amok*, an Isr.:— Amok.

5988. עַמִּיאֵל **'Ammîy'êl**, *am-mee-ale'*; from 5971 and 410; *people of God*; *Ammiël*, the name of three or four Isr.:— Ammiel.

5989. עַמִּיהוּד **'Ammîyhûwd**, *am-mee-hood'*; from 5971 and 1935; *people of splendor*; *Ammihud*, the name of three Isr.:— Ammihud.

5990. עַמִּיזָבָד **'Ammîyzâbâd**, *am-mee-zaw-bawd'*; from 5971 and 2064; *people of endowment*; *Ammizabad*, an Isr.:— Ammizabad.

5991. עַמִּיחוּר° **'Ammîychûwr**, *am-mee-khoor'*; from 5971 and 2353; *people of nobility*; *Ammichur*, a Syrian prince:— Ammihud [*from the marg.*].

5992. עַמִּינָדָב **'Ammîynâdâb**, *am-mee-naw-dawb'*; from 5971 and 5068; *people of liberality*; *Amminadab*, the name of four Isr.:— Amminadab.

5993. עַמִּי נָדִיב **'Ammîy Nâdîyb**, *am-mee' naw-deeb'*; from 5971 and 5081; *my people* (is) *liberal*; *Ammi-Nadib*, prob. an Isr.:— Amminadib.

5994. עֲמִיק **'ămîyq** (Chald.), *am-eek'*; corresp. to 6012; *profound*, i.e. unsearchable:— deep.

5995. עָמִיר **'âmîyr**, *aw-meer'*; from 6014; a *bunch* of grain:— handful, sheaf.

5996. עַמִּישַׁדָּי **'Ammîyshadday**, *am-mee-shad-dah'ee*; from 5971 and 7706; *people of* (the) *Almighty*; *Ammishaddai*, an Isr.:— Ammishaddai.

5997. עָמִית **'âmîyth**, *aw-meeth'*; from a prim. root mean. to *associate*; *companionship*; hence, (concr.) a *comrade* or kindred man:— another, fellow, neighbour.

5998. עָמַל **'âmal**, *aw-mal'*; a prim. root; to *toil*, i.e. *work severely* and with irksomeness:— [take] labour (in).

5999. עָמָל **'âmâl**, *aw-mawl'*; from 5998; *toil*, i.e. *wearing effort*; hence, *worry*, wheth. of body or mind:— grievance (-vousness), iniquity, labour, mischief, miserable (-sery), pain (-ful), perverseness, sorrow, toil, travail, trouble, wearisome, wickedness.

6000. עָמָל **'Âmâl**, *aw-mawl'*; the same as 5999; *Amal*, an Isr.:— Amal.

6001. עָמֵל **'âmêl**, *aw-male'*; from 5998; *toiling*; concr. a *laborer*; fig. *sorrowful:*— that laboureth, that is a misery, had taken [labour], wicked, workman.

6002. עֲמָלֵק **'Ămâlêq**, *am-aw-lake'*; prob. of for. or.; *Amalek*, a desc. of Esau; also his posterity and their country:— Amalek.

6003. עֲמָלֵקִי **'Ămâlêqîy**, *am-aw-lay-kee'*; patron. from 6002; an *Amalekite* (or collect. the *Amalekites*) or desc. of Amalek:— Amalekite (-s).

6004. עָמַם **'âmam**, *aw-mam'*; a prim. root; to *associate*; by impl. to *overshadow* (by *huddling* together):— become dim, hide.

6005. עִמָּנוּאֵל **'Immânûw'êl**, *im-maw-noo-ale'*; from 5973 and 410 with a pron. suff. ins.; *with us* (is) *God*; *Immanuel*, a typical name of Isaiah's son:— Immanuel.

6006. עָמַס **'âmaç**, *aw-mas'*; or

עָמַשׂ **'âmas**, *aw-mas'*; a prim. root; to *load*, i.e. *impose* a burden (or fig. infliction):— be borne, (heavy) burden (self), lade, load, put.

6007. עֲמַסְיָה **'Ămaçyâh**, *am-as-yaw'*; from 6006 and 3050; *Jah has loaded*; *Amasjah*, an Isr.:— Amasiah.

6008. עַמְעָד **'Am'âd**, *am-awd'*; from 5971 and 5703; *people of time*; *Amad*, a place in Pal.:— Amad.

6009. עָמַק **'âmaq**, *aw-mak'*; a prim. root; to *be* (caus. *make*) *deep* (lit. or fig.):— (be, have, make, seek) deep (-ly), depth, be profound.

6010. עֵמֶק **'êmeq**, *ay'-mek*; from 6009; a *vale* (i.e. broad *depression*):— dale, vale, valley [often used as a part of proper names]. See also 1025.

6011. עֹמֶק **'ômeq**, *o'-mek*; from 6009; *depth:*— depth.

6012. עָמֵק **'âmêq**, *aw-make'*; from 6009; *deep* (lit. or fig.):— deeper, depth, strange.

6013. עָמֹק 'âmôq, *aw-moke´*; from 6009; *deep* (lit. or fig.):— (× exceeding) deep (thing).

6014. עָמַר 'âmar, *aw-mar´*; a prim. root; prop. appar. to *heap*; fig. to *chastise* (as if *piling* blows); spec. (as denom. from 6016) to *gather* grain:— bind sheaves, make merchandise of.

6015. עֲמַר 'ămar (Chald.), *am-ar´*; corresp. to 6785; *wool*:— wool.

6016. עֹמֶר 'ômer, *o´-mer*; from 6014; prop. a *heap*, i.e. a *sheaf*; also an *omer*, as a dry measure:— omer, sheaf.

6017. עֲמֹרָה 'Ămôrâh, *am-o-raw´*; from 6014; a (ruined) *heap*; *Amorah*, a place in Pal.:— Gomorrah.

6018. עָמְרִי 'Omrîy, *om-ree´*; from 6014; *heaping*; *Omri*, an Isr.:— Omri.

6019. עַמְרָם 'Amrâm, *am-rawm´*; prob. from 5971 and 7311; *high people*; *Amram*, the name of two Isr.:— Amram.

6020. עַמְרָמִי 'Amrâmîy, *am-raw-mee´*; patron. from 6019; an *Amramite* or desc. of Amram:— Amramite.

עָמָשׂ 'âmas. See 6006.

6021. עֲמָשָׂא 'Ămâsâ', *am-aw-saw´*; from 6006; *burden*; *Amasa*, the name of two Isr.:— Amasa.

6022. עֲמָשַׂי 'Ămâsay, *am-aw-sah´-ee*; from 6006; *burdensome*; *Amasai*, the name of three Isr.:— Amasai.

6023. עֲמַשְׂסַי 'Ămashçay, *am-ash-sah´-ee*; prob. from 6006; *burdensome*; *Amashsay*, an Isr.:— Amashai.

6024. עֲנָב 'Ănâb, *an-awb´*; from the same as 6025; *fruit*; *Anab*, a place in Pal.:— Anab.

6025. עֵנָב 'ênâb, *ay-nawb´*; from an unused root prob. mean. to *bear* fruit; a *grape*:— (ripe) grape, wine.

6026. עָנַג 'ânag, *aw-nag´*; a prim. root; to be *soft* or *pliable*, i.e. (fig.) *effeminate* or luxurious:— delicate (-ness), (have) delight (self), sport self.

6027. עֹנֶג 'ôneg, *o´-neg*; from 6026; *luxury*:— delight, pleasant.

6028. עָנֹג 'ânôg, *aw-nogue´*; from 6026; *luxurious*:— delicate.

6029. עָנַד 'ânad, *aw-nad´*; a prim. root; to *lace* fast:— bind, tie.

6030. עָנָה 'ânâh, *aw-naw´*; a prim. root; prop. to *eye* or (gen.) to *heed*, i.e. *pay attention*; by impl. to *respond*; by extens. to *begin* to speak; spec. to *sing, shout, testify, announce*:— give account, afflict [by mistake for 6031], (cause to, give) answer, bring low [by mistake for 6031], cry, hear, Leannoth, lift up, say, × scholar, (give a) shout, sing (together by course), speak, testify, utter, (bear) witness. See also 1042, 1043.

6031. עָנָה 'ânâh, *aw-naw´*; a prim. root [possibly rather ident. with 6030 through the idea of *looking* down or *browbeating*]; to *depress* lit. or fig., tran. or intr. (in various applications, as follows):— abase self, afflict (-ion, self), answer [by mistake for 6030], chasten self, deal hardly with, defile, exercise, force, gentleness, humble (self), hurt, ravish, sing [by mistake for 6030], speak [by mistake for 6030], submit self, weaken, × in any wise.

6032. עֲנָה 'ănâh (Chald.), *an-aw´*; corresp. to 6030:— answer, speak.

6033. עֲנָה 'ănâh (Chald.), *an-aw´*; corresp. to 6031:— poor.

6034. עֲנָה 'Ănâh, *an-aw´*; prob. from 6030; an *answer*; *Anah*, the name of two Edomites and one Edomitess:— Anah.

6035. עָנָו 'ânâv, *aw-nawv´*; or [by intermixture with 6041]

עָנָיו 'ânâyv, *aw-nawv´*; from 6031; *depressed* (fig.), in mind (*gentle*) or circumstances (*needy*, espec. *saintly*):— humble, lowly, meek, poor. Comp. 6041.

6036. עָנוּב 'Ânûwb, *aw-noob´*; pass. part. from the same as 6025; *borne* (as fruit); *Anub*, an Isr.:— Anub.

6037. עַנְוָה 'anvâh, *an-vaw´*; fem. of 6035; *mildness* (royal); also (concr.) *oppressed*:— gentleness, meekness.

6038. עֲנָוָה 'ănâvâh, *an-aw-vaw´*; from 6035; *condescension*, human and subj. (*modesty*), or divine and obj. (*clemency*):— gentleness, humility, meekness.

6039. עֱנוּת 'ênûwth, *en-ooth´*; from 6031; *affliction*:— affliction.

6040. עֳנִי 'ŏnîy, *on-ee´*; from 6031; *depression*, i.e. misery:— afflicted (-ion), trouble.

6041. עָנִי 'ânîy, *aw-nee´*; from 6031; *depressed*, in mind or circumstances [practically the same as 6035, although the marg. constantly disputes this, making 6035 subj. and 6041 obj.]:— afflicted, humble, lowly, needy, poor.

6042. עֻנִּי 'Unnîy, *oon-nee´*; from 6031; *afflicted*; *Unni*, the name of two Isr.:— Unni.

6043. עֲנָיָה 'Ănâyâh, *an-aw-yaw´*; from 6030; *Jah has answered*; *Anajah*, the name of two Isr.:— Anaiah.

עָנָיו 'ânâyv See 6035.

6044. עָנִים 'Ânîym, *aw-neem´*; for plur. of 5869; *fountains*; *Anim*, a place in Pal.:— Anim.

6045. עִנְיָן 'inyân, *in-yawn´*; from 6031; *ado*, i.e. (gen.) *employment* or (spec.) an *affair*:— business, travail.

6046. עָנֵם 'Ânêm, *aw-name´*; from the dual

of 5869; *two fountains*; *Anem*, a place in Pal.:— Anem.

6047. עֲנָמִם **'Ănâmîm**, *an-aw-meem´*; as if plur. of some Eg. word; *Anamim*, a son of Mizraim and his desc., with their country:— Anamim.

6048. עֲנַמֶּלֶךְ **'Ănammelek**, *an-am-meh´-lek*; of for. or.; *Anammelek*, an Ass. deity:— Anammelech.

6049. עָנַן **'ânan**, *aw-nan´*; a prim. root; to *cover*; used only as a denom. from 6051, to *cloud* over; fig. to *act covertly*, i.e. practise magic:— × bring, enchanter, Meonemin, observe (-r of) times, soothsayer, sorcerer.

6050. עֲנַן **'ănan** (Chald.), *an-an´*; corresp. to 6051:— cloud.

6051. עָנָן **'ânân**, *aw-nawn´*; from 6049; a *cloud* (as *covering* the sky), i.e. the *nimbus* or thunder-cloud:— cloud (-y).

6052. עָנָן **'Ânân**, *aw-nawn´*; the same as 6051; *cloud*; *Anan*, an Isr.:— Anan.

6053. עֲנָנָה **'ănânâh**, *an-aw-naw´*; fem. of 6051; *cloudiness*:— cloud.

6054. עֲנָנִי **'Ănâniy**, *an-aw-nee´*; from 6051; *cloudy*; *Anani*, an Isr.:— Anani.

6055. עֲנַנְיָה **'Ănanyâh**, *an-an-yaw´*; from 6049 and 3050; *Jah has covered*; *Ananjah*, the name of an Isr. and of a place in Pal.:— Ananiah.

6056. עֲנַף **'ănaph** (Chald.), *an-af´*; or

עֶנֶף **'eneph** (Chald.), *eh´-nef*; corresp. to 6057:— bough, branch.

6057. עָנָף **'ânâph**, *aw-nawf´*; from an unused root mean. to *cover*; a *twig* (as *covering* the limbs):— bough, branch.

6058. עָנֵף **'ânêph**, *aw-nafe´*; from the same as 6057; *branching*:— full of branches.

6059. עָנַק **'ânaq**, *aw-nak´*; a prim. root; prop. to *choke*; used only as a denom. from 6060, to *collar*, i.e. adorn with a necklace; fig. to *fit out* with supplies:— compass about as a chain, furnish, liberally.

6060. עֲנָק **'ânâq**, *aw-nawk´*; from 6059; a *necklace* (as if *strangling*):— chain.

6061. עֲנָק **'Ânâq**, *aw-nawk´*; the same as 6060; *Anak*, a Canaanite:— Anak.

6062. עֲנָקִי **'Ănâqiy**, *an-aw-kee´*; patron. from 6061; an *Anakite* or desc. of Anak:— Anakim.

6063. עֵנֶר **'Ânêr**, *aw-nare´*; prob. for 5288; *Aner*, a Amorite, also a place in Pal.:— Aner.

6064. עָנַשׁ **'ânash**, *aw-nash´*; a prim. root; prop. to *urge*; by impl. to *inflict* a penalty, spec. to *fine*:— amerce, condemn, punish, × surely.

6065. עֲנַשׁ **'ănash** (Chald.), *an-ash´*; corresp. to 6066; a *mulct*:— confiscation.

6066. עֹנֶשׁ **'ônesh**, *o´-nesh*; from 6064; a *fine*:— punishment, tribute.

עֲנָת **'eneth** See 3706.

6067. עֲנָת **'Ănâth**, *an-awth´*; from 6030; *answer*; *Anath*, an Isr.:— Anath.

6068. עֲנָתוֹת **'Ănâthôwth**, *an-aw-thôth´*; plur. of 6067; *Anathoth*, the name of two Isr., also of a place in Pal.:— Anathoth.

6069. עֲנְתֹתִי **'Anthôthîy**, *an-tho-thee´*; or

עֲנְתוֹתִי **'Annᵉthôwthîy**, *an-ne-tho-thee´*; patrial from 6068; a *Antothite* or inhab. of Anathoth:— of Anathoth, Anethothite, Anetothite, Antothite.

6070. עֲנְתֹתִיָּה **'Anthôthîyâh**, *an-tho-thee-yaw´*; from the same as 6068 and 3050; *answers of Jah*; *Anthothijah*, an Isr.:— Antothijah.

6071. עָסִיס **'âçîyç**, *aw-sees´*; from 6072; *must* or fresh grape-juice (as just *trodden* out):— juice, new (sweet) wine.

6072. עָסַס **'âçaç**, *aw-sas´*; a prim. root; to *squeeze* out juice; fig. to *trample*:— tread down.

6073. עֳפֶא **'ŏphe'**, *of-eh´*; from an unused root mean. to *cover*; a *bough* (as covering the tree):— branch.

6074. עֳפִי **'ŏphiy** (Chald.), *of-ee´*; corresp. to 6073; a *twig*; bough, i.e. (collect.) *foliage*:— leaves.

6075. עָפַל **'âphal**, *aw-fal´*; a prim. root; to *swell*; fig. *be elated*:— be lifted up, presume.

6076. עֹפֶל **'ôphel**, *o´-fel*; from 6075; a *tumor*; also a *mound*, i.e. *fortress*:— emerod, fort, strong hold, tower.

6077. עֹפֶל **'Ôphel**, *o´-fel*; the same as 6076; *Ophel*, a ridge in Jerusalem:— Ophel.

6078. עָפְנִי **'Ophniy**, *of-nee´*; from an unused noun [denoting a place in Pal.; from an unused root of uncert. mean.]; an *Ophnite* (collect.) or inhab. of Ophen:— Ophni.

6079. עַפְעַף **'aph'aph**, *af-af´*; from 5774; an *eyelash* (as *fluttering*); fig. morning *ray*:— dawning, eye-lid.

6080. עָפַר **'âphar**, *aw-far´*; a prim. root: mean. either to *be gray* or perh. rather to *pulverize*; used only as denom. from 6083, to *be dust*:— cast [dust].

6081. עֵפֶר **'Êpher**, *ay´-fer*; prob. a var. of 6082; *gazelle*; *Epher*, the name of an Arabian and of two Isr.:— Epher.

6082. עֹפֶר **'ôpher**, *o´-fer*; from 6080; a *fawn* (from the *dusty* color):— young roe [hart].

6083. עָפָר **'âphâr**, *aw-fawr´*; from 6080; *dust* (as *powdered* or *gray*); hence, *clay, earth*,

Hebrew

mud:— ashes, dust, earth, ground, morter, powder, rubbish.

עְפְרָה 'Aphrâh. See 1036.

6084. עָפְרָה 'Ophrâh, *of-raw´;* fem. of 6082; *female fawn; Ophrah,* the name of an Isr. and of two places in Pal.:— Ophrah.

6085. עֶפְרוֹן 'Ephrôwn, *ef-rone´;* from the same as 6081; *fawn-like; Ephron,* the name of a Canaanite and of two places in Pal.:— Ephron, Ephrain [*from the marg.*].

עֹפֶרֶת 'ôphereth. See 5777.

6086. עֵץ 'êts, *ates;* from 6095; a *tree* (from its *firmness*); hence, *wood* (plur. *sticks*):— + carpenter, gallows, helve, + pine, plank, staff, stalk, stick, stock, timber, tree, wood.

6087. עָצַב 'âtsab, *aw-tsab´;* a prim. root; prop. to *carve,* i.e. *fabricate* or *fashion;* hence, (in a bad sense) to *worry, pain* or *anger:*— displease, grieve, hurt, make, be sorry, vex, worship, wrest.

6088. עֲצַב 'âtsab (Chald.), *ats-ab´;* corresp. to 6087; to *afflict:*— lamentable.

6089. עֶצֶב 'etseb, *eh´-tseb;* from 6087; an earthen *vessel;* usually (painful) *toil;* also a *pang* (whether of body or mind):— grievous, idol, labor, sorrow.

6090. עֹצֶב 'ôtseb, *o´-tseb;* a var. of 6089; an *idol* (as fashioned); also *pain* (bodily or mental):— idol, sorrow, × wicked.

6091. עָצָב 'âtsâb, *aw-tsawb´;* from 6087; an (idolatrous) *image:*— idol, image.

6092. עָצֵב 'âtsêb, *aw-tsabe´;* from 6087; a (hired) *workman:*— labour.

6093. עִצָּבוֹן 'itstsâbôwn, *its-tsaw-bone´;* from 6087; *worrisomeness,* i.e. *labor* or *pain:*— sorrow, toil.

6094. עַצֶּבֶת 'atstsebeth, *ats-tseh´-beth;* from 6087; an *idol;* also a *pain* or *wound:*— sorrow, wound.

6095. עָצָה 'âtsâh, *aw-tsaw´;* a prim. root; prop. to *fasten* (or *make firm*), i.e. to *close* (the eyes):— shut.

6096. עָצֶה 'âtseh, *aw-tseh´;* from 6095; the *spine* (as giving *firmness* to the body):— backbone.

6097. עֵצָה 'êtsâh, *ay-tsaw´;* fem. of 6086; *timber:*— trees.

6098. עֵצָה 'êtsâh, *ay-tsaw´;* from 3289; *advice;* by impl. *plan;* also *prudence:*— advice, advisement, counsel (l-lor|), purpose.

6099. עָצוּם 'âtsûwm, *aw-tsoom´;* or

עָצֻם 'âtsûm, *aw-tsoom´;* pass. part. of 6105; *powerful* (spec. a *paw*); by impl. *numerous:*— + feeble, great, mighty, must, strong.

6100. עֶצְיוֹן גֶּבֶר 'Etsyôwn (short.

עֶצְיֹן 'Etsyôn) Geber, *ets-yone´ gheh´ber;*

from 6096 and 1397; *backbone-like of a man; Etsjon-Geber,* a place on the Red Sea:— Ezion-gaber, Ezion-geber.

6101. עָצַל 'âtsal, *aw-tsal´;* a prim. root; to *lean* idly, i.e. to *be indolent* or *slack:*— be slothful.

6102. עָצֵל 'âtsêl, *aw-tsale´;* from 6101; *indolent:*— slothful, sluggard.

6103. עַצְלָה 'atslâh, *ats-law´;* fem. of 6102; (as abstr.) *indolence:*— slothfulness.

6104. עַצְלוּת 'atslûwth, *ats-looth´;* from 6101; *indolence:*— idleness.

6105. עָצַם 'âtsam, *aw-tsam´;* a prim. root; to *bind* fast, i.e. *close* (the eyes); intr. to *be* (caus. *make*) *powerful* or *numerous;* denom. (from 6106) to *crunch* the bones:— break the bones, close, be great, be increased, be (wax) mighty (-ier), be more, shut, be (-come, make) strong (-er).

6106. עֶצֶם 'etsem, *eh´tsem;* from 6105; a *bone* (as *strong*); by extens. the *body;* fig. the *substance,* i.e. (as pron.) *selfsame:*— body, bone, × life, (self-) same, strength, × very.

6107. עֶצֶם 'Etsem, *eh´-tsem;* the same as 6106; *bone; Etsem,* a place in Pal.:— Azem, Ezem.

6108. עֹצֶם 'ôtsem, *o´-tsem;* from 6105; *power;* hence, *body:*— might, strong, substance.

עָצֻם 'âtsûm. See 6099.

6109. עָצְמָה 'otsmâh, *ots-maw´;* fem. of 6108; *powerfulness;* by extens. *numerousness:*— abundance, strength.

6110. עַצֻּמָה 'atstsûmâh, *ats-tsoo-maw´;* fem. of 6099; a *bulwark,* i.e. (fig.) *argument:*— strong.

6111. עַצְמוֹן 'Atsmôwn, *ats-mone´;* or

עַצְמֹן 'Atsmôn, *ats-mone´;* from 6107; *bone-like; Atsmon,* a place near Pal.:— Azmon.

6112. עֶצֶן 'Êtsen, *ay´-tsen;* from an unused root mean. to *be sharp* or *strong;* a *spear:*— Eznite [*from the marg.*].

6113. עָצַר 'âtsar, *aw-tsar´;* a prim. root; to *inclose;* by anal. to *hold back;* also to *maintain, rule, assemble:*— × be able, close up, detain, fast, keep (self close, still), prevail, recover, refrain, × reign, restrain, retain, shut (up), slack, stay, stop, withhold (self).

6114. עֶצֶר 'etser, *eh´-tser;* from 6113; *restraint:*— + magistrate.

6115. עֹצֶר 'ôtser, *o´-tser;* from 6113; *closure;* also *constraint:*— × barren, oppression, × prison.

6116. עֲצָרָה 'âtsârâh, *ats-aw-raw´;* or

עֲצֶרֶת **'ătsereth,** *ats-eh´-reth;* from 6113; an *assembly,* espec. on a *festival* or *holiday:*— (solemn) assembly (meeting).

6117. עָקַב **'âqab,** *aw-kab´;* a prim. root; prop. to *swell* out or up; used only as denom. from 6119, to *seize by the heel;* fig. to *circumvent* (as if *tripping* up the heels); also to *restrain* (as if holding by the heel):— take by the heel, stay, supplant, × utterly.

6118. עֵקֶב **'êqeb,** *ay´-keb;* from 6117 in the sense of 6119; a *heel,* i.e. (fig.) the *last* of anything (used adv. *for ever*); also *result,* i.e. *compensation;* and so (adv. with prep. or rel.) on *account* of:— × because, by, end, for, if, reward.

6119. עָקֵב **'âqêb,** *aw-kabe´;* or (fem.)

עִקְּבָה **'iqq'bâh,** *ik-keb-aw´;* from 6117; a *heel* (as *protuberant*); hence, a *track;* fig. the *rear* (of an army):— heel, [horse-] hoof, last, lier in wait [by mistake for 6120], (foot-) step.

6120. עָקֵב **'âqêb,** *aw-kabe´;* from 6117 in its denom. sense; a *lier in wait:*— heel [by mistake for 6119].

6121. עָקֹב **'âqôb,** *aw-kobe´;* from 6117; in the orig. sense, a *knoll* (as *swelling* up); in the denom. sense (tran.) *fraudulent* or (intr.) *tracked:*— crooked, deceitful, polluted.

6122. עָקְבָה **'oqbâh,** *ok-baw´;* fem. of an unused form from 6117 mean. a *trick; trickery:*— subtilty.

6123. עָקַד **'âqad,** *aw-kad´;* a prim. root; to *tie* with thongs:— bind.

עֵקֶד **'Êqed.** See 1044.

6124. עָקֹד **'âqôd,** *aw-kode´;* from 6123; *striped* (with *bands*):— ring straked.

6125. עָקָה **'âqâh,** *aw-kaw´;* from 5781; *constraint:*— oppression.

6126. עַקּוּב **'Aqqûwb,** *ak-koob´;* from 6117; *insidious; Akkub,* the name of five Isr.:— Akkub.

6127. עָקַל **'âqal,** *aw-kal´;* a prim. root; to *wrest:*— wrong.

6128. עֲקַלְקַל **'ăqalqal,** *ak-al-kal´;* from 6127; *winding:*— by [-way], crooked way.

6129. עֲקַלָּתוֹן **'ăqallâthôwn,** *ak-al-law-thone´;* from 6127; *tortuous:*— crooked.

6130. עֲקָן **'Ăqân,** *aw-kawn´;* from an unused root mean. to *twist; tortuous; Akan,* an Idumæan:— Akan. Comp. 3292.

6131. עָקַר **'âqar,** *aw-kar´;* a prim. root; to *pluck* up (espec. by the roots); spec. to *hamstring;* fig. to *exterminate:*— dig down, hough, pluck up, root up.

6132. עֲקַר **'ăqar** (Chald.), *ak-ar´;* corresp. to 6131:— pluck up by the roots.

6133. עֵקֶר **'êqer,** *ay´-ker;* from 6131; fig. a *transplanted* person, i.e. naturalized citizen:— stock.

6134. עֵקֶר **'Êqer,** *ay´-ker;* the same as 6133; *Eker,* an Isr.:— Eker.

6135. עָקָר **'âqâr,** *aw-kawr´;* from 6131; *sterile* (as if *extirpated* in the generative organs):— (× male or female) barren (woman).

6136. עִקָּר **'iqqar** (Chald.), *ik-kar´;* from 6132; a *stock:*— stump.

6137. עַקְרָב **'aqrâb,** *ak-rawb´;* of uncert. der.; a *scorpion;* fig. a *scourge* or knotted whip:— scorpion.

6138. עֶקְרוֹן **'Eqrôwn,** *ek-rone´;* from 6131; *eradication; Ekron,* a place in Pal.:— Ekron.

6139. עֶקְרוֹנִי **'Eqrôwnîy,** *ek-ro-nee´;* or

עֶקְרֹנִי **'Eqrônîy,** *ek-ro-nee´;* patrial from 6138; an *Ekronite* or inhab. of Ekron:— Ekronite.

6140. עָקַשׁ **'âqash,** *aw-kash´;* a prim. root; to *knot* or *distort;* fig. to *pervert* (act or declare perverse):— make crooked, (prove, that is) perverse (-rt).

6141. עִקֵּשׁ **'iqqêsh,** *ik-kashe´;* from 6140; *distorted;* hence, *false:*— crooked, froward, perverse.

6142. עִקֵּשׁ **'Îqqêsh,** *ik-kashe´;* the same as 6141; *perverse; Ikkesh,* an Isr.:— Ikkesh.

6143. עִקְּשׁוּת **'iqq'shûwth,** *ik-kesh-ooth´;* from 6141; *perversity:*— × froward.

עָר **'âr.** See 5892.

6144. עָר **'Âr,** *awr;* the same as 5892; a *city; Ar,* a place in Moab:— Ar.

6145. עָר **'âr,** *awr;* from 5782; a *foe* (as *watchful* for mischief):— enemy.

6146. עָר **'âr** (Chald.), *awr;* corresp. to 6145:— enemy.

6147. עֵר **'Êr,** *ayr;* from 5782; *watchful; Er,* the name of two Isr.:— Er.

6148. עָרַב **'ârab,** *aw-rab´;* a prim. root; to *braid,* i.e. *intermix;* tech. to *traffic* (as if by barter); also to *give* or *be security* (as a kind of exchange):— engage, (inter-) meddle (with), mingle (self), mortgage, occupy, give pledges, be (-come, put in) surety, undertake.

6149. עָרֵב **'ârêb,** *aw-rabe´* a prim. root [rather ident. with 6148 through the idea of close *association*]; to *be agreeable:*— be pleasant (-ing), take pleasure in, be sweet.

6150. עָרַב **'ârab,** *aw-rab´;* a prim. root [rather ident. with 6148 through the idea of *covering* with a texture]; to *grow dusky* at sundown:— be darkened, (toward) evening.

6151. עֲרַב **'ărab** (Chald.), *ar-ab'*; corresp. to 6148; to *commingle:*— mingle (self), mix.

6152. עֲרָב **'Ărâb,** *ar-awb'* or

עֲרַב **'Ărab,** *ar-ab'*; from 6150 in the fig. sense of *sterility; Arab* (i.e. *Arabia*), a country E. of Pal.:— Arabia.

6153. עֶרֶב **'ereb,** *eh'-reb;* from 6150; *dusk:*— + day, even (-ing, tide), night.

6154. עֶרֶב **'êreb,** *ay'-reb;* or

עֶרֶב **'ereb** (1 Kings 10:15), (with the art. pref.), *eh'-reb;* from 6148; the *web* (or transverse threads of cloth); also a *mixture,* (or *mongrel race*):— Arabia, mingled people, mixed (multitude), woof.

6155. עֲרָב **'ărâb,** *aw-rawb';* from 6148; a *willow* (from the use of osiers as wattles):— willow.

6156. עֲרֵב **'ărêb,** *aw-rabe';* from 6149; *pleasant:*— sweet.

6157. עָרֹב **'ârôb,** *aw-robe';* from 6148; a *mosquito* (from its *swarming*):— divers sorts of flies, swarm.

6158. עֹרֵב **'ôrêb,** *o-rabe';* or

עוֹרֵב **'ôwrêb,** *o-rabe';* from 6150; a *raven* (from its *dusky* hue):— raven.

6159. עֹרֵב **'Ôrêb,** *o-rabe';* or

עוֹרֵב **'Ôwrêb,** *o-rabe';* the same as 6158; *Oreb,* the name of a Midianite and of a cliff near the Jordan:— Oreb.

6160. עֲרָבָה **'ărâbâh,** *ar-aw-baw';* from 6150 (in the sense of *sterility*); a *desert;* espec. (with the art. pref.) the (gen.) sterile valley of the Jordan and its continuation to the Red Sea:— Arabah, champaign, desert, evening, heaven, plain, wilderness. See also 1026.

6161. עֲרֻבָּה **'ărubbâh,** *ar-oob-baw';* fem. pass. part. of 6148 in the sense of a *bargain* or *exchange;* something given as *security,* i.e. (lit.) a *token* (of safety) or (metaph.) a *bondsman:*— pledge, surety.

6162. עֵרָבוֹן **'ărâbôwn,** *ar-aw-bone';* from 6148 (in the sense of *exchange*); a *pawn* (given as security):— pledge.

6163. עֲרָבִי **'Ărâbîy,** *ar-aw-bee';* or

עַרְבִי **'Arbîy,** *ar-bee';* patrial from 6152; an *Arabian* or inhab. of Arab (i.e. Arabia):— Arabian.

6164. עַרְבָתִי **'Arbâthîy,** *ar-baw-thee';* patrial from 1026; an *Arbathite* or inhab. of (Beth-) Arabah:— Arbahite.

6165. עָרַג **'ârag,** *aw-rag';* a prim. root; to *long for:*— cry, pant.

6166. עֲרָד **'Ărâd,** *ar-awd';* from an unused root mean. to *sequester* itself; *fugitive; Arad,* the name of a place near Pal., also of a Canaanite and an Isr.:— Arad.

6167. עֲרָד **'ărâd** (Chald.), *ar-awd';* corresp. to 6171; an *onager:*— wild ass.

6168. עָרָה **'ârâh,** *aw-raw';* a prim. root; to be (caus. *make*) *bare;* hence, to *empty, pour out, demolish:*— leave destitute, discover, empty, make naked, pour (out), rase, spread self, uncover.

6169. עָרָה **'ârâh,** *aw-raw';* fem. from 6168; a *naked* (i.e. *level*) *plot:*— paper reed.

6170. עֲרוּגָה **'ărûwgâh,** *ar-oo-gaw';* or

עֲרֻגָה **'ărûgâh,** *ar-oo-gaw';* fem. pass. part. of 6165; something *piled* up (as if [fig.] *raised* by mental aspiration), i.e. a *parterre:*— bed, furrow.

6171. עָרוֹד **'ârôwd,** *aw-rode';* from the same as 6166; an *onager* (from his *lonesome* habits):— wild ass.

6172. עֶרְוָה **'ervâh,** *er-vaw';* from 6168; *nudity,* lit. (espec. the *pudenda*) or fig. (*disgrace, blemish*):— nakedness, shame, unclean (-ness).

6173. עַרְוָה **'arvâh** (Chald.), *ar-vaw';* corresp. to 6172; *nakedness,* i.e. (fig.) *impoverishment:*— dishonour.

6174. עָרוֹם **'ârôwm,** *aw-rome';* or

עָרֹם **'ârôm,** *aw-rome';* from 6191 (in its orig. sense); *nude,* either partially or totally:— naked.

6175. עָרוּם **'ârûwm,** *aw-room';* pass. part. of 6191; *cunning* (usually in a bad sense):— crafty, prudent, subtil.

6176. עֲרוֹעֵר **'ărôw'êr,** *ar-o-ayr';* or

עַרְעָר **'ar'âr,** *ar-awr';* from 6209 redupl.; a *juniper* (from its *nudity* of situation):— heath.

6177. עֲרוֹעֵר **'Ărôw'êr,** *ar-o-ayr';* or

עֲרֹעֵר **'Ărô'êr,** *ar-o-ayr';* or

עַרְעוֹר **'Ar'ôwr,** *ar-ore';* the same as 6176; *nudity* of situation; *Aroër,* the name of three places in or near Pal.:— Aroer.

6178. עָרוּץ **'ărûwts,** *aw-roots';* pass. part. of 6206; *feared,* i.e. (concr.) a *horrible* place or *chasm:*— cliffs.

6179. עֵרִי **'Êrîy,** *ay-ree';* from 5782; *watchful; Eri,* an Isr.:— Eri.

6180. עֵרִי **'Êrîy,** *ay-ree';* patron. of 6179; a *Erite* (collect.) or desc. of Eri:— Erites.

6181. עֶרְיָה **'eryâh,** *er-yaw';* for 6172; *nudity:*— bare, naked, × quite.

6182. עֲרִיסָה **'ărîyçâh,** *ar-ee-saw';* from an unused root mean. to *comminute; meal:*— dough.

6183. עָרִיף **'ârîyph,** *aw-reef';* from 6201; the *sky* (as *drooping* at the horizon):— heaven.

6184. עָרִיץ **'ârîyts,** *aw-reets';* from 6206;

fearful, i.e. *powerful* or *tyrannical:*— mighty, oppressor, in great power, strong, terrible, violent.

6185. עֲרִירִי **'ărîyrîy,** *ar-e-ree´;* from 6209; *bare,* i.e. destitute (of children):— childless.

6186. עָרַךְ **'ârak,** *aw-rak´;* a prim. root; to set in a *row,* i.e. *arrange,* put in *order* (in a very wide variety of applications):— put (set) (the battle, self) in array, compare, direct, equal, esteem, estimate, expert [in war], furnish, handle, join [battle], ordain, (lay, put, reckon up, set) (in) order, prepare, tax, value.

6187. עֵרֶךְ **'êrek,** *eh´rek;* from 6186; a *pile, equipment, estimate:*— equal, estimation, (things that are set in) order, price, proportion, × set at, suit, taxation, × value[st].

6188. עָרֵל **'ârêl,** *aw-rale´;* a prim. root; prop. to *strip;* but used only as denom. from 6189; to *expose* or *remove* the prepuce, whether lit. (to *go naked*) or fig. (to *refrain* from using):— count uncircumcised, foreskin to be uncovered.

6189. עָרֵל **'ârêl,** *aw-rale´;* from 6188; prop. *exposed,* i.e. projecting loose (as to the prepuce); used only tech. *uncircumcised* (i.e. still having the prepuce uncurtailed):— uncircumcised (person).

6190. עָרְלָה **'orlâh,** *or-law´;* fem. of 6189; the *prepuce:*— foreskin, + uncircumcised.

6191. עָרַם **'âram,** *aw-ram´;* a prim. root; prop. to *be* (or *make*) *bare;* but used only in the der. sense (through the idea perh. of *smoothness*) to *be cunning* (usually in a bad sense):— × very, beware, take crafty [counsel], be prudent, deal subtilly.

6192. עָרַם **'âram,** *aw-ram´* a prim. root; to *pile* up:— gather together.

6193. עֹרֶם **'ôrem,** *o´-rem;* from 6191; a *stratagem:*— craftiness.

עֵרֹם **'Êrôm.** See 5903.

עָרֹם **'ârôm.** See 6174.

6194. עָרֵם **'ârêm** (Jer. 50:26), *aw-rame´;* or (fem.)

עֲרֵמָה **'ărêmâh,** *ar-ay-maw´;* from 6192; a *heap;* spec. a *sheaf:*— heap (of corn), sheaf.

6195. עָרְמָה **'ormâh,** *or-maw´;* fem. of 6193; *trickery;* or (in a good sense) *discretion:*— guile, prudence, subtilty, wilily, wisdom.

עֲרֵמָה **'arêmâh.** See 6194.

6196. עַרְמוֹן **'armôwn,** *ar-mone´;* prob. from 6191; the *plane* tree (from its *smooth* and shed bark):— chestnut tree.

6197. עֵרָן **'Êrân,** *ay-rawn´;* prob. from 5782; *watchful; Eran,* an Isr.:— Eran.

6198. עֵרָנִי **'Êrânîy,** *ay-raw-nee´;* patron. from 6197; an *Eranite* or desc. (collect.) of Eran:— Eranites.

עַרְעוֹר **'Ar'ôwr.** See 6177.

6199. עַרְעָר **'ar'âr,** *ar-awr´;* from 6209; *naked,* i.e. (fig.) *poor:*— destitute. See also 6176.

עֲרֹעֵר **'Ărô'êr.** See 6177.

6200. עֲרֹעֵרִי **'Ărô'êrîy,** *ar-o-ay-ree´;* patron. from 6177; an *Aroërite* or inhab. of Aroër:— Aroerite.

6201. עָרַף **'âraph,** *aw-raf´;* a prim. root; to *droop;* hence, to *drip:*— drop (down).

6202. עָרַף **'âraph,** *aw-raf´;* a prim. root [rather ident. with 6201 through the idea of *sloping*]; prop. to *bend* downward; but used only as a denom. from 6203, to *break the neck;* hence, (fig.) to *destroy:*— that is beheaded, break down, break (cut off, strike off) neck.

6203. עֹרֶף **'ôreph,** *o-ref´;* from 6202; the *nape* or back of the neck (as *declining*); hence, the *back* generally (whether lit. or fig.):— back ([stiff-] neck ([-ed]).

6204. עָרְפָּה **'Orpâh,** *or-paw´;* fem. of 6203; *mane; Orpah,* a Moabitess:— Orpah.

6205. עֲרָפֶל **'ărâphel,** *ar-aw-fel´;* prob. from 6201; *gloom* (as of a *lowering* sky):— (gross, thick) dark (cloud, -ness).

6206. עָרַץ **'ârats,** *aw-rats´;* a prim. root; to *awe* or (intr.) to *dread;* hence, to *harass:*— be affrighted (afraid, dread, feared, terrified), break, dread, fear, oppress, prevail, shake terribly.

6207. עָרַק **'âraq,** *aw-rak´;* a prim. root; to *gnaw,* i.e. (fig.) *eat* (by hyperbole); also (part.) a *pain:*— fleeing, sinew.

6208. עַרְקִי **'Arqîy,** *ar-kee´;* patrial from an unused name mean. a *tush;* an *Arkite* or inhab. of Erek:— Arkite.

6209. עָרַר **'ârar,** *aw-rar´;* a prim. root; *bare;* fig. to *demolish:*— make bare, break, raise up [perh. *by clerical err. for* raze], × utterly.

6210. עֶרֶשׂ **'eres,** *eh´res;* from an unused root mean. perh. to *arch;* a *couch* (prop. with a *canopy*):— bed (-stead), couch.

6211. עָשׁ **'âsh,** *awsh;* from 6244; a *moth:*— moth. See also 5906.

6211'. עֲשַׂב **'ăsab** (Chald.), *as-ab´;* 6212:— grass.

6212. עֶשֶׂב **'eseb,** *eh´seb;* from an unused root mean. to *glisten* (or *be green*); *grass* (or any tender shoot):— grass, herb.

6213. עָשָׂה **'âsâh,** *aw-saw´;* a prim. root; to *do* or *make,* in the broadest sense and widest application (as follows):— accomplish, advance, appoint, apt, be at, become, bear, bestow, bring forth, bruise, be busy, × certainly, have the charge of, commit, deal (with), deck, + displease, do, (ready) dress (-ed), (put in) execute (-ion), exercise, fashion, + feast, [fight-ling man, + finish, fit, fly, follow, fulfil, furnish, gather, get, go about, govern, grant, great, + hinder, hold ([a feast]), × indeed, + be industrious, + journey, keep, labour, maintain, make, be meet, observe, be occupied, offer, + officer, pare, bring (come) to pass, perform, practise, prepare, procure, provide, put, requite, × sacrifice, serve, set, shew, × sin, spend, × surely, take, × throughly, trim, × very, + vex, be [warr-] ior, work (-man), yield, use.

6214. עֲשָׂהאֵל **'Ăsâh'êl**, _as-aw-ale';_ from 6213 and 410; _God has made; Asahel,_ the name of four Isr.:— Asahel.

6215. עֵשָׂו **'Êsâv**, _ay-sawv';_ appar. a form of the pass. part. of 6213 in the orig. sense of _handling; rough_ (i.e. sensibly _felt); Esau,_ a son of Isaac, incl. his posterity:— Esau.

6216. עָשׁוֹק **'âshôwq**, _aw-shoke';_ from 6231; _oppressive_ (as noun, a _tyrant):—_ oppressor.

6217. עָשׁוּק **'âshûwq**, _aw-shook';_ or

עָשֻׁק **'âshûq**, _aw-shook';_ pass. part. of 6231; used in plur. masc. as abstr. _tyranny:—_ oppressed (-ion). [_Doubtful.]_

6218. עָשׂוֹר **'âsôwr**, _aw-sore';_ or

עָשֹׂר **'âsôr**, _aw-sore';_ from 6235; _ten;_ by abbrev. ten _strings,_ and so a _decachord:—_ (instrument of) ten (strings, -th).

6219. עֲשׁוֹת **'âshôwth**, _aw-shōth';_ from 6245; _shining,_ i.e. _polished:—_ bright.

6220. עַשְׁוָת **'Ashvâth**, _ash-vawth';_ for 6219; _bright; Ashvath,_ an Isr.:— Ashvath.

6221. עֲשִׂיאֵל **'Ăsîy'êl**, _as-ee-ale';_ from 6213 and 410; _made of God; Asiël,_ an Isr.:— Asiel.

6222. עֲשָׂיָה **'Ăsâyâh**, _aw-saw-yaw';_ from 6213 and 3050; _Jah has made; Asajah,_ the name of three or four Isr.:— Asaiah.

6223. עָשִׁיר **'âshîyr**, _aw-sheer';_ from 6238; _rich,_ whether lit. or fig. (_noble):—_ rich (man).

6224. עֲשִׂירִי **'ăsîyrîy**, _as-ee-ree';_ from 6235; _tenth;_ by abb. _tenth month_ or (fem.) _part:—_ tenth (part).

6225. עָשַׁן **'âshan**, _aw-shan';_ a prim. root; to _smoke,_ whether lit. or fig.:— be angry, (be on a) smoke.

6226. עָשֵׁן **'âshên**, _aw-shane';_ from 6225; _smoky:—_ smoking.

6227. עָשָׁן **'âshân**, _aw-shawn';_ from 6225; _smoke,_ lit. or fig. (_vapor, dust, anger):—_ smoke (-ing).

6228. עָשָׁן **'Âshân**, _aw-shawn';_ the same as 6227; _Ashan,_ a place in Pal.:— Ashan.

6229. עָשַׂק **'âsaq**, _aw-sak';_ a prim. root (ident. with 6231); to _press upon,_ i.e. _quarrel:—_ strive with.

6230. עֵשֶׂק **'Êseq**, _ay'sek;_ from 6229; _strife:—_ Esek.

6231. עָשַׁק **'âshaq**, _aw-shak';_ a prim. root (comp. 6229); to _press upon,_ i.e. _oppress, defraud, violate, overflow:—_ get deceitfully, deceive, defraud, drink up, (use) oppress ([-ion]), -or), do violence (wrong).

6232. עֵשֶׁק **'Êsheq**, _ay-shek';_ from 6231; _oppression; Eshek,_ an Isr.:— Eshek.

6233. עֹשֶׁק **'ôsheq**, _o'-shek;_ from 6231; _injury, fraud,_ (subj.) _distress,_ (concr.) _unjust gain:—_ cruelly, extortion, oppression, thing [deceitfully gotten].

עָשֻׁק **'âshûq**. See 6217.

6234. עָשְׁקָה **'oshqâh**, _osh-kaw';_ fem. of 6233; _anguish:—_ oppressed.

6235. עֶשֶׂר **'eser**, _eh'ser;_ masc.

עֲשָׂרָה **'ăsârâh**, _as-aw-raw';_ from 6237; _ten_ (as an _accumulation_ to the extent of the digits):— ten, [fif-, seven-] teen.

6236. עֲשַׂר **'ăsar** (Chald.), _as-ar';_ masc.

עֶשְׂרָה **'ăsrâh** (Chald.), _as-raw';_ corresp. to 6235; _ten:—_ ten, + twelve.

6237. עָשַׂר **'âsar**, _aw-sar';_ a prim. root (ident. with 6238); to _accumulate;_ but used only as denom. from 6235; to _tithe,_ i.e. _take_ or _give a tenth:—_ × surely, give (take) the tenth, (have, take) tithe (-ing, -s), × truly.

6238. עָשַׁר **'âshar**, _aw-shar';_ a prim. root; prop. to _accumulate;_ chiefly (spec.) to _grow_ (caus. _make) rich:—_ be (-come, en-, make, make self, wax) rich, make [1 Kings 22:48 marg.]. See 6240.

6239. עֹשֶׁר **'ôsher**, _o'-sher;_ from 6238; _wealth:—_ × far [richer], riches.

6240. עָשָׂר **'âsâr**, _aw-sawr';_ for 6235; _ten_ (only in combination), i.e. _teen;_ also (ord.) _-teenth:—_ [eigh-, fif-, four-, nine-, seven-, six-, thir-]teen (-th), + eleven (-th), + sixscore thousand, + twelve (-th).

עָשׂוֹר **'âsôr**. See 6218.

6241. עִשָּׂרוֹן **'issârôwn**, _is-saw-rone';_ or

עִשָּׂרֹן **'issârôn**, _is-saw-rone';_ from 6235; (fractional) a _tenth_ part:— tenth deal.

6242. עֶשְׂרִים **'esrîym**, _es-reem';_ from 6235; _twenty;_ also (ord.) _twentieth:—_ [six-] score, twenty (-ieth).

6243. עֶשְׂרִין **'esrîyn** (Chald.), _es-reen';_ corresp. to 6242:— twenty.

6244. עָשֵׁשׁ **'âshêsh**, _aw-shaysh';_ a prim. root; prob. to _shrink,_ i.e. _fail:—_ be consumed.

6245. עָשַׁת **'âshath**, _aw-shath';_ a prim. root; prob. to _be sleek,_ i.e. _glossy;_ hence, (through the idea of _polishing)_ to _excogi-_

tate (as if *forming* in the mind):— shine, think.

6246. עֲשִׁת **'ăshîth** (Chald.), *ash-eeth'*; corresp. to 6245; to *purpose:*— think.

6247. עֶשֶׁת **'esheth**, *eh'-sheth*; from 6245; a *fabric:*— bright.

6248. עַשְׁתוּת **'ashtûwth**, *ash-tooth'*; from 6245; *cogitation:*— thought.

6249. עַשְׁתֵּי **'ashtêy**, *ash-tay'*; appar. masc. plur. constr. of 6247 in the sense of an *afterthought* (used only in connection with 6240 in lieu of 259) *eleven* or (ord.) *eleventh:*— + eleven (-th).

6250. עֶשְׁתֹּנָה **'eshtônâh**, *esh-to-naw'*; from 6245; *thinking:*— thought.

6251. עַשְׁתְּרָה **'ashtᵉrâh**, *ash-ter-aw'*; prob. from 6238; *increase:*— flock.

6252. עַשְׁתָּרוֹת **'Ashtârôwth**, *ash-taw-rōth'*; or

עַשְׁתָּרֹת **'Ashtârôth**, *ash-taw-rōth'*; plur. of 6251; *Ashtaroth*, the name of a Sidonian deity, and of a place E. of the Jordan:— Ashtaroth, Astaroth. See also 1045, 6253, 6255.

6253. עַשְׁתֹּרֶת **'Ashtôreth**, *ash-to'reth*; prob. for 6251; *Ashtoreth*, the Phœnician goddess of love (and *increase*):— Ashtoreth.

6254. עַשְׁתְּרָתִי **'Ashtᵉrâthîy**, *ash-ter-aw-thee'*; patrial from 6252; an *Ashterathite* or inhab. of Ashtaroth:— Ashterathite.

6255. עַשְׁתְּרֹת קַרְנַיִם **'Ashtᵉrôth Qarnayim**, *ash-ter-ōth' kar-nah'-yim*; from 6252 and the dual of 7161; *Ashtaroth of* (the) *double horns* (a symbol of the deity); *Ashteroth-Karnaïm*, a place E. of the Jordan:— Ashteroth Karnaim.

6256. עֵת **'êth**, *ayth*; from 5703; *time*, espec. (adv. with prep.) *now, when*, etc.:— + after, [al-]ways, × certain, + continually, + evening, long, (due) season, so [long] as, [even-, evening-, noon-] tide, ([meal-]), what) time, when.

6257. עָתַד **'âthad**, *aw-thad'*; a prim. root; to *prepare:*— make fit, be ready to become.

עָתֻד **'attûd**. See 6260.

6258. עַתָּה **'attâh**, *at-taw'*; from 6256; at *this time*, whether adv., conjunc. or expletive:— henceforth, now, straightway, this time, whereas.

6259. עָתוּד **'âthûwd**, *aw-thood'*; pass. part. of 6257; *prepared:*— ready.

6260. עַתּוּד **'attûwd**, *at-tood'*; or

עַתֻּד **'attûd**, *at-tood'*; from 6257; *prepared*, i.e. *full grown;* spoken only (in plur.) of he-goats, or (fig.) *leaders* of the people:— chief one, (he) goat, ram.

6261. עִתִּי **'ittîy**, *it-tee'*; from 6256; *timely:*— fit.

6262. עַתַּי **'Attay**, *at-tah'ee*; for 6261; *Attai*, the name of three Isr.:— Attai.

6263. עֲתִיד **'ăthîyd** (Chald.), *ath-eed'*; corresp. to 6264; *prepared:*— ready.

6264. עָתִיד **'âthîyd**, *aw-theed'*; from 6257; *prepared;* by impl. *skilful;* fem. plur. the *future;* also *treasure:*— things that shall come, ready, treasures.

6265. עֲתָיָה **'Ăthâyâh**, *ath-aw-yaw'*; from 5790 and 3050; *Jah has helped; Athajah*, an Isr.:— Athaiah.

6266. עָתִיק **'âthîyq**, *aw-theek'*; from 6275; prop. *antique*, i.e. *venerable* or *splendid:*— durable.

6267. עַתִּיק **'attîyq**, *at-teek'*; from 6275; *removed*, i.e. *weaned;* also *antique:*— ancient, drawn.

6268. עַתִּיק **'attîyq** (Chald.), *at-teek'*; corresp. to 6267; *venerable:*— ancient.

6269. עֲתָךְ **'Ăthâk**, *ath-awk'*; from an unused root mean. to *sojourn; lodging; Athak*, a place in Pal.:— Athach.

6270. עַתְלַי **'Athlay**, *ath-lah'ee*; from an unused root mean. to *compress; constringent; Athlai*, an Isr.:— Athlai.

6271. עֲתַלְיָה **'Ăthalyâh**, *ath-al-yaw'*; or

עֲתַלְיָהוּ **'Ăthalyâhûw**, *ath-al-yaw'-hoo;* from the same as 6270 and 3050; *Jah has constrained; Athaljah*, the name of an Israelitess and two Isr.:— Athaliah.

6272. עָתַם **'âtham**, *aw-tham'*; a prim. root; prob. to *glow*, i.e. (fig.) *be desolated:*— be darkened.

6273. עָתְנִי **'Otnîy**, *oth-nee'*; from an unused root mean. to *force; forcible; Othni*, an Isr.:— Othni.

6274. עָתְנִיאֵל **'Othnîy'êl**, *oth-nee-ale'*; from the same as 6273 and 410; *force of God; Othniël*, an Isr.:— Othniel.

6275. עָתַק **'âthaq**, *aw-thak'*; a prim. root; to *remove* (intr. or tran.) fig. to *grow old;* spec. to *transcribe:*— copy out, leave off, become (wax) old, remove.

6276. עָתֵק **'âthêq**, *aw-thake'*; from 6275; *antique*, i.e. *valued:*— durable.

6277. עָתָק **'âthâq**, *aw-thawk'*; from 6275 in the sense of *license; impudent:*— arrogancy, grievous (hard) things, stiff.

6278. עֵת קָצִין **'Êth Qâtsîyn**, *ayth kaw-tseen'*; from 6256 and 7011; *time of a judge; Eth-Katsin*, a place in Pal.:— Ittah-kazin [by incl. directive enclitic].

6279. עָתַר **'âthar**, *aw-thar'*; a prim. root [rather denom. from 6281]; to *burn incense* in worship, i.e. *intercede* (recip. *listen* to prayer):— intreat, (make) pray (-er).

6280. עָתַר **'âthar**, *aw-thar'*; a prim. root; to *be* (caus. *make*) *abundant:*— deceitful, multiply.

6281. עֵתֶר **'Ether**, *eh'ther;* from 6280; *abundance; Ether*, a place in Pal.:— Ether.

6282. עָתָר **'âthâr**, *aw-thawr';* from 6280; *incense* (as increasing to a *volume* of smoke); hence, (from 6279) a *worshipper:*— suppliant, thick.

6283. עֲתֶרֶת **'ăthereth**, *ath-eh'-reth;* from 6280; *copiousness:*— abundance.

פ

אפ **pô'**. See 6311.

6284. פָּאָה **pâ'âh**, *paw-aw';* a prim. root; to *puff*, i.e. *blow* away:— scatter into corners.

6285. פֵּאָה **pê'âh**, *pay-aw';* fem. of 6311; prop. *mouth* in a fig. sense, i.e. *direction, region, extremity:*— corner, end, quarter, side.

6286. פָּאַר **pâ'ar**, *paw-ar';* a prim. root; to *gleam*, i.e. (caus.) *embellish;* fig. to *boast;* also to *explain* (i.e. make clear) oneself; denom. from 6288, to *shake* a tree:— beautify, boast self, go over the boughs, glorify (self), glory, vaunt self.

6287. פְּאֵר **pe'êr**, *peh-ayr';* from 6286; an *embellishment*, i.e. fancy *head-dress:*— beauty, bonnet, goodly, ornament, tire.

6288. פְּאֹרָה **pe'ôrâh**, *peh-o-raw';* or

פֹּרָאה **pôrâ'h**, *po-raw';* or

פֻּארָה **pu'râh**, *poo-raw';* from 6286; prop. *ornamentation*, i.e. (plur.) *foliage* (incl. the limbs) as *bright* green:— bough, branch, sprig.

6289. פָּארוּר **pâ'rûwr**, *paw-roor';* from 6286; prop. *illuminated*, i.e. a *glow;* as noun, a *flush* (of anxiety):— blackness.

6290. פָּארָן **Pâ'rân**, *paw-rawn';* from 6286; *ornamental; Paran*, a desert of Arabia:— Paran.

6291. פַּג **pag**, *pag;* from an unused root mean. to *be torpid*, i.e. *crude;* an *unripe* fig:— green fig.

6292. פִּגּוּל **piggûwl**, *pig-gool';* or

פִּגֻּל **piggûl**, *pig-gool';* from an unused root mean. to *stink;* prop. *fetid*, i.e. (fig.) *unclean* (ceremonially):— abominable (-tion, thing).

6293. פָּגַע **pâga'**, *paw-gah';* a prim. root; to *impinge*, by accident or violence, or (fig.) by importunity:— come (betwixt), cause to entreat, fall (upon), make intercession, intercessor, intreat, lay, light [upon], meet (together), pray, reach, run.

6294. פֶּגַע **pega'**, *peh'-gah;* from 6293; *impact* (casual):— chance, occurrent.

6295. פַּגְעִיאֵל **Pag'îy'êl**, *pag-ee-ale';* from 6294 and 410; *accident of God; Pagiël*, an Isr.:— Pagiel.

6296. פָּגַר **pâgar**, *paw-gar';* a prim. root; to *relax*, i.e. *become exhausted:*— be faint.

6297. פֶּגֶר **peger**, *peh'gher;* from 6296; a *carcase* (as *limp*), whether of man or beast; fig. an idolatrous *image:*— carcase (carcass), corpse, dead body.

6298. פָּגַשׁ **pâgash**, *paw-gash';* a prim. root; to *come in contact with*, whether by accident or violence; fig. to *concur:*— meet (with, together).

6299. פָּדָה **pâdâh**, *paw-daw';* a prim. root; to *sever*, i.e. *ransom;* gen. to *release, preserve:*— × at all, deliver, × by any means, ransom, (that are to be, let be) redeem (-ed), rescue, × surely.

6300. פְּדַהאֵל **Pedah'êl**, *ped-ah-ale';* from 6299 and 410; *God has ransomed; Pedahel*, an Isr.:— Pedahel.

6301. פְּדָהצוּר **Pedâhtsûwr**, *ped-aw-tsoor';* from 6299 and 6697; a *rock* (i.e. God) *has ransomed; Pedahtsur*, an Isr.:— Pedahzur.

6302. פָּדוּי **pâdûwy**, *paw-doo'-ee;* pass. part. of 6299; *ransomed* (and so occurring under 6299); as abstr. (in plur. masc.) a *ransom:*— (that are) to be (that were) redeemed.

6303. פָּדוֹן **Pâdôwn**, *paw-done';* from 6299; *ransom; Padon*, one of the Nethinim:— Padon.

6304. פְּדוּת **pedûwth**, *ped-ooth';* or

פְּדֻת **pedûth**, *ped-ooth';* from 6929; *distinction;* also *deliverance:*— division, redeem, redemption.

6305. פְּדָיָה **Pedâyâh**, *ped-aw-yaw';* or

פְּדָיָהוּ **Pedâyâhûw**, *ped-aw-yaw'-hoo;* from 6299 and 3050; *Jah has ransomed; Pedajah*, the name of six Isr.:— Pedaiah.

6306. פִּדְיוֹם **pidyôwm**, *pid-yome';* or

פִּדְיֹם **pidyôm**, *pid-yome';* also

פִּדְיוֹן **pidyôwn**, *pid-yone';* or

פִּדְיֹן **pidyôn**, *pid-yone';* from 6299; a *ransom:*— ransom, that were redeemed, redemption.

6307. פַּדָּן **Paddân**, *pad-dawn';* from an unused root mean. to *extend;* a *plateau;* or

פַּדָּן אֲרָם **Paddan 'Ărâm**, *pad-dan' ar-awm';* from the same and 758; the *table-land of Aram; Paddan* or *Paddan-Aram*, a region of Syria:— Padan, Padan-aram.

6308. פָּדַע **pâda'**, *paw-dah';* a prim. root; to *retrieve:*— deliver.

6309. פֶּדֶר **peder**, *peh'der;* from an unused root mean. to *be greasy; suet:*— fat.

פְּדֻת **pedûth**. See 6304.

6310. פֶּה **peh**, *peh;* from 6284; the *mouth* (as the means of *blowing*), whether lit. or fig. (particularly *speech;* spec. *edge, portion* or *side;* adv. (with prep.) *according to:*— accord (-ing as, -ing to), after, appointment, assent, collar, command (-ment), × eat, edge, end, entry, + file, hole, × in, mind, mouth, part, portion, × (should) say (-ing), sentence, skirt, sound, speech, × spoken, talk, tenor, × to, + two-edged, wish, word.

6311. פֹּה **pôh**, *po;* or

פֹּא **pô'** (Job 38:11), *po;* or

פֹּו **pôw**, *po;* prob. from a prim. insepa- rable particle פ **p** (of demonstr. force) and 1931; *this place* (French *içi*), i.e. *here* or *hence:*— here, hither, the one (other, this, that) side.

פֹּוא **pôw'**. See 375.

6312. פּוּאָה **Pûw'âh**, *poo-aw'* or

פֻּוָּה **Puvvâh**, *poov-vaw';* from 6284; a *blast; Puäh* or *Puvvah,* the name of two Isr.:— Phuvah, Pua, Puah.

6313. פּוּג **pûwg**, *poog;* a prim. root; to *be slug- gish:*— cease, be feeble, faint, be slacked.

6314. פּוּגָה **pûwgâh**, *poo-gaw';* from 6313; *in- termission:*— rest.

פֻּוָּה **Puvvâh**. See 6312.

6315. פּוּחַ **pûwach**, *poo'akh;* a prim. root; to *puff,* i.e. blow with the breath or air; hence, to *fan* (as a breeze), to *utter,* to *kindle* (a fire), to *scoff:*— blow (upon), break, puff, bring into a snare, speak, utter.

6316. פּוּט **Pûwṭ**, *poot;* of for. or.; *Put,* a son of Ham, also the name of his desc. or their re- gion, and of a Pers. tribe:— Phut, Put.

6317. פּוּטִיאֵל **Pûwṭîy'êl**, *poo-tee-ale';* from an unused root (prob. mean. to *disparage*) and 410; *contempt of God; Putiël,* an Isr.:— Putiel.

6318. פּוֹטִיפַר **Pôwṭiyphar**, *po-tee-far';* of Eg. der.; *Potiphar,* an Eg.:— Potiphar.

6319. פּוֹטִי פֶרַע **Pôwṭiy Phera'**, *po-tee feh'-rah;* of Eg. der.; *Poti-Phera,* an Eg.:— Poti-pherah.

6320. פּוּךְ **pûwk**, *pook;* from an unused root mean. to *paint; dye* (spec. *stibium* for the eyes):— fair colours, glistering, paint [-ed] (-ing).

6321. פּוֹל **pôwl**, *pole;* from an unused root mean. to *be thick;* a *bean* (as *plump*):— beans.

6322. פּוּל **Pûwl**, *pool;* of for. or.; *Pul,* the name of an Ass. king and of an Ethiopian tribe:— Pul.

6323. פּוּן **pûwn**, *poon;* a prim. root mean. to *turn,* i.e. *be perplexed:*— be distracted.

6324. פּוּנִי **Pûwnîy**, *poo-nee';* patron. from an unused name mean. a *turn;* a *Punite* (collect.) or desc. of an unknown *Pun:*— Punites.

6325. פּוּנֹן **Pûwnôn**, *poo-none';* from 6323; *per- plexity; Punon,* a place in the Desert:— Punon.

6326. פּוּעָה **Pûw'âh**, *poo-aw';* from an un- used root mean. to *glitter; brilliancy; Puäh,* an Israelitess:— Puah.

6327. פּוּץ **pûwts**, *poots;* a prim. root; to *dash* in pieces, lit. or fig. (espec. to *disperse*):— break (dash, shake) in (to) pieces, cast (abroad), disperse (selves), drive, retire, scatter (abroad), spread abroad.

6328. פּוּק **pûwq**, *pook;* a prim. root; to *waver:*— stumble, move.

6329. פּוּק **pûwq**, *pook;* a prim. root [rather ident. with 6328 through the idea of *drop- ping* out; comp. 5312]; to *issue,* i.e. *furnish;* caus. to *secure;* fig. to *succeed:*— afford, draw out, further, get, obtain.

6330. פּוּקָה **pûwqâh**, *poo-kaw';* from 6328; a *stumbling-block:*— grief.

6331. פּוּר **pûwr**, *poor;* a prim. root; to *crush:*— break, bring to nought, × utterly take.

6332. פּוּר **Pûwr**, *poor;* also (plur.)

פּוּרִים **Pûwrîym**, *poo-reem';* or

פֻּרִים **Pûrîym**, *poo-reem';* from 6331; a *lot* (as by means of a *broken* piece):— Pur, Purim.

6333. פּוּרָה **pûwrâh**, *poo-raw';* from 6331; a *wine-press* (as *crushing* the grapes):— winepress.

פּוּרִים **Pûwrîym**. See 6332.

6334. פּוֹרָתָא **Pôwrâthâ'**, *po-raw-thaw';* of Pers. or.; *Poratha,* a son of Haman:— Po- ratha.

6335. פּוּשׁ **pûwsh**, *poosh;* a prim. root; to *spread;* fig. *act proudly:*— grow up, be grown fat, spread selves, be scattered.

6336. פּוּתִי **Pûwthîy**, *poo-thee';* patron. from an unused name mean. a *hinge;* a *Puthite* (collect.) or desc. of an unknown *Puth:*— Puhites [as if from 6312].

6337. פָּז **pâz**, *pawz;* from 6338; *pure* (gold); hence, *gold* itself (as refined):— fine (pure) gold.

6338. פָּזַז **pâzaz**, *paw-zaz';* a prim. root; to *refine* (gold):— best [gold].

6339. פָּזַז **pâzaz**, *paw-zaz';* a prim. root [rather ident. with 6338]; to *solidify* (as if by *refining*); also to *spring* (as if *separating* the limbs):— leap, be made strong.

6340. פָּזַר **pâzar**, *paw-zar';* a prim. root; to *scatter,* whether in enmity or bounty:— dis- perse, scatter (abroad).

6341. פַּח **pach**, *pakh;* from 6351; a (metallic) *sheet* (as *pounded* thin); also a spring *net* (as spread out like a *lamina*):— gin, (thin) plate, snare.

6342. פָּחַד **pâchad**, *paw-khad';* a prim. root;

to *be startled* (by a sudden alarm); hence, to *fear* in general:— be afraid, stand in awe, (be in) fear, make to shake.

6343. פַּחַד **pachad**, *pakh´-ad*; from 6342; a (sudden) *alarm* (prop. the object feared, by impl. the feeling):— dread (-ful), fear, (thing) great [fear, -ly feared], terror.

6344. פַּחַד **pachad**, *pakh´-ad*; the same as 6343; a *testicle* (as a cause of *shame* akin to *fear*):— stone.

6345. פַּחְדָּה **pachdâh**, *pakh-daw´*; fem. of 6343; *alarm* (i.e. *awe*):— fear.

6346. פֶּחָה **pechâh**, *peh-khaw´*; of for. or.; a *prefect* (of a city or small district):— captain, deputy, governor.

6347. פֶּחָה **pechâh** (Chald.), *peh-khaw´*; corresp. to 6346:— captain, governor.

6348. פָּחַז **pâchaz**, *paw-khaz´*; a prim. root; to *bubble* up or *froth* (as boiling water), i.e. (fig.) to *be unimportant:*— light.

6349. פַּחַז **pachaz**, *pakh´-az*; from 6348; *ebullition*, i.e. froth (fig. lust):— unstable.

6350. פַּחֲזוּת **pachăzûwth**, *pakh-az-ooth´*; from 6348; *frivolity:*— lightness.

6351. פָּחַח **pâchach**, *paw-khakh´*; a prim. root; to *batter* out; but used only as denom. from 6341, to *spread a net:*— be snared.

6352. פֶּחָם **pechâm**, *peh-khawm´*; perh. from an unused root prob. mean. to *be black;* a *coal*, whether charred or live:— coals.

6353. פֶּחָר **pechâr** (Chald.), *peh-khawr´*; from an unused root prob. mean. to *fashion;* a *potter:*— potter.

6354. פַּחַת **pachath**, *pakh´-ath*; prob. from an unused root appar. mean. to *dig;* a *pit*, espec. for catching animals:— hole, pit, snare.

6355. פַּחַת מוֹאָב **Pachath Môw'âb**, *pakh´-ath mo-awb´*; from 6354 and 4124; *pit of Moâb; Pachath-Moâb*, an Isr.:— Pahath-moab.

6356. פְּחֶתֶת **pechetheth**, *pekh-eh´-theth*; from the same as 6354; a *hole* (by mildew in a garment):— fret inward.

6357. פִּטְדָה **piṭdâh**, *pit-daw´*; of for. der.; a *gem*, prob. the *topaz:*— topaz.

6358. פָּטוּר **pâṭûwr**, *paw-toor´*; pass. part. of 6362; *opened*, i.e. (as noun) a *bud:*— open.

6359. פָּטִיר **pâṭîyr**, *paw-teer´*; from 6362; *open*, i.e. *unoccupied:*— free.

6360. פַּטִּישׁ **paṭṭîysh**, *pat-teesh´*; intens. from an unused root mean. to *pound;* a *hammer:*— hammer.

6361. פַּטִּישׁ **paṭṭîysh** (Chald.), *pat-teesh´*; from a root corresp. to that of 6360; a *gown* (as if *hammered* out wide):— hose.

6362. פָּטַר **pâṭar**, *paw-tar´*; a prim. root; to *cleave* or burst through, i.e. (caus.) to *emit*,

whether lit. or fig. (*gape*):— dismiss, free, let (shoot) out, slip away.

6363. פֶּטֶר **peṭer**, *peh´-ter;* or

פִּטְרָה **piṭrâh**, *pit-raw´*; from 6362; a *fissure*, i.e. (concr.) *firstling* (as *opening* the matrix):— firstling, openeth, such as open.

6364. פִּי־בֶסֶת **Pîy-Beçeth**, *pee beh´-seth;* of Eg. or.; *Pi-Beseth*, a place in Egypt:— Pi-beseth.

6365. פִּיד **pîyd**, *peed;* from an unused root prob. mean. to *pierce;* (fig.) *misfortune:*— destruction, ruin.

6366. פֵּיָה **pêyâh**, *pay-aw´;* or

פִּיָּה **pîyâh**, *pee-yaw´*; fem. of 6310; an *edge:*— (two-) edge (-d).

6367. פִּי הַחִירֹת **Piy ha-Chîrôth**, *pee hah-khee-rōth´*; from 6310 and the fem. plur. of a noun (from the same root as 2356), with the art. interpolated; *mouth of the gorges; Pi-ha-Chiroth*, a place in Egypt:— Pi-hahiroth. [In Num. 14:19 without Pi-.]

6368. פִּיחַ **pîyach**, *pee´-akh*; from 6315; a *powder* (as easily *puffed* away), i.e. *ashes* or *dust:*— ashes.

6369. פִּיכֹל **Pîykôl**, *pee-kole´*; appar. from 6310 and 3605; *mouth of all; Picol*, a Philistine:— Phichol.

6370. פִּילֶגֶשׁ **pîylegesh**, *pee-leh´-ghesh;* or

פִּלֶּגֶשׁ **pîlegesh**, *pee-leh´-ghesh;* of uncert. der.; a *concubine;* also (masc.) a *paramour:*— concubine, paramour.

6371. פִּימָה **pîymâh**, *pee-maw´*; prob. from an unused root mean. to *be plump; obesity:*— collops.

6372. פִּינְחָס **Pîynechâç**, *pee-nekh-aws´*; appar. from 6310 and a var. of 5175; *mouth of a serpent; Pinechas*, the name of three Isr.:— Phinehas.

6373. פִּינֹן **Pîynôn**, *pee-none´*; prob. the same as 6325; *Pinon*, an Idumæan:— Pinon.

6374. פִּיפִיָּה **pîyphîyâh**, *pee-fee-yaw´*; for 6366; an *edge* or *tooth:*— tooth, × two-edged.

6375. פִּיק **pîyq**, *peek;* from 6329; a *tottering:*— smite together.

6376. פִּישׁוֹן **Pîyshôwn**, *pee-shone´*; from 6335; *dispersive; Pishon*, a river of Eden:— Pison.

6377. פִּיתוֹן **Pîythôwn**, *pee-thone´*; prob. from the same as 6596; *expansive; Pithon*, an Isr.:— Pithon.

6378. פַּךְ **pak**, *pak;* from 6379; a *flask* (from which a liquid may *flow*):— box, vial.

6379. פָּכָה **pâkâh**, *paw-kaw´*; a prim. root; to *pour:*— run out.

6380. פֹּכֶרֶת צְבָיִים **Pôkereth Tseḇâyîym**, *po-*

keh´-reth tseb-aw-yeem´; from the act. part. (of the same form as the first word) fem. of an unused root (mean. to *entrap*) and plur. of 6643; *trap of gazelles; Pokereth-Tsebajim,* one of the "servants of Solomon":— Pochereth of Zebaim.

6381. פָּלָא **pâlâ'**, *paw-law´;* a prim. root; prop. perh. to *separate,* i.e. *distinguish* (lit. or fig.); by impl. to *be* (caus. *make) great, difficult, wonderful:—* accomplish, (arise ... too, be too) hard, hidden, things too high, (be, do, do a, shew) marvelous (-ly, -els, things, work), miracles, perform, separate, make singular, (be, great, make) wonderful (-ers, -ly, things, works), wondrous (things, works, -ly).

6382. פֶּלֶא **pele'**, *peh´-leh;* from 6381; a *miracle:—* marvellous thing, wonder (-ful, -fully).

6383. פִּלְאִי **pil'îy**, *pil-ee´;* or

פָּלִיא **pâlîy'**, *paw-lee´;* from 6381; *remarkable:—* secret, wonderful.

6384. פַּלֻּאִי **Pallû'îy**, *pal-loo-ee´;* patron. from 6396; a *Palluïte* (collect.) or desc. of Pallu:— Palluites.

פְּלָאיָה **Pᵉlâ'yâh**. See 6411.

פִּלְאֶצֶר **Pil'eçer**. See 8407.

6385. פָּלַג **pâlag**, *paw-lag´;* a prim. root; to *split* (lit. or fig.):— divide.

6386. פְּלַג **pᵉlag** (Chald.), *pel-ag´;* corresp. to 6385:— divided.

6387. פְּלַג **pᵉlag** (Chald.), *pel-ag´;* from 6386; a *half:—* dividing.

6388. פֶּלֶג **peleg**, *peh´-leg;* from 6385; a *rill* (i.e. small *channel* of water, as in irrigation):— river, stream.

6389. פֶּלֶג **Peleg**, *peh´-leg;* the same as 6388; *earthquake; Peleg,* a son of Shem:— Peleg.

6390. פְּלַגָּה **pᵉlaggâh**, *pel-ag-gaw´;* from 6385; a *runlet,* i.e. *gully:—* division, river.

6391. פְּלֻגָּה **pᵉluggâh**, *pel-oog-gaw´;* from 6385; a *section:—* division.

6392. פְּלֻגָּה **pᵉluggâh** (Chald.), *pel-oog-gaw´;* corresp. to 6391:— division.

פִּלֶגֶשׁ **pîlegesh**. See 6370.

6393. פְּלָדָה **pᵉlâdâh**, *pel-aw-daw´;* from an unused root mean. to *divide;* a *cleaver,* i.e. iron *armature* (of a chariot):— torch.

6394. פִּלְדָּשׁ **Pildâsh**, *pil-dawsh´;* of uncert. der.; *Pildash,* a relative of Abraham:— Pildash.

6395. פָּלָה **pâlâh**, *paw-law´;* a prim. root; to *distinguish* (lit. or fig.):— put a difference, show marvellous, separate, set apart, sever, make wonderfully.

6396. פַּלּוּא **Pallûw'**, *pal-loo´;* from 6395; *distinguished; Pallu,* an Isr.:— Pallu, Phallu.

6397. פְּלוֹנִי **Pᵉlôwnîy**, *pel-o-nee´;* patron. from

an unused name (from 6395) mean. *separate;* a *Pelonite* or inhab. of an unknown Palon:— Pelonite.

6398. פָּלַח **pâlach**, *paw-lakh´;* a prim. root; to *slice,* i.e. *break* open or *pierce:—* bring forth, cleave, cut, shred, strike through.

6399. פְּלַח **pᵉlach** (Chald.), *pel-akh´;* corresp. to 6398; to *serve* or worship:— minister, serve.

6400. פֶּלַח **pelach**, *peh´-lakh;* from 6398; a *slice:—* piece.

6401. פִּלְחָא **Pilchâ'**, *pil-khaw´;* from 6400; *slicing; Pilcha,* an Isr.:— Pilcha.

6402. פֻּלְחָן **pŏlchân** (Chald.), *pol-khawn´;* from 6399; *worship:—* service.

6403. פָּלַט **pâlat**, *paw-lat´;* a prim. root; to *slip* out, i.e. *escape;* caus. to *deliver:—* calve, carry away safe, deliver, (cause to) escape.

6404. פֶּלֶט **Pelet**, *peh´-let;* from 6403; *escape; Pelet,* the name of two Isr.:— Pelet. See also 1046.

פָּלֵט **pâlêt**. See 6412.

6405. פַּלֵּט **pallêt**, *pal-late´;* from 6403; *escape:—* deliverance, escape.

פְּלֵטָה **pᵉlêtâh**. See 6413.

6406. פַּלְטִי **Paltîy**, *pal-tee´;* from 6403; *delivered; Palti,* the name of two Isr.:— Palti, Phalti.

6407. פַּלְטִי **Paltîy**, *pal-tee´;* patron. from 6406; a *Paltite* or desc. of Palti:— Paltite.

6408. פִּלְטַי **Piltay**, *pil-tah´-ee;* for 6407; *Piltai,* an Isr.:— Piltai.

6409. פַּלְטִיאֵל **Paltîy'êl**, *pal-tee-ale´;* from the same as 6404 and 410; *deliverance of God; Paltiël,* the name of two Isr.:— Paltiel, Phaltiel.

6410. פְּלַטְיָה **Pᵉlatyâh**, *pel-at-yaw´;* or

פְּלַטְיָהוּ **Pᵉlatyâhûw**, *pel-at-yaw´-hoo;* from 6403 and 3050; *Jah has delivered; Pelatjah,* the name of four Isr.:— Pelatiah.

פָּלִיא **pâlîy'**. See 6383.

6411. פְּלָיָה **Pᵉlâyâh**, *pel-aw-yaw´;* or

פְּלָאיָה **Pᵉlâ'yâh**, *pel-aw-yaw´;* from 6381 and 3050; *Jah has distinguished; Pelaiah,* the name of three Isr.:— Pelaiah.

6412. פָּלִיט **pâlîyt**, *paw-leet´;* or

פָּלֵיט **pâlêyt**, *paw-late´;* or

פָּלֵט **pâlêt**, *paw-late´;* from 6403; a *refugee:—* (that have) escape (-d, -th), fugitive.

6413. פְּלֵיטָה **pᵉlêytâh**, *pel-ay-taw´;* or

פְּלֵטָה **pᵉlêtâh**, *pel-ay-taw´;* fem. of 6412; *deliverance;* concr. an *escaped* portion:— deliverance, (that is) escape (-d), remnant.

6414. פָּלִיל **pâlîyl**, *paw-leel´*; from 6419; a *magistrate:*— judge.

6415. פְּלִילָה **peliylâh**, *pel-ee-law´*; fem. of 6414; *justice:*— judgment.

6416. פְּלִילִי **peliylîy**, *pel-ee-lee´*; from 6414; *judicial:*— judge.

6417. פְּלִילִיָּה **peliylîyâh**, *pel-ee-lee-yaw´*; fem. of 6416; *judicature:*— judgment.

6418. פֶּלֶךְ **pelek**, *peh´-lek*; from an unused root mean. to *be round;* a *circuit* (i.e. *district*); also a *spindle* (as *whirled*); hence, a *crutch:*— (di-) staff, part.

6419. פָּלַל **pâlal**, *paw-lal´*; a prim. root; to *judge* (officially or mentally); by extens. to *intercede, pray:*— intreat, judge (-ment), (make) pray (-er, -ing), make supplication.

6420. פָּלָל **Pâlâl**, *paw-lawl´*; from 6419; *judge; Palal,* an Isr.:— Palal.

6421. פְּלַלְיָה **Pelalyâh**, *pel-al-yaw´*; from 6419 and 3050; *Jah has judged; Pelaljah,* an Isr.:— Pelaliah.

6422. פַּלְמוֹנִי **palmôwnîy**, *pal-mo-nee´*; prob. for 6423; a *certain* one, i.e. *so-and-so:*— certain.

פִּלְנְאֶסֶר **Pilneeçer**. See 8407.

6423. פְּלֹנִי **pelônîy**, *pel-o-nee´*; from 6395; *such* a one, i.e. a specified *person:*— such.

פִּלְנֶסֶר **Pilneçer**. See 8407.

6424. פָּלַס **pâlaç**, *paw-las´*; a prim. root; prop. to *roll* flat, i.e. *prepare* (a road); also to *revolve,* i.e. *weigh* (mentally):— make, ponder, weigh.

6425. פֶּלֶס **peleç**, *peh´-les*; from 6424; a *balance:*— scales, weight.

פֶּלֶסֶר **Peleçer**. See 8407.

6426. פָּלַץ **pâlats**, *paw-lats´*; a prim. root; prop. perh. to *rend,* i.e. (by impl.) to *quiver:*— tremble.

6427. פַּלָּצוּת **pallâtsûwth**, *pal-law-tsooth´*; from 6426; *affright:*— fearfulness, horror, trembling.

6428. פָּלַשׁ **pâlash**, *paw-lash´*; a prim. root; to *roll* (in dust):— roll (wallow) self.

6429. פְּלֶשֶׁת **Pelesheth**, *pel-eh´-sheth*; from 6428; *rolling,* i.e. *migratory; Pelesheth,* a region of Syria:— Palestina, Palestine, Philistia, Philistines.

6430. פְּלִשְׁתִּי **Pelishtîy**, *pel-ish-tee´*; patrial from 6429; a *Pelishtite* or inhab. of Pelesheth:— Philistine.

6431. פֶּלֶת **Peleth**, *peh´-leth*; from an unused root mean. to *flee; swiftness; Peleth,* the name of two Isr.:— Peleth.

6432. פְּלֵתִי **Pelêthîy**, *pel-ay-thee´*; from the same form as 6431; a *courier* (collect.) or official *messenger:*— Pelethites.

6433. פֻּם **pûm** (Chald.), *poom;* prob. for 6310; the *mouth* (lit. or fig.):— mouth.

6434. פֵּן **pên**, *pane;* from an unused root mean. to *turn;* an *angle* (of a street or wall):— corner.

6435. פֶּן **pên**, *pane;* from 6437; prop. *removal;* used only (in the constr.) adv. as conjunc. *lest:*— (lest) (peradventure), that ... not.

6436. פַּנַּג **Pannag**, *pan-nag´;* of uncert. der.; prob. *pastry:*— Pannag.

6437. פָּנָה **pânâh**, *paw-naw´;* a prim. root; to *turn;* by impl. to *face,* i.e. *appear, look,* etc.:— appear, at [even-] tide, behold, cast out, come on, × corner, dawning, empty, go away, lie, look, mark, pass away, prepare, regard, (have) respect (to), (re-) turn (aside, away, back, face, self), × right [early].

פָּנֶה **pâneh**. See 6440.

6438. פִּנָּה **pinnâh**, *pin-naw´;* fem. of 6434; an *angle;* by impl. a *pinnacle;* fig. a *chieftain:*— bulwark, chief, corner, stay, tower.

6439. פְּנוּאֵל **Penûw'êl**, *pen-oo-ale´;* or (more prop.)

פְּנִיאֵל **Penîy'êl**, *pen-ee-ale´;* from 6437 and 410; *face of God; Penuël* or *Peniël,* a place E. of Jordan; also (as Penuel) the name of two Isr.:— Peniel, Penuel.

פְּנִי **pânîy**. See 6443.

6440. פָּנִים **pânîym**, *paw-neem´;* plur. (but always as sing.) of an unused noun

[פָּנֶה **pâneh**, *paw-neh´;* from 6437]; the *face* (as the part that *turns*); used in a great variety of applications (lit. and fig.); also (with prep. pref.) as a prep. (*before,* etc.):— + accept, a-(be-)fore (-time), against, anger, × as (long as), at, + battle, + because (of), + beseech, countenance, edge, + employ, endure, + enquire, face, favour, fear of, for, forefront (-part), form (-er time, -ward), from, front, heaviness, × him (-self), + honourable, + impudent, + in, it, look [-eth] (-s), × me, + meet, × more than, mouth, of, off, (of) old (time), × on, open, + out of, over against, the partial, person, + please, presence, propect, was purposed, by reason of, + regard, right forth, + serve, × shewbread, sight, state, straight, + street, × thee, × them (-selves), through (+ -out), till, time (-s) past, (un-) to (-ward), + upon, upside [+ -stand), × ye, × you.

6441. פְּנִימָה **penîymâh**, *pen-ee´-maw;* from 6440 with directive enclitic; *faceward,* i.e. *indoors:*— (with-) in (-ner part, -ward).

6442. פְּנִימִי **penîymîy**, *pen-ee-mee´;* from 6440; *interior:*— (with-) in (-ner, -ward).

6443. פָּנִין **pânîyn**, *paw-neen´;* or

פְּנִי֫° **pânîy**, *paw-nee´;* from the same as 6434; prob. a *pearl* (as *round*):— ruby.

6444. פְּנִנָּה **Pᵉninnâh**, *pen-in-naw´;* prob. fem. from 6443 contr.; *Peninnah,* an Israelitess:— Peninnah.

6445. פָּנַק **pânaq**, *paw-nak´;* a prim. root; to *enervate:*— bring up.

6446. פַּס **paç**, *pas;* from 6461; prop. the *palm* (of the hand) or *sole* (of the foot) [comp. 6447]; by impl. (plur.) a *long and sleeved* tunic (perh. simply a *wide* one; from the orig. sense of the root, i.e. of *many breadths*):— (divers) colours.

6447. פַּס **paç** (Chald.), *pas;* from a root corresp. to 6461; the *palm* (of the hand, as being *spread* out):— part.

6448. פָּסַג **pâçag**, *paw-sag´;* a prim. root; to *cut up,* i.e. (fig.) *contemplate:*— consider.

6449. פִּסְגָּה **Piçgâh**, *pis-gaw´;* from 6448; a *cleft; Pisgah,* a mountain E. of Jordan:— Pisgah.

6450. פַּס דַּמִּים **Paç Dammîym**, *pas dammeem´;* from 6446 and the plur. of 1818; *palm* (i.e. *dell*) *of bloodshed; Pas-Dammim,* a place in Pal.:— Pas-dammim. Comp. 658.

6451. פִּסָּה **piççâh**, *pis-saw´;* from 6461; *expansion,* i.e. *abundance:*— handful.

6452. פָּסַח **pâçach**, *paw-sakh´;* a prim. root; to *hop,* i.e. (fig.) *skip* over (or *spare*); by impl. to *hesitate;* also (lit.) to *limp,* to *dance:*— halt, become lame, leap, pass over.

6453. פֶּסַח **Peçach**, *peh´-sakh;* from 6452; a *pretermission,* i.e. *exemption;* used only tech. of the Jewish *Passover* (the festival or the victim):— passover (offering).

6454. פָּסֵחַ **Pâçêach**, *paw-say´-akh;* from 6452; *limping; Paseäch,* the name of two Isr.:— Paseah, Phaseah.

6455. פִּסֵּחַ **piççêach**, *pis-say´-akh;* from 6452; *lame:*— lame.

6456. פְּסִיל **pᵉçîyl**, *pes-eel´;* from 6458; an *idol:*— carved (graven) image, quarry.

6457. פָּסַךְ **Pâçak**, *paw-sak´;* from an unused root mean. to *divide; divider; Pasak,* an Isr.:— Pasach.

6458. פָּסַל **pâçal**, *paw-sal´;* a prim. root; to *carve,* whether wood or stone:— grave, hew.

6459. פֶּסֶל **peçel**, *peh´-sel;* from 6458; an *idol:*— carved (graven) image.

6460. פְּסַנְטֵרִין **pᵉçantêrîyn** (Chald.), *pes-an-tay-reen´;* or

פְּסַנְתֵּרִין **pᵉçantêrîyn**, *pes-an-tay-reen´;* a transliteration of the Gr. ψαλτήριον *psaltēriŏn;* a *lyre:*— psaltery.

6461. פָּסַס **pâçaç**, *paw-sas´;* a prim. root; prob. to *disperse,* i.e. (intr.) *disappear:*— cease.

6462. פִּסְפָּה **Piçpâh**, *pis-paw´;* perh. from 6461; *dispersion; Pispah,* an Isr.:— Pispah.

6463. פָּעָה **pâ'âh**, *paw-aw´;* a prim. root; to *scream:*— cry.

6464. פָּעוּ **Pâ'ûw**, *paw-oo´;* or

פָּעִי **Pâ'îy**, *paw-ee´;* from 6463; *screaming; Paü* or *Paï,* a place in Edom:— Pai, Pau.

6465. פְּעוֹר **Pᵉ'ôwr**, *peh-ore´;* from 6473; a *gap; Peör,* a mountain E. of Jordan; also (for 1187) a deity worshipped there:— Peor. See also 1047.

פָּעִי **Pâ'îy**. See 6464.

6466. פָּעַל **pâ'al**, *paw-al´;* a prim. root; to *do* or *make* (systematically and habitually), espec. to *practise:*— commit, [evil-] do (-er), make (-r), ordain, work (-er), wrought.

6467. פֹּעַל **pô'al**, *po´-al;* from 6466; an *act* or *work* (concr.):— act, deed, do, getting, maker, work.

6468. פְּעֻלָּה **pᵉ'ullâh**, *peh-ool-law´;* fem. pass. part. of 6466; (abstr.) *work:*— labour, reward, wages, work.

6469. פְּעֻלְּתַי **Pᵉ'ull'thay**, *peh-ool-leh-thah´-ee;* from 6468; *laborious; Peüllethai,* an Isr.:— Peulthai.

6470. פָּעַם **pâ'am**, *paw-am´;* a prim. root; to *tap,* i.e. *beat regularly;* hence, (gen.) to *impel* or *agitate:*— move, trouble.

6471. פַּעַם **pa'am**, *pah´-am;* or (fem.)

פַּעֲמָה **pa'ămâh**, *pah-am-aw´;* from 6470; a *stroke,* lit. or fig. (in various applications, as follow):— anvil, corner, foot (-step), going, [hundred-] fold, × now, (this) + once, order, rank, step, + thrice, ([often-]), second, this, two) time (-s), twice, wheel.

6472. פַּעֲמֹן **pa'ămôn**, *pah-am-one´;* from 6471; a *bell* (as *struck*):— bell.

6473. פָּעַר **pâ'ar**, *paw-ar´;* a prim. root; to *yawn,* i.e. *open* wide (lit. or fig.):— gape, open (wide).

6474. פַּעֲרַי **Pa'ăray**, *pah-ar-ah´-ee;* from 6473; *yawning; Paarai,* an Isr.:— Paarai.

6475. פָּצָה **pâtsâh**, *paw-tsaw´;* a prim. root; to *rend,* i.e. *open* (espec. the mouth):— deliver, gape, open, rid, utter.

6476. פָּצַח **pâtsach**, *paw-tsakh´;* a prim. root; to *break* out (in joyful sound):— break (forth, forth into joy), make a loud noise.

6477. פְּצִירָה **pᵉtsîyrâh**, *pets-ee-raw´;* from 6484; *bluntness:*— + file.

6478. פָּצַל **pâtsal**, *paw-tsal´;* a prim. root; to *peel:*— pill.

6479. פְּצָלָה **pᵉtsâlâh**, *pets-aw-law´;* from 6478; a *peeling:*— strake.

6480. פָּצַם **pâtsam**, *paw-tsam´*; a prim. root; to *rend* (by earthquake):— break.

6481. פָּצַע **pâtsa'**, *paw-tsah´*; a prim. root; to *split*, i.e. *wound*:— wound.

6482. פֶּצַע **petsa'**, *peh´-tsah*; from 6481; a *wound*:— wound (-ing).

פְּצַץ **Patstsets**. See 1048.

6483. פִּצֵּץ **Pitstsêts**, *pits-tsates´*; from an unused root mean. to *dissever*; *dispersive*; *Pitstsets*, a priest:— Apses [incl. the art.].

6484. פָּצַר **pâtsar**, *paw-tsar´*; a prim. root; to *peck* at, i.e. (fig.) *stun* or *dull*:— press, urge, stubbornness.

6485. פָּקַד **pâqad**, *paw-kad´*; a prim. root; to *visit* (with friendly or hostile intent); by anal. to *oversee*, *muster*, *charge*, *care for*, *miss*, *deposit*, etc.:— appoint, × at all, avenge, bestow, (appoint to have the, give a) charge, commit, count, deliver to keep, be empty, enjoin, go see, hurt, do judgment, lack, lay up, look, make, × by any means, miss, number, officer, (make) overseer, have (the) oversight, punish, reckon, (call to) remember (-brance), set (over), sum, × surely, visit, want.

פִּקֻּד **piqqûd**. See 6490.

6486. פְּקֻדָּה **pᵉquddâh**, *pek-ood-daw´*; fem. pass. part. of 6485; *visitation* (in many senses, chiefly official):— account, (that have the) charge, custody, that which ... laid up, numbers, office (-r), ordering, oversight, + prison, reckoning, visitation.

6487. פִּקָּדוֹן **piqqâdôwn**, *pik-kaw-done´*; from 6485; a *deposit*:— that which was delivered (to keep), store.

6488. פְּקִדֻת **pᵉqîdûth**, *pek-ee-dooth´*; from 6496; *supervision*:— ward.

6489. פְּקוֹד **Pᵉqôwd**, *pek-ode´*; from 6485; *punishment*; *Pekod*, a symbol. name for Bab.:— Pekod.

6490. פִּקּוּד **piqqûwd**, *pik-kood´*; or

פִּקֻּד **piqqûd**, *pik-kood´*; from 6485; prop. *appointed*, i.e. a *mandate* (of God; plur. only, collect. for the *Law*):— commandment, precept, statute.

6491. פָּקַח **pâqach**, *paw-kakh´*; a prim. root; to *open* (the senses, espec. the eyes); fig. to be *observant*:— open.

6492. פֶּקַח **Peqach**, *peh´-kakh*; from 6491; *watch*; *Pekach*, an Isr. king:— Pekah.

6493. פִּקֵּחַ **piqqêach**, *pik-kay´-akh*; from 6491; *clear-sighted*; fig. *intelligent*:— seeing, wise.

6494. פְּקַחְיָה **Pᵉqachyâh**, *pek-akh-yaw´*; from 6491 and 3050; *Jah has observed*; *Pekachjah*, an Isr. king:— Pekahiah.

6495. פְּקַח-קוֹחַ **pᵉqach-qôwach**, *pek-akh-ko´-akh*; from 6491 redoubled; *opening* (of a dun-

geon), i.e. *jail-delivery* (fig. *salvation* from sin):— opening of the prison.

6496. פָּקִיד **pâqîyd**, *paw-keed´*; from 6485; a *superintendent* (civil, military, or religious):— which had the charge, governor, office, overseer, [that] was set.

6497. פֶּקַע **peqa'**, *peh´-kah*; from an unused root mean. to *burst*; only used as an arch. term of an ornament similar to 6498, a *semi-globe*:— knop.

6498. פַּקֻּעָה **paqqu'âh**, *pak-koo-aw´*; from the same as 6497; the *wild cucumber* (from *splitting* open to shed its seeds):— gourd.

6499. פַּר **par**, *par*; or

פָּר **pâr**, *pawr*; from 6565; a *bullock* (appar. as *breaking* forth in wild strength, or perh. as *dividing* the hoof):— (+ young) bull (-ock), calf, ox.

6500. פָּרָא **pârâ'**, *paw-raw´*; a prim. root; to *bear fruit*:— be fruitful.

6501. פֶּרֶא **pere'**, *peh´-reh*; or

פֶּרֶה **pereh** (Jer. 2:24), *peh´-reh*; from 6500 in the second. sense of *running* wild; the *onager*:— wild (ass).

פֹּרָאה **pôrâ'h**. See 6288.

6502. פִּרְאָם **Pir'âm**, *pir-awm´*; from 6501; *wildly*; *Piram*, a Canaanite:— Piram.

6503. פַּרְבָּר **Parbâr**, *par-bawr´*; or

פַּרְוָר **Parvâr**, *par-vawr´*; of for. or.; *Parbar* or *Parvar*, a quarter of Jerusalem:— Parbar, suburb.

6504. פָּרַד **pârad**, *paw-rad´*; a prim. root; to *break* through, i.e. *spread* or *separate* (oneself):— disperse, divide, be out of joint, part, scatter (abroad), separate (self), sever self, stretch, sunder.

6505. פֶּרֶד **pered**, *peh´-red*; from 6504; a *mule* (perh. from his *lonely* habits):— mule.

6506. פִּרְדָּה **pirdâh**, *pir-daw´*; fem. of 6505; a *she-mule*:— mule.

6507. פְּרֻדָה **pᵉrûdâh**, *per-oo-daw´*; fem. pass. part. of 6504; something *separated*, i.e. a *kernel*:— seed.

6508. פַּרְדֵּס **pardêç**, *par-dace´*; of for. or.; a *park*:— forest, orchard.

6509. פָּרָה **pârâh**, *paw-raw´*; a prim. root; to *bear fruit* (lit. or fig.):— bear, bring forth (fruit), (be, cause to be, make) fruitful, grow, increase.

6510. פָּרָה **pârâh**, *paw-raw´*; fem. of 6499; a *heifer*:— cow, heifer, kine.

6511. פָּרָה **Pârâh**, *paw-raw´*; the same as 6510; *Parah*, a place in Pal.:— Parah.

פֶּרֶה **pereh**. See 6501.

6512. פֵּרָה **pêrâh**, *pay-raw´*; from 6331; a

hole (as *broken,* i.e. *dug*):— + mole. Comp. 2661.

6513. פֻּרָה **Pûrâh,** *poo-raw´;* for 6288; *foliage; Purah,* an Isr.:— Phurah.

6514. פְּרוּדָא **Pᵉrûwdâ',** *per-oo-daw´;* or

פְּרִידָא **Pᵉrîydâ',** *per-ee-daw´;* from 6504; *dispersion; Peruda* or *Perida,* one of "Solomon's servants":— Perida, Peruda.

פְּרוֹזִי° **pᵉrôwzîy.** See 6521.

6515. פָּרוּחַ **Pârûwach,** *paw-roo´-akh;* pass. part. of 6524; *blossomed; Paruäch,* an Isr.:— Paruah.

6516. פַּרְוַיִם **Parvayim,** *par-vah´-yim;* of for. or.; *Parvajim,* an Oriental region:— Parvaim.

6517. פָּרוּר **pârûwr,** *paw-roor´;* pass. part. of 6565 in the sense of *spreading* out [comp. 6524]; a *skillet* (as *flat* or *deep*):— pan, pot.

פַּרְוָר **Parvâr.** See 6503.

6518. פָּרָז **pârâz,** *paw-rawz´;* from an unused root mean. to *separate,* i.e. *decide;* a *chieftain:*— village.

6519. פְּרָזָה **pᵉrâzâh,** *per-aw-zaw´;* from the same as 6518; an *open* country:— (unwalled) town (without walls), unwalled village.

6520. פְּרָזוֹן **pᵉrâzôwn,** *per-aw-zone´;* from the same as 6518; *magistracy,* i.e. *leadership* (also concr. *chieftains*):— village.

6521. פְּרָזִי **pᵉrâzîy,** *per-aw-zee´;* or

פְּרוֹזִי° **pᵉrôwzîy,** *per-o-zee´;* from 6519; a *rustic:*— village.

6522. פְּרִזִּי **Pᵉrizzîy,** *per-iz-zee´;* for 6521; *inhab. of the open country;* a *Perizzite,* one of the Canaanitish tribes:— Perizzite.

6523. פַּרְזֶל **parzel** (Chald.), *par-zel´;* corresp. to 1270; *iron:*— iron.

6524. פָּרַח **pârach,** *paw-rakh´;* a prim. root; to *break* forth as a bud, i.e. *bloom;* gen. to *spread;* spec. to *fly* (as extending the wings); fig. to *flourish:*— × abroad, × abundantly, blossom, break forth (out), bud, flourish, make fly, grow, spread, spring (up).

6525. פֶּרַח **perach,** *peh´-rakh;* from 6524; a *calyx* (nat. or artif.); gen. *bloom:*— blossom, bud, flower.

6526. פִּרְחָח **pirchach,** *pir-khakh´;* from 6524; *progeny,* i.e. a *brood:*— youth.

6527. פָּרַט **pârat,** *paw-rat´;* a prim. root; to *scatter* words, i.e. *prate* (or *hum*):— chant.

6528. פֶּרֶט **peret,** *peh´-ret;* from 6527; a *stray* or *single* berry:— grape.

6529. פְּרִי **pᵉrîy,** *per-ee´;* from 6509; *fruit* (lit. or fig.):— bough, ([first-]) fruit ([-ful]), reward.

פְּרִידָא **Pᵉrîydâ'.** See 6514.

פֻּרִים **Pûrîym.** See 6332.

6530. פְּרִיץ **pᵉrîyts,** *per-eets´;* from 6555; *vio-*

lent, i.e. a *tyrant:*— destroyer, ravenous, robber.

6531. פֶּרֶךְ **perek,** *peh´-rek;* from an unused root mean. to *break* apart; *fracture,* i.e. *severity:*— cruelty, rigour.

6532. פֹּרֶכֶת **pôreketh,** *po-reh´-keth;* fem. act. part. of the same as 6531; a *separatrix,* i.e. (the sacred) *screen:*— vail.

6533. פָּרַם **pâram,** *paw-ram´;* a prim. root; to *tear:*— rend.

6534. פַּרְמַשְׁתָּא **Parmashtâ',** *par-mash-taw´;* of Pers. or.; *Parmashta,* a son of Haman:— Parmasta.

6535. פַּרְנַךְ **Parnak,** *par-nak´;* of uncert. der.; *Parnak,* an Isr.:— Parnach.

6536. פָּרַס **pâraç,** *paw-ras´;* a prim. root; to *break* in pieces, i.e. (usually without violence) to *split, distribute:*— deal, divide, have hoofs, part, tear.

6537. פְּרַס **pᵉraç** (Chald.), *per-as´;* corresp. to 6536; to *split* up:— divide, [U-] pharsin.

6538. פֶּרֶס **pereç,** *peh´-res;* from 6536; a *claw;* also a kind of *eagle:*— claw, ossifrage.

6539. פָּרָס **Pâraç,** *paw-ras´;* of for. or.; *Paras* (i.e. *Persia*), an E. country, incl. its inhab.:— Persia, Persians.

6540. פָּרַס **Pâraç** (Chald.), *paw-ras´;* corresp. to 6539:— Persia, Persians.

6541. פַּרְסָה **parçâh,** *par-saw´;* fem. of 6538; a *claw* or split *hoof:*— claw, [cloven-] footed, hoof.

6542. פַּרְסִי **Parçîy,** *par-see´;* patrial from 6539; a *Parsite* (i.e. *Persian*), or inhab. of *Peres:*— Persian.

6543. פַּרְסִי **Parçîy** (Chald.), *par-see´;* corresp. to 6542:— Persian.

6544. פָּרַע **pâra',** *paw-rah´;* a prim. root; to *loosen;* by impl. to *expose, dismiss;* fig. *absolve, begin:*— avenge, avoid, bare, go back, let, (make) naked, set at nought, perish, refuse, uncover.

6545. פֶּרַע **pera',** *peh´-rah;* from 6544; the *hair* (as *dishevelled*):— locks.

6546. פַּרְעָה **par'âh,** *par-aw´;* fem. of 6545 (in the sense of *beginning*); *leadership* (plur. concr. *leaders*):— + avenging, revenge.

6547. פַּרְעֹה **Par'ôh,** *par-o´;* of Eg. der.; *Paroh,* a gen. title of Eg. kings:— Pharaoh.

6548. פַּרְעֹה חָפְרַע **Par'ôh Chophra',** *par-o´ khof-rah´;* of Eg. der.; *Paroh-Chophra,* an Eg. king:— Pharaoh-hophra.

6549. פַּרְעֹה נְכֹה **Par'ôh Nᵉkôh,** *par-o´ nek-o´;* or

פַּרְעֹה נְכוֹ **Par'ôh Nᵉkôw,** *par-o´ nek-o´;* of Eg. der.; *Paroh-Nekoh* (or *-Neko*), an Eg. king:— Pharaoh-necho, Pharaoh-nechoh.

6550. פַּרְעֹשׁ **par'ôsh**, *par-oshe'*; prob. from 6544 and 6211; a *flea* (as the *isolated insect*):— flea.

6551. פַּרְעֹשׁ **Par'ôsh**, *par-oshe'*; the same as 6550; *Parosh*, the name of four Isr.:— Parosh, Pharosh.

6552. פִּרְעָתֹון **Pir'âthôwn**, *pir-aw-thone'*; from 6546; *chieftaincy*; *Pirathon*, a place in Pal.:— Pirathon.

6553. פִּרְעָתֹונִי **Pir'âthôwnîy**, *pir-aw-tho-nee'*; or

פִּרְעָתֹנִי **Pir'âthônîy**, *pir-aw-tho-nee'*; patrial from 6552; a *Pirathonite* or inhab. of Pirathon:— Pirathonite.

6554. פַּרְפַּר **Parpar**, *par-par'*; prob. from 6565 in the sense of *rushing; rapid*; *Parpar*, a river of Syria:— Pharpar.

6555. פָּרַץ **pârats**, *paw-rats'*; a prim. root; to *break* out (in many applications, dir. and indirect, lit. and fig.):— × abroad, (make a) breach, break (away, down, -er, forth, in, up), burst out, come (spread) abroad, compel, disperse, grow, increase, open, press, scatter, urge.

6556. פֶּרֶץ **perets**, *peh'-rets*; from 6555; a *break* (lit. or fig.):— breach, breaking forth (in), × forth, gap.

6557. פֶּרֶץ **Perets**, *peh'-rets*; the same as 6556; *Perets*, the name of two Isr.:— Perez, Pharez.

6558. פַּרְצִי **Partsîy**, *par-tsee'*; patron. from 6557; a *Partsite* (collect.) or desc. of Perets:— Pharzites.

6559. פְּרָצִים **Pᵉrâtsîym**, *per-aw-tseem'*; plur. of 6556; *breaks*; *Peratsim*, a mountain in Pal.:— Perazim.

6560. פֶּרֶץ עֻזָּא **Perets 'Uzzâ'**, *peh'-rets ooz-zaw'*; from 6556 and 5798; *break of Uzza*; *Perets-Uzza*, a place in Pal.:— Perez-uzza.

6561. פָּרַק **pâraq**, *paw-rak'*; a prim. root; to *break* off or *crunch*; fig. to *deliver*:— break (off), deliver, redeem, rend (in pieces), tear in pieces.

6562. פְּרַק **pᵉraq** (Chald.), *per-ak'*; corresp. to 6561; to *discontinue*:— break off.

6563. פֶּרֶק **pereq**, *peh'-rek*; from 6561; *rapine*; also a *fork* (in roads):— crossway, robbery.

6564. פָּרָק **pârâq**, *paw-rawk'*; from 6561; *soup* (as full of *crumbed* meat):— broth. See also 4832.

6565. פָּרַר **pârar**, *paw-rar'*; a prim. root; to *break* up (usually fig., i.e. to *violate, frustrate*:— × any ways, break (asunder), cast off, cause to cease, × clean, defeat, disannul, disappoint, dissolve, divide, make of none effect, fail, frustrate, bring (come) to nought, × utterly, make void.

6566. פָּרַשׂ **pâras**, *paw-ras'*; a prim. root; to *break* apart, *disperse*, etc.:— break, chop in pieces, lay open, scatter, spread (abroad, forth, selves, out), stretch (forth, out).

6567. פָּרַשׁ **pârash**, *paw-rash'*; a prim. root; to *separate*, lit. (to *disperse*) or fig. (to *specify*); also (by impl.) to *wound*:— scatter, declare, distinctly, shew, sting.

6568. פְּרַשׁ **pᵉrash** (Chald.), *per-ash'*; corresp. to 6567; to *specify*:— distinctly.

6569. פֶּרֶשׁ **peresh**, *peh'-resh*; from 6567; *excrement* (as *eliminated*):— dung.

6570. פֶּרֶשׁ **Peresh**, *peh'-resh*; the same as 6569; *Peresh*, an Isr.:— Peresh.

6571. פָּרָשׁ **pârâsh**, *paw-rawsh'*; from 6567; a *steed* (as *stretched* out to a vehicle, not single nor for mounting [comp. 5483]); also (by impl.) a *driver* (in a chariot), i.e. (collect.) cavalry:— horseman.

6572. פַּרְשֶׁגֶן **parshegen**, *par-sheh'-ghen*; or

פַּתְשֶׁגֶן **pathshegen**, *path-sheh'-gen*; of for. or.; a *transcript*:— copy.

6573. פַּרְשֶׁגֶן **parshegen** (Chald.), *par-sheh'-ghen*; corresp. to 6572:— copy.

6574. פַּרְשְׁדֹן **parshᵉdôn**, *par-shed-one'*; perh. by compounding 6567 and 6504 (in the sense of *straddling*) [comp. 6576]; the *crotch* (or *anus*):— dirt.

6575. פָּרָשָׁה **pârâshâh**, *paw-raw-shaw'*; from 6567; *exposition*:— declaration, sum.

6576. פַּרְשֵׁז **parshêz**, *par-shaze'*; a root appar. formed by compounding 6567 and that of 6518 [comp. 6574]; to *expand*:— spread.

6577. פַּרְשַׁנְדָּתָא **Parshandâthâ'**, *par-shan-daw-thaw'*; of Pers. or.; *Parshandatha*, a son of Haman:— Parshandatha.

6578. פְּרָת **Pᵉrâth**, *per-awth'*; from an unused root mean. to *break* forth; *rushing*; *Perath* (i.e. *Euphrates*), a river of the East:— Euphrates.

פֹּרָת **pôrâth**. See 6509.

6579. פַּרְתַם **partam**, *par-tam'*; of Pers. or.; a *grandee*:— (most) noble, prince.

6580. פַּשׁ **pash**, *pash*; prob. from an unused root mean. to *disintegrate*; *stupidity* (as a result of *grossness* or of *degeneracy*):— extremity.

6581. פָּשָׂה **pâsâh**, *paw-saw'*; a prim. root; to *spread*:— spread.

6582. פָּשַׁח **pâshach**, *paw-shakh'*; a prim. root; to *tear* in pieces:— pull in pieces.

6583. פַּשְׁחוּר **Pashchûwr**, *pash-khoor'*; prob. from 6582; *liberation*; *Pashchur*, the name of four Isr.:— Pashur.

6584. פָּשַׁט **pâshat**, *paw-shat'*; a prim. root; to *spread* out (i.e. *deploy* in hostile array); by anal. to *strip* (i.e. *unclothe, plunder, flay*, etc.):— fall upon, flay, invade, make an invasion, pull off, put off, make a road, run upon, rush, set, spoil, spread selves (abroad), strip (off, self).

6585. פָּשַׂע **pâsa'**, *paw-sah'*; a prim. root; to *stride* (from *spreading* the legs), i.e. *rush* upon:— go.

6586. פָּשַׁע **pâsha'**, *paw-shah'*; a prim. root [rather ident. with 6585 through the idea of *expansion*]; to *break* away (from just authority), i.e. *trespass, apostatize, quarrel:*— offend, rebel, revolt, transgress (-ion, -or).

6587. פֶּשַׂע **pesa'**, *peh'-sah*; from 6585; a *stride:*— step.

6588. פֶּשַׁע **pesha'**, *peh'-shah*; from 6586; a *revolt* (national, moral, or religious):— rebellion, sin, transgression, trespass.

6589. פָּשַׂק **pâsaq**, *paw-sak'*; a prim. root; to *dispart* (the feet or lips), i.e. *become licentious:*— open (wide).

6590. פְּשַׁר **p^eshar** (Chald.), *pesh-ar'*; corresp. to 6622; to *interpret:*— make [interpretations], interpreting.

6591. פְּשַׁר **p^eshar** (Chald.), *pesh-ar'*; from 6590; an *interpretation:*— interpretation.

6592. פֵּשֶׁר **pêsher**, *pay'-sher*; corresp. to 6591:— interpretation.

6593. פִּשְׁתֶּה **pishteh**, *pish-teh'*; from the same as 6580 as in the sense of *comminuting; linen* (i.e. the thread, as *carded*):— flax, linen.

6594. פִּשְׁתָּה **pishtâh**, *pish-taw'*; fem. of 6593; *flax;* by impl. a *wick:*— flax, tow.

6595. פַּת **path**, *path;* from 6626; a *bit:*— meat, morsel, piece.

6596. פֹּת **pôth**, *pohth;* or

פֹּתָה **pothâh** (Ezek. 13:19), *po-thaw';* from an unused root mean. to *open;* a *hole,* i.e. *hinge* or the female *pudenda:*— hinge, secret part.

פְּתָאִי **p^ethâ'iy**. See 6612.

6597. פִּתְאֹם **pith'ôwm**, *pith-ome';* or

פִּתְאֹם **pith'ôm**, *pith-ome';* from 6621; *instantly:*— straightway, sudden (-ly).

6598. פַּתְבַּג **pathbag**, *pathbag';* of Pers. or.; a *dainty:*— portion (provision) of meat.

6599. פִּתְגָּם **pithgâm**, *pith-gawm';* of Pers. or.; a (judicial) *sentence:*— decree, sentence.

6600. פִּתְגָּם **pithgâm** (Chald.), *pith-gawm';* corresp. to 6599; a *word, answer, letter* or *decree:*— answer, letter, matter, word.

6601. פָּתָה **pâthâh**, *paw-thaw';* a prim. root; to *open,* i.e. *be* (caus. *make) roomy;* usually fig. (in a mental or moral sense) to *be* (caus. *make) simple* or (in a sinister way) *delude:*— allure, deceive, enlarge, entice, flatter, persuade, silly (one).

6602. פְּתוּאֵל **P^ethûw'êl**, *peth-oo-ale';* from 6601

and 410; *enlarged of God; Pethuël*, an Isr.:— Pethuel.

6603. פִּתּוּחַ **pittûwach**, *pit-too'-akh;* or

פִּתֻּחַ **pittûach**, *pit-too'-akh;* pass. part. of 6605; *sculpture* (in low or high relief or even intaglio):— carved (work) (are, en-) grave (-ing, -n).

6604. פְּתוֹר **Pethôwr**, *peth-ore';* of for. or.; *Pethor*, a place in Mesopotamia:— Pethor.

6605. פָּתַח **pâthach**, *paw-thakh';* a prim. root; to *open* wide (lit. or fig.); spec. to *loosen, begin, plow, carve:*— appear, break forth, draw (out), let go free, (en-) grave (-n), loose (self), (be, be set) open (-ing), put off, ungird, unstop, have vent.

6606. פְּתַח **p^ethach** (Chald.), *peth-akh';* corresp. to 6605; to *open:*— open.

6607. פֶּתַח **pethach**, *peh'-thakh;* from 6605; an *opening* (lit.), i.e. *door* (*gate*) or *entrance* way:— door, entering (in), entrance (-ry), gate, opening, place.

6608. פֵּתַח **pêthach**, *pay'-thakh;* from 6605; *opening* (fig.) i.e. *disclosure:*— entrance.

פָּתוּחַ **pâthûach**. See 6603.

6609. פְּתִחָה **p^ethichâh**, *peth-ee-khaw';* from 6605; something *opened,* i.e. a *drawn* sword:— drawn sword.

6610. פִּתָחוֹן **pithchôwn**, *pith-khone';* from 6605; *opening* (the act):— open (-ing).

6611. פְּתַחְיָה **P^ethachyâh**, *peth-akh-yaw';* from 6605 and 3050; *Jah has opened; Pethachjah,* the name of four Isr.:— Pethakiah.

6612. פְּתִי **p^ethîy**, *peth-ee';* or

פֶּתִי **pethîy**, *peh'-thee;* or

פְּתָאִי **p^ethâ'iy**, *peth-aw-ee';* from 6601; *silly* (i.e. *seducible*):— foolish, simple (-icity, one).

6613. פְּתַי **p^ethay** (Chald.), *peth-ah'-ee;* from a root corresp. to 6601; *open,* i.e. (as noun) *width:*— breadth.

6614. פְּתִיגִיל **p^ethîygîyl**, *peth-eeg-eel';* of uncert. der.; prob. a figured *mantle* for holidays:— stomacher.

6615. פְּתַיּוּת **p^ethayûwth**, *peth-ah-yooth';* from 6612; *silliness* (i.e. *seducibility*):— simple.

6616. פָּתִיל **pâthîyl**, *paw-theel';* from 6617; *twine:*— bound, bracelet, lace, line, ribband, thread, wire.

6617. פָּתַל **pâthal**, *paw-thal';* a prim. root; to *twine,* i.e. (lit.) to *struggle* or (fig.) *be* (morally) *tortuous:*— (shew self) froward, shew self unsavoury, wrestle.

6618. פְּתַלְתֹּל **p^ethaltôl**, *peth-al-tole';* from 6617; *tortuous* (i.e. *crafty*):— crooked.

6619. פִּתֹם **Pîthôm**, *pee-thome´*; of Eg. der.; *Pithom*, a place in Egypt:— Pithom.

6620. פֶּתֶן **pethen**, *peh´-then*; from an unused root mean. to *twist*; an *asp* (from its *contortions*):— adder.

6621. פֶּתַע **petha'**, *peh´-thah*; from an unused root mean. to *open* (the eyes); a *wink*, i.e. *moment* [comp. 6597] (used only [with or without prep.] adv. *quickly* or *unexpectedly*):— at an instant, suddenly, × very.

6622. פָּתַר **pâthar**, *paw-thar´*; a prim. root; to *open* up, i.e. (fig.) *interpret* (a dream):— interpret (-ation, -er).

6623. פִּתְרוֹן **pithrôwn**, *pith-rone´*; or

פִּתְרֹן **pithrôn**, *pith-rone´*; from 6622; *interpretation* (of a dream):— interpretation.

6624. פַּתְרוֹס **Pathrôwç**, *path-roce´*; of Eg. der.; *Pathros*, a part of Egypt:— Pathros.

6625. פַּתְרֻסִי **Pathrûçîy**, *path-roo-see´*; patrial from 6624; a *Pathrusite*, or inhab. of Pathros:— Pathrusim.

פַּתְשֶׁגֶן **pathshegen**. See 6572.

6626. פָּתַת **pâthath**, *paw-thath´*; a prim. root; to *open*, i.e. *break*:— part.

צ

6627. צֵאָה **tsâ'âh**, *tsaw-aw´*; from 3318; *issue*, i.e. (human) *excrement*:— that (which) cometh from (out).

צֹאָה **tsô'âh**. See 6675.

צֵאוֹן **tsᵉ'ôwn**. See 6629.

6628. צֶאֱל **tse'el**, *tseh´-el*; from an unused root mean. to *be slender*; the *lotus* tree:— shady tree.

6629. צֹאן **tsô'n**, *tsone*; or

צֵאוֹן **tsᵉ'ôwn** (Psa. 144:13) *tseh-one´*; from an unused root mean. to *migrate*; a collect. name for a *flock* (of sheep or goats); also fig. (of men):— (small) cattle, flock (+ -s), lamb (+ -s), sheep (l-cote, -fold, -shearer, -herds]).

6630. צַאֲנָן **Tsa'ănân**, *tsah-an-awn´*; from the same as 6629 used denom.; *sheep* pasture; *Zaanan*, a place in Pal.:— Zaanan.

6631. צֶאֱצָא **tse'étsâ'**, *tseh-ets-aw´*; from 3318; *issue*, i.e. *produce*, *children*:— that which cometh forth (out), offspring.

6632. צַב **tsâb**, *tsawb*; from an unused root mean. to *establish*; a *palanquin* or *canopy* (as a *fixture*); also a species of *lizard* (prob. as *clinging* fast):— covered, litter, tortoise.

6633. צָבָא **tsâbâ'**, *tsaw-baw´*; a prim. root; to *mass* (an army or servants):— assemble, fight, perform, muster, wait upon, war.

6634. צְבָא **tsᵉbâ'** (Chald.), *tseb-aw´*; corresp. to 6633 in the fig. sense of *summoning* one's wishes; to *please*:— will, would.

6635. צָבָא **tsâbâ'**, *tsaw-baw´*; or (fem.)

צְבָאָה **tsᵉbâ'âh**, *tseb-aw-aw´*; from 6633; a *mass* of persons (or fig. things), espec. reg. organized for war (an *army*); by impl. a *campaign*, lit. or fig. (spec. *hardship, worship*):— appointed time, (+) army, (+) battle, company, host, service, soldiers, waiting upon, war (-fare).

6636. צְבֹאִים **Tsᵉbô'iym**, *tseb-o-eem´*; or (more correctly)

צְבֹיִים **Tsᵉbîyîym**, *tseb-ee-yeem´*; or

צְבֹיִם **Tsᵉbîyîm**, *tseb-ee-yeem´*; plur. of 6643; *gazelles*; *Tseboïm* or *Tsebijim*, a place in Pal.:— Zeboiim, Zeboim.

6637. צֹבֵבָה **Tsôbêbâh**, *tso-bay-baw´*; fem. act. part. of the same as 6632; the *canopier* (with the art.); *Tsobebah*, an Israelitess:— Zobebah.

6638. צָבָה **tsâbâh**, *tsaw-baw´*; a prim. root; to *amass*, i.e. *grow turgid*; spec. to *array* an army against:— fight, swell.

6639. צָבֶה **tsâbeh**, *tsaw-beh´*; from 6638; *turgid*:— swell.

צֹבָה **Tsôbâh**. See 6678.

6640. צְבוּ **tsᵉbûw** (Chald.), *tseb-oo´*; from 6634; prop. *will*; concr. an *affair* (as a matter of *determination*):— purpose.

6641. צָבוּעַ **tsâbûwa'**, *tsaw-boo-ah´*; pass. part. of the same as 6648; *dyed* (in stripes), i.e. the *hyena:*— speckled.

6642. צָבַט **tsâbat**, *tsaw-bat´*; a prim. root; to *grasp*, i.e. *hand* out:— reach.

6643. צְבִי **tsᵉbîy**, *tseb-ee´*; from 6638 in the sense of *prominence*; *splendor* (as *conspicuous*); also a *gazelle* (as *beautiful*):— beautiful (-ty), glorious (-ry), goodly, pleasant, roe (-buck).

6644. צִבְיָא **Tsibyâ'**, *tsib-yaw´*; for 6645; *Tsibja*, an Isr.:— Zibia.

6645. צִבְיָה **Tsibyâh**, *tsib-yaw´*; for 6646; *Tsibjah*, an Israelitess:— Zibiah.

6646. צְבִיָּה **tsᵉbîyâh**, *tseb-ee-yaw´*; fem. of 6643; a *female* gazelle:— roe.

צְבֹיִים **Tsᵉbîyîym**. See 6636.

צְבֹיִם **Tsᵉbâyîm**. See 6380.

6647. צְבַע **tsᵉba'** (Chald.), *tseb-ah´*; a root corresp. to that of 6648; to *dip*:— wet.

6648. צֶבַע **tseba'**, *tseh´-bah*; from an unused root mean. to *dip* (into coloring fluid); a *dye:*— divers, colours.

6649. צִבְעוֹן **Tsib'ôwn**, *tsib-one´*; from the same as 6648; *variegated*; *Tsibon*, an Idumæan:— Zibeon.

6650. צְבֹעִים **Tsᵉbô'îym**, *tseb-o-eem´*; plur. of 6641; *hyenas*; *Tseboïm*, a place in Pal.:— Zeboim.

6651. צָבַר **tsâbar**, *tsaw-bar'*; a prim. root; to *aggregate:*— gather (together), heap (up), lay up.

6652. צִבֻּר **tsibbûr**, *tsib-boor'*; from 6551; a *pile:*— heap.

6653. צֶבֶת **tsebeth**, *tseh'-beth*; from an unused root appar. mean. to *grip*; a *lock* of stalks:— handful.

6654. צַד **tsad**, *tsad*; contr. from an unused root mean. to *sidle* off; a *side*; fig. an *adversary:*— (be-) side.

6655. צַד **tsad** (Chald.), *tsad*; corresp. to 6654; used adv. (with prep.) at or upon the *side* of:— against, concerning.

6656. צְדָא **tsᵉdâ'** (Chald.), *tsed-aw'*; from an unused root corresp. to 6658 in the sense of *intentness*; a (sinister) *design:*— true.

6657. צְדָד **Tsᵉdâd**, *tsed-awd'*; from the same as 6654; a *siding*; *Tsedad*, a place near Pal.:— Zedad.

6658. צָדָה **tsâdâh**, *tsaw-daw'*; a prim. root; to *chase*; by impl. to *desolate:*— destroy, hunt, lie in wait.

צְדָה **tsᵉdâh**. See 6720.

6659. צָדוֹק **Tsâdôwq**, *tsaw-doke'*; from 6663; *just*; *Tsadok*, the name of eight or nine Isr.:— Zadok.

6660. צְדִיָּה **tsᵉdîyâh**, *tsed-ee-yaw'*; from 6658; *design* [comp. 6656]:— lying in wait.

6661. צִדִּים **Tsiddîym**, *tsid-deem'*; plur. of 6654; *sides*; *Tsiddim* (with the art.), a place in Pal.:— Ziddim.

6662. צַדִּיק **tsaddîyq**, *tsad-deek'*; from 6663; *just:*— just, lawful, righteous (man).

צִדֹנִי° **Tsîdôniy**. See 6722.

6663. צָדַק **tsâdaq**, *tsaw-dak'*; a prim. root; to be (caus. *make*) *right* (in a moral or forensic sense):— cleanse, clear self, (be, do) just (-ice, -ify, -ify self), (be, turn to) righteous (-ness).

6664. צֶדֶק **tsedeq**, *tseh'-dek*; from 6663; the *right* (nat., mor. or legal); also (abstr.) *equity* or (fig.) *prosperity:*— × even, (× that which is altogether) just (-ice), (un-) right (-eous) (cause, -ly, -ness).

6665. צִדְקָה **tsidqâh** (Chald.), *tsid-kaw'*; corresp. to 6666; *beneficence:*— righteousness.

6666. צְדָקָה **tsᵉdâqâh**, *tsed-aw-kaw'*; from 6663; *rightness* (abstr.), subj. (*rectitude*), obj. (*justice*), mor. (*virtue*) or fig. (*prosperity*):— justice, moderately, right (-eous) (act, -ly, -ness).

6667. צִדְקִיָּה **Tsidqîyâh**, *tsid-kee-yaw'*; or

צִדְקִיָּהוּ **Tsidqîyâhûw**, *tsid-kee-yaw'-hoo*; from 6664 and 3050; *right of Jah*; *Tsidkijah*, the name of six Isr.:— Zedekiah, Zidkijah.

6668. צָהַב **tsâhab**, *tsaw-hab'*; a prim. root; to *glitter*, i.e. be *golden* in color:— × fine.

6669. צָהֹב **tsâhôb**, *tsaw-obe'*; from 6668; *golden* in color:— yellow.

6670. צָהַל **tsâhal**, *tsaw-hal'*; a prim. root; to *gleam*, i.e. (fig.) be *cheerful*; by transf. to *sound* clear (of various animal or human expressions):— bellow, cry aloud (out), lift up, neigh, rejoice, make to shine, shout.

6671. צָהַר **tsâhar**, *tsaw-har'*; a prim. root; to *glisten*; used only as denom. from 3323, to *press* out oil:— make oil.

6672. צֹהַר **tsôhar**, *tso'-har*; from 6671; a *light* (i.e. *window*): dual *double light*, i.e. *noon:*— midday, noon (-day, -tide), window.

6673. צַו **tsav**, *tsav*; or

צָו **tsâv**, *tsawv*; from 6680; an *injunction:*— commandment, precept.

6674. צוֹא **tsôw'**, *tso*; or

צֹא **tsô'**, *tso*; from an unused root mean. to *issue*; *soiled* (as if *excrementitious*):— filthy.

6675. צוֹאָה **tsôw'âh**, *tso-aw'*; or

צֹאָה **tsô'âh**, *tso-aw'*: fem. of 6674; *excrement*; gen. *dirt*; fig. *pollution:*— dung, filth (-iness). [*Marg. for* 2716.]

6676. צַוַּאר **tsavva'r** (Chald.), *tsav-var'*; corresp. to 6677:— neck.

6677. צַוָּאר **tsavvâ'r**, *tsav-vawr'*; or

צַוָּר **tsavvâr** (Neh. 3:5), *tsav-vawr'*; or

צַוָּרֹן **tsavvârôn** (Cant. 4:9), *tsav-vaw-rone'*; or (fem.)

צַוָּארָה **tsavvâ'râh** (Mic. 2:3) *tsav-vaw-raw'*; intens. from 6696 in the sense of *binding*; the back of the *neck* (as that on which burdens are *bound*):— neck.

6678. צוֹבָא **Tsôwbâ'**, *tso-baw'*; or

צוֹבָה **Tsôwbâh**, *tso-baw'*; or

צֹבָה **Tsôbâh**, *tso-baw'*; from an unused root mean. to *station*; a *station*; *Zoba* or *Zobah*, a region of Syria:— Zoba, Zobah.

6679. צוּד **tsûwd**, *tsood*; a prim. root; to *lie* alongside (i.e. in wait); by impl. to *catch* an animal (fig. men); (denom. from 6718) to *victual* (for a journey):— chase, hunt, sore, take (provision).

6680. צָוָה **tsâvâh**, *tsaw-vaw'*; a prim. root; (intens.) to *constitute, enjoin:*— appoint, (for-) bid, (give a) charge, (give a, give in, send with) command (-er, -ment), send a messenger, put, (set) in order.

6681. צָוַח **tsâvach**, *tsaw-vakh'*; a prim. root; to *screech* (exultingly):— shout.

6682. צְוָחָה **tsᵉvâchâh**, *tsev-aw-khaw'*; from 6681; a *screech* (of anguish):— cry (-ing).

6683. צוּלָה **tsûwlâh**, *tsoo-law´;* from an unused root mean. to *sink;* an *abyss* (of the sea):— deep.

6684. צוּם **tsûwm**, *tsoom;* a prim. root; to *cover* over (the mouth), i.e. to *fast:*— × at all, fast.

6685. צוֹם **tsôwm**, *tsome;* or

צֹם **tsôm**, *tsome;* from 6684; a *fast:*— fast (-ing).

6686. צוּעָר **Tsûw´âr**, *tsoo-awr´;* from 6819; *small; Tsuär,* an Isr.:— Zuar.

6687. צוּף **tsûwph**, *tsoof;* a prim. root; to *overflow:*— (make to over-) flow, swim.

6688. צוּף **tsûwph**, *tsoof;* from 6687; *comb* of honey (from *dripping*):— honeycomb.

6689. צוּף **Tsûwph**, *tsoof;* or

צוֹפִי **Tsôwphay**, *tso-fah´-ee;* or

צִיף° **Tsîyph**, *tseef;* from 6688; *honeycomb; Tsuph* or *Tsophai* or *Tsiph,* the name of an Isr. and of a place in Pal.:— Zophai, Zuph.

6690. צוֹפַח **Tsôwphach**, *tso-fakh´;* from an unused root mean. to *expand, breadth; Tsophach,* an Isr.:— Zophah.

צוֹפִי **Tsôwphay.** See 6689.

6691. צוֹפַר **Tsôwphar**, *tso-far´;* from 6852; *departing; Tsophar,* a friend of Job:— Zophar.

6692. צוּץ **tsûwts**, *tsoots;* a prim. root; to *twinkle,* i.e. *glance;* by anal. to *blossom* (fig. *flourish*):— bloom, blossom, flourish, shew self.

6693. צוּק **tsûwq**, *tsook;* a prim. root; to *compress,* i.e. (fig.) *oppress, distress:*— constrain, distress, lie sore, (op-) press (-or), straiten.

6694. צוּק **tsûwq**, *tsook;* a prim. root [rather ident. with 6693 through the idea of *narrowness* (of orifice)]; to *pour* out, i.e. (fig.) *smelt, utter:*— be molten, pour.

6695. צוֹק **tsôwq**, *tsoke;* or (fem.)

צוּקָה **tsûwqâh**, *tsoo-kaw´;* from 6693; a *strait,* i.e. (fig.) *distress:*— anguish, × troublous.

6696. צוּר **tsûwr**, *tsoor;* a prim. root; to *cramp,* i.e. *confine* (in many applications, lit. and fig., formative or hostile):— adversary, assault, beset, besiege, bind (up), cast, distress, fashion, fortify, inclose, lay siege, put up in bags.

6697. צוּר **tsûwr**, *tsoor;* or

צֻר **tsûr**, *tsoor;* from 6696; prop. a *cliff* (or sharp rock, as *compressed*); gen. a *rock* or *boulder;* fig. a *refuge;* also an *edge* (as *precipitous*):— edge, × (mighty) God (one), rock, × sharp, stone, × strength, × strong. See also 1049.

6698. צוּר **Tsûwr**, *tsoor;* the same as 6697; *rock; Tsur,* the name of a Midianite and of an Isr.:— Zur.

צוֹר **Tsôwr.** See 6865.

צַוָּר **tsavvâr.** See 6677.

6699. צוּרָה **tsûwrâh**, *tsoo-raw´;* fem. of 6697; a *rock* (Job 28:10); also a *form* (as if *pressed* out):— form, rock.

צַוָּרֹן **tsavvârôn.** See 6677.

6700. צוּרִיאֵל **Tsûwrîy´êl**, *tsoo-ree-ale´;* from 6697 and 410; *rock of God; Tsuriël,* an Isr.:— Zuriel.

6701. צוּרִישַׁדָּי **Tsûwrîyshadday**, *tsoo-ree-shad-dah´-ee;* from 6697 and 7706; *rock of* (the) *Almighty; Tsurishaddai,* an Isr.:— Zurishaddai.

6702. צוּת **tsûwth**, *tsooth;* a prim. root; to *blaze:*— burn.

6703. צַח **tsach**, *tsakh;* from 6705; *dazzling,* i.e. *sunny, bright,* (fig.) *evident:*— clear, dry, plainly, white.

צְחָא **Tsîchâ´.** See 6727.

6704. צִחֶה **tsîcheh**, *tsee-kheh´;* from an unused root mean. to *glow; parched:*— dried up.

6705. צָחַח **tsâchach**, *tsaw-khakh´;* a prim. root; to *glare,* i.e. *be dazzling* white:— be whiter.

6706. צְחִיחַ **tseˢchîyach**, *tsekh-ee´-akh;* from 6705; *glaring,* i.e. *exposed* to the bright sun:— higher place, top.

6707. צְחִיחָה **tseˢchîychâh**, *tsekh-ee-khaw´;* fem. of 6706; a *parched* region, i.e. the *desert:*— dry land.

6708. צְחִיחִי° **tseˢchîychîy**, *tsekh-ee-khee´;* from 6706; *bare* spot, i.e. in the *glaring* sun:— higher place.

6709. צַחֲנָה **tsachănâh**, *tsakh-an-aw´;* from an unused root mean. to *putrefy; stench:*— ill savour.

6710. צַחְצָחָה **tsachtsâchâh**, *tsakh-tsaw-khaw´;* from 6705; a *dry* place, i.e. *desert:*— drought.

6711. צָחַק **tsâchaq**, *tsaw-khak´;* a prim. root; to *laugh* outright (in merriment or scorn); by impl. to *sport:*— laugh, mock, play, make sport.

6712. צְחֹק **tseˢchôq**, *tsekh-oke´;* from 6711; *laughter* (in pleasure or derision):— laugh (-ed to scorn).

6713. צַחַר **tsachar**, *tsakh´-ar;* from an unused root mean. to *dazzle; sheen,* i.e. *whiteness:*— white.

6714. צֹחַר **Tsôchar**, *tso´-khar;* from the same as 6713; *whiteness; Tsochar,* the name of a Hittite and of an Isr.:— Zohar. Comp. 3328.

6715. צָחֹר **tsâchôr**, *tsaw-khore´;* from the same as 6713; *white:*— white.

6716. צִי **tsîy**, *tsee;* from 6680; a *ship* (as a *fixture*):— ship.

6717. צִיבָא **Tsîybâ'**, *tsee-baw';* from the same as 6678; *station; Tsiba*, an Isr.:— Ziba.

6718. צַיִד **tsayid**, *tsah'-yid;* from a form of 6679 and mean. the same; the *chase;* also *game* (thus taken); (gen.) *lunch* (espec. for a journey):— × catcheth, food, × hunter, (that which he took in) hunting, venison, victuals.

6719. צַיָּד **tsayâd**, *tsah'-yawd;* from the same as 6718; a *huntsman:*— hunter.

6720. צֵידָה **tsêydâh**, *tsay-daw';* or

צֵדָה **tsêdâh**, *tsay-daw';* fem. of 6718; *food:*— meat, provision, venison, victuals.

6721. צִידוֹן **Tsîydôwn**, *tsee-done';* or

צִידֹן **Tsîydôn**, *tsee-done';* from 6679 in the sense of *catching* fish; *fishery; Tsidon*, the name of a son of Canaan, and of a place in Pal.:— Sidon, Zidon.

6722. צִידֹנִי **Tsîydônîy**, *tsee-do-nee';* patrial from 6721; a *Tsidonian* or inhab. of Tsidon:— Sidonian, of Sidon, Zidonian.

6723. צִיָּה **tsîyâh**, *tsee-yaw';* from an unused root mean. to *parch; aridity;* concr. a *desert:*— barren, drought, dry (land, place), solitary place, wilderness.

6724. צִיּוֹן **tsîyôwn**, *tsee-yone';* from the same as 6723; a *desert:*— dry place.

6725. צִיּוּן **tsîyûwn**, *tsee-yoon';* from the same as 6723 in the sense of *conspicuousness* [comp. 5329]; a monumental or guiding *pillar:*— sign, title, waymark.

6726. צִיּוֹן **Tsîyôwn**, *tsee-yone';* the same (reg.) as 6725; *Tsijon* (as a permanent *capital*), a mountain of Jerusalem:— Zion.

6727. צִיחָא **Tsîychâ'**, *tsee-khaw';* or

צִחָא **Tsîchâ'**, *tsee-khaw';* as if fem. of 6704; *drought; Tsicha*, the name of two Nethinim:— Ziha.

6728. צִיִּי **tsîyîy**, *tsee-ee';* from the same as 6723; a *desert-dweller*, i.e. *nomad* or wild *beast:*— wild beast of the desert, that dwell in (inhabiting) the wilderness.

6729. צִינֹק **tsîynôq**, *tsee-noke';* from an unused root mean. to *confine;* the *pillory:*— stocks.

6730. צִיעֹר **Tsîy'ôr**, *tsee-ore';* from 6819; *small; Tsior*, a place in Pal.:— Zior.

צִיף **Tsîyph**. See 6689.

6731. צִיץ **tsîyts**, *tseets;* or

צִץ **tsîts**, *tseets;* from 6692; prop. *glistening*, i.e. a burnished *plate;* also a *flower* (as bright colored); a *wing* (as gleaming in the air):— blossom, flower, plate, wing.

6732. צִיץ **Tsîyts**, *tseets;* the same as 6731; *bloom; Tsits*, a place in Pal.:— Ziz.

6733. צִיצָה **tsîytsâh**, *tsee-tsaw';* fem. of 6731; a *flower:*— flower.

6734. צִיצִת **tsîytsîth**, *tsee-tseeth';* fem. of 6731; a *floral* or *wing*-like projection, i.e. a *fore-lock* of hair, a *tassel:*— fringe, lock.

צִיקְלַג **Tsîyqᵉlag**. See 6860.

6735. צִיר **tsîyr**, *tseer;* from 6696; a *hinge* (as pressed in turning); also a *throe* (as a physical or mental *pressure*); also a *herald* or errand-doer (as *constrained* by the principal):— ambassador, hinge, messenger, pain, pang, sorrow. Comp. 6736.

6736. צִיר **tsîyr**, *tseer;* the same as 6735; a *form* (of beauty; as if *pressed* out, i.e. *carved*); hence, an (idolatrous) *image:*— beauty, idol.

6737. צָיַר **tsâyar**, *tsaw-yar';* a denom. from 6735 in the sense of *ambassador;* to *make an errand*, i.e. *betake* oneself:— make as if ... had been ambassador.

6738. צֵל **tsêl**, *tsale;* from 6751; *shade*, whether lit. or fig.:— defence, shade (-ow).

6739. צְלָא **tsᵉlâ'** (Chald.), *tsel-aw';* prob. corresp. to 6760 in the sense of *bowing; pray:*— pray.

6740. צָלָה **tsâlâh**, *tsaw-law';* a prim. root; to *roast:*— roast.

6741. צִלָּה **Tsillâh**, *tsil-law';* fem. of 6738; *Tsillah*, an antediluvian woman:— Zillah.

6742. צְלוּל **tsᵉlûwl**, *tsel-ool';* from 6749 in the sense of *rolling;* a (round or flattened) *cake:*— cake.

6743. צָלַח **tsâlach**, *tsaw-lakh';* or

צָלֵחַ **tsâlêach**, *tsaw-lay'-akh;* a prim. root; to *push* forward, in various senses (lit. or fig., tran. or intr.):— break out, come (mightily), go over, be good, be meet, be profitable, (cause to, effect, make to, send) prosper (-ity, -ous, -ously).

6744. צְלַח **tsᵉlach** (Chald.), *tsel-akh';* corresp. to 6743; to *advance* (tran. or intr.):— promote, prosper.

6745. צֵלָחָה **tsêlâchâh**, *tsay-law-khaw';* from 6743; something *protracted* or flattened out, i.e. a *platter:*— pan.

6746. צְלֹחִית **tsᵉlôchîyth**, *tsel-o-kheeth';* from 6743; something *prolonged* or tall, i.e. a *vial* or salt-*cellar:*— cruse.

6747. צַלַּחַת **tsallachath**, *tsal-lakh'-ath;* from 6743; something *advanced* or deep, i.e. a *bowl;* fig. the *bosom:*— bosom, dish.

6748. צָלִי **tsâlîy**, *tsaw-lee';* pass. part. of 6740; *roasted:*— roast.

6749. צָלַל **tsâlal**, *tsaw-lal';* a prim. root; prop. to *tumble* down, i.e. *settle* by a waving motion:— sink. Comp. 6750, 6751.

6750. צָלַל **tsâlal**, *tsaw-lal´;* a prim. root [rather ident. with 6749 through the idea of *vibration*]; to *tinkle*, i.e. *rattle* together (as the ears in *reddening* with shame, or the teeth in *chattering* with fear):— quiver, tingle.

6751. צָלַל **tsâlal**, *tsaw-lal´;* a prim. root [rather ident. with 6749 through the idea of *hovering* over (comp. 6754)]; to *shade*, as twilight or an opaque object:— begin to be dark, shadowing.

6752. צֵלֶל **tsêlel**, *tsay´-lel;* from 6751; *shade:—* shadow.

6753. צְלֶלְפּוֹנִי **Tseᵉlelpôwnîy**, *tsel-el-po-nee´;* from 6752 and the act. part. of 6437; *shade-facing; Tselelponi*, an Israelitess:— Hazelelponi [incl. *the art.*].

6754. צֶלֶם **tselem**, *tseh´-lem;* from an unused root mean. to *shade;* a *phantom*, i.e. (fig.) *illusion, resemblance;* hence, a representative *figure*, espec. an *idol:—* image, vain shew.

6755. צְלֵם **tselem** (Chald.), *tseh´-lem;* or

צְלֵם **tseᵉlem** (Chald.), *tsel-em´;* corresp. to 6754; an idolatrous *figure:—* form, image.

6756. צַלְמוֹן **Tsalmôwn**, *tsal-mone´;* from 6754; *shady; Tsalmon*, the name of a place in Pal. and of an Isr.:— Zalmon.

6757. צַלְמָוֶת **tsalmâveth**, *tsal-maw´-veth;* from 6738 and 4194; *shade of death*, i.e. the *grave* (fig. *calamity*):— shadow of death.

6758. צַלְמֹנָה **Tsalmônâh**, *tsal-mo-naw´;* fem. of 6757; *shadiness; Tsalmonah*, a place in the Desert:— Zalmonah.

6759. צַלְמֻנָּע **Tsalmunnâ´**, *tsal-moon-naw´;* from 6738 and 4513; *shade has been denied; Tsalmunna*, a Midianite:— Zalmunna.

6760. צָלַע **tsâla´**, *tsaw-lah´;* a prim. root: prob. to *curve;* used only as denom. from 6763, to *limp* (as if *one-sided*):— halt.

6761. צֶלַע **tsela´**, *tseh´-lah;* from 6760; a *limping* or *fall* (fig.):— adversity, halt (-ing).

6762. צֶלַע **Tsela´**, *tseh´-lah;* the same as 6761; *Tsela*, a place in Pal.:— Zelah.

6763. צֵלָע **tsêlâ´**, *tsay-law´;* or (fem.)

צַלְעָה **tsal'âh**, *tsal-aw´;* from 6760; a *rib* (as *curved*), lit. (of the body) or fig. (of a door, i.e. *leaf*); hence, a *side*, lit. (of a person) or fig. (of an object or the sky, i.e. *quarter*); arch. a (espec. floor or ceiling) *timber* or *plank* (single or collect., i.e. a *flooring*):— beam, board, chamber, corner, leaf, plank, rib, side (chamber).

6764. צָלָף **Tsâlâph**, *tsaw-lawf´;* from an unused root of unknown mean.; *Tsalaph*, an Isr.:— Zalaph.

6765. צְלָפְחָד **Tseᵉlophchâd**, *tsel-of-chawd´;* from the same as 6764 and 259; *Tselophchad*, an Isr.:— Zelophehad.

6766. צֶלְצַח **Tseltsach**, *tsel-tsakh´;* from 6738 and 6703; *clear shade; Tseltsach*, a place in Pal.:— Zelzah.

6767. צְלָצַל **tseᵉlâtsal**, *tsel-aw-tsal´;* from 6750 redupl.; a *clatter*, i.e. (abstr.) *whirring* (of wings); (concr.) a *cricket;* also a *harpoon* (as *rattling*), a *cymbal* (as *clanging*):— cymbal, locust, shadowing, spear.

6768. צֶלֶק **Tseleq**, *tseh´-lek;* from an unused root mean. to *split; fissure; Tselek*, an Isr.:— Zelek.

6769. צִלְּתַי **Tsilleᵉthay**, *tsil-leth-ah´-ee;* from the fem. of 6738; *shady; Tsillethai*, the name of two Isr.:— Zilthai.

צֹם **tsôm**. See 6685.

6770. צָמֵא **tsâmê´**, *tsaw-may´;* a prim. root; to *thirst* (lit. or fig.):— (be a-, suffer) thirst (-y).

6771. צָמֵא **tsâmê´**, *tsaw-may´;* from 6770; *thirsty* (lit. or fig.):— (that) thirst (-eth, -y).

6772. צָמָא **tsâmâ´**, *tsaw-maw´;* from 6770; *thirst* (lit. or fig.):— thirst (-y).

6773. צִמְאָה **tsim'âh**, *tsim-aw´;* fem. of 6772; *thirst* (fig. of *libidinousness*):— thirst.

6774. צִמָּאוֹן **tsimmâ'ôwn**, *tsim-maw-one´;* from 6771; a *thirsty* place, i.e. *desert:—* drought, dry ground, thirsty land.

6775. צָמַד **tsâmad**, *tsaw-mad´;* a prim. root; to *link*, i.e. *gird;* fig. to *serve*, (mentally) *contrive:—* fasten, frame, join (self).

6776. צֶמֶד **tsemed**, *tseh´-med;* a *yoke* or *team* (i.e. *pair*); hence, an *acre* (i.e. day's task for a yoke of cattle to plow):— acre, couple, × together, two [asses], yoke (of oxen).

6777. צַמָּה **tsammâh**, *tsam-maw´;* from an unused root mean. to *fasten* on; a *veil:—* locks.

6778. צַמּוּק **tsammûwq**, *tsam-mook´;* from 6784; a cake of *dried* grapes:— bunch (cluster) of raisins.

6779. צָמַח **tsâmach**, *tsaw-makh´;* a prim. root; to *sprout* (tran. or intr., lit. or fig.):— bear, bring forth, (cause to, make to) bud (forth), (cause to, make to) grow (again, up), (cause to) spring (forth, up).

6780. צֶמַח **tsemach**, *tseh´-makh;* from 6779; a *sprout* (usually concr.), lit. or fig.:— branch, bud, that which (where) grew (upon), spring (-ing).

6781. צָמִיד **tsâmîyd**, *tsaw-meed´;* or

צָמִד **tsâmid**, *tsaw-meed´;* from 6775; a *bracelet* or *arm-clasp;* gen. a *lid:—* bracelet, covering.

Hebrew

6782. צַמִּים **tsammîym**, *tsam-meem´;* from the same as 6777; a *noose* (as *fastening*); fig. *destruction:*— robber.

6783. צְמִיתֻת **tsᵉmîythûth**, *tsem-ee-thooth´;* or

צְמִתֻת **tsᵉmîthûth**, *tsem-ee-thooth´;* from 6789; *excision,* i.e. *destruction;* used only (adv.) with prep. pref. to *extinction,* i.e. *perpetually:*— ever.

6784. צָמַק **tsâmaq**, *tsaw-mak´;* a prim. root; to *dry* up:— dry.

6785. צֶמֶר **tsemer**, *tseh´-mer;* from an unused root prob. mean. to *be shaggy; wool:*— wool (-len).

6786. צְמָרִי **Tsᵉmârîy**, *tsem-aw-ree´;* patrial from an unused name of a place in Pal.; a *Tsemarite* or branch of the Canaanites:— Zemarite.

6787. צְמָרַיִם **Tsᵉmârayim**, *tsem-aw-rah´-yim;* dual of 6785; *double fleece; Tsemarajim,* a place in Pal.:— Zemaraim.

6788. צַמֶּרֶת **tsammereth**, *tsam-meh´-reth;* from the same as 6785; *fleeciness,* i.e. *foliage:*— highest branch, top.

6789. צָמַת **tsâmath**, *tsaw-math´;* a prim. root; to *extirpate* (lit. or fig.):— consume, cut off, destroy, vanish.

צְמִתֻת **tsᵉmîthûth**. See 6783.

6790. צִן **Tsîn**, *tseen;* from an unused root mean. to *prick;* a *crag; Tsin,* a part of the Desert:— Zin.

6791. צֵן **tsên**, *tsane;* from an unused root mean. to *be prickly;* a *thorn;* hence, a cactus-hedge:— thorn.

6792. צֹנֵא **tsônê'**, *tso-nay´;* or

צֹנֶה **tsôneh**, *tso-neh´;* for 6629; a *flock:*— sheep.

6793. צִנָּה **tsinnâh**, *tsin-naw´;* fem. of 6791; a *hook* (as *pointed*); also a (large) *shield* (as if guarding by *prickliness*); also *cold* (as *piercing*):— buckler, cold, hook, shield, target.

6794. צִנּוֹר **tsinnûwr**, *tsin-noor´;* from an unused root perh. mean. to *be hollow;* a *culvert:*— gutter, water-spout.

6795. צָנַח **tsânach**, *tsaw-nakh´;* a prim. root; to *alight;* (tran.) to *cause to descend,* i.e. *drive* down:— fasten, light [from off].

6796. צָנִין **tsânîyn**, *tsaw-neen´;* or

צָנִן **tsânîn**, *tsaw-neen´;* from the same as 6791; a *thorn:*— thorn.

6797. צָנִיף **tsânîyph**, *tsaw-neef´;* or

צָנוֹף **tsânôwph**, *tsaw-nofe´;* or (fem.)

צָנִיפָה **tsânîyphâh**, *tsaw-nee-faw´;* from 6801; a *head-dress* (i.e. piece of cloth *wrapped* around):— diadem, hood, mitre.

6798. צָנַם **tsânam**, *tsaw-nam´;* a prim. root; to *blast* or *shrink:*— withered.

6799. צְנָן **Tsᵉnân**, *tsen-awn´;* prob. for 6630; *Tsenan,* a place near Pal.:— Zenan.

צָנִן **tsânin**. See 6796.

6800. צָנַע **tsâna'**, *tsaw-nah´;* a prim. root; to *humiliate:*— humbly, lowly.

6801. צָנַף **tsânaph**, *tsaw-naf´;* a prim. root; to *wrap,* i.e. *roll* or *dress:*— be attired, × surely, violently turn.

6802. צְנֵפָה **tsᵉnêphâh**, *tsen-ay-faw´;* from 6801; a *ball:*— × toss.

6803. צִנְצֶנֶת **tsintseneth**, *tsin-tseh´-neth;* from the same as 6791; a *vase* (prob. a vial *tapering* at the top):— pot.

6804. צַנְתָּרָה **tsantârâh**, *tsan-taw-raw´;* prob. from the same as 6794; a *tube:*— pipe.

6805. צָעַד **tsâ'ad**, *tsaw-ad´;* a prim. root; to *pace,* i.e. *step* regularly; (upward) to *mount;* (along) to *march;* (down and caus.) to *hurl:*— bring, go, march (through), run over.

6806. צַעַד **tsa'ad**, *tsah´-ad;* from 6804; a *pace* or regular *step:*— pace, step.

6807. צְעָדָה **tsᵉ'âdâh**, *tseh-aw-daw´;* fem. of 6806; a *march;* (concr.) an (ornamental) *ankle-chain:*— going, ornament of the legs.

6808. צָעָה **tsâ'âh**, *tsaw-aw´;* a prim. root; to *tip* over (for the purpose of *spilling* or *pouring* out), i.e. (fig.) *depopulate;* by impl. to *imprison* or *conquer;* (refl.) to *lie down* (for coitus, sexual intercourse):— captive exile, travelling, (cause to) wander (-er).

צָעוֹר **tsâ'ôwr**. See 6810.

6809. צָעִיף **tsâ'îyph**, *tsaw-eef´;* from an unused mean. to *wrap* over; a *veil:*— vail.

6810. צָעִיר **tsâ'îyr**, *tsaw-eer´;* or

צָעוֹר **tsâ'ôwr**, *tsaw-ore´;* from 6819; *little;* (in number) *few;* (in age) *young,* (in value) *ignoble:*— least, little (one), small (one), + young (-er, -est).

6811. צָעִיר **Tsâ'îyr**, *tsaw-eer´;* the same as 6810; *Tsair,* a place in Idumæa:— Zair.

6812. צְעִירָה **tsᵉ'îyrâh**, *tseh-ee-raw´;* fem. of 6810; *smallness* (of age), i.e. *juvenility:*— youth.

6813. צָעַן **tsâ'an**, *tsaw-an´;* a prim. root; to *load* up (beasts), i.e. *migrate:*— be taken down.

6814. צֹעַן **Tsô'an**, *tso´-an;* of Eg. der.; *Tsoän,* a place in Egypt:— Zoan.

6815. צַעֲנַנִּים **Tsa'ănannîym**, *tsah-an-an-neem´;* or (dual)

צַעֲנַיִם **Tsa'ănayim**, *tsah-an-ah´-yim;* plur. from 6813; *removals; Tsaanannim* or

Tsaanajim, a place in Pal.:— Zaannannim, Zaanaim.

6816. צַעֲצֻעַ **tsa'tsûa'**, *tsah-tsoo´-ah;* from an unused root mean. to *bestrew* with carvings; *sculpture:*— image [work].

6817. צָעַק **tsa'aq**, *tsaw-ak´;* a prim. root; to *shriek;* (by impl.) to *proclaim* (an assembly):— × at all, call together, cry (out), gather (selves) (together).

6818. צְעָקָה **tsa'âqâh**, *tsah-ak-aw´;* from 6817; a *shriek:*— cry (-ing).

6819. צָעַר **tsâ'ar**, *tsaw-ar´;* a prim. root; to *be small,* i.e. (fig.) *ignoble:*— be brought low, little one, be small.

6820. צֹעַר **Tsô'ar**, *tso´ar;* from 6819; *little; Tsoär,* a place E. of the Jordan:— Zoar.

6821. צָפַד **tsâphad**, *tsaw-fad´;* a prim. root; to *adhere:*— cleave.

6822. צָפָה **tsâphâh**, *tsaw-faw´;* a prim. root; prop. to *lean* forward, i.e. to *peer* into the distance; by impl. to *observe, await:*— behold, espy, look up (well), wait for, (keep the) watch (-man).

6823. צָפָה **tsâphâh**, *tsaw-faw´;* a prim. root [prob. rather ident. with 6822 through the idea of *expansion* in outlook, transferring to act]; to *sheet* over (espec. with metal):— cover, overlay.

6824. צָפָה **tsâphâh**, *tsaw-faw´;* from 6823; an *inundation* (as *covering*):— × swimmest.

6825. צְפוֹ **Tsᵉphôw**, *tsef-o´;* or

צְפִי **Tsᵉphîy**, *tsef-ee´;* from 6822; *observant; Tsepho* or *Tsephi,* an Idumæan:— Zephi, Zepho.

6826. צִפּוּי **tsippûwy**, *tsip-poo´-ee;* from 6823; *encasement* (with metal):— covering, overlaying.

6827. צְפוֹן **Tsᵉphôwn**, *tsef-one´;* prob. for 6837; *Tsephon,* an Isr.:— Zephon.

6828. צָפוֹן **tsâphôwn**, *tsaw-fone´;* or

צָפֹן **tsâphôn**, *tsaw-fone´;* from 6845; prop. *hidden,* i.e. *dark;* used only of the *north* as a quarter (*gloomy* and *unknown*):— north (-ern, side, -ward, wind).

6829. צָפוֹן **Tsâphôwn**, *tsaw-fone´;* the same as 6828; *boreal; Tsaphon,* a place in Pal.:— Zaphon.

6830. צְפוֹנִי **tsᵉphôwnîy**, *tsef-o-nee´;* from 6828; *northern:*— northern.

6831. צְפוֹנִי **Tsᵉphôwnîy**, *tsef-o-nee´;* patron. from 6827; a *Tsephonite,* or (collect.) desc. of Tsephon:— Zephonites.

6832. צְפוּעַ **tsᵉphûwa'**, *tsef-oo´-ah;* from the same as 6848; *excrement* (as *protruded*):— dung.

6833. צִפּוֹר **tsippôwr**, *tsip-pore´;* or

צִפֹּר **tsippôr**, *tsip-pore´;* from 6852; a little *bird* (as *hopping*):— bird, fowl, sparrow.

6834. צִפּוֹר **Tsippôwr**, *tsip-pore´;* the same as 6833; *Tsippor,* a Moabite:— Zippor.

6835. צַפַּחַת **tsappachath**, *tsap-pakh´-ath;* from an unused root mean. to *expand;* a *saucer* (as *flat*):— cruse.

6836. צְפִיָּה **tsᵉphîyâh**, *tsef-ee-yaw´;* from 6822; *watchfulness:*— watching.

6837. צִפְיוֹן **Tsiphyôwn**, *tsif-yone´;* from 6822; *watch*-tower; *Tsiphjon,* an Isr.:— Ziphion. Comp. 6827.

6838. צַפִּיחִת **tsappîychîth**, *tsap-pee-kheeth´;* from the same as 6835; a flat thin *cake:*— wafer.

6839. צֹפִים **Tsôphîym**, *tso-feem´;* plur. of act. part. of 6822; *watchers; Tsophim,* a place E. of the Jordan:— Zophim.

6840. צָפִין **tsâphîyn**, *tsaw-feen´;* from 6845; a *treasure* (as *hidden*):— hid.

6841. צְפִיר **tsᵉphîyr** (Chald.), *tsef-eer´;* corresp. to 6842; a he-*goat:*— he [goat].

6842. צָפִיר **tsâphîyr**, *tsaw-feer´;* from 6852; a male *goat* (as *prancing*):— (he) goat.

6843. צְפִירָה **tsᵉphîyrâh**, *tsef-ee-raw´;* fem. formed like 6842; a *crown* (as *encircling* the head); also a *turn* of affairs (i.e. *mishap*):— diadem, morning.

6844. צָפִית **tsâphîyth**, *tsaw-feeth´;* from 6822; a *sentry:*— watchtower.

6845. צָפַן **tsâphan**, *tsaw-fan´;* a prim. root; to *hide* (by *covering* over); by impl. to *hoard* or *reserve;* fig. to *deny;* spec. (favorably) to *protect,* (unfavorably) to *lurk:*— esteem, hide (-den one, self), lay up, lurk (be set) privily, (keep) secret (-ly, place).

צָפֹן **tsâphôn**. See 6828.

6846. צְפַנְיָה **Tsᵉphanyâh**, *tsef-an-yaw´;* or

צְפַנְיָהוּ **Tsᵉphanyâhûw**, *tsef-an-yaw´-hoo;* from 6845 and 3050; *Jah has secreted; Tsephanjah,* the name of four Isr.:— Zephaniah.

6847. צָפְנַת פַּעְנֵחַ **Tsophnath Pa'nêach**, *tsof-nath´ pah-nay´-akh;* of Eg. der.; *Tsophnath-Paneäch,* Joseph's Eg. name:— Zaphnath-paaneah.

6848. צֶפַע **tsepha'**, *tseh´-fah;* or

צִפְעֹנִי **tsiph'ônîy**, *tsif-o-nee´;* from an unused root mean. to *extrude;* a *viper* (as *thrusting* out the tongue, i.e. *hissing*):— adder, cockatrice.

6849. צְפִעָה **tsᵉphî'âh**, *tsef-ee-aw´;* fem. from the same as 6848; an *outcast* thing:— issue.

צִפְעֹנִי **tsiph'ônîy**. See 6848.

6850. צָפַף **tsâphaph**, *tsaw-faf´;* a prim. root;

to *coo* or *chirp* (as a bird):— chatter, peep, whisper.

6851. צַפְצָפָה **tsaphtsâphâh**, *tsaf-tsaw-faw´*; from 6687; a *willow* (as growing in *overflowed* places):— willow tree.

6852. צָפַר **tsâphar**, *tsaw-far´*; a prim. root; to *skip* about, i.e. *return:*— depart early.

6853. צְפַר **tsᵉphar** (Chald.), *tsef-ar´*; corresp. to 6833; a *bird:*— bird.

צִפֹּר **tsippôr**. See 6833.

6854. צְפַרְדֵּעַ **tsᵉphardêa'**, *tsef-ar-day´-ah;* from 6852 and a word elsewhere unused mean. a *swamp;* a *marsh-leaper,* i.e. *frog:*— frog.

6855. צִפֹּרָה **Tsippôrâh**, *tsip-po-raw´;* fem. of 6833; *bird; Tsipporah,* Moses' wife:— Zipporah.

6856. צִפֹּרֶן **tsippôren**, *tsip-po´-ren;* from 6852 (in the denom. sense [from 6833] of *scratching*); prop. a *claw,* i.e. (human) *nail;* also the *point* of a style (or pen, tipped with adamant):— nail, point.

6857. צְפַת **Tsᵉphath**, *tsef-ath´;* from 6822; *watch*-tower; *Tsephath,* a place in Pal.:— Zephath.

6858. צֶפֶת **tsepheth**, *tseh´-feth;* from an unused root mean. to *encircle;* a *capital* of a column:— chapiter.

6859. צְפָתָה **Tsᵉphâthâh**, *tsef-aw´-thaw;* the same as 6857; *Tsephathah,* a place in Pal.:— Zephathah.

צִיץ **tsîts**. See 6732.

6860. צִקְלַג **Tsiqlâg**, *tsik-lag´;* or

צִיקְלַג **Tsîyqᵉlag** (1 Chron. 12:1, 20), *tsee-kel-ag´;* of uncert. der.: *Tsiklag* or *Tsikelag,* a place in Pal.:— Ziklag.

6861. צִקְלֹן **tsiqlôn**, *tsik-lone´;* from an unused root mean. to *wind;* a *sack* (as *tied* at the mouth):— husk.

6862. צַר **tsar**, *tsar;* or

צָר **tsâr**, *tsawr;* from 6887; *narrow;* (as a noun) a *tight* place (usually fig., i.e. *trouble*); also a *pebble* (as in 6864); (tran.) an *opponent* (as *crowding*):— adversary, afflicted (-tion), anguish, close, distress, enemy, flint, foe, narrow, small, sorrow, strait, tribulation, trouble.

6863. צֵר **Tsêr**, *tsare;* from 6887; *rock; Tser,* a place in Pal.:— Zer.

6864. צֹר **tsôr**, *tsore;* from 6696; a *stone* (as if *pressed* hard or to a point); (by impl. of use) a *knife:*— flint, sharp stone.

6865. צֹר **Tsôr**, *tsore;* or

צוֹר **Tsôwr**, *tsore;* the same as 6864; a *rock; Tsor,* a place in Pal.:— Tyre, Tyrus.

צֻר **tsûr**. See 6697.

6866. צָרַב **tsârab´**; a prim. root; to *burn:*— burn.

6867. צָרֶבֶת **tsârebeth**, *tsaw-reh´-beth;* from 6686; *conflagration* (of fire or disease):— burning, inflammation.

6868. צְרֵדָה **Tsᵉrêdâh**, *tser-ay-daw´;* or

צְרֵדָתָה **Tsᵉrêdâthâh**, *tser-ay-daw´-thaw;* appar. from an unused root mean. to *pierce; puncture; Tseredah,* a place in Pal.:— Zereda, Zeredathah.

6869. צָרָה **tsârâh**, *tsaw-raw´;* fem. of 6862; *tightness* (i.e. fig. *trouble*); tran. a female *rival:*— adversary, adversity, affliction, anguish, distress, tribulation, trouble.

6870. צְרוּיָה **Tsᵉrûwyâh**, *tser-oo-yaw´;* fem. pass. part. from the same as 6875; *wounded; Tserujah,* an Israelitess:— Zeruiah.

6871. צְרוּעָה **Tsᵉrûw'âh**, *tser-oo-aw´;* fem. pass. part. of 6879; *leprous; Tseruäh,* an Israelitess:— Zeruah.

6872. צְרוֹר **tsᵉrôwr**, *tser-ore´;* or (short.)

צְרֹר **tsᵉrôr**, *tser-ore´;* from 6887; a *parcel* (as *packed* up); also a *kernel* or *particle* (as if a *package*):— bag, × bendeth, bundle, least grain, small stone.

6873. צָרַח **tsârach**, *tsaw-rakh´;* a prim. root; to *be clear* (in tone, i.e. *shrill*), i.e. to *whoop:*— cry, roar.

6874. צְרִי **Tsᵉrîy**, *tser-ee´;* the same as 6875; *Tseri,* an Isr.:— Zeri. Comp. 3340.

6875. צְרִי **tsᵉrîy**, *tser-ee´;* or

צֳרִי **tsŏrîy**, *tsor-ee´;* from an unused root mean. to *crack* [as by *pressure*], hence, to *leak; distillation,* i.e. *balsam:*— balm.

6876. צֹרִי **Tsôrîy**, *tso-ree´;* patrial from 6865; a *Tsorite* or inhab. of Tsor (i.e. *Syrian*):— (man) of Tyre.

6877. צְרִיחַ **tsᵉrîyach**, *tser-ee´-akh;* from 6873 in the sense of *clearness* of vision; a *citadel:*— high place, hold.

6878. צֹרֶךְ **tsôrek**, *tso´-rek;* from an unused root mean. to *need; need:*— need.

6879. צָרַע **tsâra'**, *tsaw-rah´;* a prim. root; to *scourge,* i.e. (intr. and fig.) to *be stricken with leprosy:*— leper, leprous.

6880. צִרְעָה **tsir'âh**, *tsir-aw´;* from 6879; a *wasp* (as *stinging*):— hornet.

6881. צָרְעָה **Tsor'âh**, *tsor-aw´;* appar. another form for 6880; *Tsorah,* a place in Pal.:— Zareah, Zorah, Zoreah.

6882. צָרְעִי **Tsor'îy**, *tsor-ee´;* or

צָרְעָתִי **Tsor'âthîy**, *tsor-aw-thee´;* patrial from 6881; a *Tsorite* or *Tsorathite,* i.e. inhab. of Tsorah:— Zorites, Zareathites, Zorathites.

Hebrew

6883. צָרַעַת **tsâra'ath,** *tsaw-rah´-ath;* from 6879; *leprosy:*— leprosy.

6884. צָרַף **tsâraph,** *tsaw-raf´;* a prim. root; to *fuse* (metal), i.e. *refine* (lit. or fig.):— cast, (re-) fine (-er), founder, goldsmith, melt, pure, purge away, try.

6885. צֹרְפִי **Tsôrephîy,** *tso-ref-ee´;* from 6884; *refiner; Tsorephi* (with the art.), an Isr.:— goldsmith's.

6886. צָרְפַת **Tsârephath,** *tsaq-ref-ath´;* from 6884; *refinement; Tsarephath,* a place in Pal.:— Zarephath.

6887. צָרַר **tsârar,** *tsaw-rar´;* a prim. root; to *cramp,* lit. or fig., tran. or intr. (as follows):— adversary, (be in) afflict (-ion), beseige, bind (up), (be in, bring) distress, enemy, narrower, oppress, pangs, shut up, be in a strait (trouble), vex.

6888. צְרֵרָה **Tsۥrêrâh,** *tser-ay-raw´;* appar. by err. transc. for 6868; *Tsererah* for *Tseredah:*— Zererath.

6889. צֶרֶת **Tsereth,** *tseh´-reth;* perh. from 6671; *splendor; Tsereth,* an Isr.:— Zereth.

6890. צֶרֶת הַשַּׁחַר **Tsereth hash-Shachar,** *tseh´-reth hash-shakh´-ar;* from the same as 6889 and 7837 with the art. interposed; *splendor of the dawn; Tsereth-hash-Shachar,* a place in Pal.:— Zareth-shahar.

6891. צָרְתָן **Tsârethân,** *tsaw-reth-awn´;* perh. for 6868; *Tsarethan,* a place in Pal.:— Zarthan.

ק

6892. קֵא **qê',** *kay;* or

קִיא **qîy',** *kee;* from 6958; *vomit:*— vomit.

6893. קָאַת **qâ'ath,** *kaw-ath´;* from 6958; prob. the *pelican* (from *vomiting*):— cormorant.

6894. קַב **qab,** *kab;* from 6895; a *hollow,* i.e. vessel used as a (dry) *measure:*— cab.

6895. קָבַב **qâbab,** *kaw-bab´;* a prim. root; to *scoop* out, i.e. (fig.) to *malign* or *execrate* (i.e. *stab* with words):— × at all, curse.

6896. קֵבָה **qêbâh,** *kay-baw´;* from 6895; the *paunch* (as a *cavity*) or first stomach of ruminants:— maw.

6897. קֹבָה **qôbâh,** *ko´-baw;* from 6895; the *abdomen* (as a cavity):— belly.

6898. קֻבָּה **qubbâh,** *koob-baw´;* from 6895; a *pavilion* (as a domed *cavity*):— tent.

6899. קִבּוּץ **qibbûwts,** *kib-boots´;* from 6908; a *throng:*— company.

6900. קְבוּרָה **qۥbûwrâh,** *keb-oo-raw´;* or

קְבֻרָה **qۥbûrâh,** *keb-oo-raw´;* fem. pass. part. of 6912; *sepulture;* (concr.) a *sepulchre:*— burial, burying place, grave, sepulchre.

6901. קָבַל **qâbal,** *kaw-bal´;* a prim. root; to *admit,* i.e. *take* (lit. or fig.):— choose, (take) hold, receive, (under-) take.

6902. קְבַל **qۥbal** (Chald.), *keb-al´;* corresp. to 6901; to *acquire:*— receive, take.

6903. קְבֵל **qۥbêl** (Chald.), *keb-ale´;* or

קֳבֵל **qôbêl** (Chald.), *kob-ale´;* (corresp. to 6905; (adv.) *in front of;* usually (with other particles) *on account of, so as, since, hence:*— + according to, + as, + because, before, + for this cause, + forasmuch as, + by this means, over against, by reason of, + that, + therefore, + though, + wherefore.

6904. קֹבֵל **qôbel,** *ko´-bel;* from 6901 in the sense of *confronting* (as standing *opposite* in order to receive); a *battering*-ram:— war.

6905. קָבָל **qâbâl,** *kaw-bawl´;* from 6901 in the sense of *opposite* [see 6904]; the *presence,* i.e. (adv.) *in front of:*— before.

6906. קָבַע **qâba',** *kaw-bah´;* a prim. root; to *cover,* i.e. (fig.) *defraud:*— rob, spoil.

6907. קֻבַּעַת **qubba'ath,** *koob-bah´-ath;* from 6906; a *goblet* (as deep like a *cover*):— dregs.

6908. קָבַץ **qâbats,** *kaw-bats´;* a prim. root; to *grasp,* i.e. *collect:*— assemble (selves), gather (bring) (together, selves together, up), heap, resort, × surely, take up.

6909. קַבְצְאֵל **Qabtsۥ'êl,** *kab-tseh-ale´;* from 6908 and 410; *God has gathered; Kabtseël,* a place in Pal.:— Kabzeel. Comp. 3343.

6910. קְבֻצָה **qۥbûtsâh,** *keb-oo-tsaw´;* fem. pass. part. of 6908; a *hoard:*— × gather.

6911. קִבְצַיִם **Qibtsayim,** *kib-tsah´-yim;* dual from 6908; a *double heap; Kibtsajim,* a place in Pal.:— Kibzaim.

6912. קָבַר **qâbar,** *kaw-bar´;* a prim. root; to *inter:*— × in any wise, bury (-ier).

6913. קֶבֶר **qeber,** *keh´-ber;* or (fem.)

קִבְרָה **qibrâh,** *kib-raw´;* from 6912; a *sepulchre:*— burying place, grave, sepulchre.

קְבֻרָה **qۥbûrâh.** See 6900.

6914. קִבְרוֹת הַתַּאֲוָה **Qibrôwth hat-Ta'ăvâh,** *kib-rôth´ hat-tah-av-aw´;* from the fem. plur. of 6913 and 8378 with the art. interposed; *graves of the longing; Kibroth-hat-Taavh,* a place in the Desert:— Kibroth-hattaavah.

6915. קָדַד **qâdad,** *kaw-dad´;* a prim. root; to *shrivel* up, i.e. *contract* or *bend* the body (or neck) in deference:— bow (down) (the) head, stoop.

6916. קִדָּה **qiddâh,** *kid-daw´;* from 6915; *cassia* bark (as in *shrivelled* rolls):— cassia.

6917. קָדוּם **qâdûwm**, *kaw-doom´*; pass. part. of 6923; a *pristine* hero:— ancient.

6918. קָדוֹשׁ **qâdôwsh**, *kaw-doshe´*; or

קָדֹשׁ **qâdôsh**, *kaw-doshe´*; from 6942; *sacred* (cerem. or mor.); (as noun) *God* (by eminence), an *angel*, a *saint*, a *sanctuary:*— holy (One), saint.

6919. קָדַח **qâdach**, *kaw-dakh´*; a prim. root; to *inflame:*— burn, kindle.

6920. קַדַּחַת **qaddachath**, *kad-dakh´-ath*; from 6919; *inflammation*, i.e. febrile disease:— burning ague, fever.

6921. קָדִים **qâdîym**, *kaw-deem´*; or

קָדִם **qâdim**, *kaw-deem´*; from 6923; the *fore* or front part; hence, (by orientation) the *East* (often adv. *eastward*, for brevity the *east wind*):— east (-ward, wind).

6922. קַדִּישׁ **qaddîysh** (Chald.), *kad-deesh´*; corresp. to 6918:— holy (One), saint.

6923. קָדַם **qâdam**, *kaw-dam´*; a prim. root; to *project* (one self), i.e. *precede*; hence, to *anticipate, hasten, meet* (usually for help):— come (go, [flee]) before, + disappoint, meet, prevent.

6924. קֶדֶם **qedem**, *keh´-dem*; or

קֵדְמָה **qêdmâh**, *kayd´-maw*; from 6923; the *front*, of place (absolutely, the *fore part*, rel. the *East*) or time (*antiquity*); often used adv. (*before, anciently, eastward*):— aforetime, ancient (time), before, east (end, part, side, -ward), eternal, × ever (-lasting), forward, old, past. Comp. 6926.

6925. קֳדָם **qŏdâm** (Chald.), *kod-awm´*; or

קְדָם **qedâm** (Chald.) (Dan. 7:13), *ked-awm´*; corresp. to 6924; *before:*— before, × from, × I (thought), × me, + of, × it pleased, presence.

קָדִים **qâdîm**. See 6921.

6926. קִדְמָה **qidmâh**, *kid-maw´*; fem. of 6924; the *forward* part (or rel.) *East* (often adv. *on* (the) *east* or *in front*):— east (-ward).

6927. קַדְמָה **qadmâh**, *kad-maw´*; from 6923; *priority* (in time); also used adv. (*before*):— afore, antiquity, former (old) estate.

6928. קַדְמָה **qadmâh** (Chald.), *kad-maw´*; corresp. to 6927; *former* time:— afore [-time], ago.

קֵדְמָה **qêdmâh**. See 6924.

6929. קֵדְמָה **Qêdemâh**, *kayd´-maw*; from 6923; *precedence; Kedemah*, a son of Ishmael:— Kedemah.

6930. קַדְמוֹן **qadmôwn**, *kad-mone´*; from 6923; *eastern:*— east.

6931. קַדְמוֹנִי **qadmôwnîy**, *kad-mo-nee´*; or

קַדְמֹנִי **qadmŏnîy**, *kad-mo-nee´*; from 6930; (of time) *anterior* or (of place) *oriental:*— ancient, they that went before, east, (thing of) old.

6932. קְדֵמוֹת **Qedêmôwth**, *ked-ay-mothe´*; from 6923; *beginnings; Kedemoth*, a place in eastern Pal.:— Kedemoth.

6933. קַדְמַי **qadmay** (Chald.), *kad-mah´-ee*; from a root corresp. to 6923; *first:*— first.

6934. קַדְמִיאֵל **Qadmîy'êl**, *kad-mee-ale´*; from 6924 and 410; *presence of God; Kadmiël*, the name of three Isr.:— Kadmiel.

קַדְמֹנִי **qadmônîy**. See 6931.

6935. קַדְמֹנִי **Qadmônîy**, *kad-mo-nee´*; the same as 6931; *ancient*, i.e. aboriginal; *Kadmonite* (collect.), the name of a tribe in Pal.:— Kadmonites.

6936. קָדְקֹד **qodqôd**, *kod-kode´*; from 6915; the *crown* of the head (as the part most bowed):— crown (of the head), pate, scalp, top of the head.

6937. קָדַר **qâdar**, *kaw-dar´*; a prim. root; to *be ashy*, i.e. *dark*-colored; by impl. to *mourn* (in sackcloth or sordid garments):— be black (-ish), be (make) dark (-en), × heavily, (cause to) mourn.

6938. קֵדָר **Qêdâr**, *kay-dawr´*; from 6937; *dusky* (of the skin or the tent); *Kedar*, a son of Ishmael; also (collect.) *bedawin* (as his desc. or representatives):— Kedar.

6939. קִדְרוֹן **Qidrôwn**, *kid-rone´*; from 6937; *dusky* place; *Kidron*, a brook near Jerusalem:— Kidron.

6940. קַדְרוּת **qadrûwth**, *kad-rooth´*; from 6937; *duskiness:*— blackness.

6941. קְדֹרַנִּית **qedôrannîyth**, *ked-o-ran-neeth´*; adv. from 6937; *blackish ones* (i.e. *in sackcloth*); used adv. in *mourning* weeds:— mournfully.

6942. קָדַשׁ **qâdâsh**, *kaw-dash´*; a prim. root; to *be* (caus. *make, pronounce* or *observe* as) *clean* (cerem. or mor.):— appoint, bid, consecrate, dedicate, defile, hallow, (be, keep) holy (-er, place), keep, prepare, proclaim, purify, sanctify (-ied one, self), × wholly.

6943. קֶדֶשׁ **Qedesh**, *keh´-desh*; from 6942; a *sanctum; Kedesh*, the name of four places in Pal.:— Kedesh.

6944. קֹדֶשׁ **qôdesh**, *ko´-desh*; from 6942; a *sacred* place or thing; rarely abstr. *sanctity:*— consecrated (thing), dedicated (thing), hallowed (thing), holiness, (× most) holy (× day, portion, thing), saint, sanctuary.

6945. קָדֵשׁ **qâdêsh**, *kaw-dashe´*; from 6942; a (quasi) *sacred* person, i.e. (tech.) a (male) *devotee* (by prostitution) to licentious idolatry:— sodomite, unclean.

6946. קָדֵשׁ **Qâdêsh**, *kaw-dashe´*; the same

as 6945; *sanctuary; Kadesh,* a place in the Desert:— Kadesh. Comp. 6947.

קָדֹשׁ **qâdôsh.** See 6918.

6947. קָדֵשׁ בַּרְנֵעַ **Qâdêsh Barnêa',** *kaw-dashe' bar-nay'-ah;* from the same as 6946 and an otherwise unused word (appar. compounded of a correspondent to 1251 and a der. of 5128) mean. *desert of a fugitive; Kadesh of* (the) *Wilderness of Wandering; Kadesh-Barneä,* a place in the Desert:— Kadesh-barnea.

6948. קְדֵשָׁה **qᵉdêshâh,** *ked-ay-shaw';* fem. of 6945; a female *devotee* (i.e. *prostitute*):— harlot, whore.

6949. קָהָה **qâhâh,** *kaw-haw';* a prim. root; to *be dull:*— be set on edge, be blunt.

6950. קָהַל **qâhal,** *kaw-hal';* a prim. root; to *convoke:*— assemble (selves) (together), gather (selves) (together).

6951. קָהָל **qâhâl,** *kaw-hawl';* from 6950; *assemblage* (usually concr.):— assembly, company, congregation, multitude.

6952. קְהִלָּה **qᵉhillâh,** *keh-hil-law';* from 6950; an *assemblage:*— assembly, congregation.

6953. קֹהֶלֶת **qôheleth,** *ko-heh'-leth;* fem. of act. part. from 6950; a (female) *assembler* (i.e. *lecturer*): abstr. *preaching* (used as a "nom de plume", *Koheleth*):— preacher.

6954. קְהֵלָתָה **Qᵉhêlâthâh,** *keh-hay-law'-thaw;* from 6950; *convocation; Kehelathah,* a place in the Desert:— Kehelathah.

6955. קְהָת **Qᵉhâth,** *keh-hawth';* from an unused root mean. to *ally* oneself; *allied; Kehath,* an Isr.:— Kohath.

6956. קְהָתִי **Qᵉhâthîy,** *ko-haw-thee';* patron. from 6955; a *Kohathite* (collect.) or desc. of Kehath:— Kohathites.

6957. קַו **qav,** *kav;* or

קָו **qâv,** *kawv;* from 6960 [comp. 6961]; a *cord* (as *connecting*), espec. for measuring; fig. a *rule;* also a *rim,* a musical *string* or *accord:*— line. Comp. 6978.

6958. קוֹא **qôw',** *ko;* or

קָיָה **qâyâh** (Jer. 25:27), *kaw-yaw';* a prim. root; to *vomit:*— spue (out), vomit (out, up, up again).

6959. קוֹבַע **qôwba',** *ko'-bah or ko-bah';* a form collat. to 3553; a *helmet:*— helmet.

6960. קָוָה **qâvâh,** *kaw-vaw';* a prim. root; to *bind* together (perh. by *twisting*), i.e. *collect;* (fig.) to *expect:*— gather (together), look, patiently, tarry, wait (for, on, upon).

6961. קָוֶה° **qâveh,** *kaw-veh';* from 6960; a (measuring) *cord* (as if for *binding*):— line.

קֹוֵחַ **qôwach.** See 6495.

6962. קוּט **qûwṭ,** *koot;* a prim. root; prop. to *cut off,* i.e. (fig.) *detest:*— be grieved, loathe self.

6963. קוֹל **qôwl,** *kole;* or

קֹל **qôl,** *kole;* from an unused root mean. to *call* aloud; a *voice* or *sound:*— + aloud, bleating, crackling, cry (+ out), fame, lightness, lowing, noise, + hold peace, [proc-] claim, proclamation, + sing, sound, + spark, thunder (-ing), voice, + yell.

6964. קוֹלָיָה **Qôwlâyâh,** *ko-law-yaw';* from 6963 and 3050; *voice of Jah; Kolajah,* the name of two Isr.:— Kolaiah.

6965. קוּם **qûwm,** *koom;* a prim. root; to *rise* (in various applications, lit., fig., intens. and caus.):— abide, accomplish, × be clearer, confirm, continue, decree, × be dim, endure, × enemy, enjoin, get up, make good, help, hold, (help to) lift up (again), make, × but newly, ordain, perform, pitch, raise (up), rear (up), remain, (a-) rise (up) (again, against), rouse up, set (up), (e-) stablish, (make to) stand (up), stir up, strengthen, succeed, (as-, make) sure (-ly), (be) up (-hold, -rising).

6966. קוּם **qûwm** (Chald.), *koom;* corresp. to 6965:— appoint, establish, make, raise up self, (a-) rise (up), (make to) stand, set (up).

6967. קוֹמָה **qôwmâh,** *ko-maw';* from 6965; *height:*— × along, height, high, stature, tall.

6968. קוֹמְמִיּוּת **qôwmᵉmîyûwth,** *ko-mem-ee-yooth';* from 6965; *elevation,* i.e. (adv.) *erectly* (fig.):— upright.

6969. קוּן **qûwn,** *koon;* a prim. root; to *strike* a musical note, i.e. *chant* or *wail* (at a funeral):— lament, mourning woman.

6970. קוֹעַ **Qôwa',** *ko'-ah;* prob. from 6972 in the orig. sense of *cutting* off; *curtailment; Koä,* a region of Bab.:— Koa.

6971. קוֹף **qôwph,** *kofe;* or

קֹף **qôph,** *kofe;* prob. of for. or.; a *monkey:*— ape.

6972. קוּץ **qûwts,** *koots;* a prim. root; to *clip* off; used only as denom. from 7019; to *spend the harvest* season:— summer.

6973. קוּץ **qûwts,** *koots;* a prim. root [rather ident. with 6972 through the idea of *severing* oneself from (comp. 6962)]; to *be* (caus. *make*) *disgusted* or *anxious:*— abhor, be distressed, be grieved, loathe, vex, be weary.

6974. קוּץ **qûwts,** *koots;* a prim. root [rather ident. with 6972 through the idea of *abruptness* in starting up from sleep (comp. 3364)]; to *awake* (lit. or fig.):— arise, (be) (a-) wake, watch.

6975. קוֹץ **qôwts,** *kotse;* or

קֹץ **qôts,** *kotse;* from 6972 (in the sense of *pricking*); a *thorn:*— thorn.

6976. קוֹץ **Qôwts,** *kotse;* the same as 6975;

Kots, the name of two Isr.:— Koz, Hakkoz [incl. *the art.*].

6977. קְוֻצָּה **qᵉvutstsâh**, *kev-oots-tsaw´*; fem. pass. part. of 6972 in its orig. sense; a *forelock* (as *shorn*):— lock.

6978. קַו־קַו **qav-qav**, *kav-kav´*; from 6957 (in the sense of a *fastening*); *stalwart*:— × meted out.

6979. קוּר **qûwr**, *koor*; a prim. root; to *trench*; by impl. to *throw forth*; also (denom. from 7023) to *wall up*, whether lit. (to *build* a wall) or fig. (to *estop*):— break down, cast out, destroy, dig.

6980. קוּר **qûwr**, *koor*; from 6979; (only plur.) *trenches*, i.e. a *web* (as if so formed):— web.

6981. קוֹרֵא **Qôwrê´**, *ko-ray´*; or

קֹרֵא **Qôrê´** (1 Chron. 26:1), *ko-ray´*; act. part. of 7121; *crier*; *Korè*, the name of two Isr.:— Kore.

6982. קוֹרָה **qôwrâh**, *ko-raw´*; or

קֹרָה **qôrâh**, *ko-raw´*; from 6979; a *rafter* (forming *trenches* as it were); by impl. a *roof*:— beam, roof.

6983. קוֹשׁ **qôwsh**, *koshe*; a prim. root; to *bend*; used only as denom. for 3369, to *set a trap*:— lay a snare.

6984. קוּשָׁיָהוּ **Qûwshâyâhûw**, *koo-shaw-yaw´-hoo*; from the pass. part. of 6983 and 3050; *entrapped of Jah*; *Kushajah*, an Isr.:— Kushaiah.

6985. קַט **qaṭ**, *kat*; from 6990 in the sense of *abbreviation*; a *little*, i.e. (adv.) *merely*:— very.

6986. קֶטֶב **qeṭeb**, *keh´-teb*; from an unused root mean. to *cut off*; *ruin*:— destroying, destruction.

6987. קֹטֶב **qôṭeb**, *ko´-teb*; from the same as 6986; *extermination*:— destruction.

6988. קְטוֹרָה **qᵉṭôwrâh**, *ket-o-raw´*; from 6999; *perfume*:— incense.

6989. קְטוּרָה **Qᵉṭûwrâh**, *ket-oo-raw´*; fem. pass. part. of 6999; *perfumed*; *Keturah*, a wife of Abraham:— Keturah.

6990. קְטַט **qâṭaṭ**, *kaw-tat´*; a prim. root; to *clip* off, i.e. (fig.) *destroy*:— be cut off.

6991. קָטַל **qâṭal**, *kaw-tal´*; a prim. root; prop. to *cut* off, i.e. (fig.) *put to death*:— kill, slay.

6992. קְטַל **qᵉṭal** (Chald.), *ket-al´*; corresp. to 6991; to *kill*:— slay.

6993. קֶטֶל **qeṭel**, *keh´-tel*; from 6991; a *violent death*:— slaughter.

6994. קָטֹן **qâṭôn**, *kaw-tone´*; a prim. root [rather denom. from 6996]; to *diminish*, i.e. *be* (caus. *make*) *diminutive* or (fig.) *of no account*:— be a (make) small (thing), be not worthy.

6995. קֹטֶן **qôṭen**, *ko´-ten*; from 6994; a *pettiness*, i.e. the *little finger*:— little finger.

6996. קָטָן **qâṭân**, *kaw-tawn´*; or

קָטֹן **qâṭôn**, *kaw-tone´*; from 6962; abbreviated, i.e. *diminutive*, lit. (in quantity, size or number) or fig. (in age or importance):— least, less (-er), little (one), small (-est, one, quantity, thing), young (-er, -est).

6997. קָטָן **Qâṭân**, *kaw-tawn´*; the same as 6996; *small*; *Katan*, an Isr.:— Hakkatan [incl. *the art.*].

6998. קָטַף **qâṭaph**, *kaw-taf´*; a prim. root; to *strip off*:— crop off, cut down (up), pluck.

6999. קָטַר **qâṭar**, *kaw-tar´*; a prim. root [rather ident. with 7000 through the idea of fumigation in a *close* place and perh. thus *driving* out the occupants]; to *smoke*, i.e. turn into fragrance by fire (espec. as an act of worship):— burn (incense, sacrifice) (upon), (altar for) incense, kindle, offer (incense, a sacrifice).

7000. קָטַר **qâṭar**, *kaw-tar´*; a prim. root; to *inclose*:— join.

7001. קְטַר **qᵉṭar** (Chald.), *ket-ar´*; from a root corresp. to 7000; a *knot* (as *tied* up), i.e. (fig.) a *riddle*; also a *vertebra* (as if a knot):— doubt, joint.

7002. קִטֵּר **qiṭṭêr**, *kit-tare´*; from 6999; *perfume*:— incense.

7003. קִטְרוֹן **Qiṭrôwn**, *kit-rone´*; from 6999; *fumigative*; *Kitron*, a place in Pal.:— Kitron.

7004. קְטֹרֶת **qᵉṭôreth**, *ket-o´-reth*; from 6999; a *fumigation*:— (sweet) incense, perfume.

7005. קַטָּת **Qaṭṭâth**, *kat-tawth´*; from 6996; *littleness*; *Kattath*, a place in Pal.:— Kattath.

7006. קָיָה **qâyâh**, *kaw-yaw´*; a prim. root; to *vomit*:— spue.

7007. קַיִט **qâyiṭ** (Chald.), *kah´-yit*; corresp. to 7019; *harvest*:— summer.

7008. קִיטוֹר **qîyṭôwr**, *kee-tore´*; or

קִיטֹר **qîyṭôr**, *kee-tore´*; from 6999; a *fume*, i.e. *cloud*:— smoke, vapour.

7009. קִים **qîym**, *keem*; from 6965; an *opponent* (as *rising* against one), i.e. (collect.) *enemies*:— substance.

7010. קְיָם **qᵉyâm** (Chald.), *keh-yawm´*; from 6966; an *edict* (as *arising* in law):— decree, statute.

7011. קַיָּם **qayâm** (Chald.), *kah-yawm´*; from 6966; *permanent* (as *rising* firmly):— stedfast, sure.

7012. קִימָה **qîymâh**, *kee-maw´*; from 6965; an *arising*:— rising up.

קִימוֹשׁ **Qîymôwsh**. See 7057.

Hebrew

7013. קַיִן **qayin**, *kah´-yin;* from 6969 in the orig. sense of *fixity;* a *lance* (as *striking fast*):— spear.

7014. קַיִן **Qayin**, *kah´-yin;* the same as 7013 (with a play upon the affinity to 7069); *Kajin,* the name of the first child, also of a place in Pal., and of an Oriental tribe:— Cain, Kenite (-s).

7015. קִינָה **qîynâh**, *kee-naw´;* from 6969; a *dirge* (as accompanied by *beating* the breasts or on instruments):— lamentation.

7016. קִינָה **Qîynâh**, *kee-naw´;* the same as 7015; *Kinah,* a place in Pal.:— Kinah.

7017. קֵינִי **Qêynîy**, *kay-nee´;* or

קִינִי **Qîynîy** (1 Chron. 2:55) *kee-nee´;* patron. from 7014; a *Kenite* or member of the tribe of Kajin:— Kenite.

7018. קֵינָן **Qêynân**, *kay-nawn´;* from the same as 7064; *fixed; Kenan,* an antediluvian:— Cainan, Kenan.

7019. קַיִץ **qayits**, *kah´-yits;* from 6972; *harvest* (as the *crop*), whether the product (grain or fruit) or the (dry) season:— summer (fruit, house).

7020. קִיצוֹן **qîytsôwn**, *kee-tsone´;* from 6972; *terminal:*— out (utter-) most.

7021. קִיקָיוֹן **qîyqâyôwn**, *kee-kaw-yone´;* perh. from 7006; the *gourd* (as *nauseous*):— gourd.

7022. קִיקָלוֹן **qîyqâlôwn**, *kee-kaw-lone´;* from 7036; intense *disgrace:*— shameful spewing.

7023. קִיר **qîyr**, *keer;* or

קִר **qir** (Isa. 22:5), *keer;* or (fem.)

קִירָה **qîyrâh**, *kee-raw´;* from 6979; a *wall* (as built in a *trench*):— + mason, side, town, × very, wall.

7024. קִיר **Qîyr**, *keer;* the same as 7023; *fortress; Kir,* a place in Ass.; also one in Moab:— Kir. Comp. 7025.

7025. קִיר חֶרֶשׂ **Qîyr Cheres**, *keer kheh´-res;* or (fem. of the latter word)

קִיר חֲרֶשֶׂת **Qîyr Chăreseth**, *keer khar-eh´-seth;* from 7023 and 2789; *fortress of earthenware; Kir-Cheres* or *Kir-Chareseth,* a place in Moab:— Kir-haraseth, Kir-hareseth, Kir-haresh, Kir-heres.

7026. קֵירוֹס **Qêyrôç**, *kay-roce´;* or

קֵרֹס **Qêrôç**, *kay-roce´;* from the same as 7166; *ankled; Keros,* one of the Nethinim:— Keros.

7027. קִישׁ **Qîysh**, *keesh;* from 6983; a *bow; Kish,* the name of five Isr.:— Kish.

7028. קִישׁוֹן **Qîyshôwn**, *kee-shone´;* from 6983; *winding; Kishon,* a river of Pal.:— Kishon, Kison.

7029. קִישִׁי **Qîyshîy**, *kee-shee´;* from 6983; *bowed; Kishi,* an Isr.:— Kishi.

7030. קִיתָרֹס° **qîythârôç** (Chald.), *kee-thaw-roce´;* of Gr. or. (κίθαρις); a *lyre:*— harp.

7031. קַל **qal**, *kal;* contr. from 7043; *light;* (by impl.) *rapid* (also adv.):— light, swift (-ly).

7032. קָל **qâl** (Chald.), *kawl;* corresp. to 6963:— sound, voice.

קֹל **qôl**. See 6963.

7033. קָלָה **qâlâh**, *kaw-law´;* a prim. root [rather ident. with 7034 through the idea of *shrinkage* by heat]; to *toast,* i.e. *scorch* partially or slowly:— dried, loathsome, parch, roast.

7034. קָלָה **qâlâh**, *kaw-law´;* a prim. root; to *be light* (as impl. in *rapid* motion), but fig. only (*be* [caus. *hold*] *in contempt*):— base, contemn, despise, lightly esteem, set light, seem vile.

7035. קָלַהּ° **qâlahh**, *kaw-lah´;* for 6950; to *assemble:*— gather together.

7036. קָלוֹן **qâlôwn**, *kaw-lone´;* from 7034; *disgrace;* (by impl.) the *pudenda:*— confusion, dishonour, ignominy, reproach, shame.

7037. קַלַּחַת **qallachath**, *kal-lakh´-ath;* appar. but a form for 6747; a *kettle:*— caldron.

7038. קָלַט **qâlat**, *kaw-lat´;* a prim. root; to *maim:*— lacking in his parts.

7039. קָלִי **qâlîy**, *kaw-lee´;* or

קָלִיא **qâlîy'**, *kaw-lee´;* from 7033; *roasted* ears of grain:— parched corn.

7040. קַלַּי **Qallay**, *kal-lah´-ee;* from 7043; *frivolous; Kallai,* an Isr.:— Kallai.

7041. קֵלָיָה **Qêlâyâh**, *kay-law-yaw´;* from 7034; *insignificance; Kelajah,* an Isr.:— Kelaiah.

7042. קְלִיטָא **Qelîytâ'**, *kel-ee-taw´;* from 7038; *maiming; Kelita,* the name of three Isr.:— Kelita.

7043. קָלַל **qâlal**, *kaw-lal´;* a prim. root; to *be* (caus. *make*) *light,* lit. (*swift, small, sharp,* etc.) or fig. (*easy, trifling, vile,* etc.):— abate, make bright, bring into contempt, (ac-) curse, despise, (be) ease (-y, -ier), (be a, make, make somewhat, move, seem a, set) light (-en, -er, -ly, -ly afflict, -ly esteem, thing), × slight [-ly], be swift (-er), (be, be more, make, re-) vile, whet.

7044. קָלָל **qâlâl**, *kaw-lawl´;* from 7043; *brightened* (as if *sharpened*):— burnished, polished.

7045. קְלָלָה **qelâlâh**, *kel-aw-law´;* from 7043; *vilification:*— (ac-) curse (-d, -ing).

7046. קָלַס **qâlaç**, *kaw-las´;* a prim. root; to *disparage,* i.e. *ridicule:*— mock, scoff, scorn.

Hebrew

7047. קֶלֶס **qeleç**, *keh´-les*; from 7046; a *laughing-stock*:— derision.

7048. קַלָּסָה **qallâçâh**, *kal-law-saw´*; intens. from 7046; *ridicule*:— mocking.

7049. קָלַע **qâla'**, *kaw-lah´*; a prim. root: to *sling*; also to *carve* (as if a *circular* motion, or into *light* forms):— carve, sling (out).

7050. קֶלַע **qela'**, *keh´-lah*; from 7049; a *sling*; also a (door) *screen* (as if *slung* across), or the *valve* (of the door) itself:— hanging, leaf, sling.

7051. קַלָּע **qallâ'**, *kal-law´*; intens. from 7049; a *slinger*:— slinger.

7052. קְלֹקֵל **qᵉlôqêl**, *kel-o-kale´*; from 7043; *insubstantial*:— light.

7053. קִלְּשׁוֹן **qillᵉshôwn**, *kil-lesh-one´*; from an unused root mean. to *prick*; a *prong*, i.e. hay-fork:— fork.

7054. קָמָה **qâmâh**, *kaw-maw´*; fem. of act. part. of 6965; something that *rises*, i.e. a *stalk* of grain:— (standing) corn, grown up, stalk.

7055. קְמוּאֵל **Qᵉmûw'êl**, *kem-oo-ale´*; from 6965 and 410; *raised of God*; *Kemuël*, the name of a rel. of Abraham, and of two Isr.:— Kemuel.

7056. קָמוֹן **Qâmôwn**, *kaw-mone´*; from 6965; an *elevation*; *Kamon*, a place E. of the Jordan:— Camon.

7057. קִמּוֹשׁ **qimmôwsh**, *kim-moshe´*; or

קִימוֹשׁ **qîymôwsh**, *kee-moshe´*; from an unused root mean. to *sting*; a *prickly* plant:— nettle. Comp. 7063.

7058. קֶמַח **qemach**, *keh´-makh*; from an unused root prob. mean. to *grind*; *flour*:— flour, meal.

7059. קָמַט **qâmaṭ**, *kaw-mat´*; a prim. root; to *pluck*, i.e. *destroy*:— cut down, fill with wrinkles.

7060. קָמַל **qâmal**, *kaw-mal´*; a prim. root; to *wither*:— hew down, wither.

7061. קָמַץ **qâmats**, *kaw-mats´*; a prim. root; to *grasp* with the hand:— take an handful.

7062. קֹמֶץ **qômets**, *ko´mets*; from 7061; a *grasp*, i.e. *handful*:— handful.

7063. קִמָּשׁוֹן **qimmâshôwn**, *kim-maw-shone´*; from the same as 7057; a *prickly* plant:— thorn.

7064. קֵן **qên**, *kane*; contr. from 7077; a *nest* (as *fixed*), sometimes incl. the *nestlings*; fig. a *chamber* or *dwelling*:— nest, room.

7065. קָנָא **qânâ'**, *kaw-naw´*; a prim. root; to *be* (caus. *make*) *zealous*, i.e. (in a bad sense) *jealous* or *envious*:— (be) envy (-ious), be (move to, provoke to) jealous (-y), × very, (be) zeal (-ous).

7066. קְנָא **qᵉnâ'** (Chald.), *ken-aw´*; corresp. to 7069; to *purchase*:— buy.

7067. קַנָּא **qannâ'**, *kan-naw´*; from 7065; *jealous*:— jealous. Comp. 7072.

7068. קִנְאָה **qin'âh**, *kin-aw´*; from 7065; *jealousy* or *envy*:— envy (-ied), jealousy, × sake, zeal.

7069. קָנָה **qânâh**, *kaw-naw´*; a prim. root; to *erect*, i.e. *create*; by extens. to *procure*, espec. by purchase (caus. *sell*); by impl. to *own*:— attain, buy (-er), teach to keep cattle, get, provoke to jealousy, possess (-or), purchase, recover, redeem, × surely, × verily.

7070. קָנֶה **qâneh**, *kaw-neh´*; from 7069; a *reed* (as *erect*); by resemblance a *rod* (espec. for measuring), *shaft*, *tube*, *stem*, the *radius* (of the arm), *beam* (of a steelyard):— balance, bone, branch, calamus, cane, reed, × spearman, stalk.

7071. קָנָה **Qânâh**, *kaw-naw´*; fem. of 7070; *reediness*; *Kanah*, the name of a stream and of a place in Pal.:— Kanah.

7072. קַנּוֹא **qannôw'**, *kan-no´*; for 7067; *jealous* or *angry*:— jealous.

7073. קְנַז **Qᵉnaz**, *ken-az´*; prob. from an unused root mean. to *hunt*; *hunter*; *Kenaz*, the name of an Edomite and of two Isr.:— Kenaz.

7074. קְנִזִּי **Qᵉnizzîy**, *ken-iz-zee´*; patron. from 7073, a *Kenizzite* or desc. of Kenaz:— Kenezite, Kenizzites.

7075. קִנְיָן **qinyân**, *kin-yawn´*; from 7069; *creation*, i.e. (concr.) *creatures*; also *acquisition, purchase, wealth*:— getting, goods, × with money, riches, substance.

7076. קִנָּמוֹן **qinnâmôwn**, *kin-naw-mone´*; from an unused root (mean. to *erect*); *cinnamon* bark (as in *upright* rolls):— cinnamon.

7077. קָנַן **qânan**, *kaw-nan´*; a prim. root; to *erect*; but used only as denom. from 7064; to *nestle*, i.e. *build* or *occupy* as a *nest*:— make ... nest.

7078. קֶנֶץ **qenets**, *keh´-nets*; from an unused root prob. mean. to *wrench*; *perversion*:— end.

7079. קְנָת **Qᵉnâth**, *ken-awth´*; from 7069; *possession*; *Kenath*, a place E. of the Jordan:— Kenath.

7080. קָסַם **qâçam**, *kaw-sam´*; a prim. root; prop. to *distribute*, i.e. *determine* by lot or magical scroll; by impl. to *divine*:— divine (-r, -ation), prudent, soothsayer, use [divination].

7081. קֶסֶם **qeçem**, *keh´-sem*; from 7080; a *lot*; also *divination* (incl. its *fee*), *oracle*:—

(reward of) divination, divine sentence, witchcraft.

7082. קָסַס qâçaç, *kaw-sas´;* a prim. root; to *lop* off:— cut off.

7083. קֶסֶת qeçeth, *keh´-seth;* from the same as 3563 (or as 7185); prop. a *cup,* i.e. an *inkstand:*— inkhorn.

7084. קְעִילָה Qeʻîylâh, *keh-ee-law´;* perh. from 7049 in the sense of *inclosing; citadel; Keïlah,* a place in Pal.:— Keilah.

7085. קַעֲקַע qaʻăqaʻ, *kah-ak-ah´;* from the same as 6970; an *incision* or gash:— + mark.

7086. קְעָרָה qeʻârâh, *keh-aw-raw´;* prob. from 7167; a *bowl* (as *cut* out hollow):— charger, dish.

קֹף qôph. See 6971.

7087. קָפָא qâphâ', *kaw-faw´;* a prim. root; to *shrink,* i.e. *thicken* (as unracked wine, curdled milk, clouded sky, frozen water):— congeal, curdle, dark°, settle.

7088. קָפַד qâphad, *kaw-fad´;* a prim. root; to *contract,* i.e. *roll together:*— cut off.

7089. קְפָדָה qephâdâh, *kef-aw-daw´;* from 7088; *shrinking,* i.e. *terror:*— destruction.

7090. קִפּוֹד qippôwd, *kip-pode´;* or

קִפֹּד qippôd, *kip-pode´;* from 7088; a species of bird, perh. the *bittern* (from its *contracted* form):— bittern.

7091. קִפּוֹז qippôwz, *kip-poze´;* from an unused root mean. to *contract,* i.e. *spring* forward; an *arrow-snake* (as *darting* on its prey):— great owl.

7092. קָפַץ qâphats, *kaw-fats´;* a prim. root; to *draw together,* i.e. close; by impl. to *leap* (by *contracting* the limbs); spec. to *die* (from *gathering* up the feet):— shut (up), skip, stop, take out of the way.

7093. קֵץ qêts, *kates;* contr. from 7112: an *extremity;* adv. (with prep. pref.) *after:*— + after, (utmost) border, end, [in-] finite, × process.

קֹץ qôts. See 6975.

7094. קָצַב qâtsab, *kaw-tsab´;* a prim. root; to *clip,* or (gen.) *chop:*— cut down, shorn.

7095. קֶצֶב qetseb, *keh´-tseb;* from 7094; *shape* (as if *cut* out); *base* (as if there *cut* off):— bottom, size.

7096. קָצָה qâtsâh, *kaw-tsaw´;* a prim. root; to *cut* off; (fig.) to *destroy;* (partially) to *scrape* off:— cut off, cut short, scrape (off).

7097. קָצֶה qâtseh, *kaw-tseh´;* or (neg. only)

קֵצֶה qêtseh, *kay´-tseh;* from 7096: an *extremity* (used in a great variety of applications and idioms; comp. 7093):— × after, border, brim, brink, edge, end, [in-] finite, frontier, outmost coast, quarter, shore, (out-) side, × some, ut(-ter-) most (part).

7098. קָצָה qâtsâh, *kaw-tsaw´;* fem. of 7097; a *termination* (used like 7097):— coast, corner, (selv-) edge, lowest, (uttermost) part.

7099. קֶצֶו qetsev, *keh´-tsev;* and (fem.)

קִצְוָה qitsvâh, *kits-vaw´;* from 7096; a *limit* (used like 7097, but with less variety):— end, edge, uttermost part.

7100. קֶצַח qetsach, *keh´-tsakh;* from an unused root appar. mean. to *incise; fennelflower* (from its *pungency*):— fitches.

7101. קָצִין qâtsîyn, *kaw-tseen´;* from 7096 in the sense of *determining;* a *magistrate* (as *deciding*) or other *leader:*— captain, guide, prince, ruler. Comp. 6278.

7102. קְצִיעָה qetsîyʻâh, *kets-ee-aw´;* from 7106; *cassia* (as *peeled;* plur. the *bark*):— cassia.

7103. קְצִיעָה Qetsîyʻâh, *kets-ee-aw´;* the same as 7102; *Ketsiah,* a daughter of Job:— Kezia.

7104. קָצִיץ Qetsîyts, *kets-eets´;* from 7112; *abrupt; Keziz,* a valley in Pal.:— Keziz.

7105. קָצִיר qâtsîyr, *kaw-tseer´;* from 7114; *severed,* i.e. *harvest* (as *reaped*), the crop, the time, the reaper, or fig.; also a *limb* (of a tree, or simply *foliage*):— bough, branch, harvest (man).

7106. קָצַע qâtsaʻ, *kaw-tsah´;* a prim. root; to *strip* off, i.e. (partially) *scrape;* by impl. to *segregate* (as an angle):— cause to scrape, corner.

7107. קָצַף qâtsaph, *kaw-tsaf´;* a prim. root; to *crack* off, i.e. (fig.) *burst* out in rage:— (be) anger (-ry), displease, fret self, (provoke to) wrath (come), be wroth.

7108. קְצַף qetsaph (Chald.), *kets-af´;* corresp. to 7107; to *become enraged:*— be furious.

7109. קְצַף qetsaph (Chald.), *kets-af´;* from 7108; *rage:*— wrath.

7110. קֶצֶף qetseph, *keh´-tsef;* from 7107; a *splinter* (as *chipped* off); fig. *rage* or *strife:*— foam, indignation, × sore, wrath.

7111. קְצָפָה qetsâphâh, *kets-aw-faw´;* from 7107; a *fragment:*— bark [-ed].

7112. קָצַץ qâtsats, *kaw-tsats´;* a prim. root; to *chop* off (lit. or fig.):— cut (asunder, in pieces, in sunder, off), × utmost.

7113. קְצַץ qetsats (Chald.), *kets-ats´;* corresp. to 7112:— cut off.

7114. קָצַר qâtsar, *kaw-tsar´;* a prim. root; to *dock* off, i.e. *curtail* (tran. or intr., lit. or fig.); espec. to *harvest* (grass or grain):— × at all, cut down, much discouraged, grieve, harvestman, lothe, mourn, reap (-er), (be, wax) short (-en, -er), straiten, trouble, vex.

Hebrew

7115. קֹצֶר **qôtser**, *ko'-tser;* from 7114; *short-ness* (of spirit), i.e. *impatience:—* anguish.

7116. קָצֵר **qâtsêr**, *kaw-tsare';* from 7114; *short* (whether in size, number, life, strength or temper):— few, hasty, small, soon.

7117. קְצָת **q°tsâth**, *kets-awth';* from 7096; a *termination* (lit. or fig.); also (by impl.) a *portion;* adv. (with prep. pref.) *after:—* end, part, × some.

7118. קְצָת **q°tsâth** (Chald.), *kets-awth';* corresp. to 7117:— end, partly.

7119. קַר **qar**, *kar;* contr. from an unused root mean. to *chill; cool;* fig. *quiet:—* cold, excellent [*from the marg.*].

קִר **qîr**. See 7023.

7120. קֹר **qôr**, *kore;* from the same as 7119; *cold:—* cold.

7121. קָרָא **qârâ'**, *kaw-raw';* a prim. root [rather ident. with 7122 through the idea of *accosting* a person met]; to *call* out to (i.e. prop. *address* by name, but used in a wide variety of applications):— bewray [self], that are bidden, call (for, forth, self, upon), cry (unto), (be) famous, guest, invite, mention, (give) name, preach, (make) proclaim (-ation), pronounce, publish, read, re-nowned, say.

7122. קָרָא **qârâ'**, *kaw-raw';* a prim. root: to *encounter*, whether accidentally or in a hostile manner:— befall, (by) chance, (cause to) come (upon), fall out, happen, meet.

7123. קְרָא **q°râ'** (Chald.), *ker-aw';* corresp. to 7121:— call, cry, read.

7124. קֹרֵא **qôrê'**, *ko-ray';* prop. act. part. of 7121; a *caller*, i.e. *partridge* (from its *cry*):— partridge. See also 6981.

7125. קִרְאָה **qîr'âh**, *keer-aw';* from 7122; an *en-countering*, accidental, friendly or hostile (also adv. *opposite*):— × against (he come), help, meet, seek, × to, × in the way.

7126. קָרַב **qârab**, *kaw-rab';* a prim. root; to *approach* (caus. *bring near*) for whatever purpose:— (cause to) approach, (cause to) bring (forth, near), (cause to) come (near, nigh), (cause to) draw near (nigh), go (near), be at hand, join, be near, offer, present, pro-duce, make ready, stand, take.

7127. קְרֵב **q°rêb** (Chald.), *ker-abe';* corresp. to 7126:— approach, come (near, nigh), draw near.

7128. קְרָב **q°râb**, *ker-awb';* from 7126; hostile *encounter:—* battle, war.

7129. קְרָב **q°râb** (Chald.), *ker-awb';* corresp. to 7128:— war.

7130. קֶרֶב **qereb**, *keh'-reb;* from 7126; prop. the *nearest* part, i.e. the *center*, whether lit., fig. or adv. (espec. with prep.):— × among, ×

before, bowels, × unto charge, + eat (up), × heart, × him, × in, inward (× -ly, part, -s, thought), midst, + out of, purtenance, × therein, × through, × within self.

7131. קָרֵב **qârêb**, *kaw-rabe';* from 7126; *near:—* approach, come (near, nigh), draw near.

קָרוֹב **qârôb**. See 7138.

7132. קְרָבָה **q°râbâh**, *ker-aw-baw';* from 7126; *approach:—* approaching, draw near.

7133. קָרְבָּן **qorbân**, *kor-bawn';* or

קֻרְבָּן **qurbân**, *koor-bawn';* from 7126; something *brought near* the altar, i.e. a sacrificial *present:—* oblation, that is of-fered, offering.

7134. קַרְדֹּם **qardôm**, *kar-dome';* perh. from 6923 in the sense of *striking* upon; an *axe:—* ax.

7135. קָרָה **qârâh**, *kaw-raw';* fem. of 7119; *coolness:—* cold.

7136. קָרָה **qârâh**, *kaw-raw';* a prim. root; to *light upon* (chiefly by accident); caus. to *bring about;* spec. to *impose* timbers (for roof or floor):— appoint, lay (make) beams, befall, bring, come (to pass unto), floor, [hap] was, happen (unto), meet, send good speed.

7137. קָרֶה **qâreh**, *kaw-reh';* from 7136; an (unfortunate) *occurrence*, i.e. some accidental (ceremonial) *disqualification:—* un-cleanness that chanceth.

קֹרָה **qôrâh**. See 6982.

7138. קָרוֹב **qârôwb**, *kaw-robe';* or

קָרֹב **qârôb**, *kaw-robe';* from 7126; *near* (in place, kindred or time):— allied, approach, at hand, + any of kin, kinsfolk (-sman), (that is) near (of kin), neighbour, (that is) next, (them that come) nigh (at hand), more ready, short (-ly).

7139. קָרַח **qârach**, *kaw-rakh';* a prim. root; to *depilate:—* make (self) bald.

7140. קֶרַח **qerach**, *keh'-rakh;* or

קֹרַח **qôrach**, *ko'-rakh;* from 7139; *ice* (as if bald, i.e. *smooth*); hence, *hail;* by re-semblance, rock *crystal:—* crystal, frost, ice.

7141. קֹרַח **Qôrach**, *ko'rakh;* from 7139; *ice; Korach*, the name of two Edomites and three Isr.:— Korah.

7142. קֵרֵחַ **qêrêach**, *kay-ray'-akh;* from 7139; *bald* (on the back of the head):— bald (head).

7143. קָרֵחַ **Qârêach**, *kaw-ray'-akh;* from 7139; *bald; Kareäch*, an Isr.:— Careah, Kareah.

7144. קׇרְחָה **qorchâh**, *kor-khaw';* or

קָרְחָא **qorchâ'** (Ezek. 27:31), *kor-khaw´*; from 7139; *baldness:*— bald (-ness), × utterly.

7145. קָרְחִי **Qorchîy**, *kor-khee´*; patron. from 7141; a *Korchite* (collect.) or desc. of Korach:— Korahite, Korathite, sons of Kore, Korhite.

7146. קָרַחַת **qârachath**, *kaw-rakh´-ath;* from 7139; a *bald* spot (on the back of the head); fig. a *threadbare* spot (on the back side of the cloth):— bald head, bare within.

7147. קְרִי **q°rîy**, *ker-ee´;* from 7136; hostile *encounter:*— contrary.

7148. קָרִיא **qârîy'**, *kaw-ree´;* from 7121; *called,* i.e. *select:*— famous, renowned.

7149. קִרְיָא **qiryâ'** (Chald.), *keer-yaw´;* or

קִרְיָה **qiryâh** (Chald.), *keer-yaw´;* corresp. to 7151:— city.

7150. קְרִיאָה **q°rîy'âh**, *ker-ee-aw´;* from 7121; a *proclamation:*— preaching.

7151. קִרְיָה **qiryâh**, *kir-yaw´;* from 7136 in the sense of *flooring*, i.e. *building*; a *city:*— city.

7152. קְרִיּוֹת **Q°rîyôwth**, *ker-ee-yōth´;* plur. of 7151; *buildings; Kerioth*, the name of two places in Pal.:— Kerioth, Kirioth.

7153. קִרְיַת עַרְבַּע **Qiryath 'Arba'**, *keer-yath´ ar-bah´;* or (with the art. interposed)

קִרְיַת הָאַרְבַּע **Qiryath hâ-'Arba'** (Neh. 11:25), *keer-yath´ haw-ar-bah´;* from 7151 and 704 or 702; *city of Arba*, or *city of the four* (giants); *Kirjath-Arba* or *Kirjath-ha-Arba*, a place in Pal.:— Kirjath-arba.

7154. קִרְיַת בַּעַל **Qiryath Ba'al**, *keer-yath´ bah´-al;* from 7151 and 1168; *city of Baal; Kirjath-Baal*, a place in Pal.:— Kirjath-baal.

7155. קִרְיַת חֻצוֹת **Qiryath Chûtsôwth**, *keer-yath´ khoo-tsōth´;* from 7151 and the fem. plur. of 2351; *city of streets; Kirjath-Chutsoth*, a place in Moab:— Kirjath-huzoth.

7156. קִרְיָתַיִם **Qiryâthayim**, *keer-yaw-thah´-yim;* dual of 7151; *double city; Kirjathaïm*, the name of two places in Pal.:— Kiriathaim, Kirjathaim.

7157. קִרְיַת יְעָרִים **Qiryath Y°'ârîym**, *keer-yath´ yeh-aw-reem´;* or (Jer. 26:20) with the art. interposed; or (Josh. 18:28) simply the former part of the word; or

קִרְיַת עָרִים **Qiryath 'Ârîym**, *keer-yath´ aw-reem´;* from 7151 and the plur. of 3293 or 5892; *city of forests*, or *city of towns; Kirjath-Jeärim* or *Kirjath-Arim*, a place in Pal.:— Kirjath, Kirjath-jearim, Kirjath-arim.

7158. קִרְיַת סַנָּה **Qiryath Çannâh**, *keer-yath´ san-naw´;* or

קִרְיַת סֵפֶר **Qiryath Çépher**, *keer-yath´ say-fer;* from 7151 and a simpler fem. from the same as 5577, or (for the latter name) 5612; *city of branches*, or *of a book; Kirjath-*

Sannah or *Kirjath-Sepher*, a place in Pal.:— Kirjath-sannah, Kirjath-sepher.

7159. קָרַם **qâram**, *kaw-ram´;* a prim. root; to *cover:*— cover.

7160. קָרַן **qâran**, *kaw-ran´;* a prim. root; to *push* or *gore*; used only as denom. from 7161, to *shoot out horns*; fig. *rays:*— have horns, shine.

7161. קֶרֶן **qeren**, *keh´-ren;* from 7160; a *horn* (as *projecting*); by impl. a *flask, cornet*; by resembl. an elephant's *tooth* (i.e. *ivory*), a *corner* (of the altar), a *peak* (of a mountain), a *ray* (of light); fig. *power:*— × hill, horn.

7162. קֶרֶן **qeren** (Chald.), *keh´-ren;* corresp. to 7161; a *horn* (lit. or for sound):— horn, cornet.

7163. קֶרֶן הַפּוּךְ **Qeren Hap-pûwk**, *keh´-ren hap-pook´;* from 7161 and 6320; *horn of cosmetic; Keren-hap-Puk*, one of Job's daughters:— Keren-happuch.

7164. קָרַס **qâraç**, *kaw-ras´;* a prim. root; prop. to *protrude*; used only as denom. from 7165 (for alliteration with 7167), to *hunch*, i.e. be hump-backed:— stoop.

7165. קֶרֶס **qereç**, *keh´-res;* from 7164; a *knob* or belaying-pin (from its swelling form):— tache.

קֶרֶס **Qêrôç**. See 7026.

7166. קַרְסֹל **qarçôl**, *kar-sole´;* from 7164; an *ankle* (as a *protuberance* or joint):— foot.

7167. קָרַע **qâra'**, *kaw-rah´;* a prim. root; to *rend*, lit. or fig. (*revile, paint* the eyes, as if enlarging them):— cut out, rend, × surely, tear.

7168. קֶרַע **qera'**, *keh´-rah;* from 7167; a *rag:*— piece, rag.

7169. קָרַץ **qârats**, *kaw-rats´;* a prim. root; to *pinch*, i.e. (partially) to *bite* the lips, *blink* the eyes (as a gesture of malice), or (fully) to *squeeze* off (a piece of clay in order to mould a vessel from it):— form, move, wink.

7170. קְרַץ **q°rats** (Chald.), *ker-ats´;* corresp. to 7171 in the sense of a *bit* (to "eat the *morsels* of" any one, i.e. *chew* him up [fig.] by *slander*):— + accuse.

7171. קֶרֶץ **qerets**, *keh´-rets;* from 7169; *extirpation* (as if by *constriction*):— destruction.

7172. קַרְקַע **qarqa'**, *kar-kah´;* from 7167; *floor* (as if a pavement of pieces or *tesseræ*), of a building or the sea:— bottom, (× one side of the) floor.

7173. קַרְקַע **Qarqa'**, *kar-kah´;* the same as 7172; *ground-floor; Karka* (with the art. pref.), a place in Pal.:— Karkaa.

7174. קַרְקֹר **Qarqôr**, *kar-kore´;* from 6979;

foundation; *Karkor*, a place E. of the Jordan:— Karkor.

7175. קֶרֶשׁ **qeresh**, *keh´-resh;* from an unused root mean. to *split* off; a *slab* or plank; by impl. a *deck* of a ship:— bench, board.

7176. קֶרֶת **qereth**, *keh´-reth;* from 7136 in the sense of building; a *city:*— city.

7177. קַרְתָּה **Qartâh**, *kar-taw´;* from 7176; *city; Kartah*, a place in Pal.:— Kartah.

7178. קַרְתָּן **Qartân**, *kar-tawn´;* from 7176; *city-plot; Kartan*, a place in Pal.:— Kartan.

7179. קַשׁ **qash**, *kash;* from 7197; *straw* (as *dry*):— stubble.

7180. קִשֻּׁא **qishshû'**, *kish-shoo´;* from an unused root (mean. to be *hard*); a *cucumber* (from the difficulty of *digestion*):— cucumber.

7181. קָשַׁב **qâshab**, *kaw-shab´;* a prim. root; to *prick up* the ears, i.e. *hearken:*— attend, (cause to) hear (-ken), give heed, incline, mark (well), regard.

7182. קֶשֶׁב **qesheb**, *keh´-sheb;* from 7181; a *hearkening:*— × diligently, hearing, much heed, that regarded.

7183. קַשָּׁב **qashshâb**, *kash-shawb´;* or

קַשֻּׁב **qashshûb**, *kash-shoob´;* from 7181; *hearkening:*— attent(-ive).

7184. קָשָׂה **qâsâh**, *kaw-saw´;* or

קַשְׂוָה **qasvâh**, *kas-vaw´;* from an unused root mean. to be *round;* a *jug* (from its shape):— cover, cup.

7185. קָשָׁה **qâshâh**, *kaw-shaw´;* a prim. root; prop. to be *dense*, i.e. *tough* or *severe* (in various applications):— be cruel, be fiercer, make grievous, be (ask a], be in, have, seem, would) hard (-en, [labour], -ly, thing), be sore, (be, make) stiff (-en, [-necked]).

7186. קָשֶׁה **qâsheh**, *kaw-sheh´;* from 7185; *severe* (in various applications):— churlish, cruel, grievous, hard (I-hearted], thing), heavy, + impudent, obstinate, prevailed, rough (-ly), sore, sorrowful, stiff (I-necked]), stubborn, + in trouble.

7187. קְשׁוֹט **q⁰shôwṭ** (Chald.), *kesh-ote´;* or

קְשֹׁט **q⁰shôṭ** (Chald.), *kesh-ote´;* corresp. to 7189; *fidelity:*— truth.

7188. קָשַׁח **qâshach**, *kaw-shakh´;* a prim. root; to be (caus. *make*) *unfeeling:*— harden.

7189. קֹשֶׁט **qôsheṭ**, *ko´-shet;* or

קֹשְׁט **qôshṭ**, *kôsht;* from an unused root mean. to *balance; equity* (as evenly *weighed*), i.e. *reality:*— certainty, truth.

קֹשֹׁט **qôshôṭ**. See 7187.

7190. קְשִׁי **q⁰shîy**, *kesh-ee´;* from 7185; *obstinacy:*— stubbornness.

7191. קְשִׁיּוֹן **Qishyôwn**, *kish-yone´;* from 7190;

hard *ground; Kishjon*, a place in Pal.:— Kishion, Keshon.

7192. קְשִׂיטָה **q⁰sîyṭah**, *kes-ee-taw´;* from an unused root (prob. mean. to *weigh* out); an *ingot* (as def. *estimated* and stamped for a coin):— piece of money (silver).

7193. קַשְׂקֶשֶׂת **qasqeseth**, *kas-keh´-seth;* by redupl. from an unused root mean. to *shale* off as bark; a *scale* (of a fish); hence, a coat of *mail* (as composed of or covered with jointed *plates* of metal):— mail, scale.

7194. קָשַׁר **qâshar**, *kaw-shar´;* a prim. root: to *tie*, phys. (*gird, confine, compact*) or ment. (in *love, league*):— bind (up), (make a) conspire (-acy, -ator), join together, knit, stronger, work [treason].

7195. קֶשֶׁר **qesher**, *keh´-sher;* from 7194; an (unlawful) *alliance:*— confederacy, conspiracy, treason.

7196. קִשֻּׁר **qishshûr**, *kish-shoor´;* from 7194; an (ornamental) *girdle* (for women):— attire, headband.

7197. קָשַׁשׁ **qâshash**, *kaw-shash´;* a prim. root; to *become sapless* through drought; used only as denom. from 7179; to *forage* for straw, stubble or wood; fig. to *assemble:*— gather (selves) (together).

7198. קֶשֶׁת **qesheth**, *keh´-sheth;* from 7185 in the orig. sense (of 6983) of *bending;* a *bow*, for *shooting* (hence, fig. *strength*) or the *iris:*— × arch (-er), + arrow, bow (I-man, -shot]).

7199. קַשָּׁת **qashshâth**, *kash-shawth´;* intens. (as denom.) from 7198; a *bowman:*— × archer.

ר

7200. רָאָה **râ'âh**, *raw-aw´;* a prim. root; to *see*, lit. or fig. (in numerous applications, dir. and impl., tran., intr. and caus.):— advise self, appear, approve, behold, × certainly, consider, discern, (make to) enjoy, have experience, gaze, take heed, × indeed, × joyfully, lo, look (on, one another, one on another, one upon another, out, up, upon), mark, meet, × be near, perceive, present, provide, regard, (have) respect, (fore-, cause to, let) see (-r, -m, one another), shew (self), × sight of others, (e-) spy, stare, × surely, × think, view, visions.

7201. רָאָה **râ'âh**, *raw-aw´;* from 7200; a *bird* of prey (prob. the *vulture*, from its sharp *sight*):— glede. Comp. 1676.

7202. רָאֶה **râ'eh**, *raw-eh´;* from 7200; *seeing*, i.e. experiencing:— see.

7203. רֹאֶה **rô'eh**, *ro-eh´;* act. part. of 7200; a *seer* (as often rendered); but also (abstr.) a *vision:*— vision.

7204. רֹאֶה **Rô'êh**, _ro-ay´;_ for 7203; _prophet; Roëh,_ an Isr.:— Haroeh [incl. _the art._].

7205. רְאוּבֵן **Re'ûwbên**, _reh-oo-bane´;_ from the imper. of 7200 and 1121; _see ye a son; Reüben,_ a son of Jacob:— Reuben.

7206. רְאוּבֵנִי **Re'ûwbêniy**, _reh-oob-ay-nee´;_ patron. from 7205; a _Reübenite_ or desc. of Reüben:— children of Reuben, Reubenites.

7207. רַאֲוָה **ra'ăvâh**, _rah-av-aw´;_ from 7200; _sight,_ i.e. _satisfaction:—_ behold.

7208. רְאוּמָה **Re'ûwmâh**, _reh-oo-maw´;_ fem. pass. part. of 7213; _raised; Reümah,_ a Syrian woman:— Reumah.

7209. רְאִי **re'iy**, _reh-ee´;_ from 7200; a _mirror_ (as _seen_):— looking glass.

7210. רֳאִי **rŏ'iy**, _ro-ee´;_ from 7200; _sight,_ whether abstr. (_vision_) or concr. (a _spectacle_):— gazingstock, look to, (that) see (-th).

7211. רְאָיָה **Re'âyâh**, _reh-aw-yaw´;_ from 7200 and 3050; _Jah has seen; Reäjah,_ the name of three Isr.:— Reaia, Reaiah.

7212. רְאִית° **re'îyth**, _reh-eeth´;_ from 7200; _sight:—_ beholding.

7213. רָאַם **râ'am**, _raw-am´;_ a prim. root; to _rise:—_ be lifted up.

7214. רְאֵם **re'êm**, _reh-ame´;_ or

רְאֵים **re'êym**, _reh-ame´;_ or

רֵים **rêym**, _rame;_ or

רֵם **rêm**, _rame;_ from 7213; a wild _bull_ (from its _conspicuousness_):— unicorn.

7215. רָאמָה **râ'mâh**, _raw-maw´;_ from 7213; something _high_ in value, i.e. perh. _coral:—_ coral.

7216. רָאמוֹת **Râ'môwth**, _raw-môth´;_ or

רָאמֹת **Râmôth**, _raw-môth´;_ plur. of 7215; _heights; Ramoth,_ the name of two places in Pal.:— Ramoth.

7217. רֵאשׁ **rê'sh** (Chald.), _raysh;_ corresp. to 7218; the _head;_ fig. the _sum:—_ chief, head, sum.

7218. רֹאשׁ **rô'sh**, _roshe;_ from an unused root appar. mean. to _shake;_ the _head_ (as most easily _shaken_), whether lit. or fig. (in many applications, of place, time, rank, etc.):— band, beginning, captain, chapiter, chief (-est place, man, things), company, end, × every [man], excellent, first, forefront, ([be-] head, height, (on) high (-est part, [priest]), × lead, × poor, principal, ruler, sum, top.

7219. רֹאשׁ **rô'sh**, _roshe;_ or

רוֹשׁ **rôwsh** (Deut. 32:32), _roshe;_ appar. the same as 7218; a poisonous _plant,_ prob. the _poppy_ (from its conspicuous _head_); gen. _poison_ (even of serpents):— gall, hemlock, poison, venom.

7220. רֹאשׁ **Rô'sh**, _roshe;_ prob. the same as

7218; _Rosh,_ the name of an Isr. and of a for. nation:— Rosh.

רֵאשׁ **rê'sh**. See 7389.

7221. רִאשָׁה **ri'shâh**, _ree-shaw´;_ from the same as 7218; a _beginning:—_ beginning.

7222. רֹאשָׁה **rô'shâh**, _ro-shaw´;_ fem. of 7218; the _head:—_ head [-stone].

7223. רִאשׁוֹן **ri'shôwn**, _ree-shone´;_ or

רִאשֹׁן **ri'shôn**, _ree-shone´;_ from 7221; _first,_ in place, time or rank (as adj. or noun):— ancestor, (that were) before (-time), beginning, eldest, first, fore [-father] (-most), former (thing), of old time, past.

7224. רִאשֹׁנִי **ri'shôniy**, _ree-sho-nee´;_ from 7223; _first:—_ first.

7225. רֵאשִׁית **rê'shîyth**, _ray-sheeth´;_ from the same as 7218; the _first,_ in place, time, order or rank (spec. a _firstfruit_):— beginning, chief (-est), first (-fruits, part, time), principal thing.

7226. רַאֲשֹׁת **ra'ăshôth**, _rah-ash-ôth´;_ from 7218; a _pillow_ (being for the _head_):— bolster.

7227. רַב **rab**, _rab;_ by contr. from 7231; _abundant_ (in quantity, size, age, number, rank, quality):— (in) abound (-undance, -ant, -antly), captain, elder, enough, exceedingly, full, great (-ly, man, one), increase, long (enough, [time]), (do, have) many (-ifold, things, a time), ([ship-] master, mighty, more, (too, very) much, multiply (-tude), officer, often [-times], plenteous, populous, prince, process [of time], suffice (-ient).

7228. רַב **rab**, _rab;_ by contr. from 7232; an _archer_ [or perh. the same as 7227]:— archer.

7229. רַב **rab** (Chald.), _rab;_ corresp. to 7227:— captain, chief, great, lord, master, stout.

רִב **rîb**. See 7378.

7230. רֹב **rôb**, _robe;_ from 7231; _abundance_ (in any respect):— abundance (-antly), all, × common [sort], excellent, great (-ly,ness, number), huge, be increased, long, many, more in number, most, much, multitude, plenty (-ifully), × very [age].

7231. רָבַב **râbab**, _raw-bab´;_ a prim. root; prop. to _cast together_ [comp. 7241], i.e. _increase,_ espec. in number; also (as denom. from 7233) to _multiply by the myriad:—_ increase, be many (-ifold), be more, multiply, ten thousands.

7232. רָבַב **râbab**, _raw-bab´;_ a prim. root [rather ident. with 7231 through the idea of _projection_]; to _shoot_ an arrow:— shoot.

7233. רְבָבָה **r^ebâbâh**, *reb-aw-baw´;* from 7231; *abundance* (in number), i.e. (spec.) a *myriad* (whether def. or indef.):— many, million, × multiply, ten thousand.

7234. רְבַד **râbad**, *raw-bad´;* a prim. root; to *spread:*— deck.

7235. רְבָה **râbâh**, *raw-baw´;* a prim. root; to *increase* (in whatever respect):— [bring in] abundance (× -antly), + archer [by *mistake for* 7232], be in authority, bring up, × continue, enlarge, excel, exceeding (-ly), be full of, (be, make) great (-er, -ly, × -ness), grow up, heap, increase, be long, (be, give, have, make, use) many (a time), (any, be, give, give the, have) more (in number), (ask, be, be so, gather, over, take, yield) much (greater, more), (make to) multiply, nourish, plenty (-eous), × process [of time], sore, store, thoroughly, very.

7236. רְבָה **r^ebâh** (Chald.), *reb-aw´;* corresp. to 7235:— make a great man, grow.

7237. רַבָּה **Rabbâh**, *rab-baw´;* fem. of 7227; *great; Rabbah*, the name of two places in Pal., East and West:— Rabbah, Rabbath.

7238. רְבוּ **r^ebûw** (Chald.), *reb-oo´;* from a root corresp. to 7235; *increase* (of dignity):— greatness, majesty.

7239. רִבּוֹ **ribbôw**, *rib-bo´;* from 7231; or

רִבּוֹא **ribbôw'**, *rib-bo´;* from 7231; a *myr-iad*, i.e. indef. *large number:*— great things, ten [eight]-een, [for]-ty, + sixscore, + three-score, × twenty, [twen]-ty thousand.

7240. רִבּוֹ **ribbôw** (Chald.), *rib-bo´;* corresp. to 7239:— × ten thousand times ten thousand.

7241. רָבִיב **râbîyb**, *raw-beeb´;* from 7231; a *rain* (as an *accumulation* of drops):— shower.

7242. רָבִיד **râbîyd**, *raw-beed´;* from 7234; a *col-lar* (as *spread* around the neck):— chain.

7243. רְבִיעִי **r^ebîy'îy**, *reb-ee-ee´;* or

רְבִעִי **r^ebî'îy**, *reb-ee-ee´;* from 7251; *fourth;* also (fractionally) a *fourth:*— four-square, fourth (part).

7244. רְבִיעַי **r^ebîy'ay** (Chald.), *reb-ee-ah´-ee;* corresp. to 7243:— fourth.

7245. רַבִּית **Rabbîyth**, *rab-beeth´;* from 7231; *multitude; Rabbith*, a place in Pal.:— Rab-bith.

7246. רָבַךְ **râbak**, *raw-bak´;* a prim. root; to *soak* (bread in oil):— baken, (that which is) fried.

7247. רִבְלָה **Riblâh**, *rib-law´;* from an unused root mean. to *be fruitful; fertile; Riblah*, a place in Syria:— Riblah.

7248. רַב־מָג **Rab-Mâg**, *rab-mawg´;* from 7227 and a for. word for a Magian; *chief Magian; Rab-Mag*, a Bab. official:— Rab-mag.

7249. רַב־סָרִיס **Rab-Çârîyç**, *rab-saw-reece´;* from 7227 and a for. word for a eunuch; *chief chamberlain; Rab-Saris*, a Bab. offi-cial:— Rab-saris.

7250. רְבַע **râba'**, *raw-bah´;* a prim. root; to *squat* or *lie* out flat, i.e. (spec.) in copula-tion:— let gender, lie down.

7251. רְבַע **râba'**, *raw-bah´;* a prim. root [rather ident. with 7250 through the idea of *sprawling* "at all fours" (or possibly the re-verse is the order of deriv.); comp. 702]; prop. to *be four* (sided); used only as de-nom. of 7253; to *be quadrate:*— (four-) square (-d).

7252. רֶבַע **reba'**, *reh´-bah;* from 7250; *pros-tration* (for sleep):— lying down.

7253. רֶבַע **reba'**, *reh´-bah;* from 7251; a *fourth* (part or side):— fourth part, side, square.

7254. רֶבַע **Reba'**, *reh´-bah;* the same as 7253; *Reba*, a Midianite:— Reba.

7255. רֹבַע **rôba'**, *ro´-bah;* from 7251; a *quar-ter:*— fourth part.

7256. רִבֵּעַ **ribbêa'**, *rib-bay´-ah;* from 7251; a desc. of the *fourth* generation, i.e. *great great grandchild:*— fourth.

רְבִיעִי **r^ebîy'îy**. See 7243.

7257. רָבַץ **râbats**, *raw-bats´;* a prim. root; to *crouch* (on all four legs folded, like a re-cumbent animal); by impl. to *recline, re-pose, brood, lurk, imbed:*— crouch (down), fall down, make a fold, lay, (cause to, make to) lie (down), make to rest, sit.

7258. רֶבֶץ **rebets**, *reh´-bets;* from 7257; a *couch* or place of repose:— where each lay, lie down in, resting place.

7259. רִבְקָה **Ribqâh**, *rib-kaw´;* from an un-used root prob. mean. to *clog* by tying up the fetlock; *fettering* (by beauty); *Ribkah*, the wife of Isaac:— Rebekah.

7260. רַבְרַב **rabrab** (Chald.), *rab-rab´;* from 7229; *huge* (in size); *domineering* (in char-acter):— (very) great (things).

7261. רַבְרְבָן **rabr^ebân** (Chald.), *rab-reb-awn´;* from 7260; a *magnate:*— lord, prince.

7262. רַבְשָׁקֵה **Rabshâqêh**, *rab-shaw-kay´;* from 7227 and 8248; *chief butler; Rab-shakeh*, a Bab. official:— Rabshakeh.

7263. רֶגֶב **regeb**, *reh´-gheb;* from an unused root mean. to *pile* together; a *lump* of clay:— clod.

7264. רָגַז **râgaz**, *raw-gaz´;* a prim. root; to *quiver* (with any violent emotion, espec. anger or fear):— be afraid, stand in awe, disquiet, fall out, fret, move, provoke, quake, rage, shake, tremble, trouble, be wroth.

7265. רְגַז **r^egaz** (Chald.), *reg-az´*; corresp. to 7264:— provoke unto wrath.

7266. רְגַז **r^egaz** (Chald.), *reg-az´*; from 7265; violent *anger*:— rage.

7267. רֹגֶז **rôgez**, *ro´-ghez*; from 7264; *commotion, restlessness* (of a horse), *crash* (of thunder), *disquiet, anger*:— fear, noise, rage, trouble (-ing), wrath.

7268. רַגָּז **raggâz**, *rag-gawz´*; intens. from 7264; *timid*:— trembling.

7269. רָגְזָה **rogzâh**, *rog-zaw´*; fem. of 7267; *trepidation*:— trembling.

7270. רָגַל **râgal**, *raw-gal´*; a prim. root; to *walk* along; but only in spec. applications, to *reconnoiter*, to *be a tale-bearer* (i.e. *slander*); also (as denom. from 7272) to *lead about*:— backbite, search, slander, (e-) spy (out), teach to go, view.

7271. רְגַל **r^egal** (Chald.), *reg-al´*; corresp. to 7272:— foot.

7272. רֶגֶל **regel**, *reh´-gel*; from 7270; a *foot* (as used in *walking*); by impl. a *step*; by euphem. the *pudenda*:— × be able to endure, × according as, × after, × coming, × follow, (broken-) foot (-ed, -stool), × great toe, × haunt, × journey, leg, + piss, + possession, time.

7273. רַגְלִי **raglîy**, *rag-lee´*; from 7272; a *footman* (soldier):— (on) foot (-man).

7274. רֹגְלִים **Rôg^elîym**, *ro-gel-eem´*; plur. of act. part. of 7270; *fullers* (as *tramping* the cloth in washing); *Rogelim*, a place E. of the Jordan:— Rogelim.

7275. רָגַם **râgam**, *raw-gam´*; a prim. root [comp. 7263, 7321, 7551]; to *cast* together (stones), i.e. to *lapidate*:— × certainly, stone.

7276. רֶגֶם **Regem**, *reh´-gem*; from 7275; stone-heap; *Regem*, an Isr.:— Regem.

7277. רִגְמָה **rigmâh**, *rig-maw´*; fem. of the same as 7276; a *pile* (of stones), i.e. (fig.) a *throng*:— council.

7278. רֶגֶם מֶלֶךְ **Regem Melek**, *reh´-gem meh´-lek*; from 7276 and 4428; *king's heap*; *Regem-Melek*, an Isr.:— Regem-melech.

7279. רָגַן **râgan**, *raw-gan´*; a prim. root; to *grumble*, i.e. *rebel*:— murmur.

7280. רָגַע **râga´**, *raw-gah´*; a prim. root; prop. to *toss* violently and suddenly (the sea with waves, the skin with boils); fig. (in a favorable manner) to *settle*, i.e. *quiet*; spec. to *wink* (from the motion of the eye-lids):— break, divide, find ease, be a moment, (cause, give, make to) rest, make suddenly.

7281. רֶגַע **rega´**, *reh´-gah*; from 7280. a *wink* (of the eyes), i.e. a very *short space* of time:— instant, moment, space, suddenly.

7282. רָגֵעַ **râgêa´**, *raw-gay´-ah*; from 7280; *restful*, i.e. *peaceable*:— that are quiet.

7283. רָגַשׁ **râgash**, *raw-gash´*; a prim. root; to *be tumultuous*:— rage.

7284. רְגַשׁ **r^egash** (Chald.), *reg-ash´*; corresp. to 7283; to *gather* tumultuously:— assemble (together).

7285. רֶגֶשׁ **regesh**, *reh´-ghesh*; or (fem.)

רִגְשָׁה **rigshâh**, *rig-shaw´*; from 7283; a tumultuous *crowd*:— company, insurrection.

7286. רָדַד **râdad**, *raw-dad´*; a prim. root; to *tread* in pieces, i.e. (fig.) to *conquer*, or (spec.) to *overlay*:— spend, spread, subdue.

7287. רָדָה **râdâh**, *raw-daw´*; a prim. root; to *tread* down, i.e. *subjugate*; spec. to *crumble* off:— (come to, make to) have dominion, prevail against, reign, (bear, make to) rule (-r, over), take.

7288. רַדַּי **Radday**, *rad-dah´-ee*; intens. from 7287; *domineering*; *Raddai*, an Isr.:— Raddai.

7289. רָדִיד **râdîyd**, *raw-deed´*; from 7286 in the sense of *spreading*; a *veil* (as expanded):— vail, veil.

7290. רָדַם **râdam**, *raw-dam´*; a prim. root; to *stun*, i.e. *stupefy* (with sleep or death):— (be fast a-, be in a deep, cast into a dead, that) sleep (-er, -eth).

7291. רָדַף **râdaph**, *raw-daf´*; a prim. root; to *run after* (usually with hostile intent; fig. [of time] *gone by*):— chase, put to flight, follow (after, on), hunt, (be under) persecute (-ion, -or), pursue (-r).

7292. רָהַב **râhab**, *raw-hab´*; a prim. root; to *urge* severely, i.e. (fig.) *importune, embolden, capture, act insolently*:— overcome, behave self proudly, make sure, strengthen.

7293. רַהַב **rahab**, *rah´-hab*; from 7292, *bluster* (-er):— proud, strength.

7294. רַהַב **Rahab**, *rah´-hab*; the same as 7293; *Rahab* (i.e. *boaster*), an epithet of Egypt:— Rahab.

7295. רָהָב **râhâb**, *raw-hawb´*; from 7292; *insolent*:— proud.

7296. רֹהַב **rôhab**, *ro´-hab*; from 7292; *pride*:— strength.

7297. רָהָה **râhâh**, *raw-haw´*; a prim. root; to *fear*:— be afraid.

7298. רַהַט **rahaṭ**, *rah´-hat*; from an unused root appar. mean. to *hollow out*; a *channel* or *watering-box*; by resemblance a *ringlet* of hair (as forming parallel lines):— gallery, gutter, trough.

7299. רֵו **rêv** (Chald.), *rave*; from a root corresp. to 7200; *aspect*:— form.

רוב° **rûwb**. See 7378.

7300. רוּד **rûwd**, *rood;* a prim. root; to *tramp* about, i.e. *ramble* (free or disconsolate):— have the dominion, be lord, mourn, rule.

7301. רָוָה **râvâh**, *raw-vaw´;* a prim. root; to *slake* the thirst (occasionally of other appetites):— bathe, make drunk, (take the) fill, satiate, (abundantly) satisfy, soak, water (abundantly).

7302. רָוֶה **râveh**, *raw-veh´;* from 7301; *sated* (with drink):— drunkenness, watered.

7303. רֹהֲגָה° **Rôwhăgâh**, *ro-hag-aw´;* from an unused root prob. mean. to *cry* out; *outcry; Rohagah*, an Isr.:— Rohgah.

7304. רָוַח **râvach**, *raw-vakh´;* a prim. root [rather ident. with 7306]; prop. to *breathe* freely, i.e. *revive;* by impl. to *have ample room:*— be refreshed, large.

7305. רֶוַח **revach**, *reh´-vakh;* from 7304; *room,* lit. (an *interval*) or fig. (*deliverance*):— enlargement, space.

7306. רוּחַ **rûwach**, *roo´-akh;* a prim. root; prop. to *blow,* i.e. *breathe;* only (lit.) to *smell* or (by impl.) *perceive* (fig. to *anticipate, enjoy*):— accept, smell, × touch, make of quick understanding.

7307. רוּחַ **rûwach**, *roo´-akh;* from 7306; *wind;* by resemblance *breath,* i.e. a sensible (or even violent) exhalation; fig. *life, anger, unsubstantiality;* by extens. a *region* of the sky; by resemblance *spirit,* but only of a rational being (incl. its expression and functions):— air, anger, blast, breath, × cool, courage, mind, × quarter, × side, spirit ([-ual]), tempest, × vain, ([whirl-]) wind (-y).

7308. רוּחַ **rûwach** (Chald.), *roo´-akh;* corresp. to 7307:— mind, spirit, wind.

7309. רְוָחָה **revâchâh**, *rev-aw-khaw´;* fem. of 7305; *relief:*— breathing, respite.

7310. רְוָיָה **revâyâh**, *rev-aw-yaw´;* from 7301; *satisfaction:*— runneth over, wealthy.

7311. רוּם **rûwm**, *room;* a prim. root; to *be high;* act. to *rise* or *raise* (in various applications, lit. or fig.):— bring up, exalt (self), extol, give, go up, haughty, heave (up), (be, lift up on, make on, set up on, too) high (-er, one), hold up, levy, lift (-er) up, (be) lofty, (× a-) loud, mount up, offer (up), + presumptuously, (be) promote (-ion), proud, set up, tall (-er), take (away, off, up), breed worms.

7312. רוּם **rûwm**, *room;* or

      רֻם **rum**, *room;* from 7311; (lit.) *elevation* or (fig.) *elation:*— haughtiness, height, × high.

7313. רוּם **rûwm** (Chald.), *room;* corresp. to 7311; (fig. only):— extol, lift up (self), set up.

7314. רוּם **rûwm** (Chald.), *room;* from 7313; (lit.) *altitude:*— height.

7315. רוֹם **rôwm**, *rome;* from 7311; *elevation,* i.e. (adv.) *aloft:*— on high.

7316. רוּמָה **Rûwmâh**, *roo-maw´;* from 7311; *height; Rumah,* a place in Pal.:— Rumah.

7317. רוֹמָה **rôwmâh**, *ro-maw´;* fem. of 7315; *elation,* i.e. (adv.) *proudly:*— haughtily.

7318. רוֹמָם **rôwmâm**, *ro-mawm´;* from 7426; *exaltation,* i.e. (fig. and spec.) *praise:*— be extolled.

7319. רוֹמְמָה **rôwmemâh**, *ro-mem-aw´;* fem. act. part. of 7426; *exaltation,* i.e. *praise:*— high.

7320. רוֹמַמְתִּי עֶזֶר **Rôwmamtîy ʼEzer** (or

      רֹמַמְתִּי **Rômamtîy**), *ro-mam´-tee eh´-zer;* from 7311 and 5828; *I have raised* up a *help; Romamti-Ezer,* an Isr.:— Romamti-ezer.

7321. רוּעַ **rûwaʼ**, *roo-ah´;* a prim. root; to *mar* (espec. by breaking); fig. to *split* the ears (with sound), i.e. *shout* (for alarm or joy):— blow an alarm, cry (alarm, aloud, out), destroy, make a joyful noise, smart, shout (for joy), sound an alarm, triumph.

7322. רוּף **rûwph**, *roof;* a prim. root; prop. to *triturate* (in a mortar), i.e. (fig.) to *agitate* (by concussion):— tremble.

7323. רוּץ **rûwts**, *roots;* a prim. root; to *run* (for whatever reason, espec. to *rush*):— break down, divide speedily, footman, guard, bring hastily, (make) run (away, through), post, stretch out.

7324. רוּק **rûwq**, *rook;* a prim. root; to *pour* out (lit. or fig.), i.e. *empty:*— × arm, cast out, draw (out), (make) empty, pour forth (out).

7325. רוּר **rûwr**, *roor;* a prim. root; to *slaver* (with spittle), i.e. (by anal.) to *emit* a fluid (ulcerous or natural):— run.

7326. רוּשׁ **rûwsh**, *roosh;* a prim. root; to *be destitute:*— lack, needy, (make self) poor (man).

      רוֹשׁ **rôwsh**. See 7219.

7327. רוּת **Rûwth**, *rooth;* prob. for 7468; *friend; Ruth,* a Moabitess:— Ruth.

7328. רָז **râz** (Chald.), *rawz;* from an unused root prob. mean. to *attenuate,* i.e. (fig.) *hide;* a *mystery:*— secret.

7329. רָזָה **râzâh**, *raw-zaw´;* a prim. root; to *emaciate,* i.e. *make* (*become*) *thin* (lit. or fig.):— famish, wax lean.

7330. רָזֶה **râzeh**, *raw-zeh´;* from 7329; *thin:*— lean.

7331. רְזוֹן **Rezôwn**, *rez-one´;* from 7336; *prince; Rezon,* a Syrian:— Rezon.

7332. רָזוֹן **râzôwn**, *raw-zone´;* from 7329; *thinness:*— leanness, × scant.

7333. רָזוֹן **razôwn**, *raw-zone´*; from 7336; a *dignitary:*— prince.

7334. רָזִי **razîy**, *raw-zee´*; from 7329; *thinness:*— leanness.

7335. רָזַם **razam**, *raw-zam´*; a prim. root; to *twinkle* the eye (in mockery):— wink.

7336. רָזַן **razan**, *raw-zan´*; a prim. root; prob. to *be heavy*, i.e. (fig.) *honorable:*— prince, ruler.

7337. רָחַב **rachab**, *raw-khab´*; a prim. root; to *broaden* (intr. or tran., lit. or fig.):— be an-(make) large (-ing), make room, make (open) wide.

7338. רַחַב **rachab**, *rakh´-ab*; from 7337; a *width:*— breadth, broad place.

7339. רְחֹב **rechôb**, *rekh-obe´*; or

רְחוֹב **rechôwb**, *rekh-obe´*; from 7337; a *width*, i.e. (concr.) *avenue* or *area:*— broad place (way), street. See also 1050.

7340. רְחֹב **Rechôb**, *rekh-obe´*; or

רְחוֹב **Rechôwb**, *rekh-obe´*; the same as 7339; *Rechob*, the name of a place in Syria, also of a Syrian and an Isr.:— Rehob.

7341. רֹחַב **rôchab**, *ro´-khab*; from 7337; *width* (lit. or fig.):— breadth, broad, largeness, thickness, wideness.

7342. רָחָב **rachâb**, *raw-khawb´*; from 7337; *roomy*, in any (or every) direction, lit. or fig.:— broad, large, at liberty, proud, wide.

7343. רָחָב **Rachâb**, *raw-khawb´*; the same as 7342; *proud*; *Rachab*, a Canaanitess:— Rahab.

7344. רְחֹבוֹת **Rechôbôwth**, *rekh-o-bôth´*; or

רְחֹבֹת **Rechôbôth**, *rekh-o-bôth´*; plur. of 7339; *streets*; *Rechoboth*, a place in Assyria and one in Pal.:— Rehoboth.

7345. רְחַבְיָה **Rechabyâh**, *rekh-ab-yaw´*; or

רְחַבְיָהוּ **Rechabyâhûw**, *rek-ab-yaw´-hoo*; from 7337 and 3050; *Jah has enlarged*; *Rechabjah*, an Isr.:— Rehabiah.

7346. רְחַבְעָם **Rechab'âm**, *rekh-ab-awm´*; from 7337 and 5971; *a people has enlarged*; *Rechabam*, an Isr. king:— Rehoboam.

רְחֹבֹת **Rechôbôth**. See 7344.

7347. רֵחֶה **rêcheh**, *ray-kheh´*; from an unused root mean. to *pulverize*; a *mill*-stone:— mill (stone).

רְחוֹב **Rechôwb**. See 7339, 7340.

7348. רְחוּם **Rechûwm**, *rekh-oom´*; a form of 7349; *Rechum*, the name of a Pers. and of three Isr.:— Rehum.

7349. רַחוּם **rachûwm**, *rakh-oom´*; from 7355; *compassionate:*— full of compassion, merciful.

7350. רָחוֹק **râchôwq**, *raw-khoke´*; or

7351. רָחֹק **râchôq**, *raw-khoke´*; from 7368; *remote*, lit. or fig., of place or time; spec. *precious*; often used adv. (with prep.):— (a-) far (abroad, off), long ago, of old, space, great while to come.

7351. רְחִיט° **rechîyṭ**, *rekh-eet´*; from the same as 7298; a *panel* (as resembling a trough):— rafter.

7352. רַחִיק **rachîyq** (Chald.), *rakh-eek´*; corresp. to 7350:— far.

7353. רָחֵל **rachêl**, *raw-kale´*; from an unused root mean. to *journey*; a *ewe* [the *females* being the predominant element of a flock] (as a good *traveller*):— ewe, sheep.

7354. רָחֵל **Râchêl**, *raw-khale´*; the same as 7353; *Rachel*, a wife of Jacob:— Rachel.

7355. רָחַם **râcham**, *raw-kham´*; a prim. root; to *fondle*; by impl. to *love*, espec. to *compassionate:*— have compassion (on, upon), love, (find, have, obtain, shew) mercy (-iful, on, upon), (have) pity, Ruhamah, × surely.

7356. רַחַם **racham**, *rakh´-am*; from 7355; *compassion* (in the plur.); by extens. the *womb* (as *cherishing* the fetus); by impl. a *maiden:*— bowels, compassion, damsel, tender love, (great, tender) mercy, pity, womb.

7357. רַחַם **Racham**, *rakh´-am*; the same as 7356; *pity*; *Racham*, an Isr.:— Raham.

7358. רֶחֶם **rechem**, *rekh´-em*; from 7355; the *womb* [comp. 7356]:— matrix, womb.

7359. רְחֵם **rechêm** (Chald.), *rekh-ame´*; corresp. to 7356; (plur.) *pity:*— mercy.

7360. רָחָם **râchâm**, *raw-khawm´*; or (fem.)

רָחָמָה **râchâmâh**, *raw-khaw-maw´*; from 7355; a kind of *vulture* (supposed to be *tender* toward its young):— gier-eagle.

7361. רַחֲמָה **rachămâh**, *rakh-am-aw´*; fem. of 7356; a *maiden:*— damsel.

7362. רַחְמָנִי **rachmânîy**, *rakh-maw-nee´*; from 7355; *compassionate:*— pitiful.

7363. רָחַף **râchaph**, *raw-khaf´*; a prim. root; to *brood*; by impl. to *be relaxed:*— flutter, move, shake.

7364. רָחַץ **râchats**, *raw-khats´*; a prim. root; to *lave* (the whole or a part of a thing):— bathe (self), wash (self).

7365. רְחַץ **rechats** (Chald.), *rekh-ats´*; corresp. to 7364 [prob. through the accessory idea of *ministering* as a servant at the bath]; to *attend* upon:— trust.

7366. רַחַץ **rachats**, *rakh´-ats*; from 7364; a *bath:*— wash [-pot].

7367. רַחְצָה **rachtsâh**, *rakh-tsaw´*; fem. of 7366; a *bathing* place:— washing.

Hebrew

7368. רָחַק **rachaq**, *raw-khak´*; a prim. root; to *widen* (in any direction), i.e. (intr.) *recede* or (tran.) *remove* (lit. or fig., of place or relation):— (a-, be, cast, drive, get, go, keep [self], put, remove, be too, [wander], withdraw) far (away, off), loose, × refrain, very, (be) a good way (off).

7369. רָחֵק **rachêq**, *raw-khake´*; from 7368; *remote:*— that are far.

רָחֹק **rachôq**. See 7350.

7370. רָחַשׁ **rachash**, *raw-khash´*; a prim. root; to *gush:*— indite.

7371. רַחַת **rachath**, *rakh´-ath*; from 7306; a *winnowing*-fork (as *blowing* the chaff away):— shovel.

7372. רָטַב **ratab**, *raw-tab´*; a prim. root; to be *moist:*— be wet.

7373. רָטֹב **ratôb**, *raw-tobe´*; from 7372; *moist* (with sap):— green.

7374. רֶטֶט **retet**, *reh´-tet*; from an unused root mean. to *tremble; terror:*— fear.

7375. רֻטֲפַשׁ **rûwtăphash**, *roo-taf-ash´*; a root compounded from 7373 and 2954; to be *rejuvenated:*— be fresh.

7376. רָטַשׁ **ratash**, *raw-tash´*; a prim. root; to *dash* down:— dash (in pieces).

7377. רִי **rîy**, *ree*; from 7301; *irrigation*, i.e. a *shower:*— watering.

7378. רִיב **rîyb**, *reeb*; or

רוּב° **rûwb**, *roob*; a prim. root; prop. to *toss*, i.e. *grapple*; mostly fig. to *wrangle*, i.e. *hold a controversy*; (by impl.) to *defend:*— adversary, chide, complain, contend, debate, × ever, × lay wait, plead, rebuke, strive, × thoroughly.

7379. רִיב **rîyb**, *reeb*; or

רִב **rîb**, *reeb*; from 7378; a *contest* (personal or legal):— + adversary, cause, chiding, contend (-tion), controversy, multitude [from the marg.], pleading, strife, strive (-ing), suit.

7380. רִיבַי **Rîybay**, *ree-bah´-ee*; from 7378; *contentious; Ribai*, an Isr.:— Ribai.

7381. רֵיחַ **rêyach**, *ray´-akh*; from 7306; *odor* (as if *blown*):— savour, scent, smell.

7382. רֵיחַ **rêyach** (Chald.), *ray´-akh*; corresp. to 7381:— smell.

רֵים **rêym**. See 7214.

רֵיעַ **rêya'**. See 7453.

7383. רִיפָה **rîyphâh**, *ree-faw´*; or

רִפָה **rîphâh**, *ree-faw´*; from 7322; (only plur.), *grits* (as *pounded*):— ground corn, wheat.

7384. רִיפַת **Rîyphath**, *ree-fath´*; or (prob. by orth. err.)

דִיפַת **Dîyphath**, *dee-fath´*; of for. or.;

Riphath, a grandson of Japheth and his desc.:— Riphath.

7385. רִיק **rîyq**, *reek*; from 7324; *emptiness*; fig. a *worthless* thing; adv. *in vain:*— empty, to no purpose, (in) vain (thing), vanity.

7386. רֵיק **rêyq**, *rake*; or (short.)

רֵק **rêq**, *rake*; from 7324; *empty*; fig. *worthless:*— emptied (-ty), vain (fellow, man).

7387. רֵיקָם **rêyqâm**, *ray-kawm´*; from 7386; *emptily*; fig. (obj.) *ineffectually*, (subj.) *undeservedly:*— without cause, empty, in vain, void.

7388. רִיר **rîyr**, *reer*; from 7325; *saliva*; by resemblance *broth:*— spittle, white [of an egg].

7389. רֵישׁ **rêysh**, *raysh*; or

רֵאשׁ **rê'sh**, *raysh*; or

רִישׁ **rîysh**, *reesh*; from 7326; *poverty:*— poverty.

7390. רַךְ **rak**, *rak*; from 7401; *tender* (lit. or fig.); by impl. *weak:*— faint [-hearted], soft, tender ([-hearted], one), weak.

7391. רֹךְ **rôk**, *roke*; from 7401; *softness* (fig.):— tenderness.

7392. רָכַב **râkab**, *raw-kab´*; a prim. root; to *ride* (on an animal or in a vehicle); caus. to *place upon* (for riding or gen.), to *despatch:*— bring (on [horse-] back), carry, get [oneself] up, on [horse-] back, put, (cause to, make to) ride (in a chariot, on, -r), set.

7393. רֶכֶב **rekeb**, *reh´-keb*; from 7392; a *vehicle*; by impl. a *team*; by extens. *cavalry*; by anal. a *rider*, i.e. the upper millstone:— chariot, (upper) millstone, multitude [from the marg.], wagon.

7394. רֵכָב **Rêkâb**, *ray-kawb´*; from 7392; *rider; Rekab*, the name of two Arabs and of two Isr.:— Rechab.

7395. רַכָּב **rakkâb**, *rak-kawb´*; from 7392; a *charioteer:*— chariot man, driver of a chariot, horseman.

7396. רִכְבָּה **rikbâh**, *rik-baw´*; fem. of 7393; a *chariot* (collect.):— chariots.

7397. רֵכָה **Rêkâh**, *ray-kaw´*; prob. fem. from 7401; *softness; Rekah*, a place in Pal.:— Rechah.

7398. רְכוּב **rekûwb**, *rek-oob´*; from pass. part. of 7392; a *vehicle* (as *ridden* on):— chariot.

7399. רְכוּשׁ **rekûwsh**, *rek-oosh´*; or

רְכֻשׁ **rekûsh**, *rek-oosh´*; from pass. part. of 7408; *property* (as *gathered*):— good, riches, substance.

7400. רָכִיל **râkîyl**, *raw-keel´*; from 7402 a

scandal-monger (as *travelling* about):— slander, carry tales, talebearer.

7401. רָכַך **rakak**, *raw-kak´*; a prim. root; to *soften* (intr. or tran.), used fig.:— (be) faint (l-hearted|), mollify, (be, make) soft (-er), be tender.

7402. רָכַל **rakal**, *raw-kal´*; a prim. root; to *travel* for trading:— (spice) merchant.

7403. רָכָל **Rakal**, *raw-kawl´*; from 7402; *merchant; Rakal*, a place in Pal.:— Rachal.

7404. רְכֻלָּה **rekullah**, *rek-ool-law´*; fem. pass. part. of 7402; *trade* (as *peddled*):— merchandise, traffic.

7405. רָכַס **rakaç**, *raw-kas´*; a prim. root; to *tie*:— bind.

7406. רֶכֶס **rekeç**, *reh´-kes*; from 7405; a mountain *ridge* (as of *tied* summits):— rough place.

7407. רֹכֶס **rôkeç**, *ro´-kes*; from 7405; a *snare* (as of *tied* meshes):— pride.

7408. רָכַש **rakash**, *raw-kash´*; a prim. root; to *lay up*, i.e. *collect*:— gather, get.

7409. רֶכֶש **rekesh**, *reh´-kesh*; from 7408; a *relay* of animals on a post-route (as *stored* up for that purpose); by impl. a *courser*:— dromedary, mule, swift beast.

רְכֻש **rekûsh**. See 7399.

רֵם **rêm**. See 7214.

7410. רָם **Râm**, *rawm*; act. part. of 7311; *high; Ram*, the name of an Arabian and of an Isr.:— Ram. See also 1027.

רֻם **rûm**. See 7311.

7411. רָמָה **ramah**, *raw-maw´*; a prim. root; to *hurl*; spec. to *shoot*; fig. to *delude* or *betray* (as if causing to fall):— beguile, betray, |bow-| man, carry, deceive, throw.

7412. רְמָה **remah** (Chald.), *rem-aw´*; corresp. to 7411; to *throw, set*, (fig.) *assess:*— cast (down), impose.

7413. רָמָה **ramah**, *raw-maw´*; fem. act. part. of 7311; a *height* (as a seat of idolatry):— high place.

7414. רָמָה **Ramah**, *raw-maw´*; the same as 7413; *Ramah*, the name of four places in Pal.:— Ramah.

7415. רִמָּה **rimmah**, *rim-maw´*; from 7426 in the sense of *breeding* |comp. 7311|; a *maggot* (as rapidly *bred*), lit. or fig.:— worm.

7416. רִמּוֹן **rimmôwn**, *rim-mone´*; or

רִמּוֹן **rimmôn**, *rim-mone´*; from 7426; a *pomegranate*, the tree (from its *upright* growth) or the fruit (also an artificial ornament):— pomegranate.

7417. רִמּוֹן **Rimmôwn**, *rim-mone´*; or (short.)

רִמּוֹן **Rimmôn**, *rim-mone´*; or

רִמּוֹנוֹ **Rimmôwnôw** (1 Chron. 6:62 |77|),

rim-mo-no´; the same as 7416; *Rimmon*, the name of a Syrian deity, also of five places in Pal.:— Remmon, Rimmon. The addition "-methoar" (Josh. 19:13) is

הַמְּתֹאָר **ham-methô'âr**, *ham-meth-o-awr´*; pass. part. of 8388 with the art.; *the* (one) *marked off*, i.e. *which pertains*; mistaken for part of the name.

רָמוֹת **Râmôwth**. See 7418, 7433.

7418. רָמוֹת־נֶגֶב **Râmôwth-Negeb**, *raw-môth-neh´-gheb*; or

רָמַת נֶגֶב **Râmath Negeb**, *raw´-math neh´-gheb*; from the plur. or constr. form of 7413 and 5045; *heights* (or *height*) *of* (the) *South*; *Ramoth-Negeb* or *Ramath-Negeb*, a place in Pal.:— south Ramoth, Ramath of the south.

7419. רָמוּת **râmûwth**, *raw-mooth´*; from 7311; a *heap* (of carcases):— height.

7420. רֹמַח **rômach**, *ro´-makh*; from an unused root mean. to *hurl*; a *lance* (as *thrown*); espec. the iron *point*:— buckler, javelin, lancet, spear.

7421. רַמִּי **rammîy**, *ram-mee´*; for 761; a *Ramite*, i.e. Aramæan:— Syrian.

7422. רַמְיָה **Ramyâh**, *ram-yaw´*; from 7311 and 3050; *Jah has raised; Ramjah*, an Isr.:— Ramiah.

7423. רְמִיָּה **remîyâh**, *rem-ee-yaw´*; from 7411; *remissness, treachery:*— deceit (-ful, -fully), false, guile, idle, slack, slothful.

7424. רַמָּךְ **rammâk**, *ram-mawk´*; of for. or.; a brood *mare:*— dromedary.

7425. רְמַלְיָהוּ **Remalyâhûw**, *rem-al-yaw´-hoo*; from an unused root and 3050 (perh. mean. to *deck*); *Jah has bedecked; Remaljah*, an Isr.:— Remaliah.

7426. רָמַם **ramam**, *raw-mam´*; a prim. root; to *rise* (lit. or fig.):— exalt, get loneselfl up, lift up (self), mount up.

7427. רֹמֵמֻת **rômêmûth**, *ro-may-mooth´*; from the act. part. of 7426; *exaltation:*— lifting up of self.

רִמֹּן **rimmôn**. See 7416.

7428. רִמֹּן פֶּרֶץ **Rimmôn Perets**, *rim-mone´ peh´-rets*; from 7416 and 6556; *pomegranate of* (the) *breach; Rimmon-Perets*, a place in the Desert:— Rimmon-parez.

7429. רָמַס **ramaç**, *raw-mas´*; a prim. root; to *tread* upon (as a potter, in walking or abusively):— oppressor, stamp upon, trample (under feet), tread (down, upon).

7430. רָמַש **ramas**, *raw-mas´*; a prim. root; prop. to *glide* swiftly, i.e. to *crawl* or *move* with short steps; by anal. to *swarm:*— creep, move.

7431. רֶמֶשׂ **remes**, *reh´-mes*; from 7430; a

reptile or any other rapidly moving animal:— that creepeth, creeping (moving) thing.

7432. רֶמֶת **Remeth**, *reh'-meth;* from 7411; *height; Remeth*, a place in Pal.:— Remeth.

7433. רָמֹת (or רָמֹות **Râmôwth**) גִּלְעָד **Râmôth Gil'âd** (2 Chron. 22:5), *raw-moth' gil-awd';* from the plur. of 7413 and 1568; *heights of Gilad; Ramoth-Gilad*, a place E. of the Jordan:— Ramoth-gilead, Ramoth in Gilead. See also 7216.

7434. רָמַת הַמִּצְפֶּה **Râmath ham-Mitspeh**, *raw-math' ham-mits-peh';* from 7413 and 4707 with the art. interpolated; *height of the watch-tower; Ramath-ham-Mitspeh*, a place in Pal.:— Ramath-mizpeh.

7435. רָמָתִי **Râmâthîy**, *raw-maw-thee';* patron. of 7414; a *Ramathite* or inhab. of Ramah:— Ramathite.

7436. רָמָתַיִם צֹופִים **Râmâthayim Tsôwphîym**, *raw-maw-thah'-yim tso-feem';* from the dual of 7413 and the plur. of the act. part. of 6822; *double height of watchers; Ramathajim-Tsophim*, a place in Pal.:— Ramathaim-zophim.

7437. רָמַת לֶחִי **Râmath Lechîy**, *raw'-math lekh'-ee;* from 7413 and 3895; *height of (a) jaw-bone; Ramath-Lechi*, a place in Pal.:— Ramath-lehi.

רָן **Rân**. See 1028.

7438. רֹן **rôn**, *rone;* from 7442; a *shout* (of deliverance):— song.

7439. רָנָה **rânâh**, *raw-naw';* a prim. root; to *whiz:*— rattle.

7440. רִנָּה **rinnâh**, *rin-naw';* from 7442; prop. a *creaking* (or shrill sound), i.e. *shout* (of joy or grief):— cry, gladness, joy, proclamation, rejoicing, shouting, sing (-ing), triumph.

7441. רִנָּה **Rinnâh**, *rin-naw';* the same as 7440; *Rinnah*, an Isr.:— Rinnah.

7442. רָנַן **rânan**, *raw-nan';* a prim. root; prop. to *creak* (or emit a stridulous sound), i.e. to *shout* (usually for joy):— aloud for joy, cry out, be joyful (greatly, make to) rejoice, (cause to) shout (for joy), (cause to) sing (aloud, for joy, out), triumph.

7443. רֶנֶן **renen**, *reh'-nen;* from 7442; an *ostrich* (from its *wail*):— × goodly.

7444. רַנֵּן **rannên**, *ran-nane';* intens. from 7442; *shouting* (for joy):— singing.

7445. רְנָנָה **renânâh**, *ren-aw-naw';* from 7442; a *shout* (for joy):— joyful (voice), singing, triumphing.

7446. רִסָּה **Riççâh**, *ris-saw';* from 7450; a *ruin* (as *dripping* to pieces); *Rissah*, a place in the Desert:— Rissah.

7447. רָסִיס **râçîyç**, *raw-sees';* from 7450; prop. *dripping* to pieces, i.e. a *ruin;* also a *dew-drop:*— breach, drop.

7448. רֶסֶן **reçen**, *reh'-sen;* from an unused root mean. to *curb;* a *halter* (as *restraining*); by impl. the *jaw:*— bridle.

7449. רֶסֶן **Reçen**, *reh'-sen;* the same as 7448; *Resen*, a place in Ass.:— Resen.

7450. רָסַס **râçaç**, *raw-sas';* a prim. root; to *comminute;* used only as denom. from 7447, to *moisten* (with drops):— temper.

7451. רַע **ra'**, *rah;* from 7489; *bad* or (as noun) *evil* (nat. or mor.):— adversity, affliction, bad, calamity, + displease (-ure), distress, evil ([-favouredness], man, thing), + exceedingly, × great, grief (-vous), harm, heavy, hurt (-ful), ill (favoured), + mark, mischief (-vous), misery, naught (-ty), noisome, + not please, sad (-ly), sore, sorrow, trouble, vex, wicked (-ly, -ness, one), worse (-st), wretchedness, wrong. [Incl. fem.

רָעָה **râ'âh**; as adj. or noun.]

7452. רֵעַ **rêa'**, *ray'-ah;* from 7321; a *crash* (of thunder), *noise* (of war), *shout* (of joy):— × aloud, noise, shouted.

7453. רֵעַ **rêa'**, *ray'-ah;* or

רֵיעַ **rêya'**, *ray'-ah;* from 7462; an *associate* (more or less close):— brother, companion, fellow, friend, husband, lover, neighbour, × (an-) other.

7454. רֵעַ **rêa'**, *ray'-ah;* from 7462; a *thought* (as *association* of ideas):— thought.

7455. רֹעַ **rôa'**, *ro'-ah;* from 7489; *badness* (as *marring*), phys. or mor.:— × be so bad, badness, (× be so) evil, naughtiness, sadness, sorrow, wickedness.

7456. רָעֵב **râ'êb**, *raw-abe';* a prim. root; to *hunger:*— (suffer to) famish, (be, have, suffer, suffer to) hunger (-ry).

7457. רָעֵב **râ'êb**, *raw-abe';* from 7456; *hungry* (more or less intensely):— hunger bitten, hungry.

7458. רָעָב **râ'âb**, *raw-awb';* from 7456; *hunger* (more or less extensive):— dearth, famine, + famished, hunger.

7459. רְעָבֹון **re'âbôwn**, *reh-aw-bone';* from 7456; *famine:*— famine.

7460. רָעַד **râ'ad**, *raw-ad';* a prim. root: to *shudder* (more or less violently):— tremble.

7461. רַעַד **ra'ad**, *rah'-ad;* or (fem.)

רְעָדָה **re'âdâh**, *reh-aw-daw';* from 7460; a *shudder:*— trembling.

7462. רָעָה **râ'âh**, *raw-aw';* a prim. root; to *tend* a flock; i.e. *pasture* it; intr. to *graze* (lit. or fig.); gen. to *rule;* by extens. to *associate* with (as a friend):— × break, companion, keep company with, devour, eat up, evil entreat, feed, use as a friend, make friendship with, herdman, keep [sheep] (-er),

Hebrew

pastor, + shearing house, shepherd, wander, waste.

7463. רֵעֶה **rê'eh**, *ray-eh'*; from 7462; a (male) *companion:*— friend.

7464. רֵעָה **rê'âh**, *ray'-aw*; fem. of 7453; a female *associate:*— companion, fellow.

7465. רֹעָה **rô'âh**, *ro-aw'*; for 7455; *breakage:*— broken, utterly.

7466. רְעוּ **Re'ûw**, *reh-oo'*; for 7471 in the sense of 7453; *friend; Reü*, a postdiluvian patriarch:— Reu.

7467. רְעוּאֵל **Re'ûw'êl**, *reh-oo-ale'*; from the same as 7466 and 410; *friend of God; Reüel*, the name of Moses' father-in-law, also of an Edomite and an Isr.:— Raguel, Reuel.

7468. רְעוּת **re'ûwth**, *reh-ooth'*; from 7462 in the sense of 7453; a female *associate; gen.* an *additional* one:— + another, mate, neighbour.

7469. רְעוּת **re'ûwth**, *reh-ooth'*; prob. from 7462; a *feeding* upon, i.e. *grasping* after:— vexation.

7470. רְעוּת **re'ûwth** (Chald.), *reh-ooth'*; corresp. to 7469; *desire:*— pleasure, will.

7471. רְעִי **re'îy**, *reh-ee'*; from 7462; *pasture:*— pasture.

7472. רֵעִי **Rê'îy**, *ray-ee'*; from 7453; *social; Reï*, an Isr.:— Rei.

7473. רֹעִי **rô'îy**, *ro-ee'*; from act. part. of 7462; *pastoral;* as noun, a *shepherd:*— shepherd.

7474. רַעְיָה **ra'yâh**, *rah-yaw'*; fem. of 7453; a female *associate:*— fellow, love.

7475. רַעְיוֹן **ra'yôwn**, *rah-yone'*; from 7462 in the sense of 7469; *desire:*— vexation.

7476. רַעְיוֹן **ra'yôwn** (Chald.), *rah-yone'*; corresp. to 7475; a *grasp*, i.e. (fig.) mental *conception:*— cogitation, thought.

7477. רָעַל **râ'al**, *raw-al'*; a prim. root; to *reel*, i.e. (fig.) to *brandish:*— terribly shake.

7478. רַעַל **ra'al**, *rah'-al*; from 7477; a *reeling* (from intoxication):— trembling.

7479. רַעֲלָה **ra'ălâh**, *rah-al-aw'*; fem. of 7478; a long *veil* (as *fluttering*):— muffler.

7480. רְעֵלָיָה **Re'êlâyâh**, *reh-ay-law-yaw'*; from 7477 and 3050; *made to tremble* (i.e. *fearful*) *of Jah; Reëlajah*, an Isr.:— Reeliah.

7481. רָעַם **râ'am**, *raw-am'*; a prim. root; to *tumble*, i.e. *be* violently *agitated;* spec. to *crash* (of thunder); fig. to *irritate* (with anger):— make to fret, roar, thunder, trouble.

7482. רַעַם **ra'am**, *rah'-am*; from 7481; a *peal* of thunder:— thunder.

7483. רַעְמָה **ra'mâh**, *rah-maw'*; fem. of 7482; the *mane* of a horse (as *quivering* in the wind):— thunder.

7484. רַעְמָה **Ra'mâh**, *rah-maw'*; the same as 7483; *Ramah*, the name of a grandson of Ham, and of a place (perh. founded by him):— Raamah.

7485. רַעְמְיָה **Ra'amyâh**, *rah-am-yaw'*; from 7481 and 3050; *Jah has shaken; Raamjah*, an Isr.:— Raamiah.

7486. רַעְמְסֵס **Ra'meçêç**, *rah-mes-ace'*; or

רַעַמְסֵס **Ra'amçêç**, *rah-am-sace'*; of Eg. or.; *Rameses* or *Raamses*, a place in Egypt:— Raamses, Rameses.

7487. רַעֲנַן **ra'ânan** (Chald.), *rah-aw-nan'*; corresp. to 7488; *green*, i.e. (fig.) *prosperous:*— flourishing.

7488. רַעֲנָן **ra'ănân**, *rah-an-awn'*; from an unused root mean. to *be green; verdant;* by anal. *new;* fig. *prosperous:*— green, flourishing.

7489. רָעַע **râ'a'**, *raw-ah'*; a prim. root; prop. to *spoil* (lit. by *breaking* to pieces); fig. to *make* (or *be*) *good for nothing*, i.e. *bad* (physically, socially or morally):— afflict, associate selves [by mistake for 7462], break (down, in pieces), + displease, (be, bring, do) evil (doer, entreat, man), show self friendly [by mistake for 7462], do harm, (do) hurt, (behave self, deal) ill, × indeed, do mischief, punish, still, vex, (do) wicked (doer, -ly), be (deal, do) worse.

7490. רְעַע **re'a'** (Chald.), *reh-ah'*; corresp. to 7489:— break, bruise.

7491. רָעַף **râ'aph**, *raw-af'*; a prim. root; to *drip:*— distil, drop (down).

7492. רָעַץ **râ'ats**, *raw-ats'*; a prim. root; to *break* in pieces; fig. *harass:*— dash in pieces, vex.

7493. רָעַשׁ **râ'ash**, *raw-ash'*; a prim. root; to *undulate* (as the earth, the sky, etc.; also a field of grain), partic. through fear; spec. to *spring* (as a locust):— make afraid, (re-)move, quake, (make to) shake, (make to) tremble.

7494. רַעַשׁ **ra'ash**, *rah'-ash*; from 7493; *vibration, bounding, uproar:*— commotion, confused noise, earthquake, fierceness, quaking, rattling, rushing, shaking.

7495. רָפָא **râphâ'**, *raw-faw'*; or

רָפָה **râphâh**, *raw-faw'*; a prim. root; prop. to *mend* (by stitching), i.e. (fig.) to *cure:*— cure, (cause to) heal, physician, repair, × thoroughly, make whole. See 7503.

7496. רָפָא **râphâ'**, *raw-faw'*; from 7495 in the sense of 7503; prop. *lax*, i.e. (fig.) a *ghost* (as *dead;* in plur. only):— dead, deceased.

7497. רָפָא **râphâ'**, *raw-faw'*; or

רָפָה **râphâh**, *raw-faw'*; from 7495 in

the sense of *invigorating; a giant:—* giant, Rapha, Rephaim (-s). See also 1051.

7498. רָפָא **Râphâ'**, *raw-faw'; or*

רָפָה **Râphâh**, *raw-faw'; prob. the same as 7497; giant; Rapha or Raphah, the name of two Isr.:—* Rapha.

7499. רְפֻאָה **rephu'âh**, *ref-oo-aw'; fem. pass. part. of 7495; a medicament:—* heal [-ed], medicine.

7500. רִפְאוּת **riph'ûwth**, *rif-ooth'; from 7495; a cure:—* health.

7501. רְפָאֵל **Rephâ'êl**, *ref-aw-ale'; from 7495 and 410; God has cured; Rephaël, an Isr.:—* Rephael.

7502. רָפַד **râphad**, *raw-fad'; a prim. root; to spread* (a bed); by impl. to *refresh:—* comfort, make [a bed], spread.

7503. רָפָה **râphâh**, *raw-faw'; a prim. root; to slacken* (in many applications, lit. or fig.):— abate, cease, consume, draw [toward evening], fail, (be) faint, be (wax) feeble, forsake, idle, leave, let alone (go, down), (be) slack, stay, be still, be slothful, (be) weak (-en). See 7495.

7504. רָפֶה **râpheh**, *raw-feh'; from 7503; slack* (in body or mind):— weak.

רָפָה **râphâh**, **Râphâh**. See 7497, 7498.

רִפָה **riphâh**. See 7383.

7505. רָפוּא **Râphûw'**, *raw-foo'; pass. part. of 7495; cured; Raphu, an Isr.:—* Raphu.

7506. רֶפַח **Rephach**, *reh'-fakh; from an unused root appar. mean. to sustain; support; Rephach, an Isr.:—* Rephah.

7507. רְפִידָה **rephîydâh**, *ref-ee-daw'; from 7502; a railing* (as *spread* along):— bottom.

7508. רְפִידִים **Rephîydîym**, *ref-ee-deem'; plur. of the masc. of the same as 7507; ballusters; Rephidim, a place in the Desert:—* Rephidim.

7509. רְפָיָה **Rephâyâh**, *ref-aw-yaw'; from 7495 and 3050; Jah has cured; Rephajah, the name of five Isr.:—* Rephaiah.

7510. רִפְיוֹן **riphyôwn**, *rif-yone'; from 7503; slackness:—* feebleness.

7511. רָפַס **râphaç**, *raw-fas'; a prim. root; to trample, i.e. prostrate:—* humble self, submit self.

7512. רְפַס **rephaç** (Chald.), *ref-as'; corresp. to 7511:—* stamp.

7513. רַפְסֹדָה **raphçôdâh**, *raf-so-daw'; from 7511; a raft* (as *flat* on the water):— flote.

7514. רָפַק **râphaq**, *raw-fak'; a prim. root; to recline:—* lean.

7515. רָפַשׂ **râphas**, *raw-fas'; a prim. root; to trample, i.e. roil* water:— foul, trouble.

7516. רֶפֶשׁ **rephesh**, *reh'-fesh; from 7515; mud* (as *roiled*):— mire.

7517. רֶפֶת **repheth**, *reh'-feth; prob. from 7503; a stall* for cattle (from their *resting* there):— stall.

7518. רָץ **rats**, *rats; contr. from 7533; a fragment:—* piece.

7519. רָצָא **râtsâ'**, *raw-tsaw'; a prim. root; to run; also to delight* in:— accept, run.

7520. רָצַד **râtsad**, *raw-tsad'; a prim. root; prob. to look askant, i.e.* (fig.) *be jealous:—* leap.

7521. רָצָה **râtsâh**, *raw-tsaw'; a prim. root; to be pleased with; spec. to satisfy a debt:—* (be) accept (-able), accomplish, set affection, approve, consent with, delight (self), enjoy, (be, have a) favour (-able), like, observe, pardon, (be, have, take) please (-ure), reconcile self.

7522. רָצוֹן **râtsôwn**, *raw-tsone'; or*

רָצֹן **râtsôn**, *raw-tsone'; from 7521; delight* (espec. as shown):— (be) acceptable (-ance, -ed), delight, desire, favour, (good) pleasure, (own, self, voluntary) will, as ... (what) would.

7523. רָצַח **râtsach**, *raw-tsakh'; a prim. root; prop. to dash in pieces, i.e. kill* (a human being), espec. to *murder:—* put to death, kill, (man-) slay (-er), murder (-er).

7524. רֶצַח **retsach**, *reh-tsakh; from 7523; a crushing; spec. a murder-cry:—* slaughter, sword.

7525. רִצְיָא **Ritsyâ'**, *rits-yaw'; from 7521; delight; Ritsjah, an Isr.:—* Rezia.

7526. רְצִין **Retsîyn**, *rets-een'; prob. for 7522; Retsin, the name of a Syrian and of an Isr.:—* Rezin.

7527. רָצַע **râtsa'**, *raw-tsah'; a prim. root; to pierce:—* bore.

7528. רָצַף **râtsaph**, *raw-tsaf'; a denom. from 7529; to tessellate, i.e.* embroider (as if with bright stones):— pave.

7529. רֶצֶף **retseph**, *reh'-tsef; for 7565; a red-hot stone* (for baking):— coal.

7530. רֶצֶף **Retseph**, *reh'-tsef; the same as 7529; Retseph, a place in Ass.:—* Rezeph.

7531. רִצְפָּה **ritspâh**, *rits-paw'; fem. of 7529; a hot stone; also a tessellated pavement:—* live coal, pavement.

7532. רִצְפָּה **Ritspâh**, *rits-paw'; the same as 7531; Ritspah, an Israelitess:—* Rizpah.

7533. רָצַץ **râtsats**, *raw-tsats'; a prim. root; to crack in pieces, lit. or fig.:—* break, bruise, crush, discourage, oppress, struggle together.

7534. רַק **raq**, *rak; from 7556 in its orig.*

sense; *emaciated* (as if *flattened* out):— lean (l-fleshed), thin.

7535. רַק **raq,** *rak;* the same as 7534 as a noun; prop. *leanness,* i.e. (fig.) *limitation;* only adv. *merely,* or conjunc. *although:*— but, even, except, howbeit, howsoever, at the least, nevertheless, nothing but, notwithstanding, only, save, so [that], surely, yet (so), in any wise.

7536. רֹק **rôq,** *roke;* from 7556; *spittle:*— spit (-ting, -tle).

7537. רָקַב **râqab,** *raw-kab';* a prim. root; to *decay* (as by worm-eating):— rot.

7538. רָקָב **râqâb,** *raw-kawb';* from 7537; *decay* (by *caries*):— rottenness (thing).

7539. רִקָּבוֹן **riqqâbôwn,** *rik-kaw-bone';* from 7538; *decay* (by *caries*):— rotten.

7540. רָקַד **râqad,** *raw-kad';* a prim. root; prop. to *stamp,* i.e. to *spring* about (wildly or for joy):— dance, jump, leap, skip.

7541. רַקָּה **raqqâh,** *rak-kaw';* fem. of 7534; prop. *thinness,* i.e. the *side* of the head:— temple.

7542. רַקּוֹן **Raqqôwn,** *rak-kone';* from 7534; *thinness; Rakkon,* a place in Pal.:— Rakkon.

7543. רָקַח **râqach,** *raw-kakh';* a prim. root; to *perfume:*— apothecary, compound, make [ointment], prepare, spice.

7544. רֶקַח **reqach,** *reh'-kakh;* from 7543; prop. *perfumery,* i.e. (by impl.) *spicery* (for flavor):— spiced.

7545. רֹקַח **rôqach,** *ro'-kakh;* from 7542; an *aromatic:*— confection, ointment.

7546. רַקָּח **raqqâch,** *rak-kawkh';* from 7543; a male *perfumer:*— apothecary.

7547. רַקַּח **raqqûach,** *rak-koo'-akh;* from 7543; a *scented* substance:— perfume.

7548. רַקָּחָה **raqqâchâh,** *rak-kaw-khaw';* fem. of 7547; a female *perfumer:*— confectioner.

7549. רָקִיעַ **râqîya',** *raw-kee'-ah;* from 7554; prop. an *expanse,* i.e. the *firmament* or (appar.) visible arch of the sky:— firmament.

7550. רָקִיק **râqîyq,** *raw-keek';* from 7556 in its orig. sense; a thin *cake:*— cake, wafer.

7551. רָקַם **râqam,** *raw-kam';* a prim. root; to *variegate* color, i.e. *embroider;* by impl. to *fabricate:*— embroiderer, needlework, curiously work.

7552. רֶקֶם **Reqem,** *reh'-kem;* from 7551; *versi-color; Rekem,* the name of a place in Pal., also of a Midianite and an Isr.:— Rekem.

7553. רִקְמָה **riqmâh,** *rik-maw';* from 7551; *variegation* of color; spec. *embroidery:*— broidered (work), divers colours, (raiment of) needlework (on both sides).

7554. רָקַע **râqa',** *raw-kah';* a prim. root; to *pound* the earth (as a sign of passion); by anal.

to *expand* (by hammering); by impl. to *overlay* (with thin sheets of metal):— beat, make broad, spread abroad (forth, over, out, into plates), stamp, stretch.

7555. רִקֻּעַ **riqqûa',** *rik-koo-ah;* from 7554; *beaten* out, i.e. a (metallic) *plate:*— broad.

7556. רָקַק **râqaq,** *raw-kak';* a prim. root; to *spit:*— spit.

7557. רַקַּת **Raqqath,** *rak-kath';* from 7556 in its orig. sense of *diffusing; a beach* (as *expanded* shingle); *Rakkath,* a place in Pal.:— Rakkath.

7558. רִשְׁיוֹן **rîshyôwn,** *rish-yone';* from an unused root mean. to *have leave;* a *permit:*— grant.

7559. רָשַׁם **râsham,** *raw-sham';* a prim. root; to *record:*— note.

7560. רְשַׁם **resham** (Chald.), *resh-am';* corresp. to 7559:— sign, write.

7561. רָשַׁע **râsha',** *raw-shah';* a prim. root; to *be* (caus. *do* or *declare*) *wrong;* by impl. to *disturb, violate:*— condemn, make trouble, vex, be (commit, deal, depart, do) wicked (-ly, -ness).

7562. רֶשַׁע **resha',** *reh'-shah;* from 7561; a *wrong* (espec. moral):— iniquity, wicked (-ness).

7563. רָשָׁע **râshâ',** *raw-shaw';* from 7561; morally *wrong;* concr. an (actively) *bad* person:— + condemned, guilty, ungodly, wicked (man), that did wrong.

7564. רִשְׁעָה **rish'âh,** *rish-aw';* fem. of 7562; *wrong* (espec. moral):— fault, wickedly (-ness).

7565. רֶשֶׁף **resheph,** *reh'-shef;* from 8313; a live *coal;* by anal. *lightning;* fig. an *arrow,* (as *flashing* through the air); spec. *fever:*— arrow, (burning) coal, burning heat, + spark, hot thunderbolt.

7566. רֶשֶׁף **Resheph,** *reh'-shef;* the same as 7565; *Resheph,* an Isr.:— Resheph.

7567. רָשַׁשׁ **râshash,** *raw-shash';* a prim. root; to *demolish:*— impoverish.

7568. רֶשֶׁת **resheth,** *reh'-sheth;* from 3423; a *net* (as *catching* animals):— net [-work].

7569. רַתּוֹק **rattôwq,** *rat-toke';* from 7576; a *chain:*— chain.

7570. רָתַח **râthach,** *raw-thakh';* a prim. root; to *boil:*— boil.

7571. רֶתַח **rethach,** *reh'-thakh;* from 7570; a *boiling:*— × [boil] well.

7572. רַתִּיקָה° **rattîyqâh,** *rat-tee-kaw';* from 7576; a *chain:*— chain.

7573. רָתַם **râtham,** *raw-tham';* a prim. root; to *yoke* up (to the pole of a vehicle):— bind.

7574. רֶתֶם **rethem,** *reh'-them;* or

Hebrew

רֹתֶם **rôthem**, *ro´-them;* from 7573; the Spanish *broom* (from its pole-like stems):— juniper (tree).

7575. רִתְמָה **Rithmâh**, *rith-maw´;* fem. of 7574; *Rithmah*, a place in the Desert:— Rithmah.

7576. רָתַק **râthaq**, *raw-thak´;* a prim. root; to *fasten:*— bind.

7577. רְתֻקָה **rethûqâh**, *reth-oo-kaw´;* fem. pass. part. of 7576; something *fastened*, i.e. a *chain:*— chain.

7578. רְתֵת **retheth**, *reth-ayth´;* for 7374; *terror:*— trembling.

שׁ

7579. שָׁאַב **shâ'ab**, *sahw-ab´;* a prim. root; to *bale* up water:— (woman to) draw (-er, water).

7580. שָׁאַג **shâ'ag**, *shaw-ag´;* a prim. root; to *rumble* or *moan:*— × mightily, roar.

7581. שְׁאָגָה **she'âgâh**, *sheh-aw-gaw´;* from 7580; a *rumbling* or *moan:*— roaring.

7582. שָׁאָה **shâ'âh**, *shaw-aw´;* a prim. root; to *rush;* by impl. to *desolate:*— be desolate, (make a) rush (-ing), (lay) waste.

7583. שָׁאָה **shâ'âh**, *shaw-aw´;* a prim. root [rather ident. with 7582 through the idea of *whirling* to giddiness]; to *stun*, i.e. (intr.) be *astonished:*— wonder.

7584. שַׁאֲוָה **sha'ăvâh**, *shah-av-aw´;* from 7582; a *tempest* (as *rushing*):— desolation.

7585. שְׁאוֹל **she'ôwl**, *sheh-ole´;* or

שְׁאֹל **she'ôl**, *sheh-ole´;* from 7592; *hades* or the world of the dead (as if a subterranean *retreat*), incl. its accessories and inmates:— grave, hell, pit.

7586. שָׁאוּל **Shâ'ûwl**, *shaw-ool´;* pass. part. of 7592; *asked; Shaül*, the name of an Edomite and two Isr.:— Saul, Shaul.

7587. שָׁאוּלִי **Shâ'ûwlîy**, *shaw-oo-lee´;* patron. from 7856; a *Shaülite* or desc. of Shaul:— Shaulites.

7588. שָׁאוֹן **shâ'ôwn**, *shaw-one´;* from 7582; *uproar* (as of *rushing*); by impl. *destruction:*— × horrible, noise, pomp, rushing, tumult (×uous).

7589. שְׁאָט **she'ât**, *sheh-awt´;* from an unused root mean. to *push* aside; *contempt:*— despite (-ful).

7590. שָׁאט **shâ't**, *shawt;* for act. part of 7750 [comp. 7589]; one *contemning:*— that (which) despise (-d).

7591. שְׁאִיָּה **she'îyâh**, *sheh-ee-yaw´;* from 7582; *desolation:*— destruction.

7592. שָׁאַל **shâ'al**, *shaw-al´;* or

שָׁאֵל **shâ'êl**, *shaw-ale´;* a prim. root; to *inquire;* by impl. to *request;* by extens. to *de-*

mand:— ask (counsel, on), beg, borrow, lay to charge, consult, demand, desire, × earnestly, enquire, + greet, obtain leave, lend, pray, request, require, + salute, × straitly, × surely, wish.

7593. שְׁאֵל **she'êl** (Chald.), *sheh-ale´;* corresp. to 7592:— ask, demand, require.

7594. שְׁאָל **She'âl**, *sheh-awl´;* from 7592; *request; Sheäl*, an Isr.:— Sheal.

שְׁאֹל **she'ôl**. See 7585.

7595. שְׁאֵלָא **she'êlâ'** (Chald.), *sheh-ay-law´;* from 7593; prop. a *question* (at law), i.e. judicial *decision* or mandate:— demand.

7596. שְׁאֵלָה **she'êlâh**, *sheh-ay-law´;* or

שֵׁלָה **shêlâh** (1 Sam. 1:17), *shay-law´;* from 7592; a *petition;* by impl. a *loan:*— loan, petition, request.

7597. שְׁאַלְתִּיאֵל **She'altîy'êl**, *sheh-al-tee-ale´;* or

שַׁלְתִּיאֵל **Shaltîy'êl**, *shal-tee-ale´;* from 7592 and 410; *I have asked God; Sheältiël*, an Isr.:— Shalthiel, Shealtiel.

7598. שְׁאַלְתִּיאֵל **She'altîy'êl** (Chald.), *sheh-al-tee-ale´;* corresp. to 7597:— Shealtiel.

7599. שָׁאַן **shâ'an**, *shaw-an´;* a prim. root; to *loll*, i.e. *be peaceful:*— be at ease, be quiet, rest. See also 1052.

7600. שַׁאֲנָן **sha'ănân**, *shah-an-awn´;* from 7599; *secure;* in a bad sense, *haughty:*— that is at ease, quiet, tumult. Comp. 7946.

7601. שָׁאַס **shâ'aç**, *shaw-as´;* a prim. root; to *plunder:*— spoil.

7602. שָׁאַף **shâ'aph**, *shaw-af´;* a prim. root; to *inhale* eagerly; fig. to *covet;* by impl. to be *angry;* also to *hasten:*— desire (earnestly), devour, haste, pant, snuff up, swallow up.

7603. שְׂאֹר **se'ôr**, *seh-ore´;* from 7604; *barm* or yeast-cake (as *swelling* by fermentation):— leaven.

7604. שָׁאַר **shâ'ar**, *shaw-ar´;* a prim. root; prop. to *swell* up, i.e. be (caus. *make*) *redundant:*— leave, (be) left, let, remain, remnant, reserve, the rest.

7605. שְׁאָר **she'âr**, *sheh-awr´;* from 7604; a *remainder:*— × other, remnant, residue, rest.

7606. שְׁאָר **she'âr** (Chald.), *sheh-awr´;* corresp. to 7605:— × whatsoever more, residue, rest.

7607. שְׁאֵר **she'êr**, *sheh-ayr´;* from 7604; *flesh* (as *swelling* out), as living or for food; gen. *food* of any kind; fig. *kindred* by blood:— body, flesh, food, (near) kin (-sman, -swoman), near (nigh) [of kin].

7608. שַׁאֲרָה **sha'ărâh**, *shah-ar-aw´;* fem. of

7607; female *kindred* by blood:— near kins-women.

7609. שְׁאֵרָה **She'êrâh,** *sheh-er-aw´;* the same as 7608; *Sheërah,* an Israelitess:— Sherah.

7610. יָשׁוּב שְׁאָר **She'âr Yâshûwb,** *sheh-awr´ yaw-shoob´;* from 7605 and 7725; *a remnant will return; Sheär-Jashub,* the symbol. name of one of Isaiah's sons:— Shear-jashub.

7611. שְׁאֵרִית **she'êrîyth,** *sheh-ay-reeth´;* from 7604; *a remainder* or residual (surviving, final) portion:— that had escaped, be left, posterity, remain (-der), remnant, residue, rest.

7612. שֵׁאת **shê'th,** *shayth;* from 7582: *devastation:*— desolation.

7613. שְׂאֵת **se'êth,** *seh-ayth´;* from 5375; an *elevation* or leprous scab; fig. *elation* or cheerfulness; *exaltation* in rank or character:— be accepted, dignity, excellency, highness, raise up self, rising.

7614. שְׁבָא **Shebâ',** *sheb-aw´;* of for. or.; *Sheba,* the name of three early progenitors of tribes and of an Ethiopian district:— Sheba, Sabeans.

7615. שְׁבָאִי **Shebâ'îy,** *sheb-aw-ee´;* patron. from 7614; a *Shebaïte* or desc. of Sheba:— Sabean.

7616. שְׁבָב **shâbâb,** *shaw-bawb´;* from an unused root mean. to *break* up; a *fragment,* i.e. *ruin:*— broken in pieces.

7617. שָׁבָה **shâbâh,** *shaw-baw´;* a prim. root; to *transport* into captivity:— (bring away, carry, carry away, lead, lead away, take) captive (-s), drive (take) away.

7618. שְׁבוּ **shebûw,** *sheb-oo´;* from an unused root (prob. ident. with that of 7617 through the idea of *subdivision* into flashes or streamers [comp. 7632] mean. to *flame;* a gem (from its sparkle), prob. the *agate:*— agate.

7619. שְׁבוּאֵל **Shebûw'êl,** *sheb-oo-ale´;* or

שׁוּבָאֵל **Shûwbâ'êl,** *shoo-baw-ale´;* from 7617 (abbrev.) or 7725 and 410; *captive* (or *returned) of God; Shebuël* or *Shubaël,* the name of two Isr.:— Shebuel, Shubael.

7620. שָׁבוּעַ **shâbûwa',** *shaw-boo´-ah;* or

שָׁבֻעַ **shâbûa',** *shaw-boo´-ah;* also (fem.)

שְׁבֻעָה **shebû'âh,** *sheb-oo-aw´;* prop. pass. part. of 7650 as a denom. of 7651; lit. *sevened,* i.e. a *week* (spec. of years):— seven, week.

7621. שְׁבוּעָה **shebûw'âh,** *sheb-oo-aw´;* fem. pass. part. of 7650; prop. something *sworn,* i.e. an *oath:*— curse, oath, × sworn.

7622. שְׁבוּת **shebûwth,** *sheb-ooth´;* or

שְׁבִית **shebîyth,** *sheb-eeth´;* from 7617; *exile,* concr. *prisoners;* fig. a *former state* of prosperity:— captive (-ity).

7623. שָׁבַח **shâbach,** *shaw-bakh´;* a prim. root; prop. to *address* in a loud tone, i.e. (spec.) *loud;* fig. to *pacify* (as if by words):— commend, glory, keep in, praise, still, triumph.

7624. שְׁבַח **shebach** (Chald.), *sheb-akh´;* corresp. to 7623; to *adulate,* i.e. *adore:*— praise.

7625. שְׁבַט **shebat** (Chald.), *sheb-at´;* corresp. to 7626; a *clan:*— tribe.

7626. שֵׁבֶט **shêbet,** *shay´-bet;* from an unused root prob. mean. to *branch* off; a *scion,* i.e. (lit.) a *stick* (for punishing, writing, fighting, ruling, walking, etc.) or (fig.) a *clan:*— × correction, dart, rod, sceptre, staff, tribe.

7627. שְׁבָט **Shebât,** *sheb-awt´;* of for. or.; *Shebat,* a Jewish month:— Sebat.

7628. שְׁבִי **shebîy,** *sheb-ee´;* from 7618; *exiled; captured;* as noun, *exile* (abstr. or concr. and collect.); by extens. *booty:*— captive (-ity), prisoners, × take away, that was taken.

7629. שֹׁבִי **Shôbîy,** *sho-bee´;* from 7617; *captor; Shobi,* an Ammonite:— Shobi.

7630. שֹׁבַי **Shôbay,** *sho-bah´-ee;* for 7629; *Shobai,* an Isr.:— Shobai.

7631. שְׁבִיב **sebîyb** (Chald.), *seb-eeb´;* corresp. to 7632:— flame.

7632. שָׁבִיב **shâbîyb,** *shaw-beeb´;* from the same as 7616; *flame* (as *split* into tongues):— spark.

7633. שִׁבְיָה **shibyâh,** *shib-yaw´;* fem. of 7628; *exile* (abstr. or concr. and collect.):— captives (-ity).

7634. שָׁבְיָה **Shobyâh,** *shob-yaw´;* fem. of the same as 7629; *captivation; Shobjah,* an Isr.:— Shachia [*from the marg.*].

7635. שָׁבִיל **shâbîyl,** *shaw-beel´;* from the same as 7640; a *track* or passage-way (as if *flowing* along):— path.

7636. שָׁבִיס **shâbîyç,** *shaw-beece´;* from an unused root mean. to *interweave;* a *netting* for the hair:— caul.

7637. שְׁבִיעִי **shebîy'îy,** *sheb-ee-ee´;* or

שְׁבִעִי **shebî'îy,** *sheb-ee-ee´;* ord. from 7657; *seventh:*— seventh (time).

שְׁבִית **shebîyth.** See 7622.

7638. שָׂבָךְ **sâbâk,** *saw-bawk´;* from an unused root mean. to *intwine;* a *netting* (ornament to the capital of a column):— net.

שַׂבְּכָא **sabbekâ'.** See 5443.

7639. שְׂבָכָה **sebâkâh,** *seb-aw-kaw´;* fem. of 7638; a *net-work,* i.e (in hunting) a *snare,* (in arch.) a *ballustrade;* also a *reticulated* ornament to a pillar:— checker, lattice, network, snare, wreath (-enwork).

7640. שֹׁבֶל **shôbel**, *show´-bel;* from an unused root mean. to *flow;* a lady's *train* (as *trailing* after her):— leg.

7641. שִׁבֹּל **shibbôl**, *shib-bole´;* or (fem.)

שִׁבֹּלֶת **shibbôleth**, *shib-bo´-leth;* from the same as 7640; a *stream* (as *flowing*); also an *ear* of grain (as *growing* out); by anal. a *branch:*— branch, channel, ear (of corn), ([water-] flood, Shibboleth. Comp. 5451.

7642. שַׁבְלוּל **shablûwl**, *shab-lool´;* from the same as 7640; a *snail* (as if *floating* in its own slime):— snail.

שִׁבֹּלֶת **shibbôleth**. See 7641.

7643. שְׁבָם **Sᵉbâm**, *seb-awm´;* or (fem.)

שִׂבְמָה **Sibmâh**, *sib-maw´;* prob. from 1313; *spice; Sebam* or *Sibmah,* a place in Moab:— Shebam, Shibmah, Sibmah.

7644. שֶׁבְנָא **Shebnâ'**, *sheb-naw´;* or

שֶׁבְנָה **Shebnâh**, *sheb-naw´;* from an unused root mean. to *grow; growth; Shebna* or *Shebnah,* an Isr.:— Shebna, Shebnah.

7645. שְׁבַנְיָה **Sⁱᵉbanyâh**, *sheb-an-yaw´;* or

שְׁבַנְיָהוּ **Shᵉbanyâhûw**, *sheb-an-yaw´-hoo;* from the same as 7644 and 3050; *Jah has grown* (i.e. *prospered*); *Shebanjah,* the name of three or four Isr.:— Shebaniah.

7646. שָׂבַע **sâba'**, *saw-bah´;* or

שָׂבֵעַ **sâbêa'**, *saw-bay´-ah;* a prim. root; to *sate,* i.e. *fill* to satisfaction (lit. or fig.):— have enough, fill (full, self, with), be (to the) full (of), have plenty of, be satiate, satisfy (with), suffice, be weary of.

7647. שָׂבָע **sâbâ'**, *saw-baw´;* from 7646; *copiousness:*— abundance, plenteous (-ness, -ly).

7648. שֹׂבַע **sôba'**, *so´-bah;* from 7646; *satisfaction* (of food or [fig.] joy):— fill, full (-ness), satisfying, be satisfied.

7649. שָׂבֵעַ **sâbêa'**, *saw-bay´-ah;* from 7646; *satiated* (in a pleasant or disagreeable sense):— full (of), satisfied (with).

7650. שָׁבַע **shâba'**, *shaw-bah´;* a prim. root; prop. to *be complete,* but used only as a denom. from 7651; to *seven* oneself, i.e. *swear* (as if by repeating a declaration seven times):— adjure, charge (by an oath, with an oath), feed to the full [*by mistake for* 7646], take an oath, × straitly, (cause to, make to) swear.

7651. שֶׁבַע **sheba'**, *sheh´-bah;* or (masc.)

שִׁבְעָה **shib'âh**, *shib-aw´;* from 7650; a prim. cardinal number; *seven* (as the sacred *full* one); also (adv.) *seven times;* by impl. a *week;* by extens. an *indefinite* number:— (+

by) seven [-fold], -s, [-teen,teenth], -th, times). Comp. 7658.

7652. שֶׁבַע **Sheba'**, *sheh´-bah;* the same as 7651; *seven; Sheba,* the name of a place in Pal., and of two Isr.:— Sheba.

שָׁבֻעַ **shâbûa'**. See 7620.

7653. שִׂבְעָה **sib'âh**, *sib-aw´;* fem. of 7647; *satiety:*— fulness.

7654. שׂבְעָה **sob'âh**, *sob-aw´;* fem. of 7648; *satiety:*— (to have) enough, × till ... be full, [un-] satiable, satisfy, × sufficiently.

שִׁבְעָה **shib'âh**. See 7651.

7655. שִׁבְעָה **shib'âh** (Chald.), *shib-aw´;* corresp. to 7651:— seven (times).

7656. שִׁבְעָה **Shib'âh**, *shib-aw´;* masc. of 7651; *seven* (*-th*); *Shebah,* a well in Pal.:— Shebah.

שְׁבֻעָה **shᵉbû'âh**. See 7620.

שְׁבִיעִי **shᵉbîy'îy**. See 7637.

7657. שִׁבְעִים **shib'îym**, *shib-eem´;* multiple of 7651; *seventy:*— seventy, threescore and ten (+ -teen).

7658. שִׁבְעָנָה **shib'ânâh**, *shib-aw-naw´;* prol. for the masc. of 7651; *seven:*— seven.

7659. שִׁבְעָתַיִם **shib'âthayim**, *shib-aw-thah´-yim;* dual (adv.) of 7651; *seven-times:*— seven (-fold, times).

7660. שָׁבַץ **shâbats**, *shaw-bats´;* a prim. root; to *interweave* (colored) threads in squares; by impl. (*of reticulation*) to *inchase* gems in gold:— embroider, set.

7661. שָׁבָץ **shâbâts**, *shaw-bawts´;* from 7660; *intanglement,* i.e. (fig.) *perplexity:*— anguish.

7662. שְׁבַק **shᵉbaq** (Chald.), *sheb-ak´;* corresp. to the root of 7733; to *quit,* i.e. *allow to remain:*— leave, let alone.

7663. שָׂבַר **sâbar**, *saw-bar´;* err.

שָׁבַר **shâbar** (Neh. 2:13, 15), *shaw-bar´;* a prim. root; to *scrutinize;* by impl. (of *watching*) to *expect* (with hope and patience):— hope, tarry, view, wait.

7664. שֵׂבֶר **sêber**, *say´-ber;* from 7663; *expectation:*— hope.

7665. שָׁבַר **shâbar**, *shaw-bar´;* a prim. root; to *burst* (lit. or fig.):— break (down, off, in pieces, up), broken ([-hearted]), bring to the birth, crush, destroy, hurt, quench, × quite, tear, view [*by mistake for* 7663].

7666. שָׁבַר **shâbar**, *shaw-bar´;* denom. from 7668; to *deal* in grain:— buy, sell.

7667. שֶׁבֶר **sheber**, *sheh´-ber;* or

שֵׁבֶר **shêber**, *shay´-ber;* from 7665; a *fracture,* fig. *ruin;* spec. a *solution* (of a dream):— affliction, breach, breaking, broken [-footed, -handed], bruise, crashing, destruction, hurt, interpretation, vexation.

7668. שֶׁבֶר **sheber**, *sheh´-ber;* the same as 7667; *grain* (as if *broken* into kernels):— corn, victuals.

7669. שֶׁבֶר **Sheber**, *sheh´-ber;* the same as 7667; *Sheber*, an Isr.:— Sheber.

7670. שִׁבְרוֹן **shibrôwn**, *shib-rone´;* from 7665; *rupture,* i.e. a *pang;* fig. *ruin:*— breaking, destruction.

7671. שְׁבָרִים **Shebârîym**, *sheb-aw-reem´;* plur. of 7667; *ruins; Shebarim,* a place in Pal.:— Shebarim.

7672. שְׁבַשׁ **shebash** (Chald.), *sheb-ash´;* corresp. to 7660; to *intangle,* i.e. *perplex:*— be astonished.

7673. שָׁבַת **shâbath**, *shaw-bath´;* a prim. root; to *repose,* i.e. *desist* from exertion; used in many impl. relations (caus., fig. or spec.):— (cause to, let, make to) cease, celebrate, cause (make) to fail, keep (sabbath), suffer to be lacking, leave, put away (down), (make to) rest, rid, still, take away.

7674. שֶׁבֶת **shebeth**, *sheh´-beth;* from 7673; *rest, interruption, cessation:*— cease, sit still, loss of time.

7675. שֶׁבֶת **shebeth**, *sheh´-beth;* infin. of 3427; prop. *session;* but used also concr. an *abode* or *locality:*— place, seat. Comp. 3429.

7676. שַׁבָּת **shabbâth**, *shab-bawth´;* intens. from 7673; *intermission,* i.e (spec.) the *Sabbath:*— (+ every) sabbath.

7677. שַׁבָּתוֹן **shabbâthôwn**, *shab-baw-thone´;* from 7676; a *sabbatism* or special holiday:— rest, sabbath.

7678. שַׁבְּתַי **Shabbethay**, *shab-beth-ah´-ee;* from 7676; *restful; Shabbethai,* the name of three Isr.:— Shabbethai.

7679. שָׂגָא **sâgâ'**, *saw-gaw´;* a prim. root; to *grow,* i.e. (caus.) to *enlarge,* (fig.) *laud:*— increase, magnify.

7680. שְׂגָא **segâ'** (Chald.), *seg-aw´;* corresp. to 7679; to *increase:*— grow, be multiplied.

7681. שָׁגֵא **Shâgê'**, *shaw-gay´;* prob. from 7686; *erring; Shagè,* an Isr.:— Shage.

7682. שָׂגַב **sâgab**, *saw-gab´;* a prim. root; to *be* (caus. *make) lofty,* espec. *inaccessible;* by impl. *safe, strong;* used lit. and fig.— defend, exalt, be excellent, (be, set on) high, lofty, be safe, set up (on high), be too strong.

7683. שָׁגַג **shâgag**, *shaw-gag´;* a prim. root; to *stray,* i.e. (fig.) *sin* (with more or less apology):— × also for that, deceived, err, go astray, sin ignorantly.

7684. שְׁגָגָה **shegâgâh**, *sheg-aw-gaw´;* from 7683; a *mistake* or inadvertent *transgres-*

sion:— error, ignorance, at unawares, unwittingly.

7685. שָׂגָה **sâgâh**, *saw-gaw´;* a prim. root; to *enlarge* (espec. upward, also fig.):— grow (up), increase.

7686. שָׁגָה **shâgâh**, *shaw-gaw´;* a prim. root; to *stray* (caus. *mislead*), usually (fig.) to *mistake,* espec. (mor.) to *transgress;* by extens. (through the idea of intoxication) to *reel,* (fig.) *be enraptured:*— (cause to) go astray, deceive, err, be ravished, sin through ignorance, (let, make to) wander.

7687. שְׂגוּב **Segûwb**, *seg-oob´;* from 7682; *aloft; Segub,* the name of two Isr.:— Segub.

7688. שָׁגַח **shâgach**, *shaw-gakh´;* a prim. root; to *peep,* i.e. *glance* sharply at:— look (narrowly).

7689. שַׂגִּיא **saggîy'**, *sag-ghee´;* from 7679; (superl.) *mighty:*— excellent, great.

7690. שַׂגִּיא **saggîy'** (Chald.), *sag-ghee´;* corresp. to 7689; *large* (in size, quantity or number, also adv.):— exceeding, great (-ly); many, much, sore, very.

7691. שְׁגִיאָה **shegîy'âh**, *sheg-ee-aw´;* from 7686; a moral *mistake:*— error.

7692. שִׁגָּיוֹן **Shiggâyôwn**, *shig-gaw-yone´;* or

שִׁגְּיֹנָה **Shiggâyônâh**, *shig-gaw-yo-naw´;* from 7686; prop. *aberration,* i.e. (tech.) a *dithyramb* or rambling poem:— Shiggaion, Shigionoth.

7693. שָׁגַל **shâgal**, *shaw-gal´;* a prim. root; to *copulate* with:— lie with, ravish.

7694. שֵׁגָל **shêgâl**, *shay-gawl´;* from 7693; a *queen* (from cohabitation):— queen.

7695. שֵׁגָל **shêgâl** (Chald.), *shay-gawl´;* corresp. to 7694; a (legitimate) *queen:*— wife.

7696. שָׁגַע **shâga'**, *shaw-gah´;* a prim. root; to *rave* through insanity:— (be, play the) mad (man).

7697. שִׁגָּעוֹן **shiggâ'ôwn**, *shig-gaw-yone´;* from 7696; *craziness:*— furiously, madness.

7698. שֶׁגֶר **sheger**, *sheh´-ger;* from an unused root prob. mean. to *eject;* the *fetus* (as finally *expelled*):— that cometh of, increase.

7699. שַׁד **shad**, *shad;* or

שֹׁד **shôd**, *shode;* prob. from 7736 (in its orig. sense) contr.; the *breast* of a woman or animal (as *bulging*):— breast, pap, teat.

7700. שֵׁד **shêd**, *shade;* from 7736; a *demon* (as *malignant*):— devil.

7701. שֹׁד **shôd**, *shode;* or

שׁוֹד **shôwd** (Job 5:21), *shode;* from 7736; *violence, ravage:*— desolation, destruction, oppression, robbery, spoil (-ed, -er, -ing), wasting.

7702. שָׂדַד **sâdad**, *saw-dad´;* a prim. root; to *abrade,* i.e. *harrow* a field:— break clods, harrow.

7703. שָׁדַד **shâdad**, *shaw-dad´;* a prim. root; prop. to *be burly,* i.e. (fig.) *powerful* (pass. *impregnable*); by impl. to *ravage:*— dead, destroy (-er), oppress, robber, spoil (-er), × utterly, (lay) waste.

7704. שָׂדֶה **sâdeh**, *saw-deh´;* or

שָׂדַי **sâday**, *saw-dah´-ee;* from an unused root mean. to *spread* out; a *field* (as *flat*):— country, field, ground, land, soil, × wild.

7705. שִׁדָּה **shiddâh**, *shid-dah´;* from 7703; a *wife* (as *mistress* of the house):— × all sorts, musical instrument.

7706. שַׁדַּי **Shadday**, *shad-dah´-ee;* from 7703; the *Almighty:*— Almighty.

7707. שְׁדֵיאוּר **Shᵉdêyʼûwr**, *shed-ay-oor´;* from the same as 7704 and 217; *spreader of light; Shedejur,* an Isr.:— Shedeur.

7708. שִׂדִּים **Siddîym**, *sid-deem´;* plur. from the same as 7704; *flats; Siddim,* a valley in Pal.:— Siddim.

7709. שְׁדֵמָה **shᵉdêmâh**, *shed-ay-maw´;* appar. from 7704; a *cultivated field:*— blasted, field.

7710. שָׁדַף **shâdaph**, *shaw-daf´;* a prim. root; to *scorch:*— blast.

7711. שְׁדֵפָה **shᵉdêphâh**, *shed-ay-faw´;* or

שִׁדָּפוֹן **shiddâphôwn**, *shid-daw-fone´;* from 7710; *blight:*— blasted (-ing).

7712. שְׁדַר **shᵉdar** (Chald.), *shed-ar´;* a prim. root; to *endeavor:*— labour.

7713. שְׂדֵרָה **sᵉdêrâh**, *sed-ay-raw´;* from an unused root mean. to *regulate;* a *row,* i.e. *rank* (of soldiers), *story* (of rooms):— board, range.

7714. שַׁדְרַךְ **Shadrak**, *shad-rak´;* prob. of for. or.; *Shadrak,* the Bab. name of one of Daniel's companions:— Shadrach.

7715. שַׁדְרַךְ **Shadrak** (Chald.), *shad-rak´;* the same as 7714:— Shadrach.

7716. שֶׂה **seh**, *seh;* or

שֵׂי **sêy**, *say;* prob. from 7582 through the idea of *pushing* out to graze; a *member of a flock,* i.e. a *sheep* or *goat:*— (lesser, small) cattle, ewe, goat, lamb, sheep. Comp. 2089.

7717. שָׂהֵד **sâhêd**, *saw-hade´;* from an unused root mean. to *testify;* a *witness:*— record.

7718. שֹׁהַם **shôham**, *sho´-ham;* from an unused root prob. mean. to *blanch;* a *gem,* prob. the *beryl* (from its *pale* green color):— onyx.

7719. שֹׁהַם **Shôham**, *sho´-ham;* the same as 7718; *Shoham,* an Isr.:— Shoham.

7720. שַׂהֲרֹן **sahărôn**, *sah-har-one´;* from the same as 5469; a round *pendant* for the neck:— ornament, round tire like the moon.

שׁו° **shav**. See 7723.

7721. שֹׂא **sôw´**, *so;* from an unused root (akin to 5375 and 7722) mean. to *rise;* a *rising:*— arise.

7722. שׁוֹא **shôw´**, *sho;* or (fem.)

שׁוֹאָה **shôwʼâh**, *sho-aw´;* or

שֹׁאָה **shôʼâh**, *sho-aw´;* from an unused root mean. to *rush* over; a *tempest;* by impl. *devastation:*— desolate (-ion), destroy, destruction, storm, wasteness.

7723. שָׁוְא **shâvʼ**, *shawv;* or

שַׁו° **shav**, *shav;* from the same as 7722 in the sense of *desolating; evil* (as *destructive*), lit. (*ruin*) or mor. (espec. *guile*); fig. *idolatry* (as false, subj.), *uselessness* (as deceptive, obj.; also adv. in *vain*):— false (-ly), lie, lying, vain, vanity.

7724. שְׁוָא **Shᵉvâʼ**, *shev-aw´;* from the same as 7723; *false; Sheva,* an Isr.:— Sheva.

7725. שׁוּב **shûwb**, *shoob;* a prim. root; to *turn* back (hence, away) tran. or intr., lit. or fig. (not necessarily with the idea of *return* to the starting point); gen. to *retreat;* often adv. *again:*— ([break, build, circumcise, dig, do anything, do evil, feed, lay down, lie down, lodge, make, rejoice, send, take, weep]) × again, (cause to) answer (+ again), × in any case (wise), × at all, averse, bring (again, back, home again), call [to mind], carry again (back), cease, × certainly, come again (back), × consider, + continually, convert, deliver (again), + deny, draw back, fetch home again, × fro, get [oneself] (back) again, × give (again), go again (back, home), [go] out, hinder, let, [see] more, × needs, be past, × pay, pervert, pull in again, put (again, up again), recall, recompense, recover, refresh, relieve, render (again), requite, rescue, restore, retrieve, (cause to, make to) return, reverse, reward, + say nay, send back, set again, slide back, still, × surely, take back (off), (cause to, make to) turn (again, self again, away, back, back again, backward, from, off), withdraw.

שׁוּבָאֵל **Shûwbâʼêl**. See 7619.

7726. שׁוֹבָב **shôwbâb**, *sho-bawb´;* from 7725; *apostate,* i.e. *idolatrous:*— backsliding, frowardly, turn away [*from marg.*].

7727. שׁוֹבָב **Shôwbâb**, *sho-bawb´;* the same as 7726; *rebellious; Shobab,* the name of two Isr.:— Shobab.

7728. שׁוֹבֵב **shôwbêb**, *sho-babe´;* from 7725; *apostate,* i.e. *heathenish* or (actually) *heathen:*— backsliding.

7729. שׁוּבָה **shûwbâh**, *shoo-baw´;* from 7725; a *return:*— returning.

7730. שֹׂבֶךְ **sôwbek**, *so´-bek;* for 5441; a *thicket,* i.e. interlaced branches:— thick boughs.

7731. שׁוֹבָךְ **Shôwbâk**, *sho-bawk´;* perh. for 7730; *Shobak,* a Syrian:— Shobach.

7732. שׁוֹבָל **Shôwbâl**, *sho-bawl´;* from the same as 7640; *overflowing; Shobal,* the name of an Edomite and two Isr.:— Shobal.

7733. שׁוֹבֵק **Shôwbêq**, *sho-bake´;* act. part. from a prim. root mean. to *leave* (comp. 7662); *forsaking; Shobek,* an Isr.:— Shobek.

7734. שׂוּג **sûwg**, *soog;* a prim. root; to *retreat:*— turn back.

7735. שׂוּג **sûwg**, *soog;* a prim. root; to *hedge* in:— make to grow.

7736. שׁוּד **shûwd**, *shood;* a prim. root; prop. to *swell* up, i.e. fig. (by impl. of *insolence*) to *devastate:*— waste.

שׁוֹד **shôwd**. See 7699, 7701.

7737. שָׁוָה **shâvâh**, *shaw-vaw´;* a prim. root; prop. to *level,* i.e. *equalize;* fig. to *resemble;* by impl. to *adjust* (i.e. *counterbalance, be suitable, compose, place, yield,* etc.):— avail, behave, bring forth, compare, countervail, (be, make) equal, lay, be (make, a-) like, make plain, profit, reckon.

7738. שָׁוָה **shâvâh**, *shaw-vaw´;* a prim. root; to *destroy:*— × substance [*from the marg.*].

7739. שְׁוָה **shevâh** (Chald.), *shev-aw´;* corresp. to 7737; to *resemble:*— make like.

7740. שָׁוֵה **Shâvêh**, *shaw-vay´;* from 7737; *plain; Shaveh,* a place in Pal.:— Shaveh.

7741. שָׁוֵה קִרְיָתַיִם **Shâvêh Qiryâthayim**, *shaw-vay´ kir-yaw-thah´-yim;* from the same as 7740 and the dual of 7151; *plain of a double city; Shaveh-Kirjathaim,* a place E. of the Jordan:— Shaveh Kiriathaim.

7742. שׂוּחַ **sûwach**, *soo´-akh;* a prim. root; to *muse* pensively:— meditate.

7743. שׁוּחַ **shûwach**, *shoo´-akh;* a prim. root; to *sink,* lit. or fig.:— bow down, incline, humble.

7744. שׁוּחַ **Shûwach**, *shoo´-akh;* from 7743; *dell; Shuäch,* a son of Abraham:— Shuah.

7745. שׁוּחָה **shûwchâh**, *shoo-khaw´;* from 7743; a *chasm:*— ditch, pit.

7746. שׁוּחָה **Shûwchâh**, *shoo-khaw´;* the same as 7745; *Shuchah,* an Isr.:— Shuah.

7747. שׁוּחִי **Shuchîy**, *shoo-khee´;* patron. from 7744; a *Shuchite* or desc. of Shuach:— Shuhite.

7748. שׁוּחָם **Shûwchâm**, *shoo-khawm´;* from 7743; *humbly; Shucham,* an Isr.:— Shuham.

7749. שׁוּחָמִי **Shûwchâmîy**, *shoo-khaw-mee´;* patron. from 7748; a *Shuchamite* (collect.):— Shuhamites.

7750. שׂוּט **sûwṭ**, *soot;* or (by perm.)

סוּט **çûwṭ**, *soot;* a prim. root; to *detrude,* i.e. (intr. and fig.) *become derelict* (wrongly practise; namely, idolatry):— turn aside to.

7751. שׁוּט **shûwṭ**, *shoot;* a prim. root; prop. to *push* forth; (but used only fig.) to *lash,* i.e. (the sea with oars) to *row;* by impl. to *travel:*— go (about, through, to and fro), mariner, rower, run to and fro.

7752. שׁוֹט **shôwṭ**, *shote;* from 7751; a *lash* (lit. or fig.):— scourge, whip.

7753. שׂוּךְ **sûwk**, *sook;* a prim. root; to *entwine,* i.e. *shut* in (for formation, protection or restraint):— fence, (make an) hedge (up).

7754. שׂוֹךְ **sôwk**, *soke;* or (fem.)

שׂוֹכָה **sôwkâh**, *so-kaw´;* from 7753; a *branch* (as *interleaved*):— bough.

7755. שׂוֹכֹה **Sôwkôh**, *so-ko´;* or

שֹׂכֹה **Sôkôh**, *so-ko´;* or

שׂוֹכוֹ **Sôwkôw**, *so-ko´;* from 7753; *Sokoh* or *Soko,* the name of two places in Pal.:— Shocho, Shochoh, Sochoh, Soco, Socoh.

7756. שׂוּכָתִי **Sûwkâthîy**, *soo-kaw-thee´;* prob. patron. from a name corresp. to 7754 (fem.); a *Sukathite* or desc. of an unknown Isr. named Sukah:— Suchathite.

7757. שׁוּל **shûwl**, *shool;* from an unused root mean. to *hang* down; a *skirt;* by impl. a bottom *edge:*— hem, skirt, train.

7758. שׁוֹלָל **shôwlâl**, *sho-lawl´;* or

שֵׁילָל **shêylâl** (Mic. 1:8), *shay-lawl´;* from 7997; *nude* (espec. bare-foot); by impl. *captive:*— spoiled, stripped.

7759. שׁוּלַמִּית **Shûwlammîyth**, *shoo-lam-meeth´;* from 7999; *peaceful* (with the art. always pref., making it a pet name); the *Shulammith,* an epithet of Solomon's queen:— Shulamite.

7760. שׂוּם **sûwm**, *soom;* or

שִׂים **sîym**, *seem;* a prim. root; to *put* (used in a great variety of applications, lit., fig., infer. and ellip.):— × any wise, appoint, bring, call [a name], care, cast in, change, charge, commit, consider, convey, determine, + disguise, dispose, do, get, give, heap up, hold, impute, lay (down, up), leave, look, make (out), mark, + name, × on, ordain, order, + paint, place, preserve, purpose, put (on), + regard, rehearse, reward, (cause to) set (on, up), shew, + stedfastly, take, × tell, + tread down, [over-] turn, × wholly, work.

7761. שׂוּם **sûwm** (Chald.), *soom;* corresp. to

Hebrew

7760:— + command, give, lay, make, + name, + regard, set.

7762. שׁוּם **shûwm**, *shoom;* from an unused root mean. to *exhale; garlic* (from its rank *odor*):— garlic.

7763. שֹׁמֵר **Shômêr**, *sho-mare´;* or

שֹׁמֵר **Shômêr**, *sho-mare´;* act. part. of 8104; *keeper; Shomer,* the name of two Isr.:— Shomer.

7764. שׁוּנִי **Shûwnîy**, *shoo-nee´;* from an unused root mean. to *rest; quiet; Shuni,* an Isr.:— Shuni.

7765. שׁוּנִי **Shûwnîy**, *shoo-nee´;* patron. from 7764; a *Shunite* (collect.) or desc. of Shuni:— Shunites.

7766. שׁוּנֵם **Shûwnêm**, *shoo-name´;* prob. from the same as 7764; *quietly; Shunem,* a place in Pal.:— Shunem.

7767. שׁוּנַמִּית **Shûwnammîyth**, *shoo-nam-meeth´;* patrial from 7766; a *Shunammitess,* or female inhab. of Shunem:— Shunamite.

7768. שָׁוַע **shâva´**, *shaw-vah´;* a prim. root; prop. to *be free;* but used only caus. and refl. to *halloo* (for help, i.e. *freedom* from some trouble):— cry (aloud, out), shout.

7769. שׁוּעַ **shûwa´**, *shoo´-ah;* from 7768; a *halloo:*— cry, riches.

7770. שׁוּעַ **Shûwa´**, *shoo´-ah;* the same as 7769; *Shuä,* a Canaanite:— Shua, Shuah.

7771. שׁוֹעַ **shôwa´**, *sho´-ah;* from 7768 in the orig. sense of *freedom;* a *noble,* i.e. *liberal, opulent;* also (as noun in the der. sense) a *halloo:*— bountiful, crying, rich.

7772. שׁוֹעַ **Shôwa´**, *sho´-ah;* the same as 7771; *rich; Shoä,* an Oriental people:— Shoa.

7773. שֶׁוַע **sheva´**, *sheh´-vah;* from 7768; a *halloo:*— cry.

7774. שׁוּעָא **Shûwâ´**, *shoo-aw´;* from 7768; *wealth; Shuä,* an Israelitess:— Shua.

7775. שַׁוְעָה **shav´âh**, *shav-aw´;* fem. of 7773; a *hallooing:*— crying.

7776. שׁוּעָל **shûw´âl**, *shoo-awl´;* or

שֻׁעָל **shu´âl**, *shoo-awl´;* from the same as 8168; a *jackal* (as a *burrower*):— fox.

7777. שׁוּעָל **Shûw´âl**, *shoo-awl´;* the same as 7776; *Shuäl,* the name of an Isr. and of a place in Pal.:— Shual.

7778. שׁוֹעֵר **shôw´êr**, *sho-are´;* or

שֹׁעֵר **shô´êr**, *sho-are´;* act. part. of 8176 (as denom. from 8179); a *janitor:*— doorkeeper, porter.

7779. שׁוּף **shûwph**, *shoof;* a prim. root; prop. to *gape,* i.e. *snap* at; fig. to *overwhelm:*— break, bruise, cover.

7780. שׁוֹפָךְ **Shôwphâk**, *sho-fawk´;* from 8210; *poured; Shophak,* a Syrian:— Shophach.

7781. שׁוּפָמִי **Shûwphâmîy**, *shoo-faw-mee´;* patron. from 8197; a *Shuphamite* (collect.) or desc. of Shephupham:— Shuphamite.

שׁוּפָן **Shôwphân**. See 5855.

7782. שׁוֹפָר **shôwphâr**, *sho-far´;* or

שֹׁפָר **shôphâr**, *sho-far´;* from 8231 in the orig. sense of *incising;* a *cornet* (as giving a *clear* sound) or curved horn:— cornet, trumpet.

7783. שׁוּק **shûwq**, *shook;* a prim. root; to *run* after or over, i.e. *overflow:*— overflow, water.

7784. שׁוּק **shûwq**, *shook;* from 7783; a *street* (as *run* over):— street.

7785. שׁוֹק **shôwq**, *shoke;* from 7783; the (lower) *leg* (as a *runner*):— hip, leg, shoulder, thigh.

7786. שׂוּר **sûwr**, *soor;* a prim. root; prop. to *vanquish;* by impl. to *rule* (caus. *crown*):— make princes, have power, reign. See 5493.

7787. שׂוּר **sûwr**, *soor;* a prim. root [rather ident. with 7786 through the idea of *reducing* to pieces; comp. 4883]; to *saw:*— cut.

7788. שׁוּר **shûwr**, *shoor;* a prim. root; prop. to *turn,* i.e. *travel* about (as a harlot or a merchant):— go, sing. See also 7891.

7789. שׁוּר **shûwr**, *shoor;* a prim. root [rather ident. with 7788 through the idea of *going round* for inspection]; to *spy* out, i.e. (gen.) *survey,* (for evil) *lurk for,* (for good) *care for:*— behold, lay wait, look, observe, perceive, regard, see.

7790. שׁוּר **shûwr**, *shoor;* from 7889; a *foe* (as *lying in wait*):— enemy.

7791. שׁוּר **shûwr**, *shoor;* from 7788; a *wall* (as *going about*):— wall.

7792. שׁוּר **shûwr** (Chald.), *shoor;* corresp. to 7791:— wall.

7793. שׁוּר **Shûwr**, *shoor;* the same as 7791; *Shur,* a region of the Desert:— Shur.

7794. שׁוֹר **shôwr**, *shore;* from 7788; a *bullock* (as a *traveller*):— bull (-ock), cow, ox, wall [by mistake for 7791].

7795. שׂוֹרָה **sôwrâh**, *so-raw´;* from 7786 in the prim. sense of 5493; prop. a *ring,* i.e. (by anal.) a *row* (adv.):— principal.

שׂוֹרֵק **sôwrêq**. See 8321.

7796. שׂוֹרֵק **Sôwrêq**, *so-rake´;* the same as 8321; a *vine; Sorek,* a valley in Pal.:— Sorek.

7797. שׂוּשׂ **sûws**, *soos;* or

שׂיש **sîys**, *sece;* a prim. root; to *be bright,* i.e. *cheerful:*— be glad, × greatly, joy, make mirth, rejoice.

7798. שַׁוְשָׁע **Shavshâ'**, *shav-shaw´;* from 7797; *joyful; Shavsha,* an Isr.:— Shavsha.

7799. שׁוּשַׁן **shûwshan**, *shoo-shan´;* or

שׁוֹשָׁן **shôwshân**, *sho-shawn´;* or

שֹׁשָׁן **shôshân**, *sho-shawn´;* and (fem.)

שׁוֹשַׁנָּה **shôwshannâh**, *sho-shan-naw´;* from 7797; a *lily* (from its *whiteness*), as a flower or arch. ornament; also a (straight) *trumpet* (from the *tubular* shape):— lily, Shoshannim.

7800. שׁוּשַׁן **Shûwshan**, *shoo-shan´;* the same as 7799; *Shushan,* a place in Pers.:— Shushan.

7801. שׁוּשַׁנְכִי **Shûwshankîy** (Chald.), *shoo-shan-kee´;* of for. or.; a *Shushankite* (collect.) or inhab. of some unknown place in Ass.:— Susanchites.

7802. שׁוּשַׁן עֵדוּת **Shûwshan 'Êdûwth**, *shoo-shan´ ay-dooth´;* or (plur. of former)

שׁוֹשַׁנִּים עֵדוּת **Shôwshannîym 'Êdûwth**, *sho-shan-neem´ ay-dooth´;* from 7799 and 5715; *lily* (or *trumpet*) *of assemblage; Shushan-Eduth* or *Shoshannim-Eduth,* the title of a popular song:— Shoshannim-Eduth, Shushan-eduth.

שׁוּשַׁק° **Shûwshaq**. See 7895.

7803. שׁוּתֶלַח **Shûwthelach**, *shoo-theh´-lakh;* prob. from 7582 and the same as 8520; *crash of breakage; Shuthelach,* the name of two Isr.:— Shuthelah.

7804. שֵׁזַב **sheᵉzab** (Chald.), *shez-ab´;* corresp. to 5800; to *leave,* i.e. (caus.) *free:*— deliver.

7805. שָׁזַף **shâzaph**, *shaw-zaf´;* a prim. root; to *tan* (by sun-burning); fig. (as if by a piercing ray) to *scan:*— look up, see.

7806. שָׁזַר **shâzar**, *shaw-zar´;* a prim. root; to *twist* (a thread of straw):— twine.

7807. שַׁח **shach**, *shakh;* from 7817; *sunk,* i.e. *downcast:*— + humble.

7808. שֵׂחַ **sêach**, *say´-akh;* for 7879; *communion,* i.e. (refl.) *meditation:*— thought.

7809. שָׁחַד **shâchad**, *shaw-khad´;* a prim. root; to *donate,* i.e. *bribe:*— hire, give a reward.

7810. שַׁחַד **shachad**, *shakh´-ad;* from 7809; a *donation* (venal or redemptive):— bribe (-ry), gift, present, reward.

7811. שָׂחָה **sâchâh**, *saw-khaw´;* a prim. root; to *swim;* caus. to *inundate:*— (make to) swim.

7812. שָׁחָה **shâchâh**, *shaw-khaw´;* a prim. root; to *depress,* i.e. *prostrate* (espec. refl. in homage to royalty or God):— bow (self) down, crouch, fall down (flat), humbly beseech, do (make) obeisance, do reverence, make to stoop, worship.

7813. שָׂחוּ **sâchûw**, *saw´-khoo;* from 7811; a *pond* (for *swimming*):— to swim in.

7814. שְׂחוֹק **sᵉchôwq**, *sekh-oke´;* or

שְׂחֹק **sᵉchôq**, *sekh-oke´;* from 7832; *laughter* (in merriment or defiance):— derision, laughter (-ed to scorn, -ing), mocked, sport.

7815. שְׁחוֹר **shᵉchôwr**, *shekh-ore´;* from 7835; *dinginess,* i.e. perh. *soot:*— coal.

שִׁיחוֹר **shîchôwr**. See 7883.

שָׁחוֹר **shâchôwr**. See 7838.

7816. שְׁחוּת **shᵉchûwth**, *shekh-ooth´;* from 7812; *pit:*— pit.

7817. שָׁחַח **shâchach**, *shaw-khakh´;* a prim. root; to *sink* or *depress* (refl. or caus.):— bend, bow (down), bring (cast) down, couch, humble self, be (bring) low, stoop.

7818. שָׂחַט **sâchat**, *saw-khat´;* a prim. root; to *tread* out, i.e. *squeeze* (grapes):— press.

7819. שָׁחַט **shâchat**, *shaw-khat´;* a prim. root; to *slaughter* (in sacrifice or massacre):— kill, offer, shoot out, slay, slaughter.

7820. שָׁחַט **shâchat**, *shaw-khat´;* a prim. root [rather ident. with 7819 through the idea of *striking*]; to *hammer* out:— beat.

7821. שְׁחִיטָה **sᵉchîytâh**, *shekh-ee-taw´;* from 7819; *slaughter:*— killing.

7822. שְׁחִין **sᵉchîyn**, *shekh-een´;* from an unused root prob. mean. to *burn; inflammation,* i.e. an *ulcer;*— boil, botch.

7823. שָׁחִיס **shâchîyç**, *shaw-khece´;* or

סָחִישׁ **çâchîysh**, *saw-kheesh´;* from an unused root appar. mean. to *sprout; after-growth:*— (that) which springeth of the same.

7824. שָׁחִיף **shâchîyph**, *shaw-kheef´;* from the same as 7828; a *board* (as *chipped* thin):— cieled with.

7825. שְׁחִית **sᵉchîyth**, *shekh-eeth´;* from 7812; a *pit*-fall (lit. or fig.):— destruction, pit.

7826. שַׁחַל **shachal**, *shakh´-al;* from an unused root prob. mean. to *roar;* a *lion* (from his characteristic *roar*):— (fierce) lion.

7827. שְׁחֵלֶת **sᵉchêleth**, *shekh-ay´-leth;* appar. from the same as 7826 through some obscure idea, perh. that of *peeling* off by concussion of sound; a *scale* or shell, i.e. the aromatic *mussel:*— onycha.

7828. שַׁחַף **shachaph**, *shakh´-af;* from an unused root mean. to *peel,* i.e. *emaciate;* the *gull* (as *thin*):— cuckoo.

7829. שַׁחֶפֶת **shachepheth**, *shakh-eh´-feth;* from the same as 7828; *emaciation:*— consumption.

7830. שַׁחַץ **shachats**, *shakh´-ats;* from an unused root appar. mean. to *strut; haugh-*

tiness (as evinced by the attitude):— × lion, pride.

7831. שְׁחָצֹים° **Shachatsôwm**, *shakh-ats-ome´;* from the same as 7830; *proudly; Shachatsom,* a place in Pal.:— Shahazimah [*from the marg.*].

7832. שָׂחַק **sâchaq**, *saw-khak´;* a prim. root; to *laugh* (in pleasure or detraction); by impl. to *play:*— deride, have in derision, laugh, make merry, mock (-er), play, rejoice, (laugh to) scorn, be in (make) sport.

7833. שָׁחַק **shâchaq**, *shaw-khak´;* a prim. root; to *comminate* (by trituration or attrition):— beat, wear.

7834. שַׁחַק **shachaq**, *shakh´-ak;* from 7833; a *powder* (as *beaten* small): by anal. a thin *vapor;* by extens. the *firmament:*— cloud, small dust, heaven, sky.

שְׂחֹק **sᵉchôq.** See 7814.

7835. שָׁחַר **shâchar**, *shaw-khar´;* a prim. root [rather ident. with 7836 through the idea of the *duskiness* of early dawn]; to *be dim* or dark (in color):— be black.

7836. שָׁחַר **shâchar**, *shaw-khar´;* a prim. root; prop. to *dawn,* i.e. (fig.) *be* (up) *early* at any task (with the impl. of earnestness); by extens. to *search* for (with painstaking):— [do something] betimes, enquire early, rise (seek) betimes, seek (diligently) early, in the morning.

7837. שַׁחַר **shachar**, *shakh´-ar;* from 7836; *dawn* (lit., fig. or adv.):— day (-spring), early, light, morning, whence riseth.

שִׁחֹר **Shîchôr.** See 7883.

7838. שָׁחֹר **shâchôr**, *shaw-khore´;* or

שָׁחוֹר **shâchôwr**, *shaw-khore´;* from 7835; prop. *dusky,* but also (absol.) *jetty:*— black.

7839. שַׁחֲרוּת **shachărûwth**, *shakh-ar-ooth´;* from 7836; a *dawning,* i.e. (fig.) *juvenescence:*— youth.

7840. שְׁחַרְחֹרֶת **shᵉcharchôreth**, *shekh-ar-kho´-reth;* from 7835; *swarthy:*— black.

7841. שְׁחַרְיָה **Shᵉcharyâh**, *shekh-ar-yaw´;* from 7836 and 3050; *Jah has sought; Shecharjah,* an Isr.:— Shehariah.

7842. שַׁחֲרַיִם **Shachărayim**, *shakh-ar-ah´-yim;* dual of 7837; *double dawn; Shacharajim,* an Isr.:— Shaharaim.

7843. שָׁחַת **shâchath**, *shaw-khath´;* a prim. root; to *decay,* i.e. (caus.) *ruin* (lit. or fig.):— batter, cast off, corrupt (-er, thing), destroy (-er, -uction), lose, mar, perish, spill, spoiler, × utterly, waste (-r).

7844. שְׁחַת **shᵉchath** (Chald.), *shekh-ath´;* corresp. to 7843:— corrupt, fault.

7845. שַׁחַת **shachath**, *shakh´-ath;* from 7743; a

pit (espec. as a trap); fig. *destruction:*— corruption, destruction, ditch, grave, pit.

7846. שֵׂט **sêṭ**, *sayte;* or

סֵט **çêṭ**, *sayt;* from 7750; a *departure* from right, i.e. *sin:*— revolter, that turn aside.

7847. שָׂטָה **sâṭâh**, *saw-taw´;* a prim. root; to *deviate* from duty:— decline, go aside, turn.

7848. שִׁטָּה **shiṭṭâh**, *shit-taw´;* fem. of a der. [only in the plur.

שִׁטִּים **shiṭṭîym**, *shit-teem´;* mean. the *sticks* of wood] from the same as 7850; the *acacia* (from its *scourging* thorns):— shittah, shittim. See also 1029.

7849. שָׁטַח **shâṭach**, *shaw-takh´;* a prim. root; to *expand:*— all abroad, enlarge, spread, stretch out.

7850. שֹׁטֵט **shôṭêṭ**, *sho-tate´;* act. part. of an otherwise unused root mean. (prop. to *pierce;* but only as a denom. from 7752) to *flog;* a *goad:*— scourge.

7851. שִׁטִּים **Shiṭṭîym**, *shit-teem´;* the same as the plur. of 7848; *acacia* trees; *Shittim,* a place E. of the Jordan:— Shittim.

7852. שָׂטַם **sâṭam**, *saw-tam´;* a prim. root; prop. to *lurk* for, i.e. *persecute:*— hate, oppose self against.

7853. שָׂטַן **sâṭan**, *saw-tan´;* a prim. root; to *attack,* (fig.) *accuse:*— (be an) adversary, resist.

7854. שָׂטָן **sâṭân**, *saw-tawn´;* from 7853; an *opponent;* espec. (with the art. pref.) *Satan,* the arch-enemy of good:— adversary, Satan, withstand.

7855. שִׂטְנָה **siṭnâh**, *sit-naw´;* from 7853; *opposition* (by letter):— accusation.

7856. שִׂטְנָה **Siṭnâh**, *sit-naw´;* the same as 7855; *Sitnah,* the name of a well in Pal.:— Sitnah.

7857. שָׁטַף **shâṭaph**, *shaw-taf´;* a prim. root; to *gush;* by impl. to *inundate, cleanse;* by anal. to *gallop, conquer:*— drown, (over-) flow (-whelm), rinse, run, rush, (throughly) wash (away).

7858. שֶׁטֶף **sheṭeph**, *sheh´-tef;* or

שֵׁטֶף **shêṭeph**, *shay´-tef;* from 7857; a *deluge* (lit. or fig.):— flood, outrageous, overflowing.

7859. שְׁטַר **sᵉṭar** (Chald.), *set-ar´;* of uncert. der.; a *side:*— side.

7860. שֹׁטֵר **shôṭêr**, *sho-tare´;* act. part. of an otherwise unused root prob. mean. to *write;* prop. a *scribe,* i.e. (by anal. or impl.) an official *superintendent* or *magistrate:*— officer, overseer, ruler.

7861. שִׁטְרַי° **Shiṭray**, *shit-rah´-ee;* from the same as 7860; *magisterial; Shitrai,* an Isr.:— Shitrai.

7862. שַׁי **shay**, *shah´-ee;* prob. from 7737; a *gift* (as *available*):— present.

7863. שִׁיא **sîy'**, *see;* from the same as 7721 by perm.; *elevation:*— excellency.

7864. שְׁיָא° **Sheyâ'**, *sheh-yaw´;* for 7724; *Sheja,* an Isr.:— Sheva [*from the marg.*].

7865. שִׁיאֹן **Sîy'ôn**, *see-ohn´;* from 7863; *peak; Sion,* the summit of Mt. Hermon:— Sion.

7866. שִׁיאֹן **Shî'yôwn**, *shee-ohn´;* from the same as 7722; *ruin; Shijon,* a place in Pal.:— Shihon.

7867. שִׂיב **sîyb**, *seeb;* a prim. root; prop. to *become aged,* i.e. (by impl.) to *grow gray:*— (be) grayheaded.

7868. שִׂיב **sîyb** (Chald.), *seeb;* corresp. to 7867:— elder.

7869. שֵׂיב **sêyb**, *sabe;* from 7867; old *age:*— age.

7870. שִׁיבָה **shîybâh**, *shee-baw´;* by perm. from 7725; a *return* (of property):— captivity.

7871. שִׁיבָה **shîybâh**, *shee-baw´;* from 3427; *residence:*— while ... lay.

7872. שֵׂיבָה **sêybâh**, *say-baw´;* fem. of 7869; old *age:*— (be) gray (grey hoar, -y) hairs (head, -ed), old age.

7873. שִׂיג **sîyg**, *seeg;* from 7734; a *withdrawal* (into a private place):— pursuing.

7874. שִׂיד **sîyd**, *seed;* a prim. root prob. mean. to *boil* up (comp. 7736); used only as denom. from 7875; to *plaster:*— plaister.

7875. שִׂיד **sîyd**, *seed;* from 7874; *lime* (as *boiling* when slacked):— lime, plaister.

7876. שָׁיָה **shâyâh**, *shaw-yaw´;* a prim. root; to *keep* in memory:— be unmindful. [Render Deut. 32:18, "A Rock bore thee, *thou must recollect;* and (yet) thou hast forgotten," etc.]

7877. שִׁיזָא **Shîyzâ'**, *shee-zaw´;* of unknown der.; *Shiza,* an Isr.:— Shiza.

7878. שִׂיַח **sîyach**, *see´-akh;* a prim. root; to *ponder,* i.e. (by impl.) *converse* (with oneself, and hence, aloud) or (tran.) *utter:*— commune, complain, declare, meditate, muse, pray, speak, talk (with).

7879. שִׂיַח **sîyach**, *see´-akh;* from 7878; a *contemplation;* by impl. an *utterance:*— babbling, communication, complaint, meditation, prayer, talk.

7880. שִׂיַח **sîyach**, *see´-akh;* from 7878; a *shoot* (as if *uttered* or put forth), i.e. (gen.) *shrubbery:*— bush, plant, shrub.

7881. שִׂיחָה **sîychâh**, *see-khaw´;* fem. of 7879; *reflection;* by extens. *devotion:*— meditation, prayer.

7882. שִׁיחָה **shîychâh**, *shee-khaw´;* for 7745; a *pit*-fall:— pit.

7883. שִׁיחוֹר **Shîychôwr**, *shee-khore´;* or

שִׁחוֹר **Shîchôwr**, *shee-khore´;* or

שִׁחֹר **Shîchôr**, *shee-khore´;* prob. from 7835; *dark,* i.e. *turbid; Shichor,* a stream of Egypt:— Shihor, Sihor.

7884. שִׁיחוֹר לִבְנָת **Shîychôwr Libnâth**, *shee-khore´ lib-nawth´;* from the same as 7883 and 3835; *darkish whiteness; Shichor-Libnath,* a stream of Pal.:— Shihor-libnath.

7885. שַׁיִט **shayiṭ**, *shay´-yit;* from 7751; an *oar;* also (comp. 7752) a *scourge*° (fig.):— oar, scourge.

7886. שִׁילֹה **Shîylôh**, *shee-lo´;* from 7951; *tranquil; Shiloh,* an epithet of the Messiah:— Shiloh.

7887. שִׁילֹה **Shîylôh**, *shee-lo´;* or

שִׁלֹה **Shîlôh**, *shee-lo´;* or

שִׁילוֹ **Shîylôw**, *shee-lo´;* or

שִׁלוֹ **Shîlôw**, *shee-lo´;* from the same as 7886; *Shiloh,* a place in Pal.:— Shiloh.

7888. שִׁילוֹנִי **Shiylôwnîy**, *shee-lo-nee´;* or

שִׁילֹנִי **Shîylôniy**, *shee-lo-nee´;* or

שִׁלֹנִי **Shîlôniy**, *shee-lo-nee´;* from 7887; a *Shilonite* or inhab. of Shiloh:— Shilonite.

שֵׁילָל **shêylâl**. See 7758.

7889. שִׁימֹן **Shîymôwn**, *shee-mone´;* appar. for 3452; *desert; Shimon,* an Isr.:— Shimon.

7890. שַׁיִן **shayin**, *shah´-yin;* from an unused root mean. to *urinate; urine:*— piss.

7891. שִׁיר **shîyr**, *sheer;* or (the orig. form)

שׁוּר° **shûwr** (1 Sam. 18:6), *shoor;* a prim. root [rather ident. with 7788 through the idea of *strolling* minstrelsy]; to *sing:*— behold [by mistake for 7789], sing (-er, -ing man, -ing woman).

7892. שִׁיר **shîyr**, *sheer;* or fem.

שִׁירָה **shîyrâh**, *shee-raw´;* from 7891; a *song;* abstr. *singing:*— musical (-ick), × sing (-er, -ing), song.

שִׂישׂ **sîys**. See 7797.

7893. שַׁיִשׁ **shayish**, *shah´-yish;* from an unused root mean. to *bleach,* i.e. *whiten; white,* i.e. *marble:*— marble. See 8336.

7894. שִׁישָׁא **Shîyshâ'**, *shee-shaw´;* from the same as 7893; *whiteness; Shisha,* an Isr.:— Shisha.

7895. שִׁישַׁק **Shîyshaq**, *shee-shak´;* or

שׁוּשַׁק° **Shûwshaq**, *shoo-shak´;* of Eg. der.; *Shishak,* an Eg. king:— Shishak.

7896. שִׁית **shîyth**, *sheeth;* a prim. root; to *place* (in a very wide application):— apply, appoint, array, bring, consider, lay (up), let alone, × look, make, mark, put (on), + regard, set, shew, be stayed, × take.

7897. שִׁית **shîyth**, *sheeth;* from 7896; a *dress* (as *put* on):— attire.

7898. שַׁיִת **shayith**, *shahˈ-yith;* from 7896; *scrub* or *trash*, i.e. wild *growth* of weeds or briers (as if *put* on the field):— thorns.

7899. שֵׂךְ **sêk**, *sake;* from 5526 in the sense of 7753; a *brier* (as of a hedge):— prick.

7900. שֹׂךְ **sôk**, *soke;* from 5526 in the sense of 7753; a *booth* (as *interlaced*):— tabernacle.

7901. שָׁכַב **shâkab**, *shaw-kabˈ;* a prim. root; to *lie* down (for rest, sexual connection, decease or any other purpose):— × at all, cast down, ([lover-]) lay (self) (down), (make to) lie (down, down to sleep, still, with), lodge, ravish, take rest, sleep, stay.

7902. שְׁכָבָה **sheˈkâbâh**, *shek-aw-bawˈ;* from 7901; a *lying* down (of dew, or for the sexual act):— × carnally, copulation, × lay, seed.

7903. שְׁכֹבֶת **sheˈkôbeth**, *shek-oˈ-beth;* from 7901; a (sexual) *lying* with:— × lie.

7904. שָׁכָה **shâkâh**, *shaw-kawˈ;* a prim. root; to *roam* (through lust):— in the morning [by mistake for 7925].

7905. שֻׁכָּה **sukkâh**, *sook-kawˈ;* fem. of 7900 in the sense of 7899; a *dart* (as pointed like a thorn):— barbed iron.

7906. שֵׂכוּ **Sêkûw**, *sayˈ-koo;* from an unused root appar. mean. to *surmount;* an *observatory* (with the art.); *Seku*, a place in Pal.:— Sechu.

7907. שֶׂכְוִי **sekvîy**, *sek-veeˈ;* from the same as 7906; *observant*, i.e. (concr.) the *mind:*— heart.

7908. שְׁכוֹל **sheˈkôwl**, *shek-oleˈ;* infin. of 7921; *bereavement:*— loss of children, spoiling.

7909. שַׁכּוּל **shakkuwl**, *shak-koolˈ;* or

שַׁכֻּל **shakkul**, *shak-koolˈ;* from 7921; *bereaved:*— barren, bereaved (robbed) of children (whelps).

7910. שִׁכּוֹר **shikkôwr**, *shik-koreˈ;* or

שִׁכֹּר **shikkôr**, *shik-koreˈ;* from 7937; *intoxicated*, as a state or a habit:— drunk (-ard, -en, -en man).

7911. שָׁכַח **shâkach**, *shaw-kakhˈ;* or

שָׁכֵחַ **shâkêach**, *shaw-kayˈ-akh;* a prim. root; to *mislay*, i.e. to *be oblivious of*, from want of memory or attention:— × at all, (cause to) forget.

7912. שְׁכַח **sheˈkach** (Chald.), *shek-akhˈ;* corresp. to 7911 through the idea of disclosure of a *covered* or *forgotten* thing; to *discover* (lit. or fig.):— find.

7913. שָׁכֵחַ **shâkêach**, *shaw-kayˈ-akh;* from 7911; *oblivious:*— forget.

7914. שְׂכִיָּה **sekîyâh**, *sek-ee-yawˈ;* fem. from the same as 7906; a *conspicuous* object:— picture.

7915. שַׂכִּין **sakkîyn**, *sak-keenˈ;* intens. perh. from the same as 7906 in the sense of 7753; a *knife* (as *pointed* or edged):— knife.

7916. שָׂכִיר **sâkîyr**, *saw-keerˈ;* from 7936; a man *at wages* by the day or year:— hired (man, servant), hireling.

7917. שְׂכִירָה **sekîyrâh**, *sek-ee-rawˈ;* fem. of 7916; a *hiring:*— that is hired.

7918. שָׁכַךְ **shâkak**, *shaw-kakˈ;* a prim. root; to *weave* (i.e. *lay*) a trap; fig. (through the idea of *secreting*) to *allay* (passions; phys. *abate* a flood):— appease, assuage, make to cease, pacify, set.

7919. שָׂכַל **sâkal**, *saw-kalˈ;* a prim. root; to *be* (caus. *make* or *act*) *circumspect* and hence, *intelligent:*— consider, expert, instruct, prosper, (deal) prudent (-ly), (give) skill (-ful), have good success, teach, (have, make to) understand (-ing), wisdom, (be, behave self, consider, make) wise (-ly), guide wittingly.

7920. שְׂכַל **sekal** (Chald.), *sek-alˈ;* corresp. to 7919:— consider.

7921. שָׁכֹל **shâkôl**, *shaw-koleˈ;* a prim. root; prop. to *miscarry*, i.e. *suffer abortion;* by anal. to *bereave* (lit. or fig.):— bereave (of children), barren, cast calf (fruit, young), be (make) childless, deprive, destroy, × expect, lose children, miscarry, rob of children, spoil.

7922. שֶׂכֶל **sekel**, *sehˈ-kel;* or

שֵׂכֶל **sêkel**, *sayˈ-kel;* from 7919; *intelligence;* by impl. *success:*— discretion, knowledge, policy, prudence, sense, understanding, wisdom, wise.

שַׁכֻּל **shakkûl**. See 7909.

שִׂכְלוּת **siklûwth**. See 5531.

7923. שִׁכֻּלִים **shikkûlîym**, *shik-koo-leemˈ;* plur. from 7921; *childlessness* (by continued bereavements):— to have after loss of others.

7924. שָׂכְלְתָנוּ **sokleˈthânûw** (Chald.), *sok-leth-aw-nooˈ;* from 7920; *intelligence:*— understanding.

7925. שָׁכַם **shâkam**, *shaw-kamˈ;* a prim. root; prop. to *incline* (the shoulder to a burden); but used only as denom. from 7926; lit. to *load up* (on the back of man or beast), i.e. to *start early* in the morning:— (arise, be up, get [oneself] up, rise up) early (betimes), morning.

7926. שְׁכֶם **sheˈkem**, *shek-emˈ;* from 7925; the

neck (between the shoulders) as the place of burdens; fig. the *spur* of a hill:— back, × consent, portion, shoulder.

7927. שֶׁכֶם **Sh^ekem,** *shek-em´;* the same as 7926; *ridge; Shekem,* a place in Pal.:— Shechem.

7928. שֶׁכֶם **Shekem,** *sheh´-kem;* for 7926; *Shekem,* the name of a Hivite and two Isr.:— Shechem.

7929. שִׁכְמָה **shikmâh,** *shik-maw´;* fem. of 7926; the *shoulder*-bone:— shoulder blade.

7930. שִׁכְמִי **Shikmîy,** *shik-mee´;* patron. from 7928; a *Shikmite* (collect.), or desc. of Shekem:— Shichemites.

7931. שָׁכַן **shâkan,** *shaw-kan´;* a prim. root [appar. akin (by transm.) to 7901 through the idea of *lodging;* comp. 5531, 7925]; to *reside* or permanently stay (lit. or fig.):— abide, continue, (cause to, make to) dwell (-er), have habitation, inhabit, lay, place, (cause to) remain, rest, set (up).

7932. שְׁכַן **sh^ekan** (Chald.), *shek-an´;* corresp. to 7931:— cause to dwell, have habitation.

7933. שֶׁכֶן **sheken,** *sheh´-ken;* from 7931; a *residence:*— habitation.

7934. שָׁכֵן **shâkên,** *shaw-kane´;* from 7931; a *resident;* by extens. a fellow-*citizen:*— inhabitant, neighbour, nigh.

7935. שְׁכַנְיָה **Sh^ekanyâh,** *shek-an-yaw´;* or (prol.)

שְׁכַנְיָהוּ **Sh^ekanyâhûw,** *shek-an-yaw´-hoo;* from 7931 and 3050; *Jah has dwelt; Shekanjah,* the name of nine Isr.:— Shecaniah, Shechaniah.

7936. שָׂכַר **sâkar,** *saw-kar´;* or (by perm.)

סָכַר **çâkar** (Ezra 4:5), *saw-kar´;* a prim. root [appar. akin (by prosthesis) to 3739 through the idea of temporary *purchase;* comp. 7937]; to *hire:*— earn wages, hire (out self), reward, × surely.

7937. שָׁכַר **shâkar,** *shaw-kar´;* a prim. root; to *become tipsy;* in a qualified sense, to *satiate* with a stimulating drink or (fig.) influence:— (be filled with) drink (abundantly), (be, make) drunk (-en), be merry. [Superlative of 8248.]

7938. שֶׂכֶר **seker,** *seh´-ker;* from 7936; *wages:*— reward, sluices.

7939. שָׂכָר **sâkâr,** *saw-kawr´;* from 7936; *payment* of contract; concr. *salary, fare, maintenance;* by impl. *compensation, benefit:*— hire, price, reward [-ed], wages, worth.

7940. שָׂכָר **Sâkar,** *saw-kar´;* the same as 7939; *recompense; Sakar,* the name of two Isr.:— Sacar.

7941. שֵׁכָר **shêkâr,** *shay-kawr´;* from 7937; an *intoxicant,* i.e. intensely alcoholic *liquor:*— strong drink, + drunkard, strong wine.

שִׁכֹּר **shikkôr.** See 7910.

7942. שִׁכְּרוֹן **Shikk^erôwn,** *shik-ker-one´;* for 7943; *drunkenness, Shikkeron,* a place in Pal.:— Shicron.

7943. שִׁכָּרוֹן **shikkârôwn,** *shik-kaw-rone´;* from 7937; *intoxication:*— (be) drunken (-ness).

7944. שַׁל **shal,** *shal;* from 7952 abbrev.; a *fault:*— error.

7945. שֶׁל **shel,** *shel;* for the rel. 834; used with prep. pref., and often followed by some pron. aff.; on *account* of, *what*soever, *which*soever:— cause, sake.

7946. שַׁלְאֲנָן **shal'ănân,** *shal-an-awn´;* for 7600; *tranquil:*— being at ease.

7947. שָׁלַב **shâlab,** *shaw-lab´;* a prim. root; to *space* off; intens. (*evenly*) to *make equidistant:*— equally distant, set in order.

7948. שָׁלָב **shâlâb,** *shaw-lawb´;* from 7947; a *spacer* or raised *interval,* i.e. the *stile* in a frame or panel:— ledge.

7949. שָׁלַג **shâlag,** *shaw-lag´;* a prim. root; prop. mean. to *be white;* used only as denom. from 7950; to *be snow-white* (with the linen clothing of the slain):— be as snow.

7950. שֶׁלֶג **sheleg,** *sheh´-leg;* from 7949; *snow* (prob. from its *whiteness*):— snow (-y).

7951. שָׁלָה **shâlâh,** *shaw-law´;* or

שָׁלַו **shâlav** (Job 3:26), *shaw-lav´;* a prim. root; to *be tranquil,* i.e. *secure* or *successful:*— be happy, prosper, be in safety.

7952. שָׁלָה **shâlâh,** *shaw-law´;* a prim. root [prob. rather ident. with 7953 through the idea of *educing*]; to *mislead:*— deceive, be negligent.

7953. שָׁלָה **shâlâh,** *shaw-law´;* a prim. root [rather cognate (by contr.) to the base of 5394, 7997 and their congeners through the idea of *extracting*]; to *draw* out or off, i.e. *remove* (the soul by death):— take away.

7954. שְׁלָה **sh^elâh** (Chald.), *shel-aw´;* corresp. to 7951; to *be secure:*— at rest.

שִׁלֹה **Shîlôh.** See 7887.

7955. שָׁלָה° **shâlâh** (Chald.), *shaw-law´;* from a root corresp. to 7952; a *wrong:*— thing amiss.

שֵׁלָה **shêlâh.** See 7596.

7956. שֵׁלָה **Shêlâh,** *shay-law´;* the same as 7596 (short.); *request; Shelah,* the name of a postdiluvian patriarch and of an Isr.:— Shelah.

7957. שַׁלְהֶבֶת **shalhebeth,** *shal-heh´-beth;* from the same as 3851 with sibilant pref.; a *flare* of fire:— (flaming) flame.

שָׁלַו **shâlav.** See 7951.

7958. שְׂלָו° **s^elâv,** *sel-awv´;* or

שְׂלָיו **sᵉlâyv**, *sel-awv´*; by orth. var. from 7951 through the idea of *sluggishness;* the *quail* collect. (as *slow* in flight from its weight):— quails.

7959. שֶׁלֶו **shelev**, *sheh´-lev;* from 7951; *security:*— prosperity.

שִׁלוֹ **Shîlôw.** See 7887.

7960. שָׁלוּ **shâlûw** (Chald.), *shaw-loo´;* or

שָׁלוּת **shâlûwth** (Chald.), *shaw-looth´;* from the same as 7955; a *fault:*— error, × fail, thing amiss.

7961. שָׁלֵו **shâlêv**, *shaw-lave´;* or

שָׁלֵיו **shâlêyv**, *shaw-lave´;* fem.

שְׁלֵוָה **shᵉlêvâh**, *shel-ay-vaw´;* from 7951; *tranquil;* (in a bad sense) *careless;* abstr. *security:*— (being) at ease, peaceable, (in) prosper (-ity), quiet (-ness), wealthy.

7962. שַׁלְוָה **shalvâh**, *shal-vaw´;* from 7951; *security* (genuine or false):— abundance, peace (-ably), prosperity, quietness.

7963. שְׁלֵוָה **shᵉlêvâh** (Chald.), *shel-ay-vaw´;* corresp. to 7962; *safety:*— tranquillity. See also 7961.

7964. שִׁלּוּחַ **shillûwach**, *shil-loo´-akh;* or

שִׁלֻּחַ **shillûach**, *shil-loo´-akh;* from 7971; (only in plur.) a *dismissal,* i.e. (of a wife) *divorce* (espec. the document); also (of a daughter) *dower:*— presents, have sent back.

7965. שָׁלוֹם **shâlôwm**, *shaw-lome´;* or

שָׁלֹם **shâlôm**, *shaw-lome´;* from 7999; *safe,* i.e. (fig.) *well, happy, friendly;* also (abstr.) *welfare,* i.e. *health, prosperity, peace:*— × do, familiar, × fare, favour, + friend, × great, (good) health, (× perfect, such as be at) peace (-able, -ably), prosper (-ity, -ous), rest, safe (-ty), salute, welfare, (× all is, be) well, × wholly.

7966. שִׁלּוּם **shillûwm**, *shil-loom´;* or

שִׁלֻּם **shillûm**, *shil-loom´;* from 7999; a *requital,* i.e. (secure) *retribution,* (venal) a *fee:*— recompense, reward.

7967. שַׁלּוּם **Shallûwm**, *shal-loom´;* or (short.)

שַׁלֻּם **Shallûm**, *shal-loom´;* the same as 7966; *Shallum,* the name of fourteen Isr.:— Shallum.

שְׁלוֹמִית **Shᵉlôwmîyth.** See 8019.

7968. שַׁלּוּן **Shallûwn**, *shal-loon´;* prob. for 7967; *Shallun,* an Isr.:— Shallum.

7969. שָׁלוֹשׁ **shâlôwsh**, *shaw-loshe´;* or

שָׁלֹשׁ **shâlôsh**, *shaw-loshe´;* masc.

שְׁלוֹשָׁה **shᵉlôwshâh**, *shel-o-shaw´;* or

שְׁלֹשָׁה **shᵉlôshâh**, *shel-o-shaw´;* a prim. number; *three;* occasionally (ord.) *third,* or (multipl.) *thrice:*— + fork, + often [-times], third, thir[-teen, -teenth], three, + thrice. Comp. 7991.

7970. שְׁלוֹשִׁים **shᵉlôwshîym**, *shel-o-sheem´;* or

שְׁלֹשִׁים **shᵉlôshîym**, *shel-o-sheem´;* multiple of 7969; *thirty;* or (ord.) *thirtieth:*— thirty, thirtieth. Comp. 7991.

שָׁלוּת **shâlûwth.** See 7960.

7971. שָׁלַח **shâlach**, *shaw-lakh´;* a prim. root; to *send away, for,* or *out* (in a great variety of applications):— × any wise, appoint, bring (on the way), cast (away, out), conduct, × earnestly, forsake, give (up), grow long, lay, leave, let depart (down, go, loose), push away, put (away, forth, in, out), reach forth, send (away, forth, out), set, shoot (forth, out), sow, spread, stretch forth (out).

7972. שְׁלַח **shᵉlach** (Chald.), *shel-akh´;* corresp. to 7971:— put, send.

7973. שֶׁלַח **shelach**, *sheh´-lakh;* from 7971; a *missile* of attack, i.e. *spear;* also (fig.) a *shoot* of growth; i.e. *branch:*— dart, plant, × put off, sword, weapon.

7974. שֶׁלַח **Shelach**, *sheh´-lakh;* the same as 7973; *Shelach,* a postdiluvian patriarch:— Salah, Shelah. Comp. 7975.

7975. שִׁלֹחַ **Shilôach**, *shee-lo´-akh;* or (in imitation of 7974)

שֶׁלַח **Shelach** (Neh. 3:15), *sheh´-lakh;* from 7971; *rill; Shiloäch,* a fountain of Jerusalem:— Shiloah, Siloah.

שִׁלֻּחַ **shillûach.** See 7964.

7976. שִׁלֻּחָה **shilluchâh**, *shil-loo-khaw´;* fem. of 7964; a *shoot:*— branch.

7977. שִׁלְחִי **Shilchîy**, *shil-khee´;* from 7973; *missive,* i.e. *armed; Shilchi,* an Isr.:— Shilhi.

7978. שִׁלְחִים **Shilchîym**, *shil-kheem´;* plur. of 7973; *javelins* or *sprouts; Shilchim,* a place in Pal.:— Shilhim.

7979. שֻׁלְחָן **shulchân**, *shool-khawn´;* from 7971; a *table* (as *spread* out); by impl. a *meal:*— table.

7980. שָׁלַט **shâlaṭ**, *shaw-lat´;* a prim. root; to *dominate,* i.e. *govern;* by impl. to *permit:*— (bear, have) rule, have dominion, give (have) power.

7981. שְׁלֵט **shᵉlêṭ** (Chald.), *shel-ate´;* corresp. to 7980:— have the mastery, have power, bear rule, be (make) ruler.

7982. שֶׁלֶט **sheleṭ**, *sheh´-let;* from 7980; prob. a *shield* (as *controlling,* i.e. protecting the person):— shield.

7983. שִׁלְטוֹן **shilṭôwn**, *shil-tone´;* from 7980; a *potentate:*— power.

7984. שִׁלְטוֹן **shiltôwn** (Chald.), *shil-tone´*; or

שִׁלְטוֹן **shiltôn**, *shil-tone´*; corresp. to 7983:— ruler.

7985. שָׁלְטָן **sholṭân** (Chald.), *shol-tawn´*; from 7981; *empire* (abstr. or concr.):— dominion.

7986. שַׁלֶּטֶת **shalleṭeth**, *shal-leh´-teth*; fem. from 7980; a *vixen:*— imperious.

7987. שְׁלִי **shᵉlîy**, *shel-ee´*; from 7951; *privacy:*— + quietly.

7988. שִׁלְיָה **shilyâh**, *shil-yaw´*; fem. from 7953; a *fetus* or *babe* (as *extruded* in birth):— young one.

שְׁלָיו **sᵉlâyv**. See 7958.

שְׁלָיו **shaleyv**. See 7961.

7989. שַׁלִּיט **shalliyṭ**, *shal-leet´*; from 7980; *potent;* concr. a *prince* or *warrior:*— governor, mighty, that hath power, ruler.

7990. שַׁלִּיט **shalliyṭ** (Chald.), *shal-leet´*; corresp. to 7989; *mighty;* abstr. *permission;* concr. a *premier:*— captain, be lawful, rule (-r).

7991. שָׁלִישׁ **shâlîysh**, *shaw-leesh´*; or

שָׁלוֹשׁ° **shâlôwsh** (1 Chron. 11:11; 12:18), *shaw-loshe´;* or

שָׁלֹשׁ° **shâlôsh** (2 Sam. 23:13), *shaw-loshe´;* from 7969; a *triple*, i.e. (as a musical instrument) a *triangle* (or perh. rather *three*-stringed lute); also (as an indef. great quantity) a *three*-fold measure (perh. a *treble* ephah); also (as an officer) a general of the *third* rank (upward, i.e. the highest):— captain, instrument of musick, (great) lord, (great) measure, prince, three [*from marg.*].

7992. שְׁלִישִׁי **shᵉlîyshîy**, *shel-ee-shee´*; ord. from 7969; *third;* fem. a *third* (part); by extens. a *third* (day, year or time); spec. a *third*-story cell):— third (part, rank, time), three (years old).

7993. שָׁלַךְ **shâlak**, *shaw-lak;* a prim. root; to *throw* out, down or away (lit. or fig.):— adventure, cast (away, down, forth, off, out), hurl, pluck, throw.

7994. שָׁלָךְ **shâlâk**, *shaw-lawk´;* from 7993; *bird of prey*, usually thought to be the *pelican* (from *casting* itself into the sea):— cormorant.

7995. שַׁלֶּכֶת **shalleketh**, *shal-leh´-keth;* from 7993; a *felling* (of trees):— when cast.

7996. שַׁלֶּכֶת **Shalleketh**, *shal-leh´-keth;* the same as 7995; *Shalleketh*, a gate in Jerusalem:— Shalleketh.

7997. שָׁלַל **shâlal**, *shaw-lal´;* a prim. root; to *drop* or *strip;* by impl. to *plunder:*— let fall, make self a prey, × of purpose, (make a, [take]) spoil.

7998. שָׁלָל **shâlâl**, *shaw-lawl´;* from 7997; *booty:*— prey, spoil.

7999. שָׁלַם **shâlam**, *shaw-lam´;* a prim. root; to *be safe* (in mind, body or estate); fig. to *be* (caus. *make*) *completed;* by impl. to *be friendly;* by extens. to *reciprocate* (in various applications):— make amends, (make an) end, finish, full, give again, make good, (re-) pay (again), (make) (to) (be at) peace (-able), that is perfect, perform, (make) prosper (-ous), recompense, render, requite, make restitution, restore, reward, × surely.

8000. שְׁלַם **shᵉlam** (Chald.), *shel-am´;* corresp. to 7999; to *complete*, to *restore:*— deliver, finish.

8001. שְׁלָם **shᵉlâm** (Chald.), *shel-awm´;* corresp. to 7965; *prosperity:*— peace.

8002. שֶׁלֶם **shelem**, *sheh´-lem;* from 7999; prop. *requital*, i.e. a (voluntary) sacrifice in *thanks:*— peace offering.

8003. שָׁלֵם **shâlêm**, *shaw-lame´;* from 7999; *complete* (lit. or fig.); espec. *friendly:*— full, just, made ready, peaceable, perfect (-ed), quiet, Shalem [by *mistake for a name*], whole.

8004. שָׁלֵם **Shâlêm**, *shaw-lame´;* the same as 8003; *peaceful; Shalem*, an early name of Jerusalem:— Salem.

שָׁלוֹם **shâlôm**. See 7965.

8005. שִׁלֵּם **shillêm**, *shil-lame´;* from 7999; *requital:*— recompense.

8006. שִׁלֵּם **Shillêm**, *shil-lame´;* the same as 8005; *Shillem*, an Isr.:— Shillem.

שִׁלּוּם **shillûm**. See 7966.

שַׁלּוּם **Shallûm**. See 7967.

8007. שַׂלְמָא **Salmâ'**, *sal-maw´;* prob. for 8008; *clothing; Salma*, the name of two Isr.:— Salma.

8008. שַׂלְמָה **salmâh**, *sal-maw´;* transp. for 8071; a *dress:*— clothes, garment, raiment.

8009. שַׂלְמָה **Salmâh**, *sal-maw´;* the same as 8008; *clothing; Salmah*, an Isr.:— Salmon. Comp. 8012.

8010. שְׁלֹמֹה **Shᵉlômôh**, *shel-o-mo´;* from 7965; *peaceful; Shelomah*, David's successor:— Solomon.

8011. שִׁלֻּמָה **shillumâh**, *shil-loo-maw´;* fem. of 7966; *retribution:*— recompense.

8012. שַׂלְמוֹן **Salmôwn**, *sal-mone´;* from 8008; *investiture; Salmon*, an Isr.:— Salmon. Comp. 8009.

8013. שְׁלֹמוֹת **Shᵉlômôwth**, *shel-o-moth´;* fem. plur. of 7965; *pacifications; Shelomoth*, the name of two Isr.:— Shelomith [*from the marg.*], Shelomoth. Comp. 8019.

8014. שַׁלְמַי **Salmay**, *sal-mah´-ee;* from 8008; *clothed; Salmai,* an Isr.:— Shalmai.

8015. שְׁלֹמִי **Sh⁰lômîy**, *shel-o-mee´;* from 7965; *peaceable; Shelomi,* an Isr.:— Shelomi.

8016. שִׁלֵּמִי **Shillêmîy**, *shil-lay-mee´;* patron. from 8006; a *Shilemite* (collect.) or desc. of Shillem:— Shillemites.

8017. שְׁלֻמִיאֵל **Sh⁰lûmîy'êl**, *shel-oo-mee-ale´;* from 7965 and 410; *peace of God; Shelumiel,* an Isr.:— Shelumiel.

8018. שֶׁלֶמְיָה **Shelemyâh**, *shel-em-yaw´;* or

שֶׁלֶמְיָהוּ **Shelemyâhuw**, *shel-em-yaw´-hoo;* from 8002 and 3050; *thank-offering of Jah; Shelemjah,* the name of nine Isr.:— Shelemiah.

8019. שְׁלֹמִית **Sh⁰lômîyth**, *shel-o-meeth´;* or

שְׁלוֹמִית **Sh⁰lôwmiyth** (Ezra 8:10), *shel-o-meeth´;* from 7965; *peaceableness; Shelomith,* the name of five Isr. and three Israelitesses:— Shelomith.

8020. שַׁלְמַן **Shalman**, *shal-man´;* of for. der.; *Shalman,* a king appar. of Assyria:— Shalman. Comp. 8022.

8021. שַׁלְמֹן **shalmôn**, *shal-mone´;* from 7999; a *bribe:*— reward.

8022. שַׁלְמַנְאֶסֶר **Shalman'eçer**, *shal-man-eh´-ser;* of for. der.; *Shalmaneser,* an Ass. king:— Shalmaneser. Comp 8020.

8023. שִׁלֹנִי **Shîlônîy**, *shee-lo-nee´;* the same as 7888; *Shiloni,* an Isr.:— Shiloni.

8024. שֵׁלָנִי **Shêlânîy**, *shay-law-nee´;* from 7956; a *Shelanite* (collect.), or desc. of Shelah:— Shelanites.

8025. שָׁלַף **shâlaph**, *saw-laf´;* a prim. root; to *pull* out, up or off:— draw (off), grow up, pluck off.

8026. שֶׁלֶף **Sheleph**, *sheh´-lef;* from 8025; *extract; Sheleph,* a son of Jokthan:— Sheleph.

8027. שָׁלַשׁ **shâlash**, *shaw-lash´;* a prim. root perh. orig. to *intensify,* i.e. *treble;* but appar. used only as denom. from 7969, to *be* (caus. *make*) *triplicate* (by restoration, in portions, strands, days or years):— do the third time, (divide into, stay) three (days, -fold, parts, years old).

8028. שֶׁלֶשׁ **Shelesh**, *sheh´-lesh;* from 8027; *triplet; Shelesh,* an Isr.:— Shelesh.

שָׁלֹשׁ **shâlôsh**. See 7969.

8029. שִׁלֵּשׁ **shillêsh**, *shil-laysh´;* from 8027; a desc. of the *third* degree, i.e. *great grandchild:*— third [generation].

8030. שִׁלְשָׁה **Shilshâh**, *shil-shaw´;* fem. from the same as 8028; *triplication; Shilshah,* an Isr.:— Shilshah.

8031. שָׁלִשָׁה **Shâlîshâh**, *shaw-lee-shaw´;* fem. from 8027; *trebled* land; *Shalishah,* a place in Pal.:— Shalisha.

שָׁלֹשָׁה **shâlôshâh**. See 7969.

8032. שִׁלְשׁוֹם **shilshôwm**, *shil-shome´;* or

שִׁלְשֹׁם **shilshôm**, *shil-shome´;* from the same as 8028; *trebly,* i.e. (in time) *day before yesterday:*— + before (that time, -time), excellent things [from the marg.], + heretofore, three days, + time past.

שְׁלֹשִׁים **sh⁰lôshîym**. See 7970.

שַׁלְתִּיאֵל **Shaltîy'êl**. See 7597.

8033. שָׁם **shâm**, *shawm;* a prim. particle [rather from the rel. 834]; *there* (transferring to time) *then;* often *thither,* or *thence:*— in it, + thence, there (-in, + of, + out), + thither, + whither.

8034. שֵׁם **shêm**, *shame;* a prim. word [perh. rather from 7760 through the idea of def. and conspicuous *position;* comp. 8064]; an *appellation,* as a mark or memorial of individuality; by impl. *honor, authority, character:*— + base, [in-] fame [-ous], named (-d), renown, report.

8035. שֵׁם **Shêm**, *shame;* the same as 8034; *name; Shem,* a son of Noah (often includ. his posterity):— Sem, Shem.

8036. שֻׁם **shum** (Chald.), *shoom;* corresp. to 8034:— name.

8037. שַׁמָּא **Shammâ'**, *sham-maw´;* from 8074; *desolation; Shamma,* an Isr.:— Shamma.

8038. שֶׁמְאֵבֶר **Shem'êber**, *shem-ay´-ber;* appar. from 8034 and 83; *name of pinion,* i.e. *illustrious; Shemeber,* a king of Zeboim:— Shemeber.

8039. שִׁמְאָה **Shim'âh**, *shim-aw´;* perh. for 8093; *Shimah,* an Isr.:— Shimah. Comp. 8043.

8040. שְׂמֹאול **s⁰mô'wl**, *sem-ole´;* or

שְׂמֹאל **s⁰mô'l**, *sem-ole´;* a prim. word [rather perh. from the same as 8071 (by insertion of א) through the idea of *wrapping* up]; prop. *dark* (as *enveloped*), i.e. the *north;* hence (by orientation), the *left* hand:— left (hand, side).

8041. שְׂמָאל **sâma'l**, *saw-mal´;* a prim. root [rather denom. from 8040]; to *use* the *left* hand or pass in that direction):— (go, turn) (on the, to the) left.

8042. שְׂמָאלִי **s⁰mâ'lîy**, *sem-aw-lee´;* from 8040; situated on the *left* side:— left.

8043. שִׁמְאָם **Shim'âm**, *shim-awm´;* for 8039 [comp. 38]; *Shimam,* an Isr.:— Shimeam.

8044. שַׁמְגַּר **Shamgar**, *sham-gar´;* of uncert. der.; *Shamgar,* an Isr. judge:— Shamgar.

8045. שָׁמַד **shâmad**, *shaw-mad´;* a prim.

root; to *desolate:*— destroy (-uction), bring to nought, overthrow, perish, pluck down, × utterly.

8046. שְׁמַד **shemad** (Chald.), *shem-ad´;* corresp. to 8045:— consume.

שָׁמֶה **shâmeh.** See 8064.

8047. שַׁמָּה **shammâh,** *sham-maw´;* from 8074; *ruin;* by impl. *consternation:*— astonishment, desolate (-ion), waste, wonderful thing.

8048. שַׁמָּה **Shammâh,** *sham-maw´;* the same as 8047; *Shammah,* the name of an Edomite and four Isr.:— Shammah.

8049. שַׁמְהוּת **Shamhûwth,** *sham-hooth´;* for 8048; *desolation; Shamhuth,* an Isr.:— Shamhuth.

8050. שְׁמוּאֵל **Shemûw'êl,** *sehm-oo-ale´;* from the pass. part. of 8085 and 410; *heard of God; Shemuel,* the name of three Isr.:— Samuel, Shemuel.

שְׁמוֹנֶה **shemôwneh.** See 8083.

שְׁמוֹנָה **shemôwnâh.** See 8083.

שְׁמוֹנִים **shemôwnîym.** See 8084.

8051. שַׁמּוּעַ **Shammûwa',** *sham-moo´-ah;* from 8074; *renowned; Shammua,* the name of four Isr.:— Shammua, Shammuah.

8052. שְׁמוּעָה **shemûw'âh,** *sehm-oo-aw´;* fem. pass. part. of 8074; something *heard,* i.e. an *announcement:*— bruit, doctrine, fame, mentioned, news, report, rumor, tidings.

8053. שָׁמוּר° **Shâmûwr,** *shaw-moor´;* pass. part. of 8103; *observed; Shamur,* an Isr.:— Shamir [*from the marg.*].

8054. שַׁמּוֹת **Shammôwth,** *sham-môth´;* plur. of 8047; *ruins; Shammoth,* an Isr.:— Shamoth.

8055. שָׂמַח **sâmach,** *saw-makh´;* a prim. root; prob. to *brighten* up, i.e. (fig.) *be* (caus. *make*) *blithe* or *gleesome:*— cheer up, be (make) glad, (have, make) joy (-ful), be (make) merry, (cause to, make to) rejoice, × very.

8056. שָׂמֵחַ **sâmêach,** *saw-may´-akh;* from 8055; *blithe* or *gleeful:*— (be) glad, joyful, (making) merry, (l-hearted), -ily), rejoice (-ing).

8057. שִׂמְחָה **simchâh,** *sim-khaw´;* from 8056; *blithesomeness* or *glee,* (relig. or festival):— × exceeding (-ly), gladness, joy (-fulness), mirth, pleasure, rejoice (-ing).

8058. שָׁמַט **shâmaṭ,** *shaw-mat´;* a prim. root; to *fling* down; incipiently to *jostle;* fig. to *let alone, desist, remit:*— discontinue, overthrow, release, let rest, shake, stumble, throw down.

8059. שְׁמִטָּה **shemiṭṭâh,** *shem-it-taw´;* from 8058; *remission* (of debt) or *suspension* of labor):— release.

8060. שַׁמַּי **Shammay,** *sham-mah´-ee;* from

8073; *destructive; Shammai,* the name of three Isr.:— Shammai.

8061. שְׁמִידָע **Shemîydâ',** *shem-ee-daw´;* appar. from 8034 and 3045; *name of knowing; Shemida,* an Isr.:— Shemida, Shemidah.

8062. שְׁמִידָעִי **Shemîydâ'îy,** *shem-ee-daw-ee´;* patron. from 8061; a *Shemidaite* (collect.) or desc. of Shemida:— Shemidaites.

8063. שְׂמִיכָה **semîykâh,** *sem-ee-kaw´;* from 5564; a *rug* (as *sustaining* the Oriental sitter):— mantle.

8064. שָׁמַיִם **shâmayim,** *shaw-mah´-yim;* dual of an unused sing.

שָׁמֶה **shâmeh,** *shaw-meh´;* from an unused root mean. to *be lofty;* the *sky* (as *aloft;* the dual perh. alluding to the visible arch in which the clouds move, as well as to the higher ether where the celestial bodies revolve):— air, × astrologer, heaven (-s).

8065. שָׁמַיִן **shâmayin** (Chald.), *shaw-mah´-yin;* corresp. to 8064:— heaven.

8066. שְׁמִינִי **shemîynîy,** *shem-ee-nee´;* from 8083; *eight:*— eight.

8067. שְׁמִינִית **shemîynîyth,** *shem-ee-neeth´;* fem. of 8066; prob. an *eight*-stringed lyre:— Sheminith.

8068. שָׁמִיר **shâmîyr,** *shaw-meer´;* from 8104 in the orig. sense of *pricking;* a *thorn;* also (from its *keenness* for scratching) a *gem,* prob. the *diamond:*— adamant (stone), brier, diamond.

8069. שָׁמִיר **Shâmîyr,** *shaw-meer´;* the same as 8068; *Shamir,* the name of two places in Pal.:— Shamir. Comp. 8053.

8070. שְׁמִירָמוֹת **Shemîyrâmôwth,** *shem-ee-raw-môth´;* or

שְׁמַרִימוֹת **Shemârîymôwth,** *shem-aw-ree-môth´;* prob. from 8034 and plur. of 7413; *name of heights; Shemiramoth,* the name of two Isr.:— Shemiramoth.

8071. שִׂמְלָה **simlâh,** *sim-law´;* perh. by perm. for the fem. of 5566 (through the idea of a *cover* assuming the shape of the object beneath); a *dress,* espec. a *mantle:*— apparel, cloth (-es, -ing), garment, raiment. Comp. 8008.

8072. שַׂמְלָה **Samlâh,** *sam-law´;* prob. for the same as 8071; *Samlah,* an Edomite:— Samlah.

8073. שַׂמְלַי° **Shamlay,** *sham-lah´-ee;* for 8014; *Shamlai,* one of the Nethinim:— Shalmai [*from the marg.*].

8074. שָׁמֵם **shâmêm,** *shaw-mame´;* a prim. root; to *stun* (or intr. *grow numb*), i.e. *devastate* or (fig.) *stupefy* (both usually in a pass. sense):— make amazed, be astonied, (be an) astonish (-ment), (be, bring into, unto, lay, lie, make) desolate (-ion, places), be destitute, destroy (self), (lay, lie, make) waste, wonder.

8075. שְׁמַם **sh^emam** (Chald.), *shem-am´;* corresp. to 8074:— be astonied.

8076. שָׁמֵם **shâmêm,** *shaw-mame´;* from 8074; *ruined:*— desolate.

8077. שְׁמָמָה **sh^emâmâh,** *shem-aw-maw´;* or

שִׁמָמָה **shîmâmâh,** *shee-mam-aw´;* fem. of 8076; *devastation;* fig. *astonishment:*— (laid, × most) desolate (-ion), waste.

8078. שִׁמָּמוֹן **shimmâmôwn,** *shim-maw-mone´;* from 8074; *stupefaction:*— astonishment.

8079. שְׁמָמִית **s^emâmîyth,** *sem-aw-meeth´;* prob. from 8074 (in the sense of *poisoning*); a *lizard* (from the superstition of its *noxiousness*):— spider.

8080. שָׁמַן **shâman,** *shaw-man´;* a prim. root; to *shine,* i.e. (by anal.) be (caus. *make*) *oily* or *gross:*— become (make, wax) fat.

8081. שֶׁמֶן **shemen,** *sheh´-men;* from 8080; *grease,* espec. liquid (as from the olive, often perfumed); fig. *richness:*— anointing, × fat (things), × fruitful, oil (l-ed]), ointment, olive, + pine.

8082. שָׁמֵן **shâmên,** *shaw-mane´;* from 8080; *greasy,* i.e. *gross;* fig. *rich:*— fat, lusty, plenteous.

8083. שְׁמֹנֶה **sh^emôneh,** *shem-o-neh´;* or

שְׁמוֹנֶה **sh^emôwneh,** *shem-o-neh´;* fem.

שְׁמֹנָה **sh^emônâh,** *shem-o-naw´;* or

שְׁמוֹנָה **sh^emôwnâh,** *shem-o-naw´;* appar. from 8082 through the idea of *plumpness;* a cardinal number, *eight* (as if a *surplus* above the "perfect" seven); also (as ord.) *eighth:*— eight (l-een, -eenth]), eighth.

8084. שְׁמֹנִים **sh^emônîym,** *shem-o-neem´;* or

שְׁמוֹנִים **sh^emôwnîym,** *shem-o-neem´;* mult. from 8083; *eighty,* also *eightieth:*— eighty (-ieth), fourscore.

8085. שָׁמַע **shâma´,** *shaw-mah´;* a prim. root; to *hear* intelligently (often with impl. of attention, obedience, etc.; caus. to *tell,* etc.):— × attentively, call (gather) together, × carefully, × certainly, consent, consider, be content, declare, × diligently, discern, give ear, (cause to, let, make to) hear (-ken, tell), × indeed, listen, make (a) noise, (be) obedient, obey, perceive, (make a) proclaim (-ation), publish, regard, report, shew (forth), (make a) sound, × surely, tell, understand, whosoever [heareth], witness.

8086. שְׁמַע **sh^ema´** (Chald.), *shem-ah´;* corresp. to 8085:— hear, obey.

8087. שֶׁמַע **Shema´,** *sheh´-mah;* for the same

as 8088; *Shema,* the name of a place in Pal. and of four Isr.:— Shema.

8088. שֵׁמַע **shêma´,** *shay´-mah;* from 8085; something *heard,* i.e. a *sound, rumor, announcement;* abstr. *audience:*— bruit, fame, hear (-ing), loud, report, speech, tidings.

8089. שֹׁמַע **shôma´,** *sho´-mah;* from 8085; a *report:*— fame.

8090. שֶׁמָא **Sh^emâ´,** *shem-aw´;* for 8087; *Shema,* a place in Pal.:— Shema.

8091. שָׁמָע **Shâmâ´,** *shaw-maw´;* from 8085; *obedient; Shama,* an Isr.:— Shama.

8092. שִׁמְעָא **Shim´â´,** *shim-aw´;* for 8093; *Shima,* the name of four Isr.:— Shimea, Shimei, Shamma.

8093. שִׁמְעָה **Shim´âh,** *shim-aw´;* fem. of 8088; *annunciation; Shimah,* an Isr.:— Shimeah.

8094. שְׁמָעָה **Sh^emâ´âh,** *shem-aw-aw´;* for 8093; *Shemaah,* an Isr.:— Shemaah.

8095. שִׁמְעוֹן **Shim´ôwn,** *shim-one´;* from 8085; *hearing; Shimon,* one of Jacob's sons, also the tribe desc. from him:— Simeon.

8096. שִׁמְעִי **Shim´iy,** *shim-ee´;* from 8088; *famous; Shimi,* the name of twenty Isr.:— Shimeah [*from the marg.*], Shimei, Shimhi, Shimi.

8097. שִׁמְעִי **Shim´iy,** *shim-ee´;* patron. from 8096; a *Shimite* (collect.) or desc. of Shimi:— of Shimi, Shimites.

8098. שְׁמַעְיָה **Sh^ema´yâh,** *shem-aw-yaw´;* or

שְׁמַעְיָהוּ **Sh^ema´yâhûw,** *shem-aw-yaw´-hoo;* from 8085 and 3050; *Jah has heard; Shemajah,* the name of twenty-five Isr.:— Shemaiah.

8099. שִׁמְעֹנִי **Shim´ôniy,** *shim-o-nee´;* patron. from 8095; a *Shimonite* (collect.) or desc. of Shimon:— tribe of Simeon, Simeonites.

8100. שִׁמְעָת **Shim´âth,** *shim-awth´;* fem. of 8088; *annunciation; Shimath,* an Ammonitess:— Shimath.

8101. שִׁמְעָתִי **Shim´âthiy,** *shim-aw-thee´;* patron. from 8093; a *Shimathite* (collect.) or desc. of Shimah:— Shimeathites.

8102. שֶׁמֶץ **shemets,** *sheh´-mets;* from an unused root mean. to *emit* a sound; an *inkling:*— a little.

8103. שִׁמְצָה **shimtsâh,** *shim-tsaw´;* fem. of 8102; scornful *whispering* (of hostile spectators):— shame.

8104. שָׁמַר **shâmar,** *shaw-mar´;* a prim. root; prop. to *hedge* about (as with thorns), i.e. *guard;* gen. to *protect, attend to,* etc.:— beware, be circumspect, take heed (to self), keep (-er, self), mark, look narrowly, observe, preserve, regard, reserve, save (self), sure, (that lay) wait (for), watch (-man).

8105. שֶׁמֶר **shemer**, *sheh´-mer;* from 8104; something *preserved*, i.e. the *settlings* (plur. only) of wine:— dregs, (wines on the) lees.

8106. שֶׁמֶר **Shemer**, *sheh´-mer;* the same as 8105; *Shemer,* the name of three Isr.:— Shamer, Shemer.

8107. שִׁמֻּר **shimmûr**, *shim-moor´;* from 8104; an *observance:*— × be (much) observed.

שֹׁמֵר **Shômêr**. See 7763.

8108. שָׁמְרָה **shomrâh**, *shom-raw´;* fem. of an unused noun from 8104 mean. a *guard; watchfulness:*— watch.

8109. שְׁמֻרָה **shᵉmûrâh**, *shem-oo-raw´;* fem. of pass. part. of 8104; something *guarded,* i.e. an *eye-lid:*— waking.

8110. שִׁמְרוֹן **Shimrôwn**, *shim-rone´;* from 8105 in its orig. sense; *guardianship; Shimron,* the name of an Isr. and of a place in Pal.:— Shimron.

8111. שֹׁמְרוֹן **Shômᵉrown**, *sho-mer-ōne´;* from the act. part. of 8104; *watch-station; Shomeron,* a place in Pal.:— Samaria.

8112. שִׁמְרוֹן מְראוֹן **Shimrôwn Mᵉr'ôwn**, *shim-rone´ mer-one´;* from 8110 and a der. of 4754; *guard of lashing; Shimron-Meron,* a place in Pal.:— Shimon-meron.

8113. שִׁמְרִי **Shimriy**, *shim-ree´;* from 8105 in its orig. sense; *watchful; Shimri,* the name of four Isr.:— Shimri.

8114. שְׁמַרְיָה **Shᵉmaryâh**, *shem-ar-yaw´;* or

שְׁמַרְיָהוּ **Shᵉmaryâhûw**, *shem-ar-yaw´-hoo;* from 8104 and 3050; *Jah has guarded; Shemarjah,* the name of four Isr.:— Shamariah, Shemariah.

שְׁמָרִימוֹת° **Shᵉmârîymôwth**. See 8070.

8115. שָׁמְרַיִן **Shomrayin** (Chald.), *shom-rah´-yin;* corresp. to 8111; *Shomrain,* a place in Pal.:— Samaria.

8116. שִׁמְרִית **Shimrîyth**, *shim-reeth´;* fem. of 8113; *female guard; Shimrith,* a Moabitess:— Shimrith.

8117. שִׁמְרוֹנִי **Shimrôniy**, *shim-ro-nee´;* patron. from 8110; a *Shimronite* (collect.) or desc. of Shimron:— Shimronites.

8118. שֹׁמְרֹנִי **Shômᵉrôniy**, *sho-mer-o-nee´;* patrial from 8111; a *Shomeronite* (collect.) or inhab. of Shomeron:— Samaritans.

8119. שִׁמְרָת **Shimrâth**, *shim-rawth´;* from 8104; *guardship; Shimrath,* an Isr.:— Shimrath.

8120. שְׁמַשׁ **shᵉmash** (Chald.), *shem-ash´;* corresp. to the root of 8121 through the idea of *activity* impl. in day-light; to *serve:*— minister.

8121. שֶׁמֶשׁ **shemesh**, *sheh´-mesh;* from an unused root mean. to *be brilliant;* the *sun;* by

impl. the *east;* fig. a *ray,* i.e. (arch.) a notched *battlement:*— + east side (-ward), sun ([rising]), + west (-ward), window. See also 1053.

8122. שְׁמֶשׁ **shemesh** (Chald.), *sheh´-mesh;* corresp. to 8121; the *sun:*— sun.

8123. שִׁמְשׁוֹן **Shimshôwn**, *shim-shone´;* from 8121; *sunlight; Shimshon,* an Isr.:— Samson.

שִׁמְשִׁי **Shimshîy**. See 1030.

8124. שִׁמְשַׁי **Shimshay** (Chald.), *shim-shah´-ee;* from 8122; *sunny; Shimshai,* a Samaritan:— Shimshai.

8125. שַׁמְשְׁרַי **Shamshᵉray**, *sham-sher-ah´-ee;* appar. from 8121; *sunlike; Shamsherai,* an Isr.:— Shamsherai.

8126. שֻׁמָתִי **Shûmâthîy**, *shoo-maw-thee´;* patron. from an unused name from 7762 prob. mean. *garlic*-smell; a *Shumathite* (collect.) or desc. of Shumah:— Shumathites.

8127. שֵׁן **shên**, *shane;* from 8150; a *tooth* (as *sharp*); spec. (for 8143) *ivory;* fig. a *cliff:*— crag, × forefront, ivory, × sharp, tooth.

8128. שֵׁן **shên** (Chald.), *shane;* corresp. to 8127; a *tooth:*— tooth.

8129. שֵׁן **Shên**, *shane;* the same as 8127; *crag; Shen,* a place in Pal.:— Shen.

8130. שָׂנֵא **sânê'**, *saw-nay´;* a prim. root; to *hate* (personally):— enemy, foe, (be) hate (-ful, -r), odious, × utterly.

8131. שְׂנֵא **sᵉnê'** (Chald.), *sen-ay´;* corresp. to 8130:— hate.

8132. שָׁנָא **shânâ'**, *shaw-naw´;* a prim. root; to *alter:*— change.

8133. שְׁנָא **shᵉnâ'** (Chald.), *shen-aw´;* corresp. to 8132:— alter, change, (be) diverse.

שְׁנָא **shênâ'**. See 8142.

8134. שִׁנְאָב **Shin'âb**, *shin-awb´;* prob. from 8132 and 1; a *father has turned; Shinab,* a Canaanite:— Shinab.

8135. שִׂנְאָה **sin'âh**, *sin-aw´;* from 8130; *hate:*— + exceedingly, hate (-ful, -red).

8136. שִׁנְאָן **shin'ân**, *shin-awn´;* from 8132; *change,* i.e. *repetition:*— × angels.

8137. שֶׁנְאַצַּר **Shen'atstsar**, *shen-ats-tsar´;* appar. of Bab. or.; *Shenatstsar,* an Isr.:— Senazar.

8138. שָׁנָה **shânâh**, *shaw-naw´;* a prim. root; to *fold,* i.e. *duplicate* (lit. or fig.); by impl. to *transmute* (tran. or intr.):— do (speak, strike) again, alter, double, (be given to) change, disguise, (be) diverse, pervert, prefer, repeat, return, do the second time.

8139. שְׁנָה **shᵉnâh** (Chald.), *shen-aw´;* corresp. to 8142:— sleep.

Hebrew

8140. שְׁנָה **shᵉnâh** (Chald.), *shen-aw´*; corresp. to 8141:— year.

8141. שָׁנֶה **shâneh** (in plur. only), *shaw-neh´*; or (fem.)

שָׁנָה **shânâh**, *shaw-naw´*; from 8138; a *year* (as a *revolution* of time):— + whole age, × long, + old, year (× -ly).

8142. שֵׁנָה **shênâh**, *shay-naw´*; or

שֵׁנָא **shênâ'** (Psa. 127:2), *shay-naw´*; from 3462; *sleep:*— sleep.

8143. שֶׁנְהַבִּים **shenhabbîym**, *shen-hab-beem´*; from 8127 and the plur. appar. of a for. word; prob. *tooth of elephants*, i.e. *ivory tusk:*— ivory.

8144. שָׁנִי **shâniy**, *shaw-nee´*; of uncert. der.; *crimson*, prop. the insect or its color, also stuff dyed with it:— crimson, scarlet (thread).

8145. שֵׁנִי **shêniy**, *shay-nee´*; from 8138; prop. *double*, i.e. *second*; also adv. *again:*— again, either [of them], (an-) other, second (time).

8146. שָׂנִיא **sâniy'**, *saw-nee´*; from 8130; *hated:*— hated.

8147. שְׁנַיִם **shᵉnayim**, *shen-ah´-yim*; dual of 8145; fem.

שְׁתַּיִם **shᵉttayim**, *shet-tah´-yim*; *two*; also (as ord.) *twofold:*— both, couple, double, second, twain, + twelfth, + twelve, + twenty (sixscore) thousand, twice, two.

8148. שְׁנִינָה **shᵉnîynâh**, *shen-ee-naw´*; from 8150; something *pointed*, i.e. a *gibe:*— byword, taunt.

8149. שְׁנִיר **Shᵉnîyr**, *shen-eer´*; or

שְׂנִיר **Sᵉnîyr**, *sen-eer´*; from an unused root mean. to *be pointed*; *peak*; *Shenir* or *Senir*, a summit of Lebanon:— Senir, Shenir.

8150. שָׁנַן **shânan**, *shaw-nan´*; a prim. root; to *point* (tran. or intr.); intens. to *pierce*; fig. to *inculcate:*— prick, sharp (-en), teach diligently, whet.

8151. שָׁנַס **shânaç**, *shaw-nas´*; a prim. root; to *compress* (with a belt):— gird up.

8152. שִׁנְעָר **Shin'âr**, *shin-awr´*; prob. of for. der.; *Shinar*, a plain in Bab.:— Shinar.

8153. שְׁנָת **shᵉnâth**, *shen-awth´*; from 3462; *sleep:*— sleep.

8154. שָׁסָה **shâçâh**, *shaw-saw´*; or

שָׁסָה **shâsâh** (Isa. 10:13), *shaw-saw´*; a prim. root; to *plunder:*— destroyer, rob, spoil (-er).

8155. שָׁסַס **shâçaç**, *shaw-sas´*; a prim. root; to *plunder:*— rifle, spoil.

8156. שָׁסַע **shâça'**, *shaw-sah´*; a prim. root; to *split* or *tear*; fig. to *upbraid:*— cleave, (be) cloven ([-footed]), rend, stay.

8157. שֶׁסַע **sheça'**, *sheh´-sah*; from 8156; a *fissure:*— cleft, clovenfooted.

8158. שָׁסַף **shâçaph**, *shaw-saf´*; a prim. root; to *cut* in pieces, i.e. *slaughter:*— hew in pieces.

8159. שָׁעָה **shâ'âh**, *shaw-aw´*; a prim. root; to *gaze* at or about (prop. for help); by impl. to *inspect*, *consider*, *compassionate*, *be nonplussed* (as looking around in amazement) or *bewildered:*— depart, be dim, be dismayed, look (away), regard, have respect, spare, turn.

8160. שָׁעָה **shâ'âh** (Chald.), *shaw-aw´*; from a root corresp. to 8159; prop. a *look*, i.e. a *moment:*— hour.

שְׁעוֹר **sᵉ'ôwr**. See 8184.

שְׁעוֹרָה **sᵉ'ôwrâh**. See 8184.

8161. שַׁעֲטָה **sha'ăṭâh**, *shah´-at-aw´*; fem. from an unused root mean. to *stamp*; a *clatter* (of hoofs):— stamping.

8162. שַׁעַטְנֵז **sha'aṭnêz**, *shah-at-naze´*; prob. of for. der.; *linsey-woolsey*, i.e. cloth of linen and wool carded and spun together:— garment of divers sorts, linen and woollen.

8163. שָׂעִיר **sâ'îyr**, *saw-eer´*; or

שָׂעִר **sâ'ir**, *saw-eer´*; from 8175; *shaggy*; as noun, a *he-goat*; by anal. a *faun:*— devil, goat, hairy, kid, rough, satyr.

8164. שָׂעִיר **sâ'îyr**, *saw-eer´*; formed the same as 8163; a *shower* (as *tempestuous*):— small rain.

8165. שֵׂעִיר **Sê'îyr**, *say-eer´*; formed like 8163; *rough*; *Seir*, a mountain of Idumaea and its aboriginal occupants, also one in Pal.:— Seir.

8166. שְׂעִירָה **sᵉ'îyrâh**, *seh-ee-raw´*; fem. of 8163; a *she-goat:*— kid.

8167. שְׂעִירָה **Sᵉ'îyrâh**, *seh-ee-raw´*; formed as 8166; *roughness*; *Seirah*, a place in Pal.:— Seirath.

8168. שֹׁעַל **shô'al**, *sho´-al*; from an unused root mean. to *hollow* out; the *palm*; by extens. a *handful:*— handful, hollow of the hand.

שֻׁעָל **shû'âl**. See 7776.

8169. שַׁעַלְבִים **Sha'albîym**, *shah-al-beem´*; or

שַׁעֲלַבִּין **Sha'ălabbîyn**, *shah-al-ab-been´*; plur. from 7776; *fox-holes*; *Shaalbim* or *Shaalabbin*, a place in Pal.:— Shaalabbin, Shaalbim.

8170. שַׁעַלְבֹנִי **Sha'albôniy**, *shah-al-bo-nee´*; patrial from 8169; a *Shaalbonite* or inhab. of Shaalbin:— Shaalbonite.

8171. שַׁעֲלִים **Sha'ălîym**, *shah-al-eem´*; plur.

of 7776; *foxes; Shaalim*, a place in Pal.:— Shalim.

8172. שָׁעַן **shâ'an**, *shaw-an´*; a prim. root; to *support* one's self:— lean, lie, rely, rest (on, self), stay.

8173. שָׁעַע **shâ'a'**, *shaw-ah´*; a prim. root; (in a good acceptation) to *look* upon (with complacency), i.e. *fondle, please* or *amuse* (self); (in a bad one) to *look* about (in dismay), i.e. *stare:*— cry (out) [by confusion with 7768], dandle, delight (self), play, shut.

שָׂעִף **sâ'îph.** See 5587.

8174. שַׁעַף **Sha'aph**, *shah´-af*; from 5586; *fluctuation; Shaaph*, the name of two Isr.:— Shaaph.

8175. שָׂעַר **sâ'ar**, *saw-ar´*; a prim. root; to *storm*; by impl. to *shiver*, i.e. *fear:*— be (horribly) afraid, fear, hurl as a storm, be tempestuous, come like (take away as with) a whirlwind.

8176. שָׁעַר **shâ'ar**, *shaw-ar´*; a prim. root; to *split* or *open*, i.e. (lit., but only as denom. from 8179) to *act as gate-keeper* (see 7778): (fig.) to *estimate:*— think.

8177. שְׂעַר **s'ar** (Chald.), *seh-ar´*; corresp. to 8181; *hair:*— hair.

8178. שַׂעַר **sa'ar**, *sah´-ar*; from 8175; a *tempest*; also a *terror:*— affrighted, × horribly, × sore, storm. See 8181.

8179. שַׁעַר **sha'ar**, *shah´-ar*; from 8176 in its orig. sense; an *opening*, i.e. *door* or *gate:*— city, door, gate, port (× -er).

8180. שַׁעַר **sha'ar**, *shah´-ar*; from 8176; a *measure* (as a *section*):— [hundred-] fold.

שָׂעִיר **sâ'îr.** See 8163.

8181. שֵׂעָר **sê'âr**, *say-awr´*; or

שַׂעַר **sa'ar** (Isa. 7:20), *sah´-ar*; from 8175 in the sense of *dishevelling; hair* (as if tossed or bristling):— hair (-y), × rough.

שֹׁעֵר **shô'êr.** See 7778.

8182. שֹׁעָר **shô'âr**, *sho-awr´*; from 8176; *harsh* or *horrid*, i.e. *offensive:*— vile.

8183. שְׂעָרָה **s'ârâh**, *seh-aw-raw´*; fem. of 8178; a *hurricane:*— storm, tempest.

8184. שְׂעֹרָה **s'ôrâh**, *seh-o-raw´*; or

שְׂעוֹרָה **s'ôwrâh**, *seh-o-raw´* (fem. mean. the *plant*); and (masc. mean. the *grain*); also

שְׂעֹר **s'ôr**, *seh-ore´*; or

שְׂעוֹר **s'ôwr**, *seh-ore´*; from 8175 in the sense of *roughness; barley* (as *villose*):— barley.

8185. שַׂעֲרָה **sa'ărâh**, *sah-ar-aw´*; fem. of 8181; *hairiness:*— hair.

8186. שַׁעֲרוּרָה **sha'ărûwrâh**, *shah-ar-oo-raw´*; or

שַׁעֲרִירִיָּה° **sha'ăriyriyâh**, *shah-ar-ee-ree-yaw´*; or

שַׁעֲרֻרִת **sha'ărurith**, *shah-ar-oo-reeth´*; fem. from 8176 in the sense of 8175; something *fearful:*— horrible thing.

8187. שְׁעַרְיָה **Sh'aryâh**, *sheh-ar-yaw´*; from 8176 and 3050; *Jah has stormed; Shearjah*, an Isr.:— Sheariah.

8188. שְׂעֹרִים **S'ôrîym**, *seh-o-reem´*; masc. plur. of 8184; *barley* grains; *Seorim*, an Isr.:— Seorim.

8189. שַׁעֲרַיִם **Sha'ărayim**, *shah-ar-ah´-yim*; dual of 8179; *double gates; Shaarajim*, a place in Pal.:— Shaaraim.

שַׁעֲרִירִיָּה° **sha'ăriyriyâh.** See 8186.

שַׁעֲרֻרִת **sha'ărurith.** See 8186.

8190. שַׁעַשְׁגַּז **Sha'ashgaz**, *shah-ash-gaz´*; of Pers. der.; *Shaashgaz*, a eunuch of Xerxes:— Shaashgaz.

8191. שַׁעֲשֻׁעַ **sha'shûa'**, *shah-shoo´-ah*; from 8173; *enjoyment:*— delight, pleasure.

8192. שָׁפָה **shâphâh**, *shaw-faw´*; a prim. root; to *abrade*, i.e. *bare:*— high, stick out.

8193. שָׂפָה **sâphâh**, *saw-faw´*; or (in dual and plur.)

שֶׂפֶת **sepheth**, *sef-eth´*; prob. from 5595 or 8192 through the idea of *termination* (comp. 5490); the *lip* (as a nat. boundary); by impl. *language*; by anal. a *margin* (of a vessel, water, cloth, etc.):— band, bank, binding, border, brim, brink, edge, language, lip, prating, [sea-] shore, side, speech, talk, [vain] words.

8194. שָׁפָה **shâphâh**, *shaw-faw´*; from 8192 in the sense of *clarifying*; a *cheese* (as *strained* from the whey):— cheese.

8195. שְׁפוֹ **Sh'phôw**, *shef-o´*; or

שְׁפִי **Sh'phiy**, *shef-ee´*; from 8192; *baldness* [comp. 8205]; *Shepho* or *Shephi*, an Idumaean:— Shephi, Shepho.

8196. שְׁפוֹט **sh'phôwt**, *shef-ote´*; or

שְׁפוּט **sh'phûwt**, *shef-oot´*; from 8199; a judicial *sentence*, i.e. *punishment:*— judgment.

8197. שְׁפוּפָם **Sh'phûwphâm**, *shef-oo-fawm´*; or

שְׁפוּפָן **Sh'phûwphân**, *shef-oo-fawn´*; from the same as 8207; *serpent-like; Shephupham* or *Shephuphan*, an Isr.:— Shephuphan, Shupham.

8198. שִׁפְחָה **shiphchâh**, *shif-khaw´*; fem. from an unused root mean. to *spread* out (as a *family; see 4940); a *female slave* (as a member of the *household*):— (bond-, hand-) maid (-en, -servant), wench, bondwoman, womanservant.

8199. שָׁפַט **shâphaṭ**, *shaw-fat´;* a prim. root; to *judge,* i.e. pronounce *sentence* (for or against); by impl. to *vindicate* or *punish;* by extens. to *govern;* pass. to *litigate* (lit. or fig.):— + avenge, × that condemn, contend, defend, execute (judgment), (be a) judge (-ment), × needs, plead, reason, rule.

8200. שְׁפַט **shᵉphaṭ** (Chald.), *shef-at´;* corresp. to 8199; to *judge:*— magistrate.

8201. שֶׁפֶט **shephet**, *sheh´-fet;* from 8199; a *sentence,* i.e. *infliction:*— judgment.

8202. שָׁפָט **Shâphâṭ**, *shaw-fawt´;* from 8199; *judge; Shaphat,* the name of four Isr.:— Shaphat.

8203. שְׁפַטְיָה **Shᵉphaṭyâh**, *shef-at-yaw´;* or

שְׁפַטְיָהוּ **Shᵉphaṭyâhûw**, *shef-at-yaw´-hoo;* from 8199 and 3050; *Jah has judged; Shephatjah,* the name of ten Isr.:— Shephatiah.

8204. שִׁפְטָן **Shiphṭân**, *shif-tawn´;* from 8199; *judge-like; Shiphtan,* an Isr.:— Shiphtan.

8205. שְׁפִי **shᵉphîy**, *shef-ee´;* from 8192; *bareness;* concr. a *bare* hill or plain:— high place, stick out.

8206. שֻׁפִּים **Shuppîym**, *shoop-peem´;* plur. of an unused noun from the same as 8207 and mean. the same; *serpents; Shuppim,* an Isr.:— Shuppim.

8207. שְׁפִיפֹן **shᵉphîyphôn**, *shef-ee-fone´;* from an unused root mean. the same as 7779; a kind of *serpent* (as *snapping*), prob. the *cerastes* or horned adder:— adder.

8208. שָׁפִיר **Shâphîyr**, *shaf-eer´;* from 8231; *beautiful; Shaphir,* a place in Pal.:— Saphir.

8209. שַׁפִּיר **sappîyr** (Chald.), *shap-peer´;* intens. of a form corresp. to 8208; *beautiful:*— fair.

8210. שָׁפַךְ **shâphak**, *shaw-fak´;* a prim. root; to *spill* forth (blood, a libation, liquid metal; or even a solid, i.e. to *mound* up); also (fig.) to *expend* (life, soul, complaint, money, etc.); intens. to *sprawl* out:— cast (up), gush out, pour (out), shed (-der, out), slip.

8211. שֶׁפֶךְ **shephek**, *sheh´-fek;* from 8210; an *emptying* place, e.g. an ash-*heap:*— are poured out.

8212. שָׁפְכָה **shophkâh**, *shof-kaw´;* fem. of a der. from 8210; a *pipe* (for *pouring* forth, e.g. wine), i.e. the *penis:*— privy member.

8213. שָׁפֵל **shâphêl**, *shaw-fale´;* a prim. root; to *depress* or *sink* (expec. fig. to *humiliate,* intr. or tran.):— abase, bring (cast, put) down, debase, humble (self), be (bring, lay, make, put) low (-er).

8214. שְׁפַל **shᵉphal** (Chald.), *shef-al´;* corresp. to 8213:— abase, humble, put down, subdue.

8215. שְׁפַל **shᵉphal** (Chald.), *shef-al´;* from 8214; *low:*— basest.

8216. שֵׁפֶל **shêphel**, *shay´-fel;* from 8213; an *humble* rank:— low estate (place).

8217. שָׁפָל **shâphâl**, *shaw-fawl´;* from 8213; *depressed,* lit. or fig.:— base (-st), humble, low (-er, -ly).

8218. שִׁפְלָה **shiphlâh**, *shif-law´;* fem. of 8216; *depression:*— low place.

8219. שְׁפֵלָה **shᵉphêlâh**, *shef-ay-law´;* from 8213; *Lowland,* i.e. (with the art.) the maritime slope of Pal.:— low country, (low) plain, vale (-ley).

8220. שִׁפְלוּת **shiphlûwth**, *shif-looth´;* from 8213; *remissness:*— idleness.

8221. שֶׁפָם **Shᵉphâm**, *shef-awm´;* prob. from 8192; *bare spot; Shepham,* a place in or near Pal.:— Shepham.

8222. שָׂפָם **sâphâm**, *saw-fawm´;* from 8193; the *beard* (as a *lip-piece*):— beard, (upper) lip.

8223. שָׁפָם **Shâphâm**, *shaw-fawm´;* formed like 8221; *baldly; Shapham,* an Isr.:— Shapham.

8224. שִׂפְמוֹת **Siphmôwth**, *sif-môth´;* fem. plur. of 8221; *Siphmoth,* a place in Pal.:— Siphmoth.

8225. שִׁפְמִי **Shiphmîy**, *shif-mee´;* patrial from 8221; a *Shiphmite* or inhab. of Shepham:— Shiphmite.

8226. שָׂפַן **sâphan**, *saw-fan´;* a prim. root; to *conceal* (as a valuable):— treasure.

8227. שָׁפָן **shâphân**, *shaw-fawn´;* from 8226; a species of *rock-rabbit* (from its *hiding*), i.e. prob. the *hyrax:*— coney.

8228. שֶׁפַע **shepha'**, *sheh´-fah;* from an unused root mean. to *abound; resources:*— abundance.

8229. שִׁפְעָה **shiph'âh**, *shif-aw´;* fem. of 8228; *copiousness:*— abundance, company, multitude.

8230. שִׁפְעִי **Shiph'îy**, *shif-ee´;* from 8228; *copious; Shiphi,* an Isr.:— Shiphi.

שָׂפַק **sâphaq**. See 5606.

8231. שָׁפַר **shâphar**, *shaw-far´;* a prim. root; to *glisten,* i.e. (fig.) be (caus. *make*) *fair:*— × goodly.

8232. שְׁפַר **shᵉphar** (Chald.), *shef-ar´;* corresp. to 8231; to *be beautiful:*— be acceptable, please, + think good.

8233. שֶׁפֶר **shepher**, *sheh´-fer;* from 8231; *beauty:*— × goodly.

8234. שֶׁפֶר **Shepher**, *sheh´-fer;* the same as 8233; *Shepher,* a place in the Desert:— Shapper.

שׁוֹפָר **shôphâr**. See 7782.

8235. שִׁפְרָה **shiphrâh**, *shif-raw´*; from 8231; *brightness:*— garnish.

8236. שִׁפְרָה **Shiphrâh**, *shif-raw´*; the same as 8235; *Shiphrah*, an Israelitess:— Shiphrah.

8237. שְׁפִרוּר° **shaphrûwr**, *shaf-roor´*; from 8231; *splendid*, i.e. a *tapestry* or *canopy:*— royal pavilion.

8238. שְׁפַרְפַר **sheᵉpharphar** (Chald.), *shef-ar-far´*; from 8231; the *dawn* (as *brilliant* with aurora):— × very early in the morning.

8239. שָׁפַת **shâphath**, *shaw-fath´*; a prim. root; to *locate*, i.e. (gen.) *hang* on or (fig.) *establish, reduce:*— bring, ordain, set on.

8240. שָׁפָת **shâphâth**, *shaw-fawth´*; from 8239; a (double) *stall* (for cattle); also a (two-pronged) *hook* (for flaying animals on):— hook, pot.

8241. שֶׁצֶף **shetseph**, *sheh´-tsef*; from 7857 (for alliteration with 7110); an *outburst* (of anger):— little.

8242. שַׂק **saq**, *sak*; from 8264; prop. a *mesh* (as allowing a liquid to *run* through), i.e. coarse loose cloth or *sacking* (used in mourning and for bagging); hence, a *bag* (for grain, etc.):— sack (-cloth, -clothes).

8243. שָׁק **shâq** (Chald.), *shawk*; corresp. to 7785; the *leg:*— leg.

8244. שָׂקַד **sâqad**, *saw-kad´*; a prim. root; to *fasten:*— bind.

8245. שָׁקַד **shâqad**, *shaw-kad´*; a prim. root; to *be alert*, i.e. *sleepless*; hence, to *be on the lookout* (whether for good or ill):— hasten, remain, wake, watch (for).

8246. שָׁקַד **shâqad**, *shaw-kad´*; a denom. from 8247; to *be* (intens. *make*) *almond-shaped:*— make like (unto, after the fashion of) almonds.

8247. שָׁקֵד **shâqêd**, *shaw-kade´*; from 8245; the *almond* (tree or nut; as being the *earliest* in bloom):— almond (tree).

8248. שָׁקָה **shâqâh**, *shaw-kaw´*; a prim. root; to *quaff*, i.e. (caus.) to *irrigate* or *furnish a potion* to:— cause to (give, give to, let, make to) drink, drown, moisten, water. See 7937, 8354.

8249. שִׁקֻּו **shiqqûv**, *shik-koov´*; from 8248; (plur. collect.) a *draught:*— drink.

8250. שִׁקּוּי **shiqqûwy**, *shik-koo´-ee*; from 8248; a *beverage; moisture*, i.e. (fig.) *refreshment:*— drink, marrow.

8251. שִׁקּוּץ **shiqqûwts**, *shik-koots´*; or

שִׁקֻּץ **shiqqûts**, *shik-koots´*; from 8262; *disgusting*, i.e. *filthy*; espec. *idolatrous* or (concr.) an *idol:*— abominable filth (idol, -ation), detestable (thing).

8252. שָׁקַט **shâqat**, *shaw-kat´*; a prim. root; to *repose* (usually fig.):— appease, idleness, (at,

be at, be in, give) quiet (-ness), (be at, be in, give, have, take) rest, settle, be still.

8253. שֶׁקֶט **sheqet**, *sheh´-ket*; from 8252; *tranquillity:*— quietness.

8254. שָׁקַל **shâqal**, *shaw-kal´*; a prim. root; to *suspend* or *poise* (espec. in trade):— pay, receive (-r), spend, × throughly, weigh.

8255. שֶׁקֶל **sheqel**, *sheh´-kel*; from 8254; prob. a *weight*; used as a commercial standard:— shekel.

8256. שָׁקָם **shâqâm**, *shaw-kawm´*; or (fem.)

שִׁקְמָה **shiqmâh**, *shik-maw´*; of uncert. der.; a *sycamore* (usually the tree):— sycamore (fruit, tree).

8257. שָׁקַע **shâqa´**, *shaw-kah´*; (abb. o Am. 8:8); a prim. root; to *subside*; by impl. to *be overflowed, cease*; caus. to *abate, subdue:*— make deep, let down, drown, quench, sink.

8258. שְׁקַעְרוּרָה **sheᵉqa´rûwrâh**, *shek-ah-roo-raw´*; from 8257; a *depression:*— hollow strake.

8259. שָׁקַף **shâqaph**, *shaw-kaf´*; a prim. root; prop. to *lean out* (of a window), i.e. (by impl.) *peep* or *gaze* (pass. *be a spectacle*):— appear, look (down, forth, out).

8260. שֶׁקֶף **sheqeph**, *sheh´-kef*; from 8259; a *loophole* (for *looking out*), to *admit* light and air:— window.

8261. שָׁקוּף **shâqûph**, *shaw-koof´*; pass. part. of 8259; an *embrasure* or opening [comp. 8260] with bevelled jam:— light, window.

8262. שָׁקַץ **shâqats**, *shaw-kats´*; a prim. root; to *be filthy*, i.e. (intens.) to *loathe, pollute:*— abhor, make abominable, have in abomination, detest, × utterly.

8263. שֶׁקֶץ **sheqets**, *sheh´-kets*; from 8262; *filth*, i.e. (fig. and spec.) an *idolatrous* object:— abominable (-tion).

שִׁקֻּץ **shiqqûts**. See 8251.

8264. שָׁקַק **shâqaq**, *shaw-kak´*; a prim. root; to *course* (like a beast of prey); by impl. to *seek* greedily:— have appetite, justle one against another, long, range, run (to and fro).

8265. שָׂקַר **sâqar**, *saw-kar´*; a prim. root; to *ogle*, i.e. *blink* coquettishly:— wanton.

8266. שָׁקַר **shâqar**, *shaw-kar´*; a prim. root; to *cheat*, i.e. *be untrue* (usually in words):— fail, deal falsely, lie.

8267. שֶׁקֶר **sheqer**, *sheh´-ker*; from 8266; an *untruth*; by impl. a *sham* (often adv.):— without a cause, deceit (-ful), false (-hood, -ly), feignedly, liar, + lie, lying, vain (thing), wrongfully.

8268. שֹׁקֶת **shôqeth**, *sho´-keth*; from 8248; a *trough* (for *watering*):— trough.

8269. שַׂר **sar,** *sar;* from 8323; a *head* person (of any rank or class):— captain (that had rule), chief (captain), general, governor, keeper, lord, (l-task-l) master, prince (-ipal), ruler, steward.

8270. שֹׁר **shôr,** *shore;* from 8324; a *string* (as *twisted* [comp. 8306]), i.e. (spec.) the umbilical cord (also fig. as the centre of strength):— navel.

8271. שְׂרֵא **sh^erê'** (Chald.), *sher-ay´;* a root corresp. to that of 8293; to *free, separate;* fig. to *unravel, commence;* by impl. (of unloading beasts) to *reside:*— begin, dissolve, dwell, loose.

8272. שַׂרְאֶצֶר **Shar'etser,** *shar-eh´-tser;* of for. der.; *Sharetser,* the name of an Ass. and an Isr.:— Sharezer.

8273. שָׁרָב **shârâb,** *shaw-rawb´;* from an unused root mean. to *glare;* quivering *glow* (of the air), expec. the *mirage:*— heat, parched ground.

8274. שֵׁרֵבְיָה **Shêrêbyâh,** *shay-rayb-yaw´;* from 8273 and 3050; *Jah has brought heat; Sherebjah,* the name of two Isr.:— Sherebiah.

8275. שַׁרְבִיט **sharbîyṭ,** *shar-beet´;* for 7626; a *rod* of empire:— sceptre.

8276. שָׂרַג **sârag,** *saw-rag´;* a prim. root; to *intwine:*— wrap together, wreath.

8277. שָׂרַד **sârad,** *saw-rad´;* a prim. root; prop. to *puncture* [comp. 8279], i.e. (fig. through the idea of *slipping* out) to *escape* or survive:— remain.

8278. שְׂרָד **s^erâd,** *ser-awd´;* from 8277; *stitching* (as *pierced* with a needle):— service.

8279. שֶׂרֶד **sered,** *seh´-red;* from 8277; a (carpenter's) *scribing-awl* (for *pricking* or scratching measurements):— line.

8280. שָׂרָה **sârâh,** *saw-raw´;* a prim. root; to *prevail:*— have power (as a prince).

8281. שָׁרָה **shârâh,** *shaw-raw´;* a prim. root; to *free:*— direct.

8282. שָׂרָה **sârâh,** *saw-raw´;* fem. of 8269; a *mistress,* i.e. *female noble:*— lady, princess, queen.

8283. שָׂרָה **Sârâh,** *saw-raw´;* the same as 8282; *Sarah,* Abraham's wife:— Sarah.

8284. שָׁרָה **shârâh,** *shaw-raw´;* prob. fem. of 7791; a *fortification* (lit. or fig.):— sing [by mistake for 7891], wall.

8285. שֵׁרָה **shêrâh,** *shay-raw´;* from 8324 in its orig. sense of *pressing;* a wrist-*band* (as compact or *clasping*):— bracelet.

8286. שְׂרוּג **S^erûwg,** *ser-oog´;* from 8276; *tendril; Serug,* a postdiluvian patriarch:— Serug.

8287. שָׁרוּחֶן **Shârûwchen,** *shaw-roo-khen´;* prob. from 8281 (in the sense of *dwelling*

[comp. 8271] and 2580; *abode of pleasure; Sharuchen,* a place in Pal.:— Sharuhen.

8288. שְׂרוֹךְ **s^erôwk,** *ser-oke´;* from 8308; a *thong* (as *laced* or *tied*):— [shoe-] latchet.

8289. שָׁרוֹן **Shârôwn,** *shaw-rone´;* prob. abridged from 3474; *plain, Sharon,* the name of a place in Pal.:— Lasharon, Sharon.

8290. שָׁרוֹנִי **Shârôwnîy,** *shaw-ro-nee´;* patrial from 8289; a *Sharonite* or inhab. of Sharon:— Sharonite.

8291. שָׂרוּק **sarûwq,** *sar-ook´;* pass. part. from the same as 8321; a *grapevine:*— principal plant. See 8320, 8321.

8292. שְׁרוּקָה **sh^erûwqâh,** *sher-oo-kaw´;* or (by perm.)

שְׁרִיקָה **sh^erîyqâh,** *sher-ee-kaw´;* fem. pass. part. of 8319; a *whistling* (in scorn); by anal. a *piping:*— bleating, hissing.

8293. שֵׁרוּת **shêrûwth,** *shay-rooth´;* from 8281 abb.; *freedom:*— remnant.

8294. שֶׂרַח **Serach,** *seh´-rakh;* by perm. for 5629; *superfluity; Serach,* an Israelitess:— Sarah, Serah.

8295. שָׂרַט **sâraṭ,** *saw-rat´;* a prim. root; to *gash:*— cut in pieces, make [cuttings] pieces.

8296. שֶׂרֶט **sereṭ,** *seh´-ret;* and

שָׂרֶטֶת **sâreṭeth,** *saw-reh´-teth;* from 8295; an *incision:*— cutting.

8297. שָׂרַי **Sâray,** *saw-rah´-ee;* from 8269; *dominative; Sarai,* the wife of Abraham:— Sarai.

8298. שָׁרַי **Shâray,** *shaw-rah´-ee;* prob. from 8324; *hostile; Sharay,* an Isr.:— Sharai.

8299. שָׂרִיג **sârîyg,** *saw-reeg´;* from 8276; a *tendril* (as *intwining*):— branch.

8300. שָׂרִיד **sârîyd,** *saw-reed´;* from 8277; a *survivor:*— × alive, left, remain (-ing), remnant, rest.

8301. שָׂרִיד **Sârîyd,** *saw-reed´;* the same as 8300; *Sarid,* a place in Pal.:— Sarid.

8302. שִׁרְיוֹן **shiryôwn,** *shir-yone´;* or

שִׁרְיֹן **shiryôn,** *shir-yone´;* and

שִׁרְיָן **shiryân,** *shir-yawn´;* also (fem.)

שִׁרְיָה **shiryâh,** *shir-yaw´;* and

שִׁרְיוֹנָה **shiryônâh,** *shir-yo-naw´;* from 8281 in the orig. sense of *turning;* a *corslet* (as if *twisted*):— breastplate, coat of mail, habergeon, harness. See 5630.

8303. שִׁרְיוֹן **Shiryôwn,** *shir-yone´;* and

שִׂרְיֹן **Siryôn,** *sir-yone´;* the same as 8304 (i.e. *sheeted* with snow); *Shirjon* or *Sirjon,* a peak of the Lebanon:— Sirion.

8304. שְׂרָיָה **S^erâyâh,** *ser-aw-yaw´;* or

שְׁרָיָהוּ **Serâyâhûw**, *ser-aw-yaw'-hoo;* from 8280 and 3050; *Jah has prevailed; Serajah,* the name of nine Isr.:— Seraiah.

8305. שְׂרִיקָה **serîyqâh**, *ser-ee-kaw';* from the same as 8321 in the orig. sense of *piercing; hetchelling* (or combing flax), i.e. (concr.) *tow* (by extens. *linen* cloth):— fine.

8306. שָׂרִיר **shârîyr**, *shaw-reer';* from 8324 in the orig. sense as in 8270 (comp. 8326); a *cord,* i.e. (by anal.) *sinew:*— navel.

8307. שְׁרִירוּת **sherîyrûwth**, *sher-ee-rooth';* from 8324 in the sense of *twisted,* i.e. *firm; obstinacy:*— imagination, lust.

8308. שָׂרַךְ **sârak**, *saw-rak';* a prim. root; to *interlace:*— traverse.

8309. שְׂרֵמָה° **sherêmâh**, *sher-ay-maw';* prob. by an orth. err. for 7709; a *common:*— field.

8310. שַׂרְסְכִים **Sarçekîym**, *sar-seh-keem';* of for. der.; *Sarsekim,* a Bab. general:— Sarsechim.

8311. שָׂרַע **sâra'**, *saw-rah';* a prim. root; to *prolong,* i.e. (reflex.) *be deformed* by excess of members:— stretch out self, (have any) superfluous thing.

8312. שַׂרְעַף **sar'aph**, *sar-af';* for 5587; *cogitation:*— thought.

8313. שָׂרַף **sâraph**, *saw-raf';* a prim. root; to *be* (caus. *set*) *on fire:*— (cause to, make a) burn (l-ing], up) kindle, × utterly.

8314. שָׂרָף **sârâph**, *saw-rawf';* from 8313; *burning,* i.e. (fig.) *poisonous* (serpent); spec. a *saraph* or symb. creature (from their copper color):— fiery (serpent), seraph.

8315. שָׂרָף **Sâraph**, *saw-raf';* the same as 8314; *Saraph,* an Isr.:— Saraph.

8316. שְׂרֵפָה **serêphâh**, *ser-ay-faw';* from 8313; *cremation:*— burning.

8317. שָׂרַץ **shârats**, *shaw-rats';* a prim. root; to *wriggle,* i.e. (by impl.) *swarm* or *abound:*— breed (bring forth, increase) abundantly (in abundance), creep, move.

8318. שֶׁרֶץ **sherets**, *sheh'-rets;* from 8317; a *swarm,* i.e. active mass of minute animals:— creep (-ing thing), move (-ing creature).

8319. שָׁרַק **shâraq**, *shaw-rak';* a prim. root; prop. to *be shrill,* i.e. to whistle or *hiss* (as a call or in scorn):— hiss.

8320. שָׂרֻק **sâruq**, *saw-rook';* from 8319; *bright red* (as *piercing* to the sight), i.e. *bay:*— speckled. See 8291.

8321. שֹׁרֵק **sôrêq**, *so-rake';* or

שׂוֹרֵק **sôwrêq**, *so-rake';* and (fem.)

שֹׂרֵקָה **sôrêqâh**, *so-ray-kaw';* from 8319 in the sense of *redness* (comp. 8320); a *vine* stock (prop. one yielding *purple* grapes, the richest variety):— choice (-st, noble) wine. Comp. 8291.

8322. שְׁרֵקָה **sherêqâh**, *sher-ay-kaw';* from 8319; a *derision:*— hissing.

8323. שָׁרַר **sârar**, *saw-rar';* a prim. root; to *have* (tran. *exercise;* refl. *get*) *dominion:*— × altogether, make self a prince, (bear) rule.

8324. שָׁרַר **shârar**, *shaw-rar';* a prim. root; to *be hostile* (only act. part. an *opponent*):— enemy.

8325. שָׁרָר **Shârâr**, *shaw-rawr';* from 8324; *hostile; Sharar,* an Isr.:— Sharar.

8326. שֹׁרֶר **shôrer**, *sho'-rer;* from 8324 in the sense of *twisting* (comp. 8270); the umbilical *cord,* i.e. (by extens.) a *bodice:*— navel.

8327. שָׁרַשׁ **shârash**, *shaw-rash';* a prim. root; to *root,* i.e. strike into the soil, or (by impl.) to pluck from it:— (take, cause to take) root (out).

8328. שֶׁרֶשׁ **sheresh**, *sheh'-resh;* from 8327; a *root* (lit. or fig.):— bottom, deep, heel, root.

8329. שֶׁרֶשׁ **Sheresh**, *sheh'-resh;* the same as 8328; *Sheresh,* an Isr.:— Sharesh.

8330. שֹׁרֶשׁ **shôresh** (Chald.), *sho'-resh;* corresp. to 8328:— root.

8331. שַׁרְשָׁה **sharshâh**, *shar-shaw';* from 8327; a *chain* (as *rooted,* i.e. *linked*):— chain. Comp. 8333.

8332. שְׁרֹשׁוּ° **sherôshûw** (Chald.), *sher-o-shoo';* from a root corresp. to 8327; *eradication,* i.e. (fig.) *exile:*— banishment.

8333. שַׁרְשְׁרָה **sharsherâh**, *shar-sher-aw';* from 8327 [comp. 8331]; a *chain;* (arch.) prob. a *garland:*— chain.

8334. שָׁרַת **shârath**, *shaw-rath';* a prim. root; to *attend* as a menial or worshipper; fig. to *contribute* to:— minister (unto), (do) serve (-ant, -ice, -itor), wait on.

8335. שָׁרֵת **shârêth**, *shaw-rayth';* infin. of 8334; *service* (in the Temple):— minister (-ry).

8336. שֵׁשׁ **shêsh**, *shaysh;* or (for alliteration with 4897)

שְׁשִׁי **sheshiy**, *shesh-ee';* for 7893; *bleached* stuff, i.e. *white* linen or (by anal.) *marble:*— × blue, fine (ltwinedl) linen, marble, silk.

8337. שֵׁשׁ **shêsh**, *shaysh;* masc.

שִׁשָּׁה **shishshâh**, *shish-shaw';* a prim. number; *six* (as an overplus [see 7797] beyond five or the fingers of the hand); as ord. *sixth:*— six (l-teen, -teenth]), sixth.

8338. שָׁשׁוּ **shâwshâw**, *shaw-shaw';* a prim. root; appar. to *annihilate:*— leave but the sixth part [by confusion with 8341].

8339. שֵׁשְׁבַּצַּר **Shêshbatstsar**, *shaysh-batstsar';* of for. der.; *Sheshbatstsar,* Zerubbabel's Pers. name:— Sheshbazzar.

Hebrew

8340. שֵׁשְׁבַּצַּר **Shêshbatstsar** (Chald.), *shaysh-bats-tsar´;* corresp. to 8339:— Sheshbazzar.

שָׁשָׂה **shâsâh.** See 8154.

8341. שָׁשָׂה **shâshâh,** *shaw-shaw´;* a denom. from 8337; to *sixth* or divide into sixths:— give the sixth part.

8342. שָׂשׂוֹן **sâsôwn,** *saw-sone´;* or

שָׂשֹׂן **sâsôn,** *saw-sone´;* from 7797; *cheerfulness;* spec. *welcome:*— gladness, joy, mirth, rejoicing.

8343. שָׁשַׁי **Shâshay,** *shaw-shah´-ee;* perh. from 8336; *whitish; Shashai,* an Isr.:— Shashai.

8344. שֵׁשַׁי **Shêshay,** *shay-shah´-ee;* prob. for 8343; *Sheshai,* a Canaanite:— Sheshai.

8345. שִׁשִּׁי **shishshîy,** *shish-shee´;* from 8337; *sixth,* ord. or (fem.) fractional:— sixth (part).

8346. שִׁשִּׁים **shishshîym,** *shish-sheem´;* multiple of 8337; *sixty:*— sixty, three score.

8347. שֵׁשַׁךְ **Shêshak,** *shay-shak´;* of for. der.; *Sheshak,* a symbol. name of Bab.:— Sheshach.

8348. שֵׁשָׁן **Shêshân,** *shay-shawn´;* perh. for 7799; *lily; Sheshan,* an Isr.:— Sheshan.

שׁוֹשָׁן **Shôshân.** See 7799.

8349. שָׁשַׁק **Shâshaq,** *shaw-shak´;* prob. from the base of 7785; *pedestrian; Shashak,* an Isr.:— Shashak.

8350. שָׁשָׁר **shâshar,** *shaw-shar´;* perh. from the base of 8324 in the sense of that of 8320; *red* ochre (from its *piercing* color):— vermillion.

8351. שֵׁת **sheth** (Num. 24:17), *shayth;* from 7582; *tumult:*— Sheth.

8352. שֵׁת **Shêth,** *shayth;* from 7896; *put,* i.e. *substituted; Sheth,* third son of Adam:— Seth, Sheth.

8353. שֵׁת **sheth** (Chald.), *shayth;* or

שִׁת **shîth** (Chald.), *sheeth;* corresp. to 8337:— six (-th).

8354. שָׁתָה **shâthâh,** *shaw-thaw´;* a prim. root; to *imbibe* (lit. or fig.):— × assuredly, banquet, × certainly, drink (-er, -ing), drunk (× -ard), surely. [Prop. intens. of 8248.]

8355. שְׁתָה **shethâh** (Chald.), *sheth-aw´;* corresp. to 8354:— drink.

8356. שָׁתָה **shâthâh,** *shaw-thaw´;* from 7896; a *basis,* i.e. (fig.) political or moral *support:*— foundation, purpose.

8357. שֵׁתָה **shêthâh,** *shay-thaw´;* from 7896; the *seat* (of the person):— buttock.

8358. שְׁתִי **shethîy,** *sheth-ee´;* from 8354; *intoxication:*— drunkenness.

8359. שְׁתִי **shethîy,** *sheth-ee´;* from 7896; a *fixture,* i.e. the *warp* in weaving:— warp.

8360. שְׁתִיָּה **shethîyâh,** *sheth-ee-yaw´;* fem. of 8358; *potation:*— drinking.

שְׁתַּיִם **shettayim.** See 8147.

8361. שִׁתִּין **shittîyn** (Chald.), *shit-teen´;* corresp. to 8346 [comp. 8353]; *sixty:*— threescore.

8362. שָׁתַל **shâthal,** *shaw-thal´;* a prim. root; to *transplant:*— plant.

8363. שְׁתִיל **shethîyl,** *sheth-eel´;* from 8362; a *sprig* (as if *transplanted*), i.e. *sucker:*— plant.

8364. שֻׁתַלְחִי **Shûthalchîy,** *shoo-thal-kee´;* patron. from 7803; a *Shuthalchite* (collect.) or desc. of Shuthelach:— Shuthalhites.

שָׁתַם **sâtham.** See 5640.

8365. שָׁתַם **shâtham,** *shaw-tham´;* a prim. root; to *unveil* (fig.):— be open.

8366. שָׁתַן **shâthan,** *shaw-than´;* a prim. root; (caus.) to *make water,* i.e. *urinate:*— piss.

8367. שָׁתַק **shâthaq,** *shaw-thak´;* a prim. root; to *subside:*— be calm, cease, be quiet.

8368. שָׂתַר **sâthar,** *saw-thar´;* a prim. root; to *break* out (as an eruption):— have in [one's] secret parts.

8369. שֵׁתָר **Shêthâr,** *shay-thawr´;* of for. der.; *Shethar,* a Pers. satrap:— Shethar.

8370. שְׁתַר בּוֹזְנַי **Shethar Bôwzenay,** *sheth-ar´ bo-zen-ah´-ee;* of for. der.; *Shethar-Bozenai,* a Pers. officer:— Shethar-boznai.

8371. שָׁתַת **shâthath,** *shaw-thath´;* a prim. root; to *place,* i.e. *array;* reflex. to *lie:*— be laid, set.

ת

8372. תָּא **tâ',** *taw;* and (fem.)

תָּאָה **tâ'âh** (Ezek. 40:12), *taw-aw´;* from (the base of) 8376; a *room* (as *circumscribed*):— (little) chamber.

8373. תָּאַב **tâ'ab,** *taw-ab´;* a prim. root; to *desire:*— long.

8374. תָּאַב **tâ'ab,** *taw-ab´;* a prim. root [prob. rather ident. with 8373 through the idea of *puffing* disdainfully at; comp. 340]; to *loathe* (mor.):— abhor.

8375. תַּאֲבָה **ta'ăbâh,** *tah-ab-aw´;* from 8374 [comp. 15]; *desire:*— longing.

8376. תָּאָה **tâ'âh,** *taw-aw´;* a prim. root; to *mark* off, i.e. (intens.) *designate:*— point out.

8377. תְּאוֹ **te'ôw,** *teh-o´;* and

תּוֹא **tôw'** (the orig. form), *toh;* from 8376; a species of *antelope* (prob. from the white *stripe* on the cheek):— wild bull (ox).

8378. תַּאֲוָה **ta'ăvâh,** *tah-av-aw´;* from 183

(abb.); a *longing*; by impl. a *delight* (subj. *satisfaction*, obj. a *charm*):— dainty, desire, ×exceedingly, × greedily, lust (ing), pleasant. See also 6914.

8379. תַּאֲוָה **ta'ăvâh**, *tah-av-aw´*; from 8376; a *limit*, i.e. *full extent*:— utmost bound.

8380. תְּאוֹם **tâ'ôwm**, *taw-ome´*; or

תְּאֹם **tâ'ôm**, *taw-ome´*; from 8382; a *twin* (in plur. only), lit. or fig.:— twins.

8381. תַּאֲלָה **ta'ălâh**, *tah-al-aw´*; from 422; an *imprecation*:— curse.

8382. תָּאַם **tâ'am**, *taw-am´*; a prim. root; to *be complete*; but used only as denom. from 8380, to *be* (caus. *make*) *twinned*, i.e. (fig.) *duplicate* or (arch.) *jointed*:— coupled (together), bear twins.

תְּאֹם **tâ'ôm**. See 8380.

8383. תְּאֻן **te'ûn**, *teh-oon´*; from 205; *naughtiness*, i.e. *toil*:— lie.

8384. תְּאֵן **te'ên**, *teh-ane´*; or (in the sing., fem.)

תְּאֵנָה **te'ênâh**, *teh-ay-naw´*; perh. of for. der.; the *fig* (tree or fruit):— fig (tree).

8385. תַּאֲנָה **ta'ănâh**, *tah-an-aw´*; or

תֹּאֲנָה **tô'ănâh**, *to-an-aw´*; from 579; an *opportunity* or (subj.) *purpose*:— occasion.

8386. תַּאֲנִיָּה **ta'ănîyâh**, *tah-an-ee-yaw´*; from 578; *lamentation*:— heaviness, mourning.

8387. תַּאֲנַת שִׁלֹה **Ta'ănath Shîlôh**, *tah-an-ath´ shee-lo´*; from 8385 and 7887; *approach of Shiloh*; *Taanath-Shiloh*, a place in Pal.:— Taanath-shiloh.

8388. תָּאַר **tâ'ar**, *taw-ar´*; a prim. root; to *delineate*; reflex. to *extend*:— be drawn, mark out, [Rimmon-] methoar [by union with 7417].

8389. תֹּאַר **tô'ar**, *to´-ar*; from 8388; *outline*, i.e. *figure* or *appearance*:— + beautiful, × comely, countenance, + fair, × favoured, form, × goodly, × resemble, visage.

8390. תַּאֲרֵעַ **Ta'ărêa'**, *tah-ar-ay´-ah*; perh. from 772; *Taarea*, an Isr.:— Tarea. See 8475.

8391. תְּאַשּׁוּר **te'ashshûwr**, *teh-ash-shoor´*; from 833; a species of *cedar* (from its *erectness*):— box (tree).

8392. תֵּבָה **têbâh**, *tay-baw´*; perh. of for. der.; a *box*:— ark.

8393. תְּבוּאָה **tebûw'âh**, *teb-oo-aw´*; from 935; *income*, i.e. *produce* (lit. or fig.):— fruit, gain, increase, revenue.

8394. תָּבוּן **tâbûwn**, *taw-boon´*; and (fem.)

תְּבוּנָה **tebûwnâh**, *teb-oo-naw´*; or

תּוֹבֻנָה° **tôwbûnâh**, *to-boo-naw´*; from 995; *intelligence*; by impl. an *argument*; by extens. *caprice*:— discretion, reason, skilfulness, understanding, wisdom.

8395. תְּבוּסָה **tebûwçâh**, *teb-oo-saw´*; from 947; a *treading down*, i.e. *ruin*:— destruction.

8396. תָּבוֹר **Tâbôwr**, *taw-bore´*; from a root corresp. to 8406; *broken* region; *Tabor*, a mountain in Pal., also a city adjacent:— Tabor.

8397. תֶּבֶל **tebel**, *teh´-bel*; appar. from 1101; *mixture*, i.e. *unnatural* bestiality:— confusion.

8398. תֵּבֵל **têbêl**, *tay-bale´*; from 2986; the *earth* (as *moist* and therefore inhabited); by extens. the *globe*; by impl. its *inhabitants*; spec. a partic. *land*, as Babylonia, Pal.:— habitable part, world.

תֵּבֵל **Tûbal**. See 8422.

8399. תַּבְלִית **tablîyth**, *tab-leeth´*; from 1086; *consumption*:— destruction.

8400. תְּבַלֻּל **teballûl**, *teb-al-lool´*; from 1101 in the orig. sense of *flowing*:— a *cataract* (in the eye):— blemish.

8401. תֶּבֶן **teben**, *teh´-ben*; prob. from 1129; prop. *material*, i.e. (spec.) *refuse haum* or *stalks of grain* (as *chopped* in threshing and used for fodder):— chaff, straw, stubble.

8402. תִּבְנִי **Tibnîy**, *tib-nee´*; from 8401; *strawy*; *Tibni*, an Isr.:— Tibni.

8403. תַּבְנִית **tabnîyth**, *tab-neeth´*; from 1129; *structure*; by impl. a *model, resemblance*:— figure, form, likeness, pattern, similitude.

8404. תַּבְעֵרָה **Tab'êrâh**, *tab-ay-raw´*; from 1197; *burning*; *Taberah*, a place in the Desert:— Taberah.

8405. תֵּבֵץ **Têbêts**, *tay-bates´*; from the same as 948; *whiteness*; *Tebets*, a place in Pal.:— Thebez.

8406. תְּבַר **tebar** (Chald.), *teb-ar´*; corresp. to 7665; to *be fragile* (fig.):— broken.

8407. תִּגְלַת פִּלְאֶסֶר **Tiglath Pil'eçer**, *tig-lath´ pil-eh´-ser*; or

תִּגְלַת פְּלֶסֶר **Tiglath Peleçer**, *tig-lath pel-eh-ser*; or

תִּלְּגַת פִּלְנְאֶסֶר **Tilgath Pilne'eçer**, *til-gath´ pil-neh-eh´-ser*; or

תִּלְגַת פִּלְנֶסֶר **Tilgath Pilneçer**, *til-gath´ pil-neh´-ser*; of for. der.; *Tiglath-Pileser* or *Tilgath-pilneser*, an Ass. king:— Tiglath-pileser, Tilgath-pilneser.

8408. תַּגְמוּל **tagmûwl**, *tag-mool´*; from 1580; a *bestowment*:— benefit.

8409. תִּגְרָה **tigrâh**, *tig-raw´*; from 1624; *strife*, i.e. *infliction*:— blow.

תֹּגַרְמָה **Tôgarmâh**. See 8425.

8410. תִּדְהָר **tidhâr**, *tid-hawr´*; appar. from

1725; *enduring;* a species of hard-wood or *lasting* tree (perh. *oak*):— pine (tree).

8411. תְּדִירָא **t^edîyrâ'** (Chald.), *ted-ee-raw´*; from 1753 in the orig. sense of *enduring; permanence,* i.e. (adv.) *constantly:*— continually.

8412. תַּדְמֹר **Tadmôr,** *tad-more´*; or

תַּמֹּר° **Tammôr** (1 Kings 9:18), *tam-more´*; appar. from 8558; *palm*-city; *Tadmor,* a place near Pal.:— Tadmor.

8413. תִּדְעָל **Tid'âl,** *tid-awl´*; perh. from 1763; *fearfulness; Tidal,* a Canaanite:— Tidal.

8414. תֹהוּ **tôhûw,** *to´-hoo;* from an unused root mean. to lie *waste;* a *desolation* (of surface), i.e. *desert;* fig. a *worthless* thing; adv. in *vain:*— confusion, empty place, without form, nothing, (thing of) nought, vain, vanity, waste, wilderness.

8415. תְּהוֹם **t^ehôwm,** *teh-home´;* or

תְּהֹם **t^ehôm,** *teh-home´;* (usually fem.) from 1949; an *abyss* (as a *surging* mass of water), espec. the *deep* (the *main* sea or the subterranean *water-supply*):— deep (place), depth.

8416. תְּהִלָּה **t^ehillâh,** *teh-hil-law´;* from 1984; *laudation;* spec. (concr.) a *hymn:*— praise.

8417. תָּהֳלָה **tohŏlâh,** *to-hol-aw´;* fem. of an unused noun (appar. from 1984) mean. *bluster; braggadocio,* i.e. (by impl.) *fatuity:*— folly.

8418. תַּהֲלֻכָה **tahălûkâh,** *tah-hal-oo-kaw´;* from 1980; a *procession:*— × went.

תְּהֹם **t^ehôm.** See 8415.

8419. תַּהְפֻּכָה **tahpûkâh,** *tah-poo-kaw´;* from 2015; a *perversity* or *fraud:*— (very) froward (-ness, thing), perverse thing.

8420. תָו **tâv,** *tawv;* from 8427; a *mark;* by impl. a *signature:*— desire, mark.

8421. תּוּב **tûwb** (Chald.), *toob;* corresp. to 7725, to *come back;* spec. (tran. and ellip.) to *reply:*— answer, restore, return (an answer).

8422. תּוּבַל **Tûwbal,** *too-bal´;* or

תֻּבַל **Tûbal,** *too-bal´;* prob. of for. der.; *Tubal,* a postdiluvian patriarch and his posterity:— Tubal.

8423. תּוּבַל קַיִן **Tûwbal Qayin,** *too-bal´ kah´-yin;* appar. from 2986 (comp. 2981) and 7014; *offspring of Cain; Tubal-Kajin,* an antediluvian patriarch:— Tubal-cain.

תּוֹבֻנָה° **tôwbûnâh.** See 8394.

8424. תּוּגָה **tûwgâh,** *too-gaw´;* from 3013; *depression* (of spirits); concr. a *grief:*— heaviness, sorrow.

8425. תּוֹגַרְמָה **Tôwgarmâh,** *to-gar-maw´;* or

תֹּגַרְמָה **Tôgarmâh,** *to-gar-maw´;* prob. of for. der.; *Togarmah,* a son of Gomer and his posterity:— Togarmah.

8426. תּוֹדָה **tôwdâh,** *to-daw´;* from 3034; prop. an *extension* of the hand, i.e. (by impl.) *avowal,* or (usually) *adoration;* spec. a *choir* of worshippers:— confession, (sacrifice of) praise, thanks (-giving, offering).

8427. תָּוָה **tâvâh,** *taw-vaw´;* a prim. root; to *mark* out, i.e. (prim.) *scratch* or (def.) *imprint:*— scrabble, set [a mark].

8428. תָּוָה **tâvâh,** *taw-vaw´;* a prim. root [or perh. ident. with 8427 through a similar idea from *scraping* to pieces] to *grieve:*— limit [by confusion with 8427].

8429. תְּוַהּ **t^evahh** (Chald.), *tev-ah´;* corresp. to 8539 or perh. to 7582 through the idea of *sweeping* to ruin [comp. 8428]; to *amaze,* i.e. (reflex. by impl.) *take alarm:*— be astonied.

8430. תּוֹחַ **Tôwach,** *to´-akh;* from an unused root mean. to *depress; humble; Toach,* an Isr.:— Toah.

8431. תּוֹחֶלֶת **tôwcheleth,** *to-kheh´-leth;* from 3176; *expectation:*— hope.

תּוֹךְ **tôwk.** See 8496.

8432. תָּוֶךְ **tâvek,** *taw´-vek;* from an unused root mean. to *sever;* a *bisection,* i.e. (by impl.) the *centre:*— among (-st), × between, half, × (there-, where-) in (-to), middle, mid [-night], midst (among), × out (of), × through, × with (-in).

תּוּכִי **tûwkkîy.** See 8500.

8433. תּוֹכֵחָה **tôwkêchâh,** *to-kay-khaw´;* and

תּוֹכַחַת **tôwkachath,** *to-kakh´-ath;* from 3198; *chastisement;* fig. (by words) *correction, refutation, proof* (even in defence):— argument, × chastened, correction, reasoning, rebuke, reproof, × be (often) reproved.

8434. תּוֹלָד **Tôwlâd,** *to-lawd´;* from 3205; *posterity; Tolad,* a place in Pal.:— Tolad. Comp. 513.

8435. תּוֹלְדָה **tôwl^edâh,** *to-led-aw´;* or

תֹּלְדָה **tôl^edâh,** *to-led-aw´;* from 3205; (plur. only) *descent,* i.e. *family;* (fig.) *history:*— birth, generations.

8436. תּוּלוֹן° **Tûwlôn,** *too-lone´;* from 8524; *suspension; Tulon,* an Isr.:— Tilon [from the marg.].

8437. תּוֹלָל **tôwlâl,** *to-lawl´;* from 3213; *causing to howl,* i.e. an *oppressor:*— that wasted.

8438. תּוֹלָע **tôwlâ',** *to-law´;* and (fem.)

תּוֹלֵעָה **tôwlê'âh,** *to-lay-aw´;* or

תּוֹלַעַת **tôwla'ath,** *to-lah´-ath;* or

תֹּלַעַת **tôla'ath,** *to-lah´-ath;* from 3216; a *maggot* (as *voracious*); spec. (often with ellip. of 8144) the *crimson-grub,* but used

Hebrew

only (in this connection) of the color from it, and cloths dyed therewith:— crimson, scarlet, worm.

8439. תּוֹלֵע **Tôwlâ'**, *to-law´*; the same as 8438; *worm; Tola*, the name of two Isr.:— Tola.

8440. תּוֹלֵעִי **Tôwlâ'îy**, *to-law-ee´*; patron. from 8439; a *Tolaite* (collect.) or desc. of Tola:— Tolaites.

8441. תּוֹעֵבָה **tôw'êbâh**, *to-ay-baw´*; or

תֹּעֵבָה **tô'êbâh**, *to-ay-baw´*; fem. act. part. of 8581; prop. something *disgusting* (mor.), i.e. (as noun) an *abhorrence*; espec. *idolatry* or (concr.) an *idol*:— abominable (custom, thing), abomination.

8442. תּוֹעָה **tôw'âh**, *to-aw´*; fem. act. part. of 8582; *mistake*, i.e. (mor.) *impiety*, or (political) *injury*:— error, hinder.

8443. תּוֹעָפָה **tôw'âphâh**, *to-aw-faw´*; from 3286; (only in plur. collect.) *weariness*, i.e. (by impl.) *toil* (*treasure* so obtained) or *speed*:— plenty, strength.

8444. תּוֹצָאָה **tôwtsâ'âh**, *to-tsaw-aw´*; or

תֹּצָאָה **tôtsâ'âh**, *to-tsaw-aw´*; from 3318; (only in plur. collect.) *exit*, i.e. (geographical) *boundary*, or (fig.) *deliverance*, (act.) *source*:— border (-s), going (-s) forth (out), issues, outgoings.

8445. תּוֹקַהַת° **Tôwqahath**, *to-kah´-ath*; from the same as 3349; *obedience; Tokahath*, an Isr.:— Tikvath [*by correction for* 8616].

8446. תּוּר **tûwr**, *toor*; a prim. root; to *meander* (caus. *guide*) about, espec. for trade or reconnoitring:— chap [-man], sent to descry, be excellent, merchant [-man], search (out), seek, (e-) spy (out).

8447. תּוֹר **tôwr**, *tore*; or

תֹּר **tôr**, *tore*; from 8446; a *succession*, i.e. a *string* or (abstr.) *order*:— border, row, turn.

8448. תּוֹר **tôwr**, *tore*; prob. the same as 8447; a *manner* (as a sort of *turn*):— estate.

8449. תּוֹר **tôwr**, *tore*; or

תֹּר **tôr**, *tore*; prob. the same as 8447; a *ring*-dove, often (fig.) as a term of endearment:— (turtle) dove.

8450. תּוֹר **tôwr** (Chald.), *tore*; corresp. (by perm.) to 7794; a *bull*:— bullock, ox.

8451. תּוֹרָה **tôwrâh**, *to-raw´*; or

תֹּרָה **tôrâh**, *to-raw´*; from 3384; a *precept* or *statute*, espec. the *Decalogue* or *Pentateuch*:— law.

8452. תּוֹרָה **tôwrâh**, *to-raw´*; prob. fem. of 8448; a *custom*:— manner.

8453. תּוֹשָׁב **tôwshâb**, *to-shawb´*; or

תֹּשָׁב **tôshâb** (1 Kings 17:1), *to-shawb´*; from 3427; a *dweller* (but not outlandish [5237]); espec. (as distinguished from a native citizen [act. part. of 3427] and a temporary inmate [1616] or mere lodger [3885]) resident *alien*:— foreigner, inhabitant, sojourner, stranger.

8454. תּוּשִׁיָּה **tûwshîyâh**, *too-shee-yaw´*; or

תֻּשִׁיָּה **tûshîyâh**, *too-shee-yaw´*; from an unused root prob. mean. to *substantiate; support* or (by impl.) *ability*, i.e. (direct) *help*, (in purpose) an *undertaking*, (intellectual) *understanding*:— enterprise, that which (thing as it) is, substance, (sound) wisdom, working.

8455. תּוֹתָח **tôwthâch**, *to-thawkh´*; from an unused root mean. to *smite*; a *club*:— darts.

8456. תָּזַז **tâzaz**, *taw-zaz´*; a prim. root; to *lop off*:— cut down.

8457. תַּזְנוּת **taznûwth**, *taz-nooth´*; or

תַּזְנֻת **taznûth**, *taz-nooth´*; from 2181; *harlotry*, i.e. (fig.) *idolatry*:— fornication, whoredom.

8458. תַּחְבֻּלָה **tachbûlâh**, *takh-boo-law´*; or

תַּחְבּוּלָה **tachbûwlâh**, *takh-boo-law´*; from 2254 as denom. from 2256; (only in plur.) prop. *steerage* (as a management of *ropes*), i.e. (fig.) *guidance* or (by impl.) a *plan*:— good advice, (wise) counsels.

8459. תֹּחוּ **Tôchûw**, *to´-khoo*; from an unused root mean. to *depress; abasement; Tochu*, an Isr.:— Tohu.

8460. תְּחוֹת **tᵉchôwth** (Chald.), *tekh-ōth´*; or

תְּחֹת **tᵉchôth** (Chald.), *tekh-ōth´*; corresp. to 8478; *beneath*:— under.

8461. תַּחְכְּמֹנִי **Tachkᵉmônîy**, *takh-kem-o-nee´*; prob. for 2453; *sagacious; Tachkemoni*, an Isr.:— Tachmonite.

8462. תְּחִלָּה **tᵉchillâh**, *tekh-il-law´*; from 2490 in the sense of *opening*; a *commencement*; rel. *original* (adv. *-ly*):— begin (-ning), first (time).

8463. תַּחֲלוּא **tachălûw'**, *takh-al-oo´*; or

תַּחֲלֻא **tachălû'**, *takh-al-oo´*; from 2456; a *malady*:— disease, × grievous, (that are) sick (-ness).

8464. תַּחְמָס **tachmâç**, *takh-mawce´*; from 2554; a species of unclean bird (from its *violence*), perh. an *owl*:— night hawk.

8465. תַּחַן **Tachan**, *takh´-an*; prob. from 2583; *station; Tachan*, the name of two Isr.:— Tahan.

8466. תַּחֲנָה **tachănâh**, *takh-an-aw´*; from 2583; (only plur. collect.) an *encampment*:— camp.

8467. תְּחִנָּה **tᵉchinnâh**, *tekh-in-naw´*; from 2603; *graciousness*; caus. *entreaty*:— favour, grace, supplication.

8468. תְּחִנָּה **Tᵉchinnâh**, *tekh-in-naw´*; the

same as 8467; *Techinnah*, an Isr.:— Tehinnah.

8469. תַּחֲנוּן **tachănûwn**, *takh-an-oon´*; or

(fem.)

תַּחֲנוּנָה **tachănûwnâh**, *takh-an-oo-naw´*; from 2603; earnest *prayer:*— intreaty, supplication.

8470. תַּחֲנִי **Tachănîy**, *takh-an-ee´*; patron. from 8465; a *Tachanite* (collect.) or desc. of Tachan:— Tahanites.

8471. תַּחְפַּנְחֵס **Tachpanchêç**, *takh-pan-khace´*; or

תְּחַפְנְחֵס **Tᵉchaphnᵉchêç** (Ezek. 30:18), *tekh-af-nekh-ace´*; or

תַּחְפְּנֵס° **Tachpᵉnêç** (Jer. 2:16), *takh-pen-ace´*; of Eg. der.; *Tachpanches, Techaphneches* or *Tachpenes*, a place in Egypt:— Tahapanes, Tahpanhes, Tehaphnehes.

8472. תַּחְפְּנֵיס **Tachpᵉnêyç**, *takh-pen-ace´*; of Eg. der.; *Tachpenes*, an Eg. woman:— Tahpenes.

8473. תַּחְרָא **tachărâ'**, *takh-ar-aw´*; from 2734 in the orig. sense of 2352 or 2353; a linen *corslet* (as *white* or *hollow*):— habergeon.

8474. תַּחְרֶה **tachârâh**, *takh-aw-raw´*; a factitious root from 2734 through the idea of the *heat* of jealousy; to *vie* with a rival:— close, contend.

8475. תַּחְרֵעַ **Tachrêa'**, *takh-ray´-ah;* for 8390; *Tachrea*, an Isr.:— Tahrea.

8476. תַּחַשׁ **tachash**, *takh´-ash;* prob. of for. der.; a (clean) animal with fur, prob. a species of *antelope:*— badger.

8477. תַּחַשׁ **Tachash**, *takh´-ash;* the same as 8476; *Tachash*, a rel. of Abraham:— Thahash.

8478. תַּחַת **tachath**, *takh´-ath;* from the same as 8430; the *bottom* (as *depressed*); only adv. *below* (often with prep. pref. *underneath*), in *lieu of*, etc.:— as, beneath, × flat, in (-stead), (same) place (where ... is), room, for ... sake, stead of, under, × unto, × when ... was mine, whereas, [where-] fore, with.

8479. תַּחַת **tachath** (Chald.), *takh´-ath;* corresp. to 8478:— under.

8480. תַּחַת **Tachath**, *takh´-ath;* the same as 8478; *Tachath*, the name of a place in the Desert, also of three Isr.:— Tahath.

תְּחֹת **tᵉchôth**. See 8460.

8481. תַּחְתּוֹן **tachtôwn**, *takh-tone´;* or

תַּחְתֹּן **tachtôn**, *takh-tone´;* from 8478; *bottommost:*— lower (-est), nether (-most).

8482. תַּחְתִּי **tachtîy**, *takh-tee´;* from 8478; *lowermost;* as noun (fem. plur.) the *depths* (fig. a pit, the womb):— low (parts, -er, -er parts, -est), nether (part).

8483. תַּחְתִּים חָדְשִׁי **Tachtîym Chodshîy**, *takh-teem´ khod-shee´;* appar. from the plur. masc. of 8482 or 8478 and 2320; *lower* (ones) *monthly; Tachtim-Chodshi*, a place in Pal.:— Tahtim-hodshi.

8484. תִּיכוֹן **tîykôwn**, *tee-kone´;* or

תִּיכֹן **tîykôn**, *tee-kone´;* from 8432; *central:*— middle (-most), midst.

8485. תֵּימָא **Têymâ'**, *tay-maw´;* or

תֵּמָא **Têmâ'**, *tay-maw´;* prob. of for. der.; *Tema*, a son of Ishmael, and the region settled by him:— Tema.

8486. תֵּימָן **têymân**, *tay-mawn´;* or

תֵּמָן **têmân**, *tay-mawn´;* denom. from 3225; the *south* (as being on the *right* hand of a person facing the east):— south (side, -ward, wind).

8487. תֵּימָן **Têymân**, *tay-mawn´;* or

תֵּמָן **Têmân**, *tay-mawn´;* the same as 8486; *Teman*, the name of two Edomites, and of the region and desc. of one of them:— south, Teman.

8488. תֵּימְנִי **Têymᵉnîy**, *tay-men-ee´;* prob. for 8489; *Temeni*, an Isr.:— Temeni.

8489. תֵּימָנִי **Têymânîy**, *tay-maw-nee´;* patron. from 8487; a *Temanite* or desc. of Teman:— Temani, Temanite.

8490. תִּימָרָה **tîymârâh**, *tee-maw-raw´;* or

תִּמָרָה **tîmârâh**, *tee-maw-raw´;* from the same as 8558; a *column*, i.e. *cloud:*— pillar.

8491. תִּיצִי **Tîytsîy**, *tee-tsee´;* patrial or patron. from an unused noun of uncert. mean.; a *Titsite* or desc. or inhab. of an unknown Tits:— Tizite.

8492. תִּירוֹשׁ **tîyrôwsh**, *tee-roshe´;* or

תִּירֹשׁ **tîyrôsh**, *tee-roshe´;* from 3423 in the sense of *expulsion; must* or fresh grape-juice (as just *squeezed* out); by impl. (rarely) fermented *wine:*— (new, sweet) wine.

8493. תִּירְיָא **Tîyrᵉyâ'**, *tee-reh-yaw´;* prob. from 3372; *fearful, Tirja*, an Isr.:— Tiria.

8494. תִּירָס **Tîyrâç**, *tee-rawce´;* prob. of for. der.; *Tiras*, a son of Japheth:— Tiras.

תִּירֹשׁ **tîyrôsh**. See 8492.

8495. תַּיִשׁ **tayish**, *tah´-yeesh;* from an unused root mean. to *butt;* a *buck* or he-goat (as given to *butting*):— he goat.

8496. תֹּךְ **tôk**, *toke;* or

תּוֹךְ **tôwk** (Psa. 72:14), *toke;* from the same base as 8432 (in the sense of *cutting* to pieces); *oppression:*— deceit, fraud.

8497. תָּכָה **tâkâh**, *taw-kaw´;* a prim. root; to *strew*, i.e. *encamp:*— sit down.

8498. תְּכוּנָה **tᵉkûwnâh**, *tek-oo-naw´;* fem. pass. part. of 8505; *adjustment*, i.e. *structure;* by impl. *equipage:*— fashion, store.

8499. תְּכוּנָה **tᵉkûwnâh**, *tek-oo-naw´;* from 3559; or prob. ident. with 8498; something *arranged* or *fixed,* i.e. a *place:*— seat.

8500. תְּכִי **tukkîy**, *took-kee´;* or

תּוּכִּי **tûwkkîy**, *took-kee´;* prob. of for. der.; some imported creature, prob. a *peacock:*— peacock.

8501. תָּכָךְ **tâkâk**, *taw-kawk´;* from an unused root mean. to *dissever,* i.e. *crush:*— deceitful.

8502. תִּכְלָה **tiklâh**, *tik-law´;* from 3615; *completeness:*— perfection.

8503. תַּכְלִית **taklîyth**, *tak-leeth´;* from 3615; *completion;* by impl. an *extremity:*— end, perfect (-ion).

8504. תְּכֵלֶת **tᵉkêleth**, *tek-ay´-leth;* prob. for 7827; the cerulean *mussel,* i.e. the color (*violet*) obtained therefrom or stuff dyed therewith:— blue.

8505. תָּכַן **tâkan**, *taw-kan´;* a prim. root; to *balance,* i.e. *measure* out (by weight or dimension); fig. to *arrange, equalize,* through the idea of *levelling* (ment. *estimate, test*):— bear up, direct, be (un-) equal, mete, ponder, tell, weigh.

8506. תֹּכֶן **tôken**, *to´-ken;* from 8505; a fixed *quantity:*— measure, tale.

8507. תֹּכֶן **Tôken**, *to´-ken;* the same as 8506; *Token,* a place in Pal.:— Tochen.

8508. תְּכֻנִית **toknîyth**, *tok-neeth´;* from 8506; *admeasurement,* i.e. *consummation:*— pattern, sum.

8509. תַּכְרִיךְ **takrîyk**, *tak-reek´;* appar. from an unused root mean. to *encompass;* a *wrapper* or robe:— garment.

8510. תֵּל **têl**, *tale;* by contr. from 8524; a *mound:*— heap, × strength.

8511. תָּלָא **tâlâ'**, *taw-law´;* a prim. root; to *suspend;* fig. (through *hesitation*) to be *uncertain;* by impl. (of mental *dependence*) to *habituate:*— be bent, hang (in doubt).

8512. תֵּל אָבִיב **Têl 'Âbîyb**, *tale aw-beeb´;* from 8510 and 24; *mound of green* growth; *Tel-Abib,* a place in Chaldaea:— Tel-abib.

8513. תְּלָאָה **tᵉlâ'âh**, *tel-aw-aw´;* from 3811; *distress:*— travail, travel, trouble.

8514. תַּלְאוּבָה **tal'ûwbâh**, *tal-oo-baw´;* from 3851; *desiccation:*— great drought.

8515. תְּלַאשַּׂר **Tᵉla'ssar**, *tel-as-sar´;* or

תְּלַשַּׂר **Tᵉlassar**, *tel-as-sar´;* of for. der.; *Telassar,* a region of Assyria:— Telassar.

8516. תַּלְבֹּשֶׁת **talbôsheth**, *tal-bo´-sheth;* from 3847; a *garment:*— clothing.

8517. תְּלַג **tᵉlag** (Chald.), *tel-ag´;* corresp. to 7950; *snow:*— snow.

תִּלְגַת **Tilgath**. See 8407.

תּוֹלְדָה **tôlᵉdâh**. See 8435.

8518. תָּלָה **tâlâh**, *taw-law´;* a prim. root; to *suspend* (espec. to *gibbet*):— hang (up).

8519. תְּלוּנָה **tᵉlûwnâh**, *tel-oo-naw´;* or

תְּלֻנָּה **tᵉlunnâh**, *tel-oon-naw´;* from 3885 in the sense of *obstinacy;* a *grumbling:*— murmuring.

8520. תֶּלַח **Telach**, *teh´-lakh;* prob. from an unused root mean. to *dissever; breach; Telach,* an Isr.:— Telah.

8521. תֵּל חַרְשָׁא **Têl Charshâ'**, *tale kharshaw´;* from 8510 and the fem. of 2798; *mound of workmanship; Tel-Charsha,* a place in Bab.:— Tel-haresha, Tel-harsa.

8522. תְּלִי **tᵉlîy**, *tel-ee´;* prob. from 8518; a *quiver* (as *slung*):— quiver.

8523. תְּלִיתַי **tᵉlîythay** (Chald.), *tel-ee-thah´-ee;* or

תַּלְתִּי **taltîy** (Chald.), *tal-tee´;* ord. from 8532; *third:*— third.

8524. תָּלַל **tâlal**, *taw-lal´;* a prim. root; to *pile* up, i.e. *elevate:*— eminent. Comp. 2048.

8525. תֶּלֶם **telem**, *teh´-lem;* from an unused root mean. to *accumulate;* a *bank* or *terrace:*— furrow, ridge.

8526. תַּלְמַי **Talmay**, *tal-mah´-ee;* from 8525; *ridged; Talmai,* the name of a Canaanite and a Syrian:— Talmai.

8527. תַּלְמִיד **talmîyd**, *tal-meed´;* from 3925; a *pupil:*— scholar.

8528. תֵּל מֶלַח **Têl Melach**, *tale meh´-lakh;* from 8510 and 4417; *mound of salt; Tel-Melach,* a place in Bab.:— Tel-melah.

תְּלֻנָּה **tᵉlunnâh**. See 8519.

8529. תָּלַע **tâla'**, *taw-law´;* a denom. from 8438; to *crimson,* i.e. dye that color:— × scarlet.

תֹּלַעַת **tôla'ath**. See 8438.

8530. תַּלְפִּיָּה **talpîyâh**, *tal-pee-yaw´;* fem. from an unused root mean. to *tower;* something *tall,* i.e. (plur. collect.) *slenderness:*— armoury.

תְּלַשַּׂר **Tᵉlassar**. See 8515.

8531. תְּלַת **tᵉlath** (Chald.), *tel-ath´;* from 8532; a *tertiary* rank:— third.

8532. תְּלָת **tᵉlâth** (Chald.), *tel-awth´;* masc.

תְּלָתָה **tᵉlâthâh** (Chald.), *tel-aw-thaw´;* or

תְּלָתָא **tᵉlâthâ'** (Chald.), *tel-aw-thaw´;* corresp. to 7969; *three* or *third:*— third, three.

תַּלְתִּי **taltiy**. See 8523.

8533. תְּלָתִין **tᵉlâthîyn** (Chald.), *tel-aw-theen´;* mult. of 8532; *ten times three:*— thirty.

8534. תַּלְתַּל **taltal**, *tal-tal´*; by redupl. from 8524 through the idea of *vibration*; a trailing *bough* (as *pendulous*):— bushy.

8535. תָּם **tâm**, *tawm*; from 8552; *complete*; usually (mor.) *pious*; spec. *gentle, dear*:— coupled together, perfect, plain, undefiled, upright.

8536. תָּם **tâm** (Chald.), *tawm*; corresp. to 8033; *there*:— × thence, there, × where.

8537. תֹּם **tôm**, *tome*; from 8552; *completeness*; fig. *prosperity*; usually (mor.) *innocence*:— full, integrity, perfect (-ion), simplicity, upright (-ly, -ness), at a venture. See 8550.

תֵּמָא **Têmâ´**. See 8485.

8538. תֻּמָּה **tummâh**, *toom-maw´*; fem. of 8537; *innocence*:— integrity.

8539. תָּמַהּ **tâmahh**, *taw-mah´*; a prim. root; to *be in consternation*:— be amazed, be astonished, marvel (-lously), wonder.

8540. תְּמַהּ **t'mahh** (Chald.), *tem-ah´*; from a root corresp. to 8539; a *miracle*:— wonder.

8541. תִּמָּהוֹן **timmâhôwn**, *tim-maw-hone´*; from 8539; *consternation*:— astonishment.

8542. תַּמּוּז **Tammûwz**, *tam-mooz´*; of uncert. der.; *Tammuz*, a Phoenician deity:— Tammuz.

8543. תְּמוֹל **t'môwl**, *tem-ole´*; or

תְּמֹל **t'môl**, *tem-ole´*; prob. for 865; prop. *ago*, i.e. a (short or long) *time since*; espec. *yesterday*, or (with 8032) *day before* yesterday:— + before (-time), + these [three] days, + heretofore, + time past, yesterday.

8544. תְּמוּנָה **t'mûwnâh**, *tem-oo-naw´*; or

תְּמֻנָה **t'mûnâh**, *tem-oo-naw´*; from 4327; *something portioned* (i.e. *fashioned*) out, as a *shape*, i.e. (indef.) *phantom*, or (spec.) *embodiment*, or (fig.) *manifestation* (of favor):— image, likeness, similitude.

8545. תְּמוּרָה **t'mûwrâh**, *tem-oo-raw´*; from 4171; *barter, compensation*:— (ex-) change (-ing), recompense, restitution.

8546. תְּמוּתָה **t'mûwthâh**, *tem-oo-thaw´*; from 4191; *execution* (as a doom):— death, die.

8547. תֶּמַח **Temach**, *teh´-makh*; of uncert. der.; *Temach*, one of the Nethinim:— Tamah, Thamah.

8548. תָּמִיד **tâmîyd**, *taw-meed´*; from an unused root mean. to *stretch*; prop. *continuance* (as indef. *extension*); but used only (attributively as adj.) *constant* (or adv. *constantly*); ellipt. the *regular* (daily) sacrifice:— alway (-s), continual (employment, -ly), daily, [(n-)] ever (-more), perpetual.

8549. תָּמִים **tâmîym**, *taw-meem´*; from 8552; *entire* (lit., fig. or mor.); also (as noun) *integrity, truth*:— without blemish, complete, full, per-

fect, sincerely (-ity), sound, without spot, undefiled, upright (-ly), whole.

8550. תֻּמִּים **Tummîym**, *toom-meem´*; plur. of 8537; *perfections*, i.e. (tech.) one of the epithets of the objects in the high-priest's breastplate as an emblem of *complete* Truth:— Thummim.

8551. תָּמַךְ **tâmak**, *taw-mak´*; a prim. root; to *sustain*; by impl. to *obtain, keep fast*; fig. to *help, follow close*:— (take, up-) hold (up), maintain, retain, stay (up).

תְּמֹל **t'môl**. See 8543.

8552. תָּמַם **tâmam**, *taw-mam´*; a prim. root; to *complete*, in a good or a bad sense, lit. or fig., tran. or intr. (as follows):— accomplish, cease, be clean [pass-] ed, consume, have done, (come to an, have an, make an) end, fail, come to the full, be all gone, × be all here, be (make) perfect, be spent, sum, be (shew self) upright, be wasted, whole.

תֵּמָן **têmân**, **Têmân**. See 8486, 8487.

8553. תִּמְנָה **Timnâh**, *tim-naw´*; from 4487; a *portion* assigned; *Timnah*, the name of two places in Pal.:— Timnah, Timnath, Thimnathah.

תְּמֻנָה **t'mûnâh**. See 8544.

8554. תִּמְנִי **Timnîy**, *tim-nee´*; patrial from 8553; a *Timnite* or inhab. of Timnah:— Timnite.

8555. תִּמְנָע **Timnâ'**, *tim-naw´*; from 4513; *restraint*; *Timna*, the name of two Edomites:— Timna, Timnah.

8556. תִּמְנַת חֶרֶס **Timnath Chereç**, *tim-nath kheh´-res*; or

תִּמְנַת סֶרַח **Timnath Çerach**, *tim-nath seh´-rakh*; from 8553 and 2775; *portion of* (the) *sun*; *Timnath-Cheres*, a place in Pal.:— Timnath-heres, Timnath-serah.

8557. תֶּמֶס **temeç**, *teh´-mes*; from 4529; *liquefaction*, i.e. *disappearance*:— melt.

8558. תָּמָר **tâmâr**, *taw-mawr´*; from an unused root mean. to *be erect*; a *palm* tree:— palm (tree).

8559. תָּמָר **Tâmâr**, *taw-mawr´*; the same as 8558; *Tamar*, the name of three women and a place:— Tamar.

8560. תֹּמֶר **tômer**, *to´-mer*; from the same root as 8558; a *palm* trunk:— palm tree.

8561. תִּמֹּר **timmôr** (plur. only), *tim-more´*; or (fem.)

תִּמֹּרָה **timmôrâh** (sing. and plur.), *tim-mo-raw´*; from the same root as 8558; (arch.) a *palm*-like pilaster (i.e. *umbellate*):— palm tree.

תַּמֹּר **Tammôr**. See 8412.

תִּמָרָה **timârâh**. See 8490.

8562. תַּמְרוּק **tamrûwq**, *tam-rook´*; or

תַּמְרֻק **tamrûq**, *tam-rook´*; or

תַּמְרִיק° **tamrîyq**, *tam-reek´*; from 4838; prop. a *scouring*, i.e. *soap* or *perfumery* for the bath; fig. a *detergent*:— × cleanse, (thing for) purification (-fying).

8563. תַּמְרוּר **tamrûwr**, *tam-roor´*; from 4843; *bitterness* (plur. as collect.):— × most bitter (-ly).

תַּמְרֻק **tamrûq** and

תַּמְרִיק **tamrîyq**. See 8562.

8564. תַּמְרוּר **tamrûwr**, *tam-roor´*; from the same root as 8558; an *erection*, i.e. *pillar* (prob. for a guide-board):— high heap.

8565. תַּן **tan**, *tan*; from an unused root prob. mean. to *elongate*; a *monster* (as preternaturally formed), i.e. a *sea-serpent* (or other huge marine animal); also a *jackal* (or other hideous land animal):— dragon, whale. Comp. 8577.

8566. תָּנָה **tânâh**, *taw-naw´*; a prim. root; to *present* (a mercenary inducement), i.e. *bargain* with (a harlot):— hire.

8567. תָּנָה **tânâh**, *taw-naw´*; a prim. root [rather ident. with 8566 through the idea of *attributing* honor]; to *ascribe* (praise), i.e. *celebrate, commemorate:*— lament, rehearse.

8568. תַּנָּה **tannâh**, *tan-naw´*; prob. fem. of 8565; a female *jackal:*— dragon.

8569. תְּנוּאָה **tᵉnûw'âh**, *ten-oo-aw´*; from 5106; *alienation*; by impl. *enmity:*— breach of promise, occasion.

8570. תְּנוּבָה **tᵉnûwbâh**, *ten-oo-baw´*; from 5107; *produce:*— fruit, increase.

8571. תְּנוּךְ **tᵉnûwk**, *ten-ook´*; perh. from the same as 594 through the idea of *protraction*; a *pinnacle*, i.e. *extremity:*— tip.

8572. תְּנוּמָה **tᵉnûwmâh**, *ten-oo-maw´*; from 5123; *drowsiness*, i.e. *sleep:*— slumber (-ing).

8573. תְּנוּפָה **tᵉnûwphâh**, *ten-oo-faw´*; from 5130; a *brandishing* (in threat); by impl. *tumult*; spec. the official *undulation* of sacrificial offerings:— offering, shaking, wave (offering).

8574. תַּנּוּר **tannûwr**, *tan-noor´*; from 5216; a *fire-pot:*— furnace, oven.

8575. תַּנְחוּם **tanchûwm**, *tan-khoom´*; or

תַּנְחֻם **tanchûm**, *tan-khoom´*; and (fem.)

תַּנְחוּמָה **tanchûwmâh**, *tan-khoo-maw´*; from 5162; *compassion, solace:*— comfort, consolation.

8576. תַּנְחֻמֶת **Tanchûmeth**, *tan-khoo´-meth*; for 8575 (fem.); *Tanchumeth*, an Isr.:— Tanhumeth.

8577. תַּנִּין **tannîyn**, *tan-neen´*; or

תַּנִּים **tannîym** (Ezek. 29:3), *tan-neem´*; intens. from the same as 8565; a marine or land *monster*, i.e. *sea-serpent* or *jackal:*— dragon, sea-monster, serpent, whale.

8578. תִּנְיָן **tinyân** (Chald.), *tin-yawn´*; corresp. to 8147; *second:*— second.

8579. תִּנְיָנוּת **tinyânûwth** (Chald.), *tin-yaw-nooth´*; from 8578; a *second time:*— again.

8580. תַּנְשֶׁמֶת **tanshemeth**, *tan-sheh´-meth*; from 5395; prop. a hard *breather*, i.e. the name of two unclean creatures, a lizard and a bird (both perh. from changing color through their *irascibility*), prob. the *tree-toad* and the *water-hen:*— mole, swan.

8581. תָּעַב **tâ'ab**, *taw-ab´*; a prim. root; to *loathe*, i.e. (mor.) *detest:*— (make to be) abhor (-red), (be, commit more, do) abominable (-y), × utterly.

תּוֹעֵבָה **tô'êbâh**. See 8441.

8582. תָּעָה **tâ'âh**, *taw-aw´*; a prim. root; to *vacillate*, i.e. *reel* or *stray* (lit. or fig.); also caus. of both:— (cause to) go astray, deceive, dissemble, (cause to, make to) err, pant, seduce, (make to) stagger, (cause to) wander, be out of the way.

8583. תֹּעוּ **Tô'ûw**, *to´-oo*; or

תֹּעִי **Tô'îy**, *to´-ee*; from 8582; *error, Tou* or *Toi*, a Syrian king:— Toi, Tou.

8584. תְּעוּדָה **tᵉ'ûwdâh**, *teh-oo-daw´*; from 5749; *attestation*, i.e. a *precept, usage:*— testimony.

8585. תְּעָלָה **tᵉ'âlâh**, *teh-aw-law´*; from 5927; a *channel* (into which water is *raised* for irrigation); also a *bandage* or *plaster* (as placed *upon* a wound):— conduit, cured, healing, little river, trench, watercourse.

8586. תַּעֲלוּל **ta'ălûwl**, *tah-al-ool´*; from 5953; *caprice* (as a fit *coming on*), i.e. *vexation*; concr. a *tyrant:*— babe, delusion.

8587. תַּעֲלֻמָּה **ta'ălummâh**, *tah-al-oom-maw´*; from 5956; a *secret:*— thing that is hid, secret.

8588. תַּעֲנוּג **ta'ănûwg**, *tah-an-oog´*; or

תַּעֲנֻג **ta'ănûg**, *tah-an-oog´*; and (fem.)

תַּעֲנֻגָה **ta'ănûgâh**, *tah-ah-oog-aw´*; from 6026; *luxury:*— delicate, delight, pleasant.

8589. תַּעֲנִית **ta'ănîyth**, *tah-an-eeth´*; from 6031; *affliction* (of self), i.e. *fasting:*— heaviness.

8590. תַּעֲנָךְ **Ta'ănâk**, *tah-an-awk´*; or

תַּעְנָךְ **Ta'nâk**, *tah-nawk´*; of uncert. der.; *Taanak* or *Tanak*, a place in Pal.:— Taanach, Tanach.

8591. תָּעַע **tâ'a'**, *taw-ah´*; a prim. root; to

cheat; by anal. to *maltreat:*— deceive, misuse.

8592. תַּעֲצֻמָה **ta'ătsûmâh**, *tah-ats-oo-maw´*; from 6105; *might* (plur. collect.):— power.

8593. תַּעַר **ta'ar**, *tah-ar´*; from 6168; a *knife* or *razor* (as *making* bare): also a *scabbard* (as *being* bare, i.e. *empty*):— [pen-] knife, rasor, scabbard, shave, sheath.

8594. תַּעֲרֻבָה **ta'ărûbâh**, *tah-ar-oo-baw´*; from 6148; *suretyship*, i.e. (concr.) a *pledge:*— + hostage.

8595. תַּעְתֻּעַ **ta'tûa'**, *tah-too´-ah*; from 8591; a *fraud:*— error.

8596. תֹּף **tôph**, *tofe*; from 8608 contr.; a *tambourine:*— tabret, timbrel.

8597. תִּפְאָרָה **tiph'ârâh**, *tif-aw-raw´*; or

תִּפְאֶרֶת **tiph'ereth**, *tif-eh´-reth*; from 6286; *ornament* (abstr. or concr., lit. or fig.):— beauty (-iful), bravery, comely, fair, glory (-ious), honour, majesty.

8598. תַּפּוּחַ **tappûwach**, *tap-poo´-akh*; from 5301; an *apple* (from its *fragrance*), i.e. the fruit or the tree (prob. includ. others of the *pome* order, as the quince, the orange, etc.):— apple (tree). See also 1054.

8599. תַּפּוּחַ **Tappûwach**, *tap-poo´-akh*; the same as 8598; *Tappuach*, the name of two places in Pal., also of an Isr.:— Tappuah.

8600. תְּפוֹצָה **t^ephôwtsâh**, *tef-o-tsaw´*; from 6327; a *dispersal:*— dispersion.

8601. תֻּפִין **tûphîyn**, *too-feen´*; from 644; *cookery*, i.e. (concr.) a *cake:*— baked piece.

8602. תָּפֵל **tâphêl**, *taw-fale´*; from an unused root mean. to *smear*; *plaster* (as *gummy*) or *slime*; (fig.) *frivolity:*— foolish things, unsavoury, untempered.

8603. תֹּפֶל **Tôphel**, *to´-fel*; from the same as 8602; *quagmire*; *Tophel*, a place near the Desert:— Tophel.

8604. תִּפְלָה **tiphlâh**, *tif-law´*; from the same as 8602; *frivolity:*— folly, foolishly.

8605. תְּפִלָּה **t^ephillâh**, *tef-il-law´*; from 6419; *intercession, supplication*; by impl. a *hymn:*— prayer.

8606. תִּפְלֶצֶת **tiphletseth**, *tif-leh´-tseth*; from 6426; *fearfulness:*— terrible.

8607. תִּפְסַח **Tiphçach**, *tif-sakh´*; from 6452; *ford*; *Tiphsach*, a place in Mesopotamia:— Tipsah.

8608. תָּפַף **tâphaph**, *taw-faf´*; a prim. root; to *drum*, i.e. play (as) on the tambourine:— taber, play with timbrels.

8609. תָּפַר **tâphar**, *taw-far´*; a prim. root; to *sew:*— (women that) sew (together).

8610. תָּפַשׂ **tâphas**, *taw-fas´*; a prim. root; to *manipulate*, i.e. *seize*; chiefly to *capture*,

wield; spec. to *overlay*; fig. to *use* unwarrantably:— catch, handle, (lay, take) hold (on, over), stop, × surely, surprise, take.

8611. תֹּפֶת **tôpheth**, *to´-feth*; from the base of 8608; a *smiting*, i.e. (fig.) *contempt:*— tabret.

8612. תֹּפֶת **Tôpheth**, *to´-feth*; the same as 8611; *Topheth*, a place near Jerusalem:— Tophet, Topheth.

8613. תָּפְתֶּה **Tophteh**, *tof-teh´*; prob. a form of 8612; *Tophteh*, a place of cremation:— Tophet.

8614. תִּפְתַי **tiphtay** (Chald.), *tif-tah´-ee*; perh. from 8199; *judicial*, i.e. a *lawyer:*— sheriff.

תֹּצָאָה **tôtsâ'âh**. See 8444.

8615. תִּקְוָה **tiqvâh**, *tik-vaw´*; from 6960; lit. a *cord* (as an *attachment* [comp. 6961]); fig. *expectancy:*— expectation (l-ted), hope, live, thing that I long for.

8616. תִּקְוָה **Tiqvâh**, *tik-vaw´*; the same as 8615; *Tikvah*, the name of two Isr.:— Tikvah.

8617. תְּקוּמָה **t^eqûwmâh**, *tek-oo-maw´*; from 6965; *resistfulness:*— power to stand.

8618. תְּקוֹמֵם **t^eqôwmêm**, *tek-o-mame´*; from 6965; an *opponent:*— rise up against.

8619. תָּקוֹעַ **tâqôwa'**, *taw-ko´-ah*; from 8628 (in the musical sense); a *trumpet:*— trumpet.

8620. תְּקוֹעַ **T^eqôwa'**, *tek-o´-ah*; a form of 8619; *Tekoa*, a place in Pal.:— Tekoa, Tekoah.

8621. תְּקוֹעִי **T^eqôw'îy**, *tek-o-ee´*; or

תְּקֹעִי **T^eqô'îy**, *tek-o-ee´*; patron. from 8620; a *Tekoite* or inhab. of Tekoah:— Tekoite.

8622. תְּקוּפָה **t^eqûwphâh**, *tek-oo-faw´*; or

תְּקֻפָה **t^eqûphâh**, *tek-oo-faw´*; from 5362; a *revolution*, i.e. (of the sun) *course*, (of time) *lapse:*— circuit, come about, end.

8623. תַּקִּיף **taqqîyph**, *tak-keef´*; from 8630; *powerful:*— mightier.

8624. תַּקִּיף **taqqîyph** (Chald.), *tak-keef´*; corresp. to 8623:— mighty, strong.

8625. תְּקַל **t^eqal** (Chald.), *tek-al´*; corresp. to 8254; to *balance:*— Tekel, be weighed.

8626. תָּקַן **tâqan**, *taw-kan´*; a prim. root; to *equalize*, i.e. *straighten* (intr. or tran.); fig. to *compose:*— set in order, make straight.

8627. תְּקַן **t^eqan** (Chald.), *tek-an´*; corresp. to 8626; to *straighten* up, i.e. *confirm:*— establish.

8628. תָּקַע **tâqa'**, *taw-kah´*; a prim. root; to *clatter*, i.e. *slap* (the hands together), *clang* (an instrument); by anal. to *drive* (a nail or tent-pin, a dart, etc.); by impl. to *become*

Hebrew

bondsman (by handclasping):— blow ([a trumpet]), cast, clap, fasten, pitch [tent], smite, sound, strike, × suretiship, thrust.

8629. תְּקַע **têqa'**, *tay-kah´*; from 8628; a *blast* of a trumpet:— sound.

תְּקוֹעִי **Teqô'îy**. See 8621.

8630. תָּקַף **tâqaph**, *taw-kaf´*; a prim. root; to *overpower*:— prevail (against).

8631. תְּקֵף **teqêph** (Chald.), *tek-afe´*; corresp. to 8630; to *become* (caus. *make*) *mighty* or (fig.) *obstinate*:— make firm, harden, be (-come) strong.

8632. תְּקֹף **teqôph** (Chald.), *tek-ofe´*; corresp. to 8633; *power*:— might, strength.

8633. תֹּקֶף **tôqeph**, *to´-kef*; from 8630; *might* or (fig.) *positiveness*:— authority, power, strength.

תְּקֻפָה **tequphâh**. See 8622.

תּוֹר **tôr**. See 8447, 8449.

8634. תַּרְאֲלָה **Tar'ălâh**, *tar-al-aw´*; prob. for 8653; a *reeling*; *Taralah*, a place in Pal.:— Taralah.

8635. תַּרְבּוּת **tarbûwth**, *tar-booth´*; from 7235; *multiplication*, i.e. *progeny:*— increase.

8636. תַּרְבִּית **tarbîyth**, *tar-beeth´*; from 7235; *multiplication*, i.e. *percentage* or *bonus* in addition to principal:— increase, unjust gain.

8637. תִּרְגַּל **tirgal**, *teer-gal´*; a denom. from 7270; to *cause to walk:*— teach to go.

8638. תִּרְגַּם **tirgam**, *teer-gam´*; a denom. from 7275 in the sense of *throwing* over; to *transfer*, i.e. *translate:*— interpret.

תּוֹרָה **tôrâh**. See 8451.

8639. תַּרְדֵּמָה **tardêmâh**, *tar-day-maw´*; from 7290; a *lethargy* or (by impl.) *trance:*— deep sleep.

8640. תִּרְהָקָה **Tirhâqâh**, *teer-haw´-kaw*; of for. der.; *Tirhakah*, a king of Kush:— Tirhakah.

8641. תְּרוּמָה **terûwmâh**, *ter-oo-maw´*; or

תְּרֻמָה **terûmâh** (Deut. 12:11), *ter-oo-maw´*; from 7311; a *present* (as offered *up*), espec. in *sacrifice* or as *tribute:*— gift, heave offering ([shoulder]), oblation, offered (-ing).

8642. תְּרוּמִיָּה **terûwmîyâh**, *ter-oo-mee-yaw´*; formed as 8641; a sacrificial *offering:*— oblation.

8643. תְּרוּעָה **terûw'âh**, *ter-oo-aw´*; from 7321; *clamor*, i.e. *acclamation* of joy or a *battle-cry*; espec. *clangor* of trumpets, as an *alarum:*— alarm, blow (-ing) (of, the) (trumpets), joy, jubile, loud noise, rejoicing, shout (-ing), (high, joyful) sound (-ing).

8644. תְּרוּפָה **terûwphâh**, *ter-oo-faw´*; from 7322 in the sense of its congener 7495; a *remedy:*— medicine.

8645. תִּרְזָה **tirzâh**, *teer-zaw´*; prob. from 7329; a species of tree (appar. from its *slenderness*), perh. the *cypress:*— cypress.

8646. תֶּרַח **Terach**, *teh´-rakh*; of uncert. der.; *Terach*, the father of Abraham; also a place in the Desert:— Tarah, Terah.

8647. תִּרְחֲנָה **Tirchănâh**, *teer-khan-aw´*; of uncert. der.; *Tirchanah*, an Isr.:— Tirhanah.

8648. תְּרֵין **terêyn** (Chald.), *ter-ane´*; fem.

תַּרְתֵּין **tartêyn**, *tar-tane´*; corresp. to 8147; *two:*— second, + twelve, two.

8649. תָּרְמָה **tormâh**, *tor-maw´*; and

תַּרְמוּת **tarmûwth**, *tar-mooth´*; or

תַּרְמִית **tarmîyth**, *tar-meeth´*; from 7411; *fraud:*— deceit (-ful), privily.

תְּרוּמָה **terûmâh**. See 8641.

8650. תֹּרֶן **tôren**, *to´-ren*; prob. for 766; a *pole* (as a mast or flag-staff):— beacon, mast.

8651. תְּרַע **tera'** (Chald.), *ter-ah´*; corresp. to 8179; a *door*; by impl. a *palace:*— gate, mouth.

8652. תָּרָע **târâ'** (Chald.), *taw-raw´*; from 8651; a *doorkeeper:*— porter.

8653. תַּרְעֵלָה **tar'êlâh**, *tar-ay-law´*; from 7477; *reeling:*— astonishment, trembling.

8654. תִּרְעָתִי **Tir'âthîy**, *teer-aw-thee´*; patrial from an unused name mean. *gate*; a *Tirathite* or inhab. of an unknown Tirah:— Tirathite.

8655. תְּרָפִים **terâphîym**, *ter-aw-feme´*; plur. perh. from 7495; a *healer*; *Teraphim* (sing. or plur.) a family idol:— idols (-atry), images, teraphim.

8656. תִּרְצָה **Tirtsâh**, *teer-tsaw´*; from 7521; *delightsomeness*; *Tirtsah*, a place in Pal.; also an Israelitess:— Tirzah.

8657. תֶּרֶשׁ **Teresh**, *teh´-resh*; of for. der.; *Teresh*, a eunuch of Xerxes:— Teresh.

8658. תַּרְשִׁישׁ **tarshîysh**, *tar-sheesh´*; prob. of for. der. [comp. 8659]; a gem, perh. the *topaz:*— beryl.

8659. תַּרְשִׁישׁ **Tarshîysh**, *tar-sheesh´*; prob. the same as 8658 (as the region of the stone, or the reverse); *Tarshish*, a place on the Mediterranean, hence, the epithet of a *merchant* vessel (as if for or from that port); also the name of a Pers. and of an Isr.:— Tarshish, Tharshish.

8660. תִּרְשָׁתָא **Tirshâthâ'**, *teer-shaw-thaw´*; of for. der.; the title of a Pers. deputy or *governor:*— Tirshatha.

תַּרְתִּין **tartêyn**. See 8648.

8661. תַּרְתָּן **Tartân**, *tar-tawn´*; of for. der.; *Tartan*, an Ass.:— Tartan.

8662. תַּרְתָּק **Tartâq**, *tar-tawk´; of* for. der.; *Tartak*, a deity of the Avvites:— Tartak.

8663. תְּשֻׁאָה **t°shû'âh**, *tesh-oo-aw´;* from 7722; a *crashing* or loud *clamor:*— crying, noise, shouting, stir.

     תּשָׁב **tôshâb**. See 8453.

8664. תִּשְׁבִּי **Tishbîy**, *tish-bee´;* patrial from an unused name mean. *recourse;* a *Tishbite* or inhab. of Tishbeh (in Gilead):— Tishbite.

8665. תַּשְׁבֵּץ **tashbêts**, *tash-bates´;* from 7660; *checkered* stuff (as *reticulated*):— broidered.

8666. תְּשׁוּבָה **t°shûwbâh**, *tesh-oo-baw´;* or

     תְּשֻׁבָה **t°shûbâh**, *tesh-oo-baw´;* from 7725; a *recurrence* (of time or place); a *reply* (as *returned*):— answer, be expired, return.

8667. תְּשׂוּמֶת **t°sûwmeth**, *tes-oo-meth´;* from 7760; a *deposit*, i.e. *pledging:*— + fellowship.

8668. תְּשׁוּעָה **t°shûw'âh**, *tesh-oo-aw´;* or

     תְּשֻׁעָה **t°shû'âh**, *tesh-oo-aw´;* from 7768 in the sense of 3467; *rescue* (lit. or fig., pers., national or spir.):— deliverance, help, safety, salvation, victory.

8669. תְּשׁוּקָה **t°shûwqâh**, *tesh-oo-kaw´;* from 7783 in the orig. sense of *stretching* out after; a *longing:*— desire.

8670. תְּשׁוּרָה **t°shûwrâh**, *tesh-oo-raw´;* from 7788 in the sense of *arrival;* a *gift:*— present.

     תַּשְׁחֵת **tashchêth**. See 516.

     תֻּשִׁיָּה **tûshîyâh**. See 8454.

8671. תְּשִׁיעִי **t°shîy'îy**, *tesh-ee-ee´;* ord. from 8672; *ninth:*— ninth.

     תְּשֻׁעָה **t°shû'âh**. See 8668.

8672. תֵּשַׁע **têsha'**, *tay´-shah;* or (masc.)

     תִּשְׁעָה **tish'âh**, *tish-aw´;* perh. from 8159 through the idea of a *turn* to the next or full number ten; *nine* or (ord.) *ninth:*— nine (+ -teen, + -teenth, -th).

8673. תִּשְׁעִים **tish'îym**, *tish-eem´;* multiple from 8672; *ninety:*— ninety.

8674. תַּתְּנַי **Tatt°nay**, *tat-ten-ah´-ee;* of for. der.; *Tattenai*, a Pers.:— Tatnai.

❧ The NEW ❧
STRONG'S™
GREEK
DICTIONARY
of BIBLE WORDS

© 1995, 1996 Thomas Nelson Publishers, Inc.

Read this first!

How to Use the Greek Dictionary

For many people Strong's unique system of numbers continues to be *the* bridge between the original languages of the Bible and the English of the *King James Version* (AV). In order to enhance the strategic importance of *Strong's Greek Dictionary* for Bible students, it has been significantly improved in this brand-new, up-to-date edition. It is now completely re-typeset with modern, larger typefaces that are kind to the eye, and all known errors in the original typesetting have been corrected, bringing this pivotal work to a new level of usefulness and accuracy.

1. What the Dictionary Is

Strong's Greek Dictionary is a fully integrated companion to the English Index. Its compact entries contain a wealth of information about the words of the Bible in their original language. You can enrich your study of the Bible enormously if you will invest the time to understand the various elements included in each entry and their significance. The example that follows identifies many of these entry elements; and the following sections on the transliteration, abbreviations, and special symbols used offer fuller explanations. While no dictionary designed for readers who do not know biblical Greek can explain all that a faithful student of the language would know, this *Dictionary* gives the serious student of the English Bible the basic information needed to pursue infinitely deeper and broader studies of God's Word. Vast amounts of biblical insight can be gained by using this *Dictionary* alone or in conjunction with other time-proven biblical reference works, such as Thomas Nelson's *Vine's Complete Expository Dictionary of Old and New Testament Words* and *Nelson's New Illustrated Bible Dictionary*, and, of course, *The New Strong's™ Exhaustive Concordance*.

2. Using the Dictionary with the English Index

To use this *Dictionary*, locate the number listed under any word in the English Index. If the number and its transliterated word are in *italic* type, you know that it refers to the *Greek Dictionary*. For example, under "EARNEST," you find *Strong's* number *728* representing the Greek word *arrhabōn*. The English Index offers a concise definition—*pledge, security*—based on the fuller explanations of the *Dictionary*. You may view that enlarged entry on the facing page or on page 587 in this *Dictionary*. The enlarged example that follows, together with the following sections of explanation, identify the kinds of information such entries provide.

3. Using the Dictionary to Do Word Studies

Careful Bible students do word studies, and *The New Strong's™ Complete Dictionary of Bible Words* with this revised, newly-typeset *Greek Dictionary*, offers unique assistance. The English Index lists five unique *Strong's* numbers for Greek words that the King James Bible translates with the English word "earnest": *603, 728, 1972, 4056, 4710*. By looking up each of these words in the *Dictionary*, you will discover that in addition to being used as a noun, "earnest money" (as seen in the previous paragraph), earnest is also used as an adjective to describe intense emotion.

You can also study the range of meaning for each of these Greek words. At the end of each *Dictionary* entry you notice the symbol :—. Following this symbol is a listing of all the ways this word is translated in the King James Bible. Word *728*, for example, is only translated "earnest." Word *4710*, on the other hand, is translated by several words, including "carefulness," "diligence," and "haste." By looking up each of these words in the English Index, you can find a listing of all the Greek words they translate. This interaction of the English Index and the *Greek Dictionary* allows you to do thorough biblical word studies in English as well as in Greek.

Of supreme importance in word studies is examining words in their biblical contexts. To study each occurrence of any word, you would need *The New Strong's™ Exhaustive Concordance*. You may wish to take notes as you look up each occurrence of the word that goes with *603*, and then each occurrence of the word that goes with *728*, and so forth. This method gives you an excellent basis for understanding all that the New Testament signifies with the King James Version's word "earnest."

These three ways of using the *Dictionary* in conjunction with the main concordance show you only a sampling of the many ways *The New Strong's™ Complete Dictionary of Bible Words* can enrich your study of the Bible. And they show you why it is important that you take the time to become familiar with each feature in the *Dictionary* as illustrated in the example on the following page.

An Example
from the
Greek New Testament Dictionary

Strong's number in *italics*, corresponding to the numbers at the ends of the context lines in the English Index.

An unnumbered cross-reference entry.

The word as it appears in the original Greek spelling.

Where appropriate, important discussion of multiple uses and functions of the word.

The Greek word represented in English letters in **bold** type (the transliteration).

Strong's syllable-by-syllable pronunciation in *italics*, with the emphasized syllable marked by the accent.

When the Greek word relates to a Hebrew or Aramaic word from the Old Testament, the Strong's numbers is encased in square brackets [...].

Brief English definitions (shown by *italics*).

ἀπέπω **apépō**. See 550.

728. ἀρραβών **arrhabōn**, *ar-hrab-ohn´;* of Heb. or. [6162]; a *pledge*, i.e. part of the purchase-money or property given in advance as *security* for the rest:— earnest.

3360. μέχρι **mĕchri** *mekh´-ree;* or

μεχρίς **mĕchris** *mekh-ris´;* from *3372; as far as,* i.e. *up to* a certain point (as a prep. of extent [denoting the *terminus*, whereas *891* refers espec. to the *space* of time or place intervening] or a conjunc.):— till, (un-) to, until.

3361. μή **mē** *may;* a primary particle of qualified *negation* (whereas *3756* expresses an absolute denial); (adv.) *not,* (conjunc.) *lest;* also (as an interrog. implying a *neg.* answer [whereas *3756* expects an *affirmative* one]) *whether:*— any, but (that), × forbear, + God forbid, + lack, lest, neither, never, no (× wise in), none, nor, [can-] not, nothing, that not, un [-taken], without. Often used in compounds in substantially the same relations. See also *3362, 3363, 3364, 3372, 3373, 3375, 3378.*

See "Special Symbols."

Italic Strong's numbers refer to related Greek words in this Dictionary.

After the long dash (—), there is a complete, alphabetical listing of all ways this Greek word is translated in the KJV. (See also "Special Symbols").

Improved, consistent abbreviations. All abbreviations occur with their full spelling in the list of abbreviations.

Note that Greek spelling variations are conveniently indented for easy comparison.

Plan of the Greek Dictionary

1. All the original words are presented in their alphabetical order (according to Greek). They are numbered for easy matching between this Dictionary and the main part of the Concordance. Many reference books also use these same numbers which were originally created by Dr. Strong.

2. Immediately after each word, the exact equivalent of each sound (phoneme) is given in English characters, according to the transliteration system given below.

3. Next follows the precise pronunciation with the proper stress mark.

4. Then comes the etymology, root meaning, and common uses of the word, along with any other important related details.

5. In the case of proper names, the normal English spelling is given, accompanied by a few words of explanation.

6. Finally, after the colon and the dash (:—), all the different ways that the word appears in the Authorized Version (KJV) are listed in alphabetical order. When the Greek word appears in English as a phrase, the main word of the phrase is used to alphabetize it.

By looking up these words in the main concordance and by noting the passages which display the same number in the right-hand column, the reader also possesses a complete *Greek New Testament Concordance*, expressed in the words of the Authorized Version.

Transliteration and Pronunciation of the Greek

The following shows how the Greek words are transliterated into English in this Dictionary.

1. The *Alphabet* is as follows:

No.	Form upper	Name lower	Transliteration and Pronunciation	
1.	**A**	α	Alpha (*al´-fah*)	**a**, as in *Arm* or *mAn* [1]
2.	**B**	β	Bēta (*bay´-tah*)	**b**
3.	**Γ**	γ	Gamma (*gam´-mah*)	**g**, as in *Guard* [2]
4.	**Δ**	δ	Dĕlta (*del´-tah*)	**d**
5.	**E**	ε	Ĕpsilŏn (*ep´-see-lon*)	**ĕ**, as in *mEt*
6.	**Z**	ζ	Zēta (*dzay´-tah*)	**z**, as in *aDZe* [3]
7.	**H**	η	Ēta (*ay´-tah*)	**ē**, as in *thEy*
8.	**Θ**	θ	Thēta (*thay´-tah*)	**th**, as in *THin* [4]
9.	**I**	ι	Iota (*ee-o´-tah*)	**i**, as in *machIne* [5]
10.	**K**	κ	Kappa (*kap´-pah*)	**k**
11.	**Λ**	λ	Lambda (*lamb´-dah*)	**l**
12.	**M**	μ	Mu (*moo*)	**m**
13.	**N**	ν	Nu (*noo*)	**n**
14.	**Ξ**	ξ	Xi (*ksee*)	**x** = *ks*
15.	**O**	o	Omikrŏn (*om´-e-cron*)	**ŏ**, as in *not*
16.	**Π**	π	Pi (*pee or pai*)	**p**
17.	**P**	ρ	Rhō (*hro*)	**r**
18.	**Σ**	σ, final ς	Sigma (*sig´-mah*)	**s** sharp
19.	**T**	τ	Tau (*tŏw*)	**t**, as in *Tree* [6]
20.	**Υ**	υ	Upsilŏn (*u´-pse-lon*)	**u**, as in *fUll*
21.	**Φ**	φ	Phi (*fee or fai*)	**ph** = *f*
22.	**X**	χ	Chi (*khee or khai*)	German **ch** [7]
23.	**Ψ**	ψ	Psi (*psee or psai*)	**ps**
24.	**Ω**	ω	Omĕga (*o´-meg-ah*)	**ō**, as in *no*

---

[1] α, when *final*, or before a final ρ or followed by any *other* consonant, is sounded like α in *Arm*; elsewhere like α in *mAn*.

[2] γ, when followed by γ, **k**, **c**, or ξ is sounded like *ng* in *kiNG*.

[3] ζ is always sounded like *dz*.

[4] θ never has the guttural sound, like *th* in *THis*.

[5] ι has the sound of *ee* when it *ends* an *accented* syllable; in other situations a more obscure sound, like *i* in *amIable* or *Imbecile*.

[6] τ never has an s-sound, like *t* in *naTion*.

[7] From the difficulty of producing the true sound of χ, it is generally sounded like *k*.

2. The mark ', placed over the *initial* vowel of a word, is called the *Rough Breathing*, and is equivalent to the English *h*, by which we have accordingly represented it. Its *absence* over an initial vowel is indicated by the mark ', called the *Smooth Breathing*, which is silent, and is therefore not represented in our method of transliteration. [8]

3. The following are the Greek *diphthongs*, properly so called: [9]

Form	Transliteration and Pronunciation
αι	**ai** (*ah'ee*) [ă + ē]
ει	**ei**, as in *hEIght*
οι	**oi**, as in *OIl*
υι	**we**, as in *sWEet*
αυ	**ow**, as in *nOW*
ευ	**eu**, as in *fEUd*
ου	**ou**, as in *thrOUgh*

4. The *accent* (stress of voice) falls on the syllable where it is written. [10] It occurs in three forms: the *acute* ('), which is the only true accent; the *grave* (`) which is its substitute; and the *circumflex* (^), which is the union of the two. The acute may stand on any one of the last *three* syllables, and in case it occurs on the final syllable, before another word in the same sentence, it is written as a grave. The grave is understood (but never written as such) on every other syllable. The circumflex is written on any syllable (necessarily the last syllable or next to the last syllable of a word) formed by the contraction of two syllables, of which the *first* would properly have the acute accent.

5. The following *punctuation* marks are used: the comma (,), the semicolon (·), the colon or period (.), the question mark (;), and by some editors, also the exclamation mark, parentheses, and quotation marks.

Special Symbols

+ (*addition*) denotes a rendering in the A.V. of one or more Greek words in connection with the one under consideration. For example, in Rev. 17:17, No. 1106, γνώμη (**gnōmē**) is translated as a verb ("to agree"), when it is actually a noun and part of a Greek idiom that is literally translated "to do one mind."

× (*multiplication*) denotes a rendering in the A.V. that results from an idiom peculiar to the Greek. For example, in Heb. 12:21, the whole Greek phrase in which ἔντρομος, **entromos** (1790) appears is a way of expressing great anxiety. The same idiom is used about Moses in Acts 7:32.

( ) (*parentheses*), in the renderings from the A.V., denote a word or syllable which is sometimes given in connection with the principal word to which it is attached. In Mark 15:39 there are two Greek prepositions (1537 and 1727) which are used together ("over against"). One English preposition, "opposite," communicates the same idea.

[ ] (*brackets*), in the rendering from the A.V., denote the inclusion of an additional word in the Greek. For example, No. 2596 κατά (**kata**) is translated "daily" in Luke 19:47, along with No. 2250 ἡμέρα (**hēmĕra**). So, two Greek words were translated by one English word.

Italics, at the end of a rendering from the A.V., denote an explanation of the variations from the usual form.

Note

Because of some changes in the numbering system (while the original work was in progress) no Greek words are cited for 2717 or 3203-3302. These numbers were dropped altogether. This will not cause any problems in *Strong's* numbering system. **No Greek words have been left out.** Because so many other reference works use this numbering system, it has **not** been revised. If it were revised, much confusion would certainly result.

---

[8] These signs are placed over the *second* vowel of a diphthong. The same is true of the accents.

The *Rough* Breathing always belongs to an initial υ.

The *Rough* Breathing is always used with ρ, when it begins a word. If this letter is doubled in the middle of a word, the first ρ takes the Smooth Breathing mark and the second ρ takes the Rough Breathing mark.

Since these signs cannot conveniently be written above the first letter of a word, when it is a *capital*, they are placed *before* it in such cases. This observation applies also to the *accents*. The aspiration *always* begins the syllable.

Occasionally, in consequence of a contraction (*crasis*), the Smooth Breathing is made to stand in the middle of a word, and is then called *Coro'nis*.

[9] The above are combinations of two *short* vowels, and are pronounced like their respective elements, but in more rapid succession than otherwise. Thus, αι is midway between *i* in h*I*gh, and *ay* in s*A*Y.

Besides these, there are what are called *improper* diphthongs, in which the former is a *long* vowel. In these,

ᾳ	sounds like	α
ῃ	"	η
ῳ	"	ω
ηυ	"	η + υ
ωυ	"	ω + υ

the second vowel, when it is ι, is written *under* the first vowel (unless it is a capital), and is *silent*; when it is υ, is sounded separately. When the initial vowel is a capital, the ι is placed after it, but it does not take a breathing mark or any accent.

The sign ¨ is called *diær;esis*. It is placed over the *second* of two vowels, indicating that they do *not* form a diphthong.

[10] Every word (except a few monosyllables, called *Aton'ics*) must have one accent; several small words (called *Enclit'ics*) put their accent (always as an acute) on the last syllable of the preceding word (in addition to its own accent, which still has the principal stress), where this is possible.

abb. = abbreviated
  abbreviation
abstr. = abstract
  abstractly
act. = active (voice)
  actively
acc. = accusative (case) [1]
adj. = adjective
  adjectivally
adv. = adverb
  adverbial
  adverbially
aff. = affix [2]
  affixed
affin. = affinity
alt. = alternate
  alternately
anal. = analogy
appar. = apparent
  apparently
arch. = architecture
  architectural
  architecturally
art. = article [3]
artif. = artificial
  artificially
Ass. = Assyrian
A.V. = Authorized Version
  (King James Version)
Bab. = Babylon
  Babylonia
  Babylonian
caus. = causative [4]
  causatively
cerem. = ceremony
  ceremonial
  ceremonially
Chald. = Chaldee
(Aramaic)
  Chaldaism
    (Aramaism)
Chr. = Christian
collat. = collateral
  collaterally
collect. = collective
  collectively
comp. = compare [5]
  comparison
  comparative
  comparatively
concr. = concrete
  concretely
conjec. = conjecture
  conjectural
  conjecturally
conjug. = conjugation [6]
  conjugational
  conjugationally
conjunc. = conjunction
  conjunctional
  conjunctionally
constr. = construct [7]
  construction
  constructive
  constructively

contr. = contracted [8]
  contraction
correl. = correlated
  correlation
  correlative
  correlatively
corresp. = corresponding
  correspondingly
dat. = dative (case) [9]
def. = definite [10]
  definitely
demonstr. = demonstra-
tive [11]
denom. = denominative [12]
  denominatively
der. = derived
  derivation
  derivative
  derivatively
desc. = descended
  descendant
  descendants
dimin. = diminutive [13]
dir. = direct
  directly
E. = East
  Eastern
eccl. = ecclesiastical
  ecclesiastically
e.g. = for example
Eg. = Egypt
  Egyptian
  Egyptians
ellip. = ellipsis [14]
  elliptical
  elliptically
emphat. = emphatic
  emphatically
equiv. = equivalent
  equivalently
err. = error
  erroneous
  erroneously
espec. = especially
etym. = etymology [15]
  etymological
  etymologically
euphem. = euphemism [16]
  euphemistic
  euphemistically
euphon. = euphonious [17]
  euphonically
extens. = extension [18]
  extensive
extern. = external
  externally
fem. = feminine (gender)
fig. = figurative
  figuratively
for. = foreign
  foreigner
freq. = frequentative
  frequentatively
fut. = future

gen. = general
  generally
  generic
  generical
  generically
Gr. = Greek
  Graecism
gut. = guttural [19]
Heb. = Hebrew
  Hebraism
i.e. = that is
ident. = identical
  identically
immed. = immediate
  immediately
imper. = imperative [20]
  imperatively
imperf. = imperfect [21]
impers. = impersonal
  impersonally
impl. = implied
  impliedly
  implication
incept. = inceptive [22]
  inceptively
incl. = including
  inclusive
  inclusively
indef. = indefinite
  indefinitely
ind. = indicative [23]
  indicatively
indiv. = individual
  individually
infer. = inference
  inferential
  inferentially
infin. = infinitive
inhab. = inhabitant
  inhabitants
ins. = inserted
intens. = intensive
  intensively
interch. = interchangeable
intern. = internal
  internally
interj. = interjection [24]
  interjectional
  interjectionally
interrog. = interrogative [25]
  interrogatively
intr. = intransitive [26]
  intransitively
invol. = involuntary
  involuntarily
irreg. = irregular
  irregularly
Isr. = Israelite
  Israelites
  Israelitish
Lat. = Latin
Levit. = Levitical
  Levitically

lit. = literal
  literally
marg. = margin
  marginal reading
masc. = masculine (gender)
mean. = meaning
ment. = mental
  mentally
metaph. = metaphorical
  metaphorically
mid. = middle (voice) [27]
modif. = modified
  modification
mor. = moral
  morally
mult. = multiplicative [28]
nat. = natural
  naturally
neg. = negative
  negatively
neut. = neuter (gender)
obj. = object
  objective
  objectively
obs. = obsolete
ord. = ordinal [29]
or. = origin
orig. = original
  originally
orth. = orthography [30]
  orthographical
  orthographically
Pal. = Palestine
part. = participle
pass. = passive (voice)
  passively
patron. = patronymic [31]
  patronymical
  patronymically
perh. = perhaps
perm. = permutation [32] (of
  adjacent letters)
pers. = person
  personal
  personally
Pers. = Persia
  Persian
  Persians
phys. = physical
  physically
plur. = plural
poet. = poetry
  poetical
  poetically
pos. = positive
  positively
pref. = prefix
  prefixed
prep. = preposition
  prepositional
  prepositionally
prim. = primitive
prob. = probable
  probably

prol. = prolonged [33]
  prolongation
pron. = pronoun
  pronominal
  pronominally
prop. = properly
prox. = proximate
  proximately
recip. = reciprocal
  reciprocally
redupl. = reduplicated [34]
  reduplication
refl. = reflexive [35]
  reflexively
reg. = regular
rel. = relative
  relatively
relig. = religion
  religious
  religiously
Rom. = Roman
second. = secondary
  secondarily
signif. = signification
  signifying
short. = shorter
  shortened
sing. = singular
spec. = specific
  specifically
streng. = strengthening
subdiv. = subdivision
  subdivisional
  subdivisionally
subj. = subjectively
  subjective
  subject
substit. = substituted
suff. = suffix
superl. = superlative [36]
  superlatively
symb. = symbolic
  symbolical
  symbolically
tech. = technical
  technically
term. = termination
tran. = transitive [37]
  transitively
transc. = transcription
transm. = transmutation [38]
transp. = transposed [39]
  transposition
typ. = typical
  typically
uncert. = uncertain
  uncertainly
var. = various
  variation
voc. = vocative (case) [40]
vol. = voluntary
  voluntarily

---

[1] often indicating the direct object of an action verb

[2] part of a word which, when attached to the beginning of the word is called a prefix; if attaching within a word, an infix; and if at the end, a suffix

[3] "the" is the definite article; "a" and "an" are indefinite articles

[4] expressing or denoting causation

[5] the comparative of an adjective or adverb expresses a greater degree of an attribute, e.g. "higher"; "more slowly"

[6] a systematic array of various verbal forms

[7] the condition in Hebrew and Aramaic when two adjacent nouns are combined semantically as follows, e.g."sword" + "king" = "(the) sword of (the) king" or "(the) king's sword". These languages tend to throw the stress of the entire noun phrase toward the end of the whole expression.

[8] a shortened form of a word. It is made by omitting or combining some elements or by reducing vowels or syllables, e.g. "is not" becomes "isn't".

[9] often the indirect object of an action verb

[10] the definite article ("the")

[11] demonstrative pronouns which point (show), e.g. "this," "that"

[12] derived from a noun

[13] a grammatical form which expresses smallness and/or endearment

[14] a construction which leaves out understood words

[15] the historical origin of a word

[16] the use of a pleasant, polite, or harmless-sounding word or phrase to hide harsh, rude, or infamous truths, e.g. "to pass away" = "to die"

[17] a linguistic mechanism to make pronunciation easier, e.g. "an" before "hour" instead of "a"

[18] when a general term can denote an entire class of things

[19] speech sounds which are produced deep in the throat

[20] the mood which expresses a command

[21] used of a tense which expresses a continuous but unfinished action or state

[22] used of a verbal aspect which denotes the beginning of an action

[23] used of the mood which expresses a verbal action as actually occurring (not hypothetical)

[24] an exclamation which expresses emotion

[25] indicating a question

[26] referring to verbs which do not govern direct objects

[27] reflexive

[28] capable of multiplying or tending to multiply

[29] This shows the position or the order within a series, e.g. "second"; the corresponding cardinal number is "two".

[30] the written system of spelling in a given language

[31] a name derived from that of a paternal ancestor, often created by an affix in various languages

[32] a rearrangement

[33] lengthening a pronunciation

[34] the repetition of a letter or syllable to form a new, inflected word

[35] denoting an action by the subject upon itself

[36] expressing the highest degree of comparison of the quality indicated by an adjective or an adverb, e.g. "highest"; "most timely"

[37] expressing an action directed toward a person or a thing (the direct object)

[38] the change of one grammatical element to another

[39] switching word order

[40] an inflection which is used when one is addressing a person or a thing directly, e.g. "John, come here!"

GREEK DICTIONARY OF THE NEW TESTAMENT

A

N. B.—The numbers *not in italics* refer to the words in the *Hebrew Dictionary*. Significations within quotation marks are derivative representatives of the Greek.

1. **A A,** *al´-fah;* of Heb. or.; the first letter of the alphabet; fig. only (from its use as a numeral) the *first:*— Alpha. Often used (usually ἄν **an,** before a vowel) also in composition (as a contr. from *427*) in the sense of *privation;* so in many words beginning with this letter; occasionally in the sense of *union* (as a contr. of *260*).

2. Ἀαρών **Aarōn,** *ah-ar-ōhn´;* of Heb. or. [175]; *Aaron,* the brother of Moses:— Aaron.

3. Ἀβαδδών **Abaddōn,** *ab-ad-dōhn´;* of Heb. or. [11]; a destroying *angel:*— Abaddon.

4. ἀβαρής **abarēs,** *ab-ar-ace´;* from *1* (as a neg. particle) and *922; weightless,* i.e. (fig.) *not burdensome:*— fɪom being burdensome.

5. Ἀββᾶ **Abba,** *ab-bah´;* of Chald. or. [2]; *father* (as a voc.):— Abba.

6. Ἄβελ **Abĕl,** *ab´-el;* of Heb. or. [1893]; *Abel,* the son of Adam:— Abel.

7. Ἀβιά **Abia,** *ab-ee-ah´;* of Heb. or. [29]; *Abijah,* the name of two Isr.:— Abia.

8. Ἀβιάθαρ **Abiathar,** *ab-ee-ath´-ar;* of Heb. or. [54]; *Abiathar,* an Isr.:— Abiathar.

9. Ἀβιληνή **Abilēnē,** *ab-ee-lay-nay´;* of for. or. [comp. 58]; *Abilene,* a region of Syria:— Abilene.

10. Ἀβιούδ **Abiŏud,** *ab-ee-ood´;* of Heb. or. [31]; *Abihud,* an Isr.:— Abiud.

11. Ἀβραάμ **Abraam,** *ab-rah-am´;* of Heb. or. [85]; *Abraham,* the Heb. patriarch:— Abraham. [In Acts 7:16 the text should prob. read *Jacob.*]

12. ἄβυσσος **abussŏs,** *ab´-us-sos;* from *1* (as a neg. particle) and a var. of *1037; depthless,* i.e. (spec.) (infernal) "abyss":— deep, (bottomless) pit.

13. Ἄγαβος **Agabŏs,** *Ag´-ab-os;* of Heb. or. [comp. 2285]; *Agabus,* an Isr.:— Agabus.

14. ἀγαθοεργέω **agathŏĕrgĕō,** *ag-ath-o-er-gheh´-o;* from *18* and *2041;* to *work good:*— do good.

15. ἀγαθοποιέω **agathŏpŏiĕō,** *ag-ath-op-oy-eh´-o;* from *17;* to *be a well-doer* (as a favor or a duty):— (when) do good (well).

16. ἀγαθοποιΐα **agathŏpŏiïa,** *ag-ath-op-oy-ee´-ah;* from *17; well-doing,* i.e. *virtue:*— well-doing.

17. ἀγαθοποιός **agathŏpŏiŏs,** *ag-ath-op-oy-os´;* from *18* and *4160;* a *well-doer,* i.e. *virtuous:*— them that do well.

18. ἀγαθός **agathŏs,** *ag-ath-os´;* a prim. word; *"good"* (in any sense, often as noun):— benefit, good (-s, things), well. Comp. *2570.*

19. ἀγαθωσύνη **agathōsunē,** *ag-ath-o-soo´-nay;* from *18; goodness,* i.e. *virtue* or *beneficence:*— goodness.

20. ἀγαλλίασις **agalliasis,** *ag-al-lee´-as-is;* from *21; exultation;* spec. *welcome:*— gladness, (exceeding) joy.

21. ἀγαλλιάω **agalliaō,** *ag-al-lee-ah´-o;* from ἄγαν **agan** (*much*) and *242;* prop. to *jump for joy,* i.e. *exult:*— be (exceeding) glad, with exceeding joy, rejoice (greatly).

22. ἄγαμος **agamŏs,** *ag´-am-os;* from *1* (as a neg. particle) and *1062; unmarried:*— unmarried.

23. ἀγανακτέω **aganaktĕō,** *ag-an-ak-teh´-o;* from ἄγαν **agan** (*much*) and ἄχθος **achthŏs** (*grief;* akin to the base of *43*); to *be greatly afflicted,* i.e. (fig.) *indignant:*— be much (sore) displeased, have (be moved with, with) indignation.

24. ἀγανάκτησις **aganaktēsis,** *ag-an-ak´-tay-sis;* from *23; indignation:*— indignation.

25. ἀγαπάω **agapaō,** *ag-ap-ah´-o;* perh. from ἄγαν **agan** (*much*) [or comp. *5689*]; to *love* (in a social or moral sense):— (be-) love (-ed). Comp. *5368.*

26. ἀγάπη **agapē,** *ag-ah´-pay;* from *25; love,* i.e. *affection* or *benevolence;* spec. (plur.) a *love-feast:*— (feast of) charity ([-ably]), dear, love.

27. ἀγαπητός **agapētŏs,** *ag-ap-ay-tos´;* from *25; beloved:*— (dearly, well) beloved, dear.

28. Ἄγαρ **Agar,** *ag´-ar;* of Heb. or. [1904]; *Hagar,* the concubine of Abraham:— Hagar.

29. ἀγγαρεύω **aggarĕuō,** *ang-ar-yew´-o;* of for. or. [comp. *104*]; prop. to *be a courier,* i.e. (by impl.) to *press* into public service:— compel (to go).

30. ἀγγεῖον **aggĕiŏn,** *ang-eye´-on;* from ἄγγος **aggŏs** (a *pail,* perh. as *bent;* comp. the base of *43*); a *receptacle:*— vessel.

31. ἀγγελία **aggĕlia,** *ang-el-ee´-ah;* from *32;* an *announcement,* i.e. (by impl.) *precept:*— message.

32. ἄγγελος **aggĕlŏs,** *ang´-el-os;* from ἀγγέλλω **aggĕllō** [prob. der. from *71;* comp. *34*] (to *bring tidings*); a *messenger;* esp. an "angel"; by impl. a *pastor:*— angel, messenger.

33. ἄγε **agĕ,** *ag´-eh;* imper. of *71;* prop. *lead,* i.e. *come* on:— go to.

34. ἀγέλη **agĕlē,** *ag-el´-ay;* from *71* [comp. *32*]; a *drove:*— herd.

35. ἀγενεαλόγητος **agĕnĕalŏgētŏs,** *ag-en-eh-al-og´-ay-tos;* from *1* (as neg. particle)

Greek

and *1075; unregistered* as to birth:— without descent.

36. ἀγενής **agĕnēs**, *ag-en-ace´;* from *1* (as neg. particle) and *1085;* prop. *without kin,* i.e. (of unknown descent, and by impl.) *ignoble:—* base things.

37. ἁγιάζω **hagiazō**, *hag-ee-ad´-zo;* from *40;* to *make holy,* i.e. (cer.) *purify* or *consecrate;* (mentally) to *venerate:—* hallow, be holy, sanctify.

38. ἁγιασμός **hagiasmŏs**, *hag-ee-as-mos´;* from *37;* prop. *purification,* i.e. (the state) *purity;* concr. (by Heb.) a *purifier:—* holiness, sanctification.

39. ἅγιον **hagiŏn**, *hag´-ee-on;* neut. of *40;* a *sacred* thing (i.e. spot):— holiest (of all), holy place, sanctuary.

40. ἅγιος **hagiŏs**, *hag´-ee-os;* from ἅγος **hagŏs** (an *awful* thing) [comp. *53, 2282*]; *sacred* (phys. *pure,* mor. *blameless* or *religious,* cer. *consecrated*):— (most) holy (one, thing), saint.

41. ἁγιότης **hagiŏtēs**, *hag-ee-ot´-ace;* from *40; sanctity* (i.e. prop. the state):— holiness.

42. ἁγιωσύνη **hagiōsunē**, *hag-ee-o-soo´-nay;* from *40; sacredness* (i.e. prop. the quality):— holiness.

43. ἀγκάλη **agkalē**, *ang-kal´-ay;* from ἄγκος **agkŏs** (a *bend,* "ache"); an *arm* (as *curved*):— arm.

44. ἄγκιστρον **agkistrŏn**, *ang´-kis-tron;* from the same as *43;* a *hook* (as bent):— hook.

45. ἄγκυρα **agkura**, *ang´-koo-rah;* from the same as *43;* an "*anchor*" (as *crooked*):— anchor.

46. ἄγναφος **agnaphŏs**, *ag´-naf-os;* from *1* (as a neg. particle) and the same as *1102;* prop. *unfulled,* i.e. (by impl.) *new* (cloth):— new.

47. ἁγνεία **hagnĕia**, *hag-ni´-ah;* from *53; cleanliness* (the quality), i.e. (spec.) *chastity:—* purity.

48. ἁγνίζω **hagnizō**, *hag-nid´-zo;* from *53;* to *make clean,* i.e. (fig.) *sanctify* (cer. or mor.):— purify (self).

49. ἁγνισμός **hagnismŏs**, *hag-nis-mos´;* from *48;* a *cleansing* (the act), i.e. (cer.) *lustration:—* purification.

50. ἀγνοέω **agnŏĕō**, *ag-no-eh´-o;* from *1* (as a neg. particle) and *3539; not to know* (through lack of information or intelligence); by impl. to *ignore* (through disinclination):— (be) ignorant (-ly), not know, not understand, unknown.

51. ἀγνόημα **agnŏĕma**, *ag-no´-ay-mah;* from *50;* a thing *ignored,* i.e. *shortcoming:—* error.

52. ἄγνοια **agnŏia**, *ag´-noy-ah;* from *50; ignorance* (prop. the quality):— ignorance.

53. ἁγνός **hagnŏs**, *hag-nos´;* from the same as *40;* prop. *clean,* i.e. (fig.) *innocent, modest, perfect:—* chaste, clean, pure.

54. ἁγνότης **hagnŏtēs**, *hag-not´-ace;* from *53;*

cleanness (the state), i.e. (fig.) *blamelessness:—* pureness.

55. ἁγνῶς **hagnōs**, *hag-noce´;* adv. from *53; purely,* i.e. *honestly:—* sincerely.

56. ἀγνωσία **agnōsia**, *ag-no-see´-ah;* from *1* (as neg. particle) and *1108; ignorance* (prop. the state):— ignorance, not the knowledge.

57. ἄγνωστος **agnōstŏs**, *ag´-noce-tos´;* from *1* (as neg. particle) and *1110; unknown:—* unknown.

58. ἀγορά **agŏra**, *ag-or-ah´;* from ἀγείρω **agĕirō** (to *gather;* prob. akin to *1453*); prop. the *town-square* (as a place of public resort); by impl. a *market* or *thoroughfare:—* market (-place), street.

59. ἀγοράζω **agŏrazō**, *ag-or-ad´-zo;* from *58;* prop. to *go to market,* i.e. (by impl.) to *purchase;* spec. to *redeem:—* buy, redeem.

60. ἀγοραῖος **agŏraiŏs**, *ag-or-ah´-yos;* from *58; relating to the market-place,* i.e. *forensic* (times); by impl. *vulgar:—* baser sort, low.

61. ἄγρα **agra**, *ag´-rah;* from *71;* (abstr.) a *catching* (of fish); also (concr.) a *haul* (of fish):— draught.

62. ἀγράμματος **agrammatŏs**, *ag-ram-mat-os;* from *1* (as neg. particle) and *1121; unlettered,* i.e. *illiterate:—* unlearned.

63. ἀγραυλέω **agraulĕō**, *ag-row-leh´-o;* from *68* and *832* (in the sense of *833*); to *camp out:—* abide in the field.

64. ἀγρεύω **agrĕuō**, *ag-rew´-o;* from *61;* to *hunt,* i.e. (fig.) to *entrap:—* catch.

65. ἀγριέλαιος **agriĕlaiŏs**, *ag-ree-el´-ah-yos;* from *66* and *1636;* an *oleaster:—* olive tree (which is) wild.

66. ἄγριος **agriŏs**, *ag´-ree-os;* from *68; wild* (as pertaining to the *country*), lit. (*natural*) or fig. (*fierce*):— wild, raging.

67. Ἀγρίππας **Agrippas**, *ag-rip´-pas;* appar. from *66* and *2462; wild-horse* tamer; *Agrippas,* one of the Herods:— Agrippa.

68. ἀγρός **agrŏs**, *ag-ros´;* from *71;* a *field* (as a *drive* for cattle); gen. the *country;* spec. a *farm,* i.e. *hamlet:—* country, farm, piece of ground, land.

69. ἀγρυπνέω **agrupnĕō**, *ag-roop-neh´-o;* ultimately from *1* (as neg. particle) and *5258;* to *be sleepless,* i.e. *keep awake:—* watch.

70. ἀγρυπνία **agrupnia**, *ag-roop-nee´-ah;* from *69; sleeplessness,* i.e. a *keeping awake:—* watch.

71. ἄγω **agō**, *ag´-o;* a prim. verb; prop. to *lead;* by impl. to *bring, drive,* (refl.) *go,* (spec.) *pass* (time), or (fig.) *induce:—* be, bring (forth), carry, (let) go, keep, lead away, be open.

72. ἀγωγή **agōgē**, *ag-o-gay´;* redupl. from

71; a *bringing* up, i.e. *mode of living:*— manner of life.

73. ἀγών **agōn**, *ag-one´;* from *71;* prop. a place of *assembly* (as if *led*), i.e. (by impl.) a *contest* (held there); fig. an *effort* or *anxiety:*— conflict, contention, fight, race.

74. ἀγωνία **agōnia**, *ag-o-nee´-ah;* from *73;* a *struggle* (prop. the state), i.e. (fig.) *anguish:*— agony.

75. ἀγωνίζομαι **agōnizŏmai**, *ag-o-nid´-zom-ahee;* from *73;* to *struggle*, lit. to *compete* for a *prize*), fig. (to *contend* with an adversary), or gen. (to *endeavor* to accomplish something):— fight, labor fervently, strive.

76. Ἀδάμ **Adam**, *ad-am´;* of Heb. or. [121]; *Adam*, the first man; typ. (of Jesus) *man* (as his representative):— Adam.

77. ἀδάπανος **adapanŏs**, *ad-ap´-an-os;* from *1* (as neg. particle); and *1160; costless*, i.e. *gratuitous:*— without expense.

78. Ἀδδί **Addi**, *ad-dee´;* prob. of Heb. or. [comp. 5716]; *Addi*, an Isr.:— Addi.

79. ἀδελφή **adělphē**, *ad-el-fay´;* fem of *80;* a *sister* (nat. or eccl.):— sister.

80. ἀδελφός **adělphŏs**, *ad-el-fos´;* from *1* (as a connective particle) and δελφύς **dělphus** (the *womb*); a *brother* (lit. or fig.) near or remote [much like 1]:— brother.

81. ἀδελφότης **adělphŏtēs**, *ad-el-fot´-ace;* from *80; brotherhood* (prop. the feeling of *brotherliness*), i.e. the (Chr.) *fraternity:*— brethren, brotherhood.

82. ἄδηλος **adēlŏs**, *ad´-ay-los;* from *1* (as a neg. particle) and *1212; hidden*, fig. *indistinct:*— appear not, uncertain.

83. ἀδηλότης **adēlŏtēs**, *ad-ay-lot´-ace;* from *82; uncertainty:*— × uncertain.

84. ἀδήλως **adēlōs**, *ad-ay´-loce;* adv. from *82; uncertainly:*— uncertainly.

85. ἀδημονέω **adēmŏněō**, *ad-ay-mon-eh´-o;* from a der. of ἀδέω **adeo** (to be *sated* to loathing); to *be in distress* (of mind):— be full of heaviness, be very heavy.

86. ᾅδης **haidēs**, *hah´-dace;* from *1* (as neg. particle) and *1492;* prop. *unseen*, i.e. "*Hades*" or the place (state) of departed souls:— grave, hell.

87. ἀδιάκριτος **adiakritŏs**, *ad-ee-ak´-ree-tos;* from *1* (as a neg. particle) and a der. of *1252;* prop. *undistinguished*, i.e. (act.) *impartial:*— without partiality.

88. ἀδιάλειπτος **adialěiptŏs**, *ad-ee-al´-ipe-tos;* from *1* (as a neg. particle) and a der. of a compound of *1223* and *3007; unintermitted*, i.e. *permanent:*— without ceasing, continual.

89. ἀδιαλείπτως **adialěiptōs**, *ad-ee-al-ipe´-toce;* adv. from *88; uninteruptedly*, i.e. *without omission* (on an appropriate occasion):— without ceasing.

90. ἀδιαφθορία **adiaphthŏria**, *ad-ee-af-thor-*

ee´-ah; from a der. of a compound of *1* (as a neg. particle) and a der. of *1311; incorruptibleness*, i.e. (fig.) *purity* (of doctrine):— uncorruptness.

91. ἀδικέω **adikěō**, *ad-ee-keh´-o;* from *94;* to be *unjust*, i.e. (act.) *do wrong* (mor., socially or phys.):— hurt, injure, be an offender, be unjust, (do, suffer, take) wrong.

92. ἀδίκημα **adikēma**, *ad-eek´-ay-mah;* from *91;* a *wrong* done:— evil doing, iniquity, matter of wrong.

93. ἀδικία **adikia**, *ad-ee-kee´-ah;* from *94;* (legal) *injustice* (prop. the quality, by impl. the act); mor. *wrongfulness* (of character, life or act):— iniquity, unjust, unrighteousness, wrong.

94. ἄδικος **adikŏs**, *ad´-ee-kos;* from *1* (as a neg. particle) and *1349; unjust;* by extens. *wicked;* by impl. *treacherous;* spec. *heathen:*— unjust, unrighteous.

95. ἀδίκως **adikōs**, *ad-ee´-koce;* adv. from *94; unjustly:*— wrongfully.

96. ἀδόκιμος **adŏkimŏs**, *ad-ok´-ee-mos;* from *1* (as a neg. particle) and *1384; unapproved*, i.e. *rejected;* by impl. *worthless* (lit. or mor.):— castaway, rejected, reprobate.

97. ἄδολος **adŏlŏs**, *ad´-ol-os;* from *1* (as a neg. particle) and *1388; undeceitful*, i.e. (fig.) *unadulterated:*— sincere.

98. Ἀδραμυττηνός **Adramuttēnŏs**, *ad-ram-oot-tay-nos´;* from Ἀδραμύττειον **Adramuttěiŏn** (a place in Asia Minor); *Adramyttene* or belonging to *Adramyttium:*— of Adramyttium.

99. Ἀδρίας **Adrias**, *ad-ree´-as;* from Ἀδρία **Adria** (a place near its shore); the *Adriatic* sea (incl. the Ionian):— Adria.

100. ἀδρότης **hadrŏtēs**, *had-rot´-ace;* from ἁδρός **hadrŏs** (stout); *plumpness*, i.e. (fig.) *liberality:*— abundance.

101. ἀδυνατέω **adunatěō**, *ad-oo-nat-eh´-o;* from *102;* to be *unable*, i.e. (pass.) *impossible:*— be impossible.

102. ἀδύνατος **adunatŏs**, *ad-oo´-nat-os;* from *1* (as a neg. particle) and *1415; unable*, i.e. *weak* (lit. or fig.); pass. *impossible:*— could not do, impossible, impotent, not possible, weak.

103. ᾄδω **aidō**, *ad´-o´* a prim. verb; to *sing:*— sing.

104. ἀεί **aěi**, *ah-eye´;* from an obs. prim. noun (appar. mean. continued *duration*); "*ever*," by qualification *regularly;* by impl. *earnestly:*— always, ever.

105. ἀετός **aětŏs**, *ah-et-os´;* from the same as *109;* an *eagle* (from its *wind*-like flight):— eagle.

106. ἄζυμος **azumŏs**, *ad´-zoo-mos;* from *1* (as a neg. particle) and *2219; unleavened*, i.e. (fig.) *uncorrupted;* (in the neut. plur.)

spec. (by impl.) the *Passover* week:— unleavened (bread).

107. 'Αζώρ **Azōr**, *ad-zore'*; of Heb. or. [comp. 5809]; *Azor*, an Isr.:— Azor.

108. "Αζωτος **Azōtŏs**, *ad'-zo-tos*; of Heb. or. [795]; *Azotus* (i.e. Ashdod), a place in Pal.:— Azotus.

109. ἀήρ **aēr**, *ah-ayr'*; from ἄημι **aēmi** (to *breathe* unconsciously, i.e. *respire;* by anal. to *blow*); "air" (as naturally *circumambient*):— air. Comp. 5594.

ἀθά **atha**. See *3134*.

110. ἀθανασία **athanasia**, *ath-an-as-ee'-ah;* from a compound of *1* (as a neg. particle) and *2288; deathlessness:*— immortality.

111. ἀθέμιτος **athĕmitŏs**, *ath-em'-ee-tos;* from *1* (as a neg. particle) and a der. of θέμις **thĕmis** (*statute;* from the base of *5087*); *illegal;* by impl. *flagitious:*— abominable, unlawful thing.

112. ἄθεος **athĕŏs**, *ath'-eh-os;* from *1* (as a neg. particle) and *2316; godless:*— without God.

113. ἄθεσμος **athĕsmŏs**, *ath'-es-mos;* from *1* (as a neg. particle) and a der. of *5087* (in the sense of *enacting*); *lawless,* i.e. (by impl.) *criminal:*— wicked.

114. ἀθετέω **athĕtĕō**, *ath-et-eh'-o;* from a compound of *1* (as a neg. particle) and a der. of *5087;* to *set aside,* i.e. (by impl.) to *disesteem, neutralize* or *violate:*— cast off, despise, disannul, frustrate, bring to nought, reject.

115. ἀθέτησις **athĕtēsis**, *ath-et'-ay-sis;* from *114; cancellation* (lit. or fig.):— disannulling, put away.

116. 'Αθῆναι **Athēnai**, *ath-ay-nahee;* plur. of 'Αθήνη **Athēnē** (the goddess of wisdom, who was reputed to have founded the city); *Athenæ,* the capitol of Greece:— Athens.

117. 'Αθηναῖος **Athēnaiŏs**, *ath-ay-nah'-yos;* from *116;* an *Athenæan* or inhab. of Athenæ:— Athenian.

118. ἀθλέω **athlĕō**, *ath-leh'-o;* from ἆθλος **athlŏs** (a *contest* in the public lists); to *contend* in the competitive games:— strive.

119. ἄθλησις **athlēsis**, *ath'-lay-sis;* from *118;* a *struggle* (fig.):— fight.

120. ἀθυμέω **athumĕō**, *ath-oo-meh'-o;* from a comp. of *1* (as a neg. particle) and *2372;* to *be spiritless,* i.e. *disheartened:*— be dismayed.

121. ἄθωος **athōŏs**, *ath'-o-os;* from *1* (as a neg. particle) and prob. a der. of *5087* (mean. a *penalty*); *not guilty:*— innocent.

122. αἴγειος **aigĕiŏs**, *ah'-ee-ghi-os;* from αἴξ **aix** (a *goat*); belonging to a *goat:*— goat.

123. αἰγιαλός **aigialŏs**, *ahee-ghee-al-os';* from ἀΐσσω **aissō** (to *rush*) and *251* (in the sense of the *sea;* a *beach* (on which the *waves dash*):— shore.

124. Αἰγύπτιος **Aiguptiŏs**, *ahee-goop'-tee-os;* from *125;* an *Ægyptian* or inhab. of Ægyptus:— Egyptian.

125. Αἴγυπτος **Aiguptŏs**, *ah'-ee-goop-tos;* of uncert. der.; *Ægyptus,* the land of the Nile:— Egypt.

126. ἀΐδιος **aïdiŏs**, *ah-id'-ee-os;* from *104; everduring* (forward and backward, or forward only):— eternal, everlasting.

127. αἰδώς **aidōs**, *ahee-doce';* perh. from *1* (as a neg. particle) and *1492* (through the idea of *downcast* eyes); *bashfulness,* i.e. (toward men), *modesty* or (toward God) *awe:*— reverence, shamefacedness.

128. Αἰθίοψ **Aithiŏps**, *ahee-thee'-ops;* from αἴθω **aithō** (to *scorch*) and ὤψ **ōps** (the *face,* from *3700*); an *Æthiopian* (as a *blackamoor*):— Ethiopian.

129. αἷμα **haima**, *hah'-ee-mah;* of uncert. der.; *blood,* lit. (of men or animals), fig. (the *juice* of grapes) or spec. (the atoning *blood* of Christ); by impl. *bloodshed,* also *kindred:*— blood.

130. αἱματεκχυσία **haimatĕkchusia**, *hahee-mat-ek-khoo-see'-ah;* from *129* and a der. of *1632;* an *effusion of blood:*— shedding of blood.

131. αἱμορρέω **haimŏrrhĕō**, *hahee-mor-hreh'-o;* from *129* and *4482;* to *flow blood,* i.e. *have a hemorrhage:*— diseased with an issue of blood.

132. Αἰνέας **Ainĕas**, *ahee-neh'-as;* of uncert. der.; *Æneas,* an Isr.:— Æneas.

133. αἴνεσις **ainĕsis**, *ah'-ee-nes-is;* from *134;* a *praising* (the act), i.e. (spec.) a *thank* (-offering):— praise.

134. αἰνέω **ainĕō**, *ahee-neh'-o;* from *136;* to *praise* (God):— praise.

135. αἴνιγμα **ainigma**, *ah'-ee-nig-ma;* from a der. of *136* (in its prim. sense); an *obscure* saying ("enigma"), i.e. (abstr.) *obscureness:*— × darkly.

136. αἶνος **ainŏs**, *ah'-ee-nos;* appar. a prim. word; prop. a *story,* but used in the sense of *1868; praise* (of God):— praise.

137. Αἰνών **Ainōn**, *ahee-nohn';* of Heb. or. [a der. of 5869, *place of springs*]; *Ænon,* a place in Pal.:— Ænon.

138. αἱρέομαι **hairĕŏmai**, *hahee-reh'-om-ahee;* prob. akin to *142;* to *take for oneself,* i.e. to *prefer:*— choose. Some of the forms are borrowed from a cognate ἕλλομαι **hellŏmai** *hel'-lom-ahee;* which is otherwise obsolete.

139. αἵρεσις **hairĕsis**, *hah'-ee-res-is;* from *138;* prop. a *choice,* i.e. (spec.) a *party* or (abstr.) *disunion:*— heresy [which is the Gr. word itself], sect.

140. αἱρετίζω **hairĕtizō**, *hahee-ret-id'-zo;* from a der. of *138;* to *make a choice:*— choose.

141. αἱρετικός **hairĕtikŏs**, *hahee-ret-ee-kos´;* from the same as *140;* a *schismatic:*— heretic [*the Gr. word itself*].

142. αἴρω **airō**, *ah´-ee-ro;* a prim. verb; to *lift;* by impl. to *take up* or *away;* fig. to *raise* (the voice), *keep in suspense* (the mind), spec. to *sail* away (i.e. *weigh anchor*); by Heb. [comp. 5375] to *expiate* sin:— away with, bear (up), carry, lift up, loose, make to doubt, put away, remove, take (away, up).

143. αἰσθάνομαι **aisthanŏmai**, *ahee-sthan´-om-ahee;* of uncert. der.; to *apprehend* (prop. by the senses):— perceive.

144. αἴσθησις **aisthēsis**, *ah´-ee-sthay-sis;* from *143; perception*, i.e. (fig.) *discernment:*— judgment.

145. αἰσθητήριον **aisthētēriŏn**, *ahee-sthay-tay´-ree-on;* from a der. of *143;* prop. an *organ of perception*, i.e. (fig.) *judgment:*— senses.

146. αἰσχροκερδής **aischrŏkĕrdēs**, *ahee-skhrok-er-dace´;* from *150* and κέρδος **kerdos** (*gain*); *sordid:*— given to (greedy of) filthy lucre.

147. αἰσχροκερδῶς **aischrŏkĕrdōs**, *ahee-skhrok-er-doce´;* adv. from *146; sordidly:*— for filthy lucre's sake.

148. αἰσχρολογία **aischrŏlŏgia**, *ahee-skhrol-og-ee´-ah;* from *150* and *3056; vile conversation:*— filthy communication.

149. αἰσχρόν **aischrŏn**, *ahee-skhron´;* neut. of *150;* a *shameful* thing, i.e. *indecorum:*— shame.

150. αἰσχρός **aischrŏs**, *ahee-skhros´;* from the same as *153; shameful*, i.e. *base* (spec. *venal*):— filthy.

151. αἰσχρότης **aischrŏtēs**, *ahee-skhrot´-ace;* from *150; shamefulness*, i.e. *obscenity:*— filthiness.

152. αἰσχύνη **aischunē**, *ahee-skhoo´-nay;* from *153; shame* or *disgrace* (abstr. or concr.):— dishonesty, shame.

153. αἰσχύνομαι **aischunŏmai**, *ahee-skhoo´-nom-ahee;* from αἶσχος **aischŏs** (*disfigurement*, i.e. *disgrace*); to *feel shame* (for oneself):— be ashamed.

154. αἰτέω **aitĕō**, *ahee-teh´-o;* of uncert. der.; to *ask* (in gen.):— ask, beg, call for, crave, desire, require. Comp. *4441.*

155. αἴτημα **aitēma**, *ah´-ee-tay-mah;* from *154;* a *thing asked* or (abstr.) an *asking:*— petition, request, required.

156. αἰτία **aitia**, *ahee-tee´-a;* from the same as *154;* a *cause* (as if *asked* for), i.e. (logical) *reason* (motive, matter), (legal) *crime* (alleged or proved):— accusation, case, cause, crime, fault, [wh-lere[-fore].

157. αἰτίαμα **aitiama**, *ahee-tee´-am-ah;* from a der. of *156;* a *thing charged:*— complaint.

158. αἴτιον **aitiŏn**, *ah´-ee-tee-on;* neut. of *159;* a *reason* or *crime* [like *156*]:— cause, fault.

159. αἴτιος **aitiŏs**, *ah´-ee-tee-os;* from the same as *154; causative*, i.e. (concr.) a *causer:*— author.

160. αἰφνίδιος **aiphnidiŏs**, *aheef-nid´-ee-os;* from a comp. of *1* (as a neg. particle) and *5316* [comp. *1810*] (mean. *non-apparent*); *unexpected*, i.e. (adv.) *suddenly:*— sudden, unawares.

161. αἰχμαλωσία **aichmalōsia**, *aheekh-mal-o-see´-ah;* from *164; captivity:*— captivity.

162. αἰχμαλωτεύω **aichmalōtĕuō**, *aheekh-mal-o-tew´-o;* from *164;* to *capture* [like *163*]:— lead captive.

163. αἰχμαλωτίζω **aichmalōtizō**, *aheekh-mal-o-tid´-zo;* from *164;* to *make captive:*— lead away captive, bring into captivity.

164. αἰχμαλωτός **aichmalōtŏs**, *aheekh-mal-o-tos´;* from αἰχμή **aichmē** (a *spear*) and a der. of the same as *259;* prop. a *prisoner of war*, i.e. (gen.) a *captive:*— captive.

165. αἰών **aiōn**, *ahee-ohn´;* from the same as *104;* prop. an *age;* by extens. *perpetuity* (also past); by impl. the *world;* spec. (Jewish) a Messianic period (present or future):— age, course, eternal, (for) ever (-more), [n-]ever, (beginning of the, while the) world (began, without end). Comp. *5550.*

166. αἰώνιος **aiōniŏs**, *ahee-o´-nee-os;* from *165; perpetual* (also used of past time, or past and future as well):— eternal, for ever, everlasting, world (began).

167. ἀκαθαρσία **akatharsia**, *ak-ath-ar-see´-ah;* from *169; impurity* (the quality), phys. or mor.:— uncleanness.

168. ἀκαθάρτης **akathartēs**, *ak-ath-ar´-tace;* from *169; impurity* (the state), mor.:— filthiness.

169. ἀκάθαρτος **akathartŏs**, *ak-ath´-ar-tos;* from *1* (as a neg. particle) and a presumed der. of *2508* (mean. *cleansed*); *impure* (cer., mor. [lewd] or spec. [demonic]):— foul, unclean.

170. ἀκαιρέομαι **akairĕŏmai**, *ak-ahee-reh´-om-ahee;* from a comp. of *1* (as a neg. particle) and *2540* (mean. *unseasonable*); to *be inopportune* (for one-self), i.e. to *fail of a proper occasion:*— lack opportunity.

171. ἀκαίρως **akairōs**, *ak-ah´-ee-roce;* adv. from the same as *170; inopportunely:*— out of season.

172. ἄκακος **akakŏs**, *ak´-ak-os;* from *1* (as a neg. particle) and *2556; not bad*, i.e. (obj.) *innocent* or (subj.) *unsuspecting:*— harmless, simple.

173. ἄκανθα **akantha**, *ak´-an-thah;* prob. from the same as *188;* a *thorn:*— thorn.

174. ἀκάνθινος **akanthinŏs**, *ak-an´-thee-nos;* from *173; thorny:*— of thorns.

175. ἄκαρπος **akarpŏs**, *ak´-ar-pos;* from *1*

(as a neg. particle) and 2590; barren (lit. or fig.):— without fruit, unfruitful.

176. ἀκατάγνωστος akatagnōstŏs, ak-at-ag´-noce-tos; from 1 (as a neg. particle) and a der. of 2607; unblamable:— that cannot be condemned.

177. ἀκατακάλυπτος akatakaluptŏs, ak-at-ak-al´-oop-tos; from 1 (as a neg. particle) and a der. of a comp. of 2596 and 2572; unveiled:— uncovered.

178. ἀκατάκριτος akatakritŏs, ak-at-ak´-ree-tos; from 1 (as a neg. particle) and a der. of 2632; without (legal) trial:— uncondemned.

179. ἀκατάλυτος akatalutŏs, ak-at-al´-oo-tos; from 1 (as a neg. particle) and a der. of 2647; indissoluble, i.e. (fig.) permanent:— endless.

180. ἀκατάπαυστος akatapaustŏs, ak-at-ap´-ow-stos; from 1 (as a neg. particle) and a der. of 2664; unrefraining:— that cannot cease.

181. ἀκαταστασία akatastasia, ak-at-as-tah-see´-ah; from 182; instability, i.e. disorder:— commotion, confusion, tumult.

182. ἀκατάστατος akatastatŏs, ak-at-as´-tat-os; from 1 (as a neg. particle) and a der. of 2525; inconstant:— unstable.

183. ἀκατάσχετος akataschĕtŏs, ak-at-as´-khet-os; from 1 (as a neg. particle) and a der. of 2722; unrestrainable:— unruly.

184. Ἀκελδαμά Akeldama, ak-el-dam-ah´; of Chald. or. [mean. field of blood; corresp. to 2506 and 1818]; Akeldama, a place near Jerusalem:— Aceldama.

185. ἀκέραιος akĕraiŏs, ak-er´-ah-yos; from 1 (as a neg. particle) and a presumed der. of 2767; unmixed, i.e. (fig.) innocent:— harmless, simple.

186. ἀκλινής aklinēs, ak-lee-nace´; from 1 (as a neg. particle) and 2827; not leaning, i.e. (fig.) firm:— without wavering.

187. ἀκμάζω akmazō, ak-mad´-zo; from the same as 188; to make a point, i.e. (fig.) mature:— be fully ripe.

188. ἀκμήν akmēn, ak-mane´; acc. of a noun ("acme") akin to ἀκή akē (a point) and mean. the same; adv. just now, i.e. still:— yet.

189. ἀκοή akŏē, ak-o-ay´; from 191; hearing (the act, the sense or the thing heard):— audience, ear, fame, which ye heard, hearing, preached, report, rumor.

190. ἀκολουθέω akŏlŏuthĕō, ak-ol-oo-theh´-o; from 1 (as a particle of union) and κέλευθος kĕlĕuthŏs (a road); prop. to be in the same way with, i.e. to accompany (spec. as a disciple):— follow, reach.

191. ἀκούω akŏuō, ak-oo´-o; a prim. verb; to hear (in various senses):— give (in the) audience (of), come (to the ears), ([shall]) hear (-er, -ken), be noised, be reported, understand.

192. ἀκρασία akrasia, ak-ras-ee´-a; from 193; want of self-restraint:— excess, incontinency.

193. ἀκράτης akratēs, ak-rat´-ace; from 1 (as a neg. particle) and 2904; powerless, i.e. without self-control:— incontinent.

194. ἄκρατος akratŏs, ak´-rat-os; from 1 (as a neg. particle) and a presumed der. of 2767; undiluted:— without mixture.

195. ἀκρίβεια akribĕia, ak-ree´-bi-ah; from the same as 196; exactness:— perfect manner.

196. ἀκριβέστατος akribĕstatŏs, ak-ree-bes´-ta-tos; superlative of ἀκρίβης akribēs (a der. of the same as 206); most exact:— most straitest.

197. ἀκριβέστερον akribĕstĕrŏn, ak-ree-bes´-ter-on; neut. of the comparative of the same as 196; (adv.) more exactly:— more perfect (-ly).

198. ἀκριβόω akribŏō, ak-ree-bŏ´-o; from the same as 196; to be exact, i.e. ascertain:— enquire diligently.

199. ἀκριβῶς akribōs, ak-ree-boce´; adv. from the same as 196; exactly:— circumspectly, diligently, perfect (-ly).

200. ἀκρίς akris, ak-rece´; appar. from the same as 206; a locust (as pointed, or as lightning on the top of vegetation):— locust.

201. ἀκροατήριον akrŏatēriŏn, ak-rŏ-at-ay´-ree-on; from 202; an audience-room:— place of hearing.

202. ἀκροατής akrŏatēs, ak-rŏ-at-ace´; from ἀκροάομαι akrŏaŏmai (to listen; appar. an intens. of 191); a hearer (merely):— hearer.

203. ἀκροβυστία akrŏbustia, ak-rob-oos-tee´-ah; from 206 and prob. a modified form of πόσθη pŏsthē (the penis or male sexual organ); the prepuce; by impl. an uncircumcised (i.e. gentile, fig. unregenerate) state or person:— not circumcised, uncircumcised [with 2192], uncircumcision.

204. ἀκρογωνιαῖος akrŏgōniaiŏs, ak-rog-o-nee-ah´-yos; from 206 and 1137; belonging to the extreme corner:— chief corner.

205. ἀκροθίνιον akrŏthiniŏn, ak-roth-in´-ee-on; from 206 and θίς this (a heap); prop. (in the plur.) the top of the heap, i.e. (by impl.) best of the booty:— spoils.

206. ἄκρον akrŏn, ak´-ron; neut. of an adj. prob. akin to the base of 188; the extremity:— one end ... other, tip, top, uttermost part.

207. Ἀκύλας Akulas, ak-oo´-las; prob. for Lat. aquila (an eagle); Akulas, an Isr.:— Aquila.

208. ἀκυρόω akurŏō, ak-oo-rŏ´-o; from 1 (as a neg. particle) and 2964; to invalidate:— disannul, make of none effect.

Greek

209. ἀκωλύτως **akōlutōs**, *ak-o-loo´-toce;* adv. from a compound of *1* (as a neg. particle) and a der. of *2967;* in *an unhindered manner,* i.e. *freely:*— no man forbidding him.

210. ἄκων **akōn**, *ak´-ohn;* from *1* (as a neg. particle) and *1635; unwilling:*— against the will.

211. ἀλάβαστρον **alabastrŏn**, *al-ab´-as-tron;* neut. of ἀλάβαστρος **alabastrŏs** (of uncert. der.), the name of a stone; prop. an "*alabaster*" box, i.e. (by extens.) a perfume *vase* (of any material):— (alabaster) box.

212. ἀλαζονεία **alazŏnĕia**, *al-ad-zon-i´-a;* from *213;* braggadocio, i.e. (by impl.) *self-confidence:*— boasting, pride.

213. ἀλαζών **alazōn**, *al-ad-zone´;* from ἄλη **alē** (*vagrancy*); *braggart:*— boaster.

214. ἀλαλάζω **alalazō**, *al-al-ad´-zo;* from ἀλαλή **alalē** (a *shout,* "halloo"); to *vociferate,* i.e. (by impl.) to *wail;* fig. to *clang:*— tinkle, wail.

215. ἀλάλητος **alalētŏs**, *al-al´-ay-tos;* from *1* (as a neg. particle) and a der. of *2980; unspeakable:*— unutterable, which cannot be uttered.

216. ἄλαλος **alalŏs**, *al´-al-os;* from *1* (as a neg. particle) and *2980; mute:*— dumb.

217. ἅλας **halas**, *hal´-as;* from *251; salt;* fig. *prudence:*— salt.

218. ἀλείφω **alĕiphō**, *al-i´-fo;* from *1* (as particle of union) and the base of *3045;* to *oil* (with perfume):— anoint.

219. ἀλεκτοροφωνία **alektŏrŏphōnia**, *al-ek-tor-of-o-nee´-ah;* from *220* and *5456; cockcrow,* i.e. the third night-watch:— cockcrowing.

220. ἀλέκτωρ **alĕktōr**, *al-ek´-tore;* from ἀλέκω (to *ward* off); a *cock* or male fowl:— cock.

221. Ἀλεξανδρεύς **Alĕxandrĕus**, *al-ex-and-reuce´;* from Ἀλεξάνδρεια (the city so called); an *Alexandreian* or inhab. of Alexandria:— of Alexandria, Alexandrian.

222. Ἀλεξανδρῖνος **Alĕxandrinŏs**, *al-ex-an-dree´-nos;* from the same as *221; Alexandrine,* or belonging to Alexandria:— of Alexandria.

223. Ἀλέξανδρος **Alĕxandrŏs**, *al-ex´-an-dros;* from the same as (the first part of) *220* and *435; man-defender; Alexander,* the name of three Isr. and one other man:— Alexander.

224. ἄλευρον **alĕurŏn**, *al´-yoo-ron;* from ἀλέω **alĕō** (to *grind*); *flour:*— meal.

225. ἀλήθεια **alēthĕia**, *al-ay´-thi-a;* from *227; truth:*— true, × truly, truth, verity.

226. ἀληθεύω **alēthĕuō**, *al-ayth-yoo´-o;* from *227;* to *be true* (in doctrine and profession):— speak (tell) the truth.

227. ἀληθής **alēthēs**, *al-ay-thace´;* from *1* (as a neg. particle) and *2990; true* (as *not concealing*):— true, truly, truth.

228. ἀληθινός **alēthinŏs**, *al-ay-thee-nos´;* from *227; truthful:*— true.

229. ἀλήθω **alēthō**, *al-ay´-tho;* from the same as *224;* to *grind:*— grind.

230. ἀληθῶς **alēthōs**, *al-ay-thoce´;* adv. from *227; truly:*— indeed, surely, of a surety, truly, of a (in) truth, verily, very.

231. ἁλιεύς **haliĕus**, *hal-ee-yoos´;* from *251;* a *sailor* (as engaged on the *salt* water), i.e. (by impl.) a *fisher:*— fisher (-man).

232. ἁλιεύω **haliĕuō**, *hal-ee-yoo´-o;* from *231;* to *be a fisher,* i.e. (by impl.) to *fish:*— go a-fishing.

233. ἁλίζω **halizō**, *hal-id´-zo;* from *251;* to *salt:*— salt.

234. ἅλισγεμα **alisgĕma**, *al-is´-ghem-ah;* from ἀλισγέω **alisgĕō** (to *soil*); (cer.) *defilement:*— pollution.

235. ἀλλά **alla**, *al-lah´;* neut. plur. of *243;* prop. *other* things, i.e. (adv.) *contrariwise* (in many relations):— and, but (even), howbeit, indeed, nay, nevertheless, no, notwithstanding, save, therefore, yea, yet.

236. ἀλλάσσω **allassō**, *al-las´-so;* from *243;* to *make different:*— change.

237. ἀλλαχόθεν **allachŏthĕn**, *al-lakh-oth´-en;* from *243; from elsewhere:*— some other way.

238. ἀλληγορέω **allēgŏrĕō**, *al-lay-gor-eh´-o;* from *243* and ἀγορέω **agŏrĕō** (to *harangue* [comp. *58*]); to *allegorize:*— be an allegory [*the Gr. word itself*].

239. ἀλληλούϊα **allēlŏuïa**, *al-lay-loo´-ee-ah;* of Heb. or. [imper. of *1984* and *3050*]; *praise ye Jah!,* an adoring exclamation:— alleluia.

240. ἀλλήλων **allēlōn**, *al-lay´-lone;* Gen. plur. from *243* redupl.; *one another:*— each other, mutual, one another, (the other), (them-, your-) selves, (selves) together [*sometimes with 3326 or 4314*].

241. ἀλλογενής **allŏgĕnēs**, *al-log-en-ace´;* from *243* and *1085; foreign,* i.e. not a Jew:— stranger.

242. ἅλλομαι **hallŏmai**, *hal´-lom-ahee;* mid. voice of appar. a prim. verb; to *jump;* fig. to *gush:*— leap, spring up.

243. ἄλλος **allŏs**, *al´-los;* a prim. word; "*else,*" i.e. *different* (in many applications):— more, one (another), (an-, some an-) other (-s, -wise).

244. ἀλλοτριεπίσκοπος **allŏtriĕpiskŏpŏs**, *al-lot-ree-ep-is´-kop-os;* from *245* and *1985; overseeing others'* affairs, i.e. a *meddler* (spec. in Gentile customs):— busybody in other men's matters.

245. ἀλλότριος **allŏtriŏs**, *al-lot´-ree-os;* from *243; another's,* i.e. not one's own; by extens. *foreign, not akin, hostile:*— alien, (an-) other (man's, men's), strange (-r).

246. ἀλλόφυλος **allŏphulŏs**, *al-lof´-oo-los;*

from 243 and 5443; for., i.e. (spec.) Gentile:— one of another nation.

247. ἄλλως allōs, al´-loce; adv. from 243; differently:— otherwise.

248. ἀλοάω aloaō, al-o-ah´-o; from the same as 257; to tread out grain:— thresh, tread out the corn.

249. ἄλογος alŏgŏs, al´-og-os; from 1 (as a neg. particle) and 3056; irrational:— brute, unreasonable.

250. ἀλόη alŏē, al-o-ay´; of for. or. [comp. 174]; aloes (the gum):— aloes.

251. ἅλς hals, halce; a prim. word; "salt":— salt.

252. ἁλυκός halukŏs, hal-oo-kos´; from 251; briny:— salt.

253. ἀλυπότερος alupŏtĕrŏs, al-oo-pot´-er-os; comparative of a comp. of 1 (as a neg. particle) and 3077; more without grief:— less sorrowful.

254. ἄλυσις halusis, hal´-oo-sis; of uncert. der.; a fetter or manacle:— bonds, chain.

255. ἀλυσιτελής alusitĕlēs, al-oo-sit-el-ace´; from 1 (as a neg. particle) and the base of 3081; gainless, i.e. (by impl.) pernicious:— unprofitable.

256. Ἀλφαῖος Alphaiŏs, al-fah´-yos; of Heb. or. [comp. 2501]; Alphæus, an Isr.:— Alpheus.

257. ἅλων halōn, hal´-ohn; prob. from the base of 1507; a threshing-floor (as rolled hard), i.e. (fig.) the grain (and chaff, as just threshed):— floor.

258. ἀλώπηξ alōpēx, al-o´-pakes; of uncert. der.; a fox, i.e. (fig.) a cunning person:— fox.

259. ἅλωσις halōsis, hal´-o-sis; from a collat. form of 138; capture:— be taken.

260. ἅμα hama, ham´-ah; a prim. particle; prop. at the "same" time, but freely used as a prep. or adv. denoting close association:— also, and, together, with (-al).

261. ἀμαθής amathēs, am-ath-ace´; from 1 (as a neg. particle) and 3129; ignorant:— unlearned.

262. ἀμαράντινος amarantinŏs, am-ar-an´-tee-nos; from 263; "amaranthine", i.e. (by impl.) fadeless:— that fadeth not away.

263. ἀμάραντος amarantŏs, am-ar´-an-tos; from 1 (as a neg. particle) and a presumed der. of 3133; unfading, i.e. (by impl.) perpetual:— that fadeth not away.

264. ἁμαρτάνω hamartanō, ham-ar-tan´-o; perh. from 1 (as a neg. particle) and the base of 3313; prop. to miss the mark (and so not share in the prize), i.e. (fig.) to err, esp. (mor.) to sin:— for your faults, offend, sin, trespass.

265. ἁμάρτημα hamartēma, ham-ar´-tay-mah; from 264; a sin (prop. concr.):— sin.

266. ἁμαρτία hamartia, ham-ar-tee´-ah; from 264; sin (prop. abstr.):— offence, sin (-ful).

267. ἀμάρτυρος amarturŏs, am-ar´-too-ros; from 1 (as a neg. particle) and a form of 3144; unattested:— without witness.

268. ἁμαρτωλός hamartōlŏs, ham-ar-to-los´; from 264; sinful, i.e. a sinner:— sinful, sinner.

269. ἄμαχος amachŏs, am´-akh-os; from 1 (as a neg. particle) and 3163; peaceable:— not a brawler.

270. ἀμάω amaō, am-ah´-o; from 260; prop. to collect, i.e. (by impl.) reap:— reap down.

271. ἀμέθυστος amĕthustŏs, am-eth´-oos-tos; from 1 (as a neg. particle) and a der. of 3184; the "amethyst" (supposed to prevent intoxication):— amethyst.

272. ἀμελέω amĕlĕō, am-el-eh´-o; from 1 (as a neg. particle) and 3199; to be careless of:— make light of, neglect, be negligent, not regard.

273. ἄμεμπτος amĕmptŏs, am´-emp-tos; from 1 (as a neg. particle) and a der. of 3201; irreproachable:— blameless, faultless, unblamable.

274. ἀμέμπτως amĕmptŏs, am-emp´-toce; adv. from 273; faultlessly:— blameless, unblamably.

275. ἀμέριμνος amĕrimnŏs, am-er´-im-nos; from 1 (as a neg. particle) and 3308; not anxious:— without care (-fulness), secure.

276. ἀμετάθετος amĕtathĕtŏs, am-et-ath´-et-os; from 1 (as a neg. particle) and a der. of 3346; unchangeable, or (neut. as abstr.) unchangeability:— immutable (-ility).

277. ἀμετακίνητος amĕtakinētŏs, am-et-ak-in´-ay-tos; from 1 (as a neg. particle) and a der. of 3334; immovable:— unmovable.

278. ἀμεταμέλητος amĕtamĕlētŏs, am-et-am-el´-ay-tos; from 1 (as a neg. particle) and a presumed der. of 3338; irrevocable:— without repentance, not to be repented of.

279. ἀμετανόητος amĕtanŏētŏs, am-et-an-o´-ay-tos; from 1 (as a neg. particle) and a presumed der. of 3340; unrepentant:— impenitent.

280. ἄμετρος amĕtrŏs, am´-et-ros; from 1 (as a neg. particle) and 3358; immoderate:— (thing) without measure.

281. ἀμήν amēn, am-ane´; of Heb. or. [543]; prop. firm, i.e. (fig.) trustworthy; adv. surely (often as interj. so be it):— amen, verily.

282. ἀμήτωρ amētōr, am-ay´-tore; from 1 (as a neg. particle) and 3384; motherless, i.e. of unknown maternity:— without mother.

283. ἀμίαντος amiantŏs, am-ee´-an-tos; from 1 (as a neg. particle) and a der. of 3392; unsoiled, i.e. (fig.) pure:— undefiled.

284. Ἀμιναδάβ Aminadab, am-ee-nad-ab´;

of Heb. or. [5992]; *Aminadab*, an Isr.:— Aminadab.

285. ἄμμος **ammŏs**, *am'-mos;* perh. from *260; sand* (as *heaped* on the beach):— sand.

286. ἀμνός **amnŏs**, *am-nos';* appar a prim. word; a *lamb:*— lamb.

287. ἀμοιβή **amŏibē**, *am-oy-bay';* from ἀμείβω **amĕibō** (to *exchange*); *requital:*— requite.

288. ἄμπελος **ampĕlŏs**, *am'-pel-os;* prob. from the base of *297* and that of *257;* a *vine* (as *coiling about* a support):— vine.

289. ἀμπελουργός **ampĕlŏurgŏs**, *am-pel-oor-gos';* from *288* and *2041;* a *vine-worker*, i.e. *pruner:*— vine-dresser.

290. ἀμπελών **ampĕlōn**, *am-pel-ohn';* from *288;* a *vineyard:*— vineyard.

291. Ἀμπλίας **Amplias**, *am-plee'-as;* contr. for Lat. *ampliatus* [enlarged]; *Amplias*, a Rom. Chr.:— Amplias.

292. ἀμύνομαι **amunŏmai**, *am-oo'-nom-ahee;* mid. voice of a prim. verb; to *ward off* (for oneself), i.e. *protect:*— defend.

293. ἀμφίβληστρον **amphiblēstrŏn**, *am-feeb'-lace-tron;* from a comp. of the base of *297* and *906;* a (fishing) *net* (as *thrown about* the fish):— net.

294. ἀμφιέννυμι **amphiĕnnumi**, *am-fee-en'-noo-mee;* from the base of *297* and ἕννυμι **hĕnnumi** (to *invest*); to *enrobe:*— clothe.

295. Ἀμφίπολις **Amphipŏlis**, *am-fip'-ol-is;* from the base of *1* and *4172;* a *city surrounded* by a river; *Amphipolis*, a place in Macedonia:— Amphipolis.

296. ἄμφοδον **amphŏdŏn**, *am'-fod-on;* from the base of *297* and *3598;* a *fork* in the road:— where two ways meet.

297. ἀμφότερος **amphŏtĕrŏs**, *am-fot'-er-os;* comp. of ἀμφί **amphi** (*around*); (in plur.) *both:*— both.

298. ἀμώμητος **amōmētŏs**, *am-o'-may-tos;* from *1* (as a neg. particle) and a der. of *3469; unblameable:*— blameless.

299. ἄμωμος **amōmŏs**, *am'-o-mos;* from *1* (as a neg. particle) and *3470; unblemished* (lit. or fig.):— without blame (blemish, fault, spot), faultless, unblameable.

300. Ἀμών **Amōn**, *am-one';* of Heb. or. [526]; *Amon*, an Isr.:— Amon.

301. Ἀμώς **Amōs**, *am-oce';* of Heb. or. [531]; *Amos*, an Isr.:— Amos.

302. ἄν **an**, *an;* a prim. particle, denoting a *supposition, wish, possibility* or *uncertainty:*— [what-, where-, wither-, who-] soever. Usually unexpressed except by the subjunctive or potential mood. Also contr. for *1437.*

303. ἀνά **ana**, *an-ah';* a prim. prep. and adv.; prop. *up;* but (by extens.) used (distributively) *severally*, or (locally) *at* (etc.):— and, apiece, by, each, every (man), in, through. In com-

pounds (as a prefix) it often means (by impl.) *repetition, intensity, reversal*, etc.

304. ἀναβαθμός **anabathmŏs**, *an-ab-ath-mos';* from *305* [comp. *898*]; a *stairway:*— stairs.

305. ἀναβαίνω **anabainō**, *an-ab-ah'-ee-no;* from *303* and the base of *939;* to *go up* (lit. or fig.):— arise, ascend (up), climb (go, grow, rise, spring) up, come (up).

306. ἀναβάλλομαι **anaballŏmai**, *an-ab-al'-lom-ahee;* mid. voice from *303* and *906;* to *put off* (for oneself):— defer.

307. ἀναβιβάζω **anabibazō**, *an-ab-ee-bad'-zo;* from *303* and a der. of the base of *939;* to *cause to go up*, i.e. *haul* (a net):— draw.

308. ἀναβλέπω **anablĕpō**, *an-ab-lep'-o;* from *303* and *991;* to *look up;* by impl. to *recover sight:*— look (up), see, receive sight.

309. ἀνάβλεψις **anablĕpsis**, *an-ab'-lep-sis;* from *308; restoration of sight:*— recovery of sight.

310. ἀναβοάω **anabŏaō**, *an-ab-o-ah'-o;* from *303* and *994;* to *halloo:*— cry (aloud, out).

311. ἀναβολή **anabŏlē**, *an-ab-ol-ay';* from *306;* a *putting off:*— delay.

312. ἀναγγέλλω **anaggĕllō**, *an-ang-el'-lo;* from *303* and the base of *32;* to *announce* (in detail):— declare, rehearse, report, show, speak, tell.

313. ἀναγεννάω **anagĕnnaō**, *an-ag-en-nah'-o;* from *303* and *1080;* to *beget* or (by extens.) *bear (again):*— beget, (bear) × (again).

314. ἀναγινώσκω **anaginōskō**, *an-ag-in-oce'-ko;* from *303* and *1097;* to *know again*, i.e. (by extens.) to *read:*— read.

315. ἀναγκάζω **anagkazō**, *an-ang-kad'-zo;* from *318;* to *necessitate:*— compel, constrain.

316. ἀναγκαῖος **anagkaiŏs**, *an-ang-kah'-yos;* from *318; necessary;* by impl. *close* (of kin):— near, necessary, necessity, needful.

317. ἀναγκαστῶς **anagkastōs**, *an-ang-kas-toce';* adv. from a der. of *315; compulsorily:*— by constraint.

318. ἀναγκή **anagkē**, *an-ang-kay';* from *303* and the base of *43; constraint* (lit. or fig.); by impl. *distress:*— distress, must needs, (of) necessity (-sary), needeth, needful.

319. ἀναγνωρίζομαι **anagnōrizŏmai**, *an-ag-no-rid'-zom-ahee;* mid. voice from *303* and *1107;* to *make* (oneself) *known:*— be made known.

320. ἀνάγνωσις **anagnōsis**, *an-ag'-no-sis;* from *314;* (the act of) *reading:*— reading.

321. ἀνάγω **anagō**, *an-ag'-o;* from *303* and *71;* to *lead up;* by extens. to *bring out;* spec. to *sail* away:— bring (again, forth, up again), depart, launch (forth), lead (up), loose, offer, sail, set forth, take up.

322. ἀναδείκνυμι **anadĕiknumi**, *an-ad-ike'-*

noo-mee; from *303* and *1166;* to *exhibit,* i.e. (by impl.) to *indicate, appoint:*— appoint, shew.

323. ἀνάδειξις **anadĕixis**, *an-ad´-ike-sis;* from 322; (the act of) *exhibition:*— shewing.

324. ἀναδέχομαι **anadĕchŏmai**, *an-ad-ekh´-om-ahee;* from *303* and *1209;* to *entertain* (as a guest):— receive.

325. ἀναδίδωμι **anadidōmi**, *an-ad-eed´-om-ee;* from *303* and *1325;* to *hand over:*— deliver.

326. ἀναζάω **anazaō**, *an-ad-zah´-o* from *303* and *2198;* to *recover life* (lit. or fig.):— (be a-) live again, revive.

327. ἀναζητέω **anazētĕō**, *an-ad-zay-teh´-o;* from *303* and *2212;* to *search* out:— seek.

328. ἀναζώννυμι **anazōnnumi**, *an-ad-zone´-noo-mee;* from *303* and *2224;* to *gird afresh:*— gird up.

329. ἀναζωπυρέω **anazōpurĕō**, *an-ad-zo-poor-eh´-o;* from *303* and a comp. of the base of *2226* and *4442;* to *re-enkindle:*— stir up.

330. ἀναθάλλω **anathallō**, *an-ath-al´-lo;* from *303* and θάλλω **thallō** (to *flourish*); to *revive:*— flourish again.

331. ἀνάθεμα **anathĕma**, *an-ath´-em-ah;* from *394;* a (religious) *ban* or (concr.) *excommunicated* (thing or person):— accursed, anathema, curse, × great.

332. ἀναθεματίζω **anathĕmatizō**, *an-ath-em-at-id´-zo;* from *331;* to *declare* or *vow* under penalty of execration:— (bind under a) curse, bind with an oath.

333. ἀναθεωρέω **anathĕōrĕō**, *an-ath-eh-o-reh´-o;* from *303* and *2334;* to *look again* (i.e. *attentively*) at (lit. or fig.):— behold, consider.

334. ἀνάθημα **anathēma**, *an-ath´-ay-mah;* from *394* [like *331,* but in a good sense]; a *votive* offering:— gift.

335. ἀναίδεια **anaidĕia**, *an-ah´-ee-die-ah';* from a comp. of *1* (as a neg. particle [comp. *427*]) and *127; impudence,* i.e. (by impl.) *importunity:*— importunity.

336. ἀναίρεσις **anairĕsis**, *an-ah´-ee-res-is;* from *337;* (the act of) *killing:*— death.

337. ἀναιρέω **anairĕō**, *an-ahee-reh´-o;* from *303* and (the act. of) *138;* to *take up,* i.e. *adopt;* by impl. to *take away* (violently), i.e. *abolish, murder:*— put to death, kill, slay, take away, take up.

338. ἀναίτιος **anaitiŏs**, *an-ah´-ee-tee-os;* from *1* (as a neg. particle) and *159* (in the sense of *156); innocent:*— blameless, guiltless.

339. ἀνακαθίζω **anakathizō**, *an-ak-ath-id´-zo;* from *303* and *2523;* prop. to *set up,* i.e. (refl.) to *sit up:*— sit up.

340. ἀνακαινίζω **anakainizō**, *an-ak-ahee-nid´-zo;* from *303* and a der. of *2537;* to *restore:*— renew.

341. ἀνακαινόω **anakainŏō**, *an-ak-ahee-nŏ´-o;* from *303* and a der. of *2537;* to *renovate:*— renew.

342. ἀνακαίνωσις **anakainōsis**, *an-ak-ah´-ee-no-sis;* from *341; renovation:*— renewing.

343. ἀνακαλύπτω **anakaluptō**, *an-ak-al-oop´-to;* from *303* (in the sense of *reversal*) and *2572;* to *unveil:*— open, (un-)taken away.

344. ἀνακάμπτω **anakamptō**, *an-ak-amp´-to;* from *303* and *2578;* to *turn back:*— (re-)turn.

345. ἀνάκειμαι **anakĕimai**, *an-ak-i´-mahee;* from *303* and *2749;* to *recline* (as a corpse or at a meal):— guest, lean, lie, sit (down, at meat), at the table.

346. ἀνακεφαλαίομαι **anakĕphalaiŏmai**, *an-ak-ef-al-ah´-ee-om-ahee;* from *303* and *2775* (in its or. sense); to *sum up:*— briefly comprehend, gather together in one.

347. ἀνακλίνω **anaklinō**, *an-ak-lee´-no;* from *303* and *2827;* to *lean back:*— lay, (make) sit down.

348. ἀνακόπτω **anakŏptō**, *an-ak-op´-to;* from *303* and *2875;* to *beat back,* i.e. *check:*— hinder.

349. ἀνακράζω **anakrazō**, *an-ak-rad´-zo;* from *303* and *2896;* to *scream up* (aloud):— cry out.

350. ἀνακρίνω **anakrinō**, *an-ak-ree´-no;* from *303* and *2919;* prop. to *scrutinize,* i.e. (by impl.) *investigate, interrogate, determine:*— ask, question, discern, examine, judge, search.

351. ἀνάκρισις **anakrisis**, *an-ak´-ree-sis;* from *350;* a (judicial) *investigation:*— examination.

352. ἀνακύπτω **anakuptō**, *an-ak-oop´-to;* from *303* (in the sense of *reversal*) and *2955;* to *unbend,* i.e. *rise;* fig. *be elated:*— lift up, look up.

353. ἀναλαμβάνω **analambanō**, *an-al-am-ban´-o;* from *303* and *2983;* to *take up:*— receive up, take (in, unto, up).

354. ἀνάληψις **analēpsis**, *an-al´-aip-sis;* from *353; ascension:*— taking up.

355. ἀναλίσκω **analiskō**, *an-al-is´-ko;* from *303* and a form of the alt. of *138;* prop. to *use up,* i.e. *destroy:*— consume.

356. ἀναλογία **analŏgia**, *an-al-og-ee´-ah;* from a comp. of *303* and *3056; proportion:*— proportion.

357. ἀναλογίζομαι **analŏgizŏmai**, *an-al-og-id´-zom-ahee;* mid. voice from *356;* to *estimate,* i.e. (fig.) *contemplate:*— consider.

358. ἄναλος **analŏs**, *an´-al-os;* from *1* (as a neg. particle) and *251; saltless,* i.e. *insipid:*— × lose saltness.

359. ἀνάλυσις **analusis**, *an-al´-oo-sis;* from *360; departure:*— departure.

360. ἀναλύω **analuō**, *an-al-oo´-o;* from *303*

and *3089;* to *break up,* i.e. *depart* (lit. or fig.):— depart, return.

361. ἀναμάρτητος **anamartētŏs**, *an-am-ar´-tay-tos;* from *1* (as a neg. particle) and a presumed der. of *264; sinless:—* that is without sin.

362. ἀναμένω **anamĕnō**, *an-am-en´-o;* from *303* and *3306;* to *await:—* wait for.

363. ἀναμιμνήσκω **anamimnēskō**, *an-am-im-nace´-ko;* from *303* and *3403;* to *remind;* (refl.) to *recollect:—* call to mind, (bring to , call to, put in), remember (-brance).

364. ἀνάμνησις **anamnēsis**, *an-am´-nay-sis;* from *363; recollection:—* remembrance (again).

365. ἀνανεόω **ananĕŏō**, *an-an-neh-o´-o;* from *303* and a der. of *3501;* to *renovate,* i.e. *reform:—* renew.

366. ἀνανήφω **ananēphō**, *an-an-ay´-fo;* from *303* and *3525;* to become *sober again,* i.e. (fig.) *regain* (one's) *senses:—* recover self.

367. Ἀνανίας **Ananias**, *an-an-ee´-as;* of Heb. or. [2608]; *Ananias,* the name of three Isr.:— Ananias.

368. ἀναντίρρητος **anantirrhētŏs**, *an-an-tir´-hray-tos;* from *1* (as a neg. particle) and a presumed der. of a comp. of *473* and *4483; indisputable:—* cannot be spoken against.

369. ἀναντιρρήτως **anantirrhētŏs**, *an-an-tir-hray´-toce;* adv. from *368; promptly:—* without gainsaying.

370. ἀνάξιος **anaxiŏs**, *an-ax´-ee-os;* from *1* (as a neg. particle) and *514; unfit:—* unworthy.

371. ἀναξίως **anaxiŏs**, *an-ax-ee´-oce;* adv. from *370; irreverently:—* unworthily.

372. ἀνάπαυσις **anapausis**, *an-ap´-ŏw-sis;* from *373; intermission;* by impl. *recreation:—* rest.

373. ἀναπαύω **anapauō**, *an-ap-ow´-o;* from *303* and *3973;* (refl.) to *repose* (lit. or fig. [be exempt], remain); by impl. to *refresh:—* take ease, refresh, (give, take) rest.

374. ἀναπείθω **anapĕithō**, *an-ap-i´-tho;* from *303* and *3982;* to *incite:—* persuade.

375. ἀναπέμπω **anapĕmpō**, *an-ap-em´-po;* from *303* and *3992;* to *send up* or *back:—* send (again).

376. ἀνάπηρος **anapērŏs**, *an-ap´-ay-ros);* from *303* (in the sense of *intensity*) and πῆρος **pērŏs** (*maimed*); *crippled:—* maimed.

377. ἀναπίπτω **anapiptō**, *an-ap-ip´-to;* from *303* and *4098;* to *fall back,* i.e. *lie down, lean back:—* lean, sit down (to meat).

378. ἀναπληρόω **anaplērŏō**, *an-ap-lay-rŏ´-o;* from *303* and *4137;* to *complete;* by impl. to *occupy, supply;* fig. to *accomplish* (by coincidence or obedience):— fill up, fulfill, occupy, supply.

379. ἀναπολόγητος **anapŏlŏgētŏs**, *an-ap-ol-og´-ay-tos;* from *1* (as a neg. particle) and a

presumed der. of *626; indefensible:—* without excuse, inexcuseable.

380. ἀναπτύσσω **anaptussō**, *an-ap-toos´-so;* from *303* (in the sense of *reversal*) and *4428;* to *unroll* (a scroll or volume):— open.

381. ἀνάπτω **anaptō**, *an-ap´-to;* from *303* and *681;* to *enkindle:—* kindle, light.

382. ἀναρίθμητος **anarithmētŏs**, *an-ar-ith´-may-tos;* from *1* (as a neg. particle) and a der. of *705; unnumbered,* i.e. *without number:—* innumerable.

383. ἀνασείω **anasĕiō**, *an-as-i´-o;* from *303* and *4579;* fig. to *excite:—* move, stir up.

384. ἀνασκευάζω **anaskĕuazō**, *an-ask-yoo-ad´-zo;* from *303* (in the sense of *reversal*) and a der. of *4632;* prop. to *pack up* (baggage), i.e. (by impl. and fig.) to *upset:—* subvert.

385. ἀνασπάω **anaspaō**, *an-as-pah´-o;* from *303* and *4685;* to *take up* or *extricate:—* draw up, pull out.

386. ἀνάστασις **anastasis**, *an-as´-tas-is;* from *450;* a *standing up* again, i.e. (lit.) a *resurrection* from death (individual, gen. or by impl. [its author]), or (fig.) a (moral) *recovery* (of spiritual truth):— raised to life again, resurrection, rise from the dead, that should rise, rising again.

387. ἀναστατόω **anastatŏō**, *an-as-tat-ŏ´-o;* from a der. of *450* (in the sense of *removal*); prop. to *drive out* of home, i.e. (by impl.) to *disturb* (lit. or fig.):— trouble, turn upside down, make an uproar.

388. ἀνασταυρόω **anastaurŏō**, *an-as-tŏw-rŏ´-o;* from *303* and *4717;* to *recrucify* (fig.):— crucify afresh.

389. ἀναστενάζω **anastĕnazō**, *an-as-ten-ad´-zo;* from *303* and *4727;* to *sigh deeply:—* sigh deeply.

390. ἀναστρέφω **anastrĕphō**, *an-as-tref´-o;* from *303* and *4762;* to *overturn;* also to *return;* by impl. to *busy* oneself, i.e. *remain, live:—* abide, behave self, have conversation, live, overthrow, pass, return, be used.

391. ἀναστροφή **anastrŏphē**, *an-as-trof-ay´;* from *390; behavior:—* conversation.

392. ἀνατάσσομαι **anatassŏmai**, *an-at-as´-som-ahee;* from *303* and the mid. voice of *5021;* to *arrange:—* set in order.

393. ἀνατέλλω **anatĕllō**, *an-at-el´-lo;* from *303* and the base of *5056;* to (*cause* to) *arise:—* (a-, make to) rise, at the rising of, spring (up), be up.

394. ἀνατίθεμαι **anatithĕmai**, *an-at-ith´-em-ahee;* from *303* and the mid. voice of *5087;* to *set forth* (for oneself), i.e. *propound:—* communicate, declare.

395. ἀνατολή **anatŏlē**, *an-at-ol-ay´;* from *393;* a *rising* of light, i.e. *dawn* (fig.); by impl. the *east* (also in plur.):— dayspring, east, rising.

396. ἀνατρέπω **anatrĕpō**, *an-at-rep´-o;* from 303 and the base of 5157; to *overturn* (fig.):— overthrow, subvert.

397. ἀνατρέφω **anatrĕphō**, *an-at-ref´-o;* from 303 and 5142; to *rear* (phys. or ment.):— bring up, nourish (up).

398. ἀναφαίνω **anaphainō**, *an-af-ah´-ee-no;* from 303 and 5316; to *show*, i.e. (refl.) *appear*, or (pass.) to *have pointed* out:— (should) appear, discover.

399. ἀναφέρω **anaphĕrō**, *an-af-er´-o;* from 303 and 5342; to *take up* (lit. or fig.):— bear, bring (carry, lead) up, offer (up).

400. ἀναφωνέω **anaphōnĕō**, *an-af-o-neh´-o;* from 303 and 5455; to *exclaim:*— speak out.

401. ἀνάχυσις **anachusis**, *an-akh´-oo-sis;* from a comp. of 303 and χέω **chĕō** (to *pour*); prop. *effusion*, i.e. (fig.) *license:*— excess.

402. ἀναχωρέω **anachōrĕō**, *an-akh-o-reh´-o;* from 303 and 5562; to *retire:*— depart, give place, go (turn) aside, withdraw self.

403. ἀνάψυξις **anapsuxis**, *an-aps´-ook-sis;* from 404; prop. a *recovery of breath*, i.e. (fig.) *revival:*— revival.

404. ἀναψύχω **anapsuchō**, *an-aps-oo´-kho;* from 303 and 5594; prop. to *cool off*, i.e. (fig.) *relieve:*— refresh.

405. ἀνδραποδιστής **andrapŏdistēs**, *an-drap-od-is-tace´;* from a der. of a comp. of 435 and 4228; an *enslaver* (as bringing *men* to his *feet*):— menstealer.

406. Ἀνδρέας **Andrĕas**, *an-dreh´-as;* from 435; *manly; Andreas*, an Isr.:— Andrew.

407. ἀνδρίζομαι **andrizŏmai**, *an-drid´-zom-ahee;* mid. voice from 435; to *act manly:*— quit like men.

408. Ἀνδρόνικος **Andrŏnikŏs**, *an-dron´-ee-kos;* from 435 and 3534; *man of victory; Andronicos*, an Isr.:— Adronicus.

409. ἀνδροφόνος **andrŏphŏnŏs**, *an-drof-on´-os;* from 435 and 5408; a *murderer:*— manslayer.

410. ἀνέγκλητος **anĕgklētŏs**, *an-eng´-klay-tos;* from 1 (as a neg. particle) and a der. of 1458; *unaccused*, i.e. (by impl.) *irreproachable:*— blameless.

411. ἀνεκδιήγητος **anĕkdiēgētŏs**, *an-ek-dee-ay´-gay-tos;* from 1 (as a neg. particle) and a presumed der. of 1555; *not expounded* in full, i.e. *indescribable:*— unspeakable.

412. ἀνεκλάλητος **anĕklalētŏs**, *an-ek-lal´-ay-tos;* from 1 (as a neg. particle) and a presumed der. of 1583; *not spoken out*, i.e. (by impl.) *unutterable:*— unspeakable.

413. ἀνέκλειπτος **anĕklĕiptŏs**, *an-ek´-lipe-tos;* from 1 (as a neg. particle) and a presumed der. of 1587; *not left out*, i.e. (by impl.) *inexhaustible:*— that faileth not.

414. ἀνεκτότερος **anĕktŏtĕrŏs**, *an-ek-tot´-er-*

os; comp. of a der. of 430; *more endurable:*— more tolerable.

415. ἀνελεήμων **anĕlĕēmōn**, *an-eleh-ay´-mone;* from 1 (as a neg. particle) and 1655; *merciless:*— unmerciful.

416. ἀνεμίζω **anemizō**, *an-em-id´-zo;* from 417; to *toss with the wind:*— drive with the wind.

417. ἄνεμος **anĕmŏs**, *an´-em-os;* from the base of 109; *wind;* (plur.) by impl. (the four) *quarters* (of the earth):— wind.

418. ἀνένδεκτος **anĕndĕktŏs**, *an-en´-dek-tos;* from 1 (as a neg. particle) and a der. of the same as 1735; *unadmitted*, i.e. (by impl.) *not supposable:*— impossible.

419. ἀνεξερεύνητος **anĕxĕrĕunētŏs**, *an-ex-er-yoo´-nay-tos;* from 1 (as a neg. particle) and a presumed der. of 1830; *not searched out*, i.e. (by impl.) *inscrutable:*— unsearchable.

420. ἀνεξίκακος **anĕxikakŏs**, *an-ex-ik´-ak-os;* from 430 and 2556; *enduring of ill*, i.e. *forbearing:*— patient.

421. ἀνεξιχνίαστος **anĕxichniastŏs**, *an-ex-ikh-nee´-as-tos;* from 1 (as a neg. particle) and a presumed der. of a comp. of 1537 and a der. of 2487; *not tracked out*, i.e. (by impl.) *untraceable:*— past finding out; unsearchable.

422. ἀνεπαίσχυντος **anĕpaischuntŏs**, *an-ep-ah´-ee-skhoon-tos;* from 1 (as a neg. particle) and a presumed der. of a comp. of 1909 and 153; *not ashamed*, i.e. (by impl.) *irreprehensible:*— that needeth not to be ashamed.

423. ἀνεπίληπτος **anĕpilēptŏs**, *an-ep-eel´-ape-tos;* from 1 (as a neg. particle) and a der. of 1949; *not arrested*, i.e. (by impl.) *inculpable:*— blameless, unrebukeable.

424. ἀνέρχομαι **anĕrchŏmai**, *an-erkh´-om-ahee;* from 303 and 2064; to *ascend:*— go up.

425. ἄνεσις **anĕsis**, *an´-es-is;* from 447; *relaxation* or (fig.) *relief:*— eased, liberty, rest.

426. ἀνετάζω **anĕtazō**, *an-et-ad´-zo;* from 303 and ἐτάζω **ĕtazō** (to *test*); to *investigate* (judicially):— (should have) examine (-d).

427. ἄνευ **anĕu**, *an´-yoo;* a prim. particle; *without:*— without. Comp. 1.

428. ἀνεύθετος **anĕuthĕtŏs**, *an-yoo´-the-tos;* from 1 (as a neg. particle) and 2111; *not well set*, i.e. *inconvenient:*— not commodious.

429. ἀνευρίσκω **anĕuriskō**, *an-yoo-ris´-ko;* from 303 and 2147; to *find out:*— find.

430. ἀνέχομαι **anĕchŏmai**, *an-ekh´-om-ahee;* mid. voice from 303 and 2192; to *hold oneself up* against, i.e. (fig.) *put up* with:— bear with, endure, forbear, suffer.

431. ἀνέψιος **anĕpsiŏs**, *an-eps´-ee-os;* from

1 (as a particle of union) and an obs. νέπος **nĕpŏs** (a *brood*); prop. *akin*, i.e. (spec.) a *cousin:*— sister's son.

432. ἄνηθον **anēthŏn**, *an´-ay-thon;* prob. of for. or.; *dill:*— anise.

433. ἀνήκω **anēkō**, *an-ay´-ko;* from *303* and *2240;* to *attain to*, i.e. (fig.) *be proper:*— convenient, be fit.

434. ἀνήμερος **anēmĕrŏs**, *an-ay´-mer-os;* from *1* (as a neg. particle) and ἥμερος **hēmĕrŏs** (*lame*); *savage:*— fierce.

435. ἀνήρ **anēr**, *an-ayr´;* a prim. word [comp. *444*]; a *man* (prop. as an indiv. male):— fellow, husband, man, sir.

436. ἀνθίστημι **anthistēmi**, *anth-is´-tay-mee;* from *473* and *2476;* to *stand against*, i.e. *oppose:*— resist, withstand.

437. ἀνθομολογέομαι **anthŏmŏlŏgĕŏmai**, *anth-om-ol-og-eh´-om-ahee;* from *473* and the mid. voice of *3670;* to *confess in turn*, i.e. *respond* in praise:— give thanks.

438. ἄνθος **anthŏs**, *anth´-os;* a prim. word; a *blossom:*— flower.

439. ἀνθρακιά **anthrakia**, *anth-rak-ee-ah´;* from *440;* a bed of burning *coals:*— fire of coals.

440. ἄνθραξ **anthrax**, *anth´-rax;* of uncert. der.; a live *coal:*— coal of fire.

441. ἀνθρωπάρεσκος **anthrōparĕskŏs**, *anth-ro-par´-es-kos;* from *444* and *700; man-courting*, i.e. *fawning:*— men-pleaser.

442. ἀνθρώπινος **anthrōpinŏs**, *anth-ro´-pee-nos;* from *444; human:*— human, common to man, man [-kind], [man-] kind, men's, after the manner of men.

443. ἀνθρωποκτόνος **anthrōpŏktŏnŏs**, *anth-ro-pok-ton´-os;* from *444* and κτείνω **ktĕinō** (to *kill*); a *manslayer:*— murderer. Comp. *5406.*

444. ἄνθρωπος **anthrōpŏs**, *anth´-ro-pos;* from *435* and ὤψ **ōps** (the *countenance;* from *3700*); *man-faced*, i.e. a *human* being:— certain, man.

445. ἀνθυπατεύω **anthupatĕuō**, *anth-oo-pat-yoo´-o;* from *446;* to *act as a proconsul:*— be the deputy.

446. ἀνθύπατος **anthupatŏs**, *anth-oo´-pat-os;* from *473* and a superl. of *5228; instead* of the *highest* officer, i.e. (spec.) a Roman *proconsul:*— deputy.

447. ἀνίημι **aniēmi**, *an-ee´-ay-mee;* from *303* and ἵημι **hiēmi** (to *send*); to *let up*, i.e. (lit.) *slacken* or (fig.) *desert, desist* from:— forbear, leave, loose.

448. ἀνίλεως **anilĕōs**, *an-ee´-leh-oce;* from *1* (as a neg. particle) and *2436; inexorable:*— without mercy.

449. ἄνιπτος **aniptŏs**, *an´-ip-tos;* from *1* (as a neg. particle) and a presumed der. of *3538; without ablution:*— unwashen.

450. ἀνίστημι **anistēmi**, *an-is´-tay-mee;* from

303 and *2476;* to *stand up* (lit. or fig., trans. or intr.):— arise, lift up, raise up (again), rise (again), stand up (-right).

451. Ἄννα **Anna**, *an´-nah;* of Heb. or. [2584]; *Anna*, an Israelitess:— Anna.

452. Ἄννας **Annas**, *an´-nas;* of Heb. or. [2608]; *Annas* (i.e. *367*), an Isr.:— Annas.

453. ἀνόητος **anŏētŏs**, *an-o´-ay-tos;* from *1* (as a neg. particle) and a der. of *3539; unintelligent;* by impl. *sensual:*— fool (-ish), unwise.

454. ἄνοια **anŏia**, *an´-oy-ah;* from a comp. of *1* (as a neg. particle) and *3563 stupidity;* by impl. *rage:*— folly, madness.

455. ἀνοίγω **anŏigō**, *an-oy´-go;* from *303* and οἴγω **ŏigō** (to *open*); to *open up* (lit. or fig., in various applications):— open.

456. ἀνοικοδομέω **anŏikŏdŏmĕō**, *an-oy-kod-om-eh´-o;* from *303* and *3618;* to *rebuild:*— build again.

457. ἄνοιξις **anŏixis**, *an´-oix-is;* from *455; opening* (throat):— × open.

458. ἀνομία **anŏmia**, *an-om-ee´-ah;* from *459; illegality*, i.e. *violation of law* or (gen.) *wickedness:*— iniquity, × transgress (-ion of) the law, unrighteousness.

459. ἄνομος **anŏmŏs**, *an´-om-os;* from *1* (as a neg. particle) and *3551; lawless*, i.e. (neg.) *not subject to* (the Jewish) *law;* (by impl. a *Gentile*), or (pos.) *wicked:*— without law, lawless, transgressor, unlawful, wicked.

460. ἀνόμως **anŏmōs**, *an-om´-oce;* adv. from *459; lawlessly*, i.e. (spec.) *not amenable to* (the Jewish) *law:*— without law.

461. ἀνορθόω **anŏrthŏō**, *an-orth-ŏ´-o;* from *303* and a der. of the base of *3717;* to *straighten up:*— lift (set) up, make straight.

462. ἀνόσιος **anŏsiŏs**, *an-os´-ee-os;* from *1* (as a neg. particle) and *3741; wicked:*— unholy.

463. ἀνοχή **anŏchē**, *an-okh-ay´;* from *430; self-restraint*, i.e. *tolerance:*— forbearance.

464. ἀνταγωνίζομαι **antagōnizŏmai**, *an-tag-o-nid´-zom-ahee;* from *473* and *75;* to *struggle against* (fig.) ["antagonize"]:— strive against.

465. ἀντάλλαγμα **antallagma**, *an-tal´-lag-mah;* from a comp. of *473* and *236;* an *equivalent* or *ransom:*— in exchange.

466. ἀντaναπληρόω **antanaplērŏō**, *an-tan-ap-lay-rŏ´-o;* from *473* and *378;* to *supplement:*— fill up.

467. ἀντaποδίδωμι **antapŏdidōmi**, *an-tap-od-ee´-do-mee;* from *473* and *591;* to *requite* (good or evil):— recompense, render, repay.

468. ἀντaπόδομα **antapŏdŏma**, *an-tap-od´-om-ah;* from *467;* a *requital* (prop. the thing):— recompense.

469. ἀντaπόδοσις **antapŏdŏsis**, *an-tap-od-*

os-is; from *467; requital* (prop. the act):— reward.

470. ἀνταποκρίνομαι **antapŏkrinŏmai,** *an-tap-ok-ree´-nom-ahee;* from *473* and *611;* to *contradict* or *dispute:*— answer again, reply against.

471. ἀντέπω **antĕpō,** *an-tep´-o;* from *473* and *2036;* to *refute* or *deny:*— gainsay, say against.

472. ἀντέχομαι **antĕchŏmai,** *an-tekh´-om-ahee;* from *473* and the mid. voice of *2192;* to *hold* oneself *opposite* to, i.e. (by impl.) *adhere* to; by extens. to *care for:*— hold fast, hold to, support.

473. ἀντί **anti,** *an-tee´;* a prim. particle; *opposite,* i.e. *instead* or *because* of (rarely in *addition* to):— for, in the room of. Often used in composition to denote *contrast, requital, substitution, correspondence,* etc.

474. ἀντιβάλλω **antiballō,** *an-tee-bal´-lo;* from *473* and *906;* to *bandy:*— have.

475. ἀντιδιατίθεμαι **antidiatithĕmai,** *an-tee-dee-at-eeth´-em-ahee;* from *473* and *1303;* to *set* oneself *opposite,* i.e. *be disputatious:*— that oppose themselves.

476. ἀντίδικος **antidikŏs,** *an-tid´-ee-kos;* from *473* and *1349;* an *opponent* (in a lawsuit); spec. *Satan* (as the arch-enemy):— adversary.

477. ἀντίθεσις **antithĕsis,** *an-tith´-es-is;* from a comp. of *473* and *5087; opposition,* i.e. a *conflict* (of theories):— opposition.

478. ἀντικαθίστημι **antikathistēmi,** *an-tee-kath-is´-tay-mee;* from *473* and *2525;* to *set down* (troops) *against,* i.e. *withstand:*— resist.

479. ἀντικαλέω **antikalĕō,** *an-tee-kal-eh´-o;* from *473* and *2564;* to *invite in return:*— bid again.

480. ἀντίκειμαι **antikĕimai,** *an-tik´-i-mahee;* from *473* and *2749;* to *lie opposite,* i.e. *be adverse* (fig. *repugnant*) to:— adversary, be contrary, oppose.

481. ἀντικρύ **antikru,** *an-tee-kroo´;* prol. from *473; opposite:*— over against.

482. ἀντιλαμβάνομαι **antilambanŏmai,** *an-tee-lam-ban´-om-ahee;* from *473* and the mid. voice of *2983;* to *take hold of in turn,* i.e. *succor;* also to *participate:*— help, partaker, support.

483. ἀντίλεγω **antilĕgō,** *an-til´-eg-o;* from *473* and *3004;* to *dispute, refuse:*— answer again, contradict, deny, gainsay (-er), speak against.

484. ἀντίληψις **antilēpsis,** *an-til´-ape-sis;* from *482; relief:*— help.

485. ἀντιλογία **antilŏgia,** *an-tee-log-ee´-ah;* from a der. of *483; dispute, disobedience:*— contradiction, gainsaying, strife.

486. ἀντιλοιδορέω **antilŏidŏrĕō,** *an-tee-loy-dor-eh´-o;* from *473* and *3058;* to *rail in reply:*— revile again.

487. ἀντίλυτρον **antilutrŏn,** *an-til´-oo-tron;* from *473* and *3083;* a *redemption-price:*— ransom.

488. ἀντιμετρέω **antimĕtrĕō,** *an-tee-met-reh´-o;* from *473* and *3354;* to *mete in return:*— measure again.

489. ἀντιμισθία **antimisthia,** *an-tee-mis-thee´-ah;* from a comp. of *473* and *3408; requital, correspondence:*— recompense.

490. Ἀντιόχεια **Antiŏchĕia,** *an-tee-okh´-i-ah;* from Ἀντίοχυς **Antiŏchus** (a Syrian king); *Antiochia,* a place in Syria:— Antioch.

491. Ἀντιοχεύς **Antiŏchĕus,** *an-tee-okh-yoos´;* from *490;* an *Antiochian* or inhab. of Antiochia:— of Antioch.

492. ἀντιπαρέρχομαι **antiparĕrchŏmai,** *an-tee-par-er´-khom-ahee;* from *473* and *3928;* to *go along opposite:*— pass by on the other side.

493. Ἀντίπας **Antipas,** *an-tee´-pas;* contr. for a comp. of *473* and a der. of *3962; Antipas,* a Chr.:— Antipas.

494. Ἀντιπατρίς **Antipatris,** *an-tip-at-rece´;* from the same as *493; Antipatris,* a place in Pal.:— Antipatris.

495. ἀντιπέραν **antipĕran,** *an-tee-per´-an;* from *473* and *4008;* on the *opposite side:*— over against.

496. ἀντιπίπτω **antipiptō,** *an-tee-pip´-to;* from *473* and *4098* (incl. its alt.); to *oppose:*— resist.

497. ἀντιστρατεύομαι **antistratĕuŏmai,** *an-tee-strat-yoo´-om-ahee;* from *473* and *4754;* (fig.) to *attack,* i.e. (by impl.) *destroy:*— war against.

498. ἀντιτάσσομαι **antitassŏmai,** *an-tee-tas´-som-ahee;* from *473* and the mid. voice of *5021;* to *range oneself against,* i.e. *oppose:*— oppose themselves, resist.

499. ἀντίτυπον **antitupŏn,** *an-teet´-oo-pon;* neut. of a comp. of *473* and *5179; corresponding* ["antitype"], i.e. a *representative, counterpart:*— (like) figure (whereunto).

500. ἀντίχριστος **antichristŏs,** *an-tee´-khris-tos;* from *473* and *5547;* an *opponent* of the *Messiah:*— antichrist.

501. ἀντλέω **antlĕō,** *ant-leh-o;* from ἄντλος **antlŏs** (the *hold* of a ship); to *bale* up (prop. bilge water), i.e. *dip* water (with a bucket, pitcher, etc.):— draw (out).

502. ἄντλημα **antlēma,** *ant´-lay-mah;* from *501;* a *baling-vessel:*— thing to draw with.

503. ἀντοφθαλμέω **antŏphthalmĕō,** *ant-of-thal-meh´-o;* from a compound of *473* and *3788;* to *face:*— bear up into.

504. ἄνυδρος **anudrŏs,** *an´-oo-dros;* from *1* (as a neg. particle) and *5204; waterless,* i.e. *dry:*— dry, without water.

505. ἀνυπόκριτος **anupŏkritŏs,** *an-oo-pok-*

ree-tos; from *1* (as a neg. particle) and a presumed der. of *5271; undissembled,* i.e. *sincere:*— without dissimulation (hypocrisy), unfeigned.

506. ἀνυπότακτος **anupŏtaktŏs,** *an-oo-pot´-ak-tos;* from *1* (as a neg. particle) and a presumed der. of *5293; unsubdued,* i.e. *insubordinate* (in fact or temper):— disobedient, that is not put under, unruly.

507. ἄνω **anō,** *an´-o;* adv. from *473; upward* or *on the top:*— above, brim, high, up.

508. ἀνώγεον **anōgĕŏn,** *an-ogue´-eh-on* (or, ἀνάγαιον *an-ag-ahee´-on;* from *507* and *1093; above* the *ground,* i.e. (prop.) the *second floor* of a building; used for a *dome* or a *balcony* on the upper story:— upper room.

509. ἄνωθεν **anōthĕn,** *an´-o-then;* from *507; from above;* by anal. *from the first;* by impl. *anew:*— from above, again, from the beginning (very first), the top.

510. ἀνωτερικός **anōtĕrikŏs,** *an-o-ter-ee-kos´;* from *511; superior,* i.e. (locally) *more remote:*— upper.

511. ἀνώτερος **anōtĕrŏs,** *an-o´-ter-os;* comparative degree of *507; upper,* i.e. (neut. as adv.) to a *more conspicuous* place, in a *former* part of the book:— above, higher.

512. ἀνωφέλες **anōphĕlĕs,** *an-o-fel´-ace;* from *1* (as a neg. particle) and the base of *5624; useless* or (neut.) *inutility:*— unprofitable (-ness).

513. ἀξίνη **axinē,** *ax-ee´-nay;* prob. from ἄγνυμι **agnumi** (to *break;* comp. *4486);* an *axe:*— axe.

514. ἄξιος **axiŏs,** *ax´-ee-os;* prob. from *71; deserving, comparable* or *suitable* (as if *drawing* praise):— due reward, meet, [un-] worthy.

515. ἀξιόω **axiŏō,** *ax-ee-ŏ´-o;* from *514;* to *deem entitled* or *fit:*— desire, think good, count (think) worthy.

516. ἀξίως **axiōs,** *ax-ee´-oce;* adv. from *514; appropriately:*— as becometh, after a godly sort, worthily (-thy).

517. ἀόρατος **aŏratŏs,** *ah-or´-at-os;* from *1* (as a neg. particle) and *3707; invisible:*— invisible (thing).

518. ἀπαγγέλλω **apaggĕllō,** *ap-ang-el´-lo;* from *575* and the base of *32;* to *announce:*— bring word (again), declare, report, shew (again), tell.

519. ἀπάγχομαι **apagchŏmai,** *ap-ang´-khom-ahee* from *575* and ἄγχω **agchō** (to *choke;* akin to the base of *43);* to *strangle oneself off* (i.e. to *death*):— hang himself.

520. ἀπάγω **apagō,** *ap-ag´-o;* from *575* and *71;* to *take off* (in various senses):— bring, carry away, lead (away), put to death, take away.

521. ἀπαίδευτος **apaidĕutŏs,** *ap-ah´-ee-dyoo-tos;* from *1* (as a neg. particle) and a der. of *3811; uninstructed,* i.e. (fig.) *stupid:*— unlearned.

522. ἀπαίρω **apairō,** *ap-ah´-ee-ro;* from *575* and *142;* to *lift off,* i.e. *remove:*— take (away).

523. ἀπαιτέω **apaitĕō,** *ap-ah´-ee-teh-o;* from *575* and *154;* to *demand back:*— ask again, require.

524. ἀπαλγέω **apalgĕō,** *ap-alg-eh´-o;* from *575* and ἀλγέω **algĕō** (to *smart*); to *grieve out,* i.e. *become apathetic:*— be past feeling.

525. ἀπαλλάσσω **apallassō,** *ap-al-las´-so;* from *575* and *236;* to *change away,* i.e. *release,* (refl.) *remove:*— deliver, depart.

526. ἀπαλλοτριόω **apallŏtriŏō,** *ap-al-lot-ree-ŏ´-o;* from *575* and a der. of *245;* to *estrange away,* i.e. (pass. and fig.) to *be non-participant:*— alienate, be alien.

527. ἁπαλός **hapalŏs,** *hap-al-os´;* of uncert. der.; *soft:*— tender.

528. ἀπαντάω **apantaō,** *ap-an-tah´-o;* from *575* and a der. of *473;* to *meet away,* i.e. *encounter:*— meet.

529. ἀπάντησις **apantēsis,** *ap-an´-tay-sis;* from *528;* a (friendly) *encounter:*— meet.

530. ἅπαξ **hapax,** *hap´-ax;* prob. from *537; one* (or a *single*) *time* (numerically or conclusively):— once.

531. ἀπαράβατος **aparabatŏs,** *ap-ar-ab´-at-os;* from *1* (as a neg. particle) and a der. of *3845; not passing away,* i.e. *untransferable* (perpetual):— unchangeable.

532. ἀπαρασκεύαστος **aparaskĕuastŏs,** *ap-ar-ask-yoo´-as-tos;* from *1* (as a neg. particle) and a der. of *3903; unready:*— unprepared.

533. ἀπαρνέομαι **aparnĕŏmai,** *ap-ar-neh´-om-ahee;* from *575* and *720;* to *deny utterly,* i.e. *disown, abstain:*— deny.

534. ἀπάρτι **aparti,** *ap-ar´-tee;* from *575* and *737; from now,* i.e. *henceforth* (already):— from henceforth.

535. ἀπαρτισμός **apartismŏs,** *ap-ar-tis-mos´;* from a der. of *534; completion:*— finishing.

536. ἀπαρχή **aparchē,** *ap-ar-khay´;* from a compound of *575* and *756;* a *beginning* of sacrifice, i.e. the (Jewish) *first-fruit* (fig.):— first-fruits.

537. ἅπας **hapas,** *hap´-as;* from *1* (as a particle of union) and *3956; absolutely all* or (sing.) *every* one:— all (things), every (one), whole.

538. ἀπατάω **apataō,** *ap-at-ah´-o;* of uncert. der.; to *cheat,* i.e. *delude:*— deceive.

539. ἀπάτη **apatē,** *ap-at´-ay;* from *538; delusion:*— deceit (-ful,fulness), deceivableness (-ving).

540. ἀπάτωρ **apatŏr,** *ap-at´-ore;* from *1* (as a neg. particle) and *3962; fatherless,* i.e. *of unrecorded paternity:*— without father.

541. ἀπαύγασμα **apaugasma**, *ap-ŏw´-gas-mah;* from a compound of 575 and 826; an off-flash, i.e. *effulgence:*— brightness.

542. ἀπείδω **apĕidō**, *ap-i´-do;* from 575 and the same as 1492; to *see* fully:— see.

543. ἀπείθεια **apĕithĕia**, *ap-i´-thi-ah;* from 545; *disbelief* (obstinate and rebellious):— disobedience, unbelief.

544. ἀπειθέω **apĕithĕō**, *ap-i-theh´-o;* from 545; to *disbelieve* (wilfully and perversely):— not believe, disobedient, obey not, unbelieving.

545. ἀπειθής **apĕithēs**, *ap-i-thace´;* from 1 (as a neg. particle) and 3982; *unpersuadable*, i.e. *contumacious:*— disobedient.

546. ἀπειλέω **apĕilĕō**, *ap-i-leh´-o;* of uncert. der.; to *menace;* by impl. to *forbid:*— threaten.

547. ἀπειλή **apĕilē**, *ap-i-lay´;* from 546; a *menace:*— × straitly, threatening.

548. ἄπειμι **apĕimi**, *ap´-i-mee;* from 575 and 1510; to *be away:*— be absent. Comp. 549.

549. ἄπειμι **apĕimi**, *ap´-i-mee;* from 575 and εἶμι **ĕimi** (to go); to *go away:*— go. Comp. 548.

550. ἀπειπόμην **apĕipŏmēn**, *ap-i-pom´-ane;* refl. past of a compound of 575 and 2036; to *say off* for oneself, i.e. *disown:*— renounce.

551. ἀπείραστος **apĕirastŏs**, *ap-i´-ras-tos;* from 1 (as a neg. particle) and a presumed der. of 3987; *untried*, i.e. *not temptable:*— not to be tempted.

552. ἄπειρος **apĕirŏs**, *ap´-i-ros;* from 1 (as a neg. particle) and 3984; *inexperienced*, i.e. *ignorant:*— unskillful.

553. ἀπεκδέχομαι **apĕkdĕchŏmai**, *ap-ek-dekh´-om-ahee;* from 575 and 1551; to *expect fully:*— look (wait) for.

554. ἀπεκδύομαι **apĕkduŏmai**, *ap-ek-doo´-om-ahee;* mid. voice from 575 and 1562; to *divest wholly* oneself, or (for oneself) *despoil:*— put off, spoil.

555. ἀπέκδυσις **apĕkdusis**, *ap-ek´-doo-sis;* from 554; *divestment:*— putting off.

556. ἀπελαύνω **apĕlaunō**, *ap-el-ŏw´-no;* from 575 and 1643; to *dismiss:*— drive.

557. ἀπελεγμός **apĕlĕgmŏs**, *ap-el-eg-mos´;* from a compound of 575 and 1651; *refutation*, i.e. (by impl.) *contempt:*— nought.

558. ἀπελεύθερος **apĕlĕuthĕrŏs**, *ap-el-yoo´-ther-os;* from 575 and 1658; one *freed away*, i.e. a *freedman:*— freeman.

559. Ἀπελλῆς **Apĕllēs**, *ap-el-lace´;* of Lat. or.; *Apelles*, a Chr.:— Apelles.

560. ἀπελπίζω **apĕlpizō**, *ap-el-pid´-zo;* from 575 and 1679; to *hope out*, i.e. *fully expect:*— hope for again.

561. ἀπέναντι **apĕnanti**, *ap-en´-an-tee;* from 575 and 1725; *from in front*, i.e. *opposite, before* or *against:*— before, contrary, over against, in the presence of.

ἀπέπω **apĕpō**. See 550.

562. ἀπέραντος **apĕrantŏs**, *ap-er´-an-tos;* from 1 (as a neg. particle) and a second. der. of 4008; *unfinished*, i.e. (by impl.) *interminable:*— endless.

563. ἀπερισπάστως **apĕrispastōs**, *ap-er-is-pas-toce´;* adv. from a compound of 1 (as a neg. particle) and a presumed der. of 4049; *undistractedly*, i.e. *free from* (domestic) *solicitude:*— without distraction.

564. ἀπερίτμητος **apĕritmētŏs**, *ap-er-eet´-may-tos;* from 1 (as a neg. particle) and a presumed der. of 4059; *uncircumcised* (fig.):— uncircumcised.

565. ἀπέρχομαι **apĕrchŏmai**, *ap-erkh´-om-ahee;* from 575 and 2064; to *go off* (i.e. *depart), aside* (i.e. *apart*) or *behind* (i.e. *follow*), lit. or fig.:— come, depart, go (aside, away, back, out, ... ways), pass away, be past.

566. ἀπέχει **apĕchĕi**, *ap-ekh´-i;* third pers. sing. pres. ind. act. of 568 used impers.; *it is sufficient:*— it is enough.

567. ἀπέχομαι **apĕchŏmai**, *ap-ekh´-om-ahee;* mid. voice (refl.) of 568; to *hold oneself off*, i.e. *refrain:*— abstain.

568. ἀπέχω **apĕchō**, *ap-ekh´-o;* from 575 and 2192; (act.) to *have out*, i.e. *receive in full;* (intr.) to *keep* (oneself) *away*, i.e. *be distant* (lit. or fig.):— be, have, receive.

569. ἀπιστέω **apistĕō**, *ap-is-teh´-o;* from 571; to *be unbelieving*, i.e. (trans.) *disbelieve*, or (by impl.) *disobey:*— believe not.

570. ἀπιστία **apistia**, *ap-is-tee´-ah;* from 571; *faithlessness*, i.e. (neg.) *disbelief* (*want of Chr. faith*), or (pos.) *unfaithfulness* (*disobedience*):— unbelief.

571. ἄπιστος **apistŏs**, *ap´-is-tos;* from 1 (as a neg. particle) and 4103; (act.) *disbelieving*, i.e. *without* Chr. faith (spec. a *heathen*); (pass.) *untrustworthy* (person), or *incredible* (thing):— that believeth not, faithless, incredible thing, infidel, unbeliever (-ing).

572. ἁπλότης **haplŏtēs**, *hap-lot´-ace;* from 573; *singleness*, i.e. (subj.) *sincerity* (*without dissimulation* or *self-seeking*), or (obj.) *generosity* (*copious bestowal*):— bountifulness, liberal (-ity), simplicity, singleness.

573. ἁπλοῦς **haplŏus**, *hap-looce´;* prob. from 1 (as a particle of union) and the base of 4120; prop. *folded together*, i.e. *single* (fig. *clear*):— single.

574. ἁπλῶς **haplōs**, *hap-loce´;* adv. from 573 (in the obj. sense of 572); *bountifully:*— liberally.

575. ἀπό **apŏ**, *apŏ´;* a primary particle; "off," i.e. *away* (from something near), in various senses (of place, time, or relation; lit. or fig.):— (× here-) after, ago, at, because of, before, by (the space of), for (-th), from, in, (out) of, off, (up-) on (-ce), since, with. In

Greek

composition (as a prefix) it usually denotes *separation, departure, cessation, completion, reversal,* etc.

576. ἀποβαίνω **apŏbainō**, *ap-ob-ah´-ee-no;* from 575 and the base of *939;* lit. to *disembark;* fig. to *eventuate:*— become, go out, turn.

577. ἀποβάλλω **apŏballō**, *ap-ob-al´-lo;* from 575 and *906;* to *throw off;* fig. to *lose:*— cast away.

578. ἀποβλέπω **apŏblĕpō**, *ap-ob-lep´-o;* from 575 and *991;* to *look away* from everything else, i.e. (fig.) intently *regard:*— have respect.

579. ἀπόβλητος **apŏblētŏs**, *ap-ob´-lay-tos;* from 577; *cast off,* i.e. (fig.) such as to *be rejected:*— be refused.

580. ἀποβολή **apŏbŏlē**, *ap-ob-ol-ay´;* from 577; *rejection;* fig. *loss:*— casting away, loss.

581. ἀπογενόμενος **apŏgĕnŏmĕnŏs**, *ap-og-en-om´-en-os;* past part. of a compound of 575 and *1096; absent,* i.e. *deceased* (fig. *renounced):*— being dead.

582. ἀπογραφή **apŏgraphē**, *ap-og-raf-ay´;* from 583; an *enrollment;* by impl. an *assessment:*— taxing.

583. ἀπογράφω **apŏgraphō**, *ap-og-raf´-o;* from 575 and *1125;* to *write off* (a copy or list), i.e. *enroll:*— tax, write.

584. ἀποδείκνυμι **apŏdĕiknumi**, *ap-od-ike´-noo-mee;* from 575 and *1166;* to *show off,* i.e. *exhibit;* fig. to *demonstrate,* i.e. *accredit:*— (ap-) prove, set forth, shew.

585. ἀπόδειξις **apŏdĕixis**, *ap-od´-ike-sis;* from *584; manifestation:*— demonstration.

586. ἀποδεκατόω **apŏdĕkatŏō**, *ap-od-ek-at-ŏ´-o;* from 575 and *1183;* to *tithe* (as debtor or creditor):— (give, pay, take) tithe.

587. ἀπόδεκτος **apŏdĕktŏs**, *ap-od´-ek-tos;* from 588; *accepted,* i.e. *agreeable:*— acceptable.

588. ἀποδέχομαι **apŏdĕchŏmai**, *ap-od-ekh´-om-ahee;* from 575 and *1209;* to *take fully,* i.e. *welcome* (persons), *approve* (things):— accept, receive (gladly).

589. ἀποδημέω **apŏdēmĕō**, *ap-od-ay-meh´-o;* from 590; to *go abroad,* i.e. *visit a foreign land:*— go (travel) into a far country, journey.

590. ἀπόδημος **apŏdēmŏs**, *ap-od´-ay-mos;* from 575 and *1218; absent from* one's own *people,* i.e. *a foreign traveller:*— taking a far journey.

591. ἀποδίδωμι **apŏdidōmi**, *ap-od-eed´-o-mee;* from 575 and *1325;* to *give away,* i.e. *up, over, back,* etc. (in various applications):— deliver (again), give (again), (re-) pay (-ment be made), perform, recompense, render, requite, restore, reward, sell, yield.

592. ἀποδιορίζω **apŏdiŏrizō**, *ap-od-ee-or-id´-zo;* from 575 and a compound of 1223 and 3724; to *disjoin* (by a boundary, fig. a party):— separate.

593. ἀποδοκιμάζω **apŏdŏkimazō**, *ap-od-ok-ee-mad´-zo;* from 575 and *1381;* to *disapprove,* i.e. (by impl.) to *repudiate:*— disallow, reject.

594. ἀποδοχή **apŏdŏchē**, *ap-od-okh-ay´;* from 588; *acceptance:*— acceptation.

595. ἀπόθεσις **apŏthĕsis**, *ap-oth´-es-is;* from 659; a *laying aside* (lit. or fig.):— putting away (off).

596. ἀποθήκη **apŏthēkē**, *ap-oth-ay´-kay;* from 659; a *repository,* i.e. *granary:*— barn, garner.

597. ἀποθησαυρίζω **apŏthēsaurizō**, *ap-oth-ay-sŏw-rid´-zo;* from 575 and 2343; to *treasure away:*— lay up in store.

598. ἀποθλίβω **apŏthlibō**, *ap-oth-lee-bo;* from 575 and 2346; to *crowd* (from every side):— press.

599. ἀποθνήσκω **apŏthnēskō**, *ap-oth-nace´-ko;* from 575 and 2348; to *die* off (lit. or fig.):— be dead, death, die, lie a-dying, be slain (× with).

600. ἀποκαθίστημι **apŏkathistēmi**, *ap-ok-ath-is´-tay-mee;* from 575 and 2525; to *reconstitute* (in health, home or organization):— restore (again).

601. ἀποκαλύπτω **apŏkaluptō**, *ap-ok-al-oop´-to;* from 575 and 2572; to *take off the cover,* i.e. *disclose:*— reveal.

602. ἀποκάλυψις **apŏkalupsis**, *ap-ok-al´-oop-sis;* from 601; *disclosure:*— appearing, coming, lighten, manifestation, be revealed, revelation.

603. ἀποκαραδοκία **apŏkaradŏkia**, *ap-ok-ar-ad-ok-ee´-ah;* from a compound of 575 and a comp. of κάρα **kara** (the *head*) and 1380 (in the sense of *watching*); *intense anticipation:*— earnest expectation.

604. ἀποκαταλλάσσω **apŏkatallassō**, *ap-ok-at-al-las´-so;* from 575 and 2644; to *reconcile fully:*— reconcile.

605. ἀποκατάστασις **apŏkatastasis**, *ap-ok-at-as´-tas-is;* from 600; *reconstitution:*— restitution.

606. ἀπόκειμαι **apŏkĕimai**, *ap-ok´-i-mahee;* from 575 and 2749; to *be reserved;* fig. to *await:*— be appointed, (be) laid up.

607. ἀποκεφαλίζω **apŏkĕphalizō**, *ap-ok-ef-al-id´-zo;* from 575 and 2776; to *decapitate:*— behead.

608. ἀποκλείω **apŏklĕiō**, *ap-ok-li´-o;* from 575 and 2808; to *close fully:*— shut up.

609. ἀποκόπτω **apŏkŏptō**, *ap-ok-op´-to;* from 575 and 2875; to *amputate;* refl. (by irony) to *mutilate* (the privy parts):— cut off. Comp. 2699.

610. ἀπόκριμα **apŏkrima**, *ap-ok´-ree-mah;*

from *611* (in its orig. sense of *judging*); a judicial *decision:*— sentence.

611. ἀποκρίνομαι **apŏkrinŏmai,** *ap-ok-ree´-nom-ahee;* from *575* and κρίνω **krinō;** to *conclude for oneself,* i.e. (by impl.) to *respond;* by Heb. [comp. 6030] to *begin to speak* (where an address is expected):— answer.

612. ἀπόκρισις **apŏkrisis,** *ap-ok´-ree-sis;* from *611;* a *response:*— answer.

613. ἀποκρύπτω **apŏkruptō,** *ap-ok-roop´-to;* from *575* and *2928;* to *conceal away* (i.e. *fully*); fig. to *keep secret:*— hide.

614. ἀπόκρυφος **apŏkruphŏs,** *ap-ok´-roo-fos;* from *613;* *secret;* by impl. *treasured:*— hid, kept secret.

615. ἀποκτείνω **apŏktĕinō,** *ap-ok-ti´-no;* from *575* and κτείνω **ktĕinō** (to *slay*); to *kill* outright; fig. to *destroy:*— put to death, kill, slay.

616. ἀποκυέω **apŏkuĕō,** *ap-ok-oo-eh´-o;* from *575* and the base of *2949;* to *breed forth,* i.e. (by transf.) to *generate* (fig.):— beget, bring forth.

617. ἀποκυλίω **apŏkuliō,** *ap-ok-oo-lee´-o;* from *575* and *2947;* to *roll away:*— roll away (back).

618. ἀπολαμβάνω **apŏlambanō,** *ap-ol-am-ban´-o;* from *575* and *2983;* to *receive* (spec. in *full,* or as a host); also to *take aside:*— receive, take.

619. ἀπόλαυσις **apŏlausis,** *ap-ol-´ow-sis;* from a compound of *575* and λαύω **lauō** (to *enjoy*); full *enjoyment:*— enjoy (-ment).

620. ἀπολείπω **apŏlĕipō,** *ap-ol-ipe´-o;* from *575* and *3007;* to *leave* behind (pass. *remain*); by impl. to *forsake:*— leave, remain.

621. ἀπολείχω **apŏlĕichō,** *ap-ol-i´-kho;* from *575* and λείχω **lĕichō** (to "*lick*"); to *lick* clean:— lick.

622. ἀπόλλυμι **apŏllumi,** *ap-ol´-loo-mee;* from *575* and the base of *3639;* to *destroy* fully (refl. to *perish,* or *lose*), lit. or fig.:— destroy, die, lose, mar, perish.

623. Ἀπολλύων **Apŏlluōn,** *ap-ol-loo´-ohn;* act. part. of *622;* a *destroyer* (i.e. Satan):— Apollyon.

624. Ἀπολλωνία **Apŏllōnia,** *ap-ol-lo-nee´-ah;* from the pagan deity Ἀπόλλων **Apŏllōn** (i.e. the *sun;* from *622*); *Apollonia,* a place in Macedonia:— Apollonia.

625. Ἀπολλώς **Apŏllōs,** *ap-ol-loce´;* prob. from the same as *624; Apollos,* an Isr.:— Apollos.

626. ἀπολογέομαι **apŏlŏgĕŏmai,** *ap-ol-og-eh´-om-ahee;* mid. voice from a compound of *575* and *3056;* to give an *account* (legal *plea*) of oneself, i.e. *exculpate* (self):— answer (for self), make defence, excuse (self), speak for self.

627. ἀπολογία **apŏlŏgia,** *ap-ol-og-ee´-ah;* from the same as *626;* a *plea* ("apology"):— answer (for self), clearing of self, defence.

628. ἀπολούω **apŏlŏuō,** *ap-ol-oo´-o;* from *575*

and *3068;* to *wash* fully, i.e. (fig.) *have remitted* (refl.):— wash (away).

629. ἀπολύτρωσις **apŏlutrōsis,** *ap-ol-oo´-tro-sis;* from a compound of *575* and *3083;* (the act) *ransom* in full, i.e. (fig.) *riddance,* or (spec.) Chr. *salvation:*— deliverance, redemption.

630. ἀπολύω **apŏluō,** *ap-ol-oo´-o;* from *575* and *3089;* to *free* fully, i.e. (lit.) *relieve, release, dismiss* (refl. *depart*), or (fig.) *let die, pardon* or (spec.) *divorce:*— (let) depart, dismiss, divorce, forgive, let go, loose, put (send) away, release, set at liberty.

631. ἀπομάσσομαι **apŏmassŏmai,** *ap-om-as´-som-ahee;* mid. voice from *575* and μάσσω **massō** (to *squeeze, knead, smear*); to *scrape away:*— wipe off.

632. ἀπονέμω **apŏnĕmō,** *ap-on-em´-o;* from *575* and the base of *3551;* to *apportion,* i.e. *bestow:*— give.

633. ἀπονίπτω **apŏniptō,** *ap-on-ip´-to;* from *575* and *3538;* to *wash off* (refl. one's own hands symb.):— wash.

634. ἀποπίπτω **apŏpiptō,** *ap-op-ip´-to;* from *575* and *4098;* to *fall off:*— fall.

635. ἀποπλανάω **apŏplanaō,** *ap-op-lan-ah´-o;* from *575* and *4105;* to *lead astray* (fig.); pass. to *stray* (from truth):— err, seduce.

636. ἀποπλέω **apŏplĕō,** *ap-op-leh´-o;* from *575* and *4126;* to *set sail:*— sail away.

637. ἀποπλύνω **apŏplunō,** *ap-op-loo´-no;* from *575* and *4150;* to *rinse off:*— wash.

638. ἀποπνίγω **apŏpnigō,** *ap-op-nee´-go;* from *575* and *4155;* to *stifle* (by drowning or overgrowth):— choke.

639. ἀπορέω **apŏrĕō,** *ap-or-eh´-o;* from a compound of *1* (as a neg. particle) and the base of *4198;* to *have no way* out, i.e. *be at a loss* (mentally):— (stand in) doubt, be perplexed.

640. ἀπορία **apŏria,** *ap-or-ee´-a;* from the same as *639;* a (state of) *quandary:*— perplexity.

641. ἀπορρίπτω **apŏrrhiptō,** *ap-or-hrip´-to;* from *575* and *4496;* to *hurl off,* i.e. *precipitate* (oneself):— cast.

642. ἀπορφανίζω **apŏrphanizō,** *ap-or-fan-id´-zo;* from *575* and a der. of *3737;* to *bereave wholly,* i.e. (fig.) *separate* (from intercourse):— take.

643. ἀποσκευάζω **apŏskĕuazō,** *ap-osk-yoo-ad´-zo;* from *575* and a der. of *4632;* to *pack up* (one's) *baggage:*— take up ... carriages.

644. ἀποσκίασμα **apŏskiasma,** *ap-os-kee´-as-mah;* from a compound of *575* and a der. of *4639;* a *shading off,* i.e. *obscuration:*— shadow.

645. ἀποσπάω **apŏspaō,** *ap-os-pah´-o;* from *575* and *4685;* to *drag forth,* i.e. (lit.) *unsheathe* (a sword), or rel. (with a degree of force impl.) *retire* (pers. or factiously):— (with-) draw (away), after we were gotten from.

646. ἀποστασία **apŏstasia**, *ap-os-tas-ee´-ah*; fem. of the same as *647*; *defection* from truth (prop. the state) ["apostasy"]:— falling away, forsake.

647. ἀποστάσιον **apŏstasiŏn**, *ap-os-tas´-ee-on*; neut. of a (presumed) adj. from a der. of *868*; prop. something *separative*, i.e. (spec.) *divorce:*— (writing of) divorcement.

648. ἀποστεγάζω **apŏstĕgazō**, *ap-os-teg-ad´-zo*; from *575* and a der. of *4721*; to *unroof:*— uncover.

649. ἀποστέλλω **apŏstĕllō**, *ap-os-tel´-lo*; from *575* and *4724*; *set apart*, i.e. (by impl.) to *send out* (prop. on a mission) lit. or fig.:— put in, send (away, forth, out), set [at liberty].

650. ἀποστερέω **apŏstĕrĕō**, *ap-os-ter-eh´-o*; from *575* and στερέω **stĕrĕō** (to *deprive*); to *despoil:*— defraud, destitute, kept back by fraud.

651. ἀποστολή **apŏstŏlē**, *ap-os-tol-ay´*; from *649*; *commission*, i.e. (spec.) *apostolate:*— apostleship.

652. ἀπόστολος **apŏstŏlŏs**, *ap-os´-tol-os*; from *649*; a *delegate*; spec. an *ambassador* of the Gospel; officially a *commissioner* of Christ ["*apostle*"] (with miraculous powers):— apostle, messenger, he that is sent.

653. ἀποστοματίζω **apŏstŏmatizō**, *ap-os-tom-at-id´-zo*; from *575* and a (presumed) der. of *4750*; to *speak off-hand* (prop. *dictate*), i.e. to *catechize* (in an invidious manner):— provoke to speak.

654. ἀποστρέφω **apŏstrĕphō**, *ap-os-tref´-o*; from *575* and *4762*; to *turn away* or *back* (lit. or fig.):— bring again, pervert, turn away (from).

655. ἀποστυγέω **apŏstugĕō**, *ap-os-toog-eh´-o*; from *575* and the base of *4767*; to *detest* utterly:— abhor.

656. ἀποσυνάγωγος **apŏsunagōgŏs**, *ap-os-oon-ag´-o-gos*; from *575* and *4864*; *excommunicated:*— (put) out of the synagogue (-s).

657. ἀποτάσσομαι **apŏtassŏmai**, *ap-ot-as´-som-ahee*; mid. voice from *575* and *5021*; lit. to *say adieu* (by departing or dismissing); fig. to *renounce:*— bid farewell, forsake, take leave, send away.

658. ἀποτελέω **apŏtĕlĕō**, *ap-ot-el-eh´-o*; from *575* and *5055*; to *complete entirely*, i.e. *consummate:*— finish.

659. ἀποτίθημι **apŏtithēmi**, *ap-ot-eeth´-ay-mee*; from *575* and *5087*; to *put away* (lit. or fig.):— cast off, lay apart (aside, down), put away (off).

660. ἀποτινάσσω **apŏtinassō**, *ap-ot-in-as´-so*; from *575* and τινάσσω **tinassō** (to *jostle*); to *brush off:*— shake off.

661. ἀποτίνω **apŏtinō**, *ap-ot-ee´-no*; from *575* and *5099*; to *pay* in full:— repay.

662. ἀποτολμάω **apŏtŏlmaō**, *ap-ot-ol-mah´-o*; from *575* and *5111*; to *venture* plainly:— be very bold.

663. ἀποτομία **apŏtŏmia**, *ap-ot-om-ee´-ah*; from the base of *664*; (fig.) *decisiveness*, i.e. *rigor:*— severity.

664. ἀποτόμως **apŏtŏmōs**, *ap-ot-om´-oce*; adv. from a der. of a compound of *575* and τέμνω **tĕmnō** (to *cut*); *abruptly*, i.e. peremptorily:— sharply (-ness).

665. ἀποτρέπω **apŏtrĕpō**, *ap-ot-rep´-o*; from *575* and the base of *5157*; to *deflect*, i.e. (refl.) *avoid:*— turn away.

666. ἀπουσία **apŏusia**, *ap-oo-see´-ah*; from the part. of *548*; a *being away:*— absence.

667. ἀποφέρω **apŏhĕrō**, *ap-of-er´-o*; from *575* and *5342*; to *bear off* (lit. or rel.):— bring, carry (away).

668. ἀποφεύγω **apŏphĕugō**, *ap-of-yoo´-go*; from *575* and *5343*; (fig.) to *escape:*— escape.

669. ἀποφθέγγομαι **apŏphthĕggŏmai**, *ap-of-theng´-om-ahee*; from *575* and *5350*; to *enunciate* plainly, i.e. *declare:*— say, speak forth, utterance.

670. ἀποφορτίζομαι **apŏphŏrtizŏmai**, *ap-of-or-tid´-zom-ahee*; from *575* and the mid. voice of *5412*; to *unload:*— unlade.

671. ἀπόχρησις **apŏchrēsis**, *ap-okh´-ray-sis*; from a compound of *575* and *5530*; the act of *using up*, i.e. *consumption:*— using.

672. ἀποχωρέω **apŏchōrĕō**, *ap-okh-o-reh´-o*; from *575* and *5562*; to *go away:*— depart.

673. ἀποχωρίζω **apŏchōrizō**, *ap-okh-o-rid´-zo*; from *575* and *5563*; to *rend apart*; refl. to *separate:*— depart (asunder).

674. ἀποψύχω **apŏpsuchō**, *ap-ops-oo´-kho*; from *575* and *5594*; to *breathe out*, i.e. *faint:*— hearts failing.

675. Ἄππιος **'Appiŏs**, *ap´-pee-os*; of Lat. or.; (in the gen., i.e. possessive case) of *Appius*, the name of a Rom.:— Appii.

676. ἀπρόσιτος **aprŏsitŏs**, *ap-ros´-ee-tos*; from *1* (as a neg. particle) and a der. of a compound of *4314* and εἰμι **ĕimi** (to *go*); *inaccessible:*— which no man can approach.

677. ἀπρόσκοπος **aprŏskŏpŏs**, *ap-ros´-kop-os*; from *1* (as a neg. particle) and a presumed der. of *4350*; act. *inoffensive*, i.e. *not leading into sin*; pass. *faultless*, i.e. *not led into sin:*— none (void of, without) offence.

678. ἀπροσωπολήπτως **aprŏsōpŏlēptōs**, *ap-ros-o-pol-ape´-toce*; adv. from a compound of *1* (as a neg. particle) and a presumed der. of a presumed comp. of *4383* and *2983* [comp. *4381*]; in a way *not accepting* the

person, i.e. *impartially:*— without respect of persons.

679. ἄπταιστος **aptaistŏs**, *ap-tah´-ee-stos*; from *1* (as a neg. particle) and a der. of *4417*; *not stumbling*, i.e. (fig.) *without sin:*— from falling.

680. ἅπτομαι **haptŏmai**, *hap´-tom-ahee*; refl. of *681*; prop. to *attach* oneself to, i.e. to *touch* (in many impl. relations):— touch.

681. ἅπτω **haptō**, *hap´-to*; a primary verb; prop. to *fasten* to, i.e. (spec.) to *set on fire:*— kindle, light.

682. Ἀπφία **Apphia**, *ap-fee´-a*; prob. of for. or.; *Apphia*, a woman of Collosæ:— Apphia.

683. ἀπωθέομαι **apōthĕŏmai**, *ap-o-theh´-om-ahee*; or ἀπώθομαι **apōthŏmai**, *ap-o´-thom-ahee*; from *575* and the mid. voice of ὠθέω **ōthĕō** or ὤθω **ōthō** (to *shove*); to *push off*, fig. to *reject:*— cast away, put away (from), thrust away (from).

684. ἀπώλεια **apōlĕia**, *ap-o´-li-a*; from a presumed der. of *622*; *ruin* or *loss* (phys. spiritual or eternal):— damnable (-nation), destruction, die, perdition, × perish, pernicious ways, waste.

685. ἀρά **ara**, *ar-ah´*; prob. from *142*; prop. *prayer* (as *lifted* to Heaven), i.e. (by impl.) *imprecation:*— curse.

686. ἄρα **ara**, *ar´-ah*; prob. from *142* (through the idea of *drawing* a conclusion); a particle denoting an *inference* more or less decisive (as follows):— haply, (what) manner (of man), no doubt, perhaps, so be, then, therefore, truly, wherefore. Often used in connection with other particles, esp. *1065* or *3767* (after) or *1487* (before). Comp. also *687*.

687. ἆρα **ara**, *ar´-ah*; a form of *686*, denoting an *interrogation* to which a negative answer is presumed:— therefore.

688. Ἀραβία **Arabia**, *ar-ab-ee´-ah*; of Heb. or. [6152]; *Arabia*, a region of Asia:— Arabia.

ἄραγε **aragĕ**. See *686* and *1065*.

689. Ἀράμ **Aram**, *ar-am´*; of Heb. or. [7410]; *Aram* (i.e. *Ram*), an Isr.:— Aram.

690. Ἄραψ **ʼAraps**, *ar´-aps*; from *688*; an *Arab* or native of Arabia:— Arabian.

691. ἀργέω **argĕō**, *arg-eh´-o*; from *692*; to be *idle*, i.e. (fig.) to *delay:*— linger.

692. ἀργός **argŏs**, *ar-gos´*; from *1* (as a neg. particle) and *2041*; *inactive*, i.e. *unemployed*; (by impl.) *lazy, useless:*— barren, idle, slow.

693. ἀργύρεος **argurĕŏs**, *ar-goo´-reh-os*; from *696*; made *of silver:*— (of) silver.

694. ἀργύριον **arguriŏn**, *ar-goo´-ree-on*; neut. of a presumed der. of *696*; *silvery*, i.e. (by impl.) *cash*; spec. a *silverling* (i.e. *drachma* or *shekel*):— money, (piece of) silver (piece).

695. ἀργυροκόπος **argurŏkŏpŏs**, *ar-goo-rok-op´-os*; from *696* and *2875*; a *beater* (i.e. *worker*) *of silver:*— silversmith.

696. ἄργυρος **argurŏs**, *ar´-goo-ros*; from ἀργός **argŏs** (*shining*); *silver* (the metal, in the articles or coin):— silver.

697. Ἄρειος Πάγος **Arĕiŏs Pagŏs**, *ar´-i-os pag´-os*; from Ἄρης **Arēs** (the name of the Greek deity of war) and a der. of *4078*; *rock of Ares*, a place in Athens:— Areopagus, Mars' Hill.

698. Ἀρεοπαγίτης **Arĕŏpagitēs**, *ar-eh-op-ag-ee´-tace*; from *697*; an *Areopagite* or member of the court held on Mars' Hill:— Areopagite.

699. ἀρέσκεια **arĕskĕia**, *ar-es´-ki-ah*; from a der. of *700*; *complaisance:*— pleasing.

700. ἀρέσκω **arĕskō**, *ar-es´-ko*; prob. from *142* (through the idea of *exciting* emotion); to be *agreeable* (or by impl. to seek to be so):— please.

701. ἀρεστός **arĕstŏs**, *ar-es-tos´*; from *700*; *agreeable*; by impl. *fit:*— (things that) please (-ing), reason.

702. Ἀρέτας **Arĕtas**, *ar-et´-as*; of for. or.; *Aretas*, an Arabian:— Aretas.

703. ἀρέτη **arĕtē**, *ar-et´-ay*; from the same as *730*; prop. *manliness* (*valor*), i.e. *excellence* (intrinsic or attributed):— praise, virtue.

704. ἀρήν **arēn**, *ar-ane´*; perh. the same as *730*; a *lamb* (as a *male*):— lamb.

705. ἀριθμέω **arithmĕō**, *ar-ith-meh´-o*; from *706*; to *enumerate* or *count:*— number.

706. ἀριθμός **arithmŏs**, *ar-ith-mos´*; from *142*; a *number* (as reckoned *up*):— number.

707. Ἀριμαθαία **Arimathaia**, *ar-ee-math-ah´-ee-ah*; of Heb. or. [7414]; *Arimathæa* (or *Ramah*), a place in Pal.:— Arimathæa.

708. Ἀρίσταρχος **Aristarchŏs**, *ar-is´-tar-khos*; from the same as *712* and *757*; *best ruling*; *Aristarchus*, a Macedonian:— Aristarchus.

709. ἀριστάω **aristaō**, *ar-is-tah´-o*; from *712*; to *take the principle meal:*— dine.

710. ἀριστερός **aristĕrŏs**, *ar-is-ter-os´*; appar. a comparative of the same as *712*; the *left* hand (as *second-best*):— left [hand].

711. Ἀριστόβουλος **Aristŏbŏulŏs**, *ar-is-tob´-oo-los*; from the same as *712* and *1012*; *best counselling*; *Aristoboulus*, a Chr.:— Aristobulus.

712. ἄριστον **aristŏn**, *ar´-is-ton*; appar. neut. of a superl. from the same as *730*; the *best* meal [or *breakfast*; perh. from ἦρι **ēri** ("early")], i.e. *luncheon:*— dinner.

713. ἀρκετός **arkĕtŏs**, *ar-ket-os´*; from *714*; *satisfactory:*— enough, suffice (-ient).

714. ἀρκέω **arkĕō**, *ar-keh´-o*; appar. a primary verb [but prob. akin to *142* through the idea of *raising* a barrier]; prop. to *ward off*, i.e. (by impl.) to *avail* (fig. *be satisfac-*

tory):— be content, be enough, suffice, be sufficient.

715. ἄρκτος **arktŏs**, *ark´-tos;* prob. from *714;* a *bear* (as *obstructing* by ferocity):— bear.

716. ἅρμα **harma**, *har´-mah;* prob. from *142* [perh. with *1* (as a particle of union) prefixed]; a *chariot* (as *raised* or fitted *together* [comp. *719*]):— chariot.

717. Ἀρμαγεδδών **Armagĕddōn**, *ar-mag-ed-dohn´;* of Heb. or. [*2022* and *4023*]; *Armageddon* (or *Har-Meggiddon*), a symbol. name:— Armageddon.

718. ἁρμόζω **harmŏzō**, *har-mod´-zo;* from *719;* to *joint,* i.e. (fig.) to *woo* (refl. to *betroth*):— espouse.

719. ἁρμός **harmŏs**, *har-mos´;* from the same as *716;* an *articulation* (of the body):— joint.

720. ἀρνέομαι **arnĕŏmai**, *ar-neh´-om-ahee;* perh. from *1* (as a neg. particle) and the mid. voice of *4483;* to *contradict,* i.e. *disavow, reject, abnegate:*— deny, refuse.

721. ἀρνίον **arniŏn**, *ar-nee´-on;* dimin. from *704;* a *lambkin:*— lamb.

722. ἀροτριόω **arŏtriŏō**, *ar-ot-ree-o´-o;* from *723;* to *plough:*— plow.

723. ἄροτρον **arŏtrŏn**, *ar´-ot-ron;* from ἀρόω **arŏō** (to *till*); a *plow:*— plow.

724. ἁρπαγή **harpagē**, *har-pag-ay´;* from *726;* *pillage* (prop. abstr.):— extortion, ravening, spoiling.

725. ἁρπαγμός **harpagmŏs**, *har-pag-mos´;* from *726;* *plunder* (prop. concr.):— robbery.

726. ἁρπάζω **harpazō**, *har-pad´-zo;* from a der. of *138;* to *seize* (in various applications):— catch (away, up), pluck, pull, take (by force).

727. ἅρπαξ **harpax**, *har´-pax;* from *726;* *rapacious:*— extortion, ravening.

728. ἀρραβών **arrhabōn**, *ar-hrab-ohn´;* of Heb. or. [*6162*]; a *pledge,* i.e. part of the purchase-money or property given in advance as *security* for the rest:— earnest.

729. ἄρραφος **arrhaphŏs**, *ar´-hraf-os;* from *1* (as a neg. particle) and a presumed der. of the same as *4476;* *unsewed,* i.e. of a single piece:— without seam.

730. ἄρρην **arrhēn**, *ar´-hrane;* or

     ἄρσην **arsēn**, *ar´-sane;* prob. from *142;* *male* (as stronger for *lifting*):— male, man.

731. ἄρρητος **arrhētŏs**, *ar´-hray-tos;* from *1* (as a neg. particle) and the same as *4490;* *unsaid,* i.e. (by impl.) *inexpressible:*— unspeakable.

732. ἄρρωστος **arrhōstŏs**, *ar´-hroce-tos;* from *1* (as a neg. particle) and a presumed der. of *4517;* *infirm:*— sick (folk, -ly).

733. ἀρσενοκοίτης **arsĕnŏkŏitēs**, *ar-sen-ok-oy´-tace;* from *730* and *2845;* a *sodomite:*— abuser of (that defile) self with mankind.

734. Ἀρτεμάς **Artĕmas**, *ar-tem-as´;* contr. from a compound of *735* and *1435; gift of Artemis; Artemas* (or *Artemidorus*), a Chr.:— Artemas.

735. Ἄρτεμις **Artĕmis**, *ar´-tem-is;* prob. from the same as *736; prompt; Artemis,* the name of a Grecian goddess borrowed by the Asiatics for one of their deities:— Diana.

736. ἀρτέμων **artĕmōn**, *ar-tem´-ohn;* from a der. of *737;* prop. something *ready* [or else more remotely from *142* (comp. *740*); something *hung* up], i.e. (spec.) the *topsail* (rather *foresail* or *jib*) of a vessel:— mainsail.

737. ἄρτι **arti**, *ar´-tee;* adv. from a der. of *142* (comp. *740*) through the idea of *suspension;* just *now:*— this day (hour), hence [-forth], here [-after], hither [-to], (even) now, (this) present.

738. ἀρτιγέννητος **artigĕnnētŏs**, *ar-teeg-en´-nay-tos;* from *737* and *1084; just born,* i.e. (fig.) a *young convert:*— new born.

739. ἄρτιος **artiŏs**, *ar´-tee-os;* from *737; fresh,* i.e. (by impl.) *complete:*— perfect.

740. ἄρτος **artos**, *ar´-tos;* from *142; bread* (as *raised*) or a *loaf:*— (shew-) bread, loaf.

741. ἀρτύω **artuō**, *ar-too´-o;* from a presumed der. of *142;* to *prepare,* i.e. *spice* (with *stimulating* condiments):— season.

742. Ἀρφαξάδ **Arphaxad**, *ar-fax-ad´;* of Heb. or. [*775*]; *Arphaxad,* a post-diluvian patriarch:— Arphaxad.

743. ἀρχάγγελος **archaggĕlŏs**, *ar-khang´-el-os;* from *757* and *32;* a *chief angel:*— archangel.

744. ἀρχαῖος **archaiŏs**, *ar-khah´-yos;* from *746; original* or *primeval:*— (them of) old (time).

745. Ἀρχέλαος **Archĕlaŏs**, *ar-khel´-ah-os;* from *757* and *2994; people-ruling; Archelaus,* a Jewish king:— Archelaus.

746. ἀρχή **archē**, *ar-khay´;* from *756;* (prop. abstr.) a *commencement,* or (concr.) *chief* (in various applications of order, time, place, or rank):— beginning, corner, (at the, the) first (estate), magistrate, power, principality, principle, rule.

747. ἀρχηγός **archēgŏs**, *ar-khay-gos´;* from *746* and *71;* a *chief leader:*— author, captain, prince.

748. ἀρχιερατικός **archiĕratikŏs**, *ar-khee-er-at-ee-kos´;* from *746* and a der. of *2413; high-priestly:*— of the high-priest.

749. ἀρχιερεύς **archiĕrĕus**, *ar-khee-er-yuce´;* from *746* and *2409;* the *high-priest* (lit. of the Jews, typ. Christ); by extens. a *chief priest:*— chief (high) priest, chief of the priests.

750. ἀρχιποίμην **archipŏimēn**, *ar-khee-*

poy´-mane; from *746* and *4166;* a *head shepherd:*— chief shepherd.

751. Ἄρχιππος **Archippŏs,** *ar´-khip-pos;* from *746* and *2462; horse-ruler; Archippus,* a Chr.:— Archippus.

752. ἀρχισυνάγωγος **archisunagōgŏs,** *ar-khee-soon-ag´-o-gos;* from *746* and *4864; director of* the *synagogue* services:— (chief) ruler of the synagogue.

753. ἀρχιτέκτων **architĕktōn,** *ar-khee-tek´-tone;* from *746* and *5045;* a *chief constructor,* i.e. "*architect*":— masterbuilder.

754. ἀρχιτελώνης **architĕlōnēs,** *ar-khee-tel-o´-nace;* from *746* and *5057;* a *principle tax-gatherer:*— chief among the publicans.

755. ἀρχιτρίκλινος **architriklinŏs,** *ar-khee-tree´-klee-nos;* from *746* and a compound of *5140* and *2827* (a *dinner-bed,* because composed of three couches); *director of* the *entertainment:*— governor (ruler) of the feast.

756. ἄρχομαι **archŏmai,** *ar´-khom-ahee;* mid. voice of *757* (through the impl. of *precedence*); to *commence* (in order of time):— (rehearse from the) begin (-ning).

757. ἄρχω **archō,** *ar´-kho;* a primary verb; to be *first* (in political rank or power):— reign (rule) over.

758. ἄρχων **archōn,** *ar´-khone;* pres. part. of *757;* a *first* (in rank or power):— chief (ruler), magistrate, prince, ruler.

759. ἄρωμα "**arōma,**" *ar´-o-mah;* from *142* (in the sense of *sending* off scent); an *aromatic:*— (sweet) spice.

760. Ἀσά **Asa,** *as-ah´;* of Heb. or. [609]; *Asa,* an Isr.:— Asa.

761. ἀσάλευτος **asalĕutŏs,** *as-al´-yoo-tos;* from *1* (as a neg. particle) and a der. of *4531; unshaken,* i.e. (by impl.) *immovable* (fig.):— which cannot be moved, unmovable.

762. ἄσβεστος **asbĕstŏs,** *as´-bes-tos;* from *1* (as a neg. particle) and a der. of *4570; not extinguished,* i.e. (by impl.) *perpetual:*— not to be quenched, unquenchable.

763. ἀσέβεια **asĕbĕia,** *as-eb´-i-ah;* from *765; impiety,* i.e. (by impl.) *wickedness:*— ungodly (-liness).

764. ἀσεβέω **asĕbĕō,** *as-eb-eh´-o;* from *765;* to be (by impl. *act*) *impious* or *wicked:*— commit (live, that after should live) ungodly.

765. ἀσεβής **asĕbēs,** *as-eb-ace´;* from *1* (as a neg. particle) and a presumed der. of *4576; irreverent,* i.e. (by extens.) *impious* or *wicked:*— ungodly (man).

766. ἀσέλγεια **asĕlgĕia,** *as-elg´-i-a;* from a compound of *1* (as a neg. particle) and a presumed σελγής **sĕlgēs** (of uncert. der., but appar. mean. *continent*); *licentiousness* (sometimes incl. other vices):— filthy, lasciviousness, wantonness.

767. ἄσημος **asēmŏs,** *as´-ay-mos;* from *1* (as a

neg. particle) and the base of *4591; unmarked,* i.e. (fig.) *ignoble:*— mean.

768. Ἀσήρ **Asēr,** *as-ayr´;* of Heb. or. [836]; *Aser* (i.e. *Asher*), an Isr. tribe:— Aser.

769. ἀσθένεια **asthĕnĕia,** *as-then´-i-ah;* from *772; feebleness* (of body or mind); by impl. *malady;* mor. *frailty:*— disease, infirmity, sickness, weakness.

770. ἀσθενέω **asthĕnĕō,** *as-then-eh´-o;* from *772;* to *be feeble* (in any sense):— be diseased, impotent folk (man), (be) sick, (be, be made) weak.

771. ἀσθένημα **asthĕnēma,** *as-then´-ay-mah;* from *770;* a *scruple* of conscience:— infirmity.

772. ἀσθενής **asthĕnēs,** *as-then-ace´;* from *1* (as a neg. particle) and the base of *4599; strengthless* (in various applications, lit., fig. and mor.):— more feeble, impotent, sick, without strength, weak (-er, -ness, thing).

773. Ἀσία **Asia,** *as-ee´-ah;* of uncert. der.; *Asia,* i.e. *Asia Minor,* or (usually) only its western shore:— Asia.

774. Ἀσιανός **Asianŏs,** *as-ee-an-os´;* from *773;* an *Asian* (i.e. *Asiatic*) or an inhabitant of Asia:— of Asia.

775. Ἀσιάρχης **Asiarchēs,** *as-ee-ar´-khace;* from *773* and *746;* an *Asiarch* or president of the public festivities in a city of Asia Minor:— chief of Asia.

776. ἀσιτία **asitia,** *as-ee-tee´-ah;* from *777; fasting* (the state):— abstinence.

777. ἄσιτος **asitŏs,** *as´-ee-tos;* from *1* (as a neg. particle) and *4621; without* (taking) *food:*— fasting.

778. ἀσκέω **askĕō,** *as-keh´-o;* prob. from the same as *4632;* to *elaborate,* i.e. (fig.) *train* (by impl. *strive*):— exercise.

779. ἀσκός **askŏs,** *as-kos´;* from the same as *778;* a leathern (or skin) *bag* used as a bottle:— bottle.

780. ἀσμένως **asmĕnōs,** *as-men´-oce;* adv. from a der. of the base of *2237; with pleasure:*— gladly.

781. ἄσοφος **asŏphŏs,** *as´-of-os;* from *1* (as a neg. particle) and *4680; unwise:*— fool.

782. ἀσπάζομαι **aspazŏmai,** *as-pad´-zom-ahee;* from *1* (as a particle of union) and a presumed form of *4685;* to *enfold* in the arms, i.e. (by impl.) to *salute,* (fig.) to *welcome:*— embrace, greet, salute, take leave.

783. ἀσπασμός **aspasmŏs,** *as-pas-mos´;* from *782;* a *greeting* (in person or by letter):— greeting, salutation.

784. ἄσπιλος **aspilŏs,** *as´-pee-los;* from *1* (as a neg. particle) and *4695; unblemished* (phys. or mor.):— without spot, unspotted.

785. ἀσπίς **aspis,** *as-pece´;* of uncert. der.; a

buckler (or *round* shield); used of a serpent (as *coiling* itself), prob. the "*asp*":— asp.

786. ἄσπονδος **aspŏndŏs**, *as´-pon-dos;* from *1* (as a neg. particle) and a der. of *4689;* lit. *without libation* (which usually accompanied a treaty), i.e. (by impl.) *truceless:*— implacable, truce-breaker.

787. ἀσσάριον **assariŏn**, *as-sar´-ee-on;* of Lat. or.; an *assarius* or *as*, a Roman coin:— farthing.

788. ἆσσον **assŏn**, *as´-son;* neut. comparative of the base of *1451; more nearly*, i.e. *very near:*— close.

789. Ἄσσος **Assŏs**, *as´-sos;* prob. of for. or.; *Assus*, a city of Asia Minor:— Assos.

790. ἀστατέω **astatĕō**, *as-tat-eh´-o;* from *1* (as a neg. particle) and a der. of *2476;* to *be non-stationary*, i.e. (fig.) *homeless:*— have no certain dwelling-place.

791. ἀστεῖος **astĕiŏs**, *as-ti´-os;* from ἄστυ **astu** (a *city*); *urbane*, i.e. (by impl.) *handsome:*— fair.

792. ἀστήρ **astēr**, *as-tare´;* prob. from the base of *4766;* a *star* (as *strown* over the sky), lit. or fig.:— star.

793. ἀστήρικτος **astēriktŏs**, *as-tay´-rik-tos;* from *1* (as a neg. particle) and a presumed der. of *4741; unfixed*, i.e. (fig.) *vacillating:*— unstable.

794. ἄστοργος **astŏrgŏs**, *as´-tor-gos;* from *1* (as a neg. particle) and a presumed der. of στέργω **stĕrgō** (to *cherish* affectionately); *hard-hearted* toward kindred:— without natural affection.

795. ἀστοχέω **astŏchĕō**, *as-tokh-eh´-o;* from a compound of *1* (as a neg. particle) and στοῖχος **stŏichŏs** (an *aim*); to *miss* the mark, i.e. (fig.) *deviate* from truth:— err, swerve.

796. ἀστραπή **astrapē**, *as-trap-ay´;* from *797; lightning;* by anal. *glare:*— lightning, bright shining.

797. ἀστράπτω **astraptō**, *as-trap´-to;* prob. from *792;* to *flash* as lightning:— lighten, shine.

798. ἄστρον **astrŏn**, *as´-tron;* neut. from *792;* prop. a *constellation;* put for a single *star* (nat. or artif.):— star.

799. Ἀσύγκριτος **Asugkritŏs**, *as-oong´-kree-tos;* from *1* (as a neg. particle) and a der. of *4793; incomparable; Asyncritus*, a Chr.:— Asyncritus.

800. ἀσύμφωνος **asumphōnŏs**, *as-oom´-fo-nos;* from *1* (as a neg. particle) and *4859; inharmonious* (fig.):— agree not.

801. ἀσύνετος **asunĕtŏs**, *as-oon´-ay-tos;* from *1* (as a neg. particle) and *4908; unintelligent;* by impl. *wicked:*— foolish, without understanding.

802. ἀσύνθετος **asunthĕtŏs**, *as-oon´-thet-os;* from *1* (as a neg. particle) and a der. of *4934;*

prop. *not agreed*, i.e. *treacherous* to compacts:— covenant-breaker.

803. ἀσφάλεια **asphalĕia**, *as-fal´-i-ah;* from *804; security* (lit. or fig.):— certainty, safety.

804. ἀσφαλής **asphalēs**, *as-fal-ace´;* from *1* (as a neg. particle) and σφάλλω **sphallō** (to "*fail*"); *secure* (lit. or fig.):— certain (-ty), safe, sure.

805. ἀσφαλίζω **asphalizō**, *as-fal-id´-zo;* from *804;* to *render secure:*— make fast (sure).

806. ἀσφαλῶς **asphalōs**, *as-fal-oce´;* adv. from *804; securely* (lit. or fig.):— assuredly, safely.

807. ἀσχημονέω **aschēmŏnĕō**, *as-kay-mon-eh´-o;* from *809;* to *be* (i.e. *act*) *unbecoming:*— behave self uncomely (unseemly).

808. ἀσχημοσύνη **aschēmŏsunē**, *as-kay-mos-oo´-nay;* from *809;* an *indecency;* by impl. the *pudenda:*— shame, that which is unseemly.

809. ἀσχήμων **aschēmōn**, *as-kay´-mone;* from *1* (as a neg. particle) and a presumed der. of *2192* (in the sense of its congener *4976*); prop. *shapeless*, i.e. (fig.) *inelegant:*— uncomely.

810. ἀσωτία **asōtia**, *as-o-tee´-ah;* from a compound of *1* (as a neg. particle) and a presumed der. of *4982;* prop. *unsavedness*, i.e. (by impl.) *profligacy:*— excess, riot.

811. ἀσώτως **asōtōs**, *as-o´-toce;* adv. from the same as *810; dissolutely:*— riotous.

812. ἀτακτέω **ataktĕō**, *at-ak-teh´-o;* from *813;* to *be* (i.e. *act*) *irregular:*— behave self disorderly.

813. ἄτακτος **ataktŏs**, *at´-ak-tos;* from *1* (as a neg. particle) and a der. of *5021; unarranged*, i.e. (by impl.) *insubordinate* (religiously):— unruly.

814. ἀτάκτως **ataktōs**, *at-ak´-toce;* adv. from *813; irregularly* (mor.):— disorderly.

815. ἄτεκνος **atĕknŏs**, *at´-ek-nos;* from *1* (as a neg. particle) and *5043; childless:*— childless, without children.

816. ἀτενίζω **atĕnizō**, *at-en-id´-zo;* from a compound of *1* (as a particle of union) and τείνω **tĕinō** (to *stretch*); to *gaze* intently:— behold earnestly (stedfastly), fasten (eyes), look (earnestly, stedfastly, up stedfastly), set eyes.

817. ἄτερ **atĕr**, *at´-er;* a particle prob. akin to *427; aloof*, i.e. *apart* from (lit. or fig.):— in the absence of, without.

818. ἀτιμάζω **atimazō**, *at-im-ad´-zo;* from *820;* to *render infamous*, i.e. (by impl.) *contemn* or *maltreat:*— despise, dishonour, suffer shame, entreat shamefully.

819. ἀτιμία **atimia**, *at-ee-mee´-ah;* from *820; infamy*, i.e. (subj.) comparative indignity, (obj.) *disgrace:*— dishonour, reproach, shame, vile.

820. ἄτιμος **atimŏs**, *at'-ee-mos;* from *1* (as a neg. particle) and *5092;* (neg.) *unhonoured* or (pos.) *dishonoured:—* despised, without honour, less honourable [*comparative degree*].

821. ἀτιμόω **atimŏō**, *at-ee-mŏ'-o;* from *820;* used like *818,* to *maltreat:—* handle shamefully.

822. ἀτμίς **atmis**, *at-mece';* from the same as *109; mist:—* vapour.

823. ἄτομος **atŏmŏs**, *at'-om-os;* from *1* (as a neg. particle) and the base of *5114; uncut,* i.e. (by impl.) *indivisible* [an "*atom*" of time]:— moment.

824. ἄτοπος **atŏpŏs**, *at'-op-os;* from *1* (as a neg. particle) and *5117; out of place,* i.e. (fig.) *improper, injurious, wicked:—* amiss, harm, unreasonable.

825. 'Ἀττάλεια **Attalĕia**, *at-tal'-i-ah;* from "Ἄτταλος **Attalŏs** (a king of Pergamus); *Attaleia,* a place in Pamphylia:— Attalia.

826. αὐγάζω **augazō**, *ŏw-gad'-zo;* from *827;* to *beam* forth (fig.):— shine.

827. αὐγή **augē**, *ŏwg'-ay;* of uncert. der.; a *ray* of light, i.e. (by impl.) *radiance, dawn:—* break of day.

828. Αὔγουστος **Augŏustŏs**, *ŏw'-goos-tos;* from Lat. ["august"]; *Augustus,* a title of the Rom. emperor:— Augustus.

829. αὐθάδης **authadēs**, *ŏw-thad'-ace;* from *846* and the base of *2237; self-pleasing,* i.e. *arrogant:—* self-willed.

830. αὐθαίρετος **authairĕtŏs**, *ŏw-thah'-ee-ret-os;* from *846* and the same as *140; self-chosen,* i.e. (by impl.) *voluntary:—* of own accord, willing of self.

831. αὐθεντέω **authĕntĕō**, *ŏw-then-teh'-o;* from a compound of *846* and an obs. ἔντης **hĕntēs** (a *worker*); to *act of oneself,* i.e. (fig.) *dominate:—* usurp authority over.

832. αὐλέω **aulĕō**, *ŏw-leh'-o;* from *836;* to play the *flute:—* pipe.

833. αὐλή **aulē**, *ŏw-lay';* from the same as *109;* a *yard* (as open to the *wind*); by impl. a *mansion:—* court, ([sheep-]) fold, hall, palace.

834. αὐλητής **aulētēs**, *ŏw-lay-tace';* from *832;* a *flute-player:—* minstrel, piper.

835. αὐλίζομαι **aulizŏmai**, *ŏw-lid'-zom-ahee;* mid. voice from *833;* to *pass the night* (prop. in the open air):— abide, lodge.

836. αὐλός **aulŏs**, *ŏw-los';* from the same as *109;* a *flute* (as *blown*):— pipe.

837. αὐξάνω **auxanō**, *ŏwx-an'-o;* a prol. form of a primary verb; to *grow* ("*wax*"), i.e. *enlarge* (lit. or fig., act. or pass.):— grow (up), (give the) increase.

838. αὔξησις **auxēsis**, *ŏwx'-ay-sis;* from *837; growth:—* increase.

839. αὔριον **auriŏn**, *ŏw'-ree-on;* from a der. of the same as *109* (mean. a *breeze,* i.e. the morning *air*); prop. *fresh,* i.e. (adv. with ellipsis of *2250*) *to-morrow:—* (to-) morrow, next day.

840. αὐστηρός **austērŏs**, *ŏw-stay-ros';* from a (presumed) der. of the same as *109* (mean. *blown*); *rough* (prop. as a *gale*), i.e. (fig.) *severe:—* austere.

841. αὐτάρκεια **autarkeia**, *ŏw-tar'-ki-ah;* from *842; self-satisfaction,* i.e. (abstr.) *contentedness,* or (concr.) a *competence:—* contentment, sufficiency.

842. αὐτάρκης **autarkēs**, *ŏw-tar'-kace;* from *846* and *714; self-complacent,* i.e. *contented:—* content.

843. αὐτοκατάκριτος **autŏkatakritŏs**, *ŏw-tok-at-ak'-ree-tos;* from *846* and a der. or *2632; self-condemned:—* condemned of self.

844. αὐτόματος **autŏmatŏs**, *ŏw-tom'-at-os;* from *846* and the same as *3155; self-moved* ["*automatic*"], i.e. *spontaneous:—* of own accord, of self.

845. αὐτόπτης **autŏptēs**, *ŏw-top'-tace;* from *846* and *3700; self-seeing,* i.e. an *eyewitness:—* eye-witness.

846. αὐτός **autŏs**, *ŏw-tos';* from the particle αὖ **au** [perh. akin to the base of *109* through the idea of a *baffling* wind] (*backward*); the refl. pron. *self,* used (alone or in the comp. *1438*) of the third pers., and (with the proper pers. pron.) of the other persons:— her, it (-self), one, the other, (mine) own, said, ([self-], the) same, ([him-, my-, thy-]) self, [your-] selves, she, that, their (-s), them ([-selves]), there [-at, -by, -in, -into, -of, -on, -with], they, (these) things, this (man), those, together, very, which. Comp. *848.*

847. αὐτοῦ **autŏu**, *ŏw-too';* gen. (i.e. possessive) of *846,* used as an adv. of location; prop. belonging to the *same* spot, i.e. *in this* (or *that*) *place:—* (t-) here.

848. αὑτοῦ **hautŏu**, *how-too';* contr. for *1438; self* (in some oblique case or refl. relation):— her (own), (of) him (-self), his (own), of it, thee, their (own), them (-selves), they.

849. αὐτόχειρ **autŏchĕir**, *ŏw-tokh'-ire;* from *846* and *5495; self-handed,* i.e. doing *personally:—* with ... own hands.

850. αὐχμηρός **auchmērŏs**, *ŏwkh-may-ros';* from αὐχμός **auchmŏs** [prob. from a base akin to that of *109*] (*dust,* as *dried* by wind); prop. *dirty,* i.e. (by impl.) *obscure:—* dark.

851. ἀφαιρέω **aphairĕō**, *af-ahee-reh'-o;* from *575* and *138;* to *remove* (lit. or fig.):— cut (smite) off, take away.

852. ἀφανής **aphanēs**, *af-an-ace';* from *1* (as a neg. particle) and *5316; non-apparent*):— that is not manifest.

853. ἀφανίζω **aphanizō**, *af-an-id'-zo;* from *852;* to *render unapparent,* i.e. (act.) *con-*

sume (*becloud*), or (pass.) *disappear* (*be destroyed*):— corrupt, disfigure, perish, vanish away.

854. ἀφανισμός **aphanismŏs,** *af-an-is-mos´;* from 853; *disappearance,* i.e. (fig.) *abrogation:*— vanish away.

855. ἄφαντος **aphantŏs,** *af´-an-tŏs;* from 1 (as a neg. particle) and a der. of 5316; *non-manifested,* i.e. *invisible:*— vanished out of sight.

856. ἀφεδρών **aphĕdrōn,** *af-ed-rone´;* from a compound of 575 and the base of 1476; a place of *sitting apart,* i.e. a *privy:*— draught.

857. ἀφειδία **aphĕidia,** *af-i-dee´-ah;* from a compound of 1 (as a neg. particle) and 5339; *unsparingness,* i.e. *austerity* (*ascetism*):— neglecting.

858. ἀφελότης **aphĕlotēs,** *af-el-ot´-ace;* from a compound of 1 (as a neg. particle) and φέλλος **phĕllŏs** (in the sense of a *stone* as *stubbing* the foot); *smoothness,* i.e. (fig.) *simplicity:*— singleness.

859. ἄφεσις **aphĕsis,** *af´-es-is;* from 863; *freedom;* (fig.) *pardon:*— deliverance, forgiveness, liberty, remission.

860. ἀφή **haphē,** *haf-ay´;* from 680; prob. a *ligament* (as *fastening*):— joint.

861. ἀφθαρσία **aphtharsia,** *af-thar-see´-ah;* from 862; *incorruptibility;* gen. *unending existence;* (fig.) *genuineness:*— immortality, incorruption, sincerity.

862. ἄφθαρτος **aphthartŏs,** *af´-thar-tos;* from 1 (as a neg. particle) and a der. of 5351; *undecaying* (in essence or continuance):— not (in-, un-) corruptible, immortal.

863. ἀφίημι **aphiēmi,** *af-ee´-ay-mee;* from 575 and ἵημι **hiēmi** (to *send;* an intens. form of εἶμι **ĕimi,** to *go*); to *send forth,* in various applications (as follow):— cry, forgive, forsake, lay aside, leave, let (alone, be, go, have), omit, put (send) away, remit, suffer, yield up.

864. ἀφικνέομαι **aphiknĕŏmai,** *af-ik-neh´-om-ahee;* from 575 and the base of 2425; to *go* (i.e. *spread*) *forth* (by rumor):— come abroad.

865. ἀφιλάγαθος **aphilagathŏs,** *af-il-ag´-ath-os;* from 1 (as a neg. particle) and 5358; *hostile to virtue:*— despiser of those that are good.

866. ἀφιλάργυρος **aphilargurŏs,** *af-il-ar´-goo-ros;* from 1 (as a neg. particle) and 5366; *unavaricious:*— without covetousness, not greedy of filthy lucre.

867. ἄφιξις **aphixis,** *af´-ix-is;* from 864; prop. *arrival,* i.e. (by impl.) *departure:*— departing.

868. ἀφίστημι **aphistēmi,** *af-is´-tay-mee;* from 575 and 2476; to *remove,* i.e. (act.) *instigate* to revolt; usually (refl.) to *desist, desert,* etc.:— depart, draw (fall) away, refrain, withdraw self.

869. ἄφνω **aphnō,** *af´-no;* adv. from 852 (contr.); *unawares,* i.e. *unexpectedly:*— suddenly.

870. ἀφόβως **aphŏbōs,** *af-ob´-oce;* adv. from a compound of 1 (as a neg. particle) and 5401; *fearlessly:*— without fear.

871. ἀφομοιόω **aphŏmŏiŏō,** *af-om-oy-ŏ´-o;* from 575 and 3666; to *assimilate* closely:— make like.

872. ἀφοράω **aphŏraō,** *af-or-ah´-o;* from 575 and 3708; to *consider* attentively:— look.

873. ἀφορίζω **aphŏrizō,** *af-or-id´-zo;* from 575 and 3724; to *set off* by boundary, i.e. (fig.) *limit, exclude, appoint,* etc.:— divide, separate, sever.

874. ἀφορμή **aphŏrmē,** *af-or-may´;* from a compound of 575 and 3729; a *starting-point,* i.e. (fig.) an *opportunity:*— occasion.

875. ἀφρίζω **aphrizō,** *af-rid´-zo;* from 876; to *froth* at the mouth (in epilepsy):— foam.

876. ἀφρός **aphrŏs,** *af-ros´;* appar. a primary word; *froth,* i.e. *slaver:*— foaming.

877. ἀφροσύνη **aphrŏsunē,** *af-ros-oo´-nay;* from 878; *senselessness,* i.e. (euphem.) *egotism;* (mor.) *recklessness:*— folly, foolishly (-ness).

878. ἄφρων **aphrōn,** *af´-rone;* from 1 (as a neg. particle) and 5424; prop. *mindless,* i.e. *stupid,* (by impl.) *ignorant,* (spec.) *egotistic,* (practically) *rash,* or (mor.) *unbelieving:*— fool (-ish), unwise.

879. ἀφυπνόω **aphupnŏō,** *af-oop-nŏ´-o;* from a compound of 575 and 5258; prop. to *become awake,* i.e. (by impl.) to *drop* (off) in slumber:— fall asleep.

880. ἄφωνος **aphōnŏs,** *af´-o-nos;* from 1 (as a neg. particle) and 5456; *voiceless,* i.e. *mute* (by nature or choice); fig. *unmeaning:*— dumb, without signification.

881. Ἀχάζ **Achaz,** *akh-adz´;* of Heb. or. [271]; *Achaz,* an Isr.:— Achaz.

882. Ἀχαΐα **Achaïa,** *ach-ah-ee´-ah;* of uncert. der.; *Achaia* (i.e. *Greece*), a country of Europe:— Achaia.

883. Ἀχαϊκός **Achaïkŏs,** *ach-ah-ee-kos´;* from 882; an *Achaïan; Achaïcus,* a Chr.:— Achaicus.

884. ἀχάριστος **acharistŏs,** *ach-ar´-is-tos;* from 1 (as a neg. particle) and a presumed der. of 5483; *thankless,* i.e. *ungrateful:*— unthankful.

885. Ἀχείμ **Achĕim** or Ἀχίμ **Achim,** *akh-ime´;* prob. of Heb. or. [comp. 3137]; *Achim,* an Isr.:— Achim.

886. ἀχειροποίητος **achĕirŏpŏiētŏs,** *akh-i-rop-oy´-ay-tos;* from 1 (as a neg. particle) and 5499; *unmanufactured,* i.e. *inartificial:*— made without (not made with) hands.

887. ἀχλύς **achlus,** *akh-looce´;* of uncert. der.; *dimness* of sight, i.e. (prob.) a *cataract:*— mist.

888. ἀχρεῖος **achrĕiŏs,** *akh-ri´-os;* from 1 (as

Greek

a neg. particle) and a der. of *5534* [comp. *5532*]; *useless*, i.e. (euphem.) *unmeritorious*:— unprofitable.

889. ἀχρειόω **achrĕiŏō**, *akh-ri-ŏ´-o*; from *888*; to *render useless*, i.e. *spoil*:— become unprofitable.

890. ἄχρηστος **achrēstŏs**, *akh´-race-tos*; from *1* (as a neg. particle) and *5543*; *inefficient*, i.e. (by impl.) *detrimental*:— unprofitable.

891. ἄχρι **achri**, *akh´-ree*; or ἄχρις **achris**, *akh´-rece*; akin to *206* (through the idea of a *terminus*); (of time) *until* or (of place) *up to*:— as far as, for, in (-to), till, (even, un-) to, until, while. Comp. *3360*.

892. ἄχυρον **achurŏn**, *akh´-oo-ron*; perh. remotely from χέω **chĕō** (to *shed* forth); *chaff* (as *diffusive*):— chaff.

893. ἀψευδής **apsĕudēs**, *aps-yoo-dace´*; from *1* (as a neg. particle) and *5579*; *veracious*:— that cannot lie.

894. ἄψινθος **apsinthŏs**, *ap´-sin-thos*; of uncert. der.; *wormwood* (as a type of *bitterness*, i.e. [fig.] *calamity*):— wormwood.

895. ἄψυχος **apsuchŏs**, *ap´-soo-khos*; from *1* (as a neg. particle) and *5590*; *lifeless*, i.e. *inanimate* (mechanical):— without life.

B

896. Βάαλ **Baal**, *bah´-al*; of Heb. or. [1168]; *Baal*, a Phœnician deity (used as a symbol of idolatry):— Baal.

897. Βαβυλών **Babulōn**, *bab-oo-lone´*; of Heb. or. [894]; *Babylon*, the capital of Chaldæa (lit. or fig. [as a type of tyranny]):— Babylon.

898. βαθμός **bathmŏs**, *bath-mos´*; from the same as *899*; a *step*, i.e. (fig.) *grade* (of dignity):— degree.

899. βάθος **bathŏs**, *bath´-os*; from the same as *901*; *profundity*, i.e. (by impl.) *extent*; (fig.) *mystery*:— deep (-ness, things), depth.

900. βαθύνω **bathunō**, *bath-oo´-no*; from *901*; to *deepen*:— deep.

901. βαθύς **bathus**, *bath-oos´*; from the base of *939*; *profound* (as *going* down), lit. or fig.:— deep, very early.

902. βαΐον **baïŏn**, *bah-ee´-on*; a diminutive of a der. prob. of the base of *939*; a palm *twig* (as *going* out far):— branch.

903. Βαλαάμ **Balaam**, *bal-ah-am´*; of Heb. or. [1109]; *Balaam*, a Mesopotamian (symbolic of a false teacher):— Balaam.

904. Βαλάκ **Balak**, *bal-ak´*; of Heb. or. [1111]; *Balak*, a Moabite:— Balac.

905. βαλάντιον **balantiŏn**, *bal-an´-tee-on*; prob. remotely from *906* (as a *depository*); a *pouch* (for money):— bag, purse.

906. βάλλω **ballō**, *bal´-lo*; a primary verb; to *throw* (in various applications, more or less violent or intense):— arise, cast (out), × dung, lay, lie, pour, put (up), send, strike, throw (down), thrust. Comp. *4496*.

907. βαπτίζω **baptizō**, *bap-tid´-zo*; from a der. of *911*; to *make overwhelmed* (i.e. *fully wet*); used only (in the N.T.) of ceremonial ablution, espec. (tech.) of the ordinance of Chr. baptism:— baptist, baptize, wash.

908. βάπτισμα **baptisma**, *bap´-tis-mah*; from *907*; *baptism* (tech. or fig.):— baptism.

909. βαπτισμός **baptismŏs**, *bap-tis-mos´*; from *907*; *ablution* (cerem. or Chr.):— baptism, washing.

910. Βαπτιστής **Baptistēs**, *bap-tis-tace´*; from *907*; a *baptizer*, as an epithet of Christ's forerunner:— Baptist.

911. βάπτω **baptō**, *bap´-to*; a primary verb; to *overwhelm*, i.e. cover wholly with a fluid; in the N.T. only in a qualified or special sense, i.e. (lit.) to *moisten* (a part of one's person), or (by impl.) to *stain* (as with dye):— dip.

912. Βαραββᾶς **Barabbas**, *bar-ab-bas´*; of Chald. or. [1347 and 5]; *son of Abba*; *Bar-abbas*, an Isr.:— Barabbas.

913. Βαράκ **Barak**, *bar-ak´*; of Heb. or. [1301]; *Barak*, an Isr.:— Barak.

914. Βαραχίας **Barachias**, *bar-akh-ee´-as*; of Heb. or. [1296]; *Barachias* (i.e. *Berechijah*), an Isr.:— Barachias.

915. βάρβαρος **barbarŏs**, *bar´-bar-os*; of uncert. der.; a *foreigner* (i.e. *non-Greek*):— barbarian (-rous).

916. βαρέω **barĕō**, *bar-eh´-o*; from *926*; to *weigh* down (fig.):— burden, charge, heavy, press.

917. βαρέως **barĕōs**, *bar-eh´-oce*; adv. from *926*; *heavily* (fig.):— dull.

918. Βαρθολομαῖος **Barthŏlŏmaiŏs** , *bar-thol-om-ah´-yos*; of Chald. or. [1247 and 8526]; *son of Tolmai*; *Bar-tholomæus*, a Chr. apostle:— Bartholomeus.

919. Βαριησοῦς **Bariēsŏus**, *bar-ee-ay-sooce´*; of Chald. or. [1247 and 3091]; *son of Jesus* (or *Joshua*); *Bar-jesus*, an Isr.:— Barjesus.

920. Βαριωνᾶς **Bariōnas**, *bar-ee-oo-nas´*; of Chald. or. [1247 and 3124]; *son of Jonas* (or *Jonah*); *Bar-jonas*, an Isr.:— Bar-jona.

921. Βαρνάβας **Barnabas**, *bar-nab´-as*; of Chald. or. [1247 and 5029]; *son of Nabas* (i.e. *prophecy*); *Barnabas*, an Isr.:— Barnabas.

922. βάρος **barŏs**, *bar-os*; prob. from the same as *939* (through the notion of *going* down; comp. *899*); *weight*; in the N.T. only fig. a *load*, *abundance*, *authority*:— burden (-some), weight.

923. Βαρσαβᾶς **Barsabas**, *bar-sab-as´*; of Chald. or. [1247 and prob. 6634]; *son of Sabas* (or *Tsaba*); *Bar-sabas*, the name of two Isr.:— Barsabas.

924. Βαρτιμαῖος **Bartimaiŏs**, *bar-tim-ah´-yos;* of Chald. or. [1247 and 2931]; *son of Timæus* (or the *unclean*); *Bar-timæus*, an Isr.:— Bartimæeus.

925. βαρύνω **barunō**, *bar-oo´-no;* from *926;* to *burden* (fig.):— overcharge.

926. βαρύς **barus**, *bar-ooce´;* from the same as *922;* *weighty,* i.e. (fig) *burdensome, grave:*— grievous, heavy, weightier.

927. βαρύτιμος **barutimŏs**, *bar-oo´-tim-os;* from *926* and *5092;* highly *valuable:*— very precious.

928. βασανίζω **basanizō**, *bas-an-id´-zo;* from *931;* to *torture:*— pain, toil, torment, toss, vex.

929. βασανισμός **basanismŏs**, *bas-an-is-mos´;* from *928;* *torture:*— torment.

930. βασανιστής **basanistēs**, *bas-an-is-tace´;* from *928;* a *torturer:*— tormentor.

931. βάσανος **basanŏs**, *bas´-an-os;* perh. remotely from the same as *939* (through the notion of *going* to the bottom); a *touch-stone,* i.e. (by anal.) *torture:*— torment.

932. βασιλεία **basilĕia**, *bas-il-i´-ah;* from *935;* prop. *royalty,* i.e. (abstr.) *rule,* or (concr.) a *realm* (lit. or fig.):— kingdom, + reign.

933. βασίλειον **basilĕiŏn**, *bas-il´-i-on;* neut. of *934;* a *palace:*— king's court.

934. βασίλειος **basilĕiŏs**, *bas-il´-i-os;* from *935; kingly* (in nature):— royal.

935. βασιλεύς **basilĕus**, *bas-il-yooce´;* prob. from *939* (through the notion of a *foundation* of power); a *sovereign* (abstr., rel., or fig.):— king.

936. βασιλεύω **basilĕuō**, *bas-il-yoo´-o;* from *935;* to *rule* (lit. or fig.):— king, reign.

937. βασιλικός **basilikŏs**, *bas-il-ee-kos´;* from *935; regal* (in relation), i.e. (lit.) belonging to (or befitting) the sovereign (as land, dress, or a *courtier*), or (fig.) *preeminent:*— king's, nobleman, royal.

938. βασίλισσα **basilissa**, *bas-il´-is-sah;* fem. from *936;* a *queen:*— queen.

939. βάσις **basis**, *bas´-ece;* from βαίνω **bainō** (to *walk*); a *pace* ("base"), i.e. (by impl.) the *foot:*— foot.

940. βασκαίνω **baskainō**, *bas-kah´-ee-no;* akin to *5335;* to *malign,* i.e. (by extens.) to *fascinate* (by false representations):— bewitch.

941. βαστάζω **bastazō**, *bas-tad´-zo;* perh. remotely der. from the base of *939* (through the idea of *removal*); to *lift,* lit. or fig. (*endure, declare, sustain, receive,* etc.):— bear, carry, take up.

942. βάτος **batŏs**, *bat´-os;* of uncert. der.; a *brier* shrub:— bramble, bush.

943. βάτος **batŏs**, *bat´-os;* of Heb. or. [1324]; a *bath,* or measure for liquids:— measure.

944. βάτραχος **batrachŏs**, *bat´-rakh-os;* of uncert. der.; a *frog:*— frog.

945. βαττολογέω **battŏlŏgĕō**, *bat-tol-og-eh´-o;* from Βάττος **Battŏs** (a proverbial stammerer) and *3056;* to *stutter,* i.e. (by impl.) to *prate* tediously:— use vain repetitions.

946. βδέλυγμα **bdĕlugma**, *bdel´-oog-mah;* from *948;* a *detestation,* i.e. (spec.) *idolatry:*— abomination.

947. βδελυκτός **bdĕluktŏs**, *bdel-ook-tos´;* from *948; detestable,* i.e. (spec.) *idolatrous:*— abominable.

948. βδελύσσω **bdĕlussō**, *bdel-oos´-so;* from a (presumed) der. of βδέω **bdĕō** (to *stink*); to *be disgusted,* i.e. (by impl.) *detest* (esp. of idolatry):— abhor, abominable.

949. βέβαιος **bĕbaiŏs**, *beb´-ah-yos;* from the base of *939* (through the idea of *basality*); *stable* (lit. or fig.):— firm, of force, stedfast, sure.

950. βεβαιόω **bĕbaiŏō**, *beb-ah-yŏ´-o;* from *949;* to *stabilitate* (fig.):— confirm, (e-) stablish.

951. βεβαίωσις **bĕbaiōsis**, *beb-ah´-yo-sis;* from *950; stabiliment:*— confirmation.

952. βέβηλος **bĕbēlŏs**, *beb´-ay-los;* from the base of *939* and βηλός **bēlŏs** (a *threshold*); *accessible* (as by *crossing* the *door-way*), i.e. (by impl. of Jewish notions) *heathenish, wicked:*— profane (person).

953. βεβηλόω **bĕbēlŏō**, *beb-ay-lŏ´-o;* from *952;* to *desecrate:*— profane.

954. Βεελζεβούλ **Bĕĕlzĕbŏul**, *beh-el-zeb-ool´;* of Chald. or. [by parody on 1176]; *dung-god; Beelzebul,* a name of Satan:— Beelzebub.

955. Βελίαλ **Bĕlial**, *bel-ee´-al;* or Βελίαρ **Bĕliar**, *bel-ee´-ar* of Heb. or. [1100]; *worthlessness; Belial,* as an epithet of Satan:— Belial

956. βέλος **bĕlŏs**, *bel´-os;* from *906;* a *missile,* i.e. *spear* or *arrow:*— dart.

957. βελτίον **bĕltiŏn**, *bel-tee´-on;* neut. of a comparative of a der. of *906* (used for the comparative of *18*); *better:*— very well.

958. Βενιαμίν **Bĕniamin**, *ben-ee-am-een´;* of Heb. or. [1144]; *Benjamin,* an Isr.:— Benjamin.

959. Βερνίκη **Bĕrnikē**, *ber-nee´-kay;* from a provincial form of *5342* and *3529; victorious; Bernice,* a member of the Herodian family:— Bernice.

960. Βέροια **Bĕrŏia**, *ber´-oy-ah;* perh. a provincial from a der. of *4008* [Peræa, i.e. the region *beyond* the coast-line]; *Beroea,* a place in Macedonia:— Berea.

961. Βεροιαῖος **Bĕrŏiaiŏs**, *ber-oy-ah´-yos;* from *960;* a *Berœcean* or native of Beræa:— of Berea.

962. Βηθαβαρά **Bēthabara**, *bay-thab-ar-ah´;* of Heb. or. [1004 and 5679]; *ferry-house; Bethabara* (i.e. *Bethabarah*), a place on the Jordan:— Bethabara.

963. Βηθανία **Bēthania**, *bay-than-ee´-ah;* of Chald. or.; *date-house; Beth-any,* a place in Pal.:— Bethany.

964. Βηθεσδά **Bēthĕsda**, *bay-thes-dah´;* of Chald. or. [compound of 1004 and 2617]; *house of kindness; Beth-esda,* a pool in Jerusalem:— Bethesda.

965. Βηθλεέμ **Bēthlĕĕm**, *bayth-leh-em´;* of Heb. or. [1036]; *Bethleem* (i.e. *Beth-lechem),* a place in Pal.:— Bethlehem.

966. Βηθσαϊδά **Bēthsaïda**, *bayth-sahee-dah´;* of Chald. or. [compound of 1004 and 6719]; *fishing-house; Bethsaïda,* a place in Pal.:— Bethsaida.

967. Βηθφαγή **Bēthphagē**, *bayth-fag-ay´;* of Chald. or. [compound of 1004 and 6291]; *fig-house; Beth-phagè,* a place in Pal.:— Bethphage.

968. βῆμα **bēma**, *bay´-ma;* from the base of *939;* a *step,* i.e. *foot-breath;* by impl. a *rostrum,* i.e. a *tribunal:*— judgment-seat, set [foot] on, throne.

969. βήρυλλος **bĕrullŏs**, *bay´-rool-los;* of uncert. der.; a *"beryl":*— beryl.

970. βία **bia**, *bee´-ah;* prob. akin to *979* (through the idea of *vital* activity); *force:*— violence.

971. βιάζω **biazō**, *bee-ad´-zo;* from *970;* to *force,* i.e. (refl.) to *crowd oneself* (into), or (pass.) to *be seized:*— press, suffer violence.

972. βίαιος **biaiŏs**, *bee´-ah-yos;* from *970; violent:*— mighty.

973. βιαστής **biastēs**, *bee-as-tace´;* from *971;* a *forcer,* i.e. (fig.) *energetic:*— violent.

974. βιβλιαρίδιον **bibliaridiŏn**, *bib-lee-ar-id´-ee-on;* a dimin. of *975;* a *booklet:*— little book.

975. βιβλίον **bibliŏn**, *bib-lee´-on;* a dimin. of *976;* a *roll:*— bill, book, scroll, writing.

976. βίβλος **biblŏs**, *bib´-los;* prop. the inner *bark* of the papyrus plant, i.e. (by impl.) a *sheet* or *scroll* of writing:— book.

977. βιβρώσκω **bibrōskō**, *bib-ro´-sko;* a redupl. and prol. form of an obs. primary verb [perh. caus. of *1006*]; to *eat:*— eat.

978. Βιθυνία **Bithunia**, *bee-thoo-nee´-ah;* of uncert. der.; *Bithynia,* a region of Asia:— Bithynia.

979. βίος **biŏs**, *bee´-os;* a primary word; *life,* i.e. (lit.) the present state of existence; by impl. the means of *livelihood:*— good, life, living.

980. βιόω **biŏō**, *bee-ŏ´-o;* from *979;* to *spend existence:*— live.

981. βίωσις **biōsis**, *bee´-o-sis;* from *980; living* (prop. the act, by impl. the mode):— manner of life.

982. βιωτικός **biōtikŏs**, *bee-o-tee-kos´;* from a der. of *980; relating to* the present *existence:*— of (pertaining to, things that pertain to) this life.

983. βλαβερός **blabĕrŏs**, *blab-er-os´;* from *984; injurious:*— hurtful.

984. βλάπτω **blaptō**, *blap´-to;* a primary verb; prop. to *hinder,* i.e. (by impl.) to *injure:*— hurt.

985. βλαστάνω **blastanō**, *blas-tan´-o;* from βλαστός **blastŏs** (a *sprout);* to *germinate;* by impl. to *yield* fruit:— bring forth, bud, spring (up).

986. Βλάστος **Blastŏs**, *blas´-tos;* perh. the same as the base of *985; Blastus,* an officer of Herod Agrippa:— Blastus.

987. βλασφημέω **blasphēmĕō**, *blas-fay-meh´-o;* from *989;* to *vilify;* spec. to *speak impiously:*— (speak) blaspheme (-er, -mously, my), defame, rail on, revile, speak evil.

988. βλασφημία **blasphēmia**, *blas-fay-me´-ah;* from *989; vilification* (espec. against God):— blasphemy, evil speaking, railing.

989. βλάσφημος **blasphēmŏs**, *blas´-fay-mos;* from a der. of *984* and *5345; scurrilous,* i.e. *calumnious* (against man), or (spec.) *impious* (against God):— blasphemer (-mous), railing.

990. βλέμμα **blemma**, *blem´-mah;* from *991; vision* (prop. concr.; by impl. abstr.):— seeing.

991. βλέπω **blĕpō**, *blep´-o;* a primary verb; to *look* at (lit. or fig.):— behold, beware, lie, look (on, to), perceive, regard, see, sight, take heed. Comp. *3700.*

992. βλητέος **blētĕŏs**, *blay-teh´-os;* from *906;* fit *to be cast* (i.e. *applied):*— must be put.

993. Βοανεργές **Bŏanĕrgĕs**, *bŏ-an-erg-es´;* of Chald. or. [1123 and 7266]; *sons of commotion; Boänerges,* an epithet of two of the Apostles:— Boanerges.

994. βοάω **bŏaō**, *bŏ-ah´-o;* appar. a prol. form of a primary verb; to *halloo,* i.e. *shout* (for help or in a tumultuous way):— cry.

995. βοή **bŏē**, *bŏ-ay´;* from *994;* a *halloo,* i.e. *call* (for aid, etc.):— cry.

996. βοήθεια **bŏēthĕia**, *bŏ-ay´-thi-ah;* from *998; aid;* spec. a rope or chain for *frapping* a vessel:— help.

997. βοηθέω **bŏēthĕō**, *bŏ-ay-theh´-o;* from *998;* to *aid* or *relieve:*— help, succour.

998. βοηθός **bŏēthŏs**, *bŏ-ay-thos´;* from *995* and θέω **thĕō** (to *run);* a *succorer:*— helper.

999. βόθυνος **bŏthunŏs**, *both´-oo-nos;* akin to *900;* a *hole* (in the ground); spec. a *cistern:*— ditch, pit.

1000. βολή **bŏlē**, *bol-ay´;* from *906;* a *throw* (as a measure of distance):— cast.

1001. βολίζω **bŏlizō**, *bol-id´-zo;* from *1002;* to *heave* the lead:— sound.

1002. βολίς **bŏlis**, *bol-ece´;* from *906;* a *missile,* i.e. *javelin:*— dart.

1003. Βοόζ **Bŏŏz**, *bŏ-oz´;* of Heb. or. [1162]; Βοοζ, (i.e. *Boäz*), an Isr.:— Booz.

1004. βόρβορος **bŏrbŏrŏs**, *bor´-bor-os;* of uncert. der.; *mud:*— mire.

1005. βορρᾶς **borrhas**, *bor-hras´;* of uncert. der.; the *north* (prop. wind):— north.

1006. βόσκω **bŏskō**, *bos´-ko;* a prol. form of a primary verb [comp. 977, 1016]; to *pasture;* by extens. to, *fodder;* refl. to *graze:*— feed, keep.

1007. Βοσόρ **Bŏsŏr**, *bos-or´;* of Heb. or. [1160]; Bosor (i.e. *Beör*), a Moabite:— Bosor.

1008. βοτάνη **bŏtanē**, *bot-an´-ay;* from 1006; *herbage* (as if for *grazing*):— herb.

1009. βότρυς **bŏtrus**, *bot´-rooce;* of uncert. der.; a *bunch* (of grapes):— (vine) cluster (of the vine).

1010. βουλευτής **bŏulĕutēs**, *bool-yoo-tace´;* from 1011; an *adviser,* i.e. (spec.) a *councillor* or member of the Jewish Sanhedrin:— counsellor.

1011. βουλεύω **bŏulĕuō**, *bool-yoo´-o;* from 1012; to *advise,* i.e. (refl.) *deliberate,* or (by impl.) *resolve:*— consult, take counsel, determine, be minded, purpose.

1012. βουλή **bŏulē**, *boo-lay´;* from 1014; *volition,* i.e. (obj.) *advice,* or (by impl.) *purpose:*— + advise, counsel, will.

1013. βούλημα **bŏulēma**, *boo´-lay-mah;* from 1014; a *resolve:*— purpose, will.

1014. βούλομαι **bŏulŏmai**, *boo´-lom-ahee;* mid. voice of a primary verb.; to *"will,"* i.e. (refl.) *be willing:*— be disposed, minded, intend, list, (be, of own) will (-ing). Comp. 2309.

1015. βουνός **bŏunŏs**, *boo-nos´;* prob. of for. or.; a *hillock:*— hill.

1016. βοῦς **bŏus**, *booce;* prob. from the base of 1006; an *ox* (as *grazing*), i.e. an animal of that species ("beef"):— ox.

1017. βραβεῖον **brabĕiŏn**, *brab-i´-on;* from βραβεύς **brabĕus** (an *umpire;* of uncert. der.); an *award* (of arbitration), i.e. (spec.) a *prize* in the public games:— prize.

1018. βραβεύω **brabĕuō**, *brab-yoo´-o;* from the same as 1017; to *arbitrate,* i.e. (gen.) to *govern* (fig. *prevail*):— rule.

1019. βραδύνω **bradunō**, *brad-oo´-no;* from 1021; to *delay:*— be slack, tarry.

1020. βραδυπλοέω **braduplŏĕō**, *brad-oo-plŏeh´-o;* from 1021 and a prol. form of 4126; to *sail slowly:*— sail slowly.

1021. βραδύς **bradus**, *brad-ooce´;* of uncert. aff.; *slow;* fig. *dull:*— slow.

1022. βραδύτης **bradutēs**, *brad-oo´-tace;* from 1021; *tardiness:*— slackness.

1023. βραχίων **brachiōn**, *brakh-ee-own´;* prop. comp. of 1024, but appar. in the sense of βράσσω **brassō** (to *wield*); the *arm,* i.e. (fig.) *strength:*— arm.

1024. βραχύς **brachus**, *brakh-ooce´;* of uncert. aff.; *short* (of time, place, quantity, or number):— few words, little (space, while).

1025. βρέφος **brĕphŏs**, *bref´-os;* of uncert. affin.; an *infant* (prop. unborn) lit. or fig.:— babe, (young) child, infant.

1026. βρέχω **brĕchō**, *brekh´-o;* a primary verb; to *moisten* (espec. by a shower):— (send) rain, wash.

1027. βροντή **brŏntē**, *bron-tay´;* akin to βρέμω **brĕmō** (to *roar*); *thunder:*— thunder (-ing).

1028. βροχή **brŏchē**, *brokh-ay´;* from 1026; *rain:*— rain.

1029. βρόχος **brŏchŏs**, *brokh´-os;* of uncert. der.; a *noose:*— snare.

1030. βρυγμός **brugmŏs**, *broog-mos´;* from 1031; a *grating* (of the teeth):— gnashing.

1031. βρύχω **bruchō**, *broo´-kho;* a primary verb; to *grate* the teeth (in pain or rage):— gnash.

1032. βρύω **bruō**, *broo´-o;* a primary verb; to *swell* out, i.e. (by impl.) to *gush:*— send forth.

1033. βρῶμα **brōma**, *bro´-mah;* from the base of 977; *food* (lit. or fig.), espec. (cer.) articles allowed or forbidden by the Jewish law:— meat, victuals.

1034. βρώσιμος **brōsimŏs**, *bro´-sim-os;* from 1035; *eatable:*— meat.

1035. βρῶσις **brōsis**, *bro´-sis;* from the base of 977; (abstr.) *eating* (lit. or fig.); by extens. (concr.) *food* (lit. or fig.):— eating, food, meat.

1036. βυθίζω **buthizō**, *boo-thid´-zo;* from 1037; to *sink;* by impl. to *drown:*— begin to sink, drown.

1037. βυθός **buthŏs**, *boo-thos´;* a var. of 899; *depth,* i.e. (by impl.) the *sea:*— deep.

1038. βυρσεύς **bursĕus**, *boorce-yooce´;* from βύρσα **bursa** (a *hide*); a *tanner:*— tanner.

1039. βύσσινος **bussinŏs**, *boos´-see-nos;* from 1040; made of *linen* (neut. a linen *cloth*):— fine linen.

1040. βύσσος **bussŏs**, *boos´-sos;* of Heb. or. [948]; white *linen:*— fine linen.

1041. βωμός **bōmŏs**, *bo´-mos;* from the base of 939; prop. a *stand,* i.e. (spec.) an *altar:*— altar.

Γ

1042. γαββαθά **gabbatha**, *gab-bath-ah´;* of Chald. or. [comp. 1355]; *the knoll; gabbatha,* a vernacular term for the Roman tribunal in Jerusalem:— Gabbatha.

1043. Γαβριήλ **Gabriēl**, *gab-ree-ale´;* of Heb. or. [1403]; *Gabriel,* an archangel:— Gabriel.

1044. γάγγραινα **gaggraina**, *gang´-graheenah;* from γραίνω **grainō** (to *gnaw*); an *ulcer* ("gangrene"):— canker.

Greek

1045. Γάδ **Gad**, *gad;* of Heb. or. [1410]; *Gad*, a tribe of Isr.:— Gad.

1046. Γαδαρηνός **Gadarēnŏs**, *gad-ar-ay-nos´;* from Γαδαρά (a town E. of the Jordan); a *Gadarene* or inhab. of Gadara:— Gadarene.

1047. γάζα **gaza**, *gad´-zah;* of for. or.; a *treasure:*— treasure.

1048. Γάζα **Gaza**, *gad´-zah;* of Heb. or. [5804]; *Gazah* (i.e. *Azzah*), a place in Pal.:— Gaza.

1049. γαζοφυλάκιον **gazŏphulakiŏn**, *gad-zof-oo-lak´-ee-on;* from 1047 and 5438; a *treasure-house,* i.e. a court in the temple for the collection-boxes:— treasury.

1050. Γάϊος **Gaïŏs**, *gah´-ee-os;* of Lat. or.; *Gaïus* (i.e. *Caius*), a Chr.:— Gaius.

1051. γάλα **gala**, *gal´-ah;* of uncert. aff.; *milk* (fig.):— milk.

1052. Γαλάτης **Galatēs**, *gal-at´-ace;* from 1053; a *Galatian* or inhab. of Galatia:— Galatian.

1053. Γαλατία **Galatia**, *gal-at-ee´-ah;* of for. or.; *Galatia,* a region of Asia:— Galatia.

1054. Γαλατικός **Galatikŏs**, *gal-at-ee-kos´;* from 1053; *Galatic* or relating to Galatia:— of Galatia.

1055. γαλήνη **galēnē**, *gal-ay´-nay;* of uncert. der.; *tranquillity:*— calm.

1056. Γαλιλαία **Galilaia**, *gal-il-ah´-yah;* of Heb. or. [1551]; *Galilæa* (i.e. the heathen *circle*), a region of Pal.:— Galilee.

1057. Γαλιλαῖος **Galilaiŏs**, *gal-ee-lah´-yos;* from 1056; *Galilæan* or belonging to Galilæa:— Galilæan, of Galilee.

1058. Γαλλίων **Galliōn**, *gal-lee´-own;* of Lat. or.; *Gallion* (i.e. *Gallio*), a Roman officer:— Gallio.

1059. Γαμαλιήλ **Gamaliēl**, *gam-al-ee-ale´;* of Heb. or. [1583]; *Gamaliel* (i.e. *Gamliel*), an Isr.:— Gamaliel.

1060. γαμέω **gamĕō**, *gam-eh´-o;* from 1062; to *wed* (of either sex):— marry (a wife).

1061. γαμίσκω **gamiskō**, *gam-is´-ko;* from 1062; to *espouse* (a daughter to a husband):— give in marriage.

1062. γάμος **gamŏs**, *gam´-os;* of uncert. aff.; *nuptials:*— marriage, wedding.

1063. γάρ **gar**, *gar;* a primary particle; prop. assigning a *reason* (used in argument, explanation or intensification; often with other particles):— and, as, because (that), but, even, for, indeed, no doubt, seeing, then, therefore, verily, what, why, yet.

1064. γαστήρ **gastēr**, *gas-tare´;* of uncert. der.; the *stomach;* by anal. the *matrix;* fig. a *gourmand:*— belly, + with child, womb.

1065. γέ **gĕ**, *gheh;* a primary particle of *emphasis* or *qualification* (often used with other particles pref.):— and besides, doubtless, at least, yet.

1066. Γεδεών **Gĕdĕōn**, *ghed-eh-own´;* of Heb. or. [1439]; *Gedeon* (i.e. *Gidlelon*), an Isr.:— Gedeon (Gideon).

1067. γέεννα **gĕĕnna**, *gheh´-en-nah;* of Heb. or. [1516 and 2011]; *valley of* (the son of) *Hinnom; ge-henna* (or *Ge-Hinnom*), a valley of Jerusalem, used (fig.) as a name for the place (or state) of everlasting punishment:— hell.

1068. Γεθσημανῆ **Gĕthsēmanē**, *gheth-say-man-ay´;* of Chald. or. [comp. 1660 and 8081]; *oil-press; Gethsemane,* a garden near Jerusalem:— Gethsemane.

1069. γείτων **gĕitōn**, *ghi´-tone;* from 1093; a *neighbour* (as adjoining one's *ground*); by impl. a *friend:*— neighbour.

1070. γελάω **gĕlaō**, *ghel-ah´-o;* of uncert. aff.; to *laugh* (as a sign of joy or satisfaction):— laugh.

1071. γέλως **gĕlōs**, *ghel´-oce;* from 1070; *laughter* (as a mark of gratification):— laughter.

1072. γεμίζω **gĕmizō**, *ghem-id´-zo;* tran. from 1073; to *fill* entirely:— fill (be) full.

1073. γέμω **gĕmō**, *ghem´-o;* a primary verb; to *swell* out, i.e. *be full:*— be full.

1074. γενεά **gĕnĕa**, *ghen-eh-ah´;* from (a presumed der. of) 1085; a *generation;* by impl. an *age* (the period or the persons):— age, generation, nation, time.

1075. γενεαλογέω **gĕnĕalŏgĕō**, *ghen-eh-al-og-eh´-o;* from 1074 and 3056; to *reckon by generations,* i.e. *trace in genealogy:*— count by descent.

1076. γενεαλογία **gĕnĕalŏgia**, *ghen-eh-al-og-ee´-ah;* from the same as 1075; *tracing by generations,* i.e. "*genealogy*":— genealogy.

1077. γενέσια **gĕnĕsia**, *ghen-es´-ee-ah;* neut. plur. of a der. of 1078; *birthday* ceremonies:— birthday.

1078. γένεσις **gĕnĕsis**, *ghen´-es-is;* from the same as 1074; *nativity;* fig. *nature:*— generation, nature (-ral).

1079. γενετή **gĕnĕtē**, *ghen-et-ay´;* fem. of a presumed der. of the base of 1074; *birth:*— birth.

1080. γεννάω **gĕnnaō**, *ghen-nah´-o;* from a var. of 1085; to *procreate* (prop. of the father, but by extens. of the mother); fig. to *regenerate:*— bear, beget, be born, bring forth, conceive, be delivered of, gender, make, spring.

1081. γέννημα **gĕnnēma**, or γένημα **gĕnēma**, *ghen´-nay-mah;* from 1080; *offspring;* by anal. *produce* (lit. or fig.):— fruit, generation.

1082. Γεννησαρέτ **Gĕnnēsarĕt**, *ghen-nay-sar-et´;* of Heb. or. [comp. 3672]; *Gennesaret* (i.e. *Kinnereth*), a lake and plain in Pal.:— Gennesaret.

1083. γέννησις **gĕnnēsis**, *ghen´-nay-sis;* from *1080; nativity:*— birth.

1084. γεννητός **gĕnnētŏs**, *ghen-nay-tos´;* from *1080; born:*— they that are born.

1085. γένος **gĕnŏs**, *ghen´-os;* from *1096;* "*kin*" (abstr. or concr., lit. or fig., indiv. or collect.):— born, country (-man), diversity, generation, kind (-red), nation, offspring, stock.

1086. Γεργεσηνός **Gĕrgĕsēnŏs**, *gher-ghes-ay-nos´;* of Heb. or. [1622]; a *Gergesene* (i.e. *Girgashite*) or one of the aborigines of Pal.:— Gergesene.

1087. γερουσία **gĕrŏusia**, *gher-oo-see´-ah;* from *1088;* the *eldership,* i.e. (collect.) the Jewish *Sanhedrin:*— senate.

1088. γέρων **gĕrōn**, *gher´-own;* of uncert. aff. [comp. *1094*]; *aged:*— old.

1089. γεύομαι **gĕuŏmai**, *ghyoo´-om-ahee;* a primary verb; *to taste;* by impl. *to eat;* fig. to *experience* (good or ill):— eat, taste.

1090. γεωργέω **gĕōrgĕō**, *gheh-or-gheh´-o;* from *1092; to till* (the soil):— dress.

1091. γεώργιον **gĕōrgiŏn**, *gheh-ore´-ghee-on;* neut. of a (presumed) der. of *1092; cultivable,* i.e. a *farm:*— husbandry.

1092. γεωργός **gĕōrgŏs**, *gheh-ore-gos´;* from *1093* and the base of *2041;* a *land-worker,* i.e. *farmer:*— husbandman.

1093. γῆ **gē**, *ghay;* contr. from a primary word; *soil;* by extension a *region,* or the solid part or the whole of the *terrene* globe (incl. the occupants in each application):— country, earth (-ly), ground, land, world.

1094. γῆρας **gēras**, *ghay´-ras;* akin to *1088; senility:*— old age.

1095. γηράσκω **gēraskō**, *ghay-ras´-ko;* from *1094; to be senescent:*— be (wax) old.

1096. γίνομαι **ginŏmai**, *ghin´-om-ahee;* a prol. and mid. voice form of a primary verb; *to cause to be* ("*gen*"-*erate*), i.e. (refl.) to *become* (*come into being*), used with great latitude (lit., fig., intens., etc.):— arise, be assembled, be (-come, -fall, -have self), be brought (to pass), (be) come (to pass), continue, be divided, draw, be ended, fall, be finished, follow, be found, be fulfilled, + God forbid, grow, happen, have, be kept, be made, be married, be ordained to be, partake, pass, be performed, be published, require, seem, be showed, × soon as it was, sound, be taken, be turned, use, wax, will, would, be wrought.

1097. γινώσκω **ginōskō**, *ghin-oce´-ko;* a prol. form of a primary verb; to "*know*" (absolutely) in a great variety of applications and with many impl. (as follow, with others not thus clearly expressed):— allow, be aware (of), feel, (have) know (-ledge), perceive, be resolved, can speak, be sure, understand.

1098. γλεῦκος **glĕukŏs**, *glyoo´-kos;* akin to *1099; sweet* wine, i.e. (prop.) *must* (fresh juice), but used of the more saccharine (and

therefore highly inebriating) fermented *wine:*— new wine.

1099. γλυκύς **glukus**, *gloo-koos´;* of uncert. aff.; *sweet* (i.e. not bitter nor salt):— sweet, fresh.

1100. γλῶσσα **glōssa**, *gloce-sah´;* of uncert. aff.; the *tongue;* by impl. a *language* (spec., one naturally unacquired):— tongue.

1101. γλωσσόκομον **glōssŏkŏmŏn**, *gloce-sok´-om-on;* from *1100* and the base of *2889;* prop. a *case* (to keep mouthpieces of wind-instruments in) i.e. (by extens.) a *casket* or (spec.) *purse:*— bag.

1102. γναφεύς **gnaphĕus**, *gnaf-yuce´;* by var. for a der. from κνάπτω **knaptō** (to *tease* cloth); a cloth-*dresser:*— fuller.

1103. γνήσιος **gnēsiŏs**, *gnay´-see-os;* from the same as *1077; legitimate* (of birth), i.e. *genuine:*— own, sincerity, true.

1104. γνησίως **gnēsiŏs**, *gnay-see´-oce;* adv. from *1103; genuinely,* i.e. *really:*— naturally.

1105. γνόφος **gnŏphŏs**, *gnof´-os;* akin to *3509; gloom* (as of a storm):— blackness.

1106. γνώμη **gnōmē**, *gno´-may;* from *1097; cognition,* i.e. (subj.) *opinion,* or (obj.) *resolve* (*counsel, consent,* etc.):— advice, + agree, judgment, mind, purpose, will.

1107. γνωρίζω **gnōrizo**, *gno-rid´-zo;* from a der. of *1097;* to *make known;* subj. to *know:*— certify, declare, make known, give to understand, do to wit, wot.

1108. γνῶσις **gnōsis**, *gno´-sis;* from *1097; knowing* (the act), i.e. (by impl.) *knowledge:*— knowledge, science.

1109. γνώστης **gnōstēs**, *gnoce´-tace;* from *1097;* a *knower:*— expert.

1110. γνωστός **gnōstŏs**, *gnoce-tos´;* from *1097; well-known:*— acquaintance, (which may be) known, notable.

1111. γογγύζω **gŏgguzō**, *gong-good´-zo;* of uncert. der.; to *grumble:*— murmur.

1112. γογγυσμός **gŏggusmŏs**, *gong-goos-mos´;* from *1111;* a *grumbling:*— grudging, murmuring.

1113. γογγυστής **gŏggustēs**, *gong-goos-tace´;* from *1111;* a *grumbler:*— murmurer.

1114. γόης **gŏēs**, *go´-ace;* from γοάω **gŏaō** (to *wail*); prop. a *wizard* (as *muttering* spells), i.e. (by impl.) an *imposter:*— seducer.

1115. Γολγοθᾶ **Golgŏtha**, *gol-goth-ah´;* of Chald. or. [comp. *1538*]; the *skull; Golgotha,* a knoll near Jerusalem:— Golgotha.

1116. Γόμορρα **Gŏmŏrrha**, *gom´-or-hrhah;* of Heb. or. [6017]; *Gomorrha* (i.e. `Amorah*), a place near the Dead Sea:— Gomorrha.

1117. γόμος **gŏmŏs**, *gom´-os;* from *1073;* a *load* (as *filling*), i.e. (spec.) a *cargo,* or (by extens.) *wares:*— burden, merchandise.

1118. γονεύς **gŏnĕus**, *gon-yooce´;* from the base of *1096;* a *parent:*— parent.

1119. γονύ **gŏnu**, *gon-oo´;* of uncert. aff.; the "*knee*":— knee (×l).

1120. γονυπετέω **gŏnupĕtĕō**, *gon-oo-pet-eh´-o;* from a compound of *1119* and the alt. of *4098;* to *fall* on the *knee:*— bow the knee, kneel down.

1121. γράμμα **gramma**, *gram´-mah;* from *1125;* a *writing,* i.e. a *letter, note, epistle, book,* etc.; plur. *learning:*— bill, learning, letter, scripture, writing, written.

1122. γραμματεύς **grammatĕus**, *gram-mat-yooce´;* from *1121;* a *writer,* i.e. (professionally) *scribe* or *secretary:*— scribe, town-clerk.

1123. γραπτός **graptŏs**, *grap-tos´;* from *1125; inscribed* (fig.):— written.

1124. γραφή **graphē**, *graf-ay´;* from *1125;* a *document,* i.e. holy *Writ* (or its contents or a statement in it):— scripture.

1125. γράφω **graphō**, *graf´-o;* a primary verb; to "*grave,*" espec. to *write;* fig. to *describe:*— describe, write (-ing, -ten).

1126. γραώδης **graōdēs**, *grah-o´-dace;* from γραύς **graus** (an *old woman*) and *1491; crone-like,* i.e. *silly:*— old wives'.

1127. γρηγορεύω **grēgŏrĕuō**, *gray-gor-yoo´-o;* from *1453;* to *keep awake,* i.e. *watch* (lit. or fig.):— be vigilant, wake, (be) watch (-ful).

1128. γυμνάζω **gumnazō**, *goom-nad´-zo;* from *1131;* to *practise naked* (in the games), i.e. *train* (fig.):— exercise.

1129. γυμνασία **gumnasia**, *goom-nas-ee´-ah;* from *1128; training,* i.e. (fig.) *asceticism:*— exercise.

1130. γυμνητεύω **gumnētĕuō**, *goom-nayt-yoo´-o* or γυμνιτεύω **gumniteuo**, *goom-niyt-yoo´-o;* from a der. of *1131;* to *strip,* i.e. (refl.) *go poorly clad:*— be naked.

1131. γυμνός **gumnŏs**, *goom-nos´;* of uncert. aff.; *nude* (absol. or rel., lit. or fig.):— naked.

1132. γυμνότης **gumnŏtēs**, *goom-not´-ace;* from *1131; nudity* (absol. or comp.):— nakedness.

1133. γυναικάριον **gunaikariŏn**, *goo-nahee-kar´-ee-on;* a dimin. from *1135;* a *little* (i.e. *foolish*) *woman:*— silly woman.

1134. γυναικεῖος **gunaikĕiŏs**, *goo-nahee-ki´-os;* from *1135; feminine:*— wife.

1135. γυνή **gunē**, *goo-nay´;* prob. from the base of *1096;* a *woman;* spec. a *wife:*— wife, woman.

1136. Γώγ **Gōg**, *gogue;* of Heb. or. [1463]; *Gog,* a symb. name for some future Antichrist:— Gog.

1137. γωνία **gōnia**, *go-nee´-ah;* prob. akin to *1119;* an *angle:*— corner, quarter.

Δ

1138. Δαβίδ **Dabid**, *dab-eed´;* of Heb. or. [1732]; *Dabid* (i.e. *David*), the Isr. king:— David.

1139. δαιμονίζομαι **daimŏnizŏmai**, *dahee-mon-id´-zom-ahee;* mid. voice from *1142;* to *be exercised by a demon:*— have a (be vexed with, be possessed with) devil (-s).

1140. δαιμόνιον **daimŏniŏn**, *dahee-mon´-ee-on;* neut. of a der. of *1142;* a *demonic being;* by extens. a *deity:*— devil, god.

1141. δαιμονιώδης **daimŏniōdēs**, *dahee-mon-ee-o´-dace;* from *1140* and *1142; demon-like:*— devilish.

1142. δαίμων **daimōn**, *dah´-ee-mown;* from δαίω **daiō** (to *distribute* fortunes); a *demon* or supernatural spirit (of a bad nature):— devil.

1143. δάκνω **daknō**, *dak´-no;* a prol. form of a primary root; to *bite,* i.e. (fig.) *thwart:*— bite.

1144. δάκρυ **dakru**, *dak´-roo;* or

    δάκρυον **dakruŏn**, *dak´-roo-on;* of uncert. affin.; a *tear:*— tear.

1145. δακρύω **dakruō**, *dak-roo´-o;* from *1144;* to *shed tears:*— weep. Comp. *2799.*

1146. δακτύλιος **daktuliŏs**, *dak-too´-lee-os;* from *1147;* a *finger-*ring:*— ring.

1147. δάκτυλος **daktulŏs**, *dak´-too-los;* prob. from *1176;* a *finger:*— finger.

1148. Δαλμανουθά **Dalmanŏutha**, *dal-man-oo-thah´;* prob. of Chald. or.; *Dalmanūtha,* a place in Pal.:— Dalmanutha.

1149. Δαλματία **Dalmatia**, *dal-mat-ee´-ah;* prob. of for. der.; *Dalmatia,* a region of Europe:— Dalmatia.

1150. δαμάζω **damazō**, *dam-ad´-zo;* a var. of an obs. primary of the same mean.; to *tame:*— tame.

1151. δάμαλις **damalis**, *dam´-al-is;* prob. from the base of *1150;* a *heifer* (as *tame*):— heifer.

1152. Δάμαρις **Damaris**, *dam´-ar-is;* prob. from the base of *1150;* perh. *gentle; Damaris,* an Athenian woman:— Damaris.

1153. Δαμασκηνός **Damaskēnŏs**, *dam-as-kay-nos´;* from *1154;* a *Damascene* or inhab. of Damascus:— Damascene.

1154. Δαμασκός **Damaskŏs**, *dam-as-kos´;* of Heb. or. [1834]; *Damascus,* a city of Syria:— Damascus.

1155. δανείζω **danĕizō**, *dan-ayd´-zo;* or

    δανίζω **danizō**, *dan-ide´-zo* from *1156;* to *loan* on interest; refl. to *borrow:*— borrow, lend.

1156. δάνειον **danĕiŏn**, *dan´-i-on;* from δάνος **danŏs** (a *gift*); prob. akin to the base of *1325;* a *loan:*— debt.

1157. δανειστής **daněistēs**, *dan-ice-tace´*; or δανιστής **danistēs**, *dan-iys-tace´* from 1155; a *lender:*— creditor.

1158. Δανιήλ **Daniēl**, *dan-ee-ale´*; of Heb. or. [1840]; *Daniel*, an Isr.:— Daniel.

1159. δαπανάω **dapanaō**, *dap-an-ah´-o*; from 1160; to *expend*, i.e. (in a good sense) to *incur cost*, or (in a bad one) to *waste:*— be at charges, consume, spend.

1160. δαπάνη **dapanē**, *dap-an´-ay*; from δάπτω **daptō** (to *devour*); *expense* (as *consuming*):— cost.

1161. δέ **dě**, *deh*; a primary particle (adversative or continuative); *but, and*, etc.:— also, and, but, moreover, now [often *unexpressed* in English].

1162. δέησις **děēsis**, *deh´-ay-sis*; from 1189; a *petition:*— prayer, request, supplication.

1163. δεῖ **děi**, *die*; third pers. sing. act. present of 1210; also δεόν **děon**, *deh-on´*; neut. act. part. of the same; both used impers.; *it is* (*was*, etc.) *necessary* (as *binding*):— behoved, be meet, must (needs), (be) need (-ful), ought, should.

1164. δεῖγμα **děigma**, *dīgh´-mah*; from the base of 1166; a *specimen* (as *shown*):— example.

1165. δειγματίζω **děigmatizō**, *dīgh-mat-id´-zo*; from 1164; to *exhibit:*— make a shew.

1166. δεικνύω **děiknuō**, *dike-noo´-o*; a prol. form of an obs. primary of the same mean.; to *show* (lit. or fig.):— shew.

1167. δειλία **děilia**, *di-lee´-ah*; from 1169; *timidity:*— fear.

1168. δειλιάω **děiliaō**, *di-lee-ah´-o*; from 1167; to *be timid:*— be afraid.

1169. δειλός **děilǒs**, *di-los´*; from δέος **děos** (*dread*); *timid*, i.e. (by impl.) *faithless:*— fearful.

1170. δεῖνα **děina**, *di´-nah*; prob. from the same as 1171 (through the idea of forgetting the name as *fearful*, i.e. *strange*); *so and so* (when the person is not specified):— such a man.

1171. δεινῶς **děinōs**, *di-noce´*; adv. from a der. of the same as 1169; *terribly*, i.e. *excessively:*— grievously, vehemently.

1172. δειπνέω **děipněō**, *dipe-neh´-o*; from 1173; to *dine*, i.e. take the principal (or evening) meal:— sup (× -er).

1173. δεῖπνον **děipnǒn**, *dipe-non*; from the same as 1160; *dinner*, i.e. the chief meal (usually in the evening):— feast, supper.

1174. δεισιδαιμονέστερος **děisidaimǒněstěrǒs**, *dice-ee-dahee-mon-es´-ter-os*; the comparative of a der. of the base of 1169 and 1142; *more religious* than others:— too superstitious.

1175. δεισιδαιμονία **děisidaimǒnia**, *dice-ee-*

dahee-mon-ee´-ah; from the same as 1174; *relig.:*— superstition.

1176. δέκα **děka**, *dek´-ah*; a primary number; *ten:*— [eight-] een, ten.

1177. δεκαδύο **děkaduǒ**, *dek-ad-oo´-o*; from 1176 and 1417; *two* and *ten*, i.e. *twelve:*— twelve.

1178. δεκαπέντε **děkapěntě**, *dek-ap-en´-teh*; from 1176 and 4002; *ten* and *five*, i.e. *fifteen:*— fifteen.

1179. Δεκάπολις **Děkapǒlis**, *dek-ap´-ol-is*; from 1176 and 4172; the *ten-city* region; the *Decapolis*, a district in Syria:— Decapolis.

1180. δεκατέσσαρες **děkatěssarěs**, *dek-at-es´-sar-es*; from 1176 and 5064; *ten* and *four*, i.e. *fourteen:*— fourteen.

1181. δεκάτη **děkatē**, *dek-at´-ay*; fem. of 1182; a *tenth*, i.e. as a percentage or (tech.) *tithe:*— tenth (part), tithe.

1182. δέκατος **děkatǒs**, *dek´-at-os*; ordinal from 1176; *tenth:*— tenth.

1183. δεκατόω **děkatǒō**, *dek-at-ǒ´-o*; from 1181; to *tithe*, i.e. to *give* or *take a tenth:*— pay (receive) tithes.

1184. δεκτός **děktǒs**, *dek-tos´*; from 1209; *approved*; (fig.) *propitious:*— accepted (-table).

1185. δελεάζω **děleazō**, *del-eh-ad´-zo*; from the base of 1388; to *entrap*, i.e. (fig.) *delude:*— allure, beguile, entice.

1186. δένδρον **děndrǒn**, *den´-dron*; prob. from δρῦς **drus** (an *oak*); a *tree:*— tree.

1187. δεξιολάβος **děxiǒlabǒs**, *dex-ee-ol-ab´-os*; from 1188 and 2983; a *guardsman* (as if *taking the right*) or light-armed soldier:— spearman.

1188. δεξιός **děxiǒs**, *dex-ee-os´*; from 1209; the *right* side or (fem.) hand (as that which usually *takes*):— right (hand, side).

1189. δέομαι **děǒmai**, *deh´-om-ahee*; mid. voice of 1210; to *beg* (as *binding oneself*), i.e. *petition:*— beseech, pray (to), make request. Comp. 4441.

δεόν **děon**. See 1163.

1190. Δερβαῖος **Děrbaiǒs**, *der-bah´-ee-os*; from 1191; a *Derbæan* or inhab. of Derbe:— of Derbe.

1191. Δέρβη **Děrbē**, *der-bay´*; of for. or.; *Derbè*, a place in Asia Minor:— Derbe.

1192. δέρμα **děrma**, *der´-mah*; from 1194; a *hide:*— skin.

1193. δερμάτινος **děrmatinǒs**, *der-mat´-ee-nos*; from 1192; made of *hide:*— leathern, of a skin.

1194. δέρω **děrō**, *der´-o*; a primary verb; prop. to *flay*, i.e. (by impl.) to *scourge*, or (by anal.) to *thrash:*— beat, smite.

1195. δεσμεύω **děsměuō**, *des-myoo´-o*; from a (presumed) der. of 1196; to *be a binder* (*captor*), i.e. to *enchain* (a prisoner), to *tie on* (a load):— bind.

1196. δεσμέω **dĕsmĕō**, *des-meh´-o;* from *1199;* to *tie*, i.e. *shackle:*— bind.

1197. δεσμή **dĕsmē**, *des-may´;* from *1196;* a *bundle:*— bundle.

1198. δέσμιος **dĕsmiŏs**, *des´-mee-os;* from *1199;* a *captive* (as *bound*):— in bonds, prisoner.

1199. δεσμόν **dĕsmŏn**, *des-mon´;* or

     δεσμός **dĕsmŏs**, *des-mos´;* neut. and masc. respectively from *1210;* a *band*, i.e. *ligament* (of the body) or *shackle* (of a prisoner); fig. an *impediment* or *disability:*— band, bond, chain, string.

1200. δεσμοφύλαξ **dĕsmŏphulax**, *des-mof-oo´-lax;* from *1199* and *5441;* a *jailer* (as *guarding* the *prisoners*):— jailor, keeper of the prison.

1201. δεσμωτήριον **dĕsmōtēriŏn**, *des-mo-tay´-ree-on;* from a der. of *1199* (equiv. to *1196);* a *place of bondage*, i.e. a *dungeon:*— prison.

1202. δεσμώτης **dĕsmōtēs**, *des-mo´-tace;* from the same as *1201;* (pass.) a *captive:*— prisoner.

1203. δεσπότης **dĕspŏtēs**, *des-pot´-ace;* perh. from *1210* and πόσις **pŏsis** (a *husband*); an absolute *ruler* ("despot"):— Lord, master.

1204. δεῦρο **dĕurŏ**, *dyoo´-ro;* of uncert. aff.; *here;* used also imperative *hither!;* and of time, *hitherto:*— come (hither), hither [-to].

1205. δεῦτε **dĕutĕ**, *dyoo´-teh;* from *1204* and an imper. form of εἶμι **ĕimi** (to *go*); *come hither!:*— come, × follow.

1206. δευτεραῖος **dĕutĕraiŏs**, *dyoo-ter-ah´-yos;* from *1208; secondary*, i.e. (spec.) on the *second* day:— next day.

1207. δευτερόπρωτος **dĕutĕrŏprōtŏs**, *dyoo-ter-op´-ro-tos;* from *1208* and *4413; second-first*, i.e. (spec.) a designation of the Sabbath immediately after the Paschal week (being the *second* after Passover day, and the *first* of the seven Sabbaths intervening before Pentecost):— second ... after the first.

1208. δεύτερος **dĕutĕrŏs**, *dyoo´-ter-os;* as the comp. of *1417;* (ordinal) *second* (in time, place, or rank; also adv.):— afterward, again, second (-arily, time).

1209. δέχομαι **dĕchŏmai**, *dekh´-om-ahee;* mid. voice of a primary verb; to *receive* (in various applications, lit. or fig.):— accept, receive, take. Comp. *2983.*

1210. δέω **dĕō**, *deh´-o;* a primary verb; to *bind* (in various applications, lit. or fig.):— bind, be in bonds, knit, tie, wind. See also *1163, 1189.*

1211. δή **dē**, *day;* prob. akin to *1161;* a particle of emphasis or explicitness; *now, then*, etc.:— also, and, doubtless, now, therefore.

1212. δῆλος **dēlŏs**, *day´-los;* of uncert. der.; *clear:*— + bewray, certain, evident, manifest.

1213. δηλόω **dēlŏō**, *day-lŏ´-o;* from *1212;* to

make plain (by words):— declare, shew, signify.

1214. Δημᾶς **Dēmas**, *day-mas´;* prob. for *1216; Demas*, a Chr.:— Demas.

1215. δημηγορέω **dēmēgŏrĕō**, *day-may-gor-eh´-o;* from a compound of *1218* and *58;* to *be a people-gatherer*, i.e. to *address* a public assembly:— make an oration.

1216. Δημήτριος **Dēmētriŏs**, *day-may´-tree-os;* from Δημήτηρ **Dēmētēr** (*Ceres*); *Demetrius*, the name of an Ephesian and of a Chr.:— Demetrius.

1217. δημιουργός **dēmiŏurgŏs**, *day-me-oor-gos´;* from *1218* and *2041;* a *worker* for the *people*, i.e. *mechanic* (spoken of the *Creator*):— maker.

1218. δῆμος **dēmŏs**, *day´-mos;* from *1210;* the *public* (as *bound* together socially):— people.

1219. δημόσιος **dēmŏsiŏs**, *day-mos´ee-os;* from *1218; public;* (fem. sing. dat. case as adv.) *in public:*— common, openly, publickly.

1220. δηνάριον **dēnariŏn**, *day-nar´-ee-on;* of Lat. or.; a *denarius* (or *ten asses*):— pence, penny [-worth].

1221. δήποτε **dēpŏtĕ**, *day´-pot-eh;* from *1211* and *4218;* a particle of generalization; *indeed, at any time:*— (what-) soever.

1222. δήπου **dēpŏu**, *day´-poo;* from *1211* and *4225;* a particle of asseveration; *indeed doubtless:*— verily.

1223. διά **dia**, *dee-ah´;* a primary prep. denoting the *channel* of an act; *through* (in very wide applications, local, causal, or occasional):— after, always, among, at, to avoid, because of (that), briefly, by, for (cause) ... fore, from, in, by occasion of, of, by reason of, for sake, that, thereby, therefore, × though, through (-out), to, wherefore, with (-in). In composition it retains the same general import.

     Δία **Dia**. See *2203.*

1224. διαβαίνω **diabainō**, *dee-ab-ah´-ee-no;* from *1223* and the base of *939;* to *cross:*— come over, pass (through).

1225. διαβάλλω **diaballō**, *dee-ab-al´-lo;* from *1223* and *906;* (fig.) to *traduce:*— accuse.

1226. διαβεβαιόομαι **diabĕbaiŏŏmai**, *dee-ab-eb-ahee-ŏ´-om-ahee;* mid. voice of a compound of *1223* and *950;* to *confirm thoroughly* (by words), i.e. *asseverate:*— affirm constantly.

1227. διαβλέπω **diablĕpō**, *dee-ab-lep´-o;* from *1223* and *991;* to *look through*, i.e. *recover* full *vision:*— see clearly.

1228. διάβολος **diabŏlŏs**, *dee-ab´-ol-os;* from *1225;* a *traducer;* spec. *Satan* [comp. 7854]:— false accuser, devil, slanderer.

1229. διαγγέλλω **diaggĕllō**, *de-ang-gel´-lo;*

from *1223* and the base of *32;* to *herald thoroughly:*— declare, preach, signify.

1230. διαγίνομαι **diaginŏmai,** *dee-ag-in´-om-ahee;* from *1223* and *1096;* to *elapse meanwhile:*— × after, be past, be spent.

1231. διαγινώσκω **diaginōskō,** *dee-ag-in-o´-sko;* from *1223* and *1097;* to *know thoroughly,* i.e. *ascertain exactly:*— (would) enquire, know the uttermost.

1232. διαγνωρίζω **diagnōrizō,** *dee-ag-no-rid´-zo;* from *1123* and *1107;* to *tell abroad:*— make known.

1233. διάγνωσις **diagnōsis,** *dee-ag´-no-sis;* from *1231;* (magisterial) *examination* ("diagnosis"):— hearing.

1234. διαγογγύζω **diagŏgguzō,** *dee-ag-ong-good´-zo;* from *1223* and *1111;* to *complain throughout* a crowd:— murmur.

1235. διαγρηγορέω **diagrēgŏrĕō,** *dee-ag-ray-gor-eh´-o;* from *1223* and *1127;* to *waken thoroughly:*— be awake.

1236. διάγω **diagō,** *dee-ag´-o;* from *1223* and *71;* to *pass* time or life:— lead life, living.

1237. διαδέχομαι **diadĕchŏmai,** *dee-ad-ekh´-om-ahee;* from *1223* and *1209;* to *receive in turn,* i.e. (fig.) *succeed to:*— come after.

1238. διάδημα **diadēma,** *dee-ad´-ay-mah;* from a compound of *1223* and *1210;* a "*diadem*" (as *bound about* the head):— crown. Comp. *4735.*

1239. διαδίδωμι **diadidōmi,** *dee-ad-id´-o-mee;* from *1223* and *1325;* to *give throughout* a crowd, i.e. *deal out;* also to *deliver* over (as to a successor):— (make) distribute (-ion), divide, give.

1240. διάδοχος **diadŏchŏs,** *dee-ad´-okh-os;* from *1237;* a *successor* in office:— room.

1241. διαζώννυμι **diazōnnumi,** *dee-az-own´-noo-mee;* from *1223* and *2224;* to *gird tightly:*— gird.

1242. διαθήκη **diathēkē,** *dee-ath-ay´-kay;* from *1303;* prop. a *disposition,* i.e. (spec.) a *contract* (espec. a devisory *will*):— covenant, testament.

1243. διαίρεσις **diairĕsis,** *dee-ah´-ee-res-is;* from *1244;* a *distinction* or (concr.) *variety:*— difference, diversity.

1244. διαιρέω **diairĕō,** *dee-ahee-reh´-o;* from *1223* and *138;* to *separate,* i.e. *distribute:*— divide.

1245. διακαθαρίζω **diakatharizō,** *dee-ak-ath-ar-id´-zo;* from *1223* and *2511;* to *cleanse perfectly,* i.e. (spec.) *winnow:*— thoroughly purge.

1246. διακατελέγχομαι **diakatĕlĕgchŏmai,** *dee-ak-at-el-eng´-khom-ahee;* mid. voice from *1223* and a compound of *2596* and *1651;* to *prove downright,* i.e. *confute:*— convince.

1247. διακονέω **diakŏnĕō,** *dee-ak-on-eh´-o;* from *1249;* to *be an attendant,* i.e. *wait upon*

(menially or as a host, friend, or [fig.] teacher); techn. to *act as a* Chr. *deacon:*— (ad-) minister (unto), serve, use the office of a deacon.

1248. διακονία **diakŏnia,** *dee-ak-on-ee´-ah;* from *1249; attendance* (as a servant, etc.); fig. (eleemosynary) *aid,* (official) *service* (espec. of the Chr. teacher, or techn. of the *diaconate*):— (ad-) minister (-ing, -tration, -try), office, relief, service (-ing).

1249. διάκονος **diakŏnŏs,** *dee-ak´-on-os;* prob. from an obs. διάκω **diakō** (to *run* on errands; comp. *1377*); an *attendant,* i.e. (gen.) a *waiter* (at table or in other menial duties); spec. a Chr. *teacher* and *pastor* (tech. a *deacon* or *deaconess*):— deacon, minister, servant.

1250. διακόσιοι **diakŏsiŏi,** *dee-ak-os´-ee-oy;* from *1364* and *1540; two hundred:*— two hundred.

1251. διακούομαι **diakŏuŏmai,** *dee-ak-oo´-om-ahee;* mid. voice from *1223* and *191;* to *hear throughout,* i.e. *patiently listen* (to a prisoner's plea):— hear.

1252. διακρίνω **diakrinō,** *dee-ak-ree´-no;* from *1223* and *2919;* to *separate thoroughly,* i.e. (lit. and refl.) to *withdraw* from, or (by impl.) *oppose;* fig. to *discriminate* (by impl. *decide*), or (refl.) *hesitate:*— contend, make (to) differ (-ence), discern, doubt, judge, be partial, stagger, waver.

1253. διάκρισις **diakrisis,** *dee-ak´-ree-sis;* from *1252;* judicial *estimation:*— discern (-ing), disputation.

1254. διακωλύω **diakōluō,** *dee-ak-o-loo´-o;* from *1223* and *2967;* to *hinder altogether,* i.e. *utterly prohibit:*— forbid.

1255. διαλαλέω **dialalĕō,** *dee-al-al-eh´-o;* from *1223* and *2980;* to *talk throughout* a company, i.e. *converse* or (gen.) *publish:*— commune, noise abroad.

1256. διαλέγομαι **dialĕgŏmai,** *dee-al-eg´-om-ahee;* mid. voice from *1223* and *3004;* to *say thoroughly,* i.e. *discuss* (in argument or exhortation):— dispute, preach (unto), reason (with), speak.

1257. διαλείπω **dialĕipō,** *dee-al-i´-po;* from *1223* and *3007;* to *leave off in the middle,* i.e. *intermit:*— cease.

1258. διάλεκτος **dialĕktŏs,** *dee-al´-ek-tos;* from *1256;* a (mode of) discourse, i.e. "*dialect*":— language, tongue.

1259. διαλλάσσω **diallassō,** *dee-al-las´-so;* from *1223* and *236;* to *change thoroughly,* i.e. (ment.) to *conciliate:*— reconcile.

1260. διαλογίζομαι **dialŏgizŏmai,** *dee-al-og-id´-zom-ahee;* from *1223* and *3049;* to *reckon thoroughly,* i.e. (gen.) to *deliberate* (by reflection or discussion):— cast in mind, consider, dispute, muse, reason, think.

Greek

1261. διαλογισμός **dialŏgismŏs**, *dee-al-og-is-mos´*; from *1260*; *discussion*, i.e. (internal) *consideration* (by impl. *purpose*), or (external) *debate:*— dispute, doubtful (-ing), imagination, reasoning, thought.

1262. διαλύω **dialuō**, *dee-al-oo´-o*; from *1223* and *3089*; to *dissolve utterly:*— scatter.

1263. διαμαρτύρομαι **diamarturŏmai**, *dee-am-ar-too´-rom-ahee*; from *1223* and *3140*; to *attest* or *protest earnestly*, or (by impl.) *hortatively:*— charge, testify (unto), witness.

1264. διαμάχομαι **diamachŏmai**, *dee-am-akh´-om-ahee*; from *1223* and *3164*; to *fight fiercely* (in altercation):— strive.

1265. διαμένω **diamĕnō**, *dee-am-en´-o*; from *1223* and *3306*; to *stay constantly* (in being or relation):— continue, remain.

1266. διαμερίζω **diamĕrizō**, *dee-am-er-id´-zo*; from *1223* and *3307*; to *partition thoroughly* (lit. in distribution, fig. in dissension):— cloven, divide, part.

1267. διαμερισμός **diamĕrismŏs**, *dee-am-er-is-mos´*; from *1266*; *disunion* (of opinion and conduct):— division.

1268. διανέμω **dianĕmō**, *dee-an-em´-o*; from *1223* and the base of *3551*; to *distribute*, i.e. (of information) to *disseminate:*— spread.

1269. διανεύω **dianĕuō**, *dee-an-yoo´-o*; from *1223* and *3506*; to *nod* (or *express* by signs) *across* an intervening space:— beckon.

1270. διανόημα **dianŏēma**, *dee-an-o´-ay-mah*; from a compound of *1223* and *3539*; something *thought through*, i.e. a *sentiment:*— thought.

1271. διάνοια **dianŏia**, *dee-an´-oy-ah*; from *1223* and *3563*; *deep thought*, prop. the faculty (*mind* or its *disposition*), by impl. its exercise:— imagination, mind, understanding.

1272. διανοίγω **dianŏigō**, *dee-an-oy´-go*; from *1223* and *455*; to *open thoroughly*, lit. (as a first-born) or fig. (to *expound*):— open.

1273. διανυκτερεύω **dianuktĕrĕuō**, *dee-an-ook-ter-yoo´-o*; from *1223* and a der. of *3571*; to *sit up the whole night:*— continue all night.

1274. διανύω **dianuō**, *dee-an-oo´-o*; from *1223* and ἀνύω **anuō** (to *effect*); to *accomplish thoroughly:*— finish.

1275. διαπαντός **diapantŏs**, *dee-ap-an-tos´*; from *1223* and the genit. of *3956*; *through all* the time, i.e. (adv.) *constantly:*— alway (-s), continually.

1276. διαπεράω **diapĕraō**, *dee-ap-er-ah´-o*; from *1223* and a der. of the base of *4008*; to *cross entirely:*— go over, pass (over), sail over.

1277. διαπλέω **diaplĕō**, *dee-ap-leh´-o*; from *1223* and *4126*; to *sail through:*— sail over.

1278. διαπονέω **diapŏnĕō**, *dee-ap-on-eh´-o*; from *1223* and a der. of *4192*; to *toil through*, i.e. (pass.) *be worried:*— be grieved.

1279. διαπορεύομαι **diapŏrĕuŏmai**, *dee-ap-or-yoo´-om-ahee*; from *1223* and *4198*; to *travel through:*— go through, journey in, pass by.

1280. διαπορέω **diapŏrĕō**, *dee-ap-or-eh´-o*; from *1223* and *639*; to *be thoroughly nonplussed:*— (be in) doubt, be (much) perplexed.

1281. διαπραγματεύομαι **diapragmatĕuŏmai**, *dee-ap-rag-mat-yoo´-om-ahee*; from *1223* and *4231*; to *thoroughly occupy oneself*, i.e. (tran. and by impl.) to *earn* in business:— gain by trading.

1282. διαπρίω **diapriō**, *dee-ap-ree´-o*; from *1223* and the base of *4249*; to *saw asunder*, i.e. (fig.) to *exasperate:*— cut (to the heart).

1283. διαρπάζω **diarpazō**, *dee-ar-pad´-zo*; from *1223* and *726*; to *seize asunder*, i.e. *plunder:*— spoil.

1284. διαρρήσσω **diarrhēssō**, *dee-ar-hrayce´-so*; from *1223* and *4486*; to *tear asunder:*— break, rend.

1285. διασαφέω **diasaphĕō**, *dee-as-af-eh´-o*; from *1223* and σαφής **saphēs** (*clear*); to *clear thoroughly*, i.e. (fig.) *declare:*— tell unto.

1286. διασείω **diasĕiō**, *dee-as-i´-o*; from *1223* and *4579*; to *shake thoroughly*, i.e. (fig.) to *intimidate:*— do violence to.

1287. διασκορπίζω **diaskŏrpizō**, *dee-as-kor-pid´-zo*; from *1223* and *4650*; to *dissipate*, i.e. (gen.) to *rout* or *separate*; spec., to *winnow*; fig. to *squander:*— disperse, scatter (abroad), strew, waste.

1288. διασπάω **diaspaō**, *dee-as-pah´-o*; from *1223* and *4685*; to *draw apart*, i.e. *sever* or *dismember:*— pluck asunder, pull in pieces.

1289. διασπείρω **diaspĕirō**, *dee-as-pi´-ro*; from *1223* and *4687*; to *sow throughout*, i.e. (fig.) *distribute* in foreign lands:— scatter abroad.

1290. διασπορά **diaspŏra**, *dee-as-por-ah´*; from *1289*; *dispersion*, i.e. (spec. and concr.) the (converted) Isr. *resident* in Gentile countries:— (which are) scattered (abroad).

1291. διαστέλλομαι **diastĕllŏmai**, *dee-as-tel´-lom-ahee*; mid. voice from *1223* and *4724*; to *set* (oneself) *apart* (fig. *distinguish*), i.e. (by impl.) to *enjoin:*— charge, that which was (give) commanded (-ment).

1292. διάστημα **diastēma**, *dee-as´-tay-mah*; from *1339*; an *interval:*— space.

1293. διαστολή **diastŏlē**, *dee-as-tol-ay´*; from *1291*; a *variation:*— difference, distinction.

1294. διαστρέφω **diastrĕphō**, *dee-as-tref´-o*; from *1223* and *4762*; to *distort*, i.e. (fig.) *misinterpret*, or (morally) *corrupt:*— perverse (-rt), turn away.

1295. διασώζω **diasōzō**, *dee-as-odze´-o*; from *1223* and *4982*; to *save thoroughly*, i.e. (by impl. or anal.) to *cure, preserve, rescue,* etc.:— bring safe, escape (safe), heal, make perfectly whole, save.

1296. διαταγή **diatagē,** *dee-at-ag-ay´;* from *1299; arrangement,* i.e. *institution:*— instrumentality.

1297. διάταγμα **diatagma,** *dee-at´-ag-mah;* from *1299;* an *arrangement,* i.e. (authoritative) *edict:*— commandment.

1298. διαταράσσω **diatarassō,** *dee-at-ar-as´-so;* from *1223* and *5015;* to *disturb wholly,* i.e. *agitate* (with alarm):— trouble.

1299. διατάσσω **diatassō,** *dee-at-as´-so;* from *1223* and *5021;* to *arrange thoroughly,* i.e. (spec.) *institute, prescribe,* etc.:— appoint, command, give, (set in) order, ordain.

1300. διατελέω **diatĕlĕō,** *dee-at-el-eh´-o;* from *1223* and *5055;* to *accomplish thoroughly,* i.e. (subj.) to *persist:*— continue.

1301. διατηρέω **diatērĕō,** *dee-at-ay-reh´-o;* from *1223* and *5083;* to *watch thoroughly,* i.e. (pos. and tran.) to *observe* strictly, or (neg. and refl.) to *avoid* wholly:— keep.

1302. διατί **diati,** *dee-at-ee´;* from *1223* and *5101; through what* cause?, i.e. *why?:*— wherefore, why.

1303. διατίθεμαι **diatithĕmai,** *dee-at-ith´-em-ahee;* mid. voice from *1223* and *5087;* to *put apart,* i.e. (fig.) *dispose* (by assignment, compact, or bequest):— appoint, make, testator.

1304. διατρίβω **diatribō,** *dee-at-ree´-bo;* from *1223* and the base of *5147;* to *wear through* (time), i.e. *remain:*— abide, be, continue, tarry.

1305. διατροφή **diatrŏphē,** *dee-at-rof-ay´;* from a compound of *1223* and *5142; nourishment:*— food.

1306. διαυγάζω **diaugazō,** *dee-ow-gad´-zo;* from *1223* and *826;* to *glimmer* (*through*), i.e. *break* (as day):— dawn.

1307. διαφανής **diaphanēs,** *dee-af-an-ace´;* from *1223* and *5316; appearing through,* i.e. "*diaphanous*":— transparent.

1308. διαφέρω **diaphĕrō,** *dee-af-er´-o;* from *1223* and *5342;* to *bear through,* i.e. (lit.) *transport;* usually to *bear apart,* i.e. (obj.) to *toss about* (fig. *report*); subj. to "*differ,*" or (by impl.) *surpass:*— be better, carry, differ from, drive up and down, be (more) excellent, make matter, publish, be of more value.

1309. διαφεύγω **diaphĕugō,** *dee-af-yoo´-go;* from *1223* and *5343;* to *flee through,* i.e. *escape:*— escape.

1310. διαφημίζω **diaphēmizō,** *dee-af-ay-mid´-zo;* from *1223* and a der. of *5345;* to *report thoroughly,* i.e. *divulgate:*— blaze abroad, commonly report, spread abroad, fame.

1311. διαφθείρω **diaphthĕirō,** *dee-af-thi´-ro;* from *1225* and *5351;* to *rot thoroughly,* i.e. (by impl.) to *ruin* (pass. *decay* utterly, fig. *pervert*):— corrupt, destroy, perish.

1312. διαφθορά **diaphthŏra,** *dee-af-thor-ah´;* from *1311; decay:*— corruption.

1313. διάφορος **diaphŏrŏs,** *dee-af´-or-os;* from *1308; varying;* also *surpassing:*— differing, divers, more excellent.

1314. διαφυλάσσω **diaphulassō,** *dee-af-oo-las´-so;* from *1223* and *5442;* to *guard thoroughly,* i.e. *protect:*— keep.

1315. διαχειρίζομαι **diachĕirizŏmai,** *dee-akh-i-rid´-zom-ahee;* from *1223* and a der. of *5495;* to *handle thoroughly,* i.e. *lay* violent *hands* upon:— kill, slay.

1316. διαχωρίζομαι **diachōrizŏmai,** *dee-akh-o-rid´-zom-ahee;* from *1223* and the mid. voice of *5563;* to *remove* (oneself) *wholly,* i.e. *retire:*— depart.

1317. διδακτικός **didaktikŏs,** *did-ak-tik-os´;* from *1318; instructive* ("didactic"):— apt to teach.

1318. διδακτός **didaktŏs,** *did-ak-tos´;* from *1321;* (subj.) *instructed,* or (obj.) *communicated* by teaching:— taught, which ... teacheth.

1319. διδασκαλία **didaskalia,** *did-as-kal-ee´-ah;* from *1320; instruction* (the function or the information):— doctrine, learning, teaching.

1320. διδάσκαλος **didaskalŏs,** *did-as´-kal-os;* from *1321;* an *instructor* (gen. or spec.):— doctor, master, teacher.

1321. διδάσκω **didaskō,** *did-as´-ko;* a prol. (caus.) form of a primary verb δάω **daō** (to *learn*); to *teach* (in the same broad application):— teach.

1322. διδαχή **didachē,** *did-akh-ay´;* from *1321; instruction* (the act or the matter):— doctrine, hath been taught.

1323. δίδραχμον **didrachmŏn,** *did´-rakh-mon;* from *1364* and *1406;* a *double drachma* (*didrachm*):— tribute.

1324. Δίδυμος **Didumŏs,** *did´-oo-mos;* prol. from *1364; double,* i.e. *twin; Didymus,* a Chr.:— Didymus.

1325. δίδωμι **didōmi,** *did´-o-mee;* a prol. form of a primary verb (which is used as an altern. in most of the tenses); to *give* (used in a very wide application, prop. or by impl., lit. or fig.; greatly modified by the connection):— adventure, bestow, bring forth, commit, deliver (up), give, grant, hinder, make, minister, number, offer, have power, put, receive, set, shew, smite (+ with the hand), strike (+ with the palm of the hand), suffer, take, utter, yield.

1326. διεγείρω **diĕgĕirō,** *dee-eg-i´-ro;* from *1223* and *1453;* to *wake fully;* i.e. *arouse* (lit. or fig.):— arise, awake, raise, stir up.

1327. διέξοδος **diĕxŏdŏs,** *dee-ex´-od-os;* from *1223* and *1841;* an *outlet through,* i.e. prob. an open *square* (from which roads diverge):— highway.

1328. διερμηνευτής **diĕrmēnĕutēs**, *dee-er-main-yoo-tace´;* from *1329;* an *explainer:*— interpreter.

1329. διερμηνεύω **diĕrmēnĕuō**, *dee-er-main-yoo´-o;* from *1223* and *2059;* to *explain thoroughly,* by impl. to *translate:*— expound, interpret (-ation).

1330. διέρχομαι **diĕrchŏmai**, *dee-er´-khom-ahee;* from *1223* and *2064;* to *traverse* (lit.):— come, depart, go (about, abroad, everywhere, over, through, throughout), pass (by, over, through, throughout), pierce through, travel, walk through.

1331. διερωτάω **diĕrōtaō**, *dee-er-o-tah´-o;* from *1223* and *2065;* to *question throughout,* i.e. *ascertain* by interrogation:— make enquiry for.

1332. διετής **diĕtēs**, *dee-et-ace´;* from *1364* and *2094;* of *two years* (in age):— two years old.

1333. διετία **diĕtia**, *dee-et-ee´-a;* from *1332;* a space of *two years* (*biennium*):— two years.

1334. διηγέομαι **diēgĕŏmai**, *dee-ayg-eh´-om-ahee;* from *1223* and *2233;* to *relate fully:*— declare, shew, tell.

1335. διήγεσις **diēgĕsis**, *dee-ayg´-es-is;* or διήγησις **diēgēsis** *dee-ayg´-es-is;* from *1334;* a *recital:*— declaration.

1336. διηνεκές **diēnĕkĕs**, *dee-ay-nek-es´;* neut. of a compound of *1223* and a der. of an alt. of *5342; carried through,* i.e. (adv. with *1519* and *3588* pref.) *perpetually:*— + continually, for ever.

1337. διθάλασσος **dithalassŏs**, *dee-thal´-as-sos;* from *1364* and *2281; having two seas,* i.e. a *sound* with a double outlet:— where two seas meet.

1338. διϊκνέομαι **diïknĕŏmai**, *dee-ik-neh´-om-ahee;* from *1223* and the base of *2425;* to *reach through,* i.e. *penetrate:*— pierce.

1339. διΐστημι **diïstēmi**, *dee-is´-tay-mee;* from *1223* and *2476;* to *stand apart,* i.e. (refl.) to *remove, intervene:*— go further, be parted, after the space of.

1340. διϊσχυρίζομαι **diïschurizŏmai**, *dee-is-khoo-rid´-zom-ahee;* from *1223* and a der. of *2478;* to *stout it through,* i.e. *asseverate:*— confidently (constantly) affirm.

1341. δικαιοκρισία **dikaiŏkrisia**, *dik-ah-yok-ris-ee´-ah;* from *1342* and *2920;* a *just sentence:*— righteous judgment.

1342. δίκαιος **dikaiŏs**, *dik´-ah-yos;* from *1349; equitable* (in character or act); by impl. *innocent, holy* (absol. or rel.):— just, meet, right (-eous).

1343. δικαιοσύνη **dikaiŏsunē**, *dik-ah-yos-oo´-nay;* from *1342; equity* (of character or act); spec. (Chr.) *justification:*— righteousness.

1344. δικαιόω **dikaiŏō**, *dik-ah-yŏ´-o;* from *1342;* to *render* (i.e. *show* or *regard* as) *just* or *innocent:*— free, justify (-ier), be righteous.

1345. δικαίωμα **dikaiōma**, *dik-ah´-yo-mah;* from *1344;* an *equitable deed;* by impl. a *statute* or *decision:*— judgment, justification, ordinance, righteousness.

1346. δικαίως **dikaiōs**, *dik-ah´-yoce;* adv. from *1342; equitably:*— justly, (to) righteously (-ness).

1347. δικαίωσις **dikaiōsis**, *dik-ah´-yo-sis;* from *1344; acquittal* (for Christ's sake):— justification.

1348. δικαστής **dikastēs**, *dik-as-tace´;* from a der. of *1349;* a *judger:*— judge.

1349. δίκη **dikē**, *dee´-kay;* prob. from *1166; right* (as self-*evident*), i.e. *justice* (the principle, a decision, or its execution):— judgment, punish, vengeance.

1350. δίκτυον **diktuŏn**, *dik´-too-on;* prob. from a primary verb δίκω **dikō** (to *cast*); a *seine* (for fishing):— net.

1351. δίλογος **dilŏgŏs**, *dil´-og-os;* from *1364* and *3056; equivocal,* i.e. telling a different story:— double-tongued.

1352. διό **diŏ**, *dee-ŏ´;* from *1223* and *3739; through which* thing, i.e. *consequently:*— for which cause, therefore, wherefore.

1353. διοδεύω **diŏdĕuō**, *dee-od-yoo´-o;* from *1223* and *3593;* to *travel through:*— go throughout, pass through.

1354. Διονύσιος **Diŏnusiŏs**, *dee-on-oo´-see-os;* from Διόνυσος **Diŏnusŏs** (*Bacchus*); *reveller; Dionysius,* an Athenian:— Dionysius.

1355. διόπερ **diŏpĕr**, *dee-op´-er;* from *1352* and *4007; on which very account:*— wherefore.

1356. διοπετής **diŏpĕtēs**, *dee-op-et´-ace;* from the alt. of *2203* and the alt. of *4098; sky-fallen* (i.e. an *aerolite*):— which fell down from Jupiter.

1357. διόρθωσις **diŏrthōsis**, *dee-or´-tho-sis;* from a compound of *1223* and a der. of *3717,* mean. to *straighten thoroughly; rectification,* i.e. (spec.) the Messianic *restoration:*— reformation.

1358. διορύσσω **diŏrussō**, *dee-or-oos´-so;* from *1223* and *3736;* to *penetrate* burglariously:— break through (up).

Διός **Diŏs**. See *2203.*

1359. Διόσκουροι **Diŏskŏurŏi**, *dee-os´-koo-roy;* from the alt. of *2203* and a form of the base of *2877; sons of Jupiter,* i.e. the twins *Dioscuri:*— Castor and Pollux.

1360. διότι **diŏti**, *dee-ot´-ee;* from *1223* and *3754; on the very account that,* or *inasmuch as:*— because (that), for, therefore.

1361. Διοτρεφής **Diŏtrĕphēs**, *dee-ot-ref-ace´;* from the alt. of *2203* and *5142; Jove-nourished; Diotrephes,* an opponent of Christianity:— Diotrephes.

1362. διπλοῦς **diplŏus**, *dip-looce´;* or διπλόος **diploos**, *dip-loce´* from *1364* and (prob.) the base of *4119; two-fold:*— double, two-fold more.

1363. διπλόω **diplŏō**, *dip-lŏ´-o;* from *1362;* to *render two-fold:*— double.

1364. δίς **dis**, *dece;* adv. from *1417; twice:*— again, twice.

Δίς **Dis**. See *2203.*

1365. διστάζω **distazō**, *dis-tad´-zo;* from *1364;* prop. to *duplicate,* i.e. (ment.) to *waver* (in opinion):— doubt.

1366. δίστομος **distŏmŏs**, *dis´-tom-os;* from *1364* and *4750; double-edged:*— with two edges, two-edged.

1367. δισχίλιοι **dischilïoi**, *dis-khil´-ee-oy;* from *1364* and *5507; two thousand:*— two thousand.

1368. διυλίζω **diulizō**, *dee-oo-lid´-zo;* from *1223* and ὑλίζω **hulizō**, *hoo-lid´-zo* (to *filter*); to *strain out:*— strain at [prob. by misprint].

1369. διχάζω **dichazō**, *dee-khad´-zo;* from a der. of *1364;* to *make apart,* i.e. *sunder* (fig. *alienate*):— set at variance.

1370. διχοστασία **dichŏstasia**, *dee-khos-tas-ee´-ah;* from a der. of *1364* and *4714; disunion,* i.e. (fig.) *dissension:*— division, sedition.

1371. διχοτομέω **dichŏtŏmĕō**, *dee-khot-om-eh´-o;* from a compound of a der. of *1364* and a der. of τέμνω **tĕmnō** (to *cut*); to *bisect,* i.e. (by extens.) to *flog* severely:— cut asunder (in sunder).

1372. διψάω **dipsaō**, *dip-sah´-o;* from a var. of *1373;* to *thirst* for (lit. or fig.):— (be, be a-) thirst (-y).

1373. δίψος **dipsŏs**, *dip´-sos;* of uncert. aff.; *thirst:*— thirst.

1374. δίψυχος **dipsuchŏs**, *dip´-soo-khos;* from *1364* and *5590; two-spirited,* i.e. *vacillating* (in opinion or purpose):— double minded.

1375. διωγμός **diōgmŏs**, *dee-ogue-mos´;* from *1377; persecution:*— persecution.

1376. διώκτης **diōktēs**, *dee-oke´-tace;* from *1377;* a *persecutor:*— persecutor.

1377. διώκω **diōkō**, *dee-o´-ko;* a prol. (and caus.) form of a primary verb δίω **diō** (to *flee;* comp. the base of *1169* and *1249*); to *pursue* (lit. or fig.); by impl. to *persecute:*— ensue, follow (after), given to, (suffer) persecute (-ion), press toward.

1378. δόγμα **dŏgma**, *dog´-mah;* from the base of *1380;* a *law* (civil, cerem. or eccl.):— decree, ordinance.

1379. δογματίζω **dŏgmatizō**, *dog-mat-id´-zo;* from *1378;* to *prescribe* by statute, i.e. (refl.) to *submit* to cer. *rule:*— be subject to ordinances.

1380. δοκέω **dŏkĕō**, *dok-eh´-o;* a prol. form of a primary verb, δόκω **dŏkō**, *dok´-o* (used only in an alt. in certain tenses; comp. the base of *1166*) of the same mean.; to *think;* by impl. to *seem* (truthfully or uncertainly):— be ac-

counted, (of own) please (-ure), be of reputation, seem (good), suppose, think, trow.

1381. δοκιμάζω **dŏkimazō**, *dok-im-ad´-zo;* from *1384;* to *test* (lit. or fig.); by impl. to *approve:*— allow, discern, examine, × like, (ap-) prove, try.

1382. δοκιμή **dŏkimē**, *dok-ee-may´;* from the same as *1384; test* (abstr. or concr.); by impl. *trustiness:*— experience (-riment), proof, trial.

1383. δοκίμιον **dŏkimiŏn**, *dok-im´-ee-on;* neut. of a presumed der. of *1382;* a *testing;* by impl. *trustworthiness:*— trial, trying.

1384. δόκιμος **dŏkimŏs**, *dok´-ee-mos;* from *1380;* prop. *acceptable* (*current* after assayal), i.e. *approved:*— approved, tried.

1385. δοκός **dŏkŏs**, *dok-os´;* from *1209* (through the idea of *holding* up); a *stick* of timber:— beam.

δόκω **dŏkō**. See *1380.*

1386. δόλιος **dŏliŏs**, *dol´-ee-os;* from *1388; guileful:*— deceitful.

1387. δολιόω **dŏliŏō**, *dol-ee-ŏ´-o;* from *1386;* to *be guileful:*— use deceit.

1388. δόλος **dŏlŏs**, *dol´-os;* from an obs. primary verb, δέλλω **dĕllō** (prob. mean. to *decoy;* comp. *1185*); a *trick* (*bait*), i.e. (fig.) *wile:*— craft, deceit, guile, subtilty (subtlety).

1389. δολόω **dŏlŏō**, *dol-ŏ´-o;* from *1388;* to *ensnare,* i.e. (fig.) *adulterate:*— handle deceitfully.

1390. δόμα **dŏma**, *dom´-ah;* from the base of *1325;* a *present:*— gift.

1391. δόξα **dŏxa**, *dox´-ah;* from the base of *1380; glory* (as very *apparent*), in a wide application (lit. or fig., obj. or subj.):— dignity, glory (-ious), honour, praise, worship.

1392. δοξάζω **dŏxazō**, *dox-ad´-zo;* from *1391;* to *render* (or *esteem*) *glorious* (in a wide application):— (make) glorify (-ious), full of (have) glory, honour, magnify.

1393. Δορκάς **Dŏrkas**, *dor-kas´; gazelle; Dorcas,* a Chr. woman:— Dorcas.

1394. δόσις **dŏsis**, *dos´-is;* from the base of *1325;* a *giving;* by impl. (concr.) a *gift:*— gift, giving.

1395. δότης **dŏtēs**, *dot´-ace;* from the base of *1325;* a *giver:*— giver.

1396. δουλαγωγέω **dŏulagōgĕō**, *doo-lag-ogue-eh´-o;* from a presumed compound of *1401* and *71;* to *be a slave-driver,* i.e. to *enslave* (fig. *subdue*):— bring into subjection.

1397. δουλεία **dŏulĕia**, *doo-li´-ah;* from *1398; slavery* (cerem. or fig.):— bondage.

1398. δουλεύω **dŏulĕuō**, *dool-yoo´-o;* from *1401;* to *be a slave* to (lit. or fig., invol. or vol.):— be in bondage, (do) serve (-ice).

1399. δούλη **dŏulē**, *doo´-lay;* fem. of *1401;* a *female slave* (invol. or vol.):— handmaid (-en).

1400. δοῦλον **dŏulŏn**, *doo´-lon;* neut. of *1401; subservient:*— servant.

1401. δοῦλος **dŏulŏs**, *doo´-los;* from *1210;* a *slave* (lit. or fig., invol. or vol.; frequently, therefore in a qualified sense of *subjection* or *subserviency*):— bond (-man), servant.

1402. δουλόω **dŏulŏō**, *doo-lŏ´-o;* from *1401;* to *enslave* (lit. or fig.):— bring into (be under) bondage, × given, become (make) servant.

1403. δοχή **dŏchē**, *dokh-ay´;* from *1209;* a *reception,* i.e. convivial *entertainment:*— feast.

1404. δράκων **drakōn**, *drak´-own;* prob. from an alt. form of δέρκομαι **dĕrkŏmai** (to *look*); a fabulous kind of *serpent* (perh. as supposed to *fascinate*):— dragon.

1405. δράσσομαι **drassŏmai**, *dras´-som-ahee;* perh. akin to the base of *1404* (through the idea of *capturing*); to *grasp,* i.e. (fig.) *entrap:*— take.

1406. δραχμή **drachmē**, *drakh-may´;* from *1405;* a *drachma* or (silver) coin (as *handled*):— piece (of silver).

δρέμω **drĕmō**. See *5143.*

1407. δρέπανον **drĕpanŏn**, *drep´-an-on;* from δρέπω **drĕpō** (to *pluck*); a gathering *hook* (espec. for harvesting):— sickle.

1408. δρόμος **drŏmŏs**, *drom´-os;* from the alt. of *5143;* a *race,* i.e. (fig.) *career:*— course.

1409. Δρούσιλλα **Drŏusilla**, *droo´-sil-lah;* a fem. dimin. of *Drusus* (a Rom. name); *Drusilla,* a member of the Herodian family:— Drusilla.

δῦμι **dumi**. See *1416.*

1410. δύναμαι **dunamai**, *doo´-nam-ahee;* of uncert. aff.; to *be able* or *possible:*— be able, can (do, + -not), could, may, might, be possible, be of power.

1411. δύναμις **dunamis**, *doo´-nam-is;* from *1410; force* (lit. or fig.); spec. miraculous *power* (usually by impl. a *miracle* itself):— ability, abundance, meaning, might (-ily, -y, -y deed), (worker of) miracle (-s), power, strength, violence, mighty (wonderful) work.

1412. δυναμόω **dunamŏō**, *doo-nam-ŏ´-o;* from *1411;* to *enable:*— strengthen.

1413. δυνάστης **dunastēs**, *doo-nas´-tace;* from *1410;* a *ruler* or *officer:*— of great authority, mighty, potentate.

1414. δυνατέω **dunatĕō**, *doo-nat-eh´-o;* from *1415;* to *be efficient* (fig.):— be mighty.

1415. δυνατός **dunatŏs**, *doo-nat-os´;* from *1410; powerful* or *capable* (lit. or fig.); neut. *possible:*— able, could, (that is) mighty (man), possible, power, strong.

1416. δύνω **dunō**, *doo´-no;* or

δῦμι **dumi**, *doo´-mee;* prol. forms of an

obsolete primary δύω **duŏ**, *doo´-o* (to *sink*); to *go* "*down*":— set.

1417. δύο **duŏ**, *doo´-ŏ;* a primary numeral; "*two*":— both, twain, two.

1418. δυσ- **dus-**, *doos;* a primary inseparable particle of uncert. der.; used only in composition as a pref.; *hard,* i.e. *with difficulty:*— + hard, + grievous, *etc.*

1419. δυσβάστακτος **dusbastaktŏs**, *doos-bas´-tak-tos;* from *1418* and a der. of *941; oppressive:*— grievous to be borne.

1420. δυσεντερία **dusĕntĕria**, *doos-en-ter-ee´-ah;* from *1418* and a comp. of *1787* (mean. a *bowel*); a "*dysentery*":— bloody flux.

1421. δυσερμήνευτος **dusĕrmēnĕutŏs**, *doos-er-mane´-yoo-tos;* from *1418* and a presumed der. of *2059; difficult of explanation:*— hard to be uttered.

1422. δύσκολος **duskŏlŏs**, *doos´-kol-os;* from *1418* and κόλον **kŏlŏn** (*food*); prop. *fastidious about eating* (*peevish*), i.e. (gen.) *impracticable:*— hard.

1423. δυσκόλως **duskŏlōs**, *doos-kol´-oce;* adv. from *1422; impracticably:*— hardly.

1424. δυσμή **dusmē**, *doos-may´;* from *1416;* the sun-*set,* i.e. (by impl.) the *western* region:— west.

1425. δυσνόητος **dusnŏētŏs**, *doos-no´-ay-tos;* from *1418* and a der. of *3539; difficult of perception:*— hard to be understood.

1426. δυσφημία **dusphēmia**, *doos-fay-mee´-ah;* from a compound of *1418* and *5345; defamation:*— evil report.

δύω **duŏ**. See *1416.*

1427. δώδεκα **dōdĕka**, *do´-dek-ah;* from *1417* and *1176; two* and *ten,* i.e. a *dozen:*— twelve.

1428. δωδέκατος **dōdĕkatŏs**, *do-dek´-at-os;* from *1427; twelfth:*— twelfth.

1429. δωδεκάφυλον **dōdĕkaphulŏn**, *do-dek-af´-oo-lon;* from *1427* and *5443;* the *commonwealth* of Israel:— twelve tribes.

1430. δῶμα **dōma**, *do´-mah;* from δέμω **dĕmō** (to *build*); prop. an *edifice,* i.e. (spec.) a *roof:*— housetop.

1431. δωρεά **dōrĕa**, *do-reh-ah´;* from *1435;* a *gratuity:*— gift.

1432. δωρεάν **dōrĕan**, *do-reh-an´;* acc. of *1431* as adv.; *gratuitously* (lit. or fig.):— without a cause, freely, for naught, in vain.

1433. δωρέομαι **dōrĕŏmai**, *do-reh´-om-ahee;* mid. voice from *1435;* to *bestow* gratuitously:— give.

1434. δώρημα **dōrēma**, *do´-ray-mah;* from *1433;* a *bestowment:*— gift.

1435. δῶρον **dōrŏn**, *do´-ron;* a *present;* spec. a *sacrifice:*— gift, offering.

E

1436. ἔα **ĕa**, eh´-ah; appar. imper. of 1439; prop. *let it be*, i.e. (as interj.) *aha!*:— let alone.

1437. ἐάν **ĕan**, eh-an´; from 1487 and 302; a *conditional* particle; *in case that, provided,* etc.; often used in connection with other particles to denote *indefiniteness* or *uncertainty:*— before, but, except, (and) if, (if) so, (what-, whither-) soever, though, when (-soever), whether (or), to whom, [who-] so (-ever). See 3361.

ἐάν μή **ĕan mē**. See 3361 and 3362.

1438. ἑαυτοῦ **hĕautŏu**, heh-ow-too´ (incl. all other cases); from a refl. pron. otherwise obs. and the gen. (dat. or acc.) of 846; *him-* (*her-, it-, them-*, also [in conjunction with the pers. pron. of the other persons] *my-, thy-, our-, your-*) *self* (*selves*), etc.:— alone, her (own, -self), (he) himself, his (own), itself, one (to) another, our (thine) own (-selves), + that she had, their (own, own selves), (of) them (-selves), they, thyself, you, your (own, own conceits, own selves, -selves).

1439. ἐάω **ĕaō**, eh-ah´-o; of uncert. aff.; to *let be*, i.e. *permit* or *leave* alone:— commit, leave, let (alone), suffer. See also 1436.

1440. ἑβδομήκοντα **hĕbdŏmēkŏnta**, heb-dom-ay´-kon-tah; from 1442 and a modified form of 1176; *seventy:*— seventy, three score and ten.

1441. ἑβδομηκοντάκις **hĕbdŏmēkŏntakis**, heb-dom-ay-kon-tak-is; multiple adv. from 1440; *seventy times:*— seventy times.

1442. ἕβδομος **hĕbdŏmŏs**, heb´-dom-os; ord. from 2033; *seventh:*— seventh.

1443. Ἐβέρ **Ĕbĕr**, eb´-er; of Heb. or. [5677]; *Eber*, a patriarch:— Eber.

1444. Ἑβραϊκός **Hĕbraïkŏs**, heb-rah-ee-kos´; from 1443; *Hebraïc* or the *Jewish* language:— Hebrew (Aramaic).

1445. Ἑβραῖος **Hĕbraiŏs**, heb-rah´-yos; from 1443; a *Hebrǽan* (i.e. Hebrew) or *Jew:*— Hebrew.

1446. Ἑβραΐς **Hĕbraïs**, heb-rah-is´; from 1443; the *Hebraistic* (i.e. *Hebrew*) or *Jewish* (*Chaldee*) language:— Hebrew (Aramaic).

1447. Ἑβραϊστί **Hĕbraïsti**, heb-rah-is-tee´; adv. from 1446; *Hebraistically* or in the Jewish (Chaldee) language:— in (the) Hebrew (tongue).

1448. ἐγγίζω **ĕggizō**, eng-id´-zo; from 1451; to make *near*, i.e. (refl.) *approach:*— approach, be at hand, come (draw) near, be (come, draw) nigh.

1449. ἐγγράφω **ĕggraphō**, eng-graf´-o; from 1722 and 1125; to "*engrave,*" i.e. *inscribe:*— write (in).

1450. ἔγγυος **ĕgguŏs**, eng´-goo-os; from 1722 and γυῖον guiŏn (a *limb*); *pledged* (as if *articu-*

lated by a member), i.e. a *bondsman:*— surety.

1451. ἐγγύς **ĕggus**, eng-goos´; from a primary verb ἄγχω **agchō** (to *squeeze* or *throttle;* akin to the base of 43); *near* (lit. or fig., of place or time):— from, at hand, near, nigh (at hand, unto), ready.

1452. ἐγγύτερον **ĕggutĕrŏn**, eng-goo´-ter-on; neut. of the comp. of 1451; *nearer:*— nearer.

1453. ἐγείρω **ĕgeirō**, eg-i´-ro; prob. akin to the base of 58 (through the idea of *collecting* one's faculties); to *waken* (tran. or intr.), i.e. *rouse* (lit. from sleep, from sitting or lying, from disease, from death; or fig. from obscurity, inactivity, ruins, nonexistence):— awake, lift (up), raise (again, up), rear up, (a-) rise (again, up), stand, take up.

1454. ἔγερσις **ĕgĕrsis**, eg´-er-sis; from 1453; a *resurgence* (from death):— resurrection.

1455. ἐγκάθετος **ĕgkathĕtŏs**, eng-kath´-et-os; from 1722 and a der. of 2524; *subinduced,* i.e. surreptitiously *suborned* as a lier-in-wait:— spy.

1456. ἐγκαίνια **ĕgkainia**, eng-kah´-ee-nee-ah; neut. plur. of a presumed compound from 1722 and 2537; *innovatives,* i.e. (spec.) *renewal* (of relig. services after the Antiochian interruption):— dedication.

1457. ἐγκαινίζω **ĕgkainizō**, eng-kahee-nid´-zo; from 1456; to *renew,* i.e. *inaugurate:*— consecrate, dedicate.

1458. ἐγκαλέω **ĕgkalĕō**, eng-kal-eh´-o; from 1722 and 2564; to *call in* (as a debt or demand), i.e. *bring to account* (*charge, criminate,* etc.):— accuse, call in question, implead, lay to the charge.

1459. ἐγκαταλείπω **ĕgkatalĕipō**, eng-kat-al-i´-po; from 1722 and 2641; to *leave behind in* some place, i.e. (in a good sense) *let remain over,* or (in a bad sense) to *desert:*— forsake, leave.

1460. ἐγκατοικέω **ĕgkatŏikĕō**, eng-kat-oy-keh´-o; from 1722 and 2730; to *settle down in* a place, i.e. *reside:*— dwell among.

1461. ἐγκεντρίζω **ĕgkĕntrizō**, eng-ken-trid´-zo; from 1722 and a der. of 2759; to *prick in,* i.e. *ingraft:*— graff in (-to).

1462. ἔγκλημα **ĕgklēma**, eng´-klay-mah; from 1458; an *accusation,* i.e. *offence* alleged:— crime laid against, laid to charge.

1463. ἐγκομβόομαι **ĕgkŏmbŏŏmai**, eng-kom-bŏ´-om-ahee; mid. voice from 1722 and κομβόω **kŏmbŏō** (to *gird*); to *engirdle* oneself (for labor), i.e. fig. (the apron being a badge of servitude) to *wear* (in token of mutual deference):— be clothed with.

1464. ἐγκοπή **ĕgkŏpē**, eng-kop-ay´; from 1465; a *hindrance:*— × hinder.

1465. ἐγκόπτω **ĕgkŏptō**, eng-kop´-to; from

1722 and 2875; to *cut into*, i.e. (fig.) *impede, detain:*— hinder, be tedious unto.

1466. ἐγκράτεια **ĕgkratĕia**, *eng-krat´-i-ah;* from 1468; *self-control* (espec. *continence*):— temperance.

1467. ἐγκρατεύομαι **ĕgkratĕuŏmai**, *eng-krat-yoo´-om-ahee;* mid. voice from 1468; to *exercise self-restraint* (in diet and chastity):— can (I-notI) contain, be temperate.

1468. ἐγκρατής **ĕgkratēs**, *eng-krat-ace´;* from 1722 and 2904; *strong in* a thing (*masterful*), i.e. (fig. and refl.) *self-controlled* (in appetite, etc.):— temperate.

1469. ἐγκρίνω **ĕgkrinō**, *eng-kree´-no;* from 1722 and 2919; to *judge in*, i.e. *count* among:— make of the number.

1470. ἐγκρύπτω **ĕgkruptō**, *eng-kroop´-to;* from 1722 and 2928; to *conceal in*, i.e. *incorporate with:*— hid in.

1471. ἔγκυος **ĕgkuŏs**, *eng´-koo-os;* from 1722 and the base of 2949; *swelling in*side, i.e. *pregnant:*— great with child.

1472. ἐγχρίω **ĕgchriō**, *eng-khree´-o;* from 1722 and 5548; to *rub in* (oil), i.e. *besmear:*— anoint.

1473. ἐγώ **ĕgō**, *eg-o´;* a primary pron. of the first pers. *I* (only expressed when emphatic):— I, me. For the other cases and the plur. see 1691, 1698, 1700, 2248, 2249, 2254, 2257, etc.

1474. ἐδαφίζω **ĕdaphizō**, *ed-af-id´-zo;* from 1475; to *raze:*— lay even with the ground.

1475. ἔδαφος **ĕdaphŏs**, *ed´-af-os;* from the base of 1476; a *basis* (*bottom*), i.e. the *soil:*— ground.

1476. ἑδραῖος **hĕdraiŏs**, *hed-rah´-yos;* from a der. of ἕζομαι **hĕzŏmai** (to *sit*); *sedentary*, i.e. (by impl.) *immovable:*— settled, stedfast.

1477. ἑδραίωμα **hĕdraiōma**, *hed-rah´-yo-mah;* from a der. of 1476; a *support*, i.e. (fig.) *basis:*— ground.

1478. Ἐζεκίας **Ĕzĕkias**, *ed-zek-ee´-as;* of Heb. or. [2396]; *Ezekias* (i.e. *Hezekiah*), an Isr.:— Ezekias.

1479. ἐθελοθρησκεία **ĕthĕlŏthrēskĕia**, *eth-el-oth-race-ki´-ah;* from 2309 and 2356; *voluntary* (*arbitrary* and *unwarranted*) *piety*, i.e. *sanctimony:*— will worship.

ἐθέλω **ĕthĕlō**. See 2309.

1480. ἐθίζω **ĕthizō**, *eth-id´-zo;* from 1485; to *accustom*, i.e. (neut. pass. part.) *customary:*— custom.

1481. ἐθνάρχης **ĕthnarchēs**, *eth-nar´-khace;* from 1484 and 746; the *governor* [not king] of *a district:*— ethnarch.

1482. ἐθνικός **ĕthnikŏs**, *eth-nee-kos´;* from 1484; *national* ("ethnic"), i.e. (spec.) a *Gentile:*— heathen (man).

1483. ἐθνικῶς **ĕthnikōs**, *eth-nee-koce´;* adv. from 1482; *as a Gentile:*— after the manner of Gentiles.

1484. ἔθνος **ĕthnŏs**, *eth´-nos;* prob. from 1486; a *race* (as of the same *habit*), i.e. a *tribe;* spec. a *foreign* (*non-Jewish*) one (usually by impl. *pagan*):— Gentile, heathen, nation, people.

1485. ἔθος **ĕthŏs**, *eth´-os;* from 1486; a *usage* (prescribed by habit or law):— custom, manner, be wont.

1486. ἔθω **ĕthō**, *eth´-o;* a primary verb; to *be used* (by habit or conventionality); neut. perfect part. *usage:*— be custom (manner, wont).

1487. εἰ **ĕi**, *i;* a primary particle of conditionality; *if, whether, that*, etc.:— forasmuch as, if, that, (Ial-I)though, whether. Often used in connection or composition with other particles, espec. as in 1489, 1490, 1499, 1508, 1509, 1512, 1513, 1536, 1537. See also 1437.

1488. εἶ **ĕi**, *i;* second pers. sing. present of 1510; thou *art:*— art, be.

1489. εἴγε **ĕigĕ**, *i´-gheh;* from 1487 and 1065; *if indeed, seeing that, unless*, (with neg.) *otherwise:*— if (so be that, yet).

1490. εἰ δὲ μή(γε) **ĕi dĕ mē(gĕ)** *i deh may´-(gheh);* from 1487, 1161, and 3361 (sometimes with 1065 added); *but if not:*— (or) else, if (not, otherwise), otherwise.

1491. εἶδος **ĕidŏs**, *i´-dos;* from 1492; a *view*, i.e. *form* (lit. or fig.):— appearance, fashion, shape, sight.

1492. εἴδω **ĕidō**, *i´-do;* a primary verb; used only in certain past tenses, the others being borrowed from the equiv. 3700 and 3708; prop. to *see* (lit. or fig.); by impl. (in the perf. only) to *know:*— be aware, behold, × can (+ not tell), consider, (have) know (-ledge), look (on), perceive, see, be sure, tell, understand, wish, wot. Comp. 3700.

1493. εἰδωλεῖον **ĕidōlĕiŏn**, *i-do-li´-on;* neut. of a presumed der. of 1497; an *image-fane:*— idol's temple.

1494. εἰδωλόθυτον **ĕidōlŏthutŏn**, *i-do-loth´-oo-ton;* neut. of a compound of 1497 and a presumed der. of 2380; an *image-sacrifice*, i.e. part of an *idolatrous offering:*— (meat, thing that is) offered (in sacrifice, sacrificed) to (unto) idols.

1495. εἰδωλολατρεία **ĕidōlŏlatrĕia**, *i-do-lol-at-ri´-ah;* from 1497 and 2999; *image-worship* (lit. or fig.):— idolatry.

1496. εἰδωλολάτρης **ĕidōlŏlatrēs**, *i-do-lol-at´-race;* from 1497 and the base of 3000; an *image-*(*servant* or) *worshipper* (lit. or fig.):— idolater.

1497. εἴδωλον **ĕidōlŏn**, *i´-do-lon;* from 1491; an *image* (i.e. for worship); by impl. a *heathen god*, or (plur.) the *worship* of such:— idol.

1498. εἴην **ĕiēn**, *i´-ane;* optative (i.e. English subjunctive) present of 1510 (incl. the other pers.); *might* (*could, would,* or *should*) *be:*— mean, + perish, should be, was, were.

1499. εἰ καί **ĕi kai**, *i kahee;* from *1487* and *2532; if also* (or *even*):— if (that), though.

1500. εἰκῆ **ĕikē**, *i-kay´;* prob. from *1502* (through the idea of *failure*); *idly,* i.e. *without reason* (or *effect*):— without a cause, (in) vain (-ly).

1501. εἴκοσι **ĕikŏsi**, *i´-kos-ee;* of uncert. aff.; a *score:*— twenty.

1502. εἴκω **ĕikō**, *i´-ko;* appar. a primary verb; prop. to *be weak,* i.e. *yield:*— give place.

1503. εἴκω **ĕikō**, *i´-ko;* appar. a primary verb [perh. akin to *1502* through the idea of *faintness* as a copy]; to *resemble:*— be like.

1504. εἰκών **ĕikōn**, *i-kone´;* from *1503*; a *likeness,* i.e. (lit.) *statue, profile,* or (fig.) *representation, resemblance:*— image.

1505. εἰλικρίνεια **ĕilikrinĕia**, *i-lik-ree´-ni-ah;* from *1506; clearness,* i.e. (by impl.) *purity* (fig.):— sincerity.

1506. εἰλικρινής **ĕilikrinēs**, *i-lik-ree-nace´;* from εἴλη **hĕilē** (the sun's *ray*) and *2919; judged by sunlight,* i.e. tested as *genuine* (fig.):— pure, sincere.

1507. εἱλίσσω **hĕilissō**, *hi-lis´-so;* a prol. form of a primary but defective verb εἵλω **hĕilō** (of the same mean.); to *coil* or *wrap:*— roll together. See also *1667*.

1508. εἰ μή **ĕi mē**, *i may;* from *1487* and *3361; if not:*— but, except (that), if not, more than, save (only) that, saving, till.

1509. εἰ μή τι **ĕi mē ti**, *i may tee;* from *1508* and the neut. of *5100; if not somewhat:*— except.

1510. εἰμί **ĕimi**, *i-mee´;* the first pers. sing. present ind.; a prol. form of a primary and defective verb; *I exist* (used only when emphatic):— am, have been, × it is I, was. See also *1488, 1498, 1511, 2258, 2071, 2070, 2075, 2076, 2771, 2468, 5600, 5607*.

1511. εἶναι **ĕinai**, *i´-nahee;* present infin. from *1510;* to *exist:*— am, are, come, is, × lust after, × please well, there is, to be, was.

εἵνεκεν **hĕinĕkĕn**. See *1752*.

1512. εἴ περ **ĕi pĕr**, *i per;* from *1487* and *4007; if perhaps:*— if so be (that), seeing, though.

1513. εἴ πως **ĕi pōs**, *i poce;* from *1487* and *4458; if somehow:*— if by any means.

1514. εἰρηνεύω **ĕirēnĕuō**, *i-rane-yoo´-o;* from *1515;* to *be* (*act*) *peaceful:*— be at (have, live in) peace, live peaceably.

1515. εἰρήνη **ĕirēnē**, *i-ray´-nay;* prob. from a primary verb εἴρω **ĕirō** (to *join*); *peace* (lit. or fig.); by impl. *prosperity:*— one, peace, quietness, rest, + set at one again.

1516. εἰρηνικός **ĕirēnikŏs**, *i-ray-nee-kos´;* from *1515; pacific;* by impl. *salutary:*— peaceable.

1517. εἰρηνοποιέω **ĕirēnŏpŏiĕō**, *i-ray-nop-oy-eh´-o;* from *1518;* to *be a peace-maker,* i.e. (fig.) to *harmonize:*— make peace.

1518. εἰρηνοποιός **ĕirēnŏpŏiŏs**, *i-ray-nop-oy-os´;* from *1515* and *4160; pacificatory,* i.e. (subj.) *peaceable:*— peacemaker.

εἴρω **ĕirō**. See *1515, 4483, 5346*.

1519. εἰς **ĕis**, *ice;* a primary prep.; *to* or *into* (indicating the point reached or entered), of place, time, or (fig.) purpose (result, etc.); also in adv. phrases:— [abundant-] ly, against, among, as, at, [back-] ward, before, by, concerning, + continual, + far more exceeding, for [intent, purpose], fore, + forth, in (among, at, unto, -so much that,to), to the intent that, + of one mind, + never, of, (up-) on, + perish, + set at one again, (so) that, therefore (-unto), throughout, till, to (be, the end, -ward), (here-) until (-to), ... ward, [where-] fore, with. Often used in composition with the same general import, but only with verbs (etc.) expressing motion (lit. or fig.).

1520. εἷς **hĕis**, *hice;* (incl. the neut. [etc.] ἕν **hĕn**); a primary numeral; *one:*— a (-n, -ny, certain), + abundantly, man, one (another), only, other, some. See also *1527, 3367, 3391, 3762*.

1521. εἰσάγω **ĕisagō**, *ice-ag´-o;* from *1519* and *71;* to *introduce* (lit. or fig.):— bring in (-to), (+ was to) lead into.

1522. εἰσακούω **ĕisakŏuō**, *ice-ak-oo´-o;* from *1519* and *191;* to *listen* to:— hear.

1523. εἰσδέχομαι **ĕisdĕchŏmai**, *ice-dekh´-om-ahee;* from *1519* and *1209;* to *take into one's favor:*— receive.

1524. εἴσειμι **ĕisĕimi**, *ice´-i-mee;* from *1519* and εἶμι **ĕimi** (to *go*); to *enter:*— enter (go) into.

1525. εἰσέρχομαι **ĕisĕrchŏmai**, *ice-er´-khom-ahee;* from *1519* and *2064;* to *enter* (lit. or fig.):— × arise, come (in, into), enter in (-to), go in (through).

1526. εἰσί **ĕisi**, *i-see´;* third pers. plur. present ind. of *1510;* they *are:*— agree, are, be, dure, × is, were.

1527. εἷς καθ᾽ εἷς **hĕis kath' hĕis**, *hice kath hice;* from *1520* repeated with *2596* inserted; *severally:*— one by one.

1528. εἰσκαλέω **ĕiskalĕō**, *ice-kal-eh´-o;* from *1519* and *2564;* to *invite* in:— call in.

1529. εἴσοδος **ĕisŏdŏs**, *ice´-od-os;* from *1519* and *3598;* an *entrance* (lit. or fig.):— coming, enter (-ing) in (to).

1530. εἰσπηδάω **ĕispēdaō**, *ice-pay-dah´-o;* from *1519* and πηδάω **pēdaō** (to *leap*); to *rush in:*— run (spring) in.

1531. εἰσπορεύομαι **ĕispŏrĕuŏmai**, *ice-por-yoo´-om-ahee;* from *1519* and *4198;* to *enter* (lit. or fig.):— come (enter) in, go into.

1532. εἰστρέχω **ĕistrĕchō**, *ice-trekh´-o;* from *1519* and *5143;* to *hasten inward:*— run in.

1533. εἰσφέρω **ĕisphĕrō**, *ice-fer´-o;* from *1519* and *5342;* to *carry inward* (lit. or fig.):— bring (in), lead into.

1534. εἶτα **ĕita**, *i´-tah;* of uncert. aff.; a particle of *succession* (in time or logical enumeration), *then, moreover:*— after that (-ward), furthermore, then. See also *1899.*

1535. εἴτε **ĕitĕ**, *i´-teh;* from *1487* and *5037;* if *too:*— if, or, whether.

1536. εἴ τις **ĕi tis**, *i tis;* from *1487* and *5100;* if *any:*— he that, if a (-ny) man ('s, thing, from any, ought), whether any, whosoever.

1537. ἐκ **ĕk**, *ek* or

ἐξ **ĕx**, *ex;* a primary prep. denoting *origin* (the point *whence* motion or action proceeds), *from, out* (of place, time, or cause; lit. or fig.; direct or remote):— after, among, × are, at, betwixt (-yond), by (the means of), exceedingly, (+ abundantly above), for (-th), from (among, forth, up), + grudgingly, + heartily, × heavenly, × hereby, + very highly, in, ... ly, (because, by reason) of, off (from), on, out among (from, of), over, since, × thenceforth, through, × unto, × vehemently, with (-out). Often used in composition, with the same general import; often of completion.

1538. ἕκαστος **hĕkastŏs**, *hek´-as-tos;* as if a superl. of ἕκας **hĕkas** (*afar*); *each* or *every:*— any, both, each (one), every (man, one, woman), particularly.

1539. ἑκάστοτε **hĕkastŏtĕ**, *hek-as´-tot-eh;* as if from *1538* and *5119;* at *every time:*— always.

1540. ἑκατόν **hĕkatŏn**, *hek-at-on´;* of uncert. aff.; a *hundred:*— hundred.

1541. ἑκατονταέτης **hĕkatŏntaĕtēs**, *hek-at-on-tah-et´-ace;* from *1540* and *2094; centenarian:*— hundred years old.

1542. ἑκατονταπλασίων **hĕkatŏntaplasiōn**, *hek-at-on-ta-plah-see´-own;* from *1540* and a presumed der. of *4111;* a *hundred times:*— hundredfold.

1543. ἑκατοντάρχης **hĕkatŏntarchēs**, *hek-at-on-tar´-khace;* or

ἑκατόνταρχος **hĕkatŏntarchŏs**, *hek-at-on´-tar-khos;* from *1540* and *757;* the *captain of one hundred men:*— centurion.

1544. ἐκβάλλω **ĕkballō**, *ek-bal´-lo;* from *1537* and *906;* to *eject* (lit. or fig.):— bring forth, cast (forth, out), drive (out), expel, leave, pluck (pull, take, thrust) out, put forth (out), send away (forth, out).

1545. ἔκβασις **ĕkbasis**, *ek´-bas-is;* from a compound of *1537* and the base of *939* (mean. to *go out*); an *exit* (lit. or fig.):— end, way to escape.

1546. ἐκβολή **ĕkbŏlē**, *ek-bol-ay´;* from *1544;* *ejection,* i.e. (spec.) a *throwing overboard* of the cargo:— + lighten the ship.

1547. ἐκγαμίζω **ĕkgamizō**, *ek-gam-id´-zo;* from *1537* and a form of *1061* [comp. *1548*]; to *marry off* a daughter:— give in marriage.

1548. ἐκγαμίσκω **ĕkgamiskō**, *ek-gam-is´-ko;* from *1537* and *1061;* the same as *1547:*— give in marriage.

1549. ἔκγονον **ĕkgŏnŏn**, *ek´-gon-on;* neut. of a der. of a compound of *1537* and *1096;* a *descendant,* i.e. (spec.) *grandchild:*— nephew.

1550. ἐκδαπανάω **ĕkdapanaō**, *ek-dap-an-ah´-o;* from *1537* and *1159;* to *expend* (wholly), i.e. (fig.) *exhaust:*— spend.

1551. ἐκδέχομαι **ĕkdĕchŏmai**, *ek-dekh´-om-ahee;* from *1537* and *1209;* to *accept from* some source, i.e. (by impl.) to *await:*— expect, look (tarry) for, wait (for).

1552. ἔκδηλος **ĕkdēlŏs**, *ek´-day-los;* from *1537* and *1212; wholly evident:*— manifest.

1553. ἐκδημέω **ĕkdēmĕō**, *ek-day-meh´-o;* from a compound of *1537* and *1218;* to *emigrate,* i.e. (fig.) *vacate* or *quit:*— be absent.

1554. ἐκδίδωμι **ĕkdidōmi**, *ek-did-o´-mee;* from *1537* and *1325;* to *give forth,* i.e. (spec.) to *lease:*— let forth (out).

1555. ἐκδιηγέομαι **ĕkdiēgĕŏmai**, *ek-dee-ayg-eh´-om-ahee;* from *1537* and a compound of *1223* and *2233;* to *narrate* through wholly:— declare.

1556. ἐκδικέω **ĕkdikĕō**, *ek-dik-eh´-o;* from *1558;* to *vindicate, retaliate, punish:*— a (re-) venge.

1557. ἐκδίκησις **ĕkdikēsis**, *ek-dik´-ay-sis;* from *1556; vindication, retribution:*— (a-, re-) venge (-ance), punishment.

1558. ἔκδικος **ĕkdikŏs**, *ek´-dik-os;* from *1537* and *1349;* carrying *justice out,* i.e. a *punisher:*— a (re-) venger.

1559. ἐκδιώκω **ĕkdiōkō**, *ek-dee-o´-ko;* from *1537* and *1377;* to *pursue out,* i.e. *expel* or *persecute* implacably:— persecute.

1560. ἔκδοτος **ĕkdŏtŏs**, *ek´-dot-os;* from *1537* and a der. of *1325; given out* or *over,* i.e. *surrendered:*— delivered.

1561. ἐκδοχή **ĕkdŏchē**, *ek-dokh-ay´;* from *1551; expectation:*— looking for.

1562. ἐκδύω **ĕkduō**, *ek-doo´-o;* from *1537* and the base of *1416;* to cause to *sink out* of, i.e. (spec. as of clothing) to *divest:*— strip, take off from, unclothe.

1563. ἐκεῖ **ĕkĕi**, *ek-i´;* of uncert. aff.; *there;* by extens. *thither:*— there, thither (-ward), (to) yonder (place).

1564. ἐκεῖθεν **ĕkĕithĕn**, *ek-i´-then;* from *1563; thence:*— from that place, (from) thence, there.

1565. ἐκεῖνος **ĕkĕinŏs**, *ek-i´-nos;* from *1563; that* one (or [neut.] thing); often intensified by the art. prefixed:— he, it, the other (same), selfsame, that (same, very), × their, × them, they, this, those. See also *3778*.

1566. ἐκεῖσε **ĕkĕisĕ**, *ek-i´-seh;* from *1563; thither:*— there.

1567. ἐκζητέω **ĕkzētĕō**, *ek-zay-teh´-o;* from *1537* and *2212;* to *search out,* i.e. (fig.) *investigate, crave, demand,* (by Heb.) *worship:*— en-(re-) quire, seek after (carefully, diligently).

1568. ἐκθαμβέω **ĕkthambĕō**, *ek-tham-beh´-o;* from *1569;* to *astonish* utterly:— affright, greatly (sore) amaze.

1569. ἔκθαμβος **ĕkthambŏs**, *ek´-tham-bos;* from *1537* and *2285; utterly astounded:*— greatly wondering.

1570. ἔκθετος **ĕkthĕtŏs**, *ek´-thet-os;* from *1537* and a der. of *5087; put out,* i.e. *exposed* to perish:— cast out.

1571. ἐκκαθαίρω **ĕkkathairō**, *ek-kath-ah´-ee-ro;* from *1537* and *2508;* to *cleanse thoroughly:*— purge (out).

1572. ἐκκαίω **ĕkkaiō**, *ek-kah´-yo;* from *1537* and *2545;* to *inflame* deeply:— burn.

1573. ἐκκακέω **ĕkkakĕō**, *ek-kak-eh´-o* or ἐγκακέω **egkakeō** *eng-kak-eh´-o;* from *1537* and *2556;* to *be (bad* or) *weak,* i.e. (by impl.) to *fail* (in heart):— faint, be weary.

1574. ἐκκεντέω **ĕkkĕntĕō**, *ek-ken-teh´-o;* from *1537* and the base of *2759;* to *transfix:*— pierce.

1575. ἐκκλάω **ĕkklaō**, *ek-klah´-o;* from *1537* and *2806;* to *exscind:*— break off.

1576. ἐκκλείω **ĕkklĕiō**, *ek-kli´-o;* from *1537* and *2808;* to *shut out* (lit. or fig.):— exclude.

1577. ἐκκλησία **ĕkklēsia**, *ek-klay-see´-ah;* from a compound of *1537* and a der. of *2564;* a *calling out,* i.e. (concr.) a popular *meeting,* espec. a religious *congregation* (Jewish *synagogue,* or Chr. community of members on earth or saints in heaven or both):— assembly, church.

1578. ἐκκλίνω **ĕkklinō**, *ek-klee´-no;* from *1537* and *2827;* to *deviate,* i.e. (absolutely) to *shun* (lit. or fig.), or (rel.) to *decline* (from piety):— avoid, eschew, go out of the way.

1579. ἐκκολυμβάω **ĕkkŏlumbaō**, *ek-kol-oom-bah´-o;* from *1537* and *2860;* to *escape* by *swimming:*— swim out.

1580. ἐκκομίζω **ĕkkŏmizō**, *ek-kom-id´-zo;* from *1537* and *2865;* to *bear forth* (to burial):— carry out.

1581. ἐκκόπτω **ĕkkŏptō**, *ek-kop-to;* from *1537* and *2875;* to *exscind;* fig. to *frustrate:*— cut down (off, out), hew down, hinder.

1582. ἐκκρέμαμαι **ĕkkrĕmamai**, *ek-krem´-am-ahee;* mid. voice from *1537* and *2910;* to *hang upon* the lips of a speaker, i.e. *listen closely:*— be very attentive.

1583. ἐκλαλέω **ĕklalĕō**, *ek-lal-eh´-o;* from *1537* and *2980;* to *divulge:*— tell.

1584. ἐκλάμπω **ĕklampō**, *ek-lam-po;* from

1537 and *2989;* to *be resplendent:*— shine forth.

1585. ἐκλανθάνομαι **ĕklanthanŏmai**, *ek-lan-than´-om-ahee;* mid. voice from *1537* and *2990;* to *be* utterly *oblivious* of:— forget.

1586. ἐκλέγομαι **ĕklĕgŏmai**, *ek-leg´-om-ahee;* mid. voice from *1537* and *3004* (in its primary sense); to *select:*— make choice, choose (out), chosen.

1587. ἐκλείπω **ĕklĕipō**, *ek-li´-po;* from *1537* and *3007;* to *omit,* i.e. (by impl.) *cease (die):*— fail.

1588. ἐκλεκτός **ĕklĕktŏs**, *ek-lek-tos´;* from *1586; select;* by impl. *favorite:*— chosen, elect.

1589. ἐκλογή **ĕklŏgē**, *ek-log-ay´;* from *1586;* (divine) *selection* (abstr. or concr.):— chosen, election.

1590. ἐκλύω **ĕkluō**, *ek-loo´-o;* from *1537* and *3089;* to *relax* (lit. or fig.):— faint.

1591. ἐκμάσσω **ĕkmassō**, *ek-mas´-so;* from *1537* and the base of *3145;* to *knead out,* i.e. (by anal.) to *wipe dry:*— wipe.

1592. ἐκμυκτερίζω **ĕkmuktērizō**, *ek-mook-ter-id´-zo;* from *1537* and *3456;* to *sneer* outright at:— deride.

1593. ἐκνεύω **ĕknĕuō**, *ek-nyoo´-o;* from *1537* and *3506;* (by anal.) to *slip off,* i.e. quietly *withdraw:*— convey self away.

1594. ἐκνήφω **ĕknēphō**, *ek-nay´-fo;* from *1537* and *3525;* (fig.) to *rouse* (oneself) *out* of stupor:— awake.

1595. ἑκούσιον **hĕkŏusiŏn**, *hek-oo´-see-on;* neut. of a der. from *1635; voluntariness:*— willingly.

1596. ἑκουσίως **hĕkŏusiōs**, *hek-oo-see´-oce;* adv. from the same as *1595; voluntarily:*— wilfully, willingly.

1597. ἔκπαλαι **ĕkpalai**, *ek´-pal-ahee;* from *1537* and *3819; long ago, for a long while:*— of a long time, of old.

1598. ἐκπειράζω **ĕkpĕirazō**, *ek-pi-rad´-zo;* from *1537* and *3985;* to *test thoroughly:*— tempt.

1599. ἐκπέμπω **ĕkpĕmpō**, *ek-pem´-po;* from *1537* and *3992;* to *despatch:*— send away (forth).

ἐκπερισσοῦ **ĕkpĕrissŏu**. See *1537* and *4053.*

1600. ἐκπετάννυμι **ĕkpĕtannumi**, *ek-pet-an´-noo-mee;* from *1537* and a form of *4072;* to *fly out,* i.e. (by anal.) to *extend:*— stretch forth.

1601. ἐκπίπτω **ĕkpiptō**, *ek-pip´-to;* from *1537* and *4098;* to *drop away;* spec., *be driven out* of one's course; fig. to *lose, become inefficient:*— be cast, fail, fall (away, off), take none effect.

1602. ἐκπλέω **ĕkplĕō**, *ek-pleh´-o;* from *1537*

and *4126;* to *depart* by ship:— sail (away, thence).

1603. ἐκπληρόω **ĕkplērŏō,** *ek-play-rŏ´-o;* from *1537* and *4137;* to *accomplish* entirely:— fulfill.

1604. ἐκπλήρωσις **ĕkplērōsis,** *ek-play´-ro-sis;* from *1603; completion:—* accomplishment.

1605. ἐκπλήσσω **ĕkplēssō,** *ek-place´-so;* from *1537* and *4141;* to *strike* with astonishment:— amaze, astonish.

1606. ἐκπνέω **ĕkpnĕō,** *ek-pneh´-o;* from *1537* and *4154;* to *expire:—* give up the ghost.

1607. ἐκπορεύομαι **ĕkpŏrĕuŏmai,** *ek-por-yoo´-om-ahee;* from *1537* and *4198;* to *depart, be discharged, proceed, project:—* come (forth, out of), depart, go (forth, out), issue, proceed (out of).

1608. ἐκπορνεύω **ĕkpŏrnĕuō,** *ek-porn-yoo´-o;* from *1537* and *4203;* to *be utterly unchaste:—* give self over to fornication.

1609. ἐκπτύω **ĕkptuō,** *ek-ptoo´-o;* from *1537* and *4429;* to *spit out,* i.e. (fig.) *spurn:—* reject.

1610. ἐκριζόω **ĕkrizŏō,** *ek-rid-zŏ´-o;* from *1537* and *4492;* to *uproot:—* pluck up by the root, root up.

1611. ἔκστασις **ĕkstasis,** *ek´-stas-is;* from *1839;* a *displacement* of the mind, i.e. *bewilderment,* "*ecstasy*":— + be amazed, amazement, astonishment, trance.

1612. ἐκστρέφω **ĕkstrĕphō,** *ek-stref´-o;* from *1537* and *4762;* to *pervert* (fig.):— subvert.

1613. ἐκταράσσω **ĕktarassō,** *ek-tar-as´-so;* from *1537* and *5015;* to *disturb wholly:—* exceedingly trouble.

1614. ἐκτείνω **ĕktĕinō,** *ek-ti´-no;* from *1537* and τείνω **tĕinō** (to *stretch*); to *extend:—* cast, put forth, stretch forth (out).

1615. ἐκτελέω **ĕktĕlĕō,** *ek-tel-eh´-o;* from *1537* and *5055;* to *complete* fully:— finish.

1616. ἐκτένεια **ĕktĕnĕia,** *ek-ten-i´-ah;* from *1618; intentness:—* × instantly.

1617. ἐκτενέστερον **ĕktĕnĕstĕrŏn,** *ek-ten-es´-ter-on;* neut. of the comparative of *1618; more intently:—* more earnestly.

1618. ἐκτενής **ĕktĕnēs,** *ek-ten-ace´;* from *1614; intent:—* without ceasing, fervent.

1619. ἐκτενῶς **ĕktĕnōs,** *ek-ten-oce´;* adv. from *1618; intently:—* fervently.

1620. ἐκτίθημι **ĕktithēmi,** *ek-tith´-ay-mee;* from *1537* and *5087;* to *expose;* fig. to *declare:—* cast out, expound.

1621. ἐκτινάσσω **ĕktinassō,** *ek-tin-as´-so;* from *1537* and τινάσσω **tinassō** (to *swing*); to *shake* violently:— shake (off).

1622. ἐκτός **ĕktŏs,** *ek-tos´;* from *1537;* the *exterior;* fig. (as a prep.) *aside from, besides:—* but, except (-ed), other than, out of, outside, unless, without.

1623. ἔκτος **hĕktŏs,** *hek´-tos;* ordinal from *1803; sixth:—* sixth.

1624. ἐκτρέπω **ĕktrĕpō,** *ek-trep´-o;* from *1537* and the base of *5157;* to *deflect,* i.e. *turn away* (lit. or fig.):— avoid, turn (aside, out of the way).

1625. ἐκτρέφω **ĕktrĕphō,** *ek-tref´-o;* from *1537* and *5142;* to *rear up* to maturity, i.e. (gen.) to *cherish* or *train:—* bring up, nourish.

1626. ἔκτρωμα **ĕktrōma,** *ek´-tro-mah;* from a compound of *1537* and τιτρώσκω **titrōskō** (to *wound*); a *miscarriage* (*abortion*), i.e. (by anal.) *untimely birth:—* born out of due time.

1627. ἐκφέρω **ĕkphĕrō,** *ek-fer´-o;* from *1537* and *5342;* to *bear out* (lit. or fig.):— bear, bring forth, carry forth (out).

1628. ἐκφεύγω **ĕkphĕugō,** *ek-fyoo´-go;* from *1537* and *5343;* to *flee out:—* escape, flee.

1629. ἐκφοβέω **ĕkphŏbĕō,** *ek-fob-eh´-o;* from *1537* and *5399;* to *frighten utterly:—* terrify.

1630. ἔκφοβος **ĕkphŏbŏs,** *ek´-fob-os;* from *1537* and *5401; frightened out* of one's wits: sore afraid, exceedingly fear.

1631. ἐκφύω **ĕkphuō,** *ek-foo´-o;* from *1537* and *5453;* to *sprout up:—* put forth.

1632. ἐκχέω **ĕkchĕō,** *ek-kheh´-o;* or (by var.)

ἐκχύνω **ĕkchunō,** *ek-khoo´-no;* from *1537;* and χέω **chĕō** (to *pour*); to *pour forth;* fig. to *bestow:—* gush (pour) out, run greedily (out), shed (abroad, forth), spill.

1633. ἐκχωρέω **ĕkchōrĕō,** *ek-kho-reh´-o;* from *1537* and *5562;* to *depart:—* depart out.

1634. ἐκψύχω **ĕkpsuchō,** *ek-psoo´-kho;* from *1537* and *5594;* to *expire:—* give (yield) up the ghost.

1635. ἑκών **hĕkōn,** *hek-own´;* of uncert. aff.; *voluntary:—* willingly.

1636. ἐλαία **ĕlaia,** *el-ah´-yah;* fem. of a presumed der. from an obsolete primary; an *olive* (the tree or the fruit):— olive (berry, tree).

1637. ἔλαιον **ĕlaiŏn,** *el´-ah-yon;* neut. of the same as *1636;* olive *oil:—* oil.

1638. ἐλαιών **ĕlaiōn,** *el-ah-yone´;* from *1636;* an *olive-orchard,* i.e. (spec.) the *Mt.* of *Olives:—* Olivet.

1639. Ἐλαμίτης **Ĕlamitēs,** *el-am-ee´-tace;* of Heb. or. [5867]; an *Elamite* or Persian:— Elamite.

1640. ἐλάσσων **ĕlassōn,** *el-as´-sone;* or

ἐλάττων **ĕlattōn** *el-at-tone´;* comparative of the same as *1646; smaller* (in size, quantity, age or quality):— less, under, worse, younger.

1641. ἐλαττονέω **ĕlattŏnĕō,** *el-at-ton-eh-o;*

from *1640;* to *diminish,* i.e. *fall short:*— have lack.

1642. ἐλαττόω **ĕlattŏō,** *el-at-tŏ´-o;* from *1640;* to *lessen* (in rank or influence):— decrease, make lower.

1643. ἐλαύνω **ĕlaunō,** *el-ŏw´-no;* a prol. form of a primary verb (obsolete except in certain tenses as an altern. of this) of uncert. affin; to *push* (as wind, oars or demoniacal power):— carry, drive, row.

1644. ἐλαφρία **ĕlaphria,** *el-af-ree´-ah;* from *1645; levity* (fig.), i.e. *fickleness:*— lightness.

1645. ἐλαφρός **ĕlaphrŏs,** *el-af-ros´;* prob. akin to *1643* and the base of *1640; light,* i.e. *easy:*— light.

1646. ἐλάχιστος **ĕlachistŏs,** *el-akh´-is-tos;* superl. of ἐλαχυς **ĕlachus** (*short*); used as equiv. to *3398; least* (in size, amount, dignity, etc.):— least, very little (small), smallest.

1647. ἐλαχιστότερος **ĕlachistŏtĕrŏs,** *el-akh-is-tot´-er-os;* comparative of *1646; far less:*— less than the least.

1648. Ἐλεάζαρ **Ĕlĕazar,** *el-eh-ad´-zar;* of Heb. or. [499]; *Eleazar,* an Isr.:— Eleazar.

1649. ἔλεγξις **ĕlĕgxis,** *el´-eng-xis;* from *1651; refutation,* i.e. *reproof:*— rebuke.

1650. ἔλεγχος **ĕlĕgchŏs,** *el´-eng-khos;* from *1651; proof, conviction:*— evidence, reproof.

1651. ἐλέγχω **ĕlĕgchō,** *el-eng´-kho;* of uncert. aff.; to *confute, admonish:*— convict, convince, tell a fault, rebuke, reprove.

1652. ἐλεεινός **ĕlĕĕinŏs,** *el-eh-i-nos´;* from *1656; pitiable:*— miserable.

1653. ἐλεέω **ĕlĕĕō,** *el-eh-eh´-o;* from *1656;* to *compassionate* (by word or deed, spec., by divine grace):— have compassion (pity on), have (obtain, receive, shew) mercy (on).

1654. ἐλεημοσύνη **ĕlĕĕmŏsunē,** *el-eh-ay-mos-oo´-nay;* from *1656; compassionateness,* i.e. (as exercised toward the poor) *beneficence,* or (concr.) a *benefaction:*— alms (-deeds).

1655. ἐλεήμων **ĕlĕēmōn,** *el-eh-ay´-mone;* from *1653; compassionate* (actively):— merciful.

1656. ἔλεος **ĕlĕŏs,** *el´-eh-os;* of uncert. aff.; *compassion* (human or divine, espec. active):— (+ tender) mercy.

1657. ἐλευθερία **ĕlĕuthĕria,** *el-yoo-ther-ee´-ah;* from *1658; freedom* (legitimate or licentious, chiefly mor. or cerem.):— liberty.

1658. ἐλεύθερος **ĕlĕuthĕrŏs,** *el-yoo´-ther-os;* prob. from the alt. of *2064; unrestrained* (to go at pleasure), i.e. (as a citizen) *not a slave* (whether *freeborn* or *manumitted*), or (gen.) *exempt* (from obligation or liability):— free (man, woman), at liberty.

1659. ἐλευθερόω **ĕlĕuthĕrŏō,** *el-yoo-ther-ŏ´-o;* from *1658;* to *liberate,* i.e. (fig.) to *exempt* (from mor., cerem. or mortal liability):— deliver, make free.

ἐλεύθω **ĕlĕuthō.** See *2064.*

1660. ἔλευσις **ĕlĕusis,** *el´-yoo-sis;* from the alt. of *2064;* an *advent:*— coming.

1661. ἐλεφάντινος **ĕlĕphantinŏs,** *el-ef-an´-tee-nos;* from ἔλεφας **ĕlĕphas** (an "*elephant*"); *elephantine,* i.e. (by impl.) composed of *ivory:*— of ivory.

1662. Ἐλιακείμ **Ĕliakĕim,** *el-ee-ak-ehm´* or Ἐλιακίμ **Ĕliakim** *el-ee-ak-ime´;* of Heb. or. [471]; *Eliakim,* an Isr.:— Eliakim.

1663. Ἐλιέζερ **Ĕliĕzĕr,** *el-ee-ed´-zer;* of Heb. or. [461]; *Eliezer,* an Isr.:— Eliezer.

1664. Ἐλιούδ **Ĕliŏud,** *el-ee-ood´;* of Heb. or. [410 and 1935]; *God of majesty; Eliud,* an Isr.:— Eliud.

1665. Ἐλισάβετ **Ĕlisabĕt,** *el-ee-sab´-et;* of Heb. or. [472]; *Elisabet,* an Israelitess:— Elisabeth.

1666. Ἐλισσαῖος **Ĕlissaiŏs,** *el-is-sah´-yos;* of Heb. or. [477]; *Elissæus,* an Isr.:— Elissæus.

1667. ἑλίσσω **hĕlissō,** *hel-is´-so;* a form of *1507;* to *coil* or *wrap:*— fold up.

1668. ἕλκος **hĕlkŏs,** *hel´-kos;* prob. from *1670;* an *ulcer* (as if drawn together):— sore.

1669. ἑλκόω **hĕlkŏō,** *hel-kŏ´-o;* from *1668;* to *cause to ulcerate,* i.e. (pass.) *be ulcerous:*— full of sores.

1670. ἑλκύω **hĕlkuō,** *hel-koo´-o;* or

ἕλκω **hĕlkō,** *hel´-ko;* prob. akin to *138;* to *drag* (lit. or fig.):— draw. Comp. *1667.*

1671. Ἑλλάς **Hĕllas,** *hel-las´;* of uncert. aff.; *Hellas* (or *Greece*), a country of Europe:— Greece.

1672. Ἕλλην **Hĕllēn,** *hel´-lane;* from *1671;* a *Hellen* (*Grecian*) or inhab. of Hellas; by extens. a *Greek-speaking* person, espec. a *non-Jew:*— Gentile, Greek.

1673. Ἑλληνικός **Hĕllēnikŏs,** *hel-lay-nee-kos´;* from *1672; Hellenic,* i.e. *Grecian* (in language):— Greek.

1674. Ἑλληνίς **Hĕllēnis,** *hel-lay-nis´;* fem. of *1672;* a *Grecian* (i.e. *non-Jewish*) *woman:*— Greek.

1675. Ἑλληνιστής **Hĕllēnistēs,** *hel-lay-nis-tace´;* from a der. of *1672;* a *Hellenist* or Greek-speaking Jew:— Grecian.

1676. Ἑλληνιστί **Hĕllēnisti,** *hel-lay-nis-tee´;* adv. from the same as *1675; Hellenistically,* i.e. in the Grecian language:— Greek.

1677. ἐλλογέω **ĕllŏgĕō,** *el-log-eh´-o;* from *1722* and *3056* (in the sense of account); to *reckon in,* i.e. *attribute:*— impute, put on account.

ἕλλομαι **hĕllŏmai.** See *138.*

1678. Ἐλμωδάμ **Ĕlmōdam,** *el-mo-dam´;* of Heb. or. [perh. for 486]; *Elmodam,* an Isr.:— Elmodam.

1679. ἐλπίζω **ĕlpizō,** *el-pid´-zo;* from *1680;*

to *expect* or *confide:*— (have, thing) hope (-d) (for), trust.

1680. ἐλπίς **ĕlpis**, *el-pece´;* from a primary ἔλπω **ĕlpō** (to *anticipate,* usually with pleasure); *expectation* (abstr. or concr.) or *confidence:*— faith, hope.

1681. Ἐλύμας **Ĕlumas**, *el-oo´-mas;* of for. or.; *Elymas,* a wizard:— Elymas.

1682. ἐλοΐ **ĕlōï**, *el-o-ee´;* of Chald. or. [426 with pron. suff.] *my God:*— Eloi.

1683. ἐμαυτοῦ **ĕmautŏu**, *em-ŏw-too´;* gen. compound of 1700 and 846; *of myself* (so likewise the dat.

    ἐμαυτῷ **ĕmautŏi**, *em-ow-to´;* and acc.

    ἐμαυτόν **ĕmautŏn**, *em-ow-ton´:*— me, mine own (self), myself.

1684. ἐμβαίνω **ĕmbainō**, *em-ba´-hee-no;* from 1722 and the base of 939; to *walk on,* i.e. *embark* (aboard a vessel), *reach* (a pool):— come (get) into, enter (into), go (up) into, step in, take ship.

1685. ἐμβάλλω **ĕmballō**, *em-bal´-lo;* from 1722 and 906; to *throw on,* i.e. (fig.) *subject to* (eternal punishment):— cast into.

1686. ἐμβάπτω **ĕmbaptō**, *em-bap´-to;* from 1722 and 911; to *whelm on,* i.e. *wet* (a part of the person, etc.) by contact with a fluid:— dip.

1687. ἐμβατεύω **ĕmbatĕuō**, *em-bat-yoo´-o;* from 1722 and a presumed der. of the base of 939; equiv. to 1684; to *intrude on* (fig.):— intrude into.

1688. ἐμβιβάζω **ĕmbibazō**, *em-bib-ad´-zo;* from 1722 and βιβάζω **bibazō** (to *mount;* caus. of 1684); to *place on,* i.e. *transfer* (aboard a vessel):— put in.

1689. ἐμβλέπω **ĕmblĕpō**, *em-blep´-o;* from 1722 and 991; to *look on,* i.e. (rel.) to *observe* fixedly, or (absolutely) to *discern* clearly:— behold, gaze up, look upon, (could) see.

1690. ἐμβριμάομαι **ĕmbrimaŏmai**, *em-brim-ah´-om-ahee;* from 1722 and βριμάομαι **brimaŏmai** (to *snort* with anger); to have *indignation on,* i.e. (tran.) to *blame,* (intr.) to *sigh* with chagrin, (spec.) to sternly *enjoin:*— straitly charge, groan, murmur against.

1691. ἐμέ **ĕmĕ**, *em-eh´;* a prol. form of 3165; *me:*— I, me, my (-self).

1692. ἐμέω **ĕmĕō**, *em-eh´-o;* of uncert. aff.; to *vomit:*— (will) spue.

1693. ἐμμαίνομαι **ĕmmainŏmai**, *em-mah´-ee-nom-ahee;* from 1722 and 3105; to *rave on,* i.e. *rage at:*— be mad against.

1694. Ἐμμανουήλ **Ĕmmanŏuēl**, *em-man-oo-ale´;* of Heb. or. [6005]; *God with us; Emmanuel,* a name of Christ:— Emmanuel.

1695. Ἐμμαούς **Ĕmmaŏus**, *em-mah-ooce´;* prob. of Heb. or. [comp. 3222]; *Emmaüs,* a place in Pal.:— Emmaus.

1696. ἐμμένω **ĕmmĕnō**, *em-men´-o;* from 1722

and 3306; to *stay in* the same place, i.e. (fig.) *persevere:*— continue.

1697. Ἐμμόρ **Ĕmmŏr**, *em-mor´;* of Heb. or. [2544]; *Emmor* (i.e. *Chamor*), a Canaanite:— Emmor.

1698. ἐμοί **ĕmŏi**, *em-oy´;* a prol. form of 3427; *to me:*— I, me, mine, my.

1699. ἐμός **ĕmŏs**, *em-os´;* from the oblique cases of 1473 (1698, 1700, 1691); *my:*— of me, mine (own), my.

1700. ἐμοῦ **ĕmŏu**, *em-oo´;* a prol. form of 3450; *of me:*— me, mine, my.

1701. ἐμπαιγμός **ĕmpaigmŏs**, *emp-aheegmos´;* from 1702; *derision:*— mocking.

1702. ἐμπαίζω **ĕmpaizō**, *emp-aheed´-zo;* from 1722 and 3815; to *jeer at,* i.e. *deride:*— mock.

1703. ἐμπαίκτης **ĕmpaiktēs**, *emp-aheektace´;* from 1702; a *derider,* i.e. (by impl.) a *false teacher:*— mocker, scoffer.

1704. ἐμπεριπατέω **ĕmpĕripatĕō**, *em-per-ee-pat-eh´-o;* from 1722 and 4043; to *perambulate on* a place, i.e. (fig.) to *be occupied among* persons:— walk in.

1705. ἐμπίπλημι **ĕmpiplēmi**, *em-pip´-lay-mee;* or

    ἐμπλήθω **ĕmplēthō**, *em-play´-tho;* from 1722 and the base of 4118; to *fill in* (up), i.e. (by impl.) to *satisfy* (lit. or fig.):— fill.

1706. ἐμπίπτω **ĕmpiptō**, *em-pip´-to;* from 1722 and 4098; to *fall on,* i.e. (lit.) to be *entrapped by,* or (fig.) be *overwhelmed with:*— fall among (into).

1707. ἐμπλέκω **ĕmplĕkō**, *em-plek´-o;* from 1722 and 4120; to *entwine,* i.e. (fig.) *involve with:*— entangle (in, self with).

    ἐμπλήθω **ĕmplēthō**. See 1705.

1708. ἐμπλοκή **ĕmplŏkē**, *em-plok-ay´;* from 1707; elaborate *braiding* of the hair:— plaiting.

1709. ἐμπνέω **ĕmpnĕō**, *emp-neh´-o;* from 1722 and 4154; to *inhale,* i.e. (fig.) to *be animated by* (bent upon):— breathe.

1710. ἐμπορεύομαι **ĕmpŏrĕuŏmai**, *em-por-yoo´-om-ahee;* from 1722 and 4198; to *travel in* (a country as a pedlar), i.e. (by impl.) to *trade:*— buy and sell, make merchandise.

1711. ἐμπορία **ĕmpŏria**, *em-por-ee´-ah;* fem. from 1713; *traffic:*— merchandise.

1712. ἐμπόριον **ĕmpŏriŏn**, *em-por´-ee-on;* neut. from 1713; a *mart* ("emporium"):— merchandise.

1713. ἔμπορος **ĕmpŏrŏs**, *em´-por-os;* from 1722 and the base of 4198; a (wholesale) *tradesman:*— merchant.

1714. ἐμπρήθω **ĕmprēthō**, *em-pray´-tho;* from 1722 and πρήθω **prēthō** (to *blow* a flame); to *enkindle,* i.e. *set on fire:*— burn up.

1715. ἔμπροσθεν **ĕmprŏsthĕn**, *em´-pros-then;* from *1722* and *4314; in front of* (in place [lit. or fig.] or time):— against, at, before, (in presence, sight) of.

1716. ἐμπτύω **ĕmptuō**, *emp-too´-o;* from *1722* and *4429;* to *spit at* or *on:*— spit (upon).

1717. ἐμφανής **ĕmphanēs**, *em-fan-ace´;* from a compound of *1722* and *5316; apparent in self:*— manifest, openly.

1718. ἐμφανίζω **ĕmphanizo**, *em-fan-id´-zo;* from *1717;* to *exhibit* (in person) or *disclose* (by words):— appear, declare (plainly), inform, (will) manifest, shew, signify.

1719. ἔμφοβος **ĕmphŏbŏs**, *em´-fob-os;* from *1722* and *5401; in fear,* i.e. *alarmed:*— affrighted, afraid, tremble.

1720. ἐμφυσάω **ĕmphusaō**, *em-foo-sah´-o;* from *1722* and φυσάω **phusao** (to *puff*) [comp. *5453*]; to *blow at* or *on:*— breathe on.

1721. ἔμφυτος **ĕmphutŏs**, *em´-foo-tos;* from *1722* and a der. of *5453; implanted* (fig.):— engrafted.

1722. ἐν **ĕn**, *en;* a primary prep. denoting (fixed) *position* (in place, time or state), and (by impl.) *instrumentality* (medially or constructively), i.e. a relation of *rest* (intermediate between *1519* and *1537);* "*in*," *at,* (up-) *on, by,* etc.:— about, after, against, + almost, × altogether, among, × as, at, before, between, (here-) by (+ all means), for (...sake of), + give self wholly to, (here-) in (-to, wardly), × mightily, (because) of, (up-) on, [open-] ly, × outwardly, one, × quickly, × shortly, [speedi-] ly, × that, × there (-in, -on), through (-out), (un-) to (-ward), under, when, where (-with), while, with (-in). Often used in compounds, with substantially the same import; rarely with verbs of motion, and then not to indicate direction, except (elliptically) by a separate (and different) prep.

1723. ἐναγκαλίζομαι **ĕnagkalizŏmai**, *en-ang-kal-id´-zom-ahee;* from *1722* and a der. of *43;* to *take in* one's *arms,* i.e. *embrace:*— take up in arms.

1724. ἐνάλιος **ĕnaliŏs**, *en-al´-ee-os;* from *1722* and *251; in the sea,* i.e. *marine:*— thing in the sea.

1725. ἔναντι **ĕnanti**, *en´-an-tee;* from *1722* and *473; in front* (i.e. fig. *presence*) *of:*— before.

1726. ἐναντίον **ĕnantiŏn**, *en-an-tee´-on;* neut. of *1727;* (adv.) *in the presence* (*view*) *of:*— before, in the presence of.

1727. ἐναντίος **ĕnantiŏs**, *en-an-tee´-os;* from *1725; opposite;* fig. *antagonistic:*— (over) against, contrary.

1728. ἐνάρχομαι **ĕnarchŏmai**, *en-ar´-khom-ahee;* from *1722* and *756;* to *commence on:*— rule [by mistake for *757*].

1729. ἐνδεής **ĕndĕēs**, *en-deh-ace´;* from a compound of *1722* and *1210* (in the sense of *lacking*); *deficient in:*— lacking.

1730. ἔνδειγμα **ĕndĕigma**, *en´-dighe-mah;* from *1731;* an *indication* (concr.):— manifest token.

1731. ἐνδείκνυμι **ĕndĕiknumi**, *en-dike´-noo-mee;* from *1722* and *1166;* to *indicate* (by word or act):— do, show (forth).

1732. ἔνδειξις **ĕndĕixis**, *en´-dike-sis;* from *1731; indication* (abstr.):— declare, evident token, proof.

1733. ἕνδεκα **hĕndĕka**, *hen´-dek-ah;* from (the neut. of) *1520* and *1176; one and ten,* i.e. *eleven:*— eleven.

1734. ἑνδέκατος **hĕndĕkatŏs**, *hen-dek´-at-os;* ord. from *1733; eleventh:*— eleventh.

1735. ἐνδέχεται **ĕndĕchĕtai**, *en-dekh´-et-ahee;* third pers. sing. present of a compound of *1722* and *1209;* (impers.) *it is accepted in,* i.e. *admitted* (*possible*):— can (+ not) be.

1736. ἐνδημέω **ĕndēmĕō**, *en-day-meh´-o;* from a compound of *1722* and *1218;* to *be in* one's own *country,* i.e. *home* (fig.):— be at home (present).

1737. ἐνδιδύσκω **ĕndiduskō**, *en-did-oos´-ko;* a prol. form of *1746;* to *invest* (with a garment):— clothe in, wear.

1738. ἔνδικος **ĕndikŏs**, *en´-dee-kos;* from *1722* and *1349; in the right,* i.e. *equitable:*— just.

1739. ἐνδόμησις **ĕndŏmēsis**, *en-dom´-ay-sis;* from a compound of *1722* and a der. of the base of *1218;* a *housing in* (*residence*), i.e. *structure:*— building.

1740. ἐνδοξάζω **ĕndŏxazō**, *en-dox-ad´-zo;* from *1741;* to *glorify:*— glorify.

1741. ἔνδοξος **ĕndŏxŏs**, *en´-dox-os;* from *1722* and *1391; in glory,* i.e. *splendid,* (fig.) *noble:*— glorious, gorgeous [-ly], honourable.

1742. ἔνδυμα **ĕnduma**, *en´-doo-mah;* from *1746; apparel* (espec. the outer *robe*):— clothing, garment, raiment.

1743. ἐνδυναμόω **ĕndunamŏō**, *en-doo-nam-ŏ´-o;* from *1722* and *1412;* to *empower:*— enable, (increase in) strength (-en), be (make) strong.

1744. ἐνδύνω **ĕndunō**, *en-doo´-no;* from *1772* and *1416;* to *sink* (by impl. *wrap* [comp. *1746*]) *on,* i.e. (fig.) *sneak:*— creep.

1745. ἔνδυσις **ĕndusis**, *en´-doo-sis;* from *1746; investment* with clothing:— putting on.

1746. ἐνδύω **ĕnduō**, *en-doo´-o;* from *1722* and *1416* (in the sense of *sinking* into a garment); to *invest* with clothing (lit. or fig.):— array, clothe (with), endue, have (put) on.

ἐνέγκω **ĕnĕgkō**. See *5342*.

1747. ἐνέδρα **ĕnĕdra**, *en-ed´-rah;* fem. from *1722* and the base of *1476;* an *ambuscade,* i.e. (fig.) murderous *purpose:*— lay wait. See also *1749*.

1748. ἐνεδρεύω **ĕnĕdrĕuō**, *en-ed-ryoo´-o;* from *1747;* to *lurk,* i.e. (fig.) *plot* assassination:— lay wait for.

1749. ἔνεδρον **ĕnĕdrŏn**, *en´-ed-ron;* neut. of the same as *1747;* an *ambush,* i.e. (fig.) murderous *design:*— lying in wait.

1750. ἐνειλέω **ĕnĕilĕō**, *en-i-leh´-o;* from *1772* and the base of *1507;* to *enwrap:*— wrap in.

1751. ἔνειμι **ĕnĕimi**, *en´-i-mee;* from *1772* and *1510;* to *be within* (neut. part. plur.):— such things as ... have. See also *1762*.

1752. ἕνεκα **hĕnĕka**, *hen´-ek-ah;* or

ἕνεκεν **hĕnĕkĕn**, *hen´-ek-en;* or

εἵνεκεν **hĕinĕkĕn**, *hi´-nek-en;* of uncert. aff.; *on account of:*— because, for (cause, sake), (where-) fore, by reason of, that.

1753. ἐνέργεια **ĕnĕrgĕia**, *en-erg´-i-ah;* from *1756; efficiency* ("energy"):— operation, strong, (effectual) working.

1754. ἐνεργέω **ĕnĕrgĕō**, *en-erg-eh´-o;* from *1756;* to *be active, efficient:*— do, (be) effectual (fervent), be mighty in, shew forth self, work (effectually in).

1755. ἐνέργημα **ĕnĕrgēma**, *en-erg´-ay-mah;* from *1754;* an *effect:*— operation, working.

1756. ἐνεργής **ĕnĕrgēs**, *en-er-gace´;* from *1722* and *2041; active, operative:*— effectual, powerful.

1757. ἐνευλογέω **ĕnĕulŏgĕō**, *en-yoo-log-eh´-o;* from *1722* and *2127;* to *confer a benefit on:*— bless.

1758. ἐνέχω **ĕnĕchō**, *en-ekh´-o;* from *1722* and *2192;* to *hold in* or *upon,* i.e. *ensnare;* by impl. to *keep a grudge:*— entangle with, have a quarrel against, urge.

1759. ἐνθάδε **ĕnthadĕ**, *en-thad´-eh;* from a prol. form of *1722;* prop. *within,* i.e. (of place) *here, hither:*— (t-) here, hither.

1760. ἐνθυμέομαι **ĕnthumĕŏmai**, *en-thoo-meh´-om-ahee;* from a compound of *1722* and *2372;* to *be inspirited,* i.e. *ponder:*— think.

1761. ἐνθύμησις **ĕnthumēsis**, *en-thoo´-may-sis;* from *1760; deliberation:*— device, thought.

1762. ἔνι **ĕni**, *en´-ee;* contr. for the third pers. sing. pres. ind. of *1751;* impers. *there is* in or among:— be, (there) is.

1763. ἐνιαυτός **ĕniautŏs**, *en-ee-ŏw-tos´;* prol. from a primary ἔνος **ĕnŏs** (a *year*); a *year:*— year.

1764. ἐνίστημι **ĕnistēmi**, *en-is´-tay-mee;* from *1722* and *2476;* to *place on* hand, i.e. (refl.) *impend,* (part.) be *instant:*— come, be at hand, present.

1765. ἐνισχύω **ĕnischuō**, *en-is-khoo´-o;* from *1722* and *2480;* to *invigorate* (tran. or refl.):— strengthen.

1766. ἔννατος **ĕnnatŏs**, *en´-nat-os;* ord. from *1767; ninth:*— ninth.

1767. ἐννέα **ĕnnĕa**, *en-neh´-ah;* a primary number; *nine:*— nine.

1768. ἐννενηκονταεννέα **ĕnnĕnēkŏntaĕnnĕa**, *en-nen-ay-kon-tah-en-neh´-ah;* from a (tenth) multiple of *1767* and *1767* itself; *ninety-nine:*— ninety and nine.

1769. ἐννεός **ĕnnĕŏs**, *en-neh-os´;* from *1770; dumb* (as *making signs*), i.e. *silent* from astonishment:— speechless.

1770. ἐννεύω **ĕnnĕuō**, *en-nyoo´-o;* from *1722* and *3506;* to *nod at,* i.e. *beckon* or *communicate by gesture:*— make signs.

1771. ἔννοια **ĕnnŏia**, *en´-noy-ah;* from a compound of *1722* and *3563; thoughtfulness,* i.e. moral *understanding:*— intent, mind.

1772. ἔννομος **ĕnnŏmŏs**, *en´-nom-os;* from *1722* and *3551;* (subj.) *legal,* or (obj.) *subject to:*— lawful, under law.

1773. ἔννυχον **ĕnnuchŏn**, *en´-noo-khon;* neut. of a compound of *1722* and *3571;* (adv.) *by night:*— before day.

1774. ἐνοικέω **ĕnŏikĕō**, *en-oy-keh´-o;* from *1722* and *3611;* to *inhabit* (fig.):— dwell in.

1775. ἑνότης **hĕnŏtēs**, *hen-ot-ace´;* from *1520; oneness,* i.e. (fig.) *unanimity:*— unity.

1776. ἐνοχλέω **ĕnŏchlĕō**, *en-okh-leh´-o;* from *1722* and *3791;* to *crowd in,* i.e. (fig.) to *annoy:*— trouble.

1777. ἔνοχος **ĕnŏchŏs**, *en´-okh-os;* from *1758; liable* to (a condition, penalty or imputation):— in danger of, guilty of, subject to.

1778. ἔνταλμα **ĕntalma**, *en´-tal-mah;* from *1781;* an *injunction,* i.e. relig. *precept:*— commandment.

1779. ἐνταφιάζω **ĕntaphiazō**, *en-taf-ee-ad´-zo;* from a compound of *1722* and *5028;* to *inswathe* with cerements for interment:— bury.

1780. ἐνταφιασμός **ĕntaphiasmŏs**, *en-taf-ee-as-mos´;* from *1779; preparation* for interment:— burying.

1781. ἐντέλλομαι **ĕntĕllŏmai**, *en-tel´-lom-ahee;* from *1722* and the base of *5056;* to *enjoin:*— (give) charge, (give) command (-ments), injoin.

1782. ἐντεῦθεν **ĕntĕuthĕn**, *ent-yoo´-then;* from the same as *1759; hence* (lit. or fig.); (repeated) *on both sides:*— (from) hence, on either side.

1783. ἔντευξις **ĕntĕuxis**, *ent´-yook-sis;* from *1793;* an *interview,* i.e. (spec.) *supplication:*— intercession, prayer.

1784. ἔντιμος **ĕntimŏs**, *en´-tee-mos;* from *1722* and *5092; valued* (fig.):— dear, more honourable, precious, in reputation.

1785. ἐντολή **ĕntŏlē**, *en-tol-ay´;* from *1781;*

injunction, i.e. an authoritative *prescription:*— commandment, precept.

1786. ἐντόπιος **ĕntŏpiŏs,** *en-top´-ee-os;* from 1722 and 5117; a *resident:*— of that place.

1787. ἐντός **ĕntŏs,** *en-tos´;* from 1722; *inside* (adverb or noun):— within.

1788. ἐντρέπω **ĕntrĕpō,** *en-trep´-o;* from 1722 and the base of 5157; to *invert,* i.e. (fig. and refl.) in a good sense, to *respect;* or in a bad one, to *confound:*— regard, (give) reverence, shame.

1789. ἐντρέφω **ĕntrĕphō,** *en-tref´-o;* from 1722 and 5142; (fig.) to *educate:*— nourish up in.

1790. ἔντρομος **ĕntrŏmŏs,** *en´-trom-os;* from 1722 and 5156; *terrified:*— × quake, × trembled.

1791. ἐντροπή **ĕntrŏpē,** *en-trop-ay´;* from 1788; *confusion:*— shame.

1792. ἐντρυφάω **ĕntruphaō,** *en-troo-fah´-o;* from 1722 and 5171; to *revel in:*— sporting selves.

1793. ἐντυγχάνω **ĕntugchanō,** *en-toong-khan´-o;* from 1722 and 5177; to *chance upon,* i.e. (by impl.) *confer with;* by extens. to *entreat* (in favor or against):— deal with, make intercession.

1794. ἐντυλίσσω **ĕntulissō,** *en-too-lis´-so;* from 1722 and τυλίσσω *tulissō* (to *twist;* prob. akin to 1507); to *entwine,* i.e. *wind* up in:— wrap in (together).

1795. ἐντυπόω **ĕntupŏō,** *en-too-pŏ´-o;* from 1722 and a der. of 5179; to *enstamp,* i.e. *engrave:*— engrave.

1796. ἐνυβρίζω **ĕnubrizō,** *en-oo-brid´-zo;* from 1722 and 5195; to *insult:*— do despite unto.

1797. ἐνυπνιάζομαι **ĕnupniazŏmai,** *en-oop-nee-ad´-zom-ahee;* mid. voice from 1798; to *dream:*— dream (-er).

1798. ἐνύπνιον **ĕnupniŏn,** *en-oop´-nee-on;* from 1722 and 5258; something seen *in sleep,* i.e. a *dream* (*vision* in a dream):— dream.

1799. ἐνώπιον **ĕnōpiŏn,** *en-o´-pee-on;* neut. of a compound of 1722 and a der. of 3700; *in the face* of (lit. or fig.):— before, in the presence (sight) of, to.

1800. Ἐνώς **Ĕnōs,** *en-oce´;* of Heb. or. [583]; *Enos* (i.e. *Enosh*), a patriarch:— Enos.

1801. ἐνωτίζομαι **ĕnōtizŏmai,** *en-o-tid´-zom-ahee;* mid. voice from a compound of 1722 and 3775; to take *in one's ear,* i.e. to *listen:*— hearken.

1802. Ἐνώχ **Ĕnōch,** *en-oke´;* of Heb. or. [2585]; *Enoch* (i.e. *Chanok*), an antediluvian:— Enoch.

ἐξ **ĕx.** See 1537.

1803. ἕξ **hĕx,** *hex;* a primary numeral; *six:*— six.

1804. ἐξαγγέλλω **ĕxaggĕllō,** *ex-ang-el´-lo;*

from 1537 and the base of 32; to *publish,* i.e. *celebrate:*— shew forth.

1805. ἐξαγοράζω **ĕxagŏrazō,** *ex-ag-or-ad´-zo;* from 1537 and 59; to *buy up,* i.e. *ransom;* fig. to *rescue* from loss (*improve* opportunity):— redeem.

1806. ἐξάγω **ĕxagō,** *ex-ag´-o;* from 1537 and 71; to *lead forth:*— bring forth (out), fetch (lead) out.

1807. ἐξαιρέω **ĕxairĕō,** *ex-ahee-reh´-o;* from 1537 and 138; act. to *tear out;* mid. voice to *select;* fig. to *release:*— deliver, pluck out, rescue.

1808. ἐξαίρω **ĕxairō,** *ex-ah´-ee-ro;* from 1537 and 142; to *remove:*— put (take) away.

1809. ἐξαιτέομαι **ĕxaitĕŏmai,** *ex-ahee-teh´-om-ahee;* mid. voice from 1537 and 154; to *demand* (for trial):— desire.

1810. ἐξαίφνης **ĕxaiphnēs,** *ex-ah´-eef-nace;* from 1537 and the base of 160; *of a sudden* (*unexpectedly*):— suddenly. Comp. 1819.

1811. ἐξακολουθέω **ĕxakŏlŏuthĕō,** *ex-ak-ol-oo-theh´-o;* from 1537 and 190; to *follow out,* i.e. (fig.) to *imitate, obey,* yield to:— follow.

1812. ἐξακόσιοι **hĕxakŏsiŏi,** *hex-ak-os´-ee-oy;* plur. ordinal from 1803 and 1540; *six hundred:*— six hundred.

1813. ἐξαλείφω **ĕxalĕiphō,** *ex-al-i´-fo;* from 1537 and 218; to *smear out,* i.e. *obliterate* (*erase* tears, fig. *pardon* sin):— blot out, wipe away.

1814. ἐξάλλομαι **ĕxallŏmai,** *ex-al´-lom-ahee;* from 1537 and 242; to *spring forth:*— leap up.

1815. ἐξανάστασις **ĕxanastasis,** *ex-an-as´-tas-is;* from 1817; a *rising from* death:— resurrection.

1816. ἐξανατέλλω **ĕxanatĕllō,** *ex-an-at-el´-lo;* from 1537 and 393; to *start up out* of the ground, i.e. *germinate:*— spring up.

1817. ἐξανίστημι **ĕxanistēmi,** *ex-an-is´-tay-mee;* from 1537 and 450; obj. to *produce,* i.e. (fig.) *beget;* subj. to *arise,* i.e. (fig.) *object:*— raise (rise) up.

1818. ἐξαπατάω **ĕxapataō,** *ex-ap-at-ah´-o;* from 1537 and 538; to *seduce wholly:*— beguile, deceive.

1819. ἐξάπινα **ĕxapina,** *ex-ap´-ee-nah;* from 1537 and a der. of the same as 160; *of a sudden,* i.e. *unexpectedly:*— suddenly. Comp. 1810.

1820. ἐξαπορέομαι **ĕxapŏrĕŏmai,** *ex-ap-or-eh´-om-ahee;* mid. voice from 1537 and 639; to *be utterly at a loss,* i.e. *despond:*— (in) despair.

1821. ἐξαποστέλλω **ĕxapŏstĕllō,** *ex-ap-os-tel´-lo;* from 1537 and 649; to *send away forth,* i.e. (on a mission) to *despatch,* or (peremptorily) to *dismiss:*— send (away, forth, out).

1822. ἐξαρτίζω **ĕxartizō**, *ex-ar-tid´-zo;* from *1537* and a der. of *739;* to *finish out* (time); fig. to *equip fully* (a teacher):— accomplish, thoroughly furnish.

1823. ἐξαστράπτω **ĕxastraptō**, *ex-as-trap´-to;* from *1537* and *797;* to *lighten forth,* i.e. (fig.) to *be radiant* (of very white garments):— glistening.

1824. ἐξαύτης **ĕxautēs**, *ex-ow´-tace;* from *1537* and the gen. sing. fem. of *846* (*5610* being understood); *from that* hour, i.e. *instantly:—* by and by, immediately, presently, straightway.

1825. ἐξεγείρω **ĕxĕgĕirō**, *ex-eg-i´-ro;* from *1537* and *1453;* to *rouse fully,* i.e. (fig.) to *resuscitate* (from death), *release* (from infliction):— raise up.

1826. ἔξειμι **ĕxĕimi**, *ex´-i-mee;* from *1537* and εἶμι **ĕimi** (to *go*); to *issue,* i.e. *leave* (a place), *escape* (to the shore):— depart, get [to land], go out.

1827. ἐξελέγχω **ĕxĕlĕgchō**, *ex-el-eng´-kho;* from *1537* and *1651;* to *convict fully,* i.e. (by impl.) to *punish:—* convince.

1828. ἐξέλκω **ĕxĕlkō**, *ex-el´-ko;* from *1537* and *1670;* to *drag forth,* i.e. (fig.) to *entice* (to sin):— draw away.

1829. ἐξέραμα **ĕxĕrama**, *ex-er´-am-ah;* from a compound of *1537* and a presumed ἐράω **ĕraō** (to *spue*); *vomit,* i.e. *food disgorged:—* vomit.

1830. ἐξερευνάω **ĕxĕrĕunaō**, *ex-er-yoo-nah´-o;* from *1537* and *2045;* to *explore* (fig.):— search diligently.

1831. ἐξέρχομαι **ĕxĕrchŏmai**, *ex-er´-khom-ahee;* from *1537* and *2064;* to *issue* (lit. or fig.):— come (forth, out), depart (out of), escape, get out, go (abroad, away, forth, out, thence), proceed (forth), spread abroad.

1832. ἔξεστι **ĕxĕsti**, *ex´-es-tee* or ἔξεστιν **exestin**, *ex´-es-teen;* third pers. sing. pres. ind. of a compound of *1537* and *1510;* so also

ἐξόν **ĕxŏn**, *ex-on´;* neut. pres. part. of the same (with or without some form of *1510* expressed); impers. *it is right* (through the fig. idea of *being out* in public):— be lawful, let, × may (-est).

1833. ἐξετάζω **ĕxĕtazō**, *ex-et-ad´-zo;* from *1537* and ἐτάζω **ĕtazō** (to *examine*); to *test thoroughly* (by questions), i.e. *ascertain* or *interrogate:—* ask, enquire, search.

1834. ἐξηγέομαι **ĕxēgĕŏmai**, *ex-ayg-eh´-om-ahee;* from *1537* and *2233;* to *consider out* (aloud), i.e. *rehearse, unfold:—* declare, tell.

1835. ἐξήκοντα **hĕxēkŏnta**, *hex-ay´-kon-tah;* the tenth multiple of *1803; sixty:—* sixty [-fold], threescore.

1836. ἑξῆς **hĕxēs**, *hex-ace´;* from *2192* (in the sense of *taking hold of*), i.e. *adjoining; successive:—* after, following, × morrow, next.

1837. ἐξηχέομαι **ĕxēchĕŏmai**, *ex-ay-kheh´-om-ahee;* mid. voice from *1537* and *2278;* to

"echo" forth, i.e. *resound* (be generally reported):— sound forth.

1838. ἕξις **hĕxis**, *hex´-is;* from *2192; habit,* i.e. (by impl.) *practice:—* use.

1839. ἐξίστημι **ĕxistēmi**, *ex-is´-tay-mee;* from *1537* and *2476;* to *put* (*stand*) *out* of wits, i.e. *astound,* or (refl.) *become amazed,* or (refl.) *become astounded, insane:—* amaze, be (make) astonished, be beside self (selves), bewitch, wonder.

1840. ἐξισχύω **ĕxischuō**, *ex-is-khoo´-o;* from *1537* and *2480;* to *have full strength,* i.e. *be entirely competent:—* be able.

1841. ἔξοδος **ĕxŏdŏs**, *ex´-od-os;* from *1537* and *3598;* an *exit,* i.e. (fig.) *death:—* decease, departing.

1842. ἐξολοθρεύω **ĕxŏlŏthrĕuō**, *ex-ol-oth-ryoo´-o;* from *1537* and *3645;* to *extirpate:—* destroy.

1843. ἐξομολογέω **ĕxŏmŏlŏgĕō**, *ex-om-ol-og-eh´-o;* from *1537* and *3670;* to *acknowledge* or (by impl. of *assent*) *agree fully:—* confess, profess, promise.

ἐξόν **ĕxŏn**. See *1832.*

1844. ἐξορκίζω **ĕxŏrkizō**, *ex-or-kid´-zo;* from *1537* and *3726;* to *exact an oath,* i.e. *conjure:—* adjure.

1845. ἐξορκιστής **ĕxŏrkistēs**, *ex-or-kis-tace´;* from *1844;* one that binds by an oath (or *spell*), i.e. (by impl.) an *"exorcist"* (conjurer):— exorcist.

1846. ἐξορύσσω **ĕxŏrussō**, *ex-or-oos´-so;* from *1537* and *3736;* to *dig out,* i.e. (by extens.) to *extract* (an eye), *remove* (roofing):— break up, pluck out.

1847. ἐξουδενόω **ĕxŏudĕnŏō**, *ex-oo-den-ŏ´-o;* from *1537* and a der. of the neut. of *3762;* to *make utterly nothing of,* i.e. *despise:—* set at nought. See also *1848.*

1848. ἐξουθενέω **ĕxŏuthĕnĕō**, *ex-oo-then-eh´-o;* a var. of *1847* and mean. the same:— contemptible, despise, least esteemed, set at nought.

1849. ἐξουσία **ĕxŏusia**, *ex-oo-see´-ah;* from *1832* (in the sense of *ability*); *privilege,* i.e. (subj.) *force, capacity, competency, freedom,* or (obj.) *mastery* (concr. *magistrate, superhuman, potentate, token of control*), delegated *influence:—* authority, jurisdiction, liberty, power, right, strength.

1850. ἐξουσιάζω **ĕxŏusiazō**, *ex-oo-see-ad´-zo;* from *1849;* to *control:—* exercise authority upon, bring under the (have) power of.

1851. ἐξοχή **ĕxŏchē**, *ex-okh-ay´;* from a compound of *1537* and *2192* (mean. to *stand out*); *prominence* (fig.):— principal.

1852. ἐξυπνίζω **ĕxupnizō**, *ex-oop-nid´-zo;* from *1853;* to *waken:—* awake out of sleep.

1853. ἔξυπνος **ĕxupnŏs**, *ex´-oop-nos;* from 1537 and 5258; *awake:*— × out of sleep.

1854. ἔξω **ĕxō**, *ex´-o;* adv. from 1537; *out (-side, of doors),* lit. or fig.:— away, forth, (with-) out (of, -ward), strange.

1855. ἔξωθεν **ĕxōthĕn**, *ex´-o-then;* from 1854; *external (-ly):*— out (-side, -ward, -wardly), (from) without.

1856. ἐξωθέω **ĕxōthĕō**, *ex-o-theh´-o;* or

ἐξώθω **ĕxōthō**, *ex-o´-tho;* from 1537 and ὠθέω **ōthĕō** (to *push*); to *expel;* by impl. to *propel:*— drive out, thrust in.

1857. ἐξώτερος **ĕxōtĕrŏs**, *ex-o´-ter-os;* comp. of 1854; *exterior:*— outer.

1858. ἑορτάζω **hĕŏrtazō**, *heh-or-tad´-zo;* from 1859; to *observe a festival:*— keep the feast.

1859. ἑορτή **hĕŏrtē**, *heh-or-tay´;* of uncert. aff.; a *festival:*— feast, holyday.

1860. ἐπαγγελία **ĕpaggĕlia**, *ep-ang-el-ee´-ah;* from 1861; an *announcement* (for information, assent or pledge; espec. a divine *assurance* of good):— message, promise.

1861. ἐπαγγέλλω **ĕpaggĕllō**, *ep-ang-el´-lo;* from 1909 and the base of 32; to *announce upon* (refl.), i.e. (by impl.) to *engage* to do something, to *assert* something respecting oneself:— profess, (make) promise.

1862. ἐπάγγελμα **ĕpaggĕlma**, *ep-ang´-el-mah;* from 1861; a *self-committal* (by *assurance* of conferring some good):— promise.

1863. ἐπάγω **ĕpagō**, *ep-ag´-o;* from 1909 and 71; to *superinduce,* i.e. *inflict* (an evil), *charge* (a crime):— bring upon.

1864. ἐπαγωνίζομαι **ĕpagōnizŏmai**, *ep-ag-o-nid´-zom-ahee;* from 1909 and 75; to *struggle for:*— earnestly contend for.

1865. ἐπαθροίζω **ĕpathrŏizō**, *ep-ath-roid´-zo;* from 1909 and ἀθροίζω **athrŏizō** (to *assemble*); to *accumulate:*— gather thick together.

1866. Ἐπαίνετος **Ĕpainĕtŏs**, *ep-a´-hee-net-os;* from 1867; *praised; Epænetus,* a Chr.:— Epenetus.

1867. ἐπαινέω **ĕpainĕō**, *ep-ahee-neh´-o;* from 1909 and 134; to *applaud:*— commend, laud, praise.

1868. ἔπαινος **ĕpainŏs**, *ep´-ahee-nos;* from 1909 and the base of 134; *laudation;* concr. a *commendable* thing:— praise.

1869. ἐπαίρω **ĕpairō**, *ep-ahee´-ro;* from 1909 and 142; to *raise up* (lit. or fig.):— exalt self, poise (lift, take) up.

1870. ἐπαισχύνομαι **ĕpaischunŏmai**, *ep-ahee-skhoo´-nom-ahee;* from 1909 and 153; to *feel shame for* something:— be ashamed.

1871. ἐπαιτέω **ĕpaitĕō**, *ep-ahee-teh´-o;* from 1909 and 154; to *ask for:*— beg.

1872. ἐπακολουθέω **ĕpakŏlŏuthĕō**, *ep-ak-ol-oo-theh´-o;* from 1909 and 190; to *accompany:*— follow (after).

1873. ἐπακούω **ĕpakŏuō**, *ep-ak-oo´-o;* from 1909 and 191; to *hearken* (favorably) *to:*— hear.

1874. ἐπακροάομαι **ĕpakrŏaŏmai**, *ep-ak-ro-ah´-om-ahee;* from 1909 and the base of 202; to *listen* (intently) *to:*— hear.

1875. ἐπάν **ĕpan**, *ep-an´;* from 1909 and 302; a particle of indef. contemporaneousness; *whenever, as soon as:*— when.

1876. ἐπάναγκες **ĕpanagkĕs**, *ep-an´-ang-kes;* neut. of a presumed compound of 1909 and 318; (adv.) *on necessity,* i.e. *necessarily:*— necessary.

1877. ἐπανάγω **ĕpanagō**, *ep-an-ag´-o;* from 1909 and 321; to *lead up on,* i.e. (tech.) to *put out* (to sea); (intr.) to *return:*— launch (thrust) out, return.

1878. ἐπαναμιμνήσκω **ĕpanamimnēskō**, *ep-an-ah-mim-nace´-ko;* from 1909 and 363; to *remind of:*— put in mind.

1879. ἐπαναπαύομαι **ĕpanapauŏmai**, *ep-an-ah-pŏw´-om-ahee;* mid. voice from 1909 and 373; to *settle on;* lit. (*remain*) or fig. (*rely*):— rest in (upon).

1880. ἐπανέρχομαι **ĕpanĕrchŏmai**, *ep-an-er´-khom-ahee;* from 1909 and 424; to *come up on,* i.e. *return:*— come again, return.

1881. ἐπανίσταμαι **ĕpanistamai**, *ep-an-is´-tam-ahee;* mid. voice from 1909 and 450; to *stand up on,* i.e. (fig.) to *attack:*— rise up against.

1882. ἐπανόρθωσις **ĕpanŏrthōsis**, *ep-an-or´-tho-sis;* from a compound of 1909 and 461; a *straightening up again,* i.e. (fig.) *rectification* (*reformation*):— correction.

1883. ἐπάνω **ĕpanō**, *ep-an´-o;* from 1909 and 507; *up above,* i.e. *over* or *on* (of place, amount, rank, etc.):— above, more than, (up-) on, over.

1884. ἐπαρκέω **ĕparkĕō**, *ep-ar-keh´-o;* from 1909 and 714; to *avail for,* i.e. *help:*— relieve.

1885. ἐπαρχία **ĕparchia**, *ep-ar-khee´-ah* or ἐπαρχεία **ĕparchĕia**, *ep-ar-khi´-ah;* from a compound of 1909 and 757 (mean. a *governor* of a district, "eparch"); a special *region* of government, i.e. a Roman *præfecture:*— province.

1886. ἔπαυλις **ĕpaulis**, *ep´-ŏw-lis;* from 1909 and an equiv. of 833; a *hut over* the head, i.e. a *dwelling:*— habitation.

1887. ἐπαύριον **ĕpauriŏn**, *ep-ow´-ree-on;* from 1909 and 839; occurring *on the succeeding* day, i.e. (2250 being implied) *tomorrow:*— day following, morrow, next day (after).

1888. ἐπαυτοφώρῳ **ĕpautŏphōrō**;, *ep-ow-tof-o´-ro;* from 1909 and 846 and (the dat. sing. of) a der. of φώρ **phōr** (a *thief*); *in theft itself,* i.e. (by anal.) *in actual crime:*— in the very act.

1889. Ἐπαφρᾶς **Ĕpaphras**, *ep-af-ras´*; contr. from 1891; *Epaphras,* a Chr.:— Epaphras.

1890. ἐπαφρίζω **ĕpaphrizō**, *ep-af-rid´-zo;* from 1909 and 875; to *foam upon,* i.e. (fig.) to *exhibit* (a vile passion):— foam out.

1891. Ἐπαφρόδιτος **Ĕpaphrŏditŏs**, *ep-af-rod´-ee-tos;* from 1909 (in the sense of *devoted* to) and Ἀφροδίτη **Aphrŏditē** (*Venus*); *Epaphroditus,* a Chr.:— Epaphroditus. Comp. 1889.

1892. ἐπεγείρω **ĕpĕgĕirō**, *ep-eg-i´-ro;* from 1909 and 1453; to *rouse upon,* i.e. (fig.) to *excite* against:— raise, stir up.

1893. ἐπεί **ĕpĕi**, *ep-i´;* from 1909 and 1487; *thereupon,* i.e. *since* (of time or cause):— because, else, for that (then, -asmuch as), otherwise, seeing that, since, when.

1894. ἐπειδή **ĕpĕidē**, *ep-i-day´;* from 1893 and 1211; *since now,* i.e. (of time) *when,* or (of cause) *whereas:*— after that, because, for (that, -asmuch as), seeing, since.

1895. ἐπειδήπερ **ĕpĕidēpĕr**, *ep-i-day´-per;* from 1894 and 4007; *since indeed* (of cause):— forasmuch.

1896. ἐπεῖδον **ĕpĕidŏn**, *ep-i´-don;* and other moods and persons of the same tense; from 1909 and 1492; to *regard* (favorably or otherwise):— behold, look upon.

1897. ἐπείπερ **ĕpĕipĕr**, *ep-i´-per;* from 1893 and 4007; *since* indeed (of cause):— seeing.

1898. ἐπεισαγωγή **ĕpĕisagōgē**, *ep-ice-ag-o-gay´;* from a compound of 1909 and 1521; a *superintroduction:*— bringing in.

1899. ἔπειτα **ĕpĕita**, *ep´-i-tah;* from 1909 and 1534; *thereafter:*— after that (-ward), then.

1900. ἐπέκεινα **ĕpĕkĕina**, *ep-ek´-i-nah;* from 1909 and (the acc. plur. neut. of) 1565; *upon those* parts of, i.e. *on the further side of:*— beyond.

1901. ἐπεκτείνομαι **ĕpĕktĕinŏmai**, *ep-ek-ti´-nom-ahee;* mid. voice from 1909 and 1614; to *stretch* (oneself) forward *upon:*— reach forth.

1902. ἐπενδύομαι **ĕpĕnduŏmai**, *ep-en-doo´-om-ahee;* mid. voice from 1909 and 1746; to *invest upon* oneself:— be clothed upon.

1903. ἐπενδύτης **ĕpĕndutēs**, *ep-en-doo´-tace;* from 1902; a *wrapper,* i.e. outer garment:— fisher's coat.

1904. ἐπέρχομαι **ĕpĕrchŏmai**, *ep-er´-khom-ahee;* from 1909 and 2064; to *supervene,* i.e. *arrive, occur, impend, attack,* (fig.) *influence:*— come (in, upon).

1905. ἐπερωτάω **ĕpĕrōtaō**, *ep-er-o-tah´-o;* from 1909 and 2065; to *ask for,* i.e. *inquire, seek:*— ask (after, questions), demand, desire, question.

1906. ἐπερώτημα **ĕpĕrōtēma**, *ep-er-o´-tay-mah;* from 1905; an *inquiry:*— answer.

1907. ἐπέχω **ĕpĕchō**, *ep-ekh´-o;* from 1909 and 2192; to *hold upon,* i.e. (by impl.) to *retain;* (by extens.) to *detain;* (with impl. of 3563) to *pay*

attention to:— give (take) heed unto, hold forth, mark, stay.

1908. ἐπηρεάζω **ĕpērĕazō**, *ep-ay-reh-ad´-zo;* from a comp. of 1909 and (prob.) ἀρειά **arĕia** (*threats*); to *insult, slander:*— use despitefully, falsely accuse.

1909. ἐπί **ĕpi**, *ep-ee´;* a primary prep.; prop. mean. *superimposition* (of time, place, order, etc.), as a relation of *distribution* [with the gen.], i.e. *over, upon,* etc.; of *rest* (with the dat.) *at, on,* etc.; of *direction* (with the acc.) *toward, upon,* etc.:— about (the times), above, after, against, among, as long as (touching), at, beside, × have charge of, (be-, [where-]fore, in (a place, as much as, the time of, -to), (because) of, (up-) on (behalf of), over, (by, for) the space of, through (-out), (un-) to (-ward), with. In compounds it retains essentially the same import, *at, upon,* etc. (lit. or fig.).

1910. ἐπιβαίνω **ĕpibainō**, *ep-ee-bah´-ee-no;* from 1909 and the base of 939; to *walk upon,* i.e. *mount, ascend, embark, arrive:*— come (into), enter into, go abroad, sit upon, take ship.

1911. ἐπιβάλλω **ĕpiballō**, *ep-ee-bal´-lo;* from 1909 and 906; to *throw upon* (lit. or fig., tran. or refl.; usually with more or less force); spec. (with 1438 implied) to *reflect;* impers. to *belong to:*— beat into, cast (up-) on, fall, lay (on), put (unto), stretch forth, think on.

1912. ἐπιβαρέω **ĕpibarĕō**, *ep-ee-bar-eh´-o;* from 1909 and 916; to *be heavy upon,* i.e. (pecuniarily) to *be expensive to;* fig. to *be severe toward:*— be chargeable to, overcharge.

1913. ἐπιβιβάζω **ĕpibibazō**, *ep-ee-bee-bad´-zo;* from 1909 and a redupl. deriv. of the base of 939 [comp. 307]; to *cause to mount* (an animal):— set on.

1914. ἐπιβλέπω **ĕpiblĕpō**, *ep-ee-blep´-o;* from 1909 and 991; to *gaze at* (with favor, pity or partiality):— look upon, regard, have respect to.

1915. ἐπίβλημα **ĕpiblēma**, *ep-ib´-lay-mah;* from 1911; a *patch:*— piece.

1916. ἐπιβοάω **ĕpibŏaō**, *ep-ee-bo-ah´-o;* from 1909 and 994; to *exclaim against:*— cry.

1917. ἐπιβουλή **ĕpibŏulē**, *ep-ee-boo-lay´;* from a presumed compound of 1909 and 1014; a *plan against* someone, i.e. a *plot:*— laying (lying) in wait.

1918. ἐπιγαμβρεύω **ĕpigambrĕuō**, *ep-ee-gam-bryoo´-o;* from 1909 and a der. of 1062; to *form affinity with,* i.e. (spec.) in a levirate way:— marry.

1919. ἐπίγειος **ĕpigĕiŏs**, *ep-ig´-i-os;* from 1909 and 1093; *worldly* (phys. or mor.):— earthly, in earth, terrestrial.

1920. ἐπιγίνομαι **ĕpiginŏmai**, *ep-ig-in´-om-*

ahee; from *1909* and *1096;* to *arrive upon,* i.e. *spring up* (as a wind):— blow.

1921. ἐπιγινώσκω **ĕpiginōskō,** *ep-ig-in-oce´-ko;* from *1909* and *1097;* to *know upon* some mark, i.e. *recognize;* by impl. to *become fully acquainted with,* to *acknowledge:—* (ac-, have, take) know (-ledge, well), perceive.

1922. ἐπίγνωσις **ĕpignōsis,** *ep-ig´-no-sis;* from *1921; recognition,* i.e. (by impl.) full *discernment, acknowledgement:—* (ac-) knowledge (-ing, -ment).

1923. ἐπιγραφή **ĕpigraphē,** *ep-ig-raf-ay´;* from *1924;* an *inscription:—* superscription.

1924. ἐπιγράφω **ĕpigraphō,** *ep-ee-graf´-o;* from *1909* and *1125;* to *inscribe* (phys. or ment.):— inscription, write in (over, thereon).

1925. ἐπιδείκνυμι **ĕpidĕiknumi,** *ep-ee-dike´-noo-mee;* from *1909* and *1166;* to *exhibit* (phys. or ment.):— shew.

1926. ἐπιδέχομαι **ĕpidĕchŏmai,** *ep-ee-dekh´-om-ahee;* from *1909* and *1209;* to *admit* (as a guest or [fig.] teacher):— receive.

1927. ἐπιδημέω **ĕpidēmĕō,** *ep-ee-day-meh´-o;* from a compound of *1909* and *1218;* to *make oneself at home,* i.e. (by extens.) to *reside* (in a foreign country):— [be] dwelling (which were) there, stranger.

1928. ἐπιδιατάσσομαι **ĕpidiatassŏmai,** *ep-ee-dee-ah-tas´-som-ahee;* mid. voice from *1909* and *1299;* to *appoint besides,* i.e. *supplement* (as a codicil):— add to.

1929. ἐπιδίδωμι **ĕpididōmi,** *ep-ee-did´-o-mee;* from *1909* and *1325;* to *give over* (by hand or surrender):— deliver unto, give, let (+ [her drive]), offer.

1930. ἐπιδιορθόω **ĕpidiŏrthŏō,** *ep-ee-dee-or-thŏ´-o;* from *1909* and a der. of *3717;* to *straighten further,* i.e. (fig.) *arrange additionally:—* set in order.

1931. ἐπιδύω **ĕpiduō,** *ep-ee-doo´-o;* from *1909* and *1416;* to *set* fully (as the sun):— go down.

1932. ἐπιείκεια **ĕpiĕikĕia,** *ep-ee-i´-ki-ah;* from *1933; suitableness,* i.e. (by impl.) *equity, mildness:—* clemency, gentleness.

1933. ἐπιεικής **ĕpiĕikēs,** *ep-ee-i-kace´;* from *1909* and *1503; appropriate,* i.e. (by impl.) *mild:—* gentle, moderation, patient.

1934. ἐπιζητέω **ĕpizētĕō,** *ep-eed-zay-teh´-o;* from *1909* and *2212;* to *search* (inquire) *for;* intens. to *demand,* to *crave:—* desire, enquire, seek (after, for).

1935. ἐπιθανάτιος **ĕpithanatiŏs,** *ep-ee-than-at´-ee-os;* from *1909* and *2288; doomed to death:—* appointed to death.

1936. ἐπίθεσις **ĕpithĕsis,** *ep-ith´-es-is;* from *2007;* an *imposition* (of hands officially):— laying (putting) on.

1937. ἐπιθυμέω **ĕpithumĕō,** *ep-ee-thoo-meh´-o;* from *1909* and *2372;* to *set the heart upon,*

i.e. *long* for (rightfully or otherwise):— covet, desire, would fain, lust (after).

1938. ἐπιθυμητής **ĕpithumētēs,** *ep-ee-thoo-may-tace´;* from *1937;* a *craver:—* + lust after.

1939. ἐπιθυμία **ĕpithumia,** *ep-ee-thoo-mee´-ah;* from *1937;* a *longing* (espec. for what is forbidden):— concupiscence, desire, lust (after).

1940. ἐπικαθίζω **ĕpikathizō,** *ep-ee-kath-id´-zo;* from *1909* and *2523;* to *seat upon:—* set on.

1941. ἐπικαλέομαι **ĕpikalĕŏmai,** *ep-ee-kal-eh´-om-ahee;* mid. voice from *1909* and *2564;* to *entitle;* by impl. to *invoke* (for aid, worship, testimony, decision, etc.):— appeal (unto), call (on, upon), surname.

1942. ἐπικάλυμα **ĕpikaluma,** *ep-ee-kal´-oo-mah;* from *1943;* a *covering,* i.e. (fig.) *pretext:—* cloke.

1943. ἐπικαλύπτω **ĕpikaluptō,** *ep-ee-kal-oop´-to;* from *1909* and *2572;* to *conceal,* i.e. (fig.) *forgive:—* cover.

1944. ἐπικατάρατος **ĕpikataratŏs,** *ep-ee-kat-ar´-at-os;* from *1909* and a der. of *2672; imprecated,* i.e. *execrable:—* accursed.

1945. ἐπίκειμαι **ĕpikĕimai,** *ep-ik´-i-mahee;* from *1909* and *2749;* to *rest upon* (lit. or fig.):— impose, be instant, (be) laid (there-, up-) on, (when) lay (on), lie (on), press upon.

1946. Ἐπικούρειος **Ĕpikourĕiŏs,** *ep-ee-koo´-ri-os* or Ἐπικούριος **Ĕpikŏuriŏs,** *ep-ee-koo´-ree-os;* from Ἐπίκουρος **Ĕpikŏurŏs** [comp. *1947]* (a noted philosopher); an *Epicurean* or follower of Epicurus:— Epicurean.

1947. ἐπικουρία **ĕpikŏuria,** *ep-ee-koo-ree´-ah;* from a compound of *1909* and a (prol.) form of the base of *2877* (in the sense of *servant*); *assistance:—* help.

1948. ἐπικρίνω **ĕpikrinō,** *ep-ee-kree´-no;* from *1909* and *2919;* to *adjudge:—* give sentence.

1949. ἐπιλαμβάνομαι **ĕpilambanŏmai,** *ep-ee-lam-ban´-om-ahee;* mid. voice from *1909* and *2983;* to *seize* (for help, injury, attainment, or any other purpose; lit. or fig.):— catch, lay hold (up-) on, take (by, hold of) on.

1950. ἐπιλανθάνομαι **ĕpilanthanŏmai,** *ep-ee-lan-than´-om-ahee;* mid. voice from *1909* and *2990;* to *lose out* of mind; by impl. to *neglect:—* (be) forget (-ful of).

1951. ἐπιλέγομαι **ĕpilĕgŏmai,** *ep-ee-leg´-om-ahee;* mid. voice from *1909* and *3004;* to *surname, select:—* call, choose.

1952. ἐπιλείπω **ĕpilĕipō,** *ep-ee-li´-po;* from *1909* and *3007;* to *leave upon,* i.e. (fig.) to *be insufficient for:—* fail.

1953. ἐπιλησμονή **ĕpilēsmŏnē,** *ep-ee-lace-mon-ay´;* from a der. of *1950; negligence:—* × forgetful.

1954. ἐπίλοιπος **ĕpilŏipŏs**, *ep-il´-oy-pos;* from *1909* and *3062; left over,* i.e. *remaining:*— rest.

1955. ἐπίλυσις **ĕpilusis**, *ep-il´-oo-sis;* from *1956; explanation,* i.e. *application:*— interpretation.

1956. ἐπιλύω **ĕpiluō**, *ep-ee-loo´-o;* from *1909* and *3089;* to *solve further,* i.e. (fig.) to *explain, decide:*— determine, expound.

1957. ἐπιμαρτυρέω **ĕpimartureō**, *ep-ee-mar-too-reh´-o;* from *1909* and *3140;* to *attest further,* i.e. *corroborate:*— testify.

1958. ἐπιμέλεια **ĕpimĕlĕia**, *ep-ee-mel´-i-ah;* from *1959; carefulness,* i.e. kind *attention* (*hospitality*):— + refresh self.

1959. ἐπιμελέομαι **ĕpimĕlĕŏmai**, *ep-ee-mel-eh´-om-ahee;* mid. voice from *1909* and the same as *3199;* to *care for* (phys. or otherwise):— take care of.

1960. ἐπιμελῶς **ĕpimĕlōs**, *ep-ee-mel-oce´;* adv. from a der. of *1959; carefully:*— diligently.

1961. ἐπιμένω **ĕpimĕnō**, *ep-ee-men´-o;* from *1909* and *3306;* to *stay over,* i.e. *remain* (fig. *persevere*):— abide (in), continue (in), tarry.

1962. ἐπινεύω **ĕpinĕuō**, *ep-een-yoo´-o;* from *1909* and *3506;* to *nod at,* i.e. (by impl.) to *assent:*— consent.

1963. ἐπίνοια **ĕpinŏia**, *ep-in´-oy-ah;* from *1909* and *3563; attention* of the mind, i.e. (by impl.) *purpose:*— thought.

1964. ἐπιορκέω **ĕpiŏrkĕō**, *ep-ee-or-keh´-o;* from *1965;* to *commit perjury:*— forswear self.

1965. ἐπίορκος **ĕpiŏrkŏs**, *ep-ee´-or-kos;* from *1909* and *3727; on oath,* i.e. (falsely) a *forswearer:*— perjured person.

1966. ἐπιοῦσα **ĕpiŏusa**, *ep-ee-oo´-sah;* fem. sing. part. of a compound of *1909* and εἶμι **ĕimi** (to *go*); *supervening,* i.e. (*2250* or *3571* being expressed or implied) the *ensuing* day or night:— following, next.

1967. ἐπιούσιος **ĕpiŏusiŏs**, *ep-ee-oo´-see-os;* perh. from the same as *1966; tomorrow's;* but more prob. from *1909* and a der. of the pres. part. fem. of *1510; for subsistence,* i.e. *needful:*— daily.

1968. ἐπιπίπτω **ĕpipiptō**, *ep-ee-pip´-to;* from *1909* and *4098;* to *embrace* (with affection) or *seize* (with more or less violence; lit. or fig.):— fall into (on, upon) lie on, press upon.

1969. ἐπιπλήσσω **ĕpiplēssō**, *ep-ee-place´-so;* from *1909* and *4141;* to *chastise,* i.e. (with words) to *upbraid:*— rebuke.

1970. ἐπιπνίγω **ĕpipnigō**, *ep-ee-pnee´-go;* from *1909* and *4155;* to *throttle upon,* i.e. (fig.) *overgrow:*— choke.

1971. ἐπιποθέω **ĕpipŏthĕō**, *ep-ee-poth-eh´-o;* from *1909* and ποθέω **pŏthĕō** (to *yearn*); to *dote upon,* i.e. *intensely crave* possession (lawfully or wrongfully):— (earnestly) desire (greatly), (greatly) long (after), lust.

1972. ἐπιπόθησις **ĕpipŏthēsis**, *ep-ee-poth´-ay-sis;* from *1971;* a *longing for:*— earnest (vehement) desire.

1973. ἐπιπόθητος **ĕpipŏthētŏs**, *ep-ee-poth´-ay-tos;* from *1909* and a der. of the latter part of *1971; yearned upon,* i.e. *greatly loved:*— longed for.

1974. ἐπιποθία **ĕpipŏthia**, *ep-ee-poth-ee´-ah;* from *1971; intense longing:*— great desire.

1975. ἐπιπορεύομαι **ĕpipŏrĕuŏmai**, *ep-ee-por-yoo´-om-ahee;* from *1909* and *4198;* to *journey further,* i.e. *travel on* (reach):— come.

1976. ἐπιρράπτω **ĕpirrhaptō**, *ep-ir-hrap´-to;* from *1909* and the base of *4476;* to *stitch upon,* i.e. *fasten* with the needle:— sew on.

1977. ἐπιρρίπτω **ĕpirrhiptō**, *ep-ir-hrip´-to;* from *1909* and *4496;* to *throw upon* (lit. or fig.):— cast upon.

1978. ἐπίσημος **ĕpisēmŏs**, *ep-is´-ay-mos;* from *1909* and some form of the base of *4591; remarkable,* i.e. (fig.) *eminent:*— notable, of note.

1979. ἐπισιτισμός **ĕpisitismŏs**, *ep-ee-sit-is-mos´;* from a compound of *1909* and a der. of *4621;* a *provisioning,* i.e. (concr.) *food:*— victuals.

1980. ἐπισκέπτομαι **ĕpiskĕptŏmai**, *ep-ee-skep´-tom-ahee;* mid. voice from *1909* and the base of *4649;* to *inspect,* i.e. (by impl.) to *select;* by extens. to *go to see, relieve:*— look out, visit.

1981. ἐπισκηνόω **ĕpiskēnŏō**, *ep-ee-skay-nŏ´-o;* from *1909* and *4637;* to *tent upon,* i.e. (fig.) *abide with:*— rest upon.

1982. ἐπισκιάζω **ĕpiskiazō**, *ep-ee-skee-ad´-zo;* from *1909* and a der. of *4639;* to *cast a shade upon,* i.e. (by anal.) to *envelop* in a haze of brilliancy; fig. to *invest* with preternatural influence:— overshadow.

1983. ἐπισκοπέω **ĕpiskŏpĕō**, *ep-ee-skop-eh´-o;* from *1909* and *4648;* to *oversee;* by impl. to *beware:*— look diligently, take the oversight.

1984. ἐπισκοπή **ĕpiskŏpē**, *ep-is-kop-ay´;* from *1980; inspection* (for relief); by impl. *superintendence;* spec., the Chr. "*episcopate*":— the office of a "bishop," bishoprick, visitation.

1985. ἐπίσκοπος **ĕpiskŏpŏs**, *ep-is´-kop-os;* from *1909* and *4649* (in the sense of *1983*); a *superintendent,* i.e. Chr. officer in general charge of a (or the) church (lit. or fig.):— bishop, overseer.

1986. ἐπισπάομαι **ĕpispaŏmai**, *ep-ee-spah´-om-ahee;* from *1909* and *4685;* to *draw over,* i.e. (with *203* impl.) *efface* the mark of *circumcision* (by recovering with the foreskin):— become uncircumcised.

1987. ἐπίσταμαι **ĕpistamai**, *ep-is´-tam-ahee;* appar. a mid. voice of *2186* (with *3563*

Greek

implied); to *put* the mind *upon,* i.e. *compre-hend,* or *be acquainted with:*— know, understand.

1988. ἐπιστάτης **ĕpistatēs**, *ep-is-tat´-ace;* from *1909* and a presumed der. of *2476;* an *appointee over,* i.e. *commander* (*teacher*):— master.

1989. ἐπιστέλλω **ĕpistĕllō**, *ep-ee-stel´-lo;* from *1909* and *4724;* to *enjoin* (by writing), i.e. (gen.) to *communicate by letter* (for any purpose):— write (a letter, unto).

1990. ἐπιστήμων **ĕpistēmōn**, *ep-ee-stay´-mone;* from *1987; intelligent:*— endued with knowledge.

1991. ἐπιστηρίζω **ĕpistērizō**, *ep-ee-stay-rid´-zo;* from *1909* and *4741;* to *support further,* i.e. *reestablish:*— confirm, strengthen.

1992. ἐπιστολή **ĕpistŏlē**, *ep-is-tol-ay´;* from *1989;* a *written message:*— "epistle," letter.

1993. ἐπιστομίζω **ĕpistŏmizō**, *ep-ee-stom-id´-zo;* from *1909* and *4750;* to *put something over* the *mouth,* i.e. (fig.) to *silence:*— stop mouths.

1994. ἐπιστρέφω **ĕpistrĕphō**, *ep-ee-stref´-o;* from *1909* and *4762;* to *revert* (lit., fig. or mor.):— come (go) again, convert, (re-) turn (about, again).

1995. ἐπιστροφή **ĕpistrŏphē**, *ep-is-trof-ay´;* from *1994; reversion,* i.e. mor. *revolution:*— conversion.

1996. ἐπισυνάγω **ĕpisunagō**, *ep-ee-soon-ag´-o;* from *1909* and *4863;* to *collect upon* the same place:— gather (together).

1997. ἐπισυναγωγή **ĕpisunagōgē**, *ep-ee-soon-ag-o-gay´;* from *1996;* a complete *collection;* spec. a Chr. *meeting* (for worship):— assembling (gathering) together.

1998. ἐπισυντρέχω **ĕpisuntrĕchō**, *ep-ee-soon-trekh´-o;* from *1909* and *4936;* to *hasten to-gether upon* one place (or a particular occasion):— come running together.

1999. ἐπισύστασις **ĕpisustasis**, *ep-ee-soo´-stas-is;* from the mid. voice of a compound of *1909* and *4921;* a *conspiracy,* i.e. *concourse* (riotous or friendly):— that which cometh upon, + raising up.

2000. ἐπισφαλής **ĕpisphalēs**, *ep-ee-sfal-ace´;* from a compound of *1909* and σφάλλω **sphallō** (to *trip*); fig. *insecure:*— dangerous.

2001. ἐπισχύω **ĕpischuō**, *ep-is-khoo´-o;* from *1909* and *2480;* to *avail further,* i.e. (fig.) *insist stoutly:*— be the more fierce.

2002. ἐπισωρεύω **ĕpisōrĕuō**, *ep-ee-so-ryoo´-o;* from *1909* and *4987;* to *accumulate further,* i.e. (fig.) *seek* additionally:— heap.

2003. ἐπιταγή **ĕpitagē**, *ep-ee-tag-ay´;* from *2004;* an *injunction* or *decree;* by impl. *authoritativeness:*— authority, commandment.

2004. ἐπιτάσσω **ĕpitassō**, *ep-ee-tas´-so;* from

1909 and *5021;* to *arrange upon,* i.e. *order:*— charge, command, injoin.

2005. ἐπιτελέω **ĕpitelĕō**, *ep-ee-tel-eh´-o;* from *1909* and *5055;* to *fulfill further* (or *completely*), i.e. *execute;* by impl. to *termi-nate, undergo:*— accomplish, do, finish, (make) (perfect), perform (× -ance).

2006. ἐπιτήδειος **ĕpitēdĕiŏs**, *ep-ee-tay´-di-os;* from ἐπιτηδές **ĕpitēdĕs** (*enough*); *serv-iceable,* i.e. (by impl.) *requisite:*— things which are needful.

2007. ἐπιτίθημι **ĕpitithēmi**, *ep-ee-tith´-ay-mee;* from *1909* and *5087;* to *impose* (in a friendly or hostile sense):— add unto, lade, lay upon, put (up) on, set on (up), + sur-name, × wound.

2008. ἐπιτιμάω **ĕpitimaō**, *ep-ee-tee-mah´-o;* from *1909* and *5091;* to *tax upon,* i.e. *cen-sure* or *admonish;* by impl. *forbid:*— (straitly) charge, rebuke.

2009. ἐπιτιμία **ĕpitimia**, *ep-ee-tee-mee´-ah;* from a compound of *1909* and *5092;* prop. *esteem,* i.e. *citizenship;* used (in the sense of *2008*) of a *penalty:*— punishment.

2010. ἐπιτρέπω **ĕpitrĕpō**, *ep-ee-trep´-o;* from *1909* and the base of *5157;* to *turn over* (*transfer*), i.e. *allow:*— give leave (liberty, license), let, permit, suffer.

2011. ἐπιτροπή **ĕpitrŏpē**, *ep-ee-trop-ay´;* from *2010; permission,* i.e. (by impl.) full *power:*— commission.

2012. ἐπίτροπος **ĕpitrŏpŏs**, *ep-it´-rop-os;* from *1909* and *5158* (in the sense of *2011*); a *commissioner,* i.e. domestic *manager, guardian:*— steward, tutor.

2013. ἐπιτυγχάνω **ĕpitugchanō**, *ep-ee-toong-khan´-o;* from *1909* and *5177;* to *chance upon,* i.e. (by impl.) to *attain:*— obtain.

2014. ἐπιφαίνω **ĕpiphainō**, *ep-ee-fah´-ee-no;* from *1909* and *5316;* to *shine upon,* i.e. *become* (lit.) *visible* or (fig.) *known:*— appear, give light.

2015. ἐπιφάνεια **ĕpiphanĕia**, *ep-if-an´-i-ah;* from *2016;* a *manifestation,* i.e. (spec.) the *advent* of Christ (past or future):— appearing, brightness.

2016. ἐπιφανής **ĕpiphanēs**, *ep-if-an-ace´;* from *2014; conspicuous,* i.e. (fig.) *memora-ble:*— notable.

2017. ἐπιφαύω **ĕpiphauō**, *ep-ee-fŏw´-o;* a form of *2014;* to *illuminate* (fig.):— give light.

2018. ἐπιφέρω **ĕpiphĕrō**, *ep-ee-fer´-o;* from *1909* and *5342;* to *bear upon* (or *further*), i.e. *adduce* (pers. or judicially [*accuse, inflict*]), *superinduce:*— add, bring (against), take.

2019. ἐπιφωνέω **ĕpiphōnĕō**, *ep-ee-fo-neh´-o;* from *1909* and *5455;* to *call at* something, i.e. *exclaim:*— cry (against), give a shout.

2020. ἐπιφώσκω **ĕpiphōskō**, *ep-ee-foce´-ko;*

a form of 2017; to begin to *grow light:*— begin to dawn, × draw on.

2021. ἐπιχειρέω **ĕpichĕirĕō**, *ep-ee-khi-reh´-o;* from 1909 and 5495; to put the *hand upon,* i.e. *undertake:*— go about, take in hand (upon).

2022. ἐπιχέω **ĕpichĕō**, *ep-ee-kheh´-o;* from 1909 and χέω **chĕō** (to pour);—to *pour upon:*— pour in.

2023. ἐπιχορηγέω **ĕpichŏrēgĕō**, *ep-ee-khor-ayg-eh´-o;* from 1909 and 5524; to *furnish besides,* i.e. fully *supply,* (fig.) *aid* or *contribute:*— add, minister (nourishment, unto).

2024. ἐπιχορηγία **ĕpichŏrēgia**, *ep-ee-khor-ayg-ee´-ah;* from 2023; *contribution:*— supply.

2025. ἐπιχρίω **ĕpichriō**, *ep-ee-khree´-o;* from 1909 and 5548; to *smear over:*— anoint.

2026. ἐποικοδομέω **ĕpŏikŏdŏmĕō**, *ep-oy-kod-om-eh´-o;* from 1909 and 3618; to *build upon,* i.e. (fig.) to *rear up:*— build thereon (thereupon, on, upon).

2027. ἐποκέλλω **ĕpŏkĕllō**, *ep-ok-el´-lo;* from 1909 and ὀκέλλω **ŏkĕllō** (to *urge*); to *drive upon* the shore, i.e. to *beach* a vessel:— run aground.

2028. ἐπονομάζω **ĕpŏnŏmazō**, *ep-on-om-ad´-zo;* from 1909 and 3687; to *name further,* i.e. *denominate:*— call.

2029. ἐποπτεύω **ĕpŏptĕuō**, *ep-opt-yoo´-o;* from 1909 and a der. of 3700; to *inspect,* i.e. *watch:*— behold.

2030. ἐπόπτης **ĕpŏptēs**, *ep-op´-tace;* from 1909 and a presumed der. of 3700; a *looker-on:*— eye-witness.

2031. ἔπος **ĕpŏs**, *ep´-os;* from 2036; a *word:*— × say.

2032. ἐπουράνιος **ĕpŏuraniŏs**, *ep-oo-ran´-ee-os;* from 1909 and 3772; *above* the *sky:*— celestial, (in) heaven (-ly), high.

2033. ἑπτά **hĕpta**, *hep-tah´;* a primary number; *seven:*— seven.

2034. ἑπτάκις **hĕptakis**, *hep-tak-is´;* adv. from 2033; *seven times:*— seven times.

2035. ἑπτακισχίλιοι **hĕptakischiliŏi**, *hep-tak-is-khil´-ee-oy;* from 2034 and 5507; *seven times a thousand:*— seven thousand.

2036. ἔπω **ĕpō**, *ep´-o;* a primary verb (used only in the def. past tense, the others being borrowed from 2046, 4483, and 5346); to *speak* or *say* (by word or writing):— answer, bid, bring word, call, command, grant, say (on), speak, tell. Comp. 3004.

2037. Ἔραστος **Ĕrastŏs**, *er´-as-tos;* from ἐράω **ĕraō** (to *love*); *beloved; Erastus,* a Chr.:— Erastus.

ἐραυνάω **ĕraunaō**. See 2045.

2038. ἐργάζομαι **ĕrgazŏmai**, *er-gad´-zom-ahee;* mid. voice from 2041; to *toil* (as a task, occupation, etc.), (by impl.) *effect, be engaged in* or *with,* etc.:— commit, do, labor for, minister about, trade (by), work.

2039. ἐργασία **ĕrgasia**, *er-gas-ee´-ah;* from 2040; *occupation;* by impl. *profit, pains:*— craft, diligence, gain, work.

2040. ἐργάτης **ĕrgatēs**, *er-gat´-ace;* from 2041; a *toiler;* fig. a *teacher:*— labourer, worker (-men).

2041. ἔργον **ĕrgŏn**, *er´-gon;* from a primary (but obs.) ἔργω **ĕrgō** (to *work*); *toil* (as an effort or occupation); by impl. an *act:*— deed, doing, labour, work.

2042. ἐρεθίζω **ĕrĕthizō**, *er-eth-id´-zo;* from a presumed prol. form of 2054; to *stimulate* (espec. to anger):— provoke.

2043. ἐρείδω **ĕrĕidō**, *er-i´-do;* of obscure aff.; to *prop,* i.e. (refl.) *get fast:*— stick fast.

2044. ἐρεύγομαι **ĕrĕugŏmai**, *er-yoog´-om-ahee;* of uncert. aff.; to *belch,* i.e. (fig.) to *speak out:*— utter.

2045. ἐρευνάω **ĕrĕunaō**, *er-yoo-nah´-o* or ἐραυνάω **ĕraunaō**, *er-ouw-nah´-o;* appar. from 2046 (through the idea of *inquiry*); to *seek,* i.e. (fig.) to *investigate:*— search.

2046. ἐρέω **ĕrĕō**, *er-eh´-o;* prob. a fuller form of 4483; an alternate for 2036 in cert. tenses; to *utter,* i.e. *speak* or *say:*— call, say, speak (of), tell.

2047. ἐρημία **ĕrēmia**, *er-ay-mee´-ah;* from 2048; *solitude* (concr.):— desert, wilderness.

2048. ἔρημος **ĕrēmŏs**, *er´-ay-mos;* of uncert. aff.; *lonesome,* i.e. (by impl.) *waste* (usually as a noun, 5561 being implied):— desert, desolate, solitary, wilderness.

2049. ἐρημόω **ĕrēmŏō**, *er-ay-mŏ´-o;* from 2048; to *lay waste* (lit. or fig.):— (bring to, make) desolate (-ion), come to nought.

2050. ἐρήμωσις **ĕrēmōsis**, *er-ay´-mo-sis;* from 2049; *despoliation:*— desolation.

2051. ἐρίζω **ĕrizō**, *er-id´-zo;* from 2054; to *wrangle:*— strive.

2052. ἐριθεία **ĕrithĕia**, *er-ith-i´-ah;* perh. as the same as 2042; prop. *intrigue,* i.e. (by impl.) *faction:*— contention (-ious), strife.

2053. ἔριον **ĕriŏn**, *er´-ee-on;* of obscure aff.; *wool:*— wool.

2054. ἔρις **ĕris**, *er´-is;* of uncert. aff.; a *quarrel,* i.e. (by impl.) *wrangling:*— contention, debate, strife, variance.

2055. ἐρίφιον **ĕriphiŏn**, *er-if´-ee-on;* from 2056; a *kidling,* i.e. (gen.) *goat* (symbol. *wicked* person):— goat.

2056. ἔριφος **ĕriphŏs**, *er´-if-os;* perh. from the same as 2053 (through the idea of *hairiness*); a *kid* or (gen.) *goat:*— goat, kid.

2057. Ἑρμᾶς **Hĕrmas**, *her-mas´;* prob. from 2060; *Hermas,* a Chr.:— Hermas.

2058. ἑρμηνεία **hĕrmēnĕia**, *her-may-ni´-ah;* from the same as 2059; *translation:*— interpretation.

2059. ἑρμηνεύω **hĕrmēnĕuō**, *her-mayn-yoo´-o;* from a presumed der. of *2060* (as the god of language); to *translate:*— interpret.

2060. Ἑρμῆς **Hĕrmēs**, *her-mace´;* perh. from *2046; Hermes,* the name of the messenger of the Gr. deities; also of a Chr.:— Hermes, Mercury.

2061. Ἑρμογένης **Hĕrmŏgĕnēs**, *her-mog-en´-ace;* from *2060* and *1096; born of Hermes; Hermogenes,* an apostate Chr.:— Hermogenes.

2062. ἑρπετόν **hĕrpĕtŏn**, *her-pet-on´;* neut. of a der. of ἕρπω **hĕrpō** (to *creep*); a *reptile,* i.e. (by Heb. [comp. *7431*]) a small *animal:*— creeping thing, serpent.

2063. ἐρυθρός **ĕruthrŏs**, *er-oo-thros´;* of uncert. aff.; *red,* i.e. (with *2281*) the *Red* Sea:— red.

2064. ἔρχομαι **ĕrchŏmai**, *er´-khom-ahee;* mid. voice of a primary verb (used only in the present and imperfect tenses, the others being supplied by a kindred [mid. voice]

ἐλεύθομαι **ĕlĕuthŏmai**, *el-yoo´-thom-ahee;* or [act.]

ἔλθω **ĕlthō**, *el´-tho;* which do not otherwise occur); to *come* or *go* (in a great variety of applications, lit. and fig.):— accompany, appear, bring, come, enter, fall out, go, grow, × light, × next, pass, resort, be set.

2065. ἐρωτάω **ĕrōtaō**, *er-o-tah´-o;* appar. from *2046* [comp. *2045*]; to *interrogate;* by impl. to *request:*— ask, beseech, desire, intreat, pray. Comp. *4441.*

2066. ἐσθής **ĕsthēs**, *es-thace´;* from ἕννυμι **hĕnnumi** (to *clothe*); *dress:*— apparel, clothing, raiment, robe.

2067. ἔσθησις **ĕsthēsis**, *es´-thay-sis;* from a der. of *2066; clothing* (concr.):— garment.

2068. ἐσθίω **ĕsthiō**, *es-thee´-o;* strengthened for a primary ἔδω **ĕdō** (to *eat*); used only in certain tenses, the rest being supplied by *5315;* to *eat* (usually lit.):— devour, eat, live.

2069. Ἐσλί **Ĕsli**, *es-lee´;* of Heb. or. [prob. for *454*]; *Esli,* an Isr.:— Esli.

2070. ἐσμέν **ĕsmĕn**, *es-men´;* first pers. plur. ind. of *1510;* we *are:*— are, be, have our being, × have hope, + [the gospel] was [preached unto] us.

2071. ἔσομαι **ĕsŏmai**, *es´-om-ahee;* future of *1510; will be:*— shall (should) be (have), (shall) come (to pass), × may have, × fall, what would follow, × live long, × sojourn.

2072. ἔσοπτρον **ĕsŏptrŏn**, *es´-op-tron;* from *1519* and a presumed der. of *3700;* a *mirror* (for *looking into*):— glass. Comp. *2734.*

2073. ἑσπέρα **hĕspĕra**, *hes-per´-ah;* fem. of an adj. ἑσπερός **hĕspĕrŏs** (*evening*); the *eve* (*5610* being implied):— evening (-tide).

2074. Ἑσρώμ **Ĕsrōm**, *es-rome´;* of Heb. or. [*2696*]; *Esrom* (i.e. *Chetsron*), an Isr.:— Esrom.

2075. ἐστέ **ĕstĕ**, *es-teh´;* second pers. plur.

pres. ind. of *1510;* ye *are:*— be, have been, belong.

2076. ἐστί **ĕsti**, *es-tee´;* third pers. sing. pres. ind. of *1510;* he (she or it) *is;* also (with neut. plur.) they *are:*— are, be (-long), call, × can [-not], come, consisteth, × dure for a while, + follow, × have, (that) is (to say), make, meaneth, × must needs, + profit, + remaineth, + wrestle.

2077. ἔστω **ĕstō**, *es´-to;* second pers. sing. pres. imper. of *1510; be* thou; also

ἔστωσαν **ĕstōsan**, *es´-to-san;* third pers. of the same; *let* them *be:*— be.

2078. ἔσχατος **ĕschatŏs**, *es´-khat-os;* a superl. prob. from *2192* (in the sense of *contiguity*); *farthest, final* (of place or time):— ends of, last, latter end, lowest, uttermost.

2079. ἐσχάτως **ĕschatōs**, *es-khat´-oce;* adv. from *2078; finally,* i.e. (with *2192*) *at the extremity* of life:— point of death.

2080. ἔσω **ĕsō**, *es´-o;* from *1519; inside* (as prep. or adj.):— (with-) in (-ner, -to, -ward).

2081. ἔσωθεν **ĕsōthĕn**, *es´-o-then;* from *2080; from inside;* also used as equiv. to *2080* (*inside*):— inward (-ly), (from) within, without.

2082. ἐσώτερος **ĕsōtĕrŏs**, *es-o´-ter-os;* comparative of *2080; interior:*— inner, within.

2083. ἑταῖρος **hĕtairŏs**, *het-ah´-ee-ros;* from ἔτης **ĕtēs** (a *clansman*); a *comrade:*— fellow, friend.

2084. ἑτερόγλωσσος **hĕtĕrŏglōssŏs**, *het-er-og´-loce-sos;* from *2087* and *1100; other-tongued,* i.e. a *foreigner:*— man of other tongue.

2085. ἑτεροδιδασκαλέω **hĕtĕrŏdidaskalĕō**, *het-er-od-id-as-kal-eh´-o;* from *2087* and *1320;* to *instruct differently:*— teach other doctrine (-wise).

2086. ἑτεροζυγέω **hĕtĕrŏzugĕō**, *het-er-od-zoog-eh´-o;* from a compound of *2087* and *2218;* to *yoke* up *differently,* i.e. (fig.) to *associate discordantly:*— unequally yoke together with.

2087. ἕτερος **hĕtĕrŏs**, *het´-er-os;* of uncert. aff.; (an-, the) *other* or *different:*— altered, else, next (day), one, (an-) other, some, strange.

2088. ἑτέρως **hĕtĕrōs**, *het-er´-oce;* adv. from *2087; differently:*— otherwise.

2089. ἔτι **ĕti**, *et´-ee;* perh. akin to *2094;* "*yet,*" *still* (of time or degree):— after that, also, ever, (any) further, (t-) henceforth (more), hereafter, (any) longer, (any) more (-one), now, still, yet.

2090. ἑτοιμάζω **hĕtoimazō**, *het-oy-mad´-zo;* from *2092;* to *prepare:*— prepare, provide, make ready. Comp. *2680.*

2091. ἑτοιμασία **hĕtŏimasia**, *het-oy-mas-*

ee'-ah; from *2090; preparation:*— preparation.

2092. ἔτοιμος **hĕtŏimŏs**, *het'-oy-mos;* from an old noun ἔτεος **hĕtĕŏs** (*fitness*); *adjusted,* i.e. *ready:*— prepared, (made) ready (-iness, to our hand).

2093. ἑτοίμως **hĕtŏimōs**, *het-oy'-moce;* adv. from *2092; in readiness:*— ready.

2094. ἔτος **ĕtŏs**, *et'-os;* appar. a primary word; a *year:*— year.

2095. εὖ **ĕu**, *yoo;* neut. of a primary εὖς **ĕus** (*good*); (adv.) *well:*— good, well (done).

2096. Εὖα **Ĕua**, *yoo'-ah;* of Heb. or. [2332]; *Eua* (or *Eva*, i.e. *Chavvah*), the first woman:— Eve.

2097. εὐαγγελίζω **ĕuaggĕlizō**, *yoo-ang-ghel-id'-zo;* from *2095* and *32;* to *announce good news* ("evangelize") espec. the gospel:— declare, bring (declare, show) glad (good) tidings, preach (the gospel).

2098. εὐαγγέλιον **ĕuaggĕliŏn**, *yoo-ang-ghel'-ee-on;* from the same as *2097;* a *good message,* i.e. the *gospel:*— gospel.

2099. εὐαγγελιστής **ĕuaggĕlistēs**, *yoo-ang-ghel-is-tace';* from *2097;* a *preacher* of the gospel:— evangelist.

2100. εὐαρεστέω **ĕuarĕstĕō**, *yoo-ar-es-teh'-o;* from *2101;* to *gratify entirely:*— please (well).

2101. εὐάρεστος **ĕuarĕstŏs**, *yoo-ar'-es-tos;* from *2095* and *701; fully agreeable:*— acceptable (-ted), wellpleasing.

2102. εὐαρέστως **ĕuarĕstōs**, *yoo-ar-es'-toce;* adv. from *2101; quite agreeably:*— acceptably, + please well.

2103. Εὔβουλος **Ĕubŏulŏs**, *yoo'-boo-los;* from *2095* and *1014; good-willer; Eubulus,* a Chr.:— Eubulus.

2104. εὐγενής **ĕugĕnēs**, *yoog-en'-ace;* from *2095* and *1096; well born,* i.e. (lit.) *high* in rank, or (fig.) *generous:*— more noble, nobleman.

2105. εὐδία **ĕudia**, *yoo-dee'-ah;* fem. from *2095* and the alternate of *2203* (as the god of the weather); a *clear sky,* i.e. *fine weather:*— fair weather.

2106. εὐδοκέω **ĕudŏkĕō**, *yoo-dok-eh'-o;* from *2095* and *1380;* to *think well* of, i.e. *approve* (an act); spec., to *approbate* (a person or thing):— think good, (be well) please (-d), be the good (have, take) pleasure, be willing.

2107. εὐδοκία **ĕudŏkia**, *yoo-dok-ee'-ah;* from a presumed compound of *2095* and the base of *1380; satisfaction,* i.e. (subj.) *delight,* or (obj.) *kindness, wish, purpose:*— desire, good pleasure (will), × seem good.

2108. εὐεργεσία **ĕuĕrgĕsia**, *yoo-erg-es-ee'-ah;* from *2110; beneficence* (gen. or spec.):— benefit, good deed done.

2109. εὐεργετέω **ĕuĕrgĕtĕō**, *yoo-erg-et-eh'-o;* from *2110;* to *be philanthropic:*— do good.

2110. εὐεργέτης **ĕuĕrgĕtēs**, *yoo-erg-et'-ace;* from *2095* and the base of *2041;* a *worker of*

good, i.e. (spec.) a *philanthropist:*— benefactor.

2111. εὔθετος **ĕuthĕtŏs**, *yoo'-thet-os;* from *2095* and a der. of *5087; well placed,* i.e. (fig.) *appropriate:*— fit, meet.

2112. εὐθέως **ĕuthĕōs**, *yoo-theh'-oce;* adv. from *2117; directly,* i.e. *at once* or *soon:*— anon, as soon as, forthwith, immediately, shortly, straightway.

2113. εὐθυδρομέω **ĕuthudrŏmĕō**, *yoo-thoo-drom-eh'-o;* from *2117* and *1408;* to *lay a straight course,* i.e. *sail direct:*— (come) with a straight course.

2114. εὐθυμέω **ĕuthumĕō**, *yoo-thoo-meh'-o;* from *2115;* to *cheer up,* i.e. (intr.) *be cheerful;* neut. comparative (adv.) *more cheerfully:*— be of good cheer (merry).

2115. εὔθυμος **ĕuthumŏs**, *yoo'-thoo-mos;* from *2095* and *2372;* in *fine spirits,* i.e. *cheerful:*— of good cheer, the more cheerfully.

2116. εὐθύνω **ĕuthunō**, *yoo-thoo'-no;* from *2117;* to *straighten* (level); tech. to *steer:*— governor, make straight.

2117. εὐθύς **ĕuthus**, *yoo-thoos';* perh. from *2095* and *5087; straight,* i.e. (lit.) *level,* or (fig.) *true;* adv. (of time) *at once:*— anon, by and by, forthwith, immediately, straightway.

2118. εὐθύτης **ĕuthutēs**, *yoo-thoo'-tace;* from *2117; rectitude:*— righteousness.

2119. εὐκαιρέω **ĕukairĕō**, *yoo-kahee-reh'-o;* from *2121;* to *have good time,* i.e. *opportunity* or *leisure:*— have leisure (convenient time), spend time.

2120. εὐκαιρία **ĕukairia**, *yoo-kahee-ree'-ah;* from *2121;* a *favorable occasion:*— opportunity.

2121. εὔκαιρος **ĕukairŏs**, *yoo'-kahee-ros;* from *2095* and *2540; well-timed,* i.e. *opportune:*— convenient, in time of need.

2122. εὐκαίρως **ĕukairōs**, *yoo-kah'-ee-roce;* adv. from *2121; opportunely:*— conveniently, in season.

2123. εὐκοπώτερος **ĕukŏpōtĕrŏs**, *yoo-kop-o'-ter-os;* comp. of a compound of *2095* and *2873; better for toil,* i.e. *more facile:*— easier.

2124. εὐλάβεια **ĕulabĕia**, *yoo-lab'-i-ah;* from *2126;* prop. *caution,* i.e. (religiously) *reverence* (*piety*); by impl. *dread* (concr.):— fear (-ed).

2125. εὐλαβέομαι **ĕulabĕŏmai**, *yoo-lab-eh'-om-ahee;* mid. voice from *2126;* to *be circumspect,* i.e. (by impl.) to *be apprehensive;* religiously to *reverence:*— (moved with) fear.

2126. εὐλαβής **ĕulabēs**, *yoo-lab-ace';* from *2095* and *2983; taking well* (*carefully*), i.e. *circumspect* (religiously, *pious*):— devout.

2127. εὐλογέω **ĕulŏgĕō**, *yoo-log-eh´-o;* from a compound of *2095* and *3056;* to *speak well of,* i.e. (religiously) to *bless* (*thank* or *invoke a benediction upon, prosper*):— bless, praise.

2128. εὐλογητός **ĕulŏgētŏs**, *yoo-log-ay-tos´;* from *2127; adorable:*— blessed.

2129. εὐλογία **ĕulŏgia**, *yoo-log-ee´-ah;* from the same as *2127; fine speaking,* i.e. *elegance of language; commendation* ("*eulogy*"), i.e. (reverentially) *adoration;* religiously *benediction;* by impl. *consecration;* by extens. *benefit* or *largess:*— blessing (a matter of) bounty (× -tifully), fair speech.

2130. εὐμετάδοτος **ĕumĕtadŏtŏs**, *yoo-met-ad´-ot-os;* from *2095* and a presumed der. of *3330; good at imparting,* i.e. *liberal:*— ready to distribute.

2131. Εὐνίκη **Ĕunikē**, *yoo-nee´-kay;* from *2095* and *3529; victorious; Eunice,* a Jewess:— Eunice.

2132. εὐνοέω **ĕunŏĕō**, *yoo-no-eh´-o;* from a compound of *2095* and *3563;* to *be well-minded,* i.e. *reconcile:*— agree.

2133. εὔνοια **ĕunŏia**, *yoo´-noy-ah;* from the same as *2132; kindness;* euphem. *conjugal duty:*— benevolence, good will.

2134. εὐνουχίζω **ĕunŏuchizō**, *yoo-noo-khid´-zo;* from *2135;* to *castrate* (fig. *live unmarried*):— make ... eunuch.

2135. εὐνοῦχος **ĕunŏuchŏs**, *yoo-noo´-khos;* from εὐνή **ĕunē** (a *bed*) and *2192;* a *castrated* person (such being employed in Oriental bed-chambers); by extens. an *impotent* or *unmarried* man; by impl. a *chamberlain* (*state-officer*):— eunuch.

2136. Εὐοδία **Ĕuŏdia**, *yoo-od-ee´-ah;* from the same as *2137; fine travelling; Euodia,* a Chr. woman:— Euodias.

2137. εὐοδόω **ĕuŏdŏō**, *yoo-od-ŏ´-o;* from a compound of *2095* and *3598;* to *help* on the *road,* i.e. (pass.) *succeed in reaching;* fig. to *succeed* in business affairs:— (have a) prosper (-ous journey).

2138. εὐπειθής **ĕupĕithēs**, *yoo-pi-thace´;* from *2095* and *3982; good* for *persuasion,* i.e. (intr.) *compliant:*— easy to be intreated.

2139. εὐπερίστατος **ĕupĕristatŏs**, *yoo-per-is´-tat-os;* from *2095* and a der. of a presumed compound of *4012* and *2476; well standing around,* i.e. (a *competitor*) *thwarting* (a racer) in every direction (fig. of sin in gen.):— which doth so easily beset.

2140. εὐποιΐα **ĕupŏiïa**, *yoo-poy-ee´-ah;* from a compound of *2095* and *4160; well-doing,* i.e. *beneficence:*— to do good.

2141. εὐπορέω **ĕupŏrĕō**, *yoo-por-eh´-o;* from a compound of *2090* and the base of *4197;* (intr.) to *be good* for *passing* through, i.e. (fig.) *have* pecuniary *means:*— ability.

2142. εὐπορία **ĕupŏria**, *yoo-por-ee´-ah;* from the same as *2141;* pecuniary *resources:*— wealth.

2143. εὐπρέπεια **ĕuprĕpĕia**, *yoo-prep´-i-ah;* from a compound of *2095* and *4241; good suitableness,* i.e. *gracefulness:*— grace.

2144. εὐπρόσδεκτος **ĕuprŏsdĕktŏs**, *yoo-pros´-dek-tos;* from *2095* and a der. of *4327; well-received,* i.e. *approved, favorable:*— acceptable (-ted).

2145. εὐπρόσεδρος **ĕuprŏsĕdrŏs**, *yoo-pros´-ed-ros;* from *2095* and the same as *4332; sitting well toward,* i.e. (fig.) *assiduous* (neut. *diligent service*):— × attend upon.

2146. εὐπροσωπέω **ĕuprŏsōpĕō**, *yoo-pros-o-peh´-o;* from a compound of *2095* and *4383;* to *be of good countenance,* i.e. (fig.) to *make a display:*— make a fair show.

2147. εὑρίσκω **hĕuriskō**, *hyoo-ris´-ko;* a prol. form of a primary

εὕρω **hĕurō**, *hyoo´-ro;* which (together with another cognate form

εὑρέω **hĕurĕō**, *hyoo-reh´-o*) is used for it in all the tenses except the present and imperfect; to *find* (lit. or fig.):— find, get, obtain, perceive, see.

2148. Εὐροκλύδων **Ĕurŏkludōn**, *yoo-rok-loo´-dohn;* from Εὖρος **Ĕurŏs** (the *east* wind) and *2830;* a *storm from the East* (or Southeast), i.e. (in modern phrase) a *Levanter:*— Euroklydon.

2149. εὐρύχωρος **ĕuruchōrŏs**, *yoo-roo´-kho-ros;* from εὐρύς **ĕurus** (*wide*) and *5561; spacious:*— broad.

2150. εὐσέβεια **ĕusĕbĕia**, *yoo-seb´-i-ah;* from *2152; piety;* spec. the *gospel* scheme:— godliness, holiness.

2151. εὐσεβέω **ĕusĕbĕō**, *yoo-seb-eh´-o;* from *2152;* to *be pious,* i.e. (toward God) to *worship,* or (toward parents) to *respect* (*support*):— show piety, worship.

2152. εὐσεβής **ĕusĕbēs**, *yoo-seb-ace´;* from *2095* and *4576; well-reverent,* i.e. *pious:*— devout, godly.

2153. εὐσεβῶς **ĕusĕbōs**, *yoo-seb-oce´;* adv. from *2152; piously:*— godly.

2154. εὔσημος **ĕusēmŏs**, *yoo´-say-mos;* from *2095* and the base of *4591; well indicated,* i.e. (fig.) *significant:*— easy to be understood.

2155. εὔσπλαγχνος **ĕusplagchnŏs**, *yoo´-splangkh-nos;* from *2095* and *4698; well compassioned,* i.e. *sympathetic:*— pitiful, tender-hearted.

2156. εὐσχημόνως **ĕuschēmŏnōs**, *yoo-skhay-mon-oce´;* adv. from *2158; decorously:*— decently, honestly.

2157. εὐσχημοσύνη **ĕuschēmŏsunē**, *yoo-skhay-mos-oo´-nay;* from *2158; decorousness:*— comeliness.

2158. εὐσχήμων **ĕuschēmōn**, *yoo-skhay-*

Greek

mone; from *2095* and *4976; well-formed,* i.e. (fig.) *decorous, noble* (in rank):— comely, honourable.

2159. εὐτόνως **ĕutŏnōs,** *yoo-ton´-oce;* adv. from a compound of *2095* and a der. of τείνω **tĕinō** (to *stretch*); *in a well-strung manner,* i.e. (fig.) *intensely* (in a good sense, *cogently;* in a bad one, *fiercely*):— mightily, vehemently.

2160. εὐτραπελία **ĕutrapĕlia,** *yoo-trap-el-ee´-ah;* from a compound of *2095* and a der. of the base of *5157* (mean. *well-turned,* i.e. *ready at repartee, jocose*); *witticism,* i.e. (in a vulgar sense) *ribaldry:*— jesting.

2161. Εὔτυχος **Ĕutuchŏs,** *yoo´-too-khos;* from *2095* and a der. of *5177; well-fated,* i.e. *fortunate; Eutychus,* a young man:— Eutychus.

2162. εὐφημία **ĕuphēmia,** *yoo-fay-mee´-ah;* from *2163; good language* ("*euphemy*"), i.e. *praise* (*repute*):— good report.

2163. εὔφημος **ĕuphēmŏs,** *yoo´-fay-mos;* from *2095* and *5345; well spoken of,* i.e. *reputable:*— of good report.

2164. εὐφορέω **ĕuphŏrĕō,** *yoo-for-eh´-o;* from *2095* and *5409; to bear well,* i.e. *be fertile:*— bring forth abundantly.

2165. εὐφραίνω **ĕuphrainō,** *yoo-frah´-ee-no;* from *2095* and *5424; to put* (mid. or pass. *be*) *in a good frame of mind,* i.e. *rejoice:*— fare, make glad, be (make) merry, rejoice.

2166. Εὐφράτης **Ĕuphratēs,** *yoo-frat´-ace;* of for. or. [comp. *6578*]; *Euphrates,* a river of Asia:— Euphrates.

2167. εὐφροσύνη **ĕuphrŏsunē,** *yoo-fros-oo´-nay;* from the same as *2165; joyfulness:*— gladness, joy.

2168. εὐχαριστέω **ĕucharistĕō,** *yoo-khar-is-teh´-o;* from *2170; to be grateful,* i.e. (act.) to *express gratitude* (toward); spec. to *say grace* at a meal:— (give) thank (-ful, -s).

2169. εὐχαριστία **ĕucharistia,** *yoo-khar-is-tee´-ah;* from *2170; gratitude;* act. *grateful language* (to God, as an act of worship):— thankfulness, (giving of) thanks (-giving).

2170. εὐχάριστος **ĕucharistŏs,** *yoo-khar´-is-tos;* from *2095* and a der. of *5483; well favored,* i.e. (by impl.) *grateful:*— thankful.

2171. εὐχή **ĕuchē,** *yoo-khay´;* from *2172;* prop. a *wish,* expressed as a *petition* to God, or in *votive* obligation:— prayer, vow.

2172. εὔχομαι **ĕuchŏmai,** *yoo´-khom-ahee;* mid. voice of a primary verb; to *wish;* by impl. to *pray* to God:— pray, will, wish.

2173. εὔχρηστος **ĕuchrēstŏs,** *yoo´-khrays-tos;* from *2095* and *5543; easily used,* i.e. *useful:*— profitable, meet for use.

2174. εὐψυχέω **ĕupsuchĕō,** *yoo-psoo-kheh´-o;* from a compound of *2095* and *5590; to be in good spirits,* i.e. *feel encouraged:*— be of good comfort.

2175. εὐωδία **ĕuōdia,** *yoo-o-dee´-ah;* from a compound of *2095* and a der. of *3605; good-scentedness,* i.e. *fragrance:*— sweet savour (smell, -smelling).

2176. εὐώνυμος **ĕuōnumŏs,** *yoo-o´-noo-mos;* from *2095* and *3686;* prop. *well-named* (*good-omened*), i.e. the *left* (which was the *lucky* side among the pagan Greeks); neut. as adv. *at the left* hand:— (on the) left.

2177. ἐφάλλομαι **ĕphallŏmai,** *ef-al´-lom-ahee;* from *1909* and *242; to spring upon:*— leap on.

2178. ἐφάπαξ **ĕphapax,** *ef-ap´-ax;* from *1909* and *530; upon one occasion* (only):— (at) once (for all).

2179. Ἐφεσῖνος **Ĕphĕsinŏs,** *ef-es-ee´-nos;* from *2181; Ephesine,* or situated at Ephesus:— of Ephesus.

2180. Ἐφέσιος **Ĕphĕsiŏs,** *ef-es´-ee-os;* from *2181;* an *Ephesian* or inhab. of Ephesus:— Ephesian, of Ephesus.

2181. Ἔφεσος **Ĕphĕsŏs,** *ef´-es-os;* prob. of for. or.; *Ephesus,* a city of Asia Minor:— Ephesus.

2182. ἐφευρέτης **ĕphĕurĕtēs,** *ef-yoo-ret´-ace;* from a compound of *1909* and *2147;* a *discoverer,* i.e. *contriver:*— inventor.

2183. ἐφημερία **ĕphēmĕria,** *ef-ay-mer-ee´-ah;* from *2184; diurnality,* i.e. (spec.) the quotidian *rotation* or *class* of the Jewish priests' service at the Temple, as distributed by families:— course.

2184. ἐφήμερος **ĕphēmĕrŏs,** *ef-ay´-mer-os;* from *1909* and *2250; for a day* ("*ephemeral*"), i.e. *diurnal:*— daily.

2185. ἐφικνέομαι **ĕphiknĕŏmai,** *ef-ik-neh´-om-ahee;* from *1909* and a cognate of *2240;* to *arrive upon,* i.e. *extend to:*— reach.

2186. ἐφίστημι **ĕphistēmi,** *ef-is´-tay-mee;* from *1909* and *2476; to stand upon,* i.e. *be present* (in various applications, friendly or otherwise, usually lit.);—assault, come (in, to, unto, upon), be at hand (instant), present, stand (before, by, over).

2187. Ἐφραΐμ **Ĕphraïm,** *ef-rah-im´;* of Heb. or. [*669* or better *6085*]; *Ephraïm,* a place in Pal.:— Ephraim.

2188. ἐφφαθά **ĕphphatha,** *ef-fath-ah´;* of Chald. or. [*6606*]; *be opened!:*— Ephphatha.

2189. ἔχθρα **ĕchthra,** *ekh´-thrah;* fem. of *2190; hostility;* by impl. a reason for *opposition:*— enmity, hatred.

2190. ἐχθρός **ĕchthrŏs,** *ekh-thros´;* from a primary ἔχθω **ĕchthō** (to *hate*); *hateful* (pass. *odious,* or act. *hostile*); usually as a noun, an *adversary* (espec. *Satan*):— enemy, foe.

2191. ἔχιδνα **ĕchidna,** *ekh´-id-nah;* of uncert. or.; an *adder* or other poisonous snake (lit. or fig.):— viper.

2192. ἔχω **ĕchō,** *ekh´-o;* incl. an alt. form

σχέω **schĕō**, *skheh´-o;* used in certain tenses only); a primary verb; to *hold* (used in very various applications, lit. or fig., direct or remote; such as *possession; ability, contiguity, relation,* or *condition*):— be (able, × hold, possessed with), accompany, + begin to amend, can (+ -not), × conceive, count, diseased, do + eat, + enjoy, + fear, following, have, hold, keep, + lack, + go to law, lie, + must needs, + of necessity, + need, next, + recover, + reign, + rest, return, × sick, take for, + tremble, + uncircumcised, use.

2193. ἕως **hĕōs**, *heh´-oce;* of uncert. aff.; a conjunc., prep. and adv. of continuance, *until* (of time and place):— even (until, unto), (as) far (as), how long, (un-) til (-l), (hither-, un-, up) to, while (-s).

Z

2194. Ζαβουλών **Zabŏulōn**, *dzab-oo-lone´;* of Heb. or. [2074]; *Zabulon* (i.e. *Zebulon*), a region of Pal.:— Zabulon.

2195. Ζακχαῖος **Zakchaiŏs**, *dzak-chah´-ee-yos;* of Heb. or. [comp. 2140]; *Zacchæus*, an Isr.:— Zacchæus.

2196. Ζαρά **Zara**, *dzar-ah´;* of Heb. or. [2226]; *Zara,* (i.e. *Zerach*), an Isr.:— Zara.

2197. Ζαχαρίας **Zacharias**, *dzakh-ar-ee´-as;* of Heb. or. [2148]; *Zacharias* (i.e. *Zechariah*), the name of two Isr.:— Zacharias.

2198. ζάω **zaō**, *dzah´-o;* a primary verb; to *live* (lit. or fig.):— life (-time), (a-) live (-ly), quick.

2199. Ζεβεδαῖος **Zĕbĕdaiŏs**, *dzeb-ed-ah´-yos;* of Heb. or. [comp. 2067]; *Zebedæus*, an Isr.:— Zebedee.

2200. ζεστός **zĕstŏs**, *dzes-tos´;* from 2204; *boiled,* i.e. (by impl.) *calid* (fig. *fervent*):— hot.

2201. ζεῦγος **zĕugŏs**, *dzyoo´-gos;* from the same as 2218; a *couple,* i.e. a *team* (of oxen yoked together) or *brace* (of birds tied together):— yoke, pair.

2202. ζευκτηρία **zĕuktēria**, *dzook-tay-ree´-ah;* fem. of a der. (at the second stage) from the same as 2218; a *fastening* (*tiller-rope*):— band.

2203. Ζεύς **Zĕus**, *dzyooce;* of uncert. aff.; in the oblique cases there is used instead of it a (prob. cognate) name

Δίς **Dis**, *deece,* which is otherwise obs.; *Zeus* or *Dis* (among the Latins *Jupiter* or *Jove*), the supreme deity of the Greeks:— Jupiter.

2204. ζέω **zĕō**, *dzeh´-o;* a primary verb; to *be hot* (*boil,* of liquids; or *glow,* of solids), i.e. (fig.) *be fervid* (*earnest*):— be fervent.

2205. ζῆλος **zēlŏs**, *dzay´-los;* from 2204; prop. *heat,* i.e. (fig.) *"zeal"* (in a favorable sense, *ardor;* in an unfavorable one, *jealousy,* as of a husband [fig. of God], or an enemy, *malice*):— emulation, envy (-ing), fervent mind, indignation, jealousy, zeal.

2206. ζηλόω **zēlŏō** *dzay-lŏ´-o* or ζηλεύω **zēlĕuō**

dzay-loo´-o; from 2205; to *have warmth* of feeling for or against:— affect, covet (earnestly), (have) desire, (move with) envy, be jealous over, (be) zealous (-ly affect).

2207. ζηλωτής **zēlōtēs**, *dzay-lo-tace´;* from 2206; a *"zealot"*:— zealous.

2208. Ζηλωτής **Zēlōtēs**, *dzay-lo-tace´;* the same as 2208; a *Zealot,* i.e. (spec.) *partisan* for Jewish political independence:— Zelotes.

2209. ζημία **zēmia**, *dzay-mee´-ah;* prob. akin to the base of 1150 (through the idea of *violence*); *detriment:*— damage, loss.

2210. ζημιόω **zēmiŏō**, *dzay-mee-ŏ´-o;* from 2209; to *injure,* i.e. (refl. or pass.) to *experience detriment:*— be cast away, receive damage, lose, suffer loss.

2211. Ζηνᾶς **Zēnas**, *dzay-nas´;* prob. contr. from a poetic form of 2203 and 1435; *Jove-given; Zenas,* a Chr.:— Zenas.

2212. ζητέω **zētĕō**, *dzay-teh´-o;* of uncert. aff.; to *seek* (lit. or fig.); spec. (by Heb.) to *worship* (God), or (in a bad sense) to *plot* (against life):— be (go) about, desire, endeavour, enquire (for), require, (× will) seek (after, for, means). Comp. 4441.

2213. ζήτημα **zētēma**, *dzay´-tay-mah;* from 2212; a *search* (prop. concr.), i.e. (in words) a *debate:*— question.

2214. ζήτησις **zētēsis**, *dzay´-tay-sis;* from 2212; a *searching* (prop. the act), i.e. a *dispute* or its *theme:*— question.

2215. ζιζάνιον **zizaniŏn**, *dziz-an´-ee-on;* of uncert. or.; *darnel* or false grain:— tares.

2216. Ζοροβάβελ **Zŏrŏbabĕl**, *dzor-ob-ab´-el;* of Heb. or. [2216]; *Zorobabel* (i.e. *Zerubbabel*), an Isr.:— Zorobabel.

2217. ζόφος **zŏphŏs**, *dzof-os;* akin to the base of 3509; *gloom* (as shrouding like a *cloud*):— blackness, darkness, mist.

2218. ζυγός **zugŏs**, *dzoo-gos´;* from the root of ζεύγνυμι **zĕugnumi** (to *join,* espec. by a "yoke"); a *coupling,* i.e. (fig.) *servitude* (a *law* or *obligation*); also (lit.) the *beam* of the balance (as *connecting* the scales):— pair of balances, yoke.

2219. ζύμη **zumē**, *dzoo´-may;* prob. from 2204; *ferment* (as if *boiling* up):— leaven.

2220. ζυμόω **zumŏō**, *dzoo-mŏ´-o;* from 2219; to *cause to ferment:*— leaven.

2221. ζωγρέω **zōgrĕō**, *dzogue-reh´-o;* from the same as 2226 and 64; to *take alive* (*make a prisoner of war*), i.e. (fig.) to *capture* or *ensnare:*— take captive, catch.

2222. ζωή **zōē**, *dzo-ay´;* from 2198; *life* (lit. or fig.):— life (-time). Comp. 5590.

2223. ζώνη **zōnē**, *dzo´-nay;* prob. akin to the base of 2218; a *belt;* by impl. a *pocket:*— girdle, purse.

2224. ζώννυμι **zōnnumi**, *dzone´-noo-mi;*

from 2223; to *bind about* (espec. with a belt):— gird.

2225. ζωογονέω zōŏgŏnĕō, *dzo-og-on-eh´-o;* from the same as 2226 and a der. of 1096; to *engender alive,* i.e. (by anal.) to *rescue* (pass. *be saved*) from death:— live, preserve.

2226. ζῶον zōŏn, *dzo´-on;* neut. of a der. of 2198; a *live* thing, i.e. an *animal:*— beast.

2227. ζωοποιέω zōŏpŏiĕō, *dzo-op-oy-eh´-o;* from the same as 2226 and 4160; to *(re-) vitalize* (lit. or fig.):— make alive, give life, quicken.

H

2228. ἤ ē, *ay;* a primary particle of distinction between two connected terms; disjunctive, *or;* comparative, *than:*— and, but (either), (n-) either, except it be, (n-) or (else), rather, save, than, that, what, yea. Often used in connection with other particles. Comp. especially 2235, 2260, 2273.

2229. ἤ ē, *ay;* an adv. of *confirmation;* perh. intens. of 2228; used only (in the N.T.) before 3303; *assuredly:*— surely.

ἡ hē. See 3588.

ἥ hē. See 3739.

ᾗ ēi. See 5600.

2230. ἡγεμονεύω hēgĕmŏnĕuō, *hayg-em-on-yoo´-o;* from 2232; to *act as ruler:*— be governor.

2231. ἡγεμονία hēgĕmŏnia, *hayg-em-on-ee´-ah;* from 2232; *government,* i.e. (in time) official *term:*— reign.

2232. ἡγεμών hēgĕmōn, *hayg-em-ohn´;* from 2233; a *leader,* i.e. *chief* person (or fig. place) of a province:— governor, prince, ruler.

2233. ἡγέομαι hēgĕŏmai, *hayg-eh´-om-ahee;* mid. voice of a (presumed) strengthened form of 71; to *lead,* i.e. *command* (with official authority); fig. to *deem,* i.e. *consider:*— account, (be) chief, count, esteem, governor, judge, have the rule over, suppose, think.

2234. ἡδέως hēdĕōs, *hay-deh´-oce;* adv. from a der. of the base of 2237; *sweetly,* i.e. (fig.) *with pleasure:*— gladly.

2235. ἤδη ēdē, *ay´-day;* appar. from 2228 (or possibly 2229) and 1211; *even now:*— already, (even) now (already), by this time.

2236. ἥδιστα hēdista, *hay´-dis-tah;* neut. plur. of the superl. of the same as 2234; *with great pleasure:*— most (very) gladly.

2237. ἡδονή hēdŏnē, *hay-don-ay´;* from ἀνδάνω handanō (to *please*); sensual *delight;* by impl. *desire:*— lust, pleasure.

2238. ἡδύοσμον hēduŏsmŏn, *hay-doo´-os-mon;* neut. of the compound of the same as 2234 and 3744; a *sweet-scented* plant, i.e. *mint:*— mint.

2239. ἦθος ēthŏs, *ay´-thos;* a strengthened

form of 1485; *usage,* i.e. (plur.) moral *habits:*— manners.

2240. ἥκω hēkō, *hay´-ko;* a primary verb; to *arrive,* i.e. *be present* (lit. or fig.):— come.

2241. ἠλί ēli, *ay-lee´* or ἐλοι ĕloi *ay-lo´-ee;* of Heb. or. [410 with pron. suff.]; *my God:*— Eli.

2242. Ἡλί Hēli, *hay-lee´;* of Heb. or. [5941]; *Heli* (i.e. *Eli*), an Isr.:— Heli.

2243. Ἡλίας Hēlias, *hay-lee´-as;* of Heb. or. [452]; *Helias* (i.e. *Elijah*), an Isr.:— Elias.

2244. ἡλικία hēlikia, *hay-lik-ee´-ah;* from the same as 2245; *maturity* (in years or size):— age, stature.

2245. ἡλίκος hēlikŏs, *hay-lee´-kos;* from ἧλιξ hēlix (a *comrade,* i.e. one of the same *age*); *as big as,* i.e. (interjectively) *how much:*— how (what) great.

2246. ἥλιος hēliŏs, *hay´-lee-os;* from ἔλη hĕlē (a *ray;* perh. akin to the alt. of 138); the *sun;* by impl. *light:*— + east, sun.

2247. ἦλος hēlŏs, *hay´-los;* of uncert. aff.; a *stud,* i.e. *spike:*— nail.

2248. ἡμᾶς hēmas, *hay-mas´;* acc. plur. of 1473; *us:*— our, us, we.

2249. ἡμεῖς hēmĕis, *hay-mice´;* nom. plur. of 1473; *we* (only used when emphat.):— us, we (ourselves).

2250. ἡμέρα hēmĕra, *hay-mer´-ah;* fem. (with 5610 impl.) of a der. of ἧμαι hēmai (to *sit;* akin to the base of 1476) mean. *tame,* i.e. *gentle; day,* i.e. (lit.) the time space between dawn and dark, or the whole 24 hours (but several days were usually reckoned by the Jews as inclusive of the parts of both extremes); fig. a *period* (always defined more or less clearly by the context):— age, + alway, (mid-) day (by day, [-lyl), + for ever, judgment, (day) time, while, years.

2251. ἡμέτερος hēmĕtĕrŏs, *hay-met´-er-os;* from 2349; *our:*— our, your [by a different *reading*].

2252. ἤμην ēmēn, *ay´-mane;* a prol. form of 2358; *I was:*— be, was. [*Sometimes unexpressed*].

2253. ἡμιθανής hēmithanēs, *hay-mee-than-ace´;* from a presumed compound of the base of 2255 and 2348; *half dead,* i.e. *entirely exhausted:*— half dead.

2254. ἡμῖν hēmin, *hay-meen´;* dat. plur. of 1473; *to* (or *for, with, by*) *us:*— our, (for) us, we.

2255. ἥμισυ hēmisu, *hay´-mee-soo;* neut. of a der. from an inseparable pref. akin to 260 (through the idea of *partition* involved in *connection*) and mean. *semi-*; (as noun) *half:*— half.

2256. ἡμιώριον hēmiōriŏn, *hay-mee-o´-ree-on;* from the base of 2255 and 5610; a *half-hour:*— half an hour.

2257. ἡμῶν hēmōn, *hay-mone´;* gen. plur. of

1473; of (or *from*) *us:*— our (company), us, we.

2258. ἦν **ēn,** *ane;* imperf. of *1510; I* (*thou,* etc.) *was* (*wast* or *were*):— + agree, be, × have (+ charge of), hold, use, was (-t), were.

2259. ἡνίκα **hēnika,** *hay-nee´-kah;* of uncert. aff.; *at which time:*— when.

2260. ἤπερ **ēpĕr,** *ay´-per;* from *2228* and *4007; than at all* (or *than perhaps, than indeed*):— than.

2261. ἤπιος **ēpiŏs,** *ay´-pee-os;* prob. from *2031;* prop. *affable,* i.e. *mild* or *kind:*— gentle.

2262. Ἤρ **Ēr,** *ayr;* of Heb. or. [6147]; *Er,* an Isr.:— Er.

2263. ἤρεμος **ērĕmŏs,** *ay´-rem-os;* perh. by transposition from *2048* (through the idea of *stillness*); *tranquil:*— quiet.

2264. Ἡρώδης **Hērōdēs,** *hay-ro´-dace;* compound of ἥρως **hērōs** (a "*hero*") and *1491; heroic; Herod,* the name of four Jewish kings:— Herod.

2265. Ἡρῳδιανοί **Hērōdianŏi,** *hay-ro-dee-an-oy´;* plur. of a der. of *2264; Herodians,* i.e. partisans of Herod:— Herodians.

2266. Ἡρῳδιάς **Hērōdias,** *hay-ro-dee-as´;* from *2264; Herodias,* a woman of the Herodian family:— Herodias.

2267. Ἡρῳδίων **Hērōdiōn,** *hay-ro-dee´-ohn;* from *2264; Herodion,* a Chr.:— Herodion.

2268. Ἡσαΐας **Hēsaïas,** *hay-sah-ee´-as;* of Heb. or. [3470]; *Hesaias* (i.e. *Jeshajah*), an Isr.:— Esaias.

2269. Ἡσαῦ **Ēsau,** *ay-sow´;* of Heb. or. [6215]; *Esau,* an Edomite:— Esau.

2270. ἡσυχάζω **hēsuchazō,** *hay-soo-khad´-zo;* from the same as *2272;* to *keep still* (intr.), i.e. *refrain* from labor, meddlesomeness or speech:— cease, hold peace, be quiet, rest.

2271. ἡσυχία **hēsuchia,** *hay-soo-khee´-ah;* fem. of *2272;* (as noun) *stillness,* i.e. desistance from bustle or language:— quietness, silence.

2272. ἡσύχιος **hēsuchiŏs,** *hay-soo´-khee-os;* a prol. form of a compound prob. of a der. of the base of *1476* and perh. *2192;* prop. *keeping* one's *seat* (*sedentary*), i.e. (by impl.) *still* (*undisturbed, undisturbing*):— peaceable, quiet.

2273. ἤτοι **ētŏi,** *ay´-toy;* from *2228* and *5104; either indeed:*— whether.

2274. ἡττάω **hēttaō,** *hayt-tah´-o;* from the same as *2276;* to *make worse,* i.e. *vanquish* (lit. or fig.); by impl. to *rate lower:*— be inferior, overcome.

2275. ἥττημα **hēttēma,** *hayt´-tay-mah;* from *2274;* a *deterioration,* i.e. (obj.) *failure* or (subj.) *loss:*— diminishing, fault.

2276. ἧττον **hēttŏn,** *hate´-ton;* neut. of comp. of ἧκα **hēka** (*slightly*) used for that of *2556; worse* (as noun); by impl. *less* (as adv.):— less, worse.

2277. ἤτω **ētō,** *ay´-to;* third pers. sing. imper. of *1510; let him* (or *it*) *be:*— let ... be.

2278. ἠχέω **ēchĕō,** *ay-kheh´-o;* from *2279;* to *make a* loud *noise,* i.e. *reverberate:*— roar, sound.

2279. ἦχος **ēchŏs,** *ay´-khos;* of uncert. aff.; a loud or confused *noise* ("*echo*"), i.e. *roar;* fig. a *rumor:*— fame, sound.

Θ

2280. Θαδδαῖος **Thaddaiŏs,** *thad-dah´-yos;* of uncert. or.; *Thaddæus,* one of the Apostles:— Thaddæus.

2281. θάλασσα **thalassa,** *thal´-as-sah;* prob. prol. from *251;* the *sea* (gen. or spec.):— sea.

2282. θάλπω **thalpō,** *thal´-po;* prob. akin to θάλλω **thallō** (to *warm*); to *brood,* i.e. (fig.) to *foster:*— cherish.

2283. Θάμαρ **Thamar,** *tham´-ar;* of Heb. or. [8559]; *Thamar* (i.e. *Tamar*), an Israelitess:— Thamar.

2284. θαμβέω **thambĕō,** *tham-beh´-o;* from *2285;* to *stupefy* (with surprise), i.e. *astound:*— amaze, astonish.

2285. θάμβος **thambŏs,** *tham´-bos;* akin to an obs. τάφω **taphō** (to *dumbfound*); *stupefaction* (by surprise), i.e. *astonishment:*— × amazed, + astonished, wonder.

2286. θανάσιμος **thanasimŏs,** *than-as´-ee-mos;* from *2288; fatal,* i.e. *poisonous:*— deadly.

2287. θανατήφορος **thanatēphŏrŏs,** *than-at-ay´-for-os;* from (the fem. form of) *2288* and *5342; death-bearing,* i.e. *fatal:*— deadly.

2288. θάνατος **thanatŏs,** *than´-at-os;* from *2348;* (prop. an adj. used as a noun) *death* (lit. or fig.):— × deadly, (be...) death.

2289. θανατόω **thanatŏō,** *than-at-ŏ´-o;* from *2288;* to *kill* (lit. or fig.):— become dead, (cause to be) put to death, kill, mortify.

θάνω **thanō.** See *2348.*

2290. θάπτω **thaptō,** *thap´-to;* a primary verb; to *celebrate funeral rites,* i.e. *inter:*— bury.

2291. Θάρα **Thara,** *thar´-ah;* of Heb. or. [8646]; *Thara* (i.e. *Terach*), the father of Abraham:— Thara.

2292. θαρρέω **tharrhĕō,** *thar-hreh´-o;* another form for *2293;* to *exercise courage:*— be bold, × boldly, have confidence, be confident. Comp. *5111.*

2293. θαρσέω **tharsĕō,** *thar-seh´-o;* from *2294;* to *have courage:*— be of good cheer (comfort). Comp. *2292.*

2294. θάρσος **tharsŏs,** *thar´-sos;* akin (by transp.) to θράσος **thrasŏs** (*daring*); *boldness* (subj.):— courage.

2295. θαῦμα **thauma,** *thŏu´-mah;* appar.

from a form of *2300; wonder* (prop. concr.; but by impl. abstr.):— admiration.

2296. θαυμάζω **thaumazō,** *thŏu-mad´-zo;* from *2295;* to *wonder;* by impl. to *admire:*— admire, have in admiration, marvel, wonder.

2297. θαυμάσιος **thaumasiŏs,** *thŏw-mas´-ee-os;* from *2295; wondrous,* i.e. (neut. as noun) a *miracle:*— wonderful thing.

2298. θαυμαστός **thaumastŏs,** *thŏw-mas-tos´;* from *2296; wondered* at, i.e. (by impl.) *wonderful:*— marvel (-lous).

2299. θεά **thĕa,** *theh-ah´;* fem. of *2316;* a female *deity:*— goddess.

2300. θεάομαι **thĕaŏmai,** *theh-ah´-om-ahee;* a prol. form of a primary verb; to *look* closely at, i.e. (by impl.) *perceive* (lit. or fig.); by extens. to *visit:*— behold, look (upon), see. Comp. *3700.*

2301. θεατρίζω **thĕatrizō,** *theh-at-rid´-zo;* from *2302;* to *expose as a spectacle:*— make a gazing stock.

2302. θέατρον **thĕatrŏn,** *theh´-at-ron;* from *2300;* a *place for public show* ("theatre"), i.e. general *audience-room;* by impl. a *show* itself (fig.):— spectacle, theatre.

2303. θεῖον **thĕiŏn,** *thi´-on;* prob. neut. of *2304* (in its orig. sense of *flashing*); *sulphur:*— brimstone.

2304. θεῖος **thĕiŏs,** *thi´-os;* from *2316; godlike* (neut. as noun, *divinity*):— divine, godhead.

2305. θειότης **thĕiŏtēs,** *thi-ot´-ace;* from *2304; divinity* (abstr.):— godhead.

2306. θειώδης **thĕiōdēs,** *thi-o´-dace;* from *2303* and *1491; sulphur-like,* i.e. *sulphurous:*— brimstone.

θελέω **thĕlĕō.** See *2309.*

2307. θέλημα **thĕlēma,** *thel´-ay-mah;* from the prol. form of *2309;* a *determination* (prop. the thing), i.e. (act.) *choice* (spec. *purpose, decree;* abstr. *volition*) or (pass.) *inclination:*— desire, pleasure, will.

2308. θέλησις **thĕlēsis,** *thel´-ay-sis;* from *2309; determination* (prop. the act), i.e. *option:*— will.

2309. θέλω **thĕlō,** *thel´-o;* or ἐθέλω **ĕthĕlō,** *eth-el´-o;* in certain tenses θελέω **thĕlĕō,** *thel-eh´-o;* and ἐθελέω **ĕthĕlĕō,** *eth-el-eh´-o;* which are otherwise obs.; appar. strengthened from the alt. form of *138;* to *determine* (as an act. *option* from subj. impulse; whereas *1014* prop. denotes rather a pass. *acquiescence* in obj. considerations), i.e. *choose* or *prefer* (lit. or fig.); by impl. to *wish,* i.e. *be inclined* to (sometimes adv. *gladly*); impers. for the future tense, to *be about to;* by Heb. to *delight in:*— desire, be disposed (forward), intend, list, love, mean, please, have rather, (be) will (have, -ling, -ling [-ly]).

2310. θεμέλιος **thĕmĕliŏs,** *them-el´-ee-os;* from a der. of *5087; something put* down, i.e.

a *substruction* (of a building, etc.), (lit. or fig.):— foundation.

2311. θεμελιόω **thĕmĕliŏō,** *them-el-ee-ŏ´-o;* from *2310;* to *lay a basis* for, i.e. (lit.) *erect,* or (fig.) *consolidate:*— (lay the) found (-ation), ground, settle.

2312. θεοδίδακτος **thĕŏdidaktŏs,** *theh-od-id´-ak-tos;* from *2316* and *1321; divinely instructed:*— taught of God.

2312´. θεολόγος **thĕŏlŏgŏs,** *theh-ol-og´-os;* from *2316* and *3004;* a *"theologian":*— divine.

2313. θεομαχέω **thĕŏmachĕō,** *theh-o-makh-eh´-o;* from *2314;* to *resist deity:*— fight against God.

2314. θεόμαχος **thĕŏmachŏs,** *theh-om´-akh-os;* from *2316* and *3164;* an *opponent of deity:*— to fight against God.

2315. θεόπνευστος **thĕŏpnĕustŏs,** *theh-op-nyoo-stos;* from *2316* and a presumed der. of *4154; divinely breathed* in:— given by inspiration of God.

2316. θεός **thĕŏs,** *theh´-os;* of uncert. aff.; a *deity,* espec. (with *3588*) the supreme *Divinity;* fig. a *magistrate;* by Heb. *very:*— × exceeding, God, god [-ly, -ward].

2317. θεοσέβεια **thĕŏsĕbĕia,** *theh-os-eb´-i-ah;* from *2318; devoutness,* i.e. *piety:*— godliness.

2318. θεοσεβής **thĕŏsĕbēs,** *theh-os-eb-ace´;* from *2316* and *4576; reverent of God,* i.e. *pious:*— worshipper of God.

2319. θεοστυγής **thĕŏstugēs,** *theh-os-too-gace´;* from *2316* and the base of *4767; hateful to God,* i.e. *impious:*— hater of God.

2320. θεότης **thĕŏtēs,** *theh-ot´-ace;* from *2316; divinity* (abstr.):— godhead.

2321. Θεόφιλος **Thĕŏphilŏs,** *theh-of´-il-os;* from *2316* and *5384; friend of God; Theophilus,* a Chr.:— Theophilus.

2322. θεραπεία **thĕrapĕia,** *ther-ap-i´-ah;* from *2323; attendance* (spec. medical, i.e. *cure*); fig. and collec. *domestics:*— healing, household.

2323. θεραπεύω **thĕrapĕuō,** *ther-ap-yoo´-o;* from the same as *2324;* to *wait upon* menially, i.e. (fig.) to *adore* (God), or (spec.) to *relieve* (of disease):— cure, heal, worship.

2324. θεράπων **thĕrapōn,** *ther-ap´-ohn;* appar. a part. from an otherwise obs. der. of the base of *2330;* a *menial attendant* (as if *cherishing*):— servant.

2325. θερίζω **thĕrizō,** *ther-id´-zo;* from *2330* (in the sense of the *crop*); to *harvest:*— reap.

2326. θερισμός **thĕrismŏs,** *ther-is-mos´;* from *2325; reaping,* i.e. the *crop:*— harvest.

2327. θεριστής **thĕristēs,** *ther-is-tace´;* from *2325;* a *harvester:*— reaper.

2328. θερμαίνω **thĕrmainō,** *ther-mah´-ee-*

no; from *2329;* to *heat* (oneself):— (be) warm (-ed, self).

2329. θέρμη **thĕrmē,** *ther´-may;* from the base of *2330; warmth:*— heat.

2330. θέρος **thĕrŏs,** *ther´-os;* from a primary θέρω **thĕrō** (to *heat*); prop. *heat,* i.e. *summer:*— summer.

2331. Θεσσαλονικεύς **Thĕssalŏnikĕus,** *thes-sal-on-ik-yoos´;* from *2332;* a *Thessalonican,* i.e. inhab. of Thessalonice:— Thessalonian.

2332. Θεσσαλονίκη **Thĕssalŏnikē,** *thes-sal-on-ee´-kay;* from Θεσσαλός **Thĕssalŏs** (a *Thessalian*) and *3529; Thessalonice,* a place in Asia Minor:— Thessalonica.

2333. Θευδᾶς **Thĕudas,** *thyoo-das´;* of uncert. or.; *Theudas,* an Isr.:— Theudas.

θέω **thĕō.** See *5087.*

2334. θεωρέω **thĕōrĕō,** *theh-o-reh´-o;* from a der. of *2300* (perh. by add. of *3708*); to *be a spectator* of, i.e. *discern,* (lit., fig. [*experience*] or intens. [*acknowledge*]):— behold, consider, look on, perceive, see. Comp. *3700.*

2335. θεωρία **thĕōria,** *theh-o-ree´-ah;* from the same as *2334; spectatorship,* i.e. (concr.) a *spectacle:*— sight.

2336. θήκη **thēkē,** *thay´-kay;* from *5087;* a *receptacle,* i.e. *scabbard:*— sheath.

2337. θηλάζω **thēlazō,** *thay-lad´-zo;* from θηλή **thēlē** (the *nipple*); to *suckle,* (by impl.) to *suck:*— (give) suck (-ling).

2338. θῆλυς **thēlus,** *thay´-loos;* from the same as *2337; female:*— female, woman.

2339. θήρα **thēra,** *thay´-rah;* from θήρ **thēr** (a wild *animal,* as *game*); *hunting,* i.e. (fig.) *destruction:*— trap.

2340. θηρεύω **thērĕuō,** *thay-ryoo´-o;* from *2339;* to *hunt* (an animal), i.e. (fig.) to *carp at:*— catch.

2341. θηριομαχέω **thēriŏmachĕō,** *thay-ree-om-akh-eh´-o;* from a compound of *2342* and *3164;* to *be a beast-fighter* (in the gladiatorial show), i.e. (fig.) to *encounter* (furious men):— fight with wild beasts.

2342. θηρίον **thēriŏn,** *thay-ree´-on;* dimin. from the same as *2339;* a *dangerous animal:*— (venomous, wild) beast.

2343. θησαυρίζω **thēsaurizō,** *thay-sŏw-rid´-zo;* from *2344;* to *amass* or *reserve* (lit. or fig.):— lay up (treasure), (keep) in store, (heap) treasure (together, up).

2344. θησαυρός **thēsaurŏs,** *thay-sow-ros´;* from *5087;* a *deposit,* i.e. *wealth* (lit. or fig.):— treasure.

2345. θιγγάνω **thiggano,** *thing-gan´-o;* a prol. form of an obs. primary θίγω **thigō** (to *finger*); to *manipulate,* i.e. *have to do with;* by impl. to *injure:*— handle, touch.

2346. θλίβω **thlibō,** *thlee´-bo;* akin to the base of *5147;* to *crowd* (lit. or fig.):— afflict, narrow, throng, suffer tribulation, trouble.

2347. θλίψις **thlipsis,** *thlip´-sis;* from *2346; pressure* (lit. or fig.):— afflicted (-tion), anguish, burdened, persecution, tribulation, trouble.

2348. θνήσκω **thnēskō,** *thnay´-sko;* a strengthened form of a simpler primary θάνω **thanō** (which is used for it only in certain tenses); to *die* (lit. or fig.):— be dead, die.

2349. θνητός **thnētŏs,** *thnay-tos´;* from *2348; liable to die:*— mortal (-ity).

2350. θορυβέω **thŏrubĕō,** *thor-oo-beh´-o;* from *2351;* to *be in tumult,* i.e. *disturb, clamor:*— make ado (a noise), trouble self, set on an uproar.

2351. θόρυβος **thŏrubŏs,** *thor´-oo-bos;* from the base of *2360;* a *disturbance:*— tumult, uproar.

2352. θραύω **thrauō,** *throw´-o;* a primary verb; to *crush:*— bruise. Comp. *4486.*

2353. θρέμμα **thrĕmma,** *threm´-mah;* from *5142; stock* (as *raised* on a farm):— cattle.

2354. θρηνέω **thrēnĕō,** *thray-neh´-o;* from *2355;* to *bewail:*— lament, mourn.

2355. θρῆνος **thrēnŏs,** *thray´-nos;* from the base of *2360; wailing:*— lamentation.

2356. θρησκεία **thrēskĕia,** *thrace-ki´-ah;* from a der. of *2357;* ceremonial *observance:*— religion, worshipping.

2357. θρῆσκος **thrēskŏs,** *thrace´-kos;* prob. from the base of *2360; ceremonious* in worship (as *demonstrative*), i.e. *pious:*— religious.

2358. θριαμβεύω **thriambĕuō,** *three-am-byoo´-o;* from a prol. compound of the base of *2360;* and a der. of *680* (mean. a *noisy iambus,* sung in honor of Bacchus); to *make an acclamatory procession,* i.e. (fig.) to *conquer* or (by Heb.) to *give victory:*— (cause) to triumph (over).

2359. θρίξ **thrix,** *threeks;* gen. τριχός **trichŏs,** etc.; of uncert. der.; *hair:*— hair. Comp. *2864.*

2360. θροέω **thrŏĕō,** *thrŏ-eh´-o;* from θρέομαι **thrĕŏmai** to *wail;* to *clamor,* i.e. (by impl.) to *frighten:*— trouble.

2361. θρόμβος **thrŏmbŏs,** *throm´-bos;* perh. from *5142* (in the sense of *thickening*); a *clot:*— great drop.

2362. θρόνος **thrŏnŏs,** *thron´-os;* from θράω **thraō** (to *sit*); a stately *seat* ("*throne*"); by impl. *power* or (concr.) a *potentate:*— seat, throne.

2363. Θυάτειρα **Thuatĕira,** *thoo-at´-i-rah;* of uncert. der.; *Thyatira,* a place in Asia Minor:— Thyatira.

2364. θυγάτηρ **thugatēr,** *thoo-gat´-air;* appar. a primary word [comp. "daughter"]; a *female child,* or (by Heb.) *descendant* (or *inhabitant*):— daughter.

2365. θυγάτριον **thugatriŏn**, *thoo-gat´-ree-on;* from *2364;* a *daughterling:*— little (young) daughter.

2366. θύελλα **thuĕlla**, *thoo´-el-lah;* from *2380* (in the sense of *blowing*) a storm:— tempest.

2367. θύϊνος **thuïnŏs**, *thoo´-ee-nos;* from a der. of *2380* (in the sense of *blowing;* denoting a certain *fragrant* tree); made of *citron*-wood:— thyine.

2368. θυμίαμα **thumiama**, *thoo-mee´-am-ah;* from *2370;* an *aroma,* i.e. fragrant *powder* burnt in relig. service; by impl. the *burning* itself:— incense, odour.

2369. θυμιαστήριον **thumiastēriŏn**, *thoo-mee-as-tay´-ree-on;* or

θυμιατήριον **thumiatērion**, *thoo-mee-a-tay´-ree-on;* from a der. of *2370;* a *place of fumigation,* i.e. the *altar of incense* (in the Temple):— censer.

2370. θυμιάω **thumiaō**, *thoo-mee-ah´-o;* from a der. of *2380* (in the sense of *smoking*); to *fumigate,* i.e. *offer* aromatic *fumes:*— burn incense.

2371. θυμομαχέω **thumŏmachĕō**, *thoo-mom-akh-eh´-o;* from a presumed compound of *2372* and *3164;* to *be in a furious fight,* i.e. (fig.) to *be exasperated:*— be highly displeased.

2372. θυμός **thumŏs**, *thoo-mos´;* from *2380; passion* (as if *breathing* hard):— fierceness, indignation, wrath. Comp. *5590.*

2373. θυμόω **thumŏō**, *tho-mŏ´-o;* from *2372;* to *put in a passion,* i.e. *enrage:*— be wroth.

2374. θύρα **thura**, *thoo´-rah;* appar. a primary word [comp. "door"]; a *portal* or entrance (the opening or the closure, lit. or fig.):— door, gate.

2375. θυρεός **thurĕŏs**, *thoo-reh-os´;* from *2374;* a large *shield* (as *door*-shaped):— shield.

2376. θυρίς **thuris**, *thoo-rece´;* from *2374;* an *aperture,* i.e. *window:*— window.

2377. θυρωρός **thurōrŏs**, *thoo-ro-ros´;* from *2374* and οὖρος **ŏurŏs** (a *watcher*); a *gate-warden:*— that kept the door, porter.

2378. θυσία **thusia**, *thoo-see´-ah;* from *2380; sacrifice* (the act or the victim, lit. or fig.):— sacrifice.

2379. θυσιαστήριον **thusiastēriŏn**, *thoo-see-as-tay´-ree-on;* from a der. of *2378;* a *place of sacrifice,* i.e. an *altar* (spec. or gen., lit. or fig.):— altar.

2380. θύω **thuō**, *thoo´-o;* a primary verb; prop. to *rush* (*breathe* hard, *blow, smoke*), i.e. (by impl.) to *sacrifice* (prop. by fire, but gen.); by extens. to *immolate* (*slaughter* for any purpose):— kill, (do) sacrifice, slay.

2381. Θωμᾶς **Thōmas**, *tho-mas´;* of Chald. or. [comp. *8380*]; *the twin;* Thomas, a Chr.:— Thomas.

2382. θώραξ **thōrax**, *tho´-rax;* of uncert. aff.; the *chest* ("*thorax*"), i.e. (by impl.) a *corslet:*— breast-plate.

I

2383. Ἰάειρος **Iaĕirŏs**, *ee-ah´-i-ros;* or

Ἰάϊρος **Iairŏs**, *ee-ahee´-ros;* of Heb. or. [2971]; *Jaïrus* (i.e. *Jair*), an Isr.:— Jairus.

2384. Ἰακώβ **Iakōb**, *ee-ak-obe´;* of Heb. or. [3290]; *Jacob* (i.e. *Ja`akob*), the progenitor of the Isr.:— also an Isr.:— Jacob.

2385. Ἰάκωβος **Iakōbŏs**, *ee-ak´-o-bos;* the same as *2384* Græcized; *Jacobus,* the name of three Isr.:— James.

2386. ἴαμα **iama**, *ee´-am-ah;* from *2390;* a *cure* (the effect):— healing.

2387. Ἰαμβρῆς **Iambrēs**, *ee-am-brace´;* of Eg. or.; *Jambres,* an Eg.:— Jambres.

2388. Ἰαννά **Ianna**, *ee-an-nah´;* prob. of Heb. or. [comp. 3238]; *Janna,* an Isr.:— Janna.

2389. Ἰαννῆς **Iannēs**, *ee-an-nace´;* of Eg. or.; *Jannes,* an Eg.:— Jannes.

2390. ἰάομαι **iaŏmai**, *ee-ah´-om-ahee;* mid. voice of appar. a primary verb; to *cure* (lit. or fig.):— heal, make whole.

2391. Ἰάρεδ **Iarĕd**, *ee-ar´-ed* or

Ἰάρετ **Iaret**, *ee-ar´-et;* of Heb. or. [3382]; *Jared* (i.e. *Jered*), an antediluvian:— Jared.

2392. ἴασις **iasis**, *ee´-as-is;* from *2390; curing* (the act):— cure, heal (-ing).

2393. ἴασπις **iaspis**, *ee´-as-pis;* prob. of for. or. [see 3471]; "*jasper*," a gem:— jasper.

2394. Ἰάσων **Iasōn**, *ee-as´-oan;* future act. part. masc. of *2390; about to cure; Jason,* a Chr.:— Jason.

2395. ἰατρός **iatrŏs**, *ee-at-ros´;* from *2390;* a *physician:*— physician.

2396. ἴδε **idĕ**, *id´-eh;* second pers. sing. imper. act. of *1492;* used as an interj. to denote *surprise; lo!:*— behold, lo, see.

2397. ἰδέα **idĕa**, *id-eh´-ah;* from *1492;* a *sight* [comp. fig. "idea"], i.e. *aspect:*— countenance.

2398. ἴδιος **idiŏs**, *id´-ee-os;* of uncert. aff.; *pertaining to self,* i.e. one's *own;* by impl. *private* or *separate:*— × his acquaintance, when they were alone, apart, aside, due, his (own, proper, several), home, (her, our, thine, your) own (business), private (-ly), proper, severally, their (own).

2399. ἰδιώτης **idiōtēs**, *id-ee-o´-tace;* from *2398;* a *private* person, i.e. (by impl.) an *ignoramus* (comp. "idiot"):— ignorant, rude, unlearned.

2400. ἰδού **idŏu**, *id-oo´;* second pers. sing. imper. mid. voice of *1492;* used as imper. *lo!;*—behold, lo, see.

2401. Ἰδουμαία **Idŏumaia**, *id-oo-mah´-yah;*

of Heb. or. [123]; *Idumæa* (i.e. *Edom*), a region E. (and S.) of Pal.:— Idumæa.

2402. ἱδρώς **hidrōs**, *hid-roce´;* a strengthened form of a primary ἴδος **idŏs** (*sweat*); *perspiration:*— sweat.

2403. Ἰεζαβήλ **Iĕzabēl**, *ee-ed-zab-ale´;* of Heb. or. [348]; *Jezabel* (i.e. *Jezebel*), a Tyrian woman (used as a synonym of a termagant or false teacher):— Jezabel.

2404. Ἱεράπολις **Hiĕrapŏlis**, *hee-er-ap´-ol-is;* from 2413 and 4172; *holy city; Hierapolis*, a place in Asia Minor:— Hierapolis.

2405. ἱερατεία **hiĕratĕia**, *hee-er-at-i´-ah;* from 2407; *priestliness*, i.e. the *sacerdotal function:*— office of the priesthood, priest's office.

2406. ἱεράτευμα **hiĕratĕuma**, *hee-er-at´-yoo-mah;* from 2407; the *priestly fraternity*, i.e. *sacerdotal order* (fig.):— priesthood.

2407. ἱερατεύω **hiĕratĕuō**, *hee-er-at-yoo´-o;* prol. from 2409; to *be a priest*, i.e. *perform his functions:*— execute the priest's office.

2408. Ἰερεμίας **Hiĕrĕmias**, *hee-er-em-ee´-as;* of Heb. or. [3414]; *Hieremias* (i.e. *Jermijah*), an Isr.:— Jeremiah.

2409. ἱερεύς **hiĕrĕus**, *hee-er-yooce´;* from 2413; a *priest* (lit. or fig.):— (high) priest.

2410. Ἰεριχώ **Hiĕrichō**, *hee-er-ee-kho´;* of Heb. or. [3405]; *Jericho*, a place in Pal.:— Jericho.

2411. ἱερόν **hiĕrŏn**, *hee-er-on´;* neut. of 2413; a *sacred* place, i.e. the entire precincts (whereas 3485 denotes the central *sanctuary* itself) of the *Temple* (at Jerusalem or elsewhere):— temple.

2412. ἱεροπρεπής **hiĕrŏprĕpēs**, *hee-er-op-rep-ace´;* from 2413 and the same as 4241; *reverent:*— as becometh holiness.

2413. ἱερός **hiĕrŏs**, *hee-er-os´;* of uncert. aff.; *sacred:*— holy.

2414. Ἱεροσόλυμα **Hiĕrŏsŏluma**, *hee-er-os-ol´-oo-mah;* of Heb. or. [3389]; *Hierosolyma* (i.e. *Jerushalaïm*), the capital of Pal.:— Jerusalem. Comp. 2419.

2415. Ἱεροσολυμίτης **Hiĕrŏsŏlumitēs**, *hee-er-os-ol-oo-mee´-tace;* from 2414; a *Hierosolymite*, i.e. inhab. of Hierosolyma:— of Jerusalem.

2416. ἱεροσυλέω **hiĕrŏsulĕō**, *hee-er-os-ool-eh´-o;* from 2417; to *be a temple-robber* (fig.):— commit sacrilege.

2417. ἱερόσυλος **hiĕrŏsulŏs**, *hee-er-os´-oo-los;* from 2411 and 4813; a *temple-despoiler:*— robber of churches.

2418. ἱερουργέω **hiĕrŏurgĕō**, *hee-er-oorg-eh´-o;* from a compound of 2411 and the base of 2041; to *be a temple-worker*, i.e. *officiate as a priest* (fig.):— minister.

2419. Ἱερουσαλήμ **Hiĕrŏusalēm**, *hee-er-oo-sal-ame´;* of Heb. or. [3389]; *Hierusalem* (i.e. *Jerushalem*), the capital of Pal.:— Jerusalem. Comp. 2414.

2420. ἱερωσύνη **hiĕrōsunē**, *hee-er-o-soo´-nay;* from 2413; *sacredness*, i.e. (by impl.) the *priestly office:*— priesthood.

2421. Ἰεσσαί **Iĕssai**, *es-es-sah´-ee;* of Heb. or. [3448]; *Jessae* (i.e. *Jishai*), an Isr.:— Jesse.

2422. Ἰεφθάε **Iĕphthaĕ**, *ee-ef-thah´-eh;* of Heb. or. [3316]; *Jephthaë* (i.e. *Jiphtach*), an Isr.:— Jephthah.

2423. Ἰεχονίας **Iĕchŏnias**, *ee-ekh-on-ee´-as;* of Heb. or. [3204]; *Jechonias* (i.e. *Jekonjah*), an Isr.:— Jechonias.

2424. Ἰησοῦς **Iēsŏus**, *ee-ay-sooce´;* of Heb. or. [3091]; *Jesus* (i.e. *Jehoshua*), the name of our Lord and two (three) other Isr.:— Jesus.

2425. ἱκανός **hikanŏs**, *hik-an-os´;* from ἵκω **hikō** [ἱκάνω **hikanō** or ἱκνέομαι **hiknĕŏmai**, akin to 2240] (to *arrive*); *competent* (as if *coming* in season), i.e. *ample* (in amount) or *fit* (in character):— able, + content, enough, good, great, large, long (while), many, meet, much, security, sore, sufficient, worthy.

2426. ἱκανότης **hikanŏtēs**, *hik-an-ot´-ace;* from 2425; *ability:*— sufficiency.

2427. ἱκανόω **hikanŏō**, *hik-an-ŏ´-o;* from 2425; to *enable*, i.e. *qualify:*— make able (meet).

2428. ἱκετηρία **hikĕtēria**, *hik-et-ay-ree´-ah;* from a der. of the base of 2425 (through the idea of *approaching* for a favor); *intreaty:*— supplication.

2429. ἱκμάς **hikmas**, *hik-mas´;* of uncert. aff.; *dampness:*— moisture.

2430. Ἰκόνιον **Ikŏniŏn**, *ee-kon´-ee-on;* perh. from 1504; *image-like; Iconium*, a place in Asia Minor:— Iconium.

2431. ἱλαρός **hilarŏs**, *hil-ar-os´;* from the same as 2436; *propitious* or *merry* ("hilarious"), i.e. *prompt* or *willing:*— cheerful.

2432. ἱλαρότης **hilarŏtēs**, *hil-ar-ot´-ace;* from 2431; *alacrity:*— cheerfulness.

2433. ἱλάσκομαι **hilaskŏmai**, *hil-as´-kom-ahee;* mid. voice from the same as 2436; to *conciliate*, i.e. (tran.) to *atone for* (sin), or (intr.) *be propitious:*— be merciful, make reconciliation for.

2434. ἱλασμός **hilasmŏs**, *hil-as-mos´;* atonement, i.e. (concr.) an *expiator:*— propitiation.

2435. ἱλαστήριον **hilastēriŏn**, *hil-as-tay´-ree-on;* neut. of a der. of 2433; an *expiatory* (place or thing), i.e. (concr.) an atoning *victim*, or (spec.) the *lid* of the Ark (in the Temple):— mercyseat, propitiation.

2436. ἵλεως **hilĕōs**, *hil´-eh-oce;* perh. from the alt. form of 138; *cheerful* (as *attractive*), i.e. *propitious; adv.* (by Heb.) God be *gracious!,* i.e. (in averting some calamity) *far* be it:— be it far, merciful.

2437. Ἰλλυρικόν **Illurikŏn,** *il-loo-ree-kon´;* neut. of an adj. from a name of uncert. der.: (the) *Illyrican* (shore), i.e. (as a name itself) *Illyricum,* a region of Europe:— Illyricum.

2438. ἱμάς **himas,** *hee-mas´;* perh. from the same as *260;* a *strap,* i.e. (spec.) the *tie* (of a sandal) or the *lash* (of a scourge):— latchet, thong.

2439. ἱματίζω **himatizō,** *him-at-id´-zo;* from *2440;* to *dress:*— clothe.

2440. ἱμάτιον **himatiŏn,** *him-at´-ee-on;* neut. of a presumed der. of ἕννυμι **ĕnnumi** (to *put on*); a *dress* (inner or outer):— apparel, cloke, clothes, garment, raiment, robe, vesture.

2441. ἱματισμός **himatismŏs,** *him-at-is-mos´;* from *2439; clothing:*— apparel (× -led), array, raiment, vesture.

2442. ἱμείρομαι **himĕirŏmai,** *him-i´-rom-ahee;* mid. voice from ἵμερος **himĕrŏs** (a *yearning;* of uncert. aff.); to *long for:*— be affectionately desirous.

2443. ἵνα **hina,** *hin´-ah;* prob. from the same as the former part of *1438* (through the *demonstrative* idea; comp. *3588*); in order *that* (denoting the *purpose* or the *result*):— albeit, because, to the intent (that), lest, so as, (so) that, (for) to. Comp. *3363.*

ἵνα μή **hina mē.** See *3363.*

2444. ἱνατί **hinati,** *hin-at-ee´;* from *2443* and *5101; for what* reason?, i.e. *why?:*— wherefore, why.

2445. Ἰόππη **Iŏppē,** *ee-op´-pay;* of Heb. or. [3305]; *Joppe* (i.e. *Japho*), a place in Pal.:— Joppa.

2446. Ἰορδάνης **Iŏrdanēs,** *ee-or-dan´-ace;* of Heb. or. [3383]; the *Jordanes* (i.e. *Jarden*), a river of Pal.:— Jordan.

2447. ἰός **iŏs,** *ee-os´;* perh. from εἶμι **ĕimi** (to *go*) or ἵημι **hiēmi** (to *send*); *rust* (as if *emitted* by metals); also *venom* (as *emitted* by serpents):— poison, rust.

2448. Ἰουδά **Iŏuda,** *ee-oo-dah´;* of Heb. or. [3063 or perh. 3194]; *Judah* (i.e. *Jehudah* or *Juttah*), a part of (or place in) Pal.:— Judah.

2449. Ἰουδαία **Iŏudaia,** *ee-oo-dah´-yah;* fem. of *2453* (with *1093* impl.); the *Judæan* land (i.e. *Judæa*), a region of Pal.:— Judæa.

2450. Ἰουδαΐζω **Iŏudaïzō,** *ee-oo-dah-id´-zo;* from *2453;* to *become* a *Judæan,* i.e. *"Judaize":*— live as the Jews.

2451. Ἰουδαϊκός **Iŏudaïkŏs,** *ee-oo-dah-ee-kos´;* from *2453; Judaïc,* i.e. *resembling a Judæan:*— Jewish.

2452. Ἰουδαϊκῶς **Iŏudaïkōs,** *ee-oo-dah-ee-koce´;* adv. from *2451; Judaïcally* or in a *manner resembling a Judæan:*— as do the Jews.

2453. Ἰουδαῖος **Iŏudaiŏs,** *ee-oo-dah´-yos;*

from *2448* (in the sense of *2455* as a country); *Judæan,* i.e. belonging to *Jehudah:*— Jew (-ess), of Judæa.

2454. Ἰουδαϊσμός **Iŏudaismŏs,** *ee-oo-dah-is-mos´;* from *2450; "Judaïsm",* i.e. the *Jewish faith* and usages:— Jews' religion.

2455. Ἰουδάς **Iŏudas,** *ee-oo-das´;* of Heb. or. [3063]; *Judas* (i.e. *Jehudah*), the name of ten Isr.; also of the posterity of one of them and its region:— Juda (-h, -s); Jude.

2456. Ἰουλία **Iŏulia,** *ee-oo-lee´-ah;* fem. of the same as *2457; Julia,* a Chr. woman:— Julia.

2457. Ἰούλιος **Iŏuliŏs,** *ee-oo´-lee-os;* of Lat. or.; *Julius,* a centurion:— Julius.

2458. Ἰουνίας **Iŏunias,** *ee-oo-nee´-as;* of Lat. or.; *Junias,* a Chr.:— Junias.

2459. Ἰοῦστος **Iŏustŏs,** *ee-ooce´-tos;* of Lat. or. (*"just"*); *Justus,* the name of three Chr.:— Justus.

2460. ἱππεύς **hippĕus,** *hip-yooce´;* from *2462;* an *equestrian,* i.e. member of a *cavalry* corps.:— horseman.

2461. ἱππικόν **hippikŏn,** *hip-pee-kon´;* neut. of a der. of *2462;* the *cavalry* force:— horse (-men).

2462. ἵππος **hippŏs,** *hip´-pos;* of uncert. aff.; a *horse:*— horse.

2463. ἶρις **iris,** *ee´-ris;* perh. from *2046* (as a symbol of the female *messenger* of the pagan deities); a *rainbow* (*"iris"*):— rainbow.

2464. Ἰσαάκ **Isaak,** *ee-sah-ak´;* of Heb. or. [3327]; *Isaac* (i.e. *Jitschak*), the son of Abraham:— Isaac.

2465. ἰσάγγελος **isaggĕlŏs,** *ee-sang´-el-los;* from *2470* and *32; like an angel,* i.e. *angelic:*— equal unto the angels.

2466. Ἰσαχάρ **Isachar,** *ee-sakh-ar´;* of Heb. or. [3485]; *Isachar* (i.e. *Jissaskar*), a son of Jacob (fig. his desc.):— Issachar.

2467. ἴσημι **isēmi,** *is´-ay-mee;* assumed by some as the base of cert. irreg. forms of *1492;* to *know:*— know.

2468. ἴσθι **isthi,** *is´-thee;* second pers. imper. present of *1510; be* thou:— + agree, be, × give thyself wholly to.

2469. Ἰσκαριώτης **Iskariōtēs,** *is-kar-ee-o´-tace;* of Heb. or. [prob. 377 and 7149]; *inhabitant of Kerioth; Iscariotes* (i.e. *Keriothite*), an epithet of Judas the traitor:— Iscariot.

2470. ἴσος **isŏs,** *ee´-sos;* prob. from *1492* (through the idea of *seeming*); *similar* (in amount and kind):— + agree, as much, equal, like.

2471. ἰσότης **isŏtēs,** *ee-sot´-ace; likeness* (in condition or proportion); by impl. *equity:*— equal (-ity).

2472. ἰσότιμος **isŏtimŏs,** *ee-sot´-ee-mos;*

from *2470* and *5092; of equal value* or *honor:*—
like precious.

2473. ἰσόψυχος **isŏpsuchŏs**, *ee-sop´-soo-khos;*
from *2470* and *5590; of similar spirit:*—
likeminded.

2474. Ἰσραήλ **Israēl**, *is-rah-ale´;* of Heb. or.
[3478]; *Israel* (i.e. *Jisrael*), the adopted name
of Jacob, incl. his desc. (lit. or fig.):— Israel.

2475. Ἰσραηλίτης **Israēlitēs**, *is-rah-ale-ee´-*
tace; from *2474;* an *"Israelite",* i.e. desc. of
Israel (lit. or fig.):— Israelite.

2476. ἵστημι **histēmi**, *his´-tay-mee;* a prol.
form of a primary στάω **staō**, *stah´-o* (of the
same mean., and used for it in certain
tenses); to *stand* (tran. or intr.), used in various applications (lit. or fig.):— abide, appoint,
bring, continue, covenant, establish, hold up,
lay, present, set (up), stanch, stand (by, forth,
still, up). Comp. *5087.*

2477. ἱστορέω **histŏrĕō**, *his-tor-eh´-o;* from a
der. of *1492;* to *be knowing* (*learned*), i.e. (by
impl.) to *visit* for information (*interview*):—
see.

2478. ἰσχυρός **ischurŏs**, *is-khoo-ros´;* from
2479; forcible (lit. or fig.):— boisterous, mighty
(-ier), powerful, strong (-er, man), valiant.

2479. ἰσχύς **ischus**, *is-khoos´;* from a der. of ἴς
is (*force;* comp. ἔσχον **ĕschŏn**, a form of *2192*);
forcefulness (lit. or fig.):— ability, might (I-
ily]), power, strength.

2480. ἰσχύω **ischuō**, *is-khoo´-o;* from *2479;* to
have (or *exercise*) *force* (lit. or fig.):— be able,
avail, can do ([-not]), could, be good, might,
prevail, be of strength, be whole, + much
work.

2481. ἴσως **isōs**, *ee´-soce;* adv. from *2470;*
likely, i.e. *perhaps:*— it may be.

2482. Ἰταλία **Italia**, *ee-tal-ee´-ah;* prob. of for.
or.; *Italia*, a region of Europe:— Italy.

2483. Ἰταλικός **Italikŏs**, *ee-tal-ee-kos´;* from
2482; Italic, i.e. belonging to Italia:— Italian.

2484. Ἰτουραία **Itŏuraia**, *ee-too-rah´-yah;* of
Heb. or. [3195]; *Ituræa* (i.e. *Jetur*), a region of
Pal.:— Ituræa.

2485. ἰχθύδιον **ichthudiŏn**, *ikh-thoo´-dee-on;*
dimin. from *2486;* a *petty fish:*— little (small)
fish.

2486. ἰχθύς **ichthus**, *ikh-thoos´;* of uncert. aff.;
a *fish:*— fish.

2487. ἴχνος **ichnŏs**, *ikh´-nos;* from ἱκνέομαι
iknĕŏmai (to *arrive;* comp. *2240*); a *track*
(fig.):— step.

2488. Ἰωάθαμ **Iōatham**, *ee-o-ath´-am;* of Heb.
or. [3147]; *Joatham* (i.e. *Jotham*), an Isr.:—
Joatham.

2489. Ἰωάννα **Iōanna**, *ee-o-an´-nah;* fem. of
the same as *2491; Joanna*, a Chr.:— Joanna.

2490. Ἰωαννᾶς **Iōannas**, *ee-o-an-nas´;* a form
of *2491; Joannas*, an Isr.:— Joannas.

2491. Ἰωάννης **Iōannēs**, *ee-o-an´-nace;* of

Heb. or. [3110]; *Joannes* (i.e. *Jochanan*), the
name of four Isr.:— John.

2492. Ἰώβ **Iōb**, *ee-obe´;* of Heb. or. [347]; *Job*
(i.e. *Ijob*), a patriarch:— Job.

2493. Ἰωήλ **Iōēl**, *ee-o-ale´;* of Heb. or. [3100];
Joel, an Isr.:— Joel.

2494. Ἰωνάν **Iōnan**, *ee-o-nan´* or Ιωναμ
Ionam, *ee-o-nam´;* prob. for *2491* or *2495;*
Jonan, an Isr.:— Jonan (Jonam).

2495. Ἰωνᾶς **Iōnas**, *ee-o-nas´;* of Heb. or.
[3124]; *Jonas* (i.e. *Jonah*), the name of two
Isr.:— Jonas.

2496. Ἰωράμ **Iōram**, *ee-o-ram´;* of Heb. or.
[3141]; *Joram*, an Isr.:— Joram.

2497. Ἰωρείμ **Iōrĕim**, *ee-o-rime´* or Ἰωρίμ
Iōrim, *ee-o-reem´;* perh. for *2496; Jorim*, an
Isr.:— Jorim.

2498. Ἰωσαφάτ **Iōsaphat**, *ee-o-saf-at´;* of
Heb. or. [3092]; *Josaphat* (i.e. *Jehoshaphat*),
an Isr.:— Josaphat.

2499. Ἰωσή **Iōsē**, *ee-o-say´;* gen. of *2500;*
Jose, an Isr.:— Jose.

2500. Ἰωσῆς **Iōsēs**, *ee-o-sace´;* perh. for
2501; Joses, the name of two Isr.:— Joses.
Comp. *2499.*

2501. Ἰωσήφ **Iōsēph**, *ee-o-safe´;* of Heb. or.
[3130]; *Joseph*, the name of seven Isr.:—
Joseph.

2502. Ἰωσίας **Iōsias**, *ee-o-see´-as;* of Heb.
or. [2977]; *Josias* (i.e. *Joshiah*), an Isr.:—
Josias.

2503. ἰῶτα **iōta**, *ee-o´-tah;* of Heb. or. [the
tenth letter of the Heb. alphabet]; *"iota,"*
the name of the eighth letter of the Greek
alphabet, put (fig.) for a very small part of
anything:— jot.

K

2504. κἀγώ **kagō**, *kag-o´;* from *2532* and
1473 (so also the dat.

κἀμοί **kamŏi**, *kam-oy´;* and acc.

κἀμέ **kamĕ**, *kam-eh´;* and (or *also,*
even, etc.) *I*, (*to*) *me:*— (and, even, even so,
so) I (also, in like wise), both me, me also.

2505. καθά **katha**, *kath-ah´;* from *2596* and
the neut. plur. of *3739; according to which*
things, i.e. *just as:*— as.

2506. καθαίρεσις **kathairĕsis**, *kath-ah´-ee-*
res-is; from *2507; demolition;* fig. *extinc-*
tion:— destruction, pulling down.

2507. καθαιρέω **kathairĕō**, *kath-ahee-reh´-*
o; from *2596* and *138* (incl. its alt.); to *lower*
(or with violence) *demolish* (lit. or fig.):—
cast (pull, put, take) down, destroy.

2508. καθαίρω **kathairō**, *kath-ah´-ee-ro;*
from *2513;* to *cleanse*, i.e. (spec.) to *prune;*
fig. to *expiate:*— purge.

2509. καθάπερ **kathapĕr**, *kath-ap´-er;* from

2505 and 4007; *exactly as:*— (even, as well) as.

2510. καθάπτω **kathaptō**, *kath-ap´-to;* from 2596 and 680; to *seize upon:*— fasten on.

2511. καθαρίζω **katharizō**, *kath-ar-id´-zo;* from 2513; to *cleanse* (lit. or fig.):— (make) clean (-se), purge, purify.

2512. καθαρισμός **katharismŏs**, *kath-ar-is-mos´;* from 2511; a *washing* off, i.e. (cer.) *ablution*, (mor.) *expiation:*— cleansing, + purge, purification (-fying).

2513. καθαρός **katharŏs**, *kath-ar-os´;* of uncert. aff.; *clean* (lit. or fig.):— clean, clear, pure.

2514. καθαρότης **katharŏtēs**, *kath-ar-ot´-ace;* from 2513; *cleanness* (cer.):— purification.

2515. καθέδρα **kathĕdra**, *kath-ed´-rah;* from 2596 and the same as 1476; a *bench* (lit. or fig.):— seat.

2516. καθέζομαι **kathĕzŏmai**, *kath-ed´-zom-ahee;* from 2596 and the base of 1476; to *sit down.*— sit.

2517. καθεξῆς **kathĕxēs**, *kath-ex-ace´;* from 2596 and 1836; *thereafter,* i.e. *consecutively;* as a noun (by ellip. of noun) a *subsequent* person or time:— after (-ward), by (in) order.

2518. καθεύδω **kathĕudō**, *kath-yoo´-do;* from 2596 and εὕδω **hĕudō** (to *sleep*); to lie *down* to *rest,* i.e. (by impl.) to *fall asleep* (lit. or fig.):— (be a-) sleep.

2519. καθηγητής **kathēgētēs**, *kath-ayg-ay-tace´;* from a compound of 2596 and 2233; a *guide,* i.e. (fig.) a *teacher:*— master.

2520. καθήκω **kathēkō**, *kath-ay´-ko;* from 2596 and 2240; to *reach to,* i.e. (neut. of pres. act. part., fig. as adj.) *becoming:*— convenient, fit.

2521. κάθημαι **kathēmai**, *kath´-ay-mahee;* from 2596; and ἧμαι **hēmai** (to *sit;* akin to the base of 1476); to *sit down;* fig. to *remain, reside:*— dwell, sit (by, down).

2522. καθημερινός **kathēmĕrinŏs**, *kath-ay-mer-ee-nos´;* from 2596 and 2250; *quotidian:*— daily.

2523. καθίζω **kathizō**, *kath-id´-zo;* another (act.) form for 2516; to *seat down,* i.e. *set* (fig. *appoint*); intr. to *sit* (down); fig. to *settle* (*hover, dwell*):— continue, set, sit (down), tarry.

2524. καθίημι **kathiēmi**, *kath-ee´-ay-mee;* from 2596; and ἵημι **hiēmi** (to *send*); to *lower:*— let down.

2525. καθίστημι **kathistēmi**, *kath-is´-tay-mee;* from 2596 and 2476; to *place down* (permanently), i.e. (fig.) to *designate, constitute, convoy:*— appoint, be, conduct, make, ordain, set.

2526. καθό **kathŏ**, *kath-o´;* from 2596 and 3739; *according to which* thing, i.e. *precisely as,* in *proportion as:*— according to that, (inasmuch) as.

2526'. καθολικός **kathŏlikŏs**, *kath-ol-ee-kos´;* from 2527; *universal:*— general.

2527. καθόλου **kathŏlŏu**, *kath-ol´-oo;* from 2596 and 3650; *on the whole,* i.e. *entirely:*— at all.

2528. καθοπλίζω **kathŏplizō**, *kath-op-lid´-zo;* from 2596; and 3695; to *equip fully* with armor:— arm.

2529. καθοράω **kathŏraō**, *kath-or-ah´-o;* from 2596 and 3708; to *behold fully,* i.e. (fig.) *distinctly apprehend:*— clearly see.

2530. καθότι **kathŏti**, *kath-ot´-ee;* from 2596; and 3739 and 5100; *according to which* certain thing, i.e. *as far* (or *inasmuch*) *as:*— (according, forasmuch) as, because (that).

2531. καθώς **kathōs**, *kath-oce´;* from 2596 and 5613; *just* (or *inasmuch*) *as, that:*— according to, (according, even) as, how, when.

2532. καί **kai**, *kahee;* appar. a primary particle, having a *copulative* and sometimes also a *cumulative* force; *and, also, even, so, then, too,* etc.; often used in connection (or composition) with other particles or small words:— and, also, both, but, even, for, if, indeed, likewise, moreover, or, so, that, then, therefore, when, yet.

2533. Καϊάφας **Kaiaphas**, *kah-ee-af´-as;* of Chald. or.; *the dell; Caïaphas* (i.e. *Cajepha*), an Isr.:— Caiaphas.

2534. καίγε **kaigĕ**, *kah´-ee-gheh;* from 2532 and 1065; *and at least* (or *even, indeed*):— and, at least.

2535. Κάϊν **Kaïn**, *kah-in;* of Heb. or. [7014]; *Caïn,* (i.e. *Cajin*), the son of Adam:— Cain.

2536. Καϊνάν **Kaïnan**, *kah-ee-nan´* or

Καϊνάμ **Kaïnam** *kah-ee-nam´;* of Heb. or. [7018]; *Cainan* (i.e. *Kenan*), the name of two patriarchs:— Cainan (Cainam).

2537. καινός **kainŏs**, *kahee-nos´;* of uncert. aff.; *new* (espec. in *freshness;* while 3501 is prop. so with respect to *age:*— new.

2538. καινότης **kainŏtēs**, *kahee-not´-ace;* from 2537; *renewal* (fig.):— newness.

2539. καίπερ **kaipĕr**, *kah´-ee-per;* from 2532 and 4007; *and indeed,* i.e. *nevertheless* or *notwithstanding:*— and yet, although.

2540. καιρός **kairŏs**, *kahee-ros´;* of uncert. aff.; an *occasion,* i.e. *set* or *proper* time:— × always, opportunity, (convenient, due) season, (due, short, while) time, a while. Comp. 5550.

2541. Καῖσαρ **Kaisar**, *kah´-ee-sar;* of Lat. or.; *Cæsar,* a title of the Rom. emperor:— Cæsar.

2542. Καισάρεια **Kaisareia**, *kahee-sar´-i-a;* from 2541; *Cæsaria,* the name of two places in Pal.:— Cæsarea.

2543. καίτοι **kaitŏi**, *kah´-ee-toy;* from 2532 and 5104; *and yet,* i.e. *nevertheless:*— although.

2544. καίτοιγε **kaitŏigĕ**, *kah´-ee-toyg-eh;* from 2543 and 1065; *and yet indeed,* i.e. *although really:*— nevertheless, though.

2545. καίω **kaiō**, *kah´-yo;* appar. a primary verb; to *set on fire,* i.e. *kindle* or (by impl.) *consume:*— burn, light.

2546. κἀκεῖ **kakĕi**, *kak-i´;* from 2532 and 1563; *likewise in that place:*— and there, there (thither) also.

2547. κἀκεῖθεν **kakĕithĕn**, *kak-i´-then;* from 2532 and 1564; *likewise from that place* (or *time*):— and afterward (from) (thence), thence also.

2548. κἀκεῖνος **kakĕinŏs**, *kak-i´-nos;* from 2532 and 1565; *likewise that* (or *those*):— and him (other, them), even he, him also, them (also), (and) they.

2549. κακία **kakia**, *kak-ee´-ah;* from 2556; *badness,* i.e. (subj.) *depravity,* or (act.) *malignity,* or (pass.) *trouble:*— evil, malice (-ious-ness), naughtiness, wickedness.

2550. κακοήθεια **kakŏēthĕia**, *kak-ŏ-ay´-thi-ah;* from a compound of 2556 and 2239; *bad character,* i.e. (spec.) *mischievousness:*— malignity.

2551. κακολογέω **kakŏlŏgĕō**, *kak-ol-og-eh´-o;* from a compound of 2556 and 3056; to *revile:*— curse, speak evil of.

2552. κακοπάθεια **kakŏpathĕia**, *kak-op-ath´-i-ah;* from a compound of 2556 and 3806; *hardship:*— suffering affliction.

2553. κακοπαθέω **kakŏpathĕō**, *kak-op-ath-eh´-o;* from the same as 2552; to *undergo hardship:*— be afflicted, endure afflictions (hardness), suffer trouble.

2554. κακοποιέω **kakŏpŏiĕō**, *kak-op-oy-eh´-o;* from 2555; to *be a bad-doer,* i.e. (obj.) to *injure,* or (gen.) to *sin:*— do (ing) evil.

2555. κακοποιός **kakŏpŏiŏs**, *kak-op-oy-os´;* from 2556 and 4160; a *bad-doer;* (spec.) a *criminal:*— evil-doer, malefactor.

2556. κακός **kakŏs**, *kak-os´;* appar. a primary word; *worthless* (*intrinsically,* such; whereas 4190 prop. refers to *effects*), i.e. (subj.) *depraved,* or (obj.) *injurious:*— bad, evil, harm, ill, noisome, wicked.

2557. κακοῦργος **kakŏurgŏs**, *kak-oor´-gos;* from 2556 and the base of 2041; a *wrong-doer,* i.e. *criminal:*— evil-doer, malefactor.

2558. κακουχέω **kakŏuchĕō**, *kak-oo-kheh´-o;* from a presumed compound of 2556 and 2192; to *maltreat:*— which suffer adversity, torment.

2559. κακόω **kakŏō**, *kak-ŏ´-o;* from 2556; to *injure;* fig. to *exasperate:*— make evil affected, entreat evil, harm, hurt, vex.

2560. κακῶς **kakōs**, *kak-oce´;* from 2556; *badly* (phys. or mor.):— amiss, diseased, evil, grievously, miserably, sick, sore.

2561. κάκωσις **kakōsis**, *kak´-o-sis;* from 2559; *maltreatment:*— affliction.

2562. καλάμη **kalamē**, *kal-am´-ay;* fem. of 2563; a *stalk* of grain, i.e. (collect.) *stubble:*— stubble.

2563. κάλαμος **kalamŏs**, *kal´-am-os;* or uncert. aff.; a *reed* (the plant or its stem, or that of a similar plant); by impl. a *pen:*— pen, reed.

2564. καλέω **kalĕō**, *kal-eh´-o;* akin to the base of 2753; to "*call*" (prop. aloud, but used in a variety of applications, dir. or otherwise):— bid, call (forth), (whose, whose surname) name (was [called]).

2565. καλλιέλαιος **kalliĕlaiŏs**, *kal-le-el´-ah-yos;* from the base of 2566 and 1636; a *cultivated olive* tree, i.e. a *domesticated* or *improved* one:— good olive tree.

2566. καλλίον **kalliŏn**, *kal-lee´-on;* neut. of the (irreg.) comp. of 2570; (adv.) *better* than many:— very well.

2567. καλοδιδάσκαλος **kalŏdidaskalŏs**, *kal-od-id-as´-kal-os;* from 2570 and 1320; a *teacher of* the *right:*— teacher of good things.

2568. Καλοὶ Λιμένες **Kalŏi Limĕnĕs**, *kal-oy´ lee-men´-es;* plur. of 2570 and 3040; *Good Harbors,* i.e. *Fairhaven,* a bay of Crete:— fair havens.

2569. καλοποιέω **kalŏpŏiĕō**, *kal-op-oy-eh´-o;* from 2570 and 4160; to *do well,* i.e. live *virtuously:*— well doing.

2570. καλός **kalŏs**, *kal-os´;* of uncert. aff.; prop. *beautiful,* but chiefly (fig.) *good* (lit. or mor.), i.e. *valuable* or *virtuous* (for *appearance* or *use,* and thus distinguished from 18, which is prop. *intrinsic*):— × better, fair, good (-ly), honest, meet, well, worthy.

2571. κάλυμα **kaluma**, *kal´-oo-mah;* from 2572; a *cover,* i.e. *veil:*— vail.

2572. καλύπτω **kaluptō**, *kal-oop´-to;* akin to 2813 and 2928; to *cover* up (lit. or fig.):— cover, hide.

2573. καλῶς **kalōs**, *kal-oce´;* adv. from 2570; *well* (usually mor.):— (in a) good (place), honestly, + recover, (full) well.

2574. κάμηλος **kamēlŏs**, *kam´-ay-los;* of Heb. or. [1581]; a "*camel*":— camel.

2575. κάμινος **kaminŏs**, *kam´-ee-nos;* prob. from 2545; a *furnace:*— furnace.

2576. καμμύω **kammuō**, *kam-moo´-o;* from a compound of 2596 and the base of 3466; to *shut down,* i.e. *close* the eyes:— close.

2577. κάμνω **kamnō**, *kam´-no;* appar. a primary verb; prop. to *toil,* i.e. (by impl.) to *tire* (fig. *faint, sicken*):— faint, sick, be wearied.

2578. κάμπτω **kamptō**, *kamp´-to;* appar. a primary verb; to *bend:*— bow.

2579. κἄν **kan**, *kan;* from 2532 and *1437; and* (or *even*) *if:*— and (also) if (so much as), if but, at the least, though, yet.

2580. Κανᾶ **Kana**, *kan-ah´;* of Heb. or. [comp. 7071]; *Cana,* a place in Pal.:— Cana.

2581. Κανανίτης **Kananitēs**, *kan-an-ee´-tace;* of Chald. or. [comp. 7067]; *zealous; Cananitës,* an epithet:— Canaanite [*by mistake for a der. from 5477*].

2582. Κανδάκη **Kandakē**, *kan-dak´-ay;* of for. or.; *Candacë,* an Eg. queen:— Candace.

2583. κανών **kanōn**, *kan-ohn´;* from κάνη **kanē** (a straight *reed,* i.e. *rod*); a *rule* ("*canon*"), i.e. (fig.) a *standard* (of faith and practice); by impl. a *boundary,* i.e. (fig.) a *sphere* (of activity):— line, rule.

2584. Καπερναούμ **Kapĕrnaŏum**, *kap-er-nah-oom´;* of Heb. or. [prob. 3723 and 5151]; *Capernaüm* (i.e. *Caphanachum*), a place in Pal.:— Capernaum.

2585. καπηλεύω **kapēlĕuō**, *kap-ale-yoo´-o;* from κάπηλος **kapēlŏs** (a *huckster*); to *retail,* i.e. (by impl.) to *adulterate* (fig.):— corrupt.

2586. καπνός **kapnŏs**, *kap-nos´;* of uncert. aff.; *smoke:*— smoke.

2587. Καππαδοκία **Kappadŏkia**, *kap-pad-ok-ee´-ah;* of for. or.; *Cappadocia,* a region of Asia Minor:— Cappadocia.

2588. καρδία **kardia**, *kar-dee´-ah;* prol. from a primary κάρ **kar** (Lat. *cor,* "*heart*"); the *heart,* i.e. (fig.) the *thoughts* or *feelings* (*mind*); also (by anal.) the *middle:*— (+ broken-) heart (-ed).

2589. καρδιογνώστης **kardiŏgnōstēs**, *kar-dee-og-noce´-tace;* from 2588 and 1097; a *heart-knower:*— which knowest the hearts.

2590. καρπός **karpŏs**, *kar-pos´;* prob. from the base of 726; *fruit* (as *plucked*), lit. or fig.:— fruit.

2591. Κάρπος **Karpŏs**, *kar´-pos;* perh. for 2590; *Carpus,* prob. a Chr.:— Carpus.

2592. καρποφορέω **karpŏphŏrĕō**, *kar-pof-or-eh´-o;* from 2593; to *be fertile* (lit. or fig.):— be (bear, bring forth) fruit (-ful).

2593. καρποφόρος **karpŏphŏrŏs**, *kar-pof-or´-os;* from 2590 and 5342; *fruitbearing* (fig.):— fruitful.

2594. καρτερέω **kartĕrĕō**, *kar-ter-eh´-o;* from a der. of 2904 (transp.); to *be strong,* i.e. (fig.) *steadfast* (*patient*):— endure.

2595. κάρφος **karphŏs**, *kar´-fos;* from κάρφω **karphō** (to *wither*); a dry *twig* or *straw:*— mote.

2596. κατά **kata**, *kat-ah´;* a primary particle; (prep.) *down* (in place or time), in varied relations (according to the case [gen., dat. or acc.] with which it is joined):— about, according as (to), after, against, (when they were) × alone, among, and, × apart, (even, like) as (concerning, pertaining to touching), × aside,

at, before, beyond, by, to the charge of, [charita-] bly, concerning, + covered, [dai-] ly, down, every, (+ far more) exceeding, × more excellent, for, from ... to, godly, in (-asmuch, divers, every, -to, respect of), ... by, after the manner of, + by any means, beyond (out of) measure, × mightily, more, × natural, of (up-) on (× part), out (of every), over against, (+ your) × own, + particularly, so, through (-oughout, oughout every), thus, (un-) to (-gether, -ward), × uttermost, where (-by), with. In composition it retains many of these applications, and frequently denotes *opposition, distribution,* or *intensity.*

2597. καταβαίνω **katabainō**, *kat-ab-ah´-ee-no;* from 2596 and the base of 939; to *descend* (lit. or fig.):— come (get, go, step) down, descend, fall (down).

2598. καταβάλλω **kataballō**, *kat-ab-al´-lo;* from 2596 and 906; to *throw down:*— cast down, descend, fall (down), lay.

2599. καταβαρέω **katabarĕō**, *kat-ab-ar-eh´-o;* from 2596 and 916; to *impose upon:*— burden.

2600. κατάβασις **katabasis**, *kat-ab´-as-is;* from 2597; a *declivity:*— descent.

2601. καταβιβάζω **katabibazō**, *kat-ab-ib-ad´-zo;* from 2596 and a der. of the base of 939; to *cause to go down,* i.e. *precipitate:*— bring (thrust) down.

2602. καταβολή **katabŏlē**, *kat-ab-ol-ay´;* from 2598; a *deposition,* i.e. *founding;* fig. *conception:*— conceive, foundation.

2603. καταβραβεύω **katabrabĕuō**, *kat-ab-rab-yoo´-o;* from 2596 and 1018 (in its orig. sense); to *award* the price *against,* i.e. (fig.) to *defraud* (of salvation):— beguile of reward.

2604. καταγγελεύς **kataggĕlĕus**, *kat-ang-gel-yooce´;* from 2605; a *proclaimer:*— setter forth.

2605. καταγγέλλω **kataggĕllō**, *kat-ang-gel´-lo;* from 2596 and the base of 32; to *proclaim, promulgate:*— declare, preach, shew, speak of, teach.

2606. καταγελάω **katagĕlaō**, *kat-ag-el-ah´-o;* to *laugh down,* i.e. *deride:*— laugh to scorn.

2607. καταγινώσκω **kataginōskō**, *kat-ag-in-o´-sko;* from 2596 and 1097; to *note against,* i.e. *find fault with:*— blame, condemn.

2608. κατάγνυμι **katagnumi**, *kat-ag´-noo-mee;* from 2596 and the base of 4486; to *rend in pieces,* i.e. *crack apart:*— break.

2609. κατάγω **katagō**, *kat-ag´-o;* from 2596 and 71; to *lead down;* spec. to *moor* a vessel:— bring (down, forth), (bring to) land, touch.

2610. καταγωνίζομαι **katagōnizŏmai**, *kat-ag-o-nid´-zom-ahee;* from 2596 and 75; to

Greek

struggle against, i.e. (by impl.) to *overcome:*— subdue.

2611. καταδέω **katadĕō,** *kat-ad-eh´-o;* from 2596 and 1210; to *tie down,* i.e. *bandage* (a wound):— bind up.

2612. κατάδηλος **katadēlŏs,** *kat-ad´-ay-los;* from 2596 intens. and 1212; *manifest:*— far more evident.

2613. καταδικάζω **katadikazō,** *kat-ad-ik-ad´-zo;* from 2596 and a der. of 1349; to *adjudge against,* i.e. *pronounce guilty:*— condemn.

2614. καταδιώκω **katadiōkō,** *kat-ad-ee-o´-ko;* from 2596 and 1377; to *hunt down,* i.e. *search for:*— follow after.

2615. καταδουλόω **katadŏulŏō,** *kat-ad-oo-lŏ´-o;* from 2596 and 1402; to *enslave utterly:*— bring into bondage.

2616. καταδυναστεύω **katadunastĕuō,** *kat-ad-oo-nas-tyoo´-o;* from 2596 and a der. of 1413; to *exercise dominion against,* i.e. *oppress:*— oppress.

2617. καταισχύνω **kataischunō,** *kat-ahee-skhoo´-no;* from 2596 and 153; to *shame down,* i.e. *disgrace* or (by impl.) *put to the blush:*— confound, dishonour, (be a-, make a-) shame (-d).

2618. κατακαίω **katakaiō,** *kat-ak-ah´-ee-o;* from 2596 and 2545; to *burn down* (to the ground), i.e. *consume wholly:*— burn (up, utterly).

2619. κατακαλύπτω **katakaluptō,** *kat-ak-al-oop´-to;* from 2596 and 2572; to *cover wholly,* i.e. *veil:*— cover, hide.

2620. κατακαυχάομαι **katakauchaŏmai,** *kat-ak-ŏw-khah´-om-ahee;* from 2596 and 2744; to *exult against* (i.e. *over*):— boast (against), glory, rejoice against.

2621. κατάκειμαι **katakĕimai,** *kat-ak´-i-mahee;* from 2596 and 2749; to *lie down,* i.e. (by impl.) *be sick;* spec. to *recline* at a meal:— keep, lie, sit at meat (down).

2622. κατακλάω **kataklaō,** *kat-ak-lah´-o;* from 2596 and 2806; to *break down,* i.e. *divide:*— break.

2623. κατακλείω **kataklĕiō,** *kat-ak-li´-o;* from 2596 and 2808; to *shut down* (in a dungeon), i.e. *incarcerate:*— shut up.

2624. κατακληροδοτέω **kataklērŏdŏtĕō,** *kat-ak-lay-rod-ot-eh´-o;* from 2596 and a der. of a compound of 2819 and 1325; to *be a giver of lots to each,* i.e. (by impl.) to *apportion an estate:*— divide by lot.

2625. κατακλίνω **kataklinō,** *kat-ak-lee´-no;* from 2596 and 2827; to *recline down,* i.e. (spec.) to *take a place* at table:— (make) sit down (at meat).

2626. κατακλύζω **katakluzō,** *kat-ak-lood´-zo;* from 2596 and the base of 2830; to *dash (wash) down,* i.e. (by impl.) to *deluge:*— overflow.

2627. κατακλυσμός **kataklusmŏs,** *kat-ak-looce-mos´;* from 2626; an *inundation:*— flood.

2628. κατακολουθέω **katakŏlŏuthĕō,** *kat-ak-ol-oo-theh´-o;* from 2596 and 190; to *accompany closely:*— follow (after).

2629. κατακόπτω **katakŏptō,** *kat-ak-op´-to;* from 2596 and 2875; to *chop down,* i.e. *mangle:*— cut.

2630. κατακρημνίζω **katakrēmnizō,** *kat-ak-rame-nid´-zo;* from 2596 and a der. of 2911; to *precipitate down:*— cast down headlong.

2631. κατάκριμα **katakrima,** *kat-ak´-ree-mah;* from 2632; an *adverse sentence* (the verdict):— condemnation.

2632. κατακρίνω **katakrinō,** *kat-ak-ree´-no;* from 2596 and 2919; to *judge against,* i.e. *sentence:*— condemn, damn.

2633. κατάκρισις **katakrisis,** *kat-ak´-ree-sis;* from 2632; *sentencing adversely* (the act):— condemn (-ation).

2634. κατακυριεύω **katakuriĕuō,** *kat-ak-oo-ree-yoo´-o;* from 2596 and 2961; to *lord against,* i.e. *control, subjugate:*— exercise dominion over (lordship), be lord over, overcome.

2635. καταλαλέω **katalalĕō,** *kat-al-al-eh´-o;* from 2637; to *be a traducer,* i.e. to *slander:*— speak against (evil of).

2636. καταλαλία **katalalia,** *kat-al-al-ee´-ah;* from 2637; *defamation:*— backbiting, evil speaking.

2637. κατάλαλος **katalalŏs,** *kat-al´-al-os;* from 2596 and the base of 2980; *talkative against,* i.e. a *slanderer:*— backbiter.

2638. καταλαμβάνω **katalambanō,** *kat-al-am-ban´-o;* from 2596 and 2983; to *take eagerly,* i.e. *seize, possess,* etc. (lit. or fig.):— apprehend, attain, come upon, comprehend, find, obtain, perceive, (over-) take.

2639. καταλέγω **katalĕgō,** *kat-al-eg´-o;* from 2596 and 3004 (in its orig. mean.); to *lay down,* i.e. (fig.) to *enroll:*— take into the number.

2640. κατάλειμμα **katalĕimma,** *kat-al´-ime-mah;* from 2641; a *remainder,* i.e. (by impl.) *a few:*— remnant.

2641. καταλείπω **katalĕipō,** *kat-al-i´-po;* from 2596 and 3007; to *leave down,* i.e. *behind;* by impl. to *abandon, have remaining:*— forsake, leave, reserve.

2642. καταλιθάζω **katalithazō,** *kat-al-ith-ad´-zo;* from 2596 and 3034; to *stone down,* i.e. *to death:*— stone.

2643. καταλλαγή **katallagē,** *kat-al-lag-ay´;* from 2644; *exchange* (fig. *adjustment*), i.e. *restoration* to (the divine) favor:— atonement, reconciliation (-ing).

2644. καταλλάσσω **katallassō,** *kat-al-las´-so;* from 2596 and 236; to *change mutually,* i.e. (fig.) to *compound* a difference:— reconcile.

2645. κατάλοιπος **katalŏipŏs**, *kat-al´-oy-pos;* from 2596 and 3062; *left down* (*behind*), i.e. *remaining* (plur. the *rest*):— residue.

2646. κατάλυμα **kataluma**, *kat-al´-oo-mah;* from 2647; prop. a *dissolution* (breaking up of a journey), i.e. (by impl.) a *lodging-place:*— guestchamber, inn.

2647. καταλύω **kataluō**, *kat-al-oo´-o;* from 2596 and 3089; to *loosen down* (*disintegrate*), i.e. (by impl.) to *demolish* (lit. or fig.); spec. [comp. 2646] to *halt* for the night:— destroy, dissolve, be guest, lodge, come to nought, overthrow, throw down.

2648. καταμανθάνω **katamanthanō**, *kat-am-an-than´-o;* from 2596 and 3129; to *learn thoroughly*, i.e. (by impl.) to *note carefully:*— consider.

2649. καταμαρτυρέω **katammarturĕō**, *kat-am-ar-too-reh´-o;* from 2596 and 3140; to *testify against:*— witness against.

2650. καταμένω **katamĕnō**, *kat-am-en´-o;* from 2596 and 3306; to *stay fully*, i.e. *reside:*— abide.

2651. καταμόνας **katamŏnas**, *kat-am-on´-as;* from 2596 and acc. plur. fem. of 3441 (with 5561 impl.); *according to sole* places, i.e. (adv.) *separately:*— alone.

2652. κατανάθεμα **katanathĕma**, *kat-an-ath´-em-ah;* from 2596 (intens.) and 331; an *imprecation:*— curse.

2653. καταναθεματίζω **katanathĕmatizō**, *kat-an-ath-em-at-id´-zo;* from 2596 (intens.) and 332; to *imprecate:*— curse.

2654. καταναλίσκω **katanaliskō**, *kat-an-al-is´-ko;* from 2596 and 355; to *consume utterly:*— consume.

2655. καταναρκάω **katanarkaō**, *kat-an-ar-kah´-o;* from 2596 and ναρκάω **narkaō** (to *be numb*); to *grow utterly torpid*, i.e. (by impl.) *slothful* (fig. *expensive*):— be burdensome (chargeable).

2656. κατανεύω **katanĕuō**, *kat-an-yoo´-o;* from 2596 and 3506; to *nod down* (*toward*), i.e. (by anal.) to *make signs* to:— beckon.

2657. κατανοέω **katanŏĕō**, *kat-an-o-eh´-o;* from 2596 and 3539; to *observe fully:*— behold, consider, discover, perceive.

2658. καταντάω **katantaō**, *kat-an-tah´-o;* from 2596 and a der. of 473; to *meet against*, i.e. *arrive at* (lit. or fig.):— attain, come.

2659. κατάνυξις **katanuxis**, *kat-an´-oox-is;* from 2660; a *prickling* (sensation, as of the limbs *asleep*), i.e. (by impl. [perh. by some confusion with 3506 or even with 3571]) *stupor* (*lethargy*):— slumber.

2660. κατανύσσω **katanussō**, *kat-an-oos´-so;* from 2596 and 3572; to *pierce thoroughly*, i.e. (fig.) to *agitate* violently ("sting to the quick"):— prick.

2661. καταξιόω **kataxiŏō**, *kat-ax-ee-ŏ´-o;* from 2596 and 515; to *deem entirely deserving:*— (ac-) count worthy.

2662. καταπατέω **katapatĕō**, *kat-ap-at-eh´-o;* from 2596 and 3961; to *trample down;* fig. to *reject* with disdain:— trample, tread (down, underfoot).

2663. κατάπαυσις **katapausis**, *kat-ap´-ow-sis;* from 2664; *reposing down*, i.e. (by Heb.) *abode:*— rest.

2664. καταπαύω **katapauō**, *kat-ap-ŏw´-o;* from 2596 and 3973; to *settle down*, i.e. (lit.) to *colonize*, or (fig.) to (*cause to*) *desist:*— cease, (give) rest (-rain).

2665. καταπέτασμα **katapĕtasma**, *kat-ap-et´-as-mah;* from a compound of 2596 and a congener of 4072; something *spread thoroughly*, i.e. (spec.) the door *screen* (to the Most Holy Place) in the Jewish Temple:— vail.

2666. καταπίνω **katapinō**, *kat-ap-ee´-no;* from 2596 and 4095; to *drink down*, i.e. *gulp entire* (lit. or fig.):— devour, drown, swallow (up).

2667. καταπίπτω **katapiptō**, *kat-ap-ip´-to;* from 2596 and 4098; to *fall down:*— fall (down).

2668. καταπλέω **kataplĕō**, *kat-ap-leh´-o;* from 2596 and 4126; to *sail down* upon a place, i.e. to *land* at:— arrive.

2669. καταπονέω **kataponĕō**, *kat-ap-on-eh´-o;* from 2596 and a der. of 4192; to *labor down*, i.e. *wear with toil* (fig. *harass*):— oppress, vex.

2670. καταποντίζω **katapŏntizō**, *kat-ap-on-tid´-zo;* from 2596 and a der. of the same as 4195; to *plunge down*, i.e. *submerge:*— drown, sink.

2671. κατάρα **katara**, *kat-ar´-ah;* from 2596 (intens.) and 685; *imprecation*, *execration:*— curse (-d, ing).

2672. καταράομαι **kataraŏmai**, *kat-ar-ah´-om-ahee;* mid. voice from 2671; to *execrate;* by anal. to *doom:*— curse.

2673. καταργέω **katargĕō**, *kat-arg-eh´-o;* from 2596 and 691; to *be (render) entirely idle* (*useless*), lit. or fig.:— abolish, cease, cumber, deliver, destroy, do away, become (make) of no (none, without) effect, fail, loose, bring (come) to nought, put away (down), vanish away, make void.

2674. καταριθμέω **katarithmĕō**, *kat-ar-ith-meh´-o;* from 2596 and 705; to *reckon among:*— number with.

2675. καταρτίζω **katartizō**, *kat-ar-tid´-zo;* from 2596 and a der. of 739; to *complete thoroughly*, i.e. *repair* (lit. or fig.) or *adjust:*— fit, frame, mend, (make) perfect (-ly join together), prepare, restore.

2676. κατάρτισις **katartisis**, *kat-ar´-tis-is;*

from 2675; *thorough equipment* (subj.):— perfection.

2677. καταρτισμός **katartismŏs**, *kat-ar-tis-mos´*; from 2675; *complete furnishing* (obj.):— perfecting.

2678. κατασείω **katasĕiō**, *kat-as-i´-o*; from 2596 and 4579; to *sway downward*, i.e. *make a signal:*— beckon.

2679. κατασκάπτω **kataskaptō**, *kat-as-kap´-to*; from 2596 and 4626; to *undermine*, i.e. (by impl.) *destroy:*— dig down, ruin.

2680. κατασκευάζω **kataskĕuazō**, *kat-ask-yoo-ad´-zo*; from 2596 and a der. of 4632; to *prepare thoroughly* (prop. by extern. *equipment;* whereas 2090 refers rather to intern. *fitness*); by impl. to *construct, create:*— build, make, ordain, prepare.

2681. κατασκηνόω **kataskēnŏō**, *kat-as-kay-nŏ´-o*; from 2596 and 4637; to *camp down*, i.e. *haunt;* fig. to *remain:*— lodge, rest.

2682. κατασκήνωσις **kataskēnōsis**, *kat-as-kay´-no-sis;* from 2681; an *encamping*, i.e. (fig.) a *perch:*— nest.

2683. κατασκιάζω **kataskiazō**, *kat-as-kee-ad´-zo;* from 2596 and a der. of 4639; to *overshade*, i.e. *cover:*— shadow.

2684. κατασκοπέω **kataskŏpĕō**, *kat-as-kop-eh´-o;* from 2685; to *be a sentinel*, i.e. to *inspect insidiously:*— spy out.

2685. κατάσκοπος **kataskŏpŏs**, *kat-as´-kop-os;* from 2596 (intens.) and 4649 (in the sense of a *watcher*); a *reconnoiterer:*— spy.

2686. κατασοφίζομαι **katasŏphizŏmai**, *kat-as-of-id´-zom-ahee;* mid. voice from 2596 and 4679; to *be crafty against*, i.e. *circumvent:*— deal subtilly (subtly) with.

2687. καταστέλλω **katastĕllō**, *kat-as-tel´-lo;* from 2596 and 4724; to *put down*, i.e. *quell:*— appease, quiet.

2688. κατάστημα **katastēma**, *kat-as´-tay-mah;* from 2525; prop. a *position* or *condition*, i.e. (subj.) *demeanor:*— behaviour.

2689. καταστολή **katastŏlē**, *kat-as-tol-ay´;* from 2687; a *deposit*, i.e. (spec.) *costume:*— apparel.

2690. καταστρέφω **katastrĕphō**, *kat-as-tref´-o;* from 2596 and 4762; to *turn* upside *down*, i.e. *upset:*— overthrow.

2691. καταστρηνιάω **katastrēniaō**, *kat-as-tray-nee-ah´-o;* from 2596 and 4763; to *become voluptuous against:*— begin to wax wanton against.

2692. καταστροφή **katastrŏphē**, *kat-as-trof-ay´;* from 2690; an *overturn* ("catastrophe"), i.e. *demolition;* fig. *apostasy:*— overthrow, subverting.

2693. καταστρώννυμι **katastrōnnumi**, *kat-as-trone´-noo-mee;* from 2596 and 4766; to *strew down*, i.e. (by impl.) to *prostrate* (*slay*):— overthrow.

2694. κατασύρω **katasurō**, *kat-as-oo´-ro;* from 2596 and 4951; to *drag down*, i.e. *arrest* judicially:— hale.

2695. κατασφάττω **katasphattō**, *kat-as-fat´-to;* from 2596 and 4969; to *kill down*, i.e. *slaughter:*— slay.

2696. κατασφραγίζω **katasphragizō**, *kat-as-frag-id´-zo;* from 2596 and 4972; to *seal closely:*— seal.

2697. κατάσχεσις **kataschĕsis**, *kat-as´-khes-is;* from 2722; a *holding down*, i.e. *occupancy:*— possession.

2698. κατατίθημι **katatithēmi**, *kat-at-ith´-ay-mee;* from 2596 and 5087; to *place down*, i.e. *deposit* (lit. or fig.):— do, lay, shew.

2699. κατατομή **katatŏmē**, *kat-at-om-ay´;* from a compound of 2596 and τέμνω **tĕmnō** (to *cut*); a *cutting down* (*off*), i.e. *mutilation* (ironically):— concision. Comp. 609.

2700. κατατοξεύω **katatŏxĕuō**, *kat-at-ox-yoo´-o;* from 2596 and a der. of 5115; to *shoot down* with an arrow or other missile:— thrust through.

2701. κατατρέχω **katatrĕchō**, *kat-at-rekh´-o;* from 2596 and 5143; to *run down*, i.e. *hasten* from a tower:— run down.

καταφάγω **kataphagō**. See 2719.

2702. καταφέρω **kataphĕrō**, *kat-af-er´-o;* from 2596 and 5342 (incl. its alt.); to *bear down*, i.e. (fig.) *overcome* (with drowsiness); spec. to *cast* a vote:— fall, give, sink down.

2703. καταφεύγω **kataphĕugō**, *kat-af-yoo´-go;* from 2596 and 5343; to *flee down* (*away*):— flee.

2704. καταφθείρω **kataphthĕirō**, *kat-af-thi´-ro;* from 2596 and 5351; to *spoil entirely*, i.e. (lit.) to *destroy;* or (fig.) to *deprave:*— corrupt, utterly perish.

2705. καταφιλέω **kataphilĕō**, *kat-af-ee-leh´-o;* from 2596 and 5368; to *kiss earnestly:*— kiss.

2706. καταφρονέω **kataphrŏnĕō**, *kat-af-ron-eh´-o;* from 2596 and 5426; to *think against*, i.e. *disesteem:*— despise.

2707. καταφροντής **kataphrŏntēs**, *kat-af-ron-tace´;* from 2706; a *contemner:*— despiser.

2708. καταχέω **katachĕō**, *kat-akh-eh´-o;* from 2596 and χέω **chĕō** (to *pour*); to *pour down* (*out*):— pour.

2709. καταχθόνιος **katachthŏniŏs**, *kat-akh-thon´-ee-os;* from 2596 and χθών **chthōn** (the *ground*); *subterranean*, i.e. *infernal* (belonging to the world of departed spirits):— under the earth.

2710. καταχράομαι **katachraŏmai**, *kat-akh-rah´-om-ahee;* from 2596 and 5530; to *overuse*, i.e. *misuse:*— abuse.

2711. καταψύχω **katapsuchō**, *kat-ap-soo-*

kho; from 2596 and 5594; to *cool down* (*off*), i.e. *refresh:*— cool.

2712. κατείδωλος **katĕidōlŏs**, *kat-i´-do-los;* from 2596 (intens.) and 1497; *utterly idolatrous:*— wholly given to idolatry.

κατελεύθω **katĕlĕuthō**. See 2718.

2713. κατέναντι **katĕnanti**, *kat-en´-an-tee;* from 2596 and 1725; *directly opposite:*— before, over against.

κατενέγκω **katĕnĕgkō**. See 2702.

2714. κατενώπιον **katĕnōpiŏn**, *kat-en-o´-pee-on;* from 2596 and 1799; *dir. in front of:*— before (the presence of), in the sight of.

2715. κατεξουσιάζω **katĕxŏusiazō**, *kat-ex-oo-see-ad´-zo;* from 2596 and 1850; to *have* (*wield*) *full privilege over:*— exercise authority.

2716. κατεργάζομαι **katĕrgazŏmai**, *kat-er-gad´-zom-ahee;* from 2596 and 2038; do *work fully*, i.e. *accomplish;* by impl. to *finish, fashion:*— cause, do (deed), perform, work (out).

2717. Because of some changes in the numbering system (while the original work was in progress) no Greek words were cited for 2717 or 3203-3302. These numbers were dropped altogether. This will not cause any problems in Strong's numbering system. No Greek words have been left out. Because so many other reference works use this numbering system, it has not been revised. If it were revised, much confusion would certainly result.

2718. κατέρχομαι **katĕrchŏmai**, *kat-er´-khom-ahee;* from 2596 and 2064 (incl. its alt.); to *come* (or *go*) *down* (lit. or fig.):— come (down), depart, descend, go down, land.

2719. κατεσθίω **katĕsthiō**, *kat-es-thee´-o;* from 2596 and 2068 (incl. its alt.); to *eat down*, i.e. *devour* (lit. or fig.):— devour.

2720. κατευθύνω **katĕuthunō**, *kat-yoo-thoo´-no;* from 2596 and 2116; to *straighten fully*, i.e. (fig.) *direct:*— guide, direct.

2721. κατεφίστημι **katĕphistēmi**, *kat-ef-is´-tay-mee;* from 2596 and 2186; to *stand over against*, i.e. *rush upon* (*assault*):— make insurrection against.

2722. κατέχω **katĕchō**, *kat-ekh´-o;* from 2596 and 2192; to *hold down* (*fast*), in various applications (lit. or fig.):— have, hold (fast), keep (in memory), let, × make toward, possess, retain, seize on, stay, take, withhold.

2723. κατηγορέω **katēgŏrĕō**, *kat-ay-gor-eh´-o;* from 2725; to *be a plaintiff*, i.e. to *charge* with some offence:— accuse, object.

2724. κατηγορία **katēgŏria**, *kat-ay-gor-ee´-ah;* from 2725; a *complaint* ("category"), i.e. criminal *charge:*— accusation (× -ed).

2725. κατήγορος **katēgŏrŏs**, *kat-ay´-gor-os;* from 2596 and 58; *against* one in the *assembly*, i.e. a *complainant* at law; spec. *Satan:*— accuser.

2726. κατήφεια **katēphĕia**, *kat-ay´-fi-ah;* from a compound of 2596 and perh. a der. of the base of 5316 (mean. *downcast* in look); *demureness*, i.e. (by impl.) *sadness:*— heaviness.

2727. κατηχέω **katēchĕō**, *kat-ay-kheh´-o;* from 2596 and 2279; to *sound down* into the ears, i.e. (by impl.) to *indoctrinate* ("catechize") or (gen.) to *apprise* of:— inform, instruct, teach.

2728. κατιόω **katiŏō**, *kat-ee-ŏ´-o;* from 2596 and a der. of 2447; to *rust down*, i.e. *corrode:*— canker.

2729. κατισχύω **katischuō**, *kat-is-khoo´-o;* from 2596 and 2480; to *overpower:*— prevail (against).

2730. κατοικέω **katŏikĕō**, *kat-oy-keh´-o;* from 2596 and 3611; to *house permanently*, i.e. *reside* (lit. or fig.):— dwell (-er), inhabitant (-ter).

2731. κατοίκησις **katŏikēsis**, *kat-oy´-kay-sis;* from 2730; *residence* (prop. the act; but by impl. concr. the mansion):— dwelling.

2732. κατοικητήριον **katŏikētēriŏn**, *kat-oy-kay-tay´-ree-on;* from a der. of 2730; a *dwelling-place:*— habitation.

2733. κατοικία **katŏikia**, *kat-oy-kee´-ah; residence* (prop. the condition; but by impl. the abode itself):— habitation.

2734. κατοπτρίζομαι **katŏptrizŏmai**, *kat-op-trid´-zom-ahee;* mid. voice from a compound of 2596 and a der. of 3700 [comp. 2072]; to *mirror oneself*, i.e. to *see reflected* (fig.):— behold as in a glass.

2735. κατόρθωμα **katŏrthōma**, *kat-or´-tho-mah;* from a compound of 2596 and a der. of 3717 [comp. 1357]; something *made fully upright*, i.e. (fig.) *rectification* (spec. *good public administration*):— very worthy deed.

2736. κάτω **katō**, *kat´-o;* also (comparative)

κατωτέρω **katōtĕrō**, *kat-o-ter-o;* [comp. 2737]; adv. from 2596; *downwards:*— beneath, bottom, down, under.

2737. κατώτερος **katōtĕrŏs**, *kat-o´-ter-os;* comparative from 2736; *inferior* (locally, of Hades):— lower.

2738. καῦμα **kauma**, *kŏw´-mah;* from 2545; prop. a *burn* (concr.), but used (abstr.) of a *glow:*— heat.

2739. καυματίζω **kaumatizō**, *kŏw-mat-id´-zo;* from 2738; to *burn:*— scorch.

2740. καῦσις **kausis**, *kŏw´-sis;* from 2545; *burning* (the act):— be burned.

2741. καυσόω **kausŏō**, *kŏw-sŏ´-o;* from 2740; to *set on fire:*— with fervent heat.

2742. καύσων **kausōn**, *kŏw´-sone;* from 2741; a *glare:*— (burning) heat.

2743. καυτηριάζω **kautēriazō**, *kŏw-tay-ree-ad´-zo* or

καυστηριάζω **kaustēriazō** *kŏws-tay-ree-ad´-zo;* from a der. of 2545; to *brand* ("*cauterize*"), i.e. (by impl.) to *render unsensitive* (fig.):— sear with a hot iron.

2744. καυχάομαι **kauchaŏmai**, *kŏw-khah´-om-ahee;* from some (obsolete) base akin to that of αὐχέω **aucheō** (to *boast*) and 2172; to *vaunt* (in a good or a bad sense):— (make) boast, glory, joy, rejoice.

2745. καύχημα **kauchēma**, *kŏw´-khay-mah;* from 2744; a *boast* (prop. the obj.; by impl. the act) in a good or a bad sense:— boasting, (whereof) to glory (of), glorying, rejoice (-ing).

2746. καύχησις **kauchēsis**, *kŏw´-khay-sis;* from 2744; *boasting* (prop. the act; by impl. the obj.), in a good or a bad sense:— boasting, whereof I may glory, glorying, rejoicing.

2747. Κεγχρεαί **Kěgchrěai**, *keng-khreh-a´-hee;* prob. from κέγχρος **kěgchrŏs** (*millet*); *Cenchreæ*, a port of Corinth:— Cenchrea.

2748. Κεδρών **Kědrōn**, *ked-rone´;* of Heb. or. [6939]; *Cedron* (i.e. *Kidron*), a brook near Jerusalem:— Cedron.

2749. κεῖμαι **kěimai**, *ki´-mahee;* mid. voice of a primary verb; to *lie* outstretched (lit. or fig.):— be (appointed, laid up, made, set), lay, lie. Comp. 5087.

2750. κειρία **kěiria**, *ki-ree´-ah;* of uncert. aff.; a *swathe*, i.e. *winding-sheet:*— graveclothes.

2751. κείρω **kěirō**, *ki´-ro;* a primary verb; to *shear:*— shear (-er).

2752. κέλευμα **kělěuma**, *kel´-yoo-mah* or

κέλευσμα **kělěusma**, *kel´-yoos-mah;* from 2753; a *cry* of incitement:— shout.

2753. κελεύω **kělěuō**, *kel-yoo´-o;* from a primary κέλλω **kěllō** (to *urge* on); "hail;" to *incite* by word, i.e. *order:*— bid, (at, give) command (-ment).

2754. κενοδοξία **kěnŏdŏxia**, *ken-od-ox-ee´-ah;* from 2755; *empty glorying*, i.e. *self-conceit:*— vain-glory.

2755. κενόδοξος **kěnŏdŏxŏs**, *ken-od´-ox-os;* from 2756 and 1391; *vainly glorifying*, i.e. *self-conceited:*— desirous of vain-glory.

2756. κενός **kěnŏs**, *ken-os´;* appar. a primary word; *empty* (lit. or fig.):— empty, (in) vain.

2757. κενοφωνία **kěnŏphōnia**, *ken-of-o-nee´-ah;* from a presumed compound of 2756 and 5456; *empty sounding*, i.e. *fruitless discussion:*— vain.

2758. κενόω **kěnŏō**, *ken-ŏ´-o;* from 2756; to *make empty*, i.e. (fig.) to *abase, neutralize, falsify:*— make (of none effect, of no reputation, void), be in vain.

2759. κέντρον **kěntrŏn**, *ken´-tron;* from κεντέω **kěntěō** (to *prick*); a *point* ("centre"), i.e. a *sting* (fig. *poison*) or *goad* (fig. divine *impulse*):— prick, sting.

2760. κεντυρίων **kěnturiōn**, *ken-too-ree´-ohn;* of Lat. or.; a *centurion*, i.e. *captain* of one hundred soldiers:— centurion.

2761. κενῶς **kěnōs**, *ken-oce´;* adv. from 2756; *vainly*, i.e. *to no purpose:*— in vain.

2762. κεραία **kěraia**, *ker-ah´-yah;* fem. of a presumed der. of the base of 2768; something *horn-like*, i.e. (spec.) the *apex* of a Heb. letter (fig. the least *particle*):— tittle.

2763. κεραμεύς **kěraměus**, *ker-am-yooce´;* from 2766; a *potter:*— potter.

2764. κεραμικός **kěramikŏs**, *ker-am-ik-os´;* from 2766; *made of clay*, i.e. *earthen:*— of a potter.

2765. κεράμιον **kěramiŏn**, *ker-am´-ee-on;* neut. of a presumed der. of 2766; an *earthenware* vessel, i.e. *jar:*— pitcher.

2766. κέραμος **kěramŏs**, *ker´-am-os;* prob. from the base of 2767 (through the idea of *mixing* clay and water); *earthenware*, i.e. a *tile* (by anal. a thin *roof* or *awning*):— tiling.

2767. κεράννυμι **kěrannumi**, *ker-an´-noo-mee;* a prol. form of a more primary κεράω **kěraō**, *ker-ah´-o* (which is used in certain tenses); to *mingle*, i.e. (by impl.) to *pour* out (for drinking):— fill, pour out. Comp. 3396.

2768. κέρας **kěras**, *ker´-as;* from a primary κάρ **kar** (the *hair* of the head); a *horn* (lit. or fig.):— horn.

2769. κεράτιον **kěratiŏn**, *ker-at´-ee-on;* neut. of a presumed der. of 2768; something *horned*, i.e. (spec.) the *pod* of the carob-tree:— husk.

κεράω **kěraō**. See 2767.

2770. κερδαίνω **kěrdainō**, *ker-dah´-ee-no;* from 2771; to *gain* (lit. or fig.):— (get) gain, win.

2771. κέρδος **kěrdŏs**, *ker´-dos;* of uncert. aff.; *gain* (pecuniary or gen.):— gain, lucre.

2772. κέρμα **kěrma**, *ker´-mah;* from 2751; a *clipping* (bit), i.e. (spec.) a *coin:*— money.

2773. κερματιστής **kěrmatistēs**, *ker-mat-is-tace´;* from a der. of 2772; a *handler of coins*, i.e. *money-broker:*— changer of money.

2774. κεφάλαιον **kěphalaiŏn**, *kef-al´-ah-yon;* neut. of a der. of 2776; a *principal* thing, i.e. *main point;* spec. an *amount* (of money):— sum.

2775. κεφαλαιόω **kěphalaiŏō**, *kef-al-ahee-ŏ´-o;* from the same as 2774; (spec.) to *strike on the head:*— wound in the head.

2776. κεφαλή **kěphalē**, *kef-al-ay´;* prob. from the primary κάπτω **kaptō** (in the sense of *seizing*); the *head* (as the part most readily *taken* hold of), lit. or fig.:— head.

2777. κεφαλίς **kěphalis**, *kef-al-is´;* from 2776; prop. a *knob*, i.e. (by impl.) a *roll* (by extens. from the *end* of a stick on which the MS. was rolled):— volume.

2778. κῆνσος **kēnsŏs**, *kane´-sos;* of Lat. or.;

prop. an *enrollment* ("*census*"), i.e. (by impl.) a *tax*:— tribute.

2779. κῆπος **kēpŏs**, *kay´-pos;* of uncert. aff.; a *garden:*— garden.

2780. κηπουρός **kēpŏurŏs**, *kay-poo-ros´;* from *2779* and οὖρος **ŏurŏs** (a *warden*); a *garden-keeper,* i.e. *gardener:*— gardener.

2781. κηρίον **kēriŏn**, *kay-ree´-on;* dimin. from κηός **kēŏs** (*wax*); a *cell* for honey, i.e. (collect.) the *comb:*— [honey-] comb.

2782. κήρυγμα **kērugma**, *kay´-roog-mah;* from *2784;* a *proclamation* (espec. of the gospel; by impl. the *gospel* itself):— preaching.

2783. κῆρυξ **kērux**, *kay´-roox;* from *2784;* a *herald,* i.e. of divine truth (espec. of the gospel):— preacher.

2784. κηρύσσω **kērussō**, *kay-roos´-so;* of uncert. aff.; to *herald* (as a public *crier*), espec. divine truth (the gospel):— preacher (-er), proclaim, publish.

2785. κῆτος **kētŏs**, *kay´-tos;* prob. from the base of *5490;* a huge *fish* (as *gaping* for prey):— whale.

2786. Κηφᾶς **Kēphas**, *kay-fas´;* of Chald. or. [comp. 3710]; *the Rock; Cephas* (i.e. *Kepha*), a surname of Peter:— Cephas.

2787. κιβωτός **kibōtŏs**, *kib-o-tos´;* of uncert. der.; a *box,* i.e. the sacred *ark* and that of Noah:— ark.

2788. κιθάρα **kithara**, *kith-ar´-ah;* of uncert. aff.; a *lyre:*— harp.

2789. κιθαρίζω **kitharizō**, *kith-ar-id´-zo;* from *2788;* to *play on a lyre:*— harp.

2790. κιθαρῳδός **kitharŏidŏs**, *kith-ar-o´-dos;* from *2788* and a der. of the same as *5603;* a *lyre-singer* (-*player*), i.e. *harpist:*— harper.

2791. Κιλικία **Kilikia**, *kil-ik-ee´-ah;* prob. of for. or.; *Cilicia,* a region of Asia Minor:— Cilicia.

2792. κινάμωμον **kinamōmŏn**, *kin-am´-o-mon;* of for. or. [comp. 7076]; *cinnamon:*— cinnamon.

2793. κινδυνεύω **kinduněuō**, *kin-doon-yoo´-o;* from *2794;* to *undergo peril:*— be in danger, be (stand) in jeopardy.

2794. κίνδυνος **kindunŏs**, *kin´-doo-nos;* of uncert. der.; *danger:*— peril.

2795. κινέω **kinĕō**, *kin-eh´-o;* from κίω **kiō** (poetic for εἶμι **ĕimi**, to *go*); to *stir* (tran.), lit. or fig.:— (re-) move (-r), way.

2796. κίνησις **kinēsis**, *kin´-ay-sis;* from *2795;* a *stirring:*— moving.

2797. Κίς **Kis**, *kis;* of Heb. or. [7027]; *Cis* (i.e. *Kish*), an Isr.:— Cis.

κίχρημι **kichrēmi**. See *5531.*

2798. κλάδος **kladŏs**, *klad´-os;* from *2806;* a *twig* or *bough* (as if broken off):— branch.

2799. κλαίω **klaiō**, *klah´-yo;* of uncert. aff.; to *sob,* i.e. *wail* aloud (whereas *1145* is rather to *cry* silently):— bewail, weep.

2800. κλάσις **klasis**, *klas´-is;* from *2806; fracture* (the act):— breaking.

2801. κλάσμα **klasma**, *klas´-mah;* from *2806;* a *piece* (*bit*):— broken, fragment.

2802. Κλαύδη **Klaudē**, *klŏw´-day* or

Καύδη **Kaudē** *kŏw´-day;* of uncert. der.; *Claude,* an island near Crete:— Clauda (Cauda).

2803. Κλαυδία **Klaudia**, *klŏw-dee´-ah;* fem. of *2804; Claudia,* a Chr. woman:— Claudia.

2804. Κλαύδιος **Klaudiŏs**, *klŏw´-dee-os;* of Lat. or.; *Claudius,* the name of two Romans:— Claudius.

2805. κλαυθμός **klauthmŏs**, *klŏwth-mos´;* from *2799; lamentation:*— wailing, weeping, × wept.

2806. κλάω **klaō**, *klah´-o;* a primary verb; to *break* (spec. of bread):— break.

2807. κλείς **klĕis**, *klice;* from *2808;* a *key* (as *shutting* a lock), lit. or fig.:— key.

2808. κλείω **klĕiō**, *kli´-o;* a primary verb; to *close* (lit. or fig.):— shut (up).

2809. κλέμμα **klĕmma**, *klem´-mah;* from *2813; stealing* (prop. the thing stolen, but used of the act):— theft.

2810. Κλεόπας **Klĕŏpas**, *kleh-op´-as;* prob. contr. from Κλεόπατρος **Klĕŏpatrŏs** (compound of *2811* and *3962*); *Cleopas,* a Chr.:— Cleopas.

2811. κλέος **klĕŏs**, *kleh´-os;* from a short. form of *2564; renown* (as if *being called*):— glory.

2812. κλέπτης **klĕptēs**, *klep´-tace;* from *2813;* a *stealer* (lit. or fig.):— thief. Comp. *3027.*

2813. κλέπτω **klĕptō**, *klep´-to;* a primary verb; to *filch:*— steal.

2814. κλῆμα **klēma**, *klay´-mah;* from *2806;* a *limb* or *shoot* (as if *broken* off):— branch.

2815. Κλήμης **Klēmēs**, *klay´-mace;* of Lat. or.; *merciful; Clemes* (i.e. *Clemens*), a Chr.:— Clement.

2816. κληρονομέω **klērŏnŏmĕō**, *klay-ron-om-eh´-o;* from *2818;* to *be an heir* to (lit. or fig.):— be heir, (obtain by) inherit (-ance).

2817. κληρονομία **klērŏnŏmia**, *klay-ron-om-ee´-ah;* from *2818; heirship,* i.e. (concr.) a *patrimony* or (gen.) a *possession:*— inheritance.

2818. κληρονόμος **klērŏnŏmŏs**, *klay-ron-om´-os;* from *2819* and the base of *3551* (in its orig. sense of *partitioning,* i.e. [refl.] *getting* by apportionment); a *sharer by lot,* i.e. *inheritor* (lit. or fig.); by impl. a *possessor:*— heir.

2819. κλῆρος **klērŏs**, *klay´-ros;* prob. from *2806* (through the idea of using *bits* of wood, etc., for the purpose); a *die* (for drawing chances); by impl. a *portion* (as if so secured); by extens. an *acquisition* (espec. a *patrimony*, fig.):— heritage, inheritance, lot, part.

2820. κληρόω **klērŏŏ**, *klay-rŏ´-o*; from *2819;* to *allot*, i.e. (fig.) to *assign* (a privilege):— obtain an inheritance.

2821. κλῆσις **klēsis**, *klay´-sis;* from a shorter form of *2564;* an *invitation* (fig.):— calling.

2822. κλητός **klētŏs**, *klay-tos´;* from the same as *2821; invited*, i.e. *appointed*, or (spec.) a *saint:*— called.

2823. κλίβανος **klibanŏs**, *klib´-an-os;* of uncert. der.; an earthen *pot* used for baking in:— oven.

2824. κλίμα **klima**, *klee´-mah;* from *2827;* a *slope*, i.e. (spec.) a *"clime"* or *tract* of country:— part, region.

2825. κλίνη **klinē**, *klee´-nay;* from *2827;* a *couch* (for sleep, sickness, sitting or eating):— bed, table.

2826. κλινίδιον **klinidiŏn**, *kleen-eed´-ee-on;* neut. of a presumed der. of *2825;* a *pallet* or *little couch:*— bed.

2827. κλίνω **klinō**, *klee´-no;* a primary verb; to *slant* or *slope*, i.e. *incline* or *recline* (lit. or fig.):— bow (down), be far spent, lay, turn to flight, wear away.

2828. κλισία **klisia**, *klee-see´-ah;* from a der. of *2827; prop. reclination*, i.e. (concr. and spec.) a *party* at a meal:— company.

2829. κλοπή **klŏpē**, *klop-ay´;* from *2813; stealing:*— theft.

2830. κλύδων **kludōn**, *kloo´-dohn;* from κλύζω **kluzo** (to *billow* or *dash* over); a *surge* of the sea (lit. or fig.):— raging, wave.

2831. κλυδωνίζομαι **kludōnizŏmai**, *kloo-do-nid´-zom-ahee;* mid. voice from *2830;* to *surge*, i.e. (fig.) to *fluctuate:*— toss to and fro.

2832. Κλωπᾶς **Klōpas**, *klo-pas´;* of Chald. or. (corresp. to *256);* Clopas, an Isr.:— Clopas.

2833. κνήθω **knēthō**, *knay´-tho;* from a primary κνάω **knaō** (to *scrape*); to *scratch*, i.e. (by impl.) to *tickle:*— × itching.

2834. Κνίδος **Knidos**, *knee´-dos;* prob. of for. or.; Cnidus, a place in Asia Minor:— Cnidus.

2835. κοδράντης **kŏdrantēs**, *kod-ran´-tace;* of Lat. or.; a *quadrans*, i.e. the fourth part of an as:— farthing.

2836. κοιλία **kŏilia**, *koy-lee´-ah;* from κοῖλος **kŏilŏs** (*"hollow"*); a *cavity*, i.e. (spec.) the *abdomen;* by impl. the *matrix;* fig. the *heart:*— belly, womb.

2837. κοιμάω **kŏimaō**, *koy-mah´-o;* from *2749;* to *put to sleep*, i.e. (pass. or refl.) to *slumber;* fig. to *decease:*— (be a-, fall a-, fall on) sleep, be dead.

2838. κοίμησις **kŏimēsis**, *koy´-may-sis;* from

2837; sleeping, i.e. (by impl.) *repose:*— taking of rest.

2839. κοινός **kŏinŏs**, *koy-nos´;* prob. from *4862; common*, i.e. (lit.) shared by all or several, or (cer.) *profane:*— common, defiled, unclean, unholy.

2840. κοινόω **kŏinŏō**, *koy-nŏ´-o;* from *2839;* to *make* (or *consider*) *profane* (ceremon.):— call common, defile, pollute, unclean.

2841. κοινωνέω **kŏinōnĕō**, *koy-no-neh´-o;* from *2844;* to *share* with others (obj. or subj.):— communicate, distribute, be partaker.

2842. κοινωνία **kŏinōnia**, *koy-nohn-ee´-ah;* from *2844; partnership*, i.e. (lit.) *participation*, or (social) *intercourse*, or (pecuniary) *benefaction:*— (to) communicate (-ation), communion, (contri-) distribution, fellowship.

2843. κοινωνικός **kŏinōnikŏs**, *koy-no-nee-kos´;* from *2844; communicative*, i.e. (pecuniarily) *liberal:*— willing to communicate.

2844. κοινωνός **kŏinōnŏs**, *koy-no-nos´;* from *2839;* a *sharer*, i.e. *associate:*— companion, × fellowship, partaker, partner.

2845. κοίτη **kŏitē**, *koy´-tay;* from *2749;* a *couch;* by extens. *cohabitation;* by impl. the male *sperm:*— bed, chambering, × conceive.

2846. κοιτών **kŏitōn**, *koy-tone´;* from *2845;* a *bedroom:*— + chamberlain.

2847. κόκκινος **kŏkkinŏs**, *kok´-kee-nos;* from *2848* (from the *kernel*-shape of the insect); *crimson*-colored:— scarlet (colour, coloured).

2848. κόκκος **kŏkkŏs**, *kok´-kos;* appar. a primary word; a *kernel* of seed:— corn, grain.

2849. κολάζω **kŏlazō**, *kol-ad´-zo;* from κόλος **kŏlos** (*dwarf*); prop. to *curtail*, i.e. (fig.) to *chastise* (or *reserve* for infliction):— punish.

2850. κολακεία **kŏlakĕia**, *kol-ak-i´-ah;* from a der. of κόλαξ **kŏlax** (a *fawner*); *flattery:*— × flattering.

2851. κόλασις **kŏlasis**, *kol´-as-is;* from *2849;* penal *infliction:*— punishment, torment.

2852. κολαφίζω **kŏlaphizō**, *kol-af-id´-zo;* from a der. of the base of *2849;* to *rap* with the fist:— buffet.

2853. κολλάω **kŏllaō**, *kol-lah´-o;* from κόλλα **kŏlla** (*"glue"*); to *glue*, i.e. (pass. or refl.) to *stick* (fig.):— cleave, join (self), keep company.

2854. κολλούριον **kŏllŏuriŏn**, *kol-loo´-ree-on;* neut. of a presumed der. of κολλύρα **kŏllura** (a *cake;* prob akin to the base of *2853*); prop. a *poultice* (as made of or in the form

Greek

of *crackers*), i.e. (by anal.) a *plaster:*— eyesalve.

2855. κολλυβιστής **kŏllubistēs**, *kol-loo-bis-tace´;* from a presumed der. of κόλλυβος **kŏllubŏs** (a small *coin;* prob. akin to 2854); a *coin-dealer:*— (money-) changer.

2856. κολοβόω **kŏlŏbŏō**, *kol-ob-ŏ´-o;* from a der. of the base of 2849; to *dock,* i.e. (fig.) *abridge:*— shorten.

2857. Κολοσσαί **Kŏlŏssai**, *kol-os-sah´-ee;* appar. fem. plur. of κολοσσός **kŏlŏssŏs** ("*colossal*"); *Colossæ,* a place in Asia Minor:— Colosse.

2858. Κολοσσαεύς **Kŏlŏssaĕus**, *kol-os-sayoos´;* from 2857; a *Colossæan,* (i.e. inhab. of Colossæ:— Colossian.

2859. κόλπος **kŏlpŏs**, *kol´-pos;* appar. a primary word; the *bosom;* by anal. a *bay:*— bosom, creek.

2860. κολυμβάω **kŏlumbaō**, *kol-oom-bah´-o;* from κόλυμβος **kŏlumbŏs** (a *diver*); to *plunge* into water:— swim.

2861. κολυμβήθρα **kŏlumbēthra**, *kol-oom-bay´-thrah;* from 2860; a *diving-place,* i.e. *pond* for bathing (or swimming):— pool.

2862. κολωνία **kŏlōnia**, *kol-o-nee´-ah;* of Lat. or.; a Rom. "*colony*" for veterans:— colony.

2863. κομάω **kŏmaō**, *kom-ah´-o;* from 2864; to *wear tresses* of hair:— have long hair.

2864. κόμη **kŏmē**, *kom´-ay;* appar. from the same as 2865; the *hair* of the head (*locks,* as *ornamental,* and thus differing from 2359; which prop. denotes merely the *scalp*):— hair.

2865. κομίζω **kŏmizō**, *kom-id´-zo;* from a primary κομέω **kŏmĕō** (to *tend,* i.e. take care of); prop. to *provide* for, i.e. (by impl.) to *carry* off (as if from harm; generally *obtain*):— bring, receive.

2866. κομψότερον **kŏmpsŏtĕrŏn**, *komp-sot´-er-on;* neut. comparative of a der. of the base of 2865 (mean. prop. *well dressed,* i.e. *nice*); fig. *convalescent:*— + began to amend.

2867. κονιάω **kŏniaō**, *kon-ee-ah´-o;* from κονία **kŏnia** (*dust;* by anal. *lime*); to *whitewash:*— whiten.

2868. κονιορτός **kŏniŏrtŏs**, *kon-ee-or-tos´;* from the base of 2867 and ὄρνυμι **ŏrnumi** (to "*rouse*"); *pulverulence* (as *blown* about):— dust.

2869. κοπάζω **kŏpazō**, *kop-ad´-zo;* from 2873; to *tire,* i.e. (fig.) to *relax:*— cease.

2870. κοπετός **kŏpĕtŏs**, *kop-et-os´;* from 2875; *mourning* (prop. by *beating* the breast):— lamentation.

2871. κοπή **kŏpē**, *kop-ay´;* from 2875; *cutting,* i.e. *carnage:*— slaughter.

2872. κοπιάω **kŏpiaō**, *kop-ee-ah´-o;* from a der. of 2873; to *feel fatigue;* by impl. to *work hard:*— (bestow) labour, toil, be wearied.

2873. κόπος **kŏpŏs**, *kop´-os;* from 2875; a *cut,* i.e. (by anal.) *toil* (as *reducing* the strength), lit. or fig.; by impl. *pains:*— labour, + trouble, weariness.

2874. κοπρία **kŏpria**, *kop-ree´-ah;* from κόπρος **kŏprŏs** (*ordure;* perh. akin to 2875); *manure:*— dung (-hill).

2875. κόπτω **kŏptō**, *kop´-to;* a primary verb; to "*chop;*" spec. to *beat* the breast in grief:— cut down, lament, mourn, (be-) wail. Comp. the base of 5114.

2876. κόραξ **kŏrax**, *kor´-ax;* perh. from 2880; a *crow* (from its *voracity*):— raven.

2877. κοράσιον **kŏrasiŏn**, *kor-as´-ee-on;* neut. of a presumed der. of κόρη **kŏrē** (a *maiden*); a (little) *girl:*— damsel, maid.

2878. κορβᾶν **kŏrban**, *kor-ban´;* and

κορβανᾶς **kŏrbanas**, *kor-ban-as´;* of Heb. and Chald. or. respectively [7133]; a votive *offering* and *the offering;* a consecrated *present* (to the Temple fund); by extens. (the latter term) the *Treasury* itself, i.e. the room where the contribution boxes stood:— Corban, treasury.

2879. Κορέ **Kŏrĕ**, *kor-eh´;* of Heb. or. [7141]; *Corë* (i.e. *Korach*), an Isr.:— Core.

2880. κορέννυμι **kŏrĕnnumi**, *kor-en´-noo-mee;* a primary verb; to *cram,* i.e. *glut* or *sate:*— eat enough, full.

2881. Κορίνθιος **Kŏrinthiŏs**, *kor-in´-thee-os;* from 2882; a *Corinthian,* i.e. inhab. of Corinth:— Corinthian.

2882. Κόρινθος **Kŏrinthŏs**, *kor´-in-thos;* of uncert. der.; *Corinthus,* a city of Greece:— Corinth.

2883. Κορνήλιος **Kŏrnĕliŏs**, *kor-nay´-lee-os;* of Lat. or.; *Cornelius,* a Rom.:— Cornelius.

2884. κόρος **kŏrŏs**, *kor-os;* of Heb. or. [3734]; a *cor,* i.e. a spec. measure:— measure.

2885. κοσμέω **kŏsmĕō**, *kos-meh´-o;* from 2889; to *put in* proper *order,* i.e. *decorate* (lit. or fig.); spec. to *snuff* (a wick):— adorn, garnish, trim.

2886. κοσμικός **kŏsmikŏs**, *kos-mee-kos´;* from 2889 (in its second. sense); *terrene* ("*cosmic*"), lit. (*mundane*) or fig. (*corrupt*):— worldly.

2887. κόσμιος **kŏsmiŏs**, *kos´-mee-os;* from 2889 (in its primary sense); *orderly,* i.e. *decorous:*— of good behaviour, modest.

2888. κοσμοκράτωρ **kŏsmŏkratōr**, *kos-mok-rat´-ore;* from 2889 and 2902; a *world-ruler,* an epithet of Satan:— ruler.

2889. κόσμος **kŏsmŏs**, *kos´-mos;* prob. from the base of 2865; orderly *arrangement,* i.e. *decoration;* by impl. the *world* (in a wide or narrow sense, incl. its inhab., lit. or fig. [mor.]):— adorning, world.

2890. Κούαρτος **Kŏuartŏs**, *koo´-ar-tos;* of

Lat. or. (*fourth*); *Quartus*, a Chr.:— Quartus.

2891. κοῦμι **kŏumi**, *koo´-mee* or κουμ **koum**, *koom´*; of Chald. origin [6966]; *cumi* (i.e. *rise!*):— cumi.

2892. κουστωδία **kŏustōdia**, *koos-to-dee´-ah;* of Lat. or.; "*custody,*" i.e. a Rom. *sentry:*— watch.

2893. κουφίζω **kŏuphizō**, *koo-fid´-zo;* from κοῦφος **kŏuphŏs** (*light* in weight); to *unload:*— lighten.

2894. κόφινος **kŏphinŏs**, *kof´-ee-nos;* of uncert. der.; a (small) *basket:*— basket.

2895. κράββατος **krabbatŏs**, *krab´-bat-os;* prob. of for. or.; a *mattress:*— bed.

2896. κράζω **krazō**, *krad´-zo;* a primary verb; prop. to "*croak*" (as a raven) or *scream*, i.e. (gen.) to *call* aloud (*shriek, exclaim, intreat*):— cry (out).

2897. κραιπάλη **kraipalē**, *krahee-pal´-ay;* prob. from the same as *726;* prop. a *headache* (as a *seizure* of pain) from drunkenness, i.e. (by impl.) a *debauch* (by anal. a *glut*):— surfeiting.

2898. κρανίον **kraniŏn**, *kran-ee-on;* dimin. of a der. of the base of *2768;* a *skull* ("*cranium*"):— Calvary, skull.

2899. κράσπεδον **kraspĕdŏn**, *kras´-ped-on;* of uncert. der.; a *margin*, i.e. (spec.) a *fringe* or *tassel:*— border, hem.

2900. κραταιός **krataiŏs**, *krat-ah-yos´;* from *2904; powerful:*— mighty.

2901. κραταιόω **krataiŏō**, *krat-ah-yŏ´-o;* from *2900;* to *empower*, i.e. (pass.) *increase in vigor:*— be strengthened, be (wax) strong.

2902. κρατέω **kratĕō**, *krat-eh´-o;* from *2904;* to *use strength*, i.e. *seize* or *retain* (lit. or fig.):— hold (by, fast), keep, lay hand (hold) on, obtain, retain, take (by).

2903. κράτιστος **kratistŏs**, *krat´-is-tos;* superl. of a der. of *2904; strongest*, i.e. (in dignity) *very honorable:*— most excellent (noble).

2904. κράτος **kratŏs**, *krat´-os;* perh. a primary word; *vigor* ["great"] (lit. or fig.):— dominion, might [-ily], power, strength.

2905. κραυγάζω **kraugazō**, *krŏw-gad´-zo;* from *2906;* to *clamor:*— cry out.

2906. κραυγή **kraugē**, *krŏw-gay´;* from *2896;* an *outcry* (in notification, tumult or grief):— clamour, cry (-ing).

2907. κρέας **krĕas**, *kreh´-as;* perh. a primary word; (butcher's) *meat:*— flesh.

2908. κρεῖσσον **krĕissŏn**, *krice´-son;* neut. of an alt. form of *2909;* (as noun) *better*, i.e. *greater advantage:*— better.

2909. κρείττων **krĕittōn**, *krite´-tohn;* comparative of a der. of *2904; stronger*, i.e. (fig.) *better*, i.e. *nobler:*— best, better.

2910. κρεμάννυμι **krĕmannumi**, *krem-an´-noo-mee;* a prol. form of a primary verb; to *hang:*— hang.

2911. κρημνός **krēmnŏs**, *krame-nos´;* from *2910; overhanging*, i.e. a *precipice:*— steep place.

2912. Κρής **Krēs**, *krace;* from *2914;* a *Cretan*, i.e. inhab. of Crete:— Crete, Cretian.

2913. Κρήσκης **Krēskēs**, *krace´-kace;* of Lat. or.; *growing; Cresces* (i.e. *Crescens*), a Chr.:— Crescens.

2914. Κρήτη **Krētē**, *kray´-tay;* of uncert. der.; *Cretë*, an island in the Mediterranean:— Crete.

2915. κριθή **krithē**, *kree-thay´;* of uncert. der.; *barley:*— barley.

2916. κρίθινος **krithinŏs**, *kree´-thee-nos;* from *2915;* consisting of *barley:*— barley.

2917. κρίμα **krima**, *kree´-mah;* from *2919;* a *decision* (the function or the effect, for or against ["crime"]):— avenge, condemned, condemnation, damnation, + go to law, judgment.

2918. κρίνον **krinŏn**, *kree´-non;* perh. a prim word; a *lily:*— lily.

2919. κρίνω **krinō**, *kree´-no;* prop. to *distinguish*, i.e. *decide* (mentally or judicially); by impl. to *try, condemn, punish:*— avenge, conclude, condemn, damn, decree, determine, esteem, judge, go to (sue at the) law, ordain, call in question, sentence to, think.

2920. κρίσις **krisis**, *kree´-sis;* decision (subj. or obj., for or against); by extens. a *tribunal;* by impl. *justice* (spec. divine *law*):— accusation, condemnation, damnation, judgment.

2921. Κρίσπος **Krispŏs**, *kris´-pos;* of Lat. or.; "*crisp*"; *Crispus*, a Corinthian:— Crispus.

2922. κριτήριον **kritēriŏn**, *kree-tay´-ree-on;* neut. of a presumed der. of *2923;* a *rule* of judging ("*criterion*"), i.e. (by impl.) a *tribunal:*— to judge, judgment (seat).

2923. κριτής **kritēs**, *kree-tace´;* from *2919;* a *judge* (gen. or spec.):— judge.

2924. κριτικός **kritikŏs**, *krit-ee-kos´;* from *2923; decisive* ("*critical*"), i.e. *discriminative:*— discerner.

2925. κρούω **krŏuō**, *kroo´-o;* appar. a primary verb; to *rap:*— knock.

2926. κρυπτή **kruptē**, *kroop-tay´;* fem. of *2927;* a *hidden* place, i.e. *cellar* ("*crypt*"):— secret.

2927. κρυπτός **kruptŏs**, *kroop-tos´;* from *2928; concealed*, i.e. *private:*— hid (-den), inward [-ly], secret.

2928. κρύπτω **kruptō**, *kroop´-to;* a primary verb; to *conceal* (prop. by *covering*):— hide (self), keep secret, secret [-ly].

2929. κρυσταλλίζω **krustallizō**, *kroos-tallid´-zo;* from *2930;* to *make* (i.e. intr. *resemble*) *ice* ("*crystallize*"):— be clear as crystal.

2930. κρύσταλλος **krustallŏs**, *kroos´-tal-los;* from a der. of κρύος **kruos** (*frost*); *ice,* i.e. (by anal.) rock "*crystal*":— crystal.

2931. κρυφῇ **kruphē**, *kroo-fay´;* adv. from 2928; *privately:—* in secret.

2932. κτάομαι **ktaŏmai**, *ktah´-om-ahee;* a primary verb; to *get,* i.e. *acquire* (by any means; *own*):— obtain, possess, provide, purchase.

2933. κτῆμα **ktēma**, *ktay´-mah;* from 2932; an *acquirement,* i.e. *estate:—* possession.

2934. κτῆνος **ktēnŏs**, *ktay´-nos;* from 2932; *property,* i.e. (spec.) a domestic *animal:—* beast.

2935. κτήτωρ **ktētōr**, *ktay´-tore;* from 2932; an *owner:—* possessor.

2936. κτίζω **ktizō**, *ktid´-zo;* prob. akin to 2932 (through the idea of *proprietorship* of the *manufacturer*); to *fabricate,* i.e. *found* (*form orig.*):— create, Creator, make.

2937. κτίσις **ktisis**, *ktis´-is;* from 2936; orig. *formation* (prop. the act; by impl. the thing, lit. or fig.):— building, creation, creature, ordinance.

2938. κτίσμα **ktisma**, *ktis´-mah;* from 2936; an orig. *formation* (concr.), i.e. *product* (created thing):— creature.

2939. κτιστής **ktistēs**, *ktis-tace´;* from 2936; a *founder,* i.e. *God* (as author of all things):— Creator.

2940. κυβεία **kubĕia**, *koo-bi´-ah;* from κύβος **kubŏs** (a "*cube,*" i.e. *die* for playing); *gambling,* i.e. (fig.) *artifice* or *fraud:—* sleight.

2941. κυβέρνησις **kubĕrnēsis**, *koo-ber´-nay-sis;* from κυβερνάω **kubĕrnaō** (of Lat. or., to *steer*); *pilotage,* i.e. (fig.) *directorship* (in the church):— government.

2942. κυβερνήτης **kubĕrnētēs**, *koo-ber-nay´-tace;* from the same as 2941; *helmsman,* i.e. (by impl.) *captain:—* (ship) master.

2943. κυκλόθεν **kuklŏthĕn**, *koo-kloth´-en;* adv. from the same as 2945; *from the circle,* i.e. *all around:—* (round) about.

κυκλός **kuklŏs**. See 2945.

2944. κυκλόω **kuklŏō**, *koo-klŏ´-o;* from the same as 2945; to *encircle,* i.e. *surround:—* compass (about), come (stand) round about.

2945. κύκλῳ **kuklō̦i**, *koo´-klo;* as if dat. of κύκλος **kuklŏs** (a *ring,* "*cycle*"; akin to 2947); i.e. *in a circle* (by impl. of 1722), i.e. (adv.) *all around:—* round about.

2946. κύλισμα **kulisma**, *koo´-lis-mah;* from 2947; a *wallow* (the effect of *rolling*), i.e. *filth:—* wallowing.

2947. κυλιόω **kuliŏō**, *koo-lee-ŏ´-o;* from the base of 2949 (through the idea of *circularity;* comp. 2945, 1507); to *roll* about:— wallow.

2948. κυλλός **kullŏs**, *kool-los´;* from the same as 2947; *rocking* about, i.e. *crippled* (*maimed,* in feet or hands):— maimed.

2949. κῦμα **kuma**, *koo´-mah;* from κύω **kuō** (to *swell* [with young], i.e. *bend, curve*); a *billow* (as *bursting* or *toppling*):— wave.

2950. κύμβαλον **kumbalŏn**, *koom´-bal-on;* from a der. of the base of 2949; a "*cymbal*" (as *hollow*):— cymbal.

2951. κύμινον **kuminŏn**, *koo´-min-on;* of for. or. [comp. 3646]; *dill* or *fennel* ("cummin"):— cummin.

2952. κυνάριον **kunariŏn**, *koo-nar´-ee-on;* neut. of a presumed der. of 2965; a *puppy:—* dog.

2953. Κύπριος **Kupriŏs**, *koo´-pree-os;* from 2954; a *Cyprian* (*Cypriot*), i.e. inhab. of Cyprus:— of Cyprus.

2954. Κύπρος **Kuprŏs**, *koo´-pros;* of uncert. or.; *Cyprus,* an island in the Mediterranean:— Cyprus.

2955. κύπτω **kuptō**, *koop´-to;* prob. from the base of 2949; to *bend forward:—* stoop (down).

2956. Κυρηναῖος **Kurēnaiŏs**, *koo-ray-nah´-yos;* from 2957; i.e. *Cyrenæan,* i.e. inhab. of Cyrene:— of Cyrene, Cyrenian.

2957. Κυρήνη **Kurēnē**, *koo-ray´-nay;* of uncert. der.; *Cyrenë,* a region of Africa:— Cyrene.

2958. Κυρήνιος **Kurēniŏs**, *koo-ray´-nee-os;* of Lat. or.; *Cyrenius* (i.e. *Quirinus*), a Rom.:— Cyrenius.

2959. Κυρία **Kuria**, *koo-ree´-ah;* fem. of 2962; *Cyria,* a Chr. woman:— lady.

2960. κυριακός **kuriakŏs**, *koo-ree-ak-os´;* from 2962; *belonging to the Lord* (Jehovah or Jesus):— Lord's.

2961. κυριεύω **kuriĕuō**, *koo-ree-yoo´-o;* from 2962; to *rule:—* have dominion over, lord, be lord of, exercise lordship over.

2962. κύριος **kuriŏs**, *koo´-ree-os;* from κῦρος **kurŏs** (*supremacy*); *supreme* in authority, i.e. (as noun) *controller;* by impl. *Mr.* (as a respectful title):— God, Lord, master, Sir.

2963. κυριότης **kuriŏtēs**, *koo-ree-ot´-ace;* from 2962; *mastery,* i.e. (concr. and collect.) *rulers:—* dominion, government.

2964. κυρόω **kurŏō**, *koo-rŏ´-o;* from the same as 2962; to *make authoritative,* i.e. *ratify:—* confirm.

2965. κύων **kuōn**, *koo´-ohn;* a primary word; a *dog* ["*hound*"] (lit. or fig.):— dog.

2966. κῶλον **kōlŏn**, *ko´-lon;* from the base of 2849; a *limb* of the body (as if *lopped*):— carcase (carcass).

2967. κωλύω **kōluō**, *ko-loo´-o;* from the base of 2849; to *estop,* i.e. *prevent* (by word or act):— forbid, hinder, keep from, let, not suffer, withstand.

2968. κώμη **kōmē**, *ko´-may;* from 2749; a *hamlet* (as if *laid* down):— town, village.

2969. κωμόπολις **kōmŏpŏlis**, *ko-mop´-ol-is;* from 2968 and 4172; an unwalled *city:*— town.

2970. κῶμος **kōmŏs**, *ko´-mos;* from 2749; a ca-rousal (as if *letting loose*):— revelling, rioting.

2971. κώνωψ **kōnōps**, *ko´-nopes;* appar. a der. of the base of 2759 and a der. of 3700; a *mos-quito* (from its *stinging proboscis*):— gnat.

2972. Κῶς **Kōs**, *koce;* of uncert. or.; *Cos,* an island in the Mediterranean:— Cos.

2973. Κωσάμ **Kōsam**, *ko-sam´;* of Heb. or. [comp. 7081]; *Cosam* (i.e. *Kosam*) an Isr.:— Cosam.

2974. κωφός **kōphŏs**, *ko-fos´;* from 2875; *blunted,* i.e. (fig.) of hearing (*deaf*) or speech (*dumb*):— deaf, dumb, speechless.

Λ

2975. λαγχάνω **lagchanō**, *lang-khan´-o;* a prol. form of a primary verb, which is only used as an alt. in certain tenses; to *lot,* i.e. *determine* (by impl. *receive*) espec. by lot:— his lot be, cast lots, obtain.

2976. Λάζαρος **Lazarŏs**, *lad´-zar-os;* prob. of Heb. or. [499]; *Lazarus* (i.e. *Elazar*), the name of two Isr. (one imaginary):— Lazarus.

2977. λάθρα **lathra**, *lath´-rah;* adv. from 2990; *privately:*— privily, secretly.

2978. λαῖλαψ **lailaps**, *lah´-ee-laps;* of uncert. der.; a *whirlwind* (*squall*):— storm, tempest.

2979. λακτίζω **laktizō**, *lak-tid´-zo;* from adv. λάξ lax (*heelwise*); to *recalcitrate:*— kick.

2980. λαλέω **laleō**, *lal-eh´-o;* a prol. form of an otherwise obs. verb; to *talk,* i.e. *utter* words:— preach, say, speak (after), talk, tell, utter. Comp. 3004.

2981. λαλιά **lalia**, *lal-ee-ah´;* from 2980; *talk:*— saying, speech.

2982. λαμά **lama**, *lam-ah´;* or

λαμμά **lamma**, *lam-mah´;* or

λεμά **lĕma**, *leh-mah´;* of Heb. or. [4100 with prep. pref.]; *lama* (i.e. *why*):— lama.

2983. λαμβάνω **lambanō**, *lam-ban´-o;* a prol. form of a primary verb, which is use only as an alt. in certain tenses; to *take* (in very many applications, lit. and fig. [properly obj. or act., to *get hold* of; whereas 1209 is rather subj. or pass., to *have offered* to one; while 138 is more violent, to *seize* or *remove*]):— accept, + be amazed, assay, attain, bring, × when I call, catch, come on (× unto), + forget, have, hold, obtain, receive (× after), take (away, up).

2984. Λάμεχ **Lamĕch**, *lam´-ekh;* of Heb. or. [3929]; *Lamech* (i.e. *Lemek*), a patriarch:— Lamech.

λαμμᾶ **lamma**. See 2982.

2985. λαμπάς **lampas**, *lam-pas´;* from 2989; a "*lamp*" or *flambeau:*— lamp, light, torch.

2986. λαμπρός **lamprŏs**, *lam-pros´;* from the same as 2985; *radiant;* by anal. *limpid;* fig. *magnificent* or *sumptuous* (in appear-ance):— bright, clear, gay, goodly, gor-geous, white.

2987. λαμπρότης **lamprŏtēs**, *lam-prot´-ace;* from 2986; *brilliancy:*— brightness.

2988. λαμπρῶς **lampros**, *lam-proce´;* adv. from 2986; *brilliantly,* i.e. fig. *luxuriously:*— sumptuously.

2989. λάμπω **lampō**, *lam´-po;* a primary verb; to *beam,* i.e. *radiate* brilliancy (lit. or fig.):— give light, shine.

2990. λανθάνω **lanthanō**, *lan-than´-o;* a prol. form of a primary verb, which is used only an alt. in certain tenses; to *lie hid* (lit. or fig.); often used adv. *unwittingly:*— be hid, be ignorate of, unawares.

2991. λαξευτός **laxĕutŏs**, *lax-yoo-tos´;* from a compound of λᾶς las (a *stone*) and the base of 3584 (in its orig. sense of *scraping*); *rock-quarried:*— hewn in stone.

2992. λαός **laŏs**, *lah-os´;* appar. a primary word; a *people* (in general; thus differing from 1218, which denotes one's *own* popu-lace):— people.

2993. Λαοδίκεια **Laŏdikĕia**, *lah-od-ik´-i-ah;* from a compound of 2992 and 1349; *Laodi-cia,* a place in Asia Minor:— Laodicea.

2994. Λαοδικεύς **Laŏdikĕus**, *lah-od-ik-yooce´;* from 2993; a *Laodicean,* i.e. inhab. of Laodicia:— Laodicean.

2995. λάρυγξ **larugx**, *lar´-oongks;* of uncert. der.; the *throat* ("*larynx*"):— throat.

2996. Λασαία **Lasaia**, *las-ah´-yah;* of un-cert. or.; *Lasæa,* a place in Crete:— Lasea.

2997. λάσχω **laschō**, *las´-kho;* a strength-ened form of a primary verb, which only occurs in this and another prol. form as alt. in certain tenses; to *crack* open (from a fall):— burst asunder.

2998. λατομέω **latŏmĕō**, *lat-om-eh´-o;* from the same as the first part of 2991 and the base of 5114; to *quarry:*— hew.

2999. λατρεία **latrĕia**, *lat-ri´-ah;* from 3000; *ministration* of God, i.e. *worship:*— (divine) service.

3000. λατρεύω **latrĕuō**, *lat-ryoo´-o;* from λάτρις latris (a hired *menial*); to *minister* (to God), i.e. *render,* relig. *homage:*— serve, do the service, worship (-per).

3001. λάχανον **lachanŏn**, *lakh´-an-on;* from λαχαίνω lachainō (to *dig*); a *vegetable:*— herb.

3002. Λεββαῖος **Lĕbbaiŏs**, *leb-bah´-yos;* of uncert. or.; *Lebbæus,* a Chr.:— Lebbæus.

3003. λεγεών **lĕgĕōn**, *leg-eh-ohn´* or

λεγιών **lĕgiōn**, *leg-ee-ohn´;* of Lat. or.; a "*legion,*" i.e. Rom. *regiment* (fig.):— le-gion.

3004. λέγω **lĕgō**, *leg´-o;* a primary verb; prop. to "*lay*" forth, i.e. (fig.) *relate* (in words [usually of systematic or set *discourse;* whereas *2036* and *5346* generally refer to an *individual* expression or speech respectively; while *4483* is prop. to *break silence* merely, and *2980* means an *extended* or random harangue]); by impl. to *mean:*— ask, bid, boast, call, describe, give out, name, put forth, say (-ing, on), shew, speak, tell, utter.

3005. λεῖμμα **lĕimma,** *lime´-mah;* from *3007;* a *remainder:*— remnant.

3006. λεῖος **lĕiŏs,** *li´-os;* appar. a primary word; *smooth,* i.e. *"level":*— smooth.

3007. λείπω **lĕipō,** *li´-po;* a primary verb; to *leave,* i.e. (intr. or pass.) to *fail* or *be absent:*— be destitute (wanting), lack.

3008. λειτουργέω **lĕitŏurgĕō,** *li-toorg-eh´-o;* from *3011;* to be a *public servant,* i.e. (by anal.) to *perform* relig. or charitable *functions (worship, obey, relieve):*— minister.

3009. λειτουργία **lĕitŏurgia,** *li-toorg-ee´-ah;* from *3008; public function* (as priest ["liturgy"] or almsgiver):— ministration (-try), service.

3010. λειτουργικός **lĕitŏurgikŏs,** *li-toorg-ik-os´;* from the same as *3008; functional publicly* ("liturgic"); i.e. *beneficent:*— ministering.

3011. λειτουργός **lĕitŏurgŏs,** *li-toorg-os´;* from a der. of *2992* and *2041; a public servant,* i.e. a *functionary* in the Temple or Gospel, or (gen.) a *worshipper* (of God) or *benefactor* (of man):— minister (-ed).

3012. λέντιον **lĕntiŏn,** *len´-tee-on;* of Lat. or.; a *"linen"* cloth, i.e. *apron:*— towel.

3013. λεπίς **lĕpis,** *lep-is´;* from λέπω **lĕpō** (to *peel*); a *flake:*— scale.

3014. λέπρα **lĕpra,** *lep´-rah;* from the same as *3013; scaliness,* i.e. *"leprosy":*— leprosy.

3015. λεπρός **lĕprŏs,** *lep-ros´;* from the same as *3014; scaly,* i.e. *leprous* (a *leper*):— leper.

3016. λεπτόν **lĕptŏn,** *lep-ton´;* neut. of a der. of the same as *3013; something scaled (light),* i.e. a small *coin:*— mite.

3017. Λευΐ **Lĕuï,** *lyoo-ee´;* of Heb. or. [3878]; *Levi,* the name of three Isr.:— Levi. Comp. *3018.*

3018. Λευΐς **Lĕuïs,** *lyoo-is´;* a form of *3017; Lewis* (i.e. *Levi*), a Chr.:— Levi.

3019. Λευΐτης **Lĕuïtēs,** *lyoo-ee´-tace;* from *3017;* a *Levite,* i.e. desc. of Levi:— Levite.

3020. Λευϊτικός **Lĕuïtikŏs,** *lyoo-it-ee-kos´;* from *3019; Levitic,* i.e. relating to the Levites:— Levitical.

3021. λευκαίνω **lĕukainō,** *lyoo-kah´-ee-no;* from *3022;* to *whiten:*— make white, whiten.

3022. λευκός **lĕukŏs,** *lyoo-kos´;* from λύκη **lukē,** (*"light"*); *white:*— white.

3023. λέων **lĕōn,** *leh-ohn´;* a primary word; a *"lion":*— lion.

3024. λήθη **lēthē,** *lay´-thay;* from *2990; forgetfulness:*— + forget.

3025. ληνός **lēnŏs,** *lay-nos´;* appar. a primary word; a *trough,* i.e. wine-*vat:*— winepress.

3026. λῆρος **lērŏs,** *lay´-ros;* appar. a primary word; *twaddle,* i.e. an *incredible story:*— idle tale.

3027. λῃστης **lēistēs,** *lace-tace´;* from λῃζομαι **leizomai** (to *plunder*); a *brigand:*— robber, thief.

3028. λῆμψις **lēmpsis,** *lemp´-sis;* from *2983; receipt* (the act):— receiving.

3029. λίαν **lian,** *lee´-an;* of uncert. aff.; *much* (adv.):— exceeding, great (-ly), sore, very (+ chiefest).

3030. λίβανος **libanŏs,** *lib´-an-os;* of for. or. [3828]; the *incense*-tree, i.e. (by impl.) *incense* itself:— frankincense.

3031. λιβανωτός **libanōtŏs,** *lib-an-o-tos´;* from *3030; frankincense,* i.e. (by extens.) a *censer* for burning it:— censer.

3032. Λιβερτῖνος **Libĕrtinŏs,** *lib-er-tee´-nos;* of Lat. or.; a Rom. *freedman:*— Libertine.

3033. Λιβύη **Libuē,** *lib-oo´-ay;* prob. from *3047; Libye,* a region of Africa:— Libya.

3034. λιθάζω **lithazō,** *lith-ad´-zo;* from *3037;* to *lapidate:*— stone.

3035. λίθινος **lithinŏs,** *lith-ee´-nos;* from *3037; stony,* i.e. made of *stone:*— of stone.

3036. λιθοβολέω **lithŏbŏlĕō,** *lith-ob-ol-eh´-o;* from a compound of *3037* and *906;* to *throw stones,* i.e. *lapidate:*— stone, cast stones.

3037. λίθος **lithŏs,** *lee´-thos;* appar. a primary word; a *stone* (lit. or fig.):— (mill-, stumbling-) stone.

3038. λιθόστρωτος **lithŏstrōtŏs,** *lith-os´-tro-tos;* from *3037* and a der. of *4766; stone-strewed,* i.e. a tessellated *mosaic* on which the Rom. tribunal was placed:— Pavement.

3039. λικμάω **likmaō,** *lik-mah´-o;* from λικμός **likmŏs,** the equiv. of λίκνον **liknŏn** (a winnowing *fan* or basket); to *winnow,* i.e. (by anal.) to *triturate:*— grind to powder.

3040. λιμήν **limēn,** *lee-mane´;* appar. a primary word; a *harbor:*— haven. Comp. *2568.*

3041. λίμνη **limnē,** *lim´-nay;* prob. from *3040* (through the idea of nearness of shore); a *pond* (large or small):— lake.

3042. λιμός **limŏs,** *lee-mos´;* prob. from *3007* (through the idea of *destitution*); a *scarcity* of food:— dearth, famine, hunger.

3043. λίνον **linŏn,** *lee´-non;* prob. a primary word; *flax,* i.e. (by impl.) *"linen":*— linen.

3044. Λῖνος **Linŏs,** *lee´-nos;* perh. from *3043; Linus,* a Chr.:— Linus.

3045. λιπαρός **liparŏs,** *lip-ar-os´;* from λίπος **lipŏs** (*grease*); *fat,* i.e. (fig.) *sumptuous:*— dainty.

3046. λίτρα **litra**, *lee´-trah;* of Lat. or. [*libra*]; a *pound* in weight:— pound.

3047. λίψ **lips**, *leeps;* prob. from λείβω **lĕibō** (to *pour* a "libation"); the *south* (-west) wind (as bringing rain, i.e. (by extens.) the *south* quarter):— southwest.

3048. λογία **lŏgia**, *log-ee´-ah* or

λογεία **lŏgeia**, *log-i´-ah;* from 3056 (in the commercial sense); a *contribution:*— collection, gathering.

3049. λογίζομαι **lŏgizŏmai**, *log-id´-zom-ahee;* mid. voice from 3056; to *take an inventory*, i.e. *estimate* (lit. or fig.):— conclude, (ac-) count (of), + despise, esteem, impute, lay, number, reason, reckon, suppose, think (on).

3050. λογικός **lŏgikŏs**, *log-ik-os´;* from 3056; *rational* ("*logical*"):— reasonable, of the word.

3051. λόγιον **lŏgiŏn**, *log´-ee-on;* neut. of 3052; an *utterance* (of God):— oracle.

3052. λόγιος **lŏgiŏs**, *log´-ee-os;* from 3056; *fluent*, i.e. an *orator:*— eloquent.

3053. λογισμός **lŏgismŏs**, *log-is-mos´;* from 3049; *computation*, i.e. (fig.) *reasoning* (*conscience, conceit*):— imagination, thought.

3054. λογομαχέω **lŏgŏmachĕō**, *log-om-akh-eh´-o;* from a compound of 3056 and 3164; to *be disputatious* (on trifles):— strive about words.

3055. λογομαχία **lŏgŏmachia**, *log-om-akh-ee´-ah;* from the same as 3054; *disputation* about trifles ("*logomachy*"):— strife of words.

3056. λόγος **lŏgŏs**, *log´-os;* from 3004; something *said* (incl. the *thought*); by impl. a *topic* (subject of discourse), also *reasoning* (the mental faculty) or *motive;* by extens. a *computation;* spec. (with the art. in John) the Divine *Expression* (i.e. *Christ*):— account, cause, communication, × concerning, doctrine, fame, × have to do, intent, matter, mouth, preaching, question, reason, + reckon, remove, say (-ing), shew, × speaker, speech, talk, thing, + none of these things move me, tidings, treatise, utterance, word, work.

3057. λόγχη **lŏgchē**, *long´-khay;* perh. a primary word; a "*lance*":— spear.

3058. λοιδορέω **lŏidŏrĕō**, *loy-dor-eh´-o;* from 3060; to *reproach*, i.e. *vilify:*— revile.

3059. λοιδορία **lŏidŏria**, *loy-dor-ee´-ah;* from 3060; *slander* or *vituperation:*— railing, reproach [-fully].

3060. λοίδορος **lŏidŏrŏs**, *loy´-dor-os;* from λοιδός **lŏidŏs** (*mischief*); *abusive*, i.e. a *blackguard:*— railer, reviler.

3061. λοιμός **lŏimŏs**, *loy´-mos;* of uncert. aff.; a *plague* (lit. the *disease*, or fig. a *pest*):— pestilence (-t).

3062. λοιποί **lŏipŏi**, *loy-poy´;* masc. plur. of a der. of 3007; *remaining* ones:— other, which remain, remnant, residue, rest.

3063. λοιπόν **lŏipŏn**, *loy-pon´;* neut. sing. of the same as 3062; something *remaining* (adv.):— besides, finally, furthermore, (from) henceforth, moreover, now, + it remaineth, then.

3064. λοιποῦ **lŏipŏu**, *loy-poo´;* gen. sing. of the same as 3062; *remaining* time:— from henceforth.

3065. Λουκᾶς **Lŏukas**, *loo-kas´;* contr. from Lat. *Lucanus; Lucas*, a Chr.:— Lucas, Luke.

3066. Λούκιος **Lŏukiŏs**, *loo´-kee-os;* of Lat. or.; *illuminative; Lucius*, a Chr.:— Lucius.

3067. λουτρόν **lŏutrŏn**, *loo-tron´;* from 3068; a *bath*, i.e. (fig.), *baptism:*— washing.

3068. λούω **lŏuō**, *loo´-o;* a primary verb; to *bathe* (the *whole* person; whereas 3538 means to wet a *part* only, and 4150 to wash, cleanse *garments* exclusively):— wash.

3069. Λύδδα **Ludda**, *lud´-dah;* of Heb. or. [3850]; *Lydda* (i.e. *Lod*), a place in Pal.:— Lydda.

3070. Λυδία **Ludia**, *loo-dee´-ah;* prop. fem. of Λύδιος **Ludiŏs** [of for. or.] (a *Lydian*, in Asia Minor); *Lydia*, a Chr. woman:— Lydia.

3071. Λυκαονία **Lukaŏnia**, *loo-kah-on-ee´-ah;* perh. remotely from 3074; *Lycaonia*, a region of Asia Minor:— Lycaonia.

3072. Λυκαονιστί **Lukaŏnisti**, *loo-kah-on-is-tee´;* adv. from a der. of 3071; *Lycaonistically*, i.e. in the language of the Lycaonians:— in the speech of Lycaonia.

3073. Λυκία **Lukia**, *loo-kee´-ah;* prob. remotely from 3074; *Lycia*, a province of Asia Minor:— Lycia.

3074. λύκος **lukŏs**, *loo´-kos;* perh. akin to the base of 3022 (from the *whitish* hair); a *wolf:*— wolf.

3075. λυμαίνομαι **lumainŏmai**, *loo-mah´-ee-nom-ahee;* mid. voice from a prob. der. of 3089 (mean. *filth*); prop. to *soil*, i.e. (fig.) *insult* (*maltreat*):— make havock of.

3076. λυπέω **lupĕō**, *loo-peh´-o;* from 3077; to *distress;* refl. or pass. to *be sad:*— cause grief, grieve, be in heaviness, (be) sorrow (-ful), be (make) sorry.

3077. λύπη **lupē**, *loo´-pay;* appar. a primary word; *sadness:*— grief, grievous, + grudgingly, heaviness, sorrow.

3078. Λυσανίας **Lusanias**, *loo-san-ee´-as;* from 3080 and ἀνία **ania** (*trouble*); *grief-dispelling; Lysanias*, a governor of Abilene:— Lysanias.

3079. Λυσίας **Lusias**, *loo-see´-as;* of uncert. aff.; *Lysias*, a Rom.:— Lysias.

3080. λύσις **lusis**, *loo´-sis;* from 3089; a *loosening*, i.e. (spec.) *divorce:*— to be loosed.

3081. λυσιτελεῖ **lusitĕlĕi**, *loo-sit-el-i´;* third pers. sing. pres. ind. act. of a der. of a compound of *3080* and *5056;* impers. it *answers* the *purpose,* i.e. *is advantageous:*— it is better.

3082. Λύστρα **Lustra,** *loos´-trah;* of uncert. or.; *Lystra,* a place in Asia Minor:— Lystra.

3083. λύτρον **lutrŏn,** *loo´-tron;* from *3089;* something to *loosen* with, i.e. a redemption price (fig. *atonement*):— ransom.

3084. λυτρόω **lutrŏō,** *loo-trŏ´-o;* from *3083;* to *ransom* (lit. or fig.):— redeem.

3085. λύτρωσις **lutrōsis,** *loo´-tro-sis;* from *3084;* a *ransoming* (fig.):— + redeemed, redemption.

3086. λυτρωτής **lutrōtēs,** *loo-tro-tace´;* from *3084;* a *redeemer* (fig.):— deliverer.

3087. λυχνία **luchnia,** *lookh-nee´-ah;* from *3088;* a *lamp-stand* (lit. or fig.):— candlestick.

3088. λύχνος **luchnŏs,** *lookh´-nos;* from the base of *3022;* a portable *lamp* or other *illuminator* (lit. or fig.):— candle, light.

3089. λύω **luŏ,** *loo´-o;* a primary verb; to *"loosen"* (lit. or fig.):— break (up), destroy, dissolve, (un-) loose, melt, put off. Comp. *4486.*

3090. Λωΐς **Lōís,** *lo-ece´;* of uncert. or.; *Loïs,* a Chr. woman:— Lois.

3091. Λώτ **Lōt,** *lote;* of Heb. or. [3876]; *Lot,* a patriarch:— Lot.

M

3092. Μαάθ **Maath,** *mah-ath´;* prob. of Heb. or.; *Maath,* an Isr.:— Maath.

3093. Μαγδαλά **Magdala,** *mag-dal-ah´;* of Chald. or. [comp. 4026]; *the tower; Magdala* (i.e. *Migdala*), a place in Pal.:— Magdala.

3094. Μαγδαληνή **Magdalēnē,** *mag-dal-ay-nay´;* fem. of a der. of *3093;* a female *Magdalene,* i.e. inhab. of Magdala:— Magdalene.

3095. μαγεία **magĕia,** *mag-i´-ah;* from *3096;* *"magic":*— sorcery.

3096. μαγεύω **magĕuō,** *mag-yoo´-o;* from *3097;* to *practice magic:*— use sorcery.

3097. μάγος **magŏs,** *mag´-os;* of for. or. [7248]; a *Magian,* i.e. Oriental *scientist;* by impl. a *magician:*— sorcerer, wise man.

3098. Μαγώγ **Magōg,** *mag-ogue´;* of Heb. or. [4031]; *Magog,* a for. nation, i.e. (fig.) an Antichristian party:— Magog.

3099. Μαδιάν **Madian,** *mad-ee-on´* or

Μαδιάμ **Madiam,** *mad-ee-on´;* of Heb. origin [4080]; *Madian* (i.e. *Midian*), a region of Arabia:— Madian.

3100. μαθητεύω **mathĕtĕuō,** *math-ayt-yoo´-o;* from *3101;* intr. to *become a pupil;* tran. to *disciple,* i.e. enroll as scholar:— be disciple, instruct, teach.

3101. μαθητής **mathētēs,** *math-ay-tes´;* from *3129;* a *learner,* i.e. *pupil:*— disciple.

3102. μαθήτρια **mathētria,** *math-ay´-tree-ah;* fem. from *3101;* a female *pupil:*— disciple.

3103. Μαθουσάλα **Mathŏusala,** *math-oo-sal´-ah;* of Heb. or. [4968]; *Mathusala* (i.e. *Methushelach*), an antediluvian:— Mathusala.

3104. Μαϊνάν **Maïnan,** *mahee-nan´;* prob. of Heb. or.; *Maïnan,* an Isr.:— Mainan.

3105. μαίνομαι **mainŏmai,** *mah´-ee-nom-ahee;* mid. voice from a primary μάω **maō** (to *long* for; through the idea of insensate *craving*); to *rave* as a "maniac":— be beside self (mad).

3106. μακαρίζω **makarizō,** *mak-ar-id´-zo;* from *3107;* to *beatify,* i.e. *pronounce* (or *esteem*) *fortunate:*— call blessed, count happy.

3107. μακάριος **makariŏs,** *mak-ar´-ee-os;* a prol. form of the poet. μάκαρ **makar** (mean. the same); supremely *blest;* by extens. *fortunate, well off:*— blessed, happy (× -ier).

3108. μακαρισμός **makarismŏs,** *mak-ar-is-mos´;* from *3106;* *beatification,* i.e. *attribution of good fortune:*— blessedness.

3109. Μακεδονία **Makĕdŏnia,** *mak-ed-on-ee´-ah;* from *3110;* *Macedonia,* a region of Greece:— Macedonia.

3110. Μακεδών **Makĕdōn,** *mak-ed´-ohn;* of uncert. der.; a *Macedon* (*Macedonian*), i.e. inhab. of Macedonia:— of Macedonia, Macedonian.

3111. μάκελλον **makĕllŏn,** *mak´-el-lon;* of Lat. or. [macellum]; a *butcher's stall, meat market* or *provision-shop:*— shambles.

3112. μακράν **makran,** *mak-ran´;* fem. acc. sing. of *3117* (*3598* being impl.); *at a distance* (lit. or fig.):— (a-) far (off), good (great) way off.

3113. μακρόθεν **makrŏthĕn,** *mak-roth´-en;* adv. from *3117;* *from a distance* or *afar:*— afar off, from far.

3114. μακροθυμέω **makrŏthumĕō,** *mak-roth-oo-meh´-o;* from the same as *3116;* be *long-spirited,* i.e. (obj.) *forbearing* or (subj.) *patient:*— bear (suffer) long, be longsuffering, have (long) patience, be patient, patiently endure.

3115. μακροθυμία **makrŏthumia,** *mak-roth-oo-mee´-ah;* from the same as *3116;* *longanimity,* i.e. (obj.) *forbearance* or (subj.) *fortitude:*— longsuffering, patience.

3116. μακροθυμώς **makrŏthumōs,** *mak-roth-oo-moce´;* adv. of a compound of *3117* and *2372; with long* (*enduring*) *temper,* i.e. *leniently:*— patiently.

3117. μακρός **makrŏs,** *mak-ros´;* from *3372; long* (in place [*distant*] or time [neut. plur.]):— far, long.

3118. μακροχρόνιος **makrŏchrŏniŏs,** *mak-*

rokh-ron´-ee-os; from *3117* and *5550; long-timed,* i.e. *long-lived:*— live long.

3119. μαλακία **malakia,** *mal-ak-ee´-ah;* from *3120; softness,* i.e. *enervation (debility):*— disease.

3120. μαλακός **malakŏs,** *mal-ak-os´;* of uncert. aff.; *soft,* i.e. *fine* (clothing); fig. a *catamite:*— effeminate, soft.

3121. Μαλελεήλ **Malĕlĕēl,** *mal-el-eh-ale´;* of Heb. or. [4111]; *Maleleël* (i.e. *Mahalalel*), an antediluvian:— Maleleel.

3122. μάλιστα **malista,** *mal´-is-tah;* neut. plur. of the superl. of an appar. primary adv. μάλα **mala** (*very*); (adv.) *most* (*in the greatest degree*) or *particularly:*— chiefly, most of all, (e-) specially.

3123. μᾶλλον **mallŏn,** *mal´-lon;* neut. of the comparative of the same as *3122;* (adv.) *more* (*in a greater degree*) or *rather:*— + better, × far, (the) more (and more), (so) much (the more), rather.

3124. Μάλχος **Malchŏs,** *mal´-khos;* of Heb. or. [4429]; *Malchus,* an Isr.:— Malchus.

3125. μάμμη **mammē,** *mam´-may;* of nat. or. ["mammy"]; a *grandmother:*— grandmother.

3126. μαμμωνᾶς **mammōnas** *mam-mo-nas´,* or

μαμωνᾶς **mamōnas** *mam-o-nas´;* of Chald. or. (*confidence,* i.e. *wealth,* personified); *mammonas,* i.e. *avarice* (deified):— mammon.

3127. Μαναήν **Manaēn,** *man-ah-ane´;* of uncert. or.; *Manaën,* a Chr.:— Manaen.

3128. Μανασσῆς **Manassēs,** *man-as-sace´;* of Heb. or. [4519]; *Mannasses* (i.e. *Menashsheh*), an Isr.:— Manasses.

3129. μανθάνω **manthanō,** *man-than´-o;* prol. from a primary verb, another form of which, μαθέω **mathĕō,** is used as an alt. in cert. tenses; to *learn* (in any way):— learn, understand.

3130. μανία **mania,** *man-ee´-ah;* from *3105; craziness:*— [+ make] × mad.

3131. μάννα **manna,** *man´-nah;* of Heb. or. [4478]; *manna* (i.e. *man*), an edible gum:— manna.

3132. μαντεύομαι **mantĕuŏmai,** *mant-yoo´-om-ahee;* from a der. of *3105* (mean. a *prophet,* as supposed to *rave* through *inspiration*); to *divine,* i.e. *utter spells* (under pretense of foretelling:— by soothsaying.

3133. μαραίνω **marainō,** *mar-ah´-ee-no;* of uncert. aff.; to *extinguish* (as fire), i.e. (fig. and pass.) to *pass away:*— fade away.

3134. μαρὰν ἀθά **maran atha,** *mar-an´ ath-ah´;* of Chald. or. (mean. *our Lord has come*); *maranatha,* i.e. an exclamation of the approaching *divine judgment:*— Maran-atha.

3135. μαργαρίτης **margaritēs,** *mar-gar-ee´-*

tace; from μάργαρος **margarŏs** (a pearl-*oyster*); a *pearl:*— pearl.

3136. Μάρθα **Martha,** *mar´-thah;* prob. of Chald. or. (mean. *mistress*); *Martha,* a Chr. woman:— Martha.

3137. Μαρία **Maria,** *mar-ee´-ah;* or

Μαριάμ **Mariam,** *mar-ee-am´;* of Heb. or. [4813]; *Maria* or *Mariam* (i.e. *Mirjam*), the name of six Chr. females:— Mary.

3138. Μάρκος **Markŏs,** *mar´-kos;* of Lat. or.; *Marcus,* a Chr.:— Marcus, Mark.

3139. μάρμαρος **marmarŏs,** *mar´-mar-os;* from μαρμαίρω **marmairō,** (to *glisten*); *marble* (as sparkling *white*):— marble.

μάρτυρ **martur.** See *3144.*

3140. μαρτυρέω **marturĕō,** *mar-too-reh´-o;* from *3144;* to *be a witness,* i.e. *testify* (lit. or fig.):— charge, give [evidence], bear record, have (obtain, of) good (honest) report, be well reported of, testify, give (have) testimony, (be, bear, give, obtain) witness.

3141. μαρτυρία **marturia,** *mar-too-ree´-ah;* from *3144; evidence* given (judicially or gen.):— record, report, testimony, witness.

3142. μαρτύριον **marturiŏn,** *mar-too´-ree-on;* neut. of a presumed der. of *3144;* something *evidential,* i.e. (gen.) *evidence* given or (spec.) the *Decalogue* (in the sacred Tabernacle):— to be testified, testimony, witness.

3143. μαρτύρομαι **marturŏmai,** *mar-too´-rom-ahee;* mid. voice from *3144;* to *be adduced* as a *witness,* i.e. (fig.) to *obtest* (in affirmation or exhortation):— take to record, testify.

3144. μάρτυς **martus,** *mar´-toos;* of uncert. aff.; a *witness* (lit. [judicially] or fig. [gen.]); by anal. a "*martyr*":— martyr, record, witness.

3145. μασσάομαι **massaŏmai,** *mas-sah´-om-ahee;* from a primary μάσσω **massō** (to *handle* or *squeeze*); to *chew:*— gnaw.

3146. μαστιγόω **mastigŏō,** *mas-tig-ŏ´-o;* from *3148;* to *flog* (lit. or fig.):— scourge.

3147. μαστίζω **mastizō,** *mas-tid´-zo;* from *3149;* to *whip* (lit.):— scourge.

3148. μάστιξ **mastix,** *mas´-tix;* prob. from the base of *3145* (through the idea of *contact*); a *whip* (lit. the Rom. *flagellum* for criminals; fig. a *disease*):— plague, scourging.

3149. μαστός **mastŏs,** *mas-tos´;* from the base of *3145;* a (prop. female) *breast* (as if *kneaded* up):— pap.

3150. ματαιολογία **mataiŏlŏgia,** *mat-ah-yol-og-ee´-ah;* from *3151; random talk,* i.e. *babble:*— vain jangling.

3151. ματαιολόγος **mataiŏlŏgŏs,** *mat-ah-yol-og´-os;* from *3152* and *3004;* an *idle* (i.e.

senseless or *mischievous*) *talker*, i.e. a *wrangler:*— vain talker.

3152. μάταιος **mataiŏs**, *mat´-ah-yos;* from the base of 3155; *empty*, i.e. (lit.) *profitless*, or (spec.) an *idol:*— vain, vanity.

3153. ματαιότης **mataiŏtēs**, *mat-ah-yot´-ace;* from 3152; *inutility;* fig. *transientness;* mor. *depravity:*— vanity.

3154. ματαιόω **mataiŏō**, *mat-ah-yŏ´-o;* from 3152; to *render* (pass. *become*) *foolish*, i.e. (mor.) *wicked* or (spec.) *idolatrous:*— become vain.

3155. μάτην **matēn**, *mat´-ane;* accus. of a der. of the base of 3145 (through the idea of tentative *manipulation*, i.e. unsuccessful *search*, or else of *punishment*); *folly*, i.e. (adv.) to no *purpose:*— in vain.

3156. Ματθαῖος **Matthaiŏs**, *mat-thah´-yos;* or

Μαθθαῖος **Maththaiŏs**, *math-thah´-yos;* a short. form of 3161; *Matthæus* (i.e. *Matthitjah*), an Isr. and a Chr.:— Matthew.

3157. Ματθάν **Matthan**, *mat-than´;* of Heb. or. [4977]; *Matthan* (i.e. *Mattan*), an Isr.:— Matthan.

3158. Ματθάτ **Matthat**, *mat-that´;* or

Μαθθάτ **Maththat**, *math-that´;* prob. a short. form of 3161; *Matthat* (i.e. *Mattithjah*), the name of two Isr.:— Mathat.

3159. Ματθίας **Matthias** *mat-thee´-as*, or Μαθθίας **Maththias**, *math-thee´-as;* appar. a short. form of 3161; *Matthias* (i.e. *Mattithjah*), an Isr.:— Matthias.

3160. Ματταθά **Mattatha**, *mat-tath-ah´;* prob. a short. form of 3161 [comp. 4992]; *Mattatha* (i.e. *Mattithjah*), an Isr.:— Mattatha.

3161. Ματταθίας **Mattathias**, *mat-tath-ee´-as;* of Heb. or. [4993]; *Mattathias* (i.e. *Mattithjah*), an Isr. and a Chr.:— Mattathias.

3162. μάχαιρα **machaira**, *makh´-ahee-rah;* prob. fem. of a presumed der. of 3163; a *knife*, i.e. *dirk;* fig. *war*, judicial *punishment:*— sword.

3163. μάχη **machē**, *makh´-ay;* from 3164; a *battle*, i.e. (fig.) *controversy:*— fighting, strive, striving.

3164. μάχομαι **machŏmai**, *makh´-om-ahee;* mid. voice of an appar. primary verb; to *war*, i.e. (fig.) to *quarrel, dispute:*— fight, strive.

3165. μέ **mĕ**, *meh;* a short. (and prob. orig.) form of 1691; *me:*— I, me, my.

3166. μεγαλαυχέω **mĕgalauchĕō**, *meg-al-ow-kheh´-o;* from a compound of 3173 and αὐχέω **auchĕō**, (to *boast;* akin to 837 and 2744); to *talk big*, i.e. *be grandiloquent* (*arrogant, egotistic*):— boast great things.

3167. μεγαλεῖος **mĕgalĕiŏs**, *meg-al-i´-os;* from 3173; *magnificent*, i.e. (neut, plur. as noun) a conspicuous *favor*, or (subj.) *perfection:*— great things, wonderful works.

3168. μεγαλειότης **mĕgalĕiŏtēs**, *meg-al-i-ot´-*

ace; from 3167; *superbness*, i.e. *glory* or *splendor:*— magnificence, majesty, mighty power.

3169. μεγαλοπρεπής **mĕgalŏprĕpēs**, *meg-al-op-rep-ace´;* from 3173 and 4241; *befitting greatness* or *magnificence* (*majestic*):— excellent.

3170. μεγαλύνω **mĕgalunō**, *meg-al-oo´-no;* from 3173; to *make* (or *declare*) *great*, i.e. *increase* or (fig.) *extol:*— enlarge, magnify, shew great.

3171. μεγάλως **mĕgalōs**, *meg-al´-oce;* adv. from 3173; *much:*— greatly.

3172. μεγαλωσύνη **mĕgalōsunē**, *meg-al-o-soo´-nay;* from 3173; *greatness*, i.e. (fig.) *divinity* (often *God* himself):— majesty.

3173. μέγας **mĕgas**, *meg´-as;* [incl. the prol. forms, fem.

μεγάλη **mĕgalē**, plur.

μεγάλοι **mĕgalŏi**, etc.; comp. also 3176, 3187]; *big* (lit. or fig. in a very wide application):— (+ fear) exceedingly, great (-est), high, large, loud, mighty, + (be) sore (afraid), strong, × to years.

3174. μέγεθος **mĕgĕthŏs**, *meg´-eth-os;* from 3173; *magnitude* (fig.):— greatness.

3175. μεγιστᾶνες **mĕgistanĕs**, *meg-is-tan´-es;* plur. from 3176; *grandees:*— great men, lords.

3176. μέγιστος **mĕgistŏs**, *meg´-is-tos;* superl. of 3173; *greatest* or *very great:*— exceeding great.

3177. μεθερμηνεύω **mĕthĕrmēnĕuō**, *meth-er-mane-yoo´-o;* from 3326 and 2059; to *explain over*, i.e. *translate:*— (by) interpret (-ation).

3178. μέθη **mĕthē**, *meth´-ay;* appar. a primary word; an *intoxicant*, i.e. (by impl.) *intoxication:*— drunkenness.

3179. μεθίστημι **mĕthistēmi**, *meth-is´-tay-mee;* or (1 Cor. 13:2)

μεθιστάνω **mĕthistanō**, *meth-is-tan´-o;* from 3326 and 2476; to *transfer*, i.e. *carry away, depose* or (fig.) *exchange, seduce:*— put out, remove, translate, turn away.

3180. μεθοδεία **mĕthŏdĕia**, *meth-od-i´-ah;* from a compound of 3326 and 3593 [comp. "method"]; *travelling over*, i.e. *travesty* (*trickery*):— wile, lie in wait.

3181. μεθόριος **mĕthŏriŏs**, *meth-or´-ee-os;* from 3326 and 3725; *bounded alongside*, i.e. *contiguous* (neut. plur. as noun, *frontier*):— border.

3182. μεθύσκω **mĕthuskō**, *meth-oos´-ko;* a prol. (tran.) form of 3184; to *intoxicate:*— be drunk (-en).

3183. μέθυσος **mĕthusŏs**, *meth´-oo-sos;* from 3184; *tipsy*, i.e. (as noun) a *sot:*— drunkard.

3184. μεθύω **mĕthuō**, *meth-oo´-o;* from an-

Greek

other form of *3178;* to *drink* to *intoxication,* i.e. *get drunk:*— drink well, make (be) drunk (-en).

3185. μεῖζον **měizŏn,** *mide´-zon;* neut. of *3187;* (adv.) in *greater* degree:— the more.

3186. μειζότερος **měizŏtěrŏs,** *mide-zot´-er-os;* continued comparative of *3187; still larger* (fig.):— greater.

3187. μείζων **měizōn,** *mide´-zone;* irreg. comparative of *3173; larger* (lit. or fig. spec. in age):— elder, greater (-est), more.

3188. μέλαν **mělan,** *mel´-an;* neut. of *3189* as noun; *ink:*— ink.

3189. μέλας **mělas,** *mel´-as;* appar. a primary word; *black:*— black.

3190. Μελεᾶς **Mělěas,** *mel-eh-as´;* of uncert. or.; *Meleas,* an Isr.:— Meleas.

μέλει **mělěi.** See *3199.*

3191. μελετάω **mělětaō,** *mel-et-ah´-o;* from a presumed der. of *3199;* to *take care of,* i.e. (by impl.) *revolve* in the mind:— imagine, (pre-) meditate.

3192. μέλι **měli,** *mel´-ee;* appar. a primary word; *honey:*— honey.

3193. μελίσσιος **mělissiŏs,** *mel-is´-see-os;* from *3192; relating to honey,* i.e. *bee* (comb):— honeycomb.

3194. Μελίτη **Mělitē,** *mel-ee´-tay;* of uncert. or.; *Melita,* an island in the Mediterranean:— Melita.

3195. μέλλω **měllō,** *mel´-lo;* a strengthened form of *3199* (through the idea of *expectation*); to *intend,* i.e. *be about* to be, do, or suffer something (of persons or things, espec. events; in the sense of *purpose, duty, necessity, probability, possibility,* or *hesitation*):— about, after that, be (almost), (that which is, things, + which was for) to come, intend, was to (be), mean, mind, be at the point, (be) ready, + return, shall (begin), (which, that) should (after, afterwards, hereafter) tarry, which was for, will, would, be yet.

3196. μέλος **mělŏs,** *mel´-os;* of uncert. aff.; a *limb* or *part* of the body:— member.

3197. Μελχί **Mělchi,** *mel-khee´;* of Heb. or. [4428 with pron. suffix *my king*]; *Melchi* (i.e. *Malki*), the name of two Isr.:— Melchi.

3198. Μελχισεδέκ **Mělchisěděk,** *mel-khis-ed-ek´;* of Heb. or. [4442]; *Melchisedek* (i.e. *Malkitsedek*), a patriarch:— Melchisedec.

3199. μέλω **mělō,** *mel´-o;* a primary verb; to *be of interest* to, i.e. to *concern* (only third pers. sing. pres. ind. used impers. *it matters*):— (take) care.

3200. μεμβράνα **měmbrana,** *mem-bran´-ah;* of Lat. or. ("*membrane*"); a (written) sheepskin:— parchment.

3201. μέμφομαι **měmphŏmai,** *mem´-fom-ahee;* mid. voice of an appar. primary verb; to *blame:*— find fault.

3202. μεμψίμοιρος **měmpsimŏirŏs,** *mempsim´-oy-ros;* from a presumed der. of *3201* and μοῖρα **mŏira,** (*fate;* akin to the base of *3313*); *blaming fate,* i.e. *querulous* (*discontented*):— complainer.

3203–3302. Because of some changes in the numbering system (while the original work was in progress) no Greek words were cited for *2717* or *3203-3302.* These numbers were dropped altogether. This will not cause any problems in Strong's numbering system. No Greek words have been left out. Because so many other reference works use this numbering system, it has not been revised. If it were revised, much confusion would certainly result.

3303. μέν **měn,** *men;* a primary particle; prop. ind. of *affirmation* or *concession* (*in fact*); usually followed by a *contrasted* clause with *1161* (*this* one, the *former,* etc):— even, indeed, so, some, truly, verily. Often compounded with other particles in an *intens.* or *asseverative* sense.

3304. μενοῦνγε **měnŏungě,** *men-oon´-geh* or

μενοῦν **měnŏun,** *men-oon´* or

μενοῦν γε **měnŏun ge** *men-oon´ geh;* from *3203* and *3767* and *1065; so then at least:*— nay but, yea doubtless (rather, verily).

3305. μέντοι **měntŏi,** *men´-toy;* from *3303* and *5104; indeed though,* i.e. *however:*— also, but, howbeit, nevertheless, yet.

3306. μένω **měnō,** *men´-o;* a primary verb; to *stay* (in a given place, state, relation or expectancy):— abide, continue, dwell, endure, be present, remain, stand, tarry (for), × thine own.

3307. μερίζω **měrizō,** *mer-id´-zo;* from *3313;* to *part,* i.e. (lit.) to *apportion, bestow, share,* or (fig.) to *disunite, differ:*— deal, be difference between, distribute, divide, give part.

3308. μέριμνα **měrimna,** *mer´-im-nah;* from *3307* (through the idea of *distraction*); *solicitude:*— care.

3309. μεριμνάω **měrimnaō,** *mer-im-nah´-o;* from *3308;* to *be anxious* about:— (be, have) care (-ful), take thought.

3310. μερίς **měris,** *mer-ece´;* fem. of *3313;* a *portion,* i.e. *province, share* or (abstr.) *participation:*— part (× -akers).

3311. μερισμός **měrismŏs,** *mer-is-mos´;* from *3307;* a *separation* or *distribution:*— dividing asunder, gift.

3312. μεριστής **měristēs,** *mer-is-tace´;* from *3307;* an *apportioner* (*administrator*):— divider.

3313. μέρος **měrŏs,** *mer´-os;* from an obs. but more primary form of μείρομαι **měirŏmai** (to *get* as a *section* or *allotment*); a *division* or *share* (lit. or fig. in a wide application):— behalf, coast, course, craft, particular (+ -ly), part (+ -ly), piece, portion, respect, side, some sort (-what).

3314. μεσημβρία mĕsēmbria, *mes-am-e-bree´-ah;* from 3319 and 2250; *midday;* by impl. the *south:*— noon, south.

3315. μεσιτεύω mĕsitĕuō, *mes-it-yoo´-o;* from 3316; to *interpose* (as arbiter), i.e (by impl.) to *ratify* (as surety):— confirm.

3316. μεσίτης mĕsitēs, *mes-ee´-tace;* from 3319; a *go-between,* i.e. (simply) an *internunciator,* or (by impl.) a *reconciler (intercessor):*— mediator.

3317. μεσονύκτιον mĕsŏnuktiŏn, *mes-on-ook´-tee-on;* neut. of compound of 3319 and 3571; *midnight* (espec. as a watch):— midnight.

3318. Μεσοποταμία Mĕsŏpŏtamia, *mes-op-ot-am-ee´-ah;* from 3319 and 4215; *Mesopotamia* (as lying between the Euphrates and the Tigris; comp. 763), a region of Asia:— Mesopotamia.

3319. μέσος mĕsŏs, *mes´-os;* from 3326; *middle* (as an adj. or [neut.] noun):— among, × before them, between, + forth, mid [-day, night], midst, way.

3320. μεσότοιχον mĕsŏtŏichŏn, *mes-ot´-oy-khon;* from 3319 and 5109; a *partition* (fig.):— middle wall.

3321. μεσουράνημα mĕsŏuranēma, *mes-oo-ran´-ay-mah;* from a presumed compound of 3319 and 3772; *mid-sky:*— midst of heaven.

3322. μεσόω mĕsŏō, *mes-ŏ´-o;* from 3319; to *form* the *middle,* i.e. (in point of time), to *be half-way* over:— be about the midst.

3323. Μεσσίας Mĕssias, *mes-see´-as;* of Heb. or. [4899]; the *Messias* (i.e. *Mashiach*), or Christ:— Messias.

3324. μεστός mĕstŏs, *mes-tos´;* of uncert. der.; *replete* (lit. or fig.):— full.

3325. μεστόω mĕstŏō, *mes-tŏ´-o;* from 3324; to *replenish,* i.e. (by impl.) to *intoxicate:*— fill.

3326. μετά mĕta, *met-ah´;* a primary prep. (often used adv.); prop. denoting *accompaniment;* "amid" (local or causal); modif. variously according to the case (gen. *association,* or acc. *succession*) with which it is joined; occupying an intermediate position between 575 or 1537 and 1519 or 4314; less intimate than 1722 and less close than 4862):— after (-ward), × that he again, against, among, × and, + follow, hence, hereafter, in, of, (up-) on, + our, × and setting, since, (un-) to, + together, when, with (+ -out). Often used in composition, in substantially the same relations of *participation* or *proximity,* and *transfer* or *sequence.*

3327. μεταβαίνω mĕtabainō, *met-ab-ah´-ee-no;* from 3326 and the base of 939; to *change place:*— depart, go, pass, remove.

3328. μεταβάλλω mĕtaballō, *met-ab-al´-lo;*

from 3326 and 906; to *throw over,* i.e. (mid. voice fig.) to *turn about* in opinion:— change mind.

3329. μετάγω mĕtagō, *met-ag´-o;* from 3326 and 71; to *lead over,* i.e. *transfer (direct):*— turn about.

3330. μεταδίδωμι mĕtadidōmi, *met-ad-id´-o-mee;* from 3326 and 1325; to *give over,* i.e. *share:*— give, impart.

3331. μετάθεσις mĕtathĕsis, *met-ath´-es-is;* from 3346; *transp.,* i.e. *transferral* (to heaven), *disestablishment* (of a law):— change, removing, translation.

3332. μεταίρω mĕtairō, *met-ah´-ee-ro;* from 3326 and 142; to *betake* oneself, i.e. *remove* (locally):— depart.

3333. μετακαλέω mĕtakalĕō, *met-ak-al-eh´-o;* from 3326 and 2564; to *call elsewhere,* i.e. *summon:*— call (for, hither).

3334. μετακινέω mĕtakinĕō, *met-ak-ee-neh´-o;* from 3326 and 2795; to *stir* to a place elsewhere, i.e. *remove* (fig.):— move away.

3335. μεταλαμβάνω mĕtalambanō, *met-al-am-ban´-o;* from 3326 and 2983; to *participate;* generally to *accept* (and use):— eat, have, be partaker, receive, take.

3336. μετάλημψις mĕtalēmpsis, *met-al´-ampe-sis;* from 3335; *participation:*— taking.

3337. μεταλλάσσω mĕtallassō, *met-al-las´-so;* from 3326 and 236; to *exchange:*— change.

3338. μεταμέλλομαι mĕtamĕllŏmai, *met-am-el´-lom-ahee;* from 3326 and the mid. voice of 3199; to *care afterwards,* i.e. *regret:*— repent (self).

3339. μεταμορφόω mĕtamŏrphŏō, *met-am-or-fŏ´-o;* from 3326 and 3445; to *transform* (lit. or fig. "metamorphose"):— change, transfigure, transform.

3340. μετανοέω mĕtanŏĕō, *met-an-ŏ-eh´-o;* from 3326 and 3539; to *think differently* or *afterwards,* i.e. *reconsider* (mor. feel *compunction*):— repent.

3341. μετάνοια mĕtanŏia, *met-an´-oy-ah;* from 3340; (subj.) *compunction* (for guilt, incl. *reformation*); by impl. *reversal* (of [another's] decision):— repentance.

3342. μεταξύ mĕtaxu, *met-ax-oo´;* from 3326 and a form of 4862; *betwixt* (of place or pers.); (of time) as adj. *intervening,* or (by impl.) *adjoining:*— between, mean while, next.

3343. μεταπέμπω mĕtapĕmpō, *met-ap-emp´-o;* from 3326 and 3992; to *send from elsewhere,* i.e. (mid. voice) to *summon* or *invite:*— call (send) for.

3344. μεταστρέφω mĕtastrĕphō, *met-as-tref´-o;* from 3326 and 4762; to *turn across,* i.e. *transmute* or (fig.) *corrupt:*— pervert, turn.

3345. μετασχηματίζω **mĕtaschēmatizō**, *met-askh-ay-mat-id´-zo;* from 3326 and a der. of 4976; to *transfigure* or *disguise;* fig. to *apply* (by accommodation):— transfer, transform (self).

3346. μετατίθημι **mĕtatithēmi**, *met-at-ith´-ay-mee;* from 3326 and 5087; to *transfer,* i.e. (lit.) *transport,* (by impl.) *exchange* (refl.) *change sides,* or (fig.) *pervert:—* carry over, change, remove, translate, turn.

3347. μετέπειτα **mĕtĕpĕita**, *met-ep´-i-tah;* from 3326 and 1899; *thereafter:—* afterward.

3348. μετέχω **mĕtĕchō**, *met-ekh´-o;* from 3326 and 2192; to *share* or *participate;* by impl. *belong* to, *eat* (or *drink*):— be partaker, pertain, take part, use.

3349. μετεωρίζω **mĕtĕōrizō**, *met-eh-o-rid´-zo;* from a compound of 3326 and a collat. form of 142 or perh. rather 109 (comp. "meteor"); to *raise in mid-air,* i.e. (fig.) *suspend* (pass. *fluctuate* or *be anxious*):— be of doubtful mind.

3350. μετοικεσία **mĕtŏikĕsia**, *met-oy-kes-ee´-ah;* from a der. of a compound of 3326 and 3624; a *change of abode,* i.e. (spec.) *expatriation:—* × brought, carried (-ying) away (in-) to.

3351. μετοικίζω **mĕtŏikizō**, *met-oy-kid´-zo;* from the same as 3350; to *transfer* as a *settler* or *captive,* i.e *colonize* or *exile:—* carry away, remove into.

3352. μετοχή **mĕtŏchē**, *met-okh-ay´;* from 3348; *participation,* i.e. *intercourse:—* fellowship.

3353. μέτοχος **mĕtŏchŏs**, *met´-okh-os;* from 3348; *participant,* i.e. (as noun) a *sharer;* by impl. an *associate:—* fellow, partaker, partner.

3354. μετρέω **mĕtrĕō**, *met-reh´-o;* from 3358; to *measure* (i.e. ascertain in size by a fixed standard); by impl. to *admeasure* (i.e. allot by rule); fig. to *estimate:—* measure, mete.

3355. μετρητής **mĕtrētēs**, *met-ray-tace´;* from 3354; a *measurer,* i.e. (spec.) a certain standard *measure* of capacity for liquids:— firkin.

3356. μετριοπαθέω **mĕtriŏpathĕō**, *met-ree-op-ath-eh´-o;* from a compound of the base of 3357 and 3806; to *be moderate in passion,* i.e. *gentle* (to *treat indulgently*):— have compassion.

3357. μετρίως **mĕtriōs**, *met-ree´-oce;* adv. from a der. of 3358; *moderately,* i.e. *slightly:—* a little.

3358. μέτρον **mĕtrŏn**, *met´-ron;* an appar. primary word; a *measure* ("metre"), lit. or fig.; by impl. a limited *portion* (*degree*):— measure.

3359. μέτωπον **mĕtōpŏn**, *met´-o-pon* ; from 3326 and ὤψ **ōps** (the *face*); the *forehead* (as *opposite,* the *countenance*):— forehead.

3360. μέχρι **mĕchri** *mekh´-ree;* or

μεχρίς **mĕchris**, *mekh-ris´;* from 3372; *as far as,* i.e. *up to* a certain point (as a prep. of extent [denoting the *terminus,* whereas

891 refers espec. to the *space* of time or place intervening] or a conjunc.):— till, (un-) to, until.

3361. μή **mē**, *may;* a primary particle of qualified *negation* (whereas 3756 expresses an absolute denial); (adv.) *not,* (conjunc.) *lest;* also (as an interrog. implying a neg. answer [whereas 3756 expects an *affirmative* one]) *whether:—* any, but (that), × forbear, + God forbid, + lack, lest, neither, never, no (× wise in), none, nor, [can-] not, nothing, that not, un [-taken], without. Often used in compounds in substantially the same relations. See also 3362, 3363, 3364, 3372, 3373, 3375, 3378.

3362. ἐὰν μή **ĕan mē**, *eh-an´ may;* i.e. 1437 and 3361; *if not,* i.e. *unless:—* × before, but, except, if, no, (if, + whosoever) not.

3363. ἵνα μή **hina mē**, *hin´-ah may;* i.e. 2443 and 3361; *in order* (or *so*) *that not:—* albeit not, lest, that, no (-t, [-thing]).

3364. οὐ μή **ŏu mē**, *oo may;* i.e. 3756 and 3361; a double neg. streng. the denial; *not at all:—* any more, at all, by any (no) means, neither, never, no (at all), in no case (wise), nor ever, not (at all, in any wise). Comp. 3378.

3365. μηδαμῶς **mēdamōs**, *may-dam-oce´;* adv. from a compound of 3361 and ἀμός **amŏs** (*somebody*); *by no means:—* not so.

3366. μηδέ **mēdĕ**, *may-deh´;* from 3361 and 1161; *but not, not even;* in a continued negation, *nor:—* neither, nor (yet), (no) not (once, so much as).

3367. μηδείς **mēdĕis**, *may-dice´;* incl. the irreg. fem. μηδεμία **mēdĕmia** *may-dem-ee´-ah;* and the neut. μηδέν **mēdĕn**, *may-den´;* from 3361 and 1520; *not even one* (man, woman, thing):— any (man, thing), no (man), none, not (at all, any man, a whit), nothing, + without delay.

3368. μηδέποτε **mēdĕpŏtĕ**, *may-dep´-ot-eh;* from 3366 and 4218; *not even ever:—* never.

3369. μηδέπω **mēdĕpō**, *may-dep´-o;* from 3366 and 4452; *not even yet:—* not yet.

3370. Μῆδος **Mēdŏs**, *may´-dos;* of for. or. [comp. 4074]; a *Median,* or inhab. of Media:— Mede.

3371. μηκέτι **mēkĕti**, *may-ket´-ee;* from 3361 and 2089; *no further:—* any longer, (not) henceforth, hereafter, no henceforward (longer, more, soon) not any more.

3372. μῆκος **mēkŏs**, *may´-kos;* prob. akin to 3173; *length* (lit. or fig.) length.

3373. μηκύνω **mēkunō**, *may-koo´-no;* from 3372; to *lengthen,* i.e. (mid. voice) to *enlarge:—* grow up.

3374. μηλωτή **mēlōtē**, *may-lo-tay´;* from μῆλον **mēlŏn**, (a *sheep*); a *sheep-skin:—* sheepskin.

3375. μήν **mēn**, *mane;* a stronger form of *3303;* a particle of affirmation (only with *2229*); *assuredly:*— + surely.

3376. μήν **mēn**, *mane;* a primary word; a *month:*— month.

3377. μηνύω **mēnuō**, *may-noo´-o;* prob. from the same base as *3145* and *3415* (i.e. μάω **maō**, to *strive*); to *disclose* (through the idea of ment. *effort* and thus calling to *mind*), i.e. *report, declare, intimate:*— shew, tell.

3378. μὴ οὐκ **mē ŏuk**, *may ook;* i.e. *3361* and *3756;* as interrog. and neg. *is it not that?:*— neither (followed by *no*), + never, not. Comp. *3364.*

3379. μήποτε **mēpŏtĕ**, *may´-pot-eh;* or

μή ποτε **mē pŏtĕ**, *may pot´-eh;* from *3361* and *4218; not ever;* also *if* (or *lest*) *ever* (or *perhaps*):— if peradventure, lest (at any time, haply), not at all, whether or not.

3380. μήπω **mēpō**, *may´-po;* from *3361* and *4452; not yet:*— not yet.

3381. μήπως **mēpōs**, *may´-poce;* or

μή πως **mē pōs**, *may poce;* from *3361* and *4458; lest somehow:*— lest (by any means, by some means, haply, perhaps).

3382. μηρός **mērŏs**, *may-ros´;* perh. a primary word; a *thigh:*— thigh.

3383. μήτε **mētĕ**, *may´-teh;* from *3361* and *5037; not too,* i.e. (in continued negation) *neither* or *nor;* also, *not even:*— neither, (n-) or, so as much.

3384. μήτηρ **mētēr**, *may´-tare;* appar. a primary word; a "*mother*" (lit. or fig., immed. or remote):— mother.

3385. μήτι **mēti**, *may´-tee;* from *3361* and the neut. of *5100; whether at all:*— not [*the particle usually not expressed, except by the form of the question*].

3386. μήτιγε **mētigĕ**, *may´-tig-eh;* from *3385* and *1065; not at all then,* i.e. *not to say* (*the rather still*):— how much more.

3387. μήτις **mētis**, *may´-tis;* or

μή τις **mē tis** *may tis;* from *3361* and *5100; whether any:*— any [*sometimes unexpressed except by the simple interrogative form of the sentence*].

3388. μήτρα **mētra**, *may´-trah;* from *3384;* the *matrix:*— womb.

3389. μητραλῴας **mētralŏias**, *may-tral-o´-as* or

μετρολῴας **mĕtrolŏias**, *may-trol-o´-as;* from *3384* and the base of *257;* a *mother-thresher,* i.e. *matricide:*— murderer of mothers.

3390. μητρόπολις **mētrŏpŏlis**, *may-trop´-ol-is;* from *3384* and *4172;* a *mother city,* i.e. "*metropolis*":— chiefest city.

3391. μία **mia**, *mee´-ah;* irreg. fem. of *1520;* *one* or *first:*— a (certain), + agree, first, one, × other.

3392. μιαίνω **miainō**, *me-ah´-ee-no;* perh. a primary verb; to *sully* or *taint,* i.e. *contaminate* (cer. or mor.):— defile.

3393. μίασμα **miasma**, *mee´-as-mah;* from *3392* ("*miasma*"); (mor.) *foulness* (prop. the effect):— pollution.

3394. μιασμός **miasmŏs**, *mee-as-mos´;* from *3392;* (mor.) *contamination* (prop.the act):— uncleanness.

3395. μίγμα **migma**, *mig´-mah;* from *3396;* a *compound:*— mixture.

3396. μίγνυμι **mignumi**, *mig´-noo-mee;* a primary verb; to *mix:*— mingle.

3397. μικρόν **mikrŏn**, *mik-ron´;* masc. or neut. sing. of *3398* (as noun); a *small* space of *time* or *degree:*— a (little) (while).

3398. μικρός **mikrŏs**, *mik-ros´;* incl. the comp.

μικρότερος **mikrŏtĕrŏs**, *mik-rot´-er-os;* appar. a primary word; *small* (in size, quantity, number or (fig.) dignity):— least, less, little, small.

3399. Μίλητος **Milētŏs**, *mil´-ay-tos;* of uncert. or.; *Miletus,* a city of Asia Minor:— Miletus.

3400. μίλιον **miliŏn**, *mil´-ee-on;* of Lat. or.; a *thousand* paces, i.e. a "*mile*":— mile.

3401. μιμέομαι **mimĕŏmai**, *mim-eh´-om-ahee;* mid. voice from μῖμος **mimŏs** (a "*mimic*"); to *imitate:*— follow.

3402. μιμητής **mimētēs**, *mim-ay-tace´;* from *3401;* an *imitator:*— follower.

3403. μιμνήσκω **mimnēskō**, *mim-nace´-ko;* a prol. form of *3415* (from which some of the tenses are borrowed); to *remind,* i.e. (mid. voice) to *recall to mind:*— be mindful, remember.

3404. μισέω **misĕō**, *mis-eh´-o;* from a primary μῖσος **misŏs** (*hatred*); to *detest* (espec. to *persecute*); by extens. to *love less:*— hate (-ful).

3405. μισθαποδοσία **misthapŏdŏsia**, *mis-thap-od-os-ee´-ah;* from *3406; requital* (good or bad):— recompence of reward.

3406. μισθαποδότης **misthapŏdŏtēs**, *mis-thap-od-ot´-ace;* from *3409* and *591;* a *renumerator:*— rewarder.

3407. μίσθιος **misthiŏs**, *mis´-thee-os;* from *3408;* a *wage-earner:*— hired servant.

3408. μισθός **misthŏs**, *mis-thos´;* appar. a primary word; *pay* for services (lit. or fig.), good or bad:— hire, reward, wages.

3409. μισθόω **misthŏō**, *mis-thŏ´-o;* from *3408;* to *let* out for wages, i.e. (mid. voice) to *hire:*— hire.

3410. μίσθωμα **misthōma**, *mis´-tho-mah;*

from 3409; a rented building:— hired house.

3411. μισθωτός **misthŏtŏs**, *mis-tho-tos´*; from 3409; a *wage-worker* (good or bad):— hired servant, hireling.

3412. Μιτυλήνη **Mitulēnē**, *mit-oo-lay´-nay*; for μυτιλήνη **mutilēnē**, *(abounding in shell-fish)*; *Mitylene* (or *Mytilene*), a town on the island of Lesbos:— Mitylene.

3413. Μιχαήλ **Michaēl**, *mikh-ah-ale´*; of Heb. or. [4317]; *Michaël*, an archangel:— Michael.

3414. μνᾶ **mna**, *mnah*; of Lat. or.; a *mna* (i.e. *mina*), a certain *weight:*— pound.

3415. μνάομαι **mnaŏmai**, *mnah´-om-ahee*; mid. voice of a der. of 3306 or perh. of the base of 3145 (through the idea of *fixture* in the mind or of mental *grasp*); to *bear in mind*, i.e. *recollect;* by impl. to *reward* or *punish:*— be mindful, remember, come (have) in remembrance. Comp. 3403.

3416. Μνάσων **Mnasōn**, *mnah´-sohn;* of uncert. or.; *Mnason*, a Chr.:— Mnason.

3417. μνεία **mnĕia**, *mni´-ah;* from 3415 or 3403; *recollection;* by impl. *recital:*— mention, remembrance.

3418. μνῆμα **mnēma**, *mnay´-mah;* from 3415; a *memorial*, i.e. sepulchral *monument (burial-place):*— grave, sepulchre, tomb.

3419. μνημεῖον **mnēmĕiŏn**, *mnay-mi´-on;* from 3420; a *remembrance*, i.e. *cenotaph (place of interment):*— grave, sepulchre, tomb.

3420. μνήμη **mnēmē**, *mnay´-may;* from 3403; *memory:*— remembrance.

3421. μνημονεύω **mnēmŏnĕuō**, *mnay-mon-yoo´-o;* from a der. of 3420; to *exercise memory*, i.e. *recollect;* by impl. to *punish;* also to *rehearse:*— make mention; be mindful, remember.

3422. μνημόσυνον **mnēmŏsunŏn**, *mnay-mos´-oo-non;* from 3421; a *reminder (memorandum)*, i.e. *record:*— memorial.

3423. μνηστεύω **mnēstĕuō**, *mnace-tyoo´-o;* from a der. of 3415; to *give a souvenir* (engagement present), i.e. *betroth:*— espouse.

3424. μογιλάλος **mŏgilalŏs**, *mog-il-al´-os;* from 3425 and 2980; *hardly talking*, i.e. *dumb (tongue-tied):*— having an impediment in his speech.

3425. μόγις **mŏgis**, *mog´-is;* adv. from a primary μόγος **mŏgŏs**, *(toil); with difficulty:*— hardly.

3426. μόδιος **mŏdiŏs**, *mod´-ee-os;* of Lat. or.; a *modius*, i.e. certain measure for things dry (the quantity or the utensil):— bushel.

3427. μοί **mŏi**, *moy;* the simpler form of 1698; *to me:*— I, me, mine, my.

3428. μοιχαλίς **mŏichalis**, *moy-khal-is´;* a prol. form of the fem. of 3432; an *adulteress* (lit. or fig.):— adulteress (-ous, -y).

3429. μοιχάω **mŏichaō**, *moy-khah´-o;* from 3432; (mid. voice) to *commit adultery:*— commit adultery.

3430. μοιχεία **mŏichĕia**, *moy-khi´-ah;* from 3431; *adultery:*— adultery.

3431. μοιχεύω **mŏichĕuō**, *moy-khyoo´-o;* from 3432; to *commit adultery:*— commit adultery.

3432. μοιχός **mŏichŏs**, *moy-khos´;* perh. a primary word; a (male) *paramour;* fig. *apostate:*— adulterer.

3433. μόλις **mŏlis**, *mol´-is;* prob. by var. for 3425; *with difficulty:*— hardly, scarce (-ly), + with much work.

3434. Μολόχ **Mŏlŏch**, *mol-okh´;* of Heb. or. [4432]; *Moloch* (i.e. *Molek*), an idol:— Moloch.

3435. μολύνω **mŏlunō**, *mol-oo´-no;* prob. from 3189; to *soil* (fig.):— defile.

3436. μολυσμός **mŏlusmŏs**, *mol-oos-mos´;* from 3435; a *stain;* i.e. (fig.) *immorality:*— filthiness.

3437. μομφή **mŏmphē**, *mom-fay´;* from 3201; *blame*, i.e. (by impl.) a *fault:*— quarrel.

3438. μονή **mŏnē**, *mon-ay´;* from 3306; a *staying*, i.e. *residence* (the act or the place):— abode, mansion.

3439. μονογενής **mŏnŏgĕnēs**, *mon-og-en-ace´;* from 3441 and 1096; *only-born*, i.e. *sole:*— only (begotten, child).

3440. μόνον **mŏnŏn**, *mon´-on;* neut. of 3441 as adv.; *merely:*— alone, but, only.

3441. μόνος **mŏnŏs**, *mon´-os;* prob. from 3306; *remaining*, i.e. *sole* or *single;* by impl. *mere:*— alone, only, by themselves.

3442. μονόφθαλμος **mŏnŏphthalmŏs**, *mon-of´-thal-mos;* from 3441 and 3788; *one-eyed:*— with one eye.

3443. μονόω **mŏnŏō**, *mon-ŏ´-o;* from 3441; to *isolate*, i.e. *bereave:*— be desolate.

3444. μορφή **mŏrphē**, *mor-fay´;* perh. from the base of 3313 (through the idea of *adjustment* of parts); *shape;* fig. *nature:*— form.

3445. μορφόω **mŏrphŏō**, *mor-fŏ´-o;* from the same as 3444; to *fashion* (fig.):— form.

3446. μόρφωσις **mŏrphōsis**, *mor´-fo-sis;* from 3445; *formation*, i.e. (by impl.) *appearance* (*semblance* or [concr.] *formula*):— form.

3447. μοσχοποιέω **mŏschŏpŏiĕō**, *mos-khop-oy-eh´-o;* from 3448 and 4160; to *fabricate* the image of a *bullock:*— make a calf.

3448. μόσχος **mŏschŏs**, *mos´-khos;* prob. strengthened for ὄσχος **ŏschŏs** (a *shoot);* a young *bullock:*— calf.

3449. μόχθος **mŏchthŏs**, *mokh´-thos;* from the base of 3425; *toil*, i.e. (by impl.) *sadness:*— painfulness, travail.

Greek

3450. μοῦ **mŏu**, *moo;* the simpler form of 1700; *of me:*— I, me, mine (own), my.

3451. μουσικός **mŏusikŏs**, *moo-sik-os´;* from Μοῦσα **Mŏusa**, (a *Muse*); "*musical*", i.e. (as noun) a *minstrel:*— musician.

3452. μυελός **muĕlŏs**, *moo-el-os´;* perh. a primary word; the *marrow:*— marrow.

3453. μυέω **muĕō**, *moo-eh´-o;* from the base of 3466; to *initiate*, i.e. (by impl.) to *teach:*— instruct.

3454. μῦθος **muthŏs**, *moo´-thos;* perh. from the same as 3453 (through the idea of *tuition*); a *tale*, i.e. *fiction* ("*myth*"):— fable.

3455. μυκάομαι **mukaŏmai**, *moo-kah´-om-ahee;* from a presumed der. of μύζω **muzō** (to "*moo*"); to *bellow* (*roar*):— roar.

3456. μυκτηρίζω **muktērizō**, *mook-tay-rid´-zo;* from a der. of the base of 3455 (mean. *snout*, as that whence *lowing* proceeds); to *make mouths* at, i.e. *ridicule:*— mock.

3457. μυλικός **mulikŏs**, *moo-lee-kos´;* from 3458; *belonging to a mill:*— mill [-stone].

3458. μύλος **mulŏs**, *moo´-los;* prob. ultimately from the base of 3433 (through the idea of *hardship*); a "*mill*", i.e. (by impl.) a *grinder* (*millstone*):— millstone.

3459. μύλων **mulōn**, *moo´-lone;* from 3458; a *mill-house:*— mill.

3460. Μύρα **Mura**, *moo´-rah;* of uncert. der.; *Myra*, a place in Asia Minor:— Myra.

3461. μυρίας **murias**, *moo-ree´-as;* from 3463; a *ten-thousand;* by extens. a "*myriad*" or indef. number:— ten thousand.

3462. μυρίζω **murizō**, *moo-rid´-zo;* from 3464; to *apply* (perfumed) *unguent* to:— anoint.

3463. μύριοι **muriŏi**, *moo´-ree-oi;* plur. of an appar. primary word (prop. mean. *very many*); *ten thousand;* by extens. *innumerably many:*— ten thousand.

3464. μύρον **murŏn**, *moo´-ron;* prob. of for. or. [comp. 4753, 4666]; "*myrrh*", i.e. (by impl.) *perfumed oil:*— ointment.

3465. Μυσία **Musia**, *moo-see´-ah;* of uncert. or.; *Mysia*, a region of Asia Minor:— Mysia.

3466. μυστήριον **mustēriŏn**, *moos-tay´-ree-on;* from a der. of μύω **muō** (to *shut* the mouth); a *secret* or "*mystery*" (through the idea of *silence* imposed by *initiation* into relig. rites):— mystery.

3467. μυωπάζω **muōpazō**, *moo-ope-ad´-zo;* from a compound of the base of 3466 and ὤψ **ōps** (the *face;* from 3700); to *shut the eyes*, i.e. *blink* (*see indistinctly*):— cannot see far off.

3468. μώλωψ **mōlōps**, *mo´-lopes;* from μῶλος **mōlŏs**, ("*moil;*" prob. akin to the base of 3433) and prob. ὤψ **ōps**, (the *face;* from 3700); a *mole* ("black eye") or *blow-mark:*— stripe.

3469. μωμάομαι **mōmaŏmai**, *mo-mah´-om-ahee;* from 3470; to *carp* at, i.e. *censure* (*discredit*):— blame.

3470. μῶμος **mōmŏs**, *mo´-mos;* perh. from 3201; a *flaw* or *blot*, i.e. (fig.) *disgraceful person:*— blemish.

3471. μωραίνω **mōrainō**, *mo-rah´-ee-no;* from 3474; to *become insipid;* fig. to *make* (pass. *act*) as a *simpleton:*— become fool, make foolish, lose savour.

3472. μωρία **mōria**, *mo-ree´-ah;* from 3474; *silliness*, i.e. *absurdity:*— foolishness.

3473. μωρολογία **mōrŏlŏgia**, *mo-rol-og-ee´-ah;* from a compound of 3474 and 3004; *silly talk*, i.e. *buffoonery:*— foolish talking.

3474. μωρός **mōrŏs**, *mo-ros´;* prob. from the base of 3466; *dull* or *stupid* (as if *shut* up), i.e. *heedless*, (mor.) *blockhead*, (appar.) *absurd:*— fool (-ish, × -ishness).

3475. Μωσεύς **Mōsĕus**, *moce-yoos´;* or Μωσῆς **Mōsēs**, *mo-sace´;* or Μωϋσῆς **Mōusēs**, *mo-oo-sace´;* of Heb. or.; [4872]; *Moseus, Moses,* or *Moüses* (i.e. *Mosheh*), the Heb. lawgiver:— Moses.

N

3476. Ναασσών **Naassōn**, *nah-as-sone´;* of Heb. or. [5177]; *Naasson* (i.e. *Nachshon*), an Isr.:— Naasson.

3477. Ναγγαί **Naggai**, *nang-gah´-ee;* prob. of Heb. or. [comp. 5052]; *Nangæ* (i.e. perh. *Nogach*), an Isr.:— Nagge.

3478. Ναζαρέθ **Nazarĕth**, *nad-zar-eth´;* or Ναζαρέτ **Nazarĕt**, *nad-zar-et´;* of uncert. der.; *Nazareth* or *Nazaret*, a place in Pal.:— Nazareth.

3479. Ναζαρηνός **Nazarēnŏs**, *nad-zar-ay-nos´;* from 3478; a *Nazarene*, i.e. inhab. of Nazareth:— of Nazareth.

3480. Ναζωραῖος **Nazōraiŏs**, *nad-zo-rah´-yos;* from 3478; a *Nazoræan*, i.e. inhab. of Nazareth; by extens. a *Christian:*— Nazarene, of Nazareth.

3481. Ναθάν **Nathan**, *nath-an´*, or Ναθάμ **Natham**, *nath-am´;* of Heb. or. [5416]; *Nathan*, an Isr.:— Nathan (Natham).

3482. Ναθαναήλ **Nathanaēl**, *nath-an-ah-ale´;* of Heb. or. [5417]; *Nathanaël* (i.e. *Nathanel*), an Isr. and Chr.:— Nathanael.

3483. ναί **nai**, *nahee;* a primary particle of strong affirmation; *yes:*— even so, surely, truth, verily, yea, yes.

3484. Ναΐν **Naïn**, *nah-in´;* prob. of Heb. or. [comp. 4999]; *Naïn*, a place in Pal.:— Nain.

3485. ναός **naŏs**, *nah-os´;* from a primary ναίω **naiō** (to *dwell*); a *fane, shrine, temple:*— shrine, temple. Comp 2411.

3486. Ναούμ **Naŏum**, *nah-oom´;* of Heb. or. [5151]; *Naüm* (i.e. *Nachum*), an Isr.:— Naum.

3487. νάρδος **nardŏs**, *nar´dos;* of for. or. [comp. 5373]; "*nard*":— [spike-] nard.

3488. Νάρκισσος **Narkissŏs**, *nar'-kis-sos;* a flower of the same name, from νάρκη **narkē** (*stupefaction*, as a "narcotic"); *Narcissus*, a Rom.:— Narcissus.

3489. ναυαγέω **nauagĕō**, *nŏw-ag-eh'-o;* from a compound of 3491 and 71; to *be shipwrecked* (*stranded*, "navigate"), lit. or fig.:— make (suffer) shipwreck.

3490. ναύκληρος **nauklērŏs**, *nŏw'-klay-ros;* from 3491 and 2819 ("clerk"); a *captain:*— owner of a ship.

3491. ναῦς **naus**, *nŏwce;* from νάω **naō** or νέω **nĕō** (to *float*); a *boat* (of any size):— ship.

3492. ναύτης **nautēs**, *now'-tace;* from 3491; a *boatman*, i.e. *seaman:*— sailor, shipman.

3493. Ναχώρ **Nachōr**, *nakh-ore';* of Heb. or. [5152]; *Nachor*, the grandfather of Abraham:— Nachor.

3494. νεανίας **nĕanias**, *neh-an-ee'-as;* from a der. of 3501; a *youth* (up to about forty years):— young man.

3495. νεανίσκος **nĕaniskŏs**, *neh-an-is'-kos;* from the same as 3494; a *youth* (under forty):— young man.

3496. Νεάπολις **Nĕapŏlis**, *neh-ap'-ol-is;* from 3501 and 4172; *new town; Neäpolis*, a place in Macedonia:— Neapolis.

3497. Νεεμάν **Nĕĕman**, *neh-eh-man'* or

　　　Ναϊμάν **Naïman**, *nah-ee-man';* of Heb. or. [5283]; *Neëman* (i.e. *Naaman*), a Syrian:— Naaman.

3498. νεκρός **nĕkrŏs**, *nek-ros';* from an appar. primary νέκυς **nĕkus** (a *corpse*); *dead* (lit. or fig.; also as noun):— dead.

3499. νεκρόω **nĕkrŏō**, *nek-rŏ'-o;* from 3498; to *deaden*, i.e. (fig.) to *subdue:*— be dead, mortify.

3500. νέκρωσις **nĕkrōsis**, *nek'-ro-sis;* from 3499; *decease;* fig. *impotency:*— deadness, dying.

3501. νέος **nĕŏs**, *neh'-os;* incl. the comparative νεώτερος **nĕōtĕrŏs**, *neh-o'-ter-os;* a primary word; "*new*", i.e. (of persons) *youthful*, or (of things) *fresh;* fig. *regenerate:*— new, young.

3502. νεοσσός **nĕŏssŏs**, *neh-os-sos'* or

　　　νοσσός **nossos**, *nos-sos';* from 3501; a *youngling* (*nestling*):— young.

3503. νεότης **nĕŏtēs**, *neh-ot'-ace;* from 3501; *newness*, i.e. *youthfulness:*— youth.

3504. νεόφυτος **nĕŏphutŏs**, *neh-of'-oo-tos;* from 3501 and a der. of 5453; *newly planted*, i.e. (fig.) a *young convert* ("*neophyte*"):— novice.

3505. Νέρων **Nĕrōn**, *ner'-ohn;* of Lat. or.; *Neron* (i.e. *Nero*), a Rom. emperor:— Nero.

3506. νεύω **nĕuō**, *nyoo'-o;* appar. a primary verb; to "*nod*," i.e. (by anal.) *signal:*— beckon.

3507. νεφέλη **nĕphĕlē**, *nef-el'-ay;* from 3509;

prop. *cloudiness*, i.e. (concr.) a *cloud:*— cloud.

3508. Νεφθαλείμ **Nĕphthalĕim**, *nef-thal-ime';* of Heb. or. [5321]; *Nephthaleim* (i.e. *Naphthali*), a tribe in Pal.:— Nephthalim.

3509. νέφος **nĕphŏs**, *nef'-os;* appar. a primary word; a *cloud:*— cloud.

3510. νεφρός **nĕphrŏs**, *nef-ros';* of uncert. aff.; a *kidney* (plur.), i.e. (fig.) the *inmost mind:*— reins.

3511. νεωκόρος **nĕōkŏrŏs**, *neh-o-kor'-os;* from a form of 3485 and κορέω **kŏrĕō** (to *sweep*); a *temple-servant*, i.e. (by impl.) a *votary:*— worshipper.

3512. νεωτερικός **nĕōtĕrikŏs**, *neh-o-ter'-ik-os;* from the comparative of 3501; *appertaining to younger* persons, i.e. *juvenile:*— youthful.

　　　νεώτερος **nĕōtĕrŏs**. See 3501.

3513. νή **nē**, *nay;* prob. an intens. form of 3483; a particle of attestation (accompanied by the obj. invoked or appealed to in confirmation); *as sure as:*— I protest by.

3514. νήθω **nēthō**, *nay'-tho;* from νέω **nĕō** (of like mean.); to *spin:*— spin.

3515. νηπιάζω **nēpiazō**, *nay-pee-ad'-zo;* from 3516; to *act* as a *babe*, i.e. (fig.) *innocently:*— be a child.

3516. νήπιος **nēpiŏs**, *nay'-pee-os;* from an obs. particle νη- **nē-** (implying *negation*) and 2031; *not speaking*, i.e. an *infant* (*minor*); fig. a *simple-minded* person, an *immature* Christian:— babe, child (+ -ish).

3517. Νηρεύς **Nērĕus**, *nare-yoos';* appar. from a der. of the base of 3491 (mean. *wet*); *Nereus*, a Chr.:— Nereus.

3518. Νηρί **Nēri**, *nay-ree';* of Heb. or. [5374]; *Neri* (i.e. *Nerijah*), an Isr.:— Neri.

3519. νησίον **nēsiŏn**, *nay-see'-on;* dimin. of 3520; an *islet:*— island.

3520. νῆσος **nēsŏs**, *nay'-sos;* prob. from the base of 3491; an *island:*— island, isle.

3521. νηστεία **nēstĕia**, *nace-ti'-ah;* from 3522; *abstinence* (from lack of food, or vol. and relig.); spec. the *fast* of the Day of Atonement:— fast (-ing.).

3522. νηστεύω **nēstĕuō**, *nace-tyoo'-o;* from 3523; to *abstain* from food (relig.):— fast.

3523. νῆστις **nēstis**, *nace'-tis;* from the insep. neg. particle νη- **nē-**, (*not*) and 2068; *not eating*, i.e. *abstinent* from food (relig.):— fasting.

3524. νηφάλεος **nēphalĕŏs**, *nay-fal'-eh-os;* or

　　　νηφάλιος **nēphaliŏs**, *nay-fal'-ee-os;* from 3525; *sober*, i.e. (fig.) *circumspect:*— sober, vigilant.

3525. νήφω **nēphō**, *nay'-fo;* of uncert. aff.: to

abstain from wine (*keep sober*), i.e. (fig.) *be discreet:*— be sober, watch.

3526. Νίγερ **Nigĕr**, *neeg'-er;* of Lat. or.; *black;* Niger, a Chr.:— Niger.

3527. Νικάνωρ **Nikanōr**, *nik-an'-ore;* prob. from 3528; *victorious; Nicanor*, a Chr.:— Nicanor.

3528. νικάω **nikaō**, *nik-ah'-o;* from 3529; to *subdue* (lit. or fig.):— conquer, overcome, prevail, get the victory.

3529. νίκη **nikē**, *nee'-kay;* appar. a primary word; *conquest* (abstr.), i.e. (fig.) the *means of success:*— victory.

3530. Νικόδημος **Nikŏdēmŏs**, *nik-od'-ay-mos;* from 3534 and 1218; *victorious among his people; Nicodemus*, an Isr.:— Nicodemus.

3531. Νικολαΐτης **Nikŏlaïtēs**, *nik-ol-ah-ee'-tace;* from 3532; a *Nicolaïte*, i.e. adherent of *Nicolaüs:*— Nicolaitane.

3532. Νικόλαος **Nikŏlaŏs**, *nik-ol'-ah-os;* from 3534 and 2992; *victorious over the people; Nicolaüs*, a heretic:— Nicolaus.

3533. Νικόπολις **Nikŏpŏlis**, *nik-op'-ol-is;* from 3534 and 4172; *victorious city; Nicopolis*, a place in Macedonia:— Nicopolis.

3534. νῖκος **nikŏs**, *nee'-kos;* from 3529; a *conquest* (concr.), i.e. (by impl.) *triumph:*— victory.

3535. Νινευΐ **Ninĕuï**, *nin-yoo-ee';* of Heb. or. [5210]; *Ninevi* (i.e. *Nineveh*), the capital of Assyria:— Nineve.

3536. Νινευΐτης **Ninĕuïtēs**, *nin-yoo-ee'-tace;* from 3535; a *Ninevite*, i.e. inhab. of Nineveh:— of Nineve, Ninevite.

3537. νιπτήρ **niptēr**, *nip-tare';* from 3538; a *ewer:*— bason.

3538. νίπτω **niptō**, *nip'-to;* to *cleanse* (espec. the hands or the feet or the face); cerem. to *perform ablution:*— wash. Comp. 3068.

3539. νοιέω **nŏiĕō**, *noy-eh'-o;* from 3563

νοέω **nŏĕō** *no-eh'-o;* to *exercise* the *mind*, (*observe*), i.e. (fig.) to *comprehend, heed:*— consider, perceive, think, understand.

3540. νόημα **nŏēma**, *nŏ'-ay-mah;* from 3539; a *perception*, i.e. *purpose*, or (by impl.) the *intellect, disposition*, itself:— device, mind, thought.

3541. νόθος **nŏthŏs**, *noth'-os;* of uncert. aff.; a *spurious* or *illegitimate* son:— bastard.

3542. νομή **nŏmē**, *nom-ay';* fem. from the same as 3551; *pasture*, i.e. (the act) *feeding* (fig. *spreading* of a gangrene), or (the food) *pasturage:*— × eat, pasture.

3543. νομίζω **nŏmizō**, *nom-id'-zo;* from 3551; prop. to *do by law* (*usage*), i.e. to *accustom* (pass. *be usual*); by extens. to *deem* or *regard:*— suppose, thing, be wont.

3544. νομικός **nŏmikŏs**, *nom-ik-os';* from

3551; *according* (or *pertaining*) *to law*, i.e. *legal* (cer.); as noun, an *expert in* the (Mosaic) *law:*— about the law, lawyer.

3545. νομίμως **nŏmimōs**, *nom-im'-oce;* adv. from a der. of 3551; *legitimately* (spec. agreeably to the rules of the lists):— lawfully.

3546. νόμισμα **nŏmisma**, *nom'-is-mah;* from 3543; *what is reckoned* as of value (after the Lat. *numisma*), i.e. current *coin:*— money.

3547. νομοδιδάσκαλος **nŏmŏdidaskalŏs**, *nom-od-id-as'-kal-os;* from 3551 and 1320; an *expounder of* the (Jewish) *law*, i.e. a *Rabbi:*— doctor (teacher) of the law.

3548. νομοθεσία **nŏmŏthĕsia**, *nom-oth-es-ee'-ah;* from 3550; *legislation* (spec. the *institution* of the Mosaic *code*):— giving of the law.

3549. νομοθετέω **nŏmŏthĕtĕō**, *nom-oth-et-eh'-o;* from 3550; to *legislate*, i.e. (pass.) to *have* (the Mosaic) *enactments* injoined, *be sanctioned* (by them):— establish, receive the law.

3550. νομοθέτης **nŏmŏthĕtēs**, *nom-oth-et'-ace;* from 3551 and a der. of 5087; a *legislator:*— lawgiver.

3551. νόμος **nŏmŏs**, *nom'-os;* from a primary νέμω **nĕmō**, (to *parcel* out, espec. *food* or *grazing* to animals); *law* (through the idea of prescriptive *usage*), gen. (*regulation*), spec. (of Moses [incl. the volume]; also of the Gospel), or fig. (a *principle*):— law.

3552. νοσέω **nŏsĕō**, *nos-eh'-o;* from 3554; to *be sick*, i.e. (by impl. of a diseased appetite) to *hanker* after (fig. to *harp* upon):— dote.

3553. νόσημα **nŏsēma**, *nos'-ay-ma;* from 3552; an *ailment:*— disease.

3554. νόσος **nŏsŏs**, *nos'-os;* of uncert. aff.; a *malady* (rarely fig. of mor. *disability*):— disease, infirmity, sickness.

3555. νοσσιά **nŏssia**, *nos-see-ah';* from 3502; a *brood* (of chickens):— brood.

3556. νοσσίον **nŏssiŏn**, *nos-see'-on;* dimin. of 3502; a *birdling:*— chicken.

3557. νοσφίζομαι **nŏsphizŏmai**, *nos-fid'-zom-ahee;* mid. voice from νοσφί **nŏsphi** (*apart* or *clandestinely*); to *sequestrate*, for oneself, i.e. *embezzle:*— keep back, purloin.

3558. νότος **nŏtŏs**, *not'-os;* of uncert. aff.; the *south* (*-west*) *wind;* by extens. the *southern quarter* itself:— south (wind).

3559. νουθεσία **nŏuthĕsia**, *noo-thes-ee'-ah;* from 3563 and a der. of 5087; calling *attention* to, i.e. (by impl.) mild *rebuke* or *warning:*— admonition.

3560. νουθετέω **nŏuthĕtĕō**, *noo-thet-eh'-o;* from the same as 3559; to *put in mind*, i.e.

(by impl.) to *caution* or *reprove* gently:— admonish, warn.

3561. νουμηνία **nŏumēnia**, *noo-may-nee´-ah;* fem. of a compound of *3501* and *3376* (as noun by impl. of *2250*); the festival of *new moon:*— new moon.

3562. νουνεχῶς **nŏunĕchōs**, *noon-ekh-oce´;* adv. from a comp. of the acc. of *3563* and *2192;* in a *mind-having* way, i.e. *prudently:*— discreetly.

3563. νοῦς **nŏus**, *nooce;* prob. from the base of *1097;* the *intellect*, i.e. *mind* (divine or human; in thought, feeling, or will); by impl. *meaning:*— mind, understanding. Comp. *5590.*

3564. Νυμφᾶς **Numphas**, *noom-fas´;* prob. contr. for a compound of *3565* and *1435;* *nymph-given* (i.e. *-born*); *Nymphas*, a Chr.:— Nymphas.

3565. νύμφη **numphē**, *noom-fay´;* from a primary but obs. verb νύπτω **nuptō**, (to *veil* as a bride; comp. Lat. "*nupto*," to *marry*); a *young married* woman (as *veiled*), incl. a *betrothed* girl; by impl. a *son's wife:*— bride, daughter in law.

3566. νυμφίος **numphiŏs**, *noom-fee´-os;* from *3565;* a *bride-groom* (lit. or fig.):— bridegroom.

3567. νυμφών **numphōn**, *noom-fohn´;* from *3565;* the *bridal* room:— bridechamber.

3568. νῦν **nun**, *noon;* a primary particle of present time; "*now*" (as adv. of date, a transition or emphasis); also as noun or adj. *present* or *immediate:*— henceforth, + hereafter, of late, soon, present, this (time). See also *3569, 3570.*

3569. τανῦν **tanun**, *tan-oon´;* or

τὰ νῦν **ta nun** *tah noon;* from neut. plur. of *3588* and *3568; the* things *now*, i.e. (adv.) *at present:*— (but) now.

3570. νυνί **nuni**, *noo-nee´;* a prol. form of *3568* for emphasis; *just now:*— now.

3571. νύξ **nux**, *noox;* a primary word; "*night*" (lit. or fig.):— (mid-) night.

3572. νύσσω **nussō**, *noos´-so;* appar. a primary word; to *prick* ("nudge"):— pierce.

3573. νυστάζω **nustazō**, *noos-tad´-zo;* from a presumed der. of *3506;* to *nod*, i.e. (by impl.) to *fall asleep;* fig. to *delay:*— slumber.

3574. νυχθήμερον **nuchthēmĕrŏn**, *nookh-thay´-mer-on;* from *3571* and *2250;* a *day-*and-*night*, i.e. full *day* of twenty-four hours:— night and day.

3575. Νῶε **Nŏē**, *no´-eh;* of Heb. or. [5146]; *Noë*, (i.e. *Noäch*), a patriarch:— Noe.

3576. νωθρός **nōthrŏs**, *no-thros´;* from a der. of *3541; sluggish*, i.e. (lit.) *lazy*, or (fig.) *stupid:*— dull, slothful.

3577. νῶτος **nōtŏs**, *no´-tos;* of uncert. aff.; the *back:*— back.

Ξ

3578. ξενία **xĕnia**, *xen-ee´-ah;* from *3581; hospitality*, i.e. (by impl.) a *place of entertainment:*— lodging.

3579. ξενίζω **xĕnizō**, *xen-id´-zo;* from *3581;* to *be a host* (pass. a *guest*); by impl. *be (make, appear) strange:*— entertain, lodge, (think it) strange.

3580. ξενοδοχέω **xĕnŏdŏchĕō**, *xen-od-okh-eh´-o;* from a compound of *3581* and *1209;* to *be hospitable:*— lodge strangers.

3581. ξένος **xĕnŏs**, *xen´-os;* appar. a primary word; *for.* (lit. *alien*, or fig. *novel*); by impl. a *guest* or (vice-versa) *entertainer:*— host, strange (-r).

3582. ξέστης **xĕstēs**, *xes´-tace;* as if from ξέω **xĕō**, (prop. to *smooth;* by impl. [of friction] to *boil* or *heat*); a *vessel* (as *fashioned* or for *cooking*) [or perh. by corruption from the Lat. *sextarius*, the *sixth* of a modius, i.e. about a *pint*], i.e. (spec.) a *measure* for liquids or solids, (by anal. a *pitcher*):— pot.

3583. ξηραίνω **xērainō**, *xay-rah´-ee-no;* from *3584;* to *desiccate;* by impl. to *shrivel*, to *mature:*— dry up, pine away, be ripe, wither (away).

3584. ξηρός **xērŏs**, *xay-ros´;* from the base of *3582* (through the idea of *scorching*); *arid;* by impl. *shrunken, earth* (as opposed to water):— dry land, withered.

3585. ξύλινος **xulinŏs**, *xoo´-lin-os;* from *3586; wooden:*— of wood.

3586. ξύλον **xulŏn**, *xoo´-lon;* from another form of the base of *3582; timber* (as fuel or material); by impl. a *stick, club* or *tree* or other wooden art. or substance:— staff, stocks, tree, wood.

3587. ξυράω **xuraō**, *xoo-rah´-o;* from a der. of the same as *3586* (mean. a *razor*); to *shave* or "*shear*" the hair:— shave.

O

3588. ὁ **hŏ**, *hŏ;* incl. the fem.

ἡ **hē**, *hay;* and the neut.

τό **tŏ**, *tŏ;* in all their inflections; the def. art.; *the* (sometimes to be supplied, at others omitted, in English idiom):— the, this, that, one, he, she, it, etc.

ὅ **hŏ**. See *3739.*

3589. ὀγδοήκοντα **ŏgdŏēkŏnta**, *og-dŏ-ay´-kon-tah;* from *3590; ten times eight:*— fourscore.

3590. ὄγδοος **ŏgdŏŏs**, *og´-dŏ-os;* from *3638;* the *eighth:*— eighth.

3591. ὄγκος **ŏgkŏs**, *ong´-kos;* prob. from the same as *43;* a *mass* (as *bending* or *bulging* by its load), i.e. *burden* (*hindrance*):— weight.

Greek

3592. ὅδε **hŏdĕ**, *hod´-eh;* incl. the fem.

ἥδε **hēdĕ**, *hay´-deh;* and the neut.

τόδε **tŏdĕ**, *tod´-e;* from 3588 and 1161; the *same,* i.e. *this* or *that* one (plur. *these* or *those*); often used as pers. pron.:— he, she, such, these, thus.

3593. ὁδεύω **hŏdĕuō**, *hod-yoo´-o;* from 3598; to *travel:*— journey.

3594. ὁδηγέω **hŏdēgĕō**, *hod-ayg-eh´-o;* from 3595; to *show* the *way* (lit. or fig. [teach]):— guide, lead.

3595. ὁδηγός **hŏdēgŏs**, *hod-ayg-os´;* from 3598 and 2233; a *conductor* (lit. or fig. [teacher]):— guide, leader.

3596. ὁδοιπορέω **hŏdŏipŏrĕō**, *hod-oy-por-eh´-o;* from a compound of 3598 and 4198; to *be a wayfarer,* i.e. *travel:*— go on a journey.

3597. ὁδοιπορία **hŏdŏipŏria**, *hod-oy-por-ee´-ah;* from the same as 3596; *travel:*— journey (-ing).

3598. ὁδός **hŏdŏs**, *hod-os´;* appar. a primary word; a *road;* by impl. a *progress* (the route, act or distance); fig. a *mode* or *means:*— journey, (high-) way.

3599. ὀδούς **ŏdŏus**, *od-ooce;* perh. from the base of 2068; a *"tooth":*— tooth.

3600. ὀδυνάω **ŏdunaō**, *od-oo-nah´-o;* from 3601; to *grieve:*— sorrow, torment.

3601. ὀδύνη **ŏdunē**, *od-oo´-nay;* from 1416; *grief* (as dejecting):— sorrow.

3602. ὀδυρμός **ŏdurmŏs**, *od-oor-mos´;* from a der. of the base of 1416; *moaning,* i.e. *lamentation:*— mourning.

3603. ὅ ἐστι **hŏ esti**, *hŏ es-tee´* or

ὅ ἐστιν **hŏ estin**, *hŏ es-teen´;* from the neut. of 3739 and the third pers. sing. pres. ind. of 1510; *which is:*— called, which is (make), i.e. (to say).

3604. Ὀζίας **Ŏzias**, *od-zee´-as;* of Heb. or. [5818]; *Ozias* (i.e. *Uzzijah*), an Isr.:— Ozias.

3605. ὄζω **ŏzō**, *od´-zo;* a primary verb (in a strengthened form); to *scent* (usually an ill "odor"): stink.

3606. ὅθεν **hŏthĕn**, *hoth´-en;* from 3739 with the directive enclitic of source; *from which* place or source or cause (adv. or conjunc.):— from thence, (from) whence, where (-by, -fore, -upon).

3607. ὀθόνη **ŏthŏnē**, *oth-on´-ay;* of uncert. aff.; a *linen* cloth, i.e. (espec.) a *sail:*— sheet.

3608. ὀθόνιον **ŏthŏniŏn**, *oth-on´-ee-on;* neut. of a presumed der. of 3607; a linen *bandage:*— linen clothes.

3609. οἰκεῖος **ŏikĕiŏs**, *oy-ki´-os;* from 3624; *domestic,* i.e. (as noun), a *relative, adherent:*— (those) of the (his own) house (-hold).

3610. οἰκέτης **ŏikĕtēs**, *oy-ket´-ace;* from 3611; a fellow *resident,* i.e. menial *domestic:*— (household) servant.

3611. οἰκέω **ŏikĕō**, *oy-keh´-o;* from 3624; to *occupy a house,* i.e. *reside* (fig. *inhabit, remain, inhere*); by impl. to *cohabit:*— dwell. See also 3625.

3612. οἴκημα **ŏikēma**, *oy´-kay-mah;* from 3611; a *tenement,* i.e. (spec.) a *jail:*— prison.

3613. οἰκητήριον **ŏikētēriŏn**, *oy-kay-tay´-ree-on;* neut. of a presumed der. of 3611 (equiv. to 3612); a *residence* (lit. or fig.):— habitation, house.

3614. οἰκία **ŏikia**, *oy-kee´-ah;* from 3624; prop. *residence* (abstr.), but usually (concr.) an *abode* (lit. or fig.); by impl. a *family* (espec. *domestics*):— home, house (-hold).

3615. οἰκιακός **ŏikiakŏs**, *oy-kee-ak-os´;* from 3614; *familiar,* i.e. (as noun) *relatives:*— they (them) of (his own) household.

3616. οἰκοδεσποτέω **ŏikŏdĕspŏtĕō**, *oy-kod-es-pot-eh´-o;* from 3617; to *be the head of* (i.e. *rule*) *a family:*— guide the house.

3617. οἰκοδεσπότης **ŏikŏdĕspŏtēs**, *oy-kod-es-pot´-ace;* from 3624 and 1203; *the head of a family:*— goodman (of the house), householder, master of the house.

3618. οἰκοδομέω **ŏikŏdŏmĕō**, *oy-kod-om-eh´-o;* from the same as 3619; to *be a house-builder,* i.e. *construct* or (fig.) *confirm:*— (be in) build (-er, -ing, up), edify, embolden.

3619. οἰκοδομή **ŏikŏdŏmē**, *oy-kod-om-ay´;* fem. (abstr.) of a compound of 3624 and the base of 1430; *architecture,* i.e. (concr.) a *structure;* fig. *confirmation:*— building, edify (-ication, ing).

3620. οἰκοδομία **ŏikŏdŏmia**, *oy-kod-om-ee´-ah;* from the same as 3619; *confirmation:*— edifying.

3621. οἰκονομέω **ŏikŏnŏmĕō**, *oy-kon-om-eh´-o;* from 3623; to *manage* (a house, i.e. an estate):— be steward.

3622. οἰκονομία **ŏikŏnŏmia**, *oy-kon-om-ee´-ah;* from 3623; *administration* (of a household or estate); spec. a (relig.) *"economy":*— dispensation, stewardship.

3623. οἰκονόμος **ŏikŏnŏmŏs**, *oy-kon-om´-os;* from 3624 and the base of 3551; a *house-distributor* (i.e. *manager*), or *overseer,* i.e. an employee in that capacity; by extens. a fiscal *agent* (*treasurer*); fig. a *preacher* (of the Gospel):— chamberlain, governor, steward.

3624. οἶκος **ŏikŏs**, *oy´-kos;* of uncert. aff.; a *dwelling* (more or less extens., lit. or fig.); by impl. a *family* (more or less related, lit. or fig.):— home, house (-hold), temple.

3625. οἰκουμένη **ŏikŏumĕnē**, *oy-kou-men´-ay;* fem. part. pres. pass. of 3611 (as noun, by impl. of 1093); *land,* i.e. the (terrene part of the) *globe;* spec. the Rom. *empire:*— earth, world.

3626. οἰκουρός **ŏikŏurŏs**, *oy-koo-ros´* or

οἰκουργός **ŏikŏurgŏs**, *oy-koor-gos´;*

from *3624* and οὖρος **ŏurŏs** (a *guard;* be "ware"); a *stayer at home,* i.e. *domestically inclined* (a "good housekeeper"):— keeper at home.

3627. οἰκτείρω **ŏiktĕirō**, *oyk-ti´-ro;* also (in certain tenses) prol.

     οἰκτερέω **ŏiktĕrĕō**, *oyk-ter-eh´-o;* from οἶκτος **ŏiktŏs**, *(pity);* to *exercise pity:*— have compassion on.

3628. οἰκτιρμός **ŏiktirmŏs**, *oyk-tir-mos´;* from *3627; pity:*— mercy.

3629. οἰκτίρμων **ŏiktirmōn**, *oyk-tir´-mone;* from *3627; compassionate:*— merciful, of tender mercy.

     οἶμαι **ŏimai**. See *3633.*

3630. οἰνοπότης **ŏinŏpŏtēs**, *oy-nop-ot´-ace;* from *3631* and a der. of the alt. of *4095;* a *tippler:*— winebibber.

3631. οἶνος **ŏinŏs**, *oy´-nos;* a primary word (or perh. of Heb. origin [3196l]); *"wine"* (lit. or fig.):— wine.

3632. οἰνοφλυγία **ŏinŏphlugia**, *oy-nof-loog-ee´-ah;* from *3631* and a form of the base of *5397;* an *overflow* (or surplus) of *wine,* i.e. *vinolency (drunkenness):*— excess of wine.

3633. οἴομαι **ŏiŏmai**, *oy´-om-ahee;*   or (shorter)

     οἶμαι **ŏimai**, *oy´-mahee;* mid. voice appar. from *3634;* to *make like* (oneself), i.e. *imagine (be of* the *opinion):*— suppose, think.

3634. οἶος **hŏiŏs**, *hoy´-os;* prob. akin to *3588, 3739,* and *3745; such* or *what sort* of (as a correl. or exclamation); espec. the neut. (adv.) with neg. not *so:*— so (as), such as, what (manner of), which.

     οἴω **ŏiō**. See *5342.*

3635. ὀκνέω **ŏknĕō**, *ok-neh´-o;* from ὄκνος **ŏknŏs**, *(hesitation);* to *be slow* (fig. *loath):*— delay.

3636. ὀκνηρός **ŏknērŏs**, *ok-nay-ros´;* from *3635; tardy,* i.e. *indolent;* (fig.) *irksome:*— grievous, slothful.

3637. ὀκταήμερος **ŏktaēmĕrŏs**, *ok-tah-ay´-mer-os;* from *3638* and *2250;* an *eight-day* old person or act:— the eighth day.

3638. ὀκτώ **ŏktō**, *ok-to´;* a primary numeral; *"eight":*— eight.

3639. ὄλεθρος **ŏlĕthrŏs**, *ol´-eth-ros;* from a primary ὄλλυμι **ŏllumi** (to *destroy;* a prol. form); *ruin,* i.e. *death, punishment:*— destruction.

3640. ὀλιγόπιστος **ŏligŏpistŏs**, *ol-ig-op´-is-tos;* from *3641* and *4102; incredulous,* i.e. *lacking confidence* (in Christ):— of little faith.

3641. ὀλίγος **ŏligŏs**, *ol-ee´-gos;* of uncert. aff.; *puny* (in extent, degree, number, duration or value); espec. neut. (adv.) *somewhat:*— + almost, brief [-ly], few, (a) little, + long, a season, short, small, a while.

3642. ὀλιγόψυχος **ŏligŏpsuchŏs**, *ol-ig-op´-soo-*

khos; from *3641* and *6590; little-spirited,* i.e. *faint-hearted:*— feebleminded.

3643. ὀλιγωρέω **ŏligōrĕō**, *ol-ig-o-reh´-o;* from a compound of *3641* and ὥρα **ōra** *("care");* to *have little regard,* for, i.e. to *disesteem:*— despise.

3644. ὀλοθρευτής **ŏlŏthrĕutēs**, *ol-oth-ryoo-tace´;* from *3645;* a *ruiner,* i.e. (spec.) a venomous *serpent:*— destroyer.

3645. ὀλοθρεύω **ŏlŏthrĕuō**, *ol-oth-ryoo´-o;* from *3639;* to *spoil,* i.e. *slay:*— destroy.

3646. ὁλοκαύτωμα **hŏlŏkautōma**, *hol-ok-ŏw´-to-mah;* from a der. of a compound of *3650* and a der. of *2545;* a *wholly-consumed* sacrifice ("holocaust"):— (whole) burnt offering.

3647. ὁλοκληρία **hŏlŏklēria**, *hol-ok-lay-ree´-ah;* from *3648; integrity,* i.e. phys. *wholeness:*— perfect soundness.

3648. ὁλόκληρος **hŏlŏklērŏs**, *hol´-ok´-lay-ros;* from *3650* and *2819; complete* in every *part,* i.e. perfectly *sound* (in body):— entire, whole.

3649. ὀλολύζω **ŏlŏluzō**, *ol-ol-ood´-zo;* a redupl. primary verb; to *"howl"* or *"halloo",* i.e. *shriek:*— howl.

3650. ὅλος **hŏlŏs**, *hol-os;* a primary word; *"whole"* or *"all",* i.e. *complete* (in extent, amount, time or degree), espec. (neut.) as noun or adv.:— all, altogether, every whit, + throughout, whole.

3651. ὁλοτελής **hŏlŏtĕlēs**, *hol-ot-el-ace´;* from *3650* and *5056; complete* to the *end,* i.e. *absolutely perfect:*— wholly.

3652. Ὀλυμπᾶς **Olumpas**, *ol-oom-pas´;* prob. a contr. from Ὀλυμπιόδωρος **Olumpiŏdōrŏs**,   *(Olympian-bestowed,* i.e. *heaven-descended); Olympas,* a Chr.:— Olympas.

3653. ὄλυνθος **ŏlunthŏs**, *ol´-oon-thos;* of uncert. der.; an *unripe* (because out of season) *fig:*— untimely fig.

3654. ὅλως **hŏlōs**, *hol-oce;* adv. from *3650; completely,* i.e. *altogether;* (by anal.) *everywhere;* (neg.) not *by any means:*— at all, commonly, utterly.

3655. ὄμβρος **ŏmbrŏs**, *om´-bros;* of uncert. aff.; a thunder *storm:*— shower.

3656. ὁμιλέω **hŏmilĕō**, *hom-il-eh´-o;* from *3658;* to *be in company* with, i.e. (by impl.) to *converse:*— commune, talk.

3657. ὁμιλία **hŏmilia**, *hom-il-ee´-ah;* from *3658; companionship* ("homily"), i.e. (by impl.) *intercourse:*— communication.

3658. ὅμιλος **hŏmilŏs**, *hom´-il-os;* from the base of *3674* and a der. of the alt. of *138* (mean. a *crowd); association together,* i.e. a *multitude:*— company.

3659. ὄμμα **ŏmma**, *om´-mah;* from *3700;* a *sight,* i.e. (by impl.) the *eye:*— eye.

3660. ὀμνύω **ŏmnuō**, *om-noo´-o;* a prol. form of a primary but obsolete ὄμω **ŏmō**, for which another prol. form ὀμόω **ŏmŏō** *om-ŏ´-o*) is used in certain tenses; to *swear,* i.e. *take* (or *declare on*) *oath:*— swear.

3661. ὀμοθυμαδόν **hŏmŏthumadŏn**, *hom-oth-oo-mad-on´;* adv. from a compound of the base of *3674* and *2372; unanimously:*— with one accord (mind).

3662. ὀμοιάζω **hŏmŏiazō**, *hom-oy-ad´-zo;* from *3664;* to *resemble:*— agree.

3663. ὀμοιοπαθής **hŏmŏiŏpathēs**, *hom-oy-op-ath-ace´;* from *3664* and the alt. of *3958; similarly affected:*— of (subject to) like passions.

3664. ὅμοιος **hŏmŏiŏs**, *hom´-oy-os;* from the base of *3674; similar* (in appearance or character):— like, + manner.

3665. ὀμοιότης **hŏmŏiŏtēs**, *hom-oy-ot´-ace;* from *3664; resemblance:*— like as, similitude.

3666. ὀμοιόω **hŏmŏiŏō**, *hom-oy-ŏ´-o;* from *3664;* to *assimilate,* i.e. *compare;* pass. to *become similar:*— be (make) like, (in the) liken (-ess), resemble.

3667. ὀμοίωμα **hŏmŏiōma**, *hom-oy´-o-mah;* from *3666;* a *form;* abstr. *resemblance:*— made like to, likeness, shape, similitude.

3668. ὀμοίως **hŏmŏiōs**, *hom-oy´-oce;* adv. from *3664; similarly:*— likewise, so.

3669. ὀμοίωσις **hŏmŏiōsis**, *hom-oy´-o-sis;* from *3666; assimilation,* i.e. *resemblance:*— similitude.

3670. ὀμολογέω **hŏmŏlŏgeō**, *hom-ol-og-eh´-o;* from a compound of the base of *3674* and *3056;* to *assent,* i.e. *covenant, acknowledge:*— con (pro-) fess, confession is made, give thanks, promise.

3671. ὀμολογία **hŏmŏlŏgia**, *hom-ol-og-ee´-ah;* from the same as *3670; acknowledgment:*— con- (pro-) fession, professed.

3672. ὀμολογουμένως **hŏmŏlŏgŏumĕnōs**, *hom-ol-og-ŏw-men´-oce;* adv. of pres. pass. part. of *3670; confessedly:*— without controversy.

3673. ὀμότεχνος **hŏmŏtĕchnŏs**, *hom-ot´-ekh-nos;* from the base of *3674* and *5078;* a *fellow-artificer:*— of the same craft.

3674. ὀμοῦ **hŏmŏu**, *hom-oo´;* gen. of ὀμός **hŏmŏs**, (the *same;* akin to *260*) as adv.; *at the same* place or time:— together.

3675. ὀμόφρων **hŏmŏphrōn**, *hom-of´-rone;* from the base of *3674* and *5424; like-minded,* i.e. *harmonious:*— of one mind.

ὀμόω **ŏmŏō**. See *3660.*

3676. ὅμως **hŏmōs**, *hom´-oce;* adv. from the base of *3674; at the same* time, i.e. (conjunc.) *notwithstanding, yet still:*— and even, nevertheless, though but.

3677. ὄναρ **ŏnar**, *on´-ar;* of uncert. der.; a *dream:*— dream.

3678. ὀνάριον **ŏnariŏn**, *on-ar´-ee-on;* neut. of a presumed der. of *3688;* a *little ass:*— young ass.

ὀνάω **ŏnaō**. See *3685.*

3679. ὀνειδίζω **ŏnĕidizō**, *on-i-did´-zo;* from *3681;* to *defame,* i.e. *rail at, chide, taunt:*— cast in teeth, (suffer) reproach, revile, upbraid.

3680. ὀνειδισμός **ŏnĕidismŏs**, *on-i-dis-mos´;* from *3679; contumely:*— reproach.

3681. ὄνειδος **ŏnĕidŏs**, *on´-i-dos;* prob. akin to the base of *3686; notoriety,* i.e. a *taunt* (*disgrace*):— reproach.

3682. Ὀνήσιμος **Ŏnēsimŏs**, *on-ay´-sim-os;* from *3685; profitable; Onesimus,* a Chr.:— Onesimus.

3683. Ὀνησίφορος **Ŏnēsiphŏrŏs**, *on-ay-sif´-or-os;* from a der. of *3685* and *5411; profit-bearer; Onesiphorus,* a Chr.:— Onesiphorus.

3684. ὀνικός **ŏnikŏs**, *on-ik-os´;* from *3688; belonging to* an *ass,* i.e. *large* (so as to be turned by an ass):— millstone.

3685. ὀνίνημι **ŏninēmi**, *on-in´-ay-mee;* a prol. form of an appar. primary verb

(ὄνομαι **ŏnŏmai**, to *slur*); for which another prol. form (ὀνάω **ŏnaō**) is used as an alt. in some tenses [unless indeed it be ident. with the base of *3686* through the idea of *notoriety*]; to *gratify,* i.e. (mid. voice) to *derive pleasure* or *advantage* from:— have joy.

3686. ὄνομα **ŏnŏma**, *on´-om-ah;* from a presumed der. of the base of *1097* (comp. *3685*); a *"name"* (lit. or fig.) [*authority, character*]:— called, (+ sur-) name (-d).

3687. ὀνομάζω **ŏnŏmazō**, *on-om-ad´-zo;* from *3686;* to *name,* i.e. *assign an appellation;* by extens. to *utter, mention, profess:*— call, name.

3688. ὄνος **ŏnŏs**, *on´-os;* appar. a primary word; a *donkey:*— an ass.

3689. ὄντως **ŏntōs**, *on´-toce;* adv. of the oblique cases of *5607; really:*— certainly, clean, indeed, of a truth, verily.

3690. ὄξος **ŏxŏs**, *ox-os;* from *3691; vinegar,* i.e. *sour* wine:— vinegar.

3691. ὀξύς **ŏxus**, *ox-oos´;* prob. akin to the base of *188* [*"acid"*]; *keen;* by anal. *rapid:*— sharp, swift.

3692. ὀπή **ŏpē**, *op-ay´;* prob. from *3700;* a *hole* (as if for light), i.e. *cavern;* by anal. a *spring* (of water):— cave, place.

3693. ὄπισθεν **ŏpisthĕn**, *op´-is-then;* from ὄπις **ŏpis**, (*regard;* from *3700*) with enclitic of source; *from the rear* (as a secure aspect), i.e. *at the back* (adv. and prep. of place or time):— after, backside, behind.

3694. ὀπίσω **ŏpisō**, *op-is´-o;* from the same as *3693* with enclitic of direction; *to the back,* i.e. *aback* (as adv. or prep. of time or

Greek

place; or as noun):— after, back (-ward), (+ get) behind, + follow.

3695. ὁπλίζω **hŏplizō**, *hop-lid´-zo;* from 3696; to *equip* (with weapons [mid. voice and fig.]):— arm self.

3696. ὅπλον **hŏplŏn**, *hop´-lon;* prob. from a primary ἕπω **hĕpō** (to be *busy* about); an *implement,* or *utensil* or *tool* (lit. or fig., espec. offensive for war):— armour, instrument, weapon.

3697. ὁποῖος **hŏpŏiŏs**, *hop-oy´-os;* from 3739 and 4169; of *what* kind *that,* i.e. *how* (*as*) *great* (*excellent*) (spec. as an indef. correl. to the antecedent def. 5108 of quality):— what manner (sort) of, such as whatsoever.

3698. ὁπότε **hŏpŏtĕ**, *hop-ot´-eh;* from 3739 and 4218; *what* (-ever) *then,* i.e. (of time) *as soon as:*— when.

3699. ὅπου **hŏpŏu**, *hop´-oo;* from 3739 and 4225; *what* (-ever) *where,* i.e. *at whichever* spot:— in what place, where (-as, -soever), whither (+ soever).

3700. ὁπτάνομαι **ŏptanŏmai**, *op-tan´-om-ahee;* a (mid. voice) prol. form of the primary (mid. voice)

ὄπτομαι **ŏptŏmai**, *op´-tom-ahee;* which is used for it in certain tenses; and both as alternate of 3708; to *gaze* (i.e. with wide-open eyes, as at something remarkable; and thus differing from 991, which denotes simply *voluntary* observation; and from 1492, which expresses merely mechanical, passive or casual vision; while 2300, and still more emphatically its intensive 2334, signifies an earnest but more continued *inspection;* and 4648 a watching *from a distance*):— appear, look, see, shew self.

3701. ὀπτασία **ŏptasia**, *op-tas-ee´-ah;* from a presumed der. of 3700; *visuality,* i.e. (concr.) an *apparition:*— vision.

ὄπτομαι **ŏptŏmai**. See 3700.

3702. ὀπτός **ŏptŏs**, *op-tos´;* from an obs. verb akin to ἕπσω **hĕpsō** (to "*steep*"); *cooked,* i.e. *roasted:*— broiled.

3703. ὀπώρα **ŏpōra**, *op-o´-rah;* appar. from the base of 3796 and 5610; prop. *even-tide* of the (summer) season (*dog-days*), i.e. (by impl.) *ripe* fruit:— fruit.

3704. ὅπως **hŏpōs**, *hop´-oce;* from 3739 and 4459; *what* (-ever) *how,* i.e. *in the manner that* (as adv. or conjunc. of coincidence, intentional or actual):— because, how, (so) that, to, when.

3705. ὅραμα **hŏrama**, *hor´-am-ah;* from 3708; something *gazed at,* i.e. a *spectacle* (espec. *supernatural*):— sight, vision.

3706. ὅρασις **hŏrasis**, *hor´-as-is;* from 3708; the act of *gazing,* i.e. (external) an *aspect* or (intern.) an inspired *appearance:*— sight, vision, sion.

3707. ὁρατός **hŏratŏs**, *hor-at-os´;* from 3708; *gazed at,* i.e. (by impl.) *capable of being seen:*— visible.

3708. ὁράω **hŏraō**, *hor-ah´-o;* prop. to *stare* at [comp. 3700], i.e. (by impl.) to *discern* clearly (phys. or ment.); by extens. to *attend* to; by Heb. to *experience;* pass. to *appear:*— behold, perceive, see, take heed.

3709. ὀργή **ŏrgē**, *or-gay´;* from 3713; prop. *desire* (as a *reaching* forth or *excitement* of the mind), i.e. (by anal.) violent *passion* (*ire,* or [justifiable] *abhorrence*); by impl. *punishment:*— anger, indignation, vengeance, wrath.

3710. ὀργίζω **ŏrgizō**, *or-gid´-zo;* from 3709; to *provoke* or *enrage,* i.e. (pass.) *become exasperated:*— be angry (wroth).

3711. ὀργίλος **ŏrgilŏs**, *org-ee´-los;* from 3709; *irascible:*— soon angry.

3712. ὀργυιά **ŏrguia**, *org-wee-ah´;* from 3713; a *stretch* of the arms, i.e. a *fathom:*— fathom.

3713. ὀρέγομαι **ŏrĕgŏmai**, *or-eg´-om-ahee;* mid. voice of appar. a prol. form of an obs. primary [comp. 3735]; to *stretch* oneself, i.e. *reach* out after (*long* for):— covet after, desire.

3714. ὀρεινός **ŏrĕinŏs**, *or-i-nos;* from 3735; *mountainous,* i.e. (fem. by impl. of 5561) the *Highlands* (of Judæa):— hill country.

3715. ὄρεξις **ŏrĕxis**, *or´-ex-is;* from 3713; *excitement* of the mind, i.e. *longing* after:— lust.

3716. ὀρθοποδέω **ŏrthŏpŏdĕō**, *or-thop-od-eh´-o;* from a compound of 3717 and 4228; to be *straight-footed,* i.e. (fig.) to *go directly* forward:— walk uprightly.

3717. ὀρθός **ŏrthŏs**, *or-thos´;* prob. from the base of 3735; *right* (as *rising*), i.e. (perpendicularly) *erect* (fig. *honest*), or (horizontally) *level* or *direct:*— straight, upright.

3718. ὀρθοτομέω **ŏrthŏtŏmĕō**, *or-thot-om-eh´-o;* from a compound of 3717 and the base of 5114, to *make a straight cut,* i.e. (fig.) to *dissect* (*expound*) *correctly* (the divine message):— rightly divide.

3719. ὀρθρίζω **ŏrthrizō**, *or-thrid´-zo;* from 3722; to *use* the *dawn,* i.e. (by impl.) to *repair betimes:*— come early in the morning.

3720. ὀρθρινός **ŏrthrinŏs**, *or-thrin-os´;* from 3722; *relating to* the *dawn,* i.e. *matutinal* (as an epithet of Venus, espec. brilliant in the early day):— morning.

3721. ὄρθριος **ŏrthriŏs**, *or´-three-os;* from 3722; *in* the *dawn,* i.e. up *at day-break:*— early.

3722. ὄρθρος **ŏrthrŏs**, *or´-thros;* from the same as 3735; *dawn* (as *sun-rise,* *rising* of light); by extens. *morn:*— early in the morning.

3723. ὀρθῶς **ŏrthŏs**, *or-thoce´;* adv. from

3717; in a straight manner, i.e. (fig.) *correctly* (also mor.):— plain, right (-ly).

3724. ὁρίζω **hŏrizō**, *hor-id´-zo;* from 3725; to *mark* out or *bound* ("horizon"), i.e. (fig.) to *appoint, decree, specify:*— declare, determine, limit, ordain.

3725. ὅριον **hŏriŏn**, *hor´-ee-on;* neut. of a der. of an appar. primary ὅρος **hŏrŏs** (a *bound* or *limit*); a *boundary*-line, i.e. (by impl.) a *frontier (region)*:— border, coast.

3726. ὁρκίζω **hŏrkizō**, *hor-kid´-zo;* from 3727; to *put on oath*, i.e. *make swear;* by anal. to solemnly *enjoin:*— adjure, charge.

3727. ὅρκος **hŏrkŏs**, *hor´-kos;* from ἕρκος **hěrkŏs**, (a *fence;* perh. akin to 3725); a *limit*, i.e. (sacred) *restraint* (spec. an *oath*):— oath.

3728. ὁρκωμοσία **hŏrkōmŏsia**, *hor-ko-mos-ee´ah;* from a compound of 3727 and a der. of 3660; *asseveration on oath:*— oath.

3729. ὁρμάω **hŏrmaō**, *hor-mah´-o;* from 3730; to *start, spur* or *urge* on, i.e. (refl.) to *dash* or *plunge:*— run (violently), rush.

3730. ὁρμή **hŏrmē**, *hor-may´;* of uncert. aff.; a violent *impulse*, i.e. *onset:*— assault.

3731. ὅρμημα **hŏrmēma**, *hor´-may-mah;* from 3730; an *attack*, i.e. (abstr.) *precipitancy:*— violence.

3732. ὄρνεον **ŏrnĕŏn**, *or´-neh-on;* neut. of a presumed der. of 3733; a *birdling:*— bird, fowl.

3733. ὄρνις **ŏrnis**, *or´-nis;* prob. from a prol. form of the base of 3735; a *bird* (as *rising* in the air), i.e. (spec.) a *hen* (or female domestic fowl):— hen.

3734. ὁροθεσία **hŏrŏthĕsia**, *hor-oth-es-ee´-ah;* from a compound of the base of 3725 and a der. of 5087; a *limit-placing*, i.e. (concr.) *boundary-line:*— bound.

3735. ὄρος **ŏrŏs**, *or´-os;* prob. from an obs. ὄρω **ŏrō** (to *rise* or "*rear;*" perh. akin to 142; comp. 3733); a *mountain* (as *lifting* itself above the plain):— hill, mount (-ain).

3736. ὀρύσσω **ŏrussō**, *or-oos´-so;* appar. a primary verb; to "*burrow*" in the ground, i.e. *dig:*— dig.

3737. ὀρφανός **ŏrphanŏs**, *or-fan-os´;* of uncert. aff.; *bereaved* ("orphan"), i.e. *parentless:*— comfortless, fatherless.

3738. ὀρχέομαι **ŏrchĕŏmai**, *or-kheh´-om-ahee;* mid. voice from ὄρχος **ŏrchŏs** (a *row* or *ring*); to *dance*, (from the *ranklike* or *regular* motion):— dance.

3739. ὅς **hŏs**, *hos;* incl. fem.

ἥ **hē**, *hay;* and neut.

ὅ **hŏ** *hŏ;* prob. a primary word (or perh. a form of the art. 3588); the rel. (sometimes demonstr.) pron., *who, which, what, that:*— one, (an-, the) other, some, that, what, which, who (-m, -se), etc. See also 3757.

3740. ὁσάκις **hŏsakis**, *hos-ak´-is;* multiple

adv. from 3739; *how* (i.e. with 302, *so*) *many times* as:— as oft (-en) as.

3741. ὅσιος **hŏsiŏs**, *hos´-ee-os;* of uncert. aff.; prop. *right* (by intrinsic or divine character; thus distinguished from 1342, which refers rather to *human* statutes and relations; from 2413, which denotes formal *consecration;* and from 40, which relates to *purity* from defilement), i.e. *hallowed (pious, sacred, sure)*:— holy, mercy, shalt be.

3742. ὁσιότης **hŏsiŏtēs**, *hos-ee-ot´-ace;* from 3741; *piety:*— holiness.

3743. ὁσίως **hŏsiōs**, *hos-ee-oce´;* adv. from 3741; *piously:*— holily.

3744. ὀσμή **ŏsmē**, *os-may´;* from 3605; *fragrance* (lit. or fig.):— odour, savour.

3745. ὅσος **hŏsŏs**, *hos´-os;* by redupl. from 3739; *as (much, great, long,* etc.) *as:*— all (that), as (long, many, much) (as), how great (many, much), [in-] asmuch as, so many as, that (ever), the more, those things, what (great, -soever), wheresoever, wherewithsoever, which, × while, who (-soever).

3746. ὅσπερ **hŏspĕr**, *hos´-per;* from 3739 and 4007; *who especially:*— whomsoever.

3747. ὀστέον **ŏstĕŏn**, *os-teh´-on;* or contr.

ὀστοῦν **ŏstoun**, *os-toon´;* of uncert. aff.; a *bone:*— bone.

3748. ὅστις **hŏstis**, *hos´-tis;* incl. the fem.

ἥτις **hētis**, *hay´-tis;* and the neut.

ὅ,τι **hŏ,ti**, *hot´-ee;* from 3739 and 5100; *which some*, i.e. *any that;* also (def.) *which same:*— × and (they), (such) as, (they) that, in that they, what (-soever), whereas ye, (they) which, who (-soever). Comp. 3754.

3749. ὀστράκινος **ŏstrakinŏs**, *os-tra´-kin-os;* from ὄστρακον **ŏstrakŏn**, ["oyster"] (a *tile*, i.e. *terra cotta*); *earthen*-ware, i.e. *clayey;* by impl. *frail:*— of earth, earthen.

3750. ὄσφρησις **ŏsphrēsis**, *os´-fray-sis;* from a der. of 3605; *smell* (the sense):— smelling.

3751. ὀσφύς **ŏsphus**, *os-foos´;* of uncert. aff.; the *loin* (extern.), i.e. the *hip;* intern. (by extens.) *procreative power:*— loin.

3752. ὅταν **hŏtan**, *hot´-an;* from 3753 and 302; *whenever* (implying *hypothesis* or more or less *uncertainty*); also caus. (conjunc.) *inasmuch as:*— as long (soon) as, that, + till, when (-soever), while.

3753. ὅτε **hŏtĕ**, *hot´-eh;* from 3739 and 5037; *at which* (thing) *too*, i.e. *when:*— after (that), as soon as, that, when, while.

ὅ, τε **hŏ, tĕ**, *hŏ,t´-eh;* also fem.

ἥ, τε **hē, tĕ**, *hay´-teh;* and neut.

τό, τε **tŏ, tĕ**, *tot´-eh;* simply the art. 3588 followed by 5037; so written (in some editions) to distinguish them from 3752 and 5119.

3754. ὅτι **hŏti**, *hot´-ee;* neut. of 3748 as conjunc.; demonst. *that* (sometimes redundant); caus. *because:*— as concerning that, as though, because (that), for (that), how (that), (in) that, though, why.

3755. ὅτου **hŏtŏu**, *hot´-oo;* for the gen. of *3748* (as adverb); during *which same* time, i.e. *whilst:*— whiles.

3756. οὐ **ŏu**, *oo;* also (before a vowel)

οὐκ **ŏuk**, *ook;* and (before an aspirate)

οὐχ **ŏuch**, *ookh;* a primary word; the absolute neg. [comp. *3361*] adv.; *no* or *not:*— + long, nay, neither, never, no (× man), none, [can-] not, + nothing, + special, un ([-worthy]), when, + without, + yet but. See also *3364, 3372.*

3757. οὗ **ŏu**, *hoo;* gen. of *3739* as adv.; at *which* place, i.e. *where:*— where (-in), whither ([-soever]).

3758. οὐά **ŏua**, *oo-ah´;* a primary exclamation of surprise; "*ah*":— ah.

3759. οὐαί **ŏuai**, *oo-ah´-ee;* a primary exclamation of grief; "*woe*":— alas, woe.

3760. οὐδαμῶς **ŏudamōs**, *oo-dam-oce´;* adv. from (the fem.) of *3762; by no means:*— not.

3761. οὐδέ **ŏudĕ**, *oo-deh´;* from *3756* and *1161; not however,* i.e. *neither, nor, not even:*— neither (indeed), never, no (more, nor, not), nor (yet), (also, even, then) not (even, so much as), + nothing, so much as.

3762. οὐδείς **ŏudĕis**, *oo-dice´;* incl. fem.

οὐδεμία **ŏudĕmia**, *oo-dem-ee´-ah;* and neut.

οὐδέν **ŏudĕn**, *oo-den´;* from *3761* and *1520; not even one* (man, woman or thing), i.e. *none, nobody, nothing:*— any (man), aught, man, neither any (thing), never (man), no (man), none (+ of these things), not (any, at all, -thing), nought.

3763. οὐδέποτε **ŏudĕpŏtĕ**, *oo-dep´-ot-eh;* from *3761* and *4218; not even at any time,* i.e. *never at all:*— neither at any time, never, nothing at any time.

3764. οὐδέπω **ŏudĕpō**, *oo-dep´-o;* from *3761* and *4452; not even yet:*— as yet not, never before (yet), (not) yet.

3765. οὐκέτι **ŏukĕti**, *ook-et´-ee;* also (separately)

οὐκ ἔτι **ŏuk ĕti**, *ook et´-ee;* from *3756* and *2089; not yet, no longer:*— after that (not), (not) any more, henceforth (hereafter) not, no longer (more), not as yet (now), now no more (not), yet (not).

3766. οὐκοῦν **ŏukŏun**, *ook-oon´;* from *3756* and *3767; is it not therefore that,* i.e. (affirmatively) *hence* or *so:*— then.

3767. οὖν **ŏun**, *oon;* appar. a primary word; (adv.) *certainly,* or (conjunc.) *accordingly:*— and (so, truly), but, now (then), so (likewise then), then, therefore, verily, wherefore.

3768. οὔπω **ŏupō**, *oo´-po;* from *3756* and *4452; not yet:*— hitherto not, (no ...) as yet, not yet.

3769. οὐρά **ŏura**, *oo-rah´;* appar. a primary word; a *tail:*— tail.

3770. οὐράνιος **ŏuraniŏs**, *oo-ran´-ee-os;* from *3772; celestial,* i.e. *belonging to* or *coming from* the *sky:*— heavenly.

3771. οὐρανόθεν **ŏuranŏthĕn**, *oo-ran-oth´-en;* from *3772* and the enclitic of source; *from* the *sky:*— from heaven.

3772. οὐρανός **ŏuranŏs**, *oo-ran-os´;* perh. from the same as *3735* (through the idea of *elevation*); the *sky;* by extens. *heaven* (as the abode of God); by impl. *happiness, power, eternity;* spec. the *Gospel* (*Christianity*):— air, heaven (I-ly), sky.

3773. Οὐρβανός **Ŏurbanŏs**, *oor-ban-os´;* of Lat. or.; *Urbanus* (of the *city,* "*urbane*"), a Chr.:— Urbanus.

3774. Οὐρίας **Ŏurias**, *oo-ree´-as;* of Heb. or. [223]; *Urias* (i.e. *Urijah*), a Hittite:— Urias.

3775. οὖς **ŏus**, *ooce;* appar. a primary word; the *ear* (phys. or ment.):— ear.

3776. οὐσία **ŏusia**, *oo-see´-ah;* from the fem. of *5607; substance,* i.e. *property* (*possessions*):— goods, substance.

3777. οὔτε **ŏutĕ**, *oo´-teh;* from *3756* and *5037; not too,* i.e. *neither* or *nor;* by anal. *not even:*— neither, none, nor (yet), (no, yet) not, nothing.

3778. οὗτος **hŏutŏs**, *hoo´-tos;* incl. nom. masc. plur.

οὗτοι **hŏutŏi**, *hoo´-toy;* nom. fem. sing.

αὕτη **hautē**, *hŏw´-tay;* and nom. fem. plur.

αὗται **hautai**, *hŏw´-tahee;* from the art. *3588* and *846; the he* (*she* or it), i.e. *this* or *that* (often with art. repeated):— he (it was that), hereof, it, she, such as, the same, these, they, this (man, same, woman), which, who.

3779. οὕτω **hŏutō**, *hoo´-to;* or (before a vowel)

οὕτως **hŏutōs**, *hoo´-toce;* adv. from *3778; in this way* (referring to what precedes or follows):— after that, after (in) this manner, as, even (so), for all that, like (-wise), no more, on this fashion (-wise), so (in like manner), thus, what.

3780. οὐχί **ŏuchi**, *oo-khee´;* intens. of *3756; not indeed:*— nay, not.

3781. ὀφειλέτης **ŏphĕilĕtēs**, *of-i-let´-ace;* from *3784;* an *ower,* i.e. person *indebted;* fig. a *delinquent;* mor. a *transgressor* (against God):— debtor, which owed, sinner.

3782. ὀφειλή **ŏphĕilē**, *of-i-lay´;* from *3784; indebtedness,* i.e. (concr.) a *sum* owed; fig. *obligation,* i.e. (conjugal) *duty:*— debt, due.

3783. ὀφείλημα **ŏphĕilēma**, *of-i´-lay-mah;*

from (the alt. of) *3784; something owed*, i.e. (fig.) a *due;* mor. a *fault:*— debt.

3784. ὀφείλω **ŏphĕilō,** *of-i´-lo;* or (in certain tenses) its prol. form

ὀφειλέω **ŏphĕilĕō,** *of-i-leh´-o;* prob. from the base of *3786* (through the idea of *accruing*); to owe (pecuniarily); fig. to *be under obligation (ought, must, should)*; mor. to *fail* in duty:— behove, be bound, (be) debt (-or), (be) due (-ty), be guilty (indebted), (must) need (-s), ought, owe, should. See also *3785.*

3785. ὄφελον **ŏphĕlŏn,** *of´-el-on;* first pers. sing. of a past tense of *3784; I ought (wish)*, i.e. (interj.) *oh that!:*— would (to God.)

3786. ὄφελος **ŏphĕlŏs,** *of´-el-os;* from ὀφέλλω **ŏphĕllō,** (to *heap* up, i.e. *accumulate* or *benefit*); *gain:*— advantageth, profit.

3787. ὀφθαλμοδουλεία **ŏphthalmŏdŏulĕia,** *of-thal-mod-oo-li´-ah;* from *3788* and *1397; sight-labor*, i.e. that needs watching (*remissness*):— eye-service.

3788. ὀφθαλμός **ŏphthalmŏs,** *of-thal-mos´;* from *3700;* the *eye* (lit. or fig.); by impl. *vision;* fig. *envy* (from the jealous side-glance):— eye, sight.

3789. ὄφις **ŏphis,** *of´-is;* prob. from *3700* (through the idea of *sharpness* of vision); a *snake*, fig. (as a type of sly cunning) an artful *malicious* person, espec. *Satan:*— serpent.

3790. ὀφρύς **ŏphrus,** *of-roos´;* perh. from *3700* (through the idea of the shading or proximity to the organ of *vision*); the eye-"*brow*" or *forehead*, i.e. (fig.) the *brink* of a precipice:— brow.

3791. ὀχλέω **ŏchlĕō,** *okh-leh´-o;* from *3793;* to *mob*, i.e. (by impl.) to *harass:*— vex.

3792. ὀχλοποιέω **ŏchlŏpŏiĕō,** *okh-lop-oy-eh´-o;* from *3793* and *4160;* to *make a crowd*, i.e. *raise a* public *disturbance:*— gather a company.

3793. ὄχλος **ŏchlŏs,** *okh´los;* from a der. of *2192* (mean. a *vehicle*); a *throng* (as *borne* along); by impl. the *rabble;* by extens. a *class* of people; fig. a *riot:*— company, multitude, number (of people), people, press.

3794. ὀχύρωμα **ŏchurōma,** *okh-oo´-ro-mah;* from a remote der. of *2192* (mean. to *fortify*, through the idea of *holding* safely); a *castle* (fig. *argument*):— stronghold.

3795. ὀψάριον **ŏpsariŏn,** *op-sar´-ee-on;* neut. of a presumed der. of the base of *3702;* a *relish* to other food (as if cooked *sauce*), i.e. (spec.) *fish* (presumably salted and dried as a condiment):— fish.

3796. ὀψέ **ŏpsĕ,** *op-seh´;* from the same as *3694* (through the idea of *backwardness*); (adv.) *late* in the day; by extens. *after the close* of the day:— (at) even, in the end.

3797. ὄψιμος **ŏpsimŏs,** *op´-sim-os;* from *3796; later*, i.e. *vernal* (showering):— latter.

3798. ὄψιος **ŏpsiŏs,** *op´-see-os;* from *3796; late;* fem. (as noun) *afternoon* (early eve) or *nightfall* (later eve):— even (-ing, [-tide]).

3799. ὄψις **ŏpsis,** *op´-sis;* from *3700;* prop. *sight* (the act), i.e. (by impl.) the *visage*, an extern. *show:*— appearance, countenance, face.

3800. ὀψώνιον **ŏpsōniŏn,** *op-so´-nee-on;* neut. of a presumed der. of the same as *3795; rations* for a soldier, i.e. (by extens.) his *stipend* or *pay:*— wages.

3801. ὁ ὢν καί ὁ ἦν καί ὁ ἐρχόμενος **hŏ ōn kai hŏ ēn kai hŏ ĕrchŏmĕnŏs,** *hŏ own kahee hŏ ane kahee hŏ er-khom´-en-os;* a phrase combining *3588* with the pres. part. and imperf. of *1510* and the pres. part. of *2064* by means of *2532; the one being and the one that was and the one coming*, i.e. *the Eternal*, as a divine epithet of Christ:— which art (is, was), and (which) wast (is, was), and art (is) to come (shalt be).

Π

3802. παγιδεύω **pagidĕuō,** *pag-id-yoo´-o;* from *3803;* to *ensnare* (fig.):— entangle.

3803. παγίς **pagis,** *pag-ece´;* from *4078;* a *trap* (as *fastened* by a noose or notch); fig. a *trick* or *statagem (temptation)*:— snare.

Πάγος **Pagŏs.** See *697.*

3804. πάθημα **pathēma,** *path´-ay-mah;* from a presumed der. of *3806;* something *undergone*, i.e. *hardship* or *pain;* subj. an *emotion* or *influence:*— affection, affliction, motion, suffering.

3805. παθητός **pathētŏs,** *path-ay-tos´;* from the same as *3804; liable* (i.e. *doomed*) to experience *pain:*— suffer.

3806. πάθος **pathŏs,** *path´-os;* from the alt. of *3958;* prop. *suffering* ("*pathos*"), i.e. (subj.) a *passion* (espec. *concupiscence*):— (inordinate) affection, lust.

πάθω **pathō.** See *3958.*

3807. παιδαγωγός **paidagōgŏs,** *pahee-dag-o-gos´;* from *3816* and a redupl. form of *71;* a *boy-leader*, i.e. a servant whose office it was to take the children to school; (by impl. [fig.] a *tutor* ["*pædagogue*"]):— instructor, schoolmaster.

3808. παιδάριον **paidariŏn,** *pahee-dar´-ee-on;* neut. of a presumed der. of *3816;* a *little boy:*— child, lad.

3809. παιδεία **paidĕia,** *pahee-di´-ah;* from *3811; tutorage*, i.e. *education* or *training;* by impl. disciplinary *correction:*— chastening, chastisement, instruction, nurture.

3810. παιδευτής **paidĕutēs,** *pahee-dyoo-tace´;* from *3811;* a *trainer*, i.e. *teacher* or (by impl.) *discipliner:*— which corrected, instructor.

3811. παιδεύω **paidĕuō,** *pahee-dyoo´-o;* from *3816;* to *train* up a child, i.e. *educate*, or (by impl.) *discipline* (by punishment):— chasten (-ise), instruct, learn, teach.

3812. παιδιόθεν **paidiŏthĕn**, *pahee-dee-oth´-en;* adv. (of *source*) from *3813; from infancy:*— of a child.

3813. παιδίον **paidiŏn**, *pahee-dee´-on;* neut. dimin. of *3816;* a *childling* (of either sex), i.e. (prop.) an infant, or (by extens.) a half-grown *boy* or girl; fig. an *immature* Chr.:— (little, young) child, damsel.

3814. παιδίσκη **paidiskē**, *pahee-dis´-kay;* fem. dimin. of *3816;* a *girl,* i.e. (spec.) a *female slave* or *servant:*— bondmaid (-woman), damsel, maid (-en).

3815. παίζω **paizō**, *paheed´-zo;* from *3816;* to *sport* (as a boy):— play.

3816. παῖς **pais**, *paheece;* perh. from *3817;* a *boy* (as often *beaten* with impunity), or (by anal.) a *girl,* and (gen.) a *child;* spec. a *slave* or *servant* (espec. a *minister* to a king; and by eminence to God):— child, maid (-en), (man) servant, son, young man.

3817. παίω **paiō**, *pah´-yo;* a primary verb; to *hit* (as if by a single blow and less violently than *5180*); spec. to *sting* (as a scorpion):— smite, strike.

3818. Πακατιανή **Pakatianē**, *pak-at-ee-an-ay´;* fem. of an adj. of uncert. der.; *Pacatianian,* a section of Phrygia:— Pacatiana.

3819. πάλαι **palai**, *pal´-ahee;* prob. another form for *3825* (through the idea of *retrocession*); (adv.) *formerly,* or (by rel.) *sometime since;* (ellip. as adj.) *ancient:*— any while, a great while ago, (of) old, in time past.

3820. παλαιός **palaiŏs**, *pal-ah-yos´;* from *3819; antique,* i.e. *not recent, worn out:*— old.

3821. παλαιότης **palaiŏtēs**, *pal-ah-yot´-ace;* from *3820; antiquatedness:*— oldness.

3822. παλαιόω **palaiŏō**, *pal-ah-yŏ´-o;* from *3820;* to *make* (pass. *become*) *worn out,* or *declare obs.:*— decay, make (wax) old.

3823. πάλη **palē**, *pal´-ay;* from πάλλω **pallō**, (to *vibrate;* another form for *906*); *wrestling:*— + wrestle.

3824. παλιγγενεσία **paliggĕnĕsia**, *pal-ing-ghen-es-ee´-ah;* from *3825* and *1078;* (spiritual) *rebirth* (the state or the act), i.e. (fig.) spiritual *renovation;* spec. Messianic *restoration:*— regeneration.

3825. πάλιν **palin**, *pal´-in;* prob. from the same as *3823* (through the idea of *oscillatory* repetition); (adv.) *anew,* i.e. (of place) *back,* (of time) *once more,* or (conjunc.) *furthermore* or *on the other hand:*— again.

3826. παμπληθεί **pamplēthĕi**, *pam-play-thi´;* dat. (adv.) of a compound of *3956* and *4128; in full multitude,* i.e. *concertedly* or *simultaneously:*— all at once.

3827. πάμπολυς **pampŏlus**, *pam-pol-ooce;* from *3956* and *4183; full many,* i.e. *immense:*— very great.

3828. Παμφυλία **Pamphulia**, *pam-fool-ee´-ah;* from a compound of *3956* and *5443; every-tribal,* i.e. *heterogeneous* (*5561* being impl.); *Pamphylia,* a region of Asia Minor:— Pamphylia.

3829. πανδοχεῖον **pandŏchĕiŏn**, *pan-dokh-i´-on;* neut. of a presumed compound of *3956* and a der. of *1209; all-receptive,* i.e. a public *lodging*-place (*caravanserai* or *khan*):— inn.

3830. πανδοχεύς **pandŏchĕus**, *pan-dokh-yoos´;* from the same as *3829;* an *innkeeper* (*warden of a caravanserai*):— host.

3831. πανήγυρις **panēguris**, *pan-ay´-goo-ris;* from *3956* and a der. of *58;* a *mass-meeting,* i.e. (fig.) *universal companionship:*— gen. assembly.

3832. πανοικί **panŏiki**, *pan-oy-kee´* or

πανοικεί **panŏikei**, *pan-oy-ki´* adv. from *3956* and *3624; with* the *whole family:*— with all his house.

3833. πανοπλία **panŏplia**, *pan-op-lee-ah;* from a compound of *3956* and *3696; full armor* ("panoply"):— all (whole) armour.

3834. πανουργία **panŏurgia**, *pan-oorg-ee´-ah;* from *3835; adroitness,* i.e. (in a bad sense) *trickery* or *sophistry:*— (cunning) craftiness, subtilty (subtlety).

3835. πανοῦργος **panŏurgŏs**, *pan-oor´-gos;* from *3956* and *2041; all-working,* i.e. *adroit* (*shrewd*):— crafty.

3836. πανταχόθεν **pantachŏthĕn**, *pan-takh-oth´-en;* adv. (of *source*) from *3837; from all* directions:— from every quarter.

3837. πανταχοῦ **pantachŏu**, *pan-takh-oo´;* gen. (as adv. of *place*) of a presumed der. of *3956; universally:*— in all places, everywhere.

3838. παντελής **pantĕlēs**, *pan-tel-ace´;* from *3956* and *5056; full-ended,* i.e. *entire* (neut. as noun, *completion*):— + in [no] wise, uttermost.

3839. πάντη **pantē**, *pan´-tay;* adv. (of *manner*) from *3956; wholly:*— always.

3840. παντόθεν **pantŏthĕn**, *pan-toth´-en;* adv. (of *source*) from *3956; from* (i.e. *on*) *all* sides:— on every side, round about.

3841. παντοκράτωρ **pantŏkratōr**, *pan-tok-rat´-ore;* from *3956* and *2904;* the *all-ruling,* i.e. *God* (as absolute and universal sovereign):— Almighty, Omnipotent.

3842. πάντοτε **pantŏtĕ**, *pan´-tot-eh;* from *3956* and *3753; every when,* i.e. *at all* times:— alway (-s), ever (-more).

3843. πάντως **pantōs**, *pan´-toce;* adv. from *3956; entirely;* spec. *at all events,* (with neg. following) *in no event:*— by all means, altogether, at all, needs, no doubt, in [no] wise, surely.

3844. παρά **para**, *par-ah´;* a primary prep.;

Greek

prop. *near;* i.e. (with gen.) *from beside* (lit. or fig.), (with dat.) *at* (or *in*) the *vicinity* of (object or subject), (with acc.) to the *proximity* with (local [espec. *beyond* or *opposed* to] or causal [on *account* of]:— above, against, among, at, before, by, contrary to, × friend, from, + give [such things as they], + that [she] had, × his, in, more than, nigh unto, (out) of, past, save, side ... by, in the sight of, then, [there-] fore, with. In compounds it retains the same variety of application.

3845. παραβαίνω **parabainō**, *par-ab-ah´-ee-no;* from 3844 and the base of 939; to *go contrary to,* i.e. *violate* a command:— (by) transgress (-ion).

3846. παραβάλλω **paraballō**, *par-ab-al´-lo;* from 3844 and 906; to *throw alongside,* i.e. (refl.) to *reach* a place, or (fig.) to *liken:—* arrive, compare.

3847. παράβασις **parabasis**, *par-ab´-as-is;* from 3845; *violation:—* breaking, transgression.

3848. παραβάτης **parabatēs**, *par-ab-at´-ace;* from 3845; a *violator:—* breaker, transgress (-or).

3849. παραβιάζομαι **parabiazŏmai**, *par-ab-ee-ad´-zom-ahee;* from 3844 and the mid. voice of 971; to *force contrary to* (nature), i.e. *compel* (by entreaty):— constrain.

3850. παραβολή **parabŏlē**, *par-ab-ol-ay´;* from 3846; a *similitude* ("*parable*"), i.e. (symbol.) *fictitious narrative* (of common life conveying a mor.), *apothegm* or *adage:—* comparison, figure, parable, proverb.

3851. παραβουλεύομαι **parabŏuleuŏmai**, *par-ab-ool-yoo´-om-ahee* or

παραβολεύομαι **parabŏleuŏmai**, *par-ab-ol-yoo´-om-ahee* from 3844, and the mid. voice of 1011; to *misconsult,* i.e. *disregard:—* not (to) regard (-ing).

3852. παραγγελία **paraggĕlia**, *par-ang-gel-ee´-ah;* from 3853; a *mandate:—* charge, command.

3853. παραγγέλλω **paraggĕllō**, *par-ang-gel´-lo;* from 3844 and the base of 32; to *transmit a message,* i.e. (by impl.) to *enjoin:—* (give in) charge, (give) command (-ment), declare.

3854. παραγίνομαι **paraginŏmai**, *par-ag-in´-om-ahee;* from 3844 and 1096; to *become near,* i.e. *approach* (*have arrived*); by impl. to *appear* publicly:— come, go, be present.

3855. παράγω **paragō**, *par-ag´-o;* from 3844 and 71; to *lead near,* i.e. (refl. or intr.) to *go along* or *away:—* depart, pass (away, by, forth).

3856. παραδειγματίζω **paradĕigmatizō**, *par-ad-igue-mat-id´-zo;* from 3844 and 1165; to *show alongside* (the public), i.e. *expose to infamy:—* make a public example, put to an open shame.

3857. παράδεισος **paradĕisŏs**, *par-ad´-i-sos;* of Oriental or. [comp. 6508]; a *park,* i.e. (spec.) an *Eden* (place of future happiness, "*paradise*"):— paradise.

3858. παραδέχομαι **paradĕchŏmai**, *par-ad-ekh´-om-ahee;* from 3844 and 1209; to *accept near,* i.e. *admit* or (by impl.) *delight in:—* receive.

3859. παραδιατριβή **paradiatribē**, *par-ad-ee-at-ree-bay´;* from a compound of 3844 and 1304; *misemployment,* i.e. *meddlesomeness:—* perverse disputing.

3860. παραδίδωμι **paradidōmi**, *par-ad-id´-o-mee;* from 3844 and 1325; to *surrender,* i.e *yield up, intrust, transmit:—* betray, bring forth, cast, commit, deliver (up), give (over, up), hazard, put in prison, recommend.

3861. παράδοξος **paradŏxŏs**, *par-ad´-ox-os;* from 3844 and 1391 (in the sense of *seeming*); *contrary to expectation,* i.e. *extraordinary* ("*paradox*"):— strange.

3862. παράδοσις **paradŏsis**, *par-ad´-os-is;* from 3860; *transmission,* i.e. (concr.) a *precept;* spec. the Jewish *traditionary law:—* ordinance, tradition.

3863. παραζηλόω **parazēlŏō**, *par-ad-zay-lŏ´-o;* from 3844 and 2206; to *stimulate alongside,* i.e. *excite to rivalry:—* provoke to emulation (jealousy).

3864. παραθαλάσσιος **parathalassiŏs**, *par-ath-al-as´-see-os;* from 3844 and 2281; *along* the *sea,* i.e. *maritime* (*lacustrine*):— upon the sea coast.

3865. παραθεωρέω **parathĕōrĕō**, *par-ath-eh-o-reh´-o;* from 3844 and 2334; to *overlook* or *disregard:—* neglect.

3866. παραθήκη **parathēkē**, *par-ath-ay´-kay;* from 3908; a *deposit,* i.e. (fig.) *trust:—* committed unto.

3867. παραινέω **parainĕō**, *par-ahee-neh´-o;* from 3844 and 134; to *mispraise,* i.e. *recommend* or *advise* (a different course):— admonish, exhort.

3868. παραιτέομαι **paraitĕŏmai**, *par-ahee-teh´-om-ahee;* from 3844 and the mid. voice of 154; to *beg off,* i.e. *deprecate, decline, shun:—* avoid, (make) excuse, intreat, refuse, reject.

3869. παρακαθίζω **parakathizō**, *par-ak-ath-id´-zo;* from 3844 and 2523; to *sit down near:—* sit.

3870. παρακαλέω **parakalĕō**, *par-ak-al-eh´-o;* from 3844 and 2564; to *call near,* i.e. *invite, invoke* (by imploration, hortation or consolation):— beseech, call for, (be of good) comfort, desire, (give) exhort (-ation), intreat, pray.

3871. παρακαλύπτω **parakaluptō**, *par-ak-al-oop´-to;* from 3844 and 2572; to *cover alongside,* i.e. *veil* (fig.):— hide.

3872. παρακαταθήκη **parakatathēkē**, *par-ak-at-ath-ay´-kay;* from a compound of

3844 and 2698; something *put down along-side*, i.e. a *deposit* (sacred *trust*):— that (thing) which is committed (un-) to (trust).

3873. παράκειμαι **parakĕimai**, *par-ak´-i-ma-hee;* from 3844 and 2749; to *lie near,* i.e. *be at hand* (fig. *be prompt* or *easy*):— be present.

3874. παράκλησις **paraklēsis**, *par-ak´-lay-sis;* from 3870; *imploration, hortation, solace:*— comfort, consolation, exhortation, intreaty.

3875. παράκλητος **paraklētŏs**, *par-ak´-lay-tos;* an *intercessor, consoler:*— advocate, comforter.

3876. παρακοή **parakŏē**, *par-ak-ŏ-ay´;* from 3878; *inattention,* i.e. (by impl.) *disobedience:*— disobedience.

3877. παρακολουθέω **parakŏlŏuthĕō**, *par-ak-ol-oo-theh´-o;* from 3844 and 190; to *follow near,* i.e. (fig.) *attend* (as a result), *trace out, conform* to:— attain, follow, fully know, have understanding.

3878. παρακούω **parakŏuō**, *par-ak-oo´-o;* from 3844 and 191; to *mishear,* i.e. (by impl.) to *disobey:*— neglect to hear.

3879. παρακύπτω **parakuptō**, *par-ak-oop´-to;* from 3844 and 2955; to *bend beside,* i.e. *lean over* (so as to *peer within*):— look (into), stoop down.

3880. παραλαμβάνω **paralambanō**, *par-al-am-ban´-o;* from 3844 and 2983; to *receive near,* i.e. *associate with* oneself (in any familiar or intimate act or relation); by anal. to *assume* an office; fig. to *learn:*— receive, take (unto, with).

3881. παραλέγομαι **paralĕgŏmai**, *par-al-eg´-om-ahee;* from 3844 and the mid. voice of 3004 (in its orig. sense); (spec.) to *lay* one's course *near,* i.e. *sail past:*— pass, sail by.

3882. παράλιος **paraliŏs**, *par-al´-ee-os;* from 3844 and 251; *beside* the *salt* (*sea*), i.e. *maritime:*— sea coast.

3883. παραλλαγή **parallagē**, *par-al-lag-ay´;* from a compound of 3844 and 236; *transmutation* (of phase or orbit), i.e. (fig.) *fickleness:*— variableness.

3884. παραλογίζομαι **paralŏgizŏmai**, *par-al-og-id´-zom-ahee;* from 3844 and 3049; to *misreckon,* i.e. *delude:*— beguile, deceive.

3885. παραλυτικός **paralutikŏs**, *par-al-oo-tee-kos´;* from a der. of 3886; as if *dissolved,* i.e. "*paralytic*":— that had (sick of) the palsy.

3886. παραλύω **paraluō**, *par-al-oo´-o;* from 3844 and 3089; to *loosen beside,* i.e. *relax* (perf. pass. part. *paralyzed* or *enfeebled*):— feeble, sick of the (taken with) palsy.

3887. παραμένω **paramĕnō**, *par-am-en´-o;* from 3844 and 3306; to *stay near,* i.e. *remain* (lit. *tarry;* or fig. *be permanent, persevere*):— abide, continue.

3888. παραμυθέομαι **paramuthĕŏmai**, *par-am-oo-theh´-om-ahee;* from 3844 and the mid. voice of a der. of 3454; to *relate near,* i.e. (by impl.) *encourage, console:*— comfort.

3889. παραμυθία **paramuthia**, *par-am-oo-thee´-ah;* from 3888; *consolation* (prop. abstr.):— comfort.

3890. παραμύθιον **paramuthiŏn**, *par-am-oo´-thee-on;* neut. of 3889; *consolation* (prop. concr.):— comfort.

3891. παρανομέω **paranŏmĕō**, *par-an-om-eh´-o;* from a compound of 3844 and 3551; to *be opposed to law,* i.e. to *transgress:*— contrary to law.

3892. παρανομία **paranŏmia**, *par-an-om-ee´-ah;* from the same as 3891; *transgression:*— iniquity.

3893. παραπικραίνω **parapikrainō**, *par-ap-ik-rah´-ee-no;* from 3844 and 4087; to *embitter alongside,* i.e. (fig.) to *exasperate:*— provoke.

3894. παραπικρασμός **parapikrasmŏs**, *par-ap-ik-ras-mos´;* from 3893; *irritation:*— provocation.

3895. παραπίπτω **parapiptō**, *par-ap-ip´-to;* from 3844 and 4098; to *fall aside,* i.e. (fig.) to *apostatize:*— fall away.

3896. παραπλέω **paraplĕō**, *par-ap-leh´-o;* from 3844 and 4126; to *sail near:*— sail by.

3897. παραπλήσιον **paraplēsiŏn**, *par-ap-lay´-see-on;* neut. of a compound of 3844 and the base of 4139 (as adv.); *close by,* i.e. (fig.) *almost:*— nigh unto.

3898. παραπλησίως **paraplēsiŏs**, *par-ap-lay-see´-oce;* adv. from the same as 3897; in a *manner near by,* i.e. (fig.) *similarly:*— likewise.

3899. παραπορεύομαι **parapŏrĕuŏmai**, *par-ap-or-yoo´-om-ahee;* from 3844 and 4198; to *travel near:*— go, pass (by).

3900. παράπτωμα **paraptōma**, *par-ap´-to-mah;* from 3895; a *side-slip* (*lapse* or *deviation*), i.e. (unintentional) *error* or (willful) *transgression:*— fall, fault, offence, sin, trespass.

3901. παραρρυέω **pararrhuĕō**, *par-ar-hroo-eh´-o;* from 3844 and the alternate of 4482; to *flow by,* i.e. (fig.) carelessly *pass* (*miss*):— let slip.

3902. παράσημος **parasēmŏs**, *par-as´-ay-mos;* from 3844 and the base of 4591; *side-marked,* i.e. *labelled* (with a *badge* [*figure-head*] of a ship):— sign.

3903. παρασκευάζω **paraskĕuazō**, *par-ask-yoo-ad´-zo;* from 3844 and a der. of 4632; to *furnish aside,* i.e. *get ready:*— prepare self, be (make) ready.

3904. παρασκευή **paraskĕuē**, *par-ask-yoo-ay´;* as if from 3903; *readiness:*— preparation.

3905. παρατείνω **paratĕinō**, *par-at-i´-no;*

Greek

from *3844* and τείνω **tĕinō** (to stretch); to *extend along*, i.e. *prolong* (in point of time):— continue.

3906. παρατηρέω **paratēreō**, *par-at-ay-reh´-o*; from *3844* and *5083;* to *inspect alongside*, i.e. *note insidiously* or *scrupulously:*— observe, watch.

3907. παρατήρησις **paratērēsis**, *par-at-ay´-ray-sis;* from *3906; inspection*, i.e. *ocular evidence:*— observation.

3908. παρατίθημι **paratithēmi**, *par-at-ith´-ay-mee;* from *3844* and *5087;* to *place alongside*, i.e. *present* (food, truth); by impl. to *deposit* (as a trust or for protection):— allege, commend, commit (the keeping of), put forth, set before.

3909. παρατυγχάνω **paratugchanō**, *par-at-oong-khan´-o;* from *3844* and *5177;* to *chance near*, i.e. *fall in with:*— meet with.

3910. παραυτίκα **parautika**, *par-ŏw-tee´-kah;* from *3844* and a der. of *846; at the very* instant, i.e. *momentary:*— but for a moment.

3911. παραφέρω **paraphērō**, *par-af-er´-o;* from *3844* and *5342* (incl. its alt. forms); to *bear along* or *aside*, i.e. *carry off* (lit. or fig.); by impl. to *avert:*— remove, take away.

3912. παραφρονέω **paraphrŏnĕō**, *par-af-ron-eh´-o;* from *3844* and *5426;* to *misthink*, i.e. *be insane* (*silly*):— as a fool.

3913. παραφρονία **paraphrŏnia**, *par-af-ron-ee´-ah;* from *3912; insanity*, i.e. *foolhardiness:*— madness.

3914. παραχειμάζω **parachĕimazō**, *par-akh-i-mad´-zo;* from *3844* and *5492;* to *winter near*, i.e. *stay* with over the *rainy* season:— winter.

3915. παραχειμασία **parachĕimasia**, *par-akh-i-mas-ee´-ah;* from *3914;* a *wintering* over:— winter in.

3916. παραχρῆμα **parachrēma**, *par-akh-ray´-mah;* from *3844* and *5536* (in its orig. sense); *at the thing* itself, i.e. *instantly:*— forthwith, immediately, presently, straightway, soon.

3917. πάρδαλις **pardalis**, *par´-dal-is;* fem. of πάρδος **pardŏs** (a *panther*); a *leopard:*— leopard.

3918. πάρειμι **parĕimi**, *par´-i-mee;* from *3844* and *1510* (incl. its various forms); to *be near*, i.e. *at hand;* neut. pres. part. (sing.) *time being*, or (plural) *property:*— come, × have, be here, + lack, (be here) present.

3919. παρεισάγω **parĕisagō**, *par-ice-ag´-o;* from *3844* and *1521;* to *lead in aside*, i.e. *introduce surreptitiously:*— privily bring in.

3920. παρείσακτος **parĕisaktŏs**, *par-ice´-ak-tos;* from *3919; smuggled in:*— unawares brought in.

3921. παρεισδύνω **parĕisdunō**, *par-ice-doo´-no;* from *3844* and a compound of *1519* and *1416;* to *settle in alongside*, i.e. *lodge stealthily:*— creep in unawares.

3922. παρεισέρχομαι **parĕisĕrchŏmai**, *par-ice-er´-khom-ahee;* from *3844* and *1525;* to *come in alongside*, i.e. *supervene additionally* or *stealthily:*— come in privily, enter.

3923. παρεισφέρω **parĕisphērō**, *par-ice-fer´-o;* from *3844* and *1533;* to *bear in alongside*, i.e. *introduce simultaneously:*— give.

3924. παρεκτός **parĕktŏs**, *par-ek-tos´;* from *3844* and *1622; near outside*, i.e. *besides:*— except, saving, without.

3925. παρεμβολή **parĕmbŏlē**, *par-em-bol-ay´;* from a compound of *3844* and *1685;* a *throwing in beside* (*juxtaposition*), i.e. (spec.) *battle-array*, *encampment* or *barracks* (tower Antonia):— army, camp, castle.

3926. παρενοχλέω **parĕnŏchlĕō**, *par-en-okh-leh´-o;* from *3844* and *1776;* to *harass further*, i.e. *annoy:*— trouble.

3927. παρεπίδημος **parepidēmŏs**, *par-ep-id´-ay-mos;* from *3844* and the base of *1927;* an *alien alongside*, i.e. a *resident foreigner:*— pilgrim, stranger.

3928. παρέρχομαι **parĕrchŏmai**, *par-er´-khom-ahee;* from *3844* and *2064;* to *come near* or *aside*, i.e. to *approach* (*arrive*), *go by* (or *away*), (fig.) *perish* or *neglect*, (caus.) *avert:*— come (forth), go, pass (away, by, over), past, transgress.

3929. πάρεσις **parĕsis**, *par´-es-is;* from *2935; prætermission*, i.e. *toleration:*— remission.

3930. παρέχω **parĕchō**, *par-ekh´-o;* from *3844* and *2192;* to *hold near*, i.e. *present, afford, exhibit, furnish occasion:*— bring, do, give, keep, minister, offer, shew, + trouble.

3931. παρηγορία **parēgŏria**, *par-ay-gor-ee´-ah;* from a compound of *3844* and a der. of *58* (mean. to *harangue* an assembly); an *address alongside*, i.e. (spec.) *consolation:*— comfort.

3932. παρθενία **parthĕnia**, *par-then-ee´-ah;* from *3933; maidenhood:*— virginity.

3933. παρθένος **parthĕnŏs**, *par-then´-os;* of unknown or.; a *maiden;* by impl. an unmarried *daughter:*— virgin.

3934. Πάρθος **Parthŏs**, *par´-thos;* prob. of for. or.; a *Parthian*, i.e. inhab. of Parthia:— Parthian.

3935. παρίημι **pariēmi**, *par-ee´-ay-mi;* from *3844* and ἵημι **hiĕmi**, (to *send*); to *let by*, i.e. *relax:*— hang down.

3936. παρίστημι **paristēmi**, *par-is´-tay-mee;* or prol.

παριστάνω **paristanō** *par-is-tan´-o;* from *3844*, and *2476;* to *stand beside*, i.e. (tran.) to *exhibit, proffer*, (spec.) *recommend*, (fig.) *substantiate;* or (intr.) to *be at hand* (or *ready*), *aid:*— assist, bring before, command, commend, give presently, present, prove, provide, shew, stand (before, by, here, up, with), yield.

3937. Παρμενᾶς **Parmĕnas**, *par-men-as´*; prob. by contr. for Παρμενίδης **Parmĕnidēs** (a der. of a compound of *3844* and *3306*); *constant; Parmenas*, a Chr.:— Parmenas.

3938. πάροδος **parŏdŏs**, *par´-od-os;* from *3844* and *3598*; a *by-road*, i.e. (act.) a *route:*— way.

3939. παροικέω **parŏikĕō**, *par-oy-keh´-o;* from *3844* and *3611*; to *dwell near*, i.e. *reside* as a *foreigner:*— sojourn in, be a stranger.

3940. παροικία **parŏikia**, *par-oy-kee´-ah;* from *3941; foreign residence:*— sojourning, × as strangers.

3941. πάροικος **parŏikŏs**, *par´-oy-kos;* from *3844* and *3624*; having a *home near*, i.e. (as noun) a *by-dweller* (*alien resident*):— foreigner, sojourn, stranger.

3942. παροιμία **parŏimia**, *par-oy-mee´-ah;* from a compound of *3844* and perh. a der. of *3633*; appar. a state *alongside of supposition*, i.e. (concr.) an *adage;* spec. an enigmatical or fictitious *illustration:*— parable, proverb.

3943. πάροινος **parŏinŏs**, *par´-oy-nos;* from *3844* and *3631*; staying *near wine*, i.e. *tippling* (a *toper*):— given to wine.

3944. παροίχομαι **parŏichŏmai**, *par-oy´-khom-ahee;* from *3844* and οἴχομαι **ŏichŏmai** (to *depart*); to *escape along*, i.e. *be gone:*— past.

3945. παρομοιάζω **parŏmŏiazō**, *par-om-oy-ad´-zo;* from *3946*; to *resemble:*— be like unto.

3946. παρόμοιος **parŏmŏiŏs**, *par-om´-oy-os;* from *3844* and *3664; alike nearly*, i.e. *similar:*— like.

3947. παροξύνω **parŏxunō**, *par-ox-oo´-no;* from *3844* and a der. of *3691*; to *sharpen alongside*, i.e. (fig.) to *exasperate:*— easily provoke, stir.

3948. παροξυσμός **parŏxusmŏs**, *par-ox-oos-mos´;* from *3947* ("*paroxysm*"); *incitement* (to good), or *dispute* (in anger):— contention, provoke unto.

3949. παροργίζω **parŏrgizō**, *par-org-id´-zo;* from *3844* and *3710*; to *anger alongside*, i.e. *enrage:*— anger, provoke to wrath.

3950. παροργισμός **parŏrgismŏs**, *par-org-is-mos´;* from *3949; rage:*— wrath.

3951. παροτρύνω **parŏtrunō**, *par-ot-roo´-no;* from *3844* and ὀτρύνω **ŏtrunō** (to *spur*); to *urge along*, i.e. *stimulate* (to hostility):— stir up.

3952. παρουσία **parŏusia**, *par-oo-see´-ah;* from the present part. of *3918*; a *being near*, i.e. *advent* (often, *return;* spec. of Christ to punish Jerusalem, or finally the wicked); (by impl.) phys. *aspect:*— coming, presence.

3953. παροψίς **parŏpsis**, *par-op-sis´;* from *3844* and the base of *3795*; a *side-dish* (the receptacle):— platter.

3954. παῤῥησία **parrhēsia**, *par-rhay-see´-ah;* from *3956* and a der. of *4483; all outspokenness*, i.e. *frankness, bluntness, publicity;* by impl. *assurance:*— bold (× -ly, -ness, -ness of speech), confidence, × freely, × openly, × plainly (-ness).

3955. παῤῥησιάζομαι **parrhēsiazŏmai**, *par-hray-see-ad´-zom-ahee;* mid. voice from *3954;* to *be frank* in utterance, or *confident* in spirit and demeanor:— be (wax) bold, (preach, speak) boldly.

3956. πᾶς **pas** *pas;* incl. all the forms of declension; appar. a primary word; *all, any, every*, the *whole:*— all (manner of, means), alway (-s), any (one), × daily, + ever, every (one, way), as many as, + no (-thing), × thoroughly, whatsoever, whole, whosoever.

3957. πάσχα **pascha**, *pas´-khah;* of Chald. or. [comp. 6453]; the *Passover* (the meal, the day, the festival or the special sacrifices connected with it):— Easter, Passover.

3958. πάσχω **paschō**, *pas´-kho;* incl. the forms

    πάθω (**pathō**, *path´-o*) and

    πένθω (**pĕnthō**, *pen´-tho*), used only in certain tenses for it; appar. a primary verb; to *experience* a sensation or impression (usually painful):— feel, passion, suffer, vex.

3959. Πάταρα **Patara**, *pat´-ar-ah;* prob. of for. or.; *Patara*, a place in Asia Minor:— Patara.

3960. πατάσσω **patassō**, *pat-as´-so;* prob. prol. from *3817;* to *knock* (gently or with a weapon or fatally):— smite, strike. Comp. *5180.*

3961. πατέω **patĕō**, *pat-eh´-o;* from a der. prob. of *3817* (mean. a "*path*"); to *trample* (lit. or fig.):— tread (down, under foot).

3962. πατήρ **patēr**, *pat-ayr´;* appar. a primary word; a "*father*" (lit. or fig., near or more remote):— father, parent.

3963. Πάτμος **Patmŏs**, *pat´-mos;* of uncert. der.; *Patmus*, an islet in the Mediterranean:— Patmos.

3964. πατραλῴας **patralŏias**, *pat-ral-o´-as* πατρολῴας **patrŏlŏias**, *pat-rol-o´-as;* from *3962* and the same as the latter part of *3389;* a *parricide:*— murderer of fathers.

3965. πατριά **patria**, *pat-ree-ah´;* as if fem. of a der. of *3962;* paternal *descent*, i.e. (concr.) a *group* of families or a whole *race* (*nation*):— family, kindred, lineage.

3966. πατριάρχης **patriarchēs**, *pat-ree-arkh´-ace;* from *3965* and *757;* a *progenitor* ("*patriarch*"):— patriarch.

3967. πατρικός **patrikŏs**, *pat-ree-kos´;* from *3962; paternal*, i.e. *ancestral:*— of fathers.

3968. πατρίς **patris**, *pat-rece´;* from *3962;* a

Greek

father-land, i.e. *native town;* (fig.) heavenly *home:*— (own) country.

3969. Πατρόβας **Patrŏbas,** *pat-rob´-as;* perh. contr. for Πατρόβιος **Patrŏbiŏs** (a compound of 3962 and 979); *father's life; Patrobas,* a Chr.:— Patrobas.

3970. πατροπαράδοτος **patrŏparadŏtŏs,** *pat-rop-ar-ad´-ot-os;* from 3962 and a der. of 3860 (in the sense of *handing over* or *down); traditionary:*— received by tradition from fathers.

3971. πατρῷος **patrŏiŏs,** *pat-ro´-os;* from 3962; *paternal,* i.e. *hereditary:*— of fathers.

3972. Παῦλος **Paulŏs,** *pŏw´-los;* of Lat. or.; (*little;* but remotely from a der. of 3973, mean. the same); *Paulus,* the name of a Rom. and of an apostle:— Paul, Paulus.

3973. παύω **pauō,** *pŏw´-o;* a primary verb ("*pause*"); to *stop* (tran. or intr.), i.e. *restrain, quit, desist, come to an end:*— cease, leave, refrain.

3974. Πάφος **Paphŏs,** *paf´-os;* of uncert. der.; *Paphus,* a place in Cyprus:— Paphos.

3975. παχύνω **pachunō,** *pakh-oo´-no;* from a der. of 4078 (mean. *thick);* to *thicken,* i.e. (by impl.) to *fatten* (fig. *stupefy* or *render callous*):— wax gross.

3976. πέδη **pĕdē,** *ped´-ay;* ultimately from 4228; a *shackle* for the feet:— fetter.

3977. πεδινός **pĕdinŏs,** *ped-ee-nos´;* from a der. of 4228 (mean. the *ground); level* (as easy for the *feet*):— plain.

3978. πεζεύω **pĕzĕuō,** *ped-zyoo´-o;* from the same as 3979; to *foot* a journey, i.e. *travel* by land:— go afoot.

3979. πεζῇ **pĕzĕi,** *ped-zay´;* dat. fem. of a der. of 4228 (as adv.); *foot-wise,* i.e. by *walking:*— a- (on) foot.

3980. πειθαρχέω **pĕitharchĕō,** *pi-tharkh-eh´-o;* from a compound of 3982 and 757; to *be persuaded* by a *ruler,* i.e. (gen.) to *submit* to authority; by anal. to *conform* to advice:— hearken, obey (magistrates).

3981. πειθός **pĕithŏs,** *pi-thos´;* from 3982; *persuasive:*— enticing.

3982. πείθω **pĕithō,** *pi´-tho;* a primary verb; to *convince* (by argument, true or false); by anal. to *pacify* or *conciliate* (by other fair means); refl. or pass. to *assent* (to evidence or authority), to *rely* (by inward certainty):— agree, assure, believe, have confidence, be (wax) confident, make friend, obey, persuade, trust, yield.

3983. πεινάω **pĕinaō,** *pi-nah´-o;* from the same as 3993 (through the idea of pinching *toil;* "*pine*"); to *famish* (absol. or comp.); fig. to *crave:*— be an hungered.

3984. πεῖρα **pĕira,** *pi´-rah;* from the base of 4008 (through the idea of *piercing);* a *test,* i.e. *attempt, experience:*— assaying, trial.

3985. πειράζω **pĕirazō,** *pi-rad´-zo;* from 3984; to *test* (obj.), i.e. *endeavor, scrutinize, entice, discipline:*— assay, examine, go about, prove, tempt (-er), try.

3986. πειρασμός **pĕirasmŏs,** *pi-ras-mos´;* from 3985; a putting to *proof* (by experiment [of good], *experience* [of evill, solicitation, discipline or provocation); by impl. *adversity:*— temptation, × try.

3987. πειράω **pĕiraō,** *pi-rah´-o;* from 3984; to *test* (subj.), i.e. (refl.) to *attempt:*— assay.

3988. πεισμονή **pĕismŏnē,** *pice-mon-ay´;* from a presumed der. of 3982; *persuadableness,* i.e. *credulity:*— persuasion.

3989. πέλαγος **pĕlagŏs,** *pel´-ag-os;* of uncert. aff.; deep or open *sea,* i.e. the *main:*— depth, sea.

3990. πελεκίζω **pĕlĕkizō,** *pel-ek-id´-zo;* from a der. of 4141 (mean. an *axe);* to *chop* off (the head), i.e. *truncate:*— behead.

3991. πέμπτος **pĕmptŏs,** *pemp´-tos;* from 4002; *fifth:*— fifth.

3992. πέμπω **pĕmpō,** *pem´-po;* appar. a primary verb; to *dispatch* (from the subj. view or point of *departure,* whereas ἵημι **hiēmi** [as a stronger form of εἶμι **ĕimi**] refers rather to the obj. point or *terminus ad quem,* and 4724 denotes prop. the *orderly* motion involved), espec. on a temporary errand; also to *transmit, bestow,* or *wield:*— send, thrust in.

3993. πένης **pĕnēs,** *pen´-ace;* from a primary πένω **pĕnō,** (to *toil* for daily subsistence); *starving,* i.e. *indigent:*— poor. Comp. 4434.

3994. πενθερά **pĕnthĕra,** *pen-ther-ah´;* fem. of 3995; a *wife's mother:*— mother in law, wife's mother.

3995. πενθερός **pĕnthĕrŏs,** *pen-ther-os´;* of uncert. aff.; a *wife's father:*— father in law.

3996. πενθέω **pĕnthĕō,** *pen-theh´-o;* from 3997; to *grieve* (the feeling or the act):— mourn, (be-) wail.

3997. πένθος **pĕnthŏs,** *pen´-thos;* strengthened from the alt. of 3958; *grief:*— mourning, sorrow.

3998. πενιχρός **pĕnichrŏs,** *pen-ikh-ros´;* prol. from the base of 3993; *necessitous:*— poor.

3999. πεντάκις **pĕntakis,** *pen-tak-ece´;* mult. adv. from 4002; *five times:*— five times.

4000. πεντακισχίλιοι **pĕntakischiliŏi,** *pen-tak-is-khil´-ee-oy;* from 3999 and 5507; *five times a thousand:*— five thousand.

4001. πεντακόσιοι **pĕntakŏsiŏi,** *pen-tak-os´-ee-oy;* from 4002 and 1540; *five hundred:*— five hundred.

4002. πέντε **pĕntĕ,** *pen´-teh;* a primary number; "*five*":— five.

4003. πεντεκαιδέκατος **pĕntĕkaidĕkatŏs,**

pen-tek-ahee-dek´-at-os; from *4002* and *2532* and *1182; five and tenth:*— fifteenth.

4004. πεντήκοντα **pĕntēkŏnta,** *pen-tay´-kontah;* mult. of *4002; fifty:*— fifty.

4005. πεντηκοστή **pĕntēkŏstē,** *pen-tay-kostay´;* fem. of the ord. of *4004; fiftieth* (*2250* being impl.) from Passover, i.e. the festival of "*Pentecost*":— Pentecost.

4006. πεποίθησις **pĕpŏithēsis,** *pep-oy´-thaysis;* from the perfect of the alt. of *3958; reliance:*— confidence, trust.

4007. περ **pĕr,** *per;* from the base of *4008;* an enclitic particle significant of *abundance* (*thoroughness*), i.e. *emphasis; much, very* or *ever:*— [whom-] soever.

4008. πέραν **pĕran,** *per´-an;* appar. acc. of an obs. der. of πείρω **pĕirō,** (to "*pierce*"); *through* (as adv. or prep.), i.e. *across:*— beyond, farther (other) side, over.

4009. πέρας **pĕras,** *per´-as;* from the same as *4008;* an *extremity:*— end, ut-(ter-) most part.

4010. Πέργαμος **Pĕrgamŏs,** *per´-gam-os;* from *4444; fortified; Pergamus,* a place in Asia Minor:— Pergamos.

4011. Πέργη **Pĕrgē,** *perg´-ay;* prob. from the same as *4010;* a *tower; Perga,* a place in Asia Minor:— Perga.

4012. περί **pĕri,** *per-ee´;* from the base of *4008;* prop. *through* (all over), i.e. *around;* fig. *with respect* to; used in various applications, of place, cause or time (with the gen. denoting the *subject* or *occasion* or *superlative* point; with the acc. the *locality, circuit, matter, circumstance* or general *period*):— (there-) about, above, against, at, on behalf of, × and his company, which concern, (as) concerning, for, × how it will go with, ([there-, where-]) of, on, over, pertaining (to), for sake, × (e-) state, (as) touching, [where-] by (in), with. In composition it retains substantially the same meaning of circuit (*around*), excess (*beyond*), or completeness (*through*).

4013. περιάγω **pĕriagō,** *per-ee-ag´-o;* from *4012* and *71;* to *take around* (as a companion); refl. to *walk around:*— compass, go (round) about, lead about.

4014. περιαιρέω **pĕriairĕō,** *per-ee-ahee-reh´-o;* from *4012* and *138* (incl. its alt.); to *remove all around,* i.e. *unveil, cast off* (anchor); fig. to *expiate:*— take away (up).

4015. περιαστράπτω **pĕriastraptō,** *per-ee-astrap´-to;* from *4012* and *797;* to *flash all around,* i.e. *to envelop in light:*— shine round (about).

4016. περιβάλλω **pĕriballō,** *per-ee-bal´-lo;* from *4012* and *906;* to *throw all around,* i.e. *invest* (with a palisade or with clothing):— array, cast about, clothe (-d me), put on.

4017. περιβλέπω **pĕriblĕpō,** *per-ee-blep´-o;* from *4012* and *991;* to *look all around:*— look (round) about (on).

4018. περιβόλαιον **pĕribŏlaiŏn,** *per-ib-ol´-ah-yon;* neut. of a presumed der. of *4016;* something *thrown around* one, i.e. a *mantle, veil:*— covering, vesture.

4019. περιδέω **pĕridĕō,** *per-ee-deh´-o;* from *4012* and *1210;* to *bind around* one, i.e. *enwrap:*— bind about.

περιδρέμω **pĕridrĕmō.** See *4063.*

περιέλλω **pĕriĕllō.** See *4014.*

περιέλθω **pĕriĕlthō.** See *4022.*

4020. περιεργάζομαι **pĕriĕrgazŏmai,** *per-ee-er-gad´-zom-ahee;* from *4012* and *2038;* to *work all around,* i.e. *bustle about* (*meddle*):— be a busybody.

4021. περίεργος **pĕriĕrgŏs,** *per-ee´-er-gos;* from *4012* and *2041; working all around,* i.e. *officious* (*meddlesome,* neut. plur. *magic*):— busybody, curious arts.

4022. περιέρχομαι **pĕriĕrchŏmai,** *per-ee-er´-khom-ahee;* from *4012* and *2064* (incl. its alt.); to *come all around,* i.e. *stroll, vacillate, veer:*— fetch a compass, vagabond, wandering about.

4023. περιέχω **pĕriĕchō,** *per-ee-ekh´-o;* from *4012* and *2192;* to *hold all around,* i.e. *include, clasp* (fig.):— + astonished, contain, after [this manner].

4024. περιζώννυμι **pĕrizōnnumi,** *per-idzone´-noo-mee;* from *4012* and *2224;* to *gird all around,* i.e. (middle or passive voice) to *fasten on one's belt* (lit. or fig.):— gird (about, self).

4025. περίθεσις **pĕrithĕsis,** *per-ith´-es-is;* from *4060;* a *putting all around,* i.e. *decorating* oneself with:— wearing.

4026. περιΐστημι **pĕriistēmi,** *per-ee-is´-taymee;* from *4012* and *2476;* to *stand all around,* i.e. (near) to *be a bystander,* or (aloof) to *keep away* from:— avoid, shun, stand by (round about).

4027. περικάθαρμα **pĕrikatharma,** *per-ee-kath´-ar-mah;* from a compound of *4012* and *2508;* something *cleaned* off all *around,* i.e. *refuse* (fig.):— filth.

4028. περικαλύπτω **pĕrikaluptō,** *per-ee-kaloop´-to;* from *4012* and *2572;* to *cover all around,* i.e. *entirely* (the face, a surface):— blindfold, cover, overlay.

4029. περίκειμαι **pĕrikĕimai,** *per-ik´-i-mahee;* from *4012* and *2749;* to *lie all around,* i.e. *enclose, encircle, hamper* (lit. or fig.):— be bound (compassed) with, hang about.

4030. περικεφαλαία **pĕrikĕphalaia,** *per-ee-kef-al-ah´-yah;* fem. of a compound of *4012* and *2776; encirclement* of the *head,* i.e. a *helmet:*— helmet.

4031. περικρατής **pĕrikratēs,** *per-ee-krat-ace´;* from *4012* and *2904; strong all around,* i.e. a *master* (*manager*):— + come by.

4032. περικρύπτω **pĕrikruptō,** *per-ee-*

kroop´-to; from *4012* and *2928;* to *conceal* all *around,* i.e. *entirely:*— hide.

4033. περικυκλόω **pĕrikuklŏŏ,** *per-ee-koo-klŏ´-o;* from *4012* and *2944;* to *encircle* all *around,* i.e. *blockade completely:*— compass round.

4034. περιλάμπω **pĕrilampō,** *per-ee-lam´-po;* from *4012* and *2989;* to *illuminate* all *around,* i.e. *invest with a halo:*— shine round about.

4035. περιλείπω **pĕrilĕipō,** *per-ee-li´-po;* from *4012* and *3007;* to *leave* all *around,* i.e. (pass.) *survive:*— remain.

4036. περίλυπος **pĕrilupŏs,** *per-il´-oo-pos;* from *4012* and *3077;* *grieved* all *around,* i.e. *intensely sad:*— exceeding (very) sorry (-ow-ful).

4037. περιμένω **pĕrimĕnō,** *per-ee-men´-o;* from *4012* and *3306;* to *stay around,* i.e. *await:*— wait for.

4038. πέριξ **pĕrix,** *per´-ix;* adv. from *4012;* all *around,* i.e. (as an adj.) *circumjacent:*— round about.

4039. περιοικέω **pĕriŏikĕō,** *per-ee-oy-keh´-o;* from *4012* and *3611;* to *reside around,* i.e. *be a neighbor:*— dwell round about.

4040. περίοικος **pĕriŏikŏs,** *per-ee´-oy-kos;* from *4012* and *3624;* *housed around,* i.e. *neighboring* (ellip. used as a noun):— neighbour.

4041. περιούσιος **pĕriŏusiŏs,** *per-ee-oo´-see-os;* from the pres. part. fem. of a compound of *4012* and *1510; being beyond* usual, i.e. *special* (one's *own*):— peculiar.

4042. περιοχή **pĕriŏchē,** *per-ee-okh-ay´;* from *4023;* a *being held around,* i.e. (concr.) a *passage* (of Scripture, as *circumscribed*):— place.

4043. περιπατέω **pĕripatĕō,** *per-ee-pat-eh´-o;* from *4012* and *3961;* to *tread* all *around,* i.e. *walk* at large (espec. as proof of ability); fig. to *live, deport oneself, follow* (as a companion or votary):— go, be occupied with, walk (about).

4044. περιπείρω **pĕripĕirō,** *per-ee-pi´-ro;* from *4012* and the base of *4008;* to *penetrate entirely,* i.e. *transfix* (fig.):— pierce through.

4045. περιπίπτω **pĕripiptō,** *per-ee-pip´-to;* from *4012* and *4098;* to *fall* into something i.e. all *around,* i.e. *light among* or *upon, be surrounded with:*— fall among (into).

4046. περιποιέομαι **pĕripŏiĕŏmai,** *per-ee-poy-eh´-om-ahee;* mid. voice from *4012* and *4160;* to *make around oneself,* i.e. *acquire* (buy):— purchase.

4047. περιποίησις **pĕripŏiēsis,** *per-ee-poy´-ay-sis;* from *4046; acquisition* (the act or the thing); by extens. *preservation:*— obtain (-ing), peculiar, purchased, possession, saving.

4048. περιρρήγνυμι **pĕrirrhēgnumi,** *per-ir-hrayg´-noo-mee;* from *4012* and *4486;* to *tear* all *around,* i.e. *completely away:*— rend off.

4049. περισπάω **pĕrispaō,** *per-ee-spah´-o;* from *4012* and *4685;* to *drag* all *around,* i.e. (fig.) to *distract* (with care):— cumber.

4050. περισσεία **pĕrissĕia,** *per-is-si´-ah;* from *4052; surplusage,* i.e. *superabundance:*— abundance (-ant, [-ly]), superfluity.

4051. περίσσευμα **pĕrissĕuma,** *per-is´-syoo-mah;* from *4052;* a *surplus,* or *superabundance:*— abundance, that was left, over and above.

4052. περισσεύω **pĕrissĕuō,** *per-is-syoo´-o;* from *4053;* to *superabound* (in quantity or quality), *be in excess, be superfluous;* also (tran.) to *cause to superabound* or *excel:*— (make, more) abound, (have, have more) abundance (be more) abundant, be the better, enough and to spare, exceed, excel, increase, be left, redound, remain (over and above).

4053. περισσός **pĕrissŏs,** *per-is-sos´;* from *4012* (in the sense of *beyond*); *superabundant* (in quantity) or *superior* (in quality); by impl. *excessive;* adv. (with *1537*) *violently;* neut. (as noun) *preeminence:*— exceeding abundantly above, more abundantly, advantage, exceedingly, very highly, beyond measure, more, superfluous, vehement [-ly].

4054. περισσότερον **pĕrissŏtĕrŏn,** *per-is-sot´-er-on;* neut. of *4055* (as adv.); in a *more superabundant* way:— more abundantly, a great deal, far more.

4055. περισσότερος **pĕrissŏtĕrŏs,** *per-is-sot´-er-os;* comp. of *4053; more superabundant* (in number, degree or character):— more abundant, greater (much) more, overmuch.

4056. περισσοτέρως **pĕrissŏtĕrōs,** *per-is-sot-er´-oce;* adv. from *4055; more superabundantly:*— more abundant (-ly), × the more earnest, (more) exceedingly, more frequent, much more, the rather.

4057. περισσῶς **pĕrissōs,** *per-is-soce´;* adv. from *4053; superabundantly:*— exceedingly, out of measure, the more.

4058. περιστερά **pĕristĕra,** *per-is-ter-ah´;* of uncert. der.; a *pigeon:*— dove, pigeon.

4059. περιτέμνω **pĕritĕmnō,** *per-ee-tem´-no;* from *4012* and the base of *5114;* to *cut around,* i.e. (spec.) to *circumcise:*— circumcise.

4060. περιτίθημι **pĕritithēmi,** *per-ee-tith´-ay-mee;* from *4012* and *5087;* to *place around;* by impl. to *present:*— bestow upon, hedge round about, put about (on, upon), set about.

4061. περιτομή **pĕritŏmē,** *per-it-om-ay´;* from *4059; circumcision* (the rite, the condition or the people, lit. or fig.):— × circumcised, circumcision.

4062. περιτρέπω **pĕritrĕpō,** *per-ee-trep´-o;*

from *4012* and the base of *5157;* to *turn around,* i.e. (ment.) to *craze:—* + make mad.

4063. περιτρέχω **pĕritrĕchō,** *per-ee-trekh´-o;* from *4012* and *5143* (incl. its alt.); to *run around,* i.e. *traverse:—* run through.

4064. περιφέρω **pĕriphĕrō,** *per-ee-fer´-o;* from *4012* and *5342;* to *convey around,* i.e. *transport hither and thither:—* bear (carry) about.

4065. περιφρονέω **pĕriphrŏnĕō,** *per-ee-fron-eh´-o;* from *4012* and *5426;* to *think beyond,* i.e. *depreciate (contemn):—* despise.

4066. περίχωρος **pĕrichōrŏs,** *per-ikh´-o-ros;* from *4012* and *5561;* *around* the *region,* i.e. *circumjacent* (as noun, with *1093* impl. *vicinity*):— country (round) about, region (that lieth) round about.

4067. περίψωμα **pĕripsōma,** *per-ip´-so-mah* or

περίψημα **pĕripsēma,** *per-ip´-say-mah;* from a compound of *4012* and ψάω *psaō* (to *rub*); something *brushed* all *around,* i.e. *offscrapings* (fig. *scum*):— offscouring.

4068. περπερεύομαι **pĕrpĕrĕuŏmai,** *per-per-yoo´-om-ahee;* mid. voice from πέρπερος **pĕrpĕrŏs** (*braggart;* perh. by redupl. of the base of *4008*); to *boast:—* vaunt itself.

4069. Περσίς **Pĕrsis,** *per-sece´;* a *Pers.* woman; *Persis,* a Chr. female:— Persis.

4070. πέρυσι **pĕrusi,** *per´-oo-si;* adv. from *4009;* the *by-gone,* i.e. (as noun) *last year:—* + a year ago.

πετάομαι **pĕtaŏmai.** See *4072.*

4071. πετεινόν **pĕtĕinŏn,** *pet-i-non´;* neut. of a der. of *4072;* a *flying* animal, i.e. *bird:—* bird, fowl.

4072. πέτομαι **pĕtŏmai,** *pet´-om-ahee;* or prol.

πετάομαι **pĕtaŏmai,** *pet-ah´-om-ahee;* or contr. πτάομαι **ptaŏmai,** *ptah´-om-ahee;* mid. voice of a primary verb; to *fly:—* fly (-ing).

4073. πέτρα **pĕtra,** *pet´-ra;* fem. of the same as *4074;* a (mass of) *rock* (lit. or fig.):— rock.

4074. Πέτρος **Pĕtrŏs,** *pet´-ros;* appar. a primary word; a (piece of) *rock* (larger than *3037*); as a name, *Petrus,* an apostle:— Peter, rock. Comp. *2786.*

4075. πετρώδης **pĕtrōdēs,** *pet-ro´-dace;* from *4073* and *1491;* *rock-like,* i.e. *rocky:—* stony.

4076. πήγανον **pēganŏn,** *pay´-gan-on;* from *4078;* *rue* (from its *thick* or *fleshy* leaves):— rue.

4077. πηγή **pēgē,** *pay-gay´;* prob. from *4078* (through the idea of *gushing* plumply); a *fount* (lit. or fig.), i.e. *source* or *supply* (of water, blood, enjoyment) (not necessarily the orig. *spring*):— fountain, well.

4078. πήγνυμι **pēgnumi,** *payg´-noo-mee;* a prol. form of a primary verb (which in its simpler form occurs only as an alt. in certain tenses); to *fix* ("peg"), i.e. (spec.) to *set up* (a tent):— pitch.

4079. πηδάλιον **pēdaliŏn,** *pay-dal´-ee-on;* neut. of a (presumed) der. of πηδόν **pēdŏn** (the *blade* of an oar; from the same as *3976*); a "*pedal,*" i.e. *helm:—* rudder.

4080. πηλίκος **pēlikŏs,** *pay-lee´-kos;* a quantitative form (the fem.) of the base of *4225;* *how much* (as an indef.), i.e. in size or (fig.) dignity:— how great (large).

4081. πηλός **pēlŏs,** *pay-los´;* perh. a primary word; *clay:—* clay.

4082. πήρα **pēra,** *pay´-rah;* of uncert. aff.; a *wallet* or leather *pouch* for food:— scrip.

4083. πῆχυς **pēchus,** *pay´-khoos;* of uncert. aff.; the *fore-arm,* i.e. (as a measure) a *cubit:—* cubit.

4084. πιάζω **piazō,** *pee-ad´-zo;* prob. another form of *971;* to *squeeze,* i.e. *seize* (gently by the hand [*press*], or officially [*arrest*], or in hunting [*capture*]):— apprehend, catch, lay hand on, take. Comp. *4085.*

4085. πιέζω **piĕzō,** *pee-ed´-zo;* another form for *4084;* to *pack:—* press down.

4086. πιθανολογία **pithanŏlŏgia,** *pith-an-ol-og-ee´-ah;* from a compound of a der. of *3982* and *3056;* *persuasive language:—* enticing words.

4087. πικραίνω **pikrainō,** *pik-rah´-ee-no;* from *4089;* to *embitter* (lit. or fig.):— be (make) bitter.

4088. πικρία **pikria,** *pik-ree´-ah;* from *4089;* *acridity* (espec. *poison*), lit. or fig.:— bitterness.

4089. πικρός **pikrŏs,** *pik-ros´;* perh. from *4078* (through the idea of *piercing*); *sharp* (*pungent*), i.e. *acrid* (lit. or fig.):— bitter.

4090. πικρῶς **pikrōs,** *pik-roce´;* adv. from *4089;* *bitterly,* i.e. (fig.) *violently:—* bitterly.

4091. Πιλάτος **Pilatŏs,** *pil-at´-os;* of Lat. or.; *close-pressed,* i.e. *firm;* *Pilatus,* a Rom.:— Pilate.

πίμπλημι **pimplēmi.** See *4130.*

4092. πίμπρημι **pimprēmi,** *pim´-pray-mee;* a redupl. and prol. form of a primary

πρέω **prĕō,** *preh´-o;* which occurs only as an alt. in certain tenses); to *fire,* i.e. *burn* (fig. and pass. *become inflamed* with fever):— be (× should have) swollen.

4093. πινακίδιον **pinakidiŏn,** *pin-ak-id´-ee-on;* dimin. of *4094;* a *tablet* (for writing on):— writing table.

4094. πίναξ **pinax,** *pin´-ax;* appar. a form of *4109;* a *plate:—* charger, platter.

4095. πίνω **pinō,** *pee´-no;* a prol. form of

πίω **piō,** *pee´-o;* which (together with another form πόω **pŏō,** *pŏ´-o;* occurs only as an alt. in certain tenses); to *imbibe* (lit. or fig.):— drink.

4096. πιότης **piŏtēs,** *pee-ot´-ace;* from πίων **piōn,** (*fat;* perh. akin to the alt. of *4095* through the idea of *repletion*); *plumpness*, i.e. (by impl.) *richness* (*oiliness*):— fatness.

4097. πιπράσκω **pipraskō**, *pip-ras´-ko;* a redupl. and prol. form of

πράω **praō**, *prah´-o;* (which occurs only as an alt. in certain tenses); contr. from περάω **pĕraō** (to *traverse;* from the base of *4008*); to *traffic* (by *travelling*), i.e. *dispose* of as merchandise or into slavery (lit. or fig.):— sell.

4098. πίπτω **piptō**, *pip´-to;* a redupl. and contr. form of πέτω **pĕtō**, *pet´-o;* (which occurs only as an alt. in certain tenses); prob. akin to 4072 through the idea of *alighting;* to *fall* (lit. or fig.):— fail, fall (down), light on.

4099. Πισιδία **Pisidia**, *pis-id-ee´-ah;* prob. of for. or.; *Pisidia*, a region of Asia Minor:— Pisidia.

4100. πιστεύω **pistĕuō**, *pist-yoo´-o;* from *4102*; to *have faith* (in, upon, or with respect to, a person or thing), i.e. *credit;* by impl. to *entrust* (espec. one's spiritual well-being to Christ):— believe (-r), commit (to trust), put in trust with.

4101. πιστικός **pistikŏs**, *pis-tik-os´;* from *4102*; *trustworthy*, i.e. *genuine* (*unadulterated*):— spike-[nard].

4102. πίστις **pistis**, *pis´-tis;* from *3982; persuasion*, i.e. *credence;* mor. *conviction* (of *relig.* truth, or the truthfulness of God or a relig. teacher), espec. *reliance* upon Christ for salvation; abstr. *constancy* in such profession; by extension, the system of religious (Gospel) *truth* itself:— assurance, belief, believe, faith, fidelity.

4103. πιστός **pistŏs**, *pis-tos´;* from *3982*; obj. *trustworthy;* subj. *trustful:*— believe (-ing, -r), faithful (-ly), sure, true.

4104. πιστόω **pistŏō**, *pis-tŏ´-o;* from *4103;* to *assure:*— assure of.

4105. πλανάω **planaō**, *plan-ah´-o;* from *4106;* to (prop. *cause* to) *roam* (from safety, truth, or virtue):— go astray, deceive, err, seduce, wander, be out of the way.

4106. πλάνη **planē**, *plan´-ay;* fem. of *4108* (as abstr.); obj. *fraudulence;* subj. a *straying* from orthodoxy or piety:— deceit, to deceive, delusion, error.

4107. πλανήτης **planētēs**, *plan-ay´-tace;* from *4108;* a *rover* ("planet"), i.e. (fig.) an *erratic* teacher:— wandering.

4108. πλάνος **planŏs**, *plan´-os;* of uncert. aff.; *roving* (as a *tramp*), i.e. (by impl.) an *impostor* or *misleader:*— deceiver, seducing.

4109. πλάξ **plax**, *plax;* from *4111;* a *moulding-board*, i.e. *flat* surface ("*plate*", or *tablet*, lit. or fig.):— table.

4110. πλάσμα **plasma**, *plas´-mah;* from *4111;* something *moulded:*— thing formed.

4111. πλάσσω **plassō**, *plas´-so;* a primary verb; to *mould*, i.e. *shape* or *fabricate:*— form.

4112. πλαστός **plastŏs**, *plas-tos´;* from *4111; moulded*, i.e. (by impl.) *artificial* or (fig.) *fictitious* (*false*):— feigned.

4113. πλατεῖα **platĕia**, *plat-i´-ah;* fem. of *4116;* a *wide* "*plat*" or "*place*", i.e. open *square:*— street.

4114. πλάτος **platŏs**, *plat´-os;* from *4116; width:*— breadth.

4115. πλατύνω **platunō**, *plat-oo´-no;* from *4116;* to *widen* (lit. or fig.):— make broad, enlarge.

4116. πλατύς **platus**, *plat-oos´;* from *4111;* spread out "*flat*" ("plot"), i.e. *broad:*— wide.

4117. πλέγμα **plĕgma**, *pleg´-mah;* from *4120;* a *plait* (of hair):— broidered hair.

πλεῖον **plĕiŏn**. See *4119*.

4118. πλεῖστος **plĕistŏs**, *plice´-tos;* irreg. superl. of *4183;* the *largest number* or *very large:*— very great, most.

4119. πλείων **plĕiōn**, *pli-own;* neut.

πλεῖον **plĕiŏn**, *pli´-on;* or

πλέον **plĕŏn**, *pleh´-on;* comparative of *4183; more* in quantity, number, or quality; also (in plur.) the *major portion:*— × above, + exceed, more excellent, further, (very) great (-er), long (-er), (very) many, greater (more) part, + yet but.

4120. πλέκω **plĕkō**, *plek´-o;* a primary word; to *twine* or *braid:*— plait.

πλέον **plĕŏn**. See *4119*.

4121. πλεονάζω **plĕŏnazō**, *pleh-on-ad´-zo;* from *4119;* to *do, make* or *be more*, i.e. *increase* (tran. or intr.); by extens. to *superabound:*— abound, abundant, make to increase, have over.

4122. πλεονεκτέω **plĕŏnĕktĕō**, *pleh-on-ek-teh´-o;* from *4123;* to *be covetous*, i.e. (by impl.) to *over-reach:*— get an advantage, defraud, make a gain.

4123. πλεονέκτης **plĕŏnĕktēs**, *pleh-on-ek´-tace;* from *4119* and *2192; holding* (*desiring*) *more*, i.e. *eager for gain* (*avaricious*, hence, a *defrauder*):— covetous.

4124. πλεονεξία **plĕŏnĕxia**, *pleh-on-ex-ee´-ah;* from *4123; avarice*, i.e. (by impl.) *fraudulency, extortion:*— covetous (-ness) practices, greediness.

4125. πλευρά **plĕura**, *plyoo-rah´;* of uncert. aff.; a *rib*, i.e. (by extens.) *side:*— side.

4126. πλέω **plĕō**, *pleh´-o;* another form for

πλεύω **plĕuō**, *plyoo´-o;* which is used as an alt. in certain tenses; prob. a form of *4150* (through the idea of *plunging* through the water); to *pass* in a vessel:— sail. See also *4130*.

4127. πληγή **plēgē**, *play-gay´;* from *4141;* a *stroke;* by impl. a *wound;* fig. a *calamity:*— plague, stripe, wound (-ed).

4128. πλῆθος **plēthŏs**, *play´-thos;* from *4130;*

a *fulness,* i.e. a *large number, throng, populace:*— bundle, company, multitude.

4129. πληθύνω **plēthunō,** *play-thoo´-no;* from another form of *4128;* to *increase* (tran. or intr.):— abound, multiply.

4130. πλήθω **plēthō,** *play´-tho;* a prol. form of a primary πλέω **pleō,** *pleh´-o* (which appears only as an alt. in certain tenses and in the redupl. form πίμπλημι **pimplēmi**); to *"fill"* (lit. or fig. [*imbue, influence, supply*]); spec. to *fulfil* (time):— accomplish, full (...come), furnish.

4131. πλήκτης **plēktēs,** *plake´-tace;* from *4141;* a *smiter,* i.e. *pugnacious (quarrelsome):*— striker.

4132. πλημμύρα **plēmmura,** *plame-moo´-rah;* prol. from *4130; flood-tide,* i.e. (by anal.) a *freshet:*— flood.

4133. πλήν **plēn,** *plane;* from *4119; moreover (besides),* i.e. *albeit, save that, rather, yet:*— but (rather), except, nevertheless, notwithstanding, save, than.

4134. πλήρης **plērēs,** *play´-race;* from *4130; replete,* or *covered* over; by anal. *complete:*— full.

4135. πληροφορέω **plērŏphŏreō,** *play-rof-or-eh´-o;* from *4134* and *5409;* to *carry* out *fully* (in evidence), i.e. *completely assure* (or *convince*), *entirely accomplish:*— most surely believe, fully know (persuade), make full proof of.

4136. πληροφορία **plērŏphŏria,** *play-rof-or-ee´-ah;* from *4135; entire confidence:*— (full) assurance.

4137. πληρόω **plērŏō,** *play-rŏ´-o;* from *4134;* to *make replete,* i.e. (lit.) to *cram* (a net), *level* up (a hollow), or (fig.) to *furnish* (or *imbue, diffuse, influence*), *satisfy, execute* (an office), *finish* (a period or task), *verify* (or *coincide* with a prediction), etc.:— accomplish, × after, (be) complete, end, expire, fill (up), fulfil, (be, make) full (come), fully preach, perfect, supply.

4138. πλήρωμα **plērōma,** *play´-ro-mah;* from *4137; repletion* or *completion,* i.e. (subj.) what *fills* (as contents, supplement, copiousness, multitude), or (obj.) what is *filled* (as container, performance, period):— which is put in to fill up, piece that filled up, fulfilling, full, fulness.

4139. πλησίον **plēsiŏn,** *play-see´-on;* neut. of a der. of πέλας **pĕlas** (near); (adv.) *close* by; as noun, a *neighbor,* i.e. *fellow* (as man, countryman, Chr. or friend):— near, neighbour.

4140. πλησμονή **plēsmŏnē,** *place-mon-ay´;* from a presumed der. of *4130;* a *filling* up, i.e. (fig.) *gratification:*— satisfying.

4141. πλήσσω **plēssō,** *place´-so;* appar. another form of *4111* (through the idea of *flattening* out); to *pound,* i.e. (fig.) to *inflict* with (calamity):— smite. Comp. *5180.*

4142. πλοιάριον **plŏiariŏn,** *ploy-ar´-ee-on;* neut. of a presumed der. of *4143;* a *boat:*— boat, little (small) ship.

4143. πλοῖον **plŏiŏn,** *ploy-on;* from *4126;* a *sailer,* i.e. *vessel:*— ship (-ping).

4144. πλόος **plŏŏs,** *plŏ´-os;* from *4126;* a *sail,* i.e. *navigation:*— course, sailing, voyage.

4145. πλούσιος **plŏusiŏs,** *ploo´-see-os;* from *4149; wealthy;* fig. *abounding* with:— rich.

4146. πλουσίως **plŏusiŏs,** *ploo-see´-oce;* adv. from *4145; copiously:*— abundantly, richly.

4147. πλουτέω **plŏuteō,** *ploo-teh´-o;* from *4148;* to *be* (or *become*) *wealthy* (lit. or fig.):— be increased with goods, (be made, wax) rich.

4148. πλουτίζω **plŏutizō,** *ploo-tid´-zo;* from *4149;* to *make wealthy* (fig.):— en- (make) rich.

4149. πλοῦτος **plŏutŏs,** *ploo´-tos;* from the base of *4130; wealth* (as *fulness*), i.e. (lit.) *money, possessions,* or (fig.) *abundance, richness,* (spec.) valuable *bestowment:*— riches.

4150. πλύνω **plunō,** *ploo´-no;* a prol. form of an obs. πλύω **pluō,** (to *"flow"*); to *"plunge,"* i.e. *launder* clothing:— wash. Comp. *3068, 3538.*

4151. πνεῦμα **pnĕuma,** *pnyoo´-mah;* from *4154;* a *current* of air, i.e. *breath* (*blast*) or a *breeze;* by anal. or fig. a *spirit,* i.e. (human) the rational *soul,* (by impl.) *vital principle,* ment. *disposition,* etc., or (superhuman) an *angel, demon,* or (divine) *God,* Christ's *spirit,* the Holy *Spirit:*— ghost, life, spirit (-ual, -ually), mind. Comp. *5590.*

4152. πνευματικός **pnĕumatikŏs,** *pnyoo-mat-ik-os´;* from *4151; non-carnal,* i.e. (humanly) *ethereal* (as opposed to gross), or (demoniacally) a *spirit* (concr.), or (divinely) *supernatural, regenerate, religious:*— spiritual. Comp. *5591.*

4153. πνευματικῶς **pnĕumatikŏs,** *pnyoo-mat-ik-oce´;* adv. from *4152; non-physical,* i.e. *divinely, figuratively:*— spiritually.

4154. πνέω **pnĕō,** *pneh´-o;* a primary word; to *breathe* hard, i.e. *breeze:*— blow. Comp. *5594.*

4155. πνίγω **pnigō,** *pnee´-go;* strengthened from *4154;* to *wheeze,* i.e. (cause. by impl.) to *throttle* or *strangle* (*drown*):— choke, take by the throat.

4156. πνικτός **pniktŏs,** *pnik-tos´;* from *4155; throttled,* i.e. (neut. concr.) an animal *choked* to death (*not bled*):— strangled.

4157. πνοή **pnŏē,** *pno-ay´;* from *4154; respiration,* a *breeze:*— breath, wind.

4158. ποδήρης **pŏdērēs,** *pod-ay´-race;* from *4228* and another element of uncert. aff.; a *dress* (*2066* impl.) *reaching* the *ankles:*— garment down to the foot.

Greek

4159. πόθεν **pŏthĕn**, *poth´-en;* from the base of *4213* with enclitic adverb of origin; *from which* (as interr.) or *what* (as rel.) place, state, source or cause:— whence.

4160. ποιέω **pŏiĕō**, *poy-eh´-o;* appar. a prol. form of an obs. primary; to *make* or *do* (in a very wide application, more or less dir.):— abide, + agree, appoint, × avenge, + band together, be, bear, + bewray, bring (forth), cast out, cause, commit, + content, continue, deal, + without any delay, (would) do (-ing), execute, exercise, fulfil, gain, give, have, hold, × journeying, keep, + lay wait, + lighten the ship, make, × mean, + none of these things move me, observe, ordain, perform, provide, + have purged, purpose, put, + raising up, × secure, shew, × shoot out, spend, take, tarry, + transgress the law, work, yield. Comp. *4238.*

4161. ποίημα **pŏiēma**, *poy´-ay-mah;* from *4160;* a *product,* i.e. *fabric* (lit. or fig.):— thing that is made, workmanship.

4162. ποίησις **pŏiēsis**, *poy´-ay-sis;* from *4160; action,* i.e. *performance* (of the law):— deed.

4163. ποιητής **pŏiētēs**, *poy-ay-tace´;* from *4160;* a *performer;* spec. a *"poet"*:— doer, poet.

4164. ποικίλος **pŏikilŏs**, *poy-kee´-los;* of uncert. der.; *motley,* i.e. *various* in character:— divers, manifold.

4165. ποιμαίνω **pŏimainō**, *poy-mah´-ee-no;* from *4166;* to *tend* as a shepherd (or fig. *superviser*):— feed (cattle), rule.

4166. ποιμήν **pŏimēn**, *poy-mane´;* of uncert. aff.; a *shepherd* (lit. or fig.):— shepherd, pastor.

4167. ποίμνη **pŏimnē**, *poym´-nay;* contr. from *4165;* a *flock* (lit. or fig.):— flock, fold.

4168. ποίμνιον **pŏimniŏn**, *poym´-nee-on;* neut. of a presumed der. of *4167;* a *flock,* i.e. (fig.) *group* (of believers):— flock.

4169. ποῖος **pŏiŏs**, *poy´-os;* from the base of *4226* and *3634;* individualizing interr. (of character) *what* sort of, or (of number) *which* one:— what (manner of), which.

4170. πολεμέω **pŏlĕmĕō**, *pol-em-eh´-o;* from *4171;* to *be* (engaged) in *warfare,* i.e. to *battle* (lit. or fig.):— fight, (make) war.

4171. πόλεμος **pŏlĕmŏs**, *pol´-em-os;* from πέλομαι **pĕlŏmai**, (to *bustle*); *warfare* (lit. or fig.; a single encounter or a series):— battle, fight, war.

4172. πόλις **pŏlis**, *pol´-is;* prob. from the same as *4171,* or perh. from *4183;* a *town* (prop. with walls, of greater or less size):— city.

4173. πολιτάρχης **pŏlitarchēs**, *pol-it-ar´-khace;* from *4172* and *757;* a *town-officer,* i.e. *magistrate:*— ruler of the city.

4174. πολιτεία **pŏlitĕia**, *pol-ee-ti´-ah;* from *4177* ("*polity*"); *citizenship;* concr. a *commu-nity:*— commonwealth, freedom.

4175. πολίτευμα **pŏlitĕuma**, *pol-it´-yoo-mah;*

from *4176;* a *community,* i.e. (abstr.) *citi-zenship* (fig.):— conversation.

4176. πολιτεύομαι **pŏlitĕuŏmai**, *pol-it-yoo´-om-ahee;* mid. voice of a der. of *4177;* to *behave* as a citizen (fig.):— let conversation be, live.

4177. πολίτης **pŏlitēs**, *pol-ee´-tace;* from *4172;* a *townsman:*— citizen.

4178. πολλάκις **pŏllakis**, *pol-lak´-is;* mult. adv. from *4183; many times,* i.e. *fre-quently:*— oft (-en, -entimes, -times).

4179. πολλαπλασίων **pŏllaplasiōn**, *pol-lap-las-ee´-ohn;* from *4183* and prob. a der. of *4120; manifold,* i.e. (neut. as noun) *very much more:*— manifold more.

4180. πολυλογία **pŏlulŏgia**, *pol-oo-log-ee´-ah;* from a compound of *4183* and *3056; loquacity,* i.e. *prolixity:*— much speaking.

4181. πολυμέρως **pŏlumĕrōs**, *pol-oo-mer´-oce;* adv. from a compound of *4183* and *3313; in many portions,* i.e. *variously* as to time and agency (*piecemeal*):— at sundry times.

4182. πολυποίκιλος **pŏlupŏikilŏs**, *pol-oo-poy´-kil-os;* from *4183* and *4164; much vari-egated,* i.e. *multifarious:*— manifold.

4183. πολύς **pŏlus**, *pol-oos´;* incl. the forms from the alt. πολλός **pŏllŏs**; (sing.) *much* (in any respect) or (plural) *many;* neut. (sing.) as adv. *largely;* neut. (plural) as adv. or noun *often, mostly, largely:*— abundant, + altogether, common, + far (passed, spent), (+ be of a) great (age, deal, -ly, while), long, many, much, oft (-en [-times]), plenteous, sore, straitly. Comp. *4118, 4119.*

4184. πολύσπλαγχνος **pŏlusplagchnŏs**, *pol-oo´-splankh-nos;* from *4183* and *4698* (fig.); *extremely compassionate:*— very pitiful.

4185. πολυτελής **pŏlutĕlēs**, *pol-oo-tel-ace´;* from *4183* and *5056; extremely expensive:*— costly, very precious, of great price.

4186. πολύτιμος **pŏlutimŏs**, *pol-oot´-ee-mos;* from *4183* and *5092; extremely valu-able:*— very costly, of great price.

4187. πολυτρόπως **pŏlutrŏpōs**, *pol-oot-rop´-oce;* adv. from a compound of *4183* and *5158; in many ways,* i.e. *variously* as to method or form:— in divers manners.

4188. πόμα **pŏma**, *pom´-ah;* from the alt. of *4095;* a *beverage:*— drink.

4189. πονηρία **pŏnēria**, *pon-ay-ree´-ah;* from *4190; depravity,* i.e. (spec.) *malice;* plur. (concr.) *plots, sins:*— iniquity, wicked-ness.

4190. πονηρός **pŏnērŏs**, *pon-ay-ros´;* from a der. of *4192; hurtful,* i.e. *evil* (prop. in effect or influence, and thus differing from *2556,* which refers rather to *essential* character, as well as from *4550,* which indicates *de-generacy* from original virtue); fig. *calami-tous;* also (pass.) *ill,* i.e. *diseased;* but espec.

(mor.) *culpable*, i.e. *derelict, vicious, facinor-ous;* neut. (sing.) *mischief, malice,* or (plural) *guilt;* masc. (sing.) the *devil,* or (plural) *sin-ners:*— bad, evil, grievous, harm, lewd, mali-cious, wicked (-ness). See also *4191.*

4191. πονηρότερος **pŏnērŏtĕrŏs,** *pon-ay-rot´-er-os;* comp. of *4190; more evil:*— more wicked.

4192. πόνος **pŏnŏs,** *pon´-os;* from the base of *3993; toil,* i.e. (by impl.) *anguish:*— pain.

4193. Ποντικός **Pŏntikŏs,** *pon-tik-os´;* from *4195;* a *Pontican,* i.e. native of Pontus:— born in Pontus.

4194. Πόντιος **Pŏntiŏs,** *pon´-tee-os;* of Lat. or.; appar. *bridged; Pontius,* a Rom.:— Pontius.

4195. Πόντος **Pŏntŏs,** *pon´-tos;* a *sea; Pontus,* a region of Asia Minor:— Pontus.

4196. Πόπλιος **Pŏpliŏs,** *pop´-lee-os;* of Lat. or.; appar. *"popular"; Poplius* (i.e. *Publius*), a Rom.:— Publius.

4197. πορεία **pŏreia,** *por-i´-ah;* from *4198; travel* (by land); fig. (plural) *proceedings,* i.e. *career:*— journey [-ing], ways.

4198. πορεύομαι **pŏrĕuŏmai,** *por-yoo´-om-ahee;* mid. voice from a der. of the same as *3984;* to *traverse,* i.e. *travel* (lit. or fig.; espec. to *remove* [fig. *die*], *live,* etc.);—depart, go (away, forth, one's way, up), (make a, take a) journey, walk.

4199. πορθέω **pŏrthĕō,** *por-theh´-o;* prol. from πέρθω **pĕrthō,** (to *sack*); to *ravage* (fig.):— de-stroy, waste.

4200. πορισμός **pŏrismŏs,** *por-is-mos´;* from a der. of πόρος **pŏrŏs** (a *way,* i.e. *means*); *fur-nishing,* (*procuring*), i.e. (by impl.) *money-get-ting* (*acquisition*):— gain.

4201. Πόρκιος **Pŏrkiŏs,** *por´-kee-os;* of Lat. or.; appar. *swinish; Porcius,* a Rom.:— Porcius.

4202. πορνεία **pŏrnĕia,** *por-ni´-ah;* from *4203; harlotry* (incl. *adultery* and *incest*); fig. *idola-try:*— fornication.

4203. πορνεύω **pŏrnĕuō,** *porn-yoo´-o;* from *4204;* to *act* the *harlot,* i.e. (lit.) *indulge* unlaw-ful *lust* (of either sex), or (fig.) *practice idola-try:*— commit (fornication).

4204. πόρνη **pŏrnē,** *por´-nay;* fem. of *4205;* a *strumpet;* fig. an *idolater:*— harlot, whore.

4205. πόρνος **pŏrnŏs,** *por´-nos;* from πέρνημι **pĕrnēmi** (to *sell;* akin to the base of *4097*); a (male) *prostitute* (as *venal*), i.e. (by anal.) a *debauchee* (*libertine*):— fornicator, whore-monger.

4206. πόρρω **pŏrrhō,** *por´-rho;* adv. from *4253; forwards,* i.e. *at a distance:*— far, a great way off. See also *4207.*

4207. πόρρωθεν **pŏrrhŏthĕn,** *por´-rho-then;* from *4206* with adv. enclitic of source; *from far,* or (by impl.) *at a distance,* i.e. *distantly:*— afar off.

4208. πορρωτέρω **pŏrrhŏtĕrō,** *por-rho-ter´-o;*

adv. comparative of *4206; further,* i.e. *a greater distance:*— farther.

4209. πορφύρα **pŏrphura,** *por-foo´-rah;* of Lat. or.; the *"purple"* mussel, i.e. (by impl.) the *red-blue* color itself, and finally a gar-ment dyed with it:— purple.

4210. πορφυροῦς **pŏrphurŏus,** *por-foo-rooce´;* from *4209; purpureal,* i.e. *bluish red:*— purple.

4211. πορφυρόπωλις **pŏrphurŏpōlis,** *por-foo-rop´-o-lis;* fem. of a compound of *4209* and *4453;* a *female trader in purple* cloth:— seller of purple.

4212. ποσάκις **pŏsakis,** *pos-ak´-is;* mult. from *4214; how many times:*— how oft (-en).

4213. πόσις **pŏsis,** *pos´-is;* from the alt. of *4095;* a *drinking* (the act), i.e. (concr.) a *draught:*— drink.

4214. πόσος **pŏsŏs,** *pos´-os;* from an obs. πός **pŏs,** (*who, what*) and *3739;* interr. pron. (of amount) *how much* (*large, long* or [plural] *many*):— how great (large, many), what.

4215. ποταμός **pŏtamŏs,** *pot-am-os´;* prob. from a der. of the alt. of *4095* (comp. *4224*); a *current, brook* or *freshet* (as *drinkable*), i.e. *running water:*— flood, river, stream, water.

4216. ποταμοφόρητος **pŏtamŏphŏrētŏs,** *pot-am-of-or´-ay-tos;* from *4215* and a der. of *5409; river-borne,* i.e. *overwhelmed by a stream:*— carried away of the flood.

4217. ποταπός **pŏtapŏs,** *pot-ap-os´;* appar. from *4219* and the base of *4226;* interrog. *whatever,* i.e. of *what possible* sort:— what (manner of).

4218. ποτέ **pŏtĕ,** *pot-eh´;* from the base of *4225* and *5037;* indef. adv., at *some time, ever:*— afore-(any, some-) time (-s), at length (the last), (+ n-) ever, in the old time, in time past, once, when.

4219. πότε **pŏtĕ,** *pot´-eh;* from the base of *4226* and *5037;* interr. adv., at *what time:*— + how long, when.

4220. πότερον **pŏtĕrŏn,** *pot´-er-on;* neut. of a comparative of the base of *4226;* interr. as adv., *which* (of two), i.e. *is it* this or that:— whether.

4221. ποτήριον **pŏtēriŏn,** *pot-ay´-ree-on;* neut. of a der. of the alt. of *4095;* a *drinking-vessel;* by extens. the contents thereof, i.e. a *cupful* (*draught*); fig. a *lot* or *fate:*— cup.

4222. ποτίζω **pŏtizō,** *pot-id´-zo;* from a der. of the alt. of *4095;* to *furnish drink, irri-gate:*— give (make) to drink, feed, water.

4223. Ποτίολοι **Pŏtiŏlŏi,** *pot-ee´-ol-oy;* of Lat. or.; *little wells,* i.e. *mineral springs; Potioli* (i.e. *Puteoli*), a place in Italy:— Puteoli.

4224. πότος **pŏtŏs,** *pot´-os;* from the alt. of *4095;* a *drinking-bout* or *carousal:*— ban-queting.

4225. πού **pŏu**, *poo;* gen. of an indef. pron. πός **pŏs** (*some*) otherwise obs. (comp. *4214*); as adv. of place, *somewhere,* i.e. *nearly:*— about, a certain place.

4226. ποῦ **pŏu**, *poo;* gen. of an interr. pron. πός **pŏs**, (*what*) otherwise obs. (perh. the same as *4225* used with the rising slide of inquiry); as adv. of place; *at* (by impl. to) *what* locality:— where, whither.

4227. Πούδης **Pŏudēs**, *poo´-dace;* of Lat. or.; *modest; Pudes* (i.e. *Pudens*), a Chr.:— Pudens.

4228. πούς **pŏus**, *pooce;* a primary word; a "*foot*" (fig. or lit.):— foot (-stool).

4229. πρᾶγμα **pragma**, *prag´-mah;* from *4238;* a *deed;* by impl. an *affair;* by extens. an *object* (material):— business, matter, thing, work.

4230. πραγματεία **pragmatĕia**, *prag-mat-i´-ah;* from *4231;* a *transaction,* i.e. *negotiation:*— affair.

4231. πραγματεύομαι **pragmatĕuŏmai**, *prag-mat-yoo´-om-ahee;* from *4229;* to *busy oneself* with, i.e. to *trade:*— occupy.

4232. πραιτώριον **praitōriŏn**, *prahee-to´-ree-on;* of Lat. or.; the *prætorium* or governor's *court-room* (sometimes incl. the whole *edifice* and *camp*):— (common, judgment) hall (of judgment), palace, prætorium.

4233. πράκτωρ **praktōr**, *prak´-tor;* from a der. of *4238;* a *practiser,* i.e. (spec.) an official *collector:*— officer.

4234. πρᾶξις **praxis**, *prax´-is;* from *4238;* *practice,* i.e. (concr.) an *act;* by extens. a *function:*— deed, office, work.

4235. πρᾷος **praiŏs**, *prah´-os;* a form of *4239,* used in certain parts; *gentle,* i.e. *humble:*— meek.

4236. πρᾳότης **praiŏtēs**, *prah-ot´-ace;* from *4235; gentleness,* by impl. *humility:*— meekness.

4237. πρασιά **prasia**, *pras-ee-ah´;* perh. from πράσον **prasŏn** (a *leek,* and so an *onion-patch*); a *garden plot,* i.e. (by impl. of reg. *beds*) a *row* (repeated in plur. by Heb., to indicate an arrangement):— in ranks.

4238. πράσσω **prassō**, *pras-so;* a primary verb; to "*practice*", i.e. *perform repeatedly* or *habitually* (thus differing from *4160,* which prop. refers to a *single* act); by impl. to *execute, accomplish,* etc.; spec. to *collect* (dues), *fare* (personally):— commit, deeds, do, exact, keep, require, use arts.

4239. πραΰς **praüs**, *prah-ooce´;* appar. a primary word; *mild,* i.e. (by impl.) *humble:*— meek. See also *4235.*

4240. πραΰτης **praütēs**, *prah-oo´-tace;* from *4239; mildness,* i.e. (by impl.) *humility:*— meekness.

4241. πρέπω **prĕpō**, *prep´-o;* appar. a primary verb; to *tower up* (*be conspicuous*), i.e. (by impl.) to *be suitable* or *proper* (third pers. sing. pres. ind., often used impers., it is *fit* or *right*):— become, comely.

4242. πρεσβεία **prĕsbĕia**, *pres-bi´-ah;* from *4243; seniority* (*eldership*), i.e. (by impl.) an *embassy* (concr. *ambassadors*):— ambassage, message.

4243. πρεσβεύω **prĕsbĕuō**, *pres-byoo´-o;* from the base of *4245;* to be a *senior,* i.e. (by impl.) *act as a representative* (fig. *preacher*):— be an ambassador.

4244. πρεσβυτέριον **prĕsbutĕriŏn**, *pres-boo-ter´-ee-on;* neut. of a presumed der. of *4245;* the *order of elders,* i.e. (spec.) Isr. *Sanhedrin* or Chr. "*presbytery*":— (estate of) elder (-s), presbytery.

4245. πρεσβύτερος **prĕsbutĕrŏs**, *pres-boo´-ter-os;* comparative of πρέσβυς **prĕsbus** (*elderly*); *older;* as noun, a *senior;* spec. an Isr. *Sanhedrist* (also fig. member of the celestial council) or Chr. "*presbyter*":— elder (-est), old.

4246. πρεσβύτης **prĕsbutēs**, *pres-boo´-tace;* from the same as *4245;* an *old man:*— aged (man), old man.

4247. πρεσβῦτις **prĕsbutis**, *pres-boo´-tis;* fem. of *4246;* an *old woman:*— aged woman.

πρήθω **prēthō**. See *4092.*

4248. πρηνής **prēnēs**, *pray-nace´;* from *4253; leaning* (*falling*) *forward* ("*prone*"), i.e. *head foremost:*— headlong.

4249. πρίζω **prizō**, *prid´-zo;* a strengthened form of a primary πρίω **priō**, (to *saw*); to *saw in two:*— saw asunder.

4250. πρίν **prin**, *prin;* adv. from *4253; prior, sooner:*— before (that), ere.

4251. Πρίσκα **Priska**, *pris´-kah;* of Lat. or.; fem. of *Priscus, ancient; Priska,* a Chr. woman:— Prisca. See also *4252.*

4252. Πρίσκιλλα **Priskilla**, *pris´-kil-lah;* dimin. of *4251; Priscilla* (i.e. *little Prisca*), a Chr. woman:— Priscilla.

4253. πρό **prŏ**, *pro;* a primary prep.; "*fore*", i.e. *in front of, prior* (fig. *superior*) *to:*— above, ago, before, or ever. In composition it retains the same significations.

4254. προάγω **prŏagō**, *pro-ag´-o;* from *4253* and *71;* to *lead forward* (magisterially); intr. to *precede* (in place or time [part. *previous*]):— bring (forth, out), go before.

4255. προαιρέομαι **prŏairĕŏmai**, *prŏ-ahee-reh´-om-ahee;* from *4253* and *138;* to *choose for oneself before* another thing (*prefer*), i.e. (by impl.) to *propose* (*intend*):— purpose.

4256. προαιτιάομαι **prŏaitiaŏmai**, *prŏ-ahee-tee-ah´-om-ahee;* from *4253* and a der. of *156;* to *accuse already,* i.e. *previously charge:*— prove before.

4257. προακούω **prŏakŏuō**, *prŏ-ak-oo´-o;* from *4253* and *191;* to *hear already,* i.e. *anticipate:*— hear before.

4258. προαμαρτάνω **prŏamartanō**, *prŏ-am-ar-tan´-o;* from 4253 and 264; to *sin previously* (to conversion):— sin already, heretofore sin.

4259. προαύλιον **prŏauliŏn**, *prŏ-ŏw´-lee-on;* neut. of a presumed compound of 4253 and 833; a *forecourt,* i.e. *vestibule* (alley-way):— porch.

4260. προβαίνω **prŏbainō**, *prob-ah´-ee-no;* from 4253 and the base of 939; to *walk forward,* i.e. *advance* (lit. or in years):— + be of a great age, go farther (on), be well stricken.

4261. προβάλλω **prŏballō**, *prob-al´-lo;* from 4253 and 906; to *throw forward,* i.e. *push to the front, germinate:*— put forward, shoot forth.

4262. προβατικός **prŏbatikŏs**, *prob-at-ik-os´;* from 4263; *relating to sheep,* i.e. (a *gate*) through which they were led into Jerusalem:— sheep (market).

4263. πρόβατον **prŏbatŏn**, *prob´-at-on;* prob. neut. of a presumed. der. of 4260; *something that walks forward* (a *quadruped*), i.e. (spec.) a *sheep* (lit. or fig.):— sheep (l-foldl).

4264. προβιβάζω **prŏbibazō**, *prob-ib-ad´-zo;* from 4253 and a redupl. form of 971; to *force forward,* i.e. *bring to the front, instigate:*— draw, before instruct.

4265. προβλέπω **prŏblĕpō**, *prob-lep´-o;* from 4253 and 991; to *look out beforehand,* i.e. *furnish in advance:*— provide.

4266. προγίνομαι **prŏginŏmai**, *prog-in´-om-ahee;* from 4253 and 1096; to *be already,* i.e. *have previously transpired:*— be past.

4267. προγινώσκω **prŏginōskō**, *prog-in-oce´-ko;* from 4253 and 1097; to *know beforehand,* i.e. *foresee:*— foreknow (ordain), know (before).

4268. πρόγνωσις **prŏgnōsis**, *prog´-no-sis;* from 4267; *forethought:*— foreknowledge.

4269. πρόγονος **prŏgŏnŏs**, *prog´-on-os;* from 4266; an *ancestor,* (grand-) *parent:*— forefather, parent.

4270. προγράφω **prŏgraphō**, *prog-raf´-o;* from 4253 and 1125; to *write previously;* fig. to *announce, prescribe:*— before ordain, evidently set forth, write (afore, aforetime).

4271. πρόδηλος **prŏdēlŏs**, *prod´-ay-los;* from 4253 and 1212; *plain before* all men, i.e. *obvious:*— evident, manifest (open) beforehand.

4272. προδίδωμι **prŏdidōmi**, *prod-id´-o-mee;* from 4253 and 1325; to *give before* the other party has given:— first give.

4273. προδότης **prŏdŏtēs**, *prod-ot´-ace;* from 4272 (in the sense of *giving forward* into another's [the enemy's] hands); a *surrender:*— betrayer, traitor.

προδρέμω **prŏdrĕmō**. See 4390.

4274. πρόδρομος **prŏdrŏmŏs**, *prod´-rom-os;* from the alt. of 4390; a *runner ahead,* i.e. *scout* (fig. *precursor*):— forerunner.

4275. προείδω **prŏeidō**, *pro-i´-do;* from 4253 and 1492; *foresee:*— foresee, saw before.

προειρέω **prŏeirĕō**. See 4280.

4276. προελπίζω **prŏelpizō**, *pro-el-pid´-zo;* from 4253 and 1679; to *hope in advance* of other confirmation:— first trust.

4277. προέπω **prŏepō**, *prŏ-ep´-o;* from 4253 and 2036; to *say already,* to *predict:*— forewarn, say (speak, tell) before. Comp. 4280.

4278. προενάρχομαι **prŏenarchŏmai**, *prŏ-en-ar´-khom-ahee;* from 4253 and 1728; to *commence already:*— begin (before).

4279. προεπαγγέλλομαι **prŏepaggĕllŏmai**, *prŏ-ep-ang-ghel´-lom-ahee;* mid. voice from 4253 and 1861; to *promise of old:*— promise before.

4280. προερέω **prŏerĕō**, *prŏ-er-eh´-o;* from 4253 and 2046; used as alt. of 4277; to *say already, predict:*— foretell, say (speak, tell) before.

4281. προέρχομαι **prŏerchŏmai**, *prŏ-er-khom-ahee;* from 4253 and 2064 (incl. its alt.); to *go onward, precede* (in place or time):— go before (farther, forward), outgo, pass on.

4282. προετοιμάζω **prŏetŏimazō**, *pro-et-oy-mad´-zo;* from 4253 and 2090; to *fit up in advance* (lit. or fig.):— ordain before, prepare afore.

4283. προευαγγελίζομαι **prŏĕuaggĕlizŏmai**, *prŏ-yoo-ang-ghel-id´-zom-ahee;* mid. voice from 4253 and 2097; to *announce* glad news *in advance:*— preach before the gospel.

4284. προέχομαι **prŏechŏmai**, *prŏ-ekh-om-ahee;* mid. voice from 4253 and 2192; to *hold* oneself *before* others, i.e. (fig.) to *excel:*— be better.

4285. προηγέομαι **prŏēgĕŏmai**, *prŏ-ay-geh´-om-ahee;* from 4253 and 2233; to *lead the way* for others, i.e. *show deference:*— prefer.

4286. πρόθεσις **prŏthĕsis**, *proth´-es-is;* from 4388; a *setting forth,* i.e. (fig.) *proposal* (intention); spec. the *show*-bread (in the Temple) as *exposed* before God:— purpose, shew [-bread].

4287. προθέσμιος **prŏthĕsmiŏs**, *proth-es´-mee-os;* from 4253 and a der. of 5087; *fixed beforehand,* i.e. (fem. with 2250 implied) a *designated* day:— time appointed.

4288. προθυμία **prŏthumia**, *proth-oo-mee´-ah;* from 4289; *predisposition,* i.e. *alacrity:*— forwardness of mind, readiness (of mind), ready (willing) mind.

4289. πρόθυμος **prŏthumŏs**, *proth´-oo-mos;* from 4253 and 2372; *forward* in spirit, i.e. *predisposed;* neut. (as noun) *alacrity:*— ready, willing.

4290. προθύμως **prŏthumōs**, *proth-oo´-moce;* adv. from 4289; *with alacrity:*— willingly.

4291. προΐστημι **prŏïstēmi**, *prŏ-is´-tay-mee;* from *4253* and *2476;* to *stand before,* i.e. (in rank) to *preside,* or (by impl.) to *practice:—* maintain, be over, rule.

4292. προκαλέομαι **prŏkalĕŏmai**, *prok-al-eh´-om-ahee;* mid. voice from *4253* and *2564;* to *call forth to oneself* (*challenge*), i.e. (by impl.) to *irritate:—* provoke.

4293. προκαταγγέλλω **prŏkataggĕllō**, *prok-at-ang-ghel´-lo;* from *4253* and *2605;* to *announce beforehand,* i.e. *predict, promise:—* foretell, have notice, (shew) before.

4294. προκαταρτίζω **prŏkatartizō**, *prok-at-ar-tid´-zo;* from *4253* and *2675;* to *prepare in advance:—* make up beforehand.

4295. πρόκειμαι **prŏkĕimai**, *prok´-i-mahee;* from *4253* and *2749;* to *lie before* the view, i.e. (fig.) to *be present* (to the mind), to *stand forth* (as an example or reward):— be first, set before (forth).

4296. προκηρύσσω **prŏkērussō**, *prok-ay-rooce´-so;* from *4253* and *2784;* to *herald* (i.e. *proclaim*) *in advance:—* before (first) preach.

4297. προκοπή **prŏkŏpē**, *prok-op-ay´;* from *4298; progress,* i.e. *advancement* (subj. or obj.):— furtherance, profit.

4298. προκόπτω **prŏkŏptō**, *prok-op´-to;* from *4253* and *2875;* to *drive forward* (as if by beating), i.e. (fig. and intr.) to *advance* (in amount, to *grow;* in time, to *be well along*):— increase, proceed, profit, be far spent, wax.

4299. πρόκριμα **prŏkrima**, *prok´-ree-mah;* from a compound of *4253* and *2919;* a *prejudgment* (*prejudice*), i.e. *prepossession:—* prefer one before another.

4300. προκυρόω **prŏkurŏō**, *prok-oo-rŏ´-o;* from *4253* and *2964;* to *ratify previously:—* confirm before.

4301. προλαμβάνω **prŏlambanō**, *prol-am-ban´-o;* from *4253* and *2983;* to *take in advance,* i.e. (lit.) *eat before* others have an opportunity; (fig.) to *anticipate, surprise:—* come aforehand, overtake, take before.

4302. προλέγω **prŏlĕgō**, *prol-eg´-o;* from *4253* and *3004;* to *say beforehand,* i.e. *predict, forewarn:—* foretell, tell before.

4303. προμαρτύρομαι **prŏmarturŏmai**, *prom-ar-too´-rom-ahee;* from *4253* and *3143;* to *be a witness in advance,* i.e. *predict:—* testify beforehand.

4304. προμελετάω **prŏmĕlĕtaō**, *prom-el-et-ah´-o;* from *4253* and *3191;* to *premeditate:—* meditate before.

4305. προμεριμνάω **prŏmĕrimnaō**, *prom-er-im-nah´-o;* from *4253* and *3309;* to *care* (anxiously) *in advance:—* take thought beforehand.

4306. προνοέω **prŏnŏĕō**, *pron-ŏ-eh´-o;* from *4253* and *3539;* to *consider in advance,* i.e. *look* out *for beforehand* (act. by way of main-

tenance for others; mid. voice by way of *circumspection* for oneself):— provide (for).

4307. πρόνοια **prŏnŏia**, *pron´-oy-ah;* from *4306; forethought,* i.e. provident *care* or *supply:—* providence, provision.

4308. προοράω **prŏŏraō**, *prŏ-or-ah´-o;* from *4253* and *3708;* to *behold in advance,* i.e. (act.) to *notice* (another) *previously,* or (mid. voice) to *keep in* (one's own) *view:—* foresee, see before.

4309. προορίζω **prŏŏrizō**, *prŏ-or-id´-zo;* from *4253* and *3724;* to *limit in advance,* i.e. (fig.) *predetermine:—* determine before, ordain, predestinate.

4310. προπάσχω **prŏpaschō**, *prop-as´-kho;* from *4253* and *3958;* to *undergo* hardship *previously:—* suffer before.

4311. προπέμπω **prŏpĕmpō**, *prop-em´-po;* from *4253* and *3992;* to *send forward,* i.e. *escort* or *aid* in travel:— accompany, bring (forward) on journey (way), conduct forth.

4312. προπετής **prŏpĕtēs**, *prop-et-ace´;* from a compound of *4253* and *4098; falling forward,* i.e. *headlong* (fig. *precipitate*):— heady, rash [-ly].

4313. προπορεύομαι **prŏpŏrĕuŏmai**, *prop-or-yoo´-om-ahee;* from *4253* and *4198;* to *precede* (as guide or herald):— go before.

4314. πρός **prŏs**, *pros;* a strengthened form of *4253;* a prep. of direction; *forward to,* i.e. *toward* (with the gen. *the side* of, i.e. *pertaining to;* with the dat. *by the side of,* i.e. *near to;* usually with the acc., the place, time, occasion, or respect, which is the *destination* of the relation, i.e. *whither* or *for* which it is predicated):— about, according to, against, among, at, because of, before, between, (|where-|) by, for, × at thy house, in, for intent, nigh unto, of, which pertain to, that, to (the end that), + together, to (|you|) -ward, unto, with (-in). In composition it denotes essentially the same applications, namely, motion *toward,* accession *to,* or nearness *at.*

4315. προσάββατον **prŏsabbatŏn**, *pros-ab´-bat-on;* from *4253* and *4521;* a *fore-sabbath,* i.e. the *Sabbath-eve:—* day before the sabbath. Comp. *3904.*

4316. προσαγορεύω **prŏsagŏrĕuō**, *pros-ag-or-yoo´-o;* from *4314* and a der. of *58* (mean to *harangue*); to *address,* i.e. salute by *name:—* call.

4317. προσάγω **prŏsagō**, *pros-ag´-o;* from *4314* and *71;* to *lead toward,* i.e. (tran.) to *conduct near* (*summon, present*), or (intr.) to *approach:—* bring, draw near.

4318. προσαγωγή **prŏsagōgē**, *pros-ag-ogue-ay´;* from *4317* (comp. *72*); *admission:—* access.

4319. προσαιτέω **prŏsaitĕō**, *pros-ahee-teh-*

o; from *4314* and *154;* to *ask repeatedly* (im-portune), i.e. *solicit:*— beg.

4320. προσαναβαίνω **prŏsanabainō**, *pros-an-ab-ah´-ee-no;* from *4314* and *305;* to *ascend farther,* i.e. *be promoted* (take an upper [more honorable] seat):— go up.

4321. προσαναλίσκω **prŏsaliskō**, *pros-an-al-is´-ko;* from *4314* and *355;* to *expend further:*— spend.

4322. προσαναπληρόω **prŏsanaplērŏō**, *pros-an-ap-lay-ro´-o;* from *4314* and *378;* to *fill up further,* i.e. *furnish fully:*— supply.

4323. προσανατίθημι **prŏsanatithēmi**, *pros-an-at-ith´-ay-mee;* from *4314* and *394;* to *lay up in addition*, i.e. (mid. voice and fig.) to *impart* or (by impl.) to *consult:*— in conference add, confer.

4324. προσαπειλέω **prŏsapĕilĕō**, *pros-ap-i-leh´-o;* from *4314* and *546;* to *menace additionally:*— threaten further.

4325. προσδαπανάω **prŏsdapanaō**, *pros-dap-an-ah´-o;* from *4314* and *1159;* to *expend additionally:*— spend more.

4326. προσδέομαι **prŏsdĕŏmai**, *pros-deh´-om-ahee;* from *4314* and *1189;* to *require additionally,* i.e. *want further:*— need.

4327. προσδέχομαι **prŏsdĕchŏmai**, *pros-dekh´-om-ahee;* from *4314* and *1209;* to *admit* (to intercourse, hospitality, credence, or [fig.] endurance); by impl. to *await* (with confidence or patience):— accept, allow, look (wait) for, take.

4328. προσδοκάω **prŏsdŏkaō**, *pros-dok-ah´-o;* from *4314* and δοκεύω **dŏkĕuō** (to watch); to *anticipate* (in thought, hope or fear); by impl. to *await:*— (be in) expect (-ation), look (for), when looked, tarry, wait for.

4329. προσδοκία **prŏsdŏkia**, *pros-dok-ee´-ah;* from *4328; apprehension* (of evil); by impl. *infliction* anticipated:— expectation, looking after.

προσδρέμω **prŏsdrĕmō**. See *4370.*

4330. προσεάω **prŏsĕaō**, *pros-eh-ah´-o;* from *4314* and *1439;* to *permit further* progress:— suffer.

4331. προσεγγίζω **prŏsĕggizō**, *pros-eng-ghid´-zo;* from *4314* and *1448;* to *approach near:*— come nigh.

4332. προσεδρεύω **prŏsĕdrĕuō**, *pros-ed-ryoo´-o;* from a compound of *4314* and the base of *1476;* to *sit near,* i.e. *attend* as a servant:— wait at.

4333. προσεργάζομαι **prŏsĕrgazŏmai**, *pros-er-gad´-zom-ahee;* from *4314* and *2038;* to *work additionally,* i.e. (by impl.) *acquire besides:*— gain.

4334. προσέρχομαι **prŏsĕrchŏmai**, *pros-er´-khom-ahee;* from *4314* and *2064* (incl. its alt.); to *approach,* i.e. (lit.) *come near, visit,* or (fig.) *worship, assent to:*— (as soon as he) come

(unto), come thereunto, consent, draw near, go (near, to, unto).

4335. προσευχή **prŏsĕuchē**, *pros-yoo-khay´;* from *4336; prayer* (worship); by impl. an *oratory* (chapel):— × pray earnestly, prayer.

4336. προσεύχομαι **prŏsĕuchŏmai**, *pros-yoo´-khom-ahee;* from *4314* and *2172;* to *pray to* God, i.e. *supplicate, worship:*— pray (× earnestly, for), make prayer.

4337. προσέχω **prŏsĕchō**, *pros-ekh´-o;* from *4314* and *2192;* (fig.) to *hold* the mind (*3563* impl.) *toward,* i.e. *pay attention to, be cautious about, apply oneself* to, *adhere to:*— (give) attend (-ance, -ance at, -ance to, unto), beware, be given to, give (take) heed (to, unto); have regard.

4338. προσηλόω **prŏsēlŏō**, *pros-ay-lŏ´-o;* from *4314* and a der. of *2247;* to *peg to,* i.e. *spike* fast:— nail to.

4339. προσήλυτος **prŏsēlutŏs**, *pros-ay´-loo-tos;* from the alt. of *4334;* an *arriver* from a for. region, i.e. (spec.) an *acceder* (convert) to Judaism ("proselyte"):— proselyte.

4340. πρόσκαιρος **prŏskairŏs**, *pros´-kahee-ros;* from *4314* and *2540;* for the *occasion* only, i.e. *temporary:*— dur-[eth] for awhile, endure for a time, for a season, temporal.

4341. προσκαλέομαι **prŏskalĕŏmai**, *pros-kal-eh´-om-ahee;* mid. voice from *4314* and *2564;* to *call toward oneself,* i.e. *summon, invite:*— call (for, to, unto).

4342. προσκαρτερέω **prŏskartĕrĕō**, *pros-kar-ter-eh´-o;* from *4314* and *2594;* to *be earnest toward,* i.e. (to a thing) to *persevere, be constantly* diligent, or (in a place) to *attend* assiduously all the exercises, or (to a person) to *adhere* closely to (as a servitor):— attend (give self) continually (upon), continue (in, instant in, with), wait on (continually).

4343. προσκαρτέρησις **prŏskartĕrēsis**, *pros-kar-ter´-ay-sis;* from *4342; persistency:*— perseverance.

4344. προσκεφάλαιον **prŏskĕphalaiŏn**, *pros-kef-al´-ahee-on;* neut. of a presumed compound of *4314* and *2776;* something *for* the *head,* i.e. a *cushion:*— pillow.

4345. προσκληρόω **prŏsklērŏō**, *pros-klay-rŏ´-o;* from *4314* and *2820;* to *give a common lot to,* i.e. (fig.) to *associate with:*— consort with.

4346. πρόσκλισις **prŏsklisis**, *pros´-klis-is;* from a compound of *4314* and *2827;* a *leaning toward,* i.e. (fig.) *proclivity* (favoritism):— partiality.

4347. προσκολλάω **prŏskŏllaō**, *pros-kol-lah´-o;* from *4314* and *2853;* to *glue to,* i.e. (fig.) to *adhere:*— cleave, join (self).

4348. πρόσκομμα **prŏskŏmma**, *pros´-kom-mah;* from *4350;* a *stub,* i.e. (fig.) *occasion of* *apostasy:—* offence, stumbling (-block, [-stone]).

4349. προσκοπή **prŏskŏpē**, *pros-kop-ay´;* from *4350;* a *stumbling,* i.e. (fig. and concr.) *occasion of sin:—* offence.

4350. προσκόπτω **prŏskŏptō**, *pros-kop´-to;* from *4314* and *2875;* to *strike at,* i.e. *surge against* (as water); spec. to *stub on,* i.e. *trip up* (lit. or fig.):— beat upon, dash, stumble (at).

4351. προσκυλίω **prŏskuliō**, *pros-koo-lee´-o;* from *4314* and *2947;* to *roll toward,* i.e. *block against:—* roll (to).

4352. προσκυνέω **prŏskunĕō**, *pros-koo-neh´-o;* from *4314* and a probable der. of *2965* (mean. to *kiss,* like a dog *licking* his master's hand); to *fawn* or *crouch to,* i.e. (lit. or fig.) *prostrate* oneself in homage (do *reverence* to, *adore):—* worship.

4353. προσκυνητής **prŏskunētēs**, *pros-koo-nay-tace´;* from *4352;* an *adorer:—* worshipper.

4354. προσλαλέω **prŏslalĕō**, *pros-lal-eh´-o;* from *4314* and *2980;* to *talk to,* i.e. *converse with:—* speak to (with).

4355. προσλαμβάνω **prŏslambanō**, *pros-lamban´-o;* from *4314* and *2983;* to *take to* oneself, i.e. *use* (food), *lead* (aside), *admit* (to friendship or hospitality):— receive, take (unto).

4356. πρόσληψις **prŏslēpsis**, *pros´-lape-sis;* from *4355; admission:—* receiving.

4357. προσμένω **prŏsmĕnō**, *pros-men´-o;* from *4314* and *3306;* to *stay further,* i.e. *remain* in a place, with a person; fig. to *adhere to, persevere* in:— abide still, be with, cleave unto, continue in (with).

4358. προσορμίζω **prŏsŏrmizō**, *pros-or-mid´-zo;* from *4314* and a der. of the same as *3730* (mean. to *tie* [anchor] or *lull*); to *moor to,* i.e. (by impl.) *land at:—* draw to the shore.

4359. προσοφείλω **prŏsŏphĕilō**, *pros-of-i´-lo;* from *4314* and *3784;* to *be indebted additionally:—* over besides.

4360. προσοχθίζω **prŏsŏchthizō**, *pros-okh-thid´-zo;* from *4314* and a form of ὀχθέω **ŏchthĕō** (to *be vexed* with something irksome); to *feel indignant at:—* be grieved with.

4361. πρόσπεινος **prŏspĕinŏs**, *pros´-pi-nos;* from *4314* and the same as *3983; hungering further,* i.e. *intensely hungry:—* very hungry.

4362. προσπήγνυμι **prŏspēgnumi**, *pros-payg´-noo-mee;* from *4314* and *4078;* to *fasten to,* i.e. (spec.) to *impale* (on a cross):— crucify.

4363. προσπίπτω **prŏspiptō**, *pros-pip´-to;* from *4314* and *4098;* to *fall toward,* i.e. (gently) *prostrate* oneself (in supplication or homage), or (violently) to *rush* upon (in storm):— beat upon, fall (down) at (before).

4364. προσποιέομαι **prŏspŏiĕŏmai**, *pros-poy-eh´-om-ahee;* mid. voice from *4314* and *4160;* to *do forward for oneself,* i.e. *pretend* (as if about to do a thing):— make as though.

4365. προσπορεύομαι **prŏspŏrĕuŏmai**, *prospor-yoo´-om-ahee;* from *4314* and *4198;* to *journey toward,* i.e. *approach* [not the same as *4313*]:— go before.

4366. προσρήγνυμι **prŏsrēgnumi**, *prosrayg´-noo-mee;* from *4314* and *4486;* to *tear toward,* i.e. *burst upon* (as a tempest or flood):— beat vehemently against (upon).

4367. προστάσσω **prŏstassō**, *pros-tas´-so;* from *4314* and *5021;* to *arrange toward,* i.e. (fig.) *enjoin:—* bid, command.

4368. προστάτις **prŏstatis**, *pros-tat´-is;* fem. of a der. of *4291;* a *patroness,* i.e. *assistant:—* succourer.

4369. προστίθημι **prŏstithēmi**, *pros-tith´-ay-mee;* from *4314* and *5087;* to *place additionally,* i.e. *lay beside, annex, repeat:—* add, again, give more, increase, lay unto, proceed further, speak to any more.

4370. προστρέχω **prŏstrĕchō**, *pros-trekh´-o;* from *4314* and *5143* (incl. its alt.); to *run toward,* i.e. *hasten* to meet or join:— run (thither to, to).

4371. προσφάγιον **prŏsphagiŏn**, *pros-fag´-ee-on;* neut. of a presumed der. of a compound of *4314* and *5315;* something *eaten in addition* to bread, i.e. a *relish* (spec. *fish;* comp. *3795*):— meat.

4372. πρόσφατος **prŏsphatŏs**, *pros´-fat-os;* from *4253* and a der. of *4969; previously* (*recently*) *slain* (*fresh*), i.e. (fig.) *lately made:—* new.

4373. προσφάτως **prŏsphatōs**, *pros-fat´-oce;* adv. from *4372; recently:—* lately.

4374. προσφέρω **prŏsphĕrō**, *pros-fer´-o;* from *4314* and *5342* (incl. its alt.); to *bear toward,* i.e. *lead to, tender* (espec. to God), *treat:—* bring (to, unto), deal with, do, offer (unto, up), present unto, put to.

4375. προσφιλής **prŏsphilēs**, *pros-fee-lace´;* from a presumed compound of *4314* and *5368; friendly toward,* i.e. *acceptable:—* lovely.

4376. προσφορά **prŏsphŏra**, *pros-for-ah´;* from *4374; presentation;* concr. an *oblation* (bloodless) or *sacrifice:—* offering (up).

4377. προσφωνέω **prŏsphōnĕō**, *pros-fo-neh´-o;* from *4314* and *5455;* to *sound toward,* i.e. *address, exclaim, summon:—* call unto, speak (un-) to.

4378. πρόσχυσις **prŏschusis**, *pros´-khoo-sis;* from a comp. of *4314* and χέω **chĕō** (to *pour*); a *shedding forth,* i.e. *affusion:—* sprinkling.

4379. προσψαύω **prŏspsauō**, *pros-psŏw´-o;* from *4314* and ψαύω **psauō** (to *touch*); to *impinge,* i.e. *lay a finger on* (in order to relieve):— touch.

4380. προσωπολημπτέω **prŏsōpŏlēptĕō**, *proso-pol-ape-teh´-o;* from *4381;* to *favor an individual,* i.e. *show partiality:—* have respect to persons.

4381. προσωπολήπτης **prŏsōpŏlēptēs**, *pros-o-pol-ape´-tace;* from *4383* and *2983;* an *accepter* of *a face* (*individual*), i.e. (spec.) one *exhibiting partiality:*— respecter of persons.

4382. προσωποληψία **prŏsōpŏlēpsia**, *pros-o-pol-ape-see´-ah;* from *4381; partiality,* i.e. *favoritism:*— respect of persons.

4383. πρόσωπον **prŏsōpŏn**, *pros´-o-pon;* from *4314* and ὤψ **ōps** (the *visage,* from *3700*); the *front,* (as being *toward view*), i.e. the *countenance, aspect, appearance, surface;* by impl. *presence, person:*— (outward) appearance, × before, countenance, face, fashion, (men's) person, presence.

4384. προτάσσω **prŏtassō**, *prot-as´-so;* from *4253* and *5021;* to *pre-arrange,* i.e. *prescribe:*— before appoint.

4385. προτείνω **prŏtĕinō**, *prot-i´-no;* from *4253* and τείνω **tĕinō** (to *stretch*); to *protend,* i.e. *tie prostrate* (for scourging):— bind.

4386. πρότερον **prŏtĕrŏn**, *prot´-er-on;* neut. of *4387* as adv. (with or without the art.); *previously:*— before, (at the) first, former.

4387. πρότερος **prŏtĕrŏs**, *prot´-er-os;* comp. of *4253; prior* or *previous:*— former.

4388. προτίθεμαι **prŏtithĕmai**, *prot-ith´-em-ahee;* mid. voice from *4253* and *5087;* to *place before,* i.e. (for oneself) to *exhibit;* (to oneself) to *propose* (*determine*):— purpose, set forth.

4389. προτρέπομαι **prŏtrĕpŏmai**, *prot-rep´-om-ahee;* mid. voice from *4253* and the base of *5157;* to *turn forward* for oneself, i.e. *encourage:*— exhort.

4390. προτρέχω **prŏtrĕchō**, *prot-rekh´-o;* from *4253* and *5143* (incl. its alt.); to *run forward,* i.e. *outstrip, precede:*— outrun, run before.

4391. προϋπάρχω **prŏüparchō**, *prŏ-oop-ar´-kho;* from *4253* and *5225;* to *exist before,* i.e. (adv.) to *be* or *do* something *previously:*— + be before (-time).

4392. πρόφασις **prŏphasis**, *prof´-as-is;* from a compound of *4253* and *5316;* an *outward showing,* i.e. *pretext:*— cloke, colour, pretence, show.

4393. προφέρω **prŏphĕrō**, *prof-er´-o;* from *4253* and *5342;* to *bear forward,* i.e. *produce:*— bring forth.

4394. προφητεία **prŏphētĕia**, *prof-ay-ti´-ah;* from *4396* ("*prophecy*"); *prediction* (scriptural or other):— prophecy, prophesying.

4395. προφητεύω **prŏphētĕuō**, *prof-ate-yoo´-o;* from *4396;* to *foretell* events, *divine, speak* under *inspiration, exercise* the prophetic office:— prophesy.

4396. προφήτης **prŏphētēs**, *prof-ay´-tace;* from a compound of *4253* and *5346;* a *foreteller* ("*prophet*"); by anal. an *inspired speaker;* by extens. a *poet:*— prophet.

4397. προφητικός **prŏphētikŏs**, *prof-ay-tik-os´;* from *4396; pertaining to a foreteller* ("*prophetic*"):— of prophecy, of the prophets.

4398. προφῆτις **prŏphētis**, *prof-ay´-tis;* fem. of *4396;* a *female foreteller* or an *inspired woman:*— prophetess.

4399. προφθάνω **prŏphthanō**, *prof-than´-o;* from *4253* and *5348;* to *get an earlier start of,* i.e. *anticipate:*— prevent.

4400. προχειρίζομαι **prŏchĕirizŏmai**, *prokh-i-rid´-zom-ahee;* mid. voice from *4253* and a der. of *5495;* to *handle* for oneself *in advance,* i.e. (fig.) to *purpose:*— choose, make.

4401. προχειροτονέω **prŏchĕirŏtŏnĕō**, *prokh-i-rot-on-eh´-o;* from *4253* and *5500;* to *elect in advance:*— choose before.

4402. Πρόχορος **Prŏchŏrŏs**, *prokh´-or-os;* from *4253* and *5525; before* the *dance; Prochorus,* a Chr.:— Prochorus.

4403. πρύμνα **prumna**, *proom´-nah;* fem. of πρυμνύς **prumnus** (*hindmost*); the *stern* of a ship:— hinder part, stern.

4404. πρωΐ **prŏï**, *pro-ee´;* adv. from *4253;* at *dawn;* by impl. the *day-break* watch:— early (in the morning), (in the) morning.

4405. πρωΐα **prŏïa**, *pro-ee´-ah;* fem. of a der. of *4404* as noun; *day-dawn:*— early, morning.

4406. πρώϊμος **prŏïmŏs**, *pro´-ee-mos;* from *4404; dawning,* i.e. (by anal.) *autumnal* (showering, the first of the rainy season):— early.

4407. πρωϊνός **prŏïnŏs**, *pro-ee-nos´;* from *4404; pertaining to the dawn,* i.e. *matutinal:*— morning.

4408. πρώρα **prŏra**, *pro´-ra;* fem. of a presumed der. of *4253* as noun; the *prow,* i.e. *forward part of a vessel:*— forepart (-ship).

4409. πρωτεύω **prŏtĕuō**, *prote-yoo´-o;* from *4413;* to *be first* (in rank or influence):— have the preeminence.

4410. πρωτοκαθεδρία **prŏtŏkathĕdria**, *pro-tok-ath-ed-ree´-ah;* from *4413* and *2515;* a *sitting first* (in the front row), i.e. *preeminence* in council:— chief (highest, uppermost) seat.

4411. πρωτοκλισία **prŏtŏklisia**, *pro-tok-lis-ee´-ah;* from *4413* and *2828;* a *reclining first* (in the place of honor) at the dinner-bed, i.e. *preeminence* at meals:— chief (highest, uppermost) room.

4412. πρῶτον **prŏtŏn**, *pro´-ton;* neut. of *4413* as adv. (with or without *3588*); *firstly* (in time, place, order, or importance):— before, at the beginning, chiefly (at, at the) first (of all).

4413. πρῶτος **prŏtŏs**, *pro´-tos;* contr. superl. of *4253; foremost* (in time, place, order or importance):— before, beginning, best, chief (-est), first (of all), former.

4414. πρωτοστάτης **prŏtŏstatēs**, *pro-tos-tat´-ace;* from *4413* and *2476;* one *standing* *first* in the ranks, i.e. a *captain* (*champion*):— ringleader.

4415. πρωτοτόκια **prōtŏtŏkia**, *pro-tot-ok´-ee-ah;* from *4416;* *primogeniture* (as a privilege):— birthright.

4416. πρωτοτόκος **prōtŏtŏkŏs**, *pro-tot-ok´-os;* from *4413* and the alt. of *5088; first-born* (usually as noun, lit. or fig.):— firstbegotten (-born).

4417. πταίω **ptaiō**, *ptah´-yo;* a form of *4098;* to *trip*, i.e. (fig.) to *err, sin, fail* (of salvation):— fall, offend, stumble.

4418. πτέρνα **ptĕrna**, *pter´-nah;* of uncert. der.; the *heel* (fig.):— heel.

4419. πτερύγιον **ptĕrugiŏn**, *pter-oog´-ee-on;* neut. of a presumed der. of *4420;* a *winglet*, i.e. (fig.) *extremity* (top corner):— pinnacle.

4420. πτέρυξ **ptĕrux**, *pter´-oox;* from a der. of *4072* (mean. a *feather*); a *wing:*— wing.

4421. πτηνόν **ptēnŏn**, *ptay-non´;* contr. for *4071;* a *bird:*— bird.

4422. πτοέω **ptŏĕō**, *ptŏ-eh´-o;* prob. akin to the alt. of *4098* (through the idea of causing to *fall*) or to *4072* (through that of causing to *fly* away); to *scare:*— frighten.

4423. πτόησις **ptŏĕsis**, *ptŏ´-ay-sis;* from *4422; alarm:*— amazement.

4424. Πτολεμαΐς **Ptŏlĕmaïs**, *ptol-em-ah-is´;* from Πτολεμαῖος **Ptŏlĕmaïŏs** (*Ptolemy*, after whom it was named); *Ptolemaïs*, a place in Pal.:— Ptolemais.

4425. πτύον **ptuŏn**, *ptoo´-on;* from *4429;* a *winnowing-fork* (as *scattering* like spittle):— fan.

4426. πτύρω **pturō**, *ptoo´-ro;* from a presumed der. of *4429* (and thus akin to *4422*); to *frighten:*— terrify.

4427. πτύσμα **ptusma**, *ptoos´-mah;* from *4429; saliva:*— spittle.

4428. πτύσσω **ptussō**, *ptoos´-so;* prob. akin to πετάννυμι **pĕtannumi**, (to *spread;* and thus appar. allied to *4072* through the idea of *expansion*, and to *4429* through that of *flattening;* comp. *3961*); to *fold*, i.e. *furl* a scroll:— close.

4429. πτύω **ptuō**, *ptoo´-o;* a primary verb (comp. *4428*); to *spit:*— spit.

4430. πτῶμα **ptōma**, *pto´-mah;* from the alt. of *4098;* a *ruin*, i.e. (spec.) lifeless *body* (*corpse, carrion*):— dead body, carcase, corpse.

4431. πτῶσις **ptōsis**, *pto´-sis;* from the alt. of *4098;* a *crash*, i.e. *downfall* (lit. or fig.):— fall.

4432. πτωχεία **ptōchĕia**, *pto-khi´-ah;* from *4433; beggary*, i.e. *indigence* (lit. or fig.):— poverty.

4433. πτωχεύω **ptōchĕuō**, *pto-khyoo´-o;* from *4434;* to *be a beggar*, i.e. (by impl.) to *become indigent* (fig.):— become poor.

4434. πτωχός **ptōchŏs** *pto-khos´;* from πτώσσω **ptōssō**, to *crouch;* akin to *4422* and the alt. of *4098*); a *beggar* (as *cringing*), i.e. *pauper*

(strictly denoting absolute or public *mendicancy*, although also used in a qualified or relative sense; whereas *3993* prop. means only *straitened* circumstances in private), lit. (often used as a noun) or fig. (*distressed*):— beggar (-ly), poor.

4435. πυγμή **pugmē**, *poog-may´;* from a primary πύξ **pux** (the *fist*, as a weapon); the *clenched hand*, i.e. (only in dat. as adverb) *with the fist* (hard *scrubbing*):— oft.

4436. Πύθων **Puthōn**, *poo´-thone;* from Πυθώ **Puthō** (the name of the region where Delphi, the seat of the famous *oracle*, was located); a *Python*, i.e. (by anal. with the supposed *diviner* there) *inspiration* (*soothsaying*):— divination.

4437. πυκνός **puknŏs**, *pook-nos´;* from the same as *4635; clasped* (*thick*), i.e. (fig.) *frequent;* neut. plur. (as adv.) *frequently:*— often (-er).

4438. πυκτέω **puktĕō**, *pook-teh´-o;* from a der. of the same as *4435;* to *box* (with the fist), i.e. *contend* (as a boxer) at the games (fig.):— fight.

4439. πύλη **pulē**, *poo´-lay;* appar. a primary word; a *gate*, i.e. the leaf or wing of a folding *entrance* (lit. or fig.):— gate.

4440. πυλών **pulōn**, *poo-lone´;* from *4439;* a *gate-way, door-way* of a building or city; by impl. a *portal* or *vestibule:*— gate, porch.

4441. πυνθάνομαι **punthanŏmai**, *poon-than´-om-ahee;* mid. voice prol. from a primary πύθω **puthō** (which occurs only as an alt. in certain tenses); to *question*, i.e. *ascertain* by inquiry (as a matter of *information* merely; and thus differing from *2065*, which prop. means a *request* as a favor; and from *154*, which is strictly a *demand* for something due; as well as from *2212*, which implies a *search* for something hidden; and from *1189*, which involves the idea of urgent *need*); by impl. to *learn* (by casual intelligence):— ask, demand, enquire, understand.

4442. πῦρ **pur**, *poor;* a primary word; "*fire*" (lit. or fig., spec. *lightning*):— fiery, fire.

4443. πυρά **pura**, *poo-rah´;* from *4442;* a *fire* (concr.):— fire.

4444. πύργος **purgŏs**, *poor´-gos;* appar. a primary word ("*burgh*"); a *tower* or *castle:*— tower.

4445. πυρέσσω **purĕssō**, *poo-res´-so;* from *4443;* to *be on fire*, i.e. (spec.) to *have a fever:*— be sick of a fever.

4446. πυρετός **purĕtŏs**, *poo-ret-os´;* from *4445; inflamed*, i.e. (by impl.) *feverish* (as noun, *fever*):— fever.

4447. πύρινος **purinŏs**, *poo´-ree-nos;* from *4443; fiery*, i.e. (by impl.) *flaming:*— of fire.

4448. πυρόω **purŏō**, *poo-rŏ´-o;* from *4442;* to *kindle*, i.e. (pass.) to *be ignited, glow* (lit.), be refined (by impl.), or (fig.) to be inflamed (with anger, grief, lust):— burn, fiery, be on fire, try.

4449. πυῤῥάζω **purrhazō**, *poor-hrad´-zo;* from 4450; to *redden* (intr.):— be red.

4450. πυῤῥός **purrhŏs**, *poor-hros´;* from 4442; *fire-like*, i.e. (spec.) *flame-colored:*— red.

4451. πύρωσις **purōsis**, *poo´-ro-sis;* from 4448; *ignition*, i.e. (spec.) *smelting* (fig. *conflagration, calamity* as a *test*):— burning, trial.

4452. -πω **-pō**, *po;* another form of the base of 4458; an enclitic particle of indefiniteness; *yet, even;* used only in composition. See 3369, 3380, 3764, 3768, 4455.

4453. πωλέω **pōlĕō**, *po-leh´-o;* prob. ultimately from πέλομαι **pĕlŏmai** (to *be busy*, to *trade*); to *barter* (as a *pedlar*), i.e. to *sell:*— sell, whatever is sold.

4454. πῶλος **pōlŏs**, *po´-los;* appar. a primary word; a *"foal"* or *"filly"*, i.e. (spec.) a *young ass:*— colt.

4455. πώποτε **pōpŏtĕ**, *po´-pot-e;* from 4452 and 4218; *at any time*, i.e. (with neg. particle) *at no time:*— at any time, + never (... to any man), + yet, never man.

4456. πωρόω **pōrŏō**, *po-rŏ´-o;* appar. from πῶρος **pōrŏs**, (a kind of *stone*); to *petrify*, i.e. (fig.) to *indurate* (render *stupid* or *callous*):— blind, harden.

4457. πώρωσις **pōrōsis**, *po´-ro-sis;* from 4456; *stupidity* or *callousness:*— blindness, hardness.

4458. -πώς **-pōs**, *poce;* adv. from the base of 4225; an enclitic particle of indefiniteness of manner; *somehow* or *anyhow;* used only in composition:— haply, by any (some) means, perhaps. See 1513, 3381. Comp. 4459.

4459. πῶς **pōs**, *poce;* adv. from the base of 4226; an interr. particle of manner; *in what way?* (sometimes the question is indirect, *how*?); also as exclamation, *how* much!:— how, after (by) what manner (means), that. [*Occasionally unexpressed in English*].

P

4460. Ῥαάβ **Rhaab**, *hrah-ab´;* of Heb. or. [7343]; *Raab* (i.e. *Rachab*), a Canaanitess:— Rahab. See also 4477.

4461. ῥαββί **rhabbi**, *hrab-bee´;* of Heb. or. [7227 with pron. suff.]; *my master*, i.e *Rabbi*, as an official title of honor:— Master, Rabbi.

4462. ῥαββονί **rhabbŏni**, *hrab-bon-ee´;* or

ῥαββουνί **rhabbŏuni**, *hrab-boo-nee´;* of Chald. or.; corresp. to 4461:— Lord, Rabboni.

4463. ῥαβδίζω **rhabdizō**, *hrab-did´-zo;* from 4464; to *strike with a stick*, i.e. *bastinado:*— beat (with rods).

4464. ῥάβδος **rhabdŏs**, *hrab´-dos;* from the base of 4474; a *stick* or *wand* (as a *cudgel*, a cane or a *baton* of royalty):— rod, sceptre, staff.

4465. ῥαβδοῦχος **rhabdŏuchŏs**, *hrab-doo´-khos;* from 4464 and 2192; a *rod-* (the Lat. *fasces*) *holder*, i.e. a Rom. *lictor* (*constable* or *executioner*):— serjeant.

4466. Ῥαγαῦ **Rhagau**, *hrag-ŏw´;* of Heb. or. [7466]; *Ragaü* (i.e. *Reu*), a patriarch:— Ragau.

4467. ῥᾳδιούργημα **rhaïdiŏurgēma**, *hrad-ee-oorg´-ay-mah;* from a comp. of ῥᾴδιος **rhaïdiŏs** (*easy*, i.e. *reckless*) and 2041; *easy-going behavior*, i.e. (by extens.) a *crime:*— lewdness.

4468. ῥᾳδιουργία **rhaïdiŏurgia**, *hrad-ee-oorg-ee´-a;* from the same as 4467; *recklessness*, i.e. (by extens.) *malignity:*— mischief.

4469. ῥακά **rhaka**, *hrak-ah´;* of Chald. or. [comp. 7386]; O *empty* one, i.e. thou *worthless* (as a term of utter vilification):— Raca.

4470. ῥάκος **rhakŏs**, *hrak´-os;* from 4486; a *"rag,"* i.e. *piece* of cloth:— cloth.

4471. Ῥαμᾶ **Rhama**, *hram-ah´;* of Heb. or. [7414]; *Rama* (i.e. *Ramah*), a place in Pal.:— Rama.

4472. ῥαντίζω **rhantizō**, *hran-tid´-zo;* from a der. of ῥαίνω **rhainō** (to *sprinkle*); to *render besprinkled*, i.e. *asperse* (cerem. or fig.):— sprinkle.

4473. ῥαντισμός **rhantismŏs**, *hran-tis-mos´;* from 4472; *aspersion* (cerem. or fig.):— sprinkling.

4474. ῥαπίζω **rhapizō**, *hrap-id´-zo;* from a der. of a primary ῥέπω **rhĕpō** (to *let fall*, *"rap"*); to *slap:*— smite (with the palm of the hand). Comp. 5180.

4475. ῥάπισμα **rhapisma**, *hrap´-is-mah;* from 4474; a *slap:*— (+ strike with the) palm of the hand, smite with the hand.

4476. ῥαφίς **rhaphis**, *hraf-ece´;* from a primary ῥάπτω **rhaptō** (to *sew;* perh. rather akin to the base of 4474 through the idea of *puncturing*); a *needle:*— needle.

4477. Ῥαχάβ **Rhachab**, *hrakh-ab´;* from the same as 4460; *Rachab*, a Canaanitess:— Rachab.

4478. Ῥαχήλ **Rhachēl**, *hrakh-ale´;* of Heb. or. [7354]; *Rachel*, the wife of Jacob:— Rachel.

4479. Ῥεβέκκα **Rhĕbĕkka**, *hreb-bek´-kah;* of Heb. or. [7259]; *Rebecca* (i.e. *Ribkah*), the wife of Isaac:— Rebecca.

4480. ῥέδα **rhĕda**, *hred´-ah;* of Lat. or.; a *rheda*, i.e. four-wheeled *carriage* (*wagon* for riding):— chariot.

4481. Ῥεμφάν **Rhĕmphan**, *hrem-fan´* or

Ῥαιφάν **Rhaiphan**, *hrahee-fan´;* by incorrect transliteration for a word of Heb. of [3594]; *Remphan* (i.e. *Kijun*), an Eg. idol:—Remphan.

4482. ῥέω rhĕō, *hreh´-o;* a primary verb; for some tenses of which a prol. form

ῥεύω rhĕuō, *hryoo´-o* is used; to *flow* ("*run*"; as water):— flow.

4483. ῥέω rhĕō, *hreh´-o;* for certain tenses of which a prol. form

ἐρέω ĕrĕō, *er-eh´-o;* is used; and both as alt. for *2036;* perh. akin (or ident.) with *4482* (through the idea of *pouring* forth); to *utter,* i.e. *speak* or *say:*— command, make, say, speak (of). Comp. *3004.*

4484. Ῥήγιον Rhēgiŏn, *hrayg´-ee-on;* of Lat. or.; *Rhegium,* a place in Italy:— Rhegium.

4485. ῥῆγμα rhēgma, *hrayg´-mah;* from *4486;* something *torn,* i.e. a *fragment* (by impl. and abstr. a *fall*):— ruin.

4486. ῥήγνυμι rhēgnumi, *hrayg´-noo-mee;* or

ῥήσσω rhēssō, *hrace´-so;* both prol. forms of ῥήκω rhēkō (which appears only in certain forms, and is itself prob. a strengthened form of ἄγνυμι agnumi, [see in *2608*]); to "*break*", "*wreck*" or "*crack*", i.e. (espec.) to *sunder* (by *separation* of the parts; *2608* being its intensive [with the prep. in composition], and *2352* a *shattering* to minute fragments; but not a *reduction* to the constituent particles, like *3089*) or *disrupt, lacerate;* by impl. to *convulse* (with *spasms*); fig. to *give vent* to joyful emotions:— break (forth), burst, rend, tear.

4487. ῥῆμα rhēma, *hray´-mah;* from *4483;* an *utterance* (indiv., collect. or spec.); by impl. a *matter* or *topic* (espec. of narration, command or dispute); with a neg. *naught* whatever:— + evil, + nothing, saying, word.

4488. Ῥησά Rhēsa, *hray-sah´;* prob. of Heb. or. [appar. for *7509*]; *Resa* (i.e. *Rephajah*), an Isr.:— Rhesa.

4489. ῥήτωρ rhētōr, *hray´-tore;* from *4483;* a *speaker,* i.e. (by impl.) a forensic *advocate:*— orator.

4490. ῥητῶς rhētōs, *hray-toce´;* adv. from a der. of *4483;* out-*spokenly,* i.e. *distinctly:*— expressly.

4491. ῥίζα rhiza, *hrid´-zah;* appar. a primary word; a "*root*" (lit. or fig.):— root.

4492. ῥιζόω rhizŏō, *hrid-zŏ´-o;* from *4491;* to *root* (fig. *become stable*):— root.

4493. ῥιπή rhipē, *hree-pay´;* from *4496;* a *jerk* (of the eye, i.e. [by anal.] an *instant*):— twinkling.

4494. ῥιπίζω rhipizō, *hrip-id´-zo;* from a der. of *4496* (mean. a *fan* or *bellows*); to *breeze up,* i.e. (by anal.) to *agitate* (into waves):— toss.

4495. ῥιπτέω rhiptĕō, *hrip-teh´-o;* from a der. of *4496;* to *toss* up:— cast off.

4496. ῥίπτω rhiptō, *hrip´-to;* a primary verb (perh. rather akin to the base of *4474,* through the idea of sudden *motion*); to *fling* (prop. with a quick *toss,* thus differing from

906, which denotes a *deliberate* hurl; and from τείνω tĕinō, [see in *1614*], which indicates an *extended* projection); by qualification, to *deposit* (as if a load); by extens. to *disperse:*— cast (down, out), scatter abroad, throw.

4497. Ῥοβοάμ Rhŏbŏam, *hrob-ŏ-am´;* of Heb. or. [*7346*]; *Roboäm* (i.e. *Rechabam*), an Isr.:— Roboam.

4498. Ῥόδη Rhŏdē, *hrod´-ay;* prob. for ῥοδή rhŏdē, (a *rose*); *Rodë,* a servant girl:— Rhoda.

4499. Ῥόδος Rhŏdŏs, *hrod´-os;* prob. from ῥόδον rhŏdŏn, (a *rose*); *Rhodus,* an island of the Mediterranean:— Rhodes.

4500. ῥοιζηδόν rhŏizēdŏn, *hroyd-zay-don´;* adv. from a der. of ῥοῖζος rhŏizŏs (a *whir*); *whizzingly,* i.e. *with a crash:*— with a great noise.

4501. ῥομφαία rhŏmphaia, *hrom-fah´-yah;* prob. of for. or.; a *sabre,* i.e. a long and broad *cutlass* (any *weapon* of the kind, lit. or fig.):— sword.

4502. Ῥουβήν Rhŏubēn, *hroo-bane´;* of Heb. or. [*7205*]; *Ruben* (i.e. *Reuben*), an Isr.:— Reuben.

4503. Ῥούθ Rhŏuth, *hrooth;* of Heb. or. [*7327*]; *Ruth,* a Moabitess:— Ruth.

4504. Ῥοῦφος Rhŏuphŏs, *hroo´-fos;* of Lat. or.; *red; Rufus,* a Chr.:— Rufus.

4505. ῥύμη rhumē, *hroo´-may;* prol. from *4506* in its orig. sense; an *alley* or *avenue* (as crowded):— lane, street.

4506. ῥύομαι rhuŏmai, *hroo´-om-ahee;* mid. voice of an obs. verb, akin to *4482* (through the idea of a *current;* comp. *4511*); to *rush* or *draw* (for oneself), i.e. *rescue:*— deliver (-er).

4507. ῥυπαρία rhuparia, *hroo-par-ee´-ah;* from *4508; dirtiness* (mor.):— turpitude.

4508. ῥυπαρός rhuparŏs, *hroo-par-os´;* from *4509; dirty,* i.e. (rel.) *cheap* or *shabby;* mor. *wicked:*— vile.

4509. ῥύπος rhupŏs, *hroo´-pos;* of uncert. aff.; *dirt,* i.e. (mor.) *depravity:*— filth.

4510. ῥυπόω rhupŏō, *hroo-pŏ´-o;* from *4509;* to *soil,* i.e. (intr.) to *become dirty* (mor.):— be filthy.

4511. ῥύσις rhusis, *hroo´-sis;* from *4506* in the sense of its congener *4482;* a *flux* (of blood):— issue.

4512. ῥυτίς rhutis, *hroo-tece´;* from *4506;* a *fold* (as *drawing* together), i.e. a *wrinkle* (espec. on the face):— wrinkle.

4513. Ῥωμαϊκός Rhōmaïkŏs, *hro-mah-ee-kos´;* from *4514; Romaic,* i.e. *Lat.:*— Latin.

4514. Ῥωμαῖος Rhōmaiŏs, *hro-mah´-yos;* from *4516; Romæan,* i.e. *Roman* (as noun):— Roman, of Rome.

4515. Ῥωμαϊστί Rhōmaïsti, *hro-mah-is-*

tee´; adv. from a presumed der. of *4516; Romaïstically*, i.e. *in* the *Latin* language:— Latin.

4516. Ῥώμη **Rhōmē**, *hro´-may*; from the base of *4517; strength; Roma*, the capital of Italy:— Rome.

4517. ῥώννυμι **rhōnnumi**, *hrone´-noo-mee;* prol. from ῥώομαι **rhŏŏmai** (to *dart;* prob. akin to *4506*); to *strengthen*, i.e. (impers. pass.) *have health* (as a parting exclamation, *goodbye*):— farewell.

Σ

4518. σαβαχθανί **sabachthani**, *sab-akh-than-ee´*; of Chald. or [7662 with pron. suff.]; *thou hast left me; sabachthani* (i.e. *shebakthani*), a cry of distress:— sabachthani.

4519. σαβαώθ **sabaōth**, *sab-ah-owth´*; of Heb. or. [6635 in fem. plur.]; *armies; sabaoth* (i.e. *tsebaoth*), a military epithet of God:— sabaoth.

4520. σαββατισμός **sabbatismŏs**, *sab-bat-is-mos´*; from a der. of *4521;* a "*sabbatism*," i.e. (fig.) the *repose* of Christianity (as a type of heaven):— rest.

4521. σάββατον **sabbatŏn**, *sab´-bat-on;* of Heb. or. [7676]; the *Sabbath* (i.e. *Shabbath*), or day of weekly *repose* from secular avocations (also the observance or institution itself); by extens. a *se´nnight*, i.e. the interval between two Sabbaths; likewise the plural in all the above applications:— sabbath (day), week.

4522. σαγήνη **sagēnē**, *sag-ay´-nay;* from a der. of σάττω **sattō** (to *equip*) mean. *furniture*, espec. a *pack-saddle* (which in the E. is merely a bag of *netted* rope); a "*seine*" for fishing:— net.

4523. Σαδδουκαῖος **Saddŏukaiŏs**, *sad-doo-kah´-yos;* prob. from *4524;* a *Sadducæan* (i.e. *Tsadokian*), or follower of a certain heretical Isr.:— Sadducee.

4524. Σαδώκ **Sadōk**, *sad-oke´;* of Heb. or. [6659]; *Sadoc* (i.e. *Tsadok*), an Isr.:— Sadoc.

4525. σαίνω **sainō**, *sah´-ee-no;* akin to *4579;* to *wag* (as a dog its tail fawningly), i.e. (gen.) to *shake* (fig. *disturb*):— move.

4526. σάκκος **sakkŏs**, *sak´-kos;* of Heb. or. [8242]; "*sack*"-*cloth*, i.e. *mohair* (the material or garments made of it, worn as a sign of grief):— sackcloth.

4527. Σαλά **Sala**, *sal-ah´;* of Heb. or. [7974]; *Sala* (i.e. *Shelach*), a patriarch:— Sala.

4528. Σαλαθιήλ **Salathiēl**, *sal-ath-ee-ale´;* of Heb. or. [7597]; *Salathiël* (i.e. *Sheältiël*), an Isr.:— Salathiel.

4529. Σαλαμίς **Salamis**, *sal-am-ece´;* prob. from *4535* (from the *surge* on the shore); *Salamis*, a place in Cyprus:— Salamis.

4530. Σαλείμ **Salĕim**, *sal-ime´;* prob. from the same as *4531; Salim*, a place in Pal.:— Salim.

4531. σαλεύω **salĕuō**, *sal-yoo´-o;* from *4535;* to *waver*, i.e. *agitate, rock, topple* or (by impl.) *destroy;* fig. to *disturb, incite:*— move, shake (together), which can [-not] be shaken, stir up.

4532. Σαλήμ **Salēm**, *sal-ame´;* of Heb. or. [8004]; *Salem* (i.e. *Shalem*), a place in Pal.:— Salem.

4533. Σαλμών **Salmōn**, *sal-mone´;* of Heb. or. [8012]; *Salmon*, an Isr.:— Salmon.

4534. Σαλμώνη **Salmōnē**, *sal-mo´-nay;* perh. of similar or. to *4529; Salmone*, a place in Crete:— Salmone.

4535. σάλος **salŏs**, *sal´-os;* prob. from the base of *4525;* a *vibration*, i.e. (spec.) *billow:*— wave.

4536. σάλπιγξ **salpigx**, *sal´-pinx;* perh. from *4535* (through the idea of *quavering* or *reverberation*); a *trumpet:*— trump (-et).

4537. σαλπίζω **salpizō**, *sal-pid´-zo;* from *4536;* to *trumpet*, i.e. *sound a blast* (lit. or fig.):— (which are yet to) sound (a trumpet).

4538. σαλπιστής **salpistēs**, *sal-pis-tace´;* from *4537;* a *trumpeter:*— trumpeter.

4539. Σαλώμη **Salōmē**, *sal-o´-may;* prob. of Heb. or. [fem. from 7965]; *Salomè* (i.e. *Shelomah*), an Israelitess:— Salome.

4540. Σαμάρεια **Samarĕia**, *sam-ar´-i-ah;* of Heb. or. [8111]; *Samaria* (i.e. *Shomeron*), a city and region of Pal.:— Samaria.

4541. Σαμαρείτης **Samarĕitēs**, *sam-ar-i-tace* or

Σαμαρίτης **Samaritēs**, *sam-ar-ee´-tace;* from *4540;* a *Samarite*, i.e. inhab. of Samaria:— Samaritan.

4542. Σαμαρεῖτις **Samarĕitis**, *sam-ar-i´-tis* or

Σαμαρῖτις **Samaritis**, *sam-ar-ee´-tis* fem. of *4541;* a *Samaritess*, i.e. woman of Samaria:— of Samaria.

4543. Σαμοθρᾴκη **Samŏthraįkē**, *sam-oth-rak´-ay;* from *4544* and Θρᾴκη **Thraįkē** (*Thrace*); *Samo-thracè* (*Samos of Thrace*), an island in the Mediterranean:— Samothracia.

4544. Σάμος **Samŏs**, *sam´-os;* of uncert. aff.; *Samus*, an island of the Mediterranean:— Samos.

4545. Σαμουήλ **Samŏuēl**, *sam-oo-ale´;* of Heb. or. [8050]; *Samuel* (i.e. *Shemuel*), an Isr.:— Samuel.

4546. Σαμψών **Sampsōn**, *samp-sone´;* of Heb. or. [8123]; *Sampson* (i.e. *Shimshon*), an Isr.:— Samson.

4547. σανδάλιον **sandaliŏn**, *san-dal´-ee-on;* neut. of a der. of σάνδαλον **sandalŏn** (a "*sandal*"; of uncert. or.); a *slipper* or *sole-pad:*— sandal.

4548. σανίς **sanis**, *san-ece´;* of uncert. aff.; a *plank:*— board.

4549. Σαούλ **Saŏul**, *sah-ool´;* of Heb. or. [7586]; *Saül* (i.e. *Shaül*), the Jewish name of *Paul:*— Saul. Comp. 4569.

4550. σαπρός **saprŏs**, *sap-ros´;* from 4595; *rotten*, i.e. *worthless* (lit. or mor.):— bad, corrupt. Comp. 4190.

4551. Σαπφείρη **Sapphĕirē**, *sap-fi´-ray;* fem. of 4552; *Sapphirë*, an Israelitess:— Sapphira.

4552. σάπφειρος **sapphĕirŏs**, *sap´-fi-ros;* of Heb. or. [5601]; a *"sapphire"* or *lapis-lazuli* gem:— sapphire.

4553. σαργάνη **sarganē**, *sar-gan´-ay;* appar. of Heb. or. [8276]; a *basket* (as *interwoven* or *wicker*-work:— basket.

4554. Σάρδεις **Sardĕis**, *sar´-dice;* plur. of uncert. der.; *Sardis*, a place in Asia Minor:— Sardis.

4555. σάρδινος **sardinŏs**, *sar´-dee-nos;* from the same as 4556; *sardine* (3037 being impl.), i.e. a gem, so called:— sardine.

4556. σάρδιος **sardiŏs**, *sar´-dee-os;* prop. an adj. from an uncert. base; *sardian* (3037 being impl.), i.e. (as noun) the gem so called:— sardius.

4557. σαρδόνυξ **sardŏnux**, *sar-don´-oox;* from the base of 4556 and ὄνυξ **ŏnux** (the *nail* of a finger; hence, the *"onyx"* stone); a *"sardonyx"*, i.e. the gem so called:— sardonyx.

4558. Σάρεπτα **Sarĕpta**, *sar´-ep-tah;* of Heb. or. [6886]; *Sarepta* (i.e. *Tsarephath*), a place in Pal.:— Sarepta.

4559. σαρκικός **sarkikŏs**, *sar-kee-kos´;* from 4561; *pertaining to flesh*, i.e. (by extens.) *bodily, temporal*, or (by impl.) *animal, unregenerate:*— carnal, fleshly.

4560. σάρκινος **sarkinŏs**, *sar´-kee-nos;* from 4561; *similar to flesh*, i.e. (by anal.) *soft:*— fleshly.

4561. σάρξ **sarx**, *sarx;* prob. from the base of 4563; *flesh* (as *stripped* of the skin), i.e. (strictly) the *meat* of an animal (as food), or (by extens.) the *body* (as opposed to the soul [or spirit], or as the symbol of what is external, or as the means of kindred), or (by impl.) *human nature* (with its frailties [phys. or mor.] and passions), or (spec.) a *human being* (as such):— carnal (-ly, + -ly minded), flesh ([-ly]).

4562. Σαρούχ **Sarŏuch** *sa-rooch´,* or

     Σερούχ **Sĕrŏuch**, *seh-rooch´;* of Heb. or. [8286]; *Saruch* (i.e. *Serug*), a patriarch:— Saruch.

4563. σαρόω **sarŏō**, *sar-ŏ´-o;* from a der. of σαίρω **sairō** (to *brush* off; akin to 4951); mean. a *broom;* to *sweep:*— sweep.

4564. Σάρρα **Sarrha**, *sar´-hrah;* of Heb. or. [8283]; *Sarra* (i.e. *Sarah*), the wife of Abraham:— Sara, Sarah.

4565. Σάρων **Sarōn** *sar´-one;* of Heb. or. [8289]; *Saron* (i.e. *Sharon*), a district of Pal.:— Saron.

4566. Σατᾶν **Satan**, *sat-an´;* of Heb. or. [7854]; *Satan*, i.e. the *devil:*— Satan. Comp. 4567.

4567. Σατανᾶς **Satanas**, *sat-an-as´;* of Chald. or. corresp. to 4566 (with the def. aff.); *the accuser*, i.e. the *devil:*— Satan.

4568. σάτον **satŏn**, *sat´-on;* of Heb. or. [5429]; a certain *measure* for things dry:— measure.

4569. Σαῦλος **Saulŏs**, *sŏw´-los;* of Heb. or., the same as 4549; *Saulus* (i.e. *Shaül*), the Jewish name of *Paul:*— Saul.

σαυτοῦ **sautŏu**. etc. See 4572.

4570. σβέννυμι **sbĕnnumi**, *sben´-noo-mee;* a prol. form of an appar. primary verb; to *extinguish* (lit. or fig.):— go out, quench.

4571. σέ **sĕ**, *seh;* acc. sing. of 4771; *thee:*— thee, thou, × thy house.

4572. σεαυτοῦ **sĕautŏu**, *seh-ŏw-too´;* gen. from 4571 and 846; also dat. of the same,

     σεαυτῷ **sĕautŏi**, *seh-ŏw-to´;* and acc.

     σεαυτόν **sĕautŏn**, *seh-ŏw-ton´;* likewise contr.

     σαυτοῦ **sautŏu**, *sŏw-too´;*

     σαυτῷ **sautŏi**, *sŏw-to´;* and

     σαυτόν **sautŏn**, *sŏw-ton´;* respectively; *of* (*with, to*) *thyself:*— thee, thine own self, (thou) thy (-self).

4573. σεβάζομαι **sĕbazŏmai**, *seb-ad´-zom-ahee;* mid. voice from a der. of 4576; to *venerate*, i.e. *adore:*— worship.

4574. σέβασμα **sĕbasma**, *seb´-as-mah;* from 4573; something *adored*, i.e. an *object of worship* (god, altar, etc):— devotion, that is worshipped.

4575. σεβαστός **sĕbastŏs**, *seb-as-tos´;* from 4573; *venerable* (*august*), i.e. (as noun) a title of the Rom. *Emperor*, or (as adj.) *imperial:*— Augustus (-').

4576. σέβομαι **sĕbŏmai**, *seb´-om-ahee;* mid. voice of an appar. primary verb; to *revere*, i.e. *adore:*— devout, religious, worship.

4577. σειρά **sĕira**, *si-rah´;* prob. from 4951 through its congener εἴρω **ĕirō** (to *fasten;* akin to 138); a *chain*, (as *binding* or *drawing*):— chain.

4578. σεισμός **sĕismŏs**, *sice-mos´;* from 4579; a *commotion*, i.e. (of the air) a *gale*, (of the ground) an *earthquake:*— earthquake, tempest.

4579. σείω **sĕiō**, *si´-o;* appar. a primary verb; to *rock* (*vibrate*, prop. sideways or to and fro), i.e. (gen.) to *agitate* (in any direction; cause to *tremble*); fig. to throw into a *tremor* (of fear or concern):— move, quake, shake.

4580. Σεκοῦνδος **Sĕkŏundŏs**, *sek-oon´-dos;*

of Lat. or.; "second"; Secundus, a Chr.:— Secundus.

4581. Σελεύκεια Sĕlĕukĕia, sel-yook´-i-ah; from Σέλευκος Sĕlĕukŏs, (Seleucus, a Syrian king); Seleuceia, a place in Syria:— Seleucia.

4582. σελήνη sĕlēnē, sel-ay´-nay; from σέλας sĕlas, (brilliancy; prob. akin to the alt. of 138, through the idea of attractiveness); the moon:— moon.

4583. σεληνιάζομαι sĕlēniazŏmai, sel-ay-nee-ad´-zom-ahee; middle or passive voice from a presumed der. of 4582; to be moon-struck, i.e. crazy:— be a lunatic.

4584. Σεμεΐ Sĕmĕï, sem-eh-ee´ or

Σεμεΐν Sĕmĕïn, sem-eh-een´ of Heb. or. [8096]; Semeï (i.e. Shimi), an Isr.:— Semei (Semein).

4585. σεμίδαλις sĕmidalis, sem-id´-al-is; prob. of for. origin; fine wheaten flour:— fine flour.

4586. σεμνός sĕmnŏs, sem-nos´; from 4576; venerable, i.e. honorable:— grave, honest.

4587. σεμνότης sĕmnŏtēs, sem-not´-ace; from 4586; venerableness, i.e. probity:— gravity, honesty.

4588. Σέργιος Sĕrgiŏs, serg´-ee-os; of Lat. or.; Sergius, a Rom.:— Sergius.

4589. Σήθ Sēth, sayth; of Heb. or. [8352]; Seth (i.e. Sheth), a patriarch:— Seth.

4590. Σήμ Sēm, same; of Heb. or. [8035]; Sem (i.e. Shem), a patriarch:— Sem.

4591. σημαίνω sēmainō, say-mah´-ee-no; from σῆμα sēma, (a mark; of uncert. der.); to indicate:— signify.

4592. σημεῖον sēmĕiŏn, say-mi´-on; neut. of a presumed der. of the base of 4591; an indication, espec. cerem. or supernat.:— miracle, sign, token, wonder.

4593. σημειόω sēmĕiŏō, say-mi-ŏ´-o; from 4592; to distinguish, i.e. mark (for avoidance):— note.

4594. σήμερον sēmĕrŏn, say´-mer-on; neut. (as adv.) of a presumed compound of the art. 3588 (τ changed to σ) and 2250; on the (i.e. this) day (or night current or just passed); gen. now (i.e. at present, hitherto):— this (to-) day.

4595. σήπω sēpō, say´-po; appar. a primary verb; to putrefy, i.e. (fig.) perish:— be corrupted.

4596. σηρικός sērikŏs, say-ree-kos´ or

σιρικός sirikŏs, see-ree-kos´; from Σήρ Sēr, (an Indian tribe from whom silk was procured; hence, the name of the silk-worm); Seric, i.e. silken (neut. as noun, a silky fabric):— silk.

4597. σής sēs, sace; appar. of Heb. or. [5580]; a moth:— moth.

4598. σητόβρωτος sētŏbrōtŏs, say-tob´-ro-tos; from 4597 and a der. of 977; moth-eaten:— motheaten.

4599. σθενόω sthĕnŏō, sthen-ŏ´-o; from σθένος sthĕnŏs, (bodily vigor; prob. akin to the base of 2476); to strengthen, i.e. (fig.) confirm (in spiritual knowledge and power):— strengthen.

4600. σιαγών siagōn, see-ag-one´; of uncert. der.; the jaw-bone, i.e. (by impl.) the cheek or side of the face:— cheek.

4601. σιγάω sigaō, see-gah´-o; from 4602; to keep silent (tran. or intr.):— keep close (secret, silence), hold peace.

4602. σιγή sigē, see-gay´; appr. from σίζω sizō (to hiss, i.e. hist or hush); silence:— silence. Comp. 4623.

4603. σιδήρεος sidērĕŏs, sid-ay´-reh-os; from 4604; made of iron:— (of) iron.

4604. σίδηρος sidērŏs, sid´-ay-ros; of uncert. der.; iron:— iron.

4605. Σιδών Sidōn, sid-one´; of Heb. or. [6721]; Sidon (i.e. Tsidon), a place in Pal.:— Sidon.

4606. Σιδώνιος Sidōniŏs, sid-o´-nee-os; from 4605; a Sidonian, i.e. inhab. of Sidon:— of Sidon.

4607. σικάριος sikariŏs, sik-ar´-ee-os; of Lat. or.; a dagger-man or assassin; a freebooter (Jewish fanatic outlawed by the Romans):— murderer. Comp. 5406.

4608. σίκερα sikĕra, sik´-er-ah; of Heb. or. [7941]; an intoxicant, i.e. intensely fermented liquor:— strong drink.

4609. Σίλας Silas, see´-las; contr. for 4610; Silas, a Chr.:— Silas.

4610. Σιλουανός Silŏuanŏs, sil-oo-an-os´; of Lat. or.; "silvan"; Silvanus, a Chr.:— Silvanus. Comp. 4609.

4611. Σιλωάμ Silōam, sil-o-am´; of Heb. or. [7975]; Siloäm (i.e. Shiloäch), a pool of Jerusalem:— Siloam.

4612. σιμικίνθιον simikinthiŏn, sim-ee-kin´-thee-on; of Lat. or.; a semicinctium or half-girding, i.e. narrow covering (apron):— apron.

4613. Σίμων Simōn, see´-mone; of Heb. or. [8095]; Simon (i.e. Shimon), the name of nine Isr.:— Simon. Comp. 4826.

4614. Σινᾶ Sina, see-nah´; of Heb. or. [5514]; Sina (i.e. Sinai), a mountain in Arabia:— Sina.

4615. σίναπι sinapi, sin´-ap-ee; perh. from σίνομαι sinŏmai (to hurt, i.e. sting); mustard (the plant):— mustard.

4616. σινδών sindōn, sin-done´; of uncert. (perh. for.) or.; byssos, i.e. bleached linen (the cloth or a garment of it):— (fine) linen (cloth).

4617. σινιάζω siniazō, sin-ee-ad´-zo; from σινίον siniŏn, (a sieve); to riddle (fig.):— sift.

σῖτα **sita**. See *4621*.

4618. σιτευτός **sitĕutŏs**, *sit-yoo-tos´;* from a der. of *4621; grain-fed,* i.e. *fattened:*— fatted.

4619. σιτιστός **sitistŏs**, *sit-is-tos´;* from a der. of *4621; grained,* i.e. *fatted:*— fatling.

4620. σιτόμετρον **sitŏmĕtrŏn**, *sit-om´-et-ron;* from *4621* and *3358;* a *grain-measure,* i.e. (by impl.) *ration* (*allowance* of food):— portion of meat.

4621. σῖτος **sitŏs**, *see´-tos;* plur. irreg. neut. σῖτα **sita**, *see´-tah;* of uncert. der.; *grain,* espec. *wheat:*— corn, wheat.

4622. Σιών **Siōn**, *see-own´;* of Heb. or. [6726]; *Sion* (i.e. *Tsijon*), a hill of Jerusalem; fig. the *Church* (militant or triumphant):— Sion.

4623. σιωπάω **siōpaō**, *see-o-pah´-o;* from σιωπή **siōpē**, (*silence,* i.e. a *hush;* prop. *muteness,* i.e. *involuntary* stillness, or *inability* to speak; and thus differing from *4602,* which is rather a voluntary *refusal* or *indisposition* to speak, although the terms are often used synonymously); to *be dumb* (but not *deaf* also, like *2974* prop.); fig. to *be calm* (as *quiet* water):— dumb, (hold) peace.

4624. σκανδαλίζω **skandalizō**, *skan-dal-id´-zo* ("scandalize"); from *4625;* to *entrap,* i.e. *trip* up (fig. *stumble* [tran.] or *entice* to sin, apostasy or displeasure):— (make to) offend.

4625. σκάνδαλον **skandalŏn**, *skan´-dal-on* ("scandal"); prob. from a der. of *2578;* a *trap-stick* (*bent* sapling), i.e. *snare* (fig. *cause* of displeasure or sin):— occasion to fall (of stumbling), offence, thing that offends, stumblingblock.

4626. σκάπτω **skaptō**, *skap´-to;* appar. a primary verb; to *dig:*— dig.

4627. σκάφη **skaphē**, *skaf´-ay;* a "*skiff*" (as if *dug* out), or *yawl* (carried aboard a large vessel for landing):— boat.

4628. σκέλος **skĕlŏs**, *skel-os;* appar. from σκέλλω **skĕllō**, (to *parch;* through the idea of *leanness*); the *leg* (as *lank*):— leg.

4629. σκέπασμα **skĕpasma**, *skep´-as-mah;* from a der. of σκέπας **skĕpas** (a *covering;* perh. akin to the base of *4649,* through the idea of *noticeableness*); *clothing:*— raiment.

4630. Σκευᾶς **Skĕuas**, *skyoo-as´;* appar. of Lat. or.; *left-handed; Scevas* (i.e. *Scœvus*), an Isr.:— Sceva.

4631. σκευή **skĕuē**, *skyoo-ay´;* from *4632; furniture,* i.e. spare *tackle:*— tackling.

4632. σκεῦος **skĕuŏs**, *skyoo´-os;* of uncert. aff.; a *vessel, implement, equipment* or *apparatus* (lit. or fig. [spec. a *wife* as contributing to the usefulness of the husband]):— goods, sail, stuff, vessel.

4633. σκηνή **skēnē**, *skay-nay´;* appar. akin to *4632* and *4639;* a *tent* or cloth hut (lit. or fig.):— habitation, tabernacle.

4634. σκηνοπηγία **skēnŏpēgia**, *skay-nop-ayg-ee´-ah;* from *4636* and *4078;* the *Festival of Tabernacles* (so called from the custom of erecting booths for temporary homes):— tabernacles.

4635. σκηνοποιός **skēnŏpŏiŏs**, *skay-nop-oy-os´;* from *4633* and *4160;* a *manufacturer of tents:*— tent-maker.

4636. σκῆνος **skēnŏs**, *skay´-nos;* from *4633;* a *hut* or temporary residence, i.e. (fig.) the human *body* (as the abode of the spirit):— tabernacle.

4637. σκηνόω **skēnŏō**, *skay-nŏ´-o;* from *4636;* to *tent* or *encamp,* i.e. (fig.) to *occupy* (as a mansion) or (spec.) to *reside* (as God did in the Tabernacle of old, a symbol of protection and communion):— dwell.

4638. σκήνωμα **skēnōma**, *skay´-no-mah;* from *4637;* an *encampment,* i.e. (fig.) the *Temple* (as God's residence), the *body* (as a tenement for the soul):— tabernacle.

4639. σκία **skia**, *skee´-ah;* appar. a primary word; "*shade*" or a shadow (lit. or fig. [darkness of *error* or an *adumbration*]):— shadow.

4640. σκιρτάω **skirtaō**, *skeer-tah´-o;* akin to σκαίρω **skairō**, (to *skip*); to *jump,* i.e. sympathetically *move* (as the *quickening* of a fetus):— leap (for joy).

4641. σκληροκαρδία **sklērŏkardia**, *sklay-rok-ar-dee´-ah;* fem. of a compound of *4642* and *2588; hard-heartedness,* i.e. (spec.) *destitution of* (spiritual) *perception:*— hardness of heart.

4642. σκληρός **sklērŏs**, *sklay-ros´;* from the base of *4628; dry,* i.e. *hard* or *tough* (fig. *harsh, severe*):— fierce, hard.

4643. σκληρότης **sklērŏtēs**, *sklay-rot´-ace;* from *4642; callousness,* i.e. (fig.) *stubbornness:*— hardness.

4644. σκληροτράχηλος **sklērŏtrachēlŏs**, *sklay-rot-rakh´-ay-los;* from *4642* and *5137; hardnaped,* i.e. (fig.) *obstinate:*— stiffnecked.

4645. σκληρύνω **sklērunō**, *sklay-roo´-no;* from *4642;* to *indurate,* i.e. (fig.) *render stubborn:*— harden.

4646. σκολιός **skŏliŏs**, *skol-ee-os´;* from the base of *4628; warped,* i.e. *winding;* fig. *perverse:*— crooked, froward, untoward.

4647. σκόλοψ **skŏlŏps**, *skol´-ops;* perh. from the base of *4628* and *3700; withered* at the *front,* i.e. a *point* or *prickle* (fig. a bodily *annoyance* or *disability*):— thorn.

4648. σκοπέω **skŏpĕō**, *skop-eh´-o;* from *4649;* to take *aim* at (*spy*), i.e. (fig.) *regard:*— consider, take heed, look at (on), mark. Comp. *3700.*

4649. σκοπός **skŏpŏs**, *skop-os´* ("scope"); from σκέπτομαι **skĕptŏmai** (to *peer* about ["skeptic"]; perh. akin to *4626* through the idea of *concealment;* comp. *4629*); a *watch* (*sentry* or *scout*), i.e. (by impl.) a *goal:*— mark.

4650. σκορπίζω **skŏrpizō**, *skor-pid´-zo;* appar. from the same as *4651* (through the idea of *penetrating*); to *dissipate*, i.e. (fig.) *put to flight, waste, be liberal:*— disperse abroad, scatter (abroad).

4651. σκορπίος **skŏrpiŏs**, *skor-pee´-os;* prob. from an obs. σκέρπω **skĕrpō** (perh. strengthened from the base of *4649*, and mean. to *pierce*); a "*scorpion*" (from its *sting*):— scorpion.

4652. σκοτεινός **skŏtĕinŏs**, *skot-i-nos´;* from *4655; opaque*, i.e. (fig.) *benighted:*— dark, full of darkness.

4653. σκοτία **skŏtia**, *skot-ee´-ah;* from *4655; dimness, obscurity* (lit. or fig.):— dark (-ness).

4654. σκοτίζω **skŏtizō**, *skot-id-zo;* from *4655;* to *obscure* (lit. or fig.):— darken.

4655. σκότος **skŏtŏs**, *skot´-os;* from the base of *4639; shadiness*, i.e. *obscurity* (lit. or fig.):— darkness.

4656. σκοτόω **skŏtŏō**, *skot-ŏ´-o;* from *4655;* to *obscure* or *blind* (lit. or fig.):— be full of darkness.

4657. σκύβαλον **skubalŏn**, *skoo´-bal-on;* neut. of a presumed der. of *1519* and *2965* and *906;* what is *thrown* to the *dogs*, i.e. *refuse* (*ordure*):— dung.

4658. Σκύθης **Skuthēs**, *skoo´-thace;* prob. of for. or.; a *Scythene* or *Scythian*, i.e. (by impl.) a *savage:*— Scythian.

4659. σκυθρωπός **skuthrōpŏs**, *skoo-thro-pos´;* from σκυθρός **skuthrŏs**, (*sullen*) and a der. of *3700; angry-visaged*, i.e. *gloomy* or affecting a *mournful* appearance:— of a sad countenance.

4660. σκύλλω **skullō**, *skool´-lo;* appar. a primary verb; to *flay*, i.e. (fig.) to *harass:*— trouble (self).

4661. σκύλον **skulŏn**, *skoo´-lon;* neut. from *4660;* something *stripped* (as a *hide*), i.e. *booty:*— spoil.

4662. σκωληκόβρωτος **skōlēkŏbrŏtŏs**, *sko-lay-kob´-ro-tos;* from *4663* and a der. of *977; worm-eaten*, i.e. *diseased with maggots:*— eaten of worms.

4663. σκώληξ **skōlēx**, *sko´-lakes;* of uncert. der.; a *grub, maggot* or *earth-worm:*— worm.

4664. σμαράγδινος **smaragdinŏs**, *smar-ag´-dee-nos;* from *4665;* consisting *of emerald:*— emerald.

4665. σμάραγδος **smaragdŏs**, *smar´-ag-dos;* of uncert. der.; the *emerald* or green gem so called:— emerald.

4666. σμύρνα **smurna**, *smoor´-nah;* appar. strengthened for *3464; myrrh:*— myrrh.

4667. Σμύρνα **Smurna**, *smoor´-nah;* the same as *4666; Smyrna*, a place in Asia Minor:— Smyrna.

4668. Σμυρναῖος **Smurnaiŏs**, *smoor-nah´-yos;* from *4667;* a *Smyrnæan:*— in Smyrna.

4669. σμυρνίζω **smurnizō**, *smoor-nid´-zo;* from *4667;* to *tincture with myrrh*, i.e. *embitter* (as a narcotic):— mingle with myrrh.

4670. Σόδομα **Sŏdŏma**, *sod´-om-ah;* plur. of Heb. or. [5467]; *Sodoma* (i.e. *Sedom*), a place in Pal.:— Sodom.

4671. σοί **sŏi**, *soy;* dat. of *4771; to thee:*— thee, thine own, thou, thy.

4672. Σολομών or Σολομῶν **Sŏlŏmōn**, *sol-om-one´;* of Heb. or. [8010]; *Solomon* (i.e. *Shelomoh*), the son of David:— Solomon.

4673. σορός **sŏrŏs**, *sor-os´;* prob. akin to the base of *4987;* a *funereal receptacle* (*urn, coffin*), i.e. (by anal.) a *bier:*— bier.

4674. σός **sŏs**, *sos;* from *4771; thine:*— thine (own), thy (friend).

4675. σοῦ **sŏu**, *soo;* gen. of *4771; of thee, thy:*— × home, thee, thine (own), thou, thy.

4676. σουδάριον **sŏudariŏn**, *soo-dar´-ee-on;* of Lat. or.; a *sudarium* (*sweat-cloth*), i.e. *towel* (for wiping the perspiration from the face, or binding the face of a corpse):— handkerchief, napkin.

4677. Σουσάννα **Sŏusanna**, *soo-san´-nah;* of Heb. or. [7799 fem.]; *lily; Susannah* (i.e. *Shoshannah*), an Israelitess:— Susanna.

4678. σοφία **sŏphia**, *sof-ee´-ah;* from *4680; wisdom* (higher or lower, worldly or spiritual):— wisdom.

4679. σοφίζω **sŏphizō**, *sof-id´-zo;* from *4680;* to *render wise;* in a sinister acceptation, to *form "sophisms"*, i.e. *continue plausible error:*— cunningly devised, make wise.

4680. σοφός **sŏphŏs**, *sof-os´;* akin to σαφής **saphēs**, (*clear*); *wise* (in a most gen. application):— wise. Comp. *5429*.

4681. Σπανία **Spania**, *span-ee´-ah;* prob. of for. or.; *Spania*, a region of Europe:— Spain.

4682. σπαράσσω **sparassō**, *spar-as´-so;* prol. from σπαίρω **spairō** (to *gasp;* appar. strengthened from *4685*, through the idea of *spasmodic* contraction); to *mangle*, i.e. *convulse* with epilepsy:— rend, tear.

4683. σπαργανόω **sparganŏō**, *spar-gan-ŏ´-o;* from σπάργανον **sparganŏn**, (a *strip;* from a der. of the base of *4682* mean. to *strap* or *wrap* with strips); to *swathe* (an infant after the Oriental custom):— wrap in swaddling clothes.

4684. σπαταλάω **spatalaō**, *spat-al-ah´-o;* from σπατάλη **spatalē**, (*luxury*); to *be voluptuous:*— live in pleasure, be wanton.

4685. σπάω **spaō**, *spah´-o;* a primary verb; to *draw:*— draw (out).

4686. σπεῖρα **spĕira**, *spi´-rah;* of immed. Lat. or., but ultimately a der. of *138* in the sense of its cognate *1507;* a *coil* (*spira*, "spire"), i.e. (fig.) a *mass* of men (a Rom. military *cohort;* also [by anal.] a *squad* of Levitical janitors):— band.

4687. σπείρω **spĕirō**, *spi´-ro;* prob. strengthened from *4685* (through the idea of *extending*); to *scatter,* i.e. *sow* (lit. or fig.):— sow (-er), receive seed.

4688. σπεκουλάτωρ **spĕkŏulatōr**, *spek-oo-lat´-ore;* of Lat. or.; a *speculator,* i.e. military *scout* (*spy* or [by extens.] *life-guardsman*):— executioner.

4689. σπένδω **spĕndō**, *spen´-do;* appar. a primary verb; to *pour* out as a libation, i.e. (fig.) to *devote* (one's life or blood, as a sacrifice) ("*spend*"):— (be ready to) be offered.

4690. σπέρμα **spĕrma**, *sper´-mah;* from *4687;* something *sown,* i.e. *seed* (incl. the male "*sperm*"); by impl. *offspring;* spec. a *remnant* (fig. as if kept over for planting):— issue, seed.

4691. σπερμολόγος **spĕrmŏlŏgŏs**, *sper-mol-og´-os;* from *4690* and *3004;* a *seed-picker* (as the crow), i.e. (fig.) a *sponger, loafer* (spec. a *gossip* or *trifler* in talk):— babbler.

4692. σπεύδω **spĕudō**, *spyoo´-do;* prob. strengthened from *4228;* to "*speed*" ("study"), i.e. *urge* on (diligently or earnestly); by impl. to *await* eagerly:— (make, with) haste unto.

4693. σπήλαιον **spēlaiŏn**, *spay´-lah-yon;* neut. of a presumed der. of σπέος **spĕŏs** (a *grotto*); a *cavern;* by impl. a *hiding-place* or *resort:*— cave, den.

4694. σπιλάς **spilas**, *spee-las´;* of uncert. der.; a *ledge* or *reef* of rock in the sea:— spot [by confusion with *4696*].

4695. σπιλόω **spilŏō**, *spee-lŏ´-o;* from *4696;* to *stain* or *soil* (lit. or fig.):— defile, spot.

4696. σπίλος **spilŏs**, *spee´-los;* of uncert. der.; a *stain* or *blemish,* i.e. (fig.) *defect, disgrace:*— spot.

4697. σπλαγχνίζομαι **splagchnizŏmai**, *splangkh-nid´-zom-ahee;* mid. voice from *4698;* to have the *bowels* yearn, i.e. (fig.) *feel sympathy,* to *pity:*— have (be moved with) compassion.

4698. σπλάγχνον **splagchnŏn**, *splangkh´-non;* prob. strengthened from σπλήν **splēn** (the "*spleen*"); an *intestine,* (plural); fig. *pity* or *sympathy:*— bowels, inward affection, + tender mercy.

4699. σπόγγος **spŏggŏs**, *spong´-gos;* perh. of for. or.; a "*sponge*":— spunge.

4700. σποδός **spŏdŏs**, *spod-os´;* of uncert. der.; *ashes:*— ashes.

4701. σπορά **spŏra**, *spor-ah´;* from *4687;* a *sowing,* i.e. (by impl.) *parentage:*— seed.

4702. σπόριμος **spŏrimŏs**, *spor´-ee-mos;* from *4703;* *sown,* i.e. (neut. plur.) a planted *field:*— corn (-field).

4703. σπόρος **spŏrŏs**, *spor´-os;* from *4687;* a

scattering (of seed), i.e. (concr.) *seed* (as sown):— seed (× sown).

4704. σπουδάζω **spŏudazō**, *spoo-dad´-zo;* from *4710;* to *use speed,* i.e. to *make effort, be prompt* or *earnest:*— do (give) diligence, be diligent (forward), endeavour, labour, study.

4705. σπουδαῖος **spŏudaiŏs**, *spoo-dah´-yos;* from *4710; prompt, energetic, earnest:*— diligent.

4706. σπουδαιότερον **spŏudaiŏtĕrŏn**, *spoo-dah-yot´-er-on;* neut. of *4707* as adv.; *more earnestly* than others, i.e. very *promptly:*— very diligently.

4707. σπουδαιότερος **spŏudaiŏtĕrŏs**, *spoo-dah-yot´-er-os;* comparative of *4705; more prompt, more earnest:*— more diligent (forward).

4708. σπουδαιοτέρως **spŏudaiŏtĕrōs**, *spoo-dah-yot-er´-oce;* adv. from *4707; more speedily,* i.e. *sooner* than otherwise:— more carefully.

4709. σπουδαίως **spŏudaiōs**, *spoo-dah´-yoce;* adv. from *4705; earnestly, promptly:*— diligently, instantly.

4710. σπουδή **spŏudē**, *spoo-day´;* from *4692;* "*speed*", i.e. (by impl.) *despatch, eagerness, earnestness:*— business, (earnest) care (-fulness), diligence, forwardness, haste.

4711. σπυρίς **spuris**, *spoo-rece´;* from *4687* (as *woven*); a *hamper* or *lunch-receptacle:*— basket.

4712. στάδιον **stadiŏn**, *stad´-ee-on;* or masc. (in plur.) στάδιος **stadiŏs**, *stad´-ee-os;* from the base of *2476,* (as *fixed*); a *stade* or certain measure of distance; by impl. a *stadium* or *race-course:*— furlong, race.

4713. στάμνος **stamnŏs**, *stam´-nos;* from the base of *2476* (as *stationary*); a *jar* or earthen *tank:*— pot.

4714. στάσις **stasis**, *stas´-is;* from the base of *2476;* a *standing* (prop. the act), i.e. (by anal.) *position* (*existence*); by impl. a popular *uprising;* fig. *controversy:*— dissension, insurrection, × standing, uproar.

4715. στατήρ **statēr**, *stat-air´;* from the base of *2746;* a *stander* (*standard* of value), i.e. (spec.) a *stater* or certain coin:— piece of money.

4716. σταυρός **staurŏs**, *stŏw-ros´;* from the base of *2476;* a *stake* or *post* (as *set* upright), i.e. (spec.) a *pole* or *cross* (as an instrument of capital punishment); fig. *exposure to death,* i.e. *self-denial;* by impl. the *atonement* of Christ:— cross.

4717. σταυρόω **staurŏō**, *stŏw-rŏ´-o;* from *4716;* to *impale* on the cross; fig. to *extinguish* (*subdue*) passion or selfishness:— crucify.

4718. σταφυλή **staphulē**, *staf-oo-lay´;* prob.

from the base of *4735;* a *cluster* of grapes (as if *intertwined*):— grapes.

4719. στάχυς **stachus**, *stakh´-oos;* from the base of *2476;* a *head* of grain (as *standing* out from the stalk):— ear (of corn).

4720. Στάχυς **Stachus**, *stakh´-oos;* the same as *4719; Stachys,* a Chr.:— Stachys.

4721. στέγη **stĕgē**, *steg´-ay;* strengthened from a primary τέγος **tĕgŏs** (a *"thatch"* or *"deck"* of a building); a *roof:*— roof.

4722. στέγω **stĕgō**, *steg´-o;* from *4721;* to *roof* over, i.e. (fig.) to *cover* with silence (*endure* patiently):— (for-) bear, suffer.

4723. στείρος **stĕirŏs**, *sti´-ros;* a contr. from *4731* (as *stiff* and *unnatural*); *"sterile":*— barren.

4724. στέλλω **stĕllō**, *stel´-lo;* prob. strengthened from the base of *2476;* prop. to *set* fast (*"stall"*), i.e. (fig.) to *repress* (refl. *abstain* from associating with):— avoid, withdraw self.

4725. στέμμα **stĕmma**, *stem´-mah;* from the base of *4735;* a *wreath* for show:— garland.

4726. στεναγμός **stĕnagmŏs**, *sten-ag-mos´;* from *4727;* a *sigh:*— groaning.

4727. στενάζω **stĕnazō**, *sten-ad´-zo;* from *4728;* to *make* (intr. *be*) *in straits,* i.e. (by impl.) to *sigh, murmur, pray* inaudibly:— with grief, groan, grudge, sigh.

4728. στενός **stĕnŏs**, *sten-os´;* prob. from the base of *2476; narrow* (from obstacles *standing* close about):— strait.

4729. στενοχωρέω **stĕnŏchōrĕō**, *sten-okh-o-reh´-o;* from the same as *4730;* to *hem* in closely, i.e. (fig.) *cramp:*— distress, straiten.

4730. στενοχωρία **stĕnŏchōria**, *sten-okh-o-ree´-ah;* from a compound of *4728* and *5561; narrowness of room,* i.e. (fig.) *calamity:*— anguish, distress.

4731. στερεός **stĕrĕŏs**, *ster-eh-os´;* from *2476; stiff,* i.e. *solid, stable* (lit. or fig.):— stedfast, strong, sure.

4732. στερεόω **stĕrĕŏō**, *ster-eh-ŏ´-o;* from *4731;* to *solidify,* i.e. *confirm* (lit. or fig.):— establish, receive strength, make strong.

4733. στερέωμα **stĕrĕōma**, *ster-eh´-o-mah;* from *4732;* something *established,* i.e. (abstr.) *confirmation* (*stability*):— stedfastness.

4734. Στεφανᾶς **Stĕphanas**, *stef-an-as´;* prob. contr. for στεφανωτός **stĕphanōtŏs** (*crowned;* from *4737*); *Stephanas,* a Chr.:— Stephanas.

4735. στέφανος **stĕphanŏs**, *stef´-an-os;* from an appar. primary στέφω **stĕphō** (to *twine* or *wreathe*); a *chaplet,* (as a badge of royalty, a prize in the public games or a symbol of honor gen.; but more conspicuous and elaborate than the simple *fillet, 1238*), lit. or fig.:— crown.

4736. Στέφανος **Stĕphanŏs**, *stef´-an-os;* the same as *4735; Stephanus,* a Chr.:— Stephen.

4737. στεφανόω **stephanŏō**, *stef-an-ŏ´-o;* from

4735; to *adorn with* an honorary *wreath* (lit. or fig.):— crown.

4738. στῆθος **stēthŏs**, *stay´-thos;* from *2476* (as *standing* prominently); the (entire extern.) *bosom,* i.e. *chest:*— breast.

4739. στήκω **stēkō**, *stay´-ko;* from the perfect tense of *2476;* to *be stationary,* i.e. (fig.) to *persevere:*— stand (fast).

4740. στηριγμός **stērigmŏs**, *stay-rig-mos´;* from *4741; stability* (fig.):— stedfastness.

4741. στηρίζω **stērizō**, *stay-rid´-zo;* from a presumed der. of *2476* (like *4731*); to *set fast,* i.e. (lit.) to *turn resolutely* in a certain direction, or (fig.) to *confirm:*— fix, (e-) stablish, stedfastly set, strengthen.

4742. στίγμα **stigma**, *stig´-mah;* from a primary στίζω **stizō** (to *"stick"*, i.e. *prick*); a *mark* incised or punched (for recognition of ownership), i.e. (fig.) *scar* of service:— mark.

4743. στιγμή **stigmē**, *stig-may´;* fem. of *4742;* a *point* of time, i.e. an *instant:*— moment.

4744. στίλβω **stilbō**, *stil´-bo;* appar. a primary verb; to *gleam,* i.e. *flash* intensely:— shining.

4745. στοά **stŏa**, *stŏ-ah´;* prob. from *2476;* a *colonnade* or interior *piazza:*— porch.

4746. στοιβάς **stŏibas**, *stoy-bas´* or

στιβάς **stibas**, *stee-bas´;* from a primary στείβω **stĕibō** (to *"step"* or *"stamp"*); a *spread* (as if *tramped* flat) of loose materials for a couch, i.e. (by impl.) a *bough* of a tree so employed:— branch.

4747. στοιχεῖον **stŏichĕiŏn**, *stoy-khi´-on;* neut. of a presumed der. of the base of *4748;* something *orderly* in arrangement, i.e. (by impl.) a *serial* (*basal, fundamental, initial*) constituent (lit.), proposition (fig.):— element, principle, rudiment.

4748. στοιχέω **stŏichĕō**, *stoy-kheh´-o;* from a der. of στείχω **stĕichō** (to *range* in regular line); to *march,* in (military) rank (*keep step*), i.e. (fig.) to *conform* to virtue and piety:— walk (orderly).

4749. στολή **stŏlē**, *stol-ay´;* from *4724; equipment,* i.e. (spec.) a *"stole"* or long-fitting *gown* (as a mark of dignity):— long clothing (garment), (long) robe.

4750. στόμα **stŏma**, *stom´-a;* prob. strengthened from a presumed der. of the base of *5114;* the *mouth* (as if a *gash* in the face); by impl. *language* (and its relations); fig. an *opening* (in the earth); spec. the *front* or *edge* (of a weapon):— edge, face, mouth.

4751. στόμαχος **stŏmachŏs**, *stom´-akh-os;* from *4750;* an *orifice* (the *gullet*), i.e. (spec.) the *"stomach":*— stomach.

4752. στρατεία **stratĕia**, *strat-i´-ah;* from *4754;* military *service,* i.e. (fig.) the apostolic *career* (as one of hardship and danger):— warfare.

4753. στράτευμα **stratĕuma**, *strat´-yoo-mah;* from *4754;* an *armament,* i.e. (by impl.) a body of *troops* (more or less extensive or systematic):— army, soldier, man of war.

4754. στρατεύομαι **stratĕuŏmai**, *strat-yoo´-om-ahee;* mid. voice from the base of *4756;* to *serve* in a military campaign; fig. to *execute the apostolate* (with its arduous duties and functions), to *contend* with carnal inclinations:— soldier, (go to) war (-fare).

4755. στρατηγός **stratēgŏs**, *strat-ay-gos´;* from the base of *4756* and *71* or *2233;* a *general,* i.e. (by impl. or anal.) a (military) *governor* (*prætor*), the chief (præfect) of the (Levitical) temple-wardens:— captain, magistrate.

4756. στρατία **stratia**, *strat-ee´-ah;* fem. of a der. of στρατός **stratŏs**, (an *army;* from the base of *4766,* as *encamped*); *camp-likeness,* i.e. an *army,* i.e. (fig.) the *angels,* the celestial *luminaries:*— host.

4757. στρατιώτης **stratiōtēs**, *strat-ee-o´-tace;* from a presumed der. of the same as *4756;* a *camper-out,* i.e. a (common) *warrior* (lit. or fig.):— soldier.

4758. στρατολογέω **stratŏlŏgĕō**, *strat-ol-og-eh´-o;* from a compound of the base of *4756* and *3004* (in its orig. sense); to *gather* (or *select*) as a *warrior,* i.e. *enlist* in the army:— choose to be a soldier.

4759. στρατοπεδάρχης **stratŏpĕdarchēs**, *strat-op-ed-ar´-khace;* from *4760* and *757;* a *ruler of an army,* i.e. (spec.) a Prætorian *præfect:*— captain of the guard.

4760. στρατόπεδον **stratŏpĕdŏn**, *strat-op´-ed-on;* from the base of *4756* and the same as *3977;* a *camping-ground,* i.e. (by impl.) a body of *troops:*— army.

4761. στρεβλόω **strĕblŏō**, *streb-lŏ´-o;* from a der. of *4762;* to *wrench,* i.e. (spec.) to *torture* (by the rack), but only fig. to *pervert:*— wrest.

4762. στρέφω **strĕphō**, *stref´-o;* strengthened from the base of *5157;* to *twist,* i.e. *turn* quite around or *reverse* (lit. or fig.):— convert, turn (again, back again, self, self about).

4763. στρηνιάω **strēniaō**, *stray-nee-ah´-o;* from a presumed der. of *4764;* to *be luxurious:*— live deliciously.

4764. στρῆνος **strēnŏs**, *stray´-nos;* akin to *4731;* a "*straining*", "*strenuousness*" or "strength", i.e. (fig.) *luxury* (*voluptuousness*):— delicacy.

4765. στρουθίον **strŏuthiŏn**, *stroo-thee´-on;* dimin. of στρουθός **strŏuthŏs** (a *sparrow*); a *little sparrow:*— sparrow.

4766. στρώννυμι **strōnnumi**, *strone´-noo-mee;* or simpler

στρωννύω **strōnnuō**, *strone-noo´-o;* prol. from a still simpler

στρόω **strŏō**, *strŏ´-o* (used only as an alt.

in certain tenses; prob. akin to *4731* through the idea of *positing*); to "*strew*", i.e. *spread* (as a carpet or couch):— make bed, furnish, spread, strew.

4767. στυγνητός **stugnētŏs**, *stoog-nay-tos´;* from a der. of an obs. appar. primary στύγω **stugō** (to *hate*); *hated,* i.e. *odious:*— hateful.

4768. στυγνάζω **stugnazō**, *stoog-nad´-zo;* from the same as *4767;* to *render gloomy,* i.e. (by impl.) *glower* (*be overcast* with clouds, or *sombreness* of speech):— lower, be sad.

4769. στῦλος **stulŏs**, *stoo´-los;* from στύω **stuō** (to *stiffen;* prop. akin to the base of *2476*); a *post* ("*style*"), i.e. (fig.) *support:*— pillar.

4770. Στωϊκός **Stōïkŏs**, *sto-ik-os´;* from *4745;* a "*Stoïc*" (as occupying a particular porch in Athens), i.e. adherent of a certain philosophy:— Stoick.

4771. σύ **su**, *soo;* the pers. pron. of the second pers. sing.; *thou:*— thou. See also *4571, 4671, 4675;* and for the plur. *5209, 5210, 5213, 5216.*

4772. συγγένεια **suggĕnĕia**, *soong-ghen´-i-ah;* from *4773; relationship,* i.e. (concr.) *relatives:*— kindred.

4773. συγγενής **suggĕnēs**, *soong-ghen-ace´;* from *4862* and *1085;* a *relative* (by blood); by extens. a fellow *countryman:*— cousin, kin (-sfolk, -sman).

4774. συγγνώμη **suggnōmē**, *soong-gno´-may;* from a compound of *4862* and *1097; fellow knowledge,* i.e. *concession:*— permission.

4775. συγκάθημαι **sugkathēmai**, *soong-kath´-ay-mahee;* from *4862* and *2521;* to *seat oneself* in company *with:*— sit with.

4776. συγκαθίζω **sugkathizō**, *soong-kath-id´-zo;* from *4862* and *2523;* to *give* (or *take*) *a seat* in company *with:*— (make) sit (down) together.

4777. συγκακοπαθέω **sugkakŏpathĕō**, *soong-kak-op-ath-eh´-o;* from *4862* and *2553;* to *suffer hardship* in company *with:*— be partaker of afflictions.

4778. συγκακουχέω **sugkakŏuchĕō**, *soong-kak-oo-kheh´-o;* from *4862* and *2558;* to *maltreat* in company *with,* i.e. (pass.) *endure persecution together:*— suffer affliction with.

4779. συγκαλέω **sugkalĕō**, *soong-kal-eh´-o;* from *4862* and *2564;* to *convoke:*— call together.

4780. συγκαλύπτω **sugkaluptō**, *soong-kal-oop´-to;* from *4862* and *2572;* to *conceal altogether:*— cover.

4781. συγκάμπτω **sugkamptō**, *soong-kamp´-to;* from *4862* and *2578;* to *bend together,* i.e. (fig.) to *afflict:*— bow down.

4782. συγκαταβαίνω **sugkatabainō**, *soong-*

kat-ab-ah´-ee-no; from *4862* and *2597;* to *descend* in company *with:*— go down with.

4783. συγκατάθεσις **sugkatathĕsis,** *soong-kat-ath´-es-is;* from *4784;* a *deposition* (of sentiment) in company *with,* i.e. (fig.) *accord* with:— agreement.

4784. συγκατατίθεμαι **sugkatatithĕmai,** *soong-kat-at-ith´-em-ahee;* mid. from *4862* and *2698;* to *deposit* (one's vote or opinion) in company *with,* i.e. (fig.) to *accord* with:— consent.

4785. συγκαταψηφίζω **sugkatapsēphizō,** *soong-kat-aps-ay-fid´-zo;* from *4862* and a compound of *2596* and *5585;* to *count down* in company *with,* i.e. *enroll among:*— number with.

4786. συγκεράννυμι **sugkĕrannumi,** *soong-ker-an´-noo-mee;* from *4862* and *2767;* to *commingle,* i.e. (fig.) to *combine* or *assimilate:*— mix with, temper together.

4787. συγκινέω **sugkinĕō,** *soong-kin-eh´-o;* from *4682* and *2795;* to *move together,* i.e. (spec.) to *excite* as a mass (to sedition):— stir up.

4788. συγκλείω **sugklĕiō,** *soong-kli´-o;* from *4862* and *2808;* to *shut together,* i.e. *include* or (fig.) *embrace* in a common subjection to:— conclude, inclose, shut up.

4789. συγκληρονόμος **sugklērŏnŏmŏs,** *soong-klay-ron-om´-os;* from *4862* and *2818;* a *co-heir,* i.e. (by anal.) *participant in common:*— fellow (joint)-heir, heir together, heir with.

4790. συγκοινωνέω **sugkŏinōnĕō,** *soong-koy-no-neh´-o;* from *4862* and *2841;* to *share* in company *with,* i.e. *co-participate* in:— communicate (have fellowship) with, be partaker of.

4791. συγκοινωνός **sugkŏinōnŏs,** *soong-koy-no-nos´;* from *4862* and *2844;* a *co-participant:*— companion, partake (-r, -r with).

4792. συγκομίζω **sugkŏmizō,** *soong-kom-id´-zo;* from *4862* and *2865;* to *convey together,* i.e. *collect* or *bear* away in company *with* others:— carry.

4793. συγκρίνω **sugkrinō,** *soong-kree´-no;* from *4862* and *2919;* to *judge* of one thing in connection *with* another, i.e. *combine* (spiritual ideas with appropriate expressions) or *collate* (one person with another by way of contrast or resemblance):— compare among (with).

4794. συγκύπτω **sugkuptō,** *soong-koop´-to;* from *4862* and *2955;* to *stoop altogether,* i.e. *be completely overcome* by:— bow together.

4795. συγκυρία **sugkuria,** *soong-koo-ree´-ah;* from a compound of *4862* and κυρέω **kurĕō,** (to *light* or *happen;* from the base of *2962);* con*currence,* i.e. *accident:*— chance.

4796. συγχαίρω **sugchairō,** *soong-khah´-ee-ro;* from *4862* and *5463;* to *sympathize in gladness,* congratulate:— rejoice in (with).

4797. συγχέω **sugchĕō,** *soong-kheh´-o;* or

συγχύνω **sugchunō,** *soong-khoo´-no;* from *4862* and χέω **chĕō** (to *pour*) or its alt.; to *commingle,* promiscuously, i.e. (fig.) to *throw* (an assembly) *into disorder,* to *perplex* (the mind):— confound, confuse, stir up, be in an uproar.

4798. συγχράομαι **sugchraŏmai,** *soong-khrah´-om-ahee;* from *4862* and *5530;* to *use jointly,* i.e. (by impl.) to *hold intercourse in common:*— have dealings with.

4799. σύγχυσις **sugchusis,** *soong´-khoo-sis;* from *4797; commixture,* i.e. (fig.) riotous *disturbance:*— confusion.

4800. συζάω **suzaō,** *sood-zah´-o;* from *4862* and *2198;* to *continue to live* in common *with,* i.e. *co-survive* (lit. or fig.):— live with.

4801. συζεύγνυμι **suzĕugnumi,** *sood-zyoog´-noo-mee;* from *4862* and the base of *2201;* to *yoke together,* i.e. (fig.) *conjoin* (in marriage):— join together.

4802. συζητέω **suzētĕō,** *sood-zay-teh´-o;* from *4862* and *2212;* to *investigate jointly,* i.e. *discuss, controvert, cavil:*— dispute (with), enquire, question (with), reason (together).

4803. συζήτησις **suzētēsis,** *sood-zay´-tay-sis;* from *4802; mutual questioning,* i.e. *discussion:*— disputation (-ting), reasoning.

4804. συζητητής **suzētētēs,** *sood-zay-tay-tace´;* from *4802;* a *disputant,* i.e. *sophist:*— disputer.

4805. σύζυγος **suzugŏs,** *sood´-zoo-gos;* from *4801; co-yoked,* i.e. (fig.) as noun, a *colleague;* prob. rather as a proper name; *Syzygus,* a Chr.:— yokefellow.

4806. συζωοποιέω **suzōŏpŏiĕō,** *sood-zo-op-oy-eh´-o;* from *4862* and *2227;* to *reanimate conjointly* with (fig.):— quicken together with.

4807. συκάμινος **sukaminŏs,** *soo-kam´-ee-nos;* of Heb. or. [8256] in imitation of *4809;* a *sycamore*-fig tree:— sycamine tree.

4808. συκῆ **sukē,** *soo-kay´;* from *4810;* a *fig-tree:*— fig tree.

4809. συκομωραία **sukŏmōraia,** *soo-kom-o-rah´-yah;* from *4810* and μόρον **mŏrŏn** (the *mulberry*); the "*sycamore*"-fig tree:— sycamore tree. Comp. *4807.*

4810. σῦκον **sukŏn,** *soo´-kon;* appar. a primary word; a *fig:*— fig.

4811. συκοφαντέω **sukŏphantĕō,** *soo-kof-an-teh´-o;* from a compound of *4810* and a der. of *5316;* to *be a fig-informer* (reporter of the law forbidding the exportation of figs from Greece), "*sycophant*", i.e. (gen. and by extens.) to *defraud* (*exact* unlawfully, *extort*):— accuse falsely, take by false accusation.

4812. συλαγωγέω **sulagōgĕō,** *soo-lag-ogue-eh´-o;* from the base of *4813* and (the redupl. form of) 71; to *lead* away as *booty*, i.e. (fig.) *seduce:*— spoil.

4813. συλάω **sulaō**, *soo-lah´-o;* from a der. of σύλλω **sullō** (to *strip;* prob. akin to 138; comp. 4661); to *despoil:*— rob.

4814. συλλαλέω **sullaleō**, *sool-lal-eh´-o;* from 4862 and 2980; to *talk together,* i.e. *converse:*— commune (confer, talk) with, speak among.

4815. συλλαμβάνω **sullambanō**, *sool-lam-ban´-o;* from 4862 and 2983; to *clasp,* i.e. *seize* (*arrest, capture*); spec. to *conceive* (lit. or fig.); by impl. to *aid:*— catch, conceive, help, take.

4816. συλλέγω **sullĕgō**, *sool-leg´-o;* from 4862 and 3004 in its orig. sense; to *collect:*— gather (together, up).

4817. συλλογίζομαι **sullŏgizŏmai**, *sool-log-id´-zom-ahee;* from 4862 and 3049; to *reckon together* (with oneself), i.e. *deliberate:*— reason with.

4818. συλλυπέω **sullupĕō**, *sool-loop-eh´-o;* from 4862 and 3076; to *afflict jointly,* i.e. (pass.) *sorrow at* (on account of) someone:— be grieved.

4819. συμβαίνω **sumbainō**, *soom-bah´-ee-no;* from 4862 and the base of 939; to *walk* (fig. *transpire*) *together,* i.e. *concur* (*take place*):— be (-fall), happen (unto).

4820. συμβάλλω **sumballō**, *soom-bal´-lo;* from 4862 and 906; to *combine,* i.e. (in speaking) to *converse, consult, dispute,* (mentally) to *consider,* (by impl.) to *aid,* (personally) to *join, attack:*— confer, encounter, help, make, meet with, ponder.

4821. συμβασιλεύω **sumbasilĕuō**, *soom-bas-il-yoo´-o;* from 4862 and 936; to *be co-regent* (fig.):— reign with.

4822. συμβιβάζω **sumbibazō**, *soom-bib-ad´-zo;* from 4862 and βιβάζω **bibazō** (to *force;* caus. [by redupl.] of the base of 939); to *drive together,* i.e. *unite* (in association or affection), (mentally) to *infer, show, teach:*— compact, assuredly gather, intrust, knit together, prove.

4823. συμβουλεύω **sumbŏulĕuō**, *soom-bool-yoo´-o;* from 4862 and 1011; to *give* (or *take*) *advice jointly,* i.e. *recommend, deliberate* or *determine:*— consult, (give, take) counsel (together).

4824. συμβούλιον **sumbŏuliŏn**, *soom-boo´-lee-on;* neut. of a presumed der. of 4825; *advisement;* spec. a *deliberative* body, i.e. the provincial *assessors* or lay-court:— consultation, counsel, council.

4825. σύμβουλος **sumbŏulŏs**, *soom´-boo-los;* from 4862 and 1012; a *consultor,* i.e. *adviser:*— counsellor.

4826. Συμεών **Sumeōn**, *soom-eh-one´;* from the same as 4613; *Symeon* (i.e. *Shimon*), the name of five Isr.:— Simeon, Simon.

4827. συμμαθητής **summathētēs**, *soom-math-ay-tace´;* from a compound of 4862 and 3129; a *co-learner* (of Christianity):— fellowdisciple.

4828. συμμαρτυρέω **summarturĕō**, *soom-mar-too-reh´-o;* from 4862 and 3140; to *testify jointly,* i.e. *corroborate* by (concurrent) evidence:— testify unto, (also) bear witness (with).

4829. συμμερίζομαι **summĕrizŏmai**, *soom-mer-id´-zom-ahee;* mid. voice from 4862 and 3307; to *share jointly,* i.e. *participate in:*— be partaker with.

4830. συμμέτοχος **summĕtŏchŏs**, *soom-met´-okh-os;* from 4862 and 3353; a *co-participant:*— partaker.

4831. συμμιμητής **summimētēs**, *soom-mim-ay-tace´;* from a presumed compound of 4862 and 3401; a *co-imitator,* i.e. *fellow votary:*— follower together.

4832. συμμορφός **summŏrphŏs**, *soom-mor-fos´;* from 4862 and 3444; *jointly formed,* i.e. (fig.) *similar:*— conformed to, fashioned like unto.

4833. συμμορφόω **summŏrphŏō**, *soom-mor-fŏ´-o;* from 4832; to *render like,* i.e. (fig.) to *assimilate:*— make conformable unto.

4834. συμπαθέω **sumpathĕō**, *soom-path-eh´-o;* from 4835; to *feel "sympathy"* with, i.e. (by impl.) to *commiserate:*— have compassion, be touched with a feeling of.

4835. συμπαθής **sumpathēs**, *soom-path-ace´;* from 4841; *having a fellow-feeling* ("*sympathetic*"), i.e. (by impl.) *mutually commiserative:*— having compassion one of another.

4836. συμπαραγίνομαι **sumparaginŏmai**, *soom-par-ag-in´-om-ahee;* from 4862 and 3854; to *be present together,* i.e. to *convene;* by impl. to *appear in aid:*— come together, stand with.

4837. συμπαρακαλέω **sumparakalĕō**, *soom-par-ak-al-eh´-o;* from 4862 and 3870; to *console jointly:*— comfort together.

4838. συμπαραλαμβάνω **sumparalambanō**, *soom-par-al-am-ban´-o;* from 4862 and 3880; to *take along in company:*— take with.

4839. συμπαραμένω **sumparamĕnō**, *soom-par-am-en´-o;* from 4862 and 3887; to *remain in company,* i.e. *still live:*— continue with.

4840. συμπάρειμι **sumparĕimi**, *soom-par´-i-mee;* from 4862 and 3918; to *be at hand together,* i.e. *now present:*— be here present with.

4841. συμπάσχω **sumpaschō**, *soom-pas´-kho;* from 4862 and 3958 (incl. its alt.); to *experience pain jointly* or of the *same kind* (spec. *persecution;* to "*sympathize*"):— suffer with.

4842. συμπέμπω **sumpĕmpō**, *soom-pem´-*

po; from *4862* and *3992;* to *dispatch in company:*— send with.

4843. συμπεριλαμβάνω **sumpĕrilambanō**, *soom-per-ee-lam-ban´-o;* from *4862* and a compound of *4012* and *2983;* to *take by enclosing altogether,* i.e. *earnestly throw the arms about one:*— embrace.

4844. συμπίνω **sumpinō**, *soom-pee´-no;* from *4862* and *4095;* to *partake a beverage in company:*— drink with.

4845. συμπληρόω **sumplērŏō**, *soom-play-rŏ´-o;* from *4862* and *4137;* to *implenish completely,* i.e. (of space) to *swamp* (a boat), or (of time) to *accomplish* (pass. be *complete*):— (fully) come, fill up.

4846. συμπνίγω **sumpnigō**, *soom-pnee´-go;* from *4862* and *4155;* to *strangle completely,* i.e. (lit.) to *drown,* or (fig.) to *crowd:*— choke, throng.

4847. συμπολίτης **sumpŏlitēs**, *soom-pol-ee´-tace;* from *4862* and *4177;* a *native of the same town,* i.e. (fig.) *co-religionist (fellow-Christian):*— fellow-citizen.

4848. συμπορεύομαι **sumpŏrĕuŏmai**, *soom-por-yoo´-om-ahee;* from *4862* and *4198;* to *journey together;* by impl. to *assemble:*— go with, resort.

4849. συμπόσιον **sumpŏsiŏn**, *soom-pos´-ee-on;* neut. of a der. of the alt. of *4844;* a *drinking*-party *("symposium"),* i.e. (by extens.) a *room* of guests:— company.

4850. συμπρεσβύτερος **sumprĕsbutĕrŏs**, *soom-pres-boo´-ter-os;* from *4862* and *4245;* a *co-presbyter:*— presbyter, also an elder.

συμφάγω **sumphagō**. See *4906.*

4851. συμφέρω **sumphĕrō**, *soom-fer´-o;* from *4862* and *5342* (incl. its alt.); to *bear together (contribute),* i.e. (lit.) to *collect,* or (fig.) to *conduce;* espec. (neut. part. as a noun) *advantage:*— be better for, bring together, be expedient (for), be good, (be) profit (-able for).

4852. σύμφημι **sumphēmi**, *soom´-fay-mee;* from *4862* and *5346;* to *say jointly,* i.e. *assent to:*— consent unto.

4853. συμφυλέτης **sumphulĕtēs**, *soom-foo-let´-ace;* from *4862* and a der. of *5443;* a *co-tribesman,* i.e. *native of the same country:*— countryman.

4854. σύμφυτος **sumphutŏs**, *soom´-foo-tos;* from *4862* and a der. of *5453; grown* along *with (connate),* i.e. (fig.) closely *united* to:— planted together.

4855. συμφύω **sumphuō**, *soom-foo´-o;* from *4862* and *5453;* pass. to *grow jointly:*— spring up with.

4856. συμφωνέω **sumphōnĕō**, *soom-fo-neh´-o;* from *4859;* to be *harmonious,* i.e. (fig.) to *accord (be suitable, concur)* or *stipulate* (by compact):— agree (together, with).

4857. συμφώνησις **sumphōnēsis**, *soom-fo-nay-sis;* from *4856; accordance:*— concord.

4858. συμφωνία **sumphōnia**, *soom-fo-nee´-ah;* from *4859; unison* of sound ("*symphony*"), i.e. a *concert* of instruments (harmonious *note*):— music.

4859. σύμφωνος **sumphōnŏs**, *soom´-fo-nos;* from *4862* and *5456; sounding together (alike),* i.e. (fig.) *accordant* (neut. as noun, *agreement*):— consent.

4860. συμψηφίζω **sumpsēphizō**, *soom-psay-fid´-zo;* from *4862* and *5585;* to *compute jointly:*— reckon.

4861. σύμψυχος **sumpsuchŏs**, *soom´-psoo-khos;* from *4862* and *5590; co-spirited,* i.e. *similar in sentiment:*— like-minded.

4862. σύν **sun**, *soon;* a primary prep. denoting *union; with* or *together* (but much closer than *3326* or *3844*), i.e. by association, companionship, process, resemblance, possession, instrumentality, addition, etc.:— beside, with. [In composition, it has similar applications, including *completeness.*]

4863. συνάγω **sunagō**, *soon-ag´-o;* from *4862* and *71;* to *lead together,* i.e. *collect* or *convene;* spec. to *entertain* (hospitably):— + accompany, assemble (selves, together), bestow, come together, gather (selves together, up, together), lead into, resort, take in.

4864. συναγωγή **sunagōgē**, *soon-ag-o-gay´;* from (the redupl. form of) *4863;* an *assemblage* of persons; spec. a Jewish "*synagogue*" (the meeting or the place); by anal. a Christian *church:*— assembly, congregation, synagogue.

4865. συναγωνίζομαι **sunagōnizŏmai**, *soon-ag-o-nid´-zom-ahee;* from *4862* and *75;* to *struggle* in company *with,* i.e. (fig.) to *be a partner (assistant):*— strive together with.

4866. συναθλέω **sunathlĕō**, *soon-ath-leh´-o;* from *4862* and *118;* to *wrestle* in company *with,* i.e. (fig.) to *seek jointly:*— labour with, strive together for.

4867. συναθροίζω **sunathrŏizō**, *soon-ath-royd´-zo;* from *4862* and ἀθροίζω **athrŏizō** (to *hoard*); to *convene:*— call (gather) together.

4868. συναίρω **sunairō**, *soon-ah´-ee-ro;* from *4862* and *142;* to *make up together,* i.e. (fig.) to *compute* (an account):— reckon, take.

4869. συναιχμάλωτος **sunaichmalōtŏs**, *soon-aheekh-mal´-o-tos;* from *4862* and *164;* a *co-captive:*— fellowprisoner.

4870. συνακολουθέω **sunakŏlŏuthĕō**, *soon-ak-ol-oo-theh´-o;* from *4862* and *190;* to *accompany:*— follow.

4871. συναλίζω **sunalizō**, *soon-al-id´-zo;* from *4862* and ἀλίζω **halizō** (to *throng*); to *accumulate,* i.e. *convene:*— assemble together.

4872. συναναβαίνω **sunanabainō**, *soon-an-ab-ah´-ee-no;* from *4862* and *305;* to *ascend* in company *with:*— come up with.

4873. συνανάκειμαι **sunanakĕimai**, *soon-an-ak´-i-mahee;* from *4862* and *345;* to *recline* in company *with* (at a meal):— sit (down, at the table, together) with (at meat).

4874. συναναμίγνυμι **sunanamignumi**, *soon-an-am-ig´-noo-mee;* from *4862* and a compound of *303* and *3396;* to *mix up together,* i.e. (fig.) *associate with:*— (have, keep) company (with).

4875. συναναπαύομαι **sunanapauŏmai**, *soon-an-ap-ŏw´-om-ahee;* mid. voice from *4862* and *373;* to *recruit oneself* in company *with:*— refresh with.

4876. συναντάω **sunantaō**, *soon-an-tah´-o;* from *4862* and a der. of *473;* to *meet with;* fig. to *occur:*— befall, meet.

4877. συνάντησις **sunantēsis**, *soon-an´-tay-sis;* from *4876;* a *meeting with:*— meet.

4878. συναντιλαμβάνομαι **sunantilambanŏmai**, *soon-an-tee-lam-ban´-om-ahee;* from *4862* and *482;* to *take* hold of *opposite together,* i.e. *co-operate* (*assist*):— help.

4879. συναπάγω **sunapagō**, *soon-ap-ag´-o;* from *4862* and *520;* to *take off together,* i.e. *transport with* (*seduce,* pass. *yield*):— carry (lead) away with, condescend.

4880. συναποθνήσκω **sunapŏthnēskō**, *soon-ap-oth-nace´-ko;* from *4862* and *599;* to *decease* (lit.) in company *with,* or (fig.) similarly *to:*— be dead (die) with.

4881. συναπόλλυμι **sunapŏllumi**, *soon-ap-ol´-loo-mee;* from *4862* and *622;* to *destroy* (middle or passive voice be *slain*) in company *with:*— perish with.

4882. συναποστέλλω **sunapŏstĕllō**, *soon-ap-os-tel´-lo;* from *4862* and *649;* to *despatch* (on an errand) in company *with:*— send with.

4883. συναρμολογέω **sunarmŏlŏgĕō**, *soon-ar-mol-og-eh´-o;* from *4862* and a der. of a compound of *719* and *3004* (in its orig. sense of *laying*); to *render close-jointed together,* i.e. *organize compactly:*— be fitly framed (joined) together.

4884. συναρπάζω **sunarpazō**, *soon-ar-pad´-zo;* from *4862* and *726;* to *snatch together,* i.e. *seize:*— catch.

4885. συναυξάνω **sunauxanō**, *soon-ŏwx-an´-o;* from *4862* and *837;* to *increase* (*grow up*) *together:*— grow together.

4886. σύνδεσμος **sundĕsmŏs**, *soon´-des-mos;* from *4862* and *1199;* a *joint tie,* i.e. *ligament,* (fig.) *uniting principle, control:*— band, bond.

4887. συνδέω **sundĕō**, *soon-deh´-o;* from *4862* and *1210;* to *bind with,* i.e. (pass.) *be a fellow-prisoner* (fig.):— be bound with.

4888. συνδοξάζω **sundŏxazō**, *soon-dox-ad´-zo;* from *4862* and *1392;* to *exalt* to dignity in company (i.e. *similarly*) *with:*— glorify together.

4889. σύνδουλος **sundŏulŏs**, *soon´-doo-los;* from *4862* and *1401;* a *co-slave,* i.e. *servitor* or *ministrant of the same master* (human or divine):— fellowservant.

συνδρέμω **sundrĕmō**. See *4936.*

4890. συνδρομή **sundrŏmē**, *soon-drom-ay´;* from (the alt. of) *4936;* a *running together,* i.e. (riotous) *concourse:*— run together.

4891. συνεγείρω **sunĕgĕirō**, *soon-eg-i´-ro;* from *4862* and *1453;* to *rouse* (from death) in company *with,* i.e. (fig.) to *revivify* (spiritually) in resemblance to:— raise up together, rise with.

4892. συνέδριον **sunĕdriŏn**, *soon-ed´-ree-on;* neut. of a presumed der. of a compound of *4862* and the base of *1476;* a *joint session,* i.e. (spec.) the Jewish *Sanhedrin;* by anal. a subordinate *tribunal:*— council.

4893. συνείδησις **sunĕidēsis**, *soon-i´-day-sis;* from a prol. form of *4894;* co-perception, i.e. moral *consciousness:*— conscience.

4894. συνείδω **sunĕidō**, *soon-i´-do;* from *4862* and *1492;* to *see completely;* used (like its primary) only in two past tenses, respectively mean. to *understand* or *become aware,* and to *be conscious* or (clandestinely) *informed of:*— consider, know, be privy, be ware of.

4895. σύνειμι **sunĕimi**, *soon´-i-mee;* from *4862* and *1510* (incl. its various inflections); to *be in company with,* i.e. *present* at the time:— be with.

4896. σύνειμι **sunĕimi**, *soon´-i-mee;* from *4862* and εἶμι **ĕimi** (to *go*); to *assemble:*— gather together.

4897. συνεισέρχομαι **sunĕisĕrchŏmai**, *soon-ice-er´-khom-ahee;* from *4862* and *1525;* to *enter* in company *with:*— go in with, go with into.

4898. συνέκδημος **sunĕkdēmŏs**, *soon-ek´-day-mos;* from *4862* and the base of *1553;* a *co-absentee* from home, i.e. *fellow-traveller:*— companion in travel, travel with.

4899. συνεκλεκτός **sunĕklĕktŏs**, *soon-ek-lek-tos´;* from a compound of *4862* and *1586;* chosen in company *with,* i.e. *co-elect* (*fellow Christian*):— elected together with.

4900. συνελαύνω **sunĕlaunō**, *soon-el-ow´-no;* from *4862* and *1643;* to *drive together,* i.e. (fig.) *exhort* (to reconciliation):— + set at one again.

4901. συνεπιμαρτυρέω **sunĕpimarturĕō**, *soon-ep-ee-mar-too-reh´-o;* from *4862* and *1957;* to *testify further jointly,* i.e. *unite in adding evidence:*— also bear witness.

4902. συνέπομαι **sunĕpŏmai**, *soon-ep´-om-ahee;* mid. voice from *4862* and a primary ἕπω **hĕpō** (to *follow*); to *attend* (*travel*) in company *with:*— accompany.

4903. συνεργέω **sunĕrgĕō**, *soon-erg-eh´-o;* from *4904;* to *be a fellow-worker,* i.e. *co-operate:*— help (work) with, work (-er) together.

4904. συνεργός **sunĕrgŏs**, *soon-er-gos´;* from a presumed compound of *4862* and the base of *2041;* a *co-laborer,* i.e. *coadjutor:*— companion in labour, (fellow-) helper (-labourer, -worker), labourer together with, workfellow.

4905. συνέρχομαι **sunĕrchŏmai**, *soon-er´-khom-ahee;* from *4862* and *2064;* to *convene, depart* in company *with, associate* with, or (spec.) *cohabit* (conjugally):— accompany, assemble (with), come (together), come (company, go) with, resort.

4906. συνεσθίω **sunĕsthiō**, *soon-es-thee´-o;* from *4862* and *2068* (incl. its alt.); to *take food* in company *with:*— eat with.

4907. σύνεσις **sunĕsis**, *soon´-es-is;* from *4920;* a mental *putting together,* i.e. *intelligence* or (concr.) the *intellect:*— knowledge, understanding.

4908. συνετός **sunĕtŏs**, *soon-et´-os;* from *4920;* mentally *put* (or *putting*) *together,* i.e. *sagacious:*— prudent. Comp. *5429.*

4909. συνευδοκέω **sunĕudŏkĕō**, *soon-yoo-dok-eh´-o;* from *4862* and *2106;* to *think well of in common,* i.e. *assent to, feel gratified with:*— allow, assent, be pleased, have pleasure.

4910. συνευωχέω **sunĕuōchĕō**, *soon-yoo-o-kheh´-o;* from *4862* and a der. of a presumed compound of *2095* and a der. of *2192* (mean. to *be in good condition,* i.e. [by impl.] to *fare well,* or *feast*); to *entertain* sumptuously in company *with,* i.e. (middle or passive voice) to *revel together:*— feast with.

4911. συνεφίστημι **sunĕphistēmi**, *soon-ef-is´-tay-mee;* from *4862* and *2186;* to *stand up together,* i.e. to *resist* (or *assault*) *jointly:*— rise up together.

4912. συνέχω **sunĕchō**, *soon-ekh´-o;* from *4862* and *2192;* to *hold together,* i.e. to *compress* (the ears, with a crowd or siege) or *arrest* (a prisoner); fig. to *compel, perplex, afflict, preoccupy:*— constrain, hold, keep in, press, lie sick of, stop, be in a strait, straiten, be taken with, throng.

4913. συνήδομαι **sunēdŏmai**, *soon-ay´-dom-ahee;* mid. voice from *4862* and the base of *2237;* to *rejoice in with* oneself, i.e. *feel satisfaction* concerning:— delight.

4914. συνήθεια **sunēthĕia**, *soon-ay´-thi-ah;* from a compound of *4862* and *2239; mutual habituation,* i.e. *usage:*— custom.

4915. συνηλικιώτης **sunēlikiōtēs**, *soon-ay-lik-ee-o´-tace;* from *4862* and a der. of *2244;* a *co-aged* person, i.e. *alike* in years:— equal.

4916. συνθάπτω **sunthaptō**, *soon-thap´-to;* from *4862* and *2290;* to *inter* in company *with,* i.e. (fig.) to *assimilate* spiritually (to Christ by a sepulture as to sin):— bury with.

4917. συνθλάω **sunthlaō**, *soon-thlah´-o;* from

4862 and θλάω **thlaō** (to *crush*); to *dash together,* i.e. *shatter:*— break.

4918. συνθλίβω **sunthlibō**, *soon-thlee´-bo;* from *4862* and *2346;* to *compress,* i.e. *crowd* on all sides:— throng.

4919. συνθρύπτω **sunthruptō**, *soon-throop´-to;* from *4862* and θρύπτω **thruptō** (to *crumble*); to *crush together,* i.e. (fig.) to *dispirit:*— break.

4920. συνίημι **suniēmi**, *soon-ee´-ay-mee;* from *4862* and ἵημι **hiēmi** (to *send*); to *put together,* i.e. (mentally) to *comprehend;* by impl. to *act piously:*— consider, understand, be wise.

4921. συνιστάω **sunistaō**, *soon-is-tah´-o;* or (strengthened)

　　συνιστάνω **sunistanō**, *soon-is-tan´-o;* or

　　συνίστημι **sunistēmi**, *soon-is´-tay-mee;* from *4862* and *2476* (incl. its collat. forms); to *set together,* i.e. (by impl.) to *introduce* (favorably), or (fig.) to *exhibit;* intr. to *stand near,* or (fig.) to *constitute:*— approve, commend, consist, make, stand (with).

4922. συνοδεύω **sunŏdĕuō**, *soon-od-yoo´-o;* from *4862* and *3593;* to *travel* in company *with:*— journey with.

4923. συνοδία **sunŏdia**, *soon-od-ee´-ah;* from a compound of *4862* and *3598* ("*synod*"); *companionship* on a journey, i.e. (by impl.) a *caravan:*— company.

4924. συνοικέω **sunŏikĕō**, *soon-oy-keh´-o;* from *4862* and *3611;* to *reside together* (as a family):— dwell together.

4925. συνοικοδομέω **sunŏikŏdŏmĕō**, *soon-oy-kod-om-eh´-o;* from *4862* and *3618;* to *construct,* i.e. (pass.) to *compose* (in company with other Christians, fig.):— build together.

4926. συνομιλέω **sunŏmilĕō**, *soon-om-il-eh´-o;* from *4862* and *3656;* to *converse* mutually:— talk with.

4927. συνομορέω **sunŏmŏrĕō**, *soon-om-or-eh´-o;* from *4862* and a der. of a compound of the base of *3674* and the base of *3725;* to *border together,* i.e. *adjoin:*— join hard.

4928. συνοχή **sunŏchē**, *soon-okh-ay´;* from *4912; restraint,* i.e. (fig.) *anxiety:*— anguish, distress.

4929. συντάσσω **suntassō**, *soon-tas-so;* from *4862* and *5021;* to *arrange jointly,* i.e. (fig.) to *direct:*— appoint.

4930. συντέλεια **suntĕlĕia**, *soon-tel´-i-ah;* from *4931; entire completion,* i.e. *consummation* (of a dispensation):— end.

4931. συντελέω **suntĕlĕō**, *soon-tel-eh´-o;* from *4862* and *5055;* to *complete entirely;* gen. to *execute* (lit. or fig.):— end, finish, fulfil, make.

4932. συντέμνω **suntĕmnō**, *soon-tem´-no;* from *4862* and the base of *5114;* to *contract* by cutting, i.e. (fig.) *do concisely* (*speedily*):— (cut) short.

4933. συντηρέω **suntērĕō**, *soon-tay-reh´-o;* from *4862* and *5083;* to *keep* closely *together,* i.e. (by impl.) to *conserve* (from ruin); ment. to *remember* (and *obey*):— keep, observe, preserve.

4934. συντίθεμαι **suntithĕmai**, *soon-tith´-em-ahee;* mid. voice from *4862* and *5087;* to *place jointly,* i.e. (fig.) to *consent* (*bargain, stipulate*), *concur:*— agree, assent, covenant.

4935. συντόμως **suntŏmōs**, *soon-tom´-oce;* adv. from a der. of *4932; concisely* (*briefly*):— a few words.

4936. συντρέχω **suntrĕchō**, *soon-trekh´-o;* from *4862* and *5143* (incl. its alt.); to *rush together* (hastily *assemble*) or *headlong* (fig.):— run (together, with).

4937. συντρίβω **suntribō**, *soon-tree´-bo;* from *4862* and the base of *5147;* to *crush completely,* i.e. to *shatter* (lit. or fig.):— break (in pieces), broken to shivers (+ -hearted), bruise.

4938. σύντριμμα **suntrimma**, *soon-trim´-mah;* from *4937; concussion* or utter *fracture* (prop. concr.), i.e. complete *ruin:*— destruction.

4939. σύντροφος **suntrŏphŏs**, *soon´-trof-os;* from *4862* and *5162* (in a pass. sense); a *fellow-nursling,* i.e. *comrade:*— brought up with.

4940. συντυγχάνω **suntugchanō**, *soon-toong-khan´-o;* from *4862* and *5177;* to *chance together,* i.e. *meet* with (*reach*):— come at.

4941. Συντύχη **Suntuchē**, *soon-too´-khay;* from *4940;* an *accident; Syntyche,* a Chr. female:— Syntyche.

4942. συνυποκρίνομαι **sunupŏkrinŏmai**, *soon-oo-pok-rin´-om-ahee;* from *4862* and *5271;* to *act hypocritically* in concert *with:*— dissemble with.

4943. συνυπουργέω **sunupŏurgĕō**, *soon-oop-oorg-eh´-o;* from *4862* and a der. of a compound of *5259* and the base of *2041;* to *be a co-auxiliary,* i.e. *assist:*— help together.

4944. συνωδίνω **sunōdinō**, *soon-o-dee´-no;* from *4862* and *5605;* to *have* (parturition) *pangs* in company (concert, simultaneously) *with,* i.e. (fig.) to *sympathize* (in expectation of relief from suffering):— travail in pain together.

4945. συνωμοσία **sunōmŏsia**, *soon-o-mos-ee´-ah;* from a compound of *4862* and *3660;* a *swearing together,* i.e. (by impl.) a *plot:*— conspiracy.

4946. Συράκουσαι **Surakŏusai**, *soo-rak´-oo-sahee;* plur. of uncert. der.; *Syracuse,* the capital of Sicily:— Syracuse.

4947. Συρία **Suria**, *soo-ree´-ah;* prob. of Heb. or. [6865]; *Syria* (i.e. *Tsyria* or *Tyre*), a region of Asia:— Syria.

4948. Σύρος **Surŏs**, *soo´-ros;* from the same as *4947;* a *Syran* (i.e. prob. *Tyrian*), a native of Syria:— Syrian.

4949. Συροφοίνισσα **Surŏphŏinissa**, *soo-rof-oy´-nis-sah;* fem. of a compound of *4948* and the same as *5403;* a *Syro-phœnician* woman, i.e. a female native of Phœnicia in Syria:— Syrophenician.

4950. σύρτις **surtis**, *soor´-tis;* from *4951;* a *shoal* (from the sand *drawn* thither by the waves), i.e. the *Syrtis* Major or great bay on the N. coast of Africa:— quicksands.

4951. σύρω **surō**, *soo´-ro;* prob. akin to *138;* to *trail:*— drag, draw, hale.

4952. συσπαράσσω **susparassō**, *soos-par-as´-so;* from *4862* and *4682;* to *rend completely,* i.e. (by anal.) to *convulse* violently:— throw down.

4953. σύσσημον **sussēmŏn**, *soos´-say-mon;* neut. of a compound of *4862* and the base of *4591;* a *sign in common,* i.e. preconcerted *signal:*— token.

4954. σύσσωμος **sussōmŏs**, *soos´-so-mos;* from *4862* and *4983; of a joint body,* i.e. (fig.) a *fellow-member* of the Chr. community:— of the same body.

4955. συστασιαστής **sustasiastēs**, *soos-tas-ee-as-tace´;* from a compound of *4862* and a der. of *4714;* a *fellow-insurgent:*— make insurrection with.

4956. συστατικός **sustatikŏs**, *soos-tat-ee-kos´;* from a der. of *4921; introductory,* i.e. *recommendatory:*— of commendation.

4957. συσταυρόω **sustaurŏō**, *soos-tow-rŏ´-o;* from *4862* and *4717;* to *impale* in company *with* (lit. or fig.):— crucify with.

4958. συστέλλω **sustĕllō**, *soos-tel´-lo;* from *4862* and *4724;* to *send* (*draw*) *together,* i.e. *enwrap* (enshroud a corpse for burial), *contract* (an interval):— short, wind up.

4959. συστενάζω **sustĕnazō**, *soos-ten-ad´-zo;* from *4862* and *4727;* to *moan jointly,* i.e. (fig.) *experience a common calamity:*— groan together.

4960. συστοιχέω **sustŏichĕō**, *soos-toy-kheh´-o;* from *4862* and *4748;* to *file together* (as soldiers in ranks), i.e. (fig.) to *correspond* to:— answer to.

4961. συστρατιώτης **sustratiōtēs**, *soos-trat-ee-o´-tace;* from *4862* and *4757;* a *co-campaigner,* i.e. (fig.) an *associate* in Chr. toil:— fellowsoldier.

4962. συστρέφω **sustrĕphō**, *soos-tref´-o;* from *4862* and *4762;* to *twist together,* i.e. *collect* (a bundle, a crowd):— gather.

4963. συστροφή **sustrŏphē**, *soos-trof-ay´;* from *4962;* a *twisting together,* i.e. (fig.) a secret *coalition,* riotous *crowd:*— + band together, concourse.

4964. συσχηματίζω **suschēmatizō**, *soos-khay-mat-id´-zo;* from *4862* and a der. of

4976; to *fashion alike*, i.e. *conform* to the same pattern (fig.):— conform to, fashion self according to.

4965. Συχάρ **Suchar**, *soo-khar´*; of Heb. or. [7941]; *Sychar* (i.e. *Shekar*), a place in Pal.:— Sychar.

4966. Συχέμ **Suchĕm**, *soo-khem´*; of Heb. or. [7927]; *Sychem* (i.e. *Shekem*), the name of a Canaanite and of a place in Pal.:— Sychem.

4967. σφαγή **sphagē**, *sfag-ay´*; from 4969; *butchery* (of animals for food or sacrifice, or [fig.] of men [*destruction*]):— slaughter.

4968. σφάγιον **sphagiŏn**, *sfag´-ee-on*; neut. of a der. of 4967; a *victim* (in sacrifice):— slain beast.

4969. σφάζω **sphazo**, *sfad´-zo*; a primary verb; to *butcher* (espec. an animal for food or in sacrifice) or (gen.) to *slaughter*, or (spec.) to *maim* (violently):— kill, slay, wound.

4970. σφόδρα **sphŏdra**, *sfod´-rah*; neut. plur. of σφοδρός **sphŏdrŏs**, (*violent*; of uncert. der.) as adv.; *vehemently*, i.e. in a *high degree*, *much*:— exceeding (-ly), greatly, sore, very.

4971. σφοδρῶς **sphŏdrōs**, *sfod-roce´*; adv. from the same as 4970; *very much*:— exceedingly.

4972. σφραγίζω **sphragizō**, *sfrag-id´-zo*; from 4973; to *stamp* (with a signet or private mark) for security or preservation (lit. or fig.); by impl. to *keep secret*, to *attest*:— (set a, set to) seal up, stop.

4973. σφραγίς **sphragis**, *sfrag-ece´*; prob. strengthened from 5420; a *signet* (as *fencing* in or protecting from misappropriation); by impl. the *stamp* impressed (as a mark of privacy, or genuineness), lit. or fig.:— seal.

4974. σφυρόν **sphurŏn**, *sfoo-ron´*; neut. of a presumed der. prob. of the same as σφαῖρα **sphaira** (a *ball*, "*sphere*;" compare the fem. σφῦρα **sphura**, a *hammer*); the *ankle* (as *globular*):— ancle bone.

4975. σχεδόν **schĕdŏn**, *skhed-on´*; neut. of a presumed der. of the alt. of 2192 as adv.; *nigh*, i.e. *nearly*:— almost.

σχέω **schĕō**. See 2192.

4976. σχῆμα **schēma**, *skhay´-mah*; from the alt. of 2192; a *figure* (as a *mode* or *circumstance*), i.e. (by impl.) extern. *condition*:— fashion.

4977. σχίζω **schizō**, *skhid´-zo*; appar. a primary verb; to *split* or *sever* (lit. or fig.):— break, divide, open, rend, make a rent.

4978. σχίσμα **schisma**, *skhis´-mah*; from 4977; a *split* or *gap* ("*schism*"), lit. or fig.:— division, rent, schism.

4979. σχοινίον **schŏiniŏn**, *skhoy-nee´-on*; dimin. of σχοῖνος **schŏinŏs** (a *rush* or *flag*-plant; of uncert. der.); a *rushlet*, i.e. *grass-withe* or *tie* (gen.):— small cord, rope.

4980. σχολάζω **schŏlazo**, *skhol-ad´-zo*; from 4981; to *take a holiday*, i.e. *be at leisure* for (by

impl. *devote oneself* wholly to); fig. to *be vacant* (of a house):— empty, give self.

4981. σχολή **schŏlē**, *skhol-ay´*; prob. fem. of a presumed der. of the alt. of 2192; prop. *loitering* (as a *withholding* of oneself from work) or *leisure*, i.e. (by impl.) a "*school*" (as *vacation* from phys. employment):— school.

4982. σώζω **sōzō**, *sode´-zo*; from a primary σῶς **sōs** (contr. for obs. σάος **saŏs**, "*safe*"); to *save*, i.e. *deliver* or *protect* (lit. or fig.):— heal, preserve, save (self), do well, be (make) whole.

4983. σῶμα **sōma**, *so´-mah*; from 4982; the *body* (as a *sound* whole), used in a very wide application, lit. or fig.:— bodily, body, slave.

4984. σωματικός **sōmatikŏs**, *so-mat-ee-kos´*; from 4983; *corporeal* or *physical*:— bodily.

4985. σωματικῶς **sōmatikŏs**, *so-mat-ee-koce´*; adv. from 4984; *corporeally* or *physically*:— bodily.

4986. Σώπατρος **Sōpatrŏs**, *so´-pat-ros*; from the base of 4982 and 3962; *of a safe father*; *Sopatrus*, a Chr.:— Sopater. Comp. 4989.

4987. σωρεύω **sōrĕuō**, *sore-yoo´-o*; from another form of 4673; to *pile* up (lit. or fig.):— heap, load.

4988. Σωσθένης **Sōsthĕnēs**, *soce-then´-ace*; from the base of 4982 and that of 4599; *of safe strength*; *Sosthenes*, a Chr.:— Sosthenes.

4989. Σωσίπατρος **Sōsipatrŏs**, *so-sip´-at-ros*; prol. for 4986; *Sosipatrus*, a Chr.:— Sosipater.

4990. σωτήρ **sōtēr**, *so-tare´*; from 4982; a *deliverer*, i.e. God or Christ:— saviour.

4991. σωτηρία **sōtēria**, *so-tay-ree´-ah*; fem. of a der. of 4990 as (prop. abstr.) noun; *rescue* or *safety* (phys. or mor.):— deliver, health, salvation, save, saving.

4992. σωτήριον **sōtēriŏn**, *so-tay´-ree-on*; neut. of the same as 4991 as (prop. concr.) noun; *defender* or (by impl.) *defence*:— salvation.

4993. σωφρονέω **sōphrŏnĕō**, *so-fron-eh´-o*; from 4998; to *be of sound mind*, i.e. *sane*, (fig.) *moderate*:— be in right mind, be sober (minded), soberly.

4994. σωφρονίζω **sōphrŏnizō**, *so-fron-id´-zo*; from 4998; to *make of sound mind*, i.e. (fig.) to *discipline* or *correct*:— teach to be sober.

4995. σωφρονισμός **sōphrŏnismŏs**, *so-fron-is-mos´*; from 4994; *discipline*, i.e. *self-control*:— sound mind.

4996. σωφρόνως **sōphrŏnŏs**, *so-fron´-oce*; adv. from 4998; *with sound mind*, i.e. *moderately*:— soberly.

4997. σωφροσύνη **sōphrŏsunē**, *so-fros-oo-´*

nay; from *4998; soundness of mind,* i.e. (lit.) *sanity* or (fig.) *self-control:*— soberness, sobriety.

4998. σώφρων **sōphrōn,** *so´-frone;* from the base of *4982* and that of *5424; safe (sound)* in *mind,* i.e. *self-controlled (moderate* as to opinion or passion):— discreet, sober, temperate.

T

τά **ta.** See *3588.*

4999. Ταβέρναι **Tabĕrnai,** *tab-er´-nahee* or

Ταβερνῶν **Tabĕrnōn,** *tab-er-non´;* plur. of Lat. or.; *huts* or *wooden-walled* buildings; *Tabernæ:*— taverns.

5000. Ταβιθά **Tabitha,** *tab-ee-thah´;* of Chald. or. [comp. 6646]; *the gazelle; Tabitha* (i.e. *Tabjetha),* a Chr. female:— Tabitha.

5001. τάγμα **tagma,** *tag´-mah;* from *5021;* something orderly in *arrangement* (a troop), i.e. (fig.) a *series* or *succession:*— order.

5002. τακτός **taktŏs,** *tak-tos´;* from *5021; arranged,* i.e. *appointed* or *stated:*— set.

5003. ταλαιπωρέω **talaipōrĕō,** *tal-ahee-po-reh´-o;* from *5005;* to *be wretched,* i.e. *realize* one's own *misery:*— be afflicted.

5004. ταλαιπωρία **talaipōria,** *tal-ahee-po-ree´-ah;* from *5005; wretchedness,* i.e. *calamity:*— misery.

5005. ταλαίπωρος **talaipōrŏs,** *tal-ah´-ee-po-ros;* from the base of *5007* and a der. of the base of *3984; enduring trial,* i.e. *miserable:*— wretched.

5006. ταλαντιαῖος **talantiaiŏs,** *tal-an-tee-ah´-yos;* from *5007; talent-like* in weight:— weight of a talent.

5007. τάλαντον **talantŏn,** *tal´-an-ton;* neut. of a presumed der. of the orig. form of τλάω **tlaō** (to *bear;* equiv. to *5342);* a *balance* (as *supporting* weights), i.e. (by impl.) a certain *weight* (and thence a *coin* or rather *sum* of money) or "*talent*":— talent.

5008. ταλιθά **talitha,** *tal-ee-thah´;* of Chald. or. [comp. 2924]; *the fresh,* i.e. *young girl; talitha* (Ō *maiden*):— talitha.

5009. ταμεῖον **tamĕiŏn,** *tam-i´-on;* neut. contr. of a presumed der. of ταμίας **tamias** (a *dispenser* or *distributor;* akin to τέμνω **tĕmnō,** to *cut*); a *dispensary* or *magazine,* i.e. a chamber on the ground-floor or interior of an Oriental house (gen. used for *storage* or *privacy,* a spot for retirement):— secret chamber, closet, storehouse.

τανῦν **tanun.** See *3568.*

5010. τάξις **taxis,** *tax´-is;* from *5021;* reg. *arrangement,* i.e. (in time) fixed *succession* (of rank or character), official *dignity:*— order.

5011. ταπεινός **tapĕinŏs,** *tap-i-nos´;* of uncert. der.; *depressed,* i.e. (fig.) *humiliated* (in cir-

cumstances or disposition):— base, cast down, humble, of low degree (estate), lowly.

5012. ταπεινοφροσύνη **tapĕinŏphrŏsunē,** *tap-i-nof-ros-oo´-nay;* from a compound of *5011* and the base of *5424; humiliation of mind,* i.e. *modesty:*— humbleness of mind, humility (of mind), loneliness (of mind).

5013. ταπεινόω **tapĕinŏō,** *tap-i-nŏ´-o;* from *5011;* to *depress;* fig. to *humiliate* (in condition or heart):— abase, bring low, humble (self).

5014. ταπείνωσις **tapĕinōsis,** *tap-i´-no-sis;* from *5013; depression* (in rank or feeling):— humiliation, be made low, low estate, vile.

5015. ταράσσω **tarassō,** *tar-as´-so;* of uncert. aff.; to *stir* or *agitate* (*roil* water):— trouble.

5016. ταραχή **tarachē,** *tar-akh-ay´;* fem. from *5015; disturbance,* i.e. (of water) *roiling,* or (of a mob) *sedition:*— trouble (-ing).

5017. τάραχος **tarachŏs,** *tar´-akh-os;* masc. from *5015;* a *disturbance,* i.e. (popular) *tumult:*— stir.

5018. Ταρσεύς **Tarsĕus,** *tar-syoos´;* from *5019;* a *Tarsean,* i.e. native of Tarsus:— of Tarsus.

5019. Ταρσός **Tarsŏs,** *tar-sos´;* perh. the same as ταρσός **tarsŏs** (a *flat* basket); *Tarsus,* a place in Asia Minor:— Tarsus.

5020. ταρταρόω **tartarŏō,** *tar-tar-ŏ´-o;* from Τάρταρος **Tartarŏs,** (the deepest *abyss* of Hades); to *incarcerate* in eternal torment:— cast down to hell.

5021. τάσσω **tassō,** *tas´-so;* a prol. form of a primary verb (which latter appears only in certain tenses); to *arrange* in an orderly manner, i.e. *assign* or *dispose* (to a certain position or lot):— addict, appoint, determine, ordain, set.

5022. ταῦρος **taurŏs,** *tow´-ros;* appar. a primary word [comp. 8450, "*steer*"]; a *bullock:*— bull, ox.

5023. ταῦτα **tauta,** *tŏw´-tah;* nominative or acc. neut. plur. of *3778; these* things:— + afterward, follow, + hereafter, × him, the same, so, such, that, then, these, they, this, those, thus.

5024. ταὐτά **tauta,** *tŏw-tah´;* neut. plur. of *3588* and *846* as adv.; in *the same* way:— even thus, (manner) like, so.

5025. ταύταις **tautais,** *tŏw´-taheece;* and

ταύτας **tautas,** *tŏw´-tas;* dat. and acc. fem. plur. respectively of *3778;* (*to* or *with* or *by,* etc.) *these:*— hence, that, then, these, those.

5026. ταύτῃ **tautēi,** *tŏw´-tay;* and

ταύτην **tautēn,** *tŏw´-tane;* and

ταύτης **tautēs,** *tŏw´-tace;* dat., acc. and gen. respectively of the fem. sing. of

Greek

3778; (*toward* or *of*) *this:*— her, + hereof, it, that, + thereby, the (same), this (same).

5027. ταφή **taphē**, *taf-ay´;* fem. from *2290; burial* (the act):— × bury.

5028. τάφος **taphŏs**, *taf´-os;* masc. from *2290;* a *grave* (the place of interment):— sepulchre, tomb.

5029. τάχα **tacha**, *takh´-ah;* as if neut. plur. of *5036* (adv.); *shortly,* i.e. (fig.) *possibly:*— peradventure (-haps).

5030. ταχέως **tachĕōs**, *takh-eh´-oce;* adv. from *5036; briefly,* i.e. (in time) *speedily,* or (in manner) *rapidly:*— hastily, quickly, shortly, soon, suddenly.

5031. ταχινός **tachinŏs**, *takh-ee-nos´;* from *5034; curt,* i.e. *impending:*— shortly, swift.

5032. τάχιον **tachiŏn**, *takh´-ee-on;* neut. sing. of the comp. of *5036* (as adv.); *more swiftly,* i.e. (in manner) *more rapidly,* or (in time) *more speedily:*— out [run], quickly, shortly, sooner.

5033. τάχιστα **tachista**, *takh´-is-tah;* neut. plur. of the superl. of *5036* (as adv.); *most quickly,* i.e. (with *5613* pref.) *as soon* as possible:— + with all speed.

5034. τάχος **tachŏs**, *takh´-os;* from the same as *5036;* a *brief* space (of time), i.e. (with *1722* pref.) in *haste:*— + quickly, + shortly, + speedily.

5035. ταχύ **tachu**, *takh-oo´;* neut. sing. of *5036* (as adv.); *shortly,* i.e. *without delay, soon,* or (by surprise) *suddenly,* or (by impl. of ease) *readily:*— lightly, quickly.

5036. ταχύς **tachus**, *takh-oos´;* of uncert. aff.; *fleet,* i.e. (fig.) *prompt* or *ready:*— swift.

5037. τε **tĕ**, *teh;* a primary particle (enclitic) of connection or addition; *both* or *also* (prop. as correl. of *2532*):— also, and, both, even, then, whether. Often used in comp., usually as the latter part.

5038. τεῖχος **teichŏs**, *ti´-khos;* akin to the base of *5088;* a *wall* (as *formative* of a house):— wall.

5039. τεκμήριον **tĕkmēriŏn**, *tek-may´-ree-on;* neut. of a presumed der. of τεκμάρ **tĕkmar** (a *goal* or fixed *limit*); a *token,* (as *defining* a fact), i.e. *criterion* of certainty:— infallible proof.

5040. τεκνίον **tĕkniŏn**, *tek-nee´-on;* dimin. of *5043;* an *infant,* i.e. (plur. fig.) *darlings* (Chr. converts):— little children.

5041. τεκνογονέω **tĕknŏgŏnĕō**, *tek-nog-on-eh´-o;* from a compound of *5043* and the base of *1096;* to *be a child-bearer,* i.e. *parent* (*mother*):— bear children.

5042. τεκνογονία **tĕknŏgŏnia**, *tek-nog-on-ee´-ah;* from the same as *5041; childbirth* (*parentage*), i.e. (by impl.) *maternity* (the performance of *maternal duties*):— childbearing.

5043. τέκνον **tĕknŏn**, *tek´-non;* from the base

of *5098;* a *child* (as *produced*):— child, daughter, son.

5044. τεκνοτροφέω **tĕknŏtrŏphĕō**, *tek-not-rof-eh´-o;* from a compound of *5043* and *5142;* to *be a child-rearer,* i.e. *fulfil* the duties of a *female parent:*— bring up children.

5045. τέκτων **tĕktōn**, *tek´-tone;* from the base of *5098;* an *artificer* (as *producer* of fabrics), i.e. (spec.) a *craftsman* in wood:— carpenter.

5046. τέλειος **tĕlĕiŏs**, *tel-i-os;* from *5056; complete* (in various applications of labor, growth, ment. and mor. character, etc.); neut. (as noun, with *3588*) *completeness:*— of full age, man, perfect.

5047. τελειότης **tĕlĕiŏtēs**, *tel-i-ot´-ace;* from *5046;* (the state) *completeness* (ment. or mor.):— perfection (-ness).

5048. τελειόω **tĕlĕiŏō**, *tel-i-ŏ´-o;* from *5046;* to *complete,* i.e. (lit.) *accomplish,* or (fig.) *consummate* (in character):— consecrate, finish, fulfil, make) perfect.

5049. τελείως **tĕlĕiŏs**, *tel-i´-oce;* adv. from *5046; completely,* i.e. (of hope) *without wavering:*— to the end.

5050. τελείωσις **tĕlĕiōsis**, *tel-i´-o-sis;* from *5448;* (the act) *completion,* i.e. (of prophecy) *verification,* or (of expiation) *absolution:*— perfection, performance.

5051. τελειωτής **tĕlĕiōtēs**, *tel-i-o-tace´;* from *5048;* a *completer,* i.e. *consummater:*— finisher.

5052. τελεσφορέω **tĕlĕsphŏrĕō**, *tel-es-for-eh´-o;* from a compound of *5056* and *5342;* to *be a bearer to completion* (maturity), i.e. to *ripen* fruit (fig.):— bring fruit to perfection.

5053. τελευτάω **tĕlĕutaō**, *tel-yoo-tah´-o;* from a presumed der. of *5055;* to *finish* life (by impl. of *979*), i.e. *expire* (demise):— be dead, decease, die.

5054. τελευτή **tĕlĕutē**, *tel-yoo-tay´;* from *5053; decease:*— death.

5055. τελέω **tĕlĕō**, *tel-eh´-o;* from *5056;* to *end,* i.e. *complete, execute, conclude, discharge* (a debt):— accomplish, make an end, expire, fill up, finish, go over, pay, perform.

5056. τέλος **tĕlŏs**, *tel´-os;* from a primary τέλλω **tĕllō**, (to *set out* for a def. point or goal); prop. the point aimed at as a *limit,* i.e. (by impl.) the *conclusion* of an act or state (*termination* [lit., fig. or indef.], *result* [immed., ultimate or prophetic], *purpose*); spec. an *impost* or *levy* (as *paid*):— + continual, custom, end (-ing), finally, uttermost. Comp. *5411.*

5057. τελώνης **tĕlōnēs**, *tel-o´-nace;* from *5056* and *5608;* a *tax-farmer,* i.e. *collector of* public *revenue:*— publican.

5058. τελώνιον **tĕlōniŏn**, *tel-o´-nee-on;* neut.

of a presumed der. of *5057;* a *tax-gatherer's* place of business:— receipt of custom.

5059. τέρας **tĕras,** *ter´-as;* of uncert. aff.; a *prodigy* or *omen:*— wonder.

5060. Τέρτιος **Tĕrtiŏs,** *ter´-tee-os;* of Lat. or.; *third; Tertius,* a Chr.:— Tertius.

5061. Τέρτυλλος **Tĕrtullŏs,** *ter´-tool-los;* of uncert. der.; *Tertullus,* a Rom.:— Tertullus.

τέσσαρα **tĕssara.** See *5064.*

5062. τεσσαράκοντα **tĕssarakŏnta,** *tes-sar-ak´-on-tah;* the decade of *5064; forty:*— forty.

5063. τεσσαρακονταετής **tĕssarakŏntaĕtēs,** *tes-sar-ak-on-tah-et-ace´;* from *5062* and *2094; of forty years* of age:— (+ full, of) forty years (old).

5064. τέσσαρες **tĕssarĕs,** *tes´-sar-es;* neut.

τέσσαρα **tĕssara,** *tes´-sar-ah;* a plur. number; *four:*— four.

5065. τεσσαρεσκαιδέκατος **tĕssarĕskaidĕkatŏs,** *tes-sar-es-kahee-dek´-at-os;* from *5064* and *2532* and *1182; fourteenth:*— fourteenth.

5066. τεταρταῖος **tĕtartaiŏs,** *tet-ar-tah´-yos;* from *5064;* pertaining to the *fourth* day:— four days.

5067. τέταρτος **tĕtartŏs,** *tet´-ar-tos;* ord. from *5064; fourth:*— four (-th).

5068. τετράγωνος **tĕtragōnŏs,** *tet-rag´-o-nos;* from *5064* and *1137; four-cornered,* i.e. *square:*— foursquare.

5069. τετράδιον **tĕtradiŏn,** *tet-rad´-ee-on;* neut. of a presumed der. of τέτρας **tĕtras** (a *tetrad;* from *5064);* a *quaternion,* or squad (picket) of four Rom. soldiers:— quaternion.

5070. τετρακισχίλιοι **tĕtrakischiliŏi,** *tet-rak-is-khil´-ee-oy;* from the mult. adv. of *5064* and *5507; four times a thousand:*— four thousand.

5071. τετρακόσιοι **tĕtrakŏsiŏi,** *tet-rak-os´-ee-oy;* neut. τετρακόσια **tĕtrakŏsia,** *tet-rak-os´-ee- ah;* plur. from *5064* and *1540; four hundred:*— four hundred.

5072. τετράμηνον **tĕtramēnŏn,** *tet-ram´-ay-non;* neut. of a compound of *5064* and *3376;* a *four months'* space:— four months.

5073. τετραπλόος **tĕtraplŏŏs,** *tet-rap-lŏ´-os;* from *5064* and a der. of the base of *4118; quadruple:*— fourfold.

5074. τετράπους **tĕtrapŏus,** *tet-rap´-ooce;* from *5064* and *4228;* a *quadruped:*— four-footed beast.

5075. τετραρχέω **tĕtrarchĕō,** *tet-rar-kheh´-o;* from *5076;* to *be a tetrarch:*— (be) tetrarch.

5076. τετράρχης **tĕtrarchēs,** *tet-rar´-khace;* from *5064* and *757;* the *ruler of a fourth* part of a country ("*tetrarch*"):— tetrarch.

τεύχω **tĕuchō.** See *5177.*

5077. τεφρόω **tĕphrŏō,** *tef-rŏ´-o;* from τέφρα **tephra,** (*ashes*) to *incinerate,* i.e. *consume:*— turn to ashes.

5078. τέχνη **tĕchnē,** *tekh´-nay;* from the base of *5088; art* (as *productive*), i.e. (spec.) a *trade,* or (gen.) *skill:*— art, craft, occupation.

5079. τεχνίτης **tĕchnitēs,** *tekh-nee´-tace;* from *5078;* an *artisan;* fig. a *founder (Creator):*— builder, craftsman.

5080. τήκω **tēkō,** *tay´-ko;* appar. a primary verb; to *liquefy:*— melt.

5081. τηλαυγῶς **tēlaugōs,** *tay-lŏw-goce´;* adv. from a compound of a der. of *5056* and *827;* in a *far-shining* manner, i.e. *plainly:*— clearly.

5082. τηλικοῦτος **tēlikŏutŏs,** *tay-lik-oo´-tos;* fem.

τηλικαύτη **tēlikautē,** *tay-lik-ŏw´-tay;* from a compound of *3588* with *2245* and *3778; such as this,* i.e. (in [fig.] magnitude) *so vast:*— so great, so mighty.

5083. τηρέω **tērĕō,** *tay-reh´-o;* from τερός **tĕrŏs,** (a *watch;* perh. akin to *2334*); to *guard* (from *loss* or *injury,* prop. by keeping *the eye* upon; and thus differing from *5442,* which is prop. to *prevent* escaping; and from *2892,* which implies a *fortress* or full military lines of apparatus), i.e. to *note* (a prophecy); fig. to *fulfil* a command); by impl. to *detain* (in custody; fig. to *maintain);* by extens. to *withhold* (for personal ends; fig. to *keep unmarried*):— hold fast, keep (-er), (pre-, re-) serve, watch.

5084. τήρησις **tērēsis,** *tay´-ray-sis;* from *5083;* a *watching,* i.e. (fig.) *observance,* or (concr.) a *prison:*— hold.

τῇ **tēi,** τήν **tēn,** τῆς **tēs.** See *3588.*

5085. Τιβεριάς **Tibĕrias,** *tib-er-ee-as´;* from *5086; Tiberias,* the name of a town and a lake in Pal.:— Tiberias.

5086. Τιβέριος **Tibĕriŏs,** *tib-er´-ee-os;* of Lat. or.; prob. *pertaining to the* river *Tiberis* or *Tiber; Tiberius,* a Rom. emperor:— Tiberius.

5087. τίθημι **tithēmi,** *tith´-ay-mee;* a prol. form of a primary

θέω **thĕō,** *theh´-o* (which is used only as alt. in certain tenses); to *place* (in the widest application, lit. and fig.; prop. in a pass. or horizontal posture, and thus different from *2476,* which prop. denotes an upright and active position, while *2749* is prop. refl. and utterly prostrate):— + advise, appoint, bow, commit, conceive, give, × kneel down, lay (aside, down, up), make, ordain, purpose, put, set (forth), settle, sink down.

5088. τίκτω **tiktō,** *tik´-to;* a strengthened form of a primary τέκω **tekō,** *tek´-o* (which is used only as alt. in certain tenses); to *produce* (from seed, as a mother, a plant, the earth, etc.), lit. or fig.:— bear, be born, bring forth, be delivered, be in travail.

5089. τίλλω **tillō**, *til´-lo;* perh. akin to the alt. of *138,* and thus to *4951;* to *pull* off:— pluck.

5090. Τίμαιος **Timaiŏs**, *tim´-ah-yos;* prob. of Chald. or. [comp. 2931]; *Timæus* (i.e. *Timay*), an Isr.:— Timæus.

5091. τιμάω **timaō**, *tim-ah´-o;* from *5093;* to *prize,* i.e. *fix a valuation* upon; by impl. to *revere:*— honour, value.

5092. τιμή **timē**, *tee-may´;* from *5099;* a *value,* i.e. *money* paid, or (concr. and collect.) *valuables;* by anal. *esteem* (espec. of the highest degree), or the *dignity* itself:— honour, precious, price, some.

5093. τίμιος **timiŏs**, *tim´-ee-os;* including the comparative

τιμιώτερος **timiŏtĕrŏs**, *tim-ee-o´-ter-os;* and the superlative

τιμιώτατος **timiŏtatŏs**, *tim-ee-o´-tat-os;* from *5092;* *valuable,* i.e. (obj.) *costly,* or (subj.) *honored, esteemed,* or (fig.) *beloved:*— dear, honourable, (more, most) precious, had in reputation.

5094. τιμιότης **timiŏtēs**, *tim-ee-ot´-ace;* from *5093;* *expensiveness,* i.e. (by impl.) *magnificence:*— costliness.

5095. Τιμόθεος **Timŏthĕŏs**, *tee-moth´-eh-os;* from *5092* and *2316; dear to God; Timotheus,* a Chr.:— Timotheus, Timothy.

5096. Τίμων **Timōn**, *tee´-mone;* from *5092; valuable; Timon,* a Chr.:— Timon.

5097. τιμωρέω **timōrĕō**, *tim-o-reh´-o;* from a comp. of *5092* and οὖρος **ŏurŏs** (a *guard*); prop. to *protect,* i.e. *one's honor,* i.e. to *avenge (inflict a penalty):*— punish.

5098. τιμωρία **timōria**, *tee-mo-ree´-ah;* from *5097; vindication,* i.e. (by impl.) a *penalty:*— punishment.

5099. τίνω **tinō**, *tee´-no;* strengthened for a primary

τίω **tiō**, *tee´-o* (which is only used as an alt. in certain tenses); to *pay* a price, i.e. as a *penalty:*— be punished with.

5100. τίς **tis**, *tis;* an enclit. indef. pron.; *some* or *any* person or object:— a (kind of), any (man, thing, thing at all), certain (thing), divers, he (every) man, one (× thing), ought, + partly, some (man, body, -thing, -what), (+ that no-) thing, what (-soever), × wherewith, whom [-soever], whose [-soever].

5101. τίς **tis**, *tis;* prob. emphat. of *5100;* an interrog. pron., *who, which* or *what* (in direct or indirect questions):— every man, how (much), + no (-ne, thing), what (manner, thing), where ([-by, -fore, -of, -unto, -with, -withal]), whether, which, who (-m, -se), why.

5102. τίτλος **titlŏs**, *tit´-los;* of Lat. or.: a *titulus* or "title" (*placard*):— title.

5103. Τίτος **Titŏs**, *tee´-tos;* of Lat. or. but uncert. signif.; *Titus,* a Chr.:— Titus.

τίω **tiō**. See *5099.*

τό **tŏ**. See *3588.*

5104. τοί **tŏi**, *toy;* prob. for the dat. of *3588;* an enclit. particle of *asseveration* by way of contrast; *in sooth:*— [used only with other particles in comp. as *2544, 3305, 5105, 5106,* etc.].

5105. τοιγαροῦν **tŏigarŏun**, *toy-gar-oon´;* from *5104* and *1063* and *3767; truly for then,* i.e. *consequently:*— there-(where-) fore.

τοίγε **tŏigĕ**. See *2544.*

5106. τοίνυν **tŏinun**, *toy´-noon;* from *5104* and *3568; truly now,* i.e. *accordingly:*— then, therefore.

5107. τοιόσδε **tŏiŏsdĕ**, *toy-os´-deh;* (incl. the other inflections); from a der. of *5104* and *1161; such-like then,* i.e. *so great:*— such.

5108. τοιοῦτος **tŏiŏutŏs**, *toy-oo´-tos;* (incl. the other inflections); from *5104* and *3778; truly this,* i.e. *of this sort* (to denote character or individuality):— like, such (an one).

5109. τοῖχος **tŏichŏs**, *toy´-khos;* another form of *5038;* a *wall:*— wall.

5110. τόκος **tŏkŏs**, *tok´-os;* from the base of *5088; interest* on money loaned (as a *produce*):— usury.

5111. τολμάω **tŏlmaō**, *tol-mah´-o;* from τόλμα **tŏlma**, (*boldness;* prob. itself from the base of *5056* through the idea of *extreme* conduct); to *venture* (obj. or in *act;* while *2292* is rather subj. or in *feeling*); by impl. to be *courageous:*— be bold, boldly, dare, durst.

5112. τολμηρότερον **tŏlmērŏtĕrŏn**, *tol-may-rot´-er-on;* neut. of the comparative of a der. of the base of *5111* (as adv.); *more daringly,* i.e. *with greater confidence* than otherwise:— the more boldly.

5113. τολμητής **tŏlmētēs**, *tol-may-tace´;* from *5111;* a *daring* (*audacious*) *man:*— presumptuous.

5114. τομώτερος **tŏmōtĕrŏs**, *tom-o´-ter-os;* comparative of a der. of the primary τέμνω **tĕmnō** (to *cut; more* comprehensive or decisive than *2875,* as if by a *single* stroke; whereas that implies repeated blows, like *hacking*); *more keen:*— sharper.

5115. τόξον **tŏxŏn**, *tox´-on;* from the base of *5088;* a *bow* (appar. as the simplest fabric):— bow.

5116. τοπάζιον **tŏpaziŏn**, *top-ad´-zee-on;* neut. of a presumed der. (alt.) of τόπαζος **tŏpazŏs** (a "topaz"; of uncert. or.); a *gem,* prob. the *chrysolite:*— topaz.

5117. τόπος **tŏpŏs**, *top´-os;* appar. a primary word; a *spot* (gen. in *space,* but limited by occupancy; whereas *5561* is a larger but part. *locality*), i.e. *location* (as a position, home, tract, etc.); fig. *condition, opportunity;* spec. a *scabbard:*— coast, licence, place, × plain, quarter, + rock, room, where.

5118. τοσοῦτος **tŏsŏutŏs**, *tos-oo´-tos;* from τόσος **tŏsŏs**, *(so much;* appar. from 3588 and 3739) and 3778 (including its variations); so *vast as this,* i.e. *such* (in quantity, amount, number or space):— as large, so great (long, many, much), these many.

5119. τότε **tŏtĕ**, *tot´-eh;* from (the neut. of) 3588 and 3753; *the when,* i.e. *at the time that* (of the past or future, also in consecution):— that time, then.

5120. τοῦ **tŏu**, *too;* prop. the gen. of 3588; sometimes used for 5127; *of this person:*— his.

5121. τοὐναντίον **tŏunantiŏn**, *too-nan-tee´-on;* contr. for the neut. of 3588 and 1726; *on the contrary:*— contrariwise.

5122. τοὔνομα **tŏunŏma**, *too´-no-mah;* contr. for the neut. of 3588 and 3686; *the name* (is):— named.

5123. τουτέστι **tŏutĕsti**, *toot-es´-tee;* contr. for 5124 and 2076; *that is:*— that is (to say).

5124. τοῦτο **tŏutŏ**, *too´-tŏ;* neut. sing. nom. or acc. of 3778; *that* thing:— here [-untol, it, partly, self [-same], so, that (intent), the same, there [-fore, -untol, this, thus, where [-fore].

5125. τούτοις **tŏutŏis**, *too´-toice;* dat. plur. masc. or neut. of 3778; *to (for, in, with or by)* these (persons or things):— such, them, there [-in, -withl, these, this, those.

5126. τοῦτον **tŏutŏn**, *too-ton;* acc. sing. masc. of 3778; *this* (person, as obj. of verb or prep.):— him, the same, that, this.

5127. τούτου **tŏutŏu**, *too´-too;* gen. sing. masc. or neut. of 3778; *of (from or concerning) this* (person or thing):— here [-byl, him, it, + such manner of, that, thence [-forthl, thereabout, this, thus.

5128. τούτους **tŏutŏus**, *too´-tooce;* acc. plur. masc. of 3778; *these* (persons, as obj. of verb or prep.):— such, them, these, this.

5129. τούτῳ **tŏutŏi**, *too´-to;* dat. sing. masc. or neut. of 3778; *to (in, with or by) this* (person or thing):— here [-by, -inl, him, one, the same, there [-inl, this.

5130. τούτων **tŏutŏn**, *too´-tone;* gen. plur. masc. or neut. of 3778; *of (from or concerning) these* (persons or things):— such, their, these (things), they, this sort, those.

5131. τράγος **tragŏs**, *trag´-os;* from the base of 5176; a *he-goat* (as a *gnawer*):— goat.

5132. τράπεζα **trapĕza**, *trap´-ed-zah;* prob. contr. from 5064 and 3979; a *table* or *stool* (as being *four-legged*), usually for food (fig. a *meal*); also a *counter* for money (fig. a broker's *office* for loans at interest):— bank, meat, table.

5133. τραπεζίτης **trapĕzitēs**, *trap-ed-zee´-tace;* from 5132; a *money-broker* or *banker:* —exchanger.

5134. τραῦμα **trauma**, *trŏw´-mah;* from the base of τιτρώσκω **titrŏskō**, (to *wound;* akin to

the base of 2352, 5147, 5149, etc.); a *wound:*— wound.

5135. τραυματίζω **traumatizō**, *trŏw-mat-id´-zo;* from 5134; to *inflict a wound:*— wound.

5136. τραχηλίζω **trachēlizō**, *trakh-ay-lid´-zo;* from 5137; to *seize by the throat* or *neck,* i.e. to *expose* the *gullet* of a victim for killing (gen. to *lay bare*):— opened.

5137. τράχηλος **trachēlŏs**, *trakh´-ay-los;* prob. from 5143 (through the idea of *mobility*); the *throat* (*neck*), i.e. (fig.) *life:*— neck.

5138. τραχύς **trachus**, *trakh-oos´;* perh. strengthened from the base of 4486 (as if *jagged* by rents); *uneven, rocky* (*reefy*):— rock, rough.

5139. Τραχωνῖτις **Trachōnitis**, *trakh-o-nee´-tis;* from a der. of 5138; *rough* district; *Trachonitis,* a region of Syria:— Trachonitis.

5140. τρεῖς **trĕis**, *trice;* neut.

τρία **tria**, *tree´-ah;* or

τριῶν **triŏn**, *tree-on´;* a primary (plural) number; *"three":*— three.

5141. τρέμω **trĕmō**, *trem´-o;* strengthened from a primary τρέω **trĕō** (to *"dread," "terrify"*); to *"tremble"* or *fear:*— be afraid, trembling.

5142. τρέφω **trĕphō**, *tref´-o;* a primary verb (prop. θρέφω **thrĕphō**; but perhaps strengthened from the base of 5157 through the idea of *convolution*); prop. to *stiffen,* i.e. *fatten* (by impl. to *cherish* [with food, etc.], *pamper, rear*):— bring up, feed, nourish.

5143. τρέχω **trĕchō**, *trekh´-o;* appar. a primary verb (prop. θρέχω **thrĕchō**; comp. 2359); which uses δρέμω **drĕmō** (the base of 1408) as alt. in certain tenses; to *run* or *walk hastily* (lit. or fig.):— have course, run.

5144. τριάκοντα **triakŏnta**, *tree-ak´-on-tah;* the decade of 5140; *thirty:*— thirty.

5145. τριακόσιοι **triakŏsiŏi**, *tree-ak-os´-ee-oy;* plur. from 5140 and 1540; *three hundred:*— three hundred.

5146. τρίβολος **tribŏlŏs**, *trib´-ol-os;* from 5140 and 956; prop. a *crow-foot* (*three-pronged* obstruction in war), i.e. (by anal.) a *thorny* plant (*caltrop*):— brier, thistle.

5147. τρίβος **tribŏs**, *tree´-bos;* from τρίβω **tribō** (to *"rub"*; akin to τείρω **tĕirō**, τρύω **truō**, and the base of 5131, 5134); a *rut,* or worn *track:*— path.

5148. τριετία **triĕtia**, *tree-et-ee´-ah;* from a compound of 5140 and 2094; a *three years'* period (*triennium*):— space of three years.

5149. τρίζω **trizō**, *trid´-zo;* appar. a primary verb; to *creak* (*squeak*), i.e. (by anal.) to *grate* the teeth (in frenzy):— gnash.

5150. τρίμηνον **trimēnŏn**, *trim´-ay-non;* neut. of a compound of *5140* and *3376* as noun; a *three months'* space:— three months.

5151. τρίς **tris**, *trece;* adv. from *5140; three times:*— three times, thrice.

5152. τρίστεγον **tristĕgŏn**, *tris´-teg-on;* neut. of a compound of *5140* and *4721* as noun; a *third roof* (*story*):— third loft.

5153. τρισχίλιοι **trischiliŏi**, *tris-khil´-ee-oy;* from *5151* and *5507; three times a thousand:*— three thousand.

5154. τρίτος **tritŏs**, *tree´-tos;* ord. from *5140; third;* neut. (as noun) a *third part*, or (as adv.) a (or the) *third* time, *thirdly:*— third (-ly).

τρίχες **trichĕs**, etc. See 2359.

5155. τρίχινος **trichinŏs**, *trikh´-ee-nos;* from *2359; hairy*, i.e. made *of hair* (*mohair*):— of hair.

5156. τρόμος **trŏmŏs**, *trom´-os;* from *5141*; a "*trembling*", i.e. quaking with *fear:* —+ trembIe (-ing).

5157. τροπή **trŏpē**, *trop-ay´;* from an appar. primary τρέπω **trĕpō**, to *turn*); a *turn* ("trope"), i.e. *revolution* (fig. *variation*):— turning.

5158. τρόπος **trŏpŏs**, *trop´-os;* from the same as *5157;* a *turn*, i.e. (by impl.) *mode* or *style* (espec. with prep. or rel. pref. as adv. *like*); fig. *deportment* or *character:*— (even) as, conversation, [+ like] manner, (+ by any) means, way.

5159. τροποφορέω **trŏpŏphŏrĕō**, *trop-of-or-eh´-o;* from *5158* and *5409;* to *endure* one's *habits:*— suffer the manners.

5160. τροφή **trŏphē**, *trof-ay´;* from *5142; nourishment* (lit. or fig.); by impl. *rations* (*wages*):— food, meat.

5161. Τρόφιμος **Trŏphimŏs**, *trof´-ee-mos;* from *5160; nutritive; Trophimus*, a Chr.:— Trophimus.

5162. τροφός **trŏphŏs**, *trof-os´;* from *5142;* a *nourisher*, i.e. *nurse:*— nurse.

5163. τροχιά **trŏchia**, *trokh-ee-ah´;* from *5164;* a *track* (as a wheel-*rut*), i.e. (fig.) a *course* of conduct:— path.

5164. τροχός **trŏchŏs**, *trokh-os´;* from *5143;* a *wheel* (as a *runner*), i.e. (fig.) a *circuit* of phys. effects:— course.

5165. τρύβλιον **trublĭŏn**, *troob´-lee-on;* neut. of a presumed der. of uncert. aff.; a *bowl:*— dish.

5166. τρυγάω **trugaō**, *troo-gah´-o;* from a der. of τρύγω **trugō** (to *dry*) mean. ripe *fruit* (as if *dry*); to *collect* the vintage:— gather.

5167. τρυγών **trugōn**, *troo-gone´;* from τρύζω **truzō** (to *murmur;* akin to *5149*, but denoting a *duller* sound); a *turtle-dove* (as *cooing*):— turtle-dove.

5168. τρυμαλιά **trumalia**, *troo-mal-ee-ah´;* from a der. of τρύω **truō** (to *wear*, away; akin to the base of *5134, 5147* and *5176*); an *orifice*, i.e. needle's *eye:*— eye. Comp. *5169*.

5169. τρύπημα **trupēma**, *troo´-pay-mah;* from a der. of the base of *5168;* an *aperture*, i.e. a needle's *eye:*— eye.

5170. Τρύφαινα **Truphaina**, *troo´-fahee-nah;* from *5172; luxurious; Tryphæna*, a Chr. woman:— Tryphena.

5171. τρυφάω **truphaō**, *troo-fah´-o;* from *5172;* to *indulge in luxury:*— live in pleasure.

5172. τρυφή **truphē**, *troo-fay´;* from θρύπτω **thruptō** (to *break*, up or [fig.] *enfeeble*, espec. the mind and body by indulgence); *effeminacy*, i.e. *luxury* or *debauchery:*— delicately, riot.

5173. Τρυφῶσα **Truphōsa**, *troo-fo´-sah;* from *5172; luxuriating; Tryphosa*, a Chr. female:— Tryphosa.

5174. Τρωάς **Trōas**, *tro-as´;* from Τρός **Trŏs** (a *Trojan*); the *Troad* (or plain of Troy), i.e. *Troas*, a place in Asia Minor:— Troas.

5175. Τρωγύλλιον **Trōgulliŏn**, *tro-gool´-lee-on;* of uncert. der.; *Trogyllium*, a place in Asia Minor:— Trogyllium.

5176. τρώγω **trōgō**, *tro´-go;* probably strengthened from a collateral form of the base of *5134* and *5147* through the idea of *corrosion* or *wear;* or perh. rather of a base of *5167* and *5149* through the idea of a *crunching* sound; to *gnaw* or *chew*, i.e. (gen.) to *eat:*— eat.

5177. τυγχάνω **tugchanō**, *toong-khan´-o;* prob. for an obs. τύχω **tuchō** (for which the mid. voice of another alt. τεύχω **tĕuchō** [to *make ready* or *bring to pass*] is used in certain tenses; akin to the base of *5088* through the idea of *effecting;* prop. to *affect;* or (spec.) to *hit* or *light upon* (as a mark to be reached), i.e. (tran.) to *attain* or *secure* an object or end, or (intr.) to *happen* (as if *meeting* with); but in the latter application only impers. (with *1487*), i.e. *perchance;* or (pres. part.) as adj. *usual* (as if commonly *met with*, with *3756*, *extraordinary*), neut. (as adv.) *perhaps;* or (with another verb) as adv. by *accident* (*as it were*):— be, chance, enjoy, little, obtain, × refresh ... self, + special. Comp. *5180*.

5178. τυμπανίζω **tumpanizō**, *toom-pan-id´-zo;* from a der. of *5180* (mean. a *drum*, "*tympanum*"); to *stretch* on an instrument of *torture* resembling a drum, and thus *beat* to death:— torture.

5179. τύπος **tupŏs**, *too´-pos;* from *5180;* a *die* (as *struck*), i.e. (by impl.) a *stamp* or *scar;* by anal. a *shape*, i.e. a *statue*, (fig.) *style* or *resemblance;* spec. a *sampler* ("*type*"), i.e. a *model* (for imitation) or *instance* (for warning):— en- (ex-) ample, fashion, figure, form, manner, pattern, print.

5180. τύπτω **tuptō**, *toop´-to;* a primary verb (in a strengthened form); to "*thump*", i.e. *cudgel* or *pummel* (prop. with a stick or *bastinado*), but in any case by *repeated* blows; thus differing from *3817* and *3960*, which denote a [usually single] blow with the hand or any instrument, or *4141* with the *fist* [or a *hammer*], or *4474* with the *palm;* as well as from *5177*, an *accidental* collision); by impl. to *punish;* fig. to *offend* (the conscience):— beat, smite, strike, wound.

5181. Τύραννος **Turannŏs**, *too´-ran-nos;* a provincial form of the der. of the base of *2962;* a *"tyrant";* Tyrannus, an Ephesian:— Tyrannus.

5182. τυρβάζω **turbazō**, *toor-bad´-zo;* from τύρβη **turbē**, (Lat. *turba,* a *crowd;* akin to *2351*); to make *"turbid",* i.e. *disturb:*— trouble.

5183. Τύριος **Turiŏs**, *too´-ree-os;* from *5184;* a *Tyrian,* i.e. inhab. of Tyrus:— of Tyre.

5184. Τύρος **Turŏs**, *too´-ros;* of Heb. or. [6865]: *Tyrus* (i.e. *Tsor*), a place in Pal.:— Tyre.

5185. τυφλός **tuphlŏs**, *toof-los´;* from *5187; opaque* (as if *smoky*), i.e. (by anal.) *blind* (phys. or ment.):— blind.

5186. τυφλόω **tuphlŏō**, *toof-lŏ´-o;* from *5185;* to *make blind,* i.e. (fig.) to *obscure:*— blind.

5187. τυφόω **tuphŏō**, *toof-ŏ´-o;* from a der. of *5188;* to *envelop with smoke,* i.e. (fig.) to *inflate* with self-conceit:— high-minded, be lifted up with pride, be proud.

5188. τύφω **tuphō**, *too´-fo;* appar. a primary verb; to make a *smoke,* i.e. slowly *consume* without flame:— smoke.

5189. τυφωνικός **tuphōnikŏs**, *too-fo-nee-kos´;* from a der. of *5188; stormy* (as if *smoky*):— tempestuous.

5190. Τυχικός **Tuchikŏs**, *too-khee-kos´;* from a der. of *5177; fortuitous,* i.e. *fortunate; Ty-chicus,* a Chr.:— Tychicus.

Υ

5191. ὑακίνθινος **huakinthinŏs**, *hoo-ak-in´-thee-nos;* from *5192; "hyacinthine"* or *"jacinthine",* i.e. deep *blue:*— jacinth.

5192. ὑάκινθος **huakinthŏs**, *hoo-ak´-in-thos;* of uncert. der.; the *"hyacinth"* or *"jacinth",* i.e. some gem of a deep *blue* color, prob. the *zirkon:*— jacinth.

5193. ὑάλινος **hualinŏs**, *hoo-al´-ee-nos;* from *5194; glassy,* i.e. *transparent:*— of glass.

5194. ὕαλος **hualŏs**, *hoo´-al-os;* perh. from the same as *5205* (as being transparent like *rain*); *glass:*— glass.

5195. ὑβρίζω **hubrizō**, *hoo-brid´-zo;* from *5196;* to *exercise violence,* i.e. *abuse:*— use despitefully, reproach, entreat shamefully (spitefully).

5196. ὕβρις **hubris**, *hoo´-bris;* from *5228; insolence* (as *over*-bearing), i.e. *insult, injury:*— harm, hurt, reproach.

5197. ὑβριστής **hubristēs**, *hoo-bris-tace´;* from *5195;* an *insulter,* i.e. *maltreater:*— despiteful, injurious.

5198. ὑγιαίνω **hugiainō**, *hoog-ee-ah´-ee-no;* from *5199;* to *have* sound *health,* i.e. *be well* (in body); fig. to be *uncorrupt* (*true* in doctrine):— be in health, (be safe and) sound, (be) whole (-some).

5199. ὑγιής **hugiēs**, *hoog-ee-ace´;* from the base of *837; healthy,* i.e. *well* (in body); fig. *true* (in doctrine):— sound, whole.

5200. ὑγρός **hugrŏs**, *hoo-gros´;* from the base of *5205; wet* (as if with *rain*), i.e. (by impl.) *sappy* (*fresh*):— green.

5201. ὑδρία **hudria**, *hoo-dree-ah´;* from *5204;* a *water-jar,* i.e. *receptacle* for family supply:— water-pot.

5202. ὑδροποτέω **hudrŏpŏtĕō**, *hoo-drop-ot-eh´-o;* from a compound of *5204* and a der. of *4095;* to *be* a *water-drinker,* i.e. to *abstain from vinous beverages:*— drink water.

5203. ὑδρωπικός **hudrōpikŏs**, *hoo-dro-pik-os´;* from a compound of *5204* and a der. of *3700* (as if *looking watery*); to be *"dropsical":*— have the dropsy.

5204. ὕδωρ **hudōr**, *hoo´-dore;* gen.,

ὕδατος **hudatŏs**, *hoo´-dat-os,* etc.; from the base of *5205; water* (as if *rainy*) lit. or fig.:— water.

5205. ὑετός **huĕtŏs**, *hoo-et-os´;* from a primary ὕω **huō**, (to *rain*); *rain,* espec. a *shower:*— rain.

5206. υἱοθεσία **huiŏthĕsia**, *hwee-oth-es-ee´-ah;* from a presumed compound of *5207* and a der. of *5087;* the *placing* as a *son,* i.e. *adoption* (fig. Chr. *sonship* in respect to God):— adoption (of children, of sons).

5207. υἱός **huiŏs**, *hwee-os´;* appar. a primary word; a *"son"* (sometimes of animals), used very widely of immed. remote or fig. kinship:— child, foal, son.

5208. ὕλη **hulē**, *hoo´-lay;* perh. akin to *3586;* a *forest,* i.e. (by impl.) *fuel:*— matter.

5209. ὑμᾶς **humas**, *hoo-mas´;* acc. of *5210; you* (as the obj. of a verb or prep.):— ye, you (+ -ward), your (+ own).

5210. ὑμεῖς **humĕis**, *hoo-mice´;* irreg. plur. of *4771; you* (as subj. of verb):— ye (yourselves), you.

5211. Ὑμεναῖος **Humĕnaiŏs**, *hoo-men-ah´-yos;* from Ὑμήν **Humēn,** (the god of *weddings*); *"hymenæal"; Hymenæus,* an opponent of Christianity:— Hymenæus.

5212. ὑμέτερος **humĕtĕrŏs**, *hoo-met´-er-os;* from *5210; yours,* i.e. *pertaining to you:*— your (own).

5213. ὑμῖν **humin**, *hoo-min´;* irreg. dat. of *5210; to* (*with* or *by*) *you:*— ye, you, your (-selves).

5214. ὑμνέω **humnĕō**, *hoom-neh´-o;* from *5215;* to *hymn,* i.e. sing a relig. ode; by impl. to *celebrate* (God) in song:— sing a hymn (praise unto).

5215. ὕμνος **humnŏs**, *hoom'-nos;* appar. from a simpler (obs.) form of ὑδέω **huděō**, (to *celebrate;* prob. akin to *103;* comp. *5667*); a *"hymn"* or relig. ode (one of the Psalms):— hymn.

5216. ὑμῶν **humōn**, *hoo-mone';* gen. of *5210;* of (*from* or *concerning*) *you:*— ye, you, your (own, -selves).

5217. ὑπάγω **hupagō**, *hoop-ag'-o;* from *5259* and *71;* to *lead* (oneself) *under,* i.e. *withdraw* or *retire* (as if *sinking* out of sight), lit. or fig.:— depart, get hence, go (a-) way.

5218. ὑπακοή **hupakŏē**, *hoop-ak-ŏ-ay';* from *5219; attentive hearkening,* i.e. (by impl.) *compliance* or *submission:*— obedience, (make) obedient, obey (-ing).

5219. ὑπακούω **hupakŏuō**, *hoop-ak-oo'-o;* from *5259* and *191;* to *hear under* (as a *subordinate*), i.e. to *listen attentively;* by impl. to *heed* or *conform* to a command or authority:— hearken, be obedient to, obey.

5220. ὕπανδρος **hupandrŏs**, *hoop'-an-dros;* from *5259* and *435;* in subjection *under* a man, i.e. a *married* woman:— which hath an husband.

5221. ὑπαντάω **hupantaō**, *hoop-an-tah'-o;* from *5259* and a der. of *473;* to *go opposite (meet) under (quietly),* i.e. to *encounter, fall in with:*— (go to) meet.

5222. ὑπάντησις **hupantēsis**, *hoop-an'-tay-sis;* from *5221;* an *encounter* or *concurrence* (with *1519* for infin. in order to *fall in with*):— meeting.

5223. ὕπαρξις **huparxis**, *hoop'-arx-is;* from *5225; existency* or *proprietorship,* i.e. (concr.) *property, wealth:*— goods, substance.

5224. ὑπάρχοντα **huparchŏnta**, *hoop-ar'-khon-tah;* neut. plur. of pres. part. act. of *5225* as noun; things *extant* or *in hand,* i.e. *property* or *possessions:*— goods, that which one has, things which (one) possesseth, substance, that hast.

5225. ὑπάρχω **huparchō**, *hoop-ar'-kho;* from *5259* and *756;* to *begin under (quietly),* i.e. *come into existence (be present* or *at hand);* expletively, to *exist* (as copula or subordinate to an adj., part., adv. or prep., or as auxil. to principal verb):— after, behave, live.

5226. ὑπείκω **hupeikō**, *hoop-i'-ko;* from *5259* and εἴκω **ěikō** (to *yield,* be *"weak"*); to *surrender:*— submit self.

5227. ὑπεναντίος **hupěnantiŏs**, *hoop-en-an-tee'-os;* from *5259* and *1727; under (covertly) contrary to,* i.e. *opposed* or (as noun) an *opponent:*— adversary, against.

5228. ὑπέρ **hupěr**, *hoop-er';* a primary prep.; *"over",* i.e. (with the gen.) of place, *above, beyond, across,* or causal, *for the sake of, instead, regarding;* with the acc. *superior to, more than:*— (+ exceeding, abundantly) above, in (on) behalf of, beyond, by, + very chiefest, concerning, exceeding (above, -ly),

for, + very highly, more (than), of, over, on the part of, for sake of, in stead, than, to (-ward), very. [In composition, it retains many of the above applications.]

5229. ὑπεραίρομαι **hupěrairŏmai**, *hoop-er-ah'-ee-rom-ahee;* mid. voice from *5228* and *142;* to *raise* oneself *over,* i.e. (fig.) to *become haughty:*— exalt self, be exalted above measure.

5230. ὑπέρακμος **hupěrakmŏs**, *hoop-er'-ak-mos;* from *5228* and the base of *188; beyond* the *"acme",* i.e. fig. (of a daughter) *past* the *bloom (prime)* of youth:— + pass the flower of (her) age.

5231. ὑπεράνω **hupěranō**, *hoop-er-an'-o;* from *5228* and *507; above upward,* i.e. *greatly higher* (in place or rank):— far above, over.

5232. ὑπεραυξάνω **hupěrauxanō**, *hoop-er-ŏwx-an'-o;* from *5228* and *837;* to *increase above* ordinary degree:— grow exceedingly.

5233. ὑπερβαίνω **hupěrbainō**, *hoop-er-bah'-ee-no;* from *5228* and the base of *939;* to *transcend,* i.e. (fig.) to *overreach:*— go beyond.

5234. ὑπερβαλλόντως **hupěrballŏntōs**, *hoop-er-bal-lon'-toce;* adv. from pres. part. act. of *5235; excessively:*— beyond measure.

5235. ὑπερβάλλω **hupěrballō**, *hoop-er-bal'-lo;* from *5228* and *906;* to *throw beyond* the usual mark, i.e. (fig.) to *surpass* (only act. part. *supereminent*):— exceeding, excel, pass.

5236. ὑπερβολή **hupěrbŏlē**, *hoop-er-bol-ay';* from *5235;* a *throwing beyond* others, i.e. (fig.) *supereminence;* adv. (with *1519* or *2596*) *pre-eminently:*— abundance, (far more) exceeding, excellency, more excellent, beyond (out of) measure.

5237. ὑπερείδω **hupěrěidō**, *hoop-er-i'-do;* from *5228* and *1492;* to *overlook,* i.e. *not punish:*— wink at.

5238. ὑπερέκεινα **hupěrěkěina**, *hoop-er-ek'-i-nah;* from *5228* and the neut. plur. of *1565; above those* parts, i.e. *still farther:*— beyond.

5239. ὑπερεκτείνω **hupěrěktěinō**, *hoop-er-ek-ti'-no;* from *5228* and *1614;* to *extend inordinately:*— stretch beyond.

5240. ὑπερεκχύνω **hupěrěkchunō**, *hoop-er-ek-khoo'-no;* from *5228* and the alt. form of *1632;* to *pour out over,* i.e. (pass.) to *overflow:*— run over.

ὑπερεκπερισσοῦ **hupěrěkpěrissŏu**. See *5228* and *1537* and *4053.*

5241. ὑπερεντυγχάνω **hupěrěntugchanō**, *hoop-er-en-toong-khan'-o;* from *5228* and *1793;* to *intercede in behalf of:*— make intercession for.

5242. ὑπερέχω **hupěrechō**, *hoop-er-ekh'-o;*

from 5228 and 2192; to *hold* oneself *above*, i.e. (fig.) to *excel*; part. (as adj. or neut. as noun) *superior, superiority:*— better, excellency, higher, pass, supreme.

5243. ὑπερηφανία **hupĕrēphania**, *hoop-er-ay-fan-ee´-ah;* from 5244; *haughtiness:*— pride.

5244. ὑπερήφανος **hupĕrēphanŏs**, *hoop-er-ay´-fan-os;* from 5228 and 5316; *appearing above* others (*conspicuous*), i.e. (fig.) *haughty:*— proud.

ὑπερλίαν **hupĕrlian**. See 5228 and 3029.

5245. ὑπερνικάω **hupĕrnikaō**, *hoop-er-nik-ah´-o;* from 5228 and 3528; to *vanquish beyond*, i.e. *gain* a decisive *victory:*— more than conquer.

5246. ὑπέρογκος **hupĕrŏgkŏs**, *hoop-er´-ong-kos;* from 5228 and 3591; *bulging over*, i.e. (fig.) *insolent:*— great swelling.

5247. ὑπεροχή **hupĕrŏchē**, *hoop-er-okh-ay´;* from 5242; *prominence*, i.e. (fig.) *superiority* (in rank or character):— authority, excellency.

5248. ὑπερπερισσεύω **hupĕrpĕrissĕuō**, *hoop-er-per-is-syoo´-o;* from 5228 and 4052; to *super-abound:*— abound much more, exceeding.

5249. ὑπερπερισσῶς **hupĕrpĕrissōs**, *hoop-er-per-is-soce´;* from 5228 and 4057; *superabundantly*, i.e. *exceedingly:*— beyond measure.

5250. ὑπερπλεονάζω **hupĕrplĕŏnazō**, *hoop-er-pleh-on-ad´-zo;* from 5228 and 4121; to *super-abound:*— be exceeding abundant.

5251. ὑπερυψόω **hupĕrupsŏō**, *hoop-er-oop-so´-o;* from 5228 and 5312; to *elevate above* others, i.e. *raise* to the *highest* position:— highly exalt.

5252. ὑπερφρονέω **hupĕrphrŏnĕō**, *hoop-er-fron-eh´-o;* from 5228 and 5426; to *esteem* oneself *overmuch*, i.e. *be vain* or *arrogant:*— think more highly.

5253. ὑπερῷον **hupĕrōiŏn**, *hoop-er-o´-on;* neut. of a der. of 5228; a *higher* part of the house, i.e. apartment in the *third story:*— upper chamber (room).

5254. ὑπέχω **hupĕchō**, *hoop-ekh´-o;* from 5259 and 2192; to *hold* oneself *under*, i.e. *endure* with patience:— suffer.

5255. ὑπήκοος **hupēkŏŏs**, *hoop-ay´-kŏ-os;* from 5219; *attentively listening*, i.e. (by impl.) *submissive:*— obedient.

5256. ὑπηρετέω **hupērĕtĕō**, *hoop-ay-ret-eh´-o;* from 5257; to *be a subordinate*, i.e. (by impl.) *subserve:*— minister (unto), serve.

5257. ὑπηρέτης **hupērĕtēs**, *hoop-ay-ret´-ace;* from 5259 and a der. of ἐρέσσω **ĕressō** (to *row*); an *under-oarsman*, i.e. (gen.) *subordinate* (*assistant, sexton, constable*):— minister, officer, servant.

5258. ὕπνος **hupnŏs**, *hoop´-nos;* from an obs. primary (perh. akin to 5259 through the idea

of *subsilience*); *sleep*, i.e. (fig.) spiritual *torpor:*— sleep.

5259. ὑπό **hupŏ**, *hoop-ŏ´;* a primary prep.; *under*, i.e. (with the gen.) of place (*beneath*), or with verbs (the agency or means, *through*); (with the acc.) of place (whither [*underneath*] or where [*below*] or time (when [*at*]):— among, by, from, in, of, under, with. [In composition, it retains the same general applications, espec. of *inferior* position or condition, and spec. *covertly* or *moderately*.]

5260. ὑποβάλλω **hupŏballō**, *hoop-ob-al´-lo;* from 5259 and 906; to *throw* in *stealthily*, i.e. *introduce* by collusion:— suborn.

5261. ὑπογραμμός **hupŏgrammŏs**, *hoop-og-ram-mos´;* from a compound of 5259 and 1125; an *underwriting*, i.e. *copy* for imitation (fig.):— example.

5262. ὑπόδειγμα **hupŏdĕigma**, *hoop-od´-igue-mah;* from 5263; an *exhibit* for imitation or warning (fig. *specimen, adumbration*):— en- (ex-) ample, pattern.

5263. ὑποδείκνυμι **hupŏdĕiknumi**, *hoop-od-ike´-noo-mee;* from 5259 and 1166; to *exhibit under* the eyes, i.e. (fig.) to *exemplify* (*instruct, admonish*):— show, (fore-) warn.

5264. ὑποδέχομαι **hupŏdĕchŏmai**, *hoop-od-ekh´-om-ahee;* from 5259 and 1209; to *admit under* one's roof, i.e. *entertain* hospitably:— receive.

5265. ὑποδέω **hupŏdĕō**, *hoop-od-eh´-o;* from 5259 and 1210; to *bind under* one's feet, i.e. *put on* shoes or sandals:— bind on, (be) shod.

5266. ὑπόδημα **hupŏdēma**, *hoop-od´-ay-mah;* from 5265; something *bound under* the feet, i.e. a *shoe* or *sandal:*— shoe.

5267. ὑπόδικος **hupŏdikŏs**, *hoop-od´-ee-kos;* from 5259 and 1349; *under sentence*, i.e. (by impl.) *condemned:*— guilty.

5268. ὑποζύγιον **hupŏzugiŏn**, *hoop-od-zoog´-ee-on;* neut. of a compound of 5259 and 2218; an *animal under* the *yoke* (*draught-beast*), i.e. (spec.) a *donkey:*— ass.

5269. ὑποζώννυμι **hupŏzōnnumi**, *hoop-od-zone´-noo-mee;* from 5259 and 2224; to *gird under*, i.e. *frap* (a vessel with cables across the keel, sides and deck):— undergirt.

5270. ὑποκάτω **hupŏkatō**, *hoop-ok-at´-o;* from 5259 and 2736; *down under*, i.e. *beneath:*— under.

5271. ὑποκρίνομαι **hupŏkrinŏmai**, *hoop-ok-rin´-om-ahee;* mid. voice from 5259 and 2919; to *decide* (*speak* or *act*) *under* a false part, i.e. (fig.) *dissemble* (*pretend*):— feign.

5272. ὑπόκρισις **hupŏkrisis**, *hoop-ok´-ree-sis;* from 5271; *acting under* a feigned part, i.e. (fig.) *deceit* ("hypocrisy"):— condemnation, dissimulation, hypocrisy.

5273. ὑποκριτής **hupŏkritēs**, *hoop-ok-ree-*

tace´; from 5271; an *actor under* an assumed character (*stage-player*), i.e. (fig.) a *dissembler* ("*hypocrite*"):— hypocrite.

5274. ὑπολαμβάνω **hupŏlambanō**, *hoop-ol-am-ban´-o*; from 5259 and 2983; to *take* from *below*, i.e. *carry upward*; fig. to *take up*, i.e. *continue* a discourse or topic; ment. to *assume* (*presume*):— answer, receive, suppose.

5275. ὑπολείπω **hupŏlĕipō**, *hoop-ol-i´-po*; from 5295 and 3007; to *leave under* (*behind*), i.e. (pass.) to *remain* (*survive*):— be left.

5276. ὑπολήνιον **hupŏlēniŏn**, *hoop-ol-ay´-nee-on*; neut. of a presumed compound of 5259 and 3025; vessel or receptacle *under* the *press*, i.e. lower *winevat*:— winefat.

5277. ὑπολιμπάνω **hupŏlimpanō**, *hoop-ol-im-pan´-o*; a prol. form for 5275; to *leave behind*, i.e. *bequeath*:— leave.

5278. ὑπομένω **hupŏmĕnō**, *hoop-om-en´-o*; from 5259 and 3306; to *stay under* (*behind*), i.e. *remain*; fig. to *undergo*, i.e. *bear* (trials), *have fortitude, persevere*:— abide, endure, (take) patient (-ly), suffer, tarry behind.

5279. ὑπομιμνήσκω **hupŏmimnēskō**, *hoop-om-im-nace´-ko*; from 5259 and 3403; to *remind quietly*, i.e. *suggest* to the (mid. voice, one's own) memory:— put in mind, remember, bring to (put in) remembrance.

5280. ὑπόμνησις **hupŏmnēsis**, *hoop-om´-nay-sis*; from 5279; a *reminding* or (refl.) *recollection*:— remembrance.

5281. ὑπομονή **hupŏmŏnē**, *hoop-om-on-ay´*; from 5278; cheerful (or hopeful) *endurance, constancy*:— enduring, patience, patient continuance (waiting).

5282. ὑπονοέω **hupŏnŏĕō**, *hoop-on-ŏ-eh´-o*; from 5259 and 3539; to *think under* (*privately*), i.e. to *surmise* or *conjec.*:— think, suppose, deem.

5283. ὑπόνοια **hupŏnŏia**, *hoop-on´-oy-ah*; from 5282; *suspicion*:— surmising.

5284. ὑποπλέω **hupŏplĕō**, *hoop-op-leh´-o*; from 5259 and 4126; to *sail under* the lee of:— sail under.

5285. ὑποπνέω **hupŏpnĕō**, *hoop-op-neh´-o*; from 5259 and 4154; to *breathe gently*, i.e. *breeze*:— blow softly.

5286. ὑποπόδιον **hupŏpŏdiŏn**, *hoop-op-od´-ee-on*; neut. of a compound of 5259 and 4228; something *under* the *feet*, i.e. a *foot-rest* (fig.):— footstool.

5287. ὑπόστασις **hupŏstasis**, *hoop-os´-tas-is*; from a compound of 5259 and 2476; a *setting under* (*support*), i.e. (fig.) concr. *essence*, or abstr. *assurance* (obj. or subj.):— confidence, confident, person, substance.

5288. ὑποστέλλω **hupŏstĕllō**, *hoop-os-tel´-lo*; from 5259 and 4724; to *withhold under* (*out of sight*), i.e. (refl.) to *cower* or *shrink*, (fig.) to *conceal* (*reserve*):— draw (keep) back, shun, withdraw.

5289. ὑποστολή **hupŏstŏlē**, *hoop-os-tol-ay´*; from 5288; *shrinkage* (*timidity*), i.e. (by impl.) *apostasy*:— draw back.

5290. ὑποστρέφω **hupŏstrĕphō**, *hoop-os-tref´-o*; from 5259 and 4762; to *turn under* (*behind*), i.e. to *return* (lit. or fig.):— come again, return (again, back again), turn back (again).

5291. ὑποστρώννυμι **hupŏstrŏnnumi**, *hoop-os-trone´-noo-mee*; from 5259 and 4766; to *strew underneath* (the feet as a carpet):— spread.

5292. ὑποταγή **hupŏtagē**, *hoop-ot-ag-ay´*; from 5293; *subordination*:— subjection.

5293. ὑποτάσσω **hupŏtassō**, *hoop-ot-as´-so*; from 5259 and 5021; to *subordinate*; refl. to *obey*:— be under obedience (obedient), put under, subdue unto, (be, make) subj. (to, unto), be (put) in subjection (to, under), submit self unto.

5294. ὑποτίθημι **hupŏtithēmi**, *hoop-ot-ith´-ay-mee*; from 5259 and 5087; to *place underneath*, i.e. (fig.) to *hazard*, (refl.) to *suggest*:— lay down, put in remembrance.

5295. ὑποτρέχω **hupŏtrĕchō**, *hoop-ot-rekh´-o*; from 5259 and 5143 (incl. its alt.); to *run under*, i.e. (spec.) to *sail past*:— run under.

5296. ὑποτύπωσις **hupŏtupōsis**, *hoop-ot-oop´-o-sis*; from a compound of 5259 and a der. of 5179; *typification under* (*after*), i.e. (concr.) a *sketch* (fig.) for imitation:— form, pattern.

5297. ὑποφέρω **hupŏphĕrō**, *hoop-of-er´-o*; from 5259 and 5342; to *bear* from *underneath*, i.e. (fig.) to *undergo* hardship:— bear, endure.

5298. ὑποχωρέω **hupŏchōrĕō**, *hoop-okh-o-reh´-o*; from 5259 and 5562; to *vacate down*, i.e. *retire* i.e. *retire* quietly:— go aside, withdraw self.

5299. ὑπωπιάζω **hupōpiazō**, *hoop-o-pee-ad´-zo*; from a compound of 5259 and a der. of 3700; to *hit under* the *eye* (*buffet* or *disable* an antagonist as a pugilist), i.e. (fig.) to *tease* or *annoy* (into compliance), *subdue* (one's passions):— keep under, weary.

5300. ὗς **hus**, *hoos*; appar. a primary word; a *hog* ("*swine*"):— sow.

5301. ὕσσωπος **hussōpŏs**, *hoos´-so-pos*; of for. or. [2311]; "*hyssop*":— hyssop.

5302. ὑστερέω **hustĕrĕō**, *hoos-ter-eh´-o*; from 5306; to *be later*, i.e. (by impl.) to *be inferior*; gen. to *fall short* (*be deficient*):— come behind (short), be destitute, fail, lack, suffer need, (be in) want, be the worse.

5303. ὑστέρημα **hustĕrēma**, *hoos-ter´-ay-mah*; from 5302; a *deficit*; spec. *poverty*:— that which is behind, (that which was) lack (-ing), penury, want.

5304. ὑστέρησις **hustĕrēsis**, *hoos-ter´-ay-*

sis from *5302;* a *falling short,* i.e. (spec.) *penury:*— want.

5305. ὕστερον **husteron**, *hoos'-ter-on;* neut. of 5306 as adv.; *more lately,* i.e. *eventually:*— afterward, (at the) last (of all).

5306. ὕστερος **husteros**, *hoos'-ter-os;* comparative from 5259 (in the sense of *behind*); *later:*— latter.

5307. ὑφαντός **huphantos**, *hoo-fan-tos';* from ὑφαίνω **huphainō**, to *weave; woven,* i.e. (perh.) *knitted:*— woven.

5308. ὑψηλός **hupsēlos**, *hoop-say-los';* from 5311; *lofty* (in place or character):— high (-er, -ly) (esteemed).

5309. ὑψηλοφρονέω **hupsēlophronēō**, *hoop-say-lo-fron-eh'-o;* from a compound of 5308 and 5424; to *be lofty in mind,* i.e. *arrogant:*— be highminded.

5310. ὕψιστος **hupsistos**, *hoop'-sis-tos;* superl. from the base of 5311; *highest,* i.e. (masc. sing.) the *Supreme* (God), or (neut. plur.) the *heavens:*— most high, highest.

5311. ὕψος **hupsos**, *hoop'-sos;* from a der. of 5228; *elevation,* i.e. (abstr.) *altitude,* (spec.) the *sky,* or (fig.) *dignity:*— be exalted, height, (on) high.

5312. ὑψόω **hupsoō**, *hoop-so'-o;* from 5311; to *elevate* (lit. or fig.):— exalt, lift up.

5313. ὕψωμα **hupsōma**, *hoop'-so-mah;* from 5312; an *elevated* place or thing, i.e. (abstr.) *altitude,* or (by impl.) a *barrier* (fig.):— height, high thing.

Φ

5314. φάγος **phagos**, *fag'-os;* from 5315; a *glutton:*— gluttonous.

5315. φάγω **phagō**, *fag'-o;* a primary verb (used as an alt. of 2068 in certain tenses); to *eat* (lit. or fig.):— eat, meat.

φαιλόνης **phailonēs**, *fahee-lohn'-ace;* an alt. spelling of 5341 which see; found only in 2 Tim. 4:13.

5316. φαίνω **phainō**, *fah'-ee-no;* prol. for the base of 5457; to *lighten* (shine), i.e. *show* (tran. or intr., lit. or fig.):— appear, seem, be seen, shine, × think.

5317. Φάλεκ **Phalek**, *fal'-ek;* of Heb. or. [6389]; *Phalek* (i.e. *Peleg*), a patriarch:— Phalec.

5318. φανερός **phaneros**, *fan-er-os';* from 5316; *shining,* i.e. *apparent* (lit. or fig.); neut. (as adv.) *publicly, extern.:*— abroad, + appear, known, manifest, open [+ -ly], outward ([+ly]).

5319. φανερόω **phaneroō**, *fan-er-o'-o;* from 5318; to *render apparent* (lit. or fig.):— appear, manifestly declare, (make) manifest (forth), shew (self).

5320. φανερῶς **phanerōs**, *fan-er-oce';* adv. from 5318; *plainly,* i.e. *clearly* or *publicly:*— evidently, openly.

5321. φανέρωσις **phanerōsis**, *fan-er'-o-sis;* from 5319; *exhibition,* i.e. (fig.) *expression,* (by extens.) a *bestowment:*— manifestation.

5322. φανός **phanos**, *fan-os';* from 5316; a *lightener,* i.e. *light; lantern:*— lantern.

5323. Φανουήλ **Phanouēl**, *fan-oo-ale';* of Heb. or. [6439]; *Phanuël* (i.e. *Penuël*), an Isr.:— Phanuel.

5324. φαντάζω **phantazō**, *fan-tad'-zo;* from a der. of 5316; to *make apparent* i.e. (pass.) to *appear* (neut. part. as noun, a *spectacle*):— sight.

5325. φαντασία **phantasia**, *fan-tas-ee'-ah;* from a der. of 5324; (prop. abstr.) a (vain) *show* ("fantasy"):— pomp.

5326. φάντασμα **phantasma**, *fan'-tas-mah;* from 5324; (prop. concr.) a (mere) *show* ("phantasm"), i.e. *spectre:*— spirit.

5327. φάραγξ **pharagx**, *far'-anx;* prop. streng. from the base of 4008 or rather of 4486; a *gap* or *chasm,* i.e. *ravine* (*winter-torrent*):— valley.

5328. Φαραώ **Pharaō**, *far-ah-o';* of for. or. [6547]; *Pharaö* (i.e. *Pharoh*), an Eg. king:— Pharaoh.

5329. Φαρές **Phares**, *far-es';* of Heb. or. [6557]; *Phares* (i.e. *Perets*), an Isr.:— Phares.

5330. Φαρισαῖος **Pharisaios**, *far-is-ah'-yos;* of Heb. or. [comp. 6567]; a *separatist,* i.e. exclusively *relig.;* a *Pharisæan,* i.e. Jewish sectary:— Pharisee.

5331. φαρμακεία **pharmakeia**, *far-mak-i'-ah;* from 5332; *medication* ("pharmacy"), i.e. (by extens.) *magic* (lit. or fig.):— sorcery, witchcraft.

5332. φαρμακεύς **pharmakeus**, *far-mak-yoos';* from φάρμακον **pharmakon**, (a *drug,* i.e. spell-giving *potion*); a *druggist* ("pharmacist") or *poisoner,* i.e. (by extens.) a *magician:*— sorcerer.

5333. φαρμακός **pharmakos**, *far-mak-os';* the same as 5332:— sorcerer.

5334. φάσις **phasis**, *fas'-is;* from 5346 (not the same as "phase", which is from 5316); a *saying,* i.e. *report:*— tidings.

5335. φάσκω **phaskō**, *fas'-ko;* prol. from the same as 5346; to *assert:*— affirm, profess, say.

5336. φάτνη **phatnē**, *fat'-nay;* from πατέομαι **pateomai** (to *eat*); a *crib* (for fodder):— manger, stall.

5337. φαῦλος **phaulos**, *fow'-los;* appar. a primary word; "foul" or "flawy", i.e. (fig.) *wicked:*— evil.

5338. φέγγος **pheggos**, *feng'-gos;* prob. akin to the base of 5457 [comp. 5350]; *brilliancy:*— light.

5339. φείδομαι **pheidomai**, *fi'-dom-ahee;* of uncert. aff.; to *be chary* of, i.e. (subj.) to *abstain* or (obj.) to *treat leniently:*— forbear, spare.

5340. φειδομένως **pheĭdŏmĕnōs**, *fi-dom-en´-oce;* adv. from part. of 5339; *abstemiously,* i.e. *stingily:*— sparingly.

5341. φελόνης **phĕlŏnēs**, *fel-on´-ace* or

φαιλόνης **phailŏnēs**, *fayl-on´-ace;* by transp. for a der. prob. of 5316 (as *showing* outside the other garments); a *mantle (surtout):*— cloke.

5342. φέρω **phĕrō**, *fer´-o;* a primary verb (for which other and appar. not cognate ones are used in certain tenses only; namely,

οἴω **ŏiō**, *oy´-o;* and

ἐνέγκω **ĕnĕgkō**, *en-eng´-ko;* to *"bear"* or *carry* (in a very wide application, lit. and fig. as follows):— be, bear, bring (forth), carry, come, + let her drive, be driven, endure, go on, lay, lead, move, reach, rushing, uphold.

5343. φεύγω **phĕugō**, *fyoo´-go;* appar. a primary verb; to *run away* (lit. or fig.); by impl. to *shun;* by anal. to *vanish:*— escape, flee (away).

5344. Φῆλιξ **Phēlix**, *fay´-lix;* of Lat. or.; *happy; Phelix* (i.e. *Felix*), a Rom.:— Felix.

5345. φήμη **phēmē**, *fay´-may;* from 5346; a *saying,* i.e. *rumor* ("fame"):— fame.

5346. φημί **phēmi**, *fay-mee´;* prop. the same as the base of 5457 and 5316; to *show* or *make known* one's thoughts, i.e. *speak* or *say:*— affirm, say. Comp. 3004.

5347. Φῆστος **Phēstŏs**, *face´-tos;* of Lat. der.; *festal; Phestus* (i.e. *Festus*), a Rom.:— Festus.

5348. φθάνω **phthanō**, *fthan´-o;* appar. a primary verb; to *be beforehand,* i.e. *anticipate* or *precede;* by extens. to *have arrived* at:— (already) attain, come, prevent.

5349. φθαρτός **phthartŏs**, *fthar-tos´;* from 5351; *decayed,* i.e. (by impl.) *perishable:*— corruptible.

5350. φθέγγομαι **phthĕggŏmai**, *ftheng´-gom-ahee;* prob. akin to 5338 and thus to 5346; to *utter* a clear sound, i.e. (gen.) to *proclaim:*— speak.

5351. φθείρω **phthĕirō**, *fthi´-ro;* probably strengthened from φθίω **phthiō** (to *pine* or *waste*); prop. to *shrivel,* or *wither,* i.e. to *spoil* (by any process) or (gen.) to *ruin* (espec. fig., by mor. influences, to *deprave*):— corrupt (self), defile, destroy.

5352. φθινοπωρινός **phthinŏpōrinŏs**, *fthin-op-o-ree-nos´;* from der. of φθίνω **phthinō** (to *wane;* akin to the base of 5351) and 3703 (mean. *late autumn*); *autumnal* (as *stripped* of leaves):— whose fruit withereth.

5353. φθόγγος **phthŏggŏs**, *fthong´-gos;* from 5350; *utterance,* i.e. a *musical* note (vocal or instrumental):— sound.

5354. φθονέω **phthŏnĕō**, *fthon-eh´-o;* from 5355; to *be jealous* of:— envy.

5355. φθόνος **phthŏnŏs**, *fthon´-os;* prob. akin to the base of 5351; *ill-will* (as *detraction*), i.e. *jealousy (spite):*— envy.

5356. φθορά **phthŏra**, *fthor-ah´;* from 5351; *decay,* i.e. *ruin* (spontaneous or inflicted, lit. or fig.):— corruption, destroy, perish.

5357. φιάλη **phialē**, *fee-al´-ay;* of uncert. aff.; a broad shallow *cup* ("phial"):— vial.

5358. φιλάγαθος **philagathŏs**, *fil-ag´-ath-os;* from 5384 and 18; *fond to good,* i.e. a *promoter of virtue:*— love of good men.

5359. Φιλαδέλφεια **Philadĕlphĕia**, *fil-ad-el´-fee-ah;* from Φιλάδελφος **Philadĕlphŏs** (the same as 5361), a king of Pergamos; *Philadelphia,* a place in Asia Minor:— Philadelphia.

5360. φιλαδελφία **philadĕlphia**, *fil-ad-el-fee´-ah;* from 5361; *fraternal affection:*— brotherly love (kindness), love of the brethren.

5361. φιλάδελφος **philadĕlphŏs**, *fil-ad´-el-fos;* from 5384 and 80; *fond of brethren,* i.e. *fraternal:*— love as brethren.

5362. φίλανδρος **philandrŏs**, *fil´-an-dros;* from 5384 and 435; *fond of man,* i.e. *affectionate* as a wife:— love their husbands.

5363. φιλανθρωπία **philanthrōpia**, *fil-an-thro-pee´-ah;* from the same as 5364; *fondness of mankind,* i.e. *benevolence* ("philanthropy"):— kindness, love toward man.

5364. φιλανθρώπως **philanthrōpŏs**, *fil-an-thro´-poce;* adv. from a compound of 5384 and 444; *fondly to man* ("philanthropically"), i.e. *humanely:*— courteously.

5365. φιλαργυρία **philarguria**, *fil-ar-goo-ree´-ah;* from 5366; *avarice:*— love of money.

5366. φιλάργυρος **philargurŏs**, *fil-ar´-goo-ros;* from 5384 and 696; *fond of silver* (*money*), i.e. *avaricious:*— covetous.

5367. φίλαυτος **philautŏs**, *fil´-ŏw-tos;* from 5384 and 846; *fond of self,* i.e. *selfish:*— lover of own self.

5368. φιλέω **philĕō**, *fil-eh´-o;* from 5384; to *be a friend to* (*fond of* [an indiv. or an obj.]), i.e. *have affection* for (denoting *personal* attachment, as a matter of sentiment or feeling; while 25 is wider, embracing espec. the judgment and the *deliberate* assent of the will as a matter of principle, duty and propriety: the two thus stand related very much as 2309 and 1014, or as 2372 and 3563 respectively; the former being chiefly of the *heart* and the latter of the *head;* spec. to *kiss* (as a mark of tenderness):— kiss, love.

5369. φιλήδονος **philēdŏnŏs**, *fil-ay´-don-os;* from 5384 and 2237; *fond of pleasure,* i.e. *voluptuous:*— lover of pleasure.

5370. φίλημα **philēma**, *fil´-ay-mah;* from 5368; a *kiss:*— kiss.

5371. Φιλήμων **Philēmōn**, *fil-ay´-mone;* from *5368; friendly; Philemon,* a Chr.:— Philemon.

5372. Φιλητός **Philētŏs**, *fil-ay-tos´;* from *5368; amiable; Philetus,* an opposer of Christianity:— Philetus.

5373. φιλία **philia**, *fil-ee´-ah;* from *5384; fondness:—* friendship.

5374. Φιλιππήσιος **Philippēsiŏs**, *fil-ip-pay´-see-os;* from *5375;* a *Philippesian (Philippian),* i.e. native of Philippi:— Philippian.

5375. Φίλιπποι **Philippŏi**, *fil´-ip-poy;* plur. of *5376; Philippi,* a place in Macedonia:— Philippi.

5376. Φίλιππος **Philippŏs**, *fil´-ip-pos;* from *5384* and *2462; fond of horses; Philippus,* the name of four Isr.:— Philip.

5377. φιλόθεος **philŏthĕŏs**, *fil-oth´-eh-os;* from *5384* and *2316; fond of God,* i.e. *pious:—* lover of God.

5378. Φιλόλογος **Philŏlŏgŏs**, *fil-ol´-og-os;* from *5384* and *3056; fond of words,* i.e. *talkative (argumentative, learned, "philological"); Philologus,* a Chr.:— Philologus.

5379. φιλονεικία **philŏnĕikia**, *fil-on-i-kee´-ah;* from *5380; quarrelsomeness,* i.e. a *dispute:—* strife.

5380. φιλόνεικος **philŏnĕikŏs**, *fil-on´-i-kos;* from *5384* and νεῖκος **nĕikŏs** (a *quarrel;* prob. akin to *3534); fond of strife,* i.e. *disputatious:—* contentious.

5381. φιλονεξία **philŏnĕxia**, *fil-on-ex-ee´-ah;* from *5382; hospitableness:—* entertain strangers, hospitality.

5382. φιλόξενος **philŏxĕnŏs**, *fil-ox´-en-os;* from *5384* and *3581; fond of guests,* i.e. *hospitable:—* given to (lover of, use) hospitality.

5383. φιλοπρωτεύω **philŏprōtĕuō**, *fil-op-rote-yoo´-o;* from a compound of *5384* and *4413; to be fond of being first,* i.e. *ambitious* of distinction:— love to have the preeminence.

5384. φίλος **philŏs**, *fee´-los;* prop. *dear,* i.e. a *friend;* act. *fond,* i.e. *friendly* (still as a noun, an *associate, neighbor,* etc.):— friend.

5385. φιλοσοφία **philŏsŏphia**, *fil-os-of-ee´-ah;* from *5386; "philosophy",* i.e. (spec.) *Jewish sophistry:—* philosophy.

5386. φιλόσοφος **philŏsŏphŏs**, *fil-os´-of-os;* from *5384* and *4680; fond of wise* things, i.e. a *"philosopher":—* philosopher.

5387. φιλόστοργος **philŏstŏrgŏs**, *fil-os´-tor-gos;* from *5384* and στοργή **stŏrgē** (*cherishing* one's kindred, espec. parents or children); *fond of* natural *relatives,* i.e. *fraternal* toward fellow Chr.:— kindly affectioned.

5388. φιλότεκνος **philŏtĕknŏs**, *fil-ot´-ek-nos;* from *5384* and *5043; fond of* one's *children,* i.e. *maternal:—* love their children.

5389. φιλοτιμέομαι **philŏtimĕŏmai**, *fil-ot-im-eh´-om-ahee;* mid. voice from a compound of *5384* and *5092; to be fond of honor,* i.e. *emu-*

lous (*eager* or *earnest* to do something):— labour, strive, study.

5390. φιλοφρόνως **philŏphrŏnōs**, *fil-of-ron´-oce;* adv. from *5391; with friendliness of mind,* i.e. *kindly:—* courteously.

5391. φιλόφρων **philŏphrōn**, *fil-of´-rone;* from *5384* and *5424; friendly of mind,* i.e. *kind:—* courteous.

5392. φιμόω **phimŏō**, *fee-mŏ´-o;* from φιμός **phimŏs**, (a *muzzle*); to *muzzle:—* muzzle.

5393. Φλέγων **Phlĕgōn**, *fleg´-one;* act. part. of the base of *5395; blazing; Phlegon,* a Chr.:— Phlegon.

5394. φλογίζω **phlŏgizō**, *flog-id´-zo;* from *5395; to cause a blaze,* i.e. *ignite* (fig. to *inflame* with passion):— set on fire.

5395. φλόξ **phlŏx**, *flox;* from a primary φλέγω **phlĕgō**, (to *"flash"* or *"flame"*); a *blaze:* —flame (-ing).

5396. φλυαρέω **phluarĕō**, *floo-ar-eh´-o;* from *5397; to be a babbler* or *trifler,* i.e. (by impl.) to *berate* idly or mischievously:— prate against.

5397. φλύαρος **phluarŏs**, *floo´-ar-os;* from φλύω **phluō**, (to *bubble*); a *garrulous* person, i.e. *prater:—* tattler.

5398. φοβερός **phŏbĕrŏs**, *fob-er-os´;* from *5401; frightful,* i.e. (obj.) *formidable:—* fearful, terrible.

5399. φοβέω **phŏbĕō**, *fob-eh´-o;* from *5401;* to *frighten,* i.e. (pass.) to *be alarmed;* by anal. to *be in awe* of, i.e. *revere:—* be (+ sore) afraid, fear (exceedingly), reverence.

5400. φόβητρον **phŏbētrŏn**, *fob´-ay-tron;* neut. of a der. of *5399;* a *frightening* thing, i.e. *terrific* portent:— fearful sight.

5401. φόβος **phŏbŏs**, *fob´-os;* from a primary φέβομαι **phĕbŏmai** (to be put in *fear); alarm,* or *fright:—* be afraid, + exceedingly, fear, terror.

5402. Φοίβη **Phŏibē**, *foy´-bay;* fem. of φοῖβος **phŏibŏs**, (*bright;* prob. akin to the base of *5457); Phœbe,* a Chr. woman:— Phebe.

5403. Φοινίκη **Phŏinikē**, *foy-nee´-kay;* from *5404; palm*-country; *Phœnice* (or *Phœnicia*), a region of Pal.:— Phenice, Phenicia.

5404. φοῖνιξ **phŏinix**, *foy´-nix;* of uncert. der.; a *palm*-tree:— palm (tree).

5405. Φοῖνιξ **Phŏinix**, *foy´-nix;* prob. the same as *5404; Phœnix,* a place in Crete:— Phenice.

5406. φονεύς **phŏnĕus**, *fon-yooce´;* from *5408;* a *murderer* (always of *criminal* [or at least *intentional*] homicide; which *443* does not necessarily imply; while *4607* is a special term for a *public* bandit):— murderer.

5407. φονεύω **phŏnĕuō**, *fon-yoo´-o;* from *5406;* to *be a murderer* (of):— kill, do murder, slay.

5408. φόνος **phŏnŏs**, *fon´-os;* from an obs.

primary φένω **phĕnō** (to *slay*); *murder*:— murder, + be slain with, slaughter.

5409. φορέω **phŏrĕō**, *for-eh´-o;* from *5411;* to *have a burden,* i.e. (by anal.) to *wear* as clothing or a constant accompaniment:— bear, wear.

5410. Φόρον **Phŏrŏn,** *for´-on;* of Lat. or.; a *forum* or market-place; only in comparison with *675;* a *station* on the Appian road:— forum.

5411. φόρος **phŏrŏs,** *for´-os;* from *5342;* a *load* (as *borne*), i.e. (fig.) a *tax* (prop. an indiv. *assessment* on persons or property; whereas *5056* is usually a gen. *toll* on goods or travel):— tribute.

5412. φορτίζω **phŏrtizō,** *for-tid´-zo;* from *5414;* to *load* up (prop. as a vessel or animal), i.e. (fig.) to *overburden* with cerem. (or spiritual anxiety):— lade, be heavy laden.

5413. φορτίον **phŏrtiŏn,** *for-tee´-on;* dimin. of *5414;* an *invoice* (as part of *freight*), i.e. (fig.) a *task* or *service:*— burden.

5414. φόρτος **phŏrtŏs,** *for´-tos;* from *5342;* something *carried,* i.e. the *cargo* of a ship:— lading.

5415. Φορτουνάτος **Phŏrtŏunatŏs,** *for-too-nat´-os;* of Lat. or.; "*fortunate,*" Fortunatus, a Chr.:— Fortunatus.

5416. φραγέλλιον **phragĕlliŏn,** *frag-el´-le-on;* neut. of a der. from the base of *5417;* a *whip,* i.e. Rom. *lash* as a public punishment:— scourge.

5417. φραγελλόω **phragĕllŏō,** *frag-el-lŏ´-o;* from a presumed equiv. of the Lat. *flagellum;* to *whip,* i.e. *lash* as a public punishment:— scourge.

5418. φραγμός **phragmŏs´;** from *5420;* a *fence,* or inclosing *barrier* (lit. or fig.):— hedge (+ round about), partition.

5419. φράζω **phrazō,** *frad´-zo;* prob. akin to *5420* through the idea of *defining;* to *indicate* (by word or act), i.e. (spec.) to *expound:*— declare.

5420. φράσσω **phrassō,** *fras´-so;* appar. a streng. form of the base of *5424;* to *fence* or inclose, i.e. (spec.) to *block* up (fig. to *silence*):— stop.

5421. φρέαρ **phrĕar,** *freh´-ar;* of uncert. der.; a *hole* in the ground (dug for obtaining or holding water or other purposes), i.e. a *cistern* or *well;* fig. an *abyss* (as a *prison*):— well, pit.

5422. φρεναπατάω **phrĕnapataō,** *fren-ap-at-ah´-o;* from *5423;* to *be a mind-misleader,* i.e. *delude:*— deceive.

5423. φρεναπάτης **phrĕnapatēs,** *fren-ap-at´-ace;* from *5424* and *539;* a *mind-misleader,* i.e. *seducer:*— deceiver.

5424. φρήν **phrēn,** *frane;* prob. from an obs. φράω **phraō** (to *rein* in or *curb;* comp. *5420*); the *midrif* (as a *partition* of the body), i.e. (fig. and by impl. of sympathy) the *feelings* (or

sensitive nature; by extens. [also in the plur.] the *mind* or cognitive faculties):— understanding.

5425. φρίσσω **phrissō,** *fris´-so;* appar. a primary verb; to "*bristle*" or *chill,* i.e. *shudder* (*fear*):— tremble.

5426. φρονέω **phrŏnĕō,** *fron-eh´-o;* from *5424;* to *exercise* the *mind,* i.e. *entertain* or *have a sentiment* or *opinion;* by impl. to *be* (mentally) *disposed* (more or less earnestly in a certain direction); intens. to *interest oneself* in (with concern or obedience):— set the affection on, (be) care (-ful), (be like-, + be of one, + be of the same, + let this) mind (-ed), regard, savour, think.

5427. φρόνημα **phrŏnēma,** *fron´-ay-mah;* from *5426;* (mental) *inclination* or *purpose:* —(be, + be carnally, + be spiritually) mind (-ed).

5428. φρόνησις **phrŏnēsis,** *fron´-ay-sis;* from *5426;* mental *action* or *activity,* i.e. intellectual or mor. *insight:*— prudence, wisdom.

5429. φρόνιμος **phrŏnimŏs,** *fron´-ee-mos;* from *5424; thoughtful,* i.e. *sagacious* or *discreet* (implying a *cautious* character; while *4680* denotes *practical* skill or acumen; and *4908* indicates rather *intelligence* or mental *acquirement*); in a bad sense *conceited* (also in the comparative):— wise (-r).

5430. φρονίμως **phrŏnimōs,** *fron-im´-oce;* adv. from *5429; prudently:*— wisely.

5431. φροντίζω **phrŏntizō,** *fron-tid´-zo;* from a der. of *5424;* to *exercise thought,* i.e. *be anxious:*— be careful.

5432. φρουρέω **phrŏurĕō,** *froo-reh´-o;* from a compound of *4253* and *3708;* to *be a watcher in advance,* i.e. to *mount guard* as a sentinel (*post spies* at gates); fig. to *hem in, protect:*— keep (with a garrison). Comp. *5083.*

5433. φρυάσσω **phruassō,** *froo-as´-so;* akin to *1032, 1031;* to *snort* (as a spirited horse), i.e. (fig.) to *make a tumult:*— rage.

5434. φρύγανον **phruganŏn,** *froo´-gan-on;* neut. of a presumed der. of φρύγω **phrugō** (to *roast* or *parch;* akin to the base of *5395*); something *desiccated,* i.e. a dry *twig:*— stick.

5435. Φρυγία **Phrugia,** *froog-ee´-ah;* prob. of for. or.; *Phrygia,* a region of Asia Minor:— Phrygia.

5436. Φύγελλος **Phugĕllŏs,** *foog´-el-los;* prob. from *5343; fugitive; Phygellus,* an apostate Chr.:— Phygellus.

5437. φυγή **phugē,** *foog-ay´;* from *5343;* a *fleeing,* i.e. *escape:*— flight.

5438. φυλακή **phulakē,** *foo-lak-ay´;* from *5442;* a *guarding* or (concr. *guard*), the act, the person; fig. the place, the condition, or (spec.) the time (as a division of day or night), lit. or fig.:— cage, hold, (im-) prison (-ment), ward, watch.

5439. φυλακίζω **phulakizō**, *foo-lak-id´-zo;* from 5441; to *incarcerate:*— imprison.

5440. φυλακτήριον **phulaktēriŏn**, *foo-lak-tay´-ree-on;* neut. of a der. of 5442; a *guard-case,* i.e. *"phylactery"* for wearing slips of Scripture texts:— phylactery.

5441. φύλαξ **phulax**, *foo´-lax;* from 5442; a *watcher* or *sentry:*— keeper.

5442. φυλάσσω **phulassō**, *foo-las´-so;* prob. from 5443 through the idea of *isolation;* to *watch,* i.e. *be on guard* (lit. or fig.); by impl. to *preserve, obey, avoid:*— beware, keep (self), observe, save. Comp. 5083.

5443. φυλή **phulē**, *foo-lay´;* from 5453 (comp. 5444); an *offshoot,* i.e. *race* or *clan:*— kindred, tribe.

5444. φύλλον **phullŏn**, *fool´-lon;* from the same as 5443; a *sprout,* i.e. *leaf:*— leaf.

5445. φύραμα **phurama**, *foo´-ram-ah;* from a prol. form of φύρω **phurō** (to *mix* a liquid with a solid; perh. akin to 5453 through the idea of *swelling* in bulk), mean to *knead;* a *mass* of dough:— lump.

5446. φυσικός **phusikŏs**, *foo-see-kos´;* from 5449; *"physical",* i.e. (by impl.) *instinctive:*— natural. Comp. 5591.

5447. φυσικῶς **phusikōs**, *foo-see-koce´;* adv. from 5446; *"physically",* i.e. (by impl.) *instinctively:*— naturally.

5448. φυσιόω **phusiŏō**, *foo-see-ŏ´-o;* from 5449 in the primary sense of *blowing;* to *inflate,* i.e. (fig.) *make proud (haughty):*— puff up.

5449. φύσις **phusis**, *foo´-sis;* from 5453; *growth* (by *germination* or *expansion*), i.e. (by impl.) natural *production* (lineal *descent*); by extens. a *genus* or *sort;* fig. native *disposition, constitution* or *usage:*— (man-) kind, nature (l-all).

5450. φυσίωσις **phusiōsis**, *foo-see´-o-sis;* from 5448; *inflation,* i.e. (fig.) *haughtiness:*— swelling.

5451. φυτεία **phutĕia**, *foo-ti´-ah;* from 5452; trans-*planting,* i.e. (concr.) a *shrub* or *vegetable:*— plant.

5452. φυτεύω **phutĕuō**, *foot-yoo´-o;* from a der. of 5453; to *set out* in the earth, i.e. *implant;* fig. to *instil* doctrine:— plant.

5453. φύω **phuō**, *foo´-o;* a primary verb; prob. orig. to *"puff"* or *blow,* i.e. to *swell* up; but only used in the impl. sense, to *germinate* or *grow* (*sprout, produce*), lit. or fig.:— spring (up).

5454. φωλεός **phōlĕŏs**, *fo-leh-os´;* of uncert. der.; a *burrow* or *lurking-place:*— hole.

5455. φωνέω **phōnĕō**, *fo-neh´-o;* from 5456; to emit a *sound* (animal, human or instrumental); by impl. to *address* in words or by name, also in imitation:— call (for), crow, cry.

5456. φωνή **phōnē**, *fo-nay´;* prob. akin to 5316

through the idea of *disclosure; a tone* (articulate, bestial or artif.); by impl. an *address* (for any purpose), *saying* or *language:*— noise, sound, voice.

5457. φῶς **phōs**, *foce;* from an obs. φάω **phaō** (to *shine,* or make *manifest,* espec. by *rays;* comp. 5316, 5346); *luminousness* (in the widest application, nat. or artif., abstr. or concr., lit. or fig.):— fire, light.

5458. φωστήρ **phōstēr**, *foce-tare´;* from 5457; an *illuminator,* i.e. (concr.) a *luminary,* or (abstr.) *brilliancy:*— light.

5459. φωσφόρος **phōsphŏrŏs**, *foce-for´-os;* from 5457 and 5342; *light-bearing* ("phosphorus"), i.e. (spec.) the *morning-star* (fig.):— day star.

5460. φωτεινός **phōtĕinŏs**, *fo-ti-nos´;* from 5457; *lustrous,* i.e. *transparent* or *well-illuminated* (fig.):— bright, full of light.

5461. φωτίζω **phōtizō**, *fo-tid´-zo;* from 5457; to *shed rays,* i.e. to *shine* or (tran.) to *brighten* up (lit. or fig.):— enlighten, illuminate, (bring to, give) light, make to see.

5462. φωτισμός **phōtismŏs**, *fo-tis-mos´;* from 5461; *illumination* (fig.):— light.

Χ

5463. χαίρω **chairō**, *khah´-ee-ro;* a primary verb; to be *"cheer"ful,* i.e. calmly *happy* or well-off; impers. espec. as salutation (on meeting or parting), *be well:*— farewell, be glad, God speed, greeting, hall, joy (- fully), rejoice.

5464. χάλαζα **chalaza**, *khal´-ad-zah;* prob. from 5465; *hail:*— hail.

5465. χαλάω **chalaō**, *khal-ah´-o;* from the base of 5490; to *lower* (as into a *void*):— let down, strike.

5466. Χαλδαῖος **Chaldaiŏs**, *khal-dah´-yos;* prob. of Heb. or [3778]; a *Chaldæan* (i.e. *Kasdi*), or native or the region of the lower Euphrates:— Chaldæan.

5467. χαλεπός **chalĕpŏs**, *khal-ep-os´;* perh. from 5465 through the idea of *reducing* the strength; *difficult,* i.e. *dangerous,* or (by impl.) *furious:*— fierce, perilous.

5468. χαλιναγωγέω **chalinagōgĕō**, *khal-in-ag-ogue-eh´-o;* from a compound of 5469 and the redupl. form of 71; to *be a bitleader,* i.e. to *curb* (fig.):— bridle.

5469. χαλινός **chalinŏs**, *khal-ee-nos´;* from 5465; a *curb* or *head-stall* (as *curbing* the spirit):— bit, bridle.

5470. χάλκεος **chalkĕŏs**, *khal´-keh-os;* from 5475; *coppery:*— brass.

5471. χαλκεύς **chalkĕus**, *khalk-yooce´;* from 5475; a *copper-worker* or *brazier:*— coppersmith.

5472. χαλκηδών **chalkēdōn**, *khal-kay-*

dōhn'; from 5475 and perh. *1491; copper-like*, i.e. *"chalcedony"*:— chalcedony.

5473. χαλκίον **chalkiŏn**, *khal-kee'-on;* dimin. from 5475; a *copper dish:*— brazen vessel.

5474. χαλκολίβανον **chalkŏlibanŏn**, *khal-kol-ib'-an-on;* neut. of a compound of 5475 and 3030 (in the impl. mean of *whiteness* or *brilliancy*); *burnished copper*, an alloy of copper (or gold) and silver having a brilliant lustre:— fine brass.

5475. χαλκός **chalkŏs**, *khal-kos';* perh. from 5465 through the idea of *hollowing* out as a vessel (this metal being chiefly used for that purpose); *copper* (the substance, or some implement or coin made of it):— brass, money.

5476. χαμαί **chamai**, *kham-ah'-ee;* adv. perh. from the base of 5490 through the idea of a *fissure* in the soil; *earthward*, i.e. *prostrate:*— on (to) the ground.

5477. Χαναάν **Chanaan**, *khan-ah'-an;* of Heb. or. [3667]; *Chanaan* (i.e. *Kenaan*), the early name of Pal.:— Chanaan.

5478. Χαναναῖος **Chanaanaiŏs**, *khan-ah-an-ah'-yos;* from 5477; a *Chanaanæan* (i.e. *Kenaanite*), or native of Gentile Pal.:— of Canaan.

5479. χαρά **chara**, *khar-ah';* from 5463; *cheerfulness*, i.e. calm *delight:*— gladness, × greatly, (× be exceeding) joy (-ful, -fully, -fulness, -ous).

5480. χάραγμα **charagma**, *khar'-ag-mah;* from the same as 5482; a *scratch* or *etching*, i.e. *stamp* (as a *badge* of servitude), or *sculptured* figure (*statue*):— graven, mark.

5481. χαρακτήρ **charaktēr**, *khar-ak-tare';* from the same as 5482; a *graver* (the tool or the person), i.e. (by impl.) *engraving* ([*"character"*], the *figure* stamped, i.e. an exact *copy* or [fig.] *representation*):— express image.

5482. χάραξ **charax**, *khar'-ax;* from χαράσσω **charassō** (to *sharpen*, to a point; akin to 1125 through the idea of *scratching*); a *stake*, i.e. (by impl.) a *palisade* or *rampart* (military *mound* for circumvallation in a siege):— trench.

5483. χαρίζομαι **charizŏmai**, *khar-id'-zom-ahee;* mid. voice from 5485; to *grant* as a *favor*, i.e. gratuitously, in kindness, pardon or rescue:— deliver, (frankly) forgive, (freely) give, grant.

5484. χάριν **charin**, *khar'-in;* acc. of 5485 as prep.; through *favor* of, i.e. *on account* of:— be- (for) cause of, for sake of, + ... fore, × reproachfully.

5485. χάρις **charis**, *khar'-ece;* from 5463; *graciousness* (as *gratifying*), of manner or act (abstr. or concr.; lit., fig., or spiritual; espec. the divine influence upon the heart, and its reflection in the life; incl. *gratitude*):— acceptable, benefit, favour, gift, grace (-ious), joy, liberality, pleasure, thank (-s, -worthy).

5486. χάρισμα **charisma**, *khar'-is-mah;* from 5483; a (divine) *gratuity*, i.e. *deliverance* (from danger or passion); (spec.) a (spiritual) *endowment*, i.e. (subj.) relig. *qualification*, or (obj.) miraculous *faculty:*— (free) gift.

5487. χαριτόω **charitŏō**, *khar-ee-tŏ'-o;* from 5485; to *grace*, i.e. indue with special *honor:*— make accepted, be highly favoured.

5488. Χαρράν **Charrhan**, *khar-hran';* of Heb. or. [2771]; *Charrhan* (i.e. *Charan*), a place in Mesopotamia:— Charran.

5489. χάρτης **chartēs**, *khar'-tace;* from the same as 5482; a *sheet* (*"chart"*) of writing-material (as to be *scribbled* over):— paper.

5490. χάσμα **chasma**, *khas'-mah;* from a form of an obs. primary χάω **chaō**, (to *"gape"* or *"yawn"*); a *"chasm"* or *vacancy* (impassable *interval*):— gulf.

5491. χεῖλος **chĕilŏs**, *khi'-los;* from a form of the same as 5490; a *lip* (as a *pouring* place); fig. a *margin* (of water):— lip, shore.

5492. χειμάζω **chĕimazō**, *khi-mad'-zo;* from the same as 5494; to *storm*, i.e. (pass.) to *labor under a gale:*— be tossed with tempest.

5493. χείμαρρος **chĕimarrhŏs**, *khi'-mar-hros;* from the base of 5494 and 4482; a *storm-runlet*, i.e. *winter-torrent:*— brook.

5494. χειμών **chĕimōn**, *khi-mone';* from a der. of χέω **chĕō**, (to *pour;* akin to the base of 5490 through the idea of a *channel*), mean. a *storm* (as *pouring* rain); by impl. the *rainy* season, i.e. *winter:*— tempest, foul weather, winter.

5495. χείρ **chĕir**, *khire;* perh. from the base of 5494 in the sense of its congener the base of 5490 (through the idea of *hollowness* for *grasping*); the *hand* (lit. or fig. [*power*]; espec. [by Heb.] a *means* or *instrument*):— hand.

5496. χειραγωγέω **chĕiragōgĕō**, *khi-rag-ogue-eh'-o;* from 5497; to be a *hand-leader*, i.e. to *guide* (a blind person):— lead by the hand.

5497. χειραγωγός **chĕiragōgŏs**, *khi-rag-o-gos';* from 5495 and a redupl. form of 71; a *hand-leader*, i.e. personal *conductor* (of a blind person):— some to lead by the hand.

5498. χειρόγραφον **chĕirŏgraphŏn**, *khi-rog'-raf-on;* neut. of a compound of 5495 and 1125; something *hand-written* (*"chirograph"*), i.e. a *manuscript* (spec. a legal *document* or *bond* [fig.]):— handwriting.

5499. χειροποίητος **chĕirŏpŏiētŏs**, *khi-rop-oy'-ay-tos;* from 5495 and a der. of 4160; *manufactured*, i.e. of *human construction:*— made by (make with) hands.

5500. χειροτονέω **chĕirŏtŏnĕō**, *khi-rot-on-eh'-o;* from a comp. of 5495 and τείνω **tĕinō**

Greek

(to *stretch*); to be a *hand-reacher*, or *voter* (by raising the hand), i.e. (gen.) to *select* or *appoint:*— choose, ordain.

5501. χείρων **chĕirōn**, *khi´-rone;* irreg. comp. of 2556; from an obs. equiv. χέρης **chĕrēs** (of uncert. der.); *more evil* or *aggravated* (phys., ment. or mor.):— sorer, worse.

5502. χερουβίμ **chĕrŏubim**, *kher-oo-beem´;* plur. of Heb. or. [3742]; "*cherubim*" (i.e. *cherubs* or *kerubim*):— cherubims.

5503. χήρα **chēra**, *khay´-rah;* fem. of a presumed der. appar. from the base of 5490 through the idea of *deficiency;* a *widow* (as *lacking* a husband), lit. or fig.:— widow.

5504. χθές **chthĕs**, *khthes;* of uncert. der.; "*yesterday*"; by extens. *in time past* or *hitherto:*— yesterday.

5505. χιλιάς **chilias**, *khil-ee-as´;* from 5507; one *thousand* ("*chiliad*"):— thousand.

5506. χιλίαρχος **chiliarchŏs**, *khil-ee´-ar-khos;* from 5507 and 757; the *commander of a thousand* soldiers ("*chiliarch*"), i.e. *colonel:*— (chief, high) captain.

5507. χίλιοι **chiliŏi**, *khil´-ee-oy;* plur. of uncert. aff.; a *thousand:*— thousand.

5508. Χίος **Chiŏs**, *khee´-os;* of uncert. der.; *Chios*, an island in the Mediterranean:— Chios.

5509. χιτών **chitōn**, *khee-tone´;* of for. or. [3801]; a *tunic* or *shirt:*— clothes, coat, garment.

5510. χιών **chiōn**, *khee-one´;* perh. akin to the base of 5490 (5465) or 5494 (as *descending* or *empty*); *snow:*— snow.

5511. χλαμύς **chlamus**, *khlam-ooce´;* of uncert. der.; a military *cloak:*— robe.

5512. χλευάζω **chlĕuazō**, *khlyoo-ad´-zo;* from a der. prob. of 5491; to *throw out* the *lip*, i.e. *jeer* at:— mock.

5513. χλιαρός **chliarŏs**, *khlee-ar-os´;* from χλίω **chliō**, (to *warm*); *tepid:*— lukewarm.

5514. Χλόη **Chlŏē**, *khlŏ´-ay;* fem. of appar. a primary word; "*green*"; *Chloë*, a Chr. female:— Chloe.

5515. χλωρός **chlōrŏs**, *khlo-ros´;* from the same as 5514; *greenish*, i.e. *verdant, dun-colored:*— green, pale.

5516. χξϛ **chi xi stigma**, *khee xee stig´-ma;* the 22nd, 14th and an obs. letter (4742 as a *cross*) of the Greek alphabet (intermediate between the 5th and 6th), used as numbers; denoting respectively 600, 60 and 6; 666 as a numeral:— six hundred threescore and six.

5517. χοϊκός **chŏikŏs**, *khŏ-ik-os´;* from 5522; *dusty* or *dirty* (*soil*-like), i.e. (by impl.) *terrene:*— earthy.

5518. χοῖνιξ **chŏinix**, *khoy´-nix;* of uncertain der.; a *chœnix* or certain dry measure:— measure.

5519. χοῖρος **chŏirŏs**, *khoy´-ros;* of uncert. der.; a *hog:*— swine.

5520. χολάω **chŏlaō**, *khol-ah´-o;* from 5521; to *be bilious*, i.e. (by impl.) *irritable* (enraged, "choleric"):— be angry.

5521. χολή **chŏlē**, *khol-ay´;* fem. of an equiv. perh. akin to the same as 5514 (from the greenish hue); "*gall*" or *bile*, i.e. (by anal.) *poison* or an *anodyne* (wormwood, poppy, etc.):— gall.

5522. χόος **chŏŏs**, *khŏ´-os;* from the base of 5494; a *heap* (as *poured* out), i.e. *rubbish; loose dirt:*— dust.

5523. Χοραζίν **Chŏrazin**, *khor-ad-zin´;* of uncert. der.; *Chorazin*, a place in Pal.:— Chorazin.

5524. χορηγέω **chŏrēgĕō**, *khor-ayg-eh´-o;* from a compound of 5525 and 71; to *be* a *dance-leader*, i.e. (gen.) to *furnish:*— give, minister.

5525. χορός **chŏrŏs**, *khor-os´;* of uncert. der.; a *ring*, i.e. round *dance* ("choir"):— dancing.

5526. χορτάζω **chŏrtazō**, *khor-tad´-zo;* from 5528; to *fodder*, i.e. (gen.) to *gorge* (*supply food* in abundance):— feed, fill, satisfy.

5527. χόρτασμα **chŏrtasma**, *khor´-tas-mah;* from 5526; *forage*, i.e. *food:*— sustenance.

5528. χόρτος **chŏrtŏs**, *khor´-tos;* appar. a primary word; a "*court*" or "*garden*", i.e. (by impl. of *pasture*) *herbage* or *vegetation:*— blade, grass, hay.

5529. Χουζᾶς **Chŏuzas**, *khood-zas´;* of uncert. or.: *Chuzas*, an officer of Herod:— Chuza.

5530. χράομαι **chraŏmai**, *khrah´-om-ahee;* mid. voice of a primary verb (perh. rather from 5495, to *handle*); to *furnish* what is needed; (give an *oracle*, "*graze*" [touch slightly], *light* upon, etc.), i.e. (by impl.) to *employ* or (by extens.) to *act toward* one in a given manner:— entreat, use. Comp. 5531; 5534.

5531. χράω **chraō**, *khrah´-o;* prob. the same as the base of 5530; to *loan:*— lend.

5532. χρεία **chrĕia**, *khri´-ah;* from the base of 5530 or 5534; *employment*, i.e. an *affair;* also (by impl.) *occasion, demand, requirement* or *destitution:*— business, lack, necessary (-ity), need (-ful), use, want.

5533. χρεωφειλέτης **chrĕŏphĕilĕtēs**, *khreh-o-fi-let´-ace;* from a der. of 5531 and 3781; a *loan-ower*, i.e. *indebted* person:— debtor.

5534. χρή **chrē**, *khray;* third pers. sing. of the same as 5530 or 5531 used impers.; it *needs* (*must* or *should*) be:— ought.

5535. χρήζω **chrēizō**, *khrade´-zo;* from 5532; to *make* (i.e. *have*) *necessity*, i.e. *be in want of:*— (have) need.

5536. χρῆμα **chrēma**, *khray´-mah;* something *useful* or *needed,* i.e. *wealth, price:*— money, riches.

5537. χρηματίζω **chrēmatizō,** *khray-mat-id´- zo;* from *5536;* to *utter an oracle* (comp. the orig. sense of *5530*), i.e. divinely *intimate;* by impl. (comp. the secular sense of *5532*) to constitute a *firm* for business, i.e. (gen.) *bear* as a *title:*— be called, be admonished (warned) of God, reveal, speak.

5538. χρηματισμός **chrēmatismŏs,** *khray- mat-is-mos´;* from *5537;* a divine *response* or *revelation:*— answer of God.

5539. χρήσιμος **chrēsimŏs,** *khray´-see-mos;* from *5540; serviceable:*— profit.

5540. χρῆσις **chrēsis,** *khray´-sis;* from *5530; employment,* i.e. (spec.) sexual *intercourse* (as an *occupation* of the body):— use.

5541. χρηστεύομαι **chrēstĕuŏmai,** *khraste- yoo´-om-ahee;* mid. voice from *5543;* to *show oneself useful,* i.e. *act benevolently:*— be kind.

5542. χρηστολογία **chrēstŏlŏgia,** *khrase-tol- og-ee´-ah;* from a compound of *5543* and *3004; fair speech,* i.e. *plausibility:*— good words.

5543. χρηστός **chrēstŏs,** *khrase-tos´;* from *5530; employed,* i.e. (by impl.) *useful* (in manner or morals):— better, easy, good (-ness), gracious, kind.

5544. χρηστότης **chrēstŏtēs,** *khray-stot´-ace;* from *5543; usefulness,* i.e. mor. *excellence* (in character or demeanor):— gentleness, good (-ness), kindness.

5545. χρίσμα **chrisma,** *khris´-mah;* from *5548;* an *unguent* or *smearing,* i.e. (fig.) the spec. *endowment* ("chrism") of the Holy Spirit:— anointing, unction.

5546. Χριστιανός **Christianŏs,** *khris-tee-an- os´;* from *5547;* a *Christian,* i.e. follower of Christ:— Christian.

5547. Χριστός **Christŏs,** *khris-tos´;* from *5548; anointed,* i.e. the *Messiah,* an epithet of Jesus:— Christ.

5548. χρίω **chriō,** *khree´-o;* prob. akin to *5530* through the idea of *contact;* to *smear* or *rub* with oil, i.e. (by impl.) to *consecrate* to an office or relig. service:— anoint.

5549. χρονίζω **chrŏnizō,** *khron-id´-zo;* from *5550;* to *take time,* i.e. *linger:*— delay, tarry.

5550. χρόνος **chrŏnŏs,** *khron´-os;* of uncert. der.; a space of *time* (in gen., and thus prop. distinguished from *2540,* which designates a *fixed* or special occasion; and from *165,* which denotes a particular *period*) or *interval;* by extens. an indiv. *opportunity;* by impl. *de- lay:*— + years old, season, space, (× often-) time (-s), (a) while.

5551. χρονοτριβέω **chrŏnŏtribĕō,** *khron-ot- rib-eh´-o;* from a presumed compound of *5550* and the base of *5147;* to be a *time-wearer,* i.e. to *procrastinate* (*linger*):— spend time.

5552. χρύσεος **chrusĕŏs,** *khroo´-seh-os;* from *5557;* made of *gold:*— of gold, golden.

5553. χρυσίον **chrusiŏn,** *khroo-see´-on;* dimin. of *5557;* a *golden* article, i.e. gold plating, ornament, or coin:— gold.

5554. χρυσοδακτύλιος **chrusŏdaktuliŏs,** *khroo-sod-ak-too´-lee-os;* from *5557* and *1146; gold-ringed,* i.e. *wearing* a golden finger-ring or similar *jewelry:*— with a gold ring.

5555. χρυσόλιθος **chrusŏlithŏs,** *khroo-sol´- ee-thos;* from *5557* and *3037; gold-stone,* i.e. a *yellow* gem ("chrysolite"):— chrysolite.

5556. χρυσόπρασος **chrusŏprasŏs,** *khroo- sop´-ras-os;* from *5557* and πράσον **prasŏn** (a *leek*); a *greenish-yellow* gem ("chryso- prase"):— chrysoprase.

5557. χρυσός **chrusŏs,** *khroo-sos´;* perh. from the base of *5530* (through the idea of the *utility* of the metal); *gold;* by extens. a *golden* article, as an ornament or coin:— gold.

5558. χρυσόω **chrusŏō,** *khroo-sŏ´-o;* from *5557;* to *gild,* i.e. *bespangle* with golden ornaments:— deck.

5559. χρώς **chrōs,** *khroce;* prob. akin to the base of *5530* through the idea of *handling;* the *body* (prop. its *surface* or *skin*):— body.

5560. χωλός **chōlŏs,** *kho-los´;* appar. a primary word; "halt," i.e. *limping:*— cripple, halt, lame.

5561. χώρα **chōra,** *kho´-rah;* fem. of a der. of the base of *5490* through the idea of *empty* expanse; *room,* i.e. a space of *territory* (more or less extens.; often incl. its inhab.):— coast, county, fields, ground, land, region. Comp. *5117.*

5562. χωρέω **chōrĕō,** *kho-reh´-o;* from *5561;* to *be* in (*give*) *space,* i.e. (intr.) to *pass, enter,* or (tran.) to *hold, admit* (lit. or fig.):— come, contain, go, have place, (can, be room to) receive.

5563. χωρίζω **chōrizō,** *kho-rid´-zo;* from *5561;* to *place room* between, i.e. *part;* refl. to *go away:*— depart, put asunder, separate.

5564. χωρίον **chōriŏn,** *kho-ree´-on;* dimin. of *5561;* a *spot* or *plot* of ground:— field, land, parcel of ground, place, possession.

5565. χωρίς **chōris,** *kho-rece´;* adv. from *5561;* at a *space,* i.e. *separately* or *apart* from (often as prep.):— beside, by itself, without.

5566. χῶρος **chōrŏs,** *kho´-ros;* of Lat. or.; the *north-west* wind:— north west.

Ψ

5567. ψάλλω **psallō,** *psal´-lo;* probably strengthened from ψάω **psaō,** (to *rub* or *touch* the surface; comp. *5597*); to *twitch* or *twang,* i.e. to *play* on a stringed instrument (*celebrate* the divine worship *with music* and accompanying odes):— make melody, sing (psalms).

5568. ψαλμός **psalmŏs**, *psal-mos'*; from 5567; a set piece of *music*, i.e. a sacred *ode* (accompanied with the voice, harp or other instrument; a *"psalm"*); collect. the book of the *Psalms:*— psalm. Comp. 5603.

5569. ψευδάδελφος **psĕudadĕlphŏs**, *psyoo-dad'-el-fos*; from 5571 and 80; a *spurious brother*, i.e. *pretended associate:*— false brethren.

5570. ψευδαπόστολος **psĕudapŏstŏlŏs**, *psyoo-dap-os'-tol-os*; from 5571 and 652; a *spurious apostle*, i.e. *pretended preacher:*— false teacher.

5571. ψευδής **psĕudēs**, *psyoo-dace'*; from 5574; *untrue*, i.e. *erroneous, deceitful, wicked:*— false, liar.

5572. ψευδοδιδάσκαλος **psĕudŏdidaskalŏs**, *psyoo-dod-id-as'-kal-os*; from 5571 and 1320; a *spurious teacher*, i.e. *propagator of erroneous* Chr. *doctrine:*— false teacher.

5573. ψευδολόγος **psĕudŏlŏgŏs**, *psyoo-dol-og'-os*; from 5571 and 3004; *mendacious*, i.e. *promulgating erroneous* Chr. *doctrine:*— speaking lies.

5574. ψεύδομαι **psĕudŏmai**, *psyoo'-dom-ahee*; mid. voice of an appar. primary verb; to *utter an untruth* or attempt to *deceive* by falsehood:— falsely, lie.

5575. ψευδομάρτυρ **psĕudŏmartur**, *psyoo-dom-ar'-toor*; from 5571 and a kindred form of 3144; a *spurious witness*, i.e. *bearer of untrue testimony:*— false witness.

5576. ψευδομαρτυρέω **psĕudŏmarturĕō**, *psyoo-dom-ar-too-reh'-o*; from 5575; to *be an untrue testifier*, i.e. offer *falsehood in evidence:*— be a false witness.

5577. ψευδομαρτυρία **psĕudŏmarturia**, *psyoo-dom-ar-too-ree'-ah*; from 5575; *untrue testimony:*— false witness.

5578. ψευδοπροφήτης **psĕudŏprŏphētēs**, *psyoo-dop-rof-ay'-tace*; from 5571 and 4396; a *spurious prophet*, i.e. *pretended foreteller* or relig. *impostor:*— false prophet.

5579. ψεῦδος **psĕudŏs**, *psyoo'-dos*; from 5574; a *falsehood:*— lie, lying.

5580. ψευδόχριστος **psĕudŏchristŏs**, *psyoo-dokh'-ris-tos*; from 5571 and 5547; a *spurious Messiah:*— false Christ.

5581. ψευδώνυμος **psĕudōnumŏs**, *psyoo-do'-noo-mos*; from 5571 and 3686; *untruly named:*— falsely so called.

5582. ψεῦσμα **psĕusma**, *psyoos'-mah*; from 5574; a *fabrication*, i.e. *falsehood:*— lie.

5583. ψεύστης **psĕustēs**, *psyoos-tace'*; from 5574; a *falsifier:*— liar.

5584. ψηλαφάω **psēlaphaō**, *psay-laf-ah'-o*; from the base of 5567 (comp. 5586); to *ma-nipulate*, i.e. *verify* by contact; fig. to *search for:*— feel after, handle, touch.

5585. ψηφίζω **psēphizō**, *psay-fid'-zo*; from 5586; to *use pebbles* in enumeration, i.e. (gen.) to *compute:*— count.

5586. ψῆφος **psēphŏs**, *psay'-fos*; from the same as 5584; a *pebble* (as worn smooth by *handling*), i.e. (by impl. of use as a *counter* or *ballot*) a *verdict* (of acquittal) or *ticket* (of admission); a *vote:*— stone, voice.

5587. ψιθυρισμός **psithurismŏs**, *psith-oo-ris-mos'*; from a der. of ψίθος **psithŏs** (a *whisper*; by impl. a *slander*; prob. akin to 5574); *whispering*, i.e. secret *detraction:*— whispering.

5588. ψιθυριστής **psithuristēs**, *psith-oo-ris-tace'*; from the same as 5587; a secret *calumniator:*— whisperer.

5589. ψιχίον **psichiŏn**, *psikh-ee'-on*; dimin. from a der. of the base of 5567 (mean. a *crumb*); a *little bit* or *morsel:*— crumb.

5590. ψυχή **psuchē**, *psoo-khay'*; from 5594; *breath*, i.e. (by impl.) *spirit*, abstr. or concr. (the *animal* sentient principle only; thus distinguished on the one hand from 4151, which is the rational and immortal *soul*; and on the other from 2222, which is mere *vitality*, even of plants: these terms thus exactly correspond respectively to the Heb. 5315, 7307 and 2416):— heart (+ -ily), life, mind, soul, + us, + you.

5591. ψυχικός **psuchikŏs**, *psoo-khee-kos'*; from 5590; *sensitive*, i.e. *animate* (in distinction on the one hand from 4152, which is the higher or *renovated* nature; and on the other from 5446, which is the lower or *bestial* nature):— natural, sensual.

5592. ψύχος **psuchŏs**, *psoo'-khos*; from 5594; *coolness:*— cold.

5593. ψυχρός **psuchrŏs**, *psoo-chros'*; from 5592; *chilly* (lit. or fig.):— cold.

5594. ψύχω **psuchō**, *psoo'-kho*; a primary verb; to *breathe* (voluntarily but *gently*, thus differing on the one hand from 4154, which denotes prop. a *forcible* respiration; and on the other from the base of 109, which refers prop. to an inanimate *breeze*), i.e. (by impl. of reduction of temperature by evaporation) to *chill* (fig.):— wax cold.

5595. ψωμίζω **psōmizō**, *pso-mid'-zo*; from the base of 5596; to *supply* with *bits*, i.e. (gen.) to *nourish:*— (bestow to) feed.

5596. ψωμίον **psōmiŏn**, *pso-mee'-on*; dimin. from a der. of the base of 5597; a *crumb* or *morsel* (as if *rubbed* off), i.e. a *mouthful:*— sop.

5597. ψώχω **psōchō**, *pso'-kho*; prol. from the same base as 5567; to *triturate*, i.e. (by anal.) to *rub* out (kernels from husks with the fingers or hand):— rub.

Ω

5598. Ω **Ō,** i.e. ὦμεγα **ōmĕga,** *o´-meg-ah;* the last letter of the Greek alphabet, i.e. (fig.) the *finality:*— Omega.

5599. ὦ **ō,** *o;* a primary interj.; as a sign of the voc. *O;* as a note of exclamation, *oh:*— O.

5600. ὦ **ō,** *o;* incl. the oblique forms, as well as ἧς **ēs,** *ace;* ἦ **ē,** *ay;* etc.; the subjunctive of *1510;* (*may, might, can, could, would, should, must,* etc.; also with *1487* and its comp., as well as with other particles) *be:*— + appear, are, (may, might, should) be, × have, is, + pass the flower of her age, should stand, were.

5601. 'Ωβήδ **Obēd,** *o-bade´*

or 'Ιωβήδ **Iōbēd,** *yo-bade´;* of Heb. or. [5744]; *Obed,* an Isr.:— Obed.

5602. ὧδε **hōdĕ,** *ho´-deh;* from an adv. form of *3592; in this* same spot, i.e. *here* or *hither:*— here, hither, (in) this place, there.

5603. ᾠδή **ōidē,** *o-day´;* from *103; a chant* or "ode" (the gen. term for any words sung; while *5215* denotes espec. a *relig.* metrical composition, and *5568* still more spec. a *Heb.* cantillation):— song.

5604. ὠδίν **ōdin,** *o-deen´;* akin to *3601; a pang* or *throe,* espec. of childbirth:— pain, sorrow, travail.

5605. ὠδίνω **ōdinō,** *o-dee´-no;* from *5604;* to *experience* the *pains* of parturition (lit. or fig.):— travail in (birth).

5606. ὦμος **ōmŏs,** *o´-mos;* perh. from the alt. of *5342;* the *shoulder* (as that on which burdens are *borne*):— shoulder.

5607. ὤν **ōn,** *oan;* incl. the fem.

οὖσα **ŏusa,** *oo´-sah;* and the neut.

ὄν **ŏn,** *on;* pres. part. of *1510; being:*— be, come, have.

5608. ὠνέομαι **ōnĕŏmai,** *o-neh´-om-ahee;* mid. voice from an appar. primary ὦνος **ōnŏs** (a *sum* or *price*); to *purchase,* (synonymous with the earlier *4092*):— buy.

5609. ᾠόν **ōŏn,** *o-on´;* appar. a primary word; an "*egg*":— egg.

5610. ὥρα **hōra,** *ho´-rah;* appar. a primary word; an "*hour*" (lit. or fig.):— day, hour, instant, season, × short, [even-] tide, (high) time.

5611. ὡραῖος **hōraiŏs,** *ho-rah´-yos;* from *5610;* *belonging* to the right *hour* or *season* (*timely*), i.e. (by impl.) *flourishing* (*beauteous* [fig.]):— beautiful.

5612. ὠρύομαι **ōruŏmai,** *o-roo´-om-ahee;* mid. voice of an appar. primary verb; to "*roar*":— roar.

5613. ὡς **hōs,** *hoce;* prob. adv. of comparison from *3739; which how,* i.e. *in that manner* (very variously used, as follows):— about, after (that), (according) as (it had been, it were), as soon as (like), for, how (greatly), like (as, unto), since, so (that), that, to wit, unto, when ([-soever]), while, × with all speed.

5614. ὡσαννά **hōsanna,** *ho-san-nah´;* of Heb. or. [3467 and 4994]; *oh save!; hosanna* (i.e. *hoshia-na*), an exclamation of adoration:— hosanna.

5615. ὡσαύτως **hōsautōs,** *ho-sŏw´-toce;* from *5613* and an adv. from *846;* as *thus,* i.e. *in the same way:*— even so, likewise, after the same (in like) manner.

5616. ὡσεί **hōsĕi,** *ho-si´;* from *5613* and *1487; as if:*— about, as (it had been, it were), like (as).

5617. 'Ωσηέ **Hōsēĕ,** *ho-say-eh´;* of Heb. or. [1954]; *Hoseë* (i.e. *Hosheä*), an Isr.:— Osee.

5618. ὥσπερ **hōspĕr,** *hoce´-per;* from *5613* and *4007; just as,* i.e. *exactly like:*— (even, like) as.

5619. ὡσπερεί **hōspĕrĕi,** *hoce-per-i´;* from *5618* and *1487; just as if,* i.e. *as it were:*— as.

5620. ὥστε **hōstĕ,** *hoce´-teh;* from *5613* and *5037; so too,* i.e. *thus therefore* (in various relations of *consecution,* as follow):— (insomuch) as, so that (then), (insomuch) that, therefore, to, wherefore.

5621. ὠτίον **ōtiŏn,** *o-tee´-on;* dimin. of *3775;* an *earlet,* i.e. *one* of the ears, or perh. the *lobe* of the ear:— ear.

5622. ὠφέλεια **ōphĕlĕia,** *o-fel´-i-ah;* from a der. of the base of *5624; usefulness,* i.e. *benefit:*— advantage, profit.

5623. ὠφελέω **ōphĕlĕō,** *o-fel-eh´-o;* from the same as *5622;* to *be useful,* i.e. to *benefit:*— advantage, better, prevail, profit.

5624. ὠφέλιμος **ōphĕlimŏs,** *o-fel´-ee-mos;* from a form of *3786; helpful* or *serviceable,* i.e. *advantageous:*— profit (-able).